BUSINESS
LAW AND THE LEGAL
ENVIRONMENT

The Dryden Business Law Series

Allison/Prentice/Howell, *Business Law: Text and Cases,* Fifth Edition

Allison/Prentice/Howell, *Business Law,* Fifth Alternate Edition

Allison/Prentice, *The Legal Environment of Business,* Third Edition

Lieberman/Siedel, *Business Law and the Legal Environment,* Third Edition

Lieberman/Siedel, *The Legal Environment of Business*

Maurer, *Business Law,* Second Edition

Spiro, *The Dynamics of Law,* Third Edition

Warner, *The Legal Environment of Business*

THIRD EDITION

BUSINESS
LAW AND THE LEGAL
ENVIRONMENT

Jethro K. Lieberman

New York Law School

George J. Siedel

University of Michigan

THE DRYDEN PRESS

Harcourt Brace Jovanovich College Publishers

Fort Worth   Philadelphia   San Diego   New York   Orlando   Austin   San Antonio
Toronto   Montreal   London   Sydney   Tokyo

Acquisitions Editor: Tim Vertovec

Manuscript Editor: Sheila Spahn

Production Editor: Leslie Leland

Designer: Don Fujimoto

Art Editor: Judy Frazier

Production Managers: David Hough and Lesley Lenox

ISBN: 0-15-505516-X

Library of Congress Catalog Number: 91-72933

Printed in the United States of America

Copyrights and Acknowledgments appear on pages 1356–58,
which constitute a continuation of the copyright page.

PREFACE

Historian Shirley J. Burton recently suggested that law is "the dominant institution in American life, and . . . the single most important interpretive framework for the study of American history and cul ure." (Burton, 1991.) The centrality of law to American life is perhaps most evident in business, where law touches and shapes every functional field. In reaffirming the importance of law to business, the American Assembly of Collegiate Schools of Business (AACSB) in 1991 adopted an accreditation standard providing that both undergraduate and MBA curricula should provide students with coverage of **legal and regulatory issues.**

The goal in the Third Edition of this textbook remains the same as in earlier editions—to provide students with a textbook that is readable, up-to-date, and comprehensive in its coverage of legal and regulatory issues that are taught in **legal environment courses** and in more traditional **business law courses.** An introductory legal environment course, for instance, might cover Part I (The Legal Environment) and Part X (The Regulatory Environment), along with selected chapters dealing with the regulation of consumer credit transactions, intellectual property, the environment, and securities. Other units could be reserved for advanced courses covering more traditional business law topics. Use of a single textbook in a sequence of legal environment and business law courses is both efficient for instructors as well as economical for students.

New Features

The Third Edition contains several new features designed to strengthen its use in instruction and learning:

- Updated text to reflect changes in the law
- New chapters on Consumer Credit Transactions, Franchising, and Employment Law
- Updated Appendixes that include the Convention on Contracts for the International Sale of Goods and important revisions of the Uniform Commercial Code, the Revised Model Business Corporation Act, and the Revised Uniform Limited Partnership Act
- Many new cases decided in the late 1980s and 1990s
- New boxed inserts entitled "Law and Life" illustrating media coverage of contemporary legal issues
- Numerous figures depicting legal relationships and theories
- Student aids such as introductory chapter overviews, a list of key terms, pronunciation guides, self-test multiple-choice questions and a demonstration essay question
- A Manager's Legal Agenda at the end of each unit

These and other features are described in greater detail below.

The Quiet Revolution in Business Law

The late 1980s and 1990s have brought numerous changes that collectively have revolutionized the law affecting business. On the federal level, recent legislation has changed the law governing trademarks, copyrights, antitrust, fair housing, insider trading and a wide variety of other topics. In 1990 alone, Congress enacted four statutes that dramatically impact business: The Antitrust Amendments Act, the Americans with Disabilities Act, the Clean Air Act amendments, and the Securities Enforcement Remedies Act.

States, too, are becoming increasingly active in law reform. Especially noteworthy are the massive revisions of the Uniform Commercial Code, including new Articles 2A (Leases) and 4A (Funds Transfers) and revised Articles 3 (Negotiable Instruments) and 6 (Bulk Transfers). Among other state laws that are of great concern to business are the California statute (that became effective in 1991) imposing criminal liability on managers for selling defective products, statutes authorizing the creation of limited liability companies, the adoption by half the states of "other constituency" statutes that change the scope of directors' duties, the third generation of state takeover laws, and the 1990 amendment to the revised Model Business Corporation Act designed to limit directors' liability.

Law reform has also touched international business. Examples include sweeping changes in the legal systems in the Soviet Union and Eastern Europe, the adoption by many countries of the Convention on Contracts for the International Sale of Goods, and recent amendments to the Foreign Corrupt Practices Act.

These sweeping changes in the law have been incorporated into the Third Edition. The importance of statutory law is also reflected in the addition of **three new chapters** to this edition: Consumer Credit Transactions, Franchising, and Employment Law. The **Appendixes** have been updated to include new and revised Uniform Commercial Code Articles, the 1990 amendments to the Revised Model Business Corporation Act, and the Convention on Contracts for the International Sale of Goods.

Cases

Not to be outdone by legislatures, courts have continued their activism in developing and refining the law. The textbook has been updated to reflect these judicial developments. The chapter on Employment Law, for example, traces the evolution of Supreme Court approaches to employment discrimination, including the 1991 decision on company fetal protection policies.

Business law courses offer students an opportunity (not available in most other courses) to read and analyze original source material in the form of cases. Thus, in addition to cases summarized in the text, each chapter includes several edited cases. While many of these cases are **classroom classics,** a substantial number are of more **recent origin—** having been decided in the late 1980s and 1990s. One theme common to both the classics and the recent cases is that they often involve interesting personalities or controversial fact situations that lead to spirited class discussion. Cases that are new to this edition, for instance, raise the following questions:

- Should a court enforce a contract for the sale of a corporation that provides roach clips and bongs used to smoke marijuana?
- May a woman, who became pregnant after

undergoing a sterilization procedure using a Bleier clip, recover on a warranty theory from a manufacturer who was not in privity of contract?

- Should the Baltimore Orioles, Inc., be held liable when a player assaults a fan in the stadium parking lot, breaking his jaw with a bat?
- Should a limited partner—who invests in a limited partnership formed to finance a boxing match between Lyle Alzado (at the time a professional football player) and Mohammed Ali (then the world heavyweight boxing champion)—be held liable as a general partner to Alzado?
- In lawsuits against members of Judas Priest claiming that their album "Stained Class" caused suicidal behavior, does a Nevada court have jurisdiction based on the British rock band's "minimal contacts" with the state?

Boxes and Figures

As in earlier editions, the Third Edition contains numerous **boxed inserts** from newspapers, magazines, and journals. These inserts, which appear under the logo "Law and Life," add flavor, depth, and context to class discussions. Many of the inserts are new to this edition. The Bankruptcy chapter, for example, contains recent *Wall Street Journal* articles on the liberal exemptions allowed by Florida law, voidable preferences in the Drexel bankruptcy, and the practical problems faced by a company in a Chapter 11 proceeding.

Also new to this edition are dozens of **figures** that enable students to visualize legal relationships and theories. Transparency masters of these figures are available to instructors for use in class discussion.

Student Aids

In addition to the boxed inserts and figures, this edition contains five new features designed to facilitate the learning process.

1. **Chapter overviews** highlight the organization and coverage at the beginning of each chapter.
2. Chapters are followed by a list of **Key Terms** that students should understand after reading the chapter.

3. Phonetic **pronunciation guides** are included in the text for Latin terms.

4. Each chapter concludes with a series of **Self-Test Questions** in a multiple-choice format. Answers to these questions are included at the end of the chapter.

5. A **Demonstration Problem** in essay form follows the Self-Test Questions, along with a suggested answer. Like the Self-Test Questions, the Demonstration Problem provides students with instant feedback regarding their understanding of the law.

As in earlier editions the text also includes **Chapter Summaries** and numerous end-of-chapter **Problems,** some of which have been reprinted or adapted with permission from the Uniform CPA Examination, Copyright © by the American Institute of Certified Public Accountants.

Manager's Legal Agenda

Students taking business law courses frequently keep the textbook for their personal libraries. A survey of accounting graduates and faculty members, for instance, concluded that the business law textbook is one of the most valued in a personal library (Derstine and Hiltebeitel, 1991). In order to enhance the Third Edition, each unit concludes with a **Manager's Legal Agenda**—a list of practical measures a manager or business can take in order to comply with the law and prevent legal disputes.

Supplementary Materials

In addition to the **transparency masters** described earlier, a detailed **Instructor's Manual** has been prepared by Professors Ilse Hawkins of University of Cincinnati, and Bruce Rockwood of Bloomsburg University. The Instructor's Manual includes several features that will facilitate use of the textbook: case briefs, problem solutions, and an annotated outline containing teaching suggestions and enrichment materials.

The same authors have prepared a **Test Book** containing numerous true/false, multiple-choice and essay questions for each chapter. The test questions are also available from the publisher in a computerized format.

For the student, a **Study Guide** has been prepared by Professors Alvin Stauber and Patrick Maroney of Florida State University. This book contains chapter summaries and a large number of self-test questions in true/false, matching, multiple-choice and essay formats.

Acknowledgments

We wish to thank the following reviewers for their helpful comments and suggestions: Roger Barber, Northern Montana College; Caryn Beck-Dudley, Utah State University; William Bockanic, John Carroll University; Glenn Bogg, Florida State University; Mary Callaway, University of West Florida; Bill Cheek, Embry-Riddle Aeronautical University; John Collis, St. Ambrose University; Robert Congdon, University of Alaska, Anchorage; Carol Docan, California State University, Northridge; Karen Elwell, Bloomsburg University; Ilse Hawkins, University of Cincinnati; Nancy Judy, Front Range Community College; Sandra Linda, University of Delaware; Patrick Maroney, Florida State University; Raymond Matlock, University of Cincinnati; Gail McCracken, University of Michigan, Dearborn; Katrina Miller, Rowan-Cabanis Community College; Neal Phillips, University of Delaware; Durga Prasad, Southern Connecticut State College; Angela Rabatin, Trinity College; Bruce Rockwood, Bloomsburg University; Alvin Stauber, Florida State University; Dan Warner, Western Washington University; Ed Welsh, Phoenix College; John Wheeler, University of Virginia; Linda Wright, Wayne State University; and Neil Young, Florida State University. Special thanks to Jethro K. Lieberman's colleagues at New York Law School for their critical reading of various chapters: Professors Arthur S. Leonard, Park McGinty, Rudolph J. Peritz, Michael Perlin, Edward Samuels, and Marjorie Silver. Thanks also to George J. Siedel's colleague at the University of Michigan, Arthur Southwick.

In addition, we wish to acknowledge the reviewers of earlier editions of this text: Claudia G. Allen, North Carolina State University; Thomas M. Apke, California State University, Fullerton; H. M. Bohlman, Arizona State University; Tracy Dobson, Michigan State University; Mary Jane Dundas, Arizona State University; Charles Foster, North

Texas State University; Donald G. Hall, California State University, Los Angeles; James M. Jackman, Oklahoma State University; James Jurinski, Western Washington University; Edward L. Krehbiel, Grossmont College; Eric L. Richards, Indiana University; George Spiro, University of Massachusetts, Amherst; Frank Vickory, Florida State University; and Gary Watson, California State University, Los Angeles.

We deeply appreciate the support of the editorial and production teams at Harcourt Brace Jovanovich: Ken Rethmeier, Executive Editor; Tim Vertovec, Acquisitions Editor; Paul Raymond, Associate Editor; Sheila Spahn, Manuscript Editor; Leslie Leland, Production Editor; Don Fujimoto, Designer; Judy Frazier, Art Editor, and David Hough, Production Manager. Last, but certainly not least, we wish to acknowledge the research and proofreading assistance of Elizabeth K. Lieberman and Patricia Schaefer.

Jethro K. Lieberman
George J. Siedel

TO THE STUDENT

This book presents the law in two ways—through discussion in plain English of the major themes and rules, and through edited cases that discuss many of the major points in the judges' own words. The cases are integrated with the text, so that you will find each case at the appropriate place in the discussion. You should be aware that every case has been abridged, many considerably abridged (deletions within case opinions are indicated by asterisks and ellipses). If you are interested in reading any case in its entirety, the citations at the head of the case (Appendix A explains how to interpret them) will enable you to find it in any law library.

The Study of Law

As you plunge into the study of law, you will quickly discover some disconcerting features of the subject. The law is not always easy to understand. It requires a good deal of concentration and attention to murky statements sometimes written in an appallingly opaque style. Most of the time your sense that the writing is dense will not be a reflection on you, but on the law. Those who "write the law" are not always the best writers, and half the difficulty of the subject is getting through their prose. We have done our best to simplify and clarify.

Detail

The law, you will discover, is extremely detailed and often at least seemingly fussy and picky. Qualifications pile upon exasperating qualifications, so that some sentences—judges' sentences, not ours, we hope!—are choked with sharp twists and often unfathomable turns. This is not just an idiosyncracy of the writers of the law. The law corresponds to the myriad ways people go about organizing their world, and it would not be useful if it could not distinguish between two similar, but different, situations.

Consider, for example, the ordinary distinctions between interests in property. You may give away your car, or sell it, or loan it, or retain an interest in it. Merely to memorize these distinctions may seem boring, but to understand them is to understand the way in which we organize our lives. What does it mean, for instance, to say that you "own" an automobile? You may have arranged a loan from a bank to pay for it. If you fail to pay off the loan, the bank may repossess it. Do you "own" the car under those circumstances? You may loan the car to a friend for a day or park it in a garage. You may decide to give it away to a friend or to sell it. Does the friend to whom you have given it free as a gift "own" it in the same sense as the stranger to whom you sold it? Does the friend "own" it if you promise to give, but later renege on the promise? When you put your car in a garage, you are surrendering temporary possession but not title. When you sell the car, but agree to keep it in your garage for a month (with permission to use it), you are surrendering title, but not possession. When you borrow to purchase it, your bank or dealer may hold a security interest.

In all these cases, either you or the person to whom you sold or gave it owns the car, but differing consequences may flow from the way in which you disposed of it. These differences are captured in law, and a major part of your study will be to attend to the meaning and utility of the distinctions. And always bear in mind that although the law seems to create these distinctions, in reality it is the necessities of human existence that create them—and that also create the law to deal with them.

The Logic (or Illogic) of the Law

"The life of the law has not been logic; it has been experience," said the often-quoted Justice Holmes. You may find much apparent irrationality in the law—for example, an antitrust policy that forbids actions that injure competition, side-by-side a price-discrimination law that itself appears to injure competition. Law is not a monolith; it is a series of customs, conventions, rules, and aspirations that have been recognized in different places at different times for different circumstances. The law is not always consistent, in part because different judges interpret the law differently, in part because circumstances change, in part because different political majorities can persuade legislators to draw different lines in legislation at different times.

Nevertheless, a deep strain of *reasonableness* undergirds much of American law. Certain laws may be irrational or inconsistent with other laws, but as a whole the enterprise of law, at least as carried on in our time, is fundamentally built on reason. What your common sense tells you ought to be usually is. The difficulties start when the situations become too complex for common sense to guide. Then it is necessary to spend most of your energy trying to understand the situation. The facts are the most important element of any case. Once you understand them—and not until you understand them—will you be able to appreciate the law that is applied to them and to discern whether it makes sense or not.

The Complexity of Legal Relations

Legal relations are complex because law serves more than one purpose simultaneously. A given law or legal policy is directed toward certain people, not toward everyone. It controls certain behavior, not all behavior. It provides for remedies or sanctions. It may be superseded by other law, depending on the circumstances. If applied by a court, the judge's ruling can be appealed, because law is liable to be misinterpreted. There must always be a way to change the law, so no legal policy is ever final and unalterable. All these considerations complicate the study of law.

The Uncertainty of Law

For all the foregoing reasons, in the final analysis, law is never certain. Although statutes appear to be definitive, they are always subject to interpretation. Precedents of the courts are almost always ambiguous because they are couched in language that is capable of an infinite variety of meaning— "reasonable," "substantial," "unconscionable," "restraint of trade." Beware of those who claim to know definitively what the law is, for a simple change of circumstances can change the result when even the plainest law is applied. And much of the law is written in open-ended language that takes on meaning only from case to case. As Justice Holmes said: "General propositions do not decide concrete cases." Moreover, the enterprise of law is so immense—there is so much law—that for every apparently certain statement that one can make about the law (for example, "The contract of a person who is not yet eighteen years old is not binding"), it is usually possible to find another statement of law that will contradict it under some set of facts ("The minor's contract is binding if ratified after becoming eighteen"). Never say never.

The foregoing facets of the law—excessive detail, apparent illogic, complexity, and uncertainty—might appear to make the study of law dismal. They certainly may make the study frustrating. Yet these facets of law are also its great strength, for they mean that the law lives and breathes and is not forever frozen, unable to adapt to changing circumstances. Although we do not always make this point explicitly, it underlies virtually every page in this book.

Four Tips on Studying Law

Don't Argue with the Facts

Throughout this book, you will be presented with both real and hypothetical cases containing certain circumstances, but not others. The purpose of these cases is to study how the law is to be applied. *Don't argue with these facts.* Don't say: "But what if he didn't really agree with the terms of the contract?" (if in the example he did agree) or, "But what if he wasn't driving recklessly?" (if the example requires that he was). The result may certainly be different if the same law is applied to different facts, but the purpose of each example is to understand the law with reference to the facts presented. Once you understand the particular rule, then you may ask yourself—indeed, you ought to ask yourself— "Yes, but suppose the facts were different, what then? Would the rule apply or must the rule be modified?"

Don't Confuse the Legal Rule with the Proof of the Case

Frequently you may be tempted to substitute evidence for law. Don't succumb. Because a case may be difficult to prove does not mean that the law does not really apply as stated to the given facts. This is a corollary of the tip above. For example, a rule of law says that oral contracts for the sale of goods valued at less than $500 are binding. You might be tempted to think: "That's all to the good, but anyone can lie about making a deal, so how can such a contract be binding, for how can the oral agreement be proved?" This book deals in the main with the law, not with the lawyer's practical job of proving a case, although we frequently point out how attention to the practicalities can reap rich dividends. Therefore, if the case example states that an oral agreement was made, do not quarrel with that fact or reject it in your mind, and do not confuse the rule that says the agreement is binding with the admittedly difficult problem of proving at trial that an oral agreement was made. The meaning and application of the law does not depend on the existence of evidence, although winning a case in court usually does. In this book, you can assume that the facts we give are the truth, so that in most of the discussion throughout the text, the evidentiary problem does not arise.

Don't Confuse the Difficulty of Creating Factual Conditions with the Legal Relations That Govern Them

Many of the rules that you will study in this book depend on the existence of certain conditions. To take a simple illustration, the federal Arbitration Act recognizes the validity of a clause in a contract that binds the parties to take a dispute arising out of the contract to a private arbitrator for resolution, rather than to a court. The application of the Arbitration Act obviously depends on the existence of the clause in the contract. Now it may prove impossible for one party to negotiate the clause. The other party may be adamantly against it. Does that mean that the law itself is somehow invalid or not worth studying? Obviously not. We attempt to examine the whole panoply of law that affects business. But quite obviously not every business and not every person will be able to take advantage of every law and legal policy, just as not every business and not every person will be affected by them. The difficulty of conducting a particular business, the inequality of bargaining power, the different

situation from which each person starts, do not invalidate the general rules of the law.

Don't Confuse Certain Laws with Rules People Can Write for Themselves

This tip is a bit different from the others. Certain laws—most prominently, the Uniform Commercial Code—impose obligations *only in the absence of agreement between the parties*. Although we restate this principle at different points in the text, try to bear in mind as you read that not all law is always obligatory. Some law governs regardless of what people have provided for themselves. Two corporate marketing managers may agree not to be bound by the antitrust laws, but that agreement will not avail them one whit when they are prosecuted and thrown in jail for fixing their retail prices. Some law, on the other hand, governs only those situations in which people have not provided for their own rules. For example, the Uniform Commercial Code tells manufacturers that when they sell their goods they extend an implied warranty of fitness—that is, that the goods will be fit for a particular purpose to which they will be put. But the manufacturer may disclaim that warranty—for example, by stating that the goods are sold "as is." If the parties agree to the disclaimer, the Uniform Commercial Code does not apply. If the contract is silent—that is, does not disclaim the warranty—then the Code does apply. The law is not changed, only its application. It is rather like the set of instructions accompanying the board game *Monopoly*. The instructions tell you what the rules are, unless all the players agree to deviate from them.

In the end, these tips are only that. Ultimately, you will need to find your own way, the way that suits you best in mastering the manifold materials of the law. The law is unlike anything you have ever studied before. You may think it at times exasperating and frustrating. But it can also be fascinating and exhilarating. Whatever else it is, it is always very real.

Be patient, and the study will reward each hour you devote to it many times over.

SUMMARY OF CONTENTS

Contents

BUSINESS
LAW AND THE LEGAL
ENVIRONMENT

PART

I

The law touches every interest of man. Nothing that is human is alien to it.
—JUSTICE FELIX FRANKFURTER

The law is the witness and external deposit of our moral life. Its history is the history of the moral development of the race. The practice of it, in spite of popular jests, tends to make good citizens and good men.
—JUSTICE OLIVER WENDELL HOLMES, JR.

THE LEGAL ENVIRONMENT

CHAPTER OVERVIEW

Law and the Legal System

WHAT IS LAW?

The Nature of Law

*L*aw is the instrument that people use to regulate their conduct in civilized society. It is a complex of rules, institutions, and ways of thinking about and interpreting those rules and institutions, that permits civilization to exist and people to live orderly lives. A more precise definition of law is difficult, if not impossible, to give. Philosophers have been debating the nature of law for thousands of years. One line of thought—that of the "positivists"—holds that law is simply the rule-like pronouncements of the sovereign, whether king or a democratically elected legislature. According to another approach—that of the "natural law" philosophers—law is a system of reason, a set of deductions from principles of ethics, morals, or justice. Let us consider an actual case to see where the truth might lie.

Back in the 1840s in Illinois, a farmer named Seeley raised hogs on land next to that of a wheat farmer named Peters. Seeley's farm had no fences, and his hogs were free to roam the countryside. Peters fenced his own property, but poorly, and Seeley's hogs entered through breaks, trampling the crop. Peters sued Seeley, demanding that the court award him **damages** (a legal term meaning a sum of money that will recompense the victim for the injury he has suffered).

The question for the court was what law applied to the circumstances of this case. It should seem clear that some law would apply. If your neighbor breaks down your front door and walks out with your television set, common sense says that you should have a legal means of recovering for the damage done to your door and for the theft of your television. Common sense is right, of course; you are entitled to recover your legal damages. As the ancient maxim had it: for every (legal) wrong there is a remedy.

The case of *Peters* v. *Seeley*, however, was a bit more complex. A law could rationally put liability on the keeper of animals. Equally logically, however, the law could require a wheat farmer to fence his land. The trouble was that no clearly written law expressly declared one rule or the other. Instead, a law of

Illinois enacted in the early part of the nineteenth century declared that the "common law" of England was thenceforth the law in Illinois as well. We consider the nature of common law in some detail later on (pp. 31–40); for now it is sufficient to say that **common law** is the body of court rulings that governs the legal relationships among people in the absence of explicit legislative enactment. The "reception statute"—so called because the law *received* the common law of England into Illinois—did not spell out the rights and duties of hog farmers and wheat farmers toward one another.

To resolve the case, the Illinois Supreme Court began as you would begin. It asked: What is the common law governing the mutual obligations of hog and wheat farmers? The English common law had no specific rule relating to hog and wheat farmers, but it did have a firm rule that if the owner of animals fails to fence them in, he is liable for damages done by them to the property of others. Peters, the wheat farmer, thought that should be the end of the case, for the legislature had declared that the law to be used in Illinois was the common law of England, and by the common law of England, Peters was entitled to damages.

But the court went further with its analysis. The English common law rule had developed in a country where land was scarce and people lived close by one another. In the United States, however, the situation was quite the reverse, and the custom of fencing in animals had never taken hold. The court gave as the reason for this difference in custom the boundless land that the people of Illinois enjoyed. So much land and so little timber was available that "it must be many years yet before our extensive prairies can be fenced," and the grain would rot unless the cattle could feed on it. [Seeley v. Peters, 10 Ill. 130 (1848)][1] The court appeared to override the legislature's law and substituted its own judgment in order to conform law to the conditions and customs of the people in the state; in effect, the court was interpreting the statute to permit it to continue to develop the common law, just as the courts of England had always done. Peters had to fence in his wheat, not Seeley his hogs.

We can see in this example a notion that law is not only the commandment of political authority, but

a statement of rule that must comport in some way with reason and common sense. You might object that the example proves no such thing—that the political authority, in this case, was the court itself and that the law is whatever the court says it is. The noted jurist Oliver Wendell Holmes, Jr., a member of the Massachusetts Supreme Judicial Court for more than twenty years and of the United States Supreme Court for thirty (1902–1932), was of this view. In a lecture given in 1897, he declared (in a passage often quoted):

> Take the fundamental question, What constitutes the law? You will find some text writers telling you that it is something different from what is decided by the courts of Massachusetts or England, that it is a system of reason, that it is a deduction from principles of ethics or admitted axioms or what not, which may or may not coincide with the decisions. But if we take the view of our friend the bad man we shall find that he does not care two straws for the axioms or deduction, but that he does want to know what the Massachusetts or English courts are likely to do. I am much of his mind. *The prophecies of what the courts will do in fact, and nothing more pretentious, are what I mean by the law.* (emphasis added)

Holmes's view was adopted by an influential school of American scholars known as the "legal realists." They wanted to dispense with metaphysical notions of law and study what lawmaking bodies such as legislatures and courts really do.

The difficulty with this viewpoint is that if law is a prophecy of what courts do, then there must be some basis on which to make the prophecy, some underlying set of rules, or else the law is simply the outpouring of a dictator acting on whim. Suppose Seeley's lawyer had told his client: "Your case looks bad, because the common law of England clearly requires you to fence in your hogs. But here in this country the law is really what I can prophesy the courts will do. And I predict that the Illinois Supreme Court will rule in your favor because I am going to transmit to them a large bribe, which you will pay, and it is well known that they rule in favor of bribers." Obviously, this view of the law—that it is whatever anyone can cajole out of a court by any means, fair or foul—is not sustainable. There must be some set of social, political, and moral norms on which law and lawmaking are based. These norms will occupy us throughout most of this chapter and will be reflected in much of the discussion throughout the text.

---

[1] For a description of legal citations and how to read them, see Appendix A at the end of this book.

Law Distinguished from Morals and Justice

In exhorting his listeners to think about what courts actually do, Holmes was not speaking nonsense. He was attempting to clarify an important point in the debate about the nature of law—namely, that law is not the same as "what is right" or "what is just." To be sure, legal principles and principles of morality and justice overlap. Most, but not all, of the Ten Commandments are also legal precepts as well. It is morally wrong to steal and kill; it is also illegal to do so. But it is not unlawful to take the Lord's name in vain, though it may be blasphemous, and the sin of envy is no crime.

Immorality is not always unlawful, and neither is illegality always immoral. The law requires us to drive on the right side of the road, but nothing is intrinsically evil about driving on the left, and the British are not an immoral nation because they follow a different rule.

In general, the law concerns itself with the lowest common denominator of human conduct, not the highest. Law imposes on all of us certain duties and obligations to refrain from interfering with others and from injuring them by our own actions. But it does not require us to act to prevent any harm from befalling another. A common example is that of the drowning person. A child who cannot swim is thrashing about close to shore in a lake next to which you are walking. The child is a stranger to you, and you have nothing to do with the child's being in the water. You could probably save the child simply by wading several feet out, and in any event you are a strong swimmer. But you prefer not to get your Sunday clothes wet, so you walk on, and the child dies. Your failure to rescue the child would rightly be condemned as immoral, but there is no legal duty to save him. In short, the law does not tell us so much to do our best as it does to refrain from doing our worst. However, as **Box 1-1** indicates, one state has changed this ancient rule.

Likewise, law and justice overlap frequently, but not always. It is unjust to punish someone for an act lawful when committed, and the law prohibits the government from doing so. But a law that imposes a penalty of ten years' imprisonment on a starving man who stole a shopping cart full of groceries may be woefully unjust, yet it is nevertheless the law. Legislatures enact many laws that someone thinks are unjust, and courts do not invalidate laws or refuse to enforce them simply because one or more people demonstrate that they are harsh or unfair as applied.

The Language of Law

The law is frequently couched in obscure terms, jargon, and mystifying phraseology. Lawyers like to claim that this is because they write precisely, that their special words are required in order to state exactly the necessary qualifications, exceptions, and distinctions that make up so complex a subject as the law. In part this is true. Every discipline has its special language, and much of it is useful to the initiate. And the language of American law—a curious mixture of Old English, Old French, and a little Latin—is a lot less mystifying, a lot less given to archaisms, than it was even a few decades ago.

Nevertheless, mystifying words continue to abound. Lawyers' prose is often bad. The student who reads through judicial opinions and lawyers' briefs will find much to satisfy a taste for fuzziness. One reason is that, contrary to the usual assertion, the language of law is not so precise. Another is that words are beguiling; unfamiliar words that seem to have a fixed meaning can seduce the lazy or unwary into believing they say more than they do.

One reason for this is that much law is the product of political compromise. Legislators can be cajoled into backing each other's bills if the bills contain language ambiguous enough to let each side suppose it is securing what it wants. In addition, no rule can possibly anticipate every possible set of circumstances. Therefore, lawmakers must resort in most instances to language that is inherently fuzzy: "deceptive," "unreasonable," and "substantial."

Even words that seem to have a fixed meaning can be shown, on close inspection, to be susceptible to varying interpretations. Suppose that you are a legislator who wants to punish those who use guns and other weapons during the commission of a crime. You could specify each type of weapon of which you disapprove: handguns, rifles, shotguns, machine guns, bazookas, and so on. Since it is easy to omit a type you wished to include, you would probably add a phrase such as "and other dangerous weapons." But what is a weapon? Is a stick a weapon? A heavy-duty flashlight? It depends on why you were carrying the

LAW AND LIFE

BOX 1-1

Minnesota Law Mandates Bystander Help in Crises

[*Legal principles and principles of morality and justice overlap. Yet, immoral behavior is not always unlawful. One state, however, has declared being a "Good Samaritan" a duty and those who do not act to assist someone in danger of physical harm will be fined.* —AUTHORS' NOTE]

S T. PAUL, Aug. 2 (AP)—Being a "Good Samaritan" is now a duty, not an option, in Minnesota, where a new provision in state statutes provides up to a $100 fine for people who fail to aid in an emergency.

The amendment to an older law went into effect Monday. It is de-

A STATUTORY DUTY TO ACT

signed to prevent incidents such as one last week in St. Louis, where a 13-year-old girl was raped over 40 minutes by two youths as several people stood by. Police finally were summoned by an 11-year-old boy.

Previously, an expert lifeguard "could watch a 6-month-old baby crawl into the river and drown and sit by and do nothing about it and nothing would happen," said State Representative Randy Staten, an author of the measure. "That is totally unacceptable conduct for civilized society."

Many states have "Good Samaritan" laws that relieve a person of liability when they render aid in an emergency. The amendment to Min-

nesota's law goes a step further by making it a duty to assist.

Linda Close, division manager of public safety and litigation in the Minnesota Attorney General's office, said the amended statute "creates a duty to help somebody if a person is exposed to 'grave physical harm.' "

Mr. Staten, a Minneapolis Democrat, says he believes the statute is the first of its kind in the country, and he said officials from other states appear interested in enacting similar laws. The amendment was prompted by incidents far from Minnesota, he said, citing the rape of a woman on a pool table in New Bedford, Mass., as a group of people watched, and the Kitty Genovese case of many years ago, in which the Queens, N.Y., woman was fatally stabbed as people watched from apartment windows.

Source: *New York Times*, August 3, 1983

---

item and to what use it was put. No definitive list can be given.

Ultimately, any attempt to define with precision conduct that is to be outlawed must fail. A society in which all rules were absolute, stated without room for maneuver, would be an intolerable place to live for any who value freedom because the rules would almost invariably be overinclusive and restrictive. As Judge Jerome Frank noted in *Law and the Modern Mind* (1963, p. 7), "Much of the uncertainty of law is not an unfortunate accident: it is of immense social value."

Nevertheless, the uncertainty that arises through sheer linguistic sloppiness and unconscious semantic confusion is not of immense social value; to the contrary, it is of no value. Beginning in the late 1970s, a "plain English" movement to overcome the purely linguistic mystification of law gathered steam. Some simplification has resulted, though far from enough. Beginning with New York, a few states at the same time began to pass laws requiring contracts with con-

sumers—insurance policies and leases, for example—to be written in straightforward language.

CLASSIFICATION OF TYPES OF LAW

Because the "law" has so many different connotations, there is no one way to classify the different types of law. What follows is a simple fourfold classification scheme that presents law along its major dimensions: substantive, jurisdictional, governmental type, and procedural (see Figure 1-1).

The Major Types of Substantive Law

Substantive law deals with the different ways people interact. On a family tree of law the broadest "kingdoms" are criminal and civil law. These are substantive branches of law because they deal with human conduct. **Criminal law** (Chapter 3) is that body of law

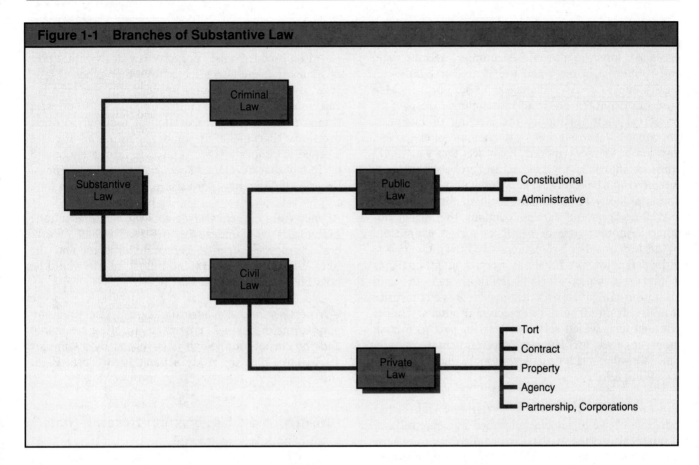

Figure 1-1   Branches of Substantive Law

that deals with violations of public order, including violent crimes (such as murder, rape, assault, and robbery), crimes against property (larceny, embezzlement), and crimes consisting of infractions of regulatory codes (income tax fraud, securities fraud, and the like). Penalties for violation of the criminal law include death, imprisonment, and monetary fines. Serious crimes, usually those punishable by imprisonment of more than one year, are called *felonies;* less serious crimes are *misdemeanors.*

Civil law governs the private relations among individuals. It might also be defined as all branches of the law not included within the criminal law. ("Civil" has a different connotation in legal systems outside the Anglo-American tradition—in those countries, the civil law refers to codes enacted by the national legislatures.

Civil law can be divided into two main branches. One is **public law**—for example, constitutional law (pp. 12–31) and administrative law (Chapter 5)—so

called because this branch (along with criminal law) deals with the relations between government and private citizens and organizations. The most significant development in twentieth-century American law is the growth of administrative or regulatory law. Examples in this category include *labor law*—the relations between unions, their members, and their employers (Chapter 51); *antitrust law*—the appropriate form of competition (Chapters 46–48); *securities law*—the code governing trading in corporate stocks (Chapter 44); and *tax law*—how the government raises money to pay for its activities.

The other principal branch is private law, which is the set of laws that spell out the duties, obligations, and responsibilities that individuals and organizations owe to each other. Within the sphere of private law are the following:

Tort Law   The word **"tort"** derives from Old French, meaning a wrong or injustice, substantially the connotation it carries today. Tort law spells out the duties of care that one person owes to another. Many *intentional* torts are also crimes: murder, assault, rape, and robbery are torts, and the victim or family can legally sue to recover damages. Other torts include false imprisonment (akin to kidnapping), trespass on property, theft (including the stealing of business, known as *unfair competition*), defamation of character, invasion of privacy—indeed, most acts that you would consider injurious to another are probably torts. A tort need not be intentional. The biggest class of tort lawsuits today—automobile accident litigation—involves *negligent*, or careless, actions that harm another. (Another type of negligent tort is *malpractice* by doctors or other professionals.) During the 1970s, a third type of tort involving neither intentional nor negligent conduct—*strict liability*—began to gain ground in the courts as a means of redressing injuries resulting from all sorts of defective products. Unlike criminal law, which serves at least in part to punish the wrongdoer, tort law serves to compensate the victim. We will consider tort law in more detail in Chapters 4 and 19.

Contract Law   Tort law spells out the rights that individuals have to remain unharmed by wrongful acts of others. It is the law that creates the duty to refrain from wrongful conduct. But people may also create their own sets of obligations toward each other by entering into contracts. A contract may impose upon an individual a liability that he would not otherwise legally have. Sometimes a contract can relieve an individual from a liability that he would have under tort law. Contract law is discussed in Part Two.

Property Law   A third category of private law is that which deals with property. In a narrow sense, the law of property deals with land and buildings (called *real property*) and personal possessions (called *personal property*). The law of real property concerns the rights of buyers, sellers, lessors, and lessees of land, houses, and other buildings (Chapters 33–34). The law of personal property deals with a range of issues that arise from the way we use our belongings—for example, the temporary possession of an automobile by a parking garage (bailment), the way we give control of money or other assets to family members or others (trusts), how we dispose of property after a death (wills and estates), and how we protect the fruits of an in-

vention (patent, trademark, and copyright, Chapter 31).

In a broader sense, property law deals with a host of issues that are also affected by other types of law. It is usually closely bound up with contract law, because much of what we contract about has to do with property. Control and operation of the myriad organizations that make up modern industrial life are steeped in property law but also are intimately bound up in law that developed specifically for this purpose; these include *agency, partnership,* and *corporation law.*

Agency Law   Agency law treats the relations among individuals who undertake to act on behalf of others—employees, agents, corporate officers, and the like. Without agency law, no industrial life would be possible. We study it in Part Seven.

Partnership and Corporation Law   The predominant forms of business enterprise are the partnership and the corporation. Each is governed by a complex set of laws that we study separately in Parts Eight and Nine.

Jurisdictional Classification: Federal, State, Local, and International

Law, as we use the term, is not a monolith. It does not spring whole from a single source, like the pronouncements of some autocratic king. Modern law is a complex affair that comes from a variety of political entities, defined both geographically and institutionally.

Geographically, law comes from several types of "jurisdictions"—that is, governments. In the United States, with its complex form of federalism, there are three types of government: federal, state, and local. The first two are semi-sovereign; the last, local government, is dependent on the other two.

Federal Law   The **federal government** is the national government, with the power to make law for the country as a whole, though its lawmaking power does not extend to everything over which government is capable of making law. The federal government consists of Congress, which functions as the national legislature; the executive branch, headed by the president and including governmental departments and administrative agencies; and the federal courts, or judicial branch. Within its sphere, federal law is superior to that of state and local law.

State Law The second semi-sovereign form of government is that of **state government.** The states also have legislative, executive, and judicial branches. Their legal power does not spring from the federal government but is rooted independently in the Constitution. Both federal and state governments are said to be "semi-sovereign" because, despite the persistence of the myth, there simply is no such thing as sovereignty in the United States—no law need forever be so, no person or institution is supreme. In our system of checks and balances, there is always a means of challenging law and political action.

Local Law The third form of government is not, however, even semi-sovereign. This is **local government:** cities, towns, villages, counties, and other political districts within the states. The powers of these governments are delegated by the states and may be modified, limited, or removed by the states. To the extent that it is authorized to do so, local government also creates law (in the form of municipal ordinances and regulations).

International Law This law is created by international organizations, by the customs and practices that prevail among nations, and by agreement. However, to the extent that international law is applicable within the United States, it is so generally because the nation has entered into *treaties* with other countries and the treaties are enforceable as part of federal law.

Law Classified by Governmental Branch Creating It

For historical as well as legal reasons, there are differences between law that comes from a legislature and law that emanates from other governmental bodies. Implicit in much of the discussion in this book is the relationship between the courts and the other branches and how that relationship affects the meaning and enforcement of law.

Statutes A law enacted by a legislature is called a *statute*. It is written and published in various forms.

Regulations Laws emanating from the executive branch—the source of administrative law—are called *regulations* or *rules;* they too are written and published. The executive branch generally derives its power to promulgate regulations and rules from the legislature. Neither statutes nor regulations stand alone. They must often be interpreted by the courts. A judicial gloss on a statute or regulation rendered in the course of a lawsuit is in effect the meaning of the statute or regulation. In most cases, members of the legislature or executive agency can always amend the statute or regulation after the court has ruled, if they are dissatisfied with the court's interpretation. The amendment will then apply to future cases.

Common Law The courts also produce a third kind of law, known as the *common law* or *unwritten law.* "Unwritten" is a misnomer; in fact, the common law has always been written down more or less, in the reports of the courts' decisions in individual cases. The vast body of judicial *opinions* constitutes the written record of the common law. Shortly, we will explore in some detail the authority of the courts to fashion the common law. For now it is enough to note that the authority is not a delegated one; it is inherent and assigned by the Constitution to the judiciary. The common law is not the exclusive province of the courts, however. The legislature may intrude and enact legislation modifying or even abolishing common law rules laid down by courts. The courts in turn have the authority to interpret the statutes that do so.

Substantive vs. Procedural Law

Still another way to classify law is by the person, group, organization, or institution to which it is addressed. Law addressed to actions and relationships among people is **substantive law.** Law that structures government by laying down procedures on how it must act—especially that which relates to the courts themselves—is known as **procedural law** or **adjective law.** For the most part, we will be concerned with that part of procedural law that shapes the legal-judicial process: how lawsuits begin and move through the courts. Every court system has its own rules of procedure, and there are often significant differences in procedure among different courts within the same system. Thus, the Federal Rules of Civil Procedure, promulgated by the Supreme Court and approved by Congress, apply to all federal courts. But each local federal court has its own set of supplementary rules with which lawyers—but not their clients—must be familiar.

SOURCES OF LAW

However law is defined and classified, it is a product of human institutions. At different times, different institutions—legislatures, courts, regulatory bodies, ad hoc conventions—create or shape laws that have varying imports and impacts on the population. Amid all this lawmaking, there are four general sources of law.

Constitutional Law

The United States Constitution is the supreme law of the land. No other law takes precedence over it, and any law that is inconsistent with it is invalid and void. In legal theory, the Constitution derives from "the people," though of necessity it was drafted by a committee of the people—those who attended the Constitutional Convention of 1787—and ratified by the people through special conventions in each state called for that purpose. We examine the Constitution in more detail later.

Although the federal Constitution is supreme, it is not the only constitution. Each state has its own. State constitutions play precisely the same role within the state that the federal Constitution plays nationally. Cities and certain other forms of municipal government have "charters" granted by the states. These charters are akin to constitutions for the municipalities.

Statutes

Statutes—the enactments of legislatures—have become our most fertile source of law during the twentieth century. Congress, the state legislatures, and city councils (whose ordinances are akin to statutes) have legislated on virtually every imaginable subject, including the conduct of war, the structure of gov-

ernment, national price controls, environmental protection, economic relations, retirement benefits, civil rights, rent control—the list is endless.

In general, there are four types of statutes. A legislature may declare a particular act or type of conduct to be unlawful and subject to severe sanctions, such as imprisonment and substantial fines. Such statutes fall within the criminal law. A statute may establish standards for judging conduct or spelling out relations between individuals and groups. For example, the legislature may decide that in automobile accident lawsuits, the negligence of the defendant must be weighed against that of the plaintiff. Such statutes fall within the realm of civil law. Or a statute may establish a governmental body or restructure an existing one and delegate to it the power to promulgate specific rules for the regulation of an industry or type of activity. Frequently, all three types of enactment are combined within a single statute—for example, environmental-protection statutes prescribe standards that people and companies must follow, permit certain classes of people to sue civilly if the standards are not followed, prescribe criminal penalties for some violations, and grant existing and new agencies the power to police the environment. The fourth type of statute is that which raises tax revenues and spends the public monies.

Administrative Law

As we have seen, administrative agencies of the executive branch of the federal and state governments promulgate rules and regulations, pursuant to power delegated by the legislatures. From at least the middle of this century, administrative law has probably been the most voluminous. Unless the agencies go beyond the scope of the power delegated to them, the rules they announce have the full force of law and are entitled to equal weight with statutes when the courts are called upon to enforce them.

Unwritten Law: The Common Law

The Constitution, statutes, and administrative law are all "written." The exact text of the rules can be consulted because they have all been published and are more or less easily accessible. But there is a vast body of law that has been called "unwritten" because it is not embodied in statutes and regulations. As we have noted, this is the *common law*, the body of law that emanates from courts and that in fact is written down in the judges' opinions in the cases they decide. To understand why there is common law, let us consider three basic functions that courts perform.

The first function is "fact-finding." Did the accused kill the victim, as charged by the prosecutor? Did the defendant promise to complete construction on the plaintiff's house by June 30? The courts sift lies from truth and attempt to sort through the ambiguities. Someone has to perform this critical function; the courts, with their elaborate procedural protections for the claimants who appear before them, do so.

The second function is "law-applying." Suppose the plaintiff, a wholesale buyer of canned tomatoes, claims that a statute gives him the right to return a defective shipload to the seller. The seller retorts that the plaintiff's interpretation of the statute is incorrect and demands the purchase price. The court must decide what the statute means and whether it applies in the circumstances of the case before it.

In most cases, both fact-finding and law-applying are required. When there is a jury, it will be responsible not only for determining what the true state of affairs was but also for applying the law to the facts. It does this by following the judge's instructions on the law. After most jury verdicts, the case is at an end. The result is a decision for one side or the other, without elaboration of the reasons. But when there is no jury, or when a case is appealed to a higher court, there will usually be a written opinion by the judge. This opinion will often be published and will usually contain a statement about the meaning of the statute in question. This opinion is significant, because it too is a source of law.

By placing its own interpretation on the literal language of a statute, the court is adding something to the law and saddling it with a meaning for the future—unless the legislature chooses to amend the statute in view of the court's decision. Those who would "look up" a statute should be wary: rarely can anyone know what the law means simply by perusing the language in the statute books, because anywhere from a handful to hundreds of published judicial opinions may interpret a particular statutory provision. These decisions cannot be disregarded, for in future cases judges will look to them as precedents to be followed.

The third type of judicial function does not involve a statute; it involves deciding whether a plaintiff's common law rights have been violated. As noted earlier, the common law is a body of legal principles enunciated by courts in the absence of statute during the past several centuries. It is not written in the statutory sense because each principle, with its corollaries and exceptions, is not set forth in one place. Rather, each principle is stated, often in lengthy prose, in judicial opinions discussing a particular case.

Where do these principles come from? The debate has been long, learned, and unending. Some say they come from God, others from reason. Still others suppose that the principles derive from the "character of the people." It seems rather more likely that the common law is a tapestry woven from age-old customs, modified by experience and new conditions, and tempered by the dictates of reason and the promptings of moral concern—and sometimes by the biases and prejudices of judges, who, after all, are the oracles of the common law.

In short, judges make law. They have made most of tort law and contract law, although large portions of contract law have been superseded by the Uniform Commercial Code and other statutes. Many rules embodied in statutes are simply articulations of common law principles. Equally important, the rules that courts use to guide them in interpreting statutes are common law rules. Inherent in the judicial power of the courts is the power to determine how to interpret.

Because the courts over the years have written millions of opinions, the search for common law principles in library stacks would be arduous. To overcome this difficulty, and to help bring order and rationality to the many conflicting decisions (for judges frequently disagree with each other), a group of lawyers and academicians—members of a private group called the American Law Institute—sat down in the 1920s to write what has become a series of "Restatements." The first was the *Restatement of the Law of Contracts*, published in 1932 after years of drafting and redrafting. Work began on its successor, *Restatement (Second) of Contracts*, in 1964; it was finally completed and published in 1981. Other Restatements include those on torts, agency law, remedies, and trusts.

The Restatements are not the law. They are statements of the law, in statutelike form, written by private citizens. But they have been extremely influential in helping to spark debate and to shape the law. They are frequently cited by judges in their opinions, and we will encounter their provisions frequently in this book.

PURPOSES OF THE U.S. CONSTITUTION

"The American Constitution is the most wonderful work ever struck off at a given time by the brain and purpose of man," British Prime Minister William Ewart Gladstone is reputed to have said, and so it very well might be. It is short, readable, and durable. Its seven articles and the Bill of Rights, as supplemented by sixteen other amendments, have endured for nearly two centuries, making it the oldest living written constitution in the world.

The Constitution performs two fundamental legal tasks: it structures the government, and it imposes limitations on the government's power to act.

The Structure of the Government

Articles I, II, and III of the Constitution set forth the structure and powers of the three branches of the federal government, as well as methods of electing or appointing officials to offices within these branches.

The first article, reflecting the Founding Fathers' belief in its paramountcy, deals with Congress, the national legislature. To Congress are given "all legislative powers herein granted." Among other powers, Congress has the authority to regulate money, enact uniform bankruptcy laws, borrow on the credit of the United States, regulate interstate and foreign commerce, and "make all laws which shall be necessary and proper for carrying into execution the foregoing powers, and all other powers vested by this Constitution in the government of the United States, or in any department or officer thereof." Not surprisingly, this "necessary and proper" clause has been called the "elastic clause."

The second article of the Constitution vests the "executive power" in the president, spells out certain functions the chief executive must perform, and enumerates a few specific roles he must play (for example, commander in chief of the military).

The third article vests "the judicial power" in the Supreme Court and "in such inferior courts as the Congress may from time to time ordain and establish."

In vesting the legislative, executive, and judicial powers in separate branches of government, the makers of the Constitution adopted the principle of "separation of powers." The theory, derived from the writings of the French social philosopher Baron de Montesquieu, is that freedom can be preserved by separating the types of governmental authority among the branches of government, which will check and balance each other, preventing any one branch from becoming too strong. It is noteworthy that the Constitution does not define "legislative," "executive," or "judicial" power. We could say that the legislative power is the power to make law, the executive power the power to carry it out, and the judicial power the power to decide cases arising under the laws. But that is too simple a view. The fact is that the powers overlap. Each branch has influence over the others. The president can veto congressional enactments and appoint judges. Congress can create executive departments. The courts can, in effect, make laws through statutory interpretation. Nor is it easy to see how it could be otherwise. But this fact makes the statement and understanding of law difficult because the law is subject to so many pressures and changes from so many directions.

The fourth article of the Constitution deals briefly with the states. It does not create the states; it accepts them as given. Under the terms of this article, each state must give "full faith and credit" to the "public acts, records, and judicial proceedings" in all the other states.

The fifth article deals with methods of amending the Constitution.

The sixth article embodies the Supremacy Clause, stated here in full: "The Constitution, and the Laws of the United States which shall be made in Pursuance thereof; and all Treaties made, or which shall be made, under the Authority of the United States, shall be the supreme Law of the Land; and the Judges in every State shall be bound thereby, any Thing in the Constitution or Laws of any State to the Contrary notwithstanding." This critical clause establishes a hierarchy of law and permits some order to be fashioned out of a republic in which dual jurisdictions frequently clash.

The seventh article provided for the ratification of the Constitution and is no longer operative.

Since 1789, when these original seven articles became effective, twenty-six amendments have been adopted. The first ten, the Bill of Rights, were adopted in 1791, in response to cries during the ratification debate that the articles insufficiently protected individual freedom. Most others deal with the structure of government, specifically concerning the right to vote and election of the president. The Thirteenth Amendment abolished slavery. The Sixteenth gave Congress the power to enact an income tax. The Eighteenth—Prohibition—was repealed by the Twenty-first. Of all the subsequent amendments, only the Fourteenth has had an immense legal as well as political impact on the nation, as noted later in this chapter.

Constitutional Limitations

In the United States, government is not sovereign; in legal theory the people are. The Constitution establishes several important limitations on the powers of government, both federal and state, to enact and enforce laws that would interfere with individual liberty.

Article I prohibits both federal and state governments from enacting any "bills of attainder" or "ex post facto" laws. A bill of attainder is a statute that imposes a penalty on a named individual. It is a means that was exercised by British monarchs to avoid trial and was universally condemned. An ex post facto law is one outlawing a particular act already performed. It too was a means of jailing persons whom the government disliked, and was likewise condemned. (A retroactive tax law, changing the tax rates or imposing new taxes on income, sales, or other activities that have already taken place, is not considered ex post facto and is not barred by the Constitution.) Article I also prohibits the federal and state governments from preferring one port of entry to another. Interstate shipments of goods are not subject to import duties, nor are foreign imports or exports subject to duties

by the states. Finally, the states—but not the federal government—are prohibited from "impairing the obligation of contracts."

Article VI prohibits any religious test from being administered to any official of the federal or state governments.

The remainder of the significant limitations on government appear in the Bill of Rights and the Fourteenth Amendment. Most of these limitations are concerned with rights of the accused in criminal trials and are explored in Chapter 3. The rest—the "preferred freedoms" of the First Amendment and the important principles of due process and equal protection of the law—we consider shortly.

Judicial Review

Before turning to these critical constitutional rights, it will be useful to consider the mechanisms by which they are secured to us as individuals. The Constitution is, after all, but a piece of paper, preserved in chemicals and under glass at the National Archives in Washington, D.C. Suppose Congress enacts a law that conflicts with a provision in the Constitution. What then?

The short answer is that we possess the right to challenge actions of the government in lawsuits—either by raising constitutional objections if we are defendants or by pleading constitutional rights as plaintiffs. If the courts conclude that the constitutional provision and the statute conflict, they are required to invalidate the statute and give priority to the Constitution. This authority is known as **judicial review**, and it distinguishes the legal system of the United States from that of every other nation in the world. Through its power to review, the U.S. Supreme Court becomes embroiled to an extent unknown by courts outside the United States in the most difficult and delicate questions of public policy. As Alexis de Tocqueville noted in a celebrated line in his *Democracy in America* (1835): "There is hardly a political question in the United States which does not sooner or later turn into a judicial one."

How the federal courts, and the Supreme Court in particular, came to claim and use this power is an oft-told tale, but one that bears repeating. In 1800, John Adams, a Federalist and advocate of strong central government, was defeated for reelection by Thomas Jefferson, an anti-Federalist whose sympathy lay toward local government. In January 1801, when the Chief Justice's seat on the Supreme Court opened up, President Adams appointed John Marshall, then secretary of state, and the Federalist Senate promptly confirmed him. Five days before the end of Adams's term, Congress rushed through a bill creating judgeships in the District of Columbia, and Adams appointed forty-two justices of the peace. The Senate confirmed the nominees on Adams's last day of office. Commissioning papers needed to be signed by the President to make their appointments official, and so into the evening Adams signed the documents (thus the term "midnight judges"). In the rush, four commissions were never dispatched. Thomas Jefferson found them the next day and forbade them to be delivered.

One of the disappointed men, William Marbury, went to the Supreme Court in December 1801 and filed suit, asserting that he was entitled to his office. He sought a *writ of mandamus* (man DAY mus), a judicial order directing a government official to take a specific action—in this case, an order to James Madison, then secretary of state, to hand over the commission to Marbury.

The Supreme Court's answer in the case of *Marbury* v. *Madison,* in an opinion by Chief Justice Marshall, was a bombshell and remains both the classic statement of the principle of judicial review and the classic example of judicial statesmanship. Marshall said that three questions had been raised. (1) Did Marbury have a right to the judicial commission he demanded? (2) If Marbury had a right to it and that right was violated, did the laws of the United States afford him a remedy? (3) If they did afford him a remedy, was it by a "mandamus issuing from the Supreme Court"?

The first two questions Marshall answered in the affirmative: (1) Marbury had been properly nominated and confirmed by the Senate, and nothing more was necessary to make Marbury a judge. (2) "The very essence of civil liberty certainly consists in the right of every individual to claim the protection of the laws, whenever he receives an injury." The law required Madison to deliver the commission, and officers of the government are bound by the law. The proper method of compelling a government official to obey the law is by a writ of mandamus.

The third question, however, Marshall answered in the negative. Marbury had a legal remedy, but the *Supreme Court* could not *constitutionally* provide it. The Judiciary Act of 1789 authorized the Supreme Court to issue writs of mandamus "in cases warranted by the principles and usages of law . . . to persons holding office under the authority of the United States." That law certainly would permit the Court to mandamus Madison, unless the law itself was invalid. The problem, Marshall said, was that Article III of the Constitution did not give the Supreme Court **original jurisdiction** over such a case. That is, in all but a rare category of cases the Constitution prohibits the Supreme Court from conducting trials, determining the facts, and applying the law to them; it can only hear appeals from trials conducted by lower courts. This prohibition certainly applied to Marbury's case. Yet here was Marbury appearing before the Supreme Court, asking it to hold a trial and issue a remedy. This, Marshall said, the Supreme Court could not do. Marbury would have to find another court to issue the writ of mandamus.

Although the Supreme Court would not strike down another federal statute for fifty-four years (and when it did, in *Dred Scott* v. *Sandford,* 19 How. 393 [1857], it foreordained the Civil War), judicial review became a fixed legal principle from which the courts have never deviated.

However, not every constitutional question pressed upon the courts, especially the Supreme Court, will receive an answer. There are a number of limitations, some constitutional and some prudential, on the power and willingness of the courts to decide constitutional issues. As summarized by Supreme Court Justice Louis D. Brandeis, here is a series of rules by which the courts try to avoid the necessity of making declarations about constitutionality:

1. The Court will not pass upon the constitutionality of legislation in a friendly, nonadversary proceeding.
2. The Court will not anticipate a question of constitutional law in advance of the necessity of deciding it.
3. The Court will not formulate a rule of constitutional law broader than is required by the precise facts to which it is to be applied.
4. The Court will not pass upon a constitutional question although properly presented by the rec-

ord, if there is also present some other ground upon which the case may be disposed of.

5. The Court will not pass upon the validity of a statute upon complaint of one who fails to show that he is injured by its operation.

6. The Court will not pass upon the constitutionality of a statute at the instance of one who has availed himself of its benefits.

7. When the validity of an act of the Congress is drawn in question, and even if a serious doubt of constitutionality is raised, it is a cardinal principle that this Court will first ascertain whether a construction of the statute is fairly possible by which the question may be avoided. [Ashwander v. Tennessee Valley Authority, 297 U.S. 288 (1937)]

These principles have their roots in *Marbury* v. *Madison*. Note that Chief Justice Marshall decided the other legal questions before passing on to the constitutional question of mandamus.

The Fourteenth Amendment

In the 1780s when the Constitution was adopted, the people did not so much fear government power as they did *central* government. Hence limitations in the Constitution, which established the national government, were for the most part applicable only to the national government. This was particularly true of the Bill of Rights, the first ten amendments adopted for the specific purpose of limiting central power. Thus the Fifth Amendment says that no person shall be denied life, liberty, or property without due process of law, but that provision did not bar the states from doing so. Many, but not all, of the states had substantially similar constitutional provisions.

This situation changed dramatically after the Civil War. In its 1857 *Dred Scott* decision, the Supreme Court had ruled that blacks could not become citizens of the United States. In 1868, with the ratification of the Fourteenth Amendment, this historical injustice was cured. Thenceforth, all persons born in the United States were automatically citizens.

The Fourteenth Amendment did not stop there. It went on to impose a significant restraint on state governments. The amendment says that no state may "deprive any person of life, liberty, or property,

without due process of law; nor deny to any person within its jurisdiction the equal protection of the laws." These words heralded an immense shift in the relationship of the states and federal government, and in time gave significant power to the federal courts, for the law meant that sooner or later people could bring suit in federal court testing the actions of state governments under the amendment.

That testing began in the 1870s and has not abated. The twists and turns of the legal doctrines that have developed fill several hundred volumes. All that we will note here is that during the past century the Supreme Court has gradually incorporated into the Fourteenth Amendment most of the various protections in the original Bill of Rights, so that the restraints that operate against the federal government for the most part operate as well against the states.

CONSTITUTIONAL LAW AND BUSINESS

Regulating Business: Federal Regulation of Interstate Commerce

The federal Constitution was written in large part because the states proved inept, after the Revolution, at regulating commerce. Each state looked to its own advantages—imposing export duties and other taxes, creating monopolies for local industry, and otherwise interfering with a truly national market. To overcome the petty jealousies of the states and their natural incentives to legislate on behalf of their own industries, the Constitution gives to Congress the power to regulate interstate and foreign commerce. This power is located in the *Commerce Clause* of Article I, which reads: "The Congress shall have Power: . . . To regulate Commerce with foreign Nations, and among the several States, . . ."

In the early years of the nation, the states originated the only business regulations, which were minimal. But in two important cases, Chief Justice Marshall embraced a nationalistic interpretation of Article I that opened the way to a broad federal power. In the first, *McCulloch* v. *Maryland* [4 Wheat. 316 (1819)], Marshall held that Congress had the power to incorporate a national bank, even though the Constitution does not spell out the power in so many words. Pointing to the clause in Article I that allows Congress to enact laws that are "necessary and proper," Marshall reasoned that Congress had great leeway in determining how it would carry out any of the powers the Constitution had given it: "Let the end be legitimate, let it be within the scope of the constitution, and all means which are appropriate, which are plainly adapted to that end, which are not prohibited, but consistent with the letter and spirit of the constitution, are constitutional."

Five years later, in *Gibbons* v. *Ogden* [6 Wheat. 1 (1824)], Marshall ruled that New York State could not grant a monopoly to operate steamboats on the state waterways. The grant (copied in other states that sought to retaliate) was intended to prevent shippers from delivering goods to and from New Jersey without securing a license from the monopolists.

The state made two arguments: first, that navigation was not part of "commerce," and, therefore, Congress could not regulate it, and second, that even if navigation was a part of "commerce," it was not part of commerce "among the states."

The first argument was that the term "commerce" is limited to buying and selling. "Navigation" is not a commercial activity itself but implies the mere carrying of commodities. Marshall responded that there was no warrant in the Constitution for narrowly reading the term "commerce" and that, indeed, the federal power to regulate navigation was "one of the primary objects for which the people of America adopted their government."

New York argued also that navigation was a local matter, not within the interstate commerce power, because navigation begins entirely within the state. Marshall responded that all commerce begins that way; there are no spaces between the states. Federal regulation of commerce may reach into local matters as long as the regulation is aimed at commerce that is not itself purely local but involves trade among the states.

In the steamboat case, Marshall pointed to a congressional enactment providing for licensing of those engaged in plying the coastal waterways. The Chief Justice ruled that the federal law was well within the federal interstate commerce power, and since there was a federal law on the subject, state laws that conflicted with it (by establishing state monopolies) were unconstitutional under the Supremacy Clause. This ruling in *Gibbons* and in other cases kept open the

flow of commerce among the states by barring state restrictions that conflicted with federal law.

With the explosive growth of industry, transportation, and national commerce in the late nineteenth century, a considerable constitutional problem arose as Congress sought to control the effects of industrial combinations and monopolies. How far does the federal commerce power extend into matters that have always been considered local? At first, the Supreme Court was inclined to narrow the scope of federal power. For example, in 1895 in an important test of the Sherman Antitrust Act, the Court dismissed a federal prosecution of the giant American Sugar Refining Company, even though the company, by acquiring other companies, controlled 98 percent of the nation's sugar refining capacity. The Court reasoned that "manufacturing" was a local activity and could never be part of interstate "commerce." [United States v. E. C. Knight Co., 1956 U.S. 1 (1985)]

But the Court soon reversed itself. For example, early in the twentieth century, the Court held that federal agencies had power to control state activities that interfered with prices on the national market. [The Shreveport Rate Case, 234 U.S. 342 (1914)] It also held that federal agencies could regulate charges and practices of such activities as stockyards because they were not the final resting place of commodities but "a throat through which the current [of commerce] flows." [Stafford v. Wallace, 258 U.S. 495 (1922)] The Court also held that Congress could prohibit the flow across state lines of illicit goods—for example, lottery tickets and adulterated foodstuffs. [Champion v. Ames, 188 U.S. 321 (1903); Hipolite Egg Co. v. United States, 220 U.S. 45 (1911)]

By the first third of this century, the immense growth in the American economy and the almost miraculous development of technology made it difficult to find any purely local commerce. With the Depression, Congress began to realize how interdependent the American economy had become and increasingly asserted jurisdiction to regulate a host of commercial interests—including transportation, trade, production, and employment—and competitive practices generally.

By the 1940s, a new theory had emerged from the cases: if a business action "affected" interstate commerce, Congress could regulate it. Large numbers of employees, for example, worked for companies that sold goods throughout the country. Was this connection sufficient to give Congress jurisdiction to enact national wage and hours standards? In the Fair Labor Standards Act of 1938, Congress set up a comprehensive scheme that prevented manufacturers from shipping certain products in interstate commerce unless they complied with minimum wage and maximum hour standards. In 1941, the Supreme Court dismissed a constitutional challenge to the law: "Congress may . . . by appropriate legislation regulate intrastate activities where they have a substantial effect on interstate commerce." [United States v. F. W. Darby Lumber Co., 312 U.S. 100 (1941)]

In the very next year, the Court upheld an application of the Agricultural Adjustment Act of 1938 to a farmer who harvested 239 bushels of wheat more than he was allotted under the act. Most of the excess wheat was consumed on the farm as food for his family and animals and was used as seed for the next year's crop. The farmer asserted that his use of the wheat was purely local, hence not within the power of Congress to reach. The Court disagreed: "Even if [the farmer's] activity be local and though it may not be regarded as commerce, it may still, whatever its nature, be reached by Congress if it exerts a substantial economic effect on interstate commerce, and this irrespective of whether such effect is what might at some earlier time have been defined as 'direct' or 'indirect'." [Wickard v. Filburn, 317 U.S. 111 (1942)] Neatly summing up the congressional commerce power in 1949, Justice Robert H. Jackson said: "If it is interstate commerce that feels the pinch, it does not matter how local the operation that applies the squeeze."

Today, the commerce power is nearly coexten-sive with the desire of the federal government to regulate private economic activity. Through dozens of agencies, the federal government oversees the national markets in securities and commodities; regulates rates and practices in communications, transportation, power generation and transmission; and sets national minimum wages and standards for millions of employees in interstate businesses. So broad is the commerce power that it has even been used to reach into the civil rights arena, once thought to be within the exclusive domain of the states by virtue of the *Civil Rights Cases* of 1883. The Court had ruled that Congress had no constitutional power to ban private acts of discrimination. But in the 1960s, finally moved to end the ancient indignities heaped upon blacks in America, Congress enacted a series of civil rights laws. One of them prohibited discrimination in public accommodations—the very subject of the law that the Court had struck down in 1883. This time Congress rested its power on the Commerce Clause, and the Supreme Court upheld the law, thus confirming congressional power to deal with private acts of racial discrimination in the economic arena. [Heart of Atlanta Motel v. United States, 379 U.S. 241 (1964)]

Recently, the Court has demonstrated anew that little commercial activity can escape the regulatory power of Congress. At issue in the following case was the power of Congress to outlaw arson, usually considered a purely local crime. The law under which the defendant had been convicted banned arson and attempted arson in any building used in interstate commerce or in any activity affecting interstate commerce. The defendant had tried to burn down a two-unit Chicago apartment.

RUSSELL v. UNITED STATES[1]
471 U.S. 858 (1985)

JUSTICE STEVENS delivered the opinion for the Court.

The question presented is whether 18 U.S.C. § 844(i) applies to a two-unit apartment building that is used as rental property.

Petitioner owns an apartment building located at 4530 South Union, Chi-

(*continued on next page*)

[1] Many court decisions discuss more than one issue of law; in order to focus specifically on the issues at hand, all cases in this text have of necessity been abridged. Asterisks within cases indicate that a paragraph or more has been deleted; deletions of less than a paragraph are indicated by ellipses. Many court opinions cite extensively to the decisions of previous courts; except where necessary to an understanding of the case, such citations and footnotes are deleted in this text, without indication of where the citations occurred.

(*continued*)

RUSSELL v. UNITED STATES[1]
471 U.S. 858 (1985)

cago, Illinois. He earned rental income from it and treated it as business property for tax purposes. In early 1983, he made an unsuccessful attempt to set fire to the building and was consequently indicted for violating § 844(i). Following a bench trial, petitioner was convicted and sentenced to 10 years' imprisonment. The District Court and the Court of Appeals both rejected his contention that the building was not commercial or business property, and therefore was not capable of being the subject of an offense under § 844(i).

Section 844(i) used broad language to define the offense. It provides:

> Whoever maliciously damages or destroys, or attempts to damage or destroy, by means of fire or an explosive, any building, vehicle, or other real or personal property used in interstate or foreign commerce or in any activity affecting interstate or foreign commerce shall be imprisoned for not more than ten years or fined not more than $10,000, or both. . . .

The reference to "any building . . . used . . . in any activity affecting interstate or foreign commerce" expresses an intent by Congress to exercise its full power under the Commerce Clause.

The legislative history indicates that Congress intended to exercise its full power to protect "business property." Moreover, after considering whether the bill as originally introduced would cover bombings of police stations or churches, the bill was revised to eliminate the words "for business purposes" from the description of covered property. Even after that change, however, the final Report on the bill emphasized the "very broad" coverage of "substantially all business property." In the floor debates on the final bill, although it was recognized that the coverage of the bill was extremely broad, the Committee Chairman, Representative Celler, expressed the opinion that "the mere bombing of a private home even under this bill would not be covered because of the question whether the Congress would have the authority under the Constitution." In sum, the legislative history suggests that Congress at least intended to protect all business property, as well as some additional property that might not fit that description, but perhaps not every private home.

By its terms, however, the statute only applies to property that is "used" in an "activity" that affects commerce. The rental of real estate is unquestionably such an activity. We need not rely on the connection between the market for residential units and "the interstate movement of people," to recognize that the local rental of an apartment unit is merely an element of a much broader commercial market in rental properties. The congressional power to regulate the class of activities that constitute the rental market for real estate includes the power to regulate individual activity within that class.

Petitioner was renting his apartment building to tenants at the time he attempted to destroy it by fire. The property was therefore being used in an activity affecting commerce within the meaning of § 844(i).

The judgment of the Court of Appeals is affirmed.

Federal Limitations on State Power over Commerce

Due Process Limitations The Commerce Clause speaks only of the power of Congress to regulate commerce among the states and with other nations. It does not deny the power to states to regulate their own commerce, and from the earliest days the states were actively engaged in economic legislation—allowing construction of canals and railroads, regulating banks, and, increasingly, forbidding numerous private economic activities thought to be deleterious to the commonweal. By 1881 in Indiana, for example, the criminal code contained dozens of prohibitions against economic crimes: shooting prairie hens out of season, falsely weighing and selling coal, using nets to prevent fish from swimming into or out of any creek emptying into the Ohio River, advertising or selling any drug that cautioned pregnant women against using it. In 1891, the state made it a punishable offense for railroads to fail to employ flagmen at crossings. In 1898, the New York Legislature prohibited labeling commodities as "sterling silver" unless they were 92.5 percent pure. Many states began to enforce dormant Sunday closing laws to give workers a day of rest.

States enacted these laws under their general "police powers"—the power to ensure the public health, safety, and morals. Unless these laws conflicted with federal commercial legislation, they were considered, almost to the end of the nineteenth century, well within the constitutional powers of the states. But for several decades, commercial lawyers had been pressing a novel argument on the Supreme Court: a state that "unreasonably" interfered with a business corporation's economic activity was violating the clause in the Fourteenth Amendment that provides: "No State shall . . . deprive any person of life, liberty or property without due process of law. . . ."

Due process of law is one of the two or three most significant concepts in our constitutional law. Although due process is capable of no precise definition—if it were, it would have exhausted its utility long ago—it connotes in general *fairness* and *freedom from arbitrary official action.* The due process clauses of both the Fifth and Fourteenth Amendments mean that the state may not execute, imprison, or fine a person without first having provided him a fair trial: the right to be heard, to have counsel, to cross-examine witnesses. In Chapter 3, on criminal law, we examine the procedural requirements of due process in greater detail.

Due process also has an important role to play in the context of civil law. The issue centers on the word "property." As we see below (pp. 29–31) the state may not take a citizen's land without compensating him for it. In addition, under the Fifth Amendment, a separate clause explicitly provides that when the federal government exercises its power of *eminent domain* (the taking of private property for public purposes—for example, to build a road), the owner must be given "just compensation." The just-compensation principle applies to the states through the Fourteenth Amendment's due process clause. But "property" is not restricted to land and tangible physical possessions. Over the years the word has been so broadly construed as to become at times synonymous with the term "liberty."

Beginning in the 1870s, businesses argued that many state economic regulations were arbitrary deprivations of property without due process. For example, in 1869 Louisiana gave a monopoly of the slaughtering trade in New Orleans to a particular company it created for the purpose. Dozens of other butchers complained that in being deprived of their livelihood (they could no longer run their own businesses), Louisiana had violated the due process clause of the Fourteenth Amendment. The Supreme Court at first said that the due process clause had no application to merely economic matters. [Slaughterhouse Cases, 16 Wall. 36 (1873)] When the operators of grain elevators protested an Illinois law regulating their rates, the Court again rejected the argument, holding that the police power permitted states to regulate the use of private property "when such regulation becomes necessary for the public good." [Munn v. Illinois, 94 U.S. 113 (1877)]

But twenty years later, a new Supreme Court capitulated to the force of complaints about the outpouring of state economic legislation. For nearly 40 years, until the late 1930s, a doctrine known as "substantive due process" reigned in the courts. This doctrine was used to invalidate numerous state and federal laws regulating commercial, industrial, and labor conditions. For example, the Supreme Court struck down a New York law limiting the numbers of hours bakers could work. The law was intended to create healthier conditions for bakers (who were forced to work more than ten hours a day six days a week), but the Court agreed with the argument of the employers that the law arbitrarily interfered with the bakers' "liberty to contract." [Lochner v. New York, 198 U.S. 45 (1905)] As Edwin S. Corwin summarized the theory, "the term 'due process of law,' in short, simply drops out of the (due process) clause, which comes to read 'no person (including corporations) shall be deprived of property,' period." The courts eventually overthrew this substantive or "economic" due process concept in the 1930s, and today it is dead. The states and the federal government are free to regulate economic activity as long as in doing so (1) they do not violate some other provision of the Constitution, and (2) the law is rationally related to the legislature's particular goal.

But a substantive notion of due process has not disappeared. Today it has a political or social, rather than economic, flavor. For instance, the Supreme Court's decisions overturning state laws that prohibit abortion are grounded at least in part on a conception of personal liberty. The Court's position is that the states cannot, consistent with due process, limit a woman's right to abort a fetus within the first trimester. Similarly, the due process clause has been used to vindicate rights of prisoners, mental patients, and students against arbitrary action by government officials.

The due process clause is also the basis for a host of civil rights decisions in which appurtenances of modern life are at stake: the right to a job; to academic tenure; and to various "privileges" granted by government—for example, a driver's license, a tax exemption, and welfare benefits. The courts have held that each of these is an incident of property which the state cannot take from any person unless the state demonstrates at a *hearing* that it has not acted arbitrarily. In the following case, the Supreme Court used the due process clause to invalidate a long-used procedure by which sellers of goods could repossess, without a hearing, the goods from customers who failed to make installment payments.

FUENTES v. SHEVIN
407 U.S. 67 (1972)

MR. JUSTICE STEWART delivered the opinion of the Court.

We here review the decisions of two three-judge federal District Courts that upheld the constitutionality of Florida and Pennsylvania laws authorizing the summary seizure of goods or chattels in a person's possession under a writ of replevin. Both statutes provide for the issuance of writs ordering state agents to seize a person's possessions, simply upon the *ex parte* application of any other person who claims a right to them and posts a security bond. Neither statute provides for notice to be given to the possessor of the property, and neither statute gives the possessor an opportunity to challenge the seizure at any kind of prior hearing. . . .

The appellant in No. 5039, Margarita Fuentes, is a resident of Florida. She purchased a gas stove and service policy from the Firestone Tire and Rubber Co. (Firestone) under a conditional sales contract calling for monthly payments over a period of time. A few months later, she purchased a stereophonic phonograph from the same company under the same sort of contract. The total cost of the stove and stereo was about $500, plus an additional financing charge of over $100. Under the contracts, Firestone retained title to the merchandise, but Mrs. Fuentes was entitled to possession unless and until she should default on her installment payments.

For more than a year, Mrs. Fuentes made her installment payments. But then, with only about $200 remaining to be paid, a dispute developed between her and Firestone over the servicing of the stove. Firestone instituted an action in a small-claims court for repossession of both the stove and the stereo, claiming that Mrs. Fuentes had refused to make her remaining payments. Simultaneously with the filing of that action and before Mrs. Fuentes had even received a summons to answer its complaint, Firestone obtained a writ of replevin ordering a sheriff to seize the disputed goods at once.

In conformance with Florida procedure, Firestone had only to fill in the blanks on the appropriate form documents and submit them to the clerk of the small-claims court. The clerk signed and stamped the documents and issued a writ of replevin. Later the same day, a local deputy sheriff and an agent of Firestone went to Mrs. Fuentes' home and seized the stove and stereo.

Shortly thereafter, Mrs. Fuentes instituted the present action in a federal district court, challenging the constitutionality of the Florida prejudgment replevin procedures under the Due Process Clause of the Fourteenth Amendment. She sought declaratory and injunctive relief against continued enforcement of the procedural provisions of the state statutes that authorize prejudgment replevin.

★   ★   ★

For more than a century the central meaning of procedural due process has been clear: "Parties whose rights are to be affected are entitled to be heard; and in order that they may enjoy that right they must first be notified." It is equally fundamental that the right to notice and an opportunity to be heard "must be granted at a meaningful time and in a meaningful manner."

The primary question in the present cases is whether these state statutes are constitutionally defective in failing to provide for hearings "at a meaningful time." The Florida replevin process guarantees an opportunity for a hearing after the seizure of goods, and the Pennsylvania process allows a post-seizure hearing if the aggrieved party shoulders the burden of initiating one. But neither the Florida nor the Pennsylvania statute provides for notice or an opportunity to be heard *before* the seizure. The issue is whether procedural due process in the context of these cases requires an opportunity for a hearing *before* the State authorizes its agents to seize property in the possession of a person upon the application of another.

The constitutional right to be heard is a basic aspect of the duty of government to follow a fair process of decision-making when it acts to deprive a person of his possessions. The purpose of this requirement is not only to ensure abstract fair play to the individual. Its purpose, more particularly, is to protect his use and possession of property from arbitrary encroachment— to minimize substantively unfair or mistaken deprivations of property, a danger that is especially great when the State seizes goods simply upon the application of and for the benefit of a private party. So viewed, the prohibition against the deprivation of property without due process of law reflects the high value, embedded in our constitutional and political history, that we place on a person's right to enjoy what is his, free of governmental interference.

(continued on next page)

(continued)

FUENTES v. SHEVIN
407 U.S. 67 (1972)

The requirement of notice and an opportunity to be heard raises no impenetrable barrier to the taking of a person's possessions. But the fair process of decision-making that it guarantees works, by itself, to protect against arbitrary deprivation of property. For when a person has an opportunity to speak up in his own defense, and when the State must listen to what he has to say, substantively unfair and simply mistaken deprivations of property interests can be prevented. It has long been recognized that "fairness can rarely be obtained by secret, one-sided determination of facts decisive of rights. . . . [And n]o better instrument has been devised for arriving at truth than to give a person in jeopardy of serious loss notice of the case against him and opportunity to meet it."

If the right to notice and a hearing is to serve its full purpose, then, it is clear that it must be granted at a time when the deprivation can still be prevented. At a later hearing, an individual's possessions can be returned to him if they were unfairly or mistakenly taken in the first place. Damages may even be awarded to him for the wrongful deprivation. But no later hearing and no damage award can undo the fact that the arbitrary taking that was subject to the right of procedural due process has already occurred. "This Court has not . . . embraced the general proposition that a wrong may be done if it can be undone."

*   *   *

We hold that the Florida and Pennsylvania prejudgment replevin provisions work a deprivation of property without due process of law insofar as they deny the right to a prior opportunity to be heard before chattels are taken from their possessor.

*   *   *

For the foregoing reasons, the judgments of the District Courts are vacated and these cases are remanded for further proceedings consistent with this opinion.

It is so ordered.

Equal Protection

Closely related to due process is the equal protection clause of the Fourteenth Amendment, quoted on p. 15. In essence, the clause means that the states may not arbitrarily or invidiously classify people in such a way that the different categories of persons will be treated unequally. This clause has had its most obvious use with respect to racial classifications. Beginning with the seminal case of *Brown* v. *Board of Education,* 347 U.S. 483 (1954) the Supreme Court has made it clear that neither the Fourteenth Amendment nor the due process clause of the Fifth Amendment will tolerate governmental classifications of individuals by race.

The equal protection clause, as interpreted from 1954 on, has had a profound impact on American society. It has led to reapportionment of state legislatures and fundamental revamping of voting laws throughout the United States. It has prompted a variety of reforms in the legal condition of women, the poor, children, ethnic and linguistic minority groups, and aliens.

Although in recent years the equal protection

clause has led the courts to transform American society in many important ways, business has found little solace in its commands. With insignificant exceptions, the courts have refused to strike down economic regulations on equal protection grounds. In general, companies have argued that in prohibiting one kind of economic activity, but allowing largely similar ones to continue, the states have unconstitutionally discriminated against the prohibited activity. For example, a New York City ordinance prohibited trucks from displaying advertisements on their sides unless the advertisements were for the regular business of the truck owners. A nationwide express delivery company, employing a fleet of 1,900 trucks in New York City alone, regularly sold display space to merchants who wished to advertise their products. The company insisted that the ordinance unfairly discriminated against it since the corner laundry truck could advertise its own business with the same distraction to traffic and pedestrians as if the fleet trucks advertised. The company argued further that "the classification which the regulation makes has no relation to the traffic problem since a violation turns not on what kind of advertisements are carried on trucks but on whose trucks they are carried." The Supreme Court rejected the argument:

> The local authorities may well have concluded that those who advertise their own wares on their trucks do not present the same traffic problem in view of the nature or extent of the advertising which they use. It would take a degree of omniscience which we lack to say that such is not the case. . . . And the fact that New York City sees fit to eliminate from traffic this kind of distraction but does not touch what may be even greater ones in a different category, such as the vivid displays on Times Square, is immaterial. It is no requirement of equal protection that all evils of the same genus be eradicated or none at all. [Railway Express Agency v. New York, 326 U.S. 106 (1949)]

State Action

With one exception, the Constitution does not apply to private conduct. It limits *government* power. (The exception is the slavery prohibition in the Thirteenth Amendment, applicable to government and private individuals alike.) A state, for example, may not pass a law prohibiting people from speaking out against (or in favor of) nuclear power, but a private company may enforce its own rule against its employees' doing so—at least insofar as the Constitution is concerned. For protection of the right to speak against private prohibitions, employees must look to state and federal statutes. Some states have begun to enact such legislation.

This rule, that the Constitution restricts only government, has equal application to the due process and equal protection clauses. In order for a court to invalidate an act claimed to violate one of these constitutional provisions, there must have been **state action**—that is, some branch of some government must have somehow been involved. It has been argued that public regulation of private activity is sufficient to convert the private into public activity, thus subjecting it to the requirements of due process. But the Supreme Court rejected this extreme view in 1974 when it refused to require private power companies, regulated by the state, to give customers a hearing before cutting off electricity for failure to pay the bill. [Jackson v. Metropolitan Edison Co., 419 U.S. 345 (1974)]

Prohibitions of Local Protectionism

Although the states are generally free to enact economic legislation under their police power to protect the public health, safety, and morals, the courts have discerned one significant constitutional limitation on state commercial regulation. That limitation stems from the Commerce Clause.

We have already seen that when Congress enacts laws regulating interstate commerce, the Supremacy Clause of Article VI preempts any conflicting state laws. Suppose Congress has not spoken. Does the Supremacy Clause grant Congress the *exclusive* power to regulate commerce? In 1851, the Court said no. The states may regulate commerce as long as they are regulating purely "local" matters even if the regulation has an incidental effect on national commerce. [Cooley v. Port of Wardens of the Port of Philadelphia, 12 How. 299 (1851)] For nearly a century, the Court had the difficult task of distinguishing between "local" and "national" subjects of regulation. The dividing line was usually indistinct. Eventually, the Court outgrew these labels and developed a "balancing test," as stated most concisely by Justice Potter Stewart:

> Where the statute regulates evenhandedly to effectuate a legitimate local public interest, and its effects on interstate commerce are only incidental, it will be upheld unless the burden imposed on such commerce is clearly excessive in relation to the putative local benefits. If a legitimate local purpose is found, then the question becomes one of degree. And the extent of the burden that will be tolerated will of course depend on the nature of the local interest involved, and on whether it could be promoted as well with a lesser impact on interstate activities. [Pike v. Bruce Church, Inc., 397 U.S. 137 (1970)]

This understanding of the Commerce Clause means that when a state (usually in alliance with a particular company or local industry) tries to protect its own residents to the detriment of consumers and businesses outside the state, the Court will be vigilant in striking down these laws. On numerous occasions, the Court has invalidated state laws that smacked of local protectionism by burdening out-of-state businesses, hindering access of competitors out of state to local markets, or otherwise discriminating against the national market. In the next case, North Carolina sought to protect its local apple growers from the sale of superior apples from the State of Washington.

HUNT v. WASHINGTON APPLE ADVERTISING COMMISSION
432 U.S. 33 (1977)

MR. CHIEF JUSTICE BURGER delivered the opinion of the Court.

In 1973, North Carolina enacted a statute which required, inter alia, all closed containers of apples sold, offered for sale, or shipped into the State to bear "no grade other than the applicable U.S. grade or standard." . . . Washington State is the Nation's largest producer of apples, its crops accounting for approximately 30% of all apples grown domestically and nearly half of all apples shipped in closed containers in interstate commerce. [Because] of the importance of the apple industry to the State, its legislature has undertaken to protect and enhance the reputation of Washington apples by establishing a stringent, mandatory inspection program [which] requires all apples shipped in interstate commerce to be tested under strict quality standards and graded accordingly. In all cases, the Washington State grades [are] the equivalent of, or superior to, the comparable grades and standards adopted by the [U.S. Dept. of] Agriculture (USDA).

[In] 1972, the North Carolina Board of Agriculture adopted an administrative regulation, unique in the 50 States, which in effect required all closed containers of apples shipped into or sold in the State to display either the applicable USDA grade or a notice indicating no classification. State grades were expressly prohibited. In addition to its obvious consequence—prohibiting the display of Washington State apple grades on containers of apples shipped into North Carolina—the regulation presented the Washington apple industry with a marketing problem of potentially nationwide significance. Washington apple growers annually ship in commerce approximately 40 million closed containers of apples, nearly 500,000 of which eventually find their way into North Carolina, stamped with the applicable Washington State variety and grade. [Compliance] with North Carolina's unique regulation would have required Washington growers to obliterate the printed labels on containers shipped to North Carolina, thus giving their product a damaged appearance. Alternatively, they could have changed their marketing practices to accommodate the needs of the North Carolina market, i.e., repack apples to be shipped to North Carolina in containers bearing only the USDA grade, and/or store the estimated portion of the harvest destined for that market in such special containers. As a last resort, they could discontinue the use of the preprinted containers entirely. None of these costly and less efficient options was very attractive to the industry. . . .

. . . [North Carolina] maintains that [the] burdens on the interstate sale of Washington apples were far outweighed by the local benefits flowing from what they contend was a valid exercise of North Carolina's [police powers]. Prior to the statute's enactment, . . . apples from 13 different States were shipped into North Carolina for sale. Seven of those States, including [Washington], had their own grading systems which, while differing in their standards, used similar descriptive labels (e.g., fancy, extra fancy, etc.). This multiplicity of inconsistent state grades [posed] dangers of deception and confusion not only in the North Carolina market, but in the Nation as a whole. The North Carolina statute, appellants claim, was enacted to eliminate this source of deception and confusion. . . .

The challenged statute has the practical effect of not only burdening interstate sales of Washington apples, but also discriminating against them. This discrimination takes various forms. The first, and most obvious, is the statute's consequence of *raising the costs* of doing business in the North Carolina market for Washington apple growers and dealers, while leaving those of their North Carolina counterparts unaffected. [This] disparate effect results from the fact that North Carolina apple producers, unlike their Washington competitors, were not forced to alter their marketing practices in order to comply with the statute. . . . Second, the statute has the effect of *stripping away* from the Washington apple industry the competitive and economic advantages it has earned for itself through its expensive inspection and grading system. The record demonstrates that the Washington apple-grading system has gained nationwide acceptance in the apple trade. [The record] contains numerous affidavits [stating a] preference [for] apples graded under the Washington, as opposed to the USDA, system because of the former's greater consistency, its emphasis on color, and its supporting mandatory inspections. Once again, the statute had no similar impact on the North Carolina apple industry and thus operated to its benefit.

Third, by *prohibiting* Washington growers and dealers from *marketing* apples under their State's grades, the statute has a *leveling effect* which insidiously operates to the advantage of local apple producers. [With] free market forces at work, Washington sellers would normally enjoy a distinct market advantage vis-à-vis local producers in those categories where the Washington grade is superior. However, because of the statute's operation, Washington apples which would otherwise qualify for and be sold under the superior Washington grades will now have to be marketed under their inferior USDA counterparts. Such "downgrading" offers the North Carolina apple industry the very sort of protection against competing out-of-state products that the Commerce Clause was designed to prohibit. . . .

(*continued on next page*)

(continued)

**HUNT v.
WASHINGTON APPLE
ADVERTISING
COMMISSION**
432 U.S. 33 (1977)

Despite the statute's facial neutrality, the Commission suggests that its discriminatory impact on interstate commerce was not an unintended by-product, and there are some indications in the record to that effect. . . . However, we need not ascribe an economic protection motive to the North Carolina Legislature to resolve this case; we conclude that the challenged statute cannot stand insofar as it prohibits the display of Washington State grades even if enacted for the declared purpose of protecting consumers from deception and fraud in the marketplace.

When discrimination against commerce of the type we have found is demonstrated, the burden falls on the State to justify it both in terms of the local benefits flowing from the statute and the unavailability of nondiscriminatory alternatives adequate to preserve the local interests at stake. North Carolina has failed to sustain that burden on both scores. [The] States unquestionably possess a substantial interest in protecting their citizens from confusion and deception in the marketing of foodstuffs, but the challenged statute does remarkably little to further that laudable goal at least with respect to Washington apples and grades. The statute [permits] the marketing of closed containers of apples under *no* grades at all. Such a result can hardly be thought to eliminate the problems of deception and confusion created by the multiplicity of differing state grades; indeed, it magnifies them by depriving purchasers of all information concerning the quality of the contents of closed apple containers. Moreover, although the statute is ostensibly a consumer protection measure, it directs its primary efforts, not at the consuming public at large, but at apple wholesalers and brokers who are the principal purchasers of closed containers of apples. And those individuals are presumably the most knowledgeable individuals in this area. Since the statute does nothing at all to purify the flow of information at the retail level, it does little to protect consumers against the problems it was designed to eliminate. . . .

In addition, it appears that nondiscriminatory alternatives to the outright ban of Washington State grades are readily available. For example, North Carolina could effectuate its goal by permitting out-of-state growers to utilize state grades only if they also marked their shipments with the applicable USDA label. In that case, the USDA grade would serve as a benchmark against which the consumer could evaluate the quality of the various state grades. . . .

[The court affirmed the lower court's holding that the North Carolina statute was unconstitutional.]

Through the Commerce Clause, the Constitution thus guarantees a truly national market against the splintering effects of local regulation. As Justice Jackson summed up the general rule and the policy that underlies it:

The Commerce Clause is one of the most prolific sources of national power and an equally prolific source of conflict with legislation of the state. While the Constitution vests in Congress the power to regulate commerce among the states, it does not say what the states may or may not do in the absence of congressional action. . . . Perhaps even more than by interpretation of its written word, this Court has advanced the solidarity and prosperity of this Nation by the meaning it has given to these great silences of the Constitution. . . . This distinction between the power of the State to shelter its people from menaces to their health or safety and from fraud, even when those dangers emanate from interstate commerce, and its lack of power to retard, burden or constrict the flow of such commerce for their economic advantage, is one deeply rooted in both our history and our law. . . . This Court consistently has rebuffed attempts of states to advance their own commercial interests by curtailing the movement of articles of commerce, either into or out of the state, while generally supporting their right to impose even burdensome regulations in the interest of local health and safety. . . . The principle that our economic unit is the Nation, which alone has the gamut of powers necessary to control the economy, including the vital power of erecting customs barriers against foreign competition, has as its corollary that the states are not separable economic units. . . . The material success that has come to inhabitants of the states which make up this federal free trade unit has been the most impressive in the history of commerce, but the established interdependence of the states only emphasizes the necessity of protecting interstate movement of goods against local burdens and repressions. We need only consider the consequences if each of the few states that produce copper, lead, high-grade iron ore, timber, cotton, oil or gas should decree that industries located in that state shall have priority. What fantastic rivalries and dislocations and reprisals would ensue if such practices are begun! Or suppose that the field of discrimination and retaliation be industry. May Michigan provide that automobiles cannot be taken out of that State until local dealers' demands are fully met? Would she not have every argument in the favor of such a statute that can be offered in support of New York's limiting sales of milk for out-of-state shipment to protect the economic interests of her competing dealers and local consumers? Could Ohio then pounce upon the rubber-tire industry, on which she has a substantial grip, to retaliate for Michigan's auto monopoly? Our system, fostered by the Commerce Clause, is that every farmer and every craftsman shall be encouraged to produce by the certainty that he will have free access to every market in the Nation, that no home embargoes will withhold his exports, and no foreign state will by customs duties or regulations exclude them. Likewise, every consumer may look to the free competition from every producing area in the Nation to protect him from exploitation by any. Such was the vision of the Founders; such has been the doctrine of this Court which has given it reality. [H.P. Hood & Sons v. Du Mond, 336 U.S. 525 (1949)]

Regulating Businesses: The Constitutional Rights of Business

Freedom of Speech and Press The First Amendment is the most significant charter of political freedom in America. In forty-five words, the First Amendment succinctly commands the government to let private individuals exercise their essential liberties:

> Congress shall make no law respecting an establishment of religion, or prohibiting the free exercise thereof; or abridging the freedom of speech, or of the press; or the right of the people peaceably to assemble, and to petition the Government for a redress of grievances.

In numerous cases, the Supreme Court (and other courts) have spelled out dozens of principles contained in these few words. Among them are the right to associate with anyone and to say or print whatever you please without first obtaining permission from the government. Freedom of speech and freedom of the press, along with the other rights guaranteed by the First Amendment, are now secure against intrusion not only by the federal government but also by the state governments. (The Court has interpreted the Fourteenth Amendment to mean that First Amendment rights apply also to intrusion by states.)

The First Amendment does not mean, however, that you can say whatever you want whenever you want to without fear of subsequent penalty. Libel and slander are actionable. Those who advertise in a false or deceptive manner can be punished. The states may regulate the time and manner of expression: you are not free in most towns to drive along residential streets at midnight blaring political slogans through a microphone. But it has long been held that the expression of political, religious, social, economic, cultural, and other ideas—no matter how obnoxious to others in the community—are protected by the First Amendment.

For many years, the mantle of protection was not thought to surround "commercial speech." Thus the courts have often struck down as unconstitutional ordinances that forbade picketing or the passing out of handbills advocating a political or religious position, but they left untouched similar laws barring the handing out of advertisements for a local retailer. Not until the 1970s did the Supreme Court reverse course and begin to protct the "purely commercial."

In *Bigelow* v. *Virginia*, 421 U.S. 809 (1975), the Supreme Court reversed a conviction of a newspaper editor in Virginia who had run an advertisement telling women they could obtain abortions in New York. The state law prohibited any published promotion or encouragement of services that would facilitate abortions in state. Virginia said that the First Amendment did not apply because the "speech" in question was purely "commercial": where and how to obtain abortions. The Supreme Court said that the First Amendment does apply even to discussions about commercial activities. The following year the Court broadened the constitutional protection for commercial speech in ruling that a state may not punish a pharmacist for advertising the price of prescription drugs. [Virginia State Board of Pharmacy v. Virginia Citizens Consumer Council, Inc., 425 U.S. 748 (1976)] For the next decade, the Court steadily broadened commercial free speech rights. It held, for example, that a state public service commission may not prohibit an electric utility from advertising designed to stimulate use of electricity, even though the commission had a legitimate purpose to conserve energy. [Central Hudson Gas v. Public Service Commission, 447 U.S. 557 (1980)] And the Court rejected an ordinance prohibiting home owners from posting "for sale" signs to promote a racially integrated community and to stem "white flight." [Linmark Associates, Inc. v. Willingboro, 431 U.S. 85 (1977)]

But in 1986, the Court began to retrench. In a much-criticized case, it agreed that Puerto Rico could constitutionally ban casinos from advertising gambling if the ads were designed to reach residents of the island. The Court seemed to be saying that legislatures may ban *advertising* of any harmful activity if the legislature could lawfully ban the *harmful activity,* even if it had not yet done so or might never do so. These activities are generally considered to include lotteries, the sale of liquor and cigarettes, and other products now legal but considered harmful. [Posadas de Puerto Rico Associates v. Tourism Co. of Puerto Rico, 478 U.S. 328 (1986)]

The question raised in the recent commercial-speech cases is how far the First Amendment protects against states that want to regulate "expression related solely to the economic interests of the speaker and its audience." In the *Central Hudson* case, the Court announced a four-pronged test: (1) The speech in question must be covered by the First Amendment; that is, it must be neither "inaccurate, [n]or relate to unlawful activity." (2) The government interest in regulating must be "substantial." (3) The regulation must "directly advance the governmental interest." (4) Finally, the restriction must be

"no more extensive than necessary." As generally understood from *Central Hudson*, the regulation must be the "least restrictive means" of carrying out the government's ends.

However, in *Board of Trustees, State University of New York* v. *Fox*, 492 U.S. 469 (1989), the Court abandoned this tough interpretation of the forth prong. The case raised the issue whether a public university may prohibit outside companies from doing business on campus—in particular, by holding "Tupperware parties" in dormitories to sell their goods. Students challenged the university's ban as unconstitutionally interfering with their free-speech rights to receive the sales pitch. The Court concluded that the sales presentations were commercial and were not entitled to special protection because the sales people also gave home economics advice. The Court agreed that the commerce was lawful, that the sales presentations were not misleading, and that the university had a substantial interest in preserving the educational atmosphere of the student's life on campus. So the question was whether the absolute ban was the least restrictive means of realizing the government's ends. In something of an about-face, the Court held that the means chosen need not be the least restrictive; rather, the means must be "narrowly tailored to achieve the desired objective." How much leeway this apparently new standard will give legislatures to curb commercial speech remains a question for courts in the 1990s. Perhaps it is reasonable to predict that advertisements will retain considerable immunity from state intrusion, except possibly for products that are generally regarded as harmful. On the other hand, direct solicitation of commercial transactions—such as door-to-door selling—will get lesser constitutional protection in the face of legislative attempts to regulate.

Advertising and commercial speech are not the only types of communications in which business is interested. Until recently, few cases had tested the power of the states to limit the right of corporations to spend their own funds to speak the "corporate mind." Few states have enacted laws that directly impinge on the freedom of companies to advertise truthfully. But some have done so, usually to limit the ability of corporations to sway voters in public referenda. In 1978, the Supreme Court finally confronted the issue head on. In First National Bank of Boston v. Bellotti (see p. 909), the Court held that states may not prohibit corporations from spending funds to influence the outcome of public referenda on issues not materially affecting their assets or business. *Bellotti* has limitations; it does not stand for the proposition that corporations may spend however they wish in taking public stands on political issues. For example, a state may limit a corporation's right to contribute money to political candidates or to advertisements that support or oppose them. Thus in 1990 the Court upheld a Michigan law that forbade companies to spend money from the general corporate treasury on political candidates. The law permits corportions to fund political candidates only if the money is used "independently" (not in cooperation with a particular campaign) and only if it comes from a segregated fund established for the purpose. The Court held that Michigan had a "compelling interest" in regulating "the corrosive and distorting effects" of corporate wealth. [Austin v. Michigan Chamber of Commerce, 58 U.S.L.W. 4371]

Other Rights of the Corporation

In 1887, without any discussion, the Supreme Court declared that corporations are "persons" within the meaning of the Fourteenth Amendment. But to say that a corporation is a person does not automatically describe what its rights are, for the courts have not accorded the corporation every right guaranteed a human being. However, the courts have concluded that corporations are entitled to the essential constitutional protections of due process. They are also entitled to Fourth Amendment protection against unreasonable search and seizure; in other words, the police must have a search warrant to enter corporate premises and look through files. The double jeopardy clause applies to criminal prosecutions of corporations; an acquittal cannot be appealed, nor can the case be retried. For purposes of the federal courts' diversity jurisdiction (see p. 44), a corporation is deemed to be a citizen both of the state in which it is incorporated and the state in which it has its principal place of business.

The cases are equally clear, though, that corporations lack certain rights that natural persons possess. For example, corporations do not have a privilege against self-incrimination, guaranteed by the Fifth and Fourteenth Amendments. In any legal proceeding, the courts may force the corporation to turn over incrim-

inating documents, even if they also incriminate officers or employees of the corporation. Corporations are not citizens under the "privileges and immunities" clause of Article IV of the Constitution, so that the states may discriminate between domestic and foreign corporations. And the corporation is not entitled to federal review of state criminal convictions, as are many individuals.

The Right to Property: Eminent Domain and Just Compensation

At common law, the sovereign could take private property for public use as long as the owner was compensated for the loss. The Fifth Amendment incorporated this power of "eminent domain," requiring the federal government to pay "just compensation" for any property it takes. Both a public purpose and a just compensation are constitutionally prerequisite to the taking.

Originally, the Fifth Amendment's command to pay just compensation applied to the federal government only, but with the ratification of the Fourteenth Amendment, the clause came to be applied to the states as well. In 1896 the Court ruled that a state may take property only for a public use, and the next year it held that just compensation is an essential element of any exercise of eminent domain.

What constitutes a public use is largely for the states themselves to say. The courts are ordinarily unwilling to contradict a state's declaration that the taking is for a public purpose. Thus, in a recent case, the Supreme Court upheld the Hawaii legislature's decision to force the seventy-two private landowners who held nearly half the state's land (almost all the rest was held by the state and federal governments) to sell to their tenants. As long as the owners were compensated, the legislature's determination to correct "the land oligopoly problem" was held to be a rational exercise of eminent domain. The land's transfer to private individuals did not invalidate the *purpose* of the taking, which was to remedy a pressing *public* problem. [Hawaii Housing Authority v. Midkiff, 467 U.S. 229 (1984)] We discuss this case further on p. 723.

The principle of just compensation is simple enough when applied to a physical taking of the property—when the state actually takes over a building or condemns a parcel of land to build a highway. A more difficult problem arises when a state does not take the property outright, but through some economic regulation, interferes with its use. Modern regulations constantly interfere with the ways we use our property; indeed, that is their very purpose. The problem of taking is thus transferred from the confiscation of title to the losses that flow from regulation.

When government regulates an activity clearly injurious to the public, the courts are unlikely to find that the owner has suffered compensable harm. A factory that pollutes the air or waterways will not find the courts receptive to its plea that it be compensated for loss of the opportunity to continue to pollute. But suppose the town council decides it wants to preserve old buildings so that the current owner is hamstrung in how the house or office may be used. Has the property been "taken," in Justice Holmes's arresting phrase, through "the petty larceny of the police power?" Holmes declared that the premise for regulation without compensation was necessity: "Government could hardly go on if to some extent values incident to property could not be diminished without paying for every such change in the general law. As long recognized, some values are enjoyed under an implied limitation and must yield to the police power. But obviously the implied limitation must have its limits." When are losses only incidental to regulation, so that no compensation need be paid? When is the regulation so severe that it amounts to a taking for which just compensation becomes a constitutional requirement?

The answer is that each case turns on its specific facts. The Court has upheld the general principle of zoning, so that a municipality may determine that some property may be used for residences and others only for business, without the municipality having to compensate owners who would rather devote their property to another use. [Euclid v. Ambler Realty Co., 272 U.S. 365 (1926)] Even when the zoning ordinance drastically limits the use of land, the Court will ordinarily uphold the ordinance if the land may be used at all. Thus, in a 1980 case, the Court upheld an ordinance that rezoned suburban land so that a developer could no longer build as many housing units as he had planned; the Court noted that the ordinance did not "prevent the best use" of the land. [Agins v. Tiburon, 447 U.S. 255 (1980).]

But in 1987, the court signaled that it may be moving in a new direction. At issue was a Los An-

geles County ordinance designed to cope with serious flooding. Heavy rainstorms had washed away an area previously devastated by fire; the ordinance banned construction in the area. A church that ran a campground for handicapped children was effectively barred from rebuilding its campsite. It sued on an "inverse condemnation" theory, a claim that the county had in effect condemned the land and thus owed the church compensation for the loss of its property. The state courts, following precedent, held that Los Angeles was not obliged to provide compensation for this regulation because at most the deprivation was merely temporary. The theory was that no compensation is due until a court has first ruled that a regulation has "taken" the property. The remedy for this "temporary taking" is the court's declaration that the taking is unconstitutional unless compensated. The jurisdiction that enacted the ordinance may then repeal the ordinance; if it does, no compensation will be due, because the taking was merely temporary. If the ordinance is not repealed, compensation must then be paid only for the time after the ruling that the owner was deprived of the use of his property. Noting that the case had taken six years in the state courts and during that entire time the church was totally barred from using its property, the Supreme Court held that the county would have to compensate the church for the loss of its use from the time the ordinance first went into effect. [First English Evangelical Lutheran Church of Glendale v. Los Angeles, 482 U.S. 304 (1987)]

The Court also ruled in 1987 that a zoning ordinance designed to protect beachfront views could not require, without compensation, beachfront owners (a married couple) to give the public an easement to the ocean across their property in return for permission to rebuild their house. The Court said that an outright denial of a permit would not have been a taking, assuming that the denial "substantially advanced" a legitimate state interest. But the easement had no relationship whatsoever to the rebuilding permit; linking the two was simply a means of extracting an easement from the owners, and the direct imposition of an easement would clearly have been a taking requiring compensation. [Nollan v. California Coastal Commission, 483 U.S. 825 (1987)]

Whether these decisions mean that legislatures everywhere must be far more wary about adopting "police power" regulations that affect the use of property remains to be seen. Such decisions may indicate that the Court will be far tougher in the future about the impact of regulations on the loss of use, or they may simply mean that the Court will look askance at any regulation that either deprives an owner of *all* use or gives physical access to others. "One thing is certain," said Justice Stevens in dissent. "The Court's decision will generate a great deal of litigation."

But even before these decisions, it was clear that the Court would not countenance actual physical invasions of property unless the taking authority paid compensation. For example, a New York ordinance required owners of rental buildings to allow cable television companies to install cables on the buildings without charge. But even though the cables occupied little space (between one-eighth and one-and-one-half cubic feet), the Court said that the cable company had to pay for any "permanent physical occupation." [Loretto v. TelePrompter Manhattan CATV Corp., 458 U.S. 419 (1982)]

The Right to Unimpaired Contracts

Article I of the Constitution prohibits states from passing any "law impairing the obligation of contracts." This clause was aimed at legislation that would absolve debtors of their financial obligations. An important provision at the time of ratification, it became relatively impotent by the mid-nineteenth century, when the Court had ruled that the states' police power (that is, the power to protect the health, safety, good order, comfort, and general welfare of the community) may not be bargained away. If you and I enter a contract for the sale of lottery tickets, the Contract Clause will not prevent the state thereafter from passing a law prohibiting such a transaction. In 1934, in the midst of the Depression, the Supreme Court went so far as to uphold a Minnesota "mortgage moratorium" law, suspending for two years the right of banks to foreclose on defaulted mortgages. The Court noted that the law was temporary and did not repudiate the debts but was limited to changes in the remedy provided in the law for breach of contract. [Home Building & Loan Ass'n v. Blaisdell, 290 U.S. 398 (1934)] The Contract Clause seemed almost dead.

But in 1977 the Court revived it, holding against New Jersey in its attempt to repeal a covenant it had enacted as security for holders of bonds of the Port Authority of New York and New Jersey. The covenant made it difficult for the Port Authority to use bond revenues to subsidize rail operations. The Court held that although courts must generally defer to states when they interfere with private contracts, the courts must scrutinize any state attempts to impair their own contractual obligations, as in this case. [United States Trust Co. v. New Jersey, 431 U.S. 1 (1977)]

In 1978, the Court expanded the reach of the Contract Clause to protect private contracts against state claims of necessity when it struck down a Minnesota law requiring employers with established pension plans to modify retroactively the obligations they assumed toward their employees. [Allied Structural Steel Co. v. Spannaus, 438 U.S. 234 (1978)] But in later cases, the Court has pulled away from the more exacting scrutiny that it seemed to have announced in 1978. Thus, in a 1983 case, the Court upheld a Kansas law that effectively blocked a private supplier of natural gas from taking advantage of a clause in a contract that required a private utility to pay more for gas whenever the federal government increased the price at which suppliers could sell gas. The Court said that when anyone asserts a Contract Clause claim, courts must undertake a three-party inquiry: (1) Was a contractual right substantially impaired? (2) If so, did the state have any significant and legitimate public purpose in regulating? (3) If it did, was the contractual modification reasonably related to the reasons justifying the legislation? Unless the complainant can show that the state had no legitimate purpose in imposing a substantial impairment or that it had failed to adjust the modification of the contract to the law's purpose, the courts must defer to the states. [Energy Reserves Group v. Kansas Power & Light Co., 459 U.S. 400 (1983)] It seems unlikely that many challenges will withstand the rigors of this test, given a Court that in modern times is generally willing to defer to legislative judgments in the economic arena. That does not mean there is no remedy. As the Court said more than a century ago: "For protection against abuses by legislatures the people must resort to the polls."

THE DEVELOPMENT OF THE COMMON LAW

The Function of Courts

One modern criticism of courts is that they are usurping lawmaking authority, that as the third branch of government they have become too involved in setting policy. However, both the anthropological and historical literature suggest that this role is hardly new, having emerged from the early desire for peace in the community.

In most primitive communities without a formal political order, every person, family, or clan believed it had a right to redress wrongs done to one of them, and a single act of killing by a hot-headed individual would often lead to a blood feud that spread geographically and persisted over time. The need to suppress the free exercise of this desire to repay one killing with another gave birth to the political ruler, whose first duty was to settle disputes. Anthropological evidence suggests that the need to resolve disputes is what motivates a political order among peoples whose relations theretofore have been merely familial or neighborly.

Certainly this was true in the society that contributed most directly to our judicial system: England. Though English society before the twelfth century was scarcely primitive, the center of political activity, where it existed, was predominantly local; there was no nation-state in the modern sense. Courts did exist, but they were virtually the private property of the nobility. The great property owners exercised a crude and self-interested justice to put down insurrection and to settle disputes among serfs, vassals, and others beholden to them. In so doing, the nobles consolidated their power as petty sovereigns. The nobles warred with each other, however, and until the kings established royal courts and substituted public sanctions and a system of compensation for blood feuds, warfare and violence reigned.

The Royal Writs

From the time of the Norman Conquest in A.D. 1066, the kings professed to be the guarantors of justice. One of the most noteworthy developments was that of the royal judicial "writs," an innovation of Henry II in the twelfth century. The writ was a formal document commanding someone to appear in the royal courts. Originally, a writ was issued to the sheriff, whose job was to summon the defendant to court. In time, plaintiffs purchased these writs—a handy source of revenue for the king. In essence, the writs permitted lawsuits to be instituted in court. Different writs

were issued for different types of complaints, and within two centuries of the Conquest they swept away the private courts that had dispensed justice on the manors.

Law and justice thus became public, and as they diffused throughout the countryside they gave birth to the nation. The royal courts were the beneficiaries of a nice symbiosis: On the one hand, the king increased his revenues by selling writs, and he consolidated his power over owners and possessors of land—the most valuable commodity in the country—by insisting that real property cases be heard in his courts. On the other hand, the people generally benefited from the steady march of royal jurisdiction. As the historian Joseph R. Strayer has written:

> Kings were quite ready to accept the idea that justice was all-important, since it was a sign of their authority and a weapon by which they might achieve supremacy in their realms. For the common folk, and even for many members of the lesser aristocracy, justice meant protection against violence and loss of lands. Thus rulers who tried to create regularly functioning law courts were assured of almost universal approval. The most warlike barons could not object to the existence of courts, though they might be very slow to obey their orders. (Strayer, 1970, p. 32)

As early as 1215, in Magna Carta—the charter of basic rights that King John was forced to grant at Runnymede—the barons themselves were insisting on a fixed place for regular courts of justice (to avoid the difficulties attendant on the peregrinations of their monarch).

The writs served as the basis for the substantive law. Writs were individual: there was one for trespass, for taking of property, for assault, and so on. The decision of the king's ministers to issue a new writ was in essence a decision that the act complained of was a legal wrong.

Stare Decisis

But by themselves, the writs were not the law. The common law ultimately was to be found in the decisions of judges in the cases that came before them. Their decisions were recorded from early days; records of judicial decisions date back to at least the thirteenth century. When questions of law arose, the judges relied on the pronouncements of their predecessors. Earlier cases served as precedent, and the great principle of **stare decisis** emerged, which means "to stand by decided cases." *Stare decisis* (STAIR ee duh SAY sus) is the source of the stability and conserving strength of the common law: once a legal principle is enunciated by a court, it is the law and is not to be overturned.

Of course, if legal judgments were too sweeping, a legal system that did not permit modifications could become inflexible and break down as social and economic conditions changed. The common law system accommodated this difficulty by requiring judges to consider only the case that was before them and to announce a principle no broader than was required by the case. If a later case presented different factual circumstances, a variant of the rule was possible. Thus lawyers became adept in the art of *distinguishing*—pointing to the vital but often subtle differences that made an earlier, unfavorable ruling inapplicable.

The Jury System

One reason for the relatively speedy acceptance of the king's justice was the change in the method of determining disputed facts. Certainly the mass of common folk welcomed procedures that substituted the knowledge of local jurors for the dreaded trials by "ordeal." Early justice did not contemplate dispassionate fact-finding, such as occurs (in theory at least) in our courts today. Instead, various methods relied on force and superstition. In the ordeal, people were forced to hold burning coals or were thrown into water; if they did not burn or sink, they were presumed innocent. This sadism was reserved for the lower classes. The aristocracy had a less painful method: **compurgation,** or swearing. After protesting his innocence, the defendant produced a number of people who swore to his good reputation. But they had to do it in a highly formal manner, and the defendant had to have a proper number of compurgators. If he did not have enough, or if they stumbled over the ritualistic formula, he was guilty. If they sailed through their set speech, however, he was free. The theory was that God tripped up those who were swearing on behalf of a guilty man. A third method was trial by battle, in which the parties fought, often to the death (the parties later were permitted to use stand-ins—hired

lances, so to speak). By the thirteenth century, a jury of witnesses was well on its way to replacing these barbarisms.

Equity

As time passed, the form of the writs tended to harden. A case had to fall within the four corners of a writ's formula, or it would be dismissed without further hearing. As the economy grew and society became more complex, many types of disputes did not easily fall within the confines of the writ system. Although the common law jurists intoned that "every wrong has a remedy," that was not always true. So people petitioned the kings for relief, and gradually a new system of law developed: **equity.** The king delegated the job of hearing these petitions to the chancellor, keeper of the royal seal and head of the king's council.

Equity removed the hard edges of the common law, softening its rigidities. Informally at first, the chancellor would do justice in individual cases for which the writs were unsuitable. For example, under common law virtually the only possible remedy was an award of money or a return of goods taken. If a seller of land reneged on his contract, the common law courts could not order transfer of title. Similarly, an **injunction,** an order to force someone to discontinue a harmful course of conduct, was not within the power of the common law courts. But the chancellor, acting from his office, known as the chancery, could decree **specific performance** of real estate contracts (direct the parties to carry them out), issue injunctions, and provide other forms of relief.

In theory, a litigant did not have a legal entitlement to equitable relief; the grant of relief was at the discretion of the chancellor, exercising the king's conscience. But in time, the **courts of chancery** developed equity into a full-fledged system of justice. Equity gave relief when there was no "adequate remedy at law."

Today, common law and equity have been merged into a unified court system, although in a few states, chancery courts or chancery divisions of the trial court still exist in name (see **Box 1-2**). A major legacy of the former division between the two concepts concerns the right to jury trial. Juries did not sit in chancery, since the chancellor was doing justice by making

LAW AND LIFE

BOX 1-2

Delaware's Sedate Chancery Court Is a Major Corporate Battlefield

By Mary Williams

[Delaware's chancery court attracts many big corporate cases. This court never empanels jurors, thereby deciding major cases quickly, while providing an informal atmosphere where judges listen to the individual cases and not "the strict letter of the law."
—AUTHORS' NOTE]

Wilmington, Del.—The lawyer for Shell Oil Co. shareholders fumbled as he argued for a preliminary injunction blocking Royal Dutch/Shell Group's $5.49 billion tender offer. He said million when he meant to say billion, then joked that the amounts were so vast he could hardly grasp them.

The judge was not amused. "We deal with that all the time," he said curtly.

It's true—despite appearances. Delaware's Court of Chancery is a small, quiet pair of courtrooms tucked at the back of a building on the Wilmington town square. Most of the time its officials handle humdrum squabbles like divvying up deceased aunts' dishes and ordering bird lovers to clean up their coops because the neighbors are complaining.

But the chancery court, a holdover from 12th-century England, has also become a major battleground in corporate fights.

*   *   *

CHANCERY: OLD-FASHIONED COURT WITH VERY MODERN TASKS

A disproportionate number of the biggest merger and takeover battles turn up here because of the laws of Delaware, which are designed to lure as many corporations as possible to the state. Delaware's low franchise fees, lenient business tax structure and do-as-you-please corporate code have already persuaded about half of the Fortune 500 companies and a third of the concerns listed on the New York Stock Exchange to incorporate here. More come every year, and with them come lawsuits. In Delaware, criminal cases and those involving monetary judgments go to superior court. But when individuals or companies sue the directors of a company incorporated in Delaware, they're usually seeking equitable relief, such as an injunction or a temporary restraining order. And those fall under the jurisdiction of the Court of Chancery.

That dual system isn't the only thing that sets the chancery court apart. It is militantly informal, and small. The whole place consists of four judges—called the chancellor and vice chancellors—two clerks, two court reporters and a half-dozen clerical workers who crank out opinions on an old hand-fed copy machine. When there's a big case, the judges have to help collate the opinions, walking round and round a table along with their secretaries.

*   *   *

Delaware officials assure companies that, if hauled into chancery, they aren't likely to get any rude surprises. The judges are experienced, and the past cases plainly lay out the law. Delaware lawyers can often predict which way the case will swing, the argument goes.

That's one reason so many big cases are filed in Delaware, even though cases against large companies can usually be filed just about anywhere. Another reason is that the chancery court, which never empanels jurors, decides major cases quickly.

*   *   *

[According to] Richard Greenfield, a Pennsylvania lawyer who specializes in shareholder suits, . . . "The judges act very often from the heart. . . . They'll listen to you, rather than the strict letter of the law."

That may be because chancery courts were set up in medieval England to help people who couldn't get justice in the common-law courts. Chancery courts back then didn't bother with formal rules or documents penned in Latin. The British imported the chancery system to America in colonial times, but most states rejected chancery courts as signs of imperial authority. Delaware, an oddball, set up a chancery court in 1792.

*   *   *

Source: *Wall Street Journal*, May 10, 1984

an exception to the hard rules of the common law. This meant that if a plaintiff sought an equitable remedy, such as an injunction or specific performance, he was not entitled to a jury trial. That distinction remains today. Cases seeking equitable relief are for judges; only in cases that were once within the jurisdiction of common law courts are the parties entitled to a jury.

Common law and equity were not the only systems of law. In the seventeenth century, one jurist counted fifteen separate systems. These included maritime law, the law merchant (an international commercial law), and ecclesiastical law (the church courts until Henry VIII's split with the Catholic Church had jurisdiction over what today we call family law, including matrimonial law). In time, equity absorbed much of these other systems.

Preexisting Law vs. Judge-made Law

In the early years, the prerogative of dispensing justice was assumed to be personal to the king; it was an attribute of kingship. By the fifteenth century, however, the press of judicial business was too large, and the kings left the administration of justice to the cadre of judges who increasingly were specially trained in law. By then, kings had become true monarchs, and the coming battles over royal sovereignty would center on the extent of their legislative and executive authority.

What was this judicial power that emanated from the king? Though King James I would insist in 1608 (and thereafter) that the king was superior to the law ("The King protecteth the law, and not the law the King," he said), his predecessors had supposed, at least since 1215, that they were bound by the law. Magna Carta, say Pollock and Maitland, the great historians of medieval English law, "means this, that the king is and shall be below the law." In short, the law—the body of rules that had become the common law—was superior and existed prior to any conscious human creation by judges hearing cases. The law simply *was*, and it was the function of judges to ascertain it, not to make it up. For a time considerably beyond the seventeenth century, even legislation was asserted to be a restoration of the old law, not a breaking of new ground, a reconfirmation of old rights, not a creation of new ones. In this, the kings and

judges acted in accordance with a universal belief of the middle ages, that law was permanent and unchanging. As Fritz Kern, the historian of medieval Europe, put it:

> Modern law is always, in one way or another, enacted by the State. Mediaeval law simply exists; it was accepted by mediaeval opinion not as being enacted by men, but as part of the Just and the Good, which are eternal. . . . Mediaeval law, . . . being neither enacted nor annulled, was not so much actual as timeless. Only good law was real law, no matter whether human law-givers or judges recognized it or ignored it, no matter whether it were positive or "only" ideal law. The attitude of law-givers and judges towards the law was only like a shadow that fell over it; it might obscure the law, but could not set it aside. (Kern, 1970, p. 156)

For several centuries, the theory of law thus developed at odds with its practice. The judges held that they were merely discovering law, even as they grandly created a huge body of common law dealing with subjects unknown to their ancestors. Precisely because it was not of human origin, this law was not to be trifled with.

This notion, that the courts sit to resolve disputes by applying preexisting law, passed into fundamental American law via Montesquieu, who articulated clearly the great principle of the separation of powers—that each of the three branches of government should be confined to its proper sphere. If separation of powers were truly observed, Montesquieu said, the judges would pose no threat: "[T]he national judges are no more than the mouth that pronounces the words of the law, mere passive beings, incapable of moderating either its force or rigour." The delegates to the Constitutional Convention studied Montesquieu; the first three articles of the Constitution owe their general structure to him. The nub of the position is that which any schoolchild can recite: rule-making is for legislators; the courts, when they try cases, are merely interpreting. This textbook view, still devoutly held by many, shades the truth considerably. Though lawmaking troubled the early judges and they frequently created extravagant fictions to persuade themselves or others that they were not deviating from the ancient customs, the courts virtually from the outset were making law. Often substantive changes were cloaked in procedural reform.

Anglo-American courts have always been rule-making institutions. The types of disputes that the common law and equity courts heard gave birth to a huge corpus of rules governing all sorts of private relations. In time these became unexceptionable, and many fields of law down to the present day are articulated largely at the hands of the judges.

Federal vs. State Common Law

The need to parse the nature of common law flows from quite practical considerations. Perhaps the clearest example of the consequences that follow from defining it one way or another is the conundrum of which "law" federal courts should apply when hearing cases based on state legal issues. As we will see in Chapter 2, the Constitution permits federal courts to hear disputes arising between citizens of different states even though no federal claims are involved. These suits would have to be lodged in state courts if the parties were citizens of the same state. Should state or federal law apply in such cases?

Under the 1789 federal Judiciary Act, federal courts are required to apply state "law." The act says: "The laws of the several States, except where the Constitution, treaties, or statutes of the United States shall otherwise require or provide, shall be regarded as rules of decision in trials at common law in the Courts of the United States in cases where they apply." Although somewhat obscure, this language was taken to mean that federal courts must look to state law. On a number of occasions during the early nineteenth century, the U.S. Supreme Court had ruled that there was no "common law of the United States." The common law exists only within each state, and the common law of each state may be different. Then, in 1842, Supreme Court Justice Joseph Story wrote an opinion that radically changed this understanding. [Swift v. Tyson, 41 U.S. 1 (1842)]

The case arose in New York and raised the question of whether the payment of a negotiable bill in return for a promise to cancel a preexisting debt constituted a valid contract. The parties were citizens of different states, so the case was brought in federal court. New York had no statute governing the question. State judicial decisions did not clearly spell out the law. So to what state law should the federal court look?

The answer turned on the fundamental meaning of "law" itself. Justice Story said that only statutes are law, not court decisions, and consequently federal courts could decide independently what the common law of a state should be. The philosophy that common law is some preexisting metaphysical concept that judges somehow discern through right reasoning has claimed the better part of Anglo-American legal history. But it was not without its detractors, and by the turn of the twentieth century critics more emphatically and cogently showed that common law is not found but made—by judges. In a characteristically acerbic and celebrated aside, Justice Oliver Wendell Holmes, dissenting in a 1917 Supreme Court case, declared that "law is not a brooding omnipresence in the sky." [Southern Pacific Co. v. Jensen, 244 U.S. 205 (1917)]

Finally, in 1938, the force of criticism by the so-called "legal realists" caught up to the Supreme Court, and Justice Story's conclusion was rejected; the ninety-six-year-old precedent was reversed. There is no general federal common law, the Court declared. In deciding a case based on diversity of citizenship, the federal judges must look to both state statutes and state court decisions, not to their own conception of "general commercial law," or some other general law. [Erie Railroad Co. v. Tompkins, 304 U.S. 64 (1938)]

NATURE OF THE JUDICIAL PROCESS

On what basis do judges interpret and declare law? Judges certainly are not free to pluck from thin air any policies they would like and simply declare them as law. Of course judges may rationalize their decisions, as a dictator cloaks his arbitrary actions in the guise of reasonableness. There is no one to stop them from doing so, except a higher court or a legislature aroused enough to enact a new law. But if they are adhering faithfully to the judicial process, how do they make their decisions?

Many judges and scholars have wrestled with this question. It is not possible to give a short or definitive answer. Judging is at bottom an art. Judges will naturally look at constitutions and statutes, and a variety of principles govern the interpretation of statutory language. (For example, an interpretation that renders consistent two provisions in a statute is to be preferred to an interpretation that makes them contradictory.) If the language of the statute does not help, judges will naturally look to precedent: *stare decisis* remains a guiding principle of our law. When the previous cases fit the facts of the present one, the decision will be easy. But few cases are so simple; when the law is clear, the parties rarely argue very long about it.

Even a precedent itself is subject to questioning, retesting, and reformulating. As Justice Benjamin N. Cardozo wrote in *The Nature of the Judicial Process*:

Fifty years ago [around 1870], I think it would have been stated as a general principle that A. may conduct his business as he pleases, even though the purpose is to cause loss to B., unless the act involves the creation of a nuisance. Spite fences were the stock illustration, and the exemption from liability in such circumstances was supposed to illustrate not the exception, but the rule. Such a rule may have been an adequate working principle to regulate the relations between individuals or classes in a simple or homogenous community. With the growing complexity of social relations, its inadequacy was revealed. As particular controversies multiplied and the attempt was made to test them by the old principle, it was found that there was something wrong in the results, and this led to a reformulation of the principle itself. Today, most judges are inclined to say that what was once thought to be the exception is the rule, and what was the rule is the exception. A. may never do anything in his business for the purpose of injuring another without reasonable and just excuse. There has been a new generalization which, applied to new particulars, yields results more in harmony with past particulars, and, what is still more important, more consistent with the social welfare. This work of modification is gradual. It goes on inch by inch. Its effects must be measured by decades and even centuries. Thus measured, they are seen to have behind them the power and the pressure of the moving glacier. (Cardozo, 1921, pp. 24–25)

Because the process of modification is gradual, few judicial opinions crystallize the moment when change has occurred. It is usually only afterward that one can look back and see how much ground has been covered. The following case, decided by the Minnesota Supreme Court, is remarkable for the way in which it reflects on the necessity for change, and even more remarkable for announcing a new rule that would apply thereafter, but not to the case in which it was decided. The opinion is a useful guide to and summary of the process of judicial reasoning and the nature of law (although the court's ultimate conclusion, that it would overrule an established legal principle only prospectively, is highly unusual).

The facts were simple. A five-year-old boy was injured on a slide in his kindergarten classroom. His father brought suit against the public school district, the school principal, and the boy's teacher, alleging that they were negligent in permitting the children to play on a defective slide. The lower court dismissed the lawsuit without trial on the grounds that a well-established legal doctrine—that of "sovereign immunity"—barred lawsuits against public agencies or its employees.

SPANEL v. MOUNDS VIEW SCHOOL DISTRICT NO. 621
264 Minn. 279, 118 N.W.2d 795 (1962)

Otis, Justice.

Plaintiff sues on behalf of his 5-year-old son to recover damages from a school district and a teacher and principal employed by it for injuries resulting from the alleged negligence of defendants in permitting a defective slide to remain in the kindergarten classroom of an elementary school.

Plaintiff appeals from an order granting a motion to dismiss the action as to defendant school district on the ground the complaint fails to state a claim upon which relief can be granted against it.

The only issue before us is whether the doctrine of governmental tort immunity shall now be overruled by judicial decision.

★   ★   ★

We hold that the order for dismissal is affirmed, with the caveat, however, that subject to the limitations we now discuss, the defense of sovereign im-

(continued on next page)

(*continued*)

SPANEL v. MOUNDS VIEW SCHOOL DISTRICT NO. 621
264 Minn. 279, 118 N.W.2d 795 (1962)

munity will no longer be available to school districts, municipal corporations, and other subdivisions of government on whom immunity has been conferred by judicial decision with respect to torts which are committed after the adjournment of the next regular session of the Minnesota Legislature.

All of the paths leading to the origin of governmental tort immunity converge on Russell v. The Men of Devon, 100 Eng.Rep. 359 (1788). This product of the English common law was left on our doorstep to become the putative ancestor of a long line of American cases beginning with Mower v. Leicester, 9 Mass. 247 (1812). Russell sued all of the male inhabitants of the County of Devon for damages occurring to his wagon by reason of a bridge being out of repair. It was apparently undisputed that the county had a duty to maintain such structures. The court held that the action would not lie because: (1) To permit it would lead to "an infinity of actions," (2) there was no precedent for attempting such a suit, (3) only the legislature should impose liability of this kind, (4) even if defendants are to be considered a corporation or quasi-corporation there is no fund out of which to satisfy the claim, (5) neither law nor reason supports the action, (6) there is a strong presumption that what has never been done cannot be done, and (7) although there is a legal principle which permits a remedy for every injury resulting from the neglect of another, a more applicable principle is "that it is better that an individual should sustain an injury than that the public should suffer an inconvenience." The court concluded that the suit should not be permitted *because the action must be brought against the public.* (Italics supplied.) There is no mention of "the king can do no wrong," but on the contrary it is suggested that plaintiff sue the county itself rather than its individual inhabitants. Every reason assigned by the court is born of expediency. The wrong to plaintiff is submerged in the convenience of the public. No moral, ethical, or rational reason for the decision is advanced by the court except the practical problem of assessing damages against individual defendants. The court's invitation to the legislature has a familiar ring. It was finally accepted as to claims against the Crown in 1947, although Russell had long since been overruled.

In 1812 when Mower's horse was killed by stepping in a hole on the Leicester bridge, counsel argued that "Men of Devon" did not apply since the town of Leicester was incorporated and had a treasury out of which to satisfy a judgment. The Massachusetts court nevertheless held that the town had no notice of the defect and that quasi-corporations are not liable for such neglect under the common law. On the authority of "Men of Devon" recovery was denied. It was on this shaky foundation that the law of governmental tort immunity was erected in Minnesota and elsewhere.

★   ★   ★

California undertook to abolish tort immunity in a suit against a public hospital district. Mr. Justice Traynor in a carefully documented and thoroughly considered opinion adverted to Borchard's comment in his classic treatise on the subject:

Nothing seems more clear than that this immunity of the King from the jurisdiction of the King's courts was purely personal. How it came to be applied in the United States of America, where the prerogative is unknown, is one of the mysteries of legal evolution.

★   ★   ★

. . . It has been argued on behalf of defendants that if immunity is abolished public schools will be deluged with claims for injuries resulting from inadequate supervision, from frostbite while waiting for buses, from blows struck by other children, from forbidden and mischievous activities impulsively and foolishly inspired, and from a host of other causes. School children have a special status in the eyes of the law, and in view of the compulsory attendance statute deserve more than ordinary protection. Operating an educational system has been described as one of the nation's biggest businesses. The fact that subdivisions of government now enjoy no immunity in a number of areas of activity has not noticeably circumscribed their usefulness or rendered them insolvent.

★   ★   ★

While the court has the right and the duty to modify rules of the common law after they have become archaic, we readily concede that the flexibility of the legislative process—which is denied the judiciary—makes the latter avenue of approach more desirable.

★   ★   ★

Counsel has assured us that members of the bar, in and out of the legislature, intend to draft and secure the introduction of bills at the forthcoming session which will give affected entities of government an opportunity to meet their new obligations. A number of procedural and substantive proposals for the orderly processing of claims have been suggested. Among them are: (1) A requirement for giving prompt notice of the claim after the occurrence of the tort, (2) a reduction in the usual period of limitations, (3) a monetary limit on the amount of liability, (4) the establishment of a special claims court or commission, or provision for trial by the court without a jury, and (5) the continuation of the defense of immunity as to some or all units of government for a limited or indefinite period of time.

★   ★   ★

On this subject Mr. Justice Cardozo has stated (109 Pa.L.Rev. 13):

> The rule that we are asked to apply is out of tune with the life about us. It has been made discordant by the forces that generate a living law. We apply it to this case because the repeal might work hardship to those who have trusted to its existence. We give notice, however, that any one trusting to it hereafter will do so at his peril.

(continued on next page)

(continued)

SPANEL v. MOUNDS VIEW SCHOOL DISTRICT NO. 621
264 Minn. 279, 118 N.W.2d 795 (1962)

It may appear unfair to deprive the present claimant of his day in court. However, we are of the opinion it would work an even greater injustice to deny defendant and other units of government a defense on which they have had a right to rely. We believe that it is more equitable if they are permitted to plan in advance by securing liability insurance or by creating funds necessary for self-insurance. In addition, provision must be made for routinely and promptly investigating personal injury and other tort claims at the time of their occurrence in order that defendants may marshal and preserve whatever evidence is available for the proper conduct of their defense.

Affirmed.

CHAPTER SUMMARY

Law is the set of rules and institutions that permit us to lead a civilized and orderly life. In a democratic society, laws must be known and understood, but complete certainty in law is not merely impossible, it is undesirable. The study of law is not like the study of chemistry or some other science; it is a discipline that requires interpretation, that calls for an understanding of human nature, philosophy, logic, and common sense. Law is a means of fixing in written form our present values and social goals.

Law can be categorized by both its substantive and its procedural aspects. One of the broadest divisions is between criminal and civil law—rules barring acts offensive to society as a whole and rules and regulations that govern our private relations.

In the United States there are several sources of law: legislative enactments, administrative regulations, and judicial decisions. These different types of law emanate from various levels: federal, state, and local. Underlying all American law is the Constitution, which regulates the relationships among the different branches of government and puts limits on their powers.

Courts play three essential roles: (1) They are the forum in which the facts of a case can be determined, (2) they apply the law to the facts, and (3) they interpret the law. The latter function gives the judiciary considerable power, for through judicial review they can void statutes that conflict with the Constitution.

The Constitution deals almost exclusively with powers of and limitations on government, rather than with private conduct. The civil liberties embodied in the First and Fourteenth Amendments have given the courts a large role to play in preserving freedoms against state intrusion. But the Constitution is not the only source of judicial authority. Courts have long independently developed the common law.

Article 1 of the U.S. Constitution gives Congress the power to regulate interstate and foreign commerce. The Supreme Court

has broadly construed the Commerce Clause. "Commerce" means more than merely buying or selling; it connotes the whole stream of activities, including the manufacture and transportation of commodities and the providing of services. Congress can reach deeply into economic matters within the states, for any activity that "affects" interstate commerce is subject to federal regulation. If Congress had enacted a law under the Commerce Clause any state law or regulation that conflicts with it is invalid.

The states continue to have a large role in business regulation. Under their "police powers," the state may enact all sorts of regulations that reasonably relate to the public health, safety, morals, and welfare. Although the Supreme Court once limited the power of states to act (by declaring certain types of economic regulations invalid under the due process clause), today the courts for the most part have recognized the constitutional validity of economic regulation, as long as the means employed rationally relate to a legitimate state goal. Wholly arbitrary laws, however, will be struck down. Moreover, before taking away property or denying some other valuable right, or permitting private individuals to do so, the state must provide a hearing to those whose property or rights are affected.

Although the equal protection clause of the Fourteenth Amendment, as interpreted in recent years, has provided women, minorities, and other groups with a powerful means of ending legalized discrimination, businesses generally cannot claim its protection. The Supreme Court almost always allows the states to distinguish among different types of economic activities when enacting laws or writing regulations.

Despite the breadth of the police power, the states may not enact regulations over commerce if the effect is to discriminate against out-of-state business or to burden interstate commerce. Local protectionism is a violation of the Commerce Clause. The theory of the Constitution is that a national market without barriers shall exist among the states to ensure the flow of trade.

Corporations enjoy certain rights available to all persons. These include the freedoms of speech and press. The government may not tell business how or what it may truthfully advertise. But companies are not entitled to every right applicable to individuals. For example, corporations do not enjoy the privilege against self-incrimination—corporations must turn over incriminating documents to the courts on demand.

The government may seize private property for a public purpose if it pays just compensation. Any sort of physical invasion or occupation is deemed a taking for payment purposes. But not every inference with the use of property amounts to a taking so that only some economic regulations require payment to those whose use or enjoyment of property is undermined by the regulation.

The Contract Clause says that the states may not impair the obligation of contracts, but for the most part the courts have held that all private contracts are subject to the reasonable exercise of the police power.

KEY TERMS

Adjective law	p. 9	Local government	p. 9
Courts of Chancery	p. 33	Original jurisdiction	p. 14
Civil law	p. 7	Private law	p. 7
Common law	p. 4	Procedural law	p. 9
Compurgation	p. 33	Public law	p. 7
Damages	p. 3	Specific performance	p. 33
Due process of law	p. 19	Stare decisis	p. 33
Equity	p. 33	State action	p. 23
Federal government	p. 31	State government	p. 9
Injunction	p. 33	Substantive law	p. 9
Judicial review	p. 13	Tort	p. 7
Law	p. 3		

SELF-TEST QUESTIONS

1. The following agencies or branches of government may make law:
   (a) a city council
   (b) the Internal Revenue Service
   (c) Congress
   (d) a state supreme court
   (e) all of the above
2. The common law is:
   (a) the same in each state
   (b) made by courts
   (c) imported from England
   (d) protected from changes by state legislatures
3. The constitutional guarantee against impairment of contract prohibits:
   (a) someone who signs a contract from breaking it
   (b) a state court from interpreting it
   (c) a state legislature from revoking an existing installment sales contract

   (d) a company from entering into an unfair contract with a consumer
4. Which of the following statements is false?
   (a) Under the Constitution, Congress may freeze the wages of soldiers and sailors.
   (b) Under the Constitution, Congress may freeze the wages of private railway workers.
   (c) Under the Constitution, Congress may freeze a child's allowance given by a parent.
   (d) Under the Constitution, Congress may prohibit sales of toys that pollute the air.
5. Which of the following statements is true?
   (a) Once it decides a constitutional question, the Supreme Court may never reverse itself.
   (b) Your state may never seize your house if all it wants to do is build a convention center.
   (c) Under the Equal Protection Clause, a state must tax every business equally.
   (d) Under the Equal Protection Clause, a state must tax every business in the same way.
   (e) All of the above.
   (d) None of the above.

DEMONSTRATION PROBLEM

You hear screams coming from your neighbor's apartment just upstairs from yours. You suspect that her husband is beating her up. However, you are afraid to become involved since her husband is large and menacing. Do you have a legal obligation to call the police? Could your neighbor sue you in federal court for failing to come to her rescue? Could she sue you in state court? Why or why not?

PROBLEMS

1. A municipal hospital had failed for many years to repair its stairways. One day a visitor caught her shoe on a particularly large crack and fell down a flight of stairs, seriously injuring herself. She sued the hospital which defended itself by invoking the doctrine of "sovereign immunity." What is that doctrine? How could the courts abolish sovereign immunity? How could the legislature abolish it?
2. Name the principal branches of substantive law and describe them briefly.
3. Under what circumstances may a federal court declare a state law unconstitutional? Under what circumstances may a state court declare a state law unconstitutional? Under what circumstances may a state court declare a federal law unconstitutional?

4. Ten years ago, the state's highest court announced as a rule of law that a mother who sees her child run over by an automobile may not recover money damages for the acute mental distress she suffered. This year, a jury has awarded a mother damages under these circumstances. The driver appeals the jury award to the state's highest court. Different judges are now sitting on that court. How must they rule? Must they throw out the jury's award? May they do so? What arguments can you find for reversing the jury? Sustaining it?

5. A congressional investigation revealed that conditions in a particular mining industry were perilous to the miners. As a result of the investigation, Congress proposed to enact a statute regulating the number of hours that workers could spend in the mines and setting forth a variety of safety measures that the mining companies would have to follow. Critics of the proposed law objected on the ground that the industry was concentrated entirely in one state and the the state for years had refused to regulate it. What source of power for Congress to regulate mining conditions could proponents of the federal law point to? What facts about the industry would have to be assumed for Congress to invoke that power?

6. A student is suspected of smoking marijuana in a local high school. The principal wishes to suspend him. Must the principal give the student a hearing before doing so? Why? A book club decides to terminate a member because she has not paid her bill. Must the club give the member a hearing before doing so? Why? What does your answer depend on? Assuming that there is no law dealing with the book club, what branch(es) of which government(s) could make one?

7. You make a deal with Fred to paint the outside of your house with a special paint that Fred prepares. It is a lead-based paint that will give your house special protection. You give Fred a down payment, but before he can start the job, your town council passes an ordinance banning, for health reasons, the use of lead-based paint on any structure. Fred refuses to use the paint, and you sue him for breach of contract. You assert that your contract with

Fred has been impaired by the ordinance and that it is therefore unconstitutional. What result?

8. Your city has a major league baseball franchise. The team threatens to move because it doesn't like the way its fans have been treating it (they boo and throw beer cans onto the infield). The city council passes a bill "seizing" the team's franchise under its power of eminent domain. What arguments could the team make in challenging the seizure? Who would win?

9. The state passes a law requiring all opticians to have a prescription from a medical doctor before selling lenses or frames to any customer. The law even requires that a customer who wants a new frame for her lenses must have a prescription before the optician can fit her current lenses into the new frame. The law exempts sellers of ready-to-wear sunglasses. What constitutional objections can the opticians make to this law? Who will win in a court test of the law?

ANSWERS TO SELF-TEST QUESTIONS

1. (e)   2. (b)   3. (c)   4. (c)   5. (e)

SUGGESTED ANSWER TO DEMONSTRATION PROBLEM

In the absence of a statute imposing a duty to report the incident or to come to someone's rescue, you have no legal obligation. A legal duty to aid someone in distress is a matter for state law, not federal law, so in any event your neighbor could not sue you in federal court. Even if a state statute imposed a general obligation to assist, it would likely provide for a small fine if you failed to do so, and would not give the victim a right to sue for damages in state court. See Box 1-1 for a description of Minnesota's statutory policy to assist people in distress.

CHAPTER OVERVIEW

The Relationship of the State and Federal Court Systems

Legal Procedure

Who May Sue

Relations with Lawyers

Alternative Means of Resolving Disputes

Courts, Lawyers, and the Legal Process

*I*n the United States, law and government are interdependent. The Constitution created the basic framework of government and imposes certain limitations on the powers of government. In turn, the various branches of government are intimately involved in the making, enforcing, and interpreting of law. Much of the law today is statutory—emanating from Congress and the state legislatures. But the student of law is concerned with the courts, because it is there that law in its broadest sense is interpreted and understood—it is up to the courts to determine what a law in a particular case actually means.

THE RELATIONSHIP OF THE STATE AND FEDERAL COURT SYSTEMS

It is sometimes said that there are two separate court systems in the United States: state and federal. The reality is more complex. In fact there are more than fifty-three court systems: those of the fifty states, the local court systems in the District of Columbia and Puerto Rico, the federal court system, and the local courts in territories outside the United States under the jurisdiction of the United States. Even the federal court system is not monolithic: in addition to the regular federal trial courts in each state, there are specialized courts, such as those in the military and for the tax system. At the same time, these different courts have several points of contact.

From the states' perspective, the local courts often must honor federal law or the laws of other states.

1. State courts are bound to uphold federal law in the face of conflicting state laws under the Supremacy Clause of the Constitution.
2. A number of claims arising under federal statutes may be tried in the state courts. In other words, the jurisdiction of the federal courts to hear cases under federal law is not always *exclusive*.
3. Under the Full Faith and Credit Clause, each state court is obligated to respect the final judgments of courts in other states. Thus, a divorce decree

handed down by an Arkansas court cannot be re-litigated in North Dakota.

4. State courts frequently must consider the laws of other states in deciding cases involving issues that cut across state lines—two drivers, each from a different state, collide in a third state. A body of law known as "conflicts of laws" dictates, under these circumstances, that courts should look to the law of the state where the accident happened.

As state courts are concerned with federal law, so federal courts often are concerned with proceedings in state courts. Because federal law is supreme, decisions of the state courts sometimes can be appealed to the federal courts. Usually appeal is from the state supreme court to the U.S. Supreme Court. In certain types of cases, a lower federal court can hear an appeal—for example, a *habeas corpus* (HAY bee us KOR pus) petition from a prisoner in a state jail complaining that his constitutional rights were violated during his trial. Federal courts also consider state claims when a case involves both state and federal issues. The federal issues permit the federal court to take jurisdiction over the whole case, including the state issues; the federal court is said to exercise "pendent jurisdiction" over the state claims.

There is also a broad category of cases heard in federal courts that concern only state legal issues—namely, cases that arise between citizens of different states. The federal courts are permitted to hear these cases under their so-called **diversity of citizenship** jurisdiction, or diversity jurisdiction. A citizen of New Jersey may sue a citizen of New York over a contract dispute in federal court, whereas if both were citizens of New Jersey, the plaintiff would be limited to the state courts. This diversity jurisdiction was established in the Constitution because it was feared that local courts would be hostile toward people from other states and that they therefore needed politically separate courts. Today, one quarter of all lawsuits filed in federal court are based on diversity of citizenship. Although it is unlikely that the outcome of many cases in state court would be affected by the citizenship of the parties, there can be advantages to pressing a suit in federal court. Federal procedures are often more efficient than state court procedures, federal dockets are often less crowded and hence a case can go forward faster, and many lawyers enjoy the generally higher status that comes in practicing before the fed-eral bench. But in any federal case based on diversity jurisdiction, the court must apply state law, whether legislative enactment or judicial decision. When the law of the state is unclear, the federal courts are not free to substitute their own independent judgment; they must attempt to predict how the state courts would rule on the issue if presented with the same case.

State Court Systems

Most lawsuits in America are brought to state courts. Despite the great variety of court systems that exist from state to state, two types of judicial *functions* are common to all: trials and appeals. A court exercising a **trial** function has *original jurisdiction*—that is, jurisdiction to determine the facts of the case and apply the law to them. A court that hears **appeals** from the trial court is said to have *appellate jurisdiction*—it must accept the facts as determined by the trial court and limit its review to the lower court's theory of the applicable law.

Limited Jurisdiction Courts   In most of the large urban states, and in many of the smaller states, there are four and sometimes five levels of courts. The lowest level is that of the **limited jurisdiction** courts. These are usually the county or municipal courts with original jurisdiction to hear minor criminal cases (petty assaults, traffic offenses, breach of peace, and the like) and civil cases involving monetary amounts up to a fixed ceiling (in most states no more than $10,000 and in many states far less). Most disputes in the United States that wind up in court are handled in the 18,000-plus limited jurisdiction courts, which are estimated to hear more than 80 percent of all cases in the states.

A variant of the limited jurisdiction court is the **small claims court,** with jurisdiction to hear civil cases involving claims for amounts ranging between $1,000 and $5,000 in about half the states and in the other states for considerably less ($500 to $1,000). The advantage of the small claims court is that its procedures are informal, it is often located in neighborhoods outside the business districts, it is usually open after business hours, and it is speedy. Lawyers are not necessary to present the case and in some states are not allowed to appear in court.

General Jurisdiction Courts All other civil and criminal cases are heard in the general trial courts, or courts of **general jurisdiction.** These go by a variety of names—often, Superior, Circuit, District, or Common Pleas Court. (New York anomalously calls its general trial court the Supreme Court.) It is to these courts that suitors seek redress for injuries suffered in automobile accidents, for breach of contract, and for all the other calamities that can befall the individual or corporation in the modern world. In these courts also the state prosecutes those accused of murder, rape, robbery, and other serious crimes. Generally at the election of the parties, the fact-finder in the courts of general jurisdiction is not the judge, as in the lower courts, but a jury of citizens.

Although courts of general jurisdiction can hear every type of case, in most states more than half the civil filings involve family matters (divorce, child custody disputes, and the like). A study conducted by the U.S. Department of Justice showed that in a specially selected sample of five general jurisdiction courts, commercial cases make up about one-third of the courts' dockets. About 12 percent of the dockets are devoted to automobile accident cases and other torts (discussed in Chapter 4).

Many states have specialized courts that hear only a certain class of cases—for example, landlord-tenant disputes or probate of wills.

By and large, cases decided by judges in the courts of limited jurisdiction are concluded at that point. Some of these cases can be retried, if one of the parties is dissatisfied with the outcome, in a court of general jurisdiction. This kind of retrial is known as a trial *de novo* (day NO vo). It is not an appeal, since the case is begun afresh.

Appellate Courts In most states, the losing party in a general jurisdiction court can take an appeal to an **intermediate appellate** court—usually called the Court of Appeals. These courts do not retry the evidence but sit instead to determine whether the trial was conducted in a procedurally proper manner and whether appropriate law was applied properly to the facts. For example, the **appellant** (the losing party who takes the appeal) might complain that the judge wrongly instructed the jury on the meaning of the law, or improperly admitted into evidence the testimony of a particular witness, or misconstrued the law in question. (The party who won in the lower court and is defending that judgment is called the **appellee.**) The appellate court can *affirm* the judgment of the lower court, *modify* it, *reverse* it, or *reverse and remand*—that is, return the case to the lower court for retrial.

The final avenue of appeal within the state court systems is to the state supreme court, which in most states sits in the state capital as a single panel of between five and nine judges. (The intermediate appellate courts usually sit in panels of three judges and are located in various parts of the state.) In a few states the highest court goes by a different name; in New York, for example, it is known as the Court of Appeals. Some types of cases may be appealed at the option of the appellant (appeal *of right*). In many states, however, the supreme court has the discretion to select the cases it wishes to hear. For most litigants, the ruling of the state supreme court is final. In a relatively narrow class of cases—those in which federal constitutional claims are made—appeal to the U.S. Supreme Court remains a possibility.

The Federal Court System

District Courts The federal judicial system is uniform throughout the United States and consists of three levels. The trial courts are known as **district** courts. Every state is divided into federal districts, ranging from one in the less populous states to four in California, Texas, and New York. The federal court with the heaviest commercial docket is the United States District Court for the Southern District of New York (Manhattan). There are 97 district courts, and Congress has authorized 575 U.S. district judges. The district judge conducts all federal trials, criminal and civil.

Courts of Appeals Cases can be appealed to the circuit courts of appeal, of which there are thirteen (Figure 2-1). Each circuit oversees the work of the district courts in several states. For example, the U.S. Court of Appeals for the Second Circuit hears appeals from the district courts in New York, Connecticut, and Vermont. The U.S. Court of Appeals for the Ninth Circuit hears appeals from the district courts in California, Oregon, Nevada, Montana, Washington, Idaho, Arizona, Alaska, Hawaii, and Guam. The U.S. Court of Appeals for the District of Columbia

Figure 2-1   The Thirteen Federal Judicial Circuits

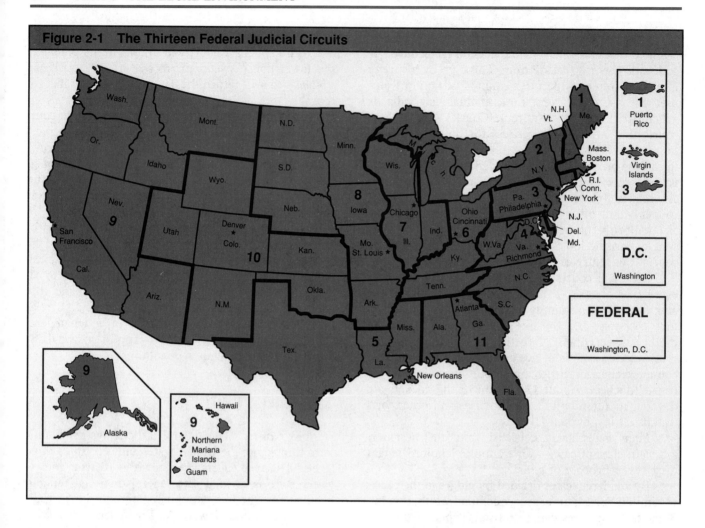

Circuit hears appeals from the district court in Washington, D.C., as well as from numerous federal administrative agencies (see Chapter 5). The U.S. Court of Appeals for the Federal Circuit, also located in Washington, D.C., hears appeals in patent and customs cases. Appeals are heard by panels of three judges. Congress has authorized 168 circuit judges.

There are also several specialized courts in the federal judicial system. These include the U.S. Tax Court and the Court of Claims.

United States Supreme Court   Overseeing the circuit courts is the U.S. Supreme Court, which sits in Washington, D.C. It consists of nine justices—the chief justice of the United States and eight associate justices. (This number is not constitutionally required; Congress can establish any number. It has been set at

nine since after the Civil War.) The Supreme Court has discretion over its docket. During its 1989–1990 term, of the 4,908 cases the Supreme Court disposed of, it granted *certiorari* (sur she uh RAIR ee)—a writ to a lower court to hand over the records in a case for review—in 205 and disposed of only 201 cases on the merits. The Supreme Court does not sit in panels. All the justices hear and consider each case together. The Supreme Court can also hear appeals from state cases. These usually are appeals from the decisions of state supreme courts, but if there is no other avenue of appeal and constitutional issues are raised, a case can be appealed even from courts of limited jurisdiction.

Unlike state judges, most of whom are elected and sit for a fixed term of years, federal judges are nominated by the president and must be confirmed by the Senate. They sit for life, although a law providing for retirement at age seventy at full pay induces most federal judges to retire and become "senior" judges. They may continue to hear cases but need not maintain a full workload. Retired judges are not counted in the totals of authorized judges, so the president may appoint a new judge when a sitting judge "takes senior status."

Federal Jurisdiction The federal judicial system hears few cases relative to the state dockets. Its jurisdiction is spelled out in the Constitution. Congress can limit the jurisdiction of federal courts—for example, until 1875, Congress did not permit the federal district courts to hear cases arising under federal law. But, as Chief Justice Marshall taught in *Marbury* v. *Madison*, Congress may not enlarge federal jurisdiction.

Today, federal courts have jurisdiction virtually coextensive with that laid down as permissible in the Constitution. That includes: (1) cases to which the United States itself is a party; (2) disputes between states, between a state and citizens of another state, between citizens of different states (diversity of citizenship, as discussed on p. 44), between a state or its citizens and a foreign government or its citizens, and disputes affecting foreign ambassadors and other such officials; (3) cases "arising under [the] Constitution, the laws of the United States, and treaties made, or which shall be made, under their authority"; and (4) admiralty and maritime cases. The first and third categories provide the bulk of the cases now in federal court. Cases "arising under" the Constitution and federal law involve claims of violations of civil rights, antitrust, environmental, patent, copyright, securities, and scores of other congressional statutes. For diversity cases, the second category above, the amount in controversy must exceed $50,000; if it is smaller, the dispute must be heard in state court.

LEGAL PROCEDURE

Adjudication and the Adversary System

Courts are not the only institutions that can resolve disputes. We examine alternative forums below (p. 66). For now, let us consider the nature of **adjudication,** the process by which courts make decisions.

Courts do not resolve disputes any which way they please. Judicial decision-making is a distinctive form of dispute resolution. In the first place, courts sit to resolve **disputes,** not problems or generalized grievances—to get the attention of a court, the litigant must make a claim of legal right or entitlement. Second, courts do not reach out for cases. A case must be brought to the court in a particular way that we will explore shortly.

Once at the court, the case will proceed through the **proofs** (submission of evidence) and **arguments** (debate about the meaning of the evidence and the law) of contesting parties. This is the essential characteristic of the **adversary system,** in which those who oppose each other may attack the other's case through proofs and cross-examination. Every person in the United States who wishes to take a case to court is entitled to hire a lawyer. In felony cases—that is, serious crimes—and in many cases involving lesser crimes (misdemeanors) the state must provide a lawyer free to a defendant who cannot afford one. The lawyer works for his client, not the court, and serves him as an advocate. The client wishes to persuade the court of the accuracy and propriety of his position. The lawyer's duty is to shape the evidence and the argument—that is, the line of reasoning about the evidence—to advance his client's cause and persuade the court of its rightness. The lawyer for the opposing **party** (as a litigant is known in court) will be doing the same thing, of course, for her client. From this crossfire of evidence and argument the judge (or, if one is sitting, the jury) must sort out the facts and reach a conclusion.

The method of adjudication has several important characteristics. (1) It places the issues in controversy in sharp focus. Tangential concerns are minimized or excluded altogether. **Relevance** is a key concept in any trial: testimony and other evidence presented in court must have some bearing on the issues being litigated. Relevance is a legal concept: a person may have had an honest motive for breaching a contract, for example, but if the law excludes motive as a justification for breach, it would be irrelevant to tell a judge or jury about the motive of the person who breached the contract. Likewise, (2) the judge is required to decide the questions presented at the trial, not to discourse on related matters that a legislature might wish to take up if the matter were before the people's elected representatives. (3) Adjudication requires that the judge's decision be reasoned, which is why judges write opinions explaining their decisions (an opinion may be omitted when the verdict comes from the jury). (4) The judge's decision must not only be reasoned, but also be **responsive** to the case presented: the judge is not free to say that the case bores him or is unimportant and that he therefore will ignore it. Unlike other branches of government that are free to ignore problems pressing upon them, judges *must* decide cases. By contrast, the legislature need not enact a law, no matter how many people petition it to do so. (5) Moreover, the court must respond in a certain way. The judge must pay attention to the parties' arguments and his decision must be an outgrowth of their proofs and arguments.

Because it must proceed from the parties' proofs and arguments, the judicial decision cannot turn on the whim of the judge or jury. Moreover, there are particular standards for determining which side must prevail, although the standards can be difficult to apply in any given case. In all cases, the **plaintiff**—the party making a claim and initiating the lawsuit (in a criminal case the plaintiff is the **prosecution**)—has the burden of proving the case. If he fails to prove it, the **defendant**—the party being sued or prosecuted— will win. This is an important point worth stressing: it is up to the plaintiff to prove why he should win; it is not up to the defendant to prove why the plaintiff should lose. Although a plaintiff in any case must satisfy the burden of proof, the nature of the burden differs in different cases. In other words, in some cases, a plaintiff must satisfy a more stringent burden of proof than in others. The government in a criminal prosecution must satisfy the highest standard of proof: the government must prove its case against the defendant *beyond a reasonable doubt.* Even if it seems more probable than not that the defendant committed the crime, as long as there remains some reasonable doubt—perhaps she was not clearly identified as the culprit, perhaps she has an alibi that could be legitimate—she must be acquitted. Certain types of civil cases, especially those involving decisions of administrative agencies of the government, call for *clear and convincing* proof. This burden, too, is higher than a more-probable-than-not standard. The burden in ordinary civil cases—those dealing with contracts, personal injuries, and most of the cases in this book—is that of a *preponderance of the evidence,* which simply means that the plaintiff's evidence of his claim that he was wrongfully injured by the defendant must outweigh the defendant's evidence casting doubt on the plaintiff's claim.

Although the plaintiff has the ultimate burden of proving the case, he does not necessarily have the burden of proving every fact at issue. For example, suppose Herb sues Ron, alleging that Ron owes him $100. Ron admits that he borrowed the money but contends that he paid Herb back. This kind of response is known as **confession and avoidance:** the defendant admits the plaintiff's premise but denies that the asserted conclusion follows. Who should have the burden of proving that Ron paid back the money? If the burden lay on the plaintiff, Herb would be in the difficult situation of trying to prove a negative: that he never received repayment. So the law places the burden on defendants in instances such as this: to demonstrate the affirmative fact that he did indeed repay the borrowed amount. The defendant should be able to do that easily enough, in this case, by presenting a receipt.

The adversary system has been praised and deplored. Its detractors stress that it values winning too highly and demeans the truth and the sensibilities of people who stand in the way of a client's victory. Moreover, an adversary system can impose high costs and long delays on the parties. When fact-finding is in the hands of the parties themselves, they can employ one artifice or another to stretch out the proceedings in an attempt to cause their opponents to lose heart or pocketbook.

At the same time, the adversary process is a bulwark of liberty in a free society. Without independent counsel, free to contest the claims of a government bent on jailing its political enemies, dissenters can rather easily be imprisoned, though they committed no crimes—as the records of the Soviet Union and of other authoritarian regimes clearly demonstrate. Likewise, without the ability to search relentlessly for facts and to probe the other side, serious wrongs would go unredressed. The law itself might be an empty shell.

Adjudication and the adversary system imply certain other characteristics of courts. (1) Judges must be impartial. Those with a personal interest in a matter before them must refuse to hear it. (2) The ruling of a court, after all appeals are exhausted, is final. This principle is known as *res judicata* (race jew dee CAW tuh) (Latin for "the thing is decided"), which means that the parties may not take up their quarrel in another court at another time. (3) Finally, a court must proceed according to a public set of formal procedural rules; a judge cannot make up the rules of the game as he goes along. To these rules we now turn.

How a Case Goes Through Court

Complaint and Summons   Beginning a lawsuit is simple and is spelled out in the rules of procedure by which each court system operates. In the federal system, the plaintiff begins a lawsuit by filing a **complaint**—a typed document spelling out in general terms his grounds for suit—with the clerk of the court. The court marshal will then serve the defendant with the complaint and a **summons,** a court document stating the name of the plaintiff and his attorney and directing the defendant to **answer** (respond to) the complaint within a fixed period. Many state court systems use the same rule. Others permit suits to be initiated by serving the defendant directly, either with the summons and complaint or sometimes with just the summons, before going to court. For ease of description, the discussion in this section speaks in terms of actions by plaintiff and defendant; in most cases, the actions will be taken by their lawyers.

The timing of the filing can be important. Virtually every possible legal complaint is governed by a federal or state **statute of limitations,** which requires a lawsuit to be filed within a certain period of time. For example, in many states a lawsuit for injuries resulting from an automobile accident must be filed within two years of the accident or the plaintiff forfeits the right to proceed.

Jurisdiction and Venue   The place of filing is equally important. Two considerations govern. The first is **jurisdiction**—the proper type of court. A claim for breach of contract, in which the amount at stake is $1 million, cannot be brought in a local county court with jurisdiction to hear cases involving sums of up to only $1,000. Likewise, a claim for copyright violation cannot be brought in state superior court, since copyright cases are within the exclusive jurisdiction of the federal courts. Jurisdiction of the courts is determined by federal and state statute.

The second consideration is **venue**—that is, the proper geographic location of the court. For example, every county in a state might have a superior court, but the plaintiff is not free to pick any county. Again, a statute will spell out to which court the plaintiff must go—for instance, the county in which she resides or the county in which the defendant resides or maintains an office.

Service of Process   The defendant must be served—that is, she must receive notice that she has been sued. Usually **service** can be done by physically presenting the defendant with a copy of the summons and complaint. But sometimes the defendant is difficult to find, or deliberately avoids the marshal or other process server. The rules spell out a variety of ways by which individuals and corporations can be served, including by mail and by service on a designated agent.

One of the most troublesome problems is service on a defendant who is out of state. The jurisdiction of a state court ordinarily reaches only those found within the state. If the plaintiff claims that an out-of-state defendant injured him in some way, must the plaintiff go to the defendant's home state? Unless the defendant had some significant contact with the plaintiff's state, the plaintiff may indeed have to. For instance, suppose a traveler from Maine stopped in at a roadside diner in Montana and ordered a slice of homemade pie that was tainted and caused him to be sick. The traveler may not simply return home and mail the diner a notice that he is suing it in a Maine court. But if out-of-state defendants have some contact with the plaintiff's state of residence, there might be grounds to bring them within the jurisdiction of the plaintiff's state courts. The basic rationale is set forth in the following case.

INTERNATIONAL SHOE CO. v. WASHINGTON
326 U.S. 310 (1945)

MR. CHIEF JUSTICE STONE delivered the opinion of the Court.

The question for decision is whether, within the limitations of the due process clause of the Fourteenth Amendment, appellant, a Delaware corporation, has by its activities in the State of Washington rendered itself amenable to proceedings in the courts of that state to recover unpaid contributions to the state unemployment compensation fund exacted by state statutes. . . .

★   ★   ★

The statutes in question set up a comprehensive scheme of unemployment compensation, the costs of which are defrayed by contributions required to be made by employers to a state unemployment compensation fund. The contributions are a specified percentage of the wages payable annually by each employer for his employees' services in the state. The assessment and collection of the contributions and the fund are administered by appellees. Section 14 (c) of the Act . . . authorizes appellee Commissioner to issue an order and notice of assessment of delinquent contributions upon prescribed personal service of the notice upon the employer if found within the state, or, if not so found, by mailing the notice to the employer by registered mail at his last known address. . . .

In this case notice of assessment for the years in question was personally served upon a sales solicitor employed by appellant in the State of Washington, and a copy of the notice was mailed by registered mail to appellant at its address in St. Louis, Missouri. Appellant appeared specially before the office of unemployment and moved to set aside the order and notice of assessment on the ground that the service upon appellant's salesman was not proper service upon appellant; that appellant was not a corporation of the State of Washington and was not doing business within the state; that it had no agent within the state upon whom service could be made; and that appellant is not an employer and does not furnish employment within the meaning of the statute.

. . . The appeal tribunal . . . denied the motion and ruled that appellee Commissioner was entitled to recover the unpaid contributions. That action was affirmed by the Commissioner; both the Superior Court and the Supreme Court affirmed. . . .

The facts as found by the appeal tribunal and accepted by the state Superior Court and Supreme Court, are not in dispute. Appellant is a Delaware corporation, having its principal place of business in St. Louis, Missouri, and is engaged in the manufacture and sale of shoes and other footwear. It maintains places of business in several states, other than Washington, at which its manufacturing is carried on and from which its merchandise is distributed interstate through several sales units or branches located outside the State of Washington.

Appellant has no office in Washington and makes no contracts either for sale or purchase of merchandise there. It maintains no stock of merchandise in that state and makes there no deliveries of goods in intrastate commerce. During the years from 1937 to 1940, now in question, appellant employed eleven to thirteen salesmen under direct supervision and control of sales managers located in St. Louis. These salesmen resided in Washington; their principal activities were confined to that state; and they were compensated by commissions based upon the amount of their sales. The commissions for each year totaled more than $31,000. Appellant supplies its salesmen with a line of samples, each consisting of one shoe of a pair, which they display to prospective purchasers. On occasion they rent permanent sample rooms, for exhibiting samples, in business buildings, or rent rooms in hotels or business buildings temporarily for that purpose. The cost of such rentals is reimbursed by appellant.

The authority of the salesmen is limited to exhibiting their samples and soliciting orders from prospective buyers, at prices and on terms fixed by appellant. The salesmen transmit the orders to appellant's office in St. Louis for acceptance or rejection, and when accepted the merchandise for filling the orders is shipped f.o.b. from points outside Washington to the purchasers within the state. All the merchandise shipped into Washington is invoiced at the place of shipment from which collections are made. No salesman has authority to enter into contracts or to make collections.

$$\star \quad \star \quad \star$$

Appellant also insists that its activities within the state were not sufficient to manifest its "presence" there. . . .

$$\star \quad \star \quad \star$$

Historically the jurisdiction of courts to render judgment *in personam* is grounded on their de facto power over the defendant's person. Hence his presence within the territorial jurisdiction of a court was prerequisite to its rendition of a judgment personally binding him. But now . . . , due process requires only that in order to subject a defendant to a judgment *in personam*, if he be not present within the territory of the forum, he have certain minimum contacts with it such that the maintenance of the suit does not offend "traditional notions of fair play and substantial justice." *Milliken* v. *Meyer*, 311 U.S. 457, 463.

Since the corporate personality is a fiction, although a fiction intended to be acted upon as though it were a fact, it is clear that unlike an individual its "presence" without, as well as within, the state of its origin can be manifested only by activities carried on in its behalf by those who are authorized to act for it. To say that the corporation is so far "present" there as to satisfy due process requirements, for purposes of taxation or the maintenance of suits against it in the courts of the state, is to beg the question to be decided. For the terms "present" or "presence" are used merely to symbolize those

(*continued on next page*)

(continued)

INTERNATIONAL SHOE CO. v. WASHINGTON
326 U.S. 310 (1945)

activities of the corporation's agent within the state which courts will deem to be sufficient to satisfy the demands of due process.

*   *   *

It is evident that the criteria by which we mark the boundary line between those activities which justify the subjection of a corporation to suit, and those which do not, cannot be simply mechanical or quantitative. The test is not merely, as has sometimes been suggested, whether the activity, which the corporation has seen fit to procure through its agents in another state, is a little more or a little less. Whether due process is satisfied must depend rather upon the quality and nature of the activity in relation to the fair and orderly administration of the laws which it was the purpose of the due process clause to insure. That clause does not contemplate that a state may make binding a judgment *in personam* against an individual or corporate defendant with which the state has no contacts, ties, or relations.

But to the extent that a corporation exercises the privilege of conducting activities within a state, it enjoys the benefits and protection of the laws of that state. The exercise of that privilege may give rise to obligations, and, so far as those obligations arise out of or are connected with the activities within the state, a procedure which requires the corporation to respond to a suit brought to enforce them can, in most instances, hardly be said to be undue.

Applying these standards, the activities carried on in behalf of appellant in the State of Washington were neither irregular nor casual. They were systematic and continuous throughout the years in question. They resulted in a large volume of interstate business, in the course of which appellant received the benefits and protection of the laws of the state, including the right to resort to the courts for the enforcement of its rights. The obligation which is here sued upon arose out of those very activities. It is evident that these operations establish sufficient contacts or ties with the state of the forum to make it reasonable and just, according to our traditional conception of fair play and substantial justice, to permit the state to enforce the obligations which appellant has incurred there. Hence we cannot say that the maintenance of the present suit in the State of Washington involves an unreasonable or undue procedure.

*   *   *

Affirmed.

Decision on the Pleadings The initial papers in a lawsuit are called the **pleadings.** These include the complaint, the answer, and the **countercomplaint,** if there is one, in which the defendant asserts counterclaims against the plaintiff. In effect, the defendant becomes the plaintiff for the claims she has against the original plaintiff. The complaint must state the nature of the plaintiff's claim, the jurisdiction of the court, and the nature of the relief that he seeks (an award of money, an injunction, a declaration of legal rights). In her answer, the defendant might deny the entire complaint, or admit to certain of its allegations and deny others. The pleadings are usually quite general and give little detail.

Cases can be decided on the pleadings alone as follows: (1) If the defendant fails to answer the complaint, the court can enter a **default judgment,** awarding the plaintiff what he seeks. (2) The defendant can move to dismiss the complaint on the grounds that the plaintiff failed to "state a claim on which relief can be granted." The defendant is saying, in effect, that even if all the plaintiff's allegations are true, they do not amount to a legal claim. For example, a claim that the defendant induced a woman to stop dating the plaintiff is not actionable, and the court will dismiss the complaint without any further proceedings. This type of dismissal is often called a **demurrer.** (3) The defendant can admit all the facts in the complaint, and either party can then move for **summary judgment.** By so doing, they are telling the court that there is no factual dispute. Each argues that he is entitled to prevail because his position is the proper one under the law. For example, the parties might stipulate that they made an oral contract for the sale of land and that the defendant-seller refuses to tender the deed. The only question is a legal one: is an oral agreement for the sale of land enforceable? The motion for summary judgment asks the court to make a legal ruling for one party or the other without the necessity of taking any evidence.

Discovery   If there is a factual dispute, the case then moves into a pretrial stage at which each party ferrets out information in the possession of the other party. This is known as **discovery.** Until around the 1940s, a lawsuit was frequently a game in which each party took advantage of the rules to surprise the other party in court. Beginning with a change in the Federal Rules of Civil Procedure, adopted by the Supreme Court in 1938 and subsequently followed by many of the states, the parties have been given considerable latitude to learn the facts of the case before trial.

The purpose of all discovery is to help the parties determine what the evidence might be, who the potential witnesses are, and what specific issues are relevant. Discovery can proceed by several methods. A party may serve an **interrogatory** on his adversary. This is written request for answers to specific questions. Or a party may **depose** the other party or a

witness. A **deposition** is a live question-and-answer session at which the witness answers questions put to him by one of the parties' lawyers. His answers are recorded verbatim and may be used at trial.

The parties are also entitled to inspect books, documents, and other physical records and tangible things in the possession of the other. This is a sweeping right, since it is not limited to evidence that is admissible at trial. Discovery of physical evidence means that a plaintiff may inspect a company's accounts, customer lists, assets, profit-and-loss statements and balance sheet, engineering and quality-control reports, sales reports, and virtually any other document.

The discovery process is run by the lawyers, not by the court. One party simply makes a written demand on the other, stating the time at which the deposition will take place or the type of documents it wishes to inspect and make copies of. The party on whom the demand is made can apply to the court for a protective order if it can show that the demand is for privileged material (for example, a party's lawyers' records are not open for inspection) or that the demand was made to harass. In complex cases between companies, the discovery of documents can run into tens of millions of pages and can take years. Depositions can consume days or even weeks of an executive's time.

Pretrial Conference   At various times during the discovery process, depending on the nature and complexity of the case, the court may hold a pretrial conference to attempt to clarify the issues and establish a timetable for proceeding. The court may also hold a settlement conference for the express purpose of seeing whether the parties can be induced to settle their differences and avoid trial altogether.

Once discovery is completed, the case moves on to trial if it has not been settled. Most cases are in fact settled before this stage; perhaps 85 percent of all civil cases are terminated before trial, and more than 90 percent of criminal prosecutions end with a guilty plea.

Trial   At trial the first order of business is to select a jury if there is to be one. The judge and sometimes the lawyers are permitted to question the jurors to be sure that they are unbiased. The questioning is known as the **voir dire** (vwahr DEER). Most juries consist of twelve regular members and two or three alternates, who will substitute for a regular juror who chances to fall ill and must leave the courtroom. Many states have begun to experiment with smaller juries in order to save time and money.

After the jury is sworn and seated, the plaintiff's lawyer makes an **opening statement,** laying out the nature of the plaintiff's claim, the facts of the case as the plaintiff sees them, and the evidence that the lawyer will present. The defendant's lawyer may also make an opening statement or may reserve his right to do so at the conclusion of the plaintiff's case.

The plaintiff's lawyer then calls witnesses and presents the physical evidence relevant to her proof. The **direct testimony** at trial is usually far from a smooth narration. The rules of evidence (governing the kinds of testimony and documents that may be introduced at trial) and the question-and-answer format ensure that the presentation of evidence is choppy and sometimes difficult to follow. Anyone who has watched an actual televised trial or a television melodrama featuring a trial scene will appreciate the nature of the trial itself: witnesses are asked questions about a number of issues that may or may not be related, the opposing lawyer will frequently jump up to object to the question or the form in which it is asked, and the jury may be sent from the room while the lawyers wrangle.

After direct testimony of each witness is concluded, the opposing lawyer may conduct **cross-examination.** This is a crucial constitutional right; in criminal cases it is enshrined in the Sixth Amendment to the Constitution, the right to confront one's accusers in open court. The stilted rules of direct testimony are relaxed, and the cross-examiner may probe the witness more informally, asking questions that may not seem immediately relevant, and pounding hard at the witness—all in an attempt to impeach the credibility of the witness, to trip her up and show that the answers she gave are false or not to be trusted. It is the use of cross-examination and the criterion of responsiveness (p. 48) that chiefly distinguish common-law courts from those of authoritarian regimes around the world. Following cross-examination, the plaintiff's lawyer may then question the witness again; this is called re-direct examination and is used to rehabilitate the witness by clarifying the answers she gave and to show that the implications suggested by the cross-examiner were unwarranted. The cross-exam-

iner may then engage the witness in re-cross-examination, and so on. The process usually stops after cross-examination or re-direct.

During the trial the judge's chief responsibility is to rule on the admissibility of evidence. If the judge rules a particular question out of order or a given document irrelevant, the lawyer proffering it has the right to appeal the ruling after the trial.

At the conclusion of the plaintiff's case the defendant presents his case, following the same procedure just outlined. Thereafter, the plaintiff is entitled to present **rebuttal** witnesses if necessary to controvert evidence that the defendant has introduced. The defendant in turn may present **surrebuttal** witnesses.

When all testimony has been introduced, either party may ask the judge for a **directed verdict**—a verdict declared by the judge without advice from the jury. This motion should be granted if the plaintiff has failed to introduce evidence legally sufficient to meet her burden of proof or if the defendant has failed to do likewise on issues on which he has the burden of proof. (For example, the plaintiff alleges that the defendant owes her money and introduces a signed promissory note. The defendant cannot show that the note is invalid. The defendant must lose the case unless he can show that the debt has been paid or otherwise discharged.) The defendant can move for a directed verdict at the close of the plaintiff's case, but the judge will usually wait to hear the entire case until deciding whether to do so. Directed verdicts are not usually granted, since it is the jury's province to determine the facts in dispute. Moreover, the parties will rarely take a weak case—one in which the facts are either unclear or unprovable—all the way to trial; they will usually settle the case outside the court.

If the judge refuses to grant a directed verdict, each lawyer will then present a **closing argument** to the jury (or, if there is no jury, to the judge alone if the latter wants to hear it). The closing argument is frequently crucial, for it is by this often dramatic presentation that the lawyer ties up the loose ends, relates the bewildering stream of seemingly unrelated facts into a smooth whole, and shows how the evidence supports his client's case.

Thereafter, the judge will **instruct** the jury. Each lawyer will have prepared in writing a set of instructions that he hopes the judge will give to the jury; these will be tailored to advance his client's case. The purpose of a jury instruction is to explain to the jurors the meaning of the law as it relates to the issues they are considering and to tell the jurors what facts they must determine if they are to give a verdict for one party or the other. Dozens or even hundreds of factual issues can be raised during the course of an even moderately complicated trial; the juror's job is not an easy or enviable one. Instructing the jury in how to go about it is likewise a tricky business. Many a verdict has been upset on appeal because a trial judge has wrongly instructed the jury. As a consequence, most judges use form instructions known as "pattern jury instructions." These are sometimes long, badly worded, and difficult to follow. But they are safe because appellate courts will approve their use if challenged on appeal.

After all instructions are given, the jury will retire to a private room and deliberate for as long as it takes to reach a unanimous verdict. (Some minor cases do not require a unanimous verdict.) If the jury cannot reach a decision (a "hung jury"), the case will have to be retried. When a jury does reach a verdict, it delivers it in open court with the parties and lawyers present, the jury is discharged, and control over the case returns to the judge. If the judge is sitting without a jury, he will usually announce his findings of fact and application of the law to those facts in a written opinion. Juries announce only their verdicts and do not state their reasons for reaching them.

Posttrial Motions   The losing party can ask the judge either for a new trial or for a *judgment notwithstanding the verdict* (often called a *judgment n.o.v.,* from the Latin initials for *non obstante veredicto* [non ob STAN tee ver ruh DIC toe]). A judge who decides that a directed verdict is appropriate usually will wait to see what the jury's verdict will be. If it is favorable to the party the judge thinks should win, he can rely on that verdict. If the verdict is for the other party, he can grant the motion for judgment n.o.v. This is a safer way to proceed because if he is reversed on appeal, there need not be a new trial. The jury's verdict always can be restored, whereas without a jury verdict (as happens when a directed verdict is granted before the case goes to the jury) the entire case must be presented to a new jury.

Appeal   If the loser's motion for a new trial or a judgment n.o.v. is denied, his only recourse is to appeal the decision, citing one of several grounds of er-

ror to the appellate court—for example, that the judge erroneously admitted evidence, failed to admit proper evidence that he should have, or wrongly instructed the jury. Enforcement of the court's **judgment**—an award of money, an injunction—is usually **stayed** (postponed) until the appellate court has ruled. As noted earlier, the party making the appeal is called the appellant; the party defending the judgment is the appellee (in some courts, they are known as petitioner and respondent).

Appellate and trial processes are different. The appellate court does not hear witnesses or accept evidence. It reviews the *record* of the case—that is, the transcript of the witnesses' testimony and the documents received into evidence at trial—in a search for legal error on a specific request of one or both of the parties. The parties' lawyers prepare **briefs**—written statements containing the facts in the case, the procedural steps taken, and the argument, or discussion of the meaning of the law and its application to the facts. At some time, perhaps months or even years later, the appellate court will hear **oral argument.** Each lawyer is given a short period of time, usually no more than thirty minutes, to present his client's case. The lawyer rarely gets a chance for an extended statement because he is usually interrupted and peppered with questions from the judges. Through this colloquy between judges and lawyers, specific legal positions can be tested and their limits explored.

Depending on its conclusion, the appellate court will *affirm* the lower court's judgment, *modify* it, *reverse* it, or *remand* it to the lower court for retrial or other action directed by the higher court. The appellate court itself does not take specific action in the case; it sits only to rule on contested issues of law. The lower court must issue the final judgment in the case. As we have already seen, there is the possibility of appealing from an intermediate appellate court to the state supreme court in twenty-nine states, and the U.S. Supreme Court from a ruling of a federal circuit court of appeal. In cases raising constitutional issues, there is also the possibility of appeal to the Supreme Court from the state courts.

Precedent   Like trial judges, appellate judges are bound by precedent. But not every previous case is a precedent for a given court. Generally speaking, decisions of higher courts must be respected only by lower courts in the same system. Courts in one state are not bound by decisions of courts in other states, nor in general are state courts bound by decisions of federal courts, except on points of federal law emanating from federal courts within the state or federal circuit in which the state court sits. State supreme courts are not bound by case law in other states, although decisions of sister supreme courts may influence the judges' reasoning. Federal district courts are bound by the decisions of the court of appeals in their circuit, but decisions by one circuit court are not precedents for courts in other circuits. Federal courts are also bound by decisions of the state supreme courts within their geographic territory in diversity jurisdiction cases. All courts are bound by decisions of the United States Supreme Court, except the Supreme Court itself.

Not everything a court says in an opinion is a precedent. Strictly speaking, only the exact **holding** is binding on the lower courts. A holding is the theory of the law that applies to the particular circumstances presented in the case. The courts may also discourse, even declare what they believe the law to be, on other points. These declarations are called **dicta** (DICK tuh) (singular: *dictum*), and the lower courts need not give them the same weight as holdings (with some exceptions; see pp. 37–40).

Judgment and Order

After all appeals are exhausted, the parties will be left with a judgment and order of the trial court. The **order,** directing the specific relief to which the parties are entitled, is usually prepared by the parties' lawyers at the conclusion of the trial. Each party offers the version that he believes best comports with the judgment or verdict, and the judge will accept or modify one and sign it as the order of the court. It is this order that the losing party must abide by.

Sometimes a contested sum of money has been paid to the court pending a decision, or a bond may have been posted. In either event, issuance of a final order will cause the money to be paid over to the winner.

If the loser is recalcitrant, the judgment can be enforced in a variety of ways. If the judgment requires one party to pay money to the other, the marshal or sheriff is authorized, upon application, to seize the loser's property to satisfy it. Subject to specific statutes, a losing party's wages or other income can be **garnished,** and the employer will be legally required to pay the winning party a certain portion of the losing party's wages until the judgment is paid off (see p. 580). If the final judgment is an injunction, failure to abide by it may subject the party against whom it is issued to a **contempt** citation, following which he may be fined or jailed.

WHO MAY SUE

Whether or not a quarrel is one that a court will hear depends, among other things, on whether it is a **legal dispute.** A legal dispute is one in which the aggrieved party asserts a **legal entitlement**—that is, a right determined by law. Not every aggrieved person has such a right. The citizen has no right to impress her views of economic policy on the Federal Reserve Board. A restaurant patron may have no legal right to prevent another patron from smoking. For a court to entertain a case, the assertion of entitlement must rest on a legal rather than political, moral, or spiritual basis.

Case or Controversy?

Courts do not render "advisory" opinions. A court may exercise its jurisdiction only if there is a dispute in which the parties are actual antagonists. A sham proceeding in which the supposed parties are not truly opposed but merely want an opinion of a court on the meaning of legislation will not be heard.

With some ingenuity, nearly any question can be converted into a dispute between two sides. For a variety of reasons, people might wish to have a court make an official pronouncement on a question of importance to them (and to others). Suppose, for example, that an organization offers a reward to anyone who comes forward with certain information (**Box 2-1**). Normally, the law of contracts would bind the organization to carry out its promise if someone supplies the information. But courts will not invariably reach such a conclusion because an inflexible rule to that effect could ultimately place every question of this nature before judges, who have enough cases to handle. In the following case, the Wisconsin Supreme Court squarely faced the question of whether every controversy is in fact a legal "case," concluding that no such generalization is possible.

LAW AND LIFE

BOX 2-1

California Judge Rules Holocaust Did Happen

[*Not all questions belong in the courtroom. Since courts do not render "advisory opinions" to parties in disagreement, a judge uses discretion when deciding if a dispute should proceed to trial.* —AUTHORS' NOTE]

LOS ANGELES, Oct. 9 (AP)—A Superior Court judge, acting on a suit filed against a group that contends the Holocaust was a myth, ruled today that "Jews were gassed to death in Auschwitz in Poland in the summer of 1944."

CASE OR CONTROVERSY?

In taking "judicial notice" of the Holocaust, Judge Thomas T. Johnson was ruling on one part of a lawsuit by Mel Mermelstein, 55 years old, a businessman from Long Beach, Calif. Mr. Mermelstein, who survived the Auschwitz concentration camp, is suing the Institute of Historical Review, a right-wing group that contends the Holocaust was fabricated by Jews.

The institute had offered a $50,000 reward to anyone who could prove the contrary, and Mr. Mermel-

stein contended the group had failed to pay off though it had seen his proof.

The judge did not rule on the question of whether the institute actually had a legal contract with the businessman.

The institute and Mr. Mermelstein had exchanged letters that William Cox, Mr. Mermelstein's attorney, contends constituted a contract.

The suit also asks for a summary judgment and payment to Mr. Mermelstein of $1 million in damages for the psychological suffering.

The institute contends that Mr. Mermelstein did not meet all the criteria for collecting the reward.

Source: *New York Times*, October 10, 1981

CUDAHY JUNIOR CHAMBER OF COMMERCE v. QUIRK
41 Wis.2d 698,
165 N.W.2d 116 (1969)

FACTS

In the spring election of 1966, the voters of the city of Cudahy were to decide by referendum whether the community water supply was to be fluoridated. A leading proponent of fluoridation was the Cudahy Junior Chamber of Commerce. A leading foe of fluoridating the water was James Quirk, working as or through The Greater Milwaukee Committee Against Fluoridation.

In the midst of the spirited campaign, Quirk "challenged" the Jaycees, offering to give them $1,000 ". . . if a daily dose of four glasses [of fluoridated water] cannot cause 'dermatologic, gastrointestinal and neurological disorders' " and adding, "If the Jaycees should find that we have misrepresented matters in this paper, we will then also pay the sum of $1,000." The Jaycees did some checking, so found to their satisfaction, demanded payment by Quirk of $1,000. When payment was refused, the Jaycees brought this action, seeking (1) a court finding that Quirk did misrepresent matters in his brochure; (2) a court finding that four glasses of fluoridated water cannot cause the mentioned disorders; (3) a court judgment for $1,000. Trial was had to a jury. The jury found misrepresentation. . . . Defendant Quirk appeals.

* * *

ROBERT W. HANSEN, J.

(continued on next page)

(continued)

**CUDAHY JUNIOR
CHAMBER OF
COMMERCE v. QUIRK**
**41 Wis.2d 698,
165 N.W.2d 116 (1969)**

★   ★   ★

What have we here? In the eyes of the law, exactly what is this sort of challenge made in the heat of an election campaign? Was it an offer that, upon acceptance, became a binding contract? Was it a reward, analogous to the sums of money offered for information leading to the arrest and conviction of the perpetrator of a crime? Was it a bet, a wagering of $1,000 against the possibility that one might be wrong?

In 2 Restatement, *Contracts*, pp. 1007, 1008, sec. 520, comment *c*, the following is stated: "A wager may relate to a trial of skill, or to *proof of an actual fact* or even to a certain event that happened in the past." (Emphasis supplied.) . . .

. . . In essence the Quirk challenge was a wager—"I'll gamble my $1,000 against your efforts to prove me wrong that my statements are correct." It is not close kin to a bet that the Green Bay Packers will best the Chicago Bears in their next gridiron encounter. It is, however, a twin to the bet that Babe Ruth once pitched for the Boston Red Sox. It is the essential nature of a transaction, rather than the label attached to it by the parties, that determines whether it is in truth and fact a wager.

Who won the bet? The jury's finding, which was sustained by the trial court, was that the Jaycees won the wager. This amounted to an acceptance of the credibility of the testimony offered by the Jaycees that Quirk had "misrepresented matters" in his brochure. We do not reach the issue of fact as to who won and who lost the wager. Our holding is that the participants in a wager may not use the court to settle their dispute because gambling debts cannot be established or collected in the courts.

The question of public policy? In addition to the judicial reluctance to hold the stakes or decide the winner in a betting situation, there are sound reasons of public policy for not having court or jury decide whose gloved fist is to be lifted in victory in this dispute. It is clear that, while $1,000 would be a welcome addition to club coffers, the primary concern of the Jaycees is to vindicate the rightness of their position that fluoridation of the Cudahy water supply involves no harmful side effects. It is at least as clear that James Quirk's principal interest is in seeking court confirmation of his contention that fluoridation of a community's drinking water risks harmful consequences. He appeared as his own counsel, and his brief and oral argument dealt only with the rightness of his antifluoridation stance. In fact, in rejecting the demand for payment of the Jaycees, he wrote, with copies to local press, "Top promoters of fluoridation will turn aghast at airing the harm and stupidity of fluoridation in open court. We welcome the opportunity of a court hearing." The time-honored explanation, "It isn't the money. It's the principle of the thing" describes both the intensity of conviction and explains the gap between the points of view of the parties to this action.

If disputants on the issue of the harmful effects of fluoridation can by the process of challenge and acceptance bring their dispute on this issue of public concern to the courts for adjudication, the list of matters in which litigants could seek determinations by the court of questions of public policy would be a long one. Dedicated crusaders for varying points of view, pro and con, by the process of challenge and response, could have courts rule on whether birth control pills have harmful side-effects, whether cigarettes cause cancer, whether sugar substitutes alter chromosomes. If there are ways of bringing such controversies to court, putting up $1,000 to be paid to anyone who can prove you wrong does not make the courts the forum or the referee. Here the true controversy is as to the effects of fluoridation. We have grave doubts as to whether this is a justiciable issue—one appropriate for judicial inquiry.

★   ★   ★

It is understandable that the Jaycees, a civic organization of young men with an established record for effective participation in civic enterprises, would want to have its presentation of facts found to be accurate, and that of its principal adversary found to be false, misleading and misrepresented. It is not the role or function of the judicial branch of our government to make that determination. Some may see it as a weakness but it is the heart of the referendum law and the democratic process that, in this situation, the voters, not judge or jury, are to bring in the verdict. We can with propriety commend all individuals and all groups who participate in securing the expressed will of an informed electorate, but it is not for us to determine whose presentation had either the greatest accuracy or greatest persuasiveness. The cases, affirmative and negative, were submitted to the jury at the polls. They were not for a jury in a courtroom to affirm or reverse.

The what, why, when and where of this case require that the judgment be reversed and the case dismissed.

Standing to Sue

A closely related question is that of **standing** to sue. Suppose you see a sixteen-wheel moving van drive across your neighbor's flowerbed, destroying her prize-winning dahlias and chrysanthemums. Since she is on vacation, you file a lawsuit against the company to recover for the economic loss she has suffered. The court will reject your suit. You do not have standing to sue because you were not injured by the moving van. Only a person whose interests are affected has the legal capacity to sue.

The "standing" doctrine is easy to understand in straightforward cases. Litigation is expensive and intrusive. The decision of whether or not to sue should be left in the hands of those who have suffered an injury and stand to gain by court action. Most of us suffer injuries from time to time that are legally redressable but that for a variety of reasons we would not go to the extreme of seeking redress for. We might want to avoid publicity, expense, discomfort; we might hope that an amicable settlement will permit us to continue in an ongoing relationship. If anyone could bring a lawsuit on our behalf, our lives would be to some degree out of our control.

Class Actions

Most lawsuits concern a dispute between one individual and another, or between an individual and a company or other organization. But a wrongdoer may injure more than one person at the same time. It is purely fortuitous whether a driver who runs a red light hits another car carrying only one person or many more. If several people are injured in the same accident, they each have the right to sue the driver for the damage that he caused them. Could they sue as a group? Ordinarily not, because the extent of the damages would not likely be the same for each person, and different facts would have to be proved at the trial. Moreover, the driver of the car that was struck might have been partially to blame, so the defendant's liability toward him might be different from his liability toward the passengers.

If, however, the potential plaintiffs were all injured in the same manner and their injuries were identical, a single lawsuit might be a far more efficient way of fixing liability and assessing financial responsibility than a host of individual lawsuits. How could such a suit be brought? All the injured parties could hire the same lawyer, who could present their common case. But with a group numbering more than a handful of people, the logistical problems could be insurmountable. How could a million stockholders allegedly defrauded by a corporation, or a million purchasers of a product allegedly overcharged because of an antitrust conspiracy, ever get together?

Consequently, there is a legal procedure that permits one person or a small group of people to serve as stand-ins for all others similarly situated. This is the **class action**. (Note that "action" means "suit," so the phrase "class action lawsuit" frequently seen in the newspapers is redundant.) The class action is provided for in the Federal Rules of Civil Procedure (Rule 23) and in the separate codes of civil procedure in the states. These rules differ and are often complex in detail, but in general, anyone may file a class action in an appropriate case subject to approval of the court. Once the class is "certified," or adjudged to be a legally adequate group complaining of common injuries, the lawyers for the named plaintiffs become in effect the lawyers for the entire class. Usually a person who does not wish to be in the class may opt out. If she does, she will not be included in an eventual judgment or settlement. But a potential plaintiff who is included in the class cannot, after a final judgment is awarded, seek to relitigate the issue if she is dissatisfied with the outcome, even though she did not participate at all in the legal proceeding.

The older rule that prohibited class actions from being used in cases in which damages are not uniform has been at least partially overcome. A case involving numerous plaintiffs presenting an identical question of liability can be tried as a class action, with separate proof of damages thereafter. Such a case may or may not be a class action in the technical sense.

RELATIONS WITH LAWYERS

The law should be the possession of every person. At times, legal topics become part of a broad public debate—as, for example, when the ways of interpreting the Constitution were spread out before a television audience during the Senate's 1987 hearings on President Reagan's nomination of Judge Robert Bork to the Supreme Court. Usually, however, the volume and complexity of law make it relatively inaccessible. The legal life of the nation is filtered, therefore, through the legal profession.

Unlike the work of particle physicists or arbitrageurs, the lawyer's job may seem generally familiar. After all, lawyers have been the staple of literature for centuries (Shakespeare and Dickens could not have done without them). For the better part of this century, in the movies America's leading actors have been cast as lawyers, whether heroes or villains. Television audiences for the past two generations have learned their law from Raymond Burr (*Perry Mason*), John Houseman (Prof. Kingsfield in *Paper Chase*), Veronica Hamel (Joyce Davenport in *Hill Street Blues*), Harry Hamlin (Michael Kuzak in *L.A. Law*), and many others. But with all the Hollywood gloss, the real work of lawyers remains largely unknown.

Organization of the Legal Profession

The number of U.S. lawyers topped the half-million mark around 1980, and by 1990 had climbed to nearly 800,000. By the end of the century, it is estimated there will be more than one million lawyers practicing law in the United States. More than 100,000 students are enrolled in the 175 accredited American law schools, and some 40,000 new lawyers graduate each year.

To practice law, a lawyer must be admitted to *the bar* of a state. In some states admission is more or less automatic following graduation from an accredited school in the state. In most states, however, the graduate must take a written examination and be screened by a character committee appointed by the supervising court.

Lawyers are admitted state by state. No general admission to practice exists in the United States. Permission to appear in the federal courts in each state is usually routine following admission to the bar of the state. When a company has a legal problem outside its home state, it will usually retain local lawyers to work with its own lawyers.

Bar associations provide a variety of services. They offer continuing professional education and public education, and work on law reform. The American Bar Association (ABA) is the largest voluntary professional association in the world, with more than 350,000 members. Its hundreds of committees are engaged in innumerable professional projects; it has a complex internal political structure through which its members debate important public issues. Its committees frequently testify on legal matters before Congress and the state legislatures. One of its most important committees is that which screens presidential nominations to the federal courts. There is a separate state bar association in each state, and in the larger states there are dozens of local bar associations. There are also several other specialty associations, such as the Association of Trial Lawyers of America, whose members are largely lawyers who litigate on behalf of plaintiffs in personal-injury and other types of lawsuits.

Lawyers practice law in assorted ways. Perhaps half the practicing lawyers in the country practice by themselves (solo) or with one or two partners. Beginning in the 1960s, law firms, as legal partnerships are known, began to grow as the needs of corporate clients mushroomed. Today, there are hundreds of firms throughout the United States with more than 100 lawyers, and dozens have more than 200 or 300 lawyers. Generally speaking, these firms have two classes of lawyers. *Partners* are like corporate officers; they run the show and split the profits. Younger lawyers are salaried and are usually called *associates*. In between the solo practitioner and the giant firm are thousands of law firms of varying sizes. Regardless of size, many firms today employ employees known as *paralegals*, or legal assistants, whose skills lie between those of legal secretaries and those of lawyers.

In addition to the *independent practitioners* (lawyers practicing by themselves or with other lawyers), increasing numbers of lawyers work as employees for government and private corporations. The head of a company's legal department is generally termed *general counsel* or *house counsel*. The *in-house* lawyer is one who is salaried by a company or other organization. Today dozens of companies employ a hundred or more lawyers to work on every conceivable type of corporate problem: litigation, securities, antitrust, real estate, taxation, personnel, and the like.

Professional Responsibility and Ethics

Lawyers serve their clients in many roles. They act as advocates in court and as negotiators, counselors, and lobbyists. As representative for the client, a lawyer is expected to work zealously in his behalf, whatever the personal consequences to the lawyer. But the lawyer is usually careful not to personally endorse the client's position. Lawyers may defend clients whose views they detest. That is the nature of the lawyer's role, and it is a frequently misunderstood one, leading lawyers to be wrongly condemned for representing those whom society despises. It is precisely those who are most despised who most need counsel, and an adversary system will ensure that they have it. Nevertheless, there are limits to the zeal that a lawyer may bring to the representation of his client's interests. These limits are spelled out in a formal code of ethics, generally known throughout the country as the Code of Professional Responsibility. Commissioned by the American Bar Association, this code is the product of many minds and drafters. It is a model code because the ABA is private and has no authority to promulgate binding rules. The code of ethics draws its legal force by being officially adopted by the state supreme courts. These courts have not adopted the model code in full; there are variations from state to state.

From the perspective of the business client, two aspects of the ethical rules are paramount: the lawyer is bound to respect the confidences of his clients, and the lawyer may not engage in a conflict of interest.

Confidentiality A lawyer may not reveal what he has learned from his client during the course of his representation. This rule has an analogue in the courtroom. Under the law of evidence, a party is protected by the **lawyer-client privilege:** a client may prevent her lawyer from testifying about facts he has learned from her and from turning over papers that he developed during the course of his representation. This is an important rule. Without it, a client might well hesitate to disclose sensitive information that could be used against her in competitive or other situations.

There is a difficulty, however. A person cannot go to a lawyer for advice about committing "the perfect crime." The rule has always contained an exception for future or continuing crimes. If the client says, "I committed a crime and I need help," the lawyer may work with her and may not disclose what the client has said. This rule has always been interpreted strictly. On the other hand, if the client says, "Help me out with this scheme to defraud the public," the confidentiality rule does not apply and the lawyer need not keep quiet. To the contrary, the lawyer might have to go public.

This latter requirement, if it is one, poses problems for corporate clients. A common example is the preparation of legal papers necessary for registration of a securities offering with the Securities and Exchange Commission. The securities laws (see Chapter 44) require companies to make a number of public disclosures about such things as assets, costs, and expenditures. The regulations are complex, and it is frequently a close question whether or not a particular item of information legally must be disclosed. If the lawyer says, "You must disclose the discovery of this new oil field," and the responsible officer refuses to do so, what should the lawyer do? In a close case, where the line between legality and illegality is difficult to draw, the lawyer is permitted to give his best advice; if the client wishes to take the risk of being brought to court by the government, it is not unethical for the lawyer to keep quiet while the client tests the case in court. To the contrary, it is probably ethically necessary for the lawyer to keep quiet. But if the client clearly steps over the line of illegality, should the lawyer speak out? There are few precedents that resolve this question, but two cases that received considerable publicity during the 1970s suggest that under certain circumstances the lawyer does indeed have a duty to speak out, or at least will not be condemned for doing so. [Securities and Exchange Commission v. National Student Marketing Corp., 457 F.Supp. 682 (D.D.C. 1978); Meyerhofer v. Empire Fire and Marine Insurance Co., 497 F.2d 1190 (2nd Cir. 1974)]

Conflict of Interest   The second important ethical consideration for the lawyer in corporate practice is the rule that prohibits any lawyer from engaging in a **conflict of interest.** This generally means that a lawyer may not represent two parties whose interests are adverse—for example, a lawyer may not represent both the plaintiff and the defendant in court.

When the clients are individuals, it is usually easy to determine whether there is a conflict of interest. Having once given legal advice to an employer in connection with a certain matter, a lawyer may not subsequently represent an employee who wishes to sue the employer over that matter. But when the lawyer represents a corporation, who exactly is the client? A corporation, after all, is a "legal fiction" (see Chapter 41); it is a collection of individuals who manage and operate the affairs of the enterprise. Is the client the chief executive officer? the board of directors? the officers as a whole?

The answer is that the client is the corporation itself, and not any of the officers, agents, or employees. Of course, in representing the corporation, the lawyer will necessarily deal with the chief executive, other officers, and to a lesser degree, the board and other employees. But they are not the client. As long as the corporation's interest and that of an individual employee are identical, the lawyer may serve them both. There will be occasions, however, when the interest of the corporation as a whole will be adverse to that of an individual who works for it. It is important to bear in mind that in a showdown, the lawyer must choose the corporation's interest over that of any individual. An officer or other employee who finds himself in such a conflict-of-interest situation will do well to retain his own independent lawyer.

The rule that the corporation or other organization, not the individual, is the client has an important bearing on the rule of confidentiality. A lawyer must respect the confidences of the client, but not those of others. If individual employees are not the client, then presumably the lawyer need not pledge to keep secret what they tell him. But a corporation as an abstract cannot talk—only people can. Does this mean that the corporate lawyer is not bound to respect corporate confidentiality? The answer is that the lawyer must keep confidential any company-related legal matters that he learns from employees. All employees? At one time, the courts employed a "control group" test: anything a lawyer learned from those who controlled the management of the company was subject to the rules regarding confidentiality and the lawyer-client privilege. For many years lower-level employees were thought not to be covered by the rule. In 1981, the Supreme Court ruled for the first time that they were.

**UPJOHN CO. v.
UNITED STATES
449 U.S. 383 (1981)**

JUSTICE REHNQUIST delivered the opinion of the Court.

* * *

Petitioner Upjohn Co. manufactures and sells pharmaceuticals here and abroad. In January 1976 independent accountants conducting an audit of one of Upjohn's foreign subsidiaries discovered that the subsidiary made payments to or for the benefit of foreign government officials in order to secure government business. The accountants so informed petitioner Mr. Gerard Thomas, Upjohn's Vice President, Secretary, and General Counsel. Thomas is a member of the Michigan and New York Bars, and has been Upjohn's General Counsel for 20 years. He consulted with outside counsel and R. T. Parfet, Jr., Upjohn's Chairman of the Board. It was decided that the company would conduct an internal investigation of what were termed "questionable payments." As part of this investigation the attorneys prepared a letter containing a questionnaire which was sent to "All Foreign General and Area Managers" over the Chairman's signature. The letter began by noting recent disclosures that several American companies made "possibly illegal" payments to foreign government officials and emphasized that the management needed full information concerning any such payments made by Upjohn. The letter indicated that the Chairman had asked Thomas, identified as "the company's General Counsel," "to conduct an investigation for the purpose of determining the nature and magnitude of any payments made by the Upjohn Company or any of its subsidiaries to any employee or official of a foreign government." The questionnaire sought detailed information concerning such payments. Managers were instructed to treat the investigation as "highly confidential" and not to discuss it with anyone other than Upjohn employees who might be helpful in providing the requested information. Responses were to be sent directly to Thomas. Thomas and outside counsel also interviewed the recipients of the questionnaire and some 33 other Upjohn officers or employees as part of the investigation.

On March 26, 1976, the company voluntarily submitted a preliminary report to the Securities and Exchange Commission on Form 8-K disclosing certain questionable payments. A copy of the report was simultaneously submitted to the Internal Revenue Service, which immediately began an investigation to determine the tax consequences of the payments. Special agents conducting the investigation were given lists by Upjohn of all those interviewed and all who had responded to the questionnaire. On November 23, 1976, the Service issued a summons pursuant to 26 U. S. C. § 7602 demanding production of:

> All files relative to the investigation conducted under the supervision of
> Gerard Thomas to identify payments to employees of foreign governments
> and any political contributions made by the Upjohn Company or any of its
> affiliates since January 1, 1971 and to determine whether any funds of the

(continued on next page)

(*continued*)

**UPJOHN CO. v.
UNITED STATES
449 U.S. 383 (1981)**

Upjohn Company had been improperly accounted for on the corporate books during the same period.

The records should include but not be limited to written questionnaires sent to managers of the Upjohn Company's foreign affiliates, and memorandums or notes of the interviews conducted in the United States and abroad with officers and employees of the Upjohn Company and its subsidiaries.

The company declined to produce the documents specified in the second paragraph on the grounds that they were protected from disclosure by the attorney-client privilege and constituted the work product of attorneys prepared in anticipation of litigation. On August 31, 1977, the United States filed a petition seeking enforcement of the summons . . . in the United States District Court for the Western District of Michigan. That court adopted the recommendation of a Magistrate who concluded that the summons should be enforced. Petitioners appealed to the Court of Appeals for the Sixth Circuit which rejected the Magistrate's finding of a waiver of the attorney-client privilege, but agreed that the privilege did not apply "[t]o the extent that the communications were made by officers and agents not responsible for directing Upjohn's actions in response to legal advice . . . for the simple reason that the communications were not the 'client's.' " The court reasoned that accepting petitioners' claim for a broader application of the privilege would encourage upper-echelon management to ignore unpleasant facts and create too broad a "zone of silence." Noting that Upjohn's counsel had interviewed officials such as the Chairman and President, the Court of Appeals remanded to the District Court so that a determination of who was within the "control group" could be made. . . .

Federal Rule of Evidence 501 provides that "the privilege of a witness . . . shall be governed by the principles of the common law as they may be interpreted by the courts of the United States in light of reason and experience." The attorney-client privilege is the oldest of the privileges for confidential communications known to the common law. Its purpose is to encourage full and frank communication between attorneys and their clients and thereby promote broader public interests in the observance of law and administration of justice. The privilege recognizes that sound legal advice or advocacy serves public ends and that such advice or advocacy depends upon the lawyer's being fully informed by the client.

★   ★   ★

In the case of the individual client the provider of information and the person who acts on the lawyer's advice are one and the same. In the corporate context, however, it will frequently be employees beyond the control group as defined by the court below—"officers and agents . . . responsible for directing [the company's] actions in response to legal advice"—who will possess the information needed by the corporation's lawyers. Middle-level—and indeed lower-level—employees can, by actions within the scope of their employment, embroil the corporation in serious legal difficulties, and it is only natural that these employees would have the relevant information needed by corporate counsel if he is adequately to advise the client with respect to such actual or potential difficulties.

★   ★   ★

The control group test adopted by the court below thus frustrates the very purpose of the privilege by discouraging the communication of relevant information by employees of the client to attorneys seeking to render legal advice to the client corporation. The attorney's advice will also frequently be more significant to noncontrol group members than to those who officially sanction the advice, and the control group test makes it more difficult to convey full and frank legal advice to the employees who will put into effect the client corporation's policy. . . .

The narrow scope given the attorney-client privilege by the court below not only makes it difficult for corporate attorneys to formulate sound advice when their client is faced with a specific legal problem but also threatens to limit the valuable efforts of corporate counsel to ensure their client's compliance with the law. In light of the vast and complicated array of regulatory legislation confronting the modern corporation, corporations, unlike most individuals, "constantly go to lawyers to find out how to obey the law," particularly since compliance with the law in this area is hardly an instinctive matter. . . .

The communications at issue were made by Upjohn employees to counsel for Upjohn acting as such, at the direction of corporate superiors in order to secure legal advice from counsel. . . . Information, not available from upper-echelon management, was needed to supply a basis for legal advice concerning compliance with securities and tax laws, foreign laws, currency regulations, duties to shareholders, and potential litigation in each of these areas. The communications concerned matters within the scope of the employees' corporate duties, and the employees themselves were sufficiently aware that they were being questioned in order that the corporation could obtain legal advice. . . . Consistent with the underlying purposes of the attorney-client privilege, these communications must be protected against compelled disclosure.

★   ★   ★

Accordingly, the judgment of the Court of Appeals is reversed, and the case remanded for further proceedings.

Legal Fees and Legal Costs

Fees   Lawyers charge for their services in one of three different ways: flat rate, hourly rate, and contingent fee. The flat rate charge is used usually when the work is relatively routine and the lawyer knows in advance approximately how long it will take to do the job. Drawing a will or doing a real estate closing on a res-

idence are the types of jobs for which lawyers are often paid a flat rate. The rate itself may be based on a percentage of the worth of the matter—1 percent of the selling price of the home, for example.

Lawyers generally charge by the hour for courtroom time and for ongoing representation in commercial matters. Virtually every sizable law firm bills its clients by hourly rates, which in many cities range from a low of perhaps $50–75 for the time of a junior associate to $150–300 and more for the time of the senior partner. The rapid climb in hourly rates has led many corporations to expand the size of their legal staffs in order to bring these costs under control. It is obviously cheaper to pay a full-time lawyer a salary than to pay high hourly rates to outside lawyers, because the lawyers' office overhead is built into these rates. Even the largest corporations cannot afford to bring all their legal work in-house, however, because from time to time legal matters crop up that call for the help of specialists who would not be used on a full-time basis. Private law firms can keep such specialists busy because they serve many different clients.

The contingent fee is one that is paid only if the lawyer wins—that is, it is contingent on success. This type of fee arrangement is used most often in personal injury cases (automobile accidents, product liability, and professional malpractice, for example). The desirability of the contingent fee is hotly debated. Trial lawyers justify it by pointing to the high cost of preparing for such lawsuits. A typical automobile accident case can cost several thousand dollars to prepare, and a complicated product liability case can cost tens of thousands of dollars. Few people have that kind of money or would be willing to spend it on the chance that they might win a lawsuit. Corporate and professional defendants complain that the contingent fee gives lawyers a license to go "big game hunting"—to file suits against "deep pocket" (wealthy) defendants in the hopes of forcing them to settle. Trial lawyers respond that the contingent fee arrangement forces them to screen cases and weed out the unmeritorious ones, because it is not worth their time to spend the hundreds of hours necessary on such cases if their chances of winning are slim or nonexistent.

Costs   In England and many other countries, the losing party must pay the legal expenses of the winning party, including attorneys' fees. That is not the general rule in the United States. Here, each party must bear most of its own costs, including, especially, the fees of lawyers. This is known as the "American rule," in contrast to the "British rule." But even in the U.S. certain relatively minor costs, such as filing fees for various documents required in court, are chargeable to the losing side at the discretion of the judge.

There are two exceptions to the American rule. By statute, Congress and the state legislatures have provided that the winning party in enumerated classes of cases may recover its full legal costs from the loser—for example, the federal antitrust laws so provide and so does the federal Equal Access to Justice Act (see **Box 2-2**). The other exception applies to litigants who either bring lawsuits in bad faith, with no expectation of winning, or who defend them in bad faith, in order to put the plaintiff to great expense. Under these circumstances, a court has the discretion to award attorneys' fees to the winner. But this rule is difficult to invoke. Generally, courts do not have *carte blanche* to award attorneys' fees in any cases they happen to think are especially meritorious.

ALTERNATIVE MEANS OF RESOLVING DISPUTES

Disputes need not be settled in court. No law requires parties who have a legal dispute to seek judicial resolution if they can resolve their disagreement privately or through some other public forum. Indeed, lawsuits frequently serve as a spur to private negotiation. Filing a lawsuit may convince one party that the other party is serious. Or the parties may decide that they do not wish to wait the three or four years it can frequently take for a case to move up on the court calendar and will come to terms privately.

Beginning around 1980, a movement toward "alternative dispute resolution" (**ADR**) has gained force throughout the United States. Corporations, private groups, and the courts themselves have begun to seek quicker and cheaper ways for litigants and potential litigants to settle many different types of quarrels than through the courts. In a number of communities, "neighborhood justice centers" or "dispute resolution centers" have sprung up to help in settling disputes, of both civil and criminal nature, that ought not to consume the time and money of courts or of the parties in lengthy proceedings.

These alternative forums use a variety of techniques, including arbitration and mediation, to bring about rapprochement. The techniques vary, and their differences are worth noting. Calling to mind the nature of the judicial process, there are two significant variables: the power to influence the process, and the

LAW AND LIFE

BOX 2-2

U.S. Must Pay Whistle-Blower's Fees

By David Lauter

[By statute, Congress has provided that winning parties recover full legal costs, including attorney fees, from the loser under the federal Equal Access to Justice Act.—AUTHORS' NOTE]

WASHINGTON—Attorneys for A. Ernest Fitzgerald, the Air Force employee who lost his job after blowing the whistle on cost overruns in the C5-A procurement program, will be able to recover their fees from the federal government, U.S. District Judge William M. Bryant has ruled.

RECOVERING ATTORNEY'S FEES

The fees probably will be "between $100,000 and $200,000," according to Mr. Fitzgerald's lead attorney, John Bodner Jr. of Washington's Howrey & Simon.

Mr. Fitzgerald sued the Air Force after officials evaded a 1972 Civil Service Commission order directing that he be restored to his old job or an equivalent position. *Fitzgerald* v. *Hampton*, 76-1486. Judge Bryant found last year that the job Mr. Fitzgerald was given was not equivalent to his original position, and a hearing will be held this May to determine whether the Air Force has yet complied with the 1972 CSC order.

On March 30, Judge Bryant ruled that the Equal Access to Justice Act entitles Mr. Fitzgerald's attorneys, who had been handling the case for the American Civil Liberties Union on a pro bono basis, to recover fees from the Air Force.

Air Force conduct in the case was "vexatious and obstructive" and exhibited "bad faith," Judge Bryant ruled.

Mr. Fitzgerald has also sued former President Richard M. Nixon and several of his associates, charging that Mr. Nixon violated his civil rights by ordering his firing. That case, *Nixon* v. *Fitzgerald*, 79-1738, is now before the Supreme Court on the question of presidential immunity.

Source: The National Law Journal, April 19, 1982

---

power to influence the outcome. The first is the degree to which the parties retain control over the shaping of the issues, the information, and the evidence that will constitute the basis for the decision. The second is the degree to which one or the other or both parties retain control to determine the outcome of the dispute unilaterally. In a court, the parties retain little control over the decision, much control over the process. In private bargaining, the parties retain total control over both process and decision (see Figure 2-2).

Arbitration

Arbitration is a species of adjudication. The parties use a private decision-maker, the **arbitrator,** and the rules of procedure are considerably more relaxed than those that apply in the courtroom. The parties may agree to resolve an existing dispute through arbitration, or they may agree in a contract before any dispute arises that all future disputes will be resolved by

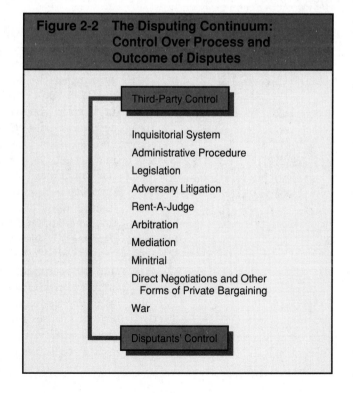

Figure 2-2   The Disputing Continuum: Control Over Process and Outcome of Disputes

Third-Party Control

Inquisitorial System
Administrative Procedure
Legislation
Adversary Litigation
Rent-A-Judge
Arbitration
Mediation
Minitrial
Direct Negotiations and Other Forms of Private Bargaining
War

Disputants' Control

arbitration. They may spell out the rules of procedure to be used and the method for choosing the arbitrator. For example, they may name the specific person, or delegate the responsibility of choosing to some neutral person, or they may each designate a person and the two designees may jointly pick a third arbitrator.

Some 40,000 arbitrations a year take place under the auspices of the American Arbitration Association (AAA), a private organization headquartered in New York, with regional offices in many other cities. The AAA uses published sets of rules for various types of arbitration (for example, labor arbitration or commercial arbitration); parties who provide in contracts for arbitration through the AAA are agreeing to be bound by the AAA rules. Judicial Arbitration & Mediation Services, Inc. (JAMS) is another significant provider of alternative dispute resolution services. JAMS is headquartered in California with regional offices throughout the west. JAMS holds 10,000 hearings a year using a panel of over 120 retired judges. Like the AAA, JAMS is establishing an industry standard and infrastructure by which civil litigants may use alternative means to settle disputes, thereby reducing costs of protracted court litigation.

Arbitration has a twofold advantage over litigation. First, it is usually much quicker, because the arbitrator does not have a backlog of cases and because the procedures are simpler. Second, in complex cases, the quality of the decision may be higher, because the parties can select an arbitrator knowledgeable in the field. Under both federal and state law, arbitration is favored, and a decision rendered by an arbitrator is by law binding and may be enforced by the courts. Judicial review of an arbitrator's decision is limited, as illustrated by the following case.

United Paperworkers is one of several recent decisions in which the Supreme Court has ruled in favor of arbitration. The Court, for instance, has decided that agreements between securities brokers and their clients to arbitrate alleged violations of securities law are enforceable. [Shearson/American Express, Inc. v. McMahon, 482 U.S. 220 (1987) and Rodriguez de Quijas v. Shearson/American Express, 109 S.Ct. 1917 (1989)] Also see the discussion of the *Mitsubishi* decision on p. 1129.

UNITED PAPERWORKERS INTERN. UNION v. MISCO, INC.
484 U.S. 29 (1987)

JUSTICE WHITE delivered the opinion of the Court.

The issue for decision involves several aspects of when a federal court may refuse to enforce an arbitration award rendered under a collective-bargaining agreement.

Misco, Inc., (Misco, or the Company) operates a paper converting plant in Monroe, Louisiana. The Company is a party to a collective-bargaining agreement with the United Paperworkers International Union, AFL-CIO, and its union local (the Union); the agreement covers the production and maintenance employees at the plant. Under the agreement, the Company or the Union may submit to arbitration any grievance that arises from the interpretation or application of its terms, and the arbitrator's decision is final and binding upon the parties. The arbitrator's authority is limited to interpretation and application of the terms contained in the agreement itself. The agreement reserves to management the right to establish, amend, and enforce "rules and regulations regulating the discipline or discharge of employees" and the procedures for imposing discipline. Such rules were to be posted and were to be in effect "until ruled on by grievance and arbitration procedures as to fairness and necessity." For about a decade, the Company's rules had listed as causes for discharge the bringing of intoxicants, narcotics, or controlled substances on to plant property or consuming any of them there, as well as reporting for work under the influence of such substances. At the time of the events involved in this case, the Company was very concerned about the use of drugs at the plant, especially among employees on the night shift.

Isiah Cooper, who worked on the night shift for Misco, was one of the employees covered by the collective-bargaining agreement. He operated a slitter-rewinder machine, which uses sharp blades to cut rolling coils of paper. The arbitrator found that this machine is hazardous and had caused numerous injuries in recent years. Cooper had been reprimanded twice in a few months for deficient performance. On January 21, 1983, one day after the second reprimand, the police searched Cooper's house pursuant to a warrant, and a substantial amount of marijuana was found. Contemporaneously, a police officer was detailed to keep Cooper's car under observation at the Company's parking lot. At about 6:30 p.m., Cooper was seen walking in the parking lot during work hours with two other men. The three men entered Cooper's car momentarily, then walked to another car, a white Cutlass, and entered it. After the other two men later returned to the plant, Cooper was apprehended by police in the backseat of this car with marijuana smoke in the air and a lighted marijuana cigarette in the front-seat ashtray. The police also searched Cooper's car and found a plastic scales case and marijuana gleanings. Cooper was arrested and charged with marijuana possession.

On January 24, Cooper told the Company that he had been arrested for possession of marijuana at his home; the Company did not learn of the marijuana cigarette in the white Cutlass until January 27. It then investigated and on February 7 discharged Cooper, asserting that in the circumstances, his presence in the Cutlass violated the rule against having drugs on the plant premises. Cooper filed a grievance protesting his discharge the same day, and the matter proceeded to arbitration. The Company was not aware until September 21, five days before the hearing before the arbitrator was scheduled, that marijuana had been found in Cooper's car. That fact did not become known to the Union until the hearing began. At the hearing it was stipulated that the issue was whether the Company had "just cause to discharge the Grievant under Rule II.1" and, "[i]f not, what if any should be the remedy."

The arbitrator upheld the grievance and ordered the Company to reinstate Cooper with backpay and full seniority. . . . In particular, the arbitrator found that the Company failed to prove that the employee had possessed or used marijuana on company property: finding Cooper in the backseat of a car and a burning cigarette in the frontseat ashtray was insufficient proof that Cooper was using or possessed marijuana on company property. The arbitrator refused to accept into evidence the fact that marijuana had been found in Cooper's car on company premises because the Company did not know of this fact when Cooper was discharged and therefore did not rely on it as a basis for the discharge.

The Company filed suit in District Court, seeking to vacate the arbitration award on several grounds, one of which was that ordering reinstatement of Cooper, who had allegedly possessed marijuana on the plant premises, was contrary to public policy. The District Court agreed that the award must be

(*continued on next page*)

(continued)

UNITED PAPERWORKERS INTERN. UNION v. MISCO, INC.
484 U.S. 29 (1987)

set aside as contrary to public policy because it ran counter to general safety concerns that arise from the operation of dangerous machinery while under the influence of drugs, as well as to state criminal laws against drug possession. The Court of Appeals affirmed. . . . The court ruled that reinstatement would violate the public policy "against the operation of dangerous machinery by persons under the influence of drugs or alcohol." The arbitrator had found that Cooper was apprehended on company premises in an atmosphere of marijuana smoke in another's car and that marijuana was found in his own car on the company lot. These facts established that Cooper had violated the Company's rules and gave the company just cause to discharge him. The arbitrator did not reach this conclusion because of a "narrow focus on Cooper's procedural rights" that led him to ignore what he "knew was in fact true: that Cooper *did* bring marijuana onto his employer's premises." Even if the arbitrator had not known of this fact at the time he entered his award, "it is doubtful that the award should be enforced today in light of what is now known."

Because the Courts of Appeals are divided on the question of when courts may set aside arbitration awards as contravening public policy, we granted the Union's petition for a writ of certiorari, and now reverse the judgment of the Court of Appeals.

★   ★   ★

Because the parties have contracted to have disputes settled by an arbitrator chosen by them rather than by a judge, it is the arbitrator's view of the facts and of the meaning of the contract that they have agreed to accept. Courts thus do not sit to hear claims of factual or legal error by an arbitrator as an appellate court does in reviewing decisions of lower courts. To resolve disputes about the application of a collective-bargaining agreement, an arbitrator must find facts and a court may not reject those findings simply because it disagrees with them. The same is true of the arbitrator's interpretation of the contract. The arbitrator may not ignore the plain language of the contract; but the parties having authorized the arbitrator to give meaning to the language of the agreement, a court should not reject an award on the ground that the arbitrator misread the contract. So, too, where it is contemplated that the arbitrator will determine remedies for contract violations that he finds, courts have no authority to disagree with his honest judgment in that respect. If the courts were free to intervene on these grounds, the speedy resolution of grievances by private mechanisms would be greatly undermined. . . .

The Company's position, simply put, is that the arbitrator committed grievous error in finding that the evidence was insufficient to prove that Cooper had possessed or used marijuana on company property. But the Court of Appeals, although it took a distinctly jaundiced view of the arbitrator's decision in this regard, was not free to refuse enforcement because it considered Cooper's presence in the white Cutlass, in the circumstances, to be ample proof that Rule II.1 was violated. No dishonesty is alleged; only improvident, even silly, factfinding is claimed. This is hardly sufficient basis for disregarding what the agent appointed by the parties determined to be the historical facts.

★   ★   ★

. . . [The Court of Appeals] held that the evidence of marijuana in Cooper's car required that the award be set aside because to reinstate a person who had brought drugs onto the property was contrary to the public policy "against the operation of dangerous machinery by persons under the influence of drugs or alcohol." We cannot affirm that judgment.

A court's refusal to enforce an arbitrator's award under a collective-bargaining agreement because it is contrary to public policy is a specific application of the more general doctrine, rooted in the common law, that a court may refuse to enforce contracts that violate law or public policy. *W. R. Grace & Co. v. Rubber Workers*, 461 U.S. 757 (1983). That doctrine derives from the basic notion that no court will lend its aid to one who founds a cause of action upon an immoral or illegal act, and is further justified by the observation that the public's interests in confining the scope of private agreements to which it is not a party will go unrepresented unless the judiciary takes account of those interests when it considers whether to enforce such agreements. In the common law of contracts, this doctrine has served as the foundation for occasional exercises of judicial power to abrogate private agreements.

In *W. R. Grace*, . . . our decision turned on our examination of whether the award created any explicit conflict with other "laws and legal precedents" rather than an assessment of "general considerations of supposed public interests." At the very least, an alleged public policy must be properly framed under the approach set out in *W. R. Grace*, and the violation of such a policy must be clearly shown if an award is not to be enforced.

As we see it, the formulation of public policy set out by the Court of Appeals did not comply with the statement that such a policy must be "ascertained 'by reference to the laws and legal precedents and not from general considerations of supposed public interests.' " The Court of Appeals made no attempt to review existing laws and legal precedents in order to demonstrate that they establish a "well defined and dominant" policy against the operation of dangerous machinery while under the influence of drugs. Although certainly such a judgment is firmly roted in common sense, we explicitly held in *W. R. Grace* that a formulation of public policy based only on "general considerations of supposed public interests" is not the sort that permits a court to set aside an arbitration award that was entered in accordance with a valid collective-bargaining agreement.

Even if the Court of Appeals' formulation of public policy is to be accepted, no violation of that policy was clearly shown in this case. In pursuing its public policy inquiry, the Court of Appeals quite properly considered the established fact that traces of marijuana had been found in Cooper's car. Yet the assumed connection between the marijuana gleanings found in Cooper's car and Cooper's actual use of drugs in the workplace is tenuous at best and provides an insufficient basis for holding that his reinstatement would ac-

(continued on next page)

(*continued*)

**UNITED
PAPERWORKERS
INTERN. UNION v.
MISCO, INC.**
484 U.S. 29 (1987)

tually violate the public policy identified by the Court of Appeals "against the operation of dangerous machinery by persons under the influence of drugs or alcohol." A refusal to enforce an award must rest on more than speculation or assumption.

In any event, it was inappropriate for the Court of Appeals itself to draw the necessary inference. To conclude from the fact that marijuana had been found in Cooper's car that Cooper had ever been or would be under the influence of marijuana while he was on the job and operating dangerous machinery is an exercise in factfinding about Cooper's use of drugs and his amenability to discipline, a task that exceeds the authority of a court asked to overturn an arbitration award. The parties did not bargain for the facts to be found by a court, but by an arbitrator chosen by them who had more opportunity to observe Cooper and to be familiar with the plant and its problems. . . .

The judgment of the Court of Appeals is reversed.

By and large, both parties must consent to submit to arbitration. But some states have experimented with "court-annexed arbitration," in which certain types of cases (in California, for instance, cases for money damages in the amount of $25,000 or less) are assigned to designated arbitrators in an attempt to save time and expense.

"Rent-a-Judge"

Most states have a statutory procedure that permits litigants to refer a lawsuit to a private judge for resolution. This procedure, dubbed "rent-a-judge" in the 1980s (but known formally as "trial by reference"), has several advantages for corporate litigants who are prepared to pay the judge's fee. The trial can be held at the parties' convenience, in private, and, in many states, without any record being kept. The judge's decision is binding and enforceable; unlike arbitration, the judge is bound to follow the ordinary rules of evidence, and the decision may be appealed to a regular appellate court. Since almost all private judges to whom cases are referred under this procedure are retired judges, the case can be scheduled far more quickly than the civil dockets of most major courts permit, and the judge can render a decision within a period agreed on by both parties. Another advantage of the reference procedure is expertise: the parties can

hire a judge who is knowledgeable in the area of the dispute—for example, patents, antitrust, or environmental litigation.

Mediation

Unlike adjudication, **mediation** gives the mediator no power to impose a decision. Instead, the mediator acts as a go-between who attempts to help the parties negotiate a solution. He can communicate the parties' positions to each other, facilitate the finding of common ground, and suggest outcomes. But the parties have complete control over both process and decision. The outcome need not be responsive to the claims initially raised, nor does it require the application of an articulated, rational standard. The parties may come up with *any* resolution of their dispute that satisfies them.

Mediation, because it is an unstructured and informal process, has no ground rules beyond those the parties themselves agree to follow. Mediation can be exceptionally helpful when (1) the emotional level is high; (2) the parties are at an impasse; (3) the issues are complex; (4) there is no one obvious right answer; (5) many parties are involved; and (6) the need to resolve the issues is urgent. Mediation works because it permits a neutral who has gained the trust of the parties "to learn intimate facts from both sides that they would never have shared with each other in the course of trial preparation. By building on the parties' trust in the mediator, the process thus allows the parties to explore workable options. With the knowledge that he gains, the mediator can learn how far apart the parties are and devise ways of bridging the gap." (Lieberman and Henry, 1986, p. 428)

The Mini-Trial

Perhaps the most celebrated corporate dispute resolution technique of the 1990s is the **"mini-trial."** This device is not in fact a trial at all, but a formalized method of settlement negotiation. During the 1980s, a host of well-known companies and even government agencies designed a mini-trial process to resolve expensive, time-consuming lawsuits. The companies included Allied Corp., Amoco, Austin Industries, Borden, Continental Can, Control Data Corp., Gillette, Honeywell, Shell Oil Co., Texaco, TRW, Union Carbide Corp., and Wisconsin Electric Power Co.; among the government agencies were NASA and the Army Corps of Engineers.

No single procedural model of the mini-trial has been universally adopted. The parties are free to design their own process. But, in general, the mini-trial has the following characteristics:

1. Preparation time is short—perhaps six weeks to two months—compared to the years of the pretrial phase of a lawsuit.
2. The hearing is highly abbreviated—no more than a day or two—compared to the months that a complex antitrust or commercial lawsuit can take in court.
3. The hearing is usually conducted before a third-party neutral known as the "neutral advisor," who has no authority to decide the dispute.
4. There is no judge or jury. The case is presented to representatives of the parties, who have the authority to settle.
5. The lawyers present their "best" case; they do not spend time on side issues.
6. Immediately after the presentations, the parties meet privately to negotiate a settlement.
7. If they fail to settle, the neutral advisor may, if agreed in advance, render an advisory opinion on how he thinks the case would come out if it went to trial. The parties might then meet again.
8. The hearings are confidential; the parties and the neutral advisor commit themselves to refrain from disclosing details of the proceeding to outsiders.

The mini-trial has several advantages: (1) costs are dramatically lower than litigation; (2) the process allows for creative problem-solving; the parties can reach resolutions not possible in court; (3) the parties are free to maintain ongoing relationships; (4) the parties can avail themselves of a knowledgeable neutral, rather than, as in court, a judge chosen at random; (5) the disputants can design whatever process and rules suit them best; (6) the entire proceedings can be kept confidential; and (7) much time can be saved over conventional legal process.

Inquisitorial Approach

Unlike the adjudicator, the decision-maker in an inquisitorial approach has power over both the outcome and the process. A familiar example of the inquisitorial approach is the legislative committee hearing. The legislative committee may listen to whomever it pleases, deny anyone it chooses the right to appear before it, and take any action it chooses (including none), regardless of the arguments made by those who appeared before it. Legislative committees do not ordinarily resolve individual disputes. One version of the inquisitorial model has caught a certain degree of public attention: the **ombudsman.** The term comes from the Scandinavian administrative system in which a public official has the power to intervene in administrative decisions on behalf of complaining citizens. In effect, the ombudsman is a people's trouble-shooter.

Legislation

If private bargaining is at one end of the dispute-resolution continuum, legislation is at the other. In private bargaining, the parties retain total power over both process and outcome. In legislation, they retain neither. The legislator neither can nor does give a hearing to all those affected by the contemplated action. No hearing at all need be held, no evidence introduced to the decision-makers. Unlike judges, legislators are not bound by any authoritative standard. Legislators may pursue political, economic, and social goals of their own choosing. Their decision need not be "rational," in the sense that the goal must follow necessarily from the means chosen. Obviously, most legislators prefer to be rational, but because they must compromise hotly contested points of view, their decisions often will not be considered rational. Moreover, there rarely are articulated standards by which the rationality of a legislative enactment can be measured, unlike a judicial decision.

Managing and Preventing Disputes

Many corporations have begun to look beyond the particular techniques for resolving disputes and are scrutinizing the ways they respond to business disputes when they first flare up—or even before. They are learning, in other words, to manage and prevent disputes, as well as to resolve them.

Managing Disputes   The philosophy of corporate dispute management is that the company law department should be considered a center for the management of investments and that litigation should be managed through tools of cost accounting and business judgment, just as other business functions are managed. Successfully implementing this philosophy requires management to understand litigation and the legal system (one of the reasons that business law courses are important) and lawyers to understand management. Beginning around 1975, the law department of Xerox Corp. developed a system of budgeting and financial planning. The result was that from 1976 to 1982, the company's outside legal expenses fell from $12 million per year to $3 million at a time of sharp inflation, and the number of in-house lawyers dropped from 152 to 70.

Among the management tools available to management-oriented lawyers are litigation budgeting and risk analysis. The lawyer looks at a lawsuit as a marketing executive looks at a product that needs to be sold. The lawyer asks: What will I get for my investment? For instance, lawyers in conventional practice handed a lawsuit might decide to take depositions of dozens of executives, without regard to cost. The manager wants to know what dividends those depositions will pay.

Preventive Law   Disputes that do not arise need never be resolved. Companies are learning to head off obvious difficulties by establishing compliance programs to ensure that employees abide by the law. Companies also are beginning to undertake litigation audits to determine, by inspecting existing lawsuits, where such companies are vulnerable and what changes in procedure might reduce their legal exposure.

A commitment to exploring alternatives to lawsuits is a form of prevention that is beginning to gain favor with some companies. When IBM settled a product-piracy suit against Hitachi, for example, the companies agreed on an elaborate arbitration system should the situation ever arise again. Knowing that their companies are bound to follow a particular procedure with tough sanctions might dissuade some executives from engaging in behavior that would invoke the process. (And, as **Box 2-3** illustrates, once a company learns that it can solve complex problems outside the courtroom, it will tend to design a dispute-resolution system invoking a variety of alternative processes to settle future disputes.)

Why ADR Might Fail

Alternative dispute resolution is not a panacea. Noncourtroom procedures may fail for a variety of reasons. First, ADR may not work because each party may be reluctant to suggest it, for fear that the opposition will perceive the suggestion as a sign of weakness. A possible solution to this difficulty is the Alternative Dispute Resolution Pledge sponsored by the Center for Public Resources in New York. More than 400 major American corporations have subscribed to this pledge (see **Box 2-4**). Each signatory undertakes to explore an alternative to litigation if the company with which it has had a dispute has also subscribed to the Policy Statement. Although lawsuits will scarcely fade away—more than 10 million cases are filed every year in the state and federal courts—there are hopeful signs that business realizes that sensible settlement is not a weakness but a strength.

Neutrals Deployed Several Kinds of ADR to Solve IBM-Fujitsu Copyright Dispute

*[The exploration of alternatives to law-suits is gaining favor with many companies. IBM and Fujitsu invoked a variety of alternative dispute resolution processes in order to settle out of the courtroom.—*AUTHORS' NOTE*]*

When IBM and Fujitsu—respectively the world's first and fourth largest computer companies—resolved their four-year fight over software copyright in mid-September, nearly all news media called the highly publicized procedure an arbitration.

But an *Alternatives* analysis of the case documents shows that not only arbitration, but also mediation, an ADR contract clause, neutral expert factfinding, negotiation by executives and attorneys, and preventive-law concepts were all deployed by the two neutrals in their ADR resolution of this complex, high-stakes battle. Moreover, the neutrals will have continuing oversight of the ongoing resolution, thus functioning very much like special masters have in large court cases.

Thus, the lessons of the case are that several kinds of ADR can be profitably employed in a dispute and, perhaps more importantly, that the failure of one ADR strategy does not mean others will be fruitless.

The nub of the dispute was IBM's claim that Fujitsu, which makes IBM-compatible hardware and software, had violated IBM's copyrights in the latter. The controversy arose gradually during the late 1970's and early 1980's, in part because U.S. copyright law was evolving. Before 1980, few thought copyrights were

MANY STRATEGIES TO RESOLVING DISPUTES OUT OF COURT

available for computer software. But in that year Congress passed the Computer Software Act, extending such protection to this intellectual property.

Global Case
The dispute was a major one in the computer market. These two multinational corporations compete in Asia, Brazil, Europe and the Pacific Rim. Hundreds of millions of dollars were at stake. So significant was the disagreement that senior officials from both companies spent eight months negotiating a settlement after IBM lodged its formal complaint with Fujitsu in October 1982.

Under that 1983 accord, Fujitsu paid substantial sums to IBM for its previous distribution of certain computer programs, and agreed to make semiannual payments for its future marketing of them. In turn, IBM granted immunity to Fujitsu, which admitted no copyright infringement, and waived all past and future claims regarding that software. The companies also set up a system for making available certain software information to each other in the future.

The 1983 agreements, however, were "confusing" and "incomplete," according to Stanford Law Prof. Robert Mnookin and retired railroad executive and computer expert John Jones, the two neutrals who orchestrated the most recent resolution. Under the weight of many disagreements about their meaning, the pacts collapsed not long after their creation.

As Messrs. Jones and Mnookin note in their September 15 opinion, the two computer makers then "attempted to negotiate a resolution of disputes through voluminous correspondence and numerous meetings of technical and business personnel." But, they observe, "None of these attempts was successful."

Two-Fold Solution
After these vain efforts to revive the 1983 agreements, the parties embarked in June 1985 on the recently concluded ADR initiative. The solution, described in an order issued by the neutrals simultaneously with their September 15 opinion, is an ongoing one, with many details to be worked out. In essence, the solution is two-fold, with the first applying to disputes over existing software and the second to potential disputes over future software.

The first part is Fujitsu's payment of a sum—yet to be determined by the neutrals—for all past and future use of an agreed-upon list of existing software programs. Mr. Jones terms this a "paid-up license" for these programs, for which Fujitsu will get a guarantee of "complete immunity" from IBM.

Second is the establishment of a "Secured Facility Regime," under which each company can examine, under elaborate safeguards, certain parts of the software of the other. In return for adequate compensation, the examining company can use the obtained information in developing its own software, and be assured of immunity from claims of copyright violations. Monitored by an independent expert and expected to last for five to ten years as the neutrals may decide, the Secured Facility Regime "will constitute the intellectual property law

(continued on next page)

Two-Fold Solution, *continued*

between these two companies," said Professor Mnookin on September 15.

In detail too profuse to recount here, the neutrals have set out the operation of this two-part decision in their September 15 opinion and award. Interested readers can obtain those documents from the American Arbitration Association, the organization under which the ADR was conducted, at 140 West 51 St., New York, NY 10020. Heard in the AAA Commercial Arbitration Tribunal, the case is titled *International Business Machines Corp. v. Fujitsu Ltd.*, No. 13T-117-0636-85.

For ADR advocates, however, the breadth of ADR devices deployed in the case may be its most interesting aspect. The following is a selected schematic of the variety of ADR strategies used in the resolution of the dispute.

ADR Contract Clause

While neutrals Mnookin and Jones had little good to say about the collapsed 1983 agreements between IBM and Fujitsu, it was in fact the ADR clause in that accord that started the ball rolling toward the September 15 resolution of the case.

The clause mandated a two-part ADR procedure: negotiation and arbitration. First, "(T)he parties agreed to submit any dispute with respect to the agreements to a meeting of responsible executives of both parties," the neutrals note in their opinion. Second, they continue, the two computer makers "agreed to submit any dispute which remained unresolved after sixty days to binding arbitration under the auspices of the AAA."

Arbitration

Two types of arbitration were used in the case. At first, the parties each

chose an arbitrator, Mr. Jones for IBM and Professor Mnookin for Fujitsu. Those two party-arbitrators appointed a third, neutral arbitrator, Donald A. Macdonald.

But at the first meeting of this panel with the parties in December 1985, "the parties and the Arbitrators agreed that all Arbitrators would serve as neutrals, that the AAA rules and ethical standards would apply, and that there would be no ex parte communications with the parties except as authorized by the Panel," neutrals Jones and Mnookin note in their opinion. Neutral Macdonald resigned in May 1987, leaving the other two to handle the case from there on.

'Mini-Trial'

The neutrals began their handling of the case in conventional arbitration fashion, hearing and deciding in February 1986 various procedural issues relating to the 1983 agreements.

But at that time the neutrals also drew on another ADR principle, the involvement of business executives, in their attempts to resolve the dispute. Messrs. Jones, Macdonald and Mnookin required that "responsible executives of both parties meet, under the guidance of the Panel, with respect to [Fujitsu's] software development process," and that "each party brief and argue, to the Panel and responsible executives, whether, and to what extent, such [Fujitsu] procedures violated IBM's rights under the 1983 agreements."

ADR advocates know that this process, the briefing and arguing of the issues before neutrals and settlement-empowered executives, followed by negotiations, is the hallmark of the mini-trial, an increasingly popular settlement procedure. (*Alternatives*, September 1986.)

Mediation

The "mini-trial" process, conducted through June and July 1986, failed. Though some ancillary issues were settled, "The fundamental dispute could not be resolved through negotiation by responsible executives," the neutrals say in their opinion. Next, the neutrals used another device favored by advocates of expedited dispute resolution: summary judgment.

And simultaneously with their rulings on the summary-judgment motions, the neutrals made the apparently crucial decision to engage the parties in yet another ADR procedure, mediation. With Messrs. Jones and Mnookin acting as mediators, the parties worked through the winter of 1986–'87.

Unlike the "mini-trial," this ADR strategy worked. "The Arbitrators' mediation efforts were successful, resulting in the execution of new agreements between the parties," the neutrals report in their opinion.

The fruits of the mediation were memorialized in two documents. In the first, the "1986 Agreement," the parties "settled all of IBM's intellectual property claims with respect to hundreds of [Fujitsu] programs," the neutrals recount. "The 1986 Agreement thereby successfully resolved almost all of the parties' disputes with respect to [Fujitsu's] past use of IBM programming material." The second accord, the "Washington Agreement," provided "a framework for the resolution of all issues remaining in dispute and the foundation for the Order," they add.

Preventive Practices

The resolution of this major software dispute, reached through a host of ADR techniques, incorporates in its Secured Facility provisions yet another ADR tactic: preventive law.

BOX 2-3

Preventive Practices, *continued*

Professor Mnookin explained these notions in full on September 15, and his description is a good summary of the advantages of the preventive approach:

"The Secured Facility regime provides a unique advantage as a means of settling complicated issues in evolving technological and legal fields. In the past, IBM could never know exactly how Fujitsu was using IBM programming material. In order to determine if some violation of its rights may have occurred, IBM had to wait until after the public release of a Fujitsu program and then conduct an elaborate technical examination of the program. Then, if it chose to pursue a claim, it was extremely expensive and time-consuming.

"Meanwhile, of course, the Fujitsu program at issue was already in the marketplace. Even the threat that IBM might at some point pursue a claim would create a potential prob-

lem for both Fujitsu and for the Fujitsu customers using a new Fujitsu program.

"The Secured Facility exposes and resolves disagreements *before* public release of software. The determination made in the facility as to what goes on the survey sheet is the final word on what material of one company can be used by the other company. Once that sheet leaves the facility, the issue is settled. IBM can be assured that only the material allowed by the instructions is being shared. Fujitsu can be assured that IBM will not make a claim with respect to the use of that material at some date in the future. And customers who license Fujitsu operating system software can be assured that no future controversy will disrupt their use of these programs."

The neutrals found use for still other ADR tools in this high-stakes, high-tech case. For example, the Secured Facility supervisor, described

at length in the neutrals' award, will function as an expert factfinder of sorts under their direction. The supervisor "shall be an experienced, unbiased, and qualified person or firm . . . with relevant systems programming experience," the neutrals order. And the neutrals themselves, who will supervise this ongoing resolution and handle any disputes that the parties alone cannot resolve, thus function as monitors or special masters.

The breadth of ADR devices used in the case should please ADR advocates. So should the simple fact that this case of global implications, involving hundreds of millions of dollars, high emotions and cultural differences, was susceptible of ADR resolution.

Source: *Alternatives to the High Cost of Litigation*, November 1987, pp. 187–90

LAW AND LIFE

BOX 2-4

THE ALTERNATIVE DISPUTE
RESOLUTION PLEDGE

RESOLVING TO TRY A SIMPLER WAY

We recognize that for many business disputes there is a less expensive, more effective method of resolution than the traditional lawsuit. Alternative dispute resolution (ADR) techniques involve collaborative techniques which often can spare businesses the high cost and wear and tear of litigation.

In recogition of the foregoing, we subscribe to the following statement of principle. In the event of a busi-

ness dispute between our corporation and another corporation which has made or will then make a similar statement, we are prepared to explore, with that other party, resolution of the dispute through negotiation or ADR techniques, before resorting to full-scale litigation. If either party believes that the dispute is not suit-

able for ADR techniques, or if such techniques do not produce results satisfactory to the disputants, either party may proceed with litigation.

X CORPORATION

_____

Chief Executive Officer

_____

Chief Legal Officer

_____

Date

A second reason for the failure of ADR may be the emotional state of the people involved. Even if there are no sound business reasons for hiring lawyers and paying the escalating legal fees, executives can be caught up in the "game." Psychologists refer to this process as "entrapment." People often spend much more of their time and money in resolving a conflict than seems justified. One study (Teger, 1979) indicates two reasons for entrapment: (1) economic reasons—the drive for the very last dollar that can be exacted; and (2) interpersonal relations, such as the desire to save face or to prove that the manager is the best. At the outset the parties might have sound economic motives for pursuing the dispute, but at some point in the litigation process the interpersonal aspects can come to the fore, and at this point a rational ADR approach will give way to the emotions of the lawsuit.

A third reason ADR might not lead away from the courtroom is that a company, for reasons of *business strategy*, might prefer litigation. Among the strategic reasons for preferring lawsuits:

- Managers attempt to avoid personal responsibility for losses by shifting responsibility to the law department or a court.
- By litigating a particular case, the company can *signal* outsiders that it is adopting an aggressive posture in certain matters. For example, some accounting firms blame increases in liability insurance rates on the willingness of other firms to settle cases rather than litigate. (*Wall Street Journal*, Nov. 8, 1984, p. 4)
- Some companies use litigation as part of their competitive strategy to hinder start-up ventures or (if they have substantial resources) to wear down or frighten off an opponent. When Computerland posted a $283 million cash bond to appeal a judgment worth over $500 million awarded a group of investors known as Micro/Vest, Computerland's president noted: "I can only say it is going to be a lot more than Micro/Vest and its speculators can afford. This ups their ante considerably." (The losing party on appeal must pay the cost of the bond—an estimated $14 million.) The Micro/Vest attorney responded: "What they're really saying is we're going to cost you a lot more money and we'll see if you can withstand the monetary gap." (*San Francisco Chronicle*, May 9, 1985, p. 33)
- A party saddled with a poor case might prefer to litigate to defer the payment of damages. In some types of cases, interest is also deferred until the court renders a judgment. For example, Federal District Judge Miles Lord accused A. H. Robins Co. of stalling Dalkon Shield litigation because ". . . the interest you earn in the interim covers the cost of the cases." (*Wall Street Journal*, Aug. 23, 1985, p.

6.) An individual manager might also have financial reasons for preferring litigation—for example, to delay posting a loss on the balance sheet until he moves on to a new position.
- A company might feel, entirely as a matter of principle, that the case is more important than its cost. According to William Langston, corporate counsel, "An executive may tell counsel, 'So and so owes us $10 million. He's a thief. Sue him. And don't tell me about the cost; this is a matter of principle.' " (*Wall Street Journal*, Dec. 13, 1982, p. 22)
- Through discovery (p. 53) in litigation, a company can obtain valuable information—for instance, it might learn about a competitor's advertising strategies, market-share trends, and product failures.
- Litigation is the only appropriate approach when a company wishes to establish a new legal theory as precedent for future cases.
- Publicity is an important part of corporate strategy—either in defending one's own reputation or besmirching a competitor's. When Maryland banned the sale of certain Gerber food products after state officials received complaints about glass in the company's jars, Gerber responded by suing the state for $150 million on the grounds that the ban was not justified. (*Ann Arbor News*, March 9, 1986, p. 37)
- Finally, litigation is often preferred when the issue—for example, the validity of a key patent—is vital to the success of a company.

But even if litigation is preferred for strategic reasons, the astute manager will not simply turn the matter over to the lawyer and wash her hands of any involvement in the litigation strategy. Like any other business activity, litigation is most sensibly pursued as an opportunity that makes sense only if cost effective. During the 1980s, smart managers and lawyers began to apply decision analysis to the realm of litigation.

Decision Analysis

Alternatives to litigation require greater management involvement than in the past. Decision tree analysis is an especially useful technique that allows management to play a more active role in legal decision-making. **Decision analysis,** a term first coined in 1963, is a discipline devoted to the systematic analysis of important decisions. **Decision tree analysis** refers to a particular technique for dealing with the uncertainty that is present in most difficult decisions. Decision tree analysis has been used for many years to analyze business decisions, and, in recent years, corporate attorneys have recognized its value in making settlement decisions. The use of decision tree analysis is especially attractive because it facilitates communication between attorneys and executives who often find it difficult to deal with the uncertainty and complexity inherent in litigation.

When used in legal decision-making, decision tree analysis requires the creation of a model of the decision, called a decision tree, that represents the value of uncertain events. A simplified decision tree depicting a $500,000 case in which the plaintiff has received a $100,000 settlement offer is presented in Figure 2-3. The plaintiff's attorney has estimated the probability of winning to be 70%. Squares are used to represent decisions (here the decision whether to settle or continue the litigation), while circles represent uncontrollable events (in this case, the court's decision). A more elaborate decision tree would include each specific issue necessary to determine whether the plaintiff is likely to win the case, along with probabilities for a range of possible recoveries.

Once created, the model can be used to calculate the value of refusing the settlement offer and continuing with the litigation, the overall probability of success, and discovery costs. As indicated in **Box 2-5**, law firms are now using software to perform these calculations.

CHAPTER SUMMARY

This chapter has provided an overview of courts and how they work. Understanding what courts are, how they operate, and what it means to "think legally" is essential to understanding any particular body of law. In the United States, the study of law is complicated by the multiplicity of court systems. There are fifty-two different court systems: the federal court system, and the court systems of each state and the District of Colum-

bia. State and federal trial courts have the authority to conduct hearings to determine the facts and to apply the law to those facts. Litigants dissatisfied with the results in the trial courts may appeal decisions in trial courts to appellate courts, which are empowered to review the lower court's application of the law. Ordinarily state courts hear state claims and federal courts hear claims based on federal law, but in some instances state courts may hear federal claims and vice versa. State supreme court decisions may be appealed on constitutional grounds to the U.S. Supreme Court.

Cases move through courts in a manner laid down by rules of procedure. The general method is known as the adversary system, operating through independent lawyers for each party to the case. Commencing with the original pleadings (complaint and answer), the lawyers for each party develop the facts of a case before going to the courtroom, where rules of evidence and procedure dictate how the facts are presented to the judge and jury. Not every quarrel can land in a courtroom. There must be a genuine controversy between two or more parties based on a claim of legal entitlement.

Lawsuits are not limited to controversies between two individuals. Cases involving dozens, or even thousands, of plaintiffs can be brought against multiple defendants. In a class action, a single plaintiff can represent an entire class of people whose claims are identical to the class representative. No one in business can afford to be ignorant of the way lawyers practice law. With nearly 800,000 lawyers, the American legal profession is the means by which people resolve or prevent most significant legal disputes.

Lawyers serve clients in a variety of roles—as advocates, negotiators, counselors, and lobbyists. The position of the client should not be imputed to the lawyer who often works for interests that she might personally dislike. But the lawyer may not do anything the client wishes; the lawyer is constrained by a formal code of ethics. One of the key provisions is that of confidentiality (unless the client seeks assistance to plan a future crime). Another key ethical provision is that a lawyer may not work for two clients whose interests conflict.

In the corporate setting, determining who is the client can

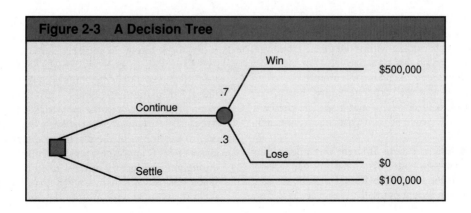

Figure 2-3   A Decision Tree

LAW AND LIFE

BOX 2-5

Decision Trees

[Many corporate attorneys have recognized the value of decision tree analysis in recent years. Such analysis enables an attorney to calculate the value of settlement over continuing litigation.
—AUTHORS' NOTE]

More lawyers are learning to apply decision-tree analysis to litigation problems, says its master teacher, lawyer Marc Victor of Menlo Park, Calif.

"It's really catching on in the legal community," Victor said. About 600 lawyers are learning what he calls "litigation-risk analysis"—double the number enrolled when Victor began teaching it in 1980.

"Litigation-risk analysis is a discipline for lawyers to get their thinking straight," Victor said. "It's most useful in cases where a lawyer does not have a wealth of previous experience to go on."

To do the analysis, lawyers must express probabilities in numbers rather than words. When trying to decide whether to try a case or settle, for example, a lawyer avoids ambiguity by telling a client the probability of winning is 70 percent rather than "very likely." Otherwise, "one lawyer may

A NEW METHOD TAKES ROOT

mean 40 percent when he says 'good possibility,' while another could mean 70 percent," Victor said.

Building a decision tree enables lawyers to assess the risks of pursuing various strategies and to put a percentage on the probability of recovery of various types of claims. "Trying to build such a picture ensures that counsel think carefully not only about the most important uncertainties in the case, but also about the interrelationships among all the important factors," Victor said.

Victor especially recommends use of decision trees in complex litigation in which "keeping track of all the factors in one's head would quickly become impossible."

In fact, plaintiffs' attorneys alleging multibillion-dollar cost overruns and construction delays in the massive South Texas nuclear project used Victor and his litigation-risk analysis to help get a tentative $750 million settlement. Defendants were Brown & Root Inc.—the architect, engineer and contractor—and its corporate parent, Dallas-based Hallibur-

ton Co.

"Lawyers are now taking decision-analysis courses at business schools, but it ought to be taught in law schools," Victor said. "Legal problems have as much uncertainty and complexity as business problems."

To help with complex legal problems, Texas Instruments has developed a decision-tree software product called Arborist. "The software can perform the decision-tree calculations," Victor said. "The computer is great for questions like: 'What if we could improve one area of research by 10 percent?' It then tells you that the value of the case would improve by X dollars. It helps you figure out whether the benefits outweigh the cost." But he cautioned that lawyers must understand decision-tree techniques before applying computer software to them.

"Software doesn't have all the answers," he said. "It can do the last 10 percent of the work, but the first 90 percent of the job for the lawyer is building the tree."

One highly automated law firm whose lawyers are using decision-tree software products is Wilmer Cutler & Pickering in Washington.

Source: *The American Bar Association Journal*, 33 (1986)

---

be a problem. Ordinarily, the lawyer represents the corporation as a whole, not the individual officers or employees. When the corporation's interests conflict with those of the employee, the employee should retain his own lawyer. For purposes of confidentiality, the lawyer is bound to protect the confidences not just of the abstract corporate entity, but of any employees who speak to the lawyer about a specific company legal problem within the scope of their particular responsibilities.

Lawyers charge their clients in different ways, depending on the type of problem—an hourly fee, a flat rate for services rendered, or a contingent fee. In the United States, the winning party is not automatically entitled to recover legal costs

(including fees paid to the lawyer) from the losing party. "Fee shifting" is permissible only if a statute specifically authorizes it (as, for example, in antitrust cases).

Litigation in court is not the only method of resolving legal disputes. Other techniques include arbitration, "rent-a-judge," mediation, and newer forms of alternative dispute resolution (ADR), such as the mini-trial. The mini-trial is a highly structured settlement negotiation in which lawyers present the case to executives of the disputing companies. Although some forms of ADR are quite ancient (arbitration has been practiced throughout the history of the United States), beginning in the 1980s business has increasingly turned to newer methods to avoid the costs and pitfalls of litigation.

Business is also learning to manage and prevent disputes at the outset. One type of preventive law is the litigation audit.

ADR is not a panacea. Alternative processes might fail because each party may fear being perceived as weak (although many companies have publicly signed a pledge to invoke ADR). Another reason for failure is that emotions get in the way of business sense. Finally, companies may avoid ADR and pursue litigation for reasons of business strategy: to wear down an opponent, minimize interest costs, obtain information, or establish a precedent.

KEY TERMS

Adjudication	p. 47	Holding	p. 56
ADR	p. 66	Instruct	p. 54
Adversary system	p. 47	Intermediate appellate	p. 45
Answer	p. 49	Interrogatory	p. 53
Appeals	p. 44	Judgment	p. 55
Appellant	p. 45	Jurisdiction	p. 49
Appellee	p. 45	Lawyer-client privilege	p. 61
Arbitrator	p. 67	Legal dispute	p. 56
Arguments	p. 47	Legal entitlement	p. 56
Briefs	p. 55	Limited jurisdiction	p. 44
Class action	p. 60	Mini-trial	p. 73
Closing argument	p. 54	Mediation	p. 72
Complaint	p. 49	Ombudsman	p. 73
Confession and avoid-	p. 48	Opening statement	p. 54
ance		Oral argument	p. 55
Conflict of interest	p. 62	Order	p. 56
Contempt	p. 56	Party	p. 47
Counter complaint	p. 52	Plaintiff	p. 48
Cross-examination	p. 54	Pleadings	p. 52
Decision analysis	p. 78	Proofs	p. 47
Decision tree analysis	p. 78	Prosecution	p. 48
Default judgment	p. 53	Rebuttal	p. 54
Defendant	p. 48	Relevance	p. 47
Demurrer	p. 53	Service	p. 49
Depose	p. 53	Small claims court	p. 44
Deposition	p. 53	Standing	p. 59
Dicta	p. 56	Statute of limitations	p. 49
Directed verdict	p. 54	Stayed	p. 55
Direct testimony	p. 54	Summary judgment	p. 53
Discovery	p. 53	Surrebuttal	p. 54
Disputes	p. 47	Summons	p. 49
District	p. 45	Trial	p. 53
Diversity of citizenship	p. 44	Venue	p. 49
Garnished	p. 56	Voir dire	p. 53
General jurisdiction	p. 45		

SELF-TEST QUESTIONS

1. Which of the following cases can be heard in a federal court?

(a) a dispute over an uncle's will
(b) a traffic accident in which the drivers were next-door neighbors
(c) prosecution of a robbery of the local convenience store
(d) prosecution on a charge of income tax evasion

2. In which of the following cases would a federal court apply state law to the case before it?

(a) a claim that a local newspaper infringed a copyright by publishing an article without permission of a resident of the same town in which the paper is published
(b) a prosecution for robbing a federally-insured bank
(c) a dispute between two people living in different states over a contract they signed
(d) a suit against the driver of a U.S. postal truck by a pedestrian who lives in the same town as the driver of the truck

3. Which of the following statements is true?

(a) The plaintiff must prove every disputed fact in the case he has brought.
(b) The defendant can have a lawsuit dismissed if the plaintiff brings it in the wrong court.
(c) The trial judge may always direct a verdict for the plaintiff even if the jury decides for the defendant.
(d) Whenever two or more people are injured in the same accident, they may bring a class action.

4. Which of the following cases can be heard in a state court?

(a) a traffic accident involving a resident of the state and a citizen of another state
(b) a prosecution for selling drugs that were brought into the United States from abroad
(c) a suit by a woman to enforce a divorce decree granted by a court in another state against her ex-husband who moved into the state after the divorce
(d) all of the above
(e) none of the above

5. Which of the following statements is true?

(a) The Supreme Court may sometimes hear cases appealed to it from lower state courts.
(b) The Supreme Court must hear every case appealed to it involving federal law.
(c) The Supreme Court may only hear cases involving the Constitution or laws passed by Congress.
(d) Congress may add or subtract to the types of cases listed in the Constitution that the Supreme Court may hear on appeal.

DEMONSTRATION

Dick sued Iris, claiming that he had an I.O.U. from her for $5,000; an I.O.U. that she had never paid. Iris said the I.O.U. was a forgery. The jury sided with Iris. Dick wants to appeal the case, contending that the jury made the wrong decision. Does he have grounds to appeal? What result?

PROBLEMS

1. What is the adversary system and what are its distinguishing characteristics?
2. Define the following terms: *jurisdiction, venue, discovery, complaint, answer, injunction, class action, directed verdict.*
3. What is a "burden of proof"? Name some different standards of proof and define them.
4. The Postal Service decides to issue a commemorative stamp honoring Elvis Presley. The Society for the Preservation of Virtue sues to enjoin it from doing so. What result? Why?
5. The Internal Revenue Service begins a tax audit of Acme Company's 1987 tax returns. In preparing the company's defense, Acme's lawyer talks to Jeremy, a vice president. Jeremy confesses to the lawyer that he has been padding his expense account. What obligations does the lawyer have to respect Jeremy's confidences and keep the information secret from the government? From the company? What difficulty might Jeremy have in relying on the company lawyer? What should Jeremy do under the circumstances?
6. Tom has a contract to buy all his scrap iron from Leslie. The contract says that the two parties must take any disputes arising out of the contract to arbitration. Leslie discovers that Tom has bought some scrap iron from someone else and threatens to take him to court. Must Tom go to court? Suppose that Leslie and Tom have their dispute arbitrated and Leslie is dissatisfied with the result. May she appeal to a court? Why or why not?
7. Frank and Joyce are neighbors. For several years, Frank's dog has been barking early in the morning, to Joyce's great annoyance. Several times she has called Frank to complain, but he has always slammed down the phone. Last week she called the police, and Frank retaliated by dumping his garbage over her fence. Joyce has now contacted a lawyer and wants to sue. The lawyer has suggested a mediator. How could the mediator help resolve this dispute? What kind of resolution would you suggest if you were the mediator?
8. For its new CAW (Computer Assisted Widget) Mobile, Ace Widgets has used Luster-Ware's new Widget-Chip, a microchip on which Luster holds a patent. Ace has paid no royalties, and Luster sues, asserting an infringement of its patent. Ace cites an agreement signed a year earlier, under which, according to Ace's interpretation, Ace could use the chip for "publicity purposes" without paying royalties. Describe the different ways Ace and Luster could resolve this dispute. What other facts might you need to know to determine which method would be most likely to succeed?
9. Alice sues her employer, Macho Products, charging the company with sex discrimination for promoting a less qualified employee—a man—to the position of sales manager. Macho's executive vice president, Sam, calls the law firm the company has used for the past fifty years. Van, the law firm's senior partner, tells Sam: "Leave it to me." Is this a good or bad idea? Why? If you think it's a bad idea, what should Sam do?

ANSWERS TO SELF-TEST QUESTIONS

1. (d)   2. (c)   3. (b)   4. (d)   5. (a)

SUGGESTED ANSWER TO DEMONSTRATION PROBLEM

A jury's finding of fact is not subject to appeal. For Dick to have grounds to appeal, he must assert that some legal mistake was made at trial. One type of legal mistake might be that one party or the other failed to meet a burden of proof. Ordinarily the plaintiff has the burden of proving the pertinent facts, but sometimes the burden will rest on a defendant. So if Dick has shown that he has a receipt from Iris and it appears to be signed by her, she will have the burden of demonstrating that her signature was forged. Therefore, Dick might be able to press an appeal by arguing that he had presented very strong evidence that she had signed the I.O.U. (for example, several witnesses might have testified that she signed it in their presence), while Iris might have presented very weak evidence of forgery (for example, suppose she merely took the stand and in a very low voice and while looking down at the floor denied she had signed it, without offering any other reason to doubt the witnesses). If the evidence was overwhelmingly on Dick's side, an appeals court might rule that Iris had failed to meet her burden of proving that the I.O.U. was forged.

CHAPTER 3

Criminal Law

THE NATURE OF CRIMINAL LAW

Criminal law is the most ancient branch of the law. The number of commentators who have attempted to define and explain it is legion, and the explanations themselves include some of the most subtle and metaphysical passages in the literature of the law. We need not be concerned with much of the criminal jurisprudence, however. Our purpose is to have a working knowledge of basic principles. We omit entirely discussion of many crimes that make up the traditional criminal law course—for example, kidnapping, rape, breach of peace—and ignore the many perplexities of criminal intent and responsibility. Similarly, though we consider certain of the constitutional rights accorded the accused, the student should note that the subject is vast and complex; space limitations alone prevent our considering more than its most basic aspects.

Criminal law is designed to deter socially harmful conduct. Crime has been defined simply as "any social harm defined and made punishable by law"

(Perkins, 1969, p. 9). "Harm to society" is a matter of definition and is not necessarily intrinsic to the act itself. For example, in a minor quarrel in the privacy of your college dormitory that results in a fistfight, the crimes of assault and battery have been committed, even though no one else knows about the fight and the people involved later make up. By contrast, when a major corporation publicly announces that it will not honor a contractual commitment, and many thousands of people must nervously contemplate whether their own contracts will be enforced, no crime has been committed. The effects on society may be much greater in the second example than in the first, but according to the law the former is the crime, not the latter.

Crimes are generally defined by statute. For constitutional reasons, courts are limited in their ability to create crimes as they have created the civil side of the common law: it would violate due process to prosecute someone for conduct that is not clearly spelled out beforehand as criminal. Of course, most people do not read statutes, and it is a commonplace that "ignorance is no excuse." Nevertheless, the legislature must set out the nature of the conduct it wishes to outlaw before the government may punish a person for breaking the law.

The statutes themselves must be clear. The courts have overturned many legislative criminal enactments because they have been vague. For example, vagrancy was long held to be a crime, but recently many courts have overturned vagrancy and "suspicious person" statutes on the grounds that they are too vague for people to know what it is they are being asked to refrain from doing.

However, not every constitutional statute defining a crime is necessarily clear the way a lay person would define clarity, and an understanding of common law and its history remains critical. Many statutes use terminology developed by the common-law courts. For example, a California statute defines murder as "the unlawful killing of a human being, with malice aforethought." If no history backed up these words, they would be unconstitutionally vague. But there is a rich history, sufficient to provide a meaning for much of the arcane language strewn about in the statute books.

Because a crime is an act that the legislature has defined as socially harmful, the parties involved cannot agree among themselves to forget a particular incident, such as a barroom brawl, if the authorities decide to prosecute. This is one of the critical distinctions between criminal and civil law. An assault is both a crime and a tort. The person who was assaulted may choose to forgive his assailant and not to sue him for damages. But he cannot force the prosecutor to refrain from prosecuting the assailant for the crime of assault. It frequently happens, though, that because of the fearfully crowded criminal court dockets that cause interminable delays, the victim may decline to "press charges" (make an official complaint). In the absence of a victim who willingly will testify, busy prosecutors usually will refrain from filing charges on their own.

Beyond the state's involvement, there are other important distinctions between crimes and torts. Crimes usually carry more severe sanctions because the law generally *punishes* the criminal defendant, whereas it generally requires the tort defendant to *remedy* his wrongdoing: a criminal defendant can go to jail; a tort defendant usually must pay a sum of money. Constitutional protections, such as the privilege against self-incrimination apply in criminal cases but not in tort cases. Finally, the government frequently prosecutes cases in which no actual physical harm has resulted (for example, assault with intent to kill when the shot entirely missed the intended target), whereas in almost all tort cases, the plaintiff must show some sort of actual injury to win a judgment.

A crime consists of an **act** and an **intent.** A person who has a burning desire to kill, but who does not act on his desire, is guilty of no crime. A person who is forced to pull a trigger against his will is not guilty of the resulting death. In recent years, legislatures have enacted criminal laws, especially those involving contaminated foods and drugs and harm to the environment, that are based on the notion of **strict liability**—a person can be found guilty of violating these laws even though no "guilty mind" has been shown (for example, see p. 103).

METHODS OF CLASSIFYING

Most classifications of crime turn on the seriousness of the act. In general, seriousness is defined by the nature or duration of the punishment set out in the statute. **Felonies** are crimes punishable (usually) by imprisonment of more than one year or by death. Crimes punishable by death are sometimes known as capital crimes; they are increasingly rare in the United States. The major felonies include murder, rape, kidnapping, armed robbery, embezzlement, and the like. All other crimes are usually known as **misdemeanors** or petty offenses. Under federal law, a petty offense is one punishable by six months' imprisonment or less or by a fine of $500 or less.

Another way of viewing crimes is by the type of social harm the statute is intended to prevent or deter. This is the classification we will employ in the following discussion (see Figure 3-1).

TYPES OF CRIMES

Offenses Against the Person

Homicide   **Homicide** is the killing of one person by another. Not every killing is criminal. When the law permits one to kill another—for example, a soldier

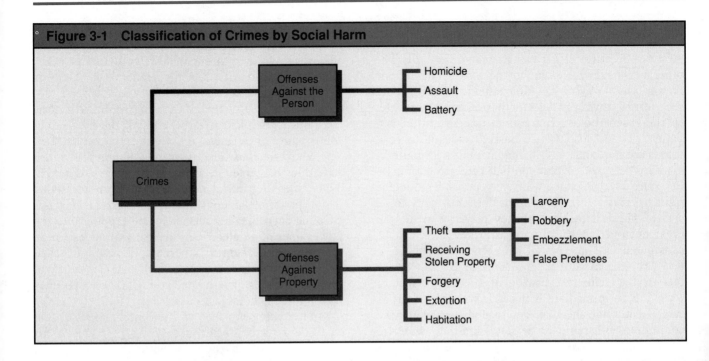

Figure 3-1   Classification of Crimes by Social Harm

killing an enemy on the battlefield during war, or a killing in self-defense—the death is said to be a **justifiable homicide.** An **excusable homicide** is one in which death results from an accident in which the killer is not at fault.

All other homicides are crimes. The most severely punished form is **murder,** defined in many states as homicide committed with **malice aforethought.** This is a term with an ancient lineage that means, in essence, an intent to kill. State statutes that use the term usually mean what is often called "second-degree" murder to distinguish it on the one hand from "first-degree" murder, in which the killing is deliberate, premeditated, and planned out in advance, and on the other hand from lesser forms of homicide such as **manslaughter** (see below). In states that have adopted the Model Penal Code, murder is defined as "killing done recklessly under circumstances manifesting extreme indifference to the value of human life." [MPC § 210.2(1)(b)] A killing need not be planned out long before the event to constitute murder; a killing is murder if it is committed an instant after the intention to do so occurs. A homicide sometimes can be murder even if the killer had no intent to kill; an intent to inflict great bodily harm or a dangerous action undertaken with wanton disregard for human life can be murder if someone dies as a result.

A killing that takes place while a felony such as armed robbery is being committed is also murder, whether or not the killer intended any harm. This is the so-called **felony murder rule.** Examples are the accidental discharge of a gun that kills an innocent bystander or the asphyxiation death of a firefighter from smoke resulting from a fire set by an arsonist. The felony murder rule is more significant than it sounds, because it also applies to the accomplices of one who does the killing. Thus, the driver of a getaway car stationed a block away from the scene of the robbery can be convicted of murder if a gun accidentally fires during the robbery and someone is killed.

Manslaughter is an act of killing that does not amount to murder. **Voluntary manslaughter** is an intentional killing but one carried out in the "sudden heat of passion" as the result of some provocation. An example is a fight that gets out of hand. **Involuntary manslaughter** entails a lesser degree of willfulness; it usually occurs when someone has taken a reckless action that results in death—for example, a death resulting from a traffic accident in which one driver wantonly runs a red light.

Assault and Battery   In common parlance, we say that a person who has struck another has assaulted him. Technically, that is a **battery**—the unlawful application of force to another person. The force need not be violent. Indeed, a man who kisses a woman is guilty of a battery if he does it against her will. The other person may consent to the force. That is one reason why surgeons require patients to sign "consent forms" giving the doctor permission to operate. In the absence of such a consent, an operation is a battery. That is also why defensive tackles in football games are not constantly being charged with battery. Those who agree to play football agree to submit to the rules of the game, which of course include the right to tackle. But the consent does not apply to all acts of physical force: a hockey player who hits an opponent over the head with a hockey stick can be prosecuted for the crime of battery.

Criminal **assault** is an *attempt* to commit a battery or the deliberate placing of another in fear of receiving an immediate battery. If you throw a rock at a friend, but she manages to dodge it, you have committed an assault. Some states limit an assault to an attempt to commit a battery by one who has a "present ability" to do so. Pointing an unloaded gun and threatening to shoot would not be an assault—nor, of course, could it be a battery. The modern tendency, however, is to define an assault as an attempt to commit a battery by one with an *apparent* ability to do so.

Assault and battery may be excused. One form of excuse is consent by the victim. Excuse may also be provided by law; for example, a bar owner may use reasonable force to remove an unruly patron.

Offenses against Property

Theft: Larceny, Robbery, Embezzlement, False Pretenses   The concept of theft is familiar enough. Less familiar is the way the law has treated various aspects of the act of stealing. Criminal law distinguishes among many different crimes that are popularly known as theft. Many technical words have entered the language—burglary, larceny, robbery—but are used loosely and often inaccurately. What follows is a brief definition of the more common terms.

The basic crime of stealing personal property is **larceny**. By its technical definition, larceny is the wrongful "taking and carrying away of the personal property of another with intent to steal the same." Its

various components gave no end of trouble under the common law. A common example is the theft of fruit. If someone walking through an orchard plucks a peach from a tree and eats it, she is not guilty of larceny because she has not taken away *personal* property—the peach is part of the land, being connected to the tree. But if she picks up a peach lying on the ground, she is guilty of larceny.

The crime of larceny is not committed unless something capable of being carried away is taken. Thus, sneaking into a movie theater without paying is not an act of larceny (though in most states it is a criminal act). Stealing electricity by tapping into the power lines of an electric utility baffled judges late in the nineteenth century, because it was not clear whether electricity is a "something" that can be taken. Modern statutes have tended to make clear that electricity can be the object of larceny.

The taking must be with an intent to steal, that is, to deprive the owner of property permanently. If you borrow your friend's car without his permission in order to go to the grocery store, intending to return it within a few minutes, and do return it, you have not committed larceny.

A particular form of larceny is **robbery**, which is defined as larceny from a person by means of violence or intimidation.

Larceny involves the taking of property from the possession of another. Suppose that a person legitimately comes to possess the property of another and wrongfully appropriates it—for example, an automobile mechanic entrusted with your car refuses to return it, or a bank teller who is entitled to temporary possession of cash in his drawer takes it home with him. The common law had trouble with such cases because the thief in these cases already had possession; his crime was in assuming ownership. Today, such wrongful conversion, known as **embezzlement**, has been made a statutory offense in all states.

Statutes against larceny and embezzlement did not cover all the gaps in the law. A conceptual problem arises in the case of one who is tricked into giving up title to property. In larceny and embezzlement, the thief gains possession or ownership without any consent of the owner or custodian of the property. Suppose, however, that an automobile dealer agrees to take his customer's present car as a trade-in. The customer says that she has full title to the car. In fact, the customer is still paying off an installment loan and the finance company has an interest in the old car. If the finance company repossesses the car, the customer—who got a new car at a discount because of her false representation—cannot be said to have taken the new car by larceny or embezzlement. Nevertheless, she tricked the dealer into selling, and the dealer will have lost the value of the repossessed car. Obviously, the customer is guilty of a criminal act; the statutes outlawing it refer to this trickery as the crime of **false pretenses**—defined as obtaining ownership of the property of another by making untrue representations of fact with intent to defraud.

A number of problems have arisen in the judicial interpretation of false pretense statutes. One concerns whether the taking is permanent or only temporary. The following case shows the subtle questions that can be presented and the dangers inherent in committing "a little fraud."

STATE v. MILLS
96 Ariz. 377, 396 P.2d 5 (1964)

LOCKWOOD, VICE CHIEF JUSTICE:

Defendants appeal from a conviction on two counts of obtaining money by false pretenses in violation of A.R.S. §§ 13-661.A.3. and 13-663.A.1.

The material facts, viewed ". . . in the light most favorable to sustaining the conviction," State v. Evans, 356 P.2d 1106, 1107 (1960) are as follows: Defendant William Mills was a builder and owned approximately 150 homes in Tucson in December, 1960. Mills conducted his business in his home. In 1960 defendant Winifred Mills, his wife, participated in the business generally by answering the telephone, typing, and receiving clients who came to the office.

In December 1960, Mills showed the complainant, Nathan Pivowar, a house at 1155 Knox Drive and another at 1210 Easy Street, and asked Pivowar if he would loan money on the Knox Drive house. Pivowar did not indicate at that time whether he would agree to such a transaction. Later in the same month Nathan Pivowar told the defendants that he and his brother, Joe Pivowar, would loan $5,000 and $4,000 on the two houses. Three or four days later Mrs. Mills, at Pivowar's request, showed him these homes again.

Mills had prepared two typed mortgages for Pivowar. Pivowar objected to the wording, so in Mills' office Mrs. Mills retyped the mortgages under Pivowar's dictation. After the mortgages had been recorded on December 31, 1960, Pivowar gave Mills a bank check for $5,791.87, some cash, and a second mortgage formerly obtained from Mills in the approximate sum of $3,000. In exchange Mills gave Pivowar two personal notes in the sums of $5,250.00 and $4,200.00 and the two mortgages as security for the loan.

Although the due date for Mills' personal notes passed without payment being made, the complainant did not present the notes for payment, did not demand that they be paid, and did not sue upon them. In 1962 the complainant learned that the mortgages which he had taken as security in the transaction were not first mortgages on the Knox Drive and Easy Street properties. These mortgages actually covered two vacant lots on which there were outstanding senior mortgages. On learning this, Pivowar signed a complaint charging the defendants with the crime of theft by false pretenses.

On appeal defendants contend that the trial court erred in denying their motion to dismiss the information. They urge that a permanent taking of

(continued on next page)

(continued)

STATE v. MILLS
96 Ariz. 377, 396 P.2d 5
(1964)

property must be proved in order to establish the crime of theft by false pretenses. Since the complainant had the right to sue on the defendants' notes, the defendants assert that complainant cannot be said to have been deprived of his property permanently.

Defendants misconceive the elements of the crime of theft by false pretenses. Stated in a different form, their argument is that although the complainant has parted with his cash, a bank check, and a second mortgage, the defendants intend to repay the loan.

Defendants admit that the proposition of law which they assert is a novel one in this jurisdiction. Respectable authority in other states persuades us that their contention is without merit. A creditor has a right to determine for himself whether he wishes to be a secured or an unsecured creditor. In the former case, he has a right to know about the security. If he extends credit in reliance upon security which is falsely represented to be adequate, he has been defrauded even if the debtor intends to repay the debt. His position is now that of an unsecured creditor; at the very least, an unreasonable risk of loss has been forced upon him by reason of the deceit. This risk which he did not intend to assume has been imposed upon him by the intentional act of the debtor, and such action constitutes an intent to defraud.

*   *   *

The cases cited by defendants in support of their contention are distinguishable from the instant case in that they involved theft by larceny. Since the crime of larceny is designed to protect a person's possessory interest in property whereas the crime of false pretenses protects one's title interest, the requirement of a permanent deprivation is appropriate to the former. Accordingly, we hold that an intent to repay a loan obtained on the basis of a false representation of the security for the loan is no defense.

*   *   *

Affirmed in part, reversed in part, and remanded for resentencing.

In the *Mills* case, the claim was that a mortgage instrument dealing with one parcel of land was used instead for another. This is a false representation of fact. Suppose, by contrast, that a person misrepresents his state of mind: "I will pay you back tomorrow," he says, knowing full well that he does not intend to. Can such a misrepresentation amount to false pretenses punishable as a criminal offense? In most jurisdictions it cannot. A false pretense violation relates to a past event or existing fact, not to a statement of intention. If it were otherwise, a person who failed to pay a debt might find himself facing criminal prosecution, and business would be less prone to take risks.

The problem of proving intent is especially difficult when a person has availed himself of the services of another without paying. A common example is absconding from a hotel or restaurant without paying for the room or meal. In most states, this is specifically defined in the statutes as **theft of services**.

Receiving Stolen Property   One who receives stolen property with knowledge that it is stolen is guilty of a felony or misdemeanor, depending on the value of the property. The receipt need not be personal; if the property is delivered to a place under the control of the receiver, then he is deemed to have received it.

"Knowledge" is construed broadly: not merely actual knowledge, but (correct) belief and suspicion (strong enough not to investigate for fear that the property will turn out to have been stolen) are sufficient for conviction.

Forgery   **Forgery** is false writing of a document with legal significance (or apparent legal significance) with intent to defraud. It includes the making up of a false document or the alteration of an existing one. The writing need not be done by hand but can be by any means—typing, printing, and so forth. Documents commonly the subject of forgery are negotiable instruments (checks, money orders, and the like), deeds, receipts, contracts, and bills of lading. The forged instrument must itself be false, not merely contain a falsehood. If you fake your neighbor's signature on one of her checks made out to cash, you have committed forgery. But if you sign a check of your own that is made out to cash, knowing that there is no money in your checking account, the instrument is not forged, though the act may be criminal if done with the intent to defraud.

The mere making of a forged instrument is unlawful. So is the **uttering**—presentation—of such an instrument, whether or not the one uttering it actually forged it.

The usual example of a false signature is by no means the only way to commit forgery. If done with intent to defraud, the backdating of a document, the modification of a corporate name, or the filling in of lines left blank on a form can all constitute forgery.

Extortion   Under common law, **extortion** could only be committed by a government official, who corruptly collected an unlawful fee under color of office. A common example is a salaried building inspector who refuses to issue a permit unless the permittee pays him. Under modern statutes, the crime of extortion has been broadened to include the wrongful collection of money or something else of value by anyone by means of a threat (short of a threat of immediate physical violence, for such a threat would make the demand an act of robbery). This kind of extortion is usually called **blackmail**. The blackmail threat commonly is to expose some fact of the victim's private life or to make a false accusation about him.

Offenses against Habitation

Burglary   **Burglary** is not a crime against property. It is defined as "the breaking and entering of the dwelling of another in the nighttime with intent to commit a felony." The intent need not be to steal; a man who sneaks into a woman's home intent on raping her has committed a burglary, even if he does not carry out the act. The astute student will note that the definition provides plenty of room for argument. What is "breaking"? (The courts do not require actual destruction; the mere opening of a closed door, even if unlocked, is enough.) What is entry? When does night begin? What kind of intent? Whose dwelling? Can a landlord burglarize the dwelling of his tenant? Yes. Can a person burglarize her own home? No.

Arson   Under common law, **arson** was the malicious burning of the dwelling of another. Burning one's own house for purposes of collecting insurance was not an act of arson under common law. The statutes today make it a felony intentionally to set fire to any building, whether or not it is a dwelling and whether or not the purpose is to collect insurance.

Other Offenses

Bribery   **Bribery** is a corrupt payment (or receipt of such a payment) for official action. The payment can be in cash or in the form of any goods, intangibles, or services that the recipient would find valuable. Under common law, only a public official could be bribed. In most states, "public official" has been given an expansive meaning, so that one performing a public function, though not an employee of the government, may be capable of being bribed.

In many states, bribery is no longer limited to payments to public officials. Purchasing agents and other agents of private enterprise can also be bribed by sellers and others. The statutes have been broadened to encompass commissions, gifts, or gratuities or promises to pay them to agents and employees in order to influence any action related to the business of their principal or employer.

Perjury   **Perjury** is the crime of giving a false oath, either orally or in writing, in a judicial or other official proceeding. Lies made in proceedings other than courts are sometimes termed "false swearing." To be perjurious, the oath must have been made corruptly—that is, with knowledge that it was false or without sincere belief that it was true. An innocent mistake is not perjury. A statement, though true, is perjury if the maker of it believes it to be false. Statements such as "I don't remember" or "to the best of my knowledge" are not sufficient to protect a person who is lying from conviction for perjury. To support a charge of perjury, however, the false statement must be **material**—that is, related to the matter in controversy.

White-collar Crime

The term "white-collar crime," as distinguished from "street crime," refers generally to fraud-related acts carried out in a nonviolent way, usually connected with business. Armed robbery is not a white-collar crime; embezzlement by a teller from a bank is. Many white-collar crimes are included within the statutory definitions of embezzlement and false pretenses. Most are violations of state law. Depending on how they are carried out, many of these same crimes are violations also of federal law. Federal statutes outlaw mail, wire, and securities fraud, for instance. Any act of fraud in which the U.S. Postal System is used or which involves interstate telephone calls is a violation of federal law. Likewise, a host of acts concerned with buying and selling of securities can run afoul of federal securities laws and give rise to criminal liability. Other white-collar crimes include tax fraud, price-fixing, violations of food, drug, and environmental laws, corporate bribery of foreign companies, and—the newest form—computer fraud. Some of these are discussed below; others are covered in later chapters.

White-collar crime is not limited to occasional acts of errant bank tellers, nor are corporations always the victims of such crime. Sometimes they are the criminals. A *Fortune* magazine study (December 1, 1980, pp. 57ff.) of major federal cases against big corporations between 1970 and 1980 showed that of the 1,043 companies prosecuted (among them were 800 of the largest corporations in America), 117 were convicted of (or otherwise settled) criminal charges, including illegal political contributions, price-fixing, and tax evasion. Among the companies were some of the most

well-known industrial names in the country, including American Airlines, Bethlehem Steel, Boise Cascade, Carnation, E. I. duPont de Nemours & Co., Gulf Oil, Gulf & Western, Litton Industries, PepsiCo, R.J. Reynolds, Rockwell International, Singer, and United Brands.

Mail and Wire Fraud Federal law prohibits the use of the mails or any interstate electronic communications medium for the purpose of furthering a "scheme or artifice to defraud." In 1987, the Supreme Court ruled that the law protects intangible as well as tangible property. As a result, the law has become a major weapon in insider trading cases in which defendants are charged with taking confidential business information. [Carpenter v. United States, 484 U.S. 19 (1987)]

Violations of Antitrust Law In Chapters 46–48, we consider the fundamentals of antitrust law, which for the most part affects the business enterprise civilly. But violations of Section 1 of the Sherman Act, which condemns activities in "restraint of trade," including price-fixing, are also crimes. The maximum fine for individual violators is $350,000, the maximum prison term three years, and corporate defendants can be fined a maximum of $10 million.

Violations of the Food and Drug Act The federal Food, Drug and Cosmetic Act prohibits any person or corporation from sending into interstate commerce any adulterated or misbranded food, drug, cosmetics, or related device. Unlike in most criminal statutes, willfulness or deliberate misconduct is not an element of the Food and Drug Act. As the *Park* case (pp. 103–106) shows, an executive can be held criminally liable even though he had no personal knowledge of the violation.

Environmental Crimes Many federal environmental statutes (discussed in Chapter 32) have criminal provisions. These include the Federal Water Pollution Control Act (commonly called the Clean Water Act), the Rivers and Harbors Act of 1899 (the Refuse Act), the Clean Air Act, the Federal Insecticide, Fungicide and Rodenticide Act (FIFRA), the Toxic Substances Control Act (TSCA), and the Resource Conservation and Recovery Act (RCRA). Under the Clean Water Act, for example, wrongful discharge of

LAW AND LIFE

BOX 3-1

Environmental Crime Can Land Executives In Prison These Days

By David Stipp

*[Anyone caught violating an environmental crime will face strict penalties under the numerous acts that now protect water, land, and air. Responsible corporate executives, for example, are specifically named as defendants in criminal prosecutions under the Clean Water Act.—*AUTHORS' NOTE]

BURLINGTON, Mass.—John Borowski, owner of a small defense contractor here, never seemed to worry much about how to dispose of the toxic wastes his plant produced. He had developed a simple, cheap method.

Using buckets, his workers would scoop fuming nitric acid and nickel wastes out of vats and pour them down a sink. When workers questioned the practice, Mr. Borowski told them not to worry because it wouldn't hurt anyone, former employees say. He knew the dumping was illegal but considered it "like not counting tips for income tax," says Peter Kruczynski, a former manager at Mr. Borowski's Borjohn Optical Technology Inc.

The federal government saw it differently. In May, Mr. Borowski became the first person convicted on charges of knowing endangerment under the federal Clean Water Act. Scheduled for sentencing in October, he could be sent to prison for years.

GETTING TOUGH WITH CORPORATE EXECUTIVES

Rashes and Sickness

Thousands of gallons of wastes went down Mr. Borowski's sink over the past decade, from there finding their way into Boston Harbor. Some of the workers in his bucket brigade developed rashes and other ailments, but Mr. Borowski attributed the problems to drinking or laziness, former employees testified at his trial. "If I had to follow every rule on the books, I'd be out of business," one worker testified Mr. Borowski told him.

Mr. Borowski won't discuss the case, except to say that he was unfairly charged because of "a clique of people who really tried to do severe harm to me and to the company." He plans an appeal.

A decade ago, the government might well have treated the dumping like minor tax cheating, at most slapping Borjohn Optical with a fine. But Uncle Sam is no longer playing Mr. Nice Guy with environmental cheaters. "A person who mugs a city by polluting should receive at least as strong a punishment as the person who mugs an individual," declares James M. Strock, the Environmental Protection Agency's criminal enforcement chief.

Judges and juries are beginning to agree. In fiscal 1989, federal courts handed out prison terms totaling about 37 years and $11.1 million in fines for environmental crimes, compared with

less than two years of sentences and $198,000 in fines five years earlier, EPA figures show.

Prosecutors are aiming higher up the corporate ladder, too. In May, Paul Tudor Jones II, president of Tudor Investment Corp. and a prominent futures trader, pleaded guilty to criminally violating the Clean Water Act by filling in wetlands to build a corporate retreat. He agreed to pay $2 million in fines and restitution and drew 18 months' probation.

Greater enforcement efforts evidently are in store. Last month the Senate passed a bill that would more than triple the number of federal investigators going after polluters, to at least 200 by 1996. And Massachusetts has formed a 30-person Environmental Crimes Strike Force.

This push began in the early 1980s, about the time the evacuations of Love Canal in Niagara, N.Y., and of dioxin-laden Times Beach, Mo., brought home the dangers of toxic waste. "On the one hand, the EPA was friendly to business during the Reagan years," says Russell Mokhiber, editor of the Corporate Crime Reporter, a newsletter in Washington, D.C. "But along with Republicans' deregulation came a law-and-order philosophy; the Justice Department had some cops who were out there enforcing the law."

If convicted, environmental-crime defendants are more likely to draw prison time now because of felony clauses added in the '80s, and also because of federal sentencing guide-

(continued on next page)

---

pollutants into navigable waters carries a fine ranging from $2,500 to $25,000 per day and imprisonment for up to one year. "Responsible corporate officers" are specifically included as potential defendants in criminal prosecutions under the act (see **Box 3-1**).

Violations of the Foreign Corrupt Practices Act As a byproduct of Watergate, federal officials at the Securities and Exchange Commission and the Internal Revenue Service uncovered numerous instances of bribes paid by major corporations to officials of for-

BOX 3-1

Rashes and Sickness, *continued*

lines set in 1987. Before the guidelines, jail terms were rare, and typically totaled 60 to 90 days. Now, "an individual convicted of an environmental felony will likely have to serve approximately two years in prison," Kevin A. Gaynor, a Washington lawyer, recently wrote in the journal Environmental Forum.

Not surprisingly, that's causing heated debate. "Environmental criminal enforcement is on the verge of spinning out of control" because of "increasingly complex regulations" and arbitrary prosecutions, charges Mr. Gaynor, who defends companies and executives in such cases and represented Mr. Jones in the wetlands case. "Now virtually any environmental violation is potentially a criminal case."

The EPA's Mr. Strock sees it differently. "The clearest evidence we have that stronger enforcement is deterring crime is the increased anxiety expressed lately by the regulated community," he says.

★   ★   ★

The typical scenario for toxic turpitude is a cash-strapped firm deciding that plugging the flow of pollutants is just too expensive. Properly disposing of a single 55-gallon barrel of toxic waste now costs as much as $1,000. For small companies, such costs can quickly become a make-or-break expense when business is weak.

Some regulators fear an environmental crime wave will hit if the economy worsens. And the new polluters might be better at covering their tracks. "Midnight dumping is essentially a thing of the past," says Andrew Savitz, Massachusetts assistant secretary for environmental law enforcement. "Now we're dealing with technical

environmental crimes . . . committed behind closed doors."

Consider Wells Metal Finishing Inc., a now-defunct company in Lowell, Mass., near the Merrimack River, a waterway federal officials have targeted for cleanup. After municipal water officials warned owner and president John Wells about illegal discharges into the river, he installed some special plumbing. It shunted waste solutions laden with cyanide and zinc past his concern's water-treatment into the sewer, and eventually into the Merrimack—which is used for drinking-water downstream from the plant. That enabled his company to freely dispose of large amounts of toxic chemicals that otherwise would have overloaded his treatmemt system, potentially tipping off employees or regulators to illegal discharges.

'Gas Chamber'

But sensors outside the company's property showed its cyanide "was turning Lowell's sewer into a gas chamber," says Brendan O'Brien, an EPA investigator. Finally, a visiting city inspector noticed the illegal bypass. Mr. Wells denied the extra pipe's purpose and promptly ordered the inspector out of his building, according to U.S. attorneys. It was too late. Now he is serving a 15-month prison term.

To counter such tricks, government agencies have assembled teams of scientists, lawyers and detectives outfitted with gear ranging from electronic sniffers to "moon suits" for poking around in sewers, but environmental violators remain hard to catch and convict. In a case in Gloucester, Mass., officials discovered a polluter's practices only after the chemicals involved blew up in the sewer, sending manhole covers flying

and forcing a downtown evacuation. Most environmental crimes escape notice until someone, often a disgruntled employee, tips off investigators.

★   ★   ★

Acting on a tip, federal agents barged into Borjohn in 1988, seizing evidence that led to Mr. Borowski being indicted for knowing endangerment under the Clean Water Act. After a four-week trial, a federal jury convicted him of two knowing-endangerment counts, each of which carries a maximum 15-year prison term and $250,000 fine.

Awaiting sentencing, Mr. Borowski now runs his company under close EPA scrutiny. His lawyer, William Codinha, argues that the government improperly prosecuted the case under environmental law, which traditionally applies to "what happens under the street or in the sewer and not in the sink." Prosecutors offered only circumstantial evidence that Borjohn's sewer discharges contained illegally high concentrations of toxic chemicals, he maintains.

Furthermore, says the lawyer, before 1987 it was only a misdemeanor to break the federal law under which Mr. Borowski was convicted. Now it's a felony. He adds that the confusion due to this "midstream" change has been compounded lately by prosecutors' crackdown on environmental crime.

"We're really dealing with a changing, fluid system here," he says.

Source: *Wall Street Journal*, September 16, 1990, p. A1

eign governments to secure contracts to do business with their countries. Congress responded in 1977 with the Foreign Corrupt Practices Act, which imposed a stringent requirement that the disposition of assets be accurately and fairly accounted for in a company's books and records. The act also made illegal the payment of bribes to foreign officials or to anyone who will transmit the money to a foreign official to assist the payor in getting business. The act is discussed in greater detail on p. 976.

Violations of the Racketeer Influenced and Corrupt Organizations Act In 1970 Congress enacted the Racketeer Influenced and Corrupt Organizations Act (RICO), aimed at ending organized crime's infiltration into legitimate business. The act tells courts to construe its language broadly "to effectuate its remedial purpose," and many who do not fall into the organized crime classification have been successfully prosecuted under the act.

RICO bans from interstate commerce anyone engaged in a "pattern of racketeering." A pattern of racketeering is broadly defined as the commission of at least two acts within ten years of any of a variety of already-existing crimes, including mail, wire, and securities fraud. Businesses that have committed (and not necessarily been convicted of) such crimes violate RICO if any proceeds from the crimes are used to enable the company to participate in interstate commerce or to acquire an interest in an enterprise engaged in interstate commerce. The act thus makes many types of fraud subject to more severe penalties than provided for by state law. In addition to imposing fines and jail sentences, the courts may order violators to forfeit any assets acquired through a violation of the act.

Criminal penalties do not exhaust RICO's potency. Congress built in a consequence more far reaching than criminal prosecution: under RICO, anyone "injured in his business or property by reason of" a pattern of racketeering may file a civil suit. A successful plaintiff can collect triple damages and recover attorney fees. During the 1980s, these provisions provided strong incentive to add RICO complaints in many commercial lawsuits, including disputes over breach of contract, wrongful discharge, lease violations, and product liability. A Justice Department survey in 1985 found that companies had filed more than 500 civil RICO suits; most were based on claims that the defendants had engaged in securities or mail fraud. Many civil RICO suits have been extremely imaginative: the state of Illinois, for example, prevailed in one such case against a company that failed to hand over sales taxes; the state's theory was that by neglecting to pay the taxes, the company had engaged in fraud, entitling it to collect triple the tax that was owed. RICO counts were also important parts of indictments against many of the well known investors and others convicted of insider-trading violations in the late 1980s and early 1990s. Because the potential liability is so large, many companies have been lobbying for changes to RICO, but so far Congress has been unwilling to budge. Moreover, many states have begun to enact similar "Little RICO" statutes.

Computer Crime No specific provision of federal law deals explicitly with computer crime, but some forty different statutes may be brought into play when computer crime has been committed. "Computer crime generally falls into four categories: (1) theft of money, financial instruments, or property; (2) misappropriation of computer time; (3) theft of programs; and (4) illegal acquisition of information. The possibilities appear to be limited only by the bounds of the perpetrator's imagination" (*Amer. Crim. L. Rev.*, 1980, p. 371). The National Center for Computer Crime has estimated that computer fraud cost the nation $555 million in 1988.

By the mid-1980s, a fifth category had appeared: interference with or destruction of computer programs and systems, usually by introducing computer "viruses" onto the user's disks. Despite the enactment of the Federal Computer Fraud and Abuse Act of 1986, and the more than 250,000 virus attacks identified through 1989, the first jury conviction came only in 1990, stemming from an incident in late 1988 when a Cornell University graduate student infected a nationwide computerized mail network that immobilized 6,000 computers for periods ranging from several hours to several days. He was sentenced to three years' probation, a $10,000 fine, and 400 hours of community service. Several bills have been introduced in Congress to make it easier to define and catch this kind of computer "terrorism."

THE NATURE OF A CRIMINAL ACT

To be guilty of a crime, you must have acted. Mental desire or intent to do so is insufficient. But what constitutes an act? This question becomes important when someone begins to commit a crime, or does so in association with others, or intends to do one thing but winds up doing something else.

Attempt

It is not necessary to commit the intended crime to be found guilty of a criminal offense. An *attempt* to commit the crime is punishable as well, though usually not as severely. For example, Bluebeard points a gun at Agatha, intending to shoot her dead. He pulls the trigger but his aim is off, and he misses her heart by four feet. He is guilty of an attempt to murder. Suppose, however, that earlier in the day, when he was preparing to shoot Agatha, Bluebeard had been overheard in his apartment muttering to himself of his intention, and that a neighbor called the police. When they arrived, he was just snapping his gun into his shoulder holster. At that point, courts in most states would not consider him guilty of an attempt because he had not passed beyond the stage of *preparation*. After having buttoned his jacket he might have reconsidered and put the gun away. Determining when the accused has passed beyond mere preparation and

taken an actual step toward *perpetrating* the crime is often difficult and is usually for the jury to decide.

Impossibility

If the defendant intends to do something that was not criminal, no act in furtherance of his intention can be an attempt. Suppose Bluebeard purchases a television set from a man on a street corner late one evening, believing the television to be stolen. In fact it was not stolen. Bluebeard cannot be convicted of an attempt to receive stolen property. Thus the following rule: "An accused cannot be convicted of an attempt to commit a crime unless he could have been convicted of the crime itself if his attempt had been successful. Where the act, if accomplished, would not constitute the crime intended, there is no indictable attempt." [Nemecek v. State, 114 P.2d 492 (Okla. 1941)]

Whether an accomplished act will result in a crime depends on the circumstances. In the following case, Hall stole electrical wire from a factory and was arrested while in possession of the wire. The police interrogated him and discovered he was intending to sell it to others. He agreed to cooperate with the police and called his prospective customers, saying he had stolen the wire and would leave the truck for them as arranged. Following their arrest for receiving stolen property, they argued that since the property was no longer stolen (because it had been recovered by the police), they could not be convicted of receiving it.

PEOPLE v. ROJAS
55 Cal.2d 252, 358 P.2d
921 (1961)

SCHAUER, JUSTICE.

In a trial by the court, after proper waiver of jury, defendants Rojas and Hidalgo were found guilty of a charge of receiving stolen property. Defendants' motions for new trial were denied. Rojas was granted probation without imposition of sentence and Hidalgo was sentenced to state prison. They appeal, respectively, from the order granting probation, the judgment, and the orders denying the motions for new trial.

Defendants urge that they were guilty of no crime (or, at most, of an attempt to receive stolen property) because when they received the property it had been recovered by the police and was no longer in a stolen condition. The attorney general argues that because the thief stole the property pursuant to prearrangement with defendants he took it as their agent, and the crime of receiving stolen property was complete when the thief began its asportation toward defendants and before the police intercepted him and recovered the property. We have concluded that defendants are guilty of attempting to receive stolen goods.

★   ★   ★

The offense with which defendants were charged and of which they were convicted was receiving "property which has been *stolen . . . , knowing the same to be so stolen.*" Pen. Code, §496, subd. 1; italics added. Defendants urge that they neither received stolen goods nor criminally attempted to do so because the conduit, when defendants received it, was not in a stolen condition but had been recovered by the police. In the Jaffe case the stolen property was recovered by the owner while it was en route to the would-be receiver and, by arrangement with the police, was delivered to such receiver as a decoy, not as property in a stolen condition. The New York Court of Appeals held that there was no attempt to receive stolen goods "because neither [defendant] nor anyone else in the world could know that the property was stolen property inasmuch as it was not in fact stolen property. . . . If all which an accused person intends to do would if done constitute no crime it cannot be a crime to attempt to do with the same purpose a part of the thing intended."

★   ★   ★

In the case at bench the criminality of the attempt is not destroyed by the fact that the goods, having been recovered by the commendably alert and efficient action of the Los Angeles police, had, unknown to defendants, lost their "stolen" status, any more than the criminality of the attempt in the case of In re Magidson (1917), 32 Cal.App. 566, 568, 163 P. 689, was destroyed by impossibility caused by the fact that the police had recovered the goods and taken them from the place where the would-be receiver went to get them. In our opinion the consequences of intent and acts such as those of defendants here should be more serious than pleased amazement that because of the timeliness of the police the projected criminality was not merely detected but also wiped out.

★   ★   ★

The orders denying defendants' motions for new trial are affirmed. The trial court's finding that defendants are guilty as charged is modified to find them guilty of the offense of attempting to receive stolen property.

Conspiracy

Under both federal and state laws, it is a separate offense to work with others toward the commission of a crime. When two or more people combine to carry out an unlawful purpose, they are engaged in a **conspiracy.** The law of conspiracy is quite broad, especially when it is used by prosecutors of white-collar crimes. Many people can be swept up in the net of conspiracy, because it is unnecessary to show that the actions they took were sufficient to constitute either the crime or an attempt. Under the usual rule, an agreement and a single overt act are sufficient to constitute the offense. Thus, if three people agree to rob a bank, and one of them goes to a store to purchase a gun to be used in the holdup, the three can be convicted of conspiracy to commit robbery. Even the purchase of an automobile to be used as the getaway car could support such a conviction. Moreover, the act of any one of the conspirators is imputed to the other members of the conspiracy. It does not matter, for instance, that only one of the bank robbers fired the gun that killed a guard. All can be convicted of murder. That is so even if one of the conspirators was stationed as a lookout several blocks away and even if he specifically told the others that his agreement to cooperate would end "just as soon as there is shooting."

Nevertheless, as the next case shows, there are limits to the connection between individuals for purposes of assessing criminal liability.

UNITED STATES v. FALCONE
109 F.2d 579 (2d Cir. 1940)

L. Hand, Circuit Judge.

These appeals are from convictions for a conspiracy to operate illicit stills.

* * *

The case against Joseph Falcone was that during the year 1937 he sold sugar to a number of grocers in Utica, who in turn sold to the distillers. He was a jobber in Utica, and bought his supply from a New York firm of sugar brokers; between March first and September 14, 1937, he bought 8,600 bags of sugar of 100 pounds each, which he disposed of to three customers: Frank Bonomo & Company, Pauline Aiello, and Alberico and Funicello, all wholesale grocers in Utica. Some of the bags in which this sugar was delivered were later found at the stills, when these were raided by the officials; and Falcone was seen on one occasion assisting in delivering the sugar at Bonomo's warehouse, when a truckload arrived. His business in sugar was far greater while the stills were active than either before they were set up, or after they were seized, and we shall assume that the evidence was enough to charge him with notice that his customers were supplying the distillers.

* * *

In the light of all this, it is apparent that the first question is whether the seller of goods, in themselves innocent, becomes a conspirator with—or, what is in substance the same thing, an abettor of—the buyer because he knows that the buyer means to use the goods to commit a crime. That came up a number of times in circuit courts of appeal while the Eighteenth Amendment was in force, and the answer was not entirely uniform.

* * *

. . . We are ourselves committed to the view of the Fifth Circuit. United States v. Peoni, 2 Cir., 100 F.2d 401. In that case we tried to trace down the doctrine as to abetting and conspiracy, as it exists in our criminal law, and concluded that the seller's knowledge was not alone enough. Civilly, a man's liability extends to any injuries which he should have apprehended to be likely to follow from his acts. If they do, he must excuse his conduct by showing that the interest which he was promoting outweighed the dangers which its protection imposed upon others; but in civil cases there has been a loss, and the only question is whether the law shall transfer it from the sufferer to another. There are indeed instances of criminal liability of the same kind, where the law imposes punishment merely because the accused did not forbear to do that from which the wrong was likely to follow; but in prosecutions for conspiracy or abetting, his attitude towards the forbidden undertaking must be more positive. It is not enough that he does not forego a normally lawful activity, of the fruits of which he knows that others will make an unlawful use; he must in some sense promote their venture himself, make it his own, have a stake in its outcome. The distinction is especially important today when so many prosecutors seek to sweep within the dragnet of conspiracy all those who have been associated in any degree whatever with the main offenders. That there are opportunities of great oppression in such a doctrine is very plain, and it is only by circumscribing the scope of such all comprehensive indictments that they can be avoided. We may agree that morally the defendants at bar should have refused to sell to illicit distillers; but, both morally and legally, to do so was toto coelo different from joining with them in running the stills.

For these reasons the prosecution did not make out a case against either of the Falcones, Alberico, or John Nole; and this is especially true of Salvatore Falcone. As to Nicholas Nole the question is closer, for when he began to do business as the "Acme Yeast Company," he hid behind the name of a cousin, whom he caused to swear falsely that the affiant was to do the business. Yet it seems to us that this was as likely to have come from a belief that it was a crime to sell the yeast and the cans to distillers as from being in fact any further involved in their business. It showed a desire to escape detection, and that was evidence of a consciousness of guilt, but the consciousness may have as well arisen from a mistake of law as from a purpose to do what the law in fact forbade. We think therefore that even as to him no case was made out.

*   *   *

[Convictions reversed.]

Agency and Corporations

A person can be guilty of a crime if he acts through another. As we have just noted, the usual reason for imputing the guilt of the actor to another is that both were engaged in a conspiracy. But imputation of guilt is not limited to a conspiracy. The agent may be innocent even though he participates. A corporate officer directs a junior employee to take a certain bag and deliver it to the officer's home. The employee reasonably believes that the officer is entitled to the bag. Unbeknownst to the employee, the bag contains money that belongs to the company, and the officer wishes to keep it. This is not a conspiracy. The employee is not guilty of larceny, the officer is—the agent's act is imputed to him (see **Box 3-2**).

Ordinarily, the imputation of crime does not work in reverse. Since intent is a necessary component of crime, an agent's intent cannot be imputed to his principal if the principal did not share the intent. The company president tells her sales manager: "Go make sure our biggest customer renews his contract for next year"—by which she meant, "Don't ignore our biggest customer." Standing before the customer's purchasing agent, the sales manager threatens to tell the purchasing agent's boss that the purchasing agent has

LAW AND LIFE

Whose Fault In Scandals?

By Andrew Pollack

[The guilt of individual employees may be imputed to the corporation. How accountable a senior manager should be for unethical conduct of a subordinate is debatable. However, managers who "look the other way" when subordinates engage in criminal activity may find themselves liable for the wrongdoing.—AUTHORS' NOTE]

In a number of recent cases involving questionable corporate practices, chief executives have chosen not to abide by Harry S. Truman's credo. The buck stopped with someone lower down.

News Analysis

The indictment last week of Eastern Airlines and nine managers for routinely ignoring maintenance and then falsifying records is not the only recent case raising the issue of how much senior management, and the top executive in particular, should be held accountable for the wrongful actions of subordinates.

On Thursday, the General Electric Company agreed to pay a $16.1 million fine to settle charges that it had overcharged the Defense Department. The Northrop Corporation paid a $17 million fine after pleading guilty in February to charges of faking tests on weapons. The Nynex Corporation admitted earlier this month that 12 purchasing managers had attended lewd parties each year with suppliers, creating the appearance of a conflict of interest.

Then cases like the Exxon Valdez oil spill have arisen. And, in the political arena there was the Iran-contra

WHERE DOES THE BUCK STOP?

affair, where questions were raised about President Ronald Reagan's role in a scheme to funnel revenues from arms sales to rebels in Nicaragua.

In such cases, is the chief executive responsible—and should that person pay a higher price? In the past, it has generally not been expected. When Robert Fomon, the former head of the E. F. Hutton Group, was asked several years ago about whether he should take some responsibility for an illegal check overdrafting scheme, he replied, "No chief executive can be held accountable for any single thing that happens in a corporation."

But some experts on ethical issues, as well as some corporate officers, say upper management must accept more responsibility. Even if those managers do not know explicitly about the actions of subordinates, they say, executives might be culpable if they have created a climate in which wrongdoing is condoned or encouraged.

"Senior management should be held accountable for unethical actions if they have put severe pressure on their employees and have not emphasized that these goals should not be achieved by cutting ethical corners," said Kirk O. Hanson, a professor at the Stanford Business School and president of the Business Enterprise Trust, a nonprofit institute at Stanford that examines issues of business ethics.

He and other experts say the pressures on companies today to improve performance pose a special risk of unethical behavior. In discussing the issue, they did not refer to Eastern, G.E. or any specific case.

Rules of Law and Evidence

Establishing criminal liability in such cases is a matter of law and evidence. Generally, a manager has to know of wrongdoing or to be willfully blind to it to be held criminally liable for the actions of a subordinate.

But beyond questions of criminal liability are the more fuzzy ethical questions. Should a good executive be expected to know what is happening in his or her organization? If the executive does not know, why not? And even if executives did not know, should they take responsibility because it happened on their watch?

"I think top corporate officers have serious moral responsibility," said Michael Josephson, the president of the Joseph and Edna Josephson Institute for the Advancement of Ethics in Los Angeles. "I think they are not stepping up to it. I think the culture is 'shift blame, take credit.' "

Different in Japan

But that is not the case in Japan, where chief executives resign after problems, even if they did not know about them. The chairman and the chief executive of the Toshiba Corporation both stepped down in 1987 for "having troubled society" after a unit was found to have illegally sold technology to the Soviet Union.

When a Japan Air Lines Boeing 747 jet crashed in 1985, killing more than 500 people, the airline's president, Yasumoto Takagi, retired after traveling across the country to express his apologies to the families of the victims. No one expected T. A. Wilson, the chief executive of the Boeing Company at the time, to resign.

Some executives in the United States have fallen on their swords.

Last year, an American Express

(continued on next page)

BOX 3-2

Different in Japan, *continued*

Company executive vice president, Harry L. Freeman, resigned to accept responsibility for a campaign by the company to discredit a business competitor, Edmund J. Safra. "Mistakes were made on my watch," Mr. Freeman said.

In 1987, Dennis P. Long, the No. 2 executive at the Anheuser-Busch Companies, quit as three subordinates were being investigated for accepting improper payments. He became a consultant to the company.

Indeed, management experts say it is impractical to expect top managers to know everything that occurs inside their organizations. "In some cases, it's like trying to hold parents responsible for all the actions of their children," Mr. Josephson said.

That is especially true in today's fast-moving business climate, where the emphasis has been on decentralizing and giving subordinates more flexibility in making decisions. It is also true in the case where the ethical violation is for personal gain, and the employee takes all precautions to conceal the action from superiors.

But trickier questions arise in a case in which the action is apparently done to help the company, not the individual. This appears to be the situation in some of the military contracting cases or in situations in which pollutants are dumped illegally to save disposal costs.

Even here, some say, top managers cannot be expected to know everything. But some executives say management should create an environment in which subordinates can report unethical activities.

"I think that top management has the responsibility to create a climate where that kind of behavior never arises," said Richard M. Rosenberg, the chairman and chief executive of the BankAmerica Corporation. "That's maybe a naïve statement, but I really believe it."

In some instances, top officers put forth performance goals with the message: "I don't care how you do it; just do it." In others, the upper executives deliberately turn a blind eye to wrongdoing or implicitly agree to it, but remain shielded from blame.

"The whole framework of plausible deniability runs throughout organizations so that the chief executive is insulated," said Abraham Zaleznik, the Konosuke Matsushita Professor of Leadership emeritus at the Harvard Business School.

In a 1986 New York Times Poll, only 33 percent of the people questioned thought that big business did an excellent or pretty good job of seeing to it that executives behave legally and ethically. But the poll found that sentiments about chief executives' accountability varied with the situation.

Some Details of Eastern Case

All the details of the case at Eastern are not known. But the 60-count Federal indictment returned last week said mechanics at the struggling airline were under pressure from executives at Eastern's headquarters to keep the planes flying. The indictment said maintenance on airplanes was not performed when it should have been and records were falsified to cover this up.

A spokesman for Frank Lorenzo, the head of Continental Airlines Holdings Inc., as Eastern's parent company is now called, did not return telephone calls last Friday, although the carrier said earlier last week that it would never condone behavior that would endanger passenger safety.

In the General Electric case, for which two men were convicted of defrauding the Pentagon, the prosecutor said evidence arose that superiors of the two men "looked the other way while fraud was committed." General Electric, which was also convicted in the case, said it thought the men were not guilty.

In cases like those of Eastern, General Electric and Northrop, the company itself is indicted and fined and its business can be injured. Eastern Airlines might lose customers, and military contractors can be barred from further Pentagon work. To the extent that the chief executive is accountable for the performance of the company, he or she might therefore suffer indirectly from such problems.

Source: *The New York Times*, July 30, 1990, p. D1

been cheating on his expense account, unless he signs a new contract. The sales manager could be convicted of blackmail, but the company president could not.

Can a corporation be guilty of a crime? The law is clear that for many types of crimes, the guilt of individual employees may be imputed to the corporation. Thus, the antitrust statutes explicitly state that the corporation may be convicted and fined for violations by employees. That is true even though the shareholders are the ones who ultimately must pay the price—and who may have had nothing to do with the crime nor power to stop it. The law of corporate criminal responsibility has been changing in recent years. The tendency is to hold the corporation criminally liable if the criminal act, such as larceny or murder, has been directed by a responsible officer or group within the corporation (the president or board of directors). And, as Box 3-2 suggests, a growing national debate on liability for corporate wrongdoing might lead to convictions of bosses for activities of subordinates.

RESPONSIBILITY

In General

For an accused to be held responsible for a criminal act, he must have a "criminal intent," often referred to as *mens rea* (mains ree ah), Latin for "guilty mind." What the state of mind must be depends on the nature of the crime and all the circumstance surrounding the act. In general, though, the requirement means that the accused must in some way have intended the criminal consequences of his act. Suppose, for example, that Bluebeard gives Agatha a poison capsule to swallow. That is the act. If Agatha dies, is Bluebeard guilty of murder? The answer depends on what his state of mind was. Obviously, if he gave it to her intending to kill her, the act was murder. What if he gave it to her knowing that the capsule was poison but believing that it would only make her mildly ill? The act is still murder, because one is liable for the consequences of a willful act in which lurks danger to others. However, if Agatha had asked Bluebeard for aspirin, and he handed her two pills that he reasonably believed to be aspirin (they came from the aspirin bottle and looked like aspirin) but that turned out to be poison, the act would not be murder, because he had neither intent nor a state of knowledge from which intent could be inferred.

Not every criminal law requires criminal intent as an ingredient of the crime. Many regulatory codes dealing with the public health and safety impose strict requirements. Failure to adhere is a violation, whether or not the violator had *mens rea*. The next two cases, both decisions of the U.S. Supreme Court, show the different considerations involved.

**MORISSETTE v.
UNITED STATES
342 U.S. 246 (1952)**

MR. JUSTICE JACKSON delivered the opinion of the Court.

*   *   *

On a large tract of uninhabited and untilled land in a wooded and sparsely populated area of Michigan, the government established a practice bombing range over which the Air Force dropped simulated bombs at ground targets. These bombs consisted of a metal cylinder about forty inches long and eight inches across, filled with sand and enough black powder to cause a smoke puff by which the strike could be located. At various places about the range signs read "Danger—Keep Out—Bombing Range." Nevertheless, the range was known as good deer country and was extensively hunted.

Spent bomb casings were cleared from the targets and thrown into piles "so that they will be out of the way." They were not stacked or piled in any order but were dumped in heaps, some of which had been accumulating for four years or upwards, were exposed to the weather and rusting away.

Morissette, in December of 1948, went hunting in this area but did not get a deer. He thought to meet expenses of the trip by salvaging some of these casings. He loaded three tons of them on his truck and took them to a nearby farm, where they were flattened by driving a tractor over them. After expending this labor and trucking them to market in Flint, he realized $84.

*   *   *

The loading, crushing and transporting of these casings were all in broad daylight, in full view of passers-by, without the slightest effort at concealment. When an investigation was started, Morissette voluntarily, promptly and candidly told the whole story to the authorities, saying that he had no intention of stealing but thought the property was abandoned, unwanted and considered of no value to the Government. He was indicted, however, on the charge that he "did unlawfully, wilfully and knowingly steal and convert" property of the United States of the value of $84, in violation of 18 U.S.C. §641, which provides that "whoever embezzles, steals, purloins, or knowingly converts" government property is punishable by fine and imprisonment. Morissette was convicted and sentenced to imprisonment for two months or to pay a fine of $200. The Court of Appeals affirmed, one judge dissenting.

On his trial, Morissette, as he had at all times told investigating officers, testified that from appearance he believed the casings were cast-off and abandoned, that he did not intend to steal the property, and took it with no wrongful or criminal intent. The trial court, however, was unimpressed, and ruled: ". . . I don't think anybody can have the defense they thought the property was abandoned on another man's piece of property." . . . The court refused to submit or to allow counsel to argue to the jury whether Morissette acted with innocent intention.

* * *

The contention that an injury can amount to a crime only when inflicted by intention is no provincial or transient notion. It is as universal and persistent in mature systems of law as belief in freedom of the human will and a consequent ability and duty of the normal individual to choose between good and evil. A relation between some mental element and punishment for a harmful act is almost as instinctive as the child's familiar exculpatory "But I didn't mean to."

* * *

Crime, as a compound concept, generally constituted only from concurrence of an evil-meaning mind with an evil-doing hand, was congenial to an intense individualism and took deep and early root in American soil. As the states codified the common law of crimes, even if their enactments were silent on the subject, their courts assumed that the omission did not signify disapproval of the principle but merely recognized that intent was so inherent in the idea of the offense that it required no statutory affirmation. . . . Courts of various jurisdictions, and for the purposes of different offenses, have devised working formulae, if not scientific ones, for the instruction of juries around such terms as "felonious intent," "criminal intent," "malice aforethought," "guilty knowledge," "fraudulent intent," "wilfulness," "*scienter*," to denote guilty knowledge, or "*mens rea*," to signify an evil purpose or mental culpability. By the use or combination of these various

(continued on next page)

(*continued*)

MORISSETTE v. UNITED STATES
342 U.S. 246 (1952)

tokens, they have sought to protect those who were not blameworthy in mind from conviction of infamous common-law crimes.

However, [certain other] offenses belong to a category of another character, with very different antecedents and origins. The crimes there involved depend on no mental element but consist only of forbidden acts or omissions. . . . The industrial revolution multiplied the number of workmen exposed to injury from increasingly powerful and complex mechanisms, driven by freshly discovered sources of energy, requiring higher precautions by employers. . . . Wide distribution of goods became an instrument of wide distribution of harm when those who dispersed food, drink, drugs, and even securities, did not comply with reasonable standards of quality, integrity, disclosure and care. Such dangers have engendered increasingly numerous and detailed regulations which heighten the duties of those in control of particular industries, trades, properties or activities that affect public health, safety or welfare.

While many of these duties are sanctioned by a more strict civil liability, lawmakers, whether wisely or not, have sought to make such regulations more effective by invoking criminal sanctions to be applied by the familiar technique of criminal prosecutions and convictions. This has confronted the courts with a multitude of prosecutions, based on statutes or administrative regulations, for what have been aptly called "public welfare offenses." . . . The accused, if he does not will the violations, usually is in a position to prevent it with no more care than society might reasonably exact from one who assumed his responsibilities. Also, penalties commonly are relatively small, and conviction does no grave damage to an offender's reputation. Under such considerations, courts have turned to construing statutes and regulations which make no mention of intent as dispensing with it and holding that the guilty act alone makes out the crime. This has not, however, been without expressions of misgiving.

★   ★   ★

Stealing, larceny, and its variants and equivalents, were among the earliest offenses known to the law that existed before legislation; they are invasions of rights of property which stir a sense of insecurity in the whole community . . . State courts of last resort, on whom fall the heaviest burden of interpreting criminal law in this country, have consistently retained the requirement of intent in larceny-type offenses. If any state has deviated, the exception has neither been called to our attention nor disclosed by our research.

★   ★   ★

The Government asks us by a feat of construction radically to change the weights and balances in the scales of justice. The purpose and obvious effect of doing away with the requirement of a guilty intent is to ease the prosecution's path to conviction, to strip the defendant of such benefit as he derived at common law from innocence of evil purpose, and to circumscribe the freedom heretofore allowed juries. Such a manifest impairment of the immunities of the individual should not be extended to common-law crimes on judicial initiative.

*   *   *

We hold that mere omission from §641 of any mention of intent will not be construed as eliminating that element from the crimes denounced.

*   *   *

Congress, by the language of this section, has been at pains to incriminate only "knowing" conversions. . . . Knowing conversion requires more than knowledge that defendant was taking the property into his possession. He must have had knowledge of the facts, though not necessarily the law, that made the taking a conversion. In the case before us, whether the mental element that Congress required be spoken of as knowledge or as intent, would not seem to alter its bearing on guilt. For it is not apparent how Morissette could have knowingly or intentionally converted property that he did not know could be converted, as would be the case if it was in fact abandoned or if he truly believed it to be abandoned and unwanted property. . . .

Of course, the jury, considering Morissette's awareness that these casings were on government property, his failure to seek any permission for their removal and his self-interest as a witness, might have disbelieved his profession of innocent intent and concluded that his assertion of a belief that the casings were abandoned was an afterthought. Had the jury convicted on proper instructions it would be the end of the matter. But juries are not bound by what seems inescapable logic to judges. They might have concluded that the heaps of spent casings left in the hinterland to rust away presented an appearance of unwanted and abandoned junk, and that lack of any conscious deprivation of property or intentional injury was indicated by Morissette's good character, the openness of the taking, crushing and transporting of the casings, and the candor with which it was all admitted. They might have refused to brand Morissette as a thief. Had they done so, that too would have been the end of the matter.

*   *   *

Reversed.

UNITED STATES v. PARK
421 U.S. 658 (1975)

MR. CHIEF JUSTICE BURGER delivered the opinion of the Court.

We granted certiorari to consider whether the jury instructions in the prosecution of a corporate officer under §301 (k) of the Federal Food, Drug, and Cosmetic Act, 52 Stat. 1042, as amended, 21 U.S.C. §331 (k), were appropriate under *United States* v. *Dotterweich*, 320 U.S. 277 (1943).

Acme Markets, Inc., is a national retail food chain with approximately 36,000 employees, 874 retail outlets, 12 general warehouses, and four special warehouses. Its headquarters, including the office of the president, respondent Park, who is chief executive officer of the corporation, are located in Philadelphia, Pa. In a five-count information filed in the United States

(continued on next page)

(*continued*)

UNITED STATES v. PARK
421 U.S. 658 (1975)

District Court for the District of Maryland, the Government charged Acme and respondent with violations of the Federal Food, Drug, and Cosmetic Act. Each count of the information alleged that the defendants had received food that had been shipped in interstate commerce and that, while the food was being held for sale in Acme's Baltimore warehouse following shipment in interstate commerce, they caused it to be held in a building accessible to rodents and to be exposed to contamination by rodents. These acts were alleged to have resulted in the food's being adulterated. . . .

Acme pleaded guilty to each count of the information. Respondent pleaded not guilty. The evidence at trial demonstrated that in April 1970 the Food and Drug Administration (FDA) advised respondent by letter of the insanitary conditions in Acme's Philadelphia warehouse. In 1971 the FDA found that similar conditions existed in the firm's Baltimore warehouse. An FDA consumer safety officer testified concerning evidence of rodent infestation and other insanitary conditions discovered during a 12-day inspection of the Baltimore warehouse in November and December 1971. He also related that a second inspection of the warehouse had been conducted in March 1972. On that occasion the inspectors found that there had been improvement in the sanitary conditions, but that "there was still evidence of rodent activity in the building and in the warehouses and we found some rodent-contaminated lots of food items."

The Government also presented testimony by the Chief of Compliance of the FDA's Baltimore office, who informed respondent by letter of the conditions at the Baltimore warehouse after the first inspection. There was testimony by Acme's Baltimore division vice president, who had responded to the letter on behalf of Acme and respondent and who described the steps taken to remedy the insanitary conditions discovered by both inspections. The Government's final witness, Acme's vice president for legal affairs and assistant secretary, identified respondent as the president and chief executive officer of the company and read a bylaw prescribing the duties of the chief executive officer. He testified that respondent functioned by delegating "normal operating duties," including sanitation, but that he retained "certain things, which are the big, broad, principles of the operation of the company," and had "the responsibility of seeing that they all work together."

At the close of the Government's case in chief, respondent moved for a judgment of acquittal on the ground that "the evidence in chief has shown that Mr. Park is not personally concerned in this Food and Drug violation." The trial judge denied the motion, stating that *United States* v. *Dotterweich*, 320 U.S. 277 (1943), was controlling.

Respondent was the only defense witness. He testified that, although all of Acme's employees were in a sense under his general direction, the company had an "organizational structure for responsibilities for certain functions" according to which different phases of its operation were "assigned to individuals who, in turn, have staff and departments under them." He identified those individuals responsible for sanitation, and related that upon receipt of the January 1972 FDA letter, he had conferred with the vice president for legal affairs, who informed him that the Baltimore division vice president "was investigating the situation immediately and would be taking corrective action and would be preparing a summary of the corrective action to reply to the letter." Respondent stated that he did not "believe there was anything [he] could have done more constructively than what [he] found was being done."

On cross-examination, respondent conceded that providing sanitary conditions for food offered for sale to the public was something that he was "responsible for in the entire operation of the company," and he stated that it was one of many phases of the company that he assigned to "dependable subordinates." Respondent . . . admitted receiving the April 1970 letter addressed to him from the FDA regarding insanitary conditions at Acme's Philadelphia warehouse. He acknowledged that, with the exception of the division vice president, the same individuals had responsibility for sanitation in both Baltimore and Philadelphia. Finally, in response to questions concerning the Philadelphia and Baltimore incidents, respondent admitted that the Baltimore problem indicated the system for handling sanitation "wasn't working perfectly" and that as Acme's chief executive officer he was responsible for "any result which occurs in our company." . . . The jury found respondent guilty on all counts of the information, and he was subsequently sentenced to pay a fine of $50 on each count.

The Court of Appeals reversed the conviction and remanded for a new trial.

★   ★   ★

The question presented by the Government's petition for certiorari in *United States* v. *Dotterweich, supra,* and the focus of this Court's opinion, was whether "the manager of a corporation, as well as the corporation itself, may be prosecuted under the Federal Food, Drug, and Cosmetic Act of 1938 for the introduction of misbranded and adulterated articles into interstate commerce." In *Dotterweich,* a jury had disagreed as to the corporation, a jobber purchasing drugs from manufacturers and shipping them in interstate commerce under its own label, but had convicted Dotterweich, the corporation's president and general manager. The Court of Appeals reversed the conviction on the ground that only the drug dealer, whether corporation or individual, was subject to the criminal provisions of the Act, and that where the dealer was a corporation, an individual connected therewith might be held personally only if he was operating the corporation "as his 'alter ego.' "

In reversing the judgment of the Court of Appeals and reinstating Dotterweich's conviction, this Court looked to the purposes of the Act and noted that they "touch phases of the lives and health of people which, in the circumstances of modern industrialism, are largely beyond self-protection." It observed that the Act is of "a now familiar type" which "dispenses with the conventional requirement for criminal conduct—awareness of some wrongdoing. In the interest of the larger good it puts the burden of acting at hazard

(*continued on next page*)

(continued)

**UNITED STATES v.
PARK**
421 U.S. 658 (1975)

upon a person otherwise innocent but standing in responsible relation to a public danger."

Central to the Court's conclusion that individuals other than proprietors are subject to the criminal provisions of the Act was the reality that "the only way in which a corporation can act is through the individuals who act on its behalf."

★   ★   ★

Thus *Dotterweich* and the cases which have followed reveal that in providing sanctions which reach and touch the individuals who execute the corporate mission—and this is by no means necessarily confined to a single corporate agent or employee—the Act imposes not only a positive duty to seek out and remedy violations when they occur but also, and primarily, a duty to implement measures that will insure that violations will not occur. The requirements of foresight and vigilance imposed on responsible corporate agents are beyond question demanding, and perhaps onerous, but they are no more stringent than the public has a right to expect of those who voluntarily assume positions of authority in business enterprises whose services and products affect the health and well-being of the public that supports them.

★   ★   ★

Reading the entire charge satisfies us that the jury's attention was adequately focused on the issue of respondent's authority with respect to the conditions that formed the basis of the alleged violations. Viewed as a whole, the charge did not permit the jury to find guilt solely on the basis of respondent's position in the corporation; rather, it fairly advised the jury that to find guilt it must find respondent "had a responsible relation to the situation," and "by virtue of his position . . . had . . . authority and responsibility" to deal with the situation. The situation referred to could only be "food . . . held in unsanitary conditions in a warehouse with the result that it consisted, in part, of filth or . . . may have been contaminated with filth."

★   ★   ★

Reversed.

Excuses That Limit or Overcome Responsibility

Mistake of Fact and Mistake of Law   Ordinarily, ignorance of the law is not an excuse. If you believe that it is permissible to turn right on a red light but the city ordinance prohibits it, your belief, even if reasonable, does not excuse your violation of the law. Under certain circumstances, however, ignorance of law will be excused. If a statute imposes criminal penalties for an action taken without a license, and the government official responsible for issuing the license formally tells you that you do not need one (though in fact you do), a conviction for violating the statute cannot stand. In rare cases, a lawyer's advice, contrary to the statute, will be held to excuse the client, but usually the client is responsible for his attorney's mistakes. Otherwise, as it is said, the lawyer would be superior to the law.

Ignorance or mistake of *fact* more frequently will serve as an excuse. If you take a coat from a restaurant, believing it to be yours, you cannot be convicted of larceny if it is not. Your honest mistake of fact negates the requisite intent. In general, the rule is that a mistaken belief of fact will excuse criminal responsibility if (1) the belief is honestly held; (2) it is reasonable to hold it; and (3) the act would not have been criminal if the facts were as they were supposed to have been.

Entrapment One common technique of criminal investigation is the use of an undercover agent or decoy—the policeman who poses as a buyer of drugs from a street dealer or the elaborate "sting" operations in which ostensibly stolen goods are "sold" to underworld "fences." Sometimes these methods are the only way by which certain kinds of crime can be rooted out and convictions secured.

But a rule against **entrapment** limits the legal ability of the police to play the role of criminals. The police are permitted to use such techniques to detect criminal activity; they are not permitted to do so to instigate crime. The distinction is usually made between a person who intends to commit a crime and one who does not. If the police provide the former with an opportunity to commit a criminal act—the sale of drugs to an undercover agent, for example—there is no defense of entrapment. But if the police knock on the door of one not known to be a drug user, and persist in a demand that he purchase drugs from them, finally overcoming his will to resist, a conviction for purchase and possession of drugs can be overturned on the ground of entrapment.

Other Excuses A number of other circumstances can limit or excuse criminal liability. These include compulsion (a gun pointed at one's head by a masked man who apparently is unafraid to use the weapon and who demands that you help him rob a store), honest consent of the "victim" (the quarterback who is tackled), adherence to the requirements of legitimate public authority lawfully exercised (a policeman directs a towing company to remove a car parked in a tow-away zone), the proper exercise of domestic authority (a parent may spank a child, within limits), and defense of self, others, property, and habitation. Each of these excuses is a complex subject in itself.

Lack of Capacity A further defense to criminal prosecution is the lack of mental capacity to commit the crime. Infants and children are considered incapable of committing a crime; under common law any child under the age of seven could not be prosecuted for any act. Today the age is governed by statutes that vary in each state. Likewise, insanity or mental disease or defect can be a complete defense, although a jury verdict of Not Guilty By Reason of Insanity often leads to post-acquittal commitment in institutions for a longer period of time than the maximum sentence that the defendant could have received had he been convicted of the underlying crime. Intoxication can be a defense to certain crimes, but the mere fact of drunkenness is not ordinarily sufficient.

PROCEDURE

The procedure followed in criminal prosecutions is complex and varies in particulars from state to state. Space here permits only the most abbreviated summary.

A criminal case begins either with an **arrest**—if the defendant is caught in the act or fleeing from the scene—or with a **warrant** for arrest. The warrant is issued by a judge or appropriate magistrate upon receiving a **complaint** detailing the charge of a specific crime against the accused. It is not enough for a police officer to go before a judge and say, "I'd like you to arrest Bluebeard because I think he's just murdered Agatha." The police officer must supply enough information to satisfy the magistrate that there is **probable cause** (reasonable grounds) to believe that the accused committed the crime. The warrant will be issued to the police or other appropriate public officer, who may then arrest the accused.

The accused will be brought before the magistrate for a **preliminary hearing** to determine whether there is sufficient reason to hold the accused for trial. If so, the accused can be sent to jail or be permitted to make **bail**. Bail is a sum of money paid to the court to secure the accused's attendance at trial. If he fails to appear, he forfeits the money. Constitutionally, bail can be withheld only if there is reason to believe that the accused will flee the jurisdiction. Although there is much pressure to permit bail to be denied if the accused presents a danger to the community, that is not now the constitutional rule.

Once the arrest is made, the case is in the hands of the **prosecutor**. In the states, prosecution is a function of the district attorney's office. These offices are usually organized on a county-by-county basis. In the federal system, criminal prosecution is handled by the office of the United States Attorney, one of whom is appointed for every federal district. Lawyers working for the district attorney or the U.S. Attorney are known as assistant district attorneys or assistant U.S. attorneys.

Following the preliminary hearing, the prosecutor must either file an **information** (a document stating the crime of which the person being held is accused) or ask the *grand jury* for an *indictment*. In many states, an information may be substituted for an indictment only for lesser crimes. The **grand jury** consists of twenty-three people who sit to determine whether there is sufficient evidence to warrant a prosecution. It does not sit to determine guilt or innocence. The **indictment** is the grand jury's formal declaration of charges on which the accused will be tried. If indicted, the accused formally becomes a **defendant.**

The defendant will then be **arraigned**—that is, brought before a judge to answer the accusation in the information or indictment. The defendant may plead guilty or not guilty. If he pleads not guilty, the case will be tried before a jury—sometimes referred to as a *petit jury* (PET ee JUR ee). The case will proceed more or less as outlined in the discussion on pp. 53–55 dealing with civil trials. One significant difference is that the jury cannot convict unless it finds the defendant guilty "beyond a reasonable doubt."

The defendant might have pleaded guilty to the offense or to a lesser charge, often referred to as a "lesser included offense." (Simple larceny, for example, is a lesser included offense of robbery because the defendant may not have used violence but nevertheless stole from the victim.) Such a plea is usually arranged through **plea bargaining** with the prosecution. In return for the plea, the prosecutor promises to recommend to the judge that the sentence be limited.

The defendant is also permitted to file a plea of *nolo contendere* (NO low kun TEN duh ree) (no contest) in prosecutions for certain crimes. In so doing, he neither affirms nor denies his guilt. He may be sentenced as though he had pleaded guilty, although usually a nolo plea is the result of a plea bargain. Why plead nolo? In some offenses, such as violations of the antitrust laws, the statutes provide that private plaintiffs may use a conviction or a guilty plea as proof

that the defendant violated the law and short-circuit a civil trial for damages. All that they need prove is the extent of their damages, not the liability of the defendant. The nolo plea permits the defendant to avoid this difficulty.

Following a guilty plea or a verdict of guilt, the judge will impose a sentence after presentencing reports are written by various court officials, often probation officers. Permissible sentences are spelled out in statutes, though these frequently give the judge a range within which to work (for example, "twenty years to life"). The judge may sentence the defendant to imprisonment, a fine, or both, or may decide to *suspend* sentence—that is, the defendant will not have to serve the sentence as long as he stays out of trouble.

Sentencing usually precedes appeal. As in civil cases, the defendant, now convicted, has the right to take at least one appeal, and frequently two or three, to higher courts, where issues of procedure and constitutional rights may be debated.

CONSTITUTIONAL RIGHTS OF THE ACCUSED

The rights of those accused of a crime are spelled out primarily in four of the ten constitutional amendments that make up the Bill of Rights (Amendments Four, Five, Six, and Eight). For the most part, these amendments have been held to apply to both the federal and state governments.

Search and Seizure

The Fourth Amendment says in part that "the right of the people to be secure in their persons, houses, papers, and effects, against unreasonable searches and seizures, shall not be violated." Although there are numerous and tricky exceptions to the general rule, ordinarily the police may not break into a person's house or confiscate papers or make an arrest unless they have a warrant to do so. This means, for instance, that a police officer cannot simply stop you on a street corner and ask to see what is in your pockets (a power the police enjoy in many other countries), nor can your home be raided without probable cause to believe that you have committed a crime. What if the police do search or seize unreasonably? The courts have devised a remedy for the use at trial of the "fruits" of an unlawful search or seizure. Evidence that is unconstitutionally seized is excluded from the trial. This is the so-called **exclusionary rule,** first made applicable in federal cases in 1914, and brought home to the states in 1961. The exclusionary rule is highly controversial and there are numerous exceptions to it. But unless the police were in "hot pursuit" or the evidence was in "plain view," it remains generally true that the prosecutor may not use evidence willfully taken by the police in the absence of a legitimate warrant.

Double Jeopardy

The Fifth Amendment prohibits the government from prosecuting a person twice for the same offense; the amendment says that no person shall be "subject for the same offense to be twice put in jeopardy of life or limb." If a defendant is acquitted, the government may not appeal. Although state and federal laws may overlap, it is not double jeopardy for both the state and federal government to prosecute a defendant for acts that violate similar federal and state statutes.

Self-incrimination

Another hotly debated right is the Fifth Amendment's right against self-incrimination (no person "shall be compelled in any criminal case to be a witness against himself"). The debate over the limits of this right has given rise to an immense literature, which cannot be summarized here. In broadest outline, the right against self-incrimination means that the prosecutor may not call a defendant to the witness stand during trial and may not comment to the jury on the defendant's failure to take the stand. Moreover, a defendant's confession must be excluded from evidence if it was not voluntarily made (if, for example, the police beat the person into giving a confession). In *Miranda* v. *Arizona* [384 U.S. 436 (1966)], the Supreme Court ruled that no confession is admissible if the police have not first advised a suspect of his constitutional rights, including the right to have a lawyer present to advise him during the questioning. These so-called *Miranda warnings* have prompted scores of follow-up cases that have made this branch of juris-

prudence especially complex—*Miranda* itself has been greatly limited in the last quarter century.

Speedy Trial

The Sixth Amendment tells the government that it must try defendants speedily. How long a delay is too long depends on the circumstances in each case. In 1975, Congress enacted the Speedy Trial Act to give priority to criminal cases in federal courts. It requires all criminal prosecutions to go to trial within seventy-five days, although the law lists many permissible reasons for delay.

Right to Cross-examine

The Sixth Amendment also states that the defendant shall have the right to confront witnesses against him. No testimony is permitted to be shown to the jury unless the person making it is present and subject to cross-examination by the defendant's counsel.

Assistance of Counsel

The Sixth Amendment guarantees criminal defendants the right to have the assistance of defense counsel. During the eighteenth century and before, the British courts frequently refused to permit defendants to have lawyers in the courtroom during trial. The right to counsel is much broader in this country, as the result of Supreme Court decisions that require the state to pay for a lawyer for indigent defendants in most criminal cases.

Cruel and Unusual Punishment

Punishment under the common law was frequently horrifying. Death was common punishment for relatively minor crimes. The unlucky defendant who found himself convicted could face brutal torture before death. The Eighth Amendment banned these actions with the words that "cruel and unusual punishments" shall not be inflicted. Virtually all such punishments either never were enacted or have been eliminated from the statute books in the United States. After the Supreme Court in 1972 declared the death penalty unconstitutional in certain states because they applied it haphazardly, many of these states rewrote their laws to meet the Court's objections. Four years later, the Court ruled that several new death-penalty statutes were constitutionally permissible. Since then, the question has been extensively litigated, and the current Supreme Court has shown itself reluctant to strike down death-penalty statutes on broad grounds.

CHAPTER SUMMARY

Criminal law is that branch of law governing offenses against society. Most criminal law requires a specific intent to commit the prohibited act, although a very few economic acts, made criminal by modern legislation, dispense with the requirement of intent. In this way, criminal law is different from much of civil law—for example, from the tort of negligence, in which carelessness, rather than intent, can result in liability.

Major crimes are known as felonies; minor ones, misdemeanors. Most people have a general notion about familiar crimes—murder, theft, and the like. But conventional knowledge does not suffice for understanding technical distinctions among related crimes such as larceny, robbery, and false pretenses. These distinctions can be important because an individual can be found guilty not merely for committing one of the acts defined in the criminal law but also for attempting or conspiring to commit such an act. It is usually easier to convict someone of an attempt or conspiracy than of the main crime, and a person involved in a conspiracy to commit a felony may find that very little is required to put him into serious trouble. Ignorance of the law is rarely an excuse, although under proper circumstances ignorance of certain facts may excuse a person who would otherwise be guilty of a crime.

Of major concern to the business executive is white-collar crime, which encompasses a host of offenses, including bribery, embezzlement, fraud, restraints of trade, and computer crime.

Persons accused of crime should know that they always have the right to consult a lawyer and should always do so.

KEY TERMS

Act	p. 84	Complaint	p. 107
Arraigned	p. 108	Conspiracy	p. 95
Arrest	p. 107	Defendant	p. 108
Arson	p. 89	Embezzlement	p. 86
Assault	p. 86	Entrapment	p. 107
Bail	p. 107	Exclusionary rule	p. 109
Battery	p. 85	Excusable homicide	p. 85
Blackmail	p. 89	Extortion	p. 89
Bribery	p. 89	False Pretenses	p. 87
Burglary	p. 89	Felonies	p. 84
Felony murder rule	p. 85	Misdemeanors	p. 84
Forgery	p. 89	Murder	p. 85
Grand jury	p. 108	Perjury	p. 89
Homicide	p. 84	Plea bargaining	p. 108
Indictment	p. 108	Preliminary hearing	p. 107
Information	p. 108	Probable cause	p. 107
Involuntary man-slaughter	p. 85	Prosecutor	p. 107
		Robbery	p. 86
Intent	p. 84	Strict liability	p. 84
Justifiable homicide	p. 85	Theft of services	p. 88
Larceny	p. 86	Uttering	p. 89
Malice aforethought	p. 85	Voluntary manslaughter	p. 85
Manslaughter	p. 85		
Material	p. 90	Warrant	p. 107

SELF-TEST QUESTIONS

1. Late at night a masked man with a gun barges into a grocery store and asks the cashier to hand over all the money in the cash register "because it's mine." The masked man is guilty of:
   (a)   false pretenses
   (b)   embezzlement
   (c)   robbery
   (d)   burglary

2. While browsing in a bookstore, you tuck a book under your arm, intending to pay for it on your way out. But you forget you have it, and walk out. You are arrested for stealing. You protest that you didn't intend to steal it. If the jury doesn't believe your story, you can be convicted of which of the following crimes:
   (a)   larceny
   (b)   robbery
   (c)   embezzlement
   (d)   none of the above

3. Willie has robbed a federally-insured bank, a crime under both federal and state law. He may be tried and convicted:
   (a)   first by the state and only then by the federal government
   (b)   first by the federal government and only then by the state
   (c)   by either the state or the federal government, but then not by the other
   (d)   by both the state and federal government, in either order

4. A manager can be convicted for a crime of a subordinate if:
   (a)   the manager directed the subordinate to commit the crime
   (b)   the manager had heard a rumor that the subordinate might commit the crime and did nothing to stop the subordinate

(c) the crime helped out the business
(d) all of the above
5. A manager on trial for helping to embezzle cash from the company can refuse to testify because:
(a) it is unlawful to commit perjury
(b) no one can be required to testify against himself involving a crime
(c) he cannot remember exactly what happened
(d) he helped out, believing that the scheme was lawful

DEMONSTRATION PROBLEM

Marilyn is arrested for arson against a nuclear utility, a crime under both state and federal law. She is acquitted in state court. Then the federal government decides to prosecute her for the same offense. The state and federal statutes are identically worded. Does she have a double-jeopardy defense against the federal prosecution? Suppose Marilyn had been convicted at the state trial and been sentenced to ten years at hard labor, whereas the maximum federal penalty would have been five years. Would she have a double-jeopardy defense in that instance?

PROBLEMS

1. Edward is accused of stealing some food from a grocery store. When the police arrested him on the street five minutes after the grocery store clerk phoned for help, he had none of the stolen goods on his person. He said he was on his way home from a movie and protested that he knew nothing about the crime. The clerk, the only witness, testified at the trial that he "thought Edward was the robber, but I can't be sure because it was dark." Should this case go to the jury? Why or why not?
2. Bill is the chief executive of a small computer manufacturing company that desperately needs funds to continue operating. One day a stranger comes to Bill to induce him to take part in a cocaine smuggling deal that would net Bill millions of dollars. Unbeknownst to Bill, the stranger is an undercover police officer. Bill tells the stranger to go away. The stranger persists, and after five months of arguing and cajoling, the stranger wears down Bill's will to resist. Bill agrees to take delivery of the cocaine and hands over a "down payment" of $10,000 to the undercover agent, who promptly arrests him for conspiracy to violate the narcotics laws. What defenses does Bill have?
3. You are the manager of a bookstore. A customer becomes irritated at having to stand in line and begins to shout at the salesclerk for refusing to wait on him. You come out of your office and ask the customer to calm down. He

shouts at you. You tell him to leave. He refuses. So you and the salesclerk pick him up and shove him bodily out the door. He calls the police to have you arrested for battery. Should the police arrest you? Assuming that they do, how would you defend yourself in court?
4. Under what circumstances can a corporation be held guilty of a crime?
5. Julian worked as a supply clerk in the warehouse of a large department store. For several days he noticed that dozens of people were returning a particular model of a well known brand of AM-FM car radio. His supervisor ordered him to "stack all those things" in a corner of the warehouse and at least twice referred to the radios as "those pieces of junk." In fact, the radios were perfectly functional; they were returned because they were last year's model sold mistakenly as the new model. After a week or so, believing that they were being abandoned, Julian began to take the radios home a few at a time. His supervisor saw him take the radios one evening but said nothing. Several weeks later, after he had taken more than 100 of the radios without objection, the police showed up at the warehouse and arrested him for theft of department store property. Julian said he thought they were abandoned and would never have taken them if he thought the store wanted them. Does Julian have a defense to a charge of larceny? How will the prosecutor respond?
6. You have been assigned the challenging job of opening up an overseas office. In preparing for the assignment, you have lengthy discussions with the company's vice president for overseas development, a person who has spent years abroad, including much time in the country where you'll be establishing your first office. The VP tells you that in order to get all the necessary permits in time, you'll need to pay a "little back-office money" to the local police chief, several police officers, and the building inspectors. You understand him to say that it is a business necessity to yield to the petty extortion of your host country. Your boss tells you, moreover, a particular way by which you can pay the bribes through a company account. He tells you not to worry; "it happens all the time." You go overseas, pay off the local officials, and open your office. Six months later, on home leave, you are arrested for violating the Foreign Corrupt Practices Act, which forbids such payments. What is your defense? Are you likely to succeed?
7. Speedy Pizza guarantees home delivery within a 2-mile radius of any of its 30 locations within 20 minutes of the time a phone order is received. As a result of this highly publicized policy, Speedy's delivery people have been ticketed for speeding on many occasions and several have been involved in minor accidents. The newspapers have given these incidents front-page coverage, and a local crusading TV reporter aired a 15-minute documentary about it on the evening news. The police have issued a statement

saying that the department will crack down on all Speedy Pizza trucks. Then real tragedy struck: a Speedy Pizza deliverer rammed his car at 75 miles per hour while intoxicated into an oncoming vehicle, killing all four people. The District Attorney wants to indict not only the driver for murder but also Speedy Pizza and Speedy's president. What are the legal arguments for and against the indictment?

ANSWERS TO SELF-TEST QUESTIONS

1. (c)   2. (a)   3. (d)   4. (a)   5. (b)

SUGGESTED ANSWER TO DEMONSTRATION PROBLEM

It is not a violation of the Constitution's double-jeopardy clause to be tried for the same crime under separate federal and state laws, even if the laws are identical, because the double-jeopardy clause protects against being prosecuted for the same "offense," and what Marilyn did constituted two separate offenses. The federal government could try her whether she was acquitted or convicted in the state trial. The length of the sentences are irrelevant, since they are determined independently under the statutes enacted by the state legislature and by Congress.

CHAPTER 4

Torts

PURPOSE OF TORT LAWS

*U*nlike criminal law, which is designed to regulate and deter conduct harmful to society and to punish those who violate its norms, tort law is concerned with the private relations among individuals. "Tort" derives from the Latin *tortus*, meaning "twisted," and came into English through the French *torquere*, meaning "wrong." At one time it was used in everyday speech; today it has been left to the lawyer.

A **tort** is usually defined as a wrong for which the law will provide redress, most often in the form of money damages but sometimes in the form of an injunction. The definition is circular. It gives no clue to the underlying principles that divide wrongs in the legal sphere from those in the moral sphere. Hurting someone's feelings may be far more devastating than saying something mildly untrue about him behind his back, yet the law will probably redress the latter but not the former.

Although the word is not popularly used, tort suits are the stuff of everyday headlines. Increasing numbers of people injured by exposure to a variety of risks seek redress. Headlines boast of multimillion-dollar lawsuits against doctors who bungled operations, against newspapers that libeled subjects of stories, and against companies that manufacture dangerous substances like asbestos, diethylstilbestrol (DES), and Agent Orange (a herbicide used in the Vietnam War). All are examples of tort suits. Tort law concepts will be discussed in several chapters—including Chapter 19 on product liability and Chapter 32 on the tort liability of a landowner.

The law of torts developed almost entirely in the common-law courts. It was made by judges and continues to be made by judges today. Through thousands of cases, the courts have fashioned a series of rules that govern the conduct of individuals in their noncontractual dealings with each other. Through contracts, individuals can shape their own rules. In the absence of agreement, tort law provides the means by which individuals can be held legally accountable for the consequences of their actions and by which those who have suffered losses at the hands of others can be compensated.

Although many acts, like homicide, are both criminal and tortious, torts and crimes are different, and the difference is worth noting. A crime is an act against the people as a whole. Society punishes the murderer; it does not usually compensate the family of the victim. Some states are beginning to adopt victim compensation programs, but the compensation is undertaken through an administrative proceeding unrelated to the criminal prosecution. Tort law, on the other hand, views the death as a private wrong for which damages are owed. The tort victim or his family, not the state, brings the action. The judgment against a defendant in a civil tort suit is, with one exception (see p. 115), not a penalty but a means of making the victim whole, or as nearly whole as possible.

Dimensions of Tort Liability

Fault   Tort principles can be viewed along different dimensions (see Figure 4-1). One is the **fault** dimension. Like criminal law, tort law requires an act for there to be liability. Unlike most criminal law, however, there need not be a specific intent. Since tort law focuses on injury to the plaintiff, it is less concerned than criminal law about the reasons for the defendant's actions. An innocent act or a relatively innocent one may still provide the basis for liability. Nevertheless, tort law for the most part relies on standards of fault, or blameworthiness.

The most obvious standard is willful conduct. If the defendant, often called the **tortfeasor** (the one committing the tort), intentionally injures another, there is little argument about tort liability. Thus all crimes resulting in injury to a person or property (murder, assault, arson, and so on) are also torts, and the plaintiff may bring a separate lawsuit to

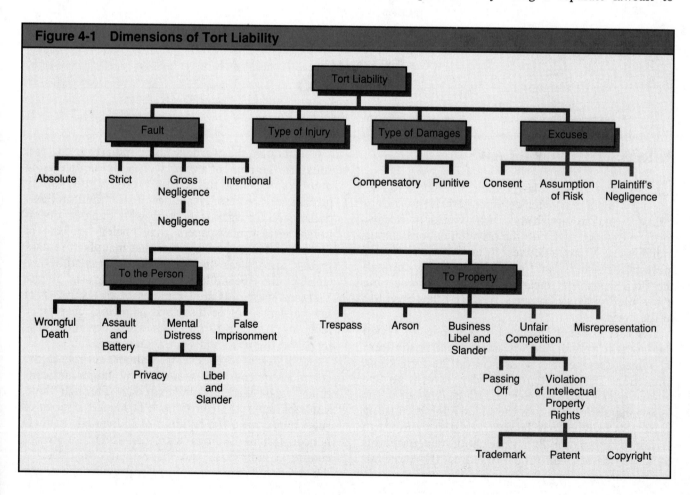

Figure 4-1   Dimensions of Tort Liability

recover damages for injuries to his person, family, or property.

Most tort suits usually do not rely on *intentional* fault. They are based, rather, on **negligence**—conduct that under the circumstances is careless or poses unreasonable risks of causing damage. Most automobile accident and medical malpractice suits are examples of negligence suits.

The fault dimension is a continuum. At one end is the deliberate desire to do injury. The middle ground is occupied by careless conduct. At the other end is conduct that most would consider entirely blameless, in the moral sense. The defendant may have observed all possible precautions and yet still be held liable. This is called **strict liability.** An example is that incurred by the manufacturer of a defective product that is placed on the market despite all possible precautions, including quality-control inspection. In many states, if the product causes injury, the manufacturer will be held liable.

Nature of Injury Another way of viewing tort liability is by the type of injury caused. The most obvious type is physical harm to the person or property— wrongful death, battery, trespass, arson, accidents caused by the defendant's negligence. Mental suffering can be redressed if it is a result of physical injury—for example, shock and depression following an automobile accident. A few states now permit recovery for mental distress alone, such as a mother's shock at seeing her child injured by a car while both were crossing the street.

Other protected interests include a person's reputation (injured by defamatory statements or writings), privacy (injured by those who divulge secrets of her personal life), and economic interests (misrepresentation to secure an economic advantage, certain forms of unfair competition).

Excuses A third element in the law of torts is the excuse for committing an apparent wrong. The law does not condemn every act that ultimately results in injury. One common rule of exculpation is **assumption of risk.** A baseball fan who sits above third base assumes the risk that a foul ball will fly toward him and strike him. He will not be permitted to complain in court that the batter should have been more careful or that the third baseman should have caught the line drive. Another excuse is negligence of the plaintiff. If two drivers are careless and hit each other on the highway, some states will refuse to permit either to recover from the other. Still another excuse is **consent:** two boxers in the ring consent to the beating that each will administer.

Damages

Since the purpose of tort law is to compensate the victim for harm actually done, damages are usually measured by the extent of the injury. Expressed in money terms, these include replacement of property destroyed, compensation for lost wages, reimbursement for medical expenses, and dollars that are supposed to approximate the pain that is suffered. Damages for these injuries are called **compensatory damages.** Because compensatory damages are intended to make the tort victim whole, they are not taxable. The plaintiff injured in a car crash who recovers $1 million in compensatory damages need pay no income tax on the award.

In certain instances, the courts will permit an award of **punitive damages.** These can be meted out as punishment for the defendant's actions. Because a punitive award, sometimes called *exemplary* damages, cuts against the general purpose of tort law, it is allowable only in aggravated situations. The law in most states permits recovery of punitive damages only when the defendant has deliberately committed a wrong with an evil intent or has otherwise done something outrageous. Punitive damages are rarely allowed in negligence cases for that reason. But if someone sets out maliciously to defame another person, punitive damages may well be appropriate. Punitive damages are intended not only to punish the wrongdoer, by exacting an additional and sometimes heavy payment (the exact amount is left to the discretion of jury and judge), but also to deter others from similar conduct. The punitive damage award has been awarded against manufacturers. One fear is that huge damage awards on behalf of a multitude of victims could swiftly bankrupt the defendant (see **Box 4-1**). Unlike compensatory damages, punitive damages are sometimes taxable.

INTENTIONAL TORTS

The analysis of most intentional torts is straightforward and parallels the substantive crimes already

LAW AND LIFE

More Punitive Damage Awards

*[Punitive damages are intended not only to punish the wrongdoer, but to deter others from similar behavior. Punitive damages have been levied against manufacturers, who face possible bankruptcy brought on by a multitude of lawsuits.—*AUTHORS' NOTE]

When she was four years old, Lee Ann Gryc leaned across an electric stove to turn off a kitchen buzzer. Her cotton pajamas accidentally brushed a lit burner, and she was instantly engulfed in flames. Within 12 seconds her mother rushed to her side to smother them, but by then it was too late: The child suffered severe second- and third-degree burns over 20% of her arms, chest, stomach, back, neck, and chin. Despite numerous skin grafts, Lee Ann, now 15, will be scarred for life. Cruelly, her Minnesota schoolmates refer to her as "Kentucky Fried Chicken," and not surprisingly she has great difficulties coping with her emotional problems.

Last May the Minnesota Supreme Court affirmed a $1.8 million award against Riegel Textile Corp., manufacturer of the pajamas. Such a figure would not ordinarily excite much comment. But in this case, $1 million of the amount was for punitive damages, and the court upheld the jury's verdict even though Riegel showed that it had complied with federal standards. In late October the U.S. Supreme Court declined to review the case, which now looms as an important precedent in the increasing number of product suits in which plaintiffs seek punitive damage judgments against U.S. businesses.

GROWING PUNITIVE DAMAGES?

No History

In legal theory, punitive damages are used to punish a defendant who intentionally or recklessly causes injury. Executives have long worried that the power to award punitive damages gives lay juries an incentive to levy outsized judgments against a corporation whenever a plaintiff is gruesomely injured. Until recently, however, the fears were largely unwarranted. A 1976 study of product liability awards by the Insurance Services Office, an industry group, declared that no conclusion could be drawn concerning punitive damage trends because there were too few cases from which to make a judgment.

That paucity of cases seems to have changed. "There is no question that since 1976 punitive damages are more commonly awarded by juries," says Malcolm E. Wheeler, a partner in the Los Angeles office of the New York-based law firm Hughes Hubbard & Reed. Wheeler, who successfully helped defend Ford Motor Co. in Indiana last year against criminal charges of reckless homicide arising out of a Pinto car crash, says that the punitive damages that the attorneys for plaintiffs ask for today are "astronomical" compared with the figures sought only five years ago.

And juries are responding. Earlier this year, for example, a Florida jury awarded a Royal Business Machines Inc. dealer $5 million, of which $3.3 million represented punitive damages, for injuries resulting from defects in one of Royal's plain-paper copiers.

New Kind of Evidence

The upsurge of punitive damage claims and awards is due to a change in "the nature of evidence" and not in the standard of proof, says Victor E. Schwartz, former chairman of the Commerce Dept.'s Task Force on Product Liability and now a professor at American University Law School and counsel to the Washington law firm of Crowell & Moring. Plaintiffs must still convince jurors that a manufacturer acted wantonly, but a company can be put in the dock for choosing between cost and safety in complex engineering matters. Ordinarily, the tradeoff may not be the basis for a punitive damage award, since at worst the choice will have been negligent. But there are exceptions, as the Gryc case shows.

Riegel made the pajamas from flannelette, a cotton material that is light, durable, inexpensive, and also, unfortunately, highly flammable. It had not been treated with flame retardant. Resolving against Riegel issues such as the practicability of the treatment and the desirability of warning consumers of flannelette's flammability would warrant a finding only that the pajamas were defective, and an award of compensatory, but not punitive, damages.

However, additional evidence showed that Riegel was aware that the standards established by the Flammable Fabrics Act were invalid and allowed unreasonably dangerous fabrics to pass the test. It was shown at trial that six lawsuits for burn accidents between 1960 and 1967 had put Riegel on notice of the potential hazard.

Minnesota is not alone in allowing punitive damages in product cases. The Wisconsin Supreme Court ruled last June that a punitive claim in the

(continued on next page)

BOX 4-1

Box 4-1, *continued*
case of an allegedly defective Mustang could proceed against Ford.

Our of Court
So far, few such awards have actually been paid. Since they are taxable to the plaintiff and not recoverable from a defendant's insurer, each party has strong incentives to compromise and settle before an appeal, according to Stuart M. Speiser, a leading New York plaintiffs trial lawyer.

Nevertheless, many corporate lawyers are apprehensive that the new trend may result in repeated, huge assessments when injuries are caused by a product that is mass marketed. "There could be 10,000 suits arising out of a single drug mishap," Schwartz says. One protection for manufacturers would be to let the jury decide on liability and let the judge determine the amount. Such a change in procedure would require legislative action.

Judicially decreed damages would not eliminate all objections, Wheeler

says. Although assessed in a civil case, punitive damages are akin to punishment, which is usually surrounded by such constitutional safeguards as grand jury indictment and the right against self-incrimination. So far, the argument has not been pressed. But, says Wheeler, "I'm just waiting for the right case."

Source: Reprinted from *Business Week*, January 12, 1981

---

discussed in Chapter 3. When physical injury or damage to property is caused, there is rarely debate over liability if the plaintiff deliberately undertook to produce the harm. Certain other intentional torts are worth noting for their relevance to business.

False Imprisonment

The tort of false imprisonment originally implied a locking up, as in a prison, but today it can occur if a person is restrained in a room or a car or even if his movements are restricted while walking down the street. People have a right to be free to go as they please, and one who without cause deprives another of personal freedom has committed a tort. Damages are allowed for time lost, discomfort and resulting ill health, mental suffering, humiliation, loss of reputation or business, and expenses such as attorneys' fees incurred as a result of the restraint (such as a false arrest). But as the following case shows, the defendant must be shown to have restrained the plaintiff in order for damages to be allowed.

LESTER v. ALBERS SUPER MARKETS, INC.
94 Ohio App. 313, 114 N.E.2d 529 (1952)

[The plaintiff, carrying a bag of rolls purchased at another store, entered the defendant's grocery store to buy some canned fruit. Seeing her bus outside, she stepped out of line and put the can on the counter. The store manager intercepted her and repeatedly demanded that she submit the bag to be searched. Finally she acquiesced, he looked inside, and said she could go. She testified that several people witnessed the scene, which lasted about 15 minutes, and that she was humiliated. The jury awarded her $800. She also testified that no one laid a hand on her nor made a move to restrain her from leaving by any one of numerous exits.]

*   *   *

MATTHEWS, JUDGE. As we view the record, it raises the fundamental question of what is imprisonment. Before any need for a determination of illegality arises there must be proof of imprisonment.

(*continued on next page*)

(continued)

LESTER v. ALBERS SUPER MARKETS, INC.
94 Ohio App. 313, 114 N.E.2d 529 (1952)

In 35 C.J.S., False Imprisonment, § 11, pages 512, 513, it is said: "Submission to the mere verbal direction of another, unaccompanied by force or by threats of any character, cannot constitute a false imprisonment, and there is no false imprisonment where an employer interviewing an employee declines to terminate the interview if no force or threat of force is used and false imprisonment may not be predicated on a person's unfounded belief that he was restrained."

Many cases are cited in support of the text.

* * *

In Fenn v. Kroger Grocery & Baking Co., Mo. Sup., 209 S.W. 885, 887, the court said:

> A case was not made out for false arrest. The plaintiff said she was intercepted as she started to leave the store; that Mr. Krause stood where she could not pass him in going out. She does not say that he made any attempt to intercept her. She says he escorted her back to the desk, that he asked her to let him see the change. . . . She does not say that she went unwillingly. . . . Evidence is wholly lacking to show that she was detained by force or threats. It was probably a disagreeable experience, a humiliating one to her, but she came out victorious and was allowed to go when she desired with the assurance of Mr. Krause that it was all right. The demurrer to the evidence on both counts was properly sustained.

The result of the cases is epitomized in 22 Am. Jr. 368, as follows:

> A customer or patron who apparently has not paid for what he has received may be detained for a reasonable time to investigate the circumstances, but upon payment of the demand, he has the unqualified right to leave the premises without restraint, so far as the proprietor is concerned, and it is false imprisonment for a private individual to detain one for an unreasonable time, or under unreasonable circumstances, for the purpose of investigating a dispute over the payment of a bill alleged to be owed by the person detained for cash services.

* * *

For these reasons, the judgment is reversed and final judgment entered for the defendant-appellant.

Intentional Infliction of Emotional Distress

Under common law there could be no recovery for acts, even though intentionally undertaken, that caused purely mental or emotional distress. For a case to go to the jury, the courts required that the mental distress result from some physical injury. In recent years, as explained in the following case, many courts have overthrown the older rule and now recognize the so-called "new tort."

ECKENRODE v. LIFE OF AMERICA INSURANCE CO.
470 F.2d 1 (7th Cir. 1972)

KILEY, CIRCUIT JUDGE. Plaintiff, a resident of Pennsylvania, filed this three count diversity complaint to recover damages for severe emotional injury suffered as a result of the deliberate refusal of Life of America Insurance Company (Insurer), of Chicago, to pay her the proceeds of Insurer's policy covering the life of her husband. The district court dismissed the suit. Plaintiff has appealed. We reverse.

★   ★   ★

Taking the allegations, properly pleaded in Counts II and III, as true, the following facts are stated: Defendant's life insurance policy covering plaintiff's husband issued September 22, 1967. Under the policy Insurer agreed to pay plaintiff $5,000 immediately upon due proof of death from "accidental causes." On December 17, 1967, insured was an accidental victim of a homicide. Plaintiff met all conditions of the policy and repeatedly demanded payment, but Insurer refused to pay. Decedent left plaintiff with several children, but no property of value. She had no money, none even for the funeral expenses. Denied payment by Insurer, she was required to borrow money to support her family, while her financial condition worsened. The family was required to live with, and accept charity from, relatives.

Further: . . . Insurer, knowing full well that plaintiff needed the proceeds of the policy to provide necessaries for her children, applied "economic coercion" in refusing to make payment on the policy, and in "inviting" plaintiff to "compromise" her claim by implying it (Insurer) had a valid defense to the claim.

The issue before us with respect to Counts II and III is whether plaintiff—beneficiary of her husband's life insurance policy—may on the foregoing "facts" recover damages for severe mental distress allegedly suffered as a result of Insurer's conduct. Illinois law controls our decision, and, in anticipation that the Illinois Supreme Court would hold as we do, we decide the issue in favor of plaintiff.

We have no doubt, in view of Knierim v. Izzo, 174 N.E.2d 157 (1961), that the Illinois Supreme Court would sustain plaintiff's complaint against Insurer's motion to dismiss.

In *Knierim*, plaintiff filed a wrongful death action alleging, inter alia, that defendant Izzo threatened her with the murder of her husband, carried out the threat, and thereby proximately caused her severe emotional distress. The trial court dismissed her complaint, but the Illinois Supreme Court reversed and held that plaintiff had stated a cause of action for an intentional causing of severe emotional distress by Izzo's "outrageous conduct."

The court recognized the "new tort" of intentional infliction of severe emotional distress, following similar recognition by an "increasing number of courts," and cited several state decisions. The court rejected reasons given by other courts not recognizing the "new tort." As to the reason that mental disturbance is incapable of financial measurement, the court pointed out that "pain and suffering" and "mental suffering" are elements of damage, respectively, in personal injury and malicious prosecution cases.

(*continued on next page*)

(continued)

ECKENRODE v. LIFE OF AMERICA INSURANCE CO.
470 F.2d 1 (7th Cir. 1972)

As to the reason that mental consequences are too evanescent for the law to deal with, the court noted that psychosomatic medicine had learned much in the past "thirty years" about the bodily effects of man's emotions, and that symptoms produced by "stronger emotions" are now visible to the professional eye. As to the reason that recognizing the "new tort" would lead to frivolous claims, the court observed that triers of fact from their own experiences would be able to draw a line between "slight hurts" and "outrageous conduct."

*   *   *

In *Knierim* the court, inter alia, relied upon State Rubbish Collectors Association v. Siliznoff, 38 Cal.2d 330, 240 P.2d 282 (1952), and Restatement, Torts § 46 (1948 Supp.). In *Siliznoff* the California Supreme Court, in an opinion by Justice Roger Traynor, recognized the "new tort" for the first time and held that Siliznoff could recover from the cross-defendant Rubbish Collectors Association for mental distress caused by the Association's severe threats to beat him up, destroy his truck and put him out of business unless Siliznoff offered to pay over certain proceeds to the Association. . . .

We think that the California court in *Fletcher*, set out correctly the elements of a prima facie case for the tort of "intentional infliction of severe emotional distress":

(1) Outrageous conduct by the defendant;
(2) The defendant's intention of causing, or reckless disregard of the probability of causing emotional distress;
(3) The plaintiff's suffering severe or extreme emotional distress; and
(4) Actual and proximate causation of the emotional distress by the defendant's outrageous conduct.

*   *   *

Here Insurer's alleged bad faith refusal to make payment on the policy, coupled with its deliberate use of "economic coercion" (*i.e.*, by delaying and refusing payment it increased plaintiff's financial distress thereby coercing her to compromise and settle) to force a settlement, clearly rises to the level of "outrageous conduct" to a person of "ordinary sensibilities."

Furthermore, it is common knowledge that one of the most frequent considerations in procuring life insurance is to ensure the continued economic and mental welfare of the beneficiaries upon the death of the insured. The very risks insured against presuppose that upon the death of the insured the beneficiary might be in difficult circumstances and thus particularly susceptible and vulnerable to high pressure tactics by an economically powerful entity. In the case before us Insurer's alleged high pressure methods (economic coercion) were aimed at the very thing insured against, and we think that the insurance company was on notice that plaintiff would be particularly vulnerable to mental distress by reason of her financial plight.

*   *   *

Reversed.

NEGLIGENCE

Physical harm need not be intentionally caused. A pedestrian knocked over by an automobile does not hurt less because the driver intended no wrong but was merely careless. The law imposes a **duty of care** on all of us in our everyday lives. Accidents caused by **negligence** are actionable.

Determining negligence is not always easy. If a driver runs a red light, we can say that she is negligent because a driver must always be careful to ascertain whether the light is red and be able to stop if it is. Suppose that the driver was carrying a badly injured person to a nearby hospital, and after slowing down at an intersection, proceeded through a red light blowing her horn, whereupon a driver to her right, seeing her, drove into the intersection anyway and crashed into her. Must one always stop at a red light? Is proof that the light was red always proof of negligence? Usually, but not always: negligence is an abstract concept that must always be applied to concrete and often widely varying sets of circumstances. Whether someone was or was not negligent is almost always a question of fact for a jury to decide. Rarely is it a legal question that a judge can settle.

Elements of Negligence

To hold the defendant liable for negligence, the plaintiff must show that the defendant breached a legal duty to be careful, measured by a particular standard of care, in conduct affecting the plaintiff and that the defendant's action caused an actual harm or injury to the plaintiff. The tort of negligence thus has four elements: (1) standard of care—how careful is the defendant required to be? (2) duty of care—is the defendant obligated to be careful toward the plaintiff? (3) causation; that is, connection between cause and injury—did the defendant's actions cause the plaintiff's injury? and (4) actual damage or loss—did the plaintiff suffer some sort of injury or loss for which compensation can be provided? Even if a plaintiff can prove each of these elements, the defendant may be able to show that the law excuses the conduct that is the basis for the tort claim. The following examines each of these elements.

Standard of Care   Not every unintentional act that causes injury is negligent. If you brake to a stop when you see a child dart out in front of your car, and the noise from your tires gives someone in a nearby house a heart attack, you have not acted negligently toward the person in the house. The purpose of the negligence standard is to protect others against the risk of injury that foreseeably would ensue from unreasonably dangerous conduct.

Given the infinite variety of human circumstances and conduct, no general statement of a reasonable standard of care is possible. Nevertheless, the law has tried to encapsulate it in the form of the famous standard of the **"reasonable person."** This fictitious person "of ordinary prudence" is the model that juries are instructed to compare in assessing whether defendants in cases before them have acted negligently. Analysis of this mythical personage has baffled several generations of commentators. How much knowledge must he have of events in the community, of technology, of cause and effect? With what physical attributes, courage, wisdom is this non-existent person supposedly endowed? If the defendant is a person with specialized knowledge, like a doctor or automobile designer, must the jury also treat the "reasonable person" as having this knowledge, even though the average person in the community will not? Answer: in most cases, yes.

Despite the many difficulties, the concept of the reasonable person is one on which most negligence cases ultimately turn. If a defendant has acted "unreasonably under the circumstances" and his conduct posed an unreasonable risk of injury, then he is liable for injury caused by his conduct. Perhaps in most instances, it is not difficult to divine what the reasonable man would do. The reasonable person stops for traffic lights and always drives at reasonable speeds, does not throw baseballs through windows, performs surgical operations according to the average standards of the medical profession, ensures that the floors of his grocery store are kept free of fluids that would cause a patron to slip and fall, takes proper precautions to avoid spillage of oil from his supertanker, and so on. But it may sometimes happen that the reasonable person would do something that no one at all in the real world has done because, in the view of courts, the circumstances make it unreasonable for anyone to fail to do so. This situation is presented in the following often-quoted opinion by the renowned jurist, Judge Learned Hand (1872–1961).

THE T. J. HOOPER
60 F.2d 737 (2d Cir. 1932)

L. HAND, CIRCUIT JUDGE.

The barges No. 17 and No. 30, belonging to the Northern Barge Company, had lifted cargoes of coal at Norfolk, Virginia, for New York in March, 1928. They were towed by two tugs of the petitioner, the "Montrose" and the "Hooper," and were lost off the Jersey Coast on March tenth, in an easterly gale. The cargo owners sued the barges under the contracts of carriage; the owner of the barges sued the tugs under the towing contract, both for its own loss and as bailee of the cargoes; the owner of the tug filed a petition to limit its liability. All the suits were joined and heard together, and the judge found that all the vessels were unseaworthy; the tugs, because they did not carry radio receiving sets by which they could have seasonably got warnings of a change in the weather which should have caused them to seek shelter in the Delaware Breakwater en route. He therefore entered an interlocutory decree holding each tug and barge jointly liable to each cargo owner, and each tug for half damages for the loss of its barge. The petitioner appealed, and the barge owner appealed and filed assignments of error.

Each tug had three ocean going coal barges in tow, the lost barge being at the end. The "Montrose," which had the No. 17, took an outside course; the "Hooper" with the No. 30, inside. The weather was fair without ominous symptoms, as the tows passed the Delaware Breakwater about midnight of March eighth, and the barges did not get into serious trouble until they were about opposite Atlantic City some sixty or seventy miles to the north. The wind began to freshen in the morning of the ninth and rose to a gale before noon; by afternoon the second barge of the Hooper's tow was out of hand and signalled the tug, which found that not only this barge needed help, but that the No. 30 was aleak. Both barges anchored and the crew of the No. 30 rode out the storm until the afternoon of the tenth, when she sank, her crew having been meanwhile taken off. The No. 17 sprang a leak about the same time; she too anchored at the Montrose's command and sank on the next morning after her crew also had been rescued. The cargoes and the tugs maintain that the barges were not fit for their service; the cargoes and the barges that the tugs should have gone into the Delaware Breakwater, and besides, did not handle their tows properly.

★   ★   ★

[The court summarized extensive evidence that the barges were unseaworthy and that had the tugs used radios to receive weather broadcasts, they would not have put to sea.] To be sure the barges would, as we have said, probably have withstood the gale, had they been well found; but a master is not justified in putting his tow to every test which she will survive, if she be fit. There is a zone in which proper caution will avoid putting her capacity to the proof; a coefficient of prudence that he should not disregard. Taking the situation as a whole, it seems to us that these masters would have taken undue chances, had they got the broadcasts.

They did not, because their private radio receiving sets, which were on board, were not in working order. These belonged to them personally, and were partly a toy, partly a part of the equipment, but neither furnished by the owner, nor supervised by it. It is not fair to say that there was a general custom among coastwise carriers so to equip their tugs. One line alone did it; as for the rest, they relied upon their crews, so far as they can be said to have relied at all. An adequate receiving set suitable for a coastwise tug can now be got at small cost and is reasonably reliable if kept up; obviously it is a source of great protection to their tows. Twice every day they can receive these predictions, based upon the widest possible information, available to every vessel within two or three hundred miles and more. Such a set is the ears of the tug to catch the spoken word, just as the master's binoculars are her eyes to see a storm signal ashore. Whatever may be said as to other vessels, tugs towing heavy coal laden barges, strung out for half a mile, have little power to manoeuvre, and do not, as this case proves, expose themselves to weather which would not turn back stauncher craft. They can have at hand protection against dangers of which they can learn in no other way.

Is it then a final answer that the business had not yet generally adopted receiving sets? There are, no doubt, cases where courts seem to make the general practice of the calling the standard of proper diligence. . . . Indeed in most cases reasonable prudence is in fact common prudence; but strictly it is never its measure; a whole calling may have unduly lagged in the adoption of new and available devices. It never may set its own tests, however persuasive be its usages. Courts must in the end say what is required; there are precautions so imperative that even their universal disregard will not excuse their omission. But here there was no custom at all as to receiving sets; some had them, some did not; the most that can be urged is that they had not yet become general. Certainly in such a case we need not pause; when some have thought a device necessary, at least we may say that they were right, and the others too slack. . . . We hold the tugs liable therefore because, had they been properly equipped, they would have got the Arlington reports. The injury was a direct consequence of this unseaworthiness.

Decree affirmed.

Duty of Care   The law does not impose on us a duty to care for every person. If the rule were otherwise, we would all, in this interdependent world, be our brothers' keepers, constantly unsure whether any action we took might subject us to liability for its effect on someone else. The law copes with this difficulty by limiting the number of people toward whom we owe a duty to be careful.

In general, the law imposes no obligation to act in a situation to which we are strangers. We may pass the drowning child without risking a lawsuit (see pp. 5, 6). But if we do act, then the law requires us to act carefully.

The law of negligence requires us to behave with due regard for the foreseeable consequences of our actions in order to avoid unreasonable risks of injury.

During the course of the twentieth century, the courts have constantly expanded the notion of **"foreseeability,"** so that today many more people are held to be within the zone of injury than was once the case. For example, it was once believed that a manufacturer or supplier owed a duty of care only to immediate purchasers, not to others who might use the product or to whom the product might be resold. This limitation was known as the rule of "privity." End users who were not immediate purchasers were said not to be "in privity" with the supplier or manufacturer. In 1916, Judge Benjamin N. Cardozo, then on the New York Court of Appeals, penned an opinion in a celebrated case that exploded the theory of privity, though it would take half a century before the last state—Mississippi in 1966—would fall in line.

**MACPHERSON v.
BUICK MOTOR CO.
217 N.Y. 382, 111 N.E.
1050 (1916)**

CARDOZO, J. The defendant is a manufacturer of automobiles. It sold an automobile to a retail dealer. The retail dealer resold to the plaintiff. While the plaintiff was in the car it suddenly collapsed. He was thrown out and injured. One of the wheels was made of defective wood, and its spokes crumbled into fragments. The wheel was not made by the defendant; it was bought from another manufacturer. There is evidence, however, that its defects could have been discovered by reasonable inspection, and that inspection was omitted. There is no claim that the defendant knew of the defect and willfully concealed it. . . . The charge is one, not of fraud, but of negligence. The question to be determined is whether the defendant owed a duty of care and vigilance to any one but the immediate purchaser.

The foundations of this branch of the law, at least in this state, were laid in Thomas v. Winchester, 6 N.Y. 397. A poison was falsely labeled. The sale was made to a druggist, who in turn sold to a customer. The customer recovered damages from the seller who affixed the label. "The defendant's negligence," it was said, "put human life in imminent danger." A poison, falsely labeled, is likely to injure any one who gets it. Because the danger is to be foreseen, there is a duty to avoid the injury.

★   ★   ★

We hold, then, that the principle of Thomas v. Winchester is not limited to poisons, explosives, and things of like nature, to things which in their normal operation are implements of destruction. If the nature of a thing is such that it is reasonably certain to place life and limb in peril when negligently made, it is then a thing of danger. Its nature gives warning of the consequences to be expected. If to the element of danger there is added knowledge that the thing will be used by persons other than the purchaser, and used without new tests, then, irrespective of contract, the manufacturer of this thing of danger is under a duty to make it carefully.

★   ★   ★

. . . In such circumstances, the presence of a known danger, attendant upon a known use, makes vigilance a duty. We have put aside the notion that the duty to safeguard life and limb, when the consequences of negligence may be foreseen, grows out of contract and nothing else. We have put the source of the obligation where it ought to be. We have put its source in the law.

From this survey of the decisions, there thus emerges a definition of the duty of a manufacturer which enables us to measure this defendant's liability. Beyond all question, the nature of an automobile gives warning of probable danger if its construction is defective. This automobile was designed to go 50 miles an hour. Unless its wheels were sound and strong, injury was almost certain. It was as much a thing of danger as a defective engine for a railroad. The defendant knew the danger. It knew also that the car would be used by persons other than the buyer. This was apparent from its size; there were seats for three persons. It was apparent also from the fact that the buyer was a dealer in cars, who bought to resell. The maker of this car supplied it for the use of purchasers from the dealer just as plainly as the contractor in Devlin v. Smith supplied the scaffold for use by the servants of the owner. The dealer was indeed the one person of whom it might be said with some approach to certainty that by him the car would not be used. Yet the defendant would have us say that he was the one person whom it was under a legal duty to protect. The law does not lead us to so inconsequent a conclusion. Precedents drawn from the days of travel by stagecoach do not fit the conditions of travel to-day. The principle that the danger must be imminent does not change, but the things subject to the principle do change. They are whatever the needs of life in a developing civilization require them to be.

* * *

We think the defendant was not absolved from a duty of inspection because it bought the wheels from a reputable manufacturer. It was not merely a dealer in automobiles. It was a manufacturer of automobiles. It was responsible for the finished product. It was not at liberty to put the finished product on the market without subjecting the component parts to ordinary and simple tests. Under the charge of the trial judge nothing more was required of it. The obligation to inspect must vary with the nature of the thing to be inspected. The more probable the danger the greater the need of caution.

* * *

The judgment should be affirmed, with costs.

Determining to whom a duty of care is owed is a vexing problem. Physicians, for example, are bound by principles of medical ethics to respect the confidences of their patients. Suppose a patient tells a psychiatrist that he intends to kill his girlfriend. Does the physician then have a higher legal duty to warn the prospective victim? The California Supreme Court has said yes. [Tarasoff v. Regents of University of California, 551 P.2d 334 (Cal. 1976)] Hotel security cases present another difficult duty-of-care issue. Is a hotel obligated to keep its guests free from physical attack by intruders? In the well-publicized case involving singer Connie Francis (see **Box 4-2**), the answer again was yes.

Causation   "For want of a nail, the kingdom was lost," as the old saying has it. Virtually any cause of an injury can be traced to some preceding cause. The problem for the law is to know when to draw the line between causes that are immediate and causes too remote for liability reasonably to be assigned to them. In tort theory, the legal phrase for the connection between the act complained of and the resulting injury is **proximate cause.** Like many legal phrases, proximate cause is virtually empty of content; it means nothing more than the boundary beyond which a person will not be held legally liable for the remote consequences of his actions. Nevertheless, proximate cause has been the subject of earnest analysis in probably thousands of cases. One generally useful rule is the *sine qua non* (sin A kwa non) or "but for" test: if an event would not have occurred but for the defendant's conduct, then the defendant is the cause of the event. This rule holds even though there are contributing causes. The person who is the substantial cause of harm cannot avoid liability by showing that other causes contributed to either the fact or the extent of the injury.

Suppose that the person who was injured was not one whom the reasonable person could have expected

LAW AND LIFE

Jury Awards Connie Francis $2.5 Million in Westbury Rape

By Max H. Seigel

[Today the notion of foreseeability has expanded to include more people within the zone of injury then was once the case. For example, a hotel may be obligated to keep its guests safe from dangerous intruders and might be liable if such measures are not enacted.—AUTHORS' NOTE]

A jury of six men awarded the singer Connie Francis $2.5 million yesterday as compensation for her rape in a Howard Johnson Motel in Westbury, L.I., on Nov. 8, 1974. Local court experts described it as one of the largest awards ever made in a rape case.

Miss Francis had contended during a month-long trial in Federal Court in Brooklyn that Howard Johnson Motor Lodges Inc. was responsible for the attack on her because it had failed to provide "a safe and secure room."

The jury also awarded Miss Francis's husband, Joseph Garzilli, $150,000 for the loss of his wife's services.

When the jury verdict was announced in court, Miss Francis, who was sitting beside her husband holding hands, burst into tears.

Letters Received

"What went through here," Miss Francis declared a few moments later, "was not easy. But if what we did here could save one girl, it was worth it."

Miss Francis said she had received letters from other women who had suffered assaults in motels all over the country.

DUTY TO PROTECT OTHERS?

Judge Thomas C. Platt, who presided over the trial, brought it more than normal publicity during its first week by barring both the press and public from the courtroom at the request of lawyers for both sides. But two of the reporters covering the trial sued, and the United States Court of Appeals for the Second Circuit overturned the judge's decision.

Miss Francis, who served as the major witness in her own behalf, testified for six days. She told how, when she was asleep in her motel room, at 4 A.M. she was assaulted by a man with a knife.

Following the attack, Miss Francis was hospitalized for four days. And she told the court, she relived the experience in recurring nightmares.

The intruder gained entry into her room, Miss Francis said, through a faulty sliding door. A police officer, who testified at the trial, said that when the sliding doors were in a locked position, they could be opened from the outside simply by a little jiggling. The officer also testified that in 1974 there had been four burglaries through sliding glass doors leading from a patio.

While not conceding that the locks had been faulty, the management of the motel had testified that it had ordered new and better locks, but that their arrival had been delayed by a United Parcel strike.

Miss Francis said yesterday that she had no plans to take up that part of her career that would place her before crowds or cause her to sleep in motels or hotels. She added that she might do some work making records.

She said: "I never received so much as a note from Mr. Howard B. Johnson saying 'We're sorry it happened.' After being shocked, I was very angry. Today, I am pleased."

Thomas S. Kirk, the lawyer representing the motel, moved to have the verdict set aside as excessive. Judge Platt said he would reserve decision pending the receipt of written briefs. He asked that these be submitted by July 12.

Judge Upholds Award by Jury To Connie Francis in L.I. Rape

A Federal judge in Brooklyn upheld yesterday a jury award of $2.5 million to Connie Francis, the singer, to compensate for her rape in a Long Island motel on Nov. 8, 1974.

But the judge, Thomas C. Platt, ruled that the $150,000 awarded Joseph Garzilli, Miss Francis's husband, was excessive and that his compensation should be cut to $25,000.

The damages were awarded the singer and her husband after Miss Francis was raped in Howard Johnson's Motel Lodge in Westbury by an intruder who was said to have easily gained access to her room through an improperly locked sliding glass door.

Following the assault, the 37-year-old singer testified, she was afraid to resume her lucrative career, which had brought her earnings of $325,000 in 1969 and $287,000 in 1970.

Thomas Kirk, lawyer for Howard Johnson's Motor Lodge, said he would appeal the judge's ruling.

Connie Francis, the entertainer, who last July was awarded a $2.5 million jury verdict as compensation after she was raped in a Howard Johnson motel in Westbury, L.I. on Nov. 8, 1974, has settled out of court with

BOX 4-2

Box 4-2, *continued*

the motel chain for $1,475,000. Richard Frank, an attorney for Miss Francis, said that the verdict had been on appeal to the Federal Court of Appeals and that he and Miss Francis

had been concerned that it would be set aside. The settlement, believed to be one of the highest ever made in a rape case, is considered "compensation for an injury" under the law—not income—and is therefore not sub-

ject to taxation. Miss Francis's original suit charged that the motel had failed to provide her with a safe and secure room.

Source: *New York Times,* July 2, 1976; September 21, 1976; February 23, 1977

to be harmed. Then, even though the defendant in some sense caused the injury, the law may nevertheless absolve him of legal responsibility. Such a situation was presented in one of the most famous American tort cases, which was, like the *MacPherson* case, also decided by Judge Cardozo. Although Judge Cardozo

persuaded four of his seven brethren to side with his position, the closeness of the case demonstrates the difficulty that unforeseeable consequences and unforeseeable plaintiffs present. The usual solution is for judges to keep hands off and put the matter in the laps of juries.

PALSGRAF v. LONG ISLAND R.R.
248 N.Y. 339, 162 N.E. 99 (1928)

CARDOZO, C. J. Plaintiff was standing on a platform of defendant's railroad after buying a ticket to go to Rockaway Beach. A train stopped at the station, bound for another place. Two men ran forward to catch it. One of the men reached the platform of the car without mishap, though the train was already moving. The other man, carrying a package, jumped aboard the car, but seemed unsteady as if about to fall. A guard on the car, who had held the door open, reached forward to help him in, and another guard on the platform pushed him from behind. In this act, the package was dislodged, and fell upon the rails. It was a package of small size, about fifteen inches long, and was covered by a newspaper. In fact it contained fireworks, but there was nothing in its appearance to give notice of its contents. The fireworks when they fell exploded. The shock of the explosion threw down some scales at the other end of the platform many feet away. The scales struck the plaintiff, causing injuries for which she sues.

The conduct of the defendant's guard, if a wrong in its relation to the holder of the package, was not a wrong in its relation to the plaintiff, standing far away. Relatively to her it was not negligence at all. Nothing in the situation gave notice that the falling package had in it the potency of peril to persons thus removed. Negligence is not actionable unless it involves the invasion of a legally protected interest, the violation of a right. "Proof of negligence in the air, so to speak, will not do." . . . If no hazard was apparent to the eye of ordinary vigilance, an act innocent and harmless, at least to outward seeming, with reference to her, did not take to itself the quality of a tort because it happened to be a wrong, though apparently not one involving the risk of bodily insecurity, with reference to someone else. . . . The plaintiff sues in her own right for a wrong personal to her, and not as the vicarious beneficiary of a breach of duty to another.

A different conclusion will involve us, and swiftly too, in a maze of

(continued on next page)

(continued)

PALSGRAF v. LONG ISLAND R.R.
248 N.Y. 339, 162 N.E. 99 (1928)

contradictions. A guard stumbles over a package which has been left upon a platform. It seems to be a bundle of newspapers. It turns out to be a can of dynamite. To the eye of ordinary vigilance, the bundle is abandoned waste, which may be kicked or trod on with impunity. Is a passenger at the other end of the platform protected by the law against the unsuspected hazard concealed beneath the waste? If not, is the result to be any different, so far as the distant passenger is concerned, when the guard stumbles over a valise which a truckman or a porter had left upon the walk? . . . The orbit of the danger as disclosed to the eye of reasonable vigilance would be the orbit of the duty. One who jostles one's neighbor in a crowd does not invade the rights of others standing at the outer fringe when the unintended contact casts a bomb upon the ground. The wrongdoer as to them is the man who carries the bomb, not the one who explodes it without suspicion of the danger. Life will have to be made over, and human nature transformed, before prevision so extravagant can be accepted as the norm of conduct, the customary standard to which behavior must conform.

The argument for the plaintiff is built upon the shifting meanings of such words as "wrong" and "wrongful," and shares their instability. What the plaintiff must show is "a wrong" to herself; i.e., a violation of her own right, and not merely a wrong to someone else, nor conduct "wrongful" because unsocial, but not "a wrong" to any one. We are told that one who drives at reckless speed through a crowded city street is guilty of a negligent act and therefore of a wrongful one, irrespective of the consequences. Negligent the act is, and wrongful in the sense that it is unsocial, but wrongful and unsocial in relation to other travelers, only because the eye of vigilance perceives the risk of damage. If the same act were to be committed on a speedway or a race course, it would lose its wrongful quality. The risk reasonably to be perceived defines the duty to be obeyed, and risk imports relation; it is risk to another or to others within the range of apprehension. This does not mean, of course, that one who launches a destructive force is always relieved of liability, if the force, though known to be destructive, pursues an unexpected path. . . . Some acts, such as shooting are so imminently dangerous to any one who may come within reach of the missile however unexpectedly, as to impose a duty of prevision not far from that of an insurer. Even to-day, and much oftener in earlier stages of the law, one acts sometimes at one's peril. . . . These cases aside, wrong is defined in terms of the natural or probable, at least when unintentional. . . .

Negligence, like risk, is thus a term of relation. Negligence in the abstract, apart from things related, is surely not a tort, if indeed it is understandable at all. . . . One who seeks redress at law does not make out a cause of action by showing without more that there has been damage to his person. If the harm was not willful, he must show that the act as to him had possibilities of danger so many and apparent as to entitle him to be protected against the doing of it though the harm was unintended.

★   ★   ★

The judgment of the Appellate Division and that of the Trial Term should be reversed, and the complaint dismissed, with costs in all courts.

Damages   For a plaintiff to win a tort case, he must allege and prove that he was injured. The fear that he might be injured in the future is not a sufficient basis for a suit. This rule has proved troublesome in medical malpractice and industrial disease cases. A doctor's negligent act or a company's negligent exposure of a worker to some form of contamination might not become manifest in the body for years. In the meantime, the tort statute of limitations might have run out, barring the victim from suing at all. An increasing number of courts have eased the plaintiff's predicament by ruling that the statute of limitations does not begin to run until the victim discovers that he has been injured or contracted a disease.

The law allows an exception to the general rule that damages must be shown when the plaintiff stands in danger of immediate injury from a hazardous activity. If you discover your neighbor experimenting with explosives in his basement, you could bring suit to enjoin him from further experimentation, even though he has not yet blown up his house—and yours.

Problems of Proof

The plaintiff in a tort suit, as in any other, has the burden of proving his allegations. He must show that the defendant took the actions complained of as negligent, demonstrate the circumstances that make the actions negligent, and prove the occurrence and extent of injury. Factual issues are for the jury to resolve. Since it is frequently difficult to make out the requisite proof, the law allows certain presumptions and rules of evidence that ease the plaintiff's task, on the ground that without them substantial injustice would be done.

One important rule goes by the Latin phrase **res ipsa loquitur** (race ipsuh LOW kwi ter), meaning "the thing speaks for itself." The best evidence is always the most direct evidence: an eyewitness account of the acts in question. But eyewitnesses are often unavailable, and in any event they frequently cannot testify directly to the reasonableness of someone's conduct, which inevitably can only be inferred from the circumstances. In many cases, therefore, **circumstantial evidence** (evidence that is indirect) will be the only evidence or will constitute the bulk of the evidence. Circumstantial evidence can often be quite telling: though no one saw anyone leave the building, muddy footprints tracing a path along the sidewalk

are fairly conclusive. *Res ipsa loquitur* is a rule of circumstantial evidence that permits the jury to draw an inference of negligence. A common statement of the rule is the following:

> There must be reasonable evidence of negligence; but where the thing is shown to be under the management of the defendant or his servants, and the accident is such as in the ordinary course of things does not happen if those who have the management use proper care, it affords reasonable evidence, in the absence of explanation by the defendants, that the accident arose from want of care. [Scott v. London & St. Katherine Docks Co., 3 H. & C. 596, 159 Eng.Rep. 665 (Q.B. 1865).]

If a barrel of flour rolls out of a factory window and hits someone, or a soda bottle explodes, or an airplane crashes, courts in every state permit juries to conclude, in the absence of contrary explanations by the defendants, that there was negligence. The plaintiff is not put to the impossible task of explaining precisely how the accident occurred. A defendant can always offer evidence that he acted reasonably—for example, that the flour barrel was securely fastened and that a bolt of lightning, for which he was not responsible, broke its bands, causing it to roll out the window. But testimony by the factory employees that they secured the barrel, in the absence of any further explanation, will not usually serve to rebut the inference.

Excuses

That the defendant was negligent does not conclude the inquiry or automatically entitle the plaintiff to a judgment. Tort law provides the defendant with several excuses, some of which are discussed briefly in this section.

Contributory and Comparative Negligence   Under an old common law rule, it was a complete defense to show that the plaintiff in a negligence suit was himself negligent. Even if the plaintiff was only mildly negligent, most of the fault being chargeable to the defendant, the court would dismiss the suit if the plaintiff's conduct contributed to his injury. In some states today, this rule of **contributory negligence** continues to hold. Although referred to as negligence, the rule encompasses a narrower form than that with which the defendant is charged, because the plaintiff's only error in such cases is in being less careful of himself than he might have been, whereas the defendant is charged with conduct careless toward others. This rule was so manifestly unjust in many cases that most states, either by statute or judicial decision, have substituted for it the rule of **comparative negligence.** Under the rule of comparative negligence, damages are apportioned according to defendant's degree of culpability. If the plaintiff has sustained a $10,000 injury and is 20 percent responsible, the defendant will be liable for $8,000 in damages.

Assumption of Risk   Assumption of risk is to defendants what *res ipsa loquitur* is to plaintiffs—a doctrine making it easier to win a case given the difficulties of proving states of mind and facts peculiarly within the knowledge of one person. Risk of injury pervades the modern world, and plaintiffs should not win a lawsuit simply because they took a risk and lost. The law provides, therefore, that when a person knowingly takes a risk he must suffer the consequences.

The **assumption of risk** doctrine comes up in three ways. The plaintiff may have formally agreed with the defendant before entering a risky situation that he will relieve the defendant of liability should injury occur. ("You can borrow my car if you agree not to sue me if the brakes fail; they're worn and I haven't had a chance to replace them.") Or the plaintiff may have entered into a relationship with the defendant knowing that the defendant is not in a position to protect him from known risks (the fan who is hit by a line drive in a ball park). Or the plaintiff may act in the face of a risky situation known in advance to have been created by the defendant's negligence (failure to leave an automobile while there was an opportunity to do so, when the driver is known to be drunk).

The difficulty in many cases is to determine the dividing line between subjectivity and objectivity. If the plaintiff had no actual knowledge of the risk, he cannot be held to have assumed it. On the other hand, it is easy to claim that you did not appreciate the danger, and the courts will apply an objective standard of community knowledge (a "but you should have known" test) in many situations. When the plaintiff has no real alternative, however, assumption of risk fails as a defense (for example, a landlord who negli-

gently fails to light the exit to the street cannot claim that his tenants assumed the risk of using it).

At the turn of the century, courts applied assumption of risk in industrial cases to bar relief to workers injured on the job. They were said to assume the risk of dangerous conditions or equipment. This rule has been abolished by workers' compensation statutes in most states.

Sovereign Immunity   It is a peculiarity of American common law that the government is held to be immune from suit on the ground that the "sovereign," the source of law, cannot be sued without its consent. If this theory made metaphorical sense in England, which for centuries suffered a monarch who did make law, it never made sense in the United States. Nevertheless, the doctrine was imported. As we saw in Chapter 1, many states have abolished sovereign immunity either by statute or by judicial decision. In the Federal Tort Claims Act, Congress has waived sovereign immunity for many classes of torts committed by federal agents.

Act of God   Technically, the rule that one is not responsible for an **"act of God,"** or *force majeure* (fawrs ma ZHUR), as it is sometimes called, is not an excuse but a defense premised on a lack of causation. If a force of nature caused the harm, then the defendant was not negligent in the first place. A marina, obligated to look after boats moored at its dock, is not liable if a sudden and fierce storm against which no precaution was possible destroys someone's vessel. However, if it is foreseeable that harm will flow from a negligent condition triggered by a natural event, then there is liability. For example, a work crew failed to remove residue explosive gas from an oil barge. Lightning hit the barge, exploded the gas, and injured several workers. The plaintiff recovered damages against the company because the negligence consisted in the failure to guard against any one of a number of chance occurrences that could ignite the gas. [Johnson v. Kosmos Portland Cement Co., 64 F.2d 193 (6th Cir. 1933)]

Imputed Negligence

Liability for negligent acts does not always end with the one who was negligent. Under certain

For the Courts, the Question of Liability

By William Glaberson

[Liability for negligence may extend beyond the one who is negligent. As the following article reports, sometimes courts have placed liability on restaurant or nightclub owners for harm done by someone else to the patrons of the owner's establishment.—AUTHORS' NOTE]

Families of those killed in the Bronx social club fire on Sunday intend to file hundreds of millions of dollars in civil lawsuits against the property owner and the landlord of the building where 87 people died, lawyers said yesterday.

Legal experts said the lawsuits would raise questions that have not been resolved by the courts about when someone can be held liable for deaths that result from someone else's criminal act. The man who the police say admitted setting the fire, Julio Gonzalez, is being held in the psychiatric prison ward at Bellevue Hospital on 87 counts of murder.

The lawsuits will ask the courts to decide how much responsibility, if any, can be assigned to the city, the property owner, the company that held a 30-year lease on the building and the club's owner, who was killed in the fire.

The legal experts said the courts would have to sort through what are likely to be complex questions about how much the property owner and landlord knew about the hazards at the Happy Land Social Club and what they might have been able to do to prevent the tragedy.

WHOM TO BLAME: OWNER OR ARSONIST? POISONER OR MANUFACTURER?

Dollar Value of a Life

Lawyers said they might have an easier case against the estate of the club owner, Elias Colon. But they said their energies were likely to be focused elsewhere because Mr. Colon's estate is not expected to be able to pay any substantial damage claims.

In preparing their cases, the lawyers, negligence experts brought into the case by lawyers who have contacts with the families, said they must weigh such issues as the dollar value the court could be expected to assign for a victim's life and what the legal damages might be for suffering death in a horrifying flash of fire.

"It's a very grisly accounting that takes place here," said Aaron J. Broder, a lawyer who said he was preparing three lawsuits.

Lawyers at five firms said they had been asked to work on groups of lawsuits. Robert G. Sullivan, a partner in the New York law firm of Sullivan & Liapakis, said he expected that the lawsuits would ask for about $10 million in damages for each victim. The lawyers said they expected survivors of most of the victims to file lawsuits.

Mr. Sullivan said his lawsuits would name Alex DiLorenzo 3d, the real-estate developer who owns the block of stores on Southern Boulevard at East Tremont Avenue where the social club stands, and Little Peach Realty, the concern that has a 30-year-lease on the property. Mr. Sullivan said he would also name Little Peach's

two principals, Jay Weiss and Morris Jaffe.

Telephone calls to Mr. DiLorenzo's office were not returned yesterday. Milton Thurm, a lawyer who said he had been retained to represent Little Peach if it was sued, said he would not comment.

Stanley M. Chesley, a Cincinnati lawyer who has handled a series of disaster cases, said he was considering making claims against the city, whose inspectors cited the illegal social club and ordered it vacated in November 1988 because it was unsafe.

But much of the attention in law offices yesterday was on the real estate transactions in which the lease on the property passed from Mr. DiLorenzo to Mr. Jaffe and Mr. Weiss, whose wife is the actress Kathleen Turner.

The legal experts said that with each step away from the immediate cause of the victims' deaths—the arson—the case would become more difficult for the plaintiffs. One critical legal question will be whether the property owner or the landlord knew or had reason to know about the dangers to the public if there were a fire. If they did know, a judge would ask a jury to determine whether a reasonable person would have done anything to prevent the risks.

Lawyers said they were investigating reports that a violations notice had been sent from the City Buildings Department to Mr. DiLorenzo, and they said they would try to find out if Mr. DiLorenzo had followed common real estate practice and informed Little Peach about problems at the building.

Little Peach's lawyers have said they never received formal notice of violations but would not say whether the concern knew about the complaints.

(continued on next page)

BOX 4-3

Box 4-3, *continued*

Lawyers for the victims' families would have to argue that the defendants were liable even though no one can reasonably protect against a criminal act. Some courts have held that a crime like arson is a "supervening cause" of a victim's injury. Therefore, those courts have held, defendants cannot be forced to pay damages even if they were negligent.

In New York in recent years, courts have come down on both sides of that question. Interpreting New York Law in 1988, Judge Gerard L. Goettel of Federal District Court dismissed a case brought by the survivors of a woman who died when she took Tylenol that had been tampered with. Judge Goettel said the grocery store where she bought the pain reliever and Johnson & Johnson, the drug's maker, could not be sued because they did not have a duty to protect the buyer from the illegal act of a third person.

Building Owner Found Liable

But last week, the Appellate Division of State Supreme Court said a man who was blinded by a shotgun blast fired from a Harlem building could sue the building owner. The appeals court said the trial court had to consider claims that the landlord "tolerated" drug trafficking in the building.

If the courts wade through all the issues in what would likely be years of litigation, they would have to turn finally to the difficult issues of computing damages. Negligence suits are intended mainly to compensate survivors for the financial loss involved in a "wrongful death."

That means the courts must assess factors like a person's training and education and the value of household chores. When measuring the dead person's "pain and suffering," the amount of time that he or she suffered must be carefully figured.

One thing that is not counted by the courts, Mr. Broder, the negligence lawyer, said, is the pain of the people who are left behind. "The real loss," he said, "is not evaluated at all."

Source: The *New York Times* March 29, 1990

circumstances, the liability is imputed to others. For example, an employer is responsible for the negligence of his employees if they were acting in the scope of employment. This rule of **vicarious liability** is often called *respondeat superior* (res pon dee ut su peer ee are), meaning that the higher authority must respond to claims brought against one of its agents. *Respondeat superior* is not limited to the employment relationship but extends to a number of other agency relationships as well.

Sometimes the courts, extending the common law, have placed liability on owners or manufacturers for harms caused by third parties to tenants, guests, or consumers. One particularly difficult dilemma arises from acts of arson or other crimes: as **Box 4-3** discusses, may the victims of an arsonist or a poisoner seek recovery from the building owner or a drug manufacturer?

Legislatures in many states have enacted laws that make people vicariously liable for acts of certain people with whom they have a relationship, though not necessarily one of agency. It is common, for example, for the owner of an automobile to be liable for the negligence of one to whom the owner lends the car. So-called "dram shop" statutes place liability on bar and tavern owners and others who serve too much alcohol to one who in an intoxicated state later causes injury to others. In these situations, although the injurious act of the drinker stemmed from negligence, the one whom the law holds vicariously liable (the bartender) is not himself necessarily negligent—the law is holding him *strictly liable*, and to this concept we now turn.

STRICT LIABILITY

To this point we have considered principles of liability that in some sense depend upon the "fault" of the tortfeasor. This fault is not synonymous with moral blame. Aside from acts intended to harm, the fault lies in a failure to live up to a standard of reasonableness or due care. But this is not the only basis for tort liability. Innocent mistakes can be a sufficient basis. One who unknowingly trespasses on another's property, for example, is liable for the damage that he does, even if he has a reasonable belief that the land is his. And it has long been held that one who engages in "ultrahazardous" (or sometimes just "hazardous") activities is liable for damage that he causes, even though he has taken every possible precaution to avoid harm to someone else. Likewise, the owner of animals that escape from their homes and do mischief elsewhere is often liable, even if the reason for their escape was beyond the power of the owner to stop (for example, a fire started by lightning that burns open a barn door). In such cases, the courts invoke the principle of **strict liability** or, as it is sometimes called, liability without fault. The reason for the **rule** is explained in the following case.

SPANO v. PERINI CORP.
25 N.Y.2d 11, 250 N.E.2d 31 (1969)

CHIEF JUDGE FULD. The principal question posed on this appeal is whether a person who has sustained property damage caused by blasting on nearby property can maintain an action for damages without a showing that the blaster was negligent. Since 1893, it has been the law of this State that proof of negligence was required unless the blast was accompanied by an actual physical invasion of the damaged property—for example, by rocks or other material being cast upon the premises. We are now asked to reconsider that rule.

The plaintiff Spano is the owner of a garage in Brooklyn which was wrecked by a blast occurring on November 27, 1962. There was then in that garage, for repairs, an automobile owned by the plaintiff Davis which he also claims was damaged by the blasting. Each of the plaintiffs brought suit against the two defendants who, as joint venturers, were engaged in constructing a tunnel in the vicinity pursuant to a contract with the City of New York. The two cases were tried together, without a jury, in the Civil Court of the City of New York, New York County, and judgments were rendered in favor of the plaintiffs. The judgments were reversed by the Appellate Term and the Appellate Division affirmed that order, granting leave to appeal to this court.

It is undisputed that, on the day in question (November 27, 1962), the defendants had set off a total of 194 sticks of dynamite at a construction site which was only 125 feet away from the damaged premises. Although both plaintiffs alleged negligence in their complaints, no attempt was made to show that the defendants had failed to exercise reasonable care or to take necessary precautions when they were blasting. Instead, they chose to rely, upon the trial, solely on the principle of absolute liability either on a tort theory or on the basis of their being third-party beneficiaries of the defendants' contract with the city. At the close of the plaintiff Spano's case, when defendants' attorney moved to dismiss the action on the ground, among others, that no negligence had been proved, the trial judge expressed the view that the defendants could be held liable even though they were not shown to have been careless. The case then proceeded, with evidence being introduced solely on the question of damages and proximate cause. Following the trial, the court awarded damages of some $4,400 to Spano and of $329 to Davis.

On appeal, a divided Appellate Term reversed that judgment, declaring that it deemed itself concluded by the established rule in this State requiring proof of negligence. . . .

The Appellate Division affirmed; it called attention to a decision in the Third Department in which the court observed that "[i]f [the established

(continued on next page)

(*continued*)

SPANO v. PERINI CORP.
25 N.Y.2d 11, 250 N.E.2d 31 (1969)

rule] is to be overruled, 'the announcement thereof should come from the authoritative source and not in the form of interpretation or prediction by an intermediate appellate court.' "

In our view, the time has come for this court to make that "announcement" and declare that one who engages in blasting must assume responsibility, and be liable without fault, for any injury he causes to neighboring property.

The concept of absolute liability in blasting cases is hardly a novel one. The overwhelming majority of American jurisdictions have adopted such a rule. . . .

We need not rely solely, however, upon out-of-state decisions in order to attain our result. Not only has the rationale of the [established rule] been overwhelmingly rejected elsewhere but it appears to be fundamentally inconsistent with earlier cases in our own court which had held . . . that a party was absolutely liable for damages to neighboring property caused by explosions.

★   ★   ★

. . . [I]t is clear that the court, in the earlier cases, was not concerned with the particular manner by which the damage was caused but by the simple fact that any explosion in a built-up area was likely to cause damage.

★   ★   ★

Such reasoning should, we venture, have led to the conclusion that the *intentional* setting off of explosives—that is, blasting—in an area in which it was likely to cause harm to neighboring property similarly results in absolute liability. However, the court [later] rejected such an extension of the rule for the reason that "[t]o exclude the defendant from blasting to adapt its lot to the contemplated uses, at the instance of the plaintiff, would not be a compromise between conflicting rights, but an extinguishment of the right of the one for the benefit of the other." The court expanded on this by stating, "This sacrifice, we think, the law does not exact. Public policy is promoted by the building up of towns and cities and the improvement of property. Any unnecessary restraint on freedom of action of a property owner hinders this."

This rationale cannot withstand analysis. . . . The question, in other words, was not *whether* it was lawful or proper to engage in blasting but *who* should bear the cost of any resulting damage—the person who engaged in the dangerous activity or the innocent neighbor injured thereby. Viewed in such a light, it clearly appears that [the 1893 case] was wrongly decided and should be forthrightly overruled.

★   ★   ★

The order appealed from should be reversed, with costs, and the matter remitted to the Appellate Division for further proceedings in accordance with this opinion.

For the student of business law, the principle of strict liability has had the greatest impact in the area of product liability—that is, the liability of manufacturers and suppliers for harm caused by defective products. The law of product liability has been changing rapidly. As recently as the early 1960s, liability was based largely on negligence. Today in most states strict liability has made deep inroads. Because of its signal importance to business, we will explore it separately in some detail (Chapter 19).

Note on Absolute Liability

Some courts and commentators use the terms "strict liability" and "absolute liability" interchangeably. This is unfortunate, because there is a distinction that the terms can usefully be made to serve. In most cases of strict liability, as the term has been used here, the defendant can be seen to have some responsibility for the harm that occurred, at least in the sense that something originally under his control went awry. By contrast, there are many kinds of injury that are truly accidental, or result from the plaintiff's negligence, or are acts of God. For example, some people are allergic to pure aspirin. To hold the manufacturer liable for the pains and costs of those who are allergic would be to impose a standard of *absolute* liability. Absolute liability is rare. Two significant examples are no-fault automobile insurance (Chapter 36) and the workers' compensation system (Chapter 37). In the latter, an employer typically pays into a compensation fund (or buys insurance) in order to insure his workers against injury on the job. Any work-related injury entitles the employee to compensation benefits from the fund. In return for this more or less automatic compensation (payments are made after papers are submitted to an administrative board; lawsuits need not be filed), workers are barred from suing their employers, even if the accident happened because of the employer's negligence.

INJURY TO ECONOMIC INTERESTS

Tort law is not confined to tangible physical harm to person or property. It also governs interference with and injury to various intangible interests. In this section, and the two that follow, we consider such torts.

Misrepresentation

Economic loss arising out of fraudulent or deceitful actions by the defendant is actionable. Because representations, including misrepresentations, are usually given during the course of contract negotiations between the parties, misrepresentation will be discussed in detail in the Contracts unit.

Unfair Competition

The freedom to compete is the touchstone of the American economic system. Although a myriad of public regulations, discussed at some length in this book, restrict or prohibit some types of economic decisions—for example, use of processes that pollute, statements made or not made in selling securities—ordinarily one business has no private right to prevent another from coming into its territory and competing head on. Centuries ago in England, it was a tort for a retailer to "steal" another retailer's customers; today in America, competition is open and wide.

Despite this general rule, not every form of competition is legally acceptable. In particular, a cluster of related acts known as "unfair competition" have led to a sizable body of tort law governing the use of deception in promoting one's products. The two main forms are **passing off** and **misappropriation.**

Passing Off The tort of passing off, sometimes known as "palming off," occurs when the seller falsely represents that his product is that of someone else. In a modern economy, passing off is typically accomplished by imitating someone else's trademark (p. 701), though it is sufficient for the tort to occur if a customer asks for goods supplied by one manufacturer and the seller secretly substitutes the goods of another, even if the goods are identical (for example, if you ask for Brand X aspirin and are given Brand Y aspirin).

The central feature of passing off is confusion of the customer. As long as the customer is not misled about the origin of a product, then it cannot be said to have been passed off (although the seller may have separately violated the trademark laws). Much of the common law of unfair competition has been absorbed by federal trademark law (Chapter 31), and so the rules governing passing off and the use of similar product names and marks has taken on a national character, at least for goods that circulate across state lines.

Misappropriation   Related to passing off, misappropriation is the imitation of an idea, design, or product, without claiming that it in fact comes from someone else. For example, suppose a baker achieved great success with a chocolate-chip cookie imaginatively shaped like a plate of spaghetti. May another baker, using her own name, sell a similar cookie? Does an actor who has a famous gesture have a right to prevent another actor from using the same gesture on camera? Does a publisher who produces a list of baseball pitchers, together with their statistics, arranged in a certain way, have a case against another publisher who appropriates the same arrangement? The answers are not easy to give, because the common law of misappropriation runs into the federal law governing copyrights and patents (Chapter 31). Because federal law preempts state law in the event of a conflict, the Supreme Court has held that when a particular product design is not copyrighted or patented, another manufacturer is free to imitate it, as long as the second user does not try to pass it off as her own. [Sears, Roebuck & Co. v. Stiffel Co., 376 U.S. 225 (1964)] Modern decisions have tended to weaken the older common law of misappropriation, leaving wide (though not unfettered) scope to the use and circulation of ideas, designs, and styles that are not otherwise protected.

Interference with Contractual Relations

Since a contract confers benefits on the parties, it is looked upon as a property right. One who interferes with that right by inducing one of the parties to break the contract has committed a tort.

By and large, the courts insist that the defendant must have intended to interfere with the contract. This tort is not based on strict liability or even, generally, on negligence. Thus, a manufacturer who contracts with a shipper to carry her goods cannot maintain a suit against a third party who negligently sinks the barge on which the goods were to be carried.

Not every act that results in a breach of contract is necessarily tortious. The courts have concluded that to protect your own legitimate interests you might have to take actions that lead to a breach of someone else's contract—for example, that of a fellow employee. Thus an employee might point out to her corporate employer the dangers in continuing the employ of another worker who is frequently drunk on the job. But the courts are leery of such justifications when uttered by competitors. Suppose someone you wish to hire is under contract to a competitor. May you hire her away? Since most employment contracts are terminable "at will," the courts generally hold that inducing someone to leave her employment for that of a competitor is not a tort. The original employer has only an expectancy that his employee will continue to work for him. Suppose the employee is also under contract not to reveal her employer's trade secrets. As a competitor, you offer to pay the employee for those secrets. You would then be liable for inducing the employee to breach her contract.

Interfering with contractual relations is not the only type of economic harm for which the law of torts provides a remedy. Numerous other acts that interfere with economic advantage can lead to damage awards. These include disparaging the quality of a plaintiff's goods or title to property, intentionally lying about a plaintiff (stating, for example, that she has gone out of business when in fact she has not), and maliciously exhorting customers to cease patronage of a competitor.

Unjustifiable Litigation

Lawsuits, whether civil or criminal, are easy to initiate, and they can be used by the unscrupulous to cause considerable annoyance, financial cost, and even loss of freedom. **Malicious prosecution** is the tort of causing someone to be prosecuted for a criminal act, knowing that there was no probable cause to believe that the plaintiff committed the crime. The plaintiff must show that the defendant acted with malice or with some purpose other than bringing the guilty to justice. A mere complaint to the authorities is insufficient to establish the tort, but any official proceeding will support the claim—for example, a warrant for the plaintiff's arrest. The criminal proceeding must terminate in the plaintiff's favor in order for his suit to be sustained.

A majority of American courts, though by no means all, permit a suit for wrongful civil proceedings.

Civil litigation is usually costly and burdensome, and one who forces another to defend himself against baseless accusations should not be permitted to saddle the one he sues with the costs of defense. However, because, as a matter of public policy, litigation is favored as the means by which legal rights can be vindicated—indeed, the Supreme Court has even ruled that individuals have a constitutional right to litigate—the plaintiff must meet a heavy burden in proving his case. The mere dismissal of the original lawsuit against the plaintiff is not sufficient proof that the suit was unwarranted. The plaintiff in a suit for wrongful civil proceedings must show that the defendant (who was the plaintiff in the original suit) filed the action for an improper purpose and had no reasonable belief that his cause was legally or factually well grounded.

LIBEL AND SLANDER

Defamation is injury to a person's good name or reputation. In general, if the harm is done through the spoken word—one person to another, by telephone, by radio or television—it is called **slander**. If the defamatory statement is published in written form, it is called **libel**.

Elements

The *Restatement (Second) of Torts* defines a defamatory communication as one that "so tends to harm the reputation of another as to lower him in the estimation of the community or to deter third persons from associating or dealing with him" (1976, Section 559).

A statement is not defamatory unless it is false. Truth is an absolute defense to a charge of libel or slander. Moreover, the statement must be "published"—that is, communicated to a third person. You cannot be libeled by one who sends you a letter full of false accusations and scurrilous statements about you, unless a third person opens it first (your secretary, perhaps). Any living person is capable of being defamed, but the dead are not. Corporations, partnerships, and other forms of associations can also be defamed, if the statements tend to injure their ability to do business or to garner contributions.

The statement must have reference to a particular person, but he need not be identified by name. A statement that "the company president is a crook" is defamatory, as is a statement that "the major network weathermen are imposters." The company president and the network weathermen could show that the words were aimed at them. But statements about large groups will not support an action for defamation (for example, "all doctors are butchers" is not defamatory of any particular doctor).

The law of defamation is largely built on strict liability. That a person did not intend to defame is ordinarily no excuse; a typographical error that converts a true statement into a false one in a newspaper, magazine, or corporate brochure can be sufficient to make out a case of libel. Even the exercise of due care is usually no excuse if the statement is in fact communicated. Repeating a libel is itself a libel; a libel cannot be justified by showing that you were quoting someone else.

Though a plaintiff may be able to prove that a statement was defamatory, he is not necessarily entitled to an award of damages. That is because the law contains a number of privileges that excuse the defamation.

Common Law Privileges

Absolute Privilege   Statements made during the course of judicial proceedings are absolutely privileged, meaning that they cannot serve as the basis for a defamation suit. Accurate accounts of judicial or other proceedings are absolutely privileged; a newspaper, for example, may pass on the slanderous utterings of a judge in court. "Judicial" is broadly construed to include most proceedings of administrative bodies of the government. The Constitution exempts members of Congress from suits for libel or slander for any statements made in connection with legislative business. The courts have constructed a similar privilege for many executive branch officials.

Qualified Privilege   Absolute privileges pertain to those in the public sector. A narrower privilege exists for private citizens. In general, a statement that would otherwise be actionable is held to be justified if made "in a reasonable manner and for a proper purpose" (Prosser, 1971, p. 786). Thus you may warn a friend to beware of dealing with a third person, and if you had reason to believe that what you said was true, you are privileged to issue the warning, even though false. Likewise, an employee may warn an employer about the conduct or character of a fellow or prospective employee, and a parent may complain to a school board about the competence or conduct of a child's teacher. There is a line to be drawn, however, and a defendant with nothing but an idle interest in the matter (an "officious intermeddler") must take the risk that his information is wrong.

Constitutional Privileges

In 1964, the Supreme Court handed down its historic decision in *New York Times* v. *Sullivan* [376 U.S. 254 (1964)], holding that under the First Amendment a libel judgment brought by a public official against a newspaper cannot stand unless the plaintiff has shown "actual malice," which in turn was defined as "knowledge that [the statement] was false or with a reckless disregard of whether it was false or not." In subsequent cases, the Court extended the constitutional doctrine further, applying it not merely to government officials but to **public figures**—people who voluntarily place themselves in the public eye or who involuntarily find themselves the objects of public scrutiny. Whether a private person is or is not a public figure is a difficult question that has so far eluded rigorous definition and has been answered only from case to case. A chief executive officer of a private corporation ordinarily will be considered a private figure, unless he puts himself in the public eye—for example, by starring in the company's TV commercials.

INVASION OF PRIVACY

The right of privacy—the right "to be let alone"—did not receive judicial recognition until the twentieth century, and its legal formulation is still evolving. In fact there is no single right of privacy. Courts and commentators have discerned at least four different types of interests: (1) the right to control the appropriation of your name and picture for commercial purposes; (2) the right to be free of intrusion on your "personal space" or seclusion; (3) freedom from public disclosure of embarrassing and intimate facts of your personal life; and (4) the right not to be presented in a "false light."

Appropriation

The earliest privacy interest to gain judicial recognition was appropriation of name or likeness: placing your photograph on a billboard or cereal box as a model, or using your name as endorsing a product or in the product name. A New York statute makes it a misdemeanor to use the name, portrait, or picture of any person for advertising purposes or for the purposes of trade (business) without first obtaining written consent. The law also permits the aggrieved person to sue for an injunction against continued use and to recover damages, including punitive damages. Because the publishing and advertising industries are concentrated heavily in New York, the statute plays an important part in advertising decisions made throughout the country. Deciding what "commercial" or "trade" purposes are is not always easy. Thus, a newsmagazine may use a baseball player's picture on its cover without first obtaining written permission, but a chocolate manufacturer could not put the player's picture on a candy wrapper without consent.

Intrusion

One form of intrusion upon a person's solitude—trespass—has long been actionable under common law. Physical invasion of home or other property is not a new tort. But in recent years, the notion of intrusion has been broadened considerably, to embrace such disparate acts as electronic eavesdropping or photographing in a private space without consent. (Photographing someone on a city street is not tortious, though subsequent use of the photograph could be.) The concept of intrusion is not limited to invading the security of a person's home or telephone. Courts have provided relief even for such acts as interviewing the plaintiff's acquaintances to cast aspersions on his beliefs and character.

Public Disclosure of Embarrassing Facts

Circulation of false statements that do injury to a person are actionable under the laws of defamation. What about true statements that might be every bit as damaging—for example, disclosure of someone's income tax return, revealing how much he earned? The general rule is that if the facts are truly private and of no "legitimate" concern to the public, then their disclosure is a violation of the right to privacy. There is a constitutional dimension to this tort, as there is to defamation. A person who is in the public eye cannot claim the same protection.

False Light

A final type of privacy invasion is that which paints a false picture. Though false, it might not be libelous, since the publication need contain nothing injurious to reputation. Indeed, the publication might even glorify the plaintiff, making him seem more heroic than he actually is. Subject to the First Amendment requirement that the plaintiff must show intent or extreme recklessness, statements that put a person in a "false light," like a fictionalized biography, are actionable.

The Right of Publicity

Although most states now recognize a right to prevent someone from capitalizing on a person's likeness, traditionally this right did not descend to a person's heirs at death. Like the rule governing defamation, the right was considered personal, not property, and expired when a person died. Thus a federal court has held that Elvis Presley's heirs could not prevent his likeness from being exploited after he died. [Memphis Development Foundation v. Factors, Etc., Inc., 616 F.2d 956 (6th Cir. 1980)] This limitation on the right of privacy gave advertisers considerable freedom to suggest that famous people endorsed their products, as anyone familiar with television commercials can attest. But in recent years, states have begun to enact statutes granting property rights in the likenesses of the deceased, as discussed in **Box 4-4.**

TORT REFORM

During the past decade, the number of tort suits has climbed dramatically, especially against doctors in medical malpractice cases and against manufacturers in product liability suits (Chapter 19). As a result, lobbying groups have mounted a strong push for statutory changes in tort law in most states. Many state legislatures have enacted caps on damage awards. In Missouri, for example, no more than $350,000 may be paid out for punitive damages and pain and suffering. Legislators have also been considering a change in the rule governing "joint-and-several liability." The rule states that when two or more defendants are responsible for causing an injury, the plaintiff may recover the entire amount of damages from any one of the defendants, even if that defendant was only minimally at fault. Many so-called "deep pocket" defendants—those with large treasuries, like corporations and governmental units—are seeking to change the rule so that they could be forced to pay only that percentage of damages corresponding to their degree of fault.

CHAPTER SUMMARY

The principles of tort law pervade modern society because they spell out the duties of care that we owe each other in our private lives. Tort law has had a significant impact on business because modern technology poses significant dangers and the modern market is so efficient at distributing goods to a wide class of consumers.

Unlike criminal law, tort law does not require the tortfeasor to have a specific intent to commit the act for which he will be held liable to pay damages. Negligence—that is, carelessness—is a major factor in tort liability. In some instances, especially in cases involving injuries caused by products, a no-fault standard called strict liability is applied.

What constitutes a legal injury depends very much on the circumstances. A person can assume a risk or consent to the particular action, thus relieving the person doing the injury from tort liability. To be liable, the tortfeasor must be the proximate cause of the injury, not a remote cause. On the other hand, certain people are held to answer for the torts of another—for example, an employer is usually liable for the torts of his employees, and a bartender might be liable for injuries caused by someone to whom he sold too many drinks. Two types of statutes—workers' compensation and no-fault

LAW AND LIFE

The Rights of Dead Celebrities

By Pamela G. Hollie

[*Several states now recognize an heir's right to prevent someone from capitalizing on the likeness of a dead celebrity. Advertisers wishing to use the likeness of a dead celebrity frequently contact the estate of the deceased for permisson in order to avoid being sued.*
—AUTHORS' NOTE]

To advertisers, certain personalities, such as John Wayne, Elvis Presley and W. C. Fields, are as bankable now as when they were alive. In some ways they are even more attractive.

Chances are that such celebrities never did commercials when they were alive and might have objected to being associated with certain endorsements. Until recently, what they would have wished could be ignored. Courts tended to rule that the commercial rights to a person's likeness and name ended with death. Manufacturers, promoters and advertisers were free to use a dead celebrity's name or likeness without penalty or payment.

But things are changing. Several states, including California, have adopted legislation that gives the heirs of celebrities more power over the use of the names and images of their dead relatives. According to new laws in Kentucky and Tennessee, the identity and name of a celebrity are considered property, like a house or a bank account, and can be willed or sold.

Large advertising agencies have routinely sought permission from estates to insure that clients are not embarrassed by a lawsuit. "We have always been careful," said Richard Pollett, vice president and assistant

PROPERTY RIGHTS AND THE DECEASED

general counsel for the J. Walter Thompson Company. "But we are more careful than ever."

★   ★   ★

However, the practice of using ghost stars is still popular. For example, Republic Airlines Inc. featured the silent film star Rudolph Valentino in a mailing to 24,000 travel agents. "We were trying to portray a thought in a few seconds," said Mary Speagh, account supervisor of Kolesar & Hartwell Inc. in Minneapolis, which handles Republic's trade services. "People know him as a lover and a charmer and a romantic. There are some parallels with what we wanted to say, and what we wanted them to feel about Republic."

Likewise, Coca-Cola U.S.A. is using the baseball great Babe Ruth, the "Sultan of Swat" who died 37 years ago, in its advertisements for Coke Classic, the revived original-formula Coke. The advertisements are intended to link Classic Coke with the classic heroes and images of the past.

The SmithKline Beckman Corporation, on the other hand, wanted to inject some humor into its mailings to doctors. It decided to substitute the heads of the Marx Brothers for those of the four Presidents on Mount Rushmore. The theme of the mailing is: "There is no substitute for the real thing."

And, the International Business Machines Corporation saw a connection between its products and Charlie Chaplin, whose "Modern Times" is a classic film about work and mechanization. In 1981, I.B.M. chose Chaplin's "Little Tramp" character

to bring humor and familiarity to the promotion of a new personal computer.

In these cases, the companies asked the permission of the celebrities' estates before using the characters. I.B.M. received a license from Bubbles Inc. in Paris before beginning its campaign. Republic paid a stock photography house for the one-time use of a Valentino photograph. "We are very careful about getting permission," Mrs. Speagh said.

★   ★   ★

The new state laws are built on years of litigation. "Ten years ago, I felt that something had to be done," said Larry Harmon, who went to court in 1976 to protect his exclusive right to portray Stan Laurel, half of the comedy team of Stan Laurel and Oliver Hardy. Mr. Harmon had purchased the rights to the character from Mr. Laurel, who died in 1965. Mr. Hardy died in 1957. Mr. Harmon won his case against Hal Roach Studios, the film company where most of the Laurel and Hardy pictures were made, in a New York court. "It was an expensive fight," he said. "It cost me $500,000."

The rights to a famous personality can also be costly—sometimes more than $10,000 for one use in a 60-second television commercial. And, the licensing process has become increasingly complicated and restrictive. "The use of a personality is very specific," said Mark Roesler, president of the Curtis Licensing Corporation, a division of the Curtis Publishing Company and the agent for the estates of seven celebrities including Buddy Holly, James Dean and Abbott and Costello.

But perhaps the most-sought-after of the Curtis line is Elvis Presley. "We have 100 different agreements

BOX 4-4

Box 4-4, *continued*
for Elvis," Mr. Roesler said adding that the Presley estate is involved in one lawsuit charging infringement. The Abbott and Costello estates have two such lawsuits pending.

"The most important thing to the families is quality control," Mr. Roesler said. "The Babe Ruth name is controlled by his two daughters and the Babe Ruth Baseball League. They agree that any use of his name be in

very good taste. For example, it is not to be used on tobacco or alcohol or be in any way associated with pornography."

Source: *New York Times*, August 9, 1985

automobile insurance—have eliminated tort liability for certain kinds of accidents and replaced it with an immediate insurance payment plan.

Among the torts of particular importance to the business community are wrongful death and personal injury caused by products or acts of employees, misrepresentation, defamation, unfair competition and interference with contractual relations.

KEY TERMS

SELF-TEST QUESTIONS

1. Without excuse or justification, a driver strikes and kills a pedestrian. He has committed the tort of:
   (a) murder
   (b) wrongful death
   (c) assault
   (d) manslaughter
2. A spark in a factory ignites some dry rubbish, and the factory burns down. The fire spreads to a nearby house, destroying it. The owner of the house sues the company that owns the factory. At trial, proof of negligence will be aided by the doctrine of:
   (a) sine qua non
   (b) contributory negligence
   (c) res ipsa loquitur
   (d) act of God
3. A woman buys a bottle of a brand-name sparkling water with a label that says "carbonated water." Unbeknownst to her or anyone else, she has a severe allergy to the carbonation and dies after drinking it. Her heirs sue the manufacturer. They will succeed on which of the following theories:
   (a) contributory negligence
   (b) assumption of risk
   (c) strict liability
   (d) none of the above
4. A photograph of the spouse of an employee taken at the company's annual holiday party is published in a company newsletter. The spouse was wearing a silly hat. The spouse can sue the company for:
   (a) libel
   (b) slander
   (c) defamation
   (d) none of the above
5. A family had a pet monkey and kept it under strict supervision in a large outdoor pen ringed with metal bars. Once while away for the day, an intruder using a hacksaw cut several of the bars and the monkey escaped, doing considerable damage to neighbors' property. The neighbors may sue on a theory of:
   (a) strict liability
   (b) res ipsa loquitur
   (c) vicarious liability
   (d) respondeat superior

DEMONSTRATION PROBLEM

While driving home one day, you notice that your brakes are squealing. The next morning you take your car to your garage mechanic, who tells you that your brakes "are shot; you need a whole new brake lining." You authorize him to make the repairs. You pick up your car on your way home from school that afternoon, after paying $125 for the repair work. On your way home, the brakes fail and you hit and seriously injure a pedestrian. It turns out that the mechanic forgot to fix your brakes after all. Who is responsible for the injury? From whom may the pedestrian recover? Suppose the pedestrian had suddenly darted out into the street against a red light?

PROBLEMS

1. What is the difference between the objectives of tort law and criminal law?
2. A woman fell ill in a store. An employee put the woman in an infirmary but provided no medical care for six hours, and she died. The woman's family sued the store for wrongful death. What arguments could the store make that it was not liable? What arguments could the family make? Which seem the stronger arguments? Why?
3. The signals on a railroad crossing are defective. Although the railroad company was notified of the problem a month earlier, the railroad inspector has failed to come by and repair them. Seeing the all-clear signal, a car drives up and stalls on the tracks as a train rounds the bend. For the past two weeks the car had been stalling, and the driver kept putting off taking the car to the shop for a tune-up. As the train rounds the bend the engineer is distracted by a conductor and does not see the car until it is too late to stop. Who is negligent? Who must bear the liability for the damage to the car and to the train?
4. Jake's Bar has been renting the ground floor of Bud's building for ten years. At the time the lease is to be renewed, Bud tells Jake that he has an offer from Mac to pay $12,000 a year for the space, double what Jake is currently paying. Afraid of risking a move, Jake signs a ten-year lease at $12,000. A year later he discovers that Mac had never made any offer at all. Jakes sues Bud. Does Jake have a case? What is his claim? What is Bud's defense? Who should win?
5. Sid's Diner has been losing market share to Leo's Diner, so Sid launches a negative advertising campaign on the local radio station. The ads say that food at Leo's is "terrible, disgusting, greasy, heavy, and unpalatable." The ads also say that Leo fries his food in butter and that all his fish are frozen. What torts, if any, has Sid committed?
6. A credit reporting agency received a report from an electronics supplier that Adam's Radios, Inc., had failed to pay for $10,000 worth of merchandise, that it had declared bankruptcy, and that Adam himself had been engaged in "unethical business practices." In fact, all these allegations were untrue. The credit agency put this report in a file, and a few weeks later released it to a finance company from whom Adam was seeking a business loan. The finance company refused the loan and told Adam why. Adam wrote the credit reporting company, demonstrating that the facts were untrue. A manager phoned Adam to say that the report would be changed, but he forgot to instruct the report clerk to destroy the old report. When Adam then sought a loan from a different finance company, it got the same old report and likewise refused Adam a loan. By the time Adam straightened the matter out, interest rates had soared and Adam was stuck having to pay six percentage points more. Adam sued the credit reporting company for having issued the report to the first finance company and to the second. What is his theory? What result? What additional facts, if any, are needed to determine liability?
7. Mississippi has a law against printing the name of a rape victim in a newspaper or broadcasting it over the air. A local radio station obtained the name of a rape victim from a police log and broadcast it. The woman sued the radio station. What is her legal theory? What result?

ANSWERS TO SELF-TEST QUESTIONS

1. (b)   2. (c)   3. (d)   4. (d)   5. (a)

SUGGESTED ANSWER TO DEMONSTRATION PROBLEM

The owner and driver of a car owe a duty of care to other drivers and pedestrians who it is reasonable to foresee will be on the public streets. So as owner and driver, you have committed a tort in hitting a pedestrian. Knowing that your brakes were failing, you had a legal duty to repair them. The obligation is personal to you, and you cannot duck your responsibility by showing that you had asked someone else to fix them. Whether the garage mechanic is also liable to the pedestrian is more difficult to answer and depends on how the courts will answer the question whether a mechanic doing routine maintenance and repair work has a duty of care toward passersby on the streets. It is possible under these circumstances that the pedestrian will succeed in a tort action against the mechanic, since he was not merely careless in how he repaired the car but forgot to do so altogether. However, regardless of the mechanic's obligation to the pedestrian, there is no question that you as owner and driver can recover from him for the damages assessed against you in the pedestrian's suit, for the mechanic was negligent toward you (and probably breached a contract as well). Whether the pedestrian's conduct absolves you depends on how egregious it was. If there is evidence that pedestrians frequently jaywalk at that point and that you know it, and especially if it can be shown that there should have been time for you to come to a stop, he may still prevail in his suit. But if the state still follows the contributory-negligence rule, and it can be shown that the pedestrian darted out without looking where he was going and in such a manner that a driver could not have anticipated his movement, his own negligence will defeat his suit.

CHAPTER

5

Administrative Law

From the 1930s on, administrative agencies, law, and procedures have virtually remade our government and much of private life. Business must deal daily with rules and decisions of administrative agencies, federal and state. Substantive administrative law is voluminous: thousands of new regulations pour forth each year. Many of the subsequent chapters in this text take up subject by subject the substance of administratively generated law.

To the lawyer, administrative law means something different: it is the study of the way in which administrative agencies work and of the means by which both the agencies and their laws can be judicially reviewed. In this chapter we consider the nature of administrative agencies and their impact on the operations of the business enterprise.

ADMINISTRATIVE AGENCIES: THEIR STRUCTURE AND POWERS

Congress created the first federal agency, the Interstate Commerce Commission (ICC), in 1887, and delegated it power to enforce federal laws against railroad rate discrimination and other unfair pricing practices. By the early part of this century, the ICC gained the power to fix rates.

Beginning with the Federal Trade Commission (FTC) in 1914, Congress has created numerous other agencies, many of them familiar actors in American government. Today more than eighty-five federal agencies have jurisdiction to regulate some form of private activity. Most were created since 1930, more than a third since 1960.

They are generally classified into two broad groups: independent agencies and executive branch agencies. In addition to the ICC and FTC, the major independent agencies are the Federal Communications Commission (1934), Securities and Exchange Commission (1934), National Labor Relations Board (1935), and Environmental Protection Agency (1970). Dozens of other agencies—the executive branch agencies—are components of the major federal departments. The Food and Drug Administration is a part of the Department of Health and Human Resources; the Nuclear Regulatory Commission (formerly the Atomic Energy Commission) and the Federal Energy Regulation Agency (formerly the Federal Power Commission), of the Department of Energy; the Occupational Safety and Health Administration, of the Department of Labor. The Department of Agriculture has broad supervisory powers over farm practices and pricing. The Internal Revenue Service, a part of the Treasury Department, plays a major role in the financial life of virtually everyone in the country.

The primary distinction between independent and executive branch agencies is in the terms of office of their members. Commissioners of the **independent agencies** serve for fixed statutory terms, and the president may not remove them except for "good cause." To some degree, therefore, they are independent of the political process. By contrast, members of executive branch agencies serve at the pleasure of the president and are therefore far more amenable to political control. One consequence of this distinction is that the rules that independent agencies promulgate may not be reviewed by the president or his staff—only Congress may directly overrule them—whereas the White House or higher authority in the various cabinet departments may oversee the work of the agencies contained within them (unless specifically denied the power by Congress).

Agencies have a variety of powers. Many of the original statutes that created them, like the Federal Communications Act, gave them licensing power. No party can enter into the productive activity covered by the act without prior license from the agency—for example, no utility can start up a nuclear power plant unless first approved by the Nuclear Regulatory Commission. In recent years, the move toward deregulation of the economy has led to diminution of some licensing power. Many agencies also have the authority to set the rates charged by companies subject to the agency's jurisdiction. Finally, the agencies can regulate business practices. The Federal Trade Commission has general jurisdiction over all business in interstate commerce to monitor and root out "unfair acts" and "deceptive practices." The Securities and Exchange Commission oversees the issuance of corporate securities and other investments and monitors the practices of the stock exchanges. The Interstate Commerce Commission continues to have broad regulatory power over railroad practices, as well as over those of truckers and interstate water carriers.

A similar growth has occurred at the state level. Most states now have dozens of regulatory agencies, many of them overlapping in function with the federal bodies.

Unlike courts, administrative agencies are charged with the responsibility of carrying out a specific assignment or reaching a goal or set of goals. They are not to remain neutral on the various issues of the day; they must act. They have been given legislative powers because in a society growing ever more complex, Congress does not know how to legislate with the kind of detail that is necessary, nor would it have the time to approach all the sectors of society even if it tried. Precisely because they are to do what general legislative bodies cannot do, agencies are specialized bodies. Through years of experience in dealing with similar problems they accumulate a body of knowledge that they can apply to accomplish their statutory duties.

All administrative agencies have two different sorts of personnel. The heads, whether a single administrator or a collegial body of commissioners, are political appointees and serve for relatively limited terms. Below them is a more or less permanent staff—the bureaucracy. Much policy-making occurs at the staff level, because these employees are in essential control of gathering facts and presenting data and argument to the commissioners, who wield the ultimate power of the agencies.

CONTROLLING ADMINISTRATIVE AGENCIES

Not surprisingly, during the course of the past fifty years a substantial debate has been conducted, often in shrill terms, about the legitimacy of administrative law-making. One criticism is that agencies are "captured" by the industry they are directed to regulate. Another is that they overregulate, stifling individual initiative and the ability to compete. During the 1960s and 1970s, a massive outpouring of federal law created many new agencies and greatly strengthened the hands of existing ones. Beginning in the late 1970s during the Carter administration and even more so under the Reagan administration, Congress began to deregulate American society. But the savings-and-loan scandal of the 1990s may lead Congress and the President to reregulate significant areas of the economy.

Administrative agencies are the focal point of controversy because they are policy-making bodies, incorporating facets of legislative, executive, and judicial power in a hybrid form that fits uneasily at best in the framework of American government (see Figure 5-1). They are necessarily at the center of tugging and hauling by legislature, executive, and courts, each of which has different means of exercising control over them.

In early 1990, for example, the Bush administration approved a Food and Drug Administration regulation that limited disease-prevention claims by food packagers, reversing a position by the Reagan Administration in 1987 permitting such claims.

Figure 5-1 Major Administrative Agencies of the United States

The major independent regulatory agencies

Consumer Product Safety Commission
Environmental Protection Agency
Equal Employment Opportunity Commission
Federal Communications Commission
Federal Deposit Insurance Corporation
Federal Energy Regulatory Commission
Federal Reserve System
Federal Trade Commission
Food and Drug Administration
Interstate Commerce Commission
National Labor Relations Board
Occupational Safety and Health Administration
Securities and Exchange Commission

The major agencies within the federal executive departments

Department of Agriculture
Farmers Home Administration
Rural Electrification Administration
Agricultural Marketing Service
Animal and Plant Health Inspection Service
Food Safety and Inspection Service
Packers and Stockyards Administration
Agricultural Stabilization and Conservation Service
Commodity Credit Corporation
Forest Service
Soil Conservation Service

Department of Commerce
Bureau of the Census
Bureau of Export Administration
International Trade Administration
Economic Development Administration
Minority Business Development Agency
National Oceanic and Atmospheric Administration
Patent and Trademark Office
National Institute of Standards and Technology (formerly Bureau of Standards)

Department of Defense
Navy/Marine Corps
Army
Air Force

Department of Education

Department of Energy
Office of Nuclear Safety
various regional power administrations

Department of Health and Human Services
Public Health Service
Alcohol, Drug Abuse, and Mental Health Administration
Centers for Disease Control
Food and Drug Administration
National Institutes of Health
Indian Health Service
Social Security Administration

Department of Housing and Urban Development
Fair Housing and Equal Opportunity
Federal Housing Commissioner
Community Planning and Development

Department of the Interior
United States Fish and Wildlife Service
National Park Service
Geological Survey
Office of Surface Mining Reclamation and Enforcement
Bureau of Indian Affairs
Minerals Management Service
Bureau of Land Management
Bureau of Reclamation

Department of Justice
Federal Bureau of Investigation
Antitrust Division
Civil Division
Civil Rights Division
Criminal Division
Environment and Natural Resources Division
Drug Enforcement Administration
Foreign Claims Settlement Commission of the United States

Department of Labor
Wage Appeals Board
Benefits Review Board
Federal Unemployment Insurance Service
Employment and Training Administration
Pension and Welfare Benefits Administration
Office of Labor-Management Standards
Employment Standards Administration
Occupational Safety and Health Administration
Mine Safety and Health Administration

Department of State
Foreign Service
Bureau of Consular Affairs

Department of Transportation
Federal Aviation Administration
Federal Highway Administration
Federal Railroad Administration
National Highway Traffic Safety Administration
Urban Mass Transportation Administration
Maritime Administration
United States Coast Guard

Department of Treasury
Bureau of Alcohol, Tobacco and Firearms
Office of the Comptroller of the Currency
United States Customs Service
Internal Revenue Service
United States Secret Service
Office of Thrift Supervision
United States Mint
Bureau of Printing and Engraving

Legislative Control

Congress can always pass a law repealing a regulation that an agency promulgates. Because this is a time-consuming process that runs counter to the reason for creating administrative bodies, it happens rarely. Another approach to controlling agencies is to reduce or threaten to reduce their appropriations. By retaining ultimate control of the purse strings, Congress can exercise considerable informal control over regulatory policy.

Executive Control

The president (or governor) can exercise considerable control over agencies that are part of his cabinet departments and that are not statutorily defined as independent. Federal agencies, moreover, are subject to the fiscal scrutiny of the Office of Management and Budget (OMB), subject to the direct control of the president. Agencies are not permitted to go directly to Congress for increases in budget; these requests must be submitted through OMB, giving the president indirect leverage over the continuation of administrators' programs and policies.

Judicial Control

Administrative agencies are creatures of law and like everyone else must obey the law. The courts have jurisdiction to hear claims that the agencies have overstepped their legal authority or have acted in some unlawful manner.

The statutory delegation of power to administrative agencies raises an initial constitutional question. Legislative power is vested in Congress, and it may not give away all of its power nor delegate power to legislate in the complete absence of standards. In 1935, in *Schechter Poultry Corp.* v. *United States* [295 U.S. 495 (1935)], the Supreme Court upset the National Industrial Recovery Act on the ground that the congressional delegation of power was too broad. Under the law, industry trade groups were granted the authority to devise a code of fair competition for the entire industry, and these codes became law if approved by the president. No administrative body was created to scrutinize the arguments for a particular code, to develop evidence, or to test one version of a code against another.

During the fifty years since the *Schechter* decision, Congress has enacted scores of laws directing agencies to carry out vaguely worded goals. The Supreme Court has never since seen fit to overturn a grant of legislative power on the ground that Congress placed too much discretion in the hands of the administrators. The reasons vary. Courts have become cautious in overturning broad economic legislation of Congress. Neither before nor since has Congress delegated power so broadly as it had in the statute that the 1935 Court upset. Finally, courts confronted with what appear to be excessively vague standards will try to save them by construing them narrowly to accord with past administrative practices and judicial precedents. Nevertheless, many administrative standards remain loose to the point of vanishing. The touchstone for officials of the Federal Communications Commission, for instance, is "public convenience, interest, or necessity."

Despite the generally cautious approach of courts, in 1986, the Supreme Court struck down the Gramm-Rudman-Hollings Act, intended to eliminate deficit spending, on the grounds that Congress had delegated to the wrong official *executive power* to determine where cuts in the federal budget must be made if Congress and the president spent more than certain target amounts. Congress gave final authority to dictate the cuts to the Comptroller General of the United States. The Comptroller General is an agent of Congress, the legislative branch of government. Since the power to make cuts was executive power, the Court said, it could be delegated only to an executive branch official. [Bowsher v. Synar, 106 S.Ct. 3181 (1986)]

Beyond the constitutional question, courts in reviewing administrative action have a variety of tools by which to control the administrative process. They can look to the statute empowering the agency to act to see whether it has exceeded its authority. They can ask whether the agency has followed its own rules and, if not, set aside the agency's action. And they can look to the Administrative Procedure Act, the general law that governs the procedures that all federal administrative agencies must follow.

THE ADMINISTRATIVE PROCEDURE ACT

In 1946, Congress enacted the Administrative Procedure Act (APA). This fundamental statute detailed for all federal administrative agencies how they must function when they are deciding cases or issuing regulations, the two basic tasks of administration. At the state level, the Model State Administrative Procedure Act, issued in 1946 and revised in 1961, has been adopted in 28 states and the District of Columbia; three states have adopted the 1981 revision. The other states have statutes that resemble the model state act to some degree.

Trial-type Hearings

Deciding cases is a major task of many agencies. Thus the FTC is empowered to charge a company with having violated the Federal Trade Commission Act—perhaps a seller is accused of making deceptive claims in its advertising. Proceeding in a manner similar to a court, staff counsel will prepare a case against the company, which can defend itself through its lawyers. The case is tried before an **administrative law judge** (ALJ), formerly known as an administrative hearing examiner. The change in nomenclature was made in 1972 to enhance ALJs' prestige and more accurately reflect their duties. Although not appointed for life as federal judges are, the ALJ must be free of assignments inconsistent with the judicial function and is not subject to supervision by anyone in the agency who carries on an investigative or prosecutorial function.

The accused parties are entitled to receive notice of the issues to be raised, to present evidence, to argue, to cross-examine, and to appear with their lawyers. *Ex parte* (eks PAR tee) communications—contacts between the ALJ and outsiders or one party when both parties are not present—are prohibited. However, the usual burden-of-proof standard followed in a civil proceeding in court does not apply: the ALJ is not bound to decide in favor of that party producing the more persuasive evidence. The rule in most administrative proceedings is "substantial evidence"—not flimsy or weak evidence, but not necessarily overwhelming evidence either. The ALJ in most cases will write an opinion. That opinion is not the decision of the agency, which can be made only by the commissioners or agency head. In effect, the ALJ's opinion is appealed to the commission itself.

Certain types of agency actions that have a direct impact on individuals need not be filtered through a full-scale hearing. Safety and quality inspections (grading of food, inspection of airplanes) can be made on the spot by skilled inspectors. Certain licenses can be administered through tests without a hearing (a test for a driver's license), and some decisions can be made by election of those affected (labor union elections).

Rule-making

Trial-type hearings generally impose on particular parties liabilities based on past or present facts. Because these cases will serve as precedents, they are a partial guide to future conduct by others. But they do not directly apply to nonparties, who may argue in a subsequent case that their conduct does not fit within the holding announced in the case. Agencies can affect future conduct far more directly by announcing rules that apply to all who come within the agency's jurisdiction.

The acts creating most of the major federal agencies expressly grant them authority to engage in **rule-making**—in essence, to legislate. The outpouring of federal regulations has been immense. As Professor Bernard Schwartz has noted:

> From its establishment in 1935, the Federal Register [see below] has in size vastly exceeded the Statutes at Large. The sheer mass of agency regulations is appalling. The Federal Register for 1974 contained 45,420 pages. But, to check all the federal regulations, one had to search the Code of Federal Regulations, with its 127 volumes, containing 65,249 pages. The C.F.R. now contains over 50 million words—seventy times as many as in the Bible and sixty times as many as in a complete Shakespeare. (Schwartz, 1976, p. 148)

The APA directs agencies about to engage in rule-making to give notice in the *Federal Register* of their intent to do so. The *Federal Register* is published daily, Monday through Friday, in Washington and contains notice of various actions, including announcements of proposed rule-making and regulations as adopted. The notice must be specific enough to identify the time, place, and nature of the rule-making and offer a description of the proposed rule or the issues involved. Any interested person or organization is entitled to participate by submitting written "data, views or arguments." Agencies are not legally required to air debate over proposed rules, though they often do so.

The procedure just described is known as "informal" rule-making. A different procedure is required for "formal" rule-making, defined as those instances in which the enabling legislation directs an agency to make rules "on the record after opportunity for an agency hearing." When engaging in formal rule-making, agencies must hold an adversary hearing.

Administrative regulations are not legally binding unless they are published. Agencies must publish in the *Federal Register* the text of final regulations, which ordinarily do not become effective until thirty days later. Every year the annual output of regulations is collected and reprinted in the *Code of Federal Regulations (CFR)*, a multivolume paperback series containing all federal rules and regulations keyed to the fifty titles of the United States Code (the compilation of all federal statutes enacted by Congress and grouped according to subject).

ADMINISTRATIVE BURDENS ON BUSINESS OPERATIONS

The administrative process is not frictionless. The interplay between government agency and private enterprise can burden business operations in a number of ways. Several of these are noted in this section.

The Paperwork Burden

Deciding whether and how to act is not a decision that government agencies reach "out of the blue." They rely heavily on information garnered from business itself. Dozens of federal agencies require corporations to keep hundreds of types of records and to file numerous periodic reports. The Commission on Federal Paperwork, established during the Ford administration to consider ways of reducing the paperwork burden, estimated in its final report in 1977 that the total annual cost of federal paperwork amounted to $50 billion and that the 10,000 largest business enterprises spent $10 billion annually on paperwork alone. The paperwork involved in licensing a single nuclear power plant, the commission said, costs upwards of $15 million.

Not surprisingly, therefore, businesses have sought ways of avoiding requests for data. Since the 1940s, the FTC has collected economic data on corporate performance from individual companies for statistical purposes. As long as each company engages in a single line of business, data are comparable. When the era of conglomerates began in the 1970s, with widely divergent types of businesses brought together under the roof of a single corporate parent, the data became useless for purposes of examining the competitive behavior of different industries. So the FTC ordered dozens of large companies to break out their economic information according to each line of business that they carried on. The companies resisted but the U.S. Court of Appeals for the District of Columbia Circuit, where much of the litigation over federal administrative action is decided, directed the companies to comply with the commission's order, holding that the Federal Trade Commission Act clearly permits the agency to collect information for investigatory purposes. [In Re: FTC Line of Business Report Litigation, 595 F.2d 685 (D.C.Cir. 1978)]

In 1980, responding to cries that businesses, individuals, and state and local governments were being swamped by federal demands for paperwork, Congress enacted the Paperwork Reduction Act. It gives power to the federal Office of Management and Budget to develop uniform policies for coordinating the gathering, storage, and transmission of all the millions of reports flowing in each year to the scores of federal departments and agencies requesting information. These reports include tax and medicare forms, financial loan and job applications, questionnaires of all sorts, compliance reports, and tax and business records. OMB was given the power also to determine whether new kinds of information are needed. In effect, any agency that wants to collect new information from outside must obtain OMB's approval.

Since OMB is part of the executive office of the President, the Paperwork Reduction Act seemed to give considerable power to the President to oversee and control the federal bureaucracy. During the 1980s, the Reagan Administration thought that it had the power under this act not only to reduce the paperwork burden but also in veto substantive regulations that government agencies adopt under powers delegated by Congress. In the next case, involving regulations requiring disclosure to employees of workplace health hazards, the Supreme Court ruled in 1990 that OMB does not have such power.

DOLE v. UNITED STEELWORKERS OF AMERICA
110 S. Ct. 929 (1990)

JUSTICE BRENNAN delivered the opinion of the Court.

Among the regulatory tools available to government agencies charged with protecting public health and safety are rules which require regulated entities to disclose information directly to employees, consumers, or others. Disclosure rules protect by providing access to information about what dangers exist and how these dangers can be avoided. Today we decide whether the Office of Management and Budget (OMB) has the authority under the Paperwork Reduction Act of 1980 (Act) to review such regulations.

In 1983, pursuant to the Occupational Safety and Health Act of 1970 (OSH Act), which authorizes the Department of Labor (DOL) to set health and safety standards for workplaces, DOL promulgated a Hazard Communications Standard. The Standard imposed various requirements on manufacturers aimed at ensuring that their employees were informed of the potential hazards posed by chemicals found at their workplace.

*   *   *

Respondent United Steelworkers of America, among others, challenged the Standard in the Court of Appeals for the Third Circuit. That court held that the Occupational Safety and Health Administration (OSHA) had not adequately explained why the regulation was limited to the manufacturing sector, in view of the OSH Act's clear directive that, to the extent feasible, OSHA is to ensure that no employee suffers material impairment of health from toxic or other harmful agents. The court directed OSHA either to apply the hazard standard rules to workplaces in other sectors or to state reasons why such application would not be feasible.

*   *   *

DOL complied by issuing a revised Hazard Communications Standard that applied to worksites in all sectors of the economy. At the same time, DOL submitted the Standard to OMB for review of any paperwork requirements. After holding a public hearing, OMB approved all but three of its provisions. OMB rejected a requirement that employees who work at multi-employer sites (such as construction sites) be provided with data sheets describing the hazardous substances to which they were likely to be exposed, through the activities of any of the companies working at the same site. . . . OMB also disapproved a provision exempting consumer products used in the workplace in the same manner, and resulting in the same frequency and duration of exposure, as in normal consumer use. . . . Finally, OMB vetoed an exemption for drugs sold in solid, final form for direct administration to patients. . . .

OMB disapproved these provisions based on its determination that the requirements were not necessary to protect employees. . . . DOL disagreed with OMB's assessment, but it published notice that the three provisions were withdrawn. DOL added its reasons for believing that the provi-

(continued on next page)

(*continued*)

DOLE v. UNITED STEELWORKERS OF AMERICA
110 S. Ct. 929 (1990)

sions were necessary, proposed that they be retained, and invited public comment. . . .

The union and its copetitioners responded by filing a motion for further relief with the Third Circuit. That court ordered DOL to reinstate the OMB-disapproved provisions. . . .

The United States sought review in this Court. We granted certiorari to answer the important question whether the Paperwork Reduction Act authorizes OMB to review and countermand agency regulations mandating disclosure by regulated entities directly to third parties. . . . We hold that the Paperwork Reduction Act does not give OMB that authority, and therefore affirm.

The Paperwork Reduction Act was enacted in response to one of the less auspicious aspects of the enormous growth of our federal bureaucracy: its seemingly insatiable appetite for data. . . . Congress designated OMB the overseer of other agencies with respect to paperwork and set forth a comprehensive scheme designed to reduce the paperwork burden. The Act charges OMB with developing uniform policies for efficient information processing, storage and transmittal systems, both within and among agencies. OMB is directed to reduce federal collection of all information by set percentages, establish a Federal Information Locator System, and develop and implement procedures for guarding the privacy of those providing confidential information. . . .

The Act prohibits any federal agency from adopting regulations which impose paperwork requirements on the public unless the information is not available to the agency from another source within the Federal Government, and the agency must formulate a plan for tabulating the information in a useful manner. Agencies are also required to minimize the burden on the public to the extent practicable. . . . In addition, the Act institutes a second layer of review by OMB for new paperwork requirements. After an agency has satisfied itself that an instrument for collecting information—termed an "information collection request"—is needed, the agency must submit the request to OMB for approval. . . . If OMB disapproves the request, the agency may not collect the information.

*   *   *

By contrast, disclosure rules do not result in information being made available for agency personnel to use. The promulgation of a disclosure rule is a final agency action that represents a substantive regulatory choice. An agency charged with protecting employees from hazardous chemicals has a variety of regulatory weapons from which to choose: It can ban the chemical altogether; it can mandate specified safety measures, such as gloves or goggles; or it can require labels or other warnings alerting users to dangers and recommended precautions. An agency chooses to impose a warning requirement because it believes that such a requirement is the least intrusive measure that will sufficiently protect the public, not because the measure is a means of acquiring information useful in performing some other agency function.

No provision of the Act expressly declares whether Congress intended the Paperwork Reduction Act to apply to disclosure rules as well as information-gathering rules.

*   *   *

Disclosure rules present none of the problems Congress sought to solve through the Paperwork Reduction Act, and none of Congress' enumerated purposes would be served by subjecting disclosure rules to the provisions of the Act. The statute makes clear that the first purpose—avoiding a burden on private parties and state and local governments—refers to avoiding "the time, effort, or financial resources expended by persons to provide information *to a Federal agency.*" . . . Because Congress expressed concern only for the burden imposed by requirements to provide information to a federal agency, and not for any burden imposed by requirements to provide information to a third party, OMB review of disclosure rules would not further this congressional aim.

Congress' second purpose—minimizing the Federal Government's cost of handling information—also would not be advanced by review of disclosure rules bcause such rules do not impose any information processing costs on the Federal Government. Because the Federal Government is not the consumer of information "requested" by a disclosure rule nor an intermediary in its dissemination, OMB review of disclosure rules would not serve Congress' third, fourth, fifth, or sixth purposes. Thus, nothing in Congress' itemized and exhaustive textual description of its reasons for enacting this particular Act indicates any legislative purpose to have OMB screen proposed disclosure rules. We find this to be strong evidence that Congress did not intend the Act to authorize OMB review of such regulations.

*   *   *

[I]ts meaning is clear: the public is protected under the Paperwork Reduction Act from paperwork regulations not issued in compliance with the Act, only when those regulations dictate that a person maintain information *for an agency* or provide information *to an agency.*

*   *   *

We affirm the judgment of the Third Circuit insofar as it held that the Paperwork Reduction Act does not give OMB the authority to review agency rules mandating disclosure by regulated entities to third parties.

Inspections

No one likes surprise inspections. A section of the Occupational Safety and Health Act of 1970 empowers agents of OSHA to search work areas for safety hazards and for violations of OSHA regulations. The act does not specify whether inspectors are required to obtain search warrants, required under the Fourth Amendment in criminal cases. For many years the government insisted that surprise inspections are not unreasonable and that the time required to obtain a warrant would defeat the surprise element. The Supreme Court finally ruled squarely on the issue in 1978. In Marshall v. Barlow's, Inc., 436 U.S. 307 (1978), the Court held that no less than private individuals, businesses are entitled to refuse police demands to search the premises unless a court has issued a search warrant.

Access to Business Information in Government Files

In 1966, Congress enacted the Freedom of Information Act (**FOIA**), opening up to the citizenry many of the files of the government. (The act was amended in 1974 and again in 1976 to overcome a tendency of many agencies to stall or refuse access to their files.) Under the FOIA, any person has a legally enforceable right of access to all government documents, with nine specific exceptions, such as classified military intelligence, medical files, and trade secrets and commercial or financial information if "obtained from a person and privileged or confidential." Without the trade-secret and financial-information exemption, business competitors could, merely by requesting it, obtain highly sensitive competitive information sitting in government files. Indeed, though proponents thought that the press and broadcast media would be the primary seekers of information under the act, in fact business corporations have sought access to government records far more often, usually to obtain competitive business data.

Many agencies have rejected requests for such information, and the issue has come up frequently in court. In a significant 1974 case, the National Park Service refused the request of the National Parks and Conservation Association, a private organization, for detailed financial information submitted by private individuals and companies operating food and other concessions in national parks. The question the court had to address was the meaning of the word "confidential." What makes information sufficiently confidential that a government agency is legally entitled to refuse access to it?

NATIONAL PARKS AND CONSERVATION ASSOCIATION v. MORTON
498 F.2d 765 (D.C.Cir. 1974)

Tamm, Circuit Judge:

Appellant brought this action under the Freedom of Information Act, 5 U.S.C. § 552 (1970), seeking to enjoin officials of the Department of the Interior from refusing to permit inspection and copying of certain agency records concerning concessions operated in the national parks. The district court granted summary judgment for the defendant on the ground that the information sought is exempt from disclosure under section 552(b)(4) of the Act which states:

(b) This section does not apply to matters that are—

*   *   *

(4) trade secrets and commercial or financial information obtained from a person and privileged or confidential. . . .

In order to bring a matter (other than a trade secret) within this exemption, it must be shown that the information is (a) commercial or financial, (b) obtained from a person, and (c) privileged or confidential. Since the parties agree that the matter in question is financial information obtained from a person and that it is not privileged, the only issue on appeal is whether the information is "confidential" within the meaning of the exemption.

Unfortunately, the statute contains no definition of the word "confidential." In the past, our decisions concerning this exemption have been guided by the following passage from the Senate Report, particularly the italicized portion:

This exception is necessary to protect the confidentiality of information which is obtained by the Government through questionnaires or other inquiries, *but which would customarily not be released to the public by the person from whom it was obtained.*

* * *

Whether particular information would customarily be disclosed to the public by the person from whom it was obtained is not the only relevant inquiry. . . . A court must also be satisfied that nondisclosure is justified by the legislative purpose which underlies the exemption.

* * *

The "financial information" exemption recognizes the need of government policymakers to have access to commercial and financial data. Unless persons having necessary information can be assured that it will remain confidential, they may decline to cooperate with officials and the ability of the Government to make intelligent, well informed decisions will be impaired.

* * *

Apart from encouraging cooperation with the Government by persons having information useful to officials, section 552(b)(4) serves another distinct but equally important purpose. It protects persons who submit financial or commercial data to government agencies from the competitive disadvantages which would result from its publication.

* * *

To summarize, commercial or financial matter is "confidential" for purposes of the exemption if disclosure of the information is likely to have either of the following effects: (1) to impair the Government's ability to obtain necessary information in the future; or (2) to cause substantial harm to the competitive position of the person from whom the information was obtained.

The financial information sought by appellant consists of audits conducted upon the books of companies operating concessions in national parks, annual financial statements filed by the concessioners with the National Park Service and other financial information. The district court concluded that this information was of the kind "that would not generally be made available for public perusal." While we discern no error in this finding, we do not think that, by itself, it supports application of the financial information exemption. The district court must also inquire into the possibility that disclosure will harm legitimate private or governmental interests in secrecy.

* * *

[Case remanded to the district court.]

Despite rulings in cases such as *National Parks* that agencies may withhold information "likely to cause substantial harm to the competitive position" of the business that submitted it, the business itself has no legal standing to intervene in the suit to object. When delivering data to the government, most companies specify those portions that they consider confidential, and most agencies notify a company whose data they

are about to disclose. But these practices are not legally required under the Freedom of Information Act.

In Chrysler Corp. v. Brown, 441 U.S. 281 (1979), Chrysler filed a "reverse FOIA suit," seeking to prevent disclosure by the Defense Logistics Agency (DLA), a branch of the U.S. Defense Department, to third parties who wanted access to records about the company's employment practices. As a defense contractor, Chrysler is required to demonstrate that it complies with affirmative action employment policies mandated by law. Chrysler argued that because FOIA continues an exemption for trade secrets, DLA was legally bound to keep the information in its hands confidential. The Court ruled otherwise: DLA could refuse to divulge the information if it chose, but Chrysler could not enjoin it from doing so.

Companies may have legal grounds for resisting disclosure (for example, the Trade Secrets Act forbids government officials from disclosing commercial trade secrets unless a law specifically permits them to be divulged), but companies rarely succeed in preventing disclosure because no general statute requires the government to tell a company that information it supplied to the government is about to be given to someone else. Beginning in the late 1980s, however, many agencies began to adopt their own rules requiring submitters to be notified when someone seeks the information.

THE SCOPE OF JUDICIAL REVIEW

Neither an administrative adjudication nor issuance of a regulation is necessarily final. Most federal agency decisions are appealable to the federal circuit courts. To get to court, the appellant must overcome numerous complex hurdles. He must have standing—that is, be in some sense directly affected by the decision or regulation. The case must be ripe for review; administrative remedies such as further appeal within the agency must have been exhausted.

Once these obstacles are cleared, the court may look at one of a series of claims. The appellant might assert that the agency's action was *ultra vires* (UL truh VI reez)—beyond the scope of its authority as set down in the statute. This attack is rarely successful. A somewhat more successful claim is that the agency did not abide by its own procedures or those imposed upon it by the Administrative Procedure Act.

In formal rule-making, the appellant also might insist that the agency lacked substantial evidence for the determination that it made. If there is virtually no evidence to support the agency's findings, the court may reverse. But findings of fact are not often upset.

Likewise, there has long been a presumption that when an agency issues a regulation it has the authority to do so: those opposing the regulation must bear a heavy burden in court to upset it. This is not a surprising rule, for otherwise courts, not administrators, would be the authors of regulations. Nevertheless, regulations cannot exceed the scope of the authority conferred by Congress on the agency. In an important 1981 case before the Supreme Court, the issue was whether the Secretary of Labor, acting through OSHA, could lawfully issue a standard limiting exposure to cotton dust in the workplace without first undertaking a cost-benefit analysis. A dozen cotton textile manufacturers and the American Textile Manufacturers Institute, representing 175 companies, asserted that the cotton dust standard was unlawful because it did not rationally relate the benefits to be derived from the standard to the costs that the standard would impose. The Supreme Court tackled the issue head on.

AMERICAN TEXTILE MANUFACTURERS INSTITUTE v. DONOVAN
452 U.S. 490 (1981)

JUSTICE BRENNAN delivered the opinion of the Court.

Congress enacted the Occupational Safety and Health Act of 1970 (Act) "to assure so far as possible every working man and woman in the Nation safe and healthful working conditions. . . ." The Act authorizes the Secretary of Labor to establish, after notice and opportunity to comment, mandatory nationwide standards governing health and safety in the workplace. In 1978, the Secretary, acting through the Occupational Safety and Health Administration (OSHA), promulgated a standard limiting occupational exposure to cotton dust, an airborne particle byproduct of the preparation and manufacture of cotton products, exposure to which induces a "constellation of respiratory effects" known as "byssinosis." This disease was one of the expressly recognized health hazards that led to passage of the Act.

Petitioners in these consolidated cases, representing the interests of the cotton industry, challenged the validity of the "Cotton Dust Standard" in the Court of Appeals for the District of Columbia Circuit pursuant to § 6 (f) of the Act, 29 U.S.C. § 655 (f). They contend in this Court, as they did below, that the Act requires OSHA to demonstrate that its Standard reflects a reasonable relationship between the costs and benefits associated with the Standard. Respondents, the Secretary of Labor and two labor organizations, counter that Congress balanced the costs and benefits in the Act itself, and that the Act should therefore be construed not to require OSHA to do so. They interpret the Act as mandating that OSHA enact the most protective standard possible to eliminate a significant risk of material health impairment, subject to the constraints of economic and technological feasibility. The Court of Appeals held that the Act did not require OSHA to compare costs and benefits.

*   *   *

The starting point of our analysis is the language of the statute itself. Section 6(b)(5) of the Act, 29 U.S.C. § 655(b)(5) (emphasis added), provides:

> The Secretary, in promulgating standards dealing with toxic materials or harmful physical agents under this subsection, shall set the standard which most adequately assures, *to the extent feasible*, on the basis of the best available evidence, that no employee will suffer material impairment of health or functional capacity even if such employee has regular exposure to the hazard dealt with by such standard for the period of his working life.

Although their interpretations differ, all parties agree that the phrase "to the extent feasible" contains the critical language in § 6(b)(5) for purposes of these cases.

The plain meaning of the word "feasible" supports respondents' interpretation of the statute. According to Webster's Third New International Dictionary of the English Language 831 (1976), "feasible" means "capable of being done, executed, or effected." . . . Thus, § 6(b)(5) directs the Secretary to issue the standard that "most adequately assures . . . that no employee will suffer material impairment of health," limited only by the extent to which this is "capable of being done." In effect then, as the Court of Appeals held, Congress itself defined the basic relationship between costs and benefits, by placing the "benefit" of worker health above all other considerations save those making attainment of this "benefit" unachievable. Any standard based on a balancing of costs and benefits by the Secretary that strikes a different balance than that struck by Congress would be inconsistent with the command set forth in § 6(b)(5). Thus, cost-benefit analysis by OSHA is not required by the statute because feasibility analysis is.

When Congress has intended that an agency engage in cost-benefit analysis, it has clearly indicated such intent on the face of the statute. One . . . example is the Outer Continental Shelf Lands Act Amendments of 1978, providing that offshore drilling operations shall use

(continued on next page)

AMERICAN TEXTILE MANUFACTURERS INSTITUTE v. DONOVAN
452 U.S. 490 (1981)

(continued)

the best available and safest technologies which the Secretary determines to be economically *feasible*, wherever failure of equipment would have a significant effect on safety, health, or the environment, except where the Secretary determines that the *incremental benefits are clearly insufficient to justify the incremental costs of using such technologies.*

These and other statutes demonstrate that Congress uses specific language when intending that an agency engage in cost-benefit analysis. Certainly in light of its ordinary meaning, the word "feasible" cannot be construed to articulate such congressional intent. We therefore reject the argument that Congress required cost-benefit analysis in § 6(b)(5).

Suing the Government

In the modern administrative state, the range of government activity is immense, and administrative agencies frequently get in the way of business enterprise. Often bureaucratic involvement is wholly legitimate, compelled by law; sometimes, however, agencies or government officials may overstep their bounds, in a fit of zeal or spite. What recourse does the private individual or company have?

Mainly for historical reasons, it has always been more difficult to sue the government than to haul private individuals into court. For one thing, the government has long had recourse to the doctrine of *sovereign immunity* (p. 37) as a shield against lawsuits. In 1976, Congress amended the Administrative Procedure Act to waive any federal claim to sovereign immunity in cases of injunctive or other non-monetary relief. In 1946 in the Federal Tort Claims Act, Congress waived sovereign immunity of the federal government for most tort claims for money damages, although the act contains several exceptions for specific agencies. (For example, one cannot sue for injuries resulting from fiscal operations of the Treasury Department, or for injuries stemming from activities of the military in wartime.) The act also contains a major exception for claims "based upon [an official's] exercise or performance or the failure to exercise or perform a discretionary function or duty." This exception prevents suits against parole boards for paroling dangerous criminals who then kill or maim in the course of another crime and against officials whose decision to ship explosive materials by public carrier leads to mass deaths and injuries following an explo-

sion en route. [Dalehite v. United States, 346 U.S. 15 (1953)]

In recent years, the Supreme Court has been stripping away the traditional immunity enjoyed by many government officials against personal suits. Some government employees—judges, prosecutors, legislators, and the president, for example—have absolute immunity against suit for official actions. But many public administrators and government employees have at best a qualified immunity. Under a provision of the Civil Rights Act of 1871 (so-called Section 1983 actions), *state* officials can be sued in federal court for money damages whenever "under color of any state law" they deprive anyone of his rights under the Constitution or federal law. In *Bivens* v. *Six Unknown Federal Narcotics Agents*, 403 U.S. 388 (1971), the Supreme Court held that *federal* agents may be sued for violating the plaintiff's Fourth Amendment rights against an unlawful search of his home. Subsequent cases have followed this logic to permit suits for violations of other constitutional provisions. This area of the law is in a state of flux, and it is likely to continue to evolve.

Sometimes damage is done to an individual or business because the government has given out erroneous information. For example, suppose that Charles, a bewildered, disabled Navy employee, is receiving a federal disability annuity. Under the regulations, he would lose his pension if he took a job that paid him in each of two succeeding years more than 80% of what he earned in his old Navy job. A few years later, Congress changed the law, making him ineligible if he earned more than 80% in any one year. For many years Charles earned considerably less than the ceiling amount. But then one year he got the opportunity to make some extra money. Not wishing to lose his pension, he called an employee relations specialist at the Navy and asked how much he could earn and still keep his pension. The specialist gave him erroneous information over the telephone and then sent him an out-of-date form that said Charles could safely take on the extra work. Unfortunately, as it turned out Charles did exceed the salary limit, and so the government cut off his pension during the time he earned too much. Charles sues to recover his lost pension. He argues that he relied to his detriment on false information supplied by the Navy and that in fairness the government should be "estopped" from denying his claim.

Unfortunately for Charles, he will lose his case. In *Office of Personnel Management* v. *Richmond*, 110 S.Ct. 2465 (1990), the Supreme Court reasoned that it would be unconstitutional to permit recovery. The Appropriations Clause of Article I says that federal money can be paid out only through an appropriation made by law. The law prevented this particular payment to be made. If the Court were to make an exception, it would permit executive officials in effect to make binding payments, even though unauthorized, simply by misrepresenting the facts. The harsh reality, therefore, is that mistakes of the government are generally held against the individual, not the government, unless the law specifically provides for recompense (as, for example, in the Federal Tort Claims Act discussed just above).

CHAPTER SUMMARY

Administrative rules and regulations constitute the largest body of laws that directly affect business. These regulations are issued by dozens of federal and state agencies that regulate virtually every aspect of modern business life, including the natural environment, corporate finance, transportation, telecommunications, energy, labor relations, and trade practices. The administrative agencies derive their power to promulgate regulations from statutes passed by Congress or state legislatures.

The agencies have a variety of powers. They can license companies to carry on certain activities or prohibit them from doing so, lay down codes of conduct, set rates that companies may charge for their services, and supervise various aspects of business.

At the federal level, administrative agencies are governed by the Administrative Procedure Act, which separates judicial functions within agencies from their rule-making functions. Many agency decisions may be appealed to the courts, which are, however, forbidden from substituting their own judgment about the worth of the regulations. The courts' role is limited to ascertaining whether the administrative regulations exceed the legislative authority delegated to the agency and whether it had sufficient evidence to make the ruling it did in a particular case.

KEY TERMS

Administrative law judge	p. 147	Independent agencies	p. 144
		Rule-making	p. 147
FOIA	p. 152		

SELF-TEST QUESTIONS

1. The Freedom of Information Act:
    (a) directs all federal agencies to open their files for public inspection
    (b) applies only to federal cabinet departments, not to independent agencies
    (c) specifies types of information that the federal government must disclose on request
    (d) lists types of information that may never be disclosed
2. The Administrative Procedure Act says that:
    (a) federal agencies may not act without first holding an evidentiary hearing
    (b) agencies must first give notice of their intention to promulgate a rule
    (c) the government may not issue a rule unless everyone who wants to has had a chance to come to Washington to testify about it
    (d) regulations are effective the instant an agency adopts them
3. Sovereign immunity is:
    (a) a federal statute preventing people from suing the government
    (b) an exception to a federal statute permitting suits for governmental negligence
    (c) an exception to the general common-law rule that plaintiffs may sue to recover damages for injuries inflicted on them negligently
    (d) a law that no one may sue the President
4. Congress cannot give the Comptroller General the power to cut the federal budget because:
    (a) the Constitution forbids delegating legislative power
    (b) the federal budget is the exclusive prerogative of the President
    (c) only the courts can cut budgets

(d) the Comptroller is a legislative officer and cutting the budget is an executive power

5. Congress may:

(a) give powers to independent federal agencies and take away powers from them

(b) not take away powers from federal agencies because they are independent

(c) authorize the President to set salaries of top agency commissioners

(d) appoint the top commissioners of federal independent agencies

DEMONSTRATION PROBLEM

Assume that the Federal Trade Commission issued a regulation stating that henceforth all used car dealers would have to tell prospective customers how many miles the car had been driven and which parts of the car were used and how old they were. To what branch or branches of government could the used-car lobby turn to eliminate the regulation? What action could other branches of the government take to eliminate the regulation?

PROBLEMS

1. Acme Insurance Company has a new type of medical benefits policy it wants to sell to former military personnel. Because of the policy's favorable terms, however, Acme does not want to ensure people who were injured or had diseases in the service. Since it doesn't trust applicants to tell the truth, Acme demands under the Freedom of Information Act that the U.S. Department of Defense (DOD) release the medical records of all discharged and retired military personnel. Must DOD turn over all the records? May it refuse to turn over any of the records? May a former member of the military force DOD under the Freedom of Information Act to keep his military records private? Must DOD turn over a medical record unless the person named in the record objects? Why or why not?

2. Suppose the State Commerce Commission, which regulates trucking, were to adopt a rule permitting any trucker who might be affected by a tariff decision to have ninety days to object after the tariff is published. Constant Truckers, Inc., objects to a tariff that sets a price of five dollars per mile maximum for hauling certain types of goods between the capital and any city in the state. When published, the tariff says it will take effect in thirty days. On the forty-fifth day, Constant objects and charges a customer ten dollars a mile. The customer complains, and the agency commences a disciplinary action against Con-

stant to see whether the trucker's license should be suspended. What is Constant's defense?

3. The Equal Employment Opportunity Commission seeks data about the racial composition of Terrific Textiles's labor force. Terrific refuses on the grounds that inadvertent disclosure of the numbers might cause certain "elements" to picket its factories. The EEOC takes Terrific to court to get the data. What result?

4. In order to police the profession, the state legislature has just passed a law permitting the State Plumbers' Association the power to hold hearings to determine whether a particular plumber has violated the plumbing code of ethics, written by the Association. Sam, a plumber, objects to the convening of a hearing when he is accused by Roger, a fellow plumber, of acting unethically by soliciting business from Roger's customers. Sam goes to court, seeking to enjoin the Association's Disciplinary Committee from holding the hearing. What result? How would you argue Sam's case? The Association's case?

5. Assume that the new President of the United States was elected overwhelmingly by pledging in his campaign to "do away with bureaucrats who interfere in your lives." The day he takes the oath of office he determines to carry out his pledge. Discuss which of the following courses may he lawfully follow: (a) Fire all incumbent commissioners of federal agencies in order to install new appointees. (b) Demand that all pending regulations being considered by federal agencies be submitted to the White House for review and redrafting, if necessary. (c) Interview potential nominees for agency positions to determine whether their regulatory philosophy is consistent with his.

6. Assume that a new Federal Banking Commission, an independent federal administrative agency, has promulgated a rule prohibiting all banks from lending more money than it has on hand in deposits on any given day. The President and many influential members of Congress fear that this rule will destroy the banking system and the economy. A special White House task force on administrative policy has just given the President a policy paper listing several options to follow: (a) The President should order the FBC to rescind the rule. (b) The President should demand that Congress pass a law abolishing the agency. (c) The President should demand that Congress pass a law repealing the rule. (d) The President should ask the commissioners of the FBC to vote to rescind the rule. The President seeks your advice, along with your reasons, about which course of action he may lawfully follow.

7. Congress wants to end the pollution of navigable waterways. The chair of a Congressional committee dealing with water pollution comes to you for advice about what to do. She tells you that the committee is considering, among other things, the following possibilities, and she wants to know whether you see any constitutional difficulties with

any of them: (a) a law establishing a new Navigable Waterways Commission, with power to "do whatever it takes to prevent all pollution in navigable waterways"; (b) a law giving the Department of Transportation power to enact rules defining the permissible level of pollution permitted by various forms of transportation on navigable waterways and by factories and others who dump wastes into waterways; (c) a law making it a crime punishable by five years in jail "to do anything that causes navigable waterways to be polluted." Discuss.

8. Prestige Pharmaceuticals applies for a one-time $10 million federal research grant to conduct tests on a promising new wonder drug to cure cancer. Under federal regulations, all applications must be received by January 1. Prestige has a letter from the head of the department responsible for the grants stating that the time to apply has been extended until March 1. Prestige does extra work on its application and mails it in on February 20. The agency receives it on February 25 and writes back that the deadline was January 1. Prestige discovers that its arch-rival, Friendly Pharmaceuticals, has bribed the head of the agency to send out the erroneous letter. Prestige wants to know whether it has a legal remedy for such actions.

ANSWERS TO SELF-TEST QUESTIONS

1. (c)   2. (b)   3. (c)   4. (d)   5. (a)

SUGGESTED ANSWER TO DEMONSTRATION PROBLEM

The used-car lobby could go to Congress and ask it to repeal the regulation. Congress could do so by enacting a law explicitly repealing the FTC's rule. The President would have to sign the bill or, as the Constitution provides, Congress could override his veto by enacting the bill by a two-thirds vote in each house. Used-car dealers might also challenge the regulation in court, asserting that the FTC does not have such authority under the law giving it power to regulate the used-car industry. The dealers would not likely prevail on this argument, since the Federal Trade Commission Act gives the FTC extensive power over interstate commerce to prevent fraud and unfair trade. The FTC itself could repeal its own rule, as new commissioners were appointed (usually by a new president) who did not agree with the policy behind the rule.

CHAPTER 6

CHAPTER OVERVIEW

Convergence of the Law and Business Ethics

Divergence of the Law and Business Ethics

The Law and Social Change

Business Ethics and Social Responsibility

*I*n Chapter 1 (p. 5) we noted the relationship between ethical principles and the law. Here we explore this relationship in greater detail and examine how it affects management decision making.

The dictionaries define ethics as a system of moral conduct, but establishing an ethical standard in specific cases is difficult because our pluralistic society has many different moral codes. To be sure, most moral codes condemn some kinds of conduct—murder, rape, theft—and thus from time immemorial legal codes have prohibited these acts. Regarding other types of conduct, society is far more equivocal.

Abortion, for example, is widely condemned as murder and widely justified as the free choice of a woman over her body. Although as individuals we can debate this issue long into the night, as a society we rarely have the luxury of embracing, or avoiding, both standards. Specific cases almost always require yes or no answers. Should the law permit women freely to seek abortions or prohibit them from doing so? When the Supreme Court considered the issue in *Roe v. Wade*, 410 U.S. 113 (1973), Justice Blackmun noted "briefly the wide divergence of thinking on this most sensitive and difficult question":

There has always been strong support of the view that life does not begin until live birth. This was the belief of the Stoics. It appears to be the predominant, though not the unanimous, attitude of the Jewish faith. It may be taken to represent also the position of a large segment of the Protestant community. . . . The Aristotelian theory of "mediate animation," that held sway throughout the Middle Ages and the Renaissance in Europe, continued to be official Roman Catholic dogma until the 19th century, despite opposition to this "ensoulment" theory from those in the Church who would recognize the existence of life from the moment of conception. The latter is now, of course, the official belief of the Catholic Church. As one brief *amicus* discloses, this is a view strongly held by many non-Catholics as well, and by many physicians.

In resolving this issue, the Court put the law onto a path that coincides with certain moral systems only because so many different approaches exist. The 7–2 majority held that secular courts cannot definitively determine when life begins and that legally the fetus has never been regarded as a whole person. Given a woman's constitutional right to control her body, the Court's answer was to recognize women's freedom to choose abortions during the first trimester of pregnancy and to permit the states to regulate the procedures of abortion thereafter and even to prohibit abortion, to preserve the potential life of the fetus in the third trimester. This is a *legal* resolution of the abortion controversy, but not an *ethical* one—a woman may have an abortion but is obviously not required to have one.

Ethical conundrums exist in the business community as well. Suppose your boss says you are doing fine work but at the moment the company cannot afford to give you a formal raise. Instead, she suggests that the company "won't look too closely at your expense accounts for a while." Is it ethical to pad your expense account on the ground that the boss has implicitly given you a raise through a different route? As we will see, the business community is split to some extent on whether this is appropriate behavior (p. 175).

Even when there is a consensus on an ethical standard, law and morality are not necessarily the same. In some cases, legal principles may mesh closely with ethical standards, even though the ethical standards are not attainable by the average person. In a famous British case, *Regina* v. *Dudley and Stephens*, 14 Q.B.D. 273 (1884), two sailors were prosecuted for murder in killing and actually eating the body of the cabin boy after nine days in a shipwreck on the high seas. The courts upheld the murder conviction, even while acknowledging that the sailors would have

died had they done anything different. Recognizing that the sailors acted from an instinct for survival, the queen commuted their sentence to six months' imprisonment. In other cases, the law may diverge from the ethical rule—as noted earlier, the law generally imposes no duty on a bystander to help someone in distress (p. 5).

In the discussion that follows, we will first examine situations in which law and business ethics converge. We will then examine two situations in which they diverge—that is, when conduct is illegal but ethical, and when it is legal but unethical. In Figure 6-1, boxes 1 and 4 represent the convergent situations, and boxes 2 and 3 the divergent settings.

CONVERGENCE OF THE LAW AND BUSINESS ETHICS

Behavior is often both legal and ethical or, conversely, illegal and unethical. Within the business community, many examples illustrate this convergence.

Contracts

Contract law imposes a duty to act in good faith. This duty is found in both the Restatement (Second) of

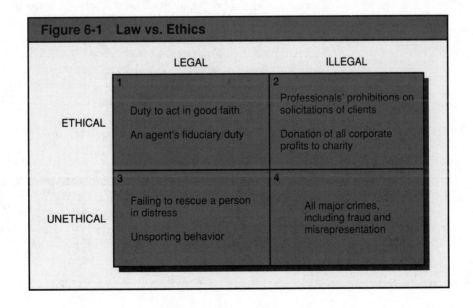

Figure 6-1   Law vs. Ethics

	LEGAL	ILLEGAL
ETHICAL	1 Duty to act in good faith An agent's fiduciary duty	2 Professionals' prohibitions on solicitations of clients Donation of all corporate profits to charity
UNETHICAL	3 Failing to rescue a person in distress Unsporting behavior	4 All major crimes, including fraud and misrepresentation

Contracts, Section 205, and the Uniform Commercial Code, Section 1–203. When this duty is breached, the aggrieved party may obtain remedies beyond those normally provided for in contract law if the contract-ing parties had a special relationship (such as that between an insurer and insured) and, in some states, even in the absence of a special relationship, as the next case demonstrates.

SEAMAN'S DIRECT BUYING SERVICE, INC. v. STANDARD OIL CO. OF CAL.
36 Cal.3d 752, 686 P.2d 1158 (1984)

[The plaintiff, Seaman's Direct Buying Service, Inc., a dealer in ship sup-plies, sued Standard Oil Company of California for breaching a marine deal-ership contract that Seaman's needed in order to lease marine space from the City of Eureka, California. When conditions in the oil industry changed and a federal allocation program went into effect, Standard told Seaman's that federal regulations prevented performance of the contract.]

In telephone calls and personal meetings with Seaman's, Standard indi-cated that the new federal regulations were the *only* barrier to the contract. "[I]f it wasn't for the [federal agency], . . . [Standard] would be willing to go ahead with the contract. . . ." "If [Seaman's could] get the federal gov-ernment to change that order so that Standard could supply [Seaman's] with fuel [Standard] would be very happy. . . ." Standard even supplied Sea-man's with the forms necessary to seek a supply authorization from the fed-eral agency and helped fill them out.

As a result of these efforts, a supply order was issued on February 4, 1974. Standard responded by changing its position. The company contended now that no binding agreement with Seaman's had ever been reached. Therefore, Standard decided to appeal the order "[b]ecause [it] did not want to take on any new business." When Seaman's learned of the appeal, it twice wrote to Standard requesting an explanation. None was forthcoming. Standard's fed-eral appeal was successful. Internal memoranda reveal Standard's reaction to this result: "[g]reat!!" "We are recommending to other div[isions] that they follow your example."

Seaman's then appealed and this decision was, in turn, reversed. The new decision provided that an order "direct[ing] [Standard] to fulfill supply obli-gations to Seaman's" would be issued upon the filing of a copy of a court decree that a valid contract existed between the parties under state law.

Seaman's asked Standard to stipulate to the existence of a contract, ex-plaining that it could not continue in operation throughout the time that a trial would take. In reply, Standard's representative laughed and said, "See you in court." Seaman's testified that if Standard had cooperated, Seaman's would have borrowed funds to remain in business until 1976 when the new marina opened.

Seaman's discontinued operations in early 1975. Soon thereafter, the com-pany filed suit against Standard, charging Standard with breach of contract, fraud, breach of the implied covenant of good faith and fair dealing, and interference with Seaman's contractual relationship with the City. The case was tried before a jury which returned a verdict for Seaman's on all but the fraud cause of action. For breach of contract, the jury awarded compensatory damages of $397,050. For tortious breach of the implied covenant of good faith and fair dealing, they awarded $397,050 in compensatory damages and $11,058,810 in punitive damages. Finally, for intentional interference with an advantageous business relationship, the jury set compensatory damages at $1,588,200 and punitive damages at $11,058,810.

Standard moved for a new trial, charging, inter alia, that the damages were excessive as a matter of law. The trial court conditionally granted the motion unless Seaman's consented to a reduction of punitive damages on the interference count to $6 million and on the good faith count to $1 million. Seaman's consented to the reduction, and judgment was entered accordingly. Standard appeals from the judgment. Seaman's has filed a cross-appeal.

★   ★   ★

The principal issue raised by this appeal is whether, and under what circumstances, a breach of the implied covenant of good faith and fair dealing in a commercial contract may give rise to an action in tort. Standard contends that a tort action for breach of the implied covenant has always been, and should continue to be, limited to cases where the underlying contract is one of insurance. Seaman's, pointing to several recent cases decided by this court and the Courts of Appeal, challenges this contention. A brief review of the development of the tort is in order.

It is well settled that, in California, the law implies in *every* contract a covenant of good faith and fair dealing. . . . Broadly stated, that covenant requires that neither party do anything which will deprive the other of the benefits of the agreement.

★   ★   ★

While the proposition that the law implies a covenant of good faith and fair dealing in all contracts is well established, the proposition advanced by Seaman's—that breach of the covenant always gives rise to an action in tort—is not so clear. In holding that a tort action is available for breach of the covenant in an insurance contract, we have emphasized the "special relationship" between insurer and insured, characterized by elements of public interest, adhesion, and fiduciary responsibility. (*Egan* v. *Mutual of Omaha Ins. Co.*, 24 Cal.3d at p. 820, 169 Cal.Rptr. 691, 620 P.2d 141.) No doubt there are other relationships with similar characteristics and deserving of similar legal treatment.

When we move from such special relationships to consideration of the tort remedy in the context of the ordinary commercial contract, we move into largely uncharted and potentially dangerous waters. Here, parties of roughly equal bargaining power are free to shape the contours of their agreement and to include provisions for attorney fees and liquidated damages in the event of breach. They may not be permitted to disclaim the covenant of good faith but they are free, within reasonable limits at least, to agree upon the standards by which application of the covenant is to be measured. In such contracts, it may be difficult to distinguish between breach of the covenant and breach of contract, and there is the risk that interjecting tort remedies will

(*continued on next page*)

(continued)

SEAMAN'S DIRECT BUYING SERVICE, INC. v. STANDARD OIL CO. OF CAL.
36 Cal.3d 752, 686 P.2d 1158 (1984)

intrude upon the expectations of the parties. This is not to say that tort remedies have no place in such a commercial context, but that it is wise to proceed with caution in determining their scope and application.

For the purposes of this case it is unnecessary to decide the broad question which Seaman's poses. Indeed, it is not even necessary to predicate liability on a breach of the implied covenant. It is sufficient to recognize that a party to a contract may incur tort remedies when, in addition to breaching the contract, it seeks to shield itself from liability by denying, in bad faith and without probable cause, that the contract exists.

It has been held that a party to a contract may be subject to tort liability, including punitive damages, if he coerces the other party to pay more than is due under the contract terms through the threat of a lawsuit, made " 'without probable cause and with no belief in the existence of the cause of action.' " (*Crater Well Drilling, Inc.* (1976) 276 Or. 789, 556 P.2d 679, 681.) There is little difference, in principle, between a contracting party obtaining excess payment in such manner, and a contracting party seeking to avoid all liability on a meritorious contract claim by adopting a "stonewall" position ("see you in court") without probable cause and with no belief in the existence of a defense. Such conduct goes beyond the mere breach of contract. It offends accepted notions of business ethics. Acceptance of tort remedies in such a situation is not likely to intrude upon the bargaining relationship or upset reasonable expectations of the contracting parties.

*   *   *

[The court reversed the judgment for Seaman's and remanded for further proceedings on the grounds that the trial judge gave erroneous instructions to the jury.]

A person making a contract has another ethical duty enshrined in law: the duty to avoid acting unconscionably. We examine later (p. 377) how courts have sought to give content to this rather amorphous term, but whatever it might mean, and however its meaning might shift from case to case, the duty is solidly rooted in law. The Uniform Commercial Code (described in Chapter 7, p. 189) empowers the courts to ignore any term of a contract that is unconscionable when made, or even to refuse to enforce the contract altogether.

Agency Law

Ethical concepts also affect the relationship between principal and agent (discussed at greater length in Chapter 37). An agent (employee) legally owes the principal (employer) a *fiduciary duty*, a duty of the highest trust and loyalty (see p. 825). Principals are also not free to act as they please; they too owe duties to agents. Quite recently, for example, some courts and legislatures have begun to recognize exceptions to the ancient "employment-at-will" doctrine (see p. 1173) that gives employers the absolute legal right to fire employees whenever they like, with or without reason. For example, a public policy exception that has developed in several states bars employers from discharging "whistleblowers"—employees who tell public authorities about illegal activities in which employers are engaged. Still, the principal is generally less legally constrained than the agent (see, for example, the *Pierce* case, p. 169).

Corporate Officers and Directors

Officers and directors of corporations owe a general fiduciary duty to shareholders and to their corporation as a separate entity. This duty arises at common law, and since the 1930s it has been embedded in federal securities laws. For example, the Securities Exchange Act of 1934 bars insider trading and requires those with inside information to disclose it to the general public before they can trade in the stock (see Chapter 44). However, this duty does not apply to everyone: There is no duty to disclose, the Supreme Court has said, in cases where the person who traded on inside information "was not [the corporation's] agent, . . . was not a fiduciary, [or] was not a person in whom the sellers [of securities] had placed their trust and confidence." [Chiarella v. United States, 445 U.S. 222 (1980)] The law thus imposes legal duties only on those who, under broad community standards, would also have an ethical duty to disclose.

Trade Regulation

With the passage of the Federal Trade Commission Act of 1914 (see Chapter 48), Congress created a federal agency, the Federal Trade Commission, to curb "unfair methods of competition" and "unfair or deceptive acts or practices." Though not defined in the legislation, it is clear that the law aims at precisely those kinds of acts that are commonly understood to be "unfair" in the moral sense. One example is the "bait and switch" advertisement, which brags of sale merchandise to lure customers into the store, only to discover that the item advertised is unavailable, and that some other, perhaps inferior, certainly more expensive, merchandise is waiting.

DIVERGENCE OF THE LAW AND BUSINESS ETHICS

When law and ethics are congruent, few have reason to complain about legal sanctions. But when they diverge, managers face a dilemma. On the one hand, managers who make decisions solely on the basis of what they perceive to be ethical conduct run the risk that their actions will be in violation of the law. On the other hand, managers who choose to adopt legal rules as the sole guide to their decision making ignore the fact that the law often embraces only minimal standards of ethical behavior. As Alexander Solzhenitsyn pointed out in his celebrated Harvard graduation address in 1978:

> I have spent all my life under a Communist regime, and I will tell you that a society without any objective legal scale is a terrible one indeed. But a society with no other scale but the legal one is not quite worthy of man either. The letter of the law is too cold and formal to have a beneficial influence on society. Whenever the tissue of life is woven of legalistic relations, there is an atmosphere of moral mediocrity, paralyzing man's noblest impulses.

Illegal but Ethical Conduct

Under various circumstances, conduct that may be considered ethical on the basis of an individual's personal or professional standards violates a principle of law. For example, under the formal canons of professional ethics of many engineering societies, members may not solicit clients from other engineers. This ethical standard is justified in part as a means to ensure that engineers do not do unsafe work because they have underbid to get a job. Unfortunately, this ethical standard violates the federal antitrust laws, as the *National Society of Professional Engineers* case shows (p. 1023).

Similarly, a personal standard can run afoul of the law. Assume that the majority shareholder of a business corporation decides that the corporation (1) should donate a substantial amount of money to her alma mater, and (2) should be run for humanitarian purposes. Could minority shareholders challenge these ethical decisions on legal grounds? As is so often the case in legal analysis, the answer is yes and no. As the following case demonstrates, corporations may engage in humanitarian activities to a limited degree.

**UNION PACIFIC
RAILROAD CO. v.
TRUSTEES, INC.
8 UTAH 2d 101, 329 P.2d
398 (1958).**

[Union Pacific Railroad Company sought a declaratory judgment that it could lawfully contribute $5,000 to a nonprofit organization for charitable, scientific, religious, or educational purposes. The lower court had held that it could not. Neither the company's charter nor the applicable state corporate statute expressly gave the corporation the power to make the contribution.]

HENRIOD, JUSTICE.

*   *   *

Directors of the plaintiff testified with singular unanimity that such new concept conceived in a shifting socio-economic atmosphere was born of new corporate business policy. It seems to be nurtured by legislative, corporate and judicial thinking. A reasonable percentage of corporate income, they urge, should be earmarked for worthy causes, as a necessary and proper item of business expense, just as funds are tagged for advertising, public relations and the like.

Mr. E. Roland Harriman, Chairman of plaintiff's Board, said "I think it is good business to do so; in the long run beneficial to our stockholders . . . I think the public has come to expect that we will support worthwhile local and national causes, and, in effect, we agree with this viewpoint." Mr. John S. Sinclair, director, said: "We have come to expect corporations to behave in the field of social consciousness as individuals would behave,—that is, with a prudent eye to its financial capacity and selectivity as to the objects of its generosity . . . Corporate donations create good will in the community."

*   *   *

It strikes us as being rather inconceivable, in what seems to be a visible, substantial national trend, that men heretofore known for their administrative and executive experience and ability, suddenly and deliberately would espouse a program on behalf of a corporation in which they are interested, and to whose shareholders they are amenable and accountable, if they were not confident that their company presently and directly, or within the foreseeable future, would receive a quid pro quo as the resultant of good will engendered by contributions.

*   *   *

The iconoclast may discount the suggestion that corporations have been endowed with a new kind of altruistic conscience, as being mythical and hardly a reason to support corporate action based on implied power, but aside from any desire to assist others without hope of reward, when a contribution to a laudable cause has been made, a real, important and serious question is posed: Why was the contribution made? We believe that if it were made with the studied and not unreasonable conviction that it would benefit the corporation, it should be the type of thing that should rest in the sound discretion of management and within the ambit of a legitimate exercise of implied authority in the ordinary course of the company's business. It is not too much unlike the sponsoring of a baseball team, subsidizing promising scholars with a view toward possibly employing them later on, giving to the local community chest, paying the salary of a public relations expert, sponsoring a concert or television program, or conducting a newspaper or radio advertising program. Such actions seldom produce any immediate and direct corporate benefits, but all involve use of corporate funds that otherwise could have gone to shareholders had such funds remained unspent. Few would venture that the company could not do all these things without express, specific authority in the charter. We think that a power once denied today may be implied under changed conditions and philosophies, and that in the light of present day industrial and business exigencies, common sense dictates that included in the implied powers of a corporation, an authority should be numbered that allows contributions of reasonable amounts to selected charitable, scientific, religious or educational institutions, if they appear reasonably designed to assure a present or foreseeable future benefit to the corporation; that management's decisions in such matters should not be rendered impotent unless arbitrary and unreasonably indefensible, or unless countermanded or eliminated by action of the shareholders at a proper meeting.

The contribution in the instant case appears to fall within implied corporate powers under such principles.

[Reversed]

Union Pacific's conclusion is now incorporated into most modern corporation statutes. But to run a business corporation entirely for humanitarian purposes, though it might be ethical by the standards of the managers, would be contrary to the law.

In a famous case, *Dodge* v. *Ford Motor Co.,* 170 N.W. 668 (Mich. 1919), reprinted on p. 935, the Dodge brothers sued the Ford Motor Company to enjoin the company from building a new plant and to force the directors to declare a dividend. During the trial, Henry Ford testified that he wanted to plow money that could otherwise be paid as dividends back into the company because he was against "awful profits." Ford's ambition, in his words, was "to employ still more men, to spread the benefits of this industrial system to the greatest possible number, to help them build up their lives and their homes. To do this we are putting the greatest share of our profits back in the business." The result: the court ordered the company to pay the dividends, since a corporation is run for its shareholders, not for humanity. (The court, however, refused to halt the corporate expansion because "judges are not business experts.")

Beyond the legal result in the *Ford* case, there is room to disagree over whether Ford was acting ethically. Father R. L. Bruckberger, a French priest, thought he was. Commenting on Ford's stance, Father Bruckberger suggested that "in all the world's universities all young people seeking some knowledge of political economy should be required to learn [Ford's philosophy] . . . by heart. It is as important in economics as the Declaration of Independence is in politics. . . . [It] should be looked upon as the businessman's Hippocratic Oath." (Lewis, 1976, pp. 101–102) But Milton Friedman, the well-known University of Chicago economist, demurs: ". . . [T]here is one and only one social responsibility of business—to use its resources and engage in activities designed to increase its profits so long as it stays within the rules of the game, which is to say, engages in open and free competition, without deception or fraud." (Friedman, 1962, p. 133)

Despite the law's traditional preference for the interests of shareholders, new laws, called "other constituency statutes," have been enacted rapidly in 25 states, beginning in 1983. As discussed in chapter

LAW AND LIFE

BOX 6-1

America's Cup Victory by San Diego Is Upheld by New York's Highest Court

[Legal but unethical conduct is often allowed by law. Whether certain behavior is considered "sporting" or "fair" has nothing to do with what is legal. However, it may take a court's opinion to determine whether legal issues are involved.—AUTHORS' NOTE]

The decision is the final word in the contentious dispute between the San Diego Yacht Club and the Mercury Bay Boating Club of New Zealand. The New Zealand challenger had claimed that San Diego violated the spirit of the 132-year-old international contest by using a catamaran to defeat New Zealand's 90-foot monohull in 1988. Mercury Bay claimed that the rules required San Diego to use a boat similar in size to the challenger's.

The New York Court of Appeals in Albany ruled that while San Diego's use of the catamaran might not have been fair, it wasn't illegal. In a 5-2 decision, the judges said the courts

NOT SPORTING, BUT LEGAL

aren't the proper forum for determining the fairness of a sport.

"The question of whether particular conduct is 'sporting' or 'fair' in the context of a particular sporting event . . . is wholly distinct from the question of whether it is legal," wrote Judge Fritz Alexander II in the majority opinion. "Questions of sportsmanship and 'fairness' with respect to sporting contests depend largely upon the rules of the particular sport and the expertise of those knowledgeable in that sport; they are not questions suitable for judicial resolution."

The court said that nowhere in the rules governing the contest is the defending yacht club required to race a vessel similar to the challenger's entry. The America's Cup is governed by New York state law because it was formed by the New York Yacht Club.

Andrew Johns, an attorney for the New Zealand club in Auckland, said Mercury Bay accepts the court's decision as final and is preparing for the next race, expected to be in 1992. "It's all systems go. We're back to an

on-the-water campaign," he said. But he added that the court's interpretation of the rules gives an unfair advantage to the defender. "What the majority has said is 'anything goes.' There is no restriction on the defender on length or any of the other factors that the challenger must give notice of," Mr. Johns said.

Harold R. Tyler Jr., an attorney for the San Diego club, said Mercury Bay's own interpretation of the rules would have put the defender at a disadvantage. Because the race has to be held 10 months after the challenge is made, the San Diego club wouldn't have had enough time to construct a 90-foot monohull to match New Zealand's entry, he said.

"Fairness is a slippery concept," Mr. Tyler said. "It's sort of like beauty—it's all in the eye of the beholder."

Both Mr. Tyler and Mr. Johns said that an agreement reached by many yacht clubs in 1988 will probably prevent similar disputes from occurring again. The lawyers said the case may also lead to changes clarifying the rules of the competition.

Source: *Wall Street Journal*, April 27, 1990

---

43 (p. 166), it is possible that courts during the 1990s will interpret these statutes as giving considerably more leeway to directors to favor interests other than shareholders in deciding what is best for the corporation.

Legal but Unethical Conduct

There is a vast range of instances in which the law has allowed conduct that many consider unethical—from unsporting behavior (see **Box 6-1**) to investment in South Africa. Individuals face special problems when confronted with this conduct because it is sanctioned by the law. For example, suppose a real estate devel-

oper hires a woman to buy homes from elderly, poor homeowners in a deteriorating neighborhood. The developer instructs her to act on his behalf as a secret agent; that is, not to disclose to any of the sellers that she is working for the developer. The woman knows that if she fully discloses the facts, property values will double. Her feeling that this activity is unethical finds no support in the law, which upholds contracts made by secret agents (Chapter 38). Consequently, she must resolve her dilemma on the basis of her personal standards. If she chooses to follow the dictates of her conscience, rather than the letter of the law, she will not—unlike Henry Ford—have violated the law. However, as the following case notes, she may still face extralegal sanctions, such as the loss of her job.

PIERCE v. ORTHO PHARMACEUTICAL CORP.
84 N.J. 58, 417 A.2d 505 (1980)

POLLOCK, J.

This case presents the question whether an employee at will has a cause of action against her employer to recover damages for the termination of her employment following her refusal to continue a project she viewed as medically unethical. . . .

Plaintiff, Dr. Grace Pierce, sued for damages after termination of her employment with defendant, Ortho Pharmaceutical Corporation. The trial judge granted defendant's motion for summary judgment. The Appellate Division reversed and remanded for a full trial. . . .

*   *   *

Ortho specializes in the development and manufacture of therapeutic and reproductive drugs. Dr. Pierce is a medical doctor who was first employed by Ortho in 1971 as an Associate Director of Medical Research. She signed no contract except a secrecy agreement, and her employment was not for a fixed term. She was an employee at will. In 1973, she became the Director of Medical Research/Therapeutics, one of three major sections of the Medical Research Department. Her primary responsibilities were to oversee development of therapeutic drugs and to establish procedures for testing those drugs for safety, effectiveness, and marketability. Her immediate supervisor was Dr. Samuel Pasquale, Executive Medical Director.

In the spring of 1975, Dr. Pierce was the only medical doctor on a project team developing loperamide, a liquid drug for treatment of diarrhea in infants, children, and elderly persons. The proposed formulation contained saccharin. Although the concentration was consistent with the formula for loperamide marketed in Europe, the project team agreed that the formula was unsuitable for use in the United States. An alternative formulation containing less saccharin might have been developed within approximately three months.

By March 28, however, the project team, except for Dr. Pierce, decided to continue with the development of loperamide. That decision was made apparently in response to a directive from the Marketing Division of Ortho. This decision meant that Ortho would file an investigational new drug application (IND) with the Federal Food and Drug Administration (FDA), continuing laboratory studies on loperamide, and begin work on a formulation. FDA approval is required before any new drug is tested clinically on humans. Therefore, loperamide would be tested on patients only if the FDA approved the saccharin formulation.

Dr. Pierce knew that the IND would have to be filed with and approved by the FDA before clinical testing could begin. Nonetheless, she continued to oppose the work being done on loperamide at Ortho. On April 21, 1975, she sent a memorandum to the project team expressing her disagreement with its decision to proceed with the development of the drug. In her opinion, there was no justification for seeking FDA permission to use the drug in light of medical controversy over the safety of saccharin.

(*continued on next page*)

(*continued*)

PIERCE v. ORTHO PHARMACEUTICAL CORP.
84 N.J. 58, 417 A.2d 505 (1980)

Dr. Pierce met with Dr. Pasquale on May 9 and informed him that she disagreed with the decision to file an IND with the FDA. She felt that by continuing to work on loperamide she would violate her interpretation of the Hippocratic oath. She concluded that the risk that saccharin might be harmful should preclude testing the formula on children or elderly persons, especially when an alternative formulation might soon be available.

Dr. Pierce recognized that she was joined in a difference of "viewpoints" or "opinion" with Dr. Pasquale and others at Ortho concerning the use of a formula containing saccharin. In her opinion, the safety of saccharin in loperamide pediatric drops was medically debatable. She acknowledged that Dr. Pasquale was entitled to his opinion to proceed with the IND. . . .

After their meeting on May 9, Dr. Pasquale informed Dr. Pierce that she would no longer be assigned to the loperamide project. On May 14, Dr. Pasquale asked Dr. Pierce to choose other projects. After Dr. Pierce returned from vacation in Finland, she met on June 16 with Dr. Pasquale to discuss other projects, but she did not choose a project at that meeting. She felt she was being demoted, even though her salary would not be decreased. . . . Viewing the matter most favorably to Dr. Pierce, we assume the sole reason for the termination of her employment was the dispute over the loperamide project. Dr. Pasquale accepted her resignation.

★   ★   ★

Under the common law, in the absence of an employment contract, employers or employees have been free to terminate the employment relationship with or without cause.

★   ★   ★

In the last century, the common law developed in a laissez-faire climate that encouraged industrial growth and approved the right of an employer to control his own business, including the right to fire without cause an employee at will. The twentieth century has witnessed significant changes in socioeconomic values that have led to reassessment of the common law rule. Businesses have evolved from small and medium size firms to gigantic corporations in which ownership is separate from management. Formerly there was a clear delineation between employers, who frequently were owners of their own businesses, and employees. The employer in the old sense has been replaced by a superior in the corporate hierarchy who is himself an employer. We are a nation of employees. Growth in the number of employees has been accompanied by increasing recognition of the need for stability in labor relations.

Commentators have questioned the compatibility of the traditional at will doctrine with the realities of modern economics and employment practices. The common law rule has been modified by the enactment of labor relations legislation. The National Labor Relations Act and other labor legislation illustrate the governmental policy of preventing employers from using the right of discharge as a means of oppression. Consistent with this policy, many states have recognized the need to protect employees who are not parties to a collective bargaining agreement or other contract from abusive practices by the employer.

Recently those states have recognized a common law cause of action for employees at will who were discharged for reasons that were in some way "wrongful." . . .

★　★　★

We hold that an employee has a cause of action for wrongful discharge when the discharge is contrary to a clear mandate of public policy. The sources of public policy include legislation; administrative rules, regulations or decisions; and judicial decisions. In certain instances, a professional code of ethics may contain an expression of public policy. However . . . unless an employee at will identifies a specific expression of public policy, he may be discharged with or without cause.

★　★　★

Viewing the matter most favorably to Dr. Pierce, the controversy at Ortho involved a difference in medical opinions. Dr. Pierce acknowledged that Dr. Pasquale was entitled to his opinion that the oath did not forbid work on loperamide. Nonetheless, implicit in Dr. Pierce's position is the contention that Dr. Pasquale and Ortho were obliged to accept her opinion. Dr. Pierce contends, in effect, that Ortho should have stopped research on loperamide because of her opinion about the controversial nature of the drug.

Dr. Pierce espouses a doctrine that would lead to disorder in drug research. Under her theory, a professional employee could redetermine the propriety of a research project even if the research did not involve a violation of a clear mandate of public policy. Chaos would result if a single doctor engaged in research were allowed to determine, according to his or her individual conscience, whether a project should continue. An employee does not have a right to continued employment when he or she refuses to conduct research simply because it would contravene his or her personal morals. An employee at will who refuses to work for an employer in answer to a call of conscience should recognize that older employees and their employer might heed a different call. However, nothing in this opinion should be construed to restrict the right of an employee at will to refuse to work on a project that he or she believes is unethical. In sum, an employer may discharge an employee who refuses to work unless the refusal is based on a clear mandate of public policy.

. . . As a matter of law, there is no public policy against conducting research on drugs that may be controversial, but potentially beneficial to mankind, particularly where continuation of the research is subject to approval by the FDA. Consequently, although we recognize an employee may maintain an action for wrongful discharge, we hold there are no issues of material fact to be resolved at trial.

(continued on next page)

PIERCE v. ORTHO PHARMACEUTICAL CORP.
84 N.J. 58, 417 A.2d 505 (1980)

(continued)

Under these circumstances, we conclude that the Hippocratic oath does not contain a clear mandate of public policy that prevented Dr. Pierce from continuing her research on loperamide. To hold otherwise would seriously impair the ability of drug manufacturers to develop new drugs according to their best judgment.

★   ★   ★

Accordingly, we reverse the judgment of the Appellate Division and remand the cause to the trial court for entry of judgment for defendant.

THE LAW AND SOCIAL CHANGE

Neither law nor ethics is static. Legal and ethical standards often develop separately and move closer to (or farther from) each other in ways difficult to predict. For example, as we saw on p. 5, under common-law rule, one person has no legal duty to help another person in trouble, although the bystander may feel a moral duty to aid the victim. As noted in Box 1-1 (p. 6), this traditional rule is now being changed by legislatures in some states: a 1983 Rhode Island law provides a penalty of up to a year in jail for any witness (other than the victim) who fails to report a rape to the police. As the following case shows, courts also are free to move in the same direction: toward a recognition that the law must enforce the moral principle that "each member of a community has a right that each other member treat him with the minimal respect due a fellow human being." (Dworkin, 1978, p. 98)

SOLDANO v. O'DANIELS
141 Cal.App.3d 443, 190 Cal.Rptr. 310 (Ct.App. 1983)

ANDREEN, ASSOCIATE JUSTICE.

Does a business establishment incur liability for wrongful death if it denies use of its telephone to a good samaritan who explains an emergency situation occurring without and wishes to call the police?

This appeal follows a judgment of dismissal of the second cause of action of a complaint for wrongful death upon a motion for summary judgment. The motion was supported only by a declaration of defense counsel. Both briefs on appeal adopt the defense averments:

"This action arises out of a shooting death occurring on August 9, 1977. Plaintiff's father [Darrell Soldano] was shot and killed by one Rudolph Villanueva on that date at defendant's Happy Jack's Saloon. This defendant owns and operates the Circle Inn which is an eating establishment located across the street from Happy Jack's. Plaintiff's second cause of action against this defendant is one for negligence.

"Plaintiff alleges that on the date of the shooting, a patron of Happy Jack's Saloon came into the Circle Inn and informed a Circle Inn employee that a man had been threatened at Happy Jack's. He requested the employee either call the police or allow him to use the Circle Inn phone to call the police. That employee allegedly refused to call the police and allegedly refused to allow the patron to use the phone to make his own call. Plaintiff alleges that the actions of the Circle Inn employee were a breach of the legal duty that the Circle Inn owed to the decedent."

We were advised at oral argument that the employee was the defendant's bartender. The state of the record is unsatisfactory in that it does not disclose the physical location of the telephone—whether on the bar, in a private office behind a closed door or elsewhere. The only factual matter before the trial court was a verified statement of the defense attorney which set forth those acts quoted above. Following normal rules applicable to motions for summary judgment, we strictly construe the defense affidavit. Accordingly, we assume the telephone was not in a private office but in a position where it could be used by a patron without inconvenience to the defendant or his guests. We also assume the call was a local one and would not result in expense to defendant.

★   ★   ★

Defendant argues that the request that its employee call the police is a request that it *do* something. He points to the established rule that one who has not created a peril ordinarily does not have a duty to take affirmative action to assist an imperiled person. It is urged that the alternative request of the patron from Happy Jack's Saloon that he be allowed to use defendant's telephone so that he personally could make the call is again a request that the defendant do something—assist another to give aid. Defendant points out that the Restatement sections which impose liability for negligent interference with a third person giving aid to another do not impose the additional duty to *aid* the good samaritan.

The refusal of the law to recognize the moral obligation of one to aid another when he is in peril and when such aid may be given without danger and at little cost in effort has been roundly criticized. . . .

"Such decisions are revolting to any moral sense. They have been denounced with vigor by legal writers." A similar rule has been termed "morally questionable" by our Supreme Court.

★   ★   ★

The consequences to the community of imposing a duty is termed "the administrative factor" by Professor Green in his analysis of determining whether a duty exists in a given case. The administrative factor is simply the pragmatic concern of fashioning a workable rule and the impact of such a rule on the judicial machinery. It is the policy of major concern in this case.

★   ★   ★

Many citizens simply "don't want to get involved." No rule should be adopted which would require a citizen to open up his or her house to a stranger so that the latter may use the telephone call for emergency assistance. As Mrs. Alexander in Anthony Burgess' A Clockwork Orange learned to her horror, such an action may be fraught with danger. It does not follow, however, that use of a telephone in a public portion of a business should be refused for a legitimate emergency call. Imposing liability for such a refusal would not subject innocent citizens to possible attack by the "good samari-

(continued on next page)

(continued)

SOLDANO v. O'DANIELS
141 Cal.App.3d 443, 190 Cal.Rptr. 310 (Ct.App. 1983)

tan," for it would be limited to an establishment open to the public during times when it is open to business, and to places within the establishment ordinarily accessible to the public. Nor would a stranger's mere assertion that an "emergency" situation is occurring create the duty to utilize an accessible telephone because the duty would arise if and only if it were clearly conveyed that there exists an imminent danger of physical harm.

Such a holding would not involve difficulties in proof, overburden the courts or unduly hamper self-determination or enterprise.

A business establishment such as the Circle Inn is open for profit. The owner encourages the public to enter, for his earnings depend on it. A telephone is a necessary adjunct to such a place. It is not unusual in such circumstances for patrons to use the telephone to call a taxicab or family member.

We acknowledge that defendant contracted for the use of his telephone, and its use is a species of property. But if it exists in a public place as defined above, there is no privacy or ownership interest in it such that the owner should be permitted to interfere with a good faith attempt to use it by a third person to come to the aid of another.

*　　*　　*

We conclude that the bartender owed a duty to the plaintiff's decedent to permit the patron from Happy Jack's to place a call to the police or to place the call himself.

It bears emphasizing that the duty in this case does not require that one must go to the aid of another. That is not the issue here. The employee was not the good samaritan intent on aiding another. The patron was.

*　　*　　*

The courts have a special responsibility to reshape, refine and guide legal doctrine they have created. As our Supreme Court summarized in *People* v. *Pierce* (1964) 61 Cal.2d 879, 882, in response to an argument that any departure from common law precedent should be left to legislative action, "In effect the contention is a request that courts abdicate their responsibility for the upkeep of the common law. That upkeep it needs continuously, as this case demonstrates."

*　　*　　*

We conclude there are sufficient justiciable issues to permit the case to go to trial and therefore reverse.

Corporate Social Responsibility

For several years, those concerned with business mores have debated a code of business ethics. The debate became especially heated in the 1970s in the wake of Watergate and Securities & Exchange Commission corporate bribery disclosures (and was renewed in the early 1990s in the wake of the savings-and-loan scandal). Spurred by enactment of the Foreign Corrupt Practices Act in 1977 (see pp. 976–978), dozens of companies began to draft codes of corporate conduct. In a 1980 survey of corporate codes of conduct, more than three-quarters of the 700 responding companies had written codes, and the larger the company the more likely that it had issued one. (White, 1980, pp. 381ff)

LAW AND LIFE

BOX 6-2

Executives Apply Stiffer Standards Than Public to Ethical Dilemmas

By Roger Ricklefs

[According to some polls, executives expect more from their employees ethically than does the general public. Many companies have enacted "codes" of business ethics, but it may be too early to determine what will result from the new wave of ethical concern.
—AUTHORS' NOTE]

It's the sort of dilemma companies encounter all the time.

An employer finds that the candidate who is by far the best qualified for a job really earned only $18,000 a year in his last job, and not the $28,000 he claimed. Should the employer hire the candidate anyway, or should he choose someone else even though that person will be considerably less qualified?

In a Gallup Organization poll conducted for The Wall Street Journal, general citizens overwhelmingly back the lenient approach: Some 63% surveyed recommend hiring the able but errant applicant, and only 27% say the employer should choose somebody else. But among the executives polled, 52% would choose somebody else, and only 47% would hire the applicant with a false claim.

As part of its poll on ethics in America, Gallup posed several dilemmas like this to find out how Americans would actually handle specific situations involving ethical issues. It found that general citizens are considerably more inclined than executives to condone wrongdoing if there are mitigating circumstances.

VARYING PERCEPTIONS OF BUSINESS ETHICS

Sometimes Gallup threw in complications. For instance, in the case of the candidate who lied about his previous salary, it asked half the members of its sample what they would do if the real salary were $25,000, only $3,000 less than the amount claimed. (In all other respects, the question was phrased the same for both subsamples.)

The general public reacts about the same as when the real salary was $18,000. Some 68% would hire the candidate and 22% wouldn't. But to executives, the amount involved matters. When the discrepancy between claimed salary and real salary was only $3,000 a year, 60% of the executives would hire the candidate and only 38% wouldn't.

To obtain this data, Gallup this summer polled a representative national general-public sample of 1,558 adults and a sample of 396 middle-level big-company executives. It interviewed the general citizens in person and mailed confidential questionnaires to the executives. The polling organization figures there is a sampling error of up to 3% in the general-public poll and up to 5% in the smaller executive poll.

Here is how the people Gallup surveyed say they would handle the dilemmas:

FAMILY VS. ETHICS

Jim, a 56-year-old middle manager with children in college, discovers that the owners of his company are cheating the government out of several thousand dollars a year in

taxes. Jim is the only employee who would be in a position to know this. Should Jim report the owners to the Internal Revenue Service at the risk of endangering his own livelihood, or disregard the discovery in order to protect his family's livelihood?

More often than not, both executives and general citizens say family responsibilities should take precedence. Roughly half—49% of the public and 52% of the executives—think Jim should disregard his discovery in order to protect his family. About 34% of both the executives and the public think he should report the owners.

The money involved "isn't worth the loss of a job," says a manufacturing executive in his 50s. "Hundreds of thousands could make a difference." A company controller urges disregarding the cheating and adds: "The IRS has auditors to catch this kind of thing."

A financial executive says that to disregard the cheating "is not my real answer, but the chances of a 56-year-old 'whistleblower' finding employment in this society might be difficult." Some executives suggest options that weren't offered in the question: resign or look for another job.

THE ROUNDABOUT RAISE

When Joe asks for a raise, his boss praises his work but says the company's rigid budget won't allow any further merit raises for the time being. Instead, the boss suggests that the company "won't look too closely at your expense accounts for a while." Should Joe take this as authorization to pad his expense account on grounds that he is simply getting the same money he deserves through a different route, or not take this roundabout "raise"?

(continued on next page)

BOX 6-2

Box 6-2, *continued*

Though the public took a permissive approach to some of the other dilemmas, it decisively rejected the roundabout raise—and the executives rejected it even more overwhelmingly. Some 65% of the general citizens and 91% of the executives say Joe should turn down the circuitous raise. Only 25% of the public and 7% of the executives think he should "take this as authorization to pad his expense account."

THE FAKED DEGREE

Bill has done a sound job for over a year. Bill's boss learns that he got the job by claiming to have a college degree, although he actually never graduated. Should his boss dismiss him for submitting a fraudulent resume or overlook the false claim since Bill has otherwise proven to be conscientious and honorable, and making an issue of the degree might ruin Bill's career?

More executives recommend dismissing Bill (50%) than suggest overlooking the claim (43%). The general public decisively recommends (66% to 22%) overlooking the false claim rather than dismissing Bill.

Within the general public, however, 33% of those with professional occupations recommend dismissal. Gallup points out that academic credentials might be particularly important to people in these occupations.

In an otherwise identical question asked of a subsample, Bill didn't merely fail to graduate—he never attended college at all. But the distinction didn't seem to matter. Both subsamples gave similar answers to the question.

SNEAKING PHONE CALLS

Helen discovers that a fellow employee regularly makes about $100 a month worth of personal long-distance telephone calls from an office telephone. Should Helen report the employee to the company or disregard the calls on the grounds that many people make personal calls at the office.

In an otherwise identical question asked of part of the sample, Gallup has the employee making only $10 a month worth of personal long-distance calls instead of $100.

The difference matters, especially to executives. When the employee is sneaking $100 a month worth of calls, 64% of the public and 76% of the executives think that Helen should report him. Some 26% of the public and 19% of the managers favor disregarding the calls.

But when the amount involved is $10 a month, only 47% of the public and 48% of the executives favor reporting the employee. About 38% of the public and 47% of the executives favor disregarding the calls.

Put another way, when $100 a month is involved, the executives are tougher than the public. But when the figure is only $10 a month, the executives are more inclined than the public to disregard the calls.

COVER-UP TEMPTATION

Bill discovers that the chemical plant he manages is creating slightly more water pollution in a nearby lake than is legally permitted. Revealing the problem will bring considerable unfavorable publicity to the plant, hurt the lakeside town's resort

business and create a scare in the community. Solving the problem will cost the company well over $100,000. It is unlikely that outsiders will discover the problem. The violation poses no danger whatever to people. At most, it will endanger a small number of fish. Should Bill reveal the problem despite the cost to his company, or consider the problem as little more than a technicality and disregard it?

The respondent can find all sorts of rationales for letting Bill disregard the pollution problem. Yet general citizens and executives alike took a tough line. Some 63% of the general public and 70% of the executives say Bill should reveal the problem and spend the money. Only 25% of the general citizens and 24% of the executives think he should disregard it as a technicality.

This is the only ethical-dilemma question in which young people are "significantly more likely to take the stricter ethical option" than their elders, observes Andrew Kohut, president of the Gallup Organization. "There are great environmental concerns among the young," he adds.

Those who worry about the ethics of young America may find at least a little welcome news in the reaction to this question. For all the permissiveness the young reveal throughout the survey, they appear quite capable of developing a stricter ethical standard on some issues than their elders. "Ethics follow values," Mr. Kohut observes.

Source: *Wall Street Journal*, November 3, 1983

LAW AND LIFE

BOX 6-3

GE's Image Makes Conviction More Jarring. Fraud Case Illustrates Difficulty of Enforcing Standards

By Douglas R. Sease

[*Even within companies where ethical behavior is a high priority, individuals go astray. Profit pressures may lead otherwise honest people to violate the law. In many cases, company loyalty, not personal gain, is the motivator behind unethical conduct.*—AUTHORS' NOTE]

For years, General Electric Co. has been regarded as one of the nation's exemplary companies, a tough but fair competitor, a breeding ground for manager's excellence and a good corporate citizen.

Along the way, it also acquired a less enviable record. Three times in the past 25 years, GE has been convicted of crimes: price fixing, bribery and fraud. The latest came in April, when GE pleaded guilty to charges of defrauding the government on missile-warhead contracts. That defense-contract investigation continues, promising to yield still more embarrassing headlines for the company.

GE wasn't the only company singled out for misconduct in any of these cases. But its carefully burnished public persona made GE's crimes particularly jarring. That they occurred at all—and how the company's top management responded—suggest how easily ethical standards can become blurred within big organizations.

Effort to Combat Crime
As the GE story shows, profit and

CORPORATE ETHICS: A CASE STUDY

time pressures can lead otherwise honest people to violate their principles—and the law. And the larger and more complex a company is, the more difficult enforcement of ethical standards becomes. Though GE years ago initiated an unusually aggressive effort to combat crime within its ranks, its size—330,000 employees making a wide variety of products in hundreds of plants—increases the likelihood of occasional lapses.

GE chairman Jack Welch concedes as much. "I am not naive enough or presumptuous enough or self-righteous enough," he says, "to think that despite our best efforts we won't have isolated incidents."

To a surprising degree, however, the public doesn't seem to care much. "In the short run, people are aware of misconduct in a corporation, but in the long run there isn't any moral outrage," says Diane Vaughan, a Boston College sociology professor who studies organizational ethics. "There is a great forgiveness rule that applies to executives and corporations."

There seems little doubt that GE means business when it comes to heading off employee crime. Ever since the 1960 price fixing case, GE lawyers have annually briefed managers to stress that sharing competitive information with rivals is a crime. Up-and-coming GE managers attending executive training sessions at GE's retreat in Croton-on-Hudson, N.Y., get a heavy dose of ethics along with other management lessons. And over the years, GE has drawn up one of corporate America's most comprehensive policies on business ethics.

More Stringent Measures
The recent Defense Department fraud conviction has inspired still more stringent measures. Mr. Welch has appointed a corporate ombudsman authorized to investigate any allegations of wrongdoing within the company. GE's thick policy manual has been expanded to ensure that strict accounting procedures are followed in government contracts and to forbid GE employees from providing gifts—including lunches—to government officials. Employee time cards now bear the warning that falsifying time charges is a crime. In the Pentagon case, GE tried to minimize cost overruns by transferring charges from one contract to another.

Workers at the Philadelphia missile-warhead plant where the fraud occurred confirm that GE is tightening accounting procedures and checking time-card charges to prevent falsifications. But they stress that plant employees were fully aware of correct procedures long before the fraud occurred.

Lest anyone doubt the seriousness of GE's intent, Mr. Welch issues a stern warning in a videotape being shown to employees. Pressure to meet corporate goals won't excuse misbehavior, he says, adding that such pressures are intensifying as GE battles competitors around the globe. He also urges employees to come forward with their suspicions of wrongdoing. "Whistle blowing, speaking out, telling it like it is, is part of what we're after," he says. "I can assure anybody who wants to talk about abuses of integrity in this company that they will be welcomed."

But rules and lectures are ineffective against an excess of loyalty to an employer. Unlike former LTV Corp. Chairman Paul Thayer or Ten-

(continued on next page)

BOX 6-3

Box 6-3, *continued*

nessee banker Jake Butcher, both of whom recently drew prison sentences for illegally using their positions to enrich themselves, the GE managers who have violated laws did so to bolster the company's fortunes, not their own.

Hoyt Steele Case

A case in point is Hoyt P. Steele, who, as GE's vice president for international sales, was charged in 1973 with authorizing a $1 million bribe to a Puerto Rican official to secure a $93 million power plant contract for GE. Mr. Steele had little to gain personally by winning the contract. At 64, he was approaching GE's then-mandatory retirement age. Nor, with an annual salary of $185,000, was he desperate for money.

But for GE the contract was crucial. An earlier bid to build a power plant of similar design in Mexico had failed, and the company wanted a prototype to help it sell the plants to other developing nations around the world.

Mr. Steele won't discuss the case today, but his testimony at his 1981 trial shows how he rationalized the scheme. He initially rejected subordinates' suggestions that a bribe might be necessary to win the contract. But after the bids were opened and GE's archrival, Westinghouse Corp., seemed to have a chance of winning the contract, Mr. Steele authorized a $300,000 payment to a Water Resources Board official who subordinates said had asked for money to ensure that GE won the contract. After the Puerto Rican official rejected that offer as insultingly low, Mr. Steele upped the ante to $1 million. He later refused a request for another $250,000.

Mr. Steele testified that he knew the payment violated GE policy. But he contended that it wasn't a crime because GE hadn't initiated the offer. "I authorized a payment, yes; not a bribe," he said. The objective "was to avoid being cheated out of an order that belonged to us." Both GE and Mr. Steele were convicted of mail fraud, wire fraud, conspiracy and interstate or foreign travel in aid of racketeering. The convictions were reversed on appeal, and three counts were ordered retried. Prosecutors settled for a no contest plea from GE to a fraud charge and dropped charges against Mr. Steele.

Source: *Wall Street Journal,* July 5, 1985

The bulk of most of the codes simply restate maxims to which lip service, if not actual adherence, has long been given—for example, proscriptions against conflicts of interest (75 percent of the codes in the survey contained such provisions), misuse of corporate assets (50 percent), and price-fixing (40 percent). Surprisingly, only 17 percent of the codes referred to the Foreign Corrupt Practices Act, although 63 percent of the codes do deal with payments to government officials and political parties. But some of their provisions are new, and include structures to ensure that they will be better policed than before—for example, a requirement that a majority of the board of directors not be in management positions in the company.

No general rule has emerged from the welter of codes. Perhaps the one to which most companies would assent was wryly put in 1976 by Arjay Miller, then dean of Stanford's Graduate School of Business: "Do that which you would feel comfortable explaining on television." (Morgenthaler & Calame, 1976, p. 1)

In Europe, many companies have gone far beyond their American counterparts in issuing "social balance sheets." Thus the Swiss food manufacturer Migros-Genossenschafts-Bund issued an eighty-nine-page printed report in the late 1970s that declared that it paid its women less than men, that many of its jobs were "extremely boring," and that it had emitted two percent more nitrous dioxide, a noxious pollutant, over the previous four years. (*Business Week,* Nov. 6, 1978, p. 175) This European trend developed in large part as a means of defusing criticism that might lead to restraining legislation.

It is perhaps still too early to determine what the long-term outlook will be for the recent flurry of concern about business ethics. There is some evidence that many executives expect more of their employees than the general public (**Box 6-2**). On the other hand, even when a company is concerned with ethical conduct, individuals often go astray (**Box 6-3**). And many executives have indicated privately that it is unlikely their companies will invariably abide by such laws as the Foreign Corrupt Practices Act when it is demonstrably necessary in certain countries to make payments to foreign officials to compete with foreign companies legally free to secure contracts in such a way.

The implicit, gloomy conclusion—that ethical conduct is harmful to profitability—is not compelling. It often results simply from laziness or incompetence. Attention to behavior that is morally appropriate can reap financial dividends. Consider, for example, DuPont's great concern with the safety of its employees. The first item on the agenda of DuPont's weekly top management meeting is safety. According to a 1982 study, DuPont's accident rate is only 4.3 percent of the American industry average, saving the company an estimated $26 million (nearly 4 percent of net profit) that it would otherwise have spent on additional compensation and other accident-related costs. (Main, 1982, p. 68) It surely is no coincidence that a moral concern for employee safety has financial benefits.

CHAPTER SUMMARY

In a pluralistic society such as the United States, there is no consensus on a single ethical code that can be concretely applied in all circumstances. The closest we come to such a guide is the law itself. But the law and some widely-held ethical precepts can diverge. The law in most states, for example, does not require bystanders to rescue people in trouble, whereas most moral codes do.

In some important instances relevant to business, the law and ethical standards converge. Examples include the contract duty to act in good faith and to avoid unconscionable terms, agents' fiduciary duty to their principals, corporate officers' and directors' fiduciary duty to their corporations, and merchants' and marketers' obligations to avoid deceptive and unfair commercial acts or practices.

In some situations, ethical standards held by certain groups (such as professional societies) diverge from legal requirements (embodied in antitrust laws, for instance). In these instances, the law will necessarily prevail. For example, the law imposes limits on the degree to which a company can devote its resources to projects that will not ultimately benefit its shareholders. The law may also permit conduct that falls short of personal ethical standards. A person who refuses to engage in such conduct risks extralegal sanctions, such as losing a job.

Because law and ethics are never static, these two general codes of conduct are a continuing influence on one another and on the society out of which they grew.

SELF-TEST QUESTIONS

1. It is wrong to make illegal every unethical act because:
   (a) it is of no concern to society how people behave morally
   (b) the law addresses minimum standards of behavior and ethics addresses higher standards
   (c) people disagree so much about the meaning of ethics that it is impossible to state any standards of appropriate behavior in the business arena
2. Which of the following is true?
   (a) It is unlawful, but never immoral, to breach a contract.
   (b) Contract law has to do with agreements, not fairness.
   (c) Some contracts may be unlawful only because they are unfair.
3. Corporations may:
   (a) give as much money as their directors agree to the Boy Scouts
   (b) contribute to the Boy Scouts only if their shareholders approve
   (c) contribute a reasonable sum to the Boy Scouts even if individual shareholders disagree
4. A corporate code of employee conduct may tell employees:
   (a) how to dress
   (b) that they must do whatever their managers tell them to do as long as they're not asked to violate a law
   (c) not to talk to a police officer investigating an incident that occurred inside the factory
   (d) all of the above
5. Which of the following statements is true? Corporate codes of ethics:
   (a) are always enforceable in court
   (b) may never be enforced in court
   (c) may be enforced by managers, who may always fire employees for failing to abide by them
   (d) may be used to weed out unfit employees

DEMONSTRATION PROBLEM

Sylvester works for a Henry's Cookies, a small manufacturer of oatmeal-rhubarb cookies cut in the shape of famous politicians. The cookies are not selling well. Kurt, the sales manager, tells Sylvester "you're going to have to sell more cookies than you've been doing if you want to keep your job." Sylvester says he's been pounding the pavement 14 hours a day looking for restaurants, bakeries, and other outlets to sell the cookies to. Kurt says Sylvester has two weeks to double his sales—"or else." Kurt then suggests that Sylvester consider bribing the managers of all the local grocery stores to buy the cookies. Kurt agrees to make $100 per manager available from corporate funds to pay each manager, "as long as you don't tell Henry" (the CEO of Henry's Cookies). Sylvester refuses, and Kurt fires him. Does Sylvester have a legal remedy against Henry's Cookies? Why or why not?

PROBLEMS

1. Velma is the secretary to the chief executive of a manufacturer of fine paper products. Her company has just acquired a huge tract of uncut timber in a remote forest. Although no law bars the company from cutting the trees, there is sentiment in the legislature for a forest preservation law that would drastically reduce the number of logs it could harvest. The company sets out to cut the trees quickly and secretly. As a member of the National Save the Tree League, Velma is outraged and leaks the plan to the local newspaper, which publishes the story. When Velma's boss learns that she has leaked the story, he fires her. Meanwhile, the legislature hurriedly debates a bill to stop the company from cutting the trees. The company rushes to put its plan into effect. The bill is enacted, and takes effect in thirty days. Figuring that by working twenty-four-hour shifts during the next month it can cut most of the lumber it needs, the company begins to saw away. Was Velma legally in the right to leak her company's plan? Morally? Was the company right (legally or ethically) in firing her? Was the company right (legally or ethically) in cutting timber, knowing the law was due to take effect in thirty days?

2. MuchdoGood Enterprises, Inc., manufacturer of quality turpets, decides to declare no dividends, although it has had an extremely profitable year. Instead, it intends to plow its profits back into the company to permit it to build a fire station for the community, not only to appear a good "corporate citizen," but also to ensure modern equipment for the extra fire hazards the town faces as a result of the chemicals it maintains at its factory. In a suit brought by enraged stockholders to force it to declare dividends, who will win and why?

3. NICOTINE (National Institute to Combat Old Tobacco Inhalers' Narcotic Enormities), a public-interest group opposed to all forms of tobacco manufacture and sale, calls on *The Bugle*, a local newspaper, to refrain from accepting cigarette advertising. *The Bugle* has frequently inveighed against the sins of smoking, but it desperately needs the considerable revenue it takes in from the tobacco companies for their ads. Asserting that the advertisements contribute to adolescent smoking, and thus eventually to many diseases, NICOTINE threatens to sue the paper to enjoin it from taking the ads. What result? Why? What should *The Bugle* do?

ANSWERS TO SELF-TEST QUESTIONS

1. (b)   2. (c)   3. (c)   4. (a)   5. (d)

SUGGESTED ANSWER TO DEMONSTRATION PROBLEM

The answer depends on whether the state in which Henry's Cookies is located has a public policy against bribery of corporate employees by suppliers. Most states do have such a policy, either explicitly in a statute or long incorporated in common law. Since Kurt told Sylvester in effect not to tell the boss, it seems reasonable to believe that Kurt knew he was doing something wrong by demanding that Sylvester engage in bribery. Even though Sylvester probably had no employee contract, the odds are that he could successfully sue to recover his job if he could show that his refusal was the only reason he was fired. Of course, in the absence of an employment contract, Kurt could have simply demanded that Sylvester double his sales and fired him if he failed to achieve Kurt's goal.

Part 1

The Manager's Legal Agenda

Don't demand certainty from your lawyers. Law is a complex social institution. In the United States there are multiple levels of laws (federal, state, county, and municipal) and multiple sources of laws within each of these levels (legislative, judicial, executive, and administrative). So most important matters are governed by overlapping sets of laws and subject to different jurisdictions. Legal questions, therefore, rarely have simple answers.

Choose the right lawyer. Because of the law's complexity, lawyers tend to specialize in one of many more or less discrete bodies of law, including criminal law, tort law (including product liability), partnership and corporation law, contract and commercial law, tax law, property and real estate law, labor and employment law, antitrust and trade regulation, and environmental law, among many others,

All managers should have a working knowledge of the particular bodies of law that affect their businesses. This knowledge is important not so that managers can do without lawyers but so that they can consult more intelligently with their lawyers.

Don't assume you know the law simply because you have read it. Although statutes and administrative regulations are primary sources of law, they cannot be read in a vacuum. The American legal system depends heavily on judicial interpretation of statutes and regulations, so familiarity with court cases is essential in every branch of law.

The worst time to look for a lawyer is when a legal difficulty arises. Managers should retain lawyers as part of doing business and talk to their lawyers regularly.

You should consult your lawyer primarily to anticipate difficulties and to prevent problems from arising. Review your business's operations and practices to ensure that the company is doing what the law requires it to do.

Never simply turn over a legal matter to your company's lawyers and hope that the problem will go away. In the end, the responsibility for deciding how to proceed is for the manager, not the lawyer.

Establish procedures in your company to ensure that communications between management and attorneys are protected by the lawyer-client privilege.

Be candid with your lawyer; lawyers cannot serve your interests if managers withhold information from them.

Whenever a dispute arises, explore with the other party the possibility of using an alternative dispute resolution procedure, such as the mini-trial.

Examine your business practices to determine whether they might lead to disputes that could be avoided.

Institute training and monitoring programs to assure that your business is doing its utmost to prevent negligent or criminal conduct on the part of all employees. With the assistance of counsel, you should regularly anticipate difficulties and devise preventive programs.

Work closely with lawyers when a government survey reaches your desk. The government often asks for information, much of which is of strategic and competitive value. Minimize the risk that that information will fall into the hands of competitors.

Bear in mind that the law is only one part of business; common sense and ethics are no less important. Legality is not always propriety, whether individual or corporate. Merely because your lawyer says that it is "legal" to do something does not automatically mean that the business enterprise should do it. That something is legal does not always make it right. Likewise, that something is morally wrong or unethical does not make it unlawful. Because people have different moral codes and ethical standards, conflicts between law and ethics frequently arise. A company should not be content simply to abide by the law, however interpreted. It should also devise an ethical code of conduct and ensure that it is known and adhered to by all employees.

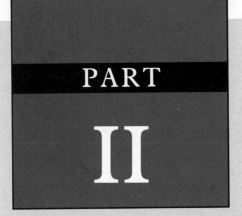

*Study your mathematics or some ac-
countant is going to beat you out of
your money. Don't wait until you get
famous to try to read a contract.*
—FORMER HEAVYWEIGHT CHAMPION
GEORGE FOREMAN

CONTRACTS

CHAPTER 7

Introduction to Contract Law

GENERAL PERSPECTIVES ON CONTRACTS

The Role of Contract in Society

Contract is probably the most familiar legal concept in our society because it is so central to a deeply held conviction about the essence of our political, economic, and social life. In common parlance, the term is used interchangeably with agreement, bargain, undertaking, or deal; but whatever the word, it embodies our notion of freedom to pursue our own lives together with others. Contract is central because it is the means by which a free society orders what would otherwise be a jostling, frenetic anarchy.

So commonplace is the concept of contract—and our freedom to make contracts with each other—that it is difficult to imagine a time when contracts were rare, an age when people's everyday associations with one another were not freely determined. Yet in historical terms, it was not so long ago that contracts were rare, entered into if at all by very few. In "primitive" societies and in the medieval Europe from which our institutions sprang, the relationships among people were largely fixed; traditions spelled out duties that each person owed to family, tribe, or manor. Though he may have oversimplified, Sir Henry Maine, a nineteenth-century historian, sketched the development of society in his classic book *Ancient Law*. As he put it:

> [F]rom a condition of society in which all the relations of Persons are summed up in the relations of Family, we seem to have steadily moved towards a phase of social order in which all these relations arise from the free agreement of Individuals. . . . Thus the status of the Slave has disappeared—it has been superseded by the contractual relation of the servant to his master. . . . The status of the Female under Tutelage . . . has also ceased to exist. . . . So too the status of the Son under Power has no true place in the law of modern European societies. If any civil obligation binds together the Parent and the child of full age, it is one to which only contract gives its legal validity. . . . If then we employ Status, agreeably with the usage of the best writers, to signify these personal conditions [arising from ancient legal privileges of the

Family] only, we may say that the movement of the progressive societies has hitherto been a movement *from Status to Contract.* ([1869] 1930, pp. 180–182)

This movement was not accidental. It went hand-in-glove with the emerging industrial order; from the fifteenth to the nineteenth centuries, as England, especially, evolved into a booming mercantile economy with all that that implies—flourishing trade, growing cities, an expanding monetary system, commercialization of agriculture, mushrooming manufacturing—contract law was created of necessity.

Contract law did not develop, however, according to a conscious, far-seeing plan. It was a response to changing conditions, and the judges who created it frequently resisted, preferring the quieter, imagined pastoral life of their forefathers. Not until the nineteenth century, in both the United States and England, did a full-fledged law of contracts arise together with and help create modern capitalism.

Contract Defined

As usual in the law, the legal definition of "**contract**" is formalistic. The Restatement says: "A contract is a promise or a set of promises for the breach of which the law gives a remedy, or the performance of which the law in some way recognizes as a duty." (*Restatement (Second) of Contracts,* Section 1.) Similarly, the Uniform Commercial Code says: " 'Contract' means the total legal obligation which results from the parties' agreement as affected by this Act and any other applicable rules of law." (Section 1-201(11).)

As operational definitions, the above are circular; in effect, contract is defined as an agreement that the law will hold the parties to. What kinds of promises or agreements the law will hold the makers to and the ways in which the law will require the makers to perform their contracts is the subject of Part II of this book.

As a preliminary note, it is important to recognize that not every promise or agreement creates a binding contract. The law takes into account the way in which contracts are made, by whom they are made, and for what purposes they are made. For example, in many states, a wager is unenforceable, even though

both parties "shake" on the bet. We will explore these wrinkles in considerable detail in the chapters to come.

A Cross-Cultural View of Contract

Because contracts are so familiar to us, it is tempting to believe that their function, and the legal rules that govern them, are universal. However, in Communist societies, contract plays a very different role. In the Soviet Union, for example, the contract does not determine the nature of an economic transaction. That transaction is first set forth by the state's planning authorities; only thereafter are the predetermined provisions set down in a written contract. This fundamental difference gives rise to a state of affairs quite difficult to imagine in the United States—litigation over what *should* be written into the contract, rather than, as in this country, over what *is* written in the contract. Such disputes arise because one of the parties—a factory perhaps—may balk at a particular term (for example, delivery date of raw materials) already dictated by the authorities and may refuse to embody it in the contract. In a capitalist economy, such a refusal would mean that there would be no contract and hence no legal rights and obligations. In a fully planned economy, the contract as such is a formality that the parties can be forced to enter into. Moreover, under such a regime, performance of most contracts can be strictly required, since most contracts are not private but imposed by the state. As we will see, U. S. courts will order specific performance of contracts only in certain circumstances.

Economic View of Contract Law

In *An Economic Analysis of Law* (1973), Judge Richard A. Posner (a former University of Chicago law professor) suggests that contract law performs three significant economic functions. First, it helps maintain incentives to individuals to exchange goods and services efficiently. Second, it reduces the costs of economic transactions because its very existence means that the parties need not go to the trouble of negotiating a variety of rules and terms already spelled out. Third, the law of contracts alerts the parties to trouble spots that have arisen in the past, thus making it easier to plan the transactions more intelligently and avoid potential pitfalls.

Overview of the Contracts Unit

Although it has countless wrinkles and nuances, contract law consists of four principal inquiries:

1. Did the parties create a *valid* contract? We will pursue this inquiry in Chapters 8–11.
2. What does the contract mean, and is it in the proper form to carry out this meaning? These questions will be raised in Chapter 12.
3. Do persons other than the contracting parties have rights or duties under the contract? Chapter 13 will look into the ways the courts have answered this question.
4. How are contractual rights enforced and, conversely, when do contractual duties terminate? Enforcement and termination are reserved for Chapters 14 and 15.

Together, the answers to these four basic inquiries determine the rights and obligations of contracting parties.

SOURCES OF CONTRACT LAW

There are four basic sources of contract law: the Constitution, federal and state statutes, federal and state case law, and administrative law. For our purposes, the most important of these, and the ones that we will examine at some length, are case law and statutes.

Case Law

Because contract law was forged in the common-law courtroom, hammered out case by case on the anvil of individual judges, it grew in the course of time to formidable proportions. By the early twentieth century, tens of thousands of contract disputes had been submitted to the courts for resolution, and the published opinions, if collected in one place, would have filled dozens of bookshelves. Clearly this mass of material was too unwieldy for efficient use. A similar problem had developed in the other leading branches of the common law. Disturbed by the profusion of cases and the resulting uncertainty of the law, a group of prominent American judges, lawyers, and teachers founded the American Law Institute in 1923 to attempt to clarify, simplify, and improve the law. One of its first projects, and ultimately one of its most successful, was the drafting of the *Restatement of the Law of Contracts*, completed in 1932. A revision—the *Restatement (Second) of Contracts*—was undertaken in 1964 and finally completed in 1979.

The Restatements (others exist in the fields of torts, agency, conflicts of laws, judgments, property, restitution, security, and trusts) are detailed analyses of the decided cases in the field. These analyses are made with an eye to discerning the various principles that have emerged from the courts, and to the maximum extent possible, the Restatements declare the law as the courts have determined it to be. The Restatements, guided by a Reporter (the director of the project) and a staff of legal scholars, go through several so-called "tentative" drafts—sometimes as many as fifteen or twenty—and are screened by various committees within the American Law Institute before they are eventually published as final documents.

The *Restatement of Contracts* won prompt respect in the courts and has been cited in innumerable cases. The Restatements are not authoritative, in the sense that they are not actual judicial precedents, but they are nevertheless weighty interpretive texts, and judges frequently look to them for guidance. They are as close to "black letter" rules of law as exist anywhere in the American legal system.

Statutory Law: The Uniform Commercial Code

Common law contract principles are still important for many types of contract disputes. But in one area they have been superseded by an important statute: the Uniform Commercial Code (UCC), especially Article 2, which deals with the sale of goods.

A Brief History The UCC is a model law developed by the American Law Institute and the National

Conference of Commissioners on Uniform State Laws; it has been adopted in one form or another in all fifty states, the District of Columbia, and the American territories. It is the only "national" law not enacted by Congress.

Before the UCC was written, commercial law varied, sometimes greatly, from state to state. This first proved a nuisance and then a serious impediment to business as the American economy became nationwide during the twentieth century. Although there had been some uniform laws concerned with commercial deals—including the Uniform Sales Act, first published in 1906—few were widely adopted and none nationally. As a result, the law governing sales of goods, negotiable instruments, warehouse receipts, securities, and other matters crucial to doing business in an industrial, market economy was a crazy quilt of untidy provisions that did not mesh well from state to state.

Initial drafting of the UCC began in 1942 and was ten years in the making, involving the efforts of hundreds of practicing lawyers, law teachers, and judges. A final draft, promulgated by the Institute and the Conference, was endorsed by the American Bar Association and published in 1951.

Pennsylvania enacted the code in its entirety in 1953. It was the only state to enact the original version, because the Law Revision Commission of the New York State legislature began to examine it line by line and had serious objections. Three years later, in 1956, a revised code was issued. This version, known as the 1957 Official Text, was enacted in Massachusetts and Kentucky. In 1958, the Conference and the Institute amended the code further and again reissued it, this time as the 1958 Official Text. Sixteen states, including Pennsylvania, adopted this version.

But in so doing, many of these states changed particular provisions. As a consequence, the Uniform Commercial Code was no longer so uniform. Responding to this development, the American Law Institute established a permanent editorial board to oversee future revisions of the code. Various subcommittees went to work redrafting, and a 1962 Official Text was eventually published. Twelve more states adopted the code, eleven of them the 1962 text. By 1966, only three states and two territories had failed to enact any version: Arizona, Idaho, Louisiana, Guam, and Puerto Rico.

Meanwhile, non-uniform provisions continued to be enacted in various states, particularly in Article 9, to which 337 such amendments had been made. In 1971, a redraft of that article was readied and the 1972 Official Text was published. By that time, Louisiana was the only holdout. Two years later, in 1974, Louisiana made the UCC a truly national law when it enacted some but not all of the 1972 text (significantly, Louisiana has not adopted Article 2). The 1972 Official Text was later amended on several occasions. These amendments are incorporated into the current version, the 1989 Official Text.

From this brief history, it is clear that the UCC is now a basic law of relevance to every business and business lawyer in the United States, even though it is not entirely uniform because different states have adopted it at various stages of its evolution—an evolution that continues still.

The Basic Framework of the UCC   The UCC consists of nine major substantive "articles," each dealing with separate though related subjects. The articles, and their places of treatment in the book, are as follows:

- Article 1: General Provisions—Parts II and III
- Article 2: Sales—Parts II and III
- Article 2A: Leases—Chapter 20
- Article 3: Commercial Paper—Chapters 21–24
- Article 4: Bank Deposits and Collections—Chapter 25
- Article 4A: Funds Transfers—Chapter 25
- Article 5: Letters of Credit—Chapter 25
- Article 6: Bulk Transfers—Chapter 17
- Article 7: Warehouse Receipts, Bills of Lading, and Other Documents of Title—Chapter 20
- Article 8: Investment Securities—Chapter 42
- Article 9: Secured Transactions—Chapter 27

Article 2 of the UCC, which deals with sales, is divided in turn into six major parts. These are: (1) Form, Formation and Readjustment of Contract; (2) General Obligation and Construction of Contract; (3) Title, Creditors and Good Faith Purchasers; (4) Performance; (5) Breach, Repudiation and Excuse; and (6) Remedies. In the contracts unit of this book, we will emphasize the first part on form, formation and readjustment. Other, more specialized topics—such as product liability, transfer of title and risk of loss, performance, and remedies—will be covered separately in the sales unit.

Article 2 applies only to the sale of goods, defined (Section 2-105) in part as "all things . . . which are movable at the time of identification to the contract for sale other than the money in which the price is to be paid. . . ." The only contracts and agreements covered by Article 2 are those relating to the present or future sale of goods.

Three Basic Contract Types: Sources of Law

The primary sources of law for the three basic types of contracts are summarized in Figure 7-1. Common law and UCC rules are often similar. For example, both require good faith in the performance of a contract. However, as we begin to study contract law, there are two general differences worth noting between the common law of contracts and the UCC's rules governing the sales of goods. First, the UCC is more liberal than the common law in upholding the existence of a contract. For example, in a sales contract (covered by the UCC), "open" terms—that is, those the parties have not agreed upon—do not require a court to rule that no contract was made. However, open terms in a *nonsales* contract will frequently result in a ruling that there is no contract. Second, although the common law of contracts applies to every person equally, under the UCC "merchants" occasionally receive special treatment. By "merchants" the UCC means persons who have special knowledge or skill in dealing in the goods involved in the transaction.

The Convention on Contracts for the International Sale of Goods

A Convention on Contracts for the International Sale of Goods was approved in 1980 at a diplomatic conference in Vienna. (A convention is a preliminary agreement that serves as the basis for a formal treaty.) The Convention has been adopted by several countries, including the United States.

The Convention is significant for three reasons. First, the Convention is a uniform law governing the sale of goods—in effect, an international Uniform

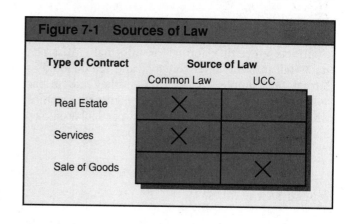

Figure 7-1 Sources of Law

Type of Contract	Source of Law	
	Common Law	UCC
Real Estate	X	
Services	X	
Sale of Goods		X

Commercial Code. The major goal of the drafters was to produce a uniform law acceptable to countries with different legal, social and economic systems. Second, although provisions in the Convention are generally consistent with the UCC, there are significant differences. For instance, under the Convention, consideration (see Chapter 9) is not required to form a contract and there is no Statute of Frauds (see Chapter 12). Finally, the Convention represents the first attempt by the Senate to reform the private law of business through its treaty powers, for the Convention preempts the UCC.

BASIC CONTRACT TAXONOMY

Contracts are not all cut from the same die. Some are written, some oral; some are explicit, some not. Because contracts can be formed, expressed, and enforced in a variety of ways, a taxonomy of contracts has developed that is useful in lumping together like legal consequences. In general, contracts are classified along five different dimensions: formality, explicitness, mutuality, enforceability, and degree of completion. **Formality** connotes the form of the contract. **Explicitness** is concerned with the degree to which the agreement is manifest to those not party to it. **Mutuality** takes into account whether promises are given by two parties or only one. **Enforceability** is the degree to which a given contract is binding. **Completion** considers whether the contract is yet to be performed or the obligations have been fully discharged by one or both parties. We will examine each of these concepts in turn.

Formality

Contracts are either formal or informal. Most contracts fall into the latter category and are denoted informal or "simple," even though they are in fact voluminous and complex. **Formal contracts** are those which, because of their form or particular subject matter, are governed by special rules.

Formal Contracts

In general, formal contracts include negotiable instruments and documents, letters of credit, and contracts under seal. The first two types of formal contracts are governed by statute; the law applicable to negotiable instruments and letters of credit is the UCC, and the special rules will be examined in Chapters 21–25.

The third type of formal contract—**contracts under seal**—originated in medieval England and developed with the common law, but the common law rules have been modified or abolished in most states. Nevertheless, a sealed contract is still recognized in many states, and its special characteristics are worth noting.

The **seal** began, in an age when few were literate, as a means of authenticating a contract without a signature. Considerable ceremony surrounded the sealing of a document with a wax impression of a signet ring. Originally use of the seal was limited to royalty, but eventually it spread to commoners. Once it was necessary to make an impression from a ring, but in time the strict formality was waived. In the United States, neither wax nor an impression was necessary. Indeed, the use of a gummed wafer, a special design or scrawl, or even the word "seal" or the letters "L.S." ("Locus Sigilli" [LOW kus see GIL lee]—which means the place where the seal is located on a docment) was recognized by American courts as sufficient to constitute a sealed contract. Today, any tangible and conventional manifestation of an intention that a document be sealed is the only requirement. Thus, a court may construe as sealed a contract with a gummed wafer affixed after the signatures, even if the contract does not recite that the parties intend it to be sealed.

In the states that continue to recognize it, the sealed contract has a significant advantage over unsealed contracts: the sealed contract is binding even though the party seeking to enforce the promise embodied in it has made no promise in return. Ordinarily, a contract requires mutual promises; for example, one party promises to pay money in return for the performance of services. But a sealed document that says simply "I promise to pay $1,000" is enforceable without what the law calls "consideration"—that is, without reciting any promise in return. In effect, the written sealed document is not merely *evidence* that a contract exists but *is* the contract. At common law, such a contract was nearly impossible to upset in court.

Today, however, the seal has lost much of its legal force. In twenty-four states, the seal has no legal effect at all, having been abolished by statute; a twenty-fifth state, Louisiana, never recognized the seal at all. Even in states that recognize the seal, lack of consideration may be a defense to a suit to enforce a contract and in many states, the only practical effect of a sealed contract is to lengthen the period of time during which a contract suit may be filed in court. Moreover, under the UCC, a purported seal on a contract for the sale of goods is ineffective; like negotiable instruments under seal, such contracts are governed by the UCC, not by the common law rules (Sections 2-203; 3-113).

Informal Contracts Most contracts are **informal contracts**. This term simply means that they are not subject to special statutory rules governing the few types of formal contracts listed above nor are they valid without consideration. The term "informal" does not mean that they are casual documents, written without regard for the sometimes intricate nuances of contract law. An informal contract can be quite formal in appearance and tone.

Although most types of contracts fall into the "informal" category, contracts still recite that they are sealed. Whether that recital is useful depends on the law of the state, as shown in the following case, in which a man attempted to avoid income taxes on the ground that his pledge to give assets to his sister amounted to a binding contract, even in the absence of any consideration, because the documents were sealed.

LINDER v. COMMISSIONER
68 T.C. 792 (1977)

OPINION

Over a period of 20 years petitioner made successive promises to his sister Rose to make sizable gifts to her. His promises for the years in issue were memorialized in bonds, executed under seal, secured by mortgages on his home. The issue before us is whether petitioner is entitled to deduct the interest which he paid to his sister on these bonds.

A deduction is generally allowed on "all interest paid or accrued within the taxable year on indebtedness." Sec. 163(a). Courts have defined indebtedness to mean an unconditional and legally enforceable obligation for the payment of money. The determination of whether an obligation is legally enforceable requires an analysis of the law of the State in which the transaction occurred, in this case New Jersey.

Since in most jurisdictions a promissory obligation executed as a gift is not legally enforceable, any interest paid on such an obligation is not deductible.

In New Jersey, as under the common law generally, a gratuitous promise to make a gift cannot normally be enforced. At common law, however, such a promise, if under seal, is enforceable. Since the gratuitous promises involved in this case were under seal, the sole issue is whether or not New Jersey retains this common law rule.

The following statutory rule applies in New Jersey:

> *In any claim upon a sealed instrument, a party may plead and set up, in defense thereto,* fraud in the consideration of the contract upon which recovery is sought, or *want or failure of consideration, as if the instrument were not sealed.* In such cases the seal shall be only presumptive evidence of sufficient consideration, which presumption may be rebutted as if the instrument were not sealed. [N.J. Stat. Ann. sec. 2A:82–3 (1976). Emphasis added.]

On its face, this statute, enacted in substantially its present form in 1900 (1900 N.J. Laws, ch. 150, sec. 15), appears to modify the common law rule and to make lack of consideration a defense to a sealed instrument. This would scarcely be surprising, for the magic of the seal has long since been legislatively exorcised in most American jurisdictions . . .

. . . Research has disclosed no recent instance in which any court in the United States has enforced a gratuitous promise under seal. Since petitioner's bonds were not in our view legally enforceable in New Jersey, interest paid thereon is nondeductible.

Explicitness

Express Contract An **express contract** is one in which the terms are spelled out directly; the parties to an express contract, whether written or oral, are conscious that they are making an enforceable agreement. For example, an agreement to purchase your neighbor's car for $500 and to take title next Monday is an express contract.

Implied Contract An **implied contract** is one that is inferred from the actions of the parties. Although no discussion of terms took place, an implied contract exists if it is clear from the conduct of both parties that they intended there be one. A delicatessen patron who asks for a "turkey sandwich to go" has made a contract and is obligated to pay when the sandwich is made. By ordering the food, the patron is implicitly agreeing to the price, whether posted or not.

The distinction between express and implied contracts has received a degree of notoriety in the so-called palimony cases, in which one member of an unmarried couple seeks a division of property after a long-standing live-together relationship has broken up. When a married couple divorces, financial rights and obligations are spelled out in a huge body of domestic relations statutes and judicial decisions. But no such laws exist for unmarried couples. Thus there appeared to be only two possible legal consequences of living together unmarried, although neither was probable in most cases. Some twenty states still have on the books statutes making fornication a crime; however, few, if any, prosecutions are brought against unmarried couples living together.

The other potential consequence is marriage: about one-third of the states recognize common law marriage, under which two people are deemed to be married if they live together with the intent to be married, regardless of their failure to have obtained a license or gone through a ceremony. But living together, by itself, is not sufficient to constitute a marriage; the intent to marry is crucial and must be shared by both.

If, however, the couple had entered into a contract, then legal consequences could still flow from the existence of the relationship. The absence of a signed agreement would not be the end of the inquiry: the actions of the couple while living together might signal their intent louder than words. The case that follows received front-page headlines in newspapers across the country when movie actor Lee Marvin was sued by his one-time companion, Michelle Marvin, who won the right to go to trial to try to prove express and implied contracts for support.

**MARVIN v. MARVIN
134 Cal.Rptr. 815, 557
P.2d 106 (1976)**

TOBRINGER, JUSTICE. Plaintiff avers that in October of 1964 she and defendant "entered into an oral agreement" that while "the parties lived together they would combine their efforts and earnings and would share equally any and all property accumulated as a result of their efforts whether individual or combined." Furthermore, they agreed to "hold themselves out to the general public as husband and wife" and that "plaintiff would further render her services as a companion, homemaker, housekeeper and cook to . . . defendant."

Shortly thereafter plaintiff agreed to "give up her lucrative career as an entertainer [and] singer" in order to "devote her full time to defendant . . . as a companion, homemaker, housekeeper and cook"; in return defendant agreed to "provide for all of plaintiff's financial support and needs for the rest of her life."

Plaintiff alleges that she lived with defendant from October of 1964 through May of 1970 and fulfilled her obligations under the agreement. During this period the parties as a result of their efforts and earnings acquired in defendant's name substantial real and personal property, including motion picture rights worth over $1 million. In May of 1970, however, defendant compelled plaintiff to leave his household. He continued to support plaintiff until November of 1971, but thereafter refused to provide further support.

On the basis of these allegations plaintiff asserts two causes of action. The first, for declaratory relief, asks the court to determine her contract and property rights; the second seeks to impose a constructive trust upon one half of the property acquired during the course of the relationship.

* * *

After hearing an argument the court granted defendant's motion [to dismiss] and entered judgment for defendant. Plaintiff moved to set aside the judgment and asked leave to amend her complaint to allege that she and defendant reaffirmed their agreement after defendant's divorce was final. The trial court denied plaintiff's motion, and she appealed from the judgment.

Plaintiff's complaint states a cause of action for breach of an express contract.

* * *

. . . [A]dults who voluntarily live together and engage in sexual relations are nonetheless as competent as any other persons to contract respecting their earnings and property rights. Of course, they cannot lawfully contract to pay for the performance of sexual services, for such a contract is, in essence, an agreement for prostitution and unlawful for that reason. But they may agree to pool their earnings and to hold all property acquired during the relationship in accord with the law governing community property; conversely they may agree that each partner's earnings and the property acquired from those earnings remains the separate property of the earning partner. So long as the agreement does not rest upon illicit meretricious consideration, the parties may order their economic affairs as they choose, and no policy precludes the courts from enforcing such agreements.

In the present instance, plaintiff alleges that the parties agreed to pool their earnings, that they contracted to share equally in all property acquired, and that defendant agreed to support plaintiff. The terms of the contract as alleged do not rest upon any unlawful consideration. We therefore conclude that the complaint furnishes a suitable basis upon which the trial court can render declaratory relief. The trial court consequently erred in granting defendant's motion for judgment on the pleadings.

Plaintiff's complaint can be amended to state a cause of action founded upon theories of implied contract or equitable relief.

* * *

We are aware that many young couples live together without the solemnization of marriage, in order to make sure that they can successfully later undertake marriage. This trial period, preliminary to marriage, serves as some assurance that the marriage will not subsequently end in dissolution to the harm of both parties. We are aware, as we have stated, of the pervasiveness of nonmarital relationships in other situations.

The mores of the society have indeed changed so radically in regard to cohabitation that we cannot impose a standard based on alleged moral considerations that have apparently been so widely abandoned by so many. Lest we be misunderstood, however, we take this occasion to point out that the structure of society itself largely depends upon the institution of marriage,

(*continued on next page*)

(continued)

MARVIN v. MARVIN
134 Cal.Rptr. 815, 557
P.2d 106 (1976)

and nothing we have said in this opinion should be taken to derogate from that institution. The joining of the man and woman in marriage is at once the most socially productive and individually fulfilling relationship that one can enjoy in the course of a lifetime.

We conclude that the judicial barriers that may stand in the way of a policy based upon the fulfillment of the reasonable expectations of the parties to a nonmarital relationship should be removed. As we have explained, the courts now hold that express agreements will be enforced unless they rest on an unlawful meretricious consideration. We add that in the absence of an express agreement, the courts may look to a variety of other remedies in order to protect the parties' lawful expectations.

The courts may inquire into the conduct of the parties to determine whether that conduct demonstrates an implied contract or implied agreement of partnership or joint venture, or some other tacit understanding between the parties. The courts may, when appropriate, employ principles of constructive trust or resulting trust. Finally, a nonmarital partner may recover in quantum merit for the reasonable value of household services rendered less the reasonable value of support received if he can show that he rendered services with the expectation of monetary reward.

Since we have determined that plaintiff's complaint states a cause of action for breach of an express contract, and, as we have explained, can be amended to state a cause of action independent of allegations of express contract, we must conclude that the trial court erred in granting defendant a judgment on the pleadings.

The judgment is reversed and the cause remanded for further proceedings consistent with the views expressed herein.

Note that Michelle Marvin had not proved that she and Lee Marvin made either an express or an implied contract. Hers was an allegation, which the state supreme court declared was entitled to be aired at trial. On "remand," Michelle failed to prove the existence of any contract; she could point to no actions that demonstrated an understanding between herself and Lee.

Contract Implied in Law: Quasi-Contract Both express and implied contracts embody an actual agreement of the parties. A **quasi-contract**, by contrast, is an obligation said to be "imposed by law" in order to avoid unjust enrichment of one person at the expense of another. In fact, a quasi-contract is not a contract at all; it is a fiction that the courts created to prevent injustice. Suppose, for example, that a carpenter mistakenly believes you have hired him to repair your porch; in fact, it is your neighbor who has

hired him. One Saturday morning he arrives at your doorstep and begins to work. Rather than stop him, you let him proceed, pleased at the prospect of having your porch fixed for free (since you have never talked to the carpenter, you figure you need not pay his bill). Although it is true there is no contract, the law implies a contract for the value of the work. The existence of this implied contract does not depend on the intention of the parties.

Mutuality

The garden-variety contract is one in which the parties make mutual promises. Each is both promisor and promisee; that is, each pledges to do something and each is the recipient of such a pledge. This type of contract is called a **bilateral contract**. But mutual promises are not necessary to constitute a contract.

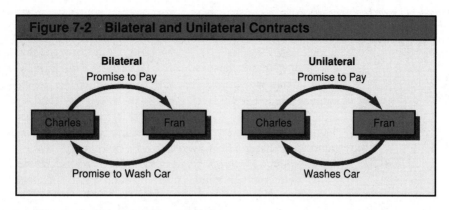

Figure 7-2 Bilateral and Unilateral Contracts

Unilateral contracts, in which one party performs an act in exchange for the other party's promise, are equally valid. If Charles says to Fran, "I will pay you five dollars if you wash my car," Charles is contractually bound to pay once Fran washes the car. Fran never makes a promise, but by actually performing she makes Charles liable to pay. See Figure 7-2. Unilateral contract theory has been used to achieve fairness when an employee is dismissed without cause, as the following case illustrates.

WOOLLEY v. HOFFMANN-LA ROCHE, INC.
99 N.J. 284, 491 A.2d 1257 (1985)

WILENTZ, C.J. The issue before us is whether certain terms in a company's employment manual may contractually bind the company. We hold that absent a clear and prominent disclaimer, an implied promise contained in an employment manual that an employee will be fired only for cause may be enforceable against an employer even when the employment is for an indefinite term and would otherwise be terminable at will.

Plaintiff, Richard Woolley, was hired by defendant, Hoffmann-La Roche, Inc., in October 1969, as an Engineering Section Head in defendant's Central Engineering Department at Nutley. There was no written employment contract between plaintiff and defendant. Plaintiff began work in mid-November 1969. Some time in December, plaintiff received and read the personnel manual on which his claims are based.

In 1976, plaintiff was promoted, and in January 1977 he was promoted again, this latter time to Group Leader for the Civil Engineering, the Piping Design, the Plant Layout, and the Standards and Systems Sections. In March 1978, plaintiff was directed to write a report to his supervisors about piping problems in one of defendant's buildings in Nutley. This report was written and submitted to plaintiff's immediate supervisor on April 5, 1978. On May 3, 1978, stating that the General Manager of defendant's Corporate Engineering Department had lost confidence in him, plaintiff's supervisors requested his resignation. Following this, by letter dated May 22, 1978, plaintiff was formally asked for his resignation, to be effective July 15, 1978.

Plaintiff refused to resign. Two weeks later defendant again requested plaintiff's resignation, and told him he would be fired if he did not resign. Plaintiff again declined, and he was fired in July.

(continued on next page)

(continued)

**WOOLLEY v.
HOFFMANN-LA
ROCHE, INC.
99 N.J. 284, 491 A.2d
1257 (1985)**

Plaintiff filed a complaint alleging breach of contract, intentional infliction of emotional distress, and defamation, but subsequently consented to the dismissal of the latter two claims. The gist of plaintiff's breach of contract claim is that the express and implied promises in defendant's employment manual created a contract under which he could not be fired at will, but rather only for cause, and then only after the procedures outlined in the manual were followed. Plaintiff contends that he was not dismissed for good cause, and that his firing was a breach of contract.

Defendant's motion for summary judgment was granted by the trial court, which held that the employment manual was not contractually binding on defendant, thus allowing defendant to terminate plaintiff's employment at will. The Appellate Division affirmed. We granted certification. 91 *N.J.* 548, 453 *A.2d* 865 (1982).

*   *   *

In order for an offer in the form of a promise to become enforceable, it must be accepted. Acceptance will depend on what the promisor bargained for: he may have bargained for a return promise that, if given, would result in a bilateral contract, both promises becoming enforceable. Or he may have bargained for some action or nonaction that, if given or withheld, would render his promise enforceable as a unilateral contract. In most of the cases involving an employer's personnel policy manual, the document is prepared without any negotiations and is voluntarily distributed to the workforce by the employer. It seeks no return promise from the employees. It is reasonable to interpret it as seeking continued work from the employees, who, in most cases, are free to quit since they are almost always employees at will, not simply in the sense that the employer can fire them without cause, but in the sense that they can quit without breaching any obligation. Thus analyzed, the manual is an offer that seeks the formation of a unilateral contract—the employees' bargained-for action needed to make the offer binding being their continued work when they have no obligation to continue.

The unilateral contract analysis is perfectly adequate for that employee who was aware of the manual and who continued to work intending that continuation to be the action in exchange for the employer's promise; it is even more helpful in support of that conclusion if, but for the employer's policy manual, the employee would have quit. *See generally* M. Petit, "Modern Unilateral Contracts," 63 *B.U.L.Rev.* 551 (1983) (judicial use of unilateral contract analysis in employment cases is widespread).

*   *   *

All that this opinion requires of an employer is that it be fair. It would be unfair to allow an employer to distribute a policy manual that makes the workforce believe that certain promises have been made and then to allow the employer to renege on those promises. What is sought here is basic honesty: if the employer, for whatever reason, does not want the manual to be capable of being construed by the court as a binding contract, there are simple ways to attain that goal. All that need be done is the inclusion in a very prominent position of an appropriate statement that there is no promise of any kind by the employer contained in the manual; that regardless of what the manual says or provides, the employer promises nothing and remains free to change wages and all other working conditions without having to consult anyone and without anyone's agreement; and that the employer continues to have the absolute power to fire anyone with or without good cause.

Reversed and remanded for trial.

Enforceability

Not every agreement between two people is a binding contract. An agreement that is lacking one of the legal elements of a contract is said to be **void**—that is, not a contract at all. An agreement that is illegal—for example, a promise to commit a crime in return for a money payment—is void. Neither party to a void "contract" may enforce it.

By contrast, a **voidable** contract is one that is unenforceable by one party but enforceable by the other. For example, a minor (any person under eighteen, in most states) may "avoid" a contract with an adult; the adult may not enforce the contract against the minor, if the minor refuses to carry out the bargain. But the adult has no choice if the minor wishes the contract to be performed. (A contract may be voidable by both parties if both are minors.) Ordinarily, the parties to a voidable contract are entitled to be restored to their original condition. Suppose you agree to buy your seventeen-year-old neighbor's car. He delivers it to you in exchange for your agreement to pay him next week. He has the legal right to terminate the deal and recover the car, in which case you will of course have no obligation to pay him. If you have already paid him, he still may legally demand a return to the *status quo ante* (stay tus kwo AN tee) (previous state of affairs). You must return the car to him; he must return the cash to you.

A voidable contract remains a valid contract until it is voided. Thus, a contract with a minor remains in force unless the minor decides he does not wish to be bound by it. When the minor reaches his majority, he may "ratify" the contract—that is, agree to be bound by it—in which case the contract will no longer be voidable and will thereafter be fully enforceable.

An **unenforceable** contract is one which some rule of law bars a court from enforcing. For example, Tom owes Pete money, but Pete has waited too long to collect it and the statute of limitations (see p. 235) has run out. The contract for repayment is unenforceable and Pete is out of luck, unless Tom makes a new promise to pay or actually pays part of the debt. (However, if Pete is holding collateral as security for the debt, he is entitled to keep it; not all rights are extinguished because a contract is unenforceable.)

Degree of Completion

In medieval England, contract—defined as set of promises—was not an intuitive concept. The courts gave relief to one who wanted to collect a debt, for in such a case the creditor presumably had already given the debtor something of value, and the failure of the debtor to pay up was seen as manifestly unjust. But the issue was less clear when neither promise had yet been fulfilled. Suppose John agrees to sell Humphrey a quantity of wheat in one month. On the appointed day, Humphrey refuses to take the wheat or to pay. The modern law of contracts holds that a valid contract exists and that Humphrey is required to pay John.

An agreement consisting of a set of promises is called an **executory** contract before either promise is carried out. Most executory contracts are enforceable. If one promise or set of terms has been fulfilled—if, for example, John had delivered the wheat to Humphrey—the contract is called **partially executed**. A contract that has been carried out fully by both parties is called an **executed** contract. The distinction between executed and executory contracts is especially important in bankruptcy proceedings—as the following case illustrates.

IN RE MUNPLE, LTD.
868 F.2d 1129 (9th Cir.
1989)

WILLIAM A. NORRIS, CIRCUIT JUDGE:

Munple entered into a representation agreement with M & M, under which M & M would act as broker for the sale of a piece of real estate owned by Munple, and would receive a $400,000 commission for the sale. Later that year, M & M found a buyer for Munple's land. A purchase agreement was executed by Munple, M & M, and the prospective buyer, which provided for a new brokerage commission of $330,000 payable to M & M at the close of escrow.

Before escrow closed, disputes arose between Munple and the buyer which culminated in Munple's filing for bankruptcy under chapter 11. After initiating the bankruptcy proceedings, Munple sought to assume the real estate purchase agreement so the escrow could close. The bankruptcy court issued an order allowing Munple to assume the purchase agreement.

Upon learning that Munple had assumed the purchase agreement, M & M submitted a demand that its $330,000 commission be paid at the close of escrow. In response, Munple filed a notion with the bankruptcy court for permission to sell the land free and clear of M & M's claim to payment.

The bankruptcy court denied Munple's motion, and entered an order directing Munple to pay the disputed commission claim upon the close of sale. On appeal by Munple, the district court affirmed, holding that the commission agreement was an executory contract that had been assumed by Munple after initiation of the chapter 11 proceedings. The district court denied M & M's request for attorneys' fees. Munple now appeals the district court's ruling on the commission agreement, while M & M cross-appeals the court's denial of attorneys' fees.

Under section 365 of the Bankruptcy Code, a debtor may assume the obligations of an executory contract subject to the bankruptcy court's approval. Whether a contract is executory within the meaning of the Bankruptcy Code is a question of federal law. In our recent decision in *Griffel v. Murphy* (*In re Wegner*), 839 F.2d 533 (9th Cir.1988), we established the following standard for determining whether a contract is executory for purposes of the code:

> Although the Code does not define "executory contract," courts have generally defined such a contract as one on which performance is due to some extent on both sides. . . . [I]n executory contracts the obligations of both parties are so far unperformed that the failure of either party to complete performance would constitute a material breach and thus excuse the performance of the other.

This means that when a party has "substantially performed" its side of the bargain, such that the party's failure to perform further would not constitute a material breach excusing performance by the other party, a contract is not executory. The party who has fully performed is thus relegated to the position of a general creditor of the bankrupt estate.

Under this standard, the commission agreement between Munple and M & M was not executory at the time that Munple assumed the purchase agreement in bankruptcy. By the time the purchase agreement was signed, M & M had completed all the performance necessary to earn its commission if and when the sale closed. M & M had procured a buyer, which was all it was required to do to earn the commission. Having found a buyer, M & M was entitled to its commission as soon as the sale closed, regardless of whether it did anything further. Thus, the commission provision in the purchase agreement was not an executory contract as defined in *Wegner*.

M & M argues on appeal that the commission provision in the purchase agreement was executory because payment of the commission was contingent on the closing of the sale. In effect, M & M argues that the condition precedent on Munple's obligation to pay the commission rendered the agreement executory. This argument confuses performance obligations and conditions precedent. Although under the terms of the agreement M & M could receive its commission only if and when Munple and the buyer closed the sale, M & M had no material obligations left to perform. The condition precedent to Munple's obligation to pay the commission imposed no further obligations on M & M, nonperformance of which would have excused Munple from paying the commission. Because M & M had done everything required of it to earn the commission, the commission provision in the purchase agreement was not executory. In so concluding, we are in line with other decisions holding that brokerage commission agreements are performed when a buyer is procured, and are not made executory by a provision conditioning payment on closing the sale.

M & M nonetheless argues that the commission provision in the purchase agreement was executory because of services M & M assertedly rendered after the signing of the purchase agreement. M & M alleges that even after the purchase agreement was signed, it "rendered substantial services and incurred expenses in connection with the sale." M & M contends that the purchase agreement "authorized" it to render such services and gave it a "strong incentive" to help close the deal because payment of the commission was contingent on closing. Even if true, these facts do not render the commission agreement executory on M & M's part after it produced the buyer. While M & M may have had both the authority and the incentive to render further services after the purchase agreement was signed, the critical question is whether M & M was *required* to perform such services in order to earn its commission. Nothing in the original representation agreement or in the later purchase agreement suggests such an obligation; and indeed, M & M does not even argue that such an obligation existed. In sum, the commission provision in the purchase agreement was plainly not executory.

★   ★   ★

[The court reversed the district court's holding that the agreement was executory.]

CHAPTER SUMMARY

In this chapter we have seen that two fundamental sources of contract law are the common law as developed in the state courts and as summarized in the *Restatement (Second) of Contracts*, and the Uniform Commercial Code for the sale of goods. In general, the UCC is more liberal than the common law in upholding the existence of a contract.

Types of contracts can be distinguished along five axes: (1) formality and informality; (2) express and implied, including quasi-contracts implied by law; (3) bilateral and unilateral; (4) enforceable and unenforceable; and (5) completed (executed) and uncompleted (executory). To understand contract law, it is necessary to master these distinctions and their nuances.

KEY TERMS

Bilateral contract	p. 196	Informal contracts	p. 192
Contract	p. 188	Implied contract	p. 193
Contracts under seal	p. 192	Mutuality	p. 191
Enforceability	p. 191	Partially executed	p. 199
Executed	p. 199	Quasi-contract	p. 196
Executory	p. 199	Seal	p. 192
Explicitness	p. 191	Unenforceable	p. 199
Express contract	p. 193	Unilateral contracts	p. 197
Formal contracts	p. 192	Void	p. 199
Formality	p. 191	Voidable	p. 199

SELF-TEST QUESTIONS

1. The major sources of contract law are:
   (a)   the Constitution
   (b)   statutes
   (c)   administrative law
   (d)   all of the above
2. The Uniform Commercial Code is an example of:
   (a)   case law
   (b)   statutory law
   (c)   constitutional law
   (d)   administrative law
3. An implied contract:
   (a)   must be in writing
   (b)   is one in which the terms are spelled out
   (c)   is one inferred from the actions of the parties
   (d)   is the same as a bilateral contract
4. The Convention on Contracts for the International Sale of Goods:
   (a)   is an annual meeting of purchasing agents
   (b)   is a form of administrative law
   (c)   is identical to the Uniform Commercial Code
   (d)   has been adopted by the United States

5. An unenforceable contract:
   (a)   is not a contract at all
   (b)   is one which a court will not enforce because of a rule of law
   (c)   is unenforceable by one party but enforceable by the other
   (c)   is unenforceable by one party but enforceable by the other
   (d)   is none of the above

DEMONSTRATION PROBLEM

Mr. and Mrs. Smith, an elderly couple, have no relatives. When Mrs. Smith became ill, the Smiths asked a friend, Henrietta, to help with various housekeeping chores, including cleaning and cooking. Although the Smiths never promised to pay her, Henrietta performed the chores for three years. Henrietta now claims that she is entitled to the reasonable value of the services performed. Is she correct? Why?

PROBLEMS

1. A letter from Bridge Builders, Inc., to the Allied Steel Company states the following:
   > We offer to purchase 10,000 tons of No. 4 steel pipe at today's quoted price for delivery two months from today. Your acceptance must be received in five days.

   Does Bridge Builders intend to create a bilateral or a unilateral contract? Why?
2. When Roscoe visited his barber for a haircut, the barber persuaded him to try a new hair cream called Kid's Stuff. Roscoe tried the product and, upon waking the next morning, discovered that all of his hair had fallen out overnight. Upon investigation he discovered that the loss of hair was due to an improper chemical compound in Kid's Stuff. If Roscoe filed a breach-of-contract action against the barber, would the case be governed by the Uniform Commercial Code? Why?
3. Rachel entered into a contract to purchase a 1954 Rambler from Hanna, who lived in the neighboring apartment. When a dispute arose over the terms of the contract, Hanna argued that, because neither she nor Rachel was a merchant, the dispute should be decided under general principles of common law. Rachel, on the other hand, argued that Hanna was legally considered to be a merchant because she sold the car for profit and that, consequently, the sale was governed by the Uniform Commercial Code. Who is correct? Why?
4. Lee and Michelle decided to become roommates. When they set up house, Michelle gave up her career and Lee

promised to share his earnings with her on a 50-50 basis. Several years later, they ended their relationship and, when Lee failed to turn over half of his earnings, Michelle filed suit on the basis of Lee's promise. Would Michelle allege breach of an express contract or an implied one? Why?

5. Hilda lost her watch. She promises Clara a $150 reward if Clara finds and returns the watch. Clara accepts the offer, promising to find the watch. Has a contract been formed? Why?

6. During Prohibition, Louie, an adult, entered into a contract to sell a case of scotch whiskey to Leroy, a minor. Is the contract void or voidable? Why?

7. James Mann owns a manufacturing plant in which radios are assembled. A CPA conducting an audit determined that several radios were missing. Theft by one or more of the workers was suspected. Accordingly, under Mann's instructions, the following sign was placed in the employees' cafeteria:

> *Reward.* I believe employees are stealing radios. I want all employees to watch other employees to see they do not steal. A reward of $500 will be paid for information given by any employee which leads to the apprehension of an employee who is stealing radios.
>
> James Mann

Waldo, a plant employee, read the notice and immediately called Mann, stating, "I accept your offer. I promise to watch other employees and to provide you with the requested information." Has a contract been formed? Why?

ANSWERS TO SELF-TEST QUESTIONS

1. (d)   2. (b)   3. (c)   4. (d)   5. (b)

SUGGESTED ANSWER TO DEMONSTRATION PROBLEM

Henrietta is correct under an implied contract theory. The Smiths asked her to perform the services and there was no reason to believe she would work free. *In re Estate of Mallas*, 241 N.E.2d 482 (Ill. 1968).

CHAPTER

8

CHAPTER OVERVIEW
The Agreement in General
The Offer
The Acceptance

The Agreement

*I*n this chapter we begin the first of the four broad inquiries of contract law (p. 189): Did the parties create a valid contract? The answer is not always obvious; the range of factors that must be taken into account can be large and their relationship subtle. Since people in business frequently conduct contract negotiations without the assistance of a lawyer, it is important to attend to the nuances to avoid legal trouble at the outset. Whether a valid contract has been formed depends in turn on whether:

1. The parties reached an agreement (the focus of this chapter);
2. Consideration was present (Chapter 9);
3. The agreement was legal (Chapter 10); and
4. The parties entered into the contract of their own free will, with knowledge of the facts, and with capacity to make a contract (Chapter 11).

THE AGREEMENT IN GENERAL

The core of a legal contract is the agreement between the parties. This is not a necessary ingredient; in Communist nations, contracts are routinely negotiated between parties who have had the terms imposed on them. But in the West, and especially in the

United States, agreement is of the essence. That is not merely a matter of convenience; it is at the heart of our received philosophical and psychological beliefs. As the great student of contract law, Samuel Williston, put it:

> It was a consequence of the emphasis laid on the ego and the individual will that the formation of a contract should seem impossible unless the wills of the parties concurred. Accordingly we find at the end of the eighteenth century, and the beginning of the nineteenth century, the prevalent idea that there must be a "meeting of the minds" (a new phrase) in order to form a contract. (1921, p. 365)

Although agreements may take any form, including unspoken conduct between the parties (UCC Section 2-204(1)), they are usually structured in terms of an offer and an acceptance. These two components will be the focus of our discussion. Note, however, that not every agreement, in the broadest sense of the word, need consist of an offer and acceptance, and it is entirely possible, therefore, for two persons to reach agreement without forming a contract. For example, people may agree that the weather is pleasant or that it would be preferable to go out for Chinese food rather than to see a foreign film; in neither case has a contract been formed. One of the major functions of the law of contracts is to sort out those agreements that are legally binding—those that are contracts—from those that are not.

In interpreting agreements, courts generally apply an objective standard. The *Restatement (Second) of Contracts* defines agreement as a "*manifestation* of mutual assent by two or more persons to one another." (Section 3.) The UCC defines agreement as "the bargain of the parties in fact as found in their language or by implication from other circumstances including course of dealing or usage of trade or course of performance." (Section 1-201(3).) The critical question is what the parties said or did, not what they thought they said or did.

The distinction between objective and subjective standards crops up occasionally when one person claims he spoke in jest. The vice president of a manufacturer of punchboards, used in gambling, testified to the Washington State Game Commission that he would pay $100,000 to anyone who found a "crooked board." Barnes, a bartender, who had purchased two that were crooked some time before, brought one to the company office, and demanded payment. The company refused, claiming that the statement was made in jest (the audience before the commission had laughed when the offer was made). The court disagreed, holding that it was reasonable to interpret the pledge of $100,000 as a means of promoting punchboards:

> [I]f the jest is not apparent and a reasonable hearer would believe that an offer was being made, then the speaker risks the formation of a contract which was not intended. It is the objective manifestations of the offeror that count and not secret, unexpressed intentions. If a party's words or acts, judged by a reasonable standard, manifest an intention to agree in regard to the matter in question, that agreement is established, and it is immaterial what may be the real but unexpressed state of the party's mind on the subject. [Barnes v. Treece, 549 P.2d 1152 (Wash. App. 1976)]

As the following case illustrates, a party's real state of mind must be expressed to the other party, rather than in an aside to one's spouse.

LUCY v. ZEHMER
196 Va. 493, 84 S.E.2d
516 (1954)

BUCHANAN, JUSTICE. This suit was instituted by W. O. Lucy and J. C. Lucy, complainants, against A. H. Zehmer and Ida S. Zehmer, his wife, defendants, to have specific performance of a contract by which it was alleged the Zehmers had sold to W. O. Lucy a tract of land owned by A. H. Zehmer in Dinwiddie county containing 471.6 acres, more or less, known as the Ferguson farm, for $50,000. J. C. Lucy, the other complainant, is a brother of W. O. Lucy, to whom W. O. Lucy transferred a half interest in his alleged purchase.

The instrument sought to be enforced was written by A. H. Zehmer on December 20, 1952, in these words: "We hereby agree to sell to W. O. Lucy the Ferguson Farm complete for $50,000.00, title satisfactory to buyer," and signed by the defendants, A. H. Zehmer and Ida S. Zehmer.

The answer of A. H. Zehmer admitted that at the time mentioned W. O. Lucy offered him $50,000 cash for the farm, but that he, Zehmer, considered that the offer was made in jest; that so thinking, and both he and Lucy having had several drinks, he wrote out "the memorandum" quoted above and induced his wife to sign it; that he did not deliver the memorandum to Lucy, but that Lucy picked it up, read it, put it in his pocket, attempted to offer Zehmer $5 to bind the bargain, which Zehmer refused to accept, and realizing for the first time that Lucy was serious, Zehmer assured

(continued on next page)

(continued)

LUCY v. ZEHMER
196 Va. 493, 84 S.E.2d 516 (1954)

him that he had no intention of selling the farm and that the whole matter was a joke. Lucy left the premises insisting that he had purchased the farm.

* * *

In his testimony Zehmer claimed that he "was high as a Georgia pine," and that the transaction "was just a bunch of two doggoned drunks bluffing to see who could talk the biggest and say the most." That claim is inconsistent with his attempt to testify in great detail as to what was said and what was done.

* * *

If it be assumed, contrary to what we think the evidence shows, that Zehmer was jesting about selling his farm to Lucy and that the transaction was intended by him to be a joke, nevertheless the evidence shows that Lucy did not so understand it but considered it to be a serious business transaction and the contract to be binding on the Zehmers as well as on himself. The very next day he arranged with his brother to put up half the money and take a half interest in the land. The day after that he employed an attorney to examine the title. The next night, Tuesday, he was back at Zehmer's place and there Zehmer told him for the first time, Lucy said, that he wasn't going to sell and he told Zehmer, "You know you sold that place fair and square." After receiving the report from his attorney that the title was good he wrote to Zehmer that he was ready to close the deal.

Not only did Lucy actually believe, but the evidence shows he was warranted in believing, that the contract represented a serious business transaction and a good faith sale and purchase of the farm.

In the field of contracts, as generally elsewhere, "We must look to the outward expression of a person as manifesting his intention rather than to his secret and unexpressed intention. 'The law imputes to a person an intention corresponding to the reasonable meaning of his words and acts.' "

At no time prior to the execution of the contract had Zehmer indicated to Lucy by word or act that he was not in earnest about selling the farm. They had argued about it and discussed its terms, as Zehmer admitted, for a long time. Lucy testified that if there was any jesting it was about paying $50,000 that night. The contract and the evidence show that he was not expected to pay the money that night. Zehmer said that after the writing was signed he laid it down on the counter in front of Lucy. Lucy said Zehmer handed it to him. In any event there had been what appeared to be a good faith offer and a good faith acceptance, followed by the execution and apparent delivery of a written contract. Both said that Lucy put the writing in his pocket and then offered Zehmer $5 to seal the bargain. Not until then, even under the defendants' evidence, was anything said or done to indicate that the matter was a joke. Both of the Zehmers testified that when Zehmer asked his wife to sign he whispered that it was a joke so Lucy wouldn't hear and that it was not intended that he should hear.

The mental assent of the parties is not requisite for the formation of a contract. If the words or other acts of one of the parties have but one reasonable meaning, his undisclosed intention is immaterial except when an unreasonable meaning which he attaches to his manifestations is known to the other party.

. . . The law, therefore, judges of an agreement between two persons exclusively from those expressions of their intentions which are communicated between them. . . . Clark on Contracts, 4 ed., § 3, p. 4.

An agreement or mutual assent is of course essential to a valid contract but the law imputes to a person an intention corresponding to the reasonable meaning of his words and acts. If his words and acts, judged by a reasonable standard, manifest an intention to agree, it is immaterial what may be the real but unexpressed state of his mind.

So a person cannot set up that he was merely jesting when his conduct and words would warrant a reasonable person in believing that he intended a real agreement.

Whether the writing signed by the defendants and now sought to be enforced by the complainants was the result of a serious offer by Lucy and a serious acceptance by the defendants, or was a serious offer by Lucy and an acceptance in secret jest by the defendants, in either event it constituted a binding contract of sale between the parties. [Judgment for W. O. Lucy and J. C. Lucy.]

Offer and acceptance may seem to be straightforward concepts, as they are when two people meet face to face. But in a commercial society, the ways of making offers and accepting them are nearly infinite. A retail store advertises its merchandise in the newspaper. A seller makes his offer by mail. A telephone caller states that his offer will stand for ten days. An offer leaves open a crucial term. An auctioneer seeks bids. An offeror gives the offeree a choice. All these situations can raise tricky questions, as can corresponding situations involving acceptances.

THE OFFER

Defined

The *Restatement (Second) of Contracts*, Section 24, defines an **offer** as "the manifestation of willingness to enter into a bargain, so made as to justify another person in understanding that his assent to that bargain is invited and will conclude it." Two key elements are implicit in that definition: the offer must be communicated, and it must be definite. Before considering these requirements, we examine the threshold question of whether an offer was intended. Let us look at proposals that may look like, but are not, offers.

Proposals That Are Not Offers

Most advertisements, price quotations, and invitations to bid are not construed as offers. A notice in the newspaper that a coat is on sale for $100 is normally intended only as an invitation to the public to come to the store to make a purchase. Similarly, a statement that a seller can "quote" a unit price to a prospective purchaser is not, by itself, of sufficient definiteness to constitute an offer: quantity, time of delivery, and other important factors are missing from such a statement. Frequently, in order to avoid construction of a statement about price and quantity as an offer, a seller or buyer may say: "Make me an offer." Such a statement suggests that no offer has yet been made. This principle usually applies in invitations for bids (for example, from contractors on a building project). Many form contracts used by sales representatives indicate that by signing the customer is making an offer to be accepted by the home office and is not himself accepting an offer made by the sales representative.

Although advertisements, price quotations, and the like are generally not offers, the facts in each case are important. Under the proper circumstances, an advertised statement can be construed as an offer, as the following case shows, in which the offended customer acted as his own lawyer and pursued an appeal to the Minnesota Supreme Court against a Minneapolis department store that took back its advertised offer.

LEFKOWITZ v. GREAT MINNEAPOLIS SURPLUS STORE
215 Minn. 188, 86 N.W.2d 689 (1957)

MURPHY, JUSTICE. This is an appeal from an order of the Municipal Court of Minneapolis denying the motion of the defendant for amended findings of fact, or, in the alternative, for a new trial. The order for judgment awarded the plaintiff the sum of $138.50 as damages for breach of contract.

This case grows out of the alleged refusal of the defendant to sell to the plaintiff a certain fur piece which it had offered for sale in a newspaper advertisement. It appears from the record that on April 6, 1956, the defendant published the following advertisement in a Minneapolis newspaper:

> "Saturday 9 A.M. Sharp
> 3 Brand New
> Fur
> Coats
> Worth to $100.00
> First Come
> First Served
> $1
> Each"

On April 13, the defendant again published an advertisement in the same newspaper as follows:

> "Saturday 9 A.M.
> 2 Brand New Pastel
> Mink 3-Skin Scarfs
> Selling for $89.50
> Out they go
> Saturday. Each. . . . $1.00
> 1 Black Lapin Stole
> Beautiful
> worth $139.50. . . . $1.00
> First Come
> First Served"

The record supports the findings of the court that on each of the Saturdays following the publication of the above-described ads the plaintiff was the first to present himself at the appropriate counter in the defendant's store and on each occasion demanded the coat and the stole so advertised and indicated his readiness to pay the sale price of $1. On both occasions, the defendant refused to sell the merchandise to the plaintiff, stating on the first occasion that by a "house rule" the offer was intended for women only and sales would not be made to men, and on the second visit that plaintiff knew defendant's house rules.

The trial court properly disallowed plaintiff's claim for the value of the fur coats since the value of these articles was speculative and uncertain. The only evidence of value was the advertisement itself to the effect that the coats were "Worth to $100.00," how much less being speculative especially in view of the price for which they were offered for sale. With reference to the offer of the defendant on April 13, 1956, to sell the "1 Black Lapin Stole . . . worth $139.50 . . ." the trial court held that the value of this article was established and granted judgment in favor of the plaintiff for that amount less the $1 quoted purchase price.

1. The defendant contends that a newspaper advertisement offering items of merchandise for sale at a named price is a "unilateral offer" which may be withdrawn without notice. He relies upon authorities which hold that, where an advertiser publishes in a newspaper that he has a certain quantity or quality of goods which he wants to dispose of at certain prices and on certain terms, such advertisements are not offers which become contracts as soon as any person to whose notice they may come signifies his acceptance by notifying the other that he will take a certain quantity of them. Such advertisements have been construed as an invitation for an offer of sale on the terms stated, which offer, when received, may be accepted or rejected and which therefore does not become a contract of sale until accepted by the seller; and until a contract has been so made, the seller may modify or revoke such prices or terms.

★　　★　　★

There are numerous authorities which hold that a particular advertisement in a newspaper or circular letter relating to a sale of articles may be construed by the court as constituting an offer, acceptance of which would complete a contract.

The test of whether a binding obligation may originate in advertisements addressed to the general public is "whether the facts show that some performance was promised in positive terms in return for something requested." 1 Williston, Contracts (Rev. ed.) § 27.

★　　★　　★

Whether in any individual instance a newspaper advertisement is an offer rather than an invitation to make an offer depends on the legal intention of the parties and the surrounding circumstances. We are of the view on the facts before us that the offer by the defendant of the sale of the Lapin fur was clear, definite, and explicit, and left nothing open for negotiation. The

(continued on next page)

(continued)

LEFKOWITZ v. GREAT MINNEAPOLIS SURPLUS STORE
215 Minn. 188, 86 N.W.2d 689 (1957)

plaintiff having successfully managed to be the first one to appear at the seller's place of business to be served, as requested by the advertisement, and having offered the stated purchase price of the article, he was entitled to performance on the part of the defendant. We think the trial court was correct in holding that there was in the conduct of the parties a sufficient mutuality of obligation to constitute a contract of sale.

2. The defendant contends that the offer was modified by a "house rule" to the effect that only women were qualified to receive the bargains advertised. The advertisement contained no such restriction. This objection may be disposed of briefly by stating that, while an advertiser has the right at any time before acceptance to modify his offer, he does not have the right, after acceptance, to impose new or arbitrary conditions not contained in the published offer.

Affirmed.

Despite the rule that advertisements are normally to be considered invitations rather than offers, legislation and government regulations may offer redress. Since 1971, retail food stores have been subject to a rule promulgated by the Federal Trade Commission that goods advertised as "specials" must be available and at the price advertised. It is unlawful for a retail chain not to have the advertised items in each of its stores and in sufficient quantity, unless the advertisement specifically states how much is stocked and which branch stores do not carry it.

When the rule was originally adopted in 1971, the FTC noted that the principles inherent in the rule apply to the advertising of other commodities in addition to food. As a result of recent studies, however, the FTC has considered amending the rule because it increases inventory costs. Regardless of potential FTC action, many states have enacted consumer protection statutes that parallel the FTC rule.

Communication

A contract is an agreement in which each party assents to the terms of the other party. Without mutual assent there cannot be a contract, and this implies that the assent each person gives must be with reference to that of the other. If Toni places several alternative offers on the table, only one of which can be accepted, and invites Sandy to choose, no contract is formed if Sandy says merely: "I accept your terms." Sandy must specify which offer she is assenting to.

From this general proposition it follows that no contract can be legally binding unless an offer is in fact communicated to the offeree. If you write a letter to a friend, offering to sell your car for a certain sum, and then forget to mail the letter, no offer has been made. If your friend coincidentally sends you a letter the following day saying that she wants to buy your car, naming the same sum, no contract has been made. Her letter to you is not an acceptance, since she did not know of your offer; her letter is, instead, an offer or an invitation to make an offer. Nor would there have been a contract if you remembered to send your letter, so that both letters crossed in the mail. Both letters would be offers, and for a valid contract to be formed it would still be necessary for one of you to accept the other's offer.

The requirement that an offer be communicated does not mean that every term must be communicated. You call up your friend and offer to sell him your car. You tell him the price and start to tell him that you will throw in the snow tires but will not pay for a new inspection and that you expect to keep the car another three weeks. Impatiently, he cuts you off and says, "Never mind about all that; I'll accept your offer on whatever terms you want." You and he have a contract.

These principles apply to unknown offers of reward. An offer of reward constitutes a unilateral contract that can be made binding only by performing the task for which the reward is offered. Suppose that Bonnie posts on a tree a sign offering a reward for returning her missing dog. If you saw the sign, found the dog, and returned it, you would have fulfilled the essentials of the offer. But if you chanced upon the dog, read the tag around its neck, and returned it without ever having been aware that a reward was offered, then you have not responded to the offer—even if you acted in the hope that the owner would reward you. There is no contractual obligation.

In many states, a different result follows from an offer of reward by a governmental entity. Commonly, local ordinances provide that a standing reward of, say, $1,000 will be paid to anyone providing information that leads to the arrest and conviction of arsonists. In order to collect the reward, it is not necessary for a person who does furnish local authorities with such information to know that a reward ordinance exists. In contract terms, the standing reward is viewed as a means of setting a climate in which people will be encouraged to act in certain ways in the expectation that they will earn unknown rewards. It is also possible to view the claim to a reward as noncontractual; the right to receive it is guaranteed, instead, by the local ordinance.

Although a completed act called for by an unknown private offer does not give rise to a contract, partial performance usually does. Suppose Apex Bakery posts a notice offering a one-week bonus to all bakers who work at least six months in the kitchen. Charlene works two months before discovering the notice on the bulletin board. Her original ignorance of the offer will not defeat her claim to the bonus if she continues working, for the offer serves as an inducement to complete the performance called for. If, however, an offeree has a legal obligation to perform a duty, a promise of a reward upon fulfillment is generally not enforceable. If you are required to finish a six-week stint in army boot camp, your drill sergeant's promise to send you to Hawaii for the balance of your required active duty "if you will only complete the course" is not binding.

Definiteness

The common law reasonably requires that an offer spell out the essential proposed terms with sufficient **definiteness** that a court could order enforcement or measure damages in the event of a breach. As it has often been put, "The law does not make contracts for the parties; it merely enforces the duties which they have undertaken" (Simpson, 1965, p. 19). Thus a supposed promise to sell "such coal as the promisor may wish to sell" is not an enforceable term because the seller undertakes no duty to sell anything.

Essential terms include price and work to be done. Not every omission is necessarily fatal; for example, as long as a missing term can be fixed by referring to some external standard—such as "no later than the first frost"—the offer is sufficiently definite. Although the requirement of definiteness is not universally necessary (as **Box 8-1** indicates, the Japanese seem to lack the need for it), it is rooted in the logic of a contract in the United States.

In major business transactions involving extensive negotiations, the parties often sign a preliminary "agreement in principle" before a detailed contract is drafted. These preliminary agreements may be definite enough to create contract liability even though they lack many of the terms found in a typical contract. For example, in 1985 a Texas jury concluded that an agreement in principle between Pennzoil Co. and Getty Oil Co. was binding and that Texaco had unlawfully interfered with their contract. As a result Texaco was held liable for over $10 billion, which was settled for $3 billion after Texaco went into bankruptcy.

Offers that state alternatives are definitive if each alternative is definite. David offers Sheila the opportunity to buy one of two automobiles at a fixed price to be delivered in two months, the choice of vehicle to be left to David. Sheila accepts. The contract is valid. If one of the cars is destroyed in the interval before delivery, David is obligated to deliver the other car. Sometimes, however, what appears to be an offer in the alternative may be something else. Charles makes a deal to sell his business to Bernie. As part of the bargain, Charles agrees not to compete with Bernie for the next two years and, if he does, to pay $25,000. Whether this is an alternative contract depends on the circumstances and intentions of the parties. If it is, then Charles is free to compete as long as he pays Bernie $25,000. On the other hand, the intention might have been to impose a fine to prevent Charles from competing in any event; hence a court could order payment of the $25,000 as damages for a breach and still order Charles to refrain from competition until the expiration of the two-year period.

LAW AND LIFE

BOX 8-1

Managing Without Lawyers

By Thomas Lifson

[Rooted in United States contract law is the requirement of definiteness. Common law reasonably requires that a contract include the essential proposed terms with sufficient definiteness that a court could order enforcement or measure damages in the event of a breach. However, this approach requires a large number of attorneys to review contract terms.—AUTHORS' NOTE]

Fed up with suits and counter-suits, tedious contracts, procedural delays and mounting legal costs, many American managers wish they could do business with fewer lawyers.

The Japanese have shown it can be done. In all of Japan, with a population of over one hundred million, there are only 15,000 lawyers, fewer than in the state of Ohio. On a per capita basis, that's one twenty-fifth the number in the United States.

This paucity of lawyers is not simply the result of management practice. The Japanese government regulates more by administrative discretion than by explicit statutes and guidelines. Compared to Americans,

WANT FEWER LAWYERS? USE FEWER CONTRACTS.

Japanese interest groups go less often to courts to seek redress.

But Japanese managers also use fewer lawyers in their dealings with other companies. In particular, they do not attach as much importance to contracts in their dealings with suppliers, partners and customers.

In America, the written word of a contract is the chief guarantee that both sides of a business relationship agree on their mutual responsibilities. Therefore, high pressure bargaining occurs at contract writing time. Every contingency imaginable must be addressed and fought over. The stakes are high, for in the face of an uncertain future both sides are locked into the terms written down.

This process requires the services of legal specialists who agree on the precise meanings of words. Once the contract is in place, the specialists are still needed to assure that each party's rights are respected. Thus, while managers are clearly responsible for the substance of a contract,

they must delegate procedural issues to lawyers who follow their own logic.

In Japan, by contrast, agreement between firms is not focused on a document. Price, quantity, delivery and other such details are seldom spelled out definitely in advance. Agreement is instead based on a vague and unspecific mutual belief in the long-run benefits of doing business together. Lacking the safeguard of a contract, Japanese managers must learn as much as possible about the other party and its likely behavior under a range of circumstances. At every level of the hierarchy, each organization must feel confident it understands and can rely on the other. . . .

The principal advantage of Japanese agreement is that the two sides are not locked into specific terms. For example, if a supplier is faced with an unexpected rise in costs beyond its control, it can often persuade its customer to accept a rise in price, on the understanding that the supplier will return a similar favor later.

In the United States, unless a provision of the contract specifically anticipated the change in costs, the supplier might have to honor its contractual obligations or risk irksome litigation. . . .

Source: *Wall Street Journal*, September 24, 1979

The UCC Approach   The UCC is generally more liberal in its approach to definiteness than the common law—at least as the common law was interpreted in the heyday of classical contract doctrine. Section 2-204(3) states the rule: "Even though one or more terms are left open a contract for sale does not fail for indefiniteness if the parties have intended to make a contract and there is a reasonably certain basis for giving an appropriate remedy."

The drafters of the UCC sought to give validity to as many contracts as possible and grounded that validity on the intention of the parties rather than on formalistic requirements. As the official comment to Section 2-204(3) notes: "If the parties intend to enter into a binding agreement, this subsection recognizes that agreement as valid in law, despite missing terms, if there is any reasonably certain basis for granting a remedy. . . . [C]ommercial standards on the point of 'indefiniteness' are intended to be applied." In other sections of the code (chiefly Sections 2-305 through 2-310), the UCC spells out rules for filling in such open provisions as price, performance, and remedies.

One of these sections, Section 2-306(1), provides that a contract term under which a buyer agrees to purchase the seller's entire output of goods (or a seller agrees to meet the buyer's requirements) means output or requirements that occur in good faith. A party to such a contract cannot offer or demand a quantity that is "unreasonably disproportionate" to a stated estimate or past quantities.

Duration of Offer

An offer need not be accepted on the spot. Because there are numerous ways of conveying an offer and numerous contingencies that may be part of the offer's subject matter, the offeror might find it necessary to give the offeree considerable time to accept or reject. By the same token, an offer cannot remain open forever so that once given it never lapses or can never be terminated. Indeed, the law recognizes seven ways by which the offer can expire: rejection by the offeree, counteroffer, acceptance as a counteroffer, lapse of time, death or insanity of a person or destruction of an essential term, illegality, and revocation. We will examine each of these in turn.

Rejection by the Offeree Rejection of an offer is effective when the offeror receives it. A subsequent change of mind by the offeree cannot revive the offer. Donna calls Chuck to reject Chuck's offer to sell his lawn mower. Chuck is then free to sell it to someone else. If Donna changes her mind and calls Chuck back to accept after all, there still is no contract, even if Chuck has made no further effort to sell the lawn mower. Having rejected the original offer, Donna, by her second call, is not accepting but making an offer to buy. Suppose Donna had written Chuck to reject, but on changing her mind decided to call to accept before the rejection letter arrives. In that case, the offer would have been accepted. (See p. 219.)

Counteroffer A counteroffer, a response that varies an offer's terms, is a rejection. Jones offers Smith a parcel of land for $10,000 and says the offer will remain open for one month. Smith responds ten days later saying he will pay $5,000. Jones's original offer has thereby been rejected. If Jones now declines Smith's counteroffer, may Smith bind Jones to his original offer by agreeing to pay the full $10,000? He may not, because once an original offer is rejected, all the terms lapse. However, an inquiry by Smith as to whether Jones would consider taking less is not a counteroffer and would not terminate the offer.

The following case illustrates the dangers in making a counter offer.

DATASERV EQUIP. v. TECHNOLOGY FINANCE LEASING
364 N.W.2d 838
(Minn.App. 1985)

WOZNIAK, JUDGE.

★   ★   ★

Appellant Technology Finance Group, Inc. (Technology), a Nevada corporation with its principal place of business in Connecticut, and Respondent Dataserv Equipment, Inc. (Dataserv), a Minnesota corporation with its principal place of business in Minneapolis, are dealers in new and used computer equipment.

On or about August 29, 1979, Dataserv's Jack Skjonsby telephoned Technology's Ron Finerty in Connecticut and proposed to sell to Technology, for the price of $100,000, certain IBM computer "features" which Dataserv had previously purchased in Canada.

As a result of long distance telephone conversations between Skjonsby and Finerty, on August 30, 1979, Finerty sent Skjonsby a written offer to purchase the features and on September 6, 1979, Dataserv sent to Technology a proposed form of contract. Dataserv's proposed contract form included a

(continued on next page)

(*continued*)

DATASERV EQUIP. v. TECHNOLOGY FINANCE LEASING
364 N.W.2d 838
(Minn.App. 1985)

nonstandard provision, appearing in the contract form as clause 8 and referred to by the parties as the "Indepth Clause." The clause provided that installation of the features would be done by Indepth, a third party. The contract also provided that "[t]his agreement is subject to acceptance by the seller . . . and shall only become effective on the date thereof," and "[t]his agreement is made subject to the terms and conditions included herein and Purchaser's acceptance is effective only to the extent that such terms and conditions are conditions herein. Any acceptance which contains conditions which are in addition to or inconsistent with the terms and conditions herein will be a counter offer and will not be binding unless agreed to in writing by the Seller."

On October 1, Finerty wrote Skjonsby that three changes "need to be made" in the contract, one of which was the deletion of clause 8. The letter closed with: "Let me know and I will make the changes and sign." Two of the changes were thereafter resolved, but the resolution of clause 8 remained in controversy.

Later in October 1979, Dataserv offered to accept, in substitution for Indepth, any other third-party installation company Technology would designate. Technology never agreed to this.

On November 8, 1979, Dataserv by telephone offered to remove the Indepth clause from the contract form. Technology responded that it was "too late," and that there was no deal.

On November 9, 1979, Finerty called Dataserv, and informed them that "the deal was not going to get done because they'd waited until too late a point in time." During this period of time, the market value of the features was dropping rapidly and Dataserv was anxious to complete the deal. It is undisputed that the market for used computer equipment, including its features, is downwardly price volatile.

By telex dated November 12, 1979, Dataserv informed Technology that the features were ready for pickup and that the pickup and payment be no later than November 15, 1979.

On November 13, 1979, Finerty responded by telex stating:

> [S]ince [Dataserv] had not responded in a positive fashion to Alanthus'
> [Alanthus is the former name of Technology Finance Group] letter request-
> ing contract changes . . . its offer to purchase [the features] was withdrawn
> on 11/9/79 via telephone conversation with Jack Skjonsby. Ten to fifteen
> days prior, I made Jack aware that this deal was dead if Dataserv did not
> agree to contract changes prior to the "Eleventh Hour".

On June 19, 1980, the features were sold by Dataserv to another party for $26,000. It then sought a judgment against Technology for the difference between the sale price of the features and the contract price.

At trial the parties stipulated that as of November 8, 1979 Dataserv telephonically offered to take out the Indepth Clause. The trial court found that this telephone call operated as an acceptance of Technology's counteroffer of October 1, 1979, thereby establishing a contract between the parties embodying the terms of Dataserv's printed standard contract dated September 6, 1979, minus clause 8 thereof. The trial court found that as of November 15, 1979, Technology breached its contract to Dataserv's damage, and awarded Dataserv $74,000 in damages, plus interest from the date of the breach.

*   *   *

Technology claims that the trial court erred in finding that the parties entered into a contract. It contends that Dataserv's response to its counteroffer operated, as a matter of law, as a rejection, terminating Dataserv's power to subsequently accept the counteroffer.

Under familiar principles of contract law, a party's rejection terminates its power of acceptance. Restatement (Second) of Contracts § 380 (1981). Once rejected, an offer is terminated and cannot subsequently be accepted without ratification by the other party.

The critical issue is whether Dataserv rejected Technology's October 1 counteroffer. Dataserv responded to Technology's October 1 counteroffer by agreeing to delete two of the three objectionable clauses, but insisting that the third be included. By refusing to accept according to the terms of the proposal, Dataserv rejected Technology's counteroffer and thus no contract was formed. Moreover, Dataserv's offer to substitute other third party installation companies, which Technology rejected, operated as a termination of its power to accept Technology's counteroffer. Dataserv's so-called "acceptance," when it offered to delete clause 8 on November 8, 1979, was without any legal effect whatsoever, except to create a new offer which Technology immediately rejected.

*   *   *

[The trial court decision is reversed.]

Acceptance as Counteroffer An acceptance that changes the terms of the offer is a counteroffer and terminates the offer. In effect, the common law imposes a "mirror image" rule: the acceptance must match the offer in all its particulars or the offer is rejected. However, if an acceptance that requests a change or addition to the offer does not require the offeror's assent, then the acceptance is valid. The Friendly Real Estate Broker offers you a house for $120,000. You accept but include in your acceptance "the vacant lot next door." Your acceptance is a counteroffer, which serves to terminate the original offer. If, instead, you had said, "It's a deal, but I prefer the vacant lot next door," then there is a contract because you are not demanding that the broker abide by your request. If you had said, "It's a deal, and I'd also like the vacant lot next door," you have a contract, because the request for the lot is a separate offer, not a counteroffer rejecting the original proposal.

The UCC is more liberal than the common law in allowing contracts to be formed despite counteroffers and in incorporating the counteroffers into the contract. Under Section 2-207, an acceptance that states additional terms or conditions operates as an acceptance unless acceptance is conditioned on the offeror's consent to the new or different terms. The new terms are construed as offers but are automatically incorporated in any contract *between merchants* for the sale of goods unless: "(a) the offer expressly limits acceptance to the terms of the offer; (b) [the terms] materially alter it; or (c) notification of objection to them has already been given or is given within a reasonable time after notice of them is received."

This UCC provision is necessary because the use of preprinted form contracts is so common. A buyer and seller send out documents accompanying or incorporating their offers and acceptances, and the provisions in each rarely correspond precisely. If the rule were otherwise, much valuable time would be wasted drafting clauses tailored to the precise wording of the routine printed forms.

An example of terms that become part of the contract without being expressly agreed to are clauses providing for interest payments on overdue bills. An example of terms that would materially alter the contract and hence would need express approval are clauses that negate the standard warranties that sellers give buyers on their merchandise.

Some sellers use contract provisions to prevent the automatic introduction of new terms. One such provision, contained in the Standard Sales Contract Guide of Dow Chemical Company, is as follows:

> *Amendments*—Any modification of this document by the Buyer, and all additional or different terms included in Buyer's purchase order or any other document responding to this offer, are hereby objected to. BY ORDERING FOR SHIPMENT THE GOODS HEREIN, BUYER AGREES TO ALL THE TERMS AND CONDITIONS CONTAINED ON BOTH SIDES OF THIS DOCUMENT.

UCC Section 2-207 is extremely pervasive, covering all sorts of contracts, ranging from those between industrial manufacturers to those between friends. In *McAfee* v. *Brewer*, 203 S.E.2d 129 (Va. 1974), the Brewers contracted to buy the plaintiff's home. Some time before the closing date on which title would change hands, the Brewers negotiated the purchase of certain items of McAfee's furniture. McAfee sent a letter listing the furnishings to be purchased and the price of each, together with a payment schedule. The letter concluded: "If the above is satisfactory please sign and return one copy with the first payment." After the closing, the Brewers sent the following letter:

> Exams were horrible but Florida was great! Enclosing a $3,000 ck.—I've misplaced the contracts. Can the secretary send another set? We're moving into Dower House on June 12—please include the red secretary on the contract for entrance foyer. I'll have to stop by sometime during the month & order a coffee table.
> Hope all is well—
> Sincerely—
> [Signed] Va. & Jack [Brewer]

McAfee responded promptly, listing the items of furniture purchased. Thereafter, the Brewers called McAfee to say that there had been a misunderstanding concerning the exact furnishings they wanted. McAfee did not return their calls. The Brewers refused to pay the balance due, and McAfee sued. At the trial, Jack Brewer testified that he had sent a check to purchase some of the listed items but not to accept McAfee's offer comprising all items on the list. McAfee argued that the Brewers' letter, together with the check and the request for the red secretary, constituted acceptance. The court agreed. Citing Section 2-207, the court noted that the Brewers had accepted McAfee's offer by letter (reasonable under the circumstances, since they had misplaced the contract); the request for the red secretary was an additional request, acceptance of which the Brewers did not expressly make as a condition of their accepting McAfee's offer.

Lapse of Time   Offers are open-ended; they lapse after some period of time. An offer may contain its own specific time limitation—for example, "until close of business today." In the absence of an expressly stated time limit, the common law rule is that the offer expires at the end of a "reasonable" time. Such a period is a factual question in each case and depends on the particular circumstances, including the nature of the service or property being contracted for, the manner in which the offer is made, and the means by which the acceptance is expected to be made.

Whenever the contract involves a speculative transaction—the sale of securities or land, for instance—the time period will depend on the nature of the security and the risk involved. In general, the greater the risk to the seller, the shorter the period of time. Karen offers to sell Gary a block of oil stocks that are fluctuating rapidly hour by hour. Gary receives the offer an hour before the market closes; he accepts by telegram two hours after the market has opened the next morning and after learning that the stock has jumped up significantly. The time period has lapsed if Gary was accepting a fixed price that Karen set, but may still be open if the price is market price at time of delivery. (Under the *Restatement (Second) of Contracts,* Section 41, an offer made by mail is "seasonally accepted if an acceptance is mailed at any time before midnight on the day on which the offer is received.")

Both the common law and the UCC require the offeree to notify the offeror that he has begun to perform the terms of a unilateral contract. Without notification, the offeror may, after a reasonable time, treat the offer as having lapsed.

Death or Destruction The death (or insanity) of the offeror, prior to acceptance, terminates the offer; the offer is said to die with the offeror. Destruction of something essential to the contract also terminates the offer. You offer to sell your car but the car is destroyed in an accident before your offer is accepted; the offer is terminated.

Post-Offer Illegality A statute making unlawful the object of the contract will terminate the offer if it takes effect after the offer was made. Thus an offer to sell a warehouse of whiskey will terminate if the governor signs a bill outlawing the sale of whiskey within the state.

Revocation The general rule, both at common law and under the UCC, is that the offeror may revoke his offer at any time, even if the offer states that it will remain open for a specified period of time. Neil offers Arlene his car for $400 and promises to keep the offer open for ten days. Two days later, Neil calls Arlene to revoke the offer. The offer is terminated and Arlene's acceptance thereafter, though within the ten days, is ineffective. But if Neil had sent his revocation by mail and before she received it, Arlene telephoned her acceptance, there would be a contract, since revocation is effective only when the offeree actually receives it. There is an exception to this rule for offers made to the public through newspaper or like advertisements. The offeror may revoke a public offering by notifying the public by the same means used to communicate the offer. If no better means of notification is reasonably available, the offer is terminated even if a particular offeree had no actual notice.

Revocation may be communicated indirectly. If Arlene had learned from a friend that Neil sold his car to someone else during the ten-day period, she would have sufficient notice. Any attempt to accept Neil's offer would be futile.

Not every type of offer is revocable. One type of offer that cannot be revoked is the **option contract,** in which the promisor explicitly agrees for consideration to limit his right to revoke. Arlene tells Neil that she cannot make up her mind in ten days but that she will pay him $25 to hold the offer open for one month. Neil agrees. Arlene has an option to buy the car for $400; if Neil should sell it to someone else during the thirty days, he will have breached the contract with Arlene. Note that the transactions involving Neil and Arlene consist of two different contracts. One is the promise of a thirty-day option for the promise of $25. It is this contract that makes the option binding and is independent of the original offer to sell the car for $400. The offer can be accepted and made part of an independent contract during the option period.

Partial performance of a unilateral contract creates an option. Although the option is not stated explicitly, it is recognized by law in the interests of justice. Otherwise, an offeror could induce the offeree to go to expense and trouble without ever being liable to fulfill his part of the bargain. Before the offeree begins to carry out the contract, the offeror is free to revoke the offer. But once performance begins, the law implies an option, allowing the offeree to complete performance according to the terms of the offer. If after a reasonable time the offeree does not fulfill the terms of the offer, then it may be revoked.

The UCC changes the common law rule for offers by merchants. Under Section 2-205, a signed offer to buy or sell goods is irrevocable (that is, an option is created) if the offer states that it will be held open. The offer must remain open for the time period stated or, if no time period is given, for a reasonable period of time, which may not exceed three months.

By law, certain types of offers may not be revoked, despite the absence of language to that effect in the offer itself. One major category of such offers is that of the contractor submitting a bid to a public agency. The general rule is that once the period of bidding opens, a bidder on a public contract may not withdraw his bid, unless the contracting authority consents. If a contractor attempts to withdraw, is awarded the contract on the basis of a withdrawn bid, and refuses to carry out the project, he can be sued for damages.

THE ACCEPTANCE

Defined Generally

To result in a legally binding contract, an offer must be accepted by the offeree. Just as the law helps define and shape an offer and its duration, so the law governs the nature and manner of acceptance. The *Restatement (Second) of Contracts* defines acceptance of an offer as "a manifestation of assent to the terms thereof made by the offeree in a manner invited or required by the offer." (Section 5.) The assent may be either by the making of a mutual promise or by performance or partial performance. If there is doubt about whether the offer requests a return promise or a return act, the *Restatement (Second) of Contracts*, Section 32, provides that the offeree may accept with either a promise or performance. The UCC also adopts this view; under Section 2-206(1)(a), "an offer to make a contract shall be construed as inviting acceptance in any manner and by any medium reasonable in the circumstances" unless the offer unambiguously requires a certain mode of acceptance.

Who May Accept?

The identity of the offeree is usually clear, even if the name is unknown. The person to whom a promise is made is ordinarily the person whom the offeror contemplates will make a return promise or perform the act requested. But this is not invariably so. A promise can be made to one person who is not expected to do anything in return. The consideration necessary to weld the offer and acceptance into a legal contract can be given by a third party. Under the common law, whoever is invited to furnish consideration to the offeror is the offeree, and only the offeree may accept the offer. A common example is sale to a minor. George promises to sell his automobile to Bartley, age seventeen, if Bartley's father will promise to pay $500 to George. Bartley is the promisee (the person to whom the promise is made) but not the offeree; Bartley can-

not legally accept George's offer. Only Bartley's father, the man who is called on to pay for the car, can accept, by making the promise requested.

When Is Acceptance Effective?

An offer, a revocation of the offer, and a rejection of the offer are not effective until received. The same rule does not always apply to the acceptance. Of course, in many instances the moment of acceptance is not in question: in face-to-face deals or transactions negotiated over the telephone, the parties extend an offer and accept it during the course of the conversation. But problems can arise in contracts negotiated through correspondence.

One common situation arises when the offeror specifies the mode of acceptance (for example, return mail, telegram, carrier pigeon). If the offeree uses the specified mode, then the acceptance is deemed effective when sent. Even though the offeror has no knowledge of the acceptance at that moment, the contract has been formed. Moreover, according to the *Restatement (Second) of Contracts*, Section 60, if the offeror says that the offer can be accepted only by the specified mode, that mode must be used.

If the offeror specifies no particular mode, then acceptance is effective when transmitted as long as the offeree uses a reasonable method of acceptance. It is implied that the offeree can use the same means used by the offeror or a means of communication customary to the industry. For example, the use of the postal service is so customary today that acceptances are considered effective when mailed, regardless of the method used to transmit the offer. Indeed, the so-called **mailbox rule** has an ancient lineage, tracing back more than 150 years to the English courts. [Adams v. Lindsell, 1 Barnewall & Alderson 681 (K.B. 1818).]

The "mailbox rule" may seem to create particular difficulties for people in business, since the acceptance is effective even though the offeror is unaware of the acceptance, and even if the letter is lost and never arrives. But the solution is the same as the rationale for the rule. In contracts negotiated through correspondence, there will always be a burden on one of the parties. If the rule were that the acceptance is not effective until received by the offeror, then the offeree would be on tenterhooks, rather than the other way around, as is the case with the present rule. As between the two, it seems fairer to place the burden on the offeror, since he alone has the power to fix the moment of effectiveness. All he need do is specify in the offer that acceptance is not effective until received.

In all other cases—that is, when the offeror fails to specify the mode of acceptance and the offeree uses a mode that is not reasonable—acceptance is deemed effective only when received. This "effective when received" rule also applies in all cases in which the offeree sends a rejection before transmitting a superseding acceptance. Suppose John offers Tom a carload of straw and says the offer will remain open for a week. On the third day, Tom writes John rejecting the straw. The following day, Tom rethinks his needs and on the morning of the fifth day sends a telegram, delivered that evening, accepting John's terms. The letter arrives the following day. Since the letter had not yet been received, the offer had not been rejected. However, the act of mailing it did deprive Tom of the power to create a contract at the moment he sent the acceptance. For there to be a valid contract, the telegraphed acceptance must arrive before the mailed rejection. If the telegram had been misdelivered, although through no fault of Tom, so that the letter arrived first, John would be correct in assuming the offer was terminated—even if the telegram arrived a minute later. See Figure 8-1.

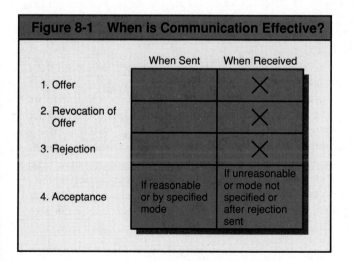

Figure 8-1	When is Communication Effective?	
	When Sent	When Received
1. Offer		X
2. Revocation of Offer		X
3. Rejection		X
4. Acceptance	If reasonable or by specified mode	If unreasonable or mode not specified or after rejection sent

Electronic Communications

Electronic communications have become increasingly common. It is estimated, for example, that the great majority of large retailers exchange data electronically. As a result, the American Bar Association established a task force to investigate emerging legal issues. The task force completed its work in 1990 with the publication of a model agreement designed for use by trading partners. The model agreement provides that an electronically-communicated offer is not effective until received by the offeree. The model agreement also requires trading partners to specify which electronic messages require acceptance and the type of "Acceptance Document" that must be used in making acceptances. (Acceptance Documents could be computer-generated responses or might require human evaluation.) The acceptance is effective only when received by the person who sent the original electronic message.

Acceptance by Silence

Ordinarily, for there to be a contract the offeree must make some positive manifestation of assent to the offeror's terms. The offeror cannot usually word his offer in such a way that the offeree's failure to respond can be construed as an acceptance. The *Restatement (Second) of Contracts*, Section 69, gives three situations, however, in which silence can operate as an acceptance. The first occurs when the offeree avails himself of services proferred by the offeror, even though he could have rejected them and had reason to know that the offeror offered them expecting compensation. The second situation occurs when the offer states that the offeree may accept without responding and the offeree, remaining silent, intends to accept. The third situation is that of previous dealings, in which only if the offeree intends not to accept is it reasonable to expect him to say so.

As an example of the first type of acceptance by silence, assume a carpenter happens by your home and sees a collapsing porch. He spots you in the front yard and points out the deterioration. "I'm a professional carpenter," he says, "and happen to be between jobs. I can fix that up for you right quick.

Somebody ought to." You say nothing. He goes to work. There is an implied contract, with the work to be done for the carpenter's usual fee.

To illustrate the second situation, let us suppose that a friend has left her car in your garage. The friend sends you a letter in which she offers you the car for $400 and adds: "If I don't hear from you, I will assume that you have accepted my offer." If you make no reply, with the intention of accepting the offer, a contract has been formed.

The third situation is illustrated by the following case, decided by Justice Oliver Wendell Holmes, Jr., when he was sitting on the Supreme Court of Massachusetts.

HOBBS v. MASSASOIT WHIP CO.
158 Mass. 194, 33 N.E. 495 (1893)

HOLMES, J. This is an action for the price of eel skins sent by the plaintiff to the defendant, and kept by the defendant some months, until they were destroyed. It must be taken that the plaintiff received no notice that the defendants declined to accept the skins. The case comes before us on exceptions to an instruction to the jury that, whether there was any prior contract or not, if skins are sent to the defendant, and it sees fit, whether it has agreed to take them or not, to lie back, and to say nothing, having reason to suppose that the man who has sent them believes that it is taking them, since it says nothing about it, then, if it fails to notify, the jury would be warranted in finding for the plaintiff.

Standing alone, and unexplained, this proposition might seem to imply that one stranger may impose a duty upon another, and make him a purchaser, in spite of himself, by sending goods to him, unless he will take the trouble, and bear the expense, of notifying the sender that he will not buy. The case was argued for the defendant on that interpretation. But, in view of the evidence, we do not understand that to have been the meaning of the judge, and we do not think that the jury can have understood that to have been his meaning. The plaintiff was not a stranger to the defendant, even if there was no contract between them. He had sent eel skins in the same way four or five times before, and they had been accepted and paid for. On the defendant's testimony, it was fair to assume that if it had admitted the eel skins to be over 22 inches in length, and fit for its business, as the plaintiff testified and the jury found that they were, it would have accepted them; that this was understood by the plaintiff; and, indeed, that there was a standing offer to him for such skins.

In such a condition of things, the plaintiff was warranted in sending the defendant skins conforming to the requirements, and even if the offer was not such that the contract was made as soon as skins corresponding to its terms were sent, sending them did impose on the defendant a duty to act about them; and silence on its part, coupled with a retention of the skins for an unreasonable time, might be found by the jury to warrant the plaintiff in assuming that they were accepted, and thus to amount to an acceptance. The proposition stands on the general principle that conduct which imports acceptance or assent is acceptance or assent, in the view of the law, whatever may have been the actual state of mind of the party,—a principle sometimes lost sight of in the cases.

Exceptions overruled.

The common-law rules governing acceptance by silence can lead to unfair tactics by unscrupulous merchants, who mail unsolicited merchandise to consumers across the country. The accompanying papers indicate that the consumer's retention of the item constitutes acceptance and makes the consumer liable for the purchase price. In fact, no contract may have been created, but many people may think so, and such tactics put many scrupulous people to the unwanted expense and trouble of mailing the items back. To ameliorate the problem, Congress and the legislatures in forty-five states have enacted special laws that declare that consumers who receive unordered merchandise may treat it as a gift. Under the federal Postal Reorganization Act, the recipient of unordered merchandise sent through the mail may "retain, use, discard, or dispose of it in any manner he sees fit without any obligation whatsoever to the sender."

CHAPTER SUMMARY

Whether a legally valid contract was formed depends on a number of factors, including whether the parties reached agreement, whether consideration was present, and whether the agreement was legal. Agreement may seem like an intuitive concept, but intuition is not a sufficient guide to the existence of agreement in legal terms. The most common way of examining an agreement for legal sufficiency is by determining whether a valid offer and acceptance were made.

An offer is a manifestation of willingness to enter into a bargain such that it would be reasonable for another individual to conclude that assent to the offer would complete the bargain. Offers must be communicated and must be definite; that is, they must spell out terms to which the offeree can assent.

An important aspect of the offer is its duration. An offer can expire in one of several ways: (1) rejection, (2) counter-offer, (3) acceptance with counter-offer, (4) lapse of time, (5) death or insanity of the offeror or destruction of an essential term, (6) illegality, and (7) revocation. No understanding of agreement is complete without a mastery of these conditions.

To constitute an agreement, an offer must be accepted. The offeree must manifest his assent to the terms of the offer in a manner invited or required by the offer. Complications arise when an offer is accepted indirectly through correspondence. Although offers and revocations of offers are not effective until received, an acceptance is deemed accepted when sent if the offeree accepts in the manner specified by the offeror. But the nuances that arise because of the "mailbox rule" and acceptance by silence require close attention to the circumstances of each agreement.

KEY TERMS

Definiteness	p. 211	Offer	p. 207
Mailbox rule	p. 218	Option contract	p. 217

SELF-TEST QUESTIONS

1. In interpreting agreements for the purpose of establishing whether a valid contract exists, courts generally apply:
   - (a) subjective standards
   - (b) objective standards
   - (c) either a subjective or objective standard
   - (d) none of the above
2. A valid offer must be:
   - (a) written
   - (b) written and intended
   - (c) communicated by letter
   - (d) communicated and definite
3. An offer:
   - (a) must specify time, place and manner of acceptance
   - (b) must be accepted immediately to be valid
   - (c) need not be accepted immediately
   - (d) remains open forever
4. An offer generally:
   - (a) is rejected by a counter-offer
   - (b) can be revoked if offeror changes her mind
   - (c) can lapse after a reasonable period of time
   - (d) all of the above
5. An acceptance is generally considered effective:
   - (a) when a letter is received by the offeror
   - (b) when a letter is mailed
   - (c) when the offeree is silent
   - (d) only when the acceptance is transmitted in writing

DEMONSTRATION PROBLEM

Ben Crazy, a senior at Big U, wanted to attend the Marcus Welby Medical School. The school sent Ben a bulletin that stated: "Students are selected on the basis of scholarship, character, and motivation without regard to race, creed, or sex." After reading the bulletin, Ben sent an application and an application fee of $15 to the school, which immediately sent him an acknowledgment and receipt. The school eventually rejected Ben's application. Ben later discovered that the school admitted students primarily on the basis of non-academic considerations such as the amount of money an applicant's family contributed to the school and family ties between the faculty and the applicant. Ben sued the school for breach of contract. Did Ben and the school form a contract? Why?

PROBLEMS

1. While reading the student newspaper one day, Oswald spotted an advertisement for "Light My Fire," a new type of cologne. According to the ad, the scent of the cologne is released by the body heat of the person using "Light My Fire." The ad also stated the price and the name of the drugstore where the product could be purchased. Thinking that he had the right kind of body heat to release the scent, Oswald immediately drove to the drugstore, walked in the door, and stated to the manager: "I accept your offer. I'll take twelve cases of 'Light My Fire'!" Does Oswald have a contract with the store? Why?

2. Mork called Mindy on the telephone and offered to sell her his stereo. She accepted the offer without asking the price. The next day Mindy changed her mind and attempted to back out of the agreement, arguing that the agreement was invalid because she and Mork had not agreed on a price. Is Mindy correct? Why?

3. On August 1, Ernie offered to sell Bert his car. Ernie promised to hold the offer open for ten days. On August 2, Ernie changed his mind and sent Bert a letter revoking the offer. On August 3, Bert sent Ernie a telegram accepting the offer; the telegram arrived the same day. Ernie's letter of revocation arrived on August 4. Is there a contract? Why?

4. On August 1, Grover decided to purchase a stereo. He visited a local store, Psychosounds, and picked out a stereo, but was not sure whether he could afford the $1,000 price. The owner of Psychosounds agreed to write up and sign an offer, which stated that it would be held open for ten days. On August 2, the owner changed his mind and sent Grover a telegram revoking the offer. Grover received the telegram the same day and on August 3 sent a reply telegram accepting the original offer. Is there a contract? Why?

5. Lucky Fasteners Corporation sent the following letter, which was signed by Donald Voltz, its sales manager. No price was specified.

> January 1, 1981
> Foster Box Company
>
> We hereby offer you 100 type #14 Lucky Fasteners. This offer will be irrevocable for 10 days.
>
> [Signed] Donald Voltz
> Sales Manager

Is this offer irrevocable for the time period stated? Why?

6. On November 26, Joe wrote to Kate offering to purchase a farm that she owned. Upon receiving the letter on November 28, Kate immediately sent Joe a letter of acceptance. However, shortly after mailing the letter, Kate had second thoughts and called Joe to advise him that she was rejecting his offer. The call was made before Joe received the letter of acceptance. Has a contract been formed? Why?

7. On the day of his business law final exam, which was to begin at 10:30 A.M., Freddy received a call from a local car dealer. The dealer stated that he was offering Freddy a brand new Lincoln Continental for $24,000 and that, if he did not hear from Freddy within the next hour, he would assume that Freddy had accepted the offer. Before Freddy had a chance to respond, the dealer hung up. Freddy immediately tried to call the dealer but the line was busy. He left for the exam and, upon returning two hours later, discovered a new Lincoln Continental in his driveway. Is he liable to the dealer for $24,000? Why?

8. The following telegrams were exchanged among Gordon, a watch merchant, Andrews, another watch merchant, and Speculator. All telegrams were signed.

September 5, 1972

(a) To Andrews: Offer you my collection of 25 original 1928 Mickey Mouse watches for $1,500. Offer will be held open until September 11.

Gordon

September 6, 1972

(b) To Gordon: Mickey Mouse market is bearish now. I am still considering your offer, will advise shortly.

Andrews

(c) To Gordon: Understand you are offering for sale 25 original 1928 Mickey Mouse watches for $1,500. I accept your offer.

Speculator

September 7, 1972

(d) To Andrews: Your judgment of market condition is wrong. Offer withdrawn.

Gordon

September 7, 1972

(e) To Speculator: You know value when you hear about it. It's a deal.

Gordon

(*f*) To Gordon: You're a hard man to deal with. Accept your offer.

Andrews

Discuss the legal effect of each telegram.

ANSWERS TO SELF-TEST QUESTIONS

1. (b)   2. (d)   3. (c)   4. (d)   5. (b)

SUGGESTED ANSWER TO DEMONSTRATION PROBLEM

Ben and the school formed a contract. The bulletin was an invitation to make an offer. Ben's application was an offer, and the school's acknoweldgment and receipt constituted acceptance. As a result of the contract the school was obligated to evaluate Ben's application according to the criteria stated in the bulletin. See *Steinberg* v. *Chicago Medical School*, 354 N.E.2d 586 (Ill. 1976).

CHAPTER 9

Consideration

*T*his chapter continues our inquiry into whether the parties created a valid contract. In the last chapter, we saw that the first requisite of a valid contract is an agreement. In this chapter we will assume that agreement has been reached and concentrate on one of its crucial aspects: the existence of **consideration.**

Consider the following three "contracts":

1. Betty offers to give a book to Lou. Lou accepts.
2. Betty offers Lou the book in exchange for Lou's promise to pay $15. Lou accepts.
3. Betty offers to give Lou the book if Lou promises to pick it up at Betty's house. Lou accepts.

The question is which, if any, is a binding contract?

In American law, only situation 2 is a binding contract, because only that contract contains a set of mutual promises in which each party agrees to give up something to the benefit of the other. This chapter will explore the meaning and rationale of that statement in depth.

The question of what constitutes a binding contract has been answered differently throughout history and in other cultures. For example, under Roman law, a contract without consideration was binding if certain formal requirements were met. And in the Anglo-American tradition, the presence of a seal was once sufficient to make a contract binding without any other consideration. In most states, the seal is no longer a substitute for consideration, although in some states it creates a presumption of consideration; in forty-nine states, the Uniform Commercial Code has abolished the seal on contracts for the sale of goods (Louisiana has not adopted UCC Article 2).

The existence of consideration is determined by examining whether the person against whom a promise is to be enforced (the **promisor**) received something in return from the person to whom he made the promise (the **promisee**). That may seem a simple enough question. But as with much in the law, the complicating situations are never very far away. The "something" that is promised or delivered cannot just be anything: a feeling of pride, warmth, amusement, friendship; it must be something known as a **legal detriment**—an act, a forebearance, or a promise of such from the promisee. The detriment need not be an actual detriment; it may in fact be a benefit to the promisee, or at least not a loss. At the same time, the "detriment" to the promisee need not confer a tangible benefit on the promisor; the promisee can agree to forego something without that something being given to the promisor. Whether consideration is legally sufficient has nothing to do with whether it is morally or economically adequate to make the bargain a fair one. Moreover, legal consideration need not even be certain; it can be a promise contingent on an event that may never happen. Consideration is a *legal* concept, and it centers on the giving up of a *legal* right or benefit.

Consideration has two elements. The first, as just outlined, is whether the promisee has incurred a legal detriment. (Some courts—although a minority—take the view that a bargained-for legal benefit to the promisor is sufficient consideration.) The second is whether the legal detriment was bargained for: did the promisor specifically intend the act, forbearance, or promise in return for his promise? Applying this two-pronged test to the three examples given at the outset of the chapter, we can easily see why only in the second is there legally sufficient consideration. In the first, Lou incurred no legal detriment; he made no pledge to act or to forbear from acting, nor did he in fact act or forbear from acting. In the third example, what might appear to be such a promise is not really so. Betty made a promise on a condition that Lou come to her house; the intent clearly is to make a gift. Betty was not seeking to induce Lou to come to her house by promising the book.

ILLUSTRATIONS OF CONSIDERATION THEORY

Actual vs. Legal Detriment

Suppose Phil offers George $100 if George will quit smoking for one year. Is Phil's promise binding? Since George is presumably benefiting by making and sticking to the agreement—surely his health will improve if he does give up smoking—how can his act be considered a legal detriment? The answer is that there is a forbearance on George's part: George is legally entitled to smoke and by contracting not to, he suffers a loss of his legal right to do so. This is a legal detriment; consideration does not require an actual detriment.

Adequacy of Consideration

Scrooge offers to buy Caspar's motorcycle, worth $700, for $10 and a shiny new fountain pen (worth $5). Caspar agrees. Is this agreement supported by adequate consideration? Yes, because both have agreed to give up something that is theirs: Scrooge the cash and the pen, Caspar the motorcycle. Courts are not generally concerned with the economic adequacy of the consideration but instead with whether it is present. As Judge Richard A. Posner puts it: "To ask whether there is consideration is simply to inquire whether the situation is one of exchange and a bargain has been struck. To go further and ask whether the consideration is adequate would require the court to do what . . . it is less well equipped to do than the parties—decide whether the price (and other essential terms) specified in the contract are reasonable" (1973, p. 46).

Normally, parties to contracts will not make such a one-sided deal as Scrooge and Caspar's. But there is a common class of contracts in which nominal consideration—usually one dollar—is recited in printed forms. Usually these are option contracts, in which "in consideration of one dollar in hand paid and receipt of which is hereby acknowledged" one party agrees to hold open the right of the other to make a purchase on agreed terms. The courts will enforce these contracts if the dollar is intended "to support a short-time option proposing an exchange on fair terms" (*Restatement (Second) of Contracts*, Section 87, comment b). If, however, the option is for an unreasonably long period of time and the underlying bargain is unfair (the Restatement gives as an example a ten-year option permitting the optionee to take phosphate rock from a widow's land at a per-ton payment of only one-fourth the prevailing rate) then the courts are unlikely to hold that the nominal consideration makes the option irrevocable.

Because the consideration on such option contracts is nominal, its recital in the written instrument is usually a mere formality, and is frequently never paid; in effect, the recital of nominal consideration is false. Nevertheless, the courts will enforce the contract—precisely because the recital has become a formality. Moreover, it would be easy enough to upset an option based on nominal consideration by falsifying oral testimony that the dollar was never paid or received. In a contest between oral testimony where the incentive to lie is strong and a written document clearly incorporating the parties' agreement, the courts prefer the latter. However, as the next case demonstrates, the state laws are not uniform on this point, and it is a safe practice always to deliver the consideration, no matter how nominal.

BOARD OF CONTROL OF EASTERN MICHIGAN UNIVERSITY v. BURGESS

45 Mich. App. 183, 206 N.W.2d 256 (1973)

R. B. BURNS, JUDGE. On February 15, 1966, defendant signed a document which purported to grant to plaintiff a 60-day option to purchase defendant's home. That document, which was drafted by plaintiff's agent, acknowledged receipt by defendant of "One and no/100 ($1.00) Dollar and other valuable consideration." Plaintiff concedes that neither the one dollar nor any other consideration was ever paid or even tendered to defendant. On April 14, 1966, plaintiff delivered to defendant written notice of its intention to exercise the option. On the closing date defendant rejected plaintiff's tender of the purchase price. Thereupon, plaintiff commenced this action for specific performance.

At trial defendant claimed that the purported option was void for want of consideration, that any underlying offer by defendant had been revoked prior to acceptance by plaintiff, and that the agreed purchase price was the product of fraud and mutual mistake. The trial judge concluded that no fraud was involved, and that any mutual mistake was not material. He also held that defendant's acknowledgment of receipt of consideration bars any subsequent contention to the contrary. Accordingly, the trial judge entered judgment for plaintiff.

Defendant appeals. She claims that acknowledgment of receipt of consideration does not bar the defense of failure of consideration. She further claims that the trial judge's findings of fact as to the absence of fraud and material mistake are in error, and that the record supports a finding that defendant was the victim of plaintiff's coercion.

Options for the purchase of land, if based on valid consideration, are contracts which may be specifically enforced. Conversely, that which purports to be an option, but which is not based on valid consideration, is not a contract and will not be enforced. One dollar is valid consideration for an option to purchase land, provided the dollar is paid or at least tendered. In the instant case defendant received no consideration for the purported option of February 15, 1966.

A written acknowledgment of receipt of consideration merely creates a rebuttable presumption that consideration has, in fact, passed. Neither the parol evidence rule nor the doctrine of estoppel bars the presentation of evidence to contradict any such acknowledgment.

It is our opinion that the document signed by defendant on February 15, 1966, is not an enforceable option, and that defendant is not barred from so asserting.

The trial court premised its holding to the contrary on Lawrence v. McCalmont, 43 U.S. (2 How.) 426, 452, 11 L.Ed. 326, 336 (1844). That case is significantly distinguishable from the instant case. Mr. Justice Story held that "[t]he guarantor acknowledged the receipt of one dollar, and is now estopped to deny it." However, in reliance upon the guaranty substantial credit had been extended to the guarantor's sons. The guarantor had received everything she bargained for, save one dollar. In the instant case defendant claims that she never received any of the consideration promised her.

That which purports to be an option for the purchase of land, but which is not based on valid consideration, is a simple offer to sell the same land. An option is a contract collateral to an offer to sell whereby the offer is made irrevocable for a specified period. Ordinarily, an offer is revocable at the will of the offeror. Accordingly, a failure of consideration affects only the collateral contract to keep the offer open, not the underlying offer.

A simple offer may be revoked for any reason or for no reason by the offeror at any time prior to its acceptance by the offeree. Thus, the question in this case becomes, "Did defendant effectively revoke her offer to sell before plaintiff accepted that offer?"

* * *

Defendant testified that within hours of signing the purported option she telephoned plaintiff's agent and informed him that she would not abide by the option unless the purchase price was increased. Defendant also testified that when plaintiff's agent delivered to her on April 14, 1966, plaintiff's notice of its intention to exercise the purported option, she told him that "the option was off."

Plaintiff's agent testified that defendant did not communicate to him any dissatisfaction until sometime in July, 1966.

If defendant is telling the truth, she effectively revoked her offer several weeks before plaintiff accepted that offer, and no contract of sale was created. If plaintiff's agent is telling the truth, defendant's offer was still open when plaintiff accepted that offer, and an enforceable contract was created. The trial judge thought it unnecessary to resolve this particular dispute. In light of our holding the dispute must be resolved.

An appellate court cannot assess the credibility of witnesses. We have neither seen nor heard them testify. Accordingly, we remand this case to the trial court for additional findings of fact based on the record already before the court.

* * *

Reversed and remanded for proceedings consistent with this opinion. Costs to defendant.

Threat of Litigation

Because every person has the legal right to file suit if he feels aggrieved, a promise to refrain from going to court is sufficient consideration to support a promise of payment or performance. In *Dedeaux* v. *Young*, 170 So.2d 561 (1965), Dedeaux purchased property and promised to make certain payments to Young, the broker. But Dedeaux thereafter failed to make these payments and Young threatened suit; had he filed papers in court, the transfer of title could have been blocked. To keep Young from suing, Dedeaux promised to pay a 5 percent commission, if Young would stay out of court. Dedeaux later resisted paying on the ground that he had never made such a promise and that even if he had, it did not amount to a contract because there was no consideration from Young. The court disagreed, holding that the evidence supported Young's contention that Dedeaux had indeed made such a promise and upholding Young's claim for the commission because "a request to forbear to exercise a legal right has been generally accepted as sufficient consideration to support a contract." If Young had had no grounds to sue—for example, if he had threatened to sue a stranger, or if it could be shown that Dedeaux had no obligation to him originally—then there would have been no consideration because Young would not have been giving up a legal right.

Accord and Satisfaction

Frequently the parties to a contract will dispute the meaning of its terms and conditions, especially the amount of money actually due. When the dispute is genuine (and not the unjustified attempt of one party to avoid paying a sum clearly due), it can be settled by the parties' agreement on a fixed sum as the amount due. This second agreement, which substitutes for the disputed first agreement, is called an **accord,** and when the payment or other term is discharged, the completed second contract is known as an **accord and satisfaction.** A suit brought for an alleged breach of the original contract could be defended by citing the later accord and satisfaction.

An accord is a contract and must therefore be supported by consideration. Suppose Jan owes Andy $7,000, due November 1. On November 1, Jan pays only $3,500 in exchange for Andy's promise to release Jan from the remainder of the debt. Has Andy (the promisor) made a binding promise? He has not because there is no consideration for the accord: Jan has incurred no detriment. But if Jan and Andy had agreed that Jan would pay the $3,500 on October 25, then there would be consideration; Jan would have incurred a legal detriment by obligating himself to make a payment earlier than the original contract required him to. If Jan had paid the $3,500 on November 11 and given Andy something else agreed to—a pen, a keg of beer, a peppercorn—the required detriment would also be present.

Unliquidated Debts   A **liquidated debt** is one that is fixed in amount, certain. A debt can be liquidated by being written down in unambiguous terms ("I.O.U. $100"), or by being mathematically ascertainable ($1 per pound of ice ordered; 60 pounds delivered; hence the liquidated debt is $60). It is also possible, however, to form a contract by which one party agrees to pay the customary or reasonable fees of the other without fixing the exact amount. It is certain that a debt is owed but it is not certain how much. The debt that is uncertain in amount is called an **unliquidated debt.** Such debts frequently occur when people consult professionals, in whose offices precise fees are rarely discussed.

Assume a patient goes to the hospital for a gall bladder operation. The cost of the operation has not been discussed beforehand in detail, although the cost in the metropolitan area is normally around $5,000. After the operation, the patient and surgeon agree on a bill of $2,500. The patient pays the bill; a month later the doctor sues for another $2,500. Judgment for whom? For the patient, who has forgone his right to challenge the reasonableness of the fee by agreeing to a fixed amount payable at a certain time. The agreement liquidating the debt is an accord and is enforceable. If, however, the patient and doctor had agreed on a $5,000 fee before the operation and the patient arbitrarily refused to pay unless the doctor agreed to cut her fee in half, then the doctor would be entitled to recover the other half in a lawsuit, since the patient would have given no consideration for the doctor's subsequent agreement to cut the fee.

Disputed Debts   As noted above, the settlement of a disputed debt lends consideration to an agreement to accept a fixed sum as payment for the amount due. Assume that in the gall bladder case the patient agrees in advance to pay $5,000. Eight months after the operation and as a result of nausea and vomiting spells, the patient undergoes a second operation; the surgeons discover a 30″ × 18″ towel embedded in the patient's intestine. The patient refuses to pay the full sum of the original surgeon's bill; they settle on $2,000, which the patient pays. This is a binding agreement because subsequent facts arose to make legitimate the patient's quarrel over his obligation to pay the full bill. As long as the dispute is based in fact and is not trumped up, as long as the promisee is acting in good faith, then consideration is present when a disputed debt is settled.

"In Full Payment" Checks   To discharge his liquidated debt for $5,000 to the doctor, the patient sends a check for $2,500 marked "payment in full." The doctor cashes it. There is no dispute. May the doctor sue for the remaining $2,500? This may appear to be an accord: by cashing the check the doctor seems to be agreeing with the patient to accept the $2,500 in full payment. But consideration is lacking. Since the

doctor is owed more than the face amount of the check, she causes the patient no legal detriment by accepting it. If the rule were otherwise, debtors could easily tempt hard-pressed creditors to accept less than the amount owed by presenting immediate cash. The key to the enforceability of a "payment in full" legend is the character of the debt. If unliquidated, or if there is a dispute, then "payment in full" can serve as accord and satisfaction when written on a check that is accepted for payment by a creditor. But if the debt is liquidated and undisputed, there is no consideration when the check is for a lesser amount. (However, it is arguable that if the check is considered to be an agreement modifying a sales contract, no consideration is necessary under Section 2-209; see page 232.)

Unforeseen Difficulties "The best-laid schemes o' mice an' men gang aft agley," sang the poet Robert Burns. So with those reduced to contract. Difficulties that no one could foresee can sometimes serve as catalyst for a further promise that may technically be without consideration but that, nevertheless, the courts will enforce. Suppose Peter contracts to build Jerry a

house for $90,000. While excavating, Peter unexpectedly discovers quicksand, the removal of which will cost an additional $10,000. To ensure that Peter does not delay, Jerry promises to pay Peter $10,000 more than originally agreed. But when the house is completed, Jerry reneges on his promise. Is Jerry liable? Logically he is not. Peter has incurred no legal detriment in exchange for the $10,000; he had already contracted to build the house. But many courts will allow Peter to recover on the theory that the original contract was terminated, either by mutual agreement or by an implied condition that the contract would be discharged if unforeseen difficulties developed. In short, the courts will enforce the parties' own mutual recognition that the unforeseen conditions had made the old contract unfair.

Preexisting Duty When the only consideration offered the promisor is an act or promise to act to carry out a preexisting duty, there is no valid contract. As the following case makes clear, the promisee suffers no legal detriment in promising to undertake that which he is already obligated to do.

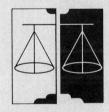

DENNEY v. REPPERT
432 S.W.2d 647 (Ky. 1968)

R. L. MYRE, SR., SPECIAL COMMISSIONER. The sole question presented in this case is which of several claimants is entitled to an award for information leading to the apprehension and conviction of certain bank robbers.

Since the learned circuit judge of the Pulaski Circuit Court correctly set out the facts and the law in this case in a written opinion, we are affirming the judgment entered in accordance thereto and are adopting, in substance, the written opinion of the circuit judge as the opinion of this court.

On June 12th or 13th, 1963, three armed men entered the First State Bank, Eubank, Kentucky, and with a display of arms and threats robbed the bank of over $30,000. Later in the day they were apprehended by State Policemen Garret Godby, Johnny Simms and Tilford Reppert, placed under arrest, and the entire loot was recovered. Later all of the prisoners were convicted and Garret Godby, Johnny Simms and Tilford Reppert appeared as witnesses at the trial.

The First State Bank of Eubank was a member of the Kentucky Bankers Association which provided and advertised a reward of $500.00 for the arrest and conviction of each bank robber. Hence the outstanding reward for the three bank robbers was $1,500.00. Many became claimants for the reward and the Kentucky State Bankers Association being unable to determine the merits of the claims for the reward asked the circuit court to determine the merits of the various claims and to adjudge who was entitled to receive the reward or share in it. All of the claimants were made defendants in the action. *(continued on next page)*

(continued)

DENNEY v. REPPERT
432 S.W.2d 647 (Ky. 1968)

At the time of the robbery the claimants Murrell Denney, Joyce Buis, Rebecca McCollum and Jewell Snyder were employees of the First State Bank of Eubank and came out of the grueling situation with great credit and glory. Each one of them deserves approbation and an accolade. They were vigilant in disclosing to the public and the peace officers the details of the crime, and in describing the culprits, and giving all the information that they possessed that would be useful in capturing the robbers. Undoubtedly, they performed a great service. It is in the evidence that the claimant Murrell Denney was conspicuous and energetic in his efforts to make known the robbery, to acquaint the officers as to the personal appearance of the criminals, and to give other pertinent facts.

The first question for determination is whether the employees of the robbed bank are eligible to receive or share in the reward? The great weight of authority answers in the negative. In Re Waggoner, 47 S.D. 401, 199 N.W. 244, 245 (1924) states the rule thusly:

> To the general rule that, when a reward is offered to the general public for the performance of some specified act, such reward may be claimed by any person who performs such act, is the exception of agents, employees and public officials who are acting within the scope of their employment or official duties.

★   ★   ★

At the time of the robbery the claimants Murrell Denney, Joyce Buis, Rebecca McCollum, and Jewell Snyder were employees of the First State Bank of Eubank. They were under duty to protect and conserve the resources and moneys of the bank, and safeguard every interest of the institution furnishing them employment. Each of these employees exhibited great courage, and cool bravery, in a time of stress and danger. The community and the county have recompensed them in commendation, admiration and high praise, and the world looks on them as heroes. But in making known the robbery and assisting in acquainting the public and the officers with details of the crime and with identification of the robbers, they performed a duty to the bank and the public, for which they cannot claim a reward.

The claims of Corbin Reynolds, Julia Reynolds, Alvie Reynolds and Gene Reynolds also must fail. According to their statements they gave valuable information to the arresting officers. However, they did not follow the procedure as set forth in the offer of reward in that they never filed a claim with the Kentucky Bankers Association. It is well established that a claimant of a reward must comply with the terms and conditions of the offer of reward.

State Policemen Garret Godby, Johnny Simms and Tilford Reppert made the arrest of the bank robbers and captured the stolen money. All participated in the prosecution. At the time of the arrest, it was the duty of the state policemen to apprehend the criminals. Under the law they cannot claim or share in the reward and they are interposing no claim to it.

This leaves the defendant, Tilford Reppert the sole eligible claimant. The record shows that at the time of the arrest he was a deputy sheriff in Rockcastle County, but the arrest and recovery of the stolen money took place in

Pulaski County. He was out of his jurisdiction, and was thus under no legal duty to make the arrest, and is thus eligible to claim and receive the reward. In Kentucky Bankers Ass'n et al. v. Cassady, 264 Ky. 351, 94 S.W.2d 622, 624, it was said:

> It is . . . well established that a public officer with the authority of the law to make an arrest may accept an offer of reward or compensation for acts or services performed outside of his bailiwick or not within the scope of his official duties. . . .

The claimant Tilford Reppert was present with Garret Godby and Johnny Simms at the time of the arrest and all cooperated in its consummation. The claimant Tilford Reppert personally recovered the stolen money. He recovered $2,000.00 more than the bank records show was stolen. This record does not reveal what became of the $2,000.00 excess.

It is manifest from the record that Tilford Reppert is the only claimant qualified and eligible to receive the reward. Therefore, it is the judgment of the circuit court that he is entitled to receive payment of the $1,500.00 reward now deposited with the Clerk of this Court.

The judgment is affirmed.

Illusory Promises

Not every promise is a pledge to do something. Some seeming promises are illusory. For example, Lydia offers to pay Juliette $10 for mowing Lydia's lawn. Juliette promises to mow the lawn if she feels like it. May Juliette enforce the contract? No, because Juliette has incurred no legal detriment; her promise is illusory, since by doing nothing she still falls within the literal wording of her promise. The doctrine that such bargains are unenforceable is sometimes referred to as the rule of **mutuality of obligation**: if one party to a contract has not made a binding obligation, neither is the other party bound.

The illusory promise presents a special problem for a class of contracts known as **exclusive dealing contracts.** In these agreements, one party (the *franchisor*) promises to deal solely with the other party (the *franchisee*)—for example, a franchisor-designer agrees to sell all of her specially designed clothes to a particular department store (the franchisee). In return, the store promises to pay a certain percentage of the sales price to the designer. On closer inspection, it may appear that the store's promise is illusory: it pays the designer only if it manages to sell dresses; it may sell none. The franchisor-designer may therefore attempt to back out of the deal by arguing that since the franchisee is not obligated to do anything, there was no consideration for her promise to deal exclusively with the store.

Courts, however, have upheld exclusive dealing contracts on the theory that the franchisee has an obligation to use reasonable efforts to promote and sell the product or services. This obligation may be spelled out in the contract or implied by its terms. In the classic statement of this concept, Judge Benjamin N. Cardozo, then on the New York Court of Appeals, in upholding such a contract, declared:

> It is true that [the franchisee] does not promise in so many words that he will use reasonable efforts to place the defendant's indorsements and market her designs. We think, however, that such a promise is fairly to be implied. The law has outgrown its primitive stage of formalism when the precise word was the sovereign talisman, and every slip was fatal. It takes a broader view today. A promise may be lacking, and yet the whole writing may be "instinct with an obligation," imperfectly expressed. . . . His promise to pay the defendant one-half of the profits and revenues resulting from the exclusive agency and to render accounts monthly, was a promise to use reasonable efforts to bring profits and revenues into existence. [Otis F. Wood v. Lucy, Lady Duff-Gordon, 118 N.E. 214 (1917).]

The UCC follows the same rule. In the absence of language specifically delineating the seller's or buyer's duties, an exclusive dealing contract under Section 2-306(2) imposes "an obligation by the seller to use best efforts to supply the goods and by the buyer to use best efforts to promote their sale."

Creditors' Composition

A **composition** is an agreement whereby two or more creditors of a debtor consent to the debtor's paying them pro rata shares of the debt due in full satisfaction of their claims. A composition agreement can be critically important to a business in trouble; through it, the business might manage to stave off bankruptcy. Even though the share accepted is less than the full amount due and is payable after the due date—so that consideration appears to be lacking—the courts routinely enforce these agreements. Either the composition is treated as an exception to the requirement of consideration, or the promise of each creditor to accept a lesser share than that owed is taken as consideration to support the promises of the others.

PROMISES ENFORCEABLE WITHOUT CONSIDERATION

For a variety of policy reasons, the courts will enforce certain types of promises even though consideration may be absent. Some of these are governed by the UCC; others are part of the established common law.

Under the UCC

The UCC permits one party to discharge, without consideration, a claim or right arising out of an alleged breach of contract by the other party. This is accomplished by delivering to the other party a signed written waiver or renunciation. (Section 1-107.) This provision applies to any contract governed by the UCC, and is not limited to the sales provisions of Article 2.

The UCC also permits a binding contract to be modified without consideration. Under Section 2-209(1), an agreement *modifying* a contract governed by Article 2 and dealing with the sale of goods is binding without consideration. A seller agrees to deliver a ton of coal within seven days. The buyer finds a need for the coal sooner and asks the seller to deliver within four days. The seller agrees to do so and pays the $100. This promise is binding.

Section 1-207 of the UCC allows a party to reserve rights while performing a contract. This section raises a difficult question when a debtor issues an "in full payment" check in payment of a disputed debt. As noted earlier in this chapter, because under the common law the creditor's acceptance of an "in full payment" check in payment of a disputed debt constitutes an accord and satisfaction, the creditor cannot collect an amount beyond the check. But what if the creditor, in cashing the check, reserves the right (under Section 1-207) to sue for an amount beyond what the debtor is offering? The following case concludes that Section 1-207 supersedes the common law and the creditor can sue for an additional amount. The opinion, however, notes that courts are split on this issue.

AFC INTERIORS v. DICELLO
46 Ohio St.3d 1 (1989)

[After the plaintiff-appellant in the case, AFC, performed interior decorating services for the defendant-appelle DiCello, a dispute developed over whether DiCello had the option to return furniture.]

SWEENEY, J. The dispositive question presented in this cause is whether an accord and satisfaction has taken place with regard to the debt owed by DiCello to AFC. The appellee, DiCello, contends that an accord and satisfaction has taken place under the instant facts. The appellant, AFC, argues however that R.C. 1301.13, which embodies Section 1-207 of the Uniform Commercial Code ("UCC"), should supercede the doctrine of accord and satisfaction in the "full payment" or "conditional check" situation where the payee reserves his or her rights to pursue the balance of the debt alleged to be owed.

Accord and satisfaction is a common-law doctrine where there is a contract between a creditor and debtor for settlement of a claim by some performance other than that which is due. Satisfaction takes place when the creditor accepts the accord.

In the cause *sub judice*, DiCello tendered a check for an amount apparently less than what AFC expected. The check carried the notation that it constituted payment in full for any and all claims that AFC may have against DiCello. AFC crossed out the notation and inserted the words "Payment on Account" and further negotiated the check. . . . Thus, the precise question before this court is whether the special endorsement of the check by AFC with knowledge of a dispute as to the amount due, and with knowledge of the conditional statement on the check, constituted an acceptance of the conditional check, *i.e.*, an accord and satisfaction. In light of the language of R.C. 1301.13, we do not believe that the special endorsement by AFC reserving its rights and subsequent negotiation of the check should continue to be recognized as an accord and satisfaction. Therefore, we reverse the decision of the court of appeals below and remand the cause for further proceedings.

★   ★   ★

The issue of whether UCC 1-207 should apply to supercede the doctrine of accord and satisfaction has been the subject of much scholarly debate. Courts in different jurisdictions are split with regard to the effect of UCC 1-207 in this context.

We are of the opinion, however, that the drafters of the UCC, and Ohio's General Assembly, promulgated UCC 1-207 in response to a perceived injustice to creditors that occurs where a creditor, under protest, deposits a check marked "paid in full" or the like, and later discovers that an accord and satisfaction has taken place which extinguished the right to demand further payment on the debt.

While this court has not applied R.C. 1301.13 (UCC 1-207) in factual situations similar to the case at bar, it appears that a discernible trend has developed whereby UCC 1-207 is used to supercede the common-law doctrine of accord and satisfaction in the "full payment" or "conditional check" situations.

★   ★   ★

As the debate concerning the scope of UCC 1-207 grew, courts around the country proceeded to make decisions concerning its application. In *Scholl* v. *Tallman* (S.D. 1976), 247 N.W. 2d 490, the South Dakota Supreme Court faced a factual situation similar to the instant cause and held that UCC 1-207 applied to the "conditional check" situation. Therein, the creditor deposited, under protest, a check marked "Settlement in Full . . ." from a debtor by scratching out the debtor's full-settlement notation and writing above his own endorsement, "Restriction of payment in full refused. $1,826.65 remains due and payable." The court stated that the creditor effected "an

(*continued on next page*)

(*continued*)

AFC INTERIORS v. DICELLO
46 Ohio St.3d 1 (1989)

explicit reservation of rights under . . . [1-207]" and thereby did not jeopardize his rights to the balance he maintained was due.

More recently, in *Horn Waterproofing Corp.* v. *Bushwick Iron & Steel Co., Inc.* (1985), 488 N.E. 2d 56, the debtor sent the creditor a check for less than the amount owed with a "full payment" notation. The creditor endorsed the check and added the notation "Under Protest," and brought an action to recover the balance alleged to be due. The court applied the UCC and held that a creditor may preserve his right to the balance of a disputed claim by explicit reservation in his endorsement of the check tendered by the debtor as full payment under UCC 1-207.

In addition to the above-cited precedents, it appears that four other jurisdictions (Delaware, Florida, Massachusetts and New Hampshire) have embraced the view that the UCC 1-207 supersedes the common-law doctrine of accord and satisfaction in the local comments to their respective versions of UCC 1-207.

While the issue is far from settled in other jurisdictions, the competing viewpoints regarding the appropriateness of applying UCC 1-207 were best summarized by White & Summers, at 691-692:

". . . Those arguing that 1-207 does not alter the common law rule typically start with the position, generally unassailable, that the offeror is 'master of his offer.' They point out that the drawer has made an offer, namely that of full payment, and they argue that allowing the payee to accept the money without the other terms of the offer is not only unfair, but also in direct conflict with the traditional notions of contract formation. Those who apply 1-207 and readily reject the common law outcome characterize the offeror as a chisler [*sic*]. He knows that he owes $10,000 and hopes to get away with $9,000. While we have no empirical basis for concluding the typical offeror is a chiseler as opposed to a legitimately aggrieved debtor, we are inclined to that view."

While we disdain characterizing any of the parties to the instant action in such a manner, we believe that the framers of the UCC drafted Section 1-207 in order to balance the interests of debtors and creditors in a more equitable manner. In any event, we are persuaded that UCC 1-207 was intended to apply in the situation confronting us in the cause *sub judice*.

*   *   *

In applying the provisions of R.C. 1301.13 to the facts of the cause *sub judice*, we find that appellant explicitly reserved its rights by crossing out DiCello's notation on the back of the check and substituting its own notation, "Payment on Account." By putting DiCello on notice in such a manner, AFC reserved its rights to collect the balance alleged to be due.

Therefore, based on the foregoing, we hold that R.C. 1301.13, which embodies UCC 1-207, supercedes the common-law doctrine of accord and satisfaction in the "full payment" or "conditional check" situation.

Moreover, we . . . further hold that pursuant to R.C. 1301.13, where a debtor tenders a check to a creditor as payment in full or less than the amount alleged to be owed on the debt, the creditor may accept the check as partial payment on the debt so long as the creditor explicitly reserves all rights by endorsing the check "under protest" or any legend sufficient to apprise the debtor that the check is not accepted as full payment on the debt. In so doing, the creditor does not thereby prejudice any rights reserved on the balance alleged to be due.

Accordingly, the judgment of the court of appeals is reversed, and the cause is remanded to the trial court for further proceedings not inconsistent with this opinion.

Past Consideration

Ordinarily, "past" consideration is not sufficient to support a promise. By **past consideration,** the courts mean an act that could have served as consideration if it had been bargained for at the time but that was not the subject of a bargain. For example, a local businessman, impressed by the diligence, intelligence, and athletic prowess of the high school valedictorian, undertakes to send her to college because he knows she is too poor to afford a good education. Four years later, she wins a lottery that pays her twice what it cost for her college education. At a dinner party after graduation, in a flush of gratitude to her benefactor, she promises to repay the $45,000 he contributed to her college expenses. He accepts her offer warmly. The following day, having sobered up from the generous amount of wine imbibed, she has second thoughts, calls her benefactor, and cancels her offer. Furious, he sues. He will lose. Even though the student might have a moral duty both to repay him and to honor her promise, there was no consideration for it. The benefactor incurred no legal detriment; his contributions were paid out before the promise, and this past consideration is invalid to support a binding contract.

However, a valid consideration, given in the past to support a promise, can be the basis for another, later contract under certain circumstances. These occur when a person's duty to act for one reason or another has become no longer binding. If the person then makes a new promise based on the unfulfilled past duty, the new promise is binding without further consideration. Three types of cases follow.

Statute of Limitations   A **statute of limitations** is a law requiring a lawsuit to be filed within a specified period of years. For example, in many states a contract claim must be sued on within six years; if the plaintiff waits longer than that, the claim will be dismissed, regardless of its merits. When the time period set forth in the statute of limitations has lapsed, the statute is said to have "run." If a debtor renews a promise to pay or acknowledges a debt after the running of a statute of limitations, then under the common law the promise is binding, although there is no consideration in the usual sense. In many states this promise or acknowledgment must be in writing and signed by the debtor. Also, in many states, the courts will imply a promise or acknowledgment if the debtor makes a partial payment after the statute has run.

Bankruptcy   The rule here is similar to that governing statutes of limitations. Traditionally, a promise to repay debts after a bankruptcy court has discharged them makes the debtor liable once again. This traditional rule gives rise to potential abuse: after undergoing the rigors of bankruptcy, a debtor could be badgered by creditors to reaffirm the debt, putting him in a worse position than before, since he must wait six years before being allowed to avail himself of bankruptcy again.

The federal Bankruptcy Reform Act includes certain procedural protections to ensure that the debtor knowingly enters into a reaffirmation of his debt. Among its provisions, the law requires the bankrupt to have reaffirmed the debt before the debtor is discharged in bankruptcy; he then has sixty days to rescind his reaffirmation. If the bankrupt party is an individual, the law also requires that a court hearing be held at which the consequences of his reaffirmation must be explained, and reaffirmation of certain consumer debts is subject to court approval if the debtor is not represented by an attorney.

Voidable Duties   Some promises that might otherwise serve as consideration are voidable by the promisor, for a variety of reasons, including minority, fraud, duress, or mistake. But a voidable contract does not automatically become void, and if the promisor has not avoided the contract but instead thereafter renews his promise, it is binding. For example, Mr. Melvin sells his bicycle to Seth, age thirteen. Seth promises to pay Mr. Melvin $100. Seth may repudiate the contract but he does not. When he turns eighteen, he renews his promise to pay the $100. This promise is binding. (However, a promise made up to the time he turned eighteen would not be binding, since he would still have been a minor.)

Promissory Estoppel

This forbidding phrase represents another type of promise that the courts will enforce without consideration. Simply stated, **promissory estoppel** means that the courts will stop the promisor from claiming that there was no consideration. The doctrine of promissory estoppel is invoked in the interests of justice when three conditions are met: (1) the promise is one that the promisor should reasonably expect to induce the promisee to take action or forbear from taking action of a definite and substantial character; (2) the action or forbearance is taken; and (3) injustice can be avoided only by enforcing the promise.

Timko serves on the board of trustees of a school. He recommends that the school purchase a building for a substantial sum of money, and to induce the trustees to vote for the purchase, he promises to help with the purchase and to pay at the end of five years the purchase price less the down payment. At the end of four years, Timko dies. The school sues his estate, which defends on the ground that there was no consideration for the promise. Timko was promised or given nothing in return, and the purchase of the building was of no direct benefit to him (which would have made the promise enforceable as a unilateral contract). The court ruled that under the three-pronged promissory estoppel test, Timko's estate was liable. [Estate of Timko v. Oral Roberts Evangelistic Assn., 215 N.W.2d 750 (Mich. App. 1974).]

As the next case illustrates, the doctrine of promissory estoppel is flexible, designed to meet the infinite variety of promises that can prompt others to act.

HOFFMAN v. RED OWL STORES, INC.
26 Wis.2d 683, 133 N.W.2d 267 (1965)

Action by Joseph Hoffman (hereinafter "Hoffman") and wife, plaintiffs, against defendants Red Owl Stores, Inc. (hereinafter "Red Owl") and Edward Lukowitz.

The complaint alleged that Lukowitz, as agent for Red Owl, represented to and agreed with plaintiffs that Red Owl would build a store building in Chilton and stock it with merchandise for Hoffman to operate in return for which plaintiffs were to put up and invest a total sum of $18,000; that in reliance upon the above mentioned agreement and representations plaintiffs sold their bakery building and business and their grocery store and business; also in reliance on the agreement and representations Hoffman purchased the building site in Chilton and rented a residence for himself and his family in Chilton; plaintiffs' actions in reliance on the representations and agreement disrupted their personal and business life; plaintiffs lost substantial amounts of income and expended large sums of money as expenses. Plaintiffs demanded recovery of damages for the breach of defendants' representations and agreements.

The action was tried to a court and jury. The facts hereafter stated are taken from the evidence adduced at the trial. Where there was a conflict in the evidence the version favorable to plaintiffs has been accepted since the verdict rendered was in favor of plaintiffs.

★   ★   ★

Sec. 90 of Restatement, 1 Contracts, provides (at p. 110):

> A promise which the promisor should reasonably expect to induce action or forbearance of a definite and substantial character on the part of the promisee and which does induce such action or forbearance is binding if injustice can be avoided only by enforcement of the promise.

★   ★   ★

The record here discloses a number of promises and assurances given to Hoffman by Lukowitz in behalf of Red Owl upon which plaintiffs relied and acted upon to their detriment.

Foremost were the promises that for the sum of $18,000 Red Owl would establish Hoffman in a store. After Hoffman had sold his grocery store and paid the $1,000 on the Chilton lot, the $18,000 figure was changed to $24,100. Then in November, 1961, Hoffman was assured that if the $24,100 figure were increased by $2,000 the deal would go through. Hoffman was induced to sell his grocery store fixtures and inventory in June, 1961, on the promise that he would be in his new store by fall. In November, plaintiffs sold their bakery building on the urging of defendants and on the assurance that this was the last step necessary to have the deal with Red Owl go through.

We determine that there was ample evidence to sustain the answers of the jury to the questions of the verdict with respect to the promissory representations made by Red Owl, Hoffman's reliance thereon in the exercise of ordinary care, and his fulfillment of the conditions required of him by the terms of the negotiations had with Red Owl.

There remains for consideration the question of law raised by defendants that agreement was never reached on essential factors necessary to establish a contract between Hoffman and Red Owl. Among these were the size, cost, design, and layout of the store building; and the terms of the lease with respect to rent, maintenance, renewal, and purchase options. This poses the question of whether the promise necessary to sustain a cause of action for promissory estoppel must embrace all essential details of a proposed transaction between promisor and promisee so as to be the equivalent of an offer that would result in a binding contract between the parties if the promisee were to accept the same.

Originally the doctrine of promissory estoppel was invoked as a substitute for consideration rendering a gratuitous promise enforceable as a contract. See Williston, Contracts (1st ed.), p. 307, sec. 139. In other words, the acts of reliance by the promisee to his detriment provided a substitute for consideration. If promissory estoppel were to be limited to only those situations

(continued on next page)

(continued)

HOFFMAN v. RED OWL STORES, INC. 26 Wis.2d 63,133 N.W.2d 267 (1965)

where the promise giving rise to the cause of action must be so definite with respect to all details that a contract would result were the promise supported by consideration, then the defendants' instant promises to Hoffman would not meet this test. However, sec. 90 of Restatement, 1 Contracts, does not impose the requirement that the promise giving rise to the cause of action must be so comprehensive in scope as to meet the requirements of an offer that would ripen into a contract if accepted by the promisee. Rather the conditions imposed are:

1. Was the promise one which the promisor should reasonably expect to induce action or forbearance of a definite and substantial character on the part of the promisee?
2. Did the promise induce such action or forbearance?
3. Can injustice be avoided only by enforcement of the promise?

We deem it would be a mistake to regard an action grounded on promissory estoppel as the equivalent of a breach of contract action. As Dean Boyer points out, it is desirable that fluidity in the application of the concept be maintained. 98 University of Pennsylvania Law Review (1950), 459, at page 497. While the first two of the above listed three requirements of promissory estoppel present issues of fact which ordinarily will be resolved by a jury, the third requirement, that the remedy can only be invoked where necessary to avoid injustice, is one that involves a policy decision by the court. Such a policy decision necessarily embraces an element of discretion.

We conclude that injustice would result here if plaintiffs were not granted some relief because of the failure of defendants to keep their promises which induced plaintiffs to act to their detriment.

Cases such as *Timko*, involving pledges of charitable contributions, have long been troublesome to courts. Recognizing the necessity to charitable institutions of such pledges, the courts have also been mindful that a mere pledge of money to the general funds of a hospital, university, or similar institution does not usually induce substantial action but is, rather, simply a promise without consideration. When the pledge does prompt a charitable institution to act, promissory estoppel is available as a remedy. In about one-quarter of the states, another doctrine is available for cases involving simple pledges: the "mutual promises" theory, whereby the pledges of many individuals are taken as consideration for each other and are binding against each promisor. This theory was not available to the plaintiff in *Timko* because his was the only promise.

Seals

As we have already seen, in some states a promise under seal is a substitute for consideration (pp. 192–93).

International Contracts

Contracts governed by the Convention on Contracts for the International Sale of Goods (see p. 191) do not require consideration to be binding.

CHAPTER SUMMARY

Most agreements are not binding contracts in the absence of what the law terms "consideration." Consideration is usually defined as a "legal detriment"—an act, a forbearance, or a promise. The act can be the payment of money, the delivery of a service, or the transfer of title to property. Always bear in mind that consideration is a legal concept and that it centers on the giving up of a legal right or benefit.

An understanding of consideration is important in many commonplace situations, including those in which (1) a debtor and creditor enter into an accord which is later disputed, (2) a duty is preexisting, (3) a promise is illusory, and (4) creditors agree to a composition.

Often promises are enforceable without consideration. These include certain promises under the UCC and other circumstances, including: (1) contracts barred by the statute of limitations, (2) promises by a bankrupt to repay debts, and (3) situations in which justice will be served by invoking the doctrine of promissory estoppel. Determining whether an agreement should be upheld despite the lack of consideration, technically defined, calls for a diligent assessment of the factual circumstances.

KEY TERMS

Accord	p. 228	Mutuality of obligation	p. 231
Accord and satisfaction	p. 228	Past consideration	p. 235
Composition	p. 232	Promisee	p. 224
Consideration	p. 224	Promisor	p. 224
Exclusive dealing contracts	p. 231	Promissory estoppel	p. 236
		Statute of limitations	p. 235
Legal detriment	p. 224	Unliquidated debt	p. 228
Liquidated debt	p. 228		

SELF-TEST QUESTIONS

1. Consideration:
   (a) can always be substituted by the presence of a seal
   (b) cannot be nominal in amount
   (c) is a bargained-for act, forbearance, or promise from the promisee
   (d) all of the above
2. An example of valid consideration is:
   (a) a promise to obey all traffic laws when driving
   (b) a promise to refrain from going to court
   (c) a promise to cook dinner if the promisor can get around to it
   (d) a promise to repay a friend for four years of free legal advice he had provided
3. An unliquidated debt is:
   (a) a debt not able to be paid
   (b) a debt not yet paid
   (c) a debt of uncertain amount
   (d) an unenforceable debt

4. The rule that if one party to a contract has not made a binding obligation, the other party is not bound is called:
   (a) revocation
   (b) mutuality of obligation
   (c) accord and satisfaction
   (d) estoppel
5. Example of promises enforceable without consideration include:
   (a) an agreement modifying a sales contract
   (b) a promise to pay a debt after the statute of limitations has run
   (c) a debtor's promise to repay a debt that has been discharged by a bankruptcy court
   (d) all of the above

DEMONSTRATION PROBLEM

Phil offers George $100 if George will promise to quit smoking marijuana for one year. George promises to quit. Is Phil's promise binding? Why?

PROBLEMS

1. Sparky, an electrical contractor, entered into a contract to do the electrical work in a dormitory that was being built by Big Builders, Inc. (BB). Sparky was to be paid $70,000 for the work. Later, a dispute arose over the scope of the work, and the parties agreed to replace the first contract with another one. Under the new contract, Sparky was to receive $65,000 but was to perform $26,000 less work. Later still, BB argued that the second contract was invalid because the consideration was inadequate in that Sparky was $21,000 better off under the agreement. Is this a good argument? Why?
2. After graduation from Big U, Bertha started her own business called Suits Unlimited. Bertha's main business activity was to visit the homes of complete strangers, knock on the door, and state to the occupants: "Hi, I'm Bertha. If you promise to pay me $5,000, I promise not to sue you." In many instances, the occupants made the requested promises. Are the promises enforceable in court? Why?
3. Hornbuckle purchased equipment from Continental Gin (CG) for $6,300. However, after some of the equipment proved defective, Hornbuckle sent CG a check for $4,000 marked "by endorsement this check is accepted in full payment." CG endorsed and deposited the check. May CG force Hornbuckle to pay the remaining $2,300? Why?
4. Raquel entered into a contract whereby she promised to deliver 100 movable widgets to Sam on December 15. Sam

promised to pay $400 for the widgets. On November 25, Sam called Raquel and asked if she could deliver the widgets on December 5. Raquel said she could, and promised delivery on the 5th. Is her promise binding? Why?

5. Magic, a minor, bought a luxury car from Kareem, an adult, promising to pay Kareem $15,000 for the car. Upon reaching the age of majority, Magic affirmed his promise to pay $15,000. Is this a binding promise, in light of the fact that the consideration (the car) had been received in the past? Why?

6. Assume in Question 6 that Magic, upon becoming an adult, affirmed the promise to pay $15,000 but did not keep his promise and that several years later Kareem's claim was barred by the statute of limitations. Nevertheless, Magic wrote to Kareem, again promising to pay the debt. Is Magic's latest promise enforceable? Why?

7. Montbanks's son, Charles, was seeking an account executive position with Dobbs, Smith & Fogarty, Inc., the largest brokerage firm in the United States. Charles was very independent and wished no interference by his father. The firm, after several weeks' deliberation, decided to hire Charles. They made him an offer on April 12, 1979, and Charles readily accepted. Montbanks feared that his son would not be hired. Being unaware of the fact that his son had been hired, Montbanks mailed a letter to Dobbs on April 13 in which he promised to give the brokerage firm $50,000 in commission business if the firm would hire his son. The letter was duly received by Dobbs, and the firm wishes to enforce it against Montbanks. May Dobbs enforce the promise? Why?

ANSWERS TO SELF-TEST QUESTIONS

1. (c)   2. (b)   3. (c)   4. (b)   5. (d)

SUGGESTED ANSWER TO DEMONSTRATION PROBLEM

Phil's promise is not binding. There was no consideration for the promise because George did not give up something that he had the right to do.

CHAPTER 10

CHAPTER OVERVIEW
Violation of Statute
Violation of Public Policy

Legality

We now turn to the third of the four requirements for a valid contract: the legality or illegality of the underlying bargain. The basic rule is that courts will not enforce an illegal contract. Why should this be? Why should the courts refuse to honor contracts made privately by people who presumably know what they are doing—for example, a wager on the World Series or the championship fight? Two reasons are usually given. One is that refusal to enforce helps discourage unlawful behavior; the other is that honoring such contracts would demean the judiciary. Are these reasons valid? Yes and no, in the opinion of one contracts scholar:

> [D]enying relief to parties who have engaged in an illegal transaction . . . helps to effectuate the public policy involved by discouraging the conduct that is disapproved. Mere denial of contractual and quasi-contractual remedy [however,] rarely has a substantial effect in discouraging illegal conduct. A man who is hired to perform a murder is not in the least deterred by the fact that the courts are not open to him to collect his fee. Such a man has other methods of enforcement, and they are in fact more effective than legal process. The same is true in varying degrees where less heinous forms of illegal conduct are involved. Even in the matter of usury it was found that mere denial of enforcement was of little value in the effort to eliminate the loan shark. And restraints of trade were not curbed to an appreciable extent until contracts in restraint of trade were made criminal.
>
> In most instances, then, the protection of the good name

of the judicial institution must provide the principal reason for the denial of a remedy to one who has trafficked in the forbidden. This is, moreover, a very good reason. The first duty of an institution is to preserve itself, and if the courts to any appreciable extent busied themselves with "justice among thieves," the community . . . would be shocked and the courts would be brought into disrepute. (Havighurst, 1952, pp. 1144–45)

Strictly enforced, the rule prohibiting courts from ordering the parties to honor illegal contracts is harsh. It means that a promisee who has already performed under the contract can neither obtain performance of the act for which he bargained nor recover the money he paid or the value of the performance he made. The court will simply leave the parties where it finds them, meaning that one of the parties will have received an uncompensated benefit.

Not surprisingly, the severity of the rule against enforcement has led courts to seek ways to moderate its impact, chiefly by modifying it according to the principle of **restitution.** In general, restitution requires that one who has conferred a benefit or suffered a loss should not unfairly be denied compensation.

Pursuing this notion, the courts have created several exceptions to the general rule. Thus a party who is excusably ignorant that his promise violates public policy and a party who is not equally in the wrong may recover. Likewise, when a party "would otherwise suffer a forfeiture that is disproportionate in relation to the contravention of public policy involved," restitution will be allowed. (*Restatement (Second) of Contracts*, Section 197 (b).) Other exceptions exist when the party seeking restitution withdraws from the transaction contemplated in the contract before the illegal purpose has been carried out and when "allowing the claim would put an end to a continuing situation that is contrary to the public interest." (*Restatement (Second) of Contracts*, Section 199(b).) An example of the latter situation occurs when two bettors place money in the hands of a stakeholder. If the wager is unlawful, the loser of the bet has the right to recover his money from the stakeholder before it is paid out to the winner.

Though by and large courts enforce contracts without considering the worth or merits of the bargain they incorporate, freedom of contract can conflict with other public policies. Tensions arise between the desire to let people pursue their own ends and the belief that certain kinds of conduct should not be encouraged. Thus, a patient may agree to be treated by a medical quack, but state laws prohibit medical care except by licensed physicians. Law and public policies against usury, gambling, obstructing justice, bribery, corrupt influence, perjury, restraint of trade,

impairment of domestic relations, and fraud all significantly affect the authority and willingness of courts to enforce contracts.

In this chapter, we will consider two types of illegality: (1) that which results from a bargain that violates a statute, and (2) that which the courts deem contrary to public policy, even though not expressly set forth in statutes.

VIOLATION OF STATUTE

In General

Any bargain that violates the criminal law—including statutes that govern gambling, licensing, doing business on Sunday, and consumer credit transactions—is illegal. Thus, determining whether contracts are lawful may seem to be an easy enough task. Clearly, whenever the statute itself explicitly forbids the making of the contract or the performance agreed upon, the bargain (such as a contract to sell drugs) is unlawful. But when the statute does not expressly prohibit the making of the contract, courts examine a number of factors, which are discussed in the following case.

BOVARD v. AMERICAN HORSE ENTERPRISES
247 Cal. Rptr. 340 (1988)

[Bovard sued Ralph and American Horse Enterprises (a corporation) to recover on promissory notes that were signed when Ralph purchased the corporation. The trial court dismissed Bovard's complaint.]

PUGLIA, PRESIDING JUSTICE.

★   ★   ★

The court found that the corporation predominantly produced paraphernalia used to smoke marijuana ["roach clips" and "bongs"] and was not engaged significantly in jewelry production, and that Bovard had recovered the corporate machinery through self-help. The parties do not challenge these findings. The court acknowledged that the manufacture of drug paraphernalia was not itself illegal in 1978 when Bovard and Ralph contracted for the sale of American Horse Enterprises, Inc. However, the court concluded a public policy against the manufacture of drug paraphernalia was implicit in the statute making the possession, use and transfer of marijuana unlawful. The trial court held the consideration for the contract was contrary to the policy of express law, and the contract was therefore illegal and void. Finally, the court found the parties were in pari delicto and thus with respect to their contractual dispute should be left as the court found them.

* * *

The trial court concluded the consideration for the contract was contrary to the policy of the law as expressed in the statute prohibiting the possession, use and transfer of marijuana. Whether a contract is contrary to public policy is a question of law to be determined from the circumstances of the particular case. Here, the critical facts are not in dispute. Whenever a court becomes aware that a contract is illegal, it has a duty to refrain from entertaining an action to enforce the contract. Furthermore the court will not permit the parties to maintain an action to settle or compromise a claim based on an illegal contract.

* * *

[There are several] factors to consider in analyzing whether a contract violates public policy: "Before labeling a contract as being contrary to public policy, courts must carefully inquire into the nature of the conduct, the extent of public harm which may be involved, and the moral quality of the conduct of the parties in light of the prevailing standards of the community [Citations.]"

These factors are more comprehensively set out in the Restatement Second of Contracts section 178:

"(1)   A promise or other term of an agreement is unenforceable on grounds of public policy if legislation provides that it is unenforceable or the interest in its enforcement is clearly outweighed in the circumstances by a public policy against the enforcement of such terms.

"(2)   In weighing the interest in the enforcement of a term, account is taken of
    "(a)   the parties' justified expectations,
    "(b)   any forfeiture that would result if enforcement were denied, and
    "(c)   any special public interest in the enforcement of the particular term.

"(3)   In weighing a public policy against enforcement of a term, account is taken of
    "(a)   the strength of that policy as manifested by legislation or judicial decisions,
    "(b)   the likelihood that a refusal to enforce the term will further that policy,
    "(c)   the seriousness of any misconduct involved and the extent to which it was deliberate, and
    "(d)   the directness of the connection between that misconduct and the term."

Applying the Restatement test to the present circumstances, we conclude the interest in enforcing this contract is very tenuous. Neither party was reasonably justified in expecting the government would not eventually act to geld American Horse Enterprises, a business harnessed to the production of paraphernalia used to facilitate the use of an illegal drug. Moreover, although

(*continued on next page*)

(continued)

BOVARD v. AMERICAN HORSE ENTERPRISES
247 Cal. Rptr. 340 (1988)

voidance of the contract imposed a forfeiture on Bovard, he did recover the corporate machinery, the only assets of the business which could be used for lawful purposes, i.e., to manufacture jewelry. Thus, the forfeiture was significantly mitigated if not negligible. Finally, there is no special public interest in the enforcement of this contract, only the general interest in preventing a party to a contract from avoiding a debt.

On the other hand, the Restatement factors favoring a public policy against enforcement of this contract are very strong. As we have explained, the public policy against manufacturing paraphernalia to facilitate the use of marijuana is strongly implied in the statutory prohibition against the possession, use, etc., of marijuana, a prohibition which dates back at least to 1929. (See Stats.1929, ch. 216, § 1, p. 380.) Obviously, refusal to enforce the instant contract will further that public policy not only in the present circumstances but by serving notice on manufacturers of drug paraphernalia that they may not resort to the judicial system to protect or advance their business interests. Moreover, it is immaterial that the business conducted by American Horse Enterprises was not expressly prohibited by law when Bovard and Ralph made their agreement since both parties knew that the corporation's products would be used primarily for purposes which were expressly illegal. We conclude the trial court correctly declared the contract contrary to the policy of express law and therefore illegal and void.

Gambling Contracts

About three months before their rematch for the world heavyweight championship fight in 1975, Muhammad Ali and Joe Frazier shook hands in the sweltering heat of Kuala Lumpur to seal a little side bet on the outcome of their fight. "Let's make a deal," said Ali. "You whip me, you get a million dollars of my money. I whip you, I get a million of your money" (*N.Y. Times*, July 2, 1975). Could the winner enforce this "contract"? In most states, the answer is clearly no. The general rule, as we have noted, is that wagers are unlawful, void, and unenforceable.

However, just because the outcome is contingent on events that lie outside the power of the parties to control does not transform a bargain into a wager. For example, if a gardener agrees to care for the grounds of a septuagenarian for life in return for an advance payment of $10,000, the uncertainty of the date of the landowner's death does not make the deal a wager. The parties have struck a bargain that accurately assesses, to the satisfaction of each, the risks of the contingency in question. Likewise, the fact that an agreement is phrased in the form of a wager does not make it one. Thus, a father says to his daughter: "I'll bet you can't get an A in organic chemistry. If

you do, I'll give you $100." This is a unilateral contract, the consideration to the father being the daughter's achieving a good grade.

Despite the general rule against enforcing wagers, there are exceptions, most statutory but some rooted in the common law. The common law permits the sale or purchase of securities or other commodities on margin (where someone other than the purchaser puts up the rest of the capital) or at a future date; an option to purchase or sell securities is not a wager. But because there are speculative elements to contracts of these types, some federal and state statutes prohibit or regulate them. In particular, an agreement in which neither party intends to part with the securities or commodities but instead is simply speculating on the rise or fall in market prices is a wager. Peter agrees to pay Paul $2 a pound for 1,000 pounds of sugar, to be delivered next May. At that time, sugar is selling for $3 a pound. If neither party intended to transfer title to the sugar, the agreement (although illegal) calls for Paul to pay Peter $1,000. (Peter tenders $2,000 to Paul for the half-ton of sugar, but Paul would have to pay $3,000 to obtain the half-ton of sugar to give him; the difference, $1,000, is what Peter has made under the contract by having shrewdly predicted the market rise.) However, if at the time the contract is made one or both of the parties intends to perform—or has the right to insist on performance—then the deal is not a wager, even if in the end neither in fact performs or insists on it.

Insurance contracts are also speculative, but unless one party has no insurable interest in the insured, the contract is not a wager. Thus, if you had taken out an insurance contract on the life of the Shah of Iran after he had fled the country, the contract would be void because you and the insurance company would have been gambling on a contingent event. If, however, you insure your home against fire or theft loss, the contingency does not make the policy a wagering agreement, because you will have suffered a direct loss should it occur. (For the definition of "insurable interest" see Chapter 36.)

Licensing Statutes

To practice most professions and carry on the trade of an increasing number of occupations, states require that providers of service possess licenses—doctors, plumbers, real estate brokers, egg inspectors; the list is long. As sometimes happens, though, a person may contract for the services of one who is unlicensed, either because he is unqualified and carrying on his business without a license or because for technical reasons (forgetting to mail in the license renewal application, for example) he does not possess a license at the moment. Robin calls Lisa, a plumber, to install the pipes for her new kitchen. Lisa, who has no license, puts in all the pipes and asks to be paid. Having discovered that Lisa is unlicensed, Robin refuses to pay. May Lisa collect?

To answer the question, a three-part analysis is necessary. First, is a license required? Some occupations may be performed without a license (lawn mowing, for example). Others may be performed with or without certain credentials, the difference lying in what the professional may tell the public. (For instance, an accountant need not be a certified public accountant to carry on most accounting functions.) Let us assume that the state requires everyone who does any sort of plumbing for pay to have a valid license.

The second step is to determine whether the licensing statute explicitly bars recovery by someone who has performed work while unlicensed. Some do; many others contain no specific provision on the point. Statutes that do bar recovery must of course govern the courts when they are presented with the question.

If the statute is silent, courts must, in the third prong of the analysis, distinguish between "regulatory" and "revenue" licenses. A **regulatory license** is intended to protect the public health, safety, and welfare. To obtain these licenses, the practitioner of the art must generally demonstrate his or her abilities by taking some sort of examination. A plumbing licensing requirement might fall into this category. A **revenue license** generally requires no such examination and is imposed purely for the sake of raising revenue. A license to deliver milk, open to anyone who applies and pays the fee, would be an example of a revenue license. (In some states, plumbing licenses are for revenue purposes only.) Generally speaking, failure to hold a regulatory license bars recovery, the absence of a revenue license does not.

As the following case illustrates, a person who fails to obtain a regulatory license may be denied recovery even when the defendant is a professional rather than a member of the public.

HARRISON & BATES, INC. v. LSR CORP.
385 S.E.2d 624 (Va. 1989)

POFF, SENIOR JUSTICE.

The principal issue framed on this appeal is whether a corporation, licensed as a real estate broker under the laws of a sister state but not under the laws of Virginia, can enforce a contract to split commissions, earned on the sale of real estate in Virginia, with a real estate broker licensed in Virginia.

The question arises from a judgment confirming the verdict of a jury that awarded LSR Corporation (LSR) half the commissions paid Harrison & Bates, Incorporated (H & B). LSR is a North Carolina corporation licensed in that state as a real estate and business brokerage firm. Sherman Kennedy and

(continued on next page)

(*continued*)

HARRISON & BATES, INC. v. LSR CORP.
385 S.E.2d 624 (Va. 1989)

William Brown are equal owners of LSR, and each is an officer and director of the corporation. Kennedy holds a North Carolina license as a real estate broker, and Brown is licensed in that state as a business broker. Neither LSR, Kennedy, nor Brown is licensed as a real estate broker in Virginia.

H & B is a Virginia corporation licensed in Virginia as a real estate broker. Bank of Virginia (now Signet Bank) granted H & B an exclusive listing for sale of the "Filer Ford" property located on West Broad Street in Richmond. In a letter dated December 30, 1981 addressed to Brown at LSR, Edward Jennings, a licensed broker with H & B, stated: "In the event you are successful in bringing forth a client with whom a sale is consummated, [H & B] agrees to split the paid gross commissions on a 50/50 basis with you."

In the months that followed, Brown and Kennedy came to Richmond with several prospective purchasers and showed them the property. When these efforts failed, they decided that the property would be more marketable if offered as a going business concern, one of a type uncommon in the Richmond community. Pursuing that decision, Brown and Kennedy obtained an option to purchase a nightclub franchise. On September 9, 1982, they formed a new Virginia corporation under the name of "2001 of Richmond, Inc." and became its sole owners, officers, and directors. Four days later, the new corporation acquired an option to purchase the Filer Ford property at a price reduced from $2 million to $1.5 million. Brown and Kennedy subscribed the document as guarantors. On October 15, 1982, the bank sold the property to 2001 of Richmond. The corporation exercised the franchise option, and the nightclub opened for business in March 1983 under the management of Brown and Kennedy.

Although all the money required to purchase the franchise and the real estate and to finance renovation of the building had been contributed by five investors assembled by Brown and Kennedy, ownership of 2001 of Richmond was divided equally among Brown, Kennedy, and the five investors. In October 1983, the investors bought the interests of Brown and Kennedy and employed new managers.

H & B was unaware of the negotiations LSR conducted with the bank until shortly before the day of sale. Jennings had supplied the bank with a list of the prospective buyers H & B had contacted, and the bank agreed to pay H & B $70,000 in commissions. Payment was made on the day of the sale.

By letter dated December 6, 1982 addressed to H & B, Kennedy stated: "As the primary broker in this transaction, LSR expects to be paid $35,000, per our contract." Kennedy explained: "LSR Corporation was the sole reason for the sale of the property. LSR brought the purchaser, helped to negotiate the purchase price, and also assisted the purchaser in negotiating financing for the property." H & B refused to pay, and LSR filed a motion for judgment claiming $35,000 in damages for breach of contract.

*   *   *

The statute in effect when this dispute occurred, former Code § 54-749 (Cum. Supp.1984) (now § 54.1-2106), is central to the principal issue stated above. In pertinent part, that statute provided:

It shall be unlawful for any person, partnership, association or corporation, to act as a real estate broker . . . without a license issued by the Virginia Real Estate Commission. No partnership, association or corporation shall be granted a license, unless every member or officer of such partnership, association or corporation, who actively participates in its brokerage business, shall hold a license as a real estate broker. . . .

★　★　★

"It is well established that, because a contract made in violation of the real estate licensing statutes is illegal, an unlicensed agent cannot recover compensation for his services in negotiating a sale under the contract." *Grenco v. Nathaniel Greene,* 237 S.E.2d 107, 109 (1977). *Grenco* cited *Massie v. Dudley,* 3 S.E.2d 176 (1939), where this Court, construing predecessors of the current real estate licensing statutes, applied this rule to a compensation agreement between a landowner and a real estate broker whose license had expired.

★　★　★

All the contracts declared illegal and unenforceable in the real estate commission cases decided by this Court were contracts between broker and client. From the two letter opinions of record, it appears that the trial court concluded, and LSR agrees, that because the licensing statutes were designed to protect the public from incompetence and fraud practiced by unregulated persons, those statutes should be interpreted to apply always to contracts between broker and client but never to contracts between broker and broker such as the contract in issue.

We disagree. Read together, Code §§ 54-749, and 54-732 apply the licensing requirement to "any person" who engages in any "act for a compensation . . . of buying or selling real estate of or for another". If the General Assembly had intended to exempt brokers who enter into commission-sharing contracts, it could have added such an exemption to the list of exemptions detailed in Code § 54-734. It did not do so, and we will not presume that the omission was a legislative inadvertence. Rather, giving the statutory language its common import, we hold that the requirement that those who act as a real estate broker in Virginia be licensed in Virginia extends not only to those who enter into a compensation contract with a seller or a purchaser but also to those who contract with each other to share commissions earned by the performance of such acts.

★　★　★

Reversed and final judgment.

Sunday Contracts

Under the common law, contracts entered into on Sundays, as well as other commercial activities, were valid and enforceable. But a separate, religious tradition that traces to the Second Commandment frowned on work performed on "the Lord's Day." In 1781 a New Haven city ordinance banning Sunday work was printed on blue paper, and since that time such laws have been known as blue laws. The first statewide blue law was enacted in the United States in 1788; it prohibited travel, work, sports and amusements, and the carrying on of any business or occupation. The only exceptions in most states throughout most of the nineteenth century were mutual promises to marry and contracts of necessity or charity. As the Puritan fervor wore off, courts began to recognize a number of exceptions to the statutory prohibitions, leading to considerable confusion. For example, if the contract were completely executed on Sunday, some courts required the transaction to be canceled; others left the parties as they were. Promises made on a "secular" day that called for performance on a Sunday were interpreted to mean performance on the next day or (if the next day was a holiday) on the day after.

As the nation became more industrial and as the amount of leisure time grew, state legislatures began to soften the blue laws. In the 1880s the bans against sports and amusements began to be repealed. In time provisions against performance of all work were relaxed, so that manufacturing and other types of labor could be conducted on Sunday. But up to the present, blue laws in many states prohibit retailing of various types. In many states, however, police widely ignore the laws and refuse to enforce them; in states where they are enforced, the police rarely enforce them in an even-handed manner (for example, supermarkets have been prosecuted but "Mom and Pop" stores left alone). Moreover, the laws are frequently wildly contradictory, distinguishing with little or no basis between classes of merchandise, allowing drugs to be sold but not cosmetics, or certain foods but not others. (In New York, the blue laws forbade the sale of thousands of items, including windshield blades, ski wax, and takeout fried chicken.)

In 1961, the U.S. Supreme Court declined to overturn the blue laws on the ground that they violate the religious establishment clause of the First Amendment. Although the blue laws unquestionably have a religious origin, the Court said that they were constitutional as long as they serve a secular purpose—for example, to control commerce or to enhance the quiet enjoyment of one day during the week.

Nevertheless, several state supreme courts began during the 1960s and 1970s to invalidate on state constitutional grounds their sometimes centuries-old blue laws. Thus the New York Court of Appeals in June 1976 largely threw out the state statute because "the gallimaufry of exceptions . . . has obliterated any natural nexus between [the section prohibiting Sunday sales] and the salutary purpose of the Sabbath

Laws" and also because the prosecution was discriminatory. [People v. Abrahams, 353 N.E.2d 574 (1976).] Legislatures also continue to repeal the laws. In 1983, for instance, Massachusetts ended a 300-year-old ban on Sunday shopping and Mississippi repealed a law that made Sunday hunting or fishing a crime. But because blue laws are still on the books in some thirty states, the retailer would do well at least to be acquainted with the policies of the enforcement agencies, which in some states continue to honor the law. (See **Box 10-1**.)

VIOLATION OF PUBLIC POLICY

In General

Public policy is expressed by courts as well as legislatures. In determining whether to enforce a contract, courts must ordinarily balance the interests at stake. To strike the proper balance, courts must weigh the parties' expectations, the forfeitures that would result from denial of enforcement, and the public interest favoring enforcement against the strength of the policy, whether denying enforcement will further the policy, the seriousness and deliberateness of the violation, and how direct the connection is between the misconduct and the contractual term to be enforced. (*Restatement (Second) of Contracts*, Section 178.)

Common Law Restraint of Trade

One of the oldest public policies evolved by courts is the common law prohibition against restraint of trade. From the early days of industrialism, the courts took a dim view of ostensible competitors who agreed among themselves to fix prices or not to sell in each others' territories. Since 1890, with the enactment of the Sherman Act, the law of restraint of trade has been absorbed by federal and state antitrust statutes (Chapter 45). But the common law prohibition still exists. Though today it is concerned almost exclusively with promises not to compete in sales of businesses and employment contracts, it can arise in other settings. For example, George's promise to Arthur never to sell the parcel of land that Arthur is selling to him is void because it unreasonably restrains trade in the land.

LAW AND LIFE

BOX 10-1

Work Hard and One Day You May Amount to Something: A Convict

By Sanford L. Jacobs

[*Many states have repealed certain blue laws which ban work or commerce on Sunday. Yet, some states still honoring blue laws take enforcement seriously.*—AUTHORS' NOTE]

Paramus, N.J., is a tough town for workaholics.

Blame it on a local 1957 ordinance that bars "worldly employment or business, except works of necessity and charity" on Sunday. Recreation-related businesses, such as movie theaters and bowling alleys, also are exempt. The purpose of the ban is to keep down traffic, the town says.

Raiding Buildings

Through the years, all kinds of professionals wanting to use their Paramus offices on Sunday have unsuc-

SUNDAY BLUES

cessfully challenged the law in court. The police take the law seriously, routinely raiding offices and removing people whose cars are spotted outside.

But last week the courts did give the law's opponents a victory—albeit a small one.

Responding to a burglar alarm last September, policemen with their guns drawn found two computer technicians at work one Sunday inside Stern's Inc.'s computer facility, which processes transactions from 28 department stores in three states. The technicians were given summonses for violating the Sunday work ban and warned that next time they would be taken to the police station. A violation carries a maximum penalty of $500 and 90 days in jail.

Stern's first requested an exemption from the ordinance for two technicians to monitor and maintain the computers, contending their work was a "necessity." The Sunday operation handles certain transactions from distant stores that are open on Sundays.

When the council rejected the request, Stern's sued to overturn the ordinance. The challenge was consolidated with complaints from a video-store operator and an office-building owner.

No to Video Tapes

Last week, Superior Court Judge David B. Follender ruled that Stern's could have two people watch the computers on Sunday because such work "is both essential and necessary." But the office-building developer was denied permission for Sunday operation for tenants. So was RKO Warner Theatres Video Inc., which wanted to rent video tapes on Sundays. The judge said that business didn't qualify as "recreation."

The video concern's attorney, Robert J. Inglima, says he fails to see the logic of the ruling since the town allows drug stores to sell blank videocassettes and movie film on Sunday. He says, however, that he hasn't decided whether it's worth appealing the decision.

Source: *Wall Street Journal,* July 18, 1988

The general rule is one of reason: not every restraint of trade is unlawful, only unreasonable ones. As the *Restatement (Second) of Contracts* puts it: "Every promise that relates to business dealings or to a professional or other gainful occupation operates as a restraint in the sense that it restricts the promisor's future activity. Such a promise is not, however, unenforceable, unless the restraint that it imposes is unreasonably detrimental to the smooth operation of a freely competitive private economy." (Section 186, comment a.) An agreement that restraints trade will be construed as unreasonable unless it is ancillary to a legitimate business interest, and is no greater than necessary to protect the legitimate interest. Restraint of trade cases usually arise in two settings: the sale of a business and an attendant agreement not to compete with the purchasers; and an employee's agreement not to compete with the employer should the employee leave for any reason.

Sale of a Business   Regina sells her lingerie store to Victoria and promises not to establish a competing store in town for one year. Since Victoria is purchasing Regina's good will, as well as her building and inventory, there is clearly a property interest to be protected. And the geographical limitation ("in town") is reasonable if that is where the store does business. But if Regina had agreed not to engage in any business in town, or to wait ten years before opening up a new store, or not to open up a new store anywhere within 100 miles of town, she could avoid the non-competition terms of the contract, because the restraint in each case (nature, duration, and geographic area of restraint) would have been broader than necessary to protect Victoria's interest. Whether the courts will uphold an agreement not to compete depends on all the circumstances of the particular case, as the Connecticut barber in the next case discovers.

MATTIS v. LALLY
138 Conn. 51, 82 A.2d 155 (1951)

BALDWIN, JUDGE. This appeal presents the question whether a restrictive clause in a bill of sale of a barber shop preventing the seller from carrying on his trade within a specified area is valid and enforceable. The court issued an injunction enforcing the restriction and the defendant appealed.

The claims of error in the finding are without merit. The facts can be summarized as follows: The defendant owned and operated in Rockville a business known as Lally's Barber Shop. In September, 1948, he sold the shop "together with all good will" to the plaintiff for $1500. The bill of sale contained the following restrictive clause: "The seller agrees in and for the consideration above named, that he will not engage in the barbering business for a period of five years from this date in the City of Rockville . . . or within a radius of one mile from Market Street in said City . . . either directly or indirectly on his own account or as partner, stockholder, employee or otherwise." The one-mile alternative was included because the limits of the town of Ellington were within a quarter of a mile of the location of the defendant's business. At the time of the sale, the defendant's condition of health was not good. He and his wife owned the four-family tenement house where they lived. The property was heavily incumbered with mortgages. Interest on these mortgages and the taxes were in arrears. The defendant was fifty-eight years old, had been a barber for forty years and was unfamiliar with any other kind of work. He was not an invalid, however, and was capable of doing some manual and physical labor. He opened a restaurant which proved unsuccessful. He gave it up and went to work for the plaintiff as a barber in his old shop. After working there about nine months he left in April, 1950, and set up a one-chair barber shop in his own home, which was not more than 300 yards from the shop he had sold to the plaintiff. There he has the patronage of old personal customers and the work is easier for him. His income is about what he received when he was working for the plaintiff. His wife has carried on a small millinery business from their home to increase the family income. He recently purchased a new Plymouth car. After the defendant left the plaintiff's employ, the business of the plaintiff did not justify the hiring of another assistant except on Saturdays. He had to work harder and his net receipts were less. Upon these facts the court concluded that the business purchased by the plaintiff required the protection of the restrictive clause, that the clause worked no undue hardship upon the defendant and that the contract was valid and enforceable.

This is a contract in restraint of trade. The test of its validity is the reasonableness of the restraint it imposes. To meet this test successfully, the restraint must be limited in its operation with respect to time and place and afford no more than a fair and just protection to the interests of the party in whose favor it is to operate, without unduly interfering with the public interest.

The plaintiff bought all the equipment in the defendant's shop "together with all good will." Good will in the sense here used means an established business at a given place with the patronage that attaches to the name and the location. It is the probability that old customers will resort to the old place. Having paid for "good will," the plaintiff was entitled to have reasonable limitations placed upon the activities of the defendant to protect his purchase. If the plaintiff could hold the patronage of the defendant's old customers and secure that of others who might be looking for the services of a barber at the established location, he would be reasonably assured of carrying on the business profitably. If, however, the defendant should open up another shop in the immediate vicinity, it was to be expected that his old personal customers and others would seek his services. There is no finding that the barber shop before the sale to the plaintiff attracted customers from the entire area covered by the restriction except as that fact is implicit in the court's finding that the plaintiff's business required the protection accorded to it. If the fact was otherwise, the burden was upon the defendant to establish it. The court correctly concluded that the limitations as to area and time were fairly and justly calculated to protect the business sold and that they were not unreasonable.

The defendant argues that this contract works an undue hardship upon him and therefore should not be enforced in equity. The court has found that the circumstances of the defendant's health and finances and the possibility that both might deteriorate in the future were known to him when he made the contract. The court found further that there was no possibility that the defendant and his wife would become public charges and that the defendant was not an invalid, although his health would be under less strain and the family finances improved if he could carry on his vocation as a barber in his home. The plaintiff, however, had purchased the business for a substantial consideration and in good faith, relying upon the restrictive clause for protection. Equity under some circumstances will hold invalid contracts which are so broad in their application that they prevent a party from carrying on his usual vocation and earning a livelihood, thus working undue hardship. Those circumstances are not present in this case. The defendant may practice his vocation anywhere except in the limited area of one town and part of another. The rest of the state and the world is open to him. To excuse him from the performance of his agreement would amount to returning to him a large part of what he has sold and would work a real hardship on the plaintiff. Nor was there any unwarranted interference with the public interest. The public is not being deprived of the defendant's services as a barber except in the area where the plaintiff is offering the same kind of service. The court correctly held that the restriction worked no undue hardship upon the defendant and was not an unreasonable interference with the public interest.

The defendant's claims that the plaintiff failed to prove irreparable damage and that he had an adequate remedy at law are of no avail. Irreparable damage would inevitably result from a violation of the defendant's promises.

There is no error.

Employment Contracts

As a condition of employment by the research division of a market research firm, Bruce, a product analyst, is required to sign an agreement in which he promises, for a period of one year after leaving the company, not to "engage, directly or indirectly, in any business competing with the company and located within 50 miles of the company's main offices." The principal reason recited in the agreement for this covenant not to compete is that, by virtue of the employment, Bruce will come to learn a variety of internal secrets, including client lists, trade or business secrets, reports, confidential business discussions, ongoing research, publications, computer programs, and related papers. Is this agreement a lawful restraint of trade?

Here both the property interest of the employer and the extent of the restraint are issues. Although the courts favor the free choice of individuals in their work, the employer undoubtedly has an important competitive interest in seeing that information not be revealed or used against it. As the following case illustrates, however, the employer's information must be secret.

**RAIN AND HAIL
INSURANCE SERVICE
v. CASPER**
902 F.2d 699 (8th Cir.
1990)

WOLLMAN, CIRCUIT JUDGE.

Rain and Hail Insurance Service, Inc. (Rain & Hail) appeals the district court's refusal to enforce a contractual non-compete clause against Paul Casper, a former Rain & Hail employee. We affirm.

Casper's employment agreement with Rain & Hail provided:

> [I]f you resign your employment with Rain and Hail Insurance Service, Inc. you agree by signing below that you will not, for a period of two years from the date of resignation, engage within your assigned territory in the marketing and servicing of any insurance lines presently represented by Rain and Hail Insurance Service, Inc. for any competitive corporation, company or firm.

Although the parties entered into the agreement in Nebraska, they agreed that the laws of the state of Iowa would apply to the agreement.

Casper resigned from Rain & Hail in November 1988. He began employment with Columbia Mutual Casualty Insurance as manager of the crop insurance division in a geographical area that overlapped the area he had worked in while employed by Rain & Hail. Rain & Hail sought preliminary injunctive relief, claiming that Casper's new employment violated the noncompete clause and would cause Rain & Hail irreparable injury.

The district court denied Rain & Hail equitable relief, finding it unlikely that Rain & Hail would succeed on the merits. Although Nebraska law generally allows parties to choose which jurisdiction's law will apply in a contract dispute (here Iowa law), the court nevertheless applied Nebraska law, reasoning that application of Iowa law would be contrary to a fundamental policy of Nebraska. Under Nebraska law, contracts in restraint of trade must be no greater than reasonably necessary to protect the employer in some legitimate interest. The district court found the restrictions of the non-compete clause overbroad because the identity of customers is not a trade secret and Rain & Hail's agreements with the customers are not exclusive. The district court also found the restriction unduly harsh and oppressive to Casper because the agreement was essentially a prerequisite to obtaining the job with Rain & Hail and because Casper had no training in other fields and needed employment.

[Judgment affirmed.]

If a covenant not to compete is ruled unlawful, the courts can pursue one of three courses by way of remedy. A court can refuse to enforce the entire covenant, freeing the employee to compete thenceforth. The court could delete from the agreement only that part which is unreasonable and enforce the remainder (the "Blue Pencil" rule). In some states, the courts have moved away from this rule and have actually taken to rewriting the objectionable clause themselves. Since the parties intended that there be some form of restriction on competition, a reasonable modification would achieve a more just result. [Raimonde v. Van Vlerah, 325 N.E.2d 544 (Ohio 1975).]

Exculpatory Clauses

The courts have long held that public policy disfavors attempts to contract out of tort liability. **Exculpatory clauses** that exempt one party from tort liability to the other for harm caused *intentionally* or *recklessly* are unenforceable without exception. A contract provision that exempts a party from tort liability for *negligence* is unenforceable under two general circumstances: (1) when it "exempts an employer from liability to an employee for injury in the course of his employment"; or (2) when it exempts one charged with a duty of public service and who is receiving compensation from liability to one to whom the duty is owed. (*Restatement (Second) of Contracts*, Section 195.) The trend is to uphold exculpatory clauses—at least in sports-injury suits. (See **Box 10-2**.)

Obstructing the Administration of Justice or Violating a Public Duty

It is well established under common law that contracts that would interfere with the administration of justice or that call upon a public official to violate a public duty are void and unenforceable. Examples of such contracts are numerous: to conceal or compound a crime, to pay for the testimony of a witness in court contingent on the court's ruling, to suppress evidence by paying a witness to leave the state or to destroy documents. Thus, in an unedifying case in Arkansas, a gambler sued a circuit court judge to recover $1,675 allegedly paid to the judge as protection money, and the Arkansas Supreme Court affirmed the dismissal of the suit, holding: "The law will not aid either party to the alleged illegal and void contract . . . 'but will leave them where it finds them, if they have been equally cognizant of the illegality.'" [Womack v. Maner, 301 S.W.2d 438 (Ark. 1957).]

Family Relations

Another broad area in which public policy intrudes on private contractual arrangements is that of undertakings between couples, either prior to or during marriage. Marriage is quintessentially a relationship defined by law, and individuals have limited ability to change its scope through legally enforceable contracts. Moreover, marriage is an institution that public policy favors, and agreements that unreasonably restrain marriage are void. Thus, a father's promise to pay his twenty-one-year-old daughter $100,000 if she refrains from marrying for ten years would be unenforceable. However, a promise in an antenuptial agreement that if the husband predeceases the wife, he will provide his wife with a fixed income for as long as she remains unmarried is valid because the offer of support is related to the need. (Upon remarriage, the need would presumably be less pressing.) Property settlements before, during, or upon the breakup of a marriage are generally enforceable, since

Liability Waivers Hold Up In More Sports-Injury Suits

By Paul M. Barrett

[Exculpatory clauses are being upheld more than ever in sports injury cases. In the past a signed waiver of rights to sue in the event of an injury or death was not enough to clear a defendant—most courts would have allowed the suit to proceed. Today, individuals must understand that they are signing away their rights to sue and that they are usually bound by everything they sign.—AUTHORS' NOTE]

During his final lesson for scuba diving certification at the Young Men's Christian Association of Metropolitan Los Angeles, Ken Sulejmanagic was left alone briefly by his instructor and drowned. When his parents sued for negligence, the YMCA demanded that the suit be thrown out because the Sulejmanag-

TREND TO UPHOLD EXCULPATORY CLAUSES

ics' 19-year-old son had signed a waiver absolving it of responsibility.

Until recently, most state courts would have allowed the suit to proceed, noting that the waiver alone was not enough to clear the defendant. But in a blunt opinion that reflects a growing trend, a state appeals court in Los Angeles last August told the trial judge to terminate the Sulejmanagic suit. It based its decision solely on the existence of the signed waiver.

Waivers are wielding more clout in the nation's courtrooms. In California, Texas, Tennessee and many other states, liability suits brought against companies involved in such activities as parachuting, diving and motorcycle racing are increasingly being blocked by judges because the plaintiffs signed releases or waivers.

"The trend is unmistakable, es-

pecially in California," where the courts often set the pattern for other states, says Jeffrey K. Riffer, a Los Angeles lawyer and adjunct professor at Pepperdine University School of Law.

'Bound by What They Sign'

Mr. Riffer, an authority on sports-injury law, says that just a few years ago, state judges tended to look skeptically at recreational-facility waivers. They "questioned whether people really understood that they were signing away their rights [to sue] or had thought about the hazards," he says. Now judges are coming to believe that "individuals generally should be bound by what they sign."

Mr. Riffer also attributes the change to the increasing number of judges who fear that liability suits have pushed recreational-facility insurance rates beyond what many companies can afford. These judges are attempting to alleviate the problem by showing that waivers do hold up in court.

Source: *Wall Street Journal,* November 11, 1988

---

property is not considered to be an essential incident of marriage. But agreements in the form of property arrangements that tend to be detrimental to marriage are void—for example, an antenuptial contract in which the wife-to-be agrees on demand of the husband-to-be to leave the marriage and renounce any claims upon the husband-to-be at any time in the future in return for which he will pay her $100,000. Separation agreements are not considered detrimental to marriage, as long as they are entered after or in contemplation of immediate separation; but a separation agreement must be "fair" under the circumstances, and judges may review them upon challenge. Similarly, child custody agreements are not left to the whim of the parents but must be consistent with the

best interest of the child, and the courts retain the power to examine this question.

CHAPTER SUMMARY

In general, illegal contracts are unenforceable. The courts must grapple with two types of illegalities: (1) statutory violations, and (2) violations of public policy not expressly declared unlawful by statute. The former include gambling contracts, contracts with unlicensed professionals, and Sunday contracts.

Contracts that violate public policy include many types of "covenants not to compete." No general rule for determining their legality can be given, except to say that the more rigid their restrictions against working or competing the less likely they will withstand judicial scrutiny. Other types of agreements that may violate public policy and hence are unenforceable include provisions that waive tort liability and contracts that interfere with family relationships.

KEY TERMS

SELF-TEST QUESTIONS

1. Gambling contracts:
   (a) are always unenforceable
   (b) are enforceable if written
   (c) are enforceable in certain situations involving the sale of securities
   (d) are always enforceable when made with insurance companies
2. In State X, plumbers must purchase a license but do not have to pass an examination. This is an example of:
   (a) a regulatory license
   (b) a revenue license
   (c) both of the above
   (d) none of the above
3. Blue laws:
   (a) are illegal under the First Amendment
   (b) have been eliminated by most states
   (c) authorize courts to use the "Blue Pencil" rule
   (d) are unconstitutional in some states
4. Exculpatory clauses are sometimes enforceable:
   (a) when they relieve someone from liability for an intentional act
   (b) when they relieve someone from liability for recklessness
   (c) when they relieve someone from liability for negligence
   (d) in all of the above situations
5. An employee's promise not to compete with the employer after leaving the company:
   (a) is never enforceable because it restrains trade
   (b) is always enforceable if in writing
   (c) is always enforceable
   (d) is enforceable if related to the employer's property interests

DEMONSTRATION PROBLEM

Richard promises John $10,000 if John will steal a secret formula belonging to his competitor. John demands payment in advance, and Richard delivers the money in cash. Thereafter, John refuses to steal the formula. Is Richard entitled to a refund? Why?

PROBLEMS

1. Speedy owned a new sports car worth $15,000. He bet a local insurance company that the car would be stolen. Under their agreement, if the car was stolen, the company promised to pay Speedy $20,000; if the car was not stolen, Speedy promised to pay the company $560 annually. Is this an illegal contract? Why?
2. In Question 1, after making the bet with the company, Speedy sold the car to a friend. However, Speedy continued to pay the company $560 per year and the company promised that, if the car was stolen, it would pay Speedy $20,000. Eventually the car was stolen from the friend. Is Speedy legally entitled to collect from the company? Why?
3. Zeke, a pre-med student at Big U, entered into a contract with the university hospital. Under the contract, Zeke agreed to act as resident surgeon in his dormitory for one semester. In his first operation, Zeke treated Sissy for acute appendicitis, performing an appendectomy. He did an outstanding job and Sissy fully recovered. But Sissy now refuses to pay Zeke and, furthermore, the hospital wants to cancel Zeke's contract. What are Zeke's legal rights under each contract? Why?
4. Ramses owned an industrial supply corporation. He decided to sell the business to Tut. Clause VIII of their Agreement of Sale provided as follows:

   As further consideration for the purchase of stock, Ramses agrees that he shall not compete, either directly or indirectly, in the same business as is conducted by the corporation in its established territory.

   Two months after the sale, Ramses opened a competing business across the street from the business now owned by Tut. Tut brought suit, asking the court to close Ramses's business on the basis of Clause VIII. What should the court decide? Why?
5. After taking a business law class at Big U, Elke entered into a contract to sell her business law book to Mac for $12. As part of the same contract she agreed to prepare a will and trust for Mac for an additional $138. Elke prepared the will and trust and sent the book to Mac, but Mac refused to pay her. Is she entitled to payment? Why?
6. Elmo, a door-to-door salesman, entered into a contract to sell the Walton family $220 worth of household products on credit. The Waltons later learned that Elmo had failed

to purchase a city license to make door-to-door sales, and refused to pay him. May Elmo collect from the Waltons? Why?

7. Philpot purchased the King Pharmacy from Golden. The contract contained a promise by Golden that he would not engage in the practice of pharmacy for one year from the date of the sale within one mile of the location of King Pharmacy. Six months later Golden opened the Queen Pharmacy within less than a mile of King Pharmacy. Is the covenant enforceable? Why?

ANSWERS TO SELF-TEST QUESTIONS

1. (c)   2. (b)   3. (d)   4. (c)   5. (d)

SUGGESTED ANSWER TO DEMONSTRATION PROBLEM

Richard is not entitled to a refund. Because the agreement is illegal, the court will leave the parties where it finds them.

CHAPTER

11

CHAPTER OVERVIEW
Duress
Undue Influence
Misrepresentation
Mistake
Capacity

Free Will, Knowledge, and Capacity

We turn now to the last of the four requirements for a valid contract. In addition to manifestation of assent, valid consideration, and legality, a party must consent to the contract freely, with adequate knowledge, and must have capacity. This raises the following major questions:

1. Did the parties enter into the contract of their own free will, or was one forced to agree under duress or undue influence?
2. Did the parties enter into the contract with full knowledge of the facts, or was one or both led to the agreement through fraud or mistake?
3. Did both parties have capacity to make a contract?

DURESS

There are two types of duress: physical and threat. A contract induced by physical violence is void; a contract entered under the compulsion of many types of threats is voidable.

Physical Duress

A door-to-door salesman rings the doorbell and demands that the occupant purchase a case of hair tonic. The occupant refuses. The salesman grabs the occupant, twists his arm behind his back, and begins to break it, saying he will stop only when the occupant signs a purchase agreement. The signed contract is void, and no later ratification by the occupant will be effective. Moreover, a subsequent purchaser who takes in good faith property sold under physical duress does not have good title. For example, a thief comes to an apartment door, terrorizes the tenant into signing a bill of sale for her diamond ring, and then sells it to a third person who has no knowledge that the ring was in effect stolen. The original owner is entitled to the ring's return, regardless of what the third party paid for it. Note that it is irrelevant whether the physical abuse is committed by a party to the contract or by a third person.

Duress by Threat

An improper threat that leaves no reasonable alternative and induces a person to assent to a contract renders the contract voidable. This rule contains a number of elements.

First, the threat must be *improper*. Second, there must be *no reasonable alternative*. If, for example, a supplier threatens to hold up shipment of necessary goods unless the buyer agrees to pay more than the contract price, this would not be duress if the buyer could purchase identical supplies from someone else. Third, the test for inducement is *subjective*. It does not matter that the person threatened is unusually timid or that a reasonable person would not have felt threatened. The question is whether the threat in fact induced assent by the victim. Such facts as the victim's belief that the threatener had the ability to carry out his threat and the length of time between the threat and assent are relevant in determining whether the threat did prompt the assent.

There are many types of improper threats: to commit a crime or a tort (for example, bodily harm or taking of property), to instigate criminal prosecution, to instigate civil proceedings when the threat is made in bad faith, and to breach a "duty of good faith and fair dealing under a contract with the recipient." (*Restatement (Second) of Contracts*, Section 176.) Having bought a lemon the day before from Mr. Oily, the local used car salesman, Jocko threatens to poison Oily if he does not buy it back for $150, the purchase price. The agreement is voidable, even though the underlying deal is fair, because Oily has no reasonable alternative and is in fact frightened into agreeing. Suppose Jocko knows that Oily has been tampering with his cars' odometers, a federal offense, and threatens to have Oily prosecuted if he will not repurchase the car. Even though Oily may be guilty, this threat makes the repurchase contract voidable, because it is a misuse for personal ends of a power (to go to the police) given each of us for other purposes. These threats having failed, suppose Jocko then tells Oily "I'm going to haul you into court and sue your pants off." If Jocko means he will sue for his purchase price, this is not an improper threat, because everyone has the right to use the courts to gain what they think is rightfully theirs. But if Jocko meant that he would fabricate damages done him by a (falsely) claimed faulty operation of the brakes, that would be an improper threat. Although Oily could defend against the suit, his reputation would suffer in the meantime from his being accused of selling a car without proper brakes.

A threat to breach a contract that induces the victim to sign a new contract could be improper. Suppose that as part of the original purchase price, Oily agrees to make all necessary repairs and replace all failed parts for the first ninety days. At the end of one month, the transmission dies, and Jocko demands a replacement. Oily refuses to repair the car unless Jocko signs a contract agreeing to buy his next car from Oily. Whether this threat is improper depends on whether Jocko has a reasonable alternative; if a replacement transmission is readily available and Jocko has the funds to pay for it, he might have an alternative in suing Oily in small claims court for the cost. But if Jocko needs the car immediately and he is impecunious, then the threat would be improper and the contract voidable. A threat to breach a contract is not necessarily improper, however. It depends on whether the new contract is fair and equitable because of unanticipated circumstances. If, for example, Oily discovers that he must purchase a replacement transmission at ten times the anticipated cost, his threat to hold up work unless Jocko agrees to pay for it might be reasonable.

UNDUE INFLUENCE

Undue influence is a milder form of duress than physical harm or threats. The Restatement characterizes it as "unfair persuasion." (*Restatement (Second) of Contracts*, Section 177.) The unfairness does not lie in any misrepresentation; rather, it occurs when the victim is under the domination of the persuader or is one who, in view of the relationship between them, is warranted in believing that the persuader will act in a manner detrimental to his welfare. Falling within this rule are such relations as husband and wife, physician and patient, lawyer and client, and parent and child. If there has been undue influence, the contract is voidable by the party who has been unfairly persuaded. Whether the relationship is one of domination and the persuasion is unfair is a factual question. The answer hinges on a host of variables, including "the unfairness of the resulting bargain, the unavailability of independent advice, and the susceptibility of the person persuaded." (*Restatement (Second) of Contracts*, Section 177, comment b.)

HODGE v. SHEA
252 So. Car. 601, 168
S.E.2d 82 (1969)

BRAILSFORD, JUSTICE. In this equitable action the circuit court decreed specific performance of a contract for the sale of land, and the defendant has appealed. The plaintiff is a physician, and the contract was prepared and executed in his medical office on August 19, 1965. The defendant had been plaintiff's patient for a number of years. On the contract date, he was seventy-five years of age, was an inebriate of long standing, and was afflicted by grievous chronic illnesses, including arteriosclerosis, cirrhosis of the liver, neuritises, arthritis of the spine and hip and varicose veins of the legs. These afflictions and others required constant medication and frequent medical attention, and rendered him infirm of body and mind, although not to the point of incompetency to contract.

During the period immediately before and after August 19, 1965, George A. Shea, the defendant, was suffering a great deal of pain in his back and hip and was having difficulty in voiding. He was attended professionally by the plaintiff, Dr. Joseph Hodge, either at the Shea home, at the doctor's office or in the hospital at least once each day from August 9 through August 26, 1965, except for August 17. The contract was signed during the morning of August 19. One of Dr. Hodge's frequent house calls was made on the afternoon of that day, and Mr. Shea was admitted to the hospital on August 21, where he remained until August 25.

Mr. Shea was separated from his wife and lived alone. He was dependent upon Dr. Hodge for house calls, which were needed from time to time. His relationship with his physician, who sometimes visited him as a friend and occasionally performed non-professional services for him, was closer than ordinarily arises from that of patient and physician.

* * *

A 125 acre tract of land near Mr. Shea's home, adjacent to land which was being developed as residential property, was one of his most valuable and readily salable assets. In 1962, the developer of this contiguous land had expressed to Mr. Shea an interest in it at $1000.00 per acre. A firm offer of this amount was made in November, 1964, and was refused by Mr. Shea on the advice of his son-in-law that the property was worth at least $1500.00 per acre. Negotiations between the developer and Mr. Ransdell commenced at that time and were in progress when Mr. Shea, at the instance of Dr. Hodge and without consulting Mr. Ransdell or anyone else, signed the contract of August 19, 1965. Under this contract Dr. Hodge claims the right to purchase twenty choice acres of the 125 acre tract for a consideration calculated by the circuit court to be the equivalent of $361.72 per acre. The

(continued on next page)

(continued)

HODGE v. SHEA
252 So. Car. 601, 168
S.E.2d 82 (1969)

market value of the land on the contract date has been fixed by an unappealed finding of the master at $1200.00 per acre.

* * *

The consideration was expressed in the contract between Dr. Hodge and Mr. Shea as follows:

> The purchase price being (Cadillac Coupe DeVille 6600) & $4000.00 Dollars, on the following terms: Dr. Joseph Hodge to give to Mr. George Shea a new $6600. coupe DeVille Cadillac which is to be registered in name of Mr. George A. Shea at absolutely no cost to him. In return, Mr. Shea will give to Dr. Joe Hodge his 1964 Cadillac coupe DeVille and shall transfer title of this vehicle to Dr. Hodge. Further, Dr. Joseph Hodge will pay to Mr. George A. Shea the balance of $4000.00 for the 20 acres of land described above subject to survey, title check, less taxes on purchase of vehicle.

* * *

The case at hand is attended by gross inadequacy of consideration, serious impairment of the grantor's mentality from age, intemperance and disease, and a confidential relationship between the grantee and grantor. Has the strong presumption of vitiating unfairness arising from this combination of circumstances been overcome by the evidence? We must conclude that it has not. The record is devoid of any evidence suggesting a reason, compatible with fairness, for Mr. Shea's assent to so disadvantageous a bargain. Disadvantageous not only because of the gross disparity between consideration and value, but because of the possibility that the sale would impede the important negotiations in which Mr. Ransdell was engaged. Unless his memory failed him, Mr. Shea knew that his son-in-law expected to sell the 125 acre tract for about $1500.00 per acre as an important step toward raising sufficient funds to satisfy the tax and judgment liens against the Shea property. These circumstances furnish strong evidence that Mr. Shea's assent to the contract, without so much as notice to Mr. Ransdell, was not the product of a deliberate exercise of an informed judgment.

* * *

Finally, on this phase of the case, it would be naive not to recognize that the 1965 Cadillac was used to entice a highly susceptible old man into a hard trade. Mr. Shea was fatuously fond of new Cadillacs, but was apparently incapable of taking care of one. His own 1964 model (he had also had a 1963 model) had been badly abused. According to Dr. Hodge, it "smelled like a toilet . . . had several fenders bumped, bullet holes in the top and the car was just filthy. . . . It was a rather foul car." There is no suggestion in the record that Dr. Hodge had any connection with an automobile business. Knowing the condition of Mr. Shea's car, his financial predicament and the activities of his son-in-law in his behalf, Dr. Hodge used the new automobile as a means of influencing Mr. Shea to agree to sell. The means was calculated to becloud Mr. Shea's judgment, and, under the circumstances, its use was unfair.

★   ★   ★

Reversed and remanded.

MISREPRESENTATION

Two Types of Fraud

An agreement in which the two parties have agreed about different things is usually a contradiction in terms. If the misunderstanding occurs because one of the parties has misrepresented some essential point under discussion, the other understandably will feel hoodwinked. Whether a contract formed under such circumstances is void, voidable, or valid depends on the nature of the misrepresentation and the intent with which it was made.

In general, the courts distinguish between what they term **fraud in the execution** and **fraud in the inducement.** When the "misrepresentation relates to the very nature of the proposed contract itself and not merely to one of its non-essential terms," the result is fraud in the execution and the contract is absolutely void. (*Restatement (Second) of Contracts*, Section 163, comment a.) The misrepresentation is said to prevent formation of the contract, because the duped party cannot effectively manifest assent to a contract whose essential terms he does not know. For example, Alphonse and Gaston decide to sign a written contract incorporating terms to which they have agreed. It is properly drawn up and Gaston reads it and approves it. Before he can sign it, however, Alphonse shrewdly substitutes a different version to which Gaston has not agreed. Gaston signs the substitute version. There is no contract. On the other hand, if the victim had the opportunity to learn the nature or essential elements of the contract and failed to do so before signing, the contract is not void (though it may be voidable, as we will see shortly). Thus, if Alphonse had prepared the original contract incorrectly but told Gaston that all was in order and that

he had no need to read it, and Gaston agreed to dispense with a reading although he could have examined it had he wished, a contract has been formed—though in some cases Gaston could later have it rescinded or reformed.

A misrepresentation that does not go to the core of the contract is said to be fraud in the inducement and renders the contract voidable at the option of the party who was misled. The misrepresentation need not in fact be fraudulent (that is, intentional); a material misrepresentation made out of ignorance is sufficient to upset the contract. This rule is subject to the important qualification that the party who was misled must have *relied* on the misrepresentation in assenting to the contract, and that reliance must be justified. We now turn to these key elements—false representation of fact, materiality, and justified reliance.

False Representation of Fact

The general rule is that any statement not in accord with the facts is a **misrepresentation.** Falsity does not depend on intent. A typist's unnoticed error in a letter (inadvertently omitting the word "not," for example, or transposing numbers) can amount to a misrepresentation on which the recipient may rely. A half-truth can amount to a misrepresentation, as, for example, when the seller of a hotel says that the income is from both permanent and transient guests but fails to disclose that the bulk of the income is from single-night stopovers by seamen using the hotel as a brothel. [Ikeda v. Curtis, 261 P.2d 684 (Wash. 1951).]

Another type of misrepresentation is **concealment,** an act that is equivalent to a statement that the facts are to the contrary and that serves to prevent the other party from learning the true statement of affairs. A common example is painting over defects in a building—by concealing the defects, the owner is misrepresenting the condition of his property. The act of concealment need not be direct; it may consist of sidetracking the other party from gaining the necessary knowledge by, for example, convincing a third person not to speak who has knowledge of the defect.

But regardless of the type, concealment is always a misrepresentation.

Finally, although generally the law imposes no obligation on anyone to speak out, **nondisclosure** of a fact can operate as a misrepresentation under certain circumstances. This occurs, for example, whenever the other party has erroneous information, or, as the following case shows, where the nondisclosure amounts to a failure to act in good faith.

REED v. KING
145 Cal. App.3d 261, 193
Cal. Rptr. 130 (1983)

BLEASE, ASSOCIATE JUSTICE.

In the sale of a house, must the seller disclose it was the site of a multiple murder? Dorris Reed purchased a house from Robert King. Neither King nor his real estate agents (the other named defendants) told Reed that a woman and her four children were murdered there ten years earlier. However, it seems "truth will come to light; murder cannot be hid long." (Shakespeare, Merchant of Venice, Act II, Scene II.) Reed learned of the gruesome episode from a neighbor after the sale. She sues seeking rescission and damages. King and the real estate agent defendants successfully demurred to her first amended complaint for failure to state a cause of action. Reed appeals the ensuing judgment of dismissal. We will reverse the judgment.

FACTS

We take all issuable facts pled in Reed's complaint as true. King and his real estate agent knew about the murders and knew the event materially affected the market value of the house when they listed it for sale. They represented to Reed the premises were in good condition and fit for an "elderly lady" living alone. They did not disclose the fact of the murders. At some point King asked a neighbor not to inform Reed of that event. Nonetheless, after Reed moved in neighbors informed her no one was interested in purchasing the house because of the stigma. Reed paid $76,000, but the house is only worth $65,000 because of its past.

★   ★   ★

Numerous cases have found non-disclosure of physical defects and legal impediments to use of real property are material. However, to our knowledge, no prior real estate sale case has faced an issue of nondisclosure of the kind presented here. Should this variety of ill-repute be required to be disclosed? Is this a circumstance where "non-disclosure of the fact amounts to a failure to act in good faith and in accordance with reasonable standards of fair dealing[?]" (Rest.2d Contracts, § 161, subd. (b).)

The paramount argument against an affirmative conclusion is it permits the camel's nose of unrestrained irrationality admission to the tent. If such an "irrational" consideration is permitted as a basis of rescission the stability of all conveyances will be seriously undermined. Any fact that might disquiet the enjoyment of some segment of the buying public may be seized upon by a disgruntled purchaser to void a bargain. In our view, keeping this genie in the bottle is not as difficult a task as these arguments assume. We do not view a decision allowing Reed to survive a demurrer in these unusual circumstances as endorsing the materiality of facts predicating peripheral, insubstantial, or fancied harms.

The murder of innocents is highly unusual in its potential for so disturbing buyers they may be unable to reside in a home where it has occurred. This fact may foreseeably deprive a buyer of the intended use of the purchase. Murder is not such a common occurrence that *buyers* should be charged with anticipating and discovering that disquieting possibility. Accordingly, the fact is not one for which a duty of inquiry and discovery can sensibly be imposed upon the buyer.

Reed alleges the fact of the murders has a quantifiable effect on the market value of the premises. We cannot say this allegation is inherently wrong and, in the pleading posture of the case, we assume it to be true. If information known or accessible only to the seller has a significant and measureable effect on market value and, as is alleged here, the seller is aware of this effect, we see no principled basis for making the duty to disclose turn upon the character of the information. Physical usefulness is not and never has been the sole criterion of valuation. Stamp collections and gold speculation would be insane activities if utilitarian considerations were the sole measure of value.

Reputation and history can have a significant effect on the value of realty. "George Washington slept here" is worth something, however physically inconsequential that consideration may be. Ill-repute or "bad will" conversely may depress the value of property. Failure to disclose such a negative fact where it will have a foreseeably depressing effect on income expected to be generated by a business is tortious. Some cases have held that *unreasonable* fears of the potential buying public that a gas or oil pipeline may rupture may depress the market value of land and entitle the owner to incremental compensation in eminent domain.

Whether Reed will be able to prove her allegation the decade-old multiple murder has a significant effect on market value we cannot determine. If she is able to do so by competent evidence she is entitled to a favorable ruling on the issues of materiality and duty to disclose. Her demonstration of objective tangible harm would still the concern that permitting her to go forward will open the floodgates to rescission on subjective and idiosyncratic grounds.

★   ★   ★

The judgment is reversed.

Sometimes a statement that is believed to be true at the time made, or was true, or was not believed to be material, turns out to have been false, or no longer true, or becomes material. In any one of these situations, failure to correct the erroneous impression is a nondisclosure that can invalidate the contract. For example, in idle chatter one day, Alphonse tells Gaston that he owns thirty acres of land. In fact, Alphonse owns only twenty-seven, but he decided to exaggerate a little. He meant no harm by it, since the conversation had no import. A year later, Gaston offers to buy the "thirty acres" from Alphonse, who does not correct the impression that Gaston has. The failure to speak is a nondisclosure that would allow Gaston to rescind a contract induced by his belief that he was purchasing thirty acres.

Materiality

Not every misrepresentation makes a contract voidable. The person making the misrepresentation must either intend to mislead or materially do so. A deliberate misrepresentation is *fraudulent* "if the maker intends his assertion to induce a party to manifest his assent and the maker (a) knows or believes that the assertion is not in accord with the facts, or (b) does not have the confidence that he states or implies in the truth of the assertion, or (c) knows that he does not have the basis that he states or implies for the assertion." (*Restatement (Second) of Contracts*, Section 162(1).) If the misrepresentation is fraudulent, the victim can avoid the contract, no matter the significance of the misrepresentation. However, as noted below, if a fraudulent misrepresentation is not material, it is unlikely that a victim will be able to prove reliance.

If a misrepresentation is not fraudulent, it cannot be the basis for rescission unless it is also material. A **material misrepresentation** is one that "would be likely to induce a reasonable person to manifest his assent" or that "the maker knows . . . would be likely to induce the recipient to do so." (*Restatement (Second) of Contracts*, Section 162(2).) An honestly mistaken statement that the house for sale was built in 1922 rather than 1923 would not be the basis for avoiding the contract, since it is not material, unless the seller knew that the buyer had sentimental or other reasons for purchasing a house built in 1922.

The question of intent often has practical consequences in terms of the remedy available to the plaintiff. If the misrepresentation is fraudulent, the plaintiff may, as an alternative to avoiding the contract, recover damages. As discussed in Chapter 15, some states would force the plaintiff to elect one of these two remedies, whereas other states would allow the plaintiff to pursue both remedies (although only one type of recovery would eventually be allowed). If the misrepresentation is not intentional, then the common law allowed the plaintiff only the remedy of rescission. But the UCC, Section 2-721, allows both remedies in contracts for the sale of goods, whether the misrepresentation is fraudulent or not, and does not require election of remedies.

Reliance

A party seeking to avoid a contract on the ground of misrepresentation must show that the misrepresentation induced his assent—that is, he relied on it. The **reliance** need not be solely on the false assertion; the defendant cannot win the case by demonstrating that the plaintiff would have assented to the contract even in the absence of the false assertion. It is sufficient to avoid the contract if the plaintiff weighed the assertion as one of the important factors leading him to make the contract, and believed it to be true. Alphonse tells Gaston, who is interested in buying his home, that he needs to paint his house only every fourth year. In fact, the paint peels immediately and he has had it repainted every spring. They discuss twenty other factors, including termites, heating bills, mortgage terms, plumbing, and the type of wood finishing, and Alphonse tells Gaston the truth about each of these. Nevertheless, Gaston may avoid the contract because the necessity of repainting is an important factor about which Alphonse deliberately misled him, and which Gaston included in the calculus that determined his decision to purchase the house.

Although materiality is not technically required whenever the misrepresentation is intentional, it is usually a crucial factor in determining whether the plaintiff did rely. Obviously, the more immaterial the false assertion, the less likely it is that the victim relied on it to his detriment. This is especially the case when the defendant knows that he does not have the basis that he states for an assertion but believes that the particular point is unimportant and therefore immaterial. Consequently, for practical purposes materiality is an important consideration in most cases.

Good-Faith Reliance   The person who asserts reliance to avoid a contract must have acted in good faith and reasonably in relying on the false assertion. Thus, if the victim failed to read documents given him that truly stated the facts, he cannot later complain that he relied on a contrary statement, as, for example, when the purchaser of a car dealership was told the inventory consisted of new cars, but the supporting papers, receipt of which he acknowledged, clearly stated how many miles each car had been driven.

[Schuler v. American Motors Sales Corp., 197 N.W.2d 493 (Mich. 1972).]

Ordinarily, the person relying on a statement need not verify it independently. However, if verification is relatively easy, or if the statement is one that concerns matters peculiarly within her purview, she may not be held to have justifiably relied on the other party's false assertion. Moreover, usually the rule of reliance applies to statements about past events or existing facts, not about the occurrence of events in the future.

Assertions of Opinion   Reliance on opinion, rather than on assertions of knowledge, is hazardous and generally not considered justifiable. If Jocko asks what condition the car is in that he wishes to buy, Mr. Oily's response of "great!" is not ordinarily a misrepresentation. As the *Restatement (Second) of Contracts* puts it: "The propensity of sellers and buyers to exaggerate the advantages to the other party of the bargains they promise is well recognized, and to some extent their assertions must be discounted." (Section 168, comment d.) Vague statements of quality, such as that a product is "good," ought suggest nothing other than that such is the personal judgment of the opinion holder.

Despite this general rule, there are certain exceptions that justify reliance on an opinion. These exceptions are for recipients who stand in a relation of trust to the person who asserts the opinion, whether because of a special relationship or because the opinion giver has special skills or knowledge about the subject matter, or for recipients who are particularly susceptible to misrepresentations. An old friend or sorority sister or neighbor who gives an opinion that would otherwise be permissible may make the contract voidable if the recipient was induced because of the relationship to rely on the opinion. Likewise, a dance studio proprietor who tells an elderly woman who has never danced before that she has "great dance potential" and that his studio can develop her into a "graceful dancer" has made an assertion that could justifiably induce her to sign up—and that would entitle her to rescind the contract later when she discovered the opinion's palpable falsity. Merely because someone is less astute than the one with whom she is bargaining does not give rise to a claim of justifiable reliance on an unwarranted opinion. But if the person is inexperienced and susceptible or gullible to blandishments, the contract can be voided, as illustrated in the following case.

VOKES v. ARTHUR MURRAY, INC.
212 So.2d 906 (Fla. 1968)

PIERCE, JUDGE. This is an appeal by Audrey E. Vokes, plaintiff below, from a final order dismissing with prejudice, for failure to state a cause of action, her fourth amended complaint, hereinafter referred to as plaintiff's complaint.

Defendant Arthur Murray, Inc., a corporation, authorizes the operation throughout the nation of dancing schools under the name of "Arthur Murray School of Dancing" through local franchised operators, one of whom was defendant J. P. Davenport whose dancing establishment was in Clearwater.

Plaintiff Mrs. Audrey E. Vokes, a widow of 51 years and without family, had a yen to be "an accomplished dancer" with the hopes of finding "new interest in life". So, on February 10, 1961, a dubious fate, with the assist of a motivated acquaintance, procured her to attend a "dance party" at Davenport's "School of Dancing" where she whiled away the pleasant hours, sometimes in a private room, absorbing his accomplished sales technique, during which her grace and poise were elaborated upon and her rosy future as "an excellent dancer" was painted for her in vivid and glowing colors. As an incident to this interlude, he sold her eight ½-hour dance lessons to be utilized within one calendar month therefrom, for the sum of $14.50 cash in hand paid, obviously a baited "come-on".

(continued on next page)

(continued)

VOKES v. ARTHUR MURRAY, INC.
212 So.2d 906 (Fla. 1968)

Thus she embarked upon an almost endless pursuit of the terpsichorean art during which, over a period of less than sixteen months, she was sold fourteen "dance courses" totalling in the aggregate 2302 hours of dancing lessons for a total cash outlay of $31,090.45, all at Davenport's dance emporium. All of these fourteen courses were evidenced by execution of a written "Enrollment Agreement—Arthur Murray's School of Dancing" with the addendum in heavy black print, "No one will be informed that you are taking dancing lessons. Your relations with us are held in strict confidence", setting forth the number of "dancing lessons" and the "lessons in rhythm sessions" currently sold to her from time to time, and always of course accompanied by payment of cash of the realm.

These dance lesson contracts and the monetary consideration therefor of over $31,000 were procured from her by means and methods of Davenport and his associates which went beyond the unsavory, yet legally permissible, perimeter of "sales puffing" and intruded well into the forbidden area of an undue influence, the suggestion of falsehood, the suppression of truth, and the free exercise of rational judgment, if what plaintiff alleged in her complaint was true. From the time of her first contact with the dancing school in February 1961, she was influenced unwittingly by a constant and continuous barrage of flattery, false praise, excessive compliments, and panegyric encomiums, to such extent it would be not only inequitable, but unconscionable, for a Court exercising inherent chancery power to allow such contracts to stand.

She was incessantly subjected to overreaching blandishment and cajolery. She was assured she had "grace and poise"; that she was "rapidly improving and developing in her dancing skill"; that the additional lessons would "make her a beautiful dancer, capable of dancing with the most accomplished dancers"; that she was "rapidly progressing in the development of her dancing skill and gracefulness", etc., etc. She was given "dance aptitude tests" for the ostensible purpose of "determining" the number of remaining hours instructions needed by her from time to time.

At one pont she was sold 545 additional hours of dancing lessons to be entitled to award of the "Bronze Medal" signifying that she had reached "the Bronze Standard", a supposed designation of dance achievement by students of Arthur Murray, Inc.

*   *   *

At another point, while she still had over 1,000 unused hours of instruction she was induced to buy 151 additional hours at a cost of $2,049.00 to be eligible for a "Student Trip to Trinidad", at her own expense as she later learned.

*   *   *

Finally, sandwiched in between other lesser sales promotions, she was influenced to buy an additional 481 hours of instruction at a cost of $6,523.81 in order to "be classified as a Gold Bar Member, the ultimate achievement of the dancing studio."

All the foregoing sales promotions, illustrative of the entire fourteen separate contracts, were procured by defendant Davenport and Arthur Murray, Inc., by false representations to her that she was improving in her dancing ability, that she had excellent potential, that she was responding to instructions in dancing grace, and that they were developing her into a beautiful dancer, whereas in truth and in fact she did not develop in her dancing ability, she had no "dance aptitude", and in fact had difficulty in "hearing the musical beat". The complaint alleged that such representations to her "were in fact false and known by the defendant to be false and contrary to the plaintiff's true ability, the truth of plaintiff's ability being fully known to the defendants, but withheld from the plaintiff for the sole and specific intent to deceive and defraud the plaintiff and to induce her in the purchasing of additional hours of dance lessons". It was averred that the lessons were sold to her "in total disregard to the true physical, rhythm, and mental ability of the plaintiff". In other words, while she first exulted that she was entering the "spring of her life", she finally was awakened to the fact there was "spring" neither in her life nor in her feet.

The complaint prayed that the Court decree the dance contracts to be null and void and to be cancelled, that an accounting be had, and judgment entered against the defendants "for that portion of the $31,090.45 not charged against specific hours of instruction given to the plaintiff". The Court held the complaint not to state a cause of action and dismissed it with prejudice. We disagree and reverse.

*   *   *

It is true that "generally a misrepresentation, to be actionable, must be one of fact rather than of opinion". But this rule has significant qualifications, applicable here. It does not apply where there is a fiduciary relationship between the parties, or where there has been some artifice or trick employed by the representor, or where the parties do not in general deal at "arm's length" as we understand the phrase, or where the representee does not have equal opportunity to become apprised of the truth or falsity of the fact represented. As stated by Judge Allen of this Court in Ramel v. Chasebrook Construction Company, Fla.App.1961, 135 So.2d 876:

> . . . A statement of a party having . . . superior knowledge may be regarded as a statement of fact although it would be considered as opinion if the parties were dealing on equal terms.

[Judgment reversed.]

Assertions of Law   Whether an assertion of law is an opinion or a statement of fact depends on the context. An assertion that "the city has repealed the sales tax" or that a court has cleared title to a parcel of land is a statement of fact; if such assertions are false, they are governed by the same rules that govern misrepresentations of fact generally. An assertion of the legal consequences of a given set of facts is generally an opinion on which the recipient relies at his peril, especially if both parties know or assume the same facts. Thus, if there is a lien on a house, the seller's statement that "the courts will throw it out, you won't be bothered by it" is an opinion, unless the seller knows that the courts will not rule as he says or is a lawyer or real estate broker, on whom a lay person may justifiably rely. (Assertions about foreign laws are generally held to be statements of fact, not opinion.)

Assertions of Intention   The law allows considerable leeway in the honesty of assertions of intention. The Restatement talks in terms of "a misrepresentation of intention . . . consistent with reasonable standards of fair dealing." (*Restatement (Second) of Contracts*, Section 171(1).) The right to misstate intentions is useful chiefly in the acquisition of land; the cases permit buyers to misrepresent the purpose of the acquisition so as not to arouse the suspicion of the seller that the land is worth considerably more than his asking price. To be a misrepresentation that will permit rescission, an assertion of intention must be false at the time made; that is, the person asserting an intention must not *then* have intended it. That later he does not carry out his stated intention is not proof that there was no intention at the time asserted. Moreover, to render a contract voidable, the false assertion of intention must be harmful in some way to other interests of the recipient. Thus, in the common example, the buyer of land tells the seller that he intends to build a residence on the lot but actually intends to put up a factory and has lied because he knows that otherwise the seller will not part with it because her own home is on an adjacent lot. The contract is voidable by the seller.

MISTAKE

In discussing fraud, we have considered the ways in which trickery by the other party makes a contract void or voidable. We now examine the ways in which the parties might "trick" themselves—by making assumptions that lead them mistakenly to believe that they have agreed to something they have not.

Mistake by One Party

Ordinarily, a contract is not voidable because one party has made a mistake about the subject matter. Mistakenly thinking that home use of video recorders has just been ruled unlawful and that they will no longer be available for sale, Linda offers Peter $1,500 for his machine, even though it is only worth $750, and Peter quickly accepts. The contract is not voidable. However, there is an exception to this rule if the mistake concerns a basic assumption and enforcement would be unconscionable or if the other party knew or had reason to know of the mistake or through his actions caused the mistake. Suppose Linda had offered $5,000 for the video recorder; a court might decide that enforcement of a contract with so large a discrepancy between price and worth would be unconscionable. Suppose Linda told Peter she understood that stores no longer were stocking video recorders, and Peter knew that she was wrong; again, the contract would be voidable if Peter kept silent or if he encouraged her in the belief in the first place. On the other hand, if the other party relies on the contract before the mistake is discovered, enforcement would not be unconscionable, even if it would be in the absence of reliance. If Peter, unaware of Linda's mistake, had used the contract for the payment of $5,000 as collateral for the purchase of property and signed an agreement, Linda could not avoid the contract.

This same rule, that one person's mistake will not invalidate the contract, is equally applicable when the mistake lies in a failure to read the written document. George offers to sell his car to Arthur, who believes that George is referring to his Mercedes. In fact, George intends to sell his Chevrolet and plainly states so in the written bill of sale. Arthur is so eager to purchase what he thinks is a Mercedes for a low price that he signs without reading. The court will hold Arthur to the contract because by signing he manifested assent to George's offer (on which George was entitled to rely), even though he did not, subjectively, assent to it.

Mutual Mistake

When both parties make a mistake about a basic assumption of the contract, it is voidable by the party who is adversely affected. The classic case was decided in 1864 when the buyer of cotton made an agreement to purchase 125 bales "to arrive ex Peerless from Bombay." Unbeknownst to the buyer and seller, there were two ships called *Peerless*, both sailing from Bombay. The ship the buyer had in mind was leaving in October; the seller was thinking of a ship called *Peerless* that would depart in December.

Figure 11-1   Mutual Mistake

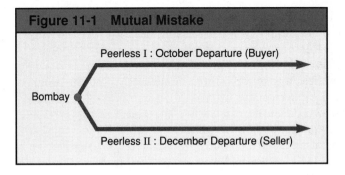

(See Figure 11-1.) The court ruled that there was no contract; since neither party was aware of the ambiguity, there was no common assent to the terms of the agreement. [Raffles v. Wichelhaus, 2 Hurlstone & Coltman 906 (1864).] Suppose, however, that the seller was aware of the ambiguity. Then there would be a contract, enforceable on the terms as understood by the buyer, who had no reason to know and did not in fact know of the ambiguity. Why? Because the seller could have clarified this crucial element of the contract but lazily (or shrewdly) did not.

The most difficult case is that which involves a mutual mistake about the subject matter of the contract. The difficulty lies in distinguishing between a mistake about the type of subject matter and a mistake as to its value. If both parties mistakenly believe they are negotiating for a specific kind of object, the contract can be avoided. Thinking that a collector owned a Stradivarius violin and a Guarnerius violin, Efrem Zimbalist, the renowned musician, offered him $8,000 for both; the collector, believing that the violins were genuine, accepted. Zimbalist took delivery, discovered they were not genuine, and refused to pay the balance of the purchase price. The collector sued and lost, because neither party had assented to the purchase or sale of ordinary violins. [Smith v. Zimbalist, 38 P.2d 170 (Colo. 1934).] (In an inflationary economy, the price of such mistakes has climbed precipitously: by the late 1970s a genuine Guarnerius violin was selling for $224,000.)

If, however, the object is of unknown value, there is no mutual mistake and the contract cannot be avoided. Assume a weekend browser sees a painting sitting on the floor of an antique shop. The owner says: "That old thing? You can have it for five bucks." The browser takes it home, dusts it off, and hangs it on the wall. A year later, a visitor, an expert in art history, recognizes the hanging as a famous lost El Greco worth $1 million. The story is headlined, the antique dealer is chagrined, and he claims the contract for sale should be voided because both parties mistakenly thought they were dickering over an "old, worthless" painting. The contract is valid because the parties in good faith assented to the sale and purchase of the particular painting, regardless of its value; in the violin case, the parties intended the sale of certain types of violins.

As the following case indicates, the law established in the *Peerless* case is still important today.

KONIC INTERNATIONAL v. SPOKANE COMPUTER SERVICES
109 Idaho 527, 708 P.2d 932 (1985)

WALTERS, CHIEF JUDGE.

The magistrate found the following facts. David Young, an employee of Spokane Computer, was instructed by his employer to investigate the possibility of purchasing a surge protector, a device which protects computers from damaging surges of electrical current. Young's investigation turned up several units priced from $50 to $200, none of which, however, were appropriate for his employer's needs. Young then contacted Konic. After discussing Spokane Computer's needs with a Konic engineer, Young was referred to one of Konic's salesmen. Later, after deciding on a certain unit, Young inquired as to the price of the selected item. The salesman responded, "fifty-six twenty." The salesman meant $5,620. Young in turn thought $56.20.

The salesman for Konic asked about Young's authority to order the equipment and was told that Young would have to get approval from one of his superiors. Young in turn prepared a purchase order for $56.20 and had it

(continued on next page)

(continued)

KONIC INTERNATIONAL v. SPOKANE COMPUTER SERVICES
109 Idaho 527, 708 P.2d 932 (1985)

approved by the appropriate authority. Young telephoned the order and purchase order number to Konic who then shipped the equipment to Spokane Computer. However, because of internal processing procedures of both parties the discrepancy in prices was not discovered immediately. Spokane Computer received the surge protector and installed it in its office. The receipt and installation of the equipment occurred while the president of Spokane Computer was on vacation. Although the president's father, who was also chairman of the board of Spokane Computer, knew of the installation, he only inquired as to what the item was and who had ordered it. The president came back from vacation the day after the surge protector had been installed and placed in operation and was told of the purchase. He immediately ordered that power to the equipment be turned off because he realized that the equipment contained parts which alone were worth more than $56 in value. Although the president then told Young to verify the price of the surge protector, Young failed to do so. Two weeks later, when Spokane Computer was processing its purchase order and Konic's invoice, the discrepancy between the amount on the invoice and the amount on the purchase order was discovered. The president of Spokane Computer then contacted Konic, told Konic that Young had no authority to order such equipment, that Spokane Computer did not want the equipment, and that Konic should remove it. Konic responded that Spokane Computer now owned the equipment and if the equipment was not paid for, Konic would sue for the price. Spokane Computer refused to pay and this litigation ensued.

Following trial, the magistrate found that Young had no actual, implied, or apparent authority to enter into the transaction and, therefore, Spokane Computer did not owe Konic for the equipment. In reaching its decision, the magistrate also noted that when Spokane Computer acquired full knowledge of the facts, it took prompt action to disaffirm Young's purchase.

*   *   *

Basically what is involved here is a failure of communication between the parties. A similar failure to communicate arose over 100 years ago in the celebrated case of *Raffles v. Wichelhaus*, 2 Hurl. 906, 159 Eng. Rep. 375 (1864) which has become better known as the case of the good ship "Peerless". In *Peerless*, the parties agreed on a sale of cotton which was to be delivered from Bombay by the ship "Peerless". In fact, there were two ships named "Peerless" and each party, in agreeing to the sale, was referring to a different ship. Because the sailing time of the two ships was materially different, neither party was willing to agree to shipment by the "other" Peerless. The court ruled that, because each party had a different ship in mind at the time of the contract, there was in fact no binding contract. The *Peerless* rule later was incorporated into section 71 of the RESTATEMENT OF CONTRACTS and has now evolved into section 20 of RESTATEMENT (SECOND) OF CONTRACTS (1981). Section 20 states in part:

(1)   There is no manifestation of mutual assent to an exchange if the parties attach materially different meanings to their manifestations and

(a)   neither knows or has reason to know the meaning attached by the other.

Comment (c) to section 20 further explains that "even though the parties manifest mutual assent to the same words of agreement, there may be no contract because of a material difference of understanding as to the terms of the exchange." Another authority, Williston, discussing situations where a mistake will prevent formation of a contract, agrees that "where a phrase of contract . . . is reasonably capable of different interpretations . . . there is no contract." 1 S. WILLISTON, CONTRACTS § 95 (3d ed. 1957).

★   ★   ★

In the present case, both parties attributed different meanings to the same term, "fifty-six twenty." Thus, there was no meeting of the minds of the parties. With a hundred fold difference in the two prices, obviously price was a material term. Because the "fifty-six twenty" designation was a material term expressed in an ambiguous form to which two meanings were obviously applied, we conclude that no contract between the parties was ever formed. [The lower court decision is affirmed.]

CAPACITY

A contract is a meeting of minds. If someone lacks mental **capacity** to understand what he is assenting to—or that he is assenting to anything—it is unreasonable to hold him to the consequences of his act. At common law there are various classes of people who are presumed to lack the requisite capacity. These include infants (minors), the mentally ill, and the intoxicated.

Minors

The general rule is that persons younger than eighteen can avoid their contracts. Although the age of majority was lowered in most states during the 1970s to correspond to the Twenty-sixth Amendment (ratified in 1971, guaranteeing the right to vote at eighteen), some states still put the age of majority at twenty-one. Legal rights for those under twenty-one remain ambiguous, however. Although eighteen-year-olds may assent to binding contracts, not all creditors and landlords believe it, and they may require parents to cosign. For those under twenty-one, there are also legal impediments to holding certain kinds of jobs, signing certain kinds of contracts, marrying, leaving home, and drinking alcohol. There is as yet no uniform set of rules.

The exact day on which the disability of minority vanishes also varies. The old common law rule put it on the day before the twenty-first birthday. Many states have changed this rule so that majority commences on the day of the eighteenth (or twenty-first) birthday.

A minor's contract is voidable, not void. A child wishing to avoid the contract need do nothing positive to disaffirm; the defense of minority to a lawsuit is sufficient. Although the adult cannot enforce the contract, the child can (which is why it is said to be voidable, not void).

When the minor becomes an adult, he has two choices: he may **ratify** the contract or **disaffirm** it. He may ratify explicitly; no further consideration is necessary. He may also do so by implication—for instance, by continuing to make payments or retaining goods for an unreasonable period of time. (In some states, a court may ratify the contract before the child becomes an adult. In California, for example, a state statute permits a movie producer to seek court approval of a contract with a child actor in order to prevent the child from disaffirming it upon reaching majority and suing for additional wages. As quid pro quo, the court can order the producer to pay a percentage of the wages into a trust fund that the child's parents or guardians cannot invade.) If the child has not disaffirmed the contract while still a minor, he may do so within a reasonable time after reaching majority.

In most cases of disavowal, the only obligation is to return the goods (if he still has them) or repay the consideration (unless it has been dissipated). However, in two situations, a minor might incur greater liability: contracts for necessities and misrepresentation of age.

Contract for Necessities   At common law, a "necessity" was defined as an essential need of a human being: food, medicine, clothing, and shelter. In recent years, however, the courts have expanded the concept, so that in many states today necessities include property and services that will enable the minor to earn a living and to provide for those dependent on him. If the contract is executory, the minor can simply disaffirm. If the contract has been executed, however, the minor must face more onerous consequences. Although he will not be required to perform under the contract, he will be liable under a theory of "quasi-contract" (Chapter 7) for the reasonable value of the necessity, as illustrated by the following case.

GASTONIA PERSONNEL CORP. v. ROGERS
276 N.C. 279, 172 S.E.2d 19 (1970)

Defendant had graduated from high school in 1966. On May 29, 1968, he was nineteen years old, emancipated and married. He needed only "one quarter or 22 hours" for completion of the courses required at Gaston Tech for an A.S. degree in civil engineering. His wife was employed as a computer programmer at First Federal Savings and Loan. He and she were living in a rented apartment. They were expecting a baby in September. Defendant had to quit school and go to work.

For assistance in obtaining suitable employment, defendant went to the office of plaintiff, an employment agency, on May 29, 1968. After talking with Maurine Finley, a personnel counselor, defendant signed a contract containing, *inter alia*, the following: "If I ACCEPT employment offered me by an employer as a result of a lead (verbal or otherwise) from you within twelve (12) months of such lead even though it may not be the position originally discussed with you, I will be obligated to pay you as per the terms of the contract." Under the contract, defendant was free to continue his own quest for employment. He was to become obligated to plaintiff only if he accepted employment from an employer to whom he was referred by plaintiff.

After making several telephone calls to employers who might need defendant's services as a draftsman, Mrs. Finley called Spratt-Seaver, Inc., in Charlotte, North Carolina. It was stipulated that defendant, as a result of his conversation with Mrs. Finley, went to Charlotte, was interviewed by Spratt-Seaver, Inc., and was employed by that company on June 6, 1968, at an annual salary of $4,784.00. The contract provided that defendant would pay plaintiff a service charge of $295.00 if the starting annual salary of accepted employment was as much as $4,680.00.

Prior to his contract with plaintiff, defendant had unsuccessfully sought employment with two other companies.

Plaintiff sued to recover a service charge of $295.00. In his answer, defendant admitted he had paid nothing to plaintiff; alleged he was not indebted to plaintiff in any amount; and, as a further answer and defense, pleaded his infancy. [The lower court granted defendant's motion to dismiss the case.]

The sole question presented is whether plaintiff offered evidence sufficient to withstand defendant's motion for nonsuit.

Under the common law, persons, whether male or female, are classified and referred to as *infants* until they attain the age of twenty-one years.

"By the fifteenth century it seems to have been well settled that an infant's bargain was in general void at his election (that is voidable), and also that he was liable for necessaries." 2 Williston, Contracts § 223 (3rd ed. 1959).

An early commentary on the common law, after the general statement that contracts made by persons (infants) before attaining the age of twenty-one "may be avoided," sets forth "some exceptions out of this generality," to wit: *"An infant may bind himselfe to pay for his necessary meat, drinke, apparell, necessary physicke, and such other necessaries, and likewise for his good teaching or instruction, whereby he may profit himselfe afterwards."* (Our italics.) Coke on Littleton, 13th ed. (1788), p. 172. The italicized portion of this excerpt from Coke on Littleton was quoted by Pearson, J. (later C. J.), in Freeman v. Bridger, 49 N.C. 1 (1856). It appears also in later decisions of this Court. If the infant married, "necessaries" included necessary food and clothing for his wife and child.

In accordance with this ancient rule of the common law, this Court has held an infant's contract, unless for "necessaries" or unless authorized by statute, is voidable by the infant, at his election, and may be disaffirmed during infancy or upon attaining the age of twenty-one.

*   *   *

This statement commands respect and approval: "Society has a moral obligation to protect the interests of infants from overreaching adults. But this protection must not become a straightjacket, stifling the economic and social advancement of infants who have the need and maturity to contract. Nor should infants be allowed to turn that protective legal shield into a weapon to wield against fair-dealing adults. It is in the interest of society to have its members contribute actively to the general economic and social welfare, if this can be accomplished consistently with the protection of those persons unable to protect themselves in the market place." Comment, Infants' Contractual Disabilities: Do Modern Sociological and Economic Trends Demand a Change in the Law? 41 Indiana Law Journal 140 et seq. (1965).

*   *   *

In general, our prior decisions are to the effect that the "necessaries" of an infant, his wife and child, include only such necessities of life as food, clothing, shelter, medical attention, etc. In our view, the concept of "necessaries" should be enlarged to include such articles of property and such services as are reasonably necessary to enable the infant to earn the money required to provide the necessities of life for himself and those who are legally dependent upon him.

(continued on next page)

*   *   *

(continued)

GASTONIA PERSONNEL CORP. v. ROGERS
276 N.C. 279, 172 S.E.2d 19 (1970)

The evidence before us tends to show that defendant, when he contracted with plaintiff, was nineteen years of age, emancipated, married, a high school graduate, within "a quarter or 22 hours" of obtaining his degree in applied science, and capable of holding a job at a starting annual salary of $4,784.00. To hold, as a matter of law, that such a person cannot obligate himself to pay for services rendered him in obtaining employment suitable to his ability, education and specialized training, enabling him to provide the necessities of life for himself, his wife and his expected child, would place him and others similarly situated under a serious economic handicap.

In the effort to protect "older minors" from improvident or unfair contracts, the law should not deny to them the opportunity and right to obligate themselves for articles of property or services which are reasonably necessary to enable them to provide for the proper support of themselves and their dependents. The minor should be held liable for the reasonable value of articles of property or services received pursuant to such contract.

Applying the foregoing legal principles, which modify *pro tanto* the ancient rule of the common law, we hold that the evidence offered by plaintiff was sufficient for submission to the jury for its determination of issues substantially as indicated below. [The lower court judgment is reversed.]

To establish liability, plaintiff must satisfy the jury by the greater weight of the evidence that defendant's contract with plaintiff was an appropriate and reasonable means for defendant to obtain suitable employment. If this issue is answered in plaintiff's favor, plaintiff must then establish by the greater weight of the evidence the reasonable value of the services received by defendant pursuant to the contract. Thus, plaintiff's recovery, if any, cannot exceed the reasonable value of its services to defendant.

Misrepresentation of Age   In most states, a minor may misrepresent his age and disaffirm in accordance with the general rule. That the adult reasonably believed the minor was also an adult is of no consequence in a contract suit. But some states have enacted statutes that make the minor liable in certain situations. A Michigan statute, for instance, prohibits a minor from disaffirming if he has signed a "separate instrument containing only the statement of age, date of signing and the signature." And some states "estop" him from claiming to be a minor if he falsely represented himself as an adult in making the contract. "Estoppel" is a refusal by the courts on equitable grounds to listen to an otherwise valid defense; unless the minor can return the consideration, the contract will be enforced.

Furthermore, the general rule is that minors are liable for their torts (for example, assault, trespass, nuisance) unless the tort suit is only an indirect method of enforcing the contract. This means in most states that the minor who has misrepresented his age can be sued for deceit; the remedy is not enforcement of the contract but recompense for the injuries caused by the fraud. As William Prosser, the noted torts scholar, said of cases to the contrary: "The effect of the decisions refusing to recognize tort liability for misrepresentation is to create a privileged class of liars who are a great trouble to the business world" (1971, p. 999).

Persons Who Are Mentally Ill

If a guardian has been legally appointed for a person who is mentally ill, any contract made by the latter is void and cannot be enforced or subsequently ratified.

This is true even though the other party may have no knowledge or reason to know of the guardianship. However, if the contract was for a necessity, the other party may have a valid claim against the estate of the one who is mentally ill in order to prevent unjust enrichment.

In other cases, whether a court will enforce a contract made with a person who is mentally ill depends on the circumstances; only if the mental illness impairs the competence of the person in the particular transaction can the contract be avoided. Upon avoidance, the mentally ill person must return any property in his possession. And if the contract was fair and the other party had no knowledge of the mental illness, the court has the power to order other relief.

Intoxicated Persons

If a person is so drunk that he has no awareness of his acts and the other person knows this, there is no contract. The intoxicated person is obligated to refund the consideration to the other party unless he dissipated it during his drunkenness. If the other person is unaware of his intoxicated state, however, an offer or acceptance of fair terms manifesting assent is binding.

If a person is only partially inebriated and has some understanding of his actions, "avoidance depends on a showing that the other party induced the drunkenness or that the consideration was inadequate or that the transaction departed from the normal pattern of similar transactions; if the particular transaction is one which a reasonably competent person might have made, it cannot be avoided even though entirely executory." (*Restatement (Second) of Contracts*, Section 16, comment b.)

Convicts

By statute in a few states, persons incarcerated in jail for conviction of crime lack capacity to form contracts. This is a result of the general suspension of civil rights, including the right to vote, imposed as a sanction on the convict, and not a comment on the mental competence of those serving time.

Married Women

At common law, married women were deemed to be lacking in the capacity to contract. This conclusion stemmed from the archaic belief that the woman was "owned" by her husband. Today, statutes in all states give married women full power to make contracts and to incur full liability in doing so.

CHAPTER SUMMARY

No agreement is enforceable if the parties did not enter into it (1) of their own free will, (2) with adequate knowledge of the terms, and (3) with the mental capacity to appreciate the relationship.

Contracts coerced through duress will void a contract if actually induced through physical harm and will make the contract voidable if entered under the compulsion of many types of threats. The threat must be improper, and leave no reasonable alternative, but the test is subjective—what did the person threatened actually fear—and not what a more reasonable person might have feared.

Misrepresentations may render an agreement void or voidable. Coming to grips with the rules relating to false representations, with all their nuances, is an important task for the student of contract law. Among the factors to be considered are whether the misrepresentation was deliberate and material. Other important factors are whether the promisee relied on the misrepresentation in good faith, whether the representation was of fact, opinion, or intention, and whether the parties had a special relationship.

Similarly, mistaken beliefs, not induced by misrepresentations, may suffice to avoid the bargain. Some mistakes on one side only make a contract voidable. More often, mutual mistakes of facts will show that there was no meeting of the minds. But the particulars of each case are exceedingly important in making such a determination.

Those who lack capacity are often entitled to avoid contract liability. Although it is possible to state the general rule, many exceptions exist—for example, in contracts for necessities, minors will be liable for the reasonable value of the goods purchased.

KEY TERMS

Capacity	p. 271	Fraud in the induce-	p. 261
Concealment	p. 261	ment	
Disaffirm	p. 271	Material misrepresen-	p. 264
Fraud in the execution	p. 261	tation	

SELF-TEST-QUESTIONS

1. Misrepresentation that does not go to the core of a contract is:
   (a) fraud in the execution
   (b) fraud in the inducement
   (c) undue influence
   (d) an example of mistake

2. In order for a misrepresentation to make a contract voidable:
   (a) there must be no intent to mislead
   (b) the party seeking to void must have relied on the misrepresentation
   (c) both of the above are required
   (d) none of the above is required

3. A mistake by one party will not invalidate a contract unless:
   (a) the other party knew of the mistake
   (b) the party making the mistake did not read the contract closely
   (c) the parties to the contract had never done business before
   (d) the party is mistaken about the law

4. Upon reaching the age of majority, a person who entered into a contract to purchase goods while a minor may:
   (a) ratify the contract and keep the goods without paying for them
   (b) disaffirm the contract and keep the goods without paying for them
   (c) avoid paying for the goods by keeping them without ratifying or disaffirming the contract
   (d) disaffirm the contract and return the goods even though he lied about his age

5. Today in some states a woman lacks capacity to form contracts if she:
   (a) is married
   (b) is a convict
   (c) marries a convict
   (d) is 21 but misrepresents her age as 17

DEMONSTRATION PROBLEM

At the end of the term Oswald, a senior at Big U, decided to sell his business law textbook. He spotted Primrose, a gullible freshman, in the library and made the following statement: "I offer you my business law notes for $12." Primrose accepted the offer. Oswald then realized that he had made a mistake in that he had offered his notes when he meant to offer his book. Primrose refused to accept the book and, when Oswald did not deliver the notes, sued him for breach of contract. Will Primrose prevail? Why?

PROBLEMS

1. Chauncey, a college student, worked part-time in a restaurant. After he had worked for several months, the owner of the restaurant discovered that Chauncey had stolen $2,000 from the cash register. The owner immediately called Chauncey's parents and told them that, if they did not sign a note for $2,000, he would initiate criminal proceedings against Chauncey. The parents signed and delivered the note to the owner but later refused to pay. May the owner collect on the note? Why?

2. Marie circulated a petition to abolish grades at Big U. Donny eagerly signed the petition. Unknown to Donny, Marie had cleverly concealed a contract beneath the petition and Donny, in fact, had signed the contract rather than the petition. The contract provided that Donny would pay Marie $5,000 a year for the rest of her life. Discuss the legal effect of the contract.

3. A restaurant advertised a steak dinner that included a "juicy, great-tasting steak, a fresh crisp salad, and a warm roll." After reading the ad, Clarence visited the restaurant and ordered the steak dinner. The steak was dry and tasted awful, the lettuce in the salad was old and limp, and the roll was frozen. May Clarence recover from the restaurant on the basis of fraud? Why?

4. Bert purchased Ernie's car. Before selling the car, Ernie had stated to Bert: "This car runs well. Last week I drove the car all the way from Chicago to San Francisco to visit my mother and back again to Chicago." In fact, Ernie was lying—he had driven the car to San Francisco to visit his paramour, not his mother. Upon discovery of the truth, may Bert avoid the contract? Why?

5. Randolph enrolled in a business law class and purchased a new business law textbook from the local bookstore. He dropped the class during the first week and sold the book to his friend Scott. Before making the sale, Randolph told Scott that he had purchased the book new and had owned it for one week. Unknown to either Randolph or Scott, the book was in fact a used one. Scott later discovered some underlining in the middle of the book and attempted to avoid the contract. Randolph refused to refund the purchase price, claiming that he had not intentionally deceived his friend. May Scott avoid the contract? Why?

6. Mary decided to purchase a house. Larry, the owner, told Mary that the annual property taxes on the house were $2,000. Mary bought the house and, when she received

her first tax bill, discovered that the annual taxes were (and always had been) $3,500. She cannot afford the additional $1,500 and now seeks to avoid the contract on grounds of fraud. Larry, who admitted that he had deliberately lied, claimed that Mary could not avoid the contract. What argument could Larry make to support his claim?

7. Duke decided to sell his car. The car's muffler had a large hole in it and, as a result, the car sounded like an airplane when Duke drove it. Before showing the car to potential buyers, Duke covered the hole with muffler tape in order to quiet the noise. Perry bought the car after test-driving it. He later discovered the faulty muffler and sought to avoid the contract, claiming fraud. Duke argued that he had not committed fraud because Perry had not asked about the muffler and Duke had made no representation of fact concerning it. Is Duke correct? Why?

ANSWERS TO SELF-TEST QUESTIONS

1. (b)   2. (b)   3. (a)   4. (d)   5. (b)

SUGGESTED ANSWER TO DEMONSTRATION PROBLEM

Primrose will probably prevail. Although there are exceptions, the general rule is that a contract is not avoidable because one party (Oswald) has made a mistake in manifesting assent.

CHAPTER 12

Form and Meaning

*I*n the first five chapters of the contracts unit, we have focused on the question of whether the parties created a valid contract and have examined the requirements of agreement, consideration, legality, free will, knowledge, and capacity. Assuming that these requirements have been met, we now turn to the form and meaning of the contract itself. Our focus here will be on three issues:

1. When must contracts be in writing?
2. If the contract is written, what effect does the writing have on prior or contemporaneous "side" agreements?
3. In case its meaning is disputed, how is the contract to be interpreted?

THE STATUTE OF FRAUDS

As a general rule, a contract need not be in writing to be enforceable (see **Box 12-1**). An oral agreement to pay a high-fashion model $1 million to pose for a photograph is as binding as if the language of the deal were printed on vellum and signed in the presence of twenty bishops. For three centuries, however, a large exception grew up around the Statute of Frauds, first enacted in England in 1677 under the formal name "An Act for the Prevention of Frauds and Perjuries." The two sections dealing with contracts read as follows:

[Sect. 4] . . . no action shall be brought whereby to charge any executor or administrator upon any special promise, to answer damages out of his own estate; (2) or whereby to charge the defendant upon any special promise to answer for the debt, default or miscarriages of another person; (3) or to charge any person upon any agreement made upon consideration of marriage; (4) or upon any contract or sale of lands, tenements or hereditaments, or any interest in or concerning them; (5) or upon any agreement that is not to be performed within the space of one year from the making thereof; (6) unless the agreement upon which such action shall be brought, or some memorandum or note thereof, shall be in writing, and signed by the party to be charged therewith, or some other person thereunto by him lawfully authorized.

[Sect. 17] . . . no contract for the sale of any goods, wares and merchandizes, for the price of ten pounds sterling or upwards, shall be allowed to be good, except the buyer shall accept part of the goods so sold, and actually

LAW AND LIFE

BOX 12-1

The Tripple Ripple Ice Cream Case

By Jill Andresky

*[Many types of oral contracts are enforceable. The following article describes a multi-million dollar oral contract that was enforceable. As this article illustrates, all agreements should be in writing, even when not required by law.—*AUTHORS' NOTE]

In the autumn of 1970 McDonald's Corp. founder and Chairman Ray Kroc came up with what he thought was one great idea. Along with Big Macs and fries, he wanted to sell combinations of vanilla, chocolate and strawberry ice cream in special, slow-dripping cones. No such cone existed at the time, so Kroc contacted Tom Cummings, the son of an old friend, whose Central Ice Cream Co. produced ice cream pops for Chicago's zoo and hospitals, and asked him to design one.

Since no contract was ever written and signed, what happened next has been debated for over 15 years. According to Cummings, Kroc promised him that if Central's "Tripple Ripple" cone passed McDonald's taste test, the fast-food chain would carry it exclusively for 20 years. McDonald's claims there was no exclusive long-term agreement, and, accordingly, the chain phased out Tripple Ripple after it bombed with customers after several years on the menu. Central Ice Cream Co., which

ARE ORAL CONTRACTS ENFORCEABLE?

had borrowed heavily to upgrade for the production of the cones, headed into Chapter 11. Cummings sued, and after a decade and a half of dispute, Central Ice Cream finally won and now stands to collect $15.5 million in damages for breach of contract and fraud.

Central Ice Cream won because Kroc and McDonald's lost sight of a basic legal principle that can cost businessmen dearly if ignored: Many business contracts do not have to be written down to be enforceable. In much the same way that Texaco was found last year to have induced Getty Oil to break an oral agreement to merge with Pennzoil, and thus wound up being hit with $10.5 billion in trial court damages, McDonald's was found to have induced Central Ice Cream to invest in reliance on a promise that McDonald's disavowed.

"Often these kinds of disputes boil down to whether you believe Sam or Joe," says Klaus Eppler, a senior partner at Proskauer Rose Goetz & Mendelsohn and an authority on contract law. "But in each case there's always the issue of whether the type of oral contract involved is as enforceable as a written one would have been, and that differs from state to state."

Generally, oral or written short-

term contracts worth only small sums of money are equally binding. Lawyers have to prove either that both parties agreed to the contract or that one party made an offer and the other party acted in reliance on it. But when contracts are worth more than $500, the Uniform Commercial Code, used in every state with minor variations, requires that agreements be in writing unless both parties admit that an oral contract existed. Moreover, the UCC holds that once a written agreement does exist, its terms supersede any past or future oral understandings on the matter.

In the Tripple Ripple case, it was up to Theodore Becker, Central Ice Cream's attorney, to prove that McDonald's admitted an oral contract existed. A Cook County, Ill. jury bought his argument. What swayed them? The fact that the two companies had been doing business for three years. "The law is full of a lot of mumbo jumbo about when your oral agreement qualifies as a contract," Becker says. "But in my experience, juries make their decisions based on whether they think bad faith was involved in the agreement." Stunned by a $52 million trial court award, McDonald's offered to settle for $15.5 million, which has been accepted.

*   *   *

When it comes to oral contracts at least, the lesson should be clear: Think before you speak. Better yet, commit your agreement to paper.

Source: *Forbes*, August 25, 1986

receive the same, or give something in earnest to bind the bargain, or in part of payment, or that some note or memorandum in writing of the said bargain be made and signed by the parties to be charged by such contract, or their agents thereunto lawfully authorized.

As may be evident from the title of the act and its language, the general purpose of the law is to provide evidence, in areas of some complexity and importance, that a contract was actually made. To a lesser degree, the law serves to caution those about to enter a contract and "to create a climate in which parties often regard their agreements as tentative until there is a signed writing." (*Restatement (Second) of Contracts* Chapter 5, statutory note.)

The Statute of Frauds has been enacted in form similar to the seventeenth-century act in every state but Maryland and New Mexico, where judicial decisions have given it legal effect, and in Louisiana. With minor exceptions in Minnesota, Wisconsin, North Carolina, and Pennsylvania, the laws all embrace the same categories of contracts that are required to be in writing (see Figure 12-1). Early in the century, Section 17 was replaced by a section of the Uniform Sales Act, and this in turn has now been replaced by provisions in the Uniform Commercial Code.

Today the Statute of Frauds is used as a technical defense in many contract actions, often with unfair results. Consequently, courts interpret the law strictly and over the years have enunciated a host of exceptions—making what appears to be simple quite complex. Indeed, after more than half a century of serious scholarly criticism, the British Parliament repealed most of the statute in 1954. As early as 1885, a British judge noted that "in the vast majority of cases [the statute's] operation is simply to enable a man to break a promise with impunity because he did not write it down with sufficient formality." A proponent of the repeal said on the floor of the House of Commons that "future students of law will, I hope, have their labours lightened by the passage of this measure." In the United States, students have no such reprieve from the Statute of Frauds, to which we now turn for examination in detail.

Types of Contracts Required in Writing

Promises to Pay Debt of Another   A promise to pay the debt of another person must be in writing if (1) the other person is obligated to a third person, (2) the promise runs to the third person in the event of the other's default, and (3) the third person knows or has reason to know of the promise. This is the **suretyship** provision of the Statute of Frauds. A surety is one who is bound to pay the debt of another, who nevertheless remains primarily liable to the third-person promisee. Unless the promise is made to the third person, however, the promisor is not a surety, and an oral promise is binding.

Some examples may make the point clearer. Suppose Lydia wishes to purchase on credit a coat at Miss Juliette's Fine Furs. Juliette thinks Lydia's creditworthiness is somewhat shaky. So Lydia's friend Jessica promises Miss Juliette's that if the store will extend Lydia credit, Jessica will pay whatever balance is due should Lydia default. Jessica is a surety for Lydia, and the agreement is subject to the Statute of Frauds; an oral promise will not be enforceable. Suppose Jessica very much wants Lydia to have the coat, so she calls the store and says: "Send Lydia the fur and I will pay for it." This agreement does not create a suretyship, because Jessica is primarily liable. To fall within the Statute of Frauds, the surety must back the debt of another person to a third-party promisee (also known as the obligee of the principal debtor). The "debt," incidentally, need not be a money obligation; it can be any contractual duty. If Lydia had promised to work as a cashier on Saturdays at Miss Juliette's in return for the coat, Jessica could

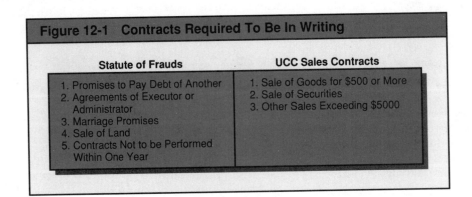

Figure 12-1 Contracts Required To Be In Writing	
Statute of Frauds	**UCC Sales Contracts**
1. Promises to Pay Debt of Another 2. Agreements of Executor or Administrator 3. Marriage Promises 4. Sale of Land 5. Contracts Not to be Performed Within One Year	1. Sale of Goods for $500 or More 2. Sale of Securities 3. Other Sales Exceeding $5000

become surety to that obligation by agreeing to work in Lydia's place if she failed to turn up. Such a promise would need to be in writing to be enforceable.

There is, however, a major exception to the surety provision of the Statute of Frauds: the **main purpose rule.** It holds that if the promisor's principal reason for acting as surety is to secure her own economic advantage, then the agreement is not bound by the Statute of Frauds writing requirement. Suppose, in the previous example, that Jessica is really the one who wants the fur coat but cannot, for reasons of prudence, let it be known that she has bought one. So she proposes that Lydia "buy" it for her and that she will guarantee Lydia's payments. Since the main purpose of Jessica's promise is to advance her own interests, an oral agreement is binding. Normally the main purpose rule comes into play when the surety desires a financial advantage to herself that cannot occur unless she provides some security. For example, the board chairman of a small company, who also owns all of the voting stock, might guarantee a printer that if his company defaulted in paying the bill for desperately needed catalogues, he would personally pay the bill. If his main purpose in giving the guarantee was to get the catalogues printed in order to stave off bankruptcy, and thus to preserve his own interest in the company, he would be bound by an oral agreement. [Stuart Studio, Inc. v. National School of Heavy Equipment, Inc., 214 S.E.2d 192 (N.C. 1975).] The same principle can be used to bind other creditors to oral agreements, as the bank discovered in the following case.

WILSON FLOORS CO. v. SCIOTA PARK, LTD.
54 Ohio St.2d 451, 377 N.E.2d 514 (1978)

In December of 1971, Wilson Floors Company (hereinafter "Wilson") entered into a contract with Unit, Inc. (hereinafter "Unit"), a Texas corporation, to furnish and install flooring materials for "The Cliffs" project, a development consisting of new apartments and an office building to be located in Columbus, Ohio. Sciota Park, Ltd., a Texas limited partnership, was the owner of the project. Unit, the general partner of Sciota Park, Ltd., was the general contractor for the project. The Pittsburgh National Bank (hereinafter the bank), as the construction lender for the project, held mortgages on The Cliffs property as security for construction loans which the bank had made to Sciota.

As the work progressed on the project Unit fell behind in making payments to Wilson for its completed work in the spring of 1973. At that time, the project was approximately two-thirds completed, the first mortgage money of seven million dollars having been fully dispersed by the bank to Sciota. Appellant thereupon stopped work in May of 1973 and informed Unit that it would not continue until payments were forthcoming. On May 15, 1973, the bank conducted a meeting with the subcontractors in The Cliffs project, including Wilson.

At the meeting, the bank sought to determine whether it would be beneficial at that stage of the project to lend more money to Sciota, foreclose on the mortgage and hire a new contractor to complete the work, or do nothing. Subcontractors were requested to furnish the bank an itemized account of what Unit owed them, and a cost estimate of future services necessary to complete their job contracts. Having reviewed the alternatives, the bank determined that it would be in its best interest to provide additional financing

(continued on next page)

(continued)

WILSON FLOORS CO. v. SCIOTA PARK, LTD.

54 Ohio St.2d 451, 377 N.E.2d 514 (1978)

for the project. The bank reasoned that to foreclose on the mortgage and hire a new contractor at this stage of construction would result in higher costs.

There is conflicting testimony in regard to whether the bank made assurances to Wilson at this meeting that it would be paid for all work to be rendered on the project. However, after the May meeting, Wilson, along with the other subcontractors, did return to work.

Payments from Unit again were not forthcoming, resulting in a second work stoppage. The bank then arranged another meeting to be conducted on June 28, 1973.

At this second meeting, there is conflicting testimony concerning the import of the statements made by the bank representative to the subcontractors. The bank representative who spoke at the meeting testified at trial that he had merely advised the subcontractors that adequate funds would be available to complete the job. However, two representatives of Wilson, also in attendance at the meeting, testified that the bank representative had assured Wilson that if it returned to work, it would be paid.

After the meeting, Wilson returned to work and continued to submit its progress billings to Unit for payment. Upon completion of its portion of The Cliffs project, Wilson submitted its final invoice of $15,584.50 to Unit. This amount was adjusted downward to $15,443.06 upon agreement of Unit and Wilson. However, Wilson was not paid this amount.

As a result of nonpayment, Wilson filed suit in the Court of Common Pleas of Franklin County against Unit, Sciota Park, Ltd., and the bank to recover the $15,443.06. On September 26, 1975, Wilson, Unit, and Sciota stipulated that judgment for the sum of $15,365.84, plus interest, be entered against Unit and Sciota. When Unit and Sciota failed to satisfy the judgment, appellant proceeded with its action against the bank. [The trial court decided in favor of Wilson, but the intermediate appellate court reversed the trial court decision.]

*   *   *

No action shall be brought whereby to charge the defendant, upon a special promise, to answer for the debt, default, or miscarriage of another person . . . unless the agreement upon which such action is brought, or some memorandum or note thereof, is in writing and signed by the party to be charged therewith or some other person thereunto by him or her lawfully authorized.

In paragraph one of the syllabus in *Crawford* v. *Edison* (1887), 45 Ohio St. 239, however, this court stated:

When the leading object of the promisor is, not to answer for another, but to subserve some pecuniary or business purpose of his own, involving a benefit to himself, or damage to the other contracting party, his promise is not within the statute of frauds, although it may be in form a promise to pay the debt of another and its performance may incidentally have the effect of extinguishing that liability.

*   *   *

Because it is unquestioned that the bank in the instant cause did not become primarily liable when it guaranteed the subcontractors that they would be paid, the court must apply the second test set forth in *Crawford* to determine the enforceability of the verbal agreement.

Under the second test, it is of no consequence that when such promise is made, the original obligor remains primarily liable or that the third party continues to look to the original obligor for payment. So long as the promisor undertakes to pay the subcontractor whatever his services are worth irrespective of what he may owe the general contractor, and so long as the main purpose of the promisor is to further his own business or pecuniary interest, the promise is enforceable. See 3 Williston on Contracts (3 Ed. 1960), 466–467, Section 481. Thus, under this test it is not required to show as a condition precedent for enforceability of the oral contract that the original debt is extinguished.

The facts in the instant cause reflect that the bank made its guarantee to Wilson to subserve its own business interest of reducing costs to complete the project. Clearly, the bank induced Wilson to remain on the job and rely on its credit for future payments. To apply the statute of frauds and hold that the bank had no contractual duty to Wilson despite its oral guarantees would not prevent the wrong which the statute's enactment was to prevent, but would in reality effectuate a wrong.

Therefore, this court affirms the finding of the Court of Common Pleas that the verbal agreement made by the bank is enforceable by Wilson, and reverses the judgment of the Court of Appeals.

Besides the main purpose rule, there is another seeming exception to the surety provision. A promise to the promisee to discharge a debt that is owed a third party need not be in writing. Suppose Miss Juliette's Fine Furs was willing to grant credit, but Lydia was unsure whether she could afford a coat. Jessica's oral promise to Lydia to pay the balance due, in return for a chance to wear the fur, does not make Jessica a surety, since she has no agreement with the store. The contract is binding, therefore, even though unwritten. Contracts to discharge the promisee's duty are not really exceptions to the surety provision because, as in this example, the promisor is not in fact a surety.

Agreements of Executor or Administrator   This section of the Statute of Frauds is analogous to the surety provision. An executor or administrator of the estate of a deceased will not be bound by an oral agreement to answer personally for the debt or other duty of the deceased. For an agreement to be covered by the statute, there must have been an obligation before the decedent's death. Thus, if the executor arranges for a funeral and guarantees payment should the estate fail to pay the fee, an oral contract is binding, because there was no pre-existing obligation. If, however, the decedent has made his own arrangements and signed a note obligating his estate to pay, the executor's promise to guarantee payment would be binding only if written. The main purpose exception to the surety provision applies to this section as well.

The Marriage Provision   If any part of the consideration for a promise is marriage or the promise to marry, the Statute of Frauds requires it to be in writing. The only exception is an agreement consisting only of mutual promises to marry. Thus if John proposes and Sally accepts one evening while staring into the sunset and Sally subsequently fails to appear at the last minute at the wedding held during the light of day, John may sue for breach of contract.

However, when the promise to marry carries with it other promises, usually those concerning property settlements, they must be in writing. John tells Sally that if she will marry him, he will give her title to his mansion. Sally accepts. After the marriage, John refuses to sign over the deed. Sally is stuck, unless she had John's promise in writing. The Statute of Frauds governs such promises regardless of who makes them. Suppose John's father had said, "If you marry Sally and settle down, I will give you $1 million," and John agrees and marries Sally. The father's promise is not enforceable unless written. On the other hand, a promise that is merely *conditional* on marriage does not fall within the Statute of Frauds. John's father and Sally's father pledge to each other that if their children marry, the two fathers will each give a wedding present of $50,000. Since in this case marriage is not a consideration for either promise (the promises are consideration for each other), the agreement is not within the Statute of Frauds and the fathers' oral pledges are binding.

That a marriage has actually taken place does not give extra force to an oral agreement subject to the Statute of Frauds, even if one party entered the marriage in reliance on the agreement. That John actually married Sally does not allow her to enforce an oral promise to transfer to her the deed to his house. However, if there has been additional reliance beyond the fact of marrying, an oral contract may be enforceable despite the statute. If John had promised Sally that he would give her the house and that Sally's mother could live with them, Sally could hold John to his promise upon a showing that her mother had sold her own home and furniture and moved across the country to take up her new residence. (Note that although written marriage contracts—especially those spelling out the duties of husband and wife—have become more popular in recent years, enforcement problems remain; as noted in Chapter 10, public policy continues to prohibit contracts that impair family relations even though the requirements of the Statute of Frauds have been met.)

Sale of Land   All "interests" in land are subject to the Statute of Frauds. An interest in land is a broad

term, to be explored at greater length in Chapter 31. In general, it includes the sale, mortgaging, and leasing of real property (including homes and buildings), profits from the land, the creation of easements, and the establishment of other interests through restrictive covenants and agreements concerning use. However, not every promise that concerns real property must necessarily be in writing to be enforceable. A license to use land can be granted orally—for example, an agreement that the owner will rent a wall for an advertisement for $100 for one month. Short-term leases, usually for a term of one year or less, are also exempt from the provision. In most states, a one-year oral lease is binding even though it may not start until some time after the contract is made.

One major exception to the land provision is the **part performance doctrine.** The name is a misnomer, since it is a doctrine of reliance, and the acts taken in reliance on the contract are not necessarily partial performances under it. As in all such cases, the rationale is that it is unjust not to give the promisee specific performance if he acted in reasonable reliance on the contract and the promisor has continued to manifest assent to its terms. An oral contract to sell land is not binding simply because the buyer has paid the purchase price; payment is not by itself reliance, and if the seller refuses to transfer title, the buyer may recover the purchase price. However, if the buyer has taken possession and made improvements on the property, courts will usually enforce the contract.

The One-Year Rule   Included within the Statute of Frauds is "any agreement that is not to be performed within the space of one year from the making thereof." This language has been universally interpreted to mean a contract that is *impossible* to be fully performed within one year; if there is even the slightest chance of carrying out the agreement completely within the year, an oral contract is enforceable. Thus, an oral agreement to pay a sum of money on a date thirteen months hence is within the statute and not enforceable, but one calling for payment "within thirteen months" would be enforceable, since it is possible under the latter contract to pay in less than a year.

If the performance depends upon a contingency, the agreement's enforceability hinges on the possibility that the contingency will occur prior to the end of one year. A common example is a promise to pay a sum of money upon the marriage of a person; ordinarily such a promise is not within the one-year rule, since it is always possible for the person to marry within the year, even if it may be improbable. If the person was more than one year below the age at which marriage is lawful, however, an oral promise would not be enforceable.

Because in many cases strict application of the statute would dictate harsh results, the courts often strain for an interpretation that finds it possible to perform the agreement within the year. As the next case shows, the courts will even hold that since any person may die within the year, a contract without a fixed term may be fully performed in under a year and does not, therefore, fall within the statute.

KOZLOWSKI v. KOZLOWSKI
164 N.J.Super. 162, 395 A.2d 913 (1978)

POLOW, J. S. C. In this case the court must resolve whether plaintiff Irma Kozlowski, who cohabited with defendant Thaddeus Kozlowski for 15 years without the benefit of marriage, may succeed on [her demands].

* * *

The dilemma may be simply stated: Is there any remedy available under our law for a woman who has devoted 15 or more years living with a man, for whom she provided the necessary household services and emotional support to permit him to successfully pursue his business career and for whom she has performed housekeeping, cleaning and shopping services, run the household, raised the children, her own as well as his, all without benefit of marriage; a woman who was literally forced out of the household with no ongoing support or wherewithal for her survival?

* * *

I have considered the testimony of the parties and observed their demeanor on the witness stand, and am satisfied that plaintiff's version is the more credible. I find that the proofs indicate that she asked him specifically about her financial situation should he predecease her, in response to which he assured her he would arrange to provide for her for the rest of her life. I am satisfied that defendant's present argument, that his obligation to provide for her was to cease if they separated, is an afterthought and was neither stated nor intended when the new agreement was reached in 1968.

Although the agreement was oral, it does not violate the statute of frauds, *N.J.S.A.* 25:1–5(c) or (e), which provides:

25:1–5. Promises or agreements not binding unless in writing
No action shall be brought upon any of the following agreements or promises, unless the agreement or promise, upon which such action shall be brought or some memorandum or note thereof, shall be brought in writing, and signed by the party to be charged therewith, or by some other person thereunto by him lawfully authorized;

* * *

c. An agreement made upon consideration of marriage;

(*continued on next page*)

(continued)

**KOZLOWSKI v.
KOZLOWSKI**
164 N.J.Super. 162, 395
A.2d 913 (1978)

* * *

e. An agreement that is not to be performed within one year from the making thereof.

The consideration here for the services rendered was not marriage but compensation by way of support which plaintiff has already received and the promise of future support. In *Eiseman* v. *Schneider,* 60 *N.J.L.* 291, 37 *A.* 623 (Sup.Ct. 1897), the trial court allowed relief to be granted on an oral agreement made 20 years earlier between a man and his mother-in-law that in consideration of certain domestic services to be performed by her, he would support and maintain her during her lifetime. In the present case plaintiff performed the agreed-upon services for 15 years, giving up for that time all other potential avenues of pursuit of career or employment as well as other possible means of providing for her future support and retirement. She has foregone any chance to develop skills or to seek out opportunities which, in the revealing light of hindsight, may well have served her better. She performed diligently and fully her part of the bargain for a significant period of her life. This court could not countenance the unconscionable result which would obtain should all relief be denied this plaintiff who was cast adrift at 63 years of age without means of support assets, and with little hope of developing support opportunities. For the reasons stated in section II thereof, the contract is enforceable.

Nor does the time requirement of the statute of frauds bar enforcement of this oral agreement which would have terminated upon the death of either party. As the court in *Smith v. Balch,* 89 *N.J.Eq.* 566, 105 *A.* 17, 19 (E. & A. 1918), authoritatively held:

> In order for this provision of the statute to apply, it must appear that the parties intended when they made the contract that it should not be performed within the year. If this does not expressly or clearly appear, and the contract is one which, taking in consideration the subject-matter, may be performed within the year, the statute does not apply, although in fact a longer time was actually taken in performance.

Accordingly, an appropriate measure of relief will be awarded plaintiff in this claim. A preliminary determination of the damage caused to plaintiff was calculated based upon the present value of the reasonable annual support payable to plaintiff, computed by reference to the life expectancy tables contained in the *Rules.* Plaintiff has demanded further opportunity to present evidence because of certain limitations imposed during pre-trial discovery. A final determination of the amount of damages to be awarded will await a further plenary hearing.

The one-year period called for in the Statute of Frauds runs from the making of the contract, usually when the offer is accepted; so an oral agreement to begin one month hence and to run for one year thereafter would not be enforceable. The year ends at midnight of the contract's anniversay date, so that it is possible for an oral contract lasting a year and a day to be enforced. (The theory is that courts disregard fractions of a day in a manner most favorable to upholding the contract.)

The law requires all promises contained in an agreement to be in writing if any one of them cannot be performed within a year, but the courts have grafted an exception onto the statute for full performance by one side. An oral agreement to repay a loan in four equal installments every six months, for example, is not within the statute if the loan is actually made at the time the contract is entered into.

UCC Provisions Requiring Written Contracts

A number of Uniform Commercial Code provisions require that an instrument be written—for example, negotiable instruments (Section 3-104) and security agreements (Section 9-203(1)(a)). But three provisions are of special importance to sales law and will be considered in order below: sale of goods, sale of securities, and sale of certain types of personal property.

Sale of Goods   Section 2-201 requires all contracts for the sale of goods for the price of $500 or more to be in writing. Oral agreements for sale of goods valued at less than $500 are thus fully enforceable without exception. And the general rule itself has four major exceptions. The first is the **reply doctrine,** which applies only to transactions between merchants: if an oral agreement is reached and one party sends the other a written statement confirming the contract, the other party has ten days to object in writing or the agreement is enforceable. (Section 2-201(2).)

MILLER v. KAYE
545 P.2d 199 (Utah 1975)

ELLETT, JUSTICE. The court found, and it is not disputed, that the parties hereto are elephant merchants. Mr. Kaye obtained an elephant from Mr. Miller pursuant to what he claims was an oral lease with an option to purchase. Mr. Miller asserts that the oral agreement was merely for the lease of the animal and that the terms thereof were embodied in a telegram sent by Mr. Kaye and that there was no mention of any option to buy contained in it.

Mr. Kaye claims and offered testimony to prove that on or about July 8 or 9, 1973, he had a phone conversation with Mr. Miller wherein he exercised the option to buy the elephant for $5,000 with the lease money theretofore paid to apply on the purchase price.

There was no written agreement to purchase, and Mr. Miller relies on Section 70A-2-201(1), U.C.A.1953 (Replacement Vol. 7B) as a basis for holding any so-called oral agreement invalid. Mr. Kaye relies on subsection (2) of the section as an exception to the rule.

The contents of an envelope mailed by Mr. Kaye to Mr. Miller July 11, 1973, are of paramount importance. It is admitted that a check in the amount of $600 was enclosed. Mr. Miller claims that it was enclosed in a folded blank sheet of paper. Mr. Kaye offered testimony to the effect that the check was enclosed with a letter in words and figures as follows:

July 11, 1973

Mr. Dory R. Miller
Carson & Barnes Circus
Post Office Box J
Hugo, Oklahoma—74743

Dear Dory:

Thank you for your letter of July 3rd.

(continued on next page)

(continued)

MILLER v. KAYE
545 P.2d 199 (Utah 1975)

Supplementing our last telephone conversation, this letter will serve as your confirmation that we agree to purchase the elephant "Peggy"—at a total cost of $5,000—in lieu of continuing our lease agreement.

Enclosed you will find a check in the amount of $600 which is to be applied to the purchase, as is our previous payment of $450, as agreed.

It is also agreed that the balance will be paid as soon as possible and that the entire balance will be paid within one year.

With warmest personal regards,

Sincerely,
PAUL V. KAYE

The trial court chose to believe that the original oral agreement was for a lease with an option to purchase; that on July 8 or 9, 1973, Mr. Kaye orally notified Mr. Miller in the phone call that he was exercising the option to purchase; and that on July 11, 1973, he enclosed the original of the letter above set out in the envelope with the $600 check.

The evidence sustains these findings, and we are obliged to honor the court's findings in such a case.

The court held that by the letter of July 11, 1973, Mr. Kaye in writing confirmed the terms of the oral contract so as to bind himself, and since Mr. Miller never at any time made any written objection to the letter, subsection (2) of the statute was applicable, and as between these two merchants the oral contract was enforceable. The court, therefore, ruled in favor of Mr. Kaye. The ruling was proper, and we affirm it. Costs are awarded to the respondent.

The second exception to the sale of goods provision is for goods **specially manufactured.** Under Section 2-201(3)(a), a seller who has manufactured goods to the buyer's specifications or who has made "either a substantial beginning of their manufacture or commitments for their procurement" will not be stuck if the buyer repudiates, assuming that the goods are unsuitable for sale to others.

The third exception, Section 2-201(3)(b), occurs when the party against whom enforcement is sought admits in testimony or legal papers that a contract was in fact made. However, the admission will not permit enforcement of all claimed terms of the contract; enforcement is limited to the quantity of goods admitted.

Finally, by Section 2-201(3)(c), an oral contract for goods in excess of $500 will be upheld if payment has already been made and accepted, or if the goods have been received and accepted.

Beyond these exceptions within the UCC, the Convention on Contracts for the International Sale of Goods (see page 191) does not require international contracts for the sale of goods to be written.

Sale of Securities Like contracts for the sale of goods, agreements for the sale of securities are not generally enforceable in the absence of a writing signed by the party against whom enforcement is sought. The written document must state the quantity of securities and the price negotiated. (Section 8-319.) Unlike the provision for the sale of goods, this section has no dollar limit. But many orders for securities are made over the telephone, and so three exceptions apply. The first arises upon delivery of or payment for the security, although an oral contract is enforceable only to the extent of the delivery or payment. The second exception concerns written confirmation: if the party against whom enforcement is sought has failed to object in writing within ten days of receipt of a written confirmation of sale or purchase, he is bound. This provision applies to all sellers and purchasers and is not limited to merchants, as is the reply doctrine in Section 2-201. The third exception, for admissions, is comparable to the rule of Section 2-201(3)(b); admissions in court or in court papers permit enforcement of the contract if a given quantity and price are stated.

Suppose that a customer calls his broker to purchase 2,000 shares of stock at a stated price; the broker does so and sends a written confirmation. Within ten days, the customer reneges by objecting that there never was an agreement as claimed by the broker. (The customer might do this because the stock had fallen in price during the interim.) In the broker's suit for the purchase price, is the customer's response valid that the suit is barred by the Statute of Frauds (UCC Section 8-319) because there was no written contract? Courts have said the customer is wrong: Section 8-319 does not apply to agreements between customers and brokers. The broker is the customer's agent; the customer's order to purchase is an instruction to his agent. Since such agency agreements (see Part VII) are not subject to Section 8-319, an oral purchase order is enforceable. [Hutton v. Zaferson, 509 S.W.2d 950 (Tex. 1974)]

Sale of Other Types of Property Certain types of property are not included within the sales and securities articles of the UCC. Without a general Statute of Frauds provision, oral agreements for the purchase and sale of these other types of property would be enforceable. So by UCC Section 1-206, the Statute of Frauds applies to all transactions exceeding $5,000. Included within this section is intangible property, such as rights to royalties, rights to mortgage payments, and other rights created by contract. For example, the authors of this textbook could not bind themselves to a transfer of their rights to royalties in excess of $5,000 unless they put it in writing.

Statutes Other Than the Statute of Frauds

In many states, other statutes require a writing as evidence for several different types of contracts. These include agreements to pay commissions to real estate brokers, to make a will, to pay debts already discharged in bankruptcy, to arbitrate rather than litigate disputes, to make loans, and to make installment sales.

Contents of the Required Writing

Given that a writing is necessary for the transactions just discussed, what must the writing contain? Recall that the Statute of Frauds says that the "agreement . . . or some memorandum or note thereof shall be in writing, and signed by the party to be charged therewith." In some states, the agreement itself must be reduced to writing; a memorandum loosely describing or referring to the agreement is insufficient. But most states follow the wording of the original statute and permit a memorandum or note concerning the agreement—a logical consequence of the statute's purpose to evidence the making of the contract. The words need not appear in a formal document; they are sufficient in any form in a will, or a check or receipt, or in longhand on the back of an envelope—so long as the document is signed by the party to be charged (that is, the party being sued on the contract).

Although the writing need not contain every term, it must recite the subject matter of the contract. It need not do so, however, in terms comprehensible to those who were not party to the negotiations; it is enough if it is understandable in context. A written agreement to buy a parcel of land is sufficiently definitive if it refers to the parcel in such a way that it could be mistaken for no other—for example, "seller's land in Tuscaloosa," assuming that the seller owned only one parcel there. Beyond the subject matter, the essential terms of promises to be performed must be written out; all details need not be. If an essential term is missing, it cannot be enforced, unless it can be inferred or imposed by rule of law. A written contract for the sale of land containing every term but the time for payment, which the parties orally agreed would be upon delivery of the deed, is sufficient. (A contract that omitted the selling price would not be.)

The parties must be named in the writing in a manner sufficient to identify them. Their whole names need not be given if initials or some other reference makes it inescapable that the writing does concern the actual parties. Reference to the agent of a party identifies the party. Possession of the writing may even be sufficient: if a seller gives a memorandum of an oral agreement for the sale of his land, stating all the terms, to the buyer, the latter may seek specific performance even though the writing omits to name or describe him or his agent. (*Restatement (Second) of Contracts*, Section 207, comment f.)

In a few states, consideration for the promise must be stated in writing, even if the consideration has already been given. Consequently, written contracts frequently contain such language as "for value received." But in most states, failure to refer to consideration already given is unnecessary: "the prevailing view is that error or omission in the recital of past events does not affect the sufficiency of a memorandum." (*Restatement (Second) of Contracts*, Section 207, comment h.) The situation is different, however, when the consideration is a return promise yet to be performed. Usually the return promise is an essential term of the agreement, and failure to state it will vitiate the writing.

Required Writing under the UCC

In contracts for the sale of goods, the writing must be signed by the party to be charged, and the parties must be sufficiently identified. Section 2-201 requires identification of the subject matter by implication (". . . not enforceable . . . beyond the quantity of goods shown in each writing"). But consideration, including the selling price, need not be set forth for the memorandum to meet the requirements of the UCC, though obviously it makes sense to do so whenever possible. By contrast, UCC Sections 1-206 and 3-319 concerning intangible personal property and investment securities require "a defined or stated price."

Electronic Communications

A model agreement covering electronic communications, which was published by an American Bar Association committee in 1990 (see page 219), includes provisions relating to the Statute of Frauds. The model agreement provides that a properly-transmitted communication containing a signature is considered to be a signed writing. In order to "sign" documents, each party uses an electronic identification—either a symbol or a code. Under the model agreement the parties agree not to challenge the validity of signed documents under the Statute of Frauds.

Effect of Noncompliance

The basic rule is that contracts governed by the Statute of Frauds are unenforceable if they are not sufficiently written down. If the agreement contains several promises, the unenforceability of any one will generally render the others unenforceable also. However, if the contract has been performed fully by both sides, its unenforceability under the statute is moot. Having fulfilled its function (neither side having repudiated the contract), the agreement cannot be rescinded on the ground that it should have been, but was not, reduced to writing.

For a partially performed contract unenforceable under the Statute of Frauds, the remedy of "quasi-contract" may be available. Suppose George agrees orally to landscape Arthur's fifteen acres, in return for which George is to receive title to one acre at the far end of the lot. George is not entitled to the acre if Arthur defaults, but he may recover for the reasonable value of the services he has performed up to the time of repudiation.

Most contracts required to be in writing may be rescinded orally. The new agreement is treated in effect as a modification of the old one, and since a complete rescission will not usually require of the parties any action that the statute requires to be in writing, the rescission becomes effective in the absence of any signed memorandum.

Some agreements, however, may not be rescinded orally. Those that by their terms preclude oral rescission are an obvious class. Under the UCC, certain agreements for the sale of goods may not be orally rescinded, depending on the circumstances. For instance, if title has already passed to the buyer under a written agreement that satisfies the statute, the contract can be rescinded only by a writing. Contracts for the sale of land are another class of agreements that generally may not be orally rescinded. If title has already been transferred, or if there has been a material change of position in reliance on the contract, oral agreements to rescind are unenforceable. But a contract that remains wholly executory, even though enforceable because in writing, may be rescinded orally in most states.

Contracts governed by the Statute of Frauds may be modified orally if the resulting contract, taken as a whole, falls outside the statute. The same rule applies under the UCC (Section 2-209(3)). Thus, a written contract for the sale of a new car worth $10,000 may be orally modified by substituting sale of a used car worth $350, but not by substituting sale of a used car worth $500 or more. The modified contract effectively rescinds the original contract. In most cases, however, an unenforceable modification prevents the rescission from taking effect so that the original contract, if enforceable, remains so. For example, a written agreement for the sale of a new car worth $10,000 specifies that payment will take place upon delivery within 60 days. Thereafter, the parties orally agree to delivery within 120 days. The oral agreement is unenforceable, but it does not rescind the original agreement. But if in the same oral agreement the parties have included two separate contracts—the first to rescind the original agreement and the second to substitute a new one—the rescission will be effective even if the substitution is unenforceable. In the previous example, if the buyer and auto dealer orally agree to rescind the contract for the original car and to substitute an entirely different car with a different price and time or delivery, the original contract, though written, is rescinded and hence unenforceable; the new agreement, because it is oral, is likewise unenforceable.

PAROL EVIDENCE RULE

The Rule Defined

Unlike Minerva sprung forth whole from the brow of Zeus, contracts do not appear at a stroke memorialized on paper. Almost invariably, negotiations of some sort precede the concluding of a deal. People write letters, talk by telephone, meet face to face, and exchange thoughts and views about what they want and how they will reciprocate. They may even lie and cajole in duplicitous ways, making promises they know they cannot or will not keep in order not to kill the contract talks. In the course of these discussions, they may reach tentative agreements, some of which will ultimately be reflected in the final contract, some of which will be discarded along the way, and some of which perhaps will not be included in the final agreement but will nevertheless not be contradicted by it. Whether any weight should be given to these prior agreements is a problem that frequently arises. The general rule is that a written contract discharges all prior or contemporaneous promises, statements, or agreements that add to, vary, or conflict with it. This rule is known as the **parol evidence rule** ("parol" means "by word of mouth"). It is a substantive rule of law, and it operates to bar the introduction of evidence intended to show that the parties had agreed to something different. It applies to prior written as well as oral agreements. Though its many apparent exceptions make the rule seem difficult to apply, its purpose is simple: to give freedom to the parties to negotiate without fear of being held to the consequences of asserting preliminary positions, and to give finality to the contract.

The parol evidence rule applies to all written contracts, whether or not the Statute of Frauds requires them to be in writing. But the rule is concerned only with events that transpired before the contract in dispute was signed. It has no bearing on agreements reached subsequently that may alter the terms of an existing contract, as illustrated below.

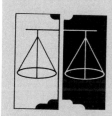

GERWIN v. CLARK
50 Ohio App.2d 331, 363 N.E.2d 602 (1977)

PER CURIAM. This cause came to be heard upon the appeal; the transcript of the docket, journal entries and original papers from the Court of Common Pleas of Hamilton County; and the assignments of error, the briefs and arguments of counsel.

On September 8, 1969, defendant-appellant entered into a written agreement with plaintiff-appellee to purchase an airplane business owned by the latter, consisting of Executaire, Inc., and its wholly owned subsidiary, Queen City Flying Service, Inc. The agreement provided that, as part of the consideration given in exchange for the sale, appellant would (1) indemnify the appellee for any loss suffered by the latter as a result of the corporations' failure to pay an outstanding promissory note given to the Provident Bank;

(continued on next page)

(continued)

GERWIN v. CLARK
50 Ohio App.2d 331, 363
N.E.2d 602 (1977)

(2) effect a release of Joan E. Gerwin and Louis Nippert as co-guarantors on an aircraft lease obligation given by the corporations to the Central Trust Company; and (3) cause the corporation to redeem any common shares owned by the appellee upon the latter's resignation from the board of directors of Executaire, Inc.

In January 1971, both corporations initiated bankruptcy proceedings, at the conclusion of which the Provident Bank obtained a personal judgment against the appellee for the balance due under the aforementioned promissory note. Appellee subsequently brought this action for breach of contract against appellant, alleging appellant's refusal to indemnify appellee for the loss suffered by such judgment and to redeem appellee's common shares following the latter's resignation from the board of directors of Executaire, Inc. Appellant denied both claims, asserting the existence of an oral agreement between the two parties in April 1970, which rescinded the three recited terms of the original agreement in exchange for the employment of appellee as vice-president of Queen City Flying Services, Inc., and as president of a third corporation, Cincinnati Aircraft, Inc., for a salary of $30,000 per year. Appellee thereafter filed a motion for summary judgment with the trial court, denying the existence of any oral agreement and arguing that the introduction of any evidence thereof was precluded, under the parol evidence rule, by a written agreement between the parties in June 1970, which assertedly incorporated the subject matter of the alleged oral agreement and which made no reference to any release by appellee of appellant's obligations under the original contract. The trial court granted the appellee's motion, and entered judgment thereon in his favor, from which judgment this appeal was timely brought, presenting four assignments of error for review.

Appellant, in his first two assignments, essentially challenges the trial court's judgment as contrary to law, asserting that the existence and terms of the alleged oral contract created a genuine issue of material fact which was wrongfully excluded from the case by the trial court's misapplication of the parol evidence rule, and which rendered disposition of the instant action by summary judgment improper under Civ. R. 56(C). We agree. While the parol evidence rule precludes the introduction of evidence of conversations or declarations which occur prior to or contemporaneous with a written contract and which attempt to vary or contradict terms contained in the writing, the rule does not bar evidence of a subsequent oral agreement which modifies a prior written agreement. Thus, where, as here, evidence is offered to prove the existence of an oral agreement which rescinds a *prior* written contract or any provision thereof, such evidence is not inadmissible by virtue of the parol evidence rule and, if otherwise relevant and competent, must be considered by the trial court in its disposition of the issues before it.

Appellee's contention that evidence of the April agreement nevertheless was properly excluded as parol evidence which varied the terms of the later June written agreement is unsupported by the record. The June agreement, which consists of a single stock purchase contract between the two parties, makes no mention of any of the employment arrangements which formed the basis of the alleged April agreement. Such an absence, from the later agreement, of any terms which are varied or contradicted by terms of the alleged oral agreement renders the parol evidence rule, as a tool to exclude proof of the latter, inapplicable in the instant case.

★　　★　　★

The judgment rendered below is hereby reversed, and the cause is remanded to the trial court for further proceedings consistent with this decision.

Despite its apparent stringency, the parol evidence rule does not negate all prior agreements or statements, nor preclude their use as evidence. A number of situations fall outside the scope of the rule and hence are not technically exceptions to it. We will consider each in turn.

Is the Agreement Integrated?

An **integrated** agreement is one that in its written form expresses the final agreement of the parties with respect to the term in question. An agreement may be fully or partially integrated. A fully integrated agreement is one in which the parties intended all terms to be contained in the writing. A partially integrated agreement is one that omits certain terms orally agreed to earlier. If the document is fully integrated, no extrinsic evidence will be permitted to modify the terms of the agreement, even if the modification is in addition to the existing terms, rather than a contradiction of them. If the contract is partially integrated, prior *consistent* additional terms may be shown. It may be necessary, therefore, to introduce evidence of prior agreements at trial, not in violation of the parol evidence rule, but for the express purpose of ascertaining whether or not the disputed agreement is integrated—that is, for the purpose of determining whether or not the parol evidence rule should be applied to the case at all. If the evidence shows that the document is integrated, then the courts will prohibit the parties from proffering other evidence to establish terms not contained in the writing.

For example, suppose the document says that a deed to land is to be delivered in 45 days. If the contract is fully integrated, the seller will not be permitted to introduce evidence tending to show that the delivery term actually negotiated was "45 days or, at the seller's option, 60 days." If the parties agreed on a delivery time but omitted to write it down, then the contract is only partially integrated and evidence of the time agreed may be considered.

Proof of integration is not always easy. It depends in the main on the form and substance of the writing itself. If the writing appears to be complete, specific, and detailed, the courts will not permit extrinsic evidence to show that there were other terms, whether or not in fact there were some. But a contract may sometimes appear complete, and only evidence of prior statements or terms can demonstrate that it is not. To rely exclusively on the "face of the document"—a test that some courts apply—would mean that in some instances the intent of the parties would be disregarded. Therefore, in an increasing number of states (today more than half), a party claiming that a term is missing from the final agreement is permitted to state the nature of his evidence. If it is of such a type that it would not normally be included in a final written document, it can be admitted into evidence. But if it is the kind of term that would generally be written down, then the parol evidence rule would bar its introduction and the party would be stuck with the terms of the final agreement.

Suppose Richard, a plumber, signs a contract to repair Pat's pipes and fails to state that new copper tubing will be used in the kitchen and the bathroom, as they had agreed in negotiating the terms. Richard thereafter proposes to install used brass piping. If the signed document was a "form" contract in which Richard had filled in various blanks, Pat might be permitted to show that the intention was to use copper pipes. (How would Pat show this? Perhaps by oral testimony of a witness who listened to the negotiations.) On the other hand, if the contract said "copper pipes to be used in kitchen," that would be a strong indication that the signed contract was integrated and that the agreement to place copper pipes in the bathroom should not be admissible to vary its terms. Why? Because such a hand-tailored contract suggests that all terms were included; it strains credulity to believe that the parties would omit mention of the bathroom while detailing work to be done in the kitchen. If Pat's evidence of an agreement to put copper in the bathroom were admitted, the parol evidence rule would be substantially undercut; one can always argue that the parties just "forgot" to include this term or that.

The parties' relationship and conduct toward each other can also help determine whether a document is fully integrated. In a Minnesota case, a Catholic priest, founder and long-time publisher and editor of the *Catholic Digest* magazine, negotiated to sell it. Before concluding a deal with a publishing company, the priest's superior in the Church directed that the *Digest* be turned over to a nonprofit institution. The priest thereupon negotiated a transfer to a Catholic college. Throughout the course of the negotiations, which lasted for eighteen months, it was agreed that the priest would continue to be editor and publisher for as long as he wished. Although the final documents omitted reference to this condition, he continued running the magazine for five years until he was dismissed. To the contention that the parol evidence rule barred extrinsic evidence of his right to maintain control over the magazine (there was a wealth of documentary evidence and oral testimony that the transfer was premised on the priest's right to continue on as editor), the court said:

> The unique circumstance of this case is that it was not the ordinary, arm's length transaction. It is instinct with the ecclesiastical relationship of the parties. . . . Plaintiff's ecclesiastical superior had impelled the transaction by instructing him to divest himself of ownership of the Digest. And when plaintiff, obedient to those instructions, ultimately dealt with defendant's agents, he was dealing with colleagues of the cloth, several of whom were of superior status. Nothing in the record indicates that in those dealings plaintiff was represented by legal counsel, but defendant was so represented. Plaintiff's "agent" was a priest, himself subject to church authority, and there is nothing to indicate that he, any more than plaintiff, was familiar with the parol evidence rule. We in no sense suggest that there was overreaching on the part of defendant

or its agents. We suggest simply that the circumstances and relationships of the parties were such that it might have been unusual if plaintiff had even hinted to defendant's agents that the alleged promises concerning permanent employment should be guarded by express incorporation into the written agreement. [Brussard v. College of St. Thomas, Inc., 200 N.W.2d 155, 162 (Minn. 1972)]

To prevent a party later from introducing extrinsic evidence to show that there were prior agreements, the contract itself can recite that there were none. Here, for example, is the final clause in the National Basketball Association Uniform Player Contract: "This agreement contains the entire agreement between the parties and there are no oral or written inducements, promises or agreements except as contained herein." Such a clause is known as a **merger.**

Invalidating Cause

Parol evidence is admissible to show the existence of grounds that would cause the contract to be invalid. Such grounds include illegality, fraud, duress, mistake, and lack of consideration. Assume that Lilly tricks Milly into signing a contract for the sale of Lilly's land by assuring her old friend that it has a large deposit of oil underneath. To prove this assertion, Lilly shows Milly a forged engineer's report. The contract recites that Milly has knowledge of the condition of the land and is not relying on any oral or written representations by Lilly (a form of merger clause). No mention is made in the agreement itself of the oil deposits. After the contract is signed, but before the deed is delivered, Milly discovers the fraud and refuses to take delivery of the deed or make further payment. When Lilly sues, Milly offers evidence of the fraud. Lilly's objection that the parol evidence rule bars admission of the forged engineer's report (since Milly stated that she did not rely on it) is unavailing. The reason is that the evidence of fraud does not vary the terms of the contract; it undercuts the very existence of a contract. As one court put it:

> A contract resting on fraud, when under attack, cannot stand. The fact that the contract has been reduced to writing does not change the rule. The contract as written was induced by the fraud. The evidence in proof of the fraud establishes the inducing or influencing cause and in

no way varies or contradicts the terms of the contract. This rule cannot be curtailed or destroyed by writing in the contract: "This contract was not procured by fraud." . . . [Nor is the contract] valid and binding to the extent that the defrauded party has agreed and unalterably committed himself to the fact that he has not relied upon any statements or representations of his adversary, but upon his own knowledge and information. . . . Such theory would permit a party to do indirectly what he could not do directly. [Ganley Bros., Inc. v. Butler Bros. Building Co., 212 N.W. 602 (Minn. 1927)]

Contracts Subject to an Oral Condition

When the parties orally agree that a written contract is contingent on the occurrence of an event or some other condition, the contract is not integrated and the oral agreement may be introduced. The classic case is that of an inventor who sells in a written contract an interest in his invention. Orally the inventor and the buyer agree that the contract is to take effect only if the buyer's engineer approves the invention. (The contract was signed in advance of approval so that the parties would not need to meet again.) The engineer did not approve it, and in a suit for performance, the court permitted the evidence of the oral agreement because it showed "that in fact there never was any agreement at all." [Pym v. Campbell, 119 Eng.Rep. 903 (Q.B. 1856)] Note that the oral condition does not contradict a term of the written contract; it negates it. The parol evidence rule will not permit evidence of an oral agreement that is inconsistent with a written term, for as to that term the contract is integrated.

Untrue Recitals or Error

The parol evidence rule does not prevent a showing that a fact stated in a contract is untrue. The rule deals with prior agreements; it cannot serve to choke off inquiry into the facts. Thus the parol evidence rule will not bar a showing that one of the parties is a minor, even if the contract recites that each party is over eighteen. Nor will it prevent a showing that a figure in the contract was typed in error—for example, a recital that the rate charged will be the plumber's "usual rate of $3 per hour" when both parties understood that the usual rate was in fact $30 per hour.

UCC Approach

Under UCC Section 2-202, a course of dealing, a usage of trade, or a course of performance can be introduced as evidence to explain or supplement any written contract for the sale of goods. A **course of dealing** is defined as "a sequence of previous conduct between the parties to a particular transaction which is fairly to be regarded as establishing a common basis of understanding for interpreting their expressions and other conduct." A **usage of trade** "is any practice or method of dealing having such regularity of observance in a place, vocation or trade as to justify an expectation that it will be observed with respect to the transaction in question." (Section 1-205.) A **course of performance** is the conduct of a party in response to a contract that calls for repeated action (for example, a purchase agreement for a factory's monthly output, or an undertaking to wash a neighbor's car weekly).

Separate Consideration

Ordinarily, an additional consistent oral term may be shown only if the contract was partially integrated. The parol evidence rule bars evidence of such a term if the contract was fully integrated. However, when there is additional consideration for the term orally agreed, it lies outside the scope of the integrated contract and may be introduced. In effect, the law treats each separate consideration as creating a new contract; the integrated written document does not undercut the separate oral agreement, as long as they are consistent. For example, the Have-a-Good-Day Ice Cream Company signs a detailed agreement with Ralph specifying all aspects of compensation, truck routes, hours, and expenses. They also agree orally that if Ralph will wash the truck weekly, he may drive it home and need not return it to the company's lot each night. The oral agreement is not superseded by the written document.

Contract Meaning

Finally, parol evidence is admissible to show the meaning of a contract. The problem of interpretation is sufficiently important that we will treat it immediately following in a separate section.

INTERPRETATION OF AGREEMENTS

As any reader knows, the meaning of words depends in part on context and in part on the skill and care of the writer. As Justice Oliver Wendell Holmes, Jr., once succinctly noted: "A word is not a crystal, transparent and unchanged; it is the skin of a living thought and may vary greatly in color and content according to the circumstances and the time in which it is used." [Towne v. Eisner, 245 U.S. 418, 425 (1917)] Words and phrases can be ambiguous, either standing alone or because they take on a different coloration from words and phrases near them. A writer can be careless and contradict himself without intending to; people often read hurriedly and easily miss errors that a more deliberate perusal might catch. Interpretation difficulties can arise for any of a number of reasons: a form contract might contain language that is inconsistent with provisions specifically annexed; the parties might use jargon that is unclear; they might forget to incorporate a necessary term; assumptions about prior usage or performance, unknown to outsiders like judges, might color their understanding of the words they do use. Because ambiguities do arise, courts are frequently called on to give content to the words on paper.

The basic rule of interpretation is that the intention of the parties governs, and if their purpose in making the contract is known or can be ascertained from all the circumstances, it will be given great weight in determining the meaning of an obscure, murky, or ambiguous provision or a pattern of conduct. Father tells the college bookstore that in consideration of its supplying his daughter, a freshman, with books for the coming year, he will guarantee payment of up to $350. Daughter purchases books totaling $400 the first semester, and father pays the bill. Midway through the second semester, the bookstore presents him with a bill for an additional $100, and he pays that. At the end of the year, he refuses to pay a third bill for $150. A court could construe his conduct as indicating a purpose to ensure that his daughter had whatever books she needed, regardless of cost, and interpret the contract to hold him liable for the final bill.

The policy of uncovering purpose has led to a number of judicial preferences in weighing one circumstance against another. Generally, the more specific the phrases or more pointed the conduct—that is, the more they relate individually to the disputing parties—the more weight they will be given. Thus a clause that is separately negotiated and added to a contract will be counted as more significant than a standard term in a form contract. Specific terms and those spelled out in detail will be given preference over general language. And in the range of language and conduct that helps in interpretation, the courts prefer the following items in the order listed: express terms, course of performance, course of dealing, and usage of trade.

PRACTICALITIES VS. LEGALITIES

In this chapter we have considered a set of generally technical legal rules that spell out the consequences of contracts that are wholly or partially oral or that, if written, are ambiguous or do not contain every term agreed upon. These rules fall within three general headings: the Statute of Frauds, the parol evidence rule, and the rules of interpretation. Obviously, the more attention paid to the contract before it is formally agreed to, the fewer the unforeseen consequences. In general, the conclusion is inescapable that a written contract will avoid a host of problems. Writing down an agreement is not always sensible or practical, but it can probably be done more often than it is. A law professor studying business practices has noted:

> Businessmen often prefer to rely on "a man's word" in a brief letter, a handshake or "common honesty and decency"—even when the transaction involves exposure to serious risks. Seven lawyers from law firms with business practices were interviewed. Five thought that businessmen often entered contracts with only a minimal degree of advanced planning. They complained that businessmen desire to "keep it simple and avoid red tape" even where large amounts of money and significant risks are involved. . . . Another said that businessmen when bargaining often talk only in pleasant generalities, think they have a contract, but fail to reach agreement on any of the hard, unpleasant questions until forced to do so by a lawyer. (Macauley, 1963, pp. 58–59)

Written contracts do not, to be sure, guarantee escape from disputes and litigation. Sometimes ambiguities are not seen; sometimes they are necessary if the parties are to reach an agreement at all. Rather than back out of the deal, it may be worth the risk to one or both parties deliberately to go along with an ambiguous provision and hope that it never arises to be tested in a dispute that winds up in court. Nevertheless, it is generally true that a written contract has at least three benefits over oral ones, even those that by law are not required to be in writing. (1) The written contract usually avoids ambiguity. (2) It can serve both as a communications device and as a device for the allocation of power, especially within large companies. By alerting various divisions to its formal requirements, the contract requires the sales, design, quality-control, and financial departments to work together. By setting forth requirements that the company must meet, it can place the power to take certain actions in the hands of one division or another. (3) Finally, should a dispute later arise, the written contract can immeasurably add to proof both of the fact that a contract was agreed to and of what its terms were.

CHAPTER SUMMARY

We are light-years away from the ancestral era that required ritual language and stylized contracts. In an age in which contract is dominant, the parties may not only make the kinds of deals they wish but they may make them in any form they wish—with some significant exceptions. The most significant issue of "form" in contract law is whether the contract must be written or may be oral and still be enforceable. The question can be answered by paying close attention to the Statute of Frauds and court decisions interpreting it. In general, as we have seen, the following types of contracts must be in writing: interests in real property, promises to pay the debt of another, certain agreements of executors and administrators, performances that cannot be completed within one year, sale of goods for $500 or more, and sale of securities.

Another significant rule that permeates all of contract law is the parol evidence rule: prior statements, agreements, or promises, whether oral or written, are often discharged by a subsequent written agreement. No matter what you were promised before you signed on the dotted line, you are stuck if you sign an integrated agreement without the promise. Again, of course, exceptions lie in wait for the unwary: Is the agreement only partially integrated? Are there grounds to invalidate the entire agreement? Is the contract subject to an oral condition? Is a fact recited in the contract untrue?

Contracts are not always clear and straightforward. Often they are murky and ambiguous. Interpreting them when the parties disagree is for the courts. To aid them in the task, the courts over the years have developed a series of guidelines—for instance: Does the agreement have a plain meaning on its face? If there is an ambiguity, against whom should it be construed? Are there usages of trade or courses of dealing or performance that would help explain the terms?

KEY TERMS

Course of dealing	p. 295	Part performance doc-	p. 284
Course of performance	p. 295	trine	
Integrated	p. 293	Reply doctrine	p. 287
Main purpose rule	p. 281	Specially manufactured	p. 288
Merger	p. 294	Suretyship	p. 280
Parol evidence rule	p. 291	Usage of trade	p. 295

SELF-TEST QUESTIONS

1. As a general rule:
   (a) contracts do not have to be in writing to be enforceable
   (b) contracts that can be performed in one year must be in writing
   (c) all oral contracts are unenforceable
   (d) a suretyship agreement need not be in writing to be enforceable
2. An exception to the UCC Statute of Frauds provision is:
   (a) the one year rule
   (b) the reply doctrine
   (c) executor agreements
   (d) all of the above
3. Rules that require certain contracts to be in writing are found in:
   (a) state statutory law
   (b) the UCC
   (c) the Statute of Frauds
   (d) all of the above
4. The parol evidence rule:
   (a) applies only when contracts must be in writing
   (b) does not apply to real estate contracts
   (c) states that a written contract discharges all prior or contemporaneous promises that add to, vary or conflict with it
   (d) is designed to hold parties to promises they made during negotiations
5. A merger clause:
   (a) is required when goods are sold for $500 or more
   (b) is used when two parcels of real estate are sold in the same contract
   (c) invalidates a contract for the sale of securities
   (d) is used to prevent the introduction of evidence about prior agreements

DEMONSTRATION PROBLEM

Sara entered into a written contract to install a mahogany bar in Alice's restaurant. Before signing the contract, Sara and Alice orally agreed that Alice's landlord had to approve the contract. Sara installed the bar without obtaining approval and now wants to recover payment. She claims that under the parol evidence rule the court should not admit evidence of the oral condition. Is she correct? Why?

PROBLEMS

1. Fred and his daughter, Dagmar, both worked for the same company. Dagmar wanted to borrow $5,000 from the company credit union, but the credit union refused to advance the money unless Fred also promised to repay the loan. Fred called the director of the credit union and stated: "You can lend the money to Dagmar. I promise to repay the loan." Dagmar later defaulted on her loan payments. May the credit union collect from Fred on the basis of his oral promise? Why?

2. Assume in problem 1 that the credit union was willing to lend the money to Dagmar without Fred's promise, but that Dagmar was reluctant to borrow such a large amount of money. Fred called Dagmar and said, "Go ahead and borrow the money—if you can't repay the debt, I will." Is Fred's oral promise enforceable? Why?

3. Cicero purchased a parcel of real estate that was land-locked. Cicero called his neighbor, Plato, and asked if he could use an abandoned drive on Plato's property to travel to his (Cicero's) property from the highway. Plato said: "Sure, anytime." Later Plato and Cicero became engaged in a dispute and Plato blockaded the drive. May Cicero enforce Plato's promise that he could use the drive "anytime"? Why?

4. Sundance, who was elderly and seriously ill, lived alone on a farm. Sundance called Butch and said: "Butch, if you will move in with me and take care of me, the farm will be yours when I die." Butch did as Sundance requested and, on Sundance's death two years later, claimed the farm on the basis of their oral agreement. Is Butch entitled to the farm? Why?

5. On February 12, Sally was hired to manage a company for a period of one year. She reported for work on February 26 but was fired two weeks later. She sued the owner of the company for breach of their one-year oral contract. May she recover? Why?

6. Bonnie entered into an oral contract to sell her 1954 Rambler to Clyde for $600. She delivered the car to Clyde, but Clyde refused to pay and now wants to return the car. Is the contract enforceable? Why?

7. Wayne, a building contractor, built a new house and offered the house and lot for sale. A young couple accepted the offer, and the parties entered into an oral agreement covering all of the terms of sale. The couple later tried to back out of the agreement. Wayne filed suit and, during the trial, the couple admitted making the contract. Is the contract enforceable? Why?

ANSWERS TO SELF-TEST QUESTIONS

1. (a)   2. (b)   3. (d)   4. (c)   5. (d)

SUGGESTED ANSWER TO DEMONSTRATION PROBLEM

Sara is not correct. The parol evidence rule does not apply to evidence of a condition showing that the parties did not intend the contract to become operative. *Washington Tent and Awning Co. v. 818 Ranch, Inc.*, 248 A.2d 126 (1968).

CHAPTER

13

Outsiders

To this point we have focused on the rights and duties of the (usually two) parties to the contract. In this chapter we will turn our attention to contracts in which outsiders acquire rights or duties, or both. Three types of outsiders merit examination:

- *Third-party beneficiaries* (outsiders who acquire rights when the original contract is made)
- *Assignees* (outsiders who acquire rights after the contract is made)
- *Delegatees* (outsiders who acquire duties after the contract is made)

THIRD-PARTY BENEFICIARIES

Until the nineteenth century, the common law recognized that two parties could by contract create rights in a third person. But early in the last century, the courts in both England and the United States substantially limited these rights. Relying on an extreme individualistic psychology, the courts could not see how a person who did not give consideration and manifested no assent could be imbued with contrac-

tually based rights. Since the promise runs from promisor to promisee, and they are the only parties to the contract, there seemed no way to connect the third-party beneficiary to the contract. But these metaphysical difficulties were resolved long ago. The courts are willing to uphold the intent of the parties, even if that intent is to give benefits to someone outside the contract.

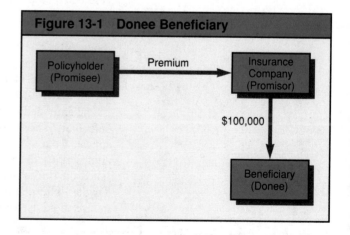

Figure 13-1 Donee Beneficiary

Two Types of Third-Party Beneficiary

In the vocabulary of the Restatement, a third person whom the parties to the contract intend to benefit is an **intended beneficiary**—that is, one who is entitled under the law of contracts to assert a right arising from a contract to which he is not a party. There are two types of intended beneficiaries. A **creditor beneficiary** is one to whom the promisor agrees to pay a debt of the promisee. A father is bound by law to support his child. If the child's uncle (the promisor) contracts with the father (the promisee) to furnish support for the child, the child is a creditor benefi-

ciary. When the promisee is not indebted to the third person but intends for him to have the benefit of the promisor's performance, the third person is a **donee beneficiary** (and the promise is sometimes called a "gift promise"). An insurance company (the promisor) promises to its policyholder (the promisee), in return for a premium, to pay $100,000 to his wife on his death; this makes the wife a donee beneficiary (see figure 13-1). The Restatement uses the general term "intended beneficiary" interchangeably for the older terminology of "creditor" and "donee" beneficiary, as the following case illustrates.

FLATTERY v. GREGORY
397 Mass. 143, 489 N.E. 2d 1257 (1986)

O'CONNOR, JUSTICE. We consider for the first time whether an insurance agent owes to a traveler on the highway, injured by the negligent driving of another, a duty to fulfill the agent's pre-accident promise to the tortfeasor to obtain optional liability coverage on the tortfeasor's motor vehicle. The case reaches us as the result of an appeal from the allowance of a motion to dismiss claims against the insurance agent.

We summarize the relevant allegations in the amended complaint. On December 24, 1979, the plaintiff was the operator of a motor vehicle which collided with a 1975 Toyota automobile. The Toyota was operated by the defendant William C. Gregory, Sr., and was owned jointly by the defendants William C. Gregory, Sr., and Joalta Gregory. As a result of injuries sustained in the collision, the plaintiff recovered a judgment against William C. Gregory, Sr., in the sum of $118,181.99.

According to the amended complaint, at the time of the collision the Gregorys owned a 1973 Mercury automobile in addition to the 1975 Toyota. The defendant William F. Borhek, an insurance agent, had procured liability coverage on the 1973 Mercury for the year 1979 with bodily injury limits of $100,000 per person and $300,000 per accident. Before 1979, Borhek had arranged for the issuance to the Gregorys of motor vehicle liability policies on their vehicles containing $100,000/$300,000 bodily injury limits. "On or about July 2, 1979," the amended complaint states, "[Borhek] caused an insurance policy to be amended and issued" to the Gregorys on the 1975 Toyota (the accident vehicle) with bodily injury limits of only $20,000 per person and $40,000 per accident.

The amended complaint is in three counts, the first of which is against the defendant The Travelers Indemnity Company and is not involved in this appeal. Count 2 alleges Borhek's liability on a theory of tort. In substance, after making the assertions recited above, the plaintiff says that the Gregorys relied on Borhek to obtain $100,000/$300,000 liability coverage on the 1975 Toyota. The plaintiff further asserts that Borhek's failure to do so and his failure to advise them that the limits were only $20,000/$40,000 constituted negligence resulting in a loss to the plaintiff. Count 3 is based on contract. It reasserts the facts set forth in count 2 and, in addition, alleges that in return for valuable consideration Borhek promised the Gregorys that he would procure a liability policy covering the 1975 Toyota with limits of $100,000/ $300,000 "for bodily injury to others, which class of individuals would have included the plaintiff," and that he failed to do so "[i]n breach of said contract."

Borhek moved that the complaint as to him be dismissed, alleging as grounds that the complaint fails to state a claim for which relief can be granted and that the plaintiff's claims are barred by the applicable statutes of limitations. A judge of the Superior Court allowed the motion, and subsequently judgment in favor of Borhek was entered under Mass.R.Civ.P. 54 (b), 365 Mass. 820 (1974). The plaintiff appealed to the Appeals Court and we granted his application for direct appellate review. We now reverse the judgment below.

*   *   *

We must inquire whether the plaintiff was "an intended beneficiary" of the service promised by Borhek as that term is used in the Restatement (Second) of Contracts § 302, and whether the promised service was "for the benefit of" the plaintiff.

"Where performance [of a promise] will benefit a person other than the promisee, that person is a beneficiary." Restatement (Second) of Contracts § 2 (1981). "A promise in a contract creates a duty in the promisor to any *intended beneficiary* to perform the promise, and the *intended beneficiary* may enforce the duty" (emphasis added). Id. at § 304. "An *incidental beneficiary* acquires by virtue of the promise no right against the promisor or the promisee" (emphasis added). *Id*. at § 315. "(1) Unless otherwise agreed between promisor and promisee, a beneficiary of a promise is an intended beneficiary if recognition of a right to performance in the beneficiary is appropriate to effectuate the intention of the parties and either (a) the performance of the promise will satisfy an obligation of the promisee to pay money to the beneficiary; or (b) the circumstances indicate that the promisee intends to give the beneficiary the benefit of the promised performance. (2) An incidental beneficiary is a beneficiary who is not an intended beneficiary." *Id*. at § 302.

The standard Massachusetts automobile liability insurance policy in 1979 contained the following language relative to optional bodily injury coverage: "Under this Part, we will pay damages to people injured or killed in accidents if you or a household member is legally responsible for the accident. . . . The damages we will pay are the amounts the injured person is entitled to collect for bodily injury through a court judgment or settlement." It is clear that the plaintiff would have benefited from Borhek's performance of his alleged contractual obligation. In the ordinary course of events the plaintiff would have received $100,000 from the insurer. Thus, the plaintiff was a "beneficiary" as described in Restatement (Second) of Contracts § 2. We also think that the plaintiff was an "intended" beneficiary under § 302. If

(*continued on next page*)

(continued)

FLATTERY v. GREGORY
397 Mass. 143, 489 N.E. 2d 1257 (1986)

the allegations of the complaint are proved, recognition of the plaintiff's right to Borhek's performance is an appropriate way to effectuate the intent of Borhek and the Gregorys that the plaintiff receive the amount of his judgment against Gregory up to $100,000, thus discharging, to that extent, "an obligation of the promisee to pay money to the beneficiary." *Id.* at § 302 (1)(a).

"It is not essential to the creation of a right in an intended beneficiary that he be identified when a contract containing the promise is made," Restatement (Second) of Contracts § 308, nor is it necessary that the promisee's obligation to pay the beneficiary be in existence when the contract is made. See Restatement (Second) of Contracts § 302, illustration 3 ("B promises A to pay whatever debts A may incur in a certain undertaking. A incurs in the undertaking debts to C, D and E. If the promise is interpreted as a promise that B will pay C, D and E, they are intended beneficiaries under Subsection [1][a]; if the money is to be paid to A in order that he may be provided with money to pay C, D and E, they are at most incidental beneficiaries"); § 308, illustration 2 ("B promises A to pay anyone to whom A may become indebted for the purchase of an automobile. A buys an automobile from C. B is under a duty to C").

[Judgment reversed.]

An **incidental beneficiary** is one who will be benefited by the performance or a contract but has no rights by virtue of it. Valuing her privacy, Greta contracts with a nursery to plant trees and flowers and landscape her back three acres. Her adjoining neighbor will certainly benefit from the land's improvement but has no legal right to require either Greta or the nursery to live up to the contract because benefit to the neighbor was not the intention of Greta or the nursery.

Duties of the Promisor to Beneficiary and to Promisee

A valid contract conferring rights on an intended beneficiary obligates the promisor to both the promisee and the beneficiary. In the case of a debt, payment will discharge the obligation to both. Peter has $100 in cash, which he is required to pay to Paul tomorrow. After the banks have closed, Mary encounters Peter and sees the cash. She asks to borrow it so she can shop at the grocery store. Peter agrees in return for Mary's promise that she will repay Paul the next day. Paul is the intended beneficiary; both he and Peter may sue Mary for the money if she defaults. Together they may collect only $100, however.

Ordinarily, promises of a gift are not enforceable because no consideration is given for them. But a **gift promise** is enforceable by the donee beneficiary. A son cannot enforce his father's promise to buy him an automobile if the father is successful in "landing a big contract" for his company. But if the father and his employer agree that if the father lands the big contract, the company will give the son an automobile, the agreement is enforceable by either the father or the son.

An intended beneficiary gains no rights if for any reason the contract between promisor and promisee is void. If the contract is voidable, the beneficiary is subject to the infirmity, and if the contract later becomes unenforceable (because, say, an event on which the contract was conditioned did not come to pass), the beneficiary loses his benefit. Thus, an oral contract by which the promisor agrees to convey land to a friend of the promisee is unenforceable under the Statute of Frauds, and the friend has no legal claim to the land. But a subsequent memorandum from the promisor reciting the terms of the agreement would suffice to give the friend the right to specific performance.

The beneficiary's rights are always limited by the express terms of the contract. A failure by the promisee to perform his part of the bargain will terminate the beneficiary's rights if the promisee's lapse terminates his own rights, unless the contract explicitly states that the beneficiary's rights are not to be modified or extinguished by the failure of the promisee to live up to the contract. An uncle promises to send his nephew on a trip if the boy's father, an accountant, will prepare the uncle's taxes. If the accountant does the tax work, the nephew has an enforceable claim against his uncle. If the accountant does not do the work, the nephew's claim fails, unless the contract said otherwise.

In a suit by the beneficiary, the promisor may avail himself of all defenses that he can assert against the promisee under the contract. But the beneficiary's right is direct, and the promisor may not assert claims and defenses against the promisee arising from other transactions, unless the contract specifically allows them.

Modification of the Beneficiary's Rights

Conferring rights on an intended beneficiary is relatively simple. Whether his rights can be modified or extinguished by subsequent agreement of the promisor and promisee is a more troublesome issue. The general rule is that the beneficiary's rights may be altered as long as the contract creating the rights does not prohibit subsequent modification and as long as the beneficiary has not in reliance on his rights materially changed his position or assented to the rights. In the nineteenth century, however, a rule was developed in life insurance cases which precluded the insured from changing the beneficiary once named in

the policy unless the policy contained language specifically reserving to the insured the right to substitute beneficiaries. Today standard policies contain such language and also allow the insured to borrow against the policy, to assign it, and to surrender it for cash.

Government Contracts

Since World War II, government contracting, once a tiny part of the public business, has become an important force in the national economy. The potential for legal problems has grown apace. It is not illogical to see a contract between the government and a company pledged to perform a service on behalf of the public as one creating rights in particular members of the public. But the consequences of such a view could be extremely costly because everyone has some interest in public works and government services.

A restaurant chain, hearing that the county was planning to build a bridge that would reroute commuter traffic, might decide to open a restaurant on one side of the bridge; if it let contracts for construction only to discover that the bridge was to be delayed or canceled, could it sue the county's contractor? In general, the answer is that it cannot. A promisor under contract to the government is not liable for the consequential damages to a member of the public arising from its failure to perform (or from a faulty performance) unless the agreement specifically calls for such liability or unless the promisee (the government) would itself be liable and a suit directly against the promisor would be consistent with the contract terms and public policy. When the government retains control over litigation or settlement of claims, or when it is easy for the public to insure itself against loss, or when the number and amount of claims would be excessive, the courts are less likely to declare individuals to be intended beneficiaries. But the service to be provided can be so tailored to the needs of particular persons that it makes sense to view them as intended beneficiaries—in the case, for example, of a service station licensed to perform emergency road repairs. As the following case shows, the beneficiary's rights might not extend to all injuries.

KORNBLUT v. CHEVRON OIL CO.
62 A.D.2d 831, 407 N.Y.S.2d 498 (1978)

HOPKINS, JUSTICE PRESIDING. The plaintiff-respondent has recovered a judgment after a jury trial in the sum of $519,855.98, including interest, costs and disbursements, against Chevron Oil Company (Chevron) and Lawrence Ettinger, Inc. (Ettinger) (hereafter collectively referred to as defendants) for damages arising from the death and injuries suffered by Fred Kornblut, her husband. The case went to the jury on the theory that the decedent was the third-party beneficiary of a contract between Chevron and the New York State Thruway Authority and a contract between Chevron and Ettinger.

★   ★   ★

On the afternoon of an extremely warm day in early August, 1970 the decedent was driving northward on the New York State Thruway. Near Sloatsburg, New York, at about 3:00 P.M., his automobile sustained a flat tire. At the time the decedent was accompanied by his wife and 12-year-old son. The decedent waited for assistance in the 92-degree temperature.

After about an hour a State Trooper, finding the disabled car, stopped and talked to the decedent. The trooper radioed Ettinger, which had the exclusive right to render service on the Thruway under an assignment of a contract between Chevron and the Thruway Authority. Thereafter, other State Troopers reported the disabled car and the decedent was told in each instance that he would receive assistance within 20 minutes.

Having not received any assistance by 6:00 P.M., the decedent attempted to change the tire himself. He finally succeeded, although he experienced difficulty and complained of chest pains to the point that his wife and son were compelled to lift the flat tire into the trunk of the automobile. The decedent drove the car to the next service area, where he was taken by ambulance to a hospital; his condition was later diagnosed as a myocardial infarction. He died 28 days later.

Plaintiff sued, *inter alia*, Chevron and Ettinger alleging in her complaint causes of action sounding in negligence and breach of contract. We need not consider the issue of negligence, since the Trial Judge instructed the jury only on the theory of breach of contract, and the plaintiff has recovered damages for wrongful death and the pain and suffering only on that theory.

★   ★   ★

We must look, then, to the terms of the contract sought to be enforced. Chevron agreed to provide "rapid and efficient roadside automotive service on a 24-hour basis from each gasoline service station facility for the areas . . . when informed by the AUTHORITY or its police personnel of a disabled vehicle on the Thruway". Chevron's vehicles are required "to be used and operated in such a manner as will produce adequate service to the public, as determined in the AUTHORITY's sole judgment and discretion". Chevron specifically covenanted that it would have "sufficient roadside automotive service vehicles, equipment and personnel to provide roadside automotive service to disabled vehicles within a maximum of thirty (30) minutes from the time a call is assigned to a service vehicle, subject to unavoidable delays due to extremely adverse weather conditions or traffic conditions."

* * *

In interpreting the contract, we must bear in mind the circumstances under which the parties bargained. The New York Thruway is a limited access toll highway, designed to move traffic at the highest legal speed, with the north and south lanes separated by green strips. Any disabled vehicle on the road impeding the flow of traffic may be a hazard and inconvenience to the other users. The income realized from tolls is generated from the expectation of the user that he will be able to travel swiftly and smoothly along the Thruway. Consequently, it is in the interest of the authority that disabled vehicles will be repaired or removed quickly to the end that any hazard and inconvenience will be minimized. Moreover, the design and purpose of the highway make difficult, if not impossible, the summoning of aid from garages not located on the Thruway. The movement of a large number of vehicles at high speed creates a risk to the operator of a vehicle who attempts to make his own repairs, as well as to the other users. These considerations clearly prompted the making of contracts with service organizations which would be located at points near in distance and time on the Thruway for the relief of distressed vehicles.

Thus, it is obvious that, although the authority had an interest in making provision for roadside calls through a contract, there was also a personal interest of the user served by the contract. Indeed, the contract provisions regulating the charges for calls and commanding refunds be paid directly to the user for overcharges, evince a protection and benefit extended to the user only. Hence, in the event of an overcharge, the user would be enabled to sue on the contract to obtain a recovery. Here the contract contemplates an individual benefit for the breach running to the user.

* * *

By choosing the theory of recovery based on contract, it became incumbent on the plaintiff to show that the injury was one which the defendants had reason to foresee as a probable result of the breach, under the ancient doctrine of *Hadley v. Baxendale* (9 Exch. R. 341), and the cases following it, in distinction to the requirement of proximate cause in tort actions (*Palsgraf v. Long Is. R.R. Co.*, 248 N.Y. 339, 346, 162 N.E. 99, 101; cf. *Pagan v. Goldberger*, 51 A.D.2d 508, 382 N.Y.S.2d 549).

. . . The death of the decedent on account of his exertion in the unusual heat of the midsummer day in changing the tire cannot be said to have been within the contemplation of the contracting parties as a reasonably foreseeable result of the failure of Chevron or its assignee to comply with the contract. . . .

The case comes down to this, then, in our view: though the decedent was the intended beneficiary to sue under certain provisions of the contract—such as the rate specified for services to be rendered—he was not the intended beneficiary to sue for consequential damages arising from personal injury because of a failure to render service promptly. Under these circumstances, the judgment must be reversed and the complaint dismissed, without costs or disbursements.

Third-Party Beneficiaries Under the UCC

Under UCC Section 2-318, the warranty of a seller of goods extends to third parties, who by law thus become intended beneficiaries. We will explore the extent and coverage of product warranty in Chapter 19, dealing with product liability.

ASSIGNEES

Centuries ago at common law, intangible rights—such as a bill of sale—could not be sold or transferred. A paper entitling its possessor to delivery of goods was personal to the purchaser; he could take possession of the goods and sell them in turn to a third person, but he could not sell the goods more simply by transferring the paper evidencing ownership. However, under the "law merchant," a body of law in use among merchants and tradesmen and enforced in special merchant tribunals, such transfers were routinely approved. By the seventeenth century, the law merchant was absorbed into the English common law, and the notion spread that other kinds of interests could be assigned as well. Today, assignments of rights are recognized in all American jurisdictions.

An especially important type of assignment—the sale of accounts—is governed by Article 9 of the UCC on secured transactions (that is, the use of personal property as collateral for a loan). Although we cover several important Article 9 provisions in this chapter, other provisions relating to the creation and perfection of security interests (see Chapter 27) also apply to the sale of accounts.

By an assignment, a promisee (referred to as the obligee) transfers a right to a third person (assignee). The assignee acquires the right to the contractual obligations of the promisor, who is referred to as the obligor (see Figure 13-2). The assignor may assign any right unless (1) doing so would materially change the obligation of the obligor, materially burden him, increase his risk, or otherwise diminish the value to him of the original contract; (2) statute or public policy forbids the assignment; or (3) the contract itself precludes assignment.

One important example of assignment of rights is **factoring**. A factor is one who purchases the right to receive income from another. In the ordinary course

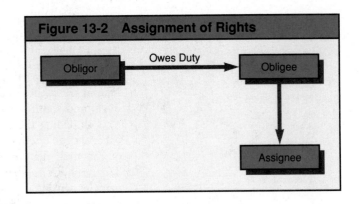

Figure 13-2   Assignment of Rights

of business, a company will have many customers that owe it money (accounts receivable). An account receivable is an asset and may be used by the company as collateral for a loan. However, the lender does not own the account receivable, and if the customer does not pay up, the company still remains indebted to its lender. The customer ordinarily will have no knowledge that its debt has been pledged to a creditor of the company. By contrast, a factor purchases the account receivable (at discount) and actually owns it. If the customer fails to pay, the loss becomes that of the factor, not the company. Moreover, the customer is told that the account receivable has been sold, and it must pay the factor rather than the company thereafter. Once the account receivable is factored, it no longer remains on the books of the company as an asset.

Method of Assignment

Manifesting Assent   In order to effect an assignment, the assignor must make known his intention to transfer the rights to the third person. The assignor's intention must be that the assignment is effective without need of any further action or any further manifestation of intention to make the assignment. In other words, the assignor must intend and understand himself to be making the assignment then and there; he is not promising to make the assignment sometime in the future.

Under the UCC, any assignments of rights in excess of $5,000 must be in writing. However, the absence of a writing is a defense only in actions between assignor and assignee. Any assignee may enforce an oral assignment against the obligor, and the obligor discharges his duty by giving performance to the assignee. Ralph has a contract to deliver to Calvin $50,000 worth of cloth. Calvin orally assigns his right to receive the cloth to Oscar. If Ralph delivers the cloth to Oscar, Calvin cannot sue Oscar for the goods because an oral assignment is effective against the obligor.

A debtor may assign to his creditor a security interest in some form of his property, including intangibles such as accounts receivable. Under the UCC (Section 9-203), a security interest cannot be enforceably conveyed unless the secured party possesses the collateral or there is a signed security agreement meeting certain formal requirements. Similarly, under many state statutes, wage assignments are absolutely void if they do not meet formal written requirements.

Acceptance   For the assignment to become effective, the assignee must manifest his acceptance under most circumstances. This is done automatically when, as is usually the case, the assignee has given consideration for the assignment (that is, if there is a contract between the assignor and assignee in which the assignment is the assignor's consideration). If a third person has given the assignor consideration for the transfer of rights, then the assignee need not accept (indeed, he need not even know about it) for the assignment to be effective. Problems of acceptance normally arise only when the assignor intends the assignment as a gift. Then, for the assignment to be irrevocable, either the assignee must manifest his acceptance or the assignor must notify a third person in writing of the assignment.

Notice   An obligor who renders performance to the assignor before receiving notice that the assignment has been made (and that performance of the contract is to be rendered therefore to the assignee) is discharged. Before notice, the assignor may also modify the obligor's duties. This rule is true both at common law and under UCC Section 9-318(3). Thus, in the above example, if Oscar had not notified Ralph of Calvin's assignment to him of the contract for cloth, Calvin could make a new agreement with Ralph (perhaps for a different type or amount of cloth to be delivered earlier or later), and Ralph would have no obligation to Oscar to fulfill the terms of the original contract.

Effect of Assignment

In general, an assignment of rights has the effect of putting the assignee into the shoes of the assignor. He gains rights against the obligor only to the extent that the assignor possessed them. An obligor who could avoid the assignor's attempt to enforce the rights could avoid a similar attempt by the assignee. Likewise, under UCC Section 9-318(1) the assignee of an account is subject to all terms of the contract between the debtor and the creditor-assignor. Suppose Ralph was required to deliver the cloth only if Calvin arranged for shipping by a certain date. Before that date Calvin assigned the contract to Oscar, who so notified Ralph. If after the date specified, Calvin failed to arrange for trucks to pick up the cloth, Ralph would be entitled to cancel delivery to Oscar, just as he would have been entitled to cancel delivery to Calvin had there been no assignment.

The "shoe rule" does not apply to two types of assignments. First, it is inapplicable to the sale of a negotiable instrument to a holder in due course (which we cover in detail in Part IV). Second, the rule may be **waived**: the obligor may agree in the original contract not to avail himself of defenses that could be used against the assignor. Under UCC Section 9-206(1) an assignee may enforce an agreement between buyers or lessees and sellers or lessors whereby the buyer or lessee agrees not to assert any claim or defense against the assignee that could be asserted against the seller or lessor. Waiver of defenses that otherwise could be asserted against a subsequent assignee is controversial, because it is a situation fraught with peril to the buyer or lessee, who may sign a contract without understanding the full import of the waiver. Under the waiver rule, for example, a farmer who buys a tractor on credit and discovers later that it does not work would still be required to pay a credit company that purchased the contract; his defense that the merchandise was shoddy would be unavailing.

There are a number of rules that limit both the holder in due course and the waiver rule. Certain defenses, the so-called "real" defenses, may be asserted. These include infancy and other incapacities, duress, illegality, fraud in the execution, and bankruptcy. The waiver clause in the contract must have been presented in good faith, and if the assignee has actual notice of a defense that the buyer or lessee could raise, then the waiver is ineffective. Moreover, in consumer transactions the rule of Section 9-206 is subject to state laws that establish a different rule for "consumer goods," which are those used primarily for personal, family, or household purposes. Many states, by statute or court decision, have made waivers of defenses ineffective and permit the consumer to raise all defenses against the assignee. Finally, effective in 1976, the Federal Trade Commission adopted a trade regulation that radically changed the ability of many sellers to pass on rights to assignees free of defenses that buyers could raise against them. This regulation, discussed in detail in Chapter 23, in essence requires that language be placed in all consumer credit contracts for the sale of consumer goods or services subjecting all subsequent holders of the contract to all claims and defenses that the debtor could assert against the seller. Because of these various limitations on the holder in due course and waiver rules, the shoe rule will govern in consumer transactions and, if there are real defenses or the assignee does not act in good faith, in business transactions as well.

Under certain circumstances, the assignee may acquire fewer rights than the assignor possessed. When the contract has not been fully performed, and the assigned right is conditional on further performance, the original contracting parties—the obligor and assignor—may modify the contract (in good faith) even after the obligor has been notified of the assignment. This rule operates both at common law and under the UCC (Section 9-318(2)). An important example of the need for such a rule is in the field of government contracting. A county might let a contract for the construction of a highway; the prime contractor who wins the bid will subcontract various aspects of the job to numerous companies and individuals. In order to obtain payment immediately, the subcontractors may assign rights to payment under these contracts to banks or other financial institutions. During the construction, before all work is complete, the county may find it necessary to change the highway specifications. The rule UCC Section 9-318(2) permits the county and the prime contractor to modify the contract and allows the prime contractor then to make the required modifications with his subcontractors, without the necessity of securing permission from all the banks and other institutions to which rights have been assigned. The assignees acquire corresponding rights under the modified contract.

Occasions When Assignments Are Not Allowed

Material Change in Duties of the Obligor   When an assignment has the effect of materially changing the duties that the obligor must perform, it is ineffective. Changing the party to whom the obligor must make a payment is not a material change of duty that will defeat an assignment, since that, of course, is the purpose behind most assignments. Nor will a minor change in the duties the obligor must perform defeat the assignment.

Several residents in the town of Centerville sign up on an annual basis with Quick-Throw Newspaper Delivery Service to receive their morning paper. A customer who is moving out of town may assign his right to receive the paper to someone else within the delivery route. As long as the assignee pays for the paper, the assignment is effective; the only relationship the obligor has to the assignee is a routine delivery in exchange for payment. But when the obligor's performance depends on a relationship with someone else that is not routine, the assignment may be fatally defective. For example, a student, seeking to earn pocket money during the school year, signs up to do research work for a professor she admires and with whom she is friendly. The professor assigns the contract to one of his colleagues with whom the student does not get along. The assignment is ineffective because the student's duties have been materially changed. Obligors can consent in the original contract, however, to a subsequent assignment of duties. Here is a clause from the World Team Tennis League contract: "It is mutually agreed that the Club shall have the right to sell, assign, trade and transfer this contract to another Club in the League, and the Player agrees to accept and be bound by such sale, exchange, assignment or transfer and to faithfully perform and carry out his or her obligations under this contract as if it had been entered into by the Player and such other Club." Consent is not necessary when the contract does not involve a personal relationship, as the following case shows.

NOLAN v. WILLIAMSON MUSIC, INC.
300 F.Supp. 1311 (S.D.N.Y. 1969)

EDELSTEIN, DISTRICT JUDGE. This action was brought by Robert Nolan, the composer of a musical composition entitled "Tumbling Tumbleweeds," and tried before the court without a jury. The plaintiff seeks, first of all, a declaration that a July 11, 1934, publishing agreement and a March 1, 1960, assignment were rescinded on May 16, 1963, and the defendants have had no rights in and to the song since that date.

* * *

Plaintiff composed "Tumbling Tumbleweeds" in 1929, and, in an agreement dated April 3, 1934, he entered into a publishing agreement with one Harry Walker, doing business as Sunset Publishing Company. However, shortly thereafter, Nolan and Walker by mutual consent rescinded their agreement, and, together with one Harry Hall, joined in an assignment of the song and its copyright to the Sam Fox Publishing Company (Sam Fox).

The assignment of Sam Fox Publishing Company was dated July 11, 1934, and it provided, *inter alia*, that the "Composers" (defined as Nolan, Walker and Hall) conveyed to the "Publisher" (defined as Sam Fox Publishing Company), its successors and assigns forever, all the right, title and interest of every kind, nature and description, including the copyright therein, throughout the world, of the Composers in 'Tumbling Tumbleweeds.' " This agreement also recites that it was the intention of the parties:

> to transfer to the Publisher all rights of every kind, nature and description (including the rights generally known in the field and musical endeavor as the moral rights of the authors) throughout the world which the Composers have, own and possess in and to the said musical composition and no right of any kind, nature or description is [to be] reserved by the Composers.

The "Composers" also agreed to renew the copyright on the song and then to assign the renewal term to the "Publisher."

* * *

Between 1934 and 1946 Sam Fox Publishing Company published and exploited "Tumbling Tumbleweeds." Subsequently, by an agreement dated January 28, 1946, Sam Fox assigned all of its right and interest in and to the song to defendant, Williamson Music, Inc., (Williamson) and agreed to use its best efforts to obtain the renewal copyright of the song and then to assign the renewal term to Williamson. Williamson was obligated to reimburse Sam Fox for any bonus or advance that the latter was required to pay in order to obtain the renewal term, provided that Williamson first approved in writing the amount involved.

* * *

The instant action followed a letter dated May 29, 1963, which Nolan sent to Fox and Williamson seeking to terminate any and all agreements relating to "Tumbling Tumbleweeds" between Nolan and Fox.

(*continued on next page*)

(*continued*)

**NOLAN v.
WILLIAMSON
MUSIC, INC.**
300 F.Supp. 1311
(S.D.N.Y. 1969)

*   *   *

The basic claim which plaintiff has urged in this suit is that he had the legal right to, and, in fact, did rescind his agreements with Fox by the May 29, 1963, notice. Plaintiff argues that rescission is justified in this case because . . . [of the] assignment of the copyright and its renewal term to Williamson.

*   *   *

The court finds that it was not a breach of contract for Sam Fox to assign the copyright to Williamson. The 1934 transfer from plaintiff to Sam Fox of "all rights of every kind, nature and description" which plaintiff had in the copyright was clearly absolute on its face. Furthermore, the agreement specifically provided that the conveyance was to the "Publisher, its successors and assigns." Whether a contract is assignable or not is, of course, a matter of contractual intent, and one must look to the language used by the parties to discern that intent. Clearly the language just quoted contemplated that the agreement was to be assignable. Williston on Contracts, § 423 (3rd ed. 1962).

The plaintiff seems to be saying, however, that this contract involved such personal elements of trust and confidence that it was not assignable without the consent of the parties despite the clear language to the contrary. This argument, though, is not premised upon any reliable evidence adduced at the trial which would demonstrate that Nolan entered into his agreement with Fox because of any personal trust and confidence which he placed in Fox. . . .

Plaintiff's assertions of fraud are based in part upon the allegation that Fox concealed from plaintiff its relationship with Williamson by never giving plaintiff actual notice of the assignment. The evidence, however, does not support a finding of fraud in this regard. It is true that Fox never gave plaintiff actual notice of the assignment, but the court has already held that the contract was assignable without Fox's first having to obtain the plaintiff's consent. Further, far from demonstrating an intent to conceal the assignment, the evidence shows that the defendants openly announced the fact of their arrangement in an advertisement placed in the trade newspaper "Variety" shortly after the assignment was made in 1946. Additionally, the assignment was registered in the Copyright Office and the Fox-Williamson relationship was noted on the copies of sheet music which were distributed.

*   *   *

It is the judgment of this court that plaintiff's agreements with Fox are not rescinded. Plaintiff is entitled to the payment of royalties due him under his 1934 and 1960 agreements with Fox and the court directs an accounting limited to the period commencing six years prior to the commencement of this action, except that this six-year limitation does not apply to the money due plaintiff for royalties derived from foreign mechanical income. The counterclaims alleged by the defendants are dismissed.

Assignment Forbidden by Statute or Public Policy
As noted in Chapter 26, the FTC prohibits the use of wage assignments in consumer credit contracts by lenders and retail installment sellers. In addition, more than forty states have statutes regulating the assignment of wages. Many of the statutes prohibit assignment of more than a certain percentage of a person's wages, or limit assignments to wages above a threshold amount, or restrict the duration of the assignment. A few states prohibit any assignment of future wages. The laws prescribe a variety of formal requirements to be observed in making the assignments. Still other states proscribe wage assignments for certain transactions, such as retail installment sales. Even in the absence of statute, public policy may prohibit wage assignments; for example, most courts would not enforce an assignment of future wages of a public official, because the knowledge that future earnings were not due him might lead the official to perform less diligently. Federal laws prohibit assigning federal contracts or claims against the United States unless they are assigned on a one-time basis to a financial institution for payment.

Contracts That Prohibit Assignment Many contracts contain general language that prohibits assignment of rights or of "the contract." Both the Restatement (Section 322) and UCC Section 2-210(3) declare that in the absence of any contrary circumstances, a provision in the agreement that prohibits assigning "the contract" bars "only the delegation to the assignee of the assignor's performance." In other words, unless the contract specifically prohibits assignment of any of its terms, a party is free to assign anything except his own duties.

Even if a contractual provision explicitly prohibits it, a right to damages for breach of the whole contract is assignable under UCC Section 2-210(2) in contracts for goods. Likewise, UCC Section 9-318(4) invalidates any contract provision that prohibits assigning sums already due or to become due. Indeed, in some states at common law a clause specifically prohibiting assignment will fail. For example, the buyer and seller agree to the sale of land and to a provision barring assignment of the rights under the contract. The buyer pays the full price, but the seller refuses to convey. The buyer then assigns to her friend the right to obtain title to the land from the seller.

The latter's objection that the contract precludes such an assignment will fall on deaf ears in some states; the assignment is effective and the friend may sue for the title.

Future Contracts The law distinguishes between assigning future rights under an existing contract and assigning rights that will arise from a future contract. Rights contingent on a future event can be assigned in exactly the same manner as existing rights, as long as the contingent rights are already incorporated in a contract. Ben has a long-standing deal with his neighbor, Mrs. Robinson, to keep the latter's walk clear of snow at $10 a snowfall. Ben is saving his money for a stereo system, but when he is $50 shy of the purchase price he becomes impatient and cajoles a friend into loaning him the balance. In return, Ben assigns his friend the earnings from the next five snowfalls. The assignment is effective. However, a right that will arise from a future contract cannot be the subject of a present assignment.

Partial Assignments

An assignor may assign part of a contractual right, but only if the obligor can perform that part of his contractual obligation separately from the remainder of his obligation. Assignment of part of a payment due is always enforceable. However, if the obligor objects, neither the assignor nor the assignee may sue him unless both are party to the suit. Mrs. Robinson owes Ben $100. Ben assigns $50 of that sum to his friend. Mrs. Robinson is perplexed by this assignment and refuses to pay until the situation is explained to her satisfaction. The friend brings suit against Mrs. Robinson. The court cannot hear the case unless Ben is also a party to the suit.

Successive Assignments

It may happen that an assignor assigns the same interest twice (see Figure 13-3). With certain exceptions, the first assignee takes precedence over any subsequent assignee. One obvious exception is when the first assignment is ineffective or revocable. A subsequent assignment has the effect of revoking a prior

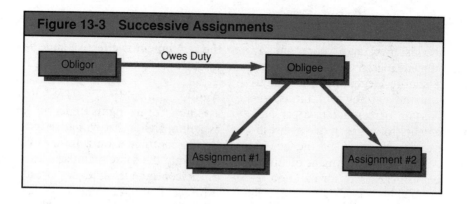

Figure 13-3   Successive Assignments

assignment that is ineffective or revocable. Another exception: if in good faith the subsequent assignee gives consideration for the assignment and has no knowledge of the prior assignment, he takes precedence whenever he obtains payment from, performance from, or a judgment against the obligor, or whenever he receives some tangible evidence from the assignor that the right has been assigned (for example, a bank deposit book or an insurance policy).

Some states follow the different English rule: the first assignee to give notice to the obligor has priority, regardless of the order in which the assignments were made. Furthermore, if the assignment falls within the filing requirements of UCC Article 9 (see Chapter 27), the first assignee to file will prevail.

Assignor's Warranties

An assignor has legal responsibilities in making assignments. He cannot blithely assign the same interests pell-mell and escape liability. Unless the contract explicitly states to the contrary, a person who assigns a right for value warrants to the assignee that he will not upset the assignment, that he has the right to make it, and that there are no defenses that will defeat it. However, the assignor does not guarantee payment; assignment does not by itself amount to a warranty that the obligor is solvent or will perform as agreed in the original contract. Mrs. Robinson owes Ben $50. Ben assigns this sum to his friend. Before the friend collects, Ben releases Mrs. Robinson from her obligation. The friend may sue Ben for the $50.

DELEGATION OF DUTIES

Basic Rules

To this point we have been considering the assignment of the assignor's rights (usually, though not solely, to money payments). But in every contract, a right connotes a corresponding duty, and these may be assigned—or **delegated,** as it is more properly called. Because most obligees are also obligors, most assignments of rights will simultaneously carry with them the delegation of duties. Unless public policy or the contract itself bars the delegation, it is legally enforceable.

In most states, at common law, duties must be expressly assigned. Under UCC Section 2-210(4) and in a minority of states at common law (as illustrated in the following case) an assignment of "the contract"

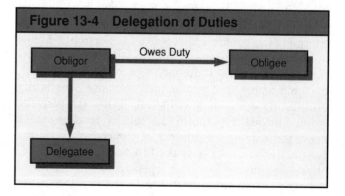

Figure 13-4   Delegation of Duties

or of "all my rights under the contract" is not only an assignment of rights but also a delegation of duties to be performed; by accepting the assignment, the assignee impliedly promises to perform the duties. The assignee would be known as a **delegatee** of the duties (see Figure 13-4).

ROSE v. VULCAN MATERIALS CO.
282 N.C. 643, 194 S.E.2d 521 (1973)

[Plaintiff instituted suit to recover damages for breach of contract. The trial court held for the plaintiff but on appeal the Court of Appeals reversed. This opinion is of the Supreme Court of North Carolina.]
HUSKINS, JUSTICE.

*   *   *

The agreement between the original parties, embodied in plaintiff's Exhibits A and B, consisted of mutual promises: Plaintiff, after leasing his quarry to J. E. Dooley and Son, Inc., promised not to engage in the rock-crushing business within an eight-mile radius of Elkin for a period of ten years. In return for this promise, J. E. Dooley and Son, Inc., promised, among other things, to furnish plaintiff stone f.o.b. the quarry site at Cycle, North Carolina, at stipulated prices for ten years. Thus, the agreement was an executory bilateral contract under which plaintiff's promise not to compete for ten years gained him a ten-year option to buy stone at specified prices.

In most states, the assignee of an executory bilateral contract is not liable to anyone for the non-performance of the assignor's duties thereunder unless he expressly promises his assignor or the other contracting party to perform, or "assume," such duties. These states refuse to *imply* a promise to perform the duties, but if the assignee expressly promises his assignor to perform, he is liable to the other contracting party on a third-party beneficiary theory. And, if the assignee makes such a promise directly to the other contracting party upon a consideration, of course he is liable to him thereon.

A minority of states holds that the assignee of an executory bilateral contract under a general assignment becomes not only assignee of the rights of the assignor but also delegatee of his duties; and that, absent a showing of contrary intent, the assignee *impliedly* promises the assignor that he will perform the duties so delegated. This rule is expressed in Restatement, Contracts, § 164 (1932) as follows:

1. Where a party under a bilateral contract which is at the time wholly or partially executory on both sides purports to assign the whole contract, his action is interpreted, in the absence of circumstances showing a contrary intention, as an assignment of the assignor's rights under the contract and a delegation of the performance of the assignor's duties.

2. Acceptance by the assignee of such an assignment is interpreted, in the absence of circumstances showing a contrary intention, as both an assent to become an assignee of the assignor's rights and as a *promise to the assignor to assume the performance of the assignor's duties.* (Emphasis added.)

(continued on next page)

(continued)

ROSE v. VULCAN MATERIALS CO.
282 N.C. 643, 194 S.E.2d 521 (1973)

* * *

We . . . adopt the Restatement rule and expressly hold that the assignee under a general assignment of an executory bilateral contract, in the absence of circumstances showing a contrary intention, becomes the delegatee of his assignor's duties and impliedly promises his assignor that he will perform such duties.

The rule we adopt and reaffirm here is regarded as the more reasonable view by legal scholars and textwriters. Professor Grismore says:

> It is submitted that the acceptance of an assignment in this form does presumptively import a tacit promise on the part of the assignee to assume the burdens of the contract, and that this presumption should prevail in the absence of the clear showing of a contrary intention. The presumption seems reasonable in view of the evident expectation of the parties. The assignment on its face indicates an intent to do more than simply to transfer the benefits assured by the contract. It purports to transfer the contract as a whole, and since the contract is made up of both benefits and burdens both must be intended to be included.

> (Grismore, Is the Assignee of a Contract Liable for the Nonperformance of Delegated Duties? 18 Mich.L.Rev. 284 (1920).)

* * *

In addition, with respect to transactions governed by the Uniform Commercial Code, an assignment of a contract in general terms is a delegation of performance of the duties of the assignor, and its acceptance by the assignee constitutes a promise by him to perform those duties. Our holding in this case maintains a desirable uniformity in the field of contract liability.

We further hold that the other party to the original contract may sue the assignee as a third-party beneficiary of his promise of performance which he impliedly makes to his assignor, under the rule above laid down, by accepting the general assignment. *Younce v. Lumber Co.*, 61 S.E. 624 (1908), holds that where the assignee makes an express promise of performance to his assignor, the other contracting party may sue him for breach thereof. We see no reason why the same result should not obtain where the assignee breaches his promise of performance *implied* under the rule of Restatement § 164. "That the assignee is liable at the suit of the third party where he expressly assumes and promises to perform delegated duties has already been decided in a few cases [citing *Younce*]. If an express promise will support such an action it is difficult to see why a tacit promise should not have the same effect." *Grismore*, supra. Parenthetically, we note that such is the rule under the Uniform Commercial Code, G.S. § 25-2-210(4).

We now apply the foregoing principles to the case at hand. The contract of 23 April 1960, Exhibit F, between defendant and J. E. Dooley and Son, Inc., under which, as stipulated by the parties, "the defendant purchased the assets and obligations of J. E. Dooley and Son, Inc.," was a general assignment of *all* the assets and obligations of J. E. Dooley and Son, Inc., including those under Exhibit B. When defendant accepted such assignment it thereby became delegatee of its assignor's duties under Exhibit B and impliedly promised to perform such duties.

When defendant later failed to perform such duties by refusing to continue sales of stone to plaintiff at the prices specified in Exhibit B, it breached its implied promise of performance and plaintiff was entitled to bring suit thereon as a third-party beneficiary.

★ ★ ★

The decision of the Court of Appeals is reversed with directions that the case be certified to the Superior Court of Forsyth County for reinstatement of the judgment of the trial court in accordance with this opinion.

Effect on Obligor   An obligor who delegates a duty does not thereby escape liability for performing the duty himself. The obligee of the duty may continue to look to the obligor for performance, unless the original contract specifically provides for substitution by delegation. The obligee may also, in many cases, look to the delegatee, because the obligee becomes an intended beneficiary of the contract between the obligor and delegatee. Of course, the obligee may subsequently agree to accept the delegatee and discharge the obligor from any further responsibility for performing the duty. A contract among three persons having this effect is called a **novation**. Fred sells his house to Lisa, who assumes his mortgage. Fred, in other words, has delegated the duty to pay the bank to Lisa. If Lisa defaults, Fred continues to be liable to the bank, unless in the original mortgage agreement a provision specifically permitted any purchaser to be substituted without recourse to Fred, or unless the bank subsequently accepts Lisa and discharges Fred.

Nondelegable Duties

Personal Promises   Personal promises are not delegable. If the contract is such that the promisee expects the obligor personally to perform the duty, the obligor may not delegate it. Suppose the Podunk Civic Opera Association hires Maria Callas to sing in its production of *Carmen* and that Callas delegates the job to her cleaning woman, who has always wanted to be on stage. The delegation is ineffective, and performance by the cleaning woman does not absolve Callas of liability for breach.

Many duties may be delegated, however. Indeed, if they could not be delegated much of the world's work would not get done. If you hire a construction company and an architect to design and build your house to certain specifications, the contractor may in turn hire individual craftspeople—plumbers, electricians, and the like—to do these specialized jobs, and as long as they are performed to specification, the contract terms will have been met.

Public Policy   Public policy may prohibit certain kinds of delegations. A public official, for example, may not delegate the duties of his office to private citizens, although various statutes generally permit the delegation of duties to his assistants and subordinates.

Barred by Contract   As we have already noted, the contract itself may bar assignment. The law generally frowns on restricting the right to assign a benefit, but it will uphold a contract provision that prohibits delegation of a duty. Thus, as we saw above, UCC Section 2-210(3) states that in a contract for sale of goods, a provision against assigning "the contract" is to be construed only as a prohibition against delegating the duties.

CHAPTER SUMMARY

The parties to a contract are not necessarily the only people who acquire rights or duties under it. One major category of persons acquiring rights are third-party beneficiaries. Only intended beneficiaries acquire rights under the contract, and these are of two types: creditor and donee beneficiaries. The rules for determining whether rights have been conferred are rather straightforward; determining whether rights can subsequently be modified or extinguished is more troublesome. Generally, as long as the contract does not prohibit change and as long as the beneficiary has not relied on the promise, the change may be made.

Contract rights may be assigned—factoring is an important example. The general rule that the promisee may assign any right is subject to exception—for example, when the promisor's obligation would be materially changed. Of course the contract itself may prohibit assignment, and sometimes statutes preclude it. Knowing how to make the assignment effective and what the consequences of the assignment are on others is worth mastering. When, for example, does the assignee not stand in the assignor's shoes? When may a future right be assigned?

Duties, as well as rights, may be transferred to third parties. Most rights (promises) contained in contracts have corresponding duties (also expressed as promises). Often when an entire contract is assigned, the duties go with it; the transferee is known, with respect to the duties, as the delegatee. The transferor himself does not necessarily escape the duty, however. Moreover, some duties are nondelegable, such as personal promises and those that public policy require to be carried out by a particular official. Without the ability to assign rights and duties, much of the modern economy would grind to a halt.

KEY TERMS

Creditor beneficiary	p. 300	Gift promise	p. 302
Delegatee	p. 313	Incidental beneficiary	p. 302
Donee beneficiary	p. 300	Intended beneficiary	p. 300
Factoring	p. 306	Novation	p. 315

SELF-TEST QUESTIONS

1. A creditor beneficiary is:
   (a) the same as a donee beneficiary
   (b) a third-party beneficiary
   (c) an incidental beneficiary
   (d) none of the above

2. Assignments are not allowed:
   (a) for rights that will arise from a future contract
   (b) when they will materially change the duties that the obliger must perform
   (c) where they are forbidden by public policy
   (d) all of the above

3. When an assignor assigns the same interest twice:
   (a) the subsequent assignee generally takes precedence
   (b) the first assignee generally takes precedence
   (c) the first assignee always takes precedence
   (d) the assignment violates public policy

4. Factoring:
   (a) is an example of delegation of duties
   (b) involves using an account receivable as collateral for a loan
   (c) involves the purchase of a right to receive income from another
   (d) all of the above

5. Personal promises:
   (a) are always delegable
   (b) are generally not delegable
   (c) are delegable if not prohibited by public policy
   (d) are delegable if not barred by the contract

DEMONSTRATION PROBLEM

Marilyn entered into a contract to sell her restaurant to Joe for $100,000. The contract provided that Joe would pay $10,000 down and sign a note for the remaining $90,000. Joe later sold the restaurant to Alice, who agreed to assume responsibility for the balance due on the note held by Marilyn. Alice then sold the restaurant to Clyde for cash, spent the money, and declared bankruptcy. Is Joe still liable to Marilyn on the note? Why?

PROBLEMS

1. Bjorn owned and operated a tennis club. Needing additional capital, he entered into an agreement to borrow $100,000 from Shady Bank. The money was to be advanced monthly, in ten installments of $10,000 each. Bjorn did not give the bank a note. Before Bjorn received the first installment payment, Shady Bank assigned its contract rights to Honest Bank for $85,000. Shortly thereafter Shady Bank went into bankruptcy. Honest Bank now claims that, because it purchased in good faith a contract right for $85,000 and became an assignee, Bjorn owes it $100,000. Bjorn claims that he owes nothing because Shady Bank did not actually make the loan as promised. Who is correct? Why?

2. In problem 1, would the result be different if Bjorn had given Shady Bank a note that was considered to be a negotiable instrument? Why?

3. Barbie rented an apartment from Hugh. Barbie's lease provided that Hugh would buy fire insurance and that Barbie would be covered by the policy. Hugh also promised to repair at his own expense any damage resulting from fire. Hugh purchased the required policy but failed to add Barbie's name. The apartment building burned down as a result of Barbie's negligence. The insurance company paid Hugh $150,000 and, in return, received an assignment of Hugh's rights. May the insurance company, in a suit against Barbie, collect the $150,000 from her? Why?

4. Sly, a book salesman, visited Franco's home. Sly stated that he represented the local school board and that Franco was required to purchase certain books for his children. Franco signed a contract to purchase the books, and the contract contained a waiver of defense clause which provided that "buyer will not assert any defenses in an action for payment which may be brought by an assignee who acquires this contract in good faith and for value." Sly immediately assigned his rights to Assignments Unlimited (A.U.), a company that had supplied Sly with contract forms which included its name and the assignment form. Franco has now learned that Sly did not represent the school board and that the books were not required. Furthermore, the books were never delivered. Must Franco pay A.U.? Why?

5. Rudy entered into a contract to sell his 1954 Rambler to Trudy for $400. Rudy assigned his right to payment of the $400 to Judy, who immediately notified Trudy of the assignment. Before the contract was performed, Trudy decided that she would rather have Rudy's 1953 Rambler. Rudy and Trudy thereupon agreed to modify the contract to provide that Trudy would receive the 1953 Rambler for $300. Is Judy entitled to $400 or $300? Why?

6. Mario owned a new Corvette, which was insured by Catch 22 Insurance Company. Mario was a safe driver and had never received a speeding ticket. Mario decided to sell the car to Johnny, who had received numerous speeding tickets and had been involved in several accidents. As part of the deal, Mario assigned his insurance contract to Johnny and sent a notice of assignment to Catch 22. Is Johnny covered by the policy? Why?

7. After graduating from Big U, Grover accepted a position with the Ford Motor Company. Grover was deeply in debt and, as a result, assigned a small percentage of his wages to his creditors. After Grover had been on the job for four months, his boss walked into the office and said: "I've got some news for you, kid. You've been traded to General Motors. Under the contract of assignment, your job responsibilities, salary, and benefits—and even the size of your office—will be identical to what you have now." When Grover started to object, the boss said: "Look, kid, you're a star. And this happens to star athletes all the time." Discuss the legality of Grover's assignment of his wages and the company's assignment of his services.

ANSWERS TO SELF-TEST QUESTIONS

1. (b)   2. (d)   3. (b)   4. (c)   5. (b)

SUGGESTED ANSWER TO DEMONSTRATION PROBLEM

Joe is still liable to Marilyn. He delegated to Alice his duty to pay but Marilyn (the obligee) never agreed to release Joe from the debt. Joe should have obtained her agreement—a novation—when the restaurant was sold to Alice.

CHAPTER OVERVIEW
Discharge of Contract Duties
Discharge of Duties in General

Discharge of Obligations

*I*n this chapter and the next we deal with the last of the four broad themes of contract law: How are contract duties discharged (that is, legally complied with); when, in other words, does a contract terminate? And, if duties are not discharged, what remedies are available to the party who failed to get the benefit or performance due him under the contract? In this chapter we will consider discharge; in the next, remedies.

Contractual duties are not the only kinds of legal obligations. A duty can arise from a breach of contract or from some other act, such as the commission of a tort. A duty, that is, can be imposed by law as well as by private agreement. We will consider discharge of duties in general, as well as the various means of discharging contractual duties in particular.

DISCHARGE OF CONTRACT DUTIES

Performance of the Duty

Full performance of the contractual obligation discharges the duty. On its face, this rule is obvious enough, but its corollary is that anything less than full performance, even a slight deviation from that which is owned, is sufficient to prevent the duty from being discharged and can amount to a breach of con-

tract. Determining when a contractual requirement has been fully performed is not always easy, and we will explore the problems of nonperformance below (and in Chapter 18 we will consider performance of sales contracts). For now, note that nonperformance does not amount to a breach unless the time has arrived for performance under the contract.

Conditions

The most common bilateral contract consists of an exchange of promises—a pledge or commitment by each party that an event will or will not occur. Andy's promise to cut Anne's lawn "over the weekend" in return for Anne's promise to pay $20 is a commitment to have the lawn mowed by Sunday night or Monday morning. Andy's promise "not to tell anyone what I saw you doing Saturday night" in return for Anne's promise to pay $100 is a commitment that an event (the revealing of a secret) will not occur. These promises are known as independent or absolute or unconditional, because their performance does not depend on any outside event. Such promises, if contractually binding, create a present duty to perform (or a duty to perform at the time stated).

Many promises are contingent on the happening of an external event. These promises are said to be conditional, and the external event is known as a **condition.** Andy's promise to cut Anne's lawn over the weekend "if it does not rain" does not create an immediate duty to perform. Indeed, there may never be a duty to perform; the duty arises only if the weather remains dry. A condition is an event the happening or nonhappening of which gives rise to a duty to perform (or discharges a duty to perform).

There are different types of conditions. Although the Restatement dispenses with many of the terms, we will refer to them in their time-honored way. If there is no duty to perform unless a particular event occurs (or does not occur), the event is known as a **condition precedent;** that is, the event precedes and gives rise to the requirement of performance. Andy's promise to mow Anne's lawn "provided that it does not rain" is subject to a condition precedent: that it not rain. If rain comes, there is no duty to cut the lawn, and Andy's failure to do so is not a breach of promise. A condition that terminates an already existing duty of performance is known as a **condition subsequent.** Thus, Andy's promise not to tell anyone what he saw Anne doing may be conditioned on Anne's return promise not to tell anyone what she saw him doing on the same evening. His duty to remain silent lasts only as long as she sticks to her pledge to do likewise. If she blabs, he is no longer bound to his promise. For most purposes, whether a condition is precedent or subsequent is irrelevant to the analysis, but the terms may help to clarify the relationship between the promises and the conditions.

A promise given in consideration of another promise can be a condition. Anne's promise to pay Andy $5 per hour to cut her grass is conditioned on Andy's actually mowing the lawn. Anne has no obligation to pay him unless he performs. Andy's promise thus creates both a duty of performance in him and a condition precedent for Anne's performance. If Andy fails to cut the grass, Anne has no obligation to pay and Andy may be liable to her for damages for breaching the contract.

Conditions can be concurrent. Many bilateral contracts are conditioned on the simultaneous performance of mutual promises—for example, the promise of a landowner to transfer title to the purchaser and of the purchaser to tender payment to the seller. The duty of each to perform is conditioned on the performance of the other. (As a practical matter, of course, someone will make the first move, proffering the deed or tendering the check.) Concurrent conditions are a special type of condition precedent.

Turning an Event into a Condition   An event can become a condition by agreement of the parties. No special language is necessary to create an express condition, but such phrases as "provided that," "on condition that," and "if" are frequently used and signal the existence of a condition. Whatever the language, the intention of the parties continues to be the touchstone in interpretation of the contract, and the purpose of the parties can determine whether a condition was intended. A contract for the sale of a house might say that "this contract is conditional on approval of buyer's mortgage from the Friendly Savings Bank." The purpose of such a clause is to excuse the buyer from having to tender the purchase price if he cannot secure a mortgage. It is a condition precedent to the buyer's obligation, not to the seller's. If Friendly Savings refuses to give the buyer a mortgage, the contract is not necessarily terminated; should the buyer come up with the purchase price elsewhere and tender it on the date set, the seller is bound to transfer title.

The nature of the event may also determine how a condition should be interpreted. The Restatement (Section 226, illustration 5) provides an example of a storekeeper insured against burglary from a safe kept on the premises. The insurance policy includes a provision that "entry be made by actual force and violence, of which there are visible marks upon the exterior of all of the doors of the safe if entry is made through such doors." Suppose a burglar picks the lock and pushes through to the inside, leaving no marks on the exterior. On its face, it may appear that the condition will defeat the storekeeper's claim. But the purpose of the condition is to prevent fraudulent claims; the requirement for visibility serves this evidentiary purpose. When palpable evidence of burglary exists, a court can interpret the condition as having occurred. (One form of evidence may be substituted for another.)

A condition also may be **implied in law,** meaning that a court will supply a term, thus making an event a condition. (Such conditions are sometimes known as **constructive conditions,** because a court adds them in construing the contract.) Bernice leases a house to Martha and agrees to keep the appliances in good repair. The lease gives Bernice no right to inspect the house from time to time. The refrigerator

LAW AND LIFE

BOX 14-1

Vain Hopes Remain Thus for Admirer Who Sued

By Les Ledbetter

[*A court may supply a term, known as a constructive condition, making an event a condition. In cases of social engagement, the promiser's ability to attend an event is always conditioned by his or her disposition towards the event.*—AUTHORS' NOTE]

SAN FRANCISCO, July 27—With quotes from Quintilian, Lord Byron and California's "anti-heart balm" statutes, a judge ruled today that a jilted accountant had no cause to sue a woman who did not keep a dinner and theater date with him earlier this year.

"The court finds that the promise to engage in a social relationship for one evening in exchange for affection and/or one evening at the theater is unenforceable under the law of contracts and torts," Judge Richard P. Figone of small claims court wrote

A DATE WITH A CONSTRUCTIVE CONDITION

in his decision on a suit filed by Tom Horsley, who had sought compensation for his time and for expenses he incurred in preparation for the date.

"The promise to attend a social engagement is always conditioned by the promiser's ability or disposition to attend the event," the judge wrote.

Sudden Pains, Other Affections

"This is particularly true within the context of a 'dating situation,'" he said, noting that the promiser may have "a sudden stomach pain" or "a headache" or "in extreme situations, showering affection elsewhere."

Judge Figone then said, "Quintilian, in the first century A.D., observed that vain hopes are often like the dreams of those who wake."

In his suit, Mr. Horsley, 41 years old, had sought $38 from Alyn Chesslet, 31, who he said failed to make a "good faith effort" to tell him she was breaking the date before he drove 40 miles from San Jose to San Francisco.

A Higher Consciousness

"If there'd been another judge it could have gone the other way," Mr. Horsley said today. "I think this judge was biased. Apparently, he relied on old law, very old law; we need a judge ruling new law. But I feel good about the whole thing, and it raised people's consciousness about this problem."

Miss Chesslet could not be reached for comment.

Judge Figone noted that the state legislature in 1939 abolished penalties for "breach of marriage promise" and in 1959 had eliminated penalties of "fraudulent promise to marry or cohabit."

Mr. Horsley, he said, did not even "reach the dubious status rendered ignominious by the legislature."

Judge Figone ordered that a red cardboard heart with a symbolic rip, tagged Exhibit A, be returned to Mr. Horsley, "mindful of Lord Byron's admonition, 'Maid of Athens, 'ere we part, oh, give me back my heart.'"

"No," the judge said later, "I don't think it should have ever been in court."

Source: *New York Times*, July 28, 1978

---

breaks. Bernice has no duty to repair it until Martha has given her notice. Martha has no duty under the contract to give notice, but her doing so is nevertheless a condition to Bernice's obligation to perform. Whether a court will infer a condition from the agreement depends upon the circumstances, as one suitor discovered when he sought judicial surcease for his aching heart (See **Box 14-1**).

Effect of Nonoccurrence of a Condition   The nonoccurrence of a condition prevents any duty subject to it from being due and (if not excused, as will be discussed shortly) negates the duty when it is no longer possible for the condition to occur. Wilbur gives $50,000 to Orville to perfect a "dripless" ice cream.

Under their agreement, Orville is to use his best efforts and is to repay Wilbur from any proceeds of the sale of his invention. Orville takes the money and tries diligently for thirty-five years to come up with ice cream that will not drip but fails and dies brokenhearted. Wilbur sues Orville's estate to recover his "loan." Since the event on which the contract was conditioned did not occur, Orville's estate has no obligation to refund the money.

Whether the nonoccurrence of the condition is a breach of contract depends on the nature of the condition. If one party's obligation hinges on the outcome of a particular event not subject to the control of the other party, the failure of the event to take place discharges the obligation and does not give rise to a suit for breach of contract. Andy's promise to cut Anne's lawn provided that it is sunny on Saturday is discharged if the day is cloudy and wet, and since the condition itself was not an obligation of performance by either party, the contract is not breached. However, if the condition was itself the promised performance of the second party, then there is a breach if he fails to carry it out. Barry agrees to drive Rachel across country for $100. Rachel says she will pay $50 extra if Barry will drive straight through and not stop off to go backpacking in New Mexico. But Barry drives to New Mexico and spends four days there. Rachel's duty to pay $50 is discharged, since this was a unilateral contract and Barry did not obligate himself to drive straight through. Suppose, however, that Barry does agree to drive nonstop, and despite this agreement he nevertheless stops off in New Mexico. Then Rachel's duty to pay is discharged, and Barry is liable for breach of contract.

The nonoccurrence of a condition can be excused—meaning that despite the nonoccurrence, the duty subject to it is due and is legally required to be performed. An excuse may be brought about in several ways: a party may promise to carry out his duty despite the failure of the condition to occur, or a party with control over the event in question may have failed to act in good faith, or it may have been impossible for the event to occur. But whether nonoccurrence is excusable depends always on the particular circumstances of the case; whenever excuse is pleaded, the courts will inquire into the reasonableness of the parties' conduct.

CITY OF WEST HAVEN v. U.S. FIDELITY & GUARANTY CO.
174 Conn. 392, 389 A.2d 741 (1978)

SPEZIALE, ASSOCIATE JUSTICE. The defendant, United States Fidelity & Guaranty Company (hereinafter USF&G), has appealed from a judgment holding it liable to the city of West Haven in the amount of $20,000. The city claimed the sum as indemnification for payments made to satisfy a judgment against it by Fred Annunziata, who was injured on city property while the city was insured under a liability insurance policy issued by the defendant. The defendant disclaimed liability on the ground that the city had failed to comply with certain conditions precedent set forth in the policy. On appeal, USF&G contends that these conditions were not met and that the trial court therefore erred in finding it liable to the plaintiff.

The underlying facts are not in dispute. The plaintiff, the city of West Haven, was insured under a liability policy issued by USF&G from July 1, 1965, to July 1, 1966. Paragraph 13 of the policy provided that no action would lie against the insurer unless, as a condition precedent, the insured fully complied with the terms of the policy, nor until the insured's obligation became finally determined either by judgment after actual trial or by written agreement of the insured, the claimant and the insurer. Paragraph 10 of the policy required that when an accident occurred, the insured would notify USF&G "as soon as practicable"; and paragraph 11 required the insured to forward "immediately" every demand, notice, summons or other process received, in the event that any claim was made or suit brought against it.

On May 10, 1966, Fred Annunziata, an employee of United Illuminating Company, was injured in a pumping station owned by the plaintiff. In July, 1966, Jack Norton, superintendent of sewers for the city, became aware of the accident when two of his men reported that photographers were in the pumping station. Norton called United Illuminating and ascertained that

(continued on next page)

(continued)

CITY OF WEST HAVEN v. U.S. FIDELITY & GUARANTY CO.
174 Conn. 392, 389 A.2d 741 (1978)

Annunziata was an employee of that company. After this conversation, Norton took no further action regarding the accident.

On May 8, 1967, a writ, summons and complaint brought by Annunziata against the city was filed with the city clerk. At that time the city was insured under a liability policy issued by Travelers Insurance Company. The writ, summons and complaint was forwarded to Travelers by letter dated June 23, 1967; but Travelers, by letter dated June 30, 1967, informed the city's corporation counsel that its insurance coverage had not commenced until July 1, 1967, and suggested that the matter be referred to the city's previous insurance carrier. The appropriate papers were sent to USF&G on September 8, 1967. In October, 1967, USF&G notified the city that the Annunziata suit had been referred to its attorneys under strict reservation of rights, and in January, 1968, it advised the city that it would offer defense only and would not satisfy any ultimate judgment entered against the city. On April 20, 1971, a judgment was entered by stipulation in favor of Annunziata; the city was represented by counsel provided by USF&G, who was present when the judgment was rendered. The judgment was paid by the city on July 1, 1971.

*   *   *

The trial court had ample grounds for determining that the information received by Norton did not constitute notice to the city and that the first notice the city had of the accident was on May 8, 1967, when the writ, summons and complaint was served upon the city clerk. The defendant's claim, therefore, that the city failed to comply with the condition requiring notice of an accident "as soon as practicable" cannot be sustained.

The defendant's next claim is that the city's four-month delay—May 8, 1967, to September 8, 1967—in forwarding the Annunziata writ, summons and complaint constituted a failure to comply with the condition requiring the insured to forward "immediately" every demand, notice, summons or other process. It should be noted that policy provisions employing terms such as "immediately" or "forthwith" are generally construed as requiring only that notice be given within a reasonable time, under the circumstances of the particular case. "[C]ircumstances may be such as to explain or excuse delay in giving notice and show it to be reasonable. . . . When the facts are undisputed and one conclusion only is reasonably possible, the question of compliance with a provision for notice is one of law; otherwise it is a question of fact." *Baker* v. *Metropolitan Casualty Ins. Co.*, supra, 153, 171 A.9.

In this case, the court found as facts that, after the city learned of the accident when suit was filed with the city clerk on May 8, 1967, it inadvertently sent the writ, summons and complaint to Travelers Insurance Company by letter dated June 23, 1967; and, after receiving notice from Travelers, in a letter dated June 30, 1967, that the matter should be referred to the city's former insurance carrier, the city did not forward notice of the accident and suit to USF&G until September 8, 1967. On the basis of these facts, the court concluded that the delay of four months was excusable and reasonable under the circumstances, and sufficient compliance with the "immediate notice" requirement of the policy. We disagree. A conclusion of the trial court will not be disturbed if it is one which could reasonably and logically be reached by the trier and if it is supported by the subordinate facts found. Here, although the subordinate facts might arguably justify a conclusion that the delay from May 8, 1967, to early July, 1967, was excusable, the finding is void of any facts which would excuse the subsequent two-month delay before notice was sent to USF&G on September 8, 1967. Because the conclusion of the court is not supported by the subordinate facts found, it cannot stand.

We hold that, on the facts as found, the four-month delay in notifying USF&G of the accident and suit was neither excusable nor reasonable. This is dispositive of the case. It is, therefore, unnecessary for us to reach the defendant's final claims relating to the plaintiff's failure to satisfy the conditions set forth in paragraph 13 of the policy.

There is error, the judgment is set aside and the case is remanded with direction to render judgment for the defendant.

Contracts can fashion conditions out of any imaginable events, but three in particular are commonplace: satisfaction, certificate of approval, and time of the essence.

Satisfaction   "You must be satisfied or your money back" reads many an advertisement in the daily papers. An obligee can require that he need not pay or otherwise carry out his undertaking unless satisfied by the obligor's performance. Andy tells Anne, a prospective customer, that he will cut her grass better than her regular gardener and that if she is not satisfied she need not pay him. Andy mows the lawn, but Anne frowns and says: "It's terrible. I hate it." Assume that Andy's work is excellent, far surpassing the usual look of Anne's lawn. Whether Anne must pay depends on the standard for judging to be employed—a standard of objective or subjective satisfaction. The objective standard is that which would satisfy the reasonable purchaser. Most courts apply this standard when the contract involves the performance of a mechanical job or the sale of a machine whose performance is capable of objective measurement. So even if the obligee requires performance to his "personal satisfaction," the courts will hold that the obligor has performed if the service performed or the goods produced are in fact satisfactory. By contrast, if the goods or services contracted for involve personal

judgment and taste, the duty to pay will be discharged if the obligee states personal (subjective) dissatisfaction. No reason at all need be given. The statement of dissatisfaction must be in good faith, however. The obligee may not claim to be dissatisfied merely to escape liability for paying. Thus, if Andy could show that Anne had told her neighbor how pleased she was with Andy's work, her expression of dissatisfaction to Andy would not defeat her duty to pay.

Architect's Certificate   Building contracts frequently make the purchaser's duty to pay conditional on the builder's receipt of an architect's certificate of compliance with all contractual terms. This condition can be onerous. The builder has already erected the structure and cannot "return" what he has done. Nevertheless, because the purchaser wants assurance that the building (obviously a major purchase) meets his specifications, the courts will hold the builder to the condition unless it is impossible to provide a certificate (the architect may have died, for example), or the architect has acted in bad faith, or the purchaser has somehow prevented the certificate from issuing.

The architect is a third person, not subject to the contract, and so her judgment is usually final. In a majority of states, if she decides that the building does not live up to the specifications, even in some minor way (wrong shade of paint, missing hardware on kitchen cabinets, basement door too large), and refuses to issue a certificate, the purchaser need not pay. In some states, minor defects will not defeat the contract. The architect's refusal to issue a certificate will be said to be unreasonable; the purchaser must pay, but he has an offset for the defects: if a window is missing, he can deduct the cost of installing it. The architect's dissatisfaction, even if unreasonable, must be honest, however. If the architect fails to inspect the work or is annoyed at the builder and simply refuses to take the time to prepare the certificate, the requirement will be excused. Similarly, if the purchaser and architect are in collusion to prevent issuance, the condition is excused.

Time Is of the Essence   It often makes a difference to the promisee whether the promisor acts on time. If Anne is having a lawn party Saturday evening, she will not be amused by Andy's excuses for having been unable to cut the grass until Sunday morning. When the timeliness of performance is material to the contract, time is said to be "of the essence" of the contract. Time as a condition can be made explicit in a clause reciting that time is of the essence. If there is no express clause, the courts will read it in when the purpose of the contract was clearly to provide for performance at or by a certain time and the promisee will gain little from late performance. But even express clauses are subject to a rule of reason, and if the promisor would suffer greatly by enforcement of the clause (and the promisee would suffer only slightly or not at all from a refusal to invoke it), the courts will generally excuse the untimely performance, as long as it was completed within a reasonable time. A builder's failure to finish a house by July 1 will not discharge the buyer's obligation to pay if the house is finished a week or even a month later, although the builder will be liable to the buyer for expenses incurred because of the lateness (storage charges for furniture, costs for housing during the interim, extra travel, and the like).

Nonperformance

One party's performance is usually a condition for the performance by the other party to the contract. When this is so, material nonperformance by the party whose obligation is prior in time has two consequences: (1) the second party's obligation is either postponed (if there is still time for the condition to be fulfilled) or discharged (if it is too late to be), and (2) the second party can sue for damages for breach of contract (this aspect will be discussed in the following chapter). A contract can contain many obligations; while a failure to carry out one duty is a breach of the contract, it is not necessarily a total breach, and the obligee may still have a duty to perform his other obligations. The failure of a condition affects only those acts subject to it. Independent duties must still be carried out. Suppose a builder and an owner have an arrangement whereby the owner is to make progress payments as the builder completes certain portions of his work. If the owner defaults on one payment, the failure is not necessarily so serious that the entire contract should be considered breached. Nevertheless, further work is contingent on payment, and the builder would be justified in ceasing work until paid. If the period of nonpayment stretches out unreasonably, then the owner's breach will have become so material that the total contract is considered breached, and the builder's obligations to complete the building will be discharged.

Under UCC Section 2-106(4), a party that ends a contract breached by the other party is said to have effected a **cancellation.** The cancelling party retains the right to seek a remedy for breach of the whole contract or any unperformed obligation. The UCC distinguishes cancellation from **termination,** which occurs when either party exercises a lawful right to end the contract other than for breach. When a contract is terminated, all executory duties are discharged on both sides, but if there has been a partial breach, the right to seek a remedy survives. (Section 2-106(3).)

When the contractual promises for exchange of performances are due simultaneously, neither party need perform unless the other party actually renders performance or is able and offers to do so. Under both the common law and the UCC, the tender of performance triggers liability, because the duty to perform is conditional on performance by the other. Andy agrees to mow Anne's lawn on Saturday in time for the big party if she will pick him up, drive him across town to her house, and pay him $10 an hour. Saturday morning, Anne is so busy she forgets to fetch him, and Andy has stayed up so late on Friday that he sleeps most of the next day away and forgets to call her. On Monday, charging that her party was ruined, Anne sues Andy for damages; Andy countersues for his hourly rate. Who wins? Both Anne's claim and Andy's counterclaim will be dismissed. Neither tendered performance: Anne failed to pick Andy up so that he could cut the grass, and Andy was not ready at the appointed time and failed to call Anne to tell her that he was ready.

Substantial Performance   Mutual performances embodied in a contract have the legal effect of a set of concurrent conditions only because the courts have read the conditions into the contract. When one party has substantially performed, the courts are willing, therefore, to modify the rule's logical requirement that each performance be completed fully before the corresponding performance is due. The other party's duty to perform ripens when the first party has substantially performed. Substantial performance thus serves to excuse the failure of the implied condition that performance be completed. If the second party's obligation was to pay, the purchase price is due, less damages for the uncompleted performance. What constitutes substantial performance is a question of fact. These rules are negated whenever the parties *expressly* agree that complete performance of one party is a condition for performance of the other party. In that case, substantial performance does not satisfy the contract and is a breach, discharging the duty of the other party to perform in turn.

As the following case illustrates, the doctrine of substantial performance is not limited to commercial contracts.

RUSSEL v. SALVE REGINA COLLEGE
890 F.2d 484 1st Cir. (1989)

TIMBERS, CIRCUIT JUDGE:

This consolidated appeal arises from the stormy relationship between Sharon L. Russell ("Russell") and Salve Regina College of Newport, Rhode Island ("Salve Regina" or "the College"), which Russell attended from 1982 to 1985. The United States District Court for the District of Rhode Island, Ronald R. Lagueux, *District Judge*, entered a directed verdict for Salve Regina on Russell's claims of invasion of privacy and intentional infliction of emotional distress at the close of plaintiff's case-in-chief, but allowed Russell's breach of contract claim to go to the jury. The jury found that Salve Regina had breached its contract with Russell by expelling her. The court entered judgment on the verdict, denying Salve Regina's motions for judgment n.o.v. and for a new trial. The court also denied Salve Regina's motion for remittitur of the damages of $30,513.40 plus interest, a total of $43,903.45, that the jury awarded Russell.

*   *   *

By all accounts, Sharon Russell was an extremely overweight young woman. In her application for admission to Salve Regina, Russell stated her weight as 280 pounds. The College apparently did not consider her condition a problem at that time, as it accepted her under an early admissions plan. From the start, Russell made it clear that her goal was admission to the College's Nursing Department.

Russell completed her freshman year without significant incident and was accepted in the College's Nursing Department starting in her sophomore year, 1983–84. Her trauma started then. The year began on a sour note when a school administrator told Russell in public that they would have trouble finding

(continued on next page)

(*continued*)

**RUSSEL v. SALVE
REGINA COLLEGE
890 F.2d 484 1st Cir.
(1989)**

a nurse's uniform to fit her. Later, during a class on how to make beds occupied by patients, the instructor had Russell serve as the patient, reasoning aloud that if the students could make a bed occupied by Russell, who weighed over 300 pounds, they would have no problem with real patients. The same instructor used Russell in similar fashion for demonstrations on injections and the taking of blood pressure.

The start of Russell's junior year, 1984–85, coincides with the time school officials began to pressure her directly to lose weight. In the first semester, they tried to get Russell to sign a "contract" stating that she would attend Weight Watchers and to prove it by submitting an attendance record. Russell offered to try to attend weekly, but refused to sign a written promise. Apparently, she did go to Weight Watchers regularly, but did not lose significant weight. One of Russell's clinical instructors gave her a failing grade in the first semester for reasons which, the jury found, were related to her weight rather than her performance.

According to the rules of the Nursing Department, failure in a clinical course generally entailed expulsion from the program. But school officials offered Russell a deal, whereby she would sign a "contract" similar to the one she rejected earlier, with the additional provision that she needed to lose at least two pounds per week to remain in good standing. The "contract" provided that the penalty for failure would be immediate withdrawal from the program. Confronting the choice of signing the agreement or being expelled, Russell signed.

Russell apparently lived up to the terms of the "contract" during the second semester by attending Weight Watchers weekly and submitting proof of attendance, but she failed to lose two pounds per week steadily. She was nevertheless allowed to complete her junior year. During the following summer, however, Russell did not maintain satisfactory contact with College officials regarding her efforts, nor did she lose any additional weight. She was asked to withdraw from the nursing program voluntarily and she did so. She transferred to a program at another school. Since that program had a two year residency requirement, Russell had to repeat her junior year, causing her nursing education to run five years rather than the usual four. Russell completed her education successfully in 1987 and is now a registered nurse.

Soon after her departure from Salve Regina, she commenced the instant action which led to this appeal.

★   ★   ★

Russell's breach of contract claim is the only one the district court submitted to the jury. The College does not dispute that a student-college relationship is essentially a contractual one. Rather, it challenges the court's jury charge regarding the terms of the contract and the duties of the parties.

From the various catalogs, manuals, handbooks, etc., that form the contract between student and institution, the district court, in its jury charge, boiled the agreement between the parties down to one in which Russell on the one hand was required to abide by disciplinary rules, pay tuition and maintain good academic standing, and the College on the other hand was required to provide her with an education until graduation. The court informed the jury that the agreement was modified by the "contract" the parties signed during Russell's junior year. The jury was told that, if Russell "substantially performed" her side of the bargain, the College's actions constituted a breach.

★   ★   ★

In this case of first impression, the district court held that the Rhode Island Supreme Court would apply the substantial performance standard to the contract in question. In view of the customary appellate deference accorded to interpretations of state law made by federal judges of that state, we hold that the district court's determination that the Rhode Island Supreme Court would apply standard contract principles is not reversible error. [The district court judgment is affirmed.]

Anticipatory Breach

General Rules   Suppose a contract calls for action to be taken in the future in return for later payment and that while the contract is still executory, one party tells the other party that he does not intend to abide by his agreement. Has the statement itself terminated the contract? If so, does the second party have the right to sue for damages immediately without having to wait until the time when performance would have been due under the contract? Such a repudiation, whether by statement or by action, does terminate the contract; in legal parlance it is known as an **anticipatory breach**. The notion that oral repudiation terminates a contract and gives rise to an immediate right to sue may seem odd; Orson Welles once thought his lawyer had invented it on the spot (see **Box 14-2**). But the doctrine had been well established for nearly a century. The general rule is that any statement indicating that the obligor will commit a breach of the type that would permit a claim for damages for total breach of the contract, or any action that renders the obligor unable (or apparently unable) to carry out his agreement, is an anticipatory breach. The repudiation alone, even though there is still time to comply with the contract terms, amounts to a total breach of the contract, gives rise to a claim for damages, and discharges the obligee from performing duties required of him under the contract. These same general

rules prevail for contracts for the sale of goods under UCC Section 2-610.

A common example of anticipatory breach, stemming from the leading 1853 British case, is that of the repudiation of an employment contract. In April, De La Tour hired Hochster as his courier, the job to commence in June. In May, De La Tour changed his mind and told Hochster not to bother to report for duty. Hochster scurried around and, before June, secured an appointment as courier to Lord Ashburton. But the second job was not to begin until July. Also in May, Hochster sued De La Tour, who argued that he should not have to pay Hochster because Hochster had not stood ready and willing to begin work in June, having already agreed to go into Lord Ashburton's employ. In an opinion by Lord Campbell, the Chief Justice of the Queen's Bench, the court ruled for Hochster:

> [I]t is surely much more rational, and more for the benefit of both parties, that, after the renunciation of the agreement by the defendant, the plaintiff should be at liberty to consider himself absolved from any future performance of it, retaining his right to sue for any damage he has suffered from the breach of it. Thus, instead of remaining idle and laying out money in preparations which must be useless, he is at liberty to seek service under another employer, which would go in mitigation of the damages to which he would otherwise be entitled for a breach of the contract. It seems strange that the defendant, after

BOX 14-2

Stylish Counselor to Broadway's Brightest

By Timothy Bay

[If a contract requires action to be taken in the future and one party tells the other party that she does not intend to uphold the agreement, the contract is terminated. This is known as an anticipatory breach and enables the second party to immediately sue.—AUTHORS' NOTE]

Arnold Weissberger became an entertainment lawyer in the mid-1930s, and it was truly a case of falling into a career by accident. After graduating from Harvard Law School, he was working as a securities specialist for a Wall Street firm. His sister, who was working with a group of young actors in a WPA workshop, called him one night and said that one of the workshop members, a struggling young actor-director, needed some legal advice. Weissberger agreed to help out, and the 21-year-old Orson Welles became his first theatrical client.

★   ★   ★

CITIZEN KANE AND ANTICIPATORY BREACH

. . . Through the years, beginning with the WPA period and extending to the present, Welles has been a close friend as well as business client. Weissberger helped his friend out during his Mercury Theater days, in his legal entanglements over *Citizen Kane*, and when he created a national furor with his "War of the Worlds" broadcast.

★   ★   ★

Citizen Kane, with the legal cross fire between William Randolph Hearst, RKO, and Orson Welles, created more work for Weissberger. One particular incident from that period stands out in the lawyer's mind. "As a result of Hearst's pressures, the head of RKO got together with Welles secretly and reached an agreement that Orson would sue RKO to release the movie. Orson then arranged a press conference at the Ambassador where he

would talk about the film and his lawsuit."

At one point, during this press conference, a reporter asked Welles when the film was going to be released. Welles told him that it was going to be released in April—it was then only January. The reporter questioned the legality of suing for breach-of-contract three months before the fact.

Welles, Weissberger recalls, "then dramatically pointed to me sitting at the back of the room. I went blank at first. Then, suddenly, I recalled something I had learned in my first year at law school—the doctrine of anticipatory breach. I told the reporter that we were going to use this rule." Before anybody could explain what this meant, Welles triumphantly continued his press conference.

Afterwards, Weissberger says, "Orson congratulated me for coming up with this 'doctrine of anticipatory breach.' He thought that it was a marvelous phrase—and that it was ingenious of me to have invented it. He really didn't believe that there was such a thing."

★   ★   ★

Source: *Juris Doctor*, June 1976, p. 22

---

renouncing the contract, and absolutely declaring that he will never act under it, should be permitted to object that faith is given to his assertion, and that an opportunity is not left to him of changing his mind. [Hochster v. De La Tour, 2 Ellis & Blackburn 678 (Q.B. 1853)]

Anticipatory breach by act, rather than statement, occurs when a seller of land, having agreed to sell the lot to one person at a date certain, sells it instead to a third party before that time. Since there would be no point to showing up at the lawyer's office when the date arrives to await the deed, the law gives a right to sue when the land is sold to the other person.

Right to Adequate Assurance After making the contract, the obligee may come upon the disquieting news that the obligor's ability to perform is rather shaky—a change in financial condition, an unknown claimant to rights in land, strike, or any of a number of situations may crop up that will interfere with the carrying out of contractual duties. Under such circumstances, the obligee has the right to demand an assurance that the obligor will perform as contractually obligated. The general reason for such a rule is given in UCC Section 2-609(1), which states that a contract "imposes an obligation on each party that the other's expectation of receiving due performance will not be impaired." Moreover, an obligee would be foolish not to make alternative arrangements if possible when it becomes obvious that his original obligor will be unable to perform.

The rule does not mean that the obligee can telephone up each day and ask nervously for a pledge that the obligor means what he said the day before about getting the job done. The obligee must have reasonable grounds to believe that the obligor will breach. Such grounds might include the discovery that the seller-obligor has faulty title to land, an obligor's offer of defective performance, and the obligor's insolvency. The fear must be that of a failure of a condition or performance that would amount to a total breach; a minor defect that can be cured and that at most would give rise to an offset in price for damages will not generally support a demand for assurances.

Under UCC Section 2-609(1), the demand must be in writing, but at common law the demand may be oral if it is reasonable in view of the circumstances. Especially when there is little time in which to ask for or receive assurances, the request for assurance can be oral. Whether the assurance is adequate and is made in timely fashion depends on all the circumstances. An obligor can give assurance by simply denying the facts that the obligee thought were true, or he can explain how he will surmount the difficulties. Assurance can also take the form of an affirmative act—for example, the posting of a bond.

If the obligee's suspicions are reasonable, he is relieved of responsibility for carrying out his own obligations until receiving an adequate assurance (except for duties for which he has already received the bargained-for exchange). And if the obligor fails within a reasonable time to give adequate assurance, the obligee may treat the failure to do so as a repudiation.

Impracticability of Performance

In General Every contract contains some element of risk: the buyer may run out of money before he can pay; the seller may run out of goods before he can deliver; the cost of raw materials may skyrocket, throwing off the manufacturer's fine financial calculations. Should the obligor's luck run sour, he is stuck with the consequences—or, in the legal phrase, his liability is strict: he must either perform or risk paying damages for breach of contract, even if his failure is due to events beyond his control. Of course, an obligor can always limit his liability through the contract itself. Instead of obligating himself to deliver one million units, he can restrict his obligation to "one million units or factory output, whichever is less." Instead of guaranteeing to finish a job by a certain date, he can agree to use his "best efforts" to do so. Similarly, damages in the event of breach can be limited. A party can even include a clause canceling the contract in the event of an untoward happening. But if these provisions are absent, the obligor is generally held to the terms of his bargain.

Exceptions do exist for some extraordinary circumstances. When there is a radical departure from the circumstances that the parties reasonably contemplated would exist at the time they entered into the contract, the courts might grant relief. They will do so when extraordinary circumstances (often called "acts of God" or *force majeure*) make it unjust to hold a party liable for performance. Although the justification for judicial relief could be found in an implied condition in all contracts that extraordinary events shall not occur, the *Restatement (Second) of Contracts*, Section 261, eschews so obvious a bootstrap logic and adopts the language of UCC Section 2-615(a), which states that the crux of the analysis is whether the nonoccurrence of the extraordinary circumstance was "a basic assumption on which the contract was made." If it was—if, that is, the parties assumed that the circumstance would not come about—then the duty is discharged if the circumstance later does come about.

When it is impossible to perform, the duty is discharged. **Impossibility** occurs when one of the parties dies before performing a personal service contract or when the subject matter of the contract is destroyed. The estate of a painter hired to do a portrait cannot be sued for damages because the painter died before she could complete the work. But **impracticability** as an excuse is not limited to cases of impossibility. When performance cannot be undertaken except with extreme difficulty or at highly unreasonable expense, it might be excused. However, "impracticable" is not the same as "impractical." The courts allow a considerable degree of fluctuation in market prices, inflation, weather, and other economic and natural conditions before holding that an extraordinary circumstance has occurred. A manufacturer that based its selling price on last year's costs for raw materials could not avoid its contracts by claiming that inflation within the historical range had made it difficult or unprofitable to meet its commitments. Examples of circumstances that could excuse might be severe limitations of supply due to war, embargo, or a natural disaster. Thus, a shipowner who contracted with a purchaser to carry goods to a foreign port would be excused if war broke out and the military authorities threatened to sink all vessels that entered the harbor. But if the shipowner had planned to steam through a canal that is subsequently closed when a hostile government seizes it, his duty is not discharged if another route is available, even if the route is longer and consequently more expensive.

Impracticability refers to the performance, not to the party doing it. Only if the performance is impracticable is the obligor discharged. The distinction is said to be the difference between "the thing cannot be done" and "I cannot do it." The former refers to that which is objectively impracticable and the latter to that which is subjectively impracticable. That a duty is **subjectively impracticable** does not excuse it. A buyer is liable for the purchase price of a house, and his inability to raise the money does not excuse him or allow him to escape from a suit for damages when the seller tenders the deed. [Christy v. Pilkinton, 273 S.W.2d 533 (1954)] If Andy promises to transport Anne to the football stadium for $5, he cannot wriggle out of his agreement because someone smashed into his car (rendering it inoperable) a half hour before he was due to pick her up. He could rent a car or take her in a taxi, even though that will cost considerably more than the sum she agreed to pay him. But if the agreement was that he would transport her *in his car*, then the circumstances make his performance **objectively impracticable** and he is excused.

Death or Incapacity As a general rule a contract does not terminate when one party dies or becomes seriously incapacitated. However, as the following case illustrates, the rule is different when the personal services of the deceased party were essential to the contract.

THOMAS YATES & CO. v. AMERICAN LEGION
370 So.2d 700 (Miss. 1979)

LEE, JUSTICE, for the Court. Thomas Yates and Company, a domestic corporation, instituted suit in the Circuit Court of the First Judicial District of Hinds County, Honorable Dan M. Lee, presiding, against the American Legion, a non-profit corporation, Association Group Insurance Administrators, a foreign corporation (AGIA), National Ben Franklin Life Insurance Company, a foreign corporation (NBF), and George P. Delivorias, and sought damages for tortious interference with a contract. The defendants filed answers and stated affirmative defenses. A separate hearing was held preliminarily on the affirmative defenses, the trial judge sustained said defenses and dismissed the declaration with thirty (30) days' leave to amend. The plaintiff declined to amend, the judgement became final, and Yates has appealed here.

Prior to March 1, 1964, Thomas Yates & Company was a sole proprietorship owned and operated by Thomas Yates, Jr. On March 1, 1964, he contracted with the American Legion to provide group insurance policies for Legion membership and he became the exclusive agent of the American Legion for that purpose. The agreement was to remain in full force and effect unless cancelled by mutual consent or cancelled on any anniversary date with one year's notice in writing prior to such anniversary date. On July 1, 1964, Thomas Yates and Company (Thomas Yates, Jr.) placed in force a master plan covering members of the American Legion.

Thomas Yates, Jr. died November 6, 1965, and the management and control of Thomas Yates & Company became vested in Thomas Yates, III. He organized the corporation, Thomas Yates and Company, September 26, 1966, and that corporation purchased all the assets of Thomas Yates and Company, the sole proprietorship. The corporation continued to provide the same insurance services to the American Legion until July, 1973, that had been performed by the senior Yates, when appellee AGIA negotiated with the American Legion and became its agent of record to procure and place group insurance coverage for the Legion's membership. Appellant charges that AGIA, acting through NBF and George Delivorias, induced the American Legion to breach its contract with appellant in violation of the notice requirement in the contract between Thomas Yates, Jr. and the American Legion, and claims damages as a result.

The appellees affirmatively state that appellant was not a party to the said contract, that the appellant corporation did not have a life insurance agent's license as required by law, and that the contract was unenforceable. Further, appellees contend that the contract between Thomas Yates, Jr. and the American Legion called for personal services from Yates, Jr. and that the contract terminated upon his death. The trial judge sustained the affirmative defenses and dismissed the declaration on the ground that the plaintiff, being a corporation, had no standing to maintain the suit.

Did the trial court err in ruling that appellant had no standing to bring the action?

The appellees contend that the contract between Thomas Yates, Jr. and the American Legion was one for personal services and that it automatically terminated upon the death of Mr. Yates approximately ten (10) months prior to the organization of the appellant corporation. Generally, the death of a party does not terminate a contract unless it is of a personal nature. 17 Am.Jr.2d *Contracts* § 413 (1964). In order to determine whether a contract is of such nature, consideration must be given to whether or not it can [be] performed by the deceased's personal representative. In *Cox* v. *Martin*, 75 Miss. 229, 21 So. 611 (1897), the Court said:

> Recurring now to the main question, it is clear that wherever the continued existence of the particular person contracted with—the contract being executory—is essential to the completion of the contract, by reason of his peculiar skill or taste, death terminates the contract; as, for example, 'contracts of authors to write books, of attorneys to render professional services, of physicians to cure particular diseases, of teachers to instruct pupils, and of masters to teach apprentices a trade or calling.' So, also, when the continued existence of a particular thing is essential to the completion of the contract, the destruction of the existence of the thing (its death) terminates, the contract—as, in contracts for the sale of specific chattels, or for the use of a building, they ceasing to exist. 1 Beach on the Modern Law of Contracts, sec. 773, p. 946, note 3, with the authorities cited. 'But where the contract with the deceased is executory, and the personal representative can fairly and fully execute it as well as the deceased himself would have done, he may do so and enforce the contract. And, on the other hand, the personal representative is bound to complete such a contract, and if he fails to do so, he may

(continued on next page)

(continued)

**THOMAS YATES &
CO. v. AMERICAN
LEGION**
370 So.2d 700 (Miss.
1979)

be compelled to pay damages out of the assets in his hands.' Note *supra*, with authorities, 22 Am.St.Rep., p. 813. 75 Miss. at 238, 21 So. at 612–613.

* * *

We are of the opinion that there was no privity of contract between appellant and the American Legion and that, although the Yates corporation continued to service the American Legion until 1973, neither the appellant nor the American Legion was bound under the agreement with Yates, Jr. We are further of the opinion that the contract between Yates, Jr. and the American Legion terminated upon the death of Yates, Jr. and that the judgment of the trial court should be affirmed.

Since the case is decided on the above question, it is not necessary to discuss the other point presented.

Affirmed.

Destruction or Deterioration of a Thing Necessary for Performance   When a specific object is necessary for the obligor's performance, its destruction or deterioration making it impracticable to be used (or its failure to come into existence) discharges the obligor's duty. Diane's Dyers contracts to buy the annual wool output of the Sheepish Ranch, but the sheep die of an epidemic disease before they can be shorn. Since the specific thing for which the contract was made has been destroyed, Sheepish is discharged from its duty to supply Diane's with wool, and Diane's has no claim against the Ranch. However, if the contract had called for a quantity of wool, without specifying that it was to be from Sheepish's flock, the duty would not be discharged; since wool is available on the open market, Sheepish could buy that and resell to Diane's.

Performance Prohibited by Government Regulation or Order   When a government promulgates a rule after a contract is made and the rule either bars performance or will make it impracticable, the obligor's duty is discharged. An obligor is not required to break the law and risk the consequences. Lotsa Lotto, Inc., makes a contract with Lancelot for the sale of lottery tickets. Lotteries are lawful in the state at the time the contract is signed. Thereafter, the state legislature enacts a law barring all forms of lotteries. Lancelot is discharged from his obligation to pay, and Lotsa Lotto is discharged from the obligation to convey the tickets. Suppose the law or regulation turns out later to have been invalid. As long as the person affected by the order complied in good faith, invalidity does not restore a duty or prevent one from having been discharged.

Impracticability Under the UCC   In Section 2-614, the code requires reasonable substitution for berthing, loading, and unloading facilities that become unavailable and for transportation and delivery systems that become "commercially impracticable." Similarly, if a government regulation bars payment in a specified manner, the buyer may provide "a means or manner of payment which is commercially a substantial equivalent." And if the seller has already delivered, the buyer may discharge his duty by paying in the manner provided by regulation "unless the regulation is discriminatory, oppressive or predatory."

By Section 2-615, the failure to deliver goods is not a breach of the seller's duty "if performance as agreed has been made impracticable by the occurrence of a contingency the non-occurrence of which was a basic assumption on which the contract was made or by compliance in good faith with any applicable foreign or domestic governmental regulation or order whether or not it later proves to be invalid." Just what circumstances constitute impracticability under this section has not been settled; few cases have been litigated through to conclusion. The code drafters note that Section 2-615 is not intended to relieve a company of liability when market conditions cause a sudden rise in prices that pain a company with fixed-price contracts, since that is the very reason the obligee sought to fix its prices in the contract. Some completely unanticipated supervening event must be the cause of impracticability. Thus, when the cost of uranium went skyhigh during the mid-1970s, Westinghouse Electric Corporation found itself obligated to deliver millions of pounds to utilities to which it had sold nuclear reactors, but it had failed to secure these amounts by negotiating long-term supply contracts with uranium processors. Westinghouse could not claim commercial impracticability solely on the grounds that the prices had risen far faster than anticipated, so it pointed to a cartel of mining companies that, Westinghouse claimed, had unlawfully forced the prices to climb precipitously. A federal judge ruled that the circumstances of the case did not amount to an excuse, but the company ultimately negotiated its way out of the lawsuits by settling with the utilities for an estimated $950 million.

Frustration of Purpose

If the parties made a basic assumption that certain circumstances would not arise, but they do arise, then a party is discharged from performing his duties if his principal purpose in making the contract has been "substantially frustrated." This is not a rule of objective impossibility. It operates even though the parties easily might be able to carry out their contractual duties. The **frustration of purpose** doctrine comes into play when circumstances make the value of one party's performance virtually worthless to the other. This rule does not permit one party to escape a contract simply because he will make less money than he had planned or because one potential benefit of the contract has disappeared. The purpose that is frustrated must be the core of the contract, known and understood by both parties, and the level of frustration must be severe; that is, the value of the contract to the party seeking to be discharged must be destroyed or nearly destroyed.

The classic illustration of frustration of purpose is the litigation that gave birth to the rule: the so-called coronation cases. In 1901, when King Edward VII was due to be crowned following the death of Queen Victoria, a parade route was announced for the ceremony. Scores of people rented rooms in buildings that lined the streets of the route in order to watch the spectacle. But the King fell ill and the procession was canceled. Many expectant viewers failed to pay, and the building owners took them to court; many lessees who had paid took the owners to court to seek refunds. The court declared that the lessees were not liable because the purpose of the contract had been frustrated by the King's illness.

Supervening government regulations, fires that destroy buildings in which an event was to take place, and business failures may all contribute to frustration of purpose. But there can be no general rule: the circumstances of each case are determinative. Suppose, for example, that a manufacturer agrees to supply a crucial circuit board to a computer maker who intends to sell his machine and software to the Soviet Union. After the contract is made but before the circuit boards are delivered, the U.S. government prohibits the sale of all computer technology to the Soviet Union. The computer manufacturer writes the circuit board maker, canceling the contract. Whether the manufacturer is discharged depends on the commercial prospects for the computer and the circuit board. If the circuit board can be used only in the particular computer, and it in turn can be sold only to the Soviets, the duty to take the boards is discharged. But if the computer can be sold elsewhere, or the circuit boards can be used in other computers that the manufacturer makes, it is liable for breach of contract, since its principal purpose—selling computers—is not frustrated.

As before, the parties can provide in the contract that the duty is absolute and that no supervening event shall give rise to discharge by reason of frustration of purpose.

Discharge by Acquisition of Correlative Rights

Every duty implies a right in someone to the performance of that duty. This is a **correlative right**. Anne has a correlative right to Andy's duty to cut her grass. The correlative right can frequently be assigned or bequeathed or transferred by operation of law. If a person obligated to perform the duty acquires the correlative right, the duty is discharged. The reason: it makes no practical sense to talk of a person owing himself a legal duty. There is a wrinkle in this rule worth noting—the person acquiring the right must do so in the same *capacity* in which he owed the duty.

Nelly borrows $1,000 from her rich Uncle Hiram. Before she has paid him back, Hiram dies, leaving all his money to Nelly. Her duty to repay the loan is discharged. Suppose, however, that Hiram had not left Nelly any money but had made her his executrix (the person who accounts for and distributes the estate to the heirs). As such, Nelly would have control over Hiram's money, but not in the same capacity as the debt owed, and she would be required to pay herself $1,000 as executrix.

Power of Avoidance

A contractual duty can be discharged if the obligor can avoid the contract. As we have seen (Chapter 11), a contract is either void or can be voided if one of the parties lacked capacity or if there has been a mistake, misrepresentation, duress, undue influence, or unfair bargaining in a fiduciary relationship.

Discharge of Sureties

As a general rule, an agreement between the principal and the third party, without the surety's consent, to modify the principal's duty to the third party discharges the surety from his contract with the principal. This situation is discussed in greater detail in Chapter 27.

Discharge by Merger

A technical form of discharge is known as **merger**. It is technical because it does not usually excuse the obligor from performing the duty; it changes only the basis on which the duty is said to be owed. A merger occurs when one duty replaces another, as for example in a judgment. Creditor and debtor have a contract whereby the debtor is required to pay the balance of a loan by a certain date. On default, the creditor sues and obtains a court judgment against the debtor. The debtor's contractual duty to pay has been merged in the judgment. When the creditor now seeks from the debtor the funds owed, his claim is based on the judgment he has won.

Once a final ruling has been handed down, the duty is determined by the court's ruling. If the court

had decided in favor of the defendant debtor that there was no duty to pay (perhaps because the debtor was a minor), the duty is discharged and the creditor may not thereafter raise it in another court. A final ruling of a court (after all appeals have been taken) is said to be *res judicata*—that is, finally adjudicated.

Occasionally, the merger rule can have an effect on the obligor's duty. Suppose Anne agrees to pay Andy out-of-pocket expenses for cutting her grass (gasoline for the lawn mower and carfare). The exact amount is not specified. Anne's obligation to Andy is **unliquidated.** Andy presents Anne with a bill for his expenses, and she says she will pay him a week hence. Andy agrees. This subsequent agreement liquidates the amount owed, and Anne's duty to pay under the original agreement is merged in the second agreement. Andy may not now claim a different amount.

DISCHARGE OF DUTIES IN GENERAL

As noted at the outset of this chapter, not all duties arise from contract. Duties may be imposed by statute or regulation or by a court, as when, for example, a plaintiff wins a tort judgment and the defendant is obligated to pay money damages. There are a number of ways by which all duties, whether contractually based or not, may be discharged. We will consider each briefly in the remainder of this chapter. (See Figure 14-1.)

Cancellation, Destruction, or Surrender

An obligee may unilaterally discharge the obligor's duty toward him by canceling, destroying, or surrendering the written document embodying the contract or other evidence of the duty. No consideration is necessary; in effect, the obligee is making a gift of the right that he possesses. No particular method of cancellation, destruction, or surrender is necessary, as long as the obligee manifests his intent that the effect of his act is to discharge the duty. The entire document can be handed over to the obligor with the words, "Here, you don't owe me anything." The obligee can tear the paper into pieces and tell the obligor that he has done so because he does not want anything more. Or he can mutilate the signatures or cross out the writing.

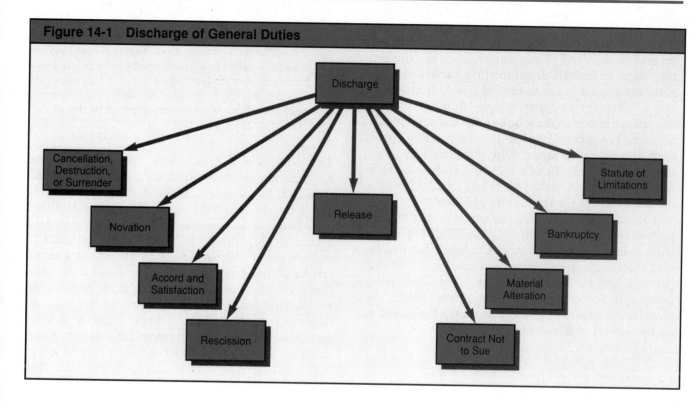

Figure 14-1 Discharge of General Duties

Novation

When by a novation a third person is substituted for the obligor, the latter is discharged. Suppose while walking down the street, Seth finds a rare Spanish gold coin that has evidently rolled down from the adjacent property. The owner sees him pick it up and truthfully says, "Hey, that's mine!" Seth is under a duty to return it. Seth wants to keep the coin, and his father speaks to the owner, who says he will take back either the coin or $1,000. The father agrees to pay $1,000 and the owner agrees to release Seth from liability. Seth is thus discharged from his obligation to return the coin.

Accord and Satisfaction

Jack sues Jill, alleging that he has loaned her $100, that she has not paid it back, and that he has not forgiven the debt. Jill admits borrowing the money and concedes that she has not repaid it. On what the-

ory would a court be correct in ruling against Jack nonetheless? On the theory of accord and satisfaction: Jill proves that because she was short of cash, Jack agreed she could work off the debt by watering his flower garden during the spring, and she has done so. Jack and Jill have made an **accord,** an agreement to substitute one performance in full satisfaction of the original duty. If the duty called for in the accord has been performed, there has been a **satisfaction** of the obligation, and it is discharged. Before the substitute performance is made, the original duty is merely suspended; if the obligor fails to perform under the accord, the obligee may enforce either the original or the substitute obligation.

Rescission

The parties may mutually agree to discharge the duties each owes the other. The *Restatement (Second) of Contracts*, Section 283, terms this an **agreement of rescission.** An agreement to rescind will be given effect even though partial performance has been made or one or both parties have a claim for partial breach. The agreement need not be in writing or even expressed in words. By their actions, such as failure to take steps to perform or enforce, the parties may signal their mutual intent to rescind. Andy is at Anne's house, pursuant to his agreement with her to mow her lawn. He begins the job, but it is unbearably hot. She sees how uncomfortable he is and readily agrees with him when he says: "Why don't we just forget the whole thing?" Andy's duty to finish mowing is discharged, as is Anne's duty to pay Andy, either for the whole job or for the part he has done.

Business executives live by contracts but they do not necessarily die by them. A sociologist who has studied business behavior under contract has discovered that in the great majority of cases in which one party wishes to "cancel an order," the other party permits it without renegotiation, even though the cancellation amounts to a repudiation of a contract. As one lawyer was quoted as saying:

Often businessmen do not feel they have "a contract"—rather they have an "order." They speak of "cancelling the order" rather than "breaching our contract." When I began practice I referred to order cancellations as breaches of contract, but my clients objected since they do not think of cancellation as wrong. Most clients, in heavy industry at least, believe that there is a right to cancel as part of the buyer-seller relationship. There is a widespread attitude that one can back out of any deal within some very vague limits. Lawyers are often surprised by this attitude. (Macauley, 1963, p. 61)

This attitude is understandable. People who depend for their economic survival on continuing relationships will be loath to react to every change in plans with a lawsuit. The legal consequences of most of these cancellations is an agreement of rescission. Under UCC Section 2-720, the use of a word like "cancellation" or "rescission" does not by itself amount to a renunciation of the right to sue for breach of a provision that occurred before the rescission. If the parties mean to discharge each other fully from all duties owed, they must say so explicitly. Actions continue to speak more loudly than words, however, and in law, so can inactions. Legal rights under contracts may be lost by both parties if they fail to act; by abandoning their claims they can effect rescission.

MADISON SQUARE GARDEN BOXING, INC. v. ALI
430 F.Supp. 679 (N.D. Ill. 1977)

CROWLEY, DISTRICT JUDGE. Madison Square Garden Boxing, Inc. (MSGB) brought this action against Muhammad Ali (Ali), the heavyweight boxing champion of the world, for breach of contract to fight Duane Bobick (Bobick) in Madison Square Garden. MSGB seeks damages and injunctive relief. The document sued upon was executed on November 25, 1976 and called for Ali to fight Bobick on a date during the period from February 1, 1977 through February 28, 1977. . . .

Ali, as heavyweight champion of the world, successfully defended his championship in September of 1976, in a contest with Ken Norton. That contest was promoted by MSGB and held at Yankee Stadium in New York, New York, pursuant to a Fighters' Agreement executed on May 13, 1976 between MSGB and Ali, not signed by Ali but signed by his manager, Muhammad.

Shortly after the conclusion of that contest, Ali, while in Istanbul, Turkey, held a press conference and, as he had on several past occasions and would again, announced his retirement from boxing.

Teddy Brenner, president and matchmaker of MSGB, continued contacts with Herbert Muhammad (Muhammad) even after Ali's announced retirement. Brenner attempted to find out if Ali was going to box again. He told Muhammad that Ali had been a great champion and had beaten every challenger except Bobick. Brenner told Muhammad that a contest between Ali and Bobick, the current "white hope" would be ideal. Muhammad, having received some criticism that he had been forcing Ali to fight, refused to make any commitment for Ali, but told Brenner that the decision to fight or not to fight was Ali's.

In mid-November of 1976, Brenner was attempting to arrange a contest between Bobick and Norton. Norton's manager was in California, so Brenner and Eddie Futch, Bobick's manager, flew to California to conduct negotiations.

On November 16, 1976, when negotiations for the Norton-Bobick fight reached an impasse, Brenner told Bobick's manager that he thought he could arrange a fight between Ali and Bobick. Futch expressed some skepticism that the fight could be arranged so Brenner placed a call to Muhammad. Futch said to Muhammad "Teddy tells me there is a possibility that Muhammad (Ali) may box again." Muhammad replied, "There is always a possibility." After this call, Brenner told Futch that if Norton-Bobick couldn't be arranged, Brenner would fly to Chicago.

★   ★   ★

[After a week of travel and negotiations] Brenner called Muhammad in the late evening hours of November 24 and told him that everything was arranged. Muhammad told Brenner that it wasn't necessary for him to come to Chicago but that he should go straight to Houston. Muhammad assured Brenner that he would advise Ali that Brenner was coming.

Armed with the document which is the subject matter of this suit, Brenner, in joyful anticipation, flew to Houston and arrived in the early morning of November 25th. He met with Ali and Ali signed the agreement. Exhausted from what one of counsel has called his "Odyssey", Brenner mistakenly inserted the date of November 24th on the agreement.

He then called Muhammad, told him he was in Houston and he was dead tired. Because it was Thanksgiving, Muhammad told him not to come to Chicago, but to return to New York and send Muhammad a copy.

★   ★   ★

On November 29th, Brenner heard that rumors were circulating that Ali would not fight. The next day he saw a newspaper article that indicated that Ali would retire. The publicity director of Madison Square Garden then told him that he had received official word that Ali was not going to fight. Brenner, Burke and McCauley then agreed to announce that the Bobick-Norton fight was going to be held in late February or early March.

Ali, at the request of the Garden's publicity director, telephonically participated in a press conference where he simultaneously announced his retirement and helped to promote the Norton-Bobick contest. Although Brenner has had several conversations with Muhammad and Ali since then, they never talked about boxing. Brenner didn't want to sacrifice a friendship and as far as he was concerned the matter was "over and done with."

(continued on next page)

(continued)

MADISON SQUARE GARDEN BOXING, INC. v. ALI
430 F.Supp. 679 (N.D. Ill. 1977)

However, this complex story did not end here. On or about December 16, 1976, Muhammad wrote to Burke and Brenner and advised them that Ali was prepared to fight Bobick. . . . He also stated that if MSGB was committed to the Norton-Bobick contest Ali would fight Bobick within four months after that contest. Muhammad stated that if an agreement wasn't signed by December 24th, the payment of the $125,000.00 would be returned. MSGB never responded to this letter, and on January 25, 1977, the $125,000.00 [an advance for training expenses] was returned to and accepted by MSGB.

* * *

Ali's claim that there was no breach must fail. When Ali again announced his retirement, it was clearly a stated intention of his refusal to perform and was at least an anticipatory breach of the contract, and MSGB would have had the right to sue for that breach.

Since MSGB did not bring an action at that time it is necessary for the Court to examine its conduct to determine if the contract was then mutually rescinded or abandoned.

MSGB, after receiving notice of Ali's then intent to retire, took no action to enforce this contract. On the contrary, the Norton-Bobick contest was reinstated and Ali's aid was solicited and accepted to promote that contest. Brenner felt the matter was "over and done with". This sentiment of Brenner was reinforced by the MSGB's subsequent conduct by accepting the return of the $125,000.00, and its failure to respond to Muhammad's letter of December 16, and its failure to bring this action until after the time for performance expired. Considering all of the circumstances and the conduct of the parties, there was mutual abandonment of the contract.

Accordingly, the defendant has established his defense of abandonment and judgment shall enter for the defendant and against the plaintiff.

An order shall enter accordingly.

Release

Just as the obligee can discharge the obligor's duty by canceling or surrendering the document, so too he can accomplish the same end by delivering to the obligor a **release,** a writing that says the obligor is discharged upon delivery of the writing or upon occurrence of a condition. But a writing that promises to discharge the obligor at some future time, not contingent on a condition, is not a release; it is only a promise of one and may be revoked. Jack owes Jill $1,000. Jill tells Jack that if he will help her with her chores, she will release him from his obligation to pay. After Jack helps her, she hands him a document that says: "I release Jack from all debts that he now owes me or may owe me in the future." A few weeks later, Jack borrows more money on condition that he will repay it. Thereafter, Jill asks Jack to repay both the $1,000 and the second sum of money. Jack does not owe the first $1,000, because Jill has released him. But the duty to pay the second sum is not discharged, because his agreement to repay operates as a modification of the earlier contract to release him from future debt.

Contract Not to Sue

An obligation may be discharged if the obligee makes a binding contract not to sue the obligor. The contract may specify that the obligee either will never sue or will not sue for a limited period of time. The obligation is discharged immediately if the contract is that the obligee will never sue. The contract not to sue for a limited period bars a suit only during the time specified.

Material Alteration

An obligee who materially and fraudulently alters a written document that either is an integrated agreement or satisfies the Statute of Frauds discharges the obligor from his duty of performance. The alteration need not be large; any change that varies the obligor's duties toward the obligee or that adversely affects the obligor's legal relationships with others is material. Alteration can include filling in blank spaces, changing dates, or substituting words. But the change must be intended to have legal effect; the mere addition of a date to a contract that had no date or correcting the spelling of a name is not by itself material. Eleanor agrees to sell Bob her land for $10,000; their written contract puts the closing on November 1. Bob fraudulently erases the date and substitutes September 1. This is a material alteration that discharges Eleanor from having to convey title at all. But if Bob had honestly believed that they had agreed on the earlier time and that the contract had been typed incorrectly, his erasure would not be fraudulent and the closing date of November 1 would still be binding.

Bankruptcy

Under the federal bankruptcy laws (Chapter 29), certain obligations are discharged once a court declares a debtor to be bankrupt. The law spells out the particular types of debts that are canceled upon bankruptcy.

Statute of Limitations

When an obligor has breached a contract, the obligee has the right to sue in court for a remedy. But that right does not last forever. Every state has statutes of limitations that establish time periods within which the suit must be brought (different time periods are spelled out for different types of legal wrongs: contract breach, various types of torts, and so on). The time period for contract actions under most statutes of limitations ranges between two and six years. The period begins to run from the day on which the suit could have been filed in court—for example, from the moment of contract breach. An obligee who waits until after the statute has run—that is, does not seek legal relief within the period prescribed by the statute of limitations—is barred from going to court thereafter, but the obligor is not thereby discharged. The effect is simply that the obligee has no legal remedy. If the parties have a continuing relationship, the obligee might be able to recoup—for example, by applying a payment for another debt to the one barred by the statute, or by offsetting a debt the obligee owes to the obligor.

CHAPTER SUMMARY

The law of contracts has many rules to determine whether obligations have been discharged. Of course, if both parties have fully performed the contract, duties will have terminated. But many duties are subject to conditions, and it is important to review the types of conditions and how they operate to bar enforcement of obligations. Among the important concepts are conditions precedent and subsequent, conditions requiring approval of the promisee or someone else, and clauses that recite time to be of the essence.

A contract obligation may be discharged if the promisor has not received the benefit of the promisee's obligation. In some cases, failure to carry out the duty completely will discharge the corresponding obligation; in other cases the substantial performance doctrine will require the other party to act.

A contract may have terminated because one of the parties tells the other in advance that he will not carry out his obligations; this is called anticipatory breach. The right to adequate assurance allows one party to determine whether the contract will be breached by the other party.

There are other events, too, that may excuse performance: impracticability (including the UCC rules governing impracticability in contracts for the sale of goods), death or incapacity of the obligor, destruction of the thing necessary for the performance, government prohibition, frustration of purpose, acquisition of correlative rights, power of avoidance, and merger.

Finally, note that not all obligations are created by contract, and the law has rules to deal with discharge of duties in general. Thus, in the appropriate cases, the obligee may cancel or surrender a written contract, may enter into an accord, may agree to rescind the agreement, or may release the obligor. Or the obligor may show a material alteration in the contract, may become bankrupt, or may plead the statute of limitations—that is, plead that the obligee waited too long to sue. Or the parties may, by word, or deed, mutually abandon the agreement. In all these ways, duties may be discharged.

KEY TERMS

Accord	p. 335	Implied in law	p. 319
Agreement of rescission	p. 335	Impossibility	p. 329
		Impracticability	p. 329
Anticipatory breach	p. 327	Merger	p. 334
Cancellation	p. 324	Objectively impracticable	p. 330
Condition	p. 319	ble	
Condition precedent	p. 319	Release	p. 338
Condition subsequent	p. 319	Satisfaction	p. 335
Constructive conditions	p. 319	Subjectively impracticable	p. 330
Correlative right	p. 333	Termination	p. 324
Frustration of purpose	p. 333	Unliquidated	p. 334

SELF-TEST QUESTIONS

1. A condition precedent:
   (a) is a condition that terminates a duty
   (b) is always within the control of one of the parties
   (c) is an event giving rise to performance
   (d) is a condition that follows performance
2. If Al and Betty have an executory contract and Betty tells Al that she will not be fulfilling her side of the bargain:
   (a) Al must wait until the date of performance to see if Betty in fact performs
   (b) Al can sue immediately for full contract damages
   (c) Al can never sue because the contract was executory when Betty notified him of nonperformance
   (d) none of the above are correct
3. Jack contracts with Anne to drive her to the airport Wednesday afternoon in his specially designed stretch limousine. On Wednesday morning Jack's limousine is hit by a drunken driver and Jack is unable to drive Ann. This is an example of:
   (a) impossibility of performance
   (b) frustration of purpose
   (c) discharge by merger
   (d) none of the above

4. Jack is ready and willing to drive Anne to the airport. But Anne's flight is cancelled and she refuses to pay. This is an example of:
   (a) impracticability of performance
   (b) frustration of purpose
   (c) discharge of merger
   (d) none of the above
5. Rescission is:
   (a) the discharge of one party to a contract through substitution of a third person
   (b) an agreement to settle for substitute performance
   (c) a mutual agreement between parties to a contract to discharge each other's contractual duties
   (d) none of the above

DEMONSTRATION PROBLEM

Tommy learned that his favorite actress, Annette, was going to attend the annual Academy Awards presentation. He reserved a hotel room across from the building where the awards would be presented so that he could watch Annette arriving at and leaving the ceremonies. He paid $500 in advance for the room. Two days before the presentation, Annette became ill and was unable to attend. Tommy canceled his reservation and demanded his money back. Is he discharged from the contract? Why?

PROBLEMS

1. To encourage the purchase of season tickets, the owner of the Hoops, a professional basketball team, promised to refund the purchase price if ticketholders did not feel that the team was exciting and competitive. During the season, the Hoops set a league scoring record and won the league title in the last game of the season in triple overtime. Over half of their games during the regular season also went into overtime. At the end of the season, Kareem, one of the season ticketholders, demanded a refund, claiming that the team had not been exciting or competitive. Is he entitled to his money back? Why?
2. Theresa hired a contractor to construct a large office building. Theresa's duty to pay the contractor was conditioned on receipt of a statement from her architect that the building complied with the terms of the contract. The contractor completed the building, but used the wrong color fixtures in the bathrooms. The architect refused to approve the work but, under state law, the contractor was considered to have substantially performed the contract. Is he entitled to payment, less damages for the improper fixtures? Why?

3. Robbie decided to purchase a car on credit. The car dealer demanded that Robbie's parents cosign the note as sureties, which they did. A few months later, Robbie and the dealer renegotiated the note without the knowledge or consent of the parents. Under the new terms, the interest rate and monthly payments were raised. What effect, if any, do these changes have on the parents' liability? Why?

4. Dr. Welby struck a pedestrian with his car while driving to work one day. Dr. Welby stopped to treat the pedestrian. In the course of treatment, Dr. Welby failed to properly clean a wound and then proceeded to stitch into the wound cinders and a button from the victim's suspenders. The victim sued Dr. Welby for causing the automobile accident and won a judgment. He then sued Dr. Welby for malpractice. Dr. Welby's defense was *res judicata*—that is, Dr. Welby argued that the victim's claim had already been adjudicated. Is this a good defense? Why?

5. Harold leased Maude's truck for three years. Shortly after the lease was signed, war was declared and the government requisitioned the truck for use in the war effort. The government agreed to pay $5,000 a year for use of the truck. Who is entitled to the money—Harold or Maude? Why?

6. Charles owned a warehouse full of No. 10 desks, a common model that could easily be purchased on the market. Diana visited the factory and selected five of the desks. Before the desks were delivered, the factory and its contents were destroyed by fire. Charles claims that as a result of the fire he is discharged from the contract. Diana argues that Charles still must perform because Charles could purchase the desks on the market and then sell them to Diana at the contract price. Who is correct? Why?

7. Leonardo, a struggling young artist, entered into a contract to sell one of his paintings to Howard for $1,200 and to paint Howard's portrait for $2,000. Before painting the portrait, Leonardo dies. Howard now demands that Leonardo's executor perform the contract by delivering the painting and doing the portrait. The executor refuses, claiming that Leonardo's contractual duties were discharged by death. Is the executor correct? Why?

ANSWERS TO SELF-TEST QUESTIONS

1. (c)   2. (b)   3. (a)   4. (b)   5. (c)

SUGGESTED ANSWER TO DEMONSTRATION PROBLEM

Tommy will be discharged if his purpose in renting the room— that is, to see Annette—was known and understood by the hotel and if the value of the contract to Tommy was virtually destroyed.

CHAPTER 15

Remedies

We come at last to the question of remedies. A valid agreement has been made, the promisor's duties have not been discharged, and the promisor has breached. When one party has failed to perform, what are the rights of the other party and the party in breach? Or when the contract has been avoided because of incapacity or misrepresentation and the like, what are the rights of the parties after disaffirmance? These questions form the focus of this chapter. Remedies for breach of contracts for the sale of goods will be considered separately in Chapter 18.

THEORY OF CONTRACT REMEDIES

Monetary awards (called "damages"), specific performance, and restitution are the three principal remedies. In view of the importance given to the intention of the parties in forming and interpreting contracts, it may seem surprising that the remedy for every breach is not a judicial order that the obligor carry out his undertakings. But it is not. Of course, some duties cannot be performed after a breach: time and circumstances will have altered their purpose and rendered many worthless. Still, there are numerous occasions on which it would be theoretically possible for courts to order the parties to carry out their contracts, yet the courts will not do it. In 1897, Justice Oliver Wendell Holmes, Jr., declared in a famous line that "the duty to keep a contract at common law means a prediction that you must pay damages if you do not keep it." By that he meant simply that the common law looks more toward compensating the promisee for his loss than toward compelling the promisor to perform. Indeed, the law of remedies often provides the parties with an incentive to break the contract. In short, the promisor has a choice: to perform or pay.

On what basis can this principle be justified? The Restatement outlines the argument:

> According to economic theory, if available goods and resources are to be utilized in their most productive manner, each good must be consumed by the person who values it most highly, and each "factory of production" must be employed in the way that produces the most valued

output. Voluntary agreements in which individuals exchange assets for those that they value more are necessary to bring about this result. A bargain from which both parties benefit results in a gain in "economic efficiency" by moving the exchanged asset to higher valued uses. Economic theory assumes that the parties to an agreement strive to maximize their own welfare and that absent some impediment such as mistake, misrepresentation or duress, each party places a value on the other's performance that is greater than the anticipated cost to him of his own performance. At the time the agreement is made, then, each party has a reasonable expectation that he will benefit from its performance.

If one party later concludes that a contract that he originally thought would be profitable will be unprofitable for him, his nonperformance cannot be said to result in a gain in efficiency unless the value to him of the gain can be said to be greater than the value to the other party of the loss. . . .

[A] breach of contract will result in a gain in "economic efficiency" if the party contemplating breach evaluates his gains at a higher figure than the value that the other party puts on his losses, and this will be so if the party contemplating breach will gain enough from the breach to have a net benefit even though he compensates the other party for his resulting loss, calculated according to the subjective preferences of that party. If this requirement is met, breach with such compensation will be advantageous to one party and not disadvantageous to the other. To prevent it by compelling performance, it is argued, would result in a less efficient distribution of wealth since the party in breach would lose more than the injured party would gain.

This conclusion accords well with the assumption of contract law that the principal purpose of the rules relating to breach is to place the injured party in as good a position as he would have been in had the contract been performed. (3 *Restatement (Second) of Contracts*, pp. 101–102.)

The logic of this position is clear in many typical cases. The computer manufacturer orders specially designed circuit boards, then discovers before the circuits are made that a competitor has built a better machine and destroyed his market. The manufacturer cancels the order. It would make little economic sense for the circuit board maker to fabricate the boards if they could not be used elsewhere. A damage remedy to compensate the maker for out-of-pocket loss or lost profits is sensible; a judicial decree forcing the computer manufacturer to pay for and take delivery of the boards would be wasteful.

PROMISEE'S INTERESTS

Contract remedies serve to protect three different interests: an *expectation* interest, a *reliance* interest, and a *restitution* interest. A promisee will have one of these and may have two or all three. An **expectation interest** is the benefit for which he bargained, and the remedy is to put him in a position as good as that which he would have been in had the contract been performed. A **reliance interest** is the loss suffered by relying on the contract and taking actions consistent with the expectation that the other party will abide by it; the remedy is reimbursement that restores the promisee to his position before the contract was made. A **restitution interest** is that which restores to the promisee any benefit he conferred on the promisor. These interests do not dictate the outcome according to a rigid formula; circumstances and the nature of the contract, as usual, will play a large role. But in general, specific performance is a remedy that addresses the expectation interest, monetary damages address all three interests, and, not surprisingly, restitution addresses the restitution interest.

Consider some simple examples. A landowner repudiates an executory contract with a builder to construct a home on her property for $100,000. The builder had anticipated a $10,000 profit (the house would have cost him $90,000 to build). What can he expect to recover in a lawsuit against the owner? The court will not order the house to be built; such an order would be wasteful, since the owner no longer wants it and may not be able to pay for it. Instead, the court will look to the builder's three possible interests. Since the builder has not yet started his work, he had given the owner nothing, and therefore has no restitution interest. Nor has he any reliance interest, since we are assuming that he has not paid out any money for supplies, hired a work crew, or advanced money to subcontractors. But he anticipated a profit, and so he has an expectation interest of $10,000.

Now suppose that the builder had dug out the foundation and poured concrete, at a cost of $15,000. His expectation interest has become $25,000 (the difference between $100,000 and $75,000, the money he will save by not having to finish the job). His reliance interest is $15,000, because this is the amount he has already spent. He may also have a restitution interest, depending on how much the foundation of the house is worth to the owner. (The value could be more or less than the sum of money actually expended to produce the foundation; for example, the builder might have had to pay his subcontractors for a greater share of the job than they had completed, and those sums therefore would not be reflected in the worth of the foundation.)

Normally, the promisee will choose which of the three interests to pursue. As is to be expected, the choice hinges on the circumstances of the case, his feelings, and the amount at stake.

DAMAGES

Compensatory Damages

General Rule   The promisee, whom we will hereafter refer to as the injured party, has the right to damages (a money award) whenever the other party has breached the contract unless, of course, the contract itself or other circumstances suspend or discharge that right. The right exists even in cases where the expectation, reliance, and restitution interests are nil. If the breach caused no loss, the plaintiff is nevertheless entitled to a minor sum, perhaps one dollar, called **nominal damages.** When, for example, a buyer could purchase the same commodity at the same price as that contracted for, without spending any extra time or money, there can be no real damages in the event of breach.

Measure of Damages   With certain exceptions and limitations that we will consider below, the usual measure of damages is the injured party's expectation interest together with incidental and consequential losses caused by the breach, less costs and losses forgone by virtue of his not having to perform his own part of the bargain. Sometimes calculating the value of the promisor's performance is easy—for example, when the injured party has ascertainable costs and profits, as in the case of the builder who would have earned $10,000 profit on a $100,000 house. When the performance is a service, a useful measure of loss is what it would cost to substitute performance by someone else. But the calculation is frequently difficult, especially when the performance is a service that is not easily duplicated. If Rembrandt breached a contract to paint your portrait, the loss could not be

measured simply by inquiring how much Van Gogh would charge to do the same thing. Nevertheless, in theory, whatever net value would ultimately have been conferred on the injured party is the proper measure of damages. An author whose publisher breaches its contract to publish the book and who cannot find another publisher is entitled to lost royalties plus the value that would have accrued from her enhanced reputation.

In addition to the expectation interest, the injured party may recover incidental and consequential loss. **Incidental loss** includes expenditures that the injured party incurs in attempting to minimize the loss that flows from the breach. To arrange for substitute goods or services, the injured party might have to pay a premium or special fees to locate another supplier or source of work. A consequential loss is that incurred by the injured party without action on his part because of the breach—for example, lost sales stemming from a failure to fix a manufacturer's machine in time or physical and property injury due to a defective machine sold by the promisor. Note, however, that one obvious, and often large, expenditure occasioned by a breach—namely, legal expenses in bringing a lawsuit to remedy the particular breach—is not an element of damages, unless the contract explicitly states that it is, and cannot be charged to the defendant. There is one situation, however, in which legal costs can be added to damages: when the breach causes the injured party to be involved in a lawsuit with someone else.

Since the injured party usually has obligations under the contract also, a breach by the other party discharges his duty to perform and may result in savings. Or he may have made substitute arrangements and realized at least a partial profit on the substitution. Or, as in the case of the builder, he may have purchased goods intended for the job that can be used elsewhere. In all these situations, the losses he has avoided—savings, profits, or value of goods—are subtracted from the losses discussed above in order to arrive at the net damages. The injured party may recover his actual losses, not more. Suppose an employer breaches a contract with a prospective employee who was to begin work for a year at a salary of $15,000. The employee quickly finds other, similar work at a salary of $10,000. Aside from whatever he might have had to spend searching for the job, his damages are limited to $5,000, the difference between what he would have earned and what he is earning.

Lost volume is a particularly troublesome problem in calculating damages. This problem arises when the injured party, a supplier of goods or services, enters another contract when the buyer repudiates. The question is whether the second contract is a substituted performance or an additional one. If it is substituted, damages may be little or nothing; if additional, the entire expectation interest may be recovered. An automobile dealer contracts to sell a car to be made in the factory and delivered in two months. The buyer repudiates the contract one month later. The dealer then sells the car to someone else. If the dealer can show that he could have sold an identical car to the second purchaser regardless of what the first purchaser did, then the second sale stands on its own and cannot be used to offset the net profit recoverable from the first purchaser. The factual inquiry in lost volume cases is whether the injured party would have engaged in the second transaction if the breach had never occurred.

To the general rule that the injured party may recover actual loss there are three general exceptions or limitations: (1) the requirement that the injured party mitigate his damages, (2) nonrecoverability of damages that were not foreseeable, and (3) exclusion of speculative damages. We will examine each in turn.

Mitigation of Damages   Contract law encourages the injured party to avoid loss wherever possible. So there can be no recovery if he had an opportunity to avoid or limit his losses and failed to take advantage of it. Such an opportunity exists as long as it does not impose, in the Restatement's words, an "undue risk, burden or humiliation." (Section 350.) The effort to **mitigate** need not be successful. As long as the injured party makes a reasonable, good-faith attempt to mitigate his losses, damages are recoverable.

Mitigation can crop up in innumerable circumstances. Thus, an injured party who continues to perform after notice that the promisor has breached or will breach may not recover for expenses incurred in continuing to perform. And losses from the use of defective goods delivered in breach of contract are not recompensable if the injured party knew before use that they were defective. Often the injured party can

make substitute arrangements—find a new job or a new employee, buy substitute goods or sell them to another buyer—and his failure to do so will limit the amount of damages he can recover from the party who breaches. Under the general rule, failure to mitigate when possible permits the promisor to deduct from damages the amount of the loss that the injured party could have avoided. When there is a readily ascertainable market price for goods, damages are equal to the difference between the contract price and the market price.

Excelsior Docu-Dramas hires Harold as cameraman for a production expected to last six months. The day before shooting is to begin, Harold announces he is leaving to meditate in Nepal. The producer could hire a comparable substitute cameraman for $100 more per week, but he does not, unreasonably declaring: "It's Harold or no one." As a result, the filming is canceled and Excelsior loses $100,000 in potential profits. Excelsior has no claim for lost profits, but its damages would include $2,600 ($100 extra salary per week for twenty-six weeks, the expected duration of shooting), assuming Harold could be found to sue. If Harold remained out of the country, the statute of limitations would stop running, so that he could be sued upon his return even if years later.

A substitute transaction is not just any possible arrangement; it must be suitable under the circumstances. Factors to be considered include the similarity, time, and place of performance, and whether the difference between the contracted-for and substitute performances can be measured and compensated. A prospective employee who cannot find substitute work within her field need not mitigate by taking a job in a wholly different one. An advertising salesperson whose employment is repudiated need not mitigate by taking a job as a taxi driver. When the only difference between the original and the substitute performances is price, the injured party must mitigate, even if the substitute performer is the original promisor.

Suppose Harold the cameraman had told Excelsior's producer that he, Harold, had made a mistake in analyzing his financial needs for the next six months and was only willing to work if he was paid an additional $100 a week. Assume Harold is an exceptional cameraman for whom there is no ready substitute. If the producer refuses, Harold is not liable for

Excelsior's lost profits, since the company could easily have mitigated. Damages are limited to $2,600, as above. If the producer had accepted Harold's terms, would this have been a new contract modifying the original, thus eliminating Excelsior's claim for damages? Obviously not: since it was entered under duress, Excelsior would still have a claim against Harold for the excess salary. Now suppose Harold had told the producer that he would work for an extra $100, but only if Excelsior would agree to surrender any claim against him for breach of contract. In that case, Excelsior would not have been obligated to mitigate, and the lost profits would be part of the company's damages.

The injured party must mitigate in timely fashion, but each case is different. If it is clear that the promisor has unconditionally repudiated before performance is due, the injured party must begin to mitigate as soon as practicable and should not wait until the day performance is due to look for an alternative.

Sometimes it may be reasonable for the injured party to continue to rely on the party who breaches. Suppose Harold fails to turn up for work on the first day of filming, but in a telephone call late that morning mumbles something about "inner ear trouble" and assures the producer he will report in "within the next four or five days." The producer says: "OK, but you had better be here then or else this whole picture will go down the tubes." The producer could hire a substitute cameraman for more money on the spot, but she prefers Harold. If Harold fails to report for duty the following week, and the picture cannot be made as a result, it is a question of fact whether the producer acted reasonably in relying on Harold's statements. (Perhaps in the past Harold had made similar promises and always lived up to them.) If the producer's failure to hire a substitute was reasonable, Harold will be liable for lost profits.

As long as the injured party makes a reasonable effort to mitigate, the success of that effort is not an issue in assessing damages. If Excelsior's producer had diligently searched for a substitute cameraman, who cost $150 extra per week, and it later came to light that the producer could have hired a cameraman for $100, the company is entitled nevertheless to damages based on the higher figure.

SHIRLEY MACLAINE PARKER v. TWENTIETH CENTURY-FOX FILM CORP.
89 Cal. Rptr. 737, 474 P.2d 689 (1970)

BURKE, JUSTICE. Defendant Twentieth Century-Fox Film Corporation appeals from a summary judgment granting to plaintiff the recovery of agreed compensation under a written contract for her services as an actress in a motion picture. As will appear, we have concluded that the trial court correctly ruled in plaintiff's favor and that the judgment should be affirmed.

Plaintiff is well known as an actress, and in the contract between plaintiff and defendant is sometimes referred to as the "Artist." Under the contract, dated August 6, 1965, plaintiff was to play the female lead in defendant's contemplated production of a motion picture entitled "Bloomer Girl." The contract provided the defendant would pay plaintiff a minimum "guaranteed compensation" of $53,471.42 per week for 14 weeks commencing May 23, 1966, for a total of $750,000. Prior to May 1966 defendant decided not to produce the picture and by a letter dated April 4, 1966, it notified plaintiff of that decision and that it would not "comply with our obligations to you under" the written contract.

By the same letter and with the professed purpose "to avoid any damage to you," defendant instead offered to employ plaintiff as the leading actress in another film tentatively entitled "Big Country, Big Man" (hereinafter, "Big Country"). The compensation offered was identical, as were 31 of the 34 numbered provisions or articles of the original contract. Unlike "Bloomer Girl," however, which was to have been a musical production, "Big Country" was a dramatic "western type" movie. "Bloomer Girl" was to have been filmed in California; "Big Country" was to be produced in Australia. Also, certain terms in the proffered contract varied from those of the original. Plaintiff was given one week within which to accept; she did not and the offer lapsed. Plaintiff then commenced this action seeking recovery of the agreed guaranteed compensation.

The complaint sets forth two causes of action. The first is for money due under the contract; the second, based upon the same allegations as the first, is for damages resulting from defendant's breach of contract. Defendant in its answer admits the existence and validity of the contract, that plaintiff complied with all the conditions, covenants and promises and stood ready to complete the performance, and that defendant breached and "anticipatorily repudiated" the contract. It denies, however, that any money is due to plaintiff either under the contract or as a result of its breach, and pleads as an affirmative defense to both causes of action plaintiff's allegedly deliberate failure to mitigate damages, asserting that she unreasonably refused to accept its offer of the leading role in "Big Country."

Plaintiff moved for summary judgment under Code of Civil Procedure section 437c, the motion was granted, and summary judgment for $750,000 plus interest was entered in plaintiff's favor. This appeal by defendant followed.

* * *

The general rule is that the measure of recovery by a wrongfully discharged employee is the amount of salary agreed upon for the period of service, less the amount which the employer affirmatively proves the employee has earned or with reasonable effort might have earned from other employment. However, before projected earnings from other employment opportunities not sought or accepted by the discharged employee can be applied in mitigation, the employer must show that the other employment was comparable, or substantially similar, to that of which the employee has been deprived; the employee's rejection of or failure to seek other available employment of a different or inferior kind may not be resorted to in order to mitigate damages.

In the present case defendant has raised no issue of *reasonableness of efforts* by plaintiff to obtain other employment; the sole issue is whether plaintiff's refusal of defendant's substitute offer of "Big Country" may be used in mitigation. Nor, if the "Big Country" offer was of employment different or inferior when compared with the original "Bloomer Girl" employment, is there an issue as to whether or not plaintiff acted reasonably in refusing the substitute offer. Despite defendant's arguments to the contrary, no case cited or which our research has discovered holds or suggests that reasonableness is an element of a wrongfully discharged employee's option to reject, or fail to seek, different or inferior employment lest the possible earnings therefrom be charged against him in mitigation of damages.

Applying the foregoing rules to the record in the present case, with all

(*continued on next page*)

(continued)

SHIRLEY MACLAINE PARKER v. TWENTIETH CENTURY-FOX FILM CORP.
89 Cal. Rptr. 737, 474 P.2d 689 (1970)

intendments in favor of the party opposing the summary judgment motion—here, defendant—it is clear that the trial court correctly ruled that plaintiff's failure to accept defendant's tendered substitute employment could not be applied in mitigation of damages because the offer of the "Big Country" lead was of employment both different and inferior, and that no factual dispute was presented on that issue. The mere circumstance that "Bloomer Girl" was to be a musical review calling upon plaintiff's talents as a dancer as well as an actress, and was to be produced in the City of Los Angeles, whereas "Big Country" was a straight dramatic role in a "Western Type" story taking place in an opal mine in Australia, demonstrates the difference in kind between the two employments; the female lead as a dramatic actress in a western style motion picture can by no stretch of imagination be considered the equivalent of or substantially similar to the lead in a song-and-dance production.

Additionally, the substitute "Big Country" offer proposed to eliminate or impair the director and screenplay approvals accorded to plaintiff under the original "Bloomer Girl" contract, and thus constituted an offer of inferior employment. No expertise or judicial notice is required in order to hold that the deprivation or infringement of an employee's rights held under an original employment contract converts the available "other employment" relied upon by the employer to mitigate damages, into inferior employment which the employee need not seek or accept.

Statements found in affidavits submitted by defendant in opposition to plaintiff's summary judgment motion, to the effect that the "Big Country" offer was not of employment different from or inferior to that under the "Bloomer Girl" contract, merely repeat the allegations of defendant's answer to the complaint in this action, constitute only conclusionary assertions with respect to undisputed facts, and do not give rise to a triable factual issue so as to defeat the motion for summary judgment.

In view of the determination that defendant failed to present any facts showing the existence of a factual issue with respect to its sole defense—plaintiff's rejection of its substitute employment offer in mitigation of damages—we need not consider plaintiff's further contention that for various reasons, including the provisions of the original contract set forth in footnote 1, *ante*, plaintiff was excused from attempting to mitigate damages.

The judgment is affirmed.

Unforeseeability Failures to act, like acts themselves, have consequences. As the old fable has it: "For want of a nail, the kingdom was lost." To put an injured party in the position he would have been in had the contract been carried out could mean, in some cases, providing compensation for a long chain of events. In many cases that would be unjust, because a person who does not anticipate a particular event when making a contract will not normally take steps to protect himself (either through limiting language in the contract or through insurance). The law is not so rigid. A loss is not compensable to the injured party unless the breaching party, at the time the contract was made, had reason to foresee it as a probable result of his breach.

Of course, the loss of the contractual benefit in the event of breach is always foreseeable. A company that signs an employment contract with a prospective employee knows full well that if it breaches, the employee will have a legitimate claim to lost salary. But it might have no reason to know that the employee's holding the job for a certain length of time was a condition of his grandfather's gift of $1 million.

The leading case, perhaps the most studied case in all the common law, is *Hadley* v. *Baxendale*, decided in England in 1854. Joseph and Jonah Hadley were proprietors of a flour mill in Gloucester. In May 1853, the shaft of the milling engine broke, stopping all milling. An employee went to Pickford and Company, a common carrier, and asked that the shaft be sent as quickly as possible to a Greenwich foundry that would use the shaft as a model to construct a new one. The carrier's agent promised delivery within two days. But through an error the shaft was shipped by canal rather than by rail and did not arrive in Greenwich for seven days. The Hadleys sued Joseph Baxendale, managing director of Pickford, for the profits they lost because of the delay. In ordering a new trial, the Court of Exchequer ruled that Baxendale was not liable because he had had no notice that the mill was stopped:

> Where two parties have made a contract which one of them has broken, the damages which the other party ought to receive in respect of such breach of contract should be such as may fairly and reasonably be considered either arising naturally, i.e., according to the usual course of things, from such breach of contract itself, or such as may reasonably be supposed to have been in the contemplation of both parties, at the time they made the contract, as the probable result of the breach of it. [Hadley v. Baxendale, 9 Ex. 341, 354, 156 Eng.Rep. 145, 151 (1854)]

Thus when the party in breach has not known and has had no reason to know that the contract entailed a special risk of loss, the burden must fall on the injured party. Damages attributable to losses that flow from events that do not occur in the ordinary course of events are known as **consequential** or **special damages.** The exact amount of a loss need not be foreseeable; it is the nature of the event that distinguishes between a claim for ordinary or consequential damages. A repair shop agrees to fix a machine that it knows is intended to be resold. Because it delays, the sale is lost. The repair shop, knowing why timeliness of performance was important, is liable for the lost profit, as long as it was reasonable. It would

not be liable for an extraordinary profit that the seller could have made because of circumstances peculiar to the particular sale unless they were disclosed.

The special circumstances need not be recited in the contract. It is enough for the party in breach to have actual knowledge of the loss that would occur through his breach. Moreover, the parol evidence rule (Chapter 12) does not bar introduction of evidence bearing on the party's knowledge before the contract was signed. So the lesson to a promisee is that the reason for the terms he bargains for should be explained to the promisor—although too much explanation could kill a contract: a messenger who is paid five dollars to deliver a letter across town is not likely to undertake the mission if he is told in advance that his failure for any reason to deliver the letter will cost the sender $1 million, liability to be placed on the messenger.

Actual knowledge is not the only criterion, because the standard of foreseeability is objective, not subjective. That means that if the party had reason to know—if a reasonable person would have understood—that a particular loss was probable should he breach, then he is liable for damages. What one has reason to know obviously depends on the circumstances of the case, the parties' prior dealings, and industry custom. A supplier selling to a middleman should know that the commodity will be resold and that delay or default may reduce profits, whereas delay in sale to an end user might not. If it was foreseeable that the breach might cause the injured party to be sued, the other party is liable for legal fees and a resulting judgment or the cost of a settlement.

Even though the breaching party may have knowledge, the courts will not always award full consequential damages. In the interests of fairness, they may impose limitations if such an award would be manifestly unfair. Such cases usually crop up when the parties have dealt informally and there is a considerable disproportion between the loss caused and the benefit the injured party had agreed to confer on the party who breached. The messenger may know that a huge sum of money rides on his prompt delivery of a letter across town, but unless he explicitly contracted to bear liability for failure to deliver, it is unlikely that the courts would force him to ante up $1 million when his fee for the service was only five dollars.

The following case represents a modern application of the rule of *Hadley* v. *Baxendale.*

WENDT v. AUTO OWNERS INS. CO.
156 Mich. App. 19, 401 N.W.2d 375 (Mich.App. 1986)

GRIBBS, JUDGE.

*   *   *

Plaintiff's vehicle jackknifed and sustained extensive collision damage while it was being driven on hazardous winter roads on February 3, 1982, in Eureka, Missouri. Plaintiff promptly notified defendant of the accident and was advised by defendant to attempt to drive the vehicle back to Menominee County in Michigan. However, the vehicle could be driven only as far as Milwaukee, Wisconsin, where the damage was adjusted by defendant.

On March 22, 1982, defendant made an offer of settlement to plaintiff. Plaintiff rejected the offer, contending that defendant refused to pay for total damages sustained, and that defendant had inappropriately applied a $1,000 deductible, contrary to the language of the insurance policy.

On April 30, 1982, approximately three months after the accident, plaintiff filed the instant suit in circuit court, alleging breach of contract (Count I), negligence in adjustment (Count II), and intentional infliction of emotional distress in wilfully failing to settle plaintiff's collision damage claim timely and properly (Count III). In addition to the damages recoverable under the policy for repair or replacement of the vehicle, plaintiff sought additional damages on all three counts for the following:

"A)   Loss of use of the settlement amount;
"B)   Default has occurred on the Note between Plaintiff and the North Menominee Credit Union under which Note the vehicle was pledged as security, and Plaintiff has incurred all costs incident thereto;
"C)   Loss of use of the vehicle or its replacement with resulting loss of revenue normally generated by said vehicle;
"D)   Plaintiff's overall business has declined, and is continuing to decline, as a direct result of the loss of revenue from this vehicle;
"E)   Storage charges have been incurred, and are continuing to be incurred, while the vehicle remains with the dealership in Milwaukee, Wisconsin, where it has been appraised by Auto-Owners."

Upon defendant's motion, the circuit court dismissed plaintiff's intentional infliction of emotional distress claim (Count III), and struck plaintiff's claims for the damages sought in A through D (hereinafter referred to as additional damages) in the remaining breach of contract and negligence claims (Counts I and II).

*   *   *

In the instant case, plaintiff pled that, knowing the hardship which would be caused to plaintiff through the loss of his vehicle, defendant intentionally and wilfully breached its contract by refusing to settle plaintiff's claim according to the terms of its contract with plaintiff. Liberally construing these allegations, we find that plaintiff alleged that defendant has breached its obligation to process plaintiff's claim in good faith. Thus plaintiff can seek damages for defendant's breach, subject to the limitations applicable to damages for breaches of commercial contracts.

Michigan follows the rule of *Hadley v. Baxendale*, 9 Exch. 341, 156 Eng.Rep. 145 (1854), that damages recoverable for breach of a contractual obligation are those that arise naturally from the breach or those that were in the contemplation of the parties at the time the contract was made. Thus, for example, lost profits resulting directly from the breach of the insurer's obligation under an insurance contract which affects a specific collateral enterprise of which both parties are aware at the time of the agreement would be recoverable.

In the instant case, plaintiff alleged that defendant was aware of the fact that plaintiff was involved in a small family trucking business and that the loss of the vehicle, or a replacement, would cause an extreme financial hardship to plaintiff and his business. Thus, we conclude that plaintiff has properly pled lost profits as an element of damages in his breach of contract claim.

With respect to the loss of use of the settlement amount, defendant's refusal to pay plaintiff's claim would logically result in a loss of the use of the settlement amount, at least until the time the settlement was paid or a complaint was filed, at which time the prejudgment statutory interest compensating plaintiff for loss of use of the settlement would be applicable if plaintiff prevailed. Thus we hold the loss of use of the settlement amount from the date it should have been paid until the date of the filing of the complaint can be said to have naturally arisen from the breach. Similarly, loss of the use of a vehicle and costs arising from the default on the note secured by the vehicle can also be viewed as natural consequences of defendant's failure to pay the settlement amount on a vehicle sustaining serious collision damage.

In summary, we find that damages in the breach of contract claim for lost profits, loss of use of the vehicle, costs arising from the default on the note secured by the vehicle, and loss of use of the settlement amount until the date of the filing of the complaint were improperly stricken. The claim for damages for loss of use of the settlement amount from the date of the filing of the complaint was properly stricken.

Affirmed in part, and reversed in part.

Uncertainty of Damages   An injured party can recover only that amount of loss which can be proved with reasonable certainty. Especially troublesome in this regard are lost profits and loss of good will. Alf is convinced that next spring the American public will be receptive to polka-dotted belts with his name monogrammed in front. He arranges for a garment factory to produce 300,000 such belts, but the factory, which takes a large deposit from him in advance, misplaces the order and does not produce the belts in time for the selling season. When Alf discovers the failure, he cannot raise more money to go elsewhere, and his project fails. He cannot recover damages for lost profits because the number is entirely speculative; no one can prove how much he would have made, if anything. He can, instead, seek restitution of the monies advanced. If he had rented a warehouse to store the belts, he would also be able to recover his reliance interest.

Proof of lost profits is not always difficult: a seller can generally demonstrate the profit he would have made on the sale to the buyer who has breached. The problem is more difficult, as Alf's case demonstrates, when it is the seller who has breached. A buyer who

Trial Strategies Often Focus On Rival Damages Theories

By Wayne E. Green

[In the past, proof of lost profits in a lawsuit between two corporations was usually dismissed by the court as "speculative." Today, however, experts using sophisticated computer programs often provide sufficient proof to show whether a company lost millions in damages or nothing at all.
—AUTHORS' NOTE]

Ask most people about a major legal battle between companies, and they're likely to focus on whether the defendant is going to be found liable.

But check the pulse of lawyers and company officials on both sides of the fight and you may get a far different perspective. In these days of huge verdicts, it is the question of damages that often dominates their thinking and dictates their strategy.

PROVING DAMAGES

"You often structure the whole lawsuit around the damages issue," says Mark Yudof, dean of the University of Texas Law School. "It's always the tail wagging the dog."

*   *   *

Time was, legal scholars say, when lost-profits theories were routinely dismissed by judges as too speculative. But that has changed as economic analysis has improved. "There's just a lot more ferment in damages than there used to be," says Charles Knapp, a law professor at New York University.

Proving and disproving damages has become a sort of cottage industry, consisting mainly of accountants and economists who are paid large fees to testify on various theories. Using sophisticated computer programs, they can construct economic models showing that a business lost millions because, say, a contract was breached— or that it lost nothing at all.

"In most cases, I can come up with five different theories of damages and they're all fair," says Joseph P. Klock, managing partner of Steel Hector & Davis, a Miami law firm.

When liabilities and damages are being tried at the same time, lawyers differ on how to counter a plaintiff's damages theory. Some argue against offering an alternative theory, since it may suggest the defendant is conceding that there were damages.

Ignoring the Issue

But others cite the Pennzoil-Texaco-case, in which **Texaco** Inc.'s lawyers avoided the damages issue, concentrating instead on proving that the company simply wasn't liable for wrongfully interfering with **Pennzoil** Co.'s agreement to acquire Getty Oil. The result was an $11.1 billion verdict against Texaco. Some say Texaco should have argued that even if it were held liable, the damages shouldn't be anything close to what Pennzoil sought.

Source: *Wall Street Journal*, May 12, 1989

---

contracts for but does not receive raw materials, supplies, and inventory cannot show definitively how much he would have netted from the use he planned to make of them. But he is permitted to prove how much money he has made in the past under similar circumstances, and he may proffer financial and market data, surveys, and expert testimony to support his claim. As **Box 15-1** indicates, proving damages has become more scientific in recent years.

When proof of profits is difficult or impossible, the courts may grant a nonmonetary award, such as specific performance, which we will examine shortly.

Liquidated Damages Precisely because damages are sometimes difficult to assess, the parties themselves may specify how much should be paid in the event of a breach. When spelled out sufficiently that the sum can be ascertained mathematically from the contract terms, such damages are said to be **liquidated damages.** Courts will enforce a liquidated damage provision as long as the sum is reasonable in light of the expected or actual harm. If the liquidated sum is unreasonably large, the excess is termed a **penalty** and is said to be against public policy and unenforceable. The following case illustrates these principles.

UNITED AIR LINES, INC. v. AUSTIN TRAVEL CORP.
867 F.2d 737 (2nd Cir. 1989)

MINER, CIRCUIT JUDGE:

Defendant-appellant Austin Travel Corp. ("Austin") appeals from a summary judgment entered in the United States District Court for the Southern District of New York (Pollack, J.) awarding plaintiff-appellee United Air Lines, Inc. ("United") $408,375 in liquidated damages and unpaid debt plus interest and costs. United sued Austin to recover (i) damages for breach of leases obligating Austin to use a United computerized reservation system ("CRS") called Apollo and a United business and accounting system known as Apollo Business System ("ABS"), and (ii) unpaid accrued rentals. Austin claimed that the liquidated damages clauses of its Apollo contracts with United were unreasonable and unenforceable and that United's CRS practices violated federal and New York State antitrust laws.

The district court held that the liquidated damages clauses were reasonable and enforceable and that Austin could not prevail on claims of monopolization, attempted monopolization, restraint of trade and price discrimination. On appeal, Austin reasserts its liquidated damages and antitrust claims. Because we hold that the liquidated damages provisions of the United–Austin contracts were at the time of execution a reasonable forecast of damages in case of breach and because there was no showing at the district court of any antitrust violation by United, we affirm the entry of summary judgment in United's favor.

* * *

It is commonplace for contracting parties to determine in advance the amount of compensation due in case of a breach of contract. A liquidated damages clause generally will be upheld by a court, unless the liquidated amount is a penalty because it is plainly or grossly disproportionate to the probable loss anticipated when the contract was executed. Liquidated damages are not penalties if they bear a "reasonable proportion to the probable loss and the amount of actual loss is incapable or difficult of precise estimation." *Leasing Service Corp. v. Justice*, 673 F.2d 70, 73 (2d Cir.1982).

The liquidated damages fixed in the Apollo contracts were, as the district court found, reasonable at the time the contracts were executed. Most of United's costs when providing Apollo service are either fixed or determined in the early stages of the contractual relationship. The few costs that United would avoid by an early termination of an Apollo contract are estimated to be "less than 20 percent of the amount of revenue from the monthly fixed usage fees and variable charges." 681 F.Supp. at 187 (emphasis omitted). The Apollo contracts' liquidated damages clauses provide for recovery by United of only 80% of the fixed and variable charges. Austin is thus provided with better than adequate credit for the costs United is able to avoid by the early removal of the Apollo CRSs from Austin premises.

[Judgment affirmed.]

Punitive Damages

Punitive damages are those awarded for the purpose of punishing a defendant in a civil action, in which criminal sanctions are of course unavailable. They are proper in cases in which the defendant has acted willfully and maliciously and are thought to deter others from acting similarly. Since the purpose of contract law is compensation, not punishment, punitive damages have not traditionally been awarded, with one exception: when the breach of contract is also a tort for which punitive damages may be recovered. Punitive damages are permitted in the law of torts (in all but four states) when the behavior is malicious or willful (reckless conduct causing physical harm, deliberate defamation of one's character, a knowingly unlawful taking of someone's property), and some kinds of contract breach are also tortious—for example, when a creditor holding collateral as security under a contract for a loan sells the collateral to a good-faith purchaser for value even though the debtor was not in default, he has breached the contract and committed the tort of conversion (see page 451). Punitive damages may be awarded, assuming the behavior was willful and not merely mistaken.

Punitive damages are not fixed by law. The judge or jury may award at its discretion whatever sum is believed necessary to redress the wrong or deter like conduct in the future. This means that a richer person may be slapped with much heavier punitive damages than a poorer one in the appropriate case. But the judge in all cases may **remit** (lower) some or all of a punitive damage award if he or she considers it excessive.

In recent years, punitive damage claims increasingly have been made in cases dealing with the refusal by insurance companies to honor their contracts. Many of these cases involve disability payments, and among the elements are charges of tortious conduct by the company's agents or employees. California has been the leader among the state courts in their growing willingness to uphold punitive damage awards that are climbing into the millions of dollars—against insurer complaints that the concept of punitive damages is but a device to permit plaintiffs to extort settlements from hapless companies. As **Box 15-2** indicates, there are signs that the courts are beginning to agree.

SPECIFIC PERFORMANCE

In General

Specific performance is a judicial order to the promisor that he undertake the performance to which he obligated himself in a contract. Specific performance is an alternative remedy to damages and may be issued at the discretion of the court, subject to a number of exceptions. (When the promisee is seeking enforcement of a contractual provision for forbearance—a promise that the promisor will refrain from doing something—an **injunction,** a judicial order not to act in a specified manner, may be the appropriate remedy.) Emily signs a contract to sell Charlotte a gold samovar, a Russian antique of great sentimental value because it once belonged to Charlotte's mother. Emily then repudiates the contract while still executory. A court may properly grant Charlotte an order of specific performance against Emily.

Adequacy of "Legal Remedy" as General Limitation

Specific performance and injunction are remedies developed historically in the courts of equity. **Equitable remedies** are flexible, designed to resolve problems to which the relatively inflexible remedies in the courts of common law (hence "legal" remedies) were unsuited. The common-law courts and courts of equity were originally separate, and they applied separate law. The rule developed that an equitable remedy would not be issued if there were an adequate remedy "at law." In its present form, the effect of the rule is to preclude specific performance or injunction if damages are adequate to protect the expectation interest of the injured party. Unlike most other matters, specific performance is not a matter that the parties can stipulate to in their contract.

"Adequacy" is, of course, a slippery term, and no hard-and-fast rule delineates those situations in which money is sufficient recompense for a contract breach. Three factors are significant in determining adequacy: the difficulty of (1) proving damages, (2) buying a substitute performance with money awarded as damages, and (3) collecting any damages awarded. Consider these cases. (1) John has a contract to buy

State Courts Shift Stance On 'Bad Faith' Damages

By Wayne E. Green

[In recent years, courts in several states have allowed punitive damage awards against insurers who do not act fairly and in good faith. But, as discussed in the following article, there is reluctance to hold other types of companies liable for punitive damages for conduct that essentially represents breach of contract.—AUTHORS' NOTE]

Until a few years ago, consumers who felt they had been stiffed on an insurance claim didn't have many options. They could forget it, or sue the insurer for breach of contract—an often costly move that promised little more than recovering the original claim.

Things changed as state courts began allowing punitive damages against insurers for such breaches of "good faith and fair dealing." Big damage awards followed. So did a wave of offshoot litigation: Borrowers suing lenders who reneged on loan commitments; employees suing employers who breached an employment contract.

Turning Back

Now, some state courts are beginning to question the wisdom of

A PUNITIVE DAMAGES RETREAT

allowing such awards. Recent cases in California and Oklahoma have rejected bad-faith claims, and key test cases loom in Wyoming and Texas.

The issue is whether such bad-faith cases should remain purely contractual disputes or whether they sometimes fall under tort law. At stake is more than the future of a legal doctrine: If courts back off from permitting punitive damages for bad-faith dealings, consumers and borrowers will lose a powerful weapon. In turn, many businesses will end up saving millions of dollars.

*   *   *

'The Only Remedy'

Courts a few years ago began turning to punitive damages because breach-of-contract remedies didn't deter some companies from refusing to honor their commitments. An insurance company, for example, could drag its feet on an apparently legitimate policy claim, then simply refuse to pay. If it was sued and lost, it usually would have to pay only the original claim, plus maybe some interest and expenses.

"Where the only remedy for these

sort of things were contract remedies, there were real injustices for plaintiffs," says Douglas Laycock, a law professor at the University of Texas.

State courts permitted people to sue for bad faith because an insurer's refusal to honor policy commitments was considered by the courts not to be just a breach of contract but also a civil wrong, or tort. But the large verdicts that followed soon stirred a backlash among insurers, already steaming over big product-liability and medical-malpractice awards. Even some legal scholars bemoaned the blurring of contract and tort law, which is based on noncontractual duties that evolved through court cases over a period of centuries.

"We went from a contract system with serious wrongs and no effective remedies to the tort system where everything gets reviewed by a jury and they award damages with essentially no standards," asserts Mr. Laycock.

The California Supreme Court, which pioneered the bad-faith doctrine, began retreating [in 1988 when] it ruled that most employees suing their employers for wrongful discharge cannot collect punitive damages. Saying the employment relationship is "fundamentally contractual," it ruled that only contractual remedies, such as recovering lost wages, should be available.

Source: *Wall Street Journal*, June 21, 1989

---

for $5,000 Tom's record album of "Abbey Road," which has the autographs of all four Beatles. Tom gets a better offer and repudiates the contract. How much the album will appreciate in value is difficult to show, and it is unlikely that John will find a similar album. Consequently, specific performance of the

contract may be granted. (2) Naomi, a local artisan, agrees to buy all of the glass scrap of Bruce's Junkyard for the next four years. After eighteen months, Bruce's repudiates. Because it is difficult to show how much scrap glass Bruce's will take in during the next thirty months, the court can issue a decree of specific performance. (3) Tessa has a sixty-day option to buy John's home. On the forty-fifth day, John offers to sell it to Charles. Tessa is entitled to an injunction barring John from offering the house for sale during the option period. (4) Arthur contracts to sell Eileen 10,000 shares of Hyflying Corp., a widely traded security listed on the stock exchanges at $10 per share. On the day delivery is due, Hyflying Corp.'s stock has risen to $10 per share. Arthur repudiates. Eileen cannot obtain specific performance, because she can always buy other shares, and money damages will compensate her for the difference in price.

Because every parcel of land is considered unique, specific performance has historically been available to both buyers and sellers when contracts for the sale of land have been breached. From the buyer's side, the argument is that no amount of money could duplicate the lot he wanted. From the seller's point of view, it might be difficult to find another buyer or to show the market price of the land in order to calculate damages.

Difficulty in Enforcement as a Limitation

Some contracts may call for complex and continuing acts stretching over long periods of time. A contractor falls behind schedule in building a 300-acre shopping mall, and the owner asks the court to lay down a voluminous plan for proceeding to meet the contract terms, including an order to the contractor to double his work force and to provide the court with weekly progress reports. The court may properly refuse specific performance: the gain from enforcement would be outweighed by the difficulty of supervision.

A similar rule applies to contracts for personal services. Not only would supervision of an ongoing relationship be difficult once disputes had riven the relationship (because the court might be called upon constantly to judge the quality of performance, likely to be poor since no one enjoys working under compulsion), but also the effect of the order would be to compel work akin to involuntary servitude in violation of the Thirteenth Amendment to the Constitution. The Metropolitan Opera signs Maria Callas to an exclusive contract for the coming season, but before the season begins Callas repudiates. The Met's demand for specific performance will be refused, even though the Met will be unable to demonstrate with any degree of certainty what its financial loss will be.

In a case involving personal services, an injunction against the party in breach may be appropriate. For example, professional athletic leagues employ so-called **negative covenants,** by which players agree in the contract either to play for the teams with which they sign or not to play at all. The theory behind the injunction is that the player has such unique skill that he is irreplaceable (the recitation of the athlete's high skill is often written into the contract) and only by barring him from playing elsewhere will he be removed from all temptation to repudiate his contract. The validity of negative covenants is discussed in the following case.

MADISON SQUARE GARDEN CORP. v. CARNERA
52 F.2d 47 (2d Cir. 1931)

CHASE, CIRCUIT JUDGE. On January 13, 1931, the plaintiff and defendant by their duly authorized agents entered into the following agreement in writing:

1. Carnera agrees that he will render services as a boxer in his next contest (which contest, hereinafter called the 'First Contest,' shall be with the winner of the proposed Schmeling-Stribling contest, or, if the same is drawn, shall be with Schmeling, and shall be deemed to be a contest for the heavyweight championship title; provided, however, that, in the event of the inability of the Garden to cause Schmeling or Stribling, as the case may be, to perform the terms of his agreement with the Garden calling for such contest, the Garden shall be without further liability to Carnera, exclusively under the auspices of the Garden, in the United States of America, or the Dominion of Canada, at such time, not, however, later than midnight of September 30, 1931, as the Garden may direct.

* * *

8. In the event that Carnera wins the First Contest, then and in such event Carnera grants an option to the Garden for his services as a boxer in his thereafter contests so long as he continues winner thereof, to be held exclusively under the auspices of the Garden, upon the same terms and conditions as herein provided, excepting the percentage applicable to such Contests shall be thirty-seven and one-half per cent (37½%) instead of twelve and one-half per cent (12½%), and the opponent in such contests shall be such as may be approved of by the Garden. Such option shall continue so long as the Garden continues to arrange a contest for Carnera when Carnera shall desire such contest, but in no event closer than thirty days apart, it being understood that should the Garden not so arrange a contest, the option shall end.

9. Carnera shall not, pending the holding of the First Contest, render services as a boxer in any major boxing contest, without the written permission of the Garden in each case had and obtained. A major contest is understood to be one with Sharkey, Baer, Campolo, Godfrey, or like grade heavyweights, or heavyweights who shall have beaten any of the above subsequent to the date hereof. If in any boxing contest engaged in by Carnera prior to the holding of the First Contest, he shall lose the same, the Garden shall at its option, to be exercised by a two weeks' notice to Carnera in writing, be without further liability under the terms of this agreement to Carnera. Carnera shall not render services during the continuance of the option referred to in paragraph 8 hereof for any person, firm or corporation other than the Garden. Carnera shall, however, at all times be permitted to engage in sparring exhibitions in which no decision is rendered and in which the heavyweight championship title is not at stake, and in which Carnera boxes not more than four rounds with any one opponent.

★ ★ ★

Thereafter the defendant, without the permission of the plantiff, written or otherwise, made a contract to engage in a boxing contest with the Sharkey mentioned in paragraph 9 of the agreement above quoted, and by the terms thereof the contest was to take place before the first contest mentioned in the defendant's contract with the plaintiff was to be held.

The plaintiff then brought this suit to restrain the defendant from carrying out his contract to box Sharkey, and obtained the preliminary injunction order, from which this appeal was taken. Jurisdiction is based on diversity of citizenship and the required amount is involved.

The District Court has found on affadivits which adequately show it that the defendant's services are unique and extraordinary. A negative covenant in a contract for such personal services is enforceable by injunction where the damages for a breach are incapable of ascertainment.

The defendant points to what is claimed to be lack of consideration for his negative promise, in that the contract is inequitable and contains no agreement to employ him. It is true that there is no promise in so many words to employ the defendant to box in a contest with Stribling or Schmeling, but

(continued on next page)

(continued)

MADISON SQUARE GARDEN CORP. v. CARNERA
52 F.2d 47 (2d Cir. 1931)

the agreement read as a whole binds the plaintiff to do just that, provided either Stribling or Schmeling becomes the contestant as the result of the match between them and can be induced to box the defendant. The defendant has agreed to "render services as a boxer" for the plaintiff exclusively, and the plaintiff has agreed to pay him a definite percentage of the gate receipts as his compensation for so doing. The promise to employ the defendant to enable him to earn the compensation agreed upon is implied to the same force and effect as though expressly stated. The fact that the plaintiff's implied promise is conditioned, with respect to the consent with the winner of the Stribling-Schmeling match, upon the contest of that performer, does not show any failure of consideration for the defendant's promise.

As we have seen, the contract is valid and enforceable. It contains a restrictive covenant which may be given effect. Whether a preliminary injunction shall be issued under such circumstances rests in the sound discretion of the court. The District Court, in its discretion, did issue the preliminary injunction and required the plaintiff as a condition upon its issuance to secure its own performance of the contract in suit with a bond for $25,000 and to give a bond in the sum of $35,000 to pay the defendant such damages as he may sustain by reason of the injunction. Such an order is clearly not an abuse of discretion.

Order affirmed.

RESTITUTION

Benefit Conferred

Restitution is a remedy applicable to several different types of cases: those in which the contract was avoided because of incapacity or misrepresentation, those in which the other party breached, and those in which the party seeking restitution breached. As the word implies, restitution is a restoring to one party of what he gave to the other. Therefore, only to the extent that the injured party conferred a benefit on the other party may the injured party be awarded restitution.

Measuring the Restitution Interest

If the claimant has given the other party a sum of money, there can be no dispute over the amount of the restitution interest. Tom gives Tim $100 to chop his tree into firewood. Tim repudiates. Tom's restitution interest is $100. But serious difficulties can arise when the benefit conferred was performance. The courts have considerable discretion to award either the cost of hiring someone else to do the work that the injured party performed (generally, the market price of the service) or the value that was added to the property of the party in breach by virtue of the claimant's performance. Mellors, a gardener, agrees to construct ten fences around Lady Chatterley's flower gardens at the market price of $2,500. After erecting three, Mellors has performed services that would cost $750, market value. Assume that he has increased the value of the Lady's grounds by $800. If the contract is repudiated, there are two measures of Mellors's restitution interest: $800, the value by which the property was enhanced; or $750, the amount it would have cost Lady Chatterley to hire someone else to do the work. Which measure to use depends on who repudiated the contract and for what reason.

In some cases, the enhancement of property or wealth measurement could lead to an award vastly exceeding the market price for the service. In such cases, the smaller measure is used. For a doctor performing lifesaving operations on a patient, restitution would recover only the market value of the doctor's services—not the monetary value of the patient's life.

If the other party breached the contract, the injured party is generally entitled to **specific restitution** of property that can be returned. Lady Chatterley gives Mellors a valuable Ming vase in return for his promise to construct the fences. Upon Mellors's breach, Lady Chatterley is entitled to specific restitution of the vase.

Applications of the Restitution Rules

When the Other Party Is in Breach   The injured party is always entitled to restitution in the event of total breach by nonperformance or repudiation, unless both parties have performed all duties except for payment by the other party of a definite sum of money for the injured party's performance. Mellors agrees to build $3,000 worth of fences for only $2,000 and completes the construction. Lady Chatterley refuses to pay. Mellors does not have a restitution right to $2,500, the market price of his services (or $3,000, the amount by which her property increased in value); he is entitled, instead, only to $2,000, his contract price. Had Lady Chatterley repudiated prior to completion, however, Mellors would then have been entitled to restitution based either on the market price of the work or the amount by which he enhanced her property.

Restitution for the Party in Breach   A party who has partially performed and then breached is entitled to restitution of a benefit conferred on the injured party, if the injured party has refused (even though justifiably) to complete his own performance owing to the other's breach. Since the party in breach is liable to the injured party for damages for loss, this rule comes into play only when the benefit conferred is greater than the amount the injured party has lost.

Restitution in Other Cases   Upon repudiation of an oral contract governed by the Statute of Frauds, the injured party is not entitled to her expectation interest, but she may recover in restitution unless the purpose of the statute would be frustrated. When one party avoids a contract owing to lack of capacity, mistake, misrepresentation, duress, or the like, she is entitled to restitution for benefit conferred on the other party. Restitution is also available if a contract duty is discharged or never arises because (1) performance was impracticable, (2) the purpose of the contract was frustrated, (3) a condition did not occur, or (4) a beneficiary disclaimed his benefit.

ELECTION OF REMEDIES

General Rule

The nature of a loss resulting from a contract breach may be such as to entitle one party to a choice of remedies. Frequently, that party will manifest his intention to pursue one of them. He is not barred from electing a different remedy unless: (1) the remedies are inconsistent, and (2) the other party relied on the manifestation to his material detriment. Lady Chatterley signs a contract to sell her gardens to Mellors. Before conveyance, she repudiates. Mellors sues her for damages. While the suit is pending, the Lady proceeds to plant several thousand dollars' worth of peonies and gladiolas. Mellors may not amend his complaint to seek specific performance.

Under the UCC

The doctrine of election of remedy has been rejected by the UCC, which means that the remedies are cumulative in nature. According to Section 2-703, comment 1: "Whether the pursuit of one remedy bars another depends entirely on the facts of the individual case." UCC Section 2-721 provides that neither demand for rescission of the contract in the case of misrepresentation or fraud, nor the return or rejection of goods, bars a claim for damages or any other remedy permitted under the UCC for nonfraudulent breach (we will examine remedies for breach of sales contracts in Chapter 18).

Tort vs. Contract Remedies

Frequently a contract breach may also amount to tortious conduct. A physician warrants her treatment as perfectly safe but performs the operation negligently, scarring the patient for life. The patient could sue for malpractice (tort) or for breach of warranty (contract). The choice involves at least four considerations:

1. *Statute of limitations.*   Most statutes of limitations prescribe longer periods for contract than for tort actions.

2. *Allowable damages.*   Punitive damages are more often permitted in tort actions, and certain kinds of injuries are compensable in tort but not in contract suits—for example, pain and suffering.

3. *Expert testimony.*   In most cases, the use of experts would be the same in either tort or contract suits, but in certain contract cases, the expert witness could be dispensed with, as, for example, in a contract case charging that the physician abandoned the patient.

4. *Insurance coverage.*   Most policies do not cover intentional torts, so a contract theory that avoids the element of willfulness would provide the plaintiff with a surer chance of recovering money damages.

Legal vs. Extralegal Remedies

A party entitled to a legal remedy is not required to pursue it. Lawsuits are disruptive, not merely to the individuals involved in the particular dispute but also to the ongoing relationships that may have grown up around the parties, especially if they are corporations or other business enterprises. Buyers must usually continue to rely on their suppliers, and sellers on their buyers. Not surprisingly, therefore, many business executives refuse to file suits even though they could, preferring to settle their disputes privately or even to ignore claims that they might easily press. Indeed, the decision whether or not to sue is not one for the lawyer but for the executive, who must analyze a number of pros and cons, many of them not legal ones at all.

CHAPTER SUMMARY

Contract remedies serve to protect three different interests: an expectation interest (the benefit bargained for), a reliance interest (loss suffered by relying on the contract), and a restitution interest (benefit conferred on the promisor). In broad terms, specific performance addresses the expectation interest, monetary damages address all three, and restitution the restitution interest.

To understand the subject of compensatory damages, one should concentrate on a number of rules and tests: how to measure damages (including the problems of lost volume and lost profits), the mitigation requirement, the unforeseeability rule, and the problem of the uncertainty of damages, including the rules that govern liquidation of damages.

When compensatory damages are inadequate, the injured party might be entitled to the equitable remedies of specific performance or injunction. But these are available for a relatively narrow range of injuries, and in many cases, while these equitable remedies might be desirable, the courts have rejected them as unworkable.

Like the expectation and reliance interests, the restitution interest can be expressed in dollar terms, but its measurement is often difficult, in part because different measures are available for the same breach. Again, it is necessary to look to the particular circumstances of each case.

The injured party may sometimes be able to elect the remedy he wishes to pursue. Knowing which he may seek (different contract remedies, or even tort remedies) and whether he may change his mind and pursue others is an important practical consideration when contracts are breached.

KEY TERMS

Consequential damages	p. 349	Nominal damages	p. 344
Equitable remedies	p. 354	Penalty	p. 352
Expectation interest	p. 343	Punitive damages	p. 354
Incidental loss	p. 344	Reliance interest	p. 343
Injunction	p. 354	Restitution interest	p. 343
Liquidated damages	p. 352	Special damages	p. 349
Lost volume	p. 345	Specific performance	p. 354
Mitigate	p. 345	Specific restitution	p. 359
Negative covenants	p. 356		

SELF-TEST QUESTIONS

1. Contract remedies protect:
   (a)   a restitution interest
   (b)   a reliance interest
   (c)   an expectation interest
   (d)   all of the above
2. A restitution interest is:
   (a)   the benefit for which the promisee bargained
   (b)   the loss suffered by relying on the contract
   (c)   that which restores any benefit one party conferred on the other
   (d)   none of the above
3. When breach of contract caused no monetary loss, the plaintiff is entitled to:
   (a)   special damages
   (b)   nominal damages
   (c)   consequential damages
   (d)   no damages
4. Damages attributable to losses that flow from events that do not occur in the ordinary course of events are:

(a) incidental damages
(b) liquidated damages
(c) consequential damages
(d) punitive damages

5. Restitution is available:
(a) when the contract was avoided because of incapacity
(b) when the other party breached
(c) when the party seeking restitution breached
(d) all of the above

DEMONSTRATION PROBLEM

While in college, Susan applied to and was accepted by a leading medical school. She did not have enough money to pay tuition and so decided to work for a year. The medical school allowed her to defer enrollment for one year. Susan was hired to work for the year on a construction crew in Alaska for $35,000. However, after working for two weeks, she was fired for no reason and was unable to find other employment. Without funds, she was unable to attend medical school the following year, and the school canceled her acceptance. She now sues the contractor who hired her for the $35,000 salary. Furthermore, Susan argues that, if not for the breach of contract by the contractor, she could have gone to medical school and would have become a physician, with lifetime earnings of $3,500,000. Consequently, she seeks damages for this amount. Result? Why?

PROBLEMS

1. Terry leased an apartment from Larry. Despite Terry's numerous complaints, Larry provided no heat or hot water, failed to repair a leaking roof, did not replace burned-out light bulbs in the hallways, and failed to replace damaged mailboxes. Finally Terry sued Larry for breach of contract and asked for $1,000 in punitive damages. Larry's defense was that punitive damages are not allowed in breach-of-contract actions. Is this a good defense? Why?

2. Dr. Casey was scheduled to perform two operations one morning. He was to perform a gallbladder operation on Millie and a breast biopsy on Tillie. The patients' charts were negligently switched, and the doctor started to perform the gallbladder operation on Tillie. He stopped the operation immediately upon discovering that the patient had a healthy gall bladder. Tillie sued the doctor, claiming $7,500 in actual damages and $75,000 in punitive damages. Should she be allowed to collect punitive damages? Why?

3. Bull, a famous college football coach, was given a ten-

year, $100,000-per-year contract by his college. After two years the college breached the contract by firing Bull. Bull did not seek other employment and, instead, sued the college for eight years remaining on the contract. May he recover? Why?

4. Tom leased an apartment from Betty for one year. After two months, Tom vacated the apartment. A prospective tenant wanted to rent the vacant apartment but Betty refused, preferring instead to collect rent from Tom for the ten months remaining on the lease. May Betty continue to collect rent from Tom? Why?

5. In 1944, Harry entered into a contract to purchase a new car from a local dealer. The dealer breached the contract, and Harry sued for specific performance. The dealer argued that the remedy of specific performance was inappropriate because cars are not unique; damages are an adequate remedy because, with damages, Harry could buy an identical car (with the same options) elsewhere. Is this a good argument? Why?

6. Danny, a promising young basketball and baseball player, signed a multi-year contract with a professional baseball team upon graduating from college. After playing baseball for one year, Danny decided that he would rather play professional basketball and decided to breach his contract with the baseball team. May the team force Danny to play by seeking the remedy of specific performance? Why?

7. In problem 6, if specific performance is refused, what alternative remedy could the team seek that might have the same effect?

ANSWERS TO SELF-TEST QUESTIONS

1. (d) 2. (c) 3. (b) 4. (c) 5. (d)

SUGGESTED ANSWER TO DEMONSTRATION PROBLEM

Susan will probably lose on her claim for future earnings. First, under the rule in *Hadley v. Baxendale*, she must prove that the contractor knew or had reason to know of the damages that would result from breach of the contract. Second, even if the contractor had reason to know of the damages, a court might decide that it would be unfair to award consequential damages that were so disproportionate to Susan's salary. Third, Susan would have difficulty proving damages with reasonable certainty. Finally, even Susan's claim for $35,000 is questionable; this amount should be reduced by any savings which result because Susan does not (we assume) have to travel to Alaska.

Part 2: Contracts

THE MANAGER'S LEGAL AGENDA

Even though many types of oral agreements are binding and many businesses depend on them, do not rely on your memory for their content. You should always record on paper your understanding of contract terms and send a letter to the other party confirming them.

Do not make jokes about what you will pay or do if the other party will only take some action; you may discover that your joke is in fact an enforceable contract.

Whenever possible, enter into written agreements. It is easier to prove the existence of a written than an oral contract.

Keep the originals of your contracts in a secure place, so that your legal relations will not be interrupted or destroyed in the event of fire, storm or other catastrophe.

Make sure that the terms you actually negotiate are included in the contract to be signed. You will not be permitted to argue later that you had agreed to additional or different terms that were not written down.

When making an offer, place a time limit for the other party to accept, especially if the other party may accept by performing; otherwise you may spend time and money arguing about whether an "unreasonable" amount of time had lapsed before performance.

A business that routinely enters into standard contracts should have a system for recording and monitoring deviations in particular contracts. Otherwise, the department or departments responsible for carrying them out will perform in the standard way and wind up breaching the contracts with different terms.

Contracts of even moderate complexity should be drafted by your lawyers or at least shown to your lawyers before signing, since many federal and state statutes will affect the validity and even legality of your undertaking.

The sales staff should undergo regular training programs to ensure that all sales personnel know about their employers' policies of honesty and fair dealing. Otherwise, a salesperson might be tempted to shade the truth or engage in some other form of fraud when inviting potential customers to sign contracts, and the employer will wind up with void or voidable contracts.

Train your service representatives and other personnel to avoid making statements suggesting to customers and others with whom you have contractual relations that your company may be anticipating breaching its contracts.

If a party to one of your contracts fails to perform, you should ensure that you promptly undertake every reasonable effort to find some other means of getting done what the other party was supposed to do under the contract. You cannot sit back and assume that you will recover your damages in a lawsuit, since the law imposes on you the duty to make good-faith efforts to mitigate.

In drafting contracts, always consider the costs and consequences to your business if the other party breaches. If at all possible, recite in the contract the type of damages for which the breaching party will be held responsible; if not possible, make sure before signing to bring to the other party's attention the benefits you are seeking under the contract and the types of losses that you will incur if the contract is breached.

Since the courts will not award compensation for every type of loss or order performance of every type of conduct required to be undertaken, whenever possible negotiate a liquidated damages clause to provide some basis for relief should the contract be breached.

PART

III

The buyer needs a hundred eyes, the seller not one.

—GEORGE HERBERT

THE SALE, STORAGE, SHIPMENT, AND LEASING OF GOODS

CHAPTER

16

CHAPTER OVERVIEW

Commercial Transactions and the UCC
Introduction to Sales Law
Scope of Article 2
General Obligations Under Article 2

Introduction to Sales

COMMERCIAL TRANSACTIONS AND THE UCC

*I*n Chapter 7 we introduced the Uniform Commercial Code. As we noted, the UCC has become a national law, adopted in every state—although Louisiana has not enacted Article 2 and several differences occur from state to state.

The UCC embraces the law of "commercial transactions," a term of some ambiguity. A commercial transaction may seem to be a series of separate transactions; it may include, for example, the making of a contract for the sale of goods, the signing of a check, the indorsement of the check, the shipment of goods under a bill of lading, and so on. However, the UCC presupposes that each of these transactions is a facet of one single transaction: the lease or sale of and payment for goods. The code deals with phases of this transaction from start to finish. These phases are organized according to the following "articles":

- *Sales* (Article 2)
- *Leases* (Article 2A)
- *Commercial Paper* (Article 3)
- *Bank Deposits and Collections* (Article 4)

- *Funds Transfers* (Article 4A)
- *Letters of Credit* (Article 5)
- *Bulk Transfers* (Article 6)
- *Warehouse Receipts, Bills of Lading, and Other Documents of Title* (Article 7)
- *Investment Securities* (Article 8)
- *Secured Transactions; Sales of Accounts and Chattel Paper* (Article 9)

Although the code comprehensively covers commercial transactions, it does not deal with every aspect of commercial law. Among the subjects it does not cover are sale of real property, mortgages, insurance contracts, suretyship transactions (unless the surety is party to a negotiable instrument), and bankruptcy. Moreover, common law principles of contract law that we examined in the preceding unit continue to apply to many transactions covered in a particular way by the UCC. These principles include capacity to contract, misrepresentation, coercion, and mistake. Many federal laws supersede the UCC; these include the Bills of Lading Act, the Consumer Credit Protection Act, the warranty provisions of the Magnuson-Moss Act, and many other regulatory statutes.

We follow the general outlines of the UCC in this unit and in Parts IV and V. In this unit we cover the law governing sales (Article 2), as well as a special type of sale, the bulk transfer (Article 6). The use of documents of title to ship and store goods is closely related to sales, and so we cover documents of title (Article 7), as well as the law of bailments and leasing (Article 2A) in this unit.

In Part IV, we cover the giving of a check, draft, or note (commercial paper) for part or all of the purchase price, and the negotiation of the commercial paper (Article 3). Related matters such as bank deposits and collections (Article 4), funds transfers (Article 4A) and letters of credit (Article 5) are also covered there.

In Part V we turn to acceptance of security by the seller or lender for financing the balance of the payment due. Key to this area is the law of secured transactions (Article 9), but other types of security (for example, mortgages and suretyship) not covered in the UCC will also be discussed in Part V. The unit includes coverage of consumer credit transactions and bankruptcy law, important topics for all creditors, even those lacking some form of security.

Finally, the specialized topic of Article 8, investment securities (for example, corporate stocks and bonds), is treated in the corporations unit of this text, Part IX.

We now turn our attention to the sale—the first facet, and the cornerstone, of the commercial transaction.

INTRODUCTION TO SALES LAW

Sales law is a special type of contract law, and many provisions of Article 2, especially those covering the form and formation of contracts, are closely related to the common law of contracts. In the contracts unit, for instance, we cover in detail certain of these UCC provisions, including:

- *Statute of Frauds* The UCC Statute of Frauds provision requires a writing to enforce a contract for the sale of goods worth $500 or more, with some exceptions (Section 2-201).
- *Parol evidence* Terms embodied in a final, written sales agreement cannot be contradicted by prior agreements or contemporaneous oral agreements, although under certain circumstances the written terms may be explained or supplemented (Section 2-202).

- *Seals* The common law of sealed instruments does not apply to written instruments for the sale of goods; seals on contracts for the sale of goods are inoperative (Section 2-203).
- *Formation in general* The UCC specifies no formal manner of making a contract, as long as the agreement can be shown to have been made (Section 2-204).
- *Firm offer* An offer signed by a merchant is irrevocable during the period in which its terms state it to be open, even if there is no consideration, as long as the period does not exceed three months (Section 2-205).

In addition to form and formation provisions (covered in Part II of this text), Article 2 covers in great detail the following key elements of the law of sales, which anyone engaged in commercial transactions must comprehend:

1. The general obligations of the parties—treated later in this chapter
2. Title, risk of loss, and insurable interest—covered in the next chapter (Chapter 17)
3. Performance of the sales contract and remedies available to the buyer and seller when the contract is not performed (Chapter 18)
4. Warranties given in a sales contract—these and related tort law concepts will be covered in Chapter 19 on product liability

SCOPE OF ARTICLE 2

Article 2 does not govern all commercial transactions, only sales. It does not cover all sales, only the sale of goods. To understand these limitations, we consider in detail the definitions of "sale" and "goods."

Sale

Defined A **sale** "consists in the passing of title from the seller to the buyer for a price" (Section 2-106(1)). The Code distinguishes a "present sale" from a "contract for sale." The former is defined as a sale "accomplished by the making of the contract"—in other words, it is a sale in which nothing more is required to effect transfer of title. A "contract for sale" includes a present sale but it also refers to a contract to sell goods in the future. Whichever type of sale is involved, the rights of the parties are the same except in a few instances stated in Article 2.

Distinguished from Gift, Bailment, Lease, and Secured Transaction   Article 2 sales should be distinguished from *gifts, bailments, leases,* and *secured transactions.* A **gift** is the transfer of title without consideration, and a "contract" for a gift of goods is unenforceable under the UCC or otherwise. A **bailment** is the transfer of possession but not title or use; parking your car in a garage often creates a bailment with the garage owner. A **lease** is a fixed-term arrangement for possession and use of something—computer equipment, for example—and does not transfer title. In a **secured transaction**, you as owner give a security interest in collateral to a creditor.

The question of whether a particular transaction is a sale subject to Article 2 arises often in cases involving injuries caused by defective products. If the product has been sold to the injured consumer, Article 2 creates certain implied warranties under which the consumer can recover damages. Although not all courts would agree, the next case notes one approach to the question of whether a sale had been made.

SHEESKIN v. GIANT FOOD, INC.
20 Md.App. 611, 318 A.2d 874 (1974)

DAVIDSON, JUDGE. Every Friday for over two years Nathan Seigel, age 73, shopped with his wife at a Giant Food Store. This complex products liability case is before us because on one of these Fridays, 23 October 1970, Mr. Seigel was carrying a six-pack carton of Coca Cola from a display bin at the Giant to a shopping cart when one or more of the bottles exploded. Mr. Seigel lost his footing, fell to the floor and was injured.

In the Circuit Court for Montgomery County, Mr. Seigel sued both the Giant Food, Inc., and the Washington Coca Cola Bottling Company, Inc., for damages resulting from their alleged negligence and breach of an implied warranty. At the conclusion of the trial Judge Walter H. Moorman, directed a verdict in favor of each defendant.

The retailer, Giant Food, Inc., contends that appellant failed to prove that an implied warranty existed between himself and the retailer because he failed to prove that there was a sale by the retailer to him or a contract of sale between the two. The retailer maintains that there was no sale or contract of sale because at the time the bottles exploded Mr. Seigel had not yet paid for them. We do not agree.

Code (1957), Art. 95B, § 2–314(1) states in pertinent part:

> Unless excluded or modified (§ 2–316), a warranty that the goods shall be merchantable is implied *in a contract for their sale* if the seller is a merchant with respect to goods of that kind. (Emphasis added.)

Thus, in order for the implied warranties of § 2–314 to be applicable there must be a "contract for sale." In Maryland it has been recognized that neither a completed "sale" nor a fully executed contract for sale is required. It is enough that there be in existence an executory contract for sale.

* * *

Here, the plaintiff has the burden of showing the existence of the warranty by establishing that at the time the bottles exploded there was a contract for

(continued on next page)

(*continued*)

SHEESKIN v. GIANT FOOD, INC.
20 Md.App. 611, 318 A.2d 874 (1974)

their sale existing between himself and the Giant. Mr. Titus, the manager of the Giant, testified that the retailer is a "self-service" store in which "the only way a customer can buy anything is to select it himself and take it to the check-out counter." He stated that there are occasions when a customer may select an item in the store and then change his mind and put the item back. There was no evidence to show that the retailer ever refused to sell an item to a customer once it had been selected by him or that the retailer did not consider himself bound to sell an item to the customer after the item had been selected. Finally, Mr. Titus said that an employee of Giant placed the six-pack of Coca Cola selected by Mr. Seigel on the shelf with the purchase price already stamped upon it. Mr. Seigel testified that he picked up the six-pack with the intent to purchase it.

We think that there is sufficient evidence to show that the retailer's act of placing the bottles upon the shelf with the price stamped upon the six-pack in which they were contained manifested an intent to offer them for sale, the terms of the offer being that it would pass title to the goods when Mr. Seigel presented them at the check-out counter and paid the stated price in cash. We also think that the evidence is sufficient to show that Mr. Seigel's act of taking physical possession of the goods with the intent to purchase them manifested an intent to accept the offer and a promise to take them to the check-out counter and pay for them there.

Code (1957), Art. 95B, § 2–206 provides in pertinent part:

> (1) Unless otherwise unambiguously indicated by the language or circumstances
> (a) An offer to make a contract shall be construed as inviting acceptance in any manner and by any medium reasonable in the circumstances. . . .

The Official Comment 1 to this section states:

> Any reasonable manner of acceptance is intended to be regarded as available unless the offeror has made quite clear that it will not be acceptable.

In our view the manner by which acceptance was to be accomplished in the transaction herein involved was not indicated by either language or circumstances. The seller did not make it clear that acceptance could not be accomplished by a promise rather than an act. Thus it is equally reasonable under the terms of this specific offer that acceptance should be accomplished in any of three ways: 1) by the act of delivering the goods to the check-out counter and paying for them; 2) by the promise to pay for the goods as evidenced by their physical delivery to the check-out counter; and 3) by the promise to deliver the goods to the check-out counter and to pay for them there as evidenced by taking physical possession of the goods by their removal from the shelf.

The fact that customers, having once selected goods with the intent to purchase them, are permitted by the seller to return them to the shelves does not preclude the possibility that a selection of the goods, as evidenced by taking physical possession of them, could constitute a reasonable mode of acceptance. Section 2–106(3) provides:

> 'Termination' occurs when either party pursuant to a power created by agreement or law puts an end to the contract otherwise than for its breach. On 'termination' all obligations which are still executory on both sides are discharged but any right based on prior breach or performance survives.

Here the evidence that the retailer permits the customer to "change his mind" indicates only an agreement between the parties to permit the consumer to end his contract with the retailer irrespective of a breach of the agreement by the retailer. It does not indicate that an agreement does not exist prior to the exercise of this option by the consumer.

★　　★　　★

[Judgment in favor of Giant Food is reversed and the case remanded for a new trial. Judgment in favor of the bottler is affirmed because the plaintiff failed to prove that the bottles were defective when they were delivered to the retailer.]

Goods

Defined Even if the transaction is considered a sale, the question still remains whether the contract concerns the sale of goods. Article 2 applies only to goods; sales of real estate and services are governed by non-UCC law. UCC Section 2-105(1) defines **goods** as "all things . . . which are movable at the time of identification to the contract for sale other than the money in which the price is to be paid. . . ." Money can be considered goods subject to Article 2 if it is the object of the contract—for example, foreign currency.

In certain cases, the courts have difficulty applying this definition because the item in question can also be viewed as realty or service. Most borderline cases raise one of two general questions: (1) Is the contract for the sale of the real estate, or is it for the sale of goods? and (2) Is the contract for the sale of goods, or is it for services?

Real Estate* vs. *Goods The dilemma is this: A landowner enters into a contract to sell crops, timber, minerals, oil, or gas. If the items have already been detached from the land (for example, the timber has been cut and the seller agrees to sell "logs"), then because the logs are clearly movable, they are "goods,"

and the UCC governs the sale. But what if, at the time the contract is made, the item is still a part of the land? Is a contract for the sale of uncut timber governed by the UCC or by real estate law?

The UCC governs under either of two circumstances: (1) if the contract calls for the seller to sever the items, or (2) if the contract calls for the buyer to sever and the goods can be severed without material harm to the real estate. (Section 2-107.) The second provision specifically includes growing crops and timber. By contrast, the law of real property governs if the buyer's severance of the items will materially harm the real estate; for example, removal of minerals, oil, gas, and structures by the buyer will cause the law of real property to govern. (See Figure 16-1.)

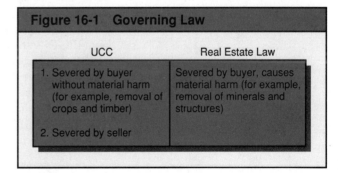

Figure 16-1　Governing Law

UCC	Real Estate Law
1. Severed by buyer without material harm (for example, removal of crops and timber) 2. Severed by seller	Severed by buyer, causes material harm (for example, removal of minerals and structures)

Goods* vs. *Services Distinguishing goods from services is the other major difficulty that arises in determining the nature of the object of a sales contract. The problem: How can goods and services be separated in contracts calling for the seller to deliver a combination of goods and services? This difficulty frequently arises in product liability cases in which the buyer sues the seller for breach of one of the UCC warranties to be discussed in Chapter 19. For example, you go to the hairdresser for a permanent and the shampoo gives you a severe scalp rash. May you recover damages on the grounds that either the hairdresser or the manufacturer breached an implied warranty in the sale of goods?

In answering this question, courts use a "predominant purpose" test—that is, they ask whether the transaction was predominantly a contract for goods or for services. The results of this analysis are not always consistent. Compare *Epstein* v. *Giannattasio*, 197 A.2d 342 (Conn. 1963), in which the court held that no sale of goods had been made because the plaintiff received a treatment in which the cosmetics were only incidentally used, with *Newmark* v. *Gimbel's Inc.*, 258 A.2d 697 (N.J. 1969), in which the court said "[i]f the permanent wave lotion were sold . . . for home consumption . . . unquestionably an implied warranty of fitness for that purpose would have been an integral incident of the sale." The New Jersey court rejected the defendant's argument that by actually applying the lotion to the patron's head the salon lessened the liability it otherwise would have had if it had simply sold her the lotion.

Another area in which the issue of goods vs. services frequently arises today is liability for the sale of computer programs, as the following case illustrates.

RRX INDUSTRIES, INC. v. LAB-CON, INC. 772 F.2d 543 (9th Cir. 1985)

EUGENE A. WRIGHT, CIRCUIT JUDGE. Thomas E. Kelly and Associates (TEKA), Lab-Con, Inc., and Thomas E. Kelly (Kelly) appeal from the district court's judgment awarding RRX Industries, Inc. general and consequential damages for breach of contract. Appellants challenge the district court's fact findings on liability and contend that the award of consequential damages was improper. We affirm.

This action arises out of a computer software contract negotiated between RRX and TEKA. TEKA agreed to supply RRX with a software system for use in its medical laboratories. The contract obligated TEKA to correct any malfunctions or "bugs" that arose in the system, but limited TEKA's liability to the contract price.

TEKA began installing the software system in January 1981 and completed it in June 1981. Bugs appeared in them soon after installation. TEKA attempted to repair the bugs by telephone patching. Subsequently, TEKA upgraded the system to make it compatible with more sophisticated hardware. The system, however, remained unreliable because defects continued to exist.

After contracting with RRX, Kelly formed Lab-Con, Inc. in order to market TEKA's software system. Lab-Con was a successor corporation to TEKA. TEKA assigned the RRX software contract to Lab-Con.

In September 1982, RRX instituted this diversity action against TEKA, Lab-Con, Kelly, and other defendants alleging breach of contract and fraud. Following a bench trial, the district court concluded that TEKA had materially breached the software contract. It found Lab-Con and Kelly individually liable and awarded RRX the amount paid under the contract, plus consequential damages. TEKA, Lab-Con, and Kelly (collectively appellants) timely appeal the judgment and award of damages.

★   ★   ★

The district court relied on the California Commercial Code to award RRX consequential damages. Such reliance was proper only if the computer software system may be characterized as a "good" rather than a service.

The California Commercial Code defines a good as "all things (including specially manufactured goods) which are movable at the time of identification to the contract for sale other than the money in which the price is to be paid, investment securities (Division 8) and things in action. . . ." Cal. Com.Code § 2105 (West 1964).

In determining whether a contract is one of sale or to provide services we look to the essence of the agreement. When a sale predominates, incidental services provided do not alter the basic transaction. Because software packages vary depending on the needs of the individual consumer, we apply a case-by-case analysis.

Here, the sales aspect of the transaction predominates. The employee training, repair services, and system upgrading were incidental to sale of the software package and did not defeat characterization of the system as a good. [Affirmed.]

In two areas, state legislatures have taken the goods vs. services issue out of the courts' hands and resolved the issue through legislation. One area involves restaurant cases, in which typically the plaintiff charges that he became ill because of tainted food. UCC Section 2-314(1) states that any seller who is regularly a merchant of the goods sold impliedly warrants their merchantability in a contract for their sale. This section explicitly declares that serving food or drink is a sale, whether they are to be consumed on or off the premises.

The second type of case involves blood transfusions, which can give a patient hepatitis, a serious and sometimes fatal disease. Hospitals and blood banks obviously face large potential liability under the UCC provision just referred to on implied warranty of merchantability. Because medical techniques cannot detect the hepatitis virus in any form of blood used, hospitals and blood banks would be in constant jeopardy, without being able to take effective action to minimize the danger. More than forty states have enacted legislation specifically providing that blood supplies to be used in transfusions are a service, not goods, thus relieving the suppliers and hospitals of an onerous burden.

GENERAL OBLIGATIONS UNDER ARTICLE 2

Once we determine that a contract provides for the sale of goods, rather than real estate or services, so what? What difference does it make that the UCC, rather than the common law of contracts applies to the transaction? This entire unit focuses on the answer to this question; that is, on the unique features of the UCC law of sales. As a prelude to more specific topics in Chapters 17, 18, and 19, we now look at two sets of general UCC provisions, one dealing with the obligations of merchants, the other with open and unfair contract terms.

Merchants

First, although the UCC applies to all sales of goods (even when you sell your used car to your neighbor), merchants often have special obligations or are governed by special rules. The code assumes that merchants should be held to particular standards because they are more experienced and have or should have special knowledge. Rules applicable to professionals ought not apply to the casual or inexperienced buyer or seller.

Who is a merchant? Section 2-104(1) defines a merchant as one "who deals in goods of the kind or otherwise by his occupation holds himself out as having knowledge or skill peculiar to the practices or goods involved in the transaction. . . ." A phrase that recurs throughout Article 2—"between merchants"—refers to any transaction in which both parties are chargeable with the knowledge or skill of merchants. (Section 2-104(3).) Not every business person is a merchant with respect to every possible transaction. But a person or institution normally not considered a merchant can be one under Article 2 if he employs an agent or broker who holds himself out as having such knowledge or skill. (Thus a university with a purchasing office can be a merchant with respect to transactions handled by that department.)

Determining whether a particular person operating a business is a merchant under Article 2 is a common problem for the courts. The following case shows how Section 2-104 is applied in practice.

LOEB AND COMPANY, INC. v. SCHREINER
321 So.2d 199 (Ala. 1975)

ALMON, JUSTICE. This is an appeal from a judgment of the Circuit Court of Lowndes County. The court decreed that the plaintiff and the defendant entered into an oral contract for the purchase and sale of one hundred fifty bales of cotton but that the contract was unenforceable under the Alabama Uniform Commercial Code because the defendant was not a "merchant" as that term is used and defined.

The plaintiff-appellant, Loeb and Company, Inc., is engaged in the marketing of raw cotton. James L. Loeb of Montgomery is President of the company and has bought cotton from the defendant-appellee, Charles Schreiner, for the past four or five years. Charles Schreiner is a cotton farmer and has been engaged in the farming of cotton and other crops since 1963.

Following a conversation on the 18th or 20th of April, 1973, with regard to the price paid by appellant company to Marlowe Reese, a neighbor of appellee, appellee telephoned appellant on April 23 and asked if the price paid Reese was available to him. He received from the president of appellant company a statement that he would pay appellee the same price. Appellant maintained at trial that appellee orally contracted with him during the telephone conversation to sell appellant company one hundred fifty bales of cotton. Appellee admitted that there were negotiations but maintained that he never agreed to sell the one hundred fifty bales.

The date, parties, terms and conditions of the alleged contract to sell were confirmed in the records of appellant company on April 23, 1973, and two copies of a confirming statement were mailed to appellee. Appellee received the confirming statement but neither signed it nor returned it, nor in any manner took exception to it until four months later when appellant telephoned him inquiring the whereabouts of the statement. In the meanwhile, the price of raw cotton had risen from the price in the alleged contract of 37¼ cents to the middle 80 cents.

When appellant company telephoned appellee and inquired about the confirming statement, appellee said that he did not intend to sign and return it and told appellant to discuss the matter with his attorney.

The trial court found that there was an oral contract but that the contract was unenforceable under the Alabama Uniform Commercial Code because the appellee was not a merchant as that term is used in Tit. 7A, §§ 2–104 and 2–201, Code of Alabama, 1940, Recompiled 1958.

Tit. 7A, § 2–201 is the section which sets out the statute of frauds for Article 2 of the Uniform Commercial Code. It governs all contracts for the sale of "goods." Cotton is included within the definition of "goods" as defined by the Code.

★   ★   ★

Appellant contends that the trial court erred in finding that the appellee cotton farmer was not a merchant and that § 2–201(2) was not applicable. If appellee is not a "merchant," § 2–201 would act as a bar to the enforcement of the contract in question. However, if appellee is a "merchant," he would be liable on the contract because he did not within ten days give notice of objection to appellant's confirming statement. Tit. 7A, § 2–104(1) defines "merchant" as follows:

> (1) 'Merchant' means a person who deals in goods of the kind or otherwise by his occupation holds himself out as having knowledge or skill peculiar to the practices or goods involved in the transaction or to whom such knowledge or skill may be attributed by his employment of an agent or broker or other intermediary who by his occupation holds himself out as having such knowledge or skill.

★   ★   ★

We hold that in the instant case the appellee was not a "merchant" within the meaning of § 2–104. We do not think the framers of the Uniform Commercial Code contemplated that a farmer should be included among those considered to be "merchants."

In order for a farmer to be included within the § 2–104 definition of "merchants," he must do one of the following:

1. deal in goods of the kind;
2. *by his occupation* hold himself out as having knowledge or skill peculiar to the practices or goods involved in the transaction; or
3. employ an agent or broker or other intermediary who by his occupation holds himself out as having such knowledge or skill.

Since the farmer in the instant case did not qualify as a merchant under 3 above, he would have to qualify under 1 or 2. It is not sufficient under 2 that one hold himself out as having knowledge or skill peculiar to the practices or goods involved, he must *by his occupation* so hold himself out. Accordingly, a person cannot be considered a "merchant" simply because he is a braggart or has a high opinion of his knowledge in a particular area. We conclude that a farmer does not solely *by his occupation* hold himself out as being a professional cotton merchant.

The remaining thing which a farmer might do to be considered a merchant is to become a dealer in goods. Although there was evidence which indicated

(*continued on next page*)

(*continued*)

LOEB AND COMPANY, INC. v. SCHREINER
321 So.2d 199 (Ala. 1975)

that the appellee here had a good deal of knowledge, this is not the test. There is not one shred of evidence that appellee ever sold anyone's cotton but his own. He was nothing more than an astute farmer selling his own product. We do not think this was sufficient to make him a dealer in goods. The official comment to § 2–104 states in part as follows:

> This Article assumes that transactions between *professionals* in a given field require special and clear rules which may not apply to a *casual or inexperienced seller or buyer*. It thus adopts a policy of expressly stating rules applicable 'between merchants' and 'as against a merchant', wherever they are needed instead of making them depend upon the circumstances of each case as in the statutes cited above. This section lays the foundation of this policy by defining those who are to be regarded as professionals or 'merchants' and by stating when a transaction is deemed to be 'between merchants'. (Emphasis added.)

Although a farmer might sell his cotton every year, we do not think that this should take him out of the category of a "casual seller" and place him in the category with "professionals."

If indeed the statute of frauds has, as claimed, permitted an injustice, it is a matter which addresses itself to the legislature.

The judgment is due to be and is hereby Affirmed.

Open and Unfair Terms

The second major feature of Article 2 that distinguishes it from the common law of contracts is how it treats open and unfair contract terms. A court has greater freedom under the code than under the common law to determine the nature of a party's general obligations when terms are left open or are unfair.

Open Terms   Under Section 2-204(3), even though one or more terms are left open, a contract for sale is not voidable for indefiniteness, as in the common law, if the parties have intended to make a contract and the court can find a reasonably certain basis for giving an appropriate remedy. Perhaps the most important and controversial example is the open price term.

The open price term is covered in detail by Section 2-305. At common law, a contract that fails to specify price or a means of accurately ascertaining price will almost always fail. Not so under this UCC provision. If the contract says nothing about price, or permits the parties to agree on price but they fail to agree, or delegates the power to fix price to a third

person who fails to do so, then Section 2-305(1) decrees that the price to be awarded is a "reasonable price at the time for delivery." When one party is permitted to fix the price, Section 2-305(2) requires that it be fixed in good faith. However, if the parties *intend* not to be bound unless the price is first fixed or agreed, and it is not fixed or agreed, then no contract results. (Section 2-305(4).)

Another illustration of the open term is in regard to particulars of performance. Section 2-311(1) provides that a contract for sale of goods is not invalid just because it leaves to one of the parties the power to specify a particular means of performing. However, "any such specification must be made in good faith and within limits set by commercial reasonableness." (Performance will be covered in greater detail in Chapter 18.)

Unfair Terms   Both the code and the common law require good faith in the performance of a contract. But what if the terms of the contract itself are unfair? At common law, the courts are obliged to respect the terms of the contract, as long as the prerequisites of contracting were met (such as capacity to contract, lack of duress, and so on). But by virtue of Section 2-302(1), the courts may tinker with a contract if they determine that it is particularly unfair. The provision reads as follows:

> If the court as a matter of law finds the contract or any clause of the contract to have been unconscionable at the time it was made the court may refuse to enforce the contract, or it may enforce the remainder of the contract without the unconscionable clause, or it may so limit the application of any unconscionable clause as to avoid any unconscionable result.

The court thus has considerable flexibility. It may refuse to enforce the entire contract, or strike a particular clause or set of clauses, or limit the application of a particular clause or set of clauses.

But what does "unconscionable" mean? The UCC provides little guidance on this crucial question. According to comment 1 to Section 2-302, the "basic test is: whether, in the light of the general commercial background and the commercial needs of the particular trade or case, the clauses involved are so one-sided as to be unconscionable under the circumstances existing at the time of the making of the contract. . . . The principle is one of the prevention of oppression and unfair surprise and not of disturbance of allocation of risks because of superior bargaining power." It should be apparent that the definition is somewhat circular. For the most part, judges have had to develop the concept with little help from the statutory language. Unconscionability is much like U.S. Supreme Court Justice Potter Stewart's famous statement about obscenity: "I can't define it, but I know it when I see it."

In the following leading case, Judge J. Skelly Wright attempted to develop a framework for analysis. He refined the meaning of unconscionability by focusing on "absence of meaningful choice" (often referred to as "procedural unconscionability") and on terms that are "unreasonably favorable" (commonly referred to as "substantive unconscionability"). An example of procedural unconscionability is the salesperson who says: "Don't worry about all that little type on the back of this form." Substantive unconscionability is the harsh term—the provision that permits the taking of a pound of flesh if the contract is not honored. (Although the UCC was not yet law in the District of Columbia when the case arose, Congress had enacted it by the time the case reached court. The Court of Appeals relied on the congressional policy to declare that the common law mirrored this provision.)

WILLIAMS v. WALKER-THOMAS FURNITURE COMPANY
350 F.2d 445 (D.C. Cir. 1965)

J. SKELLY WRIGHT, CIRCUIT JUDGE. Appellee, Walker-Thomas Furniture Company, operates a retail furniture store in the District of Columbia. During the period from 1957 to 1962 each appellant in these cases purchased a number of household items from Walker-Thomas, for which payment was to be made in installments. The terms of each purchase were contained in a printed form contract which set forth the value of the purchased item and purported to lease the item to appellant for a stipulated monthly rent payment. The contract then provided, in substance, that title would remain in Walker-Thomas until the total of all the monthly payments made equaled the stated value of the item, at which time appellants could take title. In the event of a default in the payment of any monthly installment, Walker-Thomas could repossess the item.

The contract further provided that

> the amount of each periodical installment payment to be made by [purchaser] to the Company under this present lease shall be inclusive of and not

(continued on next page)

(continued)

WILLIAMS v. WALKER-THOMAS FURNITURE COMPANY
350 F.2d 445 (D.C. Cir. 1965)

in addition to the amount of each installment payment to be made by [purchaser] under such prior leases, bills or accounts; *and all payments now and hereafter made by [purchaser] shall be credited pro rata on all outstanding leases, bills and accounts* due the Company by [purchaser] at the time each such payment is made. [Emphasis added.]

The effect of this rather obscure provision was to keep a balance due on every item purchased until the balance due on all items, whenever purchased, was liquidated. As a result, the debt incurred at the time of purchase of each item was secured by the right to repossess all the items previously purchased by the same purchaser, and each new item purchased automatically became subject to a security interest arising out of the previous dealings.

On May 12, 1962, appellant Thorne purchased an item described as a Daveno, three tables, and two lamps, having total stated value of $391.10. Shortly thereafter, he defaulted on his monthly payments and appellee sought to replevy all the items purchased since the first transaction in 1958. Similarly, on April 17, 1962, appellant Williams bought a stereo set of stated value of $514.95. She too defaulted shortly thereafter, and appellee sought to replevy all the items purchased since December, 1957. The Court of General Sessions granted judgment for appellee. The District of Columbia Court of Appeals affirmed, and we granted appellants' motion for leave to appeal to this court.

★　★　★

We do not agree that the court lacked the power to refuse enforcement to contracts found to be unconscionable. In other jurisdictions, it has been held as a matter of common law that unconscionable contracts are not enforceable. While no decision of this court so holding has been found, the notion that an unconscionable bargain should not be given full enforcement is by no means novel. In Scott v. United States, 79 U.S. (12 Wall.) 443, 445, 20 L.Ed. 438 (1870), the Supreme Court stated:

> . . . If a contract be unreasonable and unconscionable, but not void for fraud, a court of law will give to the party who sues for its breach damages, not according to its letter, but only such as he is equitably entitled to. . . .

Since we have never adopted or rejected such a rule, the question here presented is actually one of first impression.

★　★　★

Unconscionability has generally been recognized to include an absence of meaningful choice on the part of one of the parties together with contract terms which are unreasonably favorable to the other party. Whether a meaningful choice is present in a particular case can only be determined by consideration of all the circumstances surrounding the transaction. In many cases the meaningfulness of the choice is negated by a gross inequality of bargaining power. The manner in which the contract was entered is also relevant to this consideration. Did each party to the contract, considering his obvious education or lack of it, have a reasonable opportunity to understand the terms of the contract, or were the important terms hidden in a maze of fine print and minimized by deceptive sales practices? Ordinarily, one who signs an agreement without full knowledge of its terms might be held to assume the risk that he has entered a one-sided bargain. But when a party of little bargaining power, and hence little real choice, signs a commercially unreasonable contract with little or no knowledge of its terms, it is hardly likely that his consent, or even an objective manifestation of his consent, was ever given to all the terms. In such a case the usual rule that the terms of the agreement are not to be questioned should be abandoned and the court should consider whether the terms of the contract are so unfair that enforcement should be withheld.

In determining unreasonableness or fairness, the primary concern must be with the terms of the contract considered in light of the circumstances existing when the contract was made. The test is not simple, nor can it be mechanically applied. The terms are to be considered "in light of the general commercial background and the commercial needs of the particular trade or case." Corbin suggests the test as being whether the terms are "so extreme as to appear unconscionable according to the mores and business practices of the time and place." We think this formulation correctly states the test to be applied in those cases where no meaningful choice was exercised upon entering the contract.

Because the trial court and the appellate court did not feel that enforcement could be refused, no findings were made on the possible unconscionability of the contracts in these cases. Since the record is not sufficient for our deciding the issue as a matter of law, the cases must be remanded to the trial court for further proceedings.

So ordered.

Despite its fuzziness, the concept of unconscionability has had a dramatic impact in American law. In many cases, in fact, the traditional notion of *caveat emptor* (KAV ee AT EMP ter) has changed to *caveat venditor* (KAV ee AT VEN di ter) ("let the seller beware"). So important is this provision that courts in recent years have applied the doctrine in cases not involving the sale of goods.

CHAPTER SUMMARY

Sales law is a special type of contract law, governed by Article 2 of the UCC, adopted in every state but Louisiana. Article 2 governs the sale of goods only, defined as things movable at the time of identification to the contract for sale. Difficult questions sometimes arise when the subject of the contract is "goods" attached to the land. If the seller is called on to sever, or the buyer is required to sever and can do so without material harm to the land, then the items are goods subject to Article 2. When the goods are "sold" incidental to a service, the courts do not agree on whether Article 2 applies. For two categories of goods, legislation specifically answers the question: foodstuffs served by a restaurant are goods; blood supplied for transfusions is not.

In three major respects, Article 2 differs significantly from the common law of contracts. First, Article 2 frequently imposes special obligations on merchants, those who deal in goods of the kind, or who by their occupations hold themselves out as experts in the use of the goods. Second, it gives the parties greater leeway to create binding agreements with open terms, including price terms. Finally, Article 2 gives courts greater leeway than under the common law to modify contracts at the request of a party, if a clause is found to have been "unconscionable" at the time made.

KEY TERMS

Bailment	p. 369	Lease	p. 369
Gift	p. 369	Sale	p. 368
Goods	p. 371	Secured transaction	p. 369

SELF-TEST QUESTIONS

1. Among subjects the UCC does not cover are:
   (a) letters of credit
   (b) service contracts
   (c) sale of goods
   (d) bank collections
2. When a contract is unconscionable a court may:
   (a) refuse to enforce the contract
   (b) strike the unconscionable clause
   (c) limit the application of the unconscionable clause
   (d) take any of the above approaches
3. Under the UCC the definition of "merchant" is limited to:
   (a) manufacturers
   (b) retailers
   (c) wholesalers
   (d) none of the above
4. For purpose of sales law "goods":
   (a) always include items sold incidental to a service
   (b) include things moveable at the time of identification to the contract
   (c) includes blood supplied for transfusions
   (d) include all of the above
5. Article 2 differs from the common law of contracts:
   (a) in no substantial way
   (b) by disallowing parties to create agreements with open terms
   (c) by obligating courts to respect all terms of the contract
   (d) by imposing special obligations on merchants

DEMONSTRATION PROBLEM

After graduating from Big U, Heidi accepted a job as a purchasing agent for a small company. During her first day on the job, she received a telephone call from a supplier and agreed to purchase several of the supplier's products, although price was not discussed. Later she regretted making the agreement and tried to back out by asserting that the contract was too indefinite to be enforced. Is she correct? Why?

PROBLEMS

1. Ben owns fifty acres of timberland. He enters into a contract with Bunyan under which Bunyan is to cut and remove the timber from Ben's land. Bunyan enters into a contract to sell the logs to Log Cabin, Inc., a homebuilder. Are these two contracts governed by the UCC? Why?
2. Clarence agrees to sell his farm to Jud in exchange for five antique cars owned by Jud. Is this contract governed by the UCC? Why?
3. Professor Byte enters into a contract to purchase a minicomputer from Ultra-Intelligence, Inc. He also enters into a contract with a graduate student, who is to write programs which will be run on the computer. Are these two contracts governed by the UCC? Why?
4. Pat had a skin problem and went to Dr. Pore, a dermatologist, for treatment. Dr. Pore applied a salve obtained from a pharmaceutical supplier which made the problem worse. Is Dr. Pore liable under Article 2 of the UCC? Why?
5. Zanae visited the Bumbling Burrito restaurant and became seriously ill after eating tainted food. She was rushed to a local hospital where she was given a blood transfusion. Zanae developed hepatitis as a result of the transfusion. When she sues the restaurant and hospital, claiming remedies under the UCC, both defend the suit by arguing that they were providing services, not goods. Are they correct? Why?
6. Bill, the owner of Bill's Used Books, decided to go out of business. He sold two of his bookcases to Ned. Ned later discovered that the bookcases were defective and sued Bill on the theory that, as a merchant, he warranted that the bookcases were of fair, average quality. Will Ned prevail on this theory? Why?
7. Rufus visited a supermarket to purchase a bottle of soda. As he reached for a bottle on the shelf, but before he touched it, the bottle exploded. Rufus sustained serious injury and sued the supermarket, claiming breach of warranty under the UCC. Will Rufus win? Why?

ANSWERS TO SELF-TEST QUESTIONS

1. (b)   2. (d)   3. (d)   4. (b)   5. (d)

SUGGESTED ANSWER TO DEMONSTRATION PROBLEM

Heidi is not correct. Under the UCC a contract with an open price term does not fail on grounds of indefiniteness.

CHAPTER 17

CHAPTER OVERVIEW

Transfer of Title

Risk of Loss and Insurable Interest

Special Terms

Sales by Nonowners

Bulk Sales—A Special "Costa Rican" Problem

Title and Risk of Loss

*A*fter agreeing on the obvious details of a sales transaction—nature of goods, price, delivery time—buyer and seller should focus on two significant questions that lurk in the background of every sale:

1. If goods are damaged or destroyed, who must bear the loss? The answer has obvious financial significance to both. If the seller must bear the loss, then in most cases he must pay damages or send the buyer another shipment of goods. A buyer who bears the loss must pay for the goods even though they are unusable. In the absence of prior agreement, loss thus can trigger litigation between the parties.

2. When does the title pass to the buyer? This question arises more in cases involving third parties, such as creditors and tax collectors. For instance, a creditor of the seller will not be allowed to take possession of goods in the seller's warehouse if the title has already passed to the buyer.

In this chapter we cover four broad themes relating in one way or another to title and risk of loss:

1. When does the buyer acquire title?
2. When does risk of loss pass to the buyer and at what point does the buyer acquire an insurable interest?
3. Does the buyer obtain title when a nonowner sells the goods?
4. When a buyer acquires title in a "bulk sale," is the title free from claims of the seller's creditors?

TRANSFER OF TITLE

The law begins with the premise that the agreement of the parties governs. UCC Section 2-401(1) says that, in general, "title to goods passes from the seller to the buyer in any manner and on any conditions explicitly agreed on by the parties." Many companies specify in their written agreements at what moment the title will pass; here, for example, is a clause that appears in sales contracts of Dow Chemical Company: "Title and risk of loss in all goods sold hereunder shall pass to Buyer upon Seller's delivery to carrier at shipping point." Thus, Dow retains title to its goods only until it takes them to the carrier for transportation to the buyer.

In the absence of agreement, the UCC governs transfer of title. Most cases in which questions of title arise fall into one of four categories. In the first two, goods are to be physically delivered to the buyer. In the others, goods are not to be moved. The governing test in each situation is "when has the seller committed itself?"

Delta Sponge Makers, the manufacturer of industrial sponges, contracts to sell a gross of Sponge No. 2 to Very Fast Foods, Incorporated, a restaurant chain. Delta sells sponges at 1,000 to a carton, and usually uses Easy Rider Trucking Company to carry them to customers. Title can pass in one of four ways. In the first and second situations, goods are to be physically delivered; in the third and fourth, goods are "delivered" without being physically moved.

Shipment Contracts

Under Section 2-401(2), title passes to the buyer "at the time and place at which the seller completes his performance with respect to the physical delivery of the goods"—in other words, at the time and place that the seller complies with his obligation to do something with the goods. Suppose the contract calls for Delta Sponge Makers to "ship the entire lot of industrial grade Sponge No. 2 by truck or rail" and that is all that the contract says about shipment. That is a "shipment contract," and Section 2-401(2)(a) says that title passes to Very Fast Foods at the "time and place of shipment." At the moment that Delta turns over the 144 cartons of 1,000 sponges each to a trucker—perhaps Easy Rider Trucking comes to pick them up in Delta's own factory—title has passed to Very Fast Foods.

Destination Contract

Suppose the contract calls for Delta to "deliver the sponges on June 10 at the Maple Street warehouse of Very Fast Foods, Inc." This is a *destination contract,* and the seller "completes his performance with respect to the physical delivery of the goods" when it pulls up to the door of the warehouse and *tenders* the cartons. (Section 2-401(2)(b).) "Tender" means that

the party—here Delta Sponge Makers—is ready, able, and willing to perform and has notified its obligor of its readiness. When the driver of the delivery truck knocks on the warehouse door, announces that the gross of industrial Sponge No. 2 is ready for unloading and asks where the warehouse foreman wants them, Delta has tendered delivery, and title passes to Very Fast Foods.

Delivery of Documents and Title

Because it fears that the price of industrial sponges is about to soar, Very Fast wishes to acquire a large quantity long before it can use them all or even store them all. Delta does not store all of its sponges in its own plant, keeping some of them instead at Central Warehousing. Central is a **bailee,** one who has possession but not title. (A parking garage often is a bailee of its customers' cars; so is a carrier carrying a customer's goods.) Now assume that Central has issued a warehouse receipt to Delta and Delta's contract with Very Fast calls for Delta to deliver "document of title at the office of First Bank" on a particular day. When the goods are not to be physically moved, Section 2-401(3)(a) provides that title passes to Very Fast Foods "at the time when and the place where" Delta delivers the document. Section 1-201(15) says that **document of title** "includes bill of lading, dock warrant, dock receipt, warehouse receipt or order for the delivery of goods, and also any other document which in the regular course of business or financing is treated as adequately evidencing that the person in possession of it is entitled to receive, hold and dispose of the document and the goods it covers."

Delivery without Physical Movement or Documents

Suppose the contract did not specify physical transfer or exchange of documents for the purchase price. Instead, it said: "Seller agrees to sell all sponges stored on the north wall of its Orange Street warehouse, namely, the gross of industrial Sponge No. 2, in cartons marked B300–B444, to Buyer for a total purchase price of $14,000, payable in twelve equal monthly installments, beginning on the first of the month next beginning after the signing of this agreement." Then, by virtue of Section 2-401(3)(b), title passes at the time and place of contracting—that is, when Delta Sponge Makers and Very Fast Foods sign the contract.

RISK OF LOSS AND INSURABLE INTEREST

Passing the Risk of Loss

Just as title passes in accordance with the parties' agreement, so too the parties can fix the risk of loss upon one or the other. They may even devise a formula to divide the risk between themselves. If they fail to specify how the risk of loss is to be allocated or apportioned, the UCC again supplies the answers. And again we focus on four sets of circumstances, though they do not parallel precisely the four situations examined above in determining when title passes.

Shipping Goods   The contract requires Delta to ship the sponges by carrier but does not require it to deliver them at a particular destination. In this situation, risk of loss passes to Very Fast Foods when the goods are delivered to the carrier.

Delivery at a Specified Destination   If the agreement calls for Delta to deliver the sponges by carrier to a particular location, Very Fast assumes the risk of loss only when Delta's carrier tenders them at the specified place.

Goods Not to be Moved   If Delta sells to Very Fast sponges that are stored at Central Warehousing, and they are not to be moved, Section 2-509(2) sets forth three possibilities for transfer of the risk of loss:

1. The buyer receives a **negotiable document of title** covering the goods. A document of title is negotiable if by its terms goods are to be delivered to the bearer of the document or to the order of a named person.
2. The bailee acknowledges the buyer's right to take possession of the goods. Delta signs the contract for the sale of sponges and calls Central to inform it that a buyer has purchased 144 cartons and to ask it to set aside all cartons on the north wall for that purpose. Central does so, sending notice to Very Fast Foods that the goods are available. Very Fast Foods assumes risk of loss upon receipt of the notice.
3. When the seller gives the buyer a nonnegotiable document of title or a written direction to the bailee to deliver the goods and the buyer has had a reasonable time to present the document or direction.

All Other Cases   In any case that does not fit within the rules just described, risk of loss turns on whether the seller is a *merchant* (see p. 384). If he is, then the risk of loss passes to the buyer only when the buyer actually receives the goods. If the seller is not a merchant, then risk of loss passes when the seller tenders delivery of the goods—that is, when the seller stands ready, willing, and able to deliver at the time and place prescribed. (Section 2-509(3).) Cases that come within this section generally involve a buyer who is taking physical delivery from the seller's premises. A merchant who sells on those terms can be expected to insure his interest in any goods that remain under his control. The buyer is unlikely to insure goods not in his possession. The following case demonstrates how this risk of loss provision applies in a common situation, in which a customer pays for the merchandise but never actually receives his purchase because of a mishap.

RAMOS v. WHEEL SPORTS CENTER
96 Misc.2d 646, 409 N.Y.S.2d 505 (Civ. Ct. 1978)

ANTHONY MERCORELLA, JUDGE. In this non-jury action plaintiff/purchaser is seeking to recover from defendant/vendor the sum of $893, representing the payment made by plaintiff for a motorcycle.

The parties entered into a sales contract wherein defendant agreed to deliver a motorcycle to plaintiff by June 30, 1978, for the agreed price of $893. The motorcycle was subsequently stolen by looters during the infamous power blackout of July 11, 1977.

It is uncontroverted that plaintiff paid for the motorcycle in full; was given the papers necessary for registration and insurance and did in fact register the cycle and secure liability insurance prior to the loss although license plates were never affixed to the vehicle. It is also conceded that the loss occurred without any negligence on defendant's part.

Plaintiff testified that defendant's salesman was informed that plaintiff was leaving on vacation and plaintiff would come for the cycle when he returned. He further testified that he never saw or rode the vehicle. From the evidence adduced at trial it is apparent that plaintiff never exercised dominion or control over the vehicle.

Defendant's president testified that he had no knowledge of what transpired between his salesman and plaintiff nor why the cycle was not taken prior to its loss.

The sole issue presented to the Court is which party, under the facts disclosed, bears the risk of loss?

It is the opinion of this Court that defendant must bear the risk of loss under the provisions of Section 2-509(3) of the Uniform Commercial Code.

This section provides that ". . . the risk of loss passes to the buyer on his receipt of the goods if the seller is a merchant. . . ." Section 2-103(1)(c) states that receipt of goods means taking physical possession of them.

The provision tends more strongly to hold risk of loss on the seller than did the former Uniform Sales Act (1955 Law Revision Commission Report, p. 489). Whether the contract involves delivery at the seller's place of business or at the situs of the goods, a merchant seller cannot transfer risk of loss and it remains on him until actual receipt by the buyer, even though full payment has been made and the buyer notified that the goods are at his disposal. The underlying theory is that a merchant who is to make physical delivery at his own place continues meanwhile to control the goods and can be expected to insure his interest in them.

The Court is also of the opinion that no bailee/bailor relationship, constructive or otherwise, existed between the parties.

Accordingly, let judgment be entered in favor of plaintiff for the sum of $893, together with interest, costs and disbursements.

Passing the Risk of Loss in the Event of Breach

By Seller   Suppose the seller breaches the contract. Then the rules just stated are modified. Delta is obligated to deliver a gross of industrial Sponges No. 2; instead it tenders only one hundred cartons or delivers a gross of industrial No. 3. Under Section 2-510(1), the risk of loss falls on the seller whenever tender or delivery of goods fails to conform to the contract, giving the buyer a right of rejection, and remains until the seller cures the breach or until the buyer accepts despite it. Suppose Delta has breached the contract by tendering to Very Fast Foods a defective document of title. Delta cures the defect and gives the new document of title to Very Fast, but before it does so the sponges are stolen. Delta is responsible for the loss.

Suppose Very Fast had taken delivery of the sponges and only a few days later discovered that the sponges did not conform to the contract. Very Fast has the right to repudiate, and it does so. A day later its warehouse burns down and the sponges are destroyed. It then discovers that its insurance was not adequate to cover all the sponges. Who stands the loss? The seller does, under Section 2-510(2), to the extent of any deficiency in the buyer's insurance coverage.

By Buyer Suppose Very Fast Foods calls two days before the sponges are to be delivered by Delta and says, "Don't bother; we no longer have a need for them." Subsequently, while the lawyers are arguing, Delta's warehouse burns down and the sponges are destroyed. Under the rules as described above, risk of loss does not pass to the buyer until seller has delivered, which has not occurred in this case. Nevertheless, responsibility for the loss here has passed to Very Fast Foods, to the extent that the seller's insurance does not cover it. Section 2-510(3) permits the seller to treat the risk of loss as resting on the buyer for a "commercially reasonable time" when the buyer repudiates the contract before risk of loss has passed to him. This transfer of the risk can take place only when the goods are identified to the contract.

Insurable Interest

A buyer cannot legally obtain insurance unless he has an *insurable interest* in the goods. Without an insurable interest, the insurance contract would be an illegal gambling contract. For example, if you attempt to take out insurance on a ship with which you have no connection, hoping to recover a large sum if it sinks, the courts will construe the contract as a wager you have made with the insurance company that the ship is not seaworthy, and they will refuse to enforce it if the ship should sink and you try to collect. Thus this question arises: Under the UCC, at what point does the buyer acquire an insurable interest in the goods?

Of Buyer The buyer obtains a "special property and insurable interest in goods by identification of existing goods as goods to which the contract refers." (Section 2-501(1).) The parties can identify the goods in any mutually agreeable manner—for example, by branding, marking, tagging, or segregating them—and at any time.

If the parties fail to agree on when the identification should occur, then the Code spells out the following rules:

1. The goods will be considered identified at the time the contract is made if the contract is for the sale of goods that already exist and have already been identified.
2. If the contract calls for the sale of future goods, then they will be identified when the seller ships, marks, or otherwise identifies them as goods to which the contract refers.
3. If the contract is for the sale of crops or unborn animals, then the goods are identified when the crops are planted or when the young are conceived. This rule applies only to crops to be harvested within twelve months after contracting or at the next normal harvest, whichever is later, or to the sale of animals to be born within twelve months of contracting.

Of Seller As long as the seller retains title to or any security interest in the goods, he has an insurable interest.

Other Rights of Buyer The buyer's "special property" interest that arises upon identification of goods gives the buyer rights other than that to insure the goods. For example, under Section 2-502, the buyer who has paid for unshipped goods may take them from a seller who becomes insolvent within ten days after receipt of the whole payment or the first installment payment. Similarly, a buyer who has not yet taken delivery may sue a third party who has in some manner damaged the property.

SPECIAL TERMS

In discussing title and risk of loss, we noted that both can be fixed by agreement of the parties. The parties frequently do so, using one or more of the following special terms: *F.O.B.; F.A.S.* and *ex-ship; C.I.F.* and *C.F.; no arrival, no sale; sale on approval;* and *sale or return.* UCC provisions covering these terms make specific reference to risk of loss and occasionally (where noted below), title.

F.O.B.

F.O.B. means "free on board." It is shorthand for designating who must bear the expense and risk of loss in transporting to the shipper or to the destination. If a sale is said to be "F.O.B. place of shipment," the seller must pay to have the goods taken to the carrier, and the risk of loss remains with the seller until the carrier takes possession. If a sale is "F.O.B. destination," then the seller bears both the expense of transporting the goods to the buyer and the risk of loss, until the goods are tendered for delivery. The following case shows how the courts allocate risk of loss between buyer and seller.

NINTH STREET EAST, LTD. v. HARRISON
5 Conn.Cir. 597, 259 A.2d 772 (1968)

NORTON M. LEVINE, JUDGE. This is an action to recover the purchase price of merchandise sold to defendant by plaintiff. Plaintiff is a manufacturer of men's clothing, with a principal place of business in Los Angeles, California. Defendant is the owner and operator of a men's clothing store, located in Westport, Connecticut, known as "The Rage."

Pursuant to orders received by plaintiff in Los Angeles on November 28, 1966, defendant ordered a variety of clothing items from plaintiff. On November 30, 1966, plaintiff delivered the merchandise in Los Angeles to a common carrier known as Denver-Chicago Trucking Company, Inc., hereinafter called Denver, and received a bill of lading from the trucker. Simultaneously, plaintiff mailed defendant four invoices, all dated November 30, 1966, covering the clothing, in the total sum of $2216. All the invoices bore the notations that the shipment was made "F.O.B. Los Angeles" and "Via Denver-Chicago." Further, all four invoices contained the printed phrase, "Goods Shipped at Purchaser's Risk." Denver's bill of lading disclosed that the shipment was made "collect," to wit, that defendant was obligated to pay the freight charges from Los Angeles to Westport. Denver subsequently transferred the shipment to a connecting carrier known as Old Colony Transportation Company, of South Dartmouth, Massachusetts, hereinafter called Old Colony, for ultimate delivery at defendant's store in Westport. The delivery was attempted by Old Colony at defendant's store on or about December 12, 1966. A woman in charge of the store, identified as defendant's wife, requested the Old Colony truck driver to deliver the merchandise inside the door of defendant's store. The truck driver refused to do so. The dispute not having been resolved, Old Colony retained possession of the eight cartons comprising the shipment, and the truck thereupon departed from the store premises.

Defendant sent a letter, dated December 12, 1966, and received by plaintiff in Los Angeles on December 20, 1966, reporting the refusal of the truck driver to make the delivery inside defendant's store. This was the first notice to plaintiff of the non-delivery. The letter alleged that defendant needed the merchandise immediately for the holidays but that defendant nevertheless insisted that the merchandise must be delivered inside his store, as a condition of his acceptance. Plaintiff tried to reach defendant by phone, but without success. Similarly, its numerous attempts to locate the shipment were fruitless. Plaintiff filed a claim against Denver for the lost merchandise, but up to the date of trial had not been reimbursed, in whole or in part, by the carrier. Defendant never recovered possession of the merchandise at any time following the original refusal.

The sole special defense pleaded was, "The Plaintiff refused to deliver the merchandise into the Defendant's place of business." Therefore defendant claimed that he is not liable for the subsequent loss or disappearance of the shipment, or the purchase price thereof, and that the risk of loss remained with plaintiff.

The basic problem is to determine the terms and conditions of the agreement of the parties as to transportation, and the risks and hazards incident thereto. The court finds that the parties had originally agreed that the merchandise would be shipped by common carrier F.O.B. Los Angeles, as the place of shipment, and that the defendant would pay the freight charges between the two points. The notations on the invoices, and the bill of lading, previously described, make this clear. The use of the phrase "F.O.B.," meaning free on board, made this portion of the agreement not only a price term covering defendant's obligation to pay freight charges between Los Angeles and Westport but also a controlling factor as to risk of loss of the merchandise upon delivery to Denver and subsequently to Old Colony as the carriers. Title to the goods, and the right to possession, passed to defendant at Los Angeles, the F.O.B. point. Upon delivery to the common carrier at the F.O.B. point, the goods thereafter were at defendant's sole risk.

It is highly significant that all the invoices sent to defendant contained the explicit notation "Goods Shipped at Purchaser's Risk." This was, initially, a unilateral statement by plaintiff. The validity of this phrase, as expressing the understanding of both parties, was, however, never actually challenged by defendant, at the trial or in his brief. The contents of the invoices therefore confirm the statutory allocation of risk of loss on F.O.B. shipments.

*   *   *

The law erects a presumption in favor of construing the agreement as a "shipment" contract, as opposed to a "destination" contract, § 42a-2-503; Uniform Commercial Code § 2-503, comment 5. Under the presumption of a "shipment" contract, plaintiff's liability for loss or damage terminated upon delivery to the carrier at the F.O.B. point, to wit, Los Angeles. The court finds that no persuasive evidence was offered to overcome the force of the statutory presumption in the instant case. Thus, as § 42a-2-509(1) indicates, "[w]here the contract requires or authorizes the seller to ship the goods by carrier (a) if it does not require him to deliver them at a particular destination, the risk of loss passes to the buyer when the goods are duly delivered to the carrier." Accordingly, at the F.O.B. point, when the risk of loss shifted,

(continued on next page)

(continued)

NINTH STREET EAST, LTD. v. HARRISON
5 Conn.Cir. 597, 259 A.2d 772 (1968)

Denver and Old Colony, as carriers, became the agents or bailees of defendant. The risk of subsequent loss or delay rested on defendant, and not plaintiff. A disagreement arose between defendant's wife and the truck driver, resulting in nondelivery of the merchandise, retention thereof by the carrier, and, finally, disappearance of the shipment. The ensuing dispute was fundamentally a matter for resolution between defendant and the carriers, as his agents. Nothing in the outcome of that dispute could defeat or impair plaintiff's recovery against defendant.

* * *

The issues are found for plaintiff. Judgment may therefore enter for plaintiff to recover of defendant the sum of $2216, plus taxable costs.

F.A.S. and Ex-Ship

F.A.S. means "free alongside," and is used in shipment contracts to indicate where a seller's obligation to deliver ends. When used in the term "F.A.S. vessel," the seller must deliver the goods, at his own expense and risk, alongside the vessel in the port named on the contract. Once he obtains and tenders a receipt for the goods, obligating the carrier in turn to issue a bill of lading, the seller's duty is at end and the risk of loss is on the buyer.

By contrast, **ex-ship** (meaning "from the carrying vessel") is used in destination contracts; it is the reverse of F.A.S. because it places the expense and risk of loss on the seller until the goods actually reach the buyer. The term is not restricted to a particular ship, permitting delivery from any ship which has reached a place at the specified port where goods of the kind are normally unloaded. The seller is obligated to furnish the buyer with a direction to the carrier that legally obligates the carrier to release the goods. The risk of loss passes to the buyer when the goods are properly unloaded.

C.I.F. and C.F.

C.I.F. is a price term. It means that the contract price includes in a lump sum not only the cost of the goods but also insurance and freight to the named destination (hence "Cost, Insurance, and Freight"). The term **C.F.** (or C.&F.) means that the price includes cost and freight, but not insurance. When a contract states "C.I.F. destination" (for example, "C.I.F. New York") it obligates the seller, at his own expense and risk, to (1) put the goods into the hands of a carrier at the port for shipping, (2) obtain a negotiable bill of lading covering the transportation to the named destination, (3) load the goods, (4) obtain a receipt from the carrier showing that freight has been paid for, (5) obtain an insurance policy, (6) prepare an invoice, (7) ready any other documents necessary before the goods can be shipped, and (8) forward and tender "with commercial promptness" whatever documents are necessary to perfect the buyer's rights. "C.F." requires the seller to do the same except that he need not obtain insurance.

C.I.F. and C.F. clauses make the sales agreement a shipping contract. Title and risk of loss pass to the buyer once the seller has delivered the goods to the carrier and complied with the duties outlined above.

No Arrival, No Sale

The term **"no arrival, no sale"** means that the seller must ship conforming goods but he assumes no obligation that they will arrive (unless he is to blame for their failure to arrive). This is a destination contract in which the risk of loss remains on the seller. Ordinarily, "no arrival, no sale" contracts cover only losses from transportation hazards; goods that do arrive must conform to the contract. But if the seller is reselling goods to be shipped by someone over whom he has no control (for example, the seller is a middleman reselling packaged pharmaceuticals), then he is exempt from liability to the buyer even if the goods are nonconforming (if, for example, the drugs have deteriorated in their bottles).

Sale on Approval; Sale or Return

Sometimes the seller will permit the buyer to return the goods even though they conform to the contract. When the goods are intended primarily for the buyer's use, the transaction is said to be **"sale on approval."** When they are intended primarily for resale, the transaction is said to be **"sale or return."** In the usual arrangement, a buyer maintains a store in which he deals in goods of the kind. For example, when goods are delivered to the buyer's store for resale, they are deemed under such a contract to be on sale or return.

Why would a seller enter into such a contract? The usual reason is to prompt the buyer to take the goods in the first place, by minimizing the buyer's risk that he will be stuck with them if they prove not to be what he wanted or if they do not attract customers. Sale-or-return contracts are common in many retail industries; for example, most bookstores take books on a sale-or-return basis from publishers.

Under a sale-on-approval contract, risk of loss and title remain with the seller until the buyer accepts, and the buyer's trial use of the goods does not in itself constitute acceptance. If the buyer decides to return the goods, the seller bears the risk and expense of return, but a merchant buyer must follow any reasonable instructions from the seller. By contrast, under a sale-or-return contract, title and risk of loss pass to the buyer, and the buyer bears the risk and expense of returning the goods.

Occasionally the question arises whether the buyer's other creditors may claim the goods when the sales contract lets the buyer retain some rights to return the goods. The answer seems straightforward: in a sale-on-approval contract, where title remains with the seller until acceptance, the buyer does not own the goods—hence they cannot be seized by his creditors—unless he accepts them, whereas they are the buyer's goods (subject to his right to return them) in a sale-or-return contract and may be taken by creditors if they are in his possession. However, a closely related arrangement is **consignment,** in which the owner places the goods with a retailer for resale while retaining title. Section 2-326(3) says that when the buyer is reselling the goods in a place of business regularly maintained for that purpose, the goods are on sale-or-return even if the contract uses such words as "on consignment," unless it can be shown that the person conducting the business is generally known by his creditors to be substantially engaged in selling goods owned by others (for example, his store might be called "Consignment Shop" or might display a conspicuous sign stating that goods inside are on consignment) or unless the owner perfects a security interest in the goods (see Chapter 26).

Terms in Foreign Trade

Foreign trade contracts often refer to the "Revised American Foreign Trade Definitions." These are definitions adopted jointly by the Chamber of Commerce of the United States, the National Council of American Importers, and the National Foreign Trade Council. Because the various terms just examined, and others, have differing meanings in many countries, the trade groups decided to standardize trade usage. Unlike the terms defined in the UCC, the definitions have no legal standing. To be effective, importers and exporters must agree to accept them and must say so in their contracts; the terms then will be legally binding. The definitions are often much more detailed than and may even conflict with those in the UCC.

SALES BY NONOWNERS

What title does a purchaser acquire when the seller has no title or has at best only a voidable title? This question has often been difficult for courts to resolve. It typically involves a type of eternal triangle with a three-step sequence of events, as follows (see Figure 17-1): (1) The nonowner obtains possession, for example, by loan or theft; (2) the nonowner sells the goods to an innocent purchaser for cash; and (3) the nonowner then takes the money and runs to Costa Rica or some other country from which he cannot be extradited—or goes into bankruptcy. Result: two innocent parties battle over the goods, the owner usually claiming that the purchaser is guilty of *conversion*

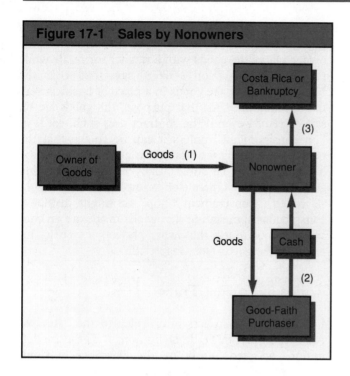

Figure 17-1   Sales by Nonowners

(that is, the unlawful assumption of ownership of property belonging to another) and claiming damages or the right to recover the goods (called a *replevin* action).

To resolve this dilemma, we begin with a basic policy of American jurisprudence: a person cannot transfer more rights than he or she owns. This policy would apply in a sale of goods case in which the nonowner had a void title or no title whatever. For example, if the nonowner stole the goods from the owner and then sold them to an innocent purchaser, the owner would be entitled to the goods or to damages. Because the thief had no title, he had none to transfer to the purchaser.

But this basic legal policy is subject to a number of exceptions. In Part IV (Commercial Paper), for instance, we discuss how certain purchasers of commercial paper ("holders in due course") will obtain greater rights than the sellers possessed. And in Part V (Debtors and Creditors) we examine how a buyer in the ordinary course of business is allowed to purchase goods free of security interests that the seller has given to creditors. Likewise, the law governing the sale of goods contains exceptions to the basic legal policy. These usually fall within one of three categories: sellers with voidable title, entrustment, and estoppel.

Sellers with a Voidable Title

Under the UCC, a person with a voidable title has the power to transfer title to a good-faith purchaser for value (see Figure 17-2). The code defines "good faith" as "honesty in fact in the conduct or transaction concerned." (Section 1-201(19).) A "purchaser" is not restricted to one who pays cash; any taking that creates an interest in property, whether by mortgage, pledge, lien, or even gift, is a purchase for purposes of the UCC. And "value" is not limited to cash or goods; a person gives value if he gives any consideration sufficient to support a simple contract, including a binding commitment to extend credit and security for a preexisting claim. Recall from Chapter 11 that a "voidable" title is one that, for policy reasons, the courts will cancel on application of one who is aggrieved. These reasons include fraud, undue influence, mistake, and lack of capacity to contract. When a person has a voidable title, it can be taken away, but if it is not, he can transfer better title than he has to a good-faith purchaser for value.

Rita, a seventeen-year-old who is a minor in the state in which she lives, decides to hold a garage sale on her graduation from high school. She sells a video game to her neighbor, Annie, who plans to give the game to her nephew. Since Rita has not attained her majority, she could rescind the contract. However, she does not. Annie discovers that her brother and sister-in-law will not permit video games in their house, so she sells the game instead to a colleague at her office, Mr. Meese. He has had no notice that Annie bought the game from a minor and has only a voidable title. He pays cash. Should Rita subsequently decide she wants the game back it would be too late: Annie has transferred good title to Mr. Meese.

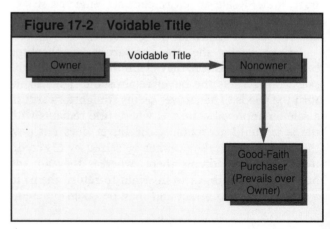

Figure 17-2   Voidable Title

Suppose Rita was an adult and Annie paid her with a check that later bounced. Does Mr. Meese still have good title? The Code says he does (Section 2-403(1)), and it identifies three other situations in which the good-faith purchaser is protected: (1) when the original transferor was deceived about the identity of the purchaser to whom he sold the goods, who then transfers to a good-faith purchaser; (2) when the orig-inal transferor was supposed to but did not receive cash from the intermediate purchaser; and (3) when "the delivery was procured through fraud punishable as larcenous under the criminal law." (Section 2-403(1)(d).)

This UCC section frequently conflicts with state motor vehicle title statutes, as illustrated by the following case.

DARTMOUTH MOTOR SALES, INC. v. WILCOX

517 A.2d 804 (N.H. 1986)

BROCK, JUSTICE.

The plaintiff, Dartmouth Motor Sales, Inc. (Dartmouth), brought an action for declaratory judgment, replevin, and injunction or rescission against Alan Wilcox, d/b/a T & T Auto Sales (Wilcox); Bruce Campbell, d/b/a Soupy's Used Cars (Campbell); Cheryl Willis (Willis); and the New Hampshire Division of Motor Vehicles. The complex set of facts relevant to the disposition of this case involves the ownership of a 1983 Chevrolet Camaro.

On January 9, 1985, Dartmouth sold the Camaro to Wilcox, who represented himself to be a dealer doing business as T & T Auto Sales. Wilcox, however, was in fact not a dealer under RSA chapter 261. Wilcox purchased the vehicle with a personal check for $6,300, and the vehicle's title was purportedly transferred by assignment. The check was later dishonored. On January 10, Campbell, a licensed dealer doing business as Soupy's Used Cars, bought the car from Wilcox for $4,300 and title to the vehicle was again transferred by assignment.

On January 15, at approximately 2:00 p.m., Dartmouth's bookkeeper telephoned Campbell and told him that Dartmouth had a potential claim against the vehicle. At about 4:00 p.m. on the same day, the bookkeeper spoke again to Campbell. According to the Master's later finding, the "substance of that conversation was that the matter was cleared up, the police had no jurisdiction, and [the bookkeeper] knew Campbell was going to sell the car and he would have to do what he would have to do." The master further found that Campbell "reasonably believed that there were no liens or adverse claims against the motor vehicle." Willis obtained a car loan and, at approximately 5:00 p.m. on that day, Campbell sold the car for $5,500 to Willis, who took possession of the Camaro, the title documents having been prepared by Mrs. Campbell. The title application was sent to the New Hampshire Title Bureau. However, it was rejected because the mileage on the sale to Dartmouth was not noted on the title certificate and also because an application for title and the required fee had to be submitted on behalf of Wilcox, as Wilcox was not a dealer.

Dartmouth filed this suit in March, and, after a hearing, the master found that Wilcox was in default and liable to Dartmouth in damages, but that Campbell had acted in good faith at all times and was not so liable. He further found the same to be true with regard to Willis. The master, having found that Willis was a *bona fide* purchaser for value, nevertheless ruled that

(continued on next page)

(continued)

DARTMOUTH MOTOR SALES, INC. v. WILCOX

517 A.2d 804 (N.H. 1986)

RSA chapter 261 superseded the relevant provisions of the Uniform Commercial Code, *see* RSA 382–A:2–403, and that therefore Dartmouth had the right of possession of and title to the Camaro because Dartmouth's title had never been transferred in accordance with RSA chapter 261. He further stated that Willis could proceed against Campbell's dealer's bond.

Campbell filed a timely motion for reconsideration, which was denied. Both the master's report and his denial of the motion for reconsideration were approved by the Superior Court.

* * *

The dispositive issue here is whether non-compliance with the described provisions of the motor vehicle title statute would render void the transfers from Dartmouth to Wilcox and from Wilcox to Campbell and therefore would render the later transfer between Campbell and Willis also void. We hold that it would not.

The intent of the title statute is "to facilitate the identification of motor vehicles, the ascertainment of their owners and the prevention of theft or fraud in their transfer." *In re Circus Time, Inc.*, 641 F.2d 39, 44 (1st Cir.1981). The purpose of RSA 382–A:2–403(1) is to encourage the free flow of goods in commerce and to lessen the impact of common-law concepts of title on sales of goods. It is evident, then, that neither statute's purpose would be served by penalizing Campbell and Willis, whom the master found to be good faith purchasers for value.

* * *

Thus, we hold that, in the following limited respect, RSA 382–A:2–403(1) takes precedence over the title statute. Where a facially valid title to a vehicle is conferred on a party who has no notice of adverse claims against the vehicle, the Code provision will take precedence over the title statute even if the title statute has not been complied with. Thus, a facially valid title certificate procured by a good faith purchaser will pass good title. In effect, "[b]y construing the statutes in this manner, both the title statutes and the Commercial Code provisions can be given effect without diminishing the effect of the other." *Island v. Warkenthien.*

Thus, since the provisions of RSA 382–A:2–403(1) govern in this limited instance, their application results in the following narrative analysis: Dartmouth sold the vehicle to Wilcox, thinking he was a licensed dealer; in fact, he was not, but this happenstance and his fraudulent purchase by use of a bad check merely resulted in the latter's receiving voidable title to the vehicle. Wilcox tranferred the vehicle and a facially valid certificate of title to Campbell, a good faith purchaser for value. Campbell later conveyed good title to Willis, also a good faith purchaser for value. Dartmouth, therefore, is not entitled to the vehicle. Rather, it should remain in the hands of Willis, who thus has no cause to proceed against Campbell's dealer's bond.

[Reversed and remanded.]

Entrustment

A merchant who deals in particular goods has the power to transfer all rights of one who entrusts to him goods of the kind to a "buyer in the ordinary course of business." (Section 2-403(2).) (See Figure 17-3.) The code defines such a buyer as a person who buys goods in an ordinary transaction from a person in the business of selling that type of goods, as long as the buyer purchases in "good faith and without knowledge that the sale to him is in violation of the ownership rights or security interest of a third party in the goods." (Section 1-201(9).) Bess takes a pearl necklace, a family heirloom, to Sportin' Life Jewelers for cleaning. The owner of Sportin' Life sells it to Clara, a buyer in the ordinary course of business, for cash, and heads for Costa Rica. As between the two

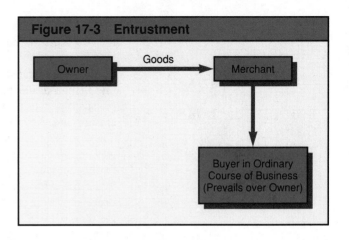

Figure 17-3   Entrustment

innocent parties, Bess and Clara (owner and purchaser), the latter prevails, as the next case explains.

FUQUA HOMES, INC. v. EVANSTON BUILDING & LOAN CO.
52 Ohio App.2d 399, 370 N.E.2d 780 (1977)

Per Curiam. This cause came on to be heard upon the appeal; the transcript of the docket, journal entries and original papers from the Court of Common Pleas of Hamilton County; and the transcript of proceedings, the briefs and the arguments of counsel.

The trial court entered a judgment against Fuqua Homes of Ohio, Inc. (hereinafter called Fuqua), a manufacturer of "modular homes," and in favor of all defendants except two. Kirk and Underhill operated a partnership known as "MMM," which constituted the middleman-dealer in the reported sale and delivery of a modular home, and had disappeared after receiving the proceeds from the purchasers. They were not served in this action. The defendants in whose favor judgment was granted were Kenneth and Wilma R. Ryan, the purchasers of the modular home (hereinafter called the Ryans), and Evanston Building & Loan Co., lender to the Ryans (hereinafter called Evanston). Such was the activity of MMM that neither the Ryans nor Evanston knew of Fuqua's claim on the modular home until after it had been placed on Ryan's real estate, and Fuqua did not know who had purchased it or where it was located. The case presents the conflicting interests of two innocent parties after the thieves have fled, taking the money with them. The trial court held that the loss must fall on the manufacturer, and we agree.

The modular home manufactured by Fuqua and purchased by the Ryans consisted of two structures, each of which is 12 feet wide and 55 feet long; each is fitted with wheels and an A-frame trailer hitch and has a temporary covering on one side to be retained during transit. The two units are separately towed to the site, where the temporary covering is removed, and

(continued on next page)

(continued)

FUQUA HOMES, INC. v. EVANSTON BUILDING & LOAN CO.
52 Ohio App.2d 399, 370 N.E.2d 780 (1977)

the two units placed side by side and so connected so as to form one weather-tight unit.

The Ryan transaction was the seventh one in which MMM acted as middleman-dealer for Fuqua products. It began, as did the others, with the purchasers' selection of a certain model of modular home from the sales literature and the plans the specifications made available by Fuqua to MMM. The Ryans entered into an agreement to buy their selection from MMM who was obligated to furnish the structure and prepare the site, including foundation, on land earlier purchased by the Ryans. MMM telephoned the order to Fuqua who mailed a written confirmation back to the dealer and then proceeded to produce and later ship the two units. Accompanying the shipment to MMM were copies of the invoice and Fuqua's "warranty documents" signed in blank but showing the model and serial number of the units. While the record does not reveal the exact content of these warranty documents, it discloses that they were delivered to the Ryans "at the closing," fully completed and signed.

Evanston financed the transaction for the Ryans, taking a mortgage on the real estate on which the structure was placed, and disbursed all funds, including those for the real estate agent (required by MMM), those for site work and other construction costs, and those due to MMM under the agreement. After receiving all but a modest sum reserved by Evanston to cover the cost of final grading and seeding, the MMM partners disappeared without having remitted any payment to Fuqua, who still holds the manufacturer's certificate of origin.

Fuqua claims that, as the unpaid holder of the certificate of origin, it has title to the modular home under R. C. Chapter 4505, the Certificate of Motor Vehicle Title Act. We disagree. That law grants a unique status to a certificate of origin (or a certificate of title), but the rights it creates in a holder of such a certificate are not absolute. A holder does not prevail against all the world under any and all circumstances.

*   *   *

The acquisition of ownership of a motor vehicle is governed by R. C. Chapter 1302 of the Ohio Uniform Commercial Code, because motor vehicles and house trailers fall within the definition of "goods" in R. C. 1302.01(A)(8). They are things "which are movable at the time of identification to the contract for sale other than the money in which the price is to be paid, investment securities and things in action." The perfection of a security interest in a motor vehicle is governed by R. C. 4505.13, and not by R. C. Chapter 1309, but in this case Fuqua asserts not a security interest in the vehicle but ownership thereof.

The sale from MMM to the Ryans is governed by R. C. 1302.44(B), which reads in full as follows:

"Any entrusting of possession of goods to a merchant who deals in goods of that kind gives him power to transfer all rights of the entruster to a buyer in ordinary course of business."

MMM is a "merchant," and the Ryans qualify as "buyers in the ordinary course of business." The transfer of the two units in a mobile state from MMM to the Ryans transferred all of Fuqua's rights, and the Ryans were thereupon entitled to have their ownership evidenced by a certificate of title.

*   *   *

The purchasers have no obligation under the law to demand or search the certificate of origin. We concur with the reasoning of the Ninth Appellate District in *Carnegie Financial Corp.* v. *Akron National Bank* that the law creates no duty in the purchaser or its financing agency to hold back the purchase price until a clear title is received. To require the purchaser or financier to receive clear title before paying would stop the free flow of commerce and impede established commercial practices in motor vehicle transactions. The floor plan financier will not release the lien (*i.e.*, the certificate of origin) until the middleman-dealer pays his promissory note and the middleman-dealer cannot pay the note until he receives funds from the purchaser or his financier. To establish the principle of law proposed by Fuqua would place the parties in a practical impasse.

*   *   *

Finding no error prejudicial to plaintiff, we affirm.

Estoppel

The UCC explicitly sets forth the two exceptions just named (transfer of voidable title and entrustment) to the general rule that a transferee cannot give his transferor better title than he had. But the UCC also makes clear that general principles of law, including the principle of estoppel, supplement the statute. In this situation, the common law principle is this: "The rightful owner may be estopped by his own acts from asserting his title. If he has invested another with the usual evidence of title, or an apparent authority to dispose of it, he will not be allowed to make claim against an innocent purchaser dealing on the faith of such apparent ownership." Suppose Sportin' Life Jewelers, a New York establishment, sent a diamond ring to Crown's Auction House of Charleston, with which it had had regular dealings over the years. The ring, worth $11,000, was sent "for examination" with the explicit understanding that Crown's had no title. The two shops had done hundreds of such transactions before. However, this time, unbeknownst to Sportin' Life, Crown's was in some financial trouble.

On receiving the ring, Crown's put it in the window and when Bess walked in, sold it to her for $12,000. Bess, who assumed Crown's owned the ring, was completely unaware of the private arrangement between the two companies. Crown's then went into bankruptcy without forwarding any money to New York. Learning of the transaction, Sportin' Life demands the ring from Bess. The principle of estoppel holds that under these circumstances, the original owner cannot complain of the actions that the auctioneer took. [Zendman v. Harry Winston, Inc., 111 N.E. 2d 871 (N.Y. 1953).]

BULK SALES—A SPECIAL "COSTA RICAN" PROBLEM

Sportin' Life sells costume jewelry and regularly buys on credit directly from Porgy Glass Works, the manufacturer. Because they have dealt with each other for years and to avoid the paperwork, Porgy has never bothered to take a security interest in the tons of glass necklaces, beads, and earrings that he ships monthly.

One day Jake, who wants to open his own jewelry store and who has no knowledge that the jewelry has not been paid for, walks into Sportin' Life Jewelers and offers to buy the entire inventory. Sportin' Life, who has not paid Porgy for several months' worth of jewelry, jumps at the chance, deposits the cash in a Swiss account, and departs that evening for a life of luxury in a villa in the Golfo del Papagayo, where he cannot be reached by the long arm of American law. What are Jake's rights against Porgy?

The usual protection offered by a security interest is unavailing in cases such as this. The Uniform Fraudulent Conveyances Act permits creditors to recover the property if they can show that the transferee had knowledge of the fraud, but that is often difficult to show and will not work, of course, against a bona fide purchaser. A sale to a creditor might be voidable under the Bankruptcy Act (Chapter 29), but rarely will the deceitful merchant sell to his own creditors. If the creditors can prove that the merchant intended to deceive and that he acted inequitably, an *equitable receivership* might be created to control distribution of the goods, but such proof is difficult to make out.

The answer is found in Article 6 of the UCC, as amended in 1989. Article 6 was developed to provide protection to creditors who might otherwise be defrauded as a result of a bulk sale. Section 6-102(1) defines a bulk sale as "a sale not in the ordinary course of the seller's business of more than half the seller's inventory . . . [if] the buyer has notice, or after reasonable inquiry would have had notice, that the seller will not continue to operate the same or a similar kind of business after the sale." Some exceptions are listed in Section 6-103. For example, the law does not apply to sales of assets having a value of less than $10,000 (which are too small to justify the costs of compliance) or greater than $25 million (which are usually well-publicized).

Under Article 6, a buyer in a bulk sale must:

1. Obtain from the seller a list of the names and addresses of the seller's creditors and the amount they are owed;
2. Prepare a schedule showing how the net contract price is to be distributed;
3. Give notice to each creditor on the list (and to other creditors known to the buyer) at least 45

days before the bulk sale and not more than 30 days after obtaining the list of creditors;
4. Distribute the net contract price according to the distribution schedule; and
5. Make the list of creditors available to creditors.

If the seller has 200 or more creditors, the buyer may file a notice of the bulk sale with the Secretary of State instead of obtaining a list of creditors from the seller.

A buyer who does not comply with the bulk sales law is liable for damages to creditors, unless the buyer acted in good faith and in a commercially reasonable manner.

The organizations who approve the UCC, while substantially revising Article 6 in 1989, also encouraged states to repeal their bulk sales laws entirely. The reason for this recommendation is that bulk sales law obligates buyers to incur costs to protect the seller's creditors and it is doubtful whether the benefits to creditors justify these costs. Consequently buyers entering into a bulk sale transaction must determine whether the law is in effect in their state.

CHAPTER SUMMARY

Two significant questions lurk in the background of any sale: (1) When does title pass, and (2) Who must bear the risk of loss if the goods are destroyed or damaged? In general, the title passes when buyer and seller agree that it passes.

If the buyer and seller fail to specify the time at which title passes, Article 2 lays down four rules. (1) Under a shipment contract, title passes when the seller places the goods with the carrier. (2) Under a destination contract, title passes when the goods are tendered at the place of delivery. (3) Under a contract calling for delivery of documents of title, title passes when the seller tenders documents of title, even if the goods are not physically moved. (4) When no physical delivery or exchange of documents is called for, title passes when the contract is signed.

Buyer and seller may also specify who must bear the risk of loss. But if they do not, Article 2 sets out these rules: (1) When the seller must ship by carrier but not to any particular destination, risk passes to the buyer when the seller delivers the goods to the carrier. (2) When the goods must be transported to a particular destination, risk passes when the carrier tenders them at that destination. (3) If the goods are held by a bailee who has issued a negotiable document of title, risk passes when the buyer receives the document. (4) In other cases, risk of loss turns on whether the seller is a merchant. If he is, risk passes when the buyer receives the goods; if he is not, when the seller tenders the goods. These rules are modified when either of the parties breaches the contract. In general, unless the breach is cured, the risk of uninsured losses lies on the party who breached.

Either party may insure the goods if it has an insurable interest in them. The buyer has an insurable interest in goods identified to the contract—for example, by marking them in some manner. The seller has an insurable interest as long as he retains title or a security interest.

In fixing passage of title and risk of loss, the parties often use shorthand terminology, whose meaning must be mastered to make sense of the contract. These terms include *F.O.B.*; *F.A.S.*; *ex-ship*; *C.I.F.*; *C.F.*; *no arrival, no sale*; *sale on approval*; and *sale or return*. Use of these terms can have a significant effect on title and risk of loss.

Sometimes goods are sold by nonowners. A person with voidable title has the power to transfer title to a good faith purchaser for value. A merchant who deals in particular goods has the power to transfer all rights of one who entrusts to him goods of the kind. And a rightful owner may be estopped by his own acts from asserting title against an innocent purchaser.

KEY TERMS

Bailee	p. 382	F.O.B.	p. 386
C.I.F.	p. 388	Negotiable document	p. 383
C.F.	p. 388	of title	
Consignment	p. 389	"No arrival, no sale"	p. 388
Document of Title	p. 382	"Sale on approval"	p. 389
Ex-ship	p. 388	"Sale or return"	p. 389
F.A.S.	p. 388		

SELF-TEST QUESTIONS

1. In general, title passes:
   (a) to a buyer when the contract is signed
   (b) when the buyer and seller agree that it passes
   (c) to a buyer when the seller receives payment for goods
   (d) none of the above
2. When a destination contract does not specify when title is to pass, it passes:
   (a) when the goods are shipped
   (b) when the contract is signed
   (c) when the buyer pays for the goods
   (d) when the seller tenders delivery
3. In a C.I.F. contract:
   (a) the seller must obtain insurance
   (b) the buyer must obtain insurance
   (c) the seller has fewer duties than with a C.F. contract
   (d) title passes to the buyer when the seller tenders delivery

4. In a sale-on-approval contract:
   (a) the goods are intended primarily for the buyer's use
   (b) the goods are intended primarily for resale
   (c) the risk of loss is on the buyer
   (d) the buyer obtains title upon receipt of the goods
5. As a general rule:
   (a) goods cannot be sold by persons with voidable title
   (b) a rightful owner cannot be estopped from asserting title against an innocent purchaser
   (c) a merchant cannot transfer the rights of a person who entrusts goods to him
   (d) a person with voidable title has the power to transfer title to a good faith purchaser for value

DEMONSTRATION PROBLEM

On July 5, Michael entered into a contract with the Stereo Shoppe for the purchase of a stereo. The contract provided that it was subject to fifteen days' free trial. During the fifteen day period, a fire destroyed Michael's house, including the stereo. Whose loss? Why?

PROBLEMS

1. Betty from Baltimore contracts to purchase 100 purple llama figurines from Sam of Syracuse. Sam is to send the goods by carrier and is not required to deliver them to Betty's Boutique, their destination. He ships them by train, which unfortunately crashes in Delaware. All of the figurines are destroyed. Whose loss? Why?
2. In problem 1, assume that the train did not crash but that Sam's creditors attempted to seize the goods before arrival. May they? Why?
3. Hattie's Head Shop signed a written agreement with the Tangerine Computer Company to supply Hattie's with a Marilyn, a 16-bit supercomputer with bubble memory, to total up its orders and pay its foreign agents. The contract provided that the computer was to be specially built and that Tangerine would deliver it by carrier to Hattie's ready to install no later than June 1. Tangerine engineers worked feverishly to comply with the contract terms. On May 25, the computer stood gleaming in the company's shipping department. That night, before the trucks could depart, a tornado struck the factory and destroyed the computer intended for Hattie's. Whose loss? Why?
4. In problem 3, assume that the tornado did not strike but that Tangerine's creditors attempted to seize the computer. May they? Why?
5. On February 17, Clancy, perpetually in debt, takes his CB radio to Lucy's repair shop. Because Lucy and Clancy

were old friends, Lucy didn't give him a receipt. On February 19, hounded by creditors, Clancy sells the CB on credit to Goober, who is to pick it up on February 21 at Lucy's, pay Lucy the repair bill, and pay the balance of the purchase price to Clancy. Who is entitled to the radio if, on February 20, Clancy's creditor walks in with the sheriff to seize the CB from Lucy? Why?

6. Assume in problem 5 that, instead of the attempted seizure of the CB by the creditor, Lucy's shop and the CB are destroyed by fire on February 20. Must Goober still pay Clancy for the radio? Why?

7. Cleo's Close-Outs, a wholesaler of discounted merchandise, offered Randy's Retailers a chance to buy all the contents of a shipment of bathtub toys just received. Cleo estimated that she had between five and six hundred rubber ducks and wrote on October 21 offering them to Randy for only one dollar each if Randy would pick them up at Cleo's. Astonishingly, Randy received the letter in the mail the next day and posted his acceptance that very day. In the wee hours of the following morning, October 23, a fire consumed Cleo's warehouse melting the ducks into an uneven soup. Assuming that Cleo's was a merchant, who bears the loss? Why?

ANSWERS TO SELF-TEST QUESTIONS

1. (b)   2. (d)   3. (a)   4. (a)   5. (d)

SUGGESTED ANSWER TO DEMONSTRATION PROBLEM

The Stereo Shoppe bears the loss. This appears to be a "sale-on-approval" contract; risk of loss and title remain with the seller until the buyer accepts.

Performance and Remedies

PERFORMANCE: INTRODUCTION

*I*n Part II, we examined contract performance and remedies under common law. In this chapter we examine performance and remedies under UCC Article 2, the law of sales. In the next chapter we cover special remedies for those injured by defective products.

The parties often set out in their contracts the details of performance. These include price terms and terms of delivery—where the goods are to be delivered, when, and how. If the parties fail to list these terms, the rules studied in this chapter will determine the parties' obligations. The operation of these rules can be obviated by specifying conditions beforehand in the contract.

Perhaps the most general rule within Article 2 is for timely performance: in the absence of agreement, any action under a sales contract shall be within a "reasonable time." (Section 2-309(1).) What is a reasonable time? It depends on the good faith of the parties and the prevailing commercial standards. Another general rule is for open price terms. Under Section 2-305, a contract can be valid even though price is not

settled; if the parties fail to set price or state that it is to be left to their future agreement, but later fail to agree, then the contract price is deemed to be "a reasonable price at the time for delivery."

PERFORMANCE BY SELLER

The focal point of the seller's obligation is, of course, the delivery of goods. Three questions that arise in the absence of controlling language in the contract are when, where, and how.

When? As noted above, the time for delivery is generally a "reasonable time." In an ordinary retail sale, the seller's duty to deliver arises when the buyer tenders payment. However, this general rule is not applicable to the great body of commercial contracts that carry credit terms, for of course in such situations the buyer has contracted for the right to pay later, after delivery of the goods.

Where? Unless the parties specify where the goods are to be delivered, the place for delivery is assumed to be the seller's place of business, or his residence if he has no separate place of business. If the goods are specially identified in the contract and the parties both know when they make the contract that the goods are in some other place, that other place is where delivery is to be made. Title documents may be delivered through customary banking channels and need not be delivered with the goods.

How? When the parties do specify delivery elsewhere than the seller's business, the manner of shipment becomes important. In a shipment contract (p. 382), Section 2-504 comes into play; it permits the seller to treat the goods as delivered once they have been put into the possession of a carrier, as long as the buyer is notified of the shipment and is supplied with the documents necessary to obtain possession from the shipper. By contrast, in a destination contract (p. 382), the seller must put the goods at the buyer's disposition at a reasonable hour and with sufficient time to permit the buyer to take delivery, though the buyer is obligated to furnish facilities reasonably suited to taking possession.

Some sales are indivisible—that is, they concern a single object that can be tendered at a particular time. When you agree to buy a television set, you have in mind taking delivery at the store or having the store deliver it to your home, at which time you will owe the purchase price. But other types of sales agreements are divisible: 100 bushels of wheat, ten desks for an office, four tires for a car. Under Section 2-307, all goods must be tendered in a single delivery, and if only a partial shipment is made, then payment is not due. The buyer may refuse to pay or to take delivery.

Sometimes, however, circumstances make it impossible to deliver the entire quantity of goods. You order ten carloads of coal, but only three cars are available to deliver it, or you do not have room to store all the coal at once. Whenever circumstances permit either party the right to make or demand delivery in lots, Section 2-307 permits the seller to demand payment for each lot, assuming that it is feasible to apportion the price.

Cure for Improper Delivery

Suppose the seller has shipped goods that do not conform to the contract and the buyer rejects them. If the goods had been shipped early and time therefore remains to ship conforming goods, the seller may notify the buyer of his intention to "cure," that is, to comply with the contract. If he does so within the time allowed, the buyer is obligated to pay. The seller may also tender nonconforming goods, reasonably expecting that the goods will be acceptable to the buyer anyway. The buyer has the right to reject them, but if the seller promptly notifies the buyer of his intention to tender conforming goods, the seller is allowed a further reasonable time in which to do so.

What are "conforming" goods? Must the seller replace defective goods or may he offer to make minor repairs to the item originally delivered? In the following case, the court determined that under this provision of the UCC, a buyer is not entitled to a refund of the purchase price if the seller in the first instance attempts to repair rather than replace the goods.

WILSON v. SCAMPOLI
228 A.2d 848 (D.C. Ct. App. 1967)

MYERS, ASSOCIATE JUDGE. This is an appeal from an order of the trial court granting rescission of a sales contract for a color television set and directing the return of the purchase price plus interest and costs.

Appellee purchased the set in question on November 4, 1965, paying the total purchase price in cash. The transaction was evidenced by a sales ticket showing the price paid and guaranteeing ninety days' free service and replacement of any defective tube and parts for a period of one year. Two days after purchase the set was delivered and uncrated, the antennae adjusted and the set plugged into an electrical outlet to "cook out." When the set was turned on however, it did not function properly, the picture having a reddish tinge. Appellant's delivery man advised the buyer's daughter, Mrs. Kolley, that it was not his duty to tune in or adjust the color but that a service representative would shortly call at her house for that purpose. After the departure of the delivery men, Mrs. Kolley unplugged the set and did not use it.

On November 8, 1965, a service representative arrived, and after spending an hour in an effort to eliminate the red cast from the picture advised Mrs. Kolley that he would have to remove the chassis from the cabinet and take it to the shop as he could not determine the cause of the difficulty from his examination at the house. He also made a written memorandum of his service call, noting that the television "Needs Shop Work (Red Screen)." Mrs. Kolley refused to allow the chassis to be removed, asserting she did not want a "repaired" set but another "brand new" set. Later she demanded the return of the purchase price, although retaining the set. Appellant refused to refund the purchase price, but renewed his offer to adjust, repair, or, if the set could not be made to function properly, to replace it. Ultimately, appellee instituted this suit against appellant seeking a refund of the purchase price. After a trial, the court ruled that "under the facts and circumstances the complaint is justified. Under the equity powers of the Court I will order the parties put back in their original status, let the $675 be returned, and the set returned to the defendant."

Appellant does not contest the jurisdiction of the trial court to order rescission in a proper case, but contends the trial judge erred in holding that rescission here was appropriate. He argues that he was always willing to comply with the terms of the sale either by correcting the malfunction by minor repairs or, in the event the set could not be made thereby properly operative, by replacement; that as he was denied the opportunity to try to correct the difficulty, he did not breach the contract of sale or any warranty thereunder, expressed or implied.

D.C. Code § 28:2-508 (Supp. V, 1966), provides

(1) Where any tender or delivery by the seller is rejected because nonconforming and the time for performance has not yet expired, the seller may seasonably notify the buyer of his intention to cure and may then within the contract time make a conforming delivery.

(2) Where the buyer rejects a non-conforming tender which the seller had reasonable grounds to believe would be acceptable with or without money allowance the seller may if he seasonably notifies the buyer have a further reasonable time to substitute a conforming tender.

A retail dealer would certainly expect and have reasonable grounds to believe that merchandise like color television sets, new and delivered as crated at the factory, would be acceptable as delivered and that, if defective in some way, he would have the right to substitute a conforming tender. The question then resolves itself to whether the dealer may conform his tender by adjustment or minor repair or whether he must conform by substituting brand new merchandise. The problem seems to be one of first impression in other jurisdictions adopting the Uniform Commercial Code as well as in the District of Columbia.

(continued on next page)

(*continued*)

WILSON v. SCAMPOLI
228 A.2d 848 (D.C. Ct.
App. 1967)

★   ★   ★

Removal of a television chassis for a short period of time in order to determine the cause of color malfunction and ascertain the extent of adjustment or correction needed to effect full operational efficiency presents no great inconvenience to the buyer. In the instant case, appellant's expert witness testified that this was not infrequently necessary with new televisions. Should the set be defective in workmanship or parts, the loss would be upon the manufacturer who warranted it free from mechanical defect. Here the adamant refusal of Mrs. Kolley, acting on behalf of appellee, to allow inspection essential to the determination of the cause of the excessive red tinge to the picture defeated any effort by the seller to provide timely repair or even replacement of the set if the difficulty could not be corrected. The cause of the defect might have been minor and easily adjusted or it may have been substantial and required replacement by another new set—but the seller was never given an adequate opportunity to make a determination.

We do not hold that appellant has no liability to appellee but as he was denied access and a reasonable opportunity to repair, appellee has not shown a breach of warranty entitling him either to a brand new set or to rescission. We therefore reverse the judgment of the trial court granting rescission and directing the return of the purchase price of the set.

Reversed.

Request for Acknowledgment of Delivery

Although not required by law, a request for an "acknowledgment of delivery" is good practice, especially in foreign trade, if goods are sold on credit. It is a common practice throughout Latin America, for example, for defendant buyers to claim that the goods were not delivered, did not conform to samples shown when the contract was made, or were defective. Without a written acknowledgment of delivery in good order, the plaintiff seller will find it nearly impossible to prove his claim for money owed.

PERFORMANCE BY BUYER

Inspection, Acceptance, and Payment

The buyer's general obligation is to accept and pay for the goods. But the buyer's duty does not spring into being unless the seller tenders delivery. That is to say, tender of delivery is a condition to the buyer's duty to accept and, unless the contract states otherwise, to pay. If the seller has properly tendered goods that conform to the contract, then the buyer's performance will normally consist of three steps: inspection, acceptance, and payment.

Step 1: Inspection   Under Sections 2-513(1) and (2), the buyer has a qualified right to inspect. That means that the buyer must be given the chance to look over the goods to determine whether they conform to the contract. If they do not, he may properly reject the goods and refuse to pay. The right to inspect is subject to these exceptions:

a. The buyer waives the right. If the parties agree that payment must be made before inspection, then the buyer must pay (unless the nonconformity is obvious without inspection). Payment under these circumstances does not constitute acceptance, and the buyer does not lose his right to inspect and reject later.
b. The delivery is to be made C.O.D.
c. Payment is to be made against documents of title.

Step 2: Acceptance   The buyer may accept goods by words, silence, or action. Section 2-606(1) defines acceptance as occurring in any one of three circumstances: (1) *words:* the buyer, after a reasonable opportunity to inspect, tells the seller either that the goods conform or that he will keep them despite any nonconformity; (2) *silence:* the buyer fails to reject, after a reasonable opportunity to inspect; or (3) *action:* the buyer does anything that is inconsistent with the seller's ownership, such as sell the goods to someone else.

Once the buyer accepts, he is obligated to pay at the contract rate, and he loses the right to reject the goods. If he knew that the goods did not conform, he cannot revoke his acceptance unless he reasonably assumed that the seller would cure the nonconformity in timely fashion. If he was ignorant of the nonconformity, he must notify the seller within a reasonable time after he discovered, or should have discovered, the nonconformity. And once the buyer accepts goods, he bears the burden thereafter to prove that the seller breached the contract with respect to those goods.

A buyer may revoke his acceptance of nonconforming goods if he had reasonably assumed that the nonconformity would be cured, but the seller refuses to do so. (Section 2-608.) Such revocation gives the buyer the same rights he would have had in rejecting the goods initially. He may also revoke if he failed initially to discover the defects in the goods because it was difficult to do so or because the seller gave false assurances that the goods were sound. The revocation must be made within a reasonable time after discovering the defects and must be made before the goods undergo any substantial change in their condition (unless the change is due to the defects). For instance, the buyer orders canned fruit, but the containers are punctured and before he discovers the defect, the fruit spoils. Since the change in conditions is attributable to the initial defect, he may revoke. In any event, a revocation does not take effect until the buyer notifies the seller that he has revoked his acceptance.

In recent years, most states have enacted "lemon" laws designed to provide remedies to purchasers of defective cars. See **Box 18-1.** The availability of these remedies depends on whether the nonconformity in the car substantially impairs its value to the consumer. Because the "substantial impairment" test is the same test used in the UCC to determine when a buyer may revoke acceptance, cases such as the following will be important to courts attempting to interpret the new "lemon" laws.

COLONIAL DODGE, INC. v. MILLER
420 Mich. 452, 362 N.W.2d 704 (1984)

KAVANAGH, JUSTICE. This case requires the Court to decide whether the failure to include a spare tire with a new automobile can constitute a substantial impairment in the value of that automobile entitling the buyer to revoke his acceptance of the vehicle under M.C.L. § 440.2608; M.S.A. § 19.2608.

We hold it may and reverse.

On April 19, 1976, defendant Clarence Miller ordered a 1976 Dodge Royal Monaco station wagon from plaintiff Colonial Dodge which included a heavy-duty trailer package with extra wide tires.

On May 28, 1976, defendant picked up the wagon, drove it a short distance where he met his wife, and exchanged it for her car. Defendant drove that car to work while his wife returned home with the new station wagon. Shortly after arriving home, Mrs. Miller noticed that their new wagon did not have a spare tire. The following morning defendant notified plaintiff that he insisted on having the tire he ordered immediately, but when told there was no spare tire then available, he informed the salesman for plaintiff that he would stop payment on the two checks that were tendered as the purchase price, and that the vehicle could be picked up from in front of his home.

(continued on next page)

(*continued*)

COLONIAL DODGE, INC. v. MILLER
420 Mich. 452, 362 N.W.2d 704 (1984)

Defendant parked the car in front of his home where it remained until the temporary ten-day registration sticker had expired, whereupon the car was towed by the St. Clair police to a St. Clair dealership. Plaintiff had applied for license plates, registration, and title in defendant's name. Defendant refused the license plates when they were delivered to him.

According to plaintiff's witness, the spare tire was not included in the delivery of the vehicle due to a nation-wide shortage caused by a labor strike. Some months later, defendant was notified his tire was available.

Plaintiff sued defendant for the purchase price of the car. On January 13, 1981, the trial court entered a judgment for plaintiff finding that defendant wrongfully revoked acceptance of the vehicle. The Court of Appeals decided that defendant never accepted the vehicle under M.C.L. § 440.2606; M.S.A. § 19.2606 of the Uniform Commercial Code and reversed. On rehearing, the Court of Appeals, noting the trial court found the parties had agreed that there was a valid acceptance, affirmed the trial court's holding there was not a substantial impairment in value sufficient to authorize defendant to revoke acceptance of the automobile.

*   *   *

Plaintiff argues the missing spare tire did not constitute a substantial impairment in the value of the automobile, within the meaning of M.C.L. § 440.2608(1); M.S.A. § 19.2608(1). Plaintiff claims a missing spare tire is a trivial defect, and a proper construction of this section of the UCC would not permit defendant to revoke under these circumstances. It maintains that since the spare tire is easy to replace and the cost of curing the nonconformity very small compared to the total contract price, there is no substantial impairment in value.

However, M.C.L. § 440.2608(1); M.S.A. § 19.2608(1) says "[t]he buyer may revoke his acceptance of a lot or commercial unit whose nonconformity substantially impairs its value *to him* * * *." (Emphasis added.) Number two of the Official Comment to M.C.L. § 440.2608; M.S.A. § 19.2608 attempts to clarify this area. It says that

> [r]evocation of acceptance is possible only where the nonconformity substantially impairs the value of the goods to the buyer. For this purpose the test is not what the seller had reason to know at the time of contracting; the question is whether the nonconformity is such as will in fact cause a substantial impairment of value to the buyer though the seller had no advance knowledge as to the buyer's particular circumstances.

We cannot accept plaintiff's interpretation of M.C.L. § 440.2608(1); M.S.A. § 19.2608(1). In order to give effect to the statute, a buyer must show the nonconformity has a special devaluing effect on him and that the buyer's assessment of it is factually correct. In this case, the defendant's concern with safety is evidenced by the fact that he ordered the special package which included special tires. The defendant's occupation demanded that he travel extensively, sometimes in excess of 150 miles per day on Detroit freeways, and often in the early morning hours. Mr. Miller testified that he was afraid of a tire going flat on a Detroit freeway at 3 a.m. Without a spare, he testified, he would be helpless until morning business hours. The dangers attendant upon a stranded motorist are common knowledge, and Mr. Miller's fears are not unreasonable.

We hold that under the circumstances the failure to include the spare tire as ordered constituted a substantial impairment in value to Mr. Miller, and that he could properly revoke his acceptance under the UCC.

That defendant did not discover this nonconformity before he accepted the vehicle does not preclude his revocation. There was testimony that the space for the spare tire was under a fastened panel, concealed from view. This out-of-sight location satisfies the requirement of M.C.L. § 440.2608(1)(b); M.S.A. § 19.2608(1)(b) that the nonconformity be difficult to discover.

M.C.L. § 440.2608(2); M.S.A. § 19.2608(2) requires that the seller be notified of the revocation of acceptance and that it occur within a reasonable time of the discovery of the nonconformity. Defendant notified plaintiff of his revocation the morning after the car was delivered to him. Notice was given within a reasonable time.

[Reversed]

Step 3: Payment The buyer may tender payment in any manner consistent with current business customs. If merchants in the area ordinarily pay their suppliers with checks, a check proffered by Mom 'n Pop's Soda Stand for a gross of colas delivered to the door is sufficient tender of payment. A supplier who refuses to accept the check and leave the colas has breached the contract. However, if the check should subsequently be dishonored, the buyer's tender is treated as conditional and as having been defeated when the check bounces. Despite business customs, a seller may demand payment in legal tender (Federal Reserve notes), but if he does demand cash he must give the buyer a reasonable extension of time to get it. He cannot make a Saturday delivery and demand $1,000 in cash when the banks are closed.

Payment is due at the time and place at which the buyer will ultimately receive the goods. That rule holds even if the agreement is a shipment contract, meaning that the place from which the goods are to be shipped is treated legally as the place of delivery. This provision is to ensure that the buyer has the right to inspect the goods before having to pay. One exception to this rule is that for delivery by documents of title, the buyer must tender payment at the time and place he is to receive the *documents*, regardless of where the *goods* are to be received. As with virtually all of the provisions in Article 2 of the UCC, these provisions are subject to agreement of the parties.

The buyer's right to retain or dispose of the goods is conditioned on making any payment due and demanded on delivery, whether the delivery is of goods or documents of title. (Section 2-507(2).)

Buyer's Options on Improper Delivery by Seller

Should the seller improperly deliver, the buyer has two options: (1) rejection of the goods, or (2) acceptance with a right to certain remedies for nonconformance.

Rejection Under Section 2-601(a) the buyer may reject the goods if the seller fails to tender delivery in conformity with the contract. The rejection must be made within a reasonable time after delivery or tender, and once it is made the buyer may not act as owner of the goods. If he has taken possession before he rejects goods in which he has no security interest, he must hold them with reasonable care to permit the seller to remove them. If the buyer is a merchant

LAW AND LIFE

BOX 18-1

These Laws Put the Squeeze on Lemons

LEMON LAWS

[The Uniform Commercial Code specifies that in some circumstances a buyer may revoke his or her acceptance of non-conforming goods. "Lemon laws" provide additional remedies to purchasers of defective cars.—AUTHORS' NOTE]

A few years ago if that plum of a new car turned out to be a lemon in disguise, about the only recourse you had was to register your complaint with the dealer, then with the manufacturer and, if that failed, take the whole mess to court.

The track record for consumers following that path was far from glorious. Litigation was both expensive and time-consuming. Today, things are clearly better. Not wonderful, mind you, but better.

A growing number of state laws say, in effect, that if your new car has a serious problem that can't be fixed in a reasonable time, either you get your money back or you get a new car. Thanks to these lemon laws and a network of industry-sponsored grievance programs, you stand a better chance of having critical new-car gripes aired and acted upon than ever before. But you have to learn how the system operates before you can hope to make it work effectively for you.

Thirty-nine states and the District of Columbia have passed lemon laws. States that haven't enacted such statutes [include] Alabama, Arkansas, Georgia, Idaho, Indiana, Kentucky, South Carolina and South Dakota.

Lemon laws vary from state to state, but basically they pinpoint types of vehicles covered, define what a lemon is, set a period during which a vehicle is eligible for consideration under the law, and establish a procedure to resolve disputes.

Most states say you've got a lemon if within its first year or 12,000 miles your vehicle is hampered by a serious defect that an authorized facility has not been able to repair in four attempts or if the vehicle has been out of service for 30 days. Some states extend the eligibility period up to 18,000 miles or two years; some reduce the number of repair attempts to three; and some cut the number of out-of-service days to only 15.

Keep in mind that lemon laws aren't meant to provide you with a way of unloading a car you decide you don't like. Generally, defects must be covered by the manufacturer's warranty and must substantially reduce the use, safety or value of the vehicle. Also, you should continue to maintain the car as required in the warranty and owner's manual.

Source: *Changing Times*, January, 1986

(Chapter 16), then the buyer has a special duty to follow reasonable instructions from the seller for disposing of the rejected goods; if the buyer receives no instructions, and the goods are perishable, then he must try to sell the goods for the seller's account. The buyer is entitled to a commission for his efforts. Whether or not a merchant, a buyer may store the goods, reship them to the seller, or resell them—and charge the seller for his services—if the seller fails to send him instructions on disposition of the goods. Storage, reshipping, and reselling do not constitute acceptance or conversion by the buyer.

It is good practice to tell the seller what the grounds for rejection are. Under Section 2-605(1)(a), failure to enumerate a particular defect, ascertainable by reasonable inspection, bars the buyer from relying on the defect in a subsequent suit if the seller could

have cured the defect. When the seller and buyer are merchants, the buyer forfeits his right to rely on the defects if after rejection he fails to respond to the seller's written request for a full and final written statement of all defects.

Acceptance of Nonconforming Goods   The buyer need not reject nonconforming goods. He may accept the whole shipment or any commercial unit and reject the rest. A "commercial unit" is defined as a unit of goods that by commercial usage is a single whole for purpose of sale; division of a commercial unit would materially impair the character, value, or use of the goods. The purpose of the rule restricting partial acceptance to commercial units is to prevent the buyer from unduly impairing the value of the goods, as for example, by taking apart a machine for some of its parts, or by accepting only one item in a suite of furniture.

Acceptance of nonconforming goods does not defeat the buyer's claim to remedies for damages (see p. 413).

Two Special Cases Involving Improper Delivery

Installment Sales A contract for an installment sale complicates the answer to the question: What right does the buyer have to accept or reject when the seller fails to deliver properly? (An installment contract is one calling for delivery of goods in separate lots with separate acceptance for each delivery.) The general answer can be found in Section 2-612, which permits the buyer to reject any nonconforming installment if the nonconformity cannot be cured and if it substantially impairs the value of that particular installment. However, the seller may avoid rejection by giving the buyer adequate assurances that he will cure the defect, unless the particular defective installment substantially impairs the value of the whole contract.

Suppose the Corner Gas Station contracts to buy 12,000 gallons of premium unleaded gasoline from Big Time Gas Supplies, deliverable in twelve monthly installments of 1,000 gallons on the first of each month, at a price of one dollar per gallon, payable three days after delivery. In the third month, Big Time is short and can deliver only 500 gallons immediately and will not have the second 500 gallons until mid-month. May Corner Gas reject this tender? The answer depends on the circumstances. The nonconformity clearly cannot be cured, since the contract calls for the full 1,000 gallons on a particular day. But the failure to make full delivery does not necessarily impair the value of that installment; for example, Corner Gas may know that it will not use up the 500 gallons until mid-month. However, if the failure will leave Corner Gas short before mid-month and unable to buy from another supplier unless it agrees to take a full 1,000 gallons (more than it could hold at once if it also took Big Time's 500 gallons), then Corner Gas is entitled to reject Big Time's tender.

Is Corner Gas entitled to reject the entire contract on the grounds that the failure to deliver impairs the value of the contract as a whole? Again, the answer depends on whether the impairment was substantial. Suppose other suppliers are willing to sell only if Corner Gas agrees to buy for a year. If Corner needed the extra gasoline right away, the contract would have been breached as whole, and Corner would be justified in rejecting all further attempted tenders of delivery from Big Time. Likewise, if the spot price of gasoline were rising, so that month-to-month purchases from other suppliers might cost it more than the original one dollar per gallon, Corner Gas would be justified in rejecting further deliveries from Big Time and fixing its costs with a supply contract from someone else. Of course, Corner Gas would have a claim against Big Time for the difference between the original contract price and what it had to pay another supplier in a rising market (see p. 412).

Casualty Losses Suppose that after the contract is made, some of the goods are destroyed through no fault of either buyer or seller. What are the rights of the buyer? The answer depends on whether the goods were identified when the contract was made. Fifi espies some perfectly adorable diamonds in the showroom of Ernie's Gems and signs a contract to buy them for $1 million, delivery to be made at Fifi's home in ten days. One day before they are due to be delivered, the diamonds are stolen from Ernie's, through no fault of the store. Because the risk of loss (see p. 383) had not yet passed to Fifi, the buyer, the contract is avoided, the loss being total. Fifi could not sue Ernie's for damages. If the loss had been partial, only some of the stones having been stolen, Fifi could inspect and either avoid the entire contract or accept the remaining goods at a price reflecting the partial delivery.

However, if the goods had not been identified when the contract was made, the seller would have breached were the diamonds to be undeliverable. For example, Fifi calls up Ernie's and says: "Send me any old diamond worth one million dollars by June 1, okay darling? I must have it for my party." Ernie's assent means that his obligation can be discharged only by tendering delivery. The theft of a particular one-million dollar diamond does not avoid the contract.

REMEDIES IN GENERAL

General Policy

The general policy of the UCC is to put the aggrieved party in as good a position as if the other party had fully performed. The code provisions are to be liberally read to achieve that result if possible. Thus the seller has a number of potential remedies when the buyer breaches; depending on the circumstances, these remedies may be cumulative: the seller may withhold delivery of any undelivered goods, stop delivery of goods already in transit, resell and recover damages or the price, and cancel the contract.

Specifying Remedies

Just as the parties may specify details of performance in the contract, so they may provide for and limit remedies in the event of breach. (Section 2-719(1).) But they are not free to eliminate all remedies. As the comment to the UCC provision puts it: "If the parties intend to conclude a contract for sale within this Article they must accept the legal consequence that there be at least a fair quantum of remedy for breach of the obligations or duties outlined in the contract." In particular, the UCC lists three exceptions from the general rule that the parties may limit remedies:

1. When the circumstances cause the agreed-on remedy to fail or be ineffective, the remedy provisions in the UCC apply.
2. Unconscionable limitation of "consequential damages" (that is, damages that flow as a result of the contract breach; for example, lost profits) is not permitted, but reasonable limitation or ex-

clusion is permissible. However, the UCC prohibits courts from enforcing any limitation of consequential damages for injury to any person arising from defects in consumer goods.

3. The parties may agree to *liquidate* damages; that is, fix in advance the amount of damages that will be paid by the party who breaches. But the amount fixed must be reasonable in light of the anticipated harm or actual harm, the difficulties of proof, and the inconvenience or impossibility of obtaining an adequate remedy otherwise. Fifi says she must have the diamond for the party or she will suffer "a million-dollar headache." Ernie's Jewelers agrees that if she doesn't get the diamond, her liquidated damages will be $1 million. The diamond is stolen and Ernie's breaches. Liquidated damages under these circumstances are not unreasonable, since who can prove how much the social embarrassment of not wearing an ostentatious diamond is worth? But the particular amount is probably unreasonable, and the court will hold it void as an unlawful "penalty."

Statute of Limitations

The UCC statute of limitations for breach of any sales contract is four years. This means that a plaintiff must file suit within four years after the breach occurs unless a warranty explicitly extends to future performance of the goods. The "future performance" exception is discussed in the following case.

WILSON v. HAMMER HOLDINGS, INC.
850 F.2d 3 (1st Cir. 1988)

COFFIN, CIRCUIT JUDGE.

In 1961, appellant Dorothy Wilson and her late husband, John, paid more than $11,000 to the Hammer Galleries for a painting that was expressly guaranteed to be an original work of art by Edouard Vuillard. In 1984, an expert deemed the painting a fake. The district court held that the Wilsons' suit for breach of warranty and negligence, filed in February 1987, was barred by the statute of limitations. We affirm.

*   *   *

The Massachusetts statute of limitations for breach of a sales contract is set out in Mass.Gen.Laws Ann. ch. 106, § 2-725. That section provides that

(1) An action for breach of any contract for sale must be commenced within four years after the cause of action has accrued. . . .

(2) A cause of action accrues when the breach occurs, regardless of the aggrieved party's lack of knowledge of the breach. A breach of warranty occurs when tender of delivery is made, except that where a warranty explicitly extends to future performance of the goods and discovery must await the time of such performance the cause of action accrues when the breach is or should have been discovered.

There is no question that the Wilsons' action was untimely under this statute if it accrued at the time they purchased the painting and received the warranty because those events occurred twenty-six years before suit was filed. The Wilsons therefore contend that this case falls within the exception to section 2-725(2), and they argue that their cause of action accrued upon their discovery in 1985 that the painting was not authentic.

★   ★   ★

Section 2-725(2) refers to a warranty of "future performance," and so the Wilsons' theory depends first on extending the concept of a "performance" to a painting. They concede that paintings, unlike consumer goods like automobiles and washing machines, generally are not purchased based on how they "perform" or "function." They suggest, however, that a painting "performs" "by being what it [is] represented to be," *Lawson v. The London Arts Group*, 708 F.2d 226, 228 (6th Cir. 1983). In this case, they say, "Femme Debout" could "perform" only by being an authentic Vuillard.

Accepting at least for the sake of argument that a painting does "perform" by being genuine, the question then becomes whether Hammer's express warranty of authenticity not only guaranteed the present "being" of the painting as an authentic Vuillard but also extended, as required by section 2-725(2), to the future existence of the painting as a Vuillard. On this point, the Wilsons argue that because the authenticity of a painting does not change over time, Hammer's warranty "necessarily guaranteed the present *and* future existence of the Painting as an authentic Vuillard." (Emphasis in original.) Therefore, they contend, explicit words warranting future performance would be superfluous in this context.

The Wilsons' argument is persuasive if one's goal is to furnish protection for art buyers equivalent to that provided expressly by section 2-725(2) to purchasers of other types of goods. Art buyers almost certainly would fail to secure a separate explicit warranty of "future performance" because a warranty that promises authenticity "now and at all times in the future" would be redundant. Therefore, it is appealing to argue that, in the circumstances of this case, the exception in section 2-725(2) should be triggered by any warranty of authenticity, which must be understood as at least an *implicit* promise of future performance.

Our difficulty with this argument, however, is that it asks us to ignore the literal language of the statute requiring an *explicit* promise of future perfor-

(*continued on next page*)

(continued)

WILSON v. HAMMER HOLDINGS, INC.
850 F.2d 3 1st Cir. (1988)

mance. The Wilsons argue essentially that because the statutory exception's requirement of an explicit prospective warranty does not make sense in the context of the sale of paintings, we should dispense with that requirement. We are reluctant, however, to waive the specific eligibility requirements established by the legislature for what, it must be remembered, is an *exception* to the general limitations rule.

* * *

We need not finally decide this issue, however, because even if we were to accept the Wilson's argument that Hammer's warranty necessarily extended to future performance of the painting, and thus met the prospective warranty requirement of section 2–725(2), we nevertheless would conclude that their action is time-barred. The statute also requires that discovery of the breach "*must* await" the time of such future performance. That is not the case here. Because of the static nature of authenticity, the Wilsons were no less capable of discovering that "Femme Debout" was a fake at the time of purchase than they were at a later time.
[Judgment affirmed.]

SELLER'S REMEDIES

To illustrate the UCC's remedy provisions, in this and the following section we assume the following facts: Howard, of Los Angeles, enters into a contract to sell and ship 100 prints of a Peter Breughel painting, plus the original, to Bunker in Dallas. Twenty-five prints have already been delivered to Bunker, another twenty-five are en route (having been shipped by common carrier), another twenty-five are finished but haven't yet been shipped, and the final twenty-five are still in production. The original is hanging on a wall in Howard's living room.

Remedies on Breach

Bunker, the buyer breaches. He sends Howard a telegram stating that he revokes the contract and will reject the goods if delivery is attempted. Howard has the following cumulative remedies; election is not required.

Withhold Further Delivery Howard may refuse to send the third batch of twenty-five prints that are awaiting shipment.

Stop Delivery Howard may also stop the shipment. If Bunker is insolvent, and Howard discovers it, Howard would be permitted to stop any shipment in the possession of a carrier or bailee. If Bunker is not insolvent, the UCC permits Howard to stop delivery only of carload, truckload, planeload, or larger shipments. The reason for limiting the right to bulk shipments in the case of noninsolvency is that stopping delivery burdens the carrier, and requiring a truck, say, to stop and find a small package, could pose a sizable burden.

Identify to the Contract Goods in Possession Howard could "identify to the contract" the twenty-five prints in his possession. Section 2-704(1) permits the seller to denote conforming goods that were not originally specified as the exact objects of the contract, if they are under his control or in his possession at the time of the breach. Assume that Howard had 1,000 prints of the Breughel. The contract did not state which 100 of those 1,000 prints he was obligated to sell, but once Bunker breached, Howard could declare that those particular prints were the ones contemplated by the contract. He has this right whether or not the identified goods could be resold. Moreover, Howard may complete production of the twenty-five unfinished prints and identify them to the contract also, if in his "reasonable commercial judgment" he could better avoid loss—for example, by reselling them. If continued production would be expensive and the chances of resale slight, the seller should cease manufacture and resell for scrap or salvage value.

Resell   Howard could resell the seventy-five prints still in his possession, as well as the original. As long as he proceeds in good faith and in a commercially reasonable manner, he is entitled to recover the difference between the resale price and the contract price, together with incidental damages (but less whatever he saved because of the buyer's breach—for example, shipping expenses). "Incidental damages" include any reasonable charges or expenses incurred because, for example, delivery had to be stopped, new transportation arranged, storage provided for, and resale commissions agreed on.

The seller may resell the goods in virtually any way he desires as long as he acts reasonably. He may resell them through a public or private sale, but if the resale is private he must give the buyer reasonable notice of his intention to resell. If the resale is public—at auction—only identified goods can be sold, unless there is a recognized market for a public sale of futures in the goods (as there is in agricultural commodities, for example). In a public resale, the seller must give the buyer notice, unless the goods are perishable or threaten to decline in value speedily. The goods must be available for inspection before the resale, and the buyer must be allowed to bid or to buy.

The seller may sell the goods item-by-item or as a unit. Although the goods must relate to the contract, it is not necessary for any or all of them to have existed or to have been identified at the time of the breach.

The seller need not account to the buyer for any profit realized from the resale. (Section 2-706(6).)

Recover Damages   The seller may recover damages equal to the difference between the market price (measured at the time and place for tender of delivery) and the unpaid contract price, plus incidental damages, but less any expenses saved because of the buyer's breach. Suppose Howard's contract price was $100 per print plus $10,000 for the original and that the market price on the day Howard was to deliver

the remaining seventy-five prints was $75 (plus $8,000 for the original). Suppose further that shipping costs (including insurance) that Howard saved when Bunker repudiated were $2,000 and that to resell them Howard would have to spend another $750. His damages, then, would be calculated as follows: original contract price ($17,500) less market price ($13,625) = $3875, less $2,000 in saved expenses = $1875, plus $750 in additional expenses = $2625 net damages recoverable by Howard, the seller.

If the above formula would not put the seller in as good a position as performance under the contract, then the measure of damages is lost profits, that is, the profit that Howard would have made had Bunker taken the original painting and prints at the contract price (again, deducting expenses saved and adding additional expenses incurred, as well as giving credit for proceeds of any resale). (Section 2-708(2).) This provision becomes especially important for so-called "lost-volume" sellers. Howard may be able to sell the remaining seventy-five prints easily and at the same price that Bunker had agreed to pay. Then why isn't Howard whole? The reason is that the second buyer was not a *substitute* buyer but an *additional* one; that is, Howard would have made that sale even if Bunker had not reneged on the contract. So Howard is still short a sale and is out a profit that he would have made had Bunker honored the contract.

Recover Price   Howard could recover from Bunker the price of the twenty-five prints that Bunker holds. Suppose they had agreed to a shipment contract, so that risk of loss passed to Bunker when Howard placed the other prints and the original with the trucker and that the trucker had crashed en route and his cargo burned up. Howard could recover the price. Or suppose there were no market for the remaining seventy-five prints and original. Howard could identify these prints to the contract and recover the contract price. If Howard did resell some, the proceeds of the sale would have to be credited to Bunker's account and deducted from any judgment. Unless sold, the prints must be held for Bunker and given to him upon his payment of the judgment.

Cancel   When Bunker repudiated, Howard could declare the contract cancelled. Cancellation entitles the injured party to any remedies for the breach of the whole contract or for any unperformed balance. That is what happens when Howard recovers damages, lost profits, or the price.

Remedies on Insolvency

The above remedies apply when the buyer *breaches* the contract. In addition to those remedies, the seller has remedies when he learns that the buyer is *insolvent*, even if the buyer has not yet breached. Insolvency results, for example, when the buyer has "ceased to pay his debts in the ordinary course of business," or the buyer "cannot pay his debts as they become due." (Section 1-201(23).)

Upon learning of Bunker's insolvency, Howard could refuse to deliver the remaining prints, unless Bunker pays cash not only for the remaining prints but for those already delivered. If Howard learned of Bunker's insolvency within ten days of delivering the first twenty-five prints, he could make a demand to reclaim them. If within three months prior to delivery Bunker had falsely represented that he was solvent, the ten-day limitation would not cut off Howard's right to reclaim. If he does seek to reclaim, Howard will lose the right to any other remedy with respect to those particular items. However, Howard cannot reclaim goods already purchased from Bunker in the ordinary course of business. Thus, a customer who buys one of the prints from Bunker's store does not risk losing it several weeks later when Bunker has become insolvent.

BUYER'S REMEDIES

In this section, let us assume that seller Howard, rather than buyer Bunker, breaches, all other circumstances being the same. That is, Howard had delivered twenty-five prints, twenty-five more were en route, the original painting hung in Howard's living room, another twenty-five finished prints were in Howard's factory, and the final twenty-five were in production.

The buyer's remedies can be divided into two general categories: (1) for goods that the buyer has not received or accepted or when he has justifiably revoked acceptance, and (2) for goods already accepted.

Goods Not Received

Cancel   If the buyer has not yet received or accepted the goods (or has justifiably rejected them or revoked the acceptance because the goods are nonconforming), he may cancel the contract.

Recover the Price   Whether or not he cancels, he is entitled to recover the price paid above the value of any prints accepted.

Under Section 2-711(1)(a), Bunker may "cover" the goods and have damages. This means that he may make a good-faith, reasonable purchase of substitute goods. He may then recover from the seller damages for the difference between the cost of cover and the contract price. This is the buyer's equivalent of the seller's right to resell. Thus, Bunker could try to purchase seventy-five additional prints of the Breughel from some other manufacturer. But his failure or inability to do so does not bar him from any other remedy open to him.

Damages for Nondelivery   Bunker could sue for damages for nondelivery. Under Section 2-713, the measure of damages is the difference between the market price at the time when the buyer learned of the breach and the contract price (plus incidental damages, less expenses saved). Suppose Bunker could have bought seventy-five prints for $125 on the day that Howard called to say that he would not be sending the rest of the order. Bunker would be entitled to $1875—the market price ($9375) less the contract price ($7500). This remedy is available even if he did not in fact purchase the substitute prints. Suppose that at the time of breach, the original painting was worth $15,000 (Howard having just sold it to someone else at that price). Bunker would be entitled to an additional $5,000, the difference between his contract price and the market price.

Recover the Goods   If the goods are unique—as in the case of the original Breughel—Bunker is entitled to specific performance, that is, recovery of the painting itself. This section is designed to give the buyer rights comparable to the seller's right to the price and modifies the old common law requirement that courts will not order specific performance except for unique goods. It permits specific performance "in other proper circumstances," and these might include particular goods contemplated under output or requirements contracts or those peculiarly available from one market source. If the remaining seventy-five prints were unavailable elsewhere because Howard is the only one manufacturing them, Bunker would be entitled to specific performance of the whole contract.

Even if the goods are not unique, the buyer is entitled to *replevy* them if they are identified to the contract and after good faith effort he cannot recover them. **Replevin** is the name of the old common law action for recovering goods that have been unlawfully taken. In our case, Bunker could replevy the twenty-five prints stopped in transit and the twenty-five prints identified and held by the seller.

Bunker also has the right to recover the goods should it turn out that Howard is insolvent. Under Section 2-502, if Howard were to become insolvent within ten days of the day on which Bunker pays the first installment of the price due, Bunker would be entitled to recover the original and the prints, as long as he tendered any unpaid portion of the price.

Security Interest in Goods Rightly Rejected If the buyer rightly rejects nonconforming goods or revokes his acceptance, he is entitled to a security interest in any goods in his possession. In other words, Bunker need not return the twenty-five prints he has already received unless Howard reimburses him for any payments made and for any expenses reasonably incurred in their inspection, receipt, transportation, care, and custody. If Howard refuses to reimburse him, Bunker may resell the goods and take from the proceeds the amount to which he is entitled.

Goods Accepted

When the buyer accepts the goods, and after the time for revocation has expired learns of a breach, he is entitled to remedies as long as he notifies the seller of the breach within a reasonable time. Bunker's remedies are twofold.

He may recover damages for any losses that in the ordinary course of events stem from the seller's breach. Suppose Howard had used inferior paper, difficult to detect, and within several weeks of acceptance the prints dissolved. Bunker is entitled to be reimbursed for the price he paid, plus **incidental** expenses such as shipping, insurance, and the like.

Bunker is also entitled to **consequential** damages resulting from the breach; these are losses resulting from general or particular requirements or needs of the buyer, needs of which the seller at the time of contracting had reason to know, and which the buyer could not reasonably prevent by cover or otherwise. Suppose Bunker is about to make a deal to resell the twenty-five prints he has accepted, only to discover that Howard used inferior inks, so that the colors have begun to fade. Howard knew that Bunker was in the business of retailing prints and therefore knew or should have known that one requirement of the goods was that they be printed in lasting ink. Because Bunker will lose the resale, he is entitled to the profits he would have made. (If Howard had not wished to take the risk of paying for consequential damages, he could have negotiated a provision limiting or excluding this remedy.) The buyer has the burden of proving consequential damages, but the UCC does not require mathematical precision. Suppose customers come to Bunker's gallery and sneer at the faded colors. If he can show that he would have sold the prints but for the fading (perhaps by showing that he had sold Breughels in the past), he would be entitled to recover a reasonable estimate of his lost profits.

Suppose Bunker discovered to his great distress that the original Breughel painting that he bought from Howard had been stolen, and the district attorney prosecuted him for the crime of receiving stolen property. Could he sue Howard to recover as consequential damages the fee for hiring an attorney to defend himself? That is the situation that arose in the following case.

DE LA HOYA v. SLIM'S GUN SHOP
80 Cal.App.3d Supp. 6,
146 Cal.Rptr. 68 (Super. 1978)

COLE, PRESIDING JUDGE. The principal issue in this case is whether an innocent buyer of personal property which turns out to have been stolen can recover as damages, from a seller, attorney's fees incurred in defending himself against criminal charges arising out of possession of the stolen property. We hold that he can and affirm the judgment below.

Respondent purchased a hand gun from appellant, a properly licensed dealer. Appellant himself had previously bought the gun from a third party, one Oehring. Appellant thereafter sold the gun to respondent. At the time he bought the gun and at the time he sold it appellant filed with the appropriate federal and state authorities all of the reports required by law, e.g., Penal Code section 12071 and 12072. Appellant did not know that the gun was stolen.

After he had purchased the gun and while using it for target shooting, respondent was questioned by an officer who traced the serial number of the weapon, determined that it had been stolen and arrested respondent. It was necessary for respondent to hire counsel to extricate himself from the criminal charges. He thereafter brought this action against appellant, seeking damages for breach of warranty of title. The trial court awarded judgment in the amount of $949, of which $140 represented the price of the gun. Included in the judgment were attorney's fees of $800.

* * *

It appears to be the general rule in those United States jurisdictions which have considered the problem that attorney fees incurred in litigation with third parties may be recoverable as damages in an action for breach of contract. We see no reason why the general rule applied elsewhere should not also be adopted in this state, and we follow it in this case.

It is, of course, true that in an action seeking damages for breach of contract, only such damages may be allowed as may reasonably be supposed to have been within the contemplation of the parties to the contract at the time they entered into the agreement. Appellant urges, in effect, that attorney fees expended in extricating respondent from his arrest were not proximately caused (Civ. Code, § 3300) and should not be allowed here. We disagree.

* * *

In the case at bench the trial court has impliedly found (there being no express findings of fact or conclusions of law) that the parties could reasonably have contemplated at the time appellant sold the hand gun to respondent that if respondent's possession of it was questioned, and the gun turned out to be stolen, respondent would be subject to arrest for receiving stolen property (Pen. Code, § 496). We cannot say that that factual finding was unwarranted, particularly considering that it was a *gun* that was involved. Once the foreseeability of arrest is established, a natural and usual consequence is that appellant would incur attorney's fees.

There remains for consideration the fact that the action was cast in the form of a buyer seeking damages for breach of warranty of title. That subject, now covered by California Uniform Commercial Code sections 2714 and 2715, was, prior to 1931, found in Civil Code section 3312 (from 1931 to 1963 when the California Uniform Commercial Code was enacted, Civ. Code, § 1789 was the operative statute). Section 3312 read: "The detriment caused by the breach of warranty of the title of personal property sold is deemed to be the value thereof to the buyer, when he is deprived of its possession, together with any costs which he has become liable to pay in an action brought for the property by the true owner."

In *Pezel* v. *Yerex*, 56 Cal.App. 304, 205 P. 475, the plaintiff had innocently bought a stolen automobile, had resold it and had been forced to pay damages to his buyer as a result of litigation brought by the latter. The appellate court denied recovery of plaintiff's attorney fees on the narrow ground that such fees were not costs within the meaning of section 3312. In view of the change in statutory language, *Pezel* v. *Yerex* has become outdated with respect to the right to include attorney fees as damages in the event of a breach of warranty of title.

"Under the Uniform Commercial Code, it would seem that the buyer may in a proper case measure damages by the loss resulting in the ordinary course of events from the seller's breach as determined in any manner which is reasonable, and this rule should apply to breach of warranty of title, as to any other breach."

The judgment is affirmed. Respondent to recover costs on appeal.

CHAPTER SUMMARY

As with most of the UCC, the parties may specify the terms of their performance. Only if they fail to do so does Article 2 provide the terms for them. In the absence of agreement, the time for delivery is a reasonable one, and the place of delivery is the seller's place of business. All goods must be tendered in a single delivery, unless circumstances permit either party the right to make or demand delivery in lots.

If the seller ships nonconforming goods but has time to meet his contractual obligation, he may notify the buyer of his intention to cure and if he does so in a timely manner the buyer must pay.

The buyer's general obligation is to accept and pay for the goods. He has the right to inspect the goods to see that they conform to the contract. If they do not he may reject them; if they do conform he is obligated to accept and pay. The buyer may pay in any manner consistent with current business customs. Payment is due at the time and place at which the buyer will ultimately receive the goods.

The general policy of the UCC is to put an aggrieved party in a position as good as he would have been in had the other party fully performed. The parties may specify or limit certain remedies, but they may not eliminate all remedies in the event of breach. However, if circumstances make a remedy agreed on inadequate, then the UCC's other remedy provisions apply. The parties may not unconscionably limit consequential damages. The parties may agree to liquidate damages, but not to unreasonable penalties.

In general, the seller may pursue the following remedies: withhold further delivery, stop delivery, identify to the contract goods in his possession, resell the goods, recover damages or the price, or cancel the contract. In addition, when it becomes apparent that the buyer is insolvent, the seller may, within certain time periods, refuse to deliver the remaining goods or reclaim goods already delivered.

The buyer, in general, has the following remedies: For goods not yet received, he may cancel the contract, recover the price paid, cover the goods and recover damages for the difference in price, recover the specific goods if they are unique or in "other proper circumstances." For goods received and accepted, the buyer may recover ordinary damages for losses that stem from the breach and consequential damages if the seller knew of the buyer's particular needs and the buyer could not reasonably cover.

KEY TERMS

Consequential   p. 413   Replevin   p. 413
Incidental   p. 413

SELF-TEST QUESTIONS

1. In the absence of agreement, the place of delivery is:
   (a) the buyer's place of business
   (b) the seller's place of business
   (c) either the buyer's place of business or the buyer's residence
   (d) any of the above
2. The UCC Statute of Limitations for breach of contract is:
   (a) two years
   (b) three years
   (c) four years
   (d) none of the above
3. Under the UCC, if buyer breaches, the seller can:
   (a) withhold further delivery
   (b) resell the goods still in seller's possession
   (c) recover damages
   (d) do all of the above
4. If the seller breaches, the buyer can generally:
   (a) recover the goods, even when the goods have not been identified to the contract and the seller is not insolvent
   (b) purchase substitute goods and recover their cost
   (c) purchase substitute goods and recover the difference between their cost and the contract price
   (d) recover punitive damages
5. Following a seller's breach, the buyer can recover the price paid:
   (a) if the buyer cancels the contract
   (b) only for goods the buyer has accepted
   (c) for all goods the buyer was to receive, whether or not the buyer accepted them
   (d) none of the above

DEMONSTRATION PROBLEM

Alex entered into a contract to deliver 5000 widgets to Betty by December 20. Alex delivered the widgets on December 19, and two days later learned that Betty could not pay her debts as they became due. May he reclaim the widgets? Why?

PROBLEMS

1. Anne entered into a contract to sell 100 cans of yellow tennis balls to Chris, delivery to be made by June 15. On June 8, Anne delivered 100 cans of white balls, which were rejected by Chris. What course of action would you recommend for Anne? Why?
2. In problem 1, assume that Anne had delivered the 100 cans of white balls on June 15; these were rejected by Chris. Under what circumstances might Anne be allowed additional time to perform the contract?
3. In problem 1, if the contract did not discuss delivery, when must Anne deliver the tennis balls?
4. In problem 1, when Anne delivers the tennis balls, does Chris have the right to inspect them? If Chris accepts the white tennis balls, may the acceptance be revoked? If so, explain the circumstances.
5. In problem 1, assume that Chris decided she could use twenty-five cans of the white balls. Could she accept twenty-five cans and reject the rest? Why?
6. Suppose in problem 1 that Anne delivered white tennis balls because a fire at her warehouse destroyed her entire stock of yellow balls. Does the fire discharge Anne's contractual duties? Why?
7. If, in problem 1, Chris rejected the white tennis balls and Anne refused to deliver yellow ones, may Chris recover damages? If so, how would they be calculated?
8. In problem 7, would Chris be entitled to specific performances? Why?

ANSWERS TO SELF-TEST PROBLEMS

1. (b)   2. (c)   3. (d)   4. (c)   5. (d)

SUGGESTED ANSWER TO DEMONSTRATION PROBLEM

Alex may reclaim the widgets. Betty is insolvent and Alex may reclaim the goods if he demands them within ten days after they were received by Betty. See UCC Section 2-702(2).

CHAPTER

19

CHAPTER OVERVIEW

Warranties

Problems with Warranty Theory

Strict Liability in Tort

Negligence

Product Liability Law Reform

Product Liability

*I*n previous chapters we discussed remedies generally. In this chapter we focus specifically on remedies available when a defective product causes personal injury or other damages. **Product liability** describes a type of claim, not a separate theory of liability. Product liability has strong emotional overtones—ranging from the pro-litigation position of consumer advocates to the conservative perspective of the manufacturers.

Consumer advocates recite the concededly distressing facts about the rate at which products cause injury. Consider this brief recital of some of the dangers that lurk in common products:

> One can hardly escape the news of the latest grisly consumer tragedy. Babies guzzling Drano or strangling in the rungs of their cribs. Children stabbing themselves blind with the sharpened sticks hidden inside their dolls. Housewives getting their sleeves too close to the burner and arriving in the emergency wards with skin seared like grilled steak. Husbands losing feet inside the savage rotors of the family lawnmower. Workers crushing their hands in unguarded machinery. Or unwitting hospital patients getting their brains bored out by defective cranial drills. (Maslow 1975, p. 27)

Product liability can also be a life-or-death matter from the manufacturer's perspective. For example, in 1974, Havir Manufacturing Company of St. Paul, Minnesota, was engulfed in a wave of lawsuits brought by operators who had lost fingers and hands in the punch presses it made. Its product liability insurance premiums, which were only $2,000 in 1970, doubled by 1974, and rose to $10,000 the next year. Its insurance company later canceled the policy. To replace the insurance would have cost $200,000, or 10 percent of the company's total sales. The company liquidated (Wysocki, 1976, p. 1).

Nor are small companies the only ones affected by the surge in litigation. In recent years, many product liability cases concern diseases resulting from the manufacture and installation of asbestos. In 1982, the nation's largest asbestos producer, the Manville Corporation, one of America's largest industrial companies, filed for bankruptcy to try to shake off more than 16,000 suits (and an anticipated 32,000 more) seeking $2 *billion* in damages (Feder, 1982, p. 1). More than 250 companies have been sued in connection with asbestos-related deaths and diseases, and the total sought is in the billions of dollars. One study predicted that employers of asbestos workers and their insurers may pay out between $38.2 billion to $92 billion in asbestos claims during the next three decades (Joseph, 1982, p. 40).

Although the debate has been heated and at times simplistic, in fact the problem of product liability is complex and most of us must regard it with a high degree of ambivalence. We are all consumers, after all, who profit greatly from living in an industrial society. Perhaps nothing illustrates this ambivalence more than the 1978 case in which a product liability defense attorney, a man who spent his professional life fighting plaintiffs who brought product liability suits against his corporate clients, sued Remington Arms Company, for paralysis resulting from an accident involving a Remington rifle during a hunting trip; the parties settled for $6.8 million, said at the time to be the largest lump-sum payment in a single personal injury case in our history (Geisel, 1978, p. 12).

In this chapter, we will examine in detail the legal theories that underlie product liability cases. In the typical product liability case, three legal theories are asserted—a contract theory and two tort theories. The contract theory is **warranty,** and the two tort theories are **strict liability** and **negligence** (see Figure 19-1). We cover them in turn in the sections that follow.

WARRANTIES

The Uniform Commercial Code (UCC) governs *express warranties* and various *implied warranties,* and until relatively recently it was the only statutory control on the use and meaning of warranties. In 1975, after years of debate, Congress passed and President Ford signed

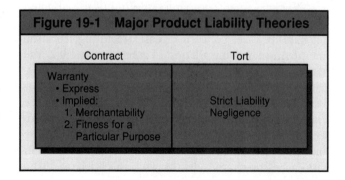

into law a federal statute, the Magnuson-Moss Act, which imposes certain requirements on manufacturers and others who warrant their goods. Our discussion of warranties will examine both the UCC and the Magnuson-Moss Act.

Express Warranty

An **express warranty** is created whenever the seller affirms that the product will have certain characteristics or will perform in a certain manner. Formal words such as "warrant" or "guarantee" are not necessary to create an express warranty. A seller may create an express warranty as part of the basis for the bargain of sale by means of (1) an affirmation of a fact or promise relating to the goods, (2) a description of the goods, or (3) a sample or model. Any of these will create an express warranty that the goods will conform to the fact, promise, description, sample, or model. Thus, a seller who stated "that the use of rustproof linings in the cans would prevent discoloration and adulteration of the Perform solution" has given an express warranty, whether he realized it or not. [Rhodes Pharmacal Co. v. Continental Can Co., 219 N.E.2d 726 (Ill. 1976)]

Nevertheless, the courts will not hold a manufacturer to every statement that could conceivably be interpreted as an express warranty. Manufacturers and sellers constantly "puff" their products, and the law is content to let them inhabit that fuzzy land without having to make good on every claim. Section 2-313(2) says that "an affirmation merely of the value of the goods or a statement purporting to be merely the seller's opinion or commendation of the goods does not create a warranty."

It is not always easy, however, to determine the line between an express warranty and a piece of puffery. A salesperson who says that a strawberry huller is "great" has probably puffed, not warranted, when it turns out that strawberries run through the huller look like victims of a massacre. But consider the classic cases of the defective used car and the faulty bull. In the former, the salesperson said the car was in "A-1 shape" and "mechanically perfect." In the latter, the seller said not only that the bull calf would "put the buyer on the map" but that "his father was the greatest living dairy bull." The car, carrying the buyer's seven-month-old child, broke down while the buyer was en route to visit her husband in the army during World War II. The court said that the salesperson had made an express warranty. [Wat Henry Pontiac Co. v. Bradley, 210 P.2d 348 (Okla. 1949)] The bull calf turned out to be sterile, putting the farmer on the judicial rather than the dairy map. The court said that the seller's spiel was trade talk, not a warranty that the bull would impregnate cows. [Frederickson v. Hackney, 198 N.W. 806 (Minn. 1924)]

Is there any qualitative difference between these decisions, other than the quarter century that separates them and the different courts that rendered them? Perhaps the most that can be said is that the more specific and measurable the statement's standards, the more likely it is that a court will hold the seller to a warranty; and that a written statement is easier to construe as a warranty than an oral one. It is also possible that courts look, if only subliminally, at how reasonable the buyer was in relying on the statement, although this ought not be the strict test. A buyer may be unreasonable in expecting a car to get 100 miles to the gallon, but if that is what the seller promised, that ought to be an enforceable warranty.

Implied Warranty

Express warranties are those over which the parties "dickered." They go to the essence of the bargain. An **implied warranty,** by contrast, is one that circumstances alone, not specific language, compel reading into the sale. In short, an implied warranty is one created by law, acting from an impulse of common sense.

Merchantability   Section 2-314 lays down the fundamental rule that goods carry an implied warranty of **merchantability** if sold by a merchant seller. What is merchantability? Section 2-314(2) says that merchantable goods are those that conform at least to the following six characteristics:

1. The trade or industry must not object to the goods being described in public as they are in the contract. Thus a microcomputer would not be merchantable under this provision if it were called a mainframe computer in the contract.
2. The goods must, if fungible, be of average quality for the type described.
3. They must be fit for ordinary purposes for which such goods are used. A steel kitchen knife that broke while being used to cut bread would not be merchantable.
4. Goods within a unit and among all units must be "of even kind, quality, and quantity," that is, must not vary too much in kind, quality, and quantity when sold in bulk.
5. They must be adequately contained, packaged, and labeled as the agreement may require.
6. They must conform to whatever factual statements are made on the container or label.

For purposes of Section 2-314 (2)(c), selling and serving food or drink for consumption on or off the premises is a sale subject to the implied warranty of merchantability—the food must be "fit for the ordinary purposes" to which it is put. The problem is common: you bite into a cherry pit in the cherry-vanilla ice cream and break a tooth, or you choke on the clam shells in the chowder. Is such food fit for the ordinary purposes to which it is put? There are two schools of thought. One asks whether the food was natural as prepared. This view adopts the seller's perspective. The other asks what the consumer's reasonable expectation was.

The first test is sometimes said to be the "natural-foreign" test. If the substance in the soup is natural to the substance—as bones are to fish—then the food is fit for consumption. The second test, relying on reasonable expectations, was followed by the court in the following opinion—although the dissenting judge questions the manner in which the test is applied.

KOPERWAS v. PUBLIX SUPERMARKETS, INC.
534 So.2d 872 (Fla.App. 3 Dist. 1988)

HELIO GOMEZ, ASSOCIATE JUDGE.

Plaintiff appeals from an adverse final judgment granting directed verdicts in favor of defendants in a personal injury action. We affirm.

Plaintiff, Tina Koperwas, purchased a can of Doxsee clam chowder at a Publix store. While eating the chowder, she injured one of her molars when she bit down on a piece of clam shell. Plaintiff filed an action against Publix and Doxsee for breach of implied warranty. In the complaint she alleged that the chowder "was not fit for use as food, but was defective, unwholesome and unfit for human consumption" and was in such a condition to be dangerous to life and health." At trial, the deposition of Doxsee's general manager was read into evidence, in which he described the "state of the art" methods Doxsee employed in manufacturing its clam chowder. At the close of plaintiff's case, the defendants moved for directed verdicts. Plaintiff argued that a jury should decide whether Doxsee used unreasonable care in the manufacture of the chowder. The trial judge disagreed and granted directed verdicts in favor of the defendants. Plaintiff now appeals.

One of the leading cases in Florida is *Zabner v. Howard Johnson's*, 201 So.2d 824 (Fla. 4th DCA 1967), which adopted the "reasonable expectation" test for determining liability. The *Zabner* court held that "[t]he question of whether food is fit for the purpose intended although it contains walnut shells or other substances must be based on what the consumer might reasonably expect to find in the food as served . . . and what is reasonably expected by a consumer is a jury question in most cases." "But where the evidence is such that all reasonable men in the exercise of an honest and impartial judgment must draw the conclusion that no breach of duty on the part of defendant[s] has been shown, it is not error to direct a verdict in defendant[s'] favor." *Messner v. Webb's City, Inc.*, 62 So.2d 66, 67 (Fla.1952).

The reasonable expectation test developed in *Zabner* supports the trial court's direction of verdicts for defendants. An occasional piece of clam shell in a bowl of clam chowder is so well known to a consumer of such product that we can say the consumer can reasonably anticipate and guard against it. *See Morrison's Cafeteria of Montgomery v. Haddox*, 431 So.2d 975 (Ala.1983) (consumer would reasonably expect to find a small bone in a fish fillet); *Webster v. Blue Ship Tea Room*, 198 N.E.2d 309 (1964) (plaintiffs should be prepared to cope with the hazards of occasional fish bones in chowder, the presence of which seems to be anticipated); *Allen v. Grafton*, 164 N.E.2d 167 (1960) (oyster shell attached to oyster can be reasonably anticipated and guarded against). Accordingly, the final judgment is affirmed.

AFFIRMED.

NESBITT, JUDGE (dissenting):

I respectfully dissent. The majority opinion purportedly follows the "reasonable expectation" test found in *Zabner v. Howard Johnson's*, 201 So.2d 824 (Fla. 4th DCA 1967), but in reality, applies the Massachusetts–New York rule (whereby the test is whether a substance found in a food rendered it unwholesome or unfit for consumption) as well as the "foreign/natural" test found in Ohio, Alabama, and other jurisdictions (whereby the test is whether the substance in the food which caused injury was foreign or natural to the food). The majority, thus, has unwittingly ruled in conflict with *Zabner* which rejected both those tests. I would follow *Zabner* and reverse. Simply because clams in their natural form come in shells does not necessarily lead one to the conclusion, as a matter of law, that a consumer of clam chowder should reasonably anticipate and guard against the presence of potentially injurious pieces of shell in the chowder he or she eats. Such is a question of fact to be determined by a jury.

Fitness for a Particular Purpose   Section 2-315 creates another implied warranty. Whenever a seller, at the time he contracts to make a sale, knows or has reason to know that the buyer is relying on the seller's skill or judgment to select a product that is suitable for the particular purpose the buyer has in mind for the goods to be sold, there is an implied warranty that the goods are fit for that purpose. You go to a hardware store and tell the salesclerk that you need a paint that will dry overnight because you are painting your front door and a thunderstorm is predicted for the next day. The clerk gives you an extremely sluggish oil-based paint that takes a week to dry. The store has breached an implied warranty of fitness.

Note the distinction between "particular" and "ordinary" purposes. Paint is made to color and when dry to protect a surface. That is its ordinary purpose, and had you said only that you wished to buy paint, no implied warranty of fitness would have been breached. It is only because you had a particular application in mind that the implied warranty arose. Suppose you had found a can of paint in a general store and told the same tale, but the proprietor had said, "I don't know anything about paint; help yourself." Not every seller has the requisite degree of skill or knowledge about every product he sells to give rise to an implied warranty. Ultimately, each case turns on its particular circumstances.

Other Warranties

Title   Article 2 contains other warranty provisions, though these do not relate specifically to product liability. Thus, under Section 2-312, unless he explicitly

excludes it, the seller warrants that he is conveying good title that is rightfully his and that the goods are transferred free of any security interest or other lien or encumbrance. In some sales (for example, a sheriff's auction), the buyer should know that the seller does not claim title in himself, nor that the title will necessarily be good as against a third party, and so subsection (2) excludes warranties in these circumstances. But the circumstances must be so obvious that no reasonable person would suppose otherwise.

In *Menzel* v. *List*, 246 N.E.2d 742 (N.Y. 1969), an art gallery in New York sold a painting by Marc Chagall that it purchased in Paris. Unfortunately, the painting had been stolen by the Germans when the original owner was forced to flee Belgium in the 1930s. Now in America, the original owner discovered that a new owner had the painting and successfully sued for its return. The customer sued the gallery, claiming that it had breached an implied warranty of title when it sold the Chagall. The court agreed and awarded damages equal to the appreciated value of the painting.

Infringement   A merchant seller warrants the goods are free of any rightful claim by a third person that the seller has infringed his rights (for example, that a gallery has not infringed a copyright in selling a reproduction). This provision applies only to a seller who regularly deals in goods of the kind in question. If you find an old print in your grandmother's attic, you do not warrant when you sell it to a neighbor that it is free of any valid infringement claims.

Other   Section 2-314(3) states that unless modified or excluded, other implied warranties may arise from a course of dealing or usage of trade. If a certain way of doing business is understood, it is not necessary for the seller to state explicitly that he will abide by the custom; it will be implied. A typical example is the obligation of a dog dealer to provide pedigree papers to prove that the dog's lineage conforms to the contract.

PROBLEMS WITH WARRANTY THEORY

It may seem that a consumer asserting a claim for breach of warranty will have a high chance of success under an express warranty or implied warranty theory of merchantability or fitness. In practice, however, consumers in many cases are denied recovery. As we saw in an earlier chapter in this unit, the consumer must prove that there was a sale and that the sale was of goods rather than real estate or services (see Chapter 16).

Moreover, the action must be brought within the time allowed by the four-year statute of limitations under UCC Article 2, rather than the longer statutes that often govern tort suits. And under Section 2-607(3)(a), the consumer who fails to give notice of breach within a reasonable time of acceptance will see his suit dismissed, and few consumers know enough to do so, except when making a complaint about a purchase of spoiled milk or about paint that wouldn't dry. In addition to these general problems, the consumer faces additional difficulties stemming directly from the warranty theory. We trace these difficulties immediately below.

Exclusion or Modification of Warranties

The UCC permits sellers to exclude or disclaim warranties in whole or in part.

Express Warranties   The simplest way for the seller to exclude express warranties is not to give them. To be sure, Section 2-316(1) forbids courts from giving operation to words in the fine print that negate or limit express warranties if doing so would unreasonably conflict with express warranties stated in the main body of the contract—as, for example, would a blanket statement that "this contract excludes all warran-

ties, express or implied." The purpose of this Code provision is to prevent consumers from being surprised by unbargained-for language.

Implied Warranties Generally   Implied warranties can be excluded easily enough also, by describing the product with language such as "as is" or "with all faults." Nor is exclusion simply a function of what the seller says. The buyer who has either examined or refused to examine the goods before entering the contract may not assert an implied warranty with regard to defects that the inspection would have revealed.

Implied Warranty of Merchantability   Section 2-316(2) permits the seller to disclaim or modify the implied warranty of merchantability, as long as the statement actually mentions merchantability and, if it is written, is "conspicuous." Note that the disclaimer need not be in writing.

Implied Warranty of Fitness   Section 2-316(2) permits the seller also to disclaim or modify an implied warranty of fitness. This disclaimer or modification must be in writing, however, and be conspicuous. It need not explicitly mention fitness; general language will do. The following sentence, for example, is sufficient to exclude all implied warranties of fitness: "There are no warranties which extend beyond the description on the face of this contract."

Here is a standard disclaimer clause found in a Dow Chemical Company agreement:

> Seller warrants that the goods supplied hereunder shall conform to the description stated on the front side hereof, that it will convey good title thereto and that such goods shall be delivered free from any lawful security interest or lien or encumbrance. SELLER MAKES NO WARRANTY OF MERCHANTABILITY OR FITNESS FOR A PARTICULAR USE. NOR IS THERE ANY OTHER EXPRESS OR IMPLIED WARRANTY.

Cumulation and Conflict   Express and implied warranties and their exclusion or limitation can often conflict. Section 2-317 provides certain rules for deciding which should prevail. In general, all warranties are to be construed as consistent with each other and as cumulative. When that assumption is unreasonable, the parties' intention governs the interpretation, according to the following rules: (a) exact or technical specifications outweigh inconsistent samples or general descriptive language; (b) a sample from an existing supply of the goods outweighs inconsistent general descriptive language; and (c) express warranties displace inconsistent implied warranties, with one exception. The exception is for an implied warranty of fitness for a particular purpose. Any inconsistency among warranties must always be resolved in favor of the implied warranty of fitness. This does not mean that the implied warranty of fitness cannot be limited or excluded altogether. The parties may do so. But in cases of doubt whether it or some other language applies, the implied warranty of fitness will have a superior claim.

The Magnuson-Moss Act and Phantom Warranties

Generally After years of debate over extending federal law to regulate warranties, Congress enacted the Magnuson-Moss Federal Trade Commission Improvement Act, and President Ford signed it into law on January 4, 1975. Its purposes were set forth by Senator Warren Magnuson in introducing the measure:

> [W]arranties have for many years confused, misled, and frequently angered American consumers. . . . Consumer anger is expected when purchasers of consumer products discover that their warranty may cover a 25-cent part but not the $100 labor charge or that there is full coverage on a piano so long as it is shipped at the purchaser's expense to the factory. . . .
>
> [T]he bill is designed to promote understanding. Far too frequently, there is a paucity of information supplied to the consumer about what in fact is offered him in that piece of paper proudly labeled "warranty." Many of the most important questions concerning the warranty are usually unanswered when there is some sort of product failure. Who should the consumer notify if his product stops working during the warranty period? What are his responsibilities after notification? How soon can he expect a fair replacement? Will repair or replacement cost him anything? There is a growing need to generate consumer understanding by clearly and conspicuously disclosing the terms and conditions of the warranty and by telling the consumer what to do if his guaranteed product becomes defective or malfunctions.

To meet these concerns, the Magnuson-Moss Act contains a variety of provisions regulating the content of warranties and the means of disclosing those contents. The act gives the Federal Trade Commission the authority to promulgate detailed regulations to interpret and enforce it.

Contents The act does not require sellers to give express warranties. The decision to offer a warranty is solely within the discretion of the seller, motivated by competitive factors. But if a seller does offer a written warranty to a consumer covering a "consumer product," the warranty must clearly and conspicuously disclose certain items. Before looking at those items, note that the act applies only to "consumers," not to every potential buyer. A consumer is defined as a buyer of a consumer product who does not use it for resale or in the ordinary course of his business, or a person to whom the buyer transferred the product (for example, to a member of his family). "Consumer product" means any tangible personal property distributed in commerce and normally used for personal, family, or household purposes. Products purchased solely for commercial or industrial use are excluded.

The FTC regulations require that any written warranty for a product actually costing a consumer more than $10 must disclose in a single document and, in readily understood language, the following nine items of information:

1. the identity of the people to whom the warranty is extended, if the warrantor intends to limit the warranty to the original purchaser or fewer than all who might come to own the product during the warranty period;
2. a clear description of products, parts, characteristics, components, or properties covered and, where necessary for clarity, a description of what is excluded;
3. a statement of what the warrantor will do in the event of a defect or a failure to conform to the warranty, including items or services the warrantor will pay for and, if necessary for clarity, those which he will not pay for;
4. a statement of when the warranty period begins and how long it runs;
5. a step-by-step explanation of what the consumer must do to get satisfaction under the warranty,

including names and addresses of those to whom the consumer must bring the product;

6. instructions to the consumer on how he can avail himself of any informal dispute settlement mechanism established by the warrantor;

7. any limitations on the duration of implied warranties—since some states do not permit such limitations, the warranty must contain a statement that says that any limitation given may not apply to the particular consumer;

8. any limitations or exclusions on relief, such as consequential damages—as above, the warranty must contain a statement explaining that some states do not permit such limitations;

9. the following statement: "This warranty gives you specific legal rights, and you may also have other rights which vary from state to state."

In addition to these requirements, the act requires that the warranty be labeled either *full* or *limited*. A **"full" warranty** means that (1) the defective product or part will be fixed or replaced free, including removal and reinstallation if necessary, (2) it will be fixed within a reasonable time after the consumer complains, (3) the consumer need do nothing unreasonable (like shipping a piano to the factory) to get warranty service, (4) the warranty is good for anyone who owns the product during the warranty period, and (5) the consumer gets his money back or a new product if the defective product cannot be fixed within a reasonable number of attempts. Despite this seeming all-inclusiveness, a full warranty need not cover the whole product; a full warranty may cover only the picture tube in the television set, for example. Of course, it must state what parts are included and excluded. A **"limited" warranty** is less inclusive. It may cover the cost of only parts, not labor; it may require the consumer to bring the product in to the store for service; it may impose a charge for handling; it may cover only the first purchaser. Both full and limited warranties may exclude consequential damages.

Disclosure   The FTC regulations require the warrantor to make the provisions of the warranty available prior to sale; this can be done in various ways. The text of the written warranty can be attached to the product or placed "in close conjunction" to it. It can be maintained in a binder kept in each department or otherwise easily accessible to the consumer. The binders must either be in plain sight or signs must be posted to call the prospective buyer's attention to them. A notice containing the text of the warranty can be posted. Or the warranty itself can be printed on the product's package or container.

Phantom Warranties   As we have seen, the UCC permits the seller to disclaim implied warranties. This authority often led sellers to give what were called "phantom warranties," that is, limited express warranties that contained disclaimers of implied warranties, thus leaving the consumer with fewer rights than if no express warranty had been given at all. In the words of the legislative report on the Magnuson-Moss Act, "The bold print giveth and the fine print taketh away." The act abolished these phantom warranties by providing that if the seller gives a written warranty, whether full or limited, he cannot disclaim or modify implied warranties. However, a seller who gives a limited warranty can limit implied warranties to the duration of the limited warranty, if the duration is reasonable.

A seller's ability to disclaim implied warranties is also limited by state law in two ways. First, a few states prohibit disclaimers whenever consumer products are sold. Second, in all states a disclaimer that is unconscionable is not allowed. (Unconscionability is discussed in Chapter 16.)

Privity

If one of the problems with warranty law is the degree to which sellers can disclaim or modify, another equally serious difficulty is the doctrine of **privity**. Privity is the legal term for the direct connection between the seller and buyer, the two contracting parties. For decades, the doctrine of privity has held that one party can have legal recourse against another only if they are in privity. But in a modern industrial economy, the product is transported through a much larger chain, as depicted in Figure 19-2. Two questions arise: (1) Is the manufacturer or wholesaler liable to the buyer under warranty theory? (2) May the buyer's family or friends assert warranty rights?

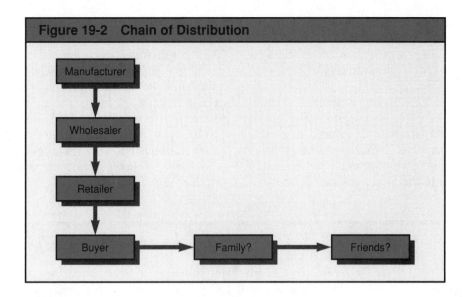

Figure 19-2   Chain of Distribution

Liability to Buyer   As just noted, the traditional rule is that remote parties are not liable; the lack of privity is a defense to a suit by a remote buyer or transferee against a remote seller. The buyer may recover damages from the retailer but not from the original manufacturer, who after all made the product and who may be much more able financially to honor the warranty. Over the past few years, however, the judicial trend has been to abolish the privity requirement. Some courts had made exceptions to the privity rule for defective foodstuffs and cosmetics that caused injury. But the fundamental shift toward abolishing the privity requirement in cases involving all products began in 1958, when the Michigan Supreme Court overturned the old theory in an opinion by Justice John D. Voelker (who also wrote the novel *Anatomy of a Murder*, under the pen name Robert Traver). [Spence v. Three Rivers Builders & Masonry Supply, Inc., 90 N.W.2d 873 (Mich. 1958)]

Despite the clear trend toward the abolition of the privity rule in warranty cases involving personal injury, privity remains a problem for the plaintiff. For example, if a purchaser suffers an economic loss (that is, lost profits as opposed to a claim based on personal injury or property damage) and sues a remote seller on an implied warranty theory, most courts hold that privity remains a defense.

Suppose the buyer, anticipating these difficul-ties, chooses to sue only the immediate seller. What recourse does the retailer, say, have against the manufacturer? Under Section 2-607(5)(a), any buyer whose seller is answerable to him for a breach of warranty (as the selling manufacturer would be answerable for breach of an implied warranty to a buying retailer) can send a notice of the suit to the seller and request that he join in the defense. This is known as "vouching in" the manufacturer or other prior seller.

Another way that retailers can be indemnified in the event that they are sued is by requiring manufacturers whose products the stores carry to sign a "vendor's broad form." This is an indemnification agreement that obligates the manufacturer to reimburse the retailer for any damages the retailer suffers in a product liability lawsuit over the manufacturer's product, as long as the store did not physically damage or alter the product.

Liability Beyond the Buyer   May the buyer's family or friends, who have not contracted with the sellers, assert warranty rights? In one of its rare instances of non-uniformity, the UCC does not dictate the result, but gives the states three choices, labeled in Section 2-318 as Alternatives A, B, and C.

Alternative A says that a seller's warranty extends "to any natural person who is in the family or household of his buyer or who is a guest in his home."

The only limitations on the seller's liability under Alternative A are these: (1) it must be reasonable to expect the person injured to use, consume, or be affected by the goods, and (2) the warranty extends only to personal injury.

Alternative B "extends to any natural person who may reasonably be expected to use, consume, or be affected by the goods, and who is injured in person by breach of the warranty." It is less restrictive than the first alternative in that it extends protection to people beyond those in the buyer's home. It does not extend protection to organizations; "natural person" refers to individuals.

Alternative C is identical to Alternative B, except that it applies not merely to any "natural person" but "to any person who is injured by breach of the warranty." This is the most liberal alternative, because it provides redress for damage to *property* as well as for *personal* injury and it extends protection to corporations and other institutional buyers.

In the following case the court interprets Alternative A.

GOWEN v. CADY
376 S.E.2d 390 (Ga.App. 1988)

SOGNIER, JUDGE.

Wanda Cady brought suit against James F. Gowen, M.D., Cryomedics, Inc. f/k/a/ Colmed, Ltd., and numerous others seeking damages stemming from her pregnancy after undergoing a voluntary sterilization procedure performed by Gowen using Bleier clips manufactured by Cryomedics. Her husband, Thomas Cady, joined her suit seeking damages for loss of consortium. . . .

*　　*　　*

The Cadys appeal from the trial court's grant of summary judgment in favor of Cryomedics. Although Mrs. Cady's action against Cryomedics (and Mr. Cady's claim for loss of consortium deriving from his wife's injuries) was originally based on theories of negligence, negligence per se, strict liability and breach of warranty, the Cadys acknowledge in their brief before this court that the only viable claim remaining on which the trial court ruled was the breach of warranty claim and it is the only claim now before this court. As to that claim, Mrs. Cady alleged in the complaint that Cryomedics was liable to her as a result of its action in selling, distributing, and introducing into the stream of commerce the Bleier clip, a device which she alleged was "defective and unfit for the purpose intended." However, the complaint contains the admission, neither amended nor withdrawn, that Cryomedics did not sell the Bleier clip to her but rather sold it to the Glynn–Brunswick Memorial Hospital Authority, which in turn sold the clip to Mrs. Cady.

" 'Generally, before a recovery may be had for breach of warranty, this state has recognized the necessity of privity between the parties where a plaintiff-purchaser of an article has been injured because of its alleged defectiveness and brings an action based on warranty. That is, if a defendant is not the seller to the plaintiff-purchaser, the plaintiff as the ultimate purchaser cannot recover on the implied or express warranty, if any, arising out of the prior sale by the defendant to the original purchaser, such as distributor or retailer from whom plaintiff purchased the product. *Thomaston v. Ft. Wayne Pools*, 352 S.E.2d 794 (1987). The evidence of record is

uncontroverted that Cryomedics did not sell the Bleir clip in question to Mrs. Cady. "Nothing contained in OCGA § 11-2-318, which extends the seller's warranties to family members and guests in the buyer's home who may reasonably be expected to use the product and who are injured thereby, eliminates the requirement that the buyer and the defendant be in privity." Id. We therefore find no error in the trial court's grant of summary judgment in favor of Cryomedics on the Cadys' claim based on breach of warranty.
JUDGMENT AFFIRMED.

Contributory Negligence, Comparative Negligence, and Assumption of Risk

Three common-law concepts remain as possible impediments to the contract-based warranty theories: *assumption of risk, contributory negligence,* and *comparative negligence.* These are discussed in Chapter 4.

Courts uniformly hold that assumption of risk is a defense for sellers against a claim of breach of warranty, while there is a split of authority over whether comparative and contributory negligence are defenses. However, the courts' use of this terminology is often conflicting and confusing. The ultimate question is really one of causation: Was the seller's breach of the warranty the cause of the plaintiff's injuries?

The UCC is not markedly helpful in clearing away the cobwebs strewn about over the years by discussions of assumption of risk and contributory negligence. Section 2-715(2)(b) says that among the forms of consequential damage for which recovery can be sought is "injury to person or property *proximately* resulting from any breach of warranty" (emphasis added). But "proximately" is a troublesome word. Indeed, ultimately it is a circular word, for it means nothing more than that the defendant must have been a direct enough cause of the injury that the courts will impose liability. Comment 5 to this section says that

[w]here the injury involved follows the use of goods without discovery of the defect causing the damage, the question of "proximate" cause turns on whether it was reasonable for the buyer to use the goods without such inspection as would have revealed the defects. If it was not reasonable for him to do so, or if he did in fact discover the defect prior to his use, the injury would not proximately result from the breach of warranty.

Obviously if a sky-diver buys a parachute and then discovers a few holes in it, his family would not likely prevail in court when they sued to recover for his death because the parachute failed to function after he jumped at 5,000 feet. But the general notion that it must have been reasonable for a buyer to use goods without inspection can make a warranty case difficult to prove.

STRICT LIABILITY IN TORT

The warranties grounded in the UCC often are ineffective in assuring recoveries for a plaintiff's injuries. The notice requirement and the ability of a seller to disclaim remain especially bothersome problems, as does the privity requirement in those states that continue to adhere to it (see Figure 19-3). To overcome the obstacles, judges have gone beyond the commercial statutes. They have fashioned a tort theory of product liability based on the principle of **strict liability.**

Defined

The formulation of strict liability that most courts use is Section 402A of the *Restatement of Torts, Second,* set out in full as follows:

1. One who sells any product in a defective condition unreasonably dangerous to the user or consumer or to his property is subject to liability for physical harm thereby caused to the ultimate user or consumer, or to his property, if
   (a) the seller is engaged in the business of selling such a product, and
   (b) it is expected to and does reach the user or

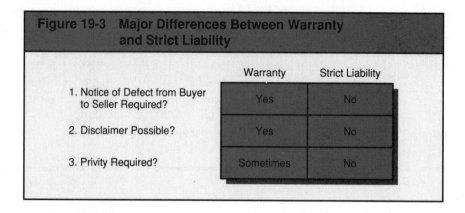

Figure 19-3   Major Differences Between Warranty and Strict Liability

	Warranty	Strict Liability
1. Notice of Defect from Buyer to Seller Required?	Yes	No
2. Disclaimer Possible?	Yes	No
3. Privity Required?	Sometimes	No

consumer without substantial change in the condition in which it is sold.

2. The rule stated in Subsection (1) applies although
   (a) the seller has exercised all possible care in the preparation and sale of his product, and
   (b) the user or consumer has not bought the product from or entered into any contractual relation with the seller.

Restatement Section 402A avoids the warranty booby traps. It states a rule of law not governed by the UCC, and so limitations and exclusions in warranties will not apply to a suit based on the Restatement theory. Nor is privity a requirement; Section 402A is not limited to buyer and seller. And the consumer is under no obligation to give notice to the seller within a reasonable time of any injuries. The above formulation of strict liability, however, is limited to physical harm. Many courts have held that a person who suffers economic loss must resort to warranty law.

Note that the *Restatement of Torts, Second,* is not a statute like the UCC. It is a private, model code of law, a statement of what the American Law Institute, a private body of lawyers and judges, thinks the law should be. Although courts in most states have adopted the concept of strict liability embodied in Section 402A, many courts depart from some of its specific elements to a consideration of which we now turn.

Section 402A Elements

"One Who Sells Any Product in a Defective Condition"   As under the UCC, sales of goods are covered but not sales of services. Furthermore, the plaintiff will not prevail if the product was safe for normal handling and consumption when sold. A glass soda bottle that is properly capped is not in a defective condition merely because it can be broken if the consumer should happen to drop it, making the jagged glass dangerous. Chocolate candy bars are not defective merely because you can become quite ill by eating too many of them at once. On the other hand, a seller would be liable for a product defectively packaged, so that it could explode or deteriorate and change its chemical composition. A product can also be in a defective condition if there is danger that could come from an anticipated wrongful use, such as a drug safe only when taken in limited doses. Under those circumstances, failure to place an adequate dosage warning on the container makes the product defective.

The plaintiff bears the burden of proving that the product is in a defective condition, and this burden can be difficult to meet. Many products are the result of complex feats of engineering. Expert witnesses are necessary to prove that the products were defectively manufactured, and these are not always easy to come by. This difficulty of proof is one reason why many cases raise the failure to warn as the dispositive issue, since in the right case that issue is far easier to prove.

As the following case demonstrates, the plaintiff cannot prevail under the theory of strict liability simply because he was injured. It is not the fact of injury that is determinative but the defective condition of the product.

ANDERSON v. ASSOCIATED GROCERS, INC.
11 Wash.App. 74, 525 P.2d 284 (1974)

GREEN, CHIEF JUDGE. Plaintiff appeals from an order granting summary judgment of dismissal in favor of the defendant, Associated Grocers, Inc. The propriety of this order presents the sole question on appeal.

Shortly after 8 a.m. on July 23, 1970, Associated Grocers delivered a pallet of produce to the back room of the Thriftway Market in Pasco. On top of the stack of produce was one cardboard box of Chiquita brand bananas. The bananas were unwrapped and the box contained breather holes. Later that morning, Tom Anderson, the produce manager, removed the box of bananas from the top of the stack. When he reached for a lug of radishes that had been under the bananas, a spider, identified as Heteropoda Venatoria, commonly called a banana spider, 6 inches in diameter, leaped from some wet burlap onto his left hand and bit him. Nine months later, April 24, 1971, Tom Anderson died of heart failure.

His wife, Johnnie Anderson, as administratrix of her husband's estate, brought this action to recover damages for the alleged wrongful death of her husband. The action is grounded upon three theories: (1) strict liability for a defect in product under Restatement (Second) of Torts § 402A (1965); (2) breach of implied warranty of merchantability and fitness based upon RCW 62A.2-314; and (3) negligence. In granting summary judgment for Associated Grocers, the trial court rejected the first two theories and found no evidence to support an issue of fact as to negligence.

On appeal, error is assigned to the granting of summary judgment in favor of defendant rather than plaintiff on the first two theories. No error having been assigned to the granting of summary judgment on the negligence theory, it is not before us.

With respect to the other two theories, plaintiff contends that the bananas delivered to the Pasco Thriftway and handled by her deceased husband were defective and thereby unfit for the ordinary purpose for which the bananas were to be used. The trial court rejected this contention because there was no showing that the bananas were in any way defective or unfit for the purpose intended. The court noted that the spider was not in the bananas nor the container, and ruled that although the container may have transported the spider, the product was not defective or unfit. We affirm.

Section 402A of the Restatement of Torts, as well as RCW 62A.2-314, and the cases cited to us by plaintiff, involve defects in the product itself. None involve transient insects or spiders. In the instant case, the spider was not in the bananas, but was on a piece of wet burlap on top of a box of radishes. There was nothing wrong with the bananas; they were edible and saleable. In these circumstances, neither the doctrine of strict liability nor breach of implied warranty of fitness applies.

Affirmed.

"Unreasonably Dangerous"   The requirement that the product be "unreasonably dangerous" has been especially troublesome. The product must be not merely dangerous, but *unreasonably* dangerous. Most products have characteristics that make them dangerous in certain circumstances. As the Restatement

commentators note, sugar is not inherently dangerous but is deadly to diabetics, and all food and drugs pose some danger, if only from overconsumption. Under Section 402A, "the article sold must be dangerous to an extent beyond that which would be contemplated by the ordinary consumer who purchases it, with the ordinary knowledge common to the community as to its characteristics." This definition is, of course, slippery. The commentator argues that "good tobacco is not unreasonably dangerous merely because the effects of smoking may be harmful," but perhaps some day, when the evidence matures on the causal connection to cancer, it will be held to be unreasonably dangerous.

Even high risks of danger are not necessarily unreasonable. Some products are unavoidably unsafe, as for example rabies vaccine, which can cause dreadful side effects. But the disease itself, almost always fatal, is worse. A product is unavoidably unsafe when it cannot be made safe for its intended purpose given the present state of human knowledge. Because important benefits may flow from the product's use, its producer or seller ought not be held liable for its danger.

However, the failure to *warn* a potential user of potential hazards can make a product defective under Section 402A, whether unreasonably dangerous or even unavoidably unsafe. The dairy farmer need not warn those with common allergies to eggs, because it will be presumed that the person with an allergic reaction to common foodstuffs will be aware of them. But when the product contains an ingredient that could cause toxic effects in a substantial number of people and its danger is not widely known (or if known, is not an ingredient that would commonly be supposed to be in the product), the lack of a warning could make the product unreasonably dangerous within the meaning of Section 402A. Many of the suits brought by asbestos workers charge exactly this point: "The utility of an insulation product containing asbestos may outweigh the known or foreseeable risk to the insulation workers and thus justify its marketing. The product could still be unreasonably dangerous, however, if unaccompanied by adequate warnings. An insulation worker, no less than any other product user, has a right to decide whether to expose himself to the risk." [Circuit Judge John Minor Wisdom, in Borel v. Fibreboard Paper Products Corp., 493 F.2d 1076 (5th Cir. 1973).] This rule of law has lately come to haunt the Manville Corporation and other producers of asbestos.

"Engaged in the Business of Selling" Section 402A(1)(a) limits liability to sellers "engaged in the business of selling such a product." The rule is intended to apply to people and entities engaged in *business*, not to casual one-time sellers. The business need not be solely in the defective product; a movie theater that sells popcorn with a razor blade inside is no less liable than a grocery store that does so. But strict liability under this rule does not attach to a private individual who sells his own automobile. In this sense, Section 402A is analogous to the UCC's limitation of the warranty of merchantability to the merchant.

The requirement that the defendant be in the business of selling stems in part from a public policy that the courts often articulate: Businesses should shoulder the cost of injuries because they are in the best position to spread the risk and distribute the expense among the public. See **Box 19-1.** A dramatic example of how judgments are ultimately assessed against the buying public came in the wake of a $5.3 million judgment against Riddell, Inc., the leading manufacturer of football helmets, in a suit brought by a high school football player who charged that a defective Riddell helmet left him paralyzed when a blow to the back of his neck severed his spinal cord. Riddell's annual product liability insurance premiums had been $40,000; three years after Riddell lost the case, its premiums had shot up to $1.5 million, or about 10 percent of its annual sales of $15 million. The premiums were said to add about $7 to the price of a $35 helmet. This same policy has been the rationale for holding bailors and lessors liable for defective equipment just as if they had been sellers, as the *Martin v. Ryder Rental, Inc.* case (p. 433) illustrates.

Reaches the User Without Change in Condition Section 402A(1)(b) limits strict liability to those defective products that are expected to and do reach the user or consumer without substantial change in the condition in which sold. A product safe when delivered cannot subject the seller to liability if it is subsequently mishandled or changed. The seller, however, must anticipate in appropriate cases that the product

Legal Mayhem

By Ronald Bailey

[Some believe that tort liability has caused the legal system to spin out of control. Already a factor in the increasing cost of living, tort liability represents a system that often compensates victims no matter who is at fault. Courts view business as vehicles for spreading risk among the public.—AUTHORS' NOTE]

WITHOUT BENEFIT of legislation or the vote of the American people, a hidden tax is levied on virtually everything we buy, sell and use. This tax costs American companies, individuals and local governments at least $80 billion a year, and some estimate as much as $300 billion. It accounts for 30% of the price of a stepladder and for over 95% of the price of childhood vaccines. One-quarter of the price of a ticket on a Long Island, N.Y. tour bus and one-third of the price of a small airplane goes to pay this tax. . . .

What is this tax? It is called tort liability.

To get a sense of the magnitude of the tax, just take a look at a few recent court cases: A jury awards $986,000 to a woman who claims she lost her psychic powers after a CAT scan; an occupant of a telephone booth crashed into by a drunk driver collects from the booth manufacturer.

FORBES has often lamented the costs to the U.S. economy of the current explosion of such cases. Now a remarkable new book, *Liability: The Legal Revolution and Its Consequences* (Basic Books, $19.95), cites some hair-raising examples of a legal system spinning dangerously out of control.

THE TORT TAX

The author, Peter Huber, brings broad credentials to the subject: He has a Ph.D. in mechanical engineering from MIT and a law degree from Harvard, and he is now a senior fellow of the Manhattan Institute, a public policy think tank.

His book shows convincingly how the expanding tort liability system is raising the cost of living and, even worse, is threatening our international competitiveness.

In the wonderful world of tort liability, old-fashioned notions of "cause" and "fault" and "contracts" have been tossed out in favor of a system that seeks to compensate victims, regardless of who is at fault, and that allocates funds from those who have them (corporations and insurers) to those who supposedly need them—and to their lawyers. In leaning toward "deep pocket" liability, U.S. courts have adopted a version of the old Marxist slogan, "From each according to his ability, to each according to his need."

Who created this mess? Who loaded such taxes on Americans?

Huber lays the blame directly on a small, but very influential, coterie of legal academicians and judges who have for 30 years been transforming traditional tort liability into the giant social lottery scheme of today. The ticket to the lottery is an injury, real or imagined. This seems a poor way to run a lottery.

Huber points the finger of blame at specific individuals. There are California Supreme Court Justice Roger Traynor and Guido Calabresi, dean of the Yale Law School. These and like-minded people, he says, impatiently

swept away a common law tradition that focused on the sanctity of contracts and their allocation of risk between buyers and sellers.

As a consequence of their presumed good intentions, courts are no longer just a forum for determining legal injury and assigning liability; they now function as middlemen disbursing insurance payments to victims.

However much fun this lottery may be for the attorneys, society is paying a price far beyond the mere dollar value of the awards and the attendant increase in insurance costs. We now have a system that adds enormous uncertainty to nearly any business decision. Writes Huber: "One thing is certain: Whether or not we stand paralyzed in the grip of tort liability, other countries around the world will not. Legal structures that promote friction and conflict among Americans most certainly also undermine our ability to compete against others."

Why does the "tort tax" add billions to the price tags of American goods sold abroad? Because every product includes the prospective costs of tort liability. In addition, U.S. tort law hampers American companies competing against foreign corporations in our domestic markets. How? Since U.S. liability costs constitute such a large portion of the overhead of new, innovative technologies, foreigners can develop their products abroad without being weighed down by this element of overhead, and then can enter the U.S. market after courts have sorted out the liability issues among American manufacturers.

U.S. research and development has been slowed, if not halted, in many areas where once we were the

(continued on next page)

BOX 19-1

Box 19-1, continued
world's leaders. For example, between 1965 and 1985 the number of vaccine manufacturers declined by more than half, and by 1986 there was only a single supplier for vaccines against polio, rubella, measles, mumps and rabies. Some universities refuse to license patents to small companies, fearing that plaintiffs suing over a patent-related product would also

reach for the deeper pockets of the university. Product development in the small aircraft and reproductive technologies industries has been dramatically slowed.

Huber: "Across the board, modern tort law weighs heavily on the spirit of innovation and enterprise. . . . Under jury pressure, the new touchstones of technological legitimacy have become age, familiarity and

ubiquity. It is the innovative and unfamiliar that is most likely to be condemned." Last year in FORBES, Huber doubted whether, under present conditions of product liability, Henry Ford would ever have been able to bring out the Model T or the Wright brothers to get off the ground.

Source: *Forbes*, November 14, 1988

---

will be stored; faulty packaging or sterilization may be the grounds for liability if the product deteriorates before being used.

Liability Despite Exercise of All Due Care   Strict liability applies under the Restatement rule even though "the seller has exercised all possible care in the preparation and sale of his product." This is the crux of "strict liability" and distinguishes it from the conventional theory of negligence. It does not matter how reasonably the seller acted or how exemplary is a manufacturer's quality control system—what matters is whether the product was defective and the user injured as a result. Suppose an automated bottle-factory manufactures 1,000 bottles an hour under exacting standards, with a rigorous and costly quality-control program designed to weed out any bottles showing even an infinitesimal amount of stress. The plant is "state of the art," and its computerized quality-control operation is the best in the world. It regularly detects the one out of every 10,000 bottles that analysis has shown will be defective. Despite this intense effort, it proves impossible to weed out every defective bottle; one out of one million, say, will still escape detection. Assume that that bottle, filled with soda, finds its way into a consumer's home, explodes when handled, sends glass shards into his eye, and

blinds him. Under strict liability, the bottler will be liable to the consumer.

Liability Without Contractual Relation   Under Section 402A(2)(b), strict liability applies even though the user has not bought the product from the seller nor entered into any contractual relation with him. In short, privity is abolished and the injured user may use the theory of strict liability against manufacturers and wholesalers as well as retailers. Here, however, the courts have announced certain limitations to the abolition of privity. For example, in some states the rule of privity still applies to bystanders. Suppose the brakes in a car are defective, and they fail while the owner is driving the car downtown. He hits a pedestrian, who sues the automobile manufacturer. Some state courts will not hold the manufacturer liable on the grounds of strict liability; the pedestrian will have to show that the manufacturer was negligent, that is, was careless in installing the brake system. The Restatement explicitly leaves open the question of the bystander's right to recover under strict liability.

The following case shows how one court tackled this question and approved the application of strict liability against a bailor truck-rental agency when a bystander was injured because of faulty brakes.

MARTIN v. RYDER TRUCK RENTAL, INC.
353 A.2d 581 (Del. 1976)

HERRMANN, CHIEF JUSTICE.

A truck was leased by the defendant, Ryder Truck Rental, Inc., to Gagliardi Brothers, Inc., in the regular course of Ryder's truck rental business. The truck, operated by a Gagliardi employee, was involved in an intersectional collision. Due to a failure of its braking system, the truck did not stop for a traffic light and struck the rear of an automobile which had stopped for the signal, causing that automobile to collide with the vehicle driven by the plaintiff, Dorothy Martin. As a result, she was injured, her car was damaged, and this suit was brought by her and her husband against Ryder.

The plaintiffs base their cause of action solely upon the doctrine of strict tort liability, *i.e.*, tort liability without proof of negligence. The Superior Court granted summary judgment in favor of Ryder, holding that the doctrine is not applicable to the factual situation here presented. We disagree.

*   *   *

Strict tort liability in the field of products liability has developed in a "step by step" process out of the law of contract warranty into the law of tort, for the purpose of the greater protection of the user and the public against defective goods by eliminating the "luggage" and "undesirable complications" of the contract-warranty remedy in direct sales transactions, such as the requirement of a sale and notice, and the provision for limitation and disclaimer, generally prescribed by the Uniform Sales Act and the UCC.

At the forefront of this development was the landmark case of *Henningsen v. Bloomfield Motors, Inc.*, 161 A.2d 69 (1960), which brought a "breakthrough" in extending strict warranty liability to products other than food and drink.

The first significant application of the strict tort liability concept in a products liability case was the landmark decision of *Greenman* v. *Yuba Power Products, Inc.*, 59 Cal.2d 57, 27 Cal. Rptr. 697, 377 P.2d 897 (1963), termed "certainly the most important decision since *Henningsen* and perhaps the most important since *MacPherson* v. *Buick* [111 N.E. 1050 (1916)]." 2 Frumer & Friedman § 16A[1], at 3-238. The defendant remote-manufacturer there sought to avoid liability for breach of warranty on a defective power tool on the ground that reasonable notice of the breach had not been given under the notice requirements of the California Sales Act governing contract warranties. The Court held otherwise, stating:

> A manufacturer is strictly liable in tort when an article he places on the market, knowing that it is to be used without inspection for defects, proves to have a defect that causes injury to a human being. . . .
>
> Although . . . strict liability has usually been based on the theory of an express or implied warranty running from the manufacturer to the plaintiff, . . . the liability is not one governed by the law of contract warranties but by the law of strict liability in tort. Accordingly, rules defining and governing warranties that were developed to meet the needs of commercial transactions cannot properly be invoked to govern the manufacturer's liability to

(continued on next page)

(continued)

MARTIN v. RYDER TRUCK RENTAL, INC.
353 A.2d 581 (Del. 1976)

those injured by their defective products unless those rules also serve the purposes for which such liability is imposed.

. . . The purpose of such liability is to insure that the costs of injuries resulting from defective products are borne by the manufacturers that put such products on the market rather than by the injured persons who are powerless to protect themselves. Sales warranties serve this purpose fitfully at best. . . .

Influenced, as were other courts, by *Yuba's* reasoning, the Supreme Court of New Jersey in 1965 abandoned the warranty terminology of *Henningsen* and embraced strict tort liability in *Santor* v. *A. and M. Karagheusian, Inc.,* 207 A.2d 305 (1965).

★   ★   ★

Since *Yuba* and *Santor*, the doctrine of strict tort liability has met with widespread acceptance throughout the country. Consequently, in the past decade, the protection afforded to a person injured by a defective product has been greatly enhanced by the steady and consistent expansion of the concept. The doctrine was developed at the outset for application against remote manufacturers for the protection of users and consumers. It has been in a constant state of refinement and extension, however. One of the extensions of the doctrine has been to bailors and lessors; another has been to injured bystanders. Once again, the leading decisions emanate from California and New Jersey.

In *Cintrone* v. *Hertz Truck Leasing, etc.,* 212 A.2d 769 (1969), the New Jersey Supreme Court applied strict liability in tort to a motor vehicle bailment situation because "[a] bailor for hire, such as a person in the U-drive-it business, puts motor vehicles in the stream of commerce in a fashion not unlike a manufacturer or retailer"; subjects such a leased vehicle "to more sustained use on the highways than most ordinary car purchasers"; and by the very nature of his business, exposes "the bailee, his employees, passengers and the traveling public . . . to a greater *quantum* of potential danger of harm from defective vehicles than usually arises out of sales by the manufacturer."

★   ★   ★

The remaining question is whether the doctrine is applicable to the case of an injured bystander.

The doctrine of strict liability in tort has been extended to injured bystanders. We endorse the rationale of *Elmore* v. *American Motors Corporation,* 451 P.2d 84 (1969):

> If anything, bystanders should be entitled to greater protection than the consumer or user where injury to bystanders from the defect is reasonably foreseeable. Consumers and users, at least, have the opportunity to inspect for defects, . . . whereas the bystander ordinarily has no such opportunities.

In short, the bystander is in greater need of protection from defective products which are dangerous, and if any distinction should be made between bystanders and users, it should be made . . . to extend greater liability in favor of the bystanders. 75 Cal.Rptr. at 657, 451 P.2d at 89.

Bystander recovery is the prevailing rule in the application of the doctrine of strict tort liability by the overwhelming weight of authority. Fairness and logic, as well as the philosophy underlying the doctrine, require that an injured bystander be covered in its application. We so hold.

[Judgment reversed.]

NEGLIGENCE

Negligence is the third theory raised in the typical product liability case. Like strict liability, it is a tort theory. We considered negligence in detail in Chapter 4. The principles discussed in that chapter apply equally in a product liability case. One question, however, should be addressed here: Why should plaintiffs bother with the negligence theory when they can use strict liability, where sellers are liable even though they have taken all possible care? The answer lies in two types of cases: those in which plaintiffs charge that the *design* of a product is defective, and those in which they charge inadequate *warnings*.

Design Cases

Manufacturers can be, and often are, held liable for injuries caused by products that were defectively designed. Although these cases are sometimes taken to be illustrations of strict liability theory, in fact most ultimately turn on the question of whether the designer used reasonable care in designing a product reasonably safe for its foreseeable use. The concern over reasonableness and standards of care are elements of negligence theory.

Design cases can pose severe problems for manufacturing and safety engineers, as the case outlined in **Box 19-2** suggests. More safety means more cost. The altered design may impair the performance of the product and make it less desirable to consumers. At what point safety comes into reasonable balance with performance, cost, and desirability (see Figure

19-4) is impossible to forecast accurately, though some factors can be taken into account. For example, if other manufacturers are marketing comparable products whose designs are intrinsically safer, the less-safe products are likely to lose a test of reasonableness in court.

Warning Cases

We noted above that a product may be defective if the manufacturer fails adequately to warn the user of potential dangers. Whether a warning should have been affixed is often a question of what is reasonably foreseeable, and the failure to affix a warning will be treated as negligent. The manufacturer of a weed killer with poisonous ingredients is certainly acting negligently when it fails to warn the consumer that the contents are potentially lethal.

The law governing the necessity to warn and the adequacy of the warnings is complex. What is reasonable turns on the degree to which a product is likely to be misused and, as the *Laaperi* case illustrates, whether the hazard is obvious.

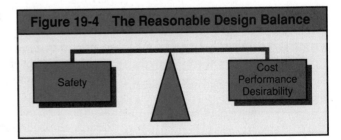

Figure 19-4   The Reasonable Design Balance

Safety

Cost Performance Desirability

WHAT HAPPENS WHEN DESIGN STANDARDS CONFLICT?

[*For manufacturers and safety engineers, lawsuits brought over a product's design can pose severe problems. Manufacturers often are held liable for injuries caused by products with faulty designs. The main focus in the courtroom is on the presence of negligence.*—AUTHORS' NOTE]

A policeman was severely injured in a Chrysler-built patrol car in New Jersey. It slammed into a steel pole and crushed him against the windshield. At the trial, his expert witnesses demonstrated that the pole pushed through the automobile in a seventeen-inch gap in its noncontinuous frame. An alternative design was possible and was known to the industry; it is a continuous frame, which, according to the expert witnesses, would have prevented the accident. The experts conceded on cross-examination, however, that the continuous frame would have cost some $300 more per car and added an additional 250 pounds. The alternative design would be more expensive and less efficient—and it would subject riders to a greater risk that they would be injured in a different kind of accident (the more rigid body would transmit the shock of collisions to persons inside, whereas a noncontinuous frame would absorb and mute the force of a collision). The vehicle conformed to federal motor vehicle safety standards. But the National Traffic and Motor Vehicle Safety Act explicitly provides that such compliance does not exempt manufacturers from common law liability. Therefore, ruled the United States Court of Appeals in Philadelphia in 1980, the jury's finding that the noncontinuous frame construction was faulty and its $2 million verdict must stand, even though it would be entirely possible for a different jury to hold the alternative continuous-frame design defective in another case. Only Congress can effect the cure for this Catch-22 situation, the court said. *Dawson v. Chrysler Corp.*, 49 L. W. 2200 (3rd. Cir. 1980).

Source: Jethro K. Lieberman, *The Litigious Society*, 1981, p. 46

LAAPERI v. SEARS, ROEBUCK & CO., INC. 787 F.2d 726 (1st Cir. 1986)

LEVIN CAMPBELL, (C.J.) In March 1976, plaintiff Albin Laaperi purchased a smoke detector from Sears. The detector, manufactured by the Pittway Corporation, was designed to be powered by AC (electrical) current. Laaperi installed the detector himself in one of the two upstairs bedrooms in his home.

Early in the morning of December 27, 1976, a fire broke out in the Laaperi home. The three boys in one of the upstairs bedrooms were killed in the blaze. Laaperi's 13-year-old daughter Janet, who was sleeping in the other upstairs bedroom, received burns over 12 percent of her body and was hospitalized for three weeks.

The uncontroverted testimony at trial was that the smoke detector did not sound an alarm on the night of the fire. The cause of the fire was later found to be a short circuit in an electrical cord that was located in a cedar closet in the boys' bedroom. The Laaperi home had two separate electrical circuits in the upstairs bedrooms: one which provided electricity to the outlets and one which powered the lighting fixtures. The smoke detector had been connected to the outlet circuit, which was the circuit that shorted and cut off. Because the circuit was shorted, the AC-operated smoke detector received no power on the night of the fire. Therefore, although the detector itself was in no sense defective (indeed, after the fire the charred detector was tested and found to be operable), no alarm sounded.

Laaperi brought this diversity action against defendants Sears and Pittway, asserting negligent design, negligent manufacture, breach of warranty, and negligent failure to warn of inherent dangers. The parties agreed that the applicable law is that of Massachusetts. Before the claims went to the jury, verdicts were directed in favor of defendants on all theories of liability other than failure to warn.

Laaperi's claim under the failure to warn theory was that he was unaware of the danger that the very short circuit which might ignite a fire in his home could, at the same time, incapacitate the smoke detector. He contended that had he been warned of this danger, he would have purchased a battery-powered smoke detector as a backup or taken some other precaution, such as wiring the detectors to a circuit of its own, in order better to protect his family in the event of an electrical fire.

The jury returned verdicts in favor of Laaperi in all four actions on the failure to warn claim. The jury assessed damages in the amount of $350,000 in each of the three actions brought on behalf of the deceased sons, and $750,000 in the action brought on behalf of Janet Laaperi. The defendants' motions for directed verdict and judgment notwithstanding the verdict were denied, and defendants appealed.

*   *   *

Defendants ask us to declare that the risk that an electrical fire could incapacitate an AC-powered smoke detector is so obvious that the average consumer would not benefit from a warning. This is not a trivial argument; in earlier—some might say sounder—days, we might have accepted it. Our sense of the current state of the tort law in Massachusetts and most other jurisdictions, however, leads us to conclude that, today, the matter before us poses a jury question; that "obviousness" in a situation such as this would be treated by the Massachusetts courts as presenting a question of fact, not of law. To be sure, it would be obvious to anyone that an electrical outage would cause this smoke detector to fail. But the average purchaser might not comprehend the specific danger that a fire-causing electrical problem can simultaneously knock out the circuit into which a smoke detector is wired, causing the detector to fail at the very moment it is needed. Thus, while the failure of a detector to function as the result of an electrical malfunction due, say, to a broken power line or a neighborhood power outage would, we think, be obvious as a matter of law, the failure that occurred here, being associated with the very risk—fire—for which the device was purchased, was not, or so a jury could find.

(continued on next page)

(continued)

LAAPERI v. SEARS, ROEBUCK & CO., INC.
787 F.2d 726 (1st Cir. 1986)

★   ★   ★

Finally, defendants contend that the award of $750,000 in damages to Janet Laaperi was excessive, and should have been overturned by the district court.

★   ★   ★

The jury undoubtedly, and understandably, felt a great deal of sympathy for a young girl who, at the age of 13, lost three brothers in a tragic fire. But by law the jury was only permitted to compensate her for those damages associated with her own injuries. Her injuries included fright and pain at the time of and after the fire, a three-week hospital stay, some minor discomfort for several weeks after discharge, and a permanent scar on her lower back.

★   ★   ★

The judgments in favor of Albin Laaperi in his capacity as administrator of the estates of his three sons are affirmed. In the action on behalf of Janet Laaperi, the verdict of the jury is set aside, the judgment of the district court vacated, and the cause remanded to that court for a new trial limited to the issue of damages.

PRODUCT LIABILITY LAW REFORM

In 1988, The Conference Board published a study that resulted from a survey of more than 500 chief executive officers from large and small companies. Table 19-1 summarizes the impacts of product liability on these companies. The study concluded that U.S. companies are less competitive in international business because of these impacts and that product liability laws must be reformed. The reform effort is underway at both the state and federal levels.

TABLE 19-1   IMPACT OF PRODUCT LIABILITY

Type of Impact	Percent of Firms Reporting Impact
Closed production plants	9
Laid off workers	16
Discontinued product lines	47
Decided against introducing new products	39
Decided against acquiring/merging	22
Discontinued product research	25
Moved production offshore	4
Lost market share	22

Source: *The Impact of Product Liability*, The Conference Board (1988).

State Reforms

Prodded by astute lobbying by manufacturing and other business trade associations, state legislatures in recent years began to respond to the audible cry of manufacturers about the hardships that the judicial transformation of the product liability lawsuit ostensibly worked on them. Most state legislatures have enacted at least one of some three dozen "reform" proposals being pressed on them. Some of these measures do little more than affirm and clarify case law. Among the most important to pass in several states are the following:

Statutes of Repose   Perhaps nothing so frightens the manufacturer as the occasional reports of cases involving products, like punch presses, that were fifty or sixty or more years old at the time they injured the plaintiff. Many states have addressed this problem by enacting the so-called *statute of repose*. This statute establishes a time period, generally ranging from six to twelve years; the manufacturer is not liable for injuries caused by the product after this time has passed.

State of the Art Defense   Several states have enacted laws that prevent advances in technology from being held against the manufacturer. The fear is that a plaintiff will convince a jury a product was defective because it did not use technology that was later available. Manufacturers have often failed to adopt new advances in technology for fear that the change will be held against them in a product liability suit. These new statutes declare that a manufacturer has a valid defense if it would have been technologically impossible to have used the new and safer technology at the time the product was manufactured.

Failure to Warn   Since it is often easier to prove that an injury resulted because the manufacturer failed to warn against a certain use than that it was caused by a defective design, manufacturers are subjected to a considerable degree of hindsight. Some of the state statutes limit the degree to which the failure to warn can be used to connect the product and the injury— for example, the manufacturer has a valid defense if it would have been impossible to foresee that the consumer might misuse the product in a certain way.

Comparative Fault for Consumer Misuse   Contributory negligence is generally not a defense in a strict liability action, while assumption of risk is. In states that have enacted so-called "comparative fault" statutes, the user's damages are pegged to the percentage of responsibility for the injury that the defendant bears. Thus, if the consumer's misuse of the product is assessed as having been 20 percent responsible for the accident (or for the extent of the injuries), the consumer is entitled to only 80 percent of damages, the amount for which the defendant manufacturer is responsible.

Criminal Penalties   Not all state reform is favorable to manufacturers. Under a California Corporate Criminal Liability Act that took effect in 1991, companies and managers must notify a state regulatory agency if they know that a product they are selling in California has a safety defect. Failure to provide notice may result in corporate and individual criminal liability.

Federal Reform

Piecemeal reform of product liability law in each state has contributed to the basic lack of uniformity from state to state, giving it a crazy-quilt effect. In the last century, this might have made little difference, but today most manufacturers sell in the national market, and are subjected to the varying requirements of the law in every state. For several years there has been talk in and out of Congress of enacting a federal product liability law that would include reforms adopted in many states, as discussed above. The U.S. Department of Commerce first proposed a draft federal bill in 1979. Since then, several other bills have been introduced in Congress, so far without success.

Congressional tort legislation is not the only possible federal action to cope with product-related injuries. In 1972, Congress created the Consumer Product Safety Commission (CPSC), and gave it broad power to act to *prevent* unsafe consumer products. The CPSC can issue mandatory safety standards governing design, construction, contents, performance, packaging, and labeling of more than 10,000 consumer products. It can recall unsafe products, recover costs on behalf of injured consumers, prosecute those who violate standards, and require manufacturers to issue warnings on hazardous products. It also regulates four federal laws previously administered by other departments: the Flammable Fabrics Act, the Hazardous Substances Act, the Poison Prevention Packaging Act, and the Refrigerator Door Safety Act. In its early years, the Commission issued standards for bicycles, power mowers, television sets, architectural glass, extension cords, book matches, pool slides, and space heaters. But the list of products is long and the Commission's record is mixed: it has come under fire for being short on regulation and for taking too long to promulgate the relatively few safety standards it has issued in a decade.

European Reform

In 1985, the Council of Ministers of the European Economic Community adopted a directive that creates new product liability risks for companies that export products to Europe. The directive embraces the concept of strict liability by allowing consumers to collect for injuries from defective products even when the manufacturer is not negligent. However, the rights of the consumer expire ten years after the product is put into circulation. The directive includes a "state of the art" defense but allows member countries (when they pass legislation that complies with the directive) to eliminate the defense. The directive further provides that a manufacturer's liability may be reduced when a consumer's negligence contributes to the injury.

CHAPTER SUMMARY

Product liability describes a type of claim—for injury caused by a defective product—and not a separate theory of liability. In the typical case, three legal doctrines may be asserted: (1) warranty, (2) strict liability, and (3) negligence.

If a seller asserts that a product will perform in a certain manner, or has certain characteristics, he has given an express warranty, and he will be held liable for damages if the warranty is breached—that is, if the goods do not live up to the warranty. Not every conceivable claim is an express warranty; the courts permit a certain degree of "puffing."

An implied warranty is one created by law. Goods sold by a merchant seller carry an implied warranty of merchantability, meaning that they must possess certain characteristics, such as being of average quality for the type described and being fit for the ordinary purposes for which they are intended.

An implied warranty of fitness for a particular purpose is created whenever a seller knows or has reason to know that the buyer is relying on the seller's knowledge and skill to select a product for the buyer's particular purposes.

Under Article 2, the seller also warrants that he is conveying good title and that the goods are free of any rightful claim by a third person.

Article 2 permits sellers to exclude or disclaim warranties in whole or in part. Thus a seller may exclude express warranties. He may also disclaim many implied warranties—for example, by noting that the sale is "as is." The Magnuson-Moss Act sets out certain types of information that must be included in any written warranty. The act requires the manufacturer or seller to label the warranty either as "full" or "limited" depending on what types of defects are covered and what the customer must do to obtain repair or replacement. The act also abolishes "phantom warranties."

Privity once stood as a bar to recovery in suits brought by those one or more steps removed in the distribution chain from the party who breached a warranty. But the nearly universal trend in the state courts has been to abolish privity as a defense.

Because various impediments stand in the way of warranty suits, most courts have adopted a tort theory of strict liability, under which a seller is liable for injuries resulting from the sale of any product in a defective condition if it is unreasonably dangerous to the user or consumer. Typical issues in strict liability cases are these: Is the defendant a seller engaged in the business of selling? Was the product sold in a defective condition? Was it unreasonably dangerous, either on its face or because of a failure to warn? Did the product reach the consumer in an unchanged condition? Strict liability applies regardless of how careful the seller was and regardless of his lack of contractual relation with the consumer or user.

Manufacturers can also be held liable for negligence—most often for faulty design of products and inadequate warnings about the hazards of using the product.

The product liability revolution has prompted many state legislatures to enact certain laws limiting to some degree the manufacturer's responsibility for defective products. These laws include statutes of repose and provide a number of other defenses.

KEY TERMS

Express warranty	p. 418	Negligence	p. 418
Full warranty	p. 424	Privity	p. 424
Implied warranty	p. 419	Product liability	p. 417
Limited warranty	p. 424	Strict liability	p. 418
Merchantability	p. 419	Warranty	p. 418

SELF-TEST QUESTIONS

1. In a product liability case:
   (a) only tort theories are typically asserted
   (b) both tort and contract theories are typically asserted
   (c) strict liability is asserted only when negligence is not asserted
   (d) breach of warranty is not asserted along with strict liability

2. An implied warranty of merchantability:
   (a) is created by an express warranty
   (b) is created by law
   (c) is impossible for a seller to disclaim
   (d) can be disclaimed by a seller only if the disclaimer is in writing

3. A possible defense to breach of warranty is:
   (a) lack of privity
   (b) absence of an express warranty
   (c) disclaimer of implied warranties
   (d) all of the above

4. Under the strict liability rule in Restatement Section 402A the seller is liable for all injuries resulting from a product:
   (a) even though all possible care has been exercised
   (b) regardless of the lack of a contract with the user
   (c) in both of the above situations
   (d) in none of the above situations

5. An individual selling her car could be liable:
   (a) for breaching the implied warranty of merchantability
   (b) under the strict liability theory
   (c) under both of the above
   (d) under neither of the above

DEMONSTRATION PROBLEM

A whiskey company manufactured a high-grade blend called Exxxtra Plus. A company employee, who had been sampling the company's product during work, carelessly poured fuel oil into one bottle. The bottle was purchased by Frank who, after three drinks, became seriously ill. Another bottle, which was not tainted with fuel oil, was purchased by Elmo, an alcoholic, who drank the bottle in one sitting and became just as ill as Frank. Both Frank and Elmo sue the company on a strict liability theory. Will they win? Why?

PROBLEMS

1. Ralph's Hardware decided to automate its accounting system and agreed to purchase a computer system from a manufacturer, Bits and Bytes (BB). During contract negotiations, BB's sales representative promised that the system was "A-1" and "perfect." However, the written contract which the parties later signed disclaimed all warranties, express and implied. After installation the computer produced only random numbers and letters, rather than the desired accounting information. Is BB liable for breaching an express warranty? Why?

2. Kate owned a small grocery store. One day John purchased a can of chip dip from the store which, unknown to Kate or John, was adulterated. John became seriously ill after eating the dip and sued Kate for damages on the grounds that she breached an implied warranty of merchantability. Is Kate liable? Why?

3. Carrie visited a neighborhood store to purchase some ham, which a salesperson cut by machine in the store. The next day she made a ham sandwich. In eating the sandwich, Carrie bit into a piece of cartilage in the ham and, as a result, lost a tooth, had to undergo root canal treatments, and must wear a full coverage crown to replace the tooth. Is the store liable for the damage? Why?

4. Clarence, a business executive, decided to hold a garage sale. At the sale, his neighbor Betty mentioned to Clarence that she was the catcher on her city-league baseball team and was having trouble catching knuckleball pitches, which required a special catcher's mitt. Clarence pulled an old mitt from a pile of items which were on sale and said, "Here, try this." Betty purchased the mitt but discovered during her next game that it didn't work. Has Clarence breached an express or implied warranty? Why?

5. Sarah purchased several elegant picture frames to hang in her dorm room. She also purchased a package of self-sticking hangers. Late one evening, while Sarah was studying business law in the library, the hangers came loose and her frames came crashing to the floor. After Sarah returned to her room and discovered the rubble, she examined the box in which the hangers were packaged and found the following language: "There are no warranties except for the description on this package and specifically there is NO IMPLIED WARRANTY OF MERCHANTABILITY." Assuming the hangers are not of fair, average, ordinary quality, would the hanger company be liable for breaching an implied warranty of merchantability? Why?

6. A thirteen-year-old boy received a "Golfing Gizmo"—a device for training novice golfers—as a gift from his mother. The label expressly states that the Gizmo is safe, but the boy is injured while using it. Should the fact that plaintiff is not in privity with the manufacturer bar his warranty claims? Why?

7. A bank repossessed a boat and sold it to Donald. During the negotiations with Donald, Donald stated that he wanted to use the boat for charter service in Florida. The bank officers handling the sale made no representations concerning the boat during negotiations. Donald later discovered that the boat was defective and sued the bank for breach of warranty. Is the bank liable? Why?

ANSWERS TO SELF-TEST QUESTIONS

1. (b)   2. (b)   3. (d)   4. (c)   5. (d)

SUGGESTED ANSWER TO DEMONSTRATION PROBLEM

Frank will win because the product is "unreasonably dangerous." Elmo will not win because, although the product is dangerous to him, it is not unreasonably dangerous to ordinary consumers.

CHAPTER

20

Bailments and the Storage, Shipment, and Leasing of Goods

Bailments: Importance Generally

*I*n this final chapter of Part III we turn to the legal relationships that buyers and sellers have with warehousers and carriers—the parties responsible for physically transferring goods from seller to buyer. This topic introduces a new branch of law, that of bailments, to which we will devote considerable attention before turning directly to warehousers and carriers.

A **bailment** is the relationship established when someone entrusts his property temporarily to someone else without intending to give up title. Although bailment has often been said to arise only through a contract, the modern definition does not require that there be an agreement. One widely quoted definition holds that a bailment is "the rightful possession of goods by one who is not the owner. It is the element of lawful possession, however created, and the duty to account for the thing as the property of another, that creates the bailment, regardless of whether such possession is based upon contract in the ordinary sense or not." [Zuppa v. Hertz, 268 A.2d 364 (N.J. 1970)]

The law of bailments is important to virtually everyone in modern society: to anyone who has ever delivered a car to a parking lot attendant, checked a coat in a restaurant, or deposited property in a safe-deposit box. In commercial transactions, bailment law governs the responsibilities of the carrier and warehouse—critical links in the movement of goods from manufacturer to the consumer.

Bailments Compared with Sales

In a sale, the buyer acquires *title* and must pay for the goods. In a bailment, the *bailee* acquires *possession* and must return the *identical* object. In most cases the distinction is clear, but difficult borderline cases can arise. Consider the sad Tale of the Leased Cows. Carpenter leased a farm for five years to Spencer. The lease included thirty cows. At the end of the term, Spencer was to give Carpenter, the owner, "cows of equal age and quality." Unfortunately, Spencer fell onto hard times, and had to borrow money from Griffin. When the time came to pay the debt, Spencer had no money, so Griffin went to court to *levy* against the cows (that is, he sought a court order giving him the cows in lieu of the money owed). Needless to say, this threatened transfer of the cows upset Carpenter, who went to court to stop Griffin from taking the cows. The question was whether Spencer was a bailee, in which case the cows would still belong to Carpenter (and Griffin could not levy against them), or a purchaser, in which case Spencer would own the cows and Griffin could levy against them. The court ruled that title had passed to Spencer—the cows were his. Why? The court reasoned that Spencer was not obligated to return the identical cows to Carpenter, hence Spencer was not a bailee. [Carpenter v. Spencer & Griffin, 37 Am. Dec. 396 (N.Y. 1841)] Section 2-304(1) of the UCC confirms this position, declaring that whenever the price of a sale is payable in goods, each party is a seller of the goods which he is to transfer.

Note the implications that flow from calling this transaction a sale. The creditor of the purchaser can seize the goods. The risk of loss is on the purchaser. The seller cannot recover the goods (to make up for the buyer's failure to pay him) or sell them to a third party.

Fungible goods (goods that are identical, like grain in a silo) present an especially troublesome problem. In many instances the goods of several owners are mingled, and the identical items are not intended to be returned. For example, the operator of a grain elevator agrees to return an equal quantity of like-quality grain but not the actual kernels deposited there. Following the rule in Carpenter's cow case, this might seem to be a sale, but it is not. Under Section 2-207, the depositors of fungible goods are "tenants in common" (see p. 737) of the goods; in other words, the goods are owned by all. This distinction between a sale and a bailment is important. When there is a loss through natural causes—for example, if the grain elevator burns—the depositors must share the loss on a pro rata basis (meaning that no single depositor is entitled to take all his grain out; if 20 percent of the grain was destroyed, then each depositor can take out no more than 80 percent of what he deposited).

ELEMENTS OF A BAILMENT

As noted above, bailment is defined as "the rightful possession of goods by one who is not the owner." For the most part, this definition is clear (and note that it does not dictate that a bailment be created by contract). Bailment law applies to the delivery of "goods," that is, to *personal property*. Personal property is usually defined as anything that can be owned other than real estate. As we have just seen in comparing bailments to sales, the definition implies a duty to return the identical goods when the bailment ends.

But one word in the definition is both critical and troublesome: *possession*. The word "bailment" derives from the French *bailler*, which means "to deliver" (that is, into the hands or possession of someone). Possession requires both a physical and a mental element. We examine these in turn.

Physical Control

In most cases, physical control is easily enough proven. A car delivered to a parking garage is obviously within the physical control of the garage. But in some instances, physical control is difficult to conceptualize. For example, you can rent a safe-deposit box in a bank to store valuable papers, stock certificates, jewelry, and the like. The box is usually housed in the bank's vault. To gain access, you sign a register and insert your key after a bank employee inserts the bank's key. You may then inspect, add to, or remove contents of the box in the privacy of a small room maintained in the vault for the purpose. Because the bank cannot gain access to the box without your key and does not know what is in the box, it might be said to have no physical control. Nevertheless, the rental of a safe-deposit box is a bailment. In so holding, a New York court pointed out that if the bank was not in possession of the box renter's property, "it is difficult to know who was. Certainly [the renter] was not, because she could not obtain access to the property without the consent and active participation of the defendant. She could not go into her safe unless the defendant used its key first, and then allowed her to open the box with her own key; thus absolutely controlling [her] access to that which she had deposited within the safe. The vault was the [company's] and was in its custody, and its contents were under the same conditions." [Lockwood v. Manhattan Storage & Warehouse Co., 50 N.Y.S. 974 (1898)] Statutes in some states, however, provide that the relationship is not a bailment but that of a landlord and tenant, and many of these statutes limit the bank's liability for losses.

Intent to Possess

In addition to physical control, the bailee must have had an *intent to possess* the goods; that is, to exercise control over them. This mental condition is difficult to prove; it almost always turns on the specific circumstances and, as a fact question, is left to the jury to determine. To illustrate the difficulty, suppose that one crisp fall day Mimi goes to Sally Jane's Boutique to try on a jacket. The sales clerk hands Mimi a jacket and watches while Mimi takes off her coat and places it on a nearby table. A few minutes later, when Mimi is finished inspecting herself in the mirror, she goes to retrieve her coat, only to discover it is missing. Who is responsible for the loss? The answer depends on whether the store is a bailee. In some sense Boutique had physical control, but did it intend to exercise that control? In a leading case, the court held that it did, even though no one said anything about guarding the coat, because a store invites its patrons to come in. Implicit in the act of trying on a garment is the removal of the garment being worn. When the customer places it in a logical place, with the knowledge of and without objection from the salesperson, the store must exercise some care in its safe-keeping. [Bunnell v. Stern, 25 N.E. 910 (N.Y. 1890)]

Now suppose that when Mimi walked in the salesperson told her to look around, try on some clothes, and to put her coat on the table. When the salesperson was finished with her present customer, she said, she would be glad to help Mimi. So Mimi tries on a jacket and minutes later discovers her coat gone. Is this a bailment? Many courts, including the New York courts, would say no. The difference? The salesperson was helping another customer. Therefore, Mimi had a better opportunity to watch over her own coat, and knew that the salesperson would not be looking out for it. This is a subtle distinction, but it has been sufficient in many cases to change the ruling. [Wamser v. Browning, King & Co., 79 N.E. 861 (N.Y. 1907)]

Questions of intent and control frequently arise in parking lot cases. As someone once said, "The key to the problem is the key itself." The key is symbolic of possession and intent to possess. If you give the attendant your key, you are a bailor and he (or the company he works for) the bailee. If you do not give him the key, no bailment arises. Many parking lot cases do not fall neatly within this rule, however. Especially common are self-service airport parking lot cases. The customer drives through a gate, takes a ticket dispensed by a machine, parks his car, locks it, and takes his key. When he leaves, he retrieves the car himself and pays at an exit gate. As a general rule, no bailment is created under these circumstances. The lot operator does not accept the vehicle nor intend to watch over it as bailee. In effect, the operator is simply renting out space. [Wall v. Airport Parking Co. of Chicago, 244 N.E.2d 190 (Ill. 1969)] But a slight change of facts can alter this legal conclusion. Suppose, for instance, that the lot had an attendant at the single point of entrance and exit, that the attendant jotted down the license number on the ticket, one portion of which he retained, and that the car owner must surrender the ticket when leaving or prove that he owns the car. These facts have been held to add up to an intention to exercise custody and control over the cars in the lot, and hence to have created a bailment. [Continental Insurance Co. v. Meyers Bros. Operations, Inc., 288 N.Y.S.2d 756 (Civ. Ct. N.Y. 1968)]

For a bailment to exist, the bailee must know or have reason to know that the property exists. When property is hidden within the main object entrusted to the bailee, lack of notice can defeat the bailment in the hidden property. For instance, a parking lot is not responsible for the disappearance of valuable golf clubs stored in the trunk of a car, nor a dance hall cloak room for the disappearance of a fur wrap inside a coat, if they did not know of their existence. [Samples v. Geary, 292 S.W. 1066 (Mo. App. 1927).] This result is usually justified by observing that when a person is unaware that goods exist or does not know their value, it is inequitable to hold him responsible for their loss since he cannot take steps to prevent it. This rule has been criticized: trunks are meant to hold things and if the car was within the garage's control, surely its contents were. Some courts soften the impact of the rule by holding that a bailee is responsible for goods that he might reasonably expect to be present, like gloves in a coat checked at a restaurant, or ordinary baggage in a car checked at a hotel.

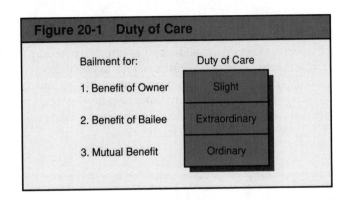

Figure 20-1   Duty of Care

Bailment for:	Duty of Care
1. Benefit of Owner	Slight
2. Benefit of Bailee	Extraordinary
3. Mutual Benefit	Ordinary

LIABILITY OF BAILEE

Duty of Care

That a bailee has accepted delivery of goods does not mean that he is responsible for their safekeeping no matter what. The law of bailments does not apply a standard of absolute liability. The bailee's liability depends on the circumstances.

While courts use a straightforward standard of "ordinary care under the circumstances," most courts use a complex, tripartite division of responsibility. If the bailment is for the benefit of the owner (bailor), the bailee—sometimes known in these circumstances as a "naked bailee"—is said to be answerable only for gross neglect or fraud. In other words, the duty of care is slight. *Example:* Your car breaks down on a dark night and you beg a passing mortorist to tow it to a gas station. On the other hand, if the goods are entrusted to the bailee for his benefit, then he owes the bailor extraordinary care. *Example:* Your neighbor begs you to let him borrow your car to go to the grocery store downtown because his car is in the shop. If the bailment is for the mutual benefit of bailee and bailor, then the ordinary negligence standard of care will govern. *Example:* You park your car in a commercial parking lot. (See Figure 20-1.)

One problem with using the majority approach is the inherent ambiguity in the standards of care. What constitutes "gross" negligence as opposed to "ordinary" negligence? The degree-of-care approach is further complicated by the tendency of the courts to take into account the value of the goods; the lesser

the value of the goods, the lesser the obligation of the bailee to watch out for them. To some degree, this approach makes sense, since it obviously behooves a person guarding diamonds to take greater precautions against theft than one holding three paperback books. But the value of the goods ought not be the whole story: some goods obviously have great value to the owner, regardless of any lack of intrinsic value.

Another problem in using the majority approach to the standard of care is determining whether or not a benefit has been conferred on the bailee when the bailor did not expressly agree to pay compensation. For example, a bank gives its customers free safe-deposit boxes. Is the bank a "gratuitous bailee," that owes its bailor only a slight degree of care, or has it made the boxes available as a commercial matter to hold onto its customers? Some courts cling to the one theory, some to the other, suggesting the difficulty with the tripartite division of the standard of care. However, in many cases, whatever the formal theory, the courts look to the actual benefits to be derived. Thus, when a customer comes to an automobile showroom and leaves her car in the lot while she test drives the new car, most courts would hold that two bailments for mutual benefit have been created—the bailment to hold the old car in the lot, the customer being the bailor; and the bailment to try out the new car, the customer being the bailee.

Burden of Proof

In a bailment case, the plaintiff bailor has the burden of proving that a loss was caused by the defendant bailee's failure to exercise due care. However, the bailor establishes a *prima facie* (PRY muh FAY she) case by showing that he delivered the goods into the bailee's hands and that the bailee did not return them or returned them damaged. At that point, a presumption of negligence arises, and to avoid liability the defendant must rebut that presumption by showing affirmatively that he was not negligent. The reason for this rule is that the bailee usually has a much better opportunity to explain why the goods were not returned or were returned damaged. To put this burden on the bailor might make it impossible for him to win a meritorious case.

The following case tests, under possibly unusual circumstances, the bailee's duty to take care of property and the standard of care required.

ANDREWS v. ALLEN
724 S.W.2d 893
(Tex.App.-Austin 1987)

GAMMAGE, JUSTICE. This is an appeal from a take-nothing judgment rendered by the district court against Joe Andrews, Sr., plaintiff, and Frontier Insurance Company, intervenor, and in favor of defendants, Ronny Ray Allen, Oak Hills Ranch, and Harold Stone. We will affirm the judgment.

Prior to March 16, 1983, Andrews delivered his quarter horse mare named "I'll Call Ya" to Oak Hills Ranch and its owner Harold Dean Stone (hereinafter collectively referred to as "Stone"), appellees, for the purposes of boarding and stabling. Stone and Oak Hills Ranch were in the business of brokering, stabling and training racehorses for profit. Several months later, Andrews asked Stone if he would arrange for "I'll Call Ya" to be transported to a trainer in Louisiana. Consequently, when Ronny Allen and his brother Billy Allen delivered two horses to Oak Hills Ranch, Stone asked them if they would haul "I'll Call Ya" back to their training stables at Silsbee, in east Texas, where the Louisiana trainer could pick her up. Andrews apparently agreed to these plans even though he did not know the Allen brothers. Ronny Allen, Billy Allen and a third brother, Ernie Allen, are co-owners of the Allen Brothers Racing Stables, also in the business of boarding and training horses for profit. Stone had previously done business with the Allen brothers.

On March 16, 1983, Ronny and Billy Allen loaded "I'll Call Ya" into their trailer and began the drive back to Silsbee. Shortly after leaving Oak Hills Ranch, the trailer became disengaged from the Allens' truck, rolled over at least once and came to rest on the side of the road. The mare was severely cut and bruised as a result of the accident and apparently lingered for several hours on the side of the road before she died without veterinary treatment.

The trial court found, and it is not disputed before this Court, that the fair market value of the horse immediately before the accident was $150,000, and the fair market value of the horse after the accident was $0.

*   *   *

Appellees argue that the court correctly found that Stone and Allen were gratuitous bailees because they received no consideration for their services, but were merely doing "favors" for friends in the horse business—in essence, that Stone was doing a favor for Andrews, and Allen was doing a favor for Stone. We disagree.

It is true that neither Stone nor Allen received any money from Andrews, although it is disputed whether they originally intended to charge Andrews for their services. The presence or absence of monetary compensation, however, is not dispositive of the issue before us. The test is whether the bailment was made as an incident of a business in which the bailee makes a profit.

> [T]he rule is that a bailment is for the mutual benefit of the bailor and the bailee, although nothing is paid directly by the bailor, where the property of the bailor is delivered by the bailor, and accepted by the bailee, as an incident of a business in which the bailee makes a profit. In such situation the bailee receives his compensation in the profits of the business in which the bailment is an incident. Therefore a business institution, which, within the scope of its business accepts and receives a bailor's property, even though no charge is made, is with respect to such property more than a mere gratuitous bailee, and should be held to the responsibilities of a bailee for mutual benefit, inasmuch as such services attract patronage. (emphasis in original) Bill Bell, Inc. v. Ramsey, 284 S.W.2d 244, 248 (Tex.Civ.App.1955, no writ).

★   ★   ★

It is undisputed that both Stone and Allen accepted delivery of "I'll Call Ya" and that both are in the business of handling horses for a profit. Both Stone and Allen testified that they typically do these "favors" for one another because it is good for business. Under the reasoning in *Bill Bell*, they each received, as consideration for the bailment, good will of others in the business and the general profits of the business to which the bailment was incident.

★   ★   ★

In a bailment for mutual benefit, a rebuttable presumption of negligence arises upon proof that the bailed chattel was destroyed or not returned. To overcome this presumption, the bailee has the burden of showing the cause of the accident or that the damage resulted from some other cause consistent with due care on his part.

The Texas Supreme Court has stated on two occasions that this presumption is "based on the just and common sense view that the party in possession or control of an article is more likely to know and more properly charged with explaining the damage to it or disappearance of it than the bailor who entrusted it to his care." The Texas Supreme Court further stated:

> A mere showing by the bailee of lack of knowledge how the loss occurred is not sufficient. The general rule is that in order to rebut the presumption of his negligence, the defaulting bailee must show how the loss occurred and that it was due to some other cause than his own neglect or negligence *or* that, however the loss occurred, it was not due to his negligence. (emphasis added) Buchanan v. Byrd [519 S.W.2d 841 (Tex. 1975).].

★   ★   ★

(continued on next page)

(continued)

ANDREWS v. ALLEN
724 S.W.2d 893
(Tex.App.-Austin 1987)

The Allen brothers testified that Billy Allen led the horse into the trailer with the help of one of Stone's employees; that Billy Allen properly secured the horse's head at the front of the trailer; that the Allen brothers used all other equipment that a reasonably prudent person would use to secure and haul the horse; that Billy Allen checked the tires and made sure the trailer hitch was properly secured; that the ball was the proper size and in good condition; that the ball was used without incident to haul other trailers after the accident; that Ronny Allen was driving at a safe speed and in a safe manner immediately before the accident; that after the accident the sleeve of the trailer hitch was still in the secured position; and that they made a reasonable effort to obtain veterinary treatment for the horse after the accident.

We find the above testimony sufficient under the second half of the Buchanan test to rebut the presumption of negligence as a matter of law. Because appellees produced evidence that they exercised ordinary care at every step of the venture, showing that no matter how the accident occurred it was not due to their negligence, they satisfied their burden of production under Buchanan thereby denying plaintiff the right to judgment as a matter of law on the issue of negligence.

[Judgment affirmed.]

Disclaimers

Bailees often attempt to disclaim their liability for loss or damage. But courts often refuse to honor the disclaimers, usually looking to one of two justifications for invalidating them.

Lack of Notice   The disclaimer must be brought to the attention of the bailor and must be unambiguous.

Thus, posted notices and receipts disclaiming or limiting liability must set forth clearly and legibly the legal effects intended. Most American courts follow the rule that the defendant bailee must show that the bailor in fact knew about the disclaimer. Language printed on the back side of a receipt will not do. However, as the following case shows, a bailor is bound by a known, unambiguous disclaimer.

**CARR v. HOOSIER
PHOTO SUPPLIES,
INC.**
441 N.E.2d 450 (S. Ct.
Ind. 1982)

GIVAN, CHIEF JUSTICE. Litigation in this cause began with the filing of a complaint in Marion Municipal Court by John R. Carr, Jr. (hereinafter "Carr"), seeking damages in the amount of $10,000 from defendants Hoosier Photo Supplies, Inc. (hereinafter "Hoosier") and Eastman Kodak Company (hereinafter "Kodak").

Carr was the beneficiary of a judgment in the amount of $1,013.60. Both sides appealed.

The Court of Appeals affirmed the trial court in its entirety.

*   *   *

The facts were established by stipulation agreement between the parties and thus are not in dispute. In the late spring or early summer of 1970, Carr purchased some Kodak film from a retailer not a party to this action, including four rolls of Kodak Ektachrome-X 135 slide film that are the subject matter of this dispute. During the month of August, 1970, Carr and his family vacationed in Europe. Using his own camera Carr took a great many photographs of the sites they saw, using among others the four rolls of film referred to earlier. Upon their return to the United States, Carr took a total of eighteen [18] rolls of exposed film to Hoosier to be developed. Only fourteen [14] of the rolls were returned to Carr after processing. All efforts to find the missing rolls or the pictures developed from them were unsuccessful. Litigation commenced when the parties were unable to negotiate a settlement.

The film Carr purchased, manufactured by Kodak, is distributed in boxes on which there is printed the following legend:

READ THIS NOTICE

This film will be replaced if defective in manufacture, labeling, or packaging, or if damaged or lost by us or any subsidiary company even though by negligence or other fault. Except for such replacement, the sale, processing, or other handling of this film for any purpose is without other warranty of liability.

In the stipulation of facts it was agreed though Carr never read this notice on the packages of film he bought, he knew there was printed on such packages "a limitation of liability similar or identical to the Eastman Kodak limitation of liability." The source of Carr's knowledge was agreed to be his years of experience as an attorney and as an amateur photographer.

When Carr took all eighteen [18] rolls of exposed film to Hoosier for processing, he was given a receipt for each roll. Each receipt contained the following language printed on the back side:

Although film price does not include processing by Kodak, the return of any film or print to us for processing or any other purpose, will constitute an agreement by you that if any such film or print is damaged or lost by us or any subsidiary company, even though by negligence or other fault, it will be replaced with an equivalent amount of Kodak film and processing and, except for such replacement, the handling of such film or prints by us for any purpose is without other warranty or liability.

Again, it was agreed though Carr did not read this notice he was aware Hoosier "[gave] to their customers at the time of accepting film for processing, receipts on which there are printed limitations of liability similar or identical to the limitation of liability printed on each receipt received by Carr from Hoosier Photo."

It was stipulated upon receipt of the eighteen [18] rolls of exposed film only fourteen [14] were returned to Hoosier by Kodak after processing. Finally, it was stipulated the four rolls of film were lost by either Hoosier or Kodak.

It is apparent upon examination of the Findings of Fact and Conclusions of Law made by the trial court that court believed this entire transaction was governed by the law of bailments and not by the Uniform Commercial Code. We agree with the trial court in this conclusion.

(continued on next page)

(continued)

CARR v. HOOSIER PHOTO SUPPLIES, INC.
441 N.E.2d 450 (S. Ct. Ind. 1982)

* * *

That either Kodak or Hoosier breached the bailment contract, by negligently losing the four rolls of film, was established in the stipulated agreement of facts. Therefore, the next issue raised is whether either or both, Hoosier or Kodak, may limit their liability as reflected on the film packages and receipts.

* * *

[A] prerequisite to finding a limitation of liability clause in a contract unconscionable and therefore void is a showing of disparity in bargaining power in favor of the party whose liability is thus limited. . . .

In the case at bar the stipulated facts foreclose a finding of disparate bargaining power between the parties or lack of knowledge or understanding of the liability clause by Carr. The facts show Carr is an experienced attorney who practices in the field of business law. . . . Moreover, it was stipulated he was aware of the limitation of liability on both the film packages and the receipts. We believe these crucial facts belie a finding of disparate bargaining power working to Carr's disadvantage.

Contrary to Carr's assertions, he was not in a "take it or leave it position" in that he had no choice but to accept the limitation of liability terms of the contract. As cross-appellants Hoosier and Kodak correctly point out, Carr and other photographers like him do have some choice in the matter of film processing. They can, for one, undertake to develop their film themselves. They can also go to independent film laboratories not a part of the Kodak Company. We do not see the availability of processing as limited to Kodak.

* * *

We hold the limitation of liability clauses operating in favor of Hoosier and Kodak were assented to by Carr; they were not unconscionable or void. Carr is, therefore, bound by such terms and is limited in his remedy to recovery of the cost of four boxes of unexposed Kodak Ektachrome-X 135 slide film.

The Court of Appeals' opinion in this case is hereby vacated. The cause is remanded to the trial court with instructions to enter a judgment in favor of appellant, John R. Carr, Jr., in the amount of $13.60, plus interest. Each party is to bear its own costs.

Public Policy Exception Even if the bailor reads the disclaimer, some courts will nevertheless hold the bailee liable on public policy grounds, especially when the bailee is a "business bailee," such as a warehouse or carrier. Indeed, to the extent that a business bailee attempts to totally disclaim liability, he will probably fail in every American jurisdiction. But the Restatement of Contracts does not go quite this far for most nonbusiness bailees. They may disclaim liability as long as the disclaimer is read and does not relieve the bailee from wanton carelessness. (*Restatement (Second) of Contracts*, Section 195(2)(b).)

Conversion

Conversion is the unlawful assumption of authority over the property of another such as to deprive him of its title or use. A bailee who assumes unlawful authority over property entrusted to him—a garage mechanic who drives a customer's car an unreasonable distance or who uses it to transport narcotics—will be held liable as an insurer, that is, for any damages.

If the bailee misdelivers the goods, the result will be the same; he will be held liable for conversion. However, he will escape liability if he delivers the goods to one who is legally entitled to possession, even if the delivery is contrary to the instructions of the bailor. Likewise, the bailee is not liable to the true owner if he redelivers the goods instead to the bailor, unless the true owner has made a demand on the bailee to redeliver the goods to him. As a practical matter, the bailee caught between a bailor and a true owner should *interplead* the two; that is, bring them both into court and let the court sort out their claims and rights.

LIABILITY OF THE BAILOR

As might be expected, most bailment cases involve the legal liability of bailees. However, a body of law on the liability of bailors is beginning to emerge.

Negligence of Bailor

A bailor may be held liable for negligence. If the bailor receives a benefit from the bailment, then he has a duty to inform the bailee of known defects and to make a reasonable inspection for other defects. Suppose the Tranquil Chemical Manufacturing Company produces an insecticide that it wants the Plattsville Chemical Storage Company to keep in tanks until sold. One of the batches is defectively acidic and oozes out of the tanks. This acidity could have been discovered through a routine inspection, but Tranquil neglects to inspect. The tanks leak and the chemical builds up on the floor until it explodes. Since Tranquil, the bailor, received a benefit from the storage, it had a duty to warn Plattsville, and its failure to do so makes it liable for all damages caused by the explosion.

If the bailor does not receive any benefit, however, then his only duty is to inform the bailee of known defects. Your neighbor begs to borrow your car. You have a duty to tell him that the brakes are weak, but you do not need to inspect the car beforehand for unknown defects.

Other Types of Liability

The theory of product liability discussed in the previous chapter is being extended to bailors. Both warranty and strict liability theories apply. The rationale for extending liability in the absence of sale is that in modern commerce, damage can be done equally by sellers or lessors of equipment. A rented car, no less than a purchased one, can inflict substantial injury.

In several states, when an automobile owner (bailor) lends a vehicle to a friend (bailee) who causes an accident, the owner is liable to third persons injured in the accident. This liability is discussed in Chapter 38 on agency law.

OTHER RIGHTS AND DUTIES

Compensation

If the bailor hires the bailee to perform services for the bailed property, then the bailee is entitled to compensation. Remember, however, that not every bailment is necessarily for compensation. The difficult question is whether the bailee is entitled to compensation when nothing explicit has been said about incidental expenses he has incurred to care for the bailed property—as, for example, if he were to repair a piece of machinery to keep it running. No firm rule can be given. Perhaps the best generalization that can be made is that, in the absence of an express agreement, ordinary repairs fall to the bailee to pay, but extraordinary repairs are the bailor's responsibility.

Because it is often difficult to distinguish between ordinary and extraordinary repairs, a bailment contract should specify the person responsible for maintenance and service. The bailor is required by federal law (the Consumer Leasing Act) to disclose this information when leasing personal property such as a car or appliances for more than four months for a personal, family, or household use.

Bailee's Lien

A **lien** is from the French, originally meaning "string" or "tie." In law it means the hold that someone has over the property of another, akin, in effect, to a security interest. A common type is the **mechanic's lien.** A carpenter builds a room on your house and you fail to pay him; he can secure a lien on your house, meaning that he has a property interest in the house and can start foreclosure proceedings if you still fail to pay. Similarly, a bailee is said to have a lien on the bailed property in his possession and need not redeliver it to the bailor until he has been paid. Try to take your car out of a parking lot without paying and see what happens. The attendant's refusal to give you the car is entirely lawful under a common law rule now more than a century and a half old. As the rule is usually stated, the common law confers the lien on the bailee if he has added value to the property through his labor, skill, or materials. But that statement of the rule is somewhat deceptive, since the person who has simply housed the goods is entitled to a lien, as is a person who has altered or repaired the goods without measurably adding value to them. Perhaps a better way of stating the rule is this: a lien is created when the bailee performs some special benefit to the goods (preserving them or repairing them, for instance.)

Many states have enacted statutes governing various types of liens. In many instances, these have broadened the bailee's common law rights. We discuss at pp. 454 and 461 two types, the liens of warehousemen and common carriers.

Rights When Goods Taken or Damaged by a Third Party

The general rule is that the bailee can recover damages in full if the bailed property is damaged or taken by a third party, but he must account in turn to the bailor. A delivery service is carrying parcels—bailed goods entrusted to the trucker for delivery—when the truck is struck from behind and it blows up. The carrier may sue the third person who caused the accident and recover for the total loss, including the value of the packages. The bailor may also recover for damages to the parcels, but not if the bailee has already recovered a judgment. Suppose the bailee has sued and lost. Does the bailor have a right to sue independently on the same grounds? Ordinarily, the principle of *res judicata* would prevent a second suit, but if the bailor did not know of and cooperate in the bailee's suit, he probably has the right to proceed on his own suit.

SPECIAL BAILMENTS

Innkeepers

The liability of an innkeeper is thought to have derived from the warlike conditions that prevailed in medieval England, where brigands and bandits roamed the countryside and the innkeeper himself might not have been above stealing from his guests. The innkeeper's liability extended not merely to loss of goods through negligence. His was an *insurer's* liability, extending to any loss, no matter how occasioned, and even to losses that occurred in the guest's room, a place where the guest had the primary right of possession. The only exception was for losses due to the guest's own negligence.

Most states have enacted statutes providing exceptions to this extraordinarily broad common law duty. Typically the statutes exempt the hotelkeeper from insurer's liability if he furnishes a safe in which the guests can leave their jewels, money, and other valuables and if he posts a notice advising the guests of its availability. He might face liability for valuables lost or stolen from the safe but not from the rooms.

Special Bailments in Commercial Transactions

In the next three sections we turn to special bailments particularly important in commercial transactions. We look first at the law governing the *storage* of goods; that is, the law governing warehousers and warehouse receipts. Second, we examine the law governing the *shipment* of goods; that is, the law governing common carriers and bills of lading. Third, we cover the negotiation and transfer of warehouse receipts and bills of lading.

The law of warehouse receipts and bills of lading is found in part in UCC Article 7, "Documents of Title." A **document of title** is defined as any document "which in the regular course of business or financing is treated as adequately evidencing that the person in possession of it is entitled to receive, hold and dispose of the document and the goods it covers." The document must say that it is issued by or addressed to a bailee and must "purport to cover goods in the bailee's possession which are either identified or are fungible portions of an identified mass" (for example, "two tons of grain from Grain Elevator #7").

The UCC provides a specific definition of bailee. Under Section 7-102(1)(a), a bailee is anyone who "acknowledges possession of goods and contracts to deliver them," when the acknowledgment is by means of a warehouse receipt, bill of lading, or other document of title.

The law governing documents of title is an appropriate area with which to conclude the sales unit because the document of title is not only a vital part of many sales transactions but is also one that shares many attributes of commercial paper, which we examine in the next unit, and because the document of title is frequently pledged as collateral for loans, a topic discussed in Part V, Secured Transactions.

STORAGE OF GOODS

Warehousing has been called the "second oldest profession," stemming from the Biblical story of Joseph, who stored grain during the seven good years against the famine of the seven bad years. Whatever its origins, warehousing is today a big business, taking in billions of dollars to stockpile foods and other goods. As noted above, the source of law governing warehousing is Article 7 of the UCC, but non-code law also can apply; Section 7-103 specifically provides that any federal statute or treaty and any state regulation or tariff supersedes the provisions of Article 7. A federal example is the United States Warehouse Act, which governs receipts for stored agricultural products.

A **warehouser** is defined in Section 7-102(h) as "a person engaged in the business of storing goods for hire," and under Section 1-201(45) a **warehouse receipt** is any receipt issued by a warehouser. The warehouse receipt is an important document because it can be used to transfer title to the goods, even while they remain in storage. No form is prescribed for the warehouse receipt, but unless it lists in its terms the

following items, the warehouser is liable to anyone who is injured by the omission of any of them:

1. location of the warehouse;
2. date receipt was issued;
3. consecutive number of the receipt;
4. statement whether the goods will be delivered to bearer, to a specified person, or "to a specified person or his order";
5. the rate of storage and handling charges;
6. description of the goods or the packages containing them;
7. signature of the warehouser, which his or her authorized agent may make;
8. the warehouser's ownership of the goods, if he or she has a sole or part ownership in them; and
9. the amount (if known, otherwise the fact) of advances made and liabilities incurred for which the warehouser claims a lien or security interest.

General Duty of Care

The warehouser's general duty of care is embodied in the tort standard for measuring negligence: he is liable for any losses or injury to the goods caused by his failure to exercise "such care in regard to them as a reasonably careful man would exercise under like circumstances." (Section 7-204(1).) However, subsection 4 declares that this section does not repeal or dilute any other state statute that imposes a higher responsibility on a warehouser. Nor does the section invalidate contractual limitations otherwise permissible under Article 7. The warehouser's duty of care under this section is considerably weaker than the carrier's duty. Determining when a warehouser becomes a carrier, if the warehouser is to act as shipper, can become an important issue.

Limitation of Liability

The warehouser may limit the amount of damages she will pay by so stating in the warehouse receipt (Section 7-204(2)), but she must strictly observe that section's requirements, under which the limitation must be stated "per article or item, or value per unit of weight." Moreover, the warehouser cannot force the bailor to accept this limitation: the bailor may demand in writing increased liability, in which event the warehouser may charge more for the storage. If the warehouser converts the goods to her own use, the limitation of liability does not apply.

Specific Types of Liability and Duties

Non-Receipt or Misdescription   Under Section 7-203, a warehouse is responsible for goods listed in a warehouse receipt which were not in fact delivered to the warehouse (or were misdescribed) and must pay damages to a good-faith purchaser of or party to a document of title. To avoid this liability, the issuer must conspicuously note on the document that he does not know whether the goods were delivered or are correctly described. One simple way is to mark on the receipt that "contents, condition, and quality are unknown."

Delivery to the Wrong Party   The bailee is obligated to deliver the goods to any person with documents that entitle him to possession, as long as the claimant pays any outstanding liens and surrenders the document so that it can be marked "cancelled" (or can be partially cancelled in the case of partial delivery). The bailee can avoid liability for nondelivery by showing that he delivered the goods to someone with a claim to possession superior to that of the claimant, that the goods were lost or destroyed through no fault of the bailee, or that certain other lawful excuses apply. (Section 7-403(1).) Suppose a thief deposits goods he has stolen with a warehouse. Discovering the theft, the warehouser turns the goods over to the rightful owner. A day later the thief arrives with a receipt and demands delivery. Because the rightful owner had the superior claim, the warehouser is not liable in damages to the thief.

Now suppose you are moving and have placed your goods at a local storage company. A few weeks later, you accidentally drop your wallet, which contains the receipt for the goods and all your identification. A thief picks up the wallet and immediately heads for the warehouse, pretending to be you. Having no suspicion that anything is amiss—it's a large place and no one can be expected to remember what you look like—the warehouse releases the goods. This time you are probably out of luck. Section 7-404 says that "a bailee who in good faith including observance of reasonable commercial standards has received goods and delivered . . . them according to the terms of

the document of title . . . is not liable." This rule is true even though the person to whom he made delivery had no authority to receive them, as in the case of the thief. However, if the warehouser had a suspicion and failed to take precautions, then he might be liable to the true owner.

Duty to Keep Goods Separate   Except for fungible goods, like grain, the warehouse must keep separate goods covered by each warehouse receipt. The purpose of this rule, which may be negated by explicit language in the receipt, is to permit the bailor to identify and take delivery of his goods at any time.

Rights of the Warehouser

Termination   A warehouser is not obligated to store goods indefinitely. Many warehouse receipts will specify the period of storage. At the termination of the period, the warehouser may notify the bailor to pay and to recover her goods. If no period is fixed in the receipt or other document of title, the warehouser may give notice to pay and remove within no less than thirty days. The bailor's failure to pay and remove permits the warehouser to sell the goods for her fee.

Suppose the goods begin to deteriorate. Sections 7-207(2) and (3) permit the warehouser to sell the goods early if necessary to recover the full amount of her lien or if the goods present a hazard. But if the rightful owner demands delivery before such a sale, the warehouser is obligated to do so.

Liens   Section 7-209(1) provides that a warehouser has a lien on goods covered by a warehouse receipt to recover the following charges and expenses: charges for storage or transportation, insurance, labor, and expenses necessary to preserve the goods. The lien is not discharged if the bailor transfers his property interest in the goods by negotiating a warehouse receipt to a purchaser in good faith, although the warehouser is limited then to an amount or a rate fixed in the receipt or to a reasonable amount or rate if none was stated. The lien attaches automatically and need not be spelled out in the warehouse receipt.

The warehouser may enforce the lien by selling the goods at a public or private sale, as long as she does so in a commercially reasonable manner, as defined in Section 7-210. All parties known to be claiming an interest in the goods must be notified of the sale and told the amount due, the nature of the sale, and its time and place. Any person who in good faith purchases the goods takes them free of any claim by the bailor, even if the warehouser failed to comply with the requirements of Section 7-210. However, her failure to comply subjects her to damages, and if she has willfully violated the provisions of this section she is liable to the bailor for conversion.

SHIPMENT OF GOODS

The shipment of goods throughout the United States and abroad is a multi-billion-dollar-a-year business, and many specialized companies have been established to undertake it, including railways, air cargo operations, trucking companies, and ocean carriers. Article 7 of the UCC applies to carriage of goods as it does to warehousing, but federal law—in particular, the Federal Bills of Lading Act (FBLA) and the so-called Carmack Amendment of 1906 to the Interstate Commerce Act—is much more important in the regulation of shipping than it is in storage. The FBLA covers *bills of lading* (see below) issued by common carriers for transportation of goods in interstate or foreign commerce (that is, from one state to another or in federal territory or to foreign countries). The Carmack Amendment covers liability of interstate carriers for loss, destruction, and damage to goods.

Two terms are particularly important in discussing shipment of goods. One is **common carrier.** The common carrier is "one who undertakes for hire or reward to transport the goods of such as choose to employ him, from place to place." [Ace High Dresses v. J. C. Trucking Co., 191 A. 536 (Conn. 1937)] This definition contains three elements: (1) the carrier must hold himself out for all in common to hire him; his business is not restricted to particular customers, but is open to all who apply for his services; (2) he must charge for his services; he is for hire; (3) the service in question must be carriage. Included within this tripartite definition are numerous types of carriers: household moving companies, taxicabs, towing companies, and even oil and gas pipelines are common carriers. Note that to be a common carrier it is not necessary to be in the business of carrying every type of good to every possible point; common carriers may limit the types of goods or the places to which they will transport them.

A **bill of lading** is any document that evidences

"the receipt of goods for shipment issued by a person engaged in the business of transporting or forwarding goods." (Section 1-206(6).) This is a comprehensive definition and includes documents used by contract carriers, that is, carriers who are not common carriers. An example of a bill of lading is depicted in Figure 20-2.

General Duty of Care

Absolute Liability Damage, destruction, and loss are major hazards of transportation for which the carrier will be liable. Who will assert the claim against the carrier depends on who bears the risk of loss. The rules governing risk of loss (examined in Chapter 17) determine whether the buyer or seller will be the plaintiff. But whoever is the plaintiff, the common carrier defendant faces *absolute liability.* With five exceptions explored below, the common carrier is an insurer of goods, and regardless of the cause of damage or loss—that is, whether or not the carrier was negligent—it must make the owner whole. This ancient common law rule is codified in both state and federal law (in the Carmack Amendment, 49 U.S.C.A. § 11707, and in the UCC, Section 7-309(1), which hold the common carrier to absolute liability to the extent that the common law of the state had previously done so).

Absolute liability was imposed in the early cases because the judges believed such a rule necessary to prevent carriers from conspiring with thieves. Since it is difficult for the owner, who was not on the scene, to prove exactly what happened, the judges reasoned that putting the burden of loss on the carrier would prompt him to take extraordinary precautions against loss (and would certainly preclude him from colluding with thieves). Note that the rules in this section govern only common carriers; contract carriers that do not hold themselves out for transport for hire are liable as ordinary bailees.

Exceptions to Absolute Liability In general, the burden or proof rests on the carrier to the advantage of the shipper. The shipper (or consignee of the shipper) can make out a *prima facie* case by showing that it delivered the goods to the carrier in good condition and that the goods either did not arrive or arrived damaged in a specified amount. Thereafter the carrier has the burden of proving that it was not negligent

Figure 20–2   A Bill of Lading Form

[*Face Side*]

UNIFORM ORDER BILL OF LADING
ORIGINAL

Shipper's No. . . . .
Agent's No. . . . .

Company

RECEIVED, subject to the classifications and tariffs in effect on the date of the issue of this Bill of Lading at . . . .

. . . . , 19 . .

from . . . .

the property described below, in apparent good order, except as noted (contents and condition of contents of packages unknown), marked, consigned, and destined to indicated below, which said company (the word company being understood throughout this contract as meaning any person or corporation in possession of the property under the contract) agrees to carry to its usual place of delivery at said destination, if on its own road or its own water line, otherwise to deliver to another carrier on the route to said destination. It is mutually agreed, as to each carrier of all or any of said property over all or any portion of said route to destination, and as to each party at any time interested in all or any of said property, that every service to be performed hereunder shall be subject to all the conditions not prohibited by law whether printed or written, herein contained, including the conditions on back hereof, which are hereby agreed to by the shipper and accepted for himself and his assigns.

The surrender of this Original ORDER Bill of Lading properly indorsed shall be required before the delivery of the property. Inspection of property covered by this bill of lading will not be permitted unless provided by law or unless permission is indorsed on this original bill of lading or given in writing by the shipper.

Consigned to ORDER of . . . .

Destination . . . . State of . . . . County of . . . .

Notify . . . .

At . . . . State of . . . . County of . . . .

Route . . . .

Delivering Carrier . . . . Car Initial . . . . Car No. . . . .

No. Pack-ages	Description of Articles, Special Marks, and Exceptions	*Weight (Subject to Correction)	Class or Rate	Check Column	Subject to Section 7 of conditions, if this shipment is to be delivered to the consignee without recourse on the consignor, the consignor shall sign the following statement:
. . . . . .	. . . .	. . . .	. . . . .	. . . .	
. . . . . .	. . . .	. . . .	. . . . .	. . . .	The carrier shall not make delivery of this shipment without payment of freight and all other lawful charges.
. . . . . .	. . . .	. . . .	. . . . .	. . . .	
. . . . . .	. . . .	. . . .	. . . . .	. . . .	
. . . . . .	. . . .	. . . .	. . . . .	. . . .	(Signature of consignor.)
. . . . . .	. . . .	. . . .	. . . . .	. . . .	
. . . . . .	. . . .	. . . .	. . . . .	. . . .	If charges are to be prepaid, write or stamp here, "To be Prepaid."
. . . . . .	. . . .	. . . .	. . . . .	. . . .	
. . . . . .	. . . .	. . . .	. . . . .	. . . .	Received $. . . . . to apply in prepayment of the charges on the property described hereon.
. . . . . .	. . . .	. . . .	. . . . .	. . . .	
. . . . . .	. . . .	. . . .	. . . . .	. . . .	Agent or Cashier.

*If the shipment moves between two ports by a carrier by water, the law requires that the bill of lading shall state whether it is "carrier's or shipper's weight."

Per . . . .
(The signature here acknowledges only the amount prepaid.)

Note.—Where the rate is dependent on value, shippers are required to state specifically in writing the agreed or declared value of the property.

The agreed or declared value of the property is hereby specifically stated by the shipper to be not exceeding

. . . . Per . . . .

Charges advanced:

$ . . . .

. . . . Shipper. . . . . Agent.

Per . . . . per . . . .

Permanent postoffice address of shipper . . . .

Source: Form 3 from UCC Section 7-301

and that the loss or damage was caused by one of the five following recognized exceptions to the rule of absolute liability.

Act of God

No one has ever succeeded in defining precisely what constitutes an act of God, but the courts seem generally agreed that it encompasses acts that are of sudden and extraordinary natural, as opposed to human, origin. Examples are earthquakes, hurricanes, and fires caused by lightning against which the carrier could not have protected itself. Rapid River Carriers contracts to transport a refrigerated cargo of beef down the Mississippi on the S.S. Rapid. En route the ship is struck by lightning, bursts into flames, and sinks. This is an act of God. But, a contributing act of negligence by a carrier overcomes the act of God exception.

Act of Public Enemy

This is a narrow exception that applies only to acts committed by pirates at high sea or by the armed forces of enemies of the state to which the carrier owes allegiance. American ships at sea that are sunk during wartime by enemy torpedoes would not be liable for losses to the owners of cargo. But an accidental bombing by American allies, mistaking the ship for an enemy vessel, would not be an excuse. Moreover, public enemies do not include lawless mobs or criminals listed on the FBI's "most wanted" list, even if federal troops are required, as in the Pullman strike of 1894, to put down the violence. In the latter case, carriers were held liable for property destroyed by violent strikers.

Act of Public Authority

When a public authority, like a sheriff or federal marshal, through lawful process, seizes goods in the carrier's possession, the carrier is excused from liability. Federal agents board the S.S. Rapid in New Orleans, as she is about to sail, show the captain a search warrant, and seize several boxes of cargo marked "beef" which turn out to hold cocaine. The owner or consignee of this illegal cargo will not prevail in a suit against the carrier to recover damages. Likewise, if the rightful owner of the goods obtains a lawful court order permitting him to attach them, the carrier is obligated to permit the goods to be taken. It is not the carrier's responsibility to contest a judicial writ or to face the consequences of resisting a court order. The courts generally agree that the carrier must notify the owner whenever goods are seized.

Act of Shipper

When goods are lost or damaged because of the shipper's negligence, the shipper is liable, not the carrier. The usual situation under this exception arises from defective packing. The shipper who packs the goods defectively is responsible for breakage unless the defect is apparent and the carrier accepts the goods anyway. For example, crystal shipped loose in boxes will inevitably be broken when driven in trucks along the highways. The trucker who knowingly accepts boxes in this condition is liable for the damage. Likewise, the carrier's negligence will overcome the exception and make him absolutely liable. A paper supplier ships several bales of fine stationery in thin cardboard boxes susceptible to moisture. Knowing their content, S.S. Rapid accepts the bales and exposes them to the elements on the upper deck. A rainstorm curdles the stationery. The carrier is liable.

Inherent Nature of the Goods

The fifth exception to the rule of absolute liability is rooted in the nature of the goods themselves. If they are inherently subject to deterioration or their inherent characteristics are such that they might be destroyed, then the loss must lie on the owner. Common examples are chemicals that can explode spontaneously and perishable fruits and vegetables. Of course, the carrier is responsible for seeing that foodstuffs are properly stored and cared for, but if they deteriorate naturally and not through the carrier's negligence, he is not liable.

Which Carrier Is Liable?

The transportation system is wondrously complex, and few goods travel from portal to portal under the care of one carrier only. In the nineteenth century, the shipper whose goods were lost had a difficult time recovering their value. Initial carriers blamed the loss on subsequent carriers, and even if the shipper could determine which carrier actually had possession of the goods when the damage or loss occurred, diverse state laws made proof burdensome. The Carmack Amendment ended the considerable confusion by placing the burden on the initial carrier; connecting carriers are deemed agents of the initial carrier. So the plaintiff, whether seller or buyer, need sue only the initial carrier, no matter where the loss occurred. Likewise, Section 7-302 of the UCC fastens liability on an initial carrier for damages or loss caused by connecting carriers.

When Does Carrier Liability Begin and End?

When a carrier's liability begins and ends is an important

issue because the same company can act both to store the goods and carry them. The carrier's liability is more stringent than the warehouser's. So the question is, when does a warehouser become a carrier and vice versa?

The basic test for the beginning of carrier liability is whether the shipper must take further action or give further instructions to the carrier before its duty to transport arises. Suppose that Cotton Picking Associates delivers 50 bales of cotton to Rapid River Carriers for transport on the S.S. Rapid. S.S. Rapid is not due back to port for two more days, so Rapid River Carrier stores the cotton in its warehouse and the following day the warehouse is struck by lightning and burns to the ground. Is Rapid River Carriers liable in its capacity as a carrier or warehouse? Since nothing was left for the owner to do, and Rapid River was storing the cotton for its own convenience awaiting the ship's arrival, it was acting as a carrier and is liable for the loss. Now suppose that when Cotton Picking delivered the 50 bales it said that another 50 bales would be coming in a week and the entire lot of 100 bales was to be shipped together. Rapid River stores the first 50 bales and lightning strikes. Since more remained for Cotton Picking to do before Rapid River was obligated to ship, the carrier was acting in its warehousing capacity and is not liable.

The carrier's absolute liability ends when it has delivered the goods to the consignee's residence or place of business, unless the agreement states otherwise (as it often does). By custom, certain carriers—notably rail and carriers by water—are not required to deliver the goods to the consignee (since rail lines and oceans do not take the carrier to the consignee's door). Instead, consignees must take delivery at the dock or some other place mutually agreed or established by custom.

When the carrier must make personal delivery to the consignee, carrier liability continues until the carrier has made reasonable efforts to deliver. An express trucking company cannot call on a corporate customer on Sunday or late at night, for instance. If reasonable efforts to deliver fail, it may store the goods in its own warehouse, in which case its liability reverts to that of a warehouser.

If personal delivery is not required (as for example in shipment by rail), the states use different approaches for determining when the carrier's liability terminates. The most popular intrastate approach provides that the carrier continues to be absolutely responsible for the goods until the consignee has been notified of their arrival and has had a reasonable opportunity to take possession of them.

Interstate shipments are governed by the Interstate Commerce Act, which generally provides that liability will be determined by language in the bill of lading filed with the Interstate Commerce Commission. The typical bill of lading provides that if the consignee does not take the goods within a stated period of time after receiving notice of their arrival, the carrier will be liable as warehouser only.

The following case discusses warehouser/carrier liability following the consignee's rejection of a shipment.

FISHER CORP. v. CONSOLIDATED FREIGHTWAYS
434 N.W.2d 17 (Neb. 1989)

CAPORALE, JUSTICE.

Plaintiff-appellant, Fisher Corporation, a manufacturer of electronic equipment, seeks to recover the value of certain video cassette recorders stolen while in the possession of defendant-appellee, Consolidated Freightways, Inc., a transporter of goods. The district court, in accordance with verdicts, dismissed Fisher's action. . . .

In its original petition, Fisher pled that it was entitled to recover on the theory that at the time of the theft, Consolidated was serving as a warehouser, or alternatively, on the theory that at the relevant time, Consolidated was serving as a common carrier. A warehouser, that is, one "engaged in the business of storing goods for hire," Neb.U.C.C. § 7-102(1)(h) (Reissue 1980), is, in the absence of a contrary agreement, liable for goods lost while in its possession only if, as detailed later in this opinion, the loss occurred through its negligence. A common carrier, on the other hand, is an insurer against loss from whatever cause, except an act of nature, of the public enemy, or of the owner of the goods. . . .

The record reveals that in June of 1984, Fisher, under a "standard bill of lading," delivered to Consolidated, at Fisher's warehouse in California, 132 recorders for shipment to World Radio, Inc., an electronics retailer, at Council Bluffs, Iowa. Consolidated divided the shipment into two parts, tendering delivery to World Radio of 60 recorders on June 29 and 72 recorders on July 6. World Radio rejected each tender as duplicative of earlier shipments.

In order to understand what follows, it is necessary to interrupt our recitation of the relevant events and review the legal significance of World Radio's rejection of the recorders. So far as we can determine from the record, the bill of lading under which the recorders came into Consolidated's possession stated nothing about Consolidated's liability for loss should it find itself unable to deliver the recorders to World Radio as Fisher had directed. Under such a circumstance, once a common carrier tenders delivery of the consigned goods to a consignee which refuses delivery, the carrier loses its status as a common carrier and becomes a warehouser. Where a common carrier turned warehouser, acting as a bailee, accepts instructions from the bailor to ship goods to a specified location, its status as a warehouser again changes to that of common carrier.

Returning to the relevant events, the record discloses that after each rejected tender, Consolidated returned the recorders to its terminal at Sarpy County, Nebraska, for storage, pending receipt of Fisher's further instructions. On the day after the second rejection, Consolidated loaded all 132 recorders onto a trailer, sealed but did not padlock the trailer doors, and placed the trailer at the south end of its terminal yard. Padlocks were not used on any trailer doors so as not to call attention to a trailer containing expensive cargo; rather, all trailers were sealed. The doors of the trailer faced away from the terminal, toward the south end of a Cyclone fence which encircled the yard.

In accordance with its usual practice, Consolidated sent Fisher a form letter notifying it of World Radio's rejection of the shipments and indicating that after 3 days, Fisher would be charged for storage unless Consolidated received disposition instructions.

At 7 a.m. on July 17, a Tuesday, Consolidated's employees discovered that 54 of the recorders were missing from the trailer. They also discovered that a large, 3-foot by 5-foot hole had been cut in the chain-link fence at the terminal's south end, and a smaller hole had been cut in the east fence. The recorders were never recovered.

The exact time the theft occurred is unknown, and witnesses' opinions vary as to when the theft took place. Maurice O'Toole, Consolidated's dock supervisor, testified that he checked the yard between 11:30 p.m. and midnight on Sunday, July 15, by walking behind all the trailers, and at that time he did not see any holes in the fence nor seals broken on the trailer containing the recorders. O'Toole claimed there was "no way [he] would have missed that hole."

(continued on next page)

(continued)

FISHER CORP. v. CONSOLIDATED FREIGHTWAYS
434 N.W.2d 17 (Neb. 1989)

★   ★   ★

The record reveals that at some point, Fisher notified Consolidated to return the rejected recorders to Fisher in California, but the record is not clear as to when that occurred. According to Fisher's evidence, it received notice from Consolidated of World Radio's rejection on Thursday, July 12, and presumably, on Friday, July 13, assigned and communicated to Consolidated a return authorization number.

★   ★   ★

All that was clear at the close of all the evidence was that at some point 54 of the recorders in Consolidated's possession were stolen and that at some point Fisher telephoned Consolidated with authorization to return all 132 recorders. However, the evidence is such that reasonable minds could reach different conclusions as to when the theft occurred and as to when Consolidated received Fisher's return instruction. Reasonable minds could conclude from the evidence that the theft occurred anytime after O'Toole's yard check on the night of Sunday, July 15, and before the theft was reported the following Tuesday, July 17. In the same manner, reasonable minds could conclude Consolidated received Fisher's oral instruction to return the recorders to it anytime between July 13 and 16.

Consequently, the evidence is sufficient to sustain the jury's special finding that Consolidated did not receive Fisher's return authorization until after the theft had taken place, thereby making Consolidated a warehouser at the time of the loss rather than a common carrier. Moreover, the evidence concerning the manner in which Consolidated stored the recorders does not compel but does support the finding implicit in the general verdict that Consolidated had not been negligent.

[Judgment affirmed.]

Disclaimers   Under neither federal nor state law may the carrier disclaim his absolute liability. He may, however, limit the damages he may have to pay under certain circumstances. Both the Carmack Amendment and UCC Section 7-309 permit the carrier to set alternate tariffs, one costing the shipper more and paying full value, the other costing less and limited to a dollar per pound or some other rate less than full value. The shipper must have a choice; the carrier may not impose a lesser tariff unilaterally on the shipper.

Specific Types of Liability

Non-Receipt or Misdescription   Under UCC Section 7-301(1), the owner of the goods (for example, a consignee) described in a bill of lading may recover damages from the issuer of the bill (the carrier) if the issuer did not actually receive the goods from the shipper, if the goods were misdescribed, or if the bill was misdated. The issuer may avoid liability by reciting in the bill of lading that she does not know whether the goods were received or conform to the description or by marking it with such words as "contents or condition of contents unknown." Even this qualifying language may be ineffective. For instance, a common carrier may not hide behind language indicating that the description was given by the shipper; the carrier must actually count the packages of goods or ascertain the kind and quantity of bulk freight.

Just because the carrier is liable to the consignee for errors in description does not mean that the shipper is free from blame. Section 7-301(5) requires the shipper to indemnify the carrier if the shipper has inaccurately described the goods in any way (including marks, labels, number, kind, quantity, condition, and weight).

Delivery to the Wrong Party The rule discussed above for warehouser applies to carriers under both state and federal law: carriers are absolutely liable for delivering the goods to the wrong party. In the classic case of *Southern Express Co.* v. *C. L. Ruth & Son,* 59 So. 538 (Ala. Ct. App. 1912), a clever imposter posed as a reputable firm and tricked the carrier into delivering a diamond ring. The court held the carrier liable, even though it was not negligent and there was no collusion. The UCC contains certain exceptions; under Section 7-303(1), the carrier is immune from liability if the holder, the consignor, or (under certain circumstances) the consignee gives instructions to deliver the goods to someone other than a person named in the bill of lading.

Carrier's Right to Lien and Enforcement of Lien

Just as the warehouser can have a lien, so too can the carrier. The lien can cover charges for storage, transportation, and preservation of goods. When someone has purchased a negotiable bill of lading, the lien is limited to charges stated in the bill, allowed under applicable tariffs, or, if none are stated, to a reasonable charge. A carrier who voluntarily delivers or unjustifiably refuses to deliver the goods loses her lien. The carrier has rights paralleling those of the warehouser to enforce her lien.

Passengers

In addition to shipping goods, common carriers also transport passengers and their baggage. The carrier owes passengers a high degree of care; a century ago the Supreme Court described the standard as "the utmost caution characteristic of very careful prudent men." [Pennsylvania Co. v. Roy, 102 U.S. 451 (1880).] This duty implies liability for a host of injuries, including mental distress occasioned by insults ("lunatic," "whore," "cheap, common scalawag") and by profane or indecent language. In the following case, the passenger was injured outside the bus company's property, illustrating the degree to which a carrier is responsible for its passenger's safety and comfort.

WERNDLI v. GREYHOUND CORPORATION
365 So.2d 177 (Fla. App. 1978)

DANAHY, JUDGE. The issue before us is whether The Greyhound Corporation was under a duty to warn appellant at the inception of her trip that the bus on which she was traveling would deposit her in a closed, locked and darkened terminal at her destination. We believe that Greyhound did have that duty and accordingly reverse the order of the trial court dismissing appellant's amended complaint.

Appellant filed suit against Greyhound seeking damages for injuries sustained as a result of an attack by a third party near the Greyhound bus terminal in Fort Myers. Her amended complaint set forth the following facts which we must accept as true:

Appellant purchased a ticket for herself and her young son at the Greyhound bus terminal in St. Petersburg for a trip which would terminate at the Greyhound bus terminal in Fort Myers. The bus departed on schedule at approximately 11:30 p.m. and, after scheduled intermediate stops, arrived at the Fort Myers terminal at approximately 4:15 a.m. When she alighted from the bus after her long ride, appellant observed that the station and restrooms were darkened, closed, and locked. Because she needed to use bathroom

(continued on next page)

(continued)

WERNDLI v. GREYHOUND CORPORATION

365 So.2d 177 (Fla. App. 1978)

facilities and also wished to obtain a cold drink for her thirsty son, appellant left the terminal facilities to cross to a lighted service station. As she walked away from the terminal, she was attacked by an unknown person who caused her severe injuries. The terminal was located in a high crime area of Fort Myers.

The trial judge dismissed the amended complaint because of the failure to allege violation of a duty which Greyhound owed appellant.

Greyhound agrees with appellant that a common carrier is required to exercise the "highest degree of care, foresight, prudence and diligence reasonably demanded at any time by the conditions or circumstances then affecting the passengers and the carrier." Greyhound maintains, however, that any duty on its part terminated absolutely when appellant left its premises after completing her trip. We find it unnecessary to address that point because Greyhound's duty arose and was breached at the time appellant purchased her ticket. A common carrier is under a duty to warn passengers of dangers which are reasonably foreseeable and which might cause harm. This is especially true in situations where the passenger would not, in the exercise of reasonable care, be likely to anticipate and apprehend the danger. Inasmuch as Greyhound knew or should have known that its Fort Myers terminal was located in a high crime area and would be darkened, closed, and locked at the time appellant was due to arrive there in the middle of the night, we believe that Greyhound should have warned or informed appellant of such a potentially dangerous condition in order that she might take that fact into consideration before purchasing her ticket and leaving St. Petersburg.

For these reasons we reverse and remand this case for reinstatement of the amended complaint and for further proceedings consistent with this opinion.

The baggage carrier is liable as an insurer unless the baggage is not in fact delivered to the carrier. A passenger who retains control over his hand luggage, by taking it with him to his seat, has not delivered the baggage to the carrier, and hence the carrier has no absolute liability for its loss or destruction. The carrier remains liable for negligence, however. When the passenger does deliver his luggage to the carrier, the question often arises whether the property so delivered is "baggage." If it is not, the carrier does not have an insurer's liability toward it. Thus, a person who transports household goods in a suitcase would not have given the carrier "baggage," as that term is usually defined (that is, something transported for the passenger's personal use or convenience). At most, the carrier would be responsible for the goods as a gratuitous bailee.

NEGOTIATION AND TRANSFER OF COMMODITY PAPER

Negotiability in General

It is a basic feature of our legal system that a person cannot transfer more rights to property than he owns. But there are certain exceptions to this rule; for example, in Chapter 17 we discussed the power of a merchant in certain circumstances to transfer title to goods, even though the merchant himself did not have title to them. A critically important exception to the general rule arises also when certain types of paper are sold. In the next unit, we discuss this rule as it relates to *commercial paper*, such as checks and notes. To conclude this unit, we discuss the rule as it applies to documents of title, sometimes known as *commodity paper.*

If a document of title is "negotiable" and is "duly negotiated," the purchaser can obtain rights greater than those of the storer or shipper. In the following discussion, we refer only to the UCC, although federal law also distinguishes between negotiable and nonnegotiable documents of title (some of the technical details in the federal law may differ, but these are beyond the scope of this book).

"Negotiable" Defined

Any document of title, including a warehouse receipt and a bill of lading, is **negotiable** if by its terms the goods are to be delivered "to bearer or to the order of" a named person. (Section 7-104(1)(a).) All other documents of title are nonnegotiable. Suppose a bill of lading says that the goods are consigned to Tom Thumb but that they may not be delivered unless Tom signs a written order that they be delivered. Under Section 7-104(2) that is not a negotiable document of title. A negotiable document of title must bear words such as the following: "Deliver to the bearer" or "deliver to the order of Tom Thumb."

"Duly Negotiated"

To transfer title effectively through negotiation of the document of title, it must be "duly negotiated." In general terms, under Section 7-501, a negotiable document of title is duly negotiated when the person named in it indorses and delivers it to a holder who purchases it in good faith and for value, without any notice that someone else might have a claim against the goods, assuming the transaction is in the regular course of business or financing. Paper made out "to bearer" is negotiated by delivery alone. A *holder* is anyone who possesses a document of title that is drawn to his order, indorsed to him, or made out "to bearer."

Effect

As a general rule, if these requirements are not met, the transferee acquires only those rights which the transferor had and nothing more. And if a nonnego-

tiable document is sold, the buyer's rights may be defeated. For example, a creditor of the transferor might be entitled to treat the sale as void.

If, however, the document is duly negotiated, then the holder acquires (1) title to the document, (2) title to the goods, (3) certain rights to the goods delivered to the bailee after the document itself was issued, and (4) the right to have the issuer of the document of title hold the goods or deliver the goods free of any defense or claim by the issuer. (Section 7-502.)

To contrast the difference between sale of goods and negotiation of the document of title, consider the plight of Lucy, the owner of presidential campaign pins and other paraphernalia. Lucy plans to hold them for ten years, and then sell them for many times their present value. She does not have the room in her cramped apartment to keep them, so she crates them up and brings them to a friend for safekeeping. The friend gives her a receipt that says simply: "Received from Lucy, five cartons; to be stored for ten years at $25 per year." Although a document of title, the receipt is not negotiable. Two years later, a browser happens on Lucy's crates, discovers their contents, and offers the friend $1,000 for them. Figuring Lucy will forget all about them, the friend sells them. As it happens, Lucy comes by a week later to check on her memorabilia, discovers what her former friend has done, and sues the browser for their return. Lucy would prevail. Now suppose instead that the friend, who has authority from Lucy to store the goods, takes the cartons to the Trusty Storage Company, receives a negotiable warehouse receipt ("deliver to bearer five cartons"), and then negotiates the receipt. This time Lucy would be out of luck. The bona fide purchaser from her friend would cut off Lucy's right to recover the goods, even though the friend never had good title to them.

But even if the requirements of negotiability are met, the document of title still will confer no rights in certain cases. For example, when a thief forges the indorsement of the owner, who held negotiable warehouse receipts, the bona fide purchaser from the thief does not obtain good title. Only if the receipts were in bearer form would the purchaser prevail in a suit by the owner. Likewise, if the owner brought his goods to a repair shop, which warehoused them without any authority and then sold the negotiable receipts received for them, the owner would prevail over the subsequent purchaser.

Another instance in which an apparent negotiation of a document of title will not give the bona fide purchaser superior rights occurs when a term in the document is altered without authorization. But if blanks are filled in without authority, the rule states different consequences for bills of lading and warehouse receipts. Under Section 7-306, any unauthorized filling in of a blank in a bill of lading leaves the bill enforceable only as it was originally. However, under Section 7-208, an unauthorized filling in of a blank in a warehouse receipt permits the good-faith purchaser with no notice that authority was lacking to treat the insertion as authorized, thus giving him good title. This section makes it dangerous for a warehouser to issue a receipt with blanks in it, because he will be liable for any losses to the owner if a good-faith purchaser takes the goods.

Finally, note that a purchaser of a document of title who is unable to get his hands on the goods—perhaps the document was forged—might have a breach of warranty action against the seller of the document. Under Section 7-507, a person who negotiates a document of title warrants to his immediate purchaser that the document is genuine, that he has no knowledge of any facts that would impair its validity, and that the negotiation is rightful and effective. Thus the purchaser of a forged warehouse receipt would not be entitled to recover the goods but could sue his transferor for breach of the warranty.

LEASE OF GOODS

The lease of goods involves billions of dollars annually, ranging from a two-hour rental of a power tool by a consumer to a long-term lease of heavy industrial equipment by a multinational corporation. Under the common law, the lease of goods is a bailment for mutual benefit. However, given the increasing importance of these leases, specific statutory guidelines were necessary and, in 1987, Article 2A on Leases was added to the Uniform Commercial Code. This was the first new article added to the UCC since it was first adopted by the states in the 1950s. In 1988, Oklahoma became the first of several states to adopt Article 4A.

Article 2A defines a lease as "a transfer of the right to possession and use of goods for a term in return for consideration." Any transaction included within this definition is a lease, regardless of its form.

Once it is determined that a transaction is a lease, the governing law in Article 2A is very similar to the law of sales discussed in Part Two and in the preceding four chapters in Part Three. The reason for this similarity is that in both transactions—the sale and the lease—an interest in goods is transferred. Thus Article 2A provisions governing unconscionability, the formation and interpretation of lease contracts, performance, and remedies draw heavily from the law of sales. Perhaps more important is the philosophy that underlies Article 2A and the rest of the UCC—freedom of contract. As noted in the Official Comment to Section 2A-101: "This codification was greatly influenced by the fundamental tenet of the common law as it has developed with respect to leases of goods: freedom of the parties to contract." As a result of this philosophy, the parties to a lease may vary most of the provisions in Article 2A.

Some expansion or revision of sales law was, of course, necessary in light of differences between sales and leases. For instance, a new Statute of Frauds rule provides that where the lease payments total $1,000 or more, the lease must be in writing.

Furthermore, special rules govern two unique lease transactions—the consumer lease and the finance lease. A consumer lease is one in which a professional lessor leases personal, family, or household goods to a lessee where the total lease payments do not exceed $25,000. Consumer lessees are given special protection. For example, courts are free to grant any relief, including attorney's fees, when a consumer lessee proves that the lease contract was induced by unconscionable conduct or the lessor used unconscionable conduct in collecting payments under the lease. Article 2A is also governed by state and federal statutes designed to protect lessees, such as the Consumer Leasing Act (see page 451).

A finance lease is one in which the role of the lessor is to provide financing rather than goods, which come from a third-party manufacturer or supplier. As a result, the primary legal responsibilities of the finance lessor relate to its financing role. The finance lessor, for instance, does not warrant that the leased goods are merchantable or that they are fit for a particular purpose—warranties that are implied in other leases and sales contracts.

CHAPTER SUMMARY

Ownership and sale of goods are not the only important legal relationships involving goods. In a modern economy, possession of goods is often temporarily surrendered without surrendering title. This creates a bailment, which is defined as the lawful possession of goods by one who is not the owner.

To create a bailment, the goods must be in the possession of the bailee. Possession requires physical control and intent. Whether the owner or someone else must bear a loss often hinges on whether the other person is or is not a bailee.

The bailee's liability for loss depends on the circumstances. Some courts use a straightforward standard of ordinary care. Others use a tripartite test, depending on whether the bailment was for the benefit of the owner (the standard then is gross negligence), for the bailee (extraordinary care), or for both (ordinary care). Bailees may disclaim liability unless they have failed to give adequate notice or unless public policy prohibits disclaimers. A bailee who converts the property will be held liable as an insurer.

A bailor may have liability toward the bailee—for example, for negligent failure to warn of hazards in the bailed property, and for strict liability if the injury was caused by a dangerous object in a defective condition.

Special bailments arise in the case of innkeepers (who have an insurer's liability toward their guests, although many state statutes provide exceptions to this general rule), warehouses, carriers, and leases.

A warehouser is defined as a person engaged in the business of storing goods for hire. The general standard of care is the same as that of ordinary negligence. Many states have statutes imposing a higher standard.

A common carrier—one who holds himself out to all for hire to transport goods—has an insurer's liability toward the goods in his possession, with five exceptions: act of God, act of public enemy, act of public authority, negligence of shipper, and inherent nature of the goods. Because many carriers are involved in most commercial shipments of goods, the law places liability on the initial carrier. The carrier's liability begins once the shipper has given all instructions and taken all action required of it. The carrier's absolute liability ends when it has delivered the goods to the consignee's place of business or residence (unless the agreement states otherwise) or, if no delivery is required, when the consignee has been notified of the arrival of the goods and has had a reasonable opportunity to take possession.

Commodity paper—any document of title—may be negotiated; that is, through proper indorsements on the paper, title may be transferred without physically touching the goods. A duly negotiated document gives the holder title to the document and to the goods, certain rights to the goods delivered to the bailee after the document was issued, and the right to take possession free of any defense or claim by the issuer of the document of title. Certain rules limit the seemingly absolute right of the holder to take title better than that held by the transferor.

Leases are governed by Article 2A of the UCC, which defines them in terms of a transfer of possession and use of goods. The law of leases and sales law, while essentially parallel, differ on occasion and special rules govern consumer leases and finance leases.

KEY TERMS

Bailment	p. 442	Mechanic's lien	p. 452
Bill of lading	p. 445	Negotiable	p. 463
Common carrier	p. 455	Warehouser	p. 453
Document of title	p. 452	Warehouse receipt	p. 453
Lien	p. 452		

SELF-TEST QUESTIONS

1. In a bailment, the bailee:
   (a) must return similar goods
   (b) must return identical goods
   (c) acquires title to the goods
   (d) must pay for the goods
2. In a bailment for the benefit of a bailee, the bailee's duty of care is:
   (a) slight
   (b) extraordinary
   (c) ordinary
   (d) all of the above
3. A disclaimer of liability by a bailee is:
   (a) never allowed
   (b) sometimes allowed
   (c) always allowed
   (d) unheard of in business
4. A bailor may be held liable to the bailee on:
   (a) a negligence theory
   (b) a warranty theory
   (c) a strict liability theory
   (d) all of the above
5. The highest duty of care is imposed on which of the following:
   (a) a common carrier
   (b) a lessee
   (c) a warehouser
   (d) an innkeeper

DEMONSTRATION PROBLEM

A shipment of jelly beans enroute from New York to California was detained at the California border by state inspectors. As a result of the delay during unbearably hot weather, the beans melted into one massive, unedible, unmarketable bean. Should the carrier be held liable? Why?

PROBLEMS

1. Jack visited his favorite restaurant, the Greasy Plate, and placed his coat on a hook near his table. After finishing his meal Jack discovered that the coat was missing. Was the restaurant a bailee of the coat? Why?
2. A campus fraternity, Phi Phi Phi, decided to allow visitors attending football games on campus to park their cars for a fee in the front yard of the fraternity. Assuming the visitors kept the keys to their cars, would the fraternity be a bailee of the cars? Why?
3. Suppose in problem 2 that the fraternity members kept the car keys. One Saturday afternoon, while the football game was still in progress, Ralph showed up at the house and claimed that he was the owner of a new luxury car which had been left in the yard by Leo, who was still at the game. Assume that Ralph, who is telling the truth, is given the keys and drives away with the car. Will the Phi Phis be liable to Leo? Why?
4. An elderly woman, who admitted that she "couldn't remember so good any more" claimed that she deposited approximately $90,000 in cash in her safe-deposit box and that, when she returned three months later, almost $40,000 was missing. During the three month period she invested approximately $40,000 in bonds. Should the safe-deposit box company be liable as bailee? Why?
5. Professor Bacon took his car to Pete's Garage for repairs. Pete finished working on the car early and decided to drive to a nearby farm to pick blueberries. He drove Bacon's car to the farm and parked the car well off the highway, in a sheltered area. Despite Pete's extraordinary care in parking the car, a drunk driver drove off the highway and plowed into the car. Is Pete liable to Bacon for damages? Why?
6. Dr. Casey drove to her tennis club to play tennis. She pulled up to the front door of the club, handed the car keys to an attendant (who parked the cars), and walked to a dressing room to put on her tennis shoes. She then walked back to her car to pick up her tennis racket. She discovered, upon arriving in the parking lot, that the car (along with the racket in the trunk) was missing. Was the tennis club a bailee of the car? Of the racket? Why?
7. Several student radicals led by Al Lyoop, who was ranked No. 3 on the FBI's most wanted list, destroyed a shipment of popcorn enroute from California to Washington. Should the carrier be held liable for the loss? Why?

ANSWERS TO SELF-TEST QUESTIONS

1. (b)   2. (b)   3. (b)   4. (d)   5. (a)

SUGGESTED ANSWER TO DEMONSTRATION PROBLEM

Carriers are not liable for acts of public authorities. However, if the carrier was negligent in storing the beans, it would be liable.

Part 3

The Manager's Legal Agenda

Any company in the business of selling, storing, shipping, or leasing goods should have a lawyer scrutinize its regular contracts to ensure that particular words used in the contract (*e.g.*, "f.o.b.," "ex-ship," and the like) do not have unexpected effects under the Uniform Commercial Code.

Likewise, since the UCC frequently specifies legal effects in the absence of certain contract terms, you should thoroughly review your sales and buying policies with your lawyer so that you can decide the appropriate level of contractual control you wish to exercise over your business.

Make sure that price and other terms are specified to avoid judicial determination of crucial open terms, as permitted under the UCC.

When selling goods, specify that title passes as early as possible, to avoid the risk of paying for lost or damaged goods that have passed beyond your control.

Similarly, when buying goods, specify that title passes as late as possible, to minimize the risk of loss.

Whether buyer or seller, check to make sure that your insurance policy covers all risks of damage or loss that you might be required to bear under your contracts.

To avoid the risk of losing goods that you own which are in the temporary possession of someone else (*e.g.*, a carrier or a storage depot), read the carrier's or bailee's disclaimers and if possible override them by entering into a specific contract with them.

Likewise, any company in the regular business of shipping and storing goods should make sure that its disclaimers are unambiguous and that it can prove the bailor has seen them.

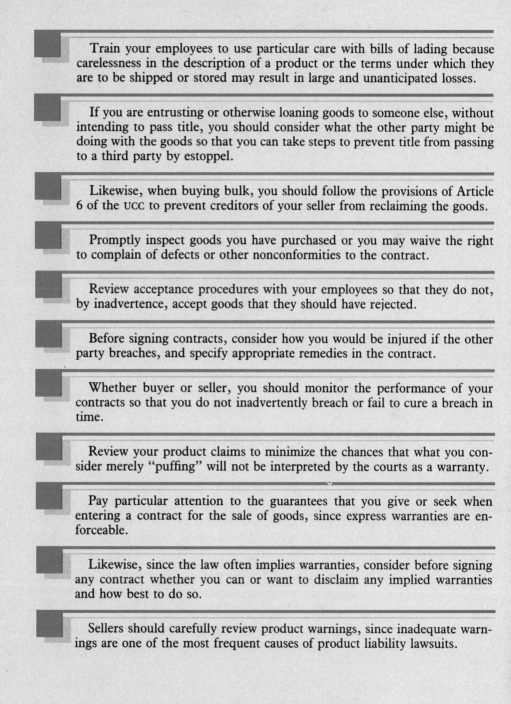

Train your employees to use particular care with bills of lading because carelessness in the description of a product or the terms under which they are to be shipped or stored may result in large and unanticipated losses.

If you are entrusting or otherwise loaning goods to someone else, without intending to pass title, you should consider what the other party might be doing with the goods so that you can take steps to prevent title from passing to a third party by estoppel.

Likewise, when buying bulk, you should follow the provisions of Article 6 of the UCC to prevent creditors of your seller from reclaiming the goods.

Promptly inspect goods you have purchased or you may waive the right to complain of defects or other nonconformities to the contract.

Review acceptance procedures with your employees so that they do not, by inadvertence, accept goods that they should have rejected.

Before signing contracts, consider how you would be injured if the other party breaches, and specify appropriate remedies in the contract.

Whether buyer or seller, you should monitor the performance of your contracts so that you do not inadvertently breach or fail to cure a breach in time.

Review your product claims to minimize the chances that what you consider merely "puffing" will not be interpreted by the courts as a warranty.

Pay particular attention to the guarantees that you give or seek when entering a contract for the sale of goods, since express warranties are enforceable.

Likewise, since the law often implies warranties, consider before signing any contract whether you can or want to disclaim any implied warranties and how best to do so.

Sellers should carefully review product warnings, since inadequate warnings are one of the most frequent causes of product liability lawsuits.

PART

IV

Just remember this: if bankers were as smart as you are, you would starve to death.

HENRY HARFIELD, ESQ., OF THE NEW YORK BAR, ADDRESSING A MEETING OF LAWYERS (*1974*)

COMMERCIAL PAPER

Nature and Form of Commercial Paper

THE IMPORTANCE OF COMMERCIAL PAPER

Commercial paper is the collective term for various instruments that include the ordinary check drawn on a commercial bank, certificates of deposit, drafts, and notes evidencing a promise to pay. Like money, commercial paper is a medium of exchange, but because it is one step removed from money, numerous difficulties arise that require a series of interlocking rules to protect both seller and buyer.

To understand the importance of commercial paper, consider the following which illustrates a distinction critical to the entire unit:

Martina runs a tennis club. She orders a truckload of new tennis rackets from Tracy, a manufacturer. The contract price of the rackets is $100,000. Tracy ships the rackets to Martina. Tracy then sells for $90,000 her contract rights (to receive the payment from Martina of $100,000) to First Bank (see Figure 21-1). Unfortunately, the rackets arrive warped at Martina's and are commercially worthless. Tracy immediately files for bankruptcy (or then departs for Costa Rica).

May the bank collect from Martina $100,000, the value of the contract rights it purchased? No. Under the contract rule discussed in Chapter 13, an assignee—here, the bank—steps into the shoes of the assignor (Tracy) and takes the assigned rights subject to any defense of the obligor (Martina). The result would be the same if Martina had given Tracy a non-negotiable note, which Tracy proceeded to sell to the bank. (By non-negotiable we do not mean that the note cannot be sold, but only that certain legal requirements to be discussed later in this chapter have not been met.)

Now let us add one fact: In addition to signing a contract, Martina gives Tracy a *negotiable* note in exchange for the rackets, and Tracy sells the note to

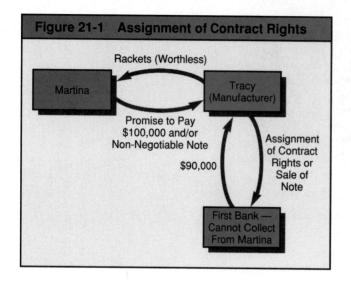

Figure 21-1   Assignment of Contract Rights

Rackets (Worthless)

Martina

Tracy (Manufacturer)

Promise to Pay $100,000 and/or Non-Negotiable Note

$90,000

Assignment of Contract Rights or Sale of Note

First Bank — Cannot Collect From Martina

the bank. By throwing in the negotiable note, Martina dramatically changes the results. Because the note is negotiable and because the bank, we assume, bought the note in good faith (that is, unaware that the rackets were warped), the bank will recover the $100,000 (see Figure 21-2).

Negotiability is the key to the central role that commercial paper plays in modern finance. Without the ability to pay and finance through commercial paper, the business world would be paralyzed. At bottom, **negotiability** is the means by which a person is empowered to transfer to another *more than what the transferor himself possesses.* In essence, this is the power to convey to the transferee the right in turn to convey

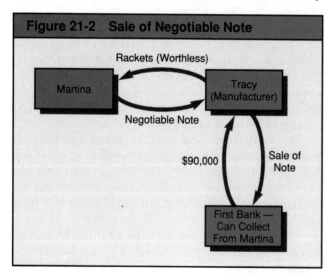

Figure 21-2   Sale of Negotiable Note

Rackets (Worthless)

Martina

Tracy (Manufacturer)

Negotiable Note

$90,000

Sale of Note

First Bank — Can Collect From Martina

clear title, when the original transferor does not have clear title.

In this chapter we examine the history and nature of commercial paper and define the types of parties and instruments. We then proceed to four fundamental issues that must be addressed to determine whether such parties as First Bank in the above example can collect:

1. Is the paper *negotiable?* That is, is the paper in the proper form? (We explore that issue in this chapter.)
2. Was the paper negotiated *properly?* (See Chapter 22.)
3. Is the purchaser of the paper a *holder in due course?* (See Chapter 23.)
4. Does the maker of the paper have available any defenses against even the holder in due course? (See Chapter 23.)

In most transactions, especially when the first three questions are answered affirmatively, the purchaser will have little trouble collecting. But when the purchaser is unable to collect, complex questions of liability arise. These questions, along with termination of liability, are discussed in Chapter 24.

Finally, in Chapter 25 we examine other legal aspects of banking, including letters of credit and electronic funds transfer.

History of Commercial Paper

Negotiable instruments are no modern invention; we know that merchants used them as long ago as the age of Hammurabi, around 2100 B.C. They fell into disuse in the Dark Ages after the collapse of the Roman Empire and then reappeared in Italy around the fourteenth century. They became more common as long-distance commerce spread. In an era before paper currency, payment in coins or bullion was awkward, especially for merchants who traveled great distances across national boundaries to attend the fairs at which most economic exchanges took place. Merchants and traders found it far more efficient to pay through paper.

Bills of exchange, today commonly known as drafts, were recognized instruments in the law merchant. The international merchant courts regularly enforced their provisions and permitted them to be transferred to others by **indorsement,** sometimes spelled *endorsement*. By the beginning of the sixteenth century, the British common-law courts began to hear cases involving bills of exchange, but it took a half century before the courts became comfortable with them and accepted them as crucial to the growing economy.

Courts were also hesitant until the end of the seventeenth century about sanctioning a transferor's assignment of a promissory note if it meant that the transferee would have better title than the transferor. One reason for the courts' reluctance to sanction assignments stemmed from the law that permitted debtors to be jailed, a law that was not repealed until 1870. The buyer of goods might have been willing originally to give a promissory note because he knew that a particular seller would not attempt to jail him for default, but who could be sure that a transferee, probably a complete stranger, would be so charitable?

The inability to negotiate promissory notes prevented a banking system from fully developing. During the English Civil War in the seventeenth century, merchants began to deposit cash with the goldsmiths, who lent it out at interest and issued the depositors promissory notes, the forerunner of bank notes. But a judicial decision in 1703 declared that promissory notes were not negotiable, whether they were made payable to the order of a specific person or to "bearer." Parliament responded the following year with the Promissory Notes Act, which for the first time permitted an assignee to sue the note's maker.

Thereafter the courts in both England and the United States began to shape the modern law of negotiable instruments. By the late nineteenth century, Parliament had codified the law of negotiable instruments in England. Codification came later in the United States. In 1896, the National Conference of Commissioners on Uniform State Laws (the National Conference) proposed the Negotiable Instruments Act, which was adopted in all states by 1924. That law eventually was superseded by the adoption of UCC Articles 3 and 4, which we study in this unit.

FUTURE OF COMMERCIAL PAPER

State Law

In 1990, the American Law Institute and the National Conference of Commissioners on Uniform State Laws approved revised Article 3, entitled "Negotiable Instruments" related amendments in Article 4. The revisions clarify and update the law without changing the basic structure presented in the chapters that follow. Because the revisions are now being considered for adoption by state legislatures, they offer a preview of future law governing commercial paper.

The revisions will have perhaps the greatest impact on the definition of negotiable paper, holder in due course requirements, and allocation of loss principles. For example, the revisions provide that paper may be negotiable even when it includes a variable interest rate or limits payment to a particular fund, in contrast to current law (see pages 482 and 484). The revisions affecting holder in due course status are both general (such as altering the good faith test by requiring "the observance of reasonable commercial standards of fair dealing" in addition to "honesty in fact;" see page 507) and specific (a check becomes overdue 90 days after its date rather than as now after 30 days; see page 510).

An especially important function of the law governing commercial paper is to allocate losses resulting from forgery. The revisions change the allocation of loss rules in several ways that affect businesses. For example, the Official Comment to revised Section 3-405 states that

> the risk of loss for fraudulent endorsements by employees who are entrusted with responsibility with respect to checks should fall on the employer rather than the bank. . . .

As a result, the employer will bear the loss even when (unlike present law covered on page 501) its negligence cannot be proven. The Official Comment summarizes the rationale as follows:

> [T]he employer is in a far better position to avoid the loss by care in choosing employees, in supervising them, and in adopting other [preventive] measures. . . .

Federal and International Preemption

State law governing commercial paper is increasingly vulnerable to federal preemption. This preemption takes two major forms. First, the Federal Reserve Board governs the activities of Federal Reserve banks.

As a result Federal Reserve regulations provide important guidelines for the check collection process. The revisions acknowledge that these regulations supersede any conflicting Article 3 provisions. Second, Article 3 might also be preempted by federal statutes. An important example is the Expedited Funds Availability Act, which became effective in 1988 (see page 550).

Federal preemption may in the future become intertwined with international law. In 1988, the United Nations General Assembly adopted the Convention on International Bills of Exchange and International Promissory Notes. This Convention, if approved by the United States as a treaty, would preempt Article 3 in cases involving international drafts and notes.

COMMERCIAL PAPER IN ECONOMICS AND FINANCE

Economics

To the economist, one type of commercial paper—the bank check—is the primary component of M1, the basic money supply. It is easy to see why. When you deposit cash in a checking account, you may either withdraw the currency—coins and bills—or draw on the account by writing out a check. If you write a check to "cash," withdraw currency, and pay a creditor, there has been no change in the money supply. But if you pay your creditor by check, the quantity of money has increased: the cash you deposited remains available and your creditor deposits the check to his own account as though it were cash. (M2, a more broadly-defined money supply, includes savings deposits at commercial banks.)

Finance

Commercial paper is defined more narrowly in finance than in law. To the corporate treasurer and other financiers, commercial paper ordinarily means short-term promissory notes sold by finance companies and large corporations for a fixed rate of interest. Maturity dates range from a low of three days to a high of nine months. It is an easy way for issuers to raise short-term money quickly. And although short-term notes are unsecured, historically they have been almost as safe as obligations of the United States government. By contrast, for legal purposes commercial paper includes long-term notes (which are often secured), drafts, checks, and certificates of deposit (CD's).

TYPES OF COMMERCIAL PAPER AND PARTIES

Coverage of Article 3

UCC Article 3 covers commercial paper, but explicitly excludes money, documents of title, and investment securities. Documents of title include bills of lading and warehouse receipts and are governed by Article 7. Investment securities are covered by Article 8. Instruments that fall within the scope of Article 3 may also be subject to Article 4 (bank deposits and collections), Article 8 (securities), and Article 9 (secured transactions). If so, the rules of these other articles supersede the provisions of Article 3 to the extent of conflict. Article 3 is a set of general provisions on negotiability; the other articles deal more narrowly with specific transactions or instruments.

Drafts

Parties   The **draft** is one of the two basic types of commercial paper; the other is the **note.** The draft is a three-party transaction. The **drawer** prepares a document—the draft—ordering the **drawee** to remit a stated sum of money to the **payee.** The drawer, drawee, and payee need not be different people; the same person may have different capacities in a single transaction. For example, a drawer (the person asking that payment be made) may also be the payee (the person to whom the payment is to be made). A drawee who signs the draft becomes an **acceptor.** By accepting, the drawee pledges to honor the draft as written. To accept, the drawee need only sign her name on the draft—usually vertically on the face, but anywhere will do. Words such as "accepted" or "good" are unnecessary. However, a drawee who indicates that she might refuse to pay will not be held to have accepted. Thus in the archetypal case, the court held that a drawee who signed his name and appended the words "Kiss my foot" did not accept the draft. [Norton v. Knapp, 19 N.W. 867 (Ia. 1884)]

Types of Drafts   Drafts can be divided into two broad subcategories: *sight drafts* and *time drafts*. A **sight draft** calls for payment "on sight"; that is, when presented. A **time draft,** not surprisingly, calls for payment on a date specified in the draft. Recall (p. 473) that Martina wished to buy tennis rackets from Tracy. Martina will not have sufficient cash to pay until she has sold them, but Tracy needs to be paid immediately. The solution: a common form of time draft known as a **trade acceptance.** Tracy, the seller, draws a draft on Martina, who thus becomes a drawee. The draft orders Martina to pay to the order of Tracy, as payee, the purchase price on a fixed date. Tracy presents the draft to Martina, who accepts it by signing her name. Tracy then can indorse the draft (by signing it) and sell it, at a discount, to her bank or some other financial institution. Tracy thus gets her money right away; the bank may collect from Martina on the date specified.

Suppose Martina had the money, but did not want to pay before delivery. Tracy, on the other hand, did not want to ship before Martina paid. The solution: a sight draft, drawn on Martina, to which would be attached an *order bill of lading* (p. 463) that Tracy received from the trucker when she shipped the rackets. The sight draft and bill of lading go to a bank in Martina's city. When the tennis rackets arrive the carrier notifies the bank, which presents the draft to Martina for payment. When she has done so, the bank gives Martina the bill of lading, entitling her to receive the shipment. The bank forwards the payment to Tracy's bank, which credits Tracy's account with the purchase amount.

Drafts in International Trade   Drafts are an international convention. Usage and customs are somewhat different outside the United States, however. In England and the British Commonwealth, drafts are called bills of exchange. In most of the world, drafts are prepared in duplicate, a custom that arose from the chancy voyages in an era of pirates and vessels far less seaworthy than ours today. One copy of the draft (*first draft*) went with the shipment, the other (*second draft*) in a different ship. Today, however, regular mail delivery is sufficiently safe that the custom of duplicate drafts is beginning to be phased out.

A widely used draft in international trade is the **banker's acceptance.** This instrument is used when an exporter agrees to extend credit to an importer. Assume Martina, the importer, is in New York; Tracy, the exporter, is in Taiwan. Tracy is willing to permit Martina to pay 90 days after shipment. Martina makes a deal with her New York bank to issue Tracy's bank in Taiwan a **letter of credit.** This tells the seller's bank that the buyer's bank is willing to accept a draft drawn on the buyer in accordance with terms spelled out in the letter of credit. To induce it to issue a letter of credit, Martina's bank may insist on a security interest in the tennis rackets, or it may conclude that Martina is creditworthy. On receipt of the letter of credit, Tracy presents her bank in Taiwan with a draft drawn on Martina's bank. That bank antes up the purchase amount (less its fees and interest), paying Tracy directly. It then forwards the draft, bill of lading, and other papers to a correspondent bank in New York, which in turn presents it to Martina's bank. If the papers are in order, that bank will "accept" the draft (sign it). The signed draft is the banker's acceptance (see Figure 21-3). It is returned to the bank in Taiwan, which can then discount the banker's acceptance if it wishes payment immediately, or else wait the 90 days to present it to the New York bank for payment. After remitting to the Chinese bank, the New York bank then demands payment from Martina.

Checks

A second type of commercial paper is the common bank **check,** a special form of draft. UCC Section 3-104(2)(b) defines a check as a "draft drawn on a bank and payable on demand." **Postdating** a check does not invalidate it, nor change its character as payable on demand. Postdating simply changes the first time at which the payee may demand payment. Like drafts, checks may be accepted by the bank. Bank acceptance of a check is called *certification;* the check is said to be **certified.** By certifying (stamping the word "certified" on the face of the check), the bank guarantees that it will honor the check when presented. It can offer this guarantee because it removes from the drawer's account the face amount of the check and holds it for payment. The payee may demand payment from the bank, but not from the drawer or

Figure 21–3   A Time Draft

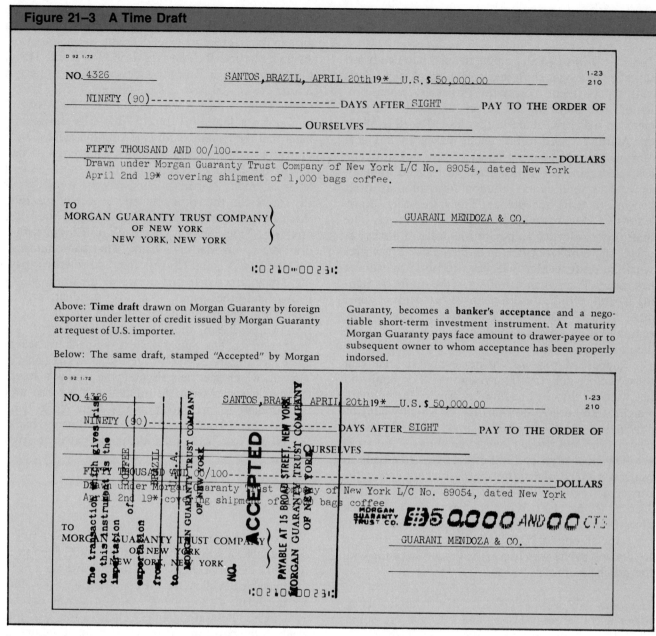

Above: **Time draft** drawn on Morgan Guaranty by foreign exporter under letter of credit issued by Morgan Guaranty at request of U.S. importer.

Below: The same draft, stamped "Accepted" by Morgan Guaranty, becomes a **banker's acceptance** and a negotiable short-term investment instrument. At maturity Morgan Guaranty pays face amount to drawer-payee or to subsequent owner to whom acceptance has been properly indorsed.

Source: From "The Financing of Exports and Imports," © 1973, 1977, 1980 by Morgan Guaranty Trust Company of New York. Used by permission.

any prior indorser of the check. Distinguish a certified check from a *cashier's* check. A **cashier's check** is drawn on the account of the bank itself and signed by an authorized bank representative in return for a cash payment from the customer. The bank guarantees payment of the cashier's check also.

Notes

A note—often called a **promissory note**—is a written promise to pay a specified sum of money on demand or at a definite time. There are two parties to a note: the **maker** (*promisor*) and the **payee** (*promisee*). For an

Figure 21–4   A Promissory Note

$25,000   Orlando, Florida
                                                                            February 17, 1991

Eight months after date I promise to pay to the order of Peter Payee
twenty-five thousand dollars.

Mike Maker
Mike Maker

example of a promissory note, see Figure 21-4. The maker might execute a promissory note in return for a money loan from a bank or other financial institution, or in return for the opportunity to make a purchase on credit.

Certificates of Deposit

A fourth type of commercial paper is the **certificate of deposit,** commonly called a *CD*. The CD is a written acknowledgment by a bank that it has received money and agrees to repay it at a time specified in the certificate. The first negotiable CD was issued in 1961 by First National City Bank of New York (now Citibank); it was designed to compete for corporate cash that companies were investing in Treasury notes and other funds. Because CDs are negotiable, they can be traded easily if the holder wants cash, though of course their price fluctuates with the market.

Other Parties to Commercial Paper

In addition to drawers, makers, drawees, and payees, there are five other capacities in which one can deal with commercial paper.

Indorser and Indorsee   The **indorser** is one who transfers ownership of a negotiable instrument by signing it. A depositor indorses a check when presenting it for deposit by signing it on the back. The bank deposits its own funds, in the amount of the check, to the depositor's account. By indorsing it, the depositor transfers ownership of the check to the bank. The depositor's bank then can present it to the drawer's bank for repayment from the drawer's funds. The **indorsee** is the one to whom a draft or note is indorsed. When a check is deposited in a bank, the bank is the indorsee.

Holder   A **holder** is a person who possesses an instrument drawn, issued, or indorsed to her, to her order, to bearer, or in blank. "Holder" is thus a generic term that embraces several of the specific types of parties already mentioned. An indorsee and a drawee can be holders. But a holder can also be someone unnamed whom the original parties did not contemplate by name; for example, the holder of a bearer note.

Holder in Due Course   A **holder in due course** is a special type of holder who, if certain requirements are met, acquires rights beyond those possessed by the transferor. We discuss the requirements for a holder in due course in Chapter 23.

Accommodation Party   An **accommodation** party is one who signs a negotiable instrument in order to lend her name to another party to the instrument. It does not matter in what capacity she signs, whether as maker or co-maker, drawer or co-drawer, or indorser. As a signatory, an accommodation party is always a surety (Chapter 26). The extent of the accommodation party's liability to pay depends on whether she has added language specifying her purposes in signing. UCC Section 3-416 distinguishes between guarantees of payment and of collection. An accommodation party who adds words such as "payment guaranteed" subjects herself to primary liability: she is guaranteeing that she will pay if the principal signatory fails to pay when the instrument is due. But if the accommodation party signs "collection guaranteed," the holder must first sue the maker and win a court judgment. Only if the judgment is unsatisfied can the holder seek to collect from the accommodation party. When words of guaranty do not specify the type, the law presumes a payment guaranty. The following case shows the difficulties that can arise if these differences are not understood.

BROWN UNIVERSITY v. LAUDATI
113 R.I. 1299, 320 A.2d 609 (1974)

PAOLINO, JUSTICE. This is a civil action to recover the balance due on a promissory note endorsed and guaranteed by the defendant. The case was heard before a justice of the Superior Court sitting with a jury and resulted in a verdict for the plaintiff in the sum of $1,788.40. The cause is before this court on the defendant's appeal from the judgment entered on the verdict.

The facts are relatively simple. On February 14, 1963, defendant's daughter Ruth signed a promissory note to Brown University under the National Defense Student Loan Program and defendant endorsed it and guaranteed full payment. Dean Gretchen Tonks, the officer in charge of the financial aid program at Pembroke College when this note was executed, testified that she explained the financial aid program to defendant and told her that if her daughter did not pay the note, defendant would be responsible for payment. Dean Tonks denied that she ever told defendant that she would not be liable under her guarantee after her daughter became twenty-one. The defendant testified that she never read the note or guarantee and that Dean Tonks told her that after her daughter became twenty-one defendant would not be responsible for the note.

* * *

[I]n the case at bar, there is competent evidence, which if believed, supports the jury's verdict. Dean Tonks' testimony that defendant had endorsed and guaranteed the note signed by her daughter is uncontradicted. The only disputed issue of fact is defendant's claim that Dean Tonks, plaintiff's agent, had misrepresented to her the legal effect of the endorsement and guarantee she signed. The defendant had the burden, as the trial justice charged, to establish such a defense of misrepresentation by clear and convincing evidence. It is obvious that the jury accepted Dean Tonks' version of what happened and rejected defendant's recollection of the events surrounding her endorsement and guarantee of the note in question. On this record we cannot fault the jury's verdict.

We come, finally, to the defendant's contention that the plaintiff should have proceeded against the defendant's daughter before suing the defendant. The trial justice had instructed the jury that the plaintiff was not required to bring legal action against the defendant's daughter prior to proceeding against the defendant. This instruction was correct. The Uniform Commercial Code provides that:

> 'Payment guaranteed' or equivalent words added to a signature mean that the signer engages that if the instrument is not paid when due he will pay it according to its tenor *without resort by the holder to any other party.* (emphasis added)

The defendant's contention that the plaintiff should have proceeded against the defendant's daughter first is clearly without merit.

The defendant's appeal is denied and dismissed, the judgment appealed from is affirmed, and the cause is remanded to the Superior Court for further proceedings.

REQUIREMENTS FOR NEGOTIABILITY

Whether or not a paper is negotiable is the first of our four major questions, and is one which nonlawyers must confront. Auditors, retailers, and financial institutions often handle notes and checks and usually must make snap judgments about negotiability. Unless the elements of UCC Section 3-104(1) are met as follows, the paper is not negotiable:

> Any writing to be a negotiable instrument within this Article must
> (a) be signed by the maker or drawer; and
> (b) contain an unconditional promise or order to pay a sum certain in money and no other promise, order, obligation or power given by the maker or drawer except as authorized by this Article; and
> (c) be payable on demand or at a definite time; and
> (d) be payable to order or to bearer.

This rule states the basic premise of a negotiable instrument: that the holder be able to ascertain all essential terms from its face. Eight crucial components of the rule are as follows:

"Any Writing"   Under Section 1-201(46), "written" or "writing" includes "printing, typewriting or any other intentional reduction to tangible form." That definition is broad—so broad, in fact, that from time to time the newspapers report checks written on materials ranging from a girdle (an Ohio resident wanted

to make his tax payment stretch) to granite (see **Box 21-1**). Since these are tangible materials, the checks meet the writing requirement. The writing can be made in any medium: ink, pencil, or even spray paint, as the angry dog-walker in Box 21-1 proved. Of course, there is a danger in using pencil or an ink that can be erased, since the drawer might be liable for alterations. For example, if you write out in pencil a check for $10 and someone erases your figures and writes in $250, you may lose your right to protest when the bank cashes it.

"Signed by the Maker or Drawer"   Signature is not limited to the personal handwriting of one's name. "Any symbol executed or adopted by a party with present intention to authenticate a writing" will serve. (Section 1-201(39).) That means that a maker or drawer may make an impression of his signature with a rubber stamp or even an "X," if he intends that by so doing he has signed. It may be typed or by thumbprint. In some cases, an appropriate letterhead may serve to make the note or draft negotiable, without any other signature. Nor does the position of the signature matter. Blackstone Kent's handwritten note, "Ten days from this note, I, Blackstone Kent, promise to pay $1,000 to the order of Webster Mews," is sufficient to make the note negotiable, even though there is no subsequent signature. Moreover, the signature may be in a trade or assumed name. (Note: special problems arise when an agent signs on behalf of a principal. We consider these problems in Chapter 24.)

LAW AND LIFE

BOX 21-1

Taking Things for Granite

By Joel Schwarz

A check meets the writing requirement when the inked, penciled, or spray-painted writing appears on any tangible material.

Joe Mallen of Sequim, Washington, wrote out a 25-pound check to the U.S. District Court in Seattle recently. It didn't bounce.

A Writing in Tangible Form

Mallen was angry after being cited for a leash law violation by the U.S. Fish and Wildlife Service for walking his dog without a leash in a federal refuge for birds. Mallen, who disputed the charge, also hadn't gotten over his irritation with a local bank clerk who had held an out-of-state check made out to Mallen for ten days without cashing it.

To vent his anger at both situations, Mallen spray painted a 25-pound stone from his front yard with three coats of white paint, and with red paint spelled out his account number, the bank's name, the payee, his leash law citation number, and his signature.

The court accepted the stone check and stamped it paid in four places.

Source: From *Student Lawyer*, December, 1981

"Contain an Unconditional Promise or Order to Pay" To be negotiable, an instrument must contain an unconditional promise or order to pay. A "promise" is an undertaking to pay and must be more than an acknowledgment of an obligation. An ordinary I.O.U. ("this is to acknowledge that I owe Blackstone Kent $400") is not a negotiable note. The note must say something like this: "I promise to [or "will"] pay $400 to Blackstone Kent on October 1." An "order" is a direction to pay and must be more than an authorization or request. A draft says "I would appreciate your paying [or, "I authorize you to pay"] Blackstone Kent $400" is not a direction but an authorization or request, and such a draft is not negotiable. The draft must say: "Pay to the order of Blackstone Kent." Words of courtesy, such as "please pay," do not negate negotiability, however.

The promise or order must be unconditional. Not: "I will pay *if* he delivers the goods," but: "I will pay." The requirement is not met "if the instrument states that it is subject to or governed by any other agreement" or if it "states that it is to be paid only out of a particular fund or source," with certain exceptions. (Section 3-105(2).) If Martina gives Tracy a note saying: "March 29, 1985. I promise to pay to the order of Tracy $10,000 to be paid only out of my savings account in First Bank," the note is not negotiable. However, if the note had simply referred to an account from which Martina expected to make the payment or indicated a particular account to be debited, the promise is unconditional and the note is negotiable.

Some exceptions: Instruments issued by a government or governmental agency do not lose negotiability if they specify that payments are limited to particular funds. Likewise, an instrument is not made conditional if it is used by or on behalf of a partnership, unincorporated association, trust, or estate, and is limited to payment out of the entire assets of one of those groups. Nor is an instrument made conditional if it merely recites the consideration or states that it is secured by a mortgage or some other device. The existence of a separate agreement between the original parties does not affect the negotiability of the instrument itself, even if the instrument refers to the separate agreement—as long as the instrument does not on its face recite that it is "subject to" the other agreement. How these rules work in practice should become clear from the following case, in which the court held that the note was subject to an underlying agreement and hence was not negotiable.

HOLLY HILL ACRES, LTD. v. CHARTER BANK OF GAINESVILLE
314 So.2d 209 (D.C.App. Fla. 1975)

SCHEB, JUDGE. Appellant/defendant appeals from a summary judgment in favor of appellee/plaintiff Bank in a suit wherein the appellee sought to foreclose a note and mortgage given by appellant.

The appellee Bank was the assignee from appellees Rogers and Blythe of a promissory note and purchase money mortgage executed and delivered by the appellant. The note, executed April 28, 1972, contains the following stipulation:

> This note with interest is secured by a mortgage on real estate, of even date herewith, made by the maker hereof in favor of the said payee, and shall be construed and enforced according to the laws of the State of Florida. *The terms of said mortgage are by this reference made a part hereof.* (Emphasis supplied.)

Rogers and Blythe assigned the promissory note and mortgage in question to the appellee to secure their own note. Appellee sued appellant and joined Rogers and Blythe as defendants alleging a default on their note as well as a default on appellant's note.

Appellant answered incorporating an affirmative defense that fraud on the part of Rogers and Blythe induced the sale which gave rise to the purchase money mortgage. Rogers and Blythe denied the fraud. In opposition to appellee Bank's motion for summary judgment, the appellant submitted an affidavit in support of its allegation of fraud on the part of agents of Rogers and Blythe. The trial court held the appellee Bank was a holder in due course of the note executed by appellant and entered a summary final judgment against the appellant.

The note having incorporated the terms of the purchase money mortgage was not negotiable. The appellee Bank was not a holder in due course, therefore, the appellant was entitled to raise against the appellee any defenses which could be raised between the appellant and Rogers and Blythe. Since appellant asserted an affirmative defense of fraud, it was incumbent on the appellee to establish the non-existence of any genuine issue of any material fact or the legal insufficiency of appellant's affirmative defense. Having failed to do so, appellee was not entitled to a judgment as a matter of law; hence, we reverse.

The note, incorporating by reference the terms of the mortgage, did not contain the unconditional promise to pay required by Fla.Stat. § 673.3-104(1)(b). Rather, the note falls within the scope of Fla.Stat. § 673.3-105(2)(a). Although negotiability is now governed by the Uniform Commercial Code, this was the Florida view even before the U.C.C. was adopted.

Appellee Bank relies upon Scott v. Taylor, 1912, 63 Fla. 62, 58 So. 30, as authority for the proposition that its note is negotiable. *Scott*, however, involved a note which stated: "this note secured by mortgage." Mere reference to a note being secured by mortgage is a common commercial practice and such reference in itself does not impede the negotiability of the note. There

(*continued on next page*)

(continued)

HOLLY HILL ACRES, LTD. v. CHARTER BANK OF GAINESVILLE
314 So.2d 209 (D.C.App. Fla. 1975)

is, however, a significant difference in a note stating that it is "secured by a mortgage" from one which provides, "the terms of said mortgage are by this reference made a part hereof." In the former instance the note merely refers to a separate agreement which does not impede its negotiability, while in the latter instance the note is rendered non-negotiable.

As a general rule the assignee of a mortgage securing a non-negotiable note, even though a bona fide purchaser for value, takes subject to all defenses available as against the mortgagee. Appellant raised the issue of fraud as between himself and other parties to the note, therefore, it was incumbent on the appellee Bank, as movant for a summary judgment, to prove the non-existence of any genuinely triable issue.

Accordingly, the entry of a summary final judgment is reversed and the cause remanded for further proceedings.

"Sum Certain"   The instrument must recite an exact amount of money that is to be paid (the "sum certain"), although the exact amount need not be expressed in a single figure. For example, the note can state that the principal is $1,000 and interest is 11.5 percent, without specifying the total amount. Or the note could state the amount in installments: twelve equal installments of $88.25. Or it could state different interest rates before and after a certain date, or depending on whether or not the maker has defaulted. It could permit the maker to take a discount if he pays before a certain date, or assess a penalty if he pays after the date. It could also provide for an attorney's fees and costs of collection on default. The fundamental rule is that for any time of payment the holder must be able to determine from the instrument itself, after the appropriate calculations, the amount then payable. A note that fixed the amount due by referring to "then prevailing market price" would not be negotiable, because the holder could not determine beforehand what that amount would be. In the next case, the holder lost on its claim that a note was negotiable because the interest was stated to be at "bank rates."

CENTERRE BANK OF BRANSON v. CAMPBELL
744 S.W.2d 490 (Mo.App. 1988)

CROW, CHIEF JUDGE.

On or about May 7, 1985, appellants ("the Campbells") signed the following document:

"PROMISSORY NOTE

$11,250.00   May 7, 1985

For value received, the undersigned jointly and severally as principals, promise to pay to the order of Strand Investment Company Eleven Thousand and Two Hundred and Fifty Dollars ($11,250.00) with interest thereon from date at the rate of 14% interest per annum, said principal and interest to be paid in annual installments as follows:

First Year—$3,750.000 +
  $1,575.000 interest $5,325.00
Second Year–$3,750.00 +
  $1,050.00 interest $4,800.00
Third Year—$3,750.00 +
  $ 525.00 interest $4275.00

Interest will be payable semi-annually.

Interest may vary with bank rates charged to Strand
Investment Company.

If default is made in the payment of any annual installment when due, then
the investor's participation in Notch Real Estate Partnership will be forfeited.

Privilege is given to pay all or any part of this note at any time without
penalty.

This note may be used as collateral to obtain funds from a financial institution.

> s/ Dowe Campbell
> Curtis D. Campbell

> s/ Debbie A. Campbell
> Debbie A. Campbell"

On May 13, 1985, the president and secretary of Strand Investment Company ("Strand") signed the following provision on the reverse side of the
above document:

> "I hereby Pledge and assign this promissory note in the amount $11,250.00
> with recourse, dated this 13th day of May, 1985, to Centerre Bank of
> Branson, Branson, Mo.

> > s/ Ben P. Gaines
> > Strand Investment Co.
> > Ben P. Gaines, President

Attest:
s/ Betty Hawkins
Secretary, Betty Hawkins"

On June 30, 1986, Centerre Bank of Branson ("Centerre") sued the Campbells.

* * *

[The Campbells] aver that the note was given for the purchase of an interest in a limited partnership to be created by Strand, that no limited partnership was thereafter created by Strand, and that by reason thereof there was
"a complete and total failure of consideration for the said promissory note."

* * *

The trial court entered judgment in favor of Centerre and against the
Campbells for $9,000, plus accrued interest and costs. The trial court filed
no findings of fact or conclusions of law, none having been requested. The
trial court did, however, include in its judgment a finding that Centerre "is
a holder in due course of the promissory note sued upon."

The Campbells appeal, briefing four points. Their first three, taken together, present a single hypothesis of error consisting of these components:
(a) the Campbells showed "by clear and convincing evidence a valid and

(continued on next page)

(continued)

CENTERRE BANK OF BRANSON v. CAMPBELL
744 S.W.2d 490 (Mo.App. 1988)

meritorious defense in that there existed a total lack and failure of consideration for the promissory note in question," (b) Centerre acquired the note subject to such defense in that Centerre was not a holder in due course, as one can be a holder in due course of a note *only if the note is a negotiable instrument,* and (c) the note was not a negotiable instrument inasmuch as "it failed to state a sum certain due the payee."

★   ★   ★

The Campbells insist that the note in the instant case is not a negotiable instrument because it contains the provision: "Interest may vary with bank rates charged to Strand Investment Company." We henceforth refer to the theory advanced by the Campbells' first three points as their "primary theory of non-liability."

★   ★   ★

Neither side has cited a Missouri case applying §§ 400.3-104 and 400.3-106 to a note containing a provision similar to: "Interest may vary with bank rates charged to Strand." Our independent research has likewise proven fruitless. There are, however, instructive decisions from other jurisdictions.

In *Taylor v. Roeder,* 360 S.E.2d 191 (1987), a note provided for interest at "[t]hree percent (3.00%) over Chase Manhattan Prime to be adjusted monthly." A second note provided for interest at "3% over Chasemanhattan [sic] prime adjusted monthly." Applying sections of the Uniform Commercial Code adopted by Virginia identical to §§ 400.3-104 and 400.3-106, RSMo 1978, the court held the notes were not negotiable instruments in that the amounts required to satisfy them could not be ascertained without reference to an extrinsic source, the varying prime rate of interest charged by Chase Manhattan Bank.

★   ★   ★

In *A. Alport & Son, Inc. v. Hotel Evans, Inc.,* 317 N.Y.S.2d 937 (Sup. Ct.1970), a note contained the notation "with interest at bank rates." Applying a section of the Uniform Commercial Code adopted by New York identical to §400.3-104, RSMo 1978, the court held the note was not a negotiable instrument in that the amount of interest had to be established by facts outside the instrument.

In the instant case, the Campbells insist that it is impossible to determine from the face of the note the amount due and payable on any payment date, as the note provides that interest may vary with bank rates charged to Strand. Consequently, say the Campbells, the note is not a negotiable instrument, as it does not contain a promise to pay a "sum certain." § 400.3-104(1)(b).

. . . We hold that under §§ 400.3-104 and 400.3-106, and the authorities discussed earlier, the provision that interest may vary with bank rates charged to Strand bars the note from being a negotiable instrument, thus no assignee thereof can be a holder in due course. The trial court therefore erred as a matter of law in ruling that Centerre was a holder in due course. [Judgment reversed.]

"In Money"   Section 1-201(24) defines money as "a medium of exchange authorized or adopted by a domestic or foreign government as a part of its currency." As long as the medium of exchange was such at the time the instrument was made, it is payable in money, even if the medium of exchange has been abolished at the time the instrument is due. An instrument payable by its terms in "currency" or "current funds" is payable in money and meets the requirements of negotiability. (Section 3-107(1).)

If the instrument says that payment may be made only in a foreign currency, the maker or drawer must honor the commitment. If it states the amount in a foreign currency but is silent about how payment is to be made, the maker or drawer has the option of paying in dollars at the exchange rate prevailing on the date due or on the day of demand.

"No Other Promise, Order, Obligation, or Power"
The only permissible promise or order in a negotiable instrument is to pay a sum certain in money. Any other promise or order negates negotiability. The reason for this rule is to prevent an instrument from having an indeterminate value. If Martina added to her promissory note that she would give Tracy a quarter interest in her business, the note would be nonnegotiable. Since it would be impossible to say exactly what the value of Martina's business would be, a present value for the note could not be fixed. The use of such an instrument would be awkward in a world of freely transferable negotiable instruments. However, when certain obligations are added to the instrument to ensure the payment of the sum due, negotiability is not defeated. Section 3-112 lists several obligations that will not defeat negotiability, for example: a promise or power to maintain or protect collateral and a term authorizing *confession of judgment* on the instrument if it is not paid when due. (A confession of judgment is a procedure that permits the plaintiff to obtain a court judgment for the sum due without having to file a lawsuit.)

"Payable on Demand or at a Definite Time"   An instrument that says it is payable on sight is payable on demand, as is one that states no time for payment. "Definite time" may be stated in several ways; it is not necessary to set out a specific date. For example, a note might say that it is payable on or before a stated date, at a fixed period after the date, at a fixed period after sight, at a definite time subject to acceleration, or at a definite time subject to extension at the option of the holder or automatically on or after the occurrence of a particular event. However, if the only time fixed is on the occurrence of a contingent event, the time is not definite, even though the event in fact has already occurred. An example of a valid acceleration clause is the following: "At the option of the holder, this note shall become immediately due and payable in the event that the maker fails to comply with any of the promises contained in this note or to pay or perform any other obligation of the maker to the holder."

Is Martina's note, "payable ten days after I give birth," negotiable? No, because the date her baby is due is uncertain. Is this note negotiable: "payable on January 1, but if the Yankees win the World Series, payable four days later"? Yes: this is a valid acceleration clause attached to a definite date.

One practical difference between a demand and time instrument is the date on which the statute of limitations begins to run. (A statute of limitations is a limit on the time a creditor has to file a lawsuit to collect the debt.) Section 3-122(1) says that "a cause of action accrues" (statute of limitations begins to run) on the day after maturity in the case of a time instrument, but on the date of the instrument in the case of a demand instrument (or on the date issued if it bears no date). As the next case demonstrates, whether the plaintiff holds a time or demand note can make a difference.

**SHIELDS v.
PRENDERGAST**
36 N.C.App. 633, 244
S.E.2d 475 (1978)

VAUGHN, JUDGE. If the note sued on is a demand instrument, a cause of action accrued against the maker on the date of the instrument, and consequently, the period of limitation began to run in favor of the maker on that date, 3 February 1970. In that event, the judge's conclusion that the suit was barred because it was not instituted within three years, would be correct.

By its terms the note is "Due At request" or payable on demand. Plaintiff contends that because of the inclusion of the term "with 30 days notice," it is not a demand instrument. We disagree. "The debt which constitutes the cause of action arises immediately on the loan. It is quite clear that a promissory note, payable on demand, is a *present debt* and is payable without any demand, and the statute begins to run from the date of it." "Instruments payable on demand include . . . those in which no time for payment is stated." G.S. 25-3-108. No time for payment is stated in the note in question, and it is, therefore, payable on demand. The provision for 30 days notice did not postpone the date upon which the period of limitation would begin to run. In *Knapp v. Greene*, 79 Hun. 264, 29 N.Y.S. 350 (1894), a New York court held that when a note was payable "on demand after three months' notice" the Statute of Limitations began to run on the day the note was executed. The court said:

> The real object [of the notice provision] was to give the debtor a reasonable time to pay the debt before the creditor could charge him with the costs of a suit. . . . 'If there was any infirmity in the consideration, or any defect in the binding character of the obligation, he might retain it until all testimony was lost, and defeat the defense. This is the mischief which the statute of limitations was intended to remedy.'

In a more recent New York case, suit was brought on a note payable "thirty days after demand." The court followed *Knapp* and said, "The note herein, being payable 'thirty days after demand', the holder was free to make his demand immediately. The notice was for the benefit of the debtor. The debtor could at any time waive the notice and tender the debt." *Environics, Inc.* v. *Pratt*, 50 A.D.2d 552, 553, 376 N.Y.S.2d 510, 511 (1975).

We hold that the note in question was payable on demand, that the period of limitation began to run on the date it was executed, and that the suit to collect on the debt was barred by the Statute of Limitations. The judgment is, therefore, affirmed.

Affirmed.

"Payable to Order or to Bearer" An instrument payable to order is one that will be paid to a particular person or organization identifiable in advance. To be payable to order, the instrument must so state, as most ordinarily do, by placing the words "payable to (the) order of" before the name of the payee. An instrument may be payable to the order of the maker, drawer, drawee, or someone else. It also may be payable to the order of two or more payees (together or in the alternative), to an estate, trust, or fund (in which case it is payable to the representative), to an office or officer, or to a partnership or unincorporated

association. Suppose a printed form says that the instrument is payable both to order and to bearer. In that event the instrument is payable only to order. However, if the words "to bearer" are handwritten or typewritten, then the instrument can be payable either to order or to bearer.

A negotiable instrument not payable to a particular person must be payable to bearer, meaning to any person who presents it. To be payable to bearer, the instrument may say: "payable to bearer" or "to the order of bearer." It may also say: "payable to John Doe or bearer." Or it may be made payable to cash or the order of cash or some other description that does not single out a specific individual (for example, "pay to the order of one keg of nails").

Missing and Ambiguous Terms

Incompleteness The rules just stated comprise the conditions for negotiability. Two additional details complete the picture. An incomplete instrument—one that is missing an essential element, like the due date or amount—can be signed before being completed if the contents at the time of signing show that the maker or drawer intends it to become a negotiable instrument. To be enforceable, however, it must first be completed—if not by the maker or drawer, then by the holder in accordance with whatever authority he has to do so.

Ambiguity When it is unclear whether the instrument is a note or draft, the holder may treat it as either. Handwritten terms are stronger than and control typewritten and printed terms, and typewritten terms control printed terms. Words control figures, unless the words themselves are ambiguous, in which case the figures control. Other provisions for dealing with ambiguity can be found in Section 3-118.

CHAPTER SUMMARY

Commercial paper is the collective term for a variety of instruments—including checks, certificates of deposit, and notes—that are used to pay for goods. The key to the central role of commercial paper is negotiability, the means by which a person is empowered to transfer to another more than what the transferor himself possesses. The law regulating negotiability is Article 3 of the UCC.

Commercial paper can be divided into two basic types: (1) the draft, and (2) the note. A draft is a document prepared by a drawer ordering the drawee to remit a stated sum of money to the payee; drafts in turn can be subdivided into two categories: sight drafts and time drafts. A note is a written promise to pay a specified sum of money on demand or at a definite time.

A special form of draft is the common bank check, a draft drawn on a bank and payable on demand. A special form of note is the certificate of deposit, a written acknowledgment by a bank that it has received money and agrees to repay it at a time specified in the certificate.

In addition to drawers, makers, drawees, and payees, one can deal with commercial paper in five other capacities: as indorser, indorsee, holder, holder in due course, and accommodation party.

A negotiable instrument must be a written document and the holder be able to ascertain all essential terms from its face. These include (1) signature of the maker or drawer, (2) an unconditional promise or order to pay (3) a sum certain (4) in money, (5) and no other promise, order, obligation, or power given by the maker or drawer, (6) payable on demand or at a definite time, and (7) payable to order or to bearer. When one of these terms is missing, the document is not negotiable, unless it is filled in before being negotiated according to authority given.

KEY TERMS

Acceptor	p. 476	Indorsee	p. 479
Accommodation	p. 479	Indorsement	p. 474
Banker's acceptance	p. 477	Indorser	p. 479
Bills of exchange	p. 474	Letter of credit	p. 477
Cashier's check	p. 478	Maker	p. 478
Certificate of deposit	p. 479	Note	p. 476
Certified	p. 477	Negotiability	p. 474
Check	p. 477	Payee	p. 476
Draft	p. 476	Postdating	p. 477
Drawee	p. 476	Promissory note	p. 478
Drawer	p. 476	Sight draft	p. 477
Holder	p. 479	Time draft	p. 477
Holder in due course	p. 479	Trade acceptance	p. 477

SELF-TEST QUESTIONS

1. A negotiable instrument must:
   (a) be signed by the payee
   (b) contain a conditional promise to pay
   (c) include a sum certain
   (d) be written on paper

2. The law regulating negotiability is found in:
   (a) Article 3 of the UCC
   (b) Article 9 of the UCC
   (c) Article 7 of the UCC
   (d) Article 8 of the UCC
3. A sight draft:
   (a) calls for payment on a specified date
   (b) calls for payment when presented
   (c) is not negotiable
   (d) is none of the above
4. The parties to a draft include:
   (a) the drawer
   (b) the payee
   (c) the drawee
   (d) all of the above
5. One to whom a draft or note is indorsed is called:
   (a) an indorser
   (b) a drawee
   (c) an accommodation party
   (d) none of the above

DEMONSTRATION PROBLEM

Sally loses $10,000 to June in a poker game, and, not having the cash in her purse to pay June, writes a check for $5,000 (the balance she has in her checking account) and signs an I.O.U. for the other $5,000. Being a very polite person, Sally writes "please" before the word "pay" on the check. June takes the check and I.O.U. to a local bank, where she attempts to transfer them for cash. Is the paper negotiable? Why?

PROBLEMS

1. Arnie manufactures golf balls. Jack orders 1,000 balls from Arnie and promises to pay $2,000 two weeks after delivery. Arnie delivers the balls, and assigns his contract rights to First Bank for $1,500. He then heads for Costa Rica. May First Bank collect $2,000 from Jack? Why?
2. Assume in problem 1 that Jack gives Arnie a non-negotiable note for $2,000 and Arnie sells the note to the bank shortly after delivering the balls. May the bank collect the

$2,000? Would the result be different if the note were negotiable? Why?
3. George decides to purchase a new stereo system on credit. He signs two documents—a contract and a note. The note states that it is given "in payment for the stereo" and "if stereo is not delivered by July 2, the note is cancelled." Is the note negotiable? Why?
4. In problem 3, assume that the note contained the first phrase ("in payment for the stereo") and the contract contained the second phrase ("if the stereo is not delivered by July 2, the note is cancelled"). Does the language used in the contract make the note non-negotiable? Why?
5. Lou enters into a contract to buy Alan's car. Lou has a checking account at First Bank and writes a check payable to Alan for the car. Alan cashes the check at a local bar. Lou, in the meantime, discovers the car is defective and stops payment on the check. When the bar owner sues Lou on the check, Lou claims the check is non-negotiable because it is payable out of a particular fund (the checking account). Is Lou correct? Why?
6. Martina signs a note payable to Tracy "ten days after I give birth." Tracy brings the note to First Bank, where she wants to sell it at a discount. You are an officer at First Bank. You recall reading in the paper that Martina gave birth to twins three days before Tracy's visit. Is the note negotiable? Why?
7. Martina signs a note payable to Tracy "one year from date but if I give birth, then payable ten days later." Does this language make the note non-negotiable? Why?

ANSWERS TO SELF-TEST QUESTIONS

1. (c)   2. (a)   3. (b)   4. (d)   5. (d)

SUGGESTED ANSWER TO DEMONSTRATION PROBLEM

The check is negotiable; writing in the word "please" does not make it non-negotiable. The I.O.U. is non-negotiable because it is an acknowledgment of debt rather than a promise to pay.

Negotiation of Commercial Paper

*I*n the last chapter, we examined the terms necessary to make a paper negotiable. In this chapter we discuss the second major question in determining whether a holder can collect: Was the paper properly *negotiated?* First we examine the distinction between *transfer* and *negotiation* of commercial paper and then we discuss

- the liability of a person who transfers paper;
- the types of indorsements and their effect; and
- special problems that arise with forged indorsements.

TRANSFER

Transfer means physical delivery of any instrument, intending to pass title. The transferee takes by as-

signment; as an assignee, the new owner of the instrument has only those rights held by the assignor. Claims that could be asserted by third parties against the assignor can be asserted against the assignee. A negotiable instrument can be transferred in this sense without being negotiated. A payee, for example, might fail to meet all the requirements of negotiation; in that event, the instrument might wind up being merely transferred (assigned). When all requirements of negotiability and negotiation have been met, the buyer is a *holder* and may (if a holder in due course; see Chapter 23) collect on the instrument without having to prove anything more. But if the instrument was not properly negotiated, the purchaser is at most a transferee and cannot collect if defenses are available, even if the paper itself is negotiable. This point is discussed in the following case.

FIRST NATIONAL BANK OF GWINNETT v. BARRETT
141 Ga.App. 161, 233 S.E.2d 24 (1977)

BELL, CHIEF JUDGE. The plaintiffs are husband and wife. Their motion for summary judgment was granted in this suit to recover for the unauthorized payment of a check.

The facts are not in dispute. On July 19, 1975, plaintiff husband issued a check in the amount of $1,500 drawn on their joint account in defendant bank which was payable to the order of a third party, Aquatic Industries. Aquatic deposited the check in the Roswell Bank on the same date and it was credited to Aquatic's account. Aquatic failed to indorse the check and the Roswell Bank also failed to supply Aquatic's missing indorsement as it was authorized to do by UCC § 4-205(1) (Code § 109A 4-205 (1)). The Roswell Bank indorsed the check and forwarded it to defendant and the latter paid it and debited plaintiffs' account for $1,500. Prior to payment by the defendant, plaintiffs had not issued a stop payment order. *Held:*

Uniform Commercial Code § 4-401(1) provides: "As against its customer, a bank may charge against his account any item which is otherwise properly payable from that account even though the charge creates an overdraft." Code § 109A 4-401(1). The question presented is whether this check when presented to defendant was "otherwise properly payable." The answer is that the check was properly payable. It was made payable to the order of a named payee and delivered to the payee. Coinciding with delivery, the check became "properly payable." That characteristic never changed and the payor bank was authorized as against its customer to charge the item to the customer's account. The absence of the payee's indorsement and the failure of the collecting Roswell Bank to supply the missing indorsement as it was authorized to do did not affect the payor bank's right to pay this check and to debit the plaintiffs' account. In absence of the indorsement of the payee the instrument was not transferred by negotiation and any subsequent transferee of the instrument could not acquire the status of a holder in due course. UCC § 3-202(1) Code § 109A 3-202(1)). Although the check was not negotiated, it was transferred from the payee to the Roswell Bank and by Roswell to the defendant bank. There is not the slightest indication that these transfers were void. The Uniform Commercial Code does not prevent transfers of negotiable order paper without indorsement. See UCC § 3-201(1) (Code § 109A 3-201(1)). Indeed, where the holder of an instrument payable to order transfers it for value without indorsing it, the transfer vests in the transferee all the title that the transferor had in the paper. The check was payable to the order of Aquatic by plaintiffs' specific instructions. The Roswell Bank paid the check to Aquatic, the party to whom payment was intended to be made, and when it was presented to the payee bank it was properly payable out of funds plaintiffs had on deposit.

Under these undisputed facts, plaintiffs were not entitled to summary judgment.

Judgment reversed.

Negotiation Defined

UCC Section 3-202(1) defines **negotiation** as "the transfer of an instrument in such form that the transferee becomes a holder." A *holder* is defined as "a person who is in possession of . . . an instrument . . . drawn, issued, or indorsed to him or his order or to bearer or in blank." (Section 1-201(20).)

Negotiation of Instrument Payable to Order To negotiate an instrument that is payable to the order of someone, it must be *indorsed* by the payee and delivered to the transferee. For example, Tracy negotiates Martina's check drawn to the order of Tracy by signing her name on the reverse of the check and giving it to the indorsee (the bank or someone to whom she owed money). The transferee is a holder (see Figure 22-1). Had Tracy neglected to indorse the check, the transferee, though in physical possession, would not be a holder.

To be effective as negotiation, an indorsement must convey the entire instrument. An indorsement that purports to convey only a portion of the sum still due amounts to a partial assignment. Tracy's signature on Martina's check together with the words "pay half to my mother" does not operate as an indorsement, and Tracy's mother becomes an assignee, not a holder. Sometimes, an indorser adds words intended to strengthen the indorsement; for example, "I hereby assign all my right, title, and interest in the within note to Daddy Warbucks." Words of assignment such as these and also words of condition, waiver, guaranty, limitation, or disclaimer of liability do not negate the effect of an indorsement.

When the instrument is made payable to a person under a misspelled name (or in a name other than his own), he may indorse in the wrong name or the right one or both. It is safer to sign in both names, and the purchaser of the instrument may demand a signature in both names.

An indorsement can be effective even though made by a person without capacity to sign. Section 3-207 declares that an indorsement transfers an instrument, even when the indorsement is made by an infant, or a corporation exceeding its powers; is obtained by fraud, duress, or mistake; is part of an illegal transaction; or is made in breach of a duty. However, unless the instrument was negotiated to a holder in due course, the indorsement can be rescinded or subjected to another appropriate legal remedy.

Payable to Bearer An instrument payable to bearer can be negotiated simply by delivering it to the transferee (see Figure 22-2). Despite this simple rule, the purchaser may require an indorsement on some bearer paper anyway. You may have noticed that sometimes you are requested to indorse your own check when you make it out to cash. That is because the indorsement increases the liability of the indorser if the holder is unable to collect.

LIABILITY OF TRANSFERORS

We discuss liability in detail in Chapter 24. However, a brief introduction to liability will help in understanding the types of indorsements discussed in this section.

Two Types of Liability Affecting Transferors

Contract Liability Persons who sign the instrument—that is, makers, acceptors, drawers, indorsers—have signed a contract and are subject to contract liabilities. Makers and acceptors are *primary parties* and are unconditionally liable to pay the instrument. Drawers and indorsers are *secondary parties* and are

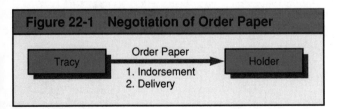

Figure 22-1 Negotiation of Order Paper

Figure 22-2 Negotiation of Bearer Paper

conditionally liable. The conditions creating liability—that is, presentment, dishonor, and notice—are discussed in Chapter 24.

Warranty Liability　The transferor's contract liability is limited. It applies only to those who sign and only if certain additional conditions are met and, as discussed below, can even be disclaimed. Consequently, a holder who has not been paid often must resort to a suit based on one of six warranties. These warranties are implied by law, which declares that any person who transfers an instrument and receives consideration for doing so has made each of these warranties:

1. he has a good title to the instrument, or is authorized to obtain payment or acceptance on behalf of someone with good title;
2. he has the right to transfer;
3. all signatures are genuine or authorized;
4. the instrument has not been materially altered;
5. no defense of any party to the instrument is good against him;
6. he has no knowledge of any insolvency proceeding against the maker, acceptor, or drawer. (UCC Section 3-417(2).)

Breach of one of these warranties must be proven at trial if there is no general contract liability.

METHODS OF TRANSFER AND INDORSEMENT

A holder can transfer negotiable paper in a variety of ways; indorsements are not identical and have differ-

ent effects. In this section we consider the various means by which an instrument can be transferred.

No Indorsement

If the instrument requires a signature, transfer without indorsement is an assignment only. Bearer paper does not require indorsement, so it can be negotiated simply by delivering it to the transferee, who becomes a holder. The transferor has no contract liability on the instrument, however, because he has not signed it. He does remain liable on the warranties, but only to the person who receives the paper, not to subsequent transferees.

Blank Indorsement

A **blank indorsement** consists of the indorser's signature alone (see Figure 22-3). A blank indorsement converts the instrument into paper closely akin to cash. Since the indorsement does not specify to whom the instrument is to be paid, it is treated like bearer paper—assuming, of course, that the first indorser is the person to whom the instrument is payable originally. A paper with blank indorsement may be negotiated by delivery alone, until such time as a holder converts it into a *special indorsement* (see p. 497) by writing over the signature any terms consistent with the indorsement. For example, a check indorsed by the payee (signed on the back) may be passed from one person to another and cashed in by any of them.

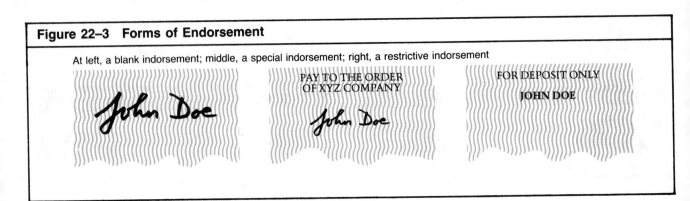

Figure 22–3　Forms of Endorsement

At left, a blank indorsement; middle, a special indorsement; right, a restrictive indorsement

PAY TO THE ORDER OF XYZ COMPANY

FOR DEPOSIT ONLY
JOHN DOE

A blank indorsement creates conditional contract liability in the indorser: he is liable to pay if the paper is dishonored. The blank indorser also has warranty liability toward subsequent holders.

In the following case, because the payee hospital indorsed a note in blank, a valid negotiation of the note back to the hospital was accomplished by delivery alone.

**WESTERLY HOSPITAL
v. HIGGINS**
106 R.I. 155, 256 A.2d
506 (1969)

ROBERTS, CHIEF JUSTICE. This civil action was brought to recover the unpaid balance alleged to be due on a promissory note made by the defendant and in which the plaintiff was named as the payee. In the superior court the plaintiff moved for a summary judgment. After hearing by a justice of that court, the motion of the defendant to strike the plaintiff's motion for a summary judgment was denied, and judgment was entered for the plaintiff for the balance due on the note together with attorney's fee for collection and costs. From that judgment the defendant has prosecuted an appeal to this court.

The record discloses that on July 13, 1967, defendant—in consideration for services performed by plaintiff hospital in connection with the birth of a child to defendant's wife—along with his wife as co-maker executed and delivered a promissory note in the amount of $527.58 payable in 18 monthly installments of $29.31 to the order of plaintiff Westerly Hospital. It further appears that thereafter a duly authorized agent of the Westerly Hospital indorsed defendant's note in blank and by delivery negotiated it to the Industrial National Bank, hereinafter referred to as Industrial, at a discount. The indorsement contained an express clause guaranteeing payment of the principal, interest, and the late charges on the note in question upon default by the maker.

Thereafter, defendant made three installment payments to Industrial, reducing the balance due on the note to $439.65. No further payments were made by defendant on the note, and, according to the pertinent provisions thereof, the entire balance of the note, principal and interest, became due and payable immediately together with all costs of collection, including a reasonable attorney's fee. After default by defendant, Industrial, as holder of the note, made a demand upon plaintiff hospital for payment of the balance due in accordance with the terms of the contract of indorsement guaranteeing payment in full to the holder in case of default by the maker. After receiving the balance due on the note, Industrial negotiated the note by delivery to plaintiff hospital.

* * *

The defendant contends that the trial justice's ruling granting summary judgment to plaintiff was in error because a genuine issue existed as to whether Westerly Hospital or Industrial was in fact the proper party to bring the instant action on the note. We cannot agree with this contention. In our opinion, the face of the instrument discloses as a matter of law that Westerly Hospital is the holder of the note in question and, therefore, a proper party

(continued on next page)

(continued)

**WESTERLY HOSPITAL
v. HIGGINS**
106 R.I. 155, 256 A.2d
506 (1969)

to bring this action. The fact of the instrument reveals that Westerly Hospital was the payee of the note made by defendant and his wife as co-makers. It further discloses that an indorsement of guarantee was executed in blank by an authorized representative of plaintiff hospital. The note was then delivered to Industrial. The pertinent provisions of the Uniform Commercial Code enacted as title 6A of G.L. 1956 by P.L. 1960, chap. 147, sec. 1, provide that where, as in the instant case, there has been a blank indorsement, mere delivery is sufficient to constitute the transferee a holder thereof and is sufficient to make the transfer a valid negotiation. § 6A-3-202; § 6A-3-204. Thereafter, when defendant defaulted, Industrial delivered the note to plaintiff in return for the payment of the remaining amount of defendant's obligation that had been guaranteed by plaintiff hospital.

*   *   *

In our opinion, then, the redelivery of the note in question by Industrial to Westerly Hospital accomplished a negotiation of the instrument. . . . It is our conclusion that in these circumstances defendant's contention that there was a genuine issue as to the identity of the proper party to bring the action on the note in question is without merit.

*   *   *

Similarly, defendant's further charge that the instrument which was signed contained blank spaces which were subsequently filled in by plaintiff is not a sufficient defense to a motion for summary judgment on a promissory note. Well-settled authority establishes the rule that one signing an instrument containing blanks is said to have conferred upon the transferee of the instrument the implied authority to complete the instrument in accordance with the understanding of the parties. Once so completed, the instrument will be in force as if it had been completed prior to the signature of the objecting party. Statutory authority for a similar result is provided for by § 6A-3-115(1) of the Uniform Commercial Code. That section states that "When a paper whose contents at the time of signing show that it is intended to become an instrument is signed while still incomplete in any necessary respect it cannot be enforced until completed, but when it is completed in accordance with authority given it is effective as completed." It is our view that since defendant does not allege that plaintiff acted in excess of his implied authority in filling in the blanks on the note in question, plaintiff would be entitled to judgment as a matter of law on the facts stated and, therefore, summary judgment was properly granted.

*   *   *

The defendant's appeal is denied and dismissed, and the judgment is affirmed.

Special Indorsement

A **special indorsement,** sometimes known as an "indorsement in full," names the transferee-holder. The payee of a check can indorse it over to a third party by writing: "Pay to the order of" the third party and then signing her name (Figure 22-3). Once specially indorsed, the check (or other instrument) can be negotiated further only when the special indorsee adds her own signature. A holder may convert a blank indorsement into a special indorsement by writing above the signature of the indorser words of a contractual nature consistent with the character of the instrument. So, for example, Martina's check to Tracy, indorsed in blank (signed by Tracy) and handed to Tracy's mother, can easily be converted into a check with special indorsement: Tracy's mother need only add the words "pay to the order of" and her name above Tracy's signature. Before doing so, she could have negotiated it simply by giving it to someone (a blank indorsement acts as bearer paper). After converting it, she must indorse it herself in order to transfer it by negotiation to someone else. The liabilities of a special indorser are the same as those of a blank indorser.

Restrictive Indorsement

An indorsement is **restrictive** if it:

1. includes words such as "for collection," "for deposit," or "pay any bank";

2. is conditional. For example, the payee indorses a note "Pay Clara if the Queen Elizabeth II arrives in New York City by May 10, 1988"; or

3. states that it is for the benefit or use of the indorser or another person. For example, Sheryl indorses a note "Pay Tex in trust for Sheryl."

With a restrictive indorsement, the indorser's liabilities are the same as with a blank indorsement. However, transferees might have additional liability if they fail to abide by the restrictions. This liability is qualified by the realities of the collection process: banks handle instruments in bulk without an opportunity to investigate restrictive indorsements. Although there are exceptions—for example, for the first bank in the process—banks may generally disregard the restrictions.

To illustrate, suppose that Kate Jones indorses her paycheck "for deposit only, Kate Jones," which is by far the most common type of restrictive indorsement (see Figure 22-3). A thief steals the check, indorses his name below the restrictive indorsement and deposits the check in Last Bank, where he has an account. The check moves through the collection process to Second Bank and then to First Bank, which pays the check. Kate has the right to recover only from Last Bank, which did not properly honor the indorsement by depositing the payment in her account.

The following case demonstrates the loss that can result from failure to use special and restrictive indorsements.

WALCOTT v. MANUFACTURERS HANOVER TRUST 507 N.Y.S. 2d 961 (1986)

IRA B. HARKAVY, JUDGE.

"Up and down the City Road,
In and out the Eagle,
That's the way the money goes—
Pop goes the Weasel!"

W. R. Mandale
Pop Goes the Weasel (c. 1853)

Plaintiff, Kenneth Walcott, alleges that on November 1, 1985, he sent his October 19, 1985 paycheck in the sum of $359.05 together with a Crossland

(continued on next page)

(*continued*)

WALCOTT v. MANUFACTURERS HANOVER TRUST
507 N.Y.S. 2d 961 (1986)

Savings Bank money order in the sum of $251.54 to Midatlantic Mortgage Company in payment of his November 1985 mortgage. He claims he signed his name to the back of the check and placed his mortgage number and the Midatlantic mailing sticker on the back of the check. He claims he then deposited the two checks in an envelope directed to Midatlantic Mortgage Company and placed the check in a United States Postal Box.

The copy of the check, introduced into evidence, shows Mr. Walcott's indorsement and the mortgage number 603052, but shows no sign of the sticker. It further shows that it was cashed by third party defendant, Bilko Check Cashing Corp. (Bilko) on November 4, 1985 and deposited into the Bilko account at defendant Manufacturers Hanover Trust (Manufacturers Hanover) on November 5, 1985.

In mid-November 1985, Mr. Walcott received a notice from Midatlantic that he was late in the November payment of his mortgage. He inquired and found that his pay check had been cashed on or about November 4, 1985 at Bilko who in turn deposited the check in their account at Manufacturers Hanover. The Crossland money order was never cashed and it was stopped by Mr. Walcott on or about November 22, 1985 and replaced by a new money order at that time.

Plaintiff claimed that an intervening thief stole the check and then cashed it at third party defendant, Bilko who in turn negotiated the check by depositing it in their account at Manufacturers Hanover. The check was finally cleared through Citibank and charged to the account of the original payor, The New York City Transit Authority.

An employee of Manufacturers Hanover testified that third party defendant Bilko had an account at the bank. She further testified that a review of the check showed that Bilko had deposited the check at Manufacturers Hanover in the Bilko account. Additional testimony revealed that once a check is deposited in the Bilko account, the bank waits three to five days for the check to clear and thereafter Bilko may use the proceeds.

The store manager of Bilko had testified previously in a prior trial of this case before this Court which ended in a mistrial. Her testimony from the prior trial was incorporated on consent of all parties into the retrial. She testified that in order for a government check to be cashed, two pieces of identification are required, usually an employee identification card containing an individual's social security number, and a drivers license. She further testified that the person presenting the check in question must have had such identification since the notations as to the calculation of the check cashing fees on the front of the check indicate that identification was shown.

The issue presented to this Court is whether plaintiff's indorsement of his paycheck was such as to be a special or restrictive indorsement, thus limiting the negotiation of the instrument or did it have the effect of creating a bearer instrument.

SPECIAL INDORSEMENT

Uniform Commercial Code § 3-204 subdivision (1) defines a special indorsement as being one that ". . . specifies the person to whom or to whose order it makes the instrument payable. Any instrument specially indorsed becomes payable to the order of the special indorsee and may be further negotiated only by his indorsement."

Examination of the back of the check, a photocopy of which, as previously stated, was introduced into evidence, reveals that Mr. Walcott did not specify any particular indorsee. In order for the alleged attached sticker to have served that purpose it must have also complied with UCC § 3-202 subdivision (2): "An indorsement must be written by or on behalf of the holder and on the instrument or a paper so firmly affixed thereto as to become a part thereof." The back of the check shows no sticker attached at all. Even if it had originally been affixed thereto, as plaintiff claims, it obviously became detached easily, thus failing to meet the indorsement requirements under the UCC to constitute a special indorsement.

RESTRICTIVE INDORSEMENT

As to the numbers written underneath plaintiff's signature, they did not have the effect of restricting plaintiff's indorsement. "An indorsement is restrictive which either

    (a) is conditional; or
    (b) purports to prohibit further transfer of the instrument; or
    (c) includes the words 'for collection,' 'for deposit,' 'pay any bank,' or like terms signifying a purpose of deposit or collection; or
    (d) otherwise states that it is for the benefit or use of the indorser or of another person." UCC § 3-205.

This section of the Uniform Commercial Code is very specific. The series of numbers representing plaintiff's mortgage account was insufficient to restrict negotiation of plaintiff's check.

BLANK INDORSEMENT

Plaintiff's indorsement had the effect of converting the check into a bearer instrument. The series of numbers having no restrictive effect, Mr. Walcott indorsed the check in blank, or otherwise stated, he simply signed his name. A blank indorsement under UCC § 3-204 subdivision (2) ". . . specifies no particular indorsee and may consist of a mere signature." Additionally, "An instrument payable to order and indorsed in blank becomes payable to bearer and may be negotiated by delivery alone. . . ." Consequently, since plaintiff failed to limit his blank indorsement, the check was properly negotiated by delivery to third party defendant Bilko and properly cashed by them.

Judgment for the defendant, Manufacturers Hanover Trust dismissing the complaint. Judgment for third party defendant, Bilko Check Cashing Corp. dismissing the complaint.

Qualified Indorsement

An indorser can limit his liability by *qualifying* the indorsement. The usual **qualified indorsement** consists of the words "without recourse," which mean that the indorser has no contract liability to subsequent holders if a maker or drawee defaults. A qualified indorsement does not impair negotiability. The qualification must be in writing by the signature on the instrument itself. By disclaiming contract liability, the qualified indorser also limits his warranty liabilities, though he does not eliminate them. Section 3-417(3) narrows the indorser's warranty that no defense of any party is good against the indorser. In its place, the qualified indorser warrants merely that he has no knowledge of any defense.

"Without recourse" indorsements can have a practical impact on the balance sheet. A company holding a promissory note can obtain cash by discounting it—indorsing it over to a bank for maturity value less the bank's discount. As an indorser, however, the company remains liable to pay the amount to subsequent holders should the maker default at maturity. The balance sheet must reflect this possibility as a *contingent liability.* However, if the note is indorsed without recourse, the company need not account for any possible default of the maker as a contingent liability.

Effect of Reacquisition

A prior party who reacquires an instrument may reissue it or negotiate it further. But doing so discharges intervening parties as to the reacquirer and as to later purchasers who are not holders in due course. Section 3-208 permits the reacquirer to cancel indorsements unnecessary to his title or ownership; in so doing, he eliminates the liability of such indorsers even to holders in due course.

Instruments Payable to Two or More Persons

A note or draft can be payable to two or more persons. In form, the payees can be listed in the alternative or jointly. When a commercial paper says "pay to the order of Tracy *or* Martina," it is stated in the alternative. Either person may negotiate (or discharge or enforce) the paper without the consent of the other. On the other hand, if the paper says "pay to the order of Tracy *and* Martina" or does not clearly state that the payees are to be paid in the alternative, then the instrument is payable to all of them and may be negotiated (or discharged or enforced) only by all of them acting together.

Instruments Payable with Words of Description

Sometimes an instrument will name a particular person as payee but indicate that that person is in reality an agent of someone else, an officer of a company, or a fiduciary. In the case of the payee as agent or officer ("Blackstone Kent, Treasurer, Services Unlimited, Ltd." or "Blackstone Kent, agent of Whitestone Kent"), the instrument is payable to the principal (Services Unlimited or Whitestone Kent), but for purposes of convenience, the agent or officer is permitted to act as if he were the holder. Thus a corporate treasurer can negotiate the check in the name of the corporation. In the case of a fiduciary ("Blackstone Kent, Trustee of the Willoughby Trust"), the instrument is payable to the fiduciary, who may negotiate, discharge, or enforce the instrument. Of course, the fiduciary remains liable for any breach of his obligations as fiduciary, and subsequent holders with notice of the breach do not become holders in due course.

Any other words purporting to describe the payee have no effect on subsequent parties, and the payee has an unconditional right to payment. Blackstone Kent may negotiate a check made payable to him as "Blackstone Kent, attorney," even if the payment is for one of his clients, and no subsequent holder will be put on notice of any fiduciary obligation. Similarly, the words "Blackstone Kent, Treasurer," are insufficient to establish agency or status as an officer. Such an instrument is freely negotiable by Blackstone Kent in his personal capacity. To list him as officer, it is necessary to name the principal as well.

FORGED INDORSEMENTS

General Rule

The Handyman Lumber Company pays its employees by check on Fridays. One employee, Sam Cedar, is in the habit each Friday afternoon of cashing the check at First State Bank, on which it is drawn. One Friday, Cedar does not notice that he has dropped the check on the work floor in the morning. A customer, seeing the check, picks it up and forges Sam Cedar's signature as an indorsement on the back. The thief takes the check to First State Bank and presents it to a busy teller who does not bother to investigate his bona fides. That afternoon, Sam Cedar discovers that the check is missing and tells Handyman's controller, who calls First State Bank to stop payment. Too late. An officer at the bank tells the controller that the check has been cashed and that the bank is charging Handyman Lumber's account. The controller replies that the bank has no authority to do so. Who is correct?

Under UCC Section 1-201(43), a forgery is an "unauthorized signature." By Section 3-404(1), any unauthorized signature is "wholly inoperative as that of the person whose name is signed." Under Section 3-419(1)(c), the general rule is that the loss is the drawee's. Consequently, the loss falls on First State Bank in the above example. However, the UCC contains some exceptions to this rule as follows.

The Negligence Exception

Any person whose negligence substantially contributes to the making of a forgery cannot assert the forgery "against a holder in due course or against a drawee or other payor who pays the instrument in good faith and in accordance with the reasonable commercial standards of the drawee's or payor's business." (Section 3-406.) Examples include the corporate drawer who uses a rubber signature stamp and carelessly leaves it unprotected, so that it is stolen; the person who has had previous notice that his signature has been forged and takes no steps to prevent reoccurrences; and the negligent mailing of a check to the wrong person having the same name as the payee.

The Imposter Rule

If one person poses as the named payee, inducing the maker or drawer to issue an instrument in the name of the payee to the imposter (or his confederate), the imposter's indorsement of the payee's name is effective. The paper can be negotiated.

If in fact the named payee is a real person, the negotiation of the instrument by the imposter has no effect on whatever obligation the drawer or maker has to the named payee. Martina owes Tracy $1,000. Knowing of the debt, Helga writes to Martina, pretending to be Tracy, and asks her to send a check to Helga's address in Tracy's name. When the check arrives, Helga indorses it by signing "pay to the order of Helga, (signed) Tracy," and then indorses it in her own name and cashes it at the drawee bank. Martina remains liable to Tracy for the money that she owes her.

Other Signatures in the Name of a Payee

The indorsement of a payee might be made by someone other than an imposter. One such situation occurs when a person signing as, or on behalf of, a maker or drawer intends the payee to have no interest whatsoever in the instrument. For example, Blackstone Kent makes a check payable in the name of Dr. Pottinger, knowing that there is no such person (or not knowing that such a person does exist). Or, knowing that there is a Dr. Pottinger, Blackstone Kent makes the check payable in his name, intending Dr. Pottinger to know nothing of the transaction. In these and similar cases, any person's indorsement of the name of Dr. Pottinger, the named payee, is effective. (Section 3-405(1)(b).) Similarly, when an agent or employee of the maker or drawer has supplied him with the name of the payee, intending the payee to have no interest, indorsement by any person of the payee's name is effective. (Section 3-405(1)(c).) An example is the corporate treasurer who adds a fictitious employee to the payroll; the treasurer's indorsement (or indorsement by anyone) of the fictitious name is effective to negotiate the check. The reason for this rule is discussed in the following case.

**NORTHBROOK PROP.
v. CITIZENS &
SOUTHERN**
361 S.E.2d 531 (Ga.App.
1987)

BEASLEY, JUDGE.

Northbrook Property and Casualty Insurance Company, as subrogee of Devin Management Company, Inc., brought suit against the Citizens and Southern National Bank seeking damages in the amount of $75,805.89. The complaint alleged that Devin's employee, Patricia Ferguson, from 1980 to 1983 cashed numerous unauthorized checks drawn by her on Devin's account and payable to fictitious individuals; that she fraudulently indorsed those checks and presented them to C & S; that C & S negligently accepted the checks and without further inquiry or authorization paid the funds to Patricia Ferguson in contravention of accepted banking practices and in violation of its contractual obligation to its depositors.

C & S moved for partial summary judgment based upon the following stipulation by the parties. Patricia Ferguson, Devin's office manager and bookkeeper, was authorized to sign the checks on behalf of the maker, Devin, and all checks for which recovery is sought were signed on Devin's behalf by her. Of the total sought of $75,805.89, checks totaling $1,892 were made payable to Patricia Ferguson or cash and $1,673 were valid or legitimate items which Devin intended to be paid. The controversy centers on checks in the amount of $71,289.00 which were made payable to fictitious persons or to actual persons who were not intended by Patricia Ferguson to have any interest in the items. During the time in question 369 checks were presented to branches of C & S for cashing, only 11 of which bore Patricia Ferguson's indorsement (the others were indorsed in the payee's name). C & S was informed of Devin's claim in February 1983.

The trial court granted C & S's motion for summary judgment finding OCGA § 11-3-405 to be controlling. Northbrook appeals to this court and contends that although OCGA § 11-3-405 is applicable, the fictitious payee/padded payroll defense contained therein is not absolute but should further involve the issue of whether the drawee bank was negligent in accepting forged items from an employee of the drawer.

* * *

Anderson, Uniform Commercial Code, p. 163 § 3-405.3 points out that Code § 3-405 "permits anyone to indorse paper made payable to a fictitious person or to one who was not intended to acquire any interest in the paper. The purpose of § 3-405 is to promote negotiability and foster the commercial reliability of paper. The rationale of UCC § 3-405 is that the employer-drawer should bear the loss caused by his dishonest employee rather than thrusting it upon the drawee bank."

The Official Code Comment to UCC § 3-405 explains that the test of subsection (1)(b) "is not whether the named payee is 'fictitious,' but whether the signer intends that he shall have no interest in the instrument. The following situations illustrate the application of the subsection. (a) The drawer of a check, for his own reasons, makes it payable to P knowing that P does not exist. . . . (c) The drawer makes the check payable to P, an existing person whom he knows, intending to receive the money himself and that P shall have no interest in the check. (d) The treasurer of a corporation draws its check payable to P, who to the knoweldge of the treasurer does not exist. (e) The treasurer of a corporation draws its check payable to P. P exists but the treasurer has fraudulently added his name to the payroll intending that he shall not receive the check."

Thus, a loss from the activities of a faithless employee must be borne by the employer rather than the drawee bank. This is accomplished by making the indorsement effective even though it is unauthorized. "The principle followed is that the loss should fall upon the employer as a risk of his business enterprise rather than upon the subsequent holder or drawee. The reasons are that the employer is normally in a better position to prevent such forgeries by reasonable care in the selection or supervision of his employees, or, if he is not, is at least in a better position to cover the loss by fidelity insurance; and that the cost of such insurance is properly an expense of his business rather than of the business of the holder or drawee." Official Code Comment, UCC § 3-405.

An overwhelming majority of the jurisdictions confronted with this issue have recognized the import of the code section to be that any loss arising from situations provided for therein should fall upon the employer and negligence on that part of the bank is irrelevant. Only bad faith by a bank prevents invoking the code section to defeat a claim.

Northbrook asks that we choose the minority position which is now viable in only one jurisdiction, California. Some strong policy arguments have been proffered in support of this position. An excellent articulation of these concerns is found in the special concurrence by Judge Cooke in *Merrill Lynch, etc., v. Chemical Bank*, 442 N.E.2d 1253. But these policy considerations are for the legislature. We are charged solely with construing the statutory language. We come to the same result finally reached by Judge Cooke that the code section makes no provison for negligence by the bank. Fortification for this plain meaning construction is implicit from the tenor of the UCC. In those situations where negligence is a factor, it invariably expressly appears in the section involved.

We therefore adopt the construction called for by the official comment and recognized by the near unanimous majority of other states which have considered the issue. Northbrook cannot recover because of mere negligence on the part of C & S.

Judgment affirmed.

CHAPTER SUMMARY

Negotiation is the transfer of an instrument in such a form that the transferee becomes a holder. There are various methods for doing so; if the procedures are not properly adhered to, the transfer is only an assignment.

An instrument payable to the order of someone must be negotiated by indorsement and delivery to the transferee. The indorsement must convey the entire instrument. An instrument payable to bearer may be negotiated simply by delivery to the transferee.

Those who sign the instrument have made a contract and are liable for its breach. Makers and acceptors are primary parties and are liable to pay the instrument. Drawers and indorsers are secondary parties and are conditionally liable. Signatories are also liable under a warranty theory.

Various forms of indorsement are possible. These include blank indorsement, special indorsement (to a named third party), restrictive indorsement (as in, "for deposit only"), and qualified indorsement ("without recourse").

As between drawer and drawee, liability for a forged instrument—one signed without authority—falls on the drawee, who paid it. There are several exceptions to this rule, including the situation in which an imposter induces the maker or drawer to issue an instrument in the name of the payee.

KEY TERMS

Blank indorsement	p. 494	Restrictive indorse-	p. 497
Negotiation	p. 493	ment	
Qualified indorsement	p. 500	Special indorsement	p. 497
		Transfer	p. 491

SELF-TEST QUESTIONS

1. A person who signs a negotiable instrument with a blank endorsement has:
   (a) warranty liability
   (b) contract liability
   (c) both of the above
   (d) neither of the above
2. "For deposit" is an example of:
   (a) a special indorsement
   (b) a restrictive indorsement
   (c) a qualified indorsement
   (d) a blank indorsement
3. "Pay to the order of XYZ Company" is an example of:
   (a) a special indorsement
   (b) a restrictive indorsement
   (c) a qualified indorsement
   (d) a blank indorsement
4. The indorser's signature alone is
   (a) a special indorsement
   (b) a restrictive indorsement
   (c) a qualified indorsement
   (d) a blank indorsement
5. Generally, liability for a forged instrument falls on:
   (a) the drawer
   (b) the drawee
   (c) both of the above
   (d) neither of the above

DEMONSTRATION PROBLEM

Bill's weekly paycheck is stolen by a thief. The thief indorses Bill's name and cashes the check at the drawee bank before Bill's employer has time to stop payment. May the drawee bank charge this payment against the drawer's account? Why?

PROBLEMS

1. Mal, a minor, purchased a stereo from Howard for $325 and gave Howard a negotiable note in that amount. Tanker, a thief, stole the note from Howard, indorsed Howard's signature and sold the note to Betty. Betty then sold the note to Carl; she did not indorse it. Carl was unable to collect on the note because Mal disaffirmed the contract. Is Betty liable to Carl on a contract or warranty theory? Why?

2. Would the result in problem 1 be different if Betty had given a qualified indorsement? Why?

3. Alphonse received a check one Friday from his employer and cashed the check at his favorite tavern, using a blank indorsement. After the tavern closed that evening, the owner, in reviewing the receipts for the evening, became concerned that, if the check were stolen and cashed by a thief, the loss would fall on the tavern. Is this concern justified? What can the owner of the tavern do for protection?

4. Martha owns a sporting goods store. She employs a bookkeeper, Bob, who is authorized to indorse checks received by the store and to deposit them in the store's bank account at Second Bank. Instead of depositing all of the checks, Bob cashes some of them and uses the proceeds for personal purposes. Martha sues the bank for her loss, claiming that the bank should have deposited the money in the store's account rather than paying Bob. Is the bank liable? Why?

5. Daniel worked as a writer in order to support himself and his wife while she earned her MBA degree. Daniel's paychecks were important, as the couple had no other source of income. One day, Daniel drove to Old Faithful State Bank to deposit his paycheck. Standing at a counter, he indorsed the check with a blank indorsement and then proceeded to fill out a deposit slip. While he was completing the slip, a thief stole the check and cashed it. Whose loss? How could the loss be avoided?

6. You are the branch manager of a bank. A well-respected local attorney walks into the bank with a check for $100,000 which he wants to deposit in the general account which his firm has at your bank. The payee on the check is an elderly widow, Hilda Jones, who received the check from the profit-sharing plan of her deceased husband, Horatio Jones. The widow indorsed the check "Pay to the order of the estate of Horatio Jones. Hilda Jones." The attorney produces court documents which show that he is the executor of the estate. After the attorney indorses the check, you deposit the check in the attorney's account. The attorney later withdraws and spends the money on a plea-

sure trip to Costa Rica, in violation of his duties as executor. Discuss the bank's liability.

7. Stephanie borrows $50,000 from Ginny and gives Ginny a negotiable note in that amount. Ginny sells the note to Roe for $45,000. Ginny's indorsement reads "For valuable consideration, I assign all of my rights in this note to Roe. Ginny." When Stephanie refuses to pay the note and skips town, Roe demands payment from Ginny, claiming contract liability on the basis of her signature. Ginny argues that she is not liable because the indorsement is qualified by the above language. Who is correct? Why?

ANSWERS TO SELF-TEST QUESTIONS

1. (c)   2. (b)   3. (a)   4. (d)   5. (b)

SUGGESTED ANSWER TO DEMONSTRATION PROBLEM

The drawee may not charge the payment against Bill's account; the general rule in cases of forged indorsements is that the drawee must bear the loss.

CHAPTER

23

Holder in Due Course and Defenses

*I*n this chapter we consider the final two questions that are raised in determining whether a holder can collect:

- Is the holder a holder in due course?
- What defenses, if any, can be asserted against the holder in due course to prevent him from collecting on the instrument?

HOLDER IN DUE COURSE

A **holder** is a person in possession of an instrument drawn, issued, or indorsed to him, or to his order, or to bearer, or in blank. In short, a holder is a person to whom an instrument has been negotiated. The holder is not necessarily an owner: An instrument may be indorsed to a person as agent for the owner of the instrument. But because the instrument was indorsed to him and he physically possesses it, the agent is a holder. Any holder may transfer, negotiate, or discharge an instrument or enforce payment in his own name.

But a holder's rights are ordinary. If a person to whom an instrument was negotiated became nothing more than a holder, the law of commercial paper would not be very significant, nor would a negotiable instrument be a particularly useful commercial device. What the holder wants is an instrument free of claims or defenses by previous possessors. A holder with such a preferred position can then treat the instrument almost as money, free from the worry that someone might show up and prove it defective.

A holder who has such a preference is a **holder in due course,** a special type of holder who takes the paper free of most defenses. The status of holder in due course is unique in the law, and is the essential purpose of negotiability. Without being a holder in due course, the holder is simply an assignee, who acquires the assignor's rights but also his liabilities; an ordinary holder must defend against claims and overcome defenses just as his assignor would.

The general rule for becoming a holder in due course is set forth in UCC Section 3-302(1): "A holder in due course is a holder who takes the instrument (a) for value; and (b) in good faith; and (c) without notice that it is overdue or has been dishonored or of any defense against or claim to it on the part of any person." We will examine the three elements of this rule in turn.

"For Value"

To become a holder in due course, the transferee must have given something of value for the instrument. Value need not be money; anything actually given in exchange for the instrument is sufficient. But "value" is not the equivalent of "consideration." An executory promise is sufficient consideration to create a binding contract, but it is not value for purposes of creating the status of holder in due course; the promise first must be carried out.

Suppose a friend has given a promissory note for $1,000 to Martina when he purchased her car. To pay for a new shipment of tennis rackets to be delivered in 30 days, Martina negotiates the note to Tracy, the seller. Tracy never sends the tennis rackets. Martina has a claim for $1,000 against Tracy, who is not a holder in due course because her promise to deliver is still executory. Assume Martina's friend has a defense against her, perhaps because the car was defective. When Tracy presents the note to the friend for payment, he may refuse to pay, raising his defense against Martina. If Tracy had been a holder in due course, he would have been obligated to pay on the note, regardless of the defense he might have had against Martina, the payee.

A taker for value can be a partial holder in due course if the consideration was only partly performed. Suppose the tennis rackets were to come in two lots, each worth $500, and Tracy delivered only one lot. Tracy would be a holder in due course only to the extent of $500, and the debtor could refuse to pay $500 of the promised sum.

Value is not limited to cash or the fulfillment of a contractual obligation. A holder who acquires a lien on or a security interest in an instrument other than by legal process has taken for value. Likewise, taking an instrument in payment of or as security for a prior claim, whether or not the claim is due, is a taking for value. Blackstone owes Webster $100, due 30 days hence. Blackstone unexpectedly receives a refund check for $100 from the Internal Revenue Service and indorses it to Webster. Webster is a holder in due course. Finally, a holder gives value when he gives another negotiable instrument or makes an irrevocable commitment to a third person, such as by a letter of credit. (Sections 3-303(b), (c).)

The rationale for the rule of value is that if the holder has not yet given anything of value in exchange for the instrument, he still has an effective remedy, should the instrument prove defective: he can rescind the transaction, given the transferor's breach of warranty.

"Good Faith"

As defined in Section 1-201(19), **good faith** "means honesty in fact in the conduct or transaction concerned." This is a subjective test. Suppose Martina had given Tracy a promissory note for the tennis rackets. Knowing that she intended to deliver defective tennis rackets and that Martina is likely to protest as soon as the shipment arrives, Tracy offers a deep discount on the note to her doctor: instead of the $1,000 face value of the note, she will give it to him in payment of an outstanding bill of $200. The doctor, being naive in commercial dealings, has no suspicion from the large discount that Tracy might be committing fraud. He has acted in good faith under the UCC test and is a holder in due course. That is not to say that no set of circumstances will ever exist to warrant a finding that there was a lack of good faith. The next case is an example of how bad faith can be inferred from the defendant's knowledge.

SECURITY CENTRAL NATIONAL BANK v. WILLIAMS
52 Ohio App.2d 175
(1976)

McCORMAC, J. Appellant sued appellee for $3,020.49 claimed to be due on a promissory note which the bank had received by assignment from Art Sales, Inc. Appellee answered denying the indebtedness and further denying that the bank was a holder in due course, alleging fraud as a defense.

The case was tried to the trial court who found that appellant was not a holder in due course and that appellee had a defense applicable against the bank. The court rendered a judgment in favor of appellee.

*　　*　　*

The assignments of error will be combined for discussion, as the sole issue presented herein is whether the bank was a holder in due course. It is clear that if the bank was not a holder in due course, that fraud and failure of consideration were established as defenses against Art Sales, Inc., which would also be applicable against the bank.

R. C. 1303.31(a) defines a holder in due course as follows:

"A holder in due course is a holder who takes the instrument:

(1)　for value; and

(2)　in good faith; and

(3)　without notice that it is overdue or has been dishonored or of any defense against or claim to it on the part of any person."

The sole area of dispute in this case is whether appellant took the instrument in question in good faith.

*　　*　　*

The facts show that Art Sales, Inc., sold equipment to appellee for making stereo tapes from master tapes for $6,039. Art Sales, Inc., promised to furnish master tapes weekly from which some 400 individual tapes could be made each week to be bought back by Art Sales, Inc., at a return to appellee of about $600 a week. Appellee purchased the equipment from Art Sales on this representation which ultimately proved to be false, only one master tape ever having been furnished. Art Sales ultimately went into bankruptcy and no recovery is possible from them.

The initial $6,039 was paid by appellee as follows: There was a cash downpayment of fifty percent or $3,019.50, and a promissory note (the one in question) was signed for the balance of $3,019.50, which with interest amounted to $3,215.08. The note was ultimately discounted to the appellant bank for approximately $500, of which $244 was interest. Obviously, there was a substantial principal discount. There were other circumstances from which knowledge of the shaky nature of Art Sales and its business could be imputed to the bank. The note was taken by the bank with recourse. The bank credit manager admitted that the note and security agreement may have been furnished to Art Sales by a member of the bank. A vice-president of the bank who handled the Art Sales account resigned shortly after Art Sales went into bankruptcy because of the Art Sales matter and several other matters. This vice-president had presumably investigated and determined Art Sales to be a reputable company. There were 33 Art Sales notes assigned to the bank in default. The sales representative of Art Sales was a former employee of the bank.

The question then is whether these circumstances and the reasonable inferences therefrom are sufficient to permit the trial court to find that appellant did not take the note by assignment in good faith, did not become a holder in due course, and thus were susceptible to defenses that were applicable against Art Sales, Inc. R. C. 1301.01 defines good faith as "honesty in fact in the conduct or transportation concerned."

This court approved the following statement in a similar case:

> . . . The basic philosophy of the holder in due course status is to encourage free negotiability of commercial paper by removing certain anxieties of one who takes the paper as an innocent purchaser knowing no reason why the paper is not as sound as its face would indicate. It would seem to follow, therefore, that the more the holder knows about the underlying transaction, and particularly the more he controls or participates or becomes involved in it, the less he fits the role of a good faith purchaser for value; the closer his relationship to the underlying agreement which is the course of the note, the less need there is for giving him the tension-free rights considered necessary in a fast-moving, credit-extending commercial world. *American Plan Corp.* v. *Woods* (1968), 16 Ohio App. 2d 1, 4.

While the facts of this case differ from those in *American Plan Corp.*, the same basic principle of law is applicable here. As stated in *American Plan Corp.*, a proper balance must be struck between the commercial need for negotiability and the individual's need for relief against fraud. That balance ending in the final determination that the consumer either is or is not able to maintain a defense against the financer must be made on a case-by-case basis. If sufficient facts exist to alert a bank or financing agent to the possibility that the original deal from which an assigned note was generated was not a completely above-board transaction, the court is justified in finding that the assignee did not take the note "in good faith" and is not entitled to the protection afforded a holder in due course.

In this case the bank had a closer than usual relationship with the dealer whose paper was taken by assignment. A former employee of the bank was a sales representative of the dealer. The bank took a substantial number of notes from the dealer by assignment, taking them with recourse and at a substantial discount rate. The vice-president of the bank who handled the notes from Art Sales resigned inferentially under pressure because of the Art Sales' deal and several other matters. The bank may have provided the note and security agreement used by Art Sales, Inc. In addition the type of business appeared to be almost inherently suspect.

Thus, it cannot be said that the trial court's finding that there was a sufficient interrelationship between the dealer and the bank to prevent the bank from attaining the status of a holder in due course was against the manifest weight of the evidence.

Appellant's assignments of error are overruled and the judgment of the trial court is affirmed.

Judgment affirmed.

"Without Notice"

It obviously would be unjust to permit a holder to enforce an instrument which, when he acquired it, he knew was defective, was subject to claims or defenses, or had been dishonored. A purchaser with knowledge cannot become a holder in due course. But proving knowledge is difficult, so the UCC (Section 3-304)(1)–(3)) lists several types of **notice** that presumptively defeat any entitlement to status as holder in due course. Notice is not limited to receipt of an explicit statement; it includes an inference that a person should have made from the circumstances.

Notice of Claim or Defense   An incomplete or altered instrument might on its face give rise to a suspicion that it is invalid and thus provide notice of a claim or defense. Section 3-304(1)(a) declares that a purchaser has notice if "the instrument is so incomplete, bears such visible evidence of forgery or alteration, or is otherwise so irregular as to call into question its validity, terms or ownership or to create an ambiguity as to the party to pay." Suppose Martina gives Tracy a demand note for $1,000. Tracy, the payee, adds a fourth zero in a different color ink, raising the sum on the face of the note to $10,000. Tracy indorses the note to a supplier whom she owes $10,000. The supplier presents the note to Martina for payment. The supplier is not a holder in due course: The alteration was obvious and irregular and therefore put the indorsee on notice; he should have known, even if he in fact paid the alteration no heed. Not every modification or incomplete term need amount to notice. The change of a date on a check, where it is obvious that the drawer made a simple mistake, is ordinarily insufficient to provide notice of a claim or defense.

The would-be holder in due course has notice of a claim or defense if he has been given notice "that the obligation of any party is voidable in whole or in part, or that all parties have been discharged." (Section 3-304(1)(b).) Notice that one party has been discharged means that the purchaser cannot be a holder in due course as to that party, but it does not operate as notice that others are discharged, so the purchaser can be a holder in due course as far as other parties are concerned.

Notice That an Instrument is Overdue   The UCC provides generally that a person who has notice that an instrument is overdue cannot be a holder in due course. What constitutes notice? When an inspection of the instrument itself would show that it was due before the purchaser acquired it, notice is presumed. A transferee to whom a promissory note due April 23 is negotiated on April 24 has notice that it was overdue and consequently is not a holder in due course. Not all paper contains a due date for the entire amount. Thus, where an installment note calls for portions of the total to be paid on different maturity dates, Section 3-304(3)(a) solves the difficulty by putting the purchaser on notice if he has reason to know "that any part of the principal amount is overdue or that there is an uncured default in payment of another instrument of the same series." Likewise, the purchaser is not a holder in due course if he should have known that acceleration of the instrument was made.

Demand paper, on the other hand, has no due date. How does one tell whether it is overdue? Section 3-304(3)(c) puts the purchaser on notice if he has reason to know that he is taking the demand instrument "after demand has been made or more than a reasonable length of time after its issue." Except for checks, the UCC does not spell out what is reasonable. The courts look to such factors as business customs and practices. The time after which a demand note is overdue might be some sixty days. However, for checks drawn and payable within the United States, the section states that the reasonable time period is presumed to be thirty days, as discussed in the following case.

AMERICAN STATE BANK v. N.W. SO. DAK. P.C.A.

404 N.W.2d 517 (S.D. 1987)

KONENKAMP, CIRCUIT JUDGE.

This is an appeal from a judgment declaring Northwest South Dakota Production Credit Association (PCA) a holder in due course of a check issued by Fort Pierre Livestock Auction, Inc. (Fort Pierre). We reverse.

On October 25, 1983, in payment for cattle sold at auction, Fort Pierre issued check number 19074 for $31,730.23 to its customer, Gene Hunt, naming as additional payees Cheyenne River Sioux Tribe Superior Court and PCA. Later Fort Pierre discovered it had miscounted the cattle and so it issued check 19331 dated October 31, 1983, for $36,343.95 to Hunt and the other payees. This check was meant to replace check 19074, but no notation to that effect was written on it. Fort Pierre did not ask Hunt to return check 19074, but attempted to issue a stop payment order. Its bank has no record of such order.

Neither check emerged for a year. Then on October 26, 1984, a PCA representative met with Hunt to arrange repayment of a huge delinquent loan. At this meeting Hunt agreed, among other things, to give PCA checks 19074 and 19331 in exchange for the forgiveness of his remaining debt. PCA did not know one check replaced the other or that Fort Pierre attempted to stop payment on check 19074.

After obtaining the checks, PCA's agent telephoned Fort Pierre's manager and told him "a couple of old [Hunt] checks were going to be deposited." The manager, in turn, called Fort Pierre's bank (American State Bank) and warned it to not accept the checks without full endorsements. The bank dutifully refused to accept one check because it had stamped, not handwritten, endorsements, but eventually, with the proper endorsements, both checks cleared through Fort Pierre's account.

Upon discovering in January 1985 that its bank had debited its account for both checks, Fort Pierre informed PCA that one check was meant to replace the other and demanded repayment for check 19074. Although PCA still had an opportunity to renegotiate its agreement with Hunt, it refused Fort Pierre's demand, choosing instead to assert holder in due course (hereafter HDC) status. Fort Pierre sued to recover the amount of check 19074.

The trial court declared check 19074 invalid: it lacked consideration because check 19331 replaced it. Nonetheless, since PCA held the check as an HDC, the court ruled it was not subject to the defense of lack of consideration; PCA's telephone call to Fort Pierre was "commercially reasonable," nullifying PCA's notice the check was overdue.

To be an HDC under SDCL 57A-3-302, a party must take the instrument for value, in good faith, and without notice that it is overdue, or dishonored, or of any defense against or claim to it by any person. The fact that PCA was a payee does not disqualify it as an HDC. If a party fails to qualify as an HDC, then under SDCL 57A-3-306 he takes the instrument subject to:

    (a)   All valid claims to it on the part of any person; and

    (b)   All defenses of any party which would be available in an action on a simple contract; and

(*continued on next page*)

(continued)

AMERICAN STATE BANK v. N.W. SO. DAK. P.C.A.
404 N.W.2d 517 (S.D. 1987)

(c) The defenses of want or failure of consideration, nonperformance of any condition precedent, nondelivery, or delivery for a special purpose (§ 57A-3-408). . . .

The holder of an instrument has the burden of proving that he is an HDC when defenses or claims are shown. PCA took check 19074 for value and in good faith, but knew it was a year old; therefore, the only issue is whether PCA had notice check 19074 was overdue. Under SDCL 57A-3-304(3):

The purchaser has notice that an instrument is overdue if he has reason to know

(a) . . .

(b) . . .

(c) That he is taking a demand instrument after demand has been made or more than a reasonable length of time after its issue. *A reasonable time for a check drawn and payable within the states and territories of the United States and District of Columbia is presumed to be thirty days.* (Emphasis added.)

This presumption is rebuttable (SDCL 57A-1-201-(31)) and we can envision instances where a delay of more than thirty days may be legitimate in the ordinary course of commerce, but PCA offered no justification for a year's delay. At the trial, PCA's representative testified he obtained the year-old check when Hunt simply pulled it out of his briefcase and handed it to him.

PCA concedes that it knew the check was a year old, but argues its telephone call to Fort Pierre warning of its imminent deposit of old Hunt checks along with Fort Pierre's apparent acquiescence overcomes the presumed notice that check 19074 was overdue. Can notice cease to be effective once it occurs? The UCC drafters expressly avoided this question. Since the UCC does not determine the time and duration under which notice ceases to be effective, the matter is left for the courts to resolve.

When a holder has no notice of a defect in an instrument at the time it comes into his hands, later events will not alter his HDC status. If knowledge acquired after the taking of an instrument is immaterial, then logically, a holder with notice that an instrument is overdue at the time it is taken should not be able to undo that notice except in the most extraordinary circumstances. When PCA's agent called Fort Pierre he made no mention of the check numbers, their amounts or dates, and Fort Pierre's manager made no comment which would lead the agent to believe the checks were not overdue, but only acknowledged the agent's intention to deposit them.

PCA's warning to Fort Pierre that it was about to deposit Hunt's "old checks" was insufficient to negate what was plainly visible on the check's face: a year-old date. Since it had notice that check 19074 was overdue PCA was not a holder in due course. The trial court's finding to the contrary was clearly erroneous.

Reversed.

Facts That Do Not Give Notice of Defense or Claim
Section 3-304(4) lists several types of facts, knowledge of which by itself does not give notice of a defense or claim. These include:

(a) That the instrument is antedated or postdated;
(b) that it was issued or negotiated in return for an executory promise or accompanied by a separate agreement, unless the purchaser has notice that a defense or claim has arisen from the terms thereof;
(c) that any party has signed for accommodation;
(d) that an incomplete instrument has been completed, unless the purchaser has notice of any improper completion;
(e) that any person negotiating the instrument is or was a fiduciary;
(f) that there has been default in payment of interest on the instrument or in payment of any other instrument, except one of the same series. (Section 3-304(4).)

Notice for other legal purposes does not necessarily amount to notice for purposes of determining whether a purchaser is a holder in due course. Section 3-304(5) states that "the filing or recording of a document does not of itself constitute notice" if a purchaser would otherwise be a holder in due course. Suppose that Blackstone buys a computer from Whitestone, and gives him a note that refers to a security interest that Whitestone retains in the computer. The security interest is recorded in a paper filed with the secretary of state. If Greenstone, who buys the note from Whitestone, were to look it up, he would find that the recording shows that Blackstone has a defense to Whitestone's demand for payment on the note, perhaps because Whitestone sent the wrong kind of computer. Section 3-304(5) ensures that the recording does not operate as "constructive notice" against Greenstone, the indorsee. The UCC does not place such a burden on holders in due course.

Payee as Holder in Due Course

In the usual circumstances, a payee would have knowledge of claims or defenses because the payee would be one of the original parties to the instrument. Nevertheless, a payee may be a holder in due course if all the prerequisites are met: acquisition for value, in good faith, and without notice as defined above. For instance, Blackstone tricks Whitestone into signing a note as co-maker. Without authority, Blackstone then delivers the note for value to Greenstone, the payee. Having taken in good faith and without notice, Greenstone is a holder in due course.

The Shelter Rule

On June 1, Clifford sells Harold the original manuscript of Benjamin Franklin's autobiography. Unbeknownst to Harold, however, the manuscript is a forgery. Harold signs a promissory note, payable to Clifford for $250,000 on August 1. Clifford negotiates the note to Betsy on July 1 for $200,000; she is unaware of the fraud. On August 2, Betsy gives the note to Al as a token of her affection. Al is Clifford's friend and knows about the scam (see Figure 23-1). May Al collect?

Begin the analysis by noting that Al is not a holder in due course. Why? For three reasons: he did not take the instrument for value (it was a gift), he did not take in good faith (he knew of the fraud), and he had notice (he acquired it after the due date). Nevertheless, Al is entitled to collect from Harold the full $250,000. His right to do so flows from Section

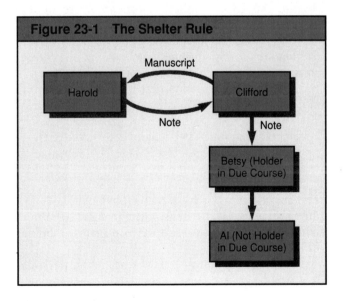

Figure 23-1 The Shelter Rule

3-201(a), which states what is usually called the **shelter rule:**

> Transfer of an instrument vests in the transferee such rights as the transferor has therein, except that a transferee who has himself been a party to any fraud or illegality affecting the instrument or who as a prior holder had notice of a defense or claim against it cannot improve his position by taking from a later holder in due course.

By virtue of the shelter rule, Al as transferee from Betsy acquires all rights that she had as transferor. Clearly Betsy is a holder in due course: she paid for the instrument, she took it in good faith, and had no notice of any claim or defense against the instrument. Since Betsy is a holder in due course, so is Al. His knowledge of the fraud does not undercut his rights as holder in due course because he was not a party to it and was not a prior holder. Now, suppose that after negotiating the instrument to Betsy, Clifford repurchased it from her. He would not be a holder in due course—and would not acquire all of Betsy's rights—because he had been a party to fraud and as a prior holder had notice of a defense. The purpose of the shelter rule is "to assure the holder in due course a free market for the paper." (Comment 3 to Section 3-201.)

DEFENSES

Despite the UCC's policy favoring holders in due course, a maker may often have a defense, even when the note is negotiable and has been properly negotiated to a person who qualifies as a holder in due course. For example, after class Lauren pulls a snub-nose .32 from her backpack, points it at Humphrey's temple, and calmly asks him to sign a negotiable note for $100,000 payable to her. He says that under the circumstances he would be delighted to honor her request and in fact does sign the note. Lauren quickly indorses and sells the note to a local bank—a holder in due course—for $90,000. She leaves town. When the bank attempts to collect, it is obvious that Humphrey will raise as a defense that he signed the note under duress. Is this a valid defense against a holder in due course?

The answer depends on whether it is a **personal defense** or a **real defense**. Personal defenses are good against holders but not holders in due course. Real defenses are good against both holders and holders in due course.

Personal Defenses

A holder who is not a holder in due course takes a negotiable instrument subject to the personal claims and defenses of numerous people. Under Section 3-306, the holder is subject to "all valid claims" on the part of *any* person, all defenses of any party available in a simple contract action, and specifically these defenses: want or failure of consideration, nonperformance of any condition precedent, nondelivery, or delivery for a special purpose. Moreover, the holder is subject to the defense "that he or a person through whom he holds the instrument acquired it by theft, or that payment or satisfaction to such holder would be inconsistent with the terms of a restrictive indorsement." These are personal defenses and are available against any holder who is not a holder in due course. The whole range of defenses to breaches of simple contracts are available in a suit in which the transferee is a mere holder. For example, suppose Lois sells Clark her car and Clark gives Lois a promissory note. Lois gives the note to Perry as a gift. Perry comes to Clark to collect on the note, but the car does not work and Clark refuses to pay. Perry is not a holder in due course and, when Perry sues, Clark may successfully raise the defense he had against Lois. Had Perry taken the note for value (and in good faith and without notice), Clark would not have been able to defend on that ground and would have had to pay Perry. Clark's only recourse then would have been against Lois in a separate suit.

Real Defenses

Real defenses are those available against a holder in due course (see Figure 23-2). These are set out in Section 3-305, as follows:

> To the extent that a holder is a holder in due course he takes the instrument free from
>   (1) all claims to it on the part of any person; and
>   (2) all defenses of any party to the instrument with whom the holder has not dealt except

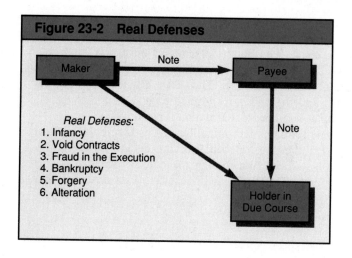

Figure 23-2 Real Defenses

Maker

Note

Payee

Real Defenses:
1. Infancy
2. Void Contracts
3. Fraud in the Execution
4. Bankruptcy
5. Forgery
6. Alteration

Note

Holder in
Due Course

(a) infancy, to the extent that it is a defense to a simple contract; and

(b) such other incapacity, or duress, or illegality of the transaction, as renders the obligation of the party a nullity; and

(c) such misrepresentation as has induced the party to sign the instrument with neither knowledge nor reasonable opportunity to obtain knowledge of its character or its essential terms; and

(d) discharge in insolvency proceedings; and

(e) any other discharge of which the holder has notice when he takes the instrument.

Infancy Whether an infant's signature on a negotiable instrument is a valid defense depends on the law of the state. In some states, for instance, an infant who misrepresents his age is estopped from asserting infancy as a defense to a breach of contract. In those states, infancy would not be available as a defense against the effort of a holder in due course to collect.

Void Contracts Section 3-305(2)(b) provides that incapacities or actions that would make a contract void are defenses against a holder in due course. These include mental incompetence, corporate acts that are beyond the powers of the corporation (ultra vires), and other incapacities specified by statute. Again,

whether a signatory lacked such capacity that the contract was void depends on state law. Duress, depending on state law, may be a personal or real defense. A serious threat, such as that at gun-point, usually renders void the agreement that it induces. In our example on p. 514, Humphrey has a defense to the bank's attempt to collect. A note signed under threat of prosecution or foreclosure may be merely voidable; hence the defense would be cut off and the holder in due course could collect.

Illegality also depends on state law. For the most part, it refers to instruments in payment of gambling debts or that incorporate usurious rates of interest.

Fraud in the Execution If a maker is tricked into signing a negotiable instrument, the transaction is void and the misrepresentation is a defense to a holder in due course. This so-called **fraud in the execution** applies to cases in which the maker thought that the paper was something other than a negotiable instrument (a receipt, for example) or if he knew that it was a negotiable instrument had no knowledge of its essential terms. The test is objective: it is not whether in fact the maker did not know but whether, considering all relevant factors (including age, intelligence, education, and business experience), the maker had a reasonable opportunity to obtain knowledge of the instrument's contents. If he did have such an opportunity, the fraud does not cut off the right of the holder in due course to collect.

By contrast, **fraud in the inducement** is a personal defense, not available in an action by a holder in due course. This kind of fraud is that which induces someone to make out a negotiable instrument with full knowledge of what he is doing. For example, Clifford's misrepresentation to Harold (p. 513) that the manuscript was in Franklin's hand is fraud in the inducement. Harold knew that he was the maker of a negotiable instrument and he knew its terms.

As the next case shows, it is a factual question whether a plaintiff has available a defense of fraud in the execution.

RICKS v. BANK OF DIXIE

352 So.2d 798 (Miss. 1977)

SUGG, JUSTICE, for the court. The Bank of Dixie, a Louisiana Corporation, as plaintiff, sued J. V. Ricks and others for collection of a promissory note in the Circuit Court of Leflore County. The court granted a peremptory instruction for plaintiff and the only issue argued on appeal is that the trial judge erred by granting a peremptory instruction for plaintiff.

A decision of the issue requires determination of this threshold question, did J. V. Ricks, Jr. sign the note on behalf of the defendants because of misrepresentation which induced him to sign the note with neither knowledge nor reasonable opportunity to obtain knowledge of its character or its essential terms?

*   *   *

Plaintiff filed an answer specifically denying every allegation of the defendants in their affirmative defenses. Defendants' first affirmative defense would relieve them from liability on the note, if supported by a preponderance of the evidence, under section 75-3-305 Mississippi Code Annotated (1972) which follows:

> To the extent that a holder is a holder in due course he takes the instrument free from
> (1) all claims to it on the part of any person; and
> (2) all defenses of any party to the instrument with whom the holder has not dealt except
>   (a) infancy, to the extent that it is a defense to a simple contract; and
>   (b) such other incapacity, or duress, or illegality of the transaction as renders the obligation of the party a nullity; and
>   (c) such misrepresentation as has induced the party to sign the instrument with neither knowledge nor reasonable opportunity to obtain knowledge of its character or its essential terms; and
>   (d) discharge in insolvency proceedings; and
>   (e) any other discharge of which the holder has notice when he takes the instrument.

The first affirmative defense was based on subsection (2) part (c) which permits defenses to be asserted against a holder in due course which were not available under the Uniform Negotiable Instruments Act. It allows the maker of an instrument to assert as a defense, "[S]uch misrepresentation as has induced the party to sign the instrument with neither knowledge nor reasonable opportunity to obtain knowledge of its character or its essential terms."

The defense authorized by section 75-3-305(2)(c) is a limited defense and may be asserted against a holder in due course only if a party was induced to sign an instrument because of misrepresentation coupled with the fact that the party signing the instrument had neither, (1) knowledge of its character or its essential terms, nor (2) reasonable opportunity to obtain knowledge of its character or essential terms. The comment pertaining to this defense found in Anderson's *Uniform Commercial Code*, Section 3-305:(1) p. 598 (1961) states:

7. Paragraph (c) of subsection (2) is new. It follows the great majority of the decisions under the original Act in recognizing the defense of 'real' or 'essential' fraud, sometimes called fraud in the essence or fraud in the factum, as effective against a holder in due course. The common illustration is that of the maker who is tricked into signing a note in the belief that it is merely a receipt or some other document. The theory of the defense is that his signature on the instrument is ineffective because he did not intend to sign such an instrument at all. Under this provision the defense extends to an instrument signed with knowledge that it is a negotiable instrument, but without knowledge of its essential terms.

The test of the defense here stated is that of excusable ignorance of the contents of the writing signed. The party must not only have been in ignorance, but must also have had no reasonable opportunity to obtain knowledge. In determining what is a reasonable opportunity all relevant factors are to be taken into account, including the age and sex of the party, his intelligence, education and business experience; his ability to read or to understand English; the representations made to him and his reason to rely on them or to have confidence in the person making them; the presence or absence of any third person who might read or explain the instrument to him, or any other possibility of obtaining independent information; and the apparent necessity, or lack of it, for acting without delay.

Unless the misrepresentation meets this test, the defense is cut off by a holder in due course.

In our opinion the above comment correctly states the factors to be considered by a trial court when it is called on to determine if a defendant is to be released from liability for signing an instrument. In order to determine if the defense in this case meets the above test, we must consider the evidence which was before the trial court.

The evidence shows without conflict that J. V. Ricks, Jr. signed a promissory note on October 7, 1974 payable to the order of Dixie Machine Works and plaintiff on behalf of all the defendants. The original note was introduced in evidence and is a negotiable instrument under the requirements of section 75-3-104 Mississippi Code Annotated (1972). Plaintiff purchased the note from Dixie Machine Works for a valuable consideration on October 21, 1974 and the note was negotiated on that date in accord with section 75-3-202 Mississippi Code Annotated (1972). Plaintiff met the requirements of section 75-3-302 and became a holder in due course.

The only witness offered by defendants was J. V. Ricks, Jr., who testified that, on the date the note was executed, he signed numerous purchase orders and he thought the note was a verification of terms. He signed all documents presented to him on that day without reading any of them. The witness has a college education and is a businessman with many years of experience. J. V. Ricks, Jr. did not use ordinary care when he signed the note without reading it and putting it into circulation; he was not prevented from reading the note; therefore, defendants' claim of misrepresentation has no legal

(continued on next page)

(continued)

RICKS v. BANK OF DIXIE
352 So.2d 798 (Miss. 1977)

substance. His testimony fails to establish that he was induced to sign the note, "[W]ith neither knowledge nor reasonable opportunity to obtain knowledge of its character or its essential terms."

★ ★ ★

. . . The trial court correctly granted the peremptory instruction for the plaintiff.

Affirmed.

Bankruptcy Drawers, makers, and subsequent indorsers are not liable to a holder in due course if they have been discharged in bankruptcy.

Forgery Under Section 3-404(1), forgery is a real defense to an action by a holder in due course. As we noted earlier (p. 501), negligence in the making or handling of a negotiable instrument may cut off this defense against a holder in due course—as, for example, when a drawer who uses a rubber signature stamp carelessly leaves it unattended.

Alteration A thief who steals two checks, both signed. One is made out to cash for $1,000; the other is blank. The thief alters the completed check to read $10,000 and completes the other check by filling in "$20,000." He transfers both checks to a bank. Can the bank recover from the drawer?

If the bank were not a holder in due course, it could not recover, because the thief's acts were fraudulent and *material*. Section 3-407(1) defines "material" as any alteration of an instrument that changes the contract of any party to it. Such changes include the number or relations of the parties, the completion of an incomplete instrument in an unau-thorized manner, and the addition or subtraction of any part of the writing as signed. Any alteration that is both fraudulent and material discharges from liability to a holder any party whose contract is changed. A nonmaterial or nonfraudulent alteration discharges no one, and the instrument may be enforced according to its original tenor or according to the authority given to complete an incomplete instrument.

The holder in due course has more protection against the defense of alteration than a mere holder. By UCC Section 3-407(3), a holder in due course may enforce the instrument according to its original tenor regardless of any alteration and may enforce an instrument as completed even if it was completed in excess of any authority given. Thus the bank, as a holder in due course, certainly may recover $1,000 on the check the thief altered; if the bank could show negligence by the drawer, it could recover the $10,000 it paid out. And by virtue of this rule, the bank may recover the full $20,000 on the completed check. Any loss owing to blanks wrongly filled in lies with the maker or drawer, not with the holder in due course.

In alteration cases, determining whether the drawer is negligent is difficult. Essentially, the issue must be decided by the judge or jury with little guidance from the UCC, as the following case notes.

RAY v. FARMERS STATE BANK OF HART
576 S.W.2d 607 (Tex. 1979)

POPE, JUSTICE. The question presented is whether Mrs. Nora Ray, the drawer, or Farmers' State Bank of Hart, Texas, the drawee, is liable for the loss occasioned by a check that a third party altered. In a case tried before the court without a jury, Mrs. Ray recovered judgment for $1,850.00, which was the amount of the alteration. The court of civil appeals reversed the judgment and rendered judgment that Mrs. Ray take nothing. We reverse the judgment of the court of civil appeals and affirm that of the trial court.

The controlling issue in the case is whether Mrs. Ray was negligent as a matter of law. On May 7, 1975, Mrs. Ray, an eighty-year-old lady, was awakened from a nap by a man who was shaking the screen to her front door. He gave his name as Robert Freeman, said he worked for the utility company, and that he needed to check the electrical system of her home because the power was off along the block. Mrs. Ray testified that when she unlatched the screen to look down the street for a utility vehicle, Freeman pushed his way inside the house. He went around the house placing a device in the electrical outlets and then went outside to check in the garage. While he was outside, as she later discovered, he cut the telephone wire to her house. Upon returning, he told Mrs. Ray that he was not through, but that he was awaiting the arrival of someone else from the utility company. He said that he was going to get a hamburger and would return after lunch, but that she should give him $1.50 for the service charge. Mrs. Ray testified that she could not see what he had done to earn $1.50 but was willing to give him the money to get him out of the house. She reached for her purse, but Freeman picked up her checkbook that was lying on the table telling her that his company required payment by check. He proceeded to fill it in, then shoved it over to her to be signed. She noted to herself that the check was for $1.50 and was in ink so it couldn't be changed. She signed the check and Freeman left.

After waiting a considerable period of time, Mrs. Ray concluded that Freeman was not going to return. She decided to phone the bank to stop payment on the check because he had not earned the money. She then discovered the phone was dead. Mrs. Ray walked down the street to use a neighbor's phone but could find nobody at home. About two hours later, when she finally talked to a lady at the bank, she learned that Freeman had cashed the check and that it was for $1,851.50 instead of $1.50.

When Freeman filled out the check at Mrs. Ray's home, he wrote the figures "1.50" far to the right of the dollar mark, leaving space in which he later added the figures "185". That made the amount appear as $1,851.50. There is some evidence that he also left space on the next line where he wrote the words "one and 50/100". He later placed in front of those words, "Eighteen Hundred & Fifty."

When Freeman presented the check at the bank, the teller required him to produce identification which he did by showing his driver's license and another identification card that showed his picture. Freeman had endorsed

(continued on next page)

(continued)

RAY v. FARMERS STATE BANK OF HART
576 S.W.2d 607 (Tex. 1979)

the check and beneath his signature he had stamped the words, "Allied Construction and Commercial-Residential."

The trial court made a number of findings of fact and also filed conclusions of law. The findings relevant to this appeal are:

1a. The Defendant Bank paid the check in question in good faith and in accordance with the reasonable commercial standards of the Bank's business.

2a. The Defendant Bank paid the check in due course of its banking business.

The relevant "conclusion of law" was that the conditions and circumstances under which Nora Ray signed and delivered the check did not amount to negligence substantially contributing to the material alteration of the instrument as required by Section 3.406 of the Uniform Commercial Code to constitute a defense.

*   *   *

Official Comment 3 to this section of the Uniform Commercial Code includes this explanation of how negligence is to be determined.

3. No attempt is made to define negligence which will contribute to an alteration. The question is left to the court or the jury upon the circumstances of the particular cases. Negligence usually has been found where spaces are left in the body of the instrument in which words or figures may be inserted.

As a general rule, the determination of negligence is the province of the trier of fact.

*   *   *

When viewed in the light most favorable to the trial court's judgment, we think there is at least some evidence of probative force to support the trial court's finding. At most, the evidence is conflicting. Under such circumstances, the trial court's finding is binding on the court of civil appeals. It is our opinion that the nature of the evidence introduced at trial was such that reasonable minds might differ as to whether Nora Ray was negligent under the circumstances. The court of civil appeals, therefore, erred in reversing the judgment of the trial court and rendering judgment that Nora Ray was negligent as a matter of law. Because of this determination, we do not reach the causation issue.

The judgment of the court of civil appeals is reversed and that of the trial court is affirmed.

CONSUMER TRANSACTIONS AND HOLDERS IN DUE COURSE

The Defrauded Consumer

The holder in due course doctrine has often worked considerable hardship to the consumer, usually as the maker of an installment note. Guiseppe, seventy-two, a lonely man who speaks English poorly, decides to take dancing lessons in the hopes that he will meet a suitable companion. The salesman for the Glide-Your-Feet Dance Studio promises that if Guiseppe signs a contract "right now" obligating him to take weekly lessons for six years, at a total cost of $23,459.62, he can always cancel after the first six weeks and obtain a total refund. Guiseppe signs the contract, which is a promissory note binding him to pay in monthly installments. The first lesson discourages Guiseppe; he is subjected to an hour of bone-jarring hopping and wrenching torso twisting, and when he asks in halting English about "a slow dance" he is laughed at ("no one does that stuff any more, Pops"). Guiseppe calls Glide-Your-Feet and says he wishes to cancel. "Fine," the bored switchboard operator tells him. The following month, a bill arrives. He ignores it. A week later, a collector from Easy Pay Credit Company duns him. He retorts that he has cancelled. The collector responds that that is no concern of the collector: He has purchased the installment note, is a holder in due course, and doesn't want to know about Guiseppe's dissatisfaction with the dance company. Under the UCC, assuming that Easy Pay took for value (at a deep discount, no doubt), without notice, and in good faith, and that the studio's actions are not considered fraud in the execution, the credit company would win a court judgment against Guiseppe for the full amount of the note.

The holder in due course doctrine thus aided and abetted garden variety consumer fraud. The courts frequently saw cases brought by credit companies against consumers who bought machines that did not work and services that did not live up to their promises. The ancient concept of a holder in due course did not square with the realities of modern commerce, in which instruments by the millions are negotiated for uncompleted transactions. The finance company that bought such commercial paper could never have honestly claimed (in the sociological sense) to be wholly ignorant that many makers will have claims against their payees (though they could and did make the claim in the legal sense).

The FTC Rule

Acting to curb abuses such as that in Guiseppe's case, the Federal Trade Commission in 1976 promulgated a trade regulation rule that in effect abolishes the holder in due course rule for consumer credit transactions. Under the FTC rule (16 CFR Section 433), the creditor becomes a mere holder and stands in the shoes of the seller, subject to all claims and defenses that the debtor could assert against the seller. Specifically, the rule requires the seller to provide notice in any consumer credit contract that the debtor is entitled to raise defenses against any subsequent purchaser of the paper. It also bars the seller from accepting any outside financing unless the loan contract between the consumer and the outside finance company contains a similar notice. (The required notice, to be printed in no less than ten-point, boldface type, is set out in Figure 23-3.) The effect of the rule is to ensure that a consumer's claim against the seller will not be defeated by a transfer of the paper. The FTC rule has this effect because the paragraph to be inserted in the consumer credit contract gives the holder notice sufficient to prevent him from becoming a holder in due course.

The rule applies only to consumer credit transactions. A consumer is defined as a natural person, not a corporation or partnership, who buys goods or services for personal, family, or household use from a seller in the ordinary course of business. Purchases of goods or services for commercial purposes and purchases of interests in real property, commodities, or securities are not affected. The rule applies to any credit extended by the seller himself (except for credit card transactions) or to any "purchase money loan." This type of loan is defined as a cash advance to the consumer applied in whole or substantial part to a

---

Figure 23-3 Notice of Defense

NOTICE

ANY HOLDER OF THIS CONSUMER CREDIT CONTRACT IS SUBJECT TO ALL CLAIMS AND DEFENSES WHICH THE DEBTOR COULD ASSERT AGAINST THE SELLER OF GOODS OR SERVICES OBTAINED PURSUANT HERETO OR WITH THE PROCEEDS HEREOF. RECOVERY HEREUNDER BY THE DEBTOR SHALL NOT EXCEED AMOUNTS PAID BY THE DEBTOR HEREUNDER.

purchase of goods or services from a seller who either (a) refers consumers to the creditor, or (b) is affiliated with the creditor. The purpose of this definition is to prevent the seller from making an end run around the rule by arranging a loan for the consumer through an outside finance company. The rule does not apply to a loan that the consumer arranges with an independent finance company entirely on his own.

The net effect of the FTC rule is this: holder in due course is virtually dead in consumer credit contracts. It remains alive and flourishing as a legal doctrine in all other business transactions.

Fair Credit Billing Act

Another development paralleling the FTC rule was the enactment of the Fair Credit Billing Act, which became effective in October, 1976. The FTC rule exempts credit card transactions from its terms. However (with certain limitations), the Fair Credit Billing Act permits purchasers to withhold payment of the balance due on credit card purchases of defective goods or services. We cover this Act in greater detail in Chapter 10.

CHAPTER SUMMARY

A holder is a holder in due course if he takes the instrument for value, in good faith, and without notice that it is overdue or has been dishonored or that any person has asserted any defense against it or claim to it. The holder in due course takes the paper free of most defenses; an ordinary holder takes the paper as an assignee, acquiring only the rights of the assignor.

Value is not the same as consideration; hence, a promise will not satisfy this criterion until it has been performed. The holder in due course must have given something of value other than a promise to give.

Good faith means honesty in fact in the conduct or transaction concerned. The test of the holder's good faith is subjective, not objective.

Notice is not limited to receipt of an explicit statement of defenses; a holder may be given notice through inferences that should be drawn from the character of the instrument. Thus an incomplete instrument, one that bears marks of forgery, or one that indicates it is overdue, may give notice on its face. Certain facts do not necessarily give notice of defense or claim: that the instrument is antedated or postdated, that the instrument was negotiated in return for an executory promise, that

any party has signed for accommodation, that an incomplete instrument has been completed, that any person negotiating the instrument is or was a fiduciary, or that there has been default in payment of interest or principal.

A person who could not have become a holder in due course directly (for example, because he had notice of a defense or claim) may become so if he takes as transferee from a holder in due course as long as he was not a party to any fraud or illegality affecting the instrument or had not previously been a holder with notice of a defense or claim. This is the "shelter rule."

Holders in due course are not immune from all defenses. A real, as opposed to a personal, defense may be asserted against the holder in due course. Personal defenses include fraud in the inducement, failure of consideration, nonperformance of a condition precedent, and the like. Real defenses consist of infancy, acts that would make a contract void (such as duress), fraud in the execution, forgery, and discharge in bankruptcy. A 1976 trade regulation rule of the Federal Trade Commission abolishes the holder in due course rule for consumer transactions.

KEY TERMS

Fraud in the execution	p. 515	Holder in due course	p. 506
Fraud in the inducement	p. 515	Notice	p. 510
		Personal defense	p. 514
Good faith	p. 507	Real defense	p. 514
Holder	p. 506	Shelter rule	p. 514

SELF-TEST QUESTIONS

1. A holder in due course takes the instrument:
   (a) for value
   (b) in good faith
   (c) without notice that it is overdue or has been dishonored
   (d) under all of the above conditions
2. The test of the holder's good faith is:
   (a) subjective
   (b) objective
   (c) not essential to determination of holder in due course status
   (d) none of the above
3. Personal defenses are:
   (a) good against both holders and holders in due course
   (b) good against holders but not holders in due course
   (c) good against holders in due course but not holders
   (d) none of the above
4. Fraud in the execution is:
   (a) a real defense
   (b) a personal defense

(c) not a defense
(d) none of the above
5. An example of a real defense might include:
(a) infancy
(b) duress
(c) forgery
(d) any of the above

DEMONSTRATION PROBLEM

Blackstone gives Whitestone twelve notes for $1,000 each, dated the first of each month of the year. By their terms, Blackstone is to pay a stated rate of interest on the fifteenth of each month. Blackstone pays up through April 1, but on April 15 fails to pay the interest due and on May 1 fails to honor the next note. A few days later, Whitestone negotiates the remainder of the notes to Greenstone. Greenstone knows that Blackstone failed to pay interest on April 15 and that Blackstone failed to make the May 1st payment. Is Greenstone a holder in due course? Why?

PROBLEMS

1. Mike signed and delivered a note in the amount of $9,000 to Paul, the payee, in exchange for Paul's tractor. Paul transferred the note to Hilda, who promised to pay $7,500 for it. After Hilda had paid Paul $5,000 of the promised $7,500, Hilda learned that Mike had a defense—the tractor was defective. Can Hilda collect from Mike on the note? How much? Why?
2. In problem 1, if Hilda had paid Paul $7,500, would your answer be different? Explain.
3. Tex fraudulently sold a boat, to which he did not have title, to Sheryl for $30,000 and received, as a deposit from her, a check in the amount of $5,000. He deposited the check in his account at First Bank, and immediately withdrew $3,000 of the proceeds. When Sheryl later discovered that Tex did not have title to the boat, she called her bank (the drawee) and stopped payment on the check. Tex, in the meantime, left for Costa Rica. First Bank now wants to collect the $3,000 from Sheryl. Sheryl claims that the bank is not a holder in due course because it did not

give value for the check in that the payment to Tex was conditional, the bank having retained the right to collect from Tex if it could not collect on the check. Is Sheryl correct? Why?
4. In problem 3, assume that Sheryl proves that First Bank did not follow standard banking practice in allowing Tex to withdraw funds before the check cleared. Sheryl argues that the bank is not a holder in due course because it lacked good faith. Is she correct? Why?
5. Suppose in problem 3 that Sheryl proves that First Bank knew that Tex was in financial difficulty and in the past had engaged in fraudulent practices. She argues that this shows that First Bank had notice which disqualifies it from becoming a holder in due course. Is she correct? Why?
6. Blackstone gives Whitestone a note for $3,000 payable on demand in return for delivery on June 10 of a home computer. The note says: "Given pursuant to our agreement that Whitestone will deliver a Talkie Home Computer on June 10." Blackstone then negotiates the note to Greenstone to pay off a debt. Does the reference to the computer agreement negate Greenstone's status as a holder in due course? Why?
7. Assume in problem 6 that Blackstone leaves blank the amount of the note and tells Whitestone to fill it in, "consistent with our conversation that the price of the Talkie Home Computer will be around $3,000." Whitestone the next day writes in "$10,000" in the presence of Greenstone, to whom he is negotiating the note. Does Greenstone's observation of the completion of the note negate his status as a holder in due course? Why?

ANSWERS TO SELF-TEST QUESTIONS

1. (d)   2. (a)   3. (b)   4. (a)   5. (d)

SUGGESTED ANSWER TO DEMONSTRATION PROBLEM

Greenstone is not a holder in due course because he knows that Blackstone failed to make the May 1 payment. (His knowledge of the failure to pay interest would not, by itself, defeat holder in due course status.)

Liability and Discharge

*I*n the preceding three chapters of this unit, we focused on the methods and consequences of negotiating commercial paper when all the proper steps are followed. For example, a maker gives a negotiable note to a payee, who properly negotiates the paper to a third-party holder in due course. As a result, this third party is entitled to collect from the maker, unless the latter has a real defense.

In this chapter, we turn to the law that applies when things go wrong: when people negotiate paper without authority or when the proper steps are not followed. We begin by examining a question especially important to management: personal liability for signing company notes and checks. Then we look in greater detail at the two general types of liability—contract and warranty—introduced in Chapter 22. We conclude the chapter by reviewing the ways in which parties are discharged from liability.

SIGNATURE BY AUTHORIZED REPRESENTATIVE

The problem of how an authorized representative should sign is one of the most frequently litigated issues in the field of commercial paper. Example: Igor

is an agent (treasurer) of Frank N. Stein, Incorporated. The corporation borrows $50,000 from First Bank, and Igor signs the note. The company later becomes bankrupt. The question: Is Igor personally liable on the note? The unhappy treasurer might be sued by the Bank—the immediate party with whom he dealt—or by a third party to whom the note was transferred (see Figure 24-1).

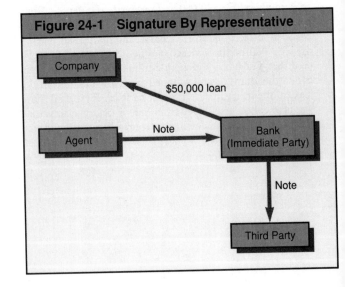

Figure 24-1 Signature By Representative

UCC Section 3-403(1) permits an agent or another authorized representative, including a corporate officer, to sign. Section 3-404(1) says that an unauthorized signature will not bind the person whose name was signed but will bind the person who did the signing. Thus, an agent is liable if the signature is not authorized, regardless of the form of signature.

In the following discussion, if we assume that in each case the company has authorized Igor to sign on behalf of the company, whether Igor is personally liable depends on the manner in which he signed the note. If Igor had signed simply "Igor," an unambiguous signature, he would be personally liable under Section 3-403(2)(a). Whenever neither the instrument nor the signature shows that the signing has been made in a representative capacity, the signatory is personally liable. Moreover, because of Section 3-401(1), the company itself would not be liable—its signature does not appear on the note if Igor signs only his own name.

Suppose that Igor had signed "Frank N. Stein, Inc. / Igor." The signature is ambiguous. Did Igor and the bank intend that both parties be held liable or was Igor signing merely as an agent? If Igor is sued by the immediate party—in this case, First Bank—he is allowed to attempt to prove in court that the parties never intended him to be liable. This situation is illustrated by the following case.

NEWPORT SEAFOOD v. NEPTUNE TRADING
555 So.2d 376 (Fla.App. 3 Dist. 1989)

GERSTEN, JUDGE.

Appellant, Newport Seafood, Inc. (Newport Seafood), appeals an order of final summary judgment in favor of appellee, Alfredo Alvarez (Alvarez), on Newport Seafood's claims against Alvarez and Neptune Trading Corporation (Neptune Trading) for tendering worthless checks. We reverse and remand.

Newport Seafood sold and delivered seafood products to Neptune Trading, which were evidenced by invoices and other statements addressed to Neptune Trading. In payment for the seafood products, three checks were tendered to Newport Seafood totalling $10,410.30. The checks were drawn on a Neptune Trading bank account, had "NEPTUNE TRADING CORPORATION" imprinted on the top, and were signed in script by Alvarez, "A. Alvarez." Alvarez was Neptune Trading's President.

After the checks were dishonored, Newport Seafood brought suit against Neptune Trading and Alvarez, individually, raising, *inter alia*, worthless check claims. Alvarez answered Newport Seafood's complaint and subsequently moved for summary judgment. Alvarez asserted in his motion for summary judgment that the invoices and other exhibits attached to Newport Seafood's complaint established that the seafood products were sold and delivered to Neptune Trading, and not to Alvarez. Alvarez also asserted that the checks were ambiguous as to the capacity in which he had signed them, in a representative capacity only. With his motion, Alvarez submitted an affidavit averring that he had signed the checks only in his capacity as president of Neptune Trading, and that he had never agreed to be personally liable to Newport Seafood on the checks.

*　　*　　*

The trial court entered final summary judgment in Alvarez's favor, from which Newport Seafood brings this appeal.

*　　*　　*

(continued on next page)

(*continued*)

NEWPORT SEAFOOD v. NEPTUNE TRADING
555 So.2d 376 (Fla.App. 3 Dist. 1989)

With respect to whether Alvarez, as well as his corporate principal, Neptune Trading, may both be held responsible to Newport Seafood, this court has recognized that a corporate principal and its representative may both be held liable on a worthless check claim.

We emphasize, however, that in order for a representative to be held liable, his personal obligation under the checks must be established. Section 673.403(2), Florida Statutes (1987), of the Uniform Commercial Code, and cases interpreting this statute, govern a representative's personal liability on worthless checks. Section 673.403(2), Florida Statutes, provides that an authorized representative who signs an instrument without indicating his representative capacity is personally obligated thereon "[e]xcept as otherwise established between the immediate parties."

In this case, Alvarez executed the checks without indicating his representative capacity. Pursuant to this statute, Alvarez is personally obligated on the checks "[e]xcept as otherwise established between the immediate parties."

Parol evidence is admissible in those cases in which an ambiguity is found on the face of the instruments regarding the capacity in which the person had signed.

Here, an ambiguity existed on the face of the checks that Alvarez signed because the name of his corporate principal, "NEPTUNE TRADING CORPORATION," was imprinted on the top of each of the checks. In *Medley Harwoods*, 346 So.2d at 1226, we held "parol evidence would be admissible at trial to show the intention of the parties" when the individual who had signed the checks had not indicated his representative capacity, and the name of his corporate principal was imprinted at the top of each check.

We therefore conclude the trial court properly considered the parol evidence offered by Alvarez, for the purpose of determining whether it had been "otherwise established between the immediate parties" that Alvarez's signing of the checks was in a representative capacity and not in his personal capacity as well. Having ruled that Alvarez's parol evidence was properly considered by the court, we do not likewise rule that summary judgment was properly entered in Alvarez's favor. Newport Seafood offered affidavits of two of its officers, attesting that at no time had an agreement been made that Alvarez would not be personally liable on the checks he signed. Embedded in the foundation of our summary judgment procedure is the fundamental precept that when a genuine issue of material fact has been raised, summary judgment is precluded.

Newport Seafood's reliance on *New York Financial, Inc. v. J & W Holding Company, Inc.*, 396 So.2d 802 (Fla. 3d DCA 1981), and *Provecasa, v. Gemini Associated Corporation*, 532 So.2d at 1106, as support for its contention that judgment should be entered in its favor, is misplaced. In *New York Financial*, the promissory note indicated that payment would be made as set forth on the reverse of the instrument. On the reverse side, under manner of payment, the defendant-appellee had signed his name without any identifying or limiting designation whatsoever. This court ruled that such unqualified and unambiguous signature imposed personal liability upon him as a matter of law. No ambiguity appeared on the face of the instrument, as in this case, which would have rendered extrinsic evidence admissible. . . .

Accordingly, the final summary judgment in favor of Alvarez is reversed and remanded for further proceedings. The issue of whether it had otherwise been established between the parties that Alvarez was executing the checks in his representative capacity and not in his personal capacity as well, should be resolved at trial.

Back to Igor. The right to prove in court that the parties did not intend the agent to be held liable will not help the agent if the plaintiff is a third party to whom the note has been sold. Under Section 3-403(2)(b), Igor will be liable to a purchaser of the note because the note failed to indicate that he signed in a representative capacity. If sued, the company also will be liable to the third party.

Now suppose that instead of writing down the company's name, Igor had only signed "Igor, Agent." Again the signature is ambiguous, and the consequences are the same as in the "Frank N. Stein/Igor" example. In this case, however, the company itself will not be liable, because no person is liable on an instrument unless his signature appears on it, and, in this example, Igor failed to sign the company's name.

Igor could have signed in a fourth manner: "Frank N. Stein, Inc." Had he done so, only the company—his principal—would have been liable. Since he was an authorized agent, he had the authority to sign the company's name, and no purchaser could have assumed Igor was holding himself out personally as liable. Of course, if he had not been authorized to sign, his signature of the company's name would fall within the rule governing forgeries, and he would be personally liable to both immediate and third parties.

The fifth and final possibility is for Igor to sign as follows: "Frank N. Stein, Inc. by Igor, Agent." This signature is unambiguous and clear. Only the company is liable.

CONTRACT LIABILITY OF PARTIES

Two types of liability can attach to those who deal in commercial paper: contract liability and warranty liability. **Contract liability** is based on a party's signature on the paper. For contract liability purposes,

signing parties are divided into two categories: *primary* parties and *secondary* parties.

Liability of Primary Parties

Maker   Two parties are primarily liable: the maker of a note and the acceptor of a draft. By signing a note, the maker promises to pay the instrument. The immediate or any subsequent holder in due course may recover from a maker.

Acceptor   Recall from Chapter 21 that acceptance is the drawee's signed engagement to honor a draft as presented. The drawee's signature on the draft is necessary and sufficient to accept. A bank certification of a check is acceptance, and the bank as acceptor becomes liable to the holder; the drawer is discharged. That is, the holder—whether a payee or indorsee—can look only to the bank, not to the drawer, for payment. If the drawee should vary the terms when accepting the draft, the holder may refuse the acceptance and treat the draft as dishonored. When that happens, the drawee is entitled to cancel its acceptance.

Liability of Secondary Parties

Parties   Unlike primary liability, secondary liability is conditional. Whether or not a secondary party is liable depends on the occurrence of three key conditions. The parties for whom these conditions are significant are the drawer and the indorsers. By virtue of Sections 3-413(2) and 3-414, drawers and indorsers engage to pay the amount of the draft to any subsequent holder or indorser who takes it up, if all of the following conditions are met: *presentment, dishonor*, and *notice of dishonor.* In addition, in certain cases, *protest* is also required.

Presentment   In order to be legally entitled to collect, a holder must first make a demand for payment or acceptance. This demand is known as **presentment.** A holder may make a *demand for payment* on the maker, acceptor, drawee, or other payor. He may make a *demand for acceptance* on the drawee. Why make such demand? Under Section 3-501(1), unless such a demand is made, the holder cannot make a legal claim against a secondary party. Martha writes Neal a check drawn on the Tertiary Bank. Neal must first present the check to the bank for payment; if he does not do so, he may not recover in a lawsuit against Martha because he has no reason to believe that he would not have been paid. However, Section 3-502 limits the drawer's discharge to situations where the bank becomes insolvent during a delay in presentment (see page 537).

Presentment may be made by mail, through a clearinghouse, at the place specified in the draft or note, or at the place of business or residence of the party on whom demand for payment or acceptance is made. When more than one maker (or acceptor, drawee, or other payor) exists, presentment need only be made on one of them. Presentment may be made also on an agent with authority to make or refuse acceptance or payment. A draft accepted by or a note payable at a bank must be presented there.

When must a presentment be made? Under certain circumstances, presentment must be made at or before a specific time. The instrument may specify the time for presentment, in which case it must be presented then. If no time for presentment is specified, presentment must be made on the date specified in the instrument for payment. In the case of sight instruments, presentment must be made within a reasonable period after date or issue, whichever is later. Likewise, when an instrument is accelerated, presentment for payment must be made within a reasonable period of time. What constitutes a reasonable time depends on customs and circumstances. The Code does specify that in the case of an uncertified check drawn and payable in the United States, thirty days is a reasonable period within which to present for payment or initiate bank collection with respect to the liability of an indorser.

The party to whom the presentment is made has certain rights under Section 3-505. She may inspect the instrument. She may demand reasonable identification of the person making presentment and ask for evidence of authority to make it when doing so on behalf of another. She may require that the instrument be presented at the place specified in it or, if no place is specified, at a reasonable one. Finally, she may demand a signed receipt on the instrument (for either partial or full payment) and require the instrument to be surrendered if paid in full. Under Section 3-506, acceptance may be deferred until the close of the next business day after presentment.

If an instrument is not paid or returned, it is said to be *converted.* If the drawee refuses to return the instrument on demand, she is liable for the face amount of the instrument. And if any other person to whom the instrument is delivered for payment refuses on demand either to pay or return it, she is liable for an amount presumed to be equal to the face amount, although she will be permitted to prove that she is liable for some other amount.

Dishonor   The second and third preconditions to secondary liability are **dishonor** and **notice of dishonor.** When acceptance or payment is refused after presentment, the instrument is said to be dishonored—although return of an instrument because it has not been properly indorsed does not constitute dishonor. The holder has an immediate right of recourse against the drawers and indorsers. But he has that right only if he has given necessary notice of the dishonor. Section 3-501(2) requires the holder to give notice to a party before the party can be charged with liability. The UCC facilitates giving notice of dishonor by permitting any party who may be compelled to pay the instrument to notify any party who may be liable on it, but each person who is to be charged with liability must actually be notified.

Suppose Ann signs a note payable to George, who indorses it to John, who in turn indorses it to Wendy. Wendy indorses it to Lisa, who presents it to Ann for payment. Ann refuses. Ann is the only primary party, so if Lisa is to be paid she must give notice of dishonor to one or more of the secondary parties, in this case, the indorsers. She knows that Wendy is rich, so she notifies only Wendy. She may collect from Wendy, but not from the others. If Wendy wishes to be reimbursed, she may notify George (the payee), and John, a prior indorser. If she fails to notify either of them, she will have no recourse. If she notifies both, she may recover from either. John in turn may collect from George, because George already will have been notified. If Wendy notifies only John, then she may collect only from him, but he must notify George or he cannot be reimbursed. Suppose Lisa notified only George. Then John and Wendy are discharged. Why? Lisa cannot proceed against them because she did not notify them. George cannot proceed against them because they indorsed subsequent to him and therefore were not contractually obligated to him. However, if mistakenly believing that he could collect from either John or Wendy, George gave each notice within the time allowed to Lisa, then she would be entitled to collect from one of them if George failed to pay, because they would have received notice. It is not necessary to receive notice from one to whom you are liable; Section 3-508(8) says that a party need be notified only once, and that notice operates for the benefit of all others who have rights against him.

The code sets deadlines for giving notice. A bank must do so by midnight of the day following the day on which it received notice of dishonor. Any other person has until midnight of the third business day after receipt of notice of dishonor. Written notice is deemed given when sent, even if it is never received.

Notice may be given in any reasonable manner. It may be given orally, although oral notice may be difficult to prove. Written terms that describe the instrument and state that it has been dishonored are sufficient. Even if misdescribed, a writing is sufficient if it does not mislead the party to whom it is given.

Protest When a draft appears on its face to be drawn or payable outside the United States, **protest** of dishonor must be made in order to charge the drawer or indorsers. This is an additional precondition to secondary liability. In form, protest is a certificate of dishonor signed and sealed by a United States consul, vice consul, notary public, or any other person authorized by the law of the place where the dishonor occurs. The certificate must identify the instrument, state that presentment was made or explain why it was excused, and declare that the draft was dishonored by nonacceptance or nonpayment. The protest is due no later than the time that notice of dishonor is due.

Mandatory protest is not necessary within the United States, although a holder may at his option make protest of either a draft or other instrument. Why would he want to do so? In the absence of the certificate, which is presumptive evidence of dishonor, a witness might have to travel considerable distance to testify to the dishonor and, at the least, might be inconvenienced in having to interrupt his work to give a deposition.

In international trade, protest simplifies the holder's ability to collect. Once protest is made, the holder can sidestep the requirements of an ordinary legal action in which the debt itself must be proved, and can avail himself of a summary procedure (known as *executive action*) that can lead to judgment in a matter of weeks rather than years.

Waived or Excused Conditions Under Section 3-511, delays in presentment, protest, or notice of dishonor are excused when the party had no notice that any was due. Delay is also excused when caused by circumstances beyond the holder's control and he diligently presents, protests, or gives notice of dishonor after the cause of the delay has ceased to operate.

Presentment, notice, and protest are excused entirely when the party to be charged has waived them; when the party himself has dishonored the instrument or has no reason to expect it will be paid; and when by reasonable diligence presentment and protest cannot be made or notice given.

Presentment by itself is also excused when the maker, acceptor, or drawee is dead or in insolvency proceedings instituted after the instrument was issued (this excuse applies to all instruments except documentary drafts), and when acceptance or payment is refused for some reason other than lack of proper presentment.

A drawee who dishonors a draft by refusing to accept it has no right to defend against suit by claiming failure to present, to protest, or to give notice of dishonor.

Secondary parties can waive the conditions necessary to hold them liable. If they waive protest, Section 3-511(5) says that they also waive presentment and notice of dishonor, even if protest is not legally required in the first place. Waiver can be written into the instrument itself; if it is, it binds all parties. However, if waiver is written in above the signature of an indorser, it binds him alone. Many bank agreements with depositors contain standard waiver clauses; for example, this one: "The depositor waives protest for and notice of the dishonor and/or nonpayment of any item deposited or cashed."

In the following case, the holder had not given the indorser notice of dishonor. The indorser argued that such notice and presentment were defenses to an action to collect on a note. The holder countered that they were unnecessary because the indorser had actual notice.

FEDERAL DEPOSIT INSURANCE CORP. v. KIRKLAND

272 So.Car. 310, 251 S.E.2d 750 (1979)

LEWIS, CHIEF JUSTICE. Among the assets coming into the hands of appellant, Federal Deposit Insurance Corporation, as the result of the closing of American Bank and Trust Company, was a note in the amount of $127,700.00, signed by Cecil Development Company, Inc., Anthony P. Cecil, and respondent, Stancel E. Kirkland, and secured by a mortgage from Cecil Development Company over certain real property on Hilton Head Island. The note was in default and appellant brought this action to collect the indebtedness through foreclosure of the mortgage and a deficiency judgment against the signers of the note. The findings of the Special Referee, to whom the issues were referred, that respondent Kirkland was liable for any deficiency on the note or indebtedness, was reversed by the lower court and this appeal followed.

This appeal involves the liability, if any, of respondent on the note. Respondent contends that he was an accommodation endorser on the note and was thus discharged due to the failure of American Bank and Trust to make presentment of the note and to give him notice of dishonor. Additionally, respondent claimed that he was discharged by reason of impairment of the collateral for the loan. We think that respondent was liable on the note and, accordingly, reverse.

In April 1973, American Bank and Trust Company made a construction loan to Cecil Development Company, Inc., to build a house on Hilton Head Island. Respondent Kirkland was an officer in the Development Company and owned 30% of the outstanding stock. In addition respondent served as the company's attorney.

The note evidencing the construction loan was signed by Cecil Development Company, Inc., and "individually," by respondent, Wilbur McLeod, and Anthony P. Cecil in 1974, when the house was still incomplete, respondent and Cecil negotiated a renewal loan with American Bank and Trust in the amount of $127,700.00. Respondent prepared the note evidencing the renewal loan and signed it; the pertinent part was as follows:

> For value received, Cecil Development Company, Inc., promised to pay to American Bank and Trust or order, the sum of one hundred twenty-seven thousand seven hundred . . . dollars, principal and interest due and payable April 3, 1974.

* * *

Cecil Development Company, Inc.

By: s/ Anthony P. Cecil
Anthony P. Cecil, President

s/ Anthony P. Cecil
Anthony P. Cecil, Individually

Stancel E. Kirkland, Individually

s/ Stancel E. Kirkland

The renewal note was due on April 3, 1974. However, on that date American Bank and Trust, Cecil Development Company, and the respondent agreed to extend the loan for an additional ninety (90) days. Although the renewal note was not paid when due, American Bank and Trust did not present the note to Cecil Development Company, nor did it give written notice of dishonor to respondent. Respondent concedes in his brief that he had "actual knowledge of default" in the payment of the note and that the maker would be unable to pay.

★   ★   ★

Although respondent signed the note in question in the lower right hand corner where a maker normally signs, both the referee and the trial judge concluded, and we agree, that respondent was an endorser and not a maker. The issues are accordingly determined in the light of respondent's status as an endorser of the note.

It is undisputed that neither presentment for payment nor notice of dishonor was made upon respondent when the note became due. Such failure would ordinarily discharge an endorser (here the respondent). However, Code Section 36-3-511(2)(b) provides that presentment and notice of dishonor is entirely excused where the endorser "has no reason to expect . . . that the instrument [will] be paid . . . ."

Respondent in this case knew that the note was not paid and that the maker, Cecil Development Company, would not pay the note. He, therefore, had full knowledge of everything that the notice of dishonor could possibly have given him. Under these circumstances, Section 36-3-511(2)(b) applied and rendered presentment and notice of dishonor unnecessary to charge respondent as endorser.

[The judgment of the lower court is reversed and the case is remanded.]

WARRANTY LIABILITY

Warranties on Transfer

In our discussion of negotiation (Chapter 22), we noted that a transferor gives five implied warranties when selling commercial paper. These warranties are important in fixing liability on a variety of transferors, because contract liability is limited, as we have seen, to those who have actually signed the instrument. Of course, secondary liability will provide a holder with sufficient grounds for recovery against a previous indorser who did not qualify his indorsement. But sometimes there is no indorsement and sometimes the indorsement is qualified. Sometimes, also, the holder fails to make timely presentment, notice of dishonor, or protest, thereby discharging a previous indorsee. In such cases, the transferee-holder can still sue a prior party on one or more of the five implied warranties.

A person who receives consideration for transferring an instrument makes the five warranties listed in Section 3-417(2). The warranty may be sued on by the immediate transferee or, if the transfer was by indorsement, by any subsequent holder who takes the instrument in good faith. The warranties thus run with the instrument. The warranties are as follows:

Good Title   The transferor warrants either that he has good title to the instrument or that he has the right to transfer title and is authorized to obtain payment or acceptance on behalf of the true title holder. If the transferor honestly believes that he has good title but in fact does not, he breaches this warranty.

Signatures Genuine   The transferor warrants that all signatures are genuine or authorized. An indorsee who indorses over a check to a creditor warrants that the drawer's signature is valid. If it happens to be forged, even though the forgery is unknown to the transferor, he has breached his warranty and his indorsee may sue him to collect. (Of course, since the transferor also was an indorsee, he may sue the person who indorsed it over to him for breach of the same warranty.) A signature that purports to be that of a principal is authorized if the person making it was an agent authorized to do so.

No Material Alteration   The transferor warrants that the instrument has not been materially altered.

No Defenses   The transferor warrants that no party has any defense to the obligation to pay him.

No Knowledge of Insolvency   Finally, the transferor warrants that he has no knowledge of any insolvency proceeding with respect to the maker or acceptor or the drawer of an unaccepted instrument. Notice that the warranty covers only "knowledge" of insolvency proceedings, not "insolvency" itself. Thus the UCC does not provide a holder protection in the form of a suit on warranty when a party is simply unable to pay.

Consider the following set of circumstances. Under duress, Ronald was forced to buy a stereo system from Nancy for $770 and to give Nancy a note payable to her order for $770. Ronald subsequently became bankrupt. Don then steals the note, raises the amount to $7700, indorses it by forging Nancy's signature, and sells the note to George, who knew of Ronald's bankruptcy. In turn, George sells and delivers (but does not indorse) the note to Jim. Jim tries to collect from Ronald but loses because Ronald has a real defense (duress). Can Jim recover instead from George? Although George has no *contract* liability to pay Jim because he was not a signatory on the instrument, he did give a set of *warranties* to Jim, his immediate transferee. And George breached all five warranties. George warranted that he had good title to the note (but it was stolen and Nancy's signature was forged), that the signatures were genuine (Nancy's was forged), that there were no material alterations (the amount of the note was wrongfully increased by ten times the proper amount), that there were no defenses (Ronald has a defense), and that he did not know of any insolvency (he knew that Ronald was bankrupt). So even in the absence of a signature and the contract liabilities that that implies, the UCC's transferor warranties can provide significant protection.

Warranties on Presentment

In an efficient commercial society the maker, bank, or other drawee who pays or accepts an instrument makes certain assumptions. The maker of a note, for example, ordinarily will assume that an indorsee who presents the note for payment is entitled to payment, that the signatures are valid, and so on. Suppose that one or more of these assumptions are erroneous. For instance, in the following classic British case, the drawee paid out on two drafts, one of which he accepted and one of which he had not. Subsequently he discovered that the drawer's signature was a forgery (the forger was hanged), and he sought to recover both payments from the indorsee to whom he had made the payments. Lord Mansfield ruled that the plaintiff was not entitled to recovery against an innocent defendant who had no knowledge of the forgery.

PRICE v. NEAL
3 Burr. 1354, 97
Eng.Rep.871 (1762)

This was a special case reserved at the sittings at Guildhall after Trinity term 1762, before Lord Mansfield.

It was an action upon the case brought by Price against Neal; wherein Price declares that the defendant Edward Neal was indebted to him in 80l. for money had and received to his the plaintiff's use: and damages were laid to 100l. The general issue was pleaded; and issue joined thereon.

It was proved at the trial, that a bill was drawn as follows—"Leicester, 22d November 1760. Sir, six weeks after date pay Mr. Rogers Ruding or order forty pounds, value received from Mr. Thomas Ploughfor; as advised by, sir, your humble servant Benjamin Sutton. To Mr. John Price in Bush-Lane Cannon-Street, London;" indorsed "R. Ruding, Antony Topham, Hammond and Laroche. Received the contents, James Watson and Son: witness Edward Neal."

That this bill was indorsed to the defendant for a valuable consideration; and notice of the bill left at the plaintiff's house, on the day it became due. Whereupon the plaintiff sent his servant to call on the defendant, to pay him the said sum of 40l. and take up the said bill: which was done accordingly.

That another bill was drawn as follows—"Leicester, 1st February 1761. Sir, six weeks after date pay Mr. Rogers Ruding or order forty pounds, value received for Mr. Thomas Ploughfor; as advised by, sir, your humble servant Benjamin Sutton. To Mr. John Price in Bush-Lane, Cannon-Street, London." That this bill was indorsed, "R. Ruding, Thomas Watson and Son. Witness for Smith, Right and Co." That the plaintiff accepted this bill, by writing on it, "Accepted John Price:" and that the plaintiff wrote on the back of it—"Messieurs Freame and Barclay, pray pay forty pounds for John Price."

That this bill being so accepted was indorsed to the defendant for a valuable consideration, and left at his bankers for payment; and was paid by order of the plaintiff, and taken up.

Both these bills were forged by one Lee, who has been since hanged for forgery.

The defendant Neal acted innocently and bonâ fide, without the least privity or suspicion of the said forgeries or of either of them; and paid the whole value of those bills.

The jury found a verdict for the plaintiff; and assessed damages 80l. and costs 10s. subject to the opinion of the Court upon this question—

"Whether the plaintiff, under the circumstances of the case, (a) can recover back, from the defendant, the money he paid on the said bills, or either of them."

*   *   *

It is an action upon the case, for money had and received to the plaintiff's use. In which action, the plaintiff can not recover the money, unless it be

(continued on next page)

(continued)

PRICE v. NEAL
3 Burr. 1354, 97
Eng.Rep.871 (1762)

against conscience in the defendant, to retain it: and great liberality is always allowed, in this sort of action.

But it can never be thought unconscientious in the defendant, to retain this money, when he has once received it upon a bill of exchange indorsed to him for a fair and valuable consideration, which he had bonâ fide paid, without the least privity or suspicion of any forgery.

Here was no fraud: no wrong. It was incumbent upon the plaintiff, to be satisfied "that the bill drawn upon him was the drawer's hand," before he accepted or paid it: but it was not incumbent upon the defendant, to inquire into it. Here was notice given by the defendant to the plaintiff of a bill drawn upon him: and he sends his servant to pay it and take it up. The other bill, he actually accepts; after which acceptance, the defendant innocently and bonâ fide discounts it. The plaintiff lies by, for a considerable time after he has paid these bills; and then found out "that they were forged:" and the forger comes to be hanged. He made no objection to them, at the time of paying them. Whatever neglect there was, was on his side. The defendant had actual encouragement from the plaintiff himself, for negotiating the second bill, from the plaintiff's having without any scruple or hesitation paid the first: and he paid the whole value, bonâ fide. It is a misfortune which has happened without the defendant's fault or neglect. If there was no neglect in the plaintiff, yet there is no reason to throw off the loss from one innocent man upon another innocent man: but, in this case, if there was any fault or negligence in any one, it certainly was in the plaintiff, and not in the defendant.

The UCC adopts Lord Mansfield's approach. A holder presenting an instrument for payment or acceptance does make certain warranties, but these are more limited than those of a transferor. Under Section 3-417(1), the holder warrants that:

1. He has good title to the instrument or is authorized to obtain payment or acceptance on behalf of the person who has good title.
2. He has no knowledge that the maker's or drawer's signature is unauthorized. Thus, if the maker's signature is unauthorized but the holder has no knowledge of that fact, he breaches no warranty in presenting the instrument for payment. A holder in due course acting in good faith does not make a warranty to the maker himself regarding the maker's own signature. Nor does he warrant the drawer's own signature to a drawer. Finally, the holder in due course does not warrant the validity of the signature to an acceptor of a draft if the holder either took the draft after acceptance or else obtained the acceptance without knowing that the drawer's signature was unauthorized.
3. The instrument has not been materially altered. Again, a holder in due course does not make such a warranty to the maker of a note, to the drawer of a draft, or to the acceptor of a draft—assuming the alteration either was made after the acceptance or was made prior to acceptance and the holder took after acceptance.

Both warranty and contract liability issues are discussed in the following case.

**FIRST NATIONAL
BANK OF
ALLENTOWN v.
MONTGOMERY**
27 UCC Rep. 164 (Pa.
1979)

DAVISON, J. This case is before the court on plaintiff's motion for summary judgment, pursuant to which the parties filed a stipulation of facts.

The parties have stipulated that on July 14, 1975, the Georgia Farm Bureau Mutual Insurance Company (maker) issued a check in the amount of $658.28, payable through the First National Bank and Trust Company in Macon, to the order of Willie Mincey, Jr. and MIC. Without indorsing it, MIC forwarded the check to Mincey for his indorsement. Mincey placed his indorsement on the check and endeavored to cash it at one of plaintiff's branches which declined to do so because Mincey was not known to bank personnel. Thereafter, Mincey returned to the bank with his uncle, defendant, and both men were told by plaintiff's branch manager that since defendant was a known depositor, the check would be cashed if defendant added his indorsement. Whereupon, defendant indorsed and plaintiff cashed the check. The funds were turned over to Mincey.

Subsequently, after plaintiff forwarded the check for collection, the maker returned the check to the Macon bank due to the lack of MIC's indorsement. The check was eventually returned to plaintiff. Since the facts are not in dispute, the litigation is ripe for summary judgment.

In order to determine defendant's liability, we must first ascertain the capacity in which he indorsed. Section 3–415(1) of the Uniform Commercial Code (UCC) of April 6, 1953, PL 3, as amended, 12A PS §3–415, provides that: "An accommodation party is one who signs the instrument in any capacity for the purpose of lending his name to another party to it." . . . We thus conclude, under the facts stipulated, that defendant was an accommodation indorser in that he received no benefit from the negotiation of the paper and that he indorsed the check solely to assist the payee.

Plaintiff's contention that defendant is liable on his indorsement is grounded on UCC §3–417. That section provides, in part, that:

"(1) Any person who obtains payment or acceptance and any prior transferor warrants to a person who in good faith pays or accepts that (a) he has a good title to the instrument or is authorized to obtain payment or acceptance on behalf of one who has a good title; . . . (2) Any person who transfers an instrument and receives consideration warrants to his transferee and if the transfer is by indorsement to any subsequent holder who takes the instrument in good faith that (a) he has a good title to the instrument or is authorized to obtain payment or acceptance on behalf of one who has a good title and the transfer is otherwise rightful; . . ."

However, §3–417 warranties are not applicable in this case, and they do not apply to accommodation indorsers generally. Section 3–417(1) sets forth warranties which run only to a party who "pays or accepts" an instrument. The only parties who "pay" an instrument are a payor bank or a maker, and the only parties who "accept" an instrument are a drawee bank or a maker.

(continued on next page)

(continued)

FIRST NATIONAL BANK OF ALLENTOWN v. MONTGOMERY
27 UCC Rep. 164 (Pa. 1979)

Here plaintiff is neither payor nor drawee; it is a mere transferee, and thus garners no benefit from §3–417(1).

Section 3–417(2) creates warranties which run to all transferees, but these warranties are given only by transferors who receive consideration. The stipulated facts clearly indicate that defendant received no consideration for his indorsement, and, in addition, it has generally been held that an accommodation indorser does not transfer the instrument.

* * *

Defendant's liability is, thus, not pursuant to any warranty, but is governed solely by his indorser's contract under §3–414. That section provides: "(1) Unless the indorsement otherwise specifies . . . every indorser engages that upon dishonor and any necessary notice of dishonor and protest he will pay the instrument . . . to the holder or to any subsequent indorser who takes it up, . . ." However, to hold defendant under this section it would be necessary to show that the check was "dishonored" and §3–507(3) specifically provides that the return of an instrument for lack of proper indorsement is *not* dishonor.

* * *

The facts having been stipulated and the law being clear, we are obliged to enter summary judgment, not, however, for the moving party, but rather in favor of the nonmoving defendant.

DISCHARGE

Article 3 lists nine ways by which the parties can be discharged from liability on an instrument. These methods, set forth in Section 3-601, are exclusive as far as the UCC is concerned but are not exclusive otherwise; Section 3-601 does not prevent a discharge in bankruptcy, for example. Moreover, by virtue of Section 3-602, no discharge of any party provided by the rules listed below operates against a subsequent holder in due course unless he has notice when he takes the instrument.

Payment or Satisfaction   A person can discharge his liability by paying or otherwise satisfying the holder, and the discharge is good even if the person knows that another has claim to the instrument. The discharge does not operate if the payment is made in bad faith to one who unlawfully obtained the instrument or if the payment or satisfaction does not conform to the terms of a restrictive indorsement.

Tender of Payment   A person who tenders full payment to a holder on or after the date due discharges any subsequent liability to pay interest, costs, and attorneys' fees. If the holder refuses to accept the tender, any party who would have had a right of recourse against the party making the tender is discharged. Mario makes a note payable to Carol, who indorses it to Ed. On the date the payment is due, Mario tenders to Ed, who refuses to accept the payment; he would rather collect from Carol. Carol is discharged: Had she been forced to pay as indorser in the event of Mario's refusal, she could have looked to him for recourse. Since Mario did tender, Ed can no longer look to Carol for payment.

Cancellation and Renunciation   The holder may discharge any party, even without consideration, by marking the face of the instrument or the indorsement in an unequivocal way, as, for example, by intentionally cancelling the instrument or the signature by destruction or mutilation or by striking out the party's signature. The holder may also renounce his rights by delivering a signed writing to that effect or by surrendering the instrument itself.

Impairment of Recourse or of Collateral   The holder will discharge a party by releasing or agreeing not to sue any third person against whom the party has a right of recourse known to the holder. Likewise, the holder will discharge a party by agreeing to suspend enforcement of the instrument or collateral against the third person. If the holder unjustifiably impairs collateral, given either by the party or by a third person against whom the party has a right of recourse, then the party is discharged also.

Reacquisition   Suppose a prior party reacquires the instrument. He may cancel any indorsement unnecessary to his title, and may also reissue or further negotiate the instrument. Any intervening party is thereby discharged from liability to the reacquiring party or to any subsequent holder not in due course. If an intervening party's indorsement is cancelled, then he is not liable even to a subsequent holder in due course.

Fraudulent and Material Alteration   Under Section 3-407, when the holder materially and fraudulently alters the instrument, he discharges any party whose contract is affected by the change.

Certification   When a drawee certifies a check for a holder, the drawer and all prior indorsers are discharged.

Acceptance Varying a Draft   Under Section 3-412, a holder may agree to the drawee's acceptance of a draft that varies its terms. Each drawer and indorser who does not affirmatively assent to the changes is discharged.

Unexcused Delay in Presentment, Notice of Dishonor, or Protest   Unexcused delay in presentment or giving notice of dishonor discharges any indorser and may (if the drawee or payor bank become insolvent) discharge any drawer, acceptor of a draft payable at a bank, or maker of a note payable at a bank. Unexcused delay in making protest (when protest is

required) discharges the drawer and all indorsers. (Section 3-502.)

CHAPTER SUMMARY

As a general rule, one who signs a note as maker or a draft as drawer is personally liable, unless he signs in a representative capacity and either the instrument or the signature shows that the signing has been made in a representative capacity. Several rules govern the various permutations of signatures when an agent and principal are involved: for example, an agent who signs as "agent" without also signing the principal's name is personally liable to persons who buy the paper and the principal is not.

The maker of a note and the acceptor of a draft have primary contract liability on the instruments. Secondarily liable are drawers and indorsers. Conditions precedent to secondary liability are: presentment, dishonor, and notice of dishonor (and in some cases a fourth condition, protest). Under the proper circumstances, any of these conditions may be waived or excused.

Presentment is a demand for payment, made on the maker, acceptor, or drawee, or a demand for acceptance on the drawee. Presentment must be made at the time specified in the instrument, unless no time is specified, in which case it must be at the time specified for payment, or within a reasonable time if a sight instrument.

Dishonor occurs when acceptance or payment is refused after presentment, at which time a holder has the right of recourse against secondary parties if he has given proper notice of dishonor. A bank must give notice by midnight of the day following the day on which it received notice of dishonor. Anyone else must give notice by midnight of the third business day after receipt of notice of dishonor.

Dishonor of a draft that appears on its face to be drawn or payable outside the United States will not create secondary liability unless the holder makes protest of dishonor. The form of protest is a certificate of dishonor signed and sealed by any person authorized by law to do so.

A seller of any commercial paper gives five implied warranties, which become valuable to a holder seeking to collect in the event that there has been no indorsement or the indorsement has been qualified. These warranties are (1) good title, (2) signatures genuine, (3) no material alteration, (4) no defenses by other parties to the obligation to pay the transferor, (5) no knowledge of insolvency of maker, acceptor, or drawer. A holder on presentment makes certain warranties also: (1) good title or authority to obtain payment or acceptance; (2) no knowledge that the maker's or drawer's signature is unauthorized; and (3) no material alteration.

Among the ways in which the parties may be discharged from their contract to honor the instrument are: (1) payment or satisfaction, (2) tender of payment, (3) cancellation and renunciation, (4) impairment of recourse or of collateral, (5) reacquisition, (6) fraudulent and material alteration, (7) certification, (8) acceptance varying a draft, and (9) unexcused delay in presentment, notice of dishonor, or protest.

KEY TERMS

SELF-TEST QUESTIONS

1. Drawers and indorsers have:
   (a) primary contract liability
   (b) secondary liability
   (c) no liability
   (d) none of the above
2. Condition(s) needed to establishing secondary liability include:
   (a) presentment
   (b) dishonor
   (c) notice of dishonor
   (d) all of the above
3. A demand for payment made on a maker, acceptor or drawee is called:
   (a) protest
   (b) notice
   (c) presentment
   (d) certification
4. An example of an implied warranty given by a seller of commercial paper includes a warranty:
   (a) of good title
   (b) that there are no material alterations
   (c) that signatures are genuine
   (d) covering all of the above
5. Under Article 3, discharge may result from:
   (a) cancellation
   (b) impairment of collateral
   (c) fraudulent alteration
   (d) all of the above

DEMONSTATION PROBLEM

Fenster has a negotiable trade acceptance in his possession. It is signed by Edwards and orders Wilberforce, a trade debtor of Edwards, to pay Fenster ten days after acceptance. Wilberforce has not yet accepted the instrument. Who has primary liability on the instrument? Why?

PROBLEMS

1. Howard Corporation has the following instrument which it purchased in good faith and for value from Luft Manufacturing, Inc.

   McHugh Wholesalers, Inc.   July 2, 1984
   Pullman, Washington

   Pay to the order of Luft Manufacturing, Inc., one thousand seven hundred dollars ($1,700) three months after acceptance.

   Peter Crandall, President
   Luft Manufacturing, Inc.

   Accepted July 12, 1984
   McHugh Wholesalers, Inc.
   By Charles Towne, President

   Crandall indorsed the instrument on the back in his capacity as president of Luft when it was transferred to Howard on July 15, 1984. What liability do McHugh and Luft have to Howard? Why?

2. An otherwise valid negotiable bearer note is signed with the forged signature of Darby. Archer, who believed he knew Darby's signature, bought the note in good faith from Harding, the forger. Archer transferred the note without indorsement to Barker, in partial payment of a debt. Barker then sold the note to Chase for 80 percent of its face amount and delivered it without indorsement. When Chase presented the note for payment at maturity, Darby refused to honor it, pleading forgery. Chase gave proper notice of dishonor to Barker and to Archer. Can Chase hold Barker liable? Why?

3. In problem 2, can Chase hold Archer liable? Why?

4. In problem 2, can Chase hold Harding liable? Why?

5. Mask stole one of Bloom's checks. The check was already signed by Bloom and made payable to Duval. The check was drawn on United Trust Company. Mask forged Duval's signature on the back of the check and cashed the check at the Corner Check Cashing Company which in turn deposited it with its bank, Town National Bank of Toka. Town National proceeded to collect on the check from United. None of the parties mentioned was negligent. Who will bear the loss assuming the amount cannot be recovered from Mask? Why?

6. Robb stole one of Markum's blank checks, made it payable to himself, and forged Markum's signature to it. The check was drawn on the Unity Trust Company. Robb cashed the check at the Friendly Check Cashing Company which in turn deposited it with its bank, the Farmer's National. Farmer's National proceeded to collect on the check from Unity Trust. The theft and forgery were quickly discovered by Markum who promptly notified Unity. None

of the parties mentioned was negligent. Who will bear the loss, assuming the amount cannot be recovered from Robb? Why?

7. Pat stole a check made out to the order of Marks. Pat forged the name of Marks on the back and made the instrument payable to herself. She then negotiated the check to Harrison for cash by signing her own name on the back of the instrument in Harrison's presence. Harrison was unaware of any of the facts surrounding the theft or forged indorsement and presented the check for payment. Central County Bank, the drawee bank, paid it. Disregarding Pat, who will bear the loss? Why?

ANSWERS TO SELF-TEST QUESTIONS

1. (b) 2. (d) 3. (c) 4. (d) 5. (d)

SUGGESTED ANSWER TO DEMONSTRATION PROBLEM

No one is primarily liable. A trade acceptance is a draft and no one has primary liability until a draft is accepted. (This problem is adapted from question 36 on the May, 1976, CPA examination.)

CHAPTER 25

CHAPTER OVERVIEW
Banks and Their Customers
Electronic Funds Transfer
Wholesale Transactions
Letters of Credit

Legal Aspects of Banking

To this point we have examined the general law of commercial paper as found in Article 3 of the UCC. Commercial paper, of course, passes through the bank collection process by the tons every day, and Article 3 applies to this flow. But there is also a separate article in the UCC, Article 4, Bank Deposits and Collections. In case of conflict with Article 3 rules, those of Article 4 govern.

In this chapter we

1. review the bank collection process;
2. examine how Article 4 governs the relationship between banks and customers;
3. look at the impact of electronic funds transfer on this relationship; and
4. discuss the letter of credit—a banking function that is especially important in international trade.

A discussion of government regulation of the financial services industry is beyond the scope of this book. Our focus is narrower: the laws that govern the operations of the banking system with respect to its depositors and customers. Although histories of banking dwell on the relationship between banks and the national government, the banking law that governs the daily operation of checking accounts is state-based—Article 4 of the UCC.

BANKS AND THEIR CUSTOMERS

The Bank Collection Process

How Checks Move   Americans write tens of billions of checks annually. You can readily imagine how complex the bank collection process must be to cope with such a flood of paper. Every check that you write must eventually come back to the bank on which it is drawn, after first having been sent to the store, say, to pay a bill, then to the store's bank, and from there through a series of intermediate banks and collection centers.

Originally, messengers physically carried the checks that arrived at their banks back to the banks on which they were drawn in order to draw out the funds. Legend has it that one day two messengers met at a coffeehouse in England and discovered that each was headed for the other's bank. They realized they could far more easily exchange their packages of checks than continue on to the other's bank. Thus was born the **clearinghouse,** an institution that physically exchanges checks, and credits and debits each bank with deposits and charges so that the banks need pay only the net difference if they are short or be credited with a net credit if there is a surplus. In America, the clearinghouse began as a local service that worked best in urban areas. Rural banks continued to have difficulties sending out checks. Eventually they established relationships with **correspondent banks** which cleared checks for them. Noncorrespondent banks charged fees when presented with out-of-town checks, so banks often developed exceedingly roundabout routes with their correspondent banks to avoid the fees. One famous story tells of the "long road from Birmingham (Alabama) to North Birmingham." The payee of a check drawn on a bank in North Birmingham deposited it four miles away in a bank in Birmingham. That bank shipped the check to a correspondent bank in Jacksonville, Florida. From there it was routed to a Philadelphia bank, which sent it south to North Birmingham. The trip took fourteen days and the check traveled 4,500 miles. Obviously so creaky a mechanism could not hope to process the current volume of checks.

The Federal Reserve System simplifies the process considerably. Any member bank of the System can use the Fed's check processing facilities. **Box 25-1** explains how the process works today.

Reason for Article 4   Not surprisingly, uniformity was the principal reason for the adoption of Article 4. Over the years, the states had begun to enact different statutes to regulate the collection process. Eighteen adopted the American Bankers Association Bank Collection Code; many others enacted Deferred Posting statutes. Article 4 absorbed many of the rules of the American Bankers Association Code and of the principles of the Deferred Posting statutes, as well as court decisions and common customs not previously codified.

Banks Covered   Article 4 covers three types of banks: **depository banks, payor banks,** and **collecting banks.** These terms are defined in Section 4-105. A depositary bank is the first bank to which an item is transferred for collection. Section 4-104 defines "item" as "any instrument for the payment of money even

though it is not negotiable," but it does not include money. A payor bank is any bank that must pay a check because it is drawn on the bank or accepted there. A depositary bank may also be a payor bank. A collecting bank is any bank except the payor bank that handles the item for collection.

Technical Rules   Detailed coverage of Parts 2 and 3 of Article 4, the substantive provisions, is beyond the scope of this book. However, Article 4 answers several specific questions that bank customers most frequently ask.

1. *What is the effect of a "pay any bank" indorsement?* The moment these words are indorsed on a check, only a bank may acquire the rights of a holder. This restriction can be lifted whenever (a) the check has been returned to the customer initiating collection or (b) the bank specially indorses the check to a person who is not a bank.

2. *May a depositary bank supply a missing indorsement?* It may supply any indorsement of the customer necessary to title unless the check contains words such as "payee's indorsement required." If the customer fails to indorse a check when depositing it in his account, the bank's notation that the check was deposited by a customer or credited to his account takes effect as the customer's indorsement. (Section 4-205(1).)

3. *Are any warranties given in the collection process?* Yes. They are identical to those provided in Article 3 (see pp. 531–536), except that they apply only to customers and collecting banks.

4. *Does the bank have the right to a charge-back or refund?* The answer turns on whether the settlement was provisional or final. A **settlement** is the proper crediting of the amount ordered to be paid by the instrument. Someone writes you a check for $1,000 drawn on First Bank, and you deposit it in Second Bank. Second Bank will make a "provisional settlement" with you—that is, it will provisionally credit your account with $1,000, and that settlement will be final when First Bank debits the check writer's account and credits Second Bank with the funds. Under Section 4-212(1), as long as the settlement was still provisional, a collecting bank has the right to a "charge-back" or

LAW AND LIFE

WHAT HAPPENS TO YOUR CHECK?

By Simona Frank

[Tens of billions of checks are written annually in the United States. Bank collection of these checks is a complex process. The following article shows how the Federal Reserve System greatly simplifies this procedure.— AUTHORS' NOTE]

You've paid the utility bills, the mortgage, the auto loan, and the charge accounts by writing checks. The following month, the same checks used to pay those bills are returned to you with bank endorsements on the back.

What happened to your checks? How were they returned to you? Checks go through several procedures from the time you write them until the time they are returned with your monthly bank statement.

When you (the drawer) write a check, you are instructing your bank (the drawee) to pay the person named on the check (the payee) a specific sum (amount of the check) out of your money on deposit with the bank. As soon as the payee deposits or cashes your check at a bank, the check begins to go through a series of basic processing steps called the collection system.

First, the check goes through proof and sorting procedures to verify that no errors have been made. The proof procedure determines that the check is properly endorsed, has not been altered in any way, and is not postdated. The sorting procedure includes categorizing checks for routing into three basic categories: "on us" checks, "other local" checks and "out-of-town" checks. An "on us" check is a check that is drawn on the bank at which it is deposited or cashed. "Other local" checks are checks which are drawn on banks in the same city or area. "Out-of-town" checks are checks that are drawn in other parts of the country.

If your check is an "on us" check, it is posted to (deducted from) your account immediately and returned to you with your monthly bank statement. The other categories of checks will eventually be posted to your account, but have to be processed through a longer route.

If your check is deposited in another local bank ("other local" check), it is routed through a process called "clearings." If it is deposited in an out-of-town bank, it is routed from proof to a process called "transit." The procedures of clearings and transit are very similar: the bank sends the check to the drawee bank for collection. However, other banks are responsible for different categories of checks and they use different methods for collecting them.

The local "clearinghouse" is an important part of the check collection operation. Banks send messengers to the clearinghouse daily to deliver and receive bundles of checks. A bundle for each of the other local banks with a list of the amounts due from other banks is delivered to the clearinghouse. The checks are exchanged and each bank is credited for other local

refund if the check "bounces" (is dishonored). However, if settlement was final, the bank cannot claim a refund. What determines whether settlement is provisional or final? Section 4-213(1) spells out four events (whichever comes first) that will convert a payor bank's provisional settlement into final settlement: When it (a) pays the item in cash; (b) settles without reserving a right to revoke and without having a right under statute, clearinghouse rule, or agreement with the customer; (c) finishes posting the item to the appropriate account; or (d) makes provisional settlement and fails to revoke the settlement in the time and manner permitted by statute, clearinghouse rule, or agreement. All clearinghouses have rules permitting revocation of settlement within certain time periods. For example, an item cleared before 10 A.M. may be returned and the settlement revoked before 2 P.M. From this section it should be apparent that a bank generally can prevent a settlement from becoming final if it chooses to do so.

BOX 25-1

checks that it brings for collection. Each bank is also debited (charged) for checks that are delivered for collection by other banks. If a bank has checks drawn on it amounting to more than it has in local checks on other banks, it owes the clearinghouse the difference. If the reverse is true, the clearinghouse owes the bank the difference. The clearinghouse receives exactly the same amount of money as it pays out. Years ago, the differences between the banks were settled in cash, but today net settlements are made in demand deposit accounts maintained by clearinghouse banks.

After your bank has received the checks from the clearinghouse, the checks are posted immediately to individual accounts and your checks are returned with your monthly statement.

The third category of checks that a bank receives for deposit or to cash is out-of-town checks. To collect these checks, transit must send them to the city where the drawee bank is located. When a bank collects an out-of-town check, it considers the speed and cost of collection. The methods

of collection are: through a correspondent bank, through a Federal Reserve bank, or by direct presentment. If a bank mails a bundle of checks drawn on an out-of-town bank directly to the drawee bank, it will be collecting these checks through direct presentment. Many banks have special arrangements with banks in other parts of the country to help collect out-of-town checks. Banks with this special arrangement are called "correspondent banks." The correspondent bank then processes the checks through the local clearinghouse or through direct presentment.

Most out-of-town checks are collected through the Federal Reserve System, which is composed of 12 Federal Reserve District banks that serve other commercial banks. For example, here's what would happen if you were to write a check drawn on your Rochester, New York, bank to a clothing store located in Sacramento, California. The clothing store deposits the check in an account at a Sacramento bank. The Sacramento bank deposits the check for credit in its account at the Federal Reserve

Bank of San Francisco, which credits the Sacramento bank's deposit account and the Sacramento bank in turn credits the clothing store's account. The Federal Reserve Bank of San Francisco sends the check to the Federal Reserve Bank of New York for collection. The Federal Reserve Bank of New York pays the Federal Reserve Bank of San Francisco by payment from its share in what is called the "Interdistrict Settlement Fund." The Federal Reserve Bank of New York forwards the check to your bank in Rochester, which deducts the amount of the check from your account. At the same time, the Federal Reserve Bank of New York deducts the amount of the check from the deposit account of the Rochester Bank with the Federal Reserve Bank. The checks are physically processed through each procedure. They may be sent by road, rail, or air, depending on which is the fastest means of transportation.

Source: FDIC *Consumer News*, May 1982

Relationship with Customers

The relationship between a bank and its customers is governed by UCC Article 4. However, Section 4-103(1) permits the bank to vary its terms, except that no bank can disclaim responsibility for failing to act in good faith or to exercise ordinary care.

Most disputes between bank and customer arise when the bank either pays or refuses to pay a check. Under several provisions of Article 4, the bank is entitled to pay, even though the payment may be adverse to the customer's interests.

Payment of Overdrafts Suppose a customer writes a check for a sum greater than the amount in her account. May the bank pay the check and charge the customer's account? Under Section 4-401(1), it may. Moreover, it may pay on an altered check and charge the customer's account for the original tenor of the check, and if a check was completed it may pay the completed amount and charge the customer's account, assuming the bank acted in good faith without knowledge that the completion was improper. May the bank obligate itself not to pay an overdraft by adopting internal policies regulating such payment? In the following case, the customer made that argument—unsuccessfully.

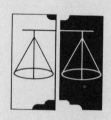

CONTINENTAL BANK v. FITTING
114 Ariz. 98, 559 P.2d 218 (1977)

SCHROEDER, PRESIDING JUDGE. The appellant, Continental Bank, brought this action to recover the amount of an overdraft which it paid on a check drawn on appellee's account. The appellee, Fitting, resisted the bank's action on the ground that the bank should not have paid the overdraft, and also counterclaimed for damages claimed to have arisen out of the wrongful dishonor by the bank of a different check. The judgment was entered in favor of Fitting on both the bank's claim on the overdraft and on Fitting's counterclaim, and the bank appeals.

The check leading to the overdraft claim was written by Fitting in the amount of $800. After writing the check, she had second thoughts and contacted the bank about the possibility of stopping payment. A bank employee advised that a stop payment order could not be submitted until the bank opened the following morning. Fitting then discussed with the bank employee the possibility of deliberately creating an overdraft situation by withdrawing enough money so that there would remain insufficient funds to cover the check in question. The bank employee indicated that in those circumstances the bank would not pay the check.

Early the next morning, Fitting proceeded to withdraw money from the account, leaving enough money to cover other checks which she had written. The bank nevertheless paid the $800 check in question, and sought recovery of the amount of the overdraft from Fitting in this action.

In defense of her judgment below, Fitting's sole reliance is upon evidence developed before the trial court showing that under the bank's usual internal procedures and policies, the bank would have known the check represented an overdraft and would not have paid it. As made clear in oral argument, Fitting does not contend that her conversations with the bank employees concerning overdraft policies constituted a contractual agreement that the check would be dishonored; nor does she claim that the bank is estopped to claim recovery of the overdraft as a result of that conversation.

In those circumstances, the sole issue with respect to the overdraft is whether the bank was lawfully entitled to pay it and to seek recourse from Fitting. The matter is governed by A.R.S. § 44-2627 [U.C.C. § 4-401] which clearly gives the bank the option to pay an overdraft and to charge the customer's account for that overdraft when the check is otherwise properly payable.

The bank, therefore, by paying the overdraft and charging the customer's account, was acting in accordance with procedures specifically authorized by law, and violated no claimed contractual agreement with its customer. Fitting offers no support for her theory that the bank's own internal policies may in and of themselves give rise to a duty to follow such policies in every case, despite provisions of the statute authorizing contrary conduct. We perceive no basis for such a holding as a matter of sound policy. As the comment to section 4-401 of the Uniform Commercial Code states:

> It is fundamental that upon proper payment of a draft the drawee may charge the account of the drawer. This is true even though the draft is an overdraft since the draft itself authorizes the payment for the drawer's account and carries an implied promise to reimburse the drawee.

The counterclaim against the bank for wrongful dishonor arises from the bank's refusal to pay a check drawn by Fitting on a trust account with the bank. There is no question that the bank erroneously dishonored the check as a result of a "hold" which it mistakenly placed on the account. The trial court awarded damages to appellee in the amount of $1,000, and the only issue before us is the correctness of the award damages. The appellant proved no specific damages as a result of the dishonor but claims rather that she is entitled to damages on the presumption that the mere fact of dishonor injuriously affected her business reputation.

Fitting, as also made clear in oral argument, agrees that the dishonor was the product of a mistake.

The subject of damages for wrongful dishonor is covered by A.R.S. § 44-2628 [U.C.C. § 4-402] which expressly provides that: "When the dishonor occurs through mistake liability is limited to actual damages proved." In arguing that she is nevertheless entitled to damages which are not actually proved appellee relies upon a case in Arizona arising prior to the adoption of that section.

We conclude that this case is no longer controlling in the face of the statute expressly requiring actual damages to be shown in the case of mistaken dishonor. A.R.S. § 44-2628 is section 4-402 of the Uniform Commercial Code, and comment 3 of that section states clearly that it "rejects decisions which have held . . . substantial damages may be awarded on the basis of defamation 'per se' without proof that damage has occurred." Since the adoption of the Code has abrogated prior Arizona law governing damages for wrongful dishonor, the trial court erred in awarding damages here.

Accordingly, the judgment in favor of Fitting on both the bank's overdraft and Fitting's counterclaim must be reversed with instructions to the trial court to enter judgment in favor of appellant bank on both claims.

Payment of Stale Checks   Section 4-404 permits a bank to refuse to pay a check that was drawn more than six months before being presented. Banks ordinarily consider such checks to be stale and will refuse to pay them, but the same section gives them the option to pay if they choose. A corporate dividend check, for example, will be presumed to be good more than six months later. The only exception to this rule is for certified checks, which must be paid whenever presented, since the customer's account was charged when the check was certified.

Payment of Deceased's or Incompetent's Checks   Suppose a customer dies or is adjudged to be incompetent. May the bank honor her checks? Section 4-405 permits banks to accept, pay, and collect an item as long as it has no notice of the death or declaration of incompetence, and has no reasonable opportunity to act on it. Even after notice of death, a bank has ten days to pay or certify checks drawn on or prior to the date of death unless someone claiming an interest in the account orders it to refrain from doing so.

Stop Payment Orders Section 4-403 expressly permits the customer to order the bank to "stop pay-

ment" on any check payable for her account, assuming the stop order arrives in enough time to reasonably permit the bank to act on it. An oral stop order is effective for fourteen days; a follow-up written confirmation within that time is effective for six months and can be renewed in writing. But, as the next case shows, if a stop order is not renewed, the bank will not be liable for paying the check, even one that is quite stale.

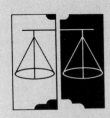

GRANITE EQUIPMENT LEASING CORP. v. HEMPSTEAD BANK
68 Misc.2d 350, 326 N.Y.S.2d 881 (1971)

BERTRAM HARNETT, JUSTICE. Under the Uniform Commercial Code, does a bank have a duty of inquiry before paying a stale check? Does it matter that the stale check had been previously stopped under a stop payment order which expired for lack of renewal? So this case goes.

Granite Equipment Leasing Corp. kept a checking account with Hempstead Bank. On October 10, 1968 Granite drew a check payable to Overseas Equipment Co., Inc. Five days later, after Overseas advised that the check had not been received, Granite wrote the Bank on October 15, 1968 to stop payment on the check. On that same day Granite authorized the Bank to wire the payee funds in the same amount as the stopped check and the Bank did so. Granite never renewed its stop payment order between October 1968 and November 10, 1969. On November 10, 1969, without notice or inquiry to Granite, the Bank accepted the original check to Overseas which had been stopped the year before, paid the indicated funds to a collecting bank, and charged Granite's account.

Granite now seeks to recover from the Bank the amount charged because of the check paid to Overseas in November 1969. The Bank defends on the ground that under UCC § 4-403 the stop payment order had expired for want of renewal, and that acting in good faith it was entitled under UCC § 4-404 to pay the stale check.

There is no doubt the check is stale. There is no doubt the stop payment order was properly given at the outset, and that it was never renewed. Granite essentially maintains the Bank had a duty to inquire into the circumstances of that stale check, and should not have paid in face of a known lapsed stop order without consulting its depositor.

The Uniform Commercial Code, which became effective in New York on September 27, 1964, provides that: "(1) A customer may by order to his bank stop payment of any item payable for his account . . . (2) . . . A written [stop] order is effective for only six months unless renewed in writing". UCC § 4-403.

The Official Comment to UCC § 4-403 notes that: "[t]he purpose of the [six-month limit] is, of course, to facilitate stopping payment by clearing the records of the drawee of accumulated unrevoked stop orders, as where the drawer has found a lost instrument or has settled his controversy with the payee, but has failed to notify the drawee. *The last sentence of subsection (2), together with the second clause in Section 4-404, rejects the reasoning of such cases as* Goldberg v. Manufacturers Trust Company, 199 Misc. 167, 102 N.Y.S.2d 144 . . .". McKinney's Uniform Commercial Code, Part 2, p. 612 (emphasis supplied).

* * *

Granite cannot be permitted to predicate liability on the part of the Bank on its failure to inquire about and find a stop payment order which had become terminated in default of renewal. Feller v. Manufacturers Trust Co., 151 N.E.2d 619, held that a drawee bank was not liable to a drawer for payment of a check two months after expiration of a stop payment order which had not been renewed. See also, William Savage, Inc. v. Manufacturers Trust Co., 20 Misc.2d 114, 189 N.Y.S.2d 308, holding a bank not liable for payment on an eleven month old check after expiration of a stop payment order.

Neither may Granite predicate a claim of liability upon the Bank's payment of a stale check. The legal principles applicable to this circumstance are codified in UCC § 4-404, which provides that: "[a] bank is under no obligation . . . to pay a check, other than a certified check, which is presented more than six months after its date, but *it may charge its customer's account for a payment made thereafter in good faith*". (emphasis supplied). Here too, the *Goldberg* case reasoning is discarded in the official commentary. There is no obligation under the statute of the Bank to search its records to discover old lapsed stop payment orders. The Bank does not have to pay a stale check, but it may pay one in "good faith." Significantly, UCC § 1-201(19) defines "good faith" as honesty in fact in the conduct or transaction concerned". In the absence of any facts which could justify a finding of dishonesty, bad faith, recklessness, or lack of ordinary care, in the face of circumstances actually known, or which should have been known, the Bank is not liable to Granite for its payment of the check drawn to Overseas.

One statute invalidates stop payment orders not renewed within six months. Another statute allows payment in good faith of stale checks. Granite cannot combine the two statutes to reach a synergistic result not contemplated by either separately.

Granite's complete remedy lies in its pending Florida action against Overseas to recover the extra payment.

Accordingly, the Court will enter judgment in favor of defendant dismissing the complaint on the merits, without costs and disbursements.

Wrongful Dishonor If a bank wrongfully dishonors an item, it is liable to the customer for all damages that are a direct consequence of ("proximately caused by") the dishonor. The bank's liability is limited to the damages actually proved; these may include damages for arrest and prosecution.

Customers' Duties In order to hold a bank liable for paying out an altered check, the customer has certain duties under Section 4-406. Primarily, the customer must act promptly in examining her statement of account and must notify the bank if any check has been altered or her signature has been forged. If the customer fails to do so, she cannot recover from the bank for an altered signature or other term if the bank can show that it suffered a loss because of the customer's slowness. Recovery may also be denied when there has been a series of forgeries and the customer did not notify the bank within two weeks after receiving the first forged item.

These rules apply to a payment made with ordinary care by the bank. If the customer can show that the bank negligently paid the item, then the customer may recover from the bank, regardless of how dilatory the customer was in notifying the bank—with two exceptions. They are: (1) from the time she first sees the statement and item, the customer has one year to tell the bank that her signature was unauthorized or that a term was altered; (2) she has three years to report an unauthorized indorsement.

The next case illustrates the nature of a customer's duties.

READ v. SOUTH CAROLINA NAT. BANK
335 S.E.2d 359 (S.C. 1985)

PER CURIAM:

Plaintiff-Appellant, Emerson B. Read, a managing partner of Lawton Bluff Company, a limited partnership, brings this action against the Defendant-Respondent, South Carolina National Bank, to recover damages allegedly due because the bank paid out monies as a result of forged signatures on checks. The complaint alleges causes of actions for negligence and for conversion.

* * *

[Plaintiff's Executive Secretary forged his signature on numerous checks by signing his name and using a rubber facsimile stamp of his signature. In late 1980, for instance, she forged his signature on fourteen checks that were drawn on the Lawton Bluff account and payable to herself. Thirteen of these checks were deposited in her son's account at the defendant bank; the remaining check was deposited at another bank. The trial court directed a verdict for the bank.]

Although the Plaintiff couched his first cause of action in negligence, the relationship between a bank and its depositor is one of contract. This contractual relationship requires that the bank pay out funds only in accordance with the orders given by the depositor. Consequently, a bank may not charge the depositor's account for any checks containing a forged or unauthorized signature of the drawer. These rules have been incorporated into the Uniform Commercial Code. South Carolina Code of Laws § 36-4-401(1) provides that a bank may charge against its customer's account only an item which is properly payable. In § 36-3-401(1) no person is liable on an instrument unless his signature appears thereon. Section 36-3-404 provides that an unauthorized signature is wholly inoperative as that of the person whose name is signed unless he ratifies it or is *precluded* from denying it. Thus, under the Code a bank breaches its agreement with its customer when it pays a check containing a forged or unauthorized signature of the drawer. It is this breach which constitutes the customer's cause of action against the bank to recover the sums paid out on checks bearing the forged signatures.

* * *

The [defense] in this case was that the Plaintiff failed in his duty to discover and promptly notify SCN of the forgeries. This duty and the effect of the customer's failure to discharge it are set forth in § 36-4-406(1) and (2).

(1) When a bank sends to its customer a statement of account accompanied by items paid in good faith in support of the debt entries or holds the statement and items pursuant to a request of instructions of its customer or otherwise in a reasonable manner makes the statement and items available to the customer, the customer must exercise reasonable care and promptness to examine the statement and items to discover his unauthorized signature or any alteration on an item and must notify the bank promptly after discovery thereof.

(2) If the bank establishes that the customer failed with respect to an item to comply with the duties imposed on the customers by subsection (1) the customer is precluded from asserting against the bank

(a) his unauthorized signature or any alteration on the item if the bank also establishes that it suffered a loss by reason of such failure; and

(b) an unauthorized signature or alteration by the same wrongdoer on any other item paid in good faith by the bank after the first item and statement was available to the customer for a reasonable period not exceeding fourteen calendar days and before the bank receives notification from the customer of any such unauthorized signature or alteration.

These provisions impose a duty on the depositor to check his monthly statement for unauthorized signatures on checks. If a depositor fails to do so, after the first forged check and statement relating thereto is sent to him, plus a reasonable period not exceeding fourteen (14) days, he is precluded from asserting the unauthorized signature against the bank, on any subsequent item containing an unauthorized signature by the same wrongdoer. The burden of proof of the depositor's negligence is on the bank.

The first forgery occurred on the Lawton Bluff account in September 1980 and would have been included in the bank statement mailed on October 1. The forgeries were not reported to SCN until January 26, 1981. Read is thus precluded from asserting forgeries which occurred after September 1980.

The preclusion under § 36-4-406(1) and (2) does not apply if the bank is negligent in paying the items.

The preclusion under subsection (2) does not apply if the customer establishes lack of ordinary care on the part of the bank in paying the item(s).
§ 36-4-406(3)

The burden of proving the bank's failure to exercise ordinary care under § 36-4-406(3) in paying the items rest squarely on the customer. The question becomes whether there was sufficient evidence to raise a jury issue as to the lack of ordinary care on the part of SCN in paying the checks. (Check paying is the determination of whether there are sufficient funds in an account and a review of the signature on the check. This process is performed

(continued on next page)

(continued)

READ v. SOUTH CAROLINA NAT. BANK
335 S.E.2d 359 (S.C. 1985)

by bank's central bookkeeping department and has nothing to do with tellers in local branches who do not have signature cards).

Employees of SCN testified that when checks drawn on SCN accounts are received by SCN for payment, they are first processed through the computer where the account is automatically debited. After this, the individual checks are received in the check paying area where the check paying clerks file the checks in account number order in file trays. The accounts in these file trays are separated by plastic dividers which contain the signature card. At the same time the checks are filed in the trays, the signature on the check is compared to the signature card in the plastic guide. Check paying clerks are assigned to file checks for certain cities so they will become familiar with the accounts and the signatures.

A quality control clerk performs a random checking behind those check paying clerks to insure that the checks are filed properly and that signatures are compared. If signatures do not match, they are pulled and placed on a return sheet and transmitted back to the local office.

A representative from C & S Bank testified that their procedure is similar to that of SCN, but that the signature cards are kept in a separate place from where the checks are filed, and that signatures are only compared on checks over $10,000.00 unless the customer requests special instructions or there is an alert on the account. A representative of First National Bank testified that the procedures used by his bank were the same as those used by SCN. Their was no other testimony of any other method of detecting forgeries employed by any other bank institution.

Although "ordinary care" is not defined in the Code, § 36-4-103(3) provides that action or nonaction consistent with general banking usage constitutes ordinary care. The only evidence as to general banking usage came from SCN and its witness from the area banks. Read presented no evidence to refute that SCN's procedure was consistent with general banking usage. On the contrary, Read's expert witness testified that SCN was more careful than the average bank in its examination of signatures. The only reasonable inference that could be drawn from the evidence is that SCN exercised ordinary care in paying the checks. [Judgment affirmed.]

The Expedited Funds Availability Act   In addition to UCC Article 4, the Expedited Funds Availability Act, which became effective in 1988, addresses the relationship between a bank and its customers. This federal statute was enacted in response to complaints by consumer groups about long delays before customers were allowed access to funds represented by checks they had deposited. The act provides that when a customer deposits a cashier's check, certified check, or a check written on an account in the same bank, the funds must be available by the next business day. Funds from other local checks (drawn on institutions within the same Federal Reserve region) must be available within two working days, while there is a maximum five-day wait for funds from out-of-town checks. In order for these time limits to be effective, the customer must endorse the check in a designated space on the back side.

ELECTRONIC FUNDS TRANSFER

Drowning in the yearly flood of billions of checks, banks have been searching for means of computerizing the check account process. The grail which they hope they have found is called **electronic funds** transfer (EFT), a system that bodes revolutionary changes in the relationships of banks and customers.

What is EFT?

In simplest terms, EFT is a method of paying by substituting an electronic signal for checks. A "debit card," inserted in the appropriate terminal, will authorize automatically the transfer of funds from your checking account, say, to the account of a store whose goods you are buying. You are doubtless familiar with some forms of EFT already; for example, the automated teller machine, which permits you to electronically transfer funds between checking and savings accounts at your bank. Other forms are telephone transfers, point of sale terminals now located in stores in some communities, and preauthorized payment plans, which permit direct electronic deposit of paychecks, Social Security checks, and dividend checks. The "short circuit" that EFT permits in the check processing cycle is illustrated in Figure 25-1.

Unlike the check collection process, EFT is virtually instantaneous: at one instant a customer has a sum of money in her account; in the next, after insertion of a plastic card in a machine or the transmission of a coded message by telephone, an electronic signal automatically debits her bank checking account and posts the amount to the bank account of the store where she is making a purchase. No checks change hands; no paper is written on. It is quiet, odorless, smudge proof. But errors are harder to trace than when a paper trail exists, and when the system fails ("our computer is down") the financial mess can be colossal. Obviously some sort of law is necessary to regulate EFT systems.

Consumer Transactions

Electronic Fund Transfer Act of 1978 Because EFT is a technology consisting of several discrete types of machines with differing purposes, its initial growth has not been guided by any signal law or even set of laws. The most important law governing consumer transactions is the Electronic Fund Transfer Act of 1978. This federal statute has been implemented and supplemented by the Federal Reserve Board's Regu-

lation E, Comptroller of the Currency guidelines on EFT, and regulations of the Federal Home Loan Bank Board. Wholesale transactions are governed by UCC Article 4A, which is discussed later in this chapter.

The EFT Act of 1978 does not embrace every type of EFT system. Included are "point-of-sale transfers, automated teller machine transactions, direct deposits or withdrawal of funds, and transfers initiated by telephone." (EFT Act Section 903(6).) Not included are such transactions as wire transfer services, automatic transfers between a customer's different accounts at the same financial institution, and "payments made by check, draft, or similar paper instrument at electronic terminals." (Reg. E, Section 205.2(g).)

Four questions present themselves to the mildly wary consumer facing the advent of EFT systems: (1) What record will I have of my transaction? (2) How can I correct errors? (3) What recourse do I have if a thief steals from my account? (4) Can anyone make me use EFT? The EFT Act, as implemented by Regulation E, answers these questions as follows.

1. *Proof of transaction* The electronic terminal itself must be equipped to provide a receipt of transfer, showing date, amount, account number, and certain other information. Perhaps more importantly, the bank or other financial institution must provide you with a monthly statement listing all electronic transfers to and from the account, including transactions made over the telephone, and must show to whom payment has been made.

2. *Correcting errors* You must call or write the financial institution whenever you believe an error has been made in your statement. You have sixty days to do so. If you call, the financial institution may require you to send in written information within ten days. The financial institution has forty-five days to investigate and correct the error. If it takes longer than ten days, however, it must credit you with the amount in dispute so that you can use the funds while it is investigating. The financial institution must either correct the error promptly or explain why it believes no error was made. You are entitled to copies of documents relied on in the investigation.

3. *Recourse for loss or theft* If you notify the issuer of your EFT card within two business days after

Figure 25-1   How EFT Replaces Checks

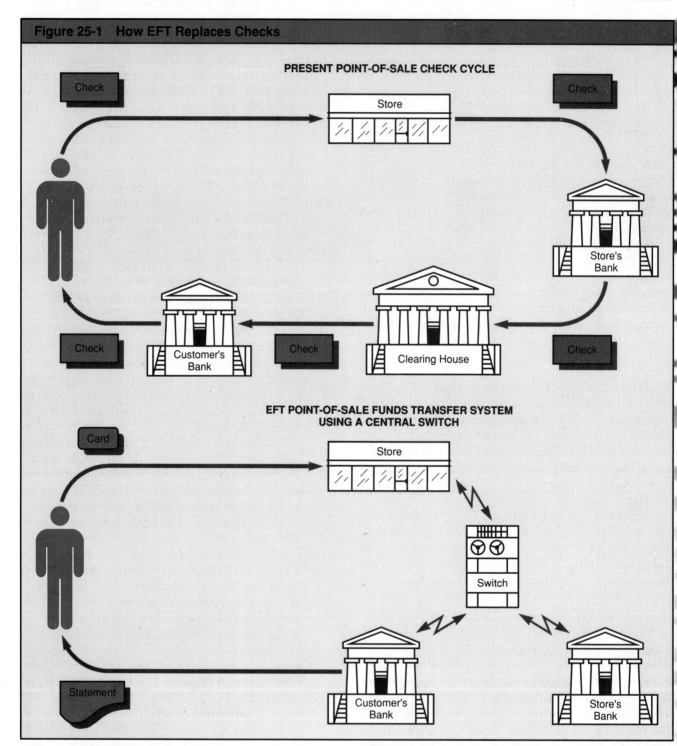

Source: Carol A. Schaller, "The Revolution of EFTS," in *The Journal of Accountancy*, October 1978. Copyright © 1978 by the American Institute of Certified Public Accountants, Inc. Adapted by permission.

learning that your card (or code number) is missing or stolen, your liability is limited to $50. If you fail to notify the issuer in this time, your liability can go as high as $500. More daunting is the prospect of loss if you fail within sixty days to notify the financial institution of an unauthorized transfer noted on your statement: after sixty days of receipt, your liability is unlimited. In other words, a thief thereafter could withdraw all your funds and use up your line of credit and you would have no recourse against the financial institution for funds withdrawn after the sixtieth day, if you failed to notify it of the unauthorized transfer.

4. *Mandatory use of EFT* Your employer or a government agency can compel you to accept a salary payment or government benefit by electronic transfer. But no creditor can insist that you repay outstanding loans or pay off other extensions of credit electronically. The act prohibits a financial institution from sending you an EFT card "valid for use" unless you specifically request one or it is replacing or renewing an expired card. The act also requires the financial institution to provide you with specific information concerning your rights and responsibilities (including how to report losses and thefts, resolve errors, and stop payment of preauthorized transfers). A financial institution may send you a card that is "not valid for use" and which you alone have the power to validate if you choose to do so, after the institution has verified that you are the person for whom the card was intended.

Enforcement A host of federal regulatory agencies oversees enforcement of the act. These include the Comptroller of the Currency (national banks), Federal Reserve District Bank (state member banks), Federal Deposit Insurance Corporation regional director (nonmember insured banks), Federal Home Loan Bank Board supervisory agent (members of the FHLB system and savings institutions insured by the Federal Savings & Loan Insurance Corporation), National Credit Union Administration (federal credit unions), Securities & Exchange Commission (brokers and dealers), and the Federal Trade Commission (retail and department stores, consumer finance companies, all nonbank debit card issuers, and certain other financial institutions). Additionally, consumers are empowered to sue (individually or as a class) for ac-

tual damages caused by any EFT system, plus penalties ranging from $100 to $1,000.

WHOLESALE TRANSACTIONS

The annual *volume* of checks greatly exceeds the number of electronic funds transfers. In a typical year, there is only one EFT transaction for every 500 checks. The annual *value* of checks written, however, is only a small percent of the value of EFT transactions, which often amount to over $2 trillion a day. Wholesale transactions—that is, transfers of funds between business or financial institutions—account for most of this value.

Before 1989, there was no comprehensive law governing wholesale transactions. In that year, Article 4A on Funds Transfers was added to the Uniform Commercial Code and has since been adopted by several states. The primary focus of Article 4A is on wholesale transactions. For instance, if any part of a funds transfer is governed by the Electronic Fund Transfer Act, Article 4A does not apply. Consistent with other UCC provisions, the rights and obligations under Article 4A may be varied by agreement of the parties.

To illustrate the operation of Article 4A, assume that Widgets International has an account in First Bank. In order to pay a supplier, Supplies Ltd., Widgets instructs First Bank to pay $2 million to the account of Supplies Ltd. in Second Bank. In the terminology of Article 4A, Widgets' instructions to its bank is a "payment order." Widgets is the "sender" of the payment order, First Bank is the "receiving bank," and Supplies Ltd. is the "beneficiary" of the order.

When First Bank performs the purchase order by instructing Second Bank to credit the account of Supplies Limited, First Bank becomes a sender of a payment order, Second Bank becomes a receiving bank, and Supplies Ltd. is still the beneficiary. This transaction is depicted in Figure 25-2. In some transactions there may also be one or more "intermediary banks" between First and Second Bank.

Three legal issues that frequently arise in funds transfer litigation are addressed in Article 4A. First, who is responsible for unauthorized payment orders? The usual practice is for banks and their customers to agree to security procedures for the verification of

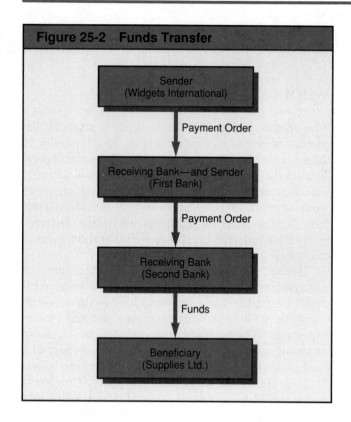

Figure 25-2   Funds Transfer

Sender
(Widgets International)

↓ Payment Order

Receiving Bank—and Sender
(First Bank)

↓ Payment Order

Receiving Bank
(Second Bank)

↓ Funds

Beneficiary
(Supplies Ltd.)

---

payment orders. If a bank establishes a commercially reasonable procedure, complies with that procedure, and acts in good faith and according to its agreement with the customer, the customer is bound by an unauthorized payment order. There is, however, an important exception to this rule. A customer will not be liable when the order is from a person unrelated to its business operations.

Second, who is responsible when the sender makes a mistake—for instance, in instructing payment greater than what was intended? The general rule is that the sender is bound by its own error. But in cases where the error would have been discovered had the bank complied with its security procedure, the receiving bank is liable for the excess over the amount intended by the sender, although the bank is allowed to recover this amount from the beneficiary.

Third, what are the consequences when the bank makes a mistake in transferring funds? Suppose, for example, that Widgets (in the situation above) instructed payment of $2 million but First Bank in turn instructed payment of $20 million. First Bank would be entitled to only $2 million from Widgets and would

then attempt to recover the remaining $18 million from Supplies Ltd. If First Bank had instructed payment to the wrong beneficiary, Widgets would have no liability and the bank would be responsible for recovering the entire payment. Unless the parties agree otherwise, however, a bank that improperly executes a payment order is not liable for consequential damages.

LETTERS OF CREDIT

Defined

A letter of credit is a statement by a bank (or some other financial institution) that it will pay specified sums of money to specified persons if certain conditions are met. Letters of credit are significant instruments in financing exports and imports.

Payment for Exports   Julius desires to sell the finest quality magic wands and other stage props to Rochelle's Gallery in Paris. Rochelle agrees to pay by letter of credit. She does so by "opening" a letter of credit at her bank, the Banque de Rue de la Houdini. She tells the bank the terms of sale, the nature and quantity of the goods, the amount to be paid, the documents she will require as proof of shipment, and an expiration date. Banque Houdini then directs its correspondent bank in the United States, First Excelsior Bank, to inform Julius that the letter of credit has been opened. For Julius to have the strongest guarantee that he will be paid, Banque Houdini can ask First Excelsior to confirm the letter of credit, thus binding both Banque Houdini and Excelsior to pay according to the terms of the letter. Once Julius is informed that the letter of credit has been issued and confirmed, he can proceed to ship the goods and draw a draft to present, along with the required documents (such as commercial invoice, bill of lading, and insurance policy), to First Excelsior, which is bound to follow to the "T" its instructions from Banque Houdini. Julius can present the draft and documents directly, through correspondent banks, or by a representative at the port from which he is shipping the goods. On presentation, First Excelsior will pay immediately if it is a sight draft or will stamp the draft "accepted" if it is a time draft (payable in thirty, sixty, or ninety days). Julius can discount an accepted time draft or hold it until it matures and cash it in for the full amount.

There are four principal types of letters of credit. The first is one issued by the foreign bank and confirmed irrevocably by the American bank, as in the example above. This binds both banks. A specimen letter of credit of this type issued by Morgan Guaranty Trust Company is shown in Figure 25-3. The second is an irrevocable letter issued by the American bank only at the request of the foreign bank. Only the American bank is bound. The third type is an irrevocable letter of credit that binds only the foreign bank; the American bank's sole role is to inform the exporter that the foreign bank has issued the letter. The American bank is not obligated to pay, and if it refuses to do so upon presentation of the drafts, the exporter must seek payment from the foreign bank. Finally, the exporter may have to be satisfied with the revocable letter of credit, which permits the importer to amend or cancel the credit unilaterally; the seller's only recourse then is to sue the importer in a foreign court.

The American or paying bank might discover that the documents do not square with the letter of credit. For instance, the draft may order a payment in excess of the credit, the insurance coverage may be inadequate, bills of lading may not carry requisite indorsements, the invoice may be unsigned, or the drafts may be presented after the date of shipment called for in the letter. The exporter can guarantee to hold the bank harmless if it pays the draft and later suffers a loss because it deviated from the terms of the letter of credit. Because this is risky, the usual practice is for the exporter to seek to amend the letter of credit to conform to the documents it has presented to the bank.

Payment for Imports   United States importers also can use the letter of credit to pay for goods bought from abroad. The importer's bank may require the importer to put up collateral to guarantee it will be reimbursed for payment of the draft. Since the letter of credit ordinarily will be irrevocable, the bank will be bound to pay the draft when presented (assuming the proper documents are attached), regardless of deficiencies ultimately found in the goods. The bank will hold the bill of lading and other documents and could hold up transfer of the goods until the importer pays, but that would saddle the bank with the burden of disposing of the goods if the importer failed to pay. If the importer's credit rating is sufficient, the bank could issue a **trust receipt**. The goods are handed over to the importer before they are paid for, but the importer then becomes trustee of the goods for the bank and must hold the proceeds for the bank up to the amount owed.

Source of Law

International   Many countries (including the United States, as we will see below) have bodies of law governing letters of credit. Sophisticated traders will agree among themselves by which body of law they choose to be governed. They can agree to be bound by the UCC, or they may decide they prefer to be governed by the Uniform Customs and Practice for Commercial Documentary Credits (UCP), a private code devised by the Congress of the International Chamber of Commerce. Suppose the parties do not stipulate a body of law for the agreement, and the various bodies of law conflict, what then? (Julius is in New York and Rochelle is in Paris; does French law or New York law govern?) The answer will depend on the particulars of the dispute. An American court must determine under the applicable principles of the law of "conflicts of law" whether New York or French law applies.

Domestic Law   The principal body of law applicable to the letter of credit in the United States is Article 5 of the UCC. Section 5-102 declares that Article 5 applies to a credit issued by a bank if the credit requires a **documentary draft** (a documentary draft is one that cannot be honored unless specified documents are presented with it). Article 5 also applies to a documentary demand for payment and to any other person issuing a credit if the credit requires that the draft or demand for payment be accompanied by a document of title. Even if a credit does not meet these terms, it will still be covered by Article 5 if it "conspicuously states that it is a letter of credit or is conspicuously so entitled." A significant principle that runs through Article 5 is freedom of contract. In fifteen places, Article 5 states that a rule is to be applied "unless otherwise agreed," thus giving the parties broad powers to stipulate the terms and conditions

Figure 25-3   A Letter of Credit

MORGAN GUARANTY TRUST COMPANY
OF NEW YORK
INTERNATIONAL BANKING DIVISION
23 WALL STREET, NEW YORK, N. Y. 10015   March 5, 19*

Smith Tool Co. Inc.
29 Bleecker Street
New York, N.Y. 10012

> On all communications please refer to
>
> NUMBER **IC** - 152647

Dear Sirs:
        We are instructed to advise you of the establishment by
  Bank of South America, Puerto Cabello, Venezuela . . . .
of their IRREVOCABLE Credit No. 19845 . . . .
in your favor, for the account of John Doe, Puerto Cabello, Venezuela . . . .
for U. S. $3,000.00 (THREE THOUSAND U. S. DOLLARS) . . . .
available upon presentation to us of your drafts at sight on us, accompanied by:

Commercial Invoice in triplicate, describing the merchandise as indicated below

Consular Invoice in triplicate, all signed and stamped by the Consul of Venezuela

Negotiable Insurance Policy and/or Underwriter's Certificate, endorsed in blank, covering
marine and war risks

Full set of straight ocean steamer Bills of Lading, showing consignment to the Bank of
South America, Puerto Cabello, stamped by Venezuelan Consul and marked "Freight Prepaid",

evidencing shipment of UNA MAQUINA DE SELLAR LATAS, C.I.F. Puerto Cabello, from United
States Port to Puerto Cabello, Venezuela

Except as otherwise expressly stated herein, this credit is subject to the Uniform Customs and Practice
for Documentary Credits (1974 revision), International Chamber of Commerce Publication No. 290.

    The above bank engages with you that all drafts drawn under and in compliance with
the terms of this advice will be duly honored if presented to our Commercial Credits
Department, 15 Broad Street, New York, N. Y. 10015, on or before March 31, 19*
on which date this credit expires.

    We confirm the foregoing and undertake that all drafts drawn and presented in
accordance with its terms will be duly honored.

Yours very truly,

Authorized Signature

Immediately upon receipt, please examine this instrument and if its terms are not clear to
you or if you need any assistance in respect to your availment of it, we would welcome your
communicating with us. Documents should be presented promptly and not later than 3 P.M.

Source: "The Financing of Exports and Imports," © 1980 by Morgan Guaranty Trust Company of New York. Used by permission.

which will bind them. Although detailed considera- tion of Article 5 is beyond the scope of this book, a distinction between guarantees and letters of credit should be noted: Article 5 applies to the latter and not the former.

In both international and domestic transactions, creditors should insist on an irrevocable letter of credit—as the football players learned in the following case.

BEATHARD v. CHICAGO FOOTBALL CLUB, INC.
419 F. Supp. 1133 (N.D.Ill. 1976)

DECKER, DISTRICT JUDGE. In this diversity action, two former football play- ers for the Chicago Football Club, Inc. (Club) seek payment of the salaries which the Club refused to pay after it was terminated as the holder of the Chicago franchise in the World Football League (WFL). Plaintiffs, Peter Beathard and Lawrence Jameson, signed player contracts with the Club in June 1975. Under the contracts Beathard was to receive a $12,000 bonus for signing and $70,000 for the 1975 season. Jameson was to receive a bonus of $10,500 and $25,000 for the 1975 season. The compensation for the season was to be paid in 18 installments—one after each game then scheduled to be played by the Club. For reasons which are now obvious, plaintiffs were con- cerned with the possibility that the Club or the WFL would not succeed, and they would not be paid their salaries. Accordingly, each contract con- tained a provision obligating the Club to either pay into escrow at an estab- lished bank of the Club's choice the amount of the player's 1975 compensation, or to secure a "domestic letter of credit" in that amount.

The Club elected to obtain letters of credit. On August 15, 1975, the Mid- City National Bank issued "Domestic Letter of Credit No. 160" to Beathard and "Domestic Letter of Credit No. 161" to Jameson.

Beathard's letter was as follows:

Domestic Letter of Credit No. 160

Date: August 15, 1975

Amount: $70,000.00
Mr. Peter Beathard
Dear Mr. Beathard:

   This letter of Credit is to guarantee payment for services rendered to the Chicago Football Club Inc. General Partner of Chicago Winds Limited Part- nership.
   You are hereby authorized to value on us for the account of Chicago Foot- ball Club Inc. General Partner of Chicago Winds Limited Partnership, 1580 North Northwest Highway, Park Ridge, Illinois up to an aggregate amount of Seventy Thousand Dollars and no/cents ($70,000.00) available in the event of default in eighteen (18) equal installments non-cumulative with the final installment due November 30, 1975.
   Drafts presented under this credit must be accompanied by a signed affi- davit of Mr. Peter Beathard stating that the Chicago Football Club, Inc. General Partner of Chicago Winds Limited Partnership has not paid Mr. Be- athard for a scheduled football game by Tuesday of the following week.

(*continued on next page*)

(continued)

**BEATHARD v.
CHICAGO FOOTBALL
CLUB, INC.**
**419 F. Supp. 1133
(N.D.Ill. 1976)**

This Letter of Credit will expire December 3, 1975.

Each draft must state on its face 'Drawn under Letter of Credit No. 160 dated August 15, 1975 of The Mid-City National Bank of Chicago, 801 West Madison Street, Chicago, Illinois 60607'.

We hereby agree with the drawers, endorsers and bona fide holders of all drafts under and in compliance with the terms of this Letter of Credit that such drafts will be duly honored upon presentation to the drawee.

This Letter of Credit is subject to the Uniform Customs and Practice for Documentary Credits (1962 Revision) International Chamber of Commerce Brochure No. 222.

THE MID-CITY NATIONAL BANK OF CHICAGO
/s/ R. R. Cadek
R. R. Cadek
Assistant Cashier
RRC:cg

Jameson's letter, No. 161, was identical except for the name and the amount.

On September 1, 1975, the WFL revoked the franchise of the Chicago Football Club, Inc., and cancelled all games scheduled between the Club and other members of the World Football League. From that date to the present, the Club has paid no salary to either plaintiff. When the Club failed to pay them their salaries, plaintiffs presented drafts under their letters of credit to the Mid-City National Bank. Plaintiffs were informed that the letters of credit had been revoked and the drafts were dishonored. This lawsuit is the product of plaintiffs' inability to collect their agreed salaries from either the Club or Mid-City. Beathard claims that he is entitled to $50,555.55 under the contract and the Letter of Credit and Jameson claims $19,440.00.

* * *

Obviously, the critical inquiry on these motions is whether the letters at issue were revocable or irrevocable. Under § 5–106(3) of the Uniform Commercial Code, Ill.Rev. Stat. ch. 26, § 5–106(3), ". . . a revocable credit . . . may be modified or revoked by the issuer without notice to or consent from the customer or beneficiary."

* * *

Clearly, if these letters of credit are found to be revocable, plaintiffs have virtually no rights under them, and they cannot succeed in their claim against the Bank.

* * *

If the letters of credit are found to be irrevocable, plaintiffs have only to show that they have complied with all of the terms of the letters to prevail on their claim against the Bank.

There is a dearth of case law on the question of what constitutes an irrevocable letter of credit. The Uniform Commercial Code is similarly silent.

The only guidance provided the court is in Article I of the Uniform Customs, which states,

all credits . . . should clearly indicate whether they are revocable or irrevocable.

In the absence of such indication the credit shall be deemed to be revocable, even though an expiry date is stipulated.

*   *   *

Plaintiffs argue that although the letters of credit do not expressly state that they are irrevocable, the language of the letters "clearly indicates" that they are. They first point to the statement in the first sentence that "This letter of Credit is to guarantee payment for services rendered to the [Club]." Plaintiffs assert that this language shows the letter to be irrevocable because only an irrevocable letter constitutes any sort of guarantee. A revocable letter, they argue, gives the beneficiary such attenuated rights that it cannot properly be called a guarantee. This argument is not correct. All letters of credit, both revocable and irrevocable, are guarantees of a sort. To be sure, the guarantee of a revocable letter of credit is considerably less valuable than that of an irrevocable letter, but a guarantee does not have to be complete and absolute to be worthy of the name. The use of this single word does not constitute a "clear indication" of irrevocability.

[The Bank's motion for summary judgment is granted.]

CHAPTER SUMMARY

Article 4 of the UCC governs a bank's relationship with its customers. Thus, it permits a bank to pay an overdraft, to pay an altered check (charging the customer's account for the original tenor of the check), to refuse to pay a six-month-old check, to pay or collect an item of a deceased person if it has no notice of death, and obligates it to honor stop payment orders. A bank is liable to the customer for damages if it wrongfully dishonors an item. The customer also has duties; primarily, the customer must inspect each statement of account and notify the bank promptly if the checks have been altered or signatures forged.

To alleviate the burden of processing millions of tons of paper, banks and other institutions are turning to electronic funds transfer (EFT). A maze of laws regulates EFT, including the federal Electronic Funds Transfer Act of 1978. Under this law, the electronic terminal must provide a receipt of transfer, the financial institution must follow certain procedures on being notified of errors, the customer's liability is limited to $50 if a card or code number is wrongfully used and the institution has been notified, and an employer or government agency can compel acceptance of salary or government benefits by EFT.

A letter of credit is a statement by a bank or other financial institution that it will pay a specified sum of money to specified persons when certain conditions are met. A letter issued by a foreign bank and confirmed irrevocably by an American bank binds both banks to pay. An irrevocable letter issued by an American bank at the request of a foreign bank binds only the American bank. When the American bank's sole role is to inform the exporter that the foreign bank has issued the letter, then only the foreign bank is bound. Letters of credit can be used by American exporters shipping goods abroad or by importers bringing goods into the country. The principal source of law governing letters of credit in the United States is Article 5 of the UCC.

KEY TERMS

Clearinghouse	p. 541	Correspondent banks	p. 541
Collecting banks	p. 541	Depository banks	p. 541

SELF-TEST QUESTIONS

1. Article 4 of the UCC permits a bank to pay:
   (a) an overdraft
   (b) an altered check
   (c) an item of a deceased person if it has no notice of death
   (d) all of the above

2. The type of banks covered by Article 4 include:
   (a) depository banks
   (b) payor banks
   (c) both of the above
   (d) none of the above

3. A bank may:
   (a) refuse to pay a check drawn more than six months before being presented
   (b) refuse to pay a check drawn more than 60 days before being presented
   (c) not refuse to pay a check drawn more than six months before being presented
   (d) do none of the above

4. Forms of electronic funds transfer include:
   (a) automated teller machines
   (b) point of sale terminals
   (c) preauthorized payment plans
   (d) all of the above

5. If you notify the issuer of your EFT card within two business days after learning that your card is missing or stolen:
   (a) your liability is limited to $50
   (b) your liability is limited to $100
   (c) your liability is limited to $500
   (d) your liability still cannot be limited

PROBLEMS

1. Winifred had a balance of $100 in her checking account at First Bank. She wrote a check payable to her landlord in the amount of $400. First Bank cashed the check and then attempted to charge her account. May it? Why?

2. Assume in problem 1 that Winifred had deposited $4,000 in her account a month before writing the check to her landlord. Her landlord altered the check by changing the amount from $400 to $4,000 and then cashed the check at First Bank. May the bank charge Winifred's account for the check? Why?

3. Assume in problem 1 that Winifred had deposited $5,000 in her account a month before writing the check but the bank misdirected her deposit, with the result that her account showed a balance of $100. Believing the landlord's check to be an overdraft, the bank refused to pay it. Was the refusal justified? Why?

4. Assume in problem 1 that, after sending the check to the landlord, Winifred decided to stop payment because she wanted to use the $100 in her account as a down payment on a stereo. She called First Bank and ordered the bank to stop payment. Four days later the bank mistakenly paid the check. Is the bank liable to Winifred? Why?

5. Assume in problem 4 that the landlord negotiated the check to a holder in due course, who presented the check to the bank for payment. Is the bank required to pay the holder in due course after the stop payment order? Why?

6. On January 15, Pru gives Ben a check in the amount of $400. Three days later she gives John a check for $600. Pru has only $700 in her account. On January 20, John cashes his check. On January 21, when Ben attempts to cash his check, the bank refuses to pay because Pru's account has insufficient funds. Must the bank honor Ben's request for payment? Why?

7. In problem 6, if the bank had paid Ben, could it charge the payment to Pru's account? Why?

DEMONSTRATION PROBLEM

On March 20, Al gave Betty a check for $1,000. On March 25, Al gave Carl a check for $1,000, which Carl immediately had certified. On October 24, when Al had $1,100 in his account, Betty presented her check for payment and the bank paid her $1,000. On October 25, Carl presented his check for payment and the bank refused to pay because of insufficient funds. Were the bank's actions proper?

ANSWERS TO SELF-TEST QUESTIONS

1. (d)   2. (c)   3. (a)   4. (d)   5. (a)

SUGGESTED ANSWER TO
DEMONSTRATION PROBLEM

The bank's payment to Betty is proper. When a check is over
six months old, a bank has the option to pay or refuse to pay.
The bank's refusal to pay Carl is improper because his check
was certified.

Part 4

THE MANAGER'S LEGAL AGENDA

Because specific words in commercial paper (or the absence of specific words) can make a large difference in creating legal relationships and in their legal consequences, your employees should not casually endorse or sign promissory notes or other commercial paper. Establish specific ground rules and language for the types of instruments that your business uses.

Develop policies for the form in which instruments will be signed or endorsed to prevent employees from becoming personally liable on your company's instruments.

Since bearer paper is just like cash, if it is lost or destroyed you may find it difficult to recover its value. If you regularly deal with large quantities of bearer paper or with bearer paper of high value, you should discuss with your insurance agent the best way to cover any risk of loss.

Commercial paper in the form of blank instruments can pose dangerous risks, since a thief or embezzler might find it all too easy simply to fill in the blanks with your business's name and negotiate the instrument for cash. You should institute policies to guard checks and other blank instruments and to ensure that without counter signatures and the like an instrument cannot take effect (*e.g.*, by stating directly on your checks that for amounts above a certain minimum no checks are valid unless accompanied by one or more additional signatures from responsible officials of your business).

To prevent liability for forgery, establish strict procedures regulating access to the business's commercial paper and to such devices as rubber stamps that could be used by unauthorized persons to endorse notes and checks.

An effective communications policy is essential to anticipate the loss of your status as a holder in due course. If an employee has knowledge of a defect or notice of a claim against an instrument about to be negotiated to your business, that knowledge might result in your inability to collect on the instrument. If the employee passes on the notice to the accounting, finance, or treasurer's office in time, a responsible official will be in a position to reject the instrument before it is too late.

Likewise, you should ensure that your employees abide by a policy of good faith and fair dealing in acquiring negotiating instruments.

Since many UCC provisions dealing with commercial paper require the transferor and transferee to act within reasonable times (and often spell out specific time limits), you should establish company-wide policies governing such matters as the depositing of checks to your bank accounts.

With the growth in electronic funds transfers, you should review with your bankers security procedures to verify payment orders. Since the bank will not be liable for unauthorized payment orders if it follows a reasonable and agreed-upon security system, you must design it with an eye to monitoring payment requests from within your company to assure that only authorized personnel make them.

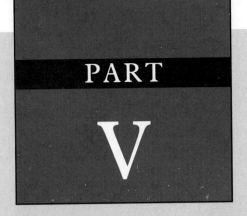

PART

V

Acquaintance: A person whom we know well enough to borrow from, but not well enough to lend to.
—AMBROSE BIERCE

DEBTORS AND CREDITORS

CHAPTER 26

CHAPTER OVERVIEW

Entering Into a Credit Transaction

Consumer Rights After a Credit Transaction

Debt-Collection Practices

Consumer Credit Transactions

Part Five is devoted to debtor-creditor relations. In this chapter we focus on the consumer credit transaction. Chapters 27 (Secured Transactions and Suretyship) and 28 (Mortgages and Nonconsensual Liens) explore different types of security that a creditor might require. Part Five concludes in Chapter 29 with an examination of debtors' and creditors' rights under bankruptcy law.

Consumer debt—the amount Americans owe to banks and mortgage lenders, stores, automobile dealers, and other merchants who sell on credit—stands at an all-time high: in the 1980s, Americans owed more than $1 *trillion*. To pay this debt, the average family spends 23 cents of every take-home (after-tax) dollar it earns. The availability of credit is thus an important factor in the American economy, and not surprisingly a number of statutes have been enacted in recent years to protect the consumer both before and after signing credit agreements.

The statutes tend to fall within three broad categories. First, several statutes are especially important when a consumer enters into a credit transaction. These include laws that regulate credit costs, the credit application, and the applicant's right to check a credit record. Second, after a consumer has contracted for credit, certain statutes give a consumer the right to cancel the contract and correct billing mistakes. Third, if the consumer fails to pay a debt, the creditor has several traditional debt collection remedies that today are tightly regulated by the government.

ENTERING INTO A CREDIT TRANSACTION

The Cost of Credit

Lenders, whether banks or retailers, are not free to charge whatever they wish for credit. Usury laws establish a maximum rate of lawful interest. The penalties for violating usury laws vary from state to state. The heaviest penalties are loss of both principal and interest, or loss of a multiple of the interest the creditor charged. The courts often interpret these laws stringently, so that even if the impetus for a usurious loan comes from the borrower, the contract can be avoided, as the next case shows.

**MATTER OF THE
ESTATE OF DANE**
55 A.D.2d 224, 390
N.Y.S.2d 249 (1976)

MAHONEY, JUSTICE. On December 17, 1968, after repeated requests by decedent that appellant loan him $10,500, the latter drew a demand note in that amount and with decedent's consent fixed the interest rate at 7½% per annum, the then maximum annual interest permitted being 7¼% (3 NYCRR 4.1). Decedent executed the note and appellant gave him the full amount of the note in cash. After letters of co-administration with the will annexed were issued to respondents on January 21, 1975, they moved for summary judgment voiding the note on the ground that it was a usurious loan. . . . The Surrogate granted the motion, voided the note and enjoined any prosecution on it thereafter. Appellant's cross motion to enforce the claim was denied.

New York's usury laws are harsh, and courts have been reluctant to extend them beyond cases that fall squarely under the statutes. Subdivision 1 of section 5-511 of the General Obligations Law makes any note for which more than the legal rate of interest is "reserved or taken" or "agreed to be reserved or taken" void. Subdivision 2 of section 5-511 commands cancellation of a note in violation of subdivision 1 of section 5-511. Here, since both sides concede that the note evidences the complete agreement between the parties, we cannot aid appellant by reliance upon the presumption that he did not make the loan at a usurious rate. The terms of the loan are not in dispute. Thus, the note itself establishes, on its face, clear evidence of usury. There is no requirement of a specific intent to violate the usury statute. A general intent to charge more than the legal rate as evidenced by the note, is all that is needed. If the lender intends to take and receive a rate in excess of the legal percentage at the time the note is made, the statute condemns the act and mandates its cancellation. The showing, as here, that the note reserves to the lender an illegal rate of interest satisfies respondents' burden of proving a usurious loan.

Next, where the rate of interest on the face of a note is in excess of the legal rate, it cannot be argued that such a loan may be saved because the borrower promoted the loan or even set the rate. The usury statutes are for the protection of the borrower and the purpose of section 5-511 of the General Obligations Law would be thwarted if the lender could avoid its consequences by asking the borrower to set the rate. Since the respondents herein asserted the defense of usury, it cannot be said that the decedent waived the defense by setting or agreeing to the 7½% rate of interest.

Finally, equitable considerations cannot be indulged when, as here, a statute specifically condemns an act. The statute fixes the law, and it must be followed.

The order should be affirmed, without costs.

Order affirmed, without costs.

Several states have eliminated interest rate limits. In other states, usury law is riddled with exceptions, making the interpretation of the statutes extremely complex. In some states, the exceptions have almost eaten up the general rule. Here are some of the more common exceptions:

- *Loans to businesses* In many states, any interest rate may be charged, although some states limit this exception to incorporated businesses.
- *Mortgage loans* Mortgage loans are often subject to special usury laws. The allowable interest rates vary, depending on whether a first mortgage or a subordinate mortgage is given.
- *Installment loans* In most states, still another set of usury laws (retail installment sales acts) governs the extension of credit by retailers and others for payment of goods purchased in fixed installments.
- *Credit card and "overdraft" checking* These common and increasingly easy forms of credit are also frequently governed by a special rate.
- *Time-price differential* Retailers may collect from buyers a so-called **time-price differential,** or sales finance charge, which means that the price of goods sold on time (credit) may be higher than those sold for cash, and the difference in most states may exceed the "normal" usury rate. The reason is that a seller who extends credit is not thought to be granting a loan, in the absence of which the usury laws do not apply.

Certain charges are not considered interest, such as fees to record documents in a public office and charges for services such as title examinations, deed preparation, credit reports, appraisals, and loan processing. But a creditor may not use these devices to cloak what is in fact a usurious bargain; it is not the form but the substance of the agreement that controls (a principle that applies in countries with cultures that reject the charging of any interest; see **Box 26-1**).

Disclosure of Credit Costs

Until 1969, lenders were generally free to disclose the true cost of money loaned or credit extended in any way they saw fit—and so they did. Financing and credit terms varied widely, and it was difficult and sometimes impossible to understand what the true cost was of a particular loan, much less to "comparison shop." After years of failure, consumer interests finally persuaded Congress to pass a national law requiring disclosure of credit costs. Officially called the Consumer Credit Protection Act, Part I of the law that took effect on July 1, 1969, is more popularly known as the **Truth-in-Lending Act.**

The act provides what its name implies: that lenders must *inform* borrowers about significant terms of the credit transaction. Truth-in-Lending does not establish maximum interest rates; these continue to be governed by state law. The two key terms that must be disclosed are the finance charge and the annual percentage rate. To see why, consider two simple loans of $1,000, each carrying interest of 10 percent, one payable at the end of twelve months and the other in twelve equal installments. Although the actual charge in each is the same—$100—the interest rate is not. Why? Because with the first loan you will have the use of the full $1,000 for the entire year; with the second, for much less than the year because you must begin repaying part of the principal within a month. In fact, with the second loan you will have use of only about half the money for the entire year, and so the actual rate of interest is closer to 15 percent. Things become much more complex when interest is compounded and stated as a monthly figure, when different rates apply to various portions of the loan, and when processing charges and other fees are stated separately.

By requiring that the finance charge and the annual percentage rate be disclosed on a uniform basis, the Truth-in-Lending law makes understanding and comparison of loans much easier. The **finance charge** is the total of all money paid for credit; it includes the interest paid over the life of the loan and all processing charges. The **annual percentage rate** is the true rate of interest for money or credit actually available to the borrower. The annual percentage rate must be calculated using the total finance charge (including all extra fees). See Figure 26-1 for an example of a disclosure form used by creditors.

In 1989, the Fair Credit and Charge Card Disclosure Act went into effect. This law amends the Truth-in-Lending Act by requiring credit card issuers to disclose in a uniform manner the annual percentage rate, annual fees, grace period, and other information on credit card applications.

Creditors who violate the Truth-in-Lending Act are subject to both criminal and civil sanctions. Of

LAW AND LIFE

BOX 26-1

The End Run Around Islamic Law

By Danielle Pletka

[*In countries with cultures that reject the charging of an interest rate, the government, often for sound financial reasons, may attempt to disguise what is, in fact, a usurious bargain.*—AUTHORS' NOTE]

When Saudi Arabia was pulling in more than $100 billion a year in oil revenues, a smile and a handshake were collateral enough for a hefty bank loan. The terms were reasonable, too: no interest. There were a few "charges and commissions," which looked something like interest. But, of course, they were not interest because that would be against the law.

The Koran states that the collection of any form of interest is usury, a major transgression of Islamic law, the only law there is in Saudi Arabia. So Saudi banks sidetracked the question with "fees." "The banks can confuse the issue by calling it any number of things: commission, services, discount. . . . But at the end of the day it's interest," says an official at one Saudi bank.

The Saudi courts agree. All those

THE ISLAMIC APPROACH

so-called signature loans that were scattered around like chicken feed when the petrodollars flowed more abundantly have left the banks scrambling to recoup the billions lost from businesses that went belly-up when the oil market collapsed. But as the banks try to force defaulters into commercial arbitration, the courts are proving of little help. Just the reverse. If the court judges that the banks' fees were equivalent to interest, not only does the defaulting borrower not have to pay back the loan, but the bank has to pay back the charges it had collected. Few cases are being taken to court anymore.

The uncompromising law has led many Saudis to look abroad for profits, chief among them the "Saudi Arabian national treasury, which places its money with organizations like Morgan Guaranty and Chase Manhattan," says the banker. For lesser folk, the local banks are happy to funnel money to their offshore affiliates, so the deposits will earn market interest rates.

Moreover, Saudi banks have created offshore mutual funds that pay the depositor market interest rates, but with gains returned in the form of shares. "By increasing the share value

of what he has, it is not construed as paying interest," one banker explains. "It is giving [the client] a reward for the use of his money, and it doesn't really violate the Koran, either."

Farming out money to foreign countries in the hope that Allah will not notice is favored by almost all, though strictly it is not condoned. The rationale is that the Koran holds sway only within the confines of the Arab world. No one has explicitly said that what is being done is illegal, and few people are asking twice. Imam Shaker el-Sayed of Washington's Islamic Center says that geography does not excuse usury, explaining that the only difference is one of legality, not religious authority.

But now the government is planning something far more daring. It will try to close the $9.6 billion budget gap by selling bonds. Bonds and religious leaders are a potentially explosive mix, and the Saudis are leery of offending their holy men. So the government must determine how to float the bonds without actually seeming to do so. Bankers are suggesting that zero coupon bonds—sharply discounted from the face value instead of paying interest—will be the most likely detour around the Koran.

Source: *Insight*, April 11, 1988

---

these, the most important are the civil remedies open to consumers. If a creditor fails to disclose the required information, a customer may sue to recover twice the finance charge, plus court costs and reasonable attorney's fees (but not less than $100 or more than $1,000).

The federal Truth-in-Lending Act is not the only statute dealing with credit disclosures. A uniform state act, the Uniform Consumer Credit Code (UCCC), is now on the books in several states. Unlike the federal

law, which does not control the amount or rate a creditor can charge, the UCCC sets maximums (36 percent per year when the principal is $300 or less, 21 percent for sums up to $1,000). It also outlaws certain types of agreements—for example, multiple sales agreements on single purchases (if a merchant could break down a higher-priced item into smaller components, the interest charge could be greater); so-called "balloon" payments (a charge, usually at the time the final payment is due, that is significantly

Big Wheel Auto   Alice Green

ANNUAL PERCENTAGE RATE	FINANCE CHARGE	Amount Financed	Total of Payments	Total Sale Price
The cost of your credit as a yearly rate	The dollar amount the credit will cost you	The amount of credit provided to you or on your behalf	The amount you will have paid after you have made all payments as scheduled	The total cost of your purchase on credit, including your downpayment of $ *1500—*
14.84 %	$ *1496.80*	$ *6107.50*	$ *7604.30*	$ *9104.30*

You have the right to receive at this time an itemization of the Amount Financed
☐ I want an itemization   ☒ I do not want an itemization

Your payment schedule will be:

Number of Payments	Amount of Payments	When Payments Are Due
36	$ *211.23*	*Monthly beginning 6-1-91*

Insurance
Credit life insurance and credit disability insurance are not required to obtain credit, and will not be provided unless you sign and agree to pay the additional cost

Type	Premium	Signature	
Credit Life	$ *120—*	I want credit life insurance	*Alice Green*
			Signature
Credit Disability		I want credit disability insurance	Signature
Credit Life and Disability		I want credit life and disability insurance	Signature

Security: You are giving a security interest in:
☒ the goods being purchased.
☐ _____

Filing fees $ *12.50*   Non-filing insurance $ _____

Late Charge: If a payment is late, you will be charged $10.

Prepayment: If you pay off early, you
☐ may   ☐ will not   have to pay a penalty.
☒ may   ☐ will not   be entitled to a refund of part of the the finance charge.

See your contract documents for any additional information about nonpayment, default, any required repayment in full before the scheduled date, and prepayment refunds and penalties.

I have received a copy of this statement.
Alice Green   *6-1-91*
Signature   Date

_____
e means an estimate

higher than the average payments); and wage assignments as security for credit. Like the federal law, though, the UCCC requires a number of identical or similar disclosures, including disclosure of the annual percentage rate and other charges. (Note: Although several states are considering adopting the UCCC, it lacks uniformity among the states that have adopted it so far.)

Applying for Credit

Through the 1960s, banks and other lending and credit-granting institutions regularly discriminated against women. Banks told single women to find a cosigner for loans. Divorced women discovered that they could not open store charge accounts because they lacked a prior credit history, even though they had contributed to the family income on which previous accounts had been based. Married couples found that the wife's earnings were not counted when they sought credit; indeed, families planning to buy homes were occasionally even told that the bank would grant a mortgage if the wife would submit to a hysterectomy. In all these cases, the premise of the refusal to treat women equally was the unstated—and usually false—belief that women would quit work to have children or simply to stay home.

By the 1970s, as women became a major factor in the labor force, Congress reacted to the manifest unfairness of the discrimination by enacting (as part of the Consumer Credit Protection Act) the **Equal Credit Opportunity Act** of 1974. The act prohibits any creditor from discriminating "against any applicant on the basis of sex or marital status with respect to any aspect of a credit transaction." In 1976, Congress broadened the law to bar discrimination (1) on the basis of race, color, religion, national origin, and age; (2) because all or a part of the applicant's income is from a public assistance program; and (3) because the applicant has exercised his or her rights under the Consumer Credit Protection Act.

Under the Equal Credit Opportunity Act, a creditor may not ask a credit applicant to state sex, race, national origin, or religion. And unless the applicant is seeking a joint loan or account or lives in a community property state, the creditor may not ask for a statement of marital status or, if you have voluntarily disclosed that you are married, for information about your spouse. All questions concerning plans for children are improper. In assessing the creditworthiness of an applicant, the creditor must consider all sources of income, including regularly received alimony and child support payments. And if credit is refused, the creditor must, on demand, tell you the specific reasons for rejection.

The wording of the law is plain and has few complications. As lenders learned early in the act's history, it means, as the following case demonstrates, exactly what it says.

MARKHAM v. COLONIAL MORTGAGE SERVICE CO., ASSOCIATES
605 F.2d 566 (D.C. Cir. 1979)

SWYGERT, CIRCUIT JUDGE. The Equal Credit Opportunity Act, 15 U.S.C. §§ 1691, *et seq.*, prohibits creditors from discriminating against applicants on the basis of sex or marital status. We are asked to decide whether this prohibition prevents creditors from refusing to aggregate the incomes of two unmarried joint mortgage applicants when determining their creditworthiness in a situation where the incomes of two similarly situated married joint applicants would have been aggregated. The plaintiffs in this action, Jerry and Marcia Markham, appeal the judgment of the district court granting defendant Illinois Federal Service Savings and Loan Association's motion for summary judgment. We reverse.

*　　*　　*

In November 1976, plaintiffs Marcia J. Harris and Jerry Markham announced their engagement and began looking for a residence in the Capitol

Hill section of Washington, D.C. One of the real estate firms which they contacted, defendant B. W. Real Estate, Inc., found suitable property for them, and in December 1976, Markham and Harris signed a contract of sale for the property.

* * *

Plaintiffs and B. W. Real Estate had decided that February 4, 1977 would be an appropriate closing date for the purchase of the Capitol Hill residence. Accordingly, plaintiffs arranged to terminate their current leases, change mailing addresses, and begin utility service at the new property. On February 1, the loan committee of Illinois Federal rejected the plaintiffs' application. On February 3, the eve of the settlement date, plaintiffs were informed through a B. W. Real Estate agent that their loan application had been denied because they were not married. They were advised that their application would be resubmitted to the "investor"—who was not identified—on February 8, but that approval would be contingent upon the submission of a marriage certificate.

On February 8, the Illinois Federal loan committee reconsidered the plaintiffs' application, but again denied it. A letter was sent that date from Illinois Federal, which letter stated that the application had been rejected with the statement: "Separate income not sufficient for loan and job tenure."

* * *

We turn to a consideration of whether the Equal Credit Opportunity Act's prohibition of discrimination on the basis of sex or marital status makes illegal Illinois Federal's refusal to aggregate plaintiffs' income when determining their creditworthiness. Illinois Federal contends that neither the purpose nor the language of the Act requires it to combine the incomes of unmarried joint applicants when making that determination.

We start, as we must, with the language of the statute itself. 15 U.S.C. § 1691(a) provides:

> It shall be unlawful for any creditor to discriminate against any applicant, with respect to any aspect of a credit transaction—
> (1) on the basis of . . . sex or marital status. . . .

* * *

This language is simple, and its meaning is not difficult to comprehend. Illinois Federal itself has correctly phrased the standard in its brief: The Act forbids discrimination "on the basis of a person's marital status, that is, to treat persons differently, all other facts being the same, because of their marital status. . . ." Brief for Defendant Illinois Federal at 18. Illinois Federal does not contend that they would not have aggregated plaintiffs' income had they been married at the time. Indeed, Illinois Federal concedes that the law

(continued on next page)

(continued)

MARKHAM v. COLONIAL MORTGAGE SERVICE CO., ASSOCIATES
605 F.2d 566 (D.C. Cir. 1979)

would have required it to do so. Thus, it is plain that Illinois Federal treated plaintiffs differently—that is, refused to aggregate their incomes—solely because of their marital status, which is precisely the sort of discrimination prohibited by section 169(a)(1) on its face.

Despite the section's clarity of language, Illinois Federal seeks to avoid a finding of prohibited discrimination by arguing that it was not the Congressional purpose to require such an aggregation of the incomes of non-married applicants. It can be assumed, *arguendo*, that one, perhaps even the main, purpose of the act was to eradicate credit discrimination waged against women, especially married women whom creditors traditionally refused to consider apart from their husbands as individually worthy of credit. But granting such an assumption does not negate the clear language of the Act itself that discrimination against *any* applicant, with respect to *any* aspect of a credit transaction, which is based on marital status is outlawed. When the plain meaning of a statute appears on its face, we need not concern ourselves with legislative history, especially when evidence of the legislation's history as has been presented to us does not argue persuasively for a narrower meaning than that which is apparent from the statutory language. We believe that the meaning of the words chosen by Congress is readily apparent.

Illinois Federal expresses the fear that a holding such as we reach today will require it to aggregate the incomes of all persons who apply for credit as a group. Lest it be misinterpreted, we note that our holding is not itself that far-reaching. It does no more than require Illinois Federal to treat plaintiffs—a couple jointly applying for credit—the same as they would be treated if married. We have not been asked to decide what the effect of the Act would have been had plaintiffs not applied for credit jointly. Nor do we have before us a question of whether the Act's marital status provision in any way applies to a situation where more than two people jointly request credit. We hold only that, under the Act Illinois Federal should have treated plaintiffs—an unmarried couple applying for credit jointly—the same as it would have treated them had they been married at the time.

*   *   *

Checking the Credit Record

Because credit is such a big business, a number of support industries have grown up around it. One of the most important is the "credit reporting" industry. Certain companies—"credit bureaus"—collect information about borrowers, holders of credit cards, store accounts, and installment purchasers. For a fee this information—currently held on tens of millions of Americans—is sold to companies anxious to know whether applicants are creditworthy. If the information is inaccurate, it can lead to rejection of a credit application that should be approved and wind up in other files where it can live to do more damage. In 1970, Congress enacted, as part of the Consumer Credit Protection Act, the **Fair Credit Reporting Act** (FCRA) to give consumers access to their credit files in order to correct errors.

Under this statute, an applicant denied credit has the right to be told the name and address of the credit bureau (called "consumer reporting agency" in the act) that prepared the report on which the denial was based. (The law covers reports used to screen insurance and job applicants as well as to determine creditworthiness.) The agency must list the nature and substance of the information (except medical information) and its sources (unless they contributed to an investigative-type report). A credit report lists such information as name, address, employer, salary history, loans outstanding, and the like; see Figure 26-2. An investigative report is one that results from personal interviews and may contain nonfinancial information, like drinking and other personal habits, character, or participation in dangerous sports. Since the investigators rely on talks with neighbors and co-workers, their reports are usually subjective and can often be misleading and inaccurate.

The agency must furnish the consumer the information free if requested within thirty days of rejection and must also specify the name and address of anyone who has received the report within the preceding six months (two years if furnished for employment purposes).

If the information turns out to be inaccurate, the agency must correct its records; if investigative material cannot be verified, it must be removed from the file. Those to whom it was distributed must be noti-

fied of the changes. When the agency and the consumer disagree about the validity of the information, the consumer's version must be placed in the file and included in future distributions of the report. After seven years, any adverse information must be removed (ten years in the case of bankruptcy).

Under the FCRA, any person who obtains information from a credit agency under false pretenses is subject to criminal penalties. The statute does not say whether a person injured by one who wrongly obtains information can sue for damages. Such a case arose under unlikely circumstances, when George Hansen, the 1974 Republican candidate for Congress in Idaho, defeated the incumbent Congressman, Orval Hansen, in the primary. A credit report on George Hansen was supplied to a Congressional committee investigating improper campaign financing procedures; Orval Hansen happened to be a committee member. George Hansen, who subsequently won the election but then pleaded guilty to violating the Federal Election Campaign Act, sued.

HANSEN v. MORGAN
582 F.2d 1214 (9th Cir. 1978)

JAMES M. CARTER, CIRCUIT JUDGE. This case grew out of a strenuous campaign for the 1974 Republican candidacy for the United States Congress in the Second District of Idaho. Orval Hansen, the incumbent congressman, was defeated in the Republican primary election by appellant George Hansen. Thereafter two Idaho citizens filed complaints with the clerk of the United States House of Representatives alleging improper campaign financing procedures by George Hansen. This caused an investigation of George Hansen by the House Administration Committee, of which incumbent Orval Hansen was a member until his term as Congressman expired.

Judith Austin, who had filed one of the above complaints, was a friend of Orval Hansen. She had a conversation with Orval Hansen in which it was discussed that a credit report on George Hansen could be interesting for what it might disclose about his campaign financing. Therefore Austin later telephoned one Rose Bowman. The substance of Austin's conversation with Bowman is in part disputed, but it is agreed that a credit report on George Hansen was discussed and that Melvin Morgan was considered as someone who might be able to obtain such a report.

Appellee Melvin Morgan is the principal stockholder and chief executive of appellee Nate Morgan Jewelers of Pocatello, a corporation. The corporation is a member of the Pocatello Credit Bureau, entitled to receive credit reports from the Bureau. On about August 10, 1974, Melvin Morgan received a telephone call from Rose Bowman which he construed to be a request for

(continued on next page)

(continued)

HANSEN v. MORGAN
582 F.2d 1214 (9th Cir. 1978)

a credit report on George Hansen. Morgan contends he agreed to obtain the report upon the belief that it was desired by Orval Hansen to assist the House Administration Committee's investigation of George Hansen. Upon Melvin Morgan's request the credit report was provided without question by the Pocatello Credit Bureau. The report was issued in the names of both George V. Hansen and his wife, Connie. It contained no information adverse to either of them.

When he received the report, Morgan delivered it personally to Orval Hansen's office in Washington D.C. Eventually the report reached the House Administration Committee.

Upon learning of the existence of the credit report, George and Connie Hansen filed suit against the Morgans and various other parties involved in the obtaining of the report. After extensive discovery, the Hansens dropped their complaint against all parties except the Morgans. Their amended complaint alleged that the Morgans, by willfully or negligently failing to comply with the requirements of § 1681b and § 1681e(a) "and other related Sections" of the FCRA, unlawfully violated the Hansens' right to privacy. Damages were sought under §§ 1681n and 1681o which authorize civil causes of action for noncompliance with the requirements of the act.

The Morgans moved for summary judgment contending as a matter of law that their conduct violated no provision of the FCRA, leaving no basis from which a civil suit based on the FCRA could be launched. In an opinion which reviewed the requirements imposed by each of the noncriminal provisions of the FCRA, the district judge agreed with the Morgans and granted their motion for summary judgment. The Hansens appeal.

*   *   *

[Sections 1681n and 1681o] create civil liability for willful (§ 1681n) or negligent (§ 1681o) noncompliance by a consumer reporting agency or user of information who fails to comply with "any requirement imposed under this subchapter with respect to any consumer. . . ." If the Morgans have negligently or willfully failed to comply with any "requirement" imposed by the FCRA on users of credit information, they can be held liable by the Hansens.

The crucial issue is what constitutes "any requirement imposed under this subchapter" for purposes of § 1681n and § 1681o. The district court apparently concluded only the noncriminal provisions of the FCRA state "requirements" for purposes of civil liability under the act. The opinion below reviewed each of the noncriminal provisions of the act which regulate conduct, concluding that no provision which applies to users of credit information, as opposed to consumer reporting agencies, had been violated by the Morgans. No mention was made of the criminal provision—§ 1681q.

However, we conclude § 1681q does state a "requirement imposed under this subchapter". 15 U.S.C. § 1681q provides:

> "Any person who knowingly and willfully obtains information on a consumer from a consumer reporting agency under false pretenses shall be fined not more than $5,000 or imprisoned not more than one year, or both."

This section requires that users of consumer information refrain from obtaining such information from credit reporting agencies under false pretenses. Its violation therefore, forms a basis of civil liability under either § 1681n or § 1681o.

The standard for determining when a consumer report has been obtained under false pretenses will usually be defined in relation to the permissible purposes of consumer reports which are enumerated in 15 U.S.C. § 1681b. This is because a consumer reporting agency can legally issue a report only for the purposes listed in § 1681b. If the agency is complying with the statute, then a user cannot utilize an account with a consumer reporting agency to obtain consumer information for a purpose not permitted by § 1681b without using a false pretense.

We hold that obtaining a consumer report in violation of the terms of the statute without disclosing the impermissible purpose for which the report is desired can constitute obtaining consumer information under false pretenses, and that the facts in this case demonstrate that the consumer report was so obtained.

This construction of the FCRA is not only consistent with the intent of Congress as revealed by the explicit language of § 1681n, the legislative history, and the stated purpose of the Act, but also comports with Supreme Court precedent relating to civil liability based on criminal provisions of federal statutes in general. When introducing the Fair Credit Reporting Bill in the Senate, Senator Proxmire stated that the bill would require:

> ". . . that credit bureaus have in effect procedures for guaranteeing the confidentiality of the information they collect and that no such information be released to noncreditors such as governmental investigative agencies without the express consent of the person involved."

As explained, § 1681q extends to users of information the requirement that they refrain from obtaining consumer information for such impermissible purposes.

The declared purpose of the FCRA is to assure that "consumer credit, personnel, insurance and other information" is collected, disseminated and used in a manner which will protect the interest of the consumer in "confidentiality, accuracy, relevancy, and proper utilization of such information. . . ." 15 U.S.C. § 1681(b). The principle mechanism for accomplishing this goal is the regulation of reporting of consumer information by consumer reporting agencies. But requirements were also placed on users of credit information. This was necessary because the objectives of the act could be defeated if users could obtain information from consumer reporting agencies under false pretenses with impunity. Even consumer reporting agencies acting in complete good faith cannot prohibit illicit use of consumer information if users are not bound to obtain consumer reports only for permissible purposes. Section 1681q is a response to this concern.

★　　★　　★

The judgment of the district court is reversed and remanded for a trial.

Figure 26–2   A Credit Report

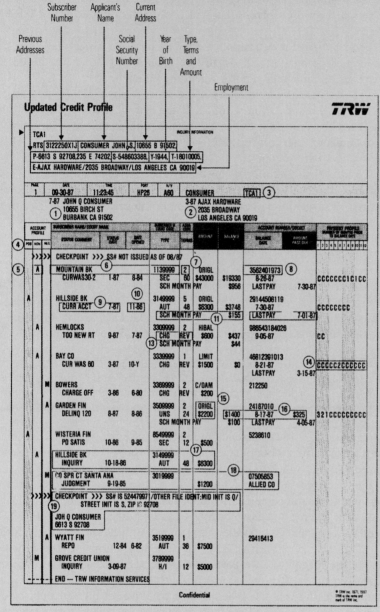

1. Name and address as recorded on automated subscriber tapes, including date of most recent update.

2. Employment name and address as reported by a subscriber through an inquiry on the date shown.

3. A code designating the TRW or Credit Bureau office nearest the consumer's current address, for your use in consumer referrals.

4. Three columns indicating positive, nonevaluated, and negative status comments.

5. A (Automated) and M (Instant Update or Manual Form) indicate the method by which the credit grantor reports information to TRW.

6. Name and number of reporting subscriber.

7. Association code describing the legal relationship to the account.

8. Account or docket number.

9. Status comment reflecting the payment condition of the account as of the status date

10. Date the account was opened.

11. Scheduled monthly payment amount.

12. Date last payment was made.

13. Type and terms of the account.

14. The applicant's payment history during the past 12 months. The code reflects the status of the account for each month, displayed for balance reporting subscribers only.
    C   —   Current
    1   —   30 days past due
    2   —   60 days past due
    3   —   90 days past due
    4   —   120 days past due
    5   —   150 days past due
    6   —   180 days past due
    — (Dash) — No history reported for that month.
    Blank —   No history maintained; see status comment.

15. The original loan amount (ORIGL), credit limit (LIMIT), historical high balance (HIBAL), or original amount charged to loss (C/OAM), represented in dollar amounts.

16. Balance owing, balance date, and amount past due, if applicable.

17. Inquiries indicate a request for the applicant's credit information—inquiring subscriber; date of inquiry; and type, terms and amount, if available.

18. Public Record: Court name, court code, docket number, type of public record, filing date, amount, and judgment creditor. This information may include bankruptcies, liens and/or judgments against the applicant.

19. Profile report messages alert the subscriber about a credit applicant's social security number, name, address, generation, or year of birth. See back page for further explanation.

CONSUMER RIGHTS AFTER A CREDIT TRANSACTION

Cancellation Rights

Ordinarily, a contract is binding when signed. But many of the newer consumer-protection laws provide an escape valve. For example, a Federal Trade Commission regulation gives consumers three days to cancel contracts made with door-to-door salespersons. Under this cooling-off provision, the cancellation is effective if made by midnight of the third business day after the date of the purchase agreement. The salesperson must notify consumers of this right and supply them with two copies of a cancellation form, and the sales agreement must contain a statement explaining the right. The purchaser cancels by returning one copy of the cancellation form to the seller, who is obligated either to pick up the goods or to pay shipping costs. The three-day cancellation privilege applies only to sales of $25 or more made either in the home or away from the seller's place of business; it does not apply to sales made by mail or telephone or to emergency repair, certain other home repair, and real estate, insurance, or securities sales.

The Truth-in-Lending Act protects consumers in a similar way. For certain "big ticket" purchases (such as installations made in the course of major home improvements), sellers sometimes require a mortgage (which is subordinate to any preexisting mortgages) on the home. The law gives such customers three days to rescind the contract. Many states have laws similar to the FTC's three-day cooling-off period, and these may apply to transactions not covered by the federal rule (for example, to purchases of less than $25 and even to certain contracts made at the seller's place of business).

Correcting Billing Mistakes

In 1975, Congress enacted the **Fair Credit Billing Act** as an amendment to the Consumer Credit Protection Act. It was intended to put to an end the phenomenon, by then a standard part of any comedian's repertoire, of the many ways a computer could insist that you pay a bill, despite errors and despite letters you might have written to complain. The act, which applies only to open-end credit and not to installment sales, sets out a procedure that creditors and customers must follow to rectify claimed errors. The customer has sixty days to notify the creditor of the nature of the error and the amount. Errors can include charges not incurred or billed with the wrong description or for goods never delivered, accounting or arithmetic errors, failure to credit payments or returns, and even billings for which you simply request additional information, including proof of sale. During the time the creditor is replying, you need not pay the questioned item or any finance charge on the disputed amount.

The creditor has thirty days to respond and ninety days to correct your account or explain why your belief that an error has been committed is incorrect. If you do turn out to be wrong, the creditor is entitled to all back finance charges and to prompt payment of the disputed amount. If you persist in disagreeing and notifying the creditor within ten days, it is obligated to tell all credit bureaus to whom it sends notices of delinquency that the bill continues to be disputed and to tell you to whom such reports have been sent; when the dispute has been settled, the creditor must notify the credit bureaus of this fact. Failure of the creditor to follow the rules, an explanation of which must be provided to each customer every six months and when a dispute arises, bars it from collecting the first $50 in dispute, plus finance charges, even if the creditor turns out to be correct.

While disputes over the quality of goods are not "billing errors," the act does apply to unsatisfactory goods or services purchased by credit card (except for store credit cards); the customer may assert against the credit card company any claims or defenses he or she may have against the seller. This means that under certain circumstances the customer may withhold payments without incurring additional finance charges. However, this right is limited to goods or services in excess of $50 that were purchased either in the home state or within 100 miles of the customer's current mailing address.

DEBT-COLLECTION PRACTICES

Banks, financial institutions, and retailers have different incentives for extending credit—for some, a loan is simply a means of making money, for others, it is an inducement to buyers. But in either case, credit is a risk because the consumer may default; the creditor needs a means of collecting when the customer fails to pay. Open-end credit is usually given without collateral. The creditor can, of course, sue, but if the consumer has no assets, collection can be troublesome. Historically, three different means of recovering the debt have evolved: garnishment, wage assignment, and confession of judgment.

Garnishment

This is a legal process by which a creditor obtains a court order directing the debtor's employer (or any party who owes money to the debtor) to pay directly to the creditor a certain portion of the employee's wages until the debt is paid. Until 1970, garnishment was regulated by state law, and its effects could be devastating—in some cases even leading to suicide (see **Box 26-2**). In 1970, Title III of the Consumer Credit Protection Act asserted federal control over garnishment proceedings for the first time. The federal wage garnishment law limits the amount of employee earnings that may be withheld in any one pay period—the lesser of 25 percent of disposable (after-tax) earnings or the amount by which disposable weekly earnings exceed thirty times the highest current federal minimum wage. The federal law covers everyone who receives personal earnings, including wages, salary, commission, bonus, and retirement income (though not tips), but it allows courts to garnish above the federal maximum in support cases (for example, alimony), in personal bankruptcy cases, and in cases of state or federal tax levies.

The federal wage garnishment law also prohibits an employer from firing any worker solely because the worker's pay has been garnished for one debt (multiple garnishments may be grounds for discharge). The penalty for violating this provision is a $1,000 fine, one year imprisonment, or both. But the law does not say that an employee fired for having one debt garnished may sue the employer for damages. In a 1980 case, the Fifth Circuit denied an employee the right to sue, holding that the statute places enforcement exclusively in the hands of the Secretary of Labor. [Smith v. Cotton Brothers Baking Co., Inc., 609 F.2d 738 (5th Cir. 1980)]

The 1970 statute is not the only limitation on the garnishment process. There is an important constitutional limitation as well. Many states permitted a creditor to garnish the employee's wages even before the case came to court; a simple form from the clerk of the court was enough to freeze a debtor's wages, often before the debtor knew a suit had been brought. In 1969, the U.S. Supreme Court held that this prejudgment garnishment procedure was unconstitutional. [Sniadach v. Family Finance Corp., 395 U.S. 337 (1969).]

Wage Assignment

A **wage assignment** is an agreement by an employee that a creditor may take future wages as security for a loan or to pay an existing debt. With a wage assignment, the creditor can collect directly from the employer. However, in some states wage assignments are unlawful and an employer need not honor the agreement (indeed, would be liable to the employee if it did). Other states regulate wage assignments in various ways—for example, by requiring that the assignment be a separate instrument, not part of the loan agreement, and by specifying that no wage assignment is valid beyond a certain period of time (two or three years).

Confession of Judgment

Because suing is at best nettlesome, many creditors have developed forms that allow them to sidestep the courthouse when debtors have defaulted. As part of the original credit agreement, the consumer or borrower waives his right to defend himself in court by signing a **confession of judgment.** This written instrument recites the debtor's agreement that a court order be automatically entered against him in the event of default. The creditor's lawyer simply takes the confession of judgment to the clerk of the court, who enters it in the judgment book of the court without ever consulting a judge. Entry of the judgment entitles the creditor to attach the debtor's assets to satisfy the debt. Like prejudgment garnishment, a confession of judgment gives the consumer no right to be heard, and it has been banned by statute or court decisions in many states.

Fair Debt Collection Practices Act

Many stores, hospitals, and other organizations attempt on their own to collect unpaid bills, but thousands of merchants, professionals, and small businesses

LAW AND LIFE

BOX 26-2

Unions, Firms, Lawyers Seek to Curb Garnishing As Its Incidence Rises

By James P. Gannon

[*Wage garnishment may give rise to devastating results. Lost jobs and even suicide are some of the possible outcomes. As a result, garnishment proceedings are now controlled by federal law.*—AUTHORS' NOTE]

CHICAGO—One payday in January, auto worker Carl W. Clark discovered his entire week's take-home pay of $112.39 had been turned over to the state of Indiana for delinquent state income taxes. Beset by debts, he asked officials at Ford Motor Co.'s plant in suburban Chicago Heights, Ill., for his accrued vacation pay to tide him over.

Next payday, he learned Indiana—the state where he used to live—had received $208.84 out of his $363.93 in wages and vacation pay. The 24-year-old father of a young boy, not knowing how much he owed Indiana tax collectors, (the two deductions actually satisfied the claim) became despondent over the pay loss. Two days later, Carl Clark placed a .22 calibre rifle under his chin and shot a bullet into his brain.

This suicide has spurred anew wide-ranging inquiries into the consequences of consumer debt problems. Under special scrutiny is the rising number of wage garnishments and other forms of pay seizure by

THE IMPACT OF GARNISHMENT

creditors, including state and Federal tax collectors. The spotlight on pay attachment also has illuminated a misery-multiplying debtor's course that runs from garnishment and loss of job to bankruptcy and going on relief.

* * *

Because the wage garnishments are issued by thousands of local courts, there aren't any national statistics on their volume. But checks of big courts in some metropolitan areas indicate more and more workers are finding part of their wages confiscated to pay overdue debts.

In Chicago, the Cook County Circuit Court issued 84,513 garnishments last year, 15% more than in 1964 and 72% more than in 1961. The marshal of the municipal courts of Los Angeles County served 114,972 wage garnishments in the fiscal year ended last June 30, up 6% from the prior year, and garnishments there this year are running at an annual rate of 122,000. Court officials in New York, Cleveland and other big cities also cite rising garnishment totals.

The figures don't disclose the full extent of pay impounding. They don't include the huge volume of wage "assignments," which are legally distinct but similar in effect to garnishments. Under a wage assignment, a debtor pledges his future wages to repay the debt if he defaults; execution of the

wage assignment doesn't normally require a court judgment, as a garnishment usually does. The garnishment figures also don't include tax levies, such as that in the Carl Clark case.

* * *

Garnishment often causes workers to lose their jobs. Many employers fire employees whose debt problems lead to excessive wage attachments, arguing that company handling of garnishment paperwork and court appearances by employees are costly and time-consuming. The Cook County Credit Bureau in Chicago surveyed 1,100 employers in 1964 and found that processing a single garnishment costs a company from $15 to $35; the estimated costs of garnishments to the surveyed employers totaled $12 million annually.

Few companies will discuss the firing of workers for garnishments. A personnel official at one General Motors Corp. plant near Chicago confirms union reports that 45 men were discharged at the plant for that reason last year. Another Chicago manufacturer admits firing "25 or 30" men for garnishments.

Union officials liken the practice of firing debt-burdened workers to the medieval custom of locking debtors in prison. "Under both practices, the debtor has a harder time paying his bills," says one. Most companies say they try to keep a man as long as he is making sincere efforts to straighten out his debts.

* * *

Source: *Wall Street Journal*, April 16, 1966

rely on collection agencies to recover accounts receivable. More than 5,000 such agencies go after debt in excess of $5 billion annually. For decades, some of these collectors used harassing tactics: posing as government agents or attorneys, calling at the debtor's

workplace, threatening physical harm or loss of property or imprisonment, using abusive language, publishing a "deadbeats" list, misrepresenting the size of the debt, and telling friends and neighbors about the debt. To provide a remedy for these abuses, Congress enacted, as part of the Consumer Credit Protection Act, the Fair Debt Collection Practices Act in 1977.

This law regulates the manner by which collection agencies may conduct their business. The law covers collection of all personal, family, and household debts by collection agencies. (It does not deal with collection by creditors like stores or banks themselves.) The collector may contact the debtor only during reasonable hours and not at work if the employer prohibits it. The debtor may write the collector to cease contact, in which case the agency is prohibited from further contact (except to confirm that there will be no further contact). In talking to others to trace the debtor's whereabouts, collectors may not tell them that the inquiry concerns a debt, and if the debtor has an attorney, only the attorney may be contacted. A denial that money is owed stops the bill collector for thirty days, and he can resume again only after the debtor is sent proof of the debt. Collectors may no longer file suit in remote places hoping for default judgments; any suit must be filed in a court where the debtor lives or where the underlying contract was signed. The use of harassing and abusive tactics, including false and misleading representations to the debtor and others, is prohibited. The federal statute gives debtors the right to sue the collector for damages for violating the statute and for causing such injuries as job loss or harm to reputation. The government is also entitled to damages, as the defendants in the following case discovered.

U.S. v. ACB SALES & SERVICE, INC.
683 F. Supp. 734 (D. Ariz. 1987)

[The FTC brought an action against ACB, its subsidaries and individual officers (Middleman and Raker) alleging violations of the Fair Debt Collection Practices Act and an FTC compliance order.]

HARDY, DISTRICT JUDGE. The Federal Debt Collection Practices Act became effective on March 20, 1978. It contained an express congressional finding that "[t]here is abundant evidence of the use of abusive, deceptive and unfair collection practices by many debt collectors." One of the stated purposes of the Act was "to eliminate abusive debt collection practices by debt collectors."

The Act does not use the term "debtor," but a "consumer" is defined as "any natural person obligated or allegedly obligated to pay any debt." Guidelines for communicating with consumers and third parties are prescribed. Section 805. Harassment or abuse of "any person in connection with a collection of a debt" is proscribed, Section 806, as are false and misleading representations in connection with the collection of a debt. Section 807.

The evidence establishes a pervasive pattern of violations so numerous they cannot be dismissed as simply the work of a few maverick collectors. In many cases managers or supervisors joined with collectors in committing violations.

The very nature of ACB's operations impels its employees to disregard the Order and the Act in attempting to collect debts. The manager of each collection office is under pressure to meet his revenue budget, the amount his office is expected to collect each month. He knows that the failure to meet his budget will result in his being removed as manager of the office. Consequently, he presses his collectors to collect more money.

A collector is under additional pressure because his income is based upon commissions. If his commissions do not meet his monthly draw, he may lose his job. If he wants to increase his income, above his draw, he must collect more money. The more quickly a collector can persuade a debtor to pay, the more time he will have to work on the collection of other accounts. When a debtor expresses an inability to pay immediately, the collector must do something to persuade the debtor that he must make payment. Collectors are instructed that debtor emotions to work on are fear, pride and sense of accomplishment. The evidence suggests that collectors work on debtors' fears more than anything else.

Any debtor who was unable or unwilling to make payment as demanded by a collector subjected himself to a torrent of abuse and harassment. He or she may have been cursed or otherwise verbally abused. Obscene and profane language was used. (But the court does not regard "damn" or "hell" as either obscene or profane.) The collector may make repeated telephone calls—many on the same day, often within minutes of each other; many day after day. In some cases collectors threaten violence to the debtors. All of these were violations of Section 806. Additionally, there are many telephone calls made by collectors between 9:00 at night and 8:00 in the morning on week days, in violation of Paragraph 8 of the Order and Section 805 of the Act.

Another standard, almost invariable tactic was to threaten, directly or impliedly, that legal proceedings would be commenced to enforce collection—filing a lawsuit, garnishing wages, attaching property, or impressing a lien upon property. Such threats were violations of Paragraphs 2 and 3 of the Order if they were "contrary to fact" and violations of Section 807 if the debt collector did not intend to take such action. There was ample evidence that debt collectors threatened legal action without intent to take such action.

Former collectors Esparza, Kreitner, Newbold and Peay testified that whenever a debtor indicated that he was unable to make immediate payment, a threat of legal action was routinely made and that only occasionally were recommendations made to commence legal proceedings. Very few of the debtors who were threatened with legal proceedings were ever sued.

At least three of ACB's clients—Denver Department of Health and Hospitals, LaSalle Extension University and North American Correspondence School—had instructed ACB not to bring suit to enforce collection against their debtors. By letter dated August 10, 1978 Denver Department of Health and Hospitals complained to ACB that "We have received repeated information that individuals were being told that, if they do not pay, the matter will be referred for legal action."

Another circumstance indicating a lack of intent is that internal procedures to initiate legal action were only occasionally commenced.

Finally, the fact that a collector earns no commission when an account is referred for legal action supports a finding that routine practices of threatening legal action were employed with no intent to actually commence such action.

In some cases collectors threatened, directly or impliedly, that criminal prosecution would be instituted against consumers, in violation of paragraph 5 of the Order and Section 807(3).

(continued on next page)

(continued)

U.S. v. ACB SALES & SERVICE, INC.
683 F. Supp. 734 (D. Ariz. 1987)

There were frequent threats to inform the debtor's employer that the debtor was not paying his bills, which was a violation of Paragraph a of the Order and Section 807(5). There were also threats to inform others of the debt, and there were occasions when the fact of debt was communicated to third persons, usually neighbors, both in violation of Paragraph b of the Order and Section 805(b). There were frequent telephone calls to debtors' places of employment after the debtors had requested that they not be called there, in violation of Paragraph 6 of the Order.

Collectors violated Paragraph 7 of the Order and Section 807 by misrepresenting that they were an attorney, a legal adviser, a friend of the debtor and an employee of a creditor. A frequent misrepresentation in violation of Section 807 was that an emergency existed that required the collector to get in touch with the debtor immediately.

Although there was evidence that debt collectors failed to disclose their identity in violation of Section 806(6), that a debt collector misrepresented himself as an attorney in violation of Section 807(3), that a debt collector misrepresented his identity in violation of paragraph 7 of the Order, and that debt collectors made false representations in violation of Section 807(10), there were not enough of these violations to establish a company-wide pattern of collection misconduct.

★　　★　　★

Mr. Middleman and Mr. Raker will each be required to pay a penalty of $25,000 for violating the Order. The ACB Companies will be required collectively to pay a penalty of $150,000 for violating the Order and a penalty of $150,000 for violating the Act.

FTC Credit Practices Rule

Under a rule that became effective in 1985, the Federal Trade Commission prohibits confessions of judgment and wage assignments in consumer credit contracts used by lenders and retail installment sellers. The purpose of the rule is to protect consumers from these and other unfair or deceptive collection practices.

ination), and the Fair Credit Reporting Act (giving consumers access to their credit files).

After entering into a credit transaction, a consumer has certain cancellation rights and may use a procedure prescribed by the Fair Credit Billing Act to correct billing errors. Traditional debt collection practices—garnishment, wage assignments and confession of judgment clauses—are now subject to federal regulation, as are the practices of collection agencies under the Fair Debt Collection Practices Act.

CHAPTER SUMMARY

The rise in consumer debt in recent years has been matched by an increase in federal regulation of consumer credit transactions. Consumers granted credit receive protection through usury laws (that establish a maximum interest rate), the Truth-in-Lending Act (requiring disclosure of credit terms), the Equal Credit Opportunity Act (prohibiting certain types of discrim-

KEY TERMS

Annual percentage rate	p. 569	Fair Credit Reporting Act	p. 574
Confession of judgment	p. 580	Finance charge	p. 569
Equal Credit Opportunity Act	p. 572	Time-price differential	p. 569
		Truth-in-Lending Act	p. 569
Fair Credit Billing Act	p. 579	Wage assignment	p. 580

SELF-TEST QUESTIONS

1. An example of a loan that is a common exception to usury law is:
   (a) a business loan
   (b) a mortgage loan
   (c) an installment loan
   (d) all of the above

2. Under the Fair Credit Reporting Act, an applicant denied credit:
   (a) has a right to a hearing
   (b) has the right to be told the name and address of the credit bureau which prepared the credit report upon which denial was based
   (c) always must pay a fee for information regarding credit denial
   (d) none of the above

3. Garnishment of wages:
   (a) is limited by Federal law
   (b) involves special rules for support cases
   (c) is a legal process where a creditor obtains a court order directing the debtor's employer to pay a portion of the debtor's wages directly to creditor
   (d) all of the above

4. A wage assignment is:
   (a) an example of garnishment
   (b) an example of confession of judgment
   (c) an exception to usury law
   (d) an agreement that a creditor may take future wages as security for a loan

5. The Truth-in-Lending Act requires disclosure of:
   (a) the annual percentage rate
   (b) the borrower's race
   (c both of the above
   (d) none of the above

DEMONSTRATION PROBLEM

Sam sells to Mary for $1,000 a painting worth $1,500 and obtains an option to repurchase it six months later for $1,250. In their state, creditors may charge a maximum interest rate of 10% per year. Does this transaction violate state law? Why?

PROBLEMS

1. Chauncey borrowed $10,000 from Victor and gave Victor a note for $13,000, which was due one year after the loan was made. Chauncey was to use the loan to run his business, which was producing dental floss. The maximum rate of interest in the state was 10 percent. Is the loan usurious? Why?

2. Sara used a credit card to make a number of purchases. She was charged the maximum interest rate allowed by law and, in addition, she paid an annual membership fee. Does the fee violate the usury law? Why?

3. Bill took his car to a mechanic after hearing a noise in the power steering. The mechanic, Roger, overhauled the steering and Bill, using his credit card, paid Roger $250. Later the same day the noise returned. When Bill immediately took the car to another mechanic, he learned that the overhaul was unnecessary because the problem was a fluid leak in the steering, which cost $200 to repair. Discuss Bill's rights against his credit card company.

4. Zeke, a welfare recipient, was convicted of welfare fraud. A county representative visited Zeke and convinced him to sign a confession of judgment, dated December 26, 1984, for an alleged overpayment of welfare benefits. Is the confession of judgment valid? Why?

5. Would the conclusion and reason in problem 4 be different if Zeke had signed the confession of judgment on December 26, 1985? Why?

6. A debt collector who had not yet decided to bring suit sent a debtor a letter that included the following language: "We are not representing either directly or by implication that legal action has been or is being taken against you at this time." Discuss the legality of this language.

ANSWERS TO SELF-TEST QUESTIONS

1. (d) 2. (b) 3. (d) 4. (d) 5. (a)

SUGGESTED ANSWER TO DEMONSTRATION PROBLEM

The transaction violates the state usury law. This is not a true sale but in effect a means of lending money at a higher rate of interest than allowed by the state usury law. Why? If Sam does not buy it back, Mary has a painting worth 50 percent more than she bought it for; Sam will lose more by leaving it with Mary than by buying it back, which is why the deal was structured this way.

CHAPTER

27

Secured Transactions and Suretyship

*I*n the real world of business transactions, most creditors are insecure: they want more from debtors than mere promissory notes. The creditor stuck holding a note may sue a defaulting debtor, but if the debtor is insolvent the creditor may wind up with nothing. A **secured** creditor, by contrast, has property he can take to satisfy the debtor's obligation. So security is an important part of many commercial transactions. Approximately two-thirds of all business loans made by Federal Reserve system banks are secured.

Creditors obtain **security** in two different ways: (1) by agreement with the debtor and (2) through the operation of law without agreement between creditor and debtor. Security obtained through agreement comes in three major types: (1) personal property (the most common form of security); (2) suretyship—the

willingness of a third party (for example, a cosigner) to pay; and (3) mortgage of real estate. Security obtained through operation of law is known as a *lien*. Derived from the French for "string" or "tie," a **lien** is the legal hold that a creditor has over the property of another in order to secure payment or discharge an obligation.

In this chapter we take up security interests in personal property and suretyship. In the next chapter we look at mortgages and nonconsensual liens.

INTRODUCTION TO SECURED TRANSACTIONS

The law of secured transactions consists of four principal components: (1) the *nature of property* that can be the subject of a security interest; (2) the *methods of creating* the security interest and *perfecting* it against claims of others; (3) *priorities* among secured and unsecured creditors—that is, who will be entitled to the secured property if more than one person asserts a legal right to it; and (4) the *rights of creditors* when the debtor defaults. After considering the source of the law and some key terminology, we examine each of these components in turn.

Source of Law

The law governing security interests in personal property is found in Article 9 of the UCC. This article covers two types of business deals, described in Section 9-102(1):

1. *sales* of accounts and chattel paper, and
2. any *transaction* intended to create a security interest in personal property (including goods, documents, instruments, general intangibles such as copyrights and goodwill, chattel paper, and accounts).

Meaning of Security Interest

Defined   Article 9 applies to any transaction "intended to create a security interest." The UCC defines "security interest" in Section 1-201(37), as "an interest in personal property or fixtures which secures payment or performance of an obligation." But this simple definition leads to a host of complexities because so many types of security interests can be created. The complexities arise in part from the state of precode law. Prior to the adoption of the code, several types of security devices, now embraced by Article 9, were governed by separate sets of laws. These included the following:

- *Pledge*   The debtor (known as the pledgor) pledged (transferred) an asset (known as *col lateral* to the creditor (known as the pledgee). The creditor could retain possession of the collateral until the pledgor paid off the debt. If the debtor failed to pay, the creditor could sell the collateral to satisfy the debt.
- *Chattel Mortgage*   With this type of security interest, the debtor was known as the mortgagor. Ordinarily used when a person wished to borrow money against assets he owned,

the debtor would give the lender a written interest—the **mortgage**—in a specific asset, although the debtor would usually retain possession of the asset. To "perfect" the mortgage against third parties (the debtor, for instance, might wrongfully try to sell the asset after he mortgaged it), the lender was required to "record" the mortgage in a public place.
- *Conditional Sale*   Here the sale was said to be conditional on the buyer's payment of the purchase price; the seller retained as security title to the goods until the price was paid, at which time full title would pass.

Other devices were also used to secure payment to manufacturers and dealers. The devices could be established with varying degrees of ease, but taken together they were subject to a number of infirmities. For one thing, although pledges, mortgages, trust receipts, and liens all had roughly the same purpose, each had a different terminology that confused business people, lawyers, and courts alike. Moreover, different laws applied to each, giving rise to different methods of creating and perfecting these security interests. Article 9 sweeps most of the archaic differences away and unifies the creation and perfection of security interests.

The "Purchase Money Security Interest"   Perhaps the simplest form of security interest is the **purchase money security interest (PMSI)**. An example of a PMSI is the security interest that the seller retains in goods sold. Suppose you want to buy this textbook on credit at your college bookstore. The manager refuses to extend you credit outright but says she will take back a PMSI—in other words, she will retain a security interest in the book itself. Contrast this situation with a counteroffer you might make: Since she tells you not to mark up the book (in the event that she has to repossess it if you default), you would rather give her some other collateral to hold—for example, your gold college signet ring. Her security interest in the ring is not a PMSI; a PMSI must be an interest in the particular goods purchased. A PMSI would also be created if you borrowed money to buy the book and gave the lender a security interest in the book (see Figure 27-1).

Leases as Security Interests   An especially confusing issue is whether a transaction is a lease or security interest. The answer depends on the facts of each case. However, a security interest is created if (1) the lessee

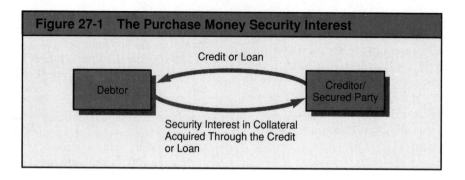

Figure 27-1   The Purchase Money Security Interest

is obligated to continue payments for the term of the lease; (2) the lessee cannot terminate the obligation; and (3) one of several economic tests, which are listed in Section 1-201 (37), is met. For example, one of the economic tests is that "the lessee has an option to become owner of the goods for no additional consideration or nominal additional consideration upon compliance with the lease agreement."

The question of lease vs. security interest is frequently litigated because of the requirements of Article 9 that a security interest be perfected in certain ways (see p. 592). If the transaction turns out to be a security interest, a lessor who fails to meet these requirements runs the risk of losing his property to a third party.

Consider this example. Ferrous Brothers Iron Works "leases" a $25,000 punch press to Millie's Machine Shop. Under the terms of the lease, Millie's must pay a yearly rental of $5,000 for five years, after which time Millie's may take title to the machine outright for the payment of one dollar. During the period of the rental, title remains in Ferrous Brothers. Is this "lease" really a security interest? Since ownership comes at nominal charge when the entire lease is satisfied, the transaction would be construed as one creating a security interest. What difference does this make? Suppose Millie's goes bankrupt in the third year of the lease, and the trustee in bankruptcy wishes to sell the punch press to satisfy debts of the machine shop. If it were a true lease, Ferrous Brothers would be entitled to reclaim the machine (unless the trustee assumed the lease.) But if the lease is really intended as a device to create a security interest, then Ferrous Brothers can recover its collateral only if it has otherwise complied with the obligations of Article 9—for example, by recording its security interest, as we will see.

Parties to a Secured Transaction

Ordinarily, the **debtor** is the person who owes payment or performance and who also owns or has rights in the collateral. But the person who owes the debt and whose property secures the debt need not be the same—for example, someone else may provide the collateral that secures the debt. In such a case, "debtor" in code sections dealing with the obligation means the person who is obligated to pay or perform and in code sections dealing with the collateral means the person who owns the collateral.

An **account debtor** is one who is obligated on an account, chattel paper, or general intangible. This is the person who is originally obligated to pay or perform.

A **secured party** is the lender, seller, or other person in whose favor a security interest was created. A person to whom accounts or chattel paper have been sold is a secured party.

PROPERTY SUBJECT TO THE SECURITY INTEREST

Collateral is the general term for property subject to the security interest. It can be divided into two broad categories: tangible property and intangible property. Tangible property has four subdivisions; intangible, five (see Figure 27-2).

Tangible Property

Tangible property refers to goods—all things which are movable at the time the security interest attaches. Goods are classified into four types:

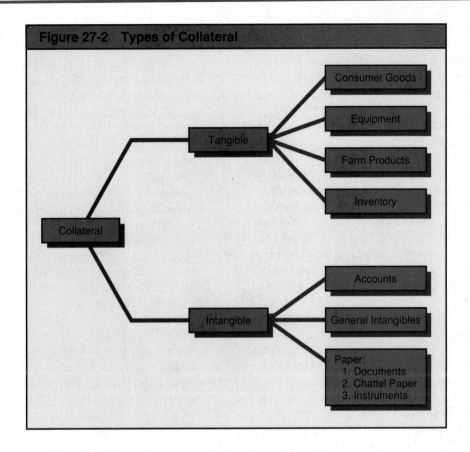

Figure 27-2   Types of Collateral

1. *Consumer Goods*   These are goods used primarily for personal, family, or household purposes—for example, a television set, family car, or dishwasher. A 1985 Federal Trade Commission Credit Practices Rule (see p. 584) prohibits finance companies and retail sellers from obtaining security interests in household goods. However, the rule does not apply to purchase-money security interests.

2. *Equipment*   This term refers to goods used primarily in business (including farming or a profession)—for example, a dentist's chair, a lawyer's books, business machinery.

3. *Farm Products*   These include crops, livestock, and supplies used or produced in farming operations and products of crops or livestock such as syrup, milk, and eggs.

4. *Inventory*   This category of goods includes raw materials, work in process, or materials used or consumed in a business, or other goods held for sale or lease—for example, books in a publisher's warehouse and vats of chemicals for use in manufacturing.

Equipment is of growing importance in secured financing. A federal study has shown that more than 27 percent of all loans are financed by equipment used as collateral, and with the increased use of robots (equipment) in factories, the percentage is sure to climb.

The four classes of goods listed above are mutually exclusive. If a particular item is equipment, it cannot be a consumer good or inventory at the same time. In close cases—a farmer's pick-up truck, for instance—the category is determined by the principal use to which it is put (for use in working on the farm or in transporting the farmer's family in lieu of a family car). The same item can fall into different categories under different possessors. A radio in a manufacturer's warehouse is inventory; if sold to a marina that uses it for listening to weather reports, it becomes equipment.

Intangible Property

As the name suggests, **intangible property** is all property that does not have an immediate tangible, corporeal form. Intangibles are divided into five types.

1. *Accounts*   An account is any right to payment for goods sold or leased or for services rendered that is not evidenced by an instrument or chattel paper, whether or not the debtor has earned the right by performance. You go to your local pharmacy to pick up a prescription and are short of cash. "Put it on my account," you say. You are recorded on the druggist's books as an account receivable; that is to say, you owe him the price of the drugs. Suppose he had asked you to sign a note promising to pay. Then your obligation to him would not be an account because it is evidenced by an instrument, namely, the promissory note.

   Note the difference between the use of an account as security and its sale (*factoring*). The holder of an account receivable can assign it to a third party as security for a loan. In that case, the original obligor on the account (the purchaser of drugs in the example above) will pay the seller and probably never know that the account was used as security—that is, that the seller (druggist) has become a borrower from someone else. If someone who owes on the account fails to pay, the holder of the account (the druggist) is still obligated to the lender to whom he pledged the account as security. By contrast, the **factor** purchases the account receivable outright. If the account is not paid, the loss falls on the factor, not on the original holder who sold it to him.

2. *General Intangibles*   This is a catch-all category that includes numerous forms of contractual, statutory, and other types of rights and that excludes goods, accounts, negotiable instruments, and money. Examples are copyrights, trademarks, patents, and goodwill.

   Three other categories of intangibles concern paper collateral, either fully negotiable or treated for some purposes as if negotiable. These are:

3. *Document*   This is a document of title, such as a warehouse receipt or bill of lading (covered in Chapter 20).

4. *Chattel Paper*   This is a general term for any writing or writings which evidence both a monetary obligation and a security interest in (or a lease of) specific goods. Chattel paper may consist of a single document that establishes both the debt and the security interest or it may be a collection of writings (a security agreement and one or more instruments). You borrow money from a friend to buy a car and sign a promissory note that gives him a security interest in the car. The note is a chattel paper.

5. *Instrument*   This means a negotiable instrument (as defined in Section 3-104; see p. 481), a certificated security (defined in Section 8-102; see p. 939), or any other writing evidencing a right to the payment of money, as long as it is not itself a security agreement or lease and as long as it can be transferred in the ordinary course of business by assignment or by delivery with any necessary indorsement.

The wide variety of property, tangible and intangible, that can become secured collateral is perhaps best illustrated by the property that the Hunt brothers were required to pledge in 1980 to stave off foreclosure in the wake of their abortive attempt to corner the silver market. Twelve banks arranged for a $1.1 *billion* line of credit. In return, the Hunts had to put up the following collateral: 69,485 head of cattle, 700 thoroughbred race horses, collections of gold and silver coins, a porcelain bird collection, a collection of Roman and Greek statues, money due from holdings in the Dallas Tornadoes soccer team and the Chicago Bulls basketball team, an art collection that included a $2.5 million painting, office equipment, cattle feeders, watercoolers, and a Rolex watch. (*Time*, June 9, 1980.)

The "Floating Lien"

The **floating lien** is made up of three key provisions in Article 9. First, after-acquired property may be included in the security agreement. Section 204(2), however, limits this right with respect to consumer goods. Second, if the collateral is sold, the security interest continues in the identifiable **proceeds,** defined as whatever is received on the sale or other disposition of the collateral. In other words, if the debtor later acquires property subject to the security agreement and sells it, the lender has an interest in the

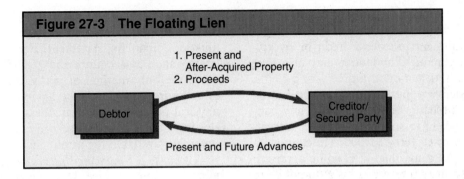

Figure 27-3   The Floating Lien

1. Present and After-Acquired Property
2. Proceeds

Debtor

Creditor/ Secured Party

Present and Future Advances

cash or noncash proceeds. Third, future advances by the lender may be included in the original security agreement. Together, these provisions constitute the floating lien—an interest that floats on the river of present and future collateral and proceeds held by the business debtor (see Figure 27-3).

The floating lien is particularly useful in loans to businesses that sell off their inventory. Without the floating lien, the lender would find its collateral steadily, perhaps rapidly, depleted as the borrowing business sells its products to its customers, until in time it would have no security at all. Through the floating lien, the borrower can be assured of retaining a security in the inventory without having to renegotiate or undertake more paperwork.

CREATION AND PERFECTION OF THE SECURITY INTEREST

The lender who seeks an enforceable security interest in collateral must enter into an agreement with the borrower to create the interest and must follow certain steps designed to ensure, first, that the interest has *attached* and, second, that it is *perfected* (see Figure 27-4).

Requirements for Attachment

Attachment is the term for the moment at which the property becomes subject to a security interest. Section 9-203 spells out the three general requirements for attachment: agreement, value, and collateral.

1. The collateral must either be in the hands of the secured party under an agreement (an arrangement that is usually called a *pledge*) or the debtor must have signed a contract known as a **security agreement.** This agreement must create or provide for a security interest. It must describe the collateral. Under Section 9-110, any description will do as long as it reasonably identifies the particular collateral.

   Unless he has the collateral in his hands, the requirement of a signed writing is absolute; the lack of a signed, written agreement will defeat the lender's attempt to enforce his claim of security interest. (It will not defeat his claim for money owed, but he will not have the extra protection of a secured interest in particular collateral.)

2. No security interest can attach if the lender fails to give value. Under Section 1-201(44), a person

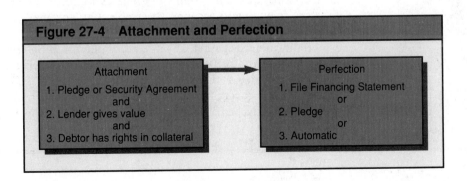

Figure 27-4   Attachment and Perfection

Attachment
1. Pledge or Security Agreement
   and
2. Lender gives value
   and
3. Debtor has rights in collateral

Perfection
1. File Financing Statement
   or
2. Pledge
   or
3. Automatic

gives value for the right to a security interest in a number of ways—for instance, by giving a binding commitment to extend credit or by giving immediate credit. The lender may also take the security in satisfaction of a preexisting claim, by making delivery pursuant to a preexisting contract for purchase, or in return for any consideration sufficient to support a simple contract. Suppose Leon owes Jerry $1,000. He cannot afford to repay the sum when due, so he agrees to give Jerry a security interest in his automobile to the extent of $1,000 in return for an extension of time to pay. That is sufficient value.

3. The debtor must have rights in the collateral. These rights need not necessarily be full title or the immediate right to possession, but they must be rights that can be conveyed.

Perfection

Creating the security interest gives the lender rights against the debtor, rights that are superior to unsecured creditors. But unless an additional set of steps is taken, the rights of the secured party might be subordinate to rights of other secured parties, certain lien creditors, and buyers who give value and who do not know of the security interest. In order to have rights superior to these, the secured party must *perfect* the security. **Perfection** is the secured party's way of announcing the security interest to the rest of the world.

Filing a Financing Statement   The most important method of perfecting a security interest is the public filing of a financing statement. For some types of collateral, such as accounts and general intangibles, filing is the only method of perfecting. The reason for this requirement should be obvious: no one can take physical possession of intangibles, so the only way of alerting others to one's security interest is to file a statement available for public inspection.

What Is a Financing Statement? A financing statement is a simple notice. It may consist of the security agreement itself, as long as it contains the information required by Section 9-402(1); namely, the names and addresses of the parties, signature of the debtor, and a description of the collateral. UCC Section 9-402(3) (see Appendix C) shows a simple but adequate financing statement.

Although the form of the financing statement is simple enough, difficulties arise when it inadequately describes the collateral. For example, the word "premises" does not embrace a debtor's inventory. Similarly, an overbroad description is troublesome because it fails to put other creditors on notice of the actual collateral in which the secured party is claiming an interest. But many courts will permit a broad term or statement such as "inventory" or "accounts receivable" to cover after-acquired property and future obligations. In the following case, the court discusses differences in the description requirements for security agreements and financing statements.

In re SOFTALK PUB. CO., INC.
856 F.2d 1328 (9th Cir. 1988)

CYNTHIA HOLCOMB HALL, CIRCUIT JUDGE.

On November 3, 1983, First City (then known as "California Citizens Bank") loaned $125,000 to the Softalk Publishing Company ("Softalk"). In exchange, Softalk gave its promissory note and a security interest in certain of its assets, including its accounts receivable. On November 16, First City filed with the California Secretary of State a UCC-1 financing statement, signed by Softalk, to perfect First City's security interest in Softalk's assets.

First City used a preprinted UCC-1 form for its financing statement. Where the form provided a blank space under the heading, "The FINANCING STATEMENT covers the following types or items of property," First City wrote, "See Attached." It then attached a separate sheet upon which was typed:

> As security for and in consideration of all present and any future advances or other obligations debtor hereby grants California Citizens Bank a security interest in all of the following types or items of property ("Collateral" herein) in which the debtor now has or hereafter acquires any right, title, or interest, or rights present and future, wheresoever located and whether in the possession of the debtor, a warehouseman, bailee, trustee or any other person, and all increases therein and products and proceeds thereof. Proceeds include but are not limited to inventory, returned merchandise, accounts, accounts receivable, chattel, paper, general intangibles, insurance proceeds, documents, money, goods, equipment, instruments, and any other tangible or intangible property arising under the sale, lease or other disposition of collateral:

Nothing followed the colon.

Softalk continued to maintain a checking account at First City, into which it deposited proceeds of accounts receivable.

Four months later, on March 1, 1984, Webb, having extended nearly $1 million in credit to Softalk, obtained a security agreement covering Softalk's accounts receivable, accounts, contract rights, and proceeds. Webb filed a financing statement on April 12, the validity of which is uncontested here. At all material times, Softalk owed Webb not less than $400,000.

On August 17, 1984, First City withdrew $78,343.14 from Softalk's account and applied the funds to an outstanding obligation of Softalk to First City. The funds included proceeds of Softalk's accounts receivable.

Softalk filed for bankruptcy under Chapter 7 on August 22, 1984. Webb filed a complaint in the bankruptcy court, contending that Webb had an interest superior to First City's in the money withdrawn by First City because First City's interest was unperfected. Webb argued that First City's financing statement failed to meet the requirements of California Commercial Code sections 9402 and 9110 because it did not provide an adequate description of the collateral. The bankruptcy court granted a partial summary judgment holding that First City's security interest was unperfected, and entered a money judgment in favor of Webb for $78,343.14 plus interest from August 17, 1984 at 10 percent per annum.

First City appealed to the BAP [Bankruptcy Appellate Panel], which affirmed the bankruptcy court. This appeal followed.

★   ★   ★

A security interest ordinarily arises upon the parties' execution of a security agreement. But to *perfect* a security interest, a creditor generally must file a financing statement. A perfected security interest gives the holder priority over holders of unperfected or subsequently perfected security interests in the same collateral.

Section 9402 states that a financing statement is sufficient if it provides the names and addresses of the debtor and the secured party, is signed by the debtor, and "contains a statement indicating the types, or describing the

(continued on next page)

(continued)

In re SOFTALK PUB. CO., INC.
856 F.2d 1328 (9th Cir. 1988)

items, of collateral." The statute mandates no particular language, nor does it insist on a strict format for compliance. "A financing statement substantially complying with the requirements is effective even though it contains minor errors which are not seriously misleading." Section 9110 sets forth the requirements for an adeqauate description. "For the purposes of [the Code] any description of personal property or real estate is sufficient whether or not it is specific if it reasonably identifies what is described."

The financing statement serves to give notice to other creditors or potential creditors that the filing creditor might have a security interest in certain assets of the named debtor. In contrast, the security agreement is a contract between a creditor and a debtor, pursuant to which the debtor encumbers its assets, granting a lien to the creditor in the specific items listed, upon the terms specified in the agreement. The differing purposes of the two documents often leads to descriptions of far less specificity in financing statements than in security agreements. The security agreement, the contract between the parties, setting forth the terms of a debt and creating legal obligations, must be adequate to its purpose. A higher degree of specificity might be necessary to define the rights of the parties. Accordingly, the Code requires that it include a "description of collateral." The financing statement, on the other hand, serves merely to alert third parties to inquire further; it therefore need not offer exhaustive details. . . .

First City's principal argument is "that its financing statement is not seriously misleading, if at all, because it contains sufficient information to put a third party on notice that the described property may be subject to a lien and that a further search is needed to determine whether a particular asset is covered by a security agreement." According to First City, compliance with the literal commands of the Code is irrelevant to the adequacy of a financing statement; a financing statement is adequate if it puts a third party on inquiry notice regardless of the extent to which it does or does not comply with the statutory requirements. We disagree.

Although we read section 9402 liberally, the statute does spell out a few minimal requisites. One of the section 9402 requisites provides that a financing statement must contain a statement identifying or describing the collateral. This statement need not be specific, and it may contain minor errors that are not seriously misleading, but its existence is mandatory. As the BAP observed, "[s]ince the UCC has reduced the formal requisites of a financing statement to a minimum, there can be no acceptable excuse for failure to comply with its provisions." We agree, and conclude that a financing statement is insufficient to perfect a security interest unless it contains a statement identifying or describing the collateral.

*   *   *

The financing statement [in this case] contains no language that literally purports to be a "statement indicating the types of collateral or describing the items of collateral." [The decision is affirmed.]

Where Must the Financing Statement be Filed? The financing statement must be publicly filed, but in one of its rare deliberate decisions not to be uniform, Article 9 permits the states to choose whether the filing is to be made in a state or local office. For example, a state might select a public office in the debtor's county for farming and consumer goods collateral, and the office of the secretary of state for other property. The debate is between the convenience for national creditors of locating records on thousands of potential borrowers in a central, statewide location and the convenience for local creditors of being able to check up in a nearby county office on local businesses seeking to borrow. The policy choice between a centralized statewide system and a local system of filing has been left to each state legislature.

The states do agree on where to file financing statements covering security interests in *fixtures*. Under Section 9-313(1)(a), **fixtures** are any goods that become so related to particular real estate that an interest in them arises under real estate law. For example, in some states a dishwasher (which standing by itself is a consumer good) becomes a fixture—that is, part of the real estate and subject to real property law—when it is hooked up to the plumbing in a house. Financing statements covering fixtures are to be filed in the office where a mortgage on the real estate concerned would be filed. Such a financing statement must describe the real estate sufficiently for someone to identify it. The mortgage itself may double as a fixture filing statement if the particular fixtures are described, the mortgage contains the other information necessary in a financing statement, and it is duly recorded in the property public office (see Chapter 28).

Whenever in doubt as to whether a local or state filing is required, the lender should always file the financing statement both locally and centrally. That way, regardless of how the courts might legally define the collateral, the lender will have perfected the security interest. Furthermore, if the collateral is shipped to another state, the lender must reperfect its interest within four months in the state to which the collateral has been moved. Otherwise, it will be in a position inferior to a subsequent buyer who has properly perfected his own security interest in the state. For moves of the collateral or of the debtor's office within a state, the Code gives the states an alternative: they may permit the first proper filing in a county office to stand or they may require the secured party to reperfect within four months in the new county.

Period Within Which Statement is Effective Under Section 9-403(2), a financing statement is effective for five years from the date of filing. The only exception is for a mortgage that doubles as a fixture filing; then it remains effective until the mortgage is released or satisfied or otherwise terminates.

Exemptions Some transactions are exempt from the filing provision. The most important category of exempt collateral is that covered by state certificate of title laws. For example, many states require automobile owners to obtain a certificate of title from the state motor vehicle office. Most of these states provide that it is not necessary to file a financing statement in order to perfect a security interest in an automobile. The reason is that the motor vehicle regulations require any security interests to be stated on the title, so that anyone attempting to buy a car in which a security interest had been created would be on notice when he took the actual title certificate.

Pledging Collateral A financing statement is one way to perfect a security interest; a second major method of perfecting is through the **pledge**—the transfer of possession of the collateral to the secured party. The general rule is stated in Section 9-305. A security interest in any of the following is perfected when the secured party takes possession: goods, instruments (other than certificated securities), money, negotiable documents, chattel paper, and letters of credit. The perfection continues only so long as the secured party retains possession. Pledges cannot be used for accounts and general intangibles.

Pledge of Instruments A security interest in instruments can be perfected only by a secured party's taking possession, except that the secured party is given a perfected security interest for twenty-one days from the time the interest attaches before having to take possession. (This grace period of twenty-one days applies only if the secured party gave new value to the debtor under a security agreement.) The secured party may also deliver an instrument to the debtor for specified purposes (such as sale, exchange, or collection) for twenty-one days without losing a perfected security interest. The reason for permitting these short-term arrangements is to avoid cluttering up public files with records of transient transactions.

This "temporary perfection" is not absolutely perfect, however; it carries risks. For example, a purchaser who gives new value for an instrument and takes possession of it in the ordinary course of business has a claim to it superior to that of the secured party if the purchaser had no knowledge that the instrument was subject to a perfected security interest—even if the interest had been filed. Likewise, a holder in due course of a negotiable instrument (see Chapter 23) and certain others will take priority over an earlier security interest even though it was perfected.

Field Warehousing   When the pawnbroker lends money, he takes possession of the goods—the watch, the ring, the camera. But when large manufacturing concerns wish to borrow against their inventory, taking physical possession is not necessarily so easy. The bank does not wish to have shipped to its Wall Street office several tons of copper mined in Colorado. Bank employees perhaps could go west to the mine and take physical control of the copper, but banks are unlikely to employ people and equipment necessary to build a warehouse on the spot. Thus this so-called *field pledge* is rare. More common is the **field warehouse.** The field warehouse can take one of two forms. An independent company can go to the site and put up a temporary structure—for example, a fence around the copper—thus establishing physical control of the collateral. Or the independent company can lease the warehouse facilities of the debtor and post signs indicating that the goods inside are within its sole custody. Either way the goods are within the physical possession of the field warehouse service. The field warehouse then segregates the goods secured to the particular bank or finance company and issues a warehouse receipt to the lender for those goods. The lender is thus assured of a security interest in the collateral.

Automatic Perfection   If a seller of consumer goods takes a purchase money security interest in the goods sold, then perfection of the security interest is automatic. But the seller may file a financial statement, and faces a risk if he fails to file and the consumer debtor sells the goods. Under Section 9-307(2), a buyer takes free of a security interest, even though perfected, if he buys without knowledge of the interest, pays value, and uses of the goods for his personal, family, or household purposes—unless the secured party has first filed a financing statement covering the goods. As the next case suggests, what constitutes "value" can be a vexing problem.

In re NICOLOSI
4 UCC Rep. 111 (S.D. Ohio 1966)

CHARLES A. ANDERSON, REFEREE in Bankruptcy.

PRELIMINARY STATEMENT AND ISSUES

This matter is before the court upon a petition by the trustee to sell a diamond ring in his possession free of liens; the evidence, and the briefs filed by the trustee, his own attorney, on April 29, 1966 and Mr. Frank Svoboda, attorney for Rike-Kumler Company, on May 11, 1966.

Even though no pleadings were filed by Rike-Kumler Company, the issue from the briefs is whether or not a valid security interest was perfected in this chattel as consumer goods, superior to the statutory title and lien of the trustee in bankruptcy.

FINDINGS OF FACT

The bankrupt purchased from the Rike-Kumler Company, on July 7, 1964, the diamond ring in question, for $1237.35, as an engagement ring for his fiancee.

He executed a purchase money security agreement, which was not filed. Also, no financing statement was filed.

The chattel was adequately described in the security agreement.

The controversy is between the trustee in bankruptcy and the party claiming a perfected security interest in the property. The recipient of the property has terminated her relationship with the bankrupt, and delivered the property to the trustee.

Conclusion of Law, Decision, and Order

If the diamond ring, purchased as an engagement ring by the bankrupt, cannot be categorized as consumer goods, and therefore exempted from the notice filing requirements of the Uniform Commercial Code as adopted in Ohio, a perfected security interest does not exist.

No judicial precedents have been cited in the briefs.

Under the commercial code, collateral is divided into tangible, intangible, and documentary categories. Certainly, a diamond ring falls into the tangible category. The classes of tangible goods are distinguished by the primary use intended. Under Revised Code § 1309.07 (UCC § 9-109), the four classes are "consumer goods," "equipment," "farm products" and "inventory."

The difficulty is that the code provisions use terms arising in commercial circles which have different semantical values from legal precedents. Does the fact that the purchaser bought the goods as a special gift to another person signify that it was not for his own "personal, family or household purposes"? The trustee urges that these special facts control under the express provisions of the commercial code.

By a process of exclusion, a diamond engagement ring purchased for one's fiancé is not "equipment" bought or used in business, "farm products" used in farming operations, or "inventory" held for sale, lease or service contracts. When the bankrupt purchased the ring, therefore, it could only have been "consumer goods" bought for use "primarily for personal use." There could be no judicial purpose to create a special class of property in derogation of the statutory principles.

Another problem is implicit, although not covered by the briefs.

By the foregoing summary analysis, it is apparent that the diamond ring, when the interest of the bankrupt attached, was consumer goods since it could have been no other class of goods. Unless the fiancee had a special status under the code provision protecting a bona fide buyer, without knowledge, for value, of consumer goods, the failure to file a financing statement is not crucial. No evidence has been adduced pertinant to the scienter question.

Is a promise, as valid contractual consideration, included under the term "value"? In other words, was the ring given to his betrothed in consideration of marriage (promise for a promise)? If so, and "value" has been given, the transferee is a "buyer" under traditional concepts.

The Uniform Commercial Code definition of "value" (because of the code purpose of being so broad as to not derogate from the ideal ubiquitous

(continued on next page)

(continued)

In re NICOLOSI
4 UCC Rep. 111 (S.D.
Ohio 1966)

secured creditor) very definitely covers a promise for a promise. The definition reads that "a person gives 'value' for rights if he acquires them . . . (4) generally, in return for any consideration sufficient to support a simple contract."

It would seem unrealistic, nevertheless, to apply contract law concepts historically developed into the law of marriage relations in the context of new concepts developed for uniform commercial practices. They are not, in reality, the same juristic manifold. The purpose of uniformity of the code should not be defeated by the obsessions of the code drafters to be all inclusive for secured creditors.

Even if the trustee, in behalf of the unsecured creditors, would feel inclined to insert love, romance and morals into commercial law, he is appearing in the wrong era, and possibly the wrong court.

Ordered, that the Rike-Kumler Company holds a perfected security interest in the diamond engagement ring, and the security interest attached to the proceeds realized from the sale of the goods by the trustee in bankruptcy.

PRIORITIES

This is the money question: Who gets what when a debtor defaults? Depending on how the priorities in the collateral were established, even a secured creditor may walk away with the collateral or with nothing.

General Rule

The general rule is "first in time, first in right." Priority dates from the earliest of two events: (1) filing of a financing statement covering the collateral; or (2) other perfection of the security interest. If neither secured party has perfected, then the first secured interest to attach has priority. Let's test this general rule against the following situations.

1. Rosemary, without having yet lent money, files a financing statement on February 1 covering certain collateral owned by Susan—Susan's fur coat. Under Article 9, a filing may be made before the security interest attaches. On March 1, Erika files a similar statement, also without having lent any

money. On April 1, Erika loans Susan $1,000, the loan being secured by the fur coat described in the statement she filed on March 1. On May 1, Rosemary also loans Susan $1,000, with the same fur coat as security. Who has priority? Rosemary does, since she filed first, even though Erica actually first extended the loan, which was perfected when made (because she had already filed). This result is dictated by the rule even though Rosemary may have known of Erica's interest when she subsequently made her loan.

2. Susan cajoles both Rosemary and Erica, each unbeknownst to the other, to loan her $1,000 secured by the fur coat, which she already owns and which hangs in her coat closet. Erika gives Susan the money a week after Rosemary, but Rosemary has not perfected and Erika does not either. A week later they find out they have each made a loan against the same coat. Who has priority? Whoever perfects first: the rule creates a race to the filing office or to Susan's closet. Whoever can submit the financing statement or actually take possession of the coat first will have priority, and the outcome does not depend on knowledge or lack of knowledge that someone else is claiming a security interest in the same collat-

eral. But what of the rule that in the absence of perfection, whichever security interest first attached has priority? This is "thought to be of merely theoretical interest," says the Code commentary, "since it is hard to imagine a situation where the case would come into litigation without [either party] having perfected his interest." And if the debtor filed a petition in bankruptcy, neither unperfected security interest could prevail against the bankruptcy trustee (see Chapter 28).

Creditors with Purchase Money Security Interests

General Rule of PMSIs   Under Section 9-312(4) a PMSI perfected within ten days after the debtor takes possession of the collateral has priority over all other types of security interests except for interests in inventory.

Suppose Susan manufactures fur coats. On February 1, Rosemary advances her $10,000 under a security agreement covering all Susan's machinery and containing an after-acquired property clause. Rosemary files a financing statement that same day. On March 1, Susan buys a new machine from Erika for $5,000 and gives her a security interest in the machine; Erika files a financing statement within ten days of the time that the machine is delivered to Susan. Who has priority if Susan defaults on her loan payments? Under the PMSI rule, Erika has priority, since she had a PMSI. Suppose, however, that Susan had not bought the machine from Erica but had merely given her a security interest in it. Then Rosemary would have priority, since her filing was prior to Erika's.

Inventory   Inventory is covered by a different rule. A perfected PMSI in inventory has priority over a conflicting security interest in the same inventory if four conditions are met: (1) the PMSI must have been perfected when the debtor receives possession of the inventory; (2) the purchase money secured party must send written notice to the holder of the conflicting security interest if the holder had filed a financing statement; (3) the notice must have come to the holder

within five years before the debtor receives the inventory; and (4) the notice must state that the person giving the notice expects to acquire or already has acquired a PMSI in the debtor's inventory, and must describe the inventory item by item. The notice requirement is aimed at protecting a secured party in the typical situation in which incoming inventory is subject to a prior agreement to make advances against it. If the original creditor gets notice that new inventory is subject to a PMSI he will be forewarned against making an advance on it; if he does not receive notice, he will have priority.

Fixture Financing   Here the first creditor is typically a mortgagee (for example, a bank) with a mortgage covering the real estate and fixtures, even fixtures added after the date of the mortgage. In accord with the general rule, the mortgagee would normally have priority if the mortgage is recorded first, as would a fixture filing if made before the mortgage was recorded.

Susan buys a furnace to put in her house. Rosemary's bank holds the mortgage, with the usual clause stating that it covers all fixtures later acquired. Erika makes an advance against the furnace and files a financing statement. Erika would have priority only if the mortgage had not previously been recorded.

But there is a major exception similar to the rule for PMSIs generally. Under Section 9-313(4)(a), a perfected security interest in the fixture has priority over a mortgage if the security interest is a PMSI and the security interest is perfected by a fixture filing before the goods become fixtures (for example, at the time the furnace is still in the store) or within ten days after.

So if Susan buys the furnace from Erika, who takes back a PMSI and files the appropriate financing statement within ten days of installation, then Erika would have priority over Rosemary's bank, even if the bank had already recorded its mortgage covering after-acquired fixtures.

The rule according priority to PMSIs over prior mortgages is justified by observing that mortgages are long-term investments. They rarely come into conflict with the relatively shorter-term financing arrangements contemplated in the granting of a PMSI for fixtures. By giving priority to the PMSI, the rule encourages improvement and modernization of the real estate, which in the long run benefits the mortgagee.

Bailees with Liens

A bailee is someone who, while in possession of goods, lacks title (see Chapter 20). A bailee has a lien on goods in his possession for which he furnishes services or materials in the ordinary course of his business (for example, a garage mechanic's repairs to a car). If the goods are subject to a security interest, the lien takes priority over a perfected security interest, unless the lien is statutory and the statute expressly provides to the contrary. (Section 9-310.)

Protection of Buyers of Goods in Ordinary Course of Business

A buyer in the ordinary course of business takes free of a security interest created by the seller even though the security interest is perfected and the buyer knows it. This provision might seem to open a large loophole in the protection accorded perfected security interests. In fact, the provision applies mainly to inventory, because "buyer in the ordinary course of business" means a buyer (except a pawnbroker) "from a person in the business of selling goods of that kind." A person who buys items from a person who is in the business of selling them is likely to be buying inventory. Moreover, a "buyer in the ordinary course of business" is one who buys "in good faith and without knowledge that the sale to him is in violation of the . . . security interest of a third party." The two provisions may appear to be contradictory. The resolution of the conflict is this: If the buyer knows merely that there is a security interest in the goods, he takes free. But if he knows that the sale violates a *term in the security agreement*, then he takes subject to the security interest.

Buyers other than in the ordinary course of business (that is, all other buyers) have a limited protection also. Section 9-307(3) says they take free of a security interest that secures future advances made (1) after the secured party learned of the purchase; or (2) more than forty-five days after the purchase, whichever occurs first.

RIGHTS OF CREDITORS ON DEFAULT

After a debtor's default (for example, by missing payments on the debt), the creditor could ignore the security interest and bring suit on the underlying debt. But creditors rarely resort to this remedy because it is time-consuming and costly. Most creditors prefer to repossess the collateral and sell it or retain possession in satisfaction of the debt.

Repossession

Section 9-503 permits the secured party to take possession of the collateral on default (unless the agreement specifies otherwise). Repossession is not as easy as it sounds. Ever since Shylock in Shakespeare's *The Merchant of Venice* demanded the right under his bond to cut out a pound of Antonio's flesh nearest the heart, the courts have answered with Portia's words that a pound of flesh he may have but no "jot of blood" (act 3, scene 1).

The provisions in Article 9 permit the creditor to seek the aid of a court in obtaining the collateral. But Section 9-503 goes further by permitting self-help: "In taking possession a secured party may proceed without judicial process if this can be done without breach of the peace." This language has given rise to a flourishing business that operates on the margin of legality (see **Box 27-1**). "Breach of peace" is language that can cover a wide variety of situations over which courts do not always agree. For example, some courts interpret a creditor's taking of the collateral despite the debtor's clear oral protest as a breach of the peace; other courts do not.

Repossession raises constitutional issues, in addition to problems in defining breach of peace. If state action (p. 23) is involved in a repossession, then the due process clause of the Fourteenth Amendment comes into play. For example, in the *Fuentes* case (p. 20), the Supreme Court held that the Fourteenth Amendment prevents state courts from allowing government officials to seize property before the debtor has had notice and an opportunity to be heard. Due process rights also come into play if an official even assists the creditor with the repossession, as discussed in the *MacLeod* case.

LAW AND LIFE

BOX 27-1

The Gentle Art of Repopping

By Tony Swan

[Repossession of collateral may proceed without judicial process as long as there is no breach of peace. As noted in the following article, "breach of peace" is not clearly defined.—AUTHORS' NOTE]

repop/rē-päp/v./colloq./1. to resume possession of in default of the payment of installments due; usually by stealth; ideally after dark; sometimes perilously.

What we have here is a capitalist morality play for grownups: If you're bad—and moneylending agencies have very fixed and narrow ideas of what "bad" is—the boogey men will come in the night and boogey off with your car.

Rich and Doug are two of the dozens of boogey men, professional auto repossessors (although they could just as easily be a pair of characters out of *Oliver Twist*), operating in the Los Angeles area, where some 50 cars are reclaimed every day. They live and operate in a legal twilight zone that's very much like a football game: There are definite rules, but many violations of the rules go unnoticed by the officials, who in this game wear badges rather than striped shirts.

Doug, who has a penchant for plain speech, puts it this way: "We're car thieves. It's as simple as that—car thieves hired by the bank."

REPOSSESSION AND THE AUTOMOBILE

In terms of the techniques he employs, Doug's assessment is as accurate as it can be. Since the repossessor enters the picture when other methods of dealing with the account have failed, he's obligated to ply his art with the same stealthy skill he'd use if he was after the crown jewels. But there's this distinction: As an indirect agent of the bank, he is operating somewhere close to the law—if not actually within its letter, at least within hailing (and/or coverup) distance of its spirit.

Most repossessors work as independent contractors for agencies licensed to perform this service for the bank or lending institution holding title to the car. (In California, as in most states, there are two names involved with the title of a vehicle: the registered owner [R.O.], which means the individual purchasing the car; and the legal owner, which is the institution holding a lien against the vehicle.) The license is issued to the agency when its owner has passed a background check and has posted a bond. Employees of the agency operate under its license.

But who could possibly want to pursue this line of work, with its strange hours, marginal reputation, and many dangers?

"Usually it's very young guys," says Bernie Finks of the Los Angeles Police Commission. "I think a lot of 'em are probably college students, because it's a good part-time hustle—there aren't any particular hours. You never see anyone starting out in it who's over 30. . . ."

The rules that govern this game—and that's the way many of the repoppers view their livelihood—seem simple enough. You may not carry a concealed weapon. You may not break and enter. But when you're out there at 3 a.m. and the dogs start barking and a light comes on in the bedroom and you've been after the car for three weeks and it's a simple matter of snipping off a padlock with bolt-cutters, then it boils down to whatever you can get away with. . . .

Perhaps the murkiest area of all in this dicey business is the matter of possession. As far as the repoppers are concerned, once they're inside the car, it's theirs. But the registered owners usually have a different opinion, one they're too often willing to back up with firearms.

As for the police: "We can take no sides unless there's a court order," says [Lieutenant] Hees [of the LAPD Burglary and Auto Division]. "We cannot interpret degrees of possession. We just try to keep the peace. It's definitely a gray area of the law and a pain [. . .] for the police officer."

Source: Reprinted by permission from *Motor Trend* magazine, March 1976

In re MacLEOD
118 B.R. 1
(Bkrtcy.D.N.H. 1990)

JAMES E. YACOS, BANKRUPTCY JUDGE.

Plaintiffs filed a Complaint against defendants for turnover of property pursuant to section 542 of the Code. They sought the turnover of a bulldozer and excavator which defendants repossessed on April 27, 1990 prior to the chapter 11 filing. A hearing was held on June 27, 1990 after which I made a bench ruling that the repossession was unlawful and ultimately entered an order directing the turnover. Today, I refine my remarks in an opinion with regard to the repossession issue since there is no case law in New Hampshire on this issue.

★   ★   ★

On April 27th a state policeman was involved due to the anticipation of possible violence with plaintiff, John MacLeod. The policeman woke John MacLeod up at 6:30 a.m., and told him that a repossession was going to take place and he was not to leave the house. MacLeod was also told not to "do something stupid." The defendants agents were able to start the equipment with the assistance of a mechanic, and took the equipment.

The defendants' attorney who was involved in the repossession on April 27th testified that if John MacLeod had told the repossessors to leave the property they would have ceased the repossession effort immediately and left the premises. I do not find this testimony credible. A person forcibly restrained by a police officer is not in the position to politely ask people to leave. In addition, I find the persistent conduct of the defendants over the repeated protests of John MacLeod inconsistent with this testimony.

A self-help repossession can only be done without a breach of the peace. This rule is stated in NHRSA 382-A:9-503 as follows:

> "Unless otherwise agreed a secured party has on default the right to take possession of the collateral. In taking possession a secured party may proceed without judicial process if this can be done without breach of the peace or may proceed by action. If the security agreement so provides the secured party may require the debtor to assemble the collateral and make it available to the secured party at a place to be designated by the secured party which is reasonably convenient to both parties. Without removal a secured party may render equipment unusable, and may dispose of collateral on the debtor's premises under Section 9-504.

The repossession was unlawful because the plaintiffs in no way *consented* to the repossession.

Yet, there is a separate and more compelling reason why a breach of the peace occurred in this case—the defendants introduced law enforcement personnel into the repossession. Cases have held that the use of law enforcement personnel for a self-help repossession renders the repossession unlawful. See *Walker v. Walthall*, 588 P.2d 863 (App.1978); *First and Farmers Bank of Somerset, Inc. v. Henderson*, 763 S.W.2d 137 (Ky.Ct.App.1988).

In the *Walker* case the repossessor went with a uniformed police officer to the debtor's home and obtained verbal consent to take an automobile. The police officer said and did nothing. The creditor had the police officer there to prevent anticipated violence. The court concluded:

> In the instant action we believe the presence of the deputy sheriff and its accompanying intimidation is the same kind of conduct condemned by the Washington court. The fact that the deputy did not say anything is not significant. Nor is it required that the possessor (Walthall here) actually indicate resistance, either verbally or physically to the uniformed and armed officer.
>
> Such a result, if left standing, would set a precedent by involving local law enforcement in self-help repossessions, and would create the very volatile situations the statute was designed to prevent.

*   *   *

> We believe, therefore, that the introduction of law enforcement officers into the area of self-help repossession, regardless of their degree of participation or nonparticipation in the actual events, would constitute the state action, thereby invalidating a repossession without proper notice and hearing.

Similarly, in *First and Farmers Bank, supra,* the Kentucky court was confronted with a case where a uniformed policeman met the creditor at the scene of the repossession when the debtor was verbally protesting the repossession to the creditor. At most the policeman answered the debtor's question whether the bank had the right to repossess by nodding his head. The court stated:

> If a creditor is allowed to unofficially use the powers of the state to squelch potential breaches of the peace, he can effectively evade or avoid the statute. The statute makes it clear that a creditor runs the risk of serious liability if he proceeds with a self-help repossession when there is a serious objection by the debtor. If the strong arm of the law is needed, then the creditor must secure judicial intervention when a police officer is carrying out or sanctioning the repossession.

*   *   *

The reasoning of these cases is persuasive. In short, if a creditor can argue that they have avoided a breach of the peace by use of law enforcement personnel, and then contend they are in a position for self-help repossession, they effectively circumvent the intent of the statute which is to give the debtor a right to object without the presence of state action.

The repossession of equipment by defendants without the consent of the plaintiffs and with the assistance of the state police was not a self-help repossession and accordingly was unlawful. Therefore, that element of plaintiff's complaint for turnover has been proven.

Disposition after Repossession

Sale   After repossession, the creditor has two options. He may sell the collateral or accept the collateral in satisfaction of the debt (see Figure 27-5). Sale is the usual method of recovering the debt. Section 9-504 permits the secured creditor to "sell, lease, or otherwise dispose of any or all of the collateral in its then condition or following any commercially reasonable preparation or processing." The collateral may be sold as a whole or in parcels, at one time or at different times. Two requirements limit the creditor's power to resell: (1) he must send notice to the debtor and (unless consumer goods are sold) to other secured parties; and (2) all aspects of the sale must be "commercially reasonable." If sale proceeds do not cover the debt, the creditor is entitled to recover the deficiency; if the proceeds exceed the debt, the excess must be paid to the debtor. To deter unreasonable sales, Section 9-507 gives the debtor the right to seek a court order against resale and even provides for damages when the goods have already been sold unreasonably. The debtor might also be relieved from liability for the deficiency, as illustrated by the case on p. 606.

Strict Foreclosure   Since resale can be a bother, the secured creditor may wish simply to accept the collateral in full satisfaction of the debt, as permitted in Section 9-505(2). This is known as **strict foreclosure.** The creditor must send the debtor written notice of his decision to do so. In the case of consumer goods, that is the only required notice. In other cases, the creditor must send notice to any other secured creditors from whom he has received a written notice claiming an interest in the collateral. The debtor or other creditors have twenty-one days to object, in which event the collateral must be sold under Section 9-504. In the absence of written objection, however, the creditor may keep the collateral in full satisfaction of the debt.

The strict foreclosure provisions contain a safety feature for consumer goods debtors. If the debtor has paid at least 60 percent of the debt, then the creditor may not use strict foreclosure—unless the debtor signs a statement *after default* renouncing his right to bar strict foreclosure and to force a sale. A consumer who refuses to sign such a statement thus forces the secured creditor to sell the collateral under Section 9-504. Should the creditor fail to sell the goods within ninety days after taking possession of the goods, he is liable to the debtor for the value of the goods in a conversion suit or may incur the liabilities set forth in Section 9-507(1), which provides for minimum damages for the consumer debtor.

Intangible Collateral

A secured party's repossession of inventory or equipment can disrupt or even close a debtor's business.

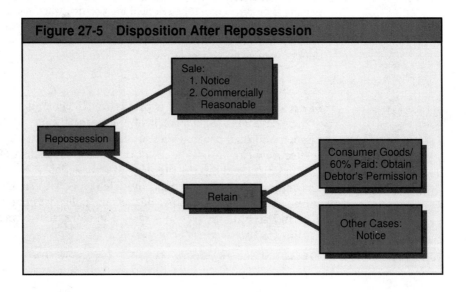

Figure 27-5   Disposition After Repossession

Repossession

Sale:
1. Notice
2. Commercially Reasonable

Retain

Consumer Goods/ 60% Paid: Obtain Debtor's Permission

Other Cases: Notice

However, when the collateral is intangible—such as accounts receivable, general intangibles, chattel paper, or instruments—collection by a secured party after the debtor's default may proceed without interrupting the business. Section 9-502 provides that on default the secured party is entitled to notify the third party—for example, a person who owes money on an account—that payment should be made to him. The secured party is accountable to the debtor for any surplus and the debtor is liable for any deficiency unless the parties have agreed otherwise.

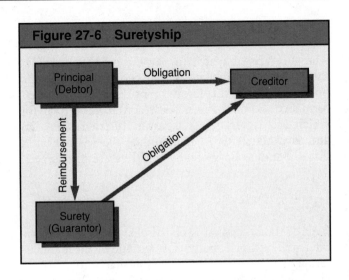

Figure 27-6 Suretyship

INTRODUCTION TO SURETYSHIP

Suretyship Defined

Suretyship is the second of the three major types of consensual security arrangements noted at the beginning of this chapter—and a common one. Creditors frequently ask the owners of small, closely held companies to guarantee their loans to the company, and parent corporations also frequently are guarantors of their subsidiaries' debts. This is the essence of suretyship, which the *Restatement of the Law of Security* defines as follows:

> Suretyship is the relation which exists where one person has undertaken an obligation and another person is also under an obligation or other duty to the obligee, who is entitled to but one performance, and as between the two who are bound, one rather than the other should perform. (Section 82.)

The **surety** is the person who is bound on an obligation from which someone else—the **principal**—should relieve him by discharging a duty, often by paying money. The **creditor** is the person to whom the surety is bound and to whom the principal is obligated to perform a duty (see Figure 27-6). Bear in mind that the surety and the principal may have no agreement between each other; the surety might have struck a deal with the creditor to act as surety without the consent or knowledge of the principal.

A **guarantor** is one who guarantees an obligation of another and for practical purposes, therefore, is synonymous with *surety;* to **guarantee** is to assume the obligation of a surety. In many states, however,

suretyship is used to describe a situation in which there is one contract binding both the surety and principal, while the term *guaranty* is used when a separate contract binds the guarantor. In these states the liability of a surety is said to be primary, while that of a guarantor is secondary.

Creation of Suretyship

Suretyship can arise only through contract. The general principles of contract law covered in Part II of this text apply to suretyship. Thus a person with the general capacity to contract has the power to become a surety. A revocable offer to be bound as a surety is revoked by the offeror's death. Eva offers to guarantee a loan Martha is contemplating making to Sarah's Pizzeria, but minutes before Martha actually makes the loan, Eva is run over by a truck and killed. Unaware of her death, Martha gives the cash to Sarah, who subsequently defaults. Eva's estate is not liable to Martha. For these general principles and others, refer to the chapters on contract law, and especially to Chapter 12, for the discussion of suretyship and the Statute of Frauds.

Suretyship contracts are affected to some extent by government regulation. Under a 1985 FTC Credit Practices Rule (see p. 584), creditors are prohibited from misrepresenting a surety's liability. Creditors must also give the surety a notice that explains the nature of the obligation and the potential liability.

THE SURETY AND CREDITOR

The surety is obligated to pay the creditor until (1) the principal or someone on her behalf discharges the obligation or (2) the surety or principal tenders performance. Sarah's Pizzeria owes Martha $5,000 for which Eva is surety. As a gesture of friendship, Diane pays Martha $5,000, intending the payment as a gift to Sarah's. Both Sarah's and Eva are discharged.

General Defenses

Even if the obligation is not discharged, the surety is often relieved of liability through one or more defenses. Thus the contract defenses available to a principal (and described in the contracts unit, Chapter 11) are also available to the surety—for instance, impossibility, illegality, fraud, and duress. However, the surety may contract with the creditor to be liable despite the principal's defense of impossibility or illegality, and a surety who has undertaken her suretyship with knowledge of the creditor's fraud or duress remains obligated, even though the principal will be discharged.

In other cases, too, the principal or surety may have a defense when the other party does not. For example, the principal may be able to defend on the ground that she lacks capacity or that she is bankrupt, but the surety will still be bound. Contrarily, the surety but not the principal might be able to assert a defense that the statute of limitations had run.

Assume a six-year statute of limitations on an agreement to repay a loan. The principal defaults but two years later makes a new promise to repay. Four years later, the debt still unpaid, the creditor sues both the principal and the surety. She would be entitled to judgment against the principal but not the surety. The principal's promise to pay tolled the statute as to the principal but not the surety.

Defenses Commonly Raised by Sureties

One common defense raised by sureties is release of the principal. Whenever a creditor releases the principal, the surety is discharged, unless the surety consents to remain liable or the creditor expressly reserves her rights against the surety.

Another general defense commonly raised by sureties is alteration of the contract. Should the creditor happen to alter the instrument sufficiently to discharge the principal, the surety is discharged as well. Likewise, when the creditor and principal modify their contract, a surety who has not consented to the modification is discharged.

A creditor who fails to file a financing statement (see p. 592) or record a mortgage (see p. 617) risks losing the security for the loan and might also inadvertently release a surety. And a creditor who fails to notify a surety when collateral is sold might also release the surety—even when the surety knew about the sale. The following case illustrates this point.

VERMONT NAT. BANK v. HAMILTON
546 A.2d 1349 (Vt. 1988)

DOOLEY, JUSTICE.

This is an action for a deficiency judgment following the sale at public auction of certain collateral. The lower court denied the deficiency because it found that the plaintiff had failed to give proper notice of the sale to defendants. The plaintiff appeals from this ruling.

The plaintiff below, and appellant in this Court, is Vermont National Bank, the secured party. The debtor, Northeast Ecology Systems, Inc., (the company) went bankrupt and the action was tried against Richard and Ann Hamilton (defendants) who were guarantors of the obligation to plaintiff. Defendant, Richard Hamilton, was the vice-president of the company.

The company purchased steel racking in order to store large trays of earthworms. The plaintiff financed the purchase and took a security interest in the racking. The company was unable to pay the plaintiff. As a result, the plaintiff brought this action against the defendants and the company, and sought an order giving it immediate possession of the steel racking as well as an award of damages. The parties were able to settle the issue of possession of the racking, and the settlement was incorporated into an order of the court of May 7, 1981.

★   ★   ★

Finally, plaintiff sold the racking at public auction on November 6, 1982. Plaintiff never notified defendants of the sale either orally or in writing. However, defendant Ann Hamilton read the auction announcement in the newspaper four or five days before the auction. She called the loan officer at plaintiff bank to confirm the sale. She attended the auction and did not bid.

The auction failed to produce sufficient proceeds to pay off the debt to plaintiff. Since the company was bankrupt, plaintiff sought damages against the defendants as guarantors. The amount sought was the remainder of the debt along with the expenses of selling the collateral and collection of the debt. Defendants raised a number of defenses related to the handling of the collateral and the sale. The trial court accepted one of these defenses—that the plaintiff failed to give proper notice of the sale to defendants as required by § 9-504(3) of the Uniform Commercial Code, 9A V.S.A. § 9-504(3). As a result, it denied plaintiff any deficiency and entered judgment for defendants.

★   ★   ★

Section 9-504 sets forth the procedures for a secured party to dispose of collateral after a default by the debtor. Among the requirements imposed by the section is that "reasonable notification of the time and place of any public sale . . . shall be sent by the secured party to the debtor. . . ." 9A V.S.A. § 9-504(3). The term debtor, for purposes of Article 9 of the UCC, is defined to include "the person who owes payment or other performance of the obligation secured, whether or not he owns or has rights in the collateral. . . ." 9A V.S.A. § 9-105(1)(d).

★   ★   ★

Thus, we must address whether plaintiff complied with § 9-504(3). In support of a finding of compliance, plaintiff emphasizes two facts—(1) it "sent" a newspaper notice; and (2) defendants had actual notice of the sale.

Neither of these facts establish compliance with § 9-504(3) as that section is worded. The statute requires that "reasonable notification" be "sent." The definition of "sent" in § 1-201(38) requires transmission by mail or other "usual means of communication." A secured party does not send a notice to the debtor when it places it in the newspaper to alert the public to an upcoming sale. . . .

We recognize that under § 1-201(25)(a) a person has notice of a fact if "he has actual knowledge of it." However, neither § 9-504(3), nor the definitions of the terms within it, indicate that the creditor complies when the debtor has actual notice of the public sale. Instead, § 9-504(3) imposes a process requirement to be complied with by the creditor irrespective of the debtor's knowledge. . . . [T]he focus of the statute is on whether the secured party has taken "reasonable steps" to notify the debtor. The secured party has not done so here. [Judgment affirmed.]

SURETY AND PRINCIPAL

Principal's General Duty

The principal's duty to the surety is to satisfy the obligation she owes the creditor, thereby discharging the surety's duty to the creditor.

Surety's Rights Against the Principal

Reimbursement   If the surety must pay the creditor because the principal has defaulted, the principal is obligated to reimburse the surety. The amount required to be reimbursed includes the surety's reasonable outlay, including interest and legal fees.

Exoneration   If, at the time a surety's obligation has matured, the principal can satisfy the obligation but refuses to do so, the surety is entitled to **exoneration**—a court order requiring the principal to perform. It would be inequitable to force the surety to perform and then to have to seek reimbursement from the principal if all along the principal is able to perform.

Subrogation   Suppose the principal's duty to the creditor is fully satisfied and that the surety has contributed to this satisfaction. Then the surety is entitled to be **subrogated** to the rights of the creditor against the principal. In other words, the surety stands in the creditor's shoes and may assert against the principal whatever rights the creditor could have asserted had the duty not been discharged. The right of subrogation includes the right to take secured interests that the creditor obtained from the principal to cover the duty. Sarah's Pizzeria owes Martha $5,000, and Martha has taken a security interest in Sarah's Mercedes. Eva is surety for the debt. Sarah defaults, and Eva pays Martha the $5,000. Eva is entitled to have the security interest in the car transferred to her.

RIGHTS AMONG CO-SURETIES

Two or more sureties who are bound to answer for the principal's default and who should share between them the loss caused by the default are known as **co-sureties**. A surety who in performing his own obligation to the creditor winds up paying more than his proportionate share is entitled to *contribution* from the co-sureties.

CHAPTER SUMMARY

The law governing security interests in personal property is Article 9 of the UCC, which defines a security interest as an interest in personal property or fixtures which secures payment or performance of an obligation. Article 9 lumps together all the former types of security devices, including the pledge, chattel mortgage, and conditional sale.

Four types of tangible property may serve as collateral: (1) consumer goods, (2) equipment, (3) farm products, and (4) inventory. Five types of intangibles may serve as collateral: (1) accounts, (2) general intangibles (for example, patents), (3) documents of title, (4) chattel paper, and (5) instruments. Article 9 expressly permits the debtor to give a security interest in after-acquired collateral.

To create an enforceable security interest, the lender and borrower must enter into an agreement establishing the interest, and the lender must follow steps to ensure that the security interest first attaches and then is perfected. There are three general requirements for attachment: (1) there must be a signed agreement (or the collateral must physically be in the lender's possession, (2) the lender must have given value, and (3) the debtor must have some rights in the collateral. Once the interest attaches, the lender has rights in the collateral superior to those of unsecured creditors. But others may defeat his interest unless he perfects the security interest. The three common ways of doing so are: (1) filing a financing statement, (2) pledging collateral, and (3) taking a purchase money security interest (PMSI) in consumer goods.

A financing statement is a simple notice, showing the parties' names and addresses, the signature of the debtor, and an adequate description of the collateral. The financing statement, effective for five years, must be filed in a public office; the location of the office varies among the states.

Security interests in instruments and negotiable documents can be perfected only by the secured party's taking possession, with twenty-one-day grace periods applicable under certain circumstances. Goods may also be secured through pledging; which is often done through field warehousing. If a seller of consumer goods takes a purchase money security interest in the goods sold, then perfection is automatic and no filing is required, although the lender may file and probably should to avoid losing seniority to a bona fide purchaser of consumer goods without knowledge of the security interest, if the goods are used for personal, family, or household purposes.

The general priority rule is "first in time, first in right." Priority dates from the earliest of two events: (1) filing of a financing statement covering the collateral, or (2) other perfection of the security interest. Several exceptions to this rule arise when creditors take a purchase money security interest. A buyer in the ordinary course of business takes free of a security interest created by the seller.

On default, a creditor may repossess the collateral. For the most part, self-help private repossession continues to be lawful but risky. After repossession, the lender may sell the collateral or accept it in satisfaction of the debt. Any excess in the selling price above the debt amount must go to the debtor.

Suretyship is a legal relationship that is created when one person has undertaken an obligation and another person is also under an obligation to the same obligee, who is entitled to only one performance and as between the two who are bound, one rather than the other should perform. The surety is bound to the creditor on an obligation that the principal should relieve him of. The surety is obligated to pay the creditor unless the principal or someone on his behalf discharges the obligation or either the surety or principal tenders performance. The surety may avail himself of the principal's contract defenses, but under various circumstances, certain defenses may be available to the one that are not available to the other. One general defense often raised by sureties is alteration of the contract. If the surety is required to perform, he has rights for reimbursement against the principal, including interest and legal fees.

KEY TERMS

Account debtor	p. 588	Mortgage	p. 587
Attachment	p. 591	Perfection	p. 592
Collateral	p. 588	Pledge	p. 595
Co-sureties	p. 608	Principal	p. 605
Creditor	p. 605	Proceeds	p. 590
Debtor	p. 588	Purchase money security interest	p. 587
Exoneration	p. 608		
Factor	p. 590	Secured	p. 586
Field warehouse	p. 596	Secured party	p. 588
Fixtures	p. 595	Security	p. 586
Floating lien	p. 590	Security agreement	p. 591
Guarantee	p. 605	Strict foreclosure	p. 604
Guarantor	p. 605	Subrogated	p. 608
Intangible property	p. 590	Surety	p. 605
Lien	p. 586		

SELF-TEST QUESTIONS

1. Creditors may obtain security:
   (a) by agreement with the debtor
   (b) through the operation of law
   (c) through both of the above
   (d) through none of the above

2. For the purposes of collateral, tangible property includes:
   (a) inventory
   (b) chattel paper
   (c) accounts
   (d) documents of title

3. To perfect a security interest, one may:
   (a) file a financing statement
   (b) pledge collateral
   (c) take a purchase money security interest in consumer goods
   (d) do any of the above

4. A financing statement:
   (a) does not have to be filed in a public office
   (b) is effective for ten years
   (c) is effective for seven years
   (d) includes a description of the collateral

5. With regard to priority:
   (a) The general rule is "first in time, first in right."
   (b) A purchase money security interest perfected within ten days after the debtor takes possession of the collateral has priority over other types of security interests except interests in inventory.
   (c) Both of the above are true.
   (d) None of the above are true.

DEMONSTRATION PROBLEM

Third Bank has a security interest in consumer goods owned by Fred. Fred defaults after paying off 90 percent of the debt. After repossessing the goods, may Third Bank use a strict foreclosure remedy? Why?

PROBLEMS

1. Tom and Mary, a married couple, own a car which they use for family purposes. Because Mary has a new job which requires extensive travel to neighboring cities, they purchase a second car. They finance the purchase at First Bank and give the bank a security interest in the second car. How is the car classified under Article 9 of the UCC? Does the bank have a purchase money security interest? Why?

2. Tom and Mary borrow money from First Bank for a vacation trip to San Diego. First Bank takes a security interest in their first car (see problem 1). How is the car classified under Article 9 of the UCC? Does the bank have a purchase money security interest? Why?

3. You are a loan officer at Second Bank. You want to take a security interest in the accounts of a local store. Must your agreement creating the security interest be written? Why?

4. In problem 3, assume that a security interest was created but that you forgot to perfect the interest. What effect does the failure to perfect have on the bank's right to enforce the security interest? Why?

5. First Bank lends $20,000 to Generic Stores, Inc. (GS), takes a security interest in GS's present and future inventory, and files a financing statement. No Name Toys sells a shipment of toys to GS on credit, takes a security interest in the toys, and files a financing statement five days after delivering them. Which security interest has priority? Why?

6. Baby Huey visits GS (see problem 5) and, being fully aware of the two security interests, buys several toys. Are Baby Huey's toys subject to either of the security interests? Why?

7. First Bank has a security interest in certain equipment owned by Urban Industries. After Urban defaults on its loan, First Bank lawfully repossesses the equipment. What options are made available to the bank after repossession? Explain.

ANSWERS TO SELF-TEST QUESTIONS

1. (c)   2. (a)   3. (d)   4. (d)   5. (c)

SUGGESTED ANSWER TO DEMONSTRATION PROBLEM

Third Bank may use strict foreclosure if Fred signs a statement after default renouncing his right to force a sale.

CHAPTER

28

Mortgages and Nonconsensual Liens

INTRODUCTION TO MORTGAGES

*H*aving discussed security interests in personal property and suretyship—two of the three common types of consensual security arrangements—in the previous chapter, we turn now to the third type of consensual security arrangement—the mortgage. We also discuss briefly various forms of nonconsensual liens (see Figure 28-1).

Definitions

In the conventional sense, a **mortgage** is a means of securing a debt with real estate. A long time ago, the mortgage was considered an actual transfer of title, to become void if the debt was paid off. The modern view, held in most states, is that the mortgage is but a lien, giving the holder in the event of default the right to sell the property and repay the debt from the proceeds. The person giving the mortgage is the **mortgagor** or borrower. In the typical home purchase, the buyer is the mortgagor. The buyer needs to borrow from a bank to finance his purchase; in exchange for the money with which to pay the seller, the buyer "takes out a mortgage" with, say, a bank. The lender is the **mortgagee,** the person or institution holding the mortgage, with the right to foreclose on the property if the debt is not timely paid. Although the law of real estate mortgages is different from the set of rules in Article 9 of the UCC that we studied in the last chapter, the circumstances are the same, except that the security is real estate rather than personal property (secured transactions) or the promise of another (suretyship).

Use of Mortgages

According to the *Statistical Abstract of the United States,* about three-quarters of all mortgages are taken out

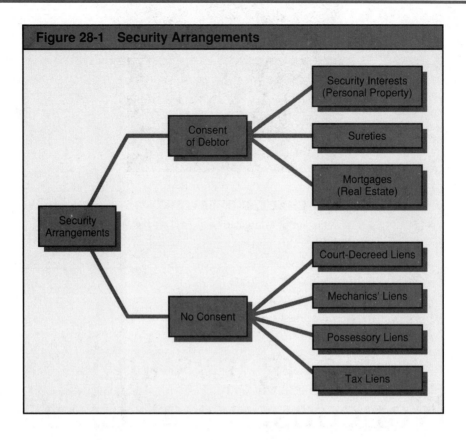

Figure 28-1   Security Arrangements

Security Arrangements

Consent of Debtor
- Security Interests (Personal Property)
- Sureties
- Mortgages (Real Estate)

No Consent
- Court-Decreed Liens
- Mechanics' Liens
- Possessory Liens
- Tax Liens

on nonfarm residential property; 18 percent are for commercial real estate, and the balance of 7 percent are farm mortgages. Corporate mortgages are similar to individual residential mortgages, but corporations can also issue **mortgage bonds.** These are the same as ordinary corporate bonds except that they are secured by a company's real property—its factories and the like.

Short History of Mortgage Law

The mortgage has ancient roots, but the form we know evolved from English land law in the Middle Ages. In the fourteenth century, the mortgage was a deed and actually transferred title to the mortgagee. If desired, the mortgagee could move into the house, occupy the property, or rent it out. But since the mortgage obligated him to apply to the mortgage debt whatever rents he collected, he seldom ousted the mortgagor. Moreover, the mortgage set a specific date

(the *law day*) on which the debt was to be repaid. If the mortgagor did so, the mortgage became void and he was entitled to recover the property. If the mortgagor failed to pay the debt, the property automatically vested in the mortgagee. No further proceedings were necessary.

This law was severe. A day's delay in paying the debt, for any reason, forfeited the land, and the courts strictly enforced the mortgage. The only possible relief was a petition to the king, who over time referred these and other kinds of petitions to the courts in equity. At first fitfully, and then as a matter of course (by the seventeenth century), the equity courts would order the mortgagee to return the land when the mortgagor stood ready to pay the debt plus interest. Thus a new right developed: the *equitable right of redemption*, known for short as the **equity of redemption.** In time the courts held that this equity of redemption was a form of property right: it could be sold and inherited. This was a powerful right; no matter how many years later, the mortgagor could always recover his land by proffering a sum of money.

Understandably, mortgagees did not warm to this interpretation of the law, because their property rights were rendered insecure. They tried to defeat the equity of redemption by having mortgagors waive and surrender it to the mortgagees, but the courts voided waiver clauses as a violation of public policy. Hence a mortgage, once a transfer of title, has become a security for debt. A mortgage as such can never be converted into a deed of title.

The law did not rest there, however. Mortgagees won a measure of relief in the development of the **foreclosure**. On default, the mortgagee would seek a court order giving the mortgagor a fixed time—perhaps six months or a year—within which to pay off the debt; under the court decree, failure meant that the mortgagor was forever foreclosed from asserting his right of redemption. This **strict foreclosure** gave the mortgagee outright title at the end of the time period. Most states follow a somewhat different approach: the mortgagee forecloses by forcing a public sale at auction. Proceeds up to the amount of the debt are the mortgagee's to keep; surplus is paid over to the mortgagor. **Foreclosure by sale** is the usual procedure in the United States. At bottom, its theory is that a mortgage is a lien on the land.

Under statutes enacted in many states, the mortgagor has one last chance to recover his property, even after foreclosure. This statutory right of redemption extends the period to repay, often by one year.

CREATION OF THE MORTGAGE

Statutory Regulation

The decision whether to lend money and take a mortgage is complicated because it will be affected by so much federal and state legislation. Thus various statutes dealing with consumer credit transactions (see Chapter 26) have a bearing on the mortgage, including usury statutes, the Truth in Lending Act, and the Equal Credit Opportunity Act.

Other statutes are directed more specifically at mortgage lending. One, enacted in 1974, is the Real Estate Settlement Procedures Act (RESPA), aimed at abuses in the settlement process—the process of obtaining the mortgage and purchasing a residence. RESPA covers all federally related first mortgage loans secured by residential properties for one to four families. In general terms, RESPA requires the lender to disclose information about settlement costs in advance of the closing day. It also outlaws what had been a common practice of giving and accepting kickbacks and referral fees. The act prohibits lenders from requiring mortgagors to use a particular company to obtain insurance, and it limits the amount of extra funds the lender can demand of the mortgagor to cover future insurance and tax charges.

Several statutes are directed at the practice of **redlining**—the refusal of lenders to make loans on property in low-income neighborhoods or imposition of stricter mortgage terms when they do make loans there. (The term derives from the supposition that lenders draw red lines on maps around ostensibly marginal neighborhoods.) Although many lenders have denied that banks and financial institutions engage in the practice, evidence has convinced Congress and several state legislatures to pass statutes that attempt to deal with the practice.

Proponents of redlining assert the right of lenders to use their own criteria to determine which customers are worth the risk. Opponents assert that the criteria are too sweeping and include such irrelevant ones as the race or sex of the customer. To get at the latter evils, Congress enacted the Home Mortgage Disclosure Act of 1975, which requires mortgage lenders to disclose annually the number and total amount of home mortgages and home improvement loans they have made in each metropolitan area throughout the country. The HMDA has no mechanism to force lenders to make loans in low-income neighborhoods, but Congress has also enacted the Community Reinvestment Act (CRA), which directs a variety of federal agencies, in considering applications for federal charters, insurance, or permission to extend operations, to take into account how well lending institutions have met community needs. Under the CRA, the institution must provide public information on its credit practices, and maintain a public file of comments about those practices. The CRA requires the Federal Deposit Insurance Corporation, a federal agency, to examine lending institutions' compliance with the CRA in routine examinations conducted every twelve to eighteen months. These examinations, together with community input, can determine whether a bank will be granted permission to open a new branch or begin operations (see **Box 28-1**).

LAW AND LIFE

Why More Banks May Start Doing the Right Thing

By Chuck Hawkins

[The Community Reinvestment Act (CRA) makes it difficult for banks and savings and loans to "redline" when deciding to lend money. As a result of changes in the law that became effective in 1990, the CRA will have a greater impact in the future.—AUTHORS' NOTE]

Two years ago, Cecelia White was on welfare and living in a Cleveland housing project. But aided by the nonprofit Cleveland Housing Network, the 35-year-old White was able to land a job as a nursing assistant and move, with her two sons, into a renovated home. White pays $225 a month in rent to the network, which

IMPACT OF THE CRA

owns the house with the help of a mortgage from Ameritrust Corp. and funds provided by private investors and the city government. The network uses part of White's payments to pay off the loan, and she will own the home in 13 years. Says White: "Our whole life has changed."

White's story is far from common, however. The Community Reinvestment Act of 1977 requires banks to make loans equitably to the communities they serve, but enforcement has been lax. Indeed, the Washington (D.C.) government issued a report in May blasting six suburban banks. City officials charge that of the $955 million in mortgages written in the District over two years, only 6% went to low-income, mostly black, areas.

That may be about to change.

For regulatory exams started after July 1 [1990], banks and savings and loans will have to disclose their new CRA ratings. Previously, the grades, which are assigned by examiners to determine compliance with the law, have been kept confidential. Now, after years of half-hearted enforcement, regulators—prodded by Congress—are getting tougher.

Harder Line
Lenders are scrambling to improve their records because they know poor CRA ratings could have devastating effects. With ratings visible for all to see, bankers fret that some big depositors, such as city and state governments and unions, may pull money from institutions with lousy grades.

Regulators are already taking a harder line. The Federal Reserve Board held up First Union Corp.'s acquisition of Florida National Bank last year in part because community groups accused the Charlotte (N.C.) acquirer of a poor community record.

The Note and the Mortgage Document

The Note If the lender decides to grant a mortgage, the mortgagor signs two critical documents at the closing: the *note* and the *mortgage*. We cover notes in Part IV, Commercial Paper. It is enough here to recall that in a note the mortgagor promises to pay a specified principal sum, plus interest, by a certain date or dates. The note is the underlying obligation for which the mortgage serves as security. Without the note, the mortgagee would have an empty document, since the mortgage would secure nothing. Without a mortgage, a note is still quite valid, evidencing the debtor's personal obligation.

One particular provision that usually appears in both mortgages and the underlying notes is the **acceleration clause.** This provides that if a debtor should default on any particular payment, the entire principal and interest will become due immediately at the lender's option. Why an acceleration clause? Without it, the lender would be powerless to foreclose the entire mortgage when the mortgagor defaulted but would have to wait until the expiration of the note's term. Although the acceleration clause is routine, it will not be enforced unless the mortgagee acts in an equitable and fair manner, as the *Harrell* case illustrates.

BOX 28-1

CRA challenges from citizen groups have also helped delay the merger of Atlanta's Citizens & Southern Corp. and Sovran Financial Corp. in Norfolk, Va.

Bankers are hardly warming to the new CRA regulations. They complain that they shouldn't be forced to lose money through social-engineering projects—especially at a time when many banks and thrifts are trying to cope with acres of bad real estate loans. Moreover, Fritz Elmendorf, executive director of the Consumer Bankers Assn. in Washington, says his members worry that CRA standards are too subjective. With four agencies enforcing the law—the Federal Reserve Board, the Federal Deposit Insurance Corp., the Office of the Comptroller of the Currency, and the Office of Thrift Supervision—regulators may not grade uniformly.

There are no hard-and-fast rules for applying CRA standards. But regulators have told banks and thrifts that they will be looking beyond lending patterns. Charitable contributions, the size of checking-account fees, and the availability of bilingual officers in branches located in ethnic areas could also be factored into the ratings. Even a director's membership in a private club that has a history of discrimination against minorities may affect a bank's CRA rating.

Lip Service

Social activists are delighted with the new regulatory posture. They say many banks and S&Ls have paid only lip service to CRA requirements because regulators weren't strict. "Bankers don't accept the notion that they lend on a prejudicial basis, but the bottom line is that not enough money is being provided to inner-city neighborhoods," says Representative Joseph P. Kennedy II (D-Mass.). He teamed up with House Banking Committee Chairman Henry B. Gonzalez (D-Tex.) to amend last summer's thrift-bailout law to include the requirement for public disclosure of CRA ratings.

Proponents of tougher CRA standards argue that banks shouldn't look at low-income lending as a losing proposition. Wells Fargo Bank says it has yet to record a default on $137 million in CRA housing loans since 1986. In March, the San Francisco bank announced a goal of $1 billion in new CRA lending, including small-business loans, through 1996. And Cleveland's Ameritrust Development Bank, a unit of Ameritrust that deals exclusively in local development projects, reported 1989 pretax profits of $800,000 on assets of $65 million.

Profits on CRA lending may not add up to a gold mine. But they don't look bad when compared with returns on Third World loans or those that financed some of the splashy takeovers of the Roaring Eighties, either. And now that CRA ratings will be public, a lot of banks could have a lot of explaining to do.

Source: *Business Week*, June 18, 1990

HARRELL v. PERKINS
216 Ark. 579, 226 S.W.2d 803 (1950)

McFADDIN, JUSTICE. The creditor filed this mortgage foreclosure suit and sought acceleration of the entire mortgage indebtedness. The only question for decision is whether the Chancery Court ruled correctly in refusing to enter a decree for such acceleration.

On April 25, 1947 C. R. Perkins, and wife, executed a mortgage, on a house and lot in the City of Little Rock, to H. H. Harrell (the appellant) to secure a note for $12,500. The note was payable in monthly installments of $82.81; and both the note and mortgage contained an acceleration clause. The one in the note reads: ". . . if default be made at any time in payment of any of said installments for a period of 60 days, all of the remaining installments not then due shall at the option of the holder at once become due and payable, for the purpose of foreclosure."

(continued on next page)

(continued)

HARRELL v. PERKINS
216 Ark. 579, 226 S.W.2d
803 (1950)

Mrs. Leola Blanchard (the only appellee) purchased the property from Mr. and Mrs. Perkins and assumed the mortgage indebtedness held by Mr. Harrell. All monthly payments were made on the note to and including March 25, 1948. Thereafter, no monthly payments were made due to the facts hereinafter to be stated.

On October 8, 1948 Mr. Harrell filed suit to foreclose his mortgage and claimed the acceleration of maturity of the entire note. Mr. and Mrs. Perkins defaulted; but Mrs. Blanchard resisted Mr. Harrell's claim to acceleration. She alleged due and proper tender to Mr. Harrell of all the past due monthly payments and interests; and she claimed that because of such tender, and because of Mr. Harrell's conduct, equity should not declare the entire indebtedness to be due. The Chancery Court entered a decree (a) allowing Mrs. Blanchard to pay all the monthly payments in default, together with interest and costs of the suit, and (b) refusing to give effect to Mr. Harrell's declaration that his entire note be due and payable. From that decree Mr. Harrell has appealed: and the only issue is his right to accelerate the maturity of the entire note.

We affirm the decree of the Chancery Court, because Mr. Harrell is estopped from claiming the acceleration of the monthly payments. The evidence discloses that in February and March, 1948, when there were no monthly payments in default, Mr. Harrell "as the aggressor" urged Mrs. Blanchard to obtain a loan elsewhere and pay off his entire note. He first offered to take a discount of $493.41; and a few days later he offered a discount of $729.98. His letter to her of February 25th shows that he clearly understood that she was to get an FHA loan and use the proceeds thereof to pay his note. After having mentioned the FHA loan, Mr. Harrell closed that letter with this language: "Will be out of town at least until Saturday, but in the meantime I thought that you might be able to go ahead with the preliminaries, and see if this can be worked out to our mutual benefit. You know, without my saying it, that I will be grateful to you for your action along this line."

In his letter to Mrs. Blanchard of March 20, 1948 (while there were no monthly payments in default) Mr. Harrell increased the offered discount to $1,000 if Mrs. Blanchard would obtain a loan and pay him in full.

As previously mentioned, Mr. Harrell understood that Mrs. Blanchard was to get an FHA loan to pay him. Because of Mr. Harrell's insistence, Mrs. Blanchard undertook to get an FHA loan but was confronted with a long series of requirements. In order to meet these, she made property improvements costing in excess of $11,000. Mr. Harrell lived adjacent to Mrs. Blanchard's property and knew all that was occurring; and while the improvements were being made Mr. Harrell admits that he told Mrs. Blanchard in June or July: ". . . just let the payments go and we will settle the whole thing at the same time"—that is, that she need not make the monthly payments until the FHA loan be consummated, and he be then paid from such proceeds.

But after Mrs. Blanchard had made improvements in excess of $11,000, and while she was awaiting the closing of the FHA loan, Mr. Harrell "changed his tune" and sought to foreclose his entire note. On October 1, 1948 Mrs. Blanchard and her attorney made a tender of all defaulted monthly payments, together with interest, but this tender was refused; and on October 8 Mr. Harrell filed the present suit. At the trial it was stipulated "that on several occasions prior to this date and on this date, that the defendant is able, ready and willing to, and does and has tendered all the monthly payments that are in arrears, together with the accrued interest", and together with all court costs.

In the light of the foregoing evidence, and other of like tenor, it is clear that it would be unconscionable for Mr. Harrell to accelerate his entire indebtedness. In Johnson v. Guaranty Bank, 177 Ark. 770, 9 S.W.2d 3, 5, we had occasion to discuss the nature of an acceleration clause; and this language is used:

> The stipulation for accelerating the time of payment of the whole debt may be waived by the mortgagee, especially when it is made to depend upon his option. A court of equity will also relieve against the effect of such provision, where the default of the debtor is the result of accident or mistake, or when it is procured by the fraud or other inequitable conduct of the creditor himself. Pomeroy's Equity Jurisprudence, 4 Ed. vol. 1, Sec. 439.

In 70 A.L.R. 993 there is an Annotation, "Grounds of relief from acceleration clause in mortgage"; and in that Annotation cases from many other jurisdictions are cited to sustain this conclusion: "It is held, apparently without dissent, that a court of equity has the power to relieve a mortgagor from the effect of an operative acceleration clause, when the default of the mortgagor was the result of some unconscionable or inequitable conduct of the mortgagee."

The case at bar comes within the last clause of the quotation from Johnson v. Guaranty Bank, supra—that is, equity will relieve against acceleration when the creditor's conduct has been responsible for the debtor's default. Mr. Harrell persuaded Mrs. Blanchard to seek an FHA loan to pay his note; he knew she was expending large sums in improvements; she offered him the monthly payments, pending the completion of the FHA loan requirements, and he refused them. Under these circumstances, equity should not decree an acceleration of maturity of the entire note.

Affirmed.

The Mortgage   Under the Statute of Frauds (Chapter 12), the mortgage must be in writing. The mortgage document itself contains a number of provisions. The mortgagor will usually make certain warranties to the mortgagee and state the amount and terms of the debt and the mortgagor's duties concerning taxes, insurance, and repairs. The New York statutory form mortgage in Figure 28-2 shows these and other provisions.

PRIORITIES

The General Rule of Recording

Recording is the act of giving public notice of changes in interests in real estate. Recording was created by statute; it did not exist at common law. The typical recording statute calls for a transfer of title or mortgage to be placed in a particular county office, usually

Figure 28–2   A Sample Mortgage Form

Mortgage
(New York Statutory Form)

This mortgage, made the _____ day of _____, 19_____, between _____, [insert residence], the mortgagor, and _____ [insert residence], the mortgagee.

Witnesseth, that to secure the payment of an indebtedness in the sum of _____ dollars, lawful money of the United States, to be paid on the _____day of _____, 19_____, with interest thereon to be computed from _____ at the rate of _____ per centum per annum, and to be paid _____, according to a certain bond or obligation bearing even date herewith, the mortgagor hereby mortgages to the mortgagee [description].

And the mortgagor covenants with the mortgagee as follows:

1. That the mortgagor will pay the indebtedness as hereinbefore provided.
2. That the mortgagor will keep the buildings on the premises insured against loss by fire for the benefit of the mortgagee; that he will assign and deliver the policies to the mortgagee; and that he will reimburse the mortgagee for any premiums paid for insurance made by the mortgagee on the mortgagor's default in so insuring the buildings or in so assigning and delivering the policies.
3. That no building on the premises shall be removed or demolished without the consent of the mortgagee.
4. That the whole of said principal sum and interest shall become due at the option of the mortgagee: after default in the payment of any installment of principal or of interest for _____ days; or after default in the payment of any tax, water rate or assessment for _____ days after notice and demand; or after default after notice and demand either in assigning and delivering the policies insuring the buildings against loss by fire or in reimbursing the mortgagee for premiums paid on such insurance, as hereinbefore provided; or after default upon request in furnishing a statement of the amount due on the mortgage and whether any offsets or defenses exist against the mortgage debt, as hereinafter provided.
5. That the holder of this mortgage, in any action to foreclose it, shall be entitled to the appointment of a receiver.
6. That the mortgagor will pay all taxes, assessments or water rates, and in default thereof, the mortgagee may pay the same.
7. That the mortgagor within _____ days upon request in person or within _____ days upon request by mail will furnish a written statement duly acknowledged of the amount due on this mortgage and whether any offsets or defenses exist against the mortgage debt.
8. That notice and demand or request may be in writing and may be served in person or by mail.
9. That the mortgagor warrants the title to the premises.

In Witness Whereof, this mortgage has been duly executed by the mortgagor.

---

the recorder's office or the register of deeds. We consider recording in more detail in Chapter 33.

A mortgage is valid between the parties whether or not it is recorded, but a mortgagee might lose to a third party—another mortgagee or a good-faith purchaser of the property—unless the mortgage is recorded. The general rule of priority is the same as that for filing of financing statements in secured transactions: first in time (to record), first in right.

Exceptions to First-in-Time Rule

Fixture Filings   The fixture filing provision in Article 9 is one exception to the general rule that the first to record has a prior claim on the property. As noted in Chapter 27, the UCC gives priority to purchase money security interests if certain requirements are met.

Future Advances A bank might make advances to the debtor subsequent to the conveying of the mortgage. If the future advances are obligatory, then the first-in-time rule applies. For example, a bank might agree to accept a mortgage on property and extend a line of credit on which the debtor could draw up to a certain limit. Or, as in the construction industry, a bank might make periodic advances to the contractors as work progresses, backed by a mortgage on the property. A second creditor might actually have loaned the debtor a sum of money, secured by the same property, before the debtor began to draw against the first line of credit. But by searching the mortgage records the second creditor should have been on notice that the first mortgage was intended as security for the entire line of credit.

However, if the future advances are not obligatory, then priority is determined by notice. For example, a bank might take a mortgage as security for an original loan and for any future loans that the bank chooses to make. A later creditor can achieve priority by notifying the bank with the first mortgage that it is making an advance. Suppose Jimmy mortgages his property to a wealthy dowager, Mrs. Calabash, in return for an immediate loan of $10,000 and they agree that the mortgage will serve as security for future loans to be arranged. The mortgage is recorded. A month later, before Mrs. Calabash loans him any more money, Jimmy gives a second mortgage to Louella in return for a loan of $5,000. Louella notifies Mrs. Calabash that she is loaning Jimmy the money. A month later, Mrs. Calabash loans Jimmy another $10,000. Jimmy then defaults, and the property turns out to be worth only $20,000. Whose claims will be honored and in what order? Mrs. Calabash will collect her original $10,000, because it was recited in the mortgage and the mortgage was recorded. Louella will collect her $5,000 next, because she notified the first mortgage holder of the advance. That leaves Mrs. Calabash in third position to collect what she can of her second advance. Mrs. Calabash could have protected herself by refusing the second loan.

In the next case, the court had to determine whether mechanics' lien claimants were entitled to priority over a lender which made future advances.

R.B. THOMPSON JR. LUMBER v. WINDSOR DEVELOPMENT
374 N.W.2d 493
(Minn.App. 1985)

FORSBERG, JUDGE. This is a consolidated appeal from judgments in four mechanics lien actions consolidated for trial.

* * *

In the Prairie East actions, C7-85-46 and C6-85-23, Rothschild [Financial Corporation] mortgages were found to precede the liens [of the claimants]. The lien claimants contend that the court erred in assigning priority based on a finding that the Rothschild loan advances were obligatory rather than optional. We reverse and remand.

Four separate parcels of real estate in two developments are involved in this appeal. All parcels were owned and developed by Windsor Development, which went out of business in October, 1983, and has made no appearance in these actions.

* * *

Rothschild began providing construction financing to Windsor from Windsor's inception in 1974. Windsor provided Rothschild with its plans for the units to be built, and the parties would enter into a mortgage on a specific

(continued on next page)

(continued)

R.B. THOMPSON JR. LUMBER v. WINDSOR DEVELOPMENT
374 N.W.2d 493
(Minn.App. 1985)

piece of property. The amount of the mortgage, however, was not immediately paid out. Rather, as Rothschild's vice-president testified, a "credit line" was established for the amount of all mortgages.

In 1982, Rothschild instituted the "new documentation," which included a loan agreement. The loan agreement provided as follows:

No. 6. Subject to the following, lender agrees to advance the proceeds of the loan for the purpose above stated in accordance with the approved plans, specifications and sworn construction statement submitted to lender by borrower for the subject property. Lender will make advances periodically *at its sole discretion* and only upon receipt of written lender's request for payment form signed by borrower. [Emphasis added].

Although the previous documentation did not include the loan agreement, Rothschild's vice-president testified that the procedure had been the same.

When Windsor submitted a draw request, Rothschild paid out the amount requested, providing it did not exceed the undisbursed balance in that particular mortgage, and providing there was money left in the overall credit line. Rothschild did not require a certain percentage completion of the construction, nor did it require that the contractors were actually paid from the advances. In fact, Rothschild knew that in some cases subcontractors were not being paid from these funds, which were going to pay operating expenses, or interest owed to Rothschild on other mortgages. Rothschild did not make inspections of the properties, nor require lien waivers from materialmen.

The overall line of credit on Windsor projects reached $2–2½ million. Rothschild's vice-president testified that all of the mortgages in this case were fully disbursed.

* * *

The trial court found that the loan advances covered by the Rothschild mortgages were obligatory rather than optional; therefore, the mortgages on the Prairie East lots had priority over the liens to the full amount of the mortgages and not merely the sums advanced up to the attachment of the liens. The trial court explained its finding as follows:

On the face of the loan documents, Rothschild reserved discretion regarding the timing and conditions of advances on the loan but it did not retain the right to refuse to advance the full amount of the loan proceeds. The advances were therefore obligatory and not optional.

The supreme court has indicated:

Whether the payments of a mortgagee are obligatory or optional must be determined from the nature of the entire transaction.

* * *

Rothschild's obligation was dependent upon the balance of the overall line of credit and the terms of its credit line agreement with Windsor. Rothschild's vice-president, however, testified that the company could choose not to advance money on a mortgage if there was no money left in the line of credit. His testimony generally established that Rothschild was more concerned with the line of credit, and Windsor's general financial condition, than with security on individual mortgages. Rothschild did not inspect properties to ensure that construction had progressed sufficiently to provide security adequate to the amounts disbursed on the mortgage, and did not require lien waivers or sworn construction statements.

Thus, we believe Rothschild's advances were not obligatory as to any individual piece of property, but were optional in nature, and had priority over the mechanics liens only for the amounts advanced up to the attachment of the liens. We remand for a determination of these amounts.

TERMINATION OF MORTGAGE

The mortgagor's liability can terminate in three ways: through *payment, assumption (with a novation)*, and *foreclosure*.

Payment

Unless he lives in the home for twenty-five or thirty years, the mortgagor usually pays off the mortgage when the property is sold. Occasionally mortgages are paid off in order to refinance. If the mortgage was taken out at a time of high interest rates and rates later drop, the homeowner might want to obtain a new mortgage at the lower rates. In many mortgages, however, this entails extra closing costs and penalties for prepaying the original mortgage. Whatever the reason, when a mortgage is paid off, the discharge should be recorded.

Assumption

The property can be sold without paying off the mortgage if the mortgage is assumed by the new buyer, who agrees to pay the seller's (the original mortgagor's) debt. This is a *novation* (p. 315) if, in approving the *assumption*, the bank releases the old mortgagor and substitutes the buyer as the new debtor.

The buyer need not assume the mortgage. If the buyer purchases the property without agreeing to be personally liable, this is a sale "subject to" the mortgage (see Figure 28-3). In the event of the seller's subsequent default, the bank can foreclose the mortgage and sell the property which the buyer has purchased, but the buyer is not liable for the deficiency.

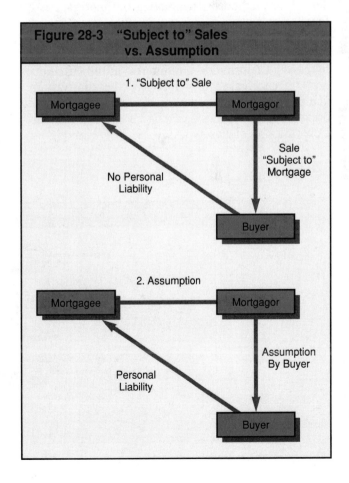

Figure 28-3 "Subject to" Sales vs. Assumption

1. "Subject to" Sale

Mortgagee — Mortgagor

No Personal Liability

Sale "Subject to" Mortgage

Buyer

2. Assumption

Mortgagee — Mortgagor

Personal Liability

Assumption By Buyer

Buyer

In recent years, assumptions of mortgages have been controversial. With rising interest rates, buyers have preferred to assume mortgages with existing low interest rates rather than obtain new mortgages at substantially higher rates. Of course, banks and other lending institutions take a dim view of assumptions when interest rates are rising, so they often include in the mortgage a **due-on-sale** clause, by which the entire principal and interest become due when the property is sold, thus forcing the purchaser to obtain financing at the higher rates. Although many state courts at one time refused to enforce the due-on-sale clause, Congress reversed this trend when it enacted the Garn-St. Germain Depository Institutions Act in 1982, which preempts state laws and upholds the validity of due-on-sale clauses.

Foreclosure

The third method of terminating the mortgage is by foreclosure when a mortgagor defaults. Even after default, the mortgagor has the right to exercise his equity of redemption, that is, to redeem the property by paying the principal and interest in full. If he does not, the mortgagee may foreclose the equity of redemption. Although strict foreclosure (p. 613) is used occasionally, in most cases the mortgagee forecloses by one of two types of sale (see Figure 28-4).

The first type is **judicial sale.** The mortgagee seeks a court order authorizing the sale to be conducted by a public official, usually the sheriff. The mortgagor is entitled to be notified of the proceeding and to a hearing. The second type of sale is that conducted under a **power-of-sale** clause, which many lenders insist be contained in the mortgage. This clause permits the mortgagee to sell the property at public auction without first going to court—although by custom or law the sale must be advertised, and typically a sheriff or other public official conducts the public sale or auction.

Once the property has been sold, it is deeded to the purchaser. In about half the states, the mortgagor still has the right to redeem the property by paying up within six months or a year—the **statutory redemption** period. Thereafter, the mortgagor has no further right to redeem.

If the sale proceeds exceed the debt, the mortgagor is entitled to the excess unless he has given second and third mortgages, in which case the junior mortgagees are entitled to recover their claims before the mortgagor. If the proceeds are less than the debt, the mortgagee is entitled to recover the deficiency from the mortgagor. However, some states have statutorily abolished deficiency judgments. Furthermore, a creditor's voluntary waiver of rights to the deficiency is often a good strategy when the sale is suspect—as the following case shows.

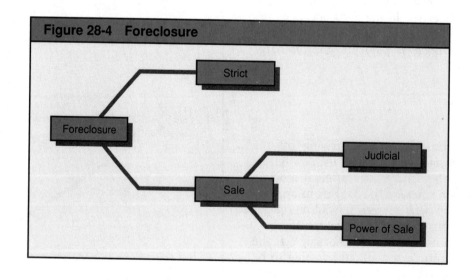

Figure 28-4   Foreclosure

GARLAND v. HILL
277 Md. 710, 357 A.2d
374 (1976)

SINGLEY, JUDGE. This litigation commenced when Thomas A. Garland, trustee, the mortgagor, filed exceptions in the Circuit Court for Charles County to the ratification of a mortgage foreclosure sale. From an order of that court (Mitchell, J.) ratifying the sale, Mr. Garland appealed to the Court of Special Appeals, which affirmed the order in *Garland v. Hill*, 28 Md.App. 622, 346 A.2d 711 (1975). We granted certiorari limited to the question, "whether an inadequate purchase price can be made adequate by the mortgagee's waiver of his right to claim a deficiency decree against the mortgagor."

On 1 November 1972, Mr. Garland, as trustee, had purchased a 359.43 acre farm in Charles County from Francis W. Hill for $359,430.00 or $1,000.00 per acre. Of the total purchase price, $72,000.00 was paid in cash; the balance was secured by a purchase money mortgage in the amount of $287,430.00. By the terms of the mortgage, the principal was to be repaid in 10 annual installments of $28,743.00, plus interest on the unpaid principal balance at the rate of 7%. When a default occurred, Mr. Hill's assignee for purposes of foreclosure instituted foreclosure proceedings on 6 November 1974, in the Circuit Court for Charles County, and the property was sold at auction at the courthouse door on 15 November.

At the time of the sale, the unpaid balance of the mortgage debt was $286,687.00, and the unpaid interest amounted to $22,000.00. There was only one bid in the amount of $25,000.00, made by Mr. Hill, the mortgagee, and the property was sold to him for that amount.

The sale was reported to the court, which entered an order nisi giving notice that the sale would be ratified unless contrary cause be shown by 24 December 1974, provided that the order be published for three successive calendar weeks commencing 9 December.

Mr. Garland excepted to the ratification of the sale, on the ground, among others, that the purchase price was "shockingly inadequate." The assignee answered, alleging that he intended, in behalf of Mr. Hill, to waive any rights to a deficiency decree against Mr. Garland, with the consequence that if the sale price and the waiver were both taken into account, the sale price would be equivalent to more than $300,000.00

When the exceptions came on for hearing, Mr. Garland testified that he had purchased the farm for $1,000.00 an acre in 1972, which he regarded as a fair and reasonable price at that time, and that in his opinion, the property had appreciated to a value of $1,200.00 per acre at the time of foreclosure.

The trial court entered a final order ratifying the sale in which it concluded that:

> The purchase price at auction was not shockingly inadequate, in view of the fact that Francis W. Hill, Mortgagee, through his counsel, M. Wayne Munday, also Assignee for the purpose of foreclosure, has waived all rights to a deficiency decree or judgment.

(continued on next page)

(continued)

GARLAND v. HILL
277 Md. 710, 357 A.2d 374 (1976)

The rule of our cases is that the mere inadequacy of the purchase price at a mortgage foreclosure sale is not enough to prevent the ratification of the sale, unless it is so grossly inadequate as to shock the conscience of the court.

If this had been a sale of the property to anyone other than the mortgagee, the sale of a farm worth $350,000.00 for $25,000.00 might well have been successfully challenged, particularly if $25,000.00 had been the only bid. Here, however, the sale was to Mr. Hill, the holder of the mortgage. Under our practice, Mr. Hill would have been entitled to an in personam decree against Mr. Garland for the difference between the sale price of $25,000.00 and the unpaid balance of the mortgage debt, $286,687.00, plus unpaid interest of $22,000.00 and the expenses of sale, in an unknown amount or $283,687.00. When Mr. Hill waived his right to the deficiency decree to which he was entitled, the result was exactly that which would have obtained had the property sold for $308,000.00. At argument before us, and before the Court of Special Appeals, counsel for Mr. Garland conceded that a bid by Mr. Hill in this amount could not have been the subject of a successful challenge.

In short, we agree with the conclusion of the Court of Special Appeals and the trial court that under the circumstances of this case, what was in effect a bid of more than $300,000.00 for the property does not shock the conscience of the court.

* * *

Judgment affirmed, costs to be paid by appellant.

OTHER METHODS OF USING REAL ESTATE AS SECURITY

Deed of Trust

The **deed of trust** is a device for securing a debt with real property; unlike the mortgage, it requires three parties. The borrower conveys the land to a third party, the trustee, to hold in trust for the lender. A deed of trust simplifies the foreclosure process by containing a provision empowering the trustee to sell the land on default. The deed of trust has certain advantages over a mortgage. It permits many lenders (bondholders of a corporation) securely to advance sums to a corporation, since foreclosure can be conducted for the benefit of all by the trustee; each different bondholder need not try to foreclose on her own mortgage. A person with a note secured by a deed of trust can easily and inexpensively sell the note; there is no need to make and record an assignment, as when the note is secured instead by a mortgage. Finally, the noteholder or bondholder may keep her ownership private, which she cannot be certain of doing if the note is secured by a mortgage.

But in many states the deed of trust has certain disadvantages as well. For example, when the debt has been fully paid, the trustee will not release the deed of trust until he sees that all notes secured by it have been marked canceled. Should the borrower have misplaced the canceled notes, he will need to procure a surety-bond to protect the trustee in case of a mistake. This can be an expensive procedure. Moreover, in some states the trustee may not sell the property on behalf of all noteholders unless the deed specifically grants the power. Without the power, the arrangements for sale are cumbersome, time-consuming, and expensive.

Installment or Land Contracts

Under the installment or **land contract,** the purchaser takes possession and agrees to pay the seller over a period of years. Until he makes the final payment, title belongs to the seller. The contract will specify the type of deed to be conveyed at closing, the terms of payment, the buyer's duty to pay taxes and insure the premises, and the seller's right to accelerate on default. The buyer's particular concern in this type of sale is whether the seller in fact has title. We consider title in Chapter 33 in the following unit on property. For now suffice it to say that the buyer can protect himself by requiring proof of title and title insurance when the contract is signed. Moreover, the buyer should record the installment contract to protect himself against the seller's attempt to convey title to an innocent third-party purchaser while the contract is in effect.

NONCONSENSUAL LIENS

The security arrangements discussed so far—security interests, suretyship, mortgages—are all obtained by the creditor with the debtor's consent. A creditor may obtain certain liens without the debtor's consent.

Court-Decreed Liens

Some nonconsensual liens are issued by courts; these include *attachment liens* and *judgment liens.*

Attachment Lien   An **attachment lien** is ordered against a person's property—real or personal—to prevent him from disposing of it during a lawsuit. To obtain an attachment lien, the plaintiff must show that the defendant likely will dispose of or hide his property; and if the court agrees with him, the plaintiff must post a bond and the court will issue a writ of attachment to the sheriff, directing her to seize the property. Attachments of real property should be recorded. Should the plaintiff win his suit, the court issues a writ of execution, directing the sheriff to sell the property to satisfy the judgment.

Judgment Lien   A **judgment lien** may be issued when a plaintiff wins a judgment in court if an attachment lien has not already been issued. Like the attachment lien, it provides a method by which the defendant's property may be seized and sold.

Mechanic's Lien

The most common nonconsensual lien on real estate is the **mechanic's lien.** A mechanic's lien can be obtained by one who furnishes labor, services, or materials to improve real estate. Thus an automobile mechanic could not obtain a mechanic's lien on a customer's house to secure payment of work he did on her car. (The lien to which the automobile mechanic is entitled is a "possessory lien" or "artisan's lien," considered on p. 627.) To qualify for a mechanic's lien, the claimant must do work that permanently improves the real estate. Building removable shelves in a store for a tenant does not entitle the builder to a lien.

A particularly difficult problem crops up when the owner has paid the contractor, who in turn fails to pay his subcontractors. In many states, the subcontractors can file a lien on the owner's property, thus forcing the owner to pay them (see Figure 28-5). To protect themselves, owners can demand a sworn statement from general contractors listing the subcontractors used on the job and from them owners can obtain a waiver of lien rights before paying the general contractor.

Procedure for Obtaining   Anyone claiming a lien against real estate must record a **lien statement** stating the amount due and the nature of the improvement. The lienor has a specified period of time (for

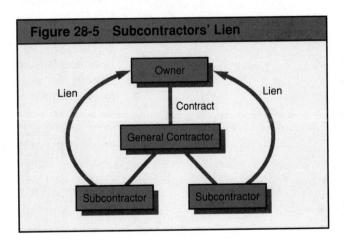

Figure 28-5   Subcontractors' Lien

instance, ninety days) to file from the time the work is finished. Recording as such does not give the lienor an automatic right to the property if the debt remains unpaid. All states specify a limited period of time, usually one year, within which the claimant must file suit to enforce the lien. Only if the court decides the lien is valid may the property be sold to satisfy the debt.

Difficult questions arise when a lien is filed against a landlord's property interests as a result of improvements and services provided to a tenant—as illustrated by the following case.

BELL v. TOLLEFSEN
782 P.2d 934 (Okla. 1989)

KAUGER, JUSTICE.
Executive Center Co. and HMS Computer Systems, Inc. negotiated a lease which provided:

". . . Tenant's suite shall be constructed per floorplan drawings and finish schedule as approved by both Tenant and Landlord at Landlord's sole cost up to a total of $16.00 per usable square foot of leased area. Tenant and Land- (sic) Landlord shall mutually agree to any excess costs and method of payment thereof prior to commencement of construction of Tenant's suite. . . ."

The question presented is whether this lease created an agency relationship subjecting the landlord's property to a mechanic's and materialmen's lien for improvements and services furnished to the tenant under the terms of a contract between the tenant and an interior decorator. We find that unless an agency relationship existed, the landlord's property interest is not subject to a mechanic's and materialman's lien for improvements and services provided to a tenant under the contract between the tenant and an interior decorator. We also find that there were material questions of fact concerning whether previous construction costs had exhausted the amount which the landlord had contracted to pay for renovation of the tenant's space, and whether there had been an agreement between the tenant and the landlord that the landlord would pay in excess of $16.00 per square foot to finish the tenant's suite. Therefore, the trial court erred in entering summary judgment.

On September 1, 1985, Chuck Tollefsen (Tollefsen/tenant), president of HMS Computer Systems, Inc. (HMS Computer), leased office space in a building owned by a partnership, Executive Center Company (Executive Center/landlord). On July 30, 1985, Tollefsen contracted with the appellee, Roseanne Bell (Bell/decorator), to provide interior decorating and other services on the leased property. On January 6, 1986, after Tollefsen had failed to pay Bell for her services, she filed a mechanic's and materialman's lien pursuant to 42 O.S.1981 § 141 in the amount of $7,886.62. The lien statement described Clyde B. Self (Self), a general partner of Executive Center, as the owner of the property.

*   *   *

Bell argues that she is entitled to enforce the mechanic's lien for labor and services rendered to Tollefsen against Executive Center's fee interest because the lease expressly authorized the improvements and obligated the landlord to reimburse the tenant for such costs. Self argues that the terms of the lease were insufficient to make Tollefsen an agent of Executive Center. Bell acknowledges that Self was not a party to the contract for improvements to the leased premises. Therefore, in order to prevail, she must establish that Tollefsen acted as Self's agent when the contract was entered.

★   ★   ★

There is a split of authority concerning whether a landlord's contribution towards improvements by a tenant is sufficient to constitute an agency relationship thus impressing a mechanic's or materialman's lien against the landlord's interest, or whether such provisions merely justify a lien against the tenant's interest. Although this narrow issue is one of first impression in Oklahoma, our decision in *Carter v. Simpson,* 302 P.2d 980, 982 (Okla.1956), aligned Oklahoma with those jurisdictions which hold that a landlord/lessor's interest in real property is not subject to a mechanic's lien claim merely because the landlord agrees to contribute to improvements to the leasehold estate absent other evidence of an agency relationship.

. . . Tollefsen's contract with Executive Center providing for a $16.00 per square foot improvement allowance will not support a lien against the landlord's interest unless: 1) either the landlord failed to spend the $16.00 per square foot allowance prior to these improvements or 2) the landlord and tenant agreed that the landlord would pay the excess costs. [The summary judgment is reversed and the case remanded to determine these fact questions.]

Priority   A mechanic's lien represents a special risk to the purchaser of real estate or to lenders who wish to take a mortgage. In most states, the mechanic's lien is given priority not from the date when the lien is recorded but from an earlier date—either the date the contractor was hired or the date construction began (see Figure 28-6). Thus a purchaser or lender might lose priority to a creditor with a mechanic's lien who filed after the sale or mortgage. A practical solution to this problem is to hold back part of the funds (purchase price or loan) or place them in escrow until the period for recording liens has expired. As discussed in the *R.B. Thompson* case, p. 619, a lender who is obligated to make future advances has priority over intervening liens.

Possessory Lien

The most common nonconsensual lien on *personal* property is the **possessory lien.** This is the right to continue to keep the goods on which work has been performed or for which materials have been supplied until the owner pays for the labor or materials. The possessory lien arises both under common law and under a variety of statutes. Because it is nonconsensual, the possessory lien is not covered by Article 9 of the UCC, which is restricted to consensual security

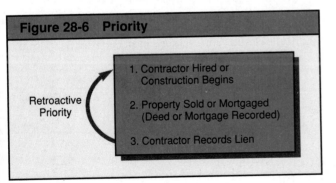

Figure 28-6   Priority

Retroactive Priority

1. Contractor Hired or Construction Begins
2. Property Sold or Mortgaged (Deed or Mortgage Recorded)
3. Contractor Records Lien

interests. Nor is it governed by the law of mechanic's liens, which are nonpossessory and relate only to work done to improve real property.

The common law rule is that anyone who, under an express or implied contract, adds value to another's chattel by labor, skill, or materials has a possessory lien for the value of his services. Moreover, the lienholder may keep the chattel until her services are paid.

Tax Lien

An important modern statutory lien is the **federal tax lien.** Once the government assesses a tax, the amount due constitutes a lien on the owner's property, whether real or personal. Until it is filed in the appropriate state office, others take priority, including purchasers, mechanics' lienors, judgment lien creditors, and holders of security interests. But once filed, the tax lien takes priority over all subsequently arising liens. Federal law exempts some property from the tax lien; for example, unemployment benefits, books and tools of a trade, workers' compensation, judgments for support of minor children, minimum amounts of wages and salary, personal effects, furniture, fuel, and provisions are exempt.

CHAPTER SUMMARY

A mortgage is a means of securing a debt with real estate. The mortgagor or borrower gives the mortgage. The lender is the mortgagee, who holds the mortgage. On default, the mortgagee may foreclose the mortgage, converting the security interest into title. In many states, the mortgagor has a statutory right of redemption after foreclosure.

Various statutes regulate the mortgage business, including the Truth in Lending Act, the Equal Credit Opportunity Act, the Real Estate Settlement Procedures Act, and the Home Mortgage Disclosure Act, which together prescribe a code of fair practices and require various disclosures to be made before the mortgage is created.

The mortgagor signs both a note and the mortgage at the closing. Without the note, the mortgage would secure nothing. Most notes and mortgages contain an acceleration clause, which calls for the entire principal and interest to be due, at the mortgagee's option, if the debtor defaults on any payment.

In most states, mortgages must be recorded for the mortgagee to be entitled to priority over third parties who might also claim an interest in the land. The general rule is "first in time, first in right," although there are exceptions for fixture filings and nonobligatory future advances. Mortgages are terminated by repayment, novation, or foreclosure, either through judicial sale or under a power-of-sale clause.

Real estate may also be used as security under a deed of trust, which permits a trustee to sell the land automatically on default.

Nonconsensual liens are security interests created by law. These include court-decreed liens, such as attachment liens and judgment liens. Other liens are mechanic's liens (for labor, services, or materials furnished in connection with someone's real property), possessory liens (for artisans working with someone else's personal property), and tax liens.

KEY TERMS

Acceleration clause	p. 614	Mechanic's lien	p. 625
Attachment lien	p. 625	Mortgage	p. 611
Deed of trust	p. 624	Mortgagee	p. 611
Due-on-sale	p. 622	Mortgage bonds	p. 612
Equity of redemption	p. 612	Mortgagor	p. 611
Federal tax lien	p. 628	Possessory lien	p. 627
Foreclosure	p. 613	Power-of-sale	p. 622
Foreclosure by sale	p. 613	Recording	p. 617
Judgment lien	p. 625	Redlining	p. 613
Judicial sale	p. 622	Statutory redemption	p. 622
Land contract	p. 625	Strict foreclosure	p. 613
Lien statement	p. 625		

SELF-TEST QUESTIONS

1. The person or institution holding a mortgage is called:
   (a) the mortgagor
   (b) the mortgagee
   (c) the debtor
   (d) none of the above
2. Mortgages are regulated by:
   (a) the Truth in Lending Act
   (b) the Equal Credit Opportunity Act
   (c) the Real Estate Settlement Procedures Act
   (d) all of the above
3. At the closing, a mortgagor signs:
   (a) only a mortgage
   (b) only a note
   (c) either a note or the mortgage
   (d) both a note and the mortgage
4. Mortgages are terminated by:
   (a) repayment
   (b) novation
   (c) foreclosure
   (d) any of the above

5. A lien ordered against a person's property to prevent disposal of that property during a lawsuit is called:
   (a) a judgment lien
   (b) an attachment lien
   (c) a possessory lien
   (d) none of the above

DEMONSTRATION PROBLEM

Bonnie holds an unsecured $10,000 note. Clyde holds a mortgage without a note on a $100,000 farm. Which is worth more—the note or the mortgage? Why?

PROBLEMS

1. Homer borrowed $75,000 from Judith. He gave Judith a note for $75,000 and a mortgage on his farm. Judith did not record the mortgage. After Homer defaulted on his payments, Judith began foreclosure proceedings. Homer argued that the mortgage was invalid because of Judith's failure to record. Judith's counter-argument is that, because a mortgage is not an interest in real estate, recording is not necessary. Who is correct? Why?

2. Assume in problem 1 that the documents did not contain an acceleration clause and that Homer missed three consecutive payments. Could Judith foreclose? Explain.

3. Sandy is negotiating the purchase of Betty's house, which has been mortgaged to Last Bank. The mortgage is not to be paid off upon the sale of the house to Sandy. If Sandy has a choice, should she assume the mortgage or take the property subject to the mortgage? Why?

4. Rupert, an automobile mechanic, does carpentry work on weekends. He builds a detached garage for Clyde for $10,000. While he is constructing the garage, he agrees to tune up Clyde's car for an additional $100. When the work is completed, Clyde fails to pay him the $10,100, and Rupert claims a mechanic's lien on the garage and car. What problems, if any, might Rupert encounter in enforcing his lien? Why?

5. In problem 4, assume that Clyde had borrowed $50,000 from First Bank and had given the bank a mortgage on the property two weeks after Rupert commenced work on the garage, but several weeks before he filed the lien. Assuming that the bank immediately recorded its mortgage and that Rupert's lien is valid, does the mortgage take priority over the lien? Why?

6. Jewel borrowed $100,000 from Second Bank and gave the bank a mortgage on her factory. The mortgage provided that the entire amount of the loan would be due twenty days after default. While Jewel was out of town on a business trip, her secretary made the monthly payment but he made an error in calculating interest. Jewel did not learn of the underpayment until twenty-one days after the payment was due and immediately tendered the correct amount. Can the bank foreclose on the factory? Why?

7. In problem 6, assuming it can foreclose, must the bank go to court during the foreclosure process? What is the last event in the process? Explain.

ANSWERS TO SELF-TEST QUESTIONS

1. (b)   2. (d)   3. (d)   4. (d)   5. (b)

SUGGESTED ANSWER TO DEMONSTRATION PROBLEM

The note is worth more. Without a note, the mortgage is an empty document.

CHAPTER 29

Bankruptcy

Bankruptcy law governs the rights of creditors and insolvent debtors who cannot pay their debts. In broadest terms, bankruptcy deals with the seizure of the debtor's assets and their distribution to the debtor's various creditors. The term derives from the Renaissance custom of Italian traders, who did their trading from benches in town marketplaces. Creditors literally "broke the bench" of a merchant who failed to pay his debts. The term *banca rotta* (broken bench) thus came to apply to business failures.

In the Victorian era, many people in both England and the United States viewed someone who became bankrupt as a wicked person. In part this attitude was prompted by the law itself, which to a greater degree in England and to a lesser degree in the United States treated the insolvent debtor as a sort of felon. Until the second half of the nineteenth century, British insolvents could be imprisoned; jail for insolvent debtors was abolished earlier in the United States. And the entire administration of bankruptcy law favored the creditor, who could with a mere filing throw the financial affairs of the alleged insolvent into complete disarray.

Today a more enlightened attitude prevails. Bankruptcy is understood as an aspect of financing, a system that permits creditors to receive an equitable distribution of the bankrupt's assets and promises new hope to debtors facing impossible financial burdens. Without such a law, we may reasonably suppose that the level of economic activity would be far less than it is, for few would be willing to risk being personally burdened forever by crushing debt.

ALTERNATIVES TO BANKRUPTCY

Assignment for Benefit of Creditors

Under a common law **assignment for the benefit of creditors,** the debtor transfers some or all of his assets to a trustee—usually someone appointed by the adjustment bureau of a local credit managers' association—who sells the assets and apportions the proceeds in some agreed manner, usually pro rata, to the creditors. Of course, not every creditor need agree with such a distribution. Strictly speaking, the common law assignment does not discharge the balance of the debt. Many state statutes attempt to address this problem either by prohibiting creditors who accept a partial payment of debt under an assignment from claiming the balance, or by permitting debtors to demand a release from creditors who accept partial payment.

Composition

A **composition** is simply an agreement by creditors to accept less than the full amount of the debt and to discharge the debtor from further liability. As a contract, composition requires consideration; the mutual agreement among creditors to accept a pro rata share of the proceeds is held to be sufficient consideration to support the discharge. The essential difference between assignment and composition lies in the creditors' agreement: an assignment implies no agreement among the creditors, whereas a composition does. Not all creditors of the particular debtor need agree to the composition for it to be valid. A creditor who does not agree to the composition remains free to attempt to collect the full sum owed; in particular, a creditor not inclined to compose the debt could attach the debtor's assets while other creditors were bargaining over the details of the composition agreement.

Receivership

A creditor may petition the court to appoint a receiver; this is a long-established procedure in equity whereby the receiver takes over the debtor's property under instructions from the court. The receiver may liquidate the property, continue to operate the business, or preserve the assets without operating the business until the court finally determines how to dispose of the debtor's property.

The difficulty with most of the alternatives to bankruptcy lies in their voluntary character: A creditor who refuses to go along with an agreement to discharge the debtor can usually manage to thwart the debtor and his fellow creditors. The only final protection, therefore, is to be found in the bankruptcy law.

THE BANKRUPTCY REFORM ACT

History of the Bankruptcy System

Constitutional Basis   The Constitution prohibits the states from impairing the "obligation of a contract." This means that no state can directly provide a means for discharging a debtor unless the debt has been entirely paid. But the Constitution in Article I, Paragraph 8, does give the federal government such a power by providing that Congress may enact a uniform bankruptcy law.

Bankruptcy Statutes   Congress passed bankruptcy laws in 1800, 1841, and 1867. These lasted only a few years each. In 1898, Congress enacted the Bankruptcy Act, which together with the Chandler Act amendments in 1938, lasted until 1978. In 1978, Congress passed the Bankruptcy Reform Act, superseding all the prior laws. This law is the subject of our chapter.

Bankruptcy Filings   At the beginning of the century, bankruptcies averaged fewer than 20,000 per year. Even in 1935, at the height of the Great Depression, bankruptcy filings in federal court climbed only to 69,000. At the end of World War II in 1945 they stood at 13,000. From 1950 on, the statistics show a steep increase. During the decade before the Bankruptcy Reform Act was passed, bankruptcy filings in court averaged 181,000 a year—reaching a high of 254,000 in 1975. In 1978, the year the act was passed, they totaled 203,000. Thereafter the numbers soared, averaging over 450,000 filings per year in the 1980s. Many commentators have suggested that the upsurge was at least partly due to the Bankruptcy Reform Act, which expanded the list and dollar value of assets—equity in homes and cars, personal property such as clothing, jewelry, and tools of one's trade—that the consumer debtor may retain after declaring bankruptcy, and which made it easier for a bankrupt business to keep its own management in charge while the company is being reorganized.

Bankruptcy Courts and Judges

Each federal judicial district has a U.S. Bankruptcy Court, whose judges are appointed by U.S. Courts of Appeal. Unless both sides agree otherwise, bankruptcy judges are to hear only bankruptcy matters (called "core proceedings").

Overview of Key Provisions

The Bankruptcy Reform Act provided for five different types of bankruptcy proceedings. Each is covered by its own chapter in the act and is usually referred to by its chapter number (see Figure 29-1).

- *Liquidation* (Chapter 7)
- *Adjustment of debts of a municipality* (Chapter 9)
- *Reorganization* (Chapter 11)
- *Adjustment of debts of a family farmer with regular annual income* (Chapter 12)
- *Adjustment of debts of an individual with regular income* (Chapter 13)

A **liquidation** is a "straight" bankruptcy proceeding. It entails selling the debtor's nonexempt assets for cash and distributing the cash to the creditors, thereby discharging the insolvent person or business from any further liability for the debt. With New York City and other municipalities on the verge of bankruptcy during the 1970s, serious questions arose over the capacity of the old bankruptcy law to deal with municipal insolvency. Chapter 9 of the Bankruptcy Reform Act provides a mechanism to adjust the debts of a municipality. (The law does not suppose that a town, city, or county will go out of existence in the wake of insolvency.) **Reorganization** is the means by which a financially troubled company can continue to operate while its financial affairs are put on a sounder basis. A business might liquidate following reorganization, but will probably take on new life after negotiations with creditors on how the old debt is to be paid off. A company may voluntarily decide to seek Chapter 11 protection in court, or it may be forced involuntarily into a Chapter 11 proceeding. Like the business, an individual may wish to negotiate a limit to his indebtedness. Chapter 13 permits an individual with regular income to establish a repayment plan, usually either a composition (see p. 631) or an extension (a stretch-out of the time for paying the entire debt). Many family farmers cannot qualify for reorganization under Chapter 13 because of the low debt ceiling (see p. 645) and, under Chapter 11, the proceeding is often complicated and expensive. As a result, Congress created Chapter 12, which applies only to farmers whose total debts do not exceed $1,500,000.

The Bankruptcy Reform Act includes three chapters that set forth the procedures to be applied to the various proceedings. Chapter 1, "General Provisions," establishes who is eligible for relief under the act. Chapter 3, "Case Administration," spells out the powers of the various officials involved in the bankruptcy proceedings and establishes the methods for instituting bankruptcy cases. Chapter 5, "Creditors, the Debtor, and the Estate," deals with the debtor's "estate"—his assets. It lays down ground-rules for determining which property is to be included in the estate, sets out the powers of the bankruptcy trustee to "avoid" (invalidate) transactions by which the debtor sought to remove property from the estate, orders the distribution of property to creditors, and sets forth the duties and benefits that accrue the debtor under the act.

To illustrate how these procedural chapters (especially Chapters 3 and 5) apply, we focus on the most common proceeding: liquidation (Chapter 7). Most of the principles of bankruptcy law discussed in connection with liquidation apply to the other types of proceedings as well. However, some principles vary, and we conclude the chapter by noting special features

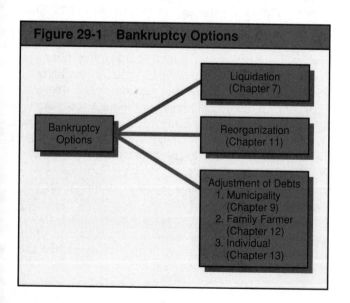

Figure 29-1   Bankruptcy Options

Bankruptcy Options

- Liquidation (Chapter 7)
- Reorganization (Chapter 11)
- Adjustment of Debts
  1. Municipality (Chapter 9)
  2. Family Farmer (Chapter 12)
  3. Individual (Chapter 13)

of two other important proceedings—Chapters 13 and 11.

LIQUIDATION

Recall that the purpose of liquidation is to convert the debtor's assets—except those exempt under the law—into cash for distribution to the creditors and thereafter to discharge the debtor from further liability. With certain exceptions any person may voluntarily file a petition to liquidate under Chapter 7. A person is defined as any individual, partnership, or corporation. The exceptions are for railroads and insurance companies, banks, savings and loan associations, credit unions, and the like.

Case Administration

For a Chapter 7 liquidation proceeding, as for bankruptcy proceedings in general, the various aspects of case administration are covered by Chapter 3. These include the rules governing commencement of the proceedings, the effect of the petition in bankruptcy, the first meeting of the creditors, and the duties and powers of trustees.

Commencement: Voluntary and Involuntary Petition   The persons noted above may file a voluntary petition in bankruptcy. To prevent "substantial abuse" of the law, the court may prohibit an individual having primarily consumer debts from using Chapter 7, as the following case illustrates.

In re BRYANT
47 B.R. 21 (W.D. No. Car. 1984)

MARVIN R. WOOTEN, Bankruptcy Judge.
　The Debtor, Mitchell W. Bryant, on October 24, 1984 filed a Voluntary Petition with this Court under Chapter 7 of the Bankruptcy Code.

*　　*　　*

　The record discloses that the Debtor and his wife own a home located in Mathews, North Carolina with an estimated fair market value of $52,500.00. The property is encumbered by the secured claims of Cameron-Brown Company and AVCO. There is some $8,000.00 of equity in the property, which would be totally offset by the Debtor and his wife's exemptions under N.C. law. The Debtor is employed by Mathews Home Furnishings, Inc; a closely-held business which is owned by his wife. His testimony indicates his family's annual income exceeds $38,000.00; his petition disclosed a monthly income of $3,420.00 or $41,400.00 annually.
　Under § 707(b) of the Code, Bankruptcy Judges are authorized to dismiss, sua sponte, cases filed by individual debtors having "primarily consumer debts", where the Court finds that to allow the case to proceed would be a "substantial abuse" of the provisions of Chapter 7. The Bankruptcy Amendments and Federal Judgeship Act (of which 707(b) is a part) failed to define the phrases "primarily consumer debts" and "substantial abuse". The section is of such recent vintage that no published cases have construed the terms.
　The Debtor has not suggested that the words "substantial abuse" should be given anything other than their ordinary, plain meaning and the court so construes them. By this definition, it is readily apparent that this case is one in which allowing the Debtor relief would constitute a substantial abuse of Chapter 7.

(continued on next page)

(continued)

In re BRYANT
47 B.R. 21 (W.D. No.
Car. 1984)

It was the philosophy of the constitutional authors and the intent of Congress in establishing the Bankruptcy Code, that this relief was to provide a fresh start for financially troubled persons. Bankruptcy was not intended to provide a means for the unscrupulous to avoid their creditors, but was designed to provide a second chance for persons who for reasons of calamity, sickness, unemployment, and the like were unable to meet their obligations. The case before the Court is not such a case.

First, this case was brought, not because of the Debtor's unemployment or an inability to pay on his part, but because he simply desired to shuck a couple of his debts. His testimony was that he had previously guaranteed a number of business debts and he filed this bankruptcy in order to "get rid" of the same. The Debtor claims he intended to pay his non-business-related debts; however, he seeks relief which would discharge *both* these guaranteed debts *and* his personal obligations.

Secondly, the Court finds on the part of the Debtor an utter disregard of his duties under the § 522 of the Code to truthfully list all of his obligations, his monthly expenses, and to disclose his general financial position to the Court.

★   ★   ★

Third, it is the opinion of the court that the Debtor's Statement of Monthly Expenses filed with his petition was done in bad faith and that these amounts were greatly overstated with the intention of misrepresenting his financial picture. For example, he avers that his average monthly expenses for feeding himself, his wife, and his two children exceeds $500.00, (excluding dining out for which he allocates another $100.00). The Debtor submits that maintaining his wife's 1984 Buick and his personal use of a "company" car costs better than $250.00 per month, discounting car payments ($381.00), rent ($50.00) and auto insurance ($50.00). Likewise, the Debtor informs the Court that while his family has no recurrent medical expenses (apart from one set of braces), his monthly medical bills exceed $200.00. Even his most diminutive bills take on gargantuan proportions—he claims to spend $100.00 per month for laundry costs although the family owns a washing machine.

★   ★   ★

In like measure, the Debtor claims expenses of $100.00 per month for dining out and for going to movies. He claims another $65.00 per month for cable television. Even if these amounts are accurate, the Court has serious questions about their appropriateness for a Debtor in Chapter 7. While Congress intended to give the Debtors relief in such cases, it was not the design of the Bankruptcy laws to allow the Debtor to lead the life of Riley while his creditors suffer on his behalf.

Therefore, in light of the Debtor's purpose in filing this petition; his fraudulent and misleading omissions in his petition; his attempts to pad his expenses statement in order to misrepresent his financial position; and the relatively exorbitant lifestyle which he seeks to maintain while taking shelter from his creditors under the Bankruptcy provisions, the Court concludes that to allow this petition would be a substantial abuse of the provisions of Chapter 7. The Bankruptcy Courts have their foundations in the Courts of Equity, and here the clean hands maxim applies: To receive equity, one must do equity. This the Debtor has not done.

In considering dismissal under 707(b) the Court must, in addition to finding "substantial abuse" determine that the Debtor's obligations were also "primarily consumer debts". As with substantial abuse, what constitutes "primarily consumer debts" was not defined in the Code and has yet to be determined by case law.

* * *

This certainly is a case involving primarily consumer debts. The Court has found the Debtor's consumer obligations to include his home mortgages and to total $46,844.97. (To this should be added his unlisted credit card debts which are of uncertain amount.) On the other hand, his nonconsumer debts total only $40,248.00. The Debtor's consumer debts outweigh his nonconsumer debts by more than seven thousand dollars and dispel the Debtor's notion that these are by amount nonconsumer debts. Similarly, with regard to number, at least twelve of the Debtor's fifteen or sixteen obligations are consumer debts, and in this respect, also, his case is one involving primarily consumer debts. [Case dismissed.]

Involuntary bankruptcy is also possible. To put anyone into bankruptcy involuntarily, the petitioning creditors must meet three conditions: (1) they must have claims for unsecured debt amounting to at least $5,000; (2) three creditors must join in the petition whenever twelve or more creditors have claims against the particular debtor—otherwise one creditor may file an involuntary petition, as long as his claim is for at least $5,000; and (3) they must have particular grounds for relief.

The Bankruptcy Reform Act specifies two grounds for relief: (1) the debtor is generally not paying his debts as they become due; (2) within 120 days of the filing, the debtor made a general assignment for the benefit of creditors. These grounds are far clearer than the "acts of bankruptcy" called for under the older bankruptcy acts.

Effect of the Petition The petition operates as a **stay** against suits or other actions against the debtor to recover claims, enforce judgments, or create liens. In other words, once the petition is filed, the debtor is freed from worry over other proceedings affecting his finances or property. Anyone with a claim, secured or unsecured, must seek relief in the bankruptcy court. This provision in the act can have dramatic consequences. Beset by tens of thousands of product liability suits for damages caused by asbestos, UNR Industries and Manville Corporation, the nation's largest asbestos producers, filed (separate) voluntary bankruptcy petitions in 1982; those filings automatically stayed all pending lawsuits.

First Meeting of Creditors Once a petition is filed, the court issues an "order of relief." In a voluntary case the petition operates as an order for relief. In an involuntary case, the order may be issued only (1) if the debtor does not contest the petition, or (2) the court determines that one or the other grounds for relief exists. If the debtor does contest the order and no grounds for relief exist, the court must dismiss the petition.

Assuming that the order has been properly issued, the creditors must meet within a reasonable time. The debtor is obligated to appear at the meeting and submit to examination under oath. The judge does not preside and, indeed, is not even entitled to attend the meeting.

When the judge issues an order for relief, he appoints an **interim trustee,** one who is authorized initially to take control of the debtor's assets. The trustee is required to collect the property, liquidate the debtor's estate, and distribute the proceeds to the creditors. The trustee may sue and be sued in the name of the estate. Under every chapter except Chapter 7, the court has sole discretion to name the trustee. Under Chapter 7, however, the creditors may select their own trustee, as long as they do so at the first meeting and follow certain voting provisions laid down in the act.

Trustee's Powers and Duties   The Bankruptcy Reform Act empowers the trustee to use, sell, or lease the debtor's property in the ordinary course of business or, after notice and a hearing, to do so even if not in the ordinary course of business. In all cases, the trustee must protect any security interests in the property. As long as the court has authorized the debtor's business to continue, the trustee may also obtain credit in the ordinary course of business. He may invest money in the estate to yield the maximum but reasonably safe return. Subject to the court's approval, he may employ various professionals, such as attorneys, accountants, and appraisers, and may, with some exceptions, assume or reject executory contracts and unexpired leases that the debtor has made. The trustee also has the authority to avoid many pre-bankruptcy transactions in order to recover property of the debtor to be included in the liquidation.

Creditors

We now turn to the three major matters covered in Chapter 5 of the Bankruptcy Reform Act: *creditors' claims, debtors' exemptions and discharge,* and the *property to be included in the estate.* We begin with the rules governing proof of claims by creditors and the priority of their claims.

Claims and Creditors   A **claim** is defined as a right to payment, whether or not it is reduced to judgment, liquidated, unliquidated, fixed, contingent, matured, unmatured, disputed, undisputed, legal, equitable, secured, or unsecured. A **creditor** is defined as any person or entity with a claim that arose no later than when the court issues the order for relief. These are very broad definitions; they are intended to give the debtor the broadest possible relief when finally discharged.

Proof of Claims   Before the trustee can distribute proceeds of the estate, creditors must file a **proof of claim,** prima facie evidence that they are owed some amount of money. Only unsecured creditors must file proof of claim, and they must do so within six months after the first date set for the first meeting of creditors. A creditor who fails to file on time will have his claim disallowed, even though the claim is valid. A party in interest, such as the trustee or creditor, may object to a proof of claim, in which case the court must determine whether to allow it. In the absence of objections, the claim is "deemed allowed." The court will not allow some claims. These include unenforceable claims, claims for unmatured interest, claims that may be offset by debts the creditor owes the debtor, and unreasonable charges by an insider or attorney.

Claims with Priority   The Bankruptcy Reform Act sets out categories of claimants and establishes priorities among them. The law is complex because it sets up different orders of priorities. In simple terms, the following rules apply. First, secured creditors are entitled to receive their security interests before anyone else is satisfied, because the security interest is not part of the property that the trustee is entitled to bring into the estate. To the extent that secured creditors have claims in excess of their collateral, they are considered to be unsecured or general creditors and are lumped in with general creditors of the appropriate class.

Second, of the six classes of claimants (see Figure 29-2 on page 644), the first is known as that of "priority" claims. It is subdivided into seven categories ranked in order of priority. The highest priority class within the general class of priority claims must be paid off in full before the next class can share in a distribution from the estate, and so on. Only if all seven subcategories of the priority class are satisfied can the remaining five classes receive a share of the estate. The seven priority classes, in the order of priorities from highest to lowest, are as follows:

- *Administration Expenses* This category includes all expenses necessary to preserve and administer the estate, such as the trustee's expenses, witness fees, expenses and fees of accountants, attorneys, appraisers, and the like.
- *"Gap" Creditor Claims* After an involuntary petition has been filed, but before a trustee is appointed or an order of relief is issued, certain creditors may have extended credit to the debtor in the ordinary course of the debtor's business. These claims, known as "gap" creditor claims, are entitled to second priority.
- *Employees' Wages, Salaries, and Commissions* To prevent undue hardship to employees, third priority goes to employees with unsecured claims for up to $2,000 in wages, salaries, or commissions, earned within ninety days of the filing of the petition or cessation of the business.
- *Contributions to Employee Benefit Plans* Fourth priority goes to unsecured claims for contributions to employee benefit plans. The act limits these claims by time (they must have been incurred within 180 days of filing or cessation) and by amount ($2,000 times the number of employees less amounts paid for wage claims).
- *Grain Producers and U.S. Fishermen* These creditors have fifth priority for unsecured claims (up to $2,000 for each individual) against debtors who own or operate grain or fish storage facilities.
- *Consumer Creditor Claims* Next in line are consumer creditors with claims of up to $900 per creditor for deposits of money for undelivered goods or unperformed services or rental of property, as long as the deposits were for goods, services, or property for nonbusiness use.
- *Taxes* The final priority category consists of claims for federal, state, and local income, property, employment, and excise taxes.

The Debtor's Exemptions and Dischargeable Debts

Exemptions The Bankruptcy Reform Act exempts certain property from the estate of an *individual* debtor, so that she will not be impoverished upon discharge. Exactly what is exempt may depend on state law, since the federal act permits the states to establish their own list of exemptions. (The liberal exemptions available in Florida and Texas are discussed in **Box 29-1**.) If a state opts out of the federal exemptions, then the debtor in the state must look to the state list and to certain federal exemptions contained in federal laws other than the Bankruptcy Reform Act. If the state has not rejected the federal list, then the debtor has the choice of the federal or state list. Most states have decided to opt out of the federal exemptions.

The federal exemptions include the following:

1. up to $7,500 in equity in a residence;
2. up to $1,200 equity in one motor vehicle;
3. up to $200 for each item of ordinary household furnishings and clothing (including household goods, books, animals, musical instruments and the like), but the total value cannot exceed $4,000;
4. up to $500 in jewelry;
5. up to $750 in books and tools used in the debtor's trade;
6. up to $400, plus up to $3,750 not used in (1) above, in any property owned by the debtor;
7. any unmatured life insurance contract owned by the debtor other than a credit life insurance contract;
8. up to $4,000 cash surrender or loan value of an unmatured life insurance contract owned by the debtor and on the debtor's life;
9. alimony and child support payments;
10. certain rights in pension and profit-sharing plans, and other annuity plans, including Social Security and veterans and disability benefits; and
11. up to $7,500 in payments from an award in a personal injury lawsuit.

Secured Property As already noted, secured creditors generally have priority, even above the priority claims. For this reason banks and other lending institutions have shifted their loan portfolios markedly from unsecured loans to secured lending. But despite the general rule, the debtor can avoid certain types of security interests. For example, the debtor can avoid a lien on property that would otherwise have been exempt if the lien is a nonpossessory, nonpurchase-money security interest in any household furnishings, goods, and the like "held primarily for the personal, family, or household use of the debtor or a dependent of the debtor."

Dischargeable Debts Once discharged, the debtor is no longer legally liable to pay any remaining un-

LAW AND LIFE

Florida Is Gaining Reputation as Haven For Debtors Who Seek to Shelter Wealth

By Martha Brannigan

[*In most cases, state law determines what property is exempt in bankruptcy. The liberal exemptions available in Florida are turning the Sunshine State into a haven for debtors—*AUTHORS' NOTE].

Florida is known nationwide as the Sunshine State. But it's also getting a reputation as a debtor's paradise.

Attracted by state laws that shield certain personal assets, individuals looking over their shoulders at creditors are streaming into Florida. It isn't clear how many people move to the state expressly to shelter their wealth, and not all such moves will survive court challenges. But bankruptcy filings have increased far more rapidly in Florida than nationally.

While the federal Bankruptcy

SUNSHINE AND BANKRUPTCY

Code applies everywhere, states can write their own rules about which assets are exempt from creditors. "In Florida, you can fashion your ownership of property so you are totally insulated from ever paying a debt," says Michael G. Williamson, an Orlando bankruptcy attorney.

Among the 50 states, only Texas comes close as a debtor's retreat. John Connally, the former Texas governor, clung to a 200-acre ranch there, leaving creditors to pick over the remains of his bankrupt estate. The Hunt Brothers also salvaged big residences despite bankruptcy. Still, Florida seems to be the favored spot for debtors on the move. "People don't want to move [to Texas] and buy these houses and see them go down 30% in value," says Lindsay Sharpe, a bankruptcy attorney in Austin.

The centerpiece of Florida's debtor protection measures is its homestead law. No matter what his debts, a homesteader—someone who declares a particular property as his

principal abode—can keep a home of unlimited value on as much as a half acre of land within a city, or on as much as 160 acres outside one.

But that's only the start. The salary of a head of household is exempt from a creditor's grasp, as are annuities, certain retirement and profit-sharing plans and individual retirement accounts. In addition, property owned by a married couple in tenancy by the entirety—a legal form in which each party is viewed as owning the whole asset—cannot be seized for debts owed by only one spouse.

Former baseball commissioner Bowie K. Kuhn, for instance, moved to Florida last December. His relocation from New Jersey came just two weeks before a bankruptcy-law filing in New York by the defunct law firm of Myerson & Kuhn, of which he was a founding, name partner. By law, individual partners can be held liable for all the debts of the partnership.

Mr. Kuhn filed papers in a Florida state court last December declaring Florida as his legal domicile—a way of establishing a homestead. He sold his home in New Jersey in January and bought a $1 million estate

paid debts (except nondischargeable debts) that arose before the court issued the order of relief. The discharge operates to void any money judgments already rendered against the debtor and to bar the judgment creditor from seeking to recover the judgment.

Some debts are not dischargeable in bankruptcy. These include

1. certain taxes and customs duties;
2. debts not listed with the court, unless the creditor had actual notice of the bankruptcy proceeding;
3. liability for the fraudulent obtaining of money while acting in a fiduciary capacity, for embezzlement, or for larceny;
4. liability for willfully and deliberately injuring another's person or property (this exclusion does not apply to liability for negligent acts);
5. fines, penalties, and forfeitures payable to a governmental entity for the benefit of the entity;
6. alimony and child support;

BOX 29-1

in Marsh Landing, an enclave in Ponte Vedra Beach, Fla., a few days later.

Mr. Kuhn says he "certainly took into consideration the debtor laws" when he moved to Florida, but also found it an attractive spot to make a fresh start because of his strong ties there and the state's professional and recreational offerings.

In the spring, Mr. Kuhn was joined in Florida by his ex-partner, Harvey D. Myerson, who also has obligations resulting from the bankruptcy of his previous firm—the defunct Finley, Kumble, Wagner, Underberg, Manley, Myerson & Casey.

Mr. Myerson put up for sale his Manhattan co-op apartment and East Hampton, N.Y., house and bought a home in Key West for $1.75 million. The Mediterranean-style, four-bedroom, six bathroom property—including an oceanfront swimming pool, gold fixtures, a coral staircase and an elevator—is tagged "the southernmost home in the continental U.S." A real estate agent's brochure describes the place as "only 88 miles from Cuba."

More to the point, grumble some of Mr. Myerson's former partners, is

that the abode is in Florida. In May, an attorney representing the bankrupt firm of Myerson & Kuhn went to federal bankruptcy court in New York for relief.

Urgent Advice

"Mr. Myerson is selling his residences in New York," Ronald Cohen, the firm's attorney, urgently advised federal bankruptcy Judge Prudence B. Abram at the hearing. "And we have learned that he is intending to purchase or maybe has already purchased . . ."

"A house in Florida," Judge Abram said, finishing the sentence. "Beyond ridiculous" was the judge's assessment of the development. "We've already got one person in Florida," she said. "I don't think we should have two."

Mr. Myerson told his Myerson & Kuhn colleagues that he wasn't trying to pull a fast one. He agreed to give them a security interest in his artwork and some New York real estate to quiet their fears. His attorney, Charles Stillman, says, "His decision to go to Florida was strictly personal and not based on creditors' rights."

For his part, Mr. Kuhn isn't home

free yet. After his move south, Marine Midland Bank, a big creditor, filed suit in a Florida court, asking for a lien on his Florida property. The bank alleges he put money into the house to dodge a personal guarantee of a $3.2 million loan to the law firm.

'An Outrage'

"It's an outrage is what it is," says Leon Marcus, a former Myerson & Kuhn partner, who calls Mr. Kuhn's move "a great test case" of the Florida homestead law. "I can't believe the intent of the Legislature was to protect people under these circumstances. I don't think you have any instance as flagrant as this one."

Just how flagrant is too flagrant isn't clear under Florida law: A certain degree of "pre-petition planning," as bankruptcy lawyers like to call it, is acceptable. However, a deliberate move to evade creditors doesn't always work, particularly if it's taken on the eve of bankruptcy. Under the federal Bankruptcy Code, if a judge finds a move was made "to hinder, delay or defraud" creditors, it will be deemed a "fraudulent transfer" and void.

Source: *Wall Street Journal*, August 3, 1990

7. debts that could have been or actually were listed in a previous bankruptcy in which the debtor waived or was denied discharge; and

8. educational loans that first became due within five years of the filing of the bankruptcy petition if they were "made, insured, or guaranteed by a governmental unit, or made under any program funded in whole or in part by a governmental unit or a nonprofit institution," unless preventing the debt from being discharged would work an "undue hardship" on the debtor or his family.

9. debts resulting from the debtor's drunk driving.

Furthermore, a debt of over $500 incurred to purchase luxury items within forty days before filing, or debts resulting from certain cash advances of more than $1,000 within twenty days before filing are presumed to be nondischargeable. This provision is designed to prevent debtors from "loading up" on luxury goods in anticipation of bankruptcy.

The nature of the "undue hardship" rule for educational loans is discussed in the following case.

In re **BURTON**
117 B.R. 167 (W.D.Pa.
1990)

BERNARD MARKOVITZ, Bankruptcy Judge.

Debtor received student loans guaranteed by PHEAA during the course of his education.

In 1975, Debtor attended Pittsburgh Art Institute. Sometime thereafter, he transferred to Ivy School of Art. In 1980, Debtor transferred to Slippery Rock State University. In 1981 or 1982, Debtor transferred to Indiana University of Pennsylvania in order to obtain a teaching certificate. Debtor discontinued his education in 1983. He never received a degree or a teaching certificate and has had an ongoing dispute with Indiana University of Pennsylvania, the details of which are neither clear nor relevant.

Debtor filed a voluntary petition under Chapter 7 of the Bankruptcy Code on July 26, 1989.

Debtor is thirty-three (33) years old and has no dependents. He presently is on public assistance and receives a cash disbursement, as well as food stamps every month. His total monthly expenses presently exceed his monthly income. Debtor also receives financial assistance from his elderly mother which enables him to meet his monthly expenses.

Debtor does not hold a steady job and has worked only sporadically since 1983. He has delivered sandwiches, done laundry, done yard work, and has been an entertainer.

The total amount presently due and owing on Debtor's school loan is approximately $15,000.000

Debtor seeks to have the indebtedness arising out of his student loans held dischargeable under the exception set forth at 11 U.S.C. § 523(a)(8)(B), which provides in pertinent part that:

> (a) A discharge under section 727, 1141, 1228(a), 1228(b), or 1328(b) of this title does not discharge an individual debtor from any debt—

> *　　*　　*

> (8) for an educational loan made, insured, or guaranteed by a governmental unit, or made under any program funded in whole or in part by a governmental unit or a nonprofit institution, unless—

> *　　*　　*

> (B) excepting such debt from discharge under this paragraph will impose an undue hardship on the debtor and the debtor's dependents.

> *　　*　　*

Several courts have adopted a tripartite test for determining whether a debt is dischargeable due to undue hardship. The test, first set forth in *In re Johnson*, 5 BCD 532 (Bankr.E.D.Pa.1979), sets forth a sequential procedure for analyzing the facts of a given case.

The tests may be termed, in order, the mechanical test, the good faith test, and the policy test.

The mechanical test, in essence, requires a debtor to show that his financial resources in the foreseeable future will not be sufficient to enable that debtor to support himself and his dependents (if any) at a subsistence level while the debtor repays the debt obligation.

*   *   *

If the debtor fails to make the showing required under the mechanical test, discharge of the debt in question must be denied. If, however, debtor does make such a showing, the court then must proceed to the second stage of analysis.

The second stage of analysis is reached if and only if the debtor has met their burden of proof with respect to the so-called "mechanical" test. Assuming that repayment of the loan would result in the requisite "undue hardship", discharge still must not be granted unless the debtor has made a "good faith attempt" to repay the loan. . . .

The third and final phase of analysis is the so-called "policy" test, which requires the court to ascertain whether debtor's attempt to discharge the loan constitutes the sort of abuse which § 523(a)(8)(B) was enacted to prevent. . . .

Debtor has failed to meet his required burden of proof. In particular, Debtor has failed to satisfy the "mechanical" test set forth above. He has failed to show, by a preponderance of the credible evidence, that his financial resources will be insufficient in the foreseeable future to enable him to support himself at a subsistence level while repaying his student loans.

Debtor presently is unemployed. However, his education and skills are such that Debtor reasonably can be expected in the foreseeable future to repay his student loans while living above the subsistence level. Debtor appears to be a talented artist with marketable skills. In addition, he has completed at least four (4) years of college and is obviously intelligent. Debtor unquestionably has the skills and training sufficient to enable him to find decent employment.

It should also be noted that Debtor is unmarried and has no family support obligations. He is required to support only himself and is not burdened with the responsibility of supporting others.

Also, Debtor has not shown that his health will prevent him from finding and retaining gainful employment in the foreseeable future. Debtor alleges that his health is poor and that his mental and physical conditions make it impossible for him to be gainfully employed. Specifically, Debtor claims that he suffers from Epstein-Barr Syndrome; that he has a severe bowel disorder which incapacitates him for approximately twenty (20) minutes of every hour; and that he is unable to concentrate due to depression.

No admissible evidence was presented that Debtor suffers from Epstein-Barr Syndrome. The only medical evidence that he does offer is contained in an uncorroborated letter authored by a person holding herself out as a licensed medical doctor and which is clearly inadmissible hearsay. Debtor merely offered a letter purportedly signed by Dr. Sarver and did not call Dr. Sarver to testify in person or by deposition as to Debtor's medical condition. Moreover, even if he does in fact suffer from this malady, Debtor has failed to

(continued on next page)

(continued)

In re BURTON
117 B.R. 167 (W.D.Pa. 1990)

show what the long-term deleterious effects of the disease are; that he can be expected to suffer those effects during the next ten (10) years or so; or, that this condition will prevent him from being gainfully employed during that time.

As for his alleged bowel disorder and inability to concentrate, the Court noticed that prior to and during the hearing that Debtor was able to remain in the courtroom for considerably longer than an hour without having to excuse himself. During said time frame, Debtor was alert and able to respond cogently while testifying.

In summary, it is clear to the Court that Debtor is a bright and articulate young man with potential well beyond his stated position. Debtor's difficulties appear to be self-inflicted. Certainly, if he immerses himself in his limitless future, as opposed to self-deprecation and/or sympathy, he can achieve substantial results. Debtor's future decades need not be bleak if he chooses advancement. Clearly that choice is his. [The debt is not discharged.]

Reaffirmation   A bankrupt may reaffirm a debt that was discharged. The Bankruptcy Reform Act provides important protection to the debtor intent on doing so. No reaffirmation is binding unless four conditions are satisfied: (1) the reaffirmation must have been made prior to the granting of the discharge; (2) the debtor must be given sixty days after the agreement is filed with the court to rescind the agreement; (3) if the debtor is an individual, the court must hold a discharge hearing at which the debtor is told about the legal consequences of reaffirmation; (4) court approval is required for reaffirmation of a debt, except for consumer debts secured by the debtor's real property, if an individual debtor is not represented by an attorney.

Property Included in the Estate

When a bankruptcy petition is filed, an estate is created consisting of all the debtor's then-existing property interests, whether legal or equitable. In addition, the estate includes any bequests, inheritances, and certain other distributions of property that the debtor receives within the next 180 days. It also includes property recovered by the trustee under certain powers granted by the Bankruptcy Reform Act.

Trustee's Avoiding Powers   The Bankruptcy Reform Act confers on the trustee certain powers to recover property for the estate that the debtor transferred before bankruptcy. One such power is to act as a **hypothetical lien creditor.** This power is best explained by an example. Suppose J. R. Ewing purchases equipment on credit from Naive Supply Company. Naive fails to perfect its security interest and a few weeks later J. R. files a bankruptcy petition. By virtue of a section conferring on the trustee the status of a hypothetical lien creditor, the trustee can act as though he had a lien on the equipment, with priority over Naive's unperfected security interest. Thus the trustee can avoid Naive's security interest, with the result that Naive would be treated as an unsecured creditor.

Another power is to avoid transactions known as **voidable preferences**—transactions highly favorable to particular creditors. A transfer of property is voidable if it was made (1) to a creditor or for his benefit, (2) on account of a debt owed before the transfer was made, (3) while the debtor was insolvent (see **Box 29-2**), (4) on or within ninety days before the filing of the petition, and (5) to enable a creditor to receive more than he would have under Chapter 7. If the creditor was an "insider"—one who had a special relationship with the debtor, for example, a relative or

Drexel Payments of Over $600 Million Before Chapter 11 May Be Recoverable

By Wade Lambert

[Trustees have the power to avoid certain transactions known as voidable preferences. As the following article illustrates, the solvency of the debtor is an important issue when trustees attempt to exercise this power.—AUTHORS' NOTE]

NEW YORK—Drexel Burnham Lambert Group Inc. made more than $600 million in payments that may be recoverable under bankruptcy law because the transactions occurred during the three months immediately prior to the company's bankruptcy-court filing.

The payments were disclosed in the company's statement of financial affairs, filed with the federal bankruptcy court in Manhattan last week. The document also lists details of millions of dollars owed to former employees who cashed in their Drexel stock in the months before Drexel

VOIDABLE PREFERENCES?

filed for protection Feb. 13 under the federal Bankruptcy Code.

The filing, released Friday, discloses that Drexel paid loans and interest totaling $621.8 million during the three months immediately prior to filing for bankruptcy-court protection. Bankruptcy lawyers say such payments, with certain exceptions, can be recovered if it is shown that a company gave preference to some creditors and if the debtor was insolvent at the time. Such money can then be redistributed to creditors.

Creditors' and shareholders' attorneys are using the statement of financial affairs as a road map to possible pockets of money to pay off Drexel's debts, according to bankruptcy lawyers familiar with the case. Creditors also are likely to examine the document for any payments to company executives, which could be recoverable if such payments were made within a year before the Chapter 11 filing and if the company was insolvent at the time of the transaction.

"The primary issue will be

whether Drexel was insolvent," said Barry Dichter, a bankruptcy partner at Cadwalader, Wickersham & Taft, who represents the Central Bank of Portugal, one of Drexel's largest creditors. "It's fair to say that determining whether Drexel Burnham Lambert Group was solvent or insolvent at the time of the transactions will be one of the toughest solvency problems ever presented to a bankruptcy court." He said the hardest task for those involved in the proceedings will be to determine the value of junk bonds held by Drexel.

"Preferences are a litigation goldmine," added Hugh M. Ray, a bankruptcy law attorney in Houston. Creditors' attorneys "will want to know who got what and when, and who knew what and when," he said.

Alan Miller, an attorney for Drexel, said: "At no point was [Drexel] insolvent." However, bankruptcy lawyers say the debtor is presumed to have been insolvent during those three months. If the Drexel creditors' committee or shareholders' committee seek to recover such payments, it will be up to the parties that were paid to prove that the company was solvent.

Source: *Wall Street Journal*, May 7, 1990

---

general partner of the debtor or a corporation which the debtor controls or serves as director or officer—then the trustee may void the transaction if it was made within one year of the filing of the petition, assuming that the debtor was insolvent at the time the transaction was made.

Some transfers that seem to fall within these provisions do not. The most important exceptions are (1) transfers made for new value (the debtor buys a refrigerator for cash one week before filing a petition; this is an exchange for new value and the trustee may

not void it); (2) a transfer that creates a purchase money security interest securing new value if the secured party perfects within ten days after the debtor receives the goods; (3) payment of a debt incurred in the ordinary course of business, on ordinary business terms; and (4) transfers totalling less than $600 by an individual whose debts are primarily consumer debts.

The trustee may also avoid **fraudulent transfers** made within one year before the date that the bankruptcy petition was filed. This provision contemplates various types of fraud. For example, while insolvent the debtor might transfer property to a relative for less than it was worth, intending to recover it after discharge. This situation should be distinguished from the voidable preference discussed above, in which the debtor pays a favored creditor what he actually owes, but in so doing cannot then pay other creditors.

Liquidation of the Estate

Except as noted, the above provisions apply to each type of bankruptcy proceeding. The following discussion is limited to certain provisions under Chapter 7.

Trustee's Duties   In addition to the duties already noted (p. 636), the trustee has other duties under Chapter 7. He must sell the property for money, close up the estate "as expeditiously as is compatible with the best interests of parties in interest," investigate the debtor's financial affairs, examine proofs of claims, reject improper ones, oppose the discharge of the debtor where doing so is advisable in the trustee's opinion, furnish a creditor with information about the estate and his administration (unless the court orders otherwise), file tax reports if the business continues to be operated, and make a final report and file it with the court.

Distribution of the Estate   After payment of claims with priority (p. 636) the trustee must distribute the estate to the remaining classes of claimants in the order given (see Figure 29-2):

1. unsecured creditors who filed their claims on time
2. unsecured creditors who were tardy in filing claims
3. persons claiming fines, penalties, forfeitures, or exemplary or punitive damages to the extent that the claims are not for actual pecuniary loss suffered by the claimant
4. all creditors, who are entitled to interest at the legal rate
5. the debtor, who receives anything remaining

Discharge   Once the estate is distributed, the court will order the debtor discharged, unless one of the following exceptions applies:

1. the debtor is not an individual
2. the debtor has concealed or destroyed property with intent to defraud, hinder, or delay within twelve months preceding filing of the petition
3. the debtor has concealed, destroyed, or falsified books and records
4. the debtor has lied under oath, knowingly given a false account, presented or used a false claim, or given or received bribes
5. the debtor has failed to explain satisfactorily any loss of assets

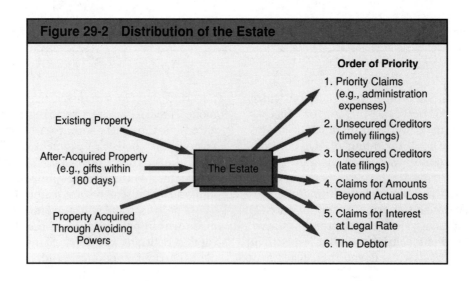

Figure 29-2   Distribution of the Estate

Existing Property

After-Acquired Property (e.g., gifts within 180 days)

Property Acquired Through Avoiding Powers

The Estate

Order of Priority
1. Priority Claims (e.g., administration expenses)
2. Unsecured Creditors (timely filings)
3. Unsecured Creditors (late filings)
4. Claims for Amounts Beyond Actual Loss
5. Claims for Interest at Legal Rate
6. The Debtor

6. the debtor has refused to obey any lawful order of the court or answer any material question approved by the court during the proceeding
7. the debtor has committed any one of the preceding acts within one year of the filing of the petition in connection with another case concerning an insider
8. another court has granted the debtor a discharge in another case commenced within the last six years
9. the court has approved a written waiver of discharge executed by the debtor after the order for relief was issued

The Bankruptcy Reform Act prohibits governmental units from discriminating against a person who has gone through bankruptcy. Debtors are also protected from discrimination by private employers; for example, a private employer may not fire a debtor because of the bankruptcy.

ADJUSTMENTS OF DEBTS OF AN INDIVIDUAL WITH REGULAR INCOME—CHAPTER 13

Anyone with a steady income who is having difficulty paying off accumulated debts may seek the protection of a bankruptcy court in a Chapter 13 proceeding. Under this chapter, the individual debtor presents a payment plan to creditors and the court appoints a trustee. If the creditors wind up with more under the plan presented than they would receive in a Chapter 7 proceeding, then the court is likely to approve it. In general, a Chapter 13 repayment plan extends the time to pay the debt and may reduce it so that the debtor need not pay it all. Typically, the debtor will pay a fixed sum monthly to the trustee, who will distribute it to the creditors. The provisions of Chapters 3 and 5 discussed above apply also to this chapter; therefore, the discussion that follows focuses on some unique features of Chapter 13.

Eligibility

Chapter 13 is voluntary only. Anyone who has a regular income, unsecured debts of less than $100,000

and secured debts of less than $350,000 is eligible to seek its protection. The debts must be unpaid and owing at the time the debtor applies for relief.

The Plan

Plans are typically extensions or compositions (p. 631). Chapter 13 limits the stretch-out period to three years, unless the court approves a longer period of up to five years. The plan must provide for payments of all future income or a sufficient portion of it to the trustee. Priority creditors are entitled to be paid in full, although they may be paid later than required under the original indebtedness. As long as the plan is being carried out, the debtor may enjoin any creditors from suing to collect the original debt.

Confirmation

The court must approve the plan if it meets certain requirements. These include (1) distribution of property to unsecured creditors whose claims are allowed in an amount no less than that which they would have received had the estate been liquidated under Chapter 7; (2) acceptance by secured creditors, with some exceptions, such as when the debtor surrenders the secured property to the creditor; and (3) proposal of the plan "in good faith." Under the 1984 amendments, however, if the trustee or an unsecured creditor objects to confirmation, the plan must meet additional tests. For example, a plan will be approved if all of the debtor's disposable income over a three-year period will be used to make payments under the plan.

Discharge

Once a debtor has made all payments called for in the plan, the court will discharge him from all debts except certain long-term debts and obligations to pay alimony, maintenance, and support. Indeed, Chapter 13 is so broad that it permits the court to discharge the debtor from many debts considered nondischargeable under Chapter 7 and to discharge him even if he has not made all the payments, assuming that (1) the failure to pay stemmed from circumstances for which he should not be held accountable, (2) the creditors received no less than what they would have received under Chapter 7, and (3) the plan would be impractical to modify.

The following case discusses both the discharge of debt resulting from a "willful and malicious injury" and the "good faith" requirement.

In re LeMAIRE
898 F.2d 1346 (8th Cir. 1990)

JOHN R. GIBSON, Circuit Judge.

On July 9, 1978, at about noon [Paul] Handeen went to pick up his son and found [the debtor] LeMaire waiting for him. When Handeen got out of his car, LeMaire shot at him nine times with a bolt action rifle. The first two shots missed Handeen, but the third struck him on the left side of his neck. Handeen then attempted to hide behind the car. LeMaire circled the car, shot at and missed Handeen twice more, and then hit him inside of his left knee. LeMaire circled again and Handeen jerked his head back to avoid the bullet at the time he thought LeMaire would pull the trigger of the rifle aimed at his head. LeMaire fired, and the bullet went through Handeen's right nostril, shattering the roof of his mouth and going through his tongue. LeMaire then fired a shot at Handeen's left arm. The bullet went through Handeen's arm and lodged on his spine. LeMarie fired a final shot through Handeen's ankle. In all, five of the nine shots fired by LeMaire struck Handeen. LeMaire declared that he had intended to kill Handeen. He pled guilty to a charge of aggravated assault and was sentenced to imprisonment for a term of one to ten years. He served twenty-seven months of his sentence and was released in 1981. LeMaire then returned to graduate school at the University of Minnesota and received his doctorate in experimental behavioral pharmacology in January 1986.

Handeen brought a civil suit against LeMaire and obtained a consent judgment. LeMaire paid $3,000 of the judgment, but made no further payments, prompting Handeen to commence garnishment proceedings to collect the $50,362.50 balance on the judgment. Soon after, on January 16, 1987, LeMaire filed this bankruptcy petition under Chapter 13.

Handeen objected to the bankruptcy court confirming LeMaire's Chapter 13 plan; the bankruptcy court, however, rejected his assertion that the civil judgment arising out of the crime was not dischargeable. The court instead confirmed LeMaire's plan, which provided that his creditors be paid approximately 42% on their claims. The plan listed three claims: (1) Handeen's judgment; (2) a student loan; and (3) a claim by LeMaire's parents for loans to LeMaire, including $3,600 expended on his legal fees, $3,000 spent in partial payment on the judgment, and $2,172 lent to buy a computer. The record reveals that LeMaire's debt to his parents was evidenced by a promissory note he signed the day before he filed his Chapter 13 petition.

Handeen appealed to the district court from the bankruptcy court's order confirming LeMaire's Chapter 13 plan. The district court affirmed and, upon appeal, a panel of this court also affirmed. We granted rehearing en banc, vacated the panel opinion, and heard oral argument. We now reverse.

Handeen vigorously argues that, as a matter of law, his civil judgment cannot be discharged because it arose from a criminal act. The panel rejected this argument and we do likewise.

Handeen's argument is based upon 11 U.S.C. § 523(a)(6) (1988), which provides that a debt arising from infliction of "willful and malicious injury by the debtor to another entity" may not be discharged under specified sections of the Bankruptcy Code. As the panel observed, there is no question that LeMaire's assault inflicted a "willful and malicious" injury upon Handeen. Handeen's reliance upon section 523(a)(6) is unavailing, however, because LeMaire filed his petition under Chapter 13, which does not include section 523(a)(6) in its list of nondischargeable debts. Although section 523(a)(6) does by its express statutory terms apply to a petition for bankruptcy under Chapter 7, its applicability does not extend to a filing under Chapter 13. Therefore, a debt which falls within the scope of section 523(a)(6), such as the debt owed to Handeen, which may not be discharged under Chapter 7, may nevertheless be discharged if the debtor meets the requirements of Chapter 13.

Alternatively, Handeen argues that the bankruptcy court should not have confirmed LeMaire's Chapter 13 plan because LeMaire did not propose it in good faith. Section 1325(a) of Title 11 of the Bankruptcy Code establishes six criteria which a debtor must meet in order to have his Chapter 13 plan confirmed by a bankruptcy court. The critical requirement, for present purposes, is that "the plan has been proposed in good faith and not by any means forbidden by law."

★   ★   ★

[695 F.2d 311] directs a bankruptcy court to consider whether the debt would be nondischargeable in a Chapter 7 filing, and the court did so here, observing that this factor is closely linked to the debtor's motivation and sincerity. Although the court was correct in this observation, our review of the record convinces us that the court accorded insufficient weight to this factor. The specific evidence in the record which persuades us that the bankruptcy court was clearly erroneous in finding that LeMaire proposed his plan in good faith is discussed below in the context of another *Estus* factor, LeMaire's motivation and sincerity in seeking Chapter 13 relief. At this point, we need only observe that this debt could not be discharged under Chapter 7.

In evaluating LeMaire's motivation and sincerity, the bankruptcy court balanced Handeen's desire to be compensated for his injuries against LeMaire's desire to have a fresh start and found the latter to outweigh the former in importance. The court noted that, while LeMaire had been unable to pay his debt to his victim, he had paid his debt to society by serving a prison sentence and had attempted to reorder his life and make a fresh start. The court found that forcing LeMaire to be burdened the rest of his life with a judgment which would continue to accrue interest, result in endless garnishments, and prevent him from accumulating property would be inimical

(*continued on next page*)

(continued)

In re LeMAIRE
898 F.2d 1346 (8th Cir. 1990)

to such a fresh start. The court concluded that LeMaire had made a whole-hearted attempt to pay Handeen as much as possible, and that LeMaire's motivation was proper and his sincerity real.

We are convinced that the court's analysis here fails to properly consider the strong public policy factors, inherent in the Bankruptcy Code, which are implicated in discharging this debt and gives undue emphasis to the fact that the statutory terms governing Chapter 13 petitions do not expressly make a debt resulting from a willful and malicious injury nondischargeable. In light of the court's clear errors both in according insufficient weight to the nondischargeability of this debt in Chapter 7, and in finding that LeMaire's motivation and sincerity in seeking Chapter 13 relief were proper, we do not believe that LeMaire has fulfilled the good faith requirement of Chapter 13. [The lower court decision is reversed and the case remanded.]

REORGANIZATION—CHAPTER 11

Chapter 11 provides a means by which corporations, partnerships, and other businesses, including sole proprietorships, can rehabilitate themselves and continue to operate free from the burden of debts that they cannot pay.

It is simple enough to apply for the protection of the court in a Chapter 11 proceeding, and in recent years, more and more large, financially ailing companies have sought shelter in Chapter 11. An increasing number of corporations have turned to Chapter 11 even though, by conventional terms, they were solvent. Doing so enables them to negotiate with creditors to reduce debt. It also may even permit courts to snuff out lawsuits that have not yet been filed.

Chapters 3 and 5 discussed above under "liquidation" apply to Chapter 11 proceedings also. Our discussion, therefore, is limited to special features of Chapter 11. For a practical perspective on a typical Chapter 11 proceeding, see **Box 29-3**.

Eligibility

Any person eligible for discharge in a Chapter 7 proceeding is eligible for a Chapter 11 proceeding, ex-cept stockbrokers and commodity brokers. Railroad corporations are also eligible for Chapter 11 protection. A company may voluntarily enter Chapter 11 or may be put there involuntarily by creditors.

Operation of Business

Unless a trustee is appointed, the debtor will retain possession of the business and may continue to operate with its own management. The court may appoint a trustee on request of any party in interest after notice and a hearing. The appointment may be made for cause—such as dishonesty, incompetence, or gross mismanagement—or if it is otherwise in the best interests of the creditors. In the *Deena* case the court states the reasons for appointing a trustee and discusses the philosophy of Chapter 11.

Pulling a Company Through Chapter 11 Is a Risky Business as Hurdles Abound

By Laurie P. Cohen

[Chapter 11 bankruptcy is a means by which corporations and other businesses attempt to rehabilitate themselves. However, in actuality one out of eight companies is able to reorganize through Chapter 11. Eventually, all the others cease operations.—AUTHORS' NOTE]

Companies that file for protection from creditors under Chapter 11 of the federal Bankruptcy Code hope to work out a way to pay off their debts and continue in operation.

But the road through bankruptcy court is a perilous one, and only one out of eight companies reorganizes successfully. The rest cease operations, according to the Federal Office of Court Administration.

A decade ago, a company that sought protection from its creditors had virtually no chance of emerging from bankruptcy. But in recent years, even such blue-chip companies as Texaco Inc. and Wickes Cos. have managed to continue operating in bankruptcy proceedings and have emerged as leaner and more viable businesses.

Here is a step-by-step look at what bankruptcy experts say a company faces once it embarks on a Chapter 11 reorganization:

- The case is assigned to a federal bankruptcy judge in the district where the filing is made. The judge's role during the case is to resolve conflicts that may arise. The bankruptcy judge doesn't have to approve company expenditures made in the ordinary course of business. The judge must, however, approve payments of all debts incurred before the Chapter 11 filing and other payments considered to be extraordinary.

- A U.S. trustee, who is employed by the Justice Department, will be appointed by the bankruptcy judge and will explain to the debtor company and its counsel the reporting and operating requirements for the district where the filing is made.

- Usually within a day of the filing, the company and its lawyers will submit to the court a list of the company's 20 largest creditors. The company must close its existing bank accounts and its books and begin new accounts and books as of the date the filing is made.

- Within days, the company's executives will meet with the company's bank lenders to work out a basis for continuing to operate. The company will attempt to negotiate a credit line with its banks that will provide funds to pay suppliers and employees. Banks are usually willing to cooperate, rather than risk losing all. Some suppliers may seek assurances that they will be paid in advance for merchandise sold while the company is in Chapter 11 proceedings. The banks will want to enable the company to make such guarantees.

- The U.S. trustee will attend to the administrative details of the bankruptcy and supervise day-to-day problems. He will then appoint one or more creditors committees, culled from the list of top creditors. These committees will appoint chairmen and will hire their own lawyers, investment bankers and accountants. There may be a committee of senior bondholders, subordinated bond holders, landlords, etc.

- If the creditors believe that the company's management isn't operating the business as a fiduciary ought to, the creditors can ask the judge to appoint an outside trustee to manage the company's affairs before it emerges from bankruptcy. This isn't a common occurence, although it did happen in the Eastern Airlines case.

- With its funds for continuing operations in place, the company can begin the task of reorganizing its operations. Its investment bankers will consider whether the company can take existing creditors' debt and restructure it on improved or extended terms. The bankers will also determine whether it may be best for the company to bring in a "white knight" partner who can provide new financing, or whether assets ought to be sold.

- The company will negotiate with its various creditor groups, and the creditors will negotiate with each other. Virtually all of the creditor groups will want to be paid out before the others, which, of course, isn't feasible. A compromise will likely be reached at the end of an arduous negotiating process.

- Finally, if all goes well, a plan of reorganization will be produced by the company's investment bankers and lawyers. The plan will be voted on by creditors and confirmed by a federal bankruptcy judge. Once confirmed, the company will be ready to emerge from Chapter 11 proceedings. In a major corporate bankruptcy, the entire process generally takes at least six months and may take as much as two years.

Source: *Wall Street Journal*, January 16, 1990

STEP-BY-STEP THROUGH CHAPTER 11

In re **DEENA PACKAGING INDUSTRIES, INC.** 29 B.R. 705 (S.D. N.Y. 1983)

EDWARD J. RYAN, BANKRUPTCY JUDGE. On July 6, 1978, Deena Packaging Industries, Inc. (Deena) filed a voluntary petition in bankruptcy under Chapter XI, section 322 of the Bankruptcy Act. At that time, Flushing Savings Bank (Flushing), as a major creditor of Deena, held a mortgage on Deena's manufacturing plant. The 200,000 square foot plant was Deena's major asset. This court confirmed a plan whereby the mortgage was extended and Deena was to pay certain sums in repayment each month to Flushing. After Deena defaulted on its August 1981 payment, Flushing obtained a foreclosure judgment against Deena in New York State Supreme Court in the amount of $1,724,141. On the eve of the foreclosure sale initiated by Flushing, however, an involuntary petition in bankruptcy was filed against Deena pursuant to section 303 of the Bankruptcy Code. Consequently the foreclosure sale was stayed.

On August 16, 1982 Deena entered into a written lease with a third party for the rental of the fourth floor of the mortgaged premises. On October 6, 1982, Deena filed a voluntary Chapter 11 petition. The above mentioned lease was not included in that petition. In November 1982 Deena executed a second lease whereby another portion of the mortgaged premises was rented. The annual rental proceeds were approximately $100,000.

Deena incurred brokerage fee liabilities in connection with these leases. The arrangement between Deena and the broker who secured the tenants was that the broker's fee would be due and owing only when rental income was received by Deena. As rental income is earned, therefore, Deena becomes liable for brokerage fees on that amount. The total broker's fees payable on these two leases is not to exceed $45,000. When Deena amended its voluntary petition on December 17, 1982, by filing additional schedules and a statement of financial affairs, it disclosed neither the leases nor the brokerage liability.

Previously, Flushing had moved to have a trustee appointed to protect its rights as a secured creditor. A trial took place on the issue of appointment on the 17th day of December 1982 and was continued through January 25, 1983. This court concludes that the appointment of a trustee is entirely appropriate in these circumstances.

The appointment of a trustee in bankruptcy is governed by 11 U.S.C. § 1104 (1978 Supp.). The court may appoint a trustee for cause, or, under section 1104(a)(2), to protect the interests of creditors. Appointing a trustee for cause is not a discretionary function and necessarily includes a showing of "fraud, dishonesty, incompetence, or gross mismanagement of the affairs of the debtor by current management, either before or after the commencement of the case." Appointing a trustee to protect the interests of creditors, however, entails equitable considerations through which the court may exercise its discretionary powers.

The appointment of a trustee in Chapter 11 cases has been held by some courts to be extraordinary relief. This is consistent with the presumption that a Chapter 11 debtor should remain in possession and continue to manage its own affairs. Indeed, no trustee need be appointed in instances of slight mismanagement or where there are no discrepancies uncovered in the accounting records of a debtor. Section 1104, however, specifically proscribes certain conduct by debtors in possession; dishonesty is one such enumerated, prohibited act.

Although the grounds for cause were not specified in Flushing's papers, the trial record reveals that Deena's failure to include relevant financial data on their original and amended schedules raises questions of dishonest conduct. Under Bankruptcy Rules 108 and 10-108, the debtor is required to list *all* its assets and liabilities with the court.

The *In re Horn & Hardart* case, 22 B.R. 668, (Bkrtcy.E.D.Pa.1982), illustrates grounds for finding cause under section 1104(a)(1). Although the specific allegation therein was gross mismanagement, the court viewed the debtor's failure to file several operating statements mandated by the bankruptcy rules as an important consideration when determining whether or not cause existed for the appointment of a trustee. The court wrote in support of its view "that the debtor has poorly fulfilled the responsibilities imposed by the Bankruptcy Code and Rules." That situation, coupled with continuing operating losses, led the court to appoint a trustee for cause.

In another recent decision, the Bankruptcy Court for the Eastern District of Pennsylvania appointed a trustee in a Chapter 11 proceeding for cause and to protect the interests of the creditors. The debtor corporation in *In re Philadelphia Athletic Club, Inc.*, 15 B.R. 60 (Bkrtcy.S.D.N.Y.1981) was found to be grossly mismanaged; the debtor could not overcome allegations of mismanagement because it had failed to keep adequate books and records. The court reasoned that full disclosure of the debtor's financial position is necessary to determine whether the debtor can operate profitably or should be liquidated.

The respective debtors' failure to file relevant post-petition financial information in the *Horn & Hardart* and the *Philadelphia Athletic Club* cases contributed to the courts' appointment of trustees. In the case at hand, Deena omitted the rental income and brokerage liability from the original and amended petitions. The debtor's omissions violate the disclosure requirements of Bankruptcy Rules 108 and 10-108. Since the debtor has proffered no justification whatsoever for the nondisclosure of the leases in the petitions, this court concludes that these omissions be characterized as dishonest conduct for the purposes of section 1104(a)(1). Consequently, the cause requirement under section 1104(a)(1) has been met.

Even if Flushing had been unable to demonstrate sufficient cause, this court is empowered under section 1104(a)(2) to appoint a trustee to protect Flushing's rights as a creditor. The ability of the debtor to profitably operate its business is a substantial concern of the creditors. Deena conceded in its post trial memorandum that the operation of the building, its only income producing activity, is "almost self-sustaining, although not yet profitable." Such a concession raises doubts as to whether Deena should continue to act as a debtor in possession or whether its assets should be liquidated and its creditors paid off.

(continued on next page)

(continued)

In re DEENA
PACKAGING
INDUSTRIES, INC.
29 B.R. 705 (S.D. N.Y.
1983)

Accurate information as to the debtor's viability must reach the court and the creditors. Because Deena has failed to provide a full and truthful statement of its financial condition, it is necessary to appoint a trustee so that the court and Deena's creditors are fully informed.

Accordingly, the United States Trustee is directed to appoint a disinterested person to serve as trustee in accordance with Code Section 1104(c). Settle an appropriate order.

Creditors' Committee

The court must appoint a committee of unsecured creditors as soon as practicable after issuing the order for relief. The committee must consist of creditors willing to serve who have the seven largest claims, unless the court decides to continue a committee formed before the filing, if the committee was fairly chosen and adequately represents the various claims. The committee has several duties, including: (1) to investigate the debtor's financial affairs; (2) to determine whether to seek appointment of a trustee or to let the business continue to operate; and (3) to consult with the debtor or trustee throughout the case.

The Reorganization Plan

The debtor may always file its own plan, whether in a voluntary or involuntary case. If the court leaves the debtor in possession without appointing a trustee, the debtor has the exclusive right to file a reorganization plan during the first 120 days. If it does file, it will then have another 60 days to obtain the creditors' acceptances. Although its exclusivity expires at the end of 180 days, the court may lengthen or shorten the period for good cause. At the end of the exclusive period, the creditors' committee, a single creditor, or a holder of equity in the debtor's property may file a plan. If the court does appoint a trustee, any party in interest may file a plan at any time.

The Bankruptcy Reform Act specifies certain features of the plan and permits others to be included. Among other things, the plan must (1) designate classes of claims and ownership interests; (2) specify which classes or interests are *impaired*—a claim or ownership interest is impaired if the creditor's legal, equitable, or contractual rights are altered under the plan; (3) specify the treatment of any class of claims or interests that is impaired under the plan; (4) provide the same treatment for each claim or interest of a particular class, unless the holder of a particular claim or interest agrees to a less favorable treatment; and (5) provide adequate means for carrying out the plan.

Acceptance of Plan

The act requires the plan to be accepted by certain proportions of each impaired class of claims and interests. A class of claims accepts a plan if creditors representing at least two-thirds of the dollar amount of claims and more than one-half the number of allowed claims vote in favor. A class of property interests accepts the plan if creditors representing two-thirds of the dollar amount of the allowed ownership interests vote in favor. Unimpaired classes of claims and interests are deemed to have accepted the plan; it is unnecessary to solicit their acceptance.

Confirmation of Plan

The final act necessary under Chapter 11 is **confirmation** by the court. Once the court confirms the plan, the plan is binding on all creditors. The rules governing confirmation are complex but, in essence, they include the following requirements:

1. The plan must have been proposed in good faith. Companies must also make a good faith attempt to negotiate modifications in their collective bargaining agreements. (See p. 1155.)
2. All provisions of the Bankruptcy Reform Act must have been complied with.

3. The court must have determined that the reorganized business will be likely to succeed and be unlikely to require further financial reorganization in the foreseeable future.

4. Impaired classes of claims and interests must have accepted the plan, unless the plan treats the impaired class in a "fair and equitable" manner, in which case consent is not required. This is sometimes referred to as the *cram-down* provision.

5. All members of every class must have received no less value than they would have in a Chapter 7 liquidation.

CHAPTER SUMMARY

The federal bankruptcy law governs the rights of creditors and insolvent debtors who cannot pay their debts. Alternatives to bankruptcy are assignment for benefit of creditors, composition (agreement by creditors to accept less than the face amount of the debt), and receivership. Since these are voluntary procedures, they are often ineffective when all parties fail to agree to them.

The Constitution lodges in Congress the power to legislate on bankruptcy. The current law is the Bankruptcy Reform Act of 1978, which provides for five types of proceedings: (1) liquidation (Chapter 7), (2) adjustment of debts of a municipality (Chapter 9), (3) reorganization (Chapter 11), (4) adjustment of debts of a family farmer with regular income, (Chapter 12), and (5) adjustment of debts of an individual with regular income (Chapter 13).

With some exceptions, any individual, partnership, or corporation seeking liquidation may file a voluntary petition in bankruptcy. An involuntary petition is also possible. Petitioning creditors in an involuntary bankruptcy must have claims for unsecured debt amounting to at least $5,000. Three creditors must join in the petition if there are twelve or more creditors, and must have particular grounds for relief.

A petition operates as a stay against suits against the debtor to recover claims or enforce judgments or liens. The judge will issue an order of relief and appoint a trustee, who takes over the debtor's property and preserves security interests. To recover monies owed, creditors must file proof of claims. The trustee has certain powers to recover property for the estate that the debtor transferred before bankruptcy. These include the power to act as a hypothetical lien creditor and to avoid fraudulent transfers and transactions known as voidable preferences.

The Bankruptcy Reform Act sets out categories of claimants and establishes priorities among them. The highest priority groups are (1) administration expenses, (2) gap creditor claims, (3) employees' wages, salaries, and commissions, (4) contributions to employee benefit plans, (5) grain producers and U.S. fishermen, (6) consumer creditor claims, and (7) taxes. After payment of these priority claims, the trustee must distribute the estate in the following order: unsecured creditors who filed claims on time, tardy unsecured creditors, persons claiming fines and the like, all other creditors, and finally the debtor.

Certain property is exempted from the estate of an individual debtor. States may opt out of a federal list of exemptions and substitute their own. Most states have opted out.

Once discharged, the debtor is no longer legally liable for most debts. However, some categories of debts are not dischargeable. Under certain conditions, a debtor may reaffirm a discharged debt.

Anyone with regular income who has difficulty paying off accumulated debts may voluntarily seek the protection of a bankruptcy court in a Chapter 13 proceeding. The individual presents a payment plan to creditors and the court appoints a trustee. The plan extends the time to pay and may reduce the size of the debt. If the creditors wind up with more in this proceeding than they would have in a Chapter 7 proceeding, the court is likely to approve the plan. The court may approve a stretch-out of five years. Chapter 13 is limited to those with regular income who have unsecured debts of less than $100,000 and secured debts of less than $350,000.

In a reorganization under Chapter 11, the debtor retains possession of the business and may continue to operate with its own management unless the court appoints a trustee. The court may do so either for cause or if it is in the best interests of the creditors. Any person eligible for discharge in Chapter 7 is eligible for Chapter 11, except stockbrokers and commodity brokers. The court must appoint a committee of unsecured creditors, who remain active throughout the proceeding. The debtor may file its own reorganization plan, and has the exclusive right to do so within 120 days if it remains in possession. The plan must be accepted by certain proportions of each impaired class of claims and interests. It is binding on all creditors and the debtor is discharged from all debts once the court confirms the plan.

KEY TERMS

Assignment for the benefit of creditors	p. 630	Hypothetical lien creditor	p. 642
Bankruptcy	p. 630	Interim trustee	p. 636
Claim	p. 636	Liquidation	p. 632
Confirmation	p. 652	Proof of claim	p. 636
Composition	p. 631	Reorganization	p. 632
Creditor	p. 636	Stay	p. 635
Fradulent transfers	p. 643	Voidable preferences	p. 642

SELF-TEST QUESTIONS

1. Alternatives to bankruptcy include:
   (a) an assignment
   (b) a composition
   (c) receivership
   (d) all of the above
2. A composition is:
   (a) a procedure whereby a receiver takes over the debtor's property
   (b) an agreement by creditors to accept less than the face amount of the debt
   (c) basically the same as an assignment
   (d) none of the above
3. A Chapter 11 bankruptcy provides for:
   (a) liquidation
   (b) reorganization
   (c) adjustment of debts of an individual with regular income
   (d) adjustment of debts of a municipality
4. An involuntary bankruptcy petition is
   (a) always allowed
   (b) never allowed
   (c) allowed if creditors meet certain conditions
   (d) filed by the debtor
5. The highest priority class set out by the Bankruptcy Reform Act includes:
   (a) administration expenses
   (b) unsecured creditors
   (c) persons claiming fines
   (d) the debtor

DEMONSTRATION PROBLEM

Sandy has filed a voluntary petition for bankruptcy under Chapter 7. One of Sandy's creditors is the federal government, which has a claim for $3,000 in unpaid federal taxes. Sandy also owes the attorney who handled the bankruptcy $750. If Sandy has only $750 in nonexempt assets, who is entitled to them—the government or the attorney? Why?

PROBLEMS

1. David has debts of $9,000 and few assets. He decides to file for bankruptcy but, because he has debts of less than $10,000, prefers to use the state court system rather than the federal system. Describe the procedure David should follow to file for bankruptcy at the state level.
2. In problem 1, assume that David has developed a plan for paying off his creditors. What type of bankruptcy proceeding should David use—Chapter 7, 11, or 13? Why?
3. Assume in problem 1 that David does not want to file for bankruptcy. He has two creditors and owes each of them $4,500. May one of the creditors force David into bankruptcy? Why?
4. Assume that David owns the following unsecured property: a $2,000 oboe, a $2,000 piano, a $500 diamond ring, a $1,000 car, and a life insurance policy with a cash surrender value of $3,500. How much of this property is available for distribution to his creditors in bankruptcy? Why?
5. If David owes his ex-wife alimony and child support, and is obligated to pay $3,000 for an educational loan, what effect will his discharge in bankruptcy have on these obligations? Why?
6. Assume that David owns a corporation which he wants to liquidate under Chapter 7. After the corporate assets are distributed to creditors, what major obstacle does David face in obtaining a court order discharging the corporation? Why?
7. Instead of using Chapter 7 (see problem 6), David decides to develop a reorganization plan for his company. What chapter of the Bankruptcy Reform Act should he use? Must all of the company's creditors approve the plan? Why?

ANSWERS TO SELF-TEST QUESTIONS

1. (d)   2. (b)   3. (b)   4. (c)   5. (a)

SUGGESTED ANSWER TO DEMONSTRATION PROBLEM

The attorney is entitled to the assets. Attorneys' fees are in the highest subcatetory within the priority class; taxes are the lowest subcategory.

Part 5

The Manager's Legal Agenda

The commercial borrowing and lending of money is no longer a simple affair; many interlocking federal and state statutes govern interest rates and their disclosure and set limits on the kinds of questions to be asked when determining whether to extend credit. Legal advice is essential.

Check for errors in billing as soon as possible. The Fair Credit Billing Act and other federal and state laws limit the time in which you can demand corrections.

If you sell goods under an installment arrangement, you should ensure that you file financing statements in a regular and timely manner to perfect a security interest in the goods you have sold. Otherwise, you may discover that your interest is secondary to that of someone else who filed first.

Because the place of filing financing statements varies from state to state and by type of property to be collateralized, make sure you file in the appropriate state or local office. Do not assume that you must file in the same place in each state. As a safety precaution, you should file both centrally and locally.

Since financing statements are effective for only five years from the date of filing, keep a "tickler" file that alerts the responsible person within the business that particular financing statements are about to expire.

Carefully evaluate agreements the business may have made to guarantee loans of employees or others, since these guarantees are contingent liabilities that could affect the balance sheet.

Ensure that payments on mortgaged business property are made on time to avoid the risk that the bank or other lending institution might invoke an acceleration clause that would require the balance of the mortgage to be paid off at once.

When considering whether to extend credit to customers backed by a mortgage on the customers' property, search the mortgage records for evidence that an existing mortgage is intended as security for an entire line of credit. If you fail to do so, you may later discover that even though your debtor took on later debt, you will have a lower priority in collecting or foreclosing, should that become necessary.

Use care in negotiating leases or other contracts permitting tenants to improve a landlord's property to avoid the possibility that as landlord you will be required to pay off a mechanic's lien should the tenant default in paying for work that benefitted the tenant only. In general, avoid any terms that suggest the tenant is operating as your agent.

If you suspect one of your debtors is insolvent or near insolvency, you should try to collect whatever is owed you immediately. If you do not collect more than three months before the debtor files for bankruptcy, the payments may be recoverable through the bankruptcy proceeding, meaning that you would be required to repay the funds to the bankruptcy trustee for redistribution to the creditors generally.

Although bankruptcy may provide a means for a business to restructure its debt and remain solvent, it is not a procedure to be undertaken lightly. Among other things, it could mean that managers will lose control of important business decisions until the reorganization plan is approved.

PART

VI

I know of no country, indeed, where the love of money has taken stronger hold on the affections of men and where a profounder contempt is expressed for the theory of the permanent equality of property.
—ALEXIS DE TOCQUEVILLE

PROPERTY, ESTATE PLANNING, AND INSURANCE

CHAPTER 30

Introduction to Property: Personal Property and Fixtures

*I*n this chapter we examine the general nature of property rights and the law relating to personal property—with special emphasis on acquisition—and fixtures. In Chapter 31, we discuss intellectual property, a class of personal property important to business. In Chapters 32 through 34, we focus on real property, including its nature and regulation, its acquisition by purchase (and some other methods), and its acquisition by lease (landlord and tenant law).

In Chapters 35 and 36, we discuss estate planning and insurance—two areas of the law that relate to both personal and real property.

THE GENERAL NATURE OF PROPERTY RIGHTS

Defined

Property, which seems so commonsense a concept, is difficult to define in an intelligible way, though philosophers have been striving to do so for the past 2,500 years. To say that property is what we own is to beg the question—or substitute a synonym for the word

we are trying to define. Blackstone's famous definition is somewhat verbose: "The right of property is that sole and despotic dominion which one man claims and exercises over the external things of the world, in total exclusion of the right of any other individual in the universe. It consists in the free use, enjoyment, and disposal of all a person's acquisitions, without any control or diminution save only by the laws of the land." Attempting a more formal and concise definition, the *Restatement of the Law of Property* defines property as the "legal relationship between persons with respect to a thing."

The Restatement's definition makes an essential point: property is a *legal relationship*, not a listing. This relationship deals with the power of one person to use objects in ways that affect others, to exclude others from the property, and to acquire and transfer property. However, the definition does not contain within itself a list of those things capable of being expressed in that relationship. We all know that we can own personal objects like radios and coats and even more complex "objects" like homes and minerals under the ground. Property also embraces objects whose worth is not so much intrinsic as representative or symbolic: ownership of stock in a corporation is valued not for the piece of paper called a stock certificate but for dividends, the power to vote for directors, and the right to sell the stock on the open market. Wholly intangible "things," like copyrights and patents and bank accounts, are capable of being owned as property. But the list of things that can be property is not fixed. Our concept of property continues to evolve. In the United States, many jobs are considered a type of property—protection against being fired, claims on pension funds, and other employment rights are converting what was once simply a contractual claim into a more solid-sounding property right. Welfare payments also are regarded as property, at least for purposes of the due process clause of the Fourteenth Amendment. A state cannot deprive a person of such payments without first holding a hearing. Likewise, some courts have even begun to recognize a person's educational degree as a property right in divorce proceedings, although most courts—as the following leading case demonstrates—have not gone that far.

In re THE MARRIAGE OF GRAHAM
194 Colo. 429, 574 P.2d 75 (1978)

LEE, JUSTICE. This case presents the novel question of whether in a marriage dissolution proceeding a master's degree in business administration (M.B.A.) constitutes marital property which is subject to division by the court. In its opinion, the Colorado Court of Appeals held that it was not. We affirm the judgment.

The Uniform Dissolution of Marriage Act requires that a court shall divide marital property, without regard to marital misconduct, in such proportions as the court deems just after considering all relevant factors. The Act defines marital property as follows:

> For purposes of this article only, 'marital property' means all property acquired by either spouse subsequent to the marriage except:
> (a) Property acquired by gift, bequest, devise, or descent;
> (b) Property acquired in exchange for property acquired prior to the marriage or in exchange for property acquired by gift, bequest, devise, or descent;
> (c) Property acquired by a spouse after a decree of legal separation; and
> (d) Property excluded by valid agreement of the parties.

The parties to this proceeding were married on August 5, 1968, in Denver, Colorado. Throughout the six-year marriage, Anne P. Graham, wife and petitioner here, was employed full-time as an airline stewardess. She is still so employed. Her husband, Dennis J. Graham, respondent, worked part-time for most of the marriage, although his main pursuit was his education. He attended school for approximately three and one-half years of the marriage, acquiring both a bachelor of science degree in engineering physics and a master's degree in business administration at the University of Colorado. Following graduation, he obtained a job as an executive assistant with a large corporation at a starting salary of $14,000 per year.

The trial court determined that during the marriage petitioner contributed seventy percent of the financial support, which was used both for family expenses and for her husband's education. No marital assets were accumulated during the marriage. In addition, the Grahams together managed an apartment house and petitioner did the majority of housework and cooked most of the meals for the couple. No children were born during the marriage.

The parties jointly filed a petition for dissolution, on February 4, 1974, in the Boulder County District Court. Petitioner did not make a claim for maintenance or for attorney fees. After a hearing on October 24, 1974, the trial court found, as a matter of law, that an education obtained by one spouse during a marriage is jointly-owned property to which the other spouse has a property right. The future earnings value of the M.B.A. to respondent was evaluated at $82,836 and petitioner was awarded $33,134 of this amount, payable in monthly installments of $100. [The court of appeals reversed.]

*   *   *

The legislature intended the term "property" to be broadly inclusive, as indicated by its use of the qualifying adjective "all" in section 14-10-113(2). Previous Colorado cases have given "property" a comprehensive meaning, as typified by the following definition: "In short it embraces anything and everything which may belong to a man and in the ownership of which he has a right to be protected by law." *Las Animas County High School District v. Raye*, 356 P.2d 237.

Nonetheless, there are necessary limits upon what may be considered "property," and we do not find any indication in the Act that the concept as used by the legislature is other than that usually understood to be embodied within the term. One helpful definition is "everything that has an exchangeable value or which goes to make up wealth or estate." *Black's Law Dictionary* 1382 (rev. 4th ed. 1968). . . .

An educational degree, such as an M.B.A., is simply not encompassed even by the broad views of the concept of "property." It does not have an exchange value or any objective transferable value on an open market. It is personal to the holder. It terminates on death of the holder and is not inheritable. It cannot be assigned, sold, transferred, conveyed, or pledged. An advanced degree is a cumulative product of many years of previous education, combined with diligence and hard work. It may not be acquired by the mere expenditure of money. It is simply an intellectual achievement that may potentially assist in the future acquisition of property. In our view, it has none of the attributes of property in the usual sense of that term.

*   *   *

A spouse who provides financial support while the other spouse acquires an education is not without a remedy. Where there is marital property to be divided, such contribution to the education of the other spouse may be taken into consideration by the court. Here, we again note that no marital property had been accumulated by the parties. Further, if maintenance is sought and a need is demonstrated, the trial court may make an award based on all relevant factors. Certainly, among the relevant factors to be considered is the contribution of the spouse seeking maintenance to the education of the other spouse from whom the maintenance is sought. Again, we note that in this case petitioner sought no maintenance from respondent.

The judgment [of the court of appeals] is affirmed.

The Economist's View

Property is not solely a legal concept, of course, and different disciplines express different philosophies about the purpose of property. To the jurist, property rights should be protected because it is just to do so. To the economist, "the legal protection of property rights has an important economic function: to create incentives to use resources efficiently" (Posner, 1973, p. 10). For a truly efficient system of property rights, the economist would require *universality* (everything is owned), *exclusivity* (the owners of each thing may exclude all others from using it), and *transferability* (owners may exchange their property). Together, these aspects of property would lead, under an appropriate economic model, to efficient production and distribution of goods. Because efficiency is a desideratum in a modern economy, the tendency may be to regard these features as necessary legal aspects of property as well. To do so would be mistaken. Rightly or wrongly, the law of property does not conform entirely to the economic conception of the ownership of productive property.

Classification of Property

Property can be classified in various ways, including tangible vs. intangible, private vs. public, and personal vs. real. **Tangible property** is that which physically exists, like a building, a ring, or a machine tool. **Intangible property** is something without physical reality that entitles the owner to certain benefits. **Public property** is that which is owned by the government; **private property** is that which is owned by anyone else, including a corporation.

Perhaps the most important distinction is between real and personal property. Essentially, **real property** is immovable; **personal property,** also known as *chattels*, is movable. Chattels that become affixed to personal property in a certain manner are called *fixtures* and are treated as real property. Fixtures are discussed later in this chapter.

Importance of the Distinction Between Real and Personal Property

In our legal system, the distinction between real and personal property is significant in several ways. For example, the sale of personal property, but not real property, is governed by Article 2 of the Uniform Commercial Code (see Chapter 7). Real estate transactions, by contrast, are governed by the general law of contracts. Suppose goods are exchanged for realty. UCC Section 2-304 says that the transfer of the goods and the seller's obligations with reference to them are subject to Article 2, but not the transfer of the interests in realty nor the transferor's obligations in connection with them.

The form of transfer depends on whether the property is real or personal. Real property is normally transferred by a deed, which must meet formal requirements. Transfer of personal property often can take place without any documents at all.

Another difference lies in the law that governs the transfer of property on death. A person's heirs must depend on the law of the state for distribution of his property if he dies *intestate*—without a will. Who the heirs are and what their share of the property will be may depend on whether it is real or personal. For example, widows may be entitled to a different percentage of real than personal property when their husbands die intestate.

Tax laws also differ in their approach to real and personal property. In particular, the rules of valuation, depreciation, and enforcement depend heavily on the character of the property. Thus, real property depreciates more slowly than personal property, and real property owners generally have a longer time than personal property owners to make good unpaid taxes before the state seizes the property.

PERSONAL PROPERTY

Most legal issues relating to personal property tend to cluster around acquisition. Acquisition of personal property by purchase is discussed in Part Three. Five remaining categories of acquisition are: (1) possession, (2) finding lost or misplaced property, (3) gift, (4) accession, and (5) confusion.

Possession

An old saying has it that "possession is nine-tenths of the law." There is an element of truth to this, but only some. For our purposes, the more important question is what is *meant* by possession. Its meaning is not intuitively obvious, as a moment's reflection will reveal. For example, if you suppose than an object is within your possession when it is physically within your control, then what do you say about the situation in which you happen inadvertently to be standing on top of someone else's diamond ring, which accidentally fell to the road? If you are not aware that it is underfoot, do you possess it? It strains credulity to suggest that you do. Possession, then, entails both *physical control* and *intention* to control.

By itself, physical domination of the object may not even be necessary. Suppose you give your diamond ring to a friend to examine. Is it in the friend's possession? No: The friend has custody, not possession; you retain the right to permit a second friend to pluck it from her hands. This is different from the case of a bailment (Chapter 20), by which the bailor gives possession of an object to the bailee. A garage (a bailee) entrusted with a car for the evening, and not the owner, has the right to exclude others from the car; the owner could not demand that the garage attendants refrain from moving the car around as necessary.

From these examples, we can see that possession or physical control must usually be understood as the power to exclude others from using the object. Otherwise, anomalies arise from the difficulty of physically controlling certain objects. It is more difficult to exercise control over a 100-foot television antenna than a diamond ring. Moreover, in what sense do you possess your household furniture when you are out of the house? Only, we suggest, in the power to exclude others. But this power is not purely a physical one, since being absent from the house you could not physically restrain anyone. Thus the concept of possession must inevitably be mixed with legal rules that do or could control others.

Possession confers ownership in a restricted class of cases only—when no person was the owner at the time the current owner took it into his possession. The most obvious categories of objects to which this rule of possession applies are wild animals and abandoned goods. The rule requires that the would-be owner actually take possession of the animal or goods; the hunter who is pursuing a particular wild animal has no legal claim until he has actually captured it. Two hunters are perfectly free to pursue the same animal, and whoever actually grabs it will be the owner.

But this simple rule is fraught with difficulties in the case both of wild animals and abandoned goods. We examine abandoned goods below. In the case of wild game, fish in the stream, and the like, the general rule is subject to rights of owners of land on which the animals are caught. Thus, even if the animals are wild, as long as they are on another's land, the landowner's rights are superior to the hunter's. Suppose a hunter captures a wild animal, which subsequently escapes, and a second hunter thereafter captures it. Does the first hunter have a claim to the animal? The usual rule is that he does not, for once an animal returns to the wild, ownership ceases.

Lost or Misplaced Property

At common law, a technical distinction arose between lost and misplaced property. An object is **lost** if the owner inadvertently and unknowingly lets it out of his possession. It is merely **misplaced** if the owner intentionally puts it down, intending to recover it, even if he subsequently forgets to retrieve it. These definitions are important in considering the old saying "finders keepers, losers weepers." This is a misconception that is, at best, only partially true, and more often false. The following hierarchy of ownership claims determines the rights of finders and losers.

First, the owner is entitled to the return of the property unless the owner has intentionally abandoned it. The finder is said to be a quasi-bailee for the true owner, and as bailee she owes the owner certain duties of care. The finder who knows who the owner is or has reasonable means of discovering the owner's identity commits larceny if she holds on to the object intending that it be hers. This rule applies only if the finder actually takes the object into her possession. If you spot someone's wallet on the street you have no obligation to pick it up, but if you do pick it up and see the owner's name in it your legal obligation is to return it to the rightful owner. The finder who returns the object is not automatically entitled to a reward, but if the loser has offered a reward the act of returning it constitutes performance of a unilateral contract. Moreover, if the finder has had expenses in connection with finding the owner and returning the property, she is entitled to reasonable reimbursement as a quasi-bailee. But the rights of the owner are frequently subject to specific statutes, such as the one discussed below in the *Bishop* case.

Second, if the owner fails to claim the property within the time allowed by statute, or has abandoned it, then the property goes to the owner of the real estate on which it was found if (1) the finder was a trespasser; (2) the goods are found in a private place (though what exactly constitutes a private place is open to question: is the aisle of a grocery store a private place? the back of the food rack? the stockroom?); (3) the goods are buried; or (4) the goods are misplaced rather than lost.

If none of these conditions apply, then the finder is the owner. These rules are considered in the next case, which involves a statute that prescribes the manner by which finders of currency buried in the ground are to advertise their discovery.

BISHOP v. ELLSWORTH
91 Ill. App.2d 386, 234 N.E.2d 50 (1968)

STOUDER, PRESIDING JUSTICE. Dwayne Bishop, plaintiff, filed a complaint alleging that on July 21, 1965, defendants, Mark and Jeff Ellsworth and David Gibson, three small boys, entered his salvage yard premises at 427 Mulberry Street in Canton, without his permission, and while there happened upon a bottle partially imbedded in the loose earth on top of a landfill, wherein they discovered the sum of $12,590.00 in United States currency. It is further alleged that said boys delivered the money to the municipal chief of police who deposited it with defendant, Canton State Bank. The complaint also alleges defendants caused preliminary notices to be given as required by Ill.Rev.Stat., Chap. 50, Subsections 27 and 28 (1965), but that such statute or compliance therewith does not affect the rights of the plaintiff. [The trial court dismissed the plaintiff's complaint.]

. . . It is defendant's contention that the provisions of Ill.Rev.Stat., Chap. 50, Subsections 27 and 28 govern this case. The relevant portions of this statute are as follows:

"27. Lost goods . . . If any person or persons find any lost goods, money, bank notes, or other choses in action, of any description whatever, such person or persons shall inform the owner thereof, if known, and shall make restitution of the same, without any compensation whatever, except the same shall be voluntarily given on the part of the owner. If the owner be unknown, and if such property found is of the value of $15 or upwards, the finder . . . shall, within 5 days after such finding . . . appear before some judge or magistrate . . . and make affidavit of the description thereof, the time and place when and where the same was found, that no alteration has been made in the appearance thereof since the finding of the same, that the owner thereof is unknown to him and that he has not secreted, withheld or disposed of any part thereof. The judge or magistrate shall enter the value of the property found as near as he can ascertain in his estray book together with the affidavit of the finder, and shall also, within 10 days after the proceedings have been entered on his estray book, transmit to the county clerk a certified copy thereof, to be by him recorded in his estray book and to file the same in his office. . . ." "28. Advertisement . . . If the value thereof exceeds the sum of $15, the county clerk, within 20 days after receiving the certified copy of the judge or magistrate's estray record shall cause an advertisement to be set up on the court house door, and in 3 other of the most public places in the county, and also a notice thereof to be published for 3 weeks successively in some public newspaper printed in this state and if the owner of such goods, money, bank notes, or other choses in action does not appear and claim the same and pay the finder's charges and expenses within one year after the advertisement thereof as aforesaid, the ownership of such property shall vest in the finder."

★   ★   ★

We think it apparent that the statute to which defendants make reference provides a means of vesting title to lost property in the finder where the prescribed search for the owner proves fruitless. This statute does not purport to provide for the disposition of property deemed mislaid or abandoned nor does it purport to describe or determine the right to possession against any party other than the true owner. The plain meaning of this statute does not support plaintiff's position that common law is wholly abrogated thereby. The provisions of the statute are designed to provide a procedure whereby the discoverer of "lost" property may be vested with the ownership of said property even as against the true owner thereof, a right which theretofore did not exist at common law. In the absence of any language in the statute from which the contrary can be inferred it must be assumed that the term "lost" was used in its generally accepted legal sense and no extension of the term was intended. Thus the right to possession of discovered property still depends upon the relative rights of the discoverer and the owner of the locus in quo and the distinctions which exist between property which is abandoned, mislaid, lost or is treasure trove. The statute assumes that the discoverer is in the rightful possession of lost property and proceedings under such statute is not a bar where the issue is a claim to the contrary.

There is a presumption that the owner or occupant of land or premises has custody of property found on it or actually imbedded in the land. The ownership or possession of the locus in quo is related to the right to possession of property discovered thereon or imbedded therein in two respects. First, if the premises on which the property is discovered are private it is deemed that the property discovered thereon is and always has been in the constructive possession of the owner of said premises and in a legal sense the property can be neither mislaid nor lost. Second, the question of whether the property is mislaid or lost in a legal sense depends upon the intent of the true owner. The ownership or possession of the premises is an important factor in determining such intent. If the property be determined to be mislaid, the owner of the premises is entitled to the possession thereof against the discoverer. It would also appear that if the discoverer is a trespasser such trespasser can have no claim to possession of such property even if it might otherwise be considered lost.

. . . The facts as alleged in substance are that the Plaintiff was the owner and in possession of real estate, that the money was discovered in a private area of said premises in a bottle partially imbedded in the soil and that such property was removed from the premises by the finders without any right or authority and in effect as trespassers. We believe the averment of facts in the complaint substantially informs the defendants of the nature of and basis for the claim and is sufficient to state a cause of action. [The trial court's dismissal of the Plaintiff's complaint is reversed and the case is remanded.]

Gift

A **gift** is a voluntary transfer of property without consideration or compensation. It is distinguished from a sale, which requires consideration. It is distinguished from a promise to give, which is a declaration of an intention to give in the future, rather than a present transfer. It is distinguished from a testamentary disposition (will), which takes effect only upon death, not upon the preparation of the documents. Two other distinctions are worth noting. An **inter vivos** (enter VYE vos) gift is one made between living persons without conditions attached. A gift **causa mortis** (KAW zuh mor duz) is made by one in contemplation of his approaching death.

Requirements   To make an effective inter vivos or causa mortis gift, the law imposes three requirements: (1) the donor must *deliver* a deed or object to the donee; (2) the donor must actually *intend* to make a gift; and (3) the donee must *accept* (see Figure 30-1).

Delivery   Although it is firmly established that the object be delivered, it is not so clear what constitutes delivery. On the face of it, the requirement seems to be that the object must be transferred to the donee's possession. Suppose your friend tells you he is making a gift to you of certain books lying in a locked trunk. If he actually gives you the trunk so that you can carry it away, a gift has been made. Suppose, however, that he had merely given you the key, so that you could come back the next day with your car. If this were the sole key, the courts would probably construe the transfer of the key as possession of the trunk. Suppose the books were in a bank vault and the friend made out an instrument giving you or him the power to take from the bank vault. This would not be a valid gift, since he retained power over the goods.

Intent   The intent to make a gift must be an intent to give the property at the present time, not later. Thus a person who has her savings account passbook put in her name and a friend's jointly, intending that on her death the friend will be able to draw out whatever money is left, has not made a gift, because she did not intend to give the money when she changed the passbook. The intent requirement can sometimes be sidestepped if legal *title* to the object is actually transferred, postponing to the donee only the *use* or *enjoyment* of the property until later. Had the passbook been made out in the name of the donee only, and delivered to a third party to hold until the death of the donor, then a valid gift could be found to have been made. Although it is sometimes difficult to discern the distinction in practice, a more accurate statement of the rule of intent is this: Intention to give in the future does not constitute the requisite intent, whereas present gifts of future interests will be upheld.

Acceptance   In the usual case, the rule requiring acceptance poses no difficulties. A friend hands you a new novel and says "I would like you to have this." Your taking the book and saying "thank you" sufficiently evidences your acceptance. Suppose, however, that the friend had given you property without your knowing it. For example, a secret admirer puts her stock certificates jointly in your name and hers without telling you. Later, you marry someone else and she asks you to transfer the certificates back to her name. This is the first you have heard of the transaction. Has a gift been made? The usual answer is that even though you had not accepted the stock when the name change was made, the transaction was a gift which takes effect immediately, subject to your right to repudiate when you find out about it. If you refuse to reject the gift, you have joint rights in the stock. Of course, if you expressly refuse to accept a gift or indicate in some manner that you might not have accepted it, then the gift is not effective. You are running for office. A lobbyist whom you despise "gives" you a donation. If you refuse the money, no gift has been made.

Most courts have decided that a gift of a bank check is not completed until acceptance or payment by the bank—for the reasons discussed in the following case.

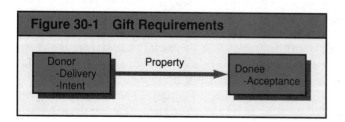

Figure 30-1   Gift Requirements

Donor
-Delivery
-Intent

Property →

Donee
-Acceptance

MATTER OF ESTATE OF BOLTON
444 N.W.2d 482 (Iowa 1989)

HARRIS, JUSTICE.

To be effective, must a gift in the form of a bank check be accepted and honored by the drawee bank prior to the death of the donor? The authorities seem nearly unanimous that the answer is yes.

The facts are straightforward and undisputed. On August 28, 1984, Arthur Bolton wrote a check for $20,000 to his daughter, Joyce Mattson, intending to make an inter vivos gift. The check was drawn on the State Bank of Wapello and was mailed to Joyce in Maryland, where she was living. Joyce received the check on or before September 1, endorsed it, and mailed it to her bank in Baltimore with instructions to use it to establish a certificate of deposit in joint tenancy with her father. The Baltimore bank apparently received the check on September 4 and subsequently complied with Joyce's instructions. On September 7 Arthur Bolton died. His death was sudden and unexpected. The check was presented to and rejected by the drawee bank in Wapello ten days after Bolton's death.

The trial court ruled that the check was void as an inter vivos gift. The court of appeals reversed and we granted further review. Although the equities clearly favor Joyce, under the clear and controlling legal principles we are obliged to agree with the trial court.

The black letter rule of law has been stated as follows:

> The general rule supported now by nearly all the cases on the subject is that the donor's check, prior to acceptance or payment by the bank, is not the subject of a valid gift either inter vivos or causa mortis. This is in accordance with the rules established by both the Uniform Negotiable Instruments Law and the Uniform Commercial Code that a check or other draft does not of itself operate as an assignment of any funds in the hands of the drawee available for its payment, and the drawee is not liable on the instrument until he accepts it. The difficulty with respect to a gift of the donor's check, if the check does not operate as an assignment, is that mere delivery of the check to the donee or to some other person for him does not place the gift beyond the donor's power of revocation, prior to payment or acceptance. Moreover, there is the further consideration, if the check does not operate as an assignment, that the death of the drawer works a revocation of the check, so that where the check is intended as a gift causa mortis and the donor dies before payment or acceptance, the death revokes the gift. Thus, the death of the drawer effects a revocation of the alleged gift of a check not presented for payment until after such death . . .

Am.Jur.2d *Gifts* § 65 at 869–70 (1968).

★   ★   ★

As noted in the language previously quoted, the rule now finds support in the uniform commercial code which states:

> A check or other draft does not of itself operate as an assignment of any funds in the hands of the drawee available for its payment, and the drawee is not liable on the instrument until the drawee accepts it.

(continued on next page)

(continued) **MATTER OF ESTATE OF BOLTON** 444 N.W.2d 482 (Iowa 1989)	Iowa Code § 554.3409(1). ★　　★　　★ We have already noted that Joyce's position has decided appeal in terms of abstract fairness. Unfortunately for her the clear rule of law which governs the dispute is against her. We are obliged to apply it. ★　　★　　★ Decision of court of appeals vacated; district court judgment affirmed.

Gifts Causa Mortis   Even though the requirements of delivery, intent, and acceptance apply to gifts *causa mortis* as well as *inter vivos*, a gift causa mortis (one made in contemplation of death) may be distinguished from a gift inter vivos on other grounds. The difference between the two lies in the power of the donor to revoke the gift before he dies; in other words, the gift is conditional on his death. Since the law does not permit gifts that take place in the future contingent on some happening, how can it be that a gift causa mortis is effective? The answer lies in the nature of the transfer: The donee takes actual title when the gift is made; should the donor not in fact die or should he revoke the gift before he dies, then and only then will the donee lose title. The difference is subtle and amounts to the difference between saying "If I die, the watch is yours" and "The watch is yours, unless I survive." In the former case, known as a **condition precedent,** there is no valid gift; in the latter case, known as a **condition subsequent,** the gift is valid.

Gifts to Minors   Every state has adopted either the Uniform Gifts to Minors Act (UGMA) or the Uniform Transfers to Minors Act (UTMA), which establish the manner by which irrevocable gifts are made to minors. Under these acts a custodian holds the gifts until the minor reaches the age of 18, 21 or 25, depending on state law. Gifts under UGMA are limited for the most part to money or securities, while UTMA allows other types of gifts as well, such as real estate or tangible personal property.

Gift Tax   The federal government and many states impose gift taxes on gifts above a certain dollar amount. We discuss gift taxes in connection with estate taxes on page 786.

Accession

An **accession** is something that is added to what one already possesses. In general, the rule is that the owner of the thing owns the additional thing that comes to be attached to it. For example, the owner of a cow owns her calves when she gives birth. But when one person adds value to another person's property, either through labor alone or by adding new materials, the rule must be stated somewhat differently. The general rule when goods are added to goods is that the owner of the principal goods becomes the owner of the enhanced product. For example, a garage uses its paint to repaint its customer's automobile. The car owner, not the painter, is the owner of the finished product. This rule has been modified, however, by UCC Section 9-314, which provides that a security interest takes priority as to affixed goods when it attaches before the goods (that is, the accessions) are affixed. An exception to this UCC rule is for subsequent purchasers or creditors with a prior perfected security interest who buy the combined goods or make advances before the security interest in the accessions has been perfected and without knowing about the security interest. In this event, the subsequent purchaser or creditor would have priority over the security interest in the accessions.

When someone has wrongfully converted—that is, taken as her own—the property of another, the owner may sue for damages, either to recover his property or its value. But a problem arises when the converter has added to the value of that property. In general the courts hold that when the conversion is willful, the owner is entitled to the full value of the goods as enhanced by the converter. Knowing that a ten-acre forest belongs to her neighbor, a carpenter enters the land, cuts down 100 trees, transports them to her shop, and cuts them up into standard lumber, thus increasing their market value. The owner is entitled to this full value, and the carpenter will get nothing for her trouble. Thus the willful converter loses the value of her labor or materials. If, on the other hand, the conversion was innocent, or at most negligent, the rule is somewhat more uncertain. Generally the courts will award the forest owner the value of the standing timber, giving the carpenter the excess attributable to her labor and transportation. A more favorable treatment of the owner is to give him the full value of the lumber as cut, remitting to the carpenter the value of her expenses.

Confusion

In accession, the goods of one owner are transformed into a more valuable commodity or inextricably united with the goods of another to form a constituent part. Still another type of joining is known as **confusion,** and it occurs when goods of different owners, while maintaining their original form, are commingled. A common example is the intermingling of grain in a silo. But goods that are identifiable as belonging to a particular person—branded cattle, for instance—are not confused, no matter how difficult it may be to separate herds that have been put together.

When the goods are identical, no particular problem of division arises. Assuming that each owner can show how much he has contributed to the confused mass, he is entitled to that quantity, and it does not matter which particular grains or kernels he extracts. So if a person, seeing a container of grain sitting on the side of the road, mistakes it for his own and empties it into a larger container in his truck, the remedy is simply to restore a like quantity to the original owner. When owners of like substances consent to have those substances combined (as in a silo), they are said to be tenants in common, holding a proportional share in the whole.

In the case of willful confusion of goods, many courts hold that the wrongdoer forfeits all his property unless he can identify his particular property. Other courts have modified this harsh rule by shifting the burden of proof to the wrongdoer, leaving it up to him to claim whatever he can establish was his. If he cannot, then he will forfeit all. Likewise, when the defendant has confused the goods negligently, without intending to do so, most courts will tend to shift

to the defendant the burden of proving how much of the mass belongs to him.

Suppose goods subject to a perfected security interest are commingled so that their original identity is lost. Prior to the UCC, some states held that the security interest was lost. However, under Section 9-315, the security interest is not lost as long as a financing statement covering the original goods also covers the product into which the goods have been manufactured, processed, or assembled.

FIXTURES

Defined

A **fixture** is an object that was once personal property and that has become so affixed to land or structures that it is considered legally a part of the real property. For example, a stove bolted to the floor of a kitchen and connected to the gas lines is usually considered a fixture, and for purposes of sale of the home, transfer at death, and taxation is treated as though it were real property.

Tests

Obviously, no clear line can be drawn between what is and is not a fixture. In general, the courts look to three tests to determine whether a particular object has become a fixture (See Figure 30-2).

Annexation   The property must be annexed or affixed to the real property. A door on a house is affixed. Suppose the door is broken and the owner has purchased a new door made to fit but which is not yet installed when the house is sold. Most courts would consider that new door a fixture under a rule of **constructive annexation.** Sometimes courts have said that

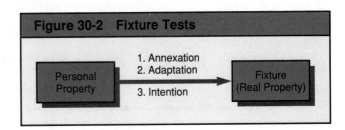

Figure 30-2   Fixture Tests

Personal Property → Fixture (Real Property)

1. Annexation
2. Adaptation
3. Intention

an item is a fixture if its removal would damage the real property, but this test is not always followed. Must the object be attached with nails, screws, glue, bolts, or some other physical device? In one case the court held that a four-ton statue was sufficiently affixed merely by its weight. [Snedeker v. Warring, 12 N.Y. 170 (1854).]

Adaptation Another test is whether the object is adapted to the use or enjoyment of the real property. Examples are home furnaces, power equipment in a mill, and computer systems in bank buildings.

Intention Recent decisions suggest that the controlling test is whether the person who actually annexes the object intends by so doing to make it a permanent part of the real estate. The intention is usually deduced from the circumstances, not from what a person might later say his intention was. If an owner installs a heating system in his house, the law will presume he intended it as a fixture because the installation was intended to benefit the house; he would not be allowed to remove the heating system when he sold the house by claiming that he had not intended to make it a fixture.

The next case illustrates the fixture tests.

CROCKER NATIONAL BANK v. SAN FRANCISCO
782 P.2d 278 (Cal. 1989)

Mosk, Justice.

We granted review to address "[o]ne of the most controversial questions of classification" for purposes of taxation in the law of fixtures, that of electronic data processing equipment.

★   ★   ★

In six actions later consolidated for discovery and trial, Crocker National Bank (hereafter Crocker) sought refund of certain real property taxes paid to the City and County of San Francisco (hereafter San Francisco) in six tax years. San Francisco had levied the taxes on certain electronic data processing equipment owned by Crocker and located in a leased building at 155 Fifth Street. For tax purposes, "real property" includes "[i]mprovements" (Rev. & Tax.Code) and "[i]mprovements" includes "fixtures." San Francisco had classified the equipment as fixtures. As a bank, Crocker was subject to taxation on its real property, but was exempt as to its personal property.

★   ★   ★

Crocker contends the Court of Appeal erred by upholding the superior court's classification of its electronic data processing equipment as fixtures for purposes of taxation. Before we can properly consider the claim, however, we must address and resolve the issues of the applicable fixtures test. . . .

★   ★   ★

. . . [I]n California "It is well settled that in determining whether an article constitutes a fixture, three criteria must be taken into consideration) the manner of its annexation to the realty; (2) its adaptability to the use and purpose for which the realty is used; and (3) the intention with which the annexation is made [citations] . . . . 'It is also settled that for tax purposes the "intention" must be determined by the physical facts or reasonably manifested outward appearances. . . .' [Citation.] [¶] In resolving whether an article placed on the premises constitutes a fixture or personal property, the aforelisted three elements do not play equal parts. In making the determination in a particular case the element of intent is regarded as a crucial and overriding factor, with the other two criteria being considered only as subsidiary ingredients relevant to the determination of the intent." (*Seatrain Terminals of California, Inc. v. County of Alameda* (1978) 147 Cal.Rptr. 578, citing cases.)

. . . [T]he test reduces itself to whether a reasonable person would consider the item to be a permanent part of the property, taking into account annexation, adaptation, and other objective manifestations of permanence.

★   ★   ★

The record establishes a number of facts beyond dispute. The equipment at issue comprises scores of separate items, including central processing units and various kinds of so-called "peripheral" devices. The superior court expressly found that "most of the . . . equipment herein can be characterized as 'general purpose,' 'off-the-shelf,' and 'fungible'. . . ." The evidence shows that the rest cannot reasonably be characterized otherwise.

As for annexation, the equipment was not physically attached to the building through permanent connections, as by means of cement, plaster, nails, bolts, or screws. Rather, it was attached merely through standardized "quick-disconnect" plugs that were inserted into the power source. Also, the items were readily movable without damage to themselves or to the building, and were in fact readily moved into, around, and out of, the structure. This was true of large central processing units, which weighed several thousand pounds and were rolled about on built-in casters; it was also true of small peripheral devices, which weighed only a few pounds and were carried by hand. Although certain pieces were connected to each other in "systems" or "groupings," they were joined not by permanent links but by standardized "quick-disconnect" cables.

As for adaptation, the equipment was not designed or modified for the building and the building was not designed or modified for the equipment. It is true that the building was planned and constructed as an operations or data processing center, and that safety, security, cooling, power, and fire-supression systems were designed into, or added onto, the structure at least in part to accommodate electronic data processing equipment. Such facts, however, are not dispositive of the question of permanence. If they were, modern office buildings would automatically transform modern office equipment, such as telecommunication and reproduction systems, into fixtures. Obviously, they do not.

★   ★   ★

Accordingly, we conclude that a reasonable person, taking into account annexation, adaptation, and other objective manifestations of permanence, would not consider the equipment at issue to constitute a permanent part of the building.

★   ★   ★

[The judgment of the Court of Appeals is reversed.]

Fixture Disputes

Because fixtures have a hybrid nature (once personal property, subsequently real property), they generate a large number of disputes. We have already examined two types of these disputes in other contexts: (1) disputes between mortgagees and secured parties (see Chapter 26), and (2) disputes over whether the sale of property attached to real estate (such as crops or a structure) but about to be severed is a sale of goods or real estate (see Chapter 16). Two other types of disputes remain.

Transfer of Real Estate   When a home owner sells her house, the problem frequently crops up whether certain items in the home have been sold or may be removed by the seller. Is a refrigerator, which simply plugs into the wall, a fixture or an item of personal property? If a dispute arises, the courts will apply the three tests above. Of course, the simplest way of avoiding the dispute is to incorporate specific reference to questionable items in the contract for sale, indicating whether buyer or seller is to keep them.

Tenant's Fixtures   Tenants frequently install fixtures in the buildings they rent or the property they occupy. A company may install tens of thousands of dollars worth of equipment; a tenant in an apartment may bolt a bookshelf into the wall or install shades over a window. Who owns the fixtures when the tenant's lease expires? The older rule was that any fixture, determined by the usual tests, must remain with the landlord. Today, however, certain types of fixtures—known as **tenant's fixtures**—stay with the tenant. These fall into three categories: (1) **trade fixtures**—articles placed on the premises to carry on the tenant's trade or business in the rented premises; (2) **agricultural fixtures**—devices installed to carry on farming activities (for example, milling plants and silos); (3) **domestic fixtures**—items that make a tenant's personal life more comfortable (carpeting, screens, doors, washing machines, bookshelves, and the like).

The three types of tenant's fixtures remain personal property and may be removed by the tenant if the following three conditions are met: (1) They must be installed for the requisite purposes of carrying on the trade or business, farming or agricultural purposes, or for making the home more comfortable. (2) They must be removable without causing substantial damage to the landlord's property. (3) They must be removed before the tenant turns over possession of the premises to the landlord. Again, any debatable points can be resolved in advance by specifying them in the written lease. It should be noted that some standard clauses in leases for apartments contain language stating that "all the improvements, alterations, repairs, and additions" belong to the landlord. Courts will often construe these provisions strictly, on the grounds that removable items are tenant's fixtures and thus not improvements or additions at all.

CHAPTER SUMMARY

Property is the legal *relationship* between persons with respect to things. The law spells out what can be owned and the degree to which one person can assert an interest in someone else's things.

Property is classified in several ways: personal vs. real, tangible vs. intangible, private vs. public. The first distinction, between real and personal, is the most important, for different legal principles often apply to each. Personal property is movable, whereas real property is immovable.

Among the ways personal property can be acquired are: (1) possession, (2) finding, (3) gift, (4) accession, and (5) confusion.

Possession means the power to exclude others from using an object. Possession confers ownership only when there is no owner at the time the current owner takes possession. "Finders keepers, losers weepers" is not a universal rule; the previous owner is entitled to return of his goods if it is reasonably possible to locate him. If not, or if the owner does not claim his property, then it goes to the owner of the real estate on which found, if the finder was a trespasser, or the goods were buried, were in a private place, or were misplaced rather than lost. If none of these conditions applies, the property goes to the finder.

A gift is a voluntary transfer of property without consideration. Two kinds are possible: inter vivos and causa mortis. To make an effective gift, (1) the donor must make out a deed or physically deliver the object to the donee, (2) the donor must intend to make a gift, and (3) the donee must accept. Delivery does not always require physical transfer; sometimes, surrender of control is sufficient. The donor must intend to give the gift now, not later.

Accession is an addition to that which is already owned—for example, the birth of calves to a cow owned by a farmer.

But when someone else, through labor or by supplying material, adds value, the accession goes to the owner of the principal goods.

Confusion is the intermingling of like goods so that each, while maintaining its form, becomes a part of a larger whole, like grain mixed in a silo. As long as the goods are identical, they can easily enough be divided among their owners.

A fixture is a type of property that ceases to be personal property, and becomes real property, when it is annexed or affixed to land or buildings on the land and adapted to the use and enjoyment of the real property. The common law rules governing fixtures do not employ clear-cut tests, and sellers and buyers can avoid many disputes by specifying in their contract what goes with the land. Tenant's fixtures remain the property of the tenant if they are for the convenience of the tenant, do not cause substantial damage to the property when removed, and are removed before possession is returned to the landlord.

KEY TERMS

SELF-TEST QUESTIONS

1. Personal property is defined as property that is:
   (a) not a chattel
   (b) owned by an individual
   (c) movable
   (d) immovable
2. Personal property can be acquired by:
   (a) accession
   (b) finding
   (c) gift
   (d) all of the above
3. A gift "causa mortis" is:
   (a) an irrevocable gift
   (b) a gift made after death
   (c) a gift made in contemplation of death
   (d) none of the above
4. To make a gift effective:
   (a) the donor must intend to make a gift
   (b) the donor must either make out a deed or deliver the gift to the donee
   (c) the donee must accept the gift
   (d) all of the above are required
5. Tenant fixtures:
   (a) remain with the landlord in all cases
   (b) remain the property of the tenant in all cases
   (c) remain the property of the tenant if they are removable without substantial damage to the landlord's property
   (d) refer to any fixture installed by a tenant

DEMONSTRATION PROBLEM

Justine had two young children. Justine wanted to make periodic gifts of stock to the children so that they would eventually have assets available to pay for college tuition. But she also realized that they would have great difficulty in buying and selling the stock before they reached the age of majority because brokers refuse to deal with minors (who can avoid their contracts). What solution would you recommend for Justine? Why?

PROBLEMS

1. Kate owns a guitar, stock in a corporation, and an antique bookcase which is built into the wall of her apartment. How is the property classified?
2. After her last business law class, Ingrid casually throws her textbook into a trash can and mutters to herself, "I'm glad I don't have to read that anymore." Tom immediately retrieves the book from the can. When Ingrid demands that he return the book, Tom refuses. Who is entitled to the book? Why?
3. In problem 2, suppose that Ingrid had accidentally left the book on a table in a restaurant. Tom finds it and, chanting "finders keepers, losers weepers," refuses to return the book. Is Ingrid entitled to the book? Why?
4. In problem 3, if the owner of the book (Ingrid) is never found, who is entitled to the book—the owner of the restaurant or Tom? Why?
5. Matilda owned an expensive necklace. On her deathbed, Matilda handed the necklace to her best friend, Sadie, saying "If I die, I want you to have this." Sadie accepted the gift and placed it in her safe-deposit box. Matilda died without a will and now her only heir, Ralph, claims the necklace. Is he entitled to it? Why?
6. Jeremy enters into a contract to purchase Waldo's house.

After the closing, when Jeremy is ready to move in, Waldo refuses to turn over the controls for the garage door opener. The controls are not mentioned in the contract of sale and Waldo claims that, because they are not annexed to the real estate, they are not fixtures. Who is entitled to the controls? Why?

7. Assume in problem 7 that Waldo owns an antique chandelier (a family heirloom) that was installed in the dining room. The contract with Jeremy does not mention the chandelier, but Waldo states that it was always his intention to take it with him when he sold the house. Who is entitled to the chandelier—Waldo or Jeremy? Why?

ANSWERS TO SELF-TEST QUESTIONS

1. (c)   2. (d)   3. (c)   4. (d)   5. (c)

SUGGESTED ANSWER TO DEMONSTRATION PROBLEM

Justine should make a gift following procedures specified in the Uniform Gifts to Minors Act or the Uniform Transfers to Minors Act. A custodian under these acts can buy and sell the stock for the minor's benefit.

CHAPTER
31

CHAPTER OVERVIEW

Types of Intellectual Property
Patents
Trade Secrets
Copyright
Trademarks

Intellectual Property

TYPES OF INTELLECTUAL PROPERTY

F ew businesses of any size could operate without being able to protect their rights to a particular type of intangible personal property interest, usually called **intellectual property**. Its major forms are patents, copyrights, and trademarks. Unlike tangible personal property (machines, inventory) or real property (land, office buildings), intellectual property has no fixed, corporeal form. It is the product of the human intellect that is embodied in the goods and services a company offers and by which the company is known.

A **patent** is the right to exclude everyone else from using or selling various types of inventions. A **copyright** is the right to exclude others from using or marketing forms of expression. A **trademark** is the right to prevent others from using a company's product name, slogan, or identifying design. Other forms of intellectual property are **trade secrets** (particular kinds of information of commercial use to a company that created it) and **right of publicity** (the right to exploit a person's name or image). Note that the property interest protected in each case is not the tan-

gible copy of the invention or writing—not the machine with a particular serial number or the book lying on someone's shelf—but the invention or words themselves. That is why intellectual property is said to be intangible: it is a right to exclude others from acting in a certain way toward objects that others may own. In this chapter we examine briefly the major types of intellectual property and the role of government regulation.

PATENTS

Source of Authority and Duration

Patent and copyright law are federal, enacted by Congress under the power given by Article I of the Constitution "to promote the Progress of Science and useful Arts, by securing for limited Times to Authors and Inventors the exclusive right to their respective Writings and Discoveries." Under current law, a patent gives an inventor exclusive rights to make, use, or sell an invention for seventeen years. In return for this limited monopoly, the inventor must fully disclose, in papers filed in the U.S. Patent and Trademark Office, a complete description of the invention.

Patentability

What May Be Patented The patent law says that "any new and useful process, machine, manufacture, or composition of matter, or any new and useful improvement thereof" may be patented. A **process** is a "means devised for the production of a given result"—for example, a process for making steel. A **machine** is a particular apparatus for achieving a certain result or carrying out a distinct process—lathes, printing presses, motors, and the cotton gin are all examples of the hundreds of thousands of machines that have received American patents since the first Patent Act in 1790. A **manufacture** is an article or product, such as a television, automobile, telephone, and light bulb. A **composition of matter** is a new arrangement of elements such that the resulting compound, such as a metal alloy, is not found in nature. In *Commissioner of Patents* v. *Chakrabarty*, 444 U.S. 1028 (1980), the Supreme Court said that even living organisms—in particular, a new "genetically engineered" bacterium that could "eat" oil spills—could be patented.

There are still other categories of patentable subjects. An **improvement** is an alteration of a process, machine, manufacture, or composition of matter that satisfies one of the tests for patentability given below. New, original, ornamental designs for articles of manufacture are patentable (like the shape of a lamp); works of art are not patentable but are protected under the copyright law. New varieties of cultivated or hybridized plants are also patentable.

What May Not Be Patented The courts have inferred from the Patent Act six categories of nonpatentable subjects: (1) printed matter (other than the design aspect); (2) naturally occurring substances; (3) methods of doing business; (4) ideas; (5) scientific principles, and (6) mental processes.

Tests for Patentability Just because an invention falls within one of the categories of patentable subjects, it is not necessarily patentable. The Patent Act and judicial interpretations have established certain tests that must first be met. A test known as **anticipation** bars a patent to any invention known or used by others in the United States or patented or described in a printed publication here or abroad before the inventor claims to have invented it. Likewise, under the **one-year rule** the Patent Office may not issue a patent if prior to one year before the application is filed the invention was described in a printed publication here or abroad or was in public use or on sale in this country. (Note the distinction between this rule and anticipation: in the former case, the test refers to the date of invention; in the latter, to the date of filing.) The rule of **priority** requires an invention to be both "new" and "useful." If an invention has already been made by someone else, it is not patentable by the later inventor, unless it can be shown that the prior inventor abandoned, suppressed, or concealed the invention or unreasonably delayed seeking a patent. An inventor will lose the right to an American patent if he patents the invention abroad before applying for a U.S. patent or if a patent is issued abroad more than a year earlier than his application for a U.S. patent. Under the **prior inventor rule,** if an invention happens to be described in a patent granted to another inventor who filed her application before the current applicant made his invention, no patent can be issued to the subsequent inventor. Moreover, only the inventor or inventors can be issued a patent.

Perhaps the most significant test of patentability is that of **obviousness.** The act says that no invention may be patented "if the differences between the subject matter sought to be patented and the prior art are such that the subject matter as a whole would have been obvious at the time the invention was made to a person having ordinary skill in the art to which said subject matter pertains." This provision of the law has produced innumerable court cases, especially over improvement patents, when those who wish to use an invention on which a patent has been issued have refused to pay royalties on the grounds that the invention was obvious to anyone who looked.

Procedures for Obtaining a Patent

An inventor cannot obtain a patent automatically; it must be approved by the U.S. Patent and Trademark Office, an arm of the U.S. Department of Commerce, located in Arlington, Virginia. Obtaining a patent is an expensive and time-consuming process, and the inventor will need the services of a patent attorney, a highly specialized practitioner. The attorney will help develop the required **specification,** a description of the invention that gives enough detail so that one skilled in the art will be able to make and use the invention. After receiving an application a Patent Office examiner will search the records and accept or reject the claim. Usually the attorney will negotiate with the examiner and will rewrite and refine the application until it is accepted. A rejection may be appealed, first to the Patent Office Board of Appeals and then, if that fails, to the federal district court in the District of Columbia or to the U.S. Court of Appeals for the Federal Circuit, the successor court to the old U.S. Court of Customs and Patent Appeals.

Once a patent application has been filed, the inventor or a company to which she has assigned the invention may put the words *patent pending* on the invention. These words have no legal effect. Anyone is free to make the invention as long as the patent has not yet been issued. But they do put others on notice that a patent has been applied for. Once the patent has been granted, infringers may be sued, even if the infringer has made the product and offered it for sale before the patent was granted.

In the world market that exists today, obtaining a U.S. patent is important, but it is not usually sufficient protection. The inventor will often need to secure patent protection in other countries as well.

Patent Ownership

The patent holder is entitled to make and market the invention and to exclude others from doing so. Because the patent is a species of property, it may be transferred. The inventor may assign part or all of his interest in the patent, or keep the property interest and license others to manufacture or use the invention in return for payments known as **royalties.** The license may be exclusive with one licensee, or the inventor may license many to exploit the invention.

One important limitation on the inventor's right to the patent interest is the so-called **shop right.** This is a right created by state courts on equitable grounds giving employers a non-exclusive royalty-free license to use any invention made by an employee on company time and with company materials. The shop right comes into play only when a company has no express or implied understanding with its employees. Most corporate laboratories have contractual agreements with employees about who owns the invention and what royalties will be paid.

Infringement and Invalidity Suits

Suits for patent infringement can arise in three ways: (1) the patent holder may seek damages and an injunction against the infringer in federal court; (2) even before being sued, the accused party may take the patent holder to court under the federal Declaratory Judgment Act, seeking a court declaration that the patent is invalid; (3) the patent holder may sue a licensee for royalties claimed to be due and the licensee may counterclaim that the patent is invalid. Such a suit, if begun in state court, may be removed to federal court.

Proving infringement can be a difficult task. Many companies employ engineers to "design around" a patent product—that is, to seek ways to alter the product to such an extent that the substitute product no longer consists of enough of the elements of the invention safeguarded by the patent. However, infringing products, processes, or machines need not be identical; as the Supreme Court said in *Sanitary Refrigerator Co.* v. *Winers*, 280 U.S. 30 (1929), "one device is an infringement of another . . . if two devices do the same work in substantially the same way, and accomplish substantially the same result, . . . even though they differ in name, form, or shape." This is known as the **doctrine of equivalents.** In an infringement suit, the court must choose between these two extremes: legitimate "design around" and infringement through some equivalent product.

An infringement suit can often be dangerous because the defendant will almost always assert in its answer that the patent is invalid. The plaintiff patent holder thus runs the risk that his entire patent will be taken away from him if the court agrees. In ruling on validity, the court may consider all the tests, such as prior art and obviousness, listed above, and rule on these independently of the conclusions drawn by the Patent Office.

Patent Misuse

Although a patent is a monopoly granted to the inventor or his assignee or licensee, the monopoly power is legally limited. An owner who misuses the patent may find that he will lose an infringement suit. One common form of misuse is to tie the patented good to some unpatented one—for example, a patented movie projector which will not be sold unless the buyer agrees to rent films supplied only by the manufacturer, or a copier manufacturer that requires buyers to purchase plain paper from it. As we will see in Chapter 46, various provisions of the federal antitrust laws, including specifically Section 3 of the Clayton Act, outlaw certain kinds of tying arrangements. Another form of patent misuse is a provision in the licensing agreement prohibiting the manufacturer from also making competing products. Although the courts have held against several other types of misuse, the general principle is that the owner may not use his patent to restrain trade in unpatented goods.

Patent Office Woes

Despite the legal system created by the federal patent law, the U.S. Patent Office is an understaffed, battered, and archaic bureaucracy several years behind in its work. More than a quarter million patent applications a year flow into the office, yet because of the staff's inefficiency, until the early 1980s more than half of all patents issued were eventually upset in court. The U.S. Court of Appeals for the Ninth Circuit, for example, ruled against patent holders in 85 percent of its cases. In 1982, however, Congress established the U.S. Court of Appeals for the Federal Circuit to hear all appeals in patent cases. By 1990, the era of contradictory rulings in the different federal circuits had ended, and the Federal Circuit has drastically changed the rate of reversals. The Federal Circuit is upholding patents in almost 80 percent of the cases it hears.

Although the Patent Office has begun to reduce its backlog, it still can take several years for a patent to be issued. Delays reduce the effective life of a patent. Consequently, many companies rely instead on keeping their innovations secret, although the law of trade secrets, to which we now turn, poses other difficulties.

TRADE SECRETS

Defined

A patent is an invention publicly disclosed in return for a monopoly. A **trade secret** is a means to a mo-

nopoly that a company hopes to maintain by preventing public disclosure. Why not always take out a patent? There are several reasons. The trade secret might be one that is not patentable, such as a customer list or an improvement that does not meet the tests of novelty or nonobviousness. A patent can be designed around; but if the trade secret is kept its owner will be the exclusive user of it. Patents are expensive to obtain and the process is extremely time-consuming. Patent protection expires in seventeen years, after which anyone is free to use the invention, but a trade secret can be maintained for as long as the secret is kept.

However, a trade secret is valuable only so long as it is kept secret. Once it is publicly revealed, by whatever means, anyone is free to use it. The critical distinction between a patent and trade secret is this: a patent gives its owner the right to enjoin anyone who infringes it from making use of it, whereas a trade secret gives its "owner" the right to sue only the person who improperly took it or revealed it.

According to the *Restatement of Torts*, Section 757, Comment b, a trade secret may consist of

> . . . any formula, pattern, device or compilation of information which is used in one's business, and which gives him an opportunity to obtain an advantage over competitors who do not know or use it. It may be a formula for a chemical compound, a process of manufacturing, treating or preserving materials, a pattern for a machine or other device, or a list of customers. . . . A trade secret is a process or device for continuous use in the operation of a business. Generally it relates to the production of goods, as, for example, a machine or formula for the production of an article.

Other types of trade secrets are customer information, pricing data, marketing methods, sources of supply, and secret technical know-how.

Elements

To be entitled to protection, a trade secret must be (1) *original*, and (2) *secret*.

Originality   The trade secret must have a certain degree of originality, although not as much as would be necessary to secure a patent. For example, a principle or technique that is common knowledge does not become a protectable trade secret merely because a particular company taught it to one of its employees who now wants to leave to work for a competitor.

Secrecy Some types of information are obviously secret, like the chemical formula that is jealously guarded through an elaborate security system within the company. But other kinds of information might not be secret, even though essential to a company's business. For instance, a list of suppliers that can be devised easily by reading through the telephone directory is not secret. Nor is a method secret simply because someone develops and uses it, if no steps are taken to guard it. A company that circulates a product description in its catalog may not claim a trade secret in the design of the product, if the description permits someone to do "reverse engineering." A company that hopes to keep its processes and designs secret should affirmatively attempt to do so—for example, by requiring employees to sign a nondisclosure agreement covering the corporate trade secrets with which they work. However, a company need not go to every extreme to guard a trade secret. As the next case demonstrates, industrial espionage is an improper means of gathering information that is arguably "public."

E. I. DUPONT DE NEMOURS & CO. v. CHRISTOPHER
431 F.2d 1012 (5th Cir. 1970); *cert. denied,* 400 U.S. 1024 (1971)

GOLDBERG, CIRCUIT JUDGE. This is a case of industrial espionage in which an airplane is the cloak and a camera the dagger. The defendants-appellants, Rolfe and Gary Christopher, are photographers in Beaumont, Texas. The Christophers were hired by an unknown third party to take aerial photographs of new construction at the Beaumont plant of E. I. duPont de Nemours & Company, Inc. Sixteen photographs of the DuPont facility were taken from the air on March 19, 1969, and these photographs were later developed and delivered to the third party.

*   *   *

. . . DuPont subsequently filed suit against the Christophers, alleging that the Christophers had wrongfully obtained photographs revealing DuPont's trade secrets which they then sold to the undisclosed third party. DuPont contended that it had developed a highly secret but unpatented process for producing methanol, a process which gave DuPont a competitive advantage over other producers. This process, DuPont alleged, was a trade secret developed after much expensive and time-consuming research, and a secret which the company had taken special precautions to safeguard. The area photographed by the Christophers was the plant designed to produce methanol by this secret process, and because the plant was still under construction parts of the process were exposed to view from directly above the construction area. Photographs of that area, DuPont alleged, would enable a skilled person to deduce the secret process for making methanol. DuPont thus contended that the Christophers had wrongfully appropriated DuPont trade secrets by taking the photographs and delivering them to the undisclosed third party. In its suit DuPont asked for damages to cover the loss it had already sustained as a result of the wrongful disclosure of the trade secret and sought temporary and permanent injunctions prohibiting any further circulation of the photographs already taken and prohibiting any additional photographing of the methanol plant.

(continued on next page)

(continued)

E. I. DUPONT DE NEMOURS & CO. v. CHRISTOPHER
431 F.2d 1012 (5th Cir. 1970); *cert. denied*, 400 U.S. 1024 (1971)

* * *

. . . The [trial] court granted DuPont's motion to compel the Christophers to divulge the name of their client. . . . Agreeing with the trial court's determination that DuPont had stated a valid claim, we affirm the decision of that court.

* * *

The Christophers argued both at trial and before this court that they committed no "actionable wrong" in photographing the DuPont facility and passing these photographs on to their client because they conducted all of their activities in public airspace, violated no government aviation standard, did not breach any confidential relation, and did not engage in any fraudulent or illegal conduct. In short, the Christophers argue that for an appropriation of trade secrets to be wrongful there must be a trespass, other illegal conduct, or breach of a confidential relationship. We disagree.

* * *

. . . [T]he Texas Supreme Court specifically adopted the rule found in the Restatement of Torts which provides:

> One who discloses or uses another's trade secret, without a privilege to do so, is liable to the other if (a) he discovered the secret by improper means, or (b) his disclosure or use constitutes a breach of confidence reposed in him by the other in disclosing the secret to him. . . . (Restatement of Torts § 757 (1939).)

Thus, although the previous cases have dealt with a breach of a confidential relationship, a trespass, or other illegal conduct, the rule is much broader than the cases heretofore encountered. Not limiting itself to specific wrongs, Texas adopted subsection (a) of the Restatement which recognizes a cause of action for the discovery of a trade secret by any "improper" means.

* * *

The question remaining, therefore, is whether aerial photography of plant construction is an improper means of obtaining another's trade secret. We conclude that it is and that the Texas courts would so hold. The Supreme Court of that state has declared that "the undoubted tendency of the law has been to recognize and enforce higher standards of commercial morality in the business world." That court has quoted with approval articles indicating that the *proper* means of gaining possession of a competitor's secret process is "through inspection and analysis" of the product in order to create a duplicate.

* * *

We think, therefore, that the Texas rule is clear. One may use his competitor's secret process if he discovers the process by reverse engineering applied to the finished product; one may use a competitor's process if he discovers it by his own independent research; but one may not avoid these labors by taking the process from the discoverer without his permission at a time when he is taking reasonable precautions to maintain its secrecy. To obtain knowledge of a process without spending the time and money to discover it independently is *improper* unless the holder voluntarily discloses it or fails to take reasonable precautions to ensure its secrecy.

★　　★　　★

In taking this position we realize that industrial espionage of the sort here perpetrated has become a popular sport in some segments of our industrial community. However, our devotion to free wheeling industrial competition must not force us into accepting the law of the jungle as the standard of morality expected in our commercial relations. Our tolerance of the espionage game must cease when the protections required to prevent another's spying cost so much that the spirit of inventiveness is dampened. Commercial privacy must be protected from espionage which could not have been reasonably anticipated or prevented. We do not mean to imply, however, that everything not in plain view is within the protected vale, nor that all information obtained through every extra optical extension is forbidden. Indeed, for our industrial competition to remain healthy there must be breathing room for observing a competing industrialist. A competitor can and must shop his competition for pricing and examine his products for quality, components, and methods of manufacture. Perhaps ordinary fences and roofs must be built to shut out incursive eyes, but we need not require the discoverer of a trade secret to guard against the unanticipated, the undetectable, or the unpreventable methods of espionage now available.

In the instant case DuPont was in the midst of constructing a plant. Although after construction the finished plant would have protected much of the process from view, during the period of construction the trade secret was exposed to view from the air. To require DuPont to put a roof over the unfinished plant to guard its secret would impose an enormous expense to prevent nothing more than a school boy's trick. We introduce here no new or radical ethic since our ethos has never given moral sanction to piracy.

★　　★　　★

The decision of the trial court is affirmed and the case remanded to that court for proceedings on the merits.

Trade secrets espionage has become a big business. Estimates put the direct loss at more than $1 billion a year and climbing. To protect industrial secrets, American corporations spend more than $15 billion on security arrangements. One security consultant has estimated that by 1995 that number will rise to more than $23 billion. Companies can fight back also through civil litigation as in *du Pont* and criminal prosecutions. In 1982, for example, the FBI set up a "sting" operation supposedly selling IBM computer secrets and wound up arresting employees of Hitachi, Ltd. and other foreign companies. Later, IBM settled civil lawsuits against Fujitsu, agreeing to a novel arrangement for resolving future disputes over trade secrets (see p. 75).

Unsolicited Ideas

Suppose you have a brilliant idea about a surefire television situation comedy. You write to the network and suggest that it put its writers to work on a series involving two secretaries who spend their evening hours searching for buried treasure in city sewers. The network never writes you back, but the following year a series called "Sewer Girls" is aired and becomes a smash success. Do you have a claim for compensation? The answer is most likely no, because, as Justice Brandeis said, "The general rule of law is, that the noblest of human productions—knowledge, truths ascertained, conceptions and ideas—become after voluntary communication to others, free as the air to common use." For an idea to be protected, it must be novel, expressed in some concrete form (a set of blueprints, a completed script), and the parties must usually have some relationship—for example, an express or implied contract, or a confidential relationship that induced the plaintiff to disclose it to the defendant.

Right of Employees to Use Trade Secrets

A perennial source of lawsuits in the trade secrets arena is the employee who is hired away by a competitor, allegedly taking trade secrets along with him (see **Box 31-1**). Companies frequently seek to prevent piracy by requiring employees to sign confidentiality agreements. An agreement not to disclose particular trade secrets learned or developed on the job is generally enforceable. Even without an agreement, an employer can often prevent disclosure under principles of agency law. Sections 395 and 396 of the *Restatement (Second) of Agency* suggest that it is an actionable breach of duty to disclose to third persons information given confidentially during the course of the agency. However, every person is held to have a right to earn a living. If the rule were strictly applied, a highly skilled person who went to another company might be barred from using his knowledge and skills. The courts do not prohibit people from using elsewhere the general knowledge and skills they developed on the job. Only specific trade secrets are protected.

To get around this difficulty, some companies require their employees to sign agreements not to compete. But unless the agreements are limited in scope and duration to protect a company against only specific misuse of trade secrets, they are unenforceable.

COPYRIGHT

Definition and Duration

Copyright is the legal protection given to "authors" for their "writings." Copyright law is federal; like patent law, its source lies in the Constitution. Copyright protects the expression of ideas in some tangible form, but it does not protect the ideas themselves. Under the 1976 Copyright Act, a copyright in any work created after January 1, 1978 begins when the work is fixed in tangible form—that is, when a book is written down or a picture is painted—and generally lasts for the life of the author plus fifty years after his death. However, knowledge of the old Copyright Act of 1909 is still necessary to determine when a copyright expires for a work created before 1978. Under that law, copyright lasted for twenty-eight years from the time of publication or registration with the U.S. Copyright Office (a branch of the Library of Congress), renewable for a second twenty-eight year term. Works copyrighted before 1978 are subject for the most part to the old rules, except that the maximum term has been increased to seventy-five years. The renewal rules are complex. An example: by the end of 1993 all works copyrighted originally in 1965 must be renewed or else they fall into the "public domain" and anyone is free to use them. A work renewed in 1993 will remain in copyright until 2040—that is, twenty-eight years for the first term, and forty-seven years for the second term, for a total of seventy-five years.

Subjects of Copyright

The Copyright Act protects a variety of "writings," some of which may not seem written at all. These include literary works (books, newspapers, and magazines), music, drama, choreography, films, art, sculpture, and sound recordings. Since copyright covers the expression and not the material or physical object, a book may be copyrighted whether it is on paper, microfilm, tape, or computer disk.

LAW AND LIFE

BOX 31-1

Protecting Corporate Secrets

[*A concern over employee appropriation of trade secrets has caused many companies in highly competitive industries to enact costly prevention methods to thwart espionage activities*—AUTHORS' NOTE]

Coca-Cola accuses Procter & Gamble of trying to uncover its confidential operational plans. Hertz charges Avis with unfair trade practices for hiring away 18 managers with knowledge of secret operational and financial information. Squibb goes to court to block Diagnostic Medical Instruments from pilfering data about its cardiac monitoring systems. S. B. Thomas sues Entemann's for filching crucial details about the equipment and ingredients used to make the famous nooks and crannies in its English muffins.

Whether the product is medicine or muffins, companies are more preoccupied than ever before with finding ways of protecting their trade secrets. American businesses this year will spend $12.5 billion on security, up from $10.7 billion in 1982. Much of it is aimed at preventing competitors from stealing proprietary information about product design, manufacturing techniques and marketing strategies. Companies install electronic locks that can be opened only with cardshaped "keys." Sensitive reports are circulated on a strict "need to know" basis. Workers are subjected to intensive background checks that include lie-detector tests and investigations by private detectives.

Such precautions and even more extreme ones do not mean that U.S. businessmen are succumbing to a kind

EMPLOYEES WHO TAKE TRADE SECRETS WITH THEM

of mass paranoia. So far, no one is known to have tapped a rival's computer over long-distance telephone lines, like Milwaukee's schoolboy 414 Gang. But the fact is that many companies, especially those in highly competitive industries, are frequently the targets of espionage activities.

Usually such intelligence gathering is done legally, if deviously, by searching trade journals or eavesdropping on conversations in airport waiting rooms. Other times it is more blatant. Tenant, a maker of floor-maintenance equipment, was awarded $500,000 in damages last April from a competitor, Advance Machine. Two managers of the rival firm admitted sifting through trash containers outside Tenant's Oakland, Calif., office for sales leads. General Motors transplanted a grove of 30-ft. evergreens to block a favored vantage point of photographers trying to shoot long-range pictures of new models at its Milford Mich., test track.

Few companies have been as persistent in cracking a case of industrial espionage as Rohm & Haas, a Philadelphia chemical manufacturer. It hired a private-detective agency and spent nearly five years tracking down the theft of a secret formula used to make latex paints. The search led to Australia, where Rohm & Haas found a firm that was duplicating its product "molecule for molecule," and then back to the U.S., where a former employee was finally detained last May after a high-speed, wrong-way car chase on a Manhattan parkway. Ex-

plaining the investigation as "perfectly consistent" with the company's security measures, Rohm & Haas Spokesman Jack Pounds says simply: "We have a lot of secrets."

Workers, especially executives, who change jobs are the biggest source of company leaks. The problem is especially acute in the electronics industry. In California's Silicon Valley, job turnover averaged 24% last year. Observes one local executive recruiter: "There's a lot of greed out there. If you can get into the right situation, you're an instant millionaire."

To reduce the amount of information that walks out the door, companies are enforcing nondisclosure agreements that prevent workers from taking secrets with them to a new job. It is not easy. Points out California Attorney James Pooley: "The most difficult area the courts have to grapple with is the distinction between your ideas and the company's property." Texas Instruments sued ten employees who left to start Compaq Computer, even though the Compaq machine, a portable that works like an IBM Personal Computer, does not use the same operating systems or software as the T.I. machines. Compaq retaliated with a $60 million suit charging Texas Instruments with restraint of trade.

IBM is perhaps the most fiercely protective company in the U.S. In a booklet distributed to employees, Chairman John Opel warns, "IBM increasingly is a target for people interested in illicitly acquiring significant business secrets. Over the years, there have been a number of actual thefts." The booklet describes an elaborate method of protecting company assets, including a four-level system for classifying documents and computer data from "IBM Internal

(continued on next page)

BOX 31-1

(Box 31-1 continued)
Use Only" to "Registered IBM Confidential." This spring IBM took three senior executives to court for revealing privileged information.

IBM is just as tough on outside suppliers. While developing software for the Personal Computer, workers at Peachtree Software in Atlanta began to refer to the company by another three initials, KGB, after IBM ordered the installation of paper shredders and locked security areas. Microsoft, which also developed soft-

ware programs for the PC, had to stiffen its procedures after IBM conducted an unannounced inspection and discovered that part of the then secret computer had been temporarily left unguarded.

Even IBM, though, could learn something from Kentucky Fried Chicken. Only two executives are entrusted with access to the recipe for Colonel Harland Sanders' original blend of eleven herbs and spices that gives the chicken its distinctive taste. To get at the formula, either man

must first use a secret key to open a strongbox that contains a combination. Then they use the combination to open a vault at the Louisville headquarters that holds a fireproof safe. After opening the safe, they face a strongbox with another combination lock. The handwritten recipe is inside the box. In one final attempt to thwart thievery, the combination to the last lock is concealed in an executive's memory.

Source: *Time*, September 19, 1983

Rights Protected

Prevent Copying   A copyright gives its holder the right to prevent others from copying. The copyright holder has the exclusive right to reproduce the work in any medium (paper, film, sound recording), to perform it (in the case of a play, for instance), or to display it (a painting or film). A copyright also gives its holder the exclusive right to prepare derivative works based on the copyrighted work. Thus a playwright could not adapt to the stage a novelist's book without the latter's permission.

Compulsory Licensing   One major exception to the exclusivity provision is for making and distributing phonorecords. The Copyright Act establishes a compulsory licensing scheme: once the music copyright holder permits a recording to be made and distributed to the public, then anyone is free to make his own recording, provided that the copier pays royalties fixed by the statute. The law does not permit a copy to be made of a prior *performance;* the copy must be an original new performance. The law also provides for compulsory licensing of jukeboxes and secondary transmissions of television cable systems.

Fair Use   Another major exception to the exclusivity of copyrights is the **fair use** doctrine. Anyone is

entitled to use material from a copyrighted work if the use is "fair," as when a book reviewer or an author quotes passages from a book. Without fair use, most writing would be useless because it could not readily be discussed. But "fair use" is not a clearly defined concept, and the courts will examine the degree to which the defendant's use of the copyrighted material will interfere with the plaintiff's right to sell it, the character and purpose of the use, the nature of the copyrighted work, and the proportion that the copied parts bear to the whole. A short passage from a long book can be copied without legal difficulty, but taking a line from a short poem or a single line from the lyric of a song might not be fair use.

The doctrine of fair use has grown more troublesome with the advent of the plain paper copiers. Suddenly it has become possible for anyone to copy virtually anything, cheaply and quickly. The 1976 act took note of the new technology, listing "teaching (including multiple copies for classroom use)" as one application of fair use. The Copyright Office follows guidelines specifying just how far the copying may go—for example, multiple copies of certain works may be made for classroom use, but copies may not be used to substitute for copyrighted anthologies. Likewise, libraries, including corporate libraries, may make single copies of whole articles for scholars or executives, but only under certain conditions spelled out in the act.

Infringement Verbatim use of a copyrighted work is easily provable. The more difficult question arises when the copyrighted work is altered in some way. As in patent law, the standard is one of substantial similarity.

Copyrightability Standards

To be subject to copyright, the writing must be "fixed" in some "tangible medium of expression." A novelist who composes a chapter of his next book in his mind and tells it to a friend before putting it on paper could not stop the friend from rushing home, writing it down, and selling it (at least the federal copyright law would offer no protection; some states might independently offer a legal remedy, however).

The work also must be creative, at least to a minimal degree. Words and phrases, like names, titles, and slogans are not copyrightable; nor are common symbols or designs familiar to the public. But an author who contributes his own creativity—like taking a photograph of nature—may copyright the resulting work, even if the basic elements of the composition were not of his making.

Finally, the work must be "original," which means simply that it must have originated with the author. The law does not require that it be novel or unique. This requirement was summarized pithily by Judge Learned Hand: "If by some magic a man who had never known it were to compose anew Keats's Ode on a Grecian Urn, he would be an author, and, if he copyrighted it, others might not copy that poem, though they might of course copy Keats's." [Sheldon v. Metro-Goldwyn Pictures Corp., 81 F.2d 49 (2d Cir. 1936)] Sometimes the claim is made that a composer, for example, just happened to compose a tune identical or strikingly similar to a copyrighted song; rather than assume the unlikely coincidence that Judge Hand hypothesized, the courts will look for evidence that the alleged copier had *access* to the copyrighted song. If he did—for example, the song was frequently played on the air—he cannot defend the copying with the claim that it was unconscious, because the work would not then have been original.

But even if the work is original, copyright does not extend to the underlying idea, nor does it cover a process, procedure, method of operation, concept, principle, or discovery. Einstein copyrighted books and monographs he wrote on the theory of relativity, but he could not copyright the famous formula $E = mc^2$, nor could he prevent others from writing about the theory. One of the most troublesome recent questions concerning expression versus ideas is whether a computer program may be copyrighted. After some years of uncertainty, the courts have accepted the copyrightability of computer programs. [Apple Computer, Inc. v. Franklin Computer Corp., 714 F.2d 1240 (3d Cir. 1983)] Now the courts are wrestling with the more difficult question of the *scope* of protection: what constitutes an "idea" and what constitutes its mere "expression" in a program, as the next case illustrates.

WHELAN v. JASLOW
797 F.2d 1222 (3d Cir. 1986), *cert. den.*
479 U.S. 1031 (1987)

BECKER, CIRCUIT JUDGE.

This appeal involves a computer program for the operation of a dental laboratory, and calls upon us to apply the principles underlying our venerable copyright laws to the relatively new field of computer technology to determine the scope of copyright protection of a computer program. More particularly, in this case of first impression in the courts of appeals, we must determine whether the structure (or sequence and organization) of a computer program is protectible by copyright, or whether the protection of the copyright law extends only as far as the literal computer code. The district court found that the copyright law covered these non-literal elements of the program, and we agree. This conclusion in turn requires us to consider whether there was sufficient evidence of substantial similarity between the structures

(continued on next page)

(continued)

WHELAN v. JASLOW
797 F.2d 1222 (3d Cir. 1986), *cert. den.* 479 U.S. 1031 (1987)

of the two programs at issue in this case to uphold the district court's finding of copyright infringement. Because we find that there was enough evidence, we affirm.

Appellant Jaslow Dental Laboratory, Inc. ("Jaslow Lab") is a Pennsylvania corporation in the business of manufacturing dental prosthetics and devices. Appellant Dentcom, Inc. ("Dentcom") is a Pennsylvania corporation in the business of developing and marketing computer programs for use by dental laboratories. . . . Individual appellants Edward Jaslow and his son Rand Jaslow are officers and shareholders in both Jaslow Lab and Dentcom. Appellants were defendants in the district court. Plaintiff-appellee Whelan Associates, Inc. ("Whelan Associates") is also a Pennsylvania corporation, engaged in the business of developing and marketing custom computer programs.

Jaslow Lab, like any other small- or medium-sized business of moderate complexity, has significant bookkeeping and administrative tasks. . . .

* * *

. . . Rand Jaslow hired the Strohl Systems Group, Inc. ("Strohl"), a small corporation that developed custom-made software to develop a program that would run on Jaslow Lab's new IBM Series One computer and take care of the Lab's business needs. Jaslow Lab and Strohl entered into an agreement providing that Strohl would design a system for Jaslow Lab's needs and that after Strohl had installed the system Strohl could market it to other dental laboratories. Jaslow Lab would receive a 10% royalty on all such sales. The person at Strohl responsible for the Jaslow Lab account was Elaine Whelan, an experienced programmer who was an officer and half-owner of Strohl.

. . . Ms. Whelan wrote a program called Dentalab for Jaslow Lab. Dentalab was written in a computer language known as EDL (Event Driven Language), so that it would work with IBM Series One machines. The program was completed and was operative at Jaslow Lab around March 1979.

. . . Ms. Whelan left Strohl in November, 1979, to form her own business, Whelan Associates, Inc., which acquired Strohl's interest in the Dentalab program. . . . Whelan Associates and Jaslow Lab entered into an agreement on July 30, 1980, according to which Jaslow Lab agreed to use its "best efforts and to act diligently in the marketing of the Dentalab package," and Whelan Associates agreed to "use its best efforts and to act diligently to improve and augment the previously successfully designed Dentalab package." The agreement stated that Jaslow Lab would receive 35% of the gross price of any programs sold and 5% of the price of any modifications to the programs. . . .

The parties' business relationship worked successfully for two years. During this time, as Rand Jaslow became more familiar with computer programming, he realized that because Dentalab was written in EDL it could not be used on computers that many of the smaller dental prosthetics firms were using, for which EDL had not been implemented. Sensing that there might be a market for a program that served essentially the same function as Dentalab but that could be used more widely, Rand Jaslow began in May or

June of 1982 to develop in his spare time a program in the BASIC language for such computers. That program, when completed, became the alleged copyright infringer in this suit; it was called the Dentcom PC program ("Dentcom program").

. . . After approximately a year of work, on May 31, 1983, his attorney sent a letter to Whelan Associates giving one month notice of termination of the agreement between Whelan Associates and Jaslow Lab. The letter stated that Jaslow Lab considered itself to be the exclusive marketer of the Dentalab program which, the letter stated, "contains valuable trade secrets of Jaslow Dental Laboratory." . . .

Approximately two months later . . . Rand Jaslow, . . . formed defendant-appellant Dentcom to sell the Dentcom program. At about the same time, Rand Jaslow and Jaslow Lab employed a professional computer programmer, Jonathan Novak, to complete the Dentcom program. The program was soon finished, and Dentcom proceeded to sell it to dental prosthetics companies that had personal computers. Dentcom sold both the Dentalab and Dentcom programs, and advertised the Dentcom program as "a new version of the Dentalab computer system."

★   ★   ★

A computer program is a set of instructions to the computer. . . .

The creation of a program often takes place in several steps, moving from the general to the specific. . . .

★   ★   ★

Once the detailed design of the program is completed, the coding begins. Each of the steps identified in the design must be turned into a language that the computer can understand. . . .

. . . The coding process is a comparatively small part of programming. By far the larger portion of the expense and difficulty in creating computer programs is attributable to the development of the structure and logic of the program, and to debugging, documentation and maintenance, rather than to the coding. . . . *See also Info World,* Nov. 11, 1985 at 13 ("the 'look and feel' of a computer software product often involves much more creativity and often is of greater commercial value than the program code which implements the product . . . ."). The evidence in this case shows that Ms. Whelan spent a tremendous amount of time studying Jaslow Labs, organizing the modules and subroutines for the Dentalab program, and working out the data arrangements, and a comparatively small amount of time actually coding the Dentalab program.

★   ★   ★

It is well, though recently, established that copyright protection extends to a program's source and object codes. . . . In this case, however, the district court did not find any copying of the source or object codes, nor did the plaintiff allege such copying. Rather, the district court held that the Den-

(continued on next page)

(continued)

WHELAN v. JASLOW
797 F.2d 1222 (3d Cir. 1986), *cert. den.*
479 U.S. 1031 (1987)

talab copyright was infringed because the *overall structure* of Dentcom was substantially similar to the overall structure of Dentalab. . . .

. . . The line between idea and expression may be drawn with reference to the end sought to be achieved by the work in question. In other words, *the purpose or function of a utilitarian work would be the work's idea, and everything that is not necessary to that purpose or function would be part of the expression of the idea.*

★   ★   ★

The rule proposed here is certainly not problem-free. The rule has its greatest force in the analysis of utilitarian or "functional" works, for the purpose of such works is easily stated and identified. By contrast, in cases involving works of literature or "non-functional" visual representations, defining the purpose of the work may be difficult. Since it may be impossible to discuss the purpose or function of a novel, poem, sculpture or painting, the rule may have little or no application to cases involving such works. The present case presents no such difficulties, for it is clear that the purpose of the utilitarian Dentalab program was to aid in the business operations of a dental laboratory. It is equally clear that the structure of the program was not essential to that task: there are other programs on the market, competitors of Dentalab and Dentcom, that perform the same functions but have different structures and designs.

This fact seems to have been dispositive for the district court:

> The mere idea or concept of a computerized program for operating a dental laboratory would not in and of itself be subject to copyright. Copyright law protects the manner in which the author expresses an idea or concept, but not the idea itself. . . . There are many ways that the same data may be organized, assembled, held, retrieved and utilized by a computer. *Different computer systems may functionally serve similar purposes without being copies of each other. There is evidence in the record that there are other software programs for the business management of dental laboratories in competition with plaintiff's program. There is no contention that any of them infringe although they may incorporate many of the same ideas and functions.* The 'expression of the idea' in a software computer program is the manner in which the program operates, controls and regulates the computer in receiving, assembling, calculating, retaining, correlating, and producing useful information either on a screen, print-out or by audio communication.

We agree. The conclusion is thus inescapable that the detailed structure of the Dentalab program is part of the expression, not the idea, of that program.

★   ★   ★

We hold that (1) copyright protection of computer programs may extend beyond the programs' literal code to their structure, sequence, and organization, and (2) the district court's finding of substantial similarity between the Dentalab and Dentcom programs was not clearly erroneous. The judgment of the district court will therefore be affirmed.

How far the copyright law will protect particular software products is a hotly debated topic, sparked by a federal district court's ruling in 1990 that the "look and feel" of Lotus 1-2-3's menu system is copyrightable and was in fact infringed by Paperback Software's VP-Planner, a competing spreadsheet. [Lotus Development Corp. v. Paperback Software International, 740 F.Supp. 37 (D.Mass. 1990)] The case has led some analysts to "fear that legal code, rather than software code, is emerging as the factor that will determine which companies and products will dominate the 1990s." (Lewis, 1990)

Who May Obtain a Copyright?

With one important exception, only the author may hold the initial copyright, although the author may assign it or license any one or more of the rights conveyed by the copyright. This is a simple principle when the author has written a book or painted a picture. But the law is unclear in the case of a motion picture or a sound recording. Is the author the script writer, the producer, the performer, the director, the engineer, or someone else? As a practical matter, all parties involved spell out their rights by contract.

The exception, which frequently covers the difficulties just enumerated, is for **works for hire.** Any person employed to write—a journalist or an advertising jingle writer, for example—is not the "author." For purposes of the statute, the employer is the author and may take out the copyright. When the employee is in fact an "independent contractor" (see p. 822) and the work in question involves any one of nine types (book, movies, etc.) spelled out in the Copyright Act, the employer and creator must spell out their entitlement to the copyright in a written agreement. [Community for Creative Non-Violence v. Reid, 109 S.Ct. 2166 (1989).]

Obtaining a Copyright

Until 1978, a work could not be copyrighted unless it was registered in the Copyright Office or was published and unless each copy of the work carried a copyright notice, consisting of the word "Copyright," the abbreviation "Copr.," or the common symbol ©

together with the date of first publication and the name of the copyright owner. Under the 1976 Act, copyright is automatic whenever the work is fixed in a ctangible medium of expression (for example, words on paper or images on film or videotape, sound on tape or compact disc), even if the work remains unpublished or undistributed. However, to retain copyright protection, the notice had to be affixed once the work was "published" and copies circulated to the public. However, after the United States entered the Berne Convention, an international treaty governing copyrights, Congress enacted the Berne Implementation Act, declaring that effective in 1989 notice, even after publication, is no longer required.

Notice does, however, confer certain benefits. In the absence of notice, a copyright holder loses the right to receive statutory damages (an amount stated in the Copyright Act and not required to be proved) if someone infringes the work. Also, although it is no longer required, an application and two copies of the work (for deposit in the Library of Congress) filed with the Copyright Office, in Washington, D.C., will enable the copyright holder to file suit should the copyright be infringed. Unlike patent registration, which requires elaborate searching of Patent Office records, copyright registration does not require a reading of the work to determine whether it is an original creation or an infringement of someone else's prior work. But copyright registration does not immunize the holder from an infringement suit. If a second work has been unlawfully copied from an earlier work, the second author's copyright will not bar the infringed author from collecting damages and obtaining an injunction.

TRADEMARKS

Defined

A **trademark** is defined by the federal Lanham Act of 1946 as "any word, name, symbol, or device or any combination thereof adopted and used by a manufacturer or merchant to identify his goods and distinguish them from goods manufactured or sold by others." Examples of well-known trademarks are "Coca-Cola," "Xerox," and "Chevrolet." A **service mark** is "used in the sale or advertising of services to identify the services of one person and distinguish them from the services of others." Examples of service marks are "McDonald's," "Mobil," and "Hilton." A **certification mark** is used in connection with products of many persons other than the owner of the mark "to certify regional or other origin, material, mode of manufacture, quality, accuracy or other characteristics of such goods or services or that the work or labor on the goods or services was performed by members of a union or other organization." Examples are "Good Housekeeping Seal of Approval" and "UL" (Underwriters' Laboratories, Incorporated, approval mark).

Extent of Trademark Protection

Kinds of Marks   Trademarks and other kinds of marks may consist of words and phrases, pictures, symbols, shapes, numerals, letters, slogans, and sounds. Trademarks are a part of our everyday world: the sounds of a radio or television network announcing itself (NBC), the shape of a whiskey bottle (Haig & Haig's Pinch Bottle), a series of initials (GE, RCA, IBM), or a growling animal (MGM's lion).

Limitations on Marks   Although trademarks abound, the law limits the subjects that may fall into one of the categories above. Not every word or shape or symbol will be protected in an infringement action. To qualify for protection, a trademark must be used to identify and distinguish. The courts employ a four-part test: (1) Is the mark so arbitrary and fanciful that it merits the widest protection? (2) Is it "suggestive" enough to warrant protection without proof of secondary meaning? (3) Is it "descriptive," warranting protection if secondary meaning is proved? (4) Is the mark generic and thus unprotectible?

These tests do not have mechanical answers; they call for judgment. Some marks are wholly fanciful, clearly identify origin of goods, and distinguish them from others—"Kodak," for example. Other marks may not be so arbitrary but may nevertheless be distinctive, either when adopted or as a result of advertising—for example, "Crest," as the name of a toothpaste.

Marks that are merely descriptive of the product are entitled to protection only if it can be shown that the mark has acquired **secondary meaning.** This term reflects a process of identification on the mark in the public mind with the originator of the product. Thus "Blue Dot," which describes a functional feature of a flash bulb, is a descriptive term that has acquired a secondary meaning and hence is protectible. However, the trademark owner of a descriptive term that has acquired secondary meaning can prevent others from using the mark only on the same kinds of goods. The mark can still be used in its primary descriptive meaning—thus, "Blue Dot" could be used as a mark for a line of polka-dotted clothing.

Some descriptive marks are more than *merely* descriptive; they *suggest* a use of the product, its nature, or one of its purposes. These may be protected even without proving that they have acquired a secondary meaning—for example, "PopCornNow," the name of a hot-air popping machine.

Certain words may not qualify at all for trademark protection. These include generic terms like "Straw Broom" (for a broom made of straw), and ordinary words like "fast food." In one case, a federal appeals court held that the word "LITE" is generic and cannot be protected by a beer manufacturer to describe a low-calorie brew. [Miller Brewing Co. v. Falstaff Brewing Corp., 655 F.2d 5 (1st Cir. 1981)]

Deceptive words will not be accepted for registration. Thus the Trademark Office denied registration to the word "Vynahyde" because it suggested that the plastic material to which it was applied came from animal skin. Geographic terms are descriptive words and may not be used as protected trademarks unless they have acquired a secondary meaning, such as "Hershey" when used for chocolates. A design that reflects a common style cannot be protected in a trademark to exclude other similar designs in the same tradition. Thus the courts have ruled that a silverware pattern that is a "functional feature" of the "baroque style" does not qualify for trademark protection (see **Box 31-2**). Finally, the Lanham Act denies federal registration to certain marks that fall within categories of words and shapes, including: the flag; the name, portrait, or signature of any living person without consent, or of a deceased U.S. president during the lifetime of his widow; and immoral, deceptive, or scandalous matter (thus "Bubby Trap" for brassieres was denied registration).

Acquiring Trademark Rights

For the first time in more than 40 years, effective in 1989 Congress changed the way in which trademarks

LAW AND LIFE

BOX 31-2

Trademark Protection Is Denied To 50-Year-Old Silver Pattern

By Deborah Squiers

*[The law has limitations on what can be protected in a trademark. As the following article notes, a federal court has ruled that a design that is a functional feature of Baroque style silverware is not protected by a trademark.—*AUTHORS' NOTE]

A BOSTON silverware manufacturer cannot assert trademark protection for a nearly 50-year-old pattern because its design is a functional feature of all Baroque style silverware, a Manhattan federal appeals court has ruled.

The appeals court last week determined that Wallace International Silversmiths Inc., of Boston, could not block a competitor, Godinger Silver Art Co., from marketing a line of silverware similar to its Grande Baroque line.

The decision, in *Wallace International Silversmiths Inc. v. Godinger Silver Art Co.*, 90-7408, held that ornamental features of the silver pattern are a "functional" part of all Baroque style silverware.

TOO COMMON FOR TRADEMARK PROTECTION

"Where an ornamental feature is claimed as a trademark and trademark protection would significantly hinder competition by limiting the range of adequate alternative designs, the aesthetic functionality doctrine denies such protection," Judge Ralph K. Winter wrote in the opinion.

The functionality doctrine precludes trademark protection for product features that are essential for its use or purpose or if it affects its cost or quality. Earlier Second Circuit decisions have held that the inquiry into whether a feature is functional should focus on its effect on competition in the marketplace.

The circuit panel, which also included Judges J. Daniel Mahoney and John M. Walker, upheld a ruling in May by Judge Charles S. Haight of the Southern District of New York. Judge Haight found the similarities between Wallace's Grand Baroque line and Godinger's recently released 20th Century Baroque were common to all baroque-style designs in silverware.

Judge Winter said Wallace International sought protection not for a "precise expression of a decorative style, but for basic elements of a style that is part of the public domain."

A Best-Seller

Introduced in the United States in 1941, Wallace International's Grande Baroque pattern is still one of the country's best selling silverware lines. A complete set of the pattern, which contains ornate designs of flowers, scrolls and curls, sells for several thousand dollars.

Wallace International owns a trademark registration for the name, Grande Baroque, but its trademark application for the design is still pending.

New York-based Godinger introduced its 20th Century Baroque pattern last spring. Like its competitor, Godinger's pattern contains the baroque elements of scrolls, curls and flowers. A four-piece setting of the silverplate pattern sells for about $20.

"The arrangements of these elements approximates Wallace's design in many ways," the opinion said, "although their dimensions are noticeably different."

Source: *New York Law Journal* October 22, 1990, p. 1

---

can be secured. Under the Lanham Act, the fundamental means of obtaining a trademark was through *use*. The manufacturer or distributor actually must have placed the mark on its product—or on related displays, labels, shipping containers, advertisements, and the like—and then have begun selling the product. If the product was sold in interstate commerce, the trademark was entitled to protection under the Lanham Act (or if not, to protection under the common law of the state in which the product was sold).

Under the Trademark Law Revision Act of 1988, trademarks now can be obtained in advance by registering with the U.S. Patent and Trademark Office an intention to use the mark within six months (the applicant can gain extensions of up to 30 more months to put the mark into use). Once obtained, the trademark will be protected for 10 years (before the 1988 revision, a federal trademark remained valid for 20 years); if the mark is still being used, the registration can be renewed. Obtaining a trademark registration

LAW AND LIFE

Protecting a Good Name is a Never-Ending Fight

[The success of a product represented by a trademark may result in the loss of exclusivity if the trademark becomes generic. As a result, manufacturers take extraordinary measures to ensure that their names are used properly.—AUTHORS' NOTE]

When thirsty restaurant patrons want a cola, they'll sometimes ask their waiter for a Coke. When a man nicks his face with a razor, he'll fumble through the medicine cabinet and, chances are, he'll mutter, "Where are the Band-Aids?" rather than, "Oh, for an adhesive bandage!" When the boss wants copies of a report, chances are, he or she will say, "Give me 10 Xeroxes," instead of, "Make ten photocopies."

THE PERILS OF TRADEMARKS

Coke, Band-Aid and Xerox—like, for example, Crisco, Fig Newtons and Kleenex—are trademarks that, according to their manufacturers, should only be used when that specific brand is requested.

This may appear to some to be "nitpicking," but the owners of trademarks—the manufacturers of products they represent—go to extraordinary lengths to ensure proper use of their good names.

Coca-Cola Co., which earned revenues of $6.8 billion in 1983, has a staff of approximately 40 trademark examiners constantly on the lookout for retailers and writers who in their estimation misuse the company's 98-year-old product name. The company also employs five in-house

trademark attorneys. Coca-Cola, which has registered its mark in 125 countries, subscribes to a clipping service and its legal department sends letters to the editors of publications that don't use the words Coca-Cola or Coke just right.

When the company suspects a retailer is offering a substitute cola and calling it Coke, it dispatches a trademark examiner to whisk a sample back to the company's Atlanta headquarters for testing. If the beverage isn't Coke, the company sends a representative to remind the retailer that the Coca-Cola name is not to be used with other sodas. If not heeded, the visit is followed by warning letters and eventually a lawsuit. Coca-Cola diligently pursues possible trademark infringers because it understands the value of a good name that the company can recognize. "If we lost all of our physical assets, we could rebuild again, based on our trademark," said Coca-Cola deputy trademark counsel Tim Hanak.

---

lies between obtaining patents and copyrights in difficulty. The Trademark Office will not routinely register a trademark; it searches its records to ensure that the mark meets several statutory tests and does not infringe another mark. Those who feel that their own marks would be hurt by registration of a proposed mark may file an **opposition proceeding** in the Trademark Office. Until 1990, the Trademark Office received about 77,000 aplications each year. With the chance in procedure, some experts predicted that applications would rise by 30 percent.

In many foreign countries, use need not be shown to obtain trademark registration. It is common for some people in these countries to register marks that they expect to be valuable so that they can sell the right to use the mark to the company that established

the mark's value. Companies that expect to market abroad should register their marks early.

Loss of Rights

Trademark owners may lose their rights if they abandon the mark, if a patent or copyright expires on which the mark is based, or if the mark becomes generic. A mark is abandoned if a company goes out of business and ceases selling the product. Some marks are based on design patents; when the patent expires, the patent holder will not be allowed to extend the patent's duration by arguing that the design or name linked with the design is a registerable trademark.

BOX 31-3

Registration Isn't Enough

Protecting one's business and product identity is not new. Ancient Egyptian craftsmen are said to have used trademarks to identify their wares. The Trademark Act of 1946, better known as the Lanham Act (15 U.S.C. 1127), is the federal statute under which trademarks used in or affecting commerce may be registered. Registration itself creates no greater right to use a particular mark than would common law, but it does confirm and supplement that right with certain procedural safeguards.

Trademarks commonly used as generic names for products

Baggies plastic bags
Con-Tact brand plastic
Cyclone chain link fence
Disposall food waste disposers
Fiberglas glass fibers
Jeep vehicles
Jell-O gelatin dessert
Kleenex tissues
Kool-Aid soft drink mix
Naugahyde vinyl coated fabrics

Ping-Pong table tennis
Plexiglas plastic
Q-tips cotton swabs
Saran Wrap plastic film
Scotch cellophane tape
Scotchgard stain repeller
Sheetrock gypsum wallboard
Styrofoam plastic foam
Tabasco pepper sauce
Teflon fluorocarbon resins
Ultrasuede fabric
Vaseline petroleum jelly

"The trademark is the principle on which trade and advertising depend," said Edith Collier, information services manager for the United States Trademark Association, a New York-based group with 1,600 corporate and lawyer members. "It is also protection for consumers. If you buy a product and don't have any source to identify that product and it's no good, who can you complain to?"

Simply registering a mark is not enough to protect it. The owner must use it in commerce and work doggedly to prevent others from using it com-petitively or generically. Many well-known, once-protected trademark names have now fallen into general public use. Aspirin, celluloid, cellophane, cube steak, dry ice, kerosene, linoleum and mimeograph—among others—have all lost their trademark protection, although aspirin and cellophane remain protected abroad. "The moral is you really have to vigorously enforce your rights," said Joseph Potenza, a Washington, D.C., trademark lawyer.

That makes it easy to understand why Xerox Corp., with $8.4 billion in revenue in 1983, becomes concerned when a newspaper or magazine editor lets the word Xerox be used as a noun or generic verb, rather than as a trademark adjective, as in "Xerox copies." The firm spends $100,000 a year advertising in legal and journalism publications to promote the proper use of its name and products, said Robert Shafter, senior trademark counsel at Xerox.

Source: Adapted from *ABA Journal*, March 1985

The most widespread difficulty that a trademark holder faces is the prospect of too much success: if a trademark comes to stand generically for the product itself, it may lose exclusivity in the mark. Famous examples are aspirin, escalator, and cellophane. As the article in **Box 31-3** demonstrates, the threat is a continual one. Trademark holders can protect themselves from their marks' becoming generic in several ways.

1. Use a descriptive term along with the trademark. Look on a jar of Vaseline and you will see that the label refers to the contents as Vaseline *petroleum jelly*.
2. Protest generic use of the mark in all publications, by writing letters and taking out advertisements.

3. Always put the words *Trademark, Registered Trademark,* or the symbol ® (meaning "registered") next to the mark itself, which should be capitalized.

CHAPTER SUMMARY

The products of the human mind are at the root of all business, but they are legally protectible only to a certain degree. Inventions that are truly novel may qualify for a seventeen-year patent; the inventor may then prohibit anyone from using the art (machine, process, manufacture, and the like) or license it on his own terms. A business may sue a person who improperly gives away its legitimate trade secrets, but it may not prevent others from using the unpatented trade secret once publicly disclosed. Writers or painters, sculptors, composers, and other creative artists may protect the expression of their ideas for the duration of their lives plus fifty years, as long as the ideas are fixed in some tangible medium. That means that they may prevent others from copying their words (or painting, etc.), but they may not prevent anyone from talking about or using their ideas. Finally, one who markets a product or service may protect its trademark—or service or other mark—that is distinctive or has taken on a secondary meaning, but may lose it if the mark becomes the generic term for the goods or services.

KEY TERMS

anticipation	p. 688	patent	p. 687
certification mark	p. 702	prior inventor rule	p. 688
composition of matter	p. 688	priority	p. 688
copyright	p. 687	process	p. 688
doctrine of equivalents	p. 689	right of publicity	p. 687
fair use	p. 696	royalties	p. 689
improvement	p. 688	secondary meaning	p. 702
intellectual property	p. 687	service mark	p. 701
machine	p. 688	shop right	p. 689
manufacture	p. 688	specification	p. 689
obviousness	p. 688	trademark	p. 687, 701
one-year rule	p. 688	trade secret	p. 687
opposition proceeding	p. 704	works for hire	p. 701

SELF-TEST QUESTIONS

1. Which of the following cannot be protected under patent, copyright, or trademark law?
   (a) a synthesized molecule
   (b) a one-line book title
   (c) a one-line advertising jingle
   (d) a one-word company name
2. Which of the following does not expire by law?
   (a) a closely-guarded trade secret not released to the public
   (b) a patent granted by the U.S. Patent Office
   (c) a copyright registered in the U.S. Copyright Office
   (d) a federal trademark registered under the Lanham Act
3. A sculptor casts a marble statue of a three-winged bird. To protect against copying, the sculptor can obtain which of the following?
   (a) a patent
   (b) a trademark
   (c) a copyright
   (d) none of the above

4. A stock analyst discovers a new system for increasing the value of a stock portfolio. He may protect against use of his system by other people by securing:
   (a) a patent
   (b) a copyright
   (c) a trademark
   (d) none of the above
5. A company prints up its customer list for use of its sales staff. The cover page carries a notice that says "confidential." A rival salesman gets a copy of the list. The company can sue to recover the list because the list is:
   (a) patented
   (b) copyrighted
   (c) a trade secret
   (d) none of the above

DEMONSTRATION PROBLEM

Bill is a programmer who has just developed and copyrighted a nifty idea for a computer software package called AnswerMe that will answer sports questions. For example, the user types in "World Series" and specifies a year and AnswerMe puts the winner on the screen. AnswerMe is knowledgeable in winners, scores, players, and other types of information in more than 20 sports. AnswerMe has a distinctive screen appearance: you type the question in a box on the left half of the screen and the answer comes up with a related picture or photo on the right half of the screen in a particular typeface and a set of border designs. A year after AnswerMe is marketed, Bill discovers that Steve has begun to market a program called TellMe. TellMe is suspiciously similar to AnswerMe. Type a sports question and it provides the answer—many of the items are the same as those that AnswerMe will give, although some are different. For example, AnswerMe does not provide the names of baseball players' wives, although TellMe does. TellMe's screen looks quite similar to AnswerMe's; although the typeface and border designs are different, they are displayed in the same fashion. Bill sues Steve. What is his argument? What is Steve's defense? Who will win?

PROBLEMS

1. Samuel Morse filed claims in the U.S. Patent Office for his invention of the telegraph and also for the "use of the motive power of the electric or galvanic current . . ., however developed, for marking or printing intelligible characters, signs or letters at any distances." For which, if any, was he entitled to a patent? Why?
2. In 1957 an inventor dreamed up and constructed a certain new kind of computer. He kept his invention a secret. Two years later, another inventor who conceived the same

machine filed a patent application. The first inventor, learning of the patent application, filed for his own patent in 1963. Who is entitled to the patent, assuming that the invention was truly novel and not obvious? Why?

3. A large company discovered that a small company was infringing one of its patents. It wrote the small company and asked it to stop. The small company denied that it was infringing. Because of personnel changes in the large company, the correspondence file was lost and only rediscovered eight years later. The large company sued. What result? Why?

4. Clifford Witter was a dance instructor at the Arthur Murray Dance Studios in Cleveland. As a condition of employment, he signed a contract not to work for a competitor. Subsequently he was hired by the Fred Astaire Dancing Studios, where he taught the method that he had learned at Arthur Murray. Arthur Murray sued to enforce the noncompete contract. What result? What additional information, if any, would you need to know to decide the case?

5. Greenberg worked for Buckingham Wax as its chief chemist, developing chemical formulas for products by testing other companies' formulas and modifying them. Brite Products bought Buckingham's goods and resold them under its own name. Greenberg went to work for Brite, where he helped Brite make chemicals substantially similar to the ones it had been buying from Buckingham. Greenberg had never made any written or oral commitment to Buckingham restricting his use of the chemical formulas he developed. May Buckingham stop Greenberg from working for Brite? May it stop him from working on formulas learned while working at Buckingham? Why?

6. Irizzary wrote the dean of Harvard Law School, suggesting that the School publish a series of books on the tax laws of various countries. After several letters, the dean declined to pursue the matter further with Irizzary. Later, the School inaugurated a "World Tax Series" in cooperation with the United Nations. Irizzary sued. What result? Why?

7. You have just purchased a VCR (videorecorder) and rush home to make a copy of your favorite movie, "Beach Blanket Bingo," being shown on television that very evening. You notice that the movie carries a copyright notice and says that it may not be recorded except with permission of the owner. Are you infringing the copyright by making a copy for your private use? Is there any difference if you decide to have your tape duplicated and sell several copies to your friends? Why?

ANSWERS TO SELF-TEST QUESTIONS

1. (b)   2. (a)   3. (c)   4. (d)   5. (c)

SUGGESTED ANSWER TO DEMONSTRATION PROBLEM

Bill will assert that Steve has infringed his copyright. He will point to the similarity in screen appearance and the substantial duplication of questions that TellMe can answer. Moreover, he may try to show that Steve has taken the "code," that is, the set of computer instructions that the program needs to function, directly from AnswerMe's code. Steve will assert that the appearance may be similar but it is not identical; for example, TellMe uses different typefaces and border designs. Steve will argue that there are only so many ways that questions can be answered on screen. He will further assert that Bill is really complaining that his *idea* has been appropriated but that ideas are not copyrightable. Anyone is legally free to develop a program to answer sports questions. If he can, he will deny that he borrowed Bill's code. Steve will win on the issue of the nature of the programs: anyone is free to play with the idea of a question-and-answer sports program. But Steve will probably lose on the issue of the screen appearance. Merely changing a typeface or a border design is not enough to avoid liability for substantially infringing the general display. The court should issue an injunction forbidding Steve to use the same screen, and Steve will have to redesign. Whether Bill or Steve will prevail on the issue of code depends on what Steve really did. If he did copy substantial portions of Bill's code, he will be enjoined from marketing TellMe until he rewrites the program.

CHAPTER

32

The Nature and Regulation of Real Estate and the Environment

INTRODUCTION

*I*n this and the next two chapters we focus on real property—immovable property, such as land and structures affixed to the land. (The law related to fixtures, which are treated as real property, was covered in Chapter 30.) Real property in the aggregate is the most valuable of all assets held in the United States; it is an important part of corporate as well as individual wealth. Corporate holdings of land, buildings, and the like amount to between $700 billion and $1.4 trillion. As a consequence, the role of the corporate real estate manager has become critically important within the corporation. The real estate manager must be aware not only of land value for purchase and sale, but also of proper lease negotiation, tax policies and assessments, zoning and land development, and environmental laws.

In this chapter we examine the nature of real estate—the thing that is being acquired—and the regulation of land use and the environment (see Figure 32-1). We divide our discussion of the nature of real estate into three major categories: (1) estates; (2) rights that are incidental to the possession and ownership of land—for example, the right to air, water, and minerals; and (3) easements—the rights in lands of others.

ESTATES

In property law, an **estate** is an interest in real property, ranging from absolute dominion and control to bare possession. Ordinarily when we think of property we think of only one kind: absolute ownership. The owner of a car has the right to drive it where and when she wants, rebuild it, repaint it, and sell it or

Figure 32-1   Chapter Overview

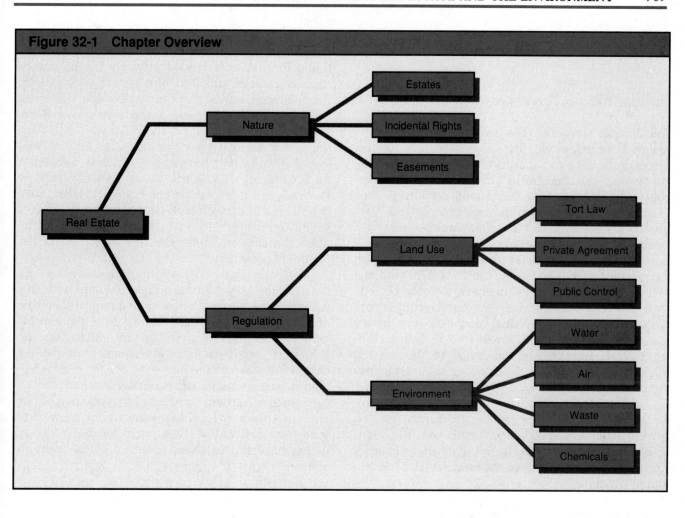

scrap it. The notion that the owner might lose her property when a particular event happens is foreign to our concept of personal property. Not so with real property. You would doubtless think it odd if you were sold a used car subject to the condition that you not paint it a different color—and that if you did, you would automatically be stripped of ownership. But land can be sold that way. Land and other real property can be divided into many categories of interests, as we will see. (Be careful not to confuse the various types of *interests* in real property with the *forms* of ownership, such as joint tenancy. An interest in real property that amounts to an estate is a measure of the *degree* to which a thing is owned; the form of ownership deals with the particular person or persons who own it.)

The common law distinguishes estates along two main axes: (1) freeholds versus leaseholds; and (2) present versus future interests. **Freehold** estates are interests in land that have an uncertain duration. The freehold can be outright ownership—in technical terms, called the **fee simple absolute**—or it can be an interest in the land for the life of the possessor; in either case it is impossible to say exactly how long the estate will last. In the case of one who owns property outright, her estate will last until she sells or transfers it; in the case of a **life estate,** it will last until the death of the owner, or another specified individual. A **leasehold** estate is one whose termination date is usually known. A one-year lease, for example, will expire precisely at the time stated in the lease agreement.

A **present estate** is one that is currently owned and enjoyed; a **future estate** is one that will come into the owner's possession upon the occurrence of a particular event. In this chapter we consider both present and future freehold interests; leasehold interests we save for Chapter 34.

Present Estates (Freeholds)

Fee Simple Absolute   The strongest form of ownership is known as the **fee simple absolute** (or *fee simple* or merely a *fee*). This is what we think of when we say that someone "owns" the land. As one court put it: "The grant of a fee in land conveys to the grantee complete ownership, immediately and forever, with the right of possession from boundary to boundary and from the center of the earth to the sky, together with all the lawful uses thereof." [Magnolia Petroleum Co. v. Thompson, 106 F.2d 217 (8th Cir. 1939).] Although the fee simple may be encumbered by a mortgage or an easement (you may borrow money against the equity in your home; you may grant someone the right to walk across your backyard), the underlying control is in the hands of the owner. Though it was once a complex matter in determining whether a person had been given a fee simple interest, today the law presumes that the estate being transferred is a fee simple, unless the conveyance expressly states to the contrary. (In his will, Big John grants his 100-acre ranch "to my Pardner Lyndon." Lyndon takes ownership of the ranch outright in fee simple absolute.)

Fee Simple Defeasible   Not every transfer of real property creates a fee simple absolute. Some transfers may limit the estate. Any transfer specifying that the ownership will terminate upon a particular happening is known as a **fee simple defeasible.** Suppose, for example, that Mr. Warbucks conveys a tract of land "to Miss Nightingale, for the purpose of operating her hospital and for no other purpose. Conveyance to be good as long as hospital remains on the property." This grant of land will remain the property of Miss Nightingale and her heirs as long as she and they maintain a hospital. When they stop doing so, the land will automatically revert to Mr. Warbucks or his heirs, without their having to do anything to regain title. Note that the conveyance of land could be perpetual, but it is not absolute, because it will remain the property of Miss Nightingale only so long as she observes the conditions in the grant.

Life Estates   An estate measured by the life of a particular person is called a **life estate.** A **conventional life estate** is created privately by the parties themselves. The simplest form is that conveyed by the following words: "to Scarlett for life." Scarlett becomes a **life tenant;** as such she is the owner of the property and may occupy it for life or lease it or even sell it, but the new tenant or buyer can acquire only as much as Scarlett has to give, which is ownership for *her* life (all she can sell, that is, is a life estate in the land, not a fee simple absolute). If Scarlett sells the house and dies a month later, the buyer's interest would terminate. A life estate may be based on the life of someone other than the life tenant: "to Scarlett for the life of Rhett."

The life tenant may use the property as though he were the owner in fee simple absolute with this exception: he may not act so as to diminish the value of the property that will ultimately go to the remainderman—the person who will become owner when the life estate terminates. The life tenant must pay for ordinary upkeep of the property, but the remainderman is responsible for extraordinary repairs.

Some life estates are created by operation of law and are known as **legal life estates.** The most common form is a widow's interest in the real property of her husband. In about one-third of the states, a woman is entitled to **dower,** a right to a percentage (often one-third) of the property of her husband when he dies. Most of these states give a widower a similar interest in the property of his deceased wife. Dower is an alternative to whatever is bequeathed in the will; the widow has the right to elect the share stated in the will or the share available under dower. To prevent the dower right from upsetting the interests of remote purchasers, the right may be waived on sale by having the spouse sign the deed.

Future Estates

To this point, we have been considering present estates. But people also can have future interests in real property. Despite the implications of its name, the future interest is *owned* now, but is not available to be used or enjoyed now. For the most part, future interests may be bought and sold, just as land held in fee simple absolute may be bought and sold. There are several classes of future interests, but in general there are two major types: **reversion** and **remainder.**

Reversion A reversion arises whenever the estate transferred has a duration less than that originally owned by the transferor. A typical example of a simple reversion is that which arises when a life estate is conveyed. The ownership conveyed is only for the life; when the life tenant dies, the ownership interest reverts to the grantor. Suppose the grantor has died in the meantime. Who gets the reversion interest? Since the reversion is a class of property that is owned now, it can be inherited, and the grantor's heirs would take the reversion at the subsequent death of the life tenant.

Remainder The transferor need not keep the reversion interest for himself. He can give that interest to someone else, in which case it is known as a **remainder** interest, because the remainder of the property is being transferred. Suppose the transferor conveys land with these words: "to Scarlett for life and then to Rhett." Scarlett has a life estate; the remainder goes to Rhett in fee simple absolute. Rhett is said to have a **vested remainder interest,** because on Scarlett's death he or his heirs will automatically become owners of the property. Some remainder interests are contingent—and are therefore known as **contingent remainder interests**—on the happening of a certain event: "to my mother for her life, then to my sister if she marries Harold before my mother dies." The transferor's sister will become the owner of the property in fee simple only if she marries Harold while her mother is alive; otherwise the property will revert to the transferor or his heirs. The number of permutations of reversions and remainders can become quite complex, far more than we have space to discuss in this text.

RIGHTS INCIDENT TO POSSESSION AND OWNERSHIP OF REAL ESTATE

Air

The traditional rule was stated by Lord Coke: "Whoever owns the soil owns up to the sky." This traditional rule remains valid today but its application can cause problems. A simple example would be a person who builds an extension to the upper story of his house so that it hangs out over the edge of his property line and thrusts into the air space of his neighbor. That would clearly be an encroachment on the neighbor's property. But is it trespass when an airplane—or an earth satellite—flies over your backyard? Obviously, the courts must balance the right to travel against landowners' rights. The next case is the leading case on the subject and illustrates this balancing process.

U.S. v. CAUSBY
328 U.S. 256 (1946)

MR. JUSTICE DOUGLAS delivered the opinion of the Court.

This is a case of first impression. The problem presented is whether respondents' property was taken within the meaning of the Fifth Amendment by frequent and regular flights of army and navy aircraft over respondents' land at low altitudes. The Court of Claims held that there was a taking and entered judgment for respondent, one judge dissenting. The case is here on a petition for a writ of certiorari which we granted because of the importance of the question presented.

Respondents own 2.8 acres near an airport outside of Greensboro, North Carolina. It has on it a dwelling house, and also various outbuildings which were mainly used for raising chickens. The end of the airport's northwest-southeast runway is 2,220 feet from the respondents' barn and 2,275 feet

(continued on next page)

(continued)

U.S. v. CAUSBY
328 U.S. 256 (1946)

from their house. The path of glide to this runway passes directly over the property—which is 100 feet wide and 1,200 feet long. . . . The use by the United States of this airport is pursuant to a lease executed in May, 1942, for a term commencing June 1, 1942 and ending June 30, 1942, with a provision for renewals until June 30, 1967, or six months after the end of the national emergency, whichever is the earlier.

Various aircraft of the United States use this airport—bombers, transports and fighters. The direction of the prevailing wind determines when a particular runway is used. The northwest-southeast runway in question is used about four per cent of the time in taking off and about seven per cent of the time in landing. Since the United States began operations in May, 1942, its four-motored heavy bombers, other planes of the heavier type, and its fighter planes have frequently passed over respondents' land and buildings in considerable numbers and rather close together. They come close enough at times to appear barely to miss the tops of the trees and at times so close to the tops of the trees as to blow the old leaves off. The noise is startling. And at night the glare from the planes brightly lights up the place. As a result of the noise, respondents had to give up their chicken business. As many as six to ten of their chickens were killed in one day by flying into the walls from fright. The total chickens lost in that manner was about 150. Production also fell off. The result was the destruction of the use of the property as a commercial chicken farm. Respondents are frequently deprived of their sleep and the family has become nervous and frightened. Although there have been no airplane accidents on respondents' property, there have been several accidents near the airport and close to respondents' place. These are the essential facts found by the Court of Claims. On the basis of these facts, it found that respondents' property had depreciated in value. It held that the United States had taken an easement over the property on June 1, 1942, and that the value of the property destroyed and the easement taken was $2,000.

*　*　*

It is an ancient doctrine that at common law ownership of the land extended to the periphery of the universe—*Cujus est solum ejus est usque ad coelum*. But that doctrine has no place in the modern world. The air is a public highway, as Congress has declared. Were that not true, every transcontinental flight would subject the operator to countless trespass suits. Common sense revolts at the idea. To recognize such private claims to the airspace would clog these highways, seriously interfere with their control and development in the public interest, and transfer into private ownership that to which only the public has a just claim.

*　*　*

We have said that the airspace is a public highway. Yet it is obvious that if the landowner is to have full enjoyment of the land, he must have exclusive control of the immediate reaches of the enveloping atmosphere. Otherwise buildings could not be erected, trees could not be planted, and even fences could not be run. The principle is recognized when the law gives a remedy in case overhanging structures are erected on adjoining land. The landowner owns at least as much of the space above the ground as he can occupy or use in connection with the land. The fact that he does not occupy it in a physical sense—by the erection of buildings and the like—is not material. As we have said, the flight of airplanes, which skim the surface but do not touch it, is as much an appropriation of the use of the land as a more conventional entry upon it. We would not doubt that if the United States erected an elevated railway over respondents' land at the precise altitude where its planes now fly, there would be a partial taking, even though none of the supports of the structure rested on the land. The reason is that there would be an intrusion so immediate and direct as to subtract from the owner's full enjoyment of the property and to limit his exploitation of it. While the owner does not in any physical manner occupy that stratum of airspace or make use of it in the conventional sense, he does use it in somewhat the same sense that space left between buildings for the purpose of light and air is used. The superadjacent airspace at this low altitude is so close to the land that continuous invasions of it affect the use of the surface of the land itself. We think that the landowner, as an incident to his ownership, has a claim to it and that invasions of it are in the same category as invasions of the surface.

★   ★   ★

The airplane is part of the modern environment of life, and the inconveniences which it causes are normally not compensable under the Fifth Amendment. The airspace, apart from the immediate reaches above the land, is part of the public domain. We need not determine at this time what those precise limits are. Flights over private land are not a taking, unless they are so low and so frequent as to be a direct and immediate interference with the enjoyment and use of the land. We need not speculate on that phase of the present case. For the findings of the Court of Claims plainly establish that there was a diminution in value of the property and that the frequent, low-level flights were the direct and immediate cause. We agree with the Court of Claims that a servitude has been imposed upon the land.

[The cause is remanded to the Court of Claims for determination whether the easement is permanent or temporary.]

Rights to the Depths

Lord Coke's dictum applies to the depths as well as the sky. The owner of the surface has the right to the oil, gas, and minerals below it, although this right can be severed and sold separately. Perplexing questions may arise in the case of oil and gas, which can flow under the surface. Some states say that oil and gas can be owned by the owner of the surface land; others say that they are not owned until actually ex-tracted—although the property owner may sell the exclusive right to extract them from his land. But states with either rule recognize that oil and gas are capable of being "captured," by drilling that causes oil or gas from under another plot of land to run toward the hole. Since the possibility of capture can lead to wasteful drilling practices, as everyone nearby rushes to capture the precious commodities, many states have enacted statutes requiring landowners to share the resources.

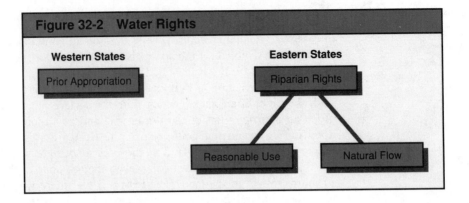

Figure 32-2   Water Rights

Water Rights

The right to determine how bodies of water will be used depends on basic property rules. Two different approaches to water use—eastern and western—have developed over time (see Figure 32-2). Eastern states, where water has historically been more plentiful, have adopted the so-called **riparian rights** theory, which itself can take two forms. "Riparian" refers to land that includes a part of the bed of a waterway or that borders on a public watercourse. A riparian owner is one who owns such land. What are the rights of upstream and downstream owners of riparian land to use the waters? One approach is the "natural flow" doctrine: Each riparian owner is entitled to have the river or other waterway maintained in its natural state. The upstream owner may use the river for drinking water or for washing, but may not divert it to irrigate his crops or to operate his mill if doing so would materially change the amount of the flow or the quality of the water. Virtually all eastern states today are not so restrictive and rely on a "reasonable use" doctrine, which permits the benefit to be derived from use of the waterway to be weighed against the gravity of the harm. This approach is illustrated in the following case.

HOOVER v. CRANE
362 Mich. 36,
106 N.W.2d 563 (1960)

EDWARDS, JUSTICE. This appeal represents a controversy between plaintiff cottage and resort owners on an inland Michigan lake and defendant, a farmer with a fruit orchard, who was using the lake water for irrigation. The chancellor who heard the matter ruled that defendant had a right to reasonable use of lake water. The decree defined such reasonable use in terms which were unsatisfactory to plaintiffs who have appealed.

The testimony taken before the chancellor pertained to the situation at Hutchins lake, in Allegan county, during the summer of 1958. Defendant is a fruit farmer who owns a 180-acre farm abutting on the lake. Hutchins lake has an area of 350 acres in a normal season. Seventy-five cottages and several farms, including defendant's, abut on it. Defendant's frontage is approximately ¼ mile, or about 10% of the frontage of the lake.

Hutchins lake is spring fed. It has no inlet but does have an outlet which drains south. Frequently in the summertime the water level falls so that the flow at the outlet ceases.

All witnesses agreed that the summer of 1958 was exceedingly dry and plaintiffs' witnesses testified that Hutchins lake's level was the lowest it had ever been in their memory. Early in August, defendant began irrigation of his 50-acre pear orchard by pumping water out of Hutchins lake. During that month the lake level fell 6 to 8 inches—the water line receded 50 to 60 feet and cottagers experienced severe difficulties with boating and swimming.

*   *   *

The tenor of plaintiffs' testimony was to attribute the 6- to 8-inch drop in the Hutchins lake level in that summer to defendant's irrigation activities. Defendant contended that the decrease was due to natural causes, that the irrigation was of great benefit to him and contributed only slightly to plaintiff's discomfiture. He suggests to us:

> One could fairly say that because plaintiffs couldn't grapple with the unknown causes that admittedly occasioned a greater part of the injury complained of, they chose to grapple mightily with the defendant because he is known and visible.

The circuit judge found it impossible to determine a normal lake level from the testimony, except that the normal summer level of the lake is lower than the level at which the lake ceases to drain into the outlet. He apparently felt that plaintiffs' problems were due much more to the abnormal weather conditions of the summer of 1958 than to defendant's irrigation activities. His opinion concluded:

> Accepting the reasonable use theory advanced by plaintiffs it appears to the court that the most equitable disposition of this case would be to allow defendant to use water from the lake until such time when his use interferes with the normal use of his neighbors. One quarter inch of water from the lake ought not to interfere with the rights and uses of defendant's neighbors and this quantity of water ought to be sufficient in time of need to service 45 acres of pears. A meter at the pump, sealed if need be, ought to be a sufficient safeguard. Pumping should not be permitted between the hours of 11 p.m. and 7 a.m. Water need be metered only at such times as there is no drainage into the outlet.
>
> The decree in this suit may provide that the case be kept open for the submission of future petitions and proofs as the conditions permit or require.

*   *   *

Michigan has adopted the reasonable-use rule in determining the conflicting rights of riparian owners to the use of lake water.

In 1874, Justice Cooley said:

> It is therefore not a diminution in the quantity of the water alone, or an alteration in its flow, or either or both of these circumstances combined with injury, that will give a right of action, if in view of all the circumstances, and having regard to equality of right in others, that which has been done and which causes the injury is not unreasonable. In other words, the injury

(continued on next page)

(continued)

HOOVER v. CRANE
362 Mich. 36,
106 N.W.2d 563 (1960)

that is incidental to a reasonable enjoyment of the common right can demand no redress. Dumont v. Kellogg, 29 Mich. 420,425

And in People v. Hulbert the Court said:

No statement can be made as to what is such reasonable use which will, without variation or qualification, apply to the facts of every case. But in determining whether a use is reasonable we must consider what the use is for; its extent, duration, necessity, and its application; the nature and size of the stream, and the several uses to which it is put; the extent of the injury to the 1 proprietor and of the benefit to the other; and all other facts which may bear upon the reasonableness of the use. [Red River] Roller Mills v. Wright, 30 Minn. 249, 15 N.W. 167, 44 Am.Rep. 194, and cases cited.

The Michigan view is in general accord with the Restatement of the Law, Torts, vol. 4, §§ 851, 852, 853.

★   ★   ★

We interpret the circuit judge's decree as affording defendant the total metered equivalent in pumpage of ¼ inch of the content of Hutchins lake to be used in any dry period in between the cessation of flow from the outlet and the date when such flow recommences. Where the decree also provides for the case to be kept open for future petitions based on changed conditions, it would seem to afford as much protection for plaintiffs as to the future as this record warrants.

Both resort use and agricultural use of the lake are entirely legitimate purposes. Neither serves to remove water from the watershed. There is, however, no doubt that the irrigation use does occasion some water loss due to increased evaporation and absorption. Indeed, extensive irrigation might constitute a threat to the very existence of the lake in which all riparian owners have a stake; and at some point the use of the water which causes loss must yield to the common good.

The question on this appeal is, of course, whether the chancellor's determination of this point was unreasonable as to plaintiffs. On this record, we cannot overrule the circuit judge's view that most of the plaintiffs' 1958 plight was due to natural causes. Nor can we say, if this be the only irrigation use intended and the only water diversion sought, that use of the amount provided in the decree during the dry season is unreasonable in respect to other riparian owners.

Affirmed. Costs to appellee.

In contrast to riparian rights doctrines, western states have adopted the **prior appropriation** doctrine. This rule looks not to equality of interests but to priority in time: first in time is first in right. The first person to use the water for a beneficial purpose has a right superior to latecomers. This rule applies even though the first user takes all the water for his own needs and even though other users are riparian owners. This rule developed in water-scarce states in which development depended on incentives to use rather than hoard. Today, the prior appropriation doctrine has come under criticism because it gives incentives to those who already have the right to the water to continue to use it profligately, rather than to those who might develop more efficient means of using it.

EASEMENTS: RIGHTS IN LAND OF OTHERS

Defined

An **easement** is an interest in land created by agreement that permits one person to make use of another's estate. This interest can extend to a *profit*, the taking of something from the other's land. Though the common law once distinguished between an easement and profit, today the distinction has faded and profits are treated as a type of easement. An easement must be distinguished from a mere **license**, which is permission, revocable at the will of the owner, to make use of the owner's land. An easement is an estate; a license is personal to the grantee, and is not assignable.

The two main types of easements are *affirmative* and *negative*. An **affirmative easement** gives the right to use the land of another (crossing it, digging under it), or to use one's own land in a way that would, but for the easement, wrongly interfere with another's land (for example, polluting the air). A **negative easement**, by contrast, prohibits the owner of the land from using his land in ways that would affect the holder of the easement. For example, the builder of a solar home would want to obtain negative easements from neighbors barring them from building structures on their land that would block sunlight from falling on the solar home. With the growth of solar energy, some states have begun to provide stronger protection by enacting laws that regulate one's ability to interfere with the enjoyment of sunlight. These laws range from a relatively weak statute in Colorado, which sets forth rules for obtaining easements, to the much stronger statute in California that says in effect that the owner of a solar device has a vested right to continue to receive the sunlight.

Another important distinction is made between easements *appurtenant* and easements *in gross*. An **easement appurtenant** benefits the owner of adjacent land. The easement is thus appurtenant to the holder's land. The benefited land is called the **dominant tenement** and the burdened land—that is, the land subject to the easement—is called the **servient tenement** (see Figure 33-3). An **easement in gross** is granted independent of the easement holder's ownership or possession of land. It is simply an independent right—for example, the right granted to a local delivery service to drive its trucks across a private roadway to gain access to homes at the other end.

Unless it is explicitly limited to the grantee, an easement appurtenant "runs with the land." That is, when the dominant tenement is sold or otherwise conveyed, the new owner automatically owns the easement. A commercial easement in gross may be transferred—for instance, easements to construct pipelines, telegraph and telephone lines, and railroad rights of way. However, most noncommercial easements in gross are not transferable, being deemed personal to the original owner of the easement. Rochelle sells her friend Mrs. Nanette an easement across her country farm to operate skimobiles during the winter. The easement is personal to Mrs. Nanette; she could not sell the easement to anyone else.

Creation

Easements may be created by express agreement, either in deeds or wills. The owner of the dominant tenement may buy the easement from the owner of the servient tenement or may reserve the easement for himself when selling his land. But courts will

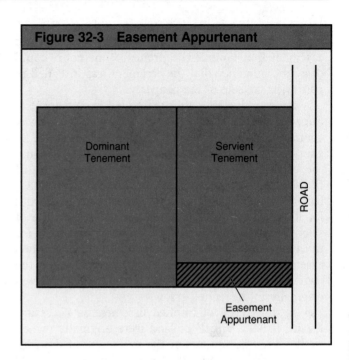

Figure 32-3 Easement Appurtenant

Dominant Tenement

Servient Tenement

ROAD

Easement Appurtenant

sometimes allow implied easements under certain circumstances. For instance, if the deed refers to an easement that bounds the premises, the court could draw the inference that the easement was intended to pass with the sale of the property.

An easement can also be implied from prior use. Suppose a seller of land has two lots, with a driveway connecting both lots to the street. The only way to gain access to the street from the back lot is to use the driveway, and the seller has always done so. If the seller now sells the back lot, the buyer can establish an easement in the driveway through the front lot if the prior use was (1) apparent at the time of sale; (2) continuous; and (3) reasonably necessary for the enjoyment of the back lot. The rule of implied easements through prior use operates only when the ownership of the dominant and servient tenements was originally in the same person.

A third type of implied easement is necessity. Again, if both parcels of land were originally owned by the same person and at the same time of the conveyance a great need for the easement existed (as would be the case if a lot were sold without direct access to the roadway), then the courts will find that an easement is implied in favor of the conveyee.

Use of the Easement

The servient owner may use the easement—remember, it is on or under or above his land—as long as his use does not interfere with the rights of the easement owner. Suppose you have an easement to walk along a path in a woods owned by your neighbor and to swim in a private lake that adjoins the woods. At the time you purchased the easement, your neighbor did not use the lake. Now he proposes to swim in it himself, and you protest. You would not have a sound case, because his swimming in the lake would not interfere with your right to do so. But if he proposed to clear the woods and build a mill on it, obliterating the path you took to the lake and polluting the lake with chemical discharges, then you could obtain an injunction to bar him from interfering with your easement.

The owner of the dominant tenement is not restricted to using his land as he was at the time he became the owner of the easement. The courts will permit him to develop the land in some "normal"

manner. For example, an easement on a private roadway for the benefit of a large estate up in the hills would not be lost if the large estate were ultimately subdivided and many new owners wished to use the roadway; the easement applies to the entire portion of the original dominant tenement, not merely to the part that abuts the easement itself. However, the owner of an easement appurtenant to one tract of land cannot use the easement on another tract of land, even if the two tracts are adjacent.

REGULATION OF LAND USE

Land use regulation falls into three broad categories: (1) restriction on the use of land through tort law; (2) private regulation by agreement; and (3) public ownership or regulation through the powers of eminent domain and zoning.

Regulation of Land Use by Tort Law

Tort law is used to regulate land use in two ways. (1) The owner may become liable for certain activities carried out on the real estate that affect others beyond the real estate. (2) The owner may be liable to persons who, upon entering the real estate, are injured.

Landowner's Activities   The two most common torts in this area are *nuisance* and *trespass*. A common-law **nuisance** is an interference with the use and enjoyment of one's land. Examples of nuisances are excessive noise (especially late at night), polluting activities, and emissions of noxious odors. But the activity must produce substantial harm, not fleeting, minor injury, and it must produce those effects on the reasonable person, not on someone who is peculiarly allergic to the complained of activity. A person who suffered migraine headaches at the sight of croquet being played on a neighbor's lawn would not likely win a nuisance lawsuit. However, the meaning of nuisance is impossible to define with any precision. As Professor William Prosser has said: "There is perhaps no more impenetrable jungle in the entire law than that which surrounds the word 'nuisance.' It has meant all things to all men, and has been applied indiscriminately to everything from an alarming advertisement to a cockroach baked in a pie. There is general agreement that it is incapable of any exact or comprehensible definition" (1971, p. 571).

A **trespass** is the wrongful physical invasion of or entry upon land possessed by another. Loud noise blaring out of speakers in the house next door might be a nuisance but could not be a trespass, because noise is not a physical invasion. But spraying pesticides on your gladiolas could constitute a trespass on your neighbor's property if the pesticide drifts across the boundary.

Nuisance and trespass are complex theories, a full explanation of which would consume far more space than we have. What is important to remember is that these torts are two-edged swords. In many situations, the landowner himself will want to use these theories to sue trespassers or persons creating a nuisance, but in many others the landowner will be liable under these theories for his own activities.

Injury to Persons Entering the Real Estate   Traditionally, liability for injury has depended on the status of the person who enters the real estate.

Trespassers   If the person is an intruder without permission—a **trespasser**—the landowner owes him no duty of care unless he knows of the intruder's presence, in which case the owner must exercise reasonable care in his activities and warn of hidden dangers of which the landowner is aware. A known trespasser is someone whom the landowner actually sees on the property or whom he knows frequently intrudes on the property, as in the case of someone who habitually walks across the land. If a landowner knows that people frequently walk across his property and one day he puts a poisonous chemical on the ground to eliminate certain insects, he is obligated to warn those who continue to walk on the grounds.

Intentional injury to known trespassers is not allowed, even if the trespasser is a criminal intent on robbery, for the law values human life above property rights. For the aftermath of one such incident, in which a farmer rigged a hidden spring-gun to prevent his farmhouse from being robbed, see **Box 32-1.**

Children   If the trespasser is a child, a different rule applies in most states. This is the doctrine of **attractive nuisance.** Originally this rule was enunciated to

deal with cases in which something on the land attracted the child to it, like a swimming pool. In recent years, most courts have dropped the requirement that the child must have been attracted to the danger. Instead, the following elements of proof are necessary to make out a case of attractive nuisance (Restatement of Torts):

1. The child must have been injured by a structure or other artificial condition.
2. The possessor of the land (not necessarily the owner) must have known or should have known that young children would be likely to trespass.
3. The possessor must have known or should have known that the artificial condition exists and that it posed an unreasonable risk of serious injury.
4. The child must have been too young to appreciate the danger that the artificial condition posed.
5. The risk to the child must have far outweighed the utility of the artificial condition to the possessor.
6. The possessor did not exercise reasonable care in protecting the children or eliminating the danger.

Suppose Farmer Brown keeps an old buggy on his front lawn, accessible from the street. A five-year-old boy clambers up the buggy one day, falls through a rotted floor board, and breaks his leg. Is Farmer Brown liable? Probably so. The child was too young to appreciate the danger posed by the buggy, a structure. The farmer should have appreciated that young children would be likely to come onto the land when they saw the buggy and that they would be likely to climb up onto the buggy. Moreover, he should have known, if he did not know in fact, that the buggy, left outside for years without being tended, would pose an unreasonable risk. The buggy's utility as a decoration was far overbalanced by the risk that it posed to children, and the farmer failed to exercise reasonable care.

Licensees   A nontrespasser who comes onto the land without being invited, or, if invited, for purposes unconnected with any business conducted on the premises, is known as a **licensee.** This class of visitors to the land consists of (1) social guests (people you invite to your home for a party), (2) a salesman not invited by the owner who wishes to sell something to

LAW AND LIFE

BOX 32-1

The Thief's Revenge

[The law values human life over property rights. For this reason a property owner may not intentionally injure a trespasser, even when the trespasser intends to commit robbery.—AUTHORS' NOTE]

One summer night in 1967, a 27-year-old gas-station-mechanic-turned-thief broke into an abandoned farmhouse near the sleepy southern Iowa village of Eddyville (population: 1,000). As he opened the door to a front room, shotgun pellets ripped through the door—and tore a 2½-inch hole through the thief's right leg. The doorknob had been wired to the trigger of a 20-gauge shotgun fixed to a bedpost in the room.

Marvin Katko later pleaded guilty to petty larceny and received a 30-day suspended sentence plus a $50 fine. But Katko, who was crippled for life

INTENTIONAL INJURY TO TRESPASSER

by the blast, thought house owner Edward Briney had been overzealous in protecting his property. He sued Briney. The judge instructed the jury that the law "placed a higher value upon human safety than upon mere rights in property." The jury awarded Katko $20,000 in actual damages and $10,000 in punitive damages. (The Iowa Supreme Court affirmed the landmark decision 8–1.)

Then a flood of sympathetic letters and contributions poured in to farmer Briney from 39 states and even Vietnam, where a U.S. soldier's wife wrote, "it makes me feel my husband is fighting for the wrong government." To help Briney pay the judgment, three of his neighbors purchased

one-quarter of his land for a modest $10,000, allowing him to rent it for taxes and bank interest.

But as the value of good Iowa soil rose over the years, this particular flame of human kindness flickered lower. Last year, Briney's three neighbors first offered to sell the land back to him—but at a price he could not afford. They then kicked him off the land and sold it for a fat profit. Charging that his erstwhile benefactors held the land effectively in trust for him, Briney has now sued them. He wants either the right to buy the land back at the original price or to collect $14,000, which he claims represents the increase in value of the land. But since Briney still owes Katko for part of the judgment, he has assigned his rights to the convicted thief. Next fall, victim and robber will go to court hand in hand against the good Samaritans.

Source: *Newsweek*, June 9, 1975

---

the owner or occupier of the property, and (3) persons visiting a building for a purpose not connected with the business on the land (for example, students who visit a factory to see how it works). The landowner owes the same duty of care to licensees that he owes to known trespassers. That is, he must warn them against hidden dangers of which he is aware, and he must exercise reasonable care in his activities to ensure that they are not injured.

Invitees   A final category of persons entering land is that of **invitee**. This is one who has been invited onto the land, usually, though not necessarily, for a business purpose of potential economic benefit to the owner or occupier of the premises. This category is confusing because it sounds as though it should include social guests (who clearly are invited onto the premises), but traditionally social guests are said to be licensees.

Invitees include customers of stores, users of athletic and other clubs, customers of repair shops, strollers through public parks, restaurant and theater patrons, hotel guests, and the like. From the owner's perspective, the major difference between licensees and invitees is that he is liable for injuries resulting to the latter from hidden dangers that he *should have been aware of*, even if he is not actually aware of the dangers. How hidden the dangers and how broad the owner's liability depend on the circumstances, but liability sometimes can be quite broad; recall the case of the woman who recovered damages from a motel that provided inadequate security against her being raped (Chapter 4). Difficult questions arise in lawsuits brought by invitees (or *business invitees*, as they are sometimes called) when the actions of persons other than the landowner contribute to the injury, as illustrated by the following case.

**DECKER v. GRAMEX
CORPORATION**
758 S.W. 59 (Mo. 1988)

BILLINGS, CHIEF JUSTICE

On December 14, 1982 Gary and Donna Decker were Christmas shopping at a shopping center in north St. Louis County containing a Schnucks market and a Grandpa Pigeon's department store. Upon returning to their car, they were forcibly abducted by two unknown assailants in the shopping center parking lot. The Deckers were both murdered after leaving the shopping center with their assailants. Donna Decker was raped and sodomized before she was killed. Both bodies were dumped in a vacant field in East St. Louis.

The son and the parents of Gary and Donna Decker filed a suit for wrongful death against Schnucks Twenty-Five, Inc. and Gramex Corporation, the owners and operators of Schnucks and Grandpa Pigeon's. They alleged defendants were negligent for failing to provide adequate security in the parking lot area, for failing to protect Gary and Donna Decker from criminal assault, abduction, and murder, and for failing to warn the Deckers of the danger of being abducted, robbed, or killed while walking in the parking lot.

Plaintiffs pleaded a history of prior crime on or about the premises of the defendants prior to the Decker murders. These crimes included one armed robbery, one purse snatching, and 45 assorted thefts. Based on these facts, plaintiffs contended that the defendants owed Gary and Donna Decker, as business invitees, a duty to exercise reasonable care for their safety while on the defendant's premises.

Defendants filed a motion for summary judgment on the ground that Missouri law did not recognize a duty on the part of a business owner to protect his patrons against the criminal conduct of unknown third persons. Plaintiffs filed an affidavit in opposition to summary judgment. In this, William J. Cira, a police chief of Bellefontaine, stated that he reviewed the records of crimes committed on the premises of Grandpa Pigeon's and Schnucks during the three years preceding the Decker murders. According to Cira, these crimes included four armed robberies, three purse snatchings, robbery second degree, attempted armed robbery, assault, assault with a deadly weapon, flourishing a deadly weapon, stealing over purse snatching [sic], and attempted purse snatching. The trial court sustained the motion for summary judgment.

*   *   *

A petition seeking damages for negligence must allege ultimate facts which, if proven, show: 1) the existence of a duty on the part of the defendant to protect the plaintiff from injury, 2) breach of that duty, 3) causation, and 4) injury to the plaintiff. Generally, there is no duty to protect business invitees from the criminal acts of unknown third persons. However, a duty to exercise care may be imposed by common law under the facts and circumstances of a given case.

Section 344 of the *Restatement (Second) of Torts* recognizes a duty on the part of a possessor of land who holds it open to the public for entry for business purposes to protect members of the public while they are on the

(*continued on next page*)

(continued)

DECKER v. GRAMEX CORPORATION
758 S.W. 59 (Mo. 1988)

land from the intentionally harmful acts of third persons or in the alternative to warn visitors so that they can avoid the harm. Under the Restatement approach, this duty may arise when the landowner knows or has reason to know from past experience that there is a likelihood of conduct on the part of third persons in general which is likely to endanger the safety of visitors, even if the landowner has no reason to expect harmful conduct on the part of any particular individual.

$\star$ $\star$ $\star$

Plaintiffs pleaded a history of prior crimes occurring on the defendants' property. These crimes included one armed robbery, one purse snatching, and multiple thefts. These allegations, by themselves, even if established at trial, might not be sufficient to establish a duty of care. However, plaintiffs also filed an affidavit in opposition to summary judgment, citing a lengthy list of prior crimes, many violent, occurring at the shopping center over a three year period. The list included four armed robberies, assault, assault with a deadly weapon, and flourishing a deadly weapon. . . .

The facts alleged in the affidavit, if established at trial, are sufficient to establish a duty of care on the part of defendants to take reasonable measures to protect their invitees from third party criminal attacks. Whether the defendants satisfied this duty of care is a question for a jury. On remand, the trial court should give plaintiffs the opportunity to amend their petition to include the facts alleged in the affidavit.

$\star$ $\star$ $\star$

Reversed and remanded for further proceedings.

The foregoing rules dealing with liability for persons entering the land are the traditional rules at common law. In recent years some courts have moved away from the rigidities and sometimes perplexing differences between trespassers, licensees, and invitees. By court decision, several states have now abolished such distinctions and hold the proprietor, owner, or occupier liable for failing to maintain the premises in a reasonably safe condition. According to the California Supreme Court:

A man's life or limb does not become less worthy of protection by the law nor a loss less worthy of compensation under the law because he has come upon the land of another without permission or with permission but without a business purpose. Reasonable people do not ordinarily vary their conduct depending upon such matters, and to focus upon the status of the injured party as a trespasser, licensee, or invitee in order to determine the question whether the landowner has a duty of care, is contrary to our modern social mores and humanitarian values. . . . Where the occupier of land is aware of a concealed condition involving in the absence of precautions an unreasonable risk of harm to those coming in contact with it and is aware that a person on the premises is about to come in contact with it, the trier of fact can reasonably conclude that a failure to warn or to repair the condition constitutes negligence. Whether or not a guest has a right to expect that his host will remedy dangerous conditions on his account, he should reasonably be entitled to rely upon a warning of the dangerous condition so that he, like the host, will be in a position to take special precautions when he comes in contact with it. [Rowland v. Christian, 443 P.2d 561 (Cal. 1968)]

Private Regulation of Land Use by Agreement

A **restrictive covenant** is an agreement regarding the use of land that "runs with the land." In effect, it is a contractual promise that becomes part of the property and that binds future owners. Violations of covenants can be redressed in court in suits for damages or injunctions but will not result in reversion of the land to the seller.

Usually courts construe restrictive covenants narrowly—that is, in a manner most conducive to free use of the land by the ultimate owner (the person against whom enforcement of the covenant is being sought). Sometimes, even when the meaning of the covenant is clear, the courts will not enforce it. For example, when the character of the neighborhood changes, the courts may declare the covenant a nullity. Thus a restriction on a one-acre parcel to residential purposes was voided when in the intervening thirty years a host of businesses grew up around it, including a bowling alley, restaurant, poolroom, and sewage disposal plant. [Norris v. Williams, 54 A.2d 331 (Md. 1947)]

An important nullification of restrictive covenants came in 1947 when the U.S. Supreme Court struck down as unconstitutional racially restrictive covenants, which barred blacks and other minorities from living on land so burdened. The Supreme Court reasoned that when a court enforces such a covenant, it acts in a discriminatory manner (barring blacks but not whites from living in a home burdened with the covenant) and thus violates the Fourteenth Amendment's guarantee of equal protection of the laws. [Shelley v. Kraemer, 334 U.S. 1 (1947)]

Public Control of Land Use Through Eminent Domain

The government may take private property for public purposes. Its power to do so is known as **eminent domain**. The power of eminent domain is subject to constitutional limitations. Under the Fifth Amendment, the property must be put to public use and the owner is entitled to "just compensation" for his loss. These requirements are sometimes difficult to apply.

Public Use   The requirement of public use normally means that the property will be useful to the public once the state has taken possession—for example, private property might be condemned to construct a highway. Although not allowed in most circumstances, the government could even condemn someone's property in order to turn around and sell it to another individual, if a legitimate public purpose could be shown. For example, a state survey in the mid-1960s showed that the government owned 49 percent of Hawaii's land. Another 47 percent was controlled by seventy-two private landowners. Because this concentration of land ownership (which dated back to feudal times) resulted in a critical shortage of residential land, the Hawaiian legislature enacted a law allowing the government to take land from large private estates and resell it in smaller parcels to homeowners. In 1984, the Supreme Court upheld the law, deciding that the land was being taken for a public use because the purpose was "to attack certain perceived evils of concentrated property ownership." [Hawaii Housing Authority v. Midkiff, 467 U.S. 229 (1984)]

Although the use must be public, the courts will not inquire into the necessity of the use or whether other property might have been better suited. It is up to government authorities to determine whether and where to build a road, not the courts.

Just Compensation   The owner is ordinarily entitled to the fair market value of land condemned under eminent domain. This value is determined by calculating the most profitable use of the land at the time of the taking, even though it was being put to a different use. The owner will have a difficult time collecting lost profits; for instance, a grocery store will not usually be entitled to collect for the profits it might have made during the next several years, in part because it can presumably move elsewhere and continue to make profits and in part because calculating future profits is inherently speculative.

Taking   The most difficult question in most modern cases is whether the government has in fact "taken" the property. This is easy to answer when the government acquires title to the property through condemnation proceedings. But more often a government action is challenged when a law or regulation inhibits the use of private land. Suppose a town promulgates a setback ordinance, requiring owners along city sidewalks to build no closer to the sidewalk than twenty feet. If the owner of a small store had only twenty-five feet of land from the sidewalk line, the ordinance would effectively prevent him from housing his enterprise, and the ordinance would be a taking. Challenging such ordinances can sometimes be difficult under traditional tort theories because the government is immune from suit in some of these cases. Instead, a theory of **inverse condemnation** has developed, in which the plaintiff private property owner asserts that the government has condemned the property, though not through the traditional mechanism of a condemnation proceeding. One example of such a claim is the *Causby* case (p. 711).

Public Control of Land Use Through Zoning

Zoning is a technique by which a city or other municipality regulates the type of activity to be permitted in geographical areas within its boundaries. Though originally limited to residential, commercial, and industrial uses, today's zoning ordinances are complex sets of regulations. A typical municipality might have the following zones: residential with a host of subcategories, such as for single-family and multiple-family dwellings, office, commercial, industrial, agricultural, and public lands. Zones may be exclusive, in which case office buildings would not be permitted in commercial zones, or they may be cumulative, so that a more restricted use would be allowed in a less restrictive zone. Zoning regulations do more than specify the type of use: they often also dictate minimum requirements for parking, open usable space, setbacks, lot sizes, and the like, and maximum requirements for height, length of side lots, and so on.

Nonconforming Uses When a zoning ordinance is enacted, it will almost always affect existing property owners, many of whom will be using their land in ways no longer permitted under the ordinance. To avoid the charge that they have thereby "taken" the property, most ordinances permit previous nonconforming uses to continue, though some ordinances limit the nonconforming uses to a specified time after becoming effective. But this permission to continue a nonconforming use is narrow; it extends only to the specific use to which the property was put before the ordinance was enacted. A manufacturer of dresses that suddenly finds itself in an area zoned residential may continue to use its sewing machines, but it could not develop a sideline in woodworking.

Variances Sometimes an owner may desire to use his property in ways not permitted under an existing zoning scheme and will ask the zoning board for a **variance**—authority to carry on a nonconforming use. The board is not free to grant a variance at its whim. The courts apply three general tests to determine the validity of a variance: (1) The land must be unable to yield a reasonable return on the uses allowed by the zoning regulation. (2) The hardship must be unique to the property, not to property generally in the area. (3) If granted, the variance must not change the essential character of the neighborhood.

Zoning as a Taking Zoning is often closely tied to the problem of governmental taking. A regulation against a particular use may make the property unprofitable from the owner's perspective. Thus inverse condemnation suits frequently grow out of new zoning requirements. Recent cases indicate that the Supreme Court might be more willing than in the past to require compensation for property owners affected by regulation. We discuss these cases on p. 30.

ENVIRONMENTAL LAW

In one sense, environmental law is very old. Medieval England had smoke control laws that established the seasons when soft coal could be burned. Nuisance laws give private individuals a limited control over polluting activities of adjacent landowners. But a comprehensive set of U.S. laws directed toward general protection of the environment is largely a product of the past quarter-century, with most of the legislative activity stemming from the late 1960s and later, when people began to perceive that the environment was systematically deteriorating from assaults by rapid population growth and greatly increased automobile driving, vast proliferation of factories that generate waste products, and a sharp rise in the production of toxic materials. Two of the most significant developments in environmental law came in 1970, when the

National Environmental Policy Act took effect and the Environmental Protection Agency became the first of a number of new federal administrative agencies to be established during the decade.

National Environmental Policy Act

Signed into law by President Nixon on January 1, 1970, the National Environmental Policy Act (NEPA) declared that it shall be the policy of the federal government, in cooperation with state and local governments, "to create and maintain conditions under which man and nature can exist in productive harmony, and fulfill the social, economic, and other requirements of present and future generations of Americans. . . . The Congress recognizes that each person should enjoy a healthful environment and that each person has a responsibility to contribute to the preservation and enhancement of the environment." The most significant aspect of NEPA is its requirement that federal agencies must prepare an **environmental impact statement** in every recommendation or report on proposals for legislation and whenever undertaking a major federal action that significantly affects environmental quality. The statement must (1) detail the environmental impact of the proposed action; (2) list any unavoidable adverse impacts should the action be taken; (3) consider alternatives to the proposed action; (4) compare short-term and long-term consequences; and (5) describe irreversible commitments of resources. Unless the impact statement is prepared, the project can be enjoined from proceeding. Note that NEPA does not apply to purely private activities but only to those proposed to be carried out in some manner by federal agencies.

The EPA

The Environmental Protection Agency (EPA) has been in the forefront of the news since its creation in 1970. Charged with monitoring environmental practices of industry, assisting the government and private business to halt environmental deterioration, promulgating regulations consistent with federal environmental policy, and policing industry for violations of the various federal environmental statutes and regulations,

the EPA has had a pervasive influence on American business. As *Business Week* noted (1977, p. 72):

> Cars rolling off Detroit's assembly line now have antipollution devices as standard equipment. The dense black smokestack emissions that used to symbolize industrial prosperity are rare, and illegal, sights. Plants that once blithely ran discharge water out of a pipe and into a river must apply for permits that are almost impossible to get unless the plants install expensive water treatment equipment. All told, the EPA has made a sizable dent in manmade environmental filth.

The EPA is especially active in regulating water and air pollution and in overseeing the disposition of toxic wastes and chemicals. To these problems we now turn.

Water Pollution

Clean Water Act   Legislation governing the nation's waterways goes back a long time. The first federal water pollution statute was the Rivers and Harbors Act of 1899. Congress enacted new laws in 1948, 1956, 1965, 1966, and 1970. But the centerpiece of water pollution enforcement is the Clean Water Act of 1972 (technically, the Federal Water Pollution Control Act Amendments of 1972), as amended in 1977 and 1981. The act is designed to restore and maintain the "chemical, physical, and biological integrity of the Nation's waters." It operates on the states, requiring them to designate the uses of every significant body of water within their borders (e.g., for drinking water, recreation, commercial fishing) and to set water quality standards to reduce pollution to levels appropriate for each use.

Private Industry   The Clean Water Act also governs private industry and imposes stringent standards on the discharge of pollutants into waterways and publicly owned sewage systems. The act created an effluent permit system known as the National Pollutant Discharge Elimination System (NPDES). To discharge any pollutants into navigable waters from a "point source" like a pipe, ditch, ship, or container, a company must obtain a certification that it meets specified standards, which are continually being tightened. For example, until 1983 industry had to use the "best practicable technology" (BPT) currently available, but after July 1, 1984 had to use the "best available technology" economically achievable (BAT). Companies must limit certain kinds of "conventional pollutants" (such as suspended solids and acidity) by so-called "best conventional control technology" (BCT).

Other EPA Water Activities   Federal law governs and the EPA regulates a number of other water control measures. Ocean dumping, for example, is the subject of the Marine Protection, Research, and Sanctuaries Act of 1972, which gives the EPA jurisdiction over wastes discharged into the oceans. The Clean Water Act gives the EPA and the U.S. Army Corps of Engineers authority to protect waters, marshlands, and other wetlands against degradation caused by dredging and fills. EPA also oversees state and local plans for restoring general water quality to acceptable levels in the face of a host of non-point source pollution. The Clean Water Act controls municipal sewage systems, which must ensure that wastewater is chemically treated before being discharged from the sewage system. The treatment requirements are expensive: by the early 1980s, Congress had appropriated more than $30 billion for the cleanup effort, and through the 1980s it is expected to spend an additional $25 billion.

Obviously, of critical importance to the nation's health is the supply of drinking water. To ensure its continuing purity, Congress enacted the Safe Drinking Water Act of 1974, with amendments passed in 1977. This law has two strategies for combating pollution of drinking water. It establishes national standards for drinking water derived from both surface reservoirs and underground aquifers. It also authorizes the EPA to regulate the injection of solid wastes into deep wells (as happens, for instance, by leakage from underground storage tanks).

Air Pollution

The centerpiece of the legislative effort to clean the atmosphere is the Clean Air Act of 1970 (as amended in 1975, 1977 and 1990). Under this act, the EPA has set two levels of National Ambient Air Quality Standards (NAAQS). The primary standards limit the ambient (that is, circulating) pollution that affects human health; secondary standards limit pollution that affects animals, plants, and property. The heart of the Clean Air Act is the requirement that, subject to EPA approval, the states implement the standards that the EPA establishes. In considering a challenge to Missouri's State Implementation Plan (SIP), the Supreme Court concluded that the Clean Air Act can force technology on a regulated source even if the technology appears at the time to be economically unfeasible. [Union Electric Co. v. EPA, 427 U.S. 246 (1976)]

Beyond the NAAQS, the EPA has established several specific standards to control different sorts of air pollution. One major type is pollution that *mobile sources* emit, mainly from automobiles. The EPA requires new cars to be equipped with catalytic converters and to use unleaded gasoline to eliminate the most noxious fumes and to keep them from escaping into the atmosphere. To minimize pollution from *stationary sources,* the EPA also imposes uniform standards on new industrial plants and those that have been substantially modernized. And to safeguard against emissions from older plants, states must promulgate and enforce SIPs.

The Clean Air Act is even more solicitous of air quality in certain parts of the nation, such as designated wilderness areas and national parks. For these areas, the EPA has set standards to prevent significant deterioration (PSD) to keep the air as pristine and clear as it was centuries ago.

The EPA also worries about chemicals so toxic that the tiniest quantities could prove fatal or extremely hazardous to health. To control emission of substances like asbestos, berylium, mercury, vinyl chloride, benzene, and arsenic, the EPA has established or proposed various National Emissions Standards for Hazardous Air Pollutants (NESHAPS).

Concern over acid rain and other types of air pollution prompted Congress to add almost 800 pages of amendments to the Clean Air Act in 1990. (The original act was 50 pages long.) As a result of these amendments, the act was modernized in a manner that parallels other environmental laws. For instance, the amendments established a permit system that is modeled after the Clean Water Act (p. 725). And the amendments provide for felony convictions for willful violations, similar to penalties incorporated into other statutes (as discussed in the *Johnson & Towers* case on p. 728).

The amendments include certain defenses for industry. Most important, companies are protected from allegations that they are violating the law by showing that they were acting in accordance with a permit. In addition to this "permit shield," the law also contains protection for workers who unintentionally violate the law while following their employers' instructions.

Waste Disposal

Though pollution of the air by highly toxic substances like benzene or vinyl chloride may seem a problem removed from that of the ordinary person, we are all in fact polluters. For we all dispose of garbage on a daily and weekly basis, and the dumping of refuse across the nation as a whole (more than five billion tons a year) poses a major burden to dump sites and surrounding areas. In the 1965 Solid Waste Disposal Act and the 1970 Resource Recovery Act, Congress sought to regulate the discharge of garbage by encouraging waste management and recycling. Federal grants were available for research and training, but the major regulatory effort was expected to come from the states and municipalities.

But shocking news prompted Congress to get tough in 1976. The plight of homeowners near Love Canal in upstate New York became a major national story as the discovery of massive underground leaks of toxic chemicals buried during the previous quarter century led to evacuation of hundreds of homes. Next came the revelation that kepone, an exceedingly toxic pesticide, had been dumped into the James River in Virginia, causing a major human health hazard and severe damage to fisheries in the James and downstream in the Chesapeake Bay. The rarely discussed industrial dumping of hazardous wastes now became an open controversy, and Congress responded in 1976 with the Resource Conservation and Recovery Act (RCRA) and the Toxic Substances Control Act (TSCA) and, in 1980, with the Comprehensive Environmental Response, Compensation, and Liability Act (CERCLA).

Resource Conservation and Recovery Act The RCRA expresses a "cradle-to-grave" philosophy: hazardous wastes must be regulated at every stage. The act gives EPA power to govern their creation, storage, transport, treatment, and disposal. Any person or company that generates hazardous wastes must obtain a permit (known as a "manifest") either to store it on its own site or ship it to an EPA-approved treatment, storage, or disposal facility. No longer can hazardous substances simply be dumped at a convenient landfill. Owners and operators of such sites must show that they can pay for damage growing out of their operations. And even after the site is closed to further dumping, they must set aside funds to monitor and maintain the site safely.

This philosophy can be severe. In 1986, the Supreme Court ruled that bankruptcy is not a sufficient reason for a company to abandon toxic waste dumps if state regulations reasonably require protection in the interest of public health or safety. The practical effect of the ruling is that trustees of the bankrupt company must first devote assets to cleaning up a dump site, and only from remaining assets may they satisfy creditors. *Midlantic National Bank* v. *New Jersey*, 474 U.S. 494 (1986). Another severity is RCRA's imposition of criminal liability, including fines of up to $25,000 a day and one-year prison sentences which can be extended beyond owners to individual employees, as the following case shows.

UNITED STATES v. JOHNSON & TOWERS, INC.

741 F.2d 662

(3d Cir. 1984)

SLOVITER, CIRCUIT JUDGE. Before us is the government's appeal from the dismissal of three counts of an indictment charging unlawful disposal of hazardous wastes under the Resource Conservation and Recovery Act. In a question of first impression regarding the statutory definition of "person," the district court concluded that the Act's criminal penalty provision imposing fines and imprisonment could not apply to the individual defendants. We will reverse.

The criminal prosecution in this case arose from the disposal of chemicals at a plant owned by Johnson & Towers in Mount Laurel, New Jersey. In its operations the company, which repairs and overhauls large motor vehicles, uses degreasers and other industrial chemicals that contain chemicals such as methylene chloride and trichlorethylene, classified as "hazardous wastes" under the Resource Conservation and Recovery Act (RCRA) and "pollutants" under the Clean Water Act. During the period relevant here, the waste chemicals from cleaning operations were drained into a holding tank and, when the tank was full, pumped into a trench. The trench flowed from the plant property into Parker's Creek, a tributary of the Delaware River. Under RCRA, generators of such wastes must obtain a permit for disposal from the Environmental Protection Agency (E.P.A.). The E.P.A. had neither issued nor received an application for a permit for Johnson & Towers' operations.

The indictment named as defendants Johnson & Towers and two of its employees, Jack Hopkins, a foreman, and Peter Angel, the service manager in the trucking department. According to the indictment, over a three-day period federal agents saw workers pump waste from the tank into the trench, and on the third day observed toxic chemicals flowing into the creek.

Count 1 of the indictment charged all three defendants with conspiracy under 18 U.S.C. § 371 (1982). Counts 2, 3, and 4 alleged violations under the RCRA criminal provision. Count 5 alleged a violation of the criminal provision of the Clean Water Act. Each substantive count also charged the individual defendants as aiders and abettors under 18 U.S.C. § 2 (1982).

The counts under RCRA charged that the defendants "did knowingly treat, store, and dispose of, and did cause to be treated, stored and disposed of hazardous wastes without having obtained a permit . . . in that the defendants discharged, deposited, injected, dumped, spilled, leaked and placed degreasers . . . into the trench. . . ." The indictment alleged that both Angel and Hopkins "managed, supervised and directed a substantial portion of Johnson & Towers' operations . . . including those related to the treatment, storage and disposal of the hazardous wastes and pollutants" and that the chemicals were discharged by "the defendants and others at their direction." The indictment did not otherwise detail Hopkins' and Angel's activities or responsibilities.

Johnson & Towers pled guilty to the RCRA counts. Hopkins and Angel pled not guilty, and then moved to dismiss counts 2, 3, and 4. The court concluded that the RCRA criminal provision applies only to "owners and operators," i.e., those obligated under the statute to obtain a permit. Since neither Hopkins nor Angel was an "owner" or "operator," the district court granted the motion as to the RCRA charges but held that the individuals could be liable on these three counts under 18 U.S.C. § 2 for aiding and abetting. The court denied the government's motion for reconsideration, and the government appealed to this court under 18 U.S.C. § 3731 (1982).

* * *

The single issue in this appeal is whether the individual defendants are subject to prosecution under RCRA's criminal provision, which applies to *[a]ny person* who—

* * *

(2)   knowingly treats, stores, or disposes of any hazardous waste identified or listed under this subchapter either—

(A)   without having obtained a permit under section 6925 of this title . . . or

(B)   in knowing violation of any material condition or requirement of such permit.

The permit provision in section 6925, referred to in section 6928(d), requires "each person owning or operating a facility for the treatment, storage, or disposal of hazardous waste identified or listed under this subchapter to have a permit" from the E.P.A.

* * *

As in any statutory analysis, we are obliged first to look to the language and then, if needed, attempt to divine Congress' specific intent with respect to the issue.

* * *

First, "person" is defined in the statute as "an individual, trust, firm, joint stock company, corporation (including a government corporation), partnership, association, State, municipality, commission, political subdivision of a State, or any interstate body." 42 U.S.C. § 6903(15) (1982). Had Congress meant in section 6928(d)(2)(A) to take aim more narrowly, it could have used more narrow language. Since it did not, we attribute to "any person" the definition given the term in section 6903(15).

Second, under the plain language of the statute the only explicit basis for exoneration is the existence of a permit covering the action. Nothing in the language of the statute suggests that we should infer another provision exonerating persons who knowingly treat, store or dispose of hazardous waste but are not owners or operators.

Finally, though the result may appear harsh, it is well established that criminal penalties attached to regulatory statutes intended to protect public health, in contrast to statutes based on common law crimes, are to be construed to effectuate the regulatory purpose.

Congress enacted RCRA in 1976 as a "cradle-to-grave" regulatory scheme

(continued on next page)

(continued)

UNITED STATES v. JOHNSON & TOWERS, INC.
741 F.2d 662
(3d Cir. 1984)

for toxic materials, providing "nationwide protection against the dangers of improper hazardous waste disposal." H.R.Rep. No. 1491, 94th Cong., 2d Sess. 11. RCRA was enacted to provide "a multifaceted approach towards solving the problems associated with the 3–4 billion tons of discarded materials generated each year, and the problems resulting from the anticipated 8% annual increase in the volume of such waste." *Id.* The committee reports accompanying legislative consideration of RCRA contain numerous statements evincing the Congressional view that improper disposal of toxic materials was a serious national problem.

The original statute made knowing disposal (but not treatment or storage) of such waste without a permit a misdemeanor. Amendments in 1978 and 1980 expanded the criminal provision to cover treatment and storage and made violation of section 6928 a felony. The fact that Congress amended the statute twice to broaden the scope of its substantive provisions and enhance the penalty is a strong indication of Congress' increasing concern about the seriousness of the prohibited conduct.

★   ★   ★

We conclude that in RCRA, no less than in the Food and Drugs Act, Congress endeavored to control hazards that, "in the circumstances of modern industrialism, are largely beyond self-protection." *United States v. Dotterweich*, 320 U.S. at 280, 64 S.Ct. at 136. It would undercut the purposes of the legislation to limit the class of potential defendants to owners and operators when others also bear responsibility for handling regulated materials. The phrase "without having obtained a permit *under section 6925*" (emphasis added) merely references the section under which the permit is required and exempts from prosecution under section 6928(d)(2)(A) anyone who has obtained a permit; we conclude that it has no other limiting effect. Therefore we reject the district court's construction limiting the substantive criminal provision by confining "any person" in section 6928(d)(2)(A) to owners and operators of facilities that store, treat or dispose of hazardous waste, as an unduly narrow view of both the statutory language and the congressional intent.

★   ★   ★

Comprehensive Environmental Response, Compensation, and Liability Act CERCLA, also known as "Superfund," gives EPA emergency powers to respond to public health or environmental dangers from faulty hazardous waste disposal, currently estimated to occur at more than 17,000 sites around the country. EPA can direct immediate removal of wastes presenting imminent danger (for example, from train wrecks, oil spills, leaking barrels, and fires). Injuries can be sudden and devastating; in 1979, for example, when a freight train derailed in Florida, 90,000 pounds of chlorine gas escaped from a punctured tank car, leaving eight motorists dead, 183 others injured, and forcing 3,500 residents within a seven-mile radius to be evacuated. EPA may also carry out "planned removals" when the danger is substantial, even if immediate removal is not necessary.

EPA prods owners who can be located to voluntarily clean up sites they have abandoned. But if the owners refuse, EPA and the states will undertake the task, drawing on a federal trust fund financed mainly by taxes on the manufacture or import of certain chemicals and petroleum (the balance of the fund comes from general revenues). States must finance 10 percent of the cost of cleaning up private sites and 50 percent of the cost of cleaning up public facilities. EPA and the states can then assess unwilling owners punitive damages up to triple the cleanup costs.

Cleanup requirements are especially controversial when applied to landowners who innocently purchased contaminated property. To deal with this problem, Congress enacted the Superfund Amendment and Reauthorization Act of 1986 (SARA), which protects innocent landowners who—at the time of purchase—made an "appropriate inquiry" into the prior uses of the property. SARA also requires companies to publicly disclose information about hazardous chemicals they use. We now turn to other laws regulating chemical hazards.

Chemical Hazards

Toxic Substances Control Act   Chemical substances that decades ago promised to improve the quality of life have lately shown their negative side—they have serious adverse side effects. For example asbestos, in use for half a century, causes cancer and asbestosis, a debilitating lung disease, in workers who breathed in fibers decades ago. The result has been crippling disease and death and more than 30,000 asbestos-related lawsuits filed nationwide. Other substances, such as polychlorinated biphenyls (PCBs) and dioxin, have caused similar tragedy. Together, the devastating effects of chemicals led to TSCA, designed to control the manufacture, processing, commercial distribution, use, and disposal of chemicals that pose unreasonable health or environmental risks. (TSCA does not apply to pesticides, tobacco, nuclear materials, firearms and ammunition, food, food additives, drugs, and cosmetics—all are regulated by other federal laws.)

TSCA gives EPA authority to screen for health and environmental risks by requiring companies to notify EPA ninety days before manufacturing or importing new chemicals. EPA may demand that the companies test the substances before marketing them and may regulate them in a number of ways, such as

requiring the manufacturer to label its products, to keep records on its manufacturing and disposal processes, and to document all significant adverse reactions in people exposed to the chemicals. EPA also has authority to ban certain especially hazardous substances, and it has banned the further production of PCBs and many uses of asbestos.

Both industry groups and consumer groups have attacked TSCA. Industry groups criticize TSCA because the enforcement mechanism requires mountainous paperwork and leads to widespread delay. Consumer groups complain because EPA has been slow to act against numerous chemical substances. The debate continues.

Pesticide Regulation   America is a major user of pesticides, substances that eliminate troublesome insects, rodents, fungi, and bacteria, consuming more than a billion pounds a year in the form of 35,000 separate chemicals. As useful as they can be, like many chemical substances, pesticides can have serious side effects on humans and plant and animal life. Beginning in the early 1970s, Congress enacted major amendments to the Federal Insecticide, Fungicide, and Rodenticide Act (FIFRA) of 1947 and the Federal Food, Drug, and Cosmetic Act (FFDCA) of 1906.

These laws direct EPA to determine whether pesticides properly balance effectiveness against safety. If the pesticide can carry out its intended function without causing unreasonable adverse effects on human health or the environment, it may remain on the market. Otherwise, EPA has authority to regulate or even ban its distribution and use. To enable EPA to carry out its functions, the laws require manufacturers to provide a wealth of data about the way individual pesticides work and their side effects. EPA is required to inspect pesticides to ensure that they conform to their labeled purposes, content, and safety, and the agency is empowered to certify pesticides for either general or restricted use. If a pesticide is restricted, only those persons certified in approved training programs may use it. Likewise, under the Pesticide Amendment to the FFDCA, EPA must establish specific tolerances for the residue of pesticides on feed crops and both raw and processed foods. The Food and Drug Administration (for agricultural commodities) and the U.S. Department of Agriculture (for meat, poultry, and fish products) enforce these provisions.

Other Types of Environmental Controls

Noise Regulation Under the Noise Regulation Act of 1972, Congress has attempted to combat a growing menace to American workers, residents, and consumers. People who live close to airports and major highways, workers who use certain kinds of machinery (for example, air compressors, rock drills, bulldozers), and consumers who use certain products, such as power mowers and air conditioners, often suffer from a variety of ailments. The Noise Act delegates to the EPA power to limit "noise emissions" from these major sources of noise. Under the act, manufacturers may not sell new products that fail to conform to the noise standards EPA sets, and users are forbidden from dismantling noise control devices installed on these products. Moreover, manufacturers must label noisy products properly. Private suits may be filed against violators, and the act also permits fines of up to $25,000 per day and a year in jail for those who seek to avoid its terms.

Radiation Controls The terrifying effects of a nuclear disaster became frighteningly clear when the Soviet Union's nuclear power plant at Chernobyl exploded in early 1986, discharging vast quantities of radiation into the world's airstream and affecting people thousands of miles away. In the United States, the most notorious nuclear accident occurred at the Three Mile Island nuclear utility in Pennsylvania in 1979, crippling the facility for years because of the extreme danger and long life of the radiation. Primary responsibility for overseeing nuclear safety rests with the Nuclear Regulatory Commission, but many other agencies and several federal laws (including the Clean Air Act, the Federal Water Pollution Control Act, the Safe Drinking Water Act, the Uranium Mill Tailings Radiation Control Act, the Marine Protection and Sanctuaries Act, the Nuclear Waste Policy Act of 1982, CERCLA, and the Ocean Dumping Act) govern the use of nuclear materials and the storage of radioactive wastes (some of which will remain severely dangerous for thousands of years). Through many of these laws, the EPA has been assigned the responsibility of setting radiation guidelines, assessing new technology, monitoring radiation in the environment, setting limits on release of radiation from nuclear utilities, developing guidance for use of X rays in medicine, and helping to plan for radiation emergencies.

CHAPTER SUMMARY

An estate is an interest in real property; it is the degree to which a thing is owned. Freehold estates are those with an uncertain duration; leaseholds are estates due to expire at a definite time. A present estate is one currently owned; a future estate is one that is owned now but not yet available for use.

Present estates are (1) the fee simple absolute; (2) the fee simple defeasible, which itself may be divided into three types; (3) the fee tail (abolished or greatly restricted in most states); and (4) the life estate.

Future estates are generally of two types: reversion and remainder. A reversion arises whenever a transferred estate will endure for a shorter time than that originally owned by the transferor. A remainder interest arises when the transferor gives the reversion interest to someone else.

Use of air, earth, and water are the major rights incident to ownership of real property. Traditionally, the owner held "up to the sky" and "down to the depths," but these rules have been modified to balance competing rights in a modern economy. The law governing water rights varies with the states; in general, the eastern states with more plentiful water have adopted either the "natural flow" version or the "reasonable use" version of the riparian rights doctrine, giving those who live along a waterway certain rights to use the water. By contrast, western states have tended to apply the prior appropriation doctrine, which holds that first in time is first in right, even if those downstream are disadvantaged.

An easement is an interest in land—created by express agreement, prior use, or by necessity—that permits one person to make use of another's estate. An affirmative easement gives one person the right to use another's land; a negative easement prevents the owner from using his land in a way that will affect another person's land. In understanding easement law, the important distinctions are between easements appurtenant and in gross, and the dominant and servient owners.

The law not only defines the nature of the property interest, it also regulates land use. Tort law regulates land use by imposing liability for (1) activities that affect those off the land, and (2) injuries caused to people who enter it. The two most important theories relating to the former are nuisance and trespass. With respect to the latter, the common law confusingly distinguishes among trespassers, licensees, and invitees. Some states are moving away from the perplexing and rigid rules of the past and simply require owners to maintain their property in a reasonably safe condition.

Land use may also be regulated by private agreement through the restrictive covenant, an agreement that "runs with the land" and that will be binding on any subsequent owner. Land use is also regulated by the government's power under eminent domain to take private land for public purposes (upon payment of just compensation), through zoning laws, and through recently enacted environmental statutes, including the National Environmental Policy Act and laws governing air, water, treatment of hazardous wastes, and chemicals.

KEY TERMS

SELF-TEST QUESTIONS

1. A freehold estate is defined as an estate:
   (a) with an uncertain duration
   (b) due to expire at a definite time
   (c) owned now but not yet available for use
   (d) that is leased or rented
2. A fee simple defeasible is a type of:
   (a) present estate
   (b) future estate
   (c) life estate
   (d) leasehold estate
3. A reversion is:
   (a) a present estate that prevents transfer of land out of the family
   (b) a form of life estate
   (c) a future estate that arises when the estate transferred

has a duration less than that originally owned by the transferor
   (d) identical to a remainder interest
4. An easement is an interest in land that may be created by:
   (a) express agreement
   (b) prior use
   (c) necessity
   (d) all of the above
5. The prior appropriation doctrine:
   (a) tends to be applied by eastern states
   (b) holds that first in time is first in right
   (c) gives those that live along a waterway special rights to use the water
   (d) all of the above

DEMONSTRATION PROBLEM

While shopping in a grocery store, Clarence was robbed and knifed by a thief. The thief was never caught and now Clarence sues the store for damages. Result? Why?

PROBLEMS

1. Dorothy deeded an acre of real estate which she owns to George for the life of Benny and then to Ernie. Describe the property interests of George, Benny, Ernie, and Dorothy.
2. In problem 1, assume that George moves into a house on the property. During a tornado the roof is destroyed and a window is smashed. Who is responsible for repairing the roof and window? Why?
3. Dennis likes to spend his weekends in his backyard, shooting his rifle across his neighbor's yard. If Dennis never sets foot on his neighbor's property and if the bullets strike neither persons nor property, has he violated the legal rights of the neighbor? Explain.
4. Dennis also drills an oil well in his backyard. He "slant drills" the well—that is, the well slants from a point on the surface in his yard to a point 400 feet beneath the surface of his neighbor's yard. Dennis has slanted the drilling in order to capture his neighbor's oil. Can he do this legally? Explain.
5. Wanda is in charge of acquisitions for her company. Realizing that water is important to company operations, Wanda buys a plant site on a river, and the company builds a plant which uses all of the river water. Downstream owners bring suit to stop the company from using any water. Result? Why?
6. Sunny decides to build a solar home. Before beginning

construction she wants to establish the legal right to prevent her neighbors from constructing buildings that will block the sunlight. She has heard that the law distinguishes between licenses and easements, easements appurtenant and in gross, and affirmative and negative easements. Which of these interests would you recommend for Sunny? Why?

7. On several occasions, thieves broke into farmer Jack's house and took his valuables. Fed up, Jack rigged up a shotgun trap in the room where he slept. While lying in bed late one night, he heard the door to the bedroom open slowly. When fully open, the door triggered the shotgun, injuring a notorious local murderer, Scarface. Scarface sues Jack for damages resulting from his injuries. Result? Why?

ANSEWERS TO SELF-TEST QUESTIONS

1. (a)   2. (a)   3. (c)   4. (d)   5. (b)

SUGGESTED ANSWER TO DEMONSTRATION PROBLEM

Clarence was an invitee. Therefore the store will be liable if the store knew or should have known of previous criminal activity and failed to take reasonable precautions. See *Earle* v. *Colonial Theater Co.*, 266 N.W.2d 466 (Mich. 1978).

CHAPTER

33

The Transfer of Real Estate by Sale

*T*his chapter follows the steps taken when real estate is transferred by sale:

1. The buyer selects a *form of ownership*.
2. The buyer searches for the real estate to be purchased. Typically in doing so the buyer will deal with *real estate brokers*.
3. After a parcel is selected, the seller and buyer will negotiate and sign a *sales agreement*.
4. The seller will normally then be required to provide *proof of title*.
5. The buyer will acquire *property insurance*.
6. The buyer will arrange *financing*.
7. Finally, the sale and purchase will be completed at a *closing*.

During this process, the buyer and seller enter into a series of contracts with each other and with third parties such as brokers, lenders, and insurance companies. In this chapter we focus on the unique features of these contracts, with the exception of mortgages (see Chapter 28) and property insurance (Chapter 36). We conclude by examining briefly adverse possession—a method of acquiring property for free.

FORMS OF OWNERSHIP

Generally

The transfer of property begins with the buyer's selection of a form of ownership. Our emphasis here is not on *what* is being acquired (the type of property interest) but on *how* the property is owned.

One form of ownership of real property is legally quite simple, although lawyers refer to it with a complicated sounding name. This is ownership by one individual, known as ownership **in severalty.** In purchasing real estate, however, buyers frequently complicate matters by grouping together—because of marriage, close friendship, or simply in order to finance the purchase more easily.

When purchasers group together for investment purposes, they often use the various forms of organization discussed in Parts VIII and IX—corporations, partnerships, limited partnerships, joint ventures, and business trusts. The most popular of these forms of organization for owning real estate is the limited partnership. A real estate limited partnership is designed to allow investors to take substantial deductions that offset current income from the partnership and other similar investments, while at the same time protecting the investor from personal liability if the venture fails.

But you do not have to form a limited partnership or other type of business in order to acquire property with others; many other forms are available for personal or investment purposes. To these we now turn.

Joint Tenancy

Joint tenancy is an estate in land owned by two or more persons. It is distinguished chiefly by the right of survivorship. If two people own land as joint tenants, then either becomes the sole owner when the other dies. For land to be owned jointly, four **unities** must co-exist: (1) **Unity of time**. The interests of the joint owners must begin at the same time. (2) **Unity of title**. The joint tenants must acquire their title in the same conveyance—that is, the same will or deed. (3) **Unity of interest**. Each owner must have the same interest in the property; for example, one may not

hold a life estate and the other the remainder interest. (4) **Unity of possession**. All parties must have an equal right to possession of the property (see Figure 33-1).

Suppose a woman owns some property and upon marriage wishes to own it jointly with her husband. She deeds it to herself and her husband "as joint tenants and not tenants in common." Strictly speaking, the common law would deny that the resulting form of ownership was joint because the unities of title and time were missing. The wife owned the property first and originally acquired title under a different conveyance. But the modern view in most states is that an owner may convey directly to herself and another in order to create a joint estate.

When one or more of the unities is destroyed, however, the joint tenancy lapses. Fritz and Gary own a farm as joint tenants. Fritz decides to sell his interest to Jesse (or, because Fritz has gone bankrupt, the sheriff auctions off his interest at a foreclosure sale). Jesse and Gary would hold as tenants in common (see p. 737) and not as joint tenants. Suppose Fritz had made out his will, leaving his interest in the farm to Reuben. On Fritz's death, would the unities be destroyed, leaving Gary and Reuben as tenants in common? No, because Gary, as joint tenant, would own the entire farm on Fritz's death, leaving nothing behind for Reuben to inherit.

Tenancy by the Entirety

About half the states permit husbands and wives to hold property as **tenants by the entirety**. This form of ownership is similar to joint tenancy, except that

Figure 33-1 Forms of Ownership and Unities

Unities	Joint Tenancy	Tenancy by Entirety	Tenancy in Common
Time	✔	✔	
Title	✔	✔	
Interest	✔	✔	
Possession	✔	✔	✔
Person		✔	

it is restricted to husbands and wives. This is sometimes described as the *unity of person*. In most of the states permitting tenancy by the entirety, acquisition by husband and wife of property as joint tenants automatically becomes a tenancy by the entirety. The fundamental importance of tenancy by the entirety is that neither spouse individually can terminate it; only a joint decision to do so will be effective. One spouse alone cannot sell or lease an interest in such property without consent of the other, and in many states a creditor of one spouse cannot seize the individual interest.

Tenancy in Common

Two or more people can hold property as **tenants in common** when the unity of possession is present, that is, when each is entitled to occupy the property. None of the other unities—of time, title, or interest—is necessary, though their existence does not impair the common ownership. Note that the tenants in common do not own a specific portion of the real estate; each has an undivided share in the whole, and each is entitled to occupy the whole estate. One tenant in common may sell, lease, or mortgage his undivided interest. When a tenant in common dies, his interest in the property passes to his heirs, not to the surviving tenants in common.

Because tenancy in common does not require a unity of interest, it has become a popular form of "mingling," by which unrelated people pool their resources to purchase a home. If they were joint tenants, each would be entitled to an equal share in the home, regardless of how much each contributed, and the survivor would become sole owner when the other owner dies. But with a tenancy in common arrangement, each can own a share in proportion to the amount invested.

Community Property

In nine states—Arizona, California, Idaho, Louisiana, Nevada, New Mexico, Texas, Washington, and Wisconsin—property acquired during a marriage is said to be **community property**. There are differences among these states, but the general theory is that, with certain exceptions, each spouse has an undivided equal interest in property acquired while the husband and wife are married to each other. The major exception is for property acquired by gift or inheritance during the marriage. (By definition, property owned by either spouse before the marriage is not community property.) Property acquired by gift of inheritance or owned before the marriage is known as **separate property**. Community property states recognize other forms of ownership; specifically, husbands and wives may hold property as joint tenants, permitting the survivor to own the whole.

The consequence of community property laws is that either the husband or the wife may manage the community property, borrow against it, and dispose of community personal property. Community real estate may only be sold or encumbered by both jointly. Each spouse may bequeath only half the community property in his or her will. In the absence of a will, the one-half property interest will pass in accordance with the laws of intestate succession. If the couple divorces, the states generally provide for an equal or near-equal division of the community property, although a few permit the court in its discretion to divide in a different proportion.

Condominiums

In popular parlance, a *condominium* is a kind of apartment building, but that is not its technical legal meaning. **Condominium** is a form of ownership, not a form of structure, and it can even apply to space—for example, to parking spaces in a garage. The word "condominium" means joint ownership or control, and it has long been used whenever land has been particularly scarce or expensive. Condominiums were popular in ancient Rome (especially near the Forum) and in the walled cities of medieval Europe.

In its modern usage, condominium refers to a form of housing involving two elements of ownership. The first is the living space itself, which may be held in common, in joint tenancy, or in any other form of ownership. The second is the common space in the building, including the roof, land under the structure, hallways, swimming pool, and the like. The common space is held by all purchasers as tenants in common. The living space may not be sold apart from the interest in the common space.

Two documents are necessary in a condominium sale, the *master deed* and the *bylaws*. The **master deed** (1) describes the condominium units, the common areas, and any restrictions that apply to them; (2) establishes the unit owner's interest in the common area, his number of votes at owners' association meetings, and his share of maintenance and operating expenses (sometimes unit owners have equal shares, sometimes their share is determined by computing the ratio of living area or market price or original price of a single unit to the whole); and (3) creates a board of directors to administer the affairs of the whole condominium. The **bylaws** usually establish the owners' association, set out voting procedures, and list the powers and duties of the officers, and the obligations of the owners for the use of the units and the common areas.

Individuals who serve on a condominium board of directors are increasingly prone to liability, as discussed in the following case.

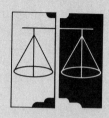

FRANCES T. v. VILLAGE GREEN OWNERS ASS'N
42 Cal.3d 490,
229 Cal.Rptr. 456,
723 P.2d 573 (1986)

BROUSSARD, JUSTICE. The question presented is whether a condominium owners association and the individual members of its board of directors may be held liable for injuries to a unit owner caused by third-party criminal conduct. Plaintiff Frances T., brought suit against the Village Green Owners Association (the Association) and individual members of its board of directors for injuries sustained when she was attacked in her condominium unit, a part of the Village Green Condominium Project (Project). Her complaint stated three causes of action: negligence, breach of contract and breach of fiduciary duty. The trial court sustained defendants' general demurrers to plaintiff's three causes of action without leave to amend and entered a judgment of dismissal. Plaintiff appealed.

On the night of October 8, 1980, an unidentified person entered plaintiff's condominium unit under cover of darkness and molested, raped and robbed her. At the time of the incident, plaintiff's unit had no exterior lighting. The manner in which her unit came to be without exterior lighting on this particular evening forms the basis of her lawsuit against the defendants.

The Association, of which plaintiff was a member, is a nonprofit corporation composed of owners of individual condominium units. The Association was formed and exists for the purposes set forth in the Project's declaration of covenants, conditions and restrictions (CC&Rs). The board of directors (board) exercises the powers of the Association and conducts, manages and controls the affairs of the Project and the Association. Among other things the Association, through its board, is authorized to enforce the regulations set forth in the CC&Rs. The Association, through the board, is also responsible for the management of the Project and for the maintenance of the Project's common areas.

* * *

[Because of what plaintiff called an "exceptional crimewave," she and other residents asked the board to install more lights in early 1980.]

By late August, the board had still taken no action. Plaintiff then installed additional exterior lighting at her unit, believing that this would protect her from crime. In a letter dated August 29, 1980, however, the site manager told plaintiff that she would have to remove the lighting because it violated the CC&Rs. Plaintiff refused to comply with this request. After appearing at a board meeting, where she requested permission to maintain her lighting until the board improved the general lighting that she believed to be a hazard, she received a communication from the board stating in part: "The Board has indicated their appreciation for your appearance on October 1, and for the information you presented to them. After deliberation, however, the Board resolved as follows: [¶] You are requested to remove the exterior lighting you added to your front door and in your patio and to restore the Association Property to its original condition on or before October 6. If this is not done on or before that date, the Association will have the work done and bill you for the costs incurred."

The site manager subsequently instructed plaintiff that pending their removal, she could not use the additional exterior lighting. The security lights had been installed using the same circuitry used for the original exterior lighting and were operated by the same switches. In order not to use her additional lighting, the plaintiff was required to forego the use of all of her exterior lights. In spite of this, however, plaintiff complied with the board's order and cut off the electric power on the circuitry controlling the exterior lighting during the daylight hours of October 8, 1980. As a result, her unit was in total darkness on October 8, 1980, the night she was raped and robbed.

★　　★　　★

The fundamental issue here is whether petitioners, the condominium Association and its individual directors, owed plaintiff the same duty of care as would a landlord in the traditional landlord-tenant relationship. We conclude that plaintiff has pleaded facts sufficient to state a cause of action for negligence against both the Association and the individual directors.

. . . The Association contends that under its own CC&Rs, it cannot permit residents to improve the security of the common areas without prior written permission, nor can it substantially increase its limited budget for common-area improvements without the approval of a majority of the members.

But regardless of these self-imposed constraints, the Association is, for all practical purposes, the Project's "landlord." And traditional tort principles impose on landlords, no less than on homeowner associations that function as a landlord in maintaining the common areas of a large condominium complex, a duty to exercise due care for the residents' safety in those areas under their control.

★　　★　　★

Under the facts as alleged by plaintiff, the directors named as defendants had specific knowledge of a hazardous condition threatening physical injury to the residents, yet they failed to take any action to avoid the harm; moreover, the action they did take may have exacerbated the risk by causing plaintiff's unit to be without any lighting on the night she was attacked.

(continued on next page)

(continued)

FRANCES T. v. VILLAGE GREEN OWNERS ASS'N
42 Cal.3d 490,
229 Cal.Rptr. 456,
723 P.2d 573 (1986)

* * *

In this case plaintiff's amended complaint alleges that each of the directors participated in the tortious activity. Under our analysis, this allegation is sufficient to withstand a demurrer. However, since only "a director who actually votes for the commission of a tort is personally liable, even though the wrongful act is performed in the name of the corporation," (*Tillman v. Wheaton-Haven Recreation Ass'n, Inc.*, 517 F.2d 1141, 1144), plaintiff will have to prove that each director acted negligently as an individual. Of course, the individual directors may then present evidence showing they opposed or did not participate in the alleged tortious conduct.

* * *

We conclude that the trial court erred in sustaining the Association's and director's demurrer to the negligence cause of action. We affirm dismissal of plaintiff's other causes of action. The judgment is therefore reversed and remanded to the trial court for further proceedings consistent with this opinion.

Cooperatives

Another popular form of owning living quarters with common areas is the **cooperative**. Unlike the person who lives in a condominium, the tenant of a cooperative does not own a particular unit. Instead, he owns a share of the entire building. Since the building is usually owned by a corporation (a cooperative corporation, hence the name), this means that the tenant owns stock in the corporation. A tenant occupies a unit under a lease from the corporation. Together, the lease and stock in the building corporation are considered personal, not real, property.

In a condominium, an owner of a unit who defaults in paying monthly mortgage bills can face foreclosure on the unit, but neighbors in the building suffer no direct financial impact—except that the defaulter probably has not paid monthly maintenance charges either. In a cooperative, however, a tenant who fails to pay monthly charges can jeopardize the entire building, because the mortgage is on the building as a whole; consequently, the others will be required to make good the payments or face foreclosure.

Timesharing

Timesharing is a method by which several people can own the same property while being entitled to occupy the premises exclusively at different times on a recurring basis. In the typical vacation property, each owner has the exclusive right to use the apartment unit or cottage for a specified period of time each year—for example, Mr. and Mrs. Smith may have possession from December 15 through December 22, Mr. and Mrs. Jones from December 23 through December 30, and so on. The property is usually owned as a condominium but need not be. The sharers may own the property in fee simple, or hold a joint lease, or even belong to a "vacation club" that sells time in the unit.

Timesharing resorts have become popular in recent years. But the lure of big money has brought unscrupulous contractors and salespersons into the market, and in their wake sharp practices and often unfinished or badly constructed buildings. As a result, about one-quarter of the states have enacted some type of consumer protection legislation, including a fifteen-day cooling-off period during which a purchaser may cancel his contract, escrowed funds that require the builder to finish the project before being paid, and use of the building by buyers even if the contractor is being sued.

REAL ESTATE BROKERS

Once a form of ownership has been selected the buyer must begin a search for the specific real estate to be purchased. This search often involves contact with a broker hired by the seller. The seller's contract with the broker, known as the **listing agreement**, is the first of the series of contracts entered into through the course of a real estate transaction. As you consider these contracts, it is important to keep in mind that despite the size of the transaction and the dire financial consequences should anything go awry, the typical person (buyer or seller) usually acts as his own attorney. As an American Bar Association committee has noted: "It is probably safe to say that in a high percentage of cases the seller is unrepresented and signs the contracts of brokerage and sale on the basis of his faith in the broker. The buyer does not employ a lawyer. He signs the contract of sale without reading it and, once financing has been obtained, leaves all the details of title search and closing to the lender or broker. The lender or broker may employ an attorney but, where title insurance is furnished by a company maintaining its own title plant, it is possible that no lawyer, not even house counsel, will appear" (1976, p. 13). Given this reality, the material that follows is especially important for nonlawyers.

Regulation of the Real Estate Business

State Licensing Real estate brokers, and the search for real estate generally, are subject to state and federal government regulation. Every state requires real estate brokers to be licensed. To obtain a license, the broker must pass an examination covering the principles of real estate practice, transactions, and instruments. Many states additionally insist that the broker take several courses in finance, appraisal, law, and real estate practice and apprentice for two years as a salesperson in a real estate broker's office.

Civil Rights Act Two federal civil rights laws also play an important role in the modern real estate transaction. These are the Civil Rights Act of 1866 and the Civil Rights Act of 1968 (Fair Housing Act). In *Jones* v. *Alfred H. Mayer Co.*, 392 U.S. 409 (1968), the Supreme Court upheld the constitutionality of the 1866 law, which expressly gives all citizens of the United States the same rights as white citizens to inherit, purchase, lease, sell, hold, and convey real and personal property. A minority buyer or renter who is discriminated against may sue for relief in federal court, which may award damages, stop the sale of the house, or even direct the seller to convey the property to the plaintiff.

The 1968 Fair Housing Act prohibits discrimination on the grounds of race, color, religion, sex, national origin, handicap, or family status (that is, no discrimination against families with children) by any one of several means, including (1) refusing to sell or rent to or negotiate with any person, (2) discriminating in the terms of sale or renting, (3) discriminating in advertising, (4) denying that the housing is available when in fact it is, (5) "blockbusting" (panicking owners into selling or renting by telling them that minority groups are moving into the neighborhood), (6) creating different terms for granting or denying home loans by commercial lenders, and (7) denying anyone the use of real estate services. However, the 1968 act contains several exemptions: (1) sale or rental of a single-family house if the seller (a) owns less than four such houses, (b) does not use a broker, (c) does not use discriminatory advertising, and (d) within two years sells no more than one house in which the seller was not the most recent occupant; (2) rentals in a building occupied by the owner as long as it houses fewer than five families and the owner did not use discriminatory advertising; (3) sale or rental of space in buildings or land restricted by religious organization owners to people of the same religion (assuming that the religion does not discriminate on the basis of race, color, or national origin), and (4) private clubs, if they limit their noncommercial rentals to members.

The net of these laws is that discrimination based on color or race is flatly prohibited, and that other types of discrimination are also barred unless one of the exemptions enumerated above applies.

Hiring the Broker: The Listing Agreement

When the seller hires a real estate broker, he will sign a **listing agreement**. (In several states, the Statute of Frauds says that the seller must sign a written agreement; however, he should do so in all states to provide evidence in the event of a later dispute.) This listing agreement provides for the broker's commission, her duties, the length of time she will serve as broker, and other terms of her *agency* relationship (see Chapters 37 and 38). Whether the seller will owe a commission if the seller or someone other than the broker finds a buyer depends on which of three types of listing agreements has been signed.

Exclusive Right to Sell If the seller agrees to an **exclusive-right-to-sell** agency, he will owe the broker the stated commission regardless of who finds the buyer. Language such as the following gives the broker an exclusive right to sell: "Should the seller or anyone acting for the seller (including his heirs) sell, lease, transfer, or otherwise dispose of the property within the time fixed for the continuance of the agency, the broker shall be entitled nevertheless to the commission as set out herein."

Exclusive Agency Somewhat less onerous from the seller's perspective (and less generous from the broker's perspective) is the **exclusive agency**. The broker has the exclusive right to sell and will be entitled to the commission if anyone other than the seller finds the buyer (in other words, the seller will owe no commission if he finds a buyer). Here is language that creates an exclusive agency: "A commission is to be paid the broker whether the purchaser is secured by the broker or by any person other than the seller."

Open Listing The third type of listing, relatively rarely used, is the **open listing**, which authorizes "the broker to act as agent in securing a purchaser for my property." The open listing calls for payment to the broker only if the broker was instrumental in finding the buyer; the broker is not entitled to her commission if anyone else, seller or otherwise, locates the buyer.

Suppose the broker finds a buyer, but the seller refuses at that point to sell. May the seller simply change his mind and avoid having to pay the broker's commission? The usual rule is that when a broker finds a buyer who is "ready, willing, and able" to purchase or lease the property, she has earned her commission. Many courts have interpreted this to mean that even if the buyers are unable to obtain financing, the commission is owed nevertheless once the prospective buyers have signed a purchase agreement. To avoid this result, the seller should insist on either a "no deal, no commission" clause in the listing agreement (entitling the broker to payment only if the sale is actually consummated) or a clause in the purchase agreement making the purchase itself contingent on the buyer's finding financing.

Broker's Duties

Once the listing agreement has been signed, the broker becomes the seller's agent—or, as occasionally happens, the buyer's agent, if hired by the buyer. A broker is not a general agent with broad authority. Rather, a broker is a special agent with authority only to show the property to potential buyers (see p. 820). Unless expressly authorized, a broker may not accept money on behalf of the seller from a prospective buyer. Suppose Eunice hires Pete's Realty to sell her house. They sign a standard exclusive agency listing, and Pete cajoles Frank into buying the house. Frank writes out a check for $10,000 as a down payment and offers it to Pete, who absconds with the money. Who must bear the loss? Ordinarily, Frank would have to bear the loss, because Pete was given no authority to accept money. Had the listing agreement explicitly recited that Pete could accept the down payment from a buyer, then the loss would fall on Eunice.

Although the broker is but a special agent, he owes the seller, his **principal**, a **fiduciary duty**. A fiduciary duty is a duty of the highest loyalty and trust. It means that the broker cannot buy the property for himself through an intermediary without full disclosure to the seller of his intentions. Nor may the broker secretly receive a commission from the buyer or suggest to a prospective buyer that the property can be purchased for less than the asking price.

THE SALES AGREEMENT

Once the buyer has selected the real estate to be acquired, an agreement of sale will be negotiated and signed. Contract law in general is discussed in Part II; our discussion here will focus on specific aspects of the real estate contract.

Required Terms

The Statute of Frauds requires that contracts for sale of real estate must be in writing. The writing must contain the following information:

Names of Buyers and Sellers The agreement must contain the names of the buyers and sellers. As long as the parties sign the agreement, however, it is not necessary for the names of buyers and sellers to be included within the body of the agreement.

Real Estate Description   The property must be described sufficiently for a court to identify the property without having to look for evidence outside the agreement. The proper address, including street, city, and state, is usually sufficient.

Price   The price terms must be clear enough for a court to enforce. A specific cash price is always clear enough. The problem usually arises when installment payments are to be made. To say "$50,000, payable monthly for fifteen years at 12 percent" is not sufficiently detailed, because it is impossible to determine whether the installments are to be equal each month, or equal principal payments with varying interest payments, declining monthly as the balance decreases.

Signature   As a matter of prudence, both buyer and seller should sign the purchase agreement. However, the Statute of Frauds requires only the signature of the party against whom the agreement is to be enforced. So if the seller has signed the agreement, he cannot avoid the agreement on the grounds that the buyer has not signed it. However, if the buyer, not having signed, refuses to go to closing and take title, the seller would be unable to enforce the agreement against him.

Other Provisions

Easements and Restrictive Covenants   Unless the contract specifically states otherwise, the seller must deliver **marketable title**. A marketable title is one that is clear of restrictions. Easements or restrictive covenants make a title unmarketable. As a general rule, if the seller fails to recite in the purchase agreement that the property is subject to easements or restrictive covenants, he is agreeing to convey marketable title. If the seller is unable to do so at the closing, he will be in breach of the agreement. Therefore, a seller must be sure to say that the property is being sold "subject to easements and restrictions of record." A buyer who sees only such language should insist that the particular easements and restrictive covenants be spelled out in the agreement before he signs.

Risk of Loss   Suppose the house burns down after the contract is signed but before the closing. Who bears the loss? Once the contract is signed, most states apply the rule of **equitable conversion**, under which the buyer's interest (his executory right to enforce the contract to take title to the property) is regarded as real property, and the seller's interest is regarded as personal property. The rule of equitable conversion stems from an old maxim of the equity courts: "That which ought to be done is regarded as done." That is, the buyer ought to have the property and the seller ought to have the money. A practical consequence of this rule is that the loss of the property falls on the buyer. Because most buyers do not purchase insurance until they take title, eleven states have adopted the Uniform Vendor and Purchaser Risk Act, which reverses the equitable conversion rule and places risk of loss on the seller. The parties may themselves reverse the application of the rule; the buyer should always insist on a clause in a contract stating that risk of loss remains with the seller until a specified date, such as the closing.

Earnest Money   As protection against the buyer's default, the seller usually insists on a down payment known as **earnest money**. This is intended to cover such immediate expenses as proof of marketable title and the broker's commission. If the buyer defaults, he forfeits the earnest money, even if the contract does not explicitly say so.

Contingencies   Performance of most real estate contracts is subject to various contingencies—that is, it is conditioned on the happening of certain events. For example, the buyer might wish to condition his agreement to buy the house on his ability to find a mortgage, or to find one at a certain rate of interest. Thus the contract for sale might read that the buyer "agrees to buy the premises for $50,000, subject to his obtaining a $40,000 mortgage at 9½ percent." The person protected by the contingency may waive it; if the lowest interest rate the buyer could find was 10 percent, he could either refuse to buy the house or waive the condition and buy it anyway at the higher rate.

Times for Performance   A frequent difficulty in contracting to purchase real estate is the length of time it takes to receive an acceptance to an offer. If the acceptance is not received in a reasonable time, the offeror may treat the offer as rejected. To avoid the uncertainty, an offeror should always state in his offer that it will be held open for a definite period of time (five working days, two weeks, or whatever). The contract also ought to spell out the times by which the following should be done: (1) seller's proof that he has title; (2) buyer's review of his evidence of title; (3) seller's correction of title defects; (4) closing date; and (5) possession by the buyer. The absence of explicit time provisions will not render the contract unenforceable—the courts will infer a reasonable time—but their absence creates the possibility of unnecessary disputes.

Types of Deeds

At common law, there are three types of deeds.

1. *General Warranty Deed*   In a warranty deed, the seller warrants to the buyer that he possesses certain types of legal rights in the property. In the general warranty deed, the seller warrants that (a) he has good title to convey (called a warranty of *seisin*); (b) the property is free from any encumbrance not stated in the deed (the warranty *against encumbrances*); and (c) the property will not be taken by someone with a better title (the warranty of *quiet enjoyment*). Breach of any of these warranties exposes the seller to damages.
2. *Special Warranty Deed*   In the special warranty deed, the seller warrants against claims arising "under, by, or through" the seller; this warranty does not apply to defects in the title created by a prior owner.
3. *Quitclaim Deed*   The simplest form of deed is the quitclaim, in which the seller makes no warranties. Instead, he simply transfers to the buyer whatever title he had, defects and all. A quitclaim deed should not be used in the ordinary purchase and sale transaction. It is usually reserved for removing a cloud on the title—for instance, a quitclaim deed by a widow who might have a dower interest in the property.

If the purchase agreement is silent about the type of deed, courts in many states will require the seller to give the buyer a quitclaim deed. It behooves the buyer, therefore, to ensure that the contract calls for a warranty deed.

Warranties

When buyers move in after the closing, they frequently discover defects (the boiler is broken, a pipe leaks, the electrical power is inadequate). To obtain recourse against such an eventuality, the buyer could attempt to negotiate a clause in the contract under which the seller gives a warranty covering named defects. However, even without an express warranty, the law implies two warranties when a buyer purchases a new house from a builder. These are warranties that (1) the house is habitable, and (2) the builder has completed the house in a workmanlike manner. Most states have refused to extend these warranties to subsequent purchasers—for example, to the buyer from a seller who had bought from the original builder. However, a few states have begun to provide limited protection to subsequent purchasers—in particular, for defects that a reasonable inspection will not reveal but that will show up only after purchase.

PROOF OF TITLE

Contracts are often formed and performed simultaneously, but in real estate transactions there is more often a gap between contract formation and performance (the closing). The reason is simple: The buyer must have time to obtain financing (see Chapter 28) and to determine whether the seller has marketable title (see Figure 33-2). That is not always easy; at least, it is not as straightforward as looking at a piece of paper. To understand how title relates to the real estate transaction, some background on *recording statutes* will be useful.

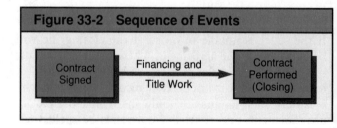

Figure 33-2   Sequence of Events

Contract Signed → Financing and Title Work → Contract Performed (Closing)

Recording Statutes

Suppose Slippery Sam owned Whispering Pines, a choice resort hotel on Lake Maguchee. On October 1, Slippery deeded Whispering Pines to Lorna for $575,000. Realizing the profit potential, Slippery decided to sell it again, and did so on November 1, without bothering to tell Malvina, the new buyer to whom he gave a new deed, that he had already sold it to Lorna. He then departed for a small island off the coast of Indonesia. When Malvina arrives on the doorstep to find Lorna already tidying up, who should prevail?

At common law, the first deed prevailed over subsequent deeds. So in our simple example, if this were a pure common law state Lorna would have title and Malvina would be out of luck, stuck with a worthless piece of paper. Her only recourse, probably futile, would be to search out and sue Slippery Sam for fraud. Most states, however, have enacted **recording statutes**, which award title to the person who has complied with the requirement to place the deed in a publicly available file in a public office in the county, often called the Recorder's Office or the Register of Deeds.

Notice Statute   Under the most common type of recording statute, called a **notice statute**, a deed must be recorded in order for the owner to prevail against a subsequent purchaser. Assume in our example that Lorna recorded her deed on November 2 and that Malvina recorded on November 4. In a notice-statute state, Malvina's claim to title would prevail over Lorna's because on the day that Malvina received title (November 1), Lorna had not yet recorded. For this rule to apply, Malvina must have been a bona fide purchaser, meaning that she must have (1) paid valuable consideration; (2) bought in good faith; and (3) had no notice of the earlier sale. If Lorna had recorded before Malvina took the deed, Lorna would prevail even though Malvina did not in fact check the public records; she *should have* checked, and the recorded deed is said to put subsequent purchasers on **constructive notice**.

Notice-Race Statute   Another common type is the **notice-race statute**. To gain priority under this statute, the subsequent bona fide purchaser must also re-

cord—that is, win the race to the recorder's office—before the earlier purchaser. So in our example, in a notice-race jurisdiction, Lorna would prevail, since she recorded before Malvina did.

Race Statute   A third, more uncommon type is the **race statute**, which gives title to whoever records first, even if the subsequent purchaser is not bona fide and has actual knowledge of the prior sale. Suppose that when she received the deed Malvina knew of the earlier sale to Lorna. Malvina got to the recording office the day she got the deed, November 1, and Lorna came in the following day. In a race-statute jurisdiction, Malvina would take title.

Chain of Title

Given the recording statutes, the buyer must check the deed on record to determine (1) whether the seller ever acquired a valid deed to the property—that is, whether a chain of title can be traced from earlier owners to the seller—and (2) whether the seller has already sold the property to another purchaser, who has recorded a deed. The two common methods for obtaining this information are *abstract and opinion* and *title insurance*.

Abstract and Opinion   An **abstract of title** is a summary of the chain of title, listing all previous deeds, mortgages, tax liens, and other instruments recorded in the county land records office. The abstract is prepared by either an attorney or a title company. Since the list itself says nothing about whether the recorded instruments are legally valid, the buyer must also have the opinion of an attorney reviewing the abstract, or based on his own search of the public records, that the seller has valid title. The attorney's opinion is known as a *title opinion* or *certificate of title*. The problem with this method of proving title is that the public records do not reveal hidden defects. One of the previous owners might have been a minor or an incompetent person who can still void his sale, or a previous deed might have been forged, or a previous seller might have claimed to be single when in fact he was married and his wife failed to sign away her dower rights. A search of the records would not detect these infirmities.

Title Insurance   To overcome these difficulties, the buyer should obtain **title insurance**. This is a one-premium policy issued by a title insurance company after a search through the same public records. When the title company is satisfied that title is valid, it will issue the insurance policy for a premium that could be as high as 1 percent of the selling price. When the buyer is taking out a mortgage, he will ordinarily purchase two policies, one to cover his investment in the property and the other to cover the mortgagee-lender's loan. In general, a title policy protects the buyer against losses that would occur if title (1) turns out to belong to someone else, (2) is subject to a lien, encumbrance, or other defect, or (3) does not give the owner access to the land. A preferred type of title policy will also insure the buyer against losses resulting from an unmarketable title.

Note that in determining whether to issue a policy, the title company goes through the same process described above of searching through the public records. The title policy as such does not guarantee that title is sound. A buyer could conceivably lose part or all of the property someday to a previous rightful owner, but if he does the title insurance company must reimburse him for his losses.

Although title insurance is usually a sound protection, most policies are subject to various exclusions and exceptions. For example, they do not provide coverage for zoning laws that restrict use of the property, or for a government's taking of the property under its power of eminent domain. Nor do the policies insure against defects created by the insured, or known by the insured but unknown to the company. Some companies will not provide coverage for mechanics' liens, public utility easements, and unpaid taxes. (If the accrued taxes are known, the insured will be presented with a list and if he pays them on or before the closing they will be covered by the final policy.) Furthermore, as the following case demonstrates, title insurance covers *title* defects only, not *physical* defects in the property.

TITLE & TRUST CO. OF FLORIDA v. BARROWS
381 So.2d 1088
(Fla.App. 1979)

McCord, Acting Chief Judge. This appeal is from a final judgment awarding money damages to appellees for breach of title insurance policy. We reverse.

Through a realtor, appellees purchased, for $12,500, a lot surrounded on three sides by land owned by others, all of which is a part of a beach subdivision. The fourth side of appellee's lot borders on a platted street called Viejo Street, the right-of-way for which has been dedicated to and accepted by St. John's County. The right-of-way line opposite appellees' lot abuts a Corps of Engineers' right-of-way in which there is a stone breakwater. The intracoastal waterway flows on the other side of the breakwater.

The realtor who sold the lot to appellees represented to them that the county would build a road in the right-of-way along Viejo Street when appellees began plans for building on their lot. There have been no street improvements in the dedicated right-of-way, and St. Johns County has no present plans for making any improvements. The "road" is merely a continuation of a sandy beach.

A year after purchasing the land appellees procured a survey which disclosed that the elevation of their lot is approximately one to three feet above the mean high water mark. They later discovered that their lot, along with the Viejo Street right-of-way abutting it, is covered by high tide water during the spring and fall of each year.

At the time appellees purchased their lot, they obtained title insurance coverage from appellant. The title policy covered:

> Any defect in or lien or encumbrance on the title to the estate or title covered hereby . . . or a lack of a right of access to and from the land; . . . .

Appellees' complaint of lack of right of access was founded on the impassable condition of the platted street. After trial without a jury, the trial court entered final judgment finding that appellees did not have access to their property and, therefore, were entitled to recover $12,500 from appellant—the face amount of the policy.

Appellant and Florida Land Title Association, appearing as amicus curiae, argue that appellant cannot be held liable on grounds of "lack of right of access to and from the land" since there is no defect shown by the public record as to their right of access; that the public record shows a dedicated and accepted public right-of-way abutting the lot. They contend that title insurance does not insure against defects in the physical condition of the land or against infirmities in legal right of access not shown by the public record. They argue that defects in the physical condition of the land such as are involved here are not covered by title insurance. We agree. Title insurance only insures against title defects.

The Supreme Court of North Carolina in *Marriott Financial Services, Inc. v. Capitol Funds, Inc.*, 288 N.C. 122, 217 S.E.2d 551 (1975), construed "right of access" to mean the right to go to and from the public right-of-way without unreasonable restrictions. Compare *Hocking v. Title Insurance & Trust Company*, 37 Cal.2d 644, 234 P.2d 625 (1951), where, in ruling that the plaintiff failed to state a cause of action in a suit brought under her title policy, the court said:

> She appears to possess fee simple title to the property for whatever it may be worth; if she has been damaged by false representations in respect to the condition and value of the land her remedy would seem to be against others than the insurers of the title she acquired.

In *Mafetone, et al., v. Forest Manor Homes, Inc., et al.*, 34 A.D.2d 566, 310 N.Y.S.2d 17 (N.Y.1970), the plaintiff brought an action against a title insurance company for damages allegedly flowing from a change in the grade of a street. There the court said:

> The title company is not responsible to plaintiffs for the damages incurred by reason of the change in elevating the abutting street to its legal grade, since the provisions of the standard title insurance policy here in question are concerned with matters affecting *title* to property and do not concern themselves with physical conditions of the abutting property *absent* a specific request by the person ordering a title report and policy. . . . (Emphasis supplied.)

(continued on next page)

(continued)

**TITLE & TRUST CO.
OF FLORIDA v.
BARROWS**
381 So.2d 1088
(Fla.App. 1979)

In *McDaniel v. Lawyers' Title Guaranty Fund*, 327 So.2d 852 (Fla. 2 D.C.A.1976), our sister court of the Second District said:

> The man on the street buys a title insurance policy to insure against defects in the record title. The title insurance company is in the business of guaranteeing the insured's title to the extent it is affected by the public records.

> In the case here before us, there is no dispute that the public record shows a legal right of access to appellees' property via the platted Viejo Street. The title insurance policy only insured against record title defects and not against physical infirmities of the platted street.
> Reversed.

THE CLOSING

Closing can be a confusing process because in most instances several contracts are being performed simultaneously:

1. The seller and purchaser are performing the sales contract.
2. The seller is paying off a mortgage, while the buyer is completing arrangements to borrow money and mortgage the property.
3. Title and other insurance arrangements will be completed.
4. The seller will pay the broker.
5. Attorneys for each party will be paid.

Despite all these transactions, the critical players are the seller, purchaser, and bank. To place the closing process in perspective, assume that one bank holds the existing (seller's) mortgage on the property and is also financing the buyer's purchase. We can visualize the three main players sitting at a table, ready to close the transaction. The key documents and the money will flow as illustrated in Figure 33-3.

The deed must satisfy two fundamental legal requirements: (1) It must be in the proper form. (2) There must be a valid delivery.

Form of the Deed

Deeds are usually prepared by attorneys, who must include not only information necessary for a valid deed but also information required in order to be able to record the deed. The following information is typically required either for a valid deed or by the recording statutes.

Grantor   The grantor—the person who is conveying the property—must be designated in some manner. Obviously, it is best to give the grantor's full name, but it is sufficient that the person or persons conveying the deed are identifiable from the document. Thus, "the heirs of Lockewood Filmer" is sufficient identification if each of the heirs signs the deed.

Grantee   Similarly, the deed should identify the grantee—the person to whom the property is being conveyed. It does not void the deed to misspell a person's name or to omit part of the name, or even not to name one of the grantees at all (as in "Lockewood Filmer and wife"). Although not technically necessary, the deed ought to detail the interests being conveyed to each grantee in order to avoid considerable legal difficulty later. "To Francis Lucas, a single man, and Joseph Lucas and Matilda Lucas, his wife" was a deed of singular opacity. Did each party have a one-third interest? Or did Joseph and Matilda hold half as tenants by the entirety and Francis have a one-half interest as a tenant in common? Or perhaps Francis had a one-third interest as tenant in common and Joseph and Matilda held two-thirds as tenants by the entirety? Or some other possible combination? The court chose the second interpretation, but considerable time and money could have been saved had the

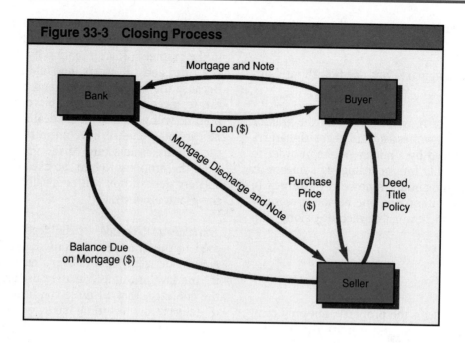

Figure 33-3   Closing Process

deed contained a few simple words of explanation. [Heatter v. Lucas, 80 A.2d 749 (Pa. 1951).]

Addresses   Addresses of the parties should be included, although their absence will not usually invalidate the deed. However, in some states, failure to note the addresses will bar the deed from being recorded.

Words of Conveyance   The deed must indicate that the grantor presently intends to convey his interest in the property to the grantee. The deed may recite that the grantor "conveys and warrants" the property (warranty deed) or "conveys and quitclaims" the property (quitclaim deed). Some deeds use the words "bargain and sell" in place of convey.

Description   The deed must contain an accurate description of the land being conveyed, a description clear enough that the land can be identified without resorting to other evidence. Four general methods are used.

1. *The U.S. Government Survey*   This is available west of the Mississippi (except Texas) and in Alabama, Florida, Illinois, Indiana, Michigan, Mississippi, Ohio, and Wisconsin. With this sur-

vey, it is possible to specify with considerable exactitude any particular plot of land in any township in these states.

2. *Metes and Bounds*   The description of metes and bounds begins with a particular designated point (called a "monument")—for example, a drainpipe, an old oak tree, or whatever—and then defines the boundary with distances and angles until returning to the monument.

3. *Plats*   Many areas have been divided into numbered lots and placed on a map called a *plat*. The plats are recorded. The deed, then, need only refer to the plat and lot number, for example "Lot 17, Appledale Subdivision, record in Liber 2 of Plats, page 62, Choctaw County Records."

4. *Informal Description*   If none of the above methods can be used, an informal description, done precisely enough, might suffice. For instance, "my home at 31 Fernwood Street, Maplewood, Idaho" would probably pass muster.

Statement of Consideration   Statutes usually require that some consideration be stated in the deed, even though a grantor may convey property as a gift. When there is a selling price, it is easy enough to state it, although the actual price need not be listed. When land is being transferred as a gift, a statement of nominal consideration—for example, one dollar—is sufficient.

Date   Dates are customary, but deeds without dates will be enforced.

Execution   The deed must be signed by the grantor and, in some states, witnesses, and these signatures must be acknowledged by a notary public in order to make the deed eligible for recording. If someone is signing for the grantor under a **power of attorney** (a written instrument authorizing one person to sign for another), the instrument must be recorded along with the deed.

Delivery

To validly convey title to the property, not only must the deed be in proper form, but it must also be *delivered*. This technical legal requirement is sometimes misunderstood. **Delivery** entails (1) physical delivery to the grantee, (2) an intention by the grantor to convey title, and (3) acceptance of title by the grantee. Because the grantor must intend to convey title, failure to meet the other elements during the grantor's lifetime will void title on his death (since at that point he cannot of course have an intention). Thus, when the grantee is unaware of the grantor's intention to deed the property to him, an executed deed sitting in a safety deposit box will be invalid if discovered after the grantor's death.

Delivery to Grantee   If the deed is physically delivered to the grantee or recorded, there is a *rebuttable presumption* that legal delivery has been made. That is, the law presumes, in the absence of evidence to the contrary, that all three conditions have been met if delivery or recording takes place. But this presumption can be rebutted, as in the following case.

HAVENS v. SCHOEN
108 Mich.App. 758, 310
N.W.2d 870 (1981)

PER CURIAM. Plaintiffs brought an action in equity seeking to set aside a deed or to impose a constructive trust on farm property which was the subject of the deed. The trial judge found no cause of action and plaintiffs appeal as a matter of right.

In 1962, plaintiff Dr. Havens purchased the Scholz family farm from the estate of her twin brother, Norman Scholz. She gave a deed of trust to her other brother Earl Scholz in 1964, naming her daughter Linda Karen Adams as the principal beneficiary. In 1969, she filed suit against Earl and Inez Scholz and, in settlement of that suit, the property was conveyed to Dr. Havens and her daughter, now deceased. On August 13, 1969, Dr. Havens executed a quit-claim deed to her daughter of her remaining interest in the farm. It is this deed which Dr. Havens wishes to set aside.

The trial court found that plaintiffs failed to meet the burden of proving an invalid conveyance. Plaintiffs claim that there was never a delivery or an intent to presently and unconditionally convey an interest in the property to the daughter. The deed was recorded but defendants presented no other evidence to prove delivery. The recording of a deed raises a presumption of delivery. The only effect of this presumption is to cast upon the opposite party the burden of moving forward with the evidence. The burden of proving delivery by a preponderance of the evidence remains with the party relying on the deed. Acknowledging that the deed was recorded, plaintiffs presented substantial evidence showing no delivery and no intent to presently and unconditionally convey an interest in the property. The deed, after recording, was returned to Dr. Havens. She continued to manage the farm and pay all expenses for it. When asked about renting the farm, the daughter told a witness to ask her mother. Plaintiffs presented sufficient evidence to dispel the presumption. We find that the trial court erred when it stated that plaintiffs had the burden of proof on all issues. The defendants had the burden of proving delivery and requisite intent.

In *Haasjes v Woldring*, 10 Mich App 100; 158 NW2d 777 (1968), *lv den* 381 Mich 756 (1968), two grandparents executed a deed to property to two grandchildren. The grandparents continued to live on the property, pay taxes on it and subsequent to the execution of the deed they made statements which this Court found inconsistent with a prior transfer of property. These circumstances combined with the fact that the deed was not placed beyond the grantors' control led the *Haasjes* Court to conclude that a valid transfer of title had not been effected. The *Haasjes* Court, citing *Wandel v Wandel*, 336 Mich 126; 57 NW2d 468 (1953), and *Resh v Fox*, 365 Mich 288; 112 NW2d 486 (1961), held that in considering whether there was a present intent to pass title, courts may look to the subsequent acts of the grantor.

⋆ ⋆ ⋆

We remand to the trial court to enter an order setting aside the August 13, 1969, deed from Norma Anderson Havens to Linda Karen Anderson Adams purporting to convey the interest of Dr. Havens in the farm. The decision of the trial court finding no justification for imposing a trust upon the property is affirmed.

Affirmed in part, reversed in part, and remanded.

Delivery to Third Party (Commercial Escrow) The grantor may deliver the deed to a third party to hold until certain conditions have been met. Thus, to avoid the problem of the deed sitting in the grantor's own safe-deposit box, he could deliver it to a third party with instructions to hold until his death and then to deliver to the grantee. This would be an effective delivery, even though the grantee could not use the property until the grantor died. For this method to be effective, the grantor must lose all control over the deed and the third party must be instructed to deliver the deed when the specified conditions occur.

This method is most frequently used in the *commercial escrow*. **Escrow** is a method by which a third party holds a document or money or both until specified conditions have been met. A typical example would be a sale in which the buyer is afraid of mechanics' liens that might be filed after the closing. The buyer would prefer to pay the seller after the time for filing mechanics' liens has lapsed. But sellers ordinarily want to ensure that they will receive their money before delivering a deed. The solution is for the buyer to pay the money into escrow (to a bank, for example) and for the seller to deliver the deed to the same escrow agent. The bank would be instructed to hold both the money and deed until the time for filing mechanics' liens has ended. If no mechanics' lien has been filed, then the money is paid out of escrow to the seller and the deed is released to the buyer. If a lien has been filed, then the money will not be paid until the seller removes the lien.

ADVERSE POSSESSION

In some instances, real property can be acquired for free—or, at least, without paying the original owner anything. (Considerable cost may be involved in meeting the requisite conditions.) This method of acquisition—known as **adverse possession**—is effective when five conditions are met: (1) the person claiming title by adverse possession must assert that he has a right to possession hostile to the interest of the original owner; (2) he must actually possess the property; (3) his possession must be "open and notorious"; (4) the possession must be continuous; (5) the possession must be exclusive.

Hostile Possession

Suppose Jean and Jacques are tenants in common of a farm. Jean announces that he no longer intends to pursue agricultural habits and leaves for the city. Jacques continues to work on the land, making improvements, and paying taxes and the mortgage. Years later Jacques files suit for title, claiming that he now owns the land outright by adverse possession. He would lose, since his possession was not hostile to Jacques. To be hostile, possession of the land must be without permission and with the intention to claim ownership. Possession by one cotenant is deemed permissive, since either or both are legally entitled to possession. Suppose, instead, that Jean and Jacques are neighboring farmers, each with title to his own acreage, and that Jean decides to fence in his property. Just to be on the safe side, he knowingly constructs the fence twenty feet over on Jacques's side. This is adverse possession, since it is clearly hostile to Jacques's possession of the land.

Actual Possession

Not only must the possession be hostile, it must also be actual. The possessor must enter onto the land and make some use of it. Many state statutes define the permissible type of possession—for example, substantial enclosure or cultivation and improvement. In other states, the courts will look to the circumstances of each case to determine whether the claimant had in fact possessed the land—grazing cattle on the land each summer, for instance.

Open and Notorious

The possessor must use the land in an open way, so that the original owner could determine by looking

that his land was being claimed and so that people in the area would know that it was being used by the adverse possessor. In the melodramatic words of one court, the adverse possessor "must unfurl his flag on the land, and keep it flying so that the owner may see, if he will, that an enemy has invaded his domains, and planted the standard of conquest." [Robin v. Brown, 162 A. 161 (Pa. 1932).] Construction of a building on the owner's property would be open and notorious; development of a cave under the owner's property would not be.

Continuous Possession

The adverse possessor must use the land continuously, not intermittently. In most states, this continuous period must last for at least twenty years. If the adverse possession is passed on to heirs, or the interest is sold, the successor adverse possessors may tack on the time they claim possession to reach the twenty years. Should the original owner sell his land, the time needed to prove continuous possession will not lapse. Of course, the original owner may interrupt the period—indeed, may terminate it—by moving to eject the adverse possessor any time before the twenty years has elapsed.

Exclusive Possession

The adverse possessor must claim exclusive possession of the land. Sharing the land with the owner is insufficient to ground a claim of legal entitlement based on adverse possession, since the sharing is not fully adverse or hostile. Jean finds a nice wooded lot to enjoy weekly picnics. The lot belongs to Jacques, who also uses it for picnics. This use would be insufficient to claim adverse possession because it is neither continuous nor exclusive.

If the five tests are met, then the adverse possessor is entitled to legal title. If any one of the tests is missing, as in the following case, the adverse possession claim will fail.

MEYERS v. MEYERS
368 N.W.2d 391
(Minn.App. 1985)

RANDALL, PRESIDING JUDGE. This appeal is from a judgment finding respondent the owner of the disputed property (family home) through adverse possession. We reverse and remand to the trial court to hold an ancillary hearing to determine ownership rights in Minnesota real estate which was not mentioned in a foreign jurisdiction divorce decree and to consider equitable claims raised by respondent.

FACTS

Respondent Bernadine Meyers and appellant Robert Meyers were married in 1940. In 1947 they moved into Robert's father's house in Winona. During that year, the Meyers, their three children, and Robert's father lived together in the house. In 1937 Robert's parents had deeded the property to him, reserving a life estate.

In 1948, Robert enlisted in the army and moved to California. His family remained in Winona, living in the home and caring for Robert's father. Robert returned for visits in December 1948 and spring 1949 and 1950.

Robert's father died in October 1950, and Robert returned to Winona for the funeral. During that visit, Robert and Bernadine argued. When the argument became violent, Bernadine called the police, and Robert was removed from the house by the authorities.

In 1954 Robert obtained a divorce in California. The decree did not mention the real estate, and no attempt at property division was made. Therefore, until this suit, neither party moved to amend the California decree or make any claims in a Minnesota court relative to the real estate.

* * *

Bernadine made significant improvements to the house in 1950. In addition, she has maintained the house and made minor repairs since that time. Robert paid the property taxes on the house through the first half of 1960, but Bernadine has paid the taxes since then.

Robert did not return to Minnesota from the time of his father's funeral in 1950 until 1979. In 1979 he indicated to Bernadine and the children that he thought he had deeded the house to the children. When informed otherwise, he told them he wanted the children to have it. When the children suggested he deed it to Bernadine instead, he said, "I'll burn it down first." Robert instructed local authorities to begin sending property tax statements to his California address, and Bernadine brought this action asking either for an equitable division of the property or reimbursement for improvements made, or for a declaration that she owned the property by virtue of adverse possession. The trial court ruled only on the adverse possession issue, finding that Bernadine owned the property.

ISSUE

Was the evidence sufficient to sustain the trial court's finding that Bernadine acquired ownership of appellant's house by adverse possession?

(*continued on next page*)

(*continued*)

MEYERS v. MEYERS
368 N.W.2d 391
(Minn.App. 1985)

ANALYSIS

To establish title by adverse possession, the adverse possessor must show by clear and convincing evidence an actual, open, hostile, continuous, and exclusive possession for 15 years. *Wojahn v. Johnson*, 297 N.W.2d 298 (Minn.1980); Minn. Stat. § 541.02 (1984). At least from 1950 to 1979, Bernadine's possession was actual, open, continuous, and exclusive. All five elements are equally necessary, however, and if her possession was not hostile to Robert's title, her claim must fail.

Robert contends Bernadine's possession of the house throughout the more than 15 years was permissive. The *Wojahn* court said:

> The general rule of law is that the existence of a family relationship between the claimant of land and the record owner . . . creates the inference, if not the presumption, that the original possession by the claimant of the other's land was permissive and not adverse . . . ; and that when such original use was thus permissive, it would be presumed permissive, rather than hostile, until the contrary was affirmatively shown.

Here, the facts, as well as the "inference" referred to in *Wojahn*, establish that Bernadine's initial possession of the property was permissive. Once initial possession is permissive, proof of the inception of possession which is hostile to the record owner's title must be clear and unequivocal.

*   *   *

The trial court found that the 1950 argument after which Robert was removed from the house was a declaration of Bernadine's adverse holding, of which Robert had notice. We disagree. Because one spouse has the other removed from the home during a domestic dispute does not mean that the spouse who remains in the home now possesses the house adversely to the ejected spouse's title. Such a holding could substantially interfere in property rights between married couples. Courts could become reluctant to allow the legitimate temporary relief of ejectment that spouses are entitled to if they show domestic abuse because of concerns over alienating title.

*   *   *

At trial, Bernadine testified that she never told Robert prior to the commencement of this lawsuit that she felt she owned the house, and that she never told anyone else that she felt she owned the house. She testified that she, in fact, never claimed to have title to the property, and that neither while raising the children nor after they grew up did she do anything different with the house that might reasonably put Robert or anyone else on notice that she was asserting an ownership claim. Bernadine has failed to show that her permissive use of the property became hostile, and thus the finding of adverse possession cannot be sustained.

Although we rule against Bernadine on her claim of adverse possession, we sympathize with her position. Bernadine was the sole parent to the parties' three children after Robert left. She maintained and improved the house by herself and paid the taxes by herself after 1960. The trial court did not rule on Bernadine's claims for equitable relief or for relief under Minnesota Statutes Chapter 518. We therefore remand this matter to the trial court so that Bernadine may have an opportunity to argue her equitable claims and present her evidence as to why there should be a division of the omitted property.

CHAPTER SUMMARY

Real property can be held in various forms of ownership. The most common forms are tenancy in common, joint tenancy, and tenancy by the entirety. Nine states recognize the community property form of ownership.

In selling real property, various common law and statutory provisions come into play—among them, the Civil Rights Acts of 1866 and 1968. These laws control the manner in which property may be listed and prohibit discrimination in sales. Sellers and buyers must also be mindful of contract and agency principles governing the listing agreement. Whether the real estate broker has an exclusive right to sell, an exclusive agency, or an open listing will have an important bearing on the fee to which the broker will be entitled when the property is sold.

The Statute of Frauds requires contracts for the sale of real property to be in writing. Such contracts must include the names of buyers and sellers, a description of the property, the price, and signatures. Unless the contract states otherwise, the seller must deliver marketable title, and the buyer will bear the loss if the property is damaged after the contract is signed but before the closing. The seller will usually insist on being paid earnest money, and the buyer will usually protect himself contractually against certain contingencies, such as failure to obtain financing. The contract should also specify the type of deed to be given to the buyer—general warranty, special warranty, or quitclaim. The first two deeds extend warranties to the buyer, who may sue if the warranties are breached.

To provide protection to subsequent buyers, most states have enacted recording statutes that require buyers to record their purchases in a county office. The statutes vary—which of two purchasers will prevail depends on whether the state has a notice, notice-race, or race statute. To protect themselves, buyers usually purchase an abstract and opinion or title insurance.

Although sale is the usual method of acquiring real property, it is possible to take legal title without the consent of the owner. That method is adverse possession, by which one who openly, continuously, and exclusively possesses property and asserts his right to do so in a manner hostile to the interest of the owner will take title in twenty years in most states.

KEY TERMS

Abstract of title	p. 745	Notice statute	p. 745
Adverse possession	p. 751	Notice-race statute	p. 745
Bylaws	p. 738	Open listing	p. 742
Community property	p. 737	Power of attorney	p. 750
Condominium	p. 737	Principal	p. 742
Constructive notice	p. 745	Race statute	p. 745
Cooperative	p. 740	Recording statutes	p. 745
Delivery	p. 750	Separate property	p. 737
Earnest money	p. 743	Tenants by the	p. 736
Equitable conversion	p. 743	entirety	
Escrow	p. 751	Tenants in common	p. 737
Exclusive agency	p. 742	Timesharing	p. 740
Exclusive-right-to-sell	p. 742	Title insurance	p. 746
Fiduciary duty	p. 742	Unities	p. 736
In severalty	p. 735	Unity of interest	p. 736
Listing agreement	p. 741	Unity of possession	p. 736
Marketable title	p. 743	Unity of time	p. 736
Master deed	p. 738	Unity of title	p. 736

SELF-TEST QUESTIONS

1. A contract for a sale of property must include:
   (a) a description of the property
   (b) price
   (c) signatures of buyer and seller
   (d) all of the above
2. If real property is damaged after a contract for sale is signed but before closing, it is generally true that the party bearing the loss is:
   (a) the seller
   (b) the buyer
   (c) both parties, who split the loss evenly
   (d) none of the above
3. The following deeds extend warranties to the buyer:
   (a) quitclaim and special warranty
   (b) quitclaim and general warranty
   (c) general and special warranty
   (d) all of the above

4. Under a notice-race statute:
   (a) whoever records first is given title, regardless of the good faith of the purchaser
   (b) whoever records first and is a bona fide purchaser is given title
   (c) either of the above may be acceptable
   (d) none of the above is acceptable
5. The elements of adverse possession do not include:
   (a) actual possession
   (b) open and notorious use
   (c) consent of the owner
   (d) continuous possession

DEMONSTRATION PROBLEM

Rufus enters into a contract to purchase the Brooklyn Bridge from Sharpy. The contract provides that Sharpy is to give Rufus a quitclaim deed at the closing. After the closing, Rufus learns that Sharpy did not own the bridge, and sues him for violating the terms of the deed. Result? Why?

PROBLEMS

1. Pancho and Cisco decide to purchase ten acres of real estate. Pancho is to provide 75 percent of the purchase price, Cisco the other 25 percent. They want to use either a joint tenancy or tenancy in common form of ownership. What do you recommend? Why?
2. Suppose in problem 1 that a friend recommends that Pancho and Cisco use a tenancy by the entirety. Would this form of ownership be appropriate? Why?
3. Richard and Elizabeth, a married couple, live in a community property state. During their marriage, they save $500,000 from Elizabeth's earnings. Richard does not work but, during the marriage, inherits $500,000. If Richard and Elizabeth are divorced, how will their property be divided? Why?

4. Jack wants to sell his house. He hires Walter, a real estate broker, to sell the house and signs an "exclusive right to sell" listing agreement. Walter finds a buyer, who signs a sales contract with Jack. However, the buyer later refuses to perform the contract because he cannot obtain financing. Does Jack owe a commission to Walter? Why?
5. Suppose in problem 4 that Jack found the buyer, that the buyer obtained financing, and that the sale was completed. Does Jack owe a commission to Walter, who provided no assistance in finding the buyer and closing the deal? Why?
6. Suppose in problem 5 that Jack's house is destroyed by fire before the closing. Who bears the loss—Jack or the buyer? Must Jack pay a commission to Walter? Why?
7. Suppose in problem 4 that the buyer paid $5,000 in earnest money when the contract was signed. Must Jack return the earnest money when the buyer learns that financing is unavailable? Why?

ANSWERS TO SELF-TEST QUESTIONS

1. (d)   2. (b)   3. (c)   4. (b)   5. (c)

ANSWER TO DEMONSTRATION PROBLEM

Sharpy wins. With the quitclaim deed, Sharpy has given Rufus no warranties; he has merely transferred to Rufus whatever rights he has in the Brooklyn Bridge.

CHAPTER 34

Landlord and Tenant Law

TYPES OF LEASEHOLDS

*I*n Chapter 32 we noted that real property can be divided into types of interests: freehold estates and leasehold estates. The freehold estate is characterized by indefinite duration, and the owner has title and the right to possess. The **leasehold estate,** by contrast, lasts for a specific period. The owner of the leasehold estate—the tenant—may take possession but does not have title to the underlying real property. When the period of the leasehold ends, the right to possession reverts to the landlord—hence the landlord's interest during the tenant's possession is known as a **reversionary interest.** Although a leasehold estate is said to be an interest in real property, the leasehold itself is in fact personal property. The law recognizes three types of leasehold estates: the *estate for years*, the *periodic tenancy*, and the *tenancy at will*.

Estate for Years

The **estate for years** is characterized by a definite beginning and a definite end. When you rent an apartment for two years, beginning September 1 and ending on the second August 31, you are the owner of an estate for years. Virtually any period will do; although it is called an estate "for years" it can last but one day or extend 1,000 years or more. Some statutes declare that any estate for years longer than a specified period—100 years in Massachusetts, for instance—is a fee simple estate.

Unless the **lease**—the agreement creating the leasehold interest—provides otherwise, the estate for years terminates automatically at midnight of the last day specified in the lease. The lease need not refer explicitly to calendar dates. It could provide that "the tenant may occupy the premises for six months to commence one week from the date of signing." Suppose the landlord and tenant sign on June 23. Then the lease term begins at 12:00 A.M. on July 1, and ends just before midnight of December 31. Unless a statute provides otherwise, the landlord is not obligated to send the tenant a notice of termination. Should the tenant die before the lease term ends, her property interest can be inherited under her will along with her other personal property or in accordance with the laws of intestate succession.

Periodic Tenancy

As its name implies, a **periodic tenancy** lasts for a period that is renewed automatically until either landlord or tenant notifies the other that it will end. The periodic tenancy is sometimes called an estate *from year to year* (or month to month, or week to week). The lease may provide explicitly for the periodic tenancy by specifying that at the expiration of, say, a one-year lease, it will be deemed renewed for another year unless one party notifies the other to the contrary within six months prior to the expiration of the term. Or the periodic tenancy may be created by implication, if the lease omits to state a term or the lease is defective but the tenant takes possession and pays rent. The usual method of creating a periodic tenancy occurs when the tenant remains on the premises ("holds over") when an estate for years under a lease has ended. The landlord may either reject the implied offer by the tenant to rent under a periodic tenancy or he may accept. If he rejects, the tenant may be ejected and the landlord is entitled to rent for the holdover period. If he accepts, the original lease determines the rent and length of the renewable period, except that no periodic tenancy may last longer than from year to year—that is, the renewable period may never be any longer than twelve months.

At common law, a party was required to give notice at least six months prior to the end of a year-to-year tenancy, and notice equal to the term for any other periodic tenancy. In most states today, the time period for giving notice is regulated by statute. In most instances, a year-to-year tenancy requires a month's notice, and shorter tenancies require notice equal to the term. To illustrate the approach typically used, suppose Simone rents from Anita on a month-to-month tenancy beginning September 15. On March 30, Simone passes her Ph.D. orals and decides to leave town. How soon may she cancel her tenancy? If she calls Anita that afternoon, she will be two weeks shy of a full month's notice for the period ending April 15, so the earliest she can finish her obligation to pay rent is May 15. Suppose her term had been from the first of each month. On April 1 she notifies Anita of her intention to leave at the end of April. She is stuck until the end of May, because notice on the first of the month is not notice for a full month. She would have had to notify Anita by March 31 to terminate the tenancy by April 30.

Tenancy at Will

If the landlord and tenant agree that the lease will last only as long as both desire it to, then they have created a **tenancy at will**. Statutes in most states require some notice of intention to terminate. Simone comes to the university to study and Anita gives her a room to stay in for free. The arrangement is a tenancy at will, and it will continue as long as both want it to. One Friday night, after dinner with classmates, Simone decides she would rather move in with Bob. She goes back to her apartment, packs her suitcase, and tells Anita she's leaving. The tenancy at will terminates that day.

CREATION OF LEASEHOLD ESTATES

Oral Leases

Leases can be created orally, unless the term of the lease exceeds the period specified by the Statute of Frauds. In most states, that period is one year. Any oral lease for a period longer than the statutory period is invalid. Suppose in a state with a one-year Statute of Frauds period, Simone orally agrees with Anita to rent her apartment for two years, at a monthly rent of $250. The lease is invalid, and either could repudiate it.

Written Leases

A lease required to be in writing under the Statute of Frauds must contain the following items or provisions: (1) It must identify the parties; (2) It must identify the premises; (3) It must specify the duration of the lease; (4) It must state the rent to be paid; and (5) It must be signed by the party against whom enforcement is sought (known as "the party to be charged").

The provisions need not be perfectly stated. As long as they satisfy the requirements listed above, they will be adequate to sustain the lease under the Statute of Frauds. For instance, the parties need not necessarily be named in the lease itself. Suppose the prospective tenant gives the landlord a month's rent in advance and the landlord gives the tenant a receipt listing the property and the terms of the lease but omitting to name the tenant. The landlord subsequently refuses to let the tenant move in. Who would prevail in court? Since the tenant had the receipt in her possession, that would be sufficient to identify her as the tenant to whom the terms of the lease were meant to apply. Likewise, the lease need not specify every aspect of the premises to be enjoyed. Thus the tenant who rents an apartment in a building will be entitled to the use of the common stairway, the roof, and so on, even though the lease is silent on these points. And as long as a specific amount is ascertainable, the rent may be stated in other than absolute dollar terms. For example, it could be expressed in terms of a cost-of-living index or as a percentage of the tenant's dollar business volume.

LANDLORD'S DUTIES AND TENANT'S RIGHTS

The law imposes a number of duties on the landlord and gives the tenant a number of corresponding rights. These include (1) possession, (2) habitable condition, and (3) noninterference with use.

Possession

The landlord must give the tenant the right of possession of the property. This duty is breached if, at the time the tenant is entitled to take possession, a third party has *paramount title* to the property and the assertion of this title would deprive the tenant of the use contemplated by the parties. **Paramount title** means any legal interest in the premises that is not terminable at the will of the landlord or at the time the tenant is entitled to take possession.

If the tenant has already taken possession and then discovers the paramount title, or if the paramount title only then comes into existence, the landlord is not automatically in breach. However, if the tenant thereafter is evicted from the premises and thus deprived of the property, then the landlord is in breach. Suppose the landlord rents a house to a doctor for ten years, knowing that the doctor intends to open a medical office in part of the home and knowing also that the lot is restricted to residential uses only. The doctor moves in. The landlord is not yet in default. The landlord will be in default if a neighbor obtains an injunction against maintaining the office. But if the landlord did not know (and could not reasonably have known) that the doctor intended to use his home for an office, then the landlord would not be in default under the lease, since the property could have been put to normal—that is, residential—use without jeopardizing the tenant's right to possession.

Warranty of Habitability

As applied to leases, the old common law doctrine of *caveat emptor* said that once the tenant has signed the lease, she must take the premises as she finds them. Since she could inspect them before signing the lease, she should not complain later. Moreover, if hidden defects come to light, they ought to be easy enough for the tenant herself to fix. Today this rule no longer applies, at least to residential rentals. Unless the parties specifically agree otherwise, the landlord is in breach of his lease if the conditions are unsuitable for residential use when the tenant is due to move in. The landlord is held to an **implied warranty of habitability**.

The change in the rule is due in part to the conditions of the modern urban setting: Tenants have little or no power to walk away from an available apartment in areas where housing is scarce. It is also due to modern construction and technology: Few tenants are capable of fixing most types of defects. As a U.S. Court of Appeals has said:

> Today's urban tenants, the vast majority of whom live in multiple dwelling houses, are interested not in the land, but solely in "a house suitable for occupation." Furthermore, today's city dweller usually has a single, specialized skill unrelated to maintenance work; he is unable to make repairs like the "jack-of-all-trades" farmer who was the common law's model of the lessee. Further, unlike his agrarian predecessor who often remained on one piece of land for his entire life, urban tenants today are more mobile than ever before. A tenant's tenure in a specific apartment will often not be sufficient to justify efforts at repairs. In addition, the increasing complexity of today's dwellings renders them much more difficult to repair than the structures of earlier times. In a multiple dwelling, repairs may require access to equipment and areas in control of the landlord. Low and middle income tenants, even

if they were interested in making repairs, would be unable to obtain financing for major repairs since they have no long-term interest in the property. [Javins v. First National Realty Corp., 428 F.2d 1071, 1078-79 (D.C. Cir.), *cert. den.*, 400 U.S. 925 (1970)]

At common law the landlord was not responsible if the premises became unsuitable once the tenant moved in. This rule was often harshly applied, even for unsuitable conditions caused by a sudden act of God, such as a tornado. Even if the premises collapsed, the tenant would be liable to pay the rent for the duration of the lease. Today, however, many states have statutorily abolished the tenant's obligation to pay the rent if a non-manmade force renders the premises unsuitable. Moreover, most states today impose on the landlord, after the tenant has moved in, the responsibility for maintaining the premises in a safe, livable condition, consistent with the safety, health, and housing codes of the jurisdiction.

These rules apply only in the absence of an express agreement between the parties. The landlord and tenant may allocate in the lease the responsibility for repairs and maintenance. But it is unlikely that any court would enforce a lease provision waiving the landlord's implied warranty of habitability for residential apartments, especially in areas where housing is relatively scarce.

These rules are examined in the following case, involving a suit by the landlord for *detainer*—that is, a suit to recover the premises from a tenant who has failed or refused to pay the rent. The tenants in the case claimed that the rent was being withheld because the landlord had breached his implied warranty of habitability.

KNIGHT v. HALLSTHAMMAR
171 Cal.Rptr. 707, 623 P.2d 268 (1981)

BIRD, CHIEF JUSTICE. This court must decide whether a residential tenant may be held to have impliedly waived a landlord's breach of implied warranty of habitability by (1) continuing to live in premises despite knowledge of the defects or (2) failing to allow a landlord a reasonable time to repair before withholding rent. There is the additional question as to whether an unlawful detainer action may be defended based on a breach of implied warranty of habitability where defects in the premises predated the current ownership of the building.

On May 18, 1977, plaintiff landlords became owners of a 30-unit apartment building at 1305 Ocean Front Walk in Venice, California. They had bought the property from a Norman Baker and his parents.

On May 19th, Western Investment Properties Inc. (hereinafter W.I.P.), which had been hired by plaintiffs to manage the property, sent a letter to the tenants indicating there would be a substantial increase in the rent. On May 26th Clara Breit, as representative of the "1305 Ocean Front Walk Tenants Association," sent a letter to W.I.P. stating that the tenants would withhold all future rent payments because of both the state of disrepair of the apartment building and the new rent increases. Neither W.I.P. nor plaintiffs responded to this letter.

When confronted in late May by tenants and the news media, an employee of W.I.P. allegedly indicated that the only repairs that would be made were to the vacant apartments and any common areas. No repairs were contemplated as to the occupied units until they became vacant. In early June, the tenants were served with three-day notices to pay the new rent or face eviction. These consolidated unlawful detainer actions by plaintiffs followed.

At the trial below, evidence was introduced by the tenants that plaintiffs had breached their implied warranty of habitability. The tenants complained of wall cracks, peeling paint, water leaks, heating and electrical fixture problems, broken or inoperable windows, rodents and cockroaches, and the lack of sufficient heat in the apartments. All of these conditions existed before plaintiffs acquired ownership. The defendants had personally complained to the manager about the conditions of their apartments before service of the three-day notices and before plaintiffs' ownership. Some complaints had also been lodged with Norman Baker. Only a portion of the complaints had resulted in corrections.

*   *   *

The jury was unable to reach a verdict with respect to three tenants but returned a verdict in favor of plaintiffs against four tenants. These appeals followed, based upon defendants' claim that the trial court erroneously gave certain instructions requested by plaintiffs while refusing to give other instructions requested by defendants.

This court must address the issue of a residential tenant who continues to live in uninhabitable premises after learning of the defects and whether this fact waives the landlord's breach of the implied warranty of habitability recognized by this court in *Green v. Superior Court* (1974), 517 P.2d 1168.

In *Green*, a landlord commenced an unlawful detainer action seeking possession of leased premises and back rent. The tenant admitted nonpayment of rent but defended on the ground that the landlord had failed to maintain the premises in an habitable condition. This court held that there is in California a common law implied warranty of habitability in residential leases, and that under this warranty a landlord "covenants that premises he leases for living quarters will be maintained in a habitable state for the duration of the lease." Further, a tenant may raise a landlord's breach of the implied warranty of habitability as a defense in an unlawful detainer proceeding. Recognizing that at least one other court had held that such a warranty generally could not be waived by any provision in the lease or rental agreement, this court in *Green* stated that "public policy requires that landlords generally not be permitted to use their superior bargaining power to negate the warranty of habitability rule." "[T]he severe shortage of low and moderate cost housing has left tenants with little bargaining power. . . . [E]ven when defects are apparent the low income tenant frequently has no realistic alternative but to accept such housing with the expectation that the landlord will make the necessary repairs."

The court also noted that "the increasing complexity of modern apartment buildings not only renders them much more difficult and expensive to repair . . . but also makes adequate inspection of the premises by a prospective tenant a virtual impossibility; complex heating, electrical and plumbing systems are hidden from view, and the landlord, who has had experience with the building, is certainly in a much better position to discover and to cure dilapidations in the premises."

*   *   *

(continued on next page)

(continued)

KNIGHT v. HALLSTHAMMAR
171 Cal.Rptr. 707, 623 P.2d 268 (1981)

Under *Green v. Superior Court, supra,* a residential tenant may not be deemed to have exempted a landlord from the implied warranty of habitability by continuing to live in uninhabitable premises, and breach of the warranty does not and should not depend upon a tenant's lack of knowledge of the conditions which make the premises uninhabitable. Further, in an unlawful detainer action, a tenant's defense that a landlord has breached an implied warranty of habitability should not depend on whether the landlord has had a "reasonable" time to repair, because the issue is whether the premises are in fact inhabitable. Nor should that defense depend on the fortuitous circumstance of a change in ownership of the premises.

The trial court's erroneous instructions to the jury and failure to set forth properly the standards of habitability were likely to mislead the jury, and therefore the judgment is reversed.

Interference with Use

In addition to maintaining the premises in a physically suitable manner, the landlord also has an obligation to the tenant not to interfere with a permissible use of the premises. Suppose Simone moves into a building with several apartments. One of the other tenants consistently plays music late in the evening, causing Simone to lose sleep. She complains to the landlord, who has a provision in the lease permitting him to terminate the lease of any tenant who persists in disturbing other tenants. If the landlord does nothing after Simone had notified him of the disturbance, he would be in breach. This right to be free of interference with permissible uses is sometimes said to arise from the landlord's implied **covenant of quiet enjoyment.**

Tenant's Remedies

When the landlord breaches one of the foregoing duties, the tenant has a choice of three basic remedies: **termination,** damages, or **rent adjustment.**

Termination of the Lease   In virtually all cases when the landlord breaches, the tenant may terminate the lease, thus ending her obligation to continue to pay rent. To terminate, the tenant must (1) actually vacate the premises during the time that she is entitled to terminate, and (2) either comply with lease provisions governing the method of terminating or else take reasonable steps to assure that the landlord knows she has terminated and why.

When the landlord physically deprives the tenant of possession, he has evicted the tenant; wrongful eviction permits the tenant to terminate the lease. Even if the landlord's conduct falls short of *actual* eviction, it may interfere substantially enough with the tenant's permissible use so that it is tantamount to eviction. This is known as **constructive eviction,** and it covers a wide variety of actions by both the landlord and those whose conduct is attributable to him, as illustrated by the following case.

**FIDELITY MUTUAL
LIFE INSURANCE CO.
v. KAMINSKY**
768 S.W.2d 818
(Tex. 1989)

MURPHY, JUSTICE.

The issue in this landlord-tenant case is whether sufficient evidence supports the jury's findings that the landlord and appellant, Fidelity Mutual Life Insurance Company ["Fidelity"], constructively evicted the tenant, Robert P. Kaminsky, M.D., P.A. ["Dr. Kaminsky"] by breaching the express covenant of quiet enjoyment contained in the parties' lease. We affirm.

Dr. Kaminsky is a gynecologist whose practice includes performing elective abortions. In May 1983, he executed a lease contract for the rental of approximately 2,861 square feet in the Red Oak Atrium Building for a two year term which began on June 1, 1983. The terms of the lease required Dr. Kaminsky to use the rented space as "an office for the practice of medicine." Fidelity owns the building and hires local companies to manage it. At some time during the lease term, Shelter Commercial Properties ["Shelter"] replaced the Horne Company as managing agents. Fidelity has not disputed either management company's capacity to act as its agent.

The parties agree that: (1) they executed a valid lease agreement; (2) Paragraph 35 of the lease contains an express covenant of quiet enjoyment conditioned on Dr. Kaminsky's paying rent when due, as he did through November 1984; Dr. Kaminsky abandoned the leased premises on or about December 3, 1984 and refused to pay additional rent; anti-abortion protestors began picketing at the building in June of 1984 and repeated and increased their demonstrations outside and inside the building until Dr. Kaminsky abandoned the premises.

When Fidelity sued for the balance due under the lease contract following Dr. Kaminsky's abandonment of the premises, he claimed that Fidelity constructively evicted him by breaching Paragraph 35 of the lease. Fidelity apparently conceded during trial that sufficient proof of the constructive eviction of Dr. Kaminsky would relieve him of his contractual liability for any remaining rent payments. Accordingly, he assumed the burden of proof and the sole issue submitted to the jury was whether Fidelity breached paragraph 35 of the lease, which reads as follows:

> *Quiet Enjoyment.*
> Lessee, on paying the said Rent, and any Additional Rent, shall and may
> peaceably and quietly have, hold and enjoy the Leased Premises for the
> said term.

A constructive eviction occurs when the tenant leaves the leased premises due to conduct by the landlord which materially interferes with the tenant's beneficial use of the premises. Texas law relieves the tenant of contractual liability for any remaining rentals due under the lease if he can establish a constructive eviction by the landlord.

★   ★   ★

(continued on next page)

(continued)

FIDELITY MUTUAL LIFE INSURANCE CO. v. KAMINSKY
768 S.W.2d 818
(Tex. 1989)

The protests took place chiefly on Saturdays, the day Dr. Kaminsky generally scheduled abortions. During the protests, the singing and chanting demonstrators picketed in the building's parking lot and inner lobby and atrium area. They approached patients to speak to them, distributed literature, discouraged patients from entering the building and often accused Dr. Kaminsky of "killing babies." As the protests increased, the demonstrators often occupied the stairs leading to Dr. Kaminsky's office and prevented patients from entering the office by blocking the doorway. Occasionally they succeeded in gaining access to the office waiting room area.

Dr. Kaminsky complained to Fidelity through its managing agents and asked for help in keeping the protestors away, but became increasingly frustrated by a lack of response to his requests. The record shows that no security personnel were present on Saturdays to exclude protestors from the building, although the lease required Fidelity to provide security service on Saturdays. The record also shows that Fidelity's attorneys prepared a written statement to be handed to the protestors soon after Fidelity hired Shelter as its managing agent. The statement tracked TEX. PENAL CODE ANN. § 30.05 (Vernon Supp. 1989) and generally served to inform trespassers that they risked criminal prosecution by failing to leave if asked to do so. Fidelity's attorneys instructed Shelter's representative to "have several of these letters printed up and be ready to distribute them and verbally demand that these people move on and off the property." The same representative conceded at trial that she did not distribute these notices. Yet when Dr. Kaminsky enlisted the aid of the Sheriff's office, officers refused to ask the protestors to leave without a directive from Fidelity or its agent. Indeed, an attorney had instructed the protestors to remain *unless* the landlord or its representative ordered them to leave. It appears that Fidelity's only response to the demonstrators was to state, through its agents, that it was aware of Dr. Kaminsky's problems.

Both action and lack of action can constitute "conduct" by the landlord which amounts to a constructive eviction. . . .

This case shows ample instances of Fidelity's failure to act in the face of repeated requests for assistance despite its having expressly covenanted Dr. Kaminsky's quiet enjoyment of the premises. These instances provided a legally sufficient basis for the jury to conclude that Dr. Kaminsky abandoned the leased premises, not because of the trespassing protestors, but because of Fidelity's lack of response to his complaints about the protestors. Under the circumstances, while it is undisputed that Fidelity did not "encourage" the demonstrators, its conduct essentially allowed them to continue to trespass. [The trial court judgment is affirmed.]

Damages Another traditional remedy is money damages, available whenever termination is an appropriate remedy. Damages may be sought after termination or as an alternative to termination. Suppose that after the landlord had refused Simone's request to repair the electrical system, Simone hired a contractor to do the job. The cost of the repair work would be recoverable from the landlord. Other recoverable costs can include the expense of relocating if the lease is terminated, moving costs, expenses connected with finding new premises, and any increase in rent over the period of the terminated lease for comparable new space. A business may recover the loss of anticipated business profits, but only if the extent of the loss is established with reasonable certainty. In the case of most new businesses, it would be almost impossible to prove loss of profits.

In all cases, the tenant's recovery will be limited to damages that would have been incurred by a tenant who took all reasonable steps to *mitigate losses*. That is, the tenant must take reasonable steps to prevent losses attributable to the landlord's breach, to find new space if terminating, to move efficiently, and so on.

Rent Remedies   Under an old common law rule, the landlord's obligation to provide the tenant with habitable space and the tenant's obligation to pay rent were **independent covenants.** If the landlord breached, the tenant was still legally bound to pay the rent; her only remedies were termination and suit for damages. But these are often difficult remedies for the tenant. Termination means the aggravation of moving, assuming that new quarters can be found, and a suit for damages is time-consuming, uncertain, and expensive. The obvious solution is to permit the tenant to withhold rent. The modern rule, adopted in several states (but not yet in most), holds that the mutual obligations of landlord and tenant are dependent. States following this approach have developed three types of remedies.

1. *Rent Withholding*   The simplest approach is for the tenant to withhold the rent until the landlord remedies the defect. In some states, the tenant may keep the money. In other states the rent must be paid each month into an escrow account or to the court, and the money in the escrow account becomes payable to the landlord when the default is cured.

2. *Rent Application*   Several state statutes permit the tenant to apply the rent money directly to remedy the defect or otherwise satisfy the landlord's performance. Thus Simone might have deducted from her rent the reasonable cost of hiring an electrician to repair the electrical system.

3. *Rent Abatement*   In some states, the rent may be reduced or even eliminated if the landlord fails to cure specific types of defects, such as violations of the housing code. The abatement will continue until the default is eliminated or the lease is terminated.

TENANT'S DUTIES AND LANDLORD'S RIGHTS

In addition to the duties of the tenant set forth in the lease itself, the common law imposes three other obligations: (1) to pay the rent *reserved* (stated) in the lease, (2) to refrain from committing waste, and (3) not to use the premises for an illegal purpose.

Duty to Pay Rent

What constitutes rent is not necessarily limited to the stated periodic payment usually denominated "rent." The tenant may also be responsible for such assessments as taxes and utilities, payable to the landlord as rent. Simone's lease calls for her to pay taxes of $500 per year, payable in quarterly installments. She pays the rent on the first of each month, and the first tax bill on January 1. On April 1 she pays the rent but defaults on the next tax bill. She has failed to pay the rent reserved in the lease.

The landlord in the majority of states is not obligated to mitigate his losses should the tenant abandon the property and fail thereafter to pay the rent. As a practical matter, this means that the landlord need not try to rent out the property but instead can let it sit vacant and sue the defaulting tenant for the balance of the rent as it becomes due. However, the tenant might notify the landlord that she has or is about to abandon and offer to surrender the property. If the landlord accepts the surrender, the lease then terminates. Unless the lease specifically provides for it, a landlord who accepts the surrender will not be able to recover from the tenant the difference between the amount of her rent obligation and the new tenant's rent obligation.

Many leases require the tenant to make a **security deposit**—a payment of a specific sum of money to secure the tenant's performance of duties under the lease. If the tenant fails to pay the rent, or otherwise defaults, the landlord may use the money to make good the tenant's performance. Whatever portion of the money is not used to satisfy the tenant's obligations must be repaid to the tenant at the end of the lease. In the absence of an agreement to the contrary, the landlord must pay interest on the security deposit when he returns the sum to the tenant at the end of the lease.

Alteration and Restoration of the Premises

In the absence of a specific agreement in the lease, the tenant is entitled to physically change the premises in order to make the best possible permissible use of the property, but she may not make structural alterations or damage (waste) the property. A residential tenant may add telephone lines, put up pictures, and affix bookshelves to the walls, but she may not remove a wall in order to enlarge a room.

The tenant must restore the property to its original condition when the lease ends, but this requirement does not include normal wear and tear. Simone rents an apartment with newly polished wooden floors. Because she likes the look of oak, she decides against covering the floors with rugs. In a few months' time, the floors lose their polish and become scuffed. Simone is not obligated to refinish the floors, because the scuffing came from normal walking, which is ordinary wear and tear.

Use of the Property for an Illegal Purpose

It is a breach of the tenant's obligation to use the property for an illegal purpose. A landlord who found a tenant running a "numbers racket," for example, or making and selling "moonshine" whisky could rightfully evict her.

Landlord's Remedies

In general, when the tenant breaches any of the duties listed above, the landlord may terminate the lease and seek damages. One common situation deserves special mention: the *holdover tenant*. When a tenant improperly overstays her lease, she is said to be a **tenant at sufferance,** meaning that she is liable to eviction. Some cultures, like Japan, exhibit a considerable pro-tenant bias, making it exceedingly difficult to move out holdover tenants who decide to stay. But in the

United States, landlords may remove tenants through summary (speedy) proceedings available in every state or, in some cases, through self-help. In general, when a state has a statute providing a summary procedure for removing a holdover tenant, neither the landlord nor the incoming tenant may resort to self-help, unless the statute specifically allows it. A provision in the lease permitting self-help in the absence of statutory authority is unenforceable. **Self-help**—entering the premises to regain possession and removal of the holdover tenant's belongings—must be peaceful, must not cause physical harm or even the expectation of harm to the tenant or anyone on the premises with his permission, and must not result in unreasonable damage to the tenant's property. Any clause in the lease attempting to waive these conditions is void.

Self-help can be risky, because some summary proceeding statutes declare it to be a criminal act and because it can subject the landlord to tort liability. Simone improperly holds over in her apartment, and with a new tenant scheduled to arrive in two days, the landlord knocks on her door the evening after her lease expires. When Simone opens the door she sees the landlord standing between two 450-pound Sumo wrestlers. He demands that she leave immediately. Fearing for her safety, she departs instantly. Since she had a reasonable expectation of harm had she not complied with the landlord's demand, Simone would be entitled to recover damages in a tort suit against her landlord, although she would not be entitled to regain possession of the apartment.

Besides summary judicial proceedings and self-help, the landlord has another possible remedy against the holdover tenant: to impose another rental term. In order to extend the lease in this manner, the landlord need simply notify the holdover tenant that she is being held to another term, usually measured by the periodic nature of the rent payment. For example, if rent was paid each month, then imposition of a new term results in a month-to-month tenancy. One year is the maximum tenancy that the landlord can create by electing to hold the tenant to another term. Equitable considerations might bar the landlord from extending the term. For instance, a strike of moving companies on the day the tenant was due to move out would be sufficient justification to stay on until she could move her possessions. Even if the landlord does not hold the tenant to a new term, he is entitled to recover from the tenant rent for the holdover period. The rent to be paid will be equal to the amount called for in the lease, unless either party can demonstrate that the rental value of the premises had increased or decreased.

TRANSFER OF LANDLORD'S OR TENANT'S INTEREST

General Rule

At common law, the interests of the landlord and tenant may be transferred freely, unless (1) the tenancy is at will; (2) the lease requires either party to perform significant personal services, which would be substantially less likely to be performed if the interest is transferred; or (3) the parties agree that the interest may not be transferred.

Landlord's Interest

When the landlord sells his interest, the purchaser takes subject to the lease. If there are tenants with leases in an apartment building, the new landlord may not evict them simply because he has taken title. The landlord may divide his interest as he sees fit, transferring all or only part of his entire interest in the property. He may assign his right to the rent or sell his reversionary interest in the premises. For instance, Simone takes a three-year lease on an apartment near the university. Simone's landlord gives his aged uncle his reversionary interest for life. This means that Simone's landlord is now the uncle, and she must pay him rent and look to him for repairs and other performances owed under the lease. When Simone's lease terminates, the uncle will be entitled to rent the premises. He does so, leasing to another student for three years. One year later, the uncle dies. His nephew (Simone's original landlord) has the reversionary interest and so once again becomes the landlord. He must perform the lease that the uncle agreed to with the new student and, when that lease expires, will be free to rent the premises as he sees fit.

Tenant's Interest

Why would a tenant be interested in transferring her leasehold interest? For at least two reasons: she might need to move before her lease expired, and she might be able to make money on the leasehold itself. In recent years, many companies in New York have discovered that their present leases were worth far more to them by moving out than staying in. They had signed long-term leases years ago when the real estate market was glutted and were paying far less than current market prices. By *subletting* the premises and moving to cheaper quarters, they could pocket the difference between their lease rate and the market rate they charged their subtenants.

The tenant can transfer her interest in the lease by assigning or by subletting. In an **assignment,** the tenant transfers all interest in the premises and all obligations. Thus the assignee-tenant is duty-bound to pay the landlord the periodic rental and to perform all other provisions in the lease. If the assignee defaulted, however, the original tenant would remain liable to the landlord. In short, with an assignment both assignor and assignee are liable under the lease, unless the landlord releases the assignor. By contrast, a **sublease** is a transfer of something less than the entire leasehold interest (see Figure 34-1). For instance, the tenant might have five years remaining on her lease and sublet the premises for two years or she might sublet the ground floor of a four-story building. Unlike an assignee, the subtenant does not step into the shoes of the tenant and is not liable to the landlord for performance of the tenant's duties. The subtenant's only obligations are to the tenant. What distinguishes the assignment from the sublease is not the name but whether or not the entire leasehold interest has been transferred. If not, the transfer is a sublease.

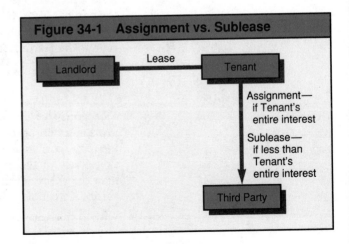

Figure 34-1   Assignment vs. Sublease

Many landlords include clauses in their leases prohibiting assignments or subleases, and these clauses are generally upheld. But the courts construe them strictly, so that a provision barring subleases will not be interpreted to bar assignments. In the following case, the landlord sought to terminate the lease when the tenant appeared to have sublet the premises without the express consent required by the lease; the court was called on to determine whether the transfer was an assignment or a sublease.

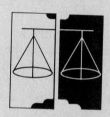

GAGNE v. HARTMEIER
271 Ark. 845, 611 S.W.2d 194 (1981)

GLAZE, JUDGE. This case involves an action for unlawful detainer. The appellants appeal from an order issued by the Sebastian County Circuit Court wherein the appellees were found entitled to a writ of possession of property owned but which had been leased by the appellees.

On August 27, 1976, the appellees, the Hartmeiers, leased property to appellant, Gagne, and his wife. The term of the lease was for ten years and the monthly rental was $1,750 plus a percentage of the gross sales of gasoline. The provision of the lease which is an issue is paragraph twelve which provides:

> LESSEES (Gagne) shall not sublease all or any part of the property herein leased without the expressed written consent of LESSORS (the Hartmeiers).

On February 4, 1980, Gagne (who was divorced at the time) entered into a written agreement designated "Contract of Sale of Personal Property and Business" with the appellants, Glosenger and Iames. Gagne entered into this agreement without obtaining the written or oral consent of the Hartmeiers, but the agreement specifically incorporated the original Hartmeier lease and made the sale subject to the lease provisions. Additionally, the terms of the transfer or sale agreement provided that the transaction was not a subletting. Glosenger and Iames then took possession of the leased property and proceeded to operate the business purchased from Gagne.

The Hartmeiers brought suit for possession of the leased property, contending that the agreement between Gagne, Glosenger and Iames was a sublease which was entered into contrary to the terms in paragraph twelve of the original lease. Gagne, Glosenger and Iames argued that the contract they entered into was an assignment rather than a sublease and the written consent of the Hartmeiers was unnecessary.

*   *   *

Most jurisdictions follow the common law distinction in determining whether a document or instrument is an assignment or sublease. Put simply, if the instrument purports to transfer the lessee's estate for the entire remainder of the term, it is an assignment, regardless of its form or the parties' intention. Conversely, if the instrument purports to transfer the lessee's estate for less than the entire term, it is a sublease, again regardless of its form or of the parties' intention. Thus, the intention of the parties to the transaction has nothing to do when applying the common law rule. The sole question is whether the lessee retained a reversionary estate. If so, the instrument would be designated a sublease.

* * *

The appellees argue Gagne did not part with his entire interest, and they relate terms in the contract of sale instrument which protect him, e.g., a right to draw funds from Glosenger's and Iames' business account, a hold harmless provision, a right of re-entry for non-payment of monies due under the agreement, a right to prohibit waste, liens and the assignment or leasing of the property. Of course, none of these rights retained by Gagne rise to the dignity of a reversionary estate. Although courts in some jurisdictions have recognized the lessee's reservation of a right of re-entry to be a reversionary estate, Arkansas has rejected this rule when the instrument is intended by the parties to be an assignment. The rights Gagne retained incidental to the sale of his business do not negate the parties' clear expression contained in the instrument that the sale contract was subject to the full Hartmeier lease agreement. We necessarily must conclude the instrument is an assignment and not a sublease.

Since we hold that the Gagne transfer or sale document is an assignment, we must then decide whether a restrictive covenant to sublease also prohibits an assignment. We find no Arkansas case on this legal issue, and none is argued in counsels' briefs. Cases do exist in other jurisdictions, however, and the prevailing rule and the better reasoned law is that a restrictive covenant contained in a lease against subletting is not violated by an assignment of the lease. This rule of law is bottomed on another but better known legal principle stated as follows:

> Covenants against assignment and underletting, being a restraint against alienation, are not favorably regarded by the courts, and are liberally construed in favor of the lessee, so as to prevent the restriction from extending any further than is necessary. [3 *Thompson on Real Property*, § 1429 (1940).]

In *Cities Service Oil Company v. Taylor* [45 S.W.2d 1039 (1932)], the court, in holding a sublease restriction did not prevent an assignment, refused to extend a sublease covenant beyond the literal requirements of a reasonable interpretation of the terms employed. Applying these principles of law to the case at bar, the Hartmeiers and Gagne could have easily inserted words in the lease agreement to have prohibited both subletting *and* assignments. They failed to do so and given the clear distinction and legal significance between these terms, we are in no position to re-write the lease to prohibit an assignment. Thus, if the trial court determined that the Gagne sale instrument was an assignment, its further decision that such an assignment would violate the sublease provision is in error.

For the above reasons, we reverse the lower court's order.

Reversed.

LANDLORD'S TORT LIABILITY

Earlier in this unit (see Chapter 32), we discussed the tort liability of the owner or occupier of real estate to persons injured on the property. As a general rule, when injury occurs on premises rented to a tenant, it is the tenant—an occupier—who is liable. The reasons for this rule seems clear: The landlord has given up all but a reversionary interest in the property; he has no further control over the premises. Indeed, he is not even permitted on the property without the tenant's permission. But over the years, certain exceptions have developed to the rule that the landlord is not liable. The primary reason for this change is the recognition that the landlord is better able to pay for repairs to his property than his relatively poorer tenants.

Exceptions to the General Rule

Hidden Dangers Known to Landlord The landlord is liable to the tenant, her family, or guests who are injured by hidden and dangerous conditions that the landlord knew about or should have known about but failed to disclose to the tenant.

Dangers to People Off the Premises The landlord is liable to people injured outside the property by defects that existed when the lease was signed. Simone rents a dilapidated house, and agrees with the landlord to keep the building repaired. She neglects to hire contractors to repair the cracked and sagging wall on the street. The building soon collapses, crushing several automobiles parked alongside. Simone can be held responsible, and so can the landlord; the tenant's contractual agreement to maintain the property is not sufficient to shift the liability away from the landlord. In a few cases, the landlord has even been held liable for activities carried on by the tenant, but only because he knew about them when the lease was signed and should have known that the injuries were probable results.

Premises Leased for Admitting the Public A landlord is responsible for injuries caused by dangerous conditions on property to be used by the public if the danger existed when the lease was made. Thus an uneven floor that might cause people to trip or a defective elevator that stops a few inches below the level of each floor would be sufficiently dangerous to pin liability on the landlord.

Landlord Retaining Control of Premises Frequently a landlord will retain control over certain areas of the property—for example, the common hallways and stairs in an apartment building. When injuries occur as a result of faulty and careless maintenance of these areas, the landlord will be responsible. In more than half the states, the landlord is liable for failure to remove ice and snow from a common walkway and stairs at the entrance. In one case the tenant even recovered damages for a broken hip caused when she fell in fright from seeing a mouse that jumped out of her stove; she successfully charged the landlord with negligence in failing to prevent mice from entering the dwelling in areas under his control. [Mangan v. F.C. Pilgrim Co., 336 N.E.2d 374 (Ill. 1975)]

Faulty Repair of Premises Landlords often have a duty to repair the premises. The duty may be statutory or may rest on an agreement in the lease. In either case, the landlord will be liable to a tenant or others for injury resulting from defects that should have been repaired. No less important, a landlord will be liable even if he has no duty to repair but negligently makes repairs that themselves turn out to be dangerous.

Modern Trend

In recent years, several courts have adopted general negligence principles in determining landlord liability, rather than limiting liability to the above exceptions. This trend is illustrated by the following case.

**STEPHENS v.
STEARNS**
106 Idaho 249,
678 P.2d 41 (1984)

DONALDSON, CHIEF JUSTICE. Plaintiff-appellant Stephens filed this suit on October 2, 1978, for personal injuries she sustained on July 15, 1977, from a fall on an interior stairway of her apartment. Plaintiff's apartment, located in a Boise apartment complex, was a "townhouse" consisting of two separate floors connected by an internal stairway.

. . . Defendant Stearns was plaintiff's landlord from the time she moved into the apartment in 1973 through the time of plaintiff's fall on July 15, 1977.

* * *

When viewed in the light most favorable to appellant, the facts are as follows: On the evening of July 15, 1977, Mrs. Stephens went to visit friends. While there she had two drinks. She returned to her apartment a little past 10:00 p.m. Mrs. Stephens turned on the television in the living room and went upstairs to change clothes. After changing her clothes, she attempted to go downstairs to watch television. As Mrs. Stephens reached the top of the stairway, she either slipped or fell forward. She testified that she "grabbed" in order to catch herself. However, Mrs. Stephens was unable to catch herself and she fell to the bottom of the stairs. As a result of the fall, she suffered serious injury. The evidence further showed that the stairway was approximately thirty-six inches wide and did not have a handrail although required by a Boise ordinance.

* * *

In granting defendant Stearns' motion for directed verdict, the trial court concluded that Stearns had not violated the common-law duty owed by a landlord to a tenant. Under the common-law rule, a landlord is generally not liable to the tenant for any damage resulting from dangerous conditions existing at the time of the leasing. However, there are a number of exceptions to the general rule depending on whether (1) there is a hidden dangerous condition on the premises of which the landlord is aware but the tenant is not; (2) the land is leased for purposes involving admission of the public; (3) the premises are still in the control of the landlord; and, (4) the landlord has negligently repaired the premises.

Rather than attempt to squeeze the facts of this case into one of the common-law exceptions, plaintiff instead has brought to our attention the modern trend of the law in this area. Under the modern trend, landlords are simply under a duty to exercise reasonable care under the circumstances. The Tennessee Supreme Court had the foresight to grasp this concept many years ago when it stated: "The ground of liability upon the part of a landlord when he demises dangerous property has nothing special to do with the relation of landlord and tenant. It is the ordinary case of liability for personal misfeasance, which runs through all the relations of individuals to each other." *Wilcox v. Hines*, 46 S.W. 297, 299 (1898). Seventy-five years later, the Supreme Court of New Hampshire followed the lead of *Wilcox. Sargent v. Ross*, 308 A.2d 528 (1973). The *Sargent* court abrogated the common-law rule and its exceptions, and adopted the reasonable care standard by stating:

(continued on next page)

(continued)

STEPHENS v. STEARNS
106 Idaho 249,
678 P.2d 41 (1984)

"We thus bring up to date the other half of landlord-tenant law. Henceforth, landlords as other persons must exercise reasonable care not to subject others to an unreasonable risk of harm. . . . A landlord must act as a reasonable person under all of the circumstances including the likelihood of injury to others, the probable seriousness of such injuries, and the burden of reducing or avoiding the risk."

Tennessee and New Hampshire are not alone in adopting this rule. As of this date, several other states have also judicially adopted a reasonable care standard for landlords.

★   ★   ★

In commenting on the common-law rule, A. James Casner, Reporter of Restatement (Second) of Property—Landlord and Tenant, has stated: "While continuing to pay lip service to the general rule, the courts have expended considerable energy and exercised great ingenuity in attempting to fit various factual settings into the recognized exceptions." We believe that the energies of the courts of Idaho should be used in a more productive manner. Therefore, after examining both the common-law rule and the modern trend, we today decide to leave the common-law rule and its exceptions behind, and we adopt the rule that a landlord is under a duty to exercise reasonable care in light of all the circumstances.

We stress that adoption of this rule is not tantamount to making the landlord an insurer for all injury occurring on the premises, but merely constitutes our removal of the landlord's common-law cloak of immunity. Those questions of hidden danger, public use, control, and duty to repair, which under the common-law were prerequisites to the consideration of the landlord's negligence, will now be relevant only inasmuch as they pertain to the elements of negligence, such as foreseeability and unreasonableness of the risk. We hold that defendant Stearns did owe a duty to plaintiff Stephens to exercise reasonable care in light of all the circumstances, and that it is for a jury to decide whether that duty was breached. Therefore, we reverse the directed verdict in favor of defendant Stearns and remand for a new trial of plaintiff's negligence action against defendant Stearns.

CHAPTER SUMMARY

A leasehold is an interest in real property that terminates on a certain date. The leasehold itself is personal property and has three major forms: (1) the estate for years, (2) the periodic tenancy, and (3) the tenancy at will. The estate for years has a definite beginning and end; it need not be measured in years. A periodic tenancy—sometimes known as an estate from year to year or month to month—is renewed automatically until either landlord or tenant notifies the other that it will end. A tenancy at will lasts only as long as both landlord and tenant desire. Oral leases are subject to the Statute of Frauds. In most states, leases to last longer than a year must be in a writing, which must identify the parties and the premises, specify the duration, state the rent, and be signed by the party to be charged.

The law imposes on the landlord certain duties toward the tenant and gives the tenant corresponding rights, including the right of possession, habitable condition, and noninterference with use. The right of possession is breached if a third party has paramount title at the time the tenant is due to take possession. In most states, a landlord is obligated not only to provide the tenant with habitable premises when he moves in but also during the entire period of the lease. The landlord must also refrain from interfering with a tenant's permissible use of the premises.

If the landlord breaches one of his obligations, the tenant has several remedies. He may terminate the lease, recover damages, or (in several but by no means all states) use a rent-related remedy (by withholding, by applying it to remedy the defect, or by abatement).

The tenant also has duties. The tenant must pay the rent and, if she abandons the property and fails to pay, most states do not require the landlord to mitigate damages. But several states are moving away from this general rule. The tenant may physically change the property to use the property to her best advantage, but she may not make structural alterations or commit waste, and must restore the property to its original condition when the lease ends. This rule does not include normal wear and tear.

Should the tenant breach any of her duties, the landlord may terminate the lease and seek damages. In the case of a holdover tenant, the landlord may elect to hold the tenant to another rental term.

The interest of either landlord or tenant may be transferred freely unless the tenancy is at will, the lease requires either party to perform significant personal services which would be substantially less likely to be performed, or the parties agree that the interest may not be transferred.

Despite the general rule that the tenant is responsible for injuries caused on the premises to outsiders, the landlord may have significant tort liability if (1) there are hidden dangers about which he knows, (2) defects that existed at the time the lease was signed injure people off the premises, (3) the premises are rented for public purposes, (4) the landlord retains control of the premises, or (5) the landlord repairs the premises in a faulty manner.

KEY TERMS

SELF-TEST QUESTIONS

1. An estate for years:
   (a) has a definite beginning and end
   (b) is a leasehold estate
   (c) usually terminates automatically at midnight of the last day specified in the lease
   (d) includes all of the above

2. Not included among the rights given to a tenant are:
   (a) paramount title
   (b) possession
   (c) habitable condition
   (d) non-interference with use

3. The interest of either landlord or tenant may be transferred freely:
   (a) unless the tenancy is at will
   (b) unless the lease requires significant personal services unlikely to be performed by someone else
   (c) both of the above
   (d) none of the above

4. When injuries are caused on the premises to outsiders:
   (a) the tenant is always liable
   (b) the landlord is always liable
   (c) the landlord may be liable if there are hidden dangers which the landlord knows about
   (d) they have no cause of action against the landlord or tenant since they have no direct contractual relationship with either party

5. Legally a tenant may:
   (a) commit waste
   (b) make some structural alterations to the property
   (c) abandon the property at any time
   (d) physically change the property to suit it to her best advantage, as long as no structural alterations are made

DEMONSTRATION PROBLEM

Matina leased the second floor of a building she owned to Scheidel. Scheidel hired a professional window washer, who was seriously injured when he fell to the ground after decayed wood in the structure failed to hold his safety belt. Is Matina liable to the window washer? Why?

PROBLEMS

1. Lanny orally agrees to rent his house to Tenny for fifteen months, at a monthly rent of $1,000. Tenny moves in and pays the first month's rent. Lanny now wants to cancel the lease. May he? Why?

2. Suppose in problem 1 that Tenny had an option to cancel after one year. Could Lanny cancel before the end of the year? Why?

3. Suppose in problem 1 that Lanny himself is a tenant and has leased the house for six months. He subleases the house to Tenny for one year. The day before Tenny is to move into the house, he learns of Lanny's six-month lease and attempts to terminate his one-year lease. May he? Why?

4. Suppose in problem 3 that Tenny learned of Lanny's lease

the day after he moved into the house. May he terminate? Why?

5. Simon owns a four-story building and rents the top floor to a college student. Simon is in the habit of burning refuse in the back yard and the smoke from the refuse is so noxious that it causes the student's eyes to water and his throat to become raw. Has Simon breached a duty to the student? Explain.

6. In problem 5, if other tenants (but not Simon) were burning refuse in the backyard, would Simon be in breach? Why?

7. Assume in problem 5 that Simon was in breach. Could the student move out of the apartment and terminate the lease? What effect would this have on the student's duty to pay rent? Explain.

8. In problem 7, assume that the tenant decides to stay in the apartment despite the discomfort caused by the smoke. Does he have any remedies against the landlord? Explain.

ANSWERS TO SELF-TEST QUESTIONS

1. (d)   2. (a)   3. (c)   4. (c)   5. (d)

ANSWER TO DEMONSTRATION PROBLEM

Matina is liable. She retained control of the outside of the building and thus falls within one of the exceptions to the general rule that landlords are not liable for torts on the leased premises. [Stumpka v. Scheidel, 56 N.W.2d 874 (1953)]

CHAPTER

35

CHAPTER OVERVIEW
Wills and Estate Administration
Trusts
Factors Affecting Both Estates and Trusts
Examples of Estate Plans

Estate Planning: Wills, Estates, and Trusts

*B*roadly defined, **estate planning** is the process by which an owner over the course of his life decides how his assets are to be passed on to others at his death. Estate planning has two general objectives: to ensure that the assets are transferred according to the owner's wishes and to minimize state and federal taxes. In this chapter we will examine estate planning tools and techniques and then integrate them by means of two sample estate plans.

Each person has at his disposal four basic estate planning tools: (1) wills, (2) trusts, (3) gifts, and (4) joint ownership (see Figure 35-1). The rules governing gifts are discussed in Chapter 30, and joint ownership is treated in Chapter 32. Consequently, we focus on the first two tools here. In addition to these tools, certain assets such as insurance (discussed in the next chapter) are also useful in estate planning.

Not only does estate planning provide for the family, the children's education, payment of the mortgage, and so on, but it also serves as the principal means by which liquidity can be guaranteed for taxes, administration expenses, and the like, while preserving the assets of the estate. And whenever

a business is formed, estate planning consequences should always be considered, for the form and structure of the business can have important tax ramifications for the individual owners.

WILLS AND ESTATE ADMINISTRATION

Defined

A **will** is the declaration of a person's wishes about the disposition of his assets on his death. Normally a written document, the will names the persons who are to receive specific items of real and personal property. Unlike a contract or a deed, a will is not binding as long as the person making the will lives. He may revoke it at any time. Wills have served their present function for virtually all of recorded history. The earliest known will stems from 1800 B.C. (see Figure 35-2). If mildly different in form, it serves the same basic function as a modern will.

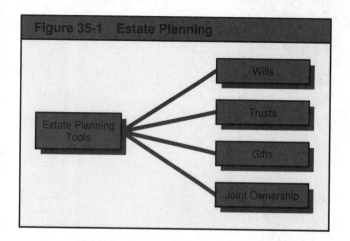

Figure 35-1   Estate Planning

Estate Planning Tools → Wills, Trusts, Gifts, Joint Ownership

Although most wills are written in a standardized form, some special types of wills are enforceable in many states.

1. A *noncupative* will is one declared orally in front of witnesses. In states where allowed, the statutes permit it to be used only when the testator is dying as he declares his will. (A **testator** is one who dies with a will.)

2. A *holographic* will is one written entirely by the testator's hand and not witnessed. At common law, a holographic will was invalid if any part of the paper on which it is written contained printing. Modern statutes tend to validate holographic wills, even with printing, as long as the testator

Figure 35-2   An Ancient Will

[*Will of Uah*] "I, Uah, devise to my wife Sheftu, the woman of Gesab called Teta, daughter of Sat Sepdu, all properties given to me by my brother Ankh-ren. She shall give it to whomsoever she may see fit of her issue born to me.

"I devise to her the Eastern slaves, 4 persons, that my brother Ankh-ren gave me. She shall give them to whomsoever she may see fit of her children.

"As to my tomb, let me be buried in it with my wife alone.

"Moreover, as to the house built for me by my brother Ankh-ren, my wife shall dwell therein and shall not be evicted by any person.

"The deputy Sebu shall act as guardian of my son. Done in the presence of these witnesses:

"Kemen, Decorator of Columns,

"Apu, Doorkeeper of the Temple,

"Senb, son of Senb, Doorkeeper of the Temple."

Source: John H. Wigmore, *A Panorama of the World's Legal Systems*, vol. 1, p. 22

who signs it puts down material provisions in his own hand.

3. *Soldiers' and sailors'* wills are usually enforceable, no matter how informal the document, if made while the soldier is on service or the sailor is at sea (although they cannot usually transfer real property without observing certain formalities).

4. A *conditional* will is one that will take effect only on the happening of a particular named event. For example, a man intending to marry might write: "This will is contingent on my marrying Miss Smithers." If he and Miss Smithers do not marry, the will can have no operational effect.

5. A *joint* will is one in which two (or more) people use the same instrument to dispose of their assets. It must be signed by each person whose assets it is to govern.

6. *Mutual* or *reciprocal* wills are two or more instruments with reciprocal terms, each written by a person who intends to dispose of his assets in favor of the others.

The Uniform Probate Code

Probate is the process by which a deceased's estate is managed under the supervision of a court. In most states, the court supervising this process is a specialized one and is often called the **probate court**. Probate practices vary widely from state to state, although they follow a general pattern in which the assets of an estate are located, added up, and disbursed according to the terms of the will or, if there is no will, according to the law of intestate succession. To attempt to bring uniformity into the conflicting sets of state laws the National Conference of Commissioners on Uniform State Laws issued the Uniform Probate Code in 1969, and it has been adopted in approximately one-third of the states to date. Our discussion of wills and estate administration is drawn primarily from the UPC, but you should note that there are variations among the states in some of the procedures standardized in the UPC.

Will Requirements and Interpretation

Capacity   Any person who is over eighteen and of "sound mind" may make a will. One who is insane may not make an enforceable will, although the degree of mental capacity necessary to sustain a will is generally said to be a "modest level of competence" and is lower than the degree of capacity a person must possess to manage his own affairs during his life. In other words, a court might order a guardian to manage the affairs of one who is mentally deficient while upholding a will that the person has written. Insanity is not the only type of mental deficiency that will disqualify a will; medication for serious physical pain that dulls the mind might lead to the conclusion that the person did not understand what he was doing when writing his will. The following case considers just such a situation.

ESTATE OF ROSEN
447 A.2d 1220 (Me. 1982)

GODFREY, JUSTICE. Phoebe Rosen and Jeffrey Rosen, widow and son of the decedent, Seymour M. Rosen, appeal from an order of the Knox County Probate Court admitting the decedent's will to probate. Appellants argue that the decedent lacked the testamentary capacity necessary to execute a valid will and that the Probate Court's finding that he did have the necessary capacity is clearly erroneous. On direct appeal from the Probate Court pursuant to section 1-308 of the Probate Code (18-AM.R.S.A. § 1-308), this Court reviews for clear error the findings of fact by the Probate Court. We affirm the judgment.

Decedent, a certified public accountant, had an accounting practice in New York City, where he had been married to Phoebe for about thirty years. Their son, Jeffrey, works in New York City. In 1973, the decedent was diagnosed as having chronic lymphatic leukemia, a disease that, as it progresses, seriously impairs the body's ability to fight infection. From 1973 on, he understood that he might die within six months. In June, 1978, he left his home and practice and moved to Maine with his secretary of two months, Robin Gordon, the appellee. He set up an accounting practice in Camden.

The leukemia progressed. The decedent was on medication and was periodically hospitalized for infections, sometimes involving septic shock, a condition described by the treating physician as akin to blood poisoning. The infections were treated with antibiotics with varying degrees of success. Despite his medical problems, the decedent continued his accounting practice, working usually three days a week, until about two months before his death on December 4, 1980. Robin Gordon lived with him and attended him until his death.

While living in New York, the decedent had executed a will leaving everything to his wife or, if she should not survive him, to his son. In November, 1979, decedent employed the services of Steven Peterson, a lawyer whose office was in the same building as decedent's, to execute a codicil to the New York will leaving all his Maine property to Robin. At about this time, decedent negotiated a property settlement with his wife, who is now living in Florida. He executed the will at issue in this proceeding on July 25, 1980, shortly after a stay in the hospital with a number of infections, and shortly before a hospitalization that marked the beginning of the decedent's final decline. This will, which revoked all earlier wills and codicils, left all

(continued on next page)

(continued)

ESTATE OF ROSEN
447 A.2d 1220 (Me. 1982)

his property, wherever located, to Robin, or to Jeffrey if Robin did not survive him.

The court admitted the 1980 will to probate over the objections of Phoebe and son, making extensive findings to support its conclusion that "the decedent clearly had testamentary capacity when he executed his Will."

The Probate Court applied the standard heretofore declared by this Court for determining whether a decedent had the mental competence necessary to execute a valid will:

> A 'disposing mind' involves the exercise of so much mind and memory as would enable a person to transact common and simple kinds of business with that intelligence which belongs to the weakest class of sound minds; and a disposing memory exists when one can recall the general nature, condition and extent of his property, and his relations to those to whom he gives, and also to those from whom he excludes, his bounty. He must have active memory enough to bring to his mind the nature and particulars of the business to be transacted, and mental power enough to appreciate them, and act with sense and judgment in regard to them. He must have sufficient capacity to comprehend the condition of his property, his relations to the persons who were or should have been the objects of his bounty, and the scope and bearing of the provisions of his will. He must have sufficient active memory to collect in his mind, without prompting, the particulars or elements of the business to be transacted, and to hold them in his mind a sufficient length of time to perceive at least their obvious relations to each other, and be able to form some rational judgment in relation to them.

Appellants portray the decedent as "a man ravaged by cancer and dulled by medication," and it is true that some evidence in the record tends to support this characterization. However, the law as set out in *In re Leonard* requires only a modest level of competence ("the weakest class of sound minds"), and there is considerable evidence of record that the decedent had at least that level of mental ability and probably more.

* * *

Appellants' principal objection to the will is that the decedent lacked the necessary knowledge of "the general nature, condition and extent of his property." *In re Leonard*, 321 A.2d at 488. The record contains testimony of Robin Gordon and lawyer Peterson that decedent did not know what his assets were or their value. However, there is other evidence, chiefly Peterson's testimony about his discussions with the decedent preliminary to the drafting of the 1980 will and, earlier, when the 1979 codicil to the New York will was being prepared, that the decedent did have knowledge of the contents of his estate. He knew that he had had a Florida condominium, although he was unsure whether this had been turned over to his wife as part of the recent property settlement; he knew that he had an interest in an oil partnership, and, although he was unable to place a value on that interest, he knew the name of an individual who could supply further information about it; he knew he had stocks and bonds, two motor vehicles, an account at the Camden National Bank, and accounts receivable from his accounting practice.

The law does not require that a testator's knowledge of his estate be highly specific in order for him to execute a valid will. It requires only that the decedent be able to recall "the general nature, condition and extent of his property." *In re Leonard*, 321 A.2d at 488. Such knowledge of one's property is an aspect of mental soundness, not an independent legal requirement as the appellants seem to suggest. Here, there was competent evidence that the decedent had a general knowledge of his estate. The Probate Court was justified in concluding that, in the circumstances, the decedent's ignorance of the precise extent of his property did not establish his mental incompetence. The decedent's uncertainty about his property was understandable in view of the fact that some of his property had been transferred to his wife in the recent property negotiations in circumstances rendering it possible that the decedent might have wanted to put the matter out of his mind. Also, there was evidence from which the court could have inferred that much of the property was of uncertain or changing value.

On the evidence of record, this Court cannot hold that the findings of the Probate Court were clearly erroneous. Where, as here, there is a choice between two permissible views of the weight of the evidence, the findings of the Probate Court must stand.

Writing   Under the UPC, wills must be in writing. The will is not confined to the specific paper called "will" and signed by the testator. It may incorporate by reference any other writing in existence when the will is made, as long as the will sufficiently identifies the other writing and manifests an intent to incorporate it. Although lawyers prepare neatly typed wills, the document can be written in pencil or pen and on any kind of paper or even on the back of an envelope. Typically, the written will has the following provisions: (1) a "publication clause," listing the testator's name and his intention to make a will; (2) a "revocation clause," revoking all previously made wills; (3) burial instructions; (4) debt payments, listing specific assets to be used; (5) **bequests,** which are gifts of personal property by will; (6) **devises,** which are gifts of real property by will; (7) a "residuary clause," disposing of all property not covered by a specific bequest or devise; (8) a "penalty clause," stating a penalty for anyone named in the will who contests the will; (9) name of minor children's guardian; and (10) name of executor. Beginning with California in 1983, several states have adopted statutory wills—simple "fill-in-the-blank" will forms that can be completed without consulting an attorney.

Signature   The testator must sign the will, and the proper place for the signature is at the end of the entire document. The testator need not sign his full name, although that is preferable; his initials or some other mark in his own hand and intended as an execution of the document will suffice. The UPC permits someone else to sign for the testator as long as the signing is done in the testator's presence and by his direction.

Witnesses   Most states require two or three witnesses to sign the will. The UPC requires two witnesses. The witnesses should observe the testator sign the will and then sign it themselves in the presence of each other. Since the witnesses might be asked to attest in court to the testator's signature, it is sound practice to avoid witnesses who are unduly elderly and to use an extra witness or two. Most states forbid a person who has an interest in the will—that is, one who is a beneficiary under the will—from witnessing.

In some states, a beneficiary who serves as a witness will lose his right to a bequest or devise. The UPC differs from the usual rule: no will or any provision of a will is invalid because an interested party witnesses it, nor does the interested witness forfeit a bequest or devise.

Revocation and Modification   Since wills are generally effective only at death, the testator may always revoke or amend a will during his lifetime. He may do so by tearing, burning, obliterating, or otherwise destroying it. A subsequent will has the effect of revoking an inconsistent prior will, and most wills expressly state that they are intended to revoke all prior wills. A written modification of or supplement to a prior will is called a **codicil.** The codicil is often necessary, because circumstances are constantly changing. The testator may have moved to a new state where he must meet different formal requirements for executing the will; one of his beneficiaries may have died; his property may have changed. Or the law, especially the tax law, may have changed.

One exception to the rule that wills are effective only at death is the so-called **living will.** Beginning with California in 1976, most states have adopted legislation permitting people to declare that they refuse further treatment should they become terminally ill and unable to tell physicians not to prolong their lives if they can survive only by being hooked up to life-preserving machines. This living will takes effect during the patient's life and must be honored by physicians unless the patient has revoked it. The patient may revoke at any time, even as he sees the doctor moving to disconnect the plug.

In most states, a later marriage revokes a prior will, but divorce does not. Under the UPC, however, a divorce or annulment revokes any disposition of property bequeathed or devised to the former spouse under a will executed prior to the divorce or annulment. A will is at least partially revoked if children are born after it is executed, unless it has either provided for subsequently born children or stated the testator's intention deliberately to disinherit such children.

Abatement   Specific bequests listed in a will might not be available in the estate when the testator dies. Suppose the testator leaves $1,000 each to "my four roommates," but when she dies her estate is worth only $2,000. The gift to each of the roommates is said to have **abated,** and each will take only $500. Abatement can pose a serious problem in wills not carefully drafted. Since circumstances can always change, a general provision providing "my dear daughter with all the rest, residue, and remainder of my estate" will do her little good if business reverses mean that the $10,000 bequest to the local hospital exhausts the estate of its assets, even though at the time the will was made the testator had assets of $1 million and supposed his daughter would be getting the bulk of it. Since specific gifts must be paid out ahead of general bequests or devises, abatement can cause the **residual legatee** (the person taking all assets not specifically distributed to named individuals) to suffer.

Ademption   Suppose that the testator bequeathed her 1923 Rolls Royce to "my faithful secretary," but that the car had been sold and she owned only a 1980 Volkswagen when she died. Since the Rolls was not part of the estate, it is said to have **adeemed** (to have been taken away). *Ademption* of a gift in a will means that the intended legatee (the person named in the will) forfeits the object because it no longer exists. An object used as a substitute by the testator will not pass to the legatee unless it is clear that she intended the legatee to have it.

Intestacy

Intestacy means dying without a will. Intestacy happens all too frequently; even those who know the consequences for their heirs often put off making a will until it is too late—Abraham Lincoln, for one, who as an experienced lawyer knew very well the hazards to heirs of dying intestate. On his death, Lincoln's property was divided one-third to his widow, one-third to a grown son, and one-third to a twelve-year-old son. Statistics show that in New York, about one-third of the people who die with estates of $5,000 or more die without wills. In every state, statutes provide for the disposition of property of decedents dying without wills. If you die without a will, the state in effect has made one for you. Although the rules vary by statute from state to state, a common distribution pattern is as follows:

Unmarried Decedent   At common law, parents of an intestate decedent could not inherit his property. Today, however, many states provide that parents will share in the property. If the parents have already died, then the estate will pass to **collateral heirs** (siblings, nieces, nephews, aunts, and uncles). If there are no collateral heirs, most state laws provide that the next surviving kin of equal degree will share the property equally (first cousins, for instance). If there are no surviving kin, the estate **escheats** (es CHEETS) (passes) to the state.

Married with No Children   In some states, the surviving spouse without children will inherit the entire estate. In other states, the spouse must share the property with the decedent's parents or, if they are deceased, with the collateral heirs as defined above.

Married with Children   In general, the surviving spouse will be entitled to one-third of the estate, and the remainder will pass in equal shares to living children of the decedent. The share of any child who died before the decedent will be divided equally among that child's offspring. These grandchildren of the decedent are said to take **per stirpes** (per STIR peas), meaning that they stand in the shoes of their parent. Suppose that the decedent left a wife, three children, and eight grandchildren (two children each of the three surviving children and two children of a fourth child who predeceased the decedent), and that the estate was worth $300,000. Under a typical intestate succession law, the widow would receive property worth $100,000. The balance of the property would be divided into four equal parts, one for each of the four children. The three surviving children would each receive $50,000. The two children of the fourth child would each receive $25,000. The other grandchildren would receive nothing. A system of distribution in which all living descendants share equally, regardless of generation, is said to be a distribution **per capita** (per KAP ah tuh). In the above example, after the widow took her share, the remaining sum would be divided into eleven parts, three for the surviving children and eight for the surviving grandchildren.

Unmarried with Children   If the decedent was a widow or widower with children, then the surviving children generally will take the entire estate.

In the real world, of course, many situations are not as neat and tidy as the above scenarios. The following case represents an attempt by the court to apply the laws of intestacy in an equitable manner when the decedent left an illegitimate son.

PRINCE v. BLACK
344 S.E.2d 411 (Ga. 1986)

SMITH, JUSTICE.

We granted certiorari from the Court of Appeals in *Black v. Prince;* . . . and we reverse.

The appellant, Reginald Prince (also known as Reginald Lumpkin) was conceived and born at a time his mother, Josephine, was cohabiting with Lorenzo Prince. Although Josephine was still legally married to Willie Lumpkin she had been separated from him for some time before she began cohabiting with Lorenzo. Lorenzo took Josephine to the hospital to have their child, visited her and his son while in the hospital, named the child Reginald Dwight, and paid all the hospital bills. When Lorenzo discovered that Josephine's husband's name appeared on the birth certificate as the father of the child, he asked if he could have the certificate changed to reflect his name, but was told that he could not do so since Josephine was legally married to Lumpkin. Lorenzo loved and cared for Reginald and was the only father that Reginald ever knew. When Reginald was six years old his mother moved to Florida and gave complete custody and control of Reginald to his father. Lorenzo registered Reginald in the public schools under the name Reginald Prince and treated Reginald as his son in every way and Reginald treated Lorenzo as his father. Prince purchased several insurance policies in

(continued on next page)

(continued)

PRINCE v. BLACK
344 S.E.2d 411 (Ga. 1986)

which he named Reginald the beneficiary and listed him as his son. Lorenzo applied to Social Security for retirement benefits for himself and Reginald as his son. On the application, he swore twice under the penalty of perjury that Reginald was his son. Reginald and his father discussed having his name formally changed to Prince, but Lorenzo died before it could be done.

Lorenzo Prince died intestate and his sister asked appellee Black to qualify as administrator of Lorenzo's estate. . . . [A] jury found that [Reginald] was the son and lawful heir of Lorenzo Prince. Appellee Black appealed to the Court of Appeals and they held that the evidence presented was sufficient to permit the jury to find that Lorenzo was Reginald's natural father, but that there was nothing to support the contention that the requirements of OCGA § 53-4-4(c) were met to enable Reginald to inherit from his father. Thus, the Court of Appeals reversed the jury's verdict.

The appellant contends that the jury's verdict can be upheld under the theory of virtual or equitable adoption.

Foster parents who intend to adopt a child so that the child can be legally recognized as their lawful heir may accomplish their objective during their lifetimes pursuant to OCGA § 19-8-8. Likewise the father of an illegitimate child who intends to have his child legally recognized so that the child may inherit from his estate as his lawful heir may accomplish his objective pursuant to OCGA § 19-7-22. If the foster parents or the father of the illegitimate child dies intestate before the formalities are completed, the child's opportunity to inherit dies with the parents. In situations in which foster parents die intestate after they have made an agreement to adopt the child and the other elements are established, the courts have allowed the child to inherit the parent's property under the doctrine of virtual or equitable adoption.

The doctrine of virtual or equitable adoption does not fit the situation in which the mother of an illegitimate child gives custody and control to the father. It is highly unlikely that the natural father would enter into an agreement with the natural mother for the father to adopt the child because: 1) the term adoption ordinarily refers to people other than the natural parents of the child and the child, and: 2) adoption has the effect of severing the relationship of parent and child between the natural parent and the child and creating a new relationship of parent and child between the adopting parent and the child. A mother who does not want to sever the parent-child relationship that she enjoys with her child would not seek to have the father adopt the child and the father would not seek to create a new relationship with the child as the relationship is already in place. Thus, it would be unusual to have a situation in which the parties can point to an agreement to adopt the child that can be enforced in equity.

There may be cases in which there is such clear and convincing evidence that the child is the natural child of the father and that the father intended for the child to share in his intestate estate, in the same manner that the child would have shared if he had been formally legitimated, that equity will consider that done which ought to have been done. Thus the father's intentions will be fulfilled by allowing the child to inherit the property that was undisposed of by will as if the child was legitimate, although the child was not formally legitimated and cannot be considered legitimate in the eyes of the law.

Here, there was clear and convincing evidence that Lorenzo was Reginald's father. The fact that Lorenzo named Reginald as his beneficiary under insurance policies and that he applied for and attained Social Security benefits for himself and Reginald as his son, clearly indicates Lorenzo's intention to allow Reginald to share in his estate as if Reginald had been formally legitimated.

Just as the doctrine of virtual or equitable adoption will allow a child to inherit from his intestate foster parents under certain conditions, the doctrine of virtual or equitable legitimation will allow an illegitimate child to inherit from his intestate father's estate when the evidence is clear and convincing as it was in this case.

Judgment reversed.

Estate Administration

To carry on the administration of an estate, a particular person must be responsible for locating the estate property and carrying out the decedent's instructions. If named in the will, this person is called an **executor.** When a woman serves she is still known in many jurisdictions as an **executrix.** If the decedent died intestate, the court will appoint an **administrator** (or administratrix), usually a close member of the family. The UPC refers to the person performing the function of executor or administrator as a *personal representative,* and we use this term. Unless excused by the will from doing so, the personal representative must post a bond, usually in an amount that exceeds the value of the decedent's personal property.

The personal representative must immediately become familiar with the decedent's business, preserve the assets, examine the books and records, check on insurance, and notify the appropriate banks.

When confirmed by the court (if necessary), the personal representative must offer the will in pro-bate—that is, file the will with the court, prove its authenticity through witnesses, and defend it against any challenges. Once the court accepts the will, it will enter a formal decree admitting the will to probate.

Traditionally, a widow could make certain elections against the will; for example, she could choose *dower* and *homestead rights.* The right of **dower** entitled the widow to a life estate in one-third of the husband's inheritable land, while a **homestead right,** is the right to the family home as measured by an amount of land (160 acres of rural land or one acre of urban land in Kansas, for example) or a specific dollar amount (for instance, $4,000).

Today, most states have eliminated traditional dower rights. These states give the surviving spouse (widow or widower) the right to reject provisions made in a will and to take a share of the decedent's estate instead. State laws that continue to give dower and homestead rights to widows only are now under attack, as illustrated by the following decision by the Arkansas Supreme Court striking down the state dower and homestead statutes.

HESS v. WIMS
272 Ark. 43, 613 S.W.2d
85 (1981)

DUDLEY, JUSTICE. Appellants challenge the constitutionality of the Arkansas laws that allow a widow, but not a widower, to take against a will and to receive dower interests, statutory allowances and homestead rights.

Mary Hess and Jean Morton, the appellants, and the decedent Hoyt Wims, were the only three children of their parents. When their mother died, Jean Morton was appointed administratrix, and the mother's Mississippi land was sold. The proceeds were given to Hoyt Wims to purchase 57 acres in St. Francis County, where the children had grown up, and their father was to be allowed to live there during his lifetime. Hoyt Wims was to leave the balance of his estate to his two sisters, if they survived him. In 1970, he had a will prepared which left all of his property to his two sisters, subject to a life estate in their father in the real estate.

The father died, and Hoyt Wims became terminally ill. In 1978, during the last year of his life, he married Geraldine Wims and moved into the home she had owned and occupied for a number of years.

After the death of Hoyt Wims in 1979 and the admittance of his will to probate, Geraldine Wims, the appellee widow, elected to take against the will and petitioned for the award of statutory allowances, dower and homestead interests. The trial court, in reliance on our gender based statutes, granted her the relief asked.

*   *   *

Appellee filed her election pursuant to Ark.Stat. Ann. § 60-501 (Repl. 1971). This statute allows a widow to take dower against the will of her husband under any condition, but allows the husband to take curtesy against the will of his wife only if her will was executed before the marriage. Dower is an inchoate right, while curtesy may be defeated. No valid compensatory purpose or justifiable governmental function can be found to sustain this gender-based discrimination. This statute must be declared in violation of the Equal Protection clause of the Fourteenth Amendment.

State and federal statutes discriminating against males upon the presumption that all males are superior to females in financial matters have been held to be unconstitutional in recent years. Most recently, in *Wengler v. Druggist Mutual Insurance Co.*, 446 U.S. 142 (1980), the United States Supreme Court held that a Missouri workers' compensation law denying a widower benefits on his wife's work-related death and providing that under the same circumstances a widow could have obtained benefits from her husband's death was an illegal sex discrimination. The Court stated that the burden is on those defending the discrimination to make out the claimed justification, and it is not sufficient that a number of years ago the Legislature thought widows to be more in need of help than widowers.

The United States Supreme Court and this court in recent years have declared invalid a number of gender based laws. In *Reed v. Reed*, 404 U.S. 71 (1971), a provision of the Idaho probate code which preferred males over females was declared void. *Califano v. Goldfarb*, 430 U.S. 199 (1977), held unconstitutional a provision of the Social Security laws denying a widower benefit from the death of his wife because he could not prove he was receiving at least one-half of his support from her, while a widow would automatically have been entitled to such benefits. *Weinberger v. Weisenfeld*, 420 U.S. 636 (1975), held unconstitutional a provision of the Social Security Act not providing for a widower to receive benefits for a minor child in his care, while a widow would be entitled to the benefits.

★   ★   ★

In this case the appellee elected to take her right of dower rather than proceed under the will. Ark.Stat.Ann. §§ 61-206, 207 and 208 (Repl. 1971) give the wife a right of dower which cannot be defeated by a husband's conveyance. The comparable curtesy statutes, Ark.Stat.Ann. §§ 61-228 and 229 (Repl. 1971), allow the wife to defeat curtesy by conveyance. These statutes provide dissimilar treatment for men and women who are similarly situated. We can find no justification for this discrimination. We hold the dower statutes applied in this case, §§ 61-206 and 208, are unconstitutional. Today, in *Stokes v. Stokes*, 613 S.W.2d 372 (1981), a case involving a widow and children, we hand down a decision invalidating the following companion statutes: §§ 61-201, 202, 203, 207 and 210.

Ark.Stat.Ann. § 62-2501 (Repl. 1971) provides allowances to a widow, but not a widower, of $2,000 plus $500 sustenance. Under the facts in this case and the language of the statute, we can find no way to extend the benefits to the disfavored class and, accordingly, we find it necessary to deny the benefits to both widowers and widows by declaring the statute unconstitutional as applied. In today's companion *Stokes* case, supra, we hold this statute is unconstitutional in the event there are minor children.

Pursuant to Article IX, Section 6 of the Arkansas Constitution, the appellee, as a widow with no children, was awarded homestead against the interest of appellants. This means that appellee, during her lifetime, is entitled to possession of the homestead and all rents and profits from the lands devised to appellants.

Our Constitution makes no comparable homestead provision for men. Had the appellee widow died before Hoyt Wims, he could not have been allowed possession of her home, even though he had none. This constitutional provision is discriminatory and we find no valid governmental function to justify this dissimilar treatment of widows and widowers. This provision as applied in this case violates the Fourteenth Amendment. There is no language in this section which will allow us to extend the homestead benefits to widowers without children, and, as a result, we hold the provision invalid as applied. We do not reach a decision on this section in the event there are children, as the State might make a valid argument that the provision is justifiable.

While dower, statutory allowances and homestead have been favored provisions of our law for nearly 150 years, it is now impermissible to presume that all females are inferior to males in financial matters. Accordingly, we find the gender based discriminatory statutes and constitutional provision relied upon to grant the election to take against the will, the widow's allowances, dower and homestead to be unconstitutional as applied in this case.

Reversed and remanded for proceedings not inconsistent with this opinion.

Once the will is admitted to probate, the personal representative must *assemble* and *inventory* all assets. This task requires the personal representative to collect debts and rent due, supervise the decedent's business, inspect the real estate, store personal and household effects, prove the death and collect proceeds of life insurance policies, take securities into custody, and ascertain whether the decedent held property in other states. Next the assets must be *appraised* as of the date of death. When inventory and appraisal are completed, the personal representative must decide how and when to dispose of the assets, by answering the following sorts of questions: Should a business be liquidated, sold, or allowed to continue to operate? Should securities be sold, and if so, when? Should the real estate be kept intact under the will or sold? To whom must the personal effects be given?

The personal representative must also handle *claims* against the estate. If the decedent had unpaid debts while alive, the estate will be responsible for paying them. In most states the personal representative is required to advertise and, when all claims have been gathered and authenticated, must pay just claims in order of priority. In general (though by no means in every state), the order of priority is as follows: (1) funeral expenses, (2) administration expenses (cost of bond, advertising expenses, filing fees, lawsuit costs, and the like), (3) family allowance, (4) claims of the federal government, (5) hospital and other expenses associated with the decedent's last illness, (6) claims of state and local governments, (7) wage claims, (8) lien claims, (9) all other debts. If the estate is too small to cover all these claims, every claim in the first category must be satisfied before the claims in the second category may be paid, and so on.

Before the estate can be distributed, the personal representative must take care of all taxes owed by the estate. She will have to file returns for both estate and income taxes, and actually pay from assets of the estate the taxes due. (She may have to sell some assets to obtain sufficient cash to do so.) **Estate taxes**—imposed by the federal government and based on the value of the estate—are nearly as old as the Republic; they date back to 1797. They were instituted originally to raise revenue, but in our time they serve also to break up large estates. Today only a small percentage of the populace is affected by estate taxes (an estimated 0.5 percent, or between 5 and 10 percent of the nation's wealth). The reason that so few are affected lies in tax law changes enacted in the early 1980s. For instance, the first $600,000 of each estate is exempt from estate taxes and all property passes to the spouse tax-free.

Although a unified tax is imposed on gifts during life and transfers at death, everyone is permitted to give away $10,000 per donee each year without paying any tax on the gift at all. A tax on sizable gifts is imposed to prevent people with large estates from giving away during their lives portions of their estate in order to escape estate taxes. Thus two grandparents with two married children and four grandchildren may give away $20,000 ($10,000 from each grandparent) to their eight descendents (children, spouses, grandchildren), for a total of $160,000 each year without paying any tax.

State governments also impose taxes at death. In many states, these are known as **inheritance taxes** and are taxes on the heir's right to receive the property. The tax rate depends on the relationship to the decedent. The closer the relation, the smaller the tax. Thus a child will pay less than a nephew or niece, and they will pay less than an unrelated friend who is named in the will.

Once the taxes are paid, a **final accounting** must be prepared, showing the remaining principal, income, and disbursements. Only at this point may the personal representative actually distribute the assets of the estate according to the will.

TRUSTS

Definitions

When the legal title to certain property is held by one person, while another has the use and benefit of it, a relationship known as a **trust** has been created. The trust developed centuries ago to get around various nuances and complexities, including taxes, of English real property law. The trustee has legal title and the beneficiary has "equitable title," since the courts of equity would enforce the obligations of the trustee to honor the terms by which the property was conveyed to him. A typical trust might provide for the trustee to manage an estate for the grantor's children, paying out income to the children until they are, say, twenty-one, at which time they become legal owners of the property.

Trusts may be created by bequest in a will, by agreement of the parties, or by a court decree. However created, the trust is governed by a set of rules that grew out of the courts of equity. Every trust involves specific property known as the *res* (rees) (Latin for "thing") and three parties, though the parties may be the same person.

Settlor or Grantor Anyone who has legal capacity to make a contract may create a trust. The creator is known as the **settlor** or **grantor.** Trusts are created for many reasons; for example, so that a minor can have the use of assets without being able to dissipate them, or so that a person can have a professional manage his money.

Trustee The trustee is the person, including a corporation, who holds the legal title to the *res*. Anyone with legal capacity to hold title to property may serve as trustee. Banks do considerable business as trustees. If the settlor should neglect to name a trustee, the court may name one. The trustee is a *fiduciary* of the trust beneficiary and will be held to the highest standard of loyalty. Not even an appearance of impropriety toward the trust property will be permitted. Thus a trustee may not loan trust property to friends, to a corporation of which he is a principal, or to himself, even if he is scrupulous to account for every penny and pays the principal back with interest.

The trustee must act prudently in administering the trust. However, as **Box 35-1** indicates, the concept of prudence is an evolving one.

Beneficiary The beneficiary is the person, institution, or other thing for which the trust has been created. Beneficiaries are not limited to one's children or close friends; an institution, corporation, or other organization such as a charity can be a beneficiary of a trust as can one's pet dogs, cats, and the like. The beneficiary may usually sell or otherwise dispose of his interest in a trust, and that interest likewise can usually be reached by creditors. Note that the settlor may create a trust of which he is the beneficiary, just as he may create a trust of which he is the trustee.

The following case considers a basic element of trust law: the settlor's power over the property once he has created the trust.

CONTINENTAL BANK & TRUST CO. v. COUNTRY CLUB MOBILE ESTATES, LTD.
632 P.2d 869 (Utah 1981)

OAKS, JUSTICE. The issue in this appeal is whether a settlor who has created a trust by conveying property that is subject to an option to sell can thereafter extend the period of the option without the participation or consent of the trustee. We hold that he cannot. For ease of reference, this opinion will refer to the plaintiff-appellant, Continental Bank & Trust Co., as the "trustee," to defendant-respondent, Country Club Mobile Estates, Ltd., as the "lessee-optionee," and to Marshall E. Huffaker, deceased, as the "settlor."

*   *   *

A trust is a form of ownership in which the legal title to property is vested in a trustee, who has equitable duties to hold and manage it for the benefit of the beneficiaries. *Restatement of Trusts, Second*, § 2 (1959). It is therefore axiomatic in trust law that the trustee under a valid trust deed has exclusive control of the trust property, subject only to the limitations imposed by law or the trust instrument, and that once the settlor has created the trust he is no longer the owner of the trust property and has only such ability to deal with it as is expressly reserved to him in the trust instrument. As stated in Bogert, *Trusts & Trustees*, § 42 (2d ed. 1965):

(*continued on next page*)

(continued)

CONTINENTAL BANK & TRUST CO. v. COUNTRY CLUB MOBILE ESTATES, LTD.
632 P.2d 869 (Utah 1981)

After a settlor has completed the creation of a trust he is, with small exceptions noted below, and except as expressly provided otherwise by the trust instrument or by statute, not in any legal relationship with the beneficiaries or the trustee, and has no liabilities or powers with regard to the trust administration.

None of the exceptions identified by Bogert applies in this case.

This is a case where a settlor created a trust and then chose to ignore it. He could have modified or revoked the trust, or directed the trustee in writing to sell or lease the trust property, but he took neither of these actions. Instead, more than two years after the creation and recording of the trust, and without any direction or notice to the trustee, the settlor gave the lessee-optionee a signed instrument purporting to extend its option to buy the trust property for another five years. The trustee did not learn of this instrument until two and one-half years later, immediately following the death of the settlor.

An extension of the option to buy would obviously have a limiting effect on the value of the reversion owned by the trust (and thus on the rights of the trust beneficiaries), which the trustee has a duty to protect. Even a revocable trust clothes beneficiaries, for the duration of the trust, with a legally enforceable right to insist that the terms of the trust be adhered to. If we gave legal effect to the settlor's extension of this option in contravention of the existence and terms of the trust, we would prejudice the interests of the beneficiaries, blur some fundamental principles of trust law, and cast doubt upon whether it is the trustee or the settlor who is empowered to manage and dispose of the trust property in a valid revocable trust.

The judgment of the district court is reversed and the cause is remanded with instructions to enter judgment for the plaintiff. Costs to appellant.

Express Trusts

Trusts are categorized into two main divisions: *express* and *implied*. Within the first category are two major subdivisions: *testamentary* trusts and *living* (or *inter vivos*) trusts. The **testamentary** trust is one created by will. It becomes effective on the testator's death. The *living* or **inter vivos** trust is one created during the lifetime of the grantor. It can be revocable or irrevocable (see Figure 35-3).

A **revocable trust** is one that the settlor can terminate at his option. On termination, legal title to the trust assets returns to the settlor. Because the settlor can reassert control over the assets whenever he wishes, the income they generate is taxed to him. Although the revocable trust permits the assets to escape probate, it is not for everyone (see **Box 35-2**).

By contrast, an **irrevocable trust** is permanent, and the settlor may not revoke or modify its terms. All income to the trust must be accumulated in the trust or paid to the beneficiaries in accordance with the trust agreement. Because income does not go to the settlor, the irrevocable trust has important income tax advantages, even though it means permanent loss of control over the assets (beyond the instructions for its use and disposition that the settlor may lay out in the trust agreement). A hybrid form is the **reversionary trust:** until the end of a fixed period, the trust is irrevocable, and the settlor may not modify its terms, but thereafter the trust assets revert

LAW AND LIFE

BOX 35-1

From Grave to Cradle

By James Lyons

[*Traditionally, the "prudent investor rule" meant that a trustee could be sued for even one bad investment. Under new rules, a trustee can make an honest mistake as long as the overall investment strategy is taken toward prudent behavior. These rules give trustees greater freedom to diversify investments.*—AUTHORS' NOTE]

It may be hard to believe, but a bunch of academics and lawyers have actually come up with something that will curb litigation, lower costs, and make life—and death—a little easier for everyone.

It's the American Law Institute's new restatement of the law on trust administration. The institute is a group of lawyers, professors and judges who periodically issue statements on various laws. The institute's views aren't binding on courts. But the old standards governing how trustees can manage funds are so outmoded—the last restatement was in 1959—that judges are likely to jump at the chance to cement the new rules into law.

THE PRUDENT INVESTOR RULE

Essentially, the new rules bring trust management into the 20th century by recognizing that even what appear to be the safest investments have risks. Think, for example, of all the supposedly safe Treasury bills that were eroded in the inflationary Seventies.

Rather than prohibiting trustees from putting money into so-called "speculative" investments such as second mortgages, the American Law Institute's new guidelines allow trustees greater freedom to diversify investments across the entire spectrum of possibilities. Now the relevant questions are whether the risk outweighs the opportunity for gain, and whether the investment fits the purposes of the trust.

Nor should individual investments be considered in isolation. Buying a stock index future may sound risky, but if it represents only 1% of your portfolio, it might be a wise choice—especially if used as an intelligent way to hedge a portfolio.

What all this gets down to is the venerable "prudent investor rule."

Derived from an 1830 Massachusetts court ruling, this rule and its variants have dominated the trust management field ever since. For the last 30 years trustees have been sued for making a single bad investment, even though the entire portfolio has done well. The new rule changes would allow trustees to make honest mistakes in single investments—as long as the investment is part of a prudent diversification strategy.

With greater freedom comes greater accountability. The new guidelines urge a trustee to delegate authority for investment strategy if he or she isn't an expert. You may think your brother Charlie is a swell guy, but what does he really know about convertible debenture strategies and the T bill futures market?

"If you put assets in a broadly diversified portfolio aimed at cutting [transaction] costs, you'll do fine," says Yale Law School Professor John Langbein, who was an adviser on the American Law Institute rules. "But if you're a trustee doing old-fashioned, small-portfolio, individual stock picking, you'll be creamed under these standards—and rightly so."

Source: *Forbes*, October 1, 1990

---

to the settlor. The reversionary trust combines tax advantages with ultimate possession of the assets.

Of the possible types of express trusts, there are five worth examining briefly: (1) *Totten* trusts, (2), *blind* trusts, (3) *Clifford* trusts, (4) *charitable* trusts, and (5) *spendthrift* trusts. The use of express trusts in business will also be noted.

Totten Trust The Totten trust, which gets its name from a New York case, *In re Totten*, 71 N.E. 748 (N.Y. 1904), is a tentative trust created when someone deposits funds in a bank as trustee for another person as beneficiary. (Usually the account will be named in the following form: "Mary, in trust for Ed.") During the person's lifetime, the grantor-depositor may withdraw funds at his discretion or revoke the trust altogether. But if the grantor-depositor dies before the beneficiary, having not revoked the trust, then the beneficiary is entitled to whatever remains in the account at the time of the depositor's death.

Blind Trust In a blind trust, the grantor transfers assets—usually stocks and bonds—to trustees who hold and manage them for the grantor as beneficiary. The trustees are not permitted to tell the grantor how they are managing the portfolio. The blind trust is used

LAW AND LIFE

Living Trust Hoopla Bears A Close Look

By Earl C. Gottschalk Jr.

[*Living trusts have received much publicity in recent years. Although the revocable trust allows the assets to escape probate, some attorneys warn that these trusts are not for every person and every situation.*—AUTHORS' NOTE]

If you haven't already heard of living trusts, the odds are you will soon.

Everyone from attorneys and charitable organizations to do-it-yourself promoters seems to be touting living trusts these days, as a way to avoid the horrors of probate court.

In San Diego, attorneys use TV ads to describe the benefits. Free seminars abound, and write-your-own-trust kits sell for as little as $29.95. There's even living-trust software.

But all that hoopla troubles a number of lawyers and others who specialize in estate planning. They express concern that living trusts are being overpromoted and misleadingly marked in an atmosphere of hype.

A living trust can, indeed, be a

LIVING TRUSTS

useful tool for someone with lots of assets, especially in states with lengthy probate procedures and high costs for settling wills, these estate-planning specialists say. But, they add, the trusts don't cut estate taxes and, if not executed properly, they can result in costly legal fees and years of litigation.

"Living trusts are overly emphasized and totally misconstrued by the general public," says Sanford J. Schlesinger, partner in the New York law firm Shea & Gould.

Adds Graydon Calder, a San Diego financial planner specializing in estate planning: "Some promoters are overdoing things and wrecking a good product."

The official name of the legal device at the center of the controversy is a revocable living trust—which means that you can transfer ownership of assets to the trust while you are alive and can alter the document's terms at any time. After your death, a successor trustee, usually a family member or friend, will distribute your assets to your beneficiaries according to your instructions in the trust document.

The biggest selling point of a

living trust is that nothing passes through probate, the often expensive and time-consuming court process for administering a will. In California, where living trusts have gained tremendous popularity, the typical will takes 18 months to two years to go through probate, says Mr. Calder.

Alexander A. Bove Jr., a Boston lawyer, says probate costs can run as high as 3% to 5% of the assets in the estate. Assets in a living trust can be disposed of more quickly and at a lower administrative cost, he says.

A living trust also avoids the publicity of probate, in which the estate becomes part of public record. And for a person who becomes incapacitated, a living trust is one way to avoid the legal proceedings required to appoint a guardian, says William Brennan, CPA partner in Ernst & Young's, Washington office.

Compared with wills, living trusts are more difficult to contest, says Mr. Brennan. "Heirs are generally more successful in challenging and setting aside wills than trusts," he says.

How smoothly a living trust can work is illustrated by the case of John Woods, a San Diego widower who died two years ago of cancer at the age of 80. Mr. Woods had previously

by high government officials who are required by the Ethics in Government Act of 1978 to put their assets in blind trusts or abstain from making decisions that affect any companies in which they have a financial stake. Once the trust is created, the grantor-beneficiary is forbidden from discussing financial matters with the trustee or even to give the trustee advice. All that the grantor-beneficiary sees is a quarterly statement indicating by how much the trust net worth has increased or decreased.

Clifford Trust   The Clifford trust, named after the settlor in a Supreme Court case, *Helvering* v. *Clifford*, 309 U.S. 331 (1940), is reversionary: the grantor establishes a trust irrevocable for at least ten years and a day. By so doing, the grantor shifts the tax burden to the beneficiary. So a person in a higher bracket can save considerable money by establishing a Clifford trust to benefit, say, his or her children. The tax savings will apply as long as the income from the trust is not devoted to needs of the children that the grantor is

BOX 35-2

transferred his home, bank accounts, stocks held at a brokerage firm, and mutual funds into a living trust with Mr. Calder, who is Mr. Woods's nephew, and another relative, as successor trustees. When Mr. Wood died, Mr. Calder says it took "only a matter of hours" to distribute the assets in the trust following Mr. Wood's instructions. The cost of the trust: $500. "It would have taken two years to administer the will in probate court," Mr. Calder says.

But living trusts aren't for everyone and every situation.

To begin with, they offer more advantages in some states than others. "Living trusts are much more accepted as basic estate planning tools in California, Florida and Massachusetts than they are in New York," says Mr. Schlesinger, the New York lawyer.

He says that in New York, probate takes only 30 days. Also, you can't place ownership of a co-op apartment in a living trust in New York, he says. In some states, bank and savings and loan officials who aren't familiar with living trusts may be reluctant to refinance property that is titled in the name of a trust, specialists say.

Setting up and funding a living trust is more complicated than drawing up a will. And they are initially more expensive. It costs $50 for a will, compared with $500 to $3,000 for a living trust, depending on the complexity of the estate, says Mr. Bove, author of "The Complete Book of Wills and Estates."

Some people try to cut corners by setting up a living trust by themselves. But Mr. Calder says cut-rate, do-it-yourself living trust kits available at book or stationery stores aren't worth your time. "Hobbies are fine," he says, "but law or brain surgery isn't one of them."

In addition, with a living trust, a person must follow through. A large number of people who pay to set up living trusts fail to place all their major assets in the trusts, limiting the device's effectiveness, estate planners say. "Some people set them up but won't go through the tedious work of changing titles and names of assets [into the trust]," says Tracy Sealer, financial analyst for Bailard, Biehl & Kaiser, a San Mateo, Calif, money management firm.

One thing living trusts won't do is cut your estate taxes. "Some marketers are claiming that living trusts

reduce your estate taxes, and they don't," says Mr. Brennan. He says that three or four clients a week ask him about a living trust, and they all erroneously think the trusts cut taxes.

So who should get a living trust? The pros say it makes sense for people who have complex estates, real estate in more than one state, who live in states with cumbersome probate procedures and high probate costs, who need to keep the details of their estate private, and who fear a battle over the provisions of their will.

The pros say it's a good idea to meet with an attorney who specializes in estate planning before going through all the time and trouble of setting up a living trust.

For a married couple with uncomplicated assets, a living trust may not be worth the effort, says Mr. Brennan. All jointly owned property, life insurance proceeds, retirement and pension plan money go directly to the named beneficiaries without passing through probate, he says. "There are people who are setting up living trusts to save their assets from probate where the money wouldn't have gone through probate anyway."

Source: *Wall Street Journal*, February 11, 1991

legally required to supply. At the expiration of the express period in the trust, legal title to the *res* reverts to the grantor. However, the Tax Reform Act of 1986 removed the tax advantages for Clifford trusts established after March, 1986. As a result, all income from such trusts is taxed to the grantor. Existing Clifford trusts were not affected by the 1986 tax law.

Charitable Trust A charitable trust is one devoted to any public purpose. The definition is broad; it can

encompass funds for research to conquer disease, to aid battered wives, to add to museum collections, or to permit a group to proselytize on behalf of a particular political or religious doctrine. The law in all states recognizes the benefits to be derived from encouraging charitable trusts, and states use the *cy pres* (see press) ("as near as possible") doctrine to further the intent of the grantor. Ordinarily, if a trust is created that proves impossible to carry out, the assets will revert to the remainderman—for example, a trust to

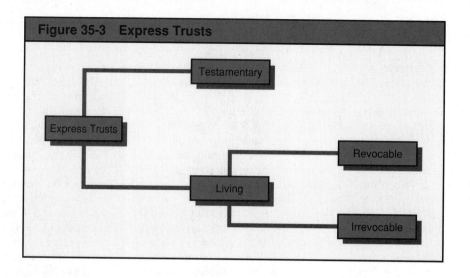

Figure 35-3   Express Trusts

pay for "my daughter's college education," if the daughter has died before going to college. But the assets of a charitable trust may be applied to a charity as similar as possible to the one chosen by the grantor.

Spendthrift Trust   A spendthrift trust is established when the settlor believes that the beneficiary is not to be trusted with whatever rights she might possess to assign the income or assets of the trust. By express provision in a trust instrument, the settlor may ensure that the trustees are legally obligated to pay only income to the beneficiary; no assignment of the assets may be made, either voluntarily by the beneficiary, or involuntarily by operation of law. Hence, the spendthrift beneficiary cannot gamble away the trust assets nor can they be reached by creditors to pay her gambling (or other) debts.

Express Trusts in Business   In addition to their use in estate planning, express trusts are also created for business purposes. The **business trust** (see Chapter 40) was popular late in the nineteenth century as a way of getting around state limitations on the corporate form and is still used today. By giving their shares to a **voting trust,** shareholders can ensure that their agreement to vote as a bloc will be carried out (see Chapter 43). But voting trusts can be dangerous. As discussed in Part Ten, agreements that result in price fixing or other restraints of trade violate the antitrust laws—for example, companies are in violation when they act collusively to fix prices by pooling voting stock under a trust agreement, as happened frequently at the turn of the century.

Implied Trusts

Trusts can be created by courts without any intent by a settlor to do so. For various reasons, a court will declare that particular property is to be held by its owner in trust for someone else. Such trusts are **implied trusts,** and are usually divided into two types: *constructive trusts* and *resulting trusts*. A **constructive trust** is one created usually to redress a fraud or to prevent unjust enrichment. Suppose you give one dollar to an agent to purchase a lottery ticket for you, but the agent buys the ticket instead in his own name and wins $1,000,000, payable into an account in amounts of $50,000 per year for twenty years. Since the agent had violated his fiduciary obligation and unjustly enriched himself, the court would impose a constructive trust on the account, and the agent would find himself holding the funds as trustee for you as beneficiary. By contrast, a **resulting trust** is one imposed to carry out the supposed intent of the parties. You give an agent $100,000 to purchase a house for you. Title is put in your agent's name at the closing, although it is clear that since she was paid for her services you did not intend to give the house to her as a gift. The court would declare that the house was to be held by the agent as trustee for you during the time that it took to have the title put in your name.

FACTORS AFFECTING BOTH ESTATES AND TRUSTS

Principal and Income

Often one person is to receive income from a trust or estate and another person, the remainderman, is to receive the remaining property when the trust or estate is terminated. In thirty-six states a uniform act, the Uniform Principal and Income Act (UPIA), defines principal and income and specifies how expenses are to be paid. If the trust agreement expressly gives the trustee power to determine what is income and what is principal, then his decision is usually unreviewable. If the agreement is silent, the trustee is bound by the provisions of the UPIA. The general rule is that *ordinary* receipts are income, whereas *extraordinary* receipts are additions to principal. **Ordinary receipts** are defined as the return of money or property derived from the use of the principal, including rent, interest, and cash dividends. **Extraordinary receipts** include stock dividends, revenues or other proceeds from the sale or exchange of trust assets, proceeds from insurance on assets, all income accrued at the testator's death, proceeds from the sale or redemption of bonds, and awards or judgments received in satisfaction of injuries to the trust property. Expenses or obligations incurred in producing or preserving income—including ordinary repairs and ordinary taxes—are chargeable to income. Expenses incurred in making permanent improvements to the property, investing the assets, and selling or purchasing trust property are chargeable to principal, as are all obligations incurred before the decedent's death.

Taxation

Estates and trusts are taxable entities under the federal income tax statute. The general rule is that all income paid out to the beneficiaries is taxable to the beneficiaries and may be deducted from the trust's or estate's gross income in arriving at its net taxable income. The trust or estate is then taxed on the balance left over—that is, on any amounts accumulated. This is known as the **conduit** rule, because the trust or estate is seen as a conduit for the income.

Power of Appointment

A power of appointment is the authority given by one person (the *donor*) to another (the *donee*) to dispose of the donor's property according to whatever instructions the donor provides. A **general power** means that the donee may give the property to anyone he wishes, including himself. A **special power** restricts distribution to a particular person or group. If properly used, the power of appointment is an important tool, because it permits the donee to react flexibly to circumstances that the donor could not have foreseen. Suppose you desire to benefit your children when they are thirty-five or forty according to whether they are wealthy or poor. The poorer children will be given more from the estate or trust than the wealthier ones. Since you will not know when you write the will or establish the trust who will be poor or rich, and how much they will have, a donee with a power of appointment will be able to make judgments impossible for the donor to make years or decades before.

EXAMPLES OF ESTATE PLANS

We have discussed several basic estate planning tools. We now see how these tools might be used together in two typical estates. We begin with a young couple, Abelard and Heloise, who have two children aged four and two. Abelard and Heloise both have life insurance through their employers ($50,000 each), and each names the other as beneficiary. They also own two cars worth $5,000 each, a house with $50,000 equity, and a bank account with $10,000. What type of estate plan is appropriate?

Some financial advisors claim that under these circumstances, Heloise and Abelard should simply put their assets in joint ownership with right of survivorship, so that when one dies the other automatically owns everything. They would thus avoid the cost of probate court and other legal expenses. But joint ownership can be risky. For example, if both died together in an automobile accident, their estates would end up in probate court, and their property would pass under the laws of intestacy. The judge would select an administrator of the estate and appoint a guardian for the children, who in most states would receive the estate assets at age eighteen. Even if Abelard and Heloise did not die together, the property might go to a surviving spouse who could not manage the assets or who might elope with a punk rock musician, leaving the children with nothing. Consequently, whether or not they hold property jointly, Heloise and Abelard should also draw up (1) wills, naming an executor of their own choice and a guardian for the children, and (2) a trust or trusts, if for no other reason than (in the event they die together) to hold and invest the property until the children are older. Of course, the trust could also be created to take effect when only one spouse dies to avoid the problem of the surviving spouse who mismanages the estate assets.

Now assume that as time passes, Heloise and Abelard find that their nest has emptied out. The children are adults and Heloise and Abelard are richer, jointly owning substantial assets: a house, a cottage, two expensive cars, several bank accounts, stocks and bonds, worth a total of $1.2 million. At this point, they face two main changes in their estate planning goals: they are no longer concerned with naming a guardian for their children, but they may have to pay estate tax. If everything passes to the survivor, because the property was held jointly, the estate tax would have no impact when one spouse dies. That is because the Internal Revenue Code allows everything to pass to the survivor tax-free. But when the surviving spouse dies, leaving an estate of $1.2 million to the children, the tax would be $235,000.

Consequently, Abelard and Heloise might decide to execute wills and trusts that would be designed in such a manner that when one spouse dies, $600,000 would go to the survivor tax-free and the other $600,000 would go to a trust tax-free (see p. 786), income from which could go to the surviving spouse. The trust property would not be part of that spouse's estate. When the surviving spouse dies, the amount in his or her estate would go to the children tax-free (if under $600,000) and whatever is left in the trust would also pass to the children at that time tax-free—for a total tax saving of $235,000. The trust arrangement would also allow for professional management of the property in the trust and would ensure that trust property eventually reached the children in the

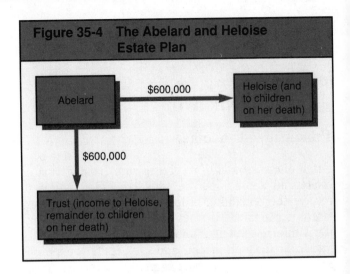

Figure 35-4   The Abelard and Heloise Estate Plan

event that the surviving spouse were to remarry. A simple schematic of the estate plan is illustrated by Figure 35-4.

When Abelard and Heloise were young, their joint ownership caused no problem, so long as it was supplemented with a will. But now joint ownership will actually defeat their estate planning goals. They can set up the will and trust arrangement described above. In theory, the plan will avoid estate taxes. But if they own property jointly with right of survivorship, all property will pass automatically to the surviving spouse (rather than half to the trust), with a resulting tax bill of $235,000. So you can see the considerable advantage they and their heirs will reap if they restructure their property ownership as their net worth grows.

Finally, note that aside from wills, trusts, and joint ownership, Heloise and Abelard may consider gifts of property while they are still living as a means of reducing the tax bite in their estates. As noted earlier, each can give away $10,000 in cash or property valued at $10,000 to each child per year without tax.

CHAPTER SUMMARY

Estate planning is the process by which an owner decides how her property is to be passed on to others. The four basic estate planning tools are wills, trusts, gifts, and joint ownership. In this chapter we examined wills and trusts. A will is the declaration of a person's wishes about the disposition of her assets on her death. The law of each state sets forth certain formalities, such as the number of witnesses, to which written wills must adhere. Wills are managed through the probate process, which varies from state to state, although many states have now adopted the Uniform Probate Code.

In general, anyone over eighteen and of sound mind may make a will. It must be signed by the testator and two or three others must witness the signature. A will may always be modified or revoked during the testator's lifetime, either expressly through a codicil, or through certain actions such as a subsequent marriage and the birth of children not contemplated by the will. Wills must be carefully drafted to avoid abatement and ademption.

The law provides for distribution in the case of intestacy. The rules vary from state to state and depend on whether the decedent was married when she died, had children or parents who survived her, or had collateral heirs.

Once a will is admitted to probate, the personal representative must assemble and inventory all assets, have them appraised, handle claims against the estate, pay taxes, prepare a final accounting, and only then distribute the assets according to the will.

A trust is a relationship in which one person holds legal title to certain property and another person has the use and benefit of it. The settlor or grantor creates the trust, giving specific property (the res) to the trustee for the benefit of the beneficiary. Trusts may be living or testamentary, revocable or irrevocable. Express trusts come in many forms, including Totten trusts, blind trusts, Clifford trusts, charitable trusts, and spendthrift trusts. Trusts may also be imposed by law; constructive and resulting trusts are designed to redress frauds, prevent unjust enrichment, or see to it that the intent of the parties is carried out.

KEY TERMS

SELF-TEST QUESTIONS

1. A will written by the testator's hand and not witnessed is called:
   - (a) a conditional will
   - (b) a noncupative will
   - (c) a holographic will
   - (d) a reciprocal will
2. A written modification or supplement to a prior will is called:
   - (a) a revocation clause
   - (b) an abatement
   - (c) a codicil
   - (d) none of the above
3. A trust created by will is called:
   - (a) an inter vivos trust
   - (b) a reversionary trust
   - (c) a Totten trust
   - (d) a testamentary trust
4. Trustees are not permitted to tell the grantor how they are managing their portfolio of assets in:
   - (a) a Clifford Trust
   - (b) a Spendthrift Trust
   - (c) a Blind Trust
   - (d) a Voting Trust
5. An example of an implied trust is:
   - (a) a Spendthrift Trust
   - (b) a Clifford Trust
   - (c) a resulting trust
   - (d) none of the above

DEMONSTRATION PROBLEM

Seymour deposits $50,000 in a bank account, ownership of which is specified as "Seymour, in trust for Fifi." What type of trust is this? Who is the settlor? The beneficiary? The trustee? May Seymour spend the money on himself? When Seymour dies does the property pass under the laws of intestacy, assuming he has no will?

PROBLEMS

1. Seymour, a resident of Rhode Island, signed a will in which he left all of his property to his close friend Fifi. Seymour and Fifi then moved to Alabama, where Seymour eventually died. Seymour's wife Hildegarde, who stayed behind in Rhode Island and who was not named in the will,

claimed that the will was revoked when Seymour moved from one state to another. Is she correct? Why?

2. Assume in problem 1 that Seymour's Rhode Island will is valid in Alabama. Is Hildegarde entitled to a part of Seymour's estate? Explain.

3. Assume in problem 1 that Seymour's Rhode Island will is valid in Alabama. Seymour and Hildegarde own, as tenants by the entirety, a cottage on the ocean. In the will Seymour specifically states that the cottage goes to Fifi on his death. Does Fifi or Hildegarde get the cottage? Or do they share it? Explain?

4. Assume in problem 1 that Seymour's Rhode Island will is not valid. Seymour's only relative, besides Hildegarde, is his nephew Chauncey, whom Seymour detests. Who is entitled to Seymour's property when he dies—Fifi, Hildegarde, or Chauncey? Explain.

5. Scrooge is in a high tax bracket. He has set aside $100,000 in a savings account, which he eventually wants to use to pay the college expenses of his tiny son Tim, who is three. The account earns $10,000 a year, of which $5,000 goes to the government in taxes. How could Scrooge lower the tax payments while retaining control of the $100,000?

6. Assume in problem 5 that Scrooge considers placing the $100,000 in trust for Tim. But he is worried that when Tim comes of age he might sell his interest in the trust. Could the trust be structured to avoid this possibility? Explain.

7. Assume that Scrooge has a substantial estate and no relatives. Is there any reason for him to consider a will or trust? Why? If he dies without a will, what will happen to his property?

ANSWERS TO SELF-TEST QUESTIONS

1. (c)   2. (c)   3. (d)   4. (c)   5. (c)

ANSWER TO DEMONSTRATION PROBLEM

This is a Totten trust. Seymour is the settlor, Fifi is the beneficiary and the bank is the trustee. Seymour may spend the money on himself, but when he dies, Fifi is entitled to whatever remains.

Insurance

We conclude the unit on property with a discussion of insurance law, not only because insurance is a means of compensating an owner for property losses, but also because the insurance contract itself represents a property right. In this chapter we begin by examining regulation of the insurance industry. We then look at legal issues relating to specific types of insurance. Finally, we examine defenses that insurance companies might raise to avoid making payments under insurance policies.

DEFINITIONS

Certain terms are usefully defined at the outset. **Insurance** is a contract of reimbursement—for example, for loss of named objects by specified perils such as fire, hurricane, or earthquake. An **insurer** is the underwriter or other company or person who promises to reimburse. The **insured** (sometimes called the *assured*) is the one who receives the payment, except in the case of life insurance: the *beneficiary* re-

ceives payments under a life insurance contract. The **premium** is the consideration paid by the insured—usually annually or semiannually—for the insurer's promise to reimburse. The contract itself is called the **policy.** The events insured against are known as **risks** or **perils.**

Alone among the major American industries, regulation of insurance is left for the most part in the hands of state, rather than federal, authorities. Under the McCarran-Ferguson Act, Congress exempted state-regulated insurance companies from the federal antitrust laws. Every state now has an insurance department that oversees insurance rates, policy standards, reserves, and other aspects of the industry. Over the years, these departments have come under fire in many states for being ineffective and "captives" of the industry. Moreover, large insurers operate in all states, and both they and consumers must contend with a "crazy-quilt" of fifty different state regulatory schemes, providing very different degrees of protection. From time to time attempts, so far unsuccessful, have been made to bring insurance under federal regulation.

Whether certain activities constitute "the business of insurance," and thus are exempt from the antitrust laws, is an issue that is raised frequently in litigation, as more and more companies and associations offer insurance plans.

TYPES OF INSURANCE

We begin with an overview of the types of insurance, from both a consumer and business perspective. Then we examine in greater detail the three most important types of insurance: property, liability, and life.

Public and Private Insurance

Sometimes a distinction is made between private and public insurance. Public (or social) insurance includes Social Security, Medicare, temporary disability insurance, and the like, funded through government plans. Private insurance plans, by contrast, are all types of coverage offered by private corporations or organizations. The focus of this chapter is private insurance.

Types of Insurance for the Individual

Life Insurance   Life insurance provides for your family or some named beneficiaries on your death. Two general types are available: **term insurance** provides coverage only during the term of the policy and pays off only on the insured's death; **whole life insurance** provides savings as well as insurance and can let the insured collect before death.

Health Insurance   Health insurance covers the cost of hospitalization, visits to the doctor's office, and prescription medicines. The most useful policies, provided by many employers, are those that cover 100 percent of the costs of being hospitalized and 80 percent of the charges for medicine and a doctor's services. Usually the policy will contain a $100 or $250 deductible, which means the insurer will not make payments until after the first $100 or $250 of charges.

Disability Insurance   A disability policy pays a certain percentage of an employee's wages (or a fixed sum) weekly or monthly if the employee becomes unable to work through illness or an accident. Premiums are lower the longer the waiting period before payments must be made: A policy that begins to pay a disabled worker within thirty days might cost twice as much as one that defers payment for six months. Social Security provides some insurance—about $1,000 a month—for the seriously disabled; the waiting period is about five months.

Homeowners' Insurance   A homeowner's policy provides insurance for damages or losses due to fire, theft, and other named perils. No policy routinely covers all perils. The homeowner must assess his needs by looking to the likely risks in his area—earthquake, storm, flooding, and so on. Homeowners' policies provide for reduced coverage if the property is not insured for at least 80 percent of its replacement costs. In inflationary times, this requirement means that the owner must adjust the policy limits upward each year or purchase a "rider" that automatically adjusts for inflation.

Automobile Insurance   Perhaps the most common type of insurance, automobile policies are required in at least minimum amounts in some states. The typical automobile policy covers liability for bodily injury and property damage, medical payments, damage to or loss of the car itself, and attorneys' fees in case of suit.

Other Liability   In this litigious society, a person can be sued for just about anything: a slip on the walk, a harsh and untrue word spoken in anger, an accident on the ballfield. A personal liability policy covers many types of these risks, and can give coverage in excess of that provided by homeowners' and automobile insurance. Such "umbrella" coverage is usually fairly inexpensive, perhaps $100 a year for $1 million in liability.

Types of Business Insurance

Workers' Compensation   Almost every business in every state must insure against injury to workers on the job. Some may do this through self-insurance—that is, by setting aside certain reserves for this contingency. Most smaller businesses purchase workers' compensation policies, available through commercial insurers, trade associations, or state funds.

Automobile Insurance   Any business that uses motor vehicles should maintain at least a minimum automobile insurance policy on the vehicles, covering personal injury, property damage, and general liability.

Property Insurance   No business should take a chance of leaving unprotected its buildings, permanent fixtures, machinery, inventory, and the like. Various property policies cover damage or loss to a company's own property or to property of others stored on the premises.

Business Interruption Insurance   Depending on the size of the business and its vulnerability to losses resulting from damage to essential operating equipment or other property, a company may wish to purchase insurance that will cover loss of earnings if the business operations are interrupted in some way—a strike, loss of power, loss of raw material supply, and so on.

Liability Insurance   Businesses face a host of risks that could result in substantial liabilities. Many types of policies are available, including owners', landlords', and tenants' (covering liability incurred on the premises); manufacturers' and contractors' (for liability incurred on all premises); products' and completed operations' (for liability that results from warranties on products or injuries caused by products); owners' and contractors' protective liability (for damages caused by independent contractors engaged by the insured); and contractual liability (for failure to abide by performances required by specific contracts).

Some years ago, different types of individual and business coverages had to be purchased separately and often from different companies. Today most insurance is available on a "package" basis through single policies that cover the most important risks. These are often called "multi-peril" policies.

PROPERTY INSURANCE

We turn now to a more detailed discussion of the law relating to the three most common types of insurance: property, liability, and life insurance.

Coverage

As we have just noted, property insurance provides coverage for real and personal property owned by a business or an individual. Property insurance is also part of automobile policies covering damage to the car caused by an accident ("collision" coverage) or by other events such as vandalism or fire ("comprehensive" coverage). Different levels of coverage are available. For example, many basic homeowners' policies cover damage resulting from the following types of perils only: fire and lightning, windstorm and hail, explosions, riots and civil commotions, aircraft and vehicular accidents, smoke, vandalism and malicious mischief, theft, and breakage of glass that is part of a building. A broader policy, known as "broad" coverage, also includes these perils: falling objects; weight of ice, snow, and sleet; collapse of buildings; sudden and accidental damage to heating systems; accidental discharge from plumbing, heating, or air-conditioning systems; freezing of heating, plumbing, and air-conditioning systems; and sudden and accidental injury from excess currents to electrical appliances and wiring. Even with the broadest form of coverage, known as "comprehensive," which covers all perils except for certain named exclusions, the homeowner can be left without protection—for example, comprehensive policies do not usually cover damage resulting from flooding, earthquakes, war, or nuclear radiation. The homeowner can purchase separate coverage for these perils, but usually at a steep premium.

Insurable Interest in Property

In order to purchase property insurance, the would-be insured must have an **insurable interest** in the property. Insurable interest is a real and substantial interest in specific property such that a loss to the insured would ensue if the property were damaged. You could not, for instance, take out an insurance policy on a motel down the block with which you have no connection. If a fire destroyed it, you would suffer no economic loss. But if you helped finance the motel and had an investment interest in it, you would be permitted to place an insurance policy on it. This requirement of an insurable interest stems from the public policy against wagering. If you could insure anything, you would in effect be betting on an accident.

To insure property, therefore, you must have a legal interest and run the risk of a pecuniary loss. Any legal interest is sufficient: a contractual right to purchase, for instance, or the right of possession (a bailee may insure). This insurable interest must exist both at the time you take out the policy and at the time the loss occurs. Moreover, coverage is limited to the extent of the interest. As a mortgagee, you could ensure only for the amount still due. In the next case, the question was whether a bona fide purchaser had an insurable interest in a stolen automobile.

BUTLER v. FARMERS INSURANCE CO. OF AMERICA
126 Ariz. 371, 616 P.2d 46 (1980)

HAYS, JUSTICE. This cause was submitted to the trial court upon the following stipulated facts: In 1976, plaintiff-appellant, James Butler, purchased a 1967 Austin-Healy for $3,500. Receiving an Arizona Certificate of Title pursuant to the sale, appellant was unaware that the vehicle had been previously stolen. Approximately two years after the purchase, the automobile was seized by Tucson police and returned to its lawful owner.

At all times relevant hereto, appellant was insured against loss of the vehicle by defendant-appellee, Farmers Insurance Co. of Arizona. It is the insurer's denial of appellant's claim for benefits under the policy which has given rise to the instant dispute.

Citing a lack of insurable interest, appellee declined to reimburse appellant for his loss, tendering instead "$55 to $56" as restitution for premiums paid. Appellant initiated suit, and cross-motions for summary judgment were filed. Although the trial court granted appellee's motion, the Court of Appeals reversed. Granting appellee's petition for review pursuant to A.R.S. § 12-120.24 (Supp. 1979), we vacate the opinion of the Court of Appeals and reverse the ruling of the trial court.

The facts as indicated previously reveal that appellee based its refusal to reimburse upon a lack of insurable interest. Although the question of whether a bona fide purchaser of stolen commodities may claim this relationship is one of first impression in Arizona, we note that the appellate courts of several jurisdictions have considered this issue and are in disagreement. Some courts, relying upon, *inter alia*, the inability of a seller of stolen property to transfer valid title, deny the innocent purchaser an interest of insurable quality. Other jurisdictions, however, cite principles of real property or public policy in finding the existence of the requisite relationship. Intending no disrespect to those courts holding otherwise, it is the considered opinion of this court that a bona fide purchaser of a stolen automobile has an interest sufficient to qualify as insurable.

Any analysis of the insurable interest principle in Arizona must focus initially upon the language of our statutes. The governing standard is set forth in A.R.S. § 20-1105(B):

"Insurable interest" . . . means any actual, lawful and substantial economic interest in the safety or preservation of the subject of the insurance free from loss, destruction or pecuniary damage or impairment.

We believe that the innocent purchaser of stolen property falls within this protection and reject any construction to the contrary.

Initially, examination of identical circumstances reveals that appellant's interest in conservation of the vehicle was both "lawful" and "substantial." The law is clear that a bona fide purchaser of stolen commodities inherits title defeasible by none other than the rightful owner. S/he possesses a valid legal claim to the property which will be given full force and effect in a court of law. Even as against the true owner, moreover, the innocent purchaser may, upon loss or destruction of the illicit merchandise, be held liable in tort for conversion, and therefore has an interest in maintaining the property in an undamaged condition.

In addition, the rule above-stated is not only sustained by the authorities, but is in accord with justice and common sense. Among the vices sought to be discouraged by the insurable interest requirement is the intentional destruction of the covered property in order to profit from the insurance proceeds. We believe this purpose will be furthered where the insured has a financial investment in the property and believes him or herself to be in lawful possession. We see no greater risk of illicit activity under these circumstances than where the insured is, in actuality, the rightful owner.

The opinion of the Court of Appeals is vacated, and this cause is remanded to the trial court for proceedings consistent with this opinion.

Subrogation

Subrogation is the substitution of one person for another in pursuit of a legal claim. When an insured is entitled to recover under a policy for property damage, the insurer is said to be subrogated to the insured's right to sue any third party who caused the damage. For example, a wrecking company negligently destroys an insured's home, mistaking it for the building it was hired to tear down. The insured has a cause of action against the wrecking company. If the insured chooses instead to collect against a homeowner's policy, the insurance company may sue the wrecking company in his place to recover the sum it was obligated to pay out under the policy (see Figure 36-1).

Figure 36-1 Subrogation

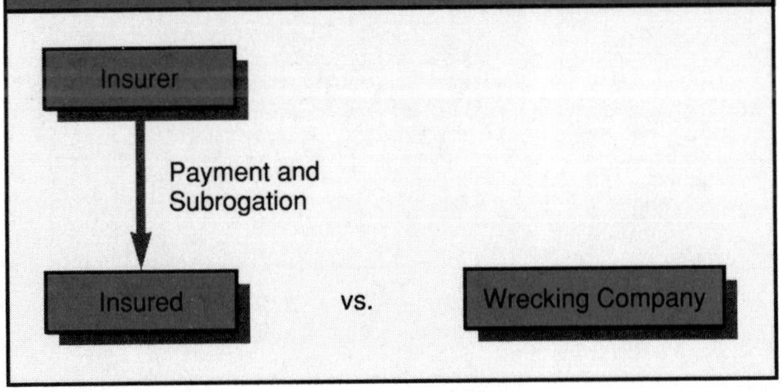

Insurer

Payment and Subrogation

Insured   vs.   Wrecking Company

Assignment

As we saw in Chapter 13, assignment is the transfer of any property right to another. In property insurance, a distinction is made between assignment of the coverage and assignment of the proceeds. Ordinarily, the insured may not assign the policy itself without the insurer's permission—that is, he may not commit the insurer to insure someone else. But the insured may assign any claims against the insurer—for example, the proceeds not yet paid out on a claim for a house that has already burned down.

Intentional Losses

Insurance is a means of spreading risk. It is economically feasible because not every house burns down, and not every car is stolen. The number that do burn down or that are stolen can be calculated and the premium set accordingly. Events that will certainly happen, like ordinary wear and tear, and destruction of property through deliberate acts such as arson, must be excluded from such calculations. The injury must result from accidental, not deliberate causes.

Coinsurance Clause

Most commercial property policies contain a so-called **coinsurance clause,** which requires the insured to maintain insurance equal to a specified percentage of the property value. It is often 80 percent, but may be higher or lower. If the property owner insures for less than that percentage, the recovery will be reduced. In effect, the owner becomes a coinsurer with the insurance company. The usual formula establishes the proportion that the insurer must pay by calculating the ratio of (1) the amount of insurance actually taken to (2) the coinsurance percentage multiplied by the total dollar value of the property. Suppose a fire causes $16,000 damage to a plant worth $100,000. The plant should have been insured for 80 percent ($80,000), but the insured took out only a $50,000 policy. He will recover only $10,000. To see why, multiply the total damages of $16,000 by the coinsurance proportion of five-eighths (total dollar value of $100,000 multiplied by the coinsurance percentage of 80 percent equals $80,000; when divided into the policy amount of $50,000, the resulting ratio is five-eighths).

LIABILITY INSURANCE

Liability insurance has taken on great importance for both the individual and business in contemporary society. Liability insurance covers specific types of legal liabilities that a homeowner, driver, professional, business executive, or business itself might incur in the round of daily activities. A business is always at risk in sending products into the marketplace. A doctor, accountant, real estate broker, insurance agent, or lawyer should obtain liability insurance to cover the risk of being sued for malpractice. A prudent homeowner will acquire liability insurance as part of a homeowner's policy, and a supplemental "umbrella" policy that insures for liability in excess of a limit of, say, $50,000 in the regular homeowner's policy. And businesses, professionals, and individuals typically acquire liability insurance for driving-related activities as part of their automobile insurance. In all cases, liability policies cover not only any settlement or award that might ultimately have to be paid, but also the cost of lawyers and related expenses in defending any claims.

Liability insurance is similar in several respects to property insurance and is often part of the same package policy. As with property insurance, subrogation is allowed with liability insurance, but assignment of the policy is not allowed (unless permission of the insurer is obtained), and intentional losses are not covered. For example, an accountant who willfully helps a client conceal fraud will not recover from his malpractice insurance policy if he is found guilty of participating in the fraud. In the following case, the court was presented with the question whether an act of self-defense that results in injury is covered by a typical homeowner's policy.

STATE FARM v. MARSHALL
554 So.2d 504 (Fla. 1989)

PER CURIAM.

This case presents the issue of whether an intentional act exclusion in a liability insurance policy excludes coverage for an act of self-defense where the insured intends to harm the attacker. We conclude that it does.

Marshall was renting the master bedroom in the home of his ex-wife, Carolyn, when he was awakened by someone pounding on his bedroom windows. He and Carolyn went to the door and saw Carolyn's son, Bailey. It was Marshall's testimony that Bailey broke a window, came in through the opening, and advanced on him wildly swinging his fists. Fearing for his life, Marshall tried to discourage Bailey by holding up a wooden club; failing in his effort, he got his semiautomatic pistol from the bedroom and threatened Bailey by firing a warning shot. When Bailey continued to advance, he placed the gun flat in the palm of his hand, with his finger away from the trigger, and struck Bailey.

The gun discharged injuring Bailey, who filed suit alleging that Marshall "did negligently discharge the aforesaid firearm," or in the alternative, that he "did intentionally shoot the Plaintiff with the intent of inflicting grievous harm." State Farm filed a separate petition for declaratory relief against Marshall and Bailey to determine its obligations under Marshall's homeowner's policy, which contained the following provision:

SECTION II—EXCLUSIONS
1. Coverage L [personal liability] and Coverage M [medical payments to others] do not apply to:
   a. bodily injury or property damage which is expected or intended by an insured. . . .

State Farm contended that because Bailey's complaint alleged that the shooting was intentional, State Farm had no duty to defend or indemnify Marshall in the action. Marshall countered by asserting that the shooting was done in self-defense. The trial court entered final summary judgment in favor of State Farm. The district court reversed, holding that an intentional act exclusion does not constitute a bar to liability coverage for an act of self-defense, and that State Farm thus was obligated to defend Marshall.

State Farm petitioned for review. . . . While the present declaratory judgment action was pending, State Farm defended Marshall under a reservation of rights. The jury found that Marshall had committed an intentional assault or battery on Bailey and that Marshall's actions were not "a reasonable use of force to prevent imminent death or great bodily harm to himself." Consistent with the jury's verdict, the trial court ordered that Bailey recover $200,000 in compensatory damages and $375,000 in punitive damages.

In the present proceeding, Marshall concedes that intentional acts are excluded from coverage under his policy and that he intended to harm his assailant, but he contends that public policy supports coverage because he

(continued on next page)

(continued)

**STATE FARM v.
MARSHALL**
554 So.2d 504 (Fla. 1989)

was acting in self-defense. We disagree. Courts have pointed out that the purpose underlying the intentional act exclusion is twofold. First, insurance companies set rates based on the random occurrence of insured events; if an insured is allowed to consciously control the occurrence of these events through the commission of intentional acts, the principle is undercut. Second, indemnification for intentional acts would stimulate persons to commit wrongful acts. Courts favoring coverage conclude that neither of these reasons apply where self-defense is concerned, since acts of self-defense are not the type of deliberate act that one would consciously undertake based on insurance coverage and such acts are not wrongful. These courts also express a concern that if the exclusion embraces self-defense, liability coverage is nonexistent for the homeowner defending his home and family, because an intentional act exclusion is present in practically every policy and is nonnegotiable.

Marshall claims that the public policy promoting self-defense is evidenced by section 776.012, Florida Statutes (1987), which authorizes the use of force in defense of one's person under certain circumstances. This argument is unpersuasive. The intent underlying an act of self-defense where the defender intends to harm the attacker is identical to that underlying an assault. In each, the actor intends to inflict harm on the other. Just as assault is often impulsive or reactive, so too is self-defense. The difference between the two lies in the motive or purpose governing the act; the motive for one is worthy, that for the other is not. Nevertheless, such acts of self-defense are undeniably intentional and have been held to be embraced within intentional act exclusions by a majority of courts.

We align ourselves with the majority of jurisdictions, which hold that self-defense is not an exception to the intentional acts exclusion and the clear terms of the policy control. In such cases, the sanctity of the parties to freely contract prevails. Members of the public may wish to insure themselves against liability incurred while lawfully defending themselves, but they must bargain for such coverage and pay for it. We will not rewrite a policy under these circumstances to provide coverage where the clear language of the policy does not; nor will we invoke public policy to override this otherwise valid contract. We quash the decision of the district court below.

It is so ordered.

No-Fault Trends

The major legal development of the century relating to liability insurance has been the elimination of liability in the two areas of greatest exposure: in the workplace and on the highway. In the next unit on agency law, we discuss the no-fault system of worker's compensation, under which a worker receives automatic benefits for workplace injuries and gives up the right to sue the employer under common law theories of liability. Here we will look briefly at the other major type of no-fault system: accidents on the highway.

"No-fault" means that recovery for damages in an accident no longer depends on who was at fault in causing it. A motorist will file a claim to recover his actual damages (medical expenses, income loss) directly from his own insurer. The no-fault system dispenses with the costly and uncertain tort system of having to prove negligence in court. Many states have adopted one form or another of no-fault automobile insurance, but even in these states the car owner must still carry other insurance. Some no-fault systems have a dollar "threshold" above which a victim may sue for medical expenses or other losses. Other states use a "verbal threshold," which permits suits for "serious" injury, defined variously as "disfigurement," "fracture," or "permanent disability." These thresholds have prevented no-fault from working as efficiently as theory predicts. Inflation has reduced the power of dollar thresholds (in some states as low as $200) to deter lawsuits, and the verbal thresholds have standards that can only be defined in court, so much litigation continues.

No state has adopted a "pure" no-fault system. A "pure" no-fault system trades away entirely the right to sue in return for the prompt payment of "first-party" insurance benefits—that is, payment by the victim's own insurance company, instead of traditional "third-party" coverage, in which the victim collects from the defendant's insurance company.

Among the criticisms of no-fault insurance is the argument that it fails to strengthen the central purpose of the tort system: to deter unsafe conduct that causes accidents. No-fault lessens, it is said, the incentive to avoid accidents (see Posner, 1973, p. 86). In any event, no-fault automobile insurance has been a major development in the insurance field since 1970 and seems destined to be a permanent fixture of insurance law.

LIFE INSURANCE

Insurable Interest

The two types of life insurance mentioned above, term and whole life policies, are important both to individuals and businesses (key employee insurance). As with property insurance, whoever takes out a life insurance policy on a person's life must have an insurable interest. Everyone has an insurable interest in his own life, and may name whomever he pleases as beneficiary; the beneficiary need not have an insurable interest. But the requirement of insurable interest restricts those who may take out insurance on someone else's life. A spouse or children have an insurable interest in a spouse or parent. Likewise, a parent has an insurable interest in any minor child. That means

that a wife, for example, may take out a life insurance policy on her husband without his consent. But she could not take out a policy on a friend or neighbor. As long as the insurable interest existed when the policy was taken out, the owner may recover when the insured dies, even if the insurable interest no longer exists. Thus a divorced wife who was married when the policy was obtained may collect when her ex-husband dies as long as she maintained the payments. Likewise, an employer has an insurable interest in his key employees and partners; such insurance policies help to pay off claims of a partner's estate and thus prevent liquidation of the business.

Subrogation

Unlike property insurance, in life insurance no subrogation is permitted. The insurer must pay the claim when the insured dies, and may not step into the shoes of anyone entitled to file a wrongful death claim against a person who caused the death. Of course, if the insured died of natural causes there would be no one to sue anyway.

Change of Beneficiary and Assignment

Unless the insured reserves the right to change beneficiaries, his initial designation is irrevocable. These days, however, most policies do reserve the right if certain formalities are observed, including written instructions to the insurer's home office to make the change and endorsement of the policy. The insured may assign the policy, but the beneficiary has priority to collect over the assignee if the right to change beneficiaries has not been reserved. If the policy permits beneficiaries to be changed, then the assignee will have priority over the original beneficiary.

Intentional Losses

Two types of intentional losses are especially important in life insurance: suicide and murder of the insured by the beneficiary.

Suicide   In a majority of states, in the absence of a suicide clause in the policy, when an insured commits suicide the insurer need not pay out if the policy is payable to the insured's estate. However, if the policy is payable to a third person (his company, for instance), payment will usually be allowed. And if an insured kills himself while insane, all states require payment, whether to the estate or a third party. Most life insurance policies today have a provision that explicitly excepts suicide from coverage for a limited period, such as two years, after the policy is issued. In other words, if the insured commits suicide within the first two years, the insurer will refund the premiums to his estate but will not pay the policy amount. After two years, suicide is treated as any other death would be.

Murder   Under the law in every state, a beneficiary who kills the insured in order to collect the life insur-ance is barred from receiving it. But the invocation of that rule does not absolve the insurer of liability to pay the policy amount. An alternate beneficiary must be found. Sometimes the policy will name contingent beneficiaries, and many but not all states require the insurer to pay the contingent beneficiaries. When there are no contingent beneficiaries, or the state law prohibits paying them, the insurer will pay the insured's estate. Not every killing is murder; the critical question is whether the beneficiary intended his conduct to eliminate the insured in order to collect the insurance. Interpreting that conduct was the question posed in the following case, in which a wife unquestionably killed her husband but was allowed to collect on the policy nevertheless.

CALAWAY v. SOUTHERN FARM BUREAU LIFE INSURANCE CO.
619 S.W.2d 301
(Ct.App. Ark. 1981)

CLONINGER, JUDGE. This is an interpleader action filed by Southern Farm Bureau Life Insurance Company, the insurer, in which the proceeds of a life insurance policy in the sum of $48,409.78 have been paid into court. The insured, Walter Calaway, Jr., was shot and killed by his wife, the appellee, Rose Marie Calaway, the primary beneficiary under the policy, and it is the contention of the appellant, Beatrice Calaway, the mother of the insured and contingent beneficiary under the policy, that the killing was under such circumstances as would disqualify appellee as beneficiary.

This appeal is from a finding by the trial court that the killing was justified and that appellee is entitled to the proceeds due under the policy. The only issue on this appeal is whether the findings of the trial court were clearly against the preponderance of the evidence.

The trial court was correct and we affirm.

At about 12:30 a.m., September 25, 1977, decedent arrived at his home, intoxicated, and he continued to drink beer until 4:30 a.m., at which time the fatal shooting occurred. During the intervening four hours, decedent alternatively talked angrily about his parents, drank beer, and threatened, slapped, choked and kicked appellee. For a period of some fifteen minutes decedent played with a loaded .44 caliber pistol, pointing it at appellee and inquiring whether she was scared of it. Shortly after 4:00 a.m. decedent staggered from the dining room to the bedroom, then returned to the dining room door and told appellee to bring the gun to him. Decedent returned to the bedroom, lay across the bed, and had propped up his head on one elbow; appellee just stood by the bed, holding the gun. Her ankle had been broken, and she was told to stop limping, and there was nothing wrong with her. Appellee testified that decedent then told her that she just didn't look bad enough; that he was going to pistol whip her and might as well kill her. Appellee stated that decedent was in the process of getting up when appellee closed her eyes, lifted the gun, and pulled the trigger. It is undisputed that appellee fired the shot, and that the shot was the cause of death. Appellee said she always did what decedent told her to do; that if she had disobeyed him or left the house he would have found her then or at a later time and would probably have killed her.

During the trouble the couple's two children, ages 2 and 1, awoke and stood at the bedroom door crying. Decedent told the children that if they didn't shut up he would whip them. Appellee put the children back to bed, and she stated that she was afraid to leave the children in the house with decedent, and that in her injured condition she could not take them with her.

Appellee testified that decedent had beaten her severely many times upon previous occasions, and that she was afraid of him. She stated: "I would not tell him it would hurt, he would just hit harder. Walter was the type of person that when he was drinking that if you didn't do what he said when he said it then it was just too bad. He would light into me and just start hitting me with his fist and slapping me and kicking me, and this wasn't just this time, it was years—years of it I mean—the time he shot my cat and shot the hole in the kitchen—I mean that he would do things like that when he was drunk. I was always required to do exactly what he said . . ."

Following the incident, appellee was in the hospital eight days. Her injuries, medically verified, included fractures to her ankle, upper leg and jaw, swollen eyes, bruises on the face, arms, back, and throat.

In Couch on Insurance 2d, § 27:154 (1960), it is stated that a beneficiary who kills the insured under such circumstances that the act is justifiable, excusable, or lawfully committed in self defense, or under such circumstances that he has no criminal responsibility for his acts, is not barred from receiving the proceeds of the policy. Thus, the beneficiary is entitled to recover when he killed the insured while acting in self defense.

It is settled law in Arkansas that when the beneficiary in a policy of life insurance wrongfully kills the insured, public policy prohibits a recovery by the beneficiary. In the case of *Metropolitan Life Insurance Company* v. *Shane*, 98 Ark. 132, 135 S.W. 836 (1911), the Court said:

> The willful, unlawful and felonious killing of the assured by the person named as beneficiary in a life policy forfeits all rights of such person therein. It is unnecessary that there should be an express exception in the contract of insurance forbidding a recovery in favor of such person in such event. On considerations of public policy the death of the insured, willfully and intentionally caused by the beneficiary of the policy, is an excepted risk so far as the person thus causing the death is concerned.

A case almost directly in point with the case at bar is *Pendergrass et al. v. New York Life Insurance Company*, 181 F.2d 136 (1950), in which the United

(continued on next page)

(continued)

**CALAWAY v.
SOUTHERN FARM
BUREAU LIFE
INSURANCE CO.**
**619 S.W.2d 301
(Ct.App. Ark. 1981)**

States Court of Appeals, 8th Circuit, in applying Arkansas law, found the homicide to be justifiable, and stated:

> At this time the deceased was violent and abusive to cross-defendant. When in the bedroom the deceased struggled with the cross-defendant and attempted to choke her. She extricated herself from his hold and flung her body across his in an attempt to hold him on the bed. The deceased threw the cross-defendant to the floor. At that time she had an urge to run but the deceased, with an oath, then demanded his gun. The cross-defendant impulsively began to execute his command as she had done many times before. Just as the cross-defendant was handing the gun to deceased, the latter, with an oath, threatened to 'kill' or 'get' the cross-defendant. He made this threat as he was arising from the bed, and at that moment the cross-defendant pulled the trigger.

*   *   *

The trial court found, and we hold, that appellee had justification to reasonably believe that decedent was about to commit a felony involving force of violence or was about to use unlawful deadly physical force.

The decision of the trial judge is affirmed.

INSURER'S DEFENSES

Types of Defenses

It is a common perception that because insurance contracts are so complex, many insureds who believe they are covered end up with uninsured losses. In other words, the large print giveth, the small print taketh away. This perception is founded, to some extent, on the use by insurance companies of three common defenses, all of which relate to a duty of good faith on the part of the insured: (1) *representations*, (2) *concealment*, and (3) *warranties*.

Representations   A **representation** is a statement made by someone seeking an insurance policy—for example, a statement that the applicant did (or did not) consult a doctor for any illness during the previous five years. An insurer has grounds to avoid the

contract if the applicant makes a false representation. The misrepresentation must have been material; that is, a false description of a person's hair coloring should not defeat a claim under an automobile accident policy. But a false statement, even if innocent, about a material fact—for instance, that no one in the family uses the car to go to work, when unbeknownst to the applicant, his wife uses the car to commute to a part-time job she hasn't told him about—will at the insurer's option defeat a claim by the insured to collect under the policy. The accident need not have arisen out of the misrepresentation to defeat the claim. In the example given, the insurance company could refuse to pay a claim for any accident in the car, even one occurring when the car was driven by the husband to go to the movies, if the insurer discovered that the car was used in a manner in which the insured had declared it was not used. The following case illustrates what happens when an insured misrepresents his smoking habits.

MUTUAL BEN. LIFE INS. CO. v. JMR ELECTRONICS CORP.
848 F.2d 30
(2nd Cir. 1988)

PER CURIAM:

JMR Electronics Corporation ("JMR") appeals from a judgment of the District Court for the Southern District of New York (Robert W. Sweet, Judge) ordering recission of a life insurance policy issued by plaintiff-appellant The Mutual Benefit Life Insurance Company ("Mutual") and dismissing JMR's counterclaim for the policy's proceeds. Judge Sweet ruled that a misrepresentation made in the policy application concerning the insured's history of cigarette smoking was material as a matter of law. Appellant contends that the misrepresentation was not material because Mutual would have provided insurance—albeit at a higher premium rate—even if the insured's smoking history had been disclosed. We agree with the District Court that summary judgment was appropriate and therefore affirm.

The basic facts are not in dispute. On June 24, 1985, JMR submitted an application to Mutual for a $250,000 "key man" life insurance policy on the life of its president, Joseph Gaon, at the non-smoker's discounted premium rate. Mutual's 1985 Ratebook provides: "The Non-Smoker rates are available when the proposed insured is at least 20 years old and has not smoked a cigarette for at least twelve months prior to the date of the application." Question 13 of the application inquired about the proposed insured's smoking history. Question 13(a) asked, "Do you smoke cigarettes? How many a day?" Gaon answered this question, "No." Question 13(b) asked, "Did you ever smoke cigarettes?" Gaon again answered, "No." Based on these representations, Mutual issued a policy on Gaon's life at the non-smoker premium rate.

Gaon died on June 22, 1986, within the period of contestability contained in the policy. Upon routine investigation of JMR's claim for proceeds under the policy, Mutual discovered that the representations made in the insurance application concerning Gaon's smoking history were untrue. JMR has stipulated that, at the time the application was submitted, Gaon in fact "had been smoking one-half of a pack of cigarettes per day for a continuous period of not less than 10 years." Mutual brought this action seeking a declaration that the policy is void. Judge Sweet granted Mutual's motion for summary judgment, dismissed JMR's counterclaim for the proceeds of the policy, and ordered recission of the insurance policy and return of JMR's premium payments, with interest.

Under New York law, which governs this diversity suit, "[i]t is the rule that even an innocent misrepresentation as to [the applicant's medical history], if material, is sufficient to allow the insurer to avoid the contract of insurance or defeat recovery thereunder." *Process Plants Corp. v. Beneficial National Life Insurance Co.*, 366 N.E.2d 1361 (1977). A "misrepresentation" is defined by statute as a false "statement as to past or present fact, made to the insurer . . . at or before the making of the insurance contract as an inducement to the making thereof." N.Y. Ins. Law § 3105(a) (McKinney 1985). A misrepresentation is "material" if "knowledge by the insurer of the

(*continued*)

(continued)

MUTUAL BEN. LIFE INS. CO. v. JMR ELECTRONICS CORP. 848 F.2d 30 (2nd Cir. 1988)

facts misrepresented would have led to a refusal by the insurer to make such contract." *Id.* § 3105(b). . . .

In the present case JMR has stipulated that Gaon's smoking history was misrepresented in the insurance application. However, JMR disputes that this misrepresentation is material as a matter of law. JMR argues that under New York law a misrepresentation is not material unless the insurer can demonstrate that, had the applicant provided complete and accurate information, coverage either would have been refused or at the very least withheld pending a more detailed underwriting examination. In JMR's view summary judgment was inappropriate on the facts of this case because a jury could reasonably have found that even "had appellee been aware of Gaon's smoking history, a policy at the smoker's premium rate would have been issued." JMR takes the position that the appropriate remedy in this situation is to permit recovery under the policy in the amount that the premium actually paid would have purchased for a smoker.

We agree with Judge Sweet that this novel theory is without basis in New York law. The plain language of the statutory definition of "materiality," found in section 3105(b), permits avoidance of liability under the policy where "knowledge of . . . the facts misrepresented would have led to a refusal by the insurer to make *such contract*." (Emphasis added). Moreover, numerous courts have observed that the materiality inquiry under New York law is made with respect to the particular policy issued in reliance upon the misrepresentation.

★　　★　　★

There is no doubt that Mutual was induced to issue the non-smoker, discounted-premium policy to JMR precisely as a result of the misrepresentations made by Gaon concerning his smoking history. That Mutual might not have refused the risk on *any* terms had it known the undisclosed facts is irrelevant. Most risks are insurable at some price. The purpose of the materiality inquiry is not to permit the jury to rewrite the terms of the insurance agreement to conform to the newly disclosed facts but to make certain that the risk insured was the risk covered by the policy agreed upon. If a fact is material to the risk, the insurer may avoid liability under a policy if that fact was misrepresented in an application for that policy whether or not the parties might have agreed to some other contractual arrangement had the critical fact been disclosed. As observed by Judge Sweet, a contrary result would reward the practice of misrepresenting facts critical to the underwriter's task because the unscrupulous (or merely negligent) applicant "would have everything to gain and nothing to lose" from making material misrepresentations in his application for insurance. Such a claimant could rest assured not only that he may demand full coverage should he survive the contestability period, but that even in the event of a contested claim, he would be entitled to the coverage that he might have contracted for had the necessary information been accurately disclosed at the outset. New York law does not permit this anomalous result. The judgment of the District Court is affirmed.

LAW AND LIFE

BOX 36-1

New Court Rulings That Raise the Risks for Insurers

[Insurance companies acting in bad faith by denying claims that they know should be paid are facing substantial punitive damage liability in court. Jurors are awarding plaintiffs outrageous sums of money with the intent to "punish" the insurance company, not just compensate the plaintiff.—AUTHORS' NOTE]

During the winter of 1981, Curtis Simmerley, a 36-year-old San Francisco accountant, suffered kidney failure and a stroke. It was then, when he needed it most, that Prudential Insurance Co. canceled his health coverage after paying out $10,000, a small portion of his hospital bill. Simmerley sued, charging that the company had acted in bad faith. Prudential denies that it deliberately refused Simmerley's valid claims. But faced with the lawsuit, Prudential decided in May to pay a $750,000 out-of-court settlement rather than take its chances before a jury.

More and more insurance companies are making that expensive decision these days. Settlements are becoming increasingly attractive as courts order insurers to pay punitive damages. In the 1970s, California courts began to change the law with a series of rulings against insurance companies. Since then more than 20 states have followed California's ex-

INSURERS AND PUNITIVE DAMAGES

ample and subjected carriers to suits for staggering sums. Across the country, jury verdicts are larger than ever. "It's hitting everybody—homeowner's, collision, medical, life—the whole business is getting clobbered," says Guy O. Kornblum, a San Francisco lawyer who represents insurance companies.

Insurance had always been viewed by the courts as a simple contract relationship. If there was a dispute about benefits, policyholders could generally get what was promised to them, but nothing more. The California courts, which often set the pace for other states, were not satisfied with the old approach. Because of the special nature of insurance, they decided to extend the remedies available in law suits against insurers. They said an insurance company that breaches its duty to deal fairly with a customer should be forced to pay damages intended to punish in addition to damages calculated merely to compensate for losses. Punitive awards have no upper limit and are likely to be measured as much by how angry the evidence makes a jury as by any other standard.

*   *   *

What insurance companies have gone through, in part, is an assault on their files by lawyers for disgruntled consumers. The punitive-damage

suits are alarming not only because of potential damage awards but also because they give policyholders the powerful weapon of court-ordered discovery. Poking around in defendants' records, some lawyers have dredged up evidence of the kind of behind-the-scenes callousness that can turn jurors into cheerleaders for plaintiffs. Although the industry insists that improper denials are rare, it must now endure the double whammy of negative publicity and multimillion-dollar verdicts.

In March, for example, a California jury awarded a Los Angeles woman, Mary Frazier, $8 million in a suit against Metropolitan Life Insurance Co. After Frazier's husband fell or jumped off a fishing boat and drowned, the company refused to pay on a $12,000 accidental-death policy that was in force at the time. The company claimed that the death was a suicide. Frazier sued, saying her husband died as a result of an accident.

Key to the case was a set of internal memos that showed how Metropolitan evaluated the claim. "While there is considerable opinion that he did commit suicide," wrote a claims agent, "I still doubt that we could sustain a denial [of benefits] in court." The agent suggested in a notation to his supervisor: "Unless you want to deny now and try for a compromise later when she complains." The supervisor's terse answer: "Deny. Refer any protest."

Source: *Business Week*, August 15, 1983

Concealment An insured is obligated to volunteer to the insurer all material facts that bear on insurability. The failure of an insured to set forth such information is a **concealment,** which is, in effect, the mirror image of a false representation. But the insured must have had a fraudulent intent to conceal the material facts. If he was ignorant of them—for instance, if he did not know that gasoline was stored in the basement—the insurer may not refuse to pay out on a fire insurance policy.

Warranties   Many insurance policies covering commercial property will contain warranties—for example, that the insured bank has installed or will install a particular type of burglar alarm system. Until recently, the rule was strictly enforced that any breach of a warranty voided the contract, even if the breach was not material—for example, the bank obtained the alarm system from a manufacturer other than the one specified, even though the alarm systems are identical. In recent years, courts or legislatures have relaxed the application of this rule. But a material breach still remains absolute grounds for the insurer to avoid the contract and refuse to pay.

Incontestable Clause

In life insurance cases, these defenses often are unavailable to the insurer because of the so-called **incontestable clause.** This states that if the insured has not died during a specified period of time in which the life insurance policy has been in effect (usually two years), then the insurer may not refuse to pay even if it is later discovered that the insured committed fraud in applying for the policy. Few nonlife policies contain an incontestable clause; it is used in life insurance because the effect on many families would be catastrophic if the insurer claimed misrepresentations or concealments that would be difficult to disprove years later when the insured himself would no longer be available to give testimony about his intentions or knowledge.

Requirement of Insurer's Good Faith

Like the insured, the insurer must act in good faith. Thus defenses may be unavailable to an insurer who has waived them or acted in such a manner as to create an estoppel. Suppose that when an insured seeks to increase his life insurance policy amount the insurance company learns that he has lied about his age on his original application. Nevertheless, the company accepts his application for an increase. The insured then dies and the insurer refuses to pay his wife any sum. A court would hold that the insurer had waived

its right to object, since it could have cancelled the policy when it learned of the misrepresentation. Moreover, an insurer that acts in bad faith by denying a claim that it knows it should pay may find itself open to substantial punitive damage liability, as suggested in **Box 36-1.**

CHAPTER SUMMARY

Insurance is an inescapable cost of doing business in a modern economy and an important service for any individual with dependents or even a modest amount of property. Most readers of this book will someday purchase automobile, homeowners', and life insurance, and many readers will deal with insurance in the course of a business career.

Most insurance questions are governed by contract law, since virtually all insurance is voluntary and entered into through written agreements. This means that the insured must pay careful attention to the wording of the policies to determine what is excluded from coverage and to ensure that he makes no warranties that he cannot keep and no misrepresentations or concealments that will void the contract. But beyond contract law, some insurance law principles—such as insurable interest and subrogation rights—are important to bear in mind. Defenses available to an insurance company may be based upon representations, concealment, or warranties, but an insurer that is over-zealous in denying coverage may find itself subject to punitive damages.

KEY TERMS

Coinsurance clause	p. 802	Perils	p. 797
Concealment	p. 811	Policy	p. 797
Incontestable clause	p. 812	Premium	p. 797
Insurance	p. 797	Representation	p. 808
Insurable interest	p. 799	Risks	p. 797
Insured	p. 797	Term insurance	p. 798
Insurer	p. 797	Whole life insurance	p. 798

SELF-TEST QUESTIONS

1. The substitution of one person for another in pursuit of a legal claim is called:
   (a)   assignment
   (b)   coinsurance
   (c)   subrogation
   (d)   none of the above
2. Most insurance questions are covered by:
   (a)   tort law
   (b)   criminal law

(c)   constitutional law

(d)   contract law

3. Common defenses used by insurance companies include:

(a)   concealment

(b)   false representation

(c)   breach of warranty

(d)   all of the above

4. A coinsurance clause:

(a)   requires the insured to be insured by more than one policy

(b)   requires the insured to maintain insurance equal to a certain percentage of the property's value

(c)   allows another beneficiary to be substituted for the insured

(d)   is none of the above

5. Property insurance typically covers:

(a)   ordinary wear and tear

(b)   damage due to theft

(c)   intentional losses

(d)   damage due to earthquakes

DEMONSTRATION PROBLEM

Myron owned a factory worth $100,000, which was covered by a $60,000 insurance policy with an 80 percent coinsurance clause. A fire caused $60,000 in damage to the factory. How much can Myron collect under his policy? Why?

PROBLEMS

1. Martin and Williams, two business partners, agreed that each would insure his life for the benefit of the other. On his application for insurance, Martin stated that he had never had any heart trouble when, in fact, he had had a mild heart attack some years before. Martin's policy contained a two year incontestability clause. Three years later, after the partnership had been dissolved but while the policy was still in force, Martin's car was struck by a car being negligently driven by Peters. Although Martin's injuries were superficial, he suffered a fatal heart attack immediately after the accident which, it was established, was caused by the excitement. The insurer has refused to pay the policy proceeds to Williams. Does the insurer have a valid defense based on Martin's misrepresentation? Explain.

2. In problem 1, was it necessary for Williams to have an insurable interest in Martin's life to recover under the policy? Why?

3. In problem 1, if Williams had taken out the policy rather than Martin, could the insurer defend the claim on the ground that, at the time of Martin's death, Williams had no insurable interest? Why?

4. If Williams had no insurable interest, would the incontestability clause prevent the company from asserting this defense? Why?

5. If the insurer pays Williams's claim, may it recover from Peters? Why?

6. Skidmore Trucking Company decided to expand its operations into the warehousing field. After examining several available properties it decided to purchase a carbarn for $100,000 from a local bus company and to convert it into a warehouse. The standard real estate purchase contract was signed by the parties. The contract obligated Skidmore to pay the seller on an apportioned basis for the prepaid premiums on the existing fire insurance policy ($100,000 extended coverage). The policy expired two years and one month from the closing date. At the closing the seller duly assigned the fire insurance policy to Skidmore in return for the payment of the apportioned amount of the prepaid premiums; but Skidmore failed to notify the insurance company of the change in ownership. Skidmore took possession of the premises and after extensive renovation began to use the building as a warehouse. Soon afterward one of Skidmore's employees negligently dropped a lighted cigarette into a trash basket and started a fire which totally destroyed the building. Was the assignment of the policy to Skidmore valid? Why?

7. In problem 6, assuming the assignment is valid, would the insurer be obligated to pay for the loss resulting from the employee's negligence? Why?

ANSWERS TO SELF-TEST QUESTIONS

1. (c)   2. (d)   3. (d)   4. (b)   5. (b)

SUGGESTED ANSWER TO DEMONSTRATION PROBLEM

Myron can collect $45,000, using the standard formula on text p. 802. The damage figure of $60,000 is multiplied by the coinsurance proportion of three-fourths (total dollar value of $100,000 multiplied by the coinsurance percentage of 80 percent equals $80,000; when divided into the policy amount of $60,000, the resulting ratio is 3/4).

Part 6

THE MANAGER'S LEGAL AGENDA

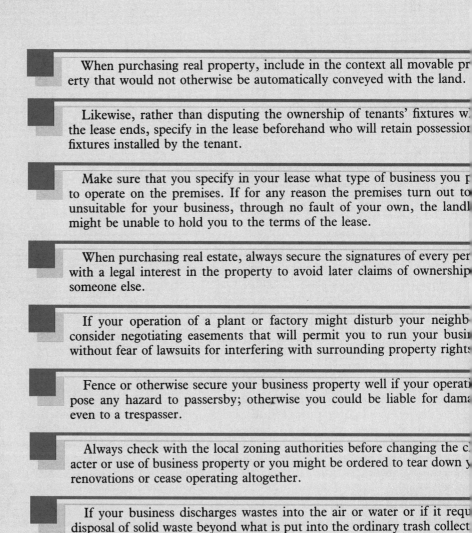

When purchasing real property, include in the context all movable pr[operty] that would not otherwise be automatically conveyed with the land.

Likewise, rather than disputing the ownership of tenants' fixtures w[hen] the lease ends, specify in the lease beforehand who will retain possessio[n of] fixtures installed by the tenant.

Make sure that you specify in your lease what type of business you p[lan] to operate on the premises. If for any reason the premises turn out to [be] unsuitable for your business, through no fault of your own, the landl[ord] might be unable to hold you to the terms of the lease.

When purchasing real estate, always secure the signatures of every per[son] with a legal interest in the property to avoid later claims of ownership [by] someone else.

If your operation of a plant or factory might disturb your neighb[ors,] consider negotiating easements that will permit you to run your busi[ness] without fear of lawsuits for interfering with surrounding property right[s.]

Fence or otherwise secure your business property well if your operati[ons] pose any hazard to passersby; otherwise you could be liable for dam[age] even to a trespasser.

Always check with the local zoning authorities before changing the c[har]acter or use of business property or you might be ordered to tear down y[our] renovations or cease operating altogether.

If your business discharges wastes into the air or water or if it requ[ires] disposal of solid waste beyond what is put into the ordinary trash collect[ion,] seek specialized advice about the environmental laws. Both federal and s[tate] authorities can levy significant fines and take other actions against violat[ors] even if the violators are inadvertent.

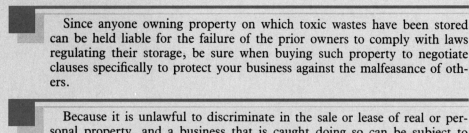

Since anyone owning property on which toxic wastes have been stored can be held liable for the failure of the prior owners to comply with laws regulating their storage, be sure when buying such property to negotiate clauses specifically to protect your business against the malfeasance of others.

Because it is unlawful to discriminate in the sale or lease of real or personal property, and a business that is caught doing so can be subject to heavy fines and damages, you should institute non-discrimination policies, train your employees, and monitor their performance to ensure that they are complying with your policies and the law.

Exchanging a deed to real property for the purchase price is not enough to guarantee legal title to the land. You should always promptly record your deed in the appropriate Recorder's Office or Register of Deeds.

When purchasing a lot, check the boundaries described in the deed to ensure that adjacent owners are not adversely possessing parts of your property. If you ignore their use for too long, you could lose that portion of your property.

Although the types and extent of insurance coverage are more a financial than a legal decision, insurance contracts demand a close reading before you sign, to avoid unintentional exclusions from coverage. But bear in mind that not every act of a company or its employees is insurable and that the business does not have an insurable interest in every employee.

Relationships Between Principal and Agent

INTRODUCTION

*A*n **agent** is a person who acts in the name of another, having been given and assumed some degree of authority to do so. Most organized human activity—and virtually all commercial activity—is carried on through agency. No corporation would be possible, even in theory, without such a concept. Likewise, partnerships and other business organizations rely extensively on agents to conduct their business. Indeed, it is not an exaggeration to say that agency is the cornerstone of enterprise organization. In a partnership (Part Eight) each partner is a general agent, while under corporation law (Part Nine) the officers and all employees are agents of the corporation.

The existence of agents does not, however, require a whole new law of torts or contracts. A tort is no less harmful for being committed by an agent; a contract is no less meant to be binding for having been negotiated by an agent. What does need to be taken into account, though, is the manner in which

an agent acts on behalf of his principal and toward a third party.

Consider John Alden, one of the most famous agents in American literature. His task, celebrated in Henry Wadsworth Longfellow's "The Courtship of Miles Standish," was to woo Priscilla, "the loveliest maiden of Plymouth," on behalf of Captain Miles Standish, a valiant soldier who grew weak at the thought of proposing marriage. Standish turned to John Alden, his young and eloquent protégé, and beseeched him to speak on his behalf, not knowing that Alden himself was madly in love with Priscilla. Alden accepted his Captain's assignment, despite the knowledge that he would thus lose Priscilla for himself, and sought the lady out. But Alden was so tongue-tied that his vaunted eloquence fell short, turned Priscilla cold toward the object of Alden's mission, and eventually led her to turn the tables in one of the most famous lines in American poetry: "Why don't you speak for yourself, John?"

Let us analyze this sequence of events in legal terms—recognizing, of course, that this example is an analogy and that the law, even today, would not impose consequences on Alden for his failure to carry out Captain Standish's wishes. Alden was the captain's agent: he was specifically authorized to speak in his name, in a manner agreed on, toward a specified end, and he accepted the assignment in consideration of the captain's friendship. He had, however, a conflict of interest. He attempted to carry out the assignment, but he did not perform according to expectations. Eventually, he wound up with the prize himself. Here are some questions to consider, the same questions that will recur throughout the discussion of agency:

1. How extensive was John's authority? Could he have made promises to Priscilla on the captain's behalf—for example, that Standish would have built her a fine house?
2. Could he have, through a tortious action, imposed liability on his principal? Suppose, for example, that he had ridden at breakneck speed to reach Priscilla's side and while en route ran into and injured a pedestrian on the road. Could the pedestrian have sued Standish?
3. Suppose Alden had injured himself on the journey. Would Standish be liable to Alden?
4. Is Alden liable to Standish for stealing the heart of Priscilla—that is, for taking the "profits" of the enterprise for himself?

As these questions suggest, agency law often involves three parties—the principal, the agent, and a third party. It therefore deals with three different relationships: between principal and agent, between principal and the third party, and between agent and third party. These relationships can be summed up in a simple diagram (see Figure 37-1).

In this chapter, we will consider the principal-agent side of the triangle. In the next chapter we will turn to relationships involving third parties.

TYPES OF AGENTS

General Agent

The **general agent** possesses the authority to carry out a broad range of transactions in the name and on behalf of the principal. The general agent may be the manager of a business or he may have a more limited

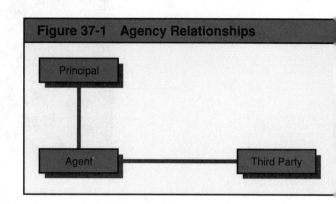

Figure 37-1   Agency Relationships

Principal

Agent

Third Party

but nevertheless ongoing role—as a purchasing agent, for example, or a life insurance agent authorized to sign up customers for the home office. In either case, the general agent has authority to alter the principal's legal relationships with third parties. One who is designated a general agent has the authority to act in any way required by the principal's business. To restrict the general agent's authority, the principal must spell out the limitations explicitly, and even so the principal may be liable for any of the agent's acts in excess of his authority (see "apparent" authority, p. 842).

Normally, the general agent is a business agent, but there are circumstances under which an individual may appoint a general agent for personal purposes. One common form of a personal general agent is the person who holds another's **power of attorney**. This is a delegation of authority to another to act in his stead; it can be accomplished by executing a simple form (see the Minnesota general form, Figure 37-2). Ordinarily, the power of attorney is used for a special purpose; for example, to sell real estate or securities in the absence of the owner. But a person facing a lengthy operation and recuperation in a hospital might give a general power of attorney to a trusted family member or friend.

Special Agent

The **special agent** is one who has authority to act only in a specifically designated instance or in a specifically designated set of transactions. For example, a real estate broker is usually a special agent hired to find a buyer for the principal's land. Suppose Sam, the seller, appoints an agent Al to find a buyer for his property. Al's commission depends on the selling price, which, Sam states in a letter to Al, "in any event may be no less than $50,000." If Al locates a buyer, Bob,

Figure 37-2   Power of Attorney

General Form of Power of Attorney

Know All Men by These Presents, that _____ of the County of _____ and State of _____, do___ by these presents hereby make, constitute and appoint _____ of the County of _____ and State of _____, _____ true and lawful Attorney in Fact for _____ and in _____ name, place and stead, to _____ granting and giving unto said Attorney in Fact full authority and power to do and perform any and all other acts necessary or incident to the performance and execution of the powers herein expressly granted, with power to do and perform all acts authorized hereby, as fully to all intents and purposes as the grantor might or could do if personally present, with full power of substitution.

   In Testimony Whereof, _____ ha ___ hereunto set _____ hand___ this _____ day of _____, 19____.

In presence of
_____   _____
_____   _____
                                      _____
                                      _____

[Acknowledgment]

Source: Minnesota Statutes Annotated § 6792

who agrees to purchase the property for $60,000, Al's signature on the contract of sale will not bind Sam. As a special agent, Al only had authority to find a buyer; he had no authority to sign the contract.

Agency Coupled with an Interest

An agent whose reimbursement depends upon his continuing to have the authority to act as an agent is said to have an **"agency coupled with an interest"** if he has a property interest in the business. A literary or author's agent, for example, customarily agrees to sell a literary work to a publisher in return for a percentage of all monies the author earns from the sale of the work. The literary agent also acts as a collection agent to ensure that his commission will be paid. By agreeing with the principal that the agency is coupled with an interest, the agent can prevent his own rights in a particular literary work from being terminated to his detriment.

Subagent

To carry out his duties, an agent will often need to appoint his own agents. These appointments may or may not be authorized by the principal. An insurance company, for example, might name a general agent to open offices in cities throughout a certain state. The agent will necessarily conduct his business through agents of his own choosing. These agents are **"subagents"** of the principal if the general agent had the express or implied authority of the principal to hire them. For legal purposes, they are agents of both the principal and the principal's general agent and both are liable for the subagent's conduct, although normally the general agent agrees to be primarily liable (see Figure 37-3).

Servant

A final category of agent is the servant or, in modern parlance, employee. The *Restatement (Second) of Agency*, Section 2, defines a servant as "an agent employed by a master [employer] to perform service in his affairs whose physical conduct in the performance of the service is controlled or is subject to the right to control by the master." A common image of the servant is the household employee with which we identify the word "servant" today; others include the factory worker, the truck driver, the farmhand. This image of the servant as un-skilled or semi-skilled laborer is no longer adequate, however. In a modern economy, most of us are servants in the eyes of the law. Even the chief managers of the largest companies are servants, because they are employees of the corporations which they serve.

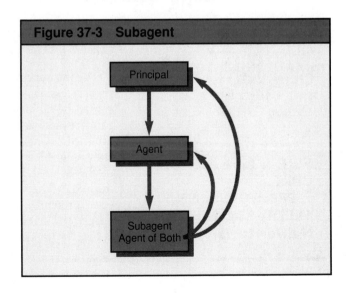

Figure 37-3   Subagent

Principal

Agent

Subagent
Agent of Both

INDEPENDENT CONTRACTORS

Not every contract for services necessarily creates a master-servant relationship. There is an important distinction made between the status of a servant and that of the **independent contractor.** According to the *Restatement (Second) of Agency*, Section 2, "an independent contractor is a person who contracts with another to do something for him but who is not controlled by the other nor subject to the other's right to control with respect to his physical conduct in the performance of the undertaking." As the name implies, the independent contractor is legally autonomous from the other contracting party. A plumber salaried to a building contractor is an employee and agent of the contractor. But a plumber who hires himself out to repair pipes in people's homes is an independent contractor.

This distinction has important legal consequences bearing on taxation, workers' compensation, and liability insurance. For example, employers are required to withhold income taxes from the paychecks of their employees. But payment to an independent contractor, such as the plumber for hire, does not require such withholding. Deciding who is an independent contractor is not always easy; there is no single factor or mechanical answer. In *Robinson* v. *New York Commodities Corp.*, 396 N.Y.S.2d 725 (App.Div. 1977), an injured salesman sought workers' compensation benefits, claiming to be an employee of the New York Commodities Corporation. But the state work-

men's compensation board ruled against him, citing a variety of factors. The claimant sold canned meats, making rounds in his car from his home. The company did not establish hours for him, did not control his movements in any way, nor did it reimburse him for mileage or any other expenses or withhold taxes from its straight commission payments to him. He reported his taxes on a form for the self-employed and hired an accountant to prepare it for him. The Appellate Division of the New York Supreme Court agreed with the compensation board that these facts established the salesman's status as an independent contractor.

It is important to bear in mind that the factual situation in each case determines whether a worker is an employee or an independent contractor. Neither the company nor the worker can establish the worker's status by agreement. As the North Dakota Workmen's Compensation Bureau put it in a bulletin to real estate brokers: "It has come to the Bureau's attention that many employers are requiring that those who work for them sign 'independent contractor' forms so that the employer does not have to pay workmen's compensation premiums for his employees. Such forms are meaningless if the worker is in fact an employee."

In addition to determining a worker's status for tax and compensation insurance purposes, it is also sometimes critical to decisions involving personal liability insurance policies, which usually exclude from coverage accidents involving employees of the insureds, as the following case shows:

GENERAL ACCIDENT FIRE & LIFE ASSUR. CORP. v. PRO GOLF ASSN.
40 Ill.App.3d 592, 352 N.E.2d 441 (1976)

KARNS, PRESIDING JUSTICE

* * *

The insurance policy in question provides certain coverage to members of the Professional Golfers Association. Gerald Hall, a professional golfer employed by the defendant-appellee Taylorville Community Pleasure Driveway District (hereinafter District), a municipal corporation, is an insured member afforded coverage under the policy. The issue presented for review concerns the applicability of a policy exclusion as to "bodily injury to any employee of the insured arising out of and in the course of his employment by the insured." The lower court determined this exclusion inapplicable, and the issue presented for review is whether the judgment of the lower court is against the manifest weight of the evidence. Also assigned as error are certain rulings of the trial court on the admission of evidence.

On June 15, 1973, Bradley Martin, age 13, was present at the golf course owned by the District to participate in junior golf league play. Gerald Hall, the golf professional employed by the District, asked a group of boys including Martin if one of them wished to retrieve or "shag" golf balls to be hit during a golf lesson Hall was to give. Martin agreed to do so. There was no conversation regarding compensation at the time. Hall testified that Martin would be compensated in some manner, "either through golf instructions or money or hot dogs or whatever." During the course of the lesson, a golf ball struck by Hall hit Martin in the eye. Martin instituted an action for damages for the injury to his eye, naming as defendants Hall and the District.

It is General Accident's position that Martin was an employee of Hall at the time of the accident and that the employee exclusion of its policy is applicable to the occurrence. The defendants argue that Martin was either an independent contractor or volunteer, and was not an employee within the meaning of the policy of insurance.

The exclusion in question is commonly referred to as the workmen's compensation exclusion. It is a standard provision of liability policies. Its purpose is to distinguish an employer's liability to his employees from liability to the general public, since the extent of the employer's liability to his employees is as provided by workmen's compensation statutes. It would be costly and redundant to insure against liability to employees under general liability policies of insurance.

We are directed to cases involving an application of the Workmen's Compensation Act to determine whether Martin was an employee of Hall at the time of occurrence. In *O'Brien* v. *Industrial Commission*, 48 Ill.2d 304, 269 N.E.2d 471 (1971), the court observed that the determination of a person's status as an employee or independent contractor "is one of the most vexatious and difficult to determine in the law of compensation." The court reviewed the customary tests of master-servant, that is, right to control the manner of doing the work; manner of payment of compensation; right to discharge; and furnishing of material, equipment or tools. Applying these tests to the instant facts, appellant argues that Martin was an employee of Hall and the contrary decision below was against the manifest weight of the evidence. Specifically, support can be found in the record that Hall had the right to control the manner in which Martin was to pick up the golf balls as the ball that struck Martin was intended as a signal to position him farther back on the practice range; that equipment, a bag and golf cart, was furnished Martin by Hall; that Martin was to be compensated in some manner as he had been compensated in the past for doing the same work, which required little skill or judgment; and that the record, while silent, supports the clear inference that Hall had the right to discharge Martin.

Appellees argue that the facts, which are not in substantial dispute, support with greater force the trial court's finding that Martin was not an employee. There was no evidence of any agreement as to compensation. Hall sometimes gave instruction or food to the boys who "shagged" golf balls,

(continued on next page)

(continued)

GENERAL ACCIDENT FIRE & LIFE ASSUR. CORP. v. PRO GOLF ASSN.
40 Ill.App.3d 592, 352 N.E.2d 441 (1976)

but there was no express understanding as to compensation. While the chore was a simple one, Martin was not instructed or directed in the manner of performing the task, and he was hired to produce a result, viz., to pick up the golf balls; no control was exercised over him, and the ball that struck him was not directing him in the manner of performing the work but was simply a signal for him to back up since balls were to be driven farther down range. No equipment other than a bag in which to place balls as picked up was required to perform the task.

*   *   *

We believe the evidence is susceptible of different inferences. The question is one of fact for the court's determination, and we cannot say that the decision of the trial court is against the manifest weight of the evidence.

*   *   *

CREATION OF AGENCY

The agency relationship can be created in two ways: by contract or by operation of law.

By Contract

The general rules of contract law covered in Part Two govern the law of agency, but two contract principles are especially important: the first is the requirement for a writing and the second concerns contractual capacity.

Most oral agency contracts are legally binding; the law does not require that they be reduced to writing. In practice, many agency contracts are written out to avoid problems of proof. And there are situations where an agency contract must be in writing: (1) if the agreed upon purpose of the agency cannot be fulfilled within one year or if the agency relationship is to last more than one year; (2) in many states, an agreement to pay a commission to a real estate broker; (3) in many states, authority given to an agent to sell real estate; and (4) in several states, contracts between companies and sales representatives.

Even when the agency contract is not required to be in writing, contracts that agents make with third parties often must be in writing. Thus Section 2-201 of the UCC specifically requires contracts for the sale of goods for the price of $500 or more to be in writing and "signed by the party against whom enforcement is sought *or by his authorized agent. . . .*"

A contract is void or voidable when one of the parties lacks capacity to make one. If both principal and agent lack capacity—for example, a minor appoints another minor to negotiate or sign an agreement—there can be no question of the contract's voidability. But suppose only one or the other lacks capacity. Generally, the law focuses on the principal. If the principal is a minor or otherwise lacks capacity, the contract can be avoided, even if the agent is fully competent. There are, however, a few situations in which the capacity of the agent is important. Thus, a mentally incompetent agent cannot bind a principal.

By Operation of Law

Most agencies spring into being contractually. But in areas of social need, courts have declared an agency to exist in the absence of an agreement. The agency relationship then is said to have been created "by operation of law." Children in most states and wives in many may purchase necessary items—food or medical services—on the father's or husband's account. Longstanding social policy deems it desirable for the head of a family to support his dependents and the courts will put the expense on the father (or the mother, if she is the family head) in order to provide for their welfare. The courts achieve this result by supposing the dependent to be the family head's agent, thus allowing creditors to sue the family head for the debt. Not every expense is a necessary, of course, and where the father is already supplying the need, the mother may not incur additional expense chargeable to the father on the ground that she prefers a different doctor or has a different conception of an adequate diet. In recent years, concern with equal rights has caused some courts to hold that wives are liable for necessaries purchased by their husbands, or that neither spouse should be liable for necessaries purchased by the other.

AGENT'S DUTIES TO PRINCIPAL

Fiduciary Duty

In a nonagency contractual situation, the parties' responsibilities terminate at the border of the contract.

There is no relationship beyond the agreement. This literalist approach is justified by the more general principle that we ought each be free to act unless we commit ourselves to a particular course.

But the agency relationship is more than a contractual one, and the agent's responsibilities go beyond the border of the contract. Agency imposes a higher duty than that simply to abide by the contract terms. It imposes a **fiduciary duty.** The law infiltrates the contract creating the agency relationship and reverses the general principle that the parties are free to act in the absence of agreement. As a fiduciary of the principal, the agent stands in a position of special trust. His responsibility is to subordinate his self-interest to that of his principal. The fiduciary responsibility is imposed by law. The absence of any clause in the contract detailing the agent's fiduciary duty does not relieve him of it, as the following case illustrates.

CHERNOW v. REYES
570 A.2d 1282
(N.J.Super. A.D. 1990)

ARNOLD M. STEIN, J.A.D.

Plaintiff appeals a non-jury verdict of no cause for action entered in favor of Angelo Reyes, his former employee, and Marc IV, Inc., Reyes' solely-owned corporation. We reverse because the soliciting and performance of competitive work during his employment constitute a breach by defendant Reyes of the implied covenant of loyalty and good faith owed to plaintiff, his employer.

Plaintiff is in the business of auditing telephone bills. An audit is first made to determine whether the customer's telephone equipment is in place, and is properly billed and in working order. Telephone bills are then checked against approved tariffs to see if there are any overcharges. Plaintiff usually receives 50% of all overcharge refunds returned to the customer by the telephone company.

On October 4, 1982, plaintiff employed defendant as an auditor. Defendant had been working as an equipment installer for New York Telephone Company where he became familiar with the equipment and services offered by telephone companies. Defendant had never previously engaged in auditing work. The agreement of hire was oral; no express restrictions against competiton were imposed as a condition of employment. Defendant did not perform any sales work for plaintiff, who had a sales force which solicited prospective customers.

(continued on next page)

(continued)

CHERNOW v. REYES
570 A.2d 1282
(N.J.Super. A.D. 1990)

According to defendant, he became disenchanted with his employment prospects early in 1983. Plaintiff refused to renegotiate defendant's salary and showed no interest in defendant's suggestions to broaden the scope of the existing business. Defendant determined to make his livelihood elsewhere. His predeparture activities are the focus of this lawsuit.

*   *   *

Defendant first acquired sole ownership of a corporation which he had formed with others in December 1982. He then copied plaintiff's retainer agreement form for clients and the authorization letter permitting examination of the client's telephone company records. Defendant then solicited and performed telephone auditing services for several companies. All this was done, of course, without plaintiff's knowledge. Defendant's clandestine efforts resulted in his obtaining three auditing contracts and the performance of work for these companies before he left plaintiff's employ. He also solicited a fourth account, United Engineering Trustees (UET), during his employment with plaintiff, but performed no work for UET until after the employment ended.

The trial judge accepted defendant's testimony that he did not attempt to solicit any of plaintiff's customers. She also found that defendant did not slacken his work efforts for plaintiff during the regular 9 to 5 workday, and that defendant's soliciting and auditing activities were conducted at night and on weekends, lunch hours and vacation days. We see no reason to disturb these findings which are amply supported by the record below.

The trial judge concluded that plaintiff was not entitled to recover damages because

> while the businesses the defendant solicited work from and performed work for before leaving the plaintiff, might have been considered to be part of a potential pool of businesses plaintiff could have been competing for, there is no evidence . . . that . . . these businesses were either then clients of the plaintiff or . . . were within the pool of businesses he was soliciting.

She also determined that defendant's conduct "did not hinder the plaintiff in any way in plaintiff's business."

We conclude that defendant's tapping of plaintiff's potential customer pool is actionable. This identifiable pool of potential business was off-limits to defendant while he remained on plaintiff's payroll. Defendant could neither solicit these prospective customers nor perform any telephone auditing services for them, even during off-work hours.

An employee owes a duty of loyalty to the employer and must not, while employed, act contrary to the employer's interest. *Auxton Computer Enterprises, Inc. v. Parker*, 416 A.2d 952 (App.Div.1980). During the period of employment, the employee has a duty not to compete with the employer's business.

*   *   *

By engaging in a competitive enterprise, defendant crossed the line drawn by *Auxton* between permissible preparation to change jobs and actionable conduct. Plaintiff was entitled to expect that a person on his payroll would not undertake to pursue competitive commercial opportunities. The protection accorded is not limited to the diversion of an employer's customers. It extends to pursuing and transacting business within the larger pool of potential customers who might have been solicited by the employer.

Defendant and his corporation are liable for any profits earned in a competitive business while he was employed by plaintiff. Under certain circumstances not present here, we would be inclined to hold the former employee liable for all profits which resulted from competition with the employer during the term of employment, even where the profits were actually earned after employment ceased. However, we limit damages in this case. Defendant was not bound by a non-competition covenant. He was free to compete with plaintiff as soon as his employment ended. None of the money earned by defendant after his employment ended came from actual customers of plaintiff solicited by defendant during the employment period. Damages will be limited to those profits actually earned by defendant and his corporation in a competing telephone auditing business up to the time that his employment ceased.

Reversed and remanded for the fixing of damages against defendants Reyes and Marc IV, Inc., and for further proceedings consistent with this opinion.

Duty to Avoid Self-Dealing A fiduciary may not lawfully profit from a conflict between his personal interest in a transaction and his principal's interest in that same transaction. A broker hired as a purchasing agent, for instance, may not sell to his principal through a company in which he or his family has a financial interest. The penalty for breach of fiduciary duty is loss of compensation and profit and possible damages for breach of trust, as the Frito-Lay suit in **Box 37-1** makes clear. The *Wall Street Journal* later reported that the Frito-Lay suit had been settled. Although the settlement terms were not disclosed, Frito-Lay reportedly was given control of American Business Management Corporation and also received $5 million in damages.

Duty to Preserve Confidential Information To further his objectives, a principal will usually need to reveal a number of secrets to his agent—how much he is willing to sell or pay for property, marketing strategies, and the like. Such information could easily be turned to the disadvantage of the principal if the agent were to compete with the principal or were to sell it to those who do. The law therefore prohibits an agent from using for his own purposes or in ways that would injure the interests of the principal information confidentially given or acquired. This prohibition extends to information gleaned from the principal though unrelated to the agent's assignment. "[A]n agent who is told by the principal of his plans, or who secretly examines books or memoranda of the employer, is not privileged to use such information at his principal's expense." (*Restatement (Second) of Agency*, Section 395.) Nor may the agent use confidential information after resigning his agency. Though he is free, in the absence of contract, to compete with his former principal, he may not use information learned in the course of his agency, such as trade secrets and customer lists.

Other Duties

In addition to fiduciary responsibility, and whatever special duties may be contained in the specific contract, the law of agency imposes other duties on an agent.

Tortilla Flap

By Bill Abrams

*[A breach of fiduciary duty can result in loss of compensation, profit, and possible damages for breach of trust. Companies today are quick to warn their employees against any self-dealing practices.—*AUTHORS' NOTE*]*

DALLAS—Authors of self-improvement success manuals usually warn you that you'll never get rich working on salary for a giant corporation. It's time they heard about James H. Stafford, who not long ago was fired by the Frito-Lay Inc. subsidiary of PepsiCo Inc., the $4 billion-a-year soft-drink and snack-food conglomerate.

Mr. Stafford is a millionaire several times over. There seems no dispute that the six-foot-four, former high-school vocational agriculture teacher, now in his late 50s, made his money during his 24 years on the Frito-Lay payroll. For the last 19 years he has been the company's commodity purchasing manager.

It takes millions of pounds of corn, vegetable oil, salt and spices to turn out all the Fritos, Doritos, Tostitos and other snacks that Frito-Lay sells; Mr. Stafford's shopping list amounted to more than $150 million

A BREACH OF FIDUCIARY DUTY

a year, making him one of the nation's largest commodity buyers.

The catch was, according to the company, that Mr. Stafford secretly owned a major interest in a West Texas company, American Business Management Corp., that was Frito-Lay's largest corn supplier; he also was receiving thousands of dollars every year in consulting fees from Lacy-Logan Co., a Dallas vegetable-oils broker that handled much of Frito-Lay's oil purchases, Frito-Lay alleges.

Frito-Lay said it didn't find out about Mr. Stafford's outside interests until this year, and when it did, it promptly fired him on Aug. 21. The following day it filed suit in Dallas County state district court against him, Grain Handling Corp. (which had acquired American Business Management), and other principals of that closely held corporation for more than $18 million in damages. The defendants have denied any wrongdoing. . . .

One ironic aspect of the case is that Frito-Lay has yet to show what

harm it has suffered as a result of Mr. Stafford's handling of commodities purchases. Frito-Lay has always been one of PepsiCo's most profitable subsidiaries. And Mr. Stafford was widely viewed by commodities sellers as one of Frito-Lay's key assets; they say he was a hard bargainer with an uncanny feel for the edible-oils market.

"He's the finest oil trader this country has ever had," says one vegetable-oil refiner. "He was rough. When you did business with Jim Stafford, you knew you'd been through a fight." Mr. Stafford, himself, claims in court papers that in the past five years he bought vegetable oil for Frito-Lay at prices "approximately $100 million less than the market price." . . .

The main ingredient in corn chips is, of course, corn. Until the mid-1960s, Frito-Lay had purchased its corn directly from farmers, some as far away as California, and had cleaned, stored and delivered the grain itself. Then the company decided to get out of the corn-handling business.

Frito-Lay says that Mr. Stafford was given the task of finding an outside corn supplier. He turned in 1968 to KornKo Inc., a company founded by Melvin N. Tekell, a Texas corn broker; Mr. Tekell's wife, and James T. Hair, an accountant. Mr. Hair also happens to be Mr. Stafford's son-in-

---

Duty of Care and Skill   An agent is usually taken on because he has special knowledge or skills that the principal wishes to tap. The agent is under a legal duty to perform his work with the care and skill that is "standard in the locality for the kind of work which he is employed to perform" (Restatement, Section 379) and to exercise any special skills, if these are greater or more refined than those prevalent among those

normally employed in the community. In short, the agent may not lawfully do a sloppy job.

Duty of Good Conduct   In the absence of an agreement, a principal may not ordinarily dictate how an agent must live his private life. An overly fastidious florist may not instruct his truck driver to steer clear of the local bar on his way home from delivering

BOX 37-1

law, the husband of the former Sherry Lynne Stafford. There was, Frito-Lay alleges, another partner in KornKo, albeit a silent one: James H. Stafford, himself. . . .

. . . Within five years, KornKo, then known as American Business Management Corp., had become Frito-Lay's single largest corn supplier, contracting to sell at least 250 million pounds in 1973 for roughly $15 million. . . .

Mr. Stafford, as an American Business Management shareholder, received nearly $19,000 in dividends between 1973 and 1976. Frito-Lay also contends that Mr. Stafford's 2,000-acre ranch, Rockbrook Farms, received "management fees" of more than $50,000 annually from the corn concern. . . .

It was Mr. Stafford's job to buy the edible oils—peanut, corn, soy or cotton oil—that were used to fry corn chips. Like most big buyers, Frito-Lay bought most of its oils through brokers who could provide up-to-date market information and conceal a buyer's identity from the marketplace.

Among oils sellers, it was common knowledge that one Dallas broker—Lacy-Logan—had, as one broker describes it, "a lock on Frito-Lay's business." . . .

Mr. Stafford became a consultant to Lacy-Logan. His fee was about $15 per carload of oil bought by Frito-Lay, according to a former Lacy-Logan employee familiar with the arrangement. This came to roughly $40,000 a year; court records show that between 1968 and 1976 Lacy-Logan paid Mr. Stafford $388,159.

In 1975 Mr. Lacy sold the company to American Business Management. One acquaintance says the reason was that Mr. Lacy "was terrified of getting caught" and upset by demands from Mr. Stafford for more money.

In 1976, American Business Management itself was sold to Quality Grain Processors Inc., later to be known as Grain Handling Corp., for $36 million in cash and notes. . . .

Mr. Stafford's immediate cash windfall as a result of the sale came to $6 million. . . .

At the time of the windfall, Mr. Stafford's salary at Frito-Lay was probably between $40,000 and $45,000, according to his former associates. Court records in the current case indicate that he may have received perhaps another $100,000 a year from kickbacks, dividends and other payments from Frito-Lay's corn and oil suppliers.

Frito-Lay is now trying to recover those monies. The company claims Mr. Stafford "placed himself in a position of conflict of interest, breached his duty of loyalty and trust and/or his fiduciary duty to Frito-Lay." . . .

Why didn't PepsiCo's internal auditors or Arthur Young & Co., PepsiCo's outside auditor since 1965, uncover the irregularities? William A. McNamara, the Arthur Young partner who coordinates PepsiCo audits, says, "This was the kind of thing that I don't think is possible to catch in a normal audit."

Mr. McNamara says Arthur Young and PepsiCo, since the Stafford affair, have been trying to come up with new controls that would prevent it from happening again. "We can't really come up with much. It was an isolated situation that happened in a subsidiary."

Since 1976, PepsiCo executives have been subject to an elaborate printed "Code of Conduct," which, among other things, bars company employees and members of their families from "any significant interest in enterprises which conduct or seek to conduct business with PepsiCo" without first obtaining a statement of clearance from the company's legal department indicating that the employee's decisions won't be influenced by his ownership of the outside interest.

Source: *Wall Street Journal*, November 14, 1978.

flowers at the end of the day. But there are some jobs on which the personal habits of the agent may have an effect. The agent is not at liberty to act with impropriety or notoriety, so as to bring disrepute on the business in which the principal is engaged. A lecturer at an anti-alcohol clinic may be directed to refrain from frequenting bars. A bank cashier who becomes known as a gambler may be fired.

Duty to Keep and Render Accounts   The agent must keep accurate financial records, take receipts, and otherwise act in conformity to standard business practices.

Duty to Act Only as Authorized   This duty states a truism, but is one for which there are limits. A principal's wishes may have been stated ambiguously or may be broad enough to confer discretion on the agent. As long as the agent acts reasonably under the circumstances, he will not be liable for damages later if the principal ultimately repudiates what the agent has done. "Only conduct which is contrary to the principal's manifestations to him, interpreted in light of what he has reason to know at the time when he acts, . . . subjects the agent to liability to the principal." (Restatement, Section 383.)

Duty Not to Attempt the Impossible or Impracticable   Principal says to Agent: "Keep working until the job is done." Agent is not obligated to go without food or sleep because the principal misapprehended how long it would take to complete the job. Nor should the agent continue to expend the principal's funds in a quixotic attempt to gain business, sign up customers, or produce inventory when it is reasonably clear that such efforts would be in vain.

Duty to Obey   As a general rule, the agent must obey reasonable directions concerning the manner of performance. What is reasonable depends on the customs of the industry or trade, prior dealings between agent and principal, and the nature of the agreement creating the agency. A principal may prescribe uniforms for various classes of employees, for instance, and a manufacturing company may tell its salesforce what sales pitch to use on customers. On the other hand, certain tasks entrusted to agents are not subject to the principal's control; for example, a lawyer may refuse to permit a client to dictate courtroom tactics.

Duty to Give Information   Because the principal cannot be every place at once—that is why agents are hired, after all—much that is vital to the principal's business comes to the attention first of agents. If the agent has actual notice or reason to know of information that is relevant to matters entrusted to him, he has a duty to inform the principal. This duty is especially critical because information in the hands of an agent is, under most circumstances, imputed to the principal, whose legal liabilities to third persons may hinge on receiving information in timely fashion. Service of process, for example, requires a defendant to answer within a certain number of days; an agent's failure to communicate to the principal that a summons has been served may bar the principal's right to defend a lawsuit. The imputation to the principal of knowledge possessed by the agent is strict: even where the agent is acting adversely to the principal's interests—for example, by trying to defraud his employer—a third party may still rely on notification to the agent, unless the third party knows the agent is acting adversely.

"Shop Rights" Doctrine   In *Grip Nut Co.* v. *Sharp,* 150 F.2d 192 (7th Cir. 1945), Sharp made a deal with Grip Nut Company that in return for a salary and bonuses as company president he would assign to the company any inventions he made. When the five-year employment contract expired, Sharp continued to serve as chief executive officer, but no new contract was negotiated concerning either pay or rights to inventions. During the next ten years, Sharp invented a number of new products and developed new machinery to manufacture them; patent rights went to the company. However, he made one invention with two other employees and they assigned the patent to him. A third employee invented a safety device and also assigned the patent to Sharp. At one time Sharp's son invented a leakproof bolt and a process to manufacture it; these, too, were assigned to Sharp. These inventions were developed in the company's plants at its expense.

When Sharp died, his family claimed the rights to the inventions on which Sharp held assignments and sued the company, which used the inventions, for patent infringement. The family reasoned that after the expiration of the employment contract, Sharp was employed only in a managerial capacity, not as an inventor. The court disagreed and invoked the "shop rights" doctrine, under which an invention "developed and perfected in [a company's] plant with its time, materials, and appliances, and wholly at its expense" may be used by the company without payment of royalties. "Because the servant uses his master's time, facilities and materials to attain a concrete result, the employer is entitled to use that which embodies his own property and to duplicate it as often as he may find occasion to employ similar appliances in his business." The company would have been given complete ownership of the patents had there been an express or implied (for example, the employee is hired to make inventions) contract to this effect between Sharp and the company.

PRINCIPAL'S DUTIES TO AGENT

Contract Duties

General Duties   The fiduciary relationship of agent to principal does not run in reverse—that is, the principal is not the agent's fiduciary. Nevertheless, the principal has a number of contractually-related obligations toward his agent. In general, these are analogues of many of the agent's duties that we have just examined. In brief: a principal has a duty "to refrain from unreasonably interfering with [an agent's] work." (Restatement, Section 434.) The principal is allowed, however, to compete with the agent, unless the agreement specifically prohibits it. The principal has a duty to inform his agent of risks of physical harm or pecuniary loss that inhere in the agent's performance of assigned tasks. Failure to warn an agent that travel in a particular neighborhood required by the job may be dangerous (a fact unknown to the agent but known to the principal) could under common law subject the principal to a suit for damages if the agent is injured while in the neighborhood performing his job. A principal is obliged to render accounts of monies due to agents; a principal's obligation to do so depends on a variety of factors, including the degree of independence of the agent, the method of compensation, and the customs of the particular business. An agent's reputation is no less valuable than a principal's, and so an agent is under no obligation to continue working for one who sullies it.

Employment at Will   Under the traditional "employment-at-will" doctrine, an employee who is not hired for a specific period can be fired at any time. This doctrine, which has come under attack in recent years, is discussed on pages 1173–1181.

Duty to Indemnify   Agents commonly spend money pursuing the principal's business. Unless the agreement explicitly provides otherwise, the principal has a duty to indemnify or reimburse the agent. A familiar form of indemnity is the employee expense account.

Tort Duties and Workers' Compensation

Andy, who works in a dynamite factory, negligently stores dynamite in the wrong shed. Andy warns his fellow employee Bill that he has done so. Bill lights up a cigarette near the shed anyway, a spark lands on the ground, the dynamite explodes, and Bill is injured. May Bill sue his employer to recover damages? At common law, the answer would be no—three times no. First, the "fellow-servant" rule would bar recovery because the employer was held not to be responsible for torts committed by one employee against another. Second, Bill's failure to heed Andy's warning and his decision to smoke near the dynamite amounted to contributory negligence. Hence, even if the dynamite had been negligently stored by the employer, rather than by a fellow employee, the claim would have been dismissed. Third, the courts might have held that Bill had "assumed the risk": since he was aware of the dangers, it would not be fair to saddle the employer with the burden of Bill's actions.

The three common-law rules just mentioned ignited intense public fury by the turn of the twentieth century. In large numbers of cases, workers who were mutilated or killed on the job found themselves and their families without recompense. Union pressure and grass roots lobbying led to workers' (originally "workmen's") compensation acts—statutory enactments that dramatically overhauled the law of torts as it affected employees.

Workers' compensation is a no-fault system. The employee gives up the right to sue the employer (and, in some states, other employees) and receives in exchange predetermined compensation for a job-related injury, regardless of who caused it. This tradeoff was felt to be equitable to employer and employee: the employee loses the right to seek damages for pain and suffering—which can be a sizable portion of any jury award—but in return he can avoid the time-consuming and uncertain judicial process and assure himself that his medical costs and a portion of his salary will be paid—and paid promptly. The employer must pay for all injuries, even those for which he is blameless, but in return he avoids the risk of losing a big lawsuit, can calculate his costs actuarially, and can spread the risks through insurance.

Most workers' compensation acts provide 100 percent of the cost of a worker's hospitalization and medical care necessary to cure the injury and relieve him from its effects. They also provide for payment of lost wages and death benefits. Even an employee who is able to work may be eligible to receive compensation for specific injuries. Table 37-1 shows the

TABLE 37-1   STATUTORY BENEFITS (TEXAS) FOR SPECIFIC INJURIES

Member	Weeks
Thumb	60
Index Finger	45
2d Finger	30
3d Finger	21
Little Finger	15
Hand	150
Arm at or above Elbow	200
Great Toe	30
Any Other Toe	10
Foot	125
Leg at or above Knee	200
Eye	100
Hearing (Both Ears)	150
Eye and Leg above Knee	350
Eye and Arm above Elbow	350
Eye and Hand	325
Eye and Foot	300

NOTE: 2d joint of thumb equivalent to ½ thumb. More than ½ of thumb equivalent to whole thumb. 3d joint of any finger equivalent to ⅓ finger. More than middle and 3d joint of any finger equivalent to whole finger. For metacarpal bone (palm) add 10 weeks to number specified for corresponding thumb, finger or fingers. For all injuries to thumb, fingers and parts of one hand compensation limited to that allowed for hand.

Source: *Employers' Handbook* of the Texas Employers' Insurance Association, 1975

table of benefits for specific injuries under the Texas statute. Assume a worker loses his arm above the elbow. He is entitled to two-thirds of his average weekly pay, not to exceed a specified maximum, for 200 weeks. If the loss is only partial (for example, partial loss of sight), the recovery is decreased by the percentage still usable. Thus a worker who loses half his sight in one eye would be limited to half the usual recovery.

Coverage   Although workers' compensation laws are on the books of every state, in a few states they are not compulsory. In states where they are elective, the employer may decline to participate, in which event the employee must seek redress in court. But in most states permitting an employer election, the old common-law defenses (fellow-servant rule, contributory negligence, and assumption of risk) have been statutorily eliminated, greatly enhancing an employee's chances of winning a suit. The incentive is therefore strong for employers to elect workers' compensation coverage.

Not all workers are covered. Those frequently excluded are farm and domestic laborers and public employees. But the trend has been to include more and more classes of workers. Approximately half the states now provide coverage for household workers, although the threshold of coverage varies widely from state to state. Some use an earnings test, the floor for coverage ranging from $200 in annual earnings to $10,000. Other states impose an hours threshold. People who fall within the domestics category include maids, babysitters, gardeners, and handymen, but generally do not include plumbers, electricians, and other independent contractors.

There are three general methods by which employers may comply with workers' compensation laws. First, they may purchase employer's liability and workers' compensation policies through private commercial insurance companies. These policies consist of two major provisions: payment by the insurer of all claims filed under workers' compensation and related laws (such as occupational disease benefits) and coverage of the costs of defending any suits filed against the employer, including any judgments awarded. Since workers' compensation statutes cut off the employee's right to sue, how can such a lawsuit be filed? The answer is that there are certain exceptions to the ban—for instance, a worker may sue if the employer deliberately injures an employee.

The second method of compliance with workers' compensation laws is to insure through a state fund established for the purpose. The third method is to self-insure. The laws specify conditions under which companies may resort to self-insurance and generally only the largest corporations qualify to do so.

Recurring Legal Issues   Workers' compensation does not cover every accident or injury. It provides payments only to employees who are injured in some work-related activity. So three issues recur in the cases: (1) Is the injury work-related? (2) Is the injured person an employee? (3) How palpable must the "injury" be for compensation to be awarded?

Is the Injury Work-Related?   As a general rule, on-the-job injuries are covered no matter what their relationship to the employee's specific duties. Although injuries resulting from drunkenness or fighting are not generally covered, there are circumstances under which they will be, as the next case shows.

CHESTER v. WORLD FOOTBALL LEAGUE
75 Mich. App. 455, 255 N.W.2d 643 (1977)

V.J. BRENNAN, J. On September 27, 1974, plaintiffs Albert and Ardis Chester brought suit against defendants jointly and severally for injuries arising out of a dispute over wages between defendant Wyche and plaintiff Albert Chester while Chester was controller for defendant Detroit Wheels [hereafter Wheels]. Defendant World Football League [hereafter League] was joined as alleged co-employer of defendant Wyche. Motion for summary judgment was filed by defendants and granted by Wayne County Circuit Judge Benjamin D. Burdick on January 30, 1976. He found the claim against Wyche and the Wheels was barred by the exclusive remedy provisions of the Workmen's Compensation Act. He found for the League on the same basis or, alternatively, because Wyche acted outside the scope of any possible agency with the League. Plaintiffs appeal as of right.

The incident giving rise to this litigation occurred on September 20, 1974. Plaintiff had been employed as controller of the Wheels through Kelly Services, Inc [hereafter Kelly]. Part of the arrangement meant that the Wheels would pay Kelly and Kelly would then pay plaintiff. However, plaintiff's deposition indicated that Kelly maintained no control over his time, duties or conduct with the Wheels.

Plaintiff had been working for the Wheels since July, 1974. Prior to September 20, 1974, the Wheels became insolvent and unable to meet their payroll. Thereupon, the League seems to have agreed to pay Wyche's salary. The last paycheck Wyche received on September 20, 1974, came from the League.

On September 20, 1974, plaintiff was working at the offices of the Wheels. Wyche and some other football players entered and engaged plaintiff in discussion about back pay due the players. The conversation became heated and Wyche grabbed plaintiff by the arm, plaintiff claiming he was thereby injured.

*   *   *

Plaintiff first contends that the trial court erred by granting summary judgment for defendant Wheels. Plaintiff maintains that he was not, as a matter of law, an employee of defendant Wheels on September 20, 1974, and so was not precluded from bringing suit against them by the exclusive remedy provisions of the Workmen's Compensation Act.

Viewing the facts most favorably to plaintiff, we must disagree. Under the act, an employee is entitled to compensation if he receives a personal injury arising out of and in the course of his employment by an employer covered by the act. In this case, there is no dispute that Chester was injured in the course of his employment or that the Wheels were an employer covered by the act. What we must decide is the legal question of whether plaintiff was an employee of the Wheels within the meaning of the act.

The device used in Michigan to determine the existence of an employment relationship is the "economic reality" test. Generally, four factors are isolated: control, payment of wages, the right to hire and fire, and the right to

(*continued on next page*)

(continued)

CHESTER v. WORLD FOOTBALL LEAGUE 75 Mich. App. 455, 255 N.W.2d 643 (1977)

discipline. Applying these factors to this case, we believe plaintiff was an employee of the Wheels.

* * *

The plaintiff in this case styles himself an independent contractor, removed from the control normally associated with an employee status. We see no distinction between the function plaintiff performed for the Wheels and similar high-level employees in other businesses who may have some control over the time, hours or duties of their employment. We believe summary judgment was properly granted in favor of defendant Wheels.

Plaintiff next argues that the trial court erred by granting summary judgment to defendant Wyche. He alleges that Wyche was not, as a matter of law, an employee of the Wheels on September 20, 1974, and so would not be protected by the exclusive remedy provisions of the Workmen's Compensation Act. We disagree.

We have determined that plaintiff was an employee of defendant Wheels for purposes of the Workmen's Compensation Act. We also recognize that defendant Wyche was an employee of the Wheels and that the act will bar suit against co-employees for injuries compensable under the act. This bar operates where the injury occurs in the regular course of employment. Therefore, the question we must decide is whether this incident developed within the course of their employment.

* * *

We find authority for the position that "injuries received in assault, either sportive or malicious, are not, by reason of such fact alone, beyond the realm of compensability". We do not believe even a favorable interpretation of the facts indicate defendant Wyche's assault "so gross and reprehensible . . . as to constitute intentional and wilful conduct". We feel the broad construction necessary and desirable for this provision justifies finding the assault within the course of the parties' employment. We perceive the incident as arising spontaneously from employee Wyche's attempt to collect salary from employee Chester. We find no error in granting summary judgment for defendant Wyche in this case.

* * *

Plaintiff's second amended complaint against the WFL asserted two separate theories of recovery. First, plaintiffs contended that the WFL was vicariously liable for Wyche's battery under the doctrine of *respondeat superior*. The second theory of liability articulated by plaintiff was that the WFL was negligent, among other reasons, in keeping Wyche, a man purportedly of known violent propensities, within the WFL organization, provoking Wyche to violence by failing to act to satisfy his grievances and failing to act to prevent those grievances from arising.

[The court held that there was no *respondeat superior* liability because Wyche was not an agent of the League. However, the court held that the League might be liable under the second theory and thus reversed the trial court's summary judgment for the WFL.]

Is the Injured Person an Employee?   Courts are apt to be liberal in construing statutes to include those who might not seem to be employed. In *Betts* v. *Ann Arbor Public Schools*, 271 N.W.2d 498 (Mich. 1978), a University of Michigan student majoring in physical education was a student teacher in a junior high school. During a four-month period he taught two physical education courses. On the last day of his student teaching, he walked into the locker room and thirty of his students grabbed him and tossed him into the swimming pool. This was traditional, but he "didn't feel like going in that morning" and put up a struggle that ended with a whistle on an elastic band hitting him in the eye, which he subsequently lost as a result of the injury. He filed a workers' compensation claim. The school board argued that he could not be classified as an employee because he received no pay. Since he was injured by students—not considered agents of the school—he would probably have been unsuccessful in filing a tort suit; hence the workers' compensation claim was his only chance of recompense. The state workers' compensation appeal board ruled against the school on the ground that payment in money was not required. "Plaintiff was paid in the form of training, college credits towards graduation, and meeting of the prerequisites of a state provisional certificate." The state supreme court affirmed the award.

How Palpable Must the "Injury" Be?   A difficult issue is whether a worker is entitled to compensation for psychological injury, including cumulative trauma. Until recently, insurance companies and compensation boards required physical injury before making an award. Claims that job stresses have led to nervous breakdowns or other mental disorders were rejected. But most courts have begun to liberalize the definition of injury and to recognize that psychological trauma can be real and that job stress can bring it on, as shown by the following case.

WOLFE v. SIBLEY, LINDSAY & CURR CO.
36 N.Y.2d 505,
369 N.Y.S.2d 637 (1975)

WACHTLER, JUDGE. This appeal involves a claim for workmen's compensation benefits for the period during which the claimant was incapacitated by severe depression caused by the discovery of her immediate supervisor's body after he had committed suicide.

The facts as adduced at a hearing before the Workmen's Compensation Board are uncontroverted. The claimant, Mrs. Diana Wolfe, began her employment with the respondent department store, Sibley, Lindsay & Curr Co. in February, 1968. After working for some time as an investigator in the security department of the store she became secretary to Mr. John Gorman, the security director. It appears from the record that as head of security, Mr. Gorman was subjected to intense pressure, especially during the Christmas holidays. Mrs. Wolfe testified that throughout the several years she worked at Sibley's Mr. Gorman reacted to this holiday pressure by becoming extremely agitated and nervous. She noted, however, that this anxiety usually disappeared when the holiday season was over. Unfortunately, Mr. Gorman's nervous condition failed to abate after the 1970 holidays.

＊　　＊　　＊

Despite the fact that he followed Mrs. Wolfe's advice to see a doctor, Mr. Gorman's mental condition continued to deteriorate. On one occasion he left work at her suggestion because he appeared to be so nervous. This condition persisted until the morning of June 9, 1971 when according to the claimant, Mr. Gorman looked much better and even smiled and "tousled her hair" when she so remarked.

(continued on next page)

(*continued*)

WOLFE v. SIBLEY, LINDSAY & CURR CO.
**36 N.Y.2d 505,
369 N.Y.S.2d 637 (1975)**

A short time later Mr. Gorman called her on the intercom and asked her to call the police to room 615. Mrs. Wolfe complied with this request and then tried unsuccessfully to reach Mr. Gorman on the intercom. She entered his office to find him lying in a pool of blood caused by a self-inflicted gunshot wound in the head. Mrs. Wolfe became extremely upset and was unable to continue working that day.

She returned to work for one week only to lock herself in her office to avoid the questions of her fellow workers. Her private physician perceiving that she was beset by feelings of guilt referred her to a psychiatrist and recommended that she leave work, which she did. While at home she ruminated about her guilt in failing to prevent the suicide and remained in bed for long periods of time staring at the ceiling. The result was that she became unresponsive to her husband and suffered a weight loss of 20 pounds. Her psychiatrist, Dr. Grinols diagnosed her condition as an acute depressive reaction.

After attempting to treat her in his office Dr. Grinols realized that the severity of her depression mandated hospitalization. Accordingly, the claimant was admitted to the hospital on July 9, 1971 where she remained for two months during which time she received psychotherapy and medication. After she was discharged, Dr. Grinols concluded that there had been no substantial remission in her depression and ruminative guilt and so had her readmitted for electroshock treatment. These treatments lasted for three weeks and were instrumental in her recovery. She was again discharged and, in mid-January, 1972, resumed her employment with Sibley, Lindsay, & Curr.

Mrs. Wolfe's claim for workmen's compensation was granted by the referee and affirmed by the Workmen's Compensation Board. On appeal the Appellate Division reversed, [concluding] that mental injury precipitated solely by psychic trauma is not compensable as a matter of law. We do not agree with this conclusion.

Workmen's compensation, as distinguished from tort liability which is essentially based on fault, is designed to shift the risk of loss of earning capacity caused by industrial accidents from the worker to industry and ultimately the consumer. In light of its beneficial and remedial character the Workmen's Compensation Law should be construed liberally in favor of the employee.

Liability under the act is predicated on accidental injury arising out of and in the course of employment. Applying these concepts to the case at bar we note that there is no issue raised concerning the causal relationship between the occurrence and the injury. The only testimony on this matter was given by Dr. Grinols who stated unequivocally that the discovery of her superior's body was the competent producing cause of her condition. Nor is there any question as to the absence of physical impact. Accordingly, the focus of our inquiry is whether or not there has been an accidental injury within the meaning of the Workmen's Compensation Law.

Since there is no statutory definition of this term we turn to the relevant decisions. These may be divided into three categories: (1) psychic trauma which produces physical injury, (2) physical impact which produces psychological injury, and (3) psychic trauma which produces psychological injury. As to the first class our court has consistently recognized the principle that an injury caused by emotional stress or shock may be accidental within the purview of the compensation law. Cases falling into the second category have uniformly sustained awards to those incurring nervous or psychological disorders as a result of physical impact. As to those cases in the third category the decisions are not as clear.

*   *   *

We hold today that psychological or nervous injury precipitated by psychic trauma is compensable to the same extent as physical injury. This determination is based on two considerations. First, as noted in the psychiatric testimony there is nothing in the nature of a stress or shock situation which ordains physical as opposed to psychological injury. The determinative factor is the particular vulnerability of an individual by virtue of his physical makeup. In a given situation one person may be susceptible to a heart attack while another may suffer a depressive reaction. In either case the result is the same—the individual is incapable of functioning properly because of an accident and should be compensated under the Workmen's Compensation Law.

Secondly, having recognized the reliability of identifying psychic trauma as a causative factor of injury in some cases and the reliability by identifying psychological injury as a resultant factor in other cases, we see no reason for limiting recovery in the latter instance to cases involving physical impact. There is nothing talismanic about physical impact.

We would note in passing that this analysis reflects the view of the majority of jurisdictions in this country and England.

[Appellate Division decision is reversed.]

CHAPTER SUMMARY

An agent is one who acts on behalf of another. The law recognizes several types of agents, including (1) the general agent, one who possesses authority to carry out a broad range of transactions in the name and on behalf of the principal; (2) the special agent, one with authority to act only in a specifically designated instance or set of transactions; (3) the agent whose agency is coupled with an interest, one who has a property interest in addition to authority to act as an agent; (4) the subagent, one appointed by an agent with authority to do so; and (5) the servant, one whose physical conduct is subject to control of the principal.

A servant should be distinguished from an independent contractor, whose work is not subject to the control of the principal. The difference is important for purposes of taxation, workers' compensation, and liability insurance.

The agency relationship is usually created by contract, and sometimes governed by the Statute of Frauds, but some agencies are created by operation of law.

An agent owes his principal the highest duty of loyalty, that of a fiduciary. The agent must avoid self-dealing, preserve confidential information, perform with skill and care, conduct his personal life so as not to bring disrepute on the business for which he acts as agent, keep and render accounts, and give appropriate information to the principal.

Although the principal is not the agent's fiduciary, the principal does have certain obligations toward the agent—for example, to refrain from interfering with the agent's work and to indemnify. The employer's common law tort liability toward his employees has been replaced by the workers' compensation system, under which the employee gives up the right to sue for damages in return for prompt payment of medical and job-loss expenses. Injuries must have been work-related and the injured person must have been an employee. Courts today allow awards for psychological trauma in the absence of physical injury.

KEY TERMS

SELF-TEST QUESTIONS

1. One who has authority to act only in a specifically designated instance or in a specifically designated set of transactions is called:
   (a) a subagent
   (b) a general agent
   (c) a special agent
   (d) none of the above
2. An agency relationship may be created by:
   (a) contract
   (b) operation of law
   (c) an oral agreement
   (d) all of the above
3. An agent's duty to the principal includes:
   (a) the duty to indemnify
   (b) the duty to warn of special dangers
   (c) the duty to avoid self dealing
   (d) all of the above
4. A person whose work is not subject to the control of the principal, but who arranges to perform a job for him is called:
   (a) a subagent
   (b) a servant
   (c) a special agent
   (d) an independent contractor
5. An employer's liability for employees' on-the-job injuries is generally governed by:
   (a) tort law
   (b) the workers' compensation system
   (c) social security
   (d) none of the above

DEMONSTRATION PROBLEM

An employee in a Rhode Island foundry inserted two coins in a coin-operated coffee machine in the company cafeteria. One coin stuck in the machine and the worker proceeded to "whack" the machine with his right arm. The arm struck a grate near the machine, rupturing the biceps muscle and causing a 10 percent loss in the use of the arm. Is the worker entitled to workers' compensation? Why?

PROBLEMS

1. A woman was involved in an automobile accident which resulted in the death of a passenger in her car. After she was charged with manslaughter, her attorney agreed to work with the claims adjuster of her insurance company in handling the case. As a result of the agreement, the woman gave a statement about the accident to the claims adjuster. When the prosecuting attorney demanded to see the statement, the woman's attorney refused on the grounds that the claims adjuster was his agent. Is the attorney correct? Why?
2. A local hotel operated under a franchise agreement with a major hotel chain. Several customers charged the banquet director of the local hotel with misconduct and harassment. They sued the hotel chain (the franchisor) for acts committed by the local hotel (the franchisee), claiming that the franchisee was the agent of the franchisor. Is an agency created under these circumstances? Why?
3. A principal hired a mortgage banking firm to obtain a loan commitment of $10,000,000 from an insurance company for the construction of a shopping center. The firm was promised a fee of $50,000 for obtaining the commitment. The firm was successful in arranging for the loan, and the insurance company, without the principal's knowledge, agreed to pay the firm a finder's fee. The principal then refused to pay the firm the promised $50,000 and the firm brought suit to recover the fee. May the firm recover the fee? Why?
4. Based on his experience as a CIA agent, a former agent published a book about certain CIA activities in South Vietnam. The CIA did not approve publication of the book although, as a condition of his employment, the agent had agreed not to publish any information relating to the CIA without specific approval of the agency. The government brought suit against the agent, claiming that all of the agent's profits from publishing the book should go to the government. Assuming that the government suffered only nominal damages because the agent published no classified information, will the government prevail? Why?
5. Upon graduation from college, Edison was hired by a major chemical company. During the time when he was employed by the company, Edison discovered a synthetic oil that could be manufactured at a very low cost. What rights, if any, does Edison's employer have to the discovery? Why?
6. An American company hired MacDonald to serve as its resident agent in Bolivia. MacDonald entered into a contract to sell cars to Bolivia and personally guaranteed performance of the contract as required by Bolivian law. The

cars delivered to Bolivia were defective and Bolivia recovered a judgment of $83,000 from MacDonald. Must the American company reimburse MacDonald for this amount? Why?

7. According to the late Professor William L. Prosser, "The theory underlying the workmen's compensation acts never has been stated better than in the old campaign slogan, 'The cost of the product should bear the blood of the workman.' " What is meant by this statement?

ANSWERS TO SELF-TEST QUESTIONS

1. (c)   2. (d)   3. (c)   4. (d)   5. (b)

SUGGESTED ANSWER TO DEMONSTRATION PROBLEM

Although the conclusion is debatable, the Rhode Island Supreme Court decided that the worker could recover under workers' compensation. The key issue here is whether the injury was work-related. The court concluded that there was a causal connection between the employment and the injury because the worker did a "permitted act in an improper manner." One justice observed that the worker's "confrontation with the balky coffee machine qualified him to join company in the Rhode Island Workers' Compensation Hall of Fame." (*Business Insurance*, September 17, 1979, at 105.)

CHAPTER

38

Liability of Principal and Agent; Termination of Agency

*I*n Chapter 37 we considered the relationship between agent and principal. Now we turn to relationships between third parties and the principal or agent. When the agent makes a contract for his principal or commits a tort in the course of his work, is the principal liable? What is the responsibility of the agent for torts committed and contracts entered into on behalf of his principal? How may the relationship be terminated, so that the principal or agent will no longer have responsibility toward or liability for the acts of the other? These are the questions addressed in this chapter.

PRINCIPAL'S CONTRACT LIABILITY

The key to determining whether a principal is liable for contracts made by his agent is **authority:** Was the agent authorized to negotiate the agreement and close the deal? Obviously, it would not be sensible to hold a contractor liable to pay for a ton of wood merely because a stranger wandered into the lumber yard claiming to represent the contractor. For there to be liability the principal must have authorized the agent in some manner to act in his behalf. There are three types of authority: *express, implied,* and *apparent* (see Figure 38-1). We will consider each in turn.

Express Authority

The strongest form of authority is that which is expressly granted, often in written form. The principal consents to the agent's actions and the third party may then rely on the document attesting to the agent's authority to deal on behalf of the principal. One common form of express authority is the standard signature card on file with banks allowing corporate agents to write checks on the company's credit. The principal bears the risk of any wrongful action of his agent, as demonstrated in *Allen A. Funt Productions, Inc.* v. *Chemical Bank,* 405 N.Y.S.2d 94 (1978). Allen A.

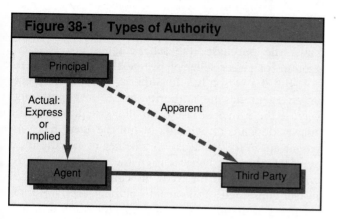

Figure 38-1 Types of Authority

Funt submitted to his bank through his production company various certificates permitting his accountant to use the company's checking accounts. In fact, for several years the accountant embezzled money from the company by writing checks to himself and depositing them in his own account. The company sued its bank, charging it with negligence, apparently for failing to monitor the amount of money taken by the accountant. But the court dismissed the negligence complaint, citing a state statute based on the common law agency principle that a third party is entitled to rely on the express authorization given to an agent; in this case, the accountant drew checks on the account within the monetary limits contained in the signature cards on file with the bank.

Implied Authority

Not every detail on an agent's work can be spelled out. It is impossible to delineate step-by-step the duties of a general agent; at best, a principal can set forth only the general nature of the duties that the agent is to perform. Even a special agent's duties are difficult to describe in such detail as to leave him without discretion. If express authority were the only valid kind, there would be no efficient way to use an agent, both because the effort to describe the duties would be too great and because the third party would be reluctant to deal with him.

But the law permits authority to be "implied" by the relationship of the parties, by the nature and customs of the business, the circumstances surrounding the act in question, the wording of the agency contract, and the knowledge that the agent has of facts relevant to the assignment. The general rule is that the agent has implied or "incidental" authority to perform acts incidental to or reasonably necessary to carrying out the transaction. Thus, if a principal instructs his agent to "deposit a check in the bank today," the agent has authority to drive to the bank, unless the principal specifically prohibits the agent from doing so.

The theory of implied authority is especially important to business in the realm of the business manager, who may be charged with running the entire business operation or only a small part of it. In either event, the business manager has a relatively large domain of implied authority. He can buy goods and services; hire, supervise, and fire employees; sell or junk inventory; take in receipts and pay debts; and in general, direct the ordinary operations of the business. The full extent of the manager's authority depends on the circumstances—what is customary in the particular industry, the particular business, and among the individuals directly concerned.

On the other hand, a manager does not have implicit authority to undertake *unusual* or *extraordinary* actions on behalf of his principal. In the absence of express permission, an agent may not sell off part of the business, start a new business, change the nature of the business, incur debt (unless borrowing is integral to the business, as in banking, for example), or move the business premises. The owner of a hotel appoints Andy manager; Andy decides to rename the hotel and commissions an artist to prepare a new logo for the hotel's stationery. Andy has no implied authority to change the name or to commission the artist, though he does have implied authority to engage a printer to replenish the stationery supply—and possibly to make some design changes in the letterhead.

Even when there is no implied authority, in an emergency the agent may act in ways that would in the normal course require specific permission from the principal. If unforeseen circumstances arise and it is impracticable to communicate with the principal to find out what his wishes would be, the agent may do "what he reasonably believes to be necessary in order to prevent substantial loss to his principal." (*Restatement (Second) of Agency*, Section 47). During World War II, Eastern Wine Corporation marketed champagne in a bottle with a diagonal red stripe that infringed the trademark of a French producer. The French company had granted licenses to an American importer to market its champagne in the United States. The contract between producer and importer required the latter to notify the French company whenever a competitor appeared to be infringing its rights and to recommend steps by which the company could put a stop to the infringement. The authority to institute suit was not expressly conferred, and ordinarily the right to do so would not be inferred. Because France was under German occupation, however, the importer was unable to communicate with the producer, its principal. The court held that the importer could file suit to enjoin Eastern Wine from continuing to display the infringing red diagonal stripe, since legal action was "essential to the preservation of the principal's property." [G.H. Mumm Champagne v. Eastern Wine Corp., 52 F.Supp. 167 (S.D.N.Y. 1943)]

The rule that a person's position can carry with it implied authority is fundamental to American business practice. But outside the United States, this rule is not applicable, and the business executive traveling abroad should be aware that in civil-law countries it is customary to present proof of authority to transact corporate business—usually in the form of a power of attorney. This is not always an easy task. Not only must the power of the traveling executive be shown, but the right of the corporate officer back in the United States to delegate authority must also be proven.

Apparent Authority

It is part and parcel of the agency relationship that through his actions in dealing with third parties the agent will affect the legal rights of the principal. What the third party knows about the agency agreement is irrelevant to the agent's legal authority to act. That authority runs from principal to agent. As long as an agent has authorization, either express or implied, he may bind the principal legally. Thus, the seller of a house may be ignorant of the buyer's true identity; the person he supposes to be the prospective purchaser actually might be the agent of an undisclosed principal. Nevertheless, if the agent is authorized to make the purchase, the seller's ignorance is not a ground for either seller or principal to void the deal.

But if a person has no authority to act as an agent, or an agent has no authority to act in a particular way, is the principal free from all consequences? The answer depends on whether or not the agent has "apparent authority"; that is, on whether or not the third person reasonably believes from the principal's words, written or spoken, or from his conduct, that he has in fact consented to the agent's actions. **Apparent authority** is a manifestation of authority communicated to the third person; it runs from principal to third party, not to the agent.

Apparent authority is sometimes said to be based on the principle of "estoppel." Estoppel is the doctrine that one should not profit from misrepresentation but should be bound by his assertions; the courts will not permit the deceitful party to deny what he has earlier said if someone else has relied to his detriment on the assertion.

Apparent authority can arise from prior business transactions. On July 10, Meggs sold his business, the right to use the trade name Rose City Sheet Metal Works, and a list of suppliers he had used. Three days later the buyer began ordering supplies from Central Supply Company, which was on Meggs's list but with which Meggs had last dealt four years previously. On September 3, Central received a letter from Meggs notifying it of the sale. The buyer failed to pay Central, which sued Meggs. The court held that Rose City Sheet Metal Works had apparent authority to buy on Meggs's credit; Meggs was liable for supplies purchased between July 10 and September 3. [Meggs v. Central Supply Co., 307 N.E.2d 288 (Ind.App. 1974)] In such cases, and in cases involving the firing of a general manager, actual notice should be given promptly to all customers. The following case illustrates other circumstances that may result in creation of apparent authority.

KANAVOS v. HANCOCK BANK & TRUST COMPANY
14 Mass. App. 326,
439 N.E.2d 311 (1982)

KASS, JUSTICE. At the close of the plaintiff's evidence, the defendant moved for a directed verdict, which the trial judge allowed. The judge's reason for so doing was that the plaintiff, in his contract action, failed to introduce sufficient evidence tending to prove that the bank officer who made the agreement with which the plaintiff sought to charge the bank had any authority to make it. Upon review of the record we are of opinion that there was evidence which, if believed, warranted a finding that the bank officer had the requisite authority or that the bank officer had apparent authority to make the agreement in controversy. We, therefore, reverse the judgment.

* * *

For approximately ten years prior to 1975, Harold Kanavos and his brother borrowed money on at least twenty occasions from the Hancock Bank & Trust Company (the Bank), and, during that period, the loan officer with whom Kanavos always dealt was James M. Brown. The aggregate loans made by the Bank to Kanavos at any given time went as high as $800,000.

Over that same decade, Brown's responsibilities at the Bank grew, and he had become executive vice-president. Brown was also the chief loan officer for the Bank, which had fourteen or fifteen branches in addition to its head office. Physically, Brown's office was at the head office, toward the rear of the main banking floor, opposite the office of the president—whose name was Kelley. Often Brown would tell Kanavos that he had to check an aspect of a loan transaction with Kelley, but Kelley always backed Brown up on those occasions.

* * *

[The plaintiff, Harold Kanavos, entered into an agreement with the defendant Bank whereby stock owned by the Kavanos brothers was sold to the Bank and the plaintiff was given an option to repurchase the stock. Kanavos' suit against the Bank was based on an amendment to the agreement offered by Brown.]

Kanavos was never permitted to introduce in evidence the terms of the offer Brown made. That offer was contained in a writing, dated July 16, 1976, on bank letterhead, which read as follows: "This letter is to confirm our conversation regarding your option to re-purchase the subject property. In lieu of your not exercising your option, we agree to pay you $40,000 representing a commission upon our sale of the subject property, and in addition, will give you the option to match the price of sale of said property to extend for a 60 day period from the time our offer is received." Brown signed the letter as executive vice-president. The basis of exclusion was that the plaintiff had not established the authority of Brown to make with Kanavos the arrangement memorialized in the July 16, 1976, letter.

* * *

(continued on next page)

(*continued*)

**KANAVOS v.
HANCOCK BANK &
TRUST COMPANY**
14 Mass. App. 326,
439 N.E.2d 311 (1982)

Whether Brown's job description impliedly authorized the right of last refusal or cash payment modification is a question of how, in the circumstances, a person in Brown's position could reasonably interpret his authority. Whether Brown had *apparent authority* to make the July 16, 1976, modification is a question of how, in the circumstances, a third person, e.g., a customer of the Bank such as Kanavos, would reasonably interpret Brown's authority in light of the manifestations of his principal, the Bank.

Titles of office generally do not establish apparent authority. Brown's status as executive vice-president was not, therefore, a badge of apparent authority to modify agreements to which the Bank was a party.

Trappings of office, e.g., office and furnishing, private secretary, while they may have some tendency to suggest executive responsibility, do not without other evidence provide a basis for finding apparent authority. Apparent authority is drawn from a variety of circumstances. Thus in *Federal Natl. Bank* v. *O'Connell*, 26 N.E.2d 539 (1940), it was held apparent authority could be found because an officer who was a director, vice-president and treasurer took an active part in directing the affairs of the bank in question and was seen by third parties talking with customers and negotiating with them. In *Costonis* v. *Medford Housing Authy.*, 176 N.E.2d 25 (1961), the executive director of a public housing authority was held to have apparent authority to vary specifications on the basis of the cumulative effect of what he had done and what the authority appeared to permit him to do.

In the instant case there was evidence of the following variety of circumstances: Brown's title of *executive* vice-president; the location of his office opposite the president; his frequent communications with the president; the long course of dealing and negotiations; the encouragement of Kanavos by the president to deal with Brown; the earlier amendment of the agreement by Brown on behalf of the Bank on material points, namely the price to be paid by the Bank for the shares and the repurchase price; the size of the Bank (fourteen or fifteen branches in addition to the main office); the secondary, rather than fundamental, nature of the change in the terms of the agreement now repudiated by the Bank, measured against the context of the overall transaction; and Brown's broad operating authority . . . all these added together would support a finding of apparent authority. When a corporate officer, as here, is allowed to exercise general executive responsibilities, the "public expectation is that the corporation should be bound to engagements made on its behalf by those who presume to have, and convincingly appear to have, the power to agree." Kempin, The Corporate Officer and the Law of Agency, 44 Va.L.Rev. 1273, 1280 (1958). This principle does not apply, of course, where in the business context, the requirement of specific authority is presumed, e.g., the sale of a major asset by a corporation or a transaction which by its nature commits the corporation to an obligation outside the scope of its usual activity. The modification agreement signed by Brown and dated July 16, 1976, should have been admitted in evidence, and a verdict should not have been directed.

Judgment reversed.

Ratification

Even if the agent possessed no actual authority, and there was no apparent authority on which the third person could rely, the principal may still be liable if he **ratifies** or adopts the agent's acts before the third person withdraws from the contract. Ratification usually relates back to the time of the undertaking, creating authority after the fact as though it had been established initially. Ratification is a voluntary act by the principal. Faced with the results of action purportedly done on his behalf but without authorization and through no fault of his own, he may affirm or disavow them as he chooses. To ratify, the principal may tell the parties concerned or by his conduct manifest that he is willing to accept the results as though the act were authorized. Or by his silence he may find under certain circumstances that he has ratified. Note that ratification does not require the usual consideration of contract law. The principal need be promised nothing extra for his decision to affirm to be binding on him. Nor does ratification depend on the position of the third party; for example, a loss stemming from his reliance on the "agent's" representations is not required.

In most situations, ratification leaves the parties where they expected to be, correcting "minor errors of agents without harm to any one," and giving "to the other party what he expected to get and to the principal what he was willing to receive" (Seavey, 1964, p. 58).

PRINCIPAL'S TORT LIABILITY

When is the principal liable for injuries that the agent causes another to suffer? Here we may make a distinction between torts prompted by the principal himself and torts of which the principal was innocent. If the principal directed the agent to commit a tort or knew that the consequences of the agent's carrying out his instructions would bring harm to someone, the principal is liable. This is an application of the general common-law principle that one cannot escape liability by delegating an unlawful act to another. The syndicate that hires a contract-killer is as culpable of murder as the man who pulls the trigger. Similarly, a principal who is negligent in his use of agents will be held liable for their negligence. This rule comes into play when the principal fails to supervise employees adequately, gives faulty directions, or hires incompetent or unsuitable people for a particular job.

Imposing liability on the principal in these cases is readily justifiable since it is the principal's own conduct that is the underlying fault. But the principle of liability for one's agent is much broader, extending as it does to acts of which the principal had no knowledge, which he had no intention to commit nor involvement in, and which he may in fact have expressly prohibited the agent from engaging in. This is the principle of **respondeat superior** ("let the master answer") or **"vicarious liability,"** under which the principal is responsible for acts committed by the agent within the scope of the employment (see Figure 38-2).

The modern basis for vicarious liability is sometimes termed the "deep pocket" theory: the principal (usually a corporation) has deeper pockets than the agent, meaning that it has the wherewithal to pay for the injuries traceable one way or another to events it set in motion. A million-dollar industrial accident is within the means of a company or its insurer; it is usually not within the means of the agent who caused it (see **Box 38-1**).

The "deep pocket" of the defendant-company is not always very deep, however. For many small businesses, in fact, the principle of *respondeat superior* is one of life or death. One example was the closing in San Francisco of the Larraburu Brothers Bakery—at the time, the world's second largest sourdough bread maker. The bakery was held liable for $2 million in

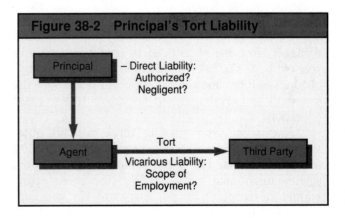

Figure 38-2   Principal's Tort Liability

Savitch Settlement

By Debra Cassandra Moss

*[The basis for vicarious liability is often called the "deep pocket" theory. Plaintiffs like to keep corporations in a lawsuit because jurors are more likely to award damages against a corporate defendant with the means to pay for injuries.—*AUTHORS' NOTE]

The estate of Jessica Savitch has reached an $8.15 million cash settlement with the *New York Post* and three other defendants for the TV newswoman's wrongful death in a car accident.

Savitch, 35, was killed Oct. 23, 1983, when riding in a car driven by *New York Post* Vice President Martin Fischbein after dining with him at a New Hope, Pa., restaurant.

In the rain and fog, Fischbein pulled out of the wrong end of the parking lot and onto a tow path along a canal, where mules once pulled barges. The car slid into the canal and flipped onto its roof.

"Since there was no role model of a female Water Cronkite, we were ready to establish through testimony

A DEEP POCKETS DEFENDANT

that Jessica Savitch was on the cutting edge, and there was no reason she would not have the same longevity and earn the same levels as a male anchor," said Arthur Raynes, lawyer for the Savitch estate.

The *Post* paid more than $7 million of the non-structured settlement. Other defendants who contributed were the Chez Odette Restaurant, Pennsylvania's Department of Environment Resources, and Fischbein's estate.

The suit alleged that the Department of Environmental Resources failed to provide barriers and adequate signs at the tow path entrance even though a similar accident happened there four years ago; that the restaurant failed to provide adequate warnings to its patrons of the danger; that Fischbein was negligent for driving into the canal and failing to see two signs prohibiting motor vehicles from entering the tow path; and that Fischbein was conducting business for the *Post*.

Philadelphia County Common Pleas Judge Bernard Goodheart de-

nied a motion for summary judgment filed by the *Post*, which claimed that it was not liable because Savitch and Fischbein were dating and not engaged in business at the time of the accident.

Raynes was able to show by income tax returns that Fischbein's car, leased by the *New York Post*, was deducted by the newspaper as a business expense. In addition, Savitch had signed a contract to write a syndicated column for the McNaught Agency, to which the *Post* subscribed.

*   *   *

Strategically, the plaintiffs preferred to keep the *Post* in the lawsuit because a jury might have been more likely to award money against a corporate defendant.

Savitch's mother, other beneficiaries, Raynes and his firm plan to establish a $500,000 trust fund from the recovery and legal fees to give scholarships to students who show excellence in journalism and broadcast news at Ithaca College, the University of Pennsylvania and Temple University, says Raynes.

Source: *ABA Journal*, June 1, 1988

damages after one of its delivery trucks injured a 6-year-old boy. The bakery's insurance policy had a limit of $1.25 million, and the bakery could not absorb the excess. The Larraburus had no choice but to cease operations.

Respondeat superior raises three difficult questions. (1) What type of agents can create tort liability for the principal? (2) Is the principal liable for the agent's intentional torts? (3) Was the agent acting within the scope of his employment? We will consider these questions in turn.

Agents for Whom Principals Are Vicariously Liable

In general, the broadest liability is imposed on the *master* in the case of tortious physical conduct by a *servant* (Chapter 37). If the servant acted within the scope of his employment—that is, if the servant's wrongful conduct occurred while performing his job—the master will be liable to the victim for damages, unless, as we have seen, the victim was another employee, in which event the workers' compensation system will be invoked. Physical injuries caused by non-servant agents are not generally chargeable to the principal. The distinction stems from the original difference between servant and agent: the servant was defined as one who did physical labor for a principal; those who were not subject to a master's control over their daily labor were non-servant agents. Because the master had an obligation to supervise those in his employ, liability was imposed when the supervision failed to prevent accidents—as, for example, when a salaried deliveryman drives too fast or runs a red light.

However, the principal might be held liable for nonphysical torts caused by agents other than servants—for example, a seller's agent who misrepresents the condition of goods can subject the seller to liability for damages.

Ordinarily, an individual or company is not vicariously liable for the tortious acts of independent contractors. The plumber who rushes to a home to repair a leak and causes a traffic accident does not subject the homeowner to liability. But there are exceptions to the rule. Generally, these exceptions fall into a category of duties that the law deems nondelegable. In some situations, one person is obligated to provide protection to or care for another. The failure to do so results in liability whether or not the harm befell the other because of an independent contractor's wrongdoing. Thus, a homeowner has a duty to ensure that physical conditions in and around the home are not unreasonably dangerous. If the owner hires an independent contracting firm to dig a sewer line and the contractor negligently fails to guard passersby against the danger of falling into an open trench, the homeowner is liable, because the duty of care in this instance cannot be delegated. (The contractor is, of course, liable to the homeowner for any damages paid to an injured passerby.)

Liability for Agents' Intentional Torts

In the nineteenth century, a principal was rarely held liable for intentional wrongdoing by the agent if the principal did not command the act complained of. The thought was that one could never infer authority to commit a willfully wrongful act. Today, liability for intentional torts is imputed to the principal whenever the agent is acting to further the principal's business. In the following case this test was not met.

SIMMONS v. BALTIMORE ORIOLES, INC.
712 F.Supp. 79
(W.D.Va. 1989)

GLEN M. WILLIAMS, SENIOR DISTRICT JUDGE.

The plaintiff brought suit against the defendants for $1,000,000 in compensatory damages and $1,000,000 in punitive damages for injuries to his face and jaw arising out of a fight with defendants Champ and Hicks, minor league baseball players employed by the Baltimore Orioles. Specifically, Simmons alleges that he was the victim of an assault by Champ and Hicks which ended with Hicks breaking Simmons' jaw with a baseball bat. Defendant Baltimore Orioles, Inc., has moved to dismiss the charges, and defendant Bluestone Security Agency has filed a motion for summary judgment. No motions are pending on behalf of Champ and Hicks individually.

Certain facts are not in dispute. Simmons, along with a friend, attended the Fourth of July, 1988 game between the Martinsville Phillies and the Bluefield Orioles, a Baltimore farm team, at Bluefield, Virginia. Bluefield was not having a good year, and whether for this or some other reason Simmons moved down to the third baseline along about the eighth inning, and started to heckle the Oriole players sitting in the bullpen. Champ stated in his deposition that Simmons was accusing the ballplayers of stealing the local

(continued on next page)

(*continued*)

**SIMMONS v.
BALTIMORE
ORIOLES, INC.**
712 F.Supp. 79
(W.D.Va. 1989)

women, and that he (Simmons) would show the Orioles what West Virginia manhood was like by blowing the players' heads off. Whatever was precisely said, the pitching coach then asked Simmons to leave.

After the game (Bluefield lost, 9–8, stranding three runners in the bottom of the ninth), Champ encountered Simmons in the parking lot. Simmons, in his complaint, offers no details of what ensued other than that he was punched and kicked by Champ and then hit in the jaw by a baseball bat wielded by Hicks, causing his jaw to be broken in two places. Champ's version was that Simmons saw him carrying a bat, made a gesture as if he were shooting Champ with his finger, and said "Oh, so you need a bat, huh?" Champ said "No, I don't," and threw his bat down. Simmons gestured toward his car and said, "Let's go over to my car, and I'll blow your head off." Another player tried to intervene, and Champ said, "Just get out of here." Simmons then advanced threateningly upon him, and Champ hit Simmons in the face. Simmons was unfazed, and Champ kicked him in the chest, causing Simmons to stagger back. According to Champ he then smiled and said "I'm drunk. I didn't feel that." Champ turned to walk away, and at that point defendant Hicks hit Simmons. Simmons says Hicks hit him with a bat, but Hicks says that he used only his fist. Hicks had not been near any of the heckling and says he intervened because he was afraid Simmons was about to pull a gun on Champ.

For the purposes of the Orioles' motion to dismiss, of course, the court accepts the plaintiff's version of the events as true. The narrow legal question is whether the Orioles breached any legal duty to Simmons.

*   *   *

The doctrine of *respondeat superior* applies only when the plaintiff proves that 1) at the time of the commission of the tort the servant was about his master's business, and 2) the servant was acting within the scope of his employment. Simmons can prove neither criterion. At the time of the assault the game was over, Champ and Hicks had left the locker room, and the altercation took place outside the confines of the ballpark. Champ and Hicks were not about any business for the Orioles, and it would be fatuous to suggest that the fight was within the scope of their employment. Therefore, no recovery can be based upon the grounds of *respondeat superior*.

The plaintiff contends, however, that Virginia has recognized the tort of "negligent hiring." *J. v. Victory Tabernacle Baptist Church*, 372 S.E.2d 391 (1988). In this case, the Virginia Supreme Court held that the mother of a ten-year-old girl who was raped by a handyman had stated a claim against the church which had employed him. Unlike *respondeat superior*, liability may be imposed even if the servant is not acting within the scope of his employment. The test is whether the employer has negligently placed "an unfit person in an employment situation involving an unreasonable risk of harm to others."

*   *   *

The plaintiff in the instant case, by contrast, makes no invidious allegations of any kind against Hicks and Champ. No previous tendency towards violence was alleged or even suggested. [The Orioles' motion to dismiss is granted.]

Deviations from Employment

It may be clear that the person causing an injury is the agent of another. But a principal cannot be responsible for every act of an agent. If an employee is following the letter of his instructions, it will be easy to determine liability. But suppose an agent deviates in some way from his job. The classic test of liability was set forth in an 1833 English case, *Joel* v. *Morison*, 6 Carrington & Payne 501. The plaintiff was run over on a highway by a speeding cart and horse. The driver was the employee of another, and inside was a fellow employee. There was no question that the driver had acted carelessly, but what they were doing on the road where the plaintiff was injured was disputed. For weeks before and after the accident, the cart had never been driven in the vicinity in which the plaintiff was walking, nor did it have any business there. The suggestion was that the employees might have gone out of their way for their own purposes. As the great English jurist, Baron Parke, put it in a famous statement: "If the servants, being on their master's business, took a detour to call upon a friend, the master will be responsible. . . . [B]ut if he was going on a frolic of his own, without being at all on his master's business, the master will not be liable." In applying this test, the court held the employer liable.

The test is thus one of degree, and it is not always easy to decide when a detour has become so great as to be transformed into a frolic. For a time, a rather mechanical rule was invoked to aid in making the decision. The courts looked to the servant's purposes in "detouring." If the servant's mind was fixed on accomplishing his own purposes, then the detour was held to be outside the scope of employment; hence the tort was not imputed to the master. But if the servant also intended to accomplish his master's purposes during his departure from the letter of his assignment, or if he committed the wrong while returning to his master's task after the completion of his frolic, then the tort was held to be within the scope of employment.

This test is not always easy to apply. If a hungry delivery man stops in at a restaurant outside the normal lunch hour, intending to continue to his next delivery after eating, he is within the scope of employment. But suppose he decides to take the truck home that evening, in violation of rules, in order to get an early start the next morning. Suppose he decides to stop by the beach, which is far away from his route. Does it make a difference if the employer knows that his truckers do this?

More recent court decisions have moved toward a different standard, one that looks to the foreseeability of the agent's conduct. By this standard, an employer may be held liable for his employee's conduct even when devoted entirely to the employee's own purposes, as long as it was foreseeable that the agent might act as he did. This is the **"zone of risk,"** the place within which, if the master were to send out a search party to find a missing employee, it would be reasonable to look. The next case illustrates this standard.

O'BOYLE v. AVIS RENT-A-CAR SYSTEM, INC.
78 A.D.2d 431,
435 N.Y.S.2d 296 (1981)

LAZER, JUSTICE. The tragic vehicular accident underlying this action occurred when a 16-year-old employee at a gasoline station from which an Avis car rental agency was being operated drove in a rental car to pick up lunch, tarried briefly with his girlfriend passenger, and during the return collided with another automobile, killing two of its occupants and seriously injuring two others. In their ensuing action, the victims or their representatives alleged, *inter alia*, that the collision was caused not only by the conduct of the employee, Robert Bruno, but also by the direct and vicarious negligence of the defendant G. Roland House, who owned the gas station and car rental agency, and the defendant Avis Rent-A-Car System, Inc., the owner of the car. At the conclusion of a trial on the issue of liability, the jury rendered a two-fold verdict [against the defendants].

★   ★   ★

On March 17, 1974 Sunday sales of gasoline were still banned due to the Arab oil embargo and the House station was open solely for the purpose of renting Avis cars. House arrived at 10:00 A.M., stayed for about an hour, and left Bruno alone and in charge for the balance of the day. At about 1:30 P.M., Greg Adams, another young House employee, appeared at the station to work on his own car and agreed to "watch the station" while Bruno and his girlfriend went to pick up a pizza which would provide lunch for Adams and Bruno. Although Adams was under the impression that Bruno was going to walk up the street to get the pizza, he saw the latter take a key off a rack and drive away in an Avis car.

After the pizza was purchased at Leonardi's, an establishment variously estimated as being one-eighth of a mile to two or three miles from the station, Bruno drove to a nursery in Armonk where he and his girlfriend "talked for about twenty minutes." When they left the nursery, it was Bruno's intention to drive the girl home and return to work, but about a mile from her house and a mile from the House station the car went out of control, entered the opposing lane of traffic, and crashed head-on with a car driven by Adele O'Boyle. Mrs. O'Boyle and her infant daughter perished while her husband and mother suffered serious injuries.

At the trial, conflicting evidence was adduced as to who was authorized to operate Avis vehicles and where and for what purpose they could be driven. House testified that he instructed Bruno "not to take an Avis car off the property under any conditions" but that he could drive Avis cars on the service station property. Although House said that this instruction was given to all employees, when asked whether he had ever authorized any licensed employee to take Avis cars off the premises, he replied that he had done so in certain emergency situations such as jump-starting a car or digging a customer out of a snow bank. House maintained that such occurrences were relatively rare and he usually would accompany his employee in rendering aid to the customer, after which the employee would drive the disabled car back to the station.

This testimony was supported by the deposition of Greg Adams, who was 14 years old and unlicensed when hired by House in 1972. Adams declared that his duties then were to "pump gas [and] rent Avis cars," that he had authority from House to drive Avis cars to and from gas pumps on the premises, and that this was observed on a number of occasions by Avis representatives. Adams asserted that on his first day on the job House advised him that there was to be "[n]o driving the Avis cars off the property" and that the direction was repeated to him at least once a week for a period of two years. Because Adams had recommended Bruno for the job, he was present during the latter's job interview and heard House say that Avis cars were not to be driven off the premises. Adams recalled only one occasion during his 22 months of employment preceding the accident when an Avis car was taken off the premises by a House employee in order to make a service call.

Countervailing evidence was offered by another part-time House employee, Perry Palazzetti, who testified at the trial. Palazzetti was 16 years old and unlicensed when hired in July, 1973, although he obtained a license shortly afterwards. In February, 1974, after closing the station, he drove an Avis car off the premises, and was apprehended in Connecticut for speeding. Palazzetti remembered some 10 to 15 instances when House had instructed him to drive Avis cars on service calls "for both purposes, Mr. House's purposes and Avis purposes" and about 10 other occasions when House directed a particular licensed employee to take an Avis car out for a service call. He was not asked, however, whether House had ever admonished him or anyone else never to take an Avis car off the premises.

*   *   *

We have deferred for last, consideration of the most troublesome issue in the case—whether Bruno's negligent act fell within the scope of his employment. Foreseeability is the State's current criterion for measuring an employer's liability for conduct of employees whose behavior is alleged to have taken them beyond the scope of their employment. In a *respondeat superior* context, foreseeability differs significantly from the " 'foreseeably unreasonable risk of harm that spells negligence' " (*Bushey & Sons v. United States*, 398 F.2d 167, 171) (2 Cir.). It is a foresight which must impel the prudent man to " 'perceive the harm likely to flow from his long-run activity in spite of all reasonable precautions on his own part.' "

*   *   *

Plainly, then, the focus of our own inquiry must be upon the foreseeability of Bruno's conduct in taking a car to get his lunch. The jury knew that House was aware of Bruno's ability to drive and it was within the jury's discretion to believe testimony that Avis cars often had been utilized in the course of the service station business. An employer takes men and women "subject to the kind of conduct normal to such beings" (*Riviello v. Waldron*,

(continued on next page)

**O'BOYLE v. AVIS
RENT-A-CAR SYSTEM,
INC.**
78 A.D.2d 431,
435 N.Y.S.2d 296 (1981)

(continued)

391 N.E.2d 1278) and, obviously, young persons subject to the kind of conduct normal to them. Whether it was foreseeable over the long run of House's operation that in the course of activities in furtherance of his employer's interest an employee—even a young one—would take an Avis car to obtain lunch was a matter for the jury to decide. Considering the evidence and the inferences drawable from it, the jury's imposition of vicarious liability upon House cannot be deemed a defiance of rationality or contrary to the weight of the evidence. [Judgment affirmed.]

Special Cases of Vicarious Liability

Vicarious liability is not limited to harm caused in the course of an agency relationship. It may also be imposed in other areas, including torts of family members, and other torts governed by statute or regulation. We will examine each in turn.

Use of Automobiles   A problem commonly arises when an automobile owner lends his vehicle to a personal friend, someone who is not an agent, and the borrower injures a third person. Is the owner liable? In many states, the owner is not liable; in other states, however, two approaches impose liability on the owner.

The first approach is legislative: "owner's consent statutes" make the owner liable when the automobile is being driven with his consent or knowledge. The second approach to placing liability on the owner is judge-made and known as the "family purpose doctrine." Under this doctrine, a family member who negligently injures someone with the car subjects the owner to liability if the family member was furthering family purposes. These are loosely defined to include virtually every use to which a child, for example, might put a car. In a Georgia case, *Dixon* v. *Phillips* 217 S.E.2d 331 (Ga. 1975), the father allowed his minor son to drive the car, but expressly forbade him from letting anyone else do so. Nevertheless, the son gave the wheel to a friend and a collision occurred while both were in the car. The court held the father liable because he made the car available for the pleasure and convenience of his son and other family members.

Torts of Family Members   At common law, the husband was liable for the torts of his wife, not be-cause she was considered an agent but because she was considered to be an extension of him. "Husband and wife were only one person in law," says Holmes and any act of the wife was supposed to have been done at the husband's direction (to which Dickens's Mr. Bumble responded, in the memorable line, "if the law supposes that, the law is a ass—a idiot"). This ancient view has been abrogated by statute or by court ruling in all the states, so that now a wife is solely responsible for her own torts unless she in fact serves as her husband's agent.

Unlike wives, children were not presumed at common law to be agents or extensions of the father so that normally parents are not vicariously liable for their children's torts. However, they can be held liable for failing to control children known to be dangerous.

Most states have statutorily changed the common law rule, making parents responsible for wilfull or malicious tortious acts of children whether or not they are known to be mischiefmakers. Thus the Illinois Parental Responsibility Law provides: "The parent or legal guardian of an unemancipated minor who resides with such parent or legal guardian is liable for actual damages for the wilful or malicious acts of such minor which cause injury to a person or property." (Ill.Rev.Stat. 1975), chapter 70, paragraph 53). Several other states impose a monetary limit on such liability.

Other Torts Governed by Statute or Regulation   There are certain types of conduct that statutes or regulation attempt to control by placing the burden of liability on those presumably in a position to prevent the unwanted conduct. An example is the "Dram Shop Act," which in many states subjects the owner f a bar to liability if the bar continues to serve an ntoxicated patron who later is involved in an accident while intoxicated.

PRINCIPAL'S CRIMINAL LIABILITY

As a general proposition, a principal will not be held liable for an agent's unauthorized criminal acts, if the crimes are those requiring specific intent. Thus a department store proprietor who tells his chief buyer to get the "best deal possible" on next fall's fashions is not liable if the buyer steals clothes from the manufacturer.

There is a narrow exception to the broad policy of immunity. Courts have ruled that under certain regulatory statutes and regulations, an agent's criminality may be imputed to the principal, just as civil liability is imputed under Dram Shop Acts. These include pure food and drug acts, speeding ordinances, building regulations, child labor rules, and minimum wage and maximum hour legislation.

AGENT'S PERSONAL LIABILITY FOR TORTS AND CONTRACTS

Tort Liability

That a principal is held vicariously liable and must pay damages to an injured third person does not excuse the agent, who actually committed the tortious acts. The agent is personally liable for his wrongful acts and must reimburse the principal for any damages he was forced to pay, as long as the principal did not authorize the wrongful conduct. The agent directed to commit a tort remains liable for his own conduct but is not obliged to repay the principal. Liability as an agent can be burdensome, sometimes perhaps more burdensome than as a principal. The latter normally purchases insurance to cover against wrongful acts of agents, but liability insurance policies frequently do not cover the employee's personal liability if named in a lawsuit individually. Thus doctors' and hospitals' malpractice policies protect a doctor from both her own mistakes and those of nurses and others that the doctor would be responsible for; nurses, however, might need their own coverage. In the absence of insurance, an agent is at serious risk in this lawsuit-conscious age.

The risk is not total. The agent is not liable for torts of other agents unless he is personally at fault— for example, by negligently supervising a junior or by giving faulty instructions. Agent, general manager for Principal, hires Brown as subordinate. Brown is competent to do the job, but by failing to exercise proper control over a machine negligently injures Ted, a visitor to the premises. Principal and Brown are liable to Ted but Agent is not.

Contract Liability

In general, an agent is not personally liable for contracts he had negotiated on behalf of a principal. There is a major exception to the general rule in some countries. For example, English law provides that an agent of a principal who resides outside England is liable, even if it is clear that he is signing the contract as an agent.

In the United States, there are the following exceptions to the general rule: (1) when the agent is serving an undisclosed or partially-disclosed principal; (2) when the agent lacks authority or exceeds his authority; and (3) if the agent entered into the contract in a personal capacity. We will consider each exception in turn.

Agent for Undisclosed (or Partially Disclosed) Principal An agent need not, and frequently will not, inform the person with whom he is negotiating that he is acting on behalf of a principal. The secret principal is usually called an **"undisclosed principal."** Or the agent may tell the other person that he is acting as an agent but not disclose the principal's name, in which event the principal is **"partially disclosed."** To understand the difficulties that occur, consider the following hypothetical but common example. A real estate developer wants to acquire several parcels of land to put up an amusement park. He is anxious to keep his identity secret because he wants to hold the land cost down. If the landowners realized that a major building project was about to be launched, their asking price would be at least as high as the ferris wheel. So he obtains two options to purchase land by using two secret agents—Bonnie and Clyde. Bonnie does not mention to sellers that she is an agent (therefore to those sellers the developer is an undisclosed principal). Clyde tells those with whom he is dealing that he is an agent but refuses to divulge the developer's name or his business interest in the land. (Thus the developer is, to the latter sellers, a partially disclosed principal.) Suppose the sellers get wind of the impending construction and want to back out of the deal. Who may enforce the contracts against them?

The developer and the agents may sue to compel transfer of title. The undisclosed or partially disclosed principal may act to enforce his rights unless the contract specifically prohibits it or there is a representation that the signatories are not signing for an undisclosed principal. The agents may also bring suit to enforce the principal's contract rights because, as agents for an undisclosed or partially disclosed principal, they are considered parties to their contracts.

Now suppose the developer attempts to call off the deal. Whom may the sellers sue? Both the developer and the agents are liable. That the sellers had no knowledge of the developer's identity—or even that there was a developer—does not invalidate the contract. If the sellers first sue agent Bonnie (or Clyde), they may still recover the purchase price from the developer as long as they had no knowledge of his identity prior to winning the first lawsuit. The developer is discharged from liability if, knowing his identity, the plaintiffs persist in a suit against the agents and recover a judgment against them anyway. Similarly, if the seller sues the principal and recovers a judgment, the agents are relieved of liability. The seller thus has a "right of election" to sue either the agent or the undisclosed principal, a right that in many states may be exercised any time before the seller collects on the judgment. In the following case, the third party elected to sue an agent who failed to disclose the principal's name.

DETROIT PURE MILK CO. v. PATTERSON
128 Mich. App. 475,
360 N.W.2d 221 (1984)

MacKenzie, Presiding Judge. Plaintiff appeals as of right from a judgment of no cause of action entered in defendant's favor by the circuit court after a bench trial. Defendant stipulated that $13,316.29 was owed to plaintiff for dairy products sold on open account to two stores, Village Variety and Village Variety Food Market. However, defendant argued that he was not personally liable; rather, the corporation which owned the two stores was liable, and the circuit court agreed.

The background facts are as follows. Defendant first became a customer of plaintiff when he owned as sole proprietor the Village Variety store. Subsequently, defendant and a partner formed and became shareholders in a corporation named V.V.F.M., Inc., which in December of 1977 purchased the Village Variety Food Market store. In January of 1979 the Village Variety store was transferred to the corporation, and in June of that same year defendant and his wife became the sole shareholders of V.V.F.M., Inc.

Defendant testified that, when the Village Variety Food Market store opened, he conveyed to plaintiff's salesmen that the store was owned by a corporation and explained the need for separate accounts for Village Variety Food Market and Village Variety, which was still a sole proprietorship owned by defendant at that time. Defendant testified that separate accounts were maintained until the Village Variety store was transferred to the corporation. Defendant couldn't recall the names used on plaintiff's invoices, stating that they could have been Village Variety or Village Variety Food Market, or Village Variety #2. Defendant admitted that he could not recall whether he ever told plaintiff's salesmen of the name of the corporation. None of the checks used to pay plaintiff were in the name of V.V.F.M., Inc., or otherwise indicated incorporation. While neither store had a sign indicating ownership by V.V.F.M., Inc., defendant testified that the sales tax and liquor licenses displayed in the Village Variety Food Market store were in the name of V.V.F.M., Inc.

Plaintiff's testifying salesman stated that he had no recollection of defendant's ever mentioning anything about a corporation. He further testified that he never looked at the sales tax or liquor licenses in the Village Variety Food Market store.

The circuit court found for defendant on the basis that defendant did nothing to mislead plaintiff either directly or indirectly, and that it was plaintiff's duty as a seller extending credit to inquire into the business structure of its customers. We agree with plaintiff that the court incorrectly stated and applied the controlling law, and erred in finding for defendant.

In contracting with plaintiff for dairy products, defendant was acting as an agent for the corporation. Where the party transacting with an agent has notice that the agent is or may be acting for a principal, but has no notice of the principal's identity, the principal is partially disclosed. Unless otherwise agreed, an agent contracting with another for a partially disclosed principal is a party to and personally liable on the contract.

In *Harmon v. Parker,* 160 N.W. 380 (1916), and *Stevens v. Graf,* 99 N.W.2d 356 (1959), the Court quoted with approval the following from 1 Mechem on Agency (2d ed.), § 1413:

> The duty rests upon the agent, if he would avoid personal liability, to disclose his agency, and not upon others to discover it. It is not, therefore, enough that the other party has the means of ascertaining the name of the principal: the agent must either bring to him actual knowledge, or, what is the same thing, that which to a reasonable man is equivalent to knowledge or the agent will be bound. There is no hardship to the agent in this rule, as he always has it in his power to relieve himself from personal liability by fully disclosing his principal and contracting only in the latter's name. If he does not do this, it may well be presumed that he intended to make himself personally responsible.

We find it unnecessary to remand to the trial court for reconsideration under the applicable law as set forth above. Even viewing the evidence in a light most favorable to defendant, no rational trier of fact could find that plaintiff had knowledge of the corporate principal's identity. Although defendant testified that he informed plaintiff's salesmen of the corporation, there was no testimony by defendant to the effect that he informed plaintiff's salesmen of the corporation's name. Nor was there any evidence showing that defendant contracted only in the corporation's name; notably the invoices sent by plaintiff were not made out to V.V.F.M., Inc. Also, there was no evidence that defendant conveyed to plaintiff's salesmen that the contractual obligation to pay for the dairy products supplied be that of the corporation only, and plaintiff's salesmen may well have believed that, notwithstanding

(continued on next page)

(continued)

DETROIT PURE MILK CO. v. PATTERSON
128 Mich. App. 475,
360 N.W.2d 221 (1984)

corporate ownership of the stores, defendant intended that his own credit, as well as that of the corporation, be relied on by plaintiff. It cannot reasonably be concluded that the licenses in the Village Variety Food Market store were alone sufficient to give plaintiff notice of the corporate principal's identity and relieve defendant of personal liability.

The trial court erred in granting a judgment for defendant, and should have granted judgment for plaintiff. We need not address the other issues raised by plaintiff on appeal.

Reversed and remanded for entry of judgment for plaintiff. Costs to plaintiff-appellant.

Lack of Authority in Agent   An agent who purports to make a contract on behalf of a principal, but who in fact has no authority to do so, is liable to the other party. The theory is that the agent has warranted to the third party that he has the requisite authority. The principal is not liable in the absence of apparent authority or ratification.

But the agent does not warrant that the principal has capacity. Thus, an agent for a minor is not liable on a contract that the minor later disavows, unless the agent expressly warranted that the principal had attained his majority. In short, the implied warranty is that the agent has authority to make a deal, not that the principal will necessarily comply with the contract once the deal is made.

Agent Acting on His Own Account   An agent will be liable on contracts made in a personal capacity as, for instance, when the agent personally guarantees repayment of a debt. The agent's intention to become personally liable is often difficult to determine on the basis of his signature on a contract. Generally, a person signing a contract can avoid personal liability only by showing that he was in fact signing as an agent. If the contract is signed "Jones, Agent," Jones can introduce evidence to show that there was never an intention to hold him personally liable. But if he signed "Jones" and neither his agency nor the principal's name is included, he will be personally liable. This can be troublesome to agents who routinely indorse checks and notes. There are special rules governing these situations, discussed in Chapter 24 dealing with commercial paper.

TERMINATION OF AGENCY

The agency relationship is not permanent. Either by action of the parties or by law, the relationship will eventually terminate.

By Act of the Parties

Termination Inferred   As with the creation of the relationship, it may be terminated either expressly or implicitly. Many agreements contain specified circumstances the occurrence of which signals the end of the agency. The most obvious of these circumstances is the expiration of a fixed period of time ("agency to terminate at the end of three months" or "on midnight, December 31"). It may also terminate on the accomplishment of a specified act ("on the sale of the house") or following a specific event ("at the conclusion of the last horse race").

There are a number of other circumstances that will spell the end of the relationship by implication. Unspecified events or changes in business conditions or the value of the subject matter of the agency might lead to a reasonable inference that the agency should be terminated or suspended; for example, the principal desires the agent to buy silver but the silver market unexpectedly rises rapidly and overnight silver doubles in price. Other circumstances that end the agency include disloyalty of the agent (for example, he accepts an appointment that is adverse to his first principal or embezzles from the principal), bankruptcy of the agent or of the principal, the outbreak of war (if it is reasonable to infer that the principal, knowing of the war, would not want the agent to continue to exercise authority), and a change in the law that makes a continued carrying out of the task illegal or seriously interferes with it.

Mutual Consent The agent and principal may at any time mutually agree to end their relationship.

Revocation or Renunciation The decision to terminate need not be mutual, however. Unless the agency is coupled with an interest, neither principal nor agent can bind the other to continue the relationship nor compel the other to perform. A principal **revokes** the agency; an agent **renounces** it. Even a contract that states the agreement is irrevocable will not be binding, although it can be the basis for a damage suit against the one who breached the agreement by revoking or renouncing it. (Recent developments relating to the employment-at-will doctrine, which allows an employer to fire an employee at any time, are discussed in Chapter 49.) If the agency is coupled with an interest, however, so that the authority to act is given to secure an interest that the agent has in the subject matter of the agency, then the principal lacks the power to revoke.

By Operation of Law

Aside from the express agreements of the parties involved, or the necessary or reasonable inferences that can be drawn from their agreements, the law voids agencies under certain circumstances. The most frequent termination by operation of law is the death of principal or agent. The death of an agent also terminates the authority of subagents he has appointed, unless the principal has expressly consented to the continuing validity of their appointment. Similarly, if the agent or principal loses capacity to enter into an agency relationship, it is suspended or terminated.

Even though authority has terminated, whether by action of the parties or operation of law, the principal may still be subject to liability. Apparent authority in many instances will still exist. It is imperative for a principal on termination of authority to notify all those who may still be in a position to deal with the agent. The only exceptions to this requirement are when termination is effected by death, loss of the principal's capacity, or an event that would make it impossible to carry out the object of the agency.

CHAPTER SUMMARY

A contract made by an agent on behalf of the principal legally binds the principal. Three types of authority may bind the principal: (1) express authority—that which is actually given and spelled out; (2) implied authority—that which may fairly be inferred from the parties' relationship and which is incidental to the agent's express authority; (3) apparent authority—that which reasonably appears to a third party under the circumstances to have been given by the principal. Even in the absence of authority, a principal may ratify the agent's acts.

The principal may be liable for tortious acts of the agent—but except under certain regulatory statutes, may not be held criminally liable for criminal acts of agents not prompted by the principal. Under the doctrine of *respondeat superior*, a principal is generally liable for acts by a servant within the scope of employment. A principal will not usually be held liable for acts of non-servant agents that cause physical damage, although he will be held liable for nonphysical torts, such as misrepresentation. The principal will not be held liable for tortious acts of independent contractors, although the principal may be liable for injuries resulting from his failure to act in situations in which he was not legally permitted to delegate a duty to act. Whenever an agent is acting to further the principal's business interests, the principal will be held vicariously liable for the agent's intentional torts. What constitutes scope of employment is not easy to determine; the modern trend is to hold a principal liable for the conduct of an agent if it was foreseeable that the agent might act as he did.

Most states have special rules of vicarious liability for special situations; for example, liability of an automobile owner for use by another. Spouses are not vicariously liable for each other, nor are parents for children, except for failing to control children known to be dangerous.

In general, an agent is not personally liable on contracts he has signed on behalf of a principal. This general rule has several exceptions recognized in most states: (1) when the agent is serving an undisclosed or partially disclosed principal; (2) when the agent lacks authority or exceeds his authority; and (3) if the agent entered into the contract in a personal capacity.

The agency relationship may be terminated by mutual consent, by express agreement of the parties that the agency will end at a certain time or on the occurrence of a certain event, or by an implied agreement arising out of the circumstances in each case. The agency may also be unilaterally revoked by the principal—unless the agency is coupled with an interest—or renounced by the agent. Finally, the agency will terminate by operation of law under certain circumstances, such as death of the principal or agent.

KEY TERMS

SELF-TEST QUESTIONS

1. Authority which legally may bind the principal includes:
   (a) implied authority
   (b) express authority
   (c) apparent authority
   (d) all of the above

2. As a general rule, a principal is not:
   (a) liable for tortious acts of an agent, even when the principal is negligent
   (b) liable for acts of a servant within the scope of employment
   (c) criminally liable for acts of the agent
   (d) liable for nondelegable duties performed by independent contractors

3. An agent may be held personally liable on contracts signed on behalf of a principal when:
   (a) the agent is serving an undisclosed or partially disclosed principal
   (b) the agent exceeds his authority
   (c) the agent entered into the contract in a personal capacity
   (d) all of the above are true

4. An agency relationship may be terminated by:
   (a) an implied agreement arising out of the circumstances
   (b) mutual consent of parties
   (c) death of the principal or agent
   (d) all of the above

5. The principal's liability for the agent's acts of which the principal had no knowledge or intention to commit is called:
   (a) contract liability
   (b) implied liability
   (c) respondeat superior
   (d) all of the above

DEMONSTRATION PROBLEM

Parke-Bernet Galleries, acting as agent for an undisclosed principal, sold a painting to Weisz. Weisz later discovered that the painting was a forgery and sued Parke-Bernet for breach of contract. In defense, Parke-Bernet argued that as a general rule, agents are not liable on contracts made for principals. Is this a good defense? Why?

PROBLEMS

1. You are the loan officer at a local bank. Patterson wants to borrow $7,000 from the bank. Bank policy requires that you obtain a loan guaranty from Patterson's employer, a milk company. The manager of the company visits the bank and signs a guaranty on behalf of the company. The last paragraph of the guaranty states: "This guaranty is signed by an officer having legal right to bind the company thru authorization of the Board of Directors." Are you satisfied with this guaranty? Would you be satisfied if the president of the company, who was also a director, affirmed that the manager had authority to sign the guaranty? Why?

2. Ralph owned a retail meat market. Ralph's agent Sam without authority but purporting to act on Ralph's behalf borrowed $3,500 from Ted. Although he never received the money, Ralph repaid $200 of the alleged loan and promised to repay the rest. If Sam had no authority to make the loan, is Ralph liable? Why?

3. A guest arrived early one morning at the Hotel Ohio. Clemens, a person in the hotel office who appeared to be in charge, walked behind the counter, registered the guest, gave him a key, and took him to his room. The guest also checked valuables (a diamond pin and money) with Clemens, who signed a receipt on behalf of the hotel. Clemens in fact was a roomer at the hotel, not an employee, and had no actual authority to act on behalf of the hotel. When Clemens absconded with the valuables, the guest sued the hotel. Is the hotel liable? Why?

4. A basketball player, playing for a professional team, punched an opposing player in the face during the course of a game. The opponent, who was seriously injured, sued the owner of the team for damages. A jury awarded the player $222,000 for medical expenses, $200,000 for physical pain, $275,000 for mental anguish, $1,000,000 for lost earnings, and $1,500,000 in punitive damages (which was $500,000 more than requested by the player). The jury also awarded $50,000 to the player's wife for loss of companionship. If we assume that the player who threw the punch acted out of personal anger and had no intention to further the business, how could the damage award against his principal be legally justified?

5. A doctor in a University of Chicago hospital seriously assaulted a patient in an examining room. The patient sued the hospital on the theory that the doctor was an agent or employee of the hospital and the assault occurred within the hospital. Is the hospital liable for the acts of its agent? Why?

6. Hector was employed by a machine shop. One day, Hector made a delivery for his employer and then proceeded back to the shop. When he was four miles from the shop and on the road where the shop was located, he turned left onto another road to visit a friend, who lived five miles west of the turnoff. On the way to the friend's house, Hector caused an accident and a person injured in the accident sued Hector's employer. Is the employer liable? Why?

7. A fourteen-year-old boy, who had no driver's license, took his parents' car without permission and caused an automobile accident. A person injured in the accident sued the boy's parents under the Illinois Parental Responsibility Law cited in the text. Are the parents liable? Why?

ANSWERS TO SELF-TEST QUESTIONS

1. (d)   2. (c)   3. (d)   4. (d)   5. (c)

SUGGESTED ANSWER TO DEMONSTRATION PROBLEM

This is not a good defense. A third party may elect to recover from an agent for an undisclosed principal. *Weisz v. Parke-Bernet Galleries, Inc.*, 325 N.Y.S.2d 576 (1971).

Part 7

THE MANAGER'S LEGAL AGEND

Because different legal consequences may flow from the type of a[g who is acting on behalf of your business, you should periodically review agency contracts to ensure that their terms are specific to the type of age you wish to create.

Similarly, you should review any powers of attorney you have grante ensure that they are limited to the functions for which they were cre and that it makes sense to continue them. If the reasons for their crea no longer exist, you should revoke them.

Since some types of agency can be created only by written contract many states, for example, agency contracts between companies and s representatives), you should ensure that your agents have signed ap priate agency contracts.

Even though, by law, an agent owes a fiduciary duty to the principal, should consider spelling out conflict-of-interest and other duties of loy in the agency agreement, both to make clear that you will not tolerate agents being influenced by outside interests and to provide you with protection, if the duty is breached, to discharge the agent.

Likewise, because the law might impute an agent's intentional wron; ing to the principal if the wrongdoing furthers the principal's business, should have a written policy that forbids your agents from undertaking tain types of actions (for example, engaging in antitrust violations) and should also be able to demonstrate that your agents have attested to knowledge of your policies and their agreement to abide by these polic

In hiring independent contractors to undertake tasks for your busir spell out in a written contract the degree of independence the contr; will have to carry out the tasks; the more independence, the greater likelihood that if there is a legal challenge later the person you hire wil held to be an independent contractor rather than an employee.

To avoid liability under the implied authority theory, you should specify in the agency contract the scope of the agent's authority.

Similarly, because an agent with apparent authority can bind the principal, you should consider the possibility that one or more of your agents might try to act in ways beyond express authority. You should, therefore, notify those with whom the agent deals about the extent of the authority you have granted.

Although some agency relationships will expire according to their internal logic (an agency to sell a house "by the end of next month" necessarily expires at the end of next month), it is more prudent to spell out precisely when and under what conditions the agency will terminate, and you should communicate the time and conditions to those with whom you anticipate the agent will deal.

PART

VIII

'Tis the only comfort of the miserable to have partners in their woes.
—CERVANTES, *DON QUIXOTE*

PARTNERSHIP

CHAPTER

39

General Characteristics and Formation

The Importance of Partnership

*I*t would be difficult to conceive of a complex society that did not operate its businesses through organizations. In this part and the next we will explore in some detail the two most common forms of organization—partnerships and corporations. We also examine other, related forms, notably limited partnerships, joint ventures, and business trusts.

When two or more people form their own business or professional practice, they usually consider becoming partners. Over 1 million business firms in the United States are partnerships and partnerships are a common form of organization among lawyers, doctors, and other professionals. According to data compiled on the accounting business, for example, 7,500 of the some 23,500 CPA firms are organized as partnerships; most of the others are sole proprietorships.

Partnerships are also popular as investment vehicles. Partnership and tax law permit an investor to put capital into a limited partnership and realize tax benefits without liability for the acts of the general partners.

Even if you do not plan to work within a partnership, it can be important to understand the law that governs it. Why? Because it is possible to become someone's partner without intending to or even realizing that a partnership has been created. Knowledge of the law can help you avoid partnership liability.

History of Partnership Law

Partnership is an ancient form of business enterprise, and special laws governing partnerships date as far back as 2300 B.C., when the Code of Hammurabi explicitly regulated the relations between partners. Partnership was an important part of Roman law, and it played a significant role in the law merchant, the international commercial law of the Middle Ages.

In the nineteenth century, both in England and the United States, partnership was a popular vehicle for business enterprise. But the law governing it was jumbled. Common-law principles were mixed with equitable standards, and the result was considerable confusion. Parliament moved to reduce the uncertainty by adopting the Partnership Act of 1890. Codification took longer in the United States. The Commissioners on Uniform State Laws undertook the task at the turn of the twentieth century, and the Uniform Partnership Act (UPA), completed in 1914, and the Uniform Limited Partnership Act (ULPA), completed in 1916, are the basis of our modern law. The UPA and the ULPA have been adopted by all states except Louisiana. Despite its name, the UPA has not been enacted uniformly among the states, however. Some states have adhered to theory that partnerships are discrete legal entities apart from the partners who comprise them.

ENTITY THEORY

Meaning of "Legal Entity"

A **legal entity** is a person or group that the law recognizes as having legal rights, such as the right to own and dispose of property, to sue and be sued, and to enter into contracts. When individuals carry out a common enterprise as partners, a threshold legal question is whether the partnership is a legal entity. The common law said no. In other words, under the common-law theory, a partnership was but a convenient name for an aggregate of individuals, and the rights and duties recognized and imposed by law are those of the individual partners. By contrast, the mercantile theory of the law merchant held that a partnership is a legal entity that can have rights and duties independent of those of its members.

During the drafting of the UPA a debate raged over which theory to adopt. The drafters resolved the debate through a compromise. In Section 6(1), the UPA provides a neutral definition of partnership ("an association of two or more persons to carry on as co-owners a business for profit") and retained the common-law theory that a partnership is an aggregation of individuals. However, a partnership does have certain entity characteristics. Before turning to them, consider the consequences of a conclusion that a partnership is not a legal entity in the following case.

PEOPLE v. ZINKE
555 N.E.2d 263 (N.Y. 1990)

KAYE, JUDGE.

Defendant, an investment adviser for small pension and profit-sharing funds, was the sole general partner in Stonehenge Investment Notes 1, Ltd., a limited partnership; defendant himself was a significant investor in the firm. In January 1987, after the limited partners and their insurers exhausted their efforts to recoup the funds defendant had allegedly embezzled, defendant was indicted for two counts of grand larceny in the second degree. Specifically, the indictment accused defendant of stealing $1,050,000 from the partnership by writing two checks on its money market account—one for $250,000 in April 1984, the other for $800,000 three months later. Defendant, who had authority under the partnership agreement to borrow firm funds, claimed that these were partnership investments.

At trial, upon the close of the People's case, defendant moved to dismiss the indictment on the ground that, as a general partner, he was a "joint or common" owner of the partnership's property and, thus, under the Penal Law could not be prosecuted for larceny even if he had misappropriated partnership property. The court reserved decision and submitted the case to the jury, which convicted defendant of both counts of the indictment. After the verdict, Supreme Court denied defendant's motion to dismiss and the Appellate Division affirmed the conviction, concluding that the general partner in a limited partnership could be prosecuted for larceny for stealing partnership property. We now reverse.

Larceny is committed when one wrongfully takes, obtains or withholds "property from an owner thereof" with intent to deprive the owner of it, or appropriate it to oneself or another (Penal Law § 155.05[1]). "Owner" is defined in Penal Law § 155.00(5) as one "who has a right to possession [of the property taken] superior to that of the taker, obtainer or withholder." This broad definition is immediately qualified by the declaration that "[a] joint or common owner of property shall not be deemed to have a right of possession thereto superior to that of any other joint or common owner thereof."

In that partners under the Partnership Law are "co-owners" of firm property (see, Partnership Law §§ 10, 51[1]), defendant contends that he cannot be charged with having committed larceny as against his limited partners, because all of the partners have an equal right of ownership.

* * *

At common law, no less than today, the requirement that the victim of a theft be an "owner" of the stolen property was an indispensable element of the crime of larceny. The idea behind this requirement was that the property alleged to be stolen had to "belong" to a party other than the accused. If the defendant was the owner of the property and entitled to possession at the time of the taking, there could be no larceny. From this principle emerged the rule that if property was owned by two or more persons, none of the owners could commit larceny from the others. In the words of Lord Hale: "Regularly a man cannot commit felony of the goods, wherein he hath a property." (Hale, History of Pleas of the Crown, at 513 [1683])

Consistent with this principle was the common-law view that a partner could not be convicted of larceny for the misappropriation of partnership assets; because each partner held title to an undivided interest in the partnership, the theory was that partners could not misappropriate what was already theirs. This view has been widely recognized throughout the common-law world. Even as States began codifying larceny, the common-law rule continued to flourish. In the absence of a legislative expression to the contrary, courts have ordinarily held that a partner cannot be guilty of larceny for misappropriating firm property, with any such defalcations left for resolution in the civil arena.

Such has been the history of the law in this State: it is surely no accident that the People cite no reported New York case where a partner has been convicted of larceny for taking partnership property. Since 1881, larceny has been defined by statute in terms of a wrongful taking or withholding from the possession of the "owner" or "true owner." For more than 80 years the Legislature made no effort to define these terms. As in other States, the courts of this State consistently regarded the common-law definition of owner as controlling, concluding that partners could not be prosecuted for stealing firm property.

* * *

(continued on next page)

(continued)

PEOPLE v. ZINKE
555 N.E.2d 263 (N.Y. 1990)

A decision not to extend the larceny statute to partnership disputes—commonly litigated in civil courts—is, moreover, consistent with the Legislature's reluctance to elevate civil wrongs to the level of criminal larceny. In particular, the Legislature was concerned both about the effects of criminalizing conduct arising out of legitimate business activities—where there can often be close questions as to intent—and the effects of offering defeated litigants in civil suits the opportunity to seek retaliation by criminal actions. Allowing larceny prosecutions against partners is, of course, contrary to those legislative concerns.

Thus, it is clear that, in New York, partners cannot be charged with larceny for misappropriating firm assets. Indeed, while not alone in this view, New York, is widely recognized as a prime example of a State that has enacted in statutory form the common-law rule that a partner "could not steal partnership property." Since 1965, "[s]everal states have followed the lead of New York on this point in recent enactments and proposals" (Model Penal Code § 223.2, revised comment, at 170, n 15 [citing statutes of Ariz., Conn., Ore., Tex., Ill.]), and many other State courts have continued to follow or have recently adopted the New York rule.

Against this backdrop, the People's arguments for criminal liability must fail. [The indictment is dismissed.]

Entity Characteristics of a Partnership

Under the UPA, a partnership does not have the general status of a legal entity, but it does have certain entity characteristics.

For Accounting Purposes   The partnership may keep business records as if it were a separate entity, and its accountants may treat it as such for purposes of preparing income statements and balance sheets.

For Purposes of Taxation   Federal tax law requires every partnership to file an informational tax return, but because partnerships are not taxable entities, they do not pay income taxes. Instead, each partner's **distributive share** which includes income or other gain, loss, deductions, and credits must be included in the partner's personal income tax return, whether or not the share is actually distributed.

For Purposes of Suing   Because the UPA conceives of a partnership as an aggregation, suits to enforce a partnership contract or some other right must be filed in the name of all the partners. Similarly, to sue a partnership the plaintiff must name and sue each of the partners. This cumbersome procedure has been modified in many states, which have enacted special statutes expressly permitting suits by and against partnerships in the firm name. In suits on a claim in federal court, a partnership may sue and be sued in its common name.

For Purposes of Bankruptcy   Under federal bankruptcy law, a partnership is an entity that may voluntarily seek the haven of a bankruptcy court or that may involuntarily be thrust into a bankruptcy proceeding by its creditors. The partnership cannot discharge its debts in a liquidation proceeding under Chapter 7 of the bankruptcy law, but it can be rehabilitated under Chapter 11 (see Chapter 29).

For Purposes of Owning Real Estate   Like a corporation, a partnership may buy, sell, and hold real property in the partnership name. (UPA Sections 8(3) and 10(1).) Real estate bought in the partnership name can be sold only in its name. The UPA provisions are permissive, not mandatory, and partnership real estate is often held in the names of one or more partners.

TESTS OF PARTNERSHIP EXISTENCE

Partnerships can come into existence quite informally. In contrast to the corporation, which is the creature of statute, partnership is a catch-all term for a large variety of working relationships, and frequently uncertainties arise about whether or not a particular relationship is that of partnership. The law can reduce the uncertainty in advance only at the price of severely restricting the flexibility of people to associate. As the chief drafter of the UPA explained: "All other business associations are statutory in origin. They are formed by the happening of an event designated in a statute as necessary to their formation. In corporations this act may be the issuing of a charter by the proper officer of the state; in limited partnerships, the filing by the associates of a specified document in a public office. On the other hand, an infinite number of combinations of circumstances may result in co-ownership of a business. Partnership is the residuum, including all forms of co-ownership, of a business except those business associations organized under a specific statute" (Lewis, 1915, p. 622). Nevertheless, a number of tests have been established that are clues to the existence of a partnership (see Figure 39-1).

Co-Ownership of a Business

Recall the UPA's definition of a partnership: "an association of two or more persons to carry on as co-owners a business for profit." If what two or more people own is clearly a *business*—including capital assets, contracts with employees or agents, an income stream, debts incurred on behalf of the operation—a partnership exists. A tougher question arises when two or more persons co-own *property*. Do they automatically become partners? The answer can be important: if one of the owners, while doing business pertinent to the property, chances to injure a stranger, the latter could sue the other owners if there is a partnership.

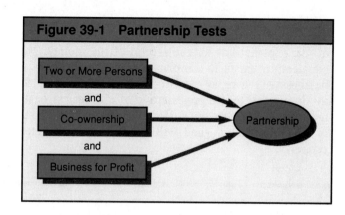

Figure 39-1   Partnership Tests

Co-ownership comes in many guises. The three most common are *joint tenancy, tenancy in common,* and *tenancy by the entireties.* In **joint tenancy,** the owners hold the property under a single instrument, such as a deed, and if one dies the others automatically become owners of the deceased's share, which does not descend to his heirs. **Tenancy in common** has the reverse rule: the survivor tenants do not take the deceased's share. Each tenant in common has a distinct estate in the property. The **tenancy by the entirety** form of ownership is limited to spouses and its effects are similar to that of joint tenancy. These concepts are discussed in more detail in relation to real property in Chapter 32.

Suppose a husband and wife who own their home as tenants by the entirety decide to spend the summer at the seashore and rent their home for three months. Is their co-ownership sufficient to establish that they are partners? The answer is no. By UPA Section 7(2), the various forms of joint ownership by themselves do not establish partnership, whether or not the co-owners share profits made by the use of the property. To establish a partnership, the ownership must be of a business, not merely of property.

Sharing of Profits

While co-ownership does not establish a partnership unless there is a business, a business, by itself, is not a partnership unless co-ownership is present. Of the tests used by courts to determine co-ownership, perhaps the most important is sharing of profits. UPA Section 7(4) provides that: "The receipt by a person of a share of the profits of a business is prima facie evidence that he is a partner in the business. . . ." That conclusion can be contradicted, however, by one of five explanations for the receipt of the money. No partnership exists if someone draws money from a business: (1) to repay a debt; (2) as wages or rent; (3) as an annuity to a representative of a deceased partner; (4) as interest on a loan; or (5) as consideration for the sale of good will of a business or other property.

Other Factors

Courts are not limited to the profit-sharing test; they also look at these factors, among others: the right to participate in decision-making, the duty to share liabilities, and the manner in which the business is operated. The following case illustrates how these factors are weighed in court.

CHAIKEN v. EMPLOYMENT SECURITY COMMISSION
274 A.2d 707 (Del. Super. Ct. 1971)

STOREY, JUDGE. The Employment Security Commission, hereinafter referred to as the Commission, levied an involuntary assessment against Richard K. Chaiken, complainant, hereinafter referred to as Chaiken, for not filing his unemployment security assessment report. Pursuant to the same statutory section, a hearing was held and a determination made by the Commission that Chaiken was the employer of two barbers in his barber shop and that he should be assessed as an employer for his share of unemployment compensation contributions. Chaiken appealed the Commission's decision.

*　　*　　*

Both in the administrative hearing and in his appeal brief Chaiken argues that he had entered into partnership agreements with each of his barbers and, therefore, was and is not subject to unemployment compensation assessment. The burden is upon the individual assessed to show that he is outside the ambit of the statutory sections requiring assessment. If Chaiken's partnership argument fails he has no secondary position and he fails to meet his burden.

Chaiken contends that he and his "partners":

1. properly registered the partnership name and names of partners in the Prothonotary's office, in accordance with 6 Del.C. § 3101,
2. properly filed federal partnership information returns and paid federal taxes quarterly on an estimated basis, and
3. duly executed partnership agreements.

Of the three factors, the last is most important. Agreements of "partnership" were executed between Chaiken and Mr. Strazella, a barber in the shop, and between Chaiken and Mr. Spitzer, similarly situated. The agreements were nearly identical. The first paragraph declared the creation of a partnership and the location of business. The second provided that Chaiken would provide barber chair, supplies, and licenses, while the other partner would provide tools of the trade. The paragraph also declared that upon dissolution of the partnership, ownership of items would revert to the party providing them. The third paragraph declared that the income of the partnership would be divided 30% for Chaiken, 70% for Strazella; 20% for Chaiken and 80% for Spitzer. The fourth paragraph declared that all partnership policy would be decided by Chaiken, whose decision was final. The fifth paragraph forbade assignment of the agreement without permission of Chaiken. The sixth paragraph required Chaiken to hold and distribute all receipts. The final paragraph stated hours of work for Strazella and Spitzer and holidays.

The mere existence of an agreement labelled "partnership" agreement and the characterization of signatories as "partners" does not conclusively prove the existence of a partnership. Rather, the intention of the parties, as explained by the wording of the agreement, is paramount.

A partnership is defined as an association of two or more persons to carry on as co-owners a business for profit. As co-owners of a business, partners have an equal right in the decision making process. But this right may be abrogated by agreement of the parties without destroying the partnership concept, provided other partnership elements are present.

Thus, while paragraph four reserves for Chaiken all right to determine partnership policy, it is not standing alone, fatal to the partnership concept. Co-owners should also contribute valuable consideration for the creation of the business. Under paragraph two, however, Chaiken provides the barber chair (and implicitly the barber shop itself), mirror, licenses and linen, while the other partners merely provide their tools and labor—nothing more than any barber-employee would furnish. Standing alone, however, mere contribution of work and skill can be valuable consideration for a partnership agreement.

Partnership interests may be assignable, although it is not a violation of partnership law to prohibit assignment in a partnership agreement. Therefore, paragraph five on assignment of partnership interests does not violate the partnership concept. On the other hand, distribution of partnership assets to the partners upon dissolution is only allowed after all partnership liabilities are satisfied. But paragraph two of the agreement, in stating the ground rules for dissolution, makes no declaration that the partnership assets will be utilized to pay partnership expenses before reversion to their original owners. This deficiency militates against a finding in favor of partnership intent since it is assumed Chaiken would have inserted such provision had he thought his lesser partners would accept such liability. Partners do accept such liability, employees do not.

Most importantly, co-owners carry on "a business for profit." The phrase has been interpreted to mean that partners share in the profits and the losses of the business. The intent to divide the profits is an indispensable requisite of partnership. Paragraph three of the agreement declares that each partner shall share in the income of the business. There is no sharing of the profits, and as the agreement is drafted, there are no profits. Merely sharing the gross returns does not establish a partnership. Nor is the sharing of profits prima facie evidence of a partnership where the profits received are in payment of wages.

The failure to share profits, therefore, is fatal to the partnership concept here.

(continued on next page)

(continued)

**CHAIKEN v.
EMPLOYMENT
SECURITY
COMMISSION**
274 A.2d 707 (Del. Super.
Ct. 1971)

Evaluating Chaiken's agreement in the light of the elements implicit in a partnership, no partnership intent can be found. The absence of the important right of decision making or the important duty to share liabilities upon dissolution individually may not be fatal to a partnership. But when both are absent, coupled with the absence of profit sharing, they become strong factors in discrediting the partnership argument. Such weighing of the elements against a partnership finding compares favorably with Fenwick v. Unemployment Compensation Commission, which decided against the partnership theory on similar facts, including the filing of partnership income tax forms.

In addition, the total circumstances of the case taken together indicate the employer-employee relationship between Chaiken and his barbers. The agreement set forth the hours of work and days off—unusual subjects for partnership agreements. The barbers brought into the relationship only the equipment required of all barber shop operators. And each barber had his own individual "partnership" with Chaiken. Furthermore, Chaiken conducted all transactions with suppliers, and purchased licenses, insurance, and the lease for the business property in his own name. Finally, the name "Richard's Barber Shop" continued to be used after the execution of the so-called partnership agreements. [The Commission's decision is affirmed.]

PARTNERSHIP BY ESTOPPEL

Ordinarily, if two people are not legally partners, then third parties cannot so regard them. Mr. Tot and Mr. Tut own equal shares of a house that they rent but do not regard it as a business and are not in fact partners. They do have a loose "understanding" that since Mr. Tot is mechanically adept, he will make necessary repairs whenever the tenants call. On his way one day to fix the boiler in the house, Mr. Tot injures a pedestrian, who sues both Mr. Tot and Mr. Tut. Since they are not partners, the pedestrian cannot sue them as if they were; hence Mr. Tut has no partnership liability.

Suppose that Mr. Tot and Mr. Tut happened to go to a lumberyard together to purchase materials that Mr. Tot intended to use to add a room to the house. Short of cash, Mr. Tot looks around and espies Mr. Tat, who greets his two friends heartily by saying

within earshot of the salesman who is debating whether to extend credit: "Well, how are my two partners this morning?" Messrs. Tot and Tut say nothing but smile faintly at the salesman, who mistakenly but reasonably believes that the two are acknowledging the partnership. The salesman knows Mr. Tat well and assumes that since Mr. Tat is rich, extending credit to the "partnership" is a "sure thing." Messrs. Tot and Tut fail to pay. The lumberyard is entitled to collect from Mr. Tat, even though he may have forgotten completely about the incident by the time suit is filed. Under UPA Section 16(1), Mr. Tat would be liable for the debt as a **partner by estoppel.** Partnership by estoppel has two elements: (1) a representation to a third party that there is in fact a partnership, and (2) reliance by the third party on the representation.

The following case shows how the courts determine whether or not a partnership by estoppel has been created.

ROSENBERGER v. HERBST

210 Pa.Super. 127, 232 A.2d 634 (1967)

HOFFMAN, JUDGE. On January 1, 1957, defendant Julius Herbst and one Eugene Parzych entered into a formal agreement relating to the operation of a farm owned by Herbst, located in Bucks County. The agreement, which is long and complex, recites Herbst's contribution of certain assets, principally the use and occupancy of the farm. It further acknowledges Parzych's indebtedness to Herbst in the amount of $6000, repayable with interest of five per cent per annum.

The actual farming operation is stated to be "under the full control of Parzych." Herbst is entitled to receive one-half of the net profits, and is bound to indemnify Parzych for one-half of any losses sustained. In a key paragraph, the agreement recites:

> Since any remuneration due hereunder to Herbst is a payment in return for his investment in the business and his capital contribution thereto, as well as in return for his leasing the Herbst Farm to Parzych without further rental payments, *the parties do not intend by this agreement to establish a partnership of any kind or type, but rather [a relation] of Debtor and Creditor and Landlord and Tenant.* [Emphasis supplied.]

Between February, 1957 and June, 1960, the plaintiffs, trading as "Clover Leaf Mill" (hereinafter "Clover Leaf") sold and delivered to Parzych large quantities of grain, feed, and fertilizer for use on the farm.

In July of 1961, Clover Leaf, for the first time, formally demanded payment from defendant Herbst for certain debts contracted by Parzych in connection with farming operations. Herbst disclaimed all liability, and this suit followed.

The court below focused exclusively on the Herbst-Parzych agreement. Concluding that the agreement constituted the two parties partners, in spite of the disclaimer clause noted above, the court directed a verdict in favor of plaintiff Clover Leaf. The defendant now appeals.

The Uniform Partnership Act of March 26, 1915, P.L. 18, § 7, 59 P.S. § 12, states the rule which governs this case: "(1) Except as provided in section sixteen [Partner by estoppel], persons who are not partners as to each other are not partners as to third persons." Two questions are therefore before us. First, did the agreement signed by Herbst and Parzych create a partnership *inter se?* Second, if it did not, is Herbst chargeable with liability as a partner, to this plaintiff, by virtue of his conduct?

The court below noted that the contractual relation between Herbst and Parzych had many of the ordinary incidents of partnership. Thus, in the words of the trial judge, the agreement provided for "the division of net profits and the sharing of losses" as well as for "a bank account on which both parties [could] draw . . . for the business operation of the farm."

Relying on the above indicia of partnership, and on a number of cases decided before the passage of the Uniform Partnership Act, supra, the lower court concluded that the parties were partners *inter se.*

(*continued on next page*)

(*continued*)

ROSENBERGER v. HERBST
210 Pa.Super. 127, 232 A.2d 634 (1967)

In relying on the profit-sharing provision of the Herbst-Parzych agreement, the lower court clearly erred. The Uniform Partnership Act, supra, 59 P.S. § 12(4), specifically provides:

> The receipt by a person of a share of the profits of a business is prima facie evidence that he is a partner in the business, *but no such inference shall be drawn if such profits were received in payment:* (a) As a debt by installment or otherwise, (b) As . . . rent to a landlord . . . (d) As interest on a loan, though the amount of payment vary with the profits of the business. . . .

As previously noted, Parzych's indebtedness to Herbst was to be repaid from the proceeds of the farming operation. Furthermore, the agreement specifically provided that Herbst's remuneration was to be considered "a payment . . . in return for his leasing the . . . Farm to Parzych without further rental payments. . . ." Accordingly, no inference of partnership may be drawn from Herbst's receipt of a fractional share of the proceeds of the farming operation.

The construction of this contract must, ultimately, be determined by reference to the intent of the parties. Paragraph Nine of the agreement clearly states that ". . . the parties do not intend to establish a partnership of any kind or type. . . ." Our Supreme Court has held: "[W]here [the parties] expressly declare that they are not partners this settles the question, for, whatever their obligations may be as to third persons, the law permits them to agree upon their legal status and relations [as between themselves]." In light of the parties' express statement of intention, coupled with the inconclusive nature of the remainder of the agreement, we hold that defendant Herbst and Eugene Parzych were not partners *inter se.*

If the plaintiff seeks to charge defendant Herbst with liability as a partner under § 16 of the Act, 59 P.S. § 38, it is his burden to show that the defendant's conduct gave rise to an estoppel. Not only did the plaintiff make no such attempt in the court below, but, in his brief on appeal, he states: "The question of partnership by estoppel was not argued in the lower court and does not require comment." We would be justified in treating this statement as a confession. Since the plaintiff may have misconceived his own position, however, we shall discuss the point briefly.

There is testimony in the record that Parzych represented himself as Herbst's partner to Clover Leaf, at some unspecified date, and that Clover Leaf allegedly relied on Herbst's credit, for some unspecified period of time. There is nothing in the record, however, to suggest that Herbst, himself, by words spoken or written or by conduct, ever made or consented to such a representation. Parzych's unauthorized statement, without more, cannot give rise to an estoppel against Herbst.

We conclude, therefore, that defendant Herbst was not estopped to deny liability as a partner for the debts contracted by Eugene Parzych. Since he and Parzych were not, in fact, partners, the judgment of the court below cannot stand.

Judgment reversed and entered for defendant.

PARTNERSHIP FORMATION

Assume that three persons have decided to form a partnership to run a bookstore business. Bob contributes $20,000. Carol contributes a house in which the business will operate. Ted contributes his services; he will manage the bookstore.

The first question is whether Bob, Carol, and Ted *must* have a partnership agreement. As should be clear from the foregoing discussion, no agreement is necessary as long as the tests of partnership are met. However, they *ought* to have an agreement in order to spell out their rights and duties among themselves.

The agreement itself is a contract and should follow the principles and rules spelled out in Part Two of this book. Because it is intended to govern the relations of the partners toward themselves and their business, every partnership contract ought to set forth clearly the following terms: (1) the name under which the partners will do business; (2) the names of the partners; (3) the nature, scope, and location of the business; (4) the capital contributions of each partner; (5) how profits and losses are to be divided; (6) how salaries, if any, are to be determined; (7) the responsibilities of each partner for managing the business; (8) limitations on the power of each partner to bind the firm; (9) the method by which a given partner may withdraw from the partnership; (10) continuation of the firm in the event of a partner's death and the formula for paying a partnership interest to his heirs; and (11) method of dissolution. In forming a partnership, three of these items merit special attention.

Who Can Be a Partner?

Recall the UPA definition that a partnership is an association of two or more *persons*. UPA Section 2 defines "person" as "individuals, partnerships, corporations, and other associations." Thus a partnership is not limited to a direct association between human beings but may also include an association between other entities, such as corporations or even partnerships themselves. Family members can be partners, and partnerships between parents and minor children are lawful, although a partner who is a minor may disaffirm the agreement.

Written vs. Oral Agreements

If the business cannot be performed within one year from the time that the agreement is entered into, the partnership agreement should be in writing to avoid invalidation under the Statute of Frauds. Most partnerships have no fixed term, however, and are partnerships "at will" and therefore not within the Statute of Frauds.

Validity of the Partnership Name

Bob, Carol, and Ted decide that it makes good business sense to choose an imposing, catchy, and well-known name for their bookstore—General Motors Corporation. There are two reasons why they cannot do so. First, their business is a partnership, not a corporation, and should not be described as one. Second, the name is deceptive because it is the name of an existing business. Furthermore, if not registered, the name would violate the *assumed* or *fictitious name statutes* of most states. These require that anyone doing business under a name other than his real name register the name, together with the names and addresses of the proprietors, in some public office. (Often the statutes require the proprietors to publish this information in the newspapers when the business is started.) As the following case shows, if a business fails to comply with the statute, it may find that it will be unable to file suit to enforce its contracts. In some states, failure to file can also lead to a monetary fine.

ARONOVITZ v. STEIN PROPERTIES
322 So.2d 74 (Fla. Dist. Ct. App. 1975)

PER CURIAM. Appellant trustee, defendant in the trial court, brings this appeal from a final judgment of the trial court awarding appellees, plaintiffs below, a money judgment pursuant to a deposit receipt contract.

On April 11, 1974, appellees filed a complaint in the Circuit Court of Dade County wherein the name of the plaintiff was set forth as "Stein Properties, a partnership." This was the only description of the plaintiff in the complaint. The record further shows that the name Stein Properties was not registered pursuant to § 865.09, Fla. Stat., F.S.A., the Florida Fictitious Name Statute.

Among the several assignments of error set forth by appellant are two which we feel are dispositive of this appeal. First, appellant contends that the trial court erred in failing to grant his motion to dismiss the complaint due to appellees' failure to register the name Stein Properties as required by the Fictitious Name Statute and, two, that the trial court erred in allowing the cause to proceed to trial where only the partnership, i.e., Stein Properties, was named as plaintiff in the complaint.

Section 865.09(3), Fla.Stat., F.S.A., provides that it shall be unlawful for any partnership to engage in business in this state under a fictitious name unless such name is properly registered with the clerk of the circuit court of the county in which its principal place of business is located. Section 865.09(5), Fla.Stat., F.S.A., provides that the penalty for the failure to comply with this law shall be that neither the business nor the members nor those interested in doing such business may maintain suit in any court of this state as a plaintiff until this law is complied with.

Here it is undisputed that Stein Properties was a partnership doing business in this state and we find that the name "Stein Properties" is a "fictitious name" as that term is defined in § 865.09(2)(b), Fla.Stat., F.S.A., because it did not reasonably reveal the names of the partners to appellant. Therefore, since the record shows that Stein Properties was not registered under the Fictitious Name Statute, it may not maintain a suit in any court of this state as plaintiff. However, the failure of appellees to comply with the statute does not prevent the trial court from taking jurisdiction of the cause, but it does act as an inhibition against allowing appellees to prosecute their complaint until the requirements of the statute are met.

Secondly, appellant contends that a partnership cannot sue in its company or firm name, but must sue in the names of the individuals comprising it. As stated above, the complaint filed by appellees designated only "Stein Properties, a partnership" as the plaintiff. We agree with appellant's contention.

Since the common law does not recognize a partnership as a legal entity distinct from and independent of the persons composing it, a partnership cannot, as such without statutory authority, sue in its firm name. All actions by a partnership must be brought in the names of its individual members. Even though our Legislature in 1972 adopted the Uniform Partnership Act, § 620.56 et seq., Fla.Stat., F.S.A., we can find no authority in the Act which would permit a partnership to sue in its firm name. In the instant case, since each partner had an interest in the deposit receipt contract sued on arising out of a partnership transaction, each partner was an indispensable party to the complaint seeking its enforcement. Therefore, the trial court should have granted appellant's motion to dismiss for failure to join an indispensable party.

We have considered the record, all points in the briefs and arguments of counsel in the light of the controlling principles of law, and have concluded that reversible error has been demonstrated. Therefore, for the reasons stated and upon the authorities cited, the judgment appealed is reversed and remanded for further action not inconsistent with this opinion.

Reversed and remanded.

CHAPTER SUMMARY

The basic law of partnership is found in two statutes, the Uniform Partnership Act and the Uniform Limited Partnership Act. At common law, a partnership was not a legal entity and could not sue or be sued in the partnership name. The UPA defines a partnership as "an association of two or more persons to carry on as co-owners a business for profit" and, although it assumes that a partnership is an aggregation of individuals, it applies a number of rules characteristic of the legal entity theory. Thus, a partnership may keep business records as if it were a legal entity, may hold real estate in the partnership name, and may sue and be sued in federal court and in many state courts in the partnership name.

Partnerships may be created informally. Among the clues to the existence of a partnership are (1) co-ownership of a business, (2) sharing of profits, (3) right to participate in decision making, (4) duty to share liabilities, and (5) manner in which the business is operated. A partnership may also be formed by estoppel when a third party reasonably relies on a representation that a partnership in fact exists.

No special rules govern the partnership agreement. As a practical matter, it should sufficiently spell out who the partners are, under what name they will conduct their business, the nature and scope of the business, capital contributions of each partner, how profits are to be divided, and similar pertinent provisions. An oral agreement to form a partnership is valid unless the business cannot be performed wholly within one year from the time that the agreement is made. However, most partnerships have no fixed terms and hence are "at will" partnerships not subject to the Statute of Frauds.

KEY TERMS

SELF-TEST QUESTIONS

1. The basic law of partnership is currently found in:
   (a) common law
   (b) Constitutional law
   (c) statutory law
   (d) none of the above
2. Existence of a partnership may be established by:
   (a) co-ownership of a business for profit
   (b) estoppel
   (c) a formal agreement
   (d) all of the above
3. It is not true that:
   (a) an oral agreement to form a partnership is valid
   (b) most partnerships have no fixed terms and are thus not subject to the Statute of Frauds
   (c) Strict statutory rules govern partnership agreements
   (d) a partnership may be formed by estoppel
4. Partnerships:
   (a) are not taxable entities
   (b) may buy, sell or hold real property in the partnership name
   (c) may file for bankruptcy
   (d) have all of the above characteristics
5. Partnerships:
   (a) are free to select any name not used by another partnership
   (b) must include the partners' names in the partnership name
   (c) can be formed by two corporations
   (d) cannot be formed by two partnerships

DEMONSTRATION PROBLEM

Jimmy, Billy, and Lillian own, as partners, a warehouse. The income from the warehouse during the current year is $180,000, two-thirds of which goes to Jimmy. Who must file a tax return listing this income—the partnership or Jimmy? Who pays the tax—the partnership or Jimmy?

PROBLEMS

1. Larry and Curly, as partners, operate a small business. They fail to pay certain state taxes. Larry dies and, there being no partnership assets, the state demands payment from the personal assets in his estate. Must the estate pay? Why?

2. Popeye, a business student, decided to lease and operate an ice cream stand during his summer vacation. Because Popeye could not afford rent payments, his landlord agreed to take 30 percent of Popeye's profits as rent. As a result of this arrangement, are the landlord and Popeye partners? Why?

3. Trish lent $20,000 to Dick. They agreed that Dick would invest the money in real estate and, when the real estate was sold, he would pay back the $20,000 plus 40 percent of the profits as interest. Does this arrangement make Trish and Dick partners? Why?

4. Betty owned a business and was indebted to First Bank in the amount of $5,000. One day she visited the bank with her friend Alice and, in a joking mood, told the bank lending officer that Alice was her partner. Alice heard the statement and said nothing. Betty defaulted on the loan and now the bank claims that Alice is liable. Is she? Why?

5. Alpha and Beta, who are neighbors, decide to purchase an acre of land together as tenants in common. Does this purchase make them partners? Explain.

6. Bonnie and Clyde decide to form a partnership. Bonnie is seventeen and Clyde is twenty-two. May they form a partnership? Explain.

7. In problem 7, assuming that Bonnie and Clyde may form a partnership, must they enter into a partnership agreement? If they do enter into an agreement, must it be written? Explain.

ANSWERS TO SELF-TEST QUESTIONS

1. (c)   2. (d)   3. (c)   4. (d)   5. (c)

SUGGESTED ANSWER TO DEMONSTRATION PROBLEM

Both Jimmy and the partnership must file returns, although the partnership return is for information purposes only. Jimmy must pay the tax. (According to *U.S. News and World Report,* June 20, 1977, p. 73, former President Jimmy Carter's 1975 share of the profits from Carter's Warehouse partnership was $119,244.47, which was reported on his individual return. He owned a two-thirds interest in the partnership; the other partners in Carter's Warehouse were his mother Lillian and brother Billy.)

CHAPTER OVERVIEW

Operation—Relations among Partners
Operation—The Partnership and Third Parties
Dissolution and Winding Up
Other Unincorporated Associations

Partnership Operation and Termination; Other Forms

*I*n this chapter, we take up three distinct themes:

1. Operation of the partnership, including the relations among partners and relations between partners and third parties.
2. Dissolution and winding up of the partnership.
3. Alternative forms of business enterprise, such as the limited partnership, that lie along a continuum between the partnership and the corporate form.

OPERATION—RELATIONS AMONG PARTNERS

Most of the rules discussed in this section apply *unless otherwise agreed* (UPA Section 18). The UPA does not dictate what the relations among partners must be; it supplies rules in the event that the partners have not done so for themselves. In this area, especially, it is important for the partners to elaborate their agreement in writing. If the partners should happen to continue their business beyond the term fixed for

it in their agreement, the terms of the agreement continue to apply.

Fiduciary Duty

Partners must treat each other as *fiduciaries*—that is, each partner must take special care that the others' interests will be fully protected. UPA Section 21(1) states:

> Every partner must account to the partnership for any benefit, and hold as trustee for it any profits derived by him without the consent of the other partners from any transaction connected with the formation, conduct, or liquidation of the partnership or from any use by him of its property.

What does it mean for a partner to act as a fiduciary? In 1893, the U.S. Supreme Court listed several "shall nots":

> [It is] well settled that one partner cannot, directly or indirectly, use partnership assets for his own benefit; that he cannot, in conducting the business of a partnership, take any profit clandestinely for himself; that he cannot

carry on the business of the partnership for his private advantage; that he cannot carry on another business in competition or rivalry with that of the firm, thereby depriving it of the benefit of his time, skill, and fidelity without being accountable to his copartners for any profit that may accrue to him therefrom; that he cannot be permitted to secure for himself that which it is his duty to obtain, if at all, for the firm of which he is a member; nor can he avail himself of knowledge or information which may be properly regarded as the property of the partnership, in the sense that it is available or useful to the firm for any purpose within the scope of the partnership business. [Latta v. Kilbourn, 150 U.S. 524, 542 (1893)]

Under UPA Section 22, any partner is entitled to a formal account (or accounting) of the partnership affairs under the following conditions:

1. if he is wrongfully excluded from the partnership business or possession of its property by his copartners;

2. if the right exists under the terms of any agreement;

3. as provided by UPA Section 21 (see above); and

4. whenever it is otherwise just and reasonable.

At common law, partners could not obtain an accounting except in the event of dissolution. But from an early date equity courts would appoint a referee, auditor, or special master to investigate the books of a business when one of the partners had grounds to complain, and the UPA has broadened considerably the right to an accounting. The court has broad power to investigate all facets of the business, to evaluate claims, declare legal rights among the parties, and order money judgments against each partner in the wrong.

In the following case, the court discusses the remedy for breach of a partner's fiduciary duty and concludes that the remedy does not include exemplary (punitive) damages.

GILROY v. CONWAY
151 Mich. App. 628, 391 N.W.2d 419 (1986)

PETERSON, JUDGE. Defendant cheated his partner and appeals from the trial court's judgment granting that partner a remedy.

Plaintiff was an established commercial photographer in Kalamazoo who also had a partnership interest in another photography business, Colonial Studios, in Coldwater. In 1974, defendant became plaintiff's partner in Colonial Studios, the name of which was changed to Skylight Studios. Under the partnership agreement, defendant was to be the operating manager of the partnership, in return for which he would have a guaranteed draw. Except for the guaranteed draw, the partnership was equal in ownership and the sharing of profits.

Prior to defendant's becoming a partner, the business had acquired a small contractual clientele of schools for which the business provided student portrait photographs. The partners agreed to concentrate on this type of business, and both partners solicited schools with success. Gross sales, which were $40,000 in 1974, increased every year and amounted to $209,085 in 1980.

In the spring of 1981, defendant offered to buy out plaintiff and some negotiations followed. On June 25, 1981, however, plaintiff was notified by the defendant that the partnership was dissolved as of July 1, 1981. Plaintiff discovered that defendant: had closed up the partnership's place of business and opened up his own business; had purchased equipment and supplies in preparation for commencing his own business and charged them to the partnership; and had taken with him the partnership employees and most of its equipment.

Defendant had also stolen the partnership's business. He had personally taken over the business of some customers by telling them that the partnership was being dissolved; in other cases he simply took over partnership contracts without telling the customers that he was then operating on his own. Plaintiff also learned that defendant's deceit had included the withdrawal, without plaintiff's knowledge, of partnership funds for defendant's personal use in 1978 in an amount exceeding $11,000.

The trial judge characterized the case as a "classic study of greed" and found that defendant had in effect appropriated the business enterprise, holding that defendant had "knowingly and wilfully violated his fiduciary relationship as a partner by converting partnership assets to his use and, in doing so, literally destroying the partnership". He also found that the partnership could have been sold as a going business on June 30, 1981, and that after a full accounting, it had a value on that date of $94,596 less accounts payable of $17,378.85, or a net value of $77,217.15. The division thereof after adjustments for plaintiff's positive equity or capital resulted in an award to plaintiff for his interest in the business of $53,779.46.

⋆   ⋆   ⋆

Plaintiff also sought exemplary damages. Count II of the complaint alleged that defendant's conduct constituted a breach of defendant's fuduciary duty to his partner under §§ 19–22 of the Uniform Partnership Act, and Count III alleged conversion of partnership property. Each count contained allegations that defendant's conduct was wilful, wanton and in reckless disregard of plaintiff's rights and that such conduct had caused injury to plaintiff's feelings, including humiliation, indignity and a sense of moral outrage. The prayer for relief sought exemplary damages therefor.

Plaintiff's testimony on the point was brief. He said:

> The effect of really the whole situation, and I think it was most apparent when I walked into the empty building, was extreme disappointment and really total outrage at the fact that something that I had given the utmost of my talent and creativity, energy, and whatever time was necessary to build, was totally destroyed and there was just nothing of any value that was left.
> . . . My business had been stolen and there wasn't a thing that I could do about it. And to me, that was very humiliating that one day I had something that I had worked 10 years on, and the next day I had absolutely nothing of any value. . . .

As noted above, the trial judge found that defendant had literally destroyed the partnership by knowingly and wilfully converting partnership assets in violation of his fiduciary duty as a partner. He also found that plaintiff had suffered a sense of outrage, indignity and humiliation and awarded him $10,000 as exemplary damages.

Defendant appeals from that award, asserting that plaintiff's cause of action arises from a breach of the partnership contract and that exemplary damages may not be awarded for breach of that contract.

(*continued on next page*)

(continued)

GILROY v. CONWAY
151 Mich. App. 628, 391
N.W.2d 419 (1986)

★   ★   ★

If it were to be assumed that a partner's breach of his fiduciary duty or appropriation of partnership equipment and business contract to his own use and profit are torts, it is clear that the duty breached arises from the partnership contract. One acquires the property interest of a co-tenant in partnership only by the contractual creation of a partnership; one becomes a fiduciary in partnership only by the contractual undertaking to become a partner. There is no tortious conduct here existing independent of the breach of the partnership contract.

Neither do we see anything in the Uniform Partnership Act to suggest that an aggrieved partner is entitled to any remedy other than to be made whole economically. The act defines identically the partnership fiduciary duty and the remedy for its breach, *i.e.*, to account:

> Sec. 21. (1) Every partner must account to the partnership for any benefit, and hold as trustee for it any profits derived by him without the consent of the other partners from any transaction connected with the formation, conduct, or liquidation of the partnership or from any use by him of its property.

So, the cases involving a partner's breach of the fiduciary duty to their partners have been concerned solely with placing the wronged partners in the economic position that they would have enjoyed but for the breach.

[Judgment for plaintiff affirmed, as modified with regard to damages.]

Sharing Profits and Losses

Profits and losses may be shared according to any formula upon which the partners agree. If no provision is stated in the partnership agreement, then UPA Section 18(a) applies. This section requires that each partner be repaid his actual contribution first, and thereafter share equally in the profits and surplus remaining after liabilities, or contribute toward losses according to his share in the profits.

Compensation

Recall the bookstore partnership of Bob, Carol, and Ted (p. 875). Is Ted, the sole "working" partner, entitled to compensation for the hours he spends in the store? In the absence of an explicit provision in the partnership agreement, he is not. Under UPA Sec-

tion 18(f), no partner, other than one who winds up the partnership's affairs on dissolution, is entitled to remuneration.

Management

All partners are entitled to share equally in the management and conduct of the business. Suppose Bob and Carol decide that the bookstore should open its doors to early commuters at 8 A.M. and close at 7 P.M. Ted, the only partner who must be at the store personally during the hours it is open, argues for a nine-hour day—9 A.M. to 6 P.M. UPA Section 18(h) permits the partners to resolve differences about "ordinary matters connected with a partnership business" by majority vote. However, the partnership agreement could be structured to delegate such decisions to the working member or could give him veto power over the decisions of nonworking partners.

Assume that the Bob–Carol–Ted partnership provides for majority rule. At their next partners' meeting, Bob and Carol vote to cut back Ted's share of the profits. May they do so? No. Under UPA Section 18(h), no act that contravenes the partnership agreement itself may be undertaken without the consent of all partners. Since the partnership agreement assures Ted an equal share, his co-partners cannot reduce it unilaterally.

Books and Information

In the absence of any other agreement, financial books and records must be kept at the partnership's principal place of business and remain open at all times for inspection and copying by any of the partners. Likewise, any partner may demand at any time information from the others concerning anything that affects the business.

Property Rights

Partnership property consists of all property originally advanced or contributed to the partnership or subsequently acquired by purchase or contribution. Unless the contrary intention can be shown, property acquired with partnership funds is partnership property. Thus, property of the Bob–Carol–Ted bookstore includes cash on hand, inventory, equipment, and the store and grounds.

The UPA recognizes two different types of partnership property rights: (1) specific property of the partnership; and (2) an interest in the partnership itself.

Rights in Specific Property   Suppose that Carol, who contributed the house and grounds from which the business is conducted, suddenly dies. Who is entitled to her share of the specific property, such as inventory, the house, and money in the cash register—her husband and children or the other partners? UPA Section 25(1) declares that the partners hold the partnership property as **tenants in partnership.** As spelled out in subsection (2), the specific property interest of a tenant in partnership vests in the surviving partners, not in the heirs. But the heirs are entitled to the deceased partner's interest in the partnership itself, so that while Bob and Ted may use the partnership property for the benefit of the partnership without consulting Carol's heirs, they must account to her heirs for her proper share of the partnership's profits. Likewise, a partner may not assign her right in specific partnership property but may assign her interest in the profits. If a third party has a claim against one of the partners, he may not attach partnership property unless the claim is for a partnership debt. The net of all this is that the partnership owns the property; the partners, individually, do not (see Figure 40-1).

Interest in the Partnership   A partner's interest in the partnership is her share of the profits and surplus, and UPA Section 26 says that it is personal property. This interest in inheritable and becomes the property of the deceased partner's heirs. The heirs do not thereby become partners, however.

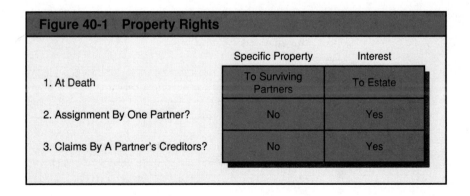

Figure 40-1 Property Rights		
	Specific Property	Interest
1. At Death	To Surviving Partners	To Estate
2. Assignment By One Partner?	No	Yes
3. Claims By A Partner's Creditors?	No	Yes

Distinction Between Specific Property and Partnership Interest The difference between the two types of property rights is virtually the same as that between an automobile manufactured by Ford Motor Company and a share of stock in the company. The former is a piece of inventory owned by the company; the latter is an interest in the entire corporation. Consider the following balance sheet of the Bob–Carol–Ted Bookstore:

ASSETS

Cash in bank	$ 1,000
Accounts receivable	7,000
Inventory	9,000
Equipment	3,000
Land and building	20,000
	40,000

CAPITAL AND LIABILITIES

Notes and accounts payable	$16,000
Capital accounts	
Bob	8,000
Carol	8,000
Ted	8,000
	40,000

The items listed under "assets" are the specific partnership property and can be used only by the partnership. The figures under the "capital" accounts represent the interest each of the partners would have in the firm if it were to be liquidated at the time the balance sheet was prepared. The distinction between specific property and the partnership interest is discussed further in the following case.

MITCHELL v. STATE
12 Ark. App. 260, 675 S.W.2d 373 (1984)

GLAZE, JUDGE. This appeal is from the property settlement provisions of a divorce decree entered May 2, 1983. The appellant contends the chancellor erred in awarding the appellee an undivided one-half interest of appellant's one-third interest in a partnership. Appellant also contends the chancellor erred in the distribution of the parties' debts, particularly partnership debts, contracted during the marriage. We agree with appellant that the chancellor erred in awarding the appellee an undivided one-sixth interest in the partnership. However, the chancellor was correct in determining that the partnership was marital property subject to being divided equally between the parties. Therefore, we modify his decision to reflect the proper manner of determining the amount to which appellee is entitled, and we remand for that determination to be made.

The appellant is in business with his father and his brother. Each owns an undivided one-third interest in J–W Foods, a retail grocery store in Huntsville. The chancellor found that the grocery business was marital property to be divided equally between the appellant and the appellee. As a part of his order, the chancellor found:

> Sue Warren [appellee] becomes the owner of an undivided one-sixth interest in such partnership and partnership assets. . . . [T]he interest of . . . Sue Warren in such partnership is subject to the liabilities of such partnership existing on the date of this order.

The appellant contends the chancellor should have awarded the appellee a sum in cash equal to one-half of appellant's net interest in the partnership. We agree. Under the Uniform Partnership Act, a partner's rights in specific partnership assets are those of a tenant in partnership. In determining at divorce the rights of a husband or wife to a spouse's partnership interest, the court cannot make specific awards of partnership assets. The court must first determine the value of the spouse's interest in the partnership, treating the accounts receivable as assets having a provable fair net present value, and then award the husband or wife a monetary decree equal to one-half that amount, the same to be enforced if necessary by a charging order on the partnership interest. We cannot make that determination ourselves on the record before us. Further proceedings will be necessary on remand to determine appellant's net interest in the partnership.

Assignment of Partner's Interest

At common law, assignment of a partner's interest in the business—for example, as a mortgage in return for a loan—would result in a legal dissolution of the partnership. Thus, in the absence of the UPA, which changed the law, Bob's decision to mortgage his interest in the bookstore in return for a $10,000 loan from his bank would mean that the three were no longer partners. UPA Section 27 declares that assignment of an interest in the partnership neither dissolves the partnership nor entitles the assignee "to interfere in the management or administration of the partnership business or affairs, or to require any information or account of partnership transactions, or to inspect the partnership books." The assignment merely entitles the assignee to receive whatever profits the assignor would have received.

Suppose a partner is sued in his personal capacity and a judgment is rendered against him. May the judgment creditor seize partnership property? UPA Section 28 permits a judgment creditor to obtain a **charging order,** which permits the partner's interest in the partnership to be charged with the unsatisfied amount of the judgment. The court may appoint a receiver to ensure that partnership proceeds are paid to the judgment creditor. But the creditor is not entitled to specific partnership property. The partner may always pay off the debt and recover his interest in the partnership. If the partner does not pay off the debt, the holder of the charging order may acquire legal ownership of the partner's interest. That confers upon the judgment creditor an important power: he may, if the partnership is one at will, dissolve the partnership and claim the partner's share of the assets. For that reason, the co-partners might wish to buy out the judgment creditor in order to preserve the partnership.

Whether an assignment of partnership interest is voluntary or involuntary, the assignee or creditor does not become a substitute partner. This is known as the doctrine of **delectus personae** (duh lek tus per sow nee): only by consent of all the partners can a third party become a partner. (UPA Section 18(g).) The freedom to select new partners, however, is not absolute. In 1984, the Supreme Court held that Title VII of the Civil Rights Act of 1964—which prohibits discrimination in employment based on race, religion, national origin, or sex—applies to partnership decisions. [Hishon v. King & Spalding, 467 U.S. 69 (1984); see Chapter 51.]

OPERATION—THE PARTNERSHIP AND THIRD PARTIES

By express terms, the law of agency applies to the UPA. Every partner is an agent of the partnership for the purpose of its business. Consequently, the following discussion will be a brief review of agency law, covered in the immediately preceding unit, as it applies to partnerships.

Contract Liability

Recall that an agent can make contracts on behalf of a principal under three types of authority: express, implied, and apparent. *Express* authority is that explicitly delegated to the agent, *implied* is that necessary to the carrying out of the express authority, and *apparent* authority is that which a third party is led to believe has been conferred by the principal on the agent even though in fact it was not, or it was revoked. When a partner has authority, the partnership is bound by contracts the partner makes on its behalf. All three types of authority are discussed in the following case.

HODGE v. GARRETT
101 Idaho 397, 614 P.2d 420 (1980)

BISTLINE, JUSTICE. Following a non-jury trial the court below granted specific performance to the plaintiff-respondent Bill Hodge. All defendants joined in a single notice of appeal, and all defendants joined in a single brief filed in this Court. Only Mr. Gatchel argued.

Hodge and defendant-appellant Rex E. Voeller, the managing partner of the Pay-Ont Drive-In Theatre, signed a contract for the sale of a small parcel of land belonging to the partnership. That parcel, although adjacent to the theater, was not used in theater operations except insofar as the east 20 feet were necessary for the operation of the theater's driveway. The agreement for the sale of land stated that it was between Hodge and the Pay-Ont Drive-In Theatre, a partnership. Voeller signed the agreement for the partnership, and written changes as to the footage and price were initialed by Voeller.

Voeller testified that he had told Hodge prior to signing that Hodge would have to present him with a plat plan which would have to be approved by the partners before the property could be sold. Hodge denied that a plat plan had ever been mentioned to him, and he testified that Voeller did not tell him that the approval of the other partners was needed until after the contract was signed. Hodge also testified that he offered to pay Voeller the full purchase price when he signed the contract, but Voeller told him that that was not necessary.

The trial court found that Voeller had actual and apparent authority to execute the contract on behalf of the partnership, and that the contract should be specifically enforced. The partners of the Pay-Ont Drive-In Theater appeal, arguing that Voeller did not have authority to sell the property and that Hodge knew that he did not have that authority.

At common law one partner could not, "without the concurrence of his copartners, convey away the real estate of the partnership, bind his partners by a deed, or transfer the title and interest of his copartners in the firm real estate." 60 Am.Jur.2d *Partnership* § 149 (1972). This rule was changed by the adoption of the Uniform Partnership Act. The relevant provisions are currently embodied in I.C. §§ 53–309(1) and 53–310(1). . . .

★   ★   ★

[According to] I.C. § 53–309(1):

> Every partner is an agent of the partnership for the purpose of its business, and the act of every partner, including the execution in the partnership

name of any instrument, for apparently carrying on in the usual way the business of the partnership of which he is a member binds the partnership, unless the partner so acting has in fact no authority to act for the partnership in the particular matter, and the person with whom he is dealing has knowledge of the fact that he has no such authority.

★   ★   ★

Thus this contract is enforceable if Voeller had the actual authority to sell the property, or, even if Voeller did not have such authority, the contract is still enforceable if the sale was in the usual way of carrying on the business and Hodge did not know that Voeller did not have this authority.

As to the question of actual authority, such authority must affirmatively appear, "for the authority of one partner to make and acknowledge a deed for the firm will not be presumed. . . ." 60 Am.Jur.2d *Partnership* § 151 (1972). Although such authority may be implied from the nature of the business or from similar past transactions, nothing in the record in this case indicates that Voeller had express or implied authority to sell real property belonging to the partnership. There is no evidence that Voeller had sold property belonging to the partnership in the past, and obviously the partnership was not engaged in the business of buying and selling real estate.

The next question, since actual authority has not been shown, is whether Voeller was conducting the partnership business in the usual way in selling this parcel of land such that the contract is binding under I.C. §§ 53–310(1) and 309(1), *i.e.*, whether Voeller had apparent authority. Here the evidence showed, and the trial court found:

★   ★   ★

That at the inception of the partnership, and at all times thereafter, Rex E. Voeller was the exclusive, managing partner of the partnership and had the full authority to make all decisions pertaining to the partnership affairs, including paying the bills, preparing profit and loss statements, income tax returns and the ordering of any goods or services necessary to the operation of the business.

The court made no finding that it was customary for Voeller to sell real property, or even personal property, belonging to the partnership. Nor was there any evidence to this effect. Nor did the court discuss whether it was in the usual course of business for the managing partner of a theater to sell real property. Yet the trial court found that Voeller had apparent authority to sell the property. From this it must be inferred that the trial court believed it to be in the usual course of business for a partner who has exclusive control of the partnership business to sell real property belonging to the partnership, where that property is not being used in the partnership business. We cannot agree with this conclusion. For a theater, "carrying on in the usual way the

(continued on next page)

(continued)

HODGE v. GARRETT
101 Idaho 397, 614 P.2d
420 (1980)

business of the partnership," I.C. § 53–309(1), means running the operations of the theater; it does not mean selling a parcel of property adjacent to the theater. Here the contract of sale stated that the land belonged to the partnership, and, even if Hodge believed that Voeller as the exclusive manager had authority to transact all business for the firm, Voeller still could not bind the partnership through a unilateral act which was not in the usual business of the partnership. We therefore hold that the trial court erred in holding that this contract was binding on the partnership.

Judgment reversed. Costs to appellant.

UPA Section 9 spells out certain types of acts the authority for doing which cannot be implied, including: disposing of the goodwill of the business, confessing a judgment, assigning partnership property to a creditor, and submitting a claim to arbitration. However, because the business of a partnership may be broad, an individual partner may have apparent authority to undertake a wide variety of acts not specifically authorized. As long as he is "apparently carrying on in the usual way the business of the partnership," he will bind his co-partners, unless he has no authority in fact and the third party knows that he does not.

Liability of Partners

The liability of the co-partners for a breach of contract is said to be **joint**. This means that the partners must be sued in a joint action brought against them all. A partner who is not named as a defendant cannot later be sued by a creditor in a separate proceeding. Thus, if the Bob–Carol–Ted Bookstore fails to pay a publisher's bill for a shipment of books, the publisher may decide to sue any of the partners individually. Although that partner could then seek a proportionate contribution from the other two, the publisher could not thereafter sue the other partners on the debt.

Notice and Admissions

If a partner has authority—express, implied, or apparent—and makes an admission or representation of

a fact within the scope of that authority, the third party may use the admission or representation as evidence against the entire partnership. Likewise, if any partner receives notice of any matter relating to partnership affairs, the notice is effective against the entire partnership unless the partner has committed fraud on the partnership.

Tort Liability

The general rule is that the partnership is liable for the tortious acts of any partner acting "in the ordinary course of the business of the partnership or with the authority of his co-partners." (UPA Section 13.) This, of course, is the general agency rule. For tortious acts, the partners are said to be **jointly and severally** liable. In this circumstance, the plaintiff may separately sue one or more partners. Even after winning a judgment, the plaintiff may sue other partners unnamed in the original action. Each and every partner is separately liable for the entire amount of the debt, although the plaintiff is not entitled to recover more than the total of his damages.

The practical impact of the rules making partners personally liable for partnership contracts and torts can be huge. In *Economics* (1973, p. 106), Professor Paul Samuelson says that unlimited liability

reveals why partnerships tend to be confined to small, personal enterprises. . . . When it becomes a question of placing their personal fortunes in jeopardy, people are reluctant to put their capital into complex ventures over which they can exercise little control. . . . In the field of

LAW AND LIFE

BOX 40-1

Laventhol Partners Face Long Process, Risk of Bankruptcy

By Laurie P. Cohen

[The general agency rule states that a partnership is liable for the tortious acts of any one partner. Plaintiffs may sue one or more partners because each and every partner is separately liable for the amount of the debt. Even in partnerships the partners have good cause to worry about liability.—AUTHORS' NOTE]

Partners of Laventhol & Horwath, which said it would file for bankruptcy court protection this week, face a long and complicated process that could lead to personal bankruptcy for some of them.

Laventhol & Horwath won't be the first accounting firm to enter bankruptcy court and then liquidate but with 350 partners, it will be the largest. And proceedings to wind up its affairs could take several years.

When a company files for bankruptcy court protection, its creditors

PERSONAL LIABILITY OF ACCOUNTING FIRM PARTNERS

are permitted only to make claims against the corporation, rather than against its shareholders. But when partnerships such as Laventhol file, creditors can sue individual partners in an effort to recover their money.

Bankruptcy law experts say that Laventhol's creditors, which include banks, landlords, suppliers and plaintiffs in litigation, are expected to try to recover money from partners, as well as from the partnership, if Laventhol is unable to satisfy their claims with its remaining assets.

If a partner was at Laventhol "when a potential liability arose, he's on the hook," said Leslie Corwin, a partner at the New York law firm of Morrison Cohen Singer & Weinstein, who is representing a Laventhol partner.

If a Laventhol partner joins an-

other accounting firm, the partner remains personally liable for his share of any Laventhol debt. However, the partner's new firm won't be responsible for any of that liability, said New York bankruptcy lawyer Joel Zweibel.

It is likely to take Laventhol a particularly long time to achieve a plan for paying off debts, largely because the firm doesn't know the extent of its liabilities. Laventhol still faces a number of lawsuits brought by former clients claiming faulty accounting practices; in one, the PTL, the religious organization of imprisoned evangelist Jim Bakker, is seeking $184 million in damages from Laventhol and other defendants.

Until such claims are settled, say bankruptcy lawyers, Laventhol won't be able to escape from bankruptcy proceedings. But, as in the filing of A.H. Robins Co., makers of the Dalkon Shield contraceptive device, bankruptcy courts have been willing to limit the total amount that claimants could recover from litigation against debtors.

Source: *Wall Street Journal*, November 20, 1990

---

investment banking, concerns like J. P. Morgan & Company used to advertise proudly 'not incorporated' so that their creditors could have extra assurance. But even these concerns have converted themselves into corporate entities. Comparatively recently, the giant brokerage concern Merrill Lynch, Pierce, Fenner & Smith incorporated itself. For a long time it had many major partners and scores of junior partners, illustrating that the barriers to running a large enterprise put up by the partnership form are not insuperable. Still, giant partnerships are now rare.

The last sentence is plainly incorrect. Many accounting and law firms boast of hundreds of partners. But

it is clear that they do worry about liability, and for good cause (see **Box 40-1**).

Criminal Liability

Criminal liability is generally personal to the miscreant. Nonparticipating copartners are ordinarily not liable for crimes if guilty intent is an element. When guilty intent is not an element, as in certain regulatory offenses, all partners may be guilty of an act committed by a partner in the course of the business.

DISSOLUTION AND WINDING UP

Dissolution

Meaning   People in business manifest considerable confusion over the meaning of **dissolution**. It does not mean the termination of the business. It has a precise legal definition, given in UPA Section 29: "The dissolution of a partnership is the change in the relation of the partners caused by any partner ceasing to be associated in the carrying on as distinguished from the winding up of the business." The partnership is not necessarily terminated on dissolution; rather, it continues until the winding up of partnership affairs is completed. (UPA Section 30.)

Causes   Partnerships can dissolve for a number of reasons. The term of the partnership agreement may have expired or the partnership may be at will and one of the partners desires to leave it. All the partners may decide that it is preferable to dissolve rather than to continue. One of the partners may have been expelled in accordance with a provision in the agreement. In none of these circumstances is the agreement violated, though its spirit surely might have been. Professor Samuelson calls to mind the example of William Dean Howells's *Silas Lapham,* who forces his partner to sell out by offering him an ultimatum: "You may buy me out or I'll buy you out." The ultimatum was given at a time when the partner could not afford to buy Lapham out and so had no choice at all.

But dissolution may also result from violation of the agreement, as when the partners decide to discharge a partner though no provision permits them to do so.

A third reason for dissolution is the occurrence of some event, such as enactment of a statute, that makes it unlawful to continue the business. Or a partner may die or one or more partners or the entire partnership may become bankrupt. Dissolution under these circumstances is said to be by **operation of law.**

Finally, dissolution may be by court order. Courts are empowered to dissolve partnerships when "on application by or for a partner" a partner is shown to be a lunatic, of unsound mind, incapable of performing his part of the agreement, "guilty of such conduct as tends to affect prejudicially the carrying on of the business," or otherwise behaves in such a way that "it is not reasonably practicable to carry on the business in partnership with him." A court may also order dissolution if the business can only be carried on at a loss or whenever equitable. In some circumstances, a court will order dissolution upon the application of a purchaser of a partner's interest. (UPA Section 32(2).)

Effect of Dissolution on Authority   For the most part, dissolution terminates the authority of the partners to act for the partnership. The only significant exceptions are for acts necessary to wind up partnership affairs or to complete transactions begun but not finished at the time of dissolution. (UPA Section 33.) Notwithstanding the latter exception, no partner can bind the partnership if it has dissolved because it has become unlawful to carry on the business or if the partner seeking to exercise authority has become bankrupt.

After Dissolution   After a partnership has dissolved, it can follow one of two paths. It can carry on business as a new partnership or it can wind up the business and cease operating (see Figure 40-2). These paths are explored in the next two sections.

Forming a New Partnership   In order to carry on the business as a new partnership, there must be an agreement, preferably as part of the original partnership agreement, that upon dissolution (for example, if a partner dies) the others will regroup and carry on. A practical difficulty for the remaining partners is how they can pay off the partnership interest to the

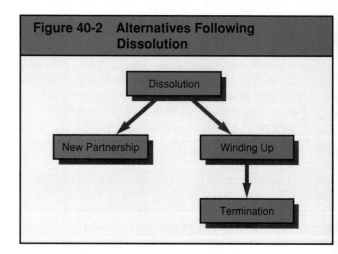

Figure 40-2   Alternatives Following Dissolution

estate of their deceased partner. Payment of a large sum might cripple or even ruin the business, and assessing the liquidation value of many types of partnerships is often exceedingly difficult. One solution is insurance.

Partnerships routinely insure the lives of the partners, who have no ownership interests in the insurance policies. The policies should bear a face amount equal to each partner's interest in the partnership and should be adjusted as the fortunes of the partnership change. Proceeds of the insurance policy are used on death to pay the purchase price of the interest inherited by the deceased's estate. If the insurance policy pays out more than the interest at stake, the partnership retains the difference. If the policy pays out less, the partnership agrees to pay the difference in periodic installments.

Another set of issues arises when the partnership changes because an old partner departs and a new one joins. Suppose that Bob leaves the bookstore business and his interest is purchased by Alice, who is then admitted to the partnership. Assume that when Bob left, the business owed Mogul Publishing Company $5,000 and Laid Back Publishers $4,000. After Bob left and Alice joined, Mogul sells another $5,000 worth of books to the store on credit, and Sizzling Paperbooks, a new creditor, advances the bookstore $3,000 worth of books. These circumstances pose four questions:

First, do creditors of the old partnership remain creditors of the new partnership? Yes. (UPA Section 41(1).)

Second, does Bob, the old partner, remain liable to the creditors of the old partnership? Yes. (UPA Section 36(1).) That could pose uncomfortable problems for Bob, who may have left the business because he lost interest in bookstores and wished to put his money into another type of investment. The last thing he wants is the threat of liability hanging over his head when he can no longer profit from the bookstore operations. That is all the more true if he had a falling out with his partners and does not trust them. The solution is given in UPA Section 36(2), which says that an old partner is discharged from liability if the creditors and the new partnership agree to discharge him.

Third, is Alice, the new partner, liable to creditors of the old partnership? Yes, but only to the extent of her capital contribution. (UPA Section 17.)

Fourth, is Bob, the old partner, liable for debts incurred after his withdrawal from the partnership? Surprisingly, yes, unless Bob takes certain action toward old and new creditors. He must provide actual notice that he has withdrawn to anyone who has extended credit in the past. Once he has done so, he has no liability to these creditors for credit extended to the partnership thereafter. Of course, it would be difficult to provide notice to future creditors, since at the time of withdrawal they would not have had a relationship with the partnership. To avoid liability to new creditors who knew of the partnership, the solution required under UPA Section 35(1)(b)(II) is to advertise his departure in a newspaper of general circulation in the place at which the partnership business was regularly carried on.

Winding Up the Partnership If the partners decide not to continue the business upon dissolution, they are obliged to wind up the business. Winding up entails concluding all unfinished business pending at the date of dissolution and payment of all debts. The partners must then settle accounts among themselves in order to distribute the remaining assets.

Determining the priority of liabilities can be problematic. For instance, debts might be incurred to both outside creditors and partners, who might have lent money to pay off certain accounts or for working capital. An agreement can spell out the order in which liabilities are to be paid, but if it does not, UPA Section 40(a) ranks them in this order: (1) to creditors other than partners, (2) to partners for liabilities other than for capital and profits, (3) to partners for capital contributions, and finally, (4) to partners for their share of profits (see Figure 40-3).

Partners are entitled to share equally in the profits and surplus remaining after all liabilities, including those owed to partners, are paid off, although the

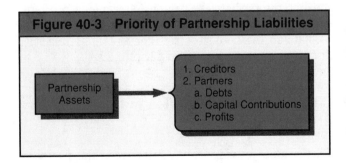

Figure 40-3   Priority of Partnership Liabilities

partnership agreement can state a different share—for example, in proportion to capital contribution. If after winding up there is a net loss, whether capital or otherwise, each partner must contribute toward it in accordance with his share in the profits, had there been any, unless the agreement states otherwise. If any of the partners is insolvent or refuses to contribute and cannot be sued, the others must contribute their own share to pay off the liabilities and in addition must contribute, in proportion to their share of the profits, the additional amount necessary to pay the liabilities of their defaulting partners.

In the event of insolvency, a court may take possession of both partnership property and individual assets of the partners. UPA Section 40(h) dictates that creditors of the partnership are entitled to priority in distribution of the partnership property, and separate creditors of the individual partners have priority in distribution of their personal assets. If particular creditors have liens on or a security interest in particular items, whether partnership or personal property, they take precedence over all other creditors. Suppose the Carol–Ted–Alice Bookstore devotes most of its shelf space to copies of this textbook, rather than to our best selling companion volume, the *Business Law Text Get-Slim-in-Only-3-Weeks Diet Plan,* and as a consequence goes bust. Assume that after the publishers reclaim the inventory and the bank forecloses the mortgage on the house, no partnership assets are left to cover a remaining $15,000 debt. The only assets are Alice's personal effects, valued at $4,000. Alice has a college tuition loan of $5,000 still outstanding. Both the college and the remaining bookstore creditor come after Alice's possessions. Who should prevail? According to UPA Section 40(h), the college is entitled to the value of her personal assets. However, if Alice files a petition in bankruptcy, the Bankruptcy Reform Act of 1978 would govern disposition of her property. The act provides that partnership and personal creditors share the personal assets on a pro rata basis, with the result that the college would receive $1,000 and the bookstore creditor $3,000. The act is discussed in greater detail in Chapter 29.

OTHER UNINCORPORATED ASSOCIATIONS

This section provides a bridge between the partnership and corporate form. Four types of associations discussed here—*limited partnerships, limited liability companies, joint ventures,* and *business trusts*—have aspects of both.

Limited Partnerships

Source   The **limited partnership** is a business form that provides limited liability to an investor, much as a corporate stockholder has limited liability, while continuing to provide the tax benefits of partnership. Limited partnerships have long been used by those seeking tax shelters. However, the Tax Reform Act of 1986 reduced the tax benefits—for example, by placing restrictions on the ability of limited partners to take tax deductions for partnership losses. As a result, the popularity of limited partnerships has diminished considerably.

The original source of limited partnership law is the Uniform Limited Partnership Act (ULPA), which was drafted in 1916. A revised version, the Revised Uniform Limited Partnership Act (RULPA), was adopted by the National Conference of Commissioners on Uniform State Laws in 1976 and is now the law in most states. Only Louisiana has adopted neither of the acts. The following discussion is based on RULPA, amended in 1985 (see Appendix G). The Uniform Partnership Act also applies to limited partnerships except where it is inconsistent with the limited partnership statutes.

Form of Partnership   A limited partnership has two categories of partners: general and limited. The general partner has the powers and liability of partners under the UPA. The limited partner is not bound by the obligations of the partnership (see Figure 40-4). With few exceptions the limited partner—which may be a corporation or another partnership—is strictly an investor. While limited partners have no say in the business, they do have the same rights as general partners to inspect and copy the business books and to demand true and full information about the business.

A limited partner may assign his interest to anyone. The assignee may or may not become a new partner. Unless the assignee becomes a new partner, known as a "substituted limited partner," his only right is to collect the assignor's share of profits or other compensation or return of capital. An assignee becomes a substituted limited partner, with all the

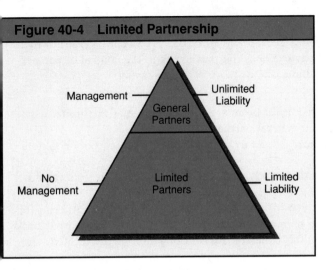

Figure 40-4   Limited Partnership

rights of a limited partner, if all the members—limited and general—consent or if the certificate explicitly gives the assignee the right to become one.

Formation   Unlike a regular partnership, a limited partnership comes into existence only when a certificate of partnership is filed with the secretary of state. The certificate must set forth certain information, including the name of the limited partnership and the names and business addresses of the general partners. The name of the partnership must include the words "limited partnership." Each general partner must sign the certificate and affirm under penalties of perjury the truth of the statements it contains.

Liability   Investors like limited partnershps because they shield them, as limited partners, from liability for the obligations of the business. However, this protection has two important qualifications. First, the name of a limited partnership may not contain the name of a limited partner unless there is a statutory exception (such as when it is also the name of a general partner). If a limited partner knowingly permits her name to be used in the limited partnership, she will be liable to any creditor who extends credit without realizing that she is not a general partner.

The second—and more important—qualification is the so-called "control" test: a limited partner who participates in the control of the business will be liable to persons who deal with the business on the reasonable belief (based on the limited partner's conduct) that she is a general partner.

The control test does not completely prohibit limited partners from participating in the business. RULPA contains several "safe harbor" provisions that exclude certain acts from the definition of control. These include (1) being a contractor for (or an agent or employee of) the limited partnership or of a general partner; (2) being an officer, director or shareholder of a corporation that is a general partner; and (3) consulting with and advising a general partner concerning the business.

When an act falls outside the safe harbors, however, RULPA provides little guidance on what constitutes control. As a result, courts must review closely the facts in each case to resolve the control issue, as discussed in the following opinion.

ALZADO v. BLINDER, ROBINSON & CO., INC.
752 P.2d 544 (Colo. 1988)

[Combat Associates was a limited partnership formed to finance an exhibition boxing match between Lyle Alzado, a professional football player, and Mohammed Ali, the world heavyweight boxing champion. A corporation was named as the general partner and plaintiff Blinder-Robinson was the sole limited partner. Combat Associates agreed to pay Alzado for the match. The fight proved to be a financial debacle. In the ensuing litigation, one issue was whether Blinder-Robinson should be treated as a general partner, which would make it liable to Alzado for his participation. A jury verdict in favor of Alzado on this issue was reversed by an intermediate appellate court. The reversal was upheld on further appeal in the following opinion.]

A limited partner may become liable to partnership creditors as a general partner if the limited partner assumes control of partnership business. § 7-

(continued on next page)

(continued)

ALZADO v. BLINDER, ROBINSON & CO., INC.
752 P.2d 544 (Colo. 1988)

61-108, 3A C.R.S. (1986); see also § 7-62-303, 3A C.R.S. (1986), which provides that a limited partner does not participate in the control of partnership business solely by doing one or more of the following:

(a)   Being a contractor for or an agent or employee of the limited partnership or of a general partner;

(b)   Being an officer, director, or shareholder of a corporate general partner;

(c)   Consulting with and advising a general partner with respect to the business of the limited partnership;

(d)   Acting as surety for the limited partnership or guaranteeing or assuming one or more specific obligations of the limited partnership or providing collateral for an obligation of the limited partnership;

(e)   Bringing an action in the right of a limited partnership to recover a judgment in its favor pursuant to part 10 or this article;

(f)   Calling, requesting, or participating in a meeting of the partners;

(g)   Proposing or approving or disapproving, by voting or otherwise, one or more of the following matters:

(I)   The dissolution and winding up or continuation of the limited partnership;

(II)   The sale, exchange, lease, mortgage, pledge, or other transfer of any assets of the limited partnership;

(III)   The incurrence of indebtedness by the limited partnership;

(IV)   A change in the nature of the business;

(V)   The admission or removal of a partner;

(VI)   A transaction or other matter involving an actual or potential conflict of interest;

(VII)   An amendment to the partnership agreement or certificate of limited partnership; or

(VIII)   Such other matters as are stated in writing in the partnership agreement;

(h)   Winding up the limited partnership pursuant to section 7-62-803; or

(i)   Exercising any right or power permitted to limited partners under this article and not specifically enumerated in this subsection (2).

Early determinations regarding whether a limited partner's conduct constituted control of partnership business were largely fact-specific and did not attempt to state general standards for determining what acts evidence such control. More recent decisions construing section 7 of the Uniform Limited Partnership Act have also failed to provide definitive interpretations of what constitutes "control." . . . Any determination of whether a limited partner's conduct amounts to control over the business affairs of the partnership must be determined by consideration of several factors, including the purpose of the partnershp, the administrative activities undertaken, the manner in which the entity actually functioned, and the nature and frequency of the limited partner's purported activities.

. . . The record here reflects that Blinder-Robinson used its Denver office as a ticket outlet, gave two parties to promote the exhibition match and provided a meeting room for many of Combat Associates' meetings. Blinder personally appeared on a television talk show and gave television interviews to promote the match. Blinder-Robinson made no investment, accounting or other financial decisions for the partnership; all such fiscal decisions were made by officers or employees of Combat Promotions, Inc., the general partner. The evidence established at most that Blinder-Robinson engaged in a few promotional activities. It does not establish that it took part in the management or control of the business affairs of the partnership. . . .

Alzado contends, in the alternative, that the actual management of the partnership's daily business activities is irrelevant to Blinder-Robinson's status for purposes of liability because Blinder-Robinson's power and authority over the partnership assets rendered it liable as a general partner. He finds this alleged unlimited authority in the expense distribution formula contained in section 4.4 of the limited partnership agreement. Alzado cites no authority, and we are aware of none, in support of the theory that provisions of a limited partnership agreement structuring expenses and establishing net profit and loss distribution formulae may themselves render a limited partner liable as a general partner for partnership debts. In theory it may be true that particular provisions of a limited partnership agreement might so circumscribe the general partners' ability to make management decisions as to constitute conclusive evidence of control by the challenged limited partner. We do not view the terms of the Combat Associates limited partnership agreement as constituting such conclusive evidence.

Alzado finally asserts that Blinder-Robinson fostered the appearance of being in control of Combat Associates, that such actions rendered Binder-Robinson liable as a general partner and that this conduct allowed third parties to believe that Blinder-Robinson was in fact a general partner. The evidence does not support this argument. Certainly, as Vice President of Combat Promotions, Inc., the general partner of Combat Associates, Alzado had no misconception concerning the function and role of Blinder-Robinson as a limited partner only. The Court of Appeals concluded that the evidence failed to establish that Blinder-Robinson exercised control over the business affairs of Combat Associates. We agree with that conclusion.

Limited Liability Companies

The control issue faced by limited partners may be avoided through the formation of a limited liability company (LLC). Two states—Wyoming and Florida—currently allow businesses to organize as LLCs, although it is likely that other states will authorize them as a result of a 1988 IRS ruling that LLCs are taxable as partnerships.

The chief characteristics of LLCs are:

1. They may be managed by designated managers or by members.

2. The manager and members are not liable for company debts.

3. An interest in a LLC can be transferred only with the unanimous consent of other members.

4. As with a partnership, dissolution may result from the death or bankruptcy of a member.

Joint Ventures

A **joint venture**—sometimes known as a joint adventure, coadventure, joint enterprise, joint undertaking, syndicate, group, or pool—is an association of persons to carry on a particular task until completed. In essence, a joint venture is a "temporary partnership."

Partnership rules generally apply, although the relationship of the joint venturers is closer to that of special than general agency (see p. 820). Joint venturers are fiduciaries toward one another. Although no formality is necessary, the associates will usually sign an agreement. The joint venture need have no group name, though it may have one. Property may be owned jointly. Profits and losses will be shared, as in a partnership, and each associate has the right to participate in management. Liability is unlimited.

Sometimes two or more businesses will form a joint venture to carry out a specific task—prospecting for oil, building a nuclear reactor, doing basic scientific research—and will incorporate the joint venture. In that case, the resulting business—known as a "joint venture corporation"—is governed by corporation law, not the law of partnership, and is not a joint venture in the sense described here. Increasingly, companies are forming joint ventures to do business abroad; foreign investors or governments own significant interests in these joint ventures.

Business Trusts

Principles and History   As discussed in Chapter 35, when a trust is created, property is given to the trustee, who holds it for the benefit of a third party. The trustee has "legal title," and the beneficiary has "equitable title," since the courts of equity would enforce the obligations of the trustee to honor the terms by which the property was conveyed to the trustee. The use of trusts for business purposes was a way

around nineteenth century restrictions on use of the corporate form. The business trust flourished particularly in Massachusetts—hence is often called the Massachusetts trust—because that state's law imposed restrictions on corporate dealing in real estate, and the trust device was a handy way around those restrictions.

After the 1920s, the popularity of the business trust declined considerably, both because corporations were given in every state, including Massachusetts, the same power to deal in real property as natural persons and partnerships, and also because state and federal law began to regulate and tax business trusts in substantially the same manner as corporations. Many investment companies remain organized as trusts, however, and since the 1960s, with a change in federal and state tax laws permitting conduit treatment of income, many *real estate investment trusts* (**REITs**) were organized. Money market funds today often use the Massachusetts business trust form because it avoids the necessity of issuing stock certificates whenever a dividend is paid.

Formation   Typically, the business trust is formed when its investors place legal title to capital in the hands of trustees through a written declaration of trust. The document sets forth the powers and duties of the trustees and interests of the beneficiaries (investors). Many states now require business trust declarations to be filed in an appropriate public office. Beneficiaries usually receive certificates that are freely transferable and that act in most respects like shares of corporate stock, but certificates are not required (see Figure 40-5).

Operation   Management is in the hands of the trustees, who are frequently self-perpetuating, although this is not a legal requirement. Trustees usually delegate day-to-day operations, if the company is at all sizable,

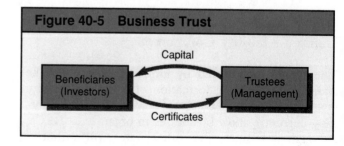

Figure 40-5   Business Trust

to employed officers. In many states, beneficiaries bear the same relationship to the trustees as do limited partners to the partnership: participating in business control causes a forfeiture of limited liability. Some states—New York is one—view strictly the beneficiary's exercise of control: even a minor attempt to control might suffice to convert the trust into a partnership or joint venture. The trustee is a fiduciary, and generally cannot enter into contracts with the trust in his private capacity.

Liability Unless beneficiaries are in a position to control, their liability in most states is limited to their capital contribution. The trustees remain liable, although in most states trustees can limit their liability by contract with outside creditors. This they can do usually by making clear that they are entering into contracts "as trustees serving in a representative capacity only and not individually." If a trustee is held personally liable for a trust's debts, he is usually entitled to indemnification from the trust estate.

Taxation Federal income tax law and many state income tax laws treat the business trust as a corporation. Trust earnings are thus taxed before dividends or other distributions are made to the beneficiaries, unlike the method of taxing partnerships. By contrast, REITs are analogous to partnerships, and serve as a conduit for income to their beneficiaries, who are taxed directly on the distribution.

Transferability of Interests Unlike the rule of *delectus personae* in partnerships, no legal impediment prevents the free transfer of trust certificates. Hence beneficiaries can sell their certificates freely on the open market. Since beneficiaries have little or no power to control the affairs of the trust, their identity is usually of no consequence to the business.

CHAPTER SUMMARY

Most of the UPA rules apply only in the absence of agreement among the partners. Under the UPA, unless the agreement states otherwise, any partner is entitled to share profits and losses equally after being repaid her actual contribution and to an equal share of the management. Ordinarily partners operate through majority vote, but no act that contravenes the partnership agreement itself may be undertaken without unanimous consent.

The partners hold specific partnership assets as tenants in partnership; these specific assets belong to the partnership, but the partnership interest is a property interest that is inheritable. The UPA specifically permits a partner to assign his interest in the partnership to an outsider, but the assignee does not thereby become a partner or gain a right to interfere in the management. A judgment creditor of a partner is not entitled to seize specific partnership property but may obtain a charging order against his partnership interest to satisfy the judgment.

A change in the relation of the partners dissolves the partnership but does not necessarily wind up the business. Dissolution may be voluntary, by violation of the agreement, by operation of law, or by court order. Dissolution terminates the authority of the partners to act for the partnership. After dissolution, a new partnership may be formed.

When a dissolved partnership is carried on as a new one, creditors of the old partnership remain creditors of the new one. A former partner remains liable to the creditors of the former partnership. A new partner is liable to the creditors of the former partnership, but only to the extent of the new partner's capital contribution. A former partner remains liable for debts incurred after his withdrawal unless he gives proper notice of his withdrawal.

Between partnerships and corporations lie a variety of the other types of association, including limited partnerships, limited liability companies, joint ventures, and business trusts. The limited partnership provides limited liability to an investor; this type of entity is governed in most states by the RULPA. The limited partner has no say in the daily operation of the business. A limited partnership comes into existence only when a certificate of partnership is filed with the secretary of state. A limited partner may forfeit his limited liability if he takes part in control or uses his name in the partnership name. The control issue can be avoided through the formation of a limited liability company, although very few states allow them.

A joint venture is a temporary partnership formed to accomplish a specific undertaking. Partnership rules generally apply. But when two businesses incorporate a joint venture between them, the resulting corporation is governed by corporation law, not partnership law.

A business trust is operated by trustees who hold legal title to the business assets and who operate the business for the beneficiaries, who hold equitable title. Although the popularity of business trusts has declined considerably, many investment companies and real estate investment trusts are business trusts. Trust certificates held by the beneficiaries may be transferred like corporate stock. Management is usually delegated to paid officers.

KEY TERMS

SELF-TEST QUESTIONS

1. Under the UPA, a partner is generally entitled to a formal accounting of partnership affairs:
   (a) whenever it is just and reasonable
   (b) if a partner is wrongfully excluded from partnership business by co-partners
   (c) if the right exists under the terms of the partnership agreement
   (d) all of the above
2. A temporary partnership formed to accomplish a specific undertaking is called:
   (a) a business trust
   (b) a limited partnership
   (c) a joint venture
   (d) none of the above
3. The doctrine that only by consent of all the partners can a third party become a partner is called:
   (a) a charging order
   (b) a tenancy in partnership
   (c) delectus personae
   (d) estoppel
4. A limited partnership:
   (a) comes into existence when a certificate of partnership is filed
   (b) always provides limited liability to an investor
   (c) gives limited partners a say in the daily operation of the business
   (d) is no longer allowed because of the Tax Reform Act of 1986
5. A trust operated by trustees who hold legal title to business assets and operate the business for beneficiaries is called a:
   (a) blind trust
   (b) business trust
   (c) revocable trust
   (d) joint venture

DEMONSTRATION PROBLEM

Butch and Sundance, as partners, commit a number of armed robberies. They agree to divide the stolen property equally. Butch feels that Sundance is keeping more than his fair share of the property and seeks an accounting in court. Result? Why?

PROBLEMS

1. Anne and Louise form a partnership. Being optimistic, they only cover division of profits in their partnership agreement. The agreement specifies that Anne will receive two-thirds of the profits, Louise one-third. The partnership sustains heavy losses. How are the losses divided?
2. Assume in problem 1 that Anne feels that they should no longer deal with one of their suppliers, while Louise disagrees. Anne tells the supplier that she will not be responsible for future sales to the partnership, but Louise continues to buy from the supplier. Is Anne liable for Louise's purchases? Explain.
3. Assume in problem 1 that Anne works long, hard hours for the partnership, while Louise spends her days pumping iron at a local health spa. Finally, tired and angry, Anne demands compensation for her services. Is she entitled to compensation? Why?
4. Two physicians, Casey and Kildare, formed a partnership. One day, while doing an appendectomy, Casey negligently forgot to remove a sponge from the patient before completing the operation. Is Kildare liable to the patient for Casey's malpractice? Why?
5. When the patient in problem 4 recovered, he visited the doctors' office and demanded compensation from Casey. Casey, in a blind rage, hit the patient and broke his jaw. Is Kildare liable? Why?
6. Assume that Casey (see problem 4) entered into a contract, on behalf of the partnership, to purchase five video games. Is Kildare liable under this contract? Why?
7. Fed up with his potential liability for Casey's activities (see problems 4, 5 and 6), Kildare decides that they should restructure the association as a limited partnership, called Casey and Kildare, Limited Partnership. Casey will be the general partner and Kildare the limited partner. Under their new arrangement, Kildare will manage the practice on Mondays and Tuesdays, while Casey will manage it on Thursdays and Fridays. (They will play golf on Wednesday.) Will the new arrangement protect Kildare from liability for Casey's activities? Why?

ANSWERS TO SELF-TEST QUESTIONS

1. (d)   2. (c)   3. (c)   4. (a)   5. (b)

SUGGESTED ANSWER TO DEMONSTRATION PROBLEM

The court will not help Butch. "We conclude that in this country, in the case of a partnership in a business confessedly illegal, . . . the decided weight of authority is that a court of equity will not entertain a bill for accounting." *Central Trust and Safe Co. v. Respass*, 66 S.W. 421 (Ky. 1902). In a celebrated English case, the Highwaymen's case (*Everet v. Williams*, 9 Law Quart. Rev. 197), the two highwaymen who sought an accounting were hanged, their attorneys were taken into custody and fined, and one was transported (*i.e.* exiled).

The Manager's Legal Agenda

In deciding whether to carry on a business as a partnership, legal advice is almost always essential. The mere size of the business or the number of principals initially involved (or who may ultimately become involved) is not usually determinative. Seek legal advice at the earliest stages of planning for the business, since even without an express agreement you may discover that once the business is underway you in fact are part of a partnership.

Although partnerships can be created quite informally and may be workable without written agreements among two or three people, both the enterprise and the individual partners will be legally more secure if they are operating under a formal contractual arrangement spelling out the terms of the partnership.

Every partnership agreement should contain, among other things, a description of each partner's responsibilities and authority to act and to bind the partnership (and limitations on those responsibilities and authority) and a method of determining how profits and losses are to be allocated.

Likewise, a partnership agreement should spell out precisely under what conditions and how a partner may withdraw from the business and how the business may continue, usually under a new partnership agreement, when a partner withdraws or dies.

Choose a partnership name wisely to avoid misleading the public or those with whom you deal. In particular, avoid any suggestion that the partnership is a corporation and keep your own name out of the partnership name if you are a limited partner.

Although the Uniform Partnership Act gives considerable power to courts to order an accounting when a partner complains that he is being cheated, a good partnership agreement should spell out the grounds under which any partner may demand an accounting, so that you will avoid the difficulty, cost, and time of a lawsuit to establish the right to one.

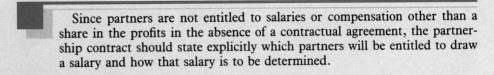

Since partners are not entitled to salaries or compensation other than a share in the profits in the absence of a contractual agreement, the partnership contract should state explicitly which partners will be entitled to draw a salary and how that salary is to be determined.

In the partnership agreement you may control how partnership decisions are to be made. If you do not wish to be governed by a rule of majority vote, you should precisely spell out the alternative.

Under partnership law, each partner is jointly liable for breach of contract. As a result, when suing a partnership, you should name all partners as defendants. Any partner not included in the action cannot be sued later.

A lawyer experienced in partnership law should review a limited partnership agreement before you sign it. And remember that you can be held liable for acts of the partnership, even while remaining a limited partner, if you begin to exercise substantial control over the affairs of the business.

Because profits of a partnership are taxed to the partners individually, you may incur a tax liability even on undistributed profits. You should always seek accounting and tax advice on profits, losses, and distribution of partnership assets.

PART

IX

Neither can a corporation be excommunicated, for it has no soul.

BLACKSTONE

CORPORATIONS

General Characteristics and Formation

We now turn to the dominant form of business enterprise in the modern world: the corporation. The corporation is a legal entity and bound by much of the law discussed in the preceding chapters. Nevertheless, as a significant institutional actor in the business world, the corporation has a host of relationships that have called forth a separate body of law. In Part IX, we take up the following broad themes:

- General nature of the corporation (Chapter 41),
- Corporate organization (Chapter 41),
- Corporate finance (Chapter 42),
- Corporate governance, including the rights and duties of directors, officers, and shareholders (Chapter 43),
- Regulation of securities, with special emphasis on insider trading (Chapter 44), and
- Corporate expansion and dissolution (Chapter 45).

Historical Background

Like partnership, the corporation is an ancient concept, recognized in the Code of Hammurabi, and to some degree a fixture in every other major legal system since then. The first corporations were not business enterprises; instead, they were associations for religious and governmental ends in which **perpetual life** was a practical requirement. It is difficult, if not impossible, to contemplate a city or church or university as an institution without legal status separate from that of its members. Some device is necessary for permitting an ongoing activity to carry on despite the death of one or more of its principals. If the mayor dies, must the city dissolve? Corporate status does the trick.

Until relatively late in legal history, kings, popes, and jurists assumed that corporations could be created only by political or ecclesiastical authority—that corporations were creatures of the state or church. By the seventeenth century, with feudalism on the wane and business enterprise becoming a growing force, kings extracted greater taxes and intervened more directly in the affairs of businesses by refusing to permit them to operate in corporate form except by royal grant. This came to be known as the "concession theory," because incorporation was a concession from the sovereign.

The most important concessions or charters were those given to the giant foreign trading companies, including the Russia Company (1554), British East India Company (1600), Hudson's Bay Company (1670, and still operating in Canada under the name "The Bay"), the South Sea Company (1711), and others. These were "joint stock" companies; that is, individuals contributed capital to the enterprise, which traded on behalf of all the stockholders. Originally, trading companies were formed for single voyages, but the advantages in a continuing fund of capital soon became apparent. Also apparent was the legal characteristic that above all led shareholders to subscribe to the stock: limited liability. They risked only the cash they put in, not their personal fortunes.

Some companies were wildly successful. The British East India Company paid its original investors a four-fold return between 1683 and 1692. But perhaps nothing excited the imagination of the British more than the discovery of a Spanish shipwreck carrying gold bullion; 150 companies were quickly formed to salvage sunken Spanish treasure. Though most of these were outright frauds, they ignited the search for easy wealth by a public unwary of the risks. In particular, the South Sea Company promised the sun and moon: in return for a monopoly over the slave-trade to the West Indies, it told a delirious public that it would retire the public debt and make every person rich. Other promoters offered schemes, among many others, "to get oil from sunflower seeds, to build ships to proceed against pirates, to cultivate silkworms in Surrey, to make a *perpetuum mobile*" (Beard, 1962, p. 437).

In 1720, a fever gripped London that sent stock prices soaring. Beggars and earls alike speculated from January to August with the enthusiasm of a child giving away play money—and then the bubble burst. Without considering the ramifications, Parliament had enacted a highly restrictive Bubble Act, which was supposed to do away with uncharted joint-stock companies. When the government prosecuted four companies under the act for having fraudulently obtained charters, the public panicked and stock prices came tumbling down, resulting in one of history's worst financial collapses.

As a consequence, corporate development was severely retarded in England. Distrustful of the chartered company, Parliament issued few corporate charters, and then only for public or quasi-public un-

dertaking, such as transportation, insurance, and banking enterprises. Corporation law languished: William Blackstone devoted less than 1 percent of his immensely influential *Commentaries on the Law of England* (1765) to corporations and omitted altogether any discussion of limited liability. In *The Wealth of Nations* (1776), Adam Smith doubted that the use of corporations would spread. England did not repeal the Bubble Act until 1825, and then because the value of true incorporation had become apparent from the experience of her former colonies.

The United States remained largely unaffected by the Bubble Act. Incorporation was granted only by special acts of state legislatures, even well into the nineteenth century, but many such acts were passed. Before the Revolution, perhaps fewer than a dozen business corporations existed throughout the thirteen colonies. During the 1790s alone, 200 businesses were incorporated, and their numbers swelled thereafter. The theory that incorporation should not be accomplished except through special legislation began to give way. As industrial development hastened in the mid-1800s, it was possible in many states to incorporate by adhering to the requirements of a general statute. Indeed, by the late nineteenth century, all but three states constitutionally *forbade* their legislatures from chartering companies through special enactments.

The U.S. Supreme Court contributed importantly to the development of corporate law. In *Paul v. Virginia*, 75 U.S. 168 (1868), the Court said that a state could prevent corporations not chartered there—**foreign corporations,** meaning from out-of-state—from coming in to engage in purely local business. The clear inference was that the states could not bar foreign corporations engaged in *interstate* business from their borders.

That decision brought about a competition in corporation laws. The early general laws had imposed numerous restrictions. The breadth of corporate enterprise was limited, ceilings were placed on total capital and indebtedness, incorporators were required to have residence in the state, often the duration of the company was not perpetual but was limited to a term of years or until a particular undertaking was completed, and the powers of management were circumscribed. These restrictions and limitations were thought to be necessary to protect the citizenry of the chartering legislature's own state. But once it became clear that companies chartered in one state could operate in others, states began in effect to "sell" incorporation for tax revenues, thus exporting the worst features of their laws. New Jersey led the way in 1875 with a general incorporation statute that greatly liberalized the powers of management and lifted many of the former restrictions. The Garden State was ultimately eclipsed by Delaware, which in 1899 enacted the most liberal corporation statute in the country, so that to the present day there are thousands of "Delaware corporations" that maintain no presence in the state other than an address on file with the secretary of state in Dover.

During the 1920s, the National Conference of Commissioners on Uniform State Laws drafted a Uniform Business Corporation Act, the final version of which was released in 1928. It was not widely adopted, but it did provide the basis during the 1930s for revisions of some state laws, including those in California, Illinois, Michigan, Minnesota, and Pennsylvania. By that time, in the midst of the Great Depression, the federal government for the first time intruded into corporate law in a major way by creating federal agencies—most notably the Securities and Exchange Commission, with power to regulate the interstate issuance of corporate stock.

Corporation Law Today

Following World War II, most states revised their general corporation laws. The most significant development was the preparation of the Model Business Corporation Act by the American Bar Association Committee on Corporate Laws. Most states have adopted all or major portions of the Model Act. The latest version of the act, the Revised Model Business Corporation Act (RMBCA) is reprinted in Appendix D and will be referred to throughout our discussion of corporation law.

PARTNERSHIPS COMPARED WITH CORPORATIONS

Let us return to our example of the Bob–Carol–Ted Bookstore, discussed in Chapters 39 and 40. Recall that Bob has contributed money, Carol real property, and Ted services. A friend has been telling them that

they ought to incorporate. What are the major factors they should consider in reaching a decision?

Ease of Formation

Partnerships are easy to form. If the business is simple enough and the partners few, the agreement need not even be written down. Creating a corporation is more complicated because formal documents must be placed on file with public authorities.

Ownership and Control

All general partners have equal rights in the management and conduct of the business. By contrast, ownership and control of corporations are, in theory, separated. In *publicly held* corporations, which have many shareholders, the separation is real. Ownership is widely dispersed because millions of shares are outstanding and it is rare that any single shareholder will own more than a tiny percentage of stock. It is difficult under the best of circumstances for shareholders to exert any form of control over corporate operations. However, in the *closely held* corporation, which has few shareholders, the officers or senior managers are usually also the shareholders, so the separation of ownership and control is less pronounced or even nonexistent.

Transferability of Interests

Transferability of an interest in a partnership is a problem because a transferee cannot become a member unless all partners consent. The problem can be addressed and overcome in the partnership agreement. Transfer of interest in a corporation through a sale of stock is much easier, but for the stock of a small corporation there might be no market or there might be contractual restrictions on transfer.

Financing

Partners have considerable flexibility in financing. They can lure potential investors by offering interests in profits and, in the case of general partnerships, control. Corporations can finance by selling freely transferable stock to the public.

Taxation

The partnership is a conduit for income and is not taxed as a separate entity. Individual partners are taxed and, although limited by the 1986 Tax Reform Act, can deduct partnership losses. Corporate earnings, on the other hand, are subject to double taxation. The corporation is first taxed as an entity on its own earnings. Then, when profits are distributed to shareholders in the form of dividends, the shareholders are taxed again. (A small corporation, with no more than thirty-five shareholders, can elect S corporation status. Because S corporations are taxed as partnerships, they avoid double taxation.) However, incorporating brings several tax benefits. For example, the corporation can take deductions for life, medical, and disability insurance coverage for its employees, whereas partners or sole proprietors cannot.

THE CORPORATE VEIL: THE CORPORATION AS LEGAL ENTITY

One last factor to be added to the list—and the one that ordinarily tips the balance in favor of incorporating—is this: the corporation is a legal entity in its own right, one that can provide a veil that protects its shareholders from personal liability (see Figure 41-1). As satirized by attorney William Gilbert and his partner Arthur Sullivan in the operetta *Utopia, Ltd.*:

> Though a Rothschild you may be in your own capacity,
>   As a company you've come to utter sorrow—
> But the liquidators say, 'Never mind, you needn't pay',
>   So you start another company tomorrow.

This crucial factor accounts for the development of much of corporate law. Unlike the individual actor in the legal system, the corporation is difficult to deal with in conventional legal terms. The business of the sole proprietor and the sole proprietor herself are one and the same. When a sole proprietor makes a decision, she risks her own capital. When the managers of a corporation take a corporate action, they are risking the capital of others—the shareholders. Thus, accountability is a major theme in the system of law constructed to cope with legal entities other than natural persons.

The Basic Rights of the Corporate "Person"

To say that a corporation is a "person" does not automatically describe what its rights are, for the courts have not accorded the corporation every right guaranteed a natural person. However, the courts have concluded that corporations are entitled to the essential constitutional protections of due process and equal protection. They are also entitled to Fourth Amendment protection against unreasonable search and seizure; in other words, the police must have a search warrant to enter corporate premises and look through files. The double jeopardy clause applies to criminal prosecutions of corporations: an acquittal cannot be appealed nor can the case be retried. For purposes of the federal courts' diversity jurisdiction (see p. 44), a corporation is deemed to be a citizen both of the state

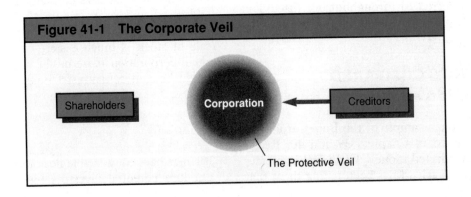

Figure 41-1   The Corporate Veil

Shareholders   Corporation ← Creditors

The Protective Veil

in which it is incorporated and the state in which it has its principal place of business.

Until relatively recently, few cases had tested the power of the state to limit the right of corporations to spend their own funds to speak the "corporate mind." Most corporate free speech cases concerned advertising and few states have enacted laws that directly impinge on the freedom of companies to advertise. But some have done so, usually to limit the ability of corporations to sway voters in public referenda. In 1978, the Supreme Court finally confronted the issue head on.

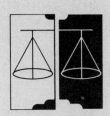

FIRST NATIONAL BANK OF BOSTON v. BELLOTTI

435 U.S. 765 (1978)

Mr. Justice Powell delivered the opinion of the Court.

In sustaining a state criminal statute that forbids certain expenditures by banks and business corporations for the purpose of influencing the vote on referendum proposals, the Massachusetts Supreme Judicial Court held that the First Amendment rights of a corporation are limited to issues that materially affect its business, property, or assets. The court rejected appellants' claim that the statute abridges freedom of speech in violation of the First and Fourteenth Amendments. The issue presented in this context is one of first impression in this Court. We postponed the question of jurisdiction to our consideration of the merits. We now reverse.

The statute at issue, Mass. Gen. Laws Ann., ch. 55, § 8 (West Supp. 1977), prohibits appellants, two national banking associations and three business corporations, from making contributions or expenditures "for the purpose of . . . influencing or affecting the vote on any question submitted to the voters, other than one materially affecting any of the property, business or assets of the corporation." The statute further specifies that "[n]o question submitted to the voters solely concerning the taxation of the income, property or transactions of individuals shall be deemed materially to affect the property, business or assets of the corporation." A corporation that violates § 8 may receive a maximum fine of $50,000; a corporate officer, director, or agent who violates the section may receive a maximum fine of $10,000 or imprisonment for up to one year, or both. Appellants wanted to spend money to publicize their views on a proposed constitutional amendment that was to be submitted to the voters as a ballot question at a general election on November 2, 1976. The amendment would have permitted the legislature to impose a graduated tax on the income of individuals. After appellee, the Attorney General of Massachusetts, informed appellants that he intended to enforce § 8 against them, they brought this action seeking to have the statute declared unconstitutional.

*   *   *

The court below framed the principal question in this case as whether and to what extent corporations have First Amendment rights. We believe that the court posed the wrong question. The Constitution often protects interests broader than those of the party seeking their vindication. The First Amendment, in particular, serves significant societal interests. The proper question therefore is not whether corporations "have" First Amendment rights and,

(continued on next page)

(*continued*)

**FIRST NATIONAL
BANK OF BOSTON v.
BELLOTTI**
435 U.S. 765 (1978)

if so, whether they are coextensive with those of natural persons. Instead, the question must be whether § 8 abridges expression that the First Amendment was meant to protect. We hold that it does.

The speech proposed by appellants is at the heart of the First Amendment's protection.

> The freedom of speech and of the press guaranteed by the Constitution embraces at the least the liberty to discuss publicly and truthfully all matters of public concern without previous restraint or fear of subsequent punishment. . . . Freedom of discussion, if it would fulfill its historic function in this nation, must embrace all issues about which information is needed or appropriate to enable the members of society to cope with the exigencies of their period. *Thornhill v. Alabama*, 310 U.S. 88, 101–102 (1940).

The referendum issue that appellants wish to address falls squarely within this description. In appellants' view, the enactment of a graduated personal income tax, as proposed to be authorized by constitutional amendment, would have a seriously adverse effect on the economy of the State. The importance of the referendum issue to the people and government of Massachusetts is not disputed. Its merits, however, are the subject of sharp disagreement.

★   ★   ★

We thus find no support in the First or Fourteenth Amendment, or in the decisions of this Court, for the proposition that speech that otherwise would be within the protection of the First Amendment loses that protection simply because its source is a corporation that cannot prove, to the satisfaction of a court, a material effect on its business or property. The "materially affecting" requirement is not an identification of the boundaries of corporate speech etched by the Constitution itself. Rather, it amounts to an impermissible legislative prohibition of speech based on the identity of the interests that spokesmen may represent in public debate over controversial issues and a requirement that the speaker have a sufficiently great interest in the subject to justify communication.

Section 8 permits a corporation to communicate to the public its views on certain referendum subjects—those materially affecting its business—but not others. It also singles out one kind of ballot question—individual taxation—as a subject about which corporations may never make their ideas public. The legislature has drawn the line between permissible and impermissible speech according to whether there is a sufficient nexus, as defined by the legislature, between the issue presented to the voters and the business interests of the speaker.

In the realm of protected speech, the legislature is constitutionally disqualified from dictating the subjects about which persons may speak and the speakers who may address a public issue. If a legislature may direct business corporations to "stick to business," it also may limit other corporations—

religious, charitable, or civic—to their respective "business" when addressing the public. Such power in government to channel the expression of views is unacceptable under the First Amendment. Especially where, as here, the legislature's suppression of speech suggests an attempt to give one side of a debatable public question an advantage in expressing its views to the people, the First Amendment is plainly offended.

★　★　★

Because that portion of § 8 challenged by appellants prohibits protected speech in a manner unjustified by a compelling state interest, it must be invalidated. The judgment of the Supreme Judicial Court is reversed.

Absence of Rights

The cases are clear that corporations lack certain rights that natural persons possess. For example, corporations do not have a privilege against self-incrimination, guaranteed by the Fifth and Fourteenth Amendments. In any legal proceeding, the courts may force the corporation to turn over incriminating documents, even if they also incriminate officers or employees of the corporation. As we explore in Chapter 45, corporations are not citizens under the privileges and immunities clause of the Constitution, so that the states can discriminate between domestic and foreign corporations. And the corporation is not entitled to federal review of state criminal convictions, as are many individuals.

Piercing the Corporate Veil

Given the importance of the corporate entity as a veil that limits shareholder liability, it is important to note that in two sets of circumstances the courts will pierce the veil: (1) when the corporation is used to commit a fraud or injustice, and (2) when the corporation does not act as if it were one.

Fraud The Felsenthal Company burned to the ground. Its president, one of the company's largest creditors and also virtually its sole owner, instigated the fire. The corporation sued the insurance company to recover the amount for which it was insured. The general rule of law is that "the willful burning of property by a stockholder in a corporation is not a defense against the collection of the insurance by the corporation, and that the corporation cannot be prevented from collecting the insurance because its agents willfully set fire to the property without the participation or authority of the corporation or of all of the stockholders." But because the fire was caused by the beneficial owner of "practically all" the stock, who also "has the absolute management of [the corporation's] affairs and its property, and is its president," the court refused to allow the company to recover the insurance money; allowing the company to recover would reward fraud. [Felsenthal Co. v. Northern Assurance Co., Ltd., 120 N.E. 268 (Ill. 1918)]

Failure to Act as a Corporation Failure to follow corporate formalities may subject stockholders to personal liability. This is a special risk that small—especially one-person—corporations run. Particular factors that bring this rule into play include inadequate capitalization, omission of regular meetings, failure to record minutes of meetings, failure to file annual reports, and commingling of corporate and personal assets. Where these factors exist, the courts may look through the corporate veil and pluck out the individual stockholder or stockholders to answer for a tort, contract breach, or the like. The classic case is the taxicab operator who incorporates several of his cabs separately and services them through still another corporation. If one of the cabs causes an accident, the corporation is usually "judgment proof" because the corporation will have few assets

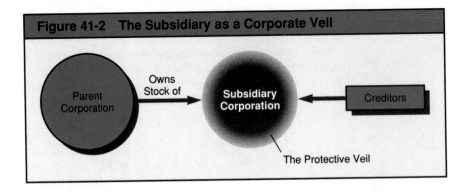

Figure 41-2   The Subsidiary as a Corporate Veil

(practically worthless cab, minimum insurance). The courts frequently permit plaintiffs to proceed against the common owner on the grounds that the particular corporation was inadequately financed.

When a corporation owns a subsidiary corpora-tion, the question frequently arises whether the subsidiary is acting as an independent entity (see Figure 41-2). In answering this question, courts have developed the **instrumentality rule,** which is applied in the following case.

DANIA JAI-ALAI PALACE, INC. v. SYKES
425 So.2d 594 (Fla. 1983)

HURLEY, JUDGE. On December 15, 1977, Gladys Sykes attempted to patronize the Dania Jai-Alai fronton. She arrived in her car and was directed into the valet parking area by a security guard employed by Dania Jai-Alai Palace, Inc. She purchased a parking ticket and turned the car over to the ticket seller who was employed by another corporation, Carrousel Concessions, Inc. Then she began to walk forward in front of her car toward the main gate of the fronton.

Ms. Sykes' car was the last in a short line of cars which were temporarily stopped near the fronton entrance waiting to be moved by parking attendants. There was about a four foot space between the Sykes' car and the one ahead. Since parking attendants were about to move the other cars in the line, the ticket seller, who was in overall charge of keeping things moving, got into Ms. Sykes' car and prepared to drive it. He looked at the gear shift indicator and moved it from "park" to "drive." As he did so, he took his foot from the brake pedal and placed it on the accelerator pedal. The car began to move forward and, at this point, he looked up and saw Ms. Sykes in front of the car, near its center. He attempted to brake, but his foot slipped and hit the accelerator. Ms. Sykes was propelled forward and crushed into the stationary car ahead; she was seriously injured.

Initially, Ms. Sykes sued Dania Jai-Alai Palace, Inc. (Dania). Later, when her attorneys discovered that Carrousel Concessions, Inc. (Carrousel) was running the valet parking, she amended her complaint to include Carrousel and to include Saturday Corporation (Saturday), the parent corporation of Dania and Carrousel. [The jury returned a verdict against all three corporate defendants for $775,000.]

*   *   *

May a parent corporation be held liable for torts committed by an employee of a wholly-owned subsidiary? In this instance, the answer is "yes." Here, the jury applied the long-established principle of Florida law that, when one corporation controls and dominates another corporation to the extent that the second corporation becomes the "mere instrumentality" of the first, the dominant corporation is liable for the torts of the subservient corporation. In light of the jury's affirmative finding, our responsibility is not to re-weigh the evidence, but only to determine whether the verdict is supported by competent substantial evidence.

At the outset, we reject appellants' contention that, in order to utilize the instrumentality doctrine, the plaintiff had to establish fraud or other wrongdoing on the part of Saturday. Although there are conflicting lines of cases on this point, we took a definitive position in *Vantage View, Inc. v. Bali East Development Corp.*, 421 So.2d 728 (Fla. 4th DCA 1982), and said that we intend to "follow the decision of the Supreme Court in *Barnes, Mayer, Aztec* and *Levenstein* which have held it sufficient to allege domination and control without the necessity of alleging improper purpose or unjust loss."

Whether a subsidiary is a mere instrumentality is normally a question of fact for the jury. "The central factual issue is control, *i.e.*, whether the parent corporation dominates the activities of the subsidiary." *Japan Petroleum Co. (Nigeria) Ltd. v. Ashland Oil, Inc.*, 456 F.Supp. 831, 841 (D.Del. 1978). The degree of control necessary to sustain liability under the instrumentality rule has been characterized as "total domination of the subservient corporation, to the extent that the subservient corporation manifests no separate corporate interests of its own and functions solely to achieve the purposes of the dominant corporation." *Krivo Industrial Supply Co. v. National Distillers & Chemical Corp.*, 483 F.2d 1098, 1106 (5th Cir. 1973). . . .

A number of courts have suggested that the following factors are relevant in determining the applicability of the instrumentality rule. (1) The parent corporation owns all or majority of the capital stock of the subsidiary. (2) The parent and subsidiary corporations have common directors or officers. (3) The parent corporation finances the subsidiary. (4) The parent corporation subscribes to all the capital stock of the subsidiary or otherwise causes its incorporation. (5) The subsidiary has grossly inadequate capital. (6) The parent corporation pays the salaries or expenses or losses of the subsidiary. (7) The subsidiary has substantially no business except with the parent corporation or no assets except those conveyed to it by the parent corporation. (8) In the papers of the parent corporation, and in the statements of its officers, "the subsidiary" is referred to as such or as a department or division. (9) The directors or executives of the subsidiary do not act independently in the interest of the subsidiary but take direction from the parent corporation. (10) The formal legal requirements of the subsidiary as a separate and independent corporation are not observed.

Turning to the evidence in the case at bar and viewing it in the light most favorable to the plaintiff/appellee, we find that Carrousel was wholly owned

(*continued on next page*)

(continued)

DANIA JAI-ALAI PALACE, INC. v. SYKES
425 So.2d 594 (Fla. 1983)

by Saturday and that they shared common officers. Furthermore, although there was testimony that the day-to-day operation of Carrousel was placed in the hands of an independent general manager, there was other testimony that the general manager regularly reported to one of the common officers and thereafter implemented his directions. Testimony also indicated that the common officer was present on the premises of the fronton and had the ability to hire and fire employees of Carrousel. The proof further demonstrated that Saturday created Carrousel and initially funded it through Dania, its other subsidiary.

A highly relevant factor in evaluating the application of the instrumentality rule is whether there is proof that the subservient corporation was being used to further the purposes of the dominant corporation to the extent that the subservient corporation in reality had no separate, independent existence of its own. In the case at bar, there was substantial proof that Carrousel existed only to serve the needs of Saturday. For example, Carrousel only operated at two frontons, both of which were owned either directly or indirectly by Saturday. Carrousel maintained its offices within the fronton and gave all outward appearances of being part of an integrated operation. In this respect, it is noteworthy that Saturday and its two subsidiary corporations filed a consolidated federal income tax return and were jointly insured. The evidence suggests that Saturday maintained a pervasive control over all aspects of the fronton's operations and, given such evidence, we cannot say that the jury's finding that Carrousel was the mere instrumentality of Saturday is clearly erroneous. Therefore, we affirm the verdict finding Saturday liable for the acts of Carrousel. [The court remanded the case for further proceedings to determine whether Ms. Sykes had been negligent.]

Other Types of Personal Liability

Even when a corporation is formed for a proper purpose and is operated as a corporation, there are instances in which individual shareholders will be personally liable. For example, if a shareholder involved in company management commits a tort or enters into a contract in a personal capacity, he will remain personally liable for the consequences of his actions. In some states, statutes give employees special rights against shareholders. For example, a New York statute permits employees to recover wages, salaries, and debts owed them by the company from the ten largest shareholders of the corporation. (Shareholders of public companies whose stock is traded on a national exchange or over the counter are exempt.) Likewise, federal law permits the IRS to recover from the "responsible persons" any withholding taxes collected by a corporation but not actually paid over to the U.S. Treasury.

CLASSIFICATIONS OF CORPORATIONS

Nonprofit Corporations

The term "corporation" embraces a variety of types (see Figure 41-3). One common type is the nonprofit or not-for-profit corporation. This is defined in the American Bar Association Model Non-Profit Corporation Act as "a corporation no part of the income of which is distributable to its members, directors or officers." Nonprofit corporations may be formed under this law for charitable, educational, civil, religious, social, and cultural purposes, among others.

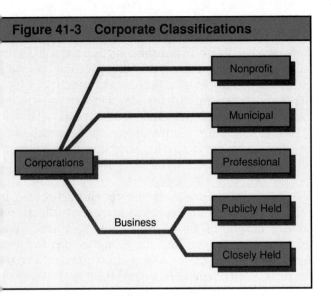

Figure 41-3   Corporate Classifications

Corporations
- Nonprofit
- Municipal
- Professional
- Business
  - Publicly Held
  - Closely Held

Public Corporation

The **public corporation** is a governmental entity. It is also called a municipal corporation, to distinguish it from the publicly *held* corporation, which is sometimes also referred to as a "public" corporation—although it is in fact private; that is, not governmental. Major cities and counties, and many towns, villages, and special governmental units, such as sewer, transportation, and public utility authorities, are incorporated. The United States Postal Service, once a cabinet-level department, is now a public corporation. These corporations are not organized for profit, do not have shareholders, and operate under different statutes than do business corporations.

Professional Corporations

Until the 1960s, lawyers, doctors, accountants, and other professionals could not practice their professions in corporate form. This inability, based on a fear of professionals' being subject to the direction of the corporate owners, was financially disadvantageous. Under the federal income tax laws then in effect, corporations could establish far better pension plans than could the self-employed. During the 1960s the states began to let professionals incorporate, but the IRS balked, denying them many tax benefits. In 1969, the IRS finally conceded that it would tax pro-

fessional corporations just as it would any other corporations, so that professionals could from that time on place a much higher proportion of tax-deductible income into a tax-deferred pension. That decision led to a burgeoning number of "professional corporations." The Model Professional Corporation Supplement (1984), developed by the American Bar Association, serves as a model for states in the development of professional corporation statutes.

Business Corporations

The Two Types   It is the business corporation proper that we focus on in this unit. There are two broad types of business corporations: *publicly held* (or *public*) and *closely held* (or *close* or *private*) corporations. Note that both types are private in the sense that they are not governmental.

The **publicly held** corporation is one in which stock is widely held or available for wide public distribution through such means as trading on a national or regional stock exchange. Its managers, if they are also owners of stock, usually constitute a small percentage of the total number of shareholders and hold a small amount of stock relative to the total shares outstanding. Few if any shareholders of public corporations know who their fellow shareholders are.

By contrast, the shareholders of the **closely held** corporation are few: perhaps only one and usually no more than thirty. Shareholders of the closely held corporation almost always share family ties or have some other association that permits each to know the others.

Though most closely held corporations are small, no economic or legal reason prevents them from being large. Some are huge, having annual sales of several billion dollars each. Roughly 95 percent of U.S. corporations are closely held.

The giant, publicly held companies with more than $1 billion in assets and sales—with initials such as IBM and GM—constitute an exclusive group of probably no more than 200. Publicly held corporations outside this elite class fall into two broad (non-legal) categories: those that are quoted on stock exchanges (perhaps 1 percent of all corporations) and others whose stock is too widely dispersed to be called closely held but which are not traded on exchanges (perhaps 4 percent of the total).

Statutory Differentiation   General principles of corporation law apply to both publicly held and closely held corporations. In addition many states have adopted specific close corporation provisions. In some states these provisions are spread throughout the corporation act; in others, a separate chapter in the act is devoted to close corporations. The Model Statutory Close Corporation Supplement (1984), developed by the American Bar Association, takes the latter approach. The supplement provides that any corporation may elect close corporation status by so stating in the articles of incorporation.

CORPORATE ORGANIZATION

If the owners of a business decide to incorporate after weighing the pros and cons discussed above, they will take the following steps.

The Corporate Charter

Function of the Charter   The ultimate goal of the incorporation process is issuance of a corporate "charter." The term varies from state to state. Most states call the basic document filed in the appropriate public office the "articles of incorporation" or "certificate of incorporation," but there are other variations. There is no legal significance to these differences in terminology.

Chartering is basically a state prerogative. Congress has chartered several enterprises, including national banks (under the National Banking Act), federal savings and loan associations, national farm loan associations, and the like, but virtually all business corporations are chartered at the state level.

Originally a legislative function, chartering is now an administrative function in every state. The secretary of state issues the final indorsement to the articles of incorporation, thus giving them legal effect.

Charter as a Contract   The charter is a contract between the state and the corporation. Under the Contracts Clause of Article I of the Constitution, no state can pass any law "impairing the obligation of contracts." In 1816 the question arose whether a state could revoke or amend a corporate charter once granted. The corporation in question was Dartmouth College. The New Hampshire legislature sought to turn the venerable private college, operating under an old royal charter, into a public institution by changing the membership of its board. The case wound up in the Supreme Court. Chief Justice Marshall ruled that the legislature's attempt was unconstitutional, because to amend a charter is to impair a contract. [Trustees of Dartmouth College v. Woodward, 17 U.S. 518 (1819)]

This decision pleased incorporators because it implied that once a corporation had been created, the state could never modify the powers it had been granted. But, in addition, the ruling seemed to favor monopolies. The theory was that by granting a charter to, say, a railroad corporation, the state was barred from creating any further railroad corporations. Why? Argued the lawyers: A competitor would cut into the first company's business, reducing the value of the charter, hence impairing the contract. Justice Story, concurring in the *Dartmouth* case, had already suggested the way out for the states: "If the legislature mean to claim such an authority [to alter or amend the charter], it must be reserved in the grant. The charter of Dartmouth College contains no such reservation." The states quickly picked up on Story's suggestion and wrote into the charter explicit language giving legislatures the authority to modify corporations' charters at their pleasure. So the potential immutability of corporate charters had little practical chance to develop.

Selection of a State

Where to Charter   Choosing the particular state in which to incorporate is the first critical decision to be made after deciding to incorporate. Over half of the Fortune 500 companies hold Delaware charters, and the article in **Box 41-1** explains why. Delaware's success has led other states to compete, and the political realities have caused the RMBCA, which was intentionally drafted to balance the interests of all significant groups (management, shareholders, and the public), to be revised from time to time so that it is more permissive from the perspective of management.

LAW AND LIFE

BOX 41-1

Delaware Works Hard to Stay a Corporate Home Sweet Home

By Lee Smith

[Over half of the Fortune 500 companies have incorporated in Delaware. The state corporation code is a consumer product in that its provisions of the code are constantly reappraised and refined to meet the demands of its management. Other states are now attempting to compete with Delaware.— AUTHORS' NOTE]

One hour is, on average, the amount of time it takes to die of exposure in the waters of the Arctic Circle or to complete a telephone call across national borders in Europe, according to *Durations, the Encyclopedia of How Long Things Take.* The book might also have noted that an hour is all the time it takes to have a business incorporated in Delaware, where chartering businesses is a flourishing industry.

The state corporation code, which makes the industry possible, is not simply a law, but also a consumer product of sorts. For that reason the 500 or so provisions of the code, which regulate everything from mergers to such minutiae as the method of determining stockholders of record, are constantly reappraised and refined, pretty much the way features on a Thunderbird or a Toronado are kept in tune with the market. "There are automobile companies that disappeared because no one paid attention to what the public wanted," observes S. Samuel Arsht, a prominent attorney who is generally regarded as the principal designer of the Delaware statute.

CHOOSING THE STATE

So expertly has Delaware met the demands of its customers—corporate managements in this case—that thousands of the nation's largest companies, including 256 of the FORTUNE 500, have come to the state over the years to incorporate. The $58 million a year they pay in franchise taxes and fees constitutes 13 percent of Delaware's total tax revenues. Moreover, the incorporation industry supports hundreds of jobs in the private sector, including a thriving legal community gathered around Wilmington's bustling Rodney Square. For generations this fraternal band has prospered on the lawsuits brought against companies incorporated in the state. "This life has all the advantages of an interesting Wall Street practice," says one leader of the local bar, "and at the same time it allows us the comforts of a small town."

*   *   *

The limited-liability corporation, which dates back to the medieval guilds, was originally conceived to be an entity with a well-defined public purpose, and that tradition came to these shores with the great English trading companies, all chartered by the Crown. Alexander Hamilton, an admirer of Adam Smith, argued, however, that a business corporation could best serve the public through the pursuit of profit, and in 1811, New York State took a big step into modern capitalism when it made the chartering of any manufacturing corporation with capital of less than $100,000 a matter of statute rather than legislative caprice. This concept

was later broadened by various states to include all corporations. The law that swept the country was the . . . New Jersey code, which allowed companies so much freedom that businesses from all over rushed to New Jersey to incorporate.

Delaware imitated New Jersey and, to make itself more appealing, undercut the New Jersey franchise tax. (Delaware's tax today ranges from a few dollars for a small corporation up to a maximum of $110,000 a year for the 117 largest companies incorporated in the state.) But Delaware's big break came in 1913 when New Jersey's Governor Woodrow Wilson, indignant that his state had become a legal haven for the notorious trusts, persuaded the legislature to write a tougher law. Delaware thus became by default the most attractive state in the incorporation business and has never surrendered its lead.

To be sure, most of the two million or so U.S. corporations are chartered in their home states. A small, closely held company has no reason to incorporate elsewhere. In most large companies, however, management and the shareholders form two distinct groups whose interests are not always identical; these companies have avoided incorporating in states whose laws and traditions have made it difficult, uncertain, or expensive to deal with querulous shareholders.

Those characteristics do not describe Delaware, where a model corporation code is reinforced by a support system widely respected not only for its orderly machinery but also for the integrity and intelligence of the people who run it. Marie C. Shultie, Corporation Administrative Officer, supervises a staff of twenty-five people

(continued on next page)

BOX 41-1

(Box 41-1 continued)

who whisk through incorporations in Dover, the state capital. Delaware's Court of Chancery on Rodney Square is one of the few surviving descendants in the U.S. of the English Courts of Equity, established primarily to settle disputes in which someone has been accused of betraying a fiduciary responsibility. The three chancellors of the court have become specialists in such matters, listening day after day as they do to shareholder accusations that the management of one corporation or another has been self-serving, inept, or unfair.

The guardians of the industry are the thirty attorneys who make up the General Corporation Law Committee of the Delaware State Bar Association and who from time to time advise the legislature on amendments to the code. Critics maintain that the committee does not *advise* the legislature but rather *tells* it what to do. "That's true," one committee member confesses. "But the law has to be written by people who know what's going on, and the Delaware legislature is not really sophisticated enough to do the job alone." He recalls an occasion several years ago when a legislator, having been persuaded to support an amendment that increased the rights of preferred shareholders, rose to demand: "Okay, when are we going to do something for the *common* shareholders?"

To be sure, twenty-six states now have laws just as attractive to management as Delaware's. Virginia and Nevada, among others, have even been able to snare some big companies, including a few formerly chartered in Delaware. However, what still gives Delaware the advantage, and a very important advantage, is its enormous body of case law—that is, applications and limitations of the statutory law that have emerged as cases have been tried before the Court of Chancery. Questions, for example, about management's freedom to change the date of an annual meeting, or to indemnify officers and directors against the costs of lawsuits, have been fully answered by a series of decisions from the bench. Therefore, companies that incorporate in Delaware know precisely what they can and cannot do in almost any situation.

Source: *Fortune*, February 13, 1978

The Promoter

Functions   Once the state of incorporation has been selected, it is time for **promoters,** the midwives of the enterprise, to go to work. Promoters have four principal functions: to seek out or discover business opportunities, to raise capital by persuading investors to sign stock subscriptions, to enter into contracts on behalf of the corporation to be formed, and to prepare the articles of incorporation.

Promoters have acquired an unsavory reputation in many quarters as fast talkers who cajole sometimes even sophisticated investors out of their money. Though some promoters fit this image, it is vastly overstated. Promotion is difficult work often carried out by the same individuals who will manage the business.

Contract Liability   Promoters face two major legal problems. First, they face possible liability on contracts made on behalf of the business before it is in-corporated. For example, suppose Bob is acting as promoter of the proposed BCT Bookstore, Incorporated. On September 15, he enters into a contract with Computogram Products to purchase computer equipment for the corporation to be formed. If the incorporation never takes place, or if the corporation is formed but refuses to accept the contract, Bob remains liable.

Now assume that the corporation is formed on October 15 and on October 18 the corporation formally accepts all the contracts that Bob has signed prior to October 15. Does Bob remain liable? In most states he does. The ratification theory of agency law will not help in many states that adhere strictly to agency rules, because there was no principal (the corporation) in existence when the contract was made—hence the promoter must remain liable. To avoid this result, Bob should seek an express novation (p. 315), although in some states, a novation will be implied. The intention of the parties should be stated as precisely as possible in the contract—as the promoters learned in the following case.

**RKO–STANLEY
WARNER THEATRES,
INC. v. GRAZIANO**
355 A.2d 830 (Pa. 1976)

EAGEN, JUSTICE. On April 30, 1970, RKO-Stanley Warner Theatres, Inc. [RKO], as seller, entered into an agreement of sale with Jack Jenofsky and Ralph Graziano, as purchasers. This agreement contemplated the sale of the Kent Theatre, a parcel of improved commercial real estate located at Cumberland and Kensington Avenues in Philadelphia, for a total purchase price of $70,000. Settlement was originally scheduled for September 30, 1970, and, at the request of Jenofsky and Graziano, continued twice, first to October 16, 1970 and then to October 21, 1970. However, Jenofsky and Graziano failed to complete settlement on the last scheduled date.

Subsequently, on November 13, 1970, RKO filed a complaint in equity seeking judicial enforcement of the agreement of sale. Although Jenofsky, in his answer to the complaint, denied personal liability for the performance of the agreement, the chancellor, after a hearing, entered a decree nisi granting the requested relief sought by RKO. . . . This appeal ensued.

At the time of the execution of this agreement, Jenofsky and Graziano were engaged in promoting the formation of a corporation to be known as Kent Enterprises, Inc. Reflecting these efforts, Paragraph 19 of the agreement, added by counsel for Jenofsky and Graziano, recited:

> It is understood by the parties hereto that it is the intention of the Purchaser to incorporate. Upon condition that such incorporation be completed by closing, all agreements, covenants, and warranties contained herein shall be construed to have been made between Seller and the resultant corporation and all documents shall reflect same.

In fact, Jenofsky and Graziano did file Articles of Incorporation for Kent Enterprises, Inc., with the State Corporation Bureau on October 9, 1971, twelve days prior to the scheduled settlement date. Jenofsky now contends the inclusion of Paragraph 19 in the agreement and the subsequent filing of incorporation papers, released him from any personal liability resulting from the non-performance of the agreement.

The legal relationship of Jenofsky to Kent Enterprises, Inc., at the date of the execution of the agreement of sale was that of promoter. As such, he is subject to the general rule that a promoter, although he may assume to act on behalf of a projected corporation and not for himself, will be held personally liable on contracts made by him for the benefit of a corporation he intends to organize. This personal liability will continue even after the contemplated corporation is formed and has received the benefits of the contract, unless there is a novation or other agreement to release liability.

The imposition of personal liability upon a promoter where that promoter has contracted on behalf of a corporation is based upon the principle that one who assumes to act for a nonexistent principal is himself liable on the contract in the absence of an agreement to the contrary. . . .

★　　★　　★

(continued on next page)

(continued)

RKO–STANLEY WARNER THEATRES, INC. v. GRAZIANO
355 A.2d 830 (Pa. 1976)

[T]here [are] three possible understandings that parties may have when an agreement is executed by a promoter on behalf of a proposed corporation:

> When a party is acting for a proposed corporation, he cannot, of course, bind it by anything he does, at the time, but he may (1) take on its behalf an offer from the other which, being accepted after the formation of the company, becomes a contract; (2) make a contract at the time binding himself, with the stipulation or understanding, that if a company is formed it will take his place and that then he shall be relieved of responsibility; or (3) bind himself personally without more and look to the proposed company, when formed, for indemnity.

Both RKO and Jenofsky concede the applicability of alternative No. 2 to the instant case. That is, they both recognize that Jenofsky (and Graziano) was to be initially personally responsible with this personal responsibility subsequently being released. Jenofsky contends the parties, by their inclusion of Paragraph 19 in the agreement, manifested an intention to release him from personal responsibility upon the mere formation of the proposed corporation, provided the incorporation was consummated prior to the scheduled closing date. However, while Paragraph 19 does make provision for recognition of the resultant corporation as to the closing documents, it makes no mention of any release of personal liability. Indeed, the entire agreement is silent as to the effect the formation of the projected corporation would have upon the personal liability of Jenofsky and Graziano. Because the agreement fails to provide expressly for the release of personal liability, it is, therefore, subject to more than one possible construction.

In *Consolidated Tile and Slate Co. v. Fox*, 410 Pa. 336, 339, 189 A.2d 228, 229 (1963), we stated that where an agreement is ambiguous and reasonably susceptible of two interpretations, "it must be construed most strongly against those who drew it." . . . Instantly, the chancellor determined that the intent of the parties to the agreement was to hold Jenofsky personally responsible until such time as a corporate entity was formed and until such time as that corporate entity adopted the agreement. We believe this construction represents the only rational and prudent interpretation of the parties' intent.

As found by the court below, this agreement was entered into on the financial strength of Jenofsky and Graziano, alone as individuals. Therefore, it would have been illogical for RKO to have consented to the release of their personal liability upon the mere formation of a resultant corporation prior to closing. For it is a well-settled rule that a contract made by a promoter, even though made for and in the name of a proposed corporation, in the absence of a subsequent adoption (either expressly or impliedly) by the corporation, will not be binding upon the corporation. If, as Jenofsky contends, the intent was to release personal responsibility upon the mere incorporation prior to closing, the effect of the agreement would have been to create the possibility that RKO, in the event of non-performance, would be able to hold no party accountable: there being no guarantee that the resultant corporation would ratify the agreement. Without express language in the agreement indicating that such was the intention of the parties, we may not attribute this intention to them.

Therefore, we hold that the intent of the parties in entering into this agreement was to have Jenofsky and Graziano personally liable until such time as the intended corporation was formed and ratified the agreement. [And there is no evidence that Kent Enterprises ratified the agreement. The decree is affirmed.]

Fiduciary Duty The promoters' other major legal concern is the duty owed to the corporation. The law is clear that promoters owe a fiduciary duty. For example, a promoter who transfers real estate worth $25,000 to the corporation in exchange for $75,000 worth of stock would be liable for $50,000 for breach of fiduciary duty.

Preincorporation Stock Subscriptions

One of the promoter's jobs is to obtain preincorporation stock subscriptions—that is, to line up offers by would-be investors to purchase stock in the corporation to be formed. Alice agrees with Bob to invest $10,000 in the BCT Bookstore, Inc., for 1,000 shares. The agreement is treated as an offer to purchase. The offer is deemed accepted at the moment the bookstore is incorporated.

The major problem for the corporation is an attempt by subscribers to revoke their offers. A basic rule of contract law is that offers are revocable before acceptance. Under RMBCA Section 6.20, however, a subscription for shares is irrevocable for six months unless the subscription agreement itself provides otherwise, or unless all the subscribers consent to revocation. In many states that have not adopted the model act, the contract rule applies and the offer is always revocable. Other states use various common-law devices to prevent revocation. For example, the subscription by one investor is held as consideration for the subscription of another, so that a binding contract has been formed.

Execution and Filing of the Articles of Incorporation

Once the business details are settled, the promoters—now known as "incorporators"—must sign and deliver the articles of incorporation to the secretary of state. The articles of incorporation typically include the corporate name, the address of its initial registered office, the period of the corporation's duration (usually perpetual), the company's purposes, the total number of shares, the classes into which they are divided and the par value of each, the limitations and rights of each class of shareholders, the authority of the directors to establish preferred or special classes of stock, provisions for preemptive rights, provisions for the regulation of the internal affairs of the corporation, including any provision restricting the transfer of shares, the number of directors constituting the initial board of directors and the names and addresses of initial members, and the name and address of each incorporator. Although compliance with these sections is largely a matter of filling in the blanks, two points deserve mention.

First, the choice of a name is often critical to the business. Under RMBCA Section 4.01, it must include one of the following words (or abbreviations): "corporation," "company," "incorporated," or "limited" ("Corp.," "Co.," "Inc.," or "Ltd."). The name is not allowed to deceive the public about the corporation's purposes, nor may it be the same as that of any other company incorporated or authorized to do business in the state.

These legal requirements are obvious; the business requirements are much harder. If the name is not descriptive of the business or does not anticipate changes, it may have to be changed and the change can be expensive. For example, when Standard Oil Company of New Jersey changed its name to Exxon in 1972, the estimated cost was over $100 million. (And, even with this expenditure, some shareholders grumbled that the new name sounded like a laxative.)

The second point to bear in mind about the articles of incorporation is that drafting the clause stating corporate purposes requires special care, because the corporation will be limited to the purposes set forth. In one famous case, the charter of Cornell University placed a limit on the amount of contributions it could receive from any one benefactor. When Jennie McGraw died in 1881, leaving the Chimes, the carillon still plays on the Ithaca campus to this day, she also bequeathed to the university her residuary estate valued at more than $1 million. This sum was greater than the ceiling placed in Cornell's charter. After lengthy litigation, the university lost in the U.S. Supreme Court, and the money went to her family. [Cornell University v. Fiske, 136 U.S. 152 (1890)] The dilemma is how to draft a clause general enough to allow the corporation to expand yet specific enough to prevent it from engaging in undesirable activities.

Some states require the purpose clauses to be specific, but the usual approach is to permit a broad statement of purposes. Section 3.01 of the RMBCA goes one step further in providing that a corporation automatically "has the purpose of engaging in any lawful business" unless the articles specify a more limited purpose.

Once completed, the articles of incorporation are delivered to the secretary of state for filing. The existence of a corporation begins once the articles have been filed.

Organizational Meeting of Directors

The first order of business, once the certificate is issued, is a meeting of the board of directors named in the articles of incorporation. They must adopt bylaws, elect officers, and transact any other business that may come before the meeting (RMBCA Section 2.05). Among the other business: accepting (ratifying) promoters' contracts, calling for the payment of stock subscriptions, and adopting bank resolution forms, giving authority to various officers to sign checks drawn on the corporation.

RMBCA Section 10.20 vests in the directors the power to alter, amend, or repeal the bylaws adopted at the initial meeting, subject to repeal or change by the shareholders. The articles of incorporation may reserve the power to modify or repeal exclusively to the shareholders. The bylaws may contain any provisions that do not conflict with the articles of incorporation or the law of the state.

Typical provisions in the bylaws include: fixing the place and time at which annual stockholders' meetings will be held, fixing a quorum, setting the method of voting, establishing the method of choosing directors, creating committees of directors, setting down the method by which board meetings may be called and the voting procedures to be followed, determining the offices to be filled by the directors and the powers with which each officer shall be vested, fixing the method of declaring dividends, establishing a fiscal year, setting out rules governing issuance and transfer of stock, and establishing the method of amending the bylaws.

Section 2.07 provides that the directors may adopt bylaws which will operate during an emergency. An emergency is a situation in which "a quorum of the corporation's directors cannot readily be assembled because of some catastrophic event."

EFFECT OF ORGANIZATION

De Jure and De Facto Corporations

If the promoters cross every "t" and dot every "i," a **de jure** (dee JUUR ee) corporation is formed—a legal entity. Because the various steps are complex, the formal prerequisites are not always met. Suppose, thinking that the incorporation has taken place, the company starts up its business. What then? Is everything it does null and void? If three conditions exist, a court might decide that a **de facto** (dee FAK toe) corporation has been formed; that is, the business will be recognized as a corporation. The state, however, has the power to force the de facto corporation to correct the defect(s) so that a de jure corporation will be created.

The three traditional elements are these: (1) a statute must exist under which the corporation could

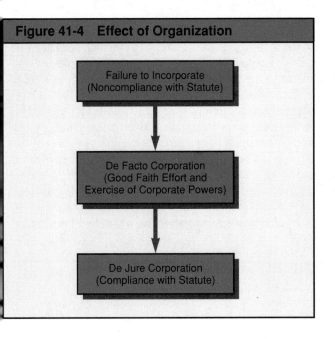

Figure 41-4   Effect of Organization

Failure to Incorporate
(Noncompliance with Statute)

↓

De Facto Corporation
(Good Faith Effort and
Exercise of Corporate Powers)

↓

De Jure Corporation
(Compliance with Statute)

on whether a de facto corporation results if every other legal requirement is met.

Corporation by Estoppel

Even if the incorporators omit important steps, it is still possible for a court under estoppel principles to treat the business as a corporation. Assume that Bob, Carol, and Ted have sought to incorporate the BCT Bookstore, Inc., but have failed to file the articles of incorporation. At the initial directors' meeting, Carol turns over to the corporation a deed to her property. A month later, Bob discovers the omission and hurriedly submits the articles of incorporation to the appropriate public office. Carol decides she wants her land back. It is clear that the corporation was not de jure at the time she surrendered her deed, and it was probably not de facto either. Can she recover the land? Under equitable principles, the answer is no. She is estopped from denying the existence of the corporation—as among her fellow incorporators and shareholders—because it would be inequitable to permit one who has conducted herself as though there were a corporation to deny its existence in order to defeat a contract into which she willingly entered. As the next case shows, the corporation-by-estoppel doctrine can also be used by the corporation against one of its creditors.

have been validly incorporated; (2) the promoters must have made a bona fide attempt to comply with the statute; and (3) corporate powers must have been used or exercised (see Figure 41-4).

A frequent cause of defective incorporation is the promoters' failure to file the articles of incorporation in the appropriate public office. The states are split

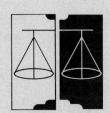

**CRANSON v.
INTERNATIONAL
BUSINESS MACHINES
CORP.**
234 Md. 477, 200 A.2d 33
(1964)

HORNEY, JUDGE. On the theory that the Real Estate Service Bureau was neither a *de jure* nor a *de facto* corporation and that Albion C. Cranson, Jr., was a partner in the business conducted by the Bureau and as such was personally liable for its debts, the International Business Machines Corporation brought this action against Cranson for the balance due on electric typewriters purchased by the Bureau. At the same time it moved for summary judgment and supported the motion by affidavit. In due course, Cranson filed a general issue plea and an affidavit in opposition to summary judgment in which he asserted in effect that the Bureau was a *de facto* corporation and that he was not personally liable for its debts.

The agreed statement of facts shows that in April 1961, Cranson was asked to invest in a new business corporation which was about to be created. Towards this purpose he met with other interested individuals and an attorney and agreed to purchase stock and become an officer and director. Thereafter,

(continued on next page)

(continued)

CRANSON v. INTERNATIONAL BUSINESS MACHINES CORP.
234 Md. 477, 200 A.2d 33 (1964)

upon being advised by the attorney that the corporation had been formed under the laws of Maryland, he paid for and received a stock certificate evidencing ownership of shares in the corporation, and was shown the corporate seal and minute book. The business of the new venture was conducted as if it were a corporation, through corporate bank accounts, with auditors maintaining corporate books and records, and under a lease entered into by the corporation for the office from which it operated its business. Cranson was elected president and all transactions conducted by him for the corporation, including the dealings with I.B.M., were made as an officer of the corporation. At no time did he assume any personal obligation or pledge his individual credit to I.B.M. Due to an oversight on the part of the attorney, of which Cranson was not aware, the certificate of incorporation, which had been signed and acknowledged prior to May 1, 1961, was not filed until November 24, 1961. Between May 17 and November 8, the Bureau purchased eight typewriters from I.B.M., on account of which partial payments were made, leaving a balance due of $4,333.40, for which this suit was brought.

Although a question is raised as to the propriety of making use of a motion for summary judgment as the means of determining the issues presented by the pleadings, we think the motion was appropriate. Since there was no genuine dispute as to the material facts, the only question was whether I.B.M. was entitled to judgment as a matter of law. The trial court found that it was, but we disagree.

The fundamental question presented by the appeal is whether an officer of a defectively incorporated association may be subjected to personal liability under the circumstances of this case. We think not.

Traditionally, two doctrines have been used by the courts to clothe an officer of a defectively incorporated association with the corporate attribute of limited liability. The first, often referred to as the doctrine of *de facto* corporations, has been applied in those cases where there are elements showing: (1) the existence of law authorizing incorporation; (2) an effort in good faith to incorporate under the existing law; and (3) actual user or exercise of corporate powers. The second, the doctrine of estoppel to deny the corporate existence, is generally employed where the person seeking to hold the officer personally liable has contracted or otherwise dealt with the association in such a manner as to recognize and in effect admit its existence as a corporate body.

★   ★   ★

. . . . There is, as we see it, a wide difference between creating a corporation by means of the *de facto* doctrine and estopping a party, due to his conduct in a particular case, from setting up the claim of no incorporation. Although some cases tend to assimilate the doctrines of incorporation *de facto* and by estoppel, each is a distinct theory and they are not dependent on one another in their application. Where there is a concurrence of the three elements necessary for the application of the *de facto* corporation doctrine, there exists an entity which is a corporation *de jure* against all persons but the state.

On the other hand, the estoppel theory is applied only to the facts of each particular case and may be invoked even where there is no corporation *de facto*. Accordingly, even though one or more of the requisites of a *de facto* corporation are absent, we think that this factor does not preclude the application of the estoppel doctrine in a proper case, such as the one at bar.

I.B.M. contends that the failure of the Bureau to file its certificate of incorporation debarred *all* corporate existence. But, in spite of the fact that the omission might have prevented the Bureau from being either a corporation *de jure* or *de facto*, Jones v. Linden Building Ass'n, we think that I.B.M. having dealt with the Bureau as if it were a corporation and relied on its credit rather than that of Cranson, is estopped to assert that the Bureau was not incorporated at the time the typewriters were purchased. In 1 Clark and Marshall, Private Corporations, § 89, it is stated:

> The doctrine in relation to estoppel is based upon the ground that it would generally be inequitable to permit the corporate existence of an association to be denied by persons who have represented it to be a corporation, or held it out as a corporation, or by any persons who have recognized it as a corporation by dealing with it as such; and by the overwhelming weight of authority, therefore, a person may be estopped to deny the legal incorporation of an association which is not even a corporation *de facto*.

In cases similar to the one at bar, involving a failure to file articles of incorporation, the courts of other jurisdictions have held that where one has recognized the corporate existence of an association, he is estopped to assert the contrary with respect to a claim arising out of such dealings.

Since I.B.M. is estopped to deny the corporate existence of the Bureau, we hold that Cranson was not liable for the balance due on account of the typewriters.

Judgment reversed; the appellee to pay the costs.

CHAPTER SUMMARY

The hallmark of the corporate form of business enterprise is limited liability for its owners. Other features of corporations are separation of ownership and management, perpetual existence, and easy transferability of interests. In the early years of the common law, corporations were thought to be creatures of sovereign power and could be created only by state grant. But by the late nineteenth century, corporations could be formed by complying with the requirements of general corporation statutes in virtually every state. Today the standard is the Revised Model Business Corporation Act.

The corporation, as a legal entity, has many of the usual rights accorded natural persons. The principle of limited liability is broad but not absolute: when the corporation is used to commit a fraud or injustice or when the corporation does not act as if it were one, the courts will pierce the corporate veil and pin liability on stockholders.

Besides the usual business corporation, there are many other forms, including not-for-profit corporations and professional corporations. Business corporations are classified into two types: publicly held and closely held corporations.

To form a corporation, the would-be stockholders must choose the state in which they wish to incorporate. The goal of the incorporation process is issuance of a corporate charter. The charter is a contract between the state and the corporation. Although the Constitution prohibits states from impairing the obligation of contracts, states reserve the right to modify corporate charters.

The corporation is created by the incorporators (or promoters), who raise capital, enter into contracts on behalf of the corporation to be formed, and prepare the articles of incorporation. The promoters are personally liable on the contracts they enter into before the corporation is formed. Incorporators owe a fiduciary duty to each other, to investors, and to the corporation.

The articles of incorporation typically contain a number of features, including the corporate name, corporate purposes, total number of shares and classes into which they are divided, par value, and the like. The name must include the word (or abbreviation) corporation, company, incorporated, or limited (Corp., Co., Inc., or Ltd.). The articles of incorporation must be filed with the secretary of state. Once they have been filed, the board of directors named in the articles must adopt bylaws, elect officers, and conduct other necessary business. The directors are empowered to alter the bylaws, subject to repeal or change by the shareholders.

Even if the formal prerequisites to incorporation are lacking, a de facto corporation will be held to have been formed if (1) a statute exists under which the corporation could have been validly incorporated, (2) the promoters made a bona fide attempt to comply with the statute, and (3) a corporate privilege was exercised. Under appropriate circumstances, a corporation will be held to exist by estoppel.

KEY TERMS

SELF-TEST QUESTIONS

1. In comparing partnerships with corporations the major factor favoring the corporate form is:
   (a) ease of formation
   (b) flexible financing
   (c) limited liability
   (d) control of the business by investors
2. A corporation with no part of its income distributable to its members, directors, or officers is called:
   (a) a publicly held corporation
   (b) a closely held corporation
   (c) a professional corporation
   (d) a nonprofit corporation
3. A corporation in which stock is widely held or available through a national or regional stock exchange is called:
   (a) a publicly held corporation
   (b) a close'y held corporation
   (c) a public corporation
   (d) none of the above

4. Essential to the formation of a de facto corporation is:
   (a) a statute under which the corporation could have been validly incorporated
   (b) promoters who make a bona fide attempt to comply with the corporation statute
   (c) the use of exercise of corporate powers
   (d) all of the above
5. Even when incorporators miss important steps, it is possible to create:
   (a) a corporation by estoppel
   (b) a de jure corporation
   (c) an S corporation
   (d) none of the above

DEMONSTRATION PROBLEM

Bunker signs written offers to purchase stock in Alpha, a corporation that is being formed, and Beta, a corporation which was formed two years ago. Two months after making these offers—and before they are accepted—Bunker changes his mind and attempts to revoke the offers. May he? Why?

PROBLEMS

1. Two young business school graduates, LaVerne and Shirley, form a consulting firm. In deciding between the partnership and corporation form of organization, they are especially concerned about personal liability for giving bad advice to their clients; that is, in the event they are sued they want to prevent plaintiffs from taking their personal assets to satisfy judgments against the firm. Which form of organization would you recommend? Why?

2. Assume that LaVerne and Shirley (see problem 1) must negotiate a large loan from a local bank in order to finance their firm. A friend advises them that they should incorporate in order to avoid personal liability for the loan. Is this good advice? Why?

3. Assume in problem 1 that LaVerne and Shirley decide to form a corporation. Before the incorporation process is complete, LaVerne enters into a contract on behalf of the corporation to purchase office furniture and equipment for $20,000. After the incorporation process has been completed, the corporation formally accepts the contract made by LaVerne. Is LaVerne personally liable on the contract before corporate acceptance? After corporate acceptance? Why?

4. Assume that LaVerne and Shirley (see problem 1) have incorporated their business. One afternoon an old college friend visits Shirley at the office. Shirley and her friend decide to go out for dinner to discuss old times. Shirley, being short of cash, takes money from a petty cash box to pay for dinner.

(She first obtains permission from LaVerne, who has done the same thing many times in the past.) Over dinner, Shirley learns that her friend is now an IRS agent and is investigating Shirley's corporation. What problems does Shirley face in the investigation? Why?

5. Assume in problem 1 that LaVerne and Shirley prepare articles of incorporation but forget to send the articles to the appropriate state office. A few months after they begin to operate their consulting business as a corporation, LaVerne visits a client. After her meeting, in driving out of a parking lot, LaVerne inadvertently backs her car over the client, causing serious bodily harm. Is Shirley liable for the accident? Why?

6. Ralph, a resident of Oklahoma, was injured when using a consumer product manufactured by a corporation whose principal offices were in Tulsa. Since his damages exceeded $10,000, he filed a product liability action against the company, which was incorporated in Delaware, in federal court. Does the federal court have jurisdiction? Why?

7. Alice is the president and only shareholder of a corporation. The IRS is investigating Alice and demands that she produce her corporate records. Alice refuses, pleading the Fifth Amendment privilege against self-incrimination. May the IRS force Alice to turn over her corporate records? Why?

ANSWER TO SELF-TEST QUESTIONS

1. (c)   2. (d)   3. (a)   4. (d)   5. (a)

SUGGESTED ANSWER TO DEMONSTRATION PROBLEM

Bunker may not revoke his preincorporation stock subscription; the RMBCA provides that such subscriptions are irrevocable for six months. (In some non-RMBCA states, however, subscriptions are as revocable as any other contract offer.) He may revoke the Beta offer under the normal contract rule that offers are revocable before acceptance.

Legal Aspects of Corporate Finance

GENERAL SOURCES OF CORPORATE FUNDS

*T*o finance growth, any ongoing business must have a source of funds. Apart from bank and trade debt, the three principal sources are *plowback, debt securities*, and *equity securities*.

Plowback

Nearly 80 percent of new funds that corporations spend on capital projects come from earnings. This source of funds is called **plowback.** Plowback is an attractive source of capital because it is subject to managerial control. No approval is necessary from government agencies for its expenditure, nor is a market of purchasers necessary, as it is when a company seeks to sell securities. Moreover, plowback saves money because it prevents the government from collecting taxes on the money that would otherwise be paid out in dividends.

Debt Securities

A second source of funds is borrowing. A note evidencing the loan—and often providing security to the lender—is a **debt security,** more commonly known as a **bond.** A bond is an IOU, a promise to repay the principal sum at the maturity date and a fixed annual amount as interest, sometimes called the **coupon** rate. Bondholders have priority over stockholders because a bond is a debt, and creditors are entitled to first call on the assets of a corporation. All interest obligations must be met before a corporation can consider paying dividends to stockholders.

Equity Securities

The third, and by far the smallest, source of new capital funds is **equity securities**—stock. Corporations derive less than 6 percent of annual new capital expenditures through the issuance of new shares. But this statistic belies the importance of equity securities to U.S. corporations. Stock is essential to the corporation in launching the business and in initial operations, and it gives the investor a bundle of legal rights—ownership, a share in earnings, transferability, and, depending on the size of the corporation and the number of shares, power to exercise control.

In this chapter we examine three topics relating to stock:

- Types of stock
- Dividends
- Transfer of securities

This is a complex, technical area of law, partly because the source of law varies. For example, stock and dividend issues are usually governed by the Revised Model Business Corporation Act (see p. 907), while the law relating to transfer of securities is found in the Uniform Commercial Code (see p. 939).

TYPES OF STOCK

Shares in a small, closely held company are often identical: each share of stock in BCT Bookstore, Incorporated, carries with it the same right to vote, to receive dividends, and to have distributed the net assets of the company upon liquidation. Most larger companies do not present so simple a picture. They might have what at first glance seems a bewildering array of stock: different classes of common stock, preferred stock, stock with par value and no-par stock, outstanding stock and treasury stock. To find out which types of stock a company has issued, look at the *shareholders'* (or *stockholders'*) *equity* section of the company's balance sheet. The discussion that follows will cover the terminology used in the example in Table 42-1.

Authorized, Issued, and Outstanding Stock

The articles of incorporation spell out how many shares of stock the corporation may issue. The corporation is not obliged to issue all **authorized shares,** but it may not issue more than the total without amending the articles of incorporation. The total of stock sold

TABLE 42-1   STOCKHOLDERS' EQUITY SHOWN ON A BALANCE SHEET

Paid-in Capital:		
7% Preferred Stock, $100 Par Value, 1,000 shares authorized, issued, and outstanding	$100,000	
Paid-in Capital in Excess of Par Value	5,000	$105,000
6% Preferred Stock, $100 Par Value, 1,000 shares authorized, issued, and outstanding	$100,000	100,000
No-Par Common Stock, Stated Value $20, 10,000 shares authorized; 5,000 shares issued and outstanding	$100,000	
Paid-In Capital in Excess of Stated Value	50,000	150,000
Total Paid-in Capital		$355,000
Retained Earnings		27,000
Total Stockholders' Equity		$382,000

to investors is the **issued stock** of the corporation and, in the hands of shareholders, is called **outstanding stock.** Outstanding stock can be traded freely, unless restrictions are noted on the certificates.

Par Value and No-Par Stock

When a value is specified on a stock certificate, it is said to be **par value.** Par value is established in the articles of incorporation and is in most states the floor price of the stock: the corporation may not accept less than par value for par value stock. Companies in most states can also issue **no-par shares.** No-par may be sold for whatever price is set by the board of directors—unless the shareholders themselves are empowered to establish the price. But many states permit (and some states require) no-par stock to have a stated value.

Once the universal practice, issuance of par value common stock is now limited. However, preferred stock usually has a par value, which is useful in determining dividend and liquidation rights.

The term **stated capital** describes the sum of the par value of the issued par value stock and the consideration received (or stated value, where used) for the no-par stock. The excess of net assets of a corporation over stated capital is its **surplus.** Surplus is divided into **earned surplus,** which is essentially the company's retained earnings, and **capital surplus,** all surplus other than earned surplus. We will return to these concepts in our discussion of dividends.

Preferred Stock

The term "preferred" has no set legal meaning. Holders of preferred stock must look to the articles of incorporation to find out what their rights are. They could include the following:

Preference to Dividends   In Table 42-1, one class of preferred stock is entitled to a 7 percent dividend. The percentage applies to the par value; if par value is $100, each share of preferred is entitled to $7 per year. Assuming the articles of incorporation say so, this stock, and the 6 percent preferred, has preference over other classes of shares for dividend payments.

Cumulative Dividends   The articles of incorporation may provide for **cumulative dividends.** The right to cumulative preferred dividends means that all unpaid dividends from prior years and from the current year must be paid before any other stockholder class can receive dividends. With a noncumulative dividend, the company may pay nonpreferred stockholders before paying preferred dividends from an earlier year, although the current year dividends must first go to the preferred holders.

Participating and Nonparticipating Shares After the preferred dividend is paid, holders of preferred shares may be entitled to a further dividend distribution. If the shares are **nonparticipating,** their holders are entitled to no distribution once the preferred dividend is paid. If they are **participating shares,** dividends will be paid out in accordance with whatever formula is set out in the articles of incorporation. For example, preferred shareholders might receive an amount of dividends equal to that paid to nonpreferred share-

holders, or the articles of incorporation might designate a ratio between the two.

Preferred stock might also be participating in another sense. That is the right to share in the distribution of assets in the event of liquidation, after having received assets under a **liquidation preference**—that is, a preference according to a predetermined formula to receive the assets of the company on liquidation ahead of other classes of shareholders.

Convertible Shares   With one exception, the articles of incorporation may grant the right to convert any class of stock into any other at the holder's option according to a fixed ratio. The exception bars conversion of stock into a class with an asset liquidation preference, although some states permit even that type of so-called "upstream" conversion to a "senior" security.

Redeemable Shares   The articles of incorporation may provide for the redemption of shares at an established price and timetable, unless in so doing the company would become insolvent. Redeemed stock is termed cancelled. Unless the articles of incorporation prohibit, the shares are considered authorized but unissued and can be reissued as the need arises. If the articles of incorporation specifically make the cancellation permanent, then the total number of authorized shares is reduced, and new shares cannot be reissued without amending the articles of incorporation.

Voting Rights   Ordinarily, the articles of incorporation provide that preferred shares do not have a voting right. Or they may provide for **contingent voting rights,** entitling preferred shareholders to vote on the happening of a particular event—for example, the nonpayment of a certain number of dividends. The articles may allow **class voting** for directors to insure that the class of preferred stockholders has some representation on the board.

Common Stock

Unless otherwise provided in the articles of incorporation, common stockholders have normal rights. These are four: (1) the right to *ratable* participation in earnings (that is, in proportion to the total shares);

(2) the right to ratable participation in the distribution of net assets on liquidation; (3) the right to vote ratably; and (4) preemptive rights (to buy stock to prevent dilution of the foregoing rights).

Treasury Shares

Defined Treasury shares are those that have originally been issued and then reacquired by the company. They are considered to be *issued* shares but not outstanding. If they are restored to the status of *authorized but unissued shares*, they are no longer treasury shares.

Consideration and Voting Treasury shares need not be sold for par value. The par value should have been received by the corporation when the shares were issued. The board of directors may denote the price of treasury shares, stated in dollars. The corporation is not permitted to vote its own treasury shares, and the shares are not included in the count to determine the total shares for purposes of fixing the size of requisite majority votes.

Purposes Corporations reacquire their shares, a process sometimes called "buyback," for a variety of reasons. If the stock market has dropped so far that the shares are worth considerably less than book value, the corporation might wish to buy its shares to prevent another company from taking it over. The company might decide that investing in itself is sounder business than making other potential investments. Treasury shares also can be used for stock options and employee stock purchase plans. And although it is essentially an accounting trick, buybacks improve a company's per-share earnings because profits need to be divided into fewer outstanding shares.

CONSIDERATION FOR STOCK

Nature of the Consideration

A stock purchaser may pay in something other than cash. Also allowable as consideration are property, whether tangible or intangible, and services or labor performed for the corporation. In most states, promissory notes and contracts for future services are not lawful forms of consideration. The following case illustrates the problems that can arise when services or promises of future delivery are intended as payment for stock.

UNITED STEEL INDUSTRIES, INC. v. MANHART
405 S.W.2d 231 (Civ.App. Tex. 1966)

McDonald, Chief Justice. This is an appeal by defendants, United Steel Industries, Inc., J. R. Hurt and W. B. Griffitts, from a judgment declaring void and cancelling 5000 shares of stock in United Steel Industries, Inc. issued to Hurt, and 4000 shares of stock in such corporation issued to Griffitts.

Plaintiffs Manhart filed this suit individually and as major stockholders against defendants United Steel Industries, Inc., Hurt, and Griffitts, alleging the corporation had issued Hurt 5000 shares of its stock in consideration of Hurt agreeing to perform CPA and bookkeeping services for the corporation for one year in the future; and had issued Griffitts 4000 shares of its stock in consideration for the promised conveyance of a 5 acre tract of land to the Corporation, which land was never conveyed to the Corporation. Plaintiffs assert the 9000 shares of stock were issued in violation of Article 2.16 Business Corporation Act, V.A.T.S. and prayed that such stock be declared void and cancelled.

(continued on next page)

(continued)

UNITED STEEL INDUSTRIES, INC. v. MANHART
405 S.W.2d 231 (Civ.App. Tex. 1966)

Trial was before the Court without a jury which, after hearing, entered judgment declaring the 5000 shares of stock issued to Hurt, and the 4000 shares issued to Griffitts, issued without valid consideration, void, and decreeing such stock cancelled.

* * *

The trial court found (on ample evidence) that the incorporators of the Corporation made an agreement with Hurt to issue him 5000 shares in consideration of Hurt's agreement to perform bookkeeping and accounting services for the Corporation for the first year of its operation. The Corporation minutes reflect the 5000 shares issued to Hurt "in consideration of labor done, services in the incorporation and organization of the Corporation." The trial court found (on ample evidence) that such minutes do not reflect the true consideration agreed upon, and that Hurt performed no services for the Corporation prior to February 1, 1965. The Articles of Incorporation were filed on January 28, 1965, and the 5000 shares were issued to Hurt on May 29, 1965. There is evidence that Hurt performed some services for the Corporation between January and May 29, 1965; but Hurt himself testified the "5000 (shares) were issued to me for services rendered or to be rendered for the first year in keeping the books. . . ."

The situation is thus one where the stock was issued to Hurt both for services already performed and for services to be rendered in the future.

The trial court concluded the promise of future services was not a valid consideration for the issuance of stock under Article 2.16 Business Corporation Act; that the issuance was void; and that since there was no apportionment of the value of future services from the value of services already rendered, the entire 5000 shares were illegally issued and void.

Article 12, Section 6, Texas Constitution, Vernon's Ann.St. provides: "No corporation shall issue stock . . . except for money paid, labor done, or property actually received. . . ." And Article 2.16 Texas Business Corporation Act provides: Payment for Shares.

A. The consideration paid for the issuance of shares shall consist of money paid, labor done, or property actually received. Shares may not be issued until the full amount of the consideration, fixed as provided by law, has been paid. . . .

B. Neither promissory notes nor the promise of future services shall constitute payment or part payment for shares of a corporation.

C. In the absence of fraud in the transaction, the judgment of the board of directors . . . as to the value of the consideration received for shares shall be conclusive.

The Fifth Circuit in Champion v. CIR, 303 F.2d 887 construing the foregoing constitutional provision and Article 2.16 of the Business Corporation Act, held:

Where it is provided that stock can be issued for labor done, as in Texas . . . the requirement is not met where the consideration for the stock is work or services to be performed in the future. . . . The situation is not changed by reason of the provision that the stock was to be given . . . for services rendered as well as to be rendered since there was no allocation or apportionment of stock between services performed and services to be performed.

The 5000 shares were issued before the future services were rendered. Such stock was illegally issued and void.

Griffitts was issued 10,000 shares partly in consideration for legal services to the Corporation and partly in exchange for the 5 acres of land. The stock was valued at $1 per share and the land had an agreed value of $4000. The trial court found (upon ample evidence) that the 4000 shares of stock issued to Griffitts was in consideration of his promise to convey the land to the Corporation; that Griffitts never conveyed the land; and the issuance of the stock was illegal and void.

The judgment of the board of directors "as to the value of consideration received for shares" is conclusive, but such does not authorize the board to issue shares contrary to the Constitution, for services to be performed in the future (as in the case of Hurt), or for property not received (as in the case of Griffitts).

The judgment is correct. Defendants' points and contentions are overruled.

Affirmed.

Evaluating the Consideration: Watered Stock

In *United Steel,* assume that attorney Griffitts's services had been thought by the corporation to be worth $6,000, but in fact were worth $1,000, and that he had received stock with par value of $6,000 (that is, 6,000 shares of $1 par value stock) in exchange for his services. Would Griffitts be liable for the difference? This is the problem of **watered stock**: the inflated consideration is in fact less than par value. The term itself comes from the ancient fraud of farmers and ranchers who increased the weight of their cattle (also known as stock) by forcing them to ingest excess water.

The *majority* approach is the **"good faith" rule.** As noted near the end of the *United Steel Industries* case on page 931, in the absence of fraud, "the judgment of the board of directors 'as to the value of consideration received for shares' is conclusive." In other words, if the directors or shareholders conclude in good faith that the consideration does fairly reflect par value, then the stock is not watered and the stock buyer cannot be assessed for the difference. The *minority* approach is the **"true value"** rule: the consideration must in fact equal par value by an objective standard at the time the shares are issued, regardless of the board's good faith judgment.

A shareholder may commence a derivative action (see Chapter 43) against a shareholder who has failed to pay full consideration under either rule to recover the difference between the value received by the corporation and the par value. Statutes in many states also allow creditors to maintain an action—the so-called "statutory obligation theory." In states which do not follow this theory, only creditors who relied upon the balance sheet may recover.

The liability of a shareholder under either rule does not extend to a good faith purchaser. To be protected, the transferee must have had no knowledge or notice that the person from whom she purchased the stock had not paid full value.

DIVIDENDS

Types

A dividend is a share of profits, a dividing up of the company's earnings. No single type is prescribed by law.

Cash Dividend   If a company's finances are such that it can declare a dividend to stockholders, a cash dividend always is permissible. It is a payment (by check, ordinarily) to the stockholders of a certain amount of money per share. A dividend is taxable as income to the recipient.

Property Dividend   Corporations occasionally pay dividends in property rather than in cash. Armand Hammer, the legendary financier and chairman and CEO of Occidental Petroleum Corporation, recounts how during World War II he founded a liquor business by buying shares of the American Distilling Company. It was giving out one barrel of whiskey per share as a dividend. Whiskey was in short supply during the war, so Hammer bought 5,000 shares and took 5,000 barrels as a dividend.

Stock Dividend   Next to cash, the most frequent type of dividend is stock itself. Normally, the corporation declares a small percentage dividend (between one and ten percent), so that a holder of 100 shares would receive four new shares on a 4 percent dividend share. Although each shareholder winds up with more stock, he realizes no personal net gain at that moment, as he would with a cash dividend, because each stockholder winds up with the same relative proportion of shares. The total outstanding stock represents no greater assets than before. The corporation may issue share dividends either from treasury stock or from authorized but unissued shares. If from treasury stock, no payment to stated capital need be made (that was done when the stock was issued). If from authorized but unissued par value stock, an amount equal to par

value must be transferred from surplus into the stated capital account. If the dividend is to be of stock without par value, the board will fix a stated value before it is issued and an amount equal to the aggregate stated value will be transferred from surplus to stated capital.

Stock Split   A *stock dividend* should be distinguished from a *stock split*. In a stock split, one share is divided into two or more shares—for example, a two-for-one split means that for every one share the stockholder owns he now has two. In the "reverse split," two or more shares are absorbed into one. The stock split has no effect on the assets of the company nor is the interest of any shareholder diluted. No transfer from surplus into stated capital is necessary. The only necessary accounting change is the adjustment of par and stated value. Because par value is being changed, many states require not only the board of directors but also the shareholders to approve a stock split.

Why split? The chief reason is to reduce the current market price of the stock in order to make it "affordable" to a much wider class of investors. For example, in 1978, IBM, whose stock was then selling for around $284, split four-for-one, reducing the price to about $70 a share. That was the lowest IBM's stock had been since 1932. Stock need not sell at stratospheric prices to be split; for example, American Telnet Corporation, whose stock cost 43¾ cents a share, declared a five-for-one split in 1980. Apparently the company felt that the stock would be more affordable at 8¾ cents a share.

Legal Limitations on Dividends

The law imposes certain limitations on cash or property dividends the corporation may disburse. Dividends may not be paid if the business is insolvent (that is, unable to pay its debts as they become due), if paying dividends would make it insolvent, or if payment would violate a restriction in the articles of incorporation. Most states also restrict the funds available for distribution to those available in earned surplus. Under this rule, a corporation that ran a deficit in the current year could still declare a dividend as long as the total earned surplus offsets the deficit.

A few states—and, significantly, Delaware is one—permit dividends to be paid out of the net of current earnings and those of the immediately preceding year, both years taken as a single period, even if the balance sheet shows a negative earned surplus. Such dividends are known as **nimble dividends.**

Distribution from Capital Surplus   Assets in the form of cash or property may be distributed from capital surplus if the articles of incorporation so provide or if shareholders approve the distribution. Such distributions must be identified to the shareholders as coming from capital surplus.

Record Date, Payment Date, Rights of Stockholders   Under securities exchange rules, the board of directors cannot simply declare a dividend payable on the date of the board meeting and authorize the treasurer to hand out cash. The board must fix two dates: a **record date** and a **payment date.** By the first, the board declares a dividend for shareholders of record as of a certain future date—perhaps ten days hence. Actual payment of the dividend is postponed until the payment date, which could be a month after the record date.

The board's action creates a debtor-creditor relationship between corporation and shareholders. The company may not revoke a cash dividend unless the shareholders consent. It may revoke a share dividend as long as the shares have not been issued.

Directors' Duties

When Directors Are Too Stingy   In every state, dividends are normally payable only at the discretion of the directors. Courts will order distribution only if they are expressly mandatory or if it can be shown that the directors abused their discretion by acting fraudulently or in a manner that was manifestly unreasonable. The following case, involving Henry Ford's refusal in 1916 to pay dividends in order to reinvest profits, is celebrated in business annals because of his testimony at trial (see **Box 42-1**), even though, as it turned out, the courts held his refusal to be an act of miserliness and an abuse of discretion.

DODGE v. FORD MOTOR CO.
204 Mich. 459, 170 N.W. 668 (1919)

[Action by John F. Dodge and Horace E. Dodge against the Ford Motor Company and its directors. The lower court ordered the directors to declare a dividend in the amount of $19,275,385.96. The court also enjoined proposed expansion of the company. The defendants appeal.]

OSTRANDER, C. J.

★   ★   ★

. . . [T]he case for plaintiffs must rest upon the claim, and the proof in support of it, that the proposed expansion of the business of the corporation, involving the further use of profits as capital, ought to be enjoined because inimical to the best interests of the company and its shareholders, and upon the further claim that in any event the withholding of the special dividend asked for by plaintiffs is arbitrary action of the directors requiring judicial interference.

The rule which will govern courts in deciding these questions is not in dispute. It is, of course, differently phrased by judges and by authors, and, as the phrasing in a particular instance may seem to lean for or against the exercise of the right of judicial interference with the actions of corporate directors, the context, or the facts before the court, must be considered.

(continued on next page)

(continued)

DODGE v. FORD MOTOR CO.
204 Mich. 459, 170 N.W. 668 (1919)

* * *

In Morawetz on Corporations (2nd Ed.) § 447, it is stated:

> Profits earned by a corporation may be divided among its shareholders, but it is not a violation of the charter if they are allowed to accumulate and remain invested in the company's business. The managing agents of a corporation are impliedly invested with a discretionary power with regard to the time and manner of distributing its profits. They may apply profits in payment of floating or funded debts, or in development of the company's business; and so long as they do not abuse their discretionary powers, or violate the company's charter, the courts cannot interfere.
>
> But it is clear that the agents of a corporation, and even the majority, cannot arbitrarily withhold profits earned by the company, or apply them to any use which is not authorized by the company's charter.

* * *

Mr. Henry Ford is the dominant force in the business of the Ford Motor Company. No plan of operations could be adopted unless he consented, and no board of directors can be elected whom he does not favor. One of the directors of the company has no stock. One share was assigned to him to qualify him for the position, but it is not claimed that he owns it. A business, one of the largest in the world, and one of the most profitable, has been built up. It employs many men, at good pay.

> "My ambition," said Mr. Ford, "is to employ still more men, to spread the benefits of this industrial system to the greatest possible number, to help them build up their lives and their homes. To do this we are putting the greatest share of our profits back in the business."
>
> "With regard to dividends, the company paid sixty percent on its capitalization of two million dollars, or $1,200,000, leaving $58,000,000 to reinvest for the growth of the company. This is Mr. Ford's policy at present, and it is understood that the other stockholders cheerfully accede to this plan."

He had made up his mind in the summer of 1916 that no dividends other than the regular dividends should be paid, "for the present."

> "Q. For how long? Had you fixed in your mind any time in the future, when you were going to pay—A. No.
> "Q. That was indefinite in the future? A. That was indefinite; yes, sir."

The record, and especially the testimony of Mr. Ford, convinces that he has to some extent the attitude towards shareholders of one who has dispensed and distributed to them large gains and that they should be content to take what he chooses to give. His testimony creates the impression, also, that he thinks the Ford Motor Company has made too much money, has had too large profits, and that, although large profits might be still earned, a sharing of them with the public, by reducing the price of the output of the company, ought to be undertaken. We have no doubt that certain sentiments, philanthropic and altruistic, creditable to Mr. Ford, had large influence in determining the policy to be pursued by the Ford Motor Company—the policy which has been herein referred to.

★   ★   ★

The difference between an incidental humanitarian expenditure of corporate funds for the benefit of the employees, like the building of a hospital for their use and the employment of agencies for the betterment of their condition, and a general purpose and plan to benefit mankind at the expense of others, is obvious. There should be no confusion (of which there is evidence) of the duties which Mr. Ford conceives that he and the stockholders owe to the general public and the duties which in law he and his codirectors owe to protesting, minority stockholders. A business corporation is organized and carried on primarily for the profit of the stockholders. The powers of the directors are to be employed for that end. The discretion of directors is to be exercised in the choice of means to attain that end, and does not extend to a change in the end itself, to the reduction of profits, or to the nondistribution of profits among shareholders in order to devote them to other purposes.

★   ★   ★

We are not, however, persuaded that we should interfere with the proposed expansion of the business of the Ford Motor Company. In view of the fact that the selling price of products may be increased at any time, the ultimate results of the larger business cannot be certainly estimated. The judges are not business experts. It is recognized that plans must often be made for a long future, for expected competition, for a continuing as well as an immediately profitable venture. The experience of the Ford Motor Company is evidence of capable management of its affairs. It may be noticed, incidentally, that it took from the public the money required for the execution of its plan, and that the very considerable salaries paid to Mr. Ford and to certain executive officers and employees were not diminished. We are not satisfied that the alleged motives of the directors, in so far as they are reflected in the conduct of the business, menace the interests of shareholders. It is enough to say, perhaps, that the court of equity is at all times open to complaining shareholders having a just grievance.

[The court affirmed the lower court's order that the company declare a dividend and reversed the lower court's injunction that halted company expansion.]

When Directors Are Too Generous Directors who vote to declare and distribute dividends in excess of those allowed by law or by provisions in the articles of incorporation personally become jointly and severally liable to the corporation. Shareholders who receive a dividend knowing it is unlawful must repay any directors held liable for voting the illegal dividends. The directors are said to be entitled to *contribution* from such shareholders. Even when directors have not been sued, some courts have held that

BOX 42-1

By David Lewis

[Dividends are normally payable only at the discretion of a corporation's directors. Courts can order distribution only if mandatory or if the directors' abuse of discretion is demonstrated. Despite his celebrated testimony, the court found Henry Ford's refusal to pay dividends in 1916 to be an abuse of discretion.—AUTHORS' NOTE]

In 1916–17, Henry Ford was involved in a lawsuit with two of the company's stockholders, John F. and Horace Dodge. The statements that Ford made in and out of court during the period of this suit were widely publicized and did much to brighten his image as an American folk hero.

The suit originated with Ford's plan, conceived in 1915 and early 1916, to double the size of the High-land Park plant, to construct a blast furnace and a foundry ten miles away on the Rouge River, and to suspend all but nominal dividends (that is, 5

HENRY FORD IN COURT

percent per month on the ridiculously low book capitalization of $2,000,000) until the indefinite date of the expansion program's completion. Ford believed that he had to increase his productive capacity and output, or risk falling behind rapidly growing competitors in the low-priced field. He was indifferent to the Dodges' medium-priced car, introduced in 1913. But the Dodges, who between them owned 10 percent of the Ford Company's stock, were thoroughly alarmed by Ford's plan. They had used several millions of dollars of Ford profits to launch their car, and they were counting upon the continued flow of impressive Ford dividends to expand production. They remonstrated with Henry, who in August 1916 replied that the company, in addition to withholding special dividends, would plow back into the business $58,000,000 of accumulated profits. The same month, Ford

slashed prices on the Model T an average of $66.00. To the Dodges, the price cuts added insult to injury. The Ford Company had been able to sell all the cars it could make. Simple arithmetic showed that at one sweep Ford had skimmed about $40,000,000 of profits from company income. The Dodges felt that he might as well have thrown the money away. They filed suit against the Ford Motor Company and Henry Ford, asking that the defendants distribute as dividends 75 percent of the company's cash surplus, or about $39,000,000. Simultaneously, they obtained a court restraining order which forbade the use of company funds for plant expansion.

Characteristically, Ford at once took his case to the public, declaring in an interview published in the *Detroit News* that his only aims in life were to enable "a large number of people to buy and enjoy the use of a car" and to give "a larger number of men employment at good wages." "And let me say right here," he continued, "that I do not believe that we

---

shareholders must repay dividends received when the corporation is insolvent or when they know that the dividends are illegal.

THE WINDS OF CHANGE

Perhaps the most dramatic innovations incorporated into the RMBCA are the financial provisions. The revisions eliminate concepts such as par value stock, no-par stock, stated capital, capital surplus, earned surplus, and treasury shares. It was felt that these concepts—notably par value and stated capital—no longer serve their original purpose of protecting creditors.

A key definition under the revisions is that of "distributions"—that is, any transfer of money or property to the shareholders. In order to make distri-

butions, a corporation must meet the traditional insolvency test and a so-called balance sheet test. Under the balance sheet test, corporate assets must be greater than or equal to liabilities and liquidation preferences on senior equity. The RMBCA also provides that promissory notes and contracts for future services may be used in payment for shares.

TRANSFER OF SECURITIES

Introduction to UCC Article 8

Partial ownership of a corporation would be an awkward investment if there were no ready means of transfer. The availability of paper certificates as tangible evidence of the ownership of equity securities

BOX 42-1

should make such an awful profit on our cars. A reasonable profit is right, but not too much. So it has been my policy to force the price of the car down as fast as production would permit, and give the benefits to users and laborers." Such statements, probably unprecedented in the business world, astonished and delighted the American public. In subsequent interviews Ford hammered home this theme, pointing out, "We could easily have maintained our price for this year and cleaned up from sixty to seventy-five millions; but I don't think it would have been right to do so; so we cut our prices and are now clearing from $1,500,000 to $2,500,000 a month, which is all any firm ought to make, maybe more—unless, as I said, the money is to be used in expansion. I have been fighting to hold down income right along. A man is not a success unless he can pay good wages and clear something for himself, but I think these wages should be paid without taking them out of the public."

Once on the witness stand, Ford gave answers which—if their purpose was to please the public—could not have been better written by any public relations expert in the land.

"Now," said Elliott G. Stevenson, the Dodges' truculent attorney, "I will ask you again, do you still think that those profits were 'awful profits?' "

"Well, I guess I do, yes," replied Ford.

"And for that reason you were not satisfied to continue to make such awful profits?" the lawyer inquired.

"We don't seem to be able to keep the profits down," apologized Ford.

". . . Are you trying to keep them down? What is the Ford Motor Company organized for except profits, will you tell me, Mr. Ford?"

"Organized to do as much good as we can, everywhere, for everybody concerned."

The dumbfounded attorney quit for the day. However, in his need to prove that a business firm's primary

responsibility is to its stockholders, he returned to the attack. "What," he asked Ford, "is the purpose of the [Ford] company?"

"To do as much as possible for everybody concerned," responded Ford, "to make money and use it, give employment, and send out the car where the people can use it . . . and incidentally to make money. . . . Business is a service not a bonanza."

"Incidentally make money?" queried the attorney.

"Yes, sir."

"But your controlling feature . . . is to employ a great army of men at high wages, to reduce the selling price of your car, so that a lot of people can buy it at a cheap price, and give everybody a car that wants one."

"If you give all that," replied Ford, who must have felt that Stevenson had admirably stated his policies, "the money will fall into your hands; you can't get out of it."

Source: *The Public Image of Henry Ford*, 1976.

solves the problem of what to transfer, but since the corporations must maintain records of their owners a set of rules is necessary to spell out how transfers are to be made. That set of rules is Article 8 of the Uniform Commercial Code (UCC).

Prior to 1977, Article 8 dealt exclusively with interests in securities represented by stock certificates. By the late 1960s, however, a "paperwork crunch" threatened to engulf the securities markets, as millions of shares began to be traded daily. One attempt to cope with the paperwork burden was the elimination or reduction of stock certificates. As *uncertificated* investment securities began to spread, there arose a need for rules governing their use. Accordingly, Article 8 was revamped in 1977. Article 8 neither authorizes nor prohibits the issuance of uncertificated securities. Their legality is left to general corporation laws. Article 8 simply sets forth the rules that must

be followed when buyers and sellers wish to transfer lawfully issued uncertificated securities.

The discussion that follows treats only selected topics under Article 8. Other aspects are treated in different chapters, including Statute of Frauds requirements (Chapter 12) and use of securities as collateral (Chapter 27).

Certificated and Uncertificated Securities Defined

A **certificated security** is a share, participation, or other interest in property, an enterprise, or an obligation of the issuer and is represented by an instrument issued in bearer or registered form. Additionally, for purposes of Article 8, the certificated security must be of a type commonly traded in securities exchanges or markets and must be one of a class or series of instruments. The most common form of the certificated security is the stock certificate.

An **uncertificated security** is a security that is not represented by an instrument. Its transfer must be registered upon books maintained for that purpose by or on behalf of the issuer.

The definition of security provided in Article 8 has no bearing on whether an interest in property or an enterprise is a security for purposes of the federal securities laws. The only purpose of the definition in Article 8 is to set out the types of interests for which Article 8 will provide protection to issuers, owners, purchasers, and creditors upon transfer, notice of claim, registration, and related transactions.

Method of Transfer

UCC Section 8-313 sets forth the basic methods of transfer. A certificated security is transferred easily enough by delivery of the certificate itself. The seller (or transferor, since a security may be given as a gift as well as sold) may deliver directly to the purchaser or transferee or to an intermediary—such as the purchaser's broker, banks, clearing corporations, and other entities that regularly maintain security accounts for their customers (collectively known as "financial intermediaries"). If transfer is made to an intermediary, the transferor must indorse the certificate to the transferee. By contrast, an uncertificated security is transferred by *registration* on the books of the issuer or of a financial intermediary. When the issuer undertakes the registration, the moment of transfer occurs at the time of registration; when an intermediary registers the transfer, the moment of transfer occurs when the intermediary acknowledges the registration.

Registration and Initial Transaction Statements

The transfer of both certificated and uncertificated securities can be registered. For certificated securities, the transferor simply presents an indorsed certificate to the issuer and requests that the transfer be registered. For uncertificated securities, the transferor instructs the issuer to make the registration. Unless the issuer and transferor have previously signed an agreement stating the means by which the instruction is to be made, the instruction must be in writing and signed by the transferor. The following case illustrates registration requirements for certificated securities.

WANLAND v. C. E. THOMPSON CO.
64 Ill. App. 3d 46, 380 N.E.2d 1012 (1978)

WILSON, J. This is an appeal from an order striking one of three counts of a complaint and dismissing the defendant named in the stricken count. The broad issue before us is whether the trial court properly struck the count and dismissed the defendant named therein, C. E. Thompson Company (hereinafter "C.E.T."), for failure to sufficiently plead ultimate facts stating a cause of action.

★   ★   ★

On October 21, 1976, plaintiff, Richard E. Wanland, filed a multi-count complaint in the court below. Count one was directed against a stockbrokerage, Shearson, Hayden, Stone, Inc. (hereinafter "Shearson"); count two, against Shearson and one of its stockbrokers, George E. Thompson; count three, against C.E.T. In count three, Wanland alleged in part that on June 18, 1973, Thompson executed an assignment of a stock certificate representing 60 shares of 4½ percent, preferred C.E.T. stock and gave the certificate to Wanland. On February 21, 1976, Thompson told Wanland that the stock certificate had to be exchanged for 60 shares of 6½ percent, preferred C.E.T. stock. Wanland gave Thompson the stock certificate in reliance upon this representation and was given a receipt in return. The 60 shares of 6½ percent C.E.T. stock were never delivered to Wanland and Thompson has refused to return the stock certificate representing 60 shares of 4½ percent stock.

Count three also alleges that Wanland has been a shareholder of C.E.T. since June 18, 1973, and consequently is entitled to receive dividends, notices of annual meetings and financial statements and reports. Nevertheless, C.E.T. has not delivered these items.

Wanland prayed for: (1) a declaratory judgment declaring him the owner of 60 shares of C.E.T. stock; (2) an order directing C.E.T. to enter Wanland's name in its stock transfer records as owner of said shares; and (3) an injunction prohibiting the transfer of the shares represented by the stock certificate to any other person.

C.E.T. responded, in part, with a motion to strike count three on the ground that it was substantially insufficient in law. In support of its motion, C.E.T. pointed to Wanland's failure to allege a condition precedent to registration of the transfer of the certificate to his name. C.E.T. explained that the transfer is governed by a Delaware statute which requires an endorsement on the certificate and presentation of the certificate for registration of a change in ownership. Wanland did not allege that he presented a properly endorsed certificate to C.E.T. for transfer of registration. Thus Wanland failed to state the conditions precedent to both his right to a transfer of a certificate, and C.E.T.'s duty to transfer it. C.E.T. went on to explain that it is required to treat Thompson, the registered owner, as such until plaintiff presents the certificate, properly endorsed, for registration of the transfer. As a result, C.E.T. moved to have count three stricken for failure to state a cause of action.

*   *   *

Under §8–401 of the Delaware Uniform Commercial Code—Investment Securities, C.E.T. has a duty to register a transfer of ownership of a security in registered form only upon satisfaction of several conditions including presentation of the security to C.E.T. with a request to register transfer. Not only did Wanland fail to allege that he presented the certificate in question to C.E.T., but he also admitted at oral argument that he never presented the certificate to C.E.T. during the period he held it. Thus, notwithstanding any question of proper endorsement, one condition precedent to C.E.T.'s obligation to transfer ownership of the shares represented by the certificate was not satisfied. Furthermore, under §8–207 of the Delaware Code, C.E.T. has the right to treat the registered owner as the person exclusively entitled to vote, receive notifications and otherwise exercise the rights and powers of an owner prior to due presentment of a security in registered form for registration of transfer.

In his complaint, Wanland alleges that Thompson has refused to return the certificate in question. As long as Thompson continues to possess the certificate, plaintiff will be unable to comply with the presentation requirement of §8–401 of the Delaware Code.

*   *   *

Affirmed.

The issuer is obligated to register the transfer when presented with an indorsed certificate or an instruction to do so in the case of uncertificated securities. However, the issuer may request reasonable assurance that the indorsements or instructions are genuine and effective. Under other laws or agreements, the issuer may be obliged first to inquire into adverse claims by a third party—whose claims would be defeated if the registration were made—and also may be obliged to collect taxes before registering the transfer.

Two days after the transfer of an uncertificated security has been registered, the issuer must send to the new registered owner an initial transaction statement describing the issue of which the security is a part, the number of shares transferred, the name and address of the new registered owner, a notation of any liens, restrictions, and adverse claims, and the date of registration. The issuer must send a similar statement to the former owner, also within two days of registering the transfer. The initial transaction statement provides the owner with proof of rights against the issuer, but it also has sharp limits: it speaks only as of the time of its issuance and runs in favor of the addressee only. Consequently, subsequent purchasers cannot rely on a previous initial transaction statement, and the statement must carry a warning to that effect.

Rights and Duties of Buyers and Sellers

Transferor's Performance   A seller of securities fulfills his duty to transfer at the time he places a certificated security in the hands of his broker or causes an uncertificated security to be registered in the name of his broker. The seller also may discharge his obligation by placing in the hands of his broker a transfer instruction for an uncertificated security, provided that the broker presents the instruction to the issuer within thirty days and the issuer does not refuse to register the requested transfer.

Warranties   A person who transfers a certificated security to a purchaser for value warrants that the transfer is effective and rightful and that the security is genuine. Substantially the same warranties are given by a person who originates an instruction to register an uncertificated security.

The Shelter Rule   A fundamental general principle of Article 8 is that a purchaser acquires all the rights of the transferor. A subsequent transferee is said to be sheltered by the lack of knowledge of his transferor. Norman purchases an uncertificated security that gives the corporate issuer the right to recall it whenever the company wants. However, Norman had no knowledge of this restriction, and the initial transaction statement mistakenly failed to disclose it. Norman, then, would acquire the security free and clear of the company's right to reacquire. Norman sells to Andy, who knows of the company's mistake. Upon receipt of Norman's instruction to register the transfer to Andy, the company wakes up and issues Andy an initial transaction statement that now discloses the restriction. Can the company legitimately do so? No. Andy can demand a "clean" statement—one without any restriction—because Andy acquires Norman's rights, and Norman was entitled to a security without any such restriction.

Bona Fide Purchase   Without notice, buyers of both certificated and uncertificated securities are entitled to take free of liens, defenses, restrictions, and adverse claims. The difference is that notice of the various types of limitations must be set forth on the face of the certificated security, whereas the purchaser of an uncertificated security receives notice only in the initial transaction statement. The buyer of the uncertificated security, therefore, would be well advised to hold on to the purchase price—or pay it over to an escrow agent—until he receives an initial transaction statement that lives up to the warranties of his transferor. If he has paid out first and receives an initial transaction statement in breach of the seller's warranties, the buyer's only recourse is a lawsuit for breach of warranty.

Lost, Destroyed, and Stolen Certificated Securities   An owner who loses a certificated security (whether the security has been misplaced, destroyed, or stolen) must notify the issuer within a reasonable period of time after he realizes the security is missing. If he does not and the issuer in the meantime has registered a transfer of the missing security—perhaps the person who stole it has sold it to an unwary customer—then the original owner has no claim against the issuer. In the following case, the court interprets the meaning of "reasonable time."

WELLER v. AMERICAN TELEPHONE & TELEGRAPH COMPANY

290 A.2d 842 (Del.Chan. 1972)

MARVEL, VICE CHANCELLOR. Plaintiff seeks the entry of a judgment against two corporations, namely American Telephone and Telegraph Company and General Electric Company, based on her claim for injuries sustained by her as a result of the alleged unauthorized registration of stock owned by her in each such company. Separate suits were filed against such issuers. However, the cases having been consolidated for trial purposes, this opinion will be filed in each case.

At the time of the acts complained of plaintiff was the registered holder of 500 shares of common stock of American Telephone and Telegraph Company and 100 shares of common stock of General Electric. Later, the shares of the latter company were split two for one.

In 1968, Gertrude L. Weller, a 94-year-old widow, was invited to live in the home of Mr. and Mrs. Kenneth Jumper. This change of residence came about because the plaintiff had known Mrs. Jumper for many years and was also acquainted with Mr. Jumper, who had performed various helpful services for her in the past. Because of her lonely circumstances and advanced age she was more than delighted to accept the Jumpers' proposal. As a token of her appreciation for their apparently unselfish gesture, Mrs. Weller, after moving in with them, made a gift of 100 shares of American Telephone and Telegraph stock to Mr. Jumper.

Thereafter, because of her age and poor health, plaintiff gradually surrendered more and more responsibility concerning the details of her business affairs to Mr. Jumper. Thus, she acquiesced when he took upon himself to open her mail, being reassured by him on numerous occasions that he was sending her stock dividend checks and other income receipts to her bank. During this period Mrs. Weller evinced complete trust in the Jumpers notwithstanding momentary worries over the fact that her mail was being opened by Mr. Jumper and that she was not actually being shown the income checks which she had received in the mail. However, she was easily convinced that there was nothing to worry about.

In February, 1970, after having moved to her nephew's to live, following disclosure to some extent of Mr. Jumper's actual nature, Mrs. Weller ascertained that for over a period of almost two years she had been systematically defrauded by Mr. Jumper. In other words she became aware for the first time of the fact that Kenneth Jumper had used a form containing her signature for the purpose of opening a joint trading account with a stockbroker, namely the third party defendant Merrill Lynch, Pierce, Fenner & Smith, Inc., and that Mr. Jumper thereafter had apparently forged her name to the stock certificates here involved for the purpose of selling them on the market.

The trial evidence is to the effect that Mr. Jumper had not only forged plaintiff's name to plaintiff's stock certificates but had also closed out her savings account and terminated her checking account by means of a forged signature. Needless to say, the income checks which Mr. Jumper had removed from Mrs. Weller's mail had also been diverted to his own use.

(continued on next page)

(continued)

WELLER v. AMERICAN TELEPHONE & TELEGRAPH COMPANY

290 A.2d 842 (Del.Chan. 1972)

Plaintiff thereupon notified the defendants American Telephone and Telegraph Company and General Electric Company on March 4, 1970 that the stock certificates representing her investments in such companies had been sold by means of forged signatures and requested the issuance to her of replacement certificates. The defendants having declined to issue such certificates as requested, this action ensued, the complaint naming as defendants the issuers of the certificates in question. Merrill Lynch was later joined as a third party defendant in its capacity as the broker which had guaranteed Mrs. Weller's signature.

★   ★   ★

§ 8-404(2) of the Uniform Commercial Code provides that where an issuer has registered a transfer of a security in the name of a person not entitled to it, such issuer on demand must deliver a like security to the true owner, provided, inter alia, the owner has acted pursuant to subsection (1) of the section which follows. § 8-404(2)(b). Subsection (1) of the following section provides that the owner of such a security must notify the issuer of the wrongful taking complained of within a reasonable time after he has notice of a lost or wrongfully taken certificate, Section 8-405(1).

Defendants argue that in the case at bar plaintiff failed to notify the issuers within a "reasonable time", as such phrase is defined in the statute. It contends that plaintiff should have known some twenty-two months before she notified the issuing corporations that Mr. Jumper had converted her stock certificates. Defendants go on to point out that had plaintiff made a casual examination of her bank book or bank statement, it would have been brought to her attention that dividend checks accruing on the shares here in issue were not being deposited to her credit.

In order to determine whether or not Mrs. Weller notified the issuer within a "reasonable time" after she had "noticed" that her shares had been transferred as a result of forgery it is necessary to determine the meaning of these two phrases as employed in the statute.

The definition section of Article 8 provides inter alia: "In addition Article 1 contains general definitions and principles of construction and interpretation applicable throughout this Article." Section 8-102(6). Article 1, provides that a person has "notice" of a fact when he has actual knowledge of it, has received notification, or ". . . from all the facts and circumstances known to him at the time in question he has reason to know that it exists." Section 1-201(25). Article 1 also provides: "What is a reasonable time for taking any action depends on the nature, purpose and circumstances of such action." Section 1-204(2).

In the case at bar we are concerned with the affairs of a 94-year-old woman, who while a guest in another's home, was persuaded to allow one of her hosts, whom she trusted, to handle her affairs. I am accordingly satisfied that Mrs. Weller, a lonely and trusting person of advanced years and of infirm mind and body, had every reasonable right to trust a family which took her in and which she had known intimately before she moved into its home. Furthermore, in light of her reliance on the perpetrator of the acts which deprived her of title to her securities and her own age and decrepitude, she having among other things broken a hip while at the Jumpers, I do not think Mrs. Weller can be charged with unreasonable action in not checking her accounts from time to time. I therefore conclude in view of all of the surrounding circumstances that Mrs. Weller did not have the required statutory notice of Mr. Jumper's dishonesty until February 19 or 20, 1970, and that she thereafter notified the issuers of her stolen securities within a reasonable time. [Judgment for plaintiff.]

If a stockholder claims that a security has been lost, destroyed or stolen—and the claim is made before the issuer has received notice that the security has been sold to a bona fide purchaser—the issuer must give the owner a new certificated security, or an equivalent uncertificated security, at the issuer's option. In return, the issuer may insist that the owner post an **indemnity bond,** holding the issuer harmless in the event that a bona fide purchaser of the missing security turns up and demands registration of transfer.

CHAPTER SUMMARY

An important way of raising capital is by the sale of stock. The articles of incorporation govern the total number of shares of stock that the corporation may issue, although it need not issue the maximum. Stock in the hands of shareholders is said to be authorized, issued, and outstanding. Stock may have a par value, which is usually the floor price of the stock. No-par shares may be sold for any price set by the directors.

Preferred stock may be: (1) entitled to cumulative dividends, (2) convertible, (3) redeemable, and (4) participating. Common stock normally has the right to (1) ratable participation in earnings, (2) ratable participation in the distribution of net assets on liquidation, and (3) ratable vote.

Ordinarily the good faith judgment of the directors concerning the fair value of the consideration received for stock is determinative. A minority of states adhere to a "true value" rule that holds to an objective standard.

Dividends may be distributed as cash, property, or stock. The law imposes certain limitations on the amount that the corporation may disburse; most states restrict the cash or property available for distribution to earned surplus. However, a few states, including Delaware, permit dividends to be paid out of the net of current earnings and those of the im-

mediately preceding year, both years taken as a single period; these are known as nimble dividends. The directors have discretion, within broad limits, to set the level of dividends; however, they will be jointly and severally liable if they approve dividends higher than allowed by law or under the articles of incorporation.

The transfer of securities is governed by Article 8 of the UCC. In essence, the law provides for transfer of certificated securities by delivery and of uncertificated securities by registration. One fundamental general principle is the shelter rule: a purchaser acquires all the rights of the transferor, so that a subsequent transferee is sheltered by the lack of knowledge of her transferor. Without notice—on the face of the certificated security or in the initial transaction statement in the case of an uncertificated security—buyers of both certificated and uncertificated securities are entitled to take free of liens, defenses, restrictions, and adverse claims.

KEY TERMS

Authorized shares	p. 929	Liquidation preference	p. 930
Bond	p. 928	Nimble dividends	p. 935
Capital surplus	p. 930	Nonparticipating	p. 930
Certificated security	p. 939	No-par shares	p. 929
Class voting	p. 930	Outstanding stock	p. 929
Contingent voting rights	p. 930	Participating shares	p. 930
		Par value	p. 929
Coupon	p. 928	Payment date	p. 935
Cumulative dividends	p. 930	Plowback	p. 928
Debt security	p. 928	Record date	p. 935
Earned surplus	p. 930	Stated capital	p. 930
Equity securities	p. 928	Surplus	p. 930
"Good faith" rule	p. 933	"True value" rule	p. 933
Indemnity bond	p. 945	Uncertificated security	p. 939
Issued stock	p. 929	Watered stock	p. 933

SELF-TEST QUESTIONS

1. Corporate funds that come from earnings are called:
   (a) equity securities
   (b) depletion
   (c) debt securities
   (d) plowback
2. When a value is specified on a stock certificate it is said to be:
   (a) par value
   (b) no-par
   (c) an authorized share
   (d) none of the above
3. Common stockholders normally:
   (a) have the right to vote ratably
   (b) do not have the right to vote ratably
   (c) never have preemptive rights
   (d) hold all of the company's treasury shares
4. Preferred stock may be:
   (a) entitled to cumulative dividends
   (b) convertible
   (c) redeemable
   (d) all of the above
5. The shelter rule relates to:
   (a) distribution of dividends
   (b) preferred stock only
   (c) the transfer of securities
   (d) plowback

DEMONSTRATION PROBLEM

BCT Bookstores, Incorporated was formed in 1989 and ran a $100,000 deficit that year. In 1990 it had a net loss of $10,000 for an accumulated net deficit of $110,000. No dividends were declared in either year. In 1991 the company finally broke into the black, earning a net profit of $50,000. Was it legally allowed to pay a dividend? Why?

PROBLEMS

1. Ralph and Alice have decided to incorporate their sewer-cleaning business under the name R & A, Inc. Their plans call for the authorization and issuance of 5000 shares of par value stock. Ralph argues that par value must be set at the estimated market value of the stock, while Alice feels that par value is the equivalent of book value—that is, assets divided by the number of shares. Who is correct? Why?
2. In problem 1, Ralph feels that, if they have a choice, par value should be set as high as possible in order to bring more capital into the business, while Alice feels that the par value should be low to encourage investment. What do you recommend? Why?
3. Ralph and Alice (see problem 1) decide to issue participating preferred stock. What does this mean?
4. Ralph and Alice (see problem 1) are also considering the issuance of redeemable preferred stock. Assuming the stock pays a 10 percent dividend and interest rates later drop to 12 percent, would there be an advantage in having the redemption option? What is the status of preferred stock that has been redeemed?
5. Assume that Ralph and Alice (see problem 1), finding it difficult to sell stock in R & A, Inc., offer one bonus share for every share of common stock purchased at par value. Slick purchases 500 shares of stock with a $10 par value for $5,000 and receives 500 bonus shares of the $10 par value stock. Discuss the legal implications.
6. Assume that 4,500 of the originally authorized 5,000 shares of R & A, Inc. (see problem 1) have been issued at a par value of $10 and are outstanding. The company repurchases 400 shares from earned surplus and later sells these 400 shares, plus an additional 600 shares, to Slick for $9 per share. Discuss the implications.
7. Irma is a business consultant who has done some work for R & A, Inc. (see problem 1), although she has not yet been paid. Irma agrees to accept 500 shares of previously unissued $10 par common stock in payment for past services. The directors of R & A, acting in good faith, estimate the value of Irma's past service at $5,000. In fact—and this can be proven if the matter comes to trial—Irma's services were worth only $3,000. Discuss the legal implications.
8. In problem 7, assume that Irma also agrees to accept 500 shares in payment for future services. The directors, again acting in good faith, estimate the value of these services at $5,000, which is an accurate estimate. Discuss the legal implications.

ANSWERS TO SELF-TEST QUESTIONS

1. (d)   2. (a)   3. (a)   4. (d)   5. (c)

SUGGESTED ANSWER TO DEMONSTRATION PROBLEM

Under the majority rule it could not, since it had no earned surplus and an accumulated deficit of $60,000. Under the nimble dividend approach it could, however. It had a net profit over the last two-year period of $40,000, and from this sum dividends would have been payable.

CHAPTER

43

CHAPTER OVERVIEW
Powers of a Corporation
Rights of Shareholders
Duties and Powers of Directors and Officers
Liability of Directors and Officers

Corporate Powers and Management

*I*n this chapter we examine three broad themes that determine the manner in which a corporation is operated and governed:

1. The power of a corporation to act
2. The rights of shareholders
3. The duties, powers, and liability of officers and directors

In the next chapter we will continue discussion of officers' and directors' liability within the context of securities regulation and insider trading.

POWERS OF A CORPORATION

Two Types of Corporate Powers

Express Powers The corporation may exercise all powers expressly given it by statute and in the articles of incorporation. RMBCA Section 3.02 sets out a number of express powers, including: to sue and be sued in the corporate name; to purchase, use, and sell land and dispose of assets to the same extent a natural person can; to make contracts, borrow money, issue notes and bonds, lend money, invest funds, make donations to the public welfare, establish pension plans; and to join in partnerships, joint ventures, trusts, or other enterprises. The powers set out in this section need not be included in the articles of incorporation.

Implied Powers Corporate powers beyond those explicitly established are **implied powers.** For example, suppose BCT Bookstore's statement of purpose reads simply: "to operate a bookstore." All acts that are necessary or appropriate to running a bookstore are permissible: hiring employees, advertising special sales, leasing trucks. Could Ted, its vice president and general manager, authorize the expenditure of funds to pay for a Sunday afternoon lecturer on the perils of nuclear war or the adventures of a professional football player? Yes, if the lectures are relevant to current books, or serve to bring people into the store—they effect the corporation's purpose.

The Ultra Vires Doctrine

Literally "beyond the powers," the **ultra vires** doctrine holds that certain legal consequences attach to an attempt by a corporation to carry out acts that are outside its lawful powers. Ultra vires is not limited to illegal acts, although it encompasses actions barred by statute as well as by the corporate charter. Under the traditional approach, either the corporation or the other party could assert ultra vires as a defense when refusing to abide by a wholly executory contract. The ultra vires doctrine loses much of its significance when corporate powers are broadly stated in the articles. Furthermore, RMBCA Section 3.04 states that "the validity of corporate action may not be challenged on the ground that the corporation lacks or lacked power to act."

Nevertheless, ultra vires retains force in three circumstances: (1) shareholders may bring suits against the corporation to enjoin it from acting beyond its powers; (2) the corporation itself, through receivers, trustees, or shareholders, may sue incumbent or former officers or directors for causing the corporation

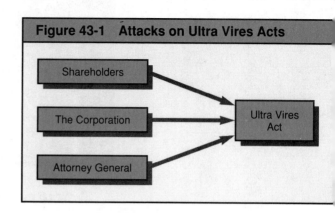

Figure 43-1   Attacks on Ultra Vires Acts

to act ultra vires; and (3) the state attorney general may assert the doctrine in a proceeding to dissolve the corporation or to enjoin it from transacting unauthorized business (see Figure 43-1). Suppose an incorporated luncheon club refuses to admit women as club members or guests. Could the ultra vires doctrine help heighten its consciousness? The next case shows how.

CROSS v. THE MIDTOWN CLUB, INC.
33 Conn.Sup. 150, 365 A.2d 1227 (1976)

STAPLETON, JUDGE. The following facts are admitted or undisputed: The plaintiff is a member in good standing of the defendant nonstock Connecticut corporation. Each of the individual defendants is a director of the corporation, and together the individual defendants constitute the entire board of directors. The certificate of incorporation sets forth that the sole purpose of the corporation is "to provide facilities for the serving of luncheon or other meals to members." Neither the certificate of incorporation nor the bylaws of the corporation contain any qualifications for membership, nor does either contain any restrictions on the luncheon guests members may bring to the club. The plaintiff sought to bring a female to lunch with him, and both he and his guest were refused seating at the luncheon facility. The plaintiff wrote twice to the president of the corporation to protest the action, but he received no reply to either letter. On three different occasions, the plaintiff submitted applications for membership on behalf of a different female, and only on the third of those occasions did the board process the application, which it then rejected. Shortly after both of the above occurrences, the board of directors conducted two separate pollings of its members, one by mail, the other by a special meeting held to vote on four alternative proposals to amending the bylaws of corporation concerning the admission of women members and guests. None of these proposed amendments to the bylaws received the required number of votes for adoption. Following that balloting, the plaintiff again wrote to the president of the corporation and asked that the directors stop interfering with his rights as a member to bring women guests to the luncheon facility and to propose women for membership. The president's reply was that "the existing bylaws, house rules and customs continue in effect, and therefore [the board] consider[s] the matter closed."

*   *   *

In addition to seeking a declaratory judgment which will inform him of his rights vis a vis the corporation and its directors, the plaintiff is also seeking injunctive relief, orders directing the admission of the plaintiff's candidate to membership and denying indemnity to the directors, money damages, and costs and expenses including reasonable attorney's fees. It should be noted at the outset that the plaintiff is not making a claim under either the federal or state civil rights or equal accommodations statutes, but that he is solely asserting his membership rights under the certificate of incorporation, the bylaws, and the statutes governing the regulation of this nonstock corporation. As such, this is a case of first impression in Connecticut.

*   *   *

Connecticut has codified the common-law right of a member to proceed against his corporation or its directors in the event of an ultra vires act. In fact, it has been done specifically under the Nonstock Corporation Act.

No powers were given to the defendant corporation in its certificate of incorporation, only a purpose, and as a result the only incidental powers which the defendant would have under the common law are those which are necessary to effect its purpose, that being to serve lunch to its members. Since the club was not formed for the purpose of having an exclusively male luncheon club, it cannot be considered necessary to its stated purpose for the club to have the implied power at common law to exclude women members.

Under the Connecticut Nonstock Corporation Act, the corporation could have set forth in its certificate of incorporation that its purpose was to engage in any lawful activity permitted that corporation. That was not done. Its corporate purposes were very narrowly stated to be solely for providing "facilities for the serving of luncheon or other meals to members." The certificate did not restrict the purpose to the serving of male members. Section 33-428 of the General Statutes provides that the corporate powers of a nonstock corporation are those set forth in the Nonstock Corporation Act, those specifically stated in the certificate of incorporation, neither of which includes the power to exclude women members, and the implied power to "exercise all legal powers necessary or convenient to effect any or all of the purposes stated in its certificate of incorporation. . . ."

We come, thus, to the nub of the controversy and the basic legal question raised by the facts in this case: is it necessary or convenient to the purpose for which this corporation was organized for it to exclude women members?

(continued on next page)

(continued)

CROSS v. THE MIDTOWN CLUB, INC.
33 Conn.Sup. 150, 365 A.2d 1227 (1976)

This court concludes that it is not. While a corporation might be organized for the narrower purpose of providing a luncheon club for men only, this one was not so organized. Its stated purpose is broader and this court cannot find that it is either necessary or convenient to that purpose for its membership to be restricted to men. It should be borne in mind that this club is one of the principal luncheon clubs for business and professional people in Stamford. It is a gathering place where a great many of the civic, business, and professional affairs of the Stamford community are discussed in an atmosphere of social intercourse. Given the scope of the entry of women today into the business and professional life of the community and the changing status of women before the law and in society, it would be anomalous indeed for this court to conclude that it is either necessary or convenient to the stated purpose for which it was organized for this club to exclude women as members or guests.

While the bylaws recognize the right of a member to bring guests to the club, the exclusion of women guests is nowhere authorized and would not appear to be any more necessary and convenient to the purpose of the club than the exclusion of women members. The bylaws at present contain no restrictions against female members or guests and even if they could be interpreted as authorizing those restrictions, they would be of no validity in light of the requirement of § 33-459(a) of the General Statutes, that the bylaws must be "reasonable [and] germane to the purposes of the corporation. . . ."

The court therefore concludes that the actions and policies of the defendants in excluding women as members and guests solely on the basis of sex is ultra vires and beyond the power of the corporation and its management under its certificate of incorporation and the Nonstock Corporation Act, and in derogation of the rights of the plaintiff as a member thereof. The plaintiff is entitled to a declaratory judgment to that effect and one may enter accordingly.

★   ★   ★

An ultra vires act is not necessarily criminal or tortious. However, every crime and tort is in some sense ultra vires because a corporation never has legal authority to commit crimes or torts. They raise special problems to which we now turn.

Criminal Acts

The early common law held that a corporation could not commit a crime because it did not have a mind and could not therefore have the requisite intent. Modern law is not so constricting. Criminal acts of its agents may be imputed to the corporation. Thus, if the board of directors specifically authorizes the company to carry out a criminal scheme, or the president instructs his employees to break a law for the benefit of the company, the corporation itself may be convicted. Of course, it is rare for people in a corporate setting to avow their criminal intentions, so in most cases courts determine the corporation's criminal liability by deciding whether an employee's crime was part of a job-related activity.

When corporations are found guilty of criminal conduct, as they occasionally are, a difficult question is how they can be punished. As long ago as 1910 Woodrow Wilson noted:

> You cannot punish corporations. Fines fall upon the wrong persons, more heavily upon the innocent than the guilty; as much upon those who knew nothing whatever of the transactions for which the fine is imposed as upon those who originated and carried them through—upon the shareholders and customers rather than upon the men who direct the policy of the business. If you dissolve the offending corporation, you throw great undertakings out of gear.

That a corporation is found guilty of criminal conduct does not excuse company officials who authorized or carried out the illegal act. They too can be prosecuted and sent to jail. Criminal provisions are being routinely added to the newer regulatory statutes, such as the Occupational Safety & Health Act, and the Toxic Substances Control Act—although prosecution depends mainly on where a particular administration wishes to spend its enforcement dollars. In recent years, as federal safety inspection of businesses has slackened, state prosecuting attorneys have become more active in filing criminal charges against management when employees are injured or die on the job. For instance, a trial court judge in Chicago sentenced a company president, plant manager, and foreman to twenty-five years in prison after they were convicted of murder following the death of a worker as a result of unsafe working conditions at a plant.

In certain cases, the criminal liability of an executive can be vicarious. The Supreme Court has affirmed the conviction of a chief executive who had no personal knowledge of a criminal violation by his company. [United States v. Park, 421 U.S. 658 (1975); see Chapter 3]

Tortious Acts

Corporations are vicariously liable for employees' and agents' torts carried out within the scope of employment. This is the rule of *respondeat superior* (see Chapter 38) and is well settled in every state. But unless they directly participated in the planning or carrying out of the torts, individual directors, officers, and shareholders are not personally liable for the acts of others within the corporations.

RIGHTS OF SHAREHOLDERS

General Management Functions

In the modern publicly held corporation, ownership and control are separated. The shareholders "own" the company through their ownership of its stock, but power to manage is vested in the directors. Typically, management and directors together own less than 3 percent of the outstanding stock of large corporations, and rarely do they own more than one-fifth. (The issue of separation and control is generally irrelevant to the closely held corporation.)

Shareholders do retain certain control functions. They elect the directors—although the spread of ownership and modern proxy rules permit a tiny fraction of shareholders to control the outcome of most elections; proxy fights are extremely difficult for insurgents to win. Shareholders also may adopt, amend, and repeal the corporation's bylaws; may adopt resolutions ratifying or refusing to ratify certain actions of the directors; and must vote on certain extraordinary matters, such as whether to amend the articles of incorporation, merge, or liquidate.

Meetings

In most states, the corporation must hold at least one meeting of shareholders each year. The board of directors or shareholders representing at least 10 percent of the stock may call a special shareholders' meeting at any time. Timely notice is required—not more than sixty days nor less than ten days before the meeting, under RMBCA Section 7.05. Shareholders may take actions without a meeting if every shareholder entitled to vote consents in writing to the action to be taken. This section is obviously useful to the closely held corporation and not to the giant public companies.

Right to Vote

Who Has the Right to Vote? A corporation—through its bylaws or by resolution of the board of directors—can set a "record date." Only the shareholders listed on the corporate records on that date receive notice of the next shareholders' meeting and have the right to vote. Every share is entitled to one vote unless the articles of incorporation state otherwise.

The one-share, one-vote principle is not followed outside the United States (see **Box 43-1**), and many U.S. companies have restructured their voting rights in an effort to repel corporate raiders. For instance, a company might decide to issue both voting and nonvoting shares, with the voting shares going to insiders who thereby control the corporation. In response to these new corporate structures the Securities and Exchange Commission (SEC) adopted a one-share, one-vote rule in 1988 that was designed to protect a shareholder's right to vote. In 1990, however, a federal appeals court overturned the SEC rule on the grounds that voting rights are governed by state law rather than by the Commission. [Business Roundtable v. SEC, 905 F.2d 406 (D.C. Cir. 1990)]

Quorum   When the articles of incorporation are silent, a shareholder quorum is a simple majority of the shares entitled to vote, whether represented in person or by proxy. Thus, if there are 1 million shares, 500,001 must be represented at the shareholder meeting. A simple majority of those shares is sufficient to carry any motion, so 250,001 shares is enough to control. The articles of incorporation may decree a different quorum but not less than one-third of the total shares.

Cumulative Voting   *Cumulative voting* means that a shareholder may distribute his total votes in any manner that he chooses—all for one candidate or several shares for different candidates. Some states permit this right unless the articles of incorporation deny it. Other states deny it unless the articles of incorporation permit it. Several states have constitutional provisions requiring cumulative voting for corporate directors.

Assume that Bob and Carol each own 2,000 shares, which they have decided to vote as a block, and Ted owns 6,000 shares. At their annual shareholder meeting they are to elect five directors. Without cumulative voting, Ted's slate of directors would win. Each of Ted's directors would receive 6,000 votes, while each of Bob and Carol's directors would receive

4,000. With cumulative voting, however, Bob and Carol could distribute their 20,000 votes (4,000 × directors) among the candidates to ensure represen-tation on the board. By placing 10,000 votes each on two of their candidates, they would be guaranteed two positions on the board. (The candidates from the two slates are not matched against each other on a one-to-one basis; instead, the five candidates with the highest number of votes are elected.) Various formula and computer programs are available to determine how votes should be allocated, but the principle underlying the calculations is this: cumulative voting is democratic in that it allows the shareholders who own 40 percent of the stock—Bob and Carol—to elect 40 percent of the board.

RMBCA Section 8.08 provides a safeguard against attempts to remove directors. Ordinarily, a director may be removed by a majority vote of the shareholders. Cumulative voting will not aid a given single director whose ouster is being sought because the majority obviously can win on a straight vote. So Section 8.08 provides: "If cumulative voting is authorized, a director may not be removed if the number of votes sufficient to elect him under cumulative voting is voted against his removal."

Voting Arrangements to Concentrate Power   Shareholders use three types of arrangements to concentrate their power: proxies, voting agreements, and voting trusts. Each of these is described as follows:

Proxies   A proxy is the representative of the shareholder. A proxy may be a person who stands in for the shareholder or may be a written instrument by which the shareholder casts his votes before the meeting. Proxies are usually solicited by and given to management, either to vote for proposals or people named in the proxy, or to vote however the proxy holder wishes. Through the proxy device, management of large companies can maintain control over the election of directors. Proxies must be signed by the shareholder and are valid for eleven months from the time they are received by the corporation, unless the proxy explicitly states otherwise. Management may use reasonable corporate funds to solicit proxies if corporate policy issues are involved, but misrepresentations in the solicitation can lead a court to nullify the proxies and to deny reimbursement for the solicitation cost. Proxies may be revoked, unless "coupled

LAW AND LIFE

BOX 43-1

Dangerous Place, Abroad

*[In 1990 a federal appeals court overturned the Securities and Exchange Commission's (SEC) rule that called for "one-share, one-vote," designed to protect a shareholder's right to vote. The court's decision is consistent with practices in other countries.—*AUTHORS' NOTE]

American shareholders fighting to get poison pills banned from the medicine-cupboard should be thankful they did not invest in Swiss Equities. A soon-to-be-released survey by the Investor Responsibility Research Centre (IRRC) reckons that Swiss shares give American investors less than a fifth of the "rights" available at home.

It is virtually impossible for non-Swiss shareholders to buy stock with full voting rights. Other countries treat both outsiders and insiders badly, too.

VOTING RIGHTS OUTSIDE UNITED STATES

In Holland, for instance, shareholders in Royal Dutch/Shell have so far been blocked from tabling a resolution calling on the company to withdraw from South Africa.

The survey ranks each country on four counts—disclosure of corporate information; voting rights (with the most points going to the country closest to one-share, one-vote); the ease with which shareholders can introduce resolutions; and shareholder notification of meetings and proxy votes. Scores were calculated using America as a standard 100%.

Like most subjective surveys, the IRRC's has its strong points and its weak. Awarding Britain only 60% for shareholder resolution procedures seems fair, because, even to be tabled, a resolution needs the backing of 5% of the shareholders, or 100 shareholders with £100 ($170)-worth of stock apiece; and the proposer(s) have to pay the costs. On the other hand, the IRRC seems unduly harsh on British shareholders' voting rights. True, a few British companies do have different classes of shares, but bad British managers and directors cannot swallow poison pills and the like.

The IRRC says that money managers may have a fiduciary duty to see that their foreign investments have voting clout. One American fund manager, Batterymarch, follows a policy of buying foreign stocks only if they have voting rights. Even when American managers have the right to vote, they often receive proxy voting forms late or not at all. When they do, some ignore them. For example, one fund with a strict non-South African policy at home does not apply the same rules to international investment.

Source: *The Economist*, April 29, 1989

---

with an interest" or "given as security." Only the last proxy given by a particular shareholder can be counted.

Proxy solicitations are regulated by the Securities and Exchange Commission. For instance, SEC rules require companies subject to the Securities Exchange Act of 1934 to file proxy materials with the SEC at least ten days before proxies are mailed to shareholders. Proxy statements must disclose all material facts and companies must use a proxy form on which shareholders can indicate whether they approve or disapprove of the proposals (see Figure 43-2).

Dissident groups opposed to management's position are entitled to solicit their own proxies at their own expense. The company must either furnish the dissidents with a list of all shareholders and addresses or mail the proxies at corporate expense. Since management usually prefers to keep the shareholder list private, dissidents can usually count on the corporation to foot the mailing bill.

Voting Agreements Unless they intend to commit fraud on a minority of stockholders, shareholders may agree in advance to vote in specific ways. These voting agreements, often called **shareholder agreements,** are generally legal. Shareholders may agree in advance, for example, to vote for specific directors; they can even agree to vote for the dissolution of the corporation in the event that a predetermined contingency occurs.

Voting Trusts To ensure that shareholder agreements will be honored, shareholders in most states

Figure 43–2   Sample Proxy Forms

UNIVERSAL
BUSINESS
CORPORATION   **Proxy**

270 Universal Center, Horizon, California 91770

This Proxy is Solicited on Behalf of the Board of Directors

The undersigned hereby appoints John Red, Mary Blue, and Lee White as Proxies, each with the power to appoint his or her substitute, and hereby authorizes them to represent and to vote, as designated below, all the shares of common stock of Universal Business held on record by the undersigned on October 23, 1980, at the annual meeting of shareholders to be held on December 20, 1980 or any adjournment thereof.

1. ELECTION OF DIRECTORS   FOR all nominees listed below   WITHHOLD AUTHORITY
(except as marked to the contrary below) ☐   to vote for all nominees listed below ☐

(INSTRUCTION: To withhold authority to vote for any individual nominee strike a line through the nominee's name in the list below.)

J. Allen, S. Brown, J. Doe, J. Green, G. Johansen, A. Jones, M. Roe, J. Smith and M. Stanton

2. PROPOSAL TO APPROVE THE APPOINTMENT OF DOLLAR AND CENTS as the independent public accountants of the corporation

☐ FOR   ☐ AGAINST   ☐ ABSTAIN

3. STOCKHOLDER PROPOSAL RELATING TO FORM AND CONTENT OF POST-MEETING REPORTS:

☐ FOR   ☐ AGAINST   ☐ ABSTAIN

4. In their discretion, the Proxies are authorized to vote upon such other business as may properly come before the meeting.

This proxy when properly executed will be voted in the manner directed herein by the undersigned stockholder. If no direction is made, this proxy will be voted for Proposals 1, 2 and 3.

Please sign exactly as name appears below. When shares are held by joint tenants, both should sign. When signing as attorney, as executor, administrator, trustee or guardian, please give full title as such. If a corporation, please sign in full corporate name by President or other authorized officer. If a partnership, please sign in partnership name by authorized person.

DATED: _____, 1984

_____
Signature

PLEASE MARK, SIGN, DATE AND RETURN THE PROXY CARD PROMPTLY USING THE ENCLOSED ENVELOPE.

_____
Signature if held jointly

Source: *Federal Register*, November 29, 1979

can create a **voting trust.** By this device, voting shares are given to voting trustees, who are empowered to vote the shares in accordance with the objectives set out in the trust agreement. RMBCA Section 7.30 limits the duration of voting trusts to ten years. The voting trust is normally irrevocable and the shareholders' stock certificates are physically transferred to the voting trustees for the duration of the trust. The voting trust agreement must be on file at the corporation, open for inspection by any shareholder.

Inspection of Books and Records

Shareholders are legally entitled to inspect a corporation's records. These include the articles of incorporation, bylaws and corporate resolutions. As a general rule, shareholders who want certain records (such as minutes of a board of directors' meeting or accounting records) must also have a "proper purpose," such as to determine the propriety of the company's dividend policy or to ascertain the company's true financial worth. *Improper* purposes include uncovering trade secrets for sale to a competitor or compilation of mailing lists for personal business purposes. A shareholder's motivation is an important factor in determining whether the purpose is proper, as the following case illustrates.

**PILLSBURY v.
HONEYWELL**
291 Minn. 322, 191
N.W.2d 406 (1971)

KELLY, JUSTICE. Petitioner appeals from an order and judgment of the district court denying all relief prayed for in a petition for writs of mandamus to compel respondent, Honeywell, Inc., (Honeywell) to produce its original shareholder ledger, current shareholder ledger, and all corporate records dealing with weapons and munitions manufacture. We must affirm.

*   *   *

Petitioner attended a meeting on July 3, 1969, of a group involved in what was known as the "Honeywell Project." Participants in the project believed that American involvement in Vietnam was wrong, that a substantial portion of Honeywell's production consisted of munitions used in that war, and that Honeywell should stop this production of munitions. Petitioner had long opposed the Vietnam war, but it was at the July 3rd meeting that he first learned of Honeywell's involvement. He was shocked at the knowledge that Honeywell had a large government contract to produce anti-personnel fragmentation bombs. Upset because of knowledge that such bombs were produced in his own community by a company which he had known and respected, petitioner determined to stop Honeywell's munitions production.

On July 14, 1969, petitioner ordered his fiscal agent to purchase 100 shares of Honeywell. He admits that the sole purpose of the purchase was to give himself a voice in Honeywell's affairs so he could persuade Honeywell to cease producing munitions. Apparently not aware of that purpose, petitioner's agent registered the stock in the name of a Pillsbury family nominee— Quad & Co. Upon discovering the nature of the registration, petitioner bought one share of Honeywell in his own name on August 11, 1969. In his deposition testimony petitioner made clear the reason for his purchase of Honeywell's shares:

"Q. . . . [D]o I understand that you requested Mr. Lacey to buy these 100 shares of Honeywell in order to follow up on the desire you had to bring to Honeywell management and to stockholders these theses that you have told us about here today?
"A. Yes. That was my motivation."

The "theses" referred to are petitioner's beliefs concerning the propriety of producing munitions for the Vietnam war.

*   *   *

(continued on next page)

(continued)

PILLSBURY v. HONEYWELL
291 Minn. 322, 191 N.W.2d 406 (1971)

Prior to the instigation of this suit, petitioner submitted two formal demands to Honeywell requesting that it produce its original shareholder ledger, current shareholder ledger, and all corporate records dealing with weapons and munitions manufacture. Honeywell refused.

* * *

The act of inspecting a corporation's shareholder ledger and business records must be viewed in its proper perspective. In terms of the corporate norm, inspection is merely the act of the concerned owner checking on what is in part his property. In the context of the large firm, inspection can be more akin to a weapon in corporate warfare. The effectiveness of the weapon is considerable:

> Considering the huge size of many modern corporations and the necessarily complicated nature of their bookkeeping, it is plain that to permit their thousands of stockholders to roam at will through their records would render impossible not only any attempt to keep their records efficiently, but the proper carrying on of their business. Cooke v. Outland, 144 S.E.2d 835, 842 (1965).

Because the power to inspect may be the power to destroy, it is important that only those with a bona fide interest in the corporation enjoy that power.

* * *

Petitioner had utterly no interest in the affairs of Honeywell before he learned of Honeywell's production of fragmentation bombs. Immediately after obtaining this knowledge, he purchased stock in Honeywell for the sole purpose of asserting ownership privileges in an effort to force Honeywell to cease such production. We agree with the court in Chas. A. Day & Co. v. Booth, 447, 123 A. 557, 558 (1924) that "where it is shown that such stockholding is only colorable, or solely for the purpose of maintaining proceedings of this kind, [we] fail to see how the petitioner can be said to be a 'person interested,' entitled as of right to inspect." But for his opposition to Honeywell's policy, petitioner probably would not have bought Honeywell stock, would not be interested in Honeywell's profits and would not desire to communicate with Honeywell's shareholders. His avowed purpose in buying Honeywell stock was to place himself in a position to try to impress his opinions favoring a reordering of priorities upon Honeywell management and its other shareholders. Such a motivation can hardly be deemed a proper purpose germane to his economic interest as a shareholder.

The fact that petitioner alleged a proper purpose in his petition will not necessarily compel a right to inspection. "A mere statement in a petition alleging a proper purpose is not sufficient. The facts in each case may be examined." Sawers v. American Phenolic Corp., 89 N.E.2d 374, 379 (1949). Neither is inspection mandated by the recitation of proper purpose in petitioner's testimony. Conversely, a company cannot defeat inspection by merely alleging an improper purpose. From the deposition, the trial court concluded that petitioner had already formed strong opinions on the immorality and the social and economic wastefulness of war long before he bought stock in Honeywell. His sole motivation was to change Honeywell's course of business because that course was incompatible with his political views. If unsuccessful, petitioner indicated that he would sell the Honeywell stock.

We do not mean to imply that a shareholder with a bona fide investment interest could not bring this suit if motivated by concern with the long- or short-term economic effects on Honeywell resulting from the production of war munitions. Similarly, this suit might be appropriate when a shareholder has a bona fide concern about the adverse effects of abstention from profitable war contracts on his investment in Honeywell.

★   ★   ★

The order of the trial court denying the writ of mandamus is affirmed.

Preemptive Rights

Assume that BCT Bookstore has outstanding 5,000 shares with par value of $10 and that Carol owns 1,000. At the annual meeting, the shareholders decide to issue an additional 1,000 shares at par and to sell them to Alice. Carol vehemently objects because her percentage of ownership will decline. She goes to court seeking an injunction against sale or, in the alternative, an order permitting her to purchase 200 of the shares (she currently has 20 percent of the total). How should the court rule?

The answer depends on the statutory provision dealing with **preemptive rights**—that is, the right of a shareholder to be protected from dilution of her percentage of ownership. In some states, shareholders have no preemptive rights unless expressly declared in the articles of incorporation, while other states give shareholders a preemptive right unless the articles of incorporation deny it. Preemptive rights were once strongly favored, but they are increasingly disappearing, especially in large public companies.

Derivative Actions

Suppose Carol discovers that Ted has been receiving kickbacks from publishers and has been splitting the proceeds with Bob. When at a directors' meeting Carol demands that the corporation file suit to recover the sums they pocketed, Bob and Ted outvote her. Carol has another remedy. She can file a **derivative action** against them. A derivative lawsuit is one brought on behalf of the corporation by a shareholder when the directors refuse to act. Although the corporation is named as a defendant in the suit, the corporation itself is the so-called real party in interest—the party entitled to recover if the plaintiff wins.

While derivative actions are subject to abuse by plaintiffs' attorneys seeking settlements that pay their fees, safeguards have been built into the law. At least ninety days before starting a derivative action, for instance, shareholders must demand in writing that the corporation take action. Shareholders may not commence derivative actions unless they were shareholders at the time of the wrongful act. And derivative actions will be dismissed if independent directors decide that the proceeding is not in the best interests of the corporation. (An independent director is a person who has no interest in the disputed transaction.)

DUTIES AND POWERS OF DIRECTORS AND OFFICERS

General Management Responsibility of the Directors

Directors derive their power to manage the corporation from the statute. RMBCA Section 8.01 states that "all corporate powers shall be exercised by or under the authority of, and the business and affairs of the corporation managed under the direction of, its board of directors." A director is a fiduciary, and, as the RMBCA puts it, must perform his duties "in good faith, with the care an ordinarily prudent person in a like position would exercise under similar circumstances." (Section 8.30.) Among the director's responsibilities: determining the mix of products and services to be offered, wages of employees and compensation of executives, prices to be charged, dividends; selection and removal of officers; delegation of operating authority to the managers; and supervising the company as a whole.

Delegation to Committees   Under RMBCA Section 8.25, the board of directors, by majority vote, may delegate its powers to various committees. This authority is limited to some degree. For example, only the full board can determine dividends, approve a merger, and amend the by-laws. The delegation of authority to a committee does not, by itself, relieve a director from the duty to exercise due care.

Delegation to Officers   The directors may delegate to officers the day-to-day authority to execute the policies established by the board (see Figure 43-3). Normally, the president is the chief executive officer to whom all other officers and employees report, but sometimes the CEO is the chairman of the board.

Number and Election of Directors

RMBCA Section 8.03 provides simply that there be one or more directors, the precise number to be fixed in the articles of incorporation or bylaws. The initial members of the board hold office until the first annual meeting and until their successors are qualified. (They are permitted to succeed themselves.) Directors are chosen to serve one-year terms, and must be elected or reelected by the shareholders annually, unless there are nine or more directors. In that case, if the articles of incorporation so provide, the board may be divided into two or three roughly equal classes and their terms staggered, so that the second class is elected at the second annual meeting and the third at the third annual meeting.

Directors' Qualifications and Characteristics

The statutes do not catalog qualifications that directors are expected to possess. In most states directors need not be residents of the state or shareholders of the corporation unless required by the articles of incorporation or bylaws, which may also set down more precise qualifications if desired.

Until the 1970s, directors tended to be a homogenous lot: white male businessmen or lawyers. Political change—rising consumer, environmental, and public interest consciousness—and embarrassment stemming from disclosures made in the wake of SEC

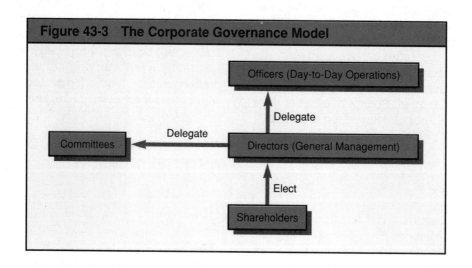

Figure 43-3   The Corporate Governance Model

Officers (Day-to-Day Operations)

Delegate

Committees   ← Delegate —   Directors (General Management)

Elect

Shareholders

investigations growing out of Watergate, prompted companies to diversify their boardrooms. Members of minority groups are being appointed in increasing numbers, although their proportion to the total is still small. Independent outside directors are becoming a potent force on corporate boards. A 1978 New York Stock Exchange survey of 993 corporate boards revealed that 824, or 83 percent, had a majority of outside directors, and the percentage has been growing.

Removal of Directors and Officers

In 1978, one week before he was scheduled to unveil the 1979 Mustang to trade journalists in person, Lee Iacocca, president of the Ford Motor Company, was summarily fired by unanimous vote of the board of directors—although his departure was billed as a "resignation." Iacocca was reported to have asked company chairman Henry Ford, "What did I do wrong?" To which Ford was supposed to have replied: "I just don't like you" (*Michigan Daily*, July 15, 1978). The story raises the question: May a corporate officer—or director, for that matter—be fired without cause?

Yes. Many state statutes expressly permit the board to fire an officer with or without cause. However, removal does not defeat an officer's rights under an employment contract. Shareholders may remove directors with or without cause at any meeting called for the purpose. A majority of the shares entitled to vote, not a majority of the shares represented at the meeting, are required for removal.

Meetings

Directors must meet, but the statutes themselves rarely prescribe how frequently. More often rules prescribing time and place are set out in the bylaws, which may permit members to participate in any meeting by conference telephone. In practice, the frequency of board meetings ranges, according to the 1981 survey of Fortune 500 companies, from three to seventeen per year.

The board or committees of the board may take action without meeting if all members of the board or committee consent in writing. A majority of the members of the board constitutes a quorum, unless the bylaws or articles of incorporation specify a larger number. Likewise, a majority present at the meeting is sufficient to carry any motion, unless the articles or bylaws specify a larger number.

Compensation

Traditionally, directors were supposed to serve without pay, as shareholder representatives. The modern practice permits the board to set its own pay, unless otherwise fixed in the articles of incorporation. A 1990 survey by the executive search firm Spencer Stuart of 100 large U.S. corporations showed that the average total annual compensation of outside directors was $45,650. Directors' compensation has risen sharply in recent years. One of the factors that accounts for this rise is the marked increase in legal risk to the director. To that topic we now turn.

LIABILITY OF DIRECTORS AND OFFICERS

Nature of the Problem

Not so long ago, boards of directors of large companies were quiescent bodies, virtual "rubber stamps" for their friends among management who put them there. By the late 1970s, with the general increase in the climate of litigiousness, one out of every nine companies on the Fortune list saw its directors or officers hit with claims for violation of their legal responsibilities (*Business Insurance*, 1979, p. 18). Serving as a director or officer was never free of business risks. Today the task is fraught with legal risk as well.

Two broad categories of obligations apply to both directors and officers. One is a *duty of loyalty*, the other the *duty of care*.

Duty of Loyalty

As a fiduciary of the corporation, the director, as well as officers and majority shareholders, owes her primary loyalty to the corporation and its stockholders. When there is a conflict between her personal interest and the interest of the corporation, she is legally bound to put the corporation's interest above her own.

Two situations commonly arise implicating the director's or officer's duty of loyalty: (1) contracts with the corporation; and (2) corporate opportunity (see Figure 43-4).

Contracts with the Corporation   The law does not bar a director from contracting with the corporation she serves. However, unless the contract or transaction is "fair to the corporation," RMBCA Section 8.61 imposes on her a stringent duty of disclosure. In the absence of a fair transaction, a contract between the corporation and one of its directors is voidable, unless the director has made full disclosure of her personal relationship or interest in the contract and disinterested board members or shareholders approve the transaction.

Corporate Opportunity   Whenever a director or officer learns of an opportunity to engage in a variety of activities or transactions that might be beneficial to the corporation, her first obligation is to present the opportunity to the corporation. The rule encompasses the chance of acquiring another corpora-

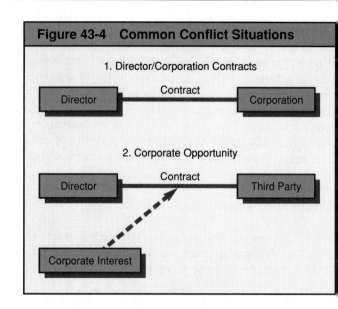

Figure 43-4   Common Conflict Situations

1. Director/Corporation Contracts

Director —— Contract —— Corporation

2. Corporate Opportunity

Director —— Contract —— Third Party

Corporate Interest

tion, purchasing property, and licensing or marketing patents or products. Whether a particular opportunity is a *corporate* opportunity can be a delicate question. The next case shows the kind of analysis that is required.

FARBER v. SERVAN LAND COMPANY, INC.
393 F.Supp. 633 (S.D. Fla. 1974)

ROETTGER, DISTRICT JUDGE.

[A minority shareholder brought suit against certain directors and majority shareholders alleging that they breached their fiduciary duty by purchasing real estate adjacent to a golf course owned by the corporation. The golf course and the adjoining acreage were later sold as a package to outside investors.]

★   ★   ★

Both as directors and majority stockholders of Servan Land Company, defendants Seriani and Savin stood in a fiduciary relationship to the corporation and to the minority shareholders as beneficiaries and by virtue of this position, defendants have the burden of proving fairness and good faith in their dealings with the corporation. As a fiduciary, an officer, director or dominant shareholder cannot use his power for his personal advantage to the detriment of the stockholders.

This court in no way takes lightly the principle that a director has an obligation to his corporation of "absolute and most scrupulous good faith." It would be easy to move from such a pious pronouncement to entering a decree in favor of plaintiff but sitting as a court of equity, this court cannot do so.

Plaintiff invokes the court's equitable powers by seeking restitution and an accounting to remedy the claimed breach of fiduciary duty occasioned by defendants' appropriation of a corporate opportunity and wrongful allocation of purchase price. Plaintiff urges that Perlman v. Feldman, 219 F.2d 173 (2nd Cir. 1955) compels a decision in his favor so that the profit personally enjoyed by defendants Seriani and Savin on the sale of the 160 acres adjacent to the corporate property be considered a corporate asset and distributed among the shareholders.

In Perlman v. Feldman the majority stockholders, in selling their controlling interest in the corporation had also sold a corporate asset—the ability to control the product. The consideration received for the sale of corporate stock included the value of the stockholders' controlling interest in the corporation which the court of appeals found to be a corporate asset. The court of appeals, in approving the intervention of equity, found that the sale of stock for excessive consideration directly harmed the corporate interests and constituted a breach of fiduciary duty.

Although this court has determined that defendants Seriani and Savin should have offered the 160 acres to the corporation before purchasing the property for themselves, the purchase of this property worked to the distinct advantage of the corporation and not to its detriment because it enhanced the value of the major corporate asset—the golf course. In fact, unlike *Perlman* where the sale of the stock for excessive consideration harmed the corporation, Servan Land Company and its stockholders, Farber included, profited from the joint sales of the 160 acres and the golf course, not only because of the increased value of the golf course but because of the defendants' overvaluation of the corporate land to the detriment of the defendants' individual land.

This case is in marked contrast to other Florida cases where courts have seen fit to invoke equitable powers and impress a trust on individual property. In Newspaper Journal Corp. v. Gore, 2 So.2d 741 (1941) the corporate officer purchased land of the "utmost importance" to the corporation—the very land on which the property of the corporation was situated—and thereafter rented the property back to the corporation at an increased rental! Not only did the increased rental fee charged by the individual corporate officers to the corporation directly harm the corporation, but the acquisition of both tracts of land by the corporation, which could have financed the purchases, would have been valuable in carrying out the business of the corporation.

Where there is a duty on the part of officers to acquire property for the corporation and in violation of the obligation they purchase it individually, as in *Gore Newspapers*, Florida law is established that the individuals cannot retain the benefit of their self-serving actions. Similarly, in Pan American Trading & Trapping v. Crown Paint, 99 So.2d 705 (Fla.1957) although the land might not have been of the utmost importance to the corporation's welfare as in *Gore* the evidence established that the land was to be acquired as a site for expansion of corporate operations, a valid and significant corporate purpose of the corporation. The equitable powers of the court were properly

(continued on next page)

(continued)

FARBER v. SERVAN LAND COMPANY, INC.
393 F.Supp. 633 (S.D. Fla. 1974)

invoked to impress a trust upon the property purchased by the individual officer in his own name instead of for the corporation.

Not only did the corporation actually profit from the personal actions of Seriani and Savin, but the 160 acres did not constitute a corporate opportunity nor was its acquisition adverse to the interests of the corporation. The mere fact that the land was adjacent to the corporate land in itself does not support a conclusion that therefore the acreage was a corporate opportunity. The property had no substantial relation to the corporation's primary purpose of operating a golf course and the individual purpose was not antagonistic to any significant corporate purpose and thus the facts do not fall within the general proposition that an officer of a corporation cannot acquire title to or an interest in property prejudicial to the corporation.

Plaintiff seeks for himself and, however involuntarily, for the other stockholders the results of Seriani and Savin's risk in purchasing the property. The argument that a corporation does not have sufficient funds to undertake the venture will not normally absolve fiduciaries of accountability for profiting from a corporate opportunity. In Irving Trust Company v. Deutsch, 73 F.2d 121 (2nd Cir. 1934) the court held that directors could not take over a corporate contract for the purchase of patent rights essential to a corporate purpose for their own profit by a claim of corporate financial inability and thereby divert corporate gains from the transaction. However, not only might Servan Land Company have been financially unable to purchase the 160 acres, but less than a year before the purchase by Seriani and Savin, the directors and stockholders declined to pursue the possibility of purchasing this very same land. . . .

The court concludes the 160 acres was not a corporate opportunity requiring that defendants must account for their profit on the risk they, but not the corporation eleven months earlier, were willing to take.

In addition, the court concludes that defendants Seriani and Savin have satisfactorily sustained the burden of explaining this transaction and establishing its propriety because of the benefit to the corporation by their holding the abutting property and being willing to aggregate it with the corporate property at the time of sale. It must be noted that the sale of the corporate property had been contemplated by the stockholders for some years.

*   *   *

Judgment is hereby entered for defendants.

When a director serves on more than one board, the problem of corporate opportunity becomes even more complex, because he may be caught in a situation of conflicting loyalties. Moreover, multiple board memberships pose another serious problem. A major study of overlapping memberships, published in 1978 following an investigation by the staff of the Senate Governmental Affairs Subcommitee on Reports, Accounting, and Management, reported that among 130 of the nation's largest companies, there were 530 direct and 12,193 indirect interlocking directors (*The Economist*, 1978, p. 129). The thirteen largest companies had 240 direct and 5,547 indirect interlocks. A **direct interlock** occurs when one person sits on the boards of two different companies; an **indirect interlock,** when directors of two different companies serve jointly on the board of a third company. The Clayton Act prohibits interlocking directorates between direct competitors. No violations of that law were uncovered in the 1978 study, but the potential for conflict of loyalties remains. For example, Citicorp, the bank holding company, had eighteen indirect links on twelve boards with its arch-rival Chase Manhattan. Citicorp also had thirty indirect ties on nineteen boards to J. P. Morgan (parent company of J. P. Morgan Trust Co.), twenty-six links on fifteen boards with Manufacturers Hanover, twenty-four on sixteen boards with Chemical New York, and fourteen on nine boards with Bankers Trust.

Duty of Care

The second major aspect of the director's responsibility is that of due care. RMBCA Section 8.30 calls on the director to perform his duties "with the care an ordinarily prudent person in a like position would exercise under similar circumstances." An "ordinarily prudent person" means one who directs his intelligence in a thoughtful way to the task at hand. The director is not held to the higher standard required of a specialist (finance, marketing) unless he is one. A director of a small, closely held corporation will not necessarily be held to the same standard as a director who is given a staff by a large, complex, diversified company. The standard of care is that which an ordinarily prudent person would use who is in "a like position" to the director in question. Moreover, the standard is not an objective, timeless one for all people in the same position. It also depends on the circumstances: a fast-moving situation calling for a snap decision will be treated differently later, if there are recriminations because it was the wrong decision, than a situation in which time was not of the essence.

What of the care itself? What kind of care would an ordinarily prudent person in *any* situation, regardless of the circumstances, be obligated to give? At a minimum, the director must *pay attention.* He must attend meetings, receive and digest information adequate to inform him about matters requiring board action, and monitor the performance of those to whom he has delegated the task of operating the corporation. Of course, documents can be misleading, reports can be slanted, information coming from self-interested management can be distorted. To what heights must suspicion be raised? To what degree must the director assume the role of Sherlock Holmes? RMBCA Section 8.30 forgives directors the necessity of playing detective whenever information, including financial data, is received in an apparently reliable manner from corporate officers or employees, or from experts such as attorneys and public accountants.

A director does not spend all his time on corporate affairs, is not omnipotent, and must be permitted to rely on the word of others. Nor can directors be infallible in making decisions. Managers work in a business environment, in which risk is a substantial factor. No decision, no matter how rigorously arrived at, is guaranteed. Accordingly, courts will not second-guess decisions made on the basis of good faith judgment and due care. This is the so-called **business judgment rule.** As described by the Delaware Supreme Court:

> The business judgment rule is an acknowledgment of the managerial prerogatives of Delaware directors. . . . It is a presumption that in making a business decision the directors of a corporation acted on an informed basis, in good faith and in the honest belief that the action taken was in the best interests of the company. [Aronson v. Lewis 473 A.2d 805, 812 (Del. 1984)]

A shareholder, as a prerequisite to filing a derivative action, must demand that the board of directors take action. If the board refuses, is its decision protected by the business judgment rule? This question—which goes to the heart of managerial power—is addressed in the following case.

SPIEGEL v. BUNTROCK

571 A.2d 767
(Del.Supr. 1990)

HOLLAND, JUSTICE:

This is an appeal from an order of the Court of Chancery dismissing a derivative action filed by the plaintiff-appellant, Ted Spiegel ("Spiegel"), a shareholder of Waste Management, Inc. ("Waste Management"). In his complaint, Spiegel alleged that Dean L. Buntrock ("Buntrock"), Chairman of the Board of Directors and Chief Executive Officer of Waste Management; Jerry E. Dempsey ("Dempsey"), Vice Chairman; Peter H. Huizenga ("Huizenga"), Vice President and Secretary; and James E. Koenig ("Koenig"), Staff Vice President (collectively "management defendants"), improperly acquired stock in ChemLawn Corporation ("ChemLawn"), based upon inside information, during the two years immediately preceding Waste Management's tender offer for ChemLawn. Spiegel sought to compel the management defendants to account to Waste Management for the personal profits they made upon the sale of their ChemLawn stock.

[Following a demand by Spiegel that the corporation take action, the Waste Management board of directors established a special committee of outside directors to investigate the matter. The committee concluded that it was not in the company's best interests to pursue the derivative action.]

*   *   *

A basic principle of the General Corportion Law of the State of Delaware is that directors, rather than shareholders, manage the business and affairs of the corporation. "The exercise of this managerial power is tempered by fundamental fiduciary obligations owed by the directors to the corporation and its shareholders." *Kaplan v. Peat, Marwick, Mitchell & Co.*, 540 A.2d at 729. The decision to bring a lawsuit or to refrain from litigating a claim on behalf of a corporation is a decision concerning the management of the corporation. Consequently, such decisions are part of the responsibility of the board of directors.

Nevertheless, a shareholder may file a derivative action to redress an alleged harm to the corporation. The nature of the derivative action is twofold.

> First, it is the equivalent of a suit by the shareholders to compel the corporation to sue. Second, it is a suit by the corporation, asserted by the shareholders on its behalf, against those liable to it.

In essence, it is a challenge to a board of directors' managerial power. Thus, by its very nature, "the derivative action impinges on the managerial freedom of directors." In fact, the United States Supreme Court has noted that the shareholder derivative action "could, if unrestrained, undermine the basic principle of corporate governance that the decisions of a corporation—including the decision to initiate litigation—should be made by the board of directors or the majority of shareholders." *Daily Income Fund, Inc. v. Fox*, 464 U.S. 523, 531 (1984).

"Because the shareholders' ability to institute an action on behalf of the corporation inherently impinges upon the directors' power to manage the affairs of the corporation the law imposes certain prerequisites on a stockholder's right to sue derivatively." *Kaplan v. Peat, Marwick, Mitchell & Co.*, 540 A.2d at 730. Chancery Court Rule 23.1 requires that shareholders seeking to assert a claim on behalf of the corporation must first exhaust intracorporate remedies by making a demand on the directors to obtain the action desired, or to plead with particularity why demand is excused.

The purpose of the pre-suit demand is to assure that the stockholder affords the corporation the opportunity to address an alleged wrong without litigation, to decide whether to invest the resources of the corporation in litigation, and to control any litigation which does occur. "[B]y promoting this form of alternate dispute resolution, rather than immediate recourse to litigation, the demand requirement is a recognition of the fundamental precept that directors manage the business and affairs of corporations." *Aronson v. Lewis*, 473 A.2d at 812.

Since a conscious decision by a board of directors to refrain from acting may be a valid exercise of business judgment, "where demand on a board had been made and refused, [courts] apply the business judgment rule in reviewing the board's refusal to act pursuant to a stockholder's demand" to file a lawsuit. *Id.* at 813. The business judgment rule is a presumption that in making a business decision, not involving self-interest, the directors of a corporation acted on an informed basis, in good faith and in the honest belief that the action taken was in the best interests of the company. "The burden is on the party challenging the decision to establish facts rebutting th[is] presumption." *Aronson v. Lewis*, 473 A.2d at 812. Thus, the business judgment rule operates as a judicial acknowledgement of a board of directors' managerial perogatives.

* * *

In this case, the Court of Chancery found there was no material dispute that the Board, through its Committee, had "function[ed] effectively . . . in a way that fully satisfies the prerequisites for the application of the business judgment rule." Consequently, the Court of Chancery concluded that, in accordance with the business judgment expressed by the Board, through its Committee, Spiegel's derivative action had to be dismissed. We agree.

In a battle for control of a corporation, directors (especially "inside" management directors) have an inherent self-interest in preserving their positions, which can lead them to block mergers that the shareholders desire. As a result Delaware courts have modified the usual business judgment presumption in this situation. In *Unocal Corp.* v. *Mesa Petroleum*, 493 A.2d 946 (Del. 1985), for instance, the court held that directors who adopt a defensive mechanism "must show that they had reasonable grounds for believing that a danger to corporate policy and effectiveness existed. . . . [T]hey satisfy that burden 'by showing good faith and reasonable investigation. . . .' "

In a widely-publicized case, the Delaware Supreme Court held that the board of Time, Inc. met the *Unocal* test. The board reasonably concluded that a tender offer by Paramount constituted a threat and acted reasonably in rejecting Paramount's offer and in merging with Warner Communications. [Paramount Communications, Inc. v. Time, Inc., 571 A.2d 1140 (1989)]

Other Constituency Statutes

Until the 1980s, the law in all the states imposed on corporate directors the obligation to advance shareholders' economic interests—to insure the long-term profitability of the corporation. Other groups—employees, local communities and neighbors, customers, suppliers, and creditors—took a back seat to this primary responsibility of directors. Of course, directors could consider the welfare of these other groups if in so doing they promoted the interests of shareholders. But directors were not legally permitted to favor the interests of others over shareholders. Thus in *Revlon Inc.* v. *MacAndrews & Forbes Holdings, Inc.,* 506 A.2d 173 (Del. 1986), the Delaware Supreme Court held that Revlon's directors had breached their fiduciary duty to the company's shareholders by attempting to side with noteholders during a hostile takeover. The court noted the prevailing rule that directors may consider the interests of other groups, as long as "there are rationally related benefits accruing to the stockholders." But when a company is about to be taken over, the object must be to sell it to the highest bidder. Then, said the court, "concern for nonstockholder interests is inappropriate."

With the wave of corporate takeovers that dotted the business landscape during the 1980s, the legislatures of 25 states, beginning with Pennsylvania in 1983, enacted laws to give directors legal authority to take account of interests other than those of shareholders in deciding how to defend against hostile mergers and acquisitions. These laws are known as **other constituency statutes,** because they permit (and in one state, Connecticut, even require) directors to take account of the interests of other constituencies of corporations.

Although the other constituency statutes are not identically worded, they are all designed to release directors from their formal legal obligation to keep paramount the interests of shareholders. The Pennsylvania and Indiana statutes make this clear; the statutes in other states are worded a bit more ambiguously, but the intent of the legislatures in enacting these laws seems clear: directors may give voice to employees worried about the loss of jobs or to communities worried about the possibility that an out-of-state acquiring company may close down a local factory to the detriment of the local economy. So broadly worded are these laws that although the motive for enacting them was to give directors a weapon in fighting hostile tender offers, in 19 of the states the principle applies to any decision by a board of directors. So, for example, it is possible that a board might legally decide to give a large charitable grant to a local community—a grant so large that it would materially decrease an annual dividend, contrary to the general rule that at some point the interests of shareholders in dividends clearly outweighs the board's power to spend corporate profits on "good works."

Because these statutes are relatively new, the courts so far have had little chance to interpret them in any depth. Critics have attacked the other constituency statutes on two major grounds: first, they substitute a clear principle of conduct for an amorphous one, because they give no guidance on how directors are supposed to weigh the interests of a corporation's various constituencies. Second, they make it more difficult for shareholders to monitor the performance of a company's board; measuring decisions against the single goal of profit maximization is far easier than against the subjective goal of "balancing" a host of competing interests. Nevertheless, since 25 states now have other constituency statutes, it is only reasonable to expect that the traditional doctrine holding shareholder interests paramount will begin to give way, as the shareholders challenge new decisions by directors that favor communities, employees, and others with an important stake in the welfare of the corporations with which they deal.

Liability Prevention and Insurance

How can a director avoid liability? Of course she can never avoid the hazard of defending a lawsuit, for in the wake of any large corporate difficulty—from a thwarted takeover bid to a bankruptcy—some group of shareholders will surely sue. But the director can immunize herself ultimately by carrying out her duties of loyalty and care. In practice, this often means that she should be prepared to document the reasonableness of her reliance on information from all sources considered. Second, if the director dissents from action that she considers mistaken or unlawful she should insure that her negative vote is recorded. Silence is construed as assent to any proposition before the board, and assent to a woefully mistaken action can be the basis for staggering liability.

Beyond these preventive techniques, another measure of protection is **indemnification** (reimbursement). In most states, the corporation *may* agree under certain circumstances to indemnify directors, officers, and employees for expenses resulting from litigation when they are made party to suits involving the corporation. In third-party actions (those brought by outsiders), the corporation may reimburse the director, officer, or employee for all expenses (including attorneys' fees), judgments, fines, and settlement amounts. In derivative actions, the corporation's power to indemnify is more limited. For example, reimbursement for litigation expenses of directors adjudged liable for negligence or misconduct is allowed only if the court approves. In both third-party and derivative actions, the corporation *must* provide indemnification expenses when the defense is successful.

Whether or not they have the power to indemnify, corporations may purchase liability insurance for directors, officers, and employees. But insurance policies do not cover every act. Most exclude "willful negligence" and criminal conduct in which intent is a necessary element of proof. Furthermore, the cost of liability insurance has increased dramatically in recent years, causing many companies to cancel their coverage. This, in turn, jeopardizes the recent movement toward outside directors because many directors are leaving or declining to serve on boards that have inadequate liability coverage. As a result, most states have enacted legislation that allows a corporation, through a charter amendment approved by shareholders, to limit the personal liability of its outside directors for failing to exercise due care. In 1990, Section 2.02 of the RMBCA was amended to provide that the articles of incorporation may include "a provision eliminating or limiting the liability of a director to the corporation or its shareholders for money damages. . . ." This section includes certain exceptions; for example, the articles may not limit liability for intentional violations of criminal law.

CHAPTER SUMMARY

A corporation may exercise two types of powers: (1) express powers, set forth by statute and in the articles of incorporation, and (2) implied powers, necessary to carry out its stated purpose. The corporation may always amend the articles of incorporation to change its purposes. Nevertheless, shareholders may enjoin their corporation from acting ultra vires, as may the state attorney general. Crimes and torts are not only ultra vires, but corporations may also be sanctioned for them. However, an individual stockholder, director, or officer—except in rare instances under certain regulatory statutes—may not be held vicariously liable if he did not participate in the crime or tort.

Because ownership and control are separated in the modern publicly held corporation, shareholders generally do not make business decisions. Shareholders who own voting stock do retain the power to elect directors, amend the bylaws, ratify or reject certain corporate actions, and vote on certain extraordinary matters, such as whether to amend the articles of incorporation, merge, or liquidate.

In voting for directors, some states permit and others require cumulative voting, with safeguards against removal of individual directors. Shareholders may use several voting arrangements that concentrate power, including proxies, voting agreements, and voting trusts. Proxies are regulated under rules promulgated by the SEC.

Corporations may deny preemptive rights—the right of a shareholder to prevent dilution of his percentage of ownership—by so stating in the articles of incorporation. Some states say that in the absence of such a provision, shareholders do have preemptive rights; others say that there are no preemptive rights unless the articles specifically include them.

Directors have the ultimate authority to run the corporation and are fiduciaries. In large corporations, directors delegate day-to-day management to salaried officers, whom they may fire, in most states, without cause. The full board of directors may by majority vote delegate its authority to committees. The board of directors may set its own pay, unless fixed in the articles of incorporation.

Directors owe the company a duty of loyalty and of care. A contract between a director and the company is voidable unless fair to the corporation, or unless all details have been disclosed and the disinterested directors or shareholders have approved. Any director or officer is obligated to inform fellow directors of any corporate opportunity that affects the company and may not act personally on it unless he has received approval. The duty of care is the obligation to act "with the care an ordinarily prudent person in a like position would exercise under similar circumstances." Directors who reasonably rely on specialist advice are absolved of wrongdoing if they turn out to be mistaken.

The corporation may agree, although not in every situation, to indemnify officers, directors, and employees for litigation expenses when they are made party to suits involving the corporation. The corporation may purchase insurance against legal expenses of directors and officers, but the policies do not cover acts of willful negligence and criminal conduct in which intent is a necessary element of proof.

KEY TERMS

SELF-TEST QUESTIONS

1. Acts that are outside a corporation's lawful powers are considered:
    (a) ultra vires
    (b) express powers
    (c) implied powers
    (d) none of the above
2. Powers set forth by statute and in the articles of incorporation are called:
    (a) implied powers
    (b) express powers
    (c) ultra vires
    (d) incorporation by estoppel
3. The principle that mistakes made by directors on the basis of good faith judgment can be forgiven:
    (a) is called the business judgment rule
    (b) depends on whether the director has exercised due care
    (c) both of the above
    (d) none of the above
4. A director of a corporation owes:
    (a) a duty of loyalty
    (b) a duty of care
    (c) both a duty of loyalty and a duty of care
    (d) none of the above
5. A corporation may purchase indemnification insurance:
    (a) to cover acts of simple negligence
    (b) to cover acts of willful negligence
    (c) to cover acts of both simple and willful negligence
    (d) to cover acts of criminal conduct

DEMONSTRATION PROBLEM

Third Corporation learned that a former officer had secretly done some consulting work for a competitor while employed by Third. Despite the consulting work, the officer had done a superb job for Third; his division was very profitable and was sold for a substantial profit after his departure. Third now sues the former officer for the compensation it paid him and the compensation he received from the competitor. Result? Why?

PROBLEMS

1. First Corporation, a Massachusetts company, decides to expend $100,000 to publicize its support of a candidate in an upcoming presidential election. A Massachusetts statute forbids corporate expenditures for the purpose of influencing the vote in elections. Chauncey, a shareholder in First Corporation, feels that the company should support a different presidential candidate and files suit to stop the company's publicizing efforts. Result? Why?
2. Assume that First Corporation (see problem 1) has all of the powers set forth in Section 3.02 of the RMBCA (see Appendix D). The directors establish a plan under which, upon the death of the company president, her husband (who was not employed by the company) will receive twice her salary for five years. Shareholder Chauncey objects to this plan and files suit to prevent it from going into effect. Result? Why?
3. In problem 1, assume that First Corporation has thirteen directors. Only seven of the directors show up for a board meeting, at which a number of important resolutions are passed by a four-to-three vote. Are these resolutions, supported by only four of the thirteen directors, valid? Why?
4. Assume in problem 1 that Chauncey is both an officer and a director of First Corporation. At a duly-called meeting of the board, the directors decide to dismiss Chauncey as an officer and director. If they had no cause for this action, is the dismissal valid? Why?
5. A book publisher that specializes in children's books has decided to publish pornographic literature for adults. Amanda, a shareholder in the company, has been active for years in an antipornography campaign. When she demands access to the publisher's books and records, the company refuses and she files suit. What arguments should Amanda raise in the litigation? Why?
6. A minority shareholder brought suit against the Chicago Cubs, a Delaware corporation, and their directors on the grounds that the directors were negligent in failing to

install lights in Wrigley Field. The shareholder specifically alleged that the majority owner, Philip Wrigley, failed to exercise good faith in that he personally believed that baseball was a daytime sport and felt that night games would cause the surrounding neighborhood to deteriorate. The shareholder accused Wrigley and the other directors of not acting in the best financial interests of the corporation. What counterarguments should the directors assert? Who will win? Why?

7. The CEO of First Bank, without prior notice to the board, announced a merger proposal during a two-hour meeting of the directors. Under the proposal the bank was to be sold to an acquiror at $55 per share. (At the time, the stock traded at $38 per share.) After the CEO discussed the proposal for twenty minutes, with no documentation to support the adequacy of the price, the board voted in favor of the proposal. Although senior management strongly opposed the proposal, it was eventually approved by the stockholders, with 70 percent in favor and 7 percent opposed. A group of stockholders later filed a class action, claiming that the directors were personally liable for the amount by which the fair value of the shares exceeded $55—an amount allegedly in excess of $100 million. Are the directors personally liable? Why?

ANSWERS TO SELF-TEST QUESTIONS

1. (a)　　2. (b)　　3. (c)　　4. (c)　　5. (a)

SUGGESTED ANSWER TO DEMONSTRATION PROBLEM

The company wins. The officer breached his fiduciary duty. "The fact that the division may have made money does not prove that no breach took place nor does it excuse one any more than a failure to make money demonstrates a breach of duty." *Wilshire Oil Co. of Texas v. Riffe*, 406 F.2d 1061 (10th Cir. 1969).

CHAPTER

44

CHAPTER OVERVIEW

Nature of Securities Regulation

Liability Under Securities Law

Securities Regulation

NATURE OF SECURITIES REGULATION

*I*n Chapter 42, we examined state law governing a corporation's issuance and transfer of stock. In Chapter 43, we covered the liability of directors and officers. This chapter extends and ties together the themes raised in chapters 42 and 43 by examining government regulation of securities and insider trading. Why is there a need for securities regulation?

What we commonly consider securities are essentially worthless pieces of paper. Their inherent value lies in the interest in property or an ongoing enterprise that they represent. This disparity between the tangible property—the stock certificate, for example—and the intangible interest it represents gives rise to several reasons for regulation. First, there is need for a mechanism to inform the buyer accurately what it is he is buying. Recall the South Sea Bubble and related schemes (see p. 906); unwary buyers discovered too late that they were investing mainly in empty air. Second, laws are necessary to prevent, and provide remedies for, deceptive and manipulative acts designed to defraud buyers and sellers. Third and finally, the evolution of stock trading on a massive scale has led to the development of numerous types of specialists and professionals, in dealings with whom the public can be at a severe disadvantage, and so the law undertakes to ensure that they do not take unfair advantage of their customers.

In this section we focus on the nature of securities regulation under two federal statutes: the Securities Act of 1933 and the Securities Exchange Act of 1934. We also look at state "Blue Sky" laws, intended to deter the kind of activity that led to the South Sea Bubble disaster. In the next section, we examine the liability that can result from violations of these laws and regulations.

The Securities Act of 1933 and the Securities Exchange Act of 1934 are vitally important, having virtually refashioned the law governing corporations during the past half century. Indeed, it is not too much to say that although they deal with securities, they have become a general federal law of corporations. This body of federal law has assumed special importance in recent years as the states have engaged in a "race to the bottom" in attempting to compete with Delaware's permissive corporation law (see Chapter 41).

What Is a Security?

Securities law questions are technical and complex and usually require professional counsel. For the nonlawyer, the critical question on which all else turns is whether the particular investment or document is a security. If it is, anyone attempting any transaction beyond the routine purchase or sale through a broker should consult legal counsel to avoid the various civil and criminal minefields that the law has strewn about.

The definition of a security in the Securities Act of 1933, set out immediately below, is comprehensive, but it does not on its face answer all questions that financiers in a dynamic market can raise. Under Section 2(1), "security" includes

> any note, stock, treasury stock, bond, debenture, evidence of indebtedness, certificate of interest or participation in any profit-sharing agreement, collateral-trust certificate, preorganization certificate or subscription, transferable share, investment contract, voting-trust certificate, certificate of deposit for a security, fractional undivided interest in oil, gas, or other mineral rights, or, in general, any interest or instrument commonly known as a "security," or any certificate of interest or participation in, temporary or interim certificate for, receipt for, guarantee of, or warrant or right to subscribe to or purchase, any of the foregoing.

Under this definition, an investment may not be a security even though it is so labeled, and may be a security even though it is called something else. For example, does a service contract—that obligates someone who has sold individual rows in an orange orchard to cultivate, harvest, and market an orange crop—involve a security subject to regulation under federal law? Yes, said the Supreme Court in *Securities & Exchange Commission v. W. J. Howey Co.*, 328 U.S. 293 (1946). The Court said the test is whether "the person invests his money in a common enterprise and is led to expect profits solely from the efforts of the promoter or a third party." Under this test, courts have liberally interpreted "investment contract" and "certificate of interest or participation in any profit-sharing agreement" to hold as securities interests in such property as real estate condominiums and cooperatives, commodity option contracts, and farm animals.

Notes that are not "investment contracts" under the *Howey* test can still be considered securities if certain factors, discussed in the next case, are present.

REVES v. ERNST & YOUNG
110 S.Ct. 945 (1990)

JUSTICE MARSHALL delivered the opinion of the Court.

This case presents the question whether certain demand notes issued by the Farmer's Cooperative of Arkansas and Oklahoma are "securities" within the meaning of § 3(a)(10) of the Securities Exchange Act of 1934. We conclude that they are.

The Co-Op is an agricultural cooperative that, at the time relevant here, had approximately 23,000 members. In order to raise money to support its general business operations, the Co-Op sold promissory notes payable on demand by the holder. Although the notes were uncollateralized and uninsured, they paid a variable rate of interest that was adjusted monthly to keep it higher than the rate paid by local financial institutions. The Co-Op offered the notes to both members and nonmembers, marketing the scheme as an "Investment Program." Advertisements for the notes, which appeared in each Co-Op newsletter, read in part: "YOUR CO-OP has more than $11,000,000 in assets to stand behind your investments. The Investment is not Federal [*sic*] insured but it is . . . Safe . . . Secure . . . and available when you need it." App. 5 (ellipses in original). Despite these assurances, the Co-Op filed for bankruptcy in 1984. At the time of the filing, over 1,600 people held notes worth a total of $10 million.

(continued on next page)

(continued)

REVES v. ERNST & YOUNG
110 S.Ct. 945 (1990)

After the Co-Op filed for bankruptcy, petitioners, a class of holders of the notes, filed suit against Arthur Young & Co., the firm that had audited the Co-Op's financial statements (and the predecessor to respondent Ernst & Young). Petitioners alleged, *inter alia*, that Arthur Young had intentionally failed to follow generally accepted accounting principles in its audit, specifically with respect to the valuation of one of the Co-Op's major assets, a gasohol plant. Petitioners claimed that Arthur Young violated these principles in an effort to inflate the assets and net worth of the Co-Op. Petitioners maintained that, had Arthur Young properly treated the plant in its audits, they would not have purchased demand notes because the Co-Op's insolvency would have been apparent. On the basis of these allegations, petitioners claimed that Arthur Young had violated the antifraud provisions of the 1934 Act as well as Arkansas' securities laws.

Petitioners prevailed at trial on both their federal and state claims, receiving a $6.1 million judgment. Arthur Young appealed, claiming that the demand notes were not "securities" under either the 1934 Act or Arkansas law, and that the statutes' antifraud provisions therefore did not apply. A panel of the Eighth Circuit, agreeing with Arthur Young on both the state and federal issues, reversed. We granted certiorari to address the federal issue and now reverse the judgment of the Court of Appeals.

*   *   *

The fundamental purpose undergirding the Securities Acts is "to eliminate serious abuses in a largely unregulated securities market." *United Housing Foundation, Inc. v. Forman,* 421 U.S. 837, 849 (1975). In defining the scope of the market that it wished to regulate, Congress painted with a broad brush. It recognized the virtually limitless scope of human ingenuity, especially in the creation of "countless and variable schemes devised by those who seek the use of the money of others on the promise of profits," *SEC v. W.J. Howey Co.,* 328 U.S. 293, 299 (1946), and determined that the best way to achieve its goal of protecting investors was "to define 'the term "security" in sufficiently broad and general terms so as to include within that definition the many types of instruments that in our commercial world fall within the ordinary concept of a security.' " *Forman, supra,* 421 U.S., at 847–848. Congress therefore did not attempt precisely to cabin the scope of the Securities Acts. Rather, it enacted a definition of "security" sufficiently broad to encompass virtually any instrument that might be sold as an investment.

*   *   *

[In deciding whether this transaction involves a "security," four factors are important.] First, we examine the transaction to assess the motivations that would prompt a reasonable seller and buyer to enter into it. If the seller's purpose is to raise money for the general use of a business enterprise or to finance substantial investments and the buyer is interested primarily in the profit the note is expected to generate, the instrument is likely to be a "security." If the note is exchanged to facilitate the purchase and sale of a minor asset or consumer good, to correct for the seller's cash-flow difficulties, or to advance some other commercial or consumer purpose, on the other hand, the note is less sensibly described as a "security." Second, we examine the "plan of distribution" of the instrument to determine whether it is an instrument in which there is "common trading for speculation or investment." Third, we examine the reasonable expectations of the investing public: The Court will consider instruments to be "securities" on the basis of such public expectations, even where an economic analysis of the circumstances of the particular transaction might suggest that the instruments are not "securities" as used in that transaction. Finally, we examine whether some factor such as the existence of another regulatory scheme significantly reduces the risk of the instrument, thereby rendering application of the Securities Acts unnecessary.

*   *   *

[W]e have little difficulty in concluding that the notes at issue here are "securities."

The Securities & Exchange Commission

Functions   The Securities & Exchange Commission is over half a century old, having been created by Congress in the Securities Exchange Act of 1934. It is an independent regulatory agency, subject to the rules of the Administrative Procedure Act (see Chapter 5). The commission is composed of five members, who have staggered five-year terms. Every June 5 the term of one of the commissioners expires. Although the president cannot remove commissioners during their term of office, he does have the power to designate the chairman from among the sitting members. The SEC is bipartisan: not more than three commissioners may be from the same political party.

The SEC's primary task is to investigate complaints or other possible violations of the law in securities transactions, and to bring enforcement proceedings when it believes that violations have occurred. It is empowered to conduct information inquiries, interview witnesses, examine brokerage records, and review trading data. If its requests are refused, it can issue subpoenas and seek compliance in federal court. Its usual leads come from complaints of investors and the general public, but it has authority to conduct surprise inspections of the books and records of brokers and dealers. Another source of leads is price fluctuations that seem to have been caused by manipulation rather than regular market forces.

Among the violations the commission searches out are these: unregistered sale of securities subject to the registration requirement of the 1933 act, fraudulent acts and practices, manipulation of market prices, carrying out of a securities business while insolvent, misappropriation of customers' funds by brokers and dealers, and other unfair dealings by broker-dealers.

When the commission believes that a violation has occurred, it can take one of three courses. First, it can refer the case to the Justice Department with a recommendation for criminal prosecution in cases of fraud or other willful violation of law.

Second, the SEC can seek a civil injunction in federal court against further violations. As a result of amendments to the securities laws in 1990 (the Securities Enforcement Remedies and Penny Stock Reform Act of 1990), the commission can also ask the court to impose civil penalties. The maximum penalty is $100,000 for each violation by an individual and $500,000 for each violation by others. Alternatively, the defendant is liable for the gain that resulted from violating securities law, if the gain exceeds the statutory penalty. The court is also authorized to bar an individual who has committed securities fraud from serving as an officer or director of a company registered under the securities law.

Third, the SEC can proceed administratively, that is, hold its own hearing, with the usual due process rights, before an administrative law judge. If the commissioners by majority vote accept the findings of the administrative law judge, after reading briefs and hearing oral argument, they can impose a variety of sanctions: suspend or expel members of exchanges; deny, suspend, or revoke the registrations of broker-dealers; censure individuals for misconduct; and bar censured individuals (temporarily or permanently) from employment with a registered firm. The 1990 securities law amendments allow the SEC to impose civil fines similar to the court-imposed fines described above. The amendments also authorize the SEC to order individuals to cease and desist from violating securities law.

Fundamental Mission of the SEC   The SEC's fundamental mission is to ensure adequate disclosure in order to facilitate informed investment decisions by the public. Whether a particular security offering is worthwhile or worthless is a decision for the public, not for the SEC, which has no legal authority to pass on the merits of an offering or to bar the sale of securities if proper disclosures are made.

One example was the 1981 sale of $274 million in limited partnership interests in a company called Petrogene Oil & Gas Associates, New York. The Petrogene offering was designed as a tax shelter. The company's filing with the SEC stated that the offering involved "a high degree of risk" and only those "who can afford the complete loss of their investment" should contemplate investing. Other disclosures: one member of the controlling group spent four months in prison for conspiracy to commit securities fraud; he and another principal were the subject of a New Mexico cease-and-desist order involving allegedly unregistered tax-shelter securities; the general partner, brother-in-law of one of the principals, had no experience in the company's proposed oil and gas operations (Petrogene planned to extract oil from plants by using radio frequencies); one of the oils to be produced was potentially carcinogenic; and the principals "stand to benefit substantially" whether or not the company fails and whether or not purchasers of shares recovered any of their investment. The prospectus went on to list specific risks. Despite this daunting compilation of troublesome details, the SEC permitted the offering because all disclosures were made (*Wall Street Journal*, December 29, 1981). It is the business of the marketplace, not the SEC, to determine whether the risk is worth taking.

Securities Act of 1933

Goals   The Securities Act of 1933 is the fundamental "truth in securities" law. Its two basic objectives, in the words of its preamble: "to provide full and fair disclosure of the character of securities sold in interstate and foreign commerce and through the mails, and to prevent frauds in the sale thereof."

Registration   The primary means for realizing these goals is the requirement of registration. Before securities subject to the act can be offered to the public, the issuer must file a registration statement and prospectus with the SEC, laying out in detail relevant and material information about the offering, as set forth in various schedules to the act. If the SEC approves the registration statement, the issuer must then provide any prospective purchaser with the prospectus. Since the SEC does not pass on the fairness of price or other terms of the offering, it is unlawful to state or imply in the prospectus that the commission has the power to disapprove securities for lack of merit, thereby suggesting that the offering is meritorious.

The SEC has prepared special forms for registering different types of issuing companies. All call for a description of the registrant's business and properties and of the significant provisions of the security to be offered, facts about how the issuing company is managed, and detailed financial statements certified by independent public accountants.

Once filed, the registration and prospectus become public and are open for public inspection. Ordinarily, the effective date of the registration statement is twenty days after filing. Until then, the offering may not be made to the public. Section 2(10) defines prospectus as any "notice, circular, advertisement, letter, or communication, written or by radio or television, which offers any security for sale or confirms the sale of any security." (An exception: brief notes advising the public of the availability of the formal prospectus.) The import of this definition is that any communication to the public about the offering of a security is unlawful unless it contains the requisite information.

The SEC staff examines the registration statement and prospectus and if they appear to be materially incomplete or inaccurate, the commission may suspend or refuse the effectiveness of the registration statement until the deficiencies are corrected. Even after the securities have gone on sale, the agency has the power to issue a **stop order** that halts trading in the stock.

Section 5(c) of the act bars any person from making any sale of any security unless it is first registered. Nevertheless, there are certain classes of exemptions from the registration requirement. Perhaps the most important of these is Section 4(3), which exempts "transactions by any person other than an issuer, underwriter or dealer." Section 4(3) also exempts most transactions of dealers. So the net is that trading in outstanding securities (the secondary market) is exempt from registration under the 1933 act: you need not file a registration statement with the SEC every time you buy or sell securities through a broker or dealer, for example. Other exemptions include: "(1) Private offerings to a limited number of persons or institutions who have access to the kind of information registration would disclose and who do not propose to redistribute the securities, (2) offerings restricted to the residents of the State in which the issuing company is organized and doing business, (3) securities of municipal, State, Federal and other government instrumentalities, of charitable institutions, of banks, and of carriers subject to the Interstate Commerce Act, (4) offerings not in excess of certain specified amounts made in compliance with regulations of the Commission . . . , and (5) offerings of 'small business investment companies' made in accordance with rules and regulations of the Commission" (*The Work of the SEC*, 1981, p. 6).

Penalties   Section 24 provides for fines not to exceed $10,000 and a prison term not to exceed five years, or both, for willful violations of any provisions of the 1933 act. This section makes these criminal penalties specifically applicable to anyone who "willfully, in a registration statement filed under this title, makes any untrue statement of a material fact or omits to state any material fact required to be stated therein or necessary to make the statements therein not misleading."

Sections 11 and 12 provide that anyone injured by false declarations in registration statements, prospectuses, or oral communications concerning the sale of the security—as well as anyone injured by the unlawful failure of an issuer to register—may file a civil suit to recover the net consideration paid for the security or for damages if the security has been sold.

Although these civil penalty provisions apply only to false statements in connection with the registration statement, prospectus, or oral communication, the Supreme Court has held that there is an "implied private right of action" for damages resulting from a violation of SEC rules under the act. [J. I. Case v. Borak, 377 U.S. 426 (1964)] The Court's ruling in the *Borak* case opened the courthouse doors to many who had been defrauded but were previously without a practical remedy.

Securities Exchange Act of 1934

Companies Covered   The 1933 act is limited, as we have just seen, to new securities issues—that is the "primary market." The trading that takes place in the secondary market is far more significant, however. In a normal year trading in outstanding stock totals some twenty times the value of new stock issues. To regulate the secondary market, Congress enacted the Securities Exchange Act of 1934. This law, which created the SEC, extended the disclosure rationale to securities listed and registered for public trading on the national securities exchanges. Amendments to the act have brought within its ambit every corporation whose equity securities are traded over the counter if the company has at least $5 million in assets and 500 or more shareholders.

Reporting; Proxy Solicitation   Any company seeking listing and registration of its stock for public trading on a national exchange—or over the counter, if the company meets the size test—must first submit a registration application to both the exchange and the SEC. The registration statement is akin to that filed by companies under the 1933 act, although the 1934 act calls for somewhat fewer disclosures. Thereafter, companies must file annual and certain other periodic reports to update information in the original filing.

The 1934 act also covers proxy solicitation. Whenever management, or a dissident minority, seeks votes of holders of registered securities for any corporate purpose, disclosures must be made to the stockholders to permit them to vote "Yes" or "No" intelligently.

Penalties   The logic of the *Borak* case (see above) also applies to this act, so that private investors may bring suit in federal court for violations of the statute that led to financial injury. Violations of any provision and the making of false statements in any of the required disclosures subject the defendant to a maximum fine of $100,000 and a maximum five-year prison sentence, but a defendant who can show that he had no knowledge of the particular rule he was convicted of violating may not be imprisoned. The maximum fine for a violation of the act by an exchange itself is $500,000. Any issuer omitting to file requisite documents and reports is liable to pay a fine of $100 for each day the failure continues.

Blue Sky Laws

Long before congressional enactment of the securities laws in the 1930s, the states had legislated securities regulations. Today, every state has enacted a "Blue Sky Law"—so called because their purpose is to prevent "speculative schemes which have no more basis than so many feet of 'blue sky'." [Hall v. Geiger-Jones Co., 242 U.S. 539 (1917)] The federal Securities Act of 1933 specifically preserves the jurisdiction of states over securities.

Blue sky laws divide into three basic types. The simplest is that which prohibits fraud in the sale of securities. Thus, at a minimum, issuers cannot mislead investors about the purpose of the investment. All blue sky laws have antifraud provisions; some have no other provisions. The second type calls for registration of broker-dealers; the third type for registration of securities. Some state laws parallel the federal laws in intent and form of proceeding, so that they overlap; other blue sky laws empower state officials (unlike the SEC) to judge the merits of the offerings. As part of a movement toward deregulation, several states have recently modified or eliminated "merit" laws.

Many of the blue sky laws are inconsistent with each other, making national uniformity difficult. In 1956, the National Conference of Commissioners on Uniform State Laws approved the Uniform Securities Act. It has not been designed to reconcile the conflicting philosophies of state regulation, but to take them into account and to make the various forms of regulation as consistent as possible. States adopt various portions of the law, depending on their regulatory philosophies. The Uniform Securities Act has antifraud, broker-dealer registration, and securities registration provisions.

LIABILITY UNDER SECURITIES LAW

The Foreign Corrupt Practices Act

One of many statutes enacted in the aftermath of Watergate, the Foreign Corrupt Practices Act of 1977 (FCPA), is incorporated into the 1934 act. Investigations by the SEC and the Watergate Special Prosecutor turned up evidence that hundreds of companies had misused corporate funds, mainly by bribing foreign officials to induce them to enter into contracts with or grant licenses to American companies. Because revealing the bribe would normally be self-defeating, and in any event could be expected to stir up immense criticism, companies paying bribes routinely hid the payments in various accounts. The SEC's legal interest in the matter was not the morality of bribery but the falsity of the financial statements that were being filed.

Congress' response, the FCPA, was much broader than necessary to treat the abuses uncovered. The FCPA prohibits an issuer (that is, any U.S. business enterprise), a stockholder acting on behalf of an issuer, and "any officer, director, employee, or agent" of an issuer from using the mails, or interstate commerce corruptly to offer, pay, or promise to pay, anything of value to foreign officials, foreign political parties, or candidates, if the purpose is to gain business by inducing the foreign official to influence an act of the government to render a decision favorable to the American corporation.

But not all payments are illegal. Under 1988 amendments to the FCPA, payments may be made to expedite routine governmental actions, such as obtaining a visa. And payments are allowed if they are lawful under the written law of a foreign country. More important than the foreign-bribe provisions, the act includes accounting provisions which broaden considerably the authority of the SEC. These provisions are discussed in the following case—the first accounting provisions case brought to trial.

S.E.C. v. WORLD-WIDE COIN INVESTMENTS, LTD.
567 F.Supp. 724 (N.D. Ga. 1983)

VINING, DISTRICT JUDGE. This is a securities fraud action in which the Securities and Exchange Commission (SEC) seeks a permanent injunction against World-Wide Coin Investments, Ltd. (World-Wide) and the individual defendants as well as an order for a full accounting and disclosure of wrongfully received benefits. . . .

World-Wide Coin Investments, Ltd., is a Delaware corporation with its principal offices in Atlanta, Georgia, and is engaged primarily in the wholesale and retail sale of rare coins, precious metals, gold and silver coins, bullion, and, until 1979, in the retail sale of camera equipment. Its operations also include the sale of Coca-Cola collector items and certain commemorative items. Its inventory of rare coins comes from its purchases of collections from estates and private individuals, purchases from dealers, purchases on domestic commodities exchanges, and purchases at coin shows.

* * *

The Foreign Corrupt Practices Act, 15 U.S.C. § 78m(b)(2) (Amend.1977) ("FCPA") was enacted by Congress as an amendment to the 1934 Securities Exchange Act and was the legislative response to numerous questionable and illegal foreign payments by United States corporations in the 1970's. Although one of the major substantive provisions of the FCPA is to require corporate disclosure of assets as a deterrent to foreign bribes, the more significant addition of the FCPA is the accounting controls or "books and records" provision, which gives the SEC authority over the entire financial management and reporting requirements of publicly held United States corporations.

The FCPA was enacted on the principle that accurate recordkeeping is an essential ingredient in promoting management responsibility and is an affirmative requirement for publicly held American corporations to strengthen the accuracy of corporate books and records, which are "the bedrock elements of our system of corporate disclosure and accountability."

* * *

The FCPA reflects a congressional determination that the scope of the federal securities laws and the SEC's authority should be expanded beyond the traditional ambit of disclosure requirements. The consequence of adding these substantive requirements governing accounting control to the federal securities laws will significantly augment the degree of federal involvement in the internal management of public corporations.

* * *

Section 13(b)(2) contains two separate requirements for issuers in complying with the FCPA's accounting provisions: (1) a company must keep accurate books and records reflecting the transactions and dispositions of the assets

(*continued on next page*)

(continued)

**S.E.C. v. WORLD-WIDE
COIN INVESTMENTS,
LTD.**
567 F.Supp. 724 (N.D.
Ga. 1983)

of the issuer, and (2) a company must maintain a reliable and adequate system of internal accounting controls. In applying these two separate requirements to the instant case, the court will examine the requirements of each provision and the problems inherent in their interpretation.

The "books and records" provision, contained in section 13(b)(2)(A) of the FCPA has three basic objectives: (1) books and records should reflect transactions in conformity with accepted methods of reporting economic events, (2) misrepresentation, concealment, falsification, circumvention, and other deliberate acts resulting in inaccurate financial books and records are unlawful, and (3) transactions should be properly reflected on books and records in such a manner as to permit the preparation of financial statements in conformity with GAAP and other criteria applicable to such statements.

* * *

The second branch of the accounting provisions—the requirement that issuers maintain a system of internal accounting controls—appears in section 13(b)(2)(B). Like the recordkeeping provisions of the Act, the internal controls provision is not limited to material transactions or to those above a specific dollar amount. While this requirement is supportive of accuracy and reliability in the auditor's review and financial disclosure process, this provision should not be analyzed solely from that point of view. The internal controls requirement is primarily designed to give statutory content to an aspect of management stewardship responsibility, that of providing shareholders with reasonable assurances that the business is adequately controlled.

* * *

The evidence in this case reveals that World-Wide, aided and abetted by Hale and Seibert, violated the provisions of section 13(b)(2) of the FCPA. As set forth in the factual background portion of this order, the internal recordkeeping and accounting controls of World-Wide has been sheer chaos since Hale took over control of the company. For example, there has been no procedure implemented with respect to writing checks: employees have had access to presigned checks; source documents were not required to be prepared when a check was drawn; employees have not been required to obtain approval before writing a check, and, even when a check was drawn to "cash," supporting documentation was usually not prepared to explain the purpose for which the check was drawn. In addition to extremely lax security measures such as leaving the vault unguarded, there has been no separation of duties in the areas of purchase and sales transactions, and valuation procedures for ending inventory. Furthermore, no promissory notes or other supporting documentation has been prepared to evidence purported loans to World-Wide by Hale or by his affiliate companies.

Since Hale obtained control of World-Wide, employees have not been required to write source documents relating to the purchase and sale of coins, bullion, or other inventory. Because of this total lack of an audit trail with respect to these transactions and the disposition of World-Wide's assets, it has been virtually impossible to determine if an item has been sold at a profit or at a loss. Furthermore, there are more than $1,700,000 worth of checks drawn to Hale or to Hale's affiliates, or to cash, for which no adequate source documentation exists. Furthermore, Hale and Seibert knew that the medallions that were sold to World-Wide by Hale in 1979 were overvalued and unmarketable. Even so, they allowed the incorrect value of the medallions to be entered on the books of World-Wide. They also knew that the company's books and records were neither accurate nor complete. Pursuant to their directives, source documents were not prepared with respect to the transfer of funds; additionally, no audit trail was maintained for the acquisition and disposition of inventory. Furthermore, it appears that there were numerous false and misleading statements and omissions in the company's numerous reports to the SEC, many of which were filed late or not at all.

[Judgment for the SEC.]

Insider Trading

Corporate insiders—directors, officers, important shareholders—can have a substantial trading advantage if they are privy to important confidential information. Learning bad news (such as financial loss, cancellation of key contracts) in advance of all other stockholders will permit the privileged few to sell shares before the price falls. Discovering good news (major oil find, unexpected profits), conversely, gives the insider a decided incentive to purchase shares before the price rises.

Because of the unfairness to those who are ignorant of inside information, federal law prohibits insider trading. Two provisions of the 1934 Securities Exchange Act are paramount: Sections 16(b) and 10(b).

Recapture of Short-Swing Profits: Section 16(b)
The Securities Exchange Act assumes that any director, officer, or shareholder owning 10 percent or more of the stock is using inside information if he or any family member makes a profit from trading activities, either buying and selling, or selling and buying, during a six-month period. Section 16(b) penalizes any such person by permitting the corporation, or a shareholder suing on its behalf, to recover the profits. The law applies to any company with more than $5 million in assets and at least 500 or more shareholders of any class of stock.

Suppose on January 1, Bob (a company officer) purchases 100 shares of BCT stock for $60 a share.

On September 1, he sells them for $100 a share. What result? Bob is in the clear, because his $4,000 profit was not realized during a six-month period. Now suppose that the price falls, and one month later, on October 1, he repurchases 100 shares at $30 a share and holds them for two years. What result? He will be forced to pay back $7,000 in profits even if he had no inside information. Why? In August, Bob held 100 shares of stock, and again on October 1—within a six-month period. His net gain on these transactions was $7,000 ($10,000 realized on the sale, less $3,000 cost of the purchase).

As a consequence of Section 16(b) and certain other provisions, trading in securities by directors, officers, and large stockholders presents numerous complexities. For instance, the law requires people in this position to make periodic reports to the SEC about their trades. As a practical matter, directors, officers, and large shareholders should not trade in their own company stock in the short-run without legal advice, as **Box 44-1** illustrates.

Insider Trading: Section 10(b) and Rule 10b-5
Section 10(b) of the Securities Exchange Act of 1934 prohibits any person from using the mails or facilities of interstate commerce "to use or employ, in connection with the purchase or sale of any security . . . any manipulative or deceptive device or contrivance in contravention of such rules and regulations as the Commission may prescribe as necessary or appropriate in the public interest or for the protection of

Your Money Matters

By Jill Bettner

[*As the following article illustrates, directors, officers, and large shareholders should not engage in "short-swing" trades within their own company without first seeking legal advice.*
—AUTHORS' NOTE]

Many corporate insiders who sold company stock earlier this year, then bought back shares at lower prices after the October stock market crash, may have violated a longstanding federal securities law barring "short-swing" profits by insiders.

Already, shareholders' lawyers have notified at least a dozen companies that corporate officials may have engaged in illegal short-swing trades. These companies could wind up in court if they don't collect the profits from those trades, and they will have to pay shareholders' lawyers hefty fees for discovering any violations.

"What we're seeing is probably just the tip of the iceberg," says Jesse Brill, a securities lawyer with Dean Witter Reynolds Inc. in San Francisco. A former Securities and Ex-

INSIDER TRADING AND THE CRASH OF 1987

change Commission lawyer, Mr. Brill tracks legal developments affecting corporate insiders for a monthly newsletter.

Most insiders whose situations have recently come to light bought company stock in the week following the Oct. 19 plunge, after selling shares at much higher prices in the preceding six months.

But the short-swing profit rule, contained in section 16(b) of the 1934 Securities and Exchange Act, works two ways: It prohibits insiders—officers, directors, and owners of 10% or more of a company's stock—not only from buying low and selling high within six months, but also from first selling high and then buying low.

"It's a profit even if the sale comes first," Mr. Brill says.

Many insiders say they learned this, to their chagrin, only after the fact. Roland C. Baer Jr., a director of Charleston, W.Va.-based Allegheny & Western Energy Corp. and presi-

dent of its Mountaineer Gas Co. unit, bought 3,000 Allegheny & Western shares Oct. 26, when the oil and natural gas company's stock stood at $10. But in July he had sold 5,000 shares at $28.50 and another 3,000 at $27.25, giving him a short-swing profit of about $55,000 before commissions.

"It was an honest mistake," he says. He plans to return his profit by year's end.

Some executives say institutional investors hurried them into buying back their companies' shares when everybody else was selling. David Downey, chairman of Downey Designs International Inc. in Indianapolis, which remounts diamonds and other gems as a while-you-wait service in department stores, says many institutional investors were "calling up in October wanting to unload, and others were saying, 'Do something.'" he says. "I started this company 24 years ago. It's my baby. I wasn't about to sit by and do nothing."

Mr. Downey blames his company's "high-priced New York lawyers for not warning me I could be doing something illegal. 'You screwed up,' they told me (afterward)," he says.

A week after the crash, when Mr. Downey bought 50,000 shares, the

---

investors." In 1942, the SEC learned of a company president who misrepresented the company's financial condition in order to buy shares at a low price from current stockholders. So the commission adopted a rule under the authority of Section 10(b). Rule 10b-5, as it was dubbed, has remained unchanged for more than forty years and spawned thousands of lawsuits and SEC proceedings. It reads as follows:

It shall be unlawful for any person, directly or indirectly, by the use of any means or instrumentality of interstate commerce, or of the mails, or of any facility of any national securities exchange,

(1) to employ any device, scheme, or artifice to defraud,

(2) to make any untrue statement of a material fact or to omit to state a material fact necessary in order to make the statements made, in the light of circumstances under which they were made, not misleading, or

(3) to engage in any act, practice, or course of business which operates or would operate as a fraud or deceit upon any person, in connection with the purchase or sale of any security.

Rule 10b-5 applies to *any* person who purchases or sells any security. It is not limited to securities registered under the 1934 act. It is not limited to publicly held companies. It applies to any security issued by any company, including the smallest closely

BOX 44-1

stock was at $3.50, well below its initial offering price of $6 on June 17. As part of the offering, Mr. Downey had sold 187,500 shares. His short-swing profit from the two transactions amounted to about $94,000 after underwriting fees and brokerage commissions.

"It seems like I am in violation of the rule," he says, "but I haven't taken any action yet. I'm waiting to hear back from my attorneys."

That he remains the company's largest stockholder "isn't much solace," he says, adding that the stock has fallen further, to $3.125, "and I can't do anything with (the shares) for another six months."

Although the short-swing rule may appear simple, securities lawyers say it has many gray areas. For example, they say court decisions haven't established a clear precedent for cases involving stock purchases by or for members of an insider's immediate family. James Moore, a vice president of California Energy Co., bought company stock in late October for his children's savings accounts. He says it could cost him $24,300.

On Sept. 9, Mr. Moore sold 7,000 shares at $6.90 in California Energy, a Santa Clara, Calif., company that is developing geothermal power plants. On Oct. 23, he bought 5,000 shares at $3.75 and four days later another 2,000 shares at $2.625.

Some federal courts have ruled that an insider has to prove that only the children benefited from such transactions, but in one case "an insider who had trusts for his kids wasn't held liable even though he was a co-trustee," says Peter Romeo, a partner in the Washington law firm of Hogan & Hartson.

Mr. Moore says, "I'm a geologist, not a lawyer, but I've learned a lot about rule 16(b) in the past month." He says preliminary responses from his own lawyer and the company's counsel hold that he didn't violate the rule. "Whatever I'm advised, I'll do," he says.

In all of these cases, the possible infractions were uncovered by lawyers who specialize in pursuing short-swing violators. In fact, enforcement of the short-swing rule effectively rests with these lawyers. That's because the 1934 law makes the courts, rather than the SEC, responsible for seeing that short-swing profits go back to the companies. But only shareholders can initiate any action against short-swing traders.

The information that leads these lawyers to possible violations is contained in Form 4 filings, required of insiders on any company stock transaction. But lawyers in the field maintain that many short-swing trades go undetected, either because they get lost in the mountain of filings or because insiders simply ignore the filing requirement and get away with it.

Typically, a lawyer first uncovers a possible case of short-swing profits, then finds a shareholder on whose behalf to act. The lawyer next notifies the company involved, which contacts the insider. Most cases involving a violation get settled without going to court: The insider simply returns the money.

The incentive for these lawyers: Companies must pay them fees of up to one-third of the amounts recovered. (When more than one lawyer finds the same violation, the fee goes to the first to notify the company.) Company shareholders, meanwhile, receive no direct payment; they gain only indirectly, through an enriched corporate treasury.

Source: *Wall Street Journal*, December 21, 1987

---

held company. In substance, it is an antifraud rule, enforcement of which seems, on its face, to be limited to action by the SEC. But over the years the courts have permitted people injured by those who violate the statute to file private damage suits. This sweeping rule has at times been referred to as the "federal law of corporations" or the "catch everybody" rule.

Insider trading ran headlong into Rule 10b-5 beginning in 1964, in a series of cases involving Texas Gulf Sulphur Company (TGS). On November 12, 1963, the company discovered a rich deposit of copper and zinc while drilling for oil near Timmins, Ontario. Keeping the discovery quiet, it proceeded to acquire mineral rights in adjacent lands. By April, 1964, word began to circulate about Texas Gulf's find.

Newspapers printed rumors, and the Toronto Stock Exchange experienced a wild speculative spree. On April 12, Charles F. Fogarty, executive vice president of TGS, issued a press release downplaying the discovery, asserting that the rumors greatly exaggerated the find, and stating that more drilling would be necessary before coming to any conclusions. Four days later, on April 16, TGS publicly announced that it had uncovered a strike of 25 million tons of ore. In the months following this announcement, TGS stock doubled in value.

The SEC charged several TGS officers and directors with having purchased or told their friends (so-called "tippees") to purchase TGS stock from November 12, 1963 through April 16, 1964 on the basis of material inside information. The SEC also alleged that the April 12, 1964 press release was deceptive. The U.S. Court of Appeals, in *SEC* v. *Texas Gulf Sulphur Co.*, 401 F.2d 833 (2d Cir. 1968), decided that the defendants who purchased the stock before the public announcement had violated Rule 10b-5. According to the court, ". . . anyone in possession of material inside information must either disclose it to the investing public, or, if he is disabled from disclosing to protect a corporate confidence, or he chooses not to do so, must abstain from trading in or recommending the securities concerned while such inside information remains undisclosed." On remand the District Court ordered certain defendants to pay $148,000 into an escrow account to be used to compensate parties injured by the insider trading.

The Court of Appeals also concluded that the press release violated Rule 10b-5 if "misleading to the reasonable investor." On remand, the District Court held that TGS failed to exercise "due diligence" in issuing the release. Sixty-nine private damage actions were subsequently filed against TGS by shareholders who claimed they sold their stock in reliance on the release. TGS settled most of these suits in late 1971 for $2.7 million.

Following the TGS episode, the Supreme Court has refined Rule 10b-5 on several fronts. First, the Court, in *Ernst & Ernst* v. *Hochfelder*, decided that proof of scienter—defined as "mental state embracing intent to deceive, manipulate, or defraud"—is required in private damage actions under Rule 10b-5. In other words, negligence alone will not result in Rule 10b-5 liability. The Supreme Court has also held that scienter must be established in SEC injunctive actions. [Aaron v. SEC, 446 U.S. 680 (1980)] The *Hochfelder* decision is reprinted and discussed in Chapter 53.

Second, the Supreme Court has placed limitations on the liability of tippees under Rule 10b-5. In 1980, the Court reversed the conviction of an employee of a company that printed tender offer and merger prospectuses. Using information obtained at work, the employee had purchased stock in target companies and later sold it for a profit when takeover attempts were publicly announced. The Court held that the employee was not an insider or fiduciary, and "a duty to disclose under Section 10(b) does not arise from the mere possession of nonpublic market information." [Chiarella v. United States, 445 U.S. 222 (1980)] This case set the stage for the following decision, which is the leading case on tippee liability.

DIRKS v. SECURITIES AND EXCHANGE COMMISSION
463 U.S. 646 (1983)

JUSTICE POWELL delivered the opinion of the Court.

Petitioner Raymond Dirks received material nonpublic information from "insiders" of a corporation with which he had no connection. He disclosed this information to investors who relied on it in trading in the shares of the corporation. The question is whether Dirks violated the antifraud provisions of the federal securities laws by this disclosure.

In 1973, Dirks was an officer of a New York broker-dealer firm who specialized in providing investment analysis of insurance company securities to institutional investors. On March 6, Dirks received information from Ronald Secrist, a former officer of Equity Funding of America. Secrist alleged that the assets of Equity Funding, a diversified corporation primarily engaged in selling life insurance and mutual funds, were vastly overstated as the result of fraudulent corporate practices. Secrist also stated that various regulatory agencies had failed to act on similar charges made by Equity Funding employees. He urged Dirks to verify the fraud and disclose it publicly.

Dirks decided to investigate the allegations. He visited Equity Funding's headquarters in Los Angeles and interviewed several officers and employees of the corporation. The senior management denied any wrongdoing, but certain corporation employees corroborated the charges of fraud. Neither Dirks nor his firm owned or traded any Equity Funding stock, but throughout his investigation he openly discussed the information he had obtained with a number of clients and investors. Some of these persons sold their holdings of Equity Funding securities, including five investment advisers who liquidated holdings of more than $16 million.

While Dirks was in Los Angeles, he was in touch regularly with William Blundell, the *Wall Street Journal*'s Los Angeles bureau chief. Dirks urged Blundell to write a story on the fraud allegations. Blundell did not believe, however, that such a massive fraud could go undetected and declined to write the story. He feared that publishing such damaging hearsay might be libelous.

During the two-week period in which Dirks pursued his investigation and spread word of Secrist's charges, the price of Equity Funding stock fell from $26 per share to less than $15 per share. This led the New York Stock Exchange to halt trading on March 27. Shortly thereafter California insurance authorities impounded Equity Funding's records and uncovered evidence of the fraud. Only then did the Securities and Exchange Commission (SEC) file a complaint against Equity Funding and only then, on April 2, did the *Wall Street Journal* publish a front-page story based largely on information assembled by Dirks. Equity Funding immediately went into receivership.

The SEC began an investigation into Dirks' role in the exposure of the fraud. The SEC concluded: "Where 'tippees'—regardless of their motivation or occupation—come into possession of material 'information that they know is confidential and know or should know came from a corporate insider,' they must either publicly disclose that information or refrain from trading." 21 S. E. C. Docket 1401, 1407 (1981) (footnote omitted) (quoting *Chiarella* v. *United States*, 445 U.S. 222, 230 n. 12 (1980)). Recognizing, however, that Dirks "played an important role in bringing [Equity Funding's] massive fraud to light," 21 S. E. C. Docket, at 1412, the SEC only censured him.

Dirks sought review in the Court of Appeals for the District of Columbia Circuit. The court entered judgment against Dirks "for the reasons stated by the Commission in its opinion."

★   ★   ★

In the seminal case of *In re Cady, Roberts & Co.*, 40 S. E. C. 907 (1961), the SEC recognized that the common law in some jurisdictions imposes on "corporate 'insiders,' particularly officers, directors, or controlling stockholders" an "affirmative duty of disclosure . . . when dealing in securities." The SEC found that not only did breach of this common-law duty also establish the elements of a Rule 10b-5 violation, but that individuals other than corporate insiders could be obligated either to disclose material nonpublic information before trading or to abstain from trading altogether.

★   ★   ★

(continued on next page)

(continued)

DIRKS v. SECURITIES AND EXCHANGE COMMISSION
463 U.S. 646 (1983)

[A] tippee assumes a fiduciary duty to the shareholders of a corporation not to trade on material nonpublic information only when the insider has breached his fiduciary duty to the shareholders by disclosing the information to the tippee and the tippee knows or should know that there has been a breach.

★   ★   ★

Whether disclosure is a breach of duty therefore depends in large part on the purpose of the disclosure. This standard was identified by the SEC itself in *Cady, Roberts:* a purpose of the securities laws was to eliminate "use of inside information for personal advantage." Thus, the test is whether the insider personally will benefit, directly or indirectly, from his disclosure. Absent some personal gain, there has been no breach of duty to stockholders. And absent a breach by the insider, there is no derivative breach.

★   ★   ★

Under the inside-trading and tipping rules set forth above, we find that there was no actionable violation by Dirks. It is undisputed that Dirks himself was a stranger to Equity Funding, with no preexisting fiduciary duty to its shareholders. He took no action, directly, or indirectly, that induced the shareholders or officers of Equity Funding to repose trust or confidence in him. There was no expectation by Dirk's sources that he would keep their information in confidence. Nor did Dirks misappropriate or illegally obtain the information about Equity Funding. Unless the insiders breached their *Cady, Roberts* duty to shareholders in disclosing the nonpublic information to Dirks, he breached no duty when he passed it on to investors as well as to the *Wall Street Journal.*

It is clear that neither Secrist nor the other Equity Funding employees violated their *Cady, Roberts* duty to the corporation's shareholders by providing information to Dirks. The tippers received no monetary or personal benefit for revealing Equity Funding's secrets, nor was their purpose to make a gift of valuable information to Dirks. As the facts of this case clearly indicate, the tippers were motivated by a desire to expose the fraud. In the absence of a breach of duty to shareholders by the insiders, there was no derivative breach by Dirks. Dirks therefore could not have been "a participant after the fact in [an] insider's breach of a fiduciary duty." *Chiarella*, 445 U.S., at 230, n. 12.

We conclude that Dirks, in the circumstances of this case, had no duty to abstain from the use of the inside information that he obtained. The judgment of the Court of Appeals therefore is reversed.

The Supreme Court has also refined Rule 10b-5 as it relates to the duty of a company to disclose material information, as discussed in the following case.

This case is also important in its discussion of the degree of reliance investors must prove to support a Rule 10b-5 action.

BASIC INC. v. LEVINSON
485 U.S. 224 (1988)

[In December, 1978, Basic Incorporated agreed to merge with Consolidated Engineering. Prior to the merger, Basic made three public statements denying it was involved in merger negotiations. Shareholders who sold their stock after the first of these statements and before the merger was announced sued Basic and its directors under Rule 10b-5, claiming that they sold their shares at depressed prices as a result of Basic's misleading statements. The District Court decided in favor of Basic on the grounds that Basic's statements were not material and therefore were not misleading. The Court of Appeals reversed and the Supreme Court granted certiorari.]

JUSTICE BLACKMUN.

We granted certiorari to resolve the split among the Courts of Appeals as to the standard of materiality applicable to preliminary merger discussions, and to determine whether the courts below properly applied a presumption of reliance in certifying the class, rather than requiring each class member to show direct reliance on Basic's statements.

*   *   *

The Court previously has addressed various positive and common-law requirements for a violation of § 10(b) or of Rule 10b-5. The Court also explicitly has defined a standard of materiality under the securities laws, see *TSC Industries, Inc. v. Northway, Inc.*, 426 U.S. 438 (1976), concluding in the proxy-solicitation context that "[a]n omitted fact is material if there is a substantial likelihood that a reasonable shareholder would consider it important in deciding how to vote." . . . We now expressly adopt the *TSC Industries* standard of materiality for the § 10(b) and Rule 10b-5 context.

The application of this materiality standard to preliminary merger discussions is not self-evident. Where the impact of the corporate development on the target's fortune is certain and clear, the *TSC Industries* materiality definition admits straight-forward application. Where, on the other hand, the event is contingent or speculative in nature, it is difficult to ascertain whether the "reasonable investor" would have considered the omitted information significant at the time. Merger negotiations, because of the ever-present possibility that the contemplated transaction will not be effectuated, fall into the latter category.

*   *   *

Even before this Court's decision in *TSC Industries*, the Second Circuit had explained the role of the materiality requirement of Rule 10b-5, with respect to contingent or speculative information or events, in a manner that gave that term meaning that is independent of the other provisions of the Rule. Under such circumstances, materiality "will depend at any given time upon a balancing of both the indicated probability that the event will occur and the anticipated magnitude of the event in light of the totality of the company activity." *SEC v. Texas Gulf Sulphur Co.*, 401 F.2d, at 849.

(*continued on next page*)

(continued)

BASIC INC. v. LEVINSON
485 U.S. 224 (1988)

*   *   *

Whether merger discussions in any particular case are material therefore depends on the facts. Generally, in order to assess the probability that the event will occur, a factfinder will need to look to indicia of interest in the transactions at the highest corporate levels. Without attempting to catalog all such possible factors, we note by way of example that board resolutions, instructions to investment bankers, and actual negotiations between principals or their intermediaries may serve as indicia of interest. To assess the magnitude of the transaction to the issuer of the securities allegedly manipulated, a factfinder will need to consider such facts as the size of the two corporate entities and of the potential premiums over market value. No particular event or factor short of closing the transaction need to be either necessary or sufficient by itself to render merger discussions material.

As we clarify today, materiality depends on the significance the reasonable investor would place on the withheld or misrepresented information. The fact-specific inquiry we endorse here is consistent with the approach a number of courts have taken in assessing the materiality of merger negotiations. Because the standard of materiality we have adopted differs from that used by both courts below, we remand the case for reconsideration of the question whether a grant of summary judgment is appropriate on this record.

We turn to the question of reliance and the fraud-on-the-market theory. Succinctly put:

> "The fraud on the market theory is based on the hypothesis that, in an open and developed securities market, the price of a company's stock is determined by the available material information regarding the company and its business. . . . Misleading statements will therefore defraud purchasers of stock even if the purchasers do not directly rely on the misstatements. . . . The causal connection between the defendants' fraud and the plaintiffs' purchase of stock in such a case is no less significant than in a case of direct reliance on misrepresentations." *Peil v. Speiser*, 806 F.2d 1154, 1160–1161 (CA3 1986).

*   *   *

We agree that reliance is an element of a Rule 10b-5 cause of action. Reliance provides the requisite causal connection between a defendant's misrepresentation and a plaintiffs misrepresentation and a plaintiff's injury. There is, however, more than one way to demonstrate the causal connection.

*   *   *

Presumptions typically serve to assist courts in managing circumstances in which direct proof, for one reason or another, is rendered difficult. The courts below accepted a presumption, created by the fraud-on-the-market theory and subject to rebuttal by petitioners, that persons who had traded Basic shares had done so in reliance on the integrity of the price set by the market, but because of petitioners' material misrepresentations that price had been fraudulently depressed. Requiring a plaintiff to show a speculative state of facts, *i.e.*, how he would have acted if omitted material information had been disclosed, or if the misrepresentation had not been made, would place an unnecessarily unrealistic evidentiary burden on the Rule 10b-5 plaintiff who has traded on an impersonal market.

Arising out of considerations of fairness, public policy, and probability, as well as judicial economy, presumptions are also useful devices for allocating the burdens of proof between parties. The presumption of reliance employed in this case is consistent with, and, by facilitating Rule 10b-5 litigation, supports, the congressional policy embodied in the 1934 Act. . . .

The presumption is also supported by common sense and probability. Recent empirical studies have tended to confirm Congress' premise that the market price of shares traded on well-developed markets reflects all publicly available information, and, hence, any material misrepresentations. It has been noted that "it is hard to imagine that there ever is a buyer or seller who does not rely on market integrity. Who would knowingly roll the dice in a crooked crap game?" *Schlanger v. Four-Phase Systems, Inc.*, 555 F.Supp. 535, 538 (SDNY 1982). . . . An investor who buys or sells stock at the price set by the market does so in reliance on the integrity of that price. Because most publicly available information is reflected in market price, an investor's reliance on any public material misrepresentations, therefore, may be presumed for purposes of a Rule 10b-5 action.

*   *   *

The judgment of the Court of Appeals is vacated and the case is remanded to that court for further proceedings consistent with this opinion.

In addition to its decisions relating to intent (*Hochfelder*), tippees (*Dirks*), and materiality (*Basic*), the Supreme Court has considered the misappropriation theory, under which a person who misappropriates information from an employer faces insider trading liability. In a leading misappropriation theory case, the Second Circuit Court of Appeals reinstated an indictment against employees who traded on the basis of inside information obtained through their work at investment banking firms. The court concluded that the employees' violation of their fiduciary duty to the firms violated securities law. [United States v. Newman, 664 F.2d 12 (2d Cir. 1981)]

In 1987, the Supreme Court affirmed the conviction of a *Wall Street Journal* reporter who leaked advanced information about the contents of his "Heard on the Street" column. The reporter, who was sentenced to eighteen months in prison, had been convicted on both mail and wire fraud (see p. 89) and securities law charges for misappropriating information. The Court upheld the mail and wire fraud conviction by an 8–0 vote and the securities law conviction by a 4–4 vote. (In effect, the tie vote affirmed the conviction.) [Carpenter v. United States, 484 U.S. 19 (1987)]

Beyond these judge-made theories of liability, Congress had been concerned about insider trading and, in 1984 and 1988, substantially increased the penalties. A person convicted of insider trading now faces a maximum criminal fine of $1 million and a possible ten-year prison term. A civil penalty of up to three times the profit made (or loss avoided) by insider trading can also be imposed. This penalty is in addition to liability for profits made through insider trading. For example, financier Ivan Boesky, who was sentenced in 1987 to a three-year prison term for insider trading, was required to disgorge $50 million profits and was liable for another $50 million as a civil penalty.

Companies that knowingly and recklessly fail to prevent insider trading by their employees are subject to a civil penalty of up to three times the profit gained or loss avoided by insider trading or $1 million, whichever is greater. Corporations are also subject to a criminal fine of up to $2.5 million.

CHAPTER SUMMARY

Beyond state corporation laws, federal statutes—most importantly, the Securities Act of 1933 and the Securities Exchange Act of 1934—regulate the issuance and trading of corporate securities. The federal definition of security is broad, encompassing most investments, even those called by other names.

The law does not prohibit risky stock offerings; it bans only those lacking adequate disclosure of risks. The primary means for realizing this goal is the registration requirement: registration statements, prospectuses, and proxy solicitations must be filed with the SEC. Penalties for violation of securities law include criminal fines and jail terms, and damages may be awarded in civil suits by both the SEC and by private individuals injured by the violation of SEC rules.

A 1977 amendment to the 1934 act is the Foreign Corrupt Practices Act, which prohibits an issuer from paying a bribe or making any other payment to foreign officials in order to gain business by inducing the foreign official to influence his government in favor of the American company. This law requires issuers to keep accurate sets of books reflecting the dispositions of their assets and to maintain internal accounting controls to ensure that transactions comport with management's authorization.

The Securities Exchange Act of 1934 presents special hazards to those trading in public stock on the basis of inside information. One provision requires reimbursement to the company of any profits made from selling and buying stock during any six-month period by directors, officers, or shareholders owning 10 percent or more of the company's stock. Under Rule 10b-5, the SEC and private parties may sue insiders who traded on information not available to the general public, thus gaining an advantage either in selling or buying the stock. Insiders include company employees.

KEY TERM

Stop order   p. 975

SELF-TEST QUESTIONS

1. The issuance of corporate securities is governed by:
   (a) various Federal statutes
   (b) state law
   (c) both of the above
   (d) none of the above
2. The law that prohibits the payment of a bribe to foreign officials to gain business is called:
   (a) the Insider Trading Act
   (b) the Blue Sky Law
   (c) the Foreign Corrupt Practices Act
   (d) none of the above
3. The primary means for banning stock offerings that inadequately disclose risks is:
   (a) the registration requirement
   (b) SEC prohibition of risky stock offerings
   (c) both of the above
   (d) none of the above
4. To enforce its prohibition on insider trading, the SEC requires reimbursement to the company of any profits made from selling and buying stock during any six month period by directors owning:
   (a) 60 percent or more of company stock
   (b) 40 percent or more of company stock
   (c) 10 percent or more of company stock
   (d) none of the above
5. Under Rule 10b-5, insiders include:
   (a) all company employees
   (b) any person who possesses non-public information
   (c) all tippees
   (d) none of the above

DEMONSTRATION PROBLEM

A corporation called Coop City ran a 200-acre housing project in New York City. In order to rent housing in the project, tenants had to purchase stock in the corporation for $25 per share. Upon expiration of their leases, tenants were required to sell the stock back to the corporation for $25. Does the stock fall within the definition of a security for purposes of federal securities law? Why?

PROBLEMS

1. Anne operated a clothing store called Anne's Rags, Inc. She owned all of the stock in the company. After several years in the clothing business, Anne sold her stock to Louise, who personally managed the business. Is the sale governed by the anti-fraud provisions of federal securities law? Why?

2. While waiting tables at a campus-area restaurant, you overhear a conversation between two corporate executives, who indicate that their company has developed a new product that will revolutionize the computer industry. The product is to be announced in three weeks. If you purchase stock in the company before the announcement, will you be liable under federal securities law? Why?

3. Eric was hired as a management consultant by a major corporation to conduct a study, which took him three months to complete. While working on the study Eric learned that someone working in research and development for the company had recently made an important discovery. Before the discovery was announced publicly, Eric purchased stock in the company. Did he violate federal securities law? Why?

4. While working for the company, Eric also learned that it was planning a takeover of another corporation. Before announcement of a tender offer, Eric purchased stock in the target company. Did he violate securities law? Why?

5. The commercial lending department of First Bank made a substantial loan to Alpha Company after obtaining a favorable confidential earnings report from Alpha. Over lunch, Heidi, the loan officer who handled the loan, mentioned the earnings report to a friend who worked in the bank's trust department. The friend proceeded to purchase stock in Alpha for several of the bank's trusts. Discuss the legal implications.

6. In problem 5, assume that a week after the loan to Alpha, First Bank financed Beta Company's takeover of Alpha. During the financing negotiations, Heidi mentioned the Alpha earnings report to Beta officials; furthermore, the report was an important factor in Heidi's decision to finance the takeover. Discuss the legal implications.

7. In problem 6, assume that after work one day, Heidi told her friend in the trust department that Alpha was Beta's takeover target. The friend proceeded to purchase additional stock in Alpha for a bank trust he administered. Discuss the legal implications.

ANSWERS TO SELF-TEST QUESTIONS

1. (c)   2. (c)   3. (a)   4. (d)   5. (a)

SUGGESTED ANSWER TO DEMONSTRATION PROBLEM

No. Even though the tenant bought "stock" it does not fall within the federal securities law definition of a security because tenants had no expectation of profit. (They had to sell the stock for the same price at which they acquired it.) *United Housing Foundation, Inc. v. Forman,* 421 U.S. 837 (1975).

CHAPTER

45

Corporate Expansion and Dissolution

*I*n this chapter we explore two broad themes:

- Corporate expansion, including growth by absorbing other companies and geographic spread across state lines.
- Corporate dissolution—the winding up and liquidation of the corporation.

CORPORATE EXPANSION

We discuss four methods of corporate expansion: (1) purchase of assets other than in the regular course of business; (2) merger; (3) consolidation; and (4) purchase of stock in another corporation. In popular usage, "merger" often is used to mean any type of expansion by which one corporation acquires part or all of another corporation. But in legal terms, merger is only one of four methods of achieving expansion other than by internal growth.

Antitrust law—an important aspect of corporate expansion—will be discussed in Chapter 47. There, in the study of Section 7 of the Clayton Act, we note the hazards of merging or consolidating with, and

purchasing the stock or assets of, a competing corporation.

Purchase of Assets

After several years of successful merchandising, a corporation formed by Bob, Carol, and Ted (BCT Bookstore, Inc.) has opened three branch stores around town and discovered its transportation costs mounting. Inventory arrives in trucks operated by the Flying Truckman Co., Inc. BCT concludes that the economics of delivery do not warrant purchasing a single truck dedicated to hauling books for its four stores alone. Then Bob learns that the owners of Flying Truckman might be willing to part with their company because it has not been earning money lately. If BCT could reorganize Flying Truckman's other routes, it could reduce its own shipping costs while making a profit on other lines of business. There is one snag. As directors, Bob and Carol are anxious to make the acquisition, but Ted is not sure of its wisdom, because the newspapers have lately made accusations about criminal elements involved in Flying Truckman's business. If BCT Bookstores were to acquire the company in toto, the bookstores might be tarred by continuing unfavorable publicity. Ted is rallying several of BCT's shareholders against the proposal.

Under the circumstances, the simplest and safest way to acquire Flying Truckman is by purchasing its assets. That way BCT would own the trucks and whatever routes it chooses, without taking upon itself the stigma of the association. It could drop the name Flying Truckman.

In most states, the boards of directors of both the seller and buyer must approve a transfer of assets. Shareholders of the selling corporation must also consent by majority vote, but shareholders of the acquiring company need not be consulted, so Ted's opposition can be effectively mooted; see Figure 45-1. (When inventory is sold in bulk, the acquiring company must also comply with the law governing bulk transfers; see Chapter 17.) By purchasing the assets—trucks, truck routes, and the trademark Flying Truckman (to prevent anyone else from using it)—the acquiring corporation can carry on the functions of the acquired company without carrying on its business as such.

One of the principal advantages of this method

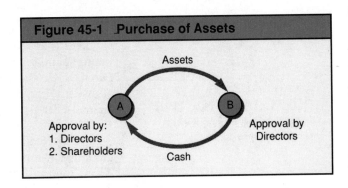

Figure 45-1 Purchase of Assets

Assets

A → B

Approval by:
1. Directors
2. Shareholders

Cash

Approval by Directors

of expansion is that the acquiring company generally is not liable for the debts of the corporation whose assets it purchased. Suppose BCT paid Flying Truckman, Inc., $250,000 for its trucks, routes, and name. With that cash, Flying Truckman, Inc., paid off several of its creditors. Its shareholders then voted to dissolve the corporation, leaving one creditor unsatisfied. The creditor can no longer sue Flying Truckman, Inc., since it does not exist. So he sues BCT Bookstores, Inc. Unless certain circumstances exist, as discussed in the following case, BCT is not liable for Flying Truckman's debts.

RAY v. ALAD CORPORATION
135 Cal.Rptr. 574, 560 P.2d 3 (1977)

WRIGHT, ASSOCIATE JUSTICE. Claiming damages for injury from a defective ladder, plaintiff asserts strict tort liability against defendant Alad Corporation (Alad II) which neither manufactured nor sold the ladder but prior to plaintiff's injury succeeded to the business of the ladder's manufacturer, the now dissolved "Alad Corporation" (Alad I), through a purchase of Alad I's assets for an adequate cash consideration. Upon acquiring Alad I's plant, equipment, inventory, trade name, and goodwill, Alad II continued to manufacture the same line of ladders under the "Alad" name, using the same equipment, designs, and personnel, and soliciting Alad I's customers through the same sales representatives with no outward indication of any change in the ownership of the business. The trial court entered summary judgment for Alad II and plaintiff appeals.

★   ★   ★

Our discussion of the law starts with the rule ordinarily applied to the determination of whether a corporation purchasing the principal assets of another corporation assumes the other's liabilities. As typically formulated the rule states that the purchaser does not assume the seller's liabilities unless

(continued on next page)

(*continued*)

RAY v. ALAD CORPORATION
135 Cal.Rptr. 574, 560
P.2d 3 (1977)

(1) there is an express or implied agreement of assumption, (2) the transaction amounts to a consolidation or merger of the two corporations, (3) the purchasing corporation is a mere continuation of the seller, or (4) the transfer of assets to the purchaser is for the fraudulent purpose of escaping liability for the seller's debts.

If this rule were determinative of Alad II's liability to plaintiff it would require us to affirm the summary judgment. None of the rule's four stated grounds for imposing liability on the purchasing corporation is present here. There was no express or implied agreement to assume liability for injury from defective products previously manufactured by Alad I. Nor is there any indication or contention that the transaction was prompted by any fraudulent purpose of escaping liability for Alad I's debts.

With respect to the second stated ground for liability, the purchase of Alad I's assets did not amount to a consolidation or merger. This exception has been invoked where one corporation takes all of another's assets without providing any consideration that could be made available to meet claims of the other's creditors or where the consideration consists wholly of shares of the purchaser's stock which are promptly distributed to the seller's shareholders in conjunction with the seller's liquidation. In the present case the sole consideration given for Alad I's assets was cash in excess of $207,000. Of this amount Alad I was paid $70,000 when the assets were transferred and at the same time a promissory note was given to Alad I for almost $114,000. Shortly before the dissolution of Alad I the note was assigned to the Hamblys, Alad I's principal stockholders, and thereafter the note was paid in full. The remainder of the consideration went for closing expenses or was paid to the Hamblys for consulting services and their agreement not to compete. There is no contention that this consideration was inadequate or that the cash and promissory note given to Alad I were not included in the assets available to meet claims of Alad I's creditors at the time of dissolution. Hence the acquisition of Alad I's assets was not in the nature of a merger or consolidation for purposes of the aforesaid rule.

Plaintiff contends that the rule's third stated ground for liability makes Alad II liable as a mere continuation of Alad I in view of Alad II's acquisition of all Alad I's operating assets, its use of those assets and of Alad I's former employees to manufacture the same line of products, and its holding itself out to customers and the public as a continuation of the same enterprise. However, California decisions holding that a corporation acquiring the assets of another corporation is the latter's mere continuation and therefore liable for its debts have imposed such liability only upon a showing of one or both of the following factual elements: (1) no adequate consideration was given for the predecessor corporation's assets and made available for meeting the claims of its unsecured creditors; (2) one or more persons were officers, directors, or stockholders of both corporations.

*   *   *

We therefore conclude that the general rule governing succession to liabilities does not require Alad II to respond to plaintiff's claim. . . .

[However,] we must decide whether the policies underlying strict tort liability for defective products call for a special exception to the rule that would otherwise insulate the present defendant from plaintiff's claim.

The purpose of the rule of strict tort liability "is to insure that the costs of injuries resulting from defective products are borne by the manufacturers that put such products on the market rather than by the injured persons who are powerless to protect themselves." However, the rule "does not rest on the analysis of the financial strength or bargaining power of the parties to the particular action. It rests, rather, on the proposition that '[t]he cost of an injury and the loss of time or health may be an overwhelming misfortune to the person injured, and a needless one, for the risk of injury can be insured by the manufacturer and distributed among the public as a cost of doing business.' (*Escola v. Coca Cola Bottling Co.*, 150 P.2d 436 [concurring opinion].)" Thus, "the paramount policy to be promoted by the rule is the protection of otherwise defenseless victims of manufacturing defects and the *spreading throughout society* of the cost of compensating them." Justification for imposing strict liability upon a *successor* to a manufacturer under the circumstances here presented rests upon (1) the virtual destruction of the plaintiff's remedies against the original manufacturer caused by the successor's acquisition of the business, (2) the successor's ability to assume the original manufacturer's risk-spreading role, and (3) the fairness of requiring the successor to assume a responsibility for defective products that was a burden necessarily attached to the original manufacturer's goodwill being enjoyed by the successor in the continued operation of the business.

* * *

We therefore conclude that a party which acquires a manufacturing business and continues the output of its line of products under the circumstances here presented assumes strict tort liability for defects in units of the same product line previously manufactured and distributed by the entity from which the business was acquired.

The judgment is reversed.

Several states, although not a majority, have adopted the *Ray* approach. The impact of this approach on small companies can be severe (see **Box 45-1**).

Merger

When the assets of a company are purchased, the company itself may or may not go out of existence. By contrast, in a **merger,** the acquired company goes out of existence by being absorbed into the acquiring company. The acquiring company receives all of the acquired company's assets, including physical property, and intangible property such as contracts, and goodwill. The acquiring company also assumes all debts of the acquired company. Unless the articles of incorporation state otherwise, majority approval by both boards of directors and by both sets of shareholders is necessary (see Figure 45-2). The shareholder majority must be of the total shares eligible to vote, not merely of the total actually represented at the special meeting called for the purpose of determining whether to merge.

BOX 45-

Changes in Products Liability Jeopardize Small Companies

By Sanford L. Jacobs

[Small companies are often hit the hardest by products liability lawsuits involving products made by equipment purchased from other companies. Insurance companies may terminate liability coverage when a client has too many lawsuits pending, forcing companies to insure themselves.—AUTHORS' NOTE]

Patrick J. Bruno never dreamed of the legal problems he was buying into in 1972 when he purchased the equipment to make die-cutting presses under the venerable Sheridan brand name. His company, Bruno Sherman Corp., has had to defend itself against more than 20 personal-injury lawsuits involving machines it didn't make. One was built before the 69-year-old Mr. Bruno was born. . . .

Mr. Bruno wasn't particularly concerned about products liability when he bought the Sheridan die-cutting press assets from Harris Corp., a big communications-equipment maker, in 1972. Harris previously had acquired T. W. & C. B. Sheridan Co.'s assets and assumed its liabilities in 1964. Mr. Bruno bought only certain assets, with $25,000 down and easy terms on the balance of about $200,000.

Mr. Bruno had a successful machine-tool repair business in Troy, N.Y., and believed he and his 35-year-old son Robert could build up Sheridan press sales. In a few years, they had annual sales of $2.5 million.

But in 1976, products liability

LIABILITY AND ACQUIRED COMPANIES

suits began to plague the company. By then, courts were liberalizing liability laws. The tendency was to award damages to a worker even if he had ignored common sense and safety warnings, foiled safety guards and was injured.

New notions about successor liability threatened to pierce the protection Bruno Sherman should have enjoyed because it didn't buy the Sheridan company or assume its liabilities. "I thought they could only blame me for what I made," Mr. Bruno says. He was wrong.

Some courts hold a company accountable for equipment built years before the company existed even if the new company's connection to the old manufacturer amounts only to continuing to use the old name. In effect, these judges are saying a company profiting from a predecessor's good will has to accept some liability, even if it doesn't buy the old concern or agree to assume its liabilities.

Victor E. Schwartz, a products liability specialist with Crowell & Moring, a Washington, D.C., law firm, says a flurry of new theories makes products liability "a little like placing a bet on roulette when the dealer has the right to change the numbers as the ball goes around."

Travelers Insurance Co. decided in 1977 it wanted out of the game. By then Bruno Sherman had nearly 20 lawsuits pending. Travelers settled some, without disclosing how much it paid, and told Mr. Bruno he must

pick a date in early 1978 for his products liability coverage to end. "I told them Feb. 23, my birthday," he says. "I never want to forget what they did."

A new company can try to protect itself against claims involving equipment it didn't make by notifying users the machinery isn't safe. Joseph A. Sherman, a Kansas City, Mo., defense attorney, says it is wise to refuse to service or sell parts for old equipment that doesn't meet current safety standards. Mr. Bruno has put owners of old Sheridan presses on notice. But his attorney, John T. Mitchell, says: "We can't really control the situation. They own the press."

For more than three years, Bruno Sherman had to insure itself because no one would cover its products liability at a reasonable premium. Legal fees for the period have run about $50,000, Mr. Bruno says. Recently, the company was able to buy $5 million of products liability insurance for a $20,000 annual premium.

The immediate future is covered. But the period without insurance isn't over, because someone injured then might bring suit sometime in the future. Plaintiff lawyers tend to sue everyone they can think of, so Bruno Sherman has been named in some suits that it eventually was able to have itself removed from—but only after spending $2,000 to $5,000 for legal costs.

Mr. Bruno's lawyer told him that publication of this column might even increase the number of lawsuits. It serves to tell more people that a company exists that is carrying on the Sheridan name.

Source: *Wall Street Journal*, November 30, 1981

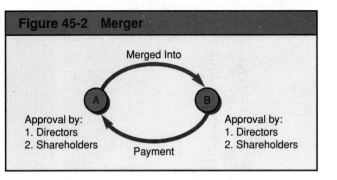

Figure 45-2   Merger

Merged Into

A → B

Approval by:
1. Directors
2. Shareholders

Payment

Approval by:
1. Directors
2. Shareholders

Consolidation

Consolidation is virtually the same as a merger. The companies merge, but the resulting entity is a new corporation. As with mergers, the board and shareholders must approve the consolidation by majority votes (see Figure 45-3). The resulting corporation becomes effective when the secretary of state issues a certificate of merger or incorporation.

Purchase of Stock

Takeovers   The fourth method of expanding, purchase of a company's stock, is more complicated. The **takeover** has become a popular method for gaining control because it does not require an affirmative vote by the target company's board of directors. The acquiring company appeals directly to the target's shareholders, by dangling before their eyes a premium above market value for their shares. The acquiring company usually need not purchase 100 percent of the shares. Indeed, if the shares are numerous and widely enough dispersed, control can be

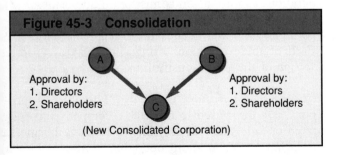

Figure 45-3   Consolidation

A → C ← B

Approval by:
1. Directors
2. Shareholders

Approval by:
1. Directors
2. Shareholders

(New Consolidated Corporation)

achieved by acquiring less than half the outstanding stock.

Tender Offers   In the case of closely held corporations, it is possible for a company bent on takeover to negotiate with each stockholder individually. That is impossible in the case of large publicly held companies. To reach all shareholders, the acquiring company must make a **tender offer.** In fact, the tender "offer" is not really an offer at all in the technical sense; it is an invitation to shareholders to tender their shares for sale at a stipulated price. The tender offer might express the price in cash or in shares of the acquiring company. Ordinarily the tender offeror will want to purchase only a controlling interest, so it will limit the tender to a specified number of shares and reserve the right not to purchase any above that number. It will also condition the tender offer on receiving a minimum number of shares so that it need buy none if stockholders do not offer a threshold number of shares for purchase.

State vs. Federal Regulation of Takeovers   Under the federal Williams Act, upon commencement of a tender offer for more than 5 percent of the target's stock, the offeror must file a statement with the Securities and Exchange Commission (SEC) stating the source of funds used in making the purchase, the purpose of the purchase, and the extent of its holdings in the target company. Even when a tender offer has not been made, any person who acquires more than 5 percent ownership must file a statement with the SEC within ten days.

Because officers and directors of the target companies have no legal say in whether stockholders will tender their shares, many states beginning in the early 1970s enacted takeover laws. The first generation of these laws acted as delaying devices by imposing lengthy waiting periods before the tender offer could be put into effect. Many of the laws expressly gave management of the target companies a right to a hearing, which could be dragged out for weeks or months, giving the target time to build up a defense. The political premise of the laws was the protection of incumbent managers from takeover by out-of-state corporations—though the "localness" of some managements was but a polite fiction. In 1982, the Supreme Court struck down the Illinois takeover law because it violated the Commerce Clause, which prohibits states from unduly regulating the flow of interstate commerce. [Edgar v. Mite Corp., 457 U.S. 624 (1982)]

Following the *Mite* decision, states began to enact a second generation of takeover laws. In 1987, the Supreme Court upheld an Indiana second-generation statute that prevents an offeror who has acquired 20 percent or more of a target's stock from voting unless other shareholders (not including management) approve. The vote to approve can be delayed for up to 50 days from the date the offeror files a statement reporting the acquisition. The Court concluded that the Commerce Clause was not violated because the Indiana law, unlike the law in *Mite,* is limited to Indiana corporations that have a substantial number of Indiana shareholders. [CTS Corporation v. Dynamics Corporation of America, 481 U.S. 69 (1987)]

Emboldened by the *CTS* decision, almost half the states have adopted a third-generation law that requires a bidder to wait several years before merging with the target company, unless the target's board agrees in advance to the merger. Because in many cases a merger is the reason for the bid, these laws are especially powerful. In 1989, the Seventh Circuit Court of Appeals upheld the Wisconsin third-generation law and the Supreme Court decided not to review the decision. [Amanda Acquisition Corp. v. Universal Foods Corp., 877 F.2d 496 (7th Cir. 1989)]

Short-Form Mergers If one company acquires 90 percent or more of the stock of another, it can merge with the target company through the so-called **short-form merger.** Only the parent's board of directors need approve the merger; consent of shareholders of either company is unnecessary (see Figure 45-4).

Appraisal Rights

A shareholder has the right to dissent from a corporate plan to merge, consolidate, or sell all or substantially all of the corporate assets. The law requires the shareholder to file with the corporation, before the vote, a notice of intention to demand the fair value of his shares. If the plan is approved and the shareholder does not vote in favor, the corporation must send a notice to the shareholder specifying procedures for obtaining payment, and the shareholder must

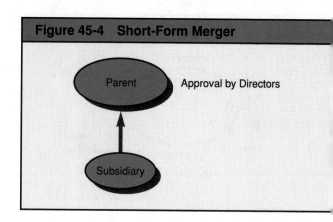

Figure 45-4   Short-Form Merger

demand payment within the time set in the notice, which cannot be less than thirty days. *Fair value* means the value of shares immediately before the effective date of the corporate action to which the shareholder has objected. Appreciation and depreciation in anticipation of the action are excluded, unless the exclusion is unfair.

If the shareholder and the company cannot agree on the fair value, the company must file a petition requesting a court to determine the fair value. The method of determining fair value depends on the circumstances. When there is a public market for stock traded on an exchange, fair value is usually the price quoted on the exchange. In some circumstances, other factors, especially net asset value and investment value—for example, earnings potential—assume greater importance.

FOREIGN CORPORATIONS

Special problems arise when corporations expand their business across state lines. We address three of these in some detail: (1) Can states impose on foreign corporations conditions on admission to do business? (2) Do state courts have jurisdiction over foreign corporations? (3) May states tax foreign corporations? Each of these questions brings into play a separate section of the U.S. Constitution.

Foreign Corporation Defined "Foreign corporation" is a term used to describe a company incorporated outside the state in which it is doing business. A Delaware corporation, operating in all states, is a foreign corporation in forty-nine of them.

Conditions on Admission to Do Business

States can impose on foreign corporations conditions on admission to do business if certain constitutional barriers are surmounted. One potential problem is the Privileges and Immunities Clause of the Constitution, which provides that "citizens shall be entitled to all privileges and immunities of citizens in the several states" (Article 4, Section 2). The Supreme Court has interpreted this murky language to mean that states may not discriminate between their own citizens and those of other states. For example, the Court voided a tax New Hampshire imposed on out-of-state commuters on the grounds that "the tax falls exclusively on the incomes of nonresidents." [Austin v. New Hampshire, 420 U.S. 656 (1975)] However, corporations are uniformly held not to be citizens for purposes of this clause, so the states may impose burdens on foreign corporations that they do not put upon companies incorporated under their laws. But these burdens may only be imposed on companies which conduct intrastate business; states may not impose them if the company is exclusively engaged in interstate commerce.

Other constitutional rights of the corporation or its members may also come into play when states attempt to license foreign corporations. Thus, when Arkansas sought to revoke the license of a Missouri construction company to do business within the state, the Supreme Court held that the state had acted unconstitutionally (violating Article III, Section 2) in conditioning the license on a waiver of the right to remove a case from the state courts to the federal courts. [Terral v. Burke Construction Co., 257 U.S. 529 (1922)]

Typical Requirements for Foreign Corporations Certain preconditions for doing business are common to most states. Foreign corporations are required to obtain from the secretary of state a "certificate of authority" to conduct business. The foreign corporation also must maintain a registered office with a registered agent who works there. The registered agent may be served with all legal process, demands, or notices required by law to be served on the corporation. Foreign corporations are generally granted every right and privilege enjoyed by domestic corporations.

These requirements must be met whenever the corporation transacts business within the state. However, some activities do not fall within the definition of "transacting business" and may be carried on even if the foreign corporation has not obtained a certificate of authority. These include filing or defending a lawsuit, holding meetings of directors or shareholders, maintaining bank accounts, maintaining offices for the transfer of the company's own securities, selling through independent contractors, soliciting orders through agents or employees (but only if the orders become binding contracts upon acceptance outside the state), creating or acquiring security interests in real or personal property, securing or collecting debts, transacting any business in interstate commerce, and "conducting an isolated transaction that is completed within 30 days and that is not one in the course of repeated transactions of a like nature." (RMBCA Section 15.01.)

Penalties for Failure to Comply with Statute A corporation may not sue in the state courts to enforce its rights until it obtains a certificate of authority. It may defend any lawsuits brought against it, however. The state attorney general has authority to collect civil penalties that vary from state to state. Other sanctions in various states include fines and penalties on taxes owed; fines and imprisonment of corporate agents, directors, and officers; nullification of corporate contracts; and personal liability on contracts by officers and directors. In some states, contracts made by a corporation that has failed to qualify are void, as illustrated by the following case.

ALLSTATE LEASING CORP. v. SCROGGINS

541 So.2d 17

(Ala.Civ.App. 1989)

INGRAM, JUDGE.

Allstate Leasing Corporation (Allstate) commenced this action against Larry and Amanda Scroggins for breach of a lease on an ice cream machine. The Scrogginses later filed a third-party complaint against Sunbelt Equipment Corporation (Sunbelt), the supplier of the leased equipment. The trial court ultimately granted summary judgment against Allstate on the ground that Allstate is a foreign corporation which has not qualified to do business in Alabama and, therefore, may not enforce its contract in our courts. Allstate now appeals from the summary judgment against it.

The Scrogginses own a retail food store in Alexander City, Alabama. They were contacted at their store about the purchase of an ice cream machine by salesmen who allegedly represented that they were agents of Allstate, a Virginia corporation, and Sunbelt, a Georgia corporation. The Scrogginses agreed to lease a machine to be placed in the store. Sunbelt was to install the equipment and sell the ingredients necessary to make the ice cream, but leasing was to be provided by Allstate.

Sunbelt thereafter delivered and installed the equipment and sold the ice cream products to the Scrogginses. At the same time, they signed a lease contract with Allstate and a certificate of equipment acceptance and tendered the first lease payment. There is some dispute about whether the salesmen represented Allstate, but we note that the contract forms were preprinted with the Allstate logo and identified Allstate as the other party to the contract. Approximately two weeks later, Allstate telephoned the Scrogginses to verify the receipt of the equipment, review the lease, and confirm the agreement. Allstate then executed the contract and purchased the leased equipment from Sunbelt. When the Scrogginses encountered mechanical difficulties with the machine, they refused to make further payments until the problems were remedied. Allstate then filed a lawsuit to enforce the lease.

A foreign corporation is required to obtain a certificate of authority from the secretary of state before transacting business in Alabama. Failure of a corporation to qualify means that any contracts it makes or enters into in this state are void and unenforceable. Nevertheless, if the unqualified corporation's activities are considered "interstate" in nature, rather than "intrastate," it is protected from the requirements of § 10-2A-247(a) by the Commerce Clause of the United States Constitution (U.S. Const. art. 1, § 8, cl. 3).

It is undisputed that Allstate is a Virginia corporation which has never obtained the requisite certificate of authority to do business in Alabama. Allstate contends on appeal, however, that it should not be subject to the qualification requirements because (1) its contract with the Scrogginses was not made or entered into in this state, and (2) it is engaged in interstate, rather than intrastate, commerce.

Our initial determination must be whether Allstate is engaged in sufficient intrastate commerce to trigger § 10-2A-247(a). The general rule is that " 'a single act of business' is sufficient to bring a foreign corporation within the purview of 'doing business' in Alabama, though acts such as delivering materials or soliciting business are generally not enough to constitute 'doing business.' " 525 So.2d at 1370. There is no inflexible rule we can apply, however, in determining whether a foreign corporation is doing business in Alabama within the meaning of § 10-2A-247(a). Each case must be decided based upon its own particular facts.

The trial court stated the following in its order granting summary judgment:

"Even if we concede that no agent of Plaintiff has ever set foot in Alabama, it is clear that Plaintiff's business consists of owning equipment and collecting rents thereon. . . . These pieces of equipment are located in Alabama, on what is intended to be a permanent basis. Alabama citizens, on an ongoing basis, pay rent with respect to that equipment. Plaintiff's activity in Alabama is not incidental to the sale, installation or servicing of the equipment. Owning that equipment in Alabama and collecting rent from citizens of Alabama are the sum and substance of Plaintiff's business. Furthermore, this is not an isolated transaction; there have, since 1984, been thirty-one (31) transactions involving about $350,000.

"We are aware of *Johnson v. MPL Leasing Corporation*, 441 So.2d 904 ([Ala.] 1983), which is quite similar to this case. In *Johnson*, however, our Supreme Court found that the only activities of the plaintiff in Alabama consisted of '(1) delivering the copying machines by common carrier and (2) filing this action.' Allstate, the Plaintiff herein, has done more than that: Allstate has owned within this state on a routine and ongoing basis many machines which it has leased to Alabama residents, and the continuing ownership of those machines in Alabama is an indispensable part of Allstate's primary business activity. These are not isolated transactions, and they are not merely incidental to another activity."

We agree and hold that Allstate's activities in this state are sufficiently intrastate in nature to subject it to the requirements of § 10-2A-247(a).

Having determined that Allstate was doing business in Alabama, it is not necessary for us to determine whether the contract was made or entered into here. The contract is not entitled to enforcement in our courts, regardless of whether it was made elsewhere to be performed in the state or made in the state and void.

Although we realize that § 10-2A-247(a) imposes stern sanctions on foreign corporations in situations like the one before us, its purpose is to provide a method by which our state can protect its residents from possible abuse by uncontrolled foreign corporations. Our duty is to uphold the principles established by our Constitution and statutes. We find that the Scrogginses were entitled to judgment as a matter of law, and that judgment must, therefore, be affirmed.

Jurisdiction over Foreign Corporations

Whether corporations are subject to state court jurisdiction depends on the extent to which they are operating within the state. If the corporation is qualified to do business within the state and has a certificate of authority or license, then state courts have jurisdiction and process may be served on the corporation's registered agent. If the corporation has failed to name an agent or is doing business without a certificate, the plaintiff may serve the secretary of state on the corporation's behalf.

Even if the corporation is not transacting enough business within the state to be required to qualify for a certificate or license, it may still be subject to suit in state courts under "long arm statutes." These laws permit state courts to exercise personal jurisdiction over a corporation that has sufficient contacts with the state.

The major constitutional limitation on long-arm statutes is the due process clause. The Supreme Court upheld the validity of long-arm statutes applied to corporations in *International Shoe Co.* v. *Washington,* 326 U.S. 310 (1945). This opinion is excerpted beginning on page 50. The "minimum contacts" test discussed in that decision is still applied today, as members of the British rock band Judas Priest and their corporations discovered in the following case. (In 1990, the trial court judge ruled in favor of the defendants on the grounds that any subliminal messages in "Stained Class" were unintentional and did not cause the suicidal actions.)

JUDAS PRIEST v. DISTRICT COURT
760 P.2d 137 (Nev. 1988)

PER CURIAM:

In the early evening hours of December 23, 1985, Raymond Belknap and James Vance took a sawed-off shotgun to an empty churchyard. They made their way to the children's play area and sat down. Raymond Belknap anchored the gun beneath his chin, pulled the trigger, and thus ended his short life. James Vance also shot himself, but survived with critical injuries.

Lawsuits were soon filed against the petitioners and others by Vance and by Belknap's mother, claiming that the Judas Priest album "Stained Class" had directly caused their suicidal actions. Petitioners herein, the individual members of Judas Priest and their corporations, have requested that we prohibit the district court from asserting *in personam* jurisdiction over them. For the reasons expressed in this opinion, we deny the writ.

A writ of prohibition is the appropriate remedy to challenge the district court's refusal to quash service of process. Under the circumstances of this case, however, we do not believe the district court exceeded its jurisdiction in refusing to quash service of process on the petitioners. A court may assert jurisdiction if there is a statutory basis for that assertion which does not contravene the due process clause of the United States Constitution. Respondents have claimed, and petitioners have denied, that jurisdiction may be asserted under two Nevada statutes, NRS 14.065(2)(a) and NRS 14.080. NRS 14.065(2)(a) provides that any person who transacts business within Nevada submits himself to the jurisdiction of Nevada courts, even if he acts through an agent; NRS 14.080 allows for service of process on any corporation which directly or indirectly supplies a product for distribution, sale or use when an injury results from such activity in the state. In our opinion, either statute allows the assertion of jurisdiction in this case.

We have held that the Nevada long-arm statutes reach the limits of due process set by the Constitution. Due process requires "minimum contacts" between the defendant and the forum state; additionally, the exercise of jurisdiction must be reasonable. *See Asahi Metal Industry Co. v. Superior Court,* 480 U.S. 102 (1987); *Burger King Corp. v. Rudzewicz,* 471 U.S. 462 (1985); *World-Wide Volkswagen Corp. v. Woodson,* 444 U.S. 286 (1980); *Internat. Shoe Co. v. Washington,* 326 U.S. 310 (1945). Because we conclude that Judas Priest has established "minimum contacts" with Nevada, and that it is reasonable to assert jurisdiction in this case, we decline to grant the writ of prohibition requested by the petitioners.

Judas Priest created and recorded the master album of "Stained Class," and entered into a licensing agreement with CBS Records, Inc. for the express purpose of distributing and selling copies of the album throughout the United States. The creator of a product is subject to personal jurisdiction where his product is sold if he is aware of and uses a national distribution system to make the sale. Jurisdiction is not destroyed simply because the product passes through a middleman. The test is whether the defendant has targeted the forum state for marketing his product, thereby purposefully availing himself of the benefits of the forum. In addition to the licensing agreement, which requires the payment of royalties to Judas Priest for each album sold, we note that the band has made two concert appearances in the state of Nevada, presumably to promote sales and increase its following. In our opinion, this activity is sufficient to show that Judas Priest has targeted Nevada as a market for sales of its products, and has thereby availed itself of the benefits of the forum.

The exercise of jurisdiction in this case is not unreasonable, because the state has a strong interest in protecting its citizens from personal injury. Furthermore, the only alternative forum available to the plaintiffs would be the courts of England. An overseas lawsuit is admittedly expensive and burdensome. While it is true that the members of Judas Priest will not be forced to defend a lawsuit in a country distant from their own, it is more equitable to place such a burden on them, and not the plaintiffs, because the band members consciously and deliberately chose to develop a world-wide market.

We are satisfied that the district court did not err by asserting *in personam* jurisdiction over the petitioners herein. We therefore deny the petition, and affirm the jurisdiction of the district court. Of course, in so doing, we are concerned only with the issue of jurisdiction, and we do not reach any question related to the merits of the cause of action respondents have attempted to allege.

In recent years the "nationalization of commerce" has given way to internationalization of commerce. This change has resulted in difficult jurisdictional questions that involve conflicting policy considerations. As **Box 45-2** indicates, the Supreme Court is divided over the resolution of these issues.

Taxing Authority

May states tax foreign corporations? Since a state may obviously tax its domestic corporations, the question might seem surprising. Why should a state ever be barred from taxing foreign corporations licensed to do business in the state? If the foreign corporation was engaged in purely local, intrastate business, no quarrel would arise. The constitutional difficulty is whether the tax constitutes an unreasonable burden on the company's interstate business, in violation of the Commerce Clause. (The Commerce Clause provides that Congress has power "to regulate Commerce . . . among the several States. . . ." [U.S. Constitution, Article I, Section 8, clause 3].) The basic approach, illustrated in the following case, is that a state can impose a tax on activities for which the state gives legal protection, so long as the tax does not unreasonably burden interstate commerce.

D.H. HOLMES CO. LTD. v. McNAMARA
486 U.S. 24 (1988)

CHIEF JUSTICE REHNQUIST delivered the opinion of the Court.

Appellant D. H. Holmes Company, Ltd., is a Louisiana corporation with its principal place of business and registered office in New Orleans. Holmes owns and operates 13 department stores in various locations throughout Louisiana that employ about 5,000 workers. It has approximately 500,000 credit card customers and an estimated 1,000,000 other customers within the State.

In 1979–1981, Holmes contracted with several New York companies for the design and printing of merchandise catalogs. The catalogs were designed in New York, but were actually printed in Atlanta, Boston, and Oklahoma City. From these locations, 82% of the catalogs were directly mailed to residents of Louisiana; the remainder of the catalogs were mailed to customers in Alabama, Mississippi, and Florida, or were sent to Holmes for distribution at its flagship store on Canal Street in New Orleans. The catalogs were shipped free of charge to the addressee, and their entire cost (about $2,000,000 for the three-year period), including mailing, was borne by Holmes. Holmes did not, however, pay any sales tax where the catalogs were designed or printed.

Although the merchandise catalogs were mailed to selected customers, they contained instructions to the postal carrier to leave them with the current resident if the addressee had moved, and to return undeliverable catalogs to appellant's Canal Street store. Holmes freely concedes that the purpose of the catalogs was to promote sales at its stores and to instill name-recognition in future buyers. The catalogs included inserts which could be used to order appellant's products by mail.

The Louisiana Department of Revenue and Taxation, of which appellee is the current Secretary, conducted an audit of Holmes' tax returns for 1979–1981 and determined that it was liable for delinquent use taxes on the value of the catalogs. The Department of Revenue and Taxation assessed the use tax pursuant to La.Rev. Stat.Ann. §§ 47:302 and 47:321 (West 1970 and Supp.1988), which are set forth in the margin. Together, §§ 47:302(A)(2) and 47:321(A)(2) impose a use tax of 3% on all tangible personal property used in Louisiana. "Use," as defined elsewhere in the statute, is the exercise of any right or power over tangible personal property incident to ownership, and includes consumption, distribution, and storage. The use tax is designed to compensate the State for sales tax that is lost when goods are purchased out-of-state and brought for use into Louisiana, and is calculated on the retail price the property would have brought when imported.

When Holmes refused to pay the use tax assessed against it, the State filed suit in Louisiana Civil District Court to collect the tax. [The lower courts held for the State.]

*   *   *

The Commerce Clause of the Constitution, Art. I, § 8, cl. 3, provides that Congress shall have the power "[t]o regulate Commerce with foreign Nations, and among the several States, and with the Indian Tribes." Even where Congress has not acted affirmatively to protect interstate commerce, the Clause prevents States from discriminating against that commerce. The "distinction between the power of the State to shelter its people from menaces to their health or safety and from fraud, even when those dangers emanate from interstate commerce, and its lack of power to retard, burden or constrict the flow of such commerce for their economic advantage, is one deeply rooted in both our history and our law." *H.P. Hood & Sons v. Du Mond*, 336 U.S. 525, 533, (1949).

One frequent source of conflict of this kind occurs when a State seeks to tax the sale or use of goods within its borders. This recurring dilemma is exemplified in what has come to be the leading case in the area, *Complete Auto Transit, Inc. v. Brady*, 430 U.S. 274, (1977). In *Complete Auto*, Mississippi imposed a tax on appellant's business of in-state transportation of motor vehicles manufactured outside the State. We found that the State's tax did not violate the Commerce Clause, because appellant's activity had a substantial nexus with Mississippi, and the tax was fairly apportioned, did not discriminate against interstate commerce, and was fairly related to benefits provided by the State.

*   *   *

Complete Auto abandoned the abstract notion that interstate commerce "itself" cannot be taxed by the States. We recognized that, with certain restrictions, interstate commerce may be required to pay its fair share of State taxes. Accordingly, in the present case, it really makes little difference for Commerce Clause purposes whether appellant's catalogs "came to rest" in the mailboxes of its Louisiana customers or whether they were still considered in the stream of interstate commerce. . . .

*   *   *

In the case before us, then, the application of Louisiana's use tax to Holmes' catalogs does not violate the Commerce Clause if the tax complies with the four prongs of *Complete Auto*. We have no doubt that the second and third elements of the test are satisfied. The Louisiana taxing scheme is fairly apportioned, for it provides a credit against its use tax for sales taxes that have been paid in other States. Holmes paid no sales tax for the catalogs where they were designed or printed; if it had, it would have been eligible for a credit against the use tax exacted. Similarly, Louisiana imposed its use tax

(*continued on next page*)

(continued)

D.H. HOLMES CO. LTD. v. McNAMARA
486 U.S. 24 (1988)

only on the 82% of the catalogs distributed in-state; it did not attempt to tax that portion of the catalogs that went to out-of-state customers.

The Louisiana tax structure likewise does not discriminate against interstate commerce. The use tax is designed to compensate the state for revenue lost when residents purchase out-of-state goods for use within the State. It is equal to the sales tax applicable to the same tangible personal property purchased in-state; in fact, both taxes are set forth in the same sections of the Louisiana statutes.

Complete Auto requires that the tax be fairly related to benefits provided by the State, but that condition is also met here. Louisiana provides a number of services that facilitate Holmes' sale of merchandise within the State: It provides fire and police protection for Holmes' stores, runs mass transit and maintains public roads which benefit appellant's customers, and supplies a number of other civic services from which Holmes profits. To be sure, many others in the State benefit from the same services; but that does not alter the fact that the use tax paid by Holmes, on catalogs designed to increase sales, is related to the advantages provided by the State which aid appellant's business.

Finally, we believe that Holmes' distribution of its catalogs reflects a substantial nexus with Louisiana. To begin with, Holmes' contention that it lacked sufficient control over the catalogs' distribution in Louisiana to be subject to the use tax verges on the nonsensical. Holmes ordered and paid for the catalogs and supplied the list of customers to whom the catalogs were sent; any catalogs that could not be delivered were returned to it. Holmes admits that it initiated the distribution to improve its sales and name-recognition among Louisiana residents. Holmes also has a significant presence in Louisiana, with 13 stores and over $100,000,000 in annual sales in the State. The distribution of catalogs to approximately 400,000 Louisiana customers was directly aimed at expanding and enhancing its Louisiana business. There is "nexus" aplenty here. [Judgment affirmed.]

State taxation of corporate income raises special concerns. In the absence of ground rules, a company doing business in many states could be liable for paying income tax to several different states on the basis of its total earnings. A company doing business in all fifty states, for example, would pay five times its earnings in income taxes if each state were to charge a 10 percent tax on those earnings. Obviously, such a result would seriously burden interstate commerce. The courts have long held, therefore, that the states may only tax that portion of the company's earnings attributable to the business carried on in the state. To compute the proportion of a company's total earnings subject to tax within the state, most states have adopted a formula based on the local percentage of the company's total sales, property, and payroll.

DISSOLUTION

In General

Dissolution is corporate death—the end of the legal existence of the corporation. It is not the same as *liquidation,* which is the process of paying the creditors and distributing the assets. Until dissolved, a corporation endures, despite the vicissitudes of the economy or its internal affairs. As Justice Cardozo said

LAW AND LIFE

BOX 45-2

Unsettled Issue of Jurisdiction

[*The issue of U.S. jurisdiction over international trade is still unsettled. Under the "stream of commerce" theory adopted in several states, a foreign manufacturer who anticipates that a product will be sold in a particular state also foresees that it can be subject to the laws and courts of that state.*— AUTHORS' NOTE]

While Gary Zurcher was driving along Interstate 80 in Solano County, Calif., eight and a half years ago, he lost control of his motorcycle and collided with a tractor rig. He was severely injured and his wife was killed.

Mr. Zurcher said a defective rear tire on his motorcycle caused the accident, so he filed a complaint in a California court against the Taiwanese manufacturer of the tire tube, the Cheng Shin Rubber Industrial Company. Cheng Shin, in turn, sought indemnification by suing the makers of the tire valve, the Asahi Metal Industry Company of Japan, in California.

Eventually, Mr. Zurcher settled his claim against Cheng Shin. But the issue remained whether a California court had jurisdiction to hear a case between *a Taiwanese tire tube manufacturer and a Japanese tire valve maker*, both of whose products could be found as components of motorcycles sold by California retailers.

* * *

Although the United States Supreme Court recently said the lower court could not hear the case, its decision about the constitutionality of

JURISDICTION AND INTERNATIONAL TRADE

certain state jurisdiction standards left more questions unresolved than it answered. The Court was dead-locked on the issue of whether a producer of goods entering the "stream of commerce" may be subject to liability in states where they are used.

As international trade burgeons, the Court is expected to be asked again to define the exact boundaries of state court authority to hear cases involving people and companies from different states and countries. In the last three terms alone, the Court has grappled on five occasions with thorny legal questions of when state courts have personal jurisdiction over out-of-state defendants.

At stake in the resolution of such jurisdictional disputes is more than just the authority of state courts. In the Asahi Metal case, for instance, foreign trade groups and companies had argued that a ruling in favor of the California court would increase the costs and uncertainties of international trade and encourage foreign governments to adopt similar statutes to reach American companies.

On the other hand, according to some legal commentators, a rule restricting state court jurisdiction could sharply curtail the ability of American consumers and companies to collect in commercial or injury disputes. Juries and product-liability laws are considered more generous in the United States than in foreign countries.

"This is not an easy question for the Court," said Maurice Rosenberg, professor of civil procedure at the Co-

lumbia Law School. "The recent trend has been towards limiting state court jurisdiction, although plaintiffs still have plenty of opportunities to sue foreign defendants."

The modern rules governing personal jurisdiction date to 1945. In a famous case, International Shoe Co. v. State of Washington, the Supreme Court said that, to be consistent with the due-process clause in the 14th Amendment to the Constitution, state courts could only assert jurisdiction over defendants who at least had "minimum contacts" with the state hearing the case.

Before the International Shoe case, courts had used such concepts as consent, physical presence or doing business in the state as the touchstones of when they could assert jurisdiction without violating the due-process clause. But as interstate commerce grew after World War I, the Court shifted the focus away from conduct within state borders and toward what it called "traditional notions of fair play and substantial justice."

Precisely how far the Court has been willing to expand this notion in an era of increasing international trade remains unclear. The present confusion among states about the requirements of the due process clause goes back to a 1980 decision.

* * *

The Court said then that a retailer who merely foresees his product will be used in another state is not subject to that state's courts. But the Court added that, if a defendant reasonably anticipates being called into another state's courts, then those courts may assert jurisdiction.

(*continued on next page*)

BOX 45-2

(Box 45-2 continued)

Meanwhile, state courts around the country have begun adopting what has become known as the stream of commerce theory of jurisdiction. Under such a theory, a court can hear a case against a foreign manufacturer if the company anticipates that the product is being marketed in the state.

The reasoning behind the theory is that, if a manufacturer anticipates his product will be sold in a state, it also foresees that it can be subject to that state's laws and courts.

In the Asahi Metal case, the Court ruled California could not hear the case because it would be "an unreasonable" assertion of jurisdiction. But it split, 4 to 4, over the constitutionality of the stream of commerce theory. The ruling, leaving the issue unresolved for now, prompted Professor Rosenberg to note that on jurisdictional matters, "the more the Justices explain, the more we don't understand."

Source: *New York Times*, March 16, 1987

---

while serving as Chief Judge of the New York Court of Appeals: "Neither bankruptcy . . . nor cessation of business . . . nor dispersion of stockholders, nor the absence of directors . . . nor all combined, will avail without more to stifle the breath of juristic personality. The corporation abides as an ideal creation, impervious to the shocks of these temporal vicissitudes. Not even the sequestration of the assets at the hands of a receiver will terminate its being." [Petrogradsky Mejdunarodny Kommerchesky Bank v. National City Bank, 170 N.E. 479, 482 (N.Y. 1930)]

Voluntary Dissolution

Any corporation may be dissolved with the unanimous written consent of the shareholders. This provision is obviously applicable primarily to closely held corporations. Dissolution can also be effected even if some shareholders dissent. The directors must first adopt a resolution by majority vote recommending the dissolution. The shareholders must then have an opportunity to vote on the resolution at a meeting after being notified of its purpose. A majority of the outstanding voting shares is necessary to carry the resolution. Although this procedure is most often used when a company has been inactive, nothing bars its use by large corporations. In 1979, UV Industries, 357th on the Fortune 500 list, with profits of $40 million annually, voted to dissolve and to distribute some $500 million to its stockholders—in part as a means of fending off a hostile takeover. "A company that's worth more dead than alive," *Fortune* magazine called it (February 26, 1979, pp. 42–44).

Once dissolution has been approved, the corporation may dissolve by filing articles of dissolution with the secretary of state. The articles may be filed as the corporation begins to wind up its affairs, or at any time thereafter. The process of winding up is known as liquidation. The company must notify all creditors of its intention to liquidate. It must collect and dispose of its assets, discharge all obligations, and distribute any remainder to its stockholders.

Involuntary Dissolution

In certain cases, dissolution can be involuntary. A state may bring an action to dissolve a corporation on one of five grounds: failure to file annual report or pay taxes, fraud in procuring incorporation, exceeding or abusing authority conferred, failure for thirty days to appoint and maintain a registered agent, and failure to notify the state of a change of registered office or agent.

Judicial Liquidation

Action by Shareholder   A shareholder may file suit to have a court dissolve the company on a showing that the company is being irreparably injured because the directors are deadlocked in the management of corporate affairs and the shareholders cannot break the deadlock. Shareholders may also sue for liquidation if corporate assets are being misapplied or wasted, or if directors or those in control are acting illegally, oppressively, or fraudulently.

Action by Creditor   A creditor also may sue to have a court liquidate the corporation on a showing that a judgment against the company has not been satisfied because the company is insolvent or the company admits in writing that the creditor's claim is due and the company is insolvent.

Claims Against A Dissolved Corporation

Under RMBCA Section 14.06 and 14.07, a dissolved corporation must provide written notice of the dissolution to its creditors. The notice must state a deadline, which must be at least 120 days after the notice, for receipt of creditors' claims. Claims not received by the deadline are barred. The corporation may also publish a notice of the dissolution in a local newspaper. Creditors who do not receive written notice or whose claim is not acted on have five years to file suit against the corporation. If the corporate assets have been distributed, shareholders are personally liable, although the liability may not exceed the assets received at liquidation.

Bankruptcy

As an alternative to dissolution, a corporation in financial trouble may look to federal bankruptcy law for relief. A corporation may use liquidation proceedings (Chapter 7 of the Bankruptcy Reform Act) or may be reorganized under Chapter 11 of the act. Both remedies are discussed in detail in Chapter 29.

CHAPTER SUMMARY

Beyond the normal operations of business, a corporation can expand in one of four ways: (1) purchase of assets, (2) merger, (3) consolidation, and (4) purchase of another corporation's stock.

When assets are purchased, the purchasing corporation is not generally liable for the debts of the corporation whose assets were sold. The purchasing corporation will be liable if it agreed to assume the debts, if the transaction was in fact a merger or consolidation, if the purchaser is merely continuing the old company, or if the acquisition was fraudulently made to escape liability for the debts. Another exception made recently in a number of courts is for product liability claims.

In a merger, the acquired company is absorbed into the acquiring company and goes out of business. The acquiring corporation assumes the other company's debts. Unless the articles of incorporation say otherwise, a majority of directors and shareholders of both corporations must approve the merger. A consolidation is virtually the same as a merger, except that the resulting entity is a new corporation.

A corporation may take over another company by purchasing a controlling interest of its stock. This is accomplished by appealing directly to the target company's shareholders. In the case of a large publicly held corporation, the appeal is known as a tender offer, which is not an offer but an invitation to shareholders to tender their stock at a stated price.

A shareholder has the right to fair value for his stock if he dissents from a plan to merge, consolidate, or sell all or substantially all of the corporate assets. If there is disagreement over the value, the shareholder has the right to a court appraisal. When one company acquires 90 percent of the stock of another, it may merge with the target through a short-form merger, which eliminates the requirement of consent of shareholders and the target company's board.

States may impose conditions on admission of a foreign corporation to do business of a purely local nature, but not if its business is exclusively interstate in character. Among the requirements are obtaining a certificate of authority from the secretary of state and maintaining a registered office with a registered agent. But certain activities do not constitute doing business—such as filing lawsuits and collecting debts—and may be carried on even if the corporation is not licensed to do business in a state. Under long-arm statutes, state courts have jurisdiction over foreign corporations, as long as the corporation has minimum contacts in the state. States may also tax corporate activities, as long as the tax does not unduly burden interstate commerce.

Dissolution is the legal termination of a corporation's existence, as distinguished from liquidation, the process of paying debts and distributing assets. A corporation may be dissolved by shareholders if they unanimously agree in writing, or by majority vote of the directors and shareholders. A corporation may also be dissolved involuntarily on one of five grounds, including failure to file an annual report or to pay taxes. Shareholders may sue for judicial liquidation on a showing that corporate assets are being wasted or directors or officers are acting illegally or fraudulently. A creditor may sue for liquidation on insolvency of the corporation.

KEY TERMS

Dissolution	p. 1004	Takeover	p. 995
Merger	p. 993	Tender offer	p. 995
Short-form merger	p. 996		

SELF-TEST QUESTIONS

1. In a merger, the acquired company:
   (a) goes out of existence
   (b) stays in existence
   (c) is consolidated into a new corporation
   (d) does none of the above
2. An offer by an acquiring company to buy shareholders' stock at a stipulated price is called:
   (a) an appraisal
   (b) a short-form merger
   (c) a tender offer
   (d) none of the above
3. The legal termination of a corporation's existence is called:
   (a) liquidation
   (b) bankruptcy
   (c) extinguishment
   (d) dissolution
4. The most important constitutional provision relating to a state's ability to tax foreign corporations is:
   (a) the Commerce Clause
   (b) the First Amendment
   (c) the due process clause
   (d) the Privileges and Immunities Clause
5. An act that is considered to be a corporation's "transacting business" in a state is:
   (a) collecting debts
   (b) holding directors' meetings
   (c) filing lawsuits
   (d) none of the above

DEMONSTRATION PROBLEM

Neva, a Nevada corporation, has enough contact with California to be subject to the jurisdiction of California courts. Does this mean that Neva must also meet California's qualification requirements? Does it mean that Neva is subject to California's corporation tax? Why?

PROBLEMS

1. Preston Corporation sold all of its assets to Adam Corporation in exchange for Adam stock. Preston then distributed the stock to its shareholders, without paying a debt of $150,000 owed to a major supplier, Corey. Corey, upon discovery that Preston is now an empty shell, attempts to recover the debt from Adam. Result? Why?

2. Would the result in problem 1 be different if Adam and Preston had merged? Why?
3. Would the result in problem 1 be different if Corey had a product liability claim against Preston? Why? What measures might you suggest for Adam to prevent potential losses from such claims?
4. In problem 1, assuming that Preston and Adam had merged, what are the rights of Graham, a shareholder who opposed the merger? Explain the procedure for enforcing his rights.
5. A bus driver from Massachusetts was injured when his seat collapsed while he was driving his bus through Maine. He brought suit in Massachusetts against the Ohio corporation that manufactured the seat. The Ohio corporation did not have an office in Massachusetts, but occasionally sent a sales representative and delivered parts to the state. Assuming that process was served on the company at its Ohio office, would a Massachusetts court have jurisdiction over the Ohio corporation? Why?
6. Assume in problem 5 that the bus driver also sued a North Dakota corporation that manufactured the bus. The North Dakota corporation had an office, regular staff, and substantial sales in Massachusetts. Massachusetts law provides that if a foreign corporation is doing business in Massachusetts, process may be served upon a Massachusetts state official. Assuming that process was served on this official, would a Massachusetts court have jurisdiction over the North Dakota corporation? Why?
7. Orego, an Oregon corporation, does business in California and has met California's qualification requirements. Is Orego subject to California's corporation tax? Why?

ANSWERS TO SELF-TEST QUESTIONS

1. (a)   2. (c)   3. (d)   4. (a)   5. (d)

SUGGESTED ANSWER TO DEMONSTRATION PROBLEM

Neva does not have to qualify merely because it is subject to the jurisdiction of California courts. The degree of business required for jurisdictional purposes is less than that required for qualification. It cannot be determined whether Neva is subject to the California tax. It is unclear whether the degree of business necessary for tax purposes is greater or less than that required for jurisdictional purposes (although both are less than that required for qualification).

Part 9

THE MANAGER'S LEGAL AGENDA

Since it is not necessary to be incorporated in the state in which a company is primarily doing business, consider the advantages and disadvantages of incorporating under the law of a state that gives more liberal powers to management or provides more certainty in the interpretation of its basic corporation statutes.

Take special care in drafting the corporate purpose for a business's articles of incorporation. Too narrow an express purpose may hamper the business in years to come; too broad a purpose may permit corporate officers to engage in activities that stockholders may consider too risky or otherwise undesirable—or give a court grounds for denying or upholding corporate activity in lawsuits by dissident stockholders or even by the attorney general of a state.

Directors have the ultimate power over the corporation, even though its officers have the managerial power. In founding a new corporation, the controlling stockholders should select directors, if other than themselves, who have broad business experience and an interest in furthering the corporate purposes.

Although for small corporations with few stockholders standard bylaws may be adequate, you should ordinarily invest time and money in having your corporation's bylaws carefully tailored to the purposes of your business.

Do not be tempted to sit on a corporate board of directors simply for the prestige or the periodic compensation. Although directors are protected against liability for simple good-faith mistakes, a director who does not attend to corporate business may find himself the target of an expensive lawsuit when something goes wrong. And you should avoid sitting on the board of any company that does not provide liability insurance coverage for its directors.

If you are a company insider, or close to someone who is, think twice about trading in the stock of the corporation after hearing a "hot tip" from the inside (or the insider). Seek legal advice. Insider-trading lawsuits and criminal prosecutions are increasing and the law is so uncertain that no one should risk trading without expert legal advice.

Likewise, payments to foreign officials are fraught with legal risks under the Foreign Corrupt Practices Act, and companies that deal with foreign governments are subject to special accounting rules. Expert advice is essential.

Because corporations as well as individuals can be held liable for failure to prevent insider trading and for bribes transmitted by their employees, you should institute strict policies regulating the use of inside information and dealings with foreign governments. You should also be able to demonstrate adequate training of all employees, monitoring, and enforement of the policies.

Among the hazards of expansion by acquisition or merger of another corporation is the potential responsiblity for the legal liabilities of the acquired company. Whether the acquiring company is at risk for acts done by the acquired company often depends on how the deal is structured. Again, you should seek expert advice on minimizing legal liability when acquiring another business.

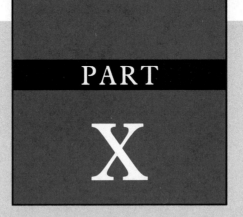

PART

X

Democracy is the recurrent suspicion that more than half the people are right more than half the time.

E. B. WHITE

THE REGULATORY ENVIRONMENT

CHAPTER 46

CHAPTER OVERVIEW

Antitrust 1: Restraints of Trade

INTRODUCTION TO GOVERNMENT REGULATION

*I*n a sense, all law is government regulation, since it is ultimately interpreted by and enforced in a court, a branch of government. But as we intend the term, government regulation differs from much of the law that we have studied to this point. The common law of torts, for example, spells out legal duties, but it tells us much more about what we should not do than about how we must act. Even the Uniform Commercial Code, a complex statute, regulates by spelling out rights and duties that, for the most part, operate only in the absence of private agreement.

Government regulation, then, refers to those sets of rules outside the common law that instruct businesses how to act or prohibit them from acting. It also refers to *federal* law primarily, for the history of business regulation during the past quarter century and more is the sometimes steady, sometimes explosive, growth of federal law and regulations in the private sector. Many state and federal regulations apply to certain types of businesses—manufacturers, for instance, or makers and sellers of flammable fabrics. But the antitrust laws apply—with some exceptions to be noted—to every business in the United States that operates in interstate commerce. Although these laws are the preserve of specialists, a general knowledge of their content and application is crucial for anyone in business.

In this chapter, we take up the origins of the federal antitrust laws and the basic rules governing restraints of trade (Section 1 of the Sherman Act and Section 3 of the Clayton Act). In Chapter 47, we turn to concentrations of market power: monopoly (Section 2 of the Sherman Act) and acquisitions and mergers (Section 7 of the Clayton Act). In Chapter 48, we explore the law of deceptive acts and unfair trade practices, both as administered by the FTC and as regulated at common law (see Figure 46-1). In Chapter 49, we survey briefly how antitrust and other laws serve to shape and regulate a major form of modern business enterprise—franchising.

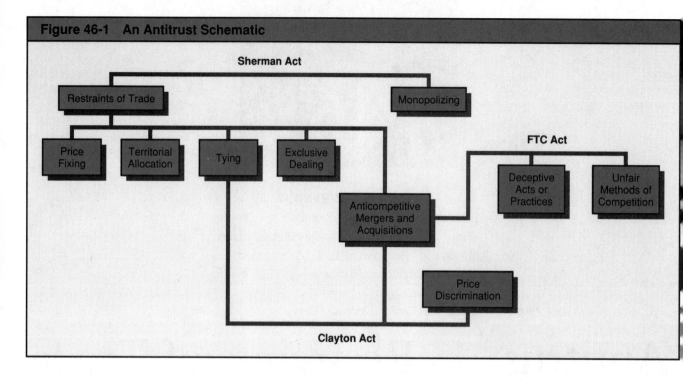

Figure 46-1   An Antitrust Schematic

HISTORY AND BASIC FRAMEWORK OF THE ANTITRUST LAWS

Why Antitrust Laws?

The antitrust laws are aimed at maintaining competition as the motive force of the U.S. economy. The very word "antitrust" implies opposition to the giant *trusts* that began to develop after the Civil War. Until then, the economy was largely local; manufacturers, distributors, and retailers were generally small. The Civil War demonstrated the utility of large-scale enterprise in meeting the military's ferocious production demands, and business owners were quick to understand the advantage of size in attracting capital. For the first time, immense fortunes could be made in industry, and adventurous entrepreneurs were quick to do so in an age that lauded the acquisitive spirit.

The first great business combinations were the railroads. To avoid ruinous price wars, railroad owners made private agreements known as "pools" through which they divided markets and offered discounts to favored shippers who agreed to ship goods on certain lines. The pools discriminated against particular shippers and certain geographic regions, and public resentment grew.

Farmers felt the effects first and hardest, and they organized politically to express their opposition. In time they succeeded in lobbying railroad regulation laws through many state houses. In *Munn* v. *Illinois,* 94 U.S. 113 (1877), the Supreme Court rejected a constitutional attack on a state law regulating the transportation and warehousing of grain; the Court declared that the "police powers" of the states permit the regulation of property put to public uses. But in time many state railroad laws were struck down because they interfered with interstate commerce, which only Congress may regulate constitutionally. The consequence was federal legislation: the Interstate Commerce Act of 1887, establishing the first federal administrative agency, the Interstate Commerce Commission.

In the meantime, the railroads had discovered that their pools lacked enforcement power. Those who nominally agreed to be bound by the pooling arrangement could and often did cheat. Ultimately, the corporate form of business enterprise would permit immense accumulations of capital to be placed under the control of a small number of managers, but in the 1870s and 1880s the corporation was not yet established as the best legal form of operation. To overcome these disadvantages, clever lawyers for John D. Rockefeller organized his Standard Oil of Ohio as a common-law *trust*. Trustees were given corporate stock certificates of various companies; by combining numerous corporations into the trust, the trustees could effectively manage and control an entire industry. Within a decade, the Cotton-oil Trust, Lead Trust, Sugar Trust, and Whiskey Trust, along with oil, telephone, steel, tobacco, and others, had become or were in the process of becoming monopolies.

Consumers howled. The political parties got the message: In 1888, both Republicans and Democrats put an antitrust plank in their platforms. In 1889, the new president, Republican Benjamin Harrison, damned monopolies as "dangerous conspiracies," and called for legislation to remedy the tendency of monopolies to "crush out" competition.

The result of all this commotion was the Sherman Antitrust Act of 1890, sponsored by Senator John Sherman of Ohio. Its two key sections forbade combinations in restraint of trade and monopolizing. Senator Sherman and its other sponsors declared that the act had roots in a common-law policy that frowned on monopolies. To an extent it had, but it added something quite important for the future of business and the American economy: the power of the federal government to enforce a national policy against monopoly and restraints of trade. Nevertheless, passage of the Sherman Act did not still the public clamor because it took fifteen years or so before a national administration began to enforce it, when President Theodore Roosevelt—the "trust buster"—sent his attorney general after the Northern Securities Corporation, a transportation holding company.

During its seven years, the Roosevelt Administration initiated fifty-four antitrust suits. The pace picked up under the Taft Administration, which in only four years filed ninety antitrust suits. But the pressure for further reform did not abate, especially when the Supreme Court, in the Standard Oil Case of 1911 (see p. 1020), declared that the Sherman Act forbids only "unreasonable" restraints of trade. A congressional investigation of U.S. Steel Corporation brought to light several practices that had gone unrestrained by the Sherman Act. It also sparked an im-

portant debate, which echoes into our own time, about the nature of national economic policy. Should it encourage competition or regulate business?

Big Business was firmly on the side of regulation, but Congress opted for the policy followed waveringly to the present: competition enforced by government, not a partnership of government and industry, must be the engine of the economy. Accordingly, in 1914 at the urging of President Woodrow Wilson, Congress enacted two more antitrust laws, the Clayton Act and the Federal Trade Commission Act. The Clayton Act outlawed specific practices, such as price discrimination, exclusive dealing and tying contracts, acquisition of a company's competitors, and interlocking directorates. The Federal Trade Commission Act outlawed "unfair methods" of competition, established the FTC as an independent administrative agency, and gave it power to enforce the antitrust laws alongside the Department of Justice.

The Sherman, Clayton, and FTC acts remain the basic texts of antitrust law. Over the years, many states have enacted antitrust laws as well; these laws govern intrastate competition and for the most part are modeled on the federal laws. The state antitrust laws are beyond the scope of this textbook.

Two additional federal statutes were adopted during the next third of a century, though both were, in form, amendments to the Clayton Act. Enacted in the midst of the Depression in 1936, the Robinson-Patman Act prohibits various forms of price discrimination. The Celler-Kefauver Act, strengthening the Clayton Act's prohibition against the acquisition of competing companies, was enacted in 1950 in the hopes of stemming what seemed to be a tide of corporate mergers and acquisitions. We examine these laws in turn.

The Basic Statutes

The Sherman Act   Section 1 of the **Sherman Act** declares: "Every contract, combination in the form of trust or otherwise, or conspiracy, in restraint of trade or commerce among the several states, or with foreign nations, is declared to be illegal." This is sweeping language. What it embraces seems to depend entirely on the meaning of the words "restraint of trade or commerce." Whatever they might mean, *every* such restraint is declared unlawful. But in fact, as we will see, the proposition cannot be stated so baldly, for in 1911 the Supreme Court limited the reach of this section to *unreasonable* restraints of trade.

What does **"restraint of trade"** mean? The Sherman Act's drafters based the act on a common-law policy against monopolies and other infringements on competition. But the common law of trade restraints had been developed in only rudimentary form, and the words have come to mean whatever the courts say they mean, following the general principles described below. In short, the antitrust laws, and the Sherman Act in particular, authorize the courts to create a federal "common law" of competition.

Section 2 of the Sherman Act proscribes monopolization: "Every person who shall monopolize, or attempt to monopolize, or combine or conspire with any other person or persons, to monopolize any part of the trade or commerce among the several states, or with foreign nations, shall be deemed guilty of a misdemeanor." In 1976, Congress upped the ante: violations of the Sherman Act are now felonies. Unlike Section 1, Section 2 does not require a combination between two or more people. A single company acting on its own can be guilty of monopolizing or attempting to monopolize.

The Clayton Act   The **Clayton Act** was enacted in 1914 to plug what many in Congress saw as loopholes in the Sherman Act. Passage of the Clayton Act was closely linked to that of the Federal Trade Commission Act. Unlike the Sherman Act, the Clayton Act is not a criminal statute; it merely declares certain defined practices as unlawful, and leaves it to the government or to private litigants to seek to enjoin them. But unlike the FTC Act, the Clayton Act does spell out undesirable practices—principally, four. Violations of the Sherman Act require an *actual* adverse impact on competition, whereas violation of the Clayton Act requires merely a *probable* adverse impact. Thus, the enforcement of the Clayton Act involves a prophecy which the defendant must rebut to escape an adverse judgment.

The four types of proscribed behavior are these:

1. Discrimination in prices charged different purchasers of the same commodities (Section 2); see pp. 1038–1043 of this chapter.
2. Conditioning the sale of one commodity on the purchaser's refraining from using or dealing in

commodities of the seller's competitors (Section 3); see pp. 1034–1038 of this chapter.
3. Acquiring the stock of a competing corporation (Section 7). Because the original language did not prohibit various types of acquisitions and mergers that had grown up with modern corporate law and finance, Congress amended this section in 1950 (the Celler-Kefauver Act) to extend its prohibition to a wide variety of acquisitions and mergers. We consider the impact of this section in the next chapter.
4. Membership by a single person on more than one corporate board of directors if the companies are or were competitors (Section 8).

The Federal Trade Commission Act   Like the Clayton Act, the FTC Act is a civil statute, involving no criminal penalties. Unlike the Clayton Act, its prohibitions are broadly worded. Its centerpiece is Section 5, which forbids "unfair methods of competition in commerce, and unfair or deceptive acts or practices in commerce." We examine Section 5 in Chapter 48.

Enforcement and Penalties

Enforcement   Four different means of enforcing the antitrust laws are available.

1. The U.S. Department of Justice may bring civil actions to enjoin violations of any section of the Sherman and Clayton Acts and may institute criminal prosecutions for violations of the Sherman Act. Both civil and criminal actions are filed by the offices of the U.S. Attorney in the appropriate federal district, under the direction of the Attorney General. In practice, the Justice Department's guidance comes through its Antitrust Division in Washington, headed by an Assistant Attorney General. With several hundred lawyers and dozens of economists and other professionals, the Antitrust Division annually files fewer than 100 civil and criminal actions, although some of the cases—*U.S.* v. *American Telephone & Telegraph* and *U.S.* v. *IBM* for example—were immensely complicated, took years to dispose of, and consumed tens of thousands of hours of staff time and tens of millions of dollars in government and defense costs.

2. The FTC hears cases under the Administrative Procedure Act, as described in Chapter 5. The Commission's decisions may be appealed to the U.S. Courts of Appeals. The FTC may also promulgate "trade regulation rules," which define fair practices in specific industries. The agency has some 500 lawyers in Washington and a dozen field offices, but only about half the lawyers are directly involved in antitrust enforcement.

3. In the Antitrust Improvements Act of 1976, Congress authorized state attorneys general to file antitrust suits in federal court for damages on behalf of its citizens; this is known as a *parens patriae* claim. Any citizen of the state who might have been injured by the defendant's actions may opt out of the suit and bring his own private action. The states have long had the authority to file antitrust suits seeking injunctive relief on behalf of their citizens.

4. Private individuals and companies may file suits for damages or injunctions if they have been directly injured by a violation of the Sherman or Clayton Acts. Private individuals or companies may not sue under the FTC Act, no matter how unfair or deceptive the behavior complained of; only the FTC may do so. In the 1980s, more than 1,500 private antitrust suits were filed in the federal courts each year, compared to fewer than 100 suits filed by the Department of Justice.

Enforcement in International Trade The Sherman and Clayton acts apply when a company's activities affect American commerce. As discussed further on pp. 1134–1137, this means that these laws apply to American companies that agree to fix the price of goods to be shipped abroad and to the acts of an American subsidiary of a foreign company.

Sanctions and Penalties for Violating the Antitrust Laws Criminal Sanctions Until 1976, violations of the Sherman Act were misdemeanors. The maximum fine was $50,000 for each count on which the defendant was convicted (only $5,000 until 1955), and the maximum jail sentence was one year. In 1976, the sanctions were increased. Today, the maximum sentence for each count is $10 million for corporations and $350,000 for individuals, and the maximum jail term is three years. Under the Criminal Fine Improvements Act of 1987, some violations of the anti-

trust laws may cost conspirators even more. Fines can range as high as double the profits that each defendant made through an antitrust conspiracy.

Forfeitures One provision in the Sherman Act, not much used, permits the government to seize any property in transit in either interstate or foreign commerce if it was the subject of a contract, combination, or conspiracy outlawed under Section 1.

Injunctions and Consent Decrees The Justice Department may enforce violations of the Sherman and Clayton Acts by seeking injunctions in federal district court. The injunction can be a complex set of instructions, listing in some detail the practices that a defendant is to avoid and even the way in which it will be required to conduct its business thereafter. Once an injunction is issued and affirmed on appeal, or the time for appeal has passed, it confers continuing jurisdiction on the court to hear complaints by those who say the defendant is violating it. In a few instances, the injunction or consent decree (see below) is in effect the basic "statute" by which an industry operates. A 1956 decree against American Telephone & Telegraph Company kept the company out of the computer business for a quarter-century until the government's monopoly suit against AT&T was settled and a new decree issued in 1983. The federal courts also have the power to break up a company convicted of monopolizing or to order divestiture when the violation consists of unlawful mergers and acquisitions.

The FTC may issue "cease and desist orders" against practices condemned under Section 5 of the FTC Act—which includes violations of the Sherman and Clayton Acts—and these orders may be appealed to the courts.

Rather than litigate a case fully, defendants may agree to **consent decrees,** in which, without admitting guilt, they agree not to carry on the activity complained of. Violations of injunctions, cease and desist orders, and consent decrees subject companies to a fine of $10,000 a day for every day the violation continues.

Use of Judgment in Private Suit Companies frequently enter into consent decrees, not just because they wish to avoid the expense and trouble of trial. Section 5 of the Clayton Act says that whenever an antitrust case brought by the federal government under either the Clayton Act or the Sherman Act goes to final judgment, the judgment can be used, in a private suit in which the same facts are at issue, as *prima facie* evidence that the violation was committed. This is a powerful provision, because it means that a private plaintiff need prove only that the violation in fact injured him. He need not prove that the defendant committed the acts that amount to antitrust violations. Since this provision makes it relatively easy for private plaintiffs to prevail in subsequent suits, defendants in government suits have a strong inducement to enter into consent decrees, because these are not considered judgments. Likewise, a guilty plea in a criminal case gives the plaintiff in a later private civil suit *prima facie* evidence of the defendant's liability. However, a plea of *nolo contendere* (see p. 108) will avoid this result. This provision has been the spur for a considerable proportion of all private antitrust suits. For example, the government's price-fixing case against the electric equipment industry that sent certain executives of General Electric to jail in the 1950s led to more than 2,200 private suits.

Treble Damages   The crux of the private suit is its unique damage award: any successful plaintiff is entitled to collect *three times* the amount of damages actually suffered—**treble damages,** as they are known—and to be paid the cost of his attorneys. These fees can be huge: defendants have had to pay out millions of dollars for attorneys' fees alone in single cases. The theory of treble damages is that they will serve as an incentive to private parties to police industry for antitrust violations, thus saving the federal government the immense expense of maintaining an adequate staff for that job.

Class Actions   One of the most important developments in antitrust law during the 1970s was the rise of the **class action.** Under liberalized rules of federal procedure, a single plaintiff may sue on behalf of the entire class of people injured by an antitrust violation. This device makes it possible to bring numerous suits that would otherwise never have been contemplated. A single individual who has paid one dollar more than he would have been charged in a competitive market obviously will not file suit. But if there are 10 million consumers like him, then in a class

action he may seek—on behalf of the entire class, of course—$30 million ($10 million trebled), plus attorneys' fees. Critics charge that the class action is a device that in the antitrust field benefits only the lawyers, who have a large incentive to find a few plaintiffs willing to have their names used in a suit run entirely by the lawyers. Nevertheless, it is true that the class action permits antitrust violations to be rooted out that could not otherwise be attacked privately. During the 1970s, suits against drug companies and the wallboard manufacturing industry were among the many large-scale antitrust class actions.

Interpreting the Laws

Vagueness   It does not take a very attentive reader to notice that the antitrust laws, and especially Section 1 of the Sherman Act, are exceedingly vague. As Chief Justice Charles Evans Hughes once put it: "The Sherman Act, as a charter of freedom, has a generality and adaptability comparable to that found to be desirable in constitutional provisions." [Appalachian Coals v. United States, 288 U.S. 344, 359 (1933)] Without the sweeping but vague language, the antitrust laws might quickly have become outdated. As written, they permit courts to adapt the law to changing circumstances.

The "Rule of Reason"   Section 1 of the Sherman Act says that "every" restraint of trade is illegal. But is a literal interpretation really possible? No, for as Justice Brandeis noted in 1918 in one of the early price-fixing cases: "Every agreement concerning trade, every regulation of trade restrains. To bind, to restrain, is of their very essence." [Chicago Board of Trade v. United States, 246 U.S. 231 (1918)] When a manufacturing company contracts to buy raw materials, trade in those goods is restrained: no one else will have access to them. But to interpret the Sherman Act to include such a contract is an absurdity. Common sense says that "every" cannot really mean *every* restraint.

Throughout this century, the courts have been occupied with this question. With the hindsight of thousands of cases, the broad outlines of the answer can be confidently stated. Beginning with *Standard Oil Co. of New Jersey* v. *United States*, 221 U.S. 1

1911), the Supreme Court has held that only *unreasonable* restraints of trade are unlawful.

Often called the "rule of reason," the interpretation of Section 1 made in *Standard Oil* itself has two possible meanings, and they have been confused over the years. The rule of reason could mean that a restraint is permissible only if it is *ancillary* to a legitimate business purpose. The standard example is a covenant not to compete. Suppose you decide to purchase a well-regarded bookstore in town. The proprietor is well-liked and has developed loyal patrons. He says he is going to retire in another state. You realize that if he changed his mind and stayed in town to open another bookstore, your new business would suffer considerably. So you negotiate as a condition of sale that he agree not to open another bookstore within ten miles of the town for the next three years. Since your intent is not to prevent him from going into business—as it would be if he had agreed never to open a bookstore anywhere—but merely to protect the value of your purchase, this restraint of trade is ancillary to your business purpose. The rule of reason holds that this is not an unlawful restraint of trade.

Another interpretation of the rule of reason is even broader. It holds that agreements that might directly impair competition are not unlawful unless the particular impairment itself is unreasonable. For example, several retailers of computer software are distraught at a burgeoning "price war" that will possibly reduce prices so low that they will not be able to offer their customers proper service. To avert this "cutthroat competition," the retailers agree to set a price floor—a floor which, under the circumstances, is reasonable. Chief Justice White, who wrote the *Standard Oil* opinion, might have found that such an agreement was reasonable because, in view of its purposes, it was not *unduly* restrictive and did not unduly restrain trade.

This latter view is not the law. "The true test of legality," Justice Brandeis wrote in 1918 in *Chicago Board of Trade*, "is whether the restraint imposed is such as merely regulates and perhaps thereby promotes competition or whether it is such as may suppress or even destroy competition." In short, the rule of reason does not attempt to distinguish between justifiable and unjustifiable impairments of competition. Rather, it requires that the courts examine whether under the circumstances it makes sense to brand the act complained of as an impairment at all.

"Per Se" Rules   Not every act or commercial practice needs to be weighed by the rule of reason. Some acts have come to be regarded as intrinsically impairing competition, so that no further analysis need be made if the plaintiff can prove that the defendant carried them out, or attempted or conspired to do so. Price-fixing is an example. Price-fixing is said to be *per se illegal* under the Sherman Act—that is, unlawful on its face. The question in a case alleging price-fixing is not whether the price was reasonable or whether it impaired or enhanced competition but whether the price in fact *was* fixed. Only the latter question can be at issue.

Under the Clayton Act   The rule of reason and the *per se* rules apply to the Sherman Act. The Clayton Act has a different standard. It speaks in terms of acts that may tend substantially to lessen competition. The courts must construe these terms too, and in the sections that follow we will see how they have done so.

"HORIZONTAL" RESTRAINTS OF TRADE

Classification of antitrust cases and principles is not self-evident because so many cases turn on complex factual circumstances. One convenient way to group the cases is to look to the relationship of those who have agreed or conspired. If the parties are competitors—whether competing manufacturers, wholesalers, retailers, or others—the resulting restraint of trade is said to be horizontal. If the parties are at different levels of the distribution chain—for example, manufacturer and retailer—their agreement is said to involve a vertical restraint of trade. These categories are not airtight: a retailer might get competing manufacturers to agree not to supply a competitor of the retailer. This is a vertical restraint with horizontal effects.

Price-fixing

Directly   Price fixing agreements are *per se* violations of Section 1 of the Sherman Act. The *per se* rule was announced explicitly in *United States* v. *Trenton Potteries*, 273 U.S. 392 (1927). In that case, twenty individuals and twenty-three corporations, makers and distributors of 82 percent of the vitreous pottery bathroom fixtures used in the United States, were found guilty of having agreed to establish and adhere to a price schedule. On appeal they did not dispute that they had combined to fix prices. They did argue that the jury should have been permitted to decide whether what they had done was reasonable. The Supreme Court disagreed, holding that any fixing of prices is a clear violation of the Sherman Act.

Twenty-four years later, the Court underscored this no-nonsense *per se* rule in *Kiefer-Stewart Co.* v. *Joseph E. Seagram & Sons*, 340 U.S. 211 (1951). The defendants were distillers who had agreed to sell liquor only to those wholesalers who agreed to resell for no more than a *maximum* price set by the distillers. The defendants argued that setting maximum prices did not violate the Sherman Act because such prices promoted rather than restrained competition. Again the Supreme Court disagreed: "[S]uch agreements, no less than those to fix minimum prices, cripple the freedom of traders and thereby restrain their ability to sell in accordance with their own judgment."

The *per se* prohibition against price-fixing is not limited to agreements that directly fix prices. Hundreds of schemes that have the effect of controlling prices have been tested in court and found wanting—some because they were *per se* restraints of trade, others because their effects were unreasonable—that is, because they impaired competition—under the circumstances. In the following sections, we examine some of these cases briefly.

Exchanging Price Information   Knowledge of competitors' prices can be an effective means of controlling prices throughout an industry. Members of a trade association of hardwood manufacturers adopted a voluntary "open competition" plan. About 90 percent of the members adhered to the plan. They accounted for one-third of the production of hardwood in the United States. Under the plan, members reported daily on sales and deliveries and monthly on production, inventory, and prices. The association in turn sent out price, sales, and production reports to the participating members. Additionally, members met from time to time to discuss these matters, and they were exhorted to refrain from excessive production in order to keep prices at profitable levels. In *American*

Column and Lumber Company v. *United States*, 257 U.S. 377 (1921), the Court condemned this plan as a *per se* violation of Section 1.

Not every exchange of information is necessarily a violation, however. In the later *Maple Flooring Manufacturers' Association* v. *United States*, 268 U.S. 563 (1925), the Court refused to find a violation in the practice of an association of twenty-two hardwood floor manufacturers in circulating a list to all members of average costs and freight rates, as well as summaries of sales, prices, and inventories. The apparent difference between *American Column and Lumber* and *Maple Flooring* was that in the latter the members did not discuss prices at their meetings and their rules permitted them to charge individually whatever they wished. It is not unlawful, therefore, for members of an industry to meet to discuss common problems or to develop statistical information about the industry through a common association, as long as the discussions do not border on price or on techniques of controlling prices, such as by restricting output. Usually it takes evidence of collusion to condemn the exchange of prices or other data.

Controlling Output   Competitors also fix prices by controlling an industry's output—for example, by agreeing to limit the amount of goods each company makes or by otherwise limiting the amount that comes to market. This latter technique was condemned in *United States* v. *Socony-Vacuum Oil Co.*, 310 U.S. 150 (1940). To prevent oil prices from dropping, dominant oil companies agreed to and did purchase from independent refiners surplus gasoline which the market was forcing them to sell at distress prices. By buying up this gasoline, the large companies created a price floor for their own product. This conduct, said the Court, is a *per se* violation.

Regulating Competitive Methods   Many companies may wish to eliminate certain business practices—such as offering discounts or trading stamps on purchase of goods. But they are afraid or powerless to do so unless their competitors also stop. The temptation is strong to agree with one's competitors to jointly end these noxious habits; doing so in most instances is unlawful when the result would be to affect the price at which the product is sold. Not every regulation of a business practice is necessarily unlawful, however. Companies might decide that it would serve their customers' interests as well as their own if the product could be standardized, so that certain names or marks signify a grade or quality of product. When no restriction is placed on what grades are to be sold or at what prices, no restraint of trade has occurred.

In the case that follows, the question is whether the practice that is the subject of the agreement violates Section 1. The practice was competitive bidding. A canon of ethics of the National Society of Professional Engineers prohibited members from making competitive bids. This type of prohibition has been common in the codes of ethics of dozens—perhaps hundreds—of occupational groups claiming professional status. These groups justify the ban by citing public benefits, though not necessarily price benefits, that flow from observance of the "ethical" rule. Note that the commerce in question was sale of a service, not of a product.

NATIONAL SOCIETY OF PROFESSIONAL ENGINEERS v. UNITED STATES
435 U.S. 679 (1978)

MR. JUSTICE STEVENS delivered the opinion of the Court.

This is a civil antitrust case brought by the United States to nullify an association's canon of ethics prohibiting competitive bidding by its members. The question is whether the canon may be justified under the Sherman Act, 15 U.S.C. § 1 *et seq.* (1976 ed.), because it was adopted by members of a learned profession for the purpose of minimizing the risk that competition would produce inferior engineering work endangering the public safety. The District Court rejected this justification without making any findings on the likelihood that competition would produce the dire consequences foreseen by the association. The Court of Appeals affirmed. We granted certiorari to decide whether the District Court should have considered the factual basis for the proffered justification before rejecting it. Because we are satisfied that the asserted defense rests on a fundamental misunderstanding of the Rule of Reason frequently applied in antitrust litigation, we affirm.

Engineering is an important and learned profession. There are over 750,000 graduate engineers in the United States, of whom about 325,000 are registered as professional engineers. Registration requirements vary from State to State, but usually require the applicant to be a graduate engineer with at least four years of practical experience and to pass a written examination. About half of those who are registered engage in consulting engineering on a fee basis. They perform services in connection with the study, design, and construction of all types of improvements to real property—bridges, office buildings, airports, and factories are examples. Engineering fees, amounting to well over $2 billion each year, constitute about 5% of total construction costs. In any given facility, approximately 50% to 80% of the cost of construction is the direct result of work performed by an engineer concerning the systems and equipment to be incorporated in the structure.

The National Society of Professional Engineers (Society) was organized in 1935 to deal with the nontechnical aspects of engineering practice, including the promotion of the professional, social, and economic interests of its members. Its present membership of 69,000 resides throughout the United States and in some foreign countries. Approximately 12,000 members are consulting engineers who offer their services to governmental, industrial, and

(*continued on next page*)

(continued)

NATIONAL SOCIETY OF PROFESSIONAL ENGINEERS v. UNITED STATES
435 U.S. 679 (1978)

private clients. Some Society members are principals or chief executive officers of some of the largest engineering firms in the country.

The charges of a consulting engineer may be computed in different ways. He may charge the client a percentage of the cost of the project, may set his fee at his actual cost plus overhead plus a reasonable profit, may charge fixed rates per hour for different types of work, may perform an assignment for a specific sum, or he may combine one or more of these approaches. . . . This case . . . involves a charge that the members of the Society have unlawfully agreed to refuse to negotiate or even to discuss the question of fees until after a prospective client has selected the engineer for a particular project. Evidence of this agreement is found in § 11(c) of the Society's Code of Ethics, adopted in July 1964.

The District Court found that the Society's Board of Ethical Review has uniformly interpreted the "ethical rules against competitive bidding for engineering services as prohibiting the submission of any form of price information to a prospective customer which would enable that customer to make a price comparison on engineering services." If the client requires that such information be provided, then § 11(c) imposes an obligation upon the engineering firm to withdraw from consideration for that job.

★   ★   ★

[P]etitioner argues that its attempt to preserve the profession's traditional method of setting fees for engineering services is a reasonable method of forestalling the public harm which might be produced by unrestrained competitive bidding. To evaluate this argument it is necessary to identify the contours of the Rule of Reason and to discuss its application to the kind of justification asserted by petitioner.

★   ★   ★

The test prescribed in *Standard Oil* is whether the challenged contracts or acts "were unreasonably restrictive of competitive conditions." Unreasonableness under that test could be based either (1) on the nature or character of the contracts, or (2) on surrounding circumstances giving rise to the inference or presumption that they were intended to restrain trade and enhance prices. Under either branch of the test, the inquiry is confined to a consideration of impact on competitive conditions.

★   ★   ★

Price is the "central nervous system of the economy," *United States* v. *Socony-Vacuum Oil Co.*, 310 U.S. 150, 226 n. 59, and an agreement that "interfere[s] with the setting of price by free market forces" is illegal on its face, *United States* v. *Container Corp.*, 393 U.S. 333, 337. In this case we are presented with an agreement among competitors to refuse to discuss prices with potential customers until after negotiations have resulted in the initial selection of an engineer. While this is not price fixing as such, no elaborate industry analysis is required to demonstrate the anticompetitive character of such an agreement. It operates as an absolute ban on competitive bidding, applying with equal force to both complicated and simple projects and to both inexperienced and sophisticated customers. As the District Court found, the ban "impedes the ordinary give and take of the market place," and substantially deprives the customer of "the ability to utilize and compare prices in selecting engineering services." On its face, this agreement restrains trade within the meaning of § 1 of the Sherman Act.

The Society's affirmative defense confirms rather than refutes the anticompetitive purpose and effect of its agreement. The Society argues that the restraint is justified because bidding on engineering services is inherently imprecise, would lead to deceptively low bids, and would thereby tempt individual engineers to do inferior work with consequent risk to public safety and health. The logic of this argument rests on the assumption that the agreement will tend to maintain the price level; if it had no such effect, it would not serve its intended purpose. The Society nonetheless invokes the Rule of Reason, arguing that its restraint on price competition ultimately inures to the public benefit by preventing the production of inferior work and by insuring ethical behavior. As the preceding discussion of the Rule of Reason reveals, this Court has never accepted such an argument.

It may be, as petitioner argues, that competition tends to force prices down and that an inexpensive item may be inferior to one that is more costly. There is some risk, therefore, that competition will cause some suppliers to market a defective product. Similarly, competitive bidding for engineering projects may be inherently imprecise and incapable of taking into account all the variables which will be involved in the actual performance of the project. Based on these considerations, a purchaser might conclude that his interest in quality—which may embrace the safety of the end product—outweighs the advantages of achieving cost savings by pitting one competitor against another. Or an individual vendor might independently refrain from price negotiation until he has satisfied himself that he fully understands the scope of his customers' needs. These decisions might be reasonable; indeed, petitioner has provided ample documentation for that thesis. But these are not reasons that satisfy the Rule; nor are such individual decisions subject to antitrust attack.

The Sherman Act does not require competitive bidding; it prohibits unreasonable restraints on competition. Petitioner's ban on competitive bidding prevents all customers from making price comparisons in the initial selection of an engineer, and imposes the Society's views of the costs and benefits of competition on the entire marketplace. It is this restraint that must be justified under the Rule of Reason, and petitioner's attempt to do so on the basis of the potential threat that competition poses to the public safety and the ethics of its profession is nothing less than a frontal assault on the basic policy of the Sherman Act.

The Sherman Act reflects a legislative judgment that ultimately competition will produce not only lower prices, but also better goods and services.

(continued on next page)

(continued)

**NATIONAL SOCIETY
OF PROFESSIONAL
ENGINEERS v.
UNITED STATES**
435 U.S. 679 (1978)

"The heart of our national economic policy long has been faith in the value of competition." *Standard Oil Co. v. FTC*, 340 U.S. 231, 248. The assumption that competition is the best method of allocating resources in a free market recognizes that all elements of a bargain—quality, service, safety, and durability—and not just the immediate cost, are favorably affected by the free opportunity to select among alternative offers. Even assuming occasional exceptions to the presumed consequences of competition, the statutory policy precludes inquiry into the question whether competition is good or bad.

* * *

In sum, the Rule of Reason does not support a defense based on the assumption that competition itself is unreasonable. Such a view of the Rule would create the "sea of doubt" on which Judge Taft refused to embark in *Addyston*, 85 F., at 284, and which this Court has firmly avoided ever since.

* * *

The judgment of the Court of Appeals is affirmed.

Non-Price Restraints of Trade

Allocating Territories   Suppose four ice cream manufacturers decided one day that their efforts to compete in all four corners of the city were costly and destructive. Why not simply strike a bargain: each will sell ice cream to retail shops in only one quadrant of the city. This is not a pricing arrangement; they are each free to sell at whatever price they desire. But it is a restraint of trade, for in carving up the territory in which each may sell, they make it impossible for grocery stores to obtain their products except in the favored quadrant. The point becomes obvious when examined on a national scale: suppose Ford and General Motors agreed that Ford would not sell its cars in New York and GM would not sell them in California?

Most cases of territorial allocation are examples of vertical restraints in which manufacturers and distributors, say, strike a bargain. But some cases deal with horizontal allocation of territories. In *United States v. Sealy*, 388 U.S. 350 (1967), the defendant company licensed manufacturers to use the Sealy trademark on beds and mattresses and restricted the territories in which the manufacturers could sell. The evidence showed that the licensees, some thirty small bedding manufacturers, actually owned the licensor

and were using the arrangement to allocate the territory. It was held to be unlawful *per se*.

Exclusionary Agreements   We said earlier that it might be permissible for manufacturers through a trade association to establish certain quality standards for the convenience of the public. As long as these standards are not exclusionary and do not reflect any control over price, they might not inhibit competition. The "UL" mark on electrical and other equipment—a mark to show that the product conforms to specifications of the private Underwriters' Laboratory—is an example. But suppose that certain widget producers establish the Scientific Safety Council, a membership association whose staff ostensibly assigns quality labels to those manufacturers who meet certain engineering and safety standards. In fact, however, the manufacturers are using the widespread public acceptance of the SSC mark to keep the market to themselves, by refusing to let nonmembers join and by refusing to let nonmembers use the SSC mark, even if their widgets conform to the announced standards. This subterfuge would be a violation of Section 1.

Boycotts   Agreements by competitors to **boycott** (refuse to deal with) those who engage in undesirable practices are unlawful. In an early case, a retailers' trade association circulated a list of wholesale distributors who sold directly to the public. The intent was to warn member retailers not to buy from those wholesalers. Although each member was free to act however he wanted, the Court saw in this blacklist a plan to promote a boycott. [Eastern State Lumber Dealers' Association v. United States, 234 U.S. 600 (1914)]

This policy remains true even if the object of the boycott is to prevent unethical or even illegal activities. Members of a garment manufacturers association agreed with a textile manufacturers association not to use any textiles that had been "pirated" from designs made by members of the textile association. The garment manufacturers also each pledged, among other things, not to sell their goods to any retailer who did not refrain from using pirated designs. The argument that this was the only way to prevent unscrupulous design pirates from operating fell on deaf judicial ears; the Supreme Court held the policy unlawful under Section 5 of the FTC Act, the case having been brought by the FTC. [Fashion Originators' Guild of America v. Federal Trade Commission, 312 U.S. 457 (1941)]

Proof of Agreement

It is vital for business managers to realize that once an agreement or conspiracy is shown to have existed, they or their companies can be convicted of violating the law even if neither agreement nor conspiracy led to concrete results. Suppose the sales manager of Extremis Widget Company sits down over a plate of fettucine with the sales manager of De Minimis Widget Company and says "Why are we working so hard? I have a plan that will let us both relax." He explains that their companies can put into operation a data exchange program that will stabilize prices. The latter does not immediately commit himself, but after lunch he goes to the stationery store and purchases a notebook in which to record the information he will get from a telephone test of the plan. That action is probably enough to establish a conspiracy to fix prices, and the government could file criminal charges at that point. Discussion with your competitors of prices, discounts, production quotas, rebates, bid rigging, trade-in allowances, commission rates, salaries, advertising, and the like is exceedingly dangerous—and can lead to criminal conduct, and potential jail terms.

Proof of Harm

It is unnecessary to show that the public is substantially harmed by a restraint of trade, as long as the plaintiff can show that the restraint injured him. In *Klor's, Inc.* v. *Broadway-Hale Stores*, 359 U.S. 207 (1959), the plaintiff was a small retail appliance shop in San Francisco. Next door to it was a competing appliance store, one of a chain of stores run by Broadway-Hale. Klor's alleged that Broadway-Hale, using its "monopolistic buying power," persuaded ten national manufacturers and their distributors, including GE, RCA, Admiral, Zenith, and Emerson, to cease selling to Klor's or to sell at discriminatory prices. The defendants did not dispute the allegations. Instead, they moved for summary judgment on the ground that even if true, the allegations did not give rise to a legal claim because the public could not conceivably have been injured as a result of their concerted refusal to deal. As evidence, they cited the uncontradicted fact that within blocks of Klor's, hundreds of household appliance retailers stood ready to sell the public the very brands Klor's was unable to stock as a result of the boycott. The district court granted the motion and dismissed Klor's complaint. The Court of Appeals affirmed. But the Supreme Court reversed:

> This combination takes from Klor's its freedom to buy appliances in an open competitive market and drives it out of business as a dealer in the defendants' products. It deprives the manufacturers and distributors of their freedom to sell to Klor's. . . . It interferes with the natural flow of interstate commerce. It clearly has, by its "nature" and "character," a "monopolistic tendency." As such it is not to be tolerated merely because the victim is just one merchant whose business is so small that his destruction makes little difference to the economy. Monopoly can surely thrive by the elimination of such small businessmen, one at a time, as it can by driving them out in large groups.

"VERTICAL" RESTRAINTS OF TRADE

We have been exploring the Sherman Act as it applies to horizontal restraints of trade—that is, restraints of trade between competitors. We now turn our attention to vertical restraints—those that are the result of agreements or conspiracies between different levels of the chain of distribution, such as manufacturer and wholesaler or wholesaler and retailer.

Resale Price Maintenance

Generally   Is it permissible for manufacturers to require distributors or retailers to sell products at a set price? The general answer is that they may not.

Why, though, would the manufacturer want to fix the price at which the retailer sells his goods? Many reasons have been advanced. For instance, long-run sales of many branded appliances and other goods depend on service by the retailer. Unless the retailer can get a fair price, it will not provide adequate service. Shoddy service will ultimately hurt the brand name and lead to fewer sales. Another argument is that unless all retailers must abide by a certain price, some goods will not be stocked at all. For instance, the argument runs, bookstores will not stock slow-selling books if they cannot be guaranteed a good price on bestsellers. Stores free to discount bestsellers will not have the profit margin to stock other types of books. To guarantee sales of bestsellers to bookstores carrying many lines of books, it is necessary to put a floor under the price of books. Still another argument is that brand-name goods are inviting targets for "loss leader" sales; if one merchant drastically discounts "Extremis" Widgets, other merchants may not want to carry the line, and the manufacturer may experience unwanted fluctuations in sales.

None of these reasons appease the critics of price fixing, including the most important critics—the federal judges. As long ago as 1910, the Supreme Court declared vertical price fixing—what has come to be called **resale price maintenance**—unlawful under the Sherman Act. Dr. Miles Medical Company required wholesalers that bought its proprietary medicines to sign an agreement in which they agreed not to sell to retailers who did not have a "retail agency contract" with Dr. Miles, and not to sell below a certain price. The retail agency contract similarly contained a price floor. Dr. Miles argued that since it was free to make or not make the medicines, it should be free to dictate the prices at which purchasers could sell it. The Supreme Court said that Dr. Miles's arrangements with more than 400 jobbers and 25,000 retailers was no different than if the wholesalers or retailers agreed among themselves to fix the price. Dr. Miles "having sold its product at prices satisfactory to itself, the public is entitled to whatever advantage may be derived from a competition in the subsequent traffic." [Dr. Miles Medical Co. v. John D. Park & Sons Co., 220 U.S. 373 (1910)]

Refusal to Deal   Nine years later, in *United States v. Colgate & Co.*, 250 U.S. 300 (1919), the Supreme Court held that a producer may announce a price at which he wants retailers to resell his product and may tell the retailers that he will refuse to deal with any who do not sell at the established price—as long as the retailers do not enter an agreement with the producer or with each other. This holding was curious because it seemed to promise an easy way to maintain resale prices. But almost from the start the Court showed that the decision was a narrow one. *Colgate* does not mean that the courts will no longer infer from the circumstances an agreement, combination, or conspiracy. All it meant was that a naked refusal to deal, even if announced in advance, is not enough by itself to violate Section 1. In a series of later cases, the Court held that surrounding circumstances may amount to an agreement. Finally, it issued the following opinion, which, though it did not overturn *Colgate*, demonstrated that the early case meant just what it said, nothing more.

**UNITED STATES v.
PARKE, DAVIS & CO.**
362 U.S. 29 (1960)

BRENNAN, J. The Government sought an injunction under § 4 of the Sherman Act against the appellee, Parke, Davis & Company on a complaint alleging that Parke Davis conspired and combined, in violation of §§ 1 and 3 of the Act, with retail and wholesale druggists in Washington, D.C., and Richmond, Virginia, to maintain the wholesale and retail prices of Parke Davis pharmaceutical products. . . . After the Government completed the presentation of its evidence at the trial, and without hearing Parke Davis in defense, the District Court for the District of Columbia dismissed the complaint . . . on the ground that upon the facts and the law the Government had not shown a right to relief. . . .

Parke Davis makes some 600 pharmaceutical products which it markets nationally through drug wholesalers and drug retailers. The retailers buy these products from the drug wholesalers or may make large quantity purchases directly from Parke Davis. Some time before 1956 Parke Davis announced a resale price maintenance policy in its wholesalers' and retailers' catalogues. The wholesalers' catalogue contained a Net Price Selling Schedule listing suggested minimum resale prices of Parke Davis products sold by wholesalers to retailers. The catalogue stated that it was Parke Davis' continuing policy to deal only with drug wholesalers who observed that schedule and who sold only to drug retailers authorized by law to fill prescriptions. Parke Davis, when selling directly to retailers, quoted the same prices listed in the wholesalers' Net Price Selling Schedule but granted retailers discounts for volume purchases. Wholesalers were not authorized to grant similar discounts. The retailers' catalogue contained a schedule of minimum retail prices applicable in States with Fair Trade Laws and stated that this schedule was suggested for use also in States not having such laws. These suggested minimum retail prices usually provided a 50% mark-up over cost on Parke Davis products purchased by retailers from wholesalers but, because of the volume discount, often in excess of 100% mark-up over cost on products purchased in large quantities directly from Parke Davis.

There are some 260 drugstores in Washington, D.C., and some 100 in Richmond, Virginia. Many of the stores are units of Peoples' Drug Stores, a large retail drug chain. There are five drug wholesalers handling Parke Davis products in the locality who do business with the drug retailers. The wholesalers observed the resale prices suggested by Parke Davis. However, during the spring and early summer of 1956 drug retailers in the two cities advertised and sold several Parke Davis vitamin products at prices substantially below the suggested minimum retail prices; in some instances the prices apparently reflected the volume discounts on direct purchases from Parke Davis since the products sold below the prices listed in the wholesalers' Net Price Selling Schedule. The Baltimore office manager of Parke Davis in charge of the sales district which included the two cities sought advice from his head office how to handle this situation. The Parke Davis attorney advised that the company could legally "enforce an adopted policy arrived at unilaterally" to sell only to customers who observed the suggested minimum resale prices.

(*continued on next page*)

(continued)

UNITED STATES v. PARKE, DAVIS & CO.
362 U.S. 29 (1960)

He further advised that this meant that "we can lawfully say 'we will sell you only so long as you observe such minimum retail prices' but cannot say 'we will sell you only if you agree to observe such minimum retail prices,' since except as permitted by Fair Trade legislations [sic] agreements as to resale price maintenance are invalid." Thereafter in July the branch manager put into effect a program for promoting observance of the suggested minimum retail prices by the retailers involved. The program contemplated the participation of the five drug wholesalers. In order to insure that retailers who did not comply would be cut off from sources of supply, representatives of Parke Davis visited the wholesalers and told them, in effect, that not only would Parke Davis refuse to sell to wholesalers who did not adhere to the policy announced in their catalogue, but also that it would refuse to sell to wholesalers who sold Parke Davis products to retailers who did not observe the suggested minimum retail prices. Each wholesaler was interviewed individually but each was informed that his competitors were also being apprised of this. The wholesalers without exception indicated a willingness to go along.

Representatives called contemporaneously upon the retailers involved, individually, and told each that if he did not observe the suggested minimum retail prices, Parke Davis would refuse to deal with him, and that furthermore he would be unable to purchase any Parke Davis products from the wholesalers. Each of the retailers was also told that his competitors were being similarly informed.

Several retailers refused to give any assurances of compliance and continued after these July interviews to advertise and sell Parke Davis products at prices below the suggested minimum retail prices. Their names were furnished by Parke Davis to the wholesalers. Thereafter Parke Davis refused to fill direct orders from such retailers and the wholesalers likewise refused to fill their orders. This ban was not limited to the Parke Davis products being sold below the suggested minimum prices but included all the company's products, even those necessary to fill prescriptions.

*   *   *

The District Court held that the Government's proofs did not establish a violation of the Sherman Act because "the actions of [Parke Davis] were properly unilateral and sanctioned by law under the doctrine laid down in the case of United States v. Colgate & Co., 250 U.S. 300, 39, S.Ct. 465, 63 L.Ed. 992. . . ."

*   *   *

The Government concedes for the purposes of this case that under the *Colgate* doctrine a manufacturer, having announced a price maintenance policy, may bring about adherence to it by refusing the deal with customers who do not observe that policy. The Government contends, however, that subsequent decisions of this Court compel the holding that what Parke Davis did here by entwining the wholesalers and retailers in a program to promote general compliance with its price maintenance policy went beyond mere customer selection and created combinations or conspiracies to enforce resale price maintenance in violation of §§ 1 and 3 of the Sherman Act.

★   ★   ★

The program upon which Parke Davis embarked to promote general compliance with its suggested resale prices plainly exceeded the limitations of the *Colgate* doctrine and . . . effected arrangements which violated the Sherman Act. Parke Davis did not content itself with announcing its policy regarding retail prices and following this with a simple refusal to have business relations with any retailers who disregarded that policy. Instead Parke Davis used the refusal to deal with the wholesalers in order to elicit their willingness to deny Parke Davis products to retailers and thereby help gain the retailers' adherence to its suggested minimum retail prices. The retailers who disregarded the price policy were promptly cut off when Parke Davis supplied the wholesalers with their names. The large retailer who said he would "abide" by the price policy, the multi-unit Peoples' Drug chain, was not cut off. In thus involving the wholesalers to stop the flow of Parke Davis products to the retailers, thereby inducing retailers' adherence to its suggested retail price, Parke Davis created a combination with the retailers and the wholesalers to maintain retail prices and violated the Sherman Act. . . .

. . . With regard to the retailers' suspension of advertising Parke Davis did not rest with the simple announcement to the trade of its policy in that regard followed by a refusal to sell to the retailers who would not observe it. First it discussed the subject with Dart Drug. When Dart indicated willingness to go along the other retailers were approached and Dart's apparent willingness to cooperate was used as the lever to gain their acquiescence in the program. Having secured those acquiescences Parke Davis returned to Dart Drug with the report of that accomplishment. Not until all this was done was the advertising suspended and sales to all the retailers resumed. In this manner Parke Davis sought assurances of compliance and got them, as well as the compliance itself. It was only by actively bringing about substantial unanimity among the competitors that Parke Davis was able to gain adherence to its policy.

★   ★   ★

The judgment is reversed and the case remanded to the District Court with directions to enter on appropriate judgment enjoining Parke Davis from further violations of the Sherman Act unless the company elects to submit evidence in defense and refutes the Government's right to injunctive relief established by the present record.

In 1988, the Supreme Court signaled that it may be on the verge of reversing the principle of *Dr. Miles* and *Parke, Davis*. Although it did not directly overturn the rule that direct resale price maintenance is a *per se* violation of Section 1 of the Sherman Act, the Court came close to doing so, as the next case, *Business Electronics Corp.* v. *Sharp Electronics Corp.*, suggests. This case stands for the proposition that a manufacturer may lawfully terminate a distributor for undercutting prices offered by other retailers, unless the terminated distributor can prove an "express or implied agreement . . . to set resale prices at some level." In other words, as long as there is no agreement to set a particular retail price, the manufacturer may agree with other distributors to discipline a price-cutting retailer.

BUSINESS ELECTRONICS CORP. v. SHARP ELECTRONICS CORP.
485 U.S. 717 (1988)

JUSTICE SCALIA delivered the opinion of the Court.

Petitioner Business Electronics Corporation seeks review of a decision of the United States Court of Appeals for the Fifth Circuit holding that a vertical restraint is *per se* illegal under § 1 of the Sherman Act, only if there is an express or implied agreement to set resale prices at some level. We granted certiorari, to resolve a conflict in the Courts of Appeals regarding the proper dividing line between the rule that vertical price restraints are illegal *per se* and the rule that vertical nonprice restraints are to be judged under the rule of reason.

In 1968, petitioner became the exclusive retailer in the Houston, Texas, area of electronic calculators manufactured by respondent Sharp Electronics Corporation. In 1972, respondent appointed Gilbert Hartwell as a second retailer in the Houston area. During the relevant period, electronic calculators were primarily sold to business customers for prices up to $1,000. . . . Respondent published a list of suggested minimum retail prices, but its written dealership agreements with petitioner and Hartwell did not obligate either to observe them, or to charge any other specific price. Petitioner's retail prices were often below respondent's suggested retail prices and generally below Hartwell's retail prices, even though Hartwell too sometimes priced below respondent's suggested retail prices. Hartwell complained to respondent on a number of occasions about petitioner's prices. In June 1973, Hartwell gave respondent the ultimatum that Hartwell would terminate his dealership unless respondent ended its relationship with petitioner within 30 days. Respondent terminated petitioner's dealership in July 1973.

Petitioner brought suit in the United States District Court for the Southern District of Texas, alleging that respondent and Hartwell had conspired to terminate petitioner and that such conspiracy was illegal *per se* under § 1 of the Sherman Act. The case was tried to a jury. The District Court submitted a liability interrogatory to the jury that asked whether "there was an agreement or understanding between Sharp Electronics Corporation and Hartwell to terminate Business Electronics as a Sharp dealer because of Business Electronics' price cutting." The District Court instructed the jury at length about this question:

★   ★   ★

"If a dealer demands that a manufacturer terminate a price cutting dealer, and the manufacturer agrees to do so, the agreement is illegal if the manufacturer's purpose is to eliminate the price cutting."

The jury answered Question 1 affirmatively and awarded $600,000 in damages. . . .

The Fifth Circuit reversed, holding that the jury interrogatory and instructions were erroneous, and remanded for a new trial. It held that, to render illegal *per se* a vertical agreement between a manufacturer and a dealer to terminate a second dealer, the first dealer "must expressly or impliedly agree to set its prices at some level, though not a specific one. The distributor cannot retain complete freedom to set whatever price it chooses."

★   ★   ★

. . . Ordinarily, whether particular concerted action violates § 1 of the Sherman Act is determined through case-by-case application of the so-called rule of reason—that is, "the factfinder weighs all of the circumstances of a case in deciding whether a restrictive practice should be prohibited as imposing an unreasonable restraint on competition." Certain categories of agreements, however, have been held to be *per se* illegal, dispensing with the need for case-by-case evaluation. We have said that *per se* rules are appropriate only for "conduct that is manifestly anticompetitive," that is, conduct " 'that would always or almost always tend to restrict competition and decrease output.' " . . .

Although vertical agreements on resale prices have been illegal *per se* since *Dr. Miles Medical Co.* v. *John D. Park & Sons Co.*, 220 U.S. 373 (1911), we have recognized that the scope of *per se* illegality should be narrow in the context of vertical restraints. In *Continental T.V., Inc.* v. *GTE Sylvania Inc.*, we refused to extend *per se* illegality to vertical nonprice restraints, specifically to a manufacturer's termination of one dealer pursuant to an exclusive territory agreement with another. We noted that especially in the vertical restraint context "departure from the rule-of-reason standard must be based on demonstrable economic effect rather than . . . upon formalistic line drawing." We concluded that vertical nonprice restraints had not been shown to have such a " 'pernicious effect on competition' " and to be so " 'lack[ing] [in] . . . redeeming value' " as to justify *per se* illegality. Rather, we found, they had real potential to stimulate interbrand competition, "the primary concern of antitrust law." . . .

Moreover, we observed that a rule of *per se* illegality for vertical nonprice restraints was not needed or effective to protect *intra*brand competition.

★   ★   ★

There has been no showing here that an agreement between a manufacturer and a dealer to terminate a "price cutter," without a further agreement on the price or price levels to be charged by the remaining dealer, almost always tends to restrict competition and reduce output. Any assistance to cartelizing that such an agreement might provide cannot be distinguished from the sort of minimal assistance that might be provided by vertical nonprice agreements like the exclusive territory agreement in *GTE Sylvania*, and is insufficient to justify a *per se* rule. Cartels are neither easy to form nor easy to maintain. . . . Without an agreement with the remaining dealer on price,

(continued on next page)

(continued)

**BUSINESS
ELECTRONICS CORP.
v. SHARP
ELECTRONICS CORP.**
485 U.S. 717 (1988)

the manufacturer both retains its incentive to cheat on any manufacturer-level cartel (since lower prices can still be passed on to consumers) and cannot as easily be used to organize and hold together a retailer-level cartel.

★   ★   ★

. . . . Petitioner contends, relying on *Albrecht* v. *Herald Co.*, 390 U.S. 145 (1968), and *United States* v. *Parke, Davis & Co.*, 362 U.S. 29 (1960), that our vertical price-fixing cases have already rejected the proposition that *per se* illegality requires setting a price or a price level. We disagree. . . .

In *Parke, Davis*, a manufacturer combined first with wholesalers and then with retailers in order to gain the "retailers' adherence to its suggested minimum retail prices." The manufacturer also brokered an agreement among its retailers not to advertise prices below its suggested retail prices, which agreement was held to be part of the *per se* illegal combination. This holding also does not support a rule that an agreement on price or price level is not required for a vertical restraint to be *per se* illegal—first, because the agreement not to advertise prices was part and parcel of the combination that contained the price agreement, and second because the agreement among retailers that the manufacturer organized was a *horizontal* conspiracy among competitors.

In sum, economic analysis supports the view, and no precedent opposes it, that a vertical restraint is not illegal *per se* unless it includes some agreement on price or price levels. Accordingly, the judgment of the Fifth Circuit is Affirmed.

Other Restrictions on Resale

Resale price maintenance is not the only kind of restriction that producers desire to place on the resale of goods. Another important class of restrictions is **territorial allocation.** To encourage its dealers—especially franchised dealers—to exert maximum effort to sell its products, a producer might wish to assign the dealer an exclusive area within which to sell the product.

The question is whether these restrictions are lawful, given that *horizontal* allocations of territory among competitors are *per se* violations of Section 1 (*Sealy;* see p. 1026). As we will see in Chapter 49, the courts follow the rule of reason—it is not a *per se* violation to allocate distributors' territory if there are sound business reasons for doing so apart from a desire to restrain trade.

Tying and Exclusive Dealing Contracts

We move now to a non-price vertical form of restraint. Suppose you went to the grocery store intent on purchasing a bag of potato chips to satisfy a late night craving. Imagine your surprise—and indignation—if the store manager waved a paper in your face and said: "I'll sell you this bag only on the condition that you sign this agreement to buy all of your potato chips in the next five years from me." Or if he said: "I'll sell only if you promise never to buy potato chips from my rival across the street." These are **exclusive dealing contracts,** and if the effect may be substantially to lessen competition they are unlawful under Section 3 of the Clayton Act. They also may be unlawful under Section 1 of the Sherman Act and Section 5 of the FTC Act. Another form of exclusive dealing, known as a **tying contract,** is also prohibited under Section 3 and the other statutes. A tying contract results when you are forced to take a certain product in order to get the product you are really after: "I'll sell you the potato chips you crave, but only if you purchase five pounds of my Grade B liver."

Section 3 of the Clayton Act declares it unlawful for any person engaged in commerce

> in the course of such commerce, to lease or make a sale or contract for sale of goods, wares, merchandise, machinery, supplies or other commodities, whether patented or unpatented, for use, consumption or resale . . . or fix a price charged therefor, or discount from or rebate upon, such price, *on the condition . . . that the lessee or purchaser . . . shall not use or deal in the goods, wares, merchandise, machinery, supplies, or other commodities of a competitor or competitors of the lessor or seller*, where the effect of such lease, sale, or contract for sale or such condition . . . may be to substantially lessen competition or tend to create a monopoly in any line of commerce [emphasis added by authors].

Tying   Under Section 3, the potato chip example is not unlawful, for you would not have much of an effect on competition nor tend to create a monopoly if you signed with your corner grocery. But the Clayton Act has serious ramifications for a producer who might wish to require a dealer to sell only its products—such as a fast-food franchisee that can carry cooking ingredients bought only from the franchisor (Chapter 49), an appliance store that can carry only one national brand of refrigerators, or an ice cream parlor that must buy ice cream supplies from the supplier of its machinery.

This latter situation came under review in *International Salt Co.* v. *United States*, 332 U.S. 392 (1947). International Salt was the largest American producer of salt for industrial uses. It held patents on two machines necessary for using salt products; one injected salt into foodstuffs during canning. It leased most of these machines to canners, and the lease required the lessees to purchase from International all salt to be used in the machines. The case was decided on summary judgment; the company did not have the chance to prove the reasonableness of its conduct. The Court held that it was not entitled to. International's valid patent on the machines did not confer on it the right to restrain trade in unpatented salt. Doing so was a violation of both Section 1 of the Sherman Act and Section 3 of the Clayton Act:

Not only is price-fixing unreasonable, *per se*, but also it is unreasonable, *per se*, to foreclose competitors from any substantial market. The volume of business affected by these contracts cannot be said to be insignificant or insubstantial, and the tendency of the arrangement to accomplishment of monopoly seems obvious. Under the law, agreements are forbidden which "tend to create a monopoly," and it is immaterial that the tendency is a creeping one rather than one that proceeds at full gallop; nor does the law await arrival at the goal before condemning the direction of the movement.

The Clayton Act applies only to "commodities." In a case involving the sale of newspaper advertising space (to purchase space in the morning paper an advertiser would have to take space in the company's afternoon paper), the government lost because it could not use the narrower standards of Section 3 and could not prove that the defendant had monopoly power over the sale of advertising space. (Another afternoon newspaper carried advertisements and its sales did not suffer.) In the course of his opinion, Justice Clark set forth the rule for determining legality of tying arrangements under both the Clayton and Sherman Acts:

> When the seller enjoys a monopolistic position in the market for the "tying" product [*i.e.*, the product that the buyer wants] or if a substantial volume of commerce in the "tied" product [*i.e.*, the product that the buyer does not want] is restrained, a tying arrangement violates the narrower standards expressed in section 3 of the Clayton Act because from either factor the requisite potential lessening of competition is inferred. And because for even a lawful monopolist it is "unreasonable *per se* to foreclose competitors from any substantial market" a tying arrangement is banned by section 1 of the Sherman Act wherever both conditions are met. [Times-Picayune Publishing Co. v. United States, 345 U.S. 594 (1953)]

This rule was broadened in 1958 in a Sherman Act case involving the Northern Pacific Railroad Company, which had received 40 million acres of land from Congress in the late nineteenth century in return for building a rail line from the Great Lakes to the Pacific. For decades Northern Pacific leased or sold the land on condition that the buyer or lessee use Northern Pacific to ship any crops grown on the land or goods manufactured there. To no avail the railroad argued that unlike International Salt's machines, the railroad's "tying product" (its land) was not patented, and that the land users were free to ship on other lines if they could find cheaper rates. Wrote Justice Black:

> [A] tying arrangement may be defined as an agreement by a party to sell one product but only on the condition that the buyer also purchases a different (or tied) product, or at least agrees that he will not purchase that product from any other supplier. Where such conditions are successfully exacted competition on the merits with respect to the tied product is inevitably curbed. . . . They deny competitors free access to the market for the tied product, not because the party imposing the tying requirements has a better product or a lower price but because of his power or leverage in another market. At the same time buyers are forced to forego their free choice between competing products. . . . *They are unreasonable in and of themselves whenever a party has sufficient economic power with respect to the tying product to appreciably restrain free competition in the market for the tied product and a "not insubstantial" amount of interstate commerce is affected.* . . . In this case . . . the undisputed facts established beyond any genuine question that the defendant possessed substantial economic power by virtue of its extensive landholdings which it used as leverage to induce large numbers of purchasers and lessees to give it preference. [Northern Pacific Railway Co. v. United States, 356 U.S. 1 (1958) (emphasis added by authors)]

Taken together, the tying cases suggest that anyone with certain market power over a commodity or other valuable (such as a trademark) runs a serious risk of violating the Clayton Act or Sherman Act or both if he insists that the buyer must also take some other product as part of the bargain.

Exclusive Dealing and Requirements Contracts

Pre-Clayton Act cases upheld many exclusive dealing arrangements under the Sherman Act rule of reason. And although after 1914 the courts took a dim view of tying arrangements, they appeared to take a more relaxed view of exclusive dealing arrangements. But in 1949, the Supreme Court rewrote the ground rules in the famous *Standard Stations* case [Standard Oil of California v. United States, 337 U.S. 293 (1949)]. In previous cases, the Supreme Court had struck down an exclusive dealership in a situation in which the seller had 40 percent of the national markets; it had upheld such an arrangement where the seller had only 1 percent. In *Standard Stations,* Standard Oil had 23 percent of the market for gasoline sales in nine Western states—7 percent was sold to its own filling stations,

7 percent to independent stations, and 9 percent to commercial users. Its 14 percent of the retail sales market compared to 42 percent shared by six major competitors. The remaining 44 percent of the market was divided by some seventy smaller refiners. Standard entered into exclusive supply contracts with the filling stations to which it sold gasoline, as did all of Standard's competitors. Under these contracts, the independent stations agreed to purchase all their requirements for gasoline and certain other products (oil, tires, tubes, batteries, and other accessories) from Standard. The company had about 8,000 supply contracts with independents. The exclusive supply contracts certainly seemed to fall within the terms of Section 3. (Reread the language of the section on p. 1035.) But the government faced one problem. Section 3 requires that the effect of the exclusivity be to substantially lessen competition or tend to create a monopoly. At most, only 14 percent of the market was involved. Certainly there was no monopoly nor likely to be. What about lessening of competition?

The Standard contracts involved some $60 million worth of gasoline. In *International Salt,* the sales totaled only some $500,000, and that was held to be a substantial enough market from which competitors were foreclosed. So the Standard arrangement must fall unless there is some logical distinction to be made between a *tying* contract and a **requirements contract**. Justice Frankfurter said that there is indeed a distinction—but as it turned out, not one that led very far. A *tying contract* has practically no justification, so the courts don't have to look very hard for evidence of a probable impact on competition. On the other hand, said Justice Frankfurter, *requirements contracts*

> may well be of economic advantage to buyers as well as to sellers, and thus indirectly of advantage to the consuming public. In the case of the buyer they may assure supply, afford protection against rises in price, enable long-term planning on the basis of known costs, and obviate the expense and risk of storage in the quantity necessary for a commodity having a fluctuating demand. From the seller's point of view, requirements contracts may make possible a substantial reduction of selling expenses, give protection against price fluctuations, and—of particular advantage to a newcomer to the field to whom it is important to know what capital expenditures are justified—offer the possibility of a predictable market. . . . They may be useful, moreover, to a seller trying to establish a foothold against the counterattacks of entrenched

competitors. . . . Since these advantages of requirements contracts may often be sufficient to account for their use, the coverage by such contracts of a substantial amount of business affords a weaker basis for the inference that competition may be lessened than would similar coverage by tying clauses, especially where the latter is combined with market control of the tying device.

That language might seem to point the way toward approving Standard's exclusive supply contracts. But it did not. For one thing, even if Standard had not improved its competitive position during the period it used these supply contracts, who could say that its position might not have deteriorated if it had not used them? Since all the major sellers used exclusive supply contracts, the effect might have been to entrench them all at the expense of the small refiners. It is not the judges' job, the Court was saying, to balance the exclusive dealing arrangement against other possible methods of distribution, for the Clayton Act says that exclusive dealing is not permissible whenever substantial competition "may be" lessened. Reasonableness of the practice does not count when the circumstances suggest, as they did here, that substantial competition may be lessened. Hence, Justice Frankfurter concluded, "the qualifying clause of Section 3 ['where the effect . . . may be substantially to lessen competition . . .'] is satisfied by *proof that competition has been foreclosed in a substantial share of the line of commerce affected* [emphasis added by authors]. . . . [E]vidence that competitive activity has not actually declined is inconclusive."

Standard Stations appeared to put the kibosh on requirements contracts, but the Supreme Court resurrected them twelve years later in *Tampa Electric Co. v. Nashville Coal Co.*, 365 U.S. 320 (1961). Tampa Electric is a Florida electric utility. It built two new plants designed to generate electricity by burning coal. To secure a supply, it made a deal with Nashville Coal to supply both plants with all the coal they could use during their first two years of operation and thereafter to supply each plant with not less than 250,000 tons each year for the succeeding twenty years. Without delivering any coal, Nashville breached the contract, claiming that it violated the antitrust laws. The district court ruled that the amount of coal consumed within "peninsular Florida" amounted to 700,000 tons, the amount that Tampa Electric would require at the end of the second year. Although some

700 coal producers served the area, the court concluded that the supply contract excluded competitors from a substantial amount of trade. The Court of Appeals affirmed. The Supreme Court reversed, holding that the lower courts had used too small a marketplace to measure the impact of the contract.

The proper "relevant competitive market" was the entire area in which Nashville competed with the other 700 producers. That area included ten states. In that market, the amount of coal tied up in the Tampa-Nashville contract was only 1 percent. Although the total contract sales amounted to $128 million, dollar volume is not the test. The question is "whether the pre-emption of competition to the extent of the tonnage involved tends to substantially foreclose competition in the relevant coal market." Measured against the 250 million tons of coal sold in the entire area, Tampa's requirement was small.

The effect of *Tampa Electric* seems to be that when the amount of commerce involved is small, requirements contracts are permissible. But that is not the end of the story, for nothing is ever simple in the field of antitrust. The marketing executive must also bear in mind Section 5 of the FTC Act, which has no clause linking the exclusive dealing to the effect on commerce. Section 5 speaks only in terms of "unfair methods of competition and unfair or deceptive acts or practices in commerce." Can Section 5 reach exclusive dealing arrangements? Yes, said the Supreme Court in a 1966 FTC case.

Brown Shoe is one of the largest shoe makers in the world and was then second largest in the United States. The company launched a Brown Franchise Stores' Program, under which it sold its shoes to 659 independent retail shoe stores on condition that they refrain from selling any competing line of shoes. In return, the stores received valuable services, including architectural plans, costly merchandising records, services of a Brown field representative, and right to participate in cheap group insurance. In an administrative proceeding under Section 5, the FTC held that the franchise program effectively foreclosed Brown's competitors from selling to a substantial number of retail outlets. The Court of Appeals set aside the Commission's cease and desist order. In *Federal Trade Commission v. Brown Shoe Co.*, 384 U.S. 316 (1966), the Supreme Court reversed, reinstating the order, even though the affected retailers accounted for only about 1 percent of the shoe dealers in the United

States—the same percentage that was held permissible in *Tampa Electric*. Justice Black explained:

> [T]he Commission has broad powers to declare trade practices unfair. The broad power of the Commission is particularly well established with regard to trade practices which conflict with the basic policies of the Sherman and Clayton Acts even though such practices may not actually violate these laws. The record in this case shows beyond doubt that Brown, the country's second largest manufacturer of shoes, has a program, which requires shoe retailers, unless faithless to their contractual obligations with Brown, substantially to limit their trade with Brown's competitors. This program obviously conflicts with the central policy of both § 1 of the Sherman Act and § 3 of the Clayton Act against contracts which take away freedom of purchasers to buy in an open market. Brown nevertheless contends that the Commission has no power to declare the franchise program unfair without proof that its effect "may be to substantially lessen competition or tend to create a monopoly" which of course would have to be proved if the Government were proceeding against Brown under § 3 of the Clayton Act or other provisions of the antitrust laws. This power of the Commission was emphatically stated in F.T.C. v. Motion Picture Advertising Service Co., 344 U.S. 392, at pp. 394–95: "It is . . . clear that the Federal Trade Commission Act was designed to supplement and bolster the Sherman Act and the Clayton Act . . . to stop in their incipience acts and practices which, when full blown, would violate those Acts . . . as well as to condemn as 'unfair methods of competition' existing violations of them." We hold that the Commission acted well within its authority in declaring the Brown franchise program unfair whether it was completely full blown or not.

PRICE DISCRIMINATION

Historical Background

If the relatively simple and straightforward language of the Sherman Act can provide litigants and courts with interpretive headaches, the law against price discrimination—the Robinson-Patman Act—can strike the student with a crippling migraine. Technically, Section 2 of the Clayton Act, the Robinson-Patman Act, has been verbally abused almost since its enactment in 1936. It has been called the "Typhoid Mary of Antitrust," a "grotesque manifestation of the scissors and paste-pot method" of draftsmanship. Critics carp at more than its language; many have asserted over the years that the act is anticompetitive because it prevents many firms from lowering their prices to attract more customers.

Despite this rhetoric, the Robinson-Patman Act has withstood numerous attempts to modify or repeal it, and it can come into play in many everyday situations. Although in recent years the Justice Department has declined to enforce it, leaving government enforcement efforts to the Federal Trade Commission, *private* plaintiffs are actively seeking treble damages in numerous cases. So whether it makes economic sense or not, the act is a living reality for marketers. This next section introduces certain problems that lurk in deciding how to price goods and how to respond to competitors' prices.

The original Section 2, enacted in 1914, was aimed at the price-cutting practice of the large trusts, which would reduce the price of products below cost where necessary in a particular location, to wipe out smaller competitors who could not long sustain such losses. But the original Clayton Act exempted from its terms any "discrimination in price . . . on account of differences in the quantity of the commodity sold." This was a gaping loophole, that made it exceedingly difficult to prove a case of price discrimination.

Not until the Depression in the 1930s did sufficient cries of alarm over price discrimination force Congress to act. The alarm was centered on the practices of large grocery chains. Their immense buying power was used as a lever to pry out price discounts from food processors and wholesalers. Unable to extract similar price concessions, the small "mom and pop" grocery stores found that they could not offer the retail customer the lower food prices set by the chains. The small shops began to fail. In 1936, Congress strengthened Section 2 by enacting the Robinson-Patman Act. Although prompted by concern about how large buyers could use their purchasing power, the act in fact places most of its restrictions on the pricing decisions of sellers.

Statutory Framework

The heart of the act is Section 2(a), which reads in pertinent part as follows:

[I]t shall be unlawful for any person engaged in commerce . . . to discriminate in price between different purchasers of commodities of like grade and quality . . . where the effect of such discrimination may be substantially to lessen competition or tend to create a monopoly in any line of commerce, or to injure, destroy or prevent competition with any person who either grants or knowingly receives the benefit of such discrimination, or with customers of either of them.

This section provides certain defenses to a charge of price discrimination. For example, differentials in price are permissible whenever they "make only due allowances for differences in the cost of manufacture, sale, or delivery resulting from the differing methods or quantities in which such commodities are to such purchasers sold or delivered." This section also permits sellers to change prices in response to changing marketing conditions or the marketability of the goods—for example, if perishable goods begin to deteriorate, the seller may drop the price in order to move the goods quickly.

Section 2(b) provides the major defense to price discrimination: any price is lawful if made in good faith to meet competition.

Discrimination by the Seller

Preliminary Matters Simultaneous Sales To be discriminatory, the different prices must have been charged in sales made at the same time or reasonably close in time. What constitutes a reasonably close time depends on the industry and the circumstances of the marketplace. The time span for dairy sales would be considerably shorter than for sales of mainframe computers, given the nature of the product, the frequency of sales, the unit cost, and the volatility of the markets.

Identity of Purchaser Another preliminary issue is the identity of the actual purchaser. A supplier who deals through a dummy wholesaler might be charged with price discrimination even though on paper only one sale appears to have been made. Under the "indirect purchaser" doctrine, a seller who deals with two or more retail customers, but passes their orders on to a single wholesaler and sells the total quantity to the wholesaler in one transaction, can be held to have vi-

olated the act. The retailers are treated as indirect purchasers of the supplier.

Sale of Commodities The act applies only to *sales of commodities*. A lease, rental, or license to use a product does not constitute a sale; hence price differentials under one of those arrangements cannot be unlawful under Robinson-Patman. Likewise, since the act applies only to commodities, tangible things, the courts have held that it does not apply to the sale of intangibles, such as rights to license or use patents, shares in a mutual fund, newspaper or television advertising, or title insurance.

Of Like Grade and Quality Only those sales involving goods of "like grade and quality" can be tested under the act for discriminatory pricing. What do these terms mean? The leading case is *FTC* v. *Borden Co.*, 383 U.S. 637 (1966), in which the Supreme Court ruled that trademarks and labels do not, for Robinson-Patman purposes, distinguish products that are otherwise the same. Grade and quality must be determined "by the characteristics of the product itself." When the products are physically or chemically identical, they are of like grade and quality, regardless of how imaginative marketing executives attempt to distinguish them. But physical differences that affect marketability can serve to denote products as being of different grade and quality, even if the differences are slight and do not affect the seller's cost in manufacturing or marketing.

Competitive Injury

To violate the Robinson-Patman Act, the seller's price discrimination must have an anticompetitive effect. The usual Clayton Act standard for measuring injury applies to Robinson-Patman violations—that is, a violation occurs when the effect may be substantially to lessen competition or tend to create a monopoly in any line of commerce. But because the Robinson-Patman Act has a more specific test of competitive injury, the general standard is rarely cited.

The more specific test measures the impact on particular persons affected. Section 2(a) says that it is unlawful to discriminate in price where the effect is "to injure, destroy, or prevent competition with any person who grants or knowingly receives the benefit of such discrimination or to customers of either of them." The effect—injury, destruction, or prevention of competition—is measured against three types of those suffering it: (1) competitors of the seller or supplier (that is, competitors of the person who "grants" the price discrimination); (2) competitors of the buyer (that is, competitors of the buyer who "knowingly receives the benefit" of the price differential); and (3) customers of either of the two types of competitors. As we will see, the third category presents many difficulties.

For purposes of our discussion, assume the following scenario. Ace Brothers Widget Company manufactures the usual sizes and styles of American domestic widgets. It competes primarily with National Widget Corporation, although several smaller companies make widgets in various parts of the country. Ace Brothers is the largest manufacturer and sells throughout the United States. National sells primarily in the western states. The industry has several forms of distribution. Many retailers buy directly from Ace and National, but several regional and national wholesalers also operate, including Widget Jobbers, Ltd. and Widget Pushers & Sons. The retailers in any particular city compete directly against each other to sell to the general public. Jobbers and Pushers are in direct competition. Jobbers also sells directly to the public, so that it is in direct competition with retailers as well as Widget Pushers. As everyone knows, widgets are extremely price sensitive, being virtually identical physically.

Primary-line Injury   Now consider the situation in California, Oregon, and Wisconsin. The competing manufacturers, Ace Brothers and National Widgets, both sell to wholesalers in California and Oregon, but only Ace has a sales arm in Wisconsin. Seeing an opportunity, Ace drops its prices to wholesalers in California and Oregon and raises them in Wisconsin, putting National at a competitive disadvantage. This situation, illustrated in Figure 46-2, is an example of **primary-line injury**—the injury is done directly to a competitor of the company that differentiates its prices. This is price discrimination, and it is prohibited under Section 2(a).

Most forms of primary-line injury have a geographical basis, but they need not. Suppose National sells exclusively to Jobbers in Northern California, and Ace Brothers sells both to Jobbers and several other wholesalers. If Ace cuts its prices to Jobbers, while charging higher prices to the other wholesalers, the

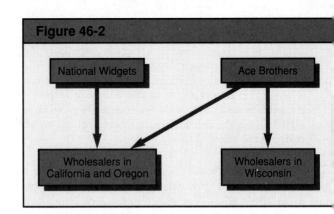

Figure 46-2

effect is also primary-line injury to National. Jobbers will obviously want to buy more from Ace at lower prices, and National's reduced business is therefore a direct injury. If Ace intends to drive National out of business, this violation of Section 2(a) could also be an attempt to monopolize in violation of Section 2 of the Sherman Act.

Secondary-line Injury   Next we consider injury done to competing buyers. Suppose that Ace Brothers favors Jobbers—or that Jobbers, a powerful and giant wholesaler, induces Ace to act favorably by threatening not to carry Ace's line of widgets otherwise. Although Ace continues to supply both Jobbers and Widget Pushers, it cuts its prices to Jobbers. As a result, Jobbers can charge its retail customers lower prices than can Pushers, so that Pushers' business begins to slack off. This is **secondary-line injury** at the buyer's level. Jobbers and Pushers are in direct competition, and by impairing Pushers' ability to compete, the requisite injury has been committed. This situation can be illustrated in Figure 46-3.

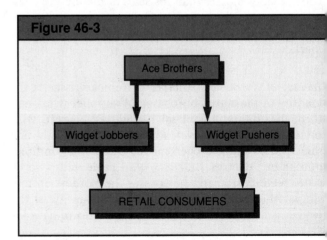

Figure 46-3

Variations on this secondary-line injury are possible. Assume Ace Brothers sells directly to Fast Widgets, a retail shop, and also to Jobbers. Jobbers sells to retail shops that compete with Fast Widgets and also directly to consumers. The situation looks like this (Figure 46-4):

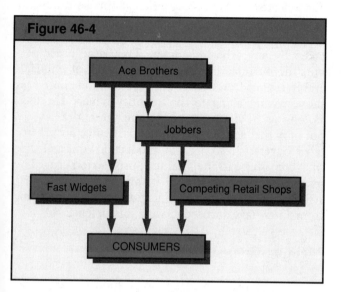

Figure 46-4

If Ace favors Jobbers by cutting its prices, discriminating against Fast Widgets, the transaction is unlawful, even though Jobbers and Fast Widgets do not compete for sales to other retailers. Their competition for the business of ultimate consumers is sufficient to establish the illegality of the discrimination. A variation on this situation was at issue in the first important case to test Section 2(a) as it affects buyers. Morton Salt sold to both wholesalers and retailers, offering quantity discounts. Its pricing policy was structured to give large buyers great savings, computed on a yearly total, not on shipments made at any one time. Only five retail chains could take advantage of the higher discounts, and as a result, these chains could sell salt to grocery shoppers at a price below that at which the chains' retail competitors could buy it from their wholesalers. See Figure 46-5 for a schematic illustration. In this case for the first time, the Supreme Court in *FTC* v. *Morton Salt Co.*, 334 U.S. 37 (1948), declared that the impact of the discrimination does not have to be actual; it is enough if there is a "reasonable *possibility*" of competitive injury.

In order to make out a case of secondary-line injury, it is necessary to show that the buyers purchasing at different prices are in fact competitors. Suppose

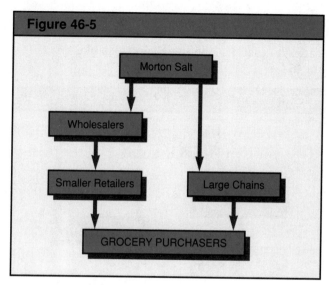

Figure 46-5

that Ace Brothers sells to Fast Widgets, the retailer, and also to Boron Enterprises, a manufacturer that incorporates widgets in most of its products. Boron does not compete against Fast Widgets, and therefore Ace Brothers may charge different prices to Boron and Fast without fearing Robinson-Patman repercussions. Here is the Boron-Fast schematic (Figure 46-6):

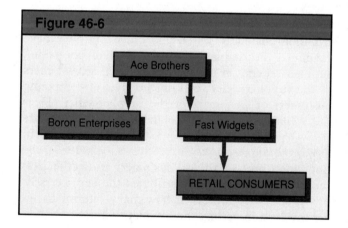

Figure 46-6

Third-line Injury   Second-line injury to buyers does not exhaust the possibilities. Robinson-Patman also works against so-called **third-line** or **tertiary-line injury.** At stake here is injury another rung down the chain of distribution. Ace Brothers sells to Pushers, which processes unfinished widgets in its own factory and sells them in turn directly to retail customers. Ace also sells to Jobbers, a wholesaler without processing facilities. Jobbers sells to retail shops that can process the goods and sell directly to consumers, thus competing with Pushers for the retail business. Schematically, that distribution chain looks like this (Figure 46-7):

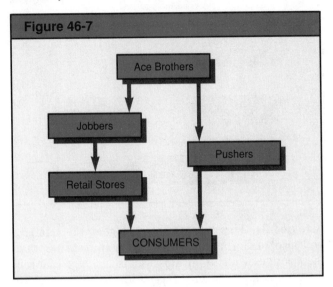

Figure 46-7

Ace Brothers

Jobbers

Pushers

Retail Stores

CONSUMERS

If Ace's price differs between Pushers and Jobbers, so that Jobbers is able to sell at a lower price to the ultimate consumers than Pushers, a Robinson-Patman violation has occurred.

Fourth-line Injury   In a complex economy, the distribution chain can go on and on. So far, we have examined discrimination on the level of competing supplier-sellers, on the level of competing customers of the supplier-seller, and on the level of competing customers of customers of the supplier-seller. Does the vigilant spotlight of Robinson-Patman penetrate below this level? The Supreme Court has said yes. In *Perkins* v. *Standard Oil Co.*, 395 U.S. 642 (1969), the Supreme Court said that "customer" in Section 2(a) means any person who distributes the supplier-seller's product, regardless of how many intermediaries are involved in getting the product to him.

Seller's Defenses

Cost Justification   Price discrimination is not *per se* unlawful. The Robinson-Patman Act allows the seller two general defenses: (1) cost justification; and (2) meeting competition. If the seller can demonstrate that sales to one particular buyer are cheaper than sales to others, a price differential is permitted, if it is based

entirely on the cost differences. For example, if one buyer is willing to have the goods packed in cheaper containers or larger crates that save money, that cost can be passed along to the buyer. Similarly, a buyer who takes over a warehousing function formerly undertaken by the seller is entitled to have the cost saving reflected in the selling price. Suppose the buyer orders his entire requirements for the year from the manufacturer, a quantity many times greater than that taken by any other customer. This large order permits the manufacturer to make the goods at a considerably reduced unit cost. May the manufacturer pass those savings along to the quantity buyer? He may, as long as he does not pass along the entire savings but only that attributable to the particular buyer. For other buyers add to his total production run, and they thus contribute to the final unit production cost. The marketing manager should be aware that the courts strictly construe cost-justification claims, and few companies have succeeded with this defense.

Meeting Competition

Lowering a price to meet competition is a complete defense to a charge of price discrimination. Assume Ace Brothers is selling widgets to retailers in Indiana and Kentucky at $100 per dozen. National Widgets suddenly enters the Kentucky market and, because it has lower manufacturing costs than Ace, sells widgets to the four Kentucky widget retailers at $85 per dozen. Ace may lower its price to that amount in Kentucky without lowering its Indiana price. However, if National's price violated the Robinson-Patman Act and Ace knew or should have known that it did, Ace may not reduce its prices. The defense of meeting competition has certain limitations. For example, the seller may not use this defense as an excuse to charge different customers a price differential over the long run. Moreover, if National's lower prices result from quantity orders, Ace may reduce its prices only for like quantities. Ace may not reduce its price for lesser quantities if National charges more for smaller orders. And, although Ace may meet National's price to a given customer, Ace may not legally charge less.

Other Prohibitions

Unlawful Brokerage Payments   Section 2(c) prohibits payment of commissions by one party in a transaction to the opposite party (or to the opposite party's agent) in a sale of goods, unless services are actually rendered for them. Suppose the buyer's broker warehouses the goods. May the seller pass along this cost to the broker in the form of a rebate? Isn't that "services rendered"? Although it might seem so, the courts have said no, because they refuse to concede that a buyer's broker or agent can perform services for the seller. Because Section 2(c) of the Robinson-Patman Act stands on its own, the plaintiff need prove only that a single payment was made. Further proof of competitive impact is unnecessary. Hence, Section 2(c) cases are relatively easy to win once the fact of a brokerage commission is uncovered.

Allowances for Merchandising and Other Services

Sections 2(d) and 2(e) prohibit sellers from granting discriminatory allowances for merchandising and from performing other services for buyers on a discriminatory basis. These sections are necessary because price alone is far from the only way to offer discounts to favored buyers. Allowances and services covered by these sections include advertising allowances, floor and window displays, warehousing, return privileges, and special packaging.

EXEMPTIONS FROM THE ANTITRUST LAWS

Regulated Industries

Congress has subjected several industries to oversight by specific regulatory agencies. These include banking, securities and commodities exchanges, communications, transportation, and fuel and energy. The question often arises whether companies within those industries are immune to antitrust attack. No simple answer can be given. As a general rule, activities that fall directly within the authority of the regulatory agency are immune. The agency is said to have exclusive jurisdiction over the conduct—for example, the rate structure of the national stock exchanges, which are supervised by the Securities & Exchange Commission. But determining whether a particular case falls within a specific power of an agency is still up to the courts, and judges tend to read the antitrust laws broadly and the regulatory laws narrowly when they seem to clash. A doctrine known as "primary jurisdiction" often dictates that the question of regulatory propriety must first be submitted to the agency before the courts will rule on an antitrust question. If the agency decides the activity complained of is otherwise impermissible, the antitrust question becomes moot.

Organized Labor

In the Clayton Act, Congress explicitly exempted labor unions from the antitrust laws in order to permit workers to band together. Section 6 says that "the labor of a human being is not a commodity or article of commerce. Nothing contained in the antitrust laws shall be construed to forbid the existence and operation of labor . . . organizations, . . . nor shall such organizations, or the members thereof, be held or construed to be illegal combinations or conspiracies in restraint of trade, under the antitrust laws." This provision was included to reverse earlier decisions of the courts that had applied the Sherman Act more against labor than business. Nevertheless, the immunity is not total, and unions have run afoul of the laws when they have combined with non-labor groups to achieve a purpose unlawful under the antitrust laws. Thus, a union could not bargain with an employer to sell its products above a certain price floor.

Insurance

Under the McCarran-Ferguson Act of 1945, insurance companies are not covered by the antitrust laws to the extent that the states regulate the business of insurance. Whether or not the states adequately regulate insurance and the degree to which the exemption applies are complex questions, and there has been some political pressure to repeal the insurance exemption.

State Action

In 1943, the Supreme Court ruled in *Parker* v. *Brown*, 317 U.S. 341 (1943), that when a valid state law regulates a particular industry practice, which the industry members are bound to follow, then they are exempt from the federal antitrust laws. Such laws include regulation of public power and licensing and regulation of the professions. This exemption for "state action" has proved troublesome and, like the other exemptions, a complex matter to apply. But it is clear that the state law must require or compel the action, and not merely permit it. No state law would be valid if it simply said: "Bakers in the state may jointly establish tariffs for the sale of cookies."

The recent trend of Supreme Court decisions is to construe the exemption as narrowly as possible. A city, county, or other subordinate unit of a state is not immune under the *Parker* doctrine. A municipality can escape the consequences of antitrust violations—for example, in its operation of utilities—only if it is carrying out express policy of the state. Even then, a state mandated price-fixing scheme may not survive a federal antitrust attack, as the next case shows. New York law required liquor retailers to charge a certain minimum price, but because the state itself did not actively supervise the policy it had established, it fell to the Supreme Court's antitrust axe.

324 LIQUOR CORP. v. DUFFY
107 S.Ct. 720 (1987)

JUSTICE POWELL delivered the opinion of the Court.

The State of New York requires retailers to charge at least 112 percent of the "posted" wholesale price for liquor, but permits wholesalers to sell to retailers at less than the "posted" price. The question presented is whether this pricing system is valid under . . . the state-action exemption from the antitrust laws. . . .

Wholesalers of liquor in the State of New York must file, or "post," monthly price schedules with the State Liquor Authority (SLA). The schedules must report, "with respect to each item," "the bottle and case price to retailers." The ABC Law itself does not require that the posted case price of an item bear any relation to its posted bottle price. The SLA, however, has promulgated a rule stating that for cases containing 48 or fewer bottles, the posted bottle price multiplied by the number of bottles in a case must exceed the posted case price by a "breakage" surcharge of $1.92.

Retailers of liquor may not sell below "cost." The statute defines "cost" as "the price of such item of liquor to the retailer plus twelve percentum of such price." "Price," in turn, is defined as the posted bottle price in effect at the time the retailer sells or offers to sell the item. Although the statute defines retail cost in terms of the wholesaler's posted bottle price, retailers generally purchase liquor by the case. The SLA expressly has authorized wholesalers to reduce, or "post off," the case price of an item without reducing the posted bottle price of the item. By reducing the case price without reducing the bottle price, wholesalers can compel retailers to charge more than 112 percent of the actual wholesale cost. Similarly, because § 101–bb(2)(b) defines "cost" in terms of the posted bottle price in effect when the retailer sells or offers to sell the item, wholesalers can sell retailers large quantities in a month when prices are low and then require the retailers to sell at an abnormally high markup by raising the bottle price in succeeding months. The New York retail pricing system thus permits wholesalers to set retail prices, and retail markups, without regard to actual retail costs. New York wholesalers advertise in trade publications that their "post offs" will guarantee retailers large markups, sometimes in excess of 30 percent. Wholesalers also advertise that buying large quantities while wholesale prices are low will result in extra retail profits after wholesale prices are raised. The effect of this complex of statutory provisions and regulations is to permit wholesalers to maintain retail prices at artificially high levels.

Appellant 324 Liquor Corporation sold two bottles of liquor to SLA investigators in June 1981 for less than 112 percent of the posted bottle price. Because the wholesalers had "posted off" their June 1981 case prices without reducing the posted bottle prices, appellant's retail prices represented an 18 percent markup over its actual wholesale cost. As a result of this violation, appellant's license was suspended for 10 days and it forfeited a $1,000 bond. Appellant sought relief from the penalties on the ground that § 101–bb violates § 1 of the Sherman Act, 15 U. S. C. § 1.

★   ★   ★

In *Parker* v. *Brown,* 317 U.S. 341 (1943), the Court held that the Sherman Act does not apply "to the anticompetitive conduct of a State acting through its legislature." *Town of Hallie* v. *City of Eau Claire,* 471 U.S. 34, 38 (1985). *Parker* v. *Brown* rests on principles of federalism and state sovereignty. Under those principles, "an unexpressed purpose to nullify a state's control over its officers and agents is not lightly to be attributed to Congress." *Parker* v. *Brown,* 317 U.S., at 351. At the same time, "a state does not give immunity to those who violate the Sherman Act by authorizing them to violate it, or by declaring that their action is lawful." Our decisions have established a two-part test for determining immunity under *Parker* v. *Brown.* "First, the challenged restraint must be 'one clearly articulated and affirmatively expressed as state policy'; second, the policy must be 'actively supervised' by the State itself." *California Retail Liquor Dealers Assn.* v. *Midcal Aluminum, Inc.,* at 105. New York's liquor pricing system meets the first requirement. The state legislature clearly has adopted a policy of resale price maintenance. Just as clearly, however, New York's liquor pricing system is not actively supervised by the State. As in *Midcal,* the State "simply authorizes price setting and enforces the prices established by private parties." New York "neither establishes prices nor reviews the reasonableness of the price schedules." New York "does not monitor market conditions or engage in any 'pointed reexamination' of the program." Each wholesaler sets its own "posted" prices; the State does not control month-to-month variations in posted prices. Nor does the State supervise the wholesaler's decision to "post off," the amount of the "post off," the corresponding decrease, if any, in the bottle price, or the frequency with which a wholesaler posts off. The State has displaced competition among liquor retailers without substituting an adequate system of regulation. "The national policy in favor of competition cannot be thwarted by casting such a gauzy cloak of state involvement over what is essentially a private price-fixing arrangement."

Reversed and remanded.

Group Solicitation of Government Action

Suppose representatives of the railroad industry lobby extensively and eventually successfully for state legislation that hampers truckers, the railroads' deadly enemies. Is this a combination or conspiracy to restrain trade? In *Eastern Railroad President's Conference* v. *Noerr Motor Freight, Inc.*, 365 U.S. 127 (1961), the Supreme Court said no. What has come to be known as the *Noerr* doctrine holds that applying the antitrust laws to such activities would violate First Amendment rights to petition the government. One exception to this rule of immunity for soliciting action by the government comes when certain groups seek to harass competitors by instituting state or federal proceedings against them if the claims are baseless or known to be false. Nor does the *Noerr* doctrine apply to horizontal boycotts even if the object is to force the government to take action. In FTC v. Superior Court Trial Lawyers Assn., 493 U.S. 411 (1990), the Supreme Court held that a group of criminal defense lawyers had clearly violated the Sherman Act when they agreed among themselves to stop handling cases on behalf of indigent defendants to force the local government to raise the lawyers' fees. The Courts rejected their claim that they had a First Amendment right to influence the government through a boycott to pay a living wage so that indigent defendants could be adequately represented.

Baseball

Baseball, the Supreme Court said back in 1923, is not "in commerce." Congress has never seen fit to overturn this doctrine. Although some inroads have been made in the way that the leagues and clubs may exercise their power, the basic decision stands. Some things are sacred.

CHAPTER SUMMARY

Four basic antitrust laws regulate the competitive activities of American business: the Sherman Act, the Clayton Act, the Federal Trade Commission Act, and the Robinson-Patman Act. The Sherman Act prohibits restraints of trade and monopolizing. The Clayton Act prohibits a variety of anticompetitive acts, including mergers and acquisitions that might tend to

lessen competition. The Federal Trade Commission Act prohibits unfair methods of competition and unfair and deceptive acts or practices in commerce. The Robinson-Patman Act—actually an amendment to the Clayton Act—prohibits a variety of price discriminations. These laws are enforced in four ways: (1) by the U.S. Department of Justice, (2) by the Federal Trade Commission, (3) by state attorneys general, and (4) by private suits.

The courts have interpreted Section 1 of the Sherman Act, prohibiting every contract, combination, or conspiracy in restraint of trade, by the lights of a rule of reason, so that reasonable restraints ancillary to a legitimate business practice are lawful. But the courts will not ask whether an act is reasonable if it is carried out in order to restrain trade; such acts necessarily violate Section 1. Some acts—price fixing, for example—are illegal *per se*.

One broad class of acts that violate Section 1 are horizontal restraints of trade: agreements or conspiracies among competitors to restrain trade in their business or industry. Condemned acts include price fixing, exchanging price information when doing so permits industry members to control prices, controlling output, regulating competitive methods, allocating territories, exclusionary agreements, and boycotts.

Vertical restraints of trade are another unlawful class of acts under Section 1. These include resale price maintenance, refusals to deal, and unreasonable territorial restrictions on distributors.

Exclusive dealing contracts and tying contracts whose effect may be to substantially lessen competition violate Section 3 of the Clayton Act and may also violate both Section 1 of the Sherman Act and Section 5 of the Federal Trade Commission Act. Requirements and supply contracts are unlawful if they tie up so much of a commodity that they tend substantially to lessen competition or might tend to do so.

The Robinson-Patman Act (Section 2 of the Clayton Act) prohibits discrimination in price for different purchasers of commodities of like grade and quality, if the effect may be substantially to (1) lessen competition or tend to create a monopoly in any line of commerce, or (2) impair competition with (a) any person who grants or (b) knowingly receives the benefit of the discrimination, or (c) with customers of either of them.

Some industries are insulated from the direct reach of the antitrust laws. These include industries separately regulated under federal law, organized labor, insurance, activities mandated under state law, group solicitation of government action, and baseball.

KEY TERMS

SELF-TEST QUESTIONS

1. Under the rule of reason, an agreement among competitors to fix prices:
   (a) is lawful as long as the price set does not unduly injure competitors
   (b) is never lawful
   (c) is lawful as long as the price set is reasonable
   (d) is lawful as long as the price set does not harm consumers

2. A tying arrangement may violate:
   (a) section 1 of the Sherman Act
   (b) section 3 of the Clayton Act
   (c) section 5 of the Federal Trade Commission Act
   (d) all of the above

3. Which of the following statements is true?
   (a) Exclusive dealing arrangements are always unlawful.
   (b) Requirements contracts are always unlawful.
   (c) Refusals to deal are always unlawful.
   (d) Express agreements to maintain resale prices are always unlawful.

4. Price discrimination is banned under:
   (a) section 2 of the Clayton Act
   (b) section 1 of the Sherman Act
   (c) section 2 of the Sherman Act
   (d) section 5 of the Federal Trade Commission Act

5. The "state action" doctrine in antitrust:
   (a) is spelled out in the Sherman Act
   (b) appears in the Clayton Act
   (c) was devised by the courts
   (d) appears in the Constitution

DEMONSTRATION PROBLEM

Illinois Brick Company manufactures concrete blocks, which it sells to masons, who in turn work on the blocks and resell them to general contractors. In the 1970s, general contractors used the enhanced blocks to fulfill state building contracts. Illinois Brick has a price-fixing agreement with other manufacturers of concrete block. The State of Illinois discovers the agreement and sues Illinois Brick for treble damages. How can the company defend itself? Suppose the masons also sue the company? What result in each case? Why?

PROBLEMS

1. To protect its businesses against ruinous price wars, the state legislature has passed a law permitting manufacturers to set a "suggested resale price" on all goods that they make and sell direct to retailers. Retailers are forbidden to undercut the resale price by more than 10 percent. A retailer who violates the law may be sued by the manufacturer for treble damages: three times the difference between the suggested resale price and the actual selling price. But out-of-state retailers are bound by no such law and are regularly discounting the goods between 35 and 40 percent. As the general manager of a large discount store located within a few miles of a city across the state line, you wish to offer the public a price of only 60 percent of the suggested retail price on items covered by the law in order to compete with the out-of-state retailers to which your customers have easy access. May you lower your price in order to compete? How would you defend yourself if sued by a manufacturer whose goods you discounted in violation of the law?

2. The DiForio Motor Car Company is a small manufacturer of automobiles and sells to three distributors in Peoria. The largest distributor, Hugh's Autos, tells DiForio that it is losing money on its dealership and will quit selling the cars unless DiForio agrees to give it an exclusive contract. DiForio tells the other distributors, whose contracts were renewed from year to year, that it will no longer sell them cars at the end of the contract year. Smith Autos, one of the other dealers, protests, but DiForio refuses to resupply it. Smith Autos sues DiForio and Hugh's. What result? Why?

3. The widget industry consists of six large manufacturers who together account for 62 percent of output, which in 1985 amounted to $2.1 billion in domestic U.S. sales. The remaining 38 percent is supplied by more than forty manufacturers. All six of the large manufacturers and thirty-one of the forty small manufacturers belong to the Widget Manufacturers Trade Association (WMTA). An officer from at least two of the six manufacturers always serves on the WMTA executive committee, which consists of seven members. The full WMTA board of directors consists of one member from each manufacturer. The executive committee meets once a month for dinner at the Widgeters Club; the full board meets semiannually at the Widget Show. The executive committee, which always meets with the association's lawyer in attendance, discusses a wide range of matters, including industry conditions, economic

trends, customer relations, technological developments, and the like, but scrupulously refrains from discussing price, territories, or output. However, after dinner at the bar, five of the seven members meet for drinks and discuss prices in an informal manner. The chairman of the executive committee concludes the discussion with the following statement: "If I had to guess, I'd guess that the unit price will increase by 5 percent the first of next month." On the first of the month, his prediction is proven to be correct among the five companies whose officers had a drink, and within a week, most of the other manufacturers likewise increase their prices. At the semiannual meeting of the full board, the WMTA chairman notes that prices have been climbing steadily and he ventures the hope that they will not continue to do so because otherwise they will face stiff competition from the Gidget industry. However, following the next several meetings of the executive committee, the price continues to rise as before. The Justice Department gets wind of these discussions and sues the companies whose officers are members of the board of directors and also sues individually the members of the executive committee and the chairman of the full board. What laws have they violated, if any, and who has violated them? What remedies or sanctions may the department seek?

4. Twenty-five local supermarket chains banded together as Topco Associates Incorporated to sell groceries under a private label. Topco was formed in 1940 to compete with the giant chains, which had the economic clout to sell private-label merchandise unavailable to the smaller chains. Topco acted as a purchasing agent for the members. By the late 1960s, Topco's members were doing a booming business: $1.3 billion in retail sales, with market share ranging from 1.5 percent to 16 percent in the markets that members served. Topco-brand groceries comprised no more than 10 percent of any store's total merchandise. Under Topco's rules, members were assigned exclusive territories in which to sell Topco-brand goods. A member chain with stores located in another member's exclusive territory could not sell Topco-brand goods in those stores. Topco argued that the market division was necessary to give each chain the economic incentive to advertise and develop brand consciousness, and thus to be able to compete more effectively against the large nonmember supermarkets' private labels. If other stores in the locality could also carry the Topco brand, then it would not be a truly "private" label and there would be no reason to tout it, since it would be like any national brand foodstuff, and Topco members did not have the funds to advertise the brand nationally. Which, if any, antitrust laws has Topco violated? Why?

5. In 1983, Panda Bears Incorporated, a small manufacturer, began to sell its patented panda bear robot dolls (they walk, smile, and eat bamboo shoots) to retail toy shops. The public took an immediate fancy to panda bears and the company found it difficult to meet the demand. Retail shops sold out even before their orders arrived. In order to allocate the limited supply fairly, while it tooled up to increase production runs, the company announced to its distributors that it would not sell to any retailers that did not also purchase its trademarked Panda Bear's Bambino Bamboos. It also announced that it would refuse to supply any retailer that sold the robots for less than $59.95. Finally, it said that it would refuse to sell unless the retailer agreed to use exclusively the company's repair services when customers brought the bears back to repair malfunctions in its delicate, patented computerized nervous system. By the following year, with demand still rising, inferior competitive products began to appear of both the robots and the bamboo shoots. Some retailers began to lower the Panda Bear price to meet the competition. The company refused to resupply them. Panda Bears Incorporated also decreed that it would refuse to sell to retailers who carried any other type of bamboo. What antitrust violations, if any, has Panda Bear Incorporated committed? What additional information might be useful in helping you to decide?

6. Sampson Company sells car tires to automotive parts stores for resale to consumers. The manager of Ace Auto Supplies is the brother of Sampson's sales manager. Ace competes with Tyler Auto Supplies. Sampson's sales manager wants to give a break to Ace by charging it 20 percent less for the same quantity of tires than the price to Tyler. But Sampson's sales manager has heard of the Robinson-Patman Act and knows that price discrimination is probably unlawful if it is not cost justified. So he calls up Fred's Tire Wholesalers and says he will be referring a substantial amount of business to the wholesaler in the future. All sales to Ace and Tyler will be made by Sampson but will be processed through Fred's, which need do nothing but fill the order. In this way, Sampson hopes to avoid charges of price discrimination, because it is only making one sale—namely, to Fred's. Is Sampson vulnerable to a price discrimination charge by Tyler? Why?

ANSWERS TO SELF-TEST QUESTIONS

1. (b)   2. (d)   3. (d)   4. (a)   5. (c)

SUGGESTED ANSWER TO DEMONSTRATION PROBLEM

In *Illinois Brick Co. v. Illinois*, 431 U.S. 720 (1977), the Supreme Court said that the state could not sue for treble damages because it was not the direct purchaser. Illinois paid for the bricks as part of the price it paid for construction done by the general contractors. However, the masons could sue the company for price-fixing, because they were directly injured by the price-fixing agreement. For several years, Congress has had before it a bill to reverse the result in this case (and thus to permit the indirect purchaser to sue), but so far the bill has not been enacted. However, as the result of the *Illinois Brick* decision, many states enacted their own laws permitting indirect-purchaser lawsuits. In a 1989 decision, *California v. ARC America Corp.*, 490 U.S. 93 (1989), the Supreme Court upheld the validity of these state laws against a challenge that they interfered with enforcement of federal antitrust law.

CHAPTER 47

CHAPTER OVERVIEW
Section 2 of the Sherman Act: The Law Against Monopolizing
Acquisitions and Mergers under Section 7 of the Clayton Act

Antitrust 2: Concentrations of Power

Monopolies and other concentrations of economic power can thwart competition. Indeed, in a pure sense, a monopoly means the lack of competition, or at least of effective competition. As the Supreme Court has long defined it, monopoly is "the power to control market prices or exclude competition." [United States v. Grinnell Corp., 384 U.S. 563, 571 (1966)] Public concern about the economic and political power of the large trusts, which tended to become monopolies in the late nineteenth century, led to Section 2 of the Sherman Act in 1890 and to Section 7 of the Clayton Act in 1914. These statutes are not limited to the behemoths of American industry such as IBM or American Telephone & Telegraph Company. A far smaller company that dominates a relatively small geographic area, or merges with another company in an area where few others compete, can be in for trouble under Sections 2 or 7. These laws, therefore, should be of concern to all businesses, not just those on the Fortune 500 list. In this chapter, we will consider how the courts have interpreted both the Section 2 prohibition against monopolizing and the Section 7 prohibition against mergers and acquisitions that tend to lessen competition or to create monopolies.

SECTION 2 OF THE SHERMAN ACT: THE LAW AGAINST MONOPOLIZING

Introduction

Section 2 of the Sherman Act reads as follows:

> Every person who shall monopolize, or attempt to monopolize, or combine or conspire with any other person or persons, to monopolize any part of the trade or commerce among the several states, or with foreign nations, shall be deemed guilty of a [felony].

We begin the analysis of Section 2 with the fundamental proposition that a monopoly is not *per se* unlawful. Section 2 itself makes this proposition inescapable: it forbids the act of *monopolizing*, not the condition or attribute of *monopoly*. Why should that be so? If monopoly power is detrimental to a functioning competitive market system, why should not the law ban the very existence of a monopoly?

The answer is that we cannot hope to have "perfect competition" but only "workable competition." Any number of circumstances might lead to monopolies that we would not want to eliminate. Demand for a product might be limited to what one company could produce, there thus being no incentive for any competitor to come into the market. A small town may be able to support only one supermarket, newspaper, or computer outlet. If a company is operating efficiently through economies of scale, we would not want to split it apart and watch the resulting companies fail. An innovator may have a field all to himself, yet we would not want to penalize the inventor for his very act of invention. Or a company might simply be smarter and more efficient, finally coming to stand alone through the very operation of competitive pressures. It would be an irony indeed if the law were to condemn a company that was forged in the fires of competition itself. As the Supreme Court has said, the Sherman Act was designed to protect competition, not competitors.

A company that has had a monopoly position "thrust upon it" is perfectly lawful. The law penalizes not the monopolist as such, but the competitor who gains his monopoly power through illegitimate means with an intent to become a monopolist, or who after having become a monopolist acts illegitimately to maintain his power.

A Section 2 case involves three essential factors:

1. What is the **relevant market** for determining dominance? The question of relevant market has two aspects, a **geographic market** dimension and a **product market** dimension. As we saw in the *Tampa Electric* case (Chapter 46), it makes a considerable difference whether the company is thought to be a competitor in ten states or only one. A large company in one state may appear tiny matched against competitors operating in many states. Likewise, if the product itself has real substitutes, it makes little sense to brand its maker a monopolist. For instance, Coca-Cola is

made by only one company, but that does not make the Coca-Cola Company a monopoly, for its soft drink competes with many in the marketplace.

2. How much **monopoly power** is too much? What share of the market must a company have to be labeled a monopoly? Is a company with 50 percent of the market a monopoly? 75 percent? 90 percent?

3. What constitutes an illegitimate means of gaining or maintaining monopoly power?

These factors are often closely intertwined, especially the first two. This makes it difficult to examine each separately, but to the extent possible we will address each factor in the order given.

Relevant Market

Product Market The monopolist never exercises power in the abstract. When exercised, monopoly power is used to set prices or exclude competition in the market for a particular product or products. Therefore it is essential in any Section 2 case to determine what products to include in the relevant market.

In the *du Pont* case below, the Court phrased the test in terms of "cross-elasticity of demand"—to what degree can a substitute be found for the product in question if the producer sets the price too high? If consumers stay with the product as its price rises, moving to a substitute only at a very high price, then the product is probably in a market by itself. If consumers shift to another product with slight rises in price, then the product market must include all such substitutes.

**UNITED STATES v.
E. I. DU PONT DE
NEMOURS & CO.
351 U.S. 377 (1956)**

MR. JUSTICE REED delivered the opinion of the Court.

The United States . . . charged du Pont with monopolizing, attempting to monopolize and conspiracy to monopolize interstate commerce in cellophane . . . in violation of Section 2 of the Sherman Act.

*   *   *

During the period that is relevant to this action, du Pont produced almost 75 percent of the cellophane sold in the United States, and cellophane constituted less than 20 percent of all "flexible packaging material" sales. This was the designation accepted at the trial. . . .

The Government contends that, by so dominating cellophane production, du Pont monopolized a "part of the trade or commerce" in violation of Section 2. Respondent agrees that cellophane is a product which constitutes "a 'part' of commerce within the meaning of Section 2." But it contends that the prohibition of Section 2 against monopolization is not violated because it does not have the power to control the price of cellophane or to exclude competitors from the market in which cellophane is sold. The court below found that the "relevant market for determining the extent of du Pont's market control is the market for flexible packaging materials," and that competition from those other materials prevented du Pont from possessing monopoly powers in its sales of cellophane.

The Government asserts that cellophane and other wrapping materials are neither substantially fungible nor like priced. For these reasons, it argues that the market for other wrappings is distinct from the market for cellophane and that the competition afforded cellophane by other wrappings is not strong enough to be considered in determining whether du Pont has monopoly powers. Market delimitation is necessary under du Pont's theory to determine whether an alleged monopolist violates Section 2. The ultimate consideration in such a determination is whether the defendants control the price and competition in the market for such part of trade or commerce as they are charged with monopolizing. Every manufacturer is the sole producer of the particular commodity it makes but its control in the above sense of the relevant market depends upon the availability of alternative commodities for buyers: i.e., whether there is a cross-elasticity of demand between cellophane and the other wrappings. This interchangeability is largely gauged by the purchase of competing products for similar uses considering the price, characteristics and adaptability of the competing commodities. The court below found that the flexible wrappings afforded such alternatives. This Court must determine whether the trial court erred in its estimate of the competition afforded cellophane by other materials. . . .

If cellophane is the "market" that du Pont is found to dominate, it may be assumed it does have monopoly power over that "market." Monopoly power is the power to control prices or exclude competition. It seems apparent that du Pont's power to set the price of cellophane has been limited only by the competition afforded by other flexible packaging materials. Moreover, it may be practically impossible for anyone to commence manufacturing cellophane without full access to du Pont's technique. However, du Pont has no power to prevent competition from other wrapping materials. The trial court consequently had to determine whether competition from the other wrappings prevented du Pont from possessing monopoly power in violation of Section 2. Price and competition are so intimately entwined that any discussion of theory must treat them as one. It is inconceivable that price could be controlled without power over competition or vice versa. This approach to the determination of monopoly power is strengthened by this Court's conclusion in prior cases, that, when an alleged monopolist has power over price and competition, an intention to monopolize in a proper case may be assumed.

★   ★   ★

Determination of the competitive market for commodities depends on how different from one another are the offered commodities in character for use, how far buyers will go to substitute one commodity for another. For example, one can think of building materials as in commodity competition but one could hardly say that brick competed with steel or wood or cement or stone in the meaning of Sherman Act litigation; the products are too different. This is the interindustry competition emphasized by some economists. On the other hand, there are certain differences in the formulae for soft drinks but one can hardly say that each one is an illegal monopoly. Whatever the market may be, we hold that control of price or competition established the existence of monopoly power under Section 2.

★   ★   ★

The Government argues:

> We do here urge that in no circumstances may competition substitute negative possession of monopolistic power over trade in a product. The decisions make it clear at the least that the courts will not consider substitutes other than those which are substantially fungible with the monopolized product and sell at substantially the same price.

But where there are market alternatives that buyers may readily use for their purposes, illegal monopoly does not exist merely because the product said to be monopolized differs from others. If it were not so, only physically identical products would be a part of the market. To accept the Government's argument, we would have to conclude that the manufacturers of plain as well as moisture-proof cellophane were monopolists, and so with films such as Pliofilm, foil, glassine, polyethylene, and Saran, for each of these wrapping materials is distinguishable. These were all exhibits in the case. New wrappings appear, generally similar to cellophane; is each a monopoly? What is called for is an appraisal of the "cross-elasticity" of demand in the trade. . . . The varying circumstances of each case determine the result. In considering what is the relevant market for determining the control of price and

(continued on next page)

(continued)

UNITED STATES v. E. I. DU PONT DE NEMOURS & CO. 351 U.S. 377 (1956)

competition, no more definite rule can be declared than that commodities reasonably interchangeable by consumers for the same purposes make up that "part of the trade or commerce," monopolization of which may be illegal. As respects flexible packaging materials, the market geographically is nationwide.

Cellophane differs from other flexible packaging materials. From some it differs more than from others. The basic materials from which the wrappings are made . . . are aluminum, cellulose, acetate, chlorides, wood pulp, rubber hydrochloride, and ethylene gas. . . .

It may be admitted that cellophane combines the desirable elements of transparency, strength and cheapness more definitely than any of the others. . . .

But despite cellophane's advantages, it has to meet competition from other materials in every one of its uses. . . . Food products are the chief outlet, with cigarettes next. The Government makes no challenge to Finding 283 that cellophane furnishes less than 7 percent of wrappings for bakery products, 25 percent for candy, 32 percent for snacks, 35 percent for meats and poultry, 27 percent for crackers and biscuits, 47 percent for fresh produce, and 34 percent for frozen foods. Seventy-five to eighty percent of cigarettes are wrapped in cellophane. . . . Thus cellophane shares the packaging market with others. The over-all result is that cellophane accounts for 17.9 percent of flexible wrapping materials, measured by the wrapping surface. . . .

Moreover a very considerable degree of functional interchangeability exists between these products . . . It will be noted, . . . that except as to permeability to gases, cellophane has no qualities that are not possessed by a number of other materials. Meat will do as an example of interchangeability. . . . Although du Pont's sales to the meat industry have reached 19,000,000 pounds annually, nearly 35 percent, this volume is attributed "to the rise of self-service retailing of fresh meat." . . . In fact, since the popularity of self-service meats, du Pont has lost "a considerable proportion" of this packaging business to Pliofilm. . . . Pliofilm is more expensive than cellophane, but its superior physical characteristics apparently offset cellophane's price advantage. While retailers shift continually between the two, the trial court found that Pliofilm is increasing its share of the business. . . .

An element for consideration as to cross-elasticity of demand between products is the responsiveness of the sales of one product to price changes of the other. If a slight decrease in the price of cellophane causes a considerable number of customers of other flexible wrappings to switch to cellophane, it would be an indication that a high cross-elasticity of demand exists between them; that the products compete in the same market. The court below held that the "[g]reat sensitivity of customers in the flexible packaging markets to price or quality changes" prevented du Pont from possessing monopoly control over price. . . . The record sustains these findings. . . .

We conclude that cellophane's interchangeability with the other materials mentioned suffices to make it a part of this flexible packaging market.

*　　*　　*

> The "market" which one must study to determine when a producer has monopoly power will vary with the part of commerce under consideration. The tests are constant. That market is composed of products that have reasonable interchangeability for the purposes for which they are produced—price, use and qualities considered. While the application of the tests remains uncertain, it seems to us that du Pont should not be found to monopolize cellophane when that product has the competition and interchangeability with other wrappings that this record shows.
>
> On the findings of the District Court, its judgment is affirmed.

Geographic Market A company need not dominate the worldwide market for a particular product or service to be held a monopolist. The Sherman Act speaks of "any part" of the trade or commerce—the "area of effective competition," as the Supreme Court has defined it. It may appear that the smaller the part the government can point to, the greater its chances of prevailing, since a company usually will have greater control over a single marketplace than a regional or national market. Hence, alleged monopolists usually argue for a broad geographic market, while the government tries to narrow it, by pointing to such factors as transportation costs and the degree to which consumers will shop outside the defined area. But this rule is not invariable. Sometimes the government will argue for a broad market because in any given regional or small market the defendant may face determined local competition or because the local market will sustain only one producer or supplier.

Monopoly Power

After the relevant product and geographic markets are defined, the next question is whether the defendant has sufficient power within them to constitute a monopoly. The usual test is the market share the putative monopolist enjoys, although no rigid rule or mathematical formula is possible. In *United States v. Aluminum Co. of America*, 148 F.2d 416 (2d Cir. 1945), Judge Learned Hand said that Alcoa's 90 percent share of the ingot market was enough to constitute a monopoly but that 64 percent would have been doubtful. In the *Cellophane* case, the Court seemed to suggest that du Pont's 75 percent share of the cellophane market would have made the company a monopoly had the relevant market been restricted to cellophane.

Monopolization: Acquiring and Maintaining a Monopoly

As noted, possessing a monopoly is not *per se* unlawful. Once a company has been found to have monopoly power in a relevant market, the final question is whether it either acquired its monopoly power in an unlawful way or has acted unlawfully to maintain it. This additional element of "deliberateness" does not mean that the government must prove that the defendant *intended* **monopolization,** in the sense that what he *desired* was the complete exclusion of all competitors. It is enough to show that the monopoly would probably result from his actions, for as Judge Hand put it: "No monopolist monopolizes unconscious of what he is doing."

What constitutes proof of unlawful acquisition or maintenance of a monopoly? In general, it consists of showing that the defendant's acts were aimed at or had the probable effect of excluding competitors from the market. Violations of Section 1 or other provisions of the antitrust laws are examples. "Predatory pricing"—charging less than cost—can be evidence that the defendant's purpose was monopolistic, for small companies cannot compete with large manufacturers, which are capable of sustaining continued losses until the competition folds up and ceases operations.

In *United States v. Lorain Journal Company*, 342 U.S. 143 (1951), the town of Lorain, Ohio, could support only one newspaper. With a circulation of

20,000, the *Lorain Journal* reached more than 99 percent of the town's families. The *Journal* had thus lawfully become a monopoly. But when a radio station was set up, the paper found itself competing directly for local and national advertising. To retaliate, the *Journal* refused to accept advertisements unless the advertiser agreed not to advertise on the local station. The Court agreed that this was an unlawful attempt to boycott, and hence was a violation of Section 2 because the paper was using its monopoly power to exclude a competitor. (Where was the *interstate* commerce? The Court said that the radio station was in interstate commerce because it broadcast national news supported by national advertising.)

Practices that help a company acquire or maintain its monopoly position need not be unlawful in themselves. In the *Aluminum* case below, Alcoa claimed its monopoly power was the result of superior business skills and techniques, which led it constantly to build plant capacity and expand output at every opportunity. But Judge Hand thought otherwise, given that for a quarter of a century other producers could not break into the market because Alcoa acted at every turn to make it impossible for them to compete, even as Alcoa increased its output by some 800 percent. Judge Hand's explanation remains the classic exposition.

UNITED STATES v. ALUMINUM COMPANY OF AMERICA
148 F.2d 416 (2d. Cir. 1945)

JUDGE LEARNED HAND.

* * *

It does not follow because "Alcoa" had such a monopoly that it "monopolized" the ingot market: it may not have achieved monopoly; monopoly may have been thrust upon it. If it had been a combination of existing smelters which united the whole industry and controlled the production of all aluminum ingot, it would certainly have "monopolized" the market. . . . We may start therefore with the premise that to have combined ninety percent of the producers of ingot would have been to "monopolize" the ingot market; and, so far as concerns the public interest, it can make no difference whether an existing competition is put an end to, or whether prospective competition is prevented. . . . Nevertheless, it is unquestionably true that from the very outset the courts have at least kept in reserve the possibility that the origin of a monopoly may be critical in determining its legality; and for this they had warrant in some of the congressional debates which accompanied the passage of the Act. . . . This notion has usually been expressed by saying that size does not determine guilt; that there must be some "exclusion" of competitors; that the growth must be something else than "natural" or "normal"; that there must be a "wrongful intent," or some other specific intent; or that some "unduly" coercive means must be used. At times there has been emphasis upon the use of the active verb, "monopolize," as the judge noted in the case at bar.

. . . A market may, for example, be so limited that it is impossible to produce at all and meet the cost of production except by a plant large enough to supply the whole demand. Or there may be changes in taste or in cost which drive out all but one purveyor. A single producer may be the survivor out of a group of active competitors, merely by virtue of his superior skill, foresight, and industry. In such cases a strong argument can be made that, although, the result may expose the public to the evils of monopoly, the Act does not mean to condemn the resultant of those very forces which it is its prime object to foster: finis opus coronat. The successful competitor, having been urged to compete, must not be turned upon when he wins.

* * *

[As] Cardozo, J., in United States v. Swift & Co., 286 U.S. 106, p. 116, 52 S. Ct. 460, 463, 76 L.Ed. 999, . . . said, "Mere size . . . is not an offense against the Sherman Act unless magnified to the point at which it amounts to a monopoly . . . but size carries with it an opportunity for abuse that is not to be ignored when the opportunity is proved to have been utilized in the past." "Alcoa's" size was "magnified" to make it a "monopoly"; indeed, it has never been anything else; and its size not only offered it an "opportunity for abuse," but it "utilized" its size for "abuse," as can easily be shown.

It would completely misconstrue "Alcoa's" position in 1940 to hold that it was the passive beneficiary of a monopoly, following upon an involuntary elimination of competitors by automatically operative economic forces. Already in 1909, when its last lawful monopoly ended, it sought to strengthen its position by unlawful practices, and these concededly continued until 1912. In that year it had two plants in New York, at which it produced less than 42 million pounds of ingot; in 1934 it had five plants (the original two, enlarged; one in Tennessee; one in North Carolina; one in Washington), and its production had risen to about 327 million pounds, an increase of almost eight-fold. Meanwhile not a pound of ingot had been produced by anyone else in the United States. This increase and this continued and undisturbed control did not fall undesigned into "Alcoa's" lap; obviously it could not have done so. It could only have resulted, as it did result, from a persistent determination to maintain the control, with which it found itself vested in 1912. There were at least one or two abortive attempts to enter the industry, but "Alcoa" effectively anticipated and forestalled all competition, and succeeded in holding the field alone. True, it stimulated demand and opened new uses for the metal, but not without making sure that it could supply what it had evoked. There is no dispute as to this; "Alcoa" avows it as evidence of the skill, energy and initiative with which it has always conducted its business: as a reason why, having won its way by fair means, it should be commended, and not dismembered. We need charge it with no moral derelictions after 1912; we may assume that all its claims for itself are true. The only question is whether it falls within the exception established in favor of those who do not seek, but cannot avoid, the control of a market. It seems to us that that question scarcely survives its statement. It was not inevitable that it should always anticipate increases in the demand for ingot and be prepared to supply them. Nothing compelled it to keep doubling and redoubling its capacity before others entered the field. It insists that it never excluded competitors; but we can think of no more effective exclusion than progressively to embrace each new opportunity as it opened, and to face

(continued on next page)

(continued)

UNITED STATES v. ALUMINUM COMPANY OF AMERICA
148 F.2d 416 (2d. Cir. 1945)

every newcomer with new capacity already geared into a great organization, having the advantage of experience, trade connections and the elite of personnel. Only in case we interpret "exclusion" as limited to manoeuvres not honestly industrial, but actuated solely by a desire to prevent competition, can such a course, indefatigably pursued, be deemed not "exclusionary." So to limit it would in our judgment emasculate the Act; would permit just such consolidations as it was designed to prevent.

*   *   *

We disregard any question of "intent." Relatively early in the history of the Act—1905—Holmes, J., in Swift & Co. v. United States, explained this aspect of the Act in a passage often quoted. Although the primary evil was monopoly, the Act also covered preliminary steps, which, if continued, would lead to it. These may do no harm of themselves; but if they are initial moves in a plan or scheme which, carried out, will result in monopoly, they are dangerous and the law will nip them in the bud. . . . In order to fall within § 2, the monopolist must have both the power to monopolize, and the intent to monopolize. To read the passage as demanding any "specific," intent, makes nonsense of it, for no monopolist monopolizes unconscious of what he is doing. So here, "Alcoa" meant to keep, and did keep, that complete and exclusive hold upon the ingot market with which it started. That was to "monopolize" that market, however innocently it otherwise proceeded. So far as the judgment held that it was not within § 2, it must be reversed.

Innovation as Evidence of Intent to Monopolize

During the 1970s, several monopolization cases seeking huge damages were filed against a number of well-known companies, including Xerox, IBM, and Eastman Kodak. In particular, IBM was hit with several suits as an outgrowth of the Justice Department's lawsuit against the computer maker. (*United States* v. *IBM* was filed in 1969 and did not terminate until 1982, when the government agreed to drop all charges, a complete victory for the company.) The plaintiffs in many of these suits—SCM Corporation against Xerox, California Computer Products Incorporated against IBM (the *Calcomp* case), Berkey Photo Incorporated against Kodak—charged that the defendants had maintained their alleged monopolies by strategically introducing key product innovations that rendered competitive products obsolete. For example, hundreds of computer companies manufacture pe-

ripheral equipment "plug-compatible" with IBM computers. Likewise, Berkey manufactured film usable in Kodak cameras. When the underlying products are changed—mainframe computers, new types of cameras—the existing manufacturers are left with unusable inventory and face a considerable time lag in designing new peripheral equipment. In some of these cases, the plaintiffs managed to obtain sizable treble damage awards—SCM won more than $110 million, IBM initially lost one case in the amount of $260 million, and Berkey bested Kodak to the tune of $87 million. Had these cases been sustained on appeal, a radical new doctrine would have been imported into the antitrust laws: that innovation for the sake of competing is unlawful.

As it happened, however, none of these cases withstood appellate scrutiny, though to date the Supreme Court has refused to hear appeals in any of the major cases, so the law has emerged entirely from decisions of the federal courts of appeals. Thus, in *ILC Peripherals Leasing Corp.* v. *International Business*

Machines (the *Memorex* case), 458 F.Supp. 423 (N.D. Cal. 1978), Memorex argued that, among other things, IBM's tactic of introducing a new generation of computer technology at lower prices constituted monopolization. The court disagreed, noting that other companies could "reverse engineer" IBM equipment much more cheaply than IBM could originally design it and that IBM computers and related products were subject to intense competition to the benefit of plug-compatible equipment users. IBM's actions undoubtedly hurt Memorex, but they were part and parcel of the competitive system, the very essence of competition. "This kind of conduct by IBM," the court said, "is precisely what the antitrust laws were meant to encourage. . . . Memorex sought to use the antitrust laws to make time stand still and preserve its very profitable position. This court will not assist it and the others who would follow after in this endeavor."

The various strands of the innovation debate are perhaps best summed up in the *Berkey* case as follows.

BERKEY PHOTO, INC. v. EASTMAN KODAK COMPANY

603 F.2d 263 (2d. Cir. 1979)

IRVING R. KAUFMAN, CHIEF JUDGE. To millions of Americans, the name Kodak is virtually synonymous with photography. . . . It is one of the giants of American enterprise, with international sales of nearly $6 billion in 1977 and pre-tax profits in excess of $1.2 billion.

This action, one of the largest and most significant private antitrust suits in history, was brought by Berkey Photo, Inc., a far smaller but still prominent participant in the industry. Berkey competes with Kodak in providing photofinishing services—the conversion of exposed film into finished prints, slides, or movies. Until 1978, Berkey sold cameras as well. It does not manufacture film, but it does purchase Kodak film for resale to its customers, and it also buys photofinishing equipment and supplies, including color print paper, from Kodak.

The two firms thus stand in a complex, multifaceted relationship, for Kodak has been Berkey's competitor in some markets and its supplier in others. In this action, Berkey claims that every aspect of the association has been infected by Kodak's monopoly power in the film, color print paper, and camera markets, willfully acquired, maintained, and exercised in violation of § 2 of the Sherman Act, 15 U.S.C. § 2. . . . Berkey alleges that these violations caused it to lose sales in the camera and photofinishing markets and to pay excessive prices to Kodak for film, color print paper, and photofinishing equipment.

*   *   *

. . . [T]he jury found for Berkey on virtually every point, awarding damages totaling $37,620,130. Judge Frankel upheld verdicts aggregating $27,154,700 for lost camera and photofinishing sales and for excessive prices on film and photofinishing equipment. . . . Trebled and supplemented by attorneys' fees and costs pursuant to § 4 of the Clayton Act, 15 U.S.C. § 15, Berkey's judgment reached a grand total of $87,091,309.47, with interest, of course, continuing to accrue.

Kodak now appeals this judgment.

(continued on next page)

(continued)

BERKEY PHOTO, INC. v. EASTMAN KODAK COMPANY

603 F.2d 263 (2d. Cir. 1979)

★   ★   ★

The principal markets relevant here, each nationwide in scope, are amateur conventional still cameras, conventional photographic film, photofinishing services, photofinishing equipment, and color print paper.

★   ★   ★

The "amateur conventional still camera" market now consists almost entirely of the so-called 110 and 126 instant-loading cameras. These are the direct descendants of the popular "box" cameras, the best-known of which was Kodak's so-called "Brownie." Small, simple, and relatively inexpensive, cameras of this type are designed for the mass market rather than for the serious photographer.

Kodak has long been the dominant firm in the market thus defined. Between 1954 and 1973 it never enjoyed less than 61% of the annual unit sales, nor less than 64% of the dollar volume, and in the peak year of 1964, Kodak cameras accounted for 90% of market revenues. Much of this success is no doubt due to the firm's history of innovation.

★   ★   ★

Berkey has been a camera manufacturer since its 1966 acquisition of the Keystone Camera Company, a producer of movie cameras and equipment. In 1968 Berkey began to sell amateur still cameras made by other firms, and the following year the Keystone Division commenced manufacturing such cameras itself. From 1970 to 1977, Berkey accounted for 8.2% of the sales in the camera market in the United States, reaching a peak of 10.2% in 1976. In 1978, Berkey sold its camera division and thus abandoned this market.

★   ★   ★

. . . One must comprehend the fundamental tension—one might almost say the paradox—that is near the heart of § 2. . . .

The conundrum was indicated in characteristically striking prose by Judge Hand, who was not able to resolve it. Having stated that Congress "did not condone 'good trusts' and condemn 'bad' ones; it forbad all," he declared with equal force, "The successful competitor, having been urged to compete, must not be turned upon when he wins." . . . We must always be mindful lest the Sherman Act be invoked perversely in favor of those who seek protection against the rigors of competition.

★   ★   ★

In sum, although the principles announced by the § 2 cases often appear to conflict, this much is clear. The mere possession of monopoly power does not *ipso facto* condemn a market participant. But, to avoid the proscriptions of § 2, the firm must refrain at all times from conduct directed at smothering competition. This doctrine has two branches. Unlawfully acquired power remains anathema even when kept dormant. And it is no less true that a firm with a legitimately achieved monopoly may not wield the resulting power to tighten its hold on the market.

★   ★   ★

As Kodak had hoped, the 110 system proved to be a dramatic success. In 1972—the system's first year—the company sold 2,984,000 Pocket Instamatics, more than 50% of its sales in the amateur conventional still camera market. The new camera thus accounted in large part for a sharp increase in total market sales, from 6.2 million units in 1971 to 8.2 million in 1972. . . .

Berkey's Keystone division was a late entrant in the 110 sweepstakes, joining the competition only in late 1973. Moreover, because of hasty design, the original models suffered from latent defects, and sales that year were a paltry 42,000. With interest in the 126 dwindling, Keystone thus suffered a net decline of 118,000 unit sales in 1973. The following year, however, it recovered strongly, in large part because improvements in its pocket cameras helped it sell 406,000 units, 7% of all 110s sold that year.

Berkey contends that the introduction of the 110 system was both an attempt to monopolize and actual monopolization of the camera market.

★   ★   ★

It will be useful at the outset to present the arguments on which Berkey asks us to uphold its verdict:

Kodak, a film and camera monopolist, was in a position to set industry standards. Rivals could not compete effectively without offering products similar to Kodak's. Moreover, Kodak persistently refused to make film available for most formats other than those in which it made cameras. Since cameras are worthless without film, this policy effectively prevented other manufacturers from introducing cameras in new formats. Because of its dominant position astride two markets, and by use of its film monopoly to distort the camera market, Kodak forfeited its own right to reap profits from such innovations without providing its rivals with sufficient advance information to enable them to enter the market with copies of the new product on the day of Kodak's introduction. This is one of several "predisclosure" arguments Berkey has advanced in the course of this litigation.

★   ★   ★

Through the 1960s, Kodak followed a checkered pattern of predisclosing innovations to various segments of the industry. Its purpose on these occasions evidently was to ensure that the industry would be able to meet consumers' demand for the complementary goods and services they would need to enjoy the new Kodak products. But predisclosure would quite obviously also diminish Kodak's share of the auxiliary markets. It was therefore, in the words of Walter Fallon, Kodak's chief executive officer, "a matter of judgment on each and every occasion" whether predisclosure would be for or against Kodak's self-interest.

(continued on next page)

(continued)

BERKEY PHOTO, INC. v. EASTMAN KODAK COMPANY
603 F.2d 263 (2d. Cir. 1979)

*   *   *

. . . Kodak decided not to release advance information about the new film and format. The decision was evidently based on the perception of Dr. Louis K. Eilers, Kodak's chief executive officer at that time, that Kodak would gain more from being first on the market for the sale of all goods and services related to the 110 system than it would lose from the inability of other photofinishers to process Kodacolor II.

*   *   *

Judge Frankel did not decide that Kodak should have disclosed the details of the 110 to other camera manufacturers prior to introduction. Instead, he left the matter to the jury. . . . We hold that this instruction was in error and that, as a matter of law, Kodak did not have a duty to predisclose information about the 110 system to competing camera manufacturers.

As Judge Frankel indicated, and as Berkey concedes, a firm may normally keep its innovations secret from its rivals as long as it wishes, forcing them to catch up on the strength of their own efforts after the new product is introduced. It is the possibility of success in the marketplace, attributable to superior performance, that provides the incentives on which the proper functioning of our competitive economy rests. . . .

Withholding from others advance knowledge of one's new products, therefore, ordinarily constitutes valid competitive conduct. Because, as we have already indicated, a monopolist is permitted, and indeed encouraged, by § 2 to compete aggressively on the merits, any success that it may achieve through "the process of invention and innovation" is clearly tolerated by the antitrust laws.

*   *   *

Moreover, enforced predisclosure would cause undesirable consequences beyond merely encouraging the sluggishness the Sherman Act was designed to prevent. A significant vice of the theory propounded by Berkey lies in the uncertainty of its application. Berkey does not contend, in the colorful phrase of Judge Frankel, that "Kodak has to live in a goldfish bowl," disclosing every innovation to the world at large. However predictable in its application, such an extreme rule would be insupportable. Rather, Berkey postulates that Kodak had a duty to disclose limited types of information to certain competitors under specific circumstances. But it is difficult to comprehend how a major corporation, accustomed though it is to making business decisions with antitrust considerations in mind, could possess the omniscience to anticipate all the instances in which a jury might one day in the future retrospectively conclude that predisclosure was warranted. And it is equally difficult to discern workable guidelines that a court might set forth to aid the firm's decision. For example, how detailed must the information conveyed be? And how far must research have progressed before it is "ripe" for disclosure? These inherent uncertainties would have an inevitable chilling effect on innovation. They go far, we believe, towards explaining why no court has ever imposed the duty Berkey seeks to create here.

* * *

We do not perceive, however, how Kodak's introduction of a new format was rendered an unlawful act of monopolization in the camera market because the firm also manufactured film to fit the cameras. The 110 system was in substantial part a camera development. . . .

Clearly, then, the policy considerations militating against predisclosure requirements for monolithic monopolists are equally applicable here. The first firm, even a monopolist, to design a new camera format has a right to the lead time that follows from its success. The mere fact that Kodak manufactured film in the new format as well, so that its customers would not be offered worthless cameras, could not deprive it of that reward. . . .

* * *

Conclusion   We have held that Kodak did not have an obligation, merely because it introduced film and camera in a new format, to make any predisclosure to its camera-making competitors. Nor did the earlier use of its film monopoly to foreclose format innovation by those competitors create of its own force such a duty where none had existed before. In awarding Berkey $15,250,000, just $828,000 short of the maximum amount demanded, the jury clearly based its calculation of lost camera profits on Berkey's central argument that it had a right to be "at the starting line when the whistle blew" for the new system. The verdict, therefore, cannot stand.

* * *

Attempts to Monopolize

Section 2 prohibits not only actual monopolization but also attempts to monopolize. An attempt need not succeed to be unlawful; a defendant who tries to exercise sway over a relevant market can take no legal comfort from failure. Of course, some people attempt the impossible, and a new company with virtually no market share can scarcely be accused of attempting to monopolize simply because it adopts market practices that would be unlawful in the hands of a company with a huge market share. In any event, the plaintiff must show a specific intent to monopolize, not merely an intent to commit the act or acts that constitute the attempt.

Remedies

Since many of the defendant's acts that constitute Section 2 monopolizing are also violations of Section 1 or of the Clayton Act, why should plaintiffs resort to Section 2 at all? What practical difference does Section 2 make? One answer is that not every act of monopolizing is a violation of another law. Leasing and pricing practices that are perfectly lawful for an ordinary competitor may be unlawful only because of Section 2. But the more important reason is the remedy provided by the Sherman Act: **divestiture.** In the right case, the courts may order the company broken up.

In the *Standard Oil* decision of 1911 (see p. 1020), the Supreme Court held that the Standard Oil Company constituted a monopoly and ordered it split apart into separate companies. Several other trusts were similarly dealt with. In many of the early cases, doing so posed no insuperable difficulties, because the companies themselves essentially consisted of separate manufacturing plants knit together by financial controls. But not every company is a loose confederation of potentially separate operating companies.

The *Alcoa* case (p. 1056) was fraught with difficult remedial issues. Judge Hand's opinion came down in 1945, but the remedial side of the case did not come up until 1950. By then the industry had changed radically, with the entrance of Reynolds and Kaiser as effective competitors, reducing Alcoa's share of the market to 50 percent. Because any aluminum producer needs considerable resources to succeed and because aluminum production is crucial to national security, the later court refused to order the company broken apart. The court ordered Alcoa to take a series of measures that would boost competition in the industry—for example, Alcoa stockholders had to divest themselves of the stock of a closely related Canadian producer in order to remove Alcoa's control of that company; and the court rendered unenforceable a patent-licensing agreement with Reynolds and Kaiser that required them to share their inventions with Alcoa, even though neither the Canadian tie nor the patent agreements were in themselves unlawful.

Although the trend has been away from breaking up the monopolist, it is still employed as a potent remedy. In perhaps the largest monopolization case ever brought—*United States* v. *American Telephone & Telegraph Company*—the government sought divestiture of several of AT&T's constituent companies, including Western Electric and the various local operating companies. To avoid prolonged litigation, AT&T agreed in 1982 to a consent decree that required it to spin off all its operating companies, companies which had been central to AT&T's decades-long monopoly.

ACQUISITIONS AND MERGERS UNDER SECTION 7 OF THE CLAYTON ACT

Neither Section 1 nor Section 2 of the Sherman Act proved particularly apt in barring mergers between companies or acquisition by one company of another. As originally written, neither did the Clayton Act, which prohibited only mergers accomplished through the sale of stock, not mergers or acquisitions carried out through acquisition of assets. In 1950 Congress amended the Clayton Act to cover the loophole concerning acquisition of assets. It also narrowed the search for relevant market; henceforth, if competition

might be lessened *in any line of commerce in any section of the country,* the merger is unlawful.

As amended, the pertinent part of Section 7 of the Clayton Act read as follows:

> [N]o corporation engaged in commerce shall acquire, directly or indirectly, the whole or any part of the stock or other share capital and no corporation subject to the jurisdiction of the Federal Trade Commission shall acquire the whole or any part of the assets of another corporation engaged also in commerce, where in any line of commerce in any section of the country, the effect of such acquisition may be substantially to lessen competition, or to tend to create a monopoly.
>
> No corporation shall acquire, directly or indirectly, the whole or any part of the stock or other share capital and no corporation subject to the jurisdiction of the Federal Trade Commission shall acquire the whole or any part of the assets of one or more corporations engaged in commerce, where in any line of commerce in any section of the country, the effect of such acquisition, of such stock or assets, or of the use of such stock by the voting or granting of proxies or otherwise, may be substantially to lessen competition, or to tend to create a monopoly.

Definitions

Mergers and Acquisitions—for the sake of brevity, we will refer to both throughout the rest of this chapter as mergers—are usually classified into three types: *horizontal, vertical,* and *conglomerate.*

Horizontal Mergers   A horizontal merger is one between competitors—for example, between two bread manufacturers or two grocery chains competing in the same locale.

Vertical Mergers   A vertical merger is that of a supplier and customer. If the customer acquires the supplier, it is known as **backward vertical integration;** if the supplier acquires the customer, it is **forward vertical integration.** For example, a book publisher that buys a paper manufacturer has engaged in backward vertical integration. Its purchase of a bookstore chain would be forward vertical integration.

Conglomerate Mergers   **Conglomerate mergers** do not have a standard definition, but generally are taken to be mergers between companies whose businesses are not directly related. Many commentators have subdivided this category into three types. In a "pure" conglomerate merger, the businesses are not related—as when a steel manufacturer acquires a movie distributor. In a **product-extension merger,** the manufacturer of one product acquires the manufacturer of a related product—for instance, a producer of household cleansers, but not of liquid bleach, acquires a producer of liquid bleach. In a **market-extension merger,** a company in one geographic market acquires a company in the same business in a different location—as when a bakery operating only in San Francisco buys a bakery operating only in Palo Alto. Since they had not competed, this would not be a horizontal merger.

General Principles

As in monopolization cases, a relevant product and geographic market must first be marked out to test the effect of the merger. But Section 7 has a market definition different from that of Section 2. Section 7 speaks of "*any line* of commerce in any *section* of the country" (emphasis added). And its test for the effect of the merger is the same as that we have already seen for exclusive dealing cases governed by Section 3: "may be substantially to lessen competition or to tend to create a monopoly." Taken together, this language makes it easier to condemn an unlawful merger than an unlawful monopoly. The relevant product market is any *line* of commerce, and the courts have taken this language to permit the plaintiff to prove the existence of "submarkets" in which the relative effect of the merger is greater. The relevant geographic market is any *section of the country*, which means that the plaintiff can show the appropriate effect in a city or a particular region and not worry about having to show the effect in a national market. Moreover, as we have seen, the effect is one of probability, not actuality. *Might* competition be substantially lessened?—not: Was it in fact substantially lessened? Or, did the merger *tend* to create a monopoly?—not: Did it in fact create one?

In *United States* v. *du Pont*, 353 U.S. 586 (1957), the government charged that du Pont's "commanding position as General Motors' supplier of automotive finishes and fabrics" was not achieved on competitive merit alone but because du Pont had ac-

quired a sizable block of GM stock, and the "consequent close intercompany relationship led to the insulation of most of the General Motors' market from free competition," in violation of Section 7. Between 1917 and 1919, du Pont took a 23 percent stock interest in GM. The district court dismissed the complaint, partly on the grounds that at least before the 1950 amendment to Section 7, the Clayton Act did not condemn vertical mergers and partly on the grounds that du Pont had not dominated GM's decision to purchase millions of dollars' worth of automotive finishes and fabrics. The Supreme Court disagreed and sent the case back to trial. The Court specifically held that even though the stock acquisition had occurred some thirty-five years earlier, the government can resort to Section 7 whenever it appears that the result of the acquisition will violate the competitive tests set forth in the section.

Defining the Market   In the seminal *Brown Shoe* case, 380 U.S. 294 (1962), the Supreme Court said that the outer boundaries of broad markets "are determined by the reasonable interchangeability of use or the cross-elasticity of demand between the product itself and substitutes for it" but that narrower "well defined submarkets" might also be appropriate lines of commerce. In drawing market boundaries, the Court said, courts should realistically reflect "[c]ompetition where, in fact, it exists." Among the factors to consider are "industry or public recognition of the submarket as a separate economic entity, the product's peculiar characteristics and uses, unique production facilities, distinct customers, distinct prices, sensitivity to price changes and specialized vendors." To select the geographic market, the court must consider both "the commercial realities" of the industry and the economic significance of the market.

The "Failing Company" Doctrine   One defense to a Section 7 case is that one of the merging companies is a **failing company.** In *Citizen Publishing Company* v. *United States*, 394 U.S. 131 (1969), the Supreme Court said that the defense is applicable if two conditions are satisfied. First, a company must be staring bankruptcy in the face; it must have virtually no chance of being resuscitated without the merger. Second, the acquiring company must be the only available purchaser, and the failing company must have made bona fide efforts to search for another purchaser.

Beneficial Effects   That a merger might produce beneficial effects is not a defense to a Section 7 case. As the Supreme Court said in *United States* v. *Philadelphia National Bank*, 374 U.S. 321, 371 (1963): "[A] merger, the effect of which 'may be substantially to lessen competition' is not saved because, on some ultimate reckoning of social or economic debits or credits, it may be deemed beneficial." And in *FTC* v. *Procter & Gamble Company*, 386 U.S. 568, 580 (1967), the Court said: "Possible economies cannot be used as a defense to illegality. Congress was also aware that some mergers which lessen competition may also result in economies but it struck the balance in favor of protecting competition."

Tests of Competitive Effect

Horizontal Mergers   Three factors are critical in assessing whether a horizontal merger may substantially lessen competition: the (1) market shares of the merging companies, (2) concentration ratios, and (3) trends in the industry toward concentration.

The first factor is self-evident. A company with 10 percent or even 5 percent of the market is in a different position from one with less than 1 percent. A **concentration ratio** refers to the number of firms that constitute an industry. An industry with only four firms is obviously much more concentrated than one with ten or seventy firms. **Concentration trends** refer to the frequency with which firms in the relevant market have been merging. The first merger in an industry with a low concentration ratio might be predicted to have no likely effect on competition, but a merger of two firms in a four-firm industry would obviously have a pronounced effect.

In the *Philadelphia Bank* case just quoted, the Court announced this test of legality in assessing the legality of a horizontal merger. "[A] merger which produces a firm controlling an undue percentage share of the relevant market, and results in a significant increase in the concentration of firms in that market is so inherently likely to lessen competition substantially that it must be enjoined in the absence of evidence clearly showing that the merger is not likely to

have such anticompetitive effects." In this case, the merger led to a 30 percent share of the commercial banking market in a four-county region around Philadelphia and an increase in concentration by more than one-third, and the Court held that those numbers amounted to a violation of Section 7. The Court also said in *Philadelphia Bank* that "if concentration is already great, the importance of preventing even slight increases in concentration and so preserving the possibility of eventual deconcentration is correspondingly great."

The Hart-Scott-Rodino Antitrust Improvements Act of 1976 requires certain companies to notify the Justice Department before actually completing mergers or acquisitions, whether by private negotiation or by public tender offer. When one of the companies has sales or assets of $100 million or more and the other company $10 million or more, pre-merger notification must be provided at least thirty days prior to completion of the deal—or fifteen days in the case of a tender offer of cash for publicly traded shares—if the resulting merger would give the acquiring company $50 million worth or 15 percent of assets or voting securities in the acquired company. The rules are complex, but they are designed to give the department time to react to a merger before it has been secretly accomplished and then announced. The 1976 act gives the department the authority to seek an injunction against the completion of any such merger, which of course greatly simplifies the remedial phase of the case should the courts ultimately hold that the merger would be unlawful. (Note: Section 7 is one of the "tools" in the kit of the lawyer who defends companies against unwelcomed takeover attempts: if the target company can point to lines of its business in which it competes with the acquiring company, it can threaten antitrust action in order to block the merger.)

Vertical Mergers   To prove a Section 7 case involving a vertical merger, the plaintiff must show that the merger forecloses competition "in a substantial share of" a substantial market. But statistical factors alone do not govern in a vertical merger. Thus in *Ford Motor Co.* v. *United States*, 405 U.S. 562 (1972), the merger between Ford and Autolite, a manufacturer of spark plugs, was held unlawful because it eliminated Ford's potential entry into the market as an independent manufacturer of spark plugs and because it foreclosed Ford "as a purchaser of about ten percent of total industry output" of spark plugs. This decision underscores the principle that a company may serve to enhance competition simply by waiting in the wings as a potential entrant to a market. If other companies feel threatened by a company the size of Ford undertaking to compete where it had not done so before, the existing manufacturers will likely keep their prices low so as not to tempt the giant in. Of course, had Ford entered the market on its own by independently manufacturing spark plugs, it might ultimately have caused weak competitors to fold. As the Court said: "Had Ford taken the internal-expansion route, there would have been no illegality; not, however, because the result necessarily would have been commendable, but simply because that course has not been proscribed."

Conglomerate Mergers   Recall the definition of a conglomerate merger (p. 1064). None of the three types listed has a direct impact on competition, so the test for illegality is more difficult to state and apply than for horizontal or vertical mergers. But they are nonetheless within the reach of Section 7. In the late 1960s and early 1970s, the government filed a number of divestiture suits against conglomerate mergers. It did not win them all, and none reached the Supreme Court; most were settled by consent decree, leading in several instances to divestiture either of the acquired company or another division of the acquiring company. Thus International Telephone & Telegraph Company agreed to divest itself of Canteen Corporation and either of the following two groups: (1) Avis, Levitt & Sons, and Hamilton Life Insurance Company or (2) Hartford Fire Insurance Company. Ling-Temco-Vought agreed to divest itself of either Jones & Laughlin Steel or Braniff Airways and Okinite Corporation. In these and other cases, the courts have looked to specific potential effects, such as raising the barriers to entry into a market and eliminating potential competition, but they have rejected the more general claim of "the rising tide of economic concentration in American industry."

Entrenching Oligopoly   One way to attack conglomerate mergers is to demonstrate that by taking over a dominant company in an oligopolistic industry, a large and strong acquiring company will further entrench the oligopoly. In *FTC* v. *Procter & Gamble Co.*, 386 U.S. 568 (1967), the government challenged P & G's

acquisition of Clorox. P & G was the leading seller of household cleansers, with annual sales of more than $1 billion. In addition, it was the "nation's largest advertiser," promoting its products so heavily that it was able to take advantage of substantial advertising discounts from the media. Clorox had more than 48 percent of national sales for liquid bleach in a heavily concentrated industry. Since all liquid bleach is chemically identical, advertising and promotion plays the dominant role in selling the product. P & G did not make or sell liquid bleach prior to the merger— hence it was a "product-extension" merger rather than a horizontal one.

The Court concluded that smaller firms would fear retaliation from P & G if they tried to compete in the liquid bleach market and that "a new entrant would be much more reluctant to face the giant Procter than it would have been to face the smaller Clorox." Hence, "the substitution of the powerful acquiring firm for the smaller, but already dominant firm may substantially reduce the competitive structure of the industry by raising entry barriers and by dissuading the smaller firms from aggressively competing." The entrenchment theory probably applies only to highly concentrated industries and dominant firms, however. Many subsequent cases have come out in favor of the defendants on a variety of grounds— that the merger led simply to a more efficient acquired firm, that the existing competitors were strong and able to compete, or even that the acquiring firm merely gives the acquired company a "deep pocket" the better to finance its operations.

Eliminating Potential Competition   This theory holds that but for the merger the acquiring company might have competed in the acquired company's market. In *Procter & Gamble*, for example, P & G might have entered the liquid bleach market itself, and thus given Clorox a "run for its money." An additional strong company would then have been in the market. When P & G bought Clorox, however, it foreclosed that possibility. This theory depends on proof of some probability that the acquiring company would have entered the market. When the acquired company is small, however, a Section 7 violation is unlikely; these so-called "toe-hold" mergers permit the acquiring company to become a competitive force in an industry without necessarily sacrificing any pre-existing competition.

Reciprocity   Many companies are both heavy buyers and sellers of products. A company may buy from its customers as well as sell to them. This practice is known in antitrust jargon as **reciprocity**. Reciprocity means the practice of a seller who uses his volume of purchases from the buyer to induce the buyer to purchase from the seller. The clearest example arose in *FTC* v. *Consolidated Foods Corp.*, 380 U.S. 592 (1965). Consolidated owned wholesale grocery outlets and retail food stores. Gentry made dehydrated onions and garlic. The Court agreed that the merger violated Section 7 because of the possibility of reciprocity: Consolidated made bulk purchases from several food processors, which were purchasers of dehydrated onions and garlic from Gentry and others. Processors who did not buy from Gentry might feel pressured to do so in order to keep Consolidated as a customer for their food supplies. If so, other onion and garlic processors would be foreclosed from competing for sales. A merger that raises the mere possibility of reciprocity is not *per se* unlawful, however. The plaintiff must demonstrate that it was probable the acquiring company would adopt the practice—for example, by conditioning future orders for supplies on the receipt of orders for onions and garlic—and that doing so would have an anticompetitive effect given the size of the reciprocating companies and their positions in the market.

Joint Ventures   Section 7 can also apply to **joint ventures**, a rule first announced in 1964. Two companies, Hooker and American Potash, dominated sales of sodium chlorate in the southeast, with 90 percent of the market. Pennsalt Chemicals Corporation produced the rest in the west and sold it in the southeast through Olin-Mathieson Chemical Corporation. The latter two decided to team up, the better to compete with the giants, and so they formed Penn-Olin, which they jointly owned. The district court dismissed the government's suit, but the Supreme Court reinstated it, saying that a joint venture can serve to blunt competition, or at least potential competition, between the parent companies. The Court said that the lower court must look to a number of criteria to determine whether the joint venture was likely to lessen competition substantially. These factors include:

> The number and power of the competitors in the relevant market; the background of their growth; the power of the joint venturers; the relationship of their lines of commerce; competition existing between them and the power of each in dealing with the competitors of the other; the setting in which the joint venture was created; the reasons and necessities for its existence; the joint venture's line of commerce and the relationship thereof to that of its parents; the adaptability of its line of commerce to non-competitive practices; the potential power of the joint venture in the relevant market; and appraisal of what the competition in the relevant market would have been if one of the joint venturers had entered it alone instead of through Penn-Olin; the effect, in the event of this occurrence, of the other joint venturer's potential competition; and such other factors as might indicate potential risk to competition in the relevant market. [United States v. Penn-Olin Chemical Co., 378 U.S. 158 (1964)]

These numerous factors illustrate how the entire economic environment surrounding the joint venture—and mergers in general—must be assessed to determine the legalities.

Remedies

The Clayton Act provides that the government may seek divestiture when an acquisition or merger violates the act. Until relatively recently, however, it was unresolved whether a private plaintiff could seek divestiture after proving a Clayton Act violation. In 1990, the Supreme Court unanimously agreed that divestiture is an available remedy in private suits, even in suits filed by a state's attorney general on behalf of consumers. [California v. American Stores, 58 U.S.L.W. 4529 (1990)] This ruling makes it more likely that anti-merger litigation will increase in the future.

The Changing Political Climate

During the years of the Reagan Administration in the 1980s, the federal government became far less active in prosecuting antitrust cases, especially merger cases, than it had in previous decades. Many giant mergers, like the merger between two oil behemoths, Texaco and Getty, resulting in a company with nearly $50 billion in assets in 1984, went unchallenged. With the arrival of the Bush Administration in 1989, the talk in Washington antitrust circles was of a renewed interest in antitrust enforcement (see **Box 47-1**).

Officials Promise to Get Tough on Antitrust Law Enforcement

By Christopher Elias

[The prosecution of antitrust cases was greatly neglected during the 1980s. Many giant mergers went unchallenged by the Justice Department and the Federal Trade Commission. The danger, some believe, in not enforcing antitrust laws is a severe threat to competition.—AUTHORS' NOTE]

For most of the 1980s, the government enforced antitrust laws at a leisurely pace, not quite yawning when a merger took place, but measuring corporate marriages in terms of economics. Mere concentration in an industry was not enough, as it had been historically, to mobilize lawyers in the Antitrust Division of the Justice Department or in the Federal Trade Commission.

Two steel companies, for example, could merge so long as they did not run afoul of something called the Herfindahl-Hirschman Index, which attempts to measure the effect of a merger on market shares. Though thousands of mergers occurred throughout the decade, only a handful were challenged (28 during one four-year period), essentially because both agencies wanted government to stay out of the way of business, as well as to prevent judges from making business decisions. This was in sharp contrast to a decades-old antitrust enforcement policy that viewed business efficiency achieved through merger as a threat to competition.

TURNING UP THE HEAT IN ANTITRUST ENFORCEMENT

The new policy enraged backers of traditional enforcement policy, sparking a vituperative debate among specialists; probably, says one cynical antitrust lawyer, because so many of his colleagues found themselves without work. There is little doubt that the "mystics," the lawyers specializing in antitrust, had less work to do. So clear were guidelines written first in 1982 by Tyler Baker, a special assistant in Justice's Antitrust Division, and revised in 1984 by Charles F. Rule, assistant attorney general in charge of antitrust, that general counsels of corporations were usually able to steer their firms away from mergers that would draw fire. Rule, who now practices antitrust law with Covington & Burling, a Washington firm, says, "We viewed the risks more as economists than lawyers, though we never said, 'Anything goes.'"

Still, there were many differences between the traditionalists and the economics-minded Chicago School, as it is called. The two sides disagree on almost everything connected to antitrust. Traditionalists equate market power with bigness and would never let two large steel firms join forces, since such horizontal mergers result in concentration. This, the reasoning goes, leads to political power and less competition. Chicago Schoolers counter that if a company has considerable market power, it probably got it by being the best.

Traditionalists further argue that pricing a product below cost is predatory, intended to eliminate compet-

itors, after which prices go sky-high. Chicago Schoolers argue that businessmen are rational and know that sky-high prices will attract competition. The two sides even disagree on the raison d'etre for antitrust law. It exists, say Chicago adherents, to improve efficiency in the markets. Traditionalists say antitrust law is intended to preserve competition. Eleanor Fox, a law professor at New York University and a leading scholar of antitrust, has remarked that the battles being fought, usually out of the public eye during bar association meetings, antitrust conferences, in studies and in legal publications, are "for the soul of antitrust."

As the Bush administration has installed its antitrust officials, the skirmishing has picked up, with all eyes on James F. Rill, who last June succeeded Rule as head of the Antitrust Division, and Janet D. Steiger, who succeeded Daniel Oliver as FTC chairman. Oliver once stunned the antitrust section of the American Bar Association, saying "the public enemy is government intervention, not private business activity." Rill and Steiger, by contrast, have been making tough speeches about renewing antitrust enforcement.

At the 23rd New England Antitrust Conference in Cambridge, Mass., in November, Rill noted "a growing perception that antitrust has lost its purpose and its potency." He revealed there were "30 active merger investigations under way" and said "some will undoubtedly mature into filed cases." He declares merger enforcement his No. 1 priority, though he says economic analysis will still be applied. "I don't look back to the days of the 1960s and 1970s. But we'll have a strong program," says Rill, who backs a House-passed bill to raise the

(continued on next page)

(Box 47-1 continued)
limit on fines for corporate felons from $1 million to $10 million.

His other priority is tough prosecution of cartels. "Price-fixing, bid rigging and other variants of cartel behavior are no more than fraud and theft from consumers," he says. As with Rule, the health care industries are high on Rill's list of targets. "We have civil investigations pending," he says, focusing on a range of cartel activities, including price-fixing and boycotting. He adds that several grand juries are examining price-fixing among competing providers, some of which may be illegally allocating patients and practice territories among themselves. "We need to be sure the health care industries are fully competitive," says Rill. "Prices are skyrocketing."

At the same Cambridge forum, Steiger, for eight years chairman of the Postal Rate Commission, said the FTC would also become a strong enforcer of antitrust policy. Enforcement "seems to ebb and flow," she said, at times repeating the views of the Reagan administration's critics in Congress, the bar associations and the states. "The FTC may have been overly cautious" in selecting merger cases, said Steiger, who promised "to reassess our techniques and methods of analysis."

Jeffrey I. Zuckerman, former director of the FTC's Bureau of Competition when Oliver was the agency's chairman, says Steiger is responding to "shrill voices saying we should have challenged more." Among those voices he says, are those of Sen. Howard M. Metzenbaum, an Ohio Democrat, and New York attorney Ira M. Millstein. Last July, a month after Rill's appointment, Millstein, as chairman of an American Bar Association task force on antitrust, submitted a report to the ABA especially critical of antitrust enforcement for the past eight years. The report charged that the Justice Department's "non-enforcement rhetoric may well have lowered respect for antitrust laws." Millstein said the task force was making "reasoned recommendations." Traditionally, antitrust policy is made by the assistant attorney general in charge of the Antitrust Division without much help from anyone else.

The ABA task force resurrected the benchmark of the 1960s and 1970s—concentration—to determine whether a merger was justified, and said "horizontal mergers that would create or enhance market power should be prevented." Zuckerman says the task force was packed with traditionalists, who profit from strict enforcement. Another antitrust attorney says, in reference to the report's recommendations, "I can't say that the motivation for more antitrust cases is related to lawyers' fees, but it's pretty bizarre for them to stand up and say, 'Sue my clients more often.'"

In Washington, Rill says that analyses of future mergers will include "market concentration" and whether a merger might make it tough for competitors to enter the merged companies' market. This is not very distant from the way the Antitrust Division under Charles Rule viewed concentration. "In the Sixties and Seventies," he says, "it was all based on concentration. In the Seventies, as an underpinning, it was wiped out. There was a problem with just using concentration. We used it as a screen to tell us when to look further, say, into market operations, price discrimination, previous market share and loss of entry into the market by competitors."

There is a pragmatic reason or two, however, for both Rill and Steiger to put new zip into antitrust

CHAPTER SUMMARY

Section 2 of the Sherman Act prohibits monopolizing or attempting to monopolize any part of interstate or foreign trade or commerce. The law does not forbid monopoly as such, but only acts or attempts or conspiracies to monopolize. The prohibition includes the monopolist who has acquired his monopoly through illegitimate means.

Three factors are essential in a Section 2 case: (1) relevant market for determining dominance, (2) the degree of monopoly power, and (3) the particular acts claimed to be illegitimate.

Relevant market has two dimensions: product and geographic. Since many goods have close substitutes, the courts look to the degree to which consumers will shift to other goods or suppliers if the price of the commodity or service in question is priced monopolistically. This test is known as cross-elasticity of demand. If the cross-elasticity is high—meaning that consumers will readily shift—then the other goods or services must be included in the product market definition, thus reducing the share of the market that the defendant will be found to have. The geographic market is not the country as a whole, because Section 2 speaks in terms of "any part" of trade or commerce. Usually the government or private

BOX 47-1

enforcement. During the Reagan administration, both staff and money were cut back considerably, consistent with the emphasis on self-policing by industry applying well-understood economic analysis. From 1980 to 1988, the number of full-time attorneys employed by the Antitrust Division fell from 464 to 258, and the number of economists from 58 to 32. Total authorized employment fell from 939 to 549. As a result, says Millstein's task force, "the division today operates much like a regulatory body with respect to mergers." Though litigation may be costly, the task force report points out, "the litigation process is public; negotiations [of a regulatory process] are not."

Millstein said that "a somewhat more vigorous and visible merger enforcement program might also enhance the division's credibility with Congress." He added, "A division that . . . joins forces with those urging ill-considered erosions in antitrust law risks further undercutting its credibility with many of its strongest supporters in and out of Congress."

In Washington, Rill acknowledges that "resources are tight across the board, largely because of the federal deficit," but he has promised strong enforcement. That has helped boost morale among his lawyers. "He has clearly sent out a signal that 'we are important and I will support you,' " says one. Under Rule, lawyers could develop a case, but if it was in opposition to economic policy, he would refuse to prosecute. Says Rule, "Jim Rill is encouraging them to be innovative, and in many ways the division is a better place to work. Rill is different. We viewed the risks more as economists, and attempted to make policy. He is a very good lawyer, much more familiar with cases, and he is there more as an enforcer. Almost all his predecessors were from academia or educated in economics. He is different in the way he speaks and in the way the words come out and, as a trial lawyer, in the way he perceives issues."

Another observer asks why Rill, "a fairly wealthy individual, independent and not doing his job to make a name," responds to criticism from the bar. He answers his own question by saying, "He's sincere and he's dedicated." Still another antitrust lawyer says of Rill's declaration of tougher enforcement: "His rhetoric is an attempt to mollify critics—the bar, for example. My guess is it's going to be difficult to beat the record in terms of numbers of cases he brings. To the bar association, that's a rotten record, probably because clients tend these days to be small, not big companies who spend big dollars. So there's dissatisfaction from the loss of fees. The Millstein report says, 'We think they [the Antitrust Division] need to change because our clients won't listen to us.' " The lawyer, who worked for the division once, says: "We wanted to make the law clear so general counsels could understand it and not hire high-priced lawyers they didn't need. An investigation generates a lot of time. Rill's attitude already has generated a lot of work for lawyers."

Rill is expected, however, to be careful in choosing which mergers to contest in court. "He's going to find that if he brings cases based on concentration alone, he's going to lose most of them," says the former division lawyer. "So he's going to look carefully at his ability to win."

Source: *Insight,* January 15, 1990

---

plaintiff will try to show that the geographic market is small, since that will tend to give the alleged monopolist a larger share of it.

Market power in general means the share of the relevant market that the alleged monopolist enjoys. The law does not lay down fixed percentages, but various decisions seem to suggest that two-thirds of a market might be too low but three-quarters high enough to constitute monopoly power.

Acts that were aimed at or had the probable effect of excluding competitors from the market are acts of monopolizing. Examples are predatory pricing and boycotts. Despite repeated claims during the 1970s and 1980s by smaller competitors, large companies have prevailed in court against the argument that innovations suddenly sprung on the market without notice are *per se* evidence of intent to monopolize.

Remedies for Section 2 violations include damages, injunction, and divestiture. These remedies are also available in Clayton Act Section 7 cases.

Section 7 prohibits mergers or acquisitions that might tend to lessen competition in any line of commerce in any section of the country. Mergers and acquisitions are usually classified in one of three ways: horizontal (between competitors), vertical (between different levels of the distribution chain), or conglomerate (between businesses that are not directly related).

The latter may be divided into product-extension and market-extension mergers. The relevant market test is different than in monopolization cases; in a Section 7 action, a relevant submarket may be proved.

In assessing horizontal mergers, the courts will look to the market shares of the merging companies, industry concentration ratios, and trends toward concentration in the industry. To prove a Section 7 vertical merger case, the plaintiff must show that the merger forecloses competition "in a substantial share of" a substantial market. Conglomerate merger cases are harder to prove, and require a showing of specific potential effects, such as raising barriers to entry into an industry, thus entrenching monopoly, or eliminating potential competition. Joint ventures may also be condemned by Section 7. The Antitrust Improvements Act of 1976 requires certain companies to give pre-merger notice to the Justice Department.

KEY TERMS

Backward vertical integration	p. 1064	Joint ventures	p. 1068
		Market-extension merger	p. 1065
Concentration ratio	p. 1066		
Concentration trends	p. 1066	Monopolization	p. 1055
Conglomerate mergers	p. 1064	Monopoly power	p. 1055
Divestiture	p. 1063	Product-extension merger	p. 1065
Failing company	p. 1065		
Forward vertical integration	p. 1064	Product market	p. 1051
		Relevant market	p. 1051
Geographic market	p. 1055		

SELF-TEST QUESTIONS

1. A company with 95 percent of the market for its product is:
   (a) a monopolist
   (b) monopolizing
   (c) violating section 2 of the Sherman Act
   (d) violating section 1 of the Sherman Act
2. Which of the following may be evidence of an intent to monopolize?
   (a) innovative practices
   (b) large market share
   (c) pricing below cost of production
   (d) low profit margins
3. A merger that lessens competition in any line of commerce is prohibited by:
   (a) section 1 of the Sherman Act
   (b) section 2 of the Sherman Act
   (c) section 7 of the Clayton Act
   (d) none of the above
4. Which of the following statements is true?
   (a) A horizontal merger is always unlawful.
   (b) A conglomerate merger between companies with unrelated products is always lawful.
   (c) A vertical merger violates section 2 of the Sherman Act.
   (d) A horizontal merger that unduly increases the concentration of firms in a particular market is always unlawful.
5. A line of commerce is a concept spelled out in:
   (a) section 7 of the Clayton Act
   (b) section 2 of the Sherman Act
   (c) section 1 of the Sherman Act
   (d) none of the above

DEMONSTRATION PROBLEM

Elmer has invented a new battery-operated car. The battery, which Elmer has patented, functions for 500 miles before needing to be recharged. The car, which he has named The Elmer, is a sensation when announced, and his factory can barely keep up with the orders. Worried about the impact, all the other car manufacturers ask Elmer for a license to use the battery in their cars. Elmer refuses because he wants the car market all to himself. Banks are eager to lend him the money to expand his production, and within three years he has gained a five-percent share of the national market for automobiles. During these years, Elmer has kept the price of The Elmer high to pay for his large costs in tooling up a factory. But then it dawns on him that he can expand his market much more rapidly if he drops his prices, so he prices the car to yield the smallest profit margin of any car being sold in the country. Its retail price is far lower than any other domestic car on the market. Business begins to boom. Within three more years, he has garnered an additional 30 percent of the market and announces at a press conference that he confidently expects to have the market "all to myself" within the next five years. Fighting for their lives now, the Big Three auto manufacturers consult their lawyers to sue Elmer for monopolizing. Do they have a case? What is Elmer's defense?

PROBLEMS

1. National Widget Company is the dominant manufacturer of widgets in the United States, with 72 percent of the market for low-priced widgets, and 89 percent of the market for high-priced widgets. Dozens of companies compete with National in the manufacture and sale of compatible peripheral equipment for use with National's widgets, including countertops, holders, sprockets and gear assemblies, instruction booklets, computer software, and

several hundred replacements parts. Revenues of these peripherals run upwards of $100 million annually. Beginning with the 1981 model year, National Widget sprang a surprise: a completely redesigned widget that made most of the peripheral equipment obsolete. Moreover, National set the price for its peripherals below that which would make economic sense for competitors to invest in new plants to tool up for producing redesigned peripherals. Five of the largest peripheral-equipment competitors sued National under Section 2 of the Sherman Act. One of these, American Widget Peripherals Inc., had an additional complaint: on making inquiries in early 1980, National's general manager assured American that it would not be redesigning any widgets until late 1985 at the earliest. On the basis of this statement, American invested $50 million in a new plant to manufacture the now obsolescent peripheral equipment and as a result will probably be forced into bankruptcy. What result? Why?

2. In 1959, The Aluminum Company of America (Alcoa) acquired the stock and assets of the Rome Cable Corporation. Alcoa and Rome both manufactured bare and insulated aluminum wire and cable, used for overhead electric power transmission lines. Rome, but not Alcoa, manufactured copper conductor, used for underground transmissions. Insulated aluminum wire and cable is quite inferior to copper, but it can be used effectively in overhead transmission, and Alcoa increased its share of annual installations from 6.5 percent in 1950 to 77.2 percent in 1959. During that time copper lost out to aluminum for overhead transmission. Aluminum and copper conductor prices do not respond to one another. As the Supreme Court summarized the facts in United States v. Aluminum Co. of America, 377 U.S. 271 (1964)

> In 1958—the year prior to the merger—Alcoa was the leading producer of aluminum conductor, with 27.8% of the market; in bare aluminum conductor, it also led the industry with 32.5%. Alcoa plus Kaiser controlled 50% of the aluminum conductor market and, with its three leading competitors, more than 76%. Only nine concerns (including Rome with 1.3%) accounted for 95.7% of the output of aluminum conductor, Alcoa was third with 11.6% and Rome was eighth with 4.7%. Five companies controlled 65.4% and four smaller ones, including Rome, added another 22.8%.

The Justice Department sued Alcoa-Rome for violation of Section 7 of the Clayton Act. What is the government's argument? What result?

3. Quality GraPhics has been buying up the stock of companies that manufacture billboards. Quality now owns or controls 23 of the 129 companies that make billboards, and their sales account for 3.2 percent of the total national market of $72 million. In Texas, Quality has acquired 27 percent of the billboard market and, in the Dallas-Ft. Worth area alone, about 25 percent. Billboard advertising accounts for only 0.001 percent of total national advertising sales—the majority goes to newspaper, magazines, television, and radio advertising. What claims could the Justice Department assert in a suit against Quality? What is Quality's defense? What result?

ANSWERS TO SELF-TEST QUESTIONS

1. (a) 2. (c) 3. (c) 4. (d) 5. (d)

SUGGESTED ANSWER TO DEMONSTRATION PROBLEM

A patent is a legal monopoly; it does not violate the Sherman Act for Elmer to exploit the natural advantages of his patent. He has no legal obligation to license others to use his invention. There are some limits to how he can exploit it, however. He may not engage in predatory pricing, defined as selling a product for less than it costs to make. But there is no evidence that Elmer is doing so (or that he has the economic wherewithal to do so); he appears to be making a tidy profit. If the growth of Elmer's market share is solely due to the demand for his product, his increasing bigness is not evidence of an intent to monopolize. The best strategy for the Big Three auto makers would be to hurry their engineers into designing their own batteries.

CHAPTER

48

CHAPTER OVERVIEW

Unfair and Deceptive Trade Practices

GENERAL POWERS OF THE FEDERAL TRADE COMMISSION

Traditionally, common law prohibited a variety of trade practices unfair either to competitors or to consumers. These included "passing off" one's products as though they were made by someone else, using a trade name confusingly similar to that of another, stealing trade secrets, and various forms of misrepresentation. In the Federal Trade Commission Act, Congress empowered a federal agency for the first time to investigate and deter acts of unfair competition.

Section 5 gave the FTC power to enforce a provision stating that "unfair methods of competition in commerce are hereby declared unlawful." By **"unfair methods of competition,"** Congress originally intended acts that constituted violations of the Sherman and Clayton antitrust acts. Nevertheless, from the outset the commissioners of the FTC took a broader view of their mandate. Specifically, they were concerned about the problem of false and deceptive ad-

vertising and promotional schemes. But the original Section 5 was confining; it seemed to authorize FTC action only when the deceptive advertising injured a competitor of the company. In 1931, the Supreme Court ruled that this was indeed the case: an advertisement that deceived the public was not within the FTC's jurisdiction unless a competitor was injured by the misrepresentation also. Congress responded in 1938 with the Wheeler-Lea amendments to the FTC Act. To the words "unfair methods of competition" were added these words: "unfair or deceptive acts or practices in commerce." Now it became clear that the FTC had a broader role to play than as a second agency enforcing the antitrust laws. Henceforth, the FTC would be the guardian also of consumers.

Deceptive practices that the FTC has prosecuted are also amenable to suit at common law. A tire manufacturer who advertises that his "special tire" is "new" when it is actually a retread has committed a common law misrepresentation, and the buyer could sue for rescission or damages. But it should be apparent that this approach is piecemeal. A lawsuit or two will not stop the determined fraud. Moreover, lawsuits such as these are expensive to bring and the amount of damages awarded is usually small, so the incentive is usually lacking to police fraudulent business practices through a common law action. Through Section 5, however, the FTC can seek far-reaching remedies against the sham and the phony; it is not limited to proving damages to individual customers case by case. So the FTC—and analogous state and municipal agencies created in many states—can serve far more effectively to regulate deceptive and unfair business practices.

As an administrative agency, the FTC has broader powers than those vested in the ordinary prosecutorial authority, such as the Department of Justice. It can initiate administrative proceedings in accordance with the Administrative Procedure Act to enforce the several statutes that it administers. It may issue cease and desist orders and enforce them in court, seek temporary and permanent injunctions, fines, and monetary damages, and promulgate *trade regulation rules* (TRRs). Although the FTC's authority to issue TRRs had long been assumed (and was approved by the U.S. Court of Appeals in Washington in 1973), Congress formalized it in 1975 in the FTC Improvement Act (part of the Magnuson-Moss Warranty Act), which gives the FTC explicit authority to prescribe rules defining unfair or deceptive acts or practices.

A **trade regulation rule** is like a statute. It is a detailed statement of procedures and substantive dos and don'ts. Before promulgating a TRR, the commission must publish its intention to do so in the Federal Register and must hold open hearings on its proposals. Draft versions of a TRR must be published to allow the public to comment. Once issued, the final version is published as part of the Code of Federal Regulations and becomes a permanent part of the law, unless modified or repealed by the FTC itself or by Congress—or overturned by a court on grounds of arbitrariness, lack of procedural regularity, or the like. A violation of a TRR is treated exactly like a violation of a federal statute. Once the FTC proves that a defendant violated a TRR no further proof is necessary that the act was unfair or deceptive. Examples of TRRs include the Retail Food Store Advertising and Marketing Practices Rule, Games of Chance in the Food Retailing and Gasoline Industries Rule, Care Labeling of Textile Wearing Apparel Rule, Mail Order Merchandise Rule, Cooling-Off Period for Door-to-

Door Sales Rule, and Use of Negative Option Plans by Sellers in Commerce.

GENERAL PRINCIPLES OF LAW GOVERNING DECEPTIVE ACTS AND PRACTICES

With a staff of some 1,600 and ten regional offices, the Federal Trade Commission is, at least from time to time, an active regulatory agency. The FTC's enforcement vigor waxes and wanes with the economic climate. The watchword for the 1990s is likely to be "tough" (see **Box 48-1**).

Critics have often charged that what the FTC chooses to investigate defies common sense because so many of the cases seem to involve trivial or at least relatively unimportant offenses: Does the nation really need a federal agency to guard us against pronouncements by singer Pat Boone on the efficacy of acne medication or the provenance of certain ostensibly native crafts sold to tourists in Alaska? One answer is that through such cases, important principles of law are declared and ratified.

To be sure, most readers of this book, unlikely to be gulled by false claims, may see a certain Alice-in-Wonderland quality to FTC enforcement. But the first principle of FTC action is that it gauges deceptive acts and practices as interpreted by the general public, not of the more sophisticated. As a U.S. Court of Appeals once said, the FTC Act was not "made for the protection of experts, but for the public—that vast multitude which includes the ignorant, the unthinking, and the credulous."

The deceptive statement or act need not actually deceive. Before 1983, it was sufficient that the statement had a "capacity to deceive." According to a standard adopted in 1983, however, the FTC will take action against deceptive advertising "if there is a representation, omission or practice that is likely to mislead the consumer acting reasonably in the circumstances, to the consumer's detriment." Critics of the new standard have charged that it will be harder to prove deception because an advertisement must be "likely to mislead" rather than merely have a "capacity to deceive." The FTC might also be put to the burden of showing that consumers reasonably interpreted the ad and that they relied on the ad. Whether

FTC Is Cracking Down on Misleading Ads

By Joanne Lipman

[In the 1990s, unlike the previous decade, the Federal Trade Commission adopted a tough posture in enforcing the law governing misleading advertisements. The current enforcement trend is illustrated by an FTC ruling regarding Kraft General Foods advertising.
—AUTHORS' NOTE]

The 1980s saw health and nutrition claims spin out of control, virtually unchecked by the federal government. When else could marketers promote candy bars as health foods or potato chips as a source of high fiber?

In the 1990s, however, the government is cracking down on misleading advertising claims. The Federal Trade Commission put advertisers on notice Friday with one of its toughest rulings yet: It found that Kraft General Foods ran deceptive advertising for its Kraft Singles cheese slices, even though Kraft only implied—never stated—the disputed calcium claim.

Clearly trying to make Kraft an example, the FTC slapped it with an order forbidding it from running misleading ads in the future. The order doesn't stick just to Kraft Singles and to calcium claims; it prohibits Kraft from misrepresenting any nutrient in any cheese-related product.

"The FTC is back in the game," notes Richard Kurnit, a New York advertising lawyer. He says Janet Steiger, who became FTC chairman in August 1989, "is continuing to fulfill her promise to put teeth back

WATCH THOSE ADS

into the FTC and take a very aggressive approach."

The FTC's ruling is sure to make advertisers think twice before making nutrition or other claims in ads. "You may see people cut back on how aggressively they make the claims," Mr. Kurnit says. Health claims won't disappear, he says, but "people who want to make them are going to be careful."

The two Kraft Singles commercials, which aired in 1985 and 1986, boasted that Kraft's cheese slices are an important source of calcium because each contains five ounces of milk. The FTC complained that the ads suggested each slice had as much calcium as five ounces of milk, when that isn't the case. In a commercial called "Class Picture," for example, as a group of kids pose for their school picture, a voiceover explains, "Kraft is made from five ounces of milk per slice. So they're concentrated with calcium."

In a second disputed commercial, called "Skimp," a mom says she buys Kraft Singles for her daughter because "imitation slices use hardly any milk. But Kraft has five ounces per slice . . . So her little bones get calcium they need to grow." The FTC ruled that commercial was deceptive because it incorrectly implied Kraft Singles have more calcium than imitation slices.

By finding the commercials misleading, the FTC upheld an administrative law judge ruling in 1989. But the FTC went even further: While the administrative law judge found "no persistent, long-term pattern of deceptive advertising," the FTC found

otherwise. It contended that a pattern of deception had been established and that, therefore, it had to impose the order prohibiting misleading nutrition claims in any cheese products.

A spokesman for Glenview, Ill.-based Kraft, a unit of **Philip Morris,** said, "We strongly disagree with interpretations which the Commission has placed upon the advertisements. We believe the ads in question . . . were both informative and truthful." He said Kraft may appeal the ruling.

The Kraft ruling is just one sign of the FTC's new approach. [Recently] . . . , it went after an ad agency for the first time; previously, it had charged only the advertisers with misleading ad messages. In that case, it claimed Lewis Galoob Toys and its ad agency, New York-based Towne, Silverstein, Rotter, misrepresented the performance of several toys. The toy company and the agency didn't admit wrongdoing but promised to avoid making deceptive ad claims in the future.

Several other major cases were recently resolved or are pending, including one against Schering-Plough Corp.'s Fibre Trim, a weight loss product. In a case that is continuing, the FTC takes issue with several Fibre Trim claims, including that it is a high-fiber supplement.

The Kraft decision "is a very important case for advertisers," says Lee Peeler, associate director for advertising practices at the FTC. "There was a perception in the past that the Commission wasn't going to deal vigorously with deceptive advertising. This is an indication that that perception was wrong."

Source: *Wall Street Journal*, February 4, 1991, p. B5

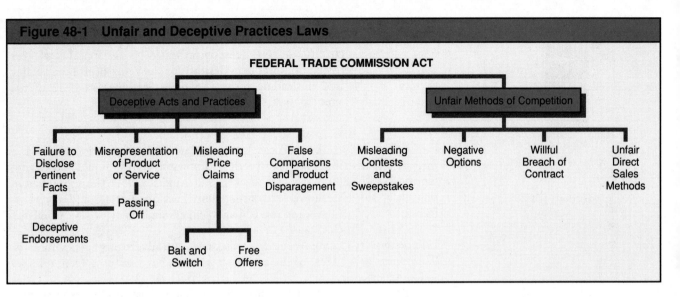

Figure 48-1   Unfair and Deceptive Practices Laws

FEDERAL TRADE COMMISSION ACT

Deceptive Acts and Practices

Unfair Methods of Competition

- Failure to Disclose Pertinent Facts
  - Deceptive Endorsements
- Misrepresentation of Product or Service
  - Passing Off
- Misleading Price Claims
  - Bait and Switch
  - Free Offers
- False Comparisons and Product Disparagement

- Misleading Contests and Sweepstakes
- Negative Options
- Willful Breach of Contract
- Unfair Direct Sales Methods

the standard will reduce the volume of FTC actions against deceptive advertising remains to be seen.

The FTC also has the authority to proceed against "unfair . . . acts or practices." These need not be deceptive, but instead are of such a character that they offend a common sense of propriety, justice, or honest way of comporting oneself. See Figure 48-1 for a diagram of the unfair and deceptive practices discussed in this chapter.

DECEPTIVE ACTS AND PRACTICES

Failure to Disclose Pertinent Facts

The business community is under no general obligation to disclose everything. Advertisers may put a bright face on their products as long as they do not make a direct material misrepresentation or misstatement. But under certain circumstances, an advertiser may be required to disclose more than it did in order not to be involved in **unfair or deceptive acts and practices.** For example, failure to state the cost of a service might constitute deception. Thus a federal court has ruled that it is deceptive for a telephone service to fail to disclose that it cost $15 per call for customers dialing a special 900 number listed in newspaper advertisements offering jobs. [FTC v. Transworld Courier Services, Inc., 59 A&TR Rpt. 174 (N.D.Ga. 1990)] Likewise, if a fact not disclosed might have a material bearing on a consumer's decision whether to purchase the product, its omission might be tantamount to deception, as the following case suggests.

J. B. WILLIAMS CO. v. FTC
381 F.2d 884 (6th Cir. 1967)

CELEBREZZE, CIRCUIT JUDGE. The question presented by this appeal is whether Petitioners' advertising of a product, Geritol, for the relief of iron deficiency anemia, is false and misleading so as to violate Sections 5 and 12 of the Federal Trade Commission Act.

* * *

The J. B. Williams Company, Inc. is a New York corporation engaged in the sale and distribution of two products known as Geritol liquid and Geritol tablets. Geritol liquid was first marketed in August, 1950; Geritol tablets in February, 1952. Geritol is sold throughout the United States and advertisements for Geritol have appeared in newspapers and on television in all the States of the United States.

Parkson Advertising Agency, Inc. has been the advertising agency for Williams since 1957. Most of the advertising money for Geritol is spent on television advertising. . . .

The Commission's Order requires that not only must the Geritol advertisements be expressly limited to those persons whose symptoms are due to an existing deficiency of one or more of the vitamins contained in the preparation, or due to an existing deficiency of iron, but also the Geritol advertisements must affirmatively disclose the negative fact that a great majority of persons who experience these symptoms do not experience them because they have a vitamin or iron deficiency; that for the great majority of people experiencing these symptoms, Geritol will be of no benefit. Closely related to this requirement is the further requirement of the Order that the Geritol advertisements refrain from representing that the symptoms are generally reliable indications of iron deficiency.

* * *

The main thrust of the Commission's Order is that the Geritol advertising must affirmatively disclose the negative fact that a great majority of persons who experience these symptoms do not experience them because there is a vitamin or iron deficiency.

The medical evidence on this issue is conflicting and the question is not one which is susceptible to precise statistical analysis.

* * *

While the advertising does not make the affirmative representation that the majority of people who are tired and rundown are so because of iron deficiency anemia and the product Geritol will be an effective cure, there is substantial evidence to support the finding of the Commission that most tired people are not so because of iron deficiency anemia, and the failure to disclose this fact is false and misleading because the advertisement creates the impression that the tired feeling is caused by something which Geritol can cure.

* * *

Here the advertisements emphasize the fact that if you are often tired and run-down you will feel stronger fast by taking Geritol. The Commission, in looking at the overall impression created by the advertisements on the general public, could reasonably find these advertisements were false and misleading. The finding that the advertisements link common, non-specific symptoms with iron deficiency anemia, and thereby create a false impression because most people with these symptoms are not suffering from iron deficiency anemia, is both reasonable and supported by substantial evidence. The Commission is not bound to the literal meaning of the words, nor must the Commission take a random sample to determine the meaning and impact of the advertisements.

Petitioners argue vigorously that the Commission does not have the legal power to require them to state the negative fact that "in the great majority of persons who experience such symptoms, these symptoms are not caused by a deficiency of one or more of the vitamins contained in the preparation or by iron deficiency or iron deficiency anemia"; and "for such persons the preparation will be of no benefit."

We believe the evidence is clear that Geritol is of no benefit in the treatment of tiredness except in those cases where tiredness has been caused by a deficiency of the ingredients contained in Geritol. The fact that the great majority of people who experience tiredness symptoms do not suffer from any deficiency of the ingredients in Geritol is a "material fact" under the meaning of that term as used in Section 15 of the Federal Trade Commission Act and Petitioners' failure to reveal this fact in this day when the consumer is influenced by mass advertising utilizing highly developed arts of persuasion, renders it difficult for the typical consumer to know whether the product will in fact meet his needs unless he is told what the product will or will not do. . . .

*   *   *

The Commission forbids the Petitioners' representation that the presence of iron deficiency anemia can be self-diagnosed or can be determined without a medical test. The danger to be remedied here has been fully and adequately taken care of in the other requirements of the Order. We can find no Congressional policy against self-medication on a trial and error basis where the consumer is fully informed and the product is safe as Geritol is conceded to be. In fact, Congressional policy is to encourage such self-help. In effect the Commission's Order 1(f) tends to place Geritol in the prescription drug field. We do not consider it within the power of the Federal Trade Commission to remove Geritol from the area of proprietary drugs and place it in the area of prescription drugs. This requirement of the Order will not be enforced. We also find this Order is not unduly vague and fairly apprises the Petitioners of what is required of them. Petition denied and, except for 1(f) of the Commission's Order, enforcement of the Order will be granted.

*   *   *

LAW AND LIFE

May Unit Illegally Deceived Customers In Its Advertising Practices, Court Rules

By James P. Miller

[The Federal Trade Commission has issued Guides Against Deceptive Pricing *which are used to judge the merit of price claims. Although they are not themselves law, as the following article reveals, these principles provide guidance to both the FTC and state courts.—*AUTHORS' NOTE]

A Colorado state court found that **May Department Stores** Co. illegally deceived customers, in a widely watched case involving the company's advertising practices.

The ruling affects only the Denver-based May D&F unit of the St. Louis department-store operator, but

REGULAR VS. "SPECIAL" PRICES

it's considered likely to have a wide impact in the retail industry, where promotional pricing practices are drawing increasing scrutiny from state officials around the nation.

May D&F said it is "disappointed" by the decision. "We believe our advertising practices are fair and appropriate," the company said, adding that it is considering an appeal.

As previously reported, Colorado Attorney General Duane Woodard claimed that May D&F duped consumers by artificially inflating its so-called original or regular prices, and then promoting discounts from those prices as bargains. The state sought an injunction against the practices, under the state's Consumer Protection Act.

May denied the charges, contending in part that its procedures comply with federal law, which would take precedence over the state statute.

But . . . , in a 17-page ruling, Judge Larry J. Naves wrote that May D&F's practices didn't comply with the Federal Trade Commission Guides Against Deceptive Pricing. The comparative price advertising policies May established in 1986 failed that test, said Judge Naves, and so, to a lesser extent, did the amended policy May adopted in 1989.

The case, which May opted to fight rather than to settle out of court as other retailers have done in similar cases, deals with the pricing of such mundane items as saucepans, rotisseries, coffee-makers, mattresses and glassware. But it has provided an intriguing view of how retail price promotions can make consumers think they're getting a better deal than they really are.

Descriptions of Products

Although certain words are considered mere puffing ("greatest," "best"), at least under certain circumstances, other words, which have more precise connotations, can cause trouble if they are misused. One example is the word "new." In most cases, the FTC has held that if a product is more than six months old, it is not new and may not lawfully be advertised as such.

The efficacy of products is perhaps their most often advertised aspect. An ad that states a product will do more than it can is almost always deceptive if the claim is specific. Common examples that the FTC continues to do battle over are claims that a cream, pill, or other substance will "rejuvenate" the body, "cure baldness," "permanently" remove wrinkles or restore the vitality of hair.

The composition of goods is another common category of deceptive claims. For example, a product advertised as "wool" had better be 100 percent wool; a mixture of wool and synthetic fabrics cannot be advertised as "wool." The FTC has lists of dozens of descriptive words with appropriate definitions.

Labeling of certain products is strictly regulated by specific statutes. Under the Food, Drug, and Cosmetic Act, artificial colors and flavors must be disclosed. Other specific federal statutes include the Wool Products Labeling Act, the Textile Fiber Products Identification Act, the Fur Products Labeling Act, and the Flammable Fabrics Act, the enforcement of which is entrusted to the FTC. In 1966, Congress enacted the Fair Packaging and Labeling Act. It governs most consumer products and gives the FTC authority to issue regulations for proper labeling of most of them. In particular, the statute is designed to help

BOX 48-2

In general, May acknowledged that in certain sections of the store it offered items at what it called the "original" or "regular" price for 10 days at the start of a six-month selling season. But few items moved at these levels. The company then would drop the price, and advertise the items as below "original price." Further discounts from those realistic prices were touted as sales prices of limited duration, as "15-hour specials" and the like. At the end of the six-month season, the items were briefly marked up again to the generally noncompetitive levels for another 10-day period that would re-establish the next 170 days' prices as "bargains."

The court found that the state "has proven by a preponderance of the evidence that May D&F violated all three" of the deceptive practices alleged in the complaint.

"May D&F's 'original' price for practically all of its merchandise in the Home Store [section] was a fictitious high price established as a reference price for the purpose of subsequently advertising bargain reductions from that price," the judge wrote. "The clear expectation of May D&F was to sell all or practically all merchandise at its 'sale' price." The company's policy as amended in 1989 was a "step in the right direction," he said, but May's "failure to disclose to the public its subjective and unique" methodology for price labeling affected consumers' choices "to their detriment."

The court enjoined May D&F from establishing a reference price for the sole purpose of figure markdowns unless it "fully and completely" discloses to consumers its method of determining those original prices at the same time, in its ads. It also is prohibited from using price terms "which have meanings unique to May D&F," unless it also publishes a glossary of such terms. The order prohibits the unit from advertising sales of limited duration "in such manner as to communicate to consumers a false sense of urgency to purchase," when similar price levels are routinely scheduled throughout a selling season.

The court ordered May D&F to pay an $8,000 fine to the state—much less than the more than $1 million the state had sought—and directed the company to pay costs and attorney fees to the state; an official at the attorney general's office estimated that would total $250,000 to $400,000.

The attorney general's office called the ruling "not only a significant decision but a major victory. The court agreed with our position in all respects." An official said such practices hurt not only consumers, but also work to the "disadvantage of small-business competitors who can't compete with these kinds of advertising shenanigans."

Source: *Wall Street Journal*, June 28, 1990

standardize quantity descriptions ("small," "medium," and "large") and to facilitate shoppers who wish to compare the value of competing goods in the stores.

Misleading Price and Savings Claims

"Buy one, get another for half price." "Suggested retail price: $25. Our price: $5.95." "Yours for only $95. You save $50." Claims such as these assault the eye and ear daily. Unless these ads are strictly true, they are violations of Section 5. To regulate deceptive price and savings claims, the FTC has issued a series of *Guides Against Deceptive Pricing* that set forth certain principles by which the commission will judge the merits of price claims. These guides are not themselves law, but they are important clues to how the FTC will act when faced with a price claim case and they may even provide guidance to state courts hearing claims of deceptive pricing ads (see **Box 48-2**).

In general, the guides deal with five claims, as follows:

1. *Comparisons of the sale price to a former price* The former price must have been offered for a substantial period of time in the near past for a seller to be justified in referring to it. A product that once had a price tag of $50, but which never actually sold for more than $40, cannot be hawked at the "former price of $50." Under the FTC guides, a reduction of at least 10 percent is necessary to make the claim true.

2. *Comparable products* "This same mattress and box springs would cost you $450 at retail." The advertisement is true only if the seller is in fact

offering the same merchandise and if the price he quoted is genuine.

3. *"Suggested" retail price* The same rules apply as those just mentioned. But in the case of a "manufacturer's suggested" price, an additional wrinkle can occur: the manufacturer might help the retailer deceive by listing a "suggested" price that is in fact considerably above the going price in the retailer's trading area. Whether it is the manufacturer who is doing his own selling, or the retailer who takes advantage of the "list price" ticket on the goods, the resulting claim of a bargain is deceptive if the product does not sell for the list price in any market or in the market of the retailer.

4. *Bargain based on purchase of something else* The usual statement in these cases is "buy one, get one free" (or at some percentage of the usual selling price). Again, the watchwords are *literal accuracy*. If the package of batteries normally sells in the advertiser's store for 99 cents, and two packages are now selling for that price, then the advertisement is unexceptionable. But advertisers are often tempted to raise the original selling price or reduce the size or quantity of the bargain product; doing so is deceptive.

5. *False claims to explain a "sale" price* "Giant clearance sale" or "going out of business" or "limited offer" are common advertising gimmicks. If true, they are legitimate, but it takes very little to make them deceptive. A "limited offer" that goes on forever (or a sale price charged beyond the date on which a sale is said to end) is deceptive. Likewise, false claims that imply the manufacturer is charging the customer a small price are illegitimate. These include claims like "wholesale price," "manufacturer's close-outs," "irregulars," or "seconds."

"Bait and Switch" Advertisements

A common sales pitch in retail is the **"bait and switch."** The retailer "baits" the prospective customer by dangling an alluring sale before his eyes. "Steinway Grand—only $1,000." But when the customer arrives at the store he finds that the advertised product has sold out. The retailer then tries to sell the disappointed customer a much higher priced product. Or the salesman may have the product, but he will disparage it—privately pointing out that it does not really live up to the advertised expectations—and will exhort the customer to buy the "better," more expensive model. These and related tactics are all violations of Section 5. In its *Guides Against Bait Advertising*, the FTC lists several such unfair practices. These include: (1) refusing to demonstrate the advertised product, (2) disparaging the product (for example, by exhibiting a visibly inferior grade of product next to higher-priced merchandise), (3) failing to stock enough of the advertised product to meet anticipated demand (although the advertiser may say "supplies limited," if that is the case), (4) stating that delivery of the advertised product will take an inordinate amount of time, (5) demonstrating a defective product, and (6) deliberately discouraging the would-be buyer from purchasing the advertised product.

Free Offers

Careless advertisers will discover that "free," perhaps the most powerful word in advertising, comes at a cost. As just noted, a product is not free if it is conditional on buying another product and the price of the "free" product is included in the purchased product ("buy one tube and get another tube free"). Just how far the commission is prepared to take this rule is clear from *F.T.C.* v. *Mary Carter Paint Co.*, 382 U.S. 46 (1965). In that case, the company offered from the time it began business to sell on a two-for-one basis: "every second can FREE, gallon or quart." The problem was that it had never priced and sold single cans of paint, so the FTC assumed that the price of the second can was included in the first, even though Mary Carter established single can prices which were comparable, it claimed, to those for paint of comparable quality sold by competing manufacturers. The Supreme Court sustained the commission's finding of deception.

Product Comparisons and Disparagements

Product disparagement—saying defamatory things about a competitor's product—is a common-law tort, redressable under state law. It is also actionable under Section 5 of the FTC Act. The FTC brands as disparagement the making of specific untrue statements about a competitor's product. The agency labels an indirect form of disparagement "comparative misrepresentation"—making false claims of superiority of one's own product. Again, the common-law puffing rule would permit the manufacturer of an over-the-counter pain reliever to make the general statement: "Our pill is the best." But the claim that a pill "works three times as fast as the leading competitor" violates Section 5 if untrue.

Truth has always been a defense to claims of product disparagement, but even that common law rule has been eroded in recent years with the application of the *significance* doctrine. A statement may be technically true but insignificant and made in such a way as to be misleading. The leading case, set out below, concerned a comparative study published in *Reader's Digest* of tar and nicotine in cigarettes. The article suggested that the differences were inconsequential to health, but the company making the cigarette with the smallest amount of tar and nicotine touted the fact anyway.

P. LORILLARD CO. v. FEDERAL TRADE COMMISSION
186 F.2d 52 (4th Cir. 1950)

PARKER, CHIEF JUDGE. This is a petition to set aside an order of the Federal Trade Commission which directed that the P. Lorillard Company cease and desist from making certain representations found to be false in the advertising of its tobacco products. The Commission has filed answer asking that its order be enforced. The company was ordered to cease and desist "from representing by any means directly or indirectly":

*   *   *

. . . That Old Gold cigarettes or the smoke therefrom contains less nicotine, or less tars and resins, or is less irritating to the throat than the cigarettes or the smoke therefrom of any of the six other leading brands of cigarettes.

*   *   *

Laboratory tests introduced in evidence show that the difference in nicotine, tars and resins of the different leading brands of cigarettes is insignificant in amount; and there is abundant testimony of medical experts that such difference as there is could result in no difference in the physiological effect upon the smoker. There is expert evidence, also, that the slight difference in the nicotine, tar and resin content of cigarettes is not constant between different brands, but varies from place to place and from time to time, and that it is a practical impossibility for the manufacturer of cigarettes to determine or to remove or substantially reduce such content or to maintain constancy of such content in the finished cigarette. This testimony gives ample support to the Commission's findings.

*   *   *

The company relies upon the truth of the advertisements complained of, saying that they merely state what had been truthfully stated in an article in the Reader's Digest. An examination of the advertisements, however, shows a perversion of the meaning of the Reader's Digest article which does little

(*continued on next page*)

(continued)

P. LORILLARD CO. v. FEDERAL TRADE COMMISSION
186 F.2d 52 (4th Cir. 1950)

credit to the company's advertising department—a perversion which results in the use of the truth in such a way as to cause the reader to believe the exact opposite of what was intended by the writer of the article. A comparison of the advertisements with the article makes this very plain. The article, after referring to laboratory tests that had been made on cigarettes of the leading brands, says:

"The laboratory's general conclusion will be sad news for the advertising copy writers, but good news for the smoker, who need no longer worry as to which cigarette can most effectively nail down his coffin. For one nail is just about as good as another. Says the laboratory report: 'The differences between brands are, practically speaking, small, and no single brand is so superior to its competitors as to justify its selection on the ground that it is less harmful.' How small the variations are may be seen from the data tabulated on page 7."

The table referred to in the article was inserted for the express purpose of showing the insignificance of the difference in the nicotine and tar content of the smoke from the various brands of cigarettes. It appears therefrom that the Old Gold cigarettes examined in the test contained less nicotine, tars and resins than the others examined, although the difference, according to the uncontradicted expert evidence, was so small as to be entirely insignificant and utterly without meaning so far as effect upon the smoker is concerned. The company proceeded to advertise this difference as though it had received a citation for public service instead of a castigation from the Reader's Digest. In the leading newspapers of the country and over the radio it advertised that the Reader's Digest had had experiments conducted and had found that Old Gold cigarettes were lowest in nicotine and lowest in irritating tars and resins, just as though a substantial difference in such content had been found. The following advertisement may be taken as typical:

"OLD GOLDS FOUND
LOWEST IN NICOTINE
OLD GOLDS FOUND
LOWEST IN THROAT-IRRITATING
TARS AND RESINS

"See Impartial Test by Reader's Digest July Issue.

"See How Your Brand Compares with Old Gold.

"Reader's Digest assigned a scientific testing laboratory to find out about cigarettes. They tested seven leading cigarettes and Reader's Digest published the results.

"The cigarette whose smoke was lowest in nicotine was Old Gold. The cigarette with the least throat-irritating tars and resins was Old Gold.

"On both these major counts Old Gold was best among all seven cigarettes tested.

"Get July Reader's Digest. Turn to Page 5. See what this highly respected magazine reports.

"You'll say, 'From now on, my cigarette is Old Gold.' Light one? Note the mild, *interesting* flavor. Easier on the throat? Sure: And *more* smoking pleasure: Yes, it's the *new* Old Gold—finer yet, since 'something new has been added'."

The fault with this advertising was not that it did not print all that the Reader's Digest article said, but that it printed a small part thereof in such a way as to create an entirely false and misleading impression, not only as to what was said in the article, but also as to the quality of the company's cigarettes. Almost anyone reading the advertisements or listening to the radio broadcasts would have gained the very definite impression that Old Gold cigarettes were less irritating to the throat and less harmful than other leading brands of cigarettes because they contained substantially less nicotine, tars and resins, and that the Reader's Digest had established this fact in impartial laboratory tests; and few would have troubled to look up the Reader's Digest to see what it really had said. The truth was exactly the opposite. There was no substantial difference in Old Gold cigarettes and the other leading brands with respect to their content of nicotine, tars and resins and this was what the Reader's Digest article plainly said. The table whose meaning the advertisements distorted for the purpose of misleading and deceiving the public was intended to prove that there was no practical difference and did prove it when properly understood. To tell less than the whole truth is a well known method of deception; and he who deceives by resorting to such method cannot excuse the deception by relying upon the truthfulness per se of the partial truth by which it has been accomplished.

In determining whether or not advertising is false or misleading within the meaning of the statute regard must be had, not to fine spun distinctions and arguments that may be made in excuse, but to the effect which it might reasonably be expected to have upon the general public. "The important criterion is the net impression which the advertisement is likely to make upon the general populace." As was well said by Judge Coxe in Florence Manufacturing Co. v. J. C. Dowd & Co., 2 Cir., 178 F. 73, 75, with reference to the law relating to trademarks: "The law is not made for the protection of experts, but for the public—that vast multitude which includes the ignorant, the unthinking and the credulous, who, in making purchases, do not stop to analyze, but are governed by appearances and general impressions."

★   ★   ★

For the reasons stated, the petition to set aside the order will be denied and the order will be enforced.

During the 1970s, to help enforce its rules against comparative misrepresentations, the FTC began to insist that advertisers fully document any quantitative claims that their products were superior to others. This meant that the advertiser should have proof of accuracy not only if the commission comes calling; the advertiser should collect the information beforehand, otherwise the claim will be held presumptively deceptive.

The FTC Act (and state laws against misleading advertising) are not the only statutes aimed at product comparisons. One important new federal law is the Trademark Law Revision Act of 1988, amending the Lanham Act. For many years, the federal courts had ruled that a provision in the Lanham Act prohibiting false statements in advertisements was limited to an advertiser's false statements about its own goods or services only. The 1988 amendments overturned that line of court cases, broadening the rule to cover false statements about someone else's goods or services as well. The amendments also prohibit false or misleading claims about another company's commercial activities, such as the nature of its warranties. The revised Lanham Act now permits a company injured by a competitor's false advertising to sue directly in federal court.

Endorsements

How wonderful to have a superstar (or maybe yesterday's superstar) appear on television drooling over your product. Presumably, millions of people would buy a throat spray if Whitney Houston swore by it, or a pair of jeans if Brooke Shields wore them, or a face cream if Catherine Deneuve blessed it. In more subtle ways, numerous products are touted every day with one form of testimonial or another: "three out of four doctors recommend . . ." or "drivers across the country use. . . ." In this area, the opportunities for deception are rife.

It is not a deception for a well-known personality to endorse a product without disclosing that she is being paid to do so. But the person giving the testimonial must in fact use the product; if she does not, the endorsement is deceptive. Suppose an astronaut just returned to earth is talked into endorsing suspenders ("they keep your pants from floating away") that he was seen to be wearing on televised shots of the orbital mission. If he has customarily worn them, he may properly endorse them. But if he stops wearing them for another brand or because he has decided to go back to wearing belts, reruns of the TV commercials must be pulled from the air.

That a particular consumer is in fact ecstatically happy about how a product helped him does not save a false statement: it is deceptive to present this glowing testimonial to the public if there are no facts to back up his claim. The assertion "I was cured by apricot pits" to market a cancer remedy would not pass FTC muster. Nor may an endorser give a testimonial involving subjects known only to experts if he is not himself that kind of expert, as shown in the following consent decree, negotiated by the FTC with singer Pat Boone.

COOGA MOOGA, INC.
Trade Reg. Rep. (CCH)
¶21,417
(FTC 1978) [1976-1979
Transfer Binder]

The FTC issued a complaint alleging that Karr Preventative Medical Products, Inc. (KPMP), Beverly Hills, Calif., and its controlling officer, Atida H. Karr, M.D., have made false and unsubstantiated claims for Acne-Statin, a mail order preparation advertised for the treatment of acne. . . .

The FTC also accepted an agreement containing a consent order entered into by Charles E. "Pat" Boone and Cooga Mooga, Inc., Los Angeles, Calif., of which Mr. Boone is president. Mr. Boone appeared in print and television advertisements for Acne-Statin in which he provided an endorsement for the product. Key provisions of the consent agreement require that Mr. Boone make a reasonable inquiry before endorsing products in the future and that he pay part of any restitution that may be ordered in this matter.

The Commission's administrative complaint against KPMP and Dr. Karr alleges in part that: (1) Acne-Statin neither will cure acne nor can eliminate its cause, as claimed; (2) they have falsely advertised that Acne-Statin is superior to all other acne preparations and to soap in the anti-bacterial treatment of acne; (3) contrary to other claims, there are time and quantity limitations on the money-back guarantee for Acne-Statin; and (4) there was no reasonable basis for claims that Acne-Statin will cure acne and result in skin free of acne blemishes or for various other performance claims.

* * *

Under their agreed-to order, Mr. Boone and Cooga Mooga, Inc. must have a reasonable basis when making any claim relating to the efficacy, performance, any characteristic or property, or the result of use of any product. Also, they must make a reasonable inquiry into the truthfulness of any proposed endorsement of this nature.

Mr. Boone must also pay his pro rata share of any restitution which might be ordered by the Commission or by a court.

The consent agreement, among other things, prohibits misrepresentations of—(a) the benefits Boone family members have derived from any product; (b) product tests or product test results; and (c) the efficacy, use or performance of any product where the use or misuse could affect the user's health and safety.

According to Albert H. Kramer, Director, Bureau of Consumer Protection, the negotiated order, while not a binding legal precedent, stands for the principle that an endorser must verify the claims made about the advertised product before the first commercial goes on the air or appears in print, or else risk FTC action. Unless the endorser is an expert on the subject, the endorser must look to independent reliable sources to validate claims, tests, or studies supplied by the advertiser. Failure to make a reasonable effort at independent evaluation could result in personal liability for the endorser.

* * *

Pictorial and Television Advertising

Pictorial representations create special problems because the picture can belie the caption or the announcer's words. A picture showing an expensive car may be deceptive if the dealer does not stock those cars or if the only readily available cars are different models. The ways of deceiving by creating false inferences through pictures are limited only by imagination. White-coated "doctors," seals of the British monarchy, and plush offices can connote various things about a product, even if the advertisement never says that the man in the white coat was a doctor, that the product was related to the British crown, or that the company had its operations in the building depicted.

Television demonstrations may also suggest nonexistent properties or qualities in a product. In one case, the commission ordered the manufacturer of a liquid cleaner to cease showing it in use near hot stoves and candles, implying falsely that it was nonflammable. A commercial showing a knife cutting through nails is deceptive if the nails were pre-cut and different knives were used for the before and after shots.

UNFAIR TRADE PRACTICES

We turn now to certain practices that, while they have deceptive elements, also operate unfairly in ways beyond mere deception. In general, these types of unfair practices will be attacked: (1) failing to substantiate material representations in advertisements before publishing them or putting them on the air; (2) failing to disclose certain material information necessary for consumers to make rational comparisons of price and quality of products; and (3) taking unconscionable advantage or exploiting the weakness of certain consumers. The FTC has enjoined many such ads of the first type. The second type of unfairness has led the commission to issue a number of TRRs setting forth what must be disclosed—for example, octane ratings of gasoline. In this section we focus briefly on the third category.

Contests and Sweepstakes

In 1971, the FTC obtained a consent order from *Reader's Digest,* barring it from promoting a mail order sweepstakes in which those responding had a chance to win large monetary or other prizes by returning numbered tickets, unless the magazine expressly disclosed how many prizes would be awarded and unless all such prizes were in fact awarded. *Reader's Digest* had heavily promoted the size and number of prizes, but few of the winning tickets were ever returned and consequently few of the prizes were ever actually awarded. [Reader's Digest Assoc., 79 F.T.C. 599 (1971)]

Beginning in the 1960s, the retail food and gasoline industries began to heavily promote games of chance. Investigations by the FTC and a House Small Business subcommittee showed that the games were rigged: winners were "picked" early by planting the winning cards early on in the distribution; winning cards were sent to geographic areas most in need of the promotional benefits of announcing winners; not all prizes were awarded before many games terminated; and local retailers could spot winning cards and cash them in or give them to favored customers. As a result of these investigations, the FTC in 1969 issued its Trade Regulation Rule for Games of Chance in the Food Retailing and Gasoline Industries, strictly regulating how the games may operate and be promoted.

Many marketers use "contests," as opposed to sweepstakes, in merchandising their products. In a contest, the consumer must actually do something other than return a ticket, such as fill in a Bingo card or come up with certain words. It is an unfair practice for the sponsoring company not to abide by its own rules in determining winners.

Door-to-door and Mail-order Selling

In 1974 the FTC promulgated a TRR requiring a three-day "cooling off" period, within which any door-to-door sales can be cancelled. The contract must state the buyer's right to the cooling-off period.

For many years, certain unscrupulous distributors would mail unsolicited merchandise and demand payment through a series of dunning letters and bills. In 1970, Congress enacted legislation that declares any unsolicited mailing and subsequent dunning to be an unfair trade practice under Section 5. Under this law, if you receive an unsolicited product in the mail, you may treat it as a gift and use it; you are under no obligation to return it or pay for it.

Another regulation of mail-order sales is the FTC's Mail-order Merchandise TRR. Any direct-mail merchandiser must deliver the promised goods within thirty days or give the consumer an option to accept delayed delivery or a prompt refund of his money— or cancellation of the order if it has not been prepaid.

Negative Option Plans

The "**negative option**" was devised in the 1920s by the Book-of-the-Month Club. It is a marketing device through which the consumer responds to the seller only if he wishes *not* to receive the product. As used by book clubs and other distributors of goods that are sent out periodically, the customer agrees when "joining" to accept and pay for all items, unless in advance of their arrival he specifically indicates he wishes to reject them. If he does nothing, he must pay. Difficulties arise when the negative option notice is late arriving in the mail or when a member quits and continues to receive the monthly notices.

In 1974, the FTC issued a TRR governing use of negative option plans by sellers. The TRR laid down specific notice requirements. Among other things, a subscriber is entitled to ten days in which to notify sellers that he has rejected the particular item about to be sent. If a customer has cancelled his membership, the seller must take back and pay the former member's mailing expenses for any merchandise mailed after cancellation. The former member may treat any shipments beyond one after cancellation as unsolicited merchandise and keep it without having to pay for it or return it.

Breach of Contract

Under certain circumstances, a company's willful breach of contract can constitute an unfair trade practice, thus violating section 5 of the FTC Act. In one recent case, a termite and pest exterminating company signed contracts with its customers guaranteeing "lifetime" protection against termite damage to structures that the company treated. The contract required a customer to renew the service each year by paying an unchanging annual fee. Five years after signing these contracts, the company notified 207,000 customers that it was increasing the annual fee because of inflation. The FTC challenged the fee hike on the ground that it was a breach of contract amounting to an unfair trade practice. The FTC's charges were sustained on appeal. The Eleventh Circuit approved the FTC's three-part test for determining unfairness: (1) the injury "must be substantial," (2) "it must not be outweighed by countervailing benefits to consumers," and (3) "it must be an injury that consumers themselves could not reasonably have avoided." In the termite case, all three parts were met: consumers were forced to pay substantially higher fees, they received no extra benefits, and they could not have anticipated or prevented the price hike, since the contract specifically precluded them. [Orkin Exterminating Co. v. FTC, 849 F.2d 1354 (11th Circ. 1988), *cert. denied*, 488 U.S. 1041 (1989)]

REMEDIES

The Federal Trade Commission has a host of weapons in its remedial arsenal. It may issue cease and desist orders against unfair and deceptive acts and practices, and "let the punishment fit the crime." For instance, the FTC can order a company to remove or modify a deceptive trade name. It may order companies to substantiate their advertising. Or, if a company fails to disclose facts about a product, the commission may order the company to affirmatively disclose the facts in future advertising. In the *J. B. Williams* case, for example (p. 1078), the court upheld the commission's order that the company tell consumers in future advertising that the condition Geritol is supposed to treat—iron-poor blood—is only rarely the cause of symptoms of tiredness that Geritol would help cure.

The FTC has often exercised its power to order affirmative disclosures during the past decade, but its power to correct advertising deceptions is even broader. In *Warner-Lambert Co. v. Federal Trade Commission,* 562 F.2d 749 (D.C. Cir. 1977), *cert. denied*, 435 U.S. 950 (1978), the U.S. Court of Appeals in Washington, using **corrective advertising,** approved the commission's power to order a company in future advertisements to *correct* its former misleading and deceptive statements regarding Listerine mouthwash, should it choose to continue to advertise the product. The court also approved the FTC's formula for determining how much the company must spend: an amount equal to the average annual expenditure on advertising the mouthwash during the ten years preceding the case.

In addition to its injunctive powers, the FTC may seek civil penalties of $10,000 for violation of final cease and desist orders, and if the violation is a continuing one—an advertising campaign that lasts for weeks or months—each day is considered a separate violation. The commission may also sue for up to $10,000 per violation, as above, for violations of its TRRs. Under the FTC Improvement Act of 1975, the commission is authorized to seek injunctions and collect monetary damages on behalf of injured consumers in cases involving violations of TRRs. It may also seek restitution for consumers in cases involving cease and desist orders, if the party continuing to commit the unfair or deceptive practice should have known that it would be dishonest or fraudulent to continue doing so. The exact reach of this power to seek restitution, which generally had not been available before 1975, remains to be tested in the courts. Unlike their rights under the antitrust statutes, however, *private* parties have no right to sue under Section 5 of the FTC Act.

Little FTC Acts

Even when consumers have no direct remedy under federal law for unfair or deceptive acts and practices, they may have recourse under state laws modeled on the FTC Act, known as Little FTC Acts. These acts are more liberal than the federal unfair trade rules, and permit consumers—and in several states, even aggrieved businesses—to sue when injured by a host of "immoral, unethical, oppressive, or unscrupulous" commercial acts. Often a successful plaintiff can recover treble damages and attorneys' fees. Unlike the current federal standard for defining deceptive acts, the state standards rest on capacity to deceive. Use of Little FTC Acts is expected to rise.

CHAPTER SUMMARY

Section 5 of the Federal Trade Commission Act gives the Federal Trade Commission the power to enforce a provision prohibiting "unfair methods of competition and unfair or deceptive acts or practices in commerce." In doing so the FTC may bring enforcement proceedings against companies on a case-by-case basis or may promulgate trade regulation rules.

A deceptive act or practice need not actually deceive, as long as it is "likely to mislead." An unfair act or practice need not deceive at all but must offend a common sense of propriety, justice, or an honest way of acting. Among the proscribed acts or practices are these: failure to disclose pertinent facts, false or misleading description of products, misleading price and savings claims, bait and switch advertisements, free offer claims, false product comparisons and disparagements, and endorsements by those who do not use the product or who have no reasonable basis for making the claims. Among the unfair trade practices that the FTC has sought to deter are certain types of contests and sweepstakes, high-pressure door-to-door and mail-order selling, and certain types of negative option plans.

The FTC has a number of remedial weapons: cease and desist orders tailored to the particular deception or unfair act (including affirmative disclosure in advertising and corrections in future advertising), civil monetary penalties, and injunctions, damages, and restitution on behalf of injured consumers. Only the FTC may sue to correct violations of Section 5; private parties have no right to sue under Section 5, but they can sue for certain kinds of false advertising under the federal trademark laws.

KEY TERMS

Bait and switch	p. 1082	Unfair methods of	p. 1074
Corrective advertising	p. 1089	competition	
Negative option	p. 1088	Unfair or deceptive	p. 1077
Product disparagement	p. 1082	acts and practices	
Trade regulation rules	p. 1075		

SELF-TEST QUESTIONS

1. Section 5 of the Federal Trade Commission Act is enforceable by:
   (a) a consumer in federal court
   (b) a consumer in state court
   (c) the Federal Trade Commission in an administrative proceeding
   (d) the Federal Trade Commission suing in a federal court
2. The Federal Trade Commission:
   (a) is an independent federal agency
   (b) is an arm of the Justice Department
   (c) supersedes Congress in defining deceptive trade practices
   (d) speaks for the President on consumer matters
3. A company falsely stated that its competitor's product "won't work." Which of the following statements is false?
   (a) The competitor may sue the company under state law.
   (b) The competitor may sue the company for violating the FTC Act.
   (c) The competitor may sue the company for violating the Lanham Act.
   (d) The Federal Trade Commission may sue the company for violating the FTC Act.
4. The FTC may order a company that violated section 5 of the FTC Act by false advertising:
   (a) to go out of business
   (b) to close down the division of the company that paid for false advertising
   (c) to issue corrective advertising
   (d) to buy back from its customers all of the products sold by the advertising
5. The ingredients in a nationally advertised cupcake must be disclosed on the package under:
   (a) state common law
   (b) a trade regulation rule promulgated by the FTC
   (c) the federal Food, Drug, and Cosmetic Act
   (d) an executive order of the President

DEMONSTRATION PROBLEM

Icebox Ike, a well-known tackle for a professional football team, was recently signed to a multimillion-dollar contract to appear in a series of nationally-televised advertisements touting the pleasures of going to the ballet and showing him in the audience watching a ballet. In fact, Icebox has never been to a ballet, although he has told his friends that he "truly believes" ballet is a "wonderful thing." The Federal Trade Commission opens an investigation to determine whether there are grounds to take legal action against Icebox and the ballet company ads. What advice can you give Icebox Ike? What remedies can the FTC seek?

PROBLEMS

1. Door-to-door salespersons of an encyclopedia company offer a complete set of encyclopedias to "selected" customers. They tell customers that their only obligation is to pay for a ten-year updating service. In fact the price of the updating service includes the cost of the encyclopedias. The Federal Trade Commission sues, charging deception under Section 5 of the FTC Act. The encyclopedia company defends on the ground that no one could

possibly have been misled because everyone must have understood that no company could afford to give away a twenty-volume set of books for free. What result?

2. Vanessa Cosmetics takes out full-page advertisements in the local newspaper stating that "this Sunday only" the Vanessa Makeup Kit will be "reduced to only $25." In fact, the regular price has been $25.50. Does this constitute deceptive advertising? Why?

3. Lilliputian Department Stores advertises a "special" on an electric carrot slicer, priced "this week only at $10." When customers come to the store, they find the carrot slicer in frayed boxes, and the advertised special is clearly inferior to a higher-grade carrot slicer priced at $25. When customers ask about the difference, the store clerk tells them that "you wouldn't want to buy the cheaper one; it wears out much too fast." What grounds, if any, exist to charge Lilliputian with violations of the FTC Act?

4. A toothpaste manufacturer advertises that special tests demonstrate that its toothpaste shows fewer cavities than a "regular toothpaste." In fact the "regular" toothpaste was not marketed, but was merely the advertiser's brand stripped of its fluoride. Various studies over the years have demonstrated, however, that fluoride in toothpaste will reduce the number of cavities a user will get. Is this advertisement deceptive under Section 5 of the FTC Act?

5. McDonald's advertises a sweepstakes through a mailing that says prizes are to be reserved for 15,610 "lucky winners." The mailing further states that "You may be [a winner] but you will never know if you don't claim your prize. All prizes not claimed will never be given away, so

hurry." The mailing does not give the odds of winning. The Federal Trade Commission sues to enjoin the mailing as deceptive. What result?

ANSWERS TO SELF-TEST QUESTIONS

1. (c)   2. (a)   3. (b)   4. (c)   5. (c)

SUGGESTED ANSWER TO DEMONSTRATION PROBLEM

Since an endorsement is deceptive if a person does not actually use the goods or services advertised, it might seem as though Icebox Ike has clearly violated the section 5 of the FTC Act. However, he may not have lied about going to the ballet but declared simply that a viewer will receive great pleasure from doing so. That is not necessarily a false statement. On the other hand, the picture of him at the ballet certainly is misleading because it suggests that he goes, or at least occasionally attends, the ballet, and that his statement about the pleasure of the ballet is a personal feeling. His statements to friends are not conclusive, since they are wholly self-serving and not capable of proof. The best thing for Icebox Ike to do is to begin to go regularly to the ballet with a smile on his face. The Federal Trade Commission can seek to enjoin the advertisements from continuing to air on television and can seek to ban Icebox Ike from endorsing the ballet in the future.

CHAPTER

49

CHAPTER OVERVIEW

Defining the Franchise Relationship

The Franchisor's Intangible Property Rights

Antitrust Considerations

Disclosure Requirements

Product Liability

Liability of Franchisor for Franchisee's Acts

Franchising Law

To facilitate the study of law and its relation to the business community, we have examined particular forms of enterprise and business activities one at a time. That has allowed us to focus on a single cluster of problems, like those facing consumers or employees. It has also simplified the discussion because many forms of business operations, such as partnerships and corporations, are subject to well-defined bodies of law—for example, the Uniform Partnership Act and the Revised Model Business Corporation Act. Likewise, certain business activities are directly regulated by particular laws. For example, many state and federal securities laws regulate the sale of stock, and both the common law of contracts and such statutes as the Uniform Commercial Code regulate contractual activities.

But business operations and activities are rarely so simple that they can be governed by a single particular law. Indeed, only by examining a host of laws can we understand the full range of legal relations of entities such as corporations. We need to look at not only the Revised Model Business Corporation Act, but also virtually the entire range of the common law (torts,

contracts, agency, and many other branches) and dozens of state and federal statutes (including environmental and labor laws).

To see how business must operate in the full legal environment (see Figure 49-1), we explore in this chapter an important method of business operation: franchising. Familiar to all Americans chiefly in the form of fast-food outlets but also in dozens of other industries as well, the franchise is not a business entity as such, like a partnership or corporation. Indeed, both franchisor and franchisee may, themselves, individually be organized as partnerships or corporations. It is, rather, a relationship between manufacturers or other suppliers and distributors—one that permits regional or even national brand identification without the huge capital accumulation required for companies that not only own central manufacturing and marketing facilities but also retail distribution outlets.

Until the 1960s, franchising was used chiefly by automobile manufacturers, soft drink bottlers, and gas stations. Then others understood the leverage that franchising could offer, and thousands of businesses

Figure 49-1   A Checklist of Franchising Law

✔ Contract law
    creation of franchise
    obligations of franchisor and franchisee to each other

✔ Intellectual property laws
    patent
    copyright
    trademark
    trade secrets

✔ Antitrust laws
    selection of franchisee
    territorial restrictions
    restrictions on purchases and sales
    termination

✔ Registration and disclosure requirements

✔ Product liability law
    liability for injuries

✔ Agency law
    responsibility of franchisor for franchisee's acts
    responsibility of franchisee for franchisor's acts

- *Distributorships or Product Franchises* (through which a manufacturer licenses a distributor to sell its products). Typically, automobile dealerships and gasoline stations operate under product franchises.
- *Business-Format Franchises* (under which the franchisee is closely identified as part of a "family" belonging to the franchisor). Fast-food chains, real estate brokerages, and many accounting firms operate under business-format franchises.
- *Manufacturing Plants* (under which the franchisor permits the franchisee actually to manufacture and market its products under standards prescribed by the franchisor). Many electronic goods are manufactured and sold under this arrangement.

The federal and state governments have promulgated many laws and regulations to cope with problems and abuses. These include the Automobile Dealers Franchise Act, the earliest federal franchise law; the Federal Trade Commission's Franchising Rule (a trade regulation rule, see p. 1075); the Petroleum Marketing Practices Act, and a host of state laws, such as the California Franchise Investment Law (1970) and the New York Franchise Disclosure Law (1980). Beyond these specific laws and regulations aimed at protecting franchisees, other federal and state laws, including those dealing with antitrust, trademarks, and consumer protection, are significant aspects of the entire body of law governing franchise operations.

Not every business relationship involving suppliers and sellers is necessarily a franchise. As opposed to franchisees, sellers may be employees of the manufacturer or independent contractors, distributors, consignees, or independent retail dealers. Three factors are crucial to the distinction between franchise and these other relationships: (1) the degree of control exercised by the supplier over the methods by which the seller conducts its business, (2) the use of the supplier's trademarks, and (3) the nature of the payment for the goods ultimately sold. For example, a person operating a perfume counter in a department store may be an independent contractor; although using the store's name on sales receipts and conforming to certain standards laid down by the store in hiring sales personnel, the operator is in reality a lessee of space, not a franchisee of the store. The operator buys products from someone else, and the store maintains no control over the operator's use of the manufacturer's trademarks. In contrast, a popcorn stand at a movie theater is usually described as a concessionaire, rather than a franchisee, because the

rushed to take advantage of a franchise arrangement. By 1990, more than one-third of all domestic retail sales—more than $600 billion worth of goods and services—were made through 533,000 franchised outlets (a number that doubled through the 1980s). Nearly seven percent of the nation's total non-agricultural labor pool works in franchised operations.

DEFINING THE FRANCHISE RELATIONSHIP

The term **"franchise"** has varied meanings in different state and federal statutes. In general, a franchise has four elements. It is (1) a contract by which in return for (2) the payment of a fee, a franchisee is granted the (3) right to sell or distribute the franchisor's goods or services in a manner substantially prescribed by the franchisor, and in which the business method involves (4) substantial use of the franchisor's trademark, trade name, or commercial symbol. The franchise is used principally in three categories of business operations:

operator merely rents space to conduct his or her own business, different from that of the lessor. Also the franchisee differs from other similar types of business relationships, such as business cooperatives, joint ventures, partnerships, merchandise brokerages, and sales agencies.

THE FRANCHISOR'S INTANGIBLE PROPERTY RIGHTS

The heart of the franchise system is the identity of the products or services offered by disparate outlets. As one court has said: "Success of this new merchandising concept [franchising] and for each Midas dealer necessitated that the American motorist recognize the Midas name and have confidence that each dealer was an exhaust specialist who handled the same quality product, provided the same clean and comfortable surroundings, gave the same prompt and dependable service and honored the same unique Midas guarantee." [Perma Life Mufflers, Inc. v. International Parts Corp., 376 F.2d 692 (7th Cir. 1967)] This means that a central concern to the franchisor is protection of the trademarks, copyrights, patents, trade secrets, or commercial symbols that tie all his distributors together into a network distinguishable from all others. We examine intangible (or intellectual) property rights in more detail in Chapter 31. Here we look briefly at those aspects of the law that give control to the franchisor.

It would do a franchisor little good to create a network of identically named products or distributors if he could not control the ingredients being used in the manufacture or sale of the final product or the method of retail operations. Subject to certain antitrust difficulties discussed on page 1099, the franchisor may, in licensing trademarks, trade secrets, or other intangible property rights, dictate how franchisees will use those rights. For example, a fast-food franchisor may instruct its myriad outlets what type of meat they may use in their hamburgers and how they may cook them.

Several distinct problems may arise depending on the type of property interest at stake. For example, a franchisor may license the use of patents, but it cannot demand royalty payments for use of the patented product or manufacturing process beyond the term of the patent itself. Patented products or processes, by definition, are open to public inspection, because the federal patent law requires that they be described in detail in the application filed in the U.S. Patent Office. By contrast, a trade secret (p. 690) is valuable only as long as it is actually kept secret. Since trade secrets (a soft-drink formula, for instance) are frequently crucial in the franchisor's business, the law permits the franchisor to control how the secrets are used to prevent public disclosure. Thus, a franchisor may by contract forbid the franchisee from disclosing the secrets publicly and may even bar the franchisee from competing in the product after the franchise term has expired.

ANTITRUST CONSIDERATIONS

Selecting the Franchisee

In general, the franchisor is free to grant or deny franchises to whomever it chooses. But that freedom is subject to particular legal limitations—for example, state and federal laws that prohibit choices made solely on the basis of race, sex, or national origin. Discriminatory motives are not the only limitation. Although a franchisor may determine in its own business interests how many (or how few) franchises to grant, it may not hide unlawful business actions behind the general rule. Thus, a franchisor cannot obtain immunity in a conspiracy with other companies to drive a particular company out of business by pointing to a general freedom to restrict the number of franchises. Such a conspiracy violates Section 1 of the Sherman Act (p. 1020), as do agreements between a franchisor and its franchisees to deny a license to an outsider to carry its goods. That was the situation in *Klor's, Inc. v. Broadway-Hale Stores, Inc.*, 359 U.S. 207 (1959), discussed on p. 1027. A manufacturer and various retail outlets agreed that Klors, a discount appliance store, should not be allowed to sell the manufacturer's goods. The Supreme Court held that the agreement was a direct violation of the Sherman Act.

Territorial Restrictions

As we noted in Chapter 46, a major issue under the antitrust laws is the right of producers to assign xclusive territories to their distributors, called **territorial restrictions,** to give them the maximum incenive to sell the goods. To maintain the exclusivity, a ranchise agreement might specify that a Chicago dealership may not move outside its assigned terriory to sell the product—for example, by opening up a new retail store in Peoria if some other retailer has been assigned that territory. This policy sacrifices maximum "intra-brand" competition for maximum "inter-brand" competition. Sellers of the Wonder-Chop Food Processor may not be allowed to compete against each other in each city, but they will feel much freer to compete against Cuisinart and other manufacturers of food processing machines. An agreement among *competing producers* or food processors to divide the selling market (e.g., Wonder-Chop to sell exclusively n Chicago, Miracle-Chop to sell exclusively in Kansas City), clearly violates the Sherman Act. As competitors, they have engaged in forbidden *horizontal* allocations of territory. But are *vertical* allocations of selling territory (that is, those decreed by a single producer for its distributors) likewise illegal *per se* (see p. 1027)?

In 1963, in *United States* v. *White Motor Co.,* 372 U.S. 253 (1963), the Supreme Court reversed a court of appeals decision holding that a *customer* allocation scheme was *per se* unlawful. White Motor struck a

bargain with its dealers requiring them to sell White trucks only to those companies with offices or purchasing headquarters within the dealer's territory. The Court said that the allocation scheme was not *per se* unlawful and that the rule of reason should be applied and sent the case back for trial to determine the effect of this restriction on competition.

Four years later, however, the Supreme Court reversed itself, and held in favor of a *per se* rule. In *United States* v. *Arnold Schwinn & Co.,* 388 U.S. 365 (1967), the Court declared vertical territorial restrictions unlawful. Schwinn's franchised retailers were allowed to sell only within their assigned territories and could not sell Schwinn bicycles to unfranchised retailers anywhere. However, the franchisees could stock bicycles other than Schwinns. Although the Court said it was following the rule of reason, the decision had the effect of a *per se* rule, because the Court reasoned that by parting with title to the Schwinn bicycles when it sold them to its franchisees, Schwinn lost the legal right to tell its purchasers how or where to sell them, regardless of the effects.

Ten years later, the Court dramatically reversed itself again, reverting to the rule of reason to analyze all vertical territorial restriction cases. The reasons for so doing and the current state of the law are set forth in the following case.

CONTINENTAL T.V., INC. v. GTE SYLVANIA, INC.
433 U.S. 36 (1977)

MR. JUSTICE POWELL delivered the opinion of the Court.

Franchise agreements between manufacturers and retailers frequently include provisions barring the retailers from selling franchised products from locations other than those specified in the agreements. This case presents important questions concerning the appropriate antitrust analysis of these restrictions under § 1 of the Sherman Act.

Respondent GTE Sylvania Inc. (Sylvania) manufactures and sells television sets through its Home Entertainment Products Division. Prior to 1962, like most other television manufacturers, Sylvania sold its televisions to independent or company-owned distributors who in turn resold to a large and diverse group of retailers. Prompted by a decline in its market share to a relatively insignificant 1% to 2% of national television sales, Sylvania conducted an intensive reassessment of its marketing strategy, and in 1962 adopted the franchise plan challenged here. Sylvania phased out its wholesale distributors and began to sell its televisions directly to a smaller and more select group of franchised retailers. An acknowledged purpose of the change was

(continued on next page)

(continued)

CONTINENTAL T.V., INC. v. GTE SYLVANIA, INC.
433 U.S. 36 (1977)

to decrease the number of competing Sylvania retailers in the hope of attracting the more aggressive and competent retailers thought necessary to the improvement of the company's market position. To this end, Sylvania limited the number of franchises granted for any given area and required each franchisee to sell his Sylvania products only from the location or locations at which he was franchised. A franchise did not constitute an exclusive territory, and Sylvania retained sole discretion to increase the number of retailers in an area in light of the success or failure of existing retailers in developing their market. The revised marketing strategy appears to have been successful during the period at issue here, for by 1965 Sylvania's share of national television sales had increased to approximately 5%, and the company ranked as the Nation's eighth largest manufacturer of color television sets.

This suit is the result of the rupture of a franchiser-franchisee relationship that had previously prospered under the revised Sylvania plan. Dissatisfied with its sales in the city of San Francisco, Sylvania decided in the spring of 1965 to franchise Young Brothers, an established San Francisco retailer of televisions, as an additional San Francisco retailer. The proposed location of the new franchise was approximately a mile from a retail outlet operated by petitioner Continental T.V., Inc. (Continental), one of the most successful Sylvania franchisees. Continental protested that the location of the new franchise violated Sylvania's marketing policy but Sylvania persisted in its plans. Continental then canceled a large Sylvania order and placed a large order with Phillips, one of Sylvania's competitors.

During this same period, Continental expressed a desire to open a store in Sacramento, Cal., a desire Sylvania attributed at least in part to Continental's displeasure over the Young Brothers decision. Sylvania believed that the Sacramento market was adequately served by the existing Sylvania retailers and denied the request. In the face of this denial, Continental advised Sylvania in early September 1965 that it was in the process of moving Sylvania merchandise from its San Jose, Cal., warehouse to a new retail location that it had leased in Sacramento. Two weeks later, allegedly for unrelated reasons, Sylvania's credit department reduced Continental's credit line from $300,000 to $50,000. In response to the reduction in credit and the generally deteriorating relations with Sylvania, Continental withheld all payments owed to John P. Maguire & Co. Inc. (Maguire), the finance company that handled the credit arrangements between Sylvania and its retailers. Shortly thereafter, Sylvania terminated Continental's franchises, and Maguire filed this diversity action in the United States District Court for the Northern District of California seeking recovery of money owed and of secured merchandise held by Continental.

The antitrust issues before us originated in cross-claims brought by Continental against Sylvania and Maguire. Most important for our purposes was the claim that Sylvania had violated § 1 of the Sherman Act by entering into and enforcing franchise agreements that prohibited the sale of Sylvania products other than from specified locations. At the close of evidence in the jury trial of Continental's claims, Sylvania requested the District Court to instruct the jury that its location restriction was illegal only if it unreasonably restrained or suppressed competition. Relying on this Court's decision in *United States* v. *Arnold Schwinn & Co.*, the District Court rejected the proffered instruction in favor of the following one:

> Therefore, if you find a preponderance of the evidence that Sylvania entered into a contract, combination or conspiracy with one or more of its dealers pursuant to which Sylvania exercised dominion or control over the products sold to the dealer, after having parted with title and risk to the products, you must find any effort thereafter to restrict outlets or store locations from which its dealers resold the merchandise which they had purchased from Sylvania to be a violation of Section 1 of the Sherman Act, regardless of the reasonableness of the location restrictions.

In answers to special interrogatories, the jury found that Sylvania had engaged "in a contract, combination or conspiracy in restraint of trade in violation of the antitrust laws with respect to location restrictions alone," and assessed Continental's damages at $591,505, which was trebled pursuant to 15 U.S.C. § 15 to produce an award of $1,774,515.

On appeal, the Court of Appeals for the Ninth Circuit, sitting en banc, reversed by a divided vote.

*   *   *

In the present case, it is undisputed that title to the television sets passed from Sylvania to Continental. Thus, the *Schwinn per se* rule applies unless Sylvania's restriction on locations falls outside *Schwinn's* prohibition against a manufacturer's attempting to restrict a "retailer's freedom as to where and to whom it will resell the products." As the Court of Appeals conceded, the language of *Schwinn* is clearly broad enough to apply to the present case. Unlike the Court of Appeals, however, we are unable to find a principled basis for distinguishing *Schwinn* from the case now before us.

*   *   *

Vertical restrictions reduce intrabrand competition by limiting the number of sellers of a particular product competing for the business of a given group of buyers. Location restrictions have this effect because of practical constraints on the effective marketing area of retail outlets. Although intrabrand competition may be reduced, the ability of retailers to exploit the resulting market may be limited both by the ability of consumers to travel to other franchised locations and, perhaps more importantly, to purchase the competing products of other manufacturers. None of these key variables, however, is affected by the form of the transaction by which a manufacturer conveys his products to the retailers.

(*continued on next page*)

(continued)

CONTINENTAL T.V., INC. v. GTE SYLVANIA, INC.
433 U.S. 36 (1977)

Vertical restrictions promote intrabrand competition by allowing the manufacturer to achieve certain efficiencies in the distribution of his products. These "redeeming virtues" are implicit in every decision sustaining vertical restrictions under the rule of reason. Economists have identified a number of ways in which manufacturers can use such restrictions to compete more effectively against other manufacturers. For example, new manufacturers and manufacturers entering new markets can use the restrictions in order to induce competent and aggressive retailers to make the kind of investment of capital and labor that is often required in the distribution of products unknown to the consumer. Established manufacturers can use them to induce retailers to engage in promotional activities or to provide service and repair facilities necessary to the efficient marketing of their products. Service and repair are vital for many products, such as automobiles and major household appliances. The availability and quality of such services affect a manufacturer's goodwill and the competitiveness of his product. Because of market imperfections such as the so-called "free rider" effect, these services might not be provided by retailers in a purely competitive situation, despite the fact that each retailer's benefit would be greater if all provided the services than if none did.

Economists also have argued that manufacturers have an economic interest in maintaining as much intrabrand competition as is consistent with the efficient distribution of their products. Although the view that the manufacturer's interest necessarily corresponds with that of the public is not universally shared, even the leading critic of vertical restrictions concedes that *Schwinn's* distinction between sale and nonsale transactions is essentially unrelated to any relevant economic impact. Indeed, to the extent that the form of the transaction is related to interbrand benefits, the Court's distinction is inconsistent with its articulated concern for the ability of smaller firms to compete effectively with larger ones. Capital requirements and administrative expenses may prevent smaller firms from using the exception for nonsale transactions.

We conclude that the distinction drawn in *Schwinn* between sale and nonsale transactions is not sufficient to justify the application of a *per se* rule in one situation and a rule of reason in the other. The question remains whether the *per se* rule stated in *Schwinn* should be expanded to include nonsale transactions or abandoned in favor of a return to the rule of reason. We have found no persuasive support for expanding the *per se* rule.

★   ★   ★

In sum, we conclude that the appropriate decision is to return to the rule of reason that governed vertical restrictions prior to *Schwinn*. When anticompetitive effects are shown to result from particular vertical restrictions they can be adequately policed under the rule of reason, the standard traditionally applied for the majority of anticompetitive practices challenged under § 1 of the Act. Accordingly, the decision of the Court of Appeals is

Affirmed.

Restricting Purchases and Sales of Non-Franchisor Products

To assure uniformity and consistent quality, the franchiser will insist that its franchisees adhere to certain standards. In food franchising, for example, the franchisor will want to assure customers that the ingredients conform to the same grade throughout all selling areas. In automobile dealerships, the manufacturer will wish to exhibit only its brand. To accomplish these objectives, the franchisor will attempt to restrict its franchisees' options in purchasing raw materials and supplies or in selling products made by someone other than the franchisor.

Such restrictions are not *per se* violations of the antitrust laws. A fast-food franchisor may lawfully demand that its outlets purchase only Grade A milk or meat. The automobile manufacturer may lawfully tell its dealers that they may not sell competitors' cars.

But the ways in which franchisors may seek to assure such quality and brand identification are nearly infinite, and not every such scheme is legal. For instance, as we saw in Chapter 46, many forms of **tying agreements** are unlawful: An agreement between a tire company and a gasoline company through which the gasoline company will require its gas stations, on pain of losing their franchises if they refuse, to sell only one brand of tires violates the antitrust laws. [Federal Trade Commission v. Texaco, 393 U.S. 223 (1968)]

In the next two cases, the courts had to wrestle with these issues. In the first case, the question was whether a take-out chicken franchisor could require its outlets to purchase food supplies from the franchisor only. In the second case, the question was whether an ice-cream franchisor could prohibit its outlets from selling such foodstuffs as hot dogs and hamburgers.

SIEGEL v. CHICKEN DELIGHT, INC.
448 F.2d 43 (9th Cir. 1971)

MERRILL, CIRCUIT JUDGE: This antitrust suit is a class action in which certain franchisees of Chicken Delight seek treble damages for injuries allegedly resulting from illegal restraints imposed by Chicken Delight's standard form franchise agreements. The restraints in question are Chicken Delight's contractual requirements that franchisees purchase certain essential cooking equipment, dry-mix food items, and trade-mark bearing packaging exclusively from Chicken Delight as a condition of obtaining a Chicken Delight trade-mark license. These requirements are asserted to constitute a tying arrangement, unlawful per se under § 1 of the Sherman Act, 15 U.S.C. § 1.

After five weeks of trial to a jury in the District Court, plaintiffs moved for a directed verdict, requesting the court to rule upon four propositions of law: (1) That the contractual requirements constituted a tying arrangement as a matter of law; (2) that the alleged tying products—the Chicken Delight name, symbols, and system of operation—possessed sufficient economic power to condemn the tying arrangement as a matter of law; (3) that the tying arrangement had not, as a matter of law, been justified; and (4) that, as a matter of law, plaintiffs as a class had been injured by the arrangement.

The court ruled in favor of plaintiffs on all issues except part of the justification defense, which it submitted to the jury. On the question submitted to it, the jury rendered special verdicts in favor of plaintiffs. . . . Chicken Delight has taken this interlocutory appeal from the trial court rulings and verdicts.

Over its eighteen years existence, Chicken Delight has licensed several hundred franchisees to operate home delivery and pick-up food stores. It

(continued on next page)

(continued)

SIEGEL v. CHICKEN DELIGHT, INC.
448 F.2d 43 (9th Cir. 1971)

charged its franchisees no franchise fee or royalties. Instead, in exchange for the license granting the franchisees the right to assume its identity and adopt its business methods and to prepare and market certain food products under its trade-mark, Chicken Delight required its franchisees to purchase a specified number of cookers and fryers and to purchase certain packaging supplies and mixes exclusively from Chicken Delight. The prices fixed for these purchases were higher than, and included a percentage markup which exceeded that of, comparable products sold by competing suppliers.

In order to establish that there exists an unlawful tying arrangement plaintiffs must demonstrate *First*, that the scheme in question involves two distinct items and provides that one (the tying product) may not be obtained unless the other (the tied product) is also purchased. *Second*, that the tying product possesses sufficient economic power appreciably to restrain competition in the tied product market. *Third*, that a "not insubstantial" amount of commerce is affected by the arrangement. Chicken Delight concedes that the third requirement has been satisfied. It disputes the existence of the first two. Further it asserts that, even if plaintiffs should prevail with respect to the first two requirements, there is a *fourth* issue: whether there exists a special justification for the particular tying arrangement in question.

The District Court ruled that the license to use the Chicken Delight name, trade-mark, and method of operations was "a tying item in the traditional sense," the tied items being the cookers and fryers, packaging products, and mixes.

★   ★   ★

The hallmark of a tie-in is that it denies competitors free access to the tied product market, not because the party imposing the arrangement has a superior product in that market, but because of the power or leverage exerted by the tying product. . . .

Chicken Delight urges us to hold that its trade-mark and franchise licenses are not items separate and distinct from the packaging, mixes, and equipment, which it says are essential components of the franchise system. To treat the combined sale of all these items as a tie-in for antitrust purposes, Chicken Delight maintains, would be like applying the antitrust rules to the sale of a car with its tires or a left shoe with the right. Therefore, concludes Chicken Delight, the lawfulness of the arrangement should not be measured by the rules governing tie-ins. We disagree.

In determining whether an aggregation of separable items should be regarded as one or more items for tie-in purposes in the normal cases of sales of products the courts must look to the function of the aggregation. Consideration is given to such questions as whether the amalgamation of products resulted in cost savings apart from those reductions in sales expenses and the like normally attendant upon any tie-in, and whether the items are normally sold or used as a unit with fixed proportions.

Where one of the products sold as part of an aggregation is a trade-mark or franchise license, new questions are injected. In determining whether the license and the remaining ("tied") items in the aggregation are to be regarded as distinct items which can be traded in distinct markets consideration must be given to the function of trade-marks.

The historical conception of a trade-mark as a strict emblem of source of the product to which it attaches has largely been abandoned. The burgeoning business of franchising has made trade-mark licensing a widespread commercial practice and has resulted in the development of a new rationale for trademarks as representations of product quality. . . . As long as the system of operation of the franchisees live up to those quality standards and remains as represented by the mark so that the public is not misled, neither the protection afforded the trade-mark by law nor the value of the trade-mark to the licensee depends upon the source of the components.

This being so, it is apparent that the goodwill of the Chicken Delight trade-mark does not attach to the multitude of separate articles used in the operation of the licensed system or in the production of its end product. It is not what is used, but how it is used and what results that have given the system and its end product their entitlement to trade-mark protection. It is to the system and the end product that the public looks with the confidence that established goodwill has created.

★   ★   ★

[A]ttempts by tie-in to extend the trade-mark protection to common articles (which the public does not and has no reason to connect with the trade-mark) simply because they are said to be essential to production of that which is the subject of the trade-mark, cannot escape antitrust scrutiny.

Chicken Delight's assertions that only a few essential items were involved in the arrangement does not give us cause to reach a different conclusion. The relevant question is not whether the items are essential to the franchise, but whether it is essential to the franchise that the items be purchased from Chicken Delight. That raises not the issue of whether there is a tie-in but rather the issue of whether the tie-in is justifiable. . . .

We conclude that the District Court was not in error in ruling as matter of law that the arrangement involved distinct tying and tied products.

★   ★   ★

The District Court ruled . . . that Chicken Delight's unique registered trade-mark, in combination with its demonstrated power to impose a tie-in, established as matter of law the existence of sufficient market power to bring the case within the Sherman Act.

We agree. . . .

It can hardly be denied that the Chicken Delight trade-mark is distinctive; that it possesses goodwill and public acceptance unique to it and not enjoyed by other fast food chains.

(*continued on next page*)

(continued)

**SIEGEL v. CHICKEN
DELIGHT, INC.
448 F.2d 43 (9th Cir.
1971)**

It is now clear that sufficient economic power is to be presumed where the tying product is patented or copyrighted.

*   *   *

Chicken Delight maintains that, even if its contractual arrangements are held to constitute a tying arrangement, it was not an unreasonable restraint under the Sherman Act. Three different bases for justification are urged.

*   *   *

The third justification Chicken Delight offers is the "marketing identity" purpose, the franchisor's preservation of the distinctiveness, uniformity and quality of its product.

In the case of a trade-mark this purpose cannot be lightly dismissed. Not only protection of the franchisor's goodwill is involved. The licensor owes an affirmative duty to the public to assure that in the hands of his licensee the trade-mark continues to represent that which it purports to represent. For a licensor, through relaxation of quality control, to permit inferior products to be presented to the public under his licensed mark might well constitute a misuse of the mark.

However, to recognize that such a duty exists is not to say that every means of meeting it is justified. Restraint of trade can be justified only in the absence of less restrictive alternatives. . . .

The District Court found factual issues to exist as to whether effective quality control could be achieved by specification in the case of the cooking machinery and the dip and spice mixes. These questions were given to the jury under instructions; and the jury, in response to special interrogatories, found against Chicken Delight.

As to the paper packaging, the court ruled as matter of law that no justification existed.

> "Defendants' showing on paper packaging is nothing more than a recitation of the need for distinctive packaging to be used uniformly by all franchisees in identifying the hot foods. This was not contested. However, the admissions in evidence clearly demonstrate that the tied packaging was easily specifiable. In fact, the only specifications required were printing and color. Moreover, defendants have admitted that any competent manufacturer of like products could consistently and satisfactorily manufacture the packaging products if defendants furnished specifications. Those suppliers could have sold to the franchisees through normal channels of distribution."

We agree. One cannot immunize a tie-in from the antitrust laws by simply stamping a trade-mark symbol on the tied product—at least where the tied product is not itself the product represented by the mark.

We conclude that the District Court was not in error in holding as matter of law (and upon the limited jury verdict) that Chicken Delight's contractual requirements constituted a tying arrangement in violation of § 1 of the Sherman Act. . . . [J]udgment is affirmed.

SUSSER v. CARVEL CORPORATION
322 F.2d 505 (2nd Cir. 1964)

LUMBARD, CHIEF JUDGE (writing for the majority in part and dissenting in part).

The plaintiffs in nine actions which were tried together in the Southern District of New York appeal from the dismissal of their complaints which alleged violations of the antitrust laws and sought treble damages from the Carvel Corporation, a New York corporation which manufactures dairy and primarily soft ice cream products, its subsidiary organizations, certain of its individual officers and attorneys, and a number of its suppliers. The plaintiffs, former and present individual operators of Carvel franchise outlets in Massachusetts, Connecticut and Pennsylvania, also charged the Carvel defendants with fraudulent misrepresentations in the franchise negotiations.

. . . The plaintiffs alleged that Carvel had unlawfully fixed the prices of the retail products sold at the franchise stores and that the franchise agreements embodied tying and exclusive dealing arrangements violative of the Sherman and Clayton acts. The complaints also charged that the contracts between Carvel and the supplier defendants embodied concerted refusals to deal with the plaintiffs violative of the antitrust laws. In a pretrial order the plaintiffs stipulated that they would rely solely upon "per se" violations of the antitrust laws as shown in certain written agreements and other documents. From a judgment which, with one exception, dismissed the complaints against all the defendants on the ground that the plaintiffs had failed to prove violations of the antitrust laws, the plaintiffs appeal.

THE CARVEL FRANCHISE SYSTEM

Although the franchise operators conduct their stores as independent businessmen, through provisions in the franchise agreement Carvel is able to maintain a chain of 400 stores uniform in appearance as well as in operation. The dealer is obligated to conduct his business in accordance with a Standard Operating Procedure Manual (Manual) which governs in great detail the general operation of the store, including the types of products which may be offered for sale, the recipes for their preparation, the nature and placement of advertising displays in the store, the color of the employees' uniforms, and the hours when the store lights must be turned on. The stores are identical in design, each featuring the Carvel crown and cone trademark on a flat slanting roof, glass walls at its front, and the name "Carvel" on its sides in neon lights. This distinctive design is protected by a design patent. The ice cream, which is processed from a mix prepared from a secret formula, is dispensed from a patented machine which bears the Carvel name or trademark. The paper containers, ice cream cones, and spoons all bear the Carvel name and in some instances are unique in design.

★   ★   ★

The appellants maintain that the franchise agreements embody violations of the Sherman and Clayton acts insofar as they require the dealer to refrain from selling any non-Carvel product. . . .

(continued on next page)

(continued)

SUSSER v. CARVEL CORPORATION
322 F.2d 505 (2nd Cir. 1964)

* * *

We do not agree.

In Tampa Electric Co. v. Nashville Co., 365 U.S. 320, 81 S.Ct. 623, 5 L.Ed.2d 580 (1961), the Supreme Court held valid a contract between Tampa, a public utility, and Nashville, a medium sized coal company, which obligated Nashville to supply Tampa's entire requirements of coal over a twenty-year period—one form of an exclusive dealing arrangement. After discussing the necessity of delineating the relevant line of commerce and the geographical market, the Court noted that requirements contracts "have not been declared illegal *per se*" and . . . further emphasized the significance of the possible economic justification for the accused arrangement, in light of the legitimate reasons for employing such a device.

. . . Instead of introducing evidence to establish the economic effects of the Carvel franchise structure, [plaintiffs] merely protest that anti-competitive effects may be inferred solely from the existence of such a network of exclusive dealerships. But the whole tenor of Tampa Electric does not permit adherence to such a stringent standard of legality.

In any event, we need not rely solely upon the appellants' failure to adduce concrete evidence concerning the relevant line of commerce and geographical market and the probable anticompetitive effects of the Carvel arrangement. For in terms of at least one factor which the Supreme Court deemed significant in Tampa Electric—that of economic justification—the Carvel exclusive dealership arrangement withstands any attack on its legality.

As Judge Dawson found, "the cornerstone of a franchise system must be the trademark or trade name of a product." The fundamental device in the Carvel franchise agreement itself is the licensing to the individual dealer of the right to employ the Carvel name in his advertising displays, on the products he sells, and on the store itself. The stores are uniform in design as well as in the public display of the ice cream machinery employed, the placement of advertising displays, and the products offered for sale. The requirement that only Carvel products be sold at Carvel outlets derives from the desirability that the public identify each Carvel outlet as one of a chain which offers identical products at a uniform standard of quality. The antitrust laws certainly do not require that the licensor of a trademark permit his licensees to associate with that trademark other products unrelated to those customarily sold under the mark. It is in the public interest that products sold under one particular trademark should be subject to the control of the trademark owner. Carvel was not required to accede to the requests of one or another of the dealers that they be permitted to sell Christmas trees or hamburgers, for example, which would have thrust upon Carvel the obligation to acquaint itself with the production and sale of these items so as to establish reasonable quality controls.

Nor do the antitrust laws proscribe a trademark owner from establishing a chain of outlets uniform in appearance and operation. Trademark licensing agreements requiring the sole use of the trademarked items have withstood attack under the antitrust laws where deemed reasonably necessary to protect the goodwill interest of the trademark owner, and such agreements certainly are not unlawful *per se* under the antitrust laws. Judge Dawson was fully warranted in concluding that in the context of the entire Carvel franchise system the requirement that no non-Carvel products be sold at the retail level is reasonably necessary for the protection of Carvel's goodwill.

★   ★   ★

Accordingly, the judgments of the district court are affirmed.

Termination

A great deal of litigation has arisen over termination of franchises. A franchisor is as free to terminate its franchisee-distributors as it is to franchise them initially, which is to say that when the franchisor decides to terminate for business reasons, the law will not stand in the way. The franchisee who fails to meet sales quotas, to invest sufficient funds in the business, or to uphold quality standards will have no legal recourse if terminated for those reasons. Standard clauses in franchise agreements that permit franchisors to terminate at the end of a stated period will pass muster; in several cases, the courts have ruled that a franchisor may even terminate all its franchises and offer the franchisees employment. [Bushie v. Stenocord Corp., 460 F.2d 116 (9th Cir. 1972)]

But it sometimes happens that franchisors have terminated their franchisees for reasons that run afoul of the antitrust laws: as part of an agreement with other franchisees, for example, to divide the territory, to raise prices, or for some other unlawful objective. Because franchisees have often sunk their life savings into their business, the courts scrutinize especially carefully cases in which it is alleged that franchisors have unfairly terminated. Many federal and state laws provide additional protection to franchisees by restricting the allowable reasons for terminating or by providing a procedure by which a franchisor must act if it intends to terminate.

In the next case, the Supreme Court discusses the distinctions—such as the difference between concerted and independent actions—that are important in termination cases in which antitrust issues are raised.

MONSANTO CO. v. SPRAY-RITE SERVICE CORP.
465 U.S. 752 (1984)

Justice Powell delivered the opinion of the Court.

This case presents a question as to the standard of proof required to find a vertical price-fixing conspiracy in violation of § 1 of the Sherman Act.

Petitioner Monsanto Co. manufactures chemical products, including agricultural herbicides. By the late 1960's, the time at issue in this case, its sales accounted for approximately 15% of the corn herbicide market and 3% of the soybean herbicide market. In the corn herbicide market, the market leader commanded a 70% share. In the soybean herbicide market, two other competitors each had between 30% and 40% of the market. Respondent Spray-Rite Service Corp. was engaged in the wholesale distribution of agricultural chemicals from 1955 to 1972. Spray-Rite was essentially a family business, whose owner and president, Donald Yapp, was also its sole salaried salesman. Spray-Rite was a discount operation, buying in large quantities and selling at a low margin.

(continued on next page)

(*continued*)

MONSANTO CO. v. SPRAY-RITE SERVICE CORP.
465 U.S. 752 (1984)

Spray-Rite was an authorized distributor of Monsanto herbicides from 1957 to 1968. In October 1967, Monsanto announced that it would appoint distributors for 1-year terms, and that it would renew distributorships according to several new criteria. Among the criteria were: (i) whether the distributor's primary activity was soliciting sales to retail dealers; (ii) whether the distributor employed trained salesmen capable of educating its customers on the technical aspects of Monsanto's herbicides; and (iii) whether the distributor could be expected "to exploit fully" the market in its geographical area of primary responsibility. Shortly thereafter, Monsanto also introduced a number of incentive programs such as making cash payments to distributors that sent salesmen to training classes, and providing free deliveries of products to customers within a distributor's area of primary responsibility.

In October 1968, Monsanto declined to renew Spray-Rite's distributorship. At that time, Spray-Rite was the 10th largest out of approximately 100 distributors of Monsanto's primary corn herbicide. Ninety percent of Spray-Rite's sales volume was devoted to herbicide sales, and 16% of its sales were of Monsanto products. After Monsanto's termination, Spray-Rite continued as a herbicide dealer until 1972. It was able to purchase some of Monsanto's products from other distributors, but not as much as it desired or as early in the season as it needed. Monsanto introduced a new corn herbicide in 1969. By 1972, its share of the corn herbicide market had increased to approximately 28%. Its share of the soybean herbicide market had grown to approximately 19%.

Spray-Rite brought this action under § 1 of the Sherman Act. It alleged that Monsanto and some of its distributors conspired to fix the resale prices of Monsanto herbicides. Its complaint further alleged that Monsanto terminated Spray-Rite's distributorship, adopted compensation programs and shipping policies, and encouraged distributors to boycott Spray-Rite in furtherance of this conspiracy. Monsanto denied the allegations of conspiracy, and asserted that Spray-Rite's distributorship had been terminated because of its failure to hire trained salesmen and promote sales to dealers adequately.

The case was tried to a jury. The District Court instructed the jury that Monsanto's conduct was *per se* unlawful if it was in furtherance of a conspiracy to fix prices. In answers to special interrogatories, the jury found that (i) the termination of Spray-Rite was pursuant to a conspiracy between Monsanto and one or more of its distributors to set resale prices, (ii) the compensation programs, areas of primary responsibility, and/or shipping policies were created by Monsanto pursuant to such a conspiracy, and (iii) Monsanto conspired with one or more distributors to limit Spray-Rite's access to Monsanto herbicides after 1968. The jury awarded $3.5 million in damages, which was trebled to $10.5 million. Only the first of the jury's findings is before us today.

The Court of Appeals for the Seventh Circuit affirmed. It held that there was sufficient evidence to satisfy Spray-Rite's burden of proving a conspiracy to set resale prices. The court stated that "proof" of termination following competitor complaints is sufficient to support an inference of concerted action."

. . . We reject the statement by the Court of Appeals for the Seventh Circuit of the standard of proof required to submit a case to the jury in distributor-termination litigation, but affirm the judgment under the standard we announce today.

This Court has drawn two important distinctions that are at the center of this and any other distributor-termination case. First, there is the basic distinction between concerted and independent action—a distinction not always clearly drawn by parties and courts. Section 1 of the Sherman Act requires that there be a "contract, combination . . . or conspiracy" between the manufacturer and other distributors in order to establish a violation. Independent action is not proscribed. A manufacturer of course generally has a right to deal, or refuse to deal, with whomever it likes, as long as it does so independently. *United States v. Colgate & Co.*, 250 U.S. 300, 307 (1919). . . .

The second important distinction in distributor-termination cases is that between concerted action to set prices and concerted action on nonprice restrictions. The former have been *per se* illegal since the early years of national antitrust enforcement. The latter are judged under the rule of reason, which requires a weighing of the relevant circumstances of a case to decide whether a restrictive practice constitutes an unreasonable restraint on competition. See *Continental T.V., Inc., v. GTE Sylvania Inc.*, 433 U.S. 36 (1977).

★   ★   ★

. . . On a claim of concerted price fixing, the antitrust plaintiff must present evidence sufficient to carry its burden of proving that there was such an agreement. If an inference of such an agreement may be drawn from highly ambiguous evidence, there is a considerable danger that the doctrines enunciated in *Sylvania* and *Colgate* will be seriously eroded.

The flaw in the evidentiary standard adopted by the Court of Appeals in this case is that it disregards this danger. Permitting an agreement to be inferred merely from the existence of complaints, or even from the fact that termination came about "in response to" complaints, could deter or penalize perfectly legitimate conduct. As Monsanto points out, complaints about price cutters "are natural—and from the manufacturer's perspective, unavoidable—reactions by distributors to the activities of their rivals." Such complaints, particularly where the manufacturer has imposed a costly set of nonprice restrictions, "arise in the normal course of business and do not indicate illegal concerted action." Roesch, Inc., v. Star Cooler Corp., 671 F.2d 1168, 1172 (CA8 1982). . . .

Thus, something more than evidence of complaints is needed. There must be evidence that tends to exclude the possibility that the manufacturer and nonterminated distributors were acting independently. . . .

(*continued on next page*)

(continued)

**MONSANTO CO. v.
SPRAY-RITE SERVICE
CORP.**
465 U.S. 752 (1984)

Applying this standard to the facts of this case, we believe there was sufficient evidence for the jury reasonably to have concluded that Monsanto and some of its distributors were parties to an "agreement" or "conspiracy" to maintain resale prices and terminate price cutters. In fact there was substantial *direct* evidence of agreements to maintain prices. There was testimony from a Monsanto district manager, for example, that Monsanto on at least two occasions in early 1969, about five months after Spray-Rite was terminated, approached price-cutting distributors and advised that if they did not maintain the suggested resale price, they would not receive adequate supplies of Monsanto's new corn herbicide. When one of the distributors did not assent, this information was referred to the Monsanto regional office, and it complained to the distributor's parent company. There was evidence that the parent instructed its subsidiary to comply, and the distributor informed Monsanto that it would charge the suggested price. Evidence of this kind plainly is relevant and persuasive as to a meeting of minds.

*   *   *

If, as the courts below reasonably could have found, there was evidence of an agreement with one or more distributors to maintain prices, the remaining question is whether the termination of Spray-Rite was of or pursuant to that agreement. It would be reasonable to find that it was, since it is necessary for competing distributors contemplating compliance with suggested prices to know that those who do not comply will be terminated. Moreover, there is some circumstantial evidence of such a link. Following the termination, there was a meeting between Spray-Rite's president and a Monsanto official. There was testimony that the first thing the official mentioned was the many complaints Monsanto had received about Spray-Rite's prices. In addition, there was reliable testimony that Monsanto never discussed with Spray-Rite prior to the termination the distributorship criteria that were the alleged basis for the action. By contrast, a former Monsanto salesman for Spray-Rite's area testified that Monsanto representatives on several occasions in 1965–1966 approached Spray-Rite, informed the distributor of complaints from other distributors—including one major and influential one—and requested that prices be maintained. Later that same year, Spray-Rite's president testified. Monsanto officials made explicit threats to terminate Spray-Rite unless it raised its prices.

We conclude that the Court of Appeals applied an incorrect standard to the evidence in this case. The correct standard is that there must be evidence that tends to exclude the possibility of independent action by the manufacturer and distributor. That is, there must be direct or circumstantial evidence that reasonably tends to prove that the manufacturer and others had a conscious commitment to a common scheme designed to achieve an unlawful objective. Under this standard, the evidence in this case created a jury issue as to whether Spray-Rite was terminated pursuant to a price-fixing conspiracy between Monsanto and its distributors.

The judgment of the court below is affirmed.

Franchise Rules: An F.T.C. View

By Barnaby J. Feder

[Although the Federal Trade Commission adopted the Franchise Disclosure Rule in 1979, most states have enacted their own laws governing what information must be disclosed before selling a franchise. Because the regulation system is now so complex, an FTC commissioner has announced the possibility of a federal takeover of all franchise regulation.—AUTHORS' NOTE]

After years of grumbling, franchisers and their attorneys have gained a sympathetic ear within the Federal Trade Commission for their complaints about the "patchwork quilt" of state and Federal regulations they face.

"Maybe everything is just wonderful but I have had people come to me and say Ray Kroc couldn't get started today," said Terry Calvani, a commission member, referring to the late founder of the McDonald's Corporation. "If that's true, we have a problem."

Mr. Calvani recently began pressing state regulators to look more closely at the costs of the lack of uniformity in their laws. To the astonishment of some experts, he also raised the possibility that the F.T.C. might pre-empt state law altogether.

"The notion of Federal preemption is a bombshell," said David J. Kaufman, a partner at the New York law firm of Kaufman, Caffey, Gildin, Rosenblum & Schaeffer. Mr. Kaufman helped write New York State's franchising rules while a special deputy attorney general. The

A FEDERAL TAKEOVER OF FRANCHISE REGULATIONS

state's rules, along with those of California and Illinois, are considered to be the most stringent in the nation.

Franchising regulation grew up in response to shady franchising schemes that flourished in the 1960's and early 1970's, costing many investors their life savings. California passed the first laws in 1971. Today, 15 states have rules governing the information that must be disclosed in a prospectus before selling a franchise, 19 states have rules covering the termination of franchises and 23 states have "business opportunity" laws that cover the sale of all new businesses.

The Federal Trade Commission has its own disclosure regulations, adopted in 1979. However, unlike many state regulations, they do not require the disclosure statement to be reviewed before a sale is made and do not give franchisees the right to file a lawsuit if the disclosure statement is defective. State regulators are scornful of the Federal commitment to enforcement in the area.

"We clean things up when they come across our desk," said Sheldon Horowitz, the special deputy attorney general who is New York State's franchise section chief. "The F.T.C. waits until the horse is stolen," he said in comments made after Mr. Calvani presented his views to franchise lawyers in New York last month.

By some estimates, more than one-third of the nation's retailing sector is affecting by this welter of regulations. Franchising traces its legal

roots in the United States to the efforts of I. M. Singer & Company to sell more sewing machines in the 1850's. It became deeply established in the automobile, gasoline and soft-drink bottling businesses before World War II but did not explode as a retailing method until the rapid expansion of the service sector in the 1950's and 1960's.

The franchisers say that the varying laws covering the sale of new franchises and the varying treatment of franchise law from state to state pile needless costs on established companies while forming costly and even prohibitive barriers to newcomers.

The burdens for large franchisers are limited in many states by exemptions based on their past performance and large capitalization. Start-up franchisers are not so lucky, according to Mr. Kaufman. "I don't know about Mr. Kroc, but Colonel Sanders certainly wouldn't have been able to get Kentucky Fried Chicken franchised today with his limited resources," Mr. Kaufman said.

The National Council of Commissioners on Uniform State Laws has proposed a "Uniform Franchise and Business Opportunities Act," but both regulators and attorneys representing franchisers agree that it would never be adopted without significant amendments.

The regulators' own trade group, the North American Security Administrators Association, has also been discussing ways to introduce more uniformity in the laws. But many are wary.

"There are different ideas about what's proper to protect franchisees in different parts of the country," said Mr. Horowitz. "Uniformity isn't necessarily the best thing."

(continued on next page)

BOX 49-1

(Box 49-1 continued)

The threat of Federal pre-emption is discounted by many franchising experts. They note that, even if Mr. Calvani and his four fellow commissioners became convinced pre-emption was a good idea, it would require rule-making procedures that could last years.

"This is a proposal that business would like but taking jurisdiction of any kind away from states is a highly charged political problem," said Louis G. Rudnick, a partner at Rudnick & Wolfe in Chicago, which is special counsel to the International Franchise Association, a Washington-based trade group.

Mr. Calvani has tried to minimize such concerns by emphasizing that his main goal is an exploration of the costs of "needless diversity." Moreover, he said, any pre-emption might well be partial. The F.T.C. might want, for instance, to leave power to enforce any national rules in the hands of the states, he added.

Source: *New York Times*, Monday, March 7, 1988

DISCLOSURE REQUIREMENTS

With the growth of franchising in the 1960s, the incidence of fraud, bad faith, and unfair dealing rose dramatically. Competition grew intense, poorly informed investors signed franchise agreements with unfair or deceptive terms that could not possibly have allowed them to become profitable, celebrities agreed to lend their names to product endorsements but—unbeknownst to many franchisees—not personally to support the product or to assure its quality. As a consequence, several states enacted franchise disclosure laws, and the Federal Trade Commission adopted the Franchise Disclosure Rule in 1979. Although differing in detail, the state laws and the federal rule in general require franchisors to make a variety of disclosures about the product or service it is franchising, the nature of the business, and the type and amount of financial investment required of the franchisee. Often franchisors must make these disclosures in the form of registration statements similar to prospectuses for stock offerings filed with the SEC. In some states, registration authorities must first screen advertising of franchise opportunities. To avoid needless duplication, most states permit the filing of a Uniform Franchising Offering Circular, which calls for a host of financial and other disclosures. The FTC rule establishes minimum federal standards for disclosure, but it does not preempt tougher state laws. The federal rule is broad in coverage: the rule governs offers of "business opportunities," even if not labeled "franchise," whenever the distributor must pay the franchisor to start the business. Like the securities laws, the state and federal franchise disclosure rules are complex. The days of amateurs creating instant businesses through franchising schemes are now past; no one should attempt to establish a franchise without a thorough review by lawyers. Indeed, so complex is the system of regulation that there has begun to be talk of a federal takeover of all franchise regulation (see **Box 49-1**).

PRODUCT LIABILITY

As we saw in Chapter 19, the old law of privity of contract, which insulated a manufacturer from legal liability to the ultimate consumer of its product, has now almost completely disappeared. Strict liability theory has given product liability law a powerful impact on all who manufacture goods. For franchisors in particular, the development of strict liability has meant that the franchisor cannot, through agreements with its franchisees, automatically disclaim liability when something goes wrong with the product—whether it is defective meat sold in a fast-food outlet or a defective automobile sold by a dealer. Whether a franchisor will be held liable depends in large part on the degree of control it exercises over how the product is manufactured and sold. In the next case, involving an exploding soda bottle, the question was whether the Seven-Up Company, the franchisor, was liable because its agreement gave it control over the design of the carton in which the bottle was sold.

KOSTERS v. SEVEN-UP CO.
595 F.2d 347 (6th Cir. 1979)

MERRITT, CIRCUIT JUDGE.

    ★   ★   ★

    The defendant, the Seven-Up Company, appeals from a $150,000 jury verdict awarded for injuries caused by an exploding 7-Up bottle. The plaintiff removed a cardboard carton containing six bottles of 7-Up from a grocery shelf, put it under her arm and headed for the check-out counter of the grocery store. She was blinded in one eye when a bottle slipped out of the carton, fell on the floor and exploded, causing a piece of glass to strike her eye as she looked down. The 7-Up carton was a so-called "over-the-crown" or "neck-thru" carton designed to be held from the top and made without a strip on the sides of the carton which would prevent a bottle from slipping out if held underneath.

    The carton was designed and manufactured by Olinkraft, Inc. Olinkraft sold it to the Brooks Bottling Company, a franchisee of the defendant, Seven-Up Company. Seven-Up retains the right to approve the design of articles used by the bottler, including cartons. The franchise agreement between Seven-Up and the Brooks Bottling Company requires that "cases, bottles, and crowns used for 7-Up will be of a type . . . and design approved by the 7-Up Company," and "any advertising . . . material . . . must be approved by the 7-Up Company before its use by the bottler."

    Using an extract provided by Seven-Up, Brooks produced the beverage and poured it into bottles. After securing Seven-Up's approval of the design under the franchise agreement, Brooks packaged the bottles in cartons selected and purchased by Brooks from various carton manufacturers, including Olinkraft. Brooks then sold cartons of 7-Up to stores in some 52 Michigan counties, including Meijers Thrifty Acres Store in Holland, Michigan, where the plaintiff picked up the carton and carried it under her arm toward the checkout counter. Plaintiff settled her claims against the bottler, the carton manufacturer and the grocer for $30,000.

    Seven-Up denied liability, insisting its approval of the cartons was only of the "graphics" and for the purpose of assuring that its trademark was properly displayed.

    ★   ★   ★

    Seven-Up Company concedes that a franchisor, like a manufacturer or supplier, may be liable to the consumer for its own negligence, without regard to privity, under the doctrine of *MacPherson v. Buick Motor Co*. Seven-Up contends, however, that it does not carry the liabilities of a supplier when it did not supply the product and that other theories of strict tort liability do not apply. Liability may not be laid on the basis of implied warranty, it says, when the franchisor did not manufacture, handle, design or require the use of the particular product. The precise question before us here is whether Michigan's principles of "strict accountability" for breach of implied warranty extend to a franchisor who retains the right of control over the product (the carton) and specifically consents to its distribution in the form sold but

(*continued on next page*)

(continued)

KOSTERS v. SEVEN-UP CO.
595 F.2d 347 (6th Cir. 1979)

does not actually manufacture, sell, handle, ship or require the use of the product.

Different questions may arise in other franchising contexts. In some instances, the franchisor may not retain the right of control or may not actually approve the form of the product. The franchisee may sell a product contrary to the instructions or without the knowledge of the franchisor. The consumer may attempt to hold the franchisor liable for the conduct of the franchisee under the agency doctrines of *respondeat superior* or apparent authority. We do not deal with these questions here.

In this case, the Seven-Up Company not only floated its franchisee and the bottles of its carbonated soft drink into the so-called "stream of commerce." The Company also assumed and exercised a degree of control over the "type, style, size and design" of the carton in which its product was to be marketed. The carton was submitted to Seven-Up for inspection. With knowledge of its design, Seven-Up consented to the entry in commerce of the carton from which the bottle fell, causing the injury. The franchisor's sponsorship, management and control of the system for distributing 7-Up, plus its specific consent to the use of the carton, in our view, places the franchisor in the position of a supplier of the product for purposes of tort liability.

We are not saying that the Seven-Up Company is absolutely liable as an insurer of the safety of the carton under the theory of implied warranty, simply by virtue of its status as a franchisor. In the first place, under Michigan's theory of implied warranty of fitness, the carton must be found to be "defective," or as the District Judge more accurately put it, "not reasonably safe." It must be harmful or unsafe because something is wrong with it, and the jury must so find. Moreover, here the franchisor inspected the carton and approved it. Thus, we need not reach the question whether the franchisor would carry the liabilities of a supplier if it had not been made aware of the product and given the opportunity to assess the risks.

When a franchisor consents to the distribution of a defective product bearing its name, the obligation of the franchisor to compensate the injured consumer for breach of implied warranty, we think, arises from several factors in combination: (1) the risk created by approving for distribution an unsafe product likely to cause injury, (2) the franchisor's ability and opportunity to eliminate the unsafe character of the product and prevent the loss, (3) the consumer's lack of knowledge of the danger, and (4) the consumer's reliance on the trade name which gives the intended impression that the franchisor is responsible for and stands behind the product. Liability is based on the franchisor's control and the public's assumption, induced by the franchisor's conduct, that it does in fact control and vouch for the product.

These are factors Michigan courts have relied on in the past in determining who may be held liable for breach of implied warranty of fitness in other products liability situations. We believe Michigan courts would apply these principles in the franchising situation presented by this case, and we therefore conclude that the case was correctly submitted to the jury to assess liability for breach of implied warranty.

[Reversed on other grounds and remanded.]

The *Kosters* case establishes that the franchisor can be liable for failure of the franchisee to assure a safe product. The reverse is also true: franchisees may be liable to some extent for failures of the franchisor. Suppose, for example, that an automobile manufacturer ships a batch of cars with defective steering wheels and that the defect is visible to the dealer on arrival. The dealer cannot avoid liability by pointing to the manufacturer's legal responsibility to manufacture safe cars. Beginning in the late 1970s, however, many states have enacted statutes requiring franchisors to indemnify franchisees for defects that originated with the franchisor or that were produced because the franchisee was required to follow specific instructions from the franchisor in assembly or repair.

is not carefully worded or if the franchisor controls too tightly how the franchisee is to operate the business, the franchisor may discover that the franchisee has become its agent for whose acts the franchisor is responsible in accordance with the agency principles covered in Chapter 38. If the franchisee is held to be an agent, the franchisor may wind up being held liable for the franchisee's debts, unpaid wages, and even, under certain circumstances, sales and other taxes. Whether a franchisee is an agent of the franchisor is ultimately a question of fact for the jury to decide, not a legal question that can be answered in the abstract by a court, as the next case shows.

LIABILITY OF FRANCHISOR FOR FRANCHISEE'S ACTS

The franchisor may assume that its franchise is simply a distributor of its products. But if the agreement

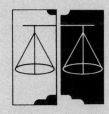

RILEY v. FORD MOTOR CO.
442 F.2d 670 (5th Cir. 1971)

ALDISERT, CIRCUIT JUDGE. A jury awarded the purchaser of a 1969 Lincoln Mark III automobile $30,000 in damages against Ford Motor Company for breach of warranty and negligent repair of certain defects. Appellant Ford insists that the district court erred in withdrawing from the jury the question whether the dealer acted as its agent, and argues that the damages were excessive as a matter of law. Having concluded that both contentions are correct, we must reverse and remand the cause for a new trial.

Appellee purchased his new automobile from a Florida dealer at a cost of $8,476.00, and Ford issued a self-styled "New Vehicle Warranty." Shortly thereafter he took the car to Robinson Brothers, an Alabama Ford dealer, for repair of a window and removal of a noise in the rear end. According to Riley these defects were not corrected. At trial he testified that in the weeks following the requested repairs, and before the car was returned to Robinson Brothers for further repairs, these additional malfunctions developed: air conditioning did not work, speed control did not function, power seats became inoperative, the radio aerial functioned spasmodically, the rear seat did not fit, headlight panels were not synchronized, the cigarette lighter was missing, windshield wipers were defective, engine knocked upon acceleration, the transmission did not function properly, gear shift lever would not function, and the left door would not close properly.

(*continued on next page*)

(continued)

RILEY v. FORD MOTOR CO.
442 F.2d 670 (5th Cir. 1971)

Dissatisfied with the car's condition, appellee wrote to Ford setting forth in detail his complaints, and requesting Ford "to direct me to a dealer employing trained service personnel, or furnish me with someone capable of overseeing service personnel available in order to insure that the defects in my automobile are properly corrected in an expert and dependable manner." Ford dispatched a Technical Service Representative who road tested the automobile, agreed that it was not functioning properly, and offered to take it to Robinson Brothers where he would personally supervise its repair. The owner believed he had a better idea. Refusing to again leave his car with Robinson's, he brought this action against Ford seeking recovery on two theories: breach of warranty and negligent repair.

Because the negligence count is predicated on the alleged negligence of Robinson Brothers, recovery against Ford depends on showing that the dealer was, in fact, an agent of the manufacturer. The evidence on this issue was conflicting. The contract between Ford and Robinson Brothers provided:

> The agreement does not, in any way, create a relationship of principal and agent between the company and the dealer and under no circumstances shall the dealer be considered to be the agent of the company. The dealer shall not act or attempt to act or represent himself directly or by implication as agent of the company or in any manner assume or create or attempt to assume or create any obligation on behalf of or in the name of the company.

Furthermore, Ford owned no stock in the dealership, paid no portion of its employees' salaries, paid no rental for the building it occupied, and had no employees stationed there for supervision or control. It is undisputed, however, that Robinson Brothers sent its mechanics to Ford's training school, received "factory campaign notices" relating to particular problems with certain models, and sold Lincoln-Mercury automobiles manufactured by Ford.

During the re-direct examination of William H. Robinson, the court interrupted testimony regarding the agency issue:

> I can't help what is in that contract. If Lincoln sells a car and says we warrant it, I don't care what is in the contract. They are acting for Ford Motor Company.

In this diversity action, we are referred to Alabama law for the relevant substantive law principles which will govern this case. It has long been the law of Alabama that "the question of agency is a matter of fact, which it is the province of the jury to determine upon, under the instructions of the court." That the district court, by its statement, "[t]hey are acting for Ford Motor Company," effectively removed the issue of agency from the jury is clear. It is equally evident that this amounted to reversible trial error.

★   ★   ★

Reversed and remanded for a new trial.

CHAPTER SUMMARY

Although differing in legal consequences from state to state, in general a franchise is created when a contract calls for a franchisee to pay a fee for the right to sell trademarked goods in a manner the franchisor substantially prescribes. The principal types of franchises are distributorships, business-format franchises, and manufacturing plants. Not all supplier-distributor relations are necessarily franchises. Other types include consignment, independent contracting, independent retail dealerships, concessions, and leases.

The franchisor's control over its trademark, trade name, or commercial symbol lies at the heart of the franchise operation. In general, the franchisor has the right to dictate to its franchises how the franchisor's intangible property rights will be used. The right to do so is subject to a large exception—one that the antitrust laws have laid down.

The franchisor may select or terminate franchisees at will unless its refusal to select a franchisee or its decision to terminate one was the consequence of an agreement violating the antitrust laws or other federal and state laws that protect franchisees.

Although allocations of territory among competitors (horizontal allocations) are *per se* violations of the Sherman Act, vertical allocations the franchisor imposes on its distributor network are not necessarily violations; the courts will follow the rule of reason before striking them down. Within antitrust limits, franchisors may also assure uniformity and consistent quality by insisting that its franchisees adhere to standards. These standards may, for example, prohibit franchises from selling products not made by the franchisor. Again, the courts follow the rule of reason and will permit the franchise practice to stand if a sound business reason can justify it.

An increasing number of states and the Federal Trade Commission regulate the promotion and sale of franchise opportunities. These laws and the FTC's Franchise Disclosure Rule generally require filing of franchise disclosure statements akin to securities registration statements.

Franchisors will generally be liable for injuries stemming from defective products, unless the assembly, installation, or repair of the product is entirely within the control of the franchisee. Franchisees may also be held liable for product defects. Whether a franchisor is liable for acts of its franchisees beyond product safety concerns depends on whether the franchisees are in fact agents of the franchisor.

KEY TERMS

Franchise	p. 1093
Territorial restriction	p. 1095
Tying agreements	p. 1099

SELF-TEST QUESTIONS

1. Franchising is a:
   (a) corporate relationship
   (b) partnership relationship
   (c) contractual relationship
   (d) common-law relationship
2. Which of the following is true? A franchisor may by contract require all franchisees to:
   (a) pay royalties on its patents forever
   (b) keep its trade secrets confidential forever
   (c) remain a franchisee forever
   (d) buy all of their supplies from the franchisor forever
3. Vertical territorial restrictions are:
   (a) unlawful *per se*
   (b) permissible under circumstances spelled out in section 1 of the Sherman Act
   (c) subject to a rule of reason
   (d) none of the above
4. A franchisor may always terminate a franchisee:
   (a) for whatever reasons it wants
   (b) as long as it has at least one other franchisee in the territory
   (c) to ensure that its other franchisees have exactly the territories they want
   (d) for sound business reasons
5. A franchisor may be responsible for actions taken by its franchisees because of:
   (a) agency law
   (b) product liability law
   (c) contract law
   (d) all of the above

DEMONSTRATION PROBLEM

Guitars, Inc., manufactures an expensive acoustical guitar and sells nationwide through a chain of franchised retail stores called Guitar-O. Throughout the 1980s, business was booming and Guitars, Inc., headquartered in El Paso, Texas, was licensing a new outlet at the rate of about one per week. In 1990, however, as the economy softened, sales began to fall off and several of the retailers pressed Guitars, Inc., to do something to help their sagging profit margins. After extensive discussions with a group of Guitar-O stores in each state, Guitars, Inc., has decided to refashion its operations by eliminating 25 percent of its stores. It has appointed the three leading Guitar-O stores in each state to decide which franchisees to terminate in that state. Is there some legal difficulty with this plan? Is there an alternative way Guitars, Inc., could accomplish the same purpose?

PROBLEMS

1. Tastee Tidbits, a national chain of snack foods, requires its distributors to buy all ingredients from a subsidiary of the parent franchisor. The franchisor also requires all 387 distributors to use the Tastee Tidbits logo and to sell Tastee's foodstuffs in distinctive huts built in the shape of a popcorn kernel. The franchise agreement specifies the cooking conditions and instructs the franchises to build their kitchens to exacting specifications. The agreement also says that each franchisee is "an independent entity for purposes of paying all taxes, hiring all personnel, and establishing all lines of bank credit." Last month Tastee Tidbits introduced Cheesy-Spicearoma, a new snack food (consisting of garlic, onions, cinnamon, and pepperoni), that it advertised extensively nationwise. Several dozen people in fourteen states became violently ill after eating a portion of Cheesy-Spicearoma and have sued the local Tastee Tidbits outlets and the parent corporation. What legal defenses, if any, do the local outlets have? What defenses, if any, does the parent franchisor have?

2. Boomerang Brothers is a manufacturer of a toy that was once a hot item in stores nationally. But lately its appeal has been waning. Boomerang had been selling its product to wholesalers for resale to general department stores and also through a chain of distributors that stocked only Boomerang's products. As sales declined, one of Boomerang's distributors suggested to the national sales manager that Boomerang stop selling to the department stores and create a single franchise in each state to market the toys. Now the sales manager discusses the idea with the company's top executives, all of whom are enthusiastic about the idea. So they announce that effective January 1, they will stop selling to department stores and will terminate all but one distributor in each state. The remaining distributor in each state will have an exclusive territory within the state to market the toys. Distributors who have been cut off file suit. With what legal violations, if any, can they charge Boomerang Brothers? What defenses, if any, does Boomerang have?

3. Ears-of-Plenty, Inc. sells juicy corn on the cob, fresh from farms daily. It requires its franchised outlets to purchase all their corn requirements from a subsidiary company organized to supply corn to all franchisees. Under the franchise agreement, the franchisees must have a variety of condiments, including butter and salt, available for customers. For more than ten years, Ears-of-Plenty has prospered selling only the delicious ears of corn. One day the Ears-of-Plenty franchise in Duluth, Minn., decides to enhance its profits by offering some other foodstuffs for sale, including fresh green vegetables, special sauces and dips, and ice cream and chocolate sauce. Ears, Inc., the franchisor, sends a letter to the Duluth franchisee, instructing it to stop selling all vegetables, sauces, dips, and ice cream. When the franchisee refuses, Ears, Inc. terminates the franchise. The Duluth outlet sues, charging the franchisor with antitrust violations. What result?

SUGGESTED ANSWER TO DEMONSTRATION PROBLEM

Although the Supreme Court has recently made clear, following *Continental T.V.*, (p. 1095), *Business Electronics* (p. 1032) and *Monsanto* (p. 1105), that vertical allocation of territories is not unlawful *per se* under section 1 of the Sherman Act, what Guitars, Inc., has proposed to do is not simply a vertical allocation. Had it unilaterally decided which franchisees to terminate then its decision would be a vertical one—manufacturer and supplier to distributor. Instead, Guitars has proposed a scheme for a horizontal allocation: allowing competing franchisees to make the decision. That is a clear violation of section 1 and both the franchisees and Guitars, Inc., would be liable to criminal prosecution and civil suits for damages. To terminate franchisees lawfully, Guitars must devise a method that does not require the agreement of competitors. For example, if it decided that the reason for termination was the contracting marketplace, then it might make sense for it to decide unilaterally to terminate the lowest 10 percent of its retailers measured by sales volume. As long as the terminations were not carried out to support a price level, even if done in order to benefit other franchisors, it may do so lawfully under the antitrust laws.

CHAPTER 50

International Legal Aspects of Doing Business

With the phenomenal growth of foreign trade and international business since World War II, the astute executive must be aware that the legal environment has an important international aspect. This international legal reality is extremely complex, because it involves three—and sometimes four—separate, though interlocking systems of law: American law, international law, and the law of the other country in which the company is doing business. The fourth system might be that of a regional association of allied countries, such as the European Common Market. In this chapter we can do no more than highlight certain basic implications of this set of interlocking legal systems.

FUNDAMENTALS OF INTERNATIONAL LAW

The Framework

As is true of any national legal system, American law deals in part with the concerns of foreigners—individual aliens who live here and foreign corporations that do business in the United States. But the international aspects of domestic law are not what is ordinarily considered **international law**. The latter is usually thought of as law that transcends national borders and that resides in some truly *inter*national sphere, some realm of affairs that governs the discourse among nations. Though such principles do exist, they require national legal systems for their observance, for there is no truly international enforcement agency. The International Court of Justice (ICJ), which was created by the United Nations and which sits in The Hague to hear cases between nations, does so only with the consent of the different nations. So international law, while real, has a different character than the law we have studied up to now, for it requires the courts of each nation to give it effect, even though it might conflict with the interests of nationals of those countries. That is a difficult burden to lay on the courts of many nations, and international law therefore meets an uneven reception around the world.

In the United States, **treaty obligations** are the

law of the land. Under Article 6 of the Constitution (the "Supremacy Clause"), any conflict between state law and federal treaties must be resolved in favor of the treaties. Although it is sometimes said that treaties create international law, their nature is perhaps closer to that of contracts: rights and obligations that flow from treaties are akin to the rights and duties created by any contract, whether between private parties or nations.

International law, in the sense of law declared by a "sovereign," is more elusive, for in the modern world, only nation-states are sovereign in the sense intended. There is no supranational state or government. The United Nations is a creature of treaty. Nevertheless, there is a supranational legal order, at least in the sense that most nations recognize certain international practices and customs, as demonstrated by the international blockade in 1990 against Iraq under a U.N. resolution adhered to by most nations of the world. These international customs include age-old conventions, such as the immunity from prosecution of diplomats in foreign jurisdictions and the mileage limit establishing a nation's territorial waters—which for centuries had been three miles and during the 1970s went to 200 miles. Other sources of international law include the rules spelled out in international treaties and the "general principles of law recognized by civilized nations," as one of the rules governing the ICJ declares. This latter source was drawn on, for example, at Nuremberg after World War II in judging high Nazi officials for "crimes against humanity."

The former source, that of treaties, is increasingly voluminous. A substantial number are bilateral; that is, treaties between two nations. But a significant number are multilateral, signed by at least three and sometimes dozens or nearly all nations. In substance, treaties range from protecting migratory birds to declaring the rights of traveling nationals, enforcing court judgments in other nations, and fixing the method of imposing customs taxes.

To differing degrees, the domestic courts of the nations invoke and respect international law. In the United States, the federal courts, led by the Supreme Court, take account of international law and principles in appropriate cases. Most international law applicable in the United States has recently been summarized in the 1986 revised Restatement of the Foreign Relations Law of the United States. The re-

sult in most cases involving foreign concerns is a blend of international and national principles. However, two very important points should be noted: (1) In the event of a conflict between a U.S. treaty obligation and the Constitution, the Constitution must prevail. [Reid v Covert, 354 U.S. 1 (1957)] (2) In the event of a conflict between a treaty and rights declared under a federal law enacted after the treaty was signed, the courts are obliged to give effect to the federal statute, even though that might mean that the United States will have breached its treaty obligations. [Edye v. Robertson (The Head Money Cases), 112 U.S. 580 (1884)]

Some International Problems in American Courts

Sovereign Immunity   It is a basic rule of international law, recognized by the federal courts, that foreign nations may not be sued without their consent. The principle of **sovereign immunity** dates back 175 years. In *The Schooner Exchange* v. *McFaddon,* (U.S. 7 Cr.) 116 (1812), the question was whether a French warship could be seized by American citizens claiming to be its true owners. (They alleged that Napoleon had seized the ship on the high seas in violation of international law; when it came into the port of Philadelphia seeking repairs, they sued for its return.) Chief Justice Marshall refused to sanction any taking by the Americans, noting that France and the United States were friendly and that the port was open to all. "National ships of war, entering the port of a friendly power open for their reception, are to be considered as exempted by the consent of that power from its jurisdiction," said Marshall. In *Ex parte Republic of Peru,* 318 U.S. 578 (1943), the Supreme Court laid down two supporting principles: (1) whether or not the courts have jurisdiction over the case, sovereign immunity still applies; and (2) the State Department has the final word on whether the property in question belongs to the foreign country; if it does, the courts must accept the Department's certification of that fact and dismiss the case.

In the early 1950s, the U.S. State Department made a critical distinction between two types of sovereign immunity. The first type confers immunity for anything that a foreign country does. The second type looks to the character of the act. If the country has acted in its sovereign or public capacity, then it is immune. But if its act was private, then it is not entitled to immunity from legal process. The State Department said that it would refuse to certify to the courts that a country should be granted immunity if it commits private acts that violate domestic law.

This basic change in policy came about with the growth of government-backed businesses that competed around the world with American business. Of course, the question remains: How can public acts be distinguished from private ones? Different criteria have been advanced: For example, can the act be undertaken only by nations and not by private individuals? An example of the former might be price regulation, an example of the latter, the selling of commodities. The trouble with this and other distinguishing criteria is that they break down quickly in real cases into semantic squabbling. Many countries, for example, operate oil companies as instrumentalities of the state, whereas in the United States oil companies are private. If an enterprise is private in the United States, must American courts consider a like enterprise owned by a foreign government private for purposes of immunity? The usual answer is no. Government operations are public and immune. In *Stone Engineering Co. v. Petroleos Mexicanos*, 42 A.2d 57 (Pa. 1945), a case involving a wholly-owned Mexican government petroleum company certified by the Secretary of State as immune from suit, the court said: "It is irrelevant here that the foreign instrumentality conducts a commercial enterprise which, it was contemplated, would show a profit. Even if that had present relevancy, the enterprise was for the development of the trade and commerce of the foreign government and to supply revenues for its treasury—appropriate concerns of that government."

Suppose the State Department has been silent. In *Victory Transport, Inc.* v. *Comisaria General*, 336 F.2d 354 (2d. Cir. 1964), the U.S. Court of Appeals in New York said that it would not recognize claims of immunity in the absence of a formal declaration from the State Department, except for acts in the following categories: (1) internal administrative acts such as an expulsion of an alien; (2) legislative acts, such as nationalization (that is, the expropriation of property); (3) acts concerning the armed forces; (4) acts concerning diplomatic activity; and (5) public loans.

The Foreign Sovereign Immunities Act of 1976   In 1976, Congress entered the sovereign immunity scene for the first time by enacting the Foreign Sovereign Immunities Act. To a large extent, this act tidies up the messy legal situation that had prevailed. In many circumstances it provides complete immunity, even for illegal acts. For example, during the conflict between Argentina and Great Britain over the Falkland islands, a commercial ship chartered in Liberia was bombed in an unprovoked attack in neutral waters by Argentinean aircraft, a clear violation of international law. Unable to obtain judicial relief in Argentina, the shipping corporation sued in federal district court in New York under the Alien Tort Act, permitting civil suits by aliens for torts "committed in violation of the law of nations or a treaty of the United States." The Supreme Court ordered the suit dismissed, holding that the Foreign Sovereign Immunities Act absolutely bars courts from exercising jurisdiction when a foreign state is entitled to immunity and that unless specifically exempted in the Act, all actions of a foreign state, even violations of international law, are immune from suit in the United States. [Argentine Republic v. Amerada Hess Shipping Corp., 488 U.S. 428 (1989)]

In the commercial arena, however, the Foreign Sovereign Immunities Act incorporated a narrowed theory of immunity into American law—commercial activities of foreign governments are not immune from suit. Under Section 1605, "A foreign state shall not be immune from the jurisdiction of courts of the United States or of the States in any case . . . in which the action is based upon a commercial activity carried on in the United States . . . [or upon certain acts performed in or outside the United States] . . . in connection with a commercial activity . . . elsewhere and that act causes a direct effect in the United States." The expropriation of private property located in the foreign nation is not a commercial activity, but a contract to buy provisions or equipment for a foreign country's armed services or to construct a government building constitutes a commercial activity. Likewise, "activities such as a foreign government's sale of a service or a product, its leasing of property, its borrowing of money, its employment or engagement of laborers, clerical staff or public relations or marketing agents, or its investment in a security of an American corporation, would be among those included within the definition" of a commercial activity. (H.Rep.No. 487, 94th Cong., 2d Sess. 16 (1976)) The activity that gives rise to a legal claim need not have occurred in the United States. American courts have jurisdiction over foreign countries if the commercial activity abroad has a "direct effect" in this country.

The act also sets out several other exceptions to sovereign immunity concerning property located in the United States. The courts have long held that property of a foreign sovereign may not be seized to satisfy a judgment, even if the sovereign had waived immunity or was otherwise subject to suit. The 1976 act continues the immunity from seizure, unless the property is used for a commercial activity in the United States. For example, automobiles used by embassy drivers in Washington could not be seized to pay off a judgment against one of the drivers for causing an accident (nor could the embassy building be attached), but if the foreign country had purchased a shipload of grain, that could be seized. Problems encountered by one U.S. citizen who attempted to seize Soviet property are discussed in **Box 50-1.**

The Foreign Sovereign Immunities Act also permits foreign countries to be sued in cases "in which rights in property taken in violation of international law are in issue and that property . . . [or its proceeds] is present in the United States." This exception seems to suggest that an uncompensated expropriation, a clear violation of international law, would not only subject the foreign sovereign to jurisdiction of American courts, but also would subject the property to seizure in the event that the plaintiffs won on the merits, at least for those classes of property covered by the 1976 act. The Supreme Court has not yet ruled definitively on this question.

Expropriation and the "Act of State" Doctrine   As the foregoing suggests, a foreign country may **expropriate** (or nationalize) private property and be immune from suit in the United States by the former owners, who might wish to sue the country directly or to seek an **order of attachment** against property in the United States owned by the foreign country. In the United States, the government may constitutionally seize private property under certain circumstances, but under the Fifth Amendment it must pay "just compensation" for any property so taken. Frequently, however, foreign governments have seized the assets of American corporations without recompensing them for the loss. Sometimes the foreign government seizes all private property in a certain in-dustry, sometimes only the property of American citizens. If the seizure violates the standards of international law—as, for example, by failing to pay just compensation—the question arises whether the former owners may sue in U.S. courts. One problem with permitting the courts to hear such claims is that by time of suit the property may have passed into the hands of bona fide purchasers, perhaps even in other countries.

The Supreme Court has enunciated a doctrine governing claims to recover for acts of expropriation. This is known as the **Act of State** doctrine. As the Supreme Court put it in 1897: "Every sovereign State is bound to respect the independence of every other sovereign State, and the courts of one country will not sit in judgment on . . . [and thereby adjudicate the legal validity of] . . . the acts of the government of another done within its own territory." [Underhill v. Hernandez, 168 U.S. 250, 252 (1897)] This means that American courts will "reject private claims based on the contention that the damaging act of another nation violates either American or international law." [Mannington Mills, Inc. v. Congoleum Corp., 595 F.2d 1287 (3rd Cir. 1979)]

Sovereign immunity and the Act of State doctrine rest on different legal principles and have different legal consequences. The doctrine of sovereign immunity bars a suit altogether: once a foreign government defendant shows that sovereign immunity applies to the claims the plaintiff has raised, the court has no jurisdiction even to consider them and must dismiss the case. By contrast, the Act of State doctrine does not require dismissal in a case properly before a court; indeed, the doctrine may be invoked by plaintiffs as well as defendants. Instead, it precludes anyone from arguing against the legal validity of an act of a foreign government. In a simple example, suppose a widow living in America is sued by her late husband's family to prevent her from inheriting his estate. They claim she was never married to the deceased. She shows that while citizens of another country, they were married by proclamation of the foreign legislature. Although legislatures do not marry people in the United States, the Act of State doctrine would bar a court from denying the legal validity of the marriage entered into in their home country.

The Supreme Court's clearest statement came in a case growing out of the 1960 expropriation of American sugar companies operating in Cuba. A sugar

Painful Shot of Sovereign Immunity

By George Archibald, Charlotte Low

[Problems arise for plaintiffs who attempt to seize the property of a foreign sovereign. Under the Foreign Sovereign Immunities Act, unless the property is used for a commercial activity in the United States, such property cannot be seized to satisfy a court judgment.—
AUTHORS' NOTE]

A U.S. citizen sues the Soviet government in a U.S. federal court when a business deal with the Soviets goes sour. The Soviets are served with legal papers but ignore them, so the U.S. citizen wins a $413,000 default judgment without having to go to trial. Deafening silence from the Soviets.

The U.S. citizen then obtains court orders for seizure of Soviet assets in the United States to satisfy the judgment. Federal marshals grab the typewriter of an Izvestia reporter. Then a federal judge orders a bank to freeze a $450,000 account held by a Soviet government entity.

Suddenly, the Kremlin takes an interest in the suit. The Soviets engage a team of lawyers to ask the judge to set aside the default judgment so their side of the case can be heard. The U.S. citizen would get another chance to prove his case but might lose this time around.

The State Department also enters the lawsuit. To back the claims of the U.S. citizen, right?

Wrong.

Welcome to the delicate, diplomatic world of the lawsuit against a foreign government. The rules are different from those in any other kind

SUING A FOREIGN GOVERNMENT

of litigation. If the suit interferes with what are perceived as optimum U.S. relations with a foreign government, the plaintiff could be out of luck.

"The U.S. government doesn't want to have private citizens interfering with its diplomatic games," says a lawyer. "Otherwise, every Soviet emigre, every guy detained in a gulag would be suing once he got over here. Nobody wants that. They'd start having their people sue us, for oppressing the masses or whatever it may be."

Such could be the case with Raphael Gregorian, a 56-year-old businessman in Palo Alto, Calif. For 14 years, Gregorian had a multimillion-dollar business in the Soviet Union as a sales representative for manufacturers of heart-lung machines and kidney dialysis equipment.

But in late 1984, the Soviet Ministry of Foreign Trade revoked his license. In a Nov. 18, 1984, article, the Soviet newspaper Izvestia accused Gregorian of selling outdated equipment and trying to get from unspecified Soviet agencies information "of interest to American intelligence."

Claiming the ouster ruined his California International Trade Corp., Gregorian brought a $320 million libel and breach-of-contract suit against Izvestia and the trade ministry in a Los Angeles federal court in January 1985. The Soviet government, although apparently properly served with legal papers, declined to respond or mount any kind of defense.

The default judgment awarded last June by U.S. District Judge David V. Kenyon—now up to about

$460,000 with interest—included $163,000 for medical equipment the Soviets allegedly received but did not pay for and $250,000 in libel damages.

In a highly publicized move, Gregorian's lawyer, Gerald L. Kroll of Los Angeles, got federal marshals to attach a Cyrillic-script manual typewriter at the home of Izvestia reporter Leonid Koryavin in Chevy Chase, Md.

But only after Kroll and the rest of his team of lawyers located a $456,413.34 account in the name of the Soviet government's Bank for Foreign Trade and Kenyon ordered the account frozen Nov. 25 did the Soviets file their request to reopen the case.

Kenyon has not yet ruled in a Jan. 28 hearing on the Soviets' request, although he has allowed the Bank for Foreign Trade to enter the case to contest the ownership of the funds, on deposit with the Bank of America's International Trade Division in New York City. What galls Kroll is that U.S officials have got involved in the case—and not on his client's side.

The State Department filed two documents called "statements of interest," direct appeals from the executive to the judicial branch. One was lodged in a New York federal court, where the Soviets initially tried to unfreeze the account, the other in Kenyon's court. In one affidavit, Thomas W. Simons Jr., deputy assistant secretary for European affairs, said the libel judgment had become a major "irritant" to U.S.-Soviet relations, particularly in arms control and trade areas.

*   *   *

(continued on next page)

BOX 50-1

(Box 50-1 continued)

Worse still, says Kroll, State and Justice officials are also helping the Soviets in a suit by Izvestia against Gregorian in a Moscow court. The Justice Department dispatched U.S. marshals to California to serve Gregorian with Soviet papers in connection with the suit. Retaliatory suits are not unusual plays in the hardball of business litigation, but Kroll says the U.S. government should not be making it so easy for the Soviets to proceed against a U.S. citizen.

*   *   *

Gregorian's problems stem from difficulties inherent in litigation against foreign governments. Until recent decades, no government, domestic or foreign, could be sued in any court without its consent. This doctrine of "sovereign immunity" stems from the ancient notion that the king could do no wrong, but it is still very much alive. Even now, injured parties can bring tort suits against most federal, state and local government entities only because special statutes allow them to do so.

Several decades ago, many European courts began relaxing the doctrine of sovereign immunity to allow merchants to sue governments that reneged on commercial contracts. The U.S. government was one of the last to follow, enacting the Foreign Sovereign Immunities Act in 1976.

The act's provisions are narrow, however, and they generally allow foreign governments to be sued only in commercial disputes. Torts, such as libel, that injure someone's person or reputation may not be covered by the act. Some lawyers believe the law may not even cover contract violations that are not strictly commercial (that is, for the sale of goods). To be on the safe side, "when one of our firm's clients enters into a contract with a foreign government, I always include a clause waiving sovereign immunity," explains Barry Sanders, an international trade lawyer with the firm Latham & Watkins in Los Angeles.

Paradoxically, says Davis R. Robinson, legal adviser to the State Department from 1981 to 1985, one of the purposes of the act was to "get the executive branch out of the business of filing statements of interest." Before the act, observers say, every time a suit was filed against a government, the foreign power would ask the department for a statement of interest, usually to urge the judge to throw out the suit.

But although most governments around the world now routinely accede to U.S. court jurisdiction in trade disputes, there are notable exceptions that cling to the old, absolutist version of sovereign immunity: the Soviet Union, the People's Republic of China and a number of Third World nations. When these countries are sued in foreign courts, international lawyers say, they often simply pretend that the suits do not exist.

*   *   *

Source: *Insight*, February 16, 1987

broker had entered into contracts with a wholly owned subsidiary of Compania Azucarera Vertientes-Camaguey de Cuba (C.A.V.), whose stock was principally owned by American residents. When the company was nationalized, sugar sold pursuant to these contracts had been loaded onto a German vessel still in Cuban waters. To sail, the skipper needed the consent of the Cuban government. That was forthcoming when the broker agreed to sign contracts with the government which provided for payment to a Cuban bank, rather than to C.A.V. The Cuban bank assigned the contracts to Banco Nacional de Cuba, an arm of the Cuban government. However, when C.A.V. notified the broker that in its opinion C.A.V. still owned the sugar, the broker agreed to turn the proceeds of the sale over to Sabbatino, appointed under New York law as receiver of C.A.V.'s assets in the state. Banco Nacional de Cuba then sued Sabbatino, alleging that the broker's refusal to pay Banco the proceeds amounted to common law conversion.

The federal district court held for Sabbatino, ruling that if Cuba had simply failed to abide by its own law, C.A.V.'s stockholders would have been entitled to no relief. But because Cuba violated international law, the federal courts did not need to respect its act of appropriation. The violation of international law, the court said, lay in Cuba's motive for the expropriation, which was retaliation for President Eisenhower's decision to lower the quota of sugars that could be imported into the United States, and not for any public purpose that would benefit the Cuban people; moreover, the expropriation did not provide for adequate compensation and was aimed at American interests only, not those of other foreign nationals operating in Cuba. The U.S. Court of Appeals affirmed the lower court's decision, holding that federal courts may always examine the validity of a foreign country's acts.

In *Banco Nacional de Cuba* v. *Sabbatino*, 376 U.S. 398 (1964), the Supreme Court reversed, relying on the Act of State doctrine. This doctrine refers, in the words of the Court, to the "validity of the public acts a recognized foreign sovereign power commit[s] within its own territory." If the foreign state exercises its own jurisdiction to give effect to its public interests, however the government defines them, the expropriated property will be held to belong to that country or to bona fide purchasers. For the doctrine to be invoked, the act of the foreign government must have been completely executed within the country; for example, by having enacted legislation expropriating the property. The Supreme Court said that the Act of State doctrine applies even though the United States had severed diplomatic relations with Cuba and even though Cuba would not reciprocally apply the Act of State doctrine in its own courts.

As with the sovereign immunity doctrine, so the Act of State doctrine has lately come—perhaps—to have an exception for purely commercial activities. In *Alfred Dunhill of London, Inc.* v. *Republic of Cuba*, 425 U.S. 682 (1976), the Court apparently held that the Act of State doctrine does not apply when the governmental acts implicate commercial activities. In a plurality opinion subscribed to by four justices, the Court said that "the concept of an act of state should not be extended to include the repudiation of a purely commercial obligation owed by a foreign sovereign or by one of its commercial instrumentalities."

Despite its consequences in cases of expropriations, the Act of State doctrine is relatively narrow. As the next case shows, it does not apply merely because a judicial inquiry in the United States might embarrass a foreign country or even interefere politically in the conduct of American foreign policy.

W.S. KIRKPATRICK & CO., INC. v. ENVIRONMENTAL TECTONICS CORP.
110 S.Ct. 701 (1990)

JUSTICE SCALIA delivered the opinion of the Court.

In this case we must decide whether the act of state doctrine bars a court in the United States from entertaining a cause of action that does not rest upon the asserted invalidity of an official act of a foreign sovereign, but that does require imputing to foreign officials an unlawful motivation (the obtaining of bribes) in the performance of such an official act.

The facts as alleged in respondent's complaint are as follows: In 1981, Harry Carpenter, who was then Chairman of the Board and Chief Executive Officer of petitioner W. S. Kirkpatrick & Co., Inc. (Kirkpatrick) learned that the Republic of Nigeria was interested in contracting for the construction and equipment of an aeromedical center at Kaduna Air Force Base in Nigeria. He made arrangements with Benson "Tunde" Akindele, a Nigerian citizen, whereby Akindele would endeavor to secure the contract for Kirkpatrick. It was agreed that, in the event the contract was awarded to Kirkpatrick, Kirkpatrick would pay to two Panamanian entities controlled by Akindele a "commission" equal to 20% of the contract price, which would in turn be given as a bribe to officials of the Nigerian Government. In accordance with this plan, the contract was awarded to petitioner W. S. Kirkpatrick & Co., International (Kirkpatrick International), a wholly owned subsidiary of Kirkpatrick; Kirkpatrick paid the promised "commission" to the appointed Panamanian entities; and those funds were disbursed as bribes. All parties agree that Nigerian law prohibits both the payment and the receipt of bribes in connection with the award of a government contract.

(continued on next page)

(continued)

**W.S. KIRKPATRICK &
CO., INC. v.
ENVIRONMENTAL
TECTONICS CORP.**
110 S.Ct. 701 (1990)

Respondent Environmental Tectonic Corporation, International, an unsuccessful bidder for the Kaduna contract, learned of the 20% "commission" and brought the matter to the attention of the Nigerian Air Force and the United States Embassy in Lagos. Following an investigation by the Federal Bureau of Investigation, the United States Attorney for the District of New Jersey brought charges against both Kirkpatrick and Carpenter for violations of the Foreign Corrupt Practices Act of 1977 and both pleaded guilty.

Respondent then brought this civil action in the United States District Court for the District of New Jersey against Carpenter, Akindele, petitioners, and others, seeking damages under the Racketeer Influenced and Corrupt Organizations Act, the Robinson-Patman Act, and the New Jersey Anti-Racketeering Act. The defendants moved to dismiss the complaint under Rule 12(b)(6) of the Federal Rules of Civil Procedure on the ground that the action was barred by the act of state doctrine.

. . . The District Court concluded that the act of state doctrine applies "if the inquiry presented for judicial determination includes the motivation of a sovereign act which would result in embarrassment to the sovereign or constitute interference in the conduct of foreign policy of the United States." Applying that principle to the facts at hand, the court held that respondent's suit had to be dismissed because in order to prevail respondents would have to show that "the defendants or certain of them intended to wrongfully influence the decision to award the Nigerian Contract by payment of a bribe, that the Government of Nigeria, its officials or other representatives knew of the offered consideration for awarding the Nigerian Contract to Kirkpatrick, that the bribe was actually received or anticipated and that 'but for' the payment or anticipation of the payment of the bribe, ETC would have been awarded the Nigerian Contract."

The Court of Appeals for the Third Circuit reversed. . . .

This Court's description of the jurisprudential foundation for the act of state doctrine has undergone some evolution over the years. . . . Some Justices have suggested possible exceptions to application of the doctrine, where one or both of the foregoing policies would seemingly not be served: an exception, for example, for acts of state that consist of commercial transactions, since neither modern international comity nor the current position of our Executive Branch accorded sovereign immunity to such acts; or an exception for cases in which the Executive Branch has represented that it has no objection to denying validity to the foreign sovereign act, since then the courts would be impeding no foreign policy goals.

. . . We find it unnecessary, however, to pursue those inquiries, since the factual predicate for application of the act of state doctrine does not exist. Nothing in the present suit requires the court to declare invalid, and thus ineffective as "a rule of decision for the courts of this country," the official act of a foreign sovereign.

In every case in which we have held the act of state doctrine applicable, the relief sought or the defense interposed would have required a court in the United States to declare invalid the official act of a foreign sovereign performed within its own territory. . . . In *Sabbatino,* upholding the defendant's claim to the funds would have required a holding that Cuba's expropriation of goods located in Havana was null and void. In the present case, by contrast, neither the claim nor any asserted defense requires a determination that Nigeria's contract with Kirkpatrick International was, or was not, effective.

Petitioners point out, however, that the facts necessary to establish respondent's claim will also establish that the contract was unlawful. Specifically, they note that in order to prevail respondent must prove that petitioner Kirkpatrick made, and Nigerian officials received, payments that violate Nigerian law, which would, they assert, support a finding that the contract is invalid under Nigerian law. Assuming that to be true, it still does not suffice. The act of state doctrine is not some vague doctrine of abstention but a *"principle of decision* binding on federal and state courts alike." As we said in *Ricaud,* "the act within its own boundaries of one sovereign State . . . becomes . . . a rule of decision for the courts of this country." Act of state issues only arise when a court *must decide*—that is, when the outcome of the case turns upon—the effect of official action by a foreign sovereign. When that question is not in the case, neither is the act of state doctrine. This is the situation here. Regardless of what the court's factual findings may suggest as to the legality of the Nigerian contract, its legality is simply not a question to be decided in the present suit, and there is thus no occasion to apply the rule of decision that the act of state doctrine requires. . . .

★   ★   ★

The short of the matter is this: Courts in the United States have the power, and ordinarily the obligation, to decide cases and controversies properly presented to them. The act of state doctrine does not establish an exception for cases and controversies that may embarrass foreign governments, but merely requires that, in the process of deciding, the acts of foreign sovereigns taken within their own jurisdictions shall be deemed valid. That doctrine has no application to the present case because the validity of no foreign sovereign act is at issue.

The judgment of the Court of Appeals for the Third Circuit is affirmed.

Compensation for Expropriations

Some expropriating countries make a bow toward the legal necessity of recompensing those whose property has been taken. Sometimes the compensation is legislated in the same act that expropriates the property. Sometimes the compensation is negotiated directly between the United States and the expropriating country. In 1949, Congress established the U.S. Foreign Claims Settlement Commission, with jurisdiction to determine the validity of claims by American residents arising out of foreign expropriations. If the United States succeeds in negotiating a lump sum payment from the foreign company that nationalized American citizens' property, the Commission will pay it out to those whose claims have been validated.

More recently, some countries have bowed to political pressures and agreed to submit expropriation claims to arbitration. Even the most outspoken political enemies of the United States, Libya and Iran, have participated in arbitrations—in Libya's case, in claims arising out of its nationalization of oil companies in the early 1970s; in Iran's case, in claims arising out of a wave of expropriations following the revolution of Ayatollah Khomeini in 1979. Throughout the 1980s, especially in arbitrations heard by the Iranian Claims Tribunal in The Hague, several arbitration panels have held that a country's right to nationalize is matched by its legal obligation to provide compensation based on something more than net book value. The appropriateness of compensation will remain a hotly-contested issue throughout the 1990s.

The Hickenlooper Amendment

Under the "Hickenlooper Amendment" to the Foreign Assistance Act of 1962, the President must suspend economic aid or other assistance to any country whose government has expropriated property of American citizens or otherwise seriously interfered with it—for example, through confiscatory taxation or discriminatory operating conditions amounting to expropriation—unless the country compensates the owners for it. American aid may not be resumed until the president is satisfied that appropriate steps are being taken to recompense the owners or to remove the confiscatory taxes or burdensome controls. As **Box 50-2** suggests, the Hickenlooper Amendment can strike with severity against countries bent on uncompensated takings.

Bilateral Investment Treaties

The United States protects private investment in some countries through bilateral "investment" treaties negotiated separately with each government. A clause in these treaties states that "each party shall permit and treat investment, and activities associated therewith, on a basis no less favorable than that accorded in like situations to investment or associated activities of its own nationals or companies, or of nationals or companies of any third country, whichever is the most favorable." In other words, if the government will not expropriate its own citizens' property without compensating them, it may not do likewise to the property of U.S. nationals. The United States has be-

gun to negotiate such treaties with a host of countries, including Egypt, Panama, Senegal, and Haiti, though to date, no treaty has been ratified in the Senate.

Overseas Private Investment Corporation To encourage private investment abroad, especially in countries with an annual per capita income of $520 or less, Congress has established the Overseas Private Investment Corporation, which insures American business abroad against the risk of expropriation, incontrovertibility of the local currency into dollars, and loss from war or revolution. To qualify for OPIC benefits, the investment must be made by an American citizen or by a company that is substantially beneficially owned by U.S. citizens (usually 50 percent or more). If property is nationalized, OPIC will not automatically honor claims to pay the insurance; the company must first seek a remedy in the expropriating country.

COMPARATIVE REVIEW OF LEGAL SYSTEMS

As important as are general considerations of international law, no business can afford to ignore the legal systems of particular nations in which it is in business or with whose nationals it is engaged in trade. The world is a place of many rules; American rules, even in the United States, are not the only ones to govern. In this text, we can provide only a thumbnail sketch of some different legal systems.

The Anglo-American System

Most countries that are today members of the British Commonwealth have adapted the common-law system to their own use. The common-law system also operates in many countries formerly colonized by Great Britain. These include Canada, Australia, India, and many African nations. Unlike England, which to this day does not have a written constitution, most of these nations have adopted a formal written constitution, but their judiciaries are not always fully independent of the executive authority.

Unlike the United States, which has only one class of lawyer, most other common law countries, includ-

LAW AND LIFE

BOX 50-2

Kalamazoo Firm's Claim Is Largest of Those Blocking Long-Term U.S. Aid

By Nancy Benac

[In retaliation for expropriation of American property by other countries, the President of the United States, under the "Hickenlooper Amendment," must suspend economic aid or assistance to that country. This is an immense price for some countries to pay; the long-term effects of such an act can be devastating for the development of the Third World.—AUTHORS' NOTE]

WASHINGTON—A decade-old standoff between the government of drought-stricken Ethiopia and a Michigan company whose plant was seized after a Marxist takeover is the main unsettled claim blocking all but emergency U.S. aid to that East African nation.

Paul Todd, a former congressman and current president of the Kalamazoo Spice Co., said Monday that his company has an $11 million claim against Ethiopia.

Todd said that was the largest chunk of roughly $30 million that U.S. individuals and companies said they lost when Marxist military rulers seized power and nationalized foreign-owned property in 1974.

THE HICKENLOOPER AMENDMENT AND FOREIGN AID

The company's plant near Addis Ababa began operation in 1970, extracting paprika, red and black peppers and tumeric, and employed about 30–40 Ethiopians when it was seized, he said.

"They just send you a letter saying, 'We're taking over,'" Todd said. "It was a total surprise."

Under a law enacted by Congress "developmental" aid from the U.S. government for efforts such as road-building, agricultural rehabilitation and education is barred to nations that have taken over U.S. property without adequately compensating owners or making a "good-faith effort" to do so.

The only U.S. aid that can be given to such countries under the so-called Hickenlooper amendment is emergency or "humanitarian" assistance, according to the State Department.

Rep. Mickey Leland, D-Texas, who chairs the House Select Commission on Hunger and returned from a trip to Ethiopia last week, said he would meet with U.S. claimants to discuss their grievances and work to resolve the claims.

"The U.S. could be doing a whole lot more" to help Ethiopia if the claims were settled, Leland said Monday, but added that the blame for the stalemate lies as much with Ethiopia's government as with anyone else.

⋆   ⋆   ⋆

Todd said he'd seen no "softening" by the Ethiopian government toward his company's claim, adding that the next move must come from them. A source with the Foreign Affairs Commission, who asked not be identified, said Kalamazoo Spice probably would be willing to settle for less than $4 million.

He said the company had no intention of agreeing to a less-than-satisfactory settlement just to start long-term aid flowing toward the nation.

"It's unfair for them to expect Americans to make all the concessions," he said.

Agreeing to forgo just compensation would discourage American businesses from investing money in foreign countries and would be a "poor principle" that is "not in the interest of the development of the Third World," Todd said.

"In the short run it's very hard to say why don't we just turn the other cheek," he conceded, but insisted that the long-term effects of such a move would hurt developing nations.

Source: *Ann Arbor News*, December 5, 1984, B5

ing Great Britain, have two classes: solicitors and barristers. Solicitors are "office lawyers"; they see clients in their offices, draw up legal instruments such as wills, and give advice, but they do not represent clients in most courts. Those who actually litigate in court are called barristers. They do not actually serve the parties directly. Barristers are retained by the solicitors, not by the clients, and so they come more directly under the control of courts than do their American counterparts.

The Continental System

In Europe, quite a different legal system developed. In classical times, Roman law spread throughout most of the known world. After the collapse of Rome and the breakup of Europe into dozens of countries and principalities, the unifying force of the Roman law was lost, and each political jurisdiction evolved its own quite different set of laws. Frequently the law within each country was tangled and inconsistent. This was true well into the eighteenth century. Voltaire wrote that in traveling through France one would come across a different set of laws as often as one changed horses. (One type of law did contain common elements from country to country: the **law merchant,** which was virtually the only functioning type of international law in medieval Europe; many of its elements were imported into the common law during the eighteenth century.)

Finally in the early nineteenth century, under the personal sponsorship of Napoleon, the law was **codified**—that is, rationalized and written down in the form of a code—in France. The spirit of the Napoleonic Code spread to other countries, where further reforms were made. **Continental law,** as European law is generally known, has been largely imported into South America, though each country has made procedural and substantive modifications over the course of time. The continental legal system survives today in vestigial form in Louisiana, which was still under French control while the Napoleonic Code was being drafted. Although the Louisiana private law stems from the continental rather than the common law tradition, the state's legal system has been heavily transformed by American constitutional requirements.

Two principal differences between common law and continental law are worth noting. The continental criminal law system is **inquisitorial** rather an **accusatorial.** The accusatorial system is our own adversary system, in which the public prosecutor accuses the defendant and must then meet a heavy burden of proof in open court. The prosecutor in our system may not question the accused against his wishes, and the accused has the legal right to representation by a lawyer who can help him plan his defense from the first moment he is arrested. In the inquisitorial system, the accused has far fewer rights to consult with a lawyer. The prosecutor has the power to hold the accused incommunicado and to question him at length without counsel present. The defendant has much less power to control the process of fact-gathering or the course of the trial than his American or English counterpart.

The second difference worth noting is that of the power of courts to make law. The continental law codes spell out legal relations and rights in much more detail than is true in the common law countries, where the law resides in judicial precedents. Theoretically, the law is complete and courts need not interpret. They simply look up the law and apply it to the facts of the case. In fact, no law can be completely given and so courts do need to fill in gaps. But their decisions do not serve as precedents the way they do in common law countries. The trial judge is much freer to interpret the law afresh; he is much less bound by the decisions of the higher courts.

Communist Legal Systems and the Revolutions of 1989

Throughout much of the 20th century, the legal systems and law of the Soviet Union, much of Eastern Europe, and China were alien to the common-law tradition in both spirit and substance. Though they contained many Western forms—such as constitutions, courts, and legislatures—in practice these institutions were fundamentally different. Despite the language of the constitutions, separation of powers was unknown because under Communism all government is subject to the will of the party. Nor can the party-dominated nation tolerate a true adversary system; the Communist lawyer is employed by the state, not the individual, though in some civil proceedings lawyers can be retained and be paid by individual clients. The judiciary is not independent, and though the party does not dictate the outcome of most cases—it has more pressing work to do—it does direct the verdict in criminal cases in which it takes an interest. The norm of responsiveness (p. 48) is thus missing: the judge need pay no attention to the proofs offered and the arguments made. Again, though Communist constitutions have spelled out what appear to be individual rights, these were granted at the sufferance of the state and tolerated only so long as they were exercised consistent with the "interests" of the state, as defined by party policy.

In 1989, a historic revolution swept across the

face of Eastern Europe and the Soviet Union, unshacking those nations from the iron hand of party members and party ideology. If not quite dead, communism lay mortally wounded as nation after nation scrambles to establish a market system to repair its shattered economy, and to devise new legal systems that will permit the economic system to operate. How these legal systems develop will be one of the most urgent and momentous stories of the 1990s. The difficulties these nations face is formidable, for as **Box 50-3** suggests, evolving market systems must mesh not only with domestic cultural norms but also a world market from which so many of these nations had long been divorced.

Even China, which clings tenaciously and brutally to its Communist political and legal system, has had to consider modernizing its legal system and harmonizing its laws with the world's. During the Chinese Great Cultural Revolution of the 1960s, the only law school in China was shut down and lawyers played no role in the affairs of the country. Today, as China once again looks toward the West, law schools have opened, a legal profession is developing, and codes of law are being drafted. This should not be surprising: commerce requires a common approach to legal problems; without it, trade and business cannot function.

Enforcing Judgments and Resolving Disputes Abroad

Conducting business around the world is risky, and perhaps the riskiest part is depending upon the legal process of other legal systems. Seeking legal satisfaction in a foreign court against a citizen or domestic company of that country can be perilous. Even if a judgment has been rendered in a U.S. court, two-thirds of the world's judicial systems will refuse to enforce it, or will impose stringent conditions on its enforcement. Some of our closest allies—for example, Australia and the United Kingdom—have been stung by the purported reach of our antitrust laws, and have enacted specific legislation barring the enforcement of American antitrust judgments upon the declaration of the nation's attorney general. Some efforts have been made through bilateral and multilateral treaties to regulate the enforcement of foreign judgments. In this regard, American courts are far more liberal than those in most other countries. State and federal courts will

routinely and conclusively recognize and enforce judgments issued by foreign courts, unless a strong public policy in the American jurisdiction prohibits it.

For this reason, most business executives prefer arbitration to resolve disputes that may arise over a contract or otherwise in the course of business. Nations of all political and ideological persuasions, including Eastern-bloc countries and China, have enacted legislation recognizing arbitration as an acceptable means of deciding disputes. Perhaps the broadest authority is the 1958 United Nations Convention on the Recognition and Enforcement of Foreign Arbitral Awards. The convention requires each adherent to enforce arbitration awards made in proceedings undertaken by arbitral clauses in the underlying contracts between the disputing parties. The convention also provides some escape clauses—for example, if enforcement of the award would be contrary to public policy of the country in which enforcement is sought. Thus, until 1983, public policy in the United States precluded parties from agreeing by contract to arbitrate a dispute over whether a patent was valid. But the Supreme Court has ruled that even a dispute that may not be legally arbitrable in the United States must be arbitrated when called for in specific private contracts. [Mitsubishi Motors Corp. v. Soler Chrysler-Plymouth, Inc., 473 U.S. 614 (1985)]

In many countries, domestic law spells out the procedures that must be followed in order for the courts to enforce any resulting award. The parties may by contract choose the set of rules under which they prefer to arbitrate. Since the publication in 1976 of the **UNCITRAL** (United Nations Commission on International Trade Law) **rules,** more and more countries are permitting their courts to enforce judgments made pursuant to them. The UNCITRAL rules allow the parties to choose their own arbitrators or, failing agreement, permit the Secretary-General of the Permanent Court of Arbitration at The Hague to select the arbitrators from a list of arbitrators maintained there.

In making international deals, more and more lawyers are insisting that their corporate clients incorporate "forum selection" and "choice of law" provisions in the arbitral clauses of the contract. The forum selection provision cites the country (and frequently the city) the arbitration will be heard in, and which set of procedural rules the arbitration will be subject

LAW AND LIFE

Soviet Law: Creaky and Uncharted

By Deborah Stead

*[The historic revolution in Eastern Europe and the Soviet Union which released these nations from the iron hand of party membership and ideology in 1989 has left a shattered economy and a murky legal system in its wake. American law firms, with offices in the Soviet Union, struggle to clarify Soviet law by meshing it with the laws of the United States.—*AUTHORS' NOTE]

MOSCOW—At Baker & McKenzie's office just off Pushkin Square, the phones are modern. But as one of the four lawyers there put it, "They're hooked into the Soviet system, so we're at the mercy of that."

The same might be said of the level of commercial law practiced by American firms here. It is sophisticated, especially by Soviet standards,

MESHING THE LAWS OF THE U.S. AND U.S.S.R.

but eventually it must hook up with the Soviet legal system—and that connection is not easy.

"The Soviets publish their laws sporadically and with great delay, so you hear about drafts through rumor, through the grapevine," said Mark Vecchio, a 31-year-old Columbia Law School graduate who is with the Moscow branch of New York-based Coudert Brothers. "You have to be in touch constantly." Coudert's clients include Estée Lauder.

Clarifying the Law

Paul Melling, a 33-year-old British lawyer who has headed Chicago-based Baker & McKenzie's office here since it opened last year, says he keeps up with legal changes "mostly through friends who are Soviet lawyers and

through reasonably good contacts with the ministries." He also reads the Soviet newspapers Pravda and Izvestia every day. (Like most of the other lawyers at American firms here, he is fluent in Russian and has an interest in Soviet culture.)

Clarifying the law, which, the lawyers say, is especially murky on currency and property deals, is a preoccupation for the dozen-or-so lawyers working for the American firms here: Coudert; Baker & McKenzie; Chadbourne & Park of New York, and Steptoe & Johnson of Washington.

Their latest concern is the country's move toward economic and political decentralization, which produced a jumble of new laws and new domains that sometimes clash. "Our office now spends 30 percent of its time on problems of legality and authority," said Richard Dean of Coudert, who has headed the Moscow office since it opened in January 1988, a year after the passage of the joint-venture law that allowed foreign in-

---

to. The forum selection clause specifies the national law that will apply—for example, "This contract shall be governed in all respects by the law of (Japan) (New York) (Belgium) (Kansas) (People's Republic of China)." Courts in different countries are split on whether to recognize and enforce these provisions, but the growing tendency is to presume the clauses valid in the absence of certain factors that would make their enforcement unreasonable—such as substantial geographic inconvenience to the parties, unavailability of appropriate relief in the forum selected, or fraud, duress, misrepresentation, or abuse of power in prompting a party to agree to the particular forum or body of law. United States courts will enforce both types of provisions in the absence of the factors just listed.

FOREIGN COMMERCIAL LEGAL SYSTEMS

Generally

Obviously, the firm doing business abroad must always be mindful of the legal system of each country in which it operates. But in the past quarter century, supranational, regional legal regimes have been established in virtually every part of the world to regulate commercial transactions that flow across the borders of member countries. The abbreviated list gives some flavor of the range of cooperation being attempted among countries around the world:

BOX 50-3

vestment in the Soviet Union if a Soviet partner was involved. Foreigners can now invest here without Soviet partners as a result of a decree issued recently by President Mikhail S. Gorbachev.

For example, Pepsico, which Baker & McKenzie represents, recently had its two Pizza Hut restaurants in Moscow temporarily closed. A newspaper said the outlets were caught in a crossfire between local authorities.

Space Shortage
Beyond the body of law are other challenges. Office space is cramped, and commercial rents are as high as $75 a square foot, more than twice Manhattan rates. Other challenges include an apartment shortage, a dearth of experienced Soviet lawyers and a recent spate of political and economic crises that could make the most stalwart Western client jumpy.

Perhaps the biggest challenge is learning how to negotiate commercial deals in the Soviet Union. Soviet law-

yers are gaining business and international experience, and some have even gone through American Bar Association training classes. But they and their clients have long been isolated from the legal traditions of free-market societies.

"The Soviet side sometimes won't get basic stuff, like calling an entity the same thing throughout the contract; they may say, 'Let's vary it; it's getting boring,' " said Robert Langer, a 30-year-old graduate of Tulane Law School who is the American lawyer at Chadbourne, Hedman, Raabe & Union of Soviet Advocates CCCP—a joint venture of American, Finnish, Austrian and Soviet lawyers.

Sometimes, to the horror of American lawyers, the Soviets will simply bring a sample contract with blank spaces for names, dates and products and suggest that it be used as the legal basis for a joint venture.

Most Soviet lawyers believe there is a "standard way of doing things, that it's not possible to diverge from that standard without causing your-

self difficulties," said Alexander Papachristou, a 32-year-old Harvard Law School graduate at Steptoe's joint-venture firm, Lex International. (U.S. Sprint and Du Pont are two clients from the American side; Lex, the private law firm on the Soviet side of the venture, brings the Bolshoi Ballet, among others.)

Lack of Understanding
Mr. Papachristou and others say the uncharted commercial climate here often makes them act as business strategists for clients, and in this role they come up against other problems.

Confidentiality, for example, "New Soviet businesses don't understand about trade secrets," said Aleksandr Minakov, Mr. Papachristou's Soviet colleague at Lex International. "When we do joint ventures with them, we have to be sure to put in a non-disclosure clause."

★   ★   ★

Source: *New York Times*, November 5, 1990, p. D1

European **Common Market** (EEC) (see Figure 50-1), whose members are Belgium, Denmark, France, Germany, Greece, Ireland, Italy, Luxembourg, Netherlands, Portugal, Spain, and the United Kingdom—with trade barriers falling in 1993, the Common Market countries are truly a "single market" larger than that of the United States (in population);
Economic and Customs Union of Central Africa (UDEAC), which includes Cameroon, Central African Republic, Chad, Congo, and Gabon;
East African Community (EAC), Kenya, Tanzania, and Uganda;
Economic Community of West African States (ECOWAS), Dahomey, Gambia, Ghana, Guinea, Guinea-Bissau, Ivory Coast, Liberia, Mali, Mauritania, Niger, Nigeria, Senegal, Sierra Leone, Togo, and Burkina Faso;
Caribbean Community (CARICOM), Barbados, Belize,

Dominica, Jamaica, Trinidad-Tobago, Grenada, St. Kitts-Nevis-Anguilla, St. Lucia, and St. Vincent;
• Andean Common Market (ANCOM), Bolivia, Colombia, Ecuador, Peru, and Venezuela, and
• Association of Southeast Asian Nations (ASEAN), Brunei, Indonesia, Malaysia, Philippines, Singapore, and Thailand.

These economic communities, and others, are attempts to break down tariff and other legal and economic barriers among their member countries, and to permit the free (or at least freer) flow of goods, capital, and workers. To varying degrees, each has conferred legislative, executive, and judicial authority on representative institutions created under the charters that established the communities. To cite the most

Figure 50-1   European Economic Community (EEC)

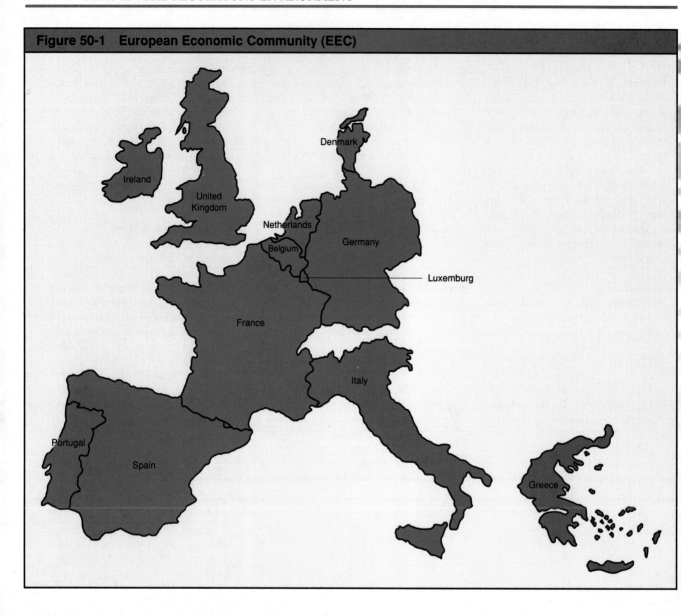

developed community, the Common Market has established the EEC Commission, which can issue regulations and decisions binding on all member countries; the Assembly, which supervises the Commission and consists of representatives elected directly in the member countries; and the Court of Justice, which hears cases involving enforcement of Commission regulations (and may interpret the provisions of the EEC's basic charter, the Treaty of Rome). Many of the "laws" of these economic communities—that is, the treaty provisions that called the communities into

being—restrict the nature and amount of foreign investment within the community.

EEC Competition Rules

The Common Market is moving closer toward the American conception of antitrust. Articles 85 and 86 of the Treaty of Rome correspond, very roughly, to Sections 1 and 2 of the Sherman Act. The EEC Commission has the authority to investigate on its own or upon complaints by any interested party or member country. The Commission may impose fines, issue injunctions, and cancel contracts. Article 85 prohibits any contract that prevents, restricts, or distorts competition or that may potentially do so. One exception not allowed under American antitrust law is for agreements that contribute to technological, production, or distribution improvements—assuming that they do not substantially eliminate competition in the particular goods in question. Despite these and a few other exceptions, Article 85 broadly prohibits price fixing, limitations on production and marketing, price discrimination, and conditioning a contract with terms unrelated to the object of the contract as, for example, a tying agreement would do.

Article 86 prohibits one or more companies with dominant positions in any market from abusing their economic position if so doing would affect trade between member countries. Under a 1978 decision, the Court of Justice said that a market share of 40 percent is sufficient to fall within Article 86. And the relevant market may be narrowly drawn. In *Europemballage Corp. & Continental Can Co.* v. *EEC Commission, 2 CCH Comm. Mkt. Rep.* 8171 (EECJ 1973), the Court ruled that metal lids for glass jars comprised a separate market.

Commission regulations permit the issuance of "negative clearances" for company practices that might be questionable; the negative clearance certifies that no grounds for prosecution exist. The Commission may also exempt certain otherwise unlawful prices on "notification" by a company. Exemption may last for up to ten years, but it applies only in the particular case and is not to be considered a precedent for other companies desiring to do the same thing. Despite these loopholes, the Commission and Court have increasingly issued regulations and applied rules resembling antitrust principles, as discussed in Chapters 46 and 47.

THE UNITED STATES IN WORLD TRADE

Tariffs

From time immemorial, the nations of the world have acted to protect their local industries by imposing customs duties on incoming goods and quotas on what might enter at all. These duties and quotas could vary from country to country. To obtain the most favorable terms, many countries enter into bilateral treaties guaranteeing them "most-favored nation" status. A most-favored nation clause assures that the signatory will be subject to no higher duties or lower quotas than those granted to the country most favorably treated. Thus, one clause in the 1850 Treaty of Friendship between the United States and Switzerland says that "each of the contracting parties hereby engages not to grant any favor in commerce to any nation, union of nations, State, or society, which shall not immediately be enjoyed by the other party."

From time to time, groups of nations join customs unions or establish free trade areas. At the present time, the most ambitious attempt to open up trade throughout the world is the General Agreement on Tariffs and Trade (**GATT**), to which 100 countries subscribe. For twenty years, participants in GATT have negotiated various "rounds" (negotiating sessions usually lasting several years—the Tokyo Round lasted from 1973 to 1979) to reduce customs duties and other burdensome tariffs by some 70 percent. Trade agreements negotiated by the United States are subject to the Trade Expansion Act of 1962 and the Trade Act of 1974, which grant the president substantial authority to enter into trade agreements and negotiate and grant concessions to other countries in the various GATT rounds.

GATT provides each signatory most-favored nation treatment—with some exceptions for preferential treatment that can be granted to developing nations. In general, GATT prohibits discrimination in import regulations and seeks to eliminate quantitative import limitations, However, the GATT articles provide several "safety valves" to protect a country against sudden increases in imports that could seriously affect domestic industries, and each nation is permitted to ban trade that affects vital national interests, such as public morals (for example, drug traffic) and national treasures (for example, ancient artifacts). Another escape clause permits a country to hike up import duties "to safeguard its external financial position and its balance of payments." GATT also deals, in complex ways, with product safety and licensing standards that can be manipulated to bar certain products from entering a national market. Finally, GATT rules cover customs declarations, procedures, and valuations, though the specifics are beyond the scope of this text.

Antidumping Laws

Just as within multiple local markets a manufacturer facing no competition in one might lower his price in the other markets in order to drive out competitors, so in international trade a seller might "dump" his products in a foreign market at lower prices than he sells at home, if his home market is protected against encroachments from abroad. In 1916, Congress enacted the first of a number of **antidumping** laws, which permitted the federal government to raise import duties on goods declared to be in violation of the law. Under the Trade Agreements Act of 1979, the Secretary of the Treasury must first determine that a class or kind of foreign merchandise is being sold or is likely to be sold in the United States at less than its fair value. The International Trade Commission (ITC), an arm of the Department of Commerce, must then determine whether an American industry has been materially injured, is being threatened with significant harm, or has been retarded because of imports of the goods. If the ITC makes such a finding, then the Secretary of the Treasury, after public notice, may impose antidumping duties on the offending goods.

The Trade Agreement Act of 1979 also permits the government to impose "countervailing duties" on imported goods if those goods were produced in a foreign country with the aid of a governmental subsidy. Determining whether a governmental program is in fact a subsidy, however, can be a difficult undertaking. Suppose that the foreign country taxes goods made by its citizens but remits the taxes if the goods are sold abroad. Is the remittance a hidden subsidy, subjecting the goods to imposition of a countervailing duty in the United States? In *Zenith Radio Corp.* v. *United States*, 437 U.S. 443 (1978), the Supreme Court said no, holding against the American company.

Export Exemption from the Antitrust Laws: The Webb-Pomerene Act

To combat foreign cartels that could more efficiently sell their goods abroad than could American companies competing with each other, Congress in 1918 enacted the Webb-Pomerene Act, shielding cooperative marketing efforts by American *exporters* from the antitrust laws. Any acts or agreements by associations of export traders are immune from prosecution or suit

under the Sherman Act, provided that the associations are not (1) restraining trade within the United States, (2) restraining the export trade of American competitors of the associations, or (3) acting to affect domestic prices of the commodities being sold by the exporters who belong to the Webb-Pomerene associations.

Although the act has been much criticized, it does not seem likely that Congress will repeal it or substantially soften its grant of immunity. To the contrary, several attempts in recent years have been made to broaden its exemption to the export of data, services, insurance, technological know-how, and other exportable intangibles not presently covered by the law.

Government-Assisted Export Programs

Two other federal laws enacted in the 1980s are intended to aid American business in the export trade. The Export Trading Company Act (ETCA) of 1982 gives banks far more power than they had previously enjoyed under American law to invest in export trading companies, specially formed to sell goods abroad. The ETCA also weakens the applicability of antitrust law to export companies through a certificate awarded after a review process. The Foreign Sales Corporation Act of 1984 gives tax incentives to U.S. companies that organize so-called foreign sales corporations (FSC).

U.S. Antitrust Law Abroad

Whether one country's laws can reach into the territory of another country has often been bitterly debated. The anomaly is easily recognizable in criminal law: a man who kills someone in France ought not be tried in an American state court, for the question whether he committed murder at all must be determined by French law. Likewise, if a person commits an act that is considered fraudulent in the United States but legal in the country where he committed it, the act's legality should be judged by the law of the place where it was committed. United States law does not reach around the world to subject to liability anyone who eventually comes into the United States. Nevertheless, one important exception to this general rule as raised the hackles of virtually every country in which Americans do business—American antitrust law.

The Sherman and Clayton Acts apply to acts in foreign commerce. If two American companies sign an agreement to fix prices of goods being shipped to foreign ports, they have clearly violated Section 1 of the Sherman Act, even if the agreement is made and signed abroad. So much may seem unexceptionable. However, in an age of multinational corporations and subsidiaries doing business worldwide, the reach of American antitrust law has antagonized most countries at one time or another. Unlike the courts in every other country with antitrust laws on the book, American courts apply the so-called "effects doctrine," under which the Sherman and Clayton Acts are said to apply if the acts, wherever committed, have had effects on American commerce. Thus, American subsidiaries of foreign companies may find themselves hauled into federal courts and subjected to treble damages under the Sherman or Clayton Acts for deeds done in their own countries. Moreover, in the course of the litigation, the federal courts may order the foreign company to disclose files under federal rules of civil procedure governing "discovery" (see p. 53).

From time to time, several nations have enacted legislation barring their nationals from cooperating with American courts—for example, by prohibiting the disclosure of corporate documents or by permitting the foreign defendant ordered by a federal court to pay treble damages to recover two-thirds of the award in a separate proceeding in his home country.

In the late 1970s, the State Department began to recognize some of the foreign concerns. It began to negotiate bilateral agreements by which each country agrees to take account of the antitrust and economic development policies of the other. Nevertheless, the reach of American antitrust law continues to be a vexing issue, and the federal courts have not yet widely relaxed their vigilant regard for federal antitrust policy, as the next case makes clear. The case was brought by Westinghouse Electric Corporation, charging several foreign uranium producers with having formed a uranium cartel in violation of U.S. antitrust laws. This case was an outgrowth of suits against Westinghouse for failure to supply uranium under long-term supply contracts. The issues posed by the uranium cartel provoked the most heated denunciation in years by foreign governments against American antitrust policy, and the debate has not yet ended.

In re **URANIUM ANTITRUST LITIGATION: WESTINGHOUSE ELEC. CORP. v. RIO ALGAM LTD.**
617 F.2d 1248 (7th Cir. 1980)

WILLIAM J. CAMPBELL, SENIOR DISTRICT JUDGE.

In October of 1976, plaintiff-appellee, Westinghouse Electric Corporation, filed a complaint alleging anti-trust violations against twenty-nine foreign and domestic uranium producers. All of the defendants were duly served with process; however, nine foreign defendants chose not to appear. On February 2, 1977, the District Court entered defaults pursuant to Rule 55(a) of the Federal Rules of Civil Procedure against each of the nine defaulting defendants. In August 1977, Westinghouse moved for entry of final judgment against the defaulters on the issue of liability. On January 3, 1979, the District Court granted the motion for entry of default judgment against the defaulting defendants.

⋆   ⋆   ⋆

The governments of Australia, Canada, South Africa and the United Kingdom of Great Britain and Northern Ireland have filed briefs as amici curiae. The principal thrust of the amici's briefs is to call into question the jurisdiction of the United States District Court over this controversy. We view the

(*continued on next page*)

(continued)

In re URANIUM
ANTITRUST
LITIGATION:
WESTINGHOUSE
ELEC. CORP. v. RIO
ALGAM LTD.
617 F.2d 1248 (7th Cir.
1980)

jurisdictional issue as two-pronged: (1) does subject matter jurisdiction exist; and (2) if so, should it be exercised?

The jurisdictional reach of the Sherman Act to conduct outside the United States was not favorably received at the outset. However, that view was later eroded, and the Act was applied to conduct outside the United States so long as some of the acts occurred within the United States and the parties were American. In *United States* v. *Aluminum Co. of America (Alcoa)*, 148 F.2d 416 (2nd Cir. 1945), Judge Learned Hand articulated what is known as the "intended effects" test. In *Alcoa* Judge Hand reasoned that agreements made outside of the United States which restrain trade or commerce within the United States have the same effect as similar agreements entered into within our borders . . . Since *Alcoa*, United States Courts have exercised jurisdiction over antitrust activity outside the United States so long as there is an intended effect on American commerce.

In its complaint Westinghouse alleges that twenty domestic and nine foreign corporations conspired to fix the price of uranium in the world market. The alleged meetings at which Westinghouse claims prices were agreed upon took place in France, Australia, South Africa, Illinois, the Canary Islands and England. At the present state of this litigation, there has been no opportunity for fact-finding. We must therefore accept all properly pleaded allegations as true for purposes of determining jurisdiction. Accordingly, the picture which emerges is one of concerted conduct both abroad and within the United States intended to affect the uranium market in this country. While the governments of the foreign participants in this alleged conspiracy are actively and admittedly sympathetic to the economic determinism of the defaulters, there is no claim that the alleged conduct of the defaulters is mandated by those governments. We therefore conclude that Westinghouse's allegations against the defaulters do fall within the jurisdictional ambit of the Sherman Act, as defined in *Alcoa*.

★   ★   ★

We turn now to the question of whether jurisdiction should be exercised in the present case.

★   ★   ★

In granting the requested default judgment, the District Court considered three factors: the complexity of the present multi-national and multi-party action; the seriousness of the charges asserted; and the recalcitrant attitude of the defaulters. The District Judge concluded that those factors all weighed heavily in favor of proceeding to judgment and damages.

The amici suggest that the District Court abused its discretion by not considering the factors set out in *Mannington Mills* in reaching this determination. While the considerations recommended in that case certainly provide an adequate framework for such a determination, we can hardly call the failure to employ those precise factors an abuse of discretion. First, the *Mannington Mills* factors are not the law of this Circuit. Second, even assuming their adoption by this Court, the circumstances here are distinct from those found in *Timberlane* and *Mannington Mills*. In those cases the defendants appeared and contested the jurisdiction of the District Court. In the present case, the defaulters have contumaciously refused to come into court and present evidence as to why the District Court should not exercise its jurisdiction. They have chosen instead to present their entire case through surrogates. Wholly owned subsidiaries of several defaulters have challenged the appropriateness of the injunctions, and shockingly to us, the governments of the defaulters have subserviently presented for them their case against the exercise of jurisdiction. If this Court were to remand the matter for further consideration of the jurisdictional question, the District Court would be placed in the impossible position of having to make specific findings with the defaulters refusing to appear and participate in discovery. We find little value in such an exercise.

We conclude that given the posture of this case, and the circumstances before the District Court, the Judge did not abuse his discretion in proceeding to exercise his jurisdiction. We therefore decline to remand the case to the District Court as requested by the amici curiae.

CHAPTER SUMMARY

International law consists of various principles and customs that regulate behavior among nations, enforceable only in the courts of each nation. In the United States, treaty obligations are the law of the land, preempting state law or older federal law in the event of a conflict. However, the U.S. Constitution and federal laws, enacted after a particular treaty was ratified, are superior to the treaty.

Under the Foreign Sovereign Immunities Act of 1976, suits against foreign governments are barred unless the activities sued over are purely commercial. The expropriation of private property in a foreign country is not considered a commercial activity. Likewise, property of a foreign government located in the United States may not be seized to satisfy a judgment unless the property itself is used for a commercial activity. Under the Act of State doctrine, American courts will not question acts committed by a foreign government on its own territory. Thus, even if a foreign country expropriates private property for no good reason and fails to pay just compensation, the former owner will find no relief in American courts. To provide a partial remedy to American interests, the Overseas Private Investment Corporation insures American businesses abroad against the risk of expropriation.

Many foreign commercial legal systems operate beyond individual countries. By treaty, many governments in various regions have created supranational legal regimes to regulate business. Perhaps the most important in commercial terms to American business at the moment is the European Common Market. The EEC is moving closer to the American conception of antitrust.

Within the United States, federal antidumping laws permit the Secretary of the Treasury to raise import duties on companies that are dumping their goods in the American market—that is, selling them below the prices sold in the home market.

Cooperative marketing efforts by American exporters are shielded from the antitrust laws if they do not restrain trade within the United States, restrain export trade of competitors of the particular export trade association, or affect domestic prices of the commodities being sold.

One of the bitterest debates in recent years in the international legal community has concerned the reach of American antitrust law abroad. By treaty, the United States has begun to take steps to moderate extreme American and foreign positions.

Enforcing legal judgments abroad is risky, so most companies doing business abroad enter into arbitration agreements with contracting parties. The broadest authority for enforcing arbitral awards is the U.N. Convention on the Recognition and Enforcement of Foreign Arbitral Awards. The most-often used set of arbitration rules are the UNCITRAL rules, which provide a means of privately adjudicating disputes according to a set of laws chosen by the parties.

KEY TERMS

SELF-TEST QUESTIONS

1. International law derives from:
   (a) the U.S. Constitution
   (b) the common law
   (c) treaties
   (d) principles recognized by many nations
2. Foreign nations are immune from suit in American courts because:
   (a) Congress says so
   (b) the Constitution says so
   (c) the United Nations says so
   (d) the Supreme Court says so
3. Expropriation of private assets by a government is:
   (a) a violation of international law
   (b) a violation of the U.S. Constitution
   (c) permitted by the domestic law of various countries
   (d) permitted under GATT
4. Arbitration of business disputes is:
   (a) permissible in every country
   (b) permissible when a country's laws permit it
   (c) permissible whenever the disputants agree to it
   (d) none of the above
5. Antidumping laws:
   (a) are required under the U.S. Constitution
   (b) violate international law
   (c) are part of the Sherman Act
   (d) can be repealed by Congress

DEMONSTRATION PROBLEM

Guns "R" Us is an American corporation that exports weapons to Asia. One of its sales representatives promised a huge shipment of "antipersonnel" machine guns to an arms dealer in a small war-torn country. The American sales representative and the foreign arms dealer did not agree on a price but anticipating that they would, Guns "R" Us shipped a boxcar full of machine guns. The deal collapsed when the foreign dealer refused to meet Guns' terms. The foreign dealer invoked a law of his country under which the local courts have jurisdiction to block the return of the weapons and to assess the appropriate price by looking at the last sales price of the weapo (which happened to be two years earlier in South America a much lower amount). Assume that a U.S. court would ha no such jurisdiction or authority to assess a fair market pri and that if the suit had been filed originally in an Americ court, the court would have held that there was no conside tion sufficient to constitute a contract because the parties ne agreed on a price. Back home, Guns "R" Us institutes a ci suit for the difference between the price paid and what it lieves it should have received, attaching property of the f eign arms dealer in the United States. What is Guns' clai What result?

PROBLEMS

1. Assume that the United States enters into a multilater treaty with several third world countries under which then existing private claims to molybdenum and certa other minerals in the United States are assigned to an ternational agency for exploitation. When the owner of American mine continues to dig for ore covered by t treaty, the Justice Department sues to enjoin further mi ing. What result? Why?
2. A foreign government enters into a contract with American company to provide computer equipment a services for the intelligence arm of its military forces. Aft the equipment has been supplied, the foreign governme refuses to pay. The American company files suit in fede court in the United States, seeking to attach an Americ bank account owned by the foreign government. The fo eign government claims that the American court has jurisdiction and that, even if it does, the government immune from suit. What result? Would the result be a different if the American company had maintained its ow equipment on a lease basis abroad and the foreign gover ment had then expropriated the equipment and refused pay the American company its just value?
3. A Japanese manufacturer of widgets sells its deluxe mod in Japan for roughly twenty-five dollars per unit and mak a profit of three dollars. To break into the United Stat market, the company prices the same widget at ten d lars, one-third below the prevailing price charged by mo American widget manufacturers. What legal violations, any, has the Japanese company committed and what ste must an American company take to seek redress?
4. The Concentrated Phosphate Export Association consis of the five largest phosphate producers. The Agency f International Development (AID) undertook to sell fert izer to Korea and solicited bids. The Association set pric and submitted a single bid on 300,000 tons. AID paid t

contract price, determined the amounts to be purchased, coordinated the procedure for buying, and undertook to resell to Korea. The Justice Department sued the Association and its members, claiming that their actions violated Section 1 of the Sherman Act. What defense might the defendants have? What result?

5. The Columbia Widget Company has just landed a multimillion dollar contract to supply the Chinese government with top-of-the-line widgets. The complex contract, negotiated over a three-year period, gives the Chinese the right to reject the widgets under special circumstances. Columbia is understandably nervous about the wording, but it wants to go ahead with the deal if it can, because it will represent a sizable part of the company's bottom line for the next five years. What advice can you give Columbia's management about how to protect its interests to minimize its risks?

ANSWERS TO SELF-TEST QUESTIONS

1. (d)   2. (a)   3. (c)   4. (b)   5. (d)

SUGGESTED ANSWER TO DEMONSTRATION PROBLEM

Guns "R" Us will claim that there was no valid contract. Because the foreign dealer kept the weapons, the American company will assert, the goods were converted and it is entitled to their fair market value. Guns will lose. It is asking an American court to rule that the procedures in the foreign country were legally invalid. Under the Act of State doctrine, an American court must respect the legal validity of acts of foreign governments and cannot permit a party to relitigate the issues.

CHAPTER
51

CHAPTER OVERVIEW

A Brief History of Labor Legislation

The National Labor Relations Board—Organization and Functions

Labor and Management Rights Under the Federal Labor Laws

Labor-Management Law

Over half a century, the federal law of labor relations has developed out of four basic statutes into an immense body of cases and precedent regulating the formation and governance of labor unions and the relationships among employers, unions, and union members. Like antitrust, labor law is a complex subject that has spawned a large class of specialized practitioners. Though specialized, it is a subject that no employer of any size can ignore, for labor law has a pervasive influence on how business is conducted throughout the United States. In this chapter we examine the basic statutory framework and the activities that it regulates.

A BRIEF HISTORY OF LABOR LEGISLATION

In the Nineteenth Century

Labor unions appeared in modern form in America in the 1790s in Boston, New York, and Philadelphia. Early in the nineteenth century, employers began to seek injunctions against union organizing and other activities. Two doctrines were employed: (1) *common law conspiracy*, and (2) *common law restraints of trade*. The first doctrine held that workers who joined together were acting criminally as conspirators, regardless of the means chosen or the objectives sought.

The second doctrine—common law restraint of trade—was also a favorite theory of the courts to use in enjoining unionizing and other joint employee activities. Workers who banded together to seek better wages or working conditions were, according to this theory, engaged in concerted activity that restrained trade in their labor. This theory made sense in a day in which conventional wisdom held that an employer was entitled to buy labor as cheaply as possible—the price would obviously rise if workers were allowed to bargain jointly rather than if they were required to offer their services individually on the open market.

Under the Antitrust Laws

The Sherman Act did nothing to change this basic judicial attitude. A number of cases decided early in the act's history condemned labor activities as violations of the antitrust law. In particular, in the *Danbury Hatters' Case*, the Supreme Court held that a "secondary boycott" (see p. 1154) against a non-unionized company violated the Sherman Act. The hatters instigated a boycott of retail stores that sold hats manufactured by a company whose workers had struck. The union was held liable for treble damages. [Loewe v. Lawlor, 208 U.S. 274 (1908)]

By 1912, labor had organized politically, and it played a pivotal role in electing Woodrow Wilson and giving him a Democratic Congress, which responded in 1914 with the Clayton Act's "labor exemption." Section 6 of the Clayton Act says that labor unions are not "illegal combinations or conspiracies in restraint of trade, under the antitrust laws." Section 20 forbids courts from issuing injunctions in cases involving strikes, boycotts, and other concerted union activities (which were declared to be lawful), as long as they arose out of disputes between employer and employees over the terms of employment.

But even the Clayton Act proved of little lasting value to the unions. In 1921 the Supreme Court again struck out against a secondary boycott that crippled the significance of the Clayton Act provisions. In the case, a machinists' union staged a boycott against an employer by whom the members were not employed in order to pressure the employer into permitting one of its factories to be unionized. The Court ruled that the Clayton Act exemptions applied only in cases involving an employer and his own employees. [Duplex Printing Press Co. v. Deering, 254 U.S. 443 (1921)] Without the ability to boycott under those circumstances free of antitrust prosecutions or treble-damage actions, labor would be hard-pressed to unionize many companies. More anti-union decisions followed.

Toward Modern Labor Legislation

Collective bargaining appeared on the national scene for the first time in 1918 with the creation of the War Labor Conference Board. A National War Labor Board was empowered to mediate or reconcile labor disputes that affected industries essential to the war. But after the war, the board was abolished.

In 1926, Congress enacted the Railway Labor Act. This statute imposed a duty on railroads to bargain in good faith with their employees' elected representatives. The act also established the National Mediation Board to mediate disputes that were not resolved in contract negotiations. The stage was set for more comprehensive national labor laws. These would come with the Great Depression.

The Norris-LaGuardia Act The first labor law of the Great Depression was the Norris-LaGuardia Act of 1932. It dealt with the propensity of federal courts to issue preliminary injunctions, often *ex parte* (that is, after hearing only the plaintiff's argument), against union activities. Even though the permanent injunction might later have been denied, the effect of the vaguely worded preliminary injunction would have been sufficient to destroy the attempt to unionize. The Norris-LaGuardia Act forbids federal courts from temporarily or permanently enjoining certain union activities, such as peaceful picketing and strikes. The act is applicable to any "labor dispute," defined as embracing "any controversy concerning terms or conditions of employment, or concerning the association or representation of persons in negotiating, fixing, maintaining, changing, or seeking to arrange terms or conditions of employment, regardless of whether or not the disputants stand in the proximate relation of employer and employee." This language thus permitted the secondary boycott that had been held a violation of the antitrust laws in *Duplex*. The act also bars the courts from enforcing so-called "yellow-dog" contracts—agreements that employees made with their employer not to join unions.

The National Labor Relations Act (the Wagner Act) In 1935, Congress finally enacted a comprehensive labor statute. The National Labor Relations Act (NLRA), often called the Wagner Act after its sponsor, Senator Robert F. Wagner, declared in Section 7 that workers in interstate commerce "have the right to self-organization, to form, join or assist labor organizations, to bargain collectively through representatives of their own choosing, and to engage in concerted activities for the purpose of collective bargaining or other mutual aid or protection." Section 8 sets out five key **"unfair labor practices."** The five employer unfair labor practices are these:

1. Interference with the rights guaranteed by Section 7
2. Interference with the organization of unions, or dominance by the employer of union administration (this section thus outlaws "company unions")

3. Discrimination against employees who belong to unions
4. Discharging or otherwise discriminating against employees who seek relief under the act
5. Refusing to bargain collectively with union representatives.

The procedures for forming a union to represent employees in an appropriate "bargaining unit" are set out in Section 9. Finally, the Wagner Act established the National Labor Relations Board (NLRB) as an independent federal administrative agency, with power to investigate and remedy unfair labor practices.

The Supreme Court upheld the constitutionality of the act in 1937 in a series of five cases. In the first, *NLRB* v. *Jones & Laughlin Steel Corp.*, 301 U.S. 1 (1937), the Court ruled that congressional power under the Commerce Clause extends to activities that might affect the flow of interstate commerce, as labor relations certainly did. Through its elaborate mechanisms for establishing collective bargaining as a basic national policy, the Wagner Act has had a profound effect on interstate commerce during the last half-century.

The Taft-Hartley Act (Labor Management Relations Act)   The Wagner Act did not attempt to restrict union activities in any way. For a dozen years, opponents of unions sought some means of curtailing the breadth of opportunity opened up to unions by the Wagner Act. After failing to obtain relief in the Supreme Court, they took their case to Congress and finally succeeded after World War II when, in 1947, Congress for the first time since 1930 had Republican majorities in both houses. Congress responded to critics of "Big Labor" with the Taft-Hartley Act, passed over President Truman's veto. Taft-Hartley—known formally as the Labor Management Relations Act—did not repeal the protections given employees and unions under the National Labor Relations Act. Instead, it balanced union power with a declaration of rights of employers. In particular, Taft-Hartley lists six unfair labor practices of unions, including secondary boycotts, strikes aimed at coercing an employer to fire an employee who refuses to join a union, and so-called "jurisdictional" strikes over which union should be entitled to do specified jobs at the worksite.

In addition to these provisions, Taft-Hartley contains several others that balance the rights of unions and employers. For example, the act guarantees both employers and unions the right to present their view on unionization and collective bargaining. Like employers, unions now became obligated to bargain in good faith. The act outlaws the "closed shop" (one in which a worker must belong to a union), gives federal courts the power to enforce collective bargaining agreements, and permits private parties to sue for damages arising out of a secondary boycott. The act also created the Federal Mediation and Conciliation Service to cope with strikes that create national emergencies, and it declared strikes by federal employees to be unlawful. It was this provision that President Reagan invoked in 1981 to fire air traffic controllers who walked off the job for higher pay.

The Landrum-Griffin Act   Congressional hearings in the 1950s brought to light union corruption and abuse and led in 1959 to the last of the major federal labor statutes, the Landrum-Griffin Act (Labor-Management Reporting and Disclosure Act). It established a series of controls on internal union procedures, including the method of electing union officers and the financial controls necessary to avoid the problems of corruption that had been encountered. Landrum-Griffin also restricted union picketing under various circumstances, narrowed the loopholes in Taft-Hartley's prohibitions against secondary boycotts, and banned "hot cargo" agreements (see p. 1155).

THE NATIONAL LABOR RELATIONS BOARD—ORGANIZATION AND FUNCTIONS

The National Labor Relations Board (NLRB) consists of five board members, appointed by the president and confirmed by the Senate, for five-year staggered terms. The president designates one of the members as chairman. The president also appoints the general counsel, who is in charge of the board's investigatory and prosecutorial functions and who represents the NLRB when it goes (or is taken) to court. The general counsel also oversees the thirty-three regional offices scattered throughout the country, each of which is headed by a regional director.

The NLRB serves two primary functions: (1) It investigates allegations of unfair labor practices and provides remedies in appropriate cases. (2) It decides in contested cases which union should serve as the exclusive bargaining agent for a particular group of employees.

Unfair Labor Practice Cases

Unfair labor practice cases are voluminous—some 40,000 a year in the early 1980s. A charge of an unfair labor practice must be presented to the board, which has no authority to initiate cases on its own. Charges are investigated at the regional level and may result in a complaint by the regional office. A regional director's failure to issue a complaint may be appealed to the general counsel, whose word is final and unappealable. A substantial number of charges are dismissed or withdrawn each year—sometimes as many as 70 percent. Once issued, the complaint is handled by an attorney from the regional office. Most cases, usually around 80 percent, are settled at this level. If not settled, the case will be tried before an administrative law judge, who will take evidence and recommend a decision and order. If no one objects, the decision and order become final as the board's opinion and order. Any party may appeal the decision to the board in Washington. The board acts on written briefs, rarely on oral argument. The board's order may be appealed to the U.S. Courts of Appeals, although its findings of fact are not reviewable "if supported by substantial evidence on the record considered as a whole." The board may also go to the Court of Appeals to seek enforcement of its orders.

Representation Cases

The NLRB is empowered to oversee representative elections—that is, elections by employees to determine whether or not to be represented by a union. The board becomes involved if at least 30 percent of the members of a potential bargaining unit petition it to do so, or if an employer petitions on being faced with a claim by a union that it exclusively represents the employees. The board determines which bargaining unit is appropriate and which employees are eligible to vote. A representative of the regional office will conduct the election itself, which is by secret ballot. The regional director may hear challenges to the election procedure to determine whether the election was valid.

LABOR AND MANAGEMENT RIGHTS UNDER THE FEDERAL LABOR LAWS

Choosing the Union as the Exclusive Bargaining Representative

Determining the Appropriate Unit As long as a union has a valid agreement with the employer, no rival union may seek an election to oust it except within sixty to ninety days before the contract expires. Nor may an election be held if an election has already been held in the bargaining unit during the preceding twelve months. To bar a new election under the valid contract rule, the agreement must be of no more than three years' duration.

Whom does the union represent? In companies of even moderate size, employees work at different tasks and have different interests. Must the secretaries, punch press operators, drivers, and clerical help all belong to the same union in a small factory? The NLRB has the authority to determine which group of employees will constitute the appropriate bargaining unit. To make its determination, the board must look at the history of collective bargaining among similar workers in the industry; the employees' duties, wages, skills, and working conditions; the relationship between the proposed unit and the structure of the employer's organization; and the desires of the employees themselves.

Two groups must be excluded from any bargaining unit—supervisory employees and independent contractors. Determining whether or not a particular employee is a supervisor is left to the discretion of the board.

Interfering with Employee Communications To conduct an organizing drive, a union must be able to communicate with the employees. But the employer has valid interests in seeing that employees and organizers do not interfere with plant operations or otherwise hinder the operation of the business. Several different problems arise from the need to balance these interests.

One problem is the protection of the employer's property rights. May nonemployee union organizers come onto the employer's property to distribute union literature—for example, by standing in the company's parking lots to hand out leaflets when employees go to and from work? May organizers, whether employees or not, picket or hand out literature in private shopping centers in order to reach the public—for example, to protest a company's policies toward its non-union employees? The interests of both employees and employers under the NLRA are twofold: (1) the right of the employees (a) to communicate with each other or the public and (b) to hear what union organizers have to say, and (2) the employer's (a) property rights, and (b) interest in managing the business efficiently and profitably.

The rules that govern in these situations are complex, but in general they appear to provide these answers: (1) If the persons doing the soliciting are not employees, the employer may bar them from entering his private property, even if they are attempting to reach employees—assuming that the employer does not discriminate and applies a rule against use of his property equally to everyone. [NLRB v. Babcock & Wilcox Co., 351 U.S. 105 (1956)] (2) If the solicitors are not employees and they are trying to reach the public, they have no right to enter the employer's private property. (3) If the solicitors are employees who are seeking to reach the public, they have the right to distribute on the employer's property—in a common case, in a shopping center—unless they have a convenient way to reach their audience on public property off the employer's premises. [Hudgens v. NLRB, 424 U.S. 507 (1976)] (4) If the solicitors are employees seeking to reach employees, the employer is permitted to limit the distribution of literature or other solicitations to avoid litter or the interruption of work, but he cannot prohibit solicitation on company property altogether.

In the leading case of *Republic Aviation Corp.* v. *NLRB*, 324 U.S. 793 (1945), the employer, a non-union plant, had a standing rule against any kind of solicitation on the premises. Thereafter, certain employees attempted to organize the plant. The employer fired one employee for soliciting on behalf of the union and three others for wearing union buttons. The Supreme Court upheld the board's determination that the discharges constituted an unfair labor practice under Section 8(a). It does not matter, the Court said, whether the employees had other means of communicating with each other or that the em-

ployer's rule against solicitation may have no effect on the union's attempt to organize the workers. In other words, the employer's intent or motive is irrelevant. The only question is whether the employer's actions might tend to interfere with the employees' exercise of their rights under the NLRA.

Regulating Campaign Statements   A union election drive is not like a polite tea-party conversation; it is, like political campaigns, full of charges and countercharges. Employers who do not want their employees unionized may warn darkly of the effect of the union on profitability; organizers may exaggerate the company's financial position. Under a 1982 NLRB case, *Midland National Life Ins. Co.*, 263 N.L.R.B. 130, the board will not set aside an election if the parties misrepresent the issues or facts, but it will do so if the statements are made in a deceptive manner, e.g., through forged documents. The board also watches for threats and promises of rewards; for example, the employer might threaten to close the plant if the union succeeds. In *NLRB* v. *Gissel Packing Co.*, 395 U.S. 575 (1969), the employer stated his worries throughout the campaign that a union would prompt a strike and force the plant to close. The board ruled that the employer's statements were an impermissible threat. To the employer's claim that he was simply exercising his First Amendment rights, the Supreme Court held that although employers do enjoy freedom of speech, it is an unfair labor practice to threaten consequences that are not rooted in economic realities.

A union campaign has become an intricate legal duel, heavily dependent on strategic considerations of law and public relations. Neither management nor labor can afford to wage a union campaign without specialized advisers, who can guide the thrust and parry of the antagonists. Labor usually has such advisers because few organizational drives are begun without outside organizers who have access to union lawyers. A business person who attempts to fight a union, like a labor organizer or employee who attempts to organize one, takes a sizable risk when acting alone, without competent advice. For example, a simple statement like "We will get the heating fixed," in response to a seemingly innocent question about the "drafty old building" at a meeting with employees, can lead to a NLRB decision to set aside an election if the union loses, because the answer can easily be construed as a promise, and under Section 8(c) of the NLRA a promise of reward or benefit during an organization campaign is an unfair labor practice by management. Few union election campaigns occur without questions, meetings, and pamphleteering carefully worked out in advance.

The results of all the electioneering are worth noting. In the 1980s, some 20 percent of the total American workforce was unionized, the lowest percentage since the two major associations of unions—American Federation of Labor (AFL) and the Congress of Industrial Organizations (CIO)—merged in 1955. Unionism was clearly on the wane. Of the 7,000 elections held annually during the first half of the decade, labor won fewer than half (about 43 percent).

Exclusivity Once selected as the bargaining representative for an appropriate group of employees, the union has the **exclusive right to bargain.** Thereafter, individual employees may not enter into separate contracts with the employer, even if they voted against the particular union or against having a union at all. The principle of exclusivity is fundamental to the collective bargaining process. Just how basic it is can be seen in the following case, in which one group of employees protested what they thought were racially discriminatory work assignments, barred under the **collective bargaining agreement,** the contract between the union and the employer. Certain of the employees filed grievances with the union, which looked into the problem more slowly than the employees thought necessary. They urged that the union permit them to picket, but the union refused. They picketed anyway, calling for a consumer boycott. The employer warned them to desist, but they continued and were fired. The question was whether they were discharged for engaging in concerted activity protected under Section 7 of the National Labor Relations Act.

EMPORIUM CAPWELL CO. v. WESTERN ADDITION COMMUNITY ORGANIZATION
420 U.S. 50 (1975)

Opinion of the Court by MR. JUSTICE MARSHALL.

* * *

The Emporium Capwell Co. (Company) operates a department store in San Francisco. At all times relevant to this litigation it was a party to the collective-bargaining agreement negotiated by the San Francisco Retailer's Council, of which it was a member, and the Department Store Employees Union (Union) which represented all stock and marketing area employees of the Company. The agreement, in which the Union was recognized as the sole collective-bargaining agency for all covered employees, prohibited employment discrimination by reason of race, color, creed, national origin, age, or sex, as well as union activity. It had a no-strike or lockout clause, and it established grievance and arbitration machinery for processing any claimed violation of the contract, including a violation of the anti-discrimination clause.

On April 3, 1968, a group of Company employees covered by the agreement met with the secretary-treasurer of the Union, Walter Johnson, to present a list of grievances including a claim that the Company was discriminating on the basis of race in making assignments and promotions. The Union official agreed to take certain of the grievances and to investigate the charge of racial discrimination. He appointed an investigating committee and prepared a report on the employees' grievances, which he submitted to the Retailer's Council and which the Council in turn referred to the Company. The report

(*continued on next page*)

(continued)

**EMPORIUM CAPWELL
CO. v. WESTERN
ADDITION
COMMUNITY
ORGANIZATION
420 U.S. 50 (1975)**

described "the possibility of racial discrimination" as perhaps the most important issue raised by the employees and termed the situation at the Company as potentially explosive if corrective action were not taken. It offered as an example of the problem the Company's failure to promote a Negro stock employee regarded by other employees as an outstanding candidate but a victim of racial discrimination.

Shortly after receiving the report, the Company's labor relations director met with Union representatives and agreed to "look into the matter" of discrimination and see what needed to be done. Apparently unsatisfied with these representations, the Union held a meeting in September attended by Union officials, Company employees, and representatives of the California Fair Employment Practices Committee (FEPC) and the local anti-poverty agency. The secretary-treasurer of the Union announced that the Union had concluded that the Company was discriminating, and that it would process every such grievance through to arbitration if necessary. Testimony about the Company's practices was taken and transcribed by a court reporter, and the next day the Union notified the Company of its formal charge and demanded that the joint union-management Adjustment Board be convened "to hear the entire case."

At the September meeting some of the Company's employees had expressed their view that the contract procedures were inadequate to handle a systemic grievance of this sort; they suggested that the Union instead begin picketing the store in protest. Johnson explained that the collective agreement bound the Union to its processes and expressed his view that successful grievants would be helping not only themselves but all others who might be the victims of invidious discrimination as well. The FEPC and anti-poverty agency representatives offered the same advice. Nonetheless, when the Adjustment Board meeting convened on October 16, James Joseph Hollins, Tom Hawkins, and two other employees whose testimony the Union had intended to elicit refused to participate in the grievance procedure. Instead, Hollins read a statement objecting to reliance on correction of individual inequities as an approach to the problem of discrimination at the store and demanding that the president of the Company meet with the four protestants to work out a broader agreement for dealing with the issue as they saw it. The four employees then walked out of the hearing.

. . . On Saturday, November 2, Hollins, Hawkins, and at least two other employees picketed the store throughout the day and distributed at the entrance handbills urging consumers not to patronize the store. Johnson encountered the picketing employees, again urged them to rely on the grievance process, and warned that they might be fired for their activities. The pickets, however, were not dissuaded, and they continued to press their demand to deal directly with the Company president.

On November 7, Hollins and Hawkins were given written warnings that a repetition of the picketing or public statements about the Company could lead to their discharge. When the conduct was repeated the following Saturday, the two employees were fired.

. . . [T]he NLRB Trial Examiner found that the discharged employees had believed in good faith that the Company was discriminating against minority employees, and that they had resorted to concerted activity on the basis of that belief. He concluded, however, that their activity was not protected by § 7 of the Act and that their discharges did not, therefore, violate § 8(a)(1).

The Board, after oral argument, adopted the findings and conclusions of its Trial Examiner and dismissed the complaint. Among the findings adopted by the Board was that the discharged employees' course of conduct

> was no mere presentation of a grievance but nothing short of a demand that the [Company] bargain with the picketing employees for the entire group of minority employees.

The Board concluded that protection of such an attempt to bargain would undermine the statutory system of bargaining through an exclusive, elected representative, impede elected unions' efforts at bettering the working conditions of minority employees, "and place on the Employer an unreasonable burden of attempting to placate self-designated representatives of minority groups while abiding by the terms of a valid bargaining agreement and attempting in good faith to meet whatever demands the bargaining representative put forth under that agreement."

On respondent's petition for review the Court of Appeals reversed and remanded. The court was of the view that concerted activity directed against racial discrimination enjoys a "unique status" by virtue of the national labor policy against discrimination . . . The issue, then, is whether such attempts to engage in separate bargaining are protected by § 7 of the Act or proscribed by § 9(a).

*   *   *

Central to the policy of fostering collective bargaining, where the employees elect that course, is the principle of majority rule. If the majority of a unit chooses union representation, the NLRA permits it to bargain with its employer to make union membership a condition of employment, thereby imposing its choice upon the minority. . . .

*   *   *

In vesting the representatives of the majority with this broad power Congress did not, of course, authorize a tyranny of the majority over minority interests. First, it confined the exercise of these powers to the context of a " 'unit appropriate' for the purposes of collective bargaining," *i.e.*, a group of employees with a sufficient commonality of circumstances to ensure against the submergence of a minority with distinctively different interests in the terms and conditions of their employment. Second, it undertook in the 1959 Landrum-Griffin amendments, to assure that minority voices are heard as

(*continued on next page*)

(continued)

EMPORIUM CAPWELL CO. v. WESTERN ADDITION COMMUNITY ORGANIZATION
420 U.S. 50 (1975)

they are in the functioning of a democratic institution. Third, we have held, by the very nature of the exclusive bargaining representative's status as representative of *all* unit employees, Congress implicitly imposed upon it a duty fairly and in good faith to represent the interests of minorities within the unit. And the Board has taken the position that a union's refusal to process grievances against racial discrimination in violation of that duty is an unfair labor practice. . . .

*   *   *

The decision by a handful of employees to bypass the grievance procedure in favor of attempting to bargain with their employer . . . may or may not be predicated upon the actual existence of discrimination. An employer confronted with bargaining demands from each of several minority groups would not necessarily, or even probably, be able to agree to remedial steps satisfactory to all at once. Competing claims on the employer's ability to accommodate each group's demands, *e.g.*, for reassignments and promotions to a limited number of positions, could only set one group against the other even if it is not the employer's intention to divide and overcome them. . . . In this instance we do not know precisely what form the demands advanced by Hollins, Hawkins, et al. would take, but the nature of the grievance that motivated them indicates that the demands would have included the transfer of some minority employees to sales areas in which higher commissions were paid. Yet the collective-bargaining agreement provided that no employee would be transferred from a higher-paying to a lower-paying classification except by consent or in the course of a layoff or reduction in force. The potential for conflict between the minority and other employees in this situation is manifest. With each group able to enforce its conflicting demands—the incumbent employees by resort to contractual processes and the minority employees by economic coercion—the probability of strife and deadlock is high; the likelihood of making headway against discriminatory practices would be minimal.

*   *   *

Accordingly, we think neither aspect of respondent's contention in support of a right to short-circuit orderly, established processes for eliminating discrimination in employment is well-founded. The policy of industrial self-determination as expressed in § 7 does not require fragmentation of the bargaining unit along racial or other lines in order to consist with the national labor policy against discrimination. And in the face of such fragmentation, whatever its effect on discriminatory practices, the bargaining process that the principle of exclusive representation is meant to lubricate could not endure unhampered.

*   *   *

Reversed.

The Duty to Bargain

In Good Faith   The NLRA holds both employer and union to a **duty to bargain** in good faith. What these words mean has long been the subject of controversy. Suppose Mr. Mardian, the company's chief negotiator, announces to Mr. Ulasewicz, the chief union negotiator, that "I will sit down and talk with you but I'll be damned if I will agree to a penny more an hour than the people are getting now." That is not a refusal to bargain: it is a statement of the company's position, and only Mardian's actual conduct during the negotiations will determine whether he was bargaining in good faith. Of course, if he refused to talk to Ulasewicz, he would have been guilty of a failure to bargain in good faith.

Suppose Mardian had steadily insisted during the bargaining sessions that the company must have complete control over every aspect of the labor relationship, including the right to hire and fire exactly as it saw fit, the right to raise or lower wages whenever it wanted, and the right to determine which employee was to do which job. The Supreme Court has said that an employer is not obligated to accept any particular term in a proposed collective bargaining agreement, and the NLRB may not second-guess any agreement eventually reached. [NLRB v. American National Insurance Co., 343 U.S. 395 (1962)] However, the employer must actually engage in bargaining, and a stubborn insistence on leaving everything entirely to the discretion of management has been construed as a failure to bargain. [NLRB v. Reed & Prince Manufacturing Co., 205 F.2d 131 (1st Cir. 1953)]

Suppose Mardian had responded to Ulasewicz's request for a ten-cent-an-hour raise: "If we do that, we'll go broke." Suppose further that Ulasewicz then demanded, on behalf of the union, that Mardian prove his contention but that Mardian refused. Under these circumstances, the Supreme Court has ruled, the Board is entitled to hold that management has failed to bargain in good faith, for once having raised the issue, the employer must in good faith demonstrate veracity. [NLRB v. Truitt Manufacturing Co., 351 U.S. 149 (1956)]

Mandatory Subjects of Bargaining   The NLRB requires employers and unions to bargain over "terms and condition of employment." Wages, hours, and working conditions—whether workers must wear uniforms, when the lunch hour begins, the type of safety equipment on hand—are well understood terms and conditions of employment. But the statutory phrase is vague, and the cases abound with debates over whether a term insisted on by union or management is within the statutory phrase. No simple rule can be stated for determining whether a desire of union or management is mandatory or nonmandatory. The cases do suggest that management retains the right to determine the scope and direction of the enterprise, so that, for example, the decision to invest in labor-saving machinery is a nonmandatory subject—meaning that a union could not insist that an employer bargain over it, although the employer may negotiate if it desires. Once a subject is incorporated in a collective bargaining agreement, neither side may demand that it be renegotiated during the term of the agreement.

The Board's Power to Compel an Agreement   A mere refusal to agree, without more, is not evidence of bad-faith bargaining. That may seem a difficult conclusion to reach in view of what has just been said. Nevertheless, the law is clear that a company may refuse to accede to a union's demand for any reason other than an unwillingness to consider the matter in the first place. If a union negotiator cannot talk management into accepting his demand, then the union may take other actions—including strikes—to try to force management to bow. As Justice Black explains in the following case, it follows from this conclusion that the NLRB has no power to *compel* agreement—even if management is guilty of negotiating in bad faith. The federal labor laws are premised on the fundamental principle that the parties are free to bargain.

**H. K. PORTER CO. v.
NLRB**
397 U.S. 99 (1970)

MR. JUSTICE BLACK delivered the opinion of the Court.

After an election respondent United Steelworkers Union was, on October 5, 1961, certified by the National Labor Relations Board as the bargaining agent for certain employees at the Danville, Virginia, plant of the petitioner, H. K. Porter Co. Thereafter negotiations commenced for a collective-bargaining agreement. Since that time the controversy has seesawed between the Board, the Court of Appeals for the District of Columbia Circuit, and this Court. This delay of over eight years is not because the case is exceedingly complex, but appears to have occurred chiefly because of the skill of the company's negotiators in taking advantage of every opportunity for delay in an act more noticeable for its generality than for its precise prescriptions. The entire lengthy dispute mainly revolves around the union's desire to have the company agree to "check off" the dues owed to the union by its members, that is, to deduct those dues periodically from the company's wage payments to the employees. The record shows, as the Board found, that the company's objection to a checkoff was not due to any general principle or policy against making deductions from employees' wages. The company does deduct charges for things like insurance, taxes, and contributions to charities, and at some other plants it has a checkoff arrangement for union dues. The evidence shows, and the court below found, that the company's objection was not because of inconvenience, but solely on the ground that the company was "not going to aid and comfort the union." Efforts by the union to obtain some kind of compromise on the checkoff request were all met with the same staccato response to the effect that the collection of union dues was the "union's business" and the company was not going to provide any assistance. Based on this and other evidence the Board found, and the Court of Appeals approved the finding, that the refusal of the company to bargain about the checkoff was not made in good faith, but was done solely to frustrate the making of any collective-bargaining agreement. In May 1966, the Court of Appeals upheld the Board's order requiring the company to cease and desist from refusing to bargain in good faith and directing it to engage in further collective bargaining, if requested by the union to do so, over the checkoff.

In the course of that opinion, the Court of Appeals intimated that the Board conceivably might have required petitioner to agree to a checkoff provision as a remedy for the prior bad-faith bargaining, although the order enforced at that time did not contain any such provision. In the ensuing negotiations the company offered to discuss alternative arrangements for collecting the union's dues, but the union insisted that the company was required to agree to the checkoff proposal without modification. . . . The union then filed in the Court of Appeals a motion for reconsideration of the earlier motion to clarify the 1966 opinion. The court granted that motion and issued a new opinion in which it held that in certain circumstances a "checkoff may be imposed as a remedy for bad faith bargaining." The case was then remanded to the Board and on July 3, 1968, the Board issued a supplemental order requiring the petitioner to "[g]rant to the Union a contract clause providing for the checkoff of union dues." The Court of Appeals affirmed this order. We granted certiorari to consider whether the Board in these circumstances has the power to remedy the unfair labor practice by requiring the company to agree to check off the dues of the workers. For reasons to be stated we hold that while the Board does have power under the National Labor Relations Act to require employers and employees to negotiate, it is without power to compel a company or a union to agree to any substantive contractual provision of a collective-bargaining agreement.

* * *

The object of this Act was not to allow governmental regulation of the terms and conditions of employment, but rather to ensure that employers and their employees could work together to establish mutually satisfactory conditions. The basic theme of the Act was that through collective bargaining the passions, arguments, and struggles of prior years would be channeled into constructive, open discussions leading, it was hoped, to mutual agreement. But it was recognized from the beginning that agreement might in some cases be impossible, and it was never intended that the Government would in such cases step in, become a party to the negotiations and impose its own views of a desirable settlement. This fundamental limitation was made abundantly clear in the legislative reports accompanying the 1935 Act. The Senate Committee on Education and Labor stated:

> The committee wishes to dispel any possible false impression that this bill is designed to compel the making of agreements or to permit governmental supervision of their terms. It must be stressed that the duty to bargain collectively does not carry with it the duty to reach an agreement, because the essence of collective bargaining is that either party shall be free to decide whether proposals made to it are satisfactory.

The discussions on the floor of Congress consistently reflected this same understanding.

* * *

. . . The parties to the instant case are agreed that this is the first time in the 35-year history of the Act that the Board has ordered either an employer or a union to agree to a substantive term of a collective-bargaining agreement.

Recognizing the fundamental principle "that the National Labor Relations Act is grounded on the premise of freedom of contract," the Court of Appeals in this case concluded that nevertheless in the circumstances presented here the Board could properly compel the employer to agree to a proposed checkoff clause. The Board had found that the refusal was based on a desire to frustrate agreement and not on any legitimate business reason. On the basis of that finding the Court of Appeals approved the further finding that the employer had not bargained in good faith, and the validity of that finding

(continued on next page)

(continued)

H. K. PORTER CO. v. NLRB
397 U.S. 99 (1970)

is not now before us. Where the record thus revealed repeated refusals by the employer to bargain in good faith on this issue, the Court of Appeals concluded that ordering agreement to the checkoff clause "may be the only means of assuring the Board, and the court, that [the employer] no longer harbors an illegal intent."

. . . It is implicit in the entire structure of the Act that the Board acts to oversee and referee the process of collective bargaining, leaving the results of the contest to the bargaining strengths of the parties. It would be anomalous indeed to hold that while § 8(d) prohibits the Board from relying on a refusal to agree as the sole evidence of bad-faith bargaining, the Act permits the Board to compel agreement in that same dispute. The Board's remedial powers under § 10 of the Act are broad, but they are limited to carrying out the policies of the Act itself. One of these fundamental policies is freedom of contract. While the parties' freedom of contract is not absolute under the Act, allowing the Board to compel agreement when the parties themselves are unable to agree would violate the fundamental premise on which the Act is based—private bargaining under governmental supervision of the procedure alone, without any official compulsion over the actual terms of the contract.

★   ★   ★

The judgment is reversed and the case is remanded to the Court of Appeals for further action consistent with this opinion.

Interference and Discrimination by the Employer

Union Activity on Company Property The employer may not issue a rule flatly prohibiting solicitation or distribution of literature during "working time" or "working hours"—a valid rule against solicitation or distribution must permit these activities during employees' free time, such as on breaks and at meals. A rule that barred solicitation on the plant floor during actual work would be presumptively valid. However, the board has the power to enjoin its enforcement if the employer used the rule to stop union soliciting but permitted employees during the forbidden times to solicit for charitable and other causes.

"Runaway Shops" A business may lawfully decide to move a factory for economic reasons, but it may not do so to discourage a union or break it apart. The removal of a plant from one location to another is known as a **runaway shop.** An employer's representative who conceals from union representatives that a move is contemplated commits an unfair labor practice because the union is deprived of the opportunity to negotiate over an important part of its members' working conditions. If a company moves a plant and it is later determined that the move was to interfere with union activity, the board may order the employer to offer affected workers employment at the new site and the cost of transportation.

Other Types of Interference Since "interference" is not a precise term but descriptive of a purpose embodied in the law, many activities fall within its scope. These include hiring professional strikebreakers to disrupt a strike, favoritism toward a particular union to discourage another one, awarding or withholding benefits to encourage or discourage unionization, misrepresentations and other acts during election campaigns, espionage and surveillance of workers, employment contracts with individual members of a union, blacklisting workers, physical or verbal attacks on union activists, and various forms of anti-union propaganda.

Discrimination against Union Members   Under Section 8(a)(3), an employer may not discriminate against employees in hiring or tenure to encourage or discourage membership in a labor organization. Thus, an employer may not refuse to hire a union activist, or fire an employee who is actively supporting the union or an organizational effort, if the employee is otherwise performing adequately on the job. Nor may an employer discriminate among employees seeking reinstatement after a strike or discriminatory layoff or *lockout* (a closing of the job site to prevent employees from coming to work), hiring only those who were less vocal in their support of the union.

The provision against employer discrimination in hiring prohibits certain types of **compulsory unionism.** Four basic types of compulsory unionism are possible: the **closed shop,** the **union shop, maintenance-of-membership agreements,** and **preferential hiring agreements.** In addition, a fifth arrangement—the **agency shop**—while not strictly compulsory unionism, has characteristics similar to it. Section 8(a)(3) prohibits the closed shop and preferential hiring. But Section 14 permits states to enact more stringent standards and thus to outlaw the union shop, agency shop, and maintenance of membership as well.

1. *Closed Shop*   This requires a potential employee to belong to the union before being hired and to remain a member during employment. It is unlawful, because it would require an employer to discriminate on the basis of membership in deciding whether to hire.
2. *Union Shop*   An employer who enters into a union shop agreement with the union may hire a non-union employee, but all employees who are hired must then become members of the union and remain members so long as they work at the job. Because the employer may hire anyone, union or non-union member, the union shop is lawful, unless barred by state law.
3. *Maintenance-of-Membership Agreements*   These require all employees who are members of the union before being hired to remain as members once they are hired, unless they take advantage of an "escape clause" to resign within a time fixed in the collective bargaining agreement. Workers who were not members of the union before being hired are not required to join once they are on the job. This type of agreement is lawful, again unless barred by state law.
4. *Preferential Hiring*   An employer who accepts a preferential hiring clause agrees to hire only union members as long as the union can supply him with a sufficient number of qualified workers. These clauses are unlawful.
5. *Agency Shop*   The agency shop is not true compulsory unionism, for it specifically permits an employee not to belong to the union. However, it does require the employee to pay into the union the same amount required as dues of members. The legality of an agency shop is determined by state law. If permissible under state law, it is permissible under federal law.

The Right to Strike

Section 13 of the NLRA says that "nothing in this Act, except as specifically provided for herein, shall be construed so as either to interfere with or impede or diminish in any way the right to strike, or to affect the limitations or qualifications on that right." The labor statutes distinguish between two types of strikes: the **economic strike** and the **unfair labor practice strike.** In the former, employees go out on strike to try to force the employer to give in to the workers' demands. In the latter, the strikes are protesting the employer's committing an unfair labor practice. The importance of the distinction lies in whether the employees are entitled to regain their jobs after it is over. In either type of strike, an employer may hire substitute employees during the strike itself. When it concludes, however, a difference arises. In *NLRB* v. *International Van Lines,* 409 U.S. 48 (1972), the Supreme Court said that an employer may hire permanent employees to take over during an economic strike, and he need not discharge the substitute employees when it is done. That is not true for unfair labor practice strikes: an employee who makes an unconditional offer to return to his job is entitled to it, even though in the meantime the employer may have replaced him.

These rules do not apply to unlawful strikes. Not every walkout by workers is permissible. Their collective bargaining agreement may contain a "no-strike" clause barring strikes during the life of the contract. Most public employees—that is, those who work for the government—are prohibited from striking. "Sit-down" strikes, in which the employees stay on the worksite, precluding the employer from using the facility, are unlawful. So are "wildcat" strikes, when a faction within the union walks out without authorization. Likewise unlawful are violent strikes, jurisdictional strikes, secondary strikes and boycotts, and strikes intended to force the employer to sign "hot cargo" agreements (p. 1155).

To combat strikes, especially when many employers are involved with a single union trying to bargain for better conditions throughout an industry, an employer may resort to a **lockout.** Typically the union will call a **whipsaw strike,** striking some of the employers but not all. The whipsaw strike puts pressure on the struck employers because their competitors are still in business. The employers who are not struck may lawfully respond by locking out all employees who belong to the multi-employer union. This is known as a **defensive lockout.** In several cases, the Supreme Court has ruled that an **offensive lockout,** which occurs when the employer, anticipating a strike, locks the employees out, is likewise permissible.

Secondary Boycotts

Section 8(b)(4), added to the NLRA by the Taft-Hartley Act, prohibits workers from engaging in **secondary boycotts**—strikes, refusals to handle goods, threats, coercion, restraints, and other actions aimed at forcing any person to refrain from performing services for or handling products of any producer other than the employer, or to stop doing business with any other person. Like the Robinson-Patman Act (Chapter 46), this section of the NLRA is extremely difficult to parse and has led to many convoluted interpretations. However, its essence is to prevent workers from picketing employers not involved in the primary labor dispute.

Suppose that the Amalgamated Widget Workers of America puts up a picket line around the Ace Widget Company to force the company to recognize the union as the exclusive bargaining agent for Ace's employees. The employees themselves do not join in the picketing, but when a delivery truck shows up at

the plant gates and discovers the pickets, it turns back because the driver's policy is never to cross a picket line. This activity falls within the literal terms of Section (8)(b)(4): it seeks to prevent the employees of Ace's suppliers from doing business with Ace. But in *NLRB* v. *International Rice Milling Co.,* 341 U.S. 665 (1951), the Supreme Court declared that this sort of **primary activity**—aimed directly at the employer involved in the primary dispute—is not unlawful. So it is permissible to throw up a picket line to attempt to stop anyone from doing business with the employer—whether suppliers, customers, or even the employer's other employees (for example, those belonging to other unions). That is why a single striking union is so often successful in closing down an entire plant: when the striking union goes out, the other unions "honor the picket line" by refusing to cross it and thus stay out of work as well. The employer might have been able to replace the striking workers if they comprised a small enough part of his labor force, but it becomes nearly impossible to replace all the workers within a dozen or more unions.

Suppose the United Sanders Union strikes the Ace Widget factory. Non-union sanders refuse to cross the picket line. So Ace sends out its unsanded widgets to Acme Sanders, a job shop across town, to do the sanding job. When the strikers learn what Ace has done, they begin to picket Acme, at which point Acme's sanders honor the picket line and refuse to enter the premises. Acme goes to court to enjoin the pickets—an exception to the Norris-LaGuardia Act permits the federal courts to enjoin picketing in cases of unlawful secondary boycotts. Should the court grant the injunction? It might seem so, but under the so-called **ally doctrine,** the court will not. Since Acme is joined with Ace to help it finish the work, the courts deem the second employer an ally (or extension) of the first. The second picket line, therefore, is not secondary.

Suppose that despite the strike Ace Widgets manages to ship its finished product to the Dime Store, which sells a variety of goods, including widgets. The union puts up a picket around the store; the picketers bear signs that urge shoppers to refrain from buying any Ace Widgets at the Dime Store. Is this an unlawful secondary boycott? Again, the answer is no. A proviso to Section 8(b)(4) permits publicity aimed at truthfully advising the public that products of a rimary employer with whom the union is on strike re being distributed by a secondary employer.

Now suppose that the picketers carried signs and rally urged shoppers not to enter the Dime Store at ll until it stopped carrying Ace's widgets. That would e unlawful: a union may not picket a secondary site o persuade consumers to refrain from purchasing any f the secondary employer's products. Likewise, the nion may not picket in order to cause the secondary mployees (the sales clerks at the Dime Store) to re-use to go to work at the secondary employer. The atter is a classic example of inducing a secondary toppage, and it is barred by Section 8(b)(4). How-ver, in *DeBartolo Corp.* v. *Florida Gulf Coast Build-ng and Construction Trades Council*, 485 U.S. 568 1988), the Supreme Court opened what may prove o be a significant loophole in the prohibition against econdary boycotts (see **Box 51-1**). Instead of picket-ng, the union distributed handbills at the entrance to a shopping mall, asking customers not to patronize any stores in the mall until the mall owner, in build-ng new stores, promised to deal only with contrac-tors paying "fair wages." Distinguishing picketing, which the Court said would constitute a secondary boycott, the Court approved the handbilling, calling it "only an attempt to persuade customers not to shop in the mall."

"Hot Cargo" Agreements

A union might find it advantageous to include in a collective bargaining agreement a provision under which the employer agrees to refrain from dealing with certain people or from purchasing their products. For example, suppose the Teamsters Union negotiates a contract with its employers that permits truckers to refuse to carry goods to an employer being struck by the Teamsters or any other union. The struck em-ployer is the primary employer; the employer who has agreed to the clause—known as a **hot cargo clause**—is the secondary employer. The Supreme Court upheld these clauses in *United Brotherhood of Carpen-ters and Joiners, Local 1976* v. *NLRB*, 357 U.S. 93 (1958), but the following year, Congress outlawed them in Section 8(e) with a partial exemption for the con-struction industry and a full exemption for garment and apparel workers.

Discrimination by Unions

A union certified as the exclusive bargaining repre-sentative in the appropriate bargaining unit is obli-gated to represent all employees within that unit, even those who are not members of the union. Various provisions of the labor statutes prohibit unions from entering into agreements with employers to discrimi-nate against nonmembers. The laws also prohibit unions from treating employees unfairly on the basis of race, creed, color, or national origin.

Jurisdictional Disputes

Ace Widget, a peaceful employer, has a distinguished labor history. It did not resist the first union, which came calling in 1936, just after the NLRA was en-acted, and by 1987 it had twenty-three different unions representing 7,200 workers at forty-eight sites throughout the United States. Then, because of in-creasingly more powerful and efficient machinery, United Widget Workers realized that it was losing jobs throughout the industry. It decided to attempt to bring within its purview jobs currently performed by mem-bers of other unions. United Widget Workers asked Ace to assign all sanding work to its members. Since sanding work was already being done by members of the United Sanders, Ace management refused. United Widget Workers decided to go on strike over the is-sue. Is the strike lawful? Under Section 8(b)(4)(D), regulating jurisdictional disputes, it is not. It is an unfair labor practice for a union to strike or engage in other concerted actions to pressure an employer to assign or reassign work to one union rather than another.

Bankruptcy and the Collective Bargaining Agreement

An employer is bound by a collective bargaining agreement to pay the wages of unionized workers specified in the agreement. But obviously no paper agreement can guarantee wages when an insolvent company goes out of business. Suppose a company files for reorganization under the bankruptcy laws (see

BOX 51-1

The Secondary Boycott Gets a Second Wind

By Aaron Bernstein and
Paul Angiolillo

[In the past, union members have been restricted by laws forbidding secondary boycotts. However, the Supreme Court has approved of handbilling, a method of secondary boycott, deeming it only "an attempt to persuade" and therefore lawful.—AUTHORS' NOTE]

Until recently, there were a surprising number of restrictions on labor unions' First Amendment rights to free speech. But a recent U.S. Supreme Court decision has done away with many of them. . . . [T]he court issued a ruling that significantly expands a union's right to conduct secondary boycotts.

PICKETING VS. HANDBILLING

The decision gives a potentially powerful new weapon to the weakened labor movement, which has been searching for alternatives in recent years as its ability to mount strikes has diminished. Already the case has prompted several unions to initiate secondary boycotts. Says Lawrence M. Cohen, an attorney for Edward J. DeBartolo Corp. in the Supreme Court case: "The court broadened the area of industrial controversy until there's no limitation on the number of parties in a labor dispute."

Handbills

The tenuous connection between DeBartolo and the union shows how far-reaching the court's decision is. In 1979, DeBartolo hired H. J. Wilson

Co. to build a store in a shopping mall it owns in Tampa, Fla. Wilson, in turn, hired a contractor, H. J. High Construction Co. The construction union thought High was paying substandard wages, so it passed out handbills asking customers not to shop at the mall's 85 stores.

Although the Taft-Hartley Act of 1947 outlaws "coercive" secondary boycotts, the Supreme Court held that the union's boycott was "only an attempt to persuade customers not to shop in the mall." While picketing would have been illegal, the court said, other forms of expression, such as handbills, are not.

That opens the door for unions to initiate boycotts against virtually any company that has a connection with a unionized employer. Already on the move is the United Paperworkers International Union, which has been on strike against International Paper Co. (IP) since last year. After getting nowhere, it hired union

---

Chapter 29). May it then ignore its contractual obligation to pay wages previously bargained for? In the early 1980s, several major companies—for example, Continental Airlines and Oklahoma-based Wilson Foods Corp.—sought the protection of federal bankruptcy law in part to cut union wages. Alarmed, Congress in 1984 amended the bankruptcy code to require companies to attempt to negotiate a modification of their contracts in good faith. If negotiations fail, a bankruptcy judge may approve only wage cuts that are necessary to a company's reorganization plan. In 1986, the U.S. Court of Appeals in Philadelphia substantially reduced the power of companies to avoid their collective bargaining agreements. The court ruled that Wheeling-Pittsburgh Steel Corp. could not modify its contract with the United Steelworkers simply because it was financially distressed. The court pointed

to the company's failure to provide a "snap-back" clause in its new agreement. Such a clause would restore wages to the higher levels of the original contract if the company made a comeback faster than anticipated. [Wheeling-Pittsburgh Steel Corp. v. United Steelworkers of America, 791 F.2d 1071 (3d Cir. 1986)] If followed in other circuits, the ruling will cool the enthusiasm of some companies to seek voluntary reorganization under the bankruptcy laws to escape their union commitments.

CHAPTER SUMMARY

Federal labor law is grounded in the National Labor Relations Act, which permits unions to organize and prohibits employers from engaging in unfair labor practices. Amendments to the NLRA, such as the Taft-Hartley Act and the Landrum-

BOX 51-1

consultant Ray Rogers, who has developed innovative nonstrike tactics against employers.

Rogers suggested secondary boycotts against IP's banks. In early June the paperworkers began boycotts against two IP lenders, Bank of Boston Corp. and Provident National Bank, which also have directors in common with IP. The banks say they aren't involved in the dispute. But Rogers says the DeBartolo decision allows unions to target an employer's financial backers.

Other unions are considering similar moves. Unions at Eastern Airlines Inc., which have been in a year-long dispute with management, decided in March to go after the company's lenders. They passed out leaflets in front of several Merrill Lynch & Co. offices, but at the time all they could do was point out that Merrill Lynch did banking for Eastern and its parent, Texas Air Corp. "Now we can be much more direct," says Jo-

seph B. Uehlein, the staff member of the AFL-CIO's Industrial Union Dept. who is coordinating the campaign. The unions are also contemplating boycotts against Equitable Life Insurance Co., a Texas Air stockholder, and Drexel Burnham Lambert Inc., one of its investment bankers.

Neighborhood Talks

The real impact of the DeBartolo decision is likely to be at the local level. While few national boycotts have succeeded in the past, the tactic works much better in small disputes. "Most strikes are local, and that is where this new weapon is likely to be most useful, when the people we're talking to are neighbors," says Laurence Gold, the AFL-CIO's general counsel.

The United Food & Commercial Workers International Union (UFCW) is already trying that strategy. Days after the DeBartolo decision, its Local 464 began a boycott against a Price Chopper supermarket that had just

opened in Newburgh, N.Y. The union, representing workers in other Newburgh stores, fears Price Chopper's lower pay rates will undermine the local wage scale.

Before, the union's only weapon would have been to try to organize Price Chopper. But labor law allows the employer to call a quick election before the union is ready. If the union loses, it can't try again for a year. Now the UFCW can launch a boycott whether it's organizing or not. "The Supreme Court ruling is like a blessing from heaven," says Local 464 President John Niccolli.

The court's decision alone isn't going to put unions back on their feet. But it may give many of them a crucial edge in their struggle to find new ways to show employers they mean business.

Source: *Business Week*, June 27, 1988

Griffin Act, declare certain acts of unions and employees also to be unfair labor practices.

The National Labor Relations Board supervises union elections and decides in contested cases which union should serve as the exclusive bargaining unit, and it also investigates allegations of unfair labor practices and provides remedies in appropriate cases.

Once elected or certified, the union is the exclusive bargaining unit for the employees it represents. Because the employer is barred from interfering with employee communications when the union is organizing for an election, he may not prohibit employees from soliciting fellow employees on company property but may limit the hours or spaces in which this may be done. The election campaign itself is an intricate legal duel; rewards, threats, and misrepresentations that affect the election are unfair labor practices.

The basic policy of the labor laws is to foster good-faith collective bargaining over wages, hours, and working conditions. The Board may not compel agreement: it may not order

the employer or the union to adopt particular provisions, but it may compel a recalcitrant company or union to bargain in the first place.

Among the unfair labor practices committed by employers are

1. Discrimination against workers or prospective workers for belonging to or joining unions. Under federal law, the closed shop and preferential hiring are unlawful. Some states outlaw also the union shop, agency shop, and maintenance-of-membership agreements.
2. Interference with strikes. Employers may hire replacement workers during a strike, but in an unfair labor practice strike, as opposed to an economic strike, the replacement workers may be temporary only; workers are entitled to their jobs back at the strike's end.

Among the unfair labor practices committed by unions are

1. Secondary boycotts. Workers may not picket employers not involved in the primary labor dispute.
2. Hot cargo agreements. An employer's agreement, under union pressure, to refrain from dealing with certain people or purchasing their products is unlawful.

KEY TERMS

Agency shop	p. 1153	Offensive lockout	p. 1154
Ally doctrine	p. 1154	Preferential hiring	p. 1153
Collective bargaining	p. 1145	agreements	
agreement		Primary activity	p. 1154
Closed shop	p. 1153	Runaway shop	p. 1152
Compulsory unionism	p. 1153	Secondary boycotts	p. 1154
Defensive lockout	p. 1154	Unfair labor practices	p. 1141
Duty to bargain	p. 1149	Unfair labor practice	p. 1153
Economic strike	p. 1153	strike	
Exclusive right to bar-	p. 1145	Union shop	p. 1153
gain		Whipsaw strike	p. 1154
Hot cargo	p. 1155		
Maintenance-of-mem-	p. 1153		
bership agreements			

SELF-TEST QUESTIONS

1. Which of the following is not a subject of mandatory bargaining?
   (a) rate of pay per hour
   (b) length of the work week
   (c) safety equipment
   (d) new product to manufacture
2. Under a union shop agreement:
   (a) an employer may not hire a non-union member
   (b) an employer must hire a non-union member
   (c) an employee must join the union after being hired
   (d) an employee must belong to the union before being hired
3. Which of the following are always unlawful under federal law?
   (a) union shop
   (b) agency shop
   (c) closed shop
   (d) runaway shop
4. An employer's agreement with its union to refrain from dealing with companies being struck by other unions is a:
   (a) secondary boycott agreement
   (b) hot cargo agreement
   (c) lockout agreement
   (d) maintenance-of-membership agreement
5. Striking employees are entitled to their jobs back when they are engaged in:
   (a) economic strikes
   (b) jurisdictional strikes
   (c) both economic and jurisdictional strikes
   (d) neither economic nor jurisdictional strikes

DEMONSTRATION PROBLEM

Amalgamated Grocery Clerks Union Local No. 362, seeking higher wages and better working conditions, is on strike against Big Stores, a supermarket chain in Centerville City. It has mounted a daily picket line around each of the stores, and sales are beginning to fall as many customers, afraid or unwilling to cross the picket line, have begun to shop at other grocery stores. To try to make its strike more effective, the Local has organized two other efforts: (1) its members are picketing Big Stores' local bank, urging customers not to do business with a bank that lends money to Big Stores; and (2) its members are passing out leaflets near the produce market that supplies Big Stores with vegetables and fruits, urging people shopping there not to buy food because the produce market also supplies Big Stores. Big Stores sues them to enjoin the union from all picketing and handbilling. What result?

PROBLEMS

1. After years of working without a union, employees of Argenta Associates began organizing for a representation election. Management did not try to prevent the employees from passing out leaflets or making speeches on company property, but the company president did send out a notice to all employees stating that in his opinion they would be better off without a union. A week before the election, he sent another notice stating that effective immediately, each employee would be entitled to a twenty-five-cents-an-hour raise. The employees voted the union down. The following day, several employees began agitating for another election. This time management threatened to fire anyone who continued talking about an election on the ground that the union had lost and the employees would have to wait a year. The employees' organizing committee filed an unfair labor practice complaint with the NLRB. What result?
2. Palooka Industries sat down with Local 308, which represented its telephone operators, to discuss renewal of the collective bargaining agreement. Palooka pressed its case for a nonstrike clause in the next contract, but Local 308 refused to discuss it at all. Exasperated, Palooka finally filed an unfair labor practice claim with the NLRB. What result?
3. Union organizers sought to organize the punch press operators at Dan's Machine Shop. The shop was located on a lot surrounded by heavily forested land from which access to employees was impossible. The only practical method of reaching employees on the site was in the company parking lot. When the organizers arrived to distribute handbills, the shop foreman, under instructions from Dan, ordered them to leave. At a hearing before the NLRB, the company said that it was not anti-union but that its

policy, which it had always strictly adhered to, forbade non-employees from being on the property if not on company business. Moreover, company policy barred any activities that would lead to littering. The company noted that the organizers could reach the employees in many other ways—meeting the employees personally in town after hours, calling them at home, writing them letters, or advertising a public meeting. The organizers responded that these methods were far less effective means of reaching the employees. What result? Why?

ANSWERS TO SELF-TEST QUESTIONS

(d)　　2. (c)　　3. (c)　　4. (b)　　5. (a)

SUGGESTED ANSWER TO DEMONSTRATION PROBLEM

Under the Norris-LaGuardia Act, federal courts may not enjoin union activities except to stop unlawful strikes or secondary boycotts. Unless there is a no-strike clause in the collective bargaining agreement between Big Stores and the union, the clerks are legally entitled to strike and put a picket line around each of the stores. However, the picketing around the banks is an unlawful secondary boycott, and so the court will enjoin the clerks from continuing their bank picketing. The leafletting near the produce market is not an unlawful secondary boycott under the *DeBartolo* case, but simply a means of persuading shoppers at the produce market not to buy produce there and is a protected form of expression.

CHAPTER 52

CHAPTER OVERVIEW
Employment Discrimination
Erosion of the Employment-at-Will Doctrine
Other Employment-Related Laws

Employment Law

*I*n the previous chapter we examined the legal relationship between the employer and the employee who belongs, or wants to belong, to a union. Although federal labor law is confined to that relationship, laws dealing with the employment relationship—both state and federal—are far broader than that. Because most employees do not belong to unions, a host of laws dealing with the many faces of discrimination shapes employers' power over and duties to their employees. Beyond discrimination, the law also controls a number of other issues—such as the extent to which an employer may terminate the relationship itself. We examine these issues in this chapter.

EMPLOYMENT DISCRIMINATION

In this section, we consider laws that prohibit discrimination in employment. Until the 1960s, Congress had intruded but little in the affairs of employers except in union relationships. A company could refuse to hire members of racial minorities, prefer men over women in its promotion policies, or pay men more than women for the same work. But with the rise of the civil rights movement in the early 1960s, Congress (and many states) began to legislate away the employer's frequently exercised power to discrim-

inate. The most important statutes are Title VII of the Civil Rights Act of 1964, the Equal Pay Act of 1963, the Age Discrimination Act of 1967, and the Americans with Disabilities Act of 1990.

Racial, Religious, Sex, and Nationality Discrimination

In Title VII of the Civil Rights Act of 1964, Congress for the first time outlawed discrimination in employment based on race, religion, sex, or national origin. The law applies to any employer whose business affects interstate commerce and who employs at least fifteen workers. Title VII declares:

> It shall be an unlawful employment practice for an employer to fail or refuse to hire or to discharge any individual, or otherwise to discriminate against any individual with respect to his compensation, terms, conditions, or privileges of employment, because of such individual's race, color, religion, sex, or national origin.

And in 1984 the Supreme Court said that Title VII applies to partnerships as well as corporations when ruling that it is illegal to discriminatorily refuse to

Figure 52-1   A Checklist of Employment Law

✔ Employment discrimination laws
  Title VII, Civil Rights Act of 1964
  Civil Rights Act of 1866
  Equal Pay Act of 1963
  Age Discrimination Act of 1967
  Pregnancy Discrimination Act of 1978
  Rehabilitation Act of 1973
  Americans with Disabilities Act of 1990

✔ Common law of employment at will

✔ Contract law

✔ Tort law

✔ Agency law

✔ Worker Adjustment and Retraining Notification Act

✔ Polygraph Protection Act

✔ Occupational Safety and Health Act

✔ Employee Retirement Income Security Act

✔ Fair Labor Standards Act

✔ Workers' Compensation laws

promote a female lawyer to partnership status in a law firm. This applies, by implication, in other fields, such as accounting. [Hishon v. King & Spalding, 467 U.S. 69 (1984)] The remedy for unlawful discrimination is back pay and hiring, reinstatement, or promotion.

Title VII established the Equal Employment Opportunity Commission (EEOC) to investigate violations of the act. A victim of discrimination who wishes to file suit must first file a complaint with the EEOC to permit that agency to attempt to conciliate the dispute. The EEOC has filed a number of lawsuits to prove statistically that a company has systematically discriminated on one of the forbidden bases. The EEOC has received perennial criticism for its extreme slowness in filing suits and for failure to handle the huge backlog of complaints with which it has had to wrestle.

The courts have come to recognize two major types of Title VII cases:

1. *Disparate Treatment* In this type of suit, the plaintiff asserts that because of race, sex, religion, or national origin, he or she has been treated less favorably within the organization than others. To prevail in a disparate treatment suit, the

plaintiff must show that the company *intended* to discriminate because of one of the factors the law forbids to be considered. Thus, in *McDonnell Douglas Corp.* v. *Green*, 411 U.S. 792 (1973), the Supreme Court held that the plaintiff had shown the company intended to discriminate by refusing to rehire him because of his race. In general there are two types of disparate treatment cases—(a) pattern-and-practice cases, in which the employee asserts that the employer systematically discriminates on the grounds of race, religion, sex, or national origins, and (b) reprisal or retaliation cases, in which the employee must show that the employer discriminated against her because she asserted her Title VII rights.

2. *Disparate Impact* In this second type of case, the employee need not show that the employer intended to discriminate but only that the effect or impact of the employer's action was discriminatory. However, to overcome the usual requirement of intent, the plaintiff must demonstrate that the reason for the employer's conduct (such as refusal to promote) was not job-related. Troublesome cases arise out of practices that appear to be neutral on the surface, such as educational requirements and tests administered to help the employer choose the most qualified candidate. In the seminal case *Griggs* v. *Duke Power Co.*, 401 U.S. 424 (1971), the Supreme Court held that under Title VII an employer is not free to use any test it pleases; the test must bear a genuine relationship to job performance. For 18 years, *Griggs* was understood to stand for the proposition that Title VII "prohibits employment practices that have discriminatory effects as well as those that are intended to discriminate." But in 1989, the Supreme Court seemed to reverse itself on what might seem a subtle procedural point. *Griggs* had said that once the plaintiff showed that an employment practice had a statistically disparate impact on minority workers, the burden falls to the defendant to demonstrate a valid business necessity for the practice. That seemed to mean that the defendant had the burden of proving that its practice did not cause the actual discrimination. However, in *Wards Cove Packing Co., Inc.* v. *Antonio*, 109 S.Ct. 2115 (1989), the Court reversed itself on the issue of burden of proof. Now, the Court said in its 5-4 decision, the burden

remains with the plaintiff to prove "that discrimination against a protected group has been caused by a specific employment practice." The defendant must still provide evidence that its employment practice is used for a business reason other than to discriminate, but it will not need to show that the practice is "necessary" to locate qualified workers. It will be sufficient for the business under attack to show that the challenged practice is useful.

Wards Cove also held that the plaintiff cannot make out a *prima facie* case of discrimination through sheer statistical data showing a disproportion of black workers in a lower-paid type of job to white workers in a higher-paid type of job within the same company. Rather, the plaintiff must compare the proportion of minorities and women in the employer's work force to the availability of qualified minorities and women in the labor pool from which the employer hires workers. Only if the plaintiff can show an imbalance and demonstrate that it is caused by a specific invalid personnel policy or practice can he or she prevail.

Title VII is not the only source of anti-discrimination legislation. In 1976, the Supreme Court ruled that a very old law, the Civil Rights Act of 1866, permits a suit against racial discrimination in the making of a contract. [Runyon v. McCrary, 427 U.S. 160 (1976)] This decision was the basis for many awards in cases showing refusals to hire based on race. But in *Patterson* v. *McLean Credit Union*, 109 S.Ct. 2363 (1989), the Court ruled that *Runyon* does not apply when plaintiffs charge racial discrimination in promotion or other employment decisions once a worker is hired.

The result of this and other decisions in the late 1980s led to a fierce debate between the President and Congress over whether to enact legislation that would effectively overturn the Court's interpretations of Title VII and the Civil Rights Act of 1866. Congress passed the Civil Rights Act of 1990 that would have done just that, but President Bush vetoed the bill, stating that its effect would be to force employers to hire minorities and women according to "quotas." Proponents of the Act argued that in 18 years no such quota system had been shown. The Senate sustained the President's veto by a thin margin. The issue remains contentious, and it does not seem likely that the Court's recent decisions will be the final word.

Discrimination Based on Religion

An employer who systematically refuses to hire Catholics, Jews, Buddhists, or members of any other religious group is obviously guilty of disparate treatment under Title VII. But refusal to deal with someone because of his religion is not the only type of violation under the law. Title VII defines religion as including religious observances and practices as well as belief and requires the employer to "reasonably accommodate to an employee's or prospective employee's religious observance or practice" unless the employer can demonstrate that a reasonable accommodation would work an "undue hardship on the conduct of the employer's business." Thus a company that refused even to consider permitting a devout Sikh to wear his religiously prescribed turban on the job would violate Title VII. But the company need not make an accommodation that would impose more than a minimal cost. For example, an employee in an airline maintenance department, open 24 hours a day, wished to avoid working on his sabbath. The employee belonged to a union, and, under the collective bargaining agreement, a rotation system determined by seniority would have put the worker into a work shift that fell on his sabbath. The Supreme Court held that the employer was not required to pay premium wages to someone whom the seniority system would not require to work on that day and could discharge the employee if he refused the assignment. [Trans World Airlines v. Hardison, 432 U.S. 63 (1977)]

Sex Discrimination

A refusal to hire or promote a woman simply because she is female is a clear violation of Title VII. Under the Pregnancy Act of 1978 Congress declared that discrimination because of pregnancy is a form of sex discrimination. In 1990, Congress passed a bill that would have required employers to grant new parents as much as eighteen weeks of unpaid leave, but

President Bush vetoed it. In the meantime, 25 states have passed some form of family leave bills, and 14 more states are contemplating doing so. The most generous law to employees is that of New Jersey, which requires employers with as few as 50 employees to grant 12 weeks of unpaid leave every other year to employees, male or female, who are having a new child (whether by birth or adoption) or are facing serious illness in their immediate families. The experience of businesses under some family leave policies has not proved as detrimental as some had feared, so it is possible that Congress will eventually report a bill satisfactory to the President and the business lobby that has so far opposed it.

Another issue of profound importance for a significant class of women are the so-called "fetal protection" policies of many businesses. Fearing possible injury to the fetuses of women of child-bearing age, many companies are barring women from holding industrial jobs that pose chemical and other hazards unless the woman can demonstrate that she is infertile. A woman's declaration that she does not intend to become pregnant is insufficient under these policies. It has been estimated that 20 million jobs could be at stake. The issue came to the Supreme Court after Johnson Controls, Inc., a Milwaukee-based manufacturer of car batteries, forbade women from working in jobs at 15 plants where lead concentration could become dangerously high in their bloodstream. On behalf of a female member, the United Auto Workers sued, charging sex discrimination. In 1991, in International Union, UAW v. Johnson Controls, Inc., 111 S.Ct. 1196 (1991), the Supreme Court held that the company's fetal protection policy was facially discriminatory because it forbade fertile women, but not fertile men, from "risk[ing], their reproductive health for a particular job." Ignoring evidence that lead exposure might harm the male reproductive system and thus injure the fetus, the company, said the Court, clearly violated the Pregnancy Discrimination Act of 1978 by preventing women from working "because of or on the basis of pregnancy, childbirth, or related medical conditions." The Court also held that

the company had failed to demonstrate that sex of an employee was a bona fide occupational qualification (BFOQ)—for the particular jobs because there was no showing that the sex discrimination "is reasonably necessary" to the "normal operation" of its business. To qualify as a BFOQ, the Court noted, a job qualification must "relate to the 'essence,' or to the 'central mission of the employer's business.' " And although there is a limited safety consideration in establishing a BFOQ, it is the safety of customers or to third persons essential to the company's business. The fetus is neither. "Our case law," the Court said, "makes clear that the safety exception is limited to instances in which sex or pregnancy actually interferes with the employee's ability to perform the job." Although a woman might risk her baby's health, that risk does not in any way interfere with her ability to work in Johnson Controls's factories.

The late 1970s brought another problem of sex discrimination to the fore: sexual harassment. The courts recognize that the age-old penchant of men to use their power to gain sexual favors is unlawful. Not only do individual supervisors violate the law if they explicitly or implicitly suggest to a woman that by submitting to sexual advances she might be hired, given a raise, promoted, or assigned to more desirable work, but a company itself is liable for back pay and reinstatement or promotion if it knows or should have known that such practices were being carried on and did nothing to stop them. The company will also be liable to a qualified person denied a raise or promotion because someone else got it by submitting to sexual advances. The law applies equally to men who are propositioned by female supervisors.

In the next case, the Supreme Court held that Title VII's ban on sexual harassment encompasses more than the trading of sexual favors for employment benefits. Unlawful sexual harassment also includes the creation of a hostile or offensive working environment, subjecting both the offending employee and the company to damage suits even if the victim was in no danger of being fired or of losing a promotion or raise.

MERITOR SAVINGS BANK v. VINSON
477 U.S. 57 (1986)

JUSTICE REHNQUIST delivered the opinion of the Court.

This case presents important questions concerning claims of workplace "sexual harassment" brought under Title VII of the Civil Rights Act of 1964.

In 1974, respondent Mechelle Vinson met Sidney Taylor, a vice president of what is now petitioner Meritor Savings Bank (the bank) and manager of one of its branch offices. When respondent asked whether she might obtain employment at the bank, Taylor gave her an application, which she completed and returned the next day; later that same day Taylor called her to say that she had been hired. With Taylor as her supervisor, respondent started as a teller-trainee, and thereafter was promoted to teller, head teller, and assistant branch manager. She worked at the same branch for four years, and it is undisputed that her advancement there was based on merit alone. In September 1978, respondent notified Taylor that she was taking sick leave for an indefinite period. On November 1, 1978, the bank discharged her for excessive use of that leave.

Respondent brought this action against Taylor and the bank, claiming that during her four years at the bank she had "constantly been subjected to sexual harassment" by Taylor in violation of Title VII. She sought injunctive relief, compensatory and punitive damages against Taylor and the bank, and attorney's fees.

At the 11-day bench trial, the parties presented conflicting testimony about Taylor's behavior during respondent's employment. Respondent testified that during her probationary period as a teller-trainee, Taylor treated her in a fatherly way and made no sexual advances. Shortly thereafter, however, he invited her out to dinner and, during the course of the meal, suggested that they go to a motel to have sexual relations. At first she refused, but out of what she described as fear of losing her job she eventually agreed. According to respondent, Taylor thereafter made repeated demands upon her for sexual favors, usually at the branch, both during and after business hours; she estimated that over the next several years she had intercourse with him some 40 to 50 times. In addition, respondent testified that Taylor fondled her in front of other employees, followed her into the women's restroom when she went there alone, exposed himself to her, and even forcibly raped her on several occasions. These activities ceased after 1977, respondent stated, when she started going with a steady boyfriend.

★   ★   ★

Finally, respondent testified that because she was afraid of Taylor she never reported his harassment to any of his supervisors and never attempted to use the bank's complaint procedure.

Taylor denied respondent's allegations of sexual activity, testifying that he never fondled her, never made suggestive remarks to her, never engaged in sexual intercourse with her and never asked her to do so. He contended instead that respondent made her accusations in response to a business-related dispute. The bank also denied respondent's allegations and asserted that any sexual harassment by Taylor was unknown to the bank and engaged in without its consent or approval.

The District Court denied relief, but did not resolve the conflicting testimony about the existence of a sexual relationship between respondent and Taylor. It found instead that

> If [respondent] and Taylor did engage in an intimate or sexual relationship during the time of [respondent's] employment with [the bank], that relationship was a voluntary one having nothing to do with her continued employment at [the bank] or her advancement or promotions at that institution.

The court ultimately found that respondent "was not the victim of sexual harassment and was not the victim of sexual discrimination" while employed at the bank.

* * *

The Court of Appeals for the District of Columbia Circuit reversed. . . . The court stated that a violation of Title VII may be predicated on either of two types of sexual harassment: harassment that involves the conditioning of concrete employment benefits on sexual favors, and harassment that, while not affecting economic benefits, creates a hostile or offensive working environment. . . .

* * *

Respondent argues, and the Court of Appeals held, that unwelcome sexual advances that create an offensive or hostile working environment violate Title VII. Without question, when a supervisor sexually harasses a subordinate because of the subordinate's sex, that supervisor "discriminate[s]" on the basis of sex. Petitioner apparently does not challenge this proposition. It contends instead that in prohibiting discrimination with respect to "compensation, terms, conditions, or privileges" of employment, Congress was concerned with what petitioner describes as "tangible loss" of "an economic character," not "purely psychological aspects of the workplace environment." In support of this claim petitioner observes that in both the legislative history of Title VII and this Court's Title VII decisions, the focus has been on tangible, economic barriers erected by discrimination.

We reject petitioner's view. First, the language of Title VII is not limited to "economic" or "tangible" discrimination. The phrase "terms, conditions, or privileges of employment" evinces a congressional intent " 'to strike at the entire spectrum of disparate treatment of men and women' " in employment. Petitioner has pointed to nothing in the Act to suggest that Congress contemplated the limitation urged here.

Second, in 1980 the EEOC issued guidelines specifying that "sexual harassment," as there defined, is a form of sex discrimination prohibited by

(continued on next page)

(continued)

MERITOR SAVINGS BANK v. VINSON
477 U.S. 57 (1986)

Title VII. As an "administrative interpretation of the Act by the enforcing agency," these guidelines, " 'while not controlling upon the courts by reason of their authority, do constitute a body of experience and informed judgment to which courts and litigants may properly resort for guidance.' " The EEOC guidelines fully support the view that harassment leading to noneconomic injury can violate Title VII.

In defining "sexual harassment," the guidelines first describe the kinds of workplace conduct that may be actionable under Title VII. These include "[u]nwelcome sexual advances, requests for sexual favors, and other verbal or physical conduct of a sexual nature." Relevant to the charges at issue in this case, the guidelines provide that such sexual misconduct constitutes prohibited "sexual harassment," whether or not it is directly linked to the grant or denial of an economic *quid pro quo*, where "such conduct has the purpose or effect of unreasonably interfering with an individual's work performance or creating an intimidating, hostile, or offensive working environment."

*   *   *

The District Court's conclusion that no actionable harassment occurred might have rested on its earlier "finding" that "[i]f [respondent] and Taylor did engage in an intimate or sexual relationship . . . , that relationship was a voluntary one." But the fact that sex-related conduct was "voluntary," in the sense that the complainant was not forced to participate against her will, is not a defense to a sexual harassment suit brought under Title VII. The gravamen of any sexual harassment claim is that the alleged sexual advances were "unwelcome." While the question whether particular conduct was indeed unwelcome presents difficult problems of proof and turns largely on credibility determinations committed to the trier of fact, the District Court in this case erroneously focused on the "voluntariness" of respondent's participation in the claimed sexual episodes. The correct inquiry is whether respondent by her conduct indicated that the alleged sexual advances were unwelcome, not whether her actual participation in sexual intercourse was voluntary.

*   *   *

Reversed and remanded.

Another sex-based problem that has been occupying the courts stems from a related law, the Equal Pay Act. This federal statute prohibits pay differentials between men and women if they are assigned to equal jobs: work requiring equal skill, effort, and responsibility. The statute seems to mean only that a woman may not be paid less than a man in the same job—flight attendant, telephone operator, sales manager. But some women have recently filed suit on a theory of **comparable worth**—a woman should be paid as much as a man if she is doing work that is comparable, even if the job is different. As **Box 52-1** suggests, the economic theory has made certain inroads even if its legal underpinnings remain weak. There are signs that at least in the public work force, comparable worth may yet gain statutory strength. At least 31 states are studying the equity of pay for men and women in municipal and state jobs, and 20 states have already enacted laws or promulgated policies that adopt some form of comparable worth for public and civil

Women Gaining Pay Equity Outside Court

By Tamar Lewin

*[The Equal Pay Act, a federal statute, prohibits men from being paid more than women if assigned equal jobs, has gained considerable ground since the birth of its campaign a decade ago. Many states are considering enacting comparable worth statutes for the public work force.—*AUTHORS' NOTE*]*

The campaign for pay equity for women, considered innovative legal theory 10 years ago, is sputtering in court but flourishing at the bargaining table, bringing multimillion-dollar pay upgrades for many jobs.

Women's rights advocates have argued for a decade that sex discrimination has resulted in lower pay for jobs usually done by women, as against men's jobs requiring similar skills, training and responsibility.

Dozens of lawsuits, mostly on behalf of government clerical workers, have asserted that employers deliberately paid women less.

"What we argue is that there was historical discrimination against women going back to the 1930s, when it was legal, and that even though the pay scales were relabeled after sex discrimination became illegal, in many

COMPARABLE WORTH IN ECONOMICS AND LAW

cases, the same basic pay structure was kept," said Winn Newman, a Washington lawyer who specializes in pay-equity litigation.

"So every day, with every paycheck, there is continuing discrimination."

In 1981 the U.S. Supreme Court legitimized the theory, saying Oregon prison matrons had grounds to sue over a pay scale that gave them $200 a month less than the deputy sheriffs who guarded male prisoners. Although the matrons settled out of court and won a raise, similar suits have racked up a string of court defeats. . . .

. . . [A] judge dismissed the California State Employees' Association's claim from a 1984 suit that the state underpaid 60,000 workers in jobs held predominantly by women. Federal District Judge Marilyn Hall Patel said the state's pay scale reflected market rates, not deliberate sex discrimination. It was the largest pay-equity suit in the nation. . . . [I]n a similar case, the United Auto Workers' claims on behalf of women who

work for the state of Michigan was also dismissed.

"Litigation in pay equity is clearly a strategy of last resort," said Claudia Wayne, director of the National Committee on Pay Equity, a 10-year-old, non-profit coalition in Washington. But, she added, "there is a strong grass-roots pay equity movement that's doing very well."

In the last eight years more than $450 million has been allocated for upgrading the pay in women's jobs, Wayne said. Twenty states have begun to make pay equity adjustments for government workers and others are in the process of re-evaluating their job classifications.

Most of the workers affected hold lower-paid positions as clerks, typists, nurses or librarians.

In a few states, particularly Minnesota, the quest for pay equity has prompted a wholesale reassessment of the public workforce. The state did a study of jobs that found a 20 percent gap between the pay of men and women. In 1982 it agreed to upgrade the women's jobs over the next four years, adding 3.7 percent to the total state payroll. Two years later, the state required all cities, counties and school districts to adjust pay to eliminate underevaluation of women's work.

At least 50 other municipalities outside Minnesota have undertaken their own such studies.

Source: *New York Times*, April 12, 1989

service jobs. In 1988, Congress enacted the Federal Equitable Pay Practices Act, which calls for a study of pay disparities in the federal work force.

Exceptions to Title VII

Although the language of Title VII is broad, the courts have allowed certain exceptions. For example, a practice or test that has a disparate impact on a racial group is allowable if the employer can prove that the practice is a business necessity or that the test is job related. Likewise, an employer may assign jobs, promotions, and benefits under a bona fide seniority system, even if it produces a discriminatory effect, as long as the employer has not designed or intended the seniority system to produce a discriminatory effect.

The courts have also allowed exceptions in cases in which religion, national origin, or sex is a **bona fide occupational qualification**—usually referred to as a BFOQ. For example, a gymnasium may legitimately hire only men to work in a men's locker room. A religious organization may lawfully employ, at least in certain positions, only those of the requisite faith. Race, however, can never be a BFOQ under Title VII.

Nor is discrimination permitted merely because the public might have certain preconceptions about the type of person who ideally should hold a certain job. For example, a person cannot be denied a job as a bank teller simply because he has an accent although that might be a disqualification if he were applying for a position as a telephone operator. Similarly, guidelines issued by the EEOC in 1978 specify that sex may be a BFOQ only when "necessary for the purpose of authenticity or genuineness." A playwright may specify a woman for a certain part in a play, but "stereotyped characterizations of the sexes" are an insufficient basis on which to rest a hiring decision. And so, although society has the notion that women generally are not adept at lifting weights, an employer may not routinely exclude women from jobs requiring this ability. He must test each individual applicant to determine whether the particular person can lift the proper amount.

Affirmative Action

Two exceedingly difficult problems, still not fully resolved, are the impact of Title VII on employment seniority and on affirmative action programs. Many union contracts require employers to rehire on the basis of seniority workers laid off for economic reasons. Those who have long been discriminated against and who only lately have been hired will obviously have far less seniority. In times of recession, they will be the ones to suffer most. Courts have been able in some cases to remedy this discriminatory effect by ordering employers to backdate the seniority to the time of the injury—that is, from the dates on which the employer first refused to hire or promote. Likewise, courts can order employers to figure seniority on a plantwide or companywide basis to alleviate the problem of the worker who was discriminatorily placed in a relatively menial position and who cannot transfer to a better job because of the limited number of openings determined by seniority.

Beginning in the 1960s, **affirmative action** programs were established in many industries, sometimes voluntarily but more often by statute or regulation. These seek to put a person where he would have been had he not been discriminated against. Because these programs use race as a criterion, they appear to violate Title VII insofar as they give preferential treatment to one race over another. Although the final chapter in this perplexing area of law is far from having been written, the Supreme Court, in *United Steelworkers* v. *Weber*, 443 U.S. 193 (1979), appeared to sanction agreements between private employers and unions that provide for voluntary affirmative action plans. The case arose when a white production worker at Kaiser Aluminum's Grammercy, Louisiana, plant sued to enjoin an affirmative action plan that provided that blacks would be accepted as craft trainees in equal numbers with whites until such time as their proportion to the company work force equaled the proportion of blacks to whites in the total workforce. Up to that time, blacks had been systematically excluded from the higher-paying craft positions. Weber, the white employee, had more seniority than many of the black workers selected for craft training, and he argued that Title VII barred the plant from adhering to a plan that discriminated against him on the basis of race. Said Justice Brennan for the five-to-two majority:

> We cannot agree with [Weber] that Congress intended to prohibit the private sector from taking effective steps to accomplish the goal that Congress designed Title VII to achieve. . . . It would be ironic indeed if a law triggered by a Nation's concern over centuries of racial injustice and intended to improve the lot of those who had 'been excluded from the American dream for so long,' constituted the first legislative prohibition of all voluntary, private, race-conscious efforts to abolish traditional patterns of racial segregation and hierarchy.

And in 1986, the Court rejected the Reagan Administration's argument that racial preferences may never be used except to redress actual victims of discrimination. In *Local 28, Sheet Metal Workers International Assn.* v. *Equal Employment Opportunity Commission*, 478 U.S. 421 (1986), a six-to-three majority held that race-conscious remedies "may be appropriate where an employer or labor union has engaged in persistent or egregious discrimination, or where necessary to dissipate the lingering effects of pervasive discrimination," even when the benefits are for members of minority groups who were not personally discriminated against. But the Court unanimously held that racial preferences could not be an automatic remedy and that courts should be sparing in approving such preferences for those who were not themselves victims of discrimination.

The Court followed *Sheet Metal Workers* in 1987 in ruling that an affirmative action plan may give preference to women over men without violating Title VII. In *Johnson* v. *Transportation Agency*, 480 U.S. 616 (1987), the Santa Clara County (California) Transportation Agency implemented a county-wide affirmative action plan designed to redress the effects of past practices in areas in which women had traditionally been underemployed or not hired at all. The plan permitted the agency to consider sex as one of many factors in hiring. Another factor was the ranking given job applicants by interviewers. The suit arose when a male applicant who scored two points higher at an interview than a female applicant lost a promotion to road dispatcher to her. The Court held that an employer is not bound strictly to rankings and test scores as long as applicants are qualified for the job. In upholding the woman's promotion, the Court stressed the flexibility of the plan:

> The Agency . . . has undertaken such a voluntary effort, and has done so in full recognition of both the difficulties and the potential for intrusion on males and non-minorities. The Agency has identified a conspicuous imbalance in job categories traditionally segregated by race and sex. It has made clear from the outset, however, that employment decisions may not be justified solely by reference to this imbalance, but must rest on a multitude of practical, realistic factors. . . . The decision [to take sex into account] was made pursuant to an affirmative action plan that represents a moderate, flexible, case-by-case approach to effecting a gradual improvement in the representation of minorities and women in the Agency's work force.

But affirmative action plans do not always trump other employment interests. In *Wygant* v. *Jackson Board of Education*, 476 U.S. 267 (1986), a 5-4 majority ruled that a voluntary affirmative action plan designed to increase the number of minority teachers

hired in the Jackson, Michigan, public schools could not be used to lay off more senior white teachers during a time of reduced budgets. Although the five-member majority could not agree on the reasons for holding that the affirmative action plan in this case violated the Equal Protection Clause of the Fourteenth Amendment (see p. 22), it is apparent that the majority was greatly troubled by the impact that such plans could have on innocent teachers, given that the affirmative action plan had not been entered into to counter intentional discrimination in the past. In 1989, the Supreme Court took this rule one step further, allowing white fire fighters in Birmingham, Alabama, to challenge an affirmative action plan embodied in a judicial consent decree, even though they had not intervened at the time of the original employment discrimination suits. [*Martin* v. *Wilks*, 109 S.Ct. 2180 (1989)] In other words, even after a court has agreed to an affirmative action plan to remedy past discrimination, persons not parties to the original discrimination suit may challenge the affirmative action plan on the grounds that they were being denied promotions in favor of less qualified applicants solely on the grounds of race.

Age Discrimination

The Age Discrimination in Employment Act of 1967 (amended in 1978 and again in 1986) prohibits discrimination based on age, and recourse to this law has been growing at a faster rate than any other federal anti-bias employment law (**Box 52-2**). In particular the act protects workers over forty and prohibits forced retirement in most jobs because of age. Until 1987, federal law had permitted mandatory retirement at age seventy, but the 1986 amendments that took effect January 1, 1987, abolished the age ceiling, except for a few jobs such as firefighters, police officers, tenured university professors, and executives with annual pensions exceeding $44,000. Like Title VII, the law has a BFOQ exception—employers may set reasonable age limitations on certain high-stress jobs requiring peak physical condition, for example.

Discrimination against the Handicapped

The federal Rehabilitation Act of 1973, while not as broad as Title VII in its coverage of employers,

Forced Exits? Companies Confront Wave of Age-discrimination Suits

By Sydney P. Freedberg

*[Age discrimination lawsuits have been growing faster than any other federal anti-bias litigation. In order to prevent these lawsuits, employers are seeking new and better ways to manage the issues deriving from an increasingly "older" work force.—*AUTHORS' NOTE]

A jury in Dade City, Fla., recently found Lykes Pasco Inc., a juice processor, guilty of age discrimination when it fired Malcolm Anderson, a 59-year-old worker with 30 years of service. The jurors awarded Mr. Anderson $196,940—about 10 times his final annual salary.

Whatever the merits of Mr. Anderson's case (the company is appealing), the outcome was typical in one respect: When juries hear age-discrimination lawsuits, the odds favor the worker.

"It's very hard to convince a jury that a nice, white-haired man who lost his job after 20 years doesn't deserve something against the big, bad corporation," says Larry Besnoff, a management lawyer in Philadelphia.

Age discrimination is the fastest-growing type of bias charge in the workplace. Last year, almost 27,000 complaints were lodged with federal and state agencies—more than twice the number filed in 1980. Although many cases never reached court, the occasional blockbuster settlement "puts the fear of God in lots of man-

NEVER TOO OLD TO SUE

agers," says J. Robert Kirk, a Washington-based management lawyer.

While some areas of the law are still being mapped, enough cases have moved through the courts to give lawyers and personnel specialists a good idea of what constitutes age discrimination—and what does and doesn't work in pursuing or fighting such charges.

An individual who is pressing a lawsuit, for example, probably wants a jury trial; a company defending against such a suit probably wants a judge. Companies can still fire older workers, as long as age itself isn't a reason. But even casual asides—such as a boss referring to an employee as "the old man"—can be proof of discrimination. Companies sometimes lose suits because they can't document that an employee's work justified dismissal. But even with good personnel records, cases often boil down to credibility contests.

"You can trot out every statistic and business explanation in the book, but if a jury thinks an older worker has been treated unfairly, they won't listen," says Jack G. Knebel, a lawyer for Miles Inc. . . . [A] San Francisco jury [recently] ordered the company to pay $1.63 million to nine older workers who had been dismissed in a company-wide layoff. Miles, maker of Alka Seltzer, is asking for a new trial.

The Law

In the area of civil rights, the Age Discrimination in Employment Act is a "favored statute" among employees and their lawyers, says Paul Brenner, a staff lawyer for the Equal Employment Opportunity Commission. That's because the age act, unlike most other civil-rights statutes, allows jury trials as well as double damages for workers who prove "willful" discrimination by an employer.

Congress passed the law in 1967, preventing employers from using age as a basis for hiring or firing people ages 40 to 65. In 1978, the age cap was lifted to 70. . . . [Later] Congress eliminated the cap for most occupations. About one-third of the states have passed companion measures that restrict mandatory retirement.

Litigants typically start by filing a charge with the Equal Employment Opportunity Commission or its state counterpart. Such agencies can file a lawsuit on behalf of an employee, but their staffs are often bogged down. Thus, most workers simply go to court themselves.

Who Sues?

The typical age-bias litigant is a white male supervisor in his 50s who was discharged in a corporate belt-tightening. A recent study by Syracuse University School of Management, which reviewed more than 10,000 age-discrimination claims, says the average litigant sees a lawsuit as his only refuge; he has no union to represent him and can't qualify for racial or sexual discrimination.

A majority of the complaints, the study says, originate in right-to-work states outside the Northeast, where employers "may be more aggressive in discharging or forcing the retirement of older workers."

Last year, a fourth of the court actions filed by the Equal Employ-

BOX 52-2

ment Opportunity Commission fell under the age act. Raymond C. Fay, a Washington lawyer specializing in discrimination cases, attributes the rise in complaints to heightened public awareness of the law and the growing numbers of workers covered by it.

In Court

Only about one age-discrimination case in five makes it to a jury. "A lot of these complaints ought not to be in court," says Christopher S. Miller, an Atlanta lawyer who co-authored the Syracuse study. "They're straight grievance claims by older workers who were the unfortunate victims of companies that were forced to cut back."

The Syracuse study says judges rule for companies about two-thirds of the time, not including those cases decided on procedural issues. Conversely, Mr. Miller says, juries side with older workers about two-thirds of the time. Says San Francisco management lawyer Victor Schachter, "Juries are inherently biased in favor of long-term employees who work for deep-pocket companies."

Rave Reviews

To avoid age-bias lawsuits, management specialists caution companies to avoid inflating performance appraisals and to ensure a thorough accurate paper trail for each employee.

Such reviews played a role in the recent judgment against Miles, which merged with Cutter Laboratories Inc. in 1983 and inherited age-bias charges. At the trial in August, Miles argued that $60 million in losses prompted Cutter to lay off 1,200 workers in 1982 and that it picked the least productive employees with the worst sales records. But the nine workers who sued claimed that the company's stan-

---

A Profile of Litigation

An analysis of 280 federal court cases involving claims under the Age Discrimination in Employment Act showed that:

- 84% were filed by white males
- 68% dealt with an employee's dismissal or involuntary retirement
- 59% were filed by managerial and professional employees
- 54% were filed by employees between the ages of 50 and 59

Sources: Syracuse University; American Association of Retired Persons

---

dards were biased against workers over 40, and their lawyer produced records showing that they had received glowing performance evaluations over the years.

The six-member District Court jury—all but one over 40 years old—believed the salespeople. What's more, the jury found the discrimination "willful" and awarded double damages—$1.63 million.

What To Do?

Any hiring or firing decision in which age has crept into the process is suspect under the law.

A company can be held liable, for instance, if an age-neutral layoff policy ends up having a disproportionate effect on older workers. An employer could also have trouble in court for involuntarily transferring an older worker who performs at a minimally acceptable level. And a company can lose a lawsuit simply on the basis of a seemingly harmless aside. In the case of Lykes Pasco, a subsidiary of Tampa, Fla.-based Lykes Bros. Inc., two secretaries testified that two executives called Mr. Anderson "the old man" and "too darned old." (The executives denied it.) In the Miles-

Cutter case, a manager allegedly commented that he preferred salespeople in their 20s. (The manager denied it.)

"Remarks like, 'We need new blood,' can be the kiss of death for a company defending against an age-bias claim," says Mr. Miller, the Atlanta lawyer.

Even a company's manuals and forms can cause trouble if they reflect any age bias. Some businesses, for example, have decided to remove the "Date of Birth" box from their job-application forms and have stopped asking what year an applicant graduated from high school or college.

Golden Handcuffs

To thwart lawsuits, some companies are starting to ask retiring employees to sign notarized releases waiving all age-discrimination claims. Some lawyers, however, debate the validity of such releases. . . . [I]n Cincinnati, a federal appeals court overturned a decision that had declared such a release illegal. The employee who had signed the release was a lawyer for NCR Corp.

(continued on next page)

BOX 52-2

(Box 52-2 continued)

Coming Attractions

The current interest in age discrimination, lawyers say, may be nothing compared to what lies ahead. By the year 2010, people age 40 or over—those protected by the law—are expected to make up half the work force. More older people with medical handicaps are likely to file suit, alleging both age and handicap bias. "More older women and more older blacks will be contending for the same jobs held by older white men," says Mr. Miller.

As more companies seek ways to streamline aging work forces, new age-discrimination issues are likely to crop up in court: When does a "voluntary" early-retirement plan become subtly coercive? Can a company fire an older, higher-salaried worker to save money? And is the fast-track method of management—in which your younger "bright stars" are transferred from department to department to broaden their experience—legal?

Source: *Wall Street Journal*, October 13, 1987, p. 37

---

nevertheless, broadly bans discrimination against handicapped persons who are otherwise qualified to hold the job. The Supreme Court has said that "otherwise qualified" means a person "who is able to meet all of a program's requirements in spite of his handicap." In one particular case, a deaf woman was held not to be otherwise qualified for a job in a nursing program because hearing was a necessary requirement to carry out the duties of the job. (Southeastern Community College v. Davis, 442 U.S. 397 (1979)]

The act applies to businesses receiving federal financial assistance and to those entering into certain kinds of contracts (such as procurement contracts) with the federal government. Among other handicaps, the following have been held to be covered by the law: blindness, congenital back problem, epilepsy, carrying a potentially contagious disease, former drug addiction, and former alcoholism. But the law excludes current alcohol or drug abuse that would hinder the performance of the employee's duties or would constitute a threat to property or safety.

Two emerging issues, far from settled, are (1) whether the Rehabilitation Act precludes drug testing on the job to determine whether an employee has a drug habit that would prevent performance of the job, and (2) whether persons with AIDS (acquired immune deficiency syndrome) are handicapped under the law's definition. If they are not, then employers are within their rights to discharge or refuse to hire those with AIDS. By 1990, several federal appeals courts had ruled that AIDS is a handicap under Section 504 of the Act. The Supreme Court has yet to rule. In 1987 in a potentially related case, the Supreme Court ruled that a person afflicted with tuberculosis, a contagious disease, may be a handicapped person within the meaning of the Rehabilitation Act; contagion, by itself, is not sufficient to remove a person from the coverage of the law. The Court said that the trial court must conduct an individualized inquiry first to assess (a) the nature of the risk, (b) the duration of the risk, (c) the severity of the risk (the potential harm to third persons), and (d) the probabilities that the victim will transmit the disease to others, and then to determine whether the employer could make a reasonable accommodation in view of the risks. If the Court adheres to this position, it is likely that it will eventually find AIDS victims to be similarly protected [Arline v. School Board, 480 U.S. 273 (1987)]

In 1990, Congress broadly extended the rationale of the Rehabilitation Act by enacting the Americans with Disabilities Act. In general, it prohibits discrimination against the disabled (a term that has replaced the earlier term) in jobs, in transportation, and in public accommodations such as restaurants and shopping malls. This far-reaching act will take years to sort out. But in broad terms, it requires employers to hire, train, and promote qualified individuals regardless of their disabilities, if they can perform essential functions of the job. The Act requires employers to reasonably accommodate individuals with disabilities, for example, by modifying equipment or restructuring jobs. The act does not protect those who are currently using illegal drugs or who suffer from certain mental diseases, such as pyromania or kleptomania, but it does cover persons infected with AIDS. However, employers may decline to hire persons with contagious diseases or infections if others would stand a significant chance of contracting the disease. Employers who can demonstrate "undue hardship" need not accommodate workers with disabilities. An undue hardship is defined as "actions requiring significant difficulty or expense" compared to the nature and cost of the accommodation, the financial condition of the employer, and the type of business. Employees who prove violations of the Act are entitled to back pay, reinstatement, attorney's fees, and injunction against further violation.

EROSION OF THE EMPLOYMENT-AT-WILL DOCTRINE

At common law, an employee without a contract guaranteeing a job for a specific period was an **"employee at will"** and could be fired at any time and for any reason, or even for no reason at all. The various federal statutes we have just examined have made inroads on the at-will doctrine. Another federal statute, the Occupational Safety and Health Act, prohibits employers from discharging employees who exercise their rights under that law.

During the 1980s, the courts and legislatures in more than 40 states have made revolutionary changes in the at-will doctrine. They have done so under three theories: tort, contract, and duty of good faith and fair dealing. To attempt to codify the changes to the older theory in a uniform and consistent way, the Commissioners on Uniform State laws are working on a proposal for a Uniform Wrongful Discharge from Employment Law.

Tort Theories

One general principle by which courts have begun to provide remedies for firings without cause is that such a discharge constitutes a tort. The wrong alleged to occur is generally that the employer has breached a public policy against wrongful discharges. There are three classes of this tort.

First, most states will find for the plaintiff employee who has been fired for refusing to commit crimes, like committing perjury to benefit the company.

Second, many states, though by no means all, will bar retaliatory discharges against employees who avail themselves of a statutory right—for example, those who file workers' compensation claims or who refuse to take lie detector tests.

Third, several states have begun to recognize a cause of action for employees dismissed for performing a public duty, such as serving on a jury. Some states have enacted so-called **whistleblower statutes,** which protect the jobs of employees who "blow the whistle" on corrupt or otherwise illegal conduct of their employers. A few states protect such a right in the absence of legislation; thus, in *Palmateer* v. *International Harvester Co.*, 421 N.E.2d 876 (Ill. 1981), the supreme court of Illinois declared that an employee may not lawfully be fired for going to the authorities with information that a fellow employee might be involved in criminal actions. Discharges motivated by special employee acts covered by statutory provisions or public policy are, relatively speaking, not a large class of cases (although as **Box 52-3** suggests, the damages in any one of these cases can be huge). In any event, the emerging statutory and public policy exceptions do not cover firings unrelated to specific employee actions such as blowing the whistle or refusing to take a lie detector test. In many cases, personality conflicts or bad management practices may lead to employees' being fired without good cause. To reach these cases, many states have turned to two other theories.

Contract Theories

An explicit employment contract, usually made only with higher-ranking employees, has always provided a legal basis for suit should the employer violate it by discharging the employee. But until the early 1980s, courts refused to give legal effect to oral statements (for example, promises made during an initial interview for employment) or policy statements in personnel manuals that said or implied the employer

LAW AND LIFE

3 Ex-Workers of Lockheed are Awarded $45 Million

By Michael Lev

[*As the following article suggests, the damages assessed in a wrongful termination case can be huge. However, this particular jury verdict was overturned two months later for reasons unrelated to the plaintiff's claims when it was revealed that one of the jurors had previously been convicted of a felony; convicted felons are ineligible to serve on juries in California.*—AUTHORS' NOTE]

Los Angeles—In one of the largest punitive damage award cases of its kind, a jury . . . awarded $45 million to three former Lockheed employees who claimed they were wrongfully dismissed after raising questions about the safety of cargo jets the company makes for the Air Force.

Lawyers who represent workers said the decision sends a far-reaching message: Companies must allow employees to raise questions about unethical practices and product safety without fear of losing their jobs.

WHISTLEBLOWERS' REWARD

"This will act as a strong incentive for individuals to continue coming forward," said Janet Goldstein, a Los Angeles lawyer who represents defense workers, but was not involved in this case.

Attorneys representing the Lockheed Corporation denied that the three workers had been wrongfully dismissed and said they would appeal.

Joseph G. Twomey, Lockheed's vice president and general counsel, said in a statement that the punitive damage award was "grossly disproportionate to the actual damages found by the jury" and "unsupportable factually and legally."

After deliberating for six days, a Superior Court jury awarded the three employees $15 million each in punitive damages and less than $400,000 in compensatory damages split among them. The punitive damage amount was so large because juries are allowed to set punitive damages based on a company's size. Lockheed has almost $10 billion in sales.

The three former Lockheed employees are Tom Benecke, 48 years old, and Terrence Schielke, 40, both internal auditors, and Clyde W. Jones Jr., 62, a quality control worker. Their case dates to 1985, when Mr. Benecke and Mr. Schielke began raising questions about the safety of the mainframe of four cargo jets built in 1983. Lockheed built 50 of the jets between 1983 and 1989 at a cost of $6.6 billion.

The trial was not intended to rule on Lockheed's competence, its ethical practices or the airworthiness of the giant C5-B cargo jets, which are being used by the Air Force to ferry troops to the Persian Gulf for Operation Desert Shield.

But Lockheed attorneys said the three employees won because their lawyers, while trying a wrongful termination case, focused attention on issues of product liability and contractor fraud.

"This was a wrongful termination case, not a False Claims Act or 'whistleblower' case," said Gordon E. Krischer, an attorney representing Lockheed. "What the other side did is try this case as a product liability

would fire only for just cause. Beginning in the early 1980s, many courts began to hold that such statements were legally binding. [Weiner v. McGraw-Hill, Inc., 433 N.E.2d 441 (N.Y. 1983)] For the employee, the contract theory might not provide long-term benefits, since the theory requires that there be some statement from which the courts can infer an agreement. An employee manual that makes no assurances, statements in manuals or other company documents that expressly disclaim any intention to deviate from the common law rule, and employees' signed acknowledgments that they serve at the will of the company will almost always operate to the employer's advantage. A contract theory requires a contract; in the absence of one, the at-will doctrine will still prevail.

BOX 52-3

case. They inflamed the jury about a defect in the airplane, which didn't exist. Lockheed was punished because the jury believed them."

Herbert Hafif, one of the plaintiffs' attorneys, said the issue of Lockheed's manufacturing quality was strongly linked to his case.

"The issue put to the jury was, Were they fired as a result of bringing attention to Lockheed's dangerous safety questions?" he said. "The answer was a resounding yes. My argument to the jury was: They made about $40 million to $60 million profit on the first four planes. Why should they keep a dime?"

While Mr. Hafif has been active in filing lawsuits under the False Claims Act claiming contractor fraud, he said he chose to pursue the issue of wrongful termination because he thought he would have a better chance of success. A False Claims Act case typically requires the Justice Department to join the prosecution.

The defendants' punitive awards of $15 million each are probably the third-largest awarded to an individual in a wrongful termination suit in the United States, said Jim Dertouzos, a senior economist with the Rand Corporation in Santa Monica, Calif. The aggregate damages of $45 million are by far the largest ever awarded in a wrongful termination suit, said Mr. Dertouzos, an expert in wrongful termination issues.

In detailing the case, Eric Jelber, one of the plaintiffs' attorneys, said Mr. Benecke and Mr. Schielke noticed hard and soft spots in mainframe metal and other defects on the planes. While officials from Lockheed and the Air Force had previously examined such complaints, the two employees felt the problem had been "swept under the rug," Mr. Jelber said.

When the two were told not to pursue the matter further, they conducted their own investigation, paying to have mainframe samples sent to an outside metallurgist, who backed up their claims. The two, joined by Mr. Jones, then wrote letters to Lawrence O. Kitchen, then Lockheed's chief executive, demanding the jets be grounded until tests could be run.

Mr. Hafif has claimed that the problems still exist, but Lockheed said the company investigated and found the alleged problems had been addressed well before the first letter arrived.

Lockheed said two of the men, Mr. Benecke and Mr. Schielke, were fired for unprofessional conduct and for violating company politics and audit procedures. In pursuing the cargo-jet investigation on their own, Lockheed said, the two men failed to follow the required procedure in reporting any potential problems they discovered. The third man, Mr. Jones, retired early and was not fired, the company said.

While the damage award could be reversed or scaled back on appeal, attorneys who represent companies in labor disputes said they were concerned by the verdict.

"The punitive damages were 113.5 times the amount of the actual economic loss suffered by the individuals," said Frank Cronin, managing partner in the Los Angeles office of Jackson, Lewis, Schnitzler and Krupman, a national labor law firm representing management.

Source: *New York Times*, November 16, 1990, P.D1

Good Faith and Fair Dealing Standard

A few states, among them Massachusetts and California, have modified the at-will doctrine in a far-reaching way by holding that every employer has entered into an implied covenant of good faith and fair dealing with its employees. That means, say the courts in these states, that it is "bad faith" and therefore unlawful to discharge employees to avoid paying commissions or pensions due them. Under this implied covenant of fair dealing, any discharge without good cause—such as incompetence, corruption, or habitual tardiness—is actionable.

As the next case shows, a single discharge can give rise to all three types of claims, and the outcome will hinge on the particular circumstances that gave rise to the suit.

**FOLEY v.
INTERACTIVE DATA
CORPORATION**
47 Cal.3d 654, 254
Cal.Rptr. 211, 765 P.2d
373 (1988)

LUCAS, CHIEF JUSTICE

After Interactive Data Corporation (defendant) fired plaintiff Daniel D. Foley, an executive employee, he filed this action seeking compensatory and punitive damages for wrongful discharge. In his second amended complaint, plaintiff asserted three distinct theories: (1) a tort cause of action alleging a discharge in violation of public policy (*Tameny v. Atlantic Richfield Co.* (1980) 610 (1330), (2) a contract cause of action for breach of an implied-in-fact promise to discharge for good cause only, . . . and (3) a cause of action alleging a tortious breach of the implied covenant of good faith and fair dealing. The trial court sustained a demurrer without leave to amend, and entered judgment for defendant.

The Court of Appeal affirmed on the grounds (1) plaintiff alleged no statutorily based breach of public policy sufficient to state a cause of action pursuant to *Tameny;* (2) plaintiff's claim for breach of the covenant to discharge only for good cause was barred by the statute of frauds; and (3) plaintiff's cause of action based on breach of the covenant of good faith and fair dealing failed because it did not allege necessary longevity of employment or express formal procedures for termination of employees. We granted review to consider each of the Court of Appeal's conclusions.

We will hold that the Court of Appeal properly found that plaintiff's particular *Tameny* cause of action could not proceed; plaintiff failed to allege facts showing a violation of a fundamental public policy. We will also conclude, however, that plaintiff has sufficiently alleged a breach of an "oral" or "implied-in-fact" contract, and that the statute of frauds does not bar his claim so that he may pursue his action in this regard. Finally, we will hold that the covenant of good faith and fair dealing applies to employment contracts and that breach of the covenant may give rise to contract but not tort damages.

FACTS

Because this appeal arose from a judgment entered after the trial court sustained defendant's demurrer, "we must, under established principles, assume the truth of all properly pleaded material allegations of the complaint in evaluating the validity" of the decision below. (*Tameny v. Atlantic Richfield Co.*, supra, 610 P.2d 1330; *Alcorn v. Anbro Engineering, Inc.* (1970) 468 P.2d 216.)

According to the complaint, plaintiff is a former employee of defendant, a wholly owned subsidiary of Chase Manhattan Bank that markets computer-based decision-support services. Defendant hired plaintiff in June 1976 as an assistant product manager at a starting salary of $18,500. As a condition of employment defendant required plaintiff to sign a "Confidential and Proprietary Information Agreement" whereby he promised not to engage in certain competition with defendant for one year after the termination of his employment for any reason. The agreement also contained a "Disclosure and Assignment of Information" provision that obliged plaintiff to disclose to defendant all computer-related information known to him, including any innovations, inventions or developments pertaining to the computer field for a period of one year following his termination. Finally, the agreement imposed on plaintiff a continuing obligation to assign to defendant all rights to his computer-related inventions or innovations for one year following termination. It did not state any limitation on the grounds for which plaintiff's employment could be terminated.

Over the next six years and nine months, plaintiff received a steady series of salary increases, promotions, bonuses, awards and superior performance evaluations. In 1979 defendant named him consultant manager of the year and in 1981 promoted him to branch manager of its Los Angeles office. His annual salary rose to $56,164 and he received an additional $6,762 merit bonus two days before his discharge in March 1983. He alleges defendant's officers made repeated oral assurances of job security so long as his performance remained adequate.

Plaintiff also alleged that during his employment, defendant maintained written "Termination Guidelines" that set forth express grounds for discharge and a mandatory seven-step pretermination procedure. Plaintiff understood that these guidelines applied not only to employees under plaintiff's supervision, but to him as well. On the basis of these representations, plaintiff alleged that he reasonably believed defendant would not discharge him except for good cause, and therefore he refrained from accepting or pursuing other job opportunities.

The event that led to plaintiff's discharge was a private conversation in January 1983 with his former supervisor, vice president Richard Earnest. During the previous year defendant had hired Robert Kuhne and subsequently named Kuhne to replace Earnest as plaintiff's immediate supervisor. Plaintiff learned that Kuhne was currently under investigation by the Federal Bureau of Investigation for embezzlement from his former employer, Bank of America. Plaintiff reported what he knew about Kuhne to Earnest, because he was "worried about working for Kuhne and having him in a supervisory position . . . , in view of Kuhne's suspected criminal conduct." Plaintiff asserted he "made this disclosure in the interest and for the benefit of his employer," allegedly because he believed that because defendant and its parent do business with the financial community on a confidential basis, the company would have a legitimate interest in knowing about a high executive's alleged prior criminal conduct.

In response, Earnest allegedly told plaintiff not to discuss "rumors" and to "forget what he heard" about Kuhne's past. In early March, Kuhne informed plaintiff that defendant had decided to replace him for "performance reasons" and that he could transfer to a position in another division in Waltham, Massachusetts. Plaintiff was told that if he did not accept a transfer, he might be demoted but not fired. One week later, in Waltham, Earnest informed plaintiff he was not doing a good job, and six days later, he notified plaintiff he could continue as a branch manager if he "agreed to go on a 'performance plan.' Plaintiff asserts he agreed to consider such an

(continued on next page)

(continued)

**FOLEY v.
INTERACTIVE DATA
CORPORATION**
47 Cal.3d 654, 254
Cal.Rptr. 211, 765 P.2d
373 (1988)

arrangement. The next day, when Kuhne met with plaintiff, purportedly to present him with a written "performance plan" proposal, Kuhne instead informed plaintiff he had a choice of resigning or being fired. Kuhne offered neither a performance plan nor an option to transfer to another position.

* * *

We turn first to plaintiff's cause of action alleging he was discharged in violation of public policy. . . .

* * *

. . . *Tameny v. Atlantic Richfield Co.* declared that a tort action for wrongful discharge may lie if the employer "condition[s] employment upon required participation in unlawful conduct by the employee." In *Tameny*, the plaintiff alleged he was fired for refusing to engage in price fixing in violation of the Cartwright Act and the Sherman Antitrust Act. . . . In upholding the claim in *Tameny*, we explained that the cause of action was not dependent on an express or implied promise in the employment contract, "but rather reflects a duty imposed by law upon all employers in order to implement the fundamental public policies embodied in the state's penal statutes.". . .

* * *

The Court of Appeal in the present case asserted, "[t]o successfully plead a cause of action under the [*Tameny*] theory, plaintiff must allege that he was terminated in retaliation for asserting his statutory rights, or for his refusal to perform an illegal act at the request of the employer, or that his employer directly violated a statute by dismissing him."

* * *

In the present case, plaintiff alleges that defendant discharged him in "sharp derogation" of a substantial public policy that imposes a legal duty on employees to report relevant business information to management. . . . Thus, plaintiff asserts, if he discovered information that might lead his employer to conclude that an employee was an embezzler, and should not be retained, plaintiff had a duty to communicate that information to his principal.

* * *

Whether or not there is a statutory duty requiring an employee to report information relevant to his employer's interest, we do not find a substantial public policy prohibiting an employer from discharging an employee for performing that duty. Past decisions recognizing a tort action for discharge in violation of public policy seek to protect the public, by protecting the employee who refuses to commit a crime. . . . No equivalent public interest bars the discharge of the present plaintiff. When the duty of an employee to disclose information to his employer serves only the private interest of the employer, the rationale underlying the *Tameny* cause of action is not implicated.

*   *   *

Plaintiff's second cause of action alleged that over the course of his nearly seven years of employment with defendant, the company's own conduct and personnel policies gave rise to an "oral contract" not to fire him without good cause. . . .

*   *   *

Although plaintiff describes his cause of action as one for breach of an oral contract, he does not allege explicit words by which the parties agreed that he would not be terminated without good cause. Instead he alleges that a course of conduct, including various oral representations, created a reasonable expectation to that effect. Thus, his cause of action is more properly described as one for breach of an implied-in-fact contract.

*   *   *

The absence of an express written or oral contract term concerning termination of employment does not necessarily indicate that the employment is actually intended by the parties to be "at will," because the presumption of at-will employment may be overcome by evidence of contrary intent. Generally, courts seek to enforce the actual understanding of the parties to a contract, and in so doing may inquire into the parties' conduct to determine if it demonstrates an implied contract. . . .

*   *   *

. . . Plaintiff here alleged repeated oral assurances of job security and consistent promotions, salary increases and bonuses during the term of his employment contributing to his reasonable expectation that he would not be discharged except for good cause.

*   *   *

Finally, plaintiff alleges that he supplied the company valuable and separate consideration by signing an agreement whereby he promised not to compete or conceal any computer-related information from defendant for one year after termination. The noncompetition agreement and its attendant "Disclosure and Assignment of Proprietary Information, Inventions, etc." may be probative evidence that "it is more probable that the parties intended a continuing relationship, with limitations upon the employer's dismissal authority [because the] employee has provided some benefit to the employer, or suffers some detriment, beyond the usual rendition of service."

In sum, plaintiff has pleaded facts which, if proved, may be sufficient for a jury to find an implied-in-fact contract limiting defendant's right to discharge him arbitrarily. . . .

We turn now to plaintiff's cause of action for tortious breach of the implied covenant of good faith and fair dealing. . . . [P]laintiff asserts we should recognize tort remedies for such a breach in the context of employment termination.

(continued on next page)

(continued)

**FOLEY v.
INTERACTIVE DATA
CORPORATION**
47 Cal.3d 654, 254
Cal.Rptr. 211, 765 P.2d
373 (1988)

The distinction between tort and contract is well grounded in common law, and divergent objectives underlie the remedies created in the two areas. Whereas contract actions are created to enforce the intentions of the parties to the agreement, tort law is primarily designed to vindicate "social policy." The covenant of good faith and fair dealing was developed in the contract arena and is aimed at making effective the agreement's promises. Plaintiff asks that we find that the breach of the implied covenant in employment contracts also gives rise to an action seeking an award of tort damages.

* * *

In our view, the underlying problem in the line of cases relied on by plaintiff lies in the decisions' uncritical incorporation of the insurance model into the employment context, without careful consideration of the fundamental policies underlying the development of tort and contract law in general or of significant differences between the insurer/insured and employer/employee relationships. When a court enforces the implied covenant it is in essence acting to protect "the interest in having promises performed"—the traditional realm of a contract action—rather than to protect some general duty to society which the law places on an employer without regard to the substance of its contractual obligations to its employee.

* * *

After review of the various commentators, and independent consideration of the similarities between the two areas, we are not convinced that a "special relationship" analogous to that between insurer and insured should be deemed to exist in the usual employment relationship which would warrant recognition of a tort action for breach of the implied covenant. Even if we were to assume that the special relationship model is an appropriate one to follow in determining whether to expand tort recovery, a breach in the employment context does not place the employee in the same economic dilemma that an insured faces when an insurer in bad faith refuses to pay a claim or to accept a settlement offer within policy limits. When an insurer takes such actions, the insured cannot turn to the marketplace to find another insurance company willing to pay for the loss already incurred. The wrongfully terminated employee, on the other hand, can (and must, in order to mitigate damages) make reasonable efforts to seek alternative employment. Moreover, the role of the employer differs from that of the "quasi-public" insurance company with whom individuals contract specifically in order to obtain protection from potential specified economic harm. The employer does not similarly "sell" protection to its employees; it is not providing a public service. . . .

* * *

We therefore conclude that the employment relationship is not sufficiently similar to that of insurer and insured to warrant judicial extension of the proposed additional tort remedies in view of the countervailing concerns about economic policy and stability, the traditional separation of tort and contract law, and finally, the numerous protections against improper terminations already afforded employees.

Our inquiry, however, does not end here. The potential effects on an individual caused by termination of employment arguably justify additional remedies for certain improper discharges. . . .

The issue is how far courts can or should go in responding to these concerns regarding the sufficiency of compensation by departing from long established principles of contract law. Significant policy judgments affecting social policies and commercial relationships are implicated in the resolution of this question in the employment termination context. Such a determination, which has the potential to alter profoundly the nature of employment, the cost of products and services, and the availability of jobs, arguably is better suited for legislative decisionmaking. . . .

*　　★　　★

We are not unmindful of the legitimate concerns of employees who fear arbitrary and improper discharges that may have a devastating effect on their economic and social status. Nor are we unaware of or unsympathetic to claims that contract remedies for breaches of contract are insufficient because they do not fully compensate due to their failure to include attorney fees and their restrictions on foreseeable damages. These defects, however, exist generally in contract situations. As discussed above, the variety of possible courses to remedy the problem is well demonstrated in the literature and include increased contract damages, provision for award of attorney fees, establishment of arbitration or other speedier and less expensive dispute resolution, or the tort remedies (the scope of which is also subject to dispute) sought by plaintiff here.

The diversity of possible solutions demonstrates the confusion that occurs when we look outside the realm of contract law in attempting to fashion remedies for a breach of a contract provision. . . . "In other words, I believe that under all the circumstances, the problem is one for the Legislature . . ."

Plaintiff may proceed with his cause of action alleging a breach of an implied-in-fact contract promise to discharge him only for good cause; his claim is not barred by the statute of frauds. His cause of action for a breach of public policy pursuant to *Tameny* was properly dismissed because the facts alleged, even if proven, would not establish a discharge in violation of public policy. Finally, as to his cause of action for tortious breach of the implied covenant of good faith and fair dealing, we hold that tort remedies are not available for breach of the implied covenant in an employment contract to employees who allege they have been discharged in violation of the covenant.

Libel Actions

The employer's power to discharge employees is constrained not only by the anti-discrimination provisions of Title VII and by erosion of the employment-will-doctrine but also by the increasing resort to common-law suits for defamation. The basic charge in most such suits by former employees is that employers have libeled or slandered them when giving references to new or prospective employers. Like plaintiffs in age discrimination suits, discharged employees find sympathetic juries when their cases eventually get that far. Although the law is different from state to state, the national statistics show that more lawyers have been getting more such cases to the juries (see **Box 52-4**).

OTHER EMPLOYMENT-RELATED LAWS

The Federal Plant Closing Act

A prime source of new jobs across America is the opening of new industrial plants—accounting for millions of jobs a year during the 1970s and 1980s. But for every 110 jobs thus created, nearly 100 have been lost annually in plant closings. In the mid-1980s alone, 2.2 million plant jobs were lost each year. As serious as these losses are for the national economy, they are no less serious for the individuals who are let go. Surveys in the 1980s showed that large numbers of companies provided little or no notice to employees that their factories were to be shut down and their jobs eliminated. Nearly a quarter of businesses with more than 100 employees provided no specific notice to their employees that their particular work site would be closed or that they would suffer mass layoffs. More than half provided two weeks' notice or less. Because programs to support dislocated workers depend heavily on the giving of advance notice, a national debate on the issue in the late 1980s culminated in 1988 in Congress's enactment of the Worker Adjustment and Retraining Notification Act, the formal name of the federal plant closing act. Under this law, businesses with 100 or more employees must give employees or their local bargaining unit, along with the local city or county government, at least 60 days' notice when-

ever (1) at least 50 employees in a single plant or office facility would lose their jobs or face long-term layoffs or reduction of more than half their working hours as the result of a shutdown, and (2) a shutdown would require long-term layoffs of 500 employees or at least a third of the work force. An employer who violates the act is liable to employees for back pay that they would have received during the notice period, and may be liable to other fines and penalties.

Polygraph Protection Act

Studies calling into question the reliability of various forms of lie detectors have led at least half the states and, in 1988, Congress to legislate against their use by private businesses. The Employee Polygraph Protection Act forbids private employers from using lie detectors for any reason (these include such devices as voice stress analyzers). Neither employees nor applicants for jobs may be required or even asked to submit to them. (The act has some exceptions for public employers, defense and intelligence businesses, private companies in the security business, and manufacturers of controlled substances.)

Use of polygraphs, machines that record changes in the subject's blood pressure, pulse, and other physiological phenomena, is strictly limited. They may be used in conjunction with an investigation into such crimes as theft, embezzlement, and industrial espionage, but in order to require the employee to submit to polygraph testing, the employer must have "reasonable suspicion" that the employee is involved in the crime, and there must be supporting evidence for the employer to discipline or discharge the employee either on the basis of the polygraph results or on the employee's refusal to submit to testing. The federal polygraph law does not preempt state laws, so if a state law absolutely bars an employer from using one, the federal law's limited authorization will be unavailable.

Occupational Safety and Health Act

In a heavily industrialized society, workplace safety is a major concern. Hundreds of studies for more than a century have documented the gruesome toll taken by hazardous working conditions in mines, on

Fired Employees Turn the Reason for Dismissal into a Legal Weapon

By Gregory Stricharchuk

[More lawyers are getting wrongful termination cases to the juries, and these juries are sympathetic to individuals who have been "put on the street" by a big company. If a lawyer proves that a fired employee was defamed, the damages can be substantial. As a result, many companies now refrain from making any negative comments about former employees.—AUTHORS' NOTE]

Companies that fire people are discovering they have to choose their final words very carefully.

Employees are turning the reason for their firing into a legal weapon: a libel charge. Because such individuals frequently are dismissed for poor performance or some form of misconduct that isn't well-documented they are able to claim that any report about their performance to others—such as from their former employer to a prospective employer—constitutes defamation.

The result is that libel suits filed by discharged employees against their former bosses today account for about a third of all defamation actions, according to Jury Verdict Research Inc. in Solon, Ohio. "These suits are the new workhorse in termination litigation," says Rodney A. Smolla, a University of Arkansas law professor and libel specialist.

The Silent Treatment
The trend is prompting many companies to refrain from making any

NEW LEGAL PERIL FOR EMPLOYERS WHO FIRE WORKERS

negative statements about former employees. But even the very act of dismissing someone can still land a company in court. If a fired worker is forced to disclose in a job interview the reason he was let go, such "compelled self-publication," as the courts define it, can also constitute defamation.

"There's no such thing as just firing someone anymore," a corporate lawyer says.

Defending such actions can take years and cost employers tens of thousands of dollars. Former workers who won their cases collected an average of almost $112,000 in 1982, the latest year for which statistics are available.

"Juries don't have a lot of sympathy for big companies putting someone on the street," says John B. Lewis, a Cleveland lawyer who defends corporations against employment-related litigation. "Juries also have a high regard for a person's reputation."

Harshly criticizing a former employee to others is perhaps the easiest way a company can make itself vulnerable to a defamation suit. Consider Larry W. Buck, who was abruptly fired from his insurance broker's job at a Frank B. Hall & Co. office in Texas. When he couldn't find new employment, he hired a private detective to find out why he had been dismissed.

According to transcripts of testimony in Harris County court in

Houston, Mr. Buck's former boss told the detective (who explained that Mr. Buck was being considered for a position of trust) that Mr. Buck was ruthless, disliked by his co-workers and a failure as a businessman. The boss described Mr. Buck as a "classical sociopath, a zero, a Jekyll-and-Hyde person who was lacking in . . . scruples."

Armed with the detective's tape-recorded interviews, Mr. Buck sued Frank B. Hall for defamation. In court, Hall executives said Mr. Buck was fired for failing to produce sufficient income, and they argued that he shouldn't recover damages because he invited their comments through hiring the investigator. But a jury agreed he had been libeled and slandered and awarded him $1.9 million. The U.S. Supreme Court upheld the award last year.

In other cases, fired employees are seeking libel damages simply because their performance was judged unsatisfactory—and that judgment was disseminated outside the company.

American Standard Corp., for example, found itself the target of a libel suit because of a letter it distributed to a state employment agency in 1978, noting that a manager had been fired for "unsatisfactory performance." The manager, Gerald F. Adler, maintained that he was dismissed for reporting alleged misdeeds at the company. (A spokesman for American Standard says the misdeeds were "vague and . . . never substantiated.")

Last January, Mr. Adler was awarded $2.8 million by a Baltimore federal jury. The judge who heard the case, however, threw out the jury's finding that Mr. Adler had been defamed and left damages related to "abusive discharge." Mr. Adler has

(continued on next page)

(continued)

appealed the decision; American Standard says it plans to appeal.

Anxious to avoid the high costs and aggravation of libel suits, many companies are sharply restricting information they will provide about former employees. Some refuse to offer anything more than a former worker's name, rank and dates of employment. But this tight-lipped approach can come back to haunt companies as they attempt to screen out incompetent and dishonest job applicants.

Arthur Silbergeld, a California lawyer, blames inadequate reference information for the high turnover of employees in that state's financial institutions. "Once on the job," he says, "the companies find that the employees can't do the job—that the skills aren't there."

An executive in TRW Inc.'s electronics and defense division recently told a U.S. Senate subcommittee that workers are able to cover up problems in their pasts and still land jobs in the defense industry because companies are wary of becoming involved in libel suits. Cleveland-based TRW, he said, would rather reject job applicants outright than confront them with negative information. Defending defamation suits, the company estimates, costs between $140,000 and $250,000 each.

Personnel consultants say one of the best ways companies can defend themselves against defamation litigation is to help discharged employees find new jobs through outplacement counseling. "People who find new jobs don't sue, while many who don't find jobs blame it on the previous employer," says Paul Thompson, a Virginia lawyer.

Companies can also help themselves by conducting regular and comprehensive performance appraisals and exit interviews. Such "progressive discipline," says John Donovan, a Buffalo, N.Y., lawyer, leaves no doubts why an employee was dismissed.

Even if a company refrains from releasing negative information about a fired employee, the company still may be vulnerable to a libel suit if the dismissal came with little warning and the reasons for the firing were unclear. If the discharged worker is forced to tell a new employer the reason he was let go, such "compelled self-publication" can constitute defamation if the reason for the firing can't be fully documented.

Disclosing the Facts

Four dental claims processors fired by Equitable Life Assurance Society in St. Paul, Minn., won a defamation suit against Equitable even though they—and not the company—disclosed they were dismissed for "gross insubordination." The four were fired after supervisors questioned expense vouchers they had submitted and ordered the women to change the vouchers.

Equitable's lawyers "laughed at us" when the suit was filed, says James W. Kenney, an attorney for the discharged employees. But a Ramsey County jury awarded the women more than $1 million.

The verdict was upheld last July by the Minnesota Supreme Court, which eliminated about $600,000 in punitive damages. Nonetheless, the ruling established in Minnesota the concept of compelled self-publication, which Georgia, Michigan and California also recognize.

Although it is unclear whether the verdict will result in a flood of similar suits, the Minnesota Supreme Court expressed such concerns in its ruling. The court said it disallowed the punitive damages because that award might stop employers from disclosing the reasons for discharging employees, which the court felt wouldn't be in the public interest.

A dissenting judge wrote, "Now the only way an employer can avoid litigation and the possible liability for substantial damages is to cease communicating the reason (for) the termination, not only to third persons, but even to the employee."

Source: Wall Street Journal, October 2, 1986, p. 31

railroads, and in factories from tools, machines, treacherous surroundings, and toxic chemicals and other substances. Studies in the late 1960s showed that more than 14,000 workers were killed annually and 2.2 million were disabled—at a cost of more than $8 billion and a loss of more than 250 million worker days. Congress responded in 1970 with the Occupational Safety and Health Act (OSHA), the primary aim of which is "to assure so far as possible every working man and woman in the Nation safe and healthful working conditions."

OSHA imposes on each employer a general duty to furnish a place of employment free from recognized hazards likely to cause death or serious physical arm to employees. It also gives the Secretary of Labor the power to establish national health and safety standards. The standard-making power has been delegated to the Occupational Safety and Health Administration (OSHA), an agency within the U.S. Department of Labor. OSHA has the authority to inspect workplaces covered by the act, whenever it receives complaints from employees or reports about fatal or multiple injuries. The agency may assess penalties and proceed administratively to enforce its standards. Criminal provisions of the act are enforced by the Justice Department.

During its first two decades, OSHA has been severely criticized for the glacial pace of its standard promulgating: fewer than 30 national workplace safety standards were issued by 1990. But not all safety enforcement is in the hands of the federal government: although OSHA standards preempt similar state standards, under the Act the Secretary may permit the states to come up with standards equal to or better than federal standards and may make grants to the states to cover half the costs of enforcement of the state safety standards.

Employee Retirement Income Security Act

More than half the American work force is covered by private pension plans for retirement. One 1988 estimate put the total held in pension funds at more than one *trillion* dollars, costing the federal treasury nearly $60 billion annually in tax write-offs. As the size of the private pension funds increased dramatically in the 1960s, Congress began to hear shocking stories of employees defrauded out of pension benefits, deprived of a lifetime's savings through various ruses (for example, by long vesting provisions and by discharges just before retirement). To put an end to such abuses, in 1974 Congress enacted the Employee Retirement Income Security Act (ERISA).

In general, ERISA governs the vesting of employees' pension rights and the funding of pension plans. Within five years of beginning employment, employees are entitled to vested interests in retirement benefits contributed on their behalf by individual employers. Multi-employer pension plans must vest their employees' interests within ten years. A variety of pension plans must be insured through a federal agency, the Pension Benefit Guaranty Corporation, to

which employers must pay annual premiums. The Corporation may assume financial control of underfunded plans and may sue to require employers to make up deficiencies. ERISA also requires pension funds to disclose financial information to beneficiaries, permits employees to sue for benefits, governs the standards of conduct of fund administrators, and forbids employers from denying employees their rights to pensions. ERISA largely preempts state law governing employee benefits.

Fair Labor Standards Act

In the midst of the Depression, Congress enacted at President Roosevelt's urging a national minimum wage law, the Fair Labor Standards Act of 1938 (FLSA). The act prohibits most forms of child labor and established a scale of minimum wages for the regular work week and a higher scale for overtime. (The original hourly minimum was 25 cents, although the Administrator of the Wage and Hour Division of the U.S. Department of Labor, a position created by the act, could raise the minimum rate industry by industry.) FLSA originally was limited to certain types of work: that which was performed in transporting goods in interstate commerce or in producing goods for shipment in interstate commerce. Employers quickly learned that they could limit the minimum wage by, for example, separating the inter- and intrastate components of their production. Within the next quarter century, the scope of FLSA was considerably broadened, so that it now covers all workers in businesses that do a particular dollar-volume of goods that move in interstate commerce, regardless of whether a particular employee actually works in the interstate component of the business. FLSA now covers between 80 and 90 percent of all persons privately employed outside of agriculture, and a lesser but substantial percentage of agricultural workers and state and local government employees. Violations of the act are investigated by the Administrator of the Wage and Hour Division, who has authority to negotiate back pay on the employee's behalf. If no settlement is reached, the Labor Department may sue on the employee's behalf or the employee, armed with a notice of the Administrator's calculations of back wages due may sue in federal or state court for back pay. Under FLSA, a successful employee will receive double the amount of back wages due.

Workers' Compensation Laws

As we note in more detail elsewhere (p. 831), since the beginning of the 20th century work-related injuries or illnesses are covered under state workers' compensation laws that provide a set amount of weekly compensation for disabilities caused by accidents and illnesses suffered on the job. The compensation plans also pay hospital and other medical expenses necessary to treat workers who are injured by or become ill from their work. In assuring workers of compensation, they eliminate the hazards and uncertainties of lawsuits by eliminating the need to prove fault. Employers fund the compensation programs by paying into statewide plans or purchasing insurance.

Other State Laws

Although it may appear that most employment law is federal, in fact employment discrimination at least is largely governed by state law because Congress has so declared. The Civil Rights Act of 1964 tells federal courts to defer to state agencies to enforce antidiscrimination provisions of parallel state statutes with remedies similar to those of the federal law. Moreover, many states have gone beyond federal law in banning certain forms of discrimination. Thus, well before enactment of the Americans with Disabilities Act, more than 40 states prohibited such discrimination in private employment. More than a dozen states ban employment discrimination based on marital status, a category not covered by federal law. And two states and more than 70 counties or municipalities ban employment discrimination on the basis of sexual orientation; most large companies have offices or plants in at least one of these jurisdictions. By contrast, federal law has no provision dealing with sexual orientation.

CHAPTER SUMMARY

For the past twenty-five years, Title VII of the Civil Rights Act of 1964 has prohibited employment discrimination based on race, religion, sex, or national origins. Any employment decision, including hiring, promotion, and discharge, based on one of these factors is unlawful and subjects the employer to an award of back pay, promotion, or reinstatement. The EEOC may file suits as may the employee—after the commission screens the complaint.

Two major types of discrimination suits are those for disparate treatment (in which the employer intended to discriminate) and disparate impact (in which, regardless of intent, the impact of a particular non-job-related practice has a discriminatory effect). In matters of religion, the employer is bound not only to refrain from discrimination based on an employee's religious beliefs or preferences but also to accommodate the employee's religious practices, to the extent that the accommodation does not impose an undue hardship on the business.

Sex discrimination, besides refusal to hire a person solely on the basis of sex, includes discrimination based on pregnancy. Sexual harassment is a form of sex discrimination, and the term includes creation of a hostile or offensive working environment. A separate statute, the Equal Pay Act, mandates equal pay for men and women assigned to the same job.

One major exception to Title VII permits hiring people of a particular religion, sex, or nationality if that feature is a bona fide occupational qualification. There is no BFOQ exception for race. Nor is a public stereotype a legitimate basis for a BFOQ.

Affirmative action plans, permitting or requiring employers to hire on the basis of race to make up for past discrimination or to bring up the level of minority workers, have been approved even though the plans may seem to conflict with Title VII. But affirmative-action plans have not been permitted to overcome bona fide seniority systems.

The Age Discrimination in Employment Act protects workers over forty from discharge solely on the basis of age. Amendments to the law have abolished the age ceiling for retirement so that most people working for employers covered by the law cannot be forced to retire.

The Rehabilitation Act prohibits discrimination based on a handicap, as long as the prospective employee is otherwise qualified to perform the job. The Americans with Disabilities Act of 1990 further extends the prohibition against discrimination based on disability to most jobs in the private sector.

At common law, an employer was free to fire an employee for any reason, or for no reason at all. In recent years, the employment-at-will doctrine has been seriously eroded. Many state courts have found against employers on the basis of implied contracts, tortious violation of public policy, or violations of an implied covenant of good faith and fair dealing.

Beyond antidiscrimination law, several other statutes have an impact on the employment relationship. These include the Plant Closing Law, the Polygraph Protection Act, the Occupational Safety and Health Act, the Employee Retirement Income Security Act, and the Fair Labor Standards Act.

KEY TERMS

SELF-TEST QUESTIONS

1. Affirmative action in employment:
   (a) is a requirement of Title VII of the Civil Rights Act of 1964
   (b) is prohibited by Title VII of the Civil Rights Act of 1964
   (c) is a federal statute enacted by Congress
   (d) depends on the circumstances of each case for validity
2. The Age Discrimination Act protects:
   (a) all workers of any age
   (b) all workers up to age 70
   (c) most workers over 40
   (d) no workers over 70
3. Federal laws barring discrimination against the handicapped and disabled:
   (a) apply to all disabilities
   (b) apply to most disabilities in private employment
   (c) apply to all disabilities in public employment
   (d) apply to most disabilities in public employment
4. Under Title VII, a bona fide occupational qualification exception may never apply to cases involving:
   (a) racial discrimination
   (b) religious discrimination
   (c) sex discrimination
   (d) age discrimination
5. The employment-at-will doctrine derives from:
   (a) Title VII of the Civil Rights Act of 1964
   (b) employment contracts
   (c) the common law
   (d) liberty of contract under the Constitution

DEMONSTRATION PROBLEM

Nancy is a waitress at Swank Restaurants, a chain of expensive French restaurants. She applies for a job as headwaiter at the branch in which she is currently serving. Swank turns her down. On investigating, Nancy discovers that Swank has never hired a female headwaiter. Noting the statistical disparity (50 percent of its ordinary serving staff is female), Nancy sues, alleging that Swank is discriminating against her and all women in violation of Title VII of the Civil Rights Act of 1964. Swank responds by saying that it has an absolute prerequisite for the job of headwaiter: all candidates must have studied at an elite school in Paris. It turns out that that school has never admitted a woman. What result?

PROBLEMS

1. Rainbow Airlines, a new air carrier headquartered in Chicago with routes from Rome to Canberra, extensively studied the psychology of passengers and determined that more than 93 percent of its passengers felt most comfortable with female flight attendants between the ages of twenty-one and thirty-four. To increase its profitability, the company issued a policy of hiring only such people for jobs in the air but opened all ground jobs to anyone who could otherwise qualify. The policy made no racial distinction and, in fact, nearly 30 percent of the stewardesses hired were black. What violations of federal law has Rainbow committed, if any?
2. Tex Olafson worked for five years as a messenger for Pressure Sell Advertising Agency, a company without a unionized work force. On his fifth anniversary with the company, Tex was called in to the president's office, given a 10 percent raise, and was complimented on his diligence. The following week, a new head of the messenger department was hired. He wanted to appoint his nephew to a messenger job, but discovered that a company-wide hiring freeze prevented him from adding another employee to the messenger ranks. So he fired Tex and hired his nephew. What remedy, if any, does Tex have? What additional facts might change the result?
3. Ernest lost both his legs in combat in Vietnam. He has applied for a job with Excelsior Products in the company's quality control lab. The job requires inspectors to randomly check products coming off the assembly line for defects. Historically, all inspectors have stood two-hour shifts. Ernest proposes to sit in his wheelchair. The company refuses to hire him because it says he will be less efficient. Ernest's previous employment record shows him to be a diligent, serious worker. Does Ernest have a legal right to be hired? What additional facts might you want to know in deciding?
4. Marlene works for Frenzied Traders, a stock-brokerage with a seat on the New York Stock Exchange. For several years Marlene has been a floor trader, spending all day in the hurly-burly of stock trading, yelling herself hoarse. Each year she has received a large bonus from the company. She has just told the company that she is pregnant. Citing a company policy, she is told she can no longer engage in trading because it is too tiring for pregnant women. Instead, she may take a backroom job, though

the company cannot guarantee that the floor job will be open after she delivers. Marlene also wants to take six months off after her child is born. The company says it cannot afford to give her that time. It has a policy of granting paid leave to anyone recuperating from a stay in the hospital and unpaid leave for four months thereafter. What legal rights does Marlene have, and what remedies is she entitled to?

5. Charlie Goodfellow works for Yum-Burger and has always commanded respect at the local franchise for being the fastest server. One day he undergoes a profound religious experience, converts to Sikhism, and changes his name to Sanjay Singh. The tenets of his religion require him to wear a beard and a turban. He lets his beard grow, puts on a turban, and his fellow workers tease him. When a regional vice president sees that Sanjay is not wearing the prescribed Yum-Burger uniform, he fires him. What rights of Sanjay, if any, has Yum-Burger violated? What remedies are available to him?

ANSWERS TO SELF-TEST QUESTIONS

1. (d)   2. (c)   3. (b)   4. (a)   5. (c)

SUGGESTED ANSWER TO DEMONSTRATION PROBLEM

Nancy may have a good case. Disparate impact, demonstrated by statistical evidence, is not sufficient to prove unlawful discrimination. But in her case, Nancy can probably show that the pool of otherwise qualified female applicants is large, and that the number of successful female candidates is zero. Moreover, Nancy can show definitively that the cause of the disparate impact is a specific employment practice, namely the requirement that head waiters attend the exclusive Paris school. The question remains whether the employment practice is valid. Swank could argue that under *Wards Cove* the employment practice need not be absolutely necessary to determining whom to hire, only that it be in some sense useful. But Nancy could counter by demonstrating that the requirement intrinsically discriminates against women for no valid purpose. There is nothing inherent about being a headwaiter or about what is taught at the school that should preclude a woman from attending. What appears to be a neutral employment practice is therefore far from neutral in effect. To prevail, Swank will probably have to demonstrate that there is no other way for Nancy to learn the things taught at the school, a demonstration that does not seem likely.

CHAPTER 53

Liability and Regulation of Accountants

The largest financial scandal in American history unfolded in the early 1990s—the collapse of hundreds, possibly thousands, of overextended savings and loan associations. The cost to taxpayers, it has been estimated, may rise to the staggering sum of $500 billion or more, as federal deposit insurance is paid to cover the bankruptcies of the S & Ls. Blame for these bank failures must no doubt be widely shared. Executives and managers stand in the front ranks: there is considerable evidence of widespread "looting" and wildly careless lending policies. Despite the criminality and gross negligence of many of the principals, the regulatory establishment might have stanched the flow of red ink far sooner if major portions of it had not been asleep—or deliberately averting its eyes—and if several U.S. senators and members of Congress, taking large contributions from influential S & L executives, had not prevailed on the regulators to go slow. But as federal agencies, prosecutors, and others finally began their investigations, a third group of culprits began to emerge: the professionals—accountants, lawyers, and other advisers—who collaborated with the S & Ls in their vast and irresponsible overextension of credit (see **Box 53-1**). One of the major questions in the aftermath of the S & L collapse, therefore, is the extent to which professionals will be held liable, both criminally and civilly, for their part in the debacle.

Although new laws may emerge from the S & L affair to provide greater accountability in banking, by both bankers and the professionals without whom they could not do business, existing federal and state law has long regulated the conduct of advisers to business. In this chapter we examine the liability of professionals and the role of regulation in policing professional conduct. We use public accounting as the illustrative case, in part because accounting is more directly subject to regulations than other professions, and in part because it is inextricably linked to business.

Of course, a public accountant has the same responsibilities as nonprofessionals. A certified public accountant (CPA) who while driving to work carelessly strikes a pedestrian is liable for negligence, just as anyone else would be. Unlike other people, however, a CPA has additional legal responsibilities and

LAW AND LIFE

BOX 53-1

Accountants Under Siege

By Paul Marcotte

*[The collapse of numerous savings and loan associations is taking its toll on professionals as well as taxpayers. Accounting and law firms are being sued by plaintiffs, including the FDIC, for their involvement with failed S&Ls.—*AUTHORS' NOTE]

Scott Univer peered around a Philadelphia hotel meeting room filled with trial lawyers waiting for him to speak about accountants' liability for work with failed thrifts.

Univer, assistant general counsel at Ernst & Young, asked how many in his audience represent clients suing accountants. Dozens of hands shot up.

"I am here to deliver a message to you," said Univer. "We're going to fight on all fronts. We are going to fight hard. We are justified in this, and we have no choice."

Fighting for Financial Lives

Univer told his surprised ABA Litigation Section audience that accountants are being forced into a "war of attrition" in these suits. Accounting firms cannot quietly hand over their insurance policies and go bare, he said, because the billions of dollars in total claims on plaintiffs' "wish lists" would devastate the profession.

"Fourteen of the 16 most major accounting firms would be bankrupt," declared Univer. "A major part of the accounting profession would be, if not destroyed, then crippled. . . . What

PROFESSIONALS FEEL THE STING

good public-policy interest does that serve?"

Elaborating on a theme of the accounting profession under siege, Univer pointed to S&L inquiries by Congressional committees, a half-dozen federal agencies, and state and local authorities.

Univer added, however, that he expects the accounting profession to survive by vigorously defending the lawsuits.

In written materials submitted at the ABA meeting, Univer highlighted the suits brought by investors and government regulators against accountants with allegations ranging from negligence, fraud and RICO to breach of contract. Among them:

- Touche Ross & Co., now merged with Deloitte, Haskins & Sells, was sued for alleged failure to properly examine Beverly Hills Savings & Loan records.
- The former Deloitte, Haskins & Sells was accused of negligence for its work with Sunrise Savings & Loan in Florida.
- Coopers & Lybrand is in U.S. district court in Oklahoma defending an audit of a borrower in a suit brought by Freedom Savings & Loan.
- Ernst & Young is accused of faulty auditing work for financial institutions in Tennessee.

Accounting firms often get sued by investors and government regulators merely because they have deep pockets, said Univer. The charge was disputed by Federal Deposit Insurance Corp. lawyer Ann Sobel, who was on the panel with Univer.

According to Sobel, the FDIC has about 30 lawsuits pending against accounting firms, 25 against lawyers, and 500 against S&L officers and directors. The agency had recovered $300 million in its lawsuits through the first eight months of 1990.

With another 1,400 S&L investigations underway, the FDIC is regularly adding staff to cope with its growing caseload.

Many FDIC suits against accountants charge negligence in conducting audits, Sobel said. Others accuse them of giving improper advice on a particular transaction or improperly auditing borrowers.

Many of the FDIC suits against lawyers also involve "plain vanilla negligence: . . . forgetting to get a security interest, failing to record a deed," said Sobel.

More serious malpractice and fraud cases involve law firms with long ties to defunct thrifts, she added. The lawyers may have helped take the S&L public or may have represented it through a change of control.

In some cases, the law firm represented the thrift in all its transactions, maintained offices in the thrift or allowed employees to work regularly on-site. A law firm is particularly vulnerable if its lawyers sat as directors of the thrift.

"Under those circumstances, it's hard for them to say we just put the papers together. That falls on deaf ears," said Sobel.

Source: *ABA Journal*, January, 1991, p. 20

liabilities arising from the practice of accounting. We examine first the common law theories of liability—breach of contract and tort—and then the impact of federal law and government regulation on public accounting practice.

COMMON LAW LIABILITY

Breach of Contract

The ordinary rules of contract law apply to agreements accountants make with clients. Failure to carry out the performance required under a contract is a breach, and the client is entitled to refuse payment. Suppose the accountant performed defectively. Some courts hold that defective performance, like nonperformance, is a breach, whereas others consider it to be negligence, a tort. The difference can be significant in some cases, since tort and contract cases are governed by different statutes of limitations, remedies, measures of damages, and standards of proof.

Tort Liability

The two usual grounds of tort liability are negligence and fraud. Negligence is usually the basis for the common *malpractice* actions against professionals.

Negligence   In judging whether a professional has acted carelessly, the courts will hold him to a higher standard than that of the mythical "reasonable man." Professional conduct will be measured by the knowledge, skills, and judgment requisite to the discipline in question. An accountant who fails to follow a generally accepted accounting principle, without good reason, in auditing a company's books is liable for the harm to stockholders and others who depend on the audit, but a nonnegligent mistake is not by itself actionable. A surgeon need not guarantee that the operation will be successful, nor must an accountant guarantee the complete accuracy of his work. His duty is simply to avoid being careless.

The public accountant's duties are therefore variable: they depend on the nature of the assignment and the developing art and practice of accounting. In this regard, one of the most vexing problems for the CPA is the degree to which he is required to ferret out fraud. Must he go behind every transaction that is recorded on the books to assure all who read his opinion that there is no possibility of fraud having been committed? At common law, he need not. As a British jurist said in an 1896 case: "An auditor is not bound to be a detective, or as was said, to approach his work with suspicion or with a foregone conclusion that there is something wrong. He is a watch-dog, but not a bloodhound." [*In re* Kingston Cotton Mill Company, 2 Ch. 279 (C.A. 1896).]

But if common law alone does not impose a duty on the auditor to detect fraud, modern professional standards do. These in turn are absorbed into common law. Thus, failure to abide by the standard of the American Institute of Certified Public Accountants (AICPA), set out below, can be the basis for a finding of negligence. The AICPA standard (Section 327.05) states:

> The independent auditor has the responsibility, within the inherent limitations of the auditing process, . . . to plan his examination . . . to search for errors or irregularities that would have a material effect on the financial statements, and to exercise due skill and care in the conduct of that examination. The auditor's search for material errors or irregularities ordinarily is accomplished by the performance of those auditing procedures that in his judgment are appropriate in the circumstances to form an opinion on the financial statements; extending auditing procedures are required if the auditor's examination indicates that material errors or irregularities may exist.

As in any negligence suit, causation must be shown: the professional's failure to conform to the requisite standard of professional conduct must be the cause of the injury that the plaintiff has suffered.

Fraud   Because they deal with facts and figures that are subject to falsification, accountants are vulnerable to the charges that they have committed the intentional tort of *fraud*. Fraud has four elements: (1) scienter; (2) false representation; (3) reliance; and (4) injury. The third and fourth elements are obvious enough: the plaintiff must have justifiably relied on the false representation (plaintiff's independent knowledge of the facts is a defense to a charge of fraud) and, as with negligence, an injury must have occurred as a result of the plaintiff's reliance.

The first two points are a bit more subtle. *Scienter* is an intention to mislead, consisting either of the knowing telling of a falsity or the making of statements with reckless disregard for whether or not they are true. Scienter exists whether or not the person making the false representation *desires* that the falsehood be communicated or relied upon; the intention is present if he knows the statement to be false or says it oblivious of its possible falsehood. It is no excuse that he honestly believes the statement to be true if he has no basis for the belief.

A false representation is not limited to a direct lie. Concealing facts that, if known, would correct a misimpression can amount to a false representation in the eyes of the law. It is sometimes said that a false statement of an opinion is not actionable as a misre-

presentation, but that conclusion does not apply to charges of fraud resulting from the expression of a professional opinion. A professional opinion is precisely what a client is paying for. The plaintiff seeks a professional opinion because he is unable to form one of his own. To say that "in my opinion, the balance sheet fairly reflects the assets and liabilities of the company" is actionable if that is not in fact the CPA's opinion or if he has no reasonable basis to offer it.

A fraud suit against an accountant may even be based on nondisclosure or complete silence. The next case shows how silence can be deceit when previous statements stand uncorrected, despite the discovery of facts that negate them.

FISCHER v. KLETZ
266 F.Supp. 180
(S.D.N.Y. 1967)

TYLER, DISTRICT JUDGE. [The defendant Peat, Marwick, Mitchell & Co. ("PMM") has moved for dismissal of part of the plaintiffs' complaint.]

* * *

Sometime early in 1964, PMM, acting as an independent public accountant, undertook the job of auditing the financial statements that Yale Express System, Inc. ("Yale"), a national transportation concern, intended to include in the annual report to its stockholders for the year ending December 31, 1963. On March 31, 1964, PMM certified the figures contained in these statements. On or about April 9, the annual report containing the certification was issued to the stockholders of Yale. Subsequently, on or about June 29, 1964, a Form 10-K Report, containing the same financial statements as the annual report, was filed with the SEC as required by that agency's rules and regulations.

At an unspecified date "early in 1964", probably shortly after the completion of the audit, Yale engaged PMM to conduct so-called "special studies" of Yale's past and current income and expenses. In the course of this special assignment, sometime presumably before the end of 1964, PMM discovered that the figures in the annual report were substantially false and misleading.

Not until May 5, 1965, however, when the results of the special studies were released, did PMM disclose this finding to the exchanges on which Yale securities were traded, to the SEC or to the public at large.

Furthermore, during the course of PMM's special studies, Yale periodically announced to PMM an intention to issue several interim statements and reports to show the company's 1964 financial performance. In at least two instances, Yale was told by PMM that figures derived from the special studies could not be used as a basis for these interim statements; in addition,

PMM recommended that the figures developed by Yale through its internal accounting procedures be used in the reports.

Yale thereupon issued several interim statements containing figures which were not compiled, audited or certified by PMM. As in the case of the annual and SEC reports, later developments revealed that the figures contained in these interim statements were materially false and misleading.

Plaintiffs allege that, from the compilation of figures for 1964 and its knowledge of the contents of the interim reports, PMM knew that the figures contained in those statements were grossly inaccurate. No disclosure of this finding has yet been made to the exchanges, the SEC or the public.

Within this alleged factual context, the plaintiffs assert that PMM is liable in damages for its failure to disclose not only that the certified financial statements in the 1963 annual report contained false and misleading figures but also that the interim statements issued by Yale were inaccurate. . . .

Plaintiffs attack PMM for its silence and inaction after its employees discovered, during the special studies, that the audited and certified figures in the financial statements reflecting Yale's 1963 performance were grossly inaccurate. They contend that inasmuch as PMM knew that its audit and certificate would be relied upon by the investing public, the accounting firm had a duty to alert the public in some way that the audited and certified statements were materially false and inaccurate. PMM counters that there is no common law or statutory basis for imposing such a duty on it as a public accounting firm retained by the officers and directors of Yale.

Strict analysis leads to the conclusion that PMM is attacked in the complaint because it wore two hats in conducting its business relations with Yale during the period in question. PMM audited and certified the financial statements in the 1963 annual report and Form 10-K as a statutory "independent public accountant" whose responsibility

> is not only to the client who pays his fee, but also to investors, creditors and others who may rely on the financial statements which he certifies. . . . The public accountant must report fairly on the facts as he finds them whether favorable or unfavorable to his client. His duty is to safeguard the public interest, not that of his client.

Following the certification, PMM switched its role to that of an accountant employed by Yale to undertake special studies which were necessitated by business demands rather than by statutory or regulatory requirements. In this sense, it can be seen that during the special studies PMM was a "dependent public accountant" whose primary obligations, under normal circumstances, were to its client and not the public.

*   *   *

Plaintiffs' claim is grounded in the common law action of deceit, albeit an unusual type in that most cases of deceit involve an affirmative misrepresentation by the defendant. Here, however, plaintiffs attack PMM's nondisclosure or silence.

(continued on next page)

(continued)

FISCHER v. KLETZ
266 F.Supp. 180
(S.D.N.Y. 1967)

* * *

The First Restatement of Torts . . . Section 551(2) lists the instances when the requisite duty to disclose arises. For present purposes, the following portion from that subsection is important:

> One party to a business transaction is under a duty to exercise reasonable care to disclose to the other before the transaction is consummated . . . (b) any subsequently acquired information which he recognizes as making untrue or misleading a previous representation which when made was true or believed to be so.

* * *

Generally speaking, I can see no reason why this duty to disclose should not be imposed upon an accounting firm which makes a representation it knows will be relied upon by investors. To be sure, certification of a financial statement does not create a formal business relationship between the accountant who certifies and the individual who relies upon the certificate for investment purposes. The act of certification, however, is similar in its effect to a representation made in a business transaction: both supply information which is naturally and justifiably relied upon by individuals for decisional purposes. Viewed in this context of the impact of nondisclosure on the injured party, it is difficult to conceive that a distinction between accountants and parties to a business transaction is warranted.

* * *

. . . The common law has long required that a person who has made a representation must correct that representation if it becomes false and if he knows people are relying on it. This duty to disclose is imposed regardless of the interest of defendant in the representation and subsequent nondisclosure. Plaintiffs have sufficiently alleged the elements of nondisclosure on the part of this "disinterested" defendant. Accordingly, they must be given an opportunity to prove those allegations.

Liability to Third Parties

Circulation of a CPA's report is rarely restricted to the corporate or other business client. Among those with a direct interest in reading audit results are current and potential owners, creditors, suppliers, managers, employees, customers, business management and taxing authorities. Those with a less direct, but nonetheless substantial interest, are financial analysts, securities exchanges, government regulators, the press, unions, and trade associations. If the auditor makes a mistake, is he liable to all for ensuing damages?

Contract law makes clear that the auditor is liable to his direct clients and any third-party beneficiaries. But these are usually the smaller portion of the total class likely to be harmed. The investing public does not hire the auditor, but millions of shareholders can be injured by an erroneous statement made in an audit report. Under older principles of common law, those not "in privity of contract" (those not party to the contract) had no rights and hence no remedies against the auditor. Today, however, courts are in agreement that the auditor guilty of fraud is liable to all third parties who might reasonably have been presumed to rely on a certified financial statement.

There remains disagreement in cases in which the accountant was not deceitful but merely negligent. For many years, the leading case was *Ultramares Corp. v.*

Touche, 174 N.E. 441 (N.Y. 1931), which held that accountants are not liable to third parties for ordinary negligence. Chief Judge Cardozo explained that the defendant accountants

> owed to their employer a duty imposed by law to make their certificate [that the balance sheet was accurate] without fraud, and a duty growing out of contract to make it with the care and caution proper to their calling. Fraud includes the pretense of knowledge when knowledge there is none. To creditors and investors to whom the employer exhibited the certificate, the defendants owed a like duty to make it without fraud, since there was notice in the circumstances of its making that the employer did not intend to keep it to himself. A different question develops when we ask whether they owed a duty to these to make it without negligence. If liability for negligence exists, a thoughtless slip or blunder, the failure to detect a theft or forgery beneath the cover of deceptive entries, may expose accountants to a liability in an indeterminate amount for an indeterminate time to an indeterminate class. The hazards of a business conducted on these terms are so extreme as to enkindle doubt whether a flaw may not exist in the implication of a duty that exposes to these consequences. . . .

In recent years, many states have abandoned the *Ultramares* rule. Section 552(1) of the *Restatement (Second) of Torts* imposes liability on anyone who, "in the course of his business, profession or employment . . . supplies false information for the guidance of others in their business transactions." This liability is limited to loss suffered (1) by any person for whose benefit or guidance the information was supplied, or with whom the accountant knew his client would share the information, and (2) "through reliance upon it in a transaction which [the accountant] intends the information to influence, or knows that the recipient so intends, or in a substantially similar transaction." (Section 552(2)(b).)

For example, suppose Acme Excelsior Corporation wishes to establish a bank credit line of $1 million and hires Riemann & Lobachevsky Company, a certified public accounting firm, to prepare an audit. Acme Excelsior tells Riemann & Lobachevsky that it intends to negotiate with the First National Bank of Centerville. Riemann & Lobachevsky neglects to consider accounts payable and thus fails to spot Acme's probable insolvency. The First National Bank may sue the accounting firm for negligence under the Restatement rule. Suppose, without telling its accountants, Acme negotiates instead with the Second National Bank of Centerville. The latter bank would not have a valid suit against the accountants, since the audit was not prepared for the Second National Bank nor did the accountants know that Acme would share the information with that bank. However, had Acme said that it intended to shop around for a bank loan, then the accountants would be liable to any bank who made the loan on the basis of the faulty audit.

A few courts have rejected both the *Ultramares* and the *Restatement* limitations of liability. The theories adopted by these courts are summarized in the following case (in which the court ultimately adopted the *Restatement* approach).

FIRST FLORIDA BANK v. MAX MITCHELL & CO.
558 So.2d 9 (Fla. 1990)

GRIMES, JUDGE.

Max Mitchell is a certified public accountant and president of Max Mitchell and Company, P.A. In April of 1985, Mitchell went to First Florida Bank for the purpose of negotiating a loan on behalf of his client, C.M. Systems, Inc. Mitchell advised Stephen Hickman, the bank vice president, that he was a certified public accountant and delivered to Hickman audited financial statements of C.M. Systems for the fiscal years ending October 31, 1983, and October 31, 1984, which had been prepared by his firm. The October 1, 1984, audited statement indicated that C.M. Systems had total assets of $3,474,336 and total liabilities of $1,296,823. It did not indicate that C.M. Systems owed money to any bank, and in a later conference with Hickman, Mitchell stated that as of April 16, 1985, C.M. Systems was not indebted to

(continued on next page)

(*continued*)

FIRST FLORIDA BANK v. MAX MITCHELL & CO.
558 So.2d 9 (Fla. 1990)

any bank. At that time, Mitchell asked Hickman to consider a $500,000 line of credit for C.M. Systems.

Over the next several weeks, Mitchell had numerous discussions with Hickman concerning various line items in Mitchell's audit of C.M. Systems. Mitchell represented that he was thoroughly familiar with the financial condition of C.M. Systems. On May 23, 1985, Hickman asked Mitchell for interim financial statements for the period which ended on April 30, 1985. Mitchell advised that they would not be available for several more weeks. Hickman asked Mitchell if there had been any material change in the company's financial condition since October 31, 1984, and Mitchell said that he was not aware of any material changes. On June 6, 1985, the bank approved the request for a $500,000 unsecured line of credit to C.M. Systems. Thereafter, C.M. Systems borrowed the entire amount of the $500,000 credit line which it has never repaid.

Subsequently, the bank discovered that the audit of C.M. Systems for the fiscal year ending October 31, 1984, had substantially overstated the assets, understated the liabilities, and overstated net income. Among other things, the audit failed to reflect that as of October 31, 1984, C.M. Systems owed at least $750,000 to several banks. In addition, several material changes had occurred in the company's balance sheet after the audit but prior to the approval of the line of credit.

The bank filed a three-count complaint against Mitchell and his firm. Because of the absence of privity between either Mitchell or his firm and the bank, the trial court granted Mitchell summary judgment on the negligence and gross negligence counts. The bank voluntarily dismisssed the count based on fraud. Believing itself bound by prior decisional law of the state, the district court of appeal affirmed.

★   ★   ★

In more than fifty years which have elapsed since *Ultramares*, the question of an accountant's liability for negligence where no privity exists has been addressed by many courts. There are now essentially four lines of authority with respect to this issue.

(1) Except in cases of fraud, an accountant is only liable to one with whom he is in privity or near privity.

(2) An accountant is liable to third parties in the absence of privity under the circumstances described in section 552, *Restatement (Second) of Torts* (1976).

★   ★   ★

(3) An accountant is liable to all persons who might reasonably be foreseen as relying upon his work product. *E.g., International Mortgage Co., v. John P. Butler Accountancy Corp.*, 177 Cal.App.3d 806, 223 Cal.Rptr. 218 (1986).

(4)   An accountant's liability to third persons shall be determined by

> the balancing of various factors, among which are the extent to which the transaction was intended to affect the plaintiff, the foreseeability of harm to him, the degree of certainty that the plaintiff suffered injury, the closeness of the connection between the defendant's conduct and the injury suffered, the moral blame attached to the defendant's conduct, and the policy of preserving future harm.

Biakanja v. Irving, 320 P.2d 16, 19 (1958).

★   ★   ★

Upon consideration, we have decided to adopt the rationale of section 552, *Restatement (Second) of Torts* (1976), as setting forth the circumstances under which accountants may be held liable in negligence to persons who are not in contractual privity. The rule shall also apply to allegations of gross negligence, but the absence of privity shall continue to be no bar to charges of fraud.

★   ★   ★

Because of the heavy reliance upon audited financial statements in the contemporary financial world, we believe permitting recovery only from those in privity or near privity is unduly restrictive. On the other hand, we are persuaded by the wisdom of the rule which limits liability to those persons or classes of persons whom an accountant "knows" will rely on his opinion rather than those he "should have known" would do so because it takes into account the fact that an accountant controls neither his client's accounting records nor the distribution of his reports.

★   ★   ★

There remains the need to apply this rule to the facts at hand. At the time Mitchell prepared the audits for C.M. Systems, it was unknown that they would be used to induce the reliance of First Florida Bank to approve a line of credit for C.M. Systems. Therefore, except for the unusual facts of this case, Mitchell could not be held liable to the bank for any negligence in preparing the audit. However, Mitchell actually negotiated the loan on behalf of his client. He personally delivered the financial statements to the bank with the knowledge that it would rely upon them in considering whether or not to make the loan. Under this unique set of facts, we believe that Mitchell vouched for the integrity of the audits and that his conduct in dealing with the bank sufficed to meet the requirements of the rule which we have adopted in this opinion.

[The lower court decision is quashed and the case is remanded.]

Common law liability does not exhaust the perils of malpractice for the modern practictioner. Federal and state statutes—especially the Securities Act of 1933 and the Securities Exchange Act of 1934—broaden considerably the potential liability of accountants for negligence and fraud. We turn now to federal statutes and regulations that have a major impact on the liability of the practicing accountant.

FEDERAL REGULATION

At least fifteen separate statutory provisions in federal securities law relate to the professional liability of the public accountant. In what follows we focus on only the most important of these. We also examine antitrust liability and the liability of tax preparers.

Liability under the Securities Act of 1933

For accountants concerned about liability, the two key provisions of the act are Sections 11 and 12(2).

Liability under Section 11—Registration Statements   This section of the Securities Act imposes third-party liability on an accountant who makes or certifies in a registration statement "an untrue statement of a material fact or [omits] to state a material fact required to be stated therein or necessary to make the statements therein not misleading." This provision applies only to registration statements and to reports and valuations used in connection with the registration statements. Registration statements are filed only for new public offerings, so the liability under this section is relatively limited. Only purchasers of the specific securities offered through the registration statement acquire rights to sue accountants; subsequent purchasers do not.

Except in one limited instance, the investor need not show reliance on the materially false statement. In other words, a purchaser who sees his investment go sour need not ever have read the registration statement. He can win a suit against the accountants by showing that the registration statement contained a misstatement or an omission of a fact that the average reasonable investor would consider important in determining whether to invest in the offering company's securities. The plaintiff must show reliance when he has made the purchase more than a year following the effective date of the registration statement and the company has issued an earnings statement covering a period of at least twelve months after the effective date.

The accountant's liability is neither strict nor absolute. He can prevail in a lawsuit by demonstrating that he has exercised **due diligence.** Through the due diligence defense, the accountant shows that he made a "reasonable investigation" and as a result had "reasonable ground to believe and did believe" that the statements contained in the registration document were true and that no material omissions had been made. Section 11 sets forth as the standard of reasonableness "that required of a prudent man in the management of his own property." Since the law requires all statements to be true as of the effective date of registration, it is necessary to carry out a second due diligence review close to the time of the date. This is commonly known as an S-1 review, after the name of SEC Form S-1 used for financial statements.

If the accountant fails the due diligence test, he is liable for the difference between the amount the investor paid for the stock and its market value at the time of suit, assuming the stock has not been sold. When the plaintiff has sold the stock prior to suit, he can recover the difference between what he paid and the sale price, but the initial offering price is a ceiling on the amount recoverable. Section 11 gives the plaintiff an incentive to sell the stock prior to suit by limiting recovery to market value at the time of filing suit. Should he subsequently sell the stock for a price even lower than that prevailing at the time of filing he is barred from recovering the decrease. Moreover, if the stock has risen in price after filing, the defendant accountant is permitted to take that rise into account in calculating his financial exposure should he lose the suit.

Under the statute of limitations, plaintiffs have one year to sue, measured from the time they discovered, or should have discovered, the falsity. No suit may be filed more than three years after the security was first offered to the public.

The best way to view the accountant's duties under the act—and what constitutes a failure to comply with them—is to scrutinize the facts in the following case, one of the leading federal cases on due diligence.

ESCOTT v. BARCHRIS CONSTRUCTION COMPANY
283 F.Supp. 643
(S.D.N.Y. 1968)

McLEAN, DISTRICT JUDGE. This is an action by purchasers of 5½ per cent convertible subordinated fifteen year debentures of BarChris Construction Corporation (BarChris). Plaintiffs purport to sue on their own behalf and "on behalf of all other present and former holders" of the debentures. When the action was begun on October 25, 1962, there were nine plaintiffs. Others were subsequently permitted to intervene. At the time of the trial, there were over sixty.

The action is brought under Section 11 of the Securities Act of 1933 (15 U.S.C. § 77k). Plaintiffs allege that the registration statement with respect to these debentures filed with the Securities and Exchange Commission, which became effective on May 16, 1961, contained material false statements and material omissions.

Defendants fall into three categories: (1) the persons who signed the registration statement; (2) the underwriters, consisting of eight investment banking firms, led by Drexel & Co. (Drexel); and (3) BarChris's auditors, Peat, Marwick, Mitchell & Co. (Peat, Marwick).

*   *   *

. . . At the time relevant here, BarChris was engaged primarily in the construction of bowling alleys, somewhat euphemistically referred to as "bowling centers." These were rather elaborate affairs. They contained not only a number of alleys or "lanes," but also, in most cases, bar and restaurant facilities.

*   *   *

By early 1961, BarChris needed additional working capital. The proceeds of the sale of the debentures involved in this action were to be devoted, in part at least, to fill that need.

The registration statement of the debentures, in preliminary form, was filed with the Securities and Exchange Commission on March 30, 1961. A first amendment was filed on May 11 and a second on May 16. The registration statement became effective on May 16. The closing of the financing took place on May 24. On that day BarChris received the net proceeds of the financing.

By that time BarChris was experiencing difficulties in collecting amounts due from some of its customers. Some of them were in arrears in payments due to factors on their discounted notes. As time went on those difficulties increased. Although BarChris continued to build alleys in 1961 and 1962, it became increasingly apparent that the industry was overbuilt. Operators of alleys, often inadequately financed, began to fail. Precisely when the tide turned is a matter of dispute, but at any rate, it was painfully apparent in 1962.

. . . In October 1962 BarChris came to the end of the road. On October 29, 1962, it filed in this court a petition for an arrangement under Chapter

(*continued on next page*)

(continued)

**ESCOTT v. BARCHRIS
CONSTRUCTION
COMPANY**
283 F.Supp. 643
(S.D.N.Y. 1968)

XI of the Bankruptcy Act. BarChris defaulted in the payment of the interest due on November 1, 1962 on the debentures.

*   *   *

Section 11(b) [of the Securities Act of 1933] provides:

> Notwithstanding the provisions of subsection (a) no person . . . shall be liable as provided therein who shall sustain the burden of proof—

*   *   *

> (3) that . . . (B) as regards any part of the registration statement purporting to be made upon his authority as an expert . . . (i) he had, after reasonable investigation, reasonable ground to believe and did believe, at the time such part of the registration statement became effective, that the statements therein were true and that there was no omission to state a material fact required to be stated therein or necessary to make the statements therein not misleading. . . .

This defines the due diligence defense for an expert. Peat, Marwick has pleaded it.

*   *   *

Peat, Marwick's work was in general charge of a member of the firm. . . . Most of the actual work was performed by a senior accountant, Berardi, who had junior assistants, one of whom was Kennedy.

Berardi was then about thirty years old. He was not yet a C.P.A. He had had no previous experience with the bowling industry. This was his first job as a senior accountant. He could hardly have been given a more difficult assignment.

*   *   *

The purpose of reviewing events subsequent to the date of a certified balance sheet (referred to as an S-1 review when made with reference to a registration statement) is to ascertain whether any material change has occurred in the company's financial position which should be disclosed in order to prevent the balance sheet figures from being misleading. The scope of such a review, under generally accepted auditing standards, is limited. It does not amount to a complete audit.

Peat, Marwick prepared a written program for such a review. I find that this program conformed to generally accepted auditing standards. . . .

*   *   *

Berardi made the S-1 review in May 1961. He devoted a little over two days to it, a total of 20½ hours. He did not discover any of the errors or omissions pertaining to the state of affairs in 1961 . . . , all of which were material. The question is whether, despite his failure to find out anything, his investigation was reasonable within the meaning of the statute.

What Berardi did was to look at a consolidating trial balance as of March 31, 1961 which had been prepared by BarChris, compare it with the audited December 31, 1960 figures, discuss . . . certain unfavorable developments which the comparison disclosed, and read certain minutes. He did not examine any "important financial records" other than the trial balance. As to minutes, he read only what minutes . . . [were given] him, which consisted only of the board of directors' minutes of BarChris. He did not read such minutes as there were of the executive committee. He did not know that there was an executive committee, hence he did not discover that . . . [there were] notes of executive committee minutes which had not been written up. He did not read the minutes of any subsidiary.

. . . He asked questions, he got answers which he considered satisfactory, and he did nothing to verify them.

★   ★   ★

Accountants should not be held to a standard higher than that recognized in their profession. I do not do so here. Berardi's review did not come up to that standard. He did not take some of the steps which Peat, Marwick's written program prescribed. He did not spend an adequate amount of time on a task of this magnitude. Most important of all, he was too easily satisfied with glib answers to his inquiries.

This is not to say that he should have made a complete audit. But there were enough danger signals in the materials which he did examine to require some further investigation on his part. Generally accepted accounting standards required such further investigation under these circumstances. It is not always sufficient merely to ask questions.

Here again, the burden of proof is on Peat, Marwick. I find that that burden has not been satisfied. I conclude that Peat, Marwick has not established its due diligence defense.

★   ★   ★

Liability under Section 12(2)—Prospectuses and Communications   Section 12(2) imposes liability on persons who sell securities for negligence in making untrue material statements or omitting material facts. Since the provision applies to sellers, accountants ordinarily are not affected by it. However, some courts have found accountants to be culpable for *aiding and abetting* the seller when the accountant knew or should have known of material misrepresentations on which investors were likely to rely. [Sandusky Land, Ltd. v. Uniplan Groups, Inc., 400 F.Supp. 440 (N.D. Ohio 1975)] Under Section 12(2), plaintiffs are entitled to return the securities for the purchase price plus interest, or to be made whole if the securities have already been sold.

Liability Under the Securities Exchange Act of 1934

The 1934 Securities Exchange Act governs the sale of securities on national exchanges, regulates proxy solicitation, and requires periodic reporting of corporate financial and other developments. Under the 1934 act, accountants are made liable to investors, creditors, and others who rely on financial statements that the accountants are required to sign. The accountant's duty is less to the client than to the investing public to certify the accuracy of the reports.

More 1934 act lawsuits are filed under Section 10(b) and the corresponding SEC Rule 10b-5 than under any other provisions. As we have seen in Chapter 44, Section 10(b) and the related rules prohibit the use of manipulative and deceptive devices to defraud anyone in connection with the sale of securities through national securities exchanges, the mails, or other instrumentalities of interstate commerce. We have already noted the use of Rule 10b-5 against insider trading (Chapter 44). Rule 10b-5 is also used as the basis for suits against accountants, who are generally charged with "aiding and abetting" others, such as insiders, who have violated the law. Accountants who accept from corporate insiders financial information that contains material errors, without under-

taking some sort of investigation into its probable truth, and without then correcting or disclosing the errors, may be held liable under Rule 10b-5 if the errors find their way into reports filed with the SEC, whether or not the accountant has been asked to carry out a full-scale audit.

During the 1970s, as more and more cases were filed under the antifraud provision of the 1934 act, accountants began to worry that they could be held liable for aiding and abetting fraud even though they had no knowledge of it and even though their failure to detect it was thus simple negligence. Finally, the Supreme Court settled the matter by ruling in the next case that there can be no private action for damages under Rule 10b-5 in the absence of a charge that the defendant intended to deceive, manipulate, or defraud. The Supreme Court later held that the SEC must establish scienter in civil enforcement actions to enjoin violations of Rule 10b-5. [Aaron v. SEC, 446 U.S. 680 (1980)]

ERNST & ERNST v. HOCHFELDER
425 U.S. 185 (1976)

MR. JUSTICE POWELL delivered the opinion of the Court.

Petitioner, Ernst & Ernst, is an accounting firm. From 1946 through 1967 it was retained by First Securities Company of Chicago (First Securities), a small brokerage firm and member of the Midwest Stock Exchange and of the National Association of Securities Dealers, to perform periodic audits of the firm's books and records. In connection with these audits Ernst & Ernst prepared for filing with the Securities and Exchange Commission (Commission) the annual reports required of First Securities under § 17(a) of the 1934 Act. It also prepared for First Securities responses to the financial questionnaires of the Midwest Stock Exchange (Exchange).

Respondents were customers of First Securities who invested in a fraudulent securities scheme perpetrated by Leston B. Nay, president of the firm and owner of 92% of its stock. Nay induced the respondents to invest funds in "escrow" accounts that he represented would yield a high rate of return. Respondents did so from 1942 through 1966 with the majority of the transactions occurring in the 1950s. In fact, there were no escrow accounts as Nay converted respondents' funds to his own use immediately upon receipt. These transactions were not in the customary form of dealings between First Securities and its customers. The respondents drew their personal checks payable to Nay or a designated bank for his account. No such escrow accounts were reflected on the books and records of First Securities, and none was shown on its periodic accounting to respondents in connection with their other investments. Nor were they included in First Securities' filings with the Commission or the Exchange.

This fraud came to light in 1968 when Nay committed suicide, leaving a note that described First Securities as bankrupt and the escrow accounts as "spurious." . . . The complaint charged that Nay's escrow scheme violated § 10(b) and Commission Rule 10b-5, and that Ernst & Ernst had "aided and abetted" Nay's violations by its "failure" to conduct proper audits of First Securities. As revealed through discovery, respondents' cause of action rested on a theory of negligent nonfeasance. The premise was that Ernst & Ernst had failed to utilize "appropriate auditing procedures" in its audits of First Securities, thereby failing to discover internal practices of the firm said to prevent an effective audit. The practice principally relied on was Nay's rule that only he could open mail addressed to him at First Securities or addressed to First Securities to his attention, even if it arrived in his absence. Respondents contended that if Ernst & Ernst had conducted a proper audit, it would have discovered this "mail rule." The existence of the rule then would have been disclosed in reports to the Exchange and to the Commission by Ernst & Ernst as an irregular procedure that prevented an effective audit. This would have led to an investigation of Nay that would have revealed the fraudulent scheme. Respondents specifically disclaimed the existence of fraud or intentional misconduct on the part of Ernst & Ernst.

* * *

The Court of Appeals for the Seventh Circuit [held] that one who breaches a duty of inquiry and disclosure owed another is liable in damages for aiding and abetting a third party's violation of Rule 10b-5 if the fraud would have been discovered or prevented but for the breach.

* * *

We granted certiorari to resolve the question whether a private cause of action for damages will lie under § 10(b) and Rule 10b-5 in the absence of any allegation of "scienter"—intent to deceive, manipulate, or defraud. We conclude that it will not and therefore we reverse.

* * *

Section 10(b) makes unlawful the use or employment of "any manipulative or deceptive device or contrivance" in contravention of Commission rules. The words "manipulative or deceptive" used in conjunction with "device or contrivance" strongly suggest that § 10(b) was intended to proscribe knowing or intentional misconduct.

In its *amicus curiae* brief, however, the Commission contends that nothing in the language "manipulative or deceptive device or contrivance" limits its operation to knowing or intentional practices. In support of its view, the Commission cites the overall congressional purpose in the 1933 and 1934 Acts to protect investors against false and deceptive practices that might injure them. The Commission then reasons that since the "effect" upon investors of given conduct is the same regardless of whether the conduct is negligent

(*continued on next page*)

(continued)

ERNST & ERNST v. HOCHFELDER
425 U.S. 185 (1976)

or intentional, Congress must have intended to bar all such practices and not just those done knowingly or intentionally. The logic of this effect oriented approach would impose liability for wholly faultless conduct where such conduct results in harm to investors, a result the Commission would be unlikely to support. But apart from where its logic might lead, the Commission would add a gloss to the operative language of the statute quite different from its commonly accepted meaning. The argument simply ignores the use of the words "manipulative," "device," and "contrivance"—terms that make unmistakable a congressional intent to proscribe a type of conduct quite different from negligence. Use of the word "manipulative" is especially significant. It is and was virtually a term of art when used in connection with securities markets. It connotes intentional or willful conduct designed to deceive or defraud investors by controlling or artificially affecting the price of securities.

★   ★   ★

We have addressed, to this point, primarily the language and history of § 10(b). The Commission contends, however, that subsections (b) and (c) of Rule 10b-5 are cast in language which—if standing alone—could encompass both intentional and negligent behavior. These subsections respectively provide that it is unlawful "[t]o make any untrue statement of a material fact or to omit to state a material fact necessary in order to make the statements made, in the light of the circumstances under which they were made, not misleading . . ." and "[t]o engage in any act, practice, or course of business which operates or would operate as a fraud or deceit upon any person . . ."

Viewed in isolation the language of subsection (b), and arguably that of subsection (c), could be read as proscribing, respectively, any type of material misstatement or omission, and any course of conduct, that has the effect of defrauding investors, whether the wrongdoing was intentional or not.

We note first that such a reading cannot be harmonized with the administrative history of the Rule, a history making clear that when the Commission adopted the Rule it was intended to apply only to activities that involved scienter. More importantly, Rule 10b-5 was adopted pursuant to authority granted the Commission under § 10(b). The rulemaking power granted to an administrative agency charged with the administration of a federal statute is not the power to make law. Rather it is " 'the power to adopt regulations to carry into effect the will of Congress as expressed by the statute.' " Thus, despite the broad view of the Rule advanced by the Commission in this case, its scope cannot exceed the power granted the Commission by Congress under § 10(b). For the reasons stated above, we think the Commission's original interpretation of Rule 10b-5 was compelled by the language and history of § 10(b) and related sections of the Acts. When a statute speaks so specifically in terms of manipulation and deception, and of implementing devices and contrivances—the commonly understood terminology of intentional wrongdoing—and when its history reflects no more expansive intent, we are quite unwilling to extend the scope of the statute to negligent conduct.

★   ★   ★

The judgment of the Court of Appeals is reversed.

Sanctions

In addition to private suits that investors can file, the accountant is subject to both civil and criminal proceedings by the government. The 1933 and 1934 acts empower the SEC to seek injunctions and civil penalties in federal court against anyone who is about to engage in or is currently engaged in violating any of the federal statutory or regulatory provisions. The SEC can refer serious cases to the U.S. Attorney for criminal prosecution that can lead to jail sentences and large monetary fines.

The SEC also has an often overlooked but important administrative sanction: the Rule 2(e) proceeding. Under Rule 2(e), the SEC may discipline errant accountants and other professionals by disqualifying them from practicing before the Commission. The SEC must give notice to the accused and hold a due process hearing before it can disqualify an accountant from practice, either temporarily or permanently. Under certain circumstances, such as conviction of a felony or revocation or suspension of a license to practice accounting, the Commission may suspend the right without a hearing. Among the reasons for disqualification are unethical or improper behavior, willful violations of the securities laws, and a finding that the auditor does not "possess the requisite qualifications to represent others" or is "lacking in character or integrity."

Although Rule 2(e) mentions only disqualification and censure, the SEC has actively devised a wide range of innovative sanctions against auditors. Many involve agreements by the auditors to employ new procedures to control their auditing practices, and to submit to independent compliance reviews. The sanctions have included peer reviews, continuing education programs, merger with larger firms, suspension of a partner from acting as such, and notification to new securities clients that the auditing firm is subject to sanction and why.

Other Federal Laws

Antitrust Liability   Until the mid-1970s, it had long been assumed that the "learned professions" were exempt from prosecution under the Sherman Act and that agreements fixing the price of *services*, as opposed to *products* put on the market, were likewise not subject to the antitrust laws. In 1975, in *Goldfarb*

v. *Virginia State Bar*, 421 U.S. 773 (1975), the U.S. Supreme Court struck down a Virginia State Bar fee schedule to which lawyers in the state were expected to adhere. The Court held that the practice of law is within the Sherman Act's meaning of "trade or commerce." Subsequent decisions have made clear that other acts also violate the antitrust laws: attempts by professionals either directly or through their professional associations and codes of ethics to fix fees, regulate advertising, set product or service standards that could exclude some practitioners from the market, and otherwise interfere with the right of individual practitioners to carry on their business in the marketplace.

Liability of Tax Preparers   The federal Revenue Acts of 1976 and 1978 established standards and liabilities for anyone, including accountants, who for compensation prepares federal tax returns for others, or who hires preparers to do so. Under these laws, the preparer must personally sign all returns he has done for compensation and include his special preparer's identification number and address. He must give a completed copy of the return or refund claim to the taxpayer no later than the moment when the preparer submits a copy to the taxpayer for signing. Employers of preparers must maintain lists of their employees, addresses, and identification numbers, and preparers themselves must maintain lists of taxpayers whose returns they filed, including taxable year, type of return or claim, and identification numbers. These lists must be kept for three years.

STATE REGULATION

State securities regulation also affects accountants. The Uniform Securities Act, adopted in many states, has a provision virtually identical to SEC Rule 10b-5. Although in many states this provision cannot be used as the basis for a suit for damages, other statutory provisions make available to private plaintiffs the right to file suits for damages for fraud and misrepresentation in the sale, purchase, and exchange of securities.

Perhaps more important, the states, far more so than the federal government, closely regulate the practice of public accounting. Most states have licensing and certification provisions that restrict the right to hold oneself out as a certified public accountant to those who meet specified standards of training and knowledge. Being certified as a certified public accountant is not a vested right: a state may revoke a license or certificate for "unprofessional conduct of the holder of such certificate or for other sufficient cause," and may issue a set of regulations that detail the proper forms of conduct and the nature of such disabling acts as conflicts of interest.

OTHER DUTIES TO CLIENTS

Privileged Communications

Accountants have professional obligations to preserve the confidentiality of communications with clients. For the most part, the confidentiality of client communications is a matter of professional ethics and is *not* protected by common law. However, several statutes do recognize the so-called **accountant-client privilege** (akin to the *lawyer-client privilege*, Chapter 2) and permit the accountant to refuse to testify in court, or in another legal proceeding, about what he has learned from the client of the client's business. Even in states recognizing the privilege, however, the communication is considered confidential only if it was intended to be confidential at the time it was made and if the client has not subsequently waived confidentiality. A communication is not considered to be intended as confidential if an outsider is present during the discussion between client and accountant; confidentiality is waived if the client subsequently volunteers any portions of the communication.

Working Papers

Working papers are the documents, notes of interviews and audits, and other papers that the auditor prepares in the course of his work for a client. In the absence of a statute or contractual agreement to the contrary, the auditor owns these papers and need not accede to a client's demand, for example, that they be transferred to a new accountant at the termination of the relationship with the original auditor. One reason that accountants are permitted to keep their working papers is to defend themselves against potential charges of malpractice or other dereliction of duty.

In states where the confidential nature of the client-auditor relationship is recognized, consent of the client is ordinarily required before the auditor can give working papers on his own to another accountant or to any other outside party. Federal law recognizes neither an accountant-client privilege nor a general right to the confidentiality of working papers. In 1984, for instance, the Supreme Court decided that an auditor's working papers are subject to subpoena by the Internal Revenue Service. [*United States v. Arthur Young & Co.,* 465 U.S. 805 (1984)]

CHAPTER SUMMARY

Accountants, like other professionals, are subject to liability under both common law and federal statutes. Thus, an accountant who fails to follow generally accepted accounting principles is guilty of malpractice, and is liable for the harm to stockholders and others. But by itself, an unintentional, non-negligent mistake is not actionable.

An auditor guilty of fraud is liable to third parties who might reasonably have been presumed to rely on certified financial statements. In several states, an accountant who is merely negligent is liable only to direct clients and third-party beneficiaries, but not to the total class who might have been harmed. However, in recent years many states have adopted a rule that pins liability on the negligent accountant for losses suffered by any person (1) to whom the audit has been supplied for benefit or guidance, or with whom the auditor knew his client would share the information, and (2) who relied on it in a transaction which the accountant intended the information to influence.

Liability may be imposed on accountants under several federal statutes. Among them:

1. Section 11, Securities Act of 1933—liability to third parties for untrue statements in registration statements. To avoid liability, the accountant must show due diligence.
2. Section 12(2), Securities Act of 1933—liability to purchasers for aiding and abetting sellers in making untrue statements in prospectuses and communications.
3. Section 10(b), Securities Exchange Act of 1934—liability to investors, creditors, and others who rely on financial statements that accountants are required to sign and file with the SEC. But there can be no private suits under Rule 10b-5 against an accountant for damages for negligence, unless the accountant can be charged with intent to deceive, manipulate, or defraud.
4. Sherman Act—liability for attempting to restrain trade by fixing fees, regulating advertising, or excluding practitioners from the profession.

In addition to private suits, accountants are subject to sanction by the government under the securities laws. In particular, the SEC may, through a Rule 2(e) proceeding,

scipline accountants by disqualifying them from practice be-
re the Commission.

Although the professional ethics of accountants require
em to maintain the confidentiality of client communications,
ost states do not protect this confidentiality by law. Like-
ise, although accountants' working papers are the property
` accountants under the laws of many states, there is no fed-
al privilege against disclosure and, if subpoenaed, the ac-
untant will be required to turn these papers over to federal
vestigators.

EY TERMS

ccountant-client priv-	p. 1206	Due diligence	p. 1198
ilege		Working papers	p. 1206

ELF-TEST QUESTIONS

1. The standards of the American Institute of Certified Public Accountants (AICPA):
   (a) derive from a federal statute enacted by Congress
   (b) derive from a model state code, enacted by various
       state legislatures
   (c) derive from the AICPA and may be the basis of
       common-law liability
   (d) derive from regulations adopted by the Securities and
       Exchange Commission
2. Scienter is an element of:
   (a) negligence
   (b) fraud
   (c) malpractice
   (d) restraint of trade
3. In some states, auditors are liable to:
   (a) direct clients
   (b) third-party beneficiaries of the audit
   (c) third parties that might reasonably have relied on
       certified financial statements
   (d) all of the above
4. For mistakes in a registration statement filed with the SEC
   an accountant is:
   (a) liable only for negligence
   (b) absolutely liable
   (c) strictly liable
   (d) liable only for gross negligence
5. Due diligence requires an accountant to:
   (a) exhaustively search every document in the files of
       the business audited
   (b) reasonably investigate the books and records of the
       business audited
   (c) investigate only those books and records specified by
       the client
   (d) none of the above

DEMONSTRATION PROBLEM

Julian Accounting Services and Acme Enterprises sign an
agreement under which Julian will provide all accounting services to Acme, including bookkeeping and preparation of profit-
and-loss statements and annual audits. The contract further
specifies that Acme will use the audits and P & Ls as the basis
for negotiating supplies from third parties. A "hold harmless"
clause in the contract says that "Julian will not be responsible
for any acts of negligence toward any third parties who might
rely on any documents prepared by Julian in the course of
complying with this contract." A year later Acme signs a long-
term supply contract with Fidelity Oil Co. In negotiating the
contract, under which Fidelity will extend millions of dollars
in credit to Acme, Fidelity relies on audits prepared by Julian.
In fact, Julian was negligent, failing to inspect Acme's accounts payable, thus overstating profits and assets and under-
stating losses and liabilities. Fidelity delivers oil to Acme on
credit. Acme goes bankrupt. Fidelity sues Julian. Julian defends by pointing to the "hold harmless" clause. What result?

PROBLEMS

1. First Corporation hired Marie, a CPA, to write up its books
   and records. In performing the write-up, Marie noticed
   suspicious circumstances, such as missing invoices, but
   failed to inform the company. Assuming that Marie was
   not hired to audit the company's books and records, but
   merely to perform the write-up, would she be liable to
   First Corporation for negligence? Why?
2. Suppose in problem 1 that the suspicious circumstances
   noted by Marie were the result of First Corporation's negligence. Would Marie be liable for negligence if the company's contributory negligence could be proven? Why?
3. Assume in problem 1 that Marie was also hired to do First
   Corporation's tax returns. Marie gave the corporation a
   guarantee that, if she made a mistake, she would pay all
   penalties and interest. Is this guarantee enforceable? Why?
4. Suppose in problem 1 that Marie is also hired to certify
   First Corporation's balance sheet. First Corporation tells
   Marie that it will use the balance sheet in an attempt to
   obtain a loan from Fifth Bank only. If the company, without telling Marie, uses the balance sheet to negotiate a
   loan with Last Bank instead of Fifth Bank, and if Marie
   is negligent in certifying the balance sheet, would she be
   liable to Last Bank? Why?
5. Suppose in problem 4 that First had told Marie that it
   expected to negotiate a bank loan but did not name the
   bank. Would Marie be liable for negligence to Last Bank?
   Why?
6. Suppose in problem 4 that First did not tell Marie that it
   was going to use the balance sheet to obtain a bank loan.
   Would Marie be liable for negligence to Last Bank? Why?

7. Suppose in problem 4 that Marie was told that First would use the balance sheet to negotiate a loan with Last Bank. After reviewing the balance sheet, Last Bank decided to merge with First Corporation. Assuming that federal and state banking regulations permit such a merger, would Marie be liable to Last Bank if she was negligent in certifying the balance sheet? Why?

ANSWERS TO SELF-TEST QUESTIONS

1. (c)   2. (b)   3. (d)   4. (a)   5. (b)

SUGGESTED ANSWER TO DEMONSTRATION PROBLEM

Julian will lose. Julian clearly has a common-law duty to both the client and any third-party beneficiaries to carry out audits and other accounting services in a non-negligent manner. It is possible that Julian may have a valid defense to a suit by Acme, since Acme explicitly agreed to waive Julian's negligence, but Julian may not avoid its liability to Fidelity since Fidelity was not a party to the Julian-Acme contract and, as a third party, is precisely within the protection of the common-law rule that accountants have a responsibility to be careful.

Part 10

The Manager's Legal Agenda

Companies should have an adequate antitrust compliance policy, one that tells employees explicitly what they are forbidden to discuss with competitors.

A company's antitrust compliance policy should be diligently enforced. A policy statement is of very low value unless the company can demonstrate that employees know its provisions and will be disciplined or fired for violating it.

Industry trade associations are a frequent meeting place for competitors, suppliers, and distributors to discuss common problems. Because the line is thin between legitimate exchange of information and unlawful conspiracy to restrain trade, you should review antitrust issues with counsel from time to time before attending such meetings.

If you plan to meet with competitors, suppliers, distributors, or even customers under circumstances in which conversations, even if innocently intended, could lead to antitrust difficulties, invite your lawyer to attend.

Throughout the 1980s, the federal government turned away from antitrust as a weapon against mergers and acquisitions. Be aware that the regulatory climate may change in the years to come. Also be aware that *state* antitrust laws may affect a merger or acquisition in your state.

A company's advertising is a source of danger in a litigious climate; consumers increasingly are suing because they perceive that companies are failing to live up to their promises. Discuss your company's advertising, in whatever form, with counsel.

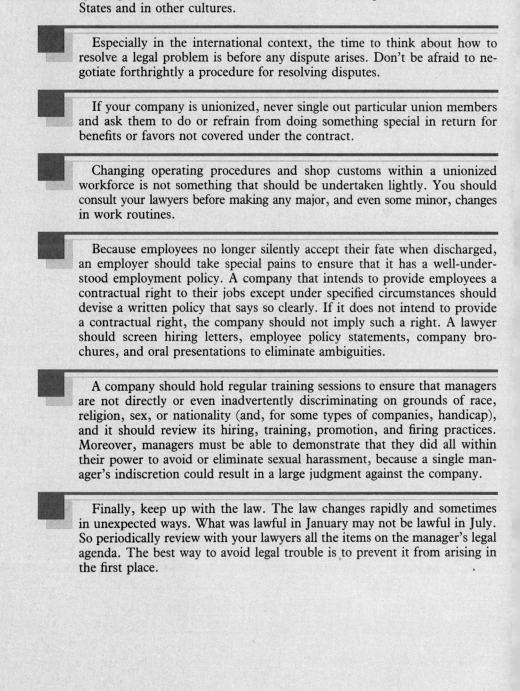

Doing business outside the United States may present special hazards. With planning, many of these can be avoided by contract. You should take special pains to negotiate contracts that will be meaningful both in the United States and in other cultures.

Especially in the international context, the time to think about how to resolve a legal problem is before any dispute arises. Don't be afraid to negotiate forthrightly a procedure for resolving disputes.

If your company is unionized, never single out particular union members and ask them to do or refrain from doing something special in return for benefits or favors not covered under the contract.

Changing operating procedures and shop customs within a unionized workforce is not something that should be undertaken lightly. You should consult your lawyers before making any major, and even some minor, changes in work routines.

Because employees no longer silently accept their fate when discharged, an employer should take special pains to ensure that it has a well-understood employment policy. A company that intends to provide employees a contractual right to their jobs except under specified circumstances should devise a written policy that says so clearly. If it does not intend to provide a contractual right, the company should not imply such a right. A lawyer should screen hiring letters, employee policy statements, company brochures, and oral presentations to eliminate ambiguities.

A company should hold regular training sessions to ensure that managers are not directly or even inadvertently discriminating on grounds of race, religion, sex, or nationality (and, for some types of companies, handicap), and it should review its hiring, training, promotion, and firing practices. Moreover, managers must be able to demonstrate that they did all within their power to avoid or eliminate sexual harassment, because a single manager's indiscretion could result in a large judgment against the company.

Finally, keep up with the law. The law changes rapidly and sometimes in unexpected ways. What was lawful in January may not be lawful in July. So periodically review with your lawyers all the items on the manager's legal agenda. The best way to avoid legal trouble is to prevent it from arising in the first place.

How to Read Legal Citations

The study of law is largely the study of legal precedents in the form of judicial opinions. These are for the most part opinions of appellate courts and are published in both official and private versions for easy reference. Cases are "cited" (referred to) by case name, volume number, the "reporter" (book series in which published), page number, and year of decision. Thus, the case of *Alyeska Pipeline Service Co.* v. *Wilderness Society*, 421 U.S. 240 (1975) can be located in volume 421 of the *United States Reports*, the official publication of the U.S. Supreme Court, beginning at page 240. The decision was handed down in 1975.

Until 1876, Supreme Court decisions were published in volumes bearing the name of the Court's Reporter of Decisions. Thus, *Marbury* v. *Madison*, 5 U.S. (1 Cr.) 137 (1803) was published in the first volume of the reports of William Cranch. For modern purposes the volumes have been given parallel citations (5 U.S.).

The U.S. Supreme Court and the supreme courts of most states publish their own official volumes. These opinions are also published in a private series known as the *National Reporter System*, published by West Publishing Company. For state cases, we cite mainly to the *National Reporter System* only; the state is indicated immediately before the date. There is no official publication of the lower federal courts; decisions of the circuit courts of appeals and district courts appear in the *National Reporter System*.

The citation to the official publication can be identified by the abbreviation of the state. Thus, "10 Ill. 2d 331" refers to volume 10 of the second series of the Illinois Supreme Court volumes, page 331. The federal citations are to "F." or "F.2d," which connote the *Federal Reporter* and the *Federal Reporter, Second Series*, containing the opinions of the U.S. Courts of Appeals; to "F.Supp.," for the *Federal Supplement*, which contains the opinions of the district courts; and to "F.R.D.," for *Federal Rules Decisions*, in which are printed opinions interpreting the Federal Rules of Civil Procedure.

Cases in the *National Reporter System* are grouped by regions. Thus, decisions of the courts in eastern states such as Maryland and Delaware appear in the Atlantic (A. and A.2d) series, those of western states such as California, Oregon, Nevada, and so on in the Pacific (P. and P.2d series). Other abbreviations are N.E. (northeast), N.W. (northwest), So. (southern), S.E. (southeast), and S.W. (southwest). Some New York and California cases now appear in separate series: N.Y.S. and Cal.Rptr.

A complete list of reporter abbreviations (and of law reviews) can be found in *Black's Law Dictionary*.

APPENDIX B

Selected Parts of the Constitution of the United States

PREAMBLE

We the People of the United States, in Order to form a more perfect Union, establish Justice, insure domestic Tranquility, provide for the common defense, promote the general Welfare, and secure the Blessings of Liberty to ourselves and our Posterity, do ordain and establish this Constitution for the United States of America.

ARTICLE 1

*   *   *

Section 8. The Congress shall have Power

[cl. 1] To lay and collect Taxes, Duties, Imposts and Excises, to pay the Debts and provide for the common Defense and general Welfare of the United States; but all Duties, Imposts and Excises shall be uniform throughout the United States;

[cl. 2] To borrow Money on the Credit of the United States;

[cl. 3] To regulate Commerce with foreign Nations, and among the several States, and with the Indian Tribes;

[cl. 4] To establish an uniform Rule of Naturalization, and uniform Laws on the subject of Bankruptcies throughout the United States;

[cl. 5] To coin Money, regulate the Value thereof, and of foreign Coin, and fix the Standard of Weights and Measures;

[cl. 6] To provide for the Punishment of counterfeiting the Securities and current Coin of the United States;

[cl. 7] To establish Post Offices and post Roads;

[cl. 8] To promote the Progress of Science and useful Arts, by securing for limited Times to Authors and Inventors the exclusive Right to their respective Writings and Discoveries;

[cl. 9] To constitute Tribunals inferior to the Supreme Court;

[cl. 10] To define and punish Piracies and Felonies committed on the high Seas; and Offences against the Law of Nations;

[cl. 11] To declare War, grant Letters of Marque and Reprisal, and make Rules concerning Captures on Land and Water;

[cl. 12] To raise and support Armies, but no Appropriation of Money to that Use shall be for a longer Term than two Years;

[cl. 13] To provide and maintain a Navy;

[cl. 14] To make Rules for the Government and Regulation of the land and naval Forces;

[cl. 15] To provide for calling forth the Militia to execute the Laws of the Union, suppress Insurrections and repel Invasions;

[cl. 16] To provide for organizing, arming, and disciplining, the Militia, and for governing such Part of them as may be employed in the Service of the United States, reserving to the States respectively, the Appointment of the Officers, and the Authority of training the Militia according to the discipline prescribed by Congress.

[cl. 17] To exercise exclusive Legislation in all Cases whatsoever, over such District (not exceeding ten Miles square) as may, by Cession of particular States, and the Acceptance of Congress become the Seat of the Government of the United States, and to exercise like Authority over all Places purchased by the Consent of the Legislature of the State in which the Same shall be, for the Erection of Forts, Magazines, Arsenals, dock-Yards, and other needful Buildings;—And

[cl. 18] To make all Laws which shall be necessary and proper for carrying into Execution the foregoing Powers, and all other Powers vested by this Constitution in the Government of the United States, or in any Department or Officer thereof.

Section 9. [cl. 1] The Migration or Importation of such persons as any of the States now existing shall think proper to admit, shall not be prohibited by the Congress prior to the Year one thousand eight hundred and eight, but a Tax or duty may be imposed on such Importation, not exceeding ten dollars for each Person.

[cl. 2] The Privilege of the Writ of Habeas Corpus shall not be suspended, unless when in Cases of Rebellion or Invasion the public Safety may require it.

[cl. 3] No Bill of Attainder or ex post facto Laws shall be passed.

[cl. 4] No Capitation, or other direct, Tax shall be laid, unless in Proportion to the Census or Enumeration herein before directed to be taken.

[cl. 5] No Tax or Duty shall be laid on Articles exported from any State.

[cl. 6] No Preference shall be given by any Regulation of Commerce or Revenue to the Ports of one State over those of another: nor shall Vessels bound to, or from, one State, be obliged to enter, clear, or pay Duties in another.

[cl. 7] No Money shall be drawn from the Treasury, but in Consequence of Appropriations made by Law; and a regular Statement and Account of the Receipts and Expenditures of all public Money shall be published from time to time.

[cl.8] No Title of Nobility shall be granted by the United States; And no Person holding any Office of Profit or Trust under them, shall, without the Consent of the Congress, accept of any present, Emolument, Office, or Title, of any kind whatever, from any King, Prince, or foreign State.

Section 10 [cl. 1] No State shall enter into any Treaty, Alliance, or Confederation; grant Letters of Marque and Reprisal; coin Money; emit Bills of Credit, make any Thing but gold and silver Coin a Tender in Payment of Debts; pass any Bill of Attainder, ex post facto Law, or Law impairing the Obligation of Contracts, or grant any Title of Nobility.

[cl. 2] No State shall, without the Consent of the Congress, lay any Imposts or Duties on Imports or Exports, except what may be absolutely necessary for executing its inspection Laws: and the net Produce of all Duties and Imposts, laid by any State on Imports or Exports, shall be for the Use of the Treasury of the United States; and all such Laws shall be subject to the Revision and Control of the Congress.

[cl. 3] No State shall, without the Consent of Congress, lay any Duty of Tonnage, keep Troops, or Ships of War in time of Peace, enter into any Agreement or Compact with another state, or with a foreign Power, or engage in War, unless actually invaded, or in such imminent Danger as will not admit of delay.

*   *   *

AMENDMENTS

(The first 10 Amendments were adopted December 15, 1791.)

Amendment 1

Congress shall make no law respecting an establishment of religion, or prohibiting the free exercise thereof; or abridging the freedom of speech, or of the press; or the right of the people peaceably to assemble, and to petition the Government for a redress of grievances.

*   *   *

Amendment 4

The right of the people to be secure in their persons, houses, papers, and effects, against unreasonable searches and seizures, shall not be violated, and no Warrants shall issue, but upon probable cause, supported by Oath or affirmation, and particularly describing the place to be searched, and the persons or things to be seized.

Amendment 5

No person shall be held to answer for a capital, or otherwise infamous crime, unless on a presentment or indictment of a Grand Jury, except in cases arising in the land or naval forces, or in the Militia, when in actual service in time of War or public danger; nor shall any person be subject for the same offence to be twice put in jeopardy of life or limb; nor shall be compelled in any criminal case to be a witness against himself, nor be deprived of life, liberty, or property, without due process of law; nor shall private property be taken for public use, without just compensation.

Amendment 6

In all criminal prosecutions, the accused shall enjoy the right to a speedy and public trial, by an impartial jury of the State and district wherein the crime shall have been committed, which district shall have been previously ascertained by law, and to be informed of the nature and cause of the accusation; to be confronted with the witnesses against him, to have compulsory process for obtaining witnesses in his favor, and to have the Assistance of Counsel for his defence.

*   *   *

Amendment 8

Excessive bail shall not be required, nor excessive fines imposed, nor cruel and unusual punishment inflicted.

*   *   *

Amendment 14
(Adopted July 28, 1868)

Section 1.   All persons born or naturalized in the United States, and subject to the jurisdiction thereof, are citizens of the United States and of the State wherein they reside. No State shall make or enforce any law which shall abridge the privileges or immunities of citizens of the United States; nor shall any State deprive any person of life, liberty, or property, without due process of law, nor deny to any person within its jurisdiction the equal protection of the laws.

*   *   *

APPENDIX C

Uniform Commercial Code*

ARTICLE 1. GENERAL PROVISIONS

Part 1. Short Title, Construction, Application and Subject Matter of the Act

§ 1-101 Short Title. This Act shall be known and may be cited as Uniform Commercial Code.

§ 1-102. Purposes; Rules of Construction; Variation by Agreement.

(1) This Act shall be liberally construed and applied to promote its underlying purposes and policies.

(2) Underlying purposes and policies of this Act are

(a) to simplify, clarify and modernize the law governing commercial transactions.

(b) to permit the continued expansion of commercial practices through custom, usage and agreement of the parties;

(c) to make uniform the law among the various jurisdictions.

(3) The effect of provisions of this Act may be varied by agreement, except as otherwise provided in this Act and except that the obligations of good faith, diligence, reasonableness and care prescribed by this Act may not be disclaimed by agreement but the parties may by agreement determine the standards by which the performance of such obligations is to be measured if such standards are not manifestly unreasonable.

(4) The presence in certain provisions of this Act of the words "unless otherwise agreed" or words of similar import does not imply that the effect of other provisions may not be varied by agreement under subsection (3).

(5) In this Act unless the context otherwise requires

(a) words in the singular number include the plural, and in the plural include the singular;

(b) words of the masculine gender include the feminine and the neuter, and when the sense so indicates words of the neuter gender may refer to any gender.

§ 1-103. Supplementary General Principles of Law Applicable. Unless displaced by the particular provisions of this Act, the principles of law and equity, including the law merchant and the law relative to capacity to contract, principal and agent, estoppel, fraud, misrepresentation, duress, coercion, mistake, bankruptcy, or other validating or invalidating cause shall supplement its provisions.

§ 1-104. Construction Against Implicit Repeal. This Act being a general act intended as a unified coverage of its subject matter, no part of it shall be deemed to be impliedly repealed by subsequent legislation if such construction can reasonably be avoided.

*Copyright 1978 by The American Law Institute and the National Conference of Commissioners on Uniform State Laws. Articles 5 and 8 of the Code are not reprinted in this Appendix.

§ 1-105. Territorial Application of the Act; Parties' Power to Choose Applicable Law.

(1) Except as provided hereafter in this section, when a transaction bears a reasonable relation to this state and also to another state or nation the parties may agree that the law either of this state or of such other state or nation shall govern their rights and duties. Failing such agreement this Act applies to transactions bearing an appropriate relation to this state.

(2) Where one of the following provisions of this Act specifies the applicable law, that provision governs and a contrary agreement is effective only to the extent permitted by the law (including the conflict of laws rules) so specified:

Rights of creditors against sold goods. Section 2-402.

Applicability of the Articles on Leases. Sections 2A-105 and 2A-106.

Applicability of the Article on Bank Deposits and Collections. Section 4-102.

Governing law in the Article on Funds Transfers. Section 4A-507.

Bulk sales subject to the Article on Bulk Sales. Section 6-103.

Applicability of the Article on Investment Securities. Section 8-106.

Perfection provisions of the Article on Secured Transactions. Section 9-103.

As amended in 1972, 1987, 1988 and 1989.

§ 1-106. Remedies to Be Liberally Administered.

(1) The remedies provided by this Act shall be liberally administered to the end that the aggrieved party may be put in as good a position as if the other party had fully performed but neither consequential or special nor penal damages may be had except as specifically provided in this Act or by other rule of law.

(2) Any right or obligation declared by this Act is enforceable by action unless the provision declaring it specifies a different and limited effect.

§ 1-107. Waiver or Renunciation of Claim or Right After Breach. Any claim or right arising out of an alleged breach can be discharged in whole or in part without consideration by a written waiver or renunciation signed and delivered by the aggrieved party.

§ 1-108. Severability. If any provision or clause of this Act or application thereof to any person or circumstances is held invalid, such invalidity shall not affect other provisions or applications of the Act which can be given effect without the invalid provision or application, and to this end the provisions of this Act are declared to be severable.

§ 1-109. Section Captions. Section captions are parts of this Act.

Part 2. General Definitions and Principles of Interpretation

§ 1-201. General Definitions. Subject to additional definitions contained in the subsequent Articles of this Act which are applicable to specific Articles or Parts thereof, and unless the context otherwise requires, in this Act:

(1) "Action" in the sense of a judicial proceeding includes recoupment, counterclaim, set-off, suit in equity and any other proceedings in which rights are determined.

(2) "Aggrieved party" means a party entitled to resort to a remedy.

(3) "Agreement" means the bargain of the parties in fact as found in their language or by implication from other circumstances including course of dealing or usage of trade or course of performance as provided

in this Act (Sections 1-205 and 2-208). Whether an agreement has legal consequences is determined by the provisions of this Act, if applicable; otherwise by the law of contracts (Section 1-103). (Compare "Contract".)

(4) "Bank" means any person engaged in the business of banking.

(5) "Bearer" means the person in possession of an instrument, document of title, or certified security payable to bearer or indorsed in blank.

(6) "Bill of lading" means a document evidencing the receipt of goods for shipment issued by a person engaged in the business of transporting or forwarding goods, and includes an airbill. "Airbill" means a document serving for air transportation as a bill of lading does for marine or rail transportation, and includes an air consignment note or air waybill.

(7) "Branch" includes a separately incorporated foreign branch of a bank.

(8) "Burden of establishing" a fact means the burden of persuading the triers of fact that the existence of the fact is more probable than its non-existence.

(9) "Buyer in ordinary course of business" means a person who in good faith and without knowledge that the sale to him is in violation of the ownership rights or security interest of a third party in the goods buys in ordinary course from a person in the business of selling goods of that kind but does not include a pawnbroker. All persons who sell minerals or the like (including oil and gas) at wellhead or minehead shall be deemed to be persons in the business of selling goods of that kind. "Buying" may be for cash or by exchange of other property or on secured or unsecured credit and includes receiving goods or documents of title under a pre-existing contract for sale but does not include a transfer in bulk or as security for or in total or partial satisfaction of a money debt.

(10) "Conspicuous": A term or clause is conspicuous when it is so written that a reasonable person against whom it is to operate ought to have noticed it. A printed heading in capitals (as: NON-NEGOTIABLE BILL OF LADING) is conspicuous. Language in the body of a form is "conspicuous" if it is in larger or other contrasting type or color. But in a telegram any stated term is "conspicuous". Whether a term or clause is "conspicuous" or not is for decision by the court.

(11) "Contract" means the total legal obligation which results from the parties' agreement as affected by this Act and any other applicable rules of law. (Compare "Agreement".)

(12) "Creditor" includes a general creditor, a secured creditor, a lien creditor and any representative of creditors, including an assignee for the benefit of creditors, a trustee in bankruptcy, a receiver in equity and an executor or administrator of an insolvent debtor's or assignor's estate.

(13) "Defendant" includes a person in the position of defendant in a cross-action or counterclaim.

(14) "Delivery" with respect to instruments, documents of title, chattel paper, or certificated securities means voluntary transfer of possession.

(15) "Document of title" includes bill of lading, dock warrant, dock receipt, warehouse receipt or order for the delivery of goods, and also any other document which in the regular course of business or financing is treated as adequately evidencing that the person in possession of it is entitled to receive, hold and dispose of the document and the goods it covers. To be a document of title a document must purport to be issued by or addressed to a bailee and purport to cover goods in the bailee's possession which are either identified or are fungible portions of a identified mass.

(16) "Fault" means wrongful act, omission or breach.

(17) "Fungible" with respect to goods or securities means goods or securities of which any unit is, by nature or usage of trade, the equivalent of any other like unit. Goods which are not fungible shall be deemed fungible for the purposes of this Act to the extent that under a particular agreement or document unlike units are treated as equivalents.

(18) "Genuine" means free of forgery or counterfeiting.

(19) "Good faith" means honesty in fact in the conduct or transaction concerned.

(20) "Holder" means a person who is in possession of a document of title or an instrument or a certificated investment security drawn, issued, or indorsed to him or his order or to bearer or in blank.

(21) To "honor" is to pay or to accept and pay, or where a credit so engages to purchase or discount a draft complying with the terms of the credit.

(22) "Insolvency proceedings" includes any assignment for the benefit of creditors or other proceedings intended to liquidate or rehabilitate the estate of the person involved.

(23) A person is "insolvent" who either has ceased to pay his debts in the ordinary course of business or cannot pay his debts as they become due or is insolvent within the meaning of the federal bankruptcy law.

(24) "Money" means a medium of exchange authorized or adopted by a domestic or foreign government as a part of its currency.

(25) A person has "notice" of a fact when

  (a) he has actual knowledge of it; or

  (b) he has received a notice or notification of it; or

  (c) from all the facts and circumstances known to him at the time in question he has reason to know that it exists.

A person "knows" or has "knowledge" of a fact when he has actual knowledge of it. "Discover" or "learn" or a word or phrase of similar import refers to knowledge rather than to reason to know. The time and circumstances under which a notice or notification may cease to be effective are not determined by this Act.

(26) A person "notifies" or "gives" a notice or notification to another by taking such steps as may be reasonably required to inform the other in ordinary course whether or not such other actually comes to know of it. A person "receives" a notice or notification when

  (a) it comes to his attention; or

  (b) it is duly delivered at the place of business through which the contract was made or at any other place held out by him as the place for receipt of such communications.

(27) Notice, knowledge or a notice or notification received by an organization is effective for a particular transaction from the time when it is brought to the attention of the individual conducting that transaction, and in any event from the time when it would have been brought to his attention if the organization had exercised due diligence. An organization exercises due diligence if it maintains reasonable routines for communicating significant information to the person conducting the transaction and there is reasonable compliance with the routines. Due diligence does not require an individual acting for the organization to communicate information unless such communication is part of his regular duties or unless he has reason to know of the transaction and that the transaction would be materially affected by the information.

(28) "Organization" includes a corporation, government or governmental subdivision or agency, business trust, estate, trust, partnership or association, two or more persons having a joint or common interest, or any other legal or commercial entity.

(29) "Party," as distinct from "third party", means a person who has engaged in a transaction or made an agreement within this Act.

(30) "Person" includes an individual or an organization (See Section 1-102).

(31) "Presumption" or "presumed" means that the trier of fact must find the existence of the fact presumed unless and until evidence is introduced which would support a finding of its non-existence.

(32) "Purchase" includes taking by sale, discount, negotiation, mortgage, pledge, lien, issue or re-issue, gift or any other voluntary transaction creating an interest in property.

(33) "Purchaser" means a person who takes by purchase.

(34) "Remedy" means any remedial right to which an aggrieved party is entitled with or without resort to a tribunal.

(35) "Representative" includes an agent, an officer of a corporation or association, and a trustee, executor or administrator of an estate, or any other person empowered to act for another.

(36) "Rights" includes remedies.

(37) "Security interest" means an interest in personal property or fixtures which secures payment or performance of an obligation. The retention or reservation of title by a seller of goods notwithstanding shipment or delivery to the buyer (Section 2-401) is limited in effect to a reservation of a "security interest". The term also includes any interest of a buyer of accounts or chattel paper which is subject to Article 9. The special property interest of a buyer of goods on identification of those goods to a contract for sale under Section 2-401 is not a "security interest", but a buyer may also acquire a "security interest" by complying with Article 9. Unless a consignment is intended as security, reservation of title thereunder is not a "security interest", but a consignment in any event is subject to the provisions on consignment sales (Section 2-326).

Whether a transaction creates a lease or security interest is determined by the facts of each case; however, a transaction creates a security interest if the consideration the lessee is to pay the lessor for the right to possession and use of the goods is an obligation for the term of the lease not subject to termination by the lessee, and

(a) the original term of the lease is equal to or greater than the remaining economic life of the goods,

(b) the lessee is bound to renew the lease for the remaining economic life of the goods or is bound to become the owner of the goods,

(c) the lessee has an option to renew the lease for the remaining economic life of the goods for no additional consideration or nominal additional consideration upon compliance with the lease agreement, or

(d) the lessee has an option to become the owner of the goods for no additional consideration or nominal additional consideration upon compliance with the lease agreement.

A transaction does not create a security interest merely because it provides that

(a) the present value of the consideration the lessee is obligated to pay the lessor for the right to possession and use of the goods is substantially equal to or is greater than the fair market value of the goods at the time the lease is entered into,

(b) the lessee assumes risk of loss of the goods, or agrees to pay taxes, insurance, filing, recording, or registration fees, or service or maintenance costs with respect to the goods,

(c) the lessee has an option to renew the lease or to become the owner of the goods,

(d) the lessee has an option to renew the lease for a fixed rent that is equal to or greater than the reasonably predictable fair market rent for the use of the goods for the term of the renewal at the time the option is to be performed, or

(e) the lessee has an option to become the owner of the goods for a fixed price that is equal to or greater than the reasonably predictable fair market value of the goods at the time the option is to be performed.

For purposes of this subsection (37):

(x) Additional consideration is not minimal if (i) when the option to renew the lease is granted to the lessee the rent is stated to be the fair market rent for the use of the goods for the term of the renewal determined at the time the option is to be performed, or (ii) when the option to become the owner of the goods is granted to the lessee the price is stated to be the fair market value of the goods determined at the time the option is to be performed. Additional consideration is nominal if it is less than the lessee's reasonably predictable cost of performing under the lease agreement if the option is not exercised;

(y) "Reasonably predictable" and "remaining economic life of the goods" are to be determined with reference to the facts and circumstances at the time the transaction is entered into; and

(z) "Present value" means the amount as of a date certain of one or more sums payable in the future, discounted to the date certain. The discount is determined by the interest rate specified by the parties if the rate is not manifestly unreasonable at the time the transaction is entered into; otherwise, the discount is determined by a commercially reasonable rate that takes into account the facts and circumstances of each case at the time the transaction was entered into.

(38) "Send" in connection with any writing or notice means to deposit in the mail or deliver for transmission by any other usual means of communication with postage or cost of transmission provided for and properly addressed and in the case of an instrument to an address specified thereon or otherwise agreed, or if there be none to any address reasonable under the circumstances. The receipt of any writing or notice within the time at which it would have arrived if properly sent has the effect of a proper sending.

(39) "Signed" includes any symbol executed or adopted by a party with present intention to authenticate a writing.

(40) "Surety" includes guarantor.

(41) "Telegram" includes a message transmitted by radio, teletype, cable, any mechanical method of transmission, or the like.

(42) "Term" means that portion of an agreement which relates to a particular matter.

(43) "Unauthorized" signature or indorsement means one made without actual, implied or apparent authority and includes a forgery.

(44) "Value". Except as otherwise provided with respect to negotiable instruments and bank collections (Sections 3-303, 4-208 and 4-209) a person gives "value" for rights if he acquires them

(a) in return for a binding commitment to extend credit or for the extension of immediately available credit whether or not drawn upon and whether or not a chargeback is provided for in the event of difficulties in collection; or

(b) as security for or in total or partial satisfaction of a pre-existing claim; or

(c) by accepting delivery pursuant to a pre-existing contract for purchase; or

(d) generally, in return for any consideration sufficient to support a simple contract.

(45) "Warehouse receipt" means a receipt issued by a person engaged in the business of storing goods for hire.

(46) "Written" or "writing" includes printing, typewriting or any other intentional reduction to tangible form. Amended in 1962, 1972, and 1977.

§ 1-202. Prima Facie Evidence by Third Party Documents.

A document in due form purporting to be a bill of lading, policy or certificate of insurance, official weigher's or inspector's certificate, consular invoice, or any other document authorized or required by the contract to be issued by a third party shall be prima facie evidence of its own authenticity and genuineness and of the facts stated in the document of the third party.

§ 1-203. Obligation of Good Faith.
Every contract or duty within this Act imposes an obligation of good faith in its peformance or enforcement.

§ 1-204. Time; Reasonable Time; "Seasonably".

(1) Whenever this Act requires any action to be taken within a reasonable time, any time which is not manifestly unreasonable may be fixed by agreement.

(2) What is a reasonable time for taking any action depends on the nature, purpose and circumstances of such action.

(3) An action is taken "seasonably" when it is taken at or within the time agreed or if no time is agreed at or within a reasonable time.

§ 1-205. Course of Dealing and Usage of Trade.

(1) A course of dealing is a sequence of previous conduct between the parties to a particular transaction which is fairly to be regarded as establishing a common basis of understanding for interpreting their expressions and other conduct.

(2) A usage of trade is any practice or method of dealing having such regularity of observance in a place, vocation or trade as to justify an expectation that it will be observed with respect to the transaction in question. The existence and scope of such a usage are to be proved as facts. If it is established that such a usage is embodied in a written trade code or similar writing the interpretation of the writing is for the court.

(3) A course of dealing between parties and any usage of trade in the vocation or trade in which they are engaged or of which they are or should be aware give particular meaning to and supplement or qualify terms of an agreement.

(4) The express terms of an agreement and an applicable course of dealing or usage of trade shall be construed wherever reasonable as consistent with each other; but when such construction is unreasonable express terms control both course of dealing and usage of trade and course of dealing controls usage of trade.

(5) An applicable usage of trade in the place where any part of performance is to occur shall be used in interpreting the agreement as to that part of the performance.

(6) Evidence of a relevant usage of trade offered by one party is not admissible unless and until he has given the other party such notice as the court finds sufficient to prevent unfair surprise to the latter.

§ 1-206. Statute of Frauds for Kinds of Personal Property Not Otherwise Covered.

(1) Except in the cases described in subsection (2) of this section a contract for the sale of personal property is not enforceable by way of action or defense beyond five thousand dollars in amount or value of remedy unless there is some writing which indicates that a contract for sale has been made between the parties at a defined or stated price, reasonably identifies the subject matter, and is signed by the party against whom enforcement is sought or by his authorized agent.

(2) Subsection (1) of this section does not apply to contracts for the sale of goods (Section 2-201) nor of securities (Section 8-319) nor to security agreements (Section 9-203).

§ 1-207. Performance or Acceptance Under Reservation of Rights.
A party who with explicit reservation of rights performs or promises performance or assents to performance in a manner demanded or offered by the other party does not thereby prejudice the rights reserved. Such words as "without prejudice", "under protest" or the like are sufficient.

§ 1-208. Option to Accelerate at Will.
A term providing that one party or his successor in interest may accelerate payment or performance or require collateral or additional collateral "at will" or "when he deems himself insecure" or in words of similar import shall be construed to mean that he shall have power to do so only if he in good faith believes that the prospect of payment or performance is impaired. The burden of establishing lack of good faith is on the party against whom the power has been exercised.

§ 1-209. Subordinated Obligations.
An obligation may be issued as subordinated to payment of another obligation of the person obliged, or a creditor may subordinate his right to payment of an obligation by agreement with either the person obligated or another creditor of the person obligated. Such a subordination does not create a security interest as against either the common debtor or a subordinated creditor. This section shall be construed as declaring the law as it existed prior to the enactment of this section and not as modifying it. Added 1966.

Note: This new section is proposed as an optional provision to make it clear that a subordination agreement does not create a security interest unless so intended.

ARTICLE 2. SALES

Part 1. Short Title, General Construction and Subject Matter

§ 2-101. Short Title.
This Article shall be known and may be cited as Uniform Commercial Code—Sales.

§ 2-102. Scope; Certain Security and Other Transactions Excluded From This Article.
Unless the context otherwise requires, this Article applies to transactions in goods; it does not apply to any transaction which although in the form of an unconditional contract to sell or present sale is intended to operate only as a security transaction nor does this Article impair or repeal any statute regulating sales to consumers, farmers or other specified classes of buyers.

§ 2-103. Definitions and Index of Definitions.

(1) In this Article unless the context otherwise requires

(a) "Buyer" means a person who buys or contracts to buy goods.

(b) "Good faith" in the case of a merchant means honesty in fact and the observance of reasonable commercial standards of fair dealing in the trade.

(c) "Receipt" of goods means taking physical possession of them.

(d) "Seller" means a person who sells or contracts to sell goods.

(2) Other definitions applying to this Article or to specified Parts thereof, and the sections in which they appear are:

"Acceptance". Section 2-606.

"Banker's credit". Section 2-325.

"Between merchants". Section 2-104.

"Cancellation". Section 2-106(4).

"Commercial unit". Section 2-105.

"Confirmed credit". Section 2-325.

"Conforming to contract". Section 2-106.

"Contract for sale". Section 2-106.

"Cover". Section 2-712.

"Entrusting". Section 2-403.

"Financing agency". Section 2-104.

"Future goods". Section 2-105.

"Goods". Section 2-105.

"Identification". Section 2-501.

"Installment contract". Section 2-612.

"Letter of Credit". Section 2-325.

"Lot". Section 2-105.

"Merchant". Section 2-104.

"Overseas". Section 2-323.

"Person in position of seller". Section 2-707.

"Present sale". Section 2-106.

"Sale". Section 2-106.

"Sale on approval". Section 2-326.

"Sale or return". Section 2-326.

"Termination". Section 2-106.

(3) The following definitions in other Articles apply to this Article:

"Check". Section 3-104.

"Consignee". Section 7-102.

"Consignor". Section 7-102.

"Consumer goods". Section 9-109.

"Dishonor". Section 3-507.

"Draft". Section 3-104.

(4) In addition Article 1 contains general definitions and principles of construction and interpretation applicable throughout this Article.

§ 2-104. Definitions: "Merchant"; "Between Merchants"; "Financing Agency."

(1) "Merchant" means a person who deals in goods of the kind or otherwise by his occupation holds himself out as having knowledge or skill peculiar to the practices or goods involved in the transaction or to whom such knowledge or skill may be attributed by his employment of an agent or broker or other intermediary who by his occupation holds himself out as having such knowledge or skill.

(2) "Financing agency" means a bank, finance company or other person who in the ordinary course of business makes advances against goods or documents of title or who by arrangement with either the seller or the buyer intervenes in ordinary course to make or collect payment due or claimed under the contract for sale, as by purchasing or paying the seller's draft or making advances against it or by merely taking it for collection whether or not documents of title accompany the draft. "Financing agency" includes also a bank or other person who similarly intervenes between persons who are in the position of seller and buyer in respect to the goods (Section 2-707).

(3) "Between merchants" means in any transaction with respect to which both parties are chargeable with the knowledge or skill of merchants.

§ 2-105. Definitions: Transferability; "Goods"; "Future" Goods; "Lot"; "Commercial Unit."

(1) "Goods" means all things (including specially manufactured goods) which are movable at the time of identification to the contract for sale other than the money in which the price is to be paid, investment securities (Article 8) and things in action. "Goods" also includes the unborn young of animals and growing crops and other identified things attached to realty as described in the section on goods to be severed from realty (Section 2-107).

(2) Goods must be both existing and identified before any interest in them can pass. Goods which are not both existing and identified are "future" goods. A purported present sale of future goods or of any interest therein operates as a contract to sell.

(3) There may be a sale of a part interest in existing identified goods.

(4) An undivided share in an identified bulk of fungible goods is sufficiently identified to be sold although the quantity of the bulk is not determined. Any agreed proportion of such a bulk or any quantity thereof agreed upon by number, weight or other measure may to the extent of the seller's interest in the bulk be sold to the buyer who then becomes an owner in common.

(5) "Lot" means a parcel or a single article which is the subject matter of a separate sale or delivery, whether or not it is sufficient to perform the contract.

(6) "Commercial unit" means such a unit of goods as by commercial usage is a single whole for purposes of sale and division of which materially impairs its character or value on the market or in use. A commercial unit may be a single article (as a machine) or a set of articles (as a suite of furniture or an assortment of sizes) or a quantity (as a bale, gross, or carload) or any other unit treated in use or in the relevant market as a single whole.

§ 2-106. Definitions: "Contract"; "Agreement"; "Contract for Sale"; "Sale"; "Present Sale"; "Conforming" to Contract; "Termination"; "Cancellation."

(1) In this Article unless the context otherwise requires "contract" and "agreement" are limited to those relating to the present or future sale of goods. "Contract for sale" includes both a present sale of goods and a contract to sell goods at a future time. A "sale" consists in the passing of title from the seller to the buyer for a price (Section 2-401). A "present sale" means a sale which is accomplished by the making of the contract.

(2) Goods or conduct including any part of a performance are "conforming" or conform to the contract when they are in accordance with the obligations under the contract.

(3) "Termination" occurs when either party pursuant to a power created by agreement or law puts an end to the contract otherwise than for its breach. On "termination" all obligations which are still executory on both sides are discharged but any right based on prior breach or performance survives.

(4) "Cancellation" occurs when either party puts an end to the contract for breach by the other and its effect is the same as that of "termination" except that the cancelling party also retains any remedy for breach of the whole contract or any unperformed balance.

§ 2-107. Goods to Be Severed From Realty: Recording.

(1) A contract for the sale of minerals or the like (including oil and gas) or a structure or its materials to be removed from realty is a contract for the sale of goods within this Article if they are to be severed by the seller but until severance a purported present sale thereof which is not effective as a transfer of an interest in land is effective only as a contract to sell.

(2) A contract for the sale apart from the land of growing crops or other things attached to realty and capable of severance without material harm thereto but not described in subsection (1) or of timber to be cut is a contract for the sale of goods within this Article whether the subject matter is to be severed by the buyer or by the seller even though it forms part of the realty at the time of contracting, and the parties can by identification effect a present sale before severance.

(3) The provisions of this section are subject to any third party rights provided by the law relating to realty records, and the contract for sale may be executed and recorded as a document transferring an

interest in land and shall then constitute notice to third parties of the buyer's rights under the contract for sale.

Part 2. Form, Formation and Readjustment of Contract

§ 2-201 Formal Requirements; Statute of Frauds.

(1) Except as otherwise provided in this section a contract for the sale of goods for the price of $500 or more is not enforceable by way of action or defense unless there is some writing sufficient to indicate that a contract for sale has been made between the parties and signed by the party against whom enforcement is sought or by his authorized agent or broker. A writing is not insufficient because if omits or incorrectly states a term agreed upon but the contract is not enforceable under this paragraph beyond the quantity of goods shown in such writing.

(2) Between merchants if within a reasonable time a writing in confirmation of the contract and sufficient against the sender is received and the party receiving it has reason to know its contents, it satisfies the requirements of subsection (1) against such party unless written notice of objection to its contents is given within ten days after it is received.

(3) A contract which does not satisfy the requirements of subsection (1) but which is valid in other respects is enforceable

    (a) if the goods are to be specially manufactured for the buyer and are not suitable for sale to others in the ordinary course of the seller's business and the seller, before notice of repudiation is received and under circumstances which reasonably indicate that the goods are for the buyer, has made either a substantial beginning of their manufacture or commitments for their procurement; or

    (b) if the party against whom enforcement is sought admits in his pleading, testimony or otherwise in court that a contract for sale was made, but the contract is not enforceable under this provision beyond the quantity of goods admitted; or

    (c) with respect to goods for which payment has been made and accepted or which have been received and accepted (Sec. 2-606).

§ 2-202. Final Written Expression: Parol or Extrinsic Evidence.

Terms with respect to which the confirmatory memoranda of the parties agree or which are otherwise set forth in a writing intended by the parties as a final expression of their agreement with respect to such terms as are included therein may not be contradicted by evidence of any prior agreement or of a contemporaneous oral agreement but may be explained or supplemented

    (a) by course of dealing or usage of trade (Section 1-205) or by course of performance (Section 2-208); and

    (b) by evidence of consistent additional terms unless the court finds the writing to have been intended also as a complete and exclusive statement of the terms of the agreement.

§ 2-203. Seals Inoperative.

The affixing of a seal to a writing evidencing a contract for sale or an offer to buy or sell goods does not constitute the writing a sealed instrument and the law with respect to sealed instruments does not apply to such a contract or offer.

§ 2-204. Formation in General.

(1) A contract for sale of goods may be made in any manner sufficient to show agreement, including conduct by both parties which recognizes the existence of such a contract.

(2) An agreement sufficient to constitute a contract for sale may be found even though the moment of its making is undermined.

(3) Even though one or more terms are left open a contract for sale does not fail for indefiniteness if the parties have intended to make a contract and there is a reasonably certain basis for giving an appropriate remedy.

§ 2-205. Firm Offers.

An offer by a merchant to buy or sell goods in a signed writing which by its terms gives assurance that it will be held open is not revocable, for lack of consideration, during the time stated or if no time is stated for a reasonable time, but in no event may such period of irrevocability exceed three months; but any such term of assurance on a form supplied by the offeree must be separately signed by the offeror.

§ 2-206. Offer and Acceptance in Formation of Contract.

(1) Unless otherwise unambiguously indicated by the language or circumstances.

    (a) an offer to make a contract shall be construed as inviting acceptance in any manner and by any medium reasonable in the circumstances;

    (b) an order or other offer to buy goods for prompt or current shipment shall be construed as inviting acceptance either by a prompt promise to ship or by the prompt or current shipment of conforming or non-conforming goods, but such a shipment of non-conforming goods does not constitute an acceptance if the seller seasonably notifies the buyer that the shipment is offered only as an accommodation to the buyer.

(2) Where the beginning of a requested performance is a reasonable mode of acceptance an offeror who is not notified of acceptance within a reasonable time may treat the offer as having lapsed before acceptance.

§ 2-207. Additional Terms in Acceptance or Confirmation.

(1) A definite and seasonable expression of acceptance or a written confirmation which is sent within a reasonable time operates as an acceptance even though it states terms additional to or different from those offered or agreed upon, unless acceptance is expressly made conditional on assent to the additional or different terms.

(2) The additional terms are to be construed as proposals for addition to the contract. Between merchants such terms become part of the contract unless:

    (a) the offer expressly limits acceptance to the terms of the offer;

    (b) they materially alter it; or

    (c) notification of objection to them has already been given or is given within a reasonable time after notice of them is received.

(3) Conduct by both parties which recognizes the existence of a contract is sufficient to establish a contract for sale although the writings of the parties do not otherwise establish a contract. In such case the terms of the particular contract consist of those terms on which the writings of the parties agree, together with any supplementary terms incorporated under any other provisions of this Act.

§ 2-208. Course of Performance or Practical Construction.

(1) Where the contract for sale involves repeated occasions for performance by either party with knowledge of the nature of the performance and opportunity for objection to it by the other, any course of performance accepted or acquiesced in without objection shall be relevant to determine the meaning of the agreement.

(2) The express terms of the agreement and any such course of performance, as well as any course of dealing and usage of trade, shall be construed whenever reasonable as consistent with each other; but when such construction is unreasonable, express terms shall control course of performance and course of performance shall control both course of dealing and usage of trade (Section 1-205).

(3) Subject to the provisions of the next section on modification and waiver, such course of performance shall be relevant to show a waiver or modification of any term inconsistent with such course of performance.

§ 2-209. Modification, Rescission and Waiver.

(1) An agreement modifying a contract within this Article needs no consideration to be binding.

(2) A signed agreement which excludes modification or rescission except by a signed writing cannot be otherwise modified or rescinded, but except as between merchants such a requirement on a form supplied by the merchant must be separately signed by the other party.

(3) The requirements of the statute of frauds section of this Article (Section 2-201) must be satisfied if the contract as modified is within its provisions.

(4) Although an attempt at modification or rescission does not satisfy the requirements of subsection (2) or (3) it can operate as a waiver.

(5) A party who has made a waiver affecting an executory portion of the contract may retract the waiver by reasonable notification received by the other party that strict performance will be required of any term waived, unless the retraction would be unjust in view of a material change of position in reliance on the waiver.

§ 2-210. Delegation of Performance; Assignment of Rights.

(1) A party may perform his duty through a delegate unless otherwise agreed or unless the other party has a substantial interest in having his original promisor perform or control the acts required by the contract. No delegation of performance relieves the party delegating of any duty to perform or any liability for breach.

(2) Unless otherwise agreed all rights of either seller or buyer can be assigned except where the assignment would materially change the duty of the other party, or increase materially the burden or risk imposed on him by his contract, or impair materially his chance of obtaining return performance. A right to damages for breach of the whole contract or a right arising out of the assignor's due performance of his entire obligation can be assigned despite agreement otherwise.

(3) Unless the circumstances indicate the contrary a prohibition of assignment of "the contract" is to be construed as barring only the delegation to the assignee of the assignor's performance.

(4) An assignment of "the contract" or of "all my rights under the contract" or an assignment in similar general terms is an assignment of rights and unless the language or the circumstances (as in an assignment for security) indicate the contrary, it is a delegation of performance of the duties of the assignor and its acceptance by the assignee constitutes a promise by him to perform those duties. This promise is enforceable by either the assignor or the other party to the original contract.

(5) The other party may treat any assignment which delegates performance as creating reasonable grounds for insecurity and may without prejudice to his rights against the assignor demand assurances from the assignee (Section 2-609).

Part 3. General Obligation and Construction of Contract

§ 2-301. General Obligations of Parties.   The obligation of the seller is to transfer and deliver and that of the buyer is to accept and pay in accordance with the contract.

§ 2-302. Unconscionable Contract or Clause.

(1) If the court as a matter of law finds the contract or any clause of the contract to have been unconscionable at the time it was made the court may refuse to enforce the contract, or it may enforce the remainder of the contract without the unconscionable clause, or it may so limit the application of any unconscionable clause as to avoid any unconscionable result.

(2) When it is claimed or appears to the court that the contract or any clause thereof may be unconscionable the parties shall be afforded a reasonable opportunity to present evidence as to its commercial setting, purpose and effect to aid the court in making the determination.

§ 2-303. Allocation or Division of Risks.   Where this Article allocates a risk or a burden as between the parties "unless otherwise agreed," the agreement may not only shift the allocation but may also divide the risk or burden.

§ 2-304. Price Payable in Money, Goods, Realty, or Otherwise.

(1) The price can be made payable in money or otherwise. If it is payable in whole or in part in goods each party is a seller of the goods which he is to transfer.

(2) Even though all or part of the price is payable in an interest in realty the transfer of the goods and the seller's obligations with reference to them are subject to the Article, but not the transfer of the interest in realty or the transferor's obligations in connection therewith.

§ 2-305. Open Price Term.

(1) The parties if they so intend can conclude a contract for sale even though the price is not settled. In such a case the price is a reasonable price at the time for delivery if

(a) nothing is said as to price; or

(b) the price is left to be agreed by the parties and they fail to agree; or

(c) the price is to be fixed in terms of some agreed market or other standard as set or recorded by a third person or agency and it is not so set or recorded.

(2) A price to be fixed by the seller or by the buyer means a price for him to fix in good faith.

(3) When a price left to be fixed otherwise than by agreement of the parties fails to be fixed through fault of one party the other may at his option treat the contract as cancelled or himself fix a reasonable price.

(4) Where, however, the parties intend not to be bound unless the price be fixed or agreed and it is not fixed or agreed there is no contract. In such a case the buyer must return any goods already received or if unable so to do must pay their reasonable value at the time of delivery and the seller must return any portion of the price paid on account.

§ 2-306. Output, Requirements and Exclusive Dealings.

(1) A term which measures the quantity by the output of the seller or the requirements of the buyer means such actual output or requirements as may occur in good faith, except that no quantity unreasonably disproportionate to any stated estimate or in the absence of a stated estimate to any normal or otherwise comparable prior output or requirements may be tendered or demanded.

(2) A lawful agreement by either the seller or the buyer for exclusive dealing in the kind of goods concerned imposes unless otherwise agreed an obligation by the seller to use best efforts to supply the goods and by the buyer to use best efforts to promote their sale.

§ 2-307. Delivery in Single Lot or Several Lots.   Unless otherwise agreed all goods called for by a contract for sale must be tendered in a single delivery and payment is due only on such tender but where the circumstances give either party the right to make or demand delivery in lots the price if it can be apportioned may be demanded for each lot.

§ 2-308. Absence of Specified Place for Delivery.   Unless otherwise agreed

(a) the place for delivery of goods is the seller's place of business or if he has none his residence; but

(b) in a contract for sale of identified goods which to the knowledge of the parties at the time of contracting are in some other place, that place is the place for their delivery; and

(c) documents of title may be delivered through customary banking channels.

§ 2-309. Absence of Specific Time Provisions; Notice of Termination.

(1) The time for shipment or delivery or any other action under a contract if not provided in this Article or agreed upon shall be a reasonable time.

(2) Where the contract provides for successive performances but is indefinite in duration it is valid for a reasonable time but unless otherwise agreed may be terminated at any time by either party.

(3) Termination of a contract by one party except on the happening of an agreed event requires that reasonable notification be received by the other party and an agreement dispensing with notification is invalid if its operation would be unconscionable.

§ 2-310. Open Time for Payment or Running of Credit; Authority to Ship Under Reservation.   Unless otherwise agreed

(a) payment is due at the time and place at which the buyer is to receive the goods even though the place of shipment is the place of delivery; and

(b) if the seller is authorized to send the goods he may ship them under reservation, and may tender the documents of title, but the buyer may inspect the goods after their arrival before payment is due unless such inspection is inconsistent with the terms of the contract (Section 2-513); and

(c) if delivery is authorized and made by way of documents of title otherwise than by subsection (b) then payment is due at the time and place at which the buyer is to receive the documents regardless of where the goods are to be received; and

(d) where the seller is required or authorized to ship the goods on credit the credit period runs from the time of shipment but post-dating the invoice or delaying its dispatch will correspondingly delay the starting of the credit period.

§ 2-311. Options and Cooperation Respecting Performance.

(1) An agreement for sale which is otherwise sufficiently definite (subsection (3) of Section 2-204) to be a contract is not made invalid by the fact that it leaves particulars of performance to be specified by one of the parties. Any such specification must be made in good faith and within limits set by commercial reasonableness.

(2) Unless otherwise agreed specifications relating to assortment of the goods are at the buyer's option and except as otherwise provided in subsections (1)(c) and (3) of Section 2-319 specifications or arrangements relating to shipment are at the seller's option.

(3) Where such specification would materially affect the other party's performance but is not seasonably made or where one party's cooperation is necessary to the agreed performance of the other but is not seasonably forthcoming, the other party in addition to all other remedies

(a) is excused for any resulting delay in his own performance; and

(b) may also either proceed to perform in any reasonable manner or after the time for a material part of his own performance treat the failure to specify or to cooperate as a breach by failure to deliver or accept the goods.

§ 2-312. Warranty of Title and Against Infringement; Buyer's Obligation Against Infringement.

(1) Subject to subsection (2) there is in a contract for sale a warranty by the seller that

(a) the title conveyed shall be good, and its transfer rightful; and

(b) the goods shall be delivered free from any security interest or other lien or encumbrance of which the buyer at the time of contracting has no knowledge.

(2) A warranty under subsection (1) will be excluded or modified only by specific language or by circumstances which give the buyer reason to know that the person selling does not claim title in himself or that he is purporting to sell only such right or title as he or a third person may have.

(3) Unless otherwise agreed a seller who is a merchant regularly dealing in goods of the kind warrants that the goods shall be delivered free of the rightful claim of any third person by way of infringement or the like but a buyer who furnishes specifications to the seller must hold the seller harmless against any such claim which arises out of compliance with the specifications.

§ 2-313. Express Warranties by Affirmation, Promise, Description, Sample.

(1) Express warranties by the seller are created as follows:

(a) Any affirmation of fact or promise made by the seller to the buyer which relates to the goods and becomes part of the basis of the bargain creates an express warranty that the goods shall conform to the affirmation or promise.

(b) Any description of the goods which is made part of the basis of the bargain creates an express warranty that the goods shall conform to the description.

(c) Any description of the goods which is made part of the basis of the bargain creates an express warranty that the whole of the goods shall conform to the sample or model.

(2) It is not necessary to the creation of an express warranty that the seller use formal words such as "warrant" or "guarantee" or that he have a specific intention to make a warranty, but an affirmation merely of the value of the goods or a statement purporting to be merely the seller's opinion or commendation of the goods does not create a warranty.

§ 2-314. Implied Warranty: Merchantability; Usage of Trade.

(1) Unless excluded or modified (Section 2-316), a warranty that the goods shall be merchantable is implied in a contract for their sale if the seller is a merchant with respect to goods of that kind. Under this section the serving for value of food or drink to be consumed either on the premises or elsewhere is a sale.

(2) Goods to be merchantable must be at least such as

(a) pass without objection in the trade under the contract description; and

(b) in the case of fungible goods, are of fair average quality within the description; and

(c) are fit for the ordinary purposes for which such goods are used; and

(d) run, within the variations permitted by the agreement, of even kind, quality and quantity within each unit and among all units involved; and

(e) are adequately contained, packaged, and labeled as the agreement may require; and

(f) conform to the promises or affirmations of fact made on the container or label if any.

(3) Unless excluded or modified (Section 2-316) other implied warranties may arise from course of dealing or usage of trade.

§ 2-315. Implied Warranty: Fitness for Particular Purpose.   Where the seller at the time of contracting has reason to know any particular purpose for which the goods are required and that the buyer is relying

on the seller's skill or judgment to select or furnish suitable goods, there is unless excluded or modified under the next section an implied warranty that the goods shall be fit for such purpose.

§ 2-316. Exclusion or Modification of Warranties.

(1) Words or conduct relevant to the creation of an express warranty and words or conduct tending to negate or limit warranty shall be construed wherever reasonable as consistent with each other; but subject to the provisions of this Article on parol or extrinsic evidence (Section 2-202) negation or limitation is inoperative to the extent that such construction is unreasonable.

(2) Subject to subsection (2), to exclude or modify the implied warranty of merchantability or any part of it the language must mention merchantability and in case of a writing must be conspicuous, and to exclude or modify any implied warranty of fitness the exclusion must be by a writing and conspicuous. Language to exclude all implied warranties of fitness is sufficient if it states, for example, that "There are no warranties which extend beyond the description on the face hereof."

(3) Notwithstanding subsection (2)

(a) unless the circumstances indicate otherwise, all implied warranties are excluded by expressions like "as is", "with all faults" or other language which in common understanding calls the buyer's attention to the exclusion of warranties and makes plain that there is no implied warranty; and

(b) when the buyer entering into the contract has examined the goods or the sample or model as fully as he desired or has refused to examine the goods there is no implied warranty with regard to defects which an examination ought in the circumstances to have revealed to him; and

(c) an implied warranty can also be excluded or modified by course of dealing or course of performance or usage of trade.

(4) Remedies for breach of warranty can be limited in accordance with the provisions of this Article on liquidation or limitation of damages and on contractual modification of remedy (Section 2-718 and 2-719).

§ 2-317. Cumulation and Conflict of Warranties Express or Implied.

Warranties whether express or implied shall be construed as consistent with each other and as cumulative, but if such construction is unreasonable the intention of the parties shall determine which warranty is dominant. In ascertaining that intention the following rules apply:

(a) Exact or technical specifications displace an inconsistent sample or model or general language of description.

(b) A sample from an existing bulk displaces inconsistent general language of description.

(c) Express warranties displace inconsistent implied warranties other than an implied warranty of fitness for a particular purpose.

§ 2-318. Third Party Beneficiaries of Warranties Express or Implied.

Note: If this Act is introduced in the Congress of the United States this section should be omitted. (States to select one alternative.)

Alternative A   A seller's warranty whether express or implied extends to any natural person who is in the family or household of his buyer or who is a guest in his home if it is reasonable to expect that such person may use, consume or be affected by the goods and who is injured in person by breach of the warranty. A seller may not exclude or limit the operation of this section.

Alternative B   A seller's warranty whether express or implied extends to any natural person who may reasonably be expected to use, consume or be affected by the goods and who is injured in person by breach of the warranty. A seller may not exclude or limit the operation of this section.

Alternative C   A seller's warranty whether express or implied extends to any person who may reasonably be expected to use, consume or be affected by the goods and who is injured by breach of the warranty. A seller may not exclude or limit the operation of this section with respect to injury to the person of an individual to whom the warranty extends. As amended 1966.

§ 2-319. F.O.B. and F.A.S. Terms.

(1) Unless otherwise agreed the term F.O.B. (which means "free on board") at a named place, even though used only in connection with the stated price, is a delivery term under which

(a) when the term is F.O.B. the place of shipment, the seller must at that place ship the goods in the manner provided in this Article (Section 2-504) and bear the expense and risk of putting them into the possession of the carrier; or

(b) when the term is F.O.B. the place of destination, the seller must at his own expense and risk transport the goods to that place and there tender delivery of them in the manner provided in this Article (Section 2-503);

(c) when under either (a) or (b) the term is also F.O.B. vessel, car or other vehicle, the seller must in addition at his own expense and risk load the goods on board. If the term is F.O.B. vessel the buyer must name the vessel and in an appropriate case the seller must comply with the provisions of this Article on the form of bill of lading (Section 2-323).

(2) Unless otherwise agreed the term F.A.S. vessel (which means "free alongside") at a named port, even though used only in connection with the stated price, is a delivery term under which the seller must

(a) at his own expense and risk deliver the goods alongside the vessel in the manner usual in that port or on a dock designated and provided by the buyer; and

(b) obtain and tender a receipt for the goods in exchange for which the carrier is under a duty to issue a bill of lading.

(3) Unless otherwise agreed in any case falling within subsection (1)(a) or (c) or subsection (2) the buyer must seasonably give any needed instructions for making delivery, including when the term is F.A.S. or F.O.B. the loading berth of the vessel and in an appropriate case its name and sailing date. The seller may treat the failure of needed instructions as a failure of cooperation under this Article (Section 2-311). He may also at his option move the goods in any reasonable manner preparatory to delivery or shipment.

(4) Under the term F.O.B. vessel or F.A.S. unless otherwise agreed the buyer must make payment against tender of the required documents and the seller may not tender nor the buyer demand delivery of the goods in substitution for the documents.

§ 2-320. C.I.F. and C. & F. Terms.

(1) The term C.I.F. means that the price includes in a lump sum the cost of the goods and the insurance and freight to the named destination. The terms C. & F. or C.F. means that the price so includes cost and freight to the named destination.

(2) Unless otherwise agreed and even though used only in connection with the stated price and destination, the term C.I.F. destination or its equivalent requires the seller at his own expense and risk to

(a) put the goods into the possession of a carrier at the port for shipment and obtain a negotiable bill or bills of lading covering the entire transportation to the named destination; and

(b) load the goods and obtain a receipt from the carrier which may be contained in the bill of lading) showing that the freight has been paid or provided for; and

(c) obtain a policy or certificate of insurance, including any war risk insurance, of a kind and on terms then current at the port of shipment in the usual amount, in the currency of the contract, shown to cover the same goods covered by the bill of lading and providing for payment of loss to the order of the buyer or for the account of whom it may concern; but the seller may add to the price the amount of the premium for any such war risk insurance; and

(d) prepare an invoice of the goods and procure any other documents required to effect shipment or to comply with the contract, and

(e) forward and tender with commercial promptness all the documents in due form and with any indorsement necessary to perfect the buyer's rights.

(3) Unless otherwise agreed the term C. & F. or its equivalent has the same effect and imposes upon the seller the same obligations and risks as a C.I.F. term except the obligation as to insurance.

(4) Under the term C.I.F. or C. & F. unless otherwise agreed the buyer must make payment against tender of the required documents and the seller may not tender nor the buyer demand delivery of the goods in substitution for the documents.

§ 2-321. C.I.F. or C. & F.: "Net Landed Weights"; "Payment on Arrival"; Warranty of Condition on Arrival. Under a contract containing a term C.I.F. or C. & F.

(1) Where the price is based on or is to be adjusted according to "net landed weights", "delivered weights", "out turn" quantity or quality or the like, unless otherwise agreed the seller must reasonably estimate the price. The payment due on tender of the documents called for by the contract is the amount so estimated, but after final adjustment of the price a settlement must be made with commercial promptness.

(2) An agreement described in subsection (1) or any warranty of quality or condition of the goods on arrival places upon the seller the risk of ordinary deterioration, shrinkage and the like in transportation but has no effect on the place or time of identification to the contract for sale or delivery or on the passing of the risk of loss.

(3) Unless otherwise agreed where the contract provides for payment on or after arrival of the goods the seller must before payment allow such preliminary inspection as is feasible; but if the goods are lost delivery of the documents and payment are due when the goods should have arrived.

§ 2-322. Delivery "Ex-Ship."

(1) Unless otherwise agreed a term for delivery of goods "ex-ship" (which means from the carrying vessel or in equivalent language is not restricted to a particular ship and requires delivery from a ship which has reached a place at the named port of destination where goods of the kind are usually discharged.

(2) Under such a term unless otherwise agreed

(a) the seller must discharge all liens arising out of the carriage and furnish the buyer with a direction which puts the carrier under a duty to deliver the goods; and

(b) the risk of loss does not pass to the buyer until the goods leave the ship's tackle or are otherwise properly unloaded.

§ 2-323. Form of Bill of Lading Required in Overseas Shipment; "Overseas."

(1) Where the contract contemplates overseas shipment and contains a term C.I.F. or C. & F. or F.O.B. vessel, the seller unless otherwise agreed must obtain a negotiable bill of lading stating that the goods have been loaded on board or, in the case of a term C.I.F. or C. & F., received for shipment.

(2) Where in a case within subsection (1) a bill of lading has been issued in a set of parts, unless otherwise agreed if the documents are not to be sent from abroad the buyer may demand tender of the full set; otherwise only one part of the bill of lading need be tendered. Even if the agreement expressly requires a full set

(a) due tender of a single part is acceptable within the provisions of this Article on cure of improper delivery (subsection (1) of Section 2-508); and

(b) even though the full set is demanded, if the documents are sent from abroad the person tendering an incomplete set may nevertheless require payment upon furnishing an indemnity which the buyer in good faith deems adequate.

(3) A shipment by water or by air or a contract contemplating such shipments is "overseas" insofar as by usage of trade or agreement it is subject to the commercial, financing or shipping practices characteristic of international deep water commerce.

§ 2-324. "No Arrival, No Sale" Term. Under a term "no arrival, no sale" or terms of like meaning, unless otherwise agreed,

(a) the seller must properly ship conforming goods and if they arrive by any means he must tender them on arrival but he assumes no obligation that the goods will arrive unless he has caused the non-arrival; and

(b) where without fault of the seller the goods are in part lost or have so deteriorated as no longer to conform to the contract or arrive after the contract time, the buyer may proceed as if there had been casualty to identified goods (Section 2-613).

§ 2-325. "Letter of Credit" Term; "Confirmed Credit."

(1) Failure of the buyer seasonably to furnish an agreed letter of credit is a breach of the contract for sale.

(2) The delivery to seller of a proper letter of credit suspends the buyer's obligation to pay. If the letter of credit is dishonored, the seller may on seasonable notification to the buyer require payment directly from him.

(3) Unless otherwise agreed the term "letter of credit" or "banker's credit" in a contract for sale means an irrevocable credit issued by a financing agency of good repute and, where the shipment is overseas, of good international repute. The term "confirmed credit" means that the credit must also carry the direct obligation of such an agency which does business in the seller's financial market.

§ 2-326. Sale on Approval and Sale or Return; Consignment Sales and Rights of Creditors.

(1) Unless otherwise agreed, if delivered goods may be returned by the buyer even though they conform to the contract, the transaction is

(a) a "sale on approval" if the goods are delivered primarily for use, and

(b) a "sale or return" if the goods are delivered primarily for resale.

(2) Except as provided in subsection (3), goods held on approval are not subject to the claims of the buyer's creditors until acceptance; goods held on sale or return are subject to such claims while in the buyer's possession.

(3) Where goods are delivered to a person for sale and such person maintains a place of business at which he deals in goods of the kind involved, under a name other than the name of the person making delivery, then with respect to claims of creditors of the person conducting the business the goods are deemed to be on sale or return. The provisons of this subsection are applicable even though an agreement purports to reserve title to the person making delivery until payment or resale or uses such words as "on consignment" or "on memorandum". However, this subsection is not applicable if the person making delivery

(a) complies with an applicable law providing for a consignor's interest or the like to be evidenced by a sign, or

(b) establishes that the person conducting the business is generally known by his creditors to be substantially engaged in selling the goods of others, or

(c) complies with the filing provisions of the Article on Secured Transactions (Article 9).

(4) Any "or return" term of a contract for sale is to be treated as a separate contract for sale within the statute of frauds section of this Article (Section 2-201) and as contradicting the sale aspect of the contract within the provisions of this Article on parol or extrinsic evidence (Section 2-202).

§ 2-327. Special Incidents of Sale on Approval and Sale or Return.

(1) Under a sale on approval unless otherwise agreed

(a) although the goods are identified to the contract the risk of loss and the title do not pass to the buyer until acceptance; and

(b) use of the goods consistent with the purpose of trial is not acceptance but failure seasonably to notify the seller of election to return the goods is acceptance, and if the goods conform to the contract acceptance of any part is acceptance of the whole; and

(c) after due notification of election to return, the return is at the seller's risk and expense but a merchant buyer must follow any reasonable instructions.

(2) Under a sale or return unless otherwise agreed

(a) the option to return extends to the whole or any commercial unit of the goods while in substantially their original condition, but must be exercised seasonably; and

(b) the return is at the buyer's risk and expense.

§ 2-328. Sale by Auction.

(1) In a sale by auction if goods are put up in lots each lot is the subject of a separate sale.

(2) A sale by auction is complete when the auctioneer so announces by the fall of the hammer or in other customary manner. Where a bid is made while the hammer is falling in acceptance of a pride bid the auctioneer may in his discretion reopen the bidding or declare the goods sold under the bid on which the hammer was falling.

(3) Such a sale is with reserve unless the goods are in explicit terms put up without reserve. In an auction with reserve the auctioneer may withdraw the goods at any time until he announces completion of the sale. In an auction without reserve, after the auctioneer calls for bids on an article or lot, that article or lot cannot be withdrawn unless no bid is made within a reasonable time. In either case a bidder may retract his bid until the auctioneer's announcement of completion of the sale, but a bidder's retraction does not revive any previous bid.

(4) If the auctioneer knowingly receives a bid on the seller's behalf or the seller makes or procures such a bid, and notice has not been given that liberty for such bidding is reserved, the buyer may at his option avoid the sale or take the goods at the price of the last good faith bid prior to the completion of the sale. This subsection shall not apply to any bid at a forced sale.

Part 4. Title, Creditors and Good Faith Purchasers

§ 2-401. Passing of Title; Reservation for Security; Limited Application of This Section. Each provision of this Article with regard to the rights, obligations and remedies of the seller, the buyer, purchasers or other third parties applies irrespective of title to the goods except where the provision refers to such title. Insofar as situations are not covered by the other provisions of this Article and matters concerning title become material the following rules apply:

(1) Title to goods cannot pass under a contract for sale prior to their identification to the contract (Section 2-501), and unless otherwise explicitly agreed the buyer acquires by their identification a special property as limited by this Act. Any retention or reservation by the seller of the title (property) in goods shipped or delivered to the buyer is limited in effect to a reservation of a security interest. Subject to these provisions and to the provisions of the Article on Secured Transactions (Article 9), title to goods passes from the seller to the buyer in any manner and on any conditions explicitly agreed on by the parties.

(2) Unless otherwise explicitly agreed title passes to the buyer at the time and place at which the seller completes his performance with reference to the physical delivery of the goods, despite any reservation of a security interest and even though a document of title is to be delivered at a different time or place; and in particular and despite any reservation of a security interest by the bill of lading

(a) if the contract requires or authorizes the seller to send the goods to the buyer but does not require him to deliver them at destination, title passes to the buyer at the time and place of shipment; but

(b) if the contract requires delivery at destination, title passes on tender there.

(3) Unless otherwise explicitly agreed where delivery is to be made without moving the goods,

(a) if the seller is to deliver a document of title, title passes at the time when and the place where he delivers such documents; or

(b) if the goods are at the time of contracting already identified and no documents are to be delivered, title passes at the time and place of contracting.

(4) A rejection or other refusal by the buyer to receive or retain the goods, whether or not justified, or a justified revocation of acceptance revests title to the goods in the seller. Such revesting occurs by operation of law and is not a "sale".

§ 2-402. Rights of Seller's Creditors Against Sold Goods.

(1) Except as provided in subsections (2) and (3), rights of unsecured creditors of the seller with respect to goods which have been identified to a contract for sale are subject to the buyer's rights to recover the goods under this Article (Section 2-502 and 2-716).

(2) A creditor of the seller may treat a sale or an identification of goods to a contract for sale as void if as against him a retention of possession by the seller is fraudulent under any rule of law of the state where the goods are situated, except that retention of possession in good faith and current course of trade by a merchant-seller for a commercially reasonable time after a sale or identification is not fraudulent.

(3) Nothing in this Article shall be deemed to impair the rights of creditors of the seller

(a) under the provisions of the Article on Secured Transactions (Article 9); or

(b) where identification to the contract or delivery is made not in current course of trade but in satisfaction of or as security for a pre-existing claim for money, security or the like and is made under circumstances which under any rule of law of the state where the goods are situated would apart from this Article constitute the transaction a fraudulent transfer or voidable preference.

§ 2-403. Power to Transfer; Good Faith Purchase of Goods; "Entrusting".

(1) A purchaser of goods acquires all title which his transferor had or had power to transfer except that a purchaser of a limited interest acquires rights only to the extent of the interest purchased. A person with voidable title has power to transfer a good title to a good faith

purchaser for value. When goods have been delivered under a transaction of purchase the purchaser has such power even though

(a) the transferor was deceived as to the identity of the purchaser, or

(b) the delivery was in exchange for a check which is later dishonored, or

(c) it was agreed that the transaction was to be a "cash sale", or

(d) the delivery was procured through fraud punishable as larcenous under the criminal law.

(2) Any entrusting of possession of goods to a merchant who deals in goods of that kind gives him power to transfer all rights of the entruster to a buyer in ordinary course of business.

(3) "Entrusting" includes any delivery and any acquiescence in retention of possession regardless of any condition expressed between the parties to the delivery or acquiescence and regardless of whether the procurement of the entrusting or the possessor's disposition of the goods have been such as to be larcenous under the criminal law.

(4) The rights of other purchasers of goods and of lien creditors are governed by the Articles on Secured Transactions (Article 9), Bulk Sales (Article 6) and Documents of Title (Article 7).

Part 5. Performance

§ 2-501. Insurable Interest in Goods; Manner of Identification of Goods.

(1) The buyer obtains a special property and an insurable interest in goods by identification of existing goods as goods to which the contract refers even though the goods so identified are non-conforming and he has an option to return or reject them. Such identification can be made at any time and in any manner explicitly agreed to by the parties. In the absence of explicit agreement identification occurs

(a) when the contract is made if it is for the sale of goods already existing and identified;

(b) if the contract is for the sale of future goods other than those described in paragraph (c), when goods are shipped, marked or otherwise designated by the seller as goods to which the contract refers;

(c) when the crops are planted or otherwise become growing crops or the young are conceived if the contract is for the sale of unborn young to be born within twelve months after contracting or for the sale of crops to be harvested within twelve months or the next normal harvest season after contracting whichever is longer.

(2) The seller retains an insurable interest in goods so long as title to or any security interest in the goods remains in him and where the identification is by the seller alone he may until default or insolvency or notification to the buyer that the identification is final substitute other goods for those identified.

(3) Nothing in this section impairs any insurable interest recognized under any other statute or rule of law.

§ 2-502. Buyer's Right to Goods on Seller's Insolvency.

(1) Subject to subsection (2) and even though the goods have not been shipped a buyer who has paid a part or all of the price of goods in which he has a special property under the provisions of the immediately preceding section may on making and keeping good a tender of any unpaid portion of their price recover them from the seller if the seller becomes insolvent within ten days after receipt of the first installment on their price.

(2) If the identification creating his special property has been made by the buyer he acquires the right to recover the goods only if they conform to the contract for sale.

§ 2-503. Manner of Seller's Tender of Delivery.

(1) Tender of delivery requires that the seller put and hold conforming goods at the buyer's disposition and give the buyer any notification reasonably necessary to enable him to take delivery. The manner, time and place for tender are determined by the agreement and this Article, and in particular

(a) tender must be at a reasonable hour, and if it is of goods they must be kept available for the period reasonably necessary to enable the buyer to take possession; but

(b) unless otherwise agreed the buyer must furnish facilities reasonably suited to the receipt of the goods.

(2) Where the case is within the next section respecting shipment tender requires that the seller comply with its provisions.

(3) Where the seller is required to deliver at a particular destination tender requires that he comply with subsection (2) and also in any appropriate case tender documents as described in subsections (4) and (5) of this section.

(4) Where goods are in the possession of a bailee and are to be delivered without being moved

(a) tender requires that the seller either tender a negotiable document of title covering such goods or procure acknowledgment by the bailee of the buyer's right to possession of the goods; but

(b) tender to the buyer of a non-negotiable document of title or of a written direction to the bailee to deliver is sufficient tender unless the buyer seasonably objects, and receipt by the bailee of notification of the buyer's rights fixes those rights as against the bailee and all third persons; but risk of loss of the goods and of any failure by the bailee to honor the non-negotiable document of title or to obey the direction remains on the seller until the buyer has had a reasonable time to present the document or direction, and a refusal by the bailee to honor the document or to obey the direction defeats the tender.

(5) Where the contract requires the seller to deliver documents

(a) he must tender all such documents in correct form, except as provided in this Article with respect to bills of lading in a set (subsection (2) of Section 2-323); and

(b) tender through customary banking channels is sufficient and dishonor of a draft accompanying the documents constitutes non-acceptance or rejection.

§ 2-504. Shipment by Seller.

Where the seller is required or authorized to send the goods to the buyer and the contract does not require him to deliver them at a particular destination, then unless otherwise agreed he must

(a) put the goods in the possession of such a carrier and make such a contract for their transportation as may be reasonable having regard to the nature of the goods and other circumstances of the case; and

(b) obtain and promptly deliver or tender in due form any document necessary to enable the buyer to obtain possession of the goods or otherwise required by the agreement or by usage of trade; and

(c) promptly notify the buyer of the shipment.

Failure to notify the buyer under paragraph (c) or to make a proper contract under paragraph (a) is a ground for rejection only if material delay or loss ensues.

§ 2-505. Seller's Shipment Under Reservation.

(1) Where the seller has identified goods to the contract by or before shipment:

(a) his procurement of a negotiable bill of lading to his own order or otherwise reserves in him a security interest in the goods. His procurement of the bill to the order of a financing agency or of the buyer indicates in addition only the seller's expectation of transferring that interest to the person named.

(b) a non-negotiable bill of lading to himself or his nominee reserves possession of the goods as security but except in a case of conditional delivery (subsection (2) of Section 2-507) a non-negotiable bill of lading naming the buyer as consignee reserves no security interest even though the seller retains possession of the bill of lading.

(2) When shipment by the seller with reservation of a security interest is in violation of the contract for sale it constitutes an improper contract for transportation within the preceding section but impairs neither the rights given to the buyer by shipment and identification of the goods to the contract nor the seller's powers as a holder of a negotiable document.

§ 2-506. Rights of Financing Agency.

(1) A financing agency by paying or purchasing for value a draft which relates to a shipment of goods acquires to the extent of the payment or purchase and in addition to its own rights under the draft and any document of title securing it any rights of the shipper in the goods including the right to stop delivery and the shipper's right to have the draft honored by the buyer.

(2) The right to reimbursement of a financing agency which has in good faith honored or purchased the draft under commitment to or authority from the buyer is not impaired by subsequent discovery of defects with reference to any relevant document which was apparently regular on its face.

§ 2-507. Effect of Seller's Tender; Delivery on Condition.

(1) Tender of delivery is a condition to the buyer's duty to accept the goods and, unless otherwise agreed, to his duty to pay for them. Tender entitles the seller to acceptance of the goods and to payment according to the contract.

(2) Where payment is due and demanded on the delivery to the buyer of goods or documents of title, his right as against the seller to retain or dispose of them is conditional upon his making the payment due.

§ 2-508. Cure by Seller of Improper Tender or Delivery; Replacement.

(1) Where any tender or delivery by the seller is rejected because nonconforming and the time for performance has not yet expired, the seller may seasonably notify the buyer of his intention to cure and may then within the contract time make a conforming delivery.

(2) Where the buyer rejects a non-conforming tender which the seller had reasonable grounds to believe would be acceptable with or without money allowance the seller may if he seasonably notifies the buyer have a further reasonable time to substitute a conforming tender.

§ 2-509. Risk of Loss in the Absence of Breach.

(1) Where the contract requires or authorizes the seller to ship the goods by carrier

(a) if it does not require him to deliver them at a particular destination, the risk of loss passes to the buyer when the goods are duly delivered to the carrier even though the shipment is under reservation (Section 2-505); but

(b) if it does require him to deliver them at a particular destination and the goods are there duly tendered while in the possession of the carrier, the risk of loss passes to the buyer when the goods are there duly so tendered as to enable the buyer to take delivery.

(2) Where the goods are held by a bailee to be delivered without being moved, the risk of loss passes to the buyer

(a) on his receipt of a negotiable document of title covering the goods; or

(b) on acknowledgment by the bailee of the buyer's right to possession of the goods; or

(c) after his receipt of a non-negotiable document of title or other written direction to deliver, as provided in subsection (4)(b) of Section 2-503.

(3) In any case not within subsection (1) or (2), the risk of loss passes to the buyer on his receipt of the goods if the seller is a merchant; otherwise the risk passes to the buyer on tender of delivery.

(4) The provisions of this section are subject to contrary agreement of the parties and to the provisions of this Article on sale on approval (Section 2-327) and on effect of breach on risk of loss (Section 2-510).

§ 2-510. Effect of Breach on Risk of Loss.

(1) Where a tender or delivery of goods so fails to conform to the contract as to give a right of rejection the risk of their loss remains on the seller until cure or acceptance.

(2) Where the buyer rightfully revokes acceptance he may to the extent of any deficiency in his effective insurance coverage treat the risk of loss as having rested on the seller from the beginning.

(3) Where the buyer as to conforming goods already identified to the contract for sale repudiates or is otherwise in breach before risk of their loss has passed to him, the seller may to the extent of any deficiency in his effective insurance coverage treat the risk of loss as resting on the buyer for a commercially reasonable time.

§ 2-511. Tender of Payments by Buyer; Payment by Check.

(1) Unless otherwise agreed tender of payment is a condition to the seller's duty to tender and complete any delivery.

(2) Tender of payment is sufficient when made by any means or in any manner current in the ordinary course of business unless the seller demands payment in legal tender and gives any extension of time reasonably necessary to produce it.

(3) Subject to the provisions of this Act on the effect of an instrument on an obligation (Section 3-802), payment by check is conditional and is defeated as between the parties by dishonor of the check on due presentment.

§ 2-512. Payment by Buyer Before Inspection.

(1) Where the contract requires payment before inspection non-conformity of the goods does not excuse the buyer from so making payment unless

(a) the non-conformity appears without inspection; or

(b) despite tender of the required documents the circumstances would justify injunction against honor under the provisions of this Act (Section 5-114).

(2) Payment pursuant to subsection (1) does not constitute an acceptance of goods or impair the buyer's right to inspect or any of his remedies.

§ 2-513. Buyer's Right to Inspection of Goods.

(1) Unless otherwise agreed and subject to subsection (3), where goods are tendered or delivered or identified to the contract for sale, the buyer has a right before payment or acceptance to inspect them at any reasonable place and time and in any reasonable manner. When the seller is required or authorized to send the goods to the buyer, the inspection may be after their arrival.

(2) Expenses of inspection must be borne by the buyer but may be recovered from the seller if the goods do not conform and are rejected.

(3) Unless otherwise agreed and subject to the provisions of this Article on C.I.F. contracts (subsection (3) of Section 2-321), the buyer is not

entitled to inspect the goods before payment of the price when the contract provides

(a) for delivery "C.O.D." or on other like terms; or

(b) for payment against documents of title, except where such payment is due only after the goods are to become available for inspection.

(4) A place or method of inspection fixed by the parties is presumed to be exclusive but unless otherwise expressly agreed it does not postpone identification or shift the place for delivery or for passing the risk of loss. If compliance becomes impossible, inspection shall be as provided in this section unless the place or method fixed was clearly intended as an indispensable condition failure of which avoids the contract.

§ 2-514. When Documents Deliverable on Acceptance; When on Payment.
Unless otherwise agreed documents against which a draft is drawn are to be delivered to the drawee on acceptance of the draft if it is payable more than three days after presentment; otherwise, only on payment.

§ 2-515. Preserving Evidence of Goods in Dispute.
In furtherance of the adjustment of any claim or dispute

(a) either party on reasonable notification to the other and for the purpose of ascertaining the facts and preserving evidence has the right to inspect, test and sample the goods including such of them as may be in the possession or control of the other; and

(b) the parties may agree to a third party inspection or survey to determine the conformity or condition of the goods and may agree that the findings shall be binding upon them in any subsequent litigation or adjustment.

Part 6. Breach, Repudiation and Excuse

§ 2-601. Buyer's Rights on Improper Delivery.
Subject to the provisions of this Article on breach in installment contracts (Section 2-612) and unless agreed under the sections on contractual limitations of remedy (Sections 2-718 and 2-719), if the goods or the tender of delivery fail in any respect to conform to the contract, the buyer may

(a) reject the whole; or

(b) accept the whole; or

(c) accept any commercial unit or units and reject the rest.

§ 2-602. Manner and Effect of Rightful Rejection.

(1) Rejection of goods must be within a reasonable time after their delivery or tender. It is ineffective unless the buyer seasonably notifies the seller.

(2) Subject to the provisions of the two following sections on rejected goods (Sections 2-603 and 2-604),

(a) after rejection any exercise of ownership by the buyer with respect to any commercial unit is wrongful as against the seller, and

(b) if the buyer has before rejection taken physical possession of goods in which he does not have a security interest under the provisions of this Article (subsection (3) of Section 2-711), he is under a duty after rejection to hold them with reasonable care at the seller's disposition for a time sufficient to permit the seller to remove them; but

(c) the buyer has no further obligations with regard to goods rightfully rejected.

(3) The seller's rights with respect to goods wrongfully rejected are governed by the provisions of this Article on seller's remedies in general (Section 2-703).

§ 2-603. Merchant Buyer's Duties as to Rightfully Rejected Goods.
(1) Subject to any security interest in the buyer (subsection (3) of Section 2-711), when the seller has no agent or place of business at the market of rejection a merchant buyer is under a duty after rejection of goods in his possession or control to follow any reasonable instructions received from the seller with respect to the goods and in the absence of such instructions to make reasonable efforts to sell them for the seller's account if they are perishable or threaten to decline in value speedily. Instructions are not reasonable if on demand indemnity for expenses is not forthcoming.

(2) When the buyer sells goods under subsection (1), he is entitled to reimbursement from the seller or out of the proceeds for reasonable expenses of caring for and selling them, and if the expenses include no selling commission then to such commission as is usual in the trade or if there is none to a reasonable sum not exceeding ten per cent on the gross proceeds.

(3) In complying with this section the buyer is held only to good faith and good faith conduct hereunder is neither acceptance nor conversion nor the basis of an action for damages.

§ 2-604. Buyer's Options as to Salvage of Rightfully Rejected Goods.
Subject to the provisions of the immediately preceding section on perishables if the seller gives no instructions within a reasonable time after notification of rejection the buyer may store the rejected goods for the seller's account or reship them to him or resell them for the seller's account with reimbursement as provided in the preceding section. Such action is not acceptance or conversion.

§ 2-605. Waiver of Buyer's Objections by Failure to Particularize.

(1) The buyer's failure to state in connection with rejection a particular defect which is ascertainable by reasonable inspection precludes him from relying on the unstated defect to justify rejection or to establish breach

(a) where the seller could have cured it if stated seasonably; or

(b) between merchants when the seller has after rejection made a request in writing for a full and final written statement of all defects on which the buyer proposes to rely.

(2) Payment against documents made without reservation of rights precludes recovery of the payment for defects apparent on the face of the documents.

§ 2-606. What Constitutes Acceptance of Goods.

(1) Acceptance of goods occurs when the buyer

(a) after a reasonable opportunity to inspect the goods signifies to the seller that the goods are conforming or that he will take or retain them in spite of their nonconformity; or

(b) fails to make an effective rejection (subsection (1) of Section 2-602), but such acceptance does not occur until the buyer has had a reasonable opportunity to inspect them; or

(c) does any act inconsistent with the seller's ownership; but if such act is wrongful as against the seller it is an acceptance only if ratified by him.

(2) Acceptance of a part of any commercial unit is acceptance of that entire unit.

§ 2-607. Effect of Acceptance; Notice of Breach; Burden of Establishing Breach After Acceptance; Notice of Claim or Litigation to Person Answerable Over.

(1) The buyer must pay at the contract rate for any goods accepted.

(2) Acceptance of goods by the buyer precludes rejection of the goods accepted and if made with knowledge of a non-conformity cannot be revoked because of it unless the acceptance was on the reasonable

assumption that the non-conformity would be seasonally cured but acceptance does not of itself impair any other remedy provided by this Article for non-conformity.

(3) Where a tender has been accepted

(a) the buyer must within a reasonable time after he discovers or should have discovered any breach notify the seller of breach or be barred from any remedy; and

(b) if the claim is one for infringement or the like (subsection (3) of Section 2-312) and the buyer is sued as a result of such a breach he must so notify the seller within a reasonable time after he receives notice of the litigation or be barred from any remedy over for liability established by the litigation.

(4) The burden is on the buyer to establish any breach with respect to the goods accepted.

(5) Where the buyer is sued for breach of a warranty or other obligation for which his seller is answerable over

(a) he may give his seller written notice of the litigation. If the notice states that the seller may come in and defend and that if the seller does not do so he will be bound in any action against him by his buyer by any determination of fact common to the two litigations, then unless the seller after seasonable receipt of the notice does come in and defend he is so bound.

(b) if the claim is one for infringement or the like (subsection (3) of Section 2-312) the original seller may demand in writing that his buyer turn over to him control of the litigation including settlement or else be barred from any remedy over and if he also agrees to bear all expense and to satisfy any adverse judgment, then unless the buyer after seasonable receipt of the demand does turn over control the buyer is so barred.

(6) The provisions of subsections (3), (4) and (5) apply to any obligation of a buyer to hold the seller harmless against infringement or the like (subsection (3) of Section 2-312).

§ 2-608. Revocation of Acceptance in Whole or in Part.

(1) The buyer may revoke his acceptance of a lot or commercial unit whose non-conformity substantially impairs its value to him if he has accepted it

(a) on the reasonable assumption that its non-conformity would be cured and it has not been seasonably cured; or

(b) without discovery of such non-conformity if his acceptance was reasonably induced either by the difficulty of discovery before acceptance or by the seller's assurances.

(2) Revocation of acceptance must occur within a reasonable time after the buyer discovers or should have discovered the ground for it and before any substantial change in condition of the goods which is not caused by their own defects. It is not effective until the buyer notifies the seller of it.

(3) A buyer who so revokes has the same rights and duties with regard to the goods involved as if he had rejected them.

§ 2-609. Right to Adequate Assurance of Performance.

(1) A contract for sale imposes an obligation on each party that the other's expectation of receiving due performance will not be impaired. When reasonable grounds for insecurity arise with respect to the performance of either party the other may in writing demand adequate assurance of due performance and until he receives such assurance may if commercially reasonable suspend any performance for which he has not already received the agreed return.

(2) Between merchants the reasonableness of grounds for insecurity and the adequacy of any assurance offered shall be determined according to commercial standards.

(3) Acceptance of any improper delivery or payment does not prejudice the aggrieved party's right to demand adequate assurance of future performance.

(4) After receipt of a justified demand failure to provide within a reasonable time not exceeding thirty days such assurance of due performance as is adequate under the circumstances of the particular case is a repudiation of the contract.

§ 2-610. Anticipatory Repudiation.
When either party repudiates the contract with respect to a performance not yet due the loss of which will substantially impair the value of the contract to the other, the aggrieved party may

(a) for a commercially reasonable time await performance by the repudiating party; or

(b) resort to any remedy for breach (Section 2-703 or Section 2-711), even though he has notified the repudiating party that he would await the latter's performance and has urged retraction; and

(c) in either case suspend his own performance or proceed in accordance with the provisions of this Article on the seller's right to identify goods to the contract notwithstanding breach or to salvage unfinished goods (Section 2-704).

§ 2-611. Retraction of Anticipatory Repudiation.

(1) Until the repudiating party's next performance is due he can retract his repudiation unless the aggrieved party has since the repudiation cancelled or materially changed his position or otherwise indicated that he considers the repudiation final.

(2) Retraction may be by any method which clearly indicates to the aggrieved party that the repudiating party intends to perform, but must include any assurance justifiably demanded under the provisions of this Article (Section 2-609).

(3) Retraction reinstates the repudiating party's rights under the contract with due excuse and allowance to the aggrieved party for any delay occasioned by the repudiation.

§ 2-612. "Installment Contract"; Breach.

(1) An "installment contract" is one which requires or authorizes the delivery of goods in separate lots to be separately accepted, even though the contract contains a clause "each delivery is a separate contract" or its equivalent.

(2) The buyer may reject any installment which is nonconforming if the non-conformity substantially impairs the value of that installment and cannot be cured or if the non-conformity is a defect in the required documents; but if the non-conformity does not fall within subsection (3) and the seller gives adequate assurance of its cure the buyer must accept that installment.

(3) Whenever non-conformity or default with respect to one or more installments substantially impairs the value of the whole contract there is a breach of the whole. But the aggrieved party reinstates the contract if he accepts a non-conforming installment without seasonably notifying of cancellation or if he brings an action with respect only to past installments or demands performance as to future installments.

§ 2-613. Casualty to Identified Goods.
Where the contract requires for its performance goods identified when the contract is made, and the goods suffer casualty without fault of either party before the risk of loss passes to the buyer, or in a proper case under a "no arrival, no sale" term (Section 2-324) then

(a) if the loss is total the contract is avoided; and

(b) if the loss is partial or the goods have so deteriorated as no longer to conform to the contract the buyer may nevertheless demand inspection and at his option either treat the contract as avoided or accept the goods with due allowance from the contract price for the deterioration or the deficiency in quantity but without further right against the seller.

§ 2-614. Substituted Performance.

(1) Where without fault of either party the agreed berthing, loading, or unloading facilities fail or an agreed type of carrier becomes unavailable or the agreed manner of delivery otherwise becomes commercially impracticable but a commercially reasonable substitute is available, such substitute performance must be tendered and accepted.

(2) If the agreed means or manner of payment fails because of domestic or foreign governmental regulation, the seller may withhold or stop delivery unless the buyer provides a means or manner of payment which is commercially a substantial equivalent. If delivery has already been taken, payment by the means or in the manner provided by the regulation discharges the buyer's obligation unless the regulation is discriminatory, oppressive or predatory.

§ 2-615. Excuse by Failure of Presupposed Conditions.

Except so far as a seller may have assumed a greater obligation and subject to the preceding section on substituted performance:

(a) Delay in delivery or non-delivery in whole or in part by a seller who complies with paragraphs (b) and (c) is not a breach of his duty under a contract for sale if performance as agreed has been made impracticable by the occurrence of a contingency the nonoccurrence of which was a basic assumption on which the contract was made or by compliance in good faith with any applicable foreign or domestic governmental regulation or order whether or not it later proves to be invalid.

(b) Where the causes mentioned in paragraph (a) affect only a part of the seller's capacity to perform, he must allocate production and deliveries among his customers but may at his option include regular customers not then under contract as well as his own requirements for further manufacture. He may so allocate in any manner which is fair and reasonable.

(c) The seller must notify the buyer seasonably that there will be delay or non-delivery and, when allocation is required under paragraph (b), of the estimated quota thus made available for the buyer.

§ 2-616. Procedure on Notice Claiming Excuse.

(1) Where the buyer receives notification of a material or indefinite delay or an allocation justified under the preceding section he may by written notification to the seller as to any delivery concerned, and where the prospective deficiency substantially impairs the value of the whole contract under the provisions of this Article relating to breach of installment contracts (Section 2-612), then also as to the whole,

(a) terminate and thereby discharge any unexecuted portion of the contract; or

(b) modify the contract by agreeing to take his available quota in substitution.

(2) If after receipt of such notification from the seller the buyer fails so to modify the contract within a reasonable time not exceeding thirty days the contract lapses with respect to any deliveries affected.

(3) The provisions of this section may not be negated by agreement except in so far as the seller has assumed a greater obligation under the preceding section.

Part 7. Remedies

§ 2-701. Remedies for Breach of Collateral Contracts Not Impaired. Remedies for breach of any obligation or promise collateral or ancillary to a contract for sale are not impaired by the provisions of this Article.

§ 2-702. Seller's Remedies on Discovery of Buyer's Insolvency.

(1) Where the seller discovers the buyer to be insolvent he may refuse delivery except for cash including payment for all goods theretofore delivered under the contract, and stop delivery under this Article (Section 2-705).

(2) Where the seller discovers that the buyer has received goods on credit while insolvent he may reclaim the goods upon demand made within ten days after the receipt, but if misrepresentation of solvency has been made to the particular seller in writing within three months before delivery the ten day limitation does not apply. Except as provided in this subsection the seller may not base a right to reclaim goods on the buyer's fraudulent or innocent misrepresentation of solvency or of intent to pay.

(3) The seller's right to reclaim under subsection (2) is subject to the rights of a buyer in ordinary course or other good faith purchaser under this Article (Section 2-403). Successful reclamation of goods excludes all other remedies with respect to them.

§ 2-703. Seller's Remedies in General. Where the buyer wrongfully rejects or revokes acceptance of goods or fails to make a payment due on or before delivery or repudiates with respect to a part or the whole, then with respect to any goods directly affected and, if the breach is of the whole contract (Section 2-612), then also with respect to the whole undelivered balance, the aggrieved seller may

(a) withhold delivery of such goods;

(b) stop delivery by any bailee as hereafter provided (Section 2-705);

(c) proceed under the next section respecting goods still unidentified to the contract;

(d) resell and recover damages as hereafter provided (Section 2-706);

(e) recover damages for non-acceptance (Section 2-708) or in a proper case the price (Section 2-709);

(f) cancel.

§ 2-704. Seller's Right to Identify Goods to the Contract Notwithstanding Breach or to Salvage Unfinished Goods.

(1) An aggrieved seller under the preceding section may

(a) identify to the contract conforming goods not already identified if at the time he learned of the breach they are in his possession or control;

(b) treat as the subject of resale goods which have demonstrably been intended for the particular contract even though those goods are unfinished.

(2) Where the goods are unfinished an aggrieved seller may in the exercize of reasonable commercial judgment for the purposes of avoiding loss and of effective realization either complete the manufacture and wholly identify the goods to the contract or cease manufacture and resell for scrap or salvage value or proceed in any other reasonable manner.

§ 2-705. Seller's Stoppage of Delivery in Transit or Otherwise.

(1) The seller may stop delivery of goods in the possession of a carrier or other bailee when he discovers the buyer to be insolvent (Section 2-702) and may stop delivery of carload, truckload, planeload or larger shipments of express or freight when the buyer repudiates or fails to make a payment due before delivery or if for any other reason the seller has a right to withhold or reclaim the goods.

(2) As against such buyer the seller may stop delivery until

(a) receipt of the goods by the buyer; or

(b) acknowledgment to the buyer by any bailee of the goods except a carrier that the bailee holds the goods for the buyer; or

(c) such acknowledgment to the buyer by a carrier by reshipment or as warehouseman; or

(d) negotiation to the buyer of any negotiable document of title covering the goods.

(3) (a) To stop delivery the seller must so notify as to enable the bailee by reasonable diligence to prevent delivery of the goods.

(b) After such notification the bailee must hold and deliver the goods according to the directions of the seller but the seller is liable to the bailee for any ensuing charges or damages.

(c) If a negotiable document of title has been issued for goods the bailee is not obliged to obey a notification to stop until surrender of the document.

(d) A carrier who has issued a non-negotiable bill of lading is not obliged to obey a notification to stop received from a person other than the consignor.

§ 2-706. Seller's Resale Including Contract for Resale.

(1) Under the conditions stated in Section 2-703 on seller's remedies, the seller may resell the goods concerned or the undelivered balance thereof. Where the resale is made in good faith and in a commercially reasonable manner the seller may recover the difference between the resale price and the contract price together with any incidental damages allowed under the provisions of this Article (Section 2-710), but less expenses saved in consequence of the buyer's breach.

(2) Except as otherwise provided in subsection (3) or unless otherwise agreed resale may be at public or private sale including sale by way of one or more contracts to sell or of identification to an existing contract of the seller. Sale may be as a unit or in parcels and at any time and place and on any terms but every aspect of the sale including the method, manner, time, place and terms must be commercially reasonable. The resale must be reasonably identified as referring to the broken contract, but it is not necessary that the goods be in existence or that any or all of them have been identified to the contract before the breach.

(3) Where the resale is at private sale the seller must give the buyer reasonable notification of his intention to resell.

(4) Where the resale is at public sale

(a) only identified goods can be sold except where there is a recognized market for a public sale of futures in goods of the kind; and

(b) it must be made at a usual place or market for public sale if one is reasonably available and except in the case of goods which are perishable or threaten to decline in value speedily the seller must give the buyer reasonable notice of time and place of the resale; and

(c) if the goods are not to be within the view of those attending the sale the notification of sale must state the place where the goods are located and provide for their reasonable inspection by prospective bidders; and

(d) the seller may buy.

(5) A purchaser who buys in good faith at a resale takes the goods free of any rights of the original buyer even though the seller fails to comply with one or more of the requirements of this section.

(6) The seller is not accountable to the buyer for any profit made on any resale. A person in the position of a seller (Section 2-707) or a buyer who has rightfully rejected or justifiably revoked acceptance must account for any excess over the amount of his security interest, as hereinafter defined (subsection (3) of Section 2-711).

§ 2-707. "Person in the Position of a Seller."

(1) A "person in the position of a seller" includes as against a principal an agent who has paid or become responsible for the price of goods on behalf of his principal or anyone who otherwise holds a security interest or other right in goods similar to that of a seller.

(2) A person in the position of a seller may as provided in this Article withhold or stop delivery (Section 2-705) and resell (Section 2-706) and recover incidental damages (Section 2-710).

§ 2-708. Seller's Damages for Non-Acceptance or Repudiation.

1. Subject to subsection (2) and to the provisions of this Article with respect to proof of market price (Section 2-723), the measure of damages for non-acceptance or repudiation by the buyer is the difference between the market price at the time and place for tender and the unpaid contract price together with any incidental damages provided in this Article (Section 2-710), but less expenses saved in consequence of the buyer's breach.

(2) If the measure of damages provided in subsection (1) is inadequate to put the seller in as good a position as performance would have done then the measure of damages is the profit (including reasonable overhead) which the seller would have made from full performance by the buyer, together with any incidental damages provided in this Article (Section 2-710), due allowance for costs reasonably incurred and due credit for payments or proceeds of resale.

§ 2-709. Action for the Price.

(1) When the buyer fails to pay the price as it becomes due the seller may recover, together with any incidental damages under the next section, the price

(a) of goods accepted or of conforming goods lost or damaged within a commercially reasonable time after risk of their loss has passed to the buyer; and

(b) of goods identified to the contract if the seller is unable after reasonable effort to resell them at a reasonable price or the circumstances reasonably indicate that such effort will be unavailing.

(2) Where the seller sues for the price he must hold for the buyer any goods which have been identified to the contract and are still in his control except that if resale becomes possible he may resell them at any time prior to the collection of the judgment. The net proceeds of any such resale must be credited to the buyer and payment of the judgment entitles him to any goods not resold.

(3) After the buyer has wrongfully rejected or revoked acceptance of the goods or has failed to make a payment due or has repudiated (Section 2-610), a seller who is held not entitled to the price under this section shall nevertheless be awarded damages for non-acceptance under the preceding section.

§ 2-710. Seller's Incidental Damages.
Incidental damages to an aggrieved seller include any commercially reasonable charges, expenses or commissions incurred in stopping delivery, in the transportation, care and custody of goods after the buyer's breach, in connection with return or resale of the goods or otherwise resulting from the breach.

§ 2-711. Buyer's Remedies in General; Buyer's Security Interest in Rejected Goods.

(1) Where the seller fails to make delivery or repudiates or the buyer rightfully rejects or justifiably revokes acceptance then with respect to any goods involved, and with respect to the whole if the breach goes to the whole contract (Section 2-612), the buyer may cancel and whether or not he has done so may in addition to recovering so much of the price as has been paid

(a) "cover" and have damages under the next section as to all the goods affected whether or not they have been identified to the contract, or

(b) recover damages for non-delivery as provided in this Article (Section 2-713).

(2) Where the seller fails to deliver or repudiates the buyer may also

(a) if the goods have been identified recover them as provided in this Article (Section 2-502); or

(b) in a proper case obtain specific performance or replevy the goods as provided in this Article (Section 2-716).

3) On rightful rejection or justifiable revocation of acceptance a buyer has a security interest in goods in his possession or control for any payments made on their price and any expenses reasonably incurred in their inspection, receipt, transportation, care and custody and may hold such goods and resell them in like manner as an aggrieved seller (Section 2-706).

§ 2-712. "Cover"; Buyer's Procurement of Substitute Goods.

1) After a breach within the preceding section the buyer may "cover" by making in good faith and without unreasonable delay any reasonable purchase of or contract to purchase goods in substitution for those due from the seller.

2) The buyer may recover from the seller as damages the difference between the cost of cover and the contract price together with any incidental or consequential damages as hereinafter defined (Section 2-715), but less expenses saved in consequence of the seller's breach.

3) Failure of the buyer to effect cover within this section does not bar him from any other remedy.

§ 2-713. Buyer's Damages for Non-Delivery or Repudiation.

(1) Subject to the provisions of this Article with respect to proof of market price (Section 2-723), the measure of damages for non-delivery or repudiation by the seller is the difference between the market price at the time when the buyer learned of the breach and the contract price together with any incidental and consequential damages provided in this Article (Section 2-715), but less expenses saved in consequence of the seller's breach.

(2) Market price is to be determined as of the place for tender or, in cases of rejection after arrival or revocation of acceptance, as of the place of arrival.

§ 2-714. Buyer's Damages for Breach in Regard to Accepted Goods.

(1) Where the buyer has accepted goods and given notification (subsection (3) of Section 2-607) he may recover as damages for any nonconformity of tender the loss resulting in the ordinary course of events from the seller's breach as determined in any manner which is reasonable.

(2) The measure of damages for breach of warranty is the difference at the time and place of acceptance between the value of the goods accepted and the value they would have had if they had been as warranted, unless special circumstances show proximate damages of a different amount.

(3) In a proper case any incidental and consequential damages under the next section may also be recovered.

§ 2-715. Buyer's Incidental and Consequential Damages.

(1) Incidental damages resulting from the seller's breach include expenses reasonably incurred in inspection, receipt, transportation and care and custody of goods rightfully rejected, any commercially reasonable charges, expenses or commissions in connection with effecting cover and any other reasonable expense incident to the delay or other breach.

(2) Consequential damages resulting from the seller's breach include

(a) any loss resulting from general or particular requirements and needs of which the seller at the time of contracting had reason to know and which could not reasonably be prevented by cover or otherwise; and

(b) injury to person or property proximately resulting from any breach of warranty.

§ 2-716. Buyer's Right to Specific Performance or Replevin.

(1) Specific performance may be decreed where the goods are unique or in other proper circumstances.

(2) The decree for specific performance may include such terms and conditions as to payment of the price, damages, or other relief as the court may deem just.

(3) The buyer has a right of replevin for goods identified to the contract if after reasonable effort he is unable to effect cover for such goods or the circumstances reasonably indicate that such effort will be unavailing or if the goods have been shipped under reservation and satisfaction of the security interest in them has been made or tendered.

§ 2-717. Deduction of Damages From the Price. The buyer on notifying the seller of his intention to do so may deduct all or any part of the damages resulting from any breach of the contract from any part of the price still due under the same contract.

§ 2-718. Liquidation or Limitation of Damages; Deposits.

(1) Damages for breach by either party may be liquidated in the agreement but only at an amount which is reasonable in the light of the anticipated or actual harm caused by the breach, the difficulties of proof of loss, and the inconvenience or nonfeasibility of otherwise obtaining an adequate remedy. A term fixing unreasonably large liquidated damages is void as a penalty.

(2) Where the seller justifiably withholds delivery of goods because of the buyer's breach, the buyer is entitled to restitution of any amount by which the sum of his payments exceeds

(a) the amount to which the seller is entitled by virtue of terms liquidating the seller's damages in accordance with subsection (1), or

(b) in the absence of such terms, twenty per cent of the value of the total performance for which the buyer is obligated under the contract or $500, whichever is smaller.

(3) The buyer's right to restitution under subsection (2) is subject to offset to the extent that the seller establishes

(a) a right to recover damages under the provisions of this Article other than subsection (1), and

(b) the amount or value of any benefits received by the buyer directly or indirectly by reason of the contract.

(4) Where a seller has received payment in goods their reasonable value or the proceeds of their resale shall be treated as payments for the purposes of subsection (2); but if the seller has notice of the buyer's breach before reselling goods received in part performance, his resale is subject to the conditions laid down in this Article on resale by an aggrieved seller (Section 2-706).

§ 2-719. Contractual Modification or Limitation of Remedy.

(1) Subject to the provisions of subsections (2) and (3) of this section and of the preceding section on liquidation and limitation of damages,

(a) the agreement may provide for remedies in addition to or in substitution for those provided in this Article and may limit or alter the measure of damages recoverable under this Article, as by limiting the buyer's remedies to return of the goods and repayment of the price or to repair and replacement of non-conforming goods or parts; and

(b) resort to a remedy as provided is optional unless the remedy is expressly agreed to be exclusive, in which case it is the sole remedy.

(2) Where circumstances cause an exclusive or limited remedy to fail of its essential purpose, remedy may be had as provided in this Act.

(3) Consequential damages may be limited or excluded unless the limitation or exclusion is unconscionable. Limitation of consequential damages for injury to the person in the case of consumer goods is prima facie unconscionable but limitation of damages where the loss is commercial is not.

§ 2-720. **Effect of "Cancellation" or "Rescission" on Claims for Antecedent Breach.** Unless the contrary intention clearly appears, expressions of "cancellation" or "rescission" of the contract or the like shall not be construed as a renunciation or discharge of any claim in damages for an antecedent breach.

§ 2-721. **Remedies for Fraud.** Remedies for material misrepresentation or fraud include all remedies available under this Article for non-fraudulent breach. Neither rescission or a claim for rescission of the contract for sale nor rejection or return of the goods shall bar or be deemed inconsistent with a claim for damages or other remedy.

§ 2-272. **Who Can Sue Third Parties for Injury to Goods.**
Where a third party so deals with goods which have been identified to a contract for sale as to cause actionable injury to a party to that contract

(a) a right of action against the third party is in either party to the contract for sale who has title to or a security interest or a special property or an insurable interest in the goods; and if the goods have been destroyed or converted a right of action is also in the party who either bore the risk of loss under the contract for sale or has since the injury assumed that risk as against the other;

(b) if at the time of the injury the party plaintiff did not bear the risk of loss as against the other party to the contract for sale and there is no arrangement between them for disposition of the recovery, his suit or settlement is, subject to his own interest, as a fiduciary for the other party to the contract;

(c) either party may with the consent of the other sue for the benefit of whom it may concern.

§ 2-723. **Proof of Market Price: Time and Place.**
(1) If an action based on anticipatory repudiation comes to trial before the time for performance with respect to some or all of the goods, any damages based on market price (Section 2-708 or Section 2-713) shall be determined according to the price of such goods prevailing at the time when the aggrieved party learned of the repudiation.

(2) If evidence of a price prevailing at the times or places described in this Article is not readily available the price prevailing within any reasonable time before or after the time described or at any other place which in commercial judgment or under usage of trade would serve as a reasonable substitute for the one described may be used, making any proper allowance for the cost of transporting the goods to or from such other place.

(3) Evidence of a relevant price prevailing at a time or place other than the one described in this Article offered by one party is not admissible unless and until he has given the other party such notice as the court finds sufficient to prevent unfair surprise.

§ 2-724. **Admissibility of Market Quotations.** Whenever the prevailing price or value of any goods regularly bought and sold in any established commodity market is in issue, reports in official publications or trade journals or in newspapers or periodicals of general circulation published as the reports of such market shall be admissible in evidence. The circumstances of the preparation of such a report may be shown to affect its weight but not its admissibility.

§ 2-725. **Statute of Limitations in Contracts for Sale.**
(1) An action for breach of any contract for sale must be commenced within four years after the cause of action has accrued. By the original agreement the parties may reduce the period of limitation to not less than one year but may not extend it.

(2) A cause of action accrues when the breach occurs, regardless of the aggrieved party's lack of knowledge of the breach. A breach of warranty occurs when tender of delivery is made, except that where a warranty explicitly extends to future performance of the goods and discovery of the breach must await the time of such performance the cause of action accrues when the breach is or should have been discovered.

(3) Where an action commenced within the time limited by subsection (1) is so terminated as to leave available a remedy by another action for the same breach such other action may be commenced after the expiration of the time limited and within six months after the termination of the first action unless the termination resulted from voluntary discontinuance or from dismissal for failure or neglect to prosecute.

(4) This section does not alter the law on tolling of the statute of limitations nor does it apply to causes of action which have accrued before this Act becomes effective.

ARTICLE 2A LEASES

Part 1. General Provisions

§ 2A-101. **Short Title.** This Article shall be known and may be cited as the Uniform Commercial Code—Leases.

§ 2A-102. **Scope.** This Article applies to any transaction, regardless of form, that creates a lease.

§ 2A-103. **Definitions and Index of Definitions.**
(1) In this Article unless the context otherwise requires:

(a) "Buyer in ordinary course of business" means a person who in good faith and without knowledge that the sale to him [or her] is in violation of the ownership rights or security interest or leasehold interest of a third party in the goods buys in ordinary course from a person in the business of selling goods of that kind but does not include a pawnbroker. "Buying" may be for cash or by exchange of other property or on secured or unsecured credit and includes receiving goods or documents of title under a pre-existing contract for sale but does not include a transfer in bulk or as security for or in total or partial satisfaction of a money debt.

(b) "Cancellation" occurs when either party puts an end to the lease contract for default by the other party.

(c) "Commercial unit" means such a unit of goods as by commercial usage is a single whole for purposes of lease and division of which materially impairs its character or value on the market or in use. A commercial unit may be a single article, as a machine, or a set of articles, as a suite of furniture or a line of machinery, or a quantity, as a gross or carload, or any other unit treated in use or in the relevant market as a single whole.

(d) "Conforming" goods or performance under a lease contract means goods or performance that are in accordance with the obligations under the lease contract.

(e) "Consumer lease" means a lease that a lessor regularly engaged in the business of leasing or selling makes to a lessee, except an organization, who takes under the lease primarily for a personal, family, or household purpose, if the total payments to be made under the lease contract, excluding payments for options to renew or buy, do not exceed $25,000.

(f) "Fault" means wrongful act, omission, breach, or default.

(g) "Finance lease" means a lease in which (i) the lessor does not select, manufacture or supply the goods, (ii) the lessor acquires the goods or the right to possession and use of the goods in connection with the lease, and (iii) either the lessee receives a copy of the contract evidencing the lessor's purchase of the goods on or before signing the lease contract, or the lessee's approval of the contract evidencing the lessor's purchase of the goods is a condition to effectiveness of the lease contract.

(h) "Goods" means all things that are movable at the time of identification to the lease contract, or are fixtures (Section 2A-309), but the term does not include money, documents, instruments, accounts, chattel paper, general intangibles, or minerals or the like, including oil and gas, before extraction. The term also includes the unborn young of animals.

(i) "Installment lease contract" means a lease contract that authorizes or requires the delivery of goods in separate lots to be separately accepted, even though the lease contract contains a clause "each delivery is a separate lease" or its equivalent.

(j) "Lease" means a transfer of the right to possession and use of goods for a term in return for consideration, but a sale, including a sale on approval or a sale or return, or retention or creation of a security interest is not a lease. Unless the context clearly indicates otherwise, the term includes a sublease.

(k) "Lease agreement" means the bargain, with respect to the lease, of the lessor and the lessee in fact as found in their language or by implication from other circumstances including course of dealing or usage of trade or course of performance as provided in this Article. Unless the context clearly indicates otherwise, the term includes a sublease agreement.

(l) "Lease contract" means the total legal obligation that results from the lease agreement as affected by this Article and any other applicable rules of law. Unless the context clearly indicates otherwise, the term includes a sublease contract.

(m) "Leasehold interest" means the interest of the lessor or the lessee under a lease contract.

(n) "Lessee" means a person who acquires the right to possession and use of goods under a lease. Unless the context clearly indicates otherwise, the term includes a sublessee.

(o) "Lessee in ordinary course of business" means a person who in good faith and without knowledge that the lease to him [or her] is in violation of the ownership rights or security interest or leasehold interest of a third party in the goods, leases in ordinary course from a person in the business of selling or leasing goods of that kind but does not include a pawnbroker. "Leasing" may be for cash or by exchange of other property or on secured or unsecured credit and includes receiving goods or documents of title under a pre-existing lease contract but does not include a transfer in bulk or as security for or in total or partial satisfaction of a money debt.

(p) "Lessor" means a person who transfers the right to possession and use of goods under a lease. Unless the context clearly indicates otherwise, the term includes a sublessor.

(q) "Lessor's residual interest" means the lessor's interest in the goods after expiration, termination, or cancellation of the lease contract.

(r) "Lien" means a charge against or interest in goods to secure payment of a debt or performance of an obligation, but the term does not include a security interest.

(s) "Lot" means a parcel or a single article that is the subject matter of a separate lease or delivery, whether or not it is sufficient to perform the lease contract.

(t) "Merchant lessee" means a lessee that is a merchant with respect to goods of the kind subject to the lease.

(u) "Present value" means the amount as of a date certain of one or more sums payable in the future, discounted to the date certain. The discount is determined by the interest rate specified by the parties if the rate was not manifestly unreasonable at the time the transaction was entered into; otherwise, the discount is determined by a commercially reasonable rate that takes into account the facts and circumstances of each case at the time the transaction was entered into.

(v) "Purchase" includes taking by sale, lease, mortgage, security interest, pledge, gift, or any other voluntary transaction creating an interest in goods.

(w) "Sublease" means a lease of goods the right to possession and use of which was acquired by the lessor as a lessee under an existing lease.

(x) "Supplier" means a person from whom a lessor buys or leases goods to be leased under a finance lease.

(y) "Supply contract" means a contract under which a lessor buys or leases goods to be leased.

(z) "Termination" occurs when either party pursuant to a power created by agreement or law puts an end to the lease contract otherwise than for default.

(2) Other definitions applying to this Article and the sections in which they appear are:

"Accessions". Section 2A-310(1).

"Construction mortgage". Section 2A-309(1)(d).

"Encumbrance". Section 2A-309(1)(e).

"Fixtures". Section 2A-309(1)(a).

"Fixture filing". Section 2A-309(1)(b).

"Purchase money lease". Section 2A-309(1)(c).

(3) The following definitions in other Articles apply to this Article:

"Accounts". Section 9-106.

"Between merchants". Section 2-104(3).

"Buyer". Section 2-103(1)(a).

"Chattel paper". Section 9-105(1)(b).

"Consumer goods". Section 9-109(1).

"Documents". Section 9-105(1)(f).

"Entrusting". Section 9-403(3).

"General intangibles". Section 9-106.

"Good faith". Section 2-103(1)(b).

"Instruments". Section 9-105(1)(i).

"Merchant". Section 2-104(1).

"Mortgage". Section 9-105(1)(j).

"Pursuant to commitment". Section 9-105(1)(k).

"Receipt". Section 2-103(1)(c).

"Sale". Section 2-106(1).

"Sale on approval". Section 2-326.

"Sale or return". Section 2-326.

"Seller". Section 2-103(1)(d).

(4) In addition Article 1 contains general definitions and principles of construction and interpretation applicable throughout this Article.

§ 2A-104. Leases Subject to Other Statutes.

(1) A lease, although subject to this Article, is also subject to any applicable:

(a) statute of the United States;

(b) certificate of title statute of this State: (list any certificate of title statutes covering automobiles, trailers, mobile homes, boats, farm tractors, and the like);

(c) certificate of title statute of another jurisdiction (Section 2A-105); or

(d) consumer protection statute of this State.

(2) In case of conflict between the provisions of this Article, other than Sections 2A-105, 2A-304(3) and 2A-305(3), and any statute referred to in subsection (1), the provisions of that statute control.

(3) Failure to comply with any applicable statute has only the effect specified therein.

§ 2A-105. Territorial Application of Article to Goods Covered by Certificate of Title.

Subject to the provisions of Sections 2A-304(3) and 2A-305(3), with respect to goods covered by a certificate of title issued under a statute of this State or of another jurisdiction, compliance and the effect of compliance or noncompliance with a certificate of title statute are governed by the law (including the conflict of laws rules) of the jurisdiction issuing the certificate until the earlier of (a) surrender of the certificate, or (b) four months after the goods are removed from that jurisdiction and thereafter until a new certificate of title is issued by another jurisdiction.

§ 2A-106. Limitation on Power of Parties to Consumer Lease to Choose Applicable Law and Judicial Forum.

(1) If the law chosen by the parties to a consumer lease is that of a jurisdiction other than a jurisdiction in which the lessee resides at the time the lease agreement becomes enforceable or within 30 days thereafter or in which the goods are to be used, the choice is not enforceable.

(2) If the judicial forum chosen by the parties to a consumer lease is a forum that would not otherwise have jurisdiction over the lessee, the choice is not enforceable.

§ 2A-107. Waiver or Renunciation of Claim or Right After Default.

Any claim or right arising out of an alleged default or breach of warranty may be discharged in whole or in part without consideration by a written waiver or renunciation signed and delivered by the aggrieved party.

§ 2A-108. Unconscionability.

(1) If the court as a matter of law finds a lease contract or any clause of a lease contract to have been unconscionable at the time it was made the court may refuse to enforce the lease contract, or it may enforce the remainder of the lease contract without the unconscionable clause, or it may so limit the application of any unconscionable clause as to avoid any unconscionable result.

(2) With respect to a consumer lease, if the court as a matter of law finds that a lease contract or any clause of a lease contract has been induced by unconscionable conduct or that unconscionable conduct has occurred in the collection of a claim arising from a lease contract, the court may grant appropriate relief.

(3) Before making a finding of unconscionability under subsection (1) or (2), the court, on its own motion or that of a party, shall afford the parties a reasonable opportunity to present evidence as to the setting, purpose, and effect of the lease contract or clause thereof, or of the conduct.

(4) In an action in which the lessee claims unconscionability with respect to a consumer lease:

(a) If the court finds unconscionability under subsection (1) or (2), the court shall award reasonable attorney's fees to the lessee.

(b) If the court does not find unconscionability and the lessee claiming unconscionability has brought or maintained an action he [or she] knew to be groundless, the court shall award reasonable attorney's fees to the party against whom the claim is made.

(c) In determining attorney's fees, the amount of the recovery on behalf of the claimant under subsections (1) and (2) is not controlling.

§ 2A-109. Option to Accelerate at Will.

(1) A term providing that one party or his [or her] successor in interest may accelerate payment or performance or require collateral or additional collateral "at will" or "when he [or she] deems himself [or herself] insecure" or in words of similar import must be construed to mean that he [or she] has power to do so only if he [or she] in good faith believes that the prospect of payment or performance is impaired.

(2) With respect to a consumer lease, the burden of establishing good faith under subsection (1) is on the party who exercised the power; otherwise the burden of establishing lack of good faith is on the party against whom the power has been exercised.

Part 2. Formation and Construction of Lease Contract

§ 2A-201. Statute of Frauds.

(1) A lease contract is not enforceable by way of action or defense unless:

(a) the total payments to be made under the lease contract, excluding payments for options to renew or buy, are less than $1,000; or

(b) there is a writing, signed by the party against whom enforcement is sought or by that party's authorized agent, sufficient to indicate that a lease contract has been made between the parties and to describe the goods leased and the lease term.

(2) Any description of leased goods or of the lease term is sufficient and satisfies subsection (1)(b), whether or not it is specific, if it reasonably identifies what is described.

(3) A writing is not sufficient because it omits or incorrectly states a term agreed upon, but the lease contract is not enforceable under subsection (1)(b) beyond the lease term and the quantity of goods shown in the writing.

(4) A lease contract that does not satisfy the requirements of subsection (1), but which is valid in other respects, is enforceable:

(a) if the goods are to be specially manufactured or obtained for the lessee and are not suitable for lease or sale to others in the ordinary course of the lessor's business, and the lessor, before notice of repudiation is received and under circumstances that reasonably indicate that the goods are for the lessee, has made either a substantial beginning of their manufacture or commitments for their procurement;

(b) if the party against whom enforcement is sought admits in that party's pleading, testimony or otherwise in court that a lease contract was made, but the lease contract is not enforceable under this provision beyond the quantity of goods admitted; or

(c) with respect to goods that have been received and accepted by the lessee.

(5) The lease term under a lease contract referred to in subsection (4) is:

(a) if there is a writing signed by the party against whom enforcement is sought or by that party's authorized agent specifying the lease term, the term so specified;

(b) if the party against whom enforcement is sought admits in that party's pleading, testimony, or otherwise in court a lease term, the term so admitted; or

(c) a reasonable lease term.

§ 2A-202. Final Written Expression: Parol or Extrinsic Evidence.

Terms with respect to which the confirmatory memoranda of the parties agree or which are otherwise set forth in a writing intended by the parties as a final expression of their agreement with respect to such terms as are included therein may not be contradicted by evidence of any prior agreement or of a contemporaneous oral agreement but may be explained or supplemented:

(a) by course of dealing or usage of trade or by course of performance; and

(b) by evidence of consistent additional terms unless the court finds the writing to have been intended also as a complete and exclusive statement of the terms of the agreement.

§ 2A-203. Seals Inoperative.

The affixing of a seal to a writing evidencing a lease contract or an offer to enter into a lease contract does not render the writing a sealed instrument and the law with respect to sealed instruments does not apply to the lease contract or offer.

§ 2A-204. Formation in General.

(1) A lease contract may be made in any manner sufficient to show agreement, including conduct by both parties which recognizes the existence of a lease contract.

(2) An agreement sufficient to constitute a lease contract may be found although the moment of its making is undetermined.

(3) Although one or more terms are left open, a lease contract does not fail for indefiniteness if the parties have intended to make a lease contract and there is a reasonably certain basis for giving an appropriate remedy.

§ 2A-205. Firm Offers.

An offer by a merchant to lease goods to or from another person in a signed writing that by its terms gives assurance it will be held open is not revocable, for lack of consideration, during the time stated or, if no time is stated, for a reasonable time, but in no event may the period of irrevocability exceed 3 months. Any such term of assurance on a form supplied by the offeree must be separately signed by the offeror.

§ 2A-206. Offer and Acceptance in Formation of Lease Contract.

(1) Unless otherwise unambiguously indicated by the language or circumstances, an offer to make a lease contract must be construed as inviting acceptance in any manner and by any medium reasonable in the circumstances.

(2) If the beginning of a requested performance is a reasonable mode of acceptance, an offeror who is not notified of acceptance within a reasonable time may treat the offer as having lapsed before acceptance.

§ 2A-207. Course of Performance or Practical Construction.

(1) If a lease contract involves repeated occasions for performance by either party with knowledge of the nature of the performance and opportunity for objection to it by the other, any course of performance accepted or acquiesced in without objection is relevant to determine the meaning of the lease agreement.

(2) The express terms of a lease agreement and any course of performance, as well as any course of dealing and usage of trade, must be construed whenever reasonable as consistent with each other; but if that construction is unreasonable, express terms control course of performance, course of performance controls both course of dealing and usage of trade, and course of dealing controls usage of trade.

(3) Subject to the provisions of Section 2A-208 on modification and waiver, course of performance is relevant to show a waiver or modification of any term inconsistent with the course of performance.

§ 2A-208. Modification, Rescission and Waiver.

(1) An agreement modifying a lease contract needs no consideration to be binding.

(2) A signed lease agreement that excludes modification or rescission except by a signed writing may not be otherwise modified or rescinded, but, except as between merchants, such a requirement on a form supplied by a merchant must be separately signed by the other party.

(3) Although an attempt at modification or rescission does not satisfy the requirements of subsection (2), it may operate as a waiver.

(4) A party who has made a waiver affecting an executory portion of a lease contract may retract the waiver by reasonable notification received by the other party that strict performance will be required of any term waived, unless the retraction would be unjust in view of a material change of position in reliance on the waiver.

§ 2A-209. Lessee Under Finance Lease as Beneficiary of Supply Contract.

(1) The benefit of the supplier's promises to the lessor under the supply contract and of all warranties, whether express or implied, under the supply contract, extends to the lessee to the extent of the lessee's leasehold interest under a finance lease related to the supply contract, but subject to the terms of the supply contract and all of the supplier's defenses or claims arising therefrom.

(2) The extension of the benefit of the supplier's promises and warranties to the lessee (Section 2A-209(1)) does not: (a) modify the rights and obligations of the parties to the supply contract, whether arising therefrom or otherwise, or (b) impose any duty or liability under the supply contract on the lessee.

(3) Any modification or rescission of the supply contract by the supplier and the lessor is effective against the lessee unless, prior to the modification or rescission, the supplier has received notice that the lessee has entered into a finance lease related to the supply contract. If the supply contract is modified or rescinded after the lessee enters the finance lease, the lessee has a cause of action against the lessor, and against the supplier if the supplier has notice of the lessee's entering the finance lease when the supply contract is modified or rescinded. The lessee's recovery from such action shall put the lessee in as good a position as if the modification or rescission had not occurred.

§ 2A-210. Express Warranties.

(1) Express warranties by the lessor are created as follows:

(a) Any affirmation of fact or promise made by the lessor to the lessee which relates to the goods and becomes part of the basis of the bargain creates an express warranty that the goods will conform to the affirmation or promise.

(b) Any description of the goods which is made part of the basis of the bargain creates an express warranty that the goods will conform to the description.

(c) Any sample or model that is made part of the basis of the bargain creates an express warranty that the whole of the goods will conform to the sample or model.

(2) It is not necessary to the creation of an express warranty that the lessor use formal words, such as "warrant" or "guarantee," or that the lessor have a specific intention to make a warranty, but an affirmation merely of the value of the goods or a statement purporting to be merely the lessor's opinion or commendation of the goods does not create a warranty.

§ 2A-211. Warranties Against Interference and Against Infringement; Lessee's Obligation Against Infringement.

(1) There is in a lease contract a warranty that for the lease term no person holds a claim to or interest in the goods that arose from an act or omission of the lessor, other than a claim by way of infringement or the like, which will interfere with the lessee's enjoyment of its leasehold interest.

(2) Except in a finance lease there is in a lease contract by a lessor who is a merchant regularly dealing in goods of the kind a warranty that the goods are delivered free of the rightful claim of any person by way of infringement or the like.

(3) A lessee who furnishes specifications to a lessor or a supplier shall hold the lessor and the supplier harmless against any claim by way of infringement or the like that arises out of compliance with the specifications.

§ 2A-212. Implied Warranty of Merchantability.

(1) Except in a finance lease, a warranty that the goods will be merchantable is implied in a lease contract if the lessor is a merchant with respect to goods of that kind.

(2) Goods to be merchantable must be at least such as

(a) pass without objection in the trade under the description in the lease agreement;

(b) in the case of fungible goods, are of fair average quality within the description;

(c) are fit for the ordinary purposes for which goods of that type are used;

(d) run, within the variation permitted by the lease agreement, of even kind, quality, and quantity within each unit and among all units involved;

(e) are adequately contained, packaged, and labeled as the lease agreement may require; and

(f) conform to any promises or affirmations of fact made on the container or label.

(3) Other implied warranties may arise from course of dealing or usage of trade.

§ 2A-213. Implied Warranty of Fitness for Particular Purpose.

Except in a finance lease, if the lessor at the time the lease contract is made has reason to know of any particular purpose for which the goods are required and that the lessee is relying on the lessor's skill or judgment to select or furnish suitable goods, there is in the lease contract an implied warranty that the goods will be fit for that purpose.

§ 2A-214. Exclusion or Modification of Warranties.

(1) Words or conduct relevant to the creation of an express warranty and words or conduct tending to negate or limit a warranty must be construed wherever reasonable as consistent with each other; but, subject to the provisions of Section 2A-202 on parol or extrinsic evidence, negation or limitation is inoperative to the extent that the construction is unreasonable.

(2) Subject to subsection (3), to exclude or modify the implied warranty of merchantability or any part of it the language must mention "merchantability", be by a writing, and be conspicuous. Subject to subsection (3), to exclude or modify any implied warranty of fitness the exclusion must be by a writing and be conspicuous. Language to exclude all implied warranties of fitness is sufficient if it is in writing, is conspicuous and states, for example, "There is no warranty that the goods will be fit for a particular purpose."

(3) Notwithstanding subsection (2), but subject to subsection (4),

(a) unless the circumstances indicate otherwise, all implied warranties are excluded by expressions like "as is," or "with all faults," or by other language that in common understanding calls the lessee's attention to the exclusion of warranties and makes plain that there is no implied warranty, if in writing and conspicuous;

(b) if the lessee before entering into the lease contract has examined the goods or the sample or model as fully as desired or has refused to examine the goods, there is no implied warranty with regard to defects that an examination ought in the circumstances to have revealed; and

(c) an implied warranty may also be excluded or modified by course of dealing, course of performance, or usage of trade.

(4) To exclude or modify a warranty against interference or against infringement (Section 2A-211) or any part of it, the language must be specific, be by a writing, and be conspicuous, unless the circumstances, including course of performance, course of dealing, or usage of trade, give the lessee reason to know that the goods are being leased subject to a claim or interest of any person.

§ 2A-215. Cumulation and Conflict of Warranties Express or Implied.

Warranties, whether express or implied, must be construed as consistent with each other and as cumulative, but if that construction is unreasonable, the intention of the parties determines which warranty is dominant. In ascertaining that intention the following rules apply:

(a) Exact or technical specifications displace an inconsistent sample or model or general language of description.

(b) A sample from an existing bulk displaces inconsistent general language of description.

(c) Express warranties displace inconsistent implied warranties other than an implied warranty of fitness for a particular purpose.

§ 2A-216. Third-Party Beneficiaries of Express and Implied Warranties.

Alternative A

A warranty to or for the benefit of a lessee under this Article, whether express or implied, extends to any natural person who is in the family or household of the lessee or who is a guest in the lessee's home if it is reasonable to expect that such person may use, consume, or be affected by the goods and who is injured in person by breach of the warranty. This section does not displace principles of law and equity that extend a warranty to or for the benefit of a lessee to other persons. The operation of this section may not be excluded, modified, or limited, but an exclusion, modification, or limitation of the warranty, including any with respect to rights and remedies, effective against the lessee is also effective against any beneficiary designated under this section.

Alternative B

A warranty to or for the benefit of a lessee under this Article, whether express or implied, extends to any natural person who may reasonably be expected to use, consume, or be affected by the goods and who is injured in person by breach of the warranty. This section does not displace principles of law and equity that extend a warranty to or for the benefit of a lessee to other persons. The operation of this section may not be excluded, modified, or limited, but an exclusion, modification, or limitation of the warranty, including any with respect to rights and remedies, effective against the lessee is also effective against the beneficiary designated under this section.

Alternative C

A warranty to or for the benefit of a lessee under this Article, whether express or implied, extends to any person who may reasonably be expected to use, consume, or be affected by the goods and who is injured by breach of the warranty. The operation of this section may not be excluded, modified, or limited with respect to injury to the person of an individual to whom the warranty extends, but an exclusion, modification, or limitation of the warranty, including any with respect to rights and remedies, effective against the lessee is also effective against the beneficiary designated under this section.

§ 2A-217. Identification.

Identification of goods as goods to which a lease contract refers may be made at any time and in any manner explicitly agreed to by the parties. In the absence of explicit agreement, identification occurs:

(a) when the lease contract is made if the lease contract is for a lease of goods that are existing and identified;

(b) when the goods are shipped, marked, or otherwise designated by the lessor as goods to which the lease contract refers, if the lease contract is for a lease of goods that are not existing and identified; or

(c) when the young are conceived, if the lease contract is for a lease of unborn young of animals.

§ 2A-218. Insurance and Proceeds.

(1) A lessee obtains an insurable interest when existing goods are identified to the lease contract even though the goods identified are nonconforming and the lessee has an option to reject them.

(2) If a lessee has an insurable interest only by reason of the lessor's identification of the goods, the lessor, until default or insolvency or notification to the lessee that identification is final, may substitute other goods for those identified.

(3) Notwithstanding a lessee's insurable interest under subsections (1) and (2), the lessor retains an insurable interest until an option to buy has been exercised by the lessee and risk of loss has passed to the lessee.

(4) Nothing in this section impairs any insurable interest recognized under any other statute or rule of law.

(5) The parties by agreement may determine that one or more parties have an obligation to obtain and pay for insurance covering the goods and by agreement may determine the beneficiary of the proceeds of the insurance.

§ 2A-219. Risk of Loss.

(1) Except in the case of a finance lease, risk of loss is retained by the lessor and does not pass to the lessee. In one case of a finance lease, risk of loss passes to the lessee.

(2) Subject to the provisions of this Article on the effect of default on risk of loss (Section 2A-220), if risk of loss is to pass to the lessee and the time of passage is not stated, the following rules apply:

(a) If the lease contract requires or authorizes the goods to be shipped by carrier

(i) and it does not require delivery at a particular destination, the risk of loss passes to the lessee when the goods are duly delivered to the carrier; but

(ii) if it does require delivery at a particular destination and the goods are there duly tendered while in the possession of the carrier, the risk of loss passes to the lessee when the goods are there duly so tendered as to enable the lessee to take delivery.

(b) If the goods are held by a bailee to be delivered without being moved, the risk of loss passes to the lessee on acknowledgment by the bailee of the lessee's right to possession of the goods.

(c) In any case not within subsection (a) or (b), the risk of loss passes to the lessee on the lessee's receipt of the goods if the lessor, or, in the case of a finance lease, the supplier, is a merchant; otherwise the risk passes to the lessee on tender of delivery.

§ 2A-220. Effect of Default on Risk of Loss.

(1) Where risk of loss is to pass to the lessee and the time of passage is not stated:

(a) If a tender or delivery of goods so fails to conform to the lease contract as to give a right of rejection, the risk of their loss remains with the lessor, or, in the case of a finance lease, the supplier, until cure or acceptance.

(b) If the lessee rightfully revokes acceptance, he [or she], to the extent of any deficiency in his [or her] effective insurance coverage, may treat the risk of loss as having remained with the lessor from the beginning.

(2) Whether or not risk of loss is to pass to the lessee, if the lessee as to conforming goods already identified to a lease contract repudiates or is otherwise in default under the lease contract, the lessor, or, in the case of a finance lease, the supplier, to the extent of any deficiency in his [or her] effective insurance coverage may treat the risk of loss as resting on the lessee for a commercially reasonable time.

§ 2A-221. Casualty to Identified Goods.

If a lease contract requires goods identified when the lease contract is made, and the goods suffer casualty without fault of the lessee, the lessor or the supplier before delivery, or the goods suffer casualty before risk of loss passes to the lessee pursuant to the lease agreement or Section 2A-219, then;

(a) if the loss is total, the lease contract is avoided; and

(b) if the loss is partial or the goods have so deteriorated as to no longer conform to the lease contract, the lessee may nevertheless demand inspection and at his [or her] option either treat the lease contract as avoided or, except in a finance lease that is not a consumer lease, accept the goods with due allowance from the rent payable for the balance of the lease term for the deterioration or the deficiency in quantity but without further right against the lessor.

Part 3. Effect of Lease Contract

§ 2A-301. Enforceability of Lease Contract.

Except as otherwise provided in this Article, a lease contract is effective and enforceable according to its terms between the parties, against purchasers of the goods and against creditors of the parties.

§ 2A-302. Title to and Possession of Goods.

Except as otherwise provided in this Article, each provision of this Article applies whether the lessor or a third party has title to the goods, and whether the lessor, the lessee, or a third party has possession of the goods, notwithstanding any statute or rule of law that possession or the absence of possession is fraudulent.

§ 2A-303. Alienability of Party's Interest Under Lease Contract or of Lessor's Residual Interest in Goods; Delegation of Performance; Assignment of Rights.

(1) Any interest of a party under a lease contract and the lessor's residual interest in the goods may be transferred unless

(a) the transfer is voluntary and the lease contract prohibits the transfer; or

(b) the transfer materially changes the duty of or materially increases the burden or risk imposed on the other party to the lease contract, and within a reasonable time after notice of the transfer the other party demands that the transferee comply with subsection (2) and the transferee fails to comply.

(2) Within a reasonable time after demand pursuant to subsection (1)(b), the transferee shall:

(a) cure or provide adequate assurance that he [or she] will promptly cure any default other than one arising from the transfer;

(b) compensate or provide adequate assurance that he [or she] will promptly compensate the other party to the lease contract and any other person holding an interest in the lease contract, except the party whose interest is being transferred, for any loss to that party resulting from the transfer;

(c) provide adequate assurance of future due performance under the lease contract; and

(d) assume the lease contract.

(3) Demand pursuant to subsection (1)(b) is without prejudice to the other party's rights against the transferee and the party whose interest is transferred.

(4) An assignment of "the lease" or of "all my rights under the lease" or an assignment in similar general terms is a transfer of rights, and unless the language or the circumstances, as in an assignment for security, indicate the contrary, the assignment is a delegation of duties by the assignor to the assignee and acceptance by the assignee constitutes a promise by him [or her] to perform those duties. This promise is enforceable by either the assignor or the other party to the lease contract.

(5) Unless otherwise agreed by the lessor and the lessee, no delegation of performance relieves the assignor as against the other party of any duty to perform or any liability for default.

(6) A right to damages for default with respect to the whole lease contract or a right arising out of the assignor's due performance of his [or her] entire obligation can be assigned despite agreement otherwise.

(7) To prohibit the transfer of an interest of a party under a lease contract, the language of prohibition must be specific, by a writing, and conspicuous.

§ 2A-304. Subsequent Lease of Goods by Lessor.

(1) Subject to the provisions of Section 2A-303, a subsequent lessee from a lessor of goods under an existing lease contract obtains, to the extent of the leasehold interest transferred, the leasehold interest in the goods that the lessor had or had power to transfer, and except as provided in subsection (2) and Section 2A-527(4), takes subject to the existing lease contract. A lessor with voidable title has power to transfer a good leasehold interest to a good faith subsequent lessee for value, but only to the extent set forth in the preceding sentence. When goods have been delivered under a transaction of purchase the lessor has that power even though:

(a) the lessor's transferor was deceived as to the identity of the lessor;

(b) the delivery was in exchange for a check which is later dishonored;

(c) it was agreed that the transaction was to be a "cash sale"; or

(d) the delivery was procured through fraud punishable as larcenous under the criminal law.

(2) A subsequent lessee in the ordinary course of business from a lessor who is a merchant dealing in goods of that kind to whom the goods were entrusted by the existing lessee before the interest of the subsequent lessee became enforceable against the lessor obtains, to the extent of the leasehold interest transferred, all of the lessor's and the existing lessee's rights to the goods, and takes free of the existing lease contract.

(3) A subsequent lessee from the lessor of goods that are subject to an existing lease contract and are covered by a certificate of title issued under a statute of this State or of another jurisdiction takes no greater rights than those provided both by this section and by the certificate of title statute.

§ 2A-305. Sale or Sublease of Goods by Lessee.

(1) Subject to the provisions of Section 2A-303, a buyer or sublessee from the lessee of goods under an existing lease contract obtains, to the extent of the interest transferred, the leasehold interest in the goods that the lessee had or had power to transfer, and except as provided in subsection (2) and Section 2A-511(4), takes subject to the existing lease contract. A lessee with a voidable leasehold interest has power to transfer a good leasehold interest to a good faith buyer for value or a good faith sublessee for value, but only to the extent set forth in the preceding sentence. When goods have been delivered under a transaction of lease the lessee has that power even though:

(a) the lessor was deceived as to the identity of the lessee;

(b) the delivery was in exchange for a check which is later dishonored; or

(c) the delivery was procured through fraud punishable as larcenous under the criminal law.

(2) A buyer in the ordinary course of business or a sublessee in the ordinary course of business from a lessee who is a merchant dealing in goods of that kind to whom the goods were entrusted by the lessor obtains, to the extent of the interest transferred, all of the lessor's and lessee's rights to the goods, and takes free of the existing lease contract.

(3) A buyer or sublessee from the lessee of goods that are subject to an existing lease contract and are covered by a certificate of title issued under a statute of this State or of another jurisdiction takes no greater rights than those provided both by this section and by the certificate of title statute.

§ 2A-306. Priority of Certain Liens Arising by Operation of Law.

If a person in the ordinary course of his [or her] business furnishes services or materials with respect to goods subject to a lease contract a lien upon those goods in the possession of that person given by statute or rule of law for those materials or services takes priority over any interest of the lessor or lessee under the lease contract or this Article unless the lien is created by statute and the statute provides otherwise or unless the lien is created by rule of law and the rule of law provides otherwise.

§ 2A-307. Priority of Liens Arising by Attachment or Levy on Security Interests in, and Other Claims to Goods.

(1) Except as otherwise provided in Section 2A-306, a creditor of a lessee takes subject to the lease contract.

(2) Except as otherwise provided in subsections (3) and (4) of this section and in Sections 2A-306 and 2A-308, a creditor of a lessor takes subject to the lease contract:

(a) unless the creditor holds a lien that attached to the goods before the lease contract became enforceable, or

(b) unless the creditor holds a security interest in the goods that under the Article on Secured Transactions (Article 9) would have priority over any other security interest in the goods perfected by filing covering the goods and made at the time the lease contract became enforceable, whether or not any other security interest existed.

(3) A lessee in the ordinary course of business takes the leasehold interest free of a security interest in the goods created by the lessor even though the security interest is perfected and the lessee knows of its existence.

(4) A lessee other than a lessee in the ordinary course of business takes the leasehold interest free of a security interest to the extent that it secures future advances made after the secured party acquires knowledge of the lease or more than 45 days after the lease contract becomes enforceable, whichever first occurs, unless the future advances are made pursuant to a commitment entered into without knowledge of the lease and before the expiration of the 45-day period.

§ 2A-308. Special Rights of Creditors.

(1) A creditor of a lessor in possession of goods subject to a lease contract may treat the lease contract as void if as against the creditor retention of possession by the lessor is fraudulent under any statute or rule of law, but retention of possession in good faith and current course of trade by the lessor for a commercially reasonable time after the lease contract becomes enforceable is not fraudulent.

(2) Nothing in this Article impairs the rights of creditors of a lessor if the lease contract (a) becomes enforceable, not in current course of trade but in satisfaction of or as security for a pre-existing claim for money, security, or the like, and (b) is made under circumstances which under any statute or rule of law apart from this Article would constitute the transaction a fraudulent transfer or voidable preference.

(3) A creditor of a seller may treat a sale or an identification of goods to a contract for sale as void if as against the creditor retention of possession by the seller is fraudulent under any statute or rule of law, but retention of possession of the goods pursuant to a lease contract entered into by the seller as lessee and the buyer as lessor in connection with the sale or identification of the goods is not fraudulent if the buyer bought for value and in good faith.

§ 2A-309. Lessor's and Lessee's Rights When Goods Become Fixtures.

(1) In this section:

(a) goods are "fixtures" when they become so related to particular real estate that an interest in them arises under real estate law;

(b) a "fixture filing" is the filing, in the office where a mortgage on the real estate would be recorded or registered, of a financing statement concerning goods that are or are to become fixtures and conforming to the requirements of subsection (5) of Section 9-402;

(c) a lease is a "purchase money issue" unless the lessee has possession or use of the goods or the right to possession or use of the goods before the lease agreement is enforceable;

(d) a mortgage is a "construction mortgage" to the extent it secures an obligation incurred for the construction of an improvement on land including the acquisition cost of the land, if the recorded writing so indicates; and

(e) "encumbrance" includes real estate mortgages and other liens on real estate and all other rights in real estate that are not ownership interests.

(2) Under this Article a lease may be of goods that are fixtures or may continue in goods that become fixtures, but no lease exists under this Article of ordinary building materials incorporated into an improvement on land.

(3) This Article does not prevent creation of a lease of fixtures pursuant to real estate law.

(4) The perfected interest of a lessor of fixtures has priority over a conflicting interest of an encumbrancer or owner of the real estate if:

(a) the lease is a purchase money lease, the conflicting interest of the encumbrancer or owner arises before the goods become fixtures, the interest of the lessor is perfected by a fixture filing before the goods become fixtures or within ten days thereafter, and the lessee has an interest of record in the real estate or is in possession of the real estate; or

(b) the interest of the lessor is perfected by a fixture filing before the interest of the encumbrancer or owner is of record, the lessor's interest has priority over any conflicting interest of a predecessor in title of the encumbrancer or owner, and the lessee has an interest of record in the real estate or is in possession of the real estate.

(5) The interest of a lessor of fixtures, whether or not perfected, has priority over the conflicting interest of an encumbrancer or owner of the real estate if:

(a) the fixtures are readily removable factory or office machines, readily removable equipment that is not primarily used or leased for use in the operation of the real estate, or readily removable replacements of domestic appliances that are goods subject to a consumer lease, and before the goods become fixtures the lease contract is enforceable; or

(b) the conflicting interest is a lien on the real estate obtained by legal or equitable proceedings after the lease contract is enforceable; or

(c) the encumbrancer or owner has consented in writing to the lease or has disclaimed an interest in the goods as fixtures; or

(d) the lessee has a right to remove the goods as against the encumbrancer or owner. If the lessee's right to remove terminates, the priority of the interest of the lessor continues for a reasonable time.

(6) Notwithstanding paragraph (a) of subsection (4) but otherwise subject to subsections (4) and (5), the interest of a lessor of fixtures is subordinate to the conflicting interest of an encumbrancer of the real estate under a construction mortgage recorded before the goods become fixtures if the goods become fixtures before the completion of the construction. To the extent given to refinance a construction mortgage, the conflicting interest of an encumbrancer of the real estate under a mortgage has this priority to the same extent as the encumbrancer of the real estate under the construction mortgage.

(7) In cases not within the preceding subsections, priority between the interest of a lessor of fixtures and the conflicting interest of an encumbrancer or owner of the real estate who is not the lessee is determined by the priority rules governing conflicting interests in real estate.

(8) If the interest of a lessor has priority over all conflicting interests of all owners and encumbrancers of the real estate, the lessor or the lessee may (a) on default, expiration, termination, or cancellation of the lease agreement by the other party but subject to the provisions of the lease agreement and this Article, or (b) if necessary to enforce his [or her] other rights and remedies under this Article, remove the goods from the real estate, free and clear of all conflicting interests of all owners and encumbrancers of the real estate, but he [or she] must reimburse any encumbrancer or owner of the real estate who is not the lessee and who has not otherwise agreed for the cost of repair of any physical injury, but not for any diminution in value of the real estate caused by the absence of the goods removed or by any necessity of replacing them. A person entitled to reimbursement may refuse permission to remove until the party seeking removal gives adequate security for the performance of this obligation.

(9) Even though the lease agreement does not create a security interest, the interest of a lessor of fixtures is perfected by filing a financing statement as a fixture filing for leased goods that are or are to become fixtures in accordance with the relevant provisions of the Article on Secured Transactions (Article 9).

§ 2A-310. Lessor's and Lessee's Rights When Goods Become Accessions.

(1) Goods are "accessions" when they are installed in or affixed to other goods.

(2) The interest of a lessor or a lessee under a lease contract entered into before the goods became accessions is superior to all interests in the whole except as stated in subsection (4).

(3) The interest of a lessor or a lessee under a lease contract entered into at the time or after the goods became accessions is superior to all subsequently acquired interests in the whole except as stated in subsection (4) but is subordinate to interests in the whole existing at the time the lease contract was made unless the holders of such interests in the whole have in writing consented to the lease or disclaimed an interest in the goods as part of the whole.

(4) The interest of a lessor or a lessee under a lease contract described in subsection (2) or (3) is subordinate to the interest of

(a) a buyer in the ordinary course of business or a lessee in the ordinary course of business of any interest in the whole acquired after the goods become accessions; or

(b) a creditor with a security interest in the whole perfected before the lease contract was made to the extent that the creditor makes subsequent advances without knowledge of the lease contract.

(5) When under subsections (2) or (3) and (4) a lessor or a lessee of accessions holds an interest that is superior to all interests in the whole, the lessor or the lessee may (a) on default, expiration, termination, or cancellation of the lease contract by the other party but subject to the provisions of the lease contract and this Article, or (b) if necessary to enforce his [or her] other rights and remedies under this Article, remove the goods from the whole, free and clear of all interests in the whole, but he [or she] must reimburse any holder of an interest in the whole who is not the lessee and who has not otherwise agreed for the cost of repair of any physical injury but not for any diminution in value of the whole caused by the absence of the goods removed or by any necessity for replacing them. A person entitled to reimbursement may refuse permission to remove until the party seeking removal gives adequate security for the performance of this obligation.

Part 4. Performance of Lease Contract: Repudiated, Substituted and Excused

§ 2A-401. Insecurity: Adequate Assurance of Performance.

(1) A lease contract imposes an obligation on each party that the other's expectation of receiving due performance will not be impaired.

(2) If reasonable grounds for insecurity arise with respect to the performance of either party, the insecure party may demand in writing adequate assurance of due performance. Until the insecure party receives that assurance, if commercially reasonable the insecure party may suspend any performance for which he [or she] has not already received the agreed return.

(3) A repudiation of the lease contract occurs if assurance of due performance adequate under the circumstances of the particular case is not provided to the insecure party within a reasonable time, not to exceed 30 days after receipt of a demand by the other party.

(4) Between merchants, the reasonableness of grounds for insecurity and the adequacy of any assurance offered must be determined according to commercial standards.

(5) Acceptance of any nonconforming delivery or payment does not prejudice the aggrieved party's right to demand adequate assurance of future performance.

§ 2A-402. Anticipatory Repudiation.

If either party repudiates a lease contract with respect to a performance not yet due under the lease contract, the loss of which performance will substantially impair the value of the lease contract to the other, the aggrieved party may:

(a) for a commercially reasonable time, await retraction of repudiation and performance by the repudiating party;

(b) make demand pursuant to Section 2A-401 and await assurance of future performance adequate under the circumstances of the particular case; or

(c) resort to any right or remedy upon default under the lease contract or this Article, even though the aggrieved party has notified the repudiating party that the aggrieved party would await the repudiating party's performance and assurance and has urged retraction. In addition, whether or not the aggrieved party is pursuing one of the foregoing remedies, the aggrieved party may suspend performance or, if the aggrieved party is the lessor, proceed in

accordance with the provisions of this Article on the lessor's rig to identify goods to the lease contract notwithstanding default or salvage unfinished goods (Section 2A-524).

§ 2A-403. Retraction of Anticipatory Repudiation.

(1) Until the repudiating party's next performance is due, the rep diating party can retract the repudiation unless, since the repudiatic the aggrieved party has cancelled the lease contract or materia changed the aggrieved party's position or otherwise indicated that t aggrieved party considers the repudiation final.

(2) Retraction may be by any method that clearly indicates to t aggrieved party that the repudiating party intends to perform und the lease contract and includes any assurance demanded under Secti 2A-401.

(3) Retraction reinstates a repudiating party's rights under a lea contract with due excuse and allowing to the aggrieved party for a delay occasioned by the repudiation.

§ 2A-404. Substituted Performance.

(1) If without fault of the lessee, the lessor and the supplier, the agre berthing, loading, or unloading facilities fail or the agreed type carrier becomes unavailable or the agreed manner of delivery otherw becomes commercially impracticable, but a commercially reasonal substitute is available, the substitute performance must be tender and accepted.

(2) If the agreed means or manner of payment fails because of domes or foreign governmental regulation:

(a) the lessor may withhold or stop delivery or cause the suppli to withhold or stop delivery unless the lessee provides a means manner of payment that is commercially a substantial equivale and

(b) if delivery has already been taken, payment by the means or the manner provided by the regulation discharges the lessee's ob gation unless the regulation is discriminatory, oppressive, or pre atory

§ 2A-405. Excused Performance.

Subject to Section 2A-404 on substituted performance, the followi rules apply:

(a) Delay in delivery or nondelivery in whole or in part by a less or a supplier who complies with paragraphs (b) and (c) is not default under the lease contract if performance as agreed has be made impracticable by the occurrence of a contingency the nonc currence of which was a basic assumption on which the lease contra was made or by compliance in good faith with any applicable forei or domestic governmental regulation or order, whether or not t regulation or order later proves to be invalid.

(b) If the causes mentioned in paragraph (a) affect only part of t lessor's or the supplier's capacity to perform, he [or she] shall alloca production and deliveries among his [or her] customers but at h [or her] option may include regular customers not then und contract for sale or lease as well as his [or her] own requiremen for further manufacture. He [or she] may so allocate in any mann that is fair and reasonable.

(c) The lessor seasonably shall notify the lessee and in the case o finance lease the supplier seasonably shall notify the lessor and t lessee, if known, that there will be delay or nondelivery and, allocation is required under paragraph (b), of the estimated quo thus made available for the lessee.

§ 2A-406. Procedure on Excused Performance.

(1) If the lessee receives notification of a material or indefinite del or an allocation justified under Section 2A-405, the lessee may

written notification to the lessor as to any goods involved, and with respect to all of the goods if under an installment lease contract the value of the whole lease contract is substantially impaired (Section 2A-510):

(a) terminate the lease contract (Section 2A-505(2)); or

(b) except in a finance lease that is not a consumer lease, modify the lease contract by accepting the available quota in substitution, with due allowance from the rent payable for the balance of the lease term for the deficiency but without further right against the lessor.

(2) If, after receipt of a notification from the lessor under Section 2A-405, the lessee fails so to modify the lease agreement within a reasonable time not exceeding 30 days, the lease contract lapses with respect to any deliveries affected.

§ 2A-407. Irrevocable Promises: Finance Leases.

(1) In the case of a finance lease that is not a consumer lease the lessee's promises under the lease contract become irrevocable and independent upon the lessee's acceptance of the goods.

(2) A promise that has become irrevocable and independent under subsection (1):

(a) is effective and enforceable between the parties, and by or against third parties including assignees of the parties, and

(b) is not subject to cancellation, termination, modification, repudiation, excuse, or substitution without the consent of the party to whom the promise runs.

Part 5. Default

A. In General

§ 2A-501. Default: Procedure.

(1) Whether the lessor or the lessee is in default under a lease contract is determined by the lease agreement and this Article.

(2) If the lessor or the lessee is in default under the lease contract, the party seeking enforcement has rights and remedies as provided in this Article and, except as limited by this Article, as provided in the lease agreement.

(3) If the lessor or the lessee is in default under the lease contract, the party seeking enforcement may reduce the party's claim to judgment, or otherwise enforce the lease contract by self-help or any available judicial procedure or nonjudicial procedure, including administrative proceeding, arbitration, or the like, in accordance with this Article.

(4) Except as otherwise provided in this Article or the lease agreement, the rights and remedies referred to in subsections (2) and (3) are cumulative.

(5) If the lease agreement covers both real property and goods, the party seeking enforcement may proceed under this Part as to the goods, or under other applicable law as to both the real property and the goods in accordance with his [or her] rights and remedies in respect of the real property, in which case this Part does not apply.

§ 2A-502. Notice After Default.

Except as otherwise provided in this Article or the lease agreement, the lessor or lessee in default under the lease contract is not entitled to notice of default or notice of enforcement from the other party to the lease agreement.

§ 2A-503. Modification or Impairment of Rights and Remedies.

(1) Except as otherwise provided in this Article, the lease agreement may include rights and remedies for default in addition to or in substitution for those provided in this Article and may limit or alter the measure of damages recoverable under this Article.

(2) Resort to a remedy provided under this Article or in the lease agreement is optional unless the remedy is expressly agreed to be exclusive. If circumstances cause an exclusive or limited remedy to fail of its essential purpose, or provision for an exclusive remedy is unconscionable, remedy may be had as provided in this Article.

(3) Consequential damages may be liquidated under Section 2A-504, or may otherwise be limited, altered, or excluded unless the limitation, alteration, or exclusion is unconscionable. Limitations of consequential damages for injury to the person in the case of consumer goods is prima facie unconscionable but limitation of damages where the loss is commercial is not.

(4) Rights and remedies on default by the lessor or the lessee with respect to any obligation or promise collateral or ancillary to the lease contract are not impaired by this Article.

§ 2A-504. Liquidation of Damages.

(1) Damages payable by either party for default, or any other act or omission, including indemnity for loss or diminution of anticipated tax benefits or loss or damage to lessor's residual interest, may be liquidated in the lease agreement but only at an amount or by a formula that is reasonable in light of the then anticipated harm caused by the default or other act or omission.

(2) If the lease agreement provides for liquidation of damages, and such provision does not comply with subsection (1), or such provision is an exclusive or limited remedy that circumstances cause to fail of its essential purpose, remedy may be had as provided in this Article.

(3) If the lessor justifiably withholds or stops delivery of goods because of the lessee's default or insolvency (Section 2A-525 or 2A-526), the lessee is entitled to restitution of any amount by which the sum of his [or her] payments exceeds:

(a) the amount to which the lessor is entitled by virtue of terms liquidating the lessor's damages in accordance with subsection (1); or

(b) in the absence of those terms, 20 percent of the then present value of the total rent the lessee was obligated to pay for the balance of the lease term, or, in the case of a consumer lease, the lesser of such amount or $500.

(4) A lessee's right to restitution under subsection (3) is subject to offset to the extent the lessor establishes:

(a) a right to recover damages under the provisions of this Article other than subsection (1); and

(b) the amount or value of any benefits received by the lessee directly or indirectly by reason of the lease contract.

§ 2A-505. Cancellation and Termination and Effect of Cancellation, Termination, Rescission, or Fraud on Rights and Remedies.

(1) On cancellation of the lease contract, all obligations that are still executory on both sides are discharged, but any right based on prior default or performance survives, and the cancelling party also retains any remedy for default of the whole lease contract or any unperformed balance.

(2) On termination of the lease contract, all obligations that are still executory on both sides are discharged, but any right based on prior default or performance survives.

(3) Unless the contrary intention clearly appears, expressions of "cancellation," "rescission," or the like of the lease contract may not be construed as a renunciation or discharge of any claim in damages for an antecedent default.

(4) Rights and remedies for material misrepresentation or fraud include all rights and remedies available under this Article for default.

(5) Neither rescission nor claim for rescission of the lease contract nor

rejection or return of the goods may bar or be deemed inconsistent with a claim for damages or other right or remedy.

§ 2A-506. Statute of Limitations.

(1) An action for default under a lease contract, including breach of warranty or indemnity, must be commenced within 4 years after the cause of action accrued. By the original lease contract the parties may reduce the period of limitation to not less than one year.

(2) A cause of action for default accrues when the act or omission on which the default or breach of warranty is based is or should have been discovered by the aggrieved party, or when the default occurs, whichever is later. A cause of action for indemnity accrues when the act or omission on which the claim for indemnity is based is or should have been discovered by the indemnified party, whichever is later.

(3) If an action commenced within the time limited by subsection (1) is so terminated as to leave available a remedy by another action for the same default or breach of warranty or indemnity, the other action may be commenced after the expiration of the time limited and within 6 months after the termination of the first action unless the termination resulted from voluntary discontinuance or from dismissal for failure or neglect to prosecute.

(4) This section does not alter the law on tolling of the statute of limitations nor does it apply to causes of action that have accrued before this Article becomes effective.

§ 2A-507. Proof of Market Rent: Time and Place.

(1) Damages based on market rent (Section 2A-519 or 2A-528) are determined according to the rent for the use of the goods concerned for a lease term identical to the remaining lease term of the original lease agreement and prevailing at the time of the default.

(2) If evidence of rent for the use of the goods concerned for a lease term identical to the remaining lease term of the original lease agreement and prevailing at the times or places described in this Article is not readily available, the rent prevailing within any reasonable time before or after the time described or at any other place or for a different lease term which in commercial judgment or under usage of trade would serve as a reasonable substitute for the one described may be used, making any proper allowance for the difference, including the cost of transporting the goods to or from the other place.

(3) Evidence of a relevant rent prevailing at a time or place or for a lease term other than the one described in this Article offered by one party is not admissible unless and until he [or she] has given the other party notice the court finds sufficient to prevent unfair surprise.

(4) If the prevailing rent or value of any goods regularly leased in any established market is in issue, reports in official publications or trade journals or in newspapers or periodicals of general circulation published as the reports of that market are admissible in evidence. The circumstances of the preparation of the report may be shown to affect its weight but not its admissibility.

B. Default by Lessor

§ 2A-508. Lessee's Remedies.

(1) If a lessor fails to deliver the goods in conformity to the lease contract (Section 2A-509) or repudiates the lease contract (Section 2A-402), or a lessee rightfully rejects the goods (Section 2A-509) or justifiably revokes acceptance of the goods (Section 2A-517), then with respect to any goods involved, and with respect to all of the goods if under an installment lease contract the value of the whole lease contract is substantially impaired (Section 2A-510), the lessor is in default under the lease contract and the lessee may:

(a) cancel the lease contract (Section 2A-505(1));

(b) recover so much of the rent and security as has been paid, but in the case of an installment lease contract the recovery is that which is just under the circumstances;

(c) cover and recover damages as to all goods affected whether or not they have been identified to the lease contract (Sections 2A-518 and 2A-520), or recover damages for nondelivery (Sections 2A-519 and 2A-520).

(2) If a lessor fails to deliver the goods in conformity to the lease contract or repudiates the lease contract, the lessee may also:

(a) if the goods have been identified, recover them (Section 2A-522); or

(b) in a proper case, obtain specific performances or replevy the goods (Section 2A-521).

(3) If a lessor is otherwise in default under a lease contract, the lessee may exercise the rights and remedies provided in the lease contract and this Article.

(4) If a lessor has breached a warranty, whether express or implied, the lessee may recover damages (Section 2A-519(4)).

(5) On rightful rejection or justifiable revocation of acceptance, a lessee has a security interest in goods in the lessee's possession or control for any rent and security that has been paid and any expenses reasonably incurred in their inspection, receipt, transportation, and care and custody and may hold those goods and dispose of them in good faith and in a commercially reasonable manner, subject to the provisions of Section 2A-527(5).

(6) Subject to the provisions of Section 2A-407, a lessee, on notifying the lessor of the lessee's intention to do so, may deduct all or any part of the damages resulting from any default under the lease contract from any part of the rent still due under the same lease contract.

§ 2A-509. Lessee's Rights on Improper Delivery; Rightful Rejection.

(1) Subject to the provisions of Section 2A-510 on default in installment lease contracts, if the goods or the tender or delivery fail in any respect to conform to the lease contract, the lessee may reject or accept the goods or accept any commercial unit or units and reject the rest of the goods.

(2) Rejection of goods is ineffective unless it is within a reasonable time after tender or delivery of the goods and the lessee seasonably notifies the lessor.

§ 2A-510. Installment Lease Contracts: Rejection and Default.

(1) Under an installment lease contract a lessee may reject any delivery that is nonconforming if the nonconformity substantially impairs the value of that delivery and cannot be cured or the nonconformity is a defect in the required documents; but if the nonconformity does not fall within subsection (2) and the lessor or the supplier gives adequate assurance of its cure, the lessee must accept that delivery.

(2) Whenever nonconformity or default with respect to one or more deliveries substantially impairs the value of the installment lease contract as a whole there is a default with respect to the whole. But, the aggrieved party reinstates the installment lease contract as a whole if the aggrieved party accepts a nonconforming delivery without seasonably notifying of cancellation or brings an action with respect only to past deliveries or demands performance as to future deliveries.

§ 2A-511. Merchant Lessee's Duties as to Rightfully Rejected Goods.

(1) Subject to any security interest or a lessee (Section 2A-508(5)), if a lessor or a supplier has no agent or place of business at the market of rejection, a merchant lessee, after rejection of goods in his [or her] possession or control, shall follow any reasonable instructions received from the lessor or the supplier with respect to the goods. In the

absence of those instructions, a merchant lessee shall make reasonable efforts to sell, lease, or otherwise dispose of the goods for the lessor's account if they threaten to decline in value speedily. Instructions are not reasonable if on demand indemnity for expenses is not forthcoming.

(2) If a merchant lessee (subsection (1)) or any other lessee (Section 2A-512) disposes of goods, he [or she] is entitled to reimbursement either from the lessor or the supplier or out of the proceeds for reasonable expenses of caring for and disposing of the goods and, if the expenses include no disposition commission, to such commission as is usual in the trade, or if there is none, to a reasonable sum not exceeding 10 percent of the gross proceeds.

(3) In complying with this section or Section 2A-512, the lessee is held only to good faith. Good faith conduct hereunder is neither acceptance or conversion nor the basis of an action for damages.

(4) A purchaser who purchases in good faith from a lessee pursuant to this section or Section 2A-512 takes the goods free of any rights of the lessor and the supplier even though the lessee fails to comply with one or more of the requirements of this Article.

§ 2A-512. Lessee's Duties as to Rightfully Rejected Goods.

(1) Except as otherwise provided with respect to goods that threaten to decline in value speedily (Section 2A-511) and subject to any security interest of a lessee (Section 2A-508(5)):

(a) the lessee, after rejection of goods in the lessee's possession, shall hold them with reasonable care at the lessor's or the supplier's disposition for a reasonable time after the lessee's seasonable notification of rejection;

(b) if the lessor or the supplier gives no instructions within a reasonable time after notification of rejection, the lessee may store the rejected goods for the lessor's or the supplier's account or ship them to the lessor or the supplier or dispose of them for the lessor's or the supplier's account with reimbursement in the manner provided in Section 2A-511; but

(c) the lessee has no further obligations with regard to goods rightfully rejected.

(2) Action by the lessee pursuant to subsection (1) is not acceptance or conversion.

§ 2A-513. Cure by Lessor of Improper Tender or Delivery; Replacement.

(1) If any tender or delivery by the lessor or the supplier is rejected because nonconforming and the time for performance has not yet expired, the lessor or the supplier may seasonably notify the lessee of the lessor's or the supplier's intention to cure and may then make a conforming delivery within the time provided in the lease contract.

(2) If the lessee rejects a nonconforming tender that the lessor or the supplier had reasonable grounds to believe would be acceptable with or without money allowance, the lessor or the supplier may have a further reasonable time to substitute a conforming tender if he [or she] seasonably notifies the lessee.

§ 2A-514. Waiver of Lessee's Objections.

(1) In rejecting goods, a lessee's failure to state a particular defect that is ascertainable by reasonable inspection precludes the lessee from relying on the defect to justify rejection or to establish default;

(a) if, stated seasonably, the lessor or the supplier could have cured it (Section 2A-513); or

(b) between merchants if the lessor or the supplier after rejection has made a request in writing for a full and final written statement of all defects on which the lessee proposes to rely.

(2) A lessee's failure to reserve rights when paying rent or other consideration against documents precludes recovery of the payment for defects apparent on the face of the documents.

§ 2A-515. Acceptance of Goods.

(1) Acceptance of goods occurs after the lessee has had a reasonable opportunity to inspect the goods and

(a) the lessee signifies or acts with respect to the goods in a manner that signifies to the lessor or the supplier that the goods are conforming or that the lessee will take or retain them in spite of their nonconformity; or

(b) the lessee fails to make an effective rejection of the goods (Section 2A-509(2)).

(2) Acceptance of a part of any commercial unit is acceptance of that entire unit.

§ 2A-516. Effect of Acceptance of Goods; Notice of Default; Burden of Establishing Default After Acceptance; Notice of Claim or Litigation to Person Answerable Over.

(1) A lessee must pay rent for any goods accepted in accordance with the lease contract, with due allowance for goods rightfully rejected or not delivered.

(2) A lessee's acceptance of goods precludes rejection of the goods accepted. In the case of a finance lease, if made with knowledge of a nonconformity, acceptance cannot be revoked because of it. In any other case, if made with knowledge of a nonconformity, acceptance cannot be revoked because of it unless the acceptance was on the reasonable assumption that the nonconformity would be seasonably cured. Acceptance does not of itself impair any other remedy provided by this Article or the lease agreement for nonconformity.

(3) If a tender has been accepted:

(a) within a reasonable time after the lessee discovers or should have discovered any default, the lessee shall notify the lessor and the supplier, or be barred from any remedy;

(b) except in the case of a consumer lease, within a reasonable time after the lessee receives notice of litigation for infringement or the like (Section 2A-211) the lessee shall notify the lessor or be barred from any remedy over for liability established by the litigation; and

(c) the burden is on the lessee to establish any default.

(4) If a lessee is sued for breach of a warranty or other obligation for which a lessor or a supplier is answerable over:

(a) The lessee may give the lessor or the supplier written notice of the litigation. If the notice states that the lessor or the supplier may come in and defend and that if the lessor or the supplier does not do so he [or she] will be bound in any action against him [or her] by the lessee by any determination of fact common to the two litigations, then unless the lessor or the supplier after seasonable receipt of the notice does come in and defend he [or she] is so bound.

(b) The lessor or the supplier may demand in writing that the lessee turn over control of the litigation including settlement if the claim is one for infringement or the like (Section 2A-211) or else be barred from any remedy over. If the demand states that the lessor or the supplier agrees to bear all expense and to satisfy any adverse judgment, then unless the lessee after seasonable receipt of the demand does turn over control the lessee is so barred.

(5) The provisions of subsections (3) and (4) apply to any obligation of a lessee to hold the lessor or the supplier harmless against infringement or the like (Section 2A-211).

§ 2A-517. Revocation of Acceptance of Goods.

(1) A lessee may revoke acceptance of a lot or commercial unit whose nonconformity substantially impairs its value to the lessee if he [or she] has accepted it:

(a) except in the case of a finance lease, on the reasonable assumption that its nonconformity would be cured and it has not been seasonably cured; or

(b) without discovery of the nonconformity if the lessee's acceptance was reasonably induced either by the lessor's assurances or, except in the case of a finance lease, by the difficulty of discovery before acceptance.

(2) Revocation of acceptance must occur within a reasonable time after the lessee discovers or should have discovered the ground for it and before any substantial change in condition of the goods which is not caused by the nonconformity. Revocation is not effective until the lessee notifies the lessor.

(3) A lessee who so revokes has the same rights and duties with regard to the goods involved as if the lessee had rejected them.

§ 2A-518. Cover; Substitute Goods.

(1) After default by a lessor under the lease contract (Section 2A-508(1)), the lessee may cover by making any purchase or lease of or contract to purchase or lease goods in substitution for those due from the lessor.

(2) Except as otherwise provided with respect to damages liquidated in the lease agreement (Section 2A-504) or determined by agreement of the parties (Section 1-102(3)), if a lessee's cover is by lease agreement substantially similar to the original lease agreement and the lease agreement is made in good faith and in a commercially reasonable manner, the lessee may recover from the lessor as damages (a) the present value, as of the date of default, of the difference between the total rent for the lease term of the new lease agreement and the total rent for the remaining lease term of the original lease agreement and (b) any incidental or consequential damages less expenses saved in consequence of the lessor's default.

(3) If a lessee's cover is by lease agreement that for any reason does not qualify for treatment under subsection (2), or is by purchase or otherwise, the lessee may recover from the lessor as if the lessee had elected not to cover and Section 2A-519 governs.

§ 2A-519. Lessee's Damages for Non-delivery, Repudiation, Default and Breach of Warranty in Regard to Accepted Goods.

(1) Except as otherwise provided with respect to damages liquidated in the lease agreement (Section 2A-504) or determined by agreement of the parties (Section 1-102(3)), if a lessee elects not to cover or a lessee elects to cover and the cover is by lease agreement that for any reason does not qualify for treatment under Section 2A-518(2), or is by purchase or otherwise, the measure of damages for non-delivery or repudiation by the lessor or for rejection or revocation of acceptance by the lessee is the present value as of the date of the default of the difference between the then market rent and the original rent, computed for the remaining lease term of the original lease agreement together with incidental and consequential damages, less expenses saved in consequence of the lessor's default.

(2) Market rent is to be determined as of the place for tender or, in cases of rejection after arrival or revocation of acceptance, as of the place of arrival.

(3) If the lessee has accepted goods and given notification (Section 2A-516(3)), the measure of damages for non-conforming tender or delivery by a lessor is the loss resulting in the ordinary course of events from the lessor's default as determined in any manner that is reasonable together with incidental and consequential damages, less expenses saved in consequence of the lessor's default.

(4) The measure of damages for breach of warranty is the present value at the time and place of acceptance of the difference between the value of the use of the goods accepted and the value if they had been as warranted for the lease term, unless special circumstances show proximate damages of a different amount, together with incidental and consequential damages, less expenses saved in consequence of the lessor's default or breach of warranty.

§ 2A-520. Lessee's Incidental and Consequential Damages.

(1) Incidental damages resulting from a lessor's default include expenses reasonably incurred in inspection, receipt, transportation, and care and custody of goods rightfully rejected or goods the acceptance of which is justifiably revoked, any commercially reasonable charges, expenses or commissions in connection with effecting cover, and any other reasonable expense incident to the default.

(2) Consequential damages resulting from a lessor's default include:

(a) any loss resulting from general or particular requirements and needs of which the lessor at the time of contracting had reason to know and which could not reasonably be prevented by cover or otherwise; and

(b) injury to person or property proximately resulting from any breach of warranty.

§ 2A-521. Lessee's Right to Specific Performance or Replevin.

(1) Specific performance may be decreed if the goods are unique or in other proper circumstances.

(2) A decree for specific performance may include any terms and conditions as to payment of the rent, damages, or other relief that the court deems just.

(3) A lessee has a right of replevin, detinue, sequestration, claim and delivery, or the like for goods identified to the lease contract if after reasonable effort the lessee is unable to effect cover for those goods or the circumstances reasonably indicate that the effort will be unavailing.

§ 2A-522. Lessee's Right to Goods on Lessor's Insolvency.

(1) Subject to subsection (2) and even though the goods have not been shipped, a lessee who has paid a part or all of the rent and security for goods identified to a lease contract (Section 2A-217) on making and keeping good a tender of any unpaid portion of the rent and security due under the lease contract may recover the goods identified from the lessor if the lessor becomes insolvent within 10 days after receipt of the first installment of rent and security.

(2) A lessee acquires the right to recover goods identified to a lease contract only if they conform to the lease contrast.

C. Default by Lessee

§ 2A-523. Lessor's Remedies.

(1) If a lessee wrongfully rejects or revokes acceptance of goods or fails to make a payment when due or repudiation with respect to a part or the whole, then, with respect to any goods involved, and with respect to all the goods if under an installment lease contract the value of the whole lease contract is substantially impaired (Section 2A-510), the lessee is in default under the lease contract and the lessor may:

(a) cancel the lease contract (Section 2A-505(1));

(b) proceed respecting goods not identified to the lease contract (Section 2A-524);

(c) withhold delivery of the goods and take possession of goods previously delivered (Section 2A-525);

(d) stop delivery of the goods by any bailee (Section 2A-526);

(e) dispose of the goods and recover damages (Section 2A-527), or retain the goods and recover damages (Section 2A-528), or in a proper case recover rent (Section 2A-529).

(2) If a lessee is otherwise in default under a lease contract, the lessor may exercise the rights and remedies provided in the lease contract and this Article.

§ 2A-524. Lessor's Right to Identify Goods to Lease Contract.

(1) A lessor aggrieved under Section 2A-523(1) may:

(a) identify to the lease contract conforming goods not already identified if at the time the lessor learned of the default they were in the lessor's or the supplier's possession or control; and

(b) dispose of goods (Section 2A-527(1)) that demonstrably have been intended for the particular lease contract even though those goods are unfinished.

(2) If the goods are unfinished, in the exercise of reasonable commercial judgment for the purposes of avoiding loss and of effective realization, an aggrieved lessor or the supplier may either complete manufacture and wholly identify the goods to the lease contract or cease manufacture and lease, sell, or otherwise dispose of the goods for scrap or salvage value or proceed in any other reasonable manner.

§ 2A-525. Lessor's Right to Possession of Goods.

(1) If a lessor discovers the lessee to be insolvent, the lessor may refuse to deliver the goods.

(2) The lessor has on default by the lessee under the lease contract the right to take possession of the goods. If the lease contract so provides, the lessor may require the lessee to assemble the goods and make them available to the lessor at a place to be designated by the lessor which is reasonably convenient to both parties. Without removal, the lessor may render unusable any goods employed in trade or business, and may dispose of goods on the lessee's premises (Section 2A-527).

(3) The lessor may proceed under subsection (2) without judicial process if that can be done without breach of the peace or the lessor may proceed by action.

§ 2A-526. Lessor's Stoppage of Delivery in Transit or Otherwise.

(1) A lessor may stop delivery of goods in the possession of a carrier in other bailee if the lessor discovers the lessee to be insolvent and may stop delivery of carload, truckload, planeload, or larger shipments of express or freight if the lessee repudiates or fails to make a payment due before delivery, whether for rent, security or otherwise under the lease contract, or for any other reason the lessor has a right to withhold or take possession of the goods.

(2) In pursuing its remedies under subdivision (1), the lessor may stop delivery until

(a) receipt of the goods by the lessee;

(b) acknowledgment to the lessee by any bailee of the goods, except a carrier, that the bailee holds the goods for the lessee; or

(c) such an acknowledgment to the lessee by a carrier via reshipment or as warehouseman.

(3)(a) To stop delivery, a lessor shall so notify as to enable the bailee by reasonable diligence to prevent delivery of the goods.

(b) After notification, the bailee shall hold and deliver the goods according to the directions of the lessor, but the lessor is liable to the bailee for any ensuing charges or damages.

(c) A carrier who has issued a nonnegotiable bill of lading is not obliged to obey a notification to stop received from a person other than the consignor.

§ 2A-527. Lessor's Rights to Dispose of Goods.

(1) After a default by a lessee under the lease contract (Section 2A-523(1)) or after the lessor refuses to deliver or takes possession of goods (Section 2A-525 or 2A-526), the lessor may dispose of the goods concerned or the undelivered balance thereof by lease, sale or otherwise.

(2) Except as otherwise provided with respect to damages liquidated in the lease agreement (Section 2A-504) or determined by agreement of the parties (Section 1-102(3)), if the disposition is by lease agreement substantially similar to the original lease agreement and the lease agreement is made in good faith and in a commercially reasonable manner, the lessor may recover from the lessee as damages (a) accrued and unpaid rent as of the date of default, (b) the present value as of the date of default of the difference between the total rent for the remaining lease term of the original lease agreement and the total rent for the lease term of the new lease agreement, and (c) any incidental damages allowed under Section 2A-530, less expenses saved in consequence of the lessee's default.

(3) If the lessor's disposition is by lease agreement that for any reason does not qualify for treatment under subsection (2), or is by sale or otherwise, the lessor may recover from the lessee as if the lessor had elected not to dispose of the goods and Section 2A-528 governs.

(4) A subsequent buyer or lessee who buys or leases from the lessor in good faith for value as a result of a disposition under this section takes the goods free of the original lease contract and any rights of the original lessee even though the lessor fails to comply with one or more of the requirements of this Article.

(5) The lessor is not accountable to the lessee for any profit made on any disposition. A lessee who has rightfully rejected or justifiably revoked acceptance shall account to the lessor for any excess over the amount of the lessee's security interest (Section 2A-508(5)).

§ 2A-528. Lessor's Damages for Non-acceptance or Repudiation.

(1) Except as otherwise provided with respect to damages liquidated in the lease agreement (Section 2A-504) or determined by agreement of the parties (Section 1-102(3)), if a lessor elects to retain the goods or a lessor elects to dispose of the goods and disposition is by lease agreement that for any reason does not qualify for treatment under Section 2A-527(2), or is by sale or otherwise, the lessor may recover from the lessee as damages for non-acceptance or repudiation by the lessee (a) accrued and unpaid rent as of the date of default, (b) the present value as of the date of default of the difference between the total rent for the remaining lease term of the original lease agreement and the market rent at the time and place for tender computed for the same lease term, and (c) any incidental damages allowed under Section 2A-530, less expenses saved in consequence of the lessee's default.

(2) If the measure of damages provided in subsection (1) is inadequate to put a lessor in as good a position as performance would have, the measure of damages if the profit, including reasonable overhead, the lessor would have made from full performance by the lessee, together with any incidental damages allowed under Section 2A-530, due allowance for costs reasonably incurred and due credit for payments or proceeds of disposition.

§ 2A-529. Lessor's Action for the Rent.

(1) After default by the lessee under the lease contract (Section 2A-523(1)), if the lessor complies with subsection (2), the lessor may recover from the lessee as damages:

(a) for goods accepted by the lessee and for conforming goods lost or damaged within a commercially reasonable time after risk of loss passes to the lessee (Section 2A-219), (i) accrued and unpaid rent as of the date of default, (ii) the present value as of the date of default of the rent for the remaining lease term of the lease agreement, and

(iii) any incidental damages allowed under Section 2A-530, less expenses saved in consequence of the lessee's default; and

(b) for goods identified to the lease contract if the lessor is unable after reasonable effort to dispose of them at a reasonable price or the circumstances reasonably indicate that effort will be unavailing, (i) accrued and unpaid rent as of the date of default, (ii) the present value as of the date of default of the rent for the remaining lease term of the lease agreement, and (iii) any incidental damages allowed under Section 2A-530, less expenses saved in consequence of the lessee's default.

(2) Except as provided in subsection (3), the lessor shall hold for the lessee for the remaining lease term of the lease agreement any goods that have been identified to the lease contract and are in the lessor's control.

(3) The lessor may dispose of the goods at any time before collection of the judgment for damages obtained pursuant to subsection (1). If the disposition is before the end of the remaining lease term of the lease agreement, the lessor's recovery against the lessee for damages will be governed by Section 2A-527 or Section 2A-528.

(4) Payment of the judgment for damages obtained pursuant to subsection (1) entitles the lessee to use and possession of the goods not then disposed of for the remaining lease term of the lease agreement.

(5) After a lessee has wrongfully rejected or revoked acceptance of goods, has failed to pay rent then due, or has repudiated (Section 2A-402), a lessor who is held not entitled to rent under this section must nevertheless be awarded damages for non-acceptance under Sections 2A-527 and 2A-528.

§ 2A-530. Lessor's Incidental Damages.

Incidental damages to an aggrieved lessor include any commercially reasonable charges, expenses, or commissions incurred in stopping delivery, in the transportation, care and custody of goods after the lessee's default, in connection with return or disposition of the goods, or otherwise resulting from the default.

§ 2A-531. Standing to Sue Third Parties for Injury to Goods.

(1) If a third party so deals with goods that have been identified to a lease contract as to cause actionable injury to a party to the lease contract (a) the lessor has a right of action against the third party, and (b) the lessee also has a right of action against the third party if the lessee:

(i) has a security interest in the goods;

(ii) has an insurable interest in the goods; or

(iii) bears the risk of loss under the lease contract or has since the injury assumed that risk as against the lessor and the goods have been converted or destroyed.

(2) If at the time of the injury the party plaintiff did not bear the risk of loss as against the other party to the lease contract and there is no arrangement between them for disposition of the recovery, his [or her] suit or settlement, subject to his [or her] own interest, is as a fiduciary for the other party to the lease contract.

(3) Either party with the consent of the other may sue for the benefit of whom it may concern.

ARTICLE 3. COMMERCIAL PAPER

Part 1. Short Title, Form and Interpretation

§ 3-101. Short Title.   This Article shall be known and may be cited as Uniform Commercial Code—Commercial Paper.

§ 3-102. Definitions and Index of Definitions.

(1) In this Article unless the context otherwise requires

(a) "Issue" means the first delivery of an instrument to a holder or a remitter.

(b) An "order" is a direction to pay and must be more than an authorization or request. It must identify the person to pay with reasonable certainty. It may be addressed to one or more such persons jointly or in the alternative but not in succession.

(c) A "promise" is an undertaking to pay and must be more than an acknowledgment of an obligation.

(d) "Secondary party" means a drawer or indorser.

(e) "Instrument" means a negotiable instrument.

(2) Other definitions applying to this Article and the sections in which they appear are:

"Acceptance". Section 3-410.

"Accommodation party". Section 3-415.

"Alteration". Section 3-407.

"Certificate of deposit". Section 3-104.

"Certification". Section 3-411.

"Check". Section 3-104.

"Definite time". Section 3-109.

"Dishonor". Section 3-507.

"Draft". Section 3-104.

"Holder in due course". Section 3-302.

"Negotiation". Section 3-202.

"Note". Section 3-104.

"Notice of dishonor". Section 3-508.

"On demand". Section 3-108.

"Presentment". Section 3-504.

"Protest". Section 3-509.

"Restrictive Indorsement". Section 3-205.

"Signature". Section 3-401.

(3) The following definitions in other Articles apply to this Article:

"Account". Section 4-104.

"Banking Day". Section 4-104.

"Clearing House". Section 4-104.

"Collecting Bank". Section 4-105.

"Customer". Section 4-104.

"Depository Bank". Section 4-105.

"Documentary Draft". Section 4-104.

"Intermediary Bank". Section 4-105.

"Item". Section 4-104.

"Midnight deadline". Section 4-104.

"Payor Bank". Section 4-105.

(4) In addition Article 1 contains general definitions and principles of construction and interpretation applicable throughout this Article.

§ 3-103. Limitations on Scope of Article.

(1) This Article does not apply to money, documents of title or investment securities.

(2) The provisions of this Article are subject to the provisions of the Article on Bank Deposits and Collections (Article 4) and Secured Transactions (Article 9).

§ 3-104. Form of Negotiable Instruments; "Draft"; "Check"; "Certificate of Deposit"; "Note."

(1) Any writing to be a negotiable instrument within this Article must

(a) be signed by the maker or drawer; and

(b) contain an unconditional promise or order to pay a sum certain in money and no other promise, order, obligation or power given by the maker or drawer except as authorized by this Article; and

(c) be payable on demand or at a definite time; and

(d) be payable to order or to bearer.

(2) A writing which complies with the requirements of this section is

(a) a "draft" ("bill of exchange") if it is an order;

(b) a "check" if it is a draft drawn on a bank and payable on demand;

(c) a "certificate of deposit" if it is an acknowledgment by a bank of receipt of money with an engagement to repay it;

(d) a "note" if it is a promise other than a certificate of deposit.

(3) As used in other Articles of this Act, and as the context may require, the terms "draft", "check", "certificate of deposit" and "note" may refer to instruments which are not negotiable within this Article as well as to instruments which are so negotiable.

§ 3-105. When Promise or Order Unconditional.

(1) A promise or order otherwise unconditional is not made conditional by the fact that the instrument

(a) is subject to implied or constructive conditions; or

(b) states its consideration, whether performed or promised, or the transaction which gave rise to the instrument, or that the promise or order is made or the instrument matures in accordance with or "as per" such transaction; or

(c) refers to or states that it arises out of a separate agreement or refers to a separate agreement for rights as to prepayment or acceleration; or

(d) states that it is drawn under a letter of credit; or

(e) states that it is secured, whether by mortgage, reservation of title or otherwise; or

(f) indicates a particular account to be debited or any other fund or source from which reimbursement is expected; or

(g) is limited to payment out of a particular fund or the proceeds of a particular source, if the instrument is issued by a government or governmental agency or unit; or

(h) is limited to payment out of the entire assets of a partnership, unincorporated association, trust or estate by or on behalf of which the instrument is issued.

(2) A promise or order is not unconditional if the instrument

(a) states that it is subject to or governed by any other agreement; or

(b) states that it is to be paid only out of a particular fund or source except as provided in this section.

§ 3-106. Sum Certain.

(1) The sum payable is a sum certain even though it is to be paid

(a) with stated interest or by stated installments; or

(b) with stated different rates of interest before and after default or a specified date; or

(c) with a stated discount or addition if paid before or after the date fixed for payment; or

(d) with exchange or less exchange, whether at a fixed rate or at the current rate; or

(e) with costs of collection or an attorney's fee or both upon default.

(2) Nothing in this section shall validate any term which is otherwise illegal.

§ 3-107. Money.

(1) An instrument is payable in money if the medium of exchange in which it is payable is money at the time the instrument is made. An instrument payable in "currency" or "current funds" is payable in money.

(2) A promise or order to pay a sum stated in a foreign currency is for a sum certain in money and, unless a different medium of payment is specified in the instrument, may be satisfied by payment of that number of dollars which the stated foreign currency will purchase at the buying sight rate for that currency on the day on which the instrument is payable or, if payable on demand, on the day of demand. If such an instrument specifies a foreign currency as the medium of payment the instrument is payable in that currency.

§ 3-108. Payable on Demand.

Instruments payable on demand include those payable at sight or on presentation and those in which no time for payment is stated.

§ 3-109. Definite Time.

(1) An instrument is payable at a definite time if by its terms it is payable

(a) on or before a stated date or at a fixed period after a stated date; or

(b) at a fixed period after sight; or

(c) at a definite time subject to any acceleration; or

(d) at a definite time subject to extension at the option of the holder, or to extension to a further definite time at the option of the maker or acceptor or automatically upon or after a specified act or event.

(2) An instrument which by its terms is otherwise payable only upon an act or event uncertain as to time of occurrence is not payable at a definite time even though the act or event has occurred.

§ 3-110. Payable to Order.

(1) An instrument is payable to order when by its terms it is payable to the order or assigns of any person therein specified with reasonable certainty, or to him or his order, or when it is conspicuously designated on its face as "exchange" or the like and names a payee. It may be payable to the order of

(a) the maker or drawer; or

(b) the drawee; or

(c) a payee who is not maker, drawer or drawee; or

(d) two or more payees together or in the alternative; or

(e) an estate, trust or fund, in which case it is payable to the order of the representative of such estate, trust or fund or his successors; or

(f) an office, or an officer by his title as such in which case it is payable to the principal but the incumbent of the office or his successors may act as if he or they were the holder; or

(g) a partnership or unincorporated association, in which case it is payable to the partnership or association and may be indorsed or transferred by any person thereto authorized.

(2) An instrument not payable to order is not made so payable by such words as "payable upon return of this instrument properly indorsed."

(3) An instrument made payable both to order and to bearer is payable to order unless the bearer words are handwritten or typewritten.

§ **3-111. Payable to Bearer.**   An instrument is payable to bearer when by its terms it is payable to

(a) bearer or the order of bearer; or

(b) a specified person or bearer; or

(c) "cash" or the order of "cash", or any other indication which does not purport to designate a specific payee.

§ **3-112. Terms and Omissions Not Affecting Negotiability.**

(1) The negotiability of an instrument is not affected by

(a) the omission of a statement of any consideration or of the place where the instrument is drawn or payable; or

(b) a statement that collateral has been given to secure obligations either on the instrument or otherwise of an obligor on the instrument or that in case of default on those obligations the holder may realize on or dispose of the collateral; or

(c) a promise or power to maintain or protect collateral or to give additional collateral; or

(d) a term authorizing a confession of judgment on the instrument if it is not paid when due; or

(e) a term purporting to waive the benefit of any law intended for the advantage or protection of any obligor; or

(f) a term in a draft providing that the payee by indorsing or cashing it acknowledges full satisfaction of an obligation of the drawer; or

(g) a statement in a draft drawn in a set of parts (Section 3-801) to the effect that the order is effective only if no other part has been honored.

(2) Nothing in this section shall validate any term which is otherwise illegal.

§ **3-113. Seal.**   An instrument otherwise negotiable is within this Article even though it is under a seal.

§ **3-114. Date, Antedating, Postdating.**

(1) The negotiability of an instrument is not affected by the fact that it is undated, antedated or postdated.

(2) Where an instrument is antedated or postdated the time when it is payable is determined by the stated date if the instrument is payable on demand or at a fixed period after date.

(3) Where the instrument or any signature thereon is dated, the date is presumed to be correct.

§ **3-115. Incomplete Instruments.**

(1) When a paper whose contents at the time of signing show that it is intended to become an instrument is signed while still incomplete in any necessary respect it cannot be enforced until completed, but when it is completed in accordance with authority given it is effective as completed.

(2) If the completion is unauthorized the rules as to material alteration apply (Section 3-407), even though the paper was not delivered by the maker or drawer; but the burden of establishing that any completion is unauthorized is on the party so asserting.

§ **3-116. Instruments Payable to Two or More Persons.**

An instrument payable to the order of two or more persons

(a) if in the alternative is payable to any one of them and may be negotiated, discharged or enforced by any of them who has possession of it;

(b) if not in the alternative is payable to all of them and may be negotiated, discharged or enforced only by all of them.

§ **3-117. Instruments Payable With Words of Description.**   An instrument made payable to a named person with the addition of words describing him

(a) as agent or officer of a specified person is payable to his principal but the agent or officer may act as if he were the holder;

(b) as any other fiduciary for a specified person or purpose is payable to the payee and may be negotiated, discharged or enforced by him;

(c) in any other manner is payable to the payee unconditionally and the additional words are without effect on subsequent parties.

§ **3-118. Ambiguous Terms and Rules of Construction.**

The following rules apply to every instrument:

(a) Where there is doubt whether the instrument is a draft or a note the holder may treat it as either. A draft drawn on the drawer is effective as a note.

(b) Handwritten terms control typewritten and printed terms, and typewritten control printed.

(c) Words control figures except that if the words are ambiguous figures control.

(d) Unless otherwise specified a provision for interest means interest at the judgment rate at the place of payment from the date of the instrument, or if it is undated from the date of issue.

(e) Unless the instrument otherwise specifies two or more persons who sign as maker, acceptor or drawer or indorser and as a part of the same transaction are jointly and severally liable even though the instrument contains such words as "I promise to pay."

(f) Unless otherwise specified consent to extension authorizes a single extension for not longer than the original period. A consent to extension, expressed in the instrument, is binding on secondary parties and accommodation makers. A holder may not exercise his option to extend an instrument over the objection of a maker or acceptor or other party who in accordance with Section 3-604 tenders full payment when the instrument is due.

§ **3-119. Other Writings Affecting Instrument.**

(1) As between the obligor and his immediate obligee or any transferee the terms of an instrument may be modified or affected by any other written agreement executed as a part of the same transaction, except that a holder in due course is not affected by any limitation of his rights arising out of the separate written agreement if he had no notice of the limitation when he took the instrument.

(2) A separate agreement does not affect the negotiability of an instrument.

§ **3-120. Instruments "Payable Through" Bank.**   An instrument which states that it is "payable through" a bank or the like designates that bank as a collecting bank to make presentment but does not of itself authorize the bank to pay the instrument.

§ **3-121. Instruments Payable at Bank.**

Note: *If this Act is introduced in the Congress of the United States this section should be omitted. (States to select either alternative)*

Alternative A   A note or acceptance which states that it is payable at a bank is the equivalent of a draft drawn on the bank payable when it falls due out of any funds of the maker or acceptor in current account or otherwise available for such payment.

Alternative B   A note or acceptance which states that it is payable at a bank is not of itself an order or authorization to the bank to pay it.

§ 3-122. Accrual of Cause of Action.

(1) A cause of action against a maker or an acceptor accrues

(a) in the case of time instrument on the day after maturity;

(b) in the case of a demand instrument upon its date or, if no date is stated, on the date of issue.

(2) A cause of action against the obligor of a demand or time certificate of deposit accrues upon demand, but demand on a time certificate may not be made until on or after the date of maturity.

(3) A cause of action against a drawer of a draft or an indorser of any instrument accrues upon demand following dishonor of the instrument. Notice of dishonor is a demand.

(4) Unless an instrument provides otherwise, interest runs at the rate provided by law for a judgment

(a) in the case of a maker, acceptor or other primary obligor of a demand instrument, from the date of demand;

(b) in all other cases from the date of accrual of the cause of action.

Part 2. Transfer and Negotiation

§ 3-201. Transfer: Right to Indorsement.

(1) Transfer of an instrument vests in the transferee such rights as the transferor has therein, except that a transferee who has himself been a party to any fraud or illegality affecting the instrument or who as a prior holder had notice of a defense or claim against it cannot improve his position by taking from a later holder in due course.

(2) A transfer of a security interest in an instrument vests the foregoing rights in the transferee to the extent of the interest transferred.

(3) Unless otherwise agreed any transfer for value of an instrument not then payable to bearer gives the transferee the specifically enforceable right to have the unqualified indorsement of the transferor. Negotiation takes effect only when the indorsement is made and until that time there is no presumption that the transferee is the owner.

§ 3-202. Negotiation.

(1) Negotiation is the transfer of an instrument in such form that the transferee becomes a holder. If the instrument is payable to order it is negotiated by delivery with any necessary indorsement; if payable to bearer it is negotiated by delivery.

(2) An indorsement must be written by or on behalf of the holder and on the instrument or on a paper so firmly affixed thereto as to become a part thereof.

(3) An indorsement is effective for negotiation only when it conveys the entire instrument or any unpaid residue. If it purports to be of less it operates only as a partial assignment.

(4) Words of assignment, condition, waiver, guaranty, limitation or disclaimer of liability and the like accompanying an indorsement do not affect its character as an indorsement.

§ 3-203. Wrong or Misspelled Name.

Where an instrument is made payable to a person under a misspelled name or one other than his own he may indorse in that name or his own or both; but signature in both names may be required by a person paying or giving value for the instrument.

§ 3-204. Special Indorsement; Blank Indorsement.

(1) A special indorsement specifies the person to whom or to whose order it makes the instrument payable. Any instrument specially indorsed becomes payable to the order of the special indorsee and may be further negotiated only by his indorsement.

(2) An indorsement in blank specifies no particular indorsee and may consist of a mere signature. An instrument payable to order and indorsed in blank becomes payable to bearer and may be negotiated by delivery alone until specially indorsed.

(3) The holder may convert a blank indorsement into a special indorsement by writing over the signature of the indorser in blank any contract consistent with the character of the indorsement.

§ 3-205. Restrictive Indorsements.

An indorsement is restrictive which either

(a) is conditional; or

(b) purports to prohibit further transfer of the instrument; or

(c) includes the words "for collection," "for deposit," "pay any bank," or like terms signifying a purpose of deposit or collection; or

(d) otherwise states that it is for the benefit or use of the indorser or of another person.

§ 3-206. Effect of Restrictive Indorsement.

(1) No restrictive indorsement prevents further transfer or negotiation of the instrument.

(2) An intermediary bank, or a payor bank which is not the depositary bank, is neither given notice nor otherwise affected by a restrictive indorsement of any person except the bank's immediate transferor or the person presenting for payment.

(3) Except for an intermediary bank, any transferee under an indorsement which is conditional or includes the words "for collection," "for deposit," "pay any bank," or like terms (sub-paragraphs (a) and (c) of Section 3-205) must pay or apply any value given by him for or on the security of the instrument consistently with the indorsement and to the extent that he does so he becomes a holder for value. In addition such transferee is a holder in due course if he otherwise complies with the requirements of Section 3-302 on what constitutes a holder in due course.

(4) The first taker under an indorsement for the benefit of the indorser or another person (subparagraph (d) of Section 3-205) must pay or apply any value given by him for or on the security of the instrument consistently with the indorsement and to the extent that he does so he becomes a holder for value. In addition such taker is a holder in due course if he otherwise complies with the requirements of Section 3-302 on what constitutes a holder in due course. A later holder for value is neither given notice nor otherwise affected by such restrictive indorsement unless he has knowledge that a fiduciary or other person has negotiated the instrument in any transaction for his own benefit or otherwise in breach of duty (subsection (2) of Section 3-304).

§ 3-207. Negotiation Effective Although It May Be Rescinded.

(1) Negotiation is effective to transfer the instrument although the negotiation is

(a) made by an infant, a corporation exceeding its powers, or any other person without capacity; or

(b) obtained by fraud, duress or mistake of any kind; or

(c) part of an illegal transaction; or

(d) made in breach of duty.

(2) Except as against a subsequent holder in due course such negotiation is in an appropriate case subject to rescission, the declaration of a constructive trust or any other remedy permitted by law.

§ 3-208. Reacquisition.

Where an instrument is returned to or reacquired by a prior party he may cancel any indorsement which is not necessary to his title and reissue or further negotiate the instrument, but any intervening party is discharged as against the reacquiring party and subsequent holders not in due course and if his indorsement has been cancelled is discharged as against subsequent holders in due course as well.

Part 3. Rights of a Holder

§ 3-301. Rights of a Holder. The holder of an instrument whether or not he is the owner may transfer or negotiate it and, except as otherwise provided in Section 3-603 on payment or satisfaction, discharge it or enforce payment in his own name.

§ 3-302. Holder in Due Course.

(1) A holder in due course is a holder who takes the instrument

    (a) for value; and

    (b) in good faith; and

    (c) without notice that it is overdue or has been dishonored or of any defense against or claim to it on the part of any person.

(2) A payee may be a holder in due course.

(3) A holder does not become a holder in due course of an instrument:

    (a) by purchase of it at judicial sale or by taking it under legal process; or

    (b) by acquiring it in taking over an estate; or

    (c) by purchasing it as part of a bulk transaction not in regular course of business of the transferor.

(4) A purchase of a limited interest can be a holder in due course only to the extent of the interest purchased.

§ 3-303. Taking for Value. A holder takes the instrument for value

    (a) to the extent that the agreed consideration has been performed or that he acquires a security interest in or a lien on the instrument otherwise than by legal process; or

    (b) when he takes the instrument in payment of or as security for an antecedent claim against any person whether or not the claim is due; or

    (c) when he gives a negotiable instrument for it or makes an irrevocable commitment to a third person.

§ 3-304. Notice to Purchaser.

(1) The purchaser has notice of a claim or defense if

    (a) the instrument is so incomplete, bears such visible evidence of forgery or alteration, or is otherwise so irregular as to call into question its validity, terms or ownership or to create an ambiguity as to the party to pay; or

    (b) the purchaser has notice that the obligation of any party is voidable in whole or in part, or that all parties have been discharged.

(2) The purchaser has notice of a claim against the instrument when he has knowledge that a fiduciary has negotiated the instrument in payment of or as security for his own debt or in any transaction for his own benefit or otherwise in breach of duty.

(3) The purchaser has notice that an instrument is overdue if he has reason to know

    (a) that any part of the principal amount is overdue or that there is an uncured default in payment of another instrument of the same series; or

    (b) that acceleration of the instrument has been made; or

    (c) that he is taking a demand instrument after demand has been made or more than a reasonable length of time after its issue. A reasonable time for a check drawn and payable within the states and territories of the United States and the District of Columbia is presumed to be thirty days.

(4) Knowledge of the following facts does not of itself give the purchaser notice of a defense or claim

    (a) that the instrument is antedated or postdated;

    (b) that it was issued or negotiated in return for an executory promise or accompanied by a separate agreement, unless the purchaser has notice that a defense or claim has arisen from the terms thereof;

    (c) that any party has signed for accommodation;

    (d) that an incomplete instrument has been completed, unless the purchaser has notice of any improper completion.

    (e) that any person negotiating the instrument is or was a fiduciary;

    (f) that there has been default in payment of interest on the instrument or in payment of any other instrument, except one of the same series.

(5) The filing or recording of a document does not of itself constitute notice within the provisions of this Article to a person who would otherwise be a holder in due course.

(6) To be effective notice must be received at such time and in such manner as to give a reasonable opportunity to act on it.

§ 3-305. Rights of a Holder in Due Course. To the extent that a holder is a holder in due course he takes the instrument free from

(1) all claims to it on the part of any person; and

(2) all defenses of any party to the instrument with whom the holder has not dealt except

    (a) infancy, to the extent that it is a defense to a simple contract; and

    (b) such other incapacity, or duress, or illegality of the transaction, as renders the obligation of the party a nullity; and

    (c) such misrepresentation as has induced the party to sign the instrument with neither knowledge nor reasonable opportunity to obtain knowledge of its character or its essential terms; and

    (d) discharge in insolvency proceedings; and

    (e) any other discharge of which the holder has notice when he takes the instrument.

§ 3-306. Rights of One Not Holder in Due Course. Unless he has the rights of a holder in due course any person takes the instrument subject to

    (a) all valid claims to it on the part of any person; and

    (b) all defenses of any party which would be available in an action on a simple contract; and

    (c) the defenses of want or failure of consideration, non-performance of any condition precedent, nondelivery, or delivery for a special purpose (Section 3-408); and

    (d) the defense that he or a person through whom he holds the instrument acquired it by theft, or that payment or satisfaction to such holder would be inconsistent with the terms of a restrictive indorsement. The claim of any third person to the instrument is not otherwise available as a defense to any party liable thereon unless the third person himself defends the action for such party.

§ 3-307. Burden of Establishing Signatures, Defenses and Due Course.

(1) Unless specifically denied in the pleadings each signature on an instrument is admitted. When the effectiveness of a signature is put in issue

    (a) the burden of establishing it is on the party claiming under the signature; but

    (b) the signature is presumed to be genuine or authorized except where the action is to enforce the obligation of a purported signer who has died or become incompetent before proof is required.

(2) When signatures are admitted or established, production of the instrument entitles a holder to recover on it unless the defendant establishes a defense.

(3) After it is shown that a defense exists a person claiming the rights of a holder in due course has the burden of establishing that he or some person under whom he claims is in all respects a holder in due course.

Part 4. Liability of Parties

§ 3-401. Signature.

(1) No person is liable on an instrument unless his signature appears thereon.

(2) A signature is made by use of any name, including any trade or assumed name, upon an instrument, or by any word or mark used in lieu of a written signature.

§ 3-402. Signature in Ambiguous Capacity. Unless the instrument clearly indicates that a signature is made in some other capacity it is an indorsement.

§ 3-403. Signature by Authorized Representative.

(1) A signature may be made by an agent or other representative, and his authority to make it may be established as in other cases of representation. No particular form of appointment is necessary to establish such authority.

(2) An authorized representative who signs his own name to an instrument

(a) is personally obligated if the instrument neither names the person represented nor shows that the representative signed in a representative capacity;

(b) except as otherwise established between the immediate parties, is personally obligated if the instrument names the person represented but does not show that the representative signed in a representative capacity, or if the instrument does not name the person represented but does show that the representative signed in a representative capacity.

(3) Except as otherwise established the name of an organization preceded or followed by the name and office of an authorized individual is a signature made in a representative capacity.

§ 3-404. Unauthorized Signatures.

(1) Any unauthorized signature is wholly inoperative as that of the person whose name is signed unless he ratifies it or is precluded from denying it; but it operates as the signature of the unauthorized signer in favor of any person who in good faith pays the instrument or takes it for value.

(2) Any unauthorized signature may be ratified for all purposes of this Article. Such ratification does not of itself affect any rights of the person ratifying against the actual signer.

§ 3-405. Imposters; Signature in Name of Payee.

(1) An indorsement by any person in the name of a named payee is effective if

(a) an imposter by use of the mails or otherwise has induced the maker or drawer to issue the instrument to him or his confederate in the name of the payee; or

(b) the person signing as or on behalf of a maker or drawer intends the payee to have no interest in the instrument; or

(c) an agent or employee of the maker or drawer has supplied him with the name of the payee intending the latter to have no such interest.

(2) Nothing in this section shall affect the criminal or civil liability of the person so indorsing.

§ 3-406. Negligence Contributing to Alteration or Unauthorized Signature. Any person who by his negligence substantially contributes to a material alteration of the instrument or to the making of an unauthorized signature is precluded from asserting the alteration or lack of authority against a holder in due course or against a drawee or other payor who pays the instrument in good faith and in accordance with the reasonable commercial standards of the drawee's or payor's business.

§ 3-407. Alteration.

(1) Any alteration of an instrument is material which changes the contract of any party thereto in any respect, including any such change in

(a) the number or relations of the parties; or

(b) an incomplete instrument, by completing it otherwise than as authorized; or

(c) the writing as signed, by adding to it or by removing any part of it.

(2) As against any person other than a subsequent holder in due course

(a) alteration by the holder which is both fraudulent and material discharges any party whose contract is thereby changed unless that party assents or is precluded from asserting the defense;

(b) no other alteration discharges any party and the instrument may be enforced according to its original tenor, or as to incomplete instruments according to the authority given.

(3) A subsequent holder in due course may in all cases enforce the instrument according to its original tenor, and when an incomplete instrument has been completed, he may enforce it as completed.

§ 3-408. Consideration. Want or failure of consideration is a defense as against any person not having the rights of a holder in due course (Section 3-305), except that no consideration is necessary for an instrument or obligation thereon given in payment of or as security for an antecedent obligation of any kind. Nothing in this section shall be taken to displace any statute outside this Act under which a promise is enforceable notwithstanding lack or failure of consideration. Partial failure of consideration is a defense pro tanto whether or not the failure is in an ascertained or liquidated amount.

§ 3-409. Draft Not an Assignment.

(1) A check or other draft does not of itself operate as an assignment of any funds in the hands of the drawee available for its payment, and the drawee is not liable on the instrument until he accepts it.

(2) Nothing in this section shall affect any liability in contract, tort, or otherwise arising from any letter of credit or other obligation or representation which is not an acceptance.

§ 3-410. Definition and Operation of Acceptance.

(1) Acceptance is the drawee's signed engagement to honor the draft as presented. It must be written on the draft, and may consist of his signature alone. It becomes operative when completed by delivery or notification.

(2) A draft may be accepted although it has not been signed by the drawer or is otherwise incomplete or is overdue or has been dishonored.

(3) Where the draft is payable at a fixed period after sight and the acceptor fails to date his acceptance the holder may complete it by supplying a date in good faith.

§ 3-411. Certification of a Check.

(1) Certification of a check is acceptance. Where a holder procures certification the drawer and all prior indorsers are discharged.

(2) Unless otherwise agreed a bank has no obligation to certify a check.

(3) A bank may certify a check before returning it for lack of proper indorsement. If it does so the drawer is discharged.

§ 3-412. Acceptance Varying Draft.

(1) Where the drawee's proffered acceptance in any manner varies the draft as presented the holder may refuse the acceptance and treat the draft as dishonored in which case the drawee is entitled to have his acceptance cancelled.

(2) The terms of the draft are not varied by an acceptance to pay at any particular bank or place in the United States, unless the acceptance states that the draft is to be paid only at such bank or place.

(3) Where the older assents to an acceptance varying the terms of the draft each drawer and indorser who does not affirmatively assent is discharged.

§ 3-413. Contract of Maker, Drawer and Acceptor.

(1) The maker or acceptor engages that he will pay the instrument according to its tenor at the time of his engagement or as completed pursuant to Section 3-115 on incomplete instruments.

(2) The drawer engages that upon dishonor of the draft and any necessary notice of dishonor or protest he will pay the amount of the draft to the holder or to any indorser who takes it up. The drawer may disclaim this liability by drawing without recourse.

(3) By making, drawing or accepting the party admits as against all subsequent parties including the drawee the existence of the payee and his then capacity to indorse.

§ 3-414. Contract of Indorser; Order of Liability.

(1) Unless the indorsement otherwise specifies (as by such words as "without recourse") every indorser engages that upon dishonor and any necessary notice of dishonor and protest he will pay the instrument according to its tenor at the time of his indorsement to the holder or to any subsequent indorser who takes it up, even though the indorser who takes it up was not obligated to do so.

(2) Unless they otherwise agree indorsers are liable to one another in the order in which they indorse, which is presumed to be the order in which their signatures appear on the instrument.

§ 3-415. Contract of Accommodation Party.

(1) An accommodation party is one who signs the instrument in any capacity for the purpose of lending his name to another party to it.

(2) When the instrument has been taken for value before it is due the accommodation party is liable in the capacity in which he has signed even though the taker knows of the accommodation.

(3) As against a holder in due course and without notice of the accommodation oral proof of the accommodation is not admissible to give the accommodation party the benefit of discharges dependent on his character as such. In other cases the accommodation character may be shown by oral proof.

(4) An indorsement which shows that it is not in the chain of title is notice of its accommodation character.

(5) An accommodation party is not liable to the party accommodated, and if he pays the instrument has a right of recourse on the instrument against such party.

§ 3-416. Contract of Guarantor.

(1) "Payment guaranteed" or equivalent words added to a signatu mean that the signer engages that if the instrument is not paid whe due he will pay it according to its tenor without resort by the hold to any other party.

(2) "Collection guaranteed" or equivalent words added to a signatu mean that the signer engages that if the instrument is not paid whe due he will pay it according to its tenor, but only after the holder h reduced his claim against the maker or acceptor to judgment an execution has been returned insolvent or it is otherwise apparent th it is useless to proceed against him.

(3) Words of guaranty which do not otherwise specify guarant payment.

(4) No words of guaranty added to the signature of a sole maker o acceptor affect his liability on the instrument. Such words added the signature of one of two or more makers or acceptors create presumption that the signature is for the accommodation of the others

(5) When words of guaranty are used presentment, notice of dishon and protest are not necessary to charge the user.

(6) Any guaranty written on the instrument is enforceable notwith standing any statute of frauds.

§ 3-417. Warranties on Presentment and Transfer.

(1) Any person who obtains payment or acceptance and any pric transferor warrants to a person who in good faith pays or accepts tha

(a) he has a good title to the instrument or is authorized to obtai payment or acceptance on behalf of one who has a good title; and

(b) he has no knowledge that the signature of the maker or drawe is unauthorized, except that this warranty is not given by a holde in due course acting in good faith

(i) to a maker with respect to the maker's own signature; or

(ii) to a drawer with respect to the drawer's own signature whether or not the drawer is also the drawee; or

(iii) to an acceptor of a draft if the holder in due course took th draft after the acceptance or obtained the acceptance withou knowledge that the drawer's signature was unauthorized; and

(c) the instrument has not been materially altered, except that th warranty is not given by a holder in due course acting in good fait

(i) to the maker of a note; or

(ii) to the drawer of a draft whether or not the drawer is also th drawee; or

(iii) to the acceptor of a draft with respect to an alteration mad prior to the acceptance if the holder in due course took the dra after the acceptance, even though the acceptance provided "pay able as originally drawn" or equivalent terms; or

(iv) to the acceptor of a draft with respect to an alteration mad after the acceptance.

(2) Any person who transfers an instrument and receives consideratio warrants to his transferee and if the transfer is by indorsement to an subsequent holder who takes the instrument in good faith that

(a) he has a good title to the instrument or is authorized to obtai payment or acceptance on behalf of one who has a good title an the transfer is otherwise rightful; and

(b) all signatures are genuine or authorized; and

(c) the instrument has not been materially altered; and

(d) no defense of any party is good against him; and

(e) he has no knowledge of any insolvency proceeding institute with respect to the maker or acceptor or the drawer of an unaccepte instrument.

(3) By transferring "without recourse" the transferor limits the obligation stated in subsection (2)(d) to a warranty that he has no knowledge of such a defense.

(4) A selling agent or broker who does not disclose the fact that he is acting only as such gives the warranties provided in this section, but if he makes such disclosure warrants only his good faith and authority.

3-418. Finality of Payment or Acceptance. Except for recovery of bank payments as provided in the Article on Bank Deposits and Collections (Article 4) and except for liability for breach of warranty on presentment under the preceding section, payment or acceptance of any instrument is final in favor of a holder in due course, or a person who has in good faith changed his position in reliance on the payment.

3-419. Conversion of Instrument; Innocent Representative.

(1) An instrument is converted when

(a) a drawee to whom it is delivered for acceptance refuses to return it on demand; or

(b) any person to whom it is delivered for payment refuses on demand either to pay or to return it; or

(c) it is paid on a forged indorsement.

(2) In an action against a drawee under subsection (1) the measure of the drawee's liability is the face amount of the instrument. In any other action under subsection (1) the measure of liability is presumed to be the face amount of the instrument.

(3) Subject to the provisions of this Act concerning restrictive indorsements a representative, including a depositary or collecting bank, who has in good faith and in accordance with the reasonable commercial standards applicable to the business of such representative dealt with an instrument or its proceeds on behalf of one who was not the true owner is not liable in conversion or otherwise to the true owner beyond the amount of any proceeds remaining in his hands.

(4) An intermediary bank or payor bank which is not a depositary bank is not liable in conversion solely by reason of the fact that proceeds of an item indorsed restrictively (Sections 3-205 and 3-206) are not paid or applied consistently with the restrictive indorsement of an indorser other than its immediate transferor.

Part 5. Presentment, Notice of Dishonor and Protest

§ 3-501. When Presentment, Notice of Dishonor, and Protest Necessary or Permissible.

(1) Unless excused (Section 3-511) presentment is necessary to charge secondary parties as follows:

(a) presentment for acceptance is necessary to charge the drawer and indorsers of a draft where the draft so provides, or is payable elsewhere than at the residence or place of business of the drawee, or its date of payment depends upon such presentment. The holder may at his option present for acceptance any other draft payable at a stated date;

(b) presentment for payment is necessary to charge any indorser;

(c) in the case of any drawer, the acceptor of a draft payable at a bank or the maker of a note payable at a bank, presentment for payment is necessary, but failure to make presentment discharges such drawer, acceptor or maker only as stated in Section 3-502(1)(b).

(2) Unless excused (Section 3-511)

(a) notice of any dishonor is necessary to charge any indorser;

(b) in the case of any drawer, the acceptor of a draft payable at a bank or the maker of a note payable at a bank, notice of any dishonor is necessary, but failure to give such notice discharges such drawer, acceptor or maker only as stated in Section 3-502(1)(b)

(3) Unless excused (Section 3-511) protest of any dishonor is necessary to charge the drawer and indorsers of any draft which on its face appears to be drawn or payable outside of the states, territories, dependencies and possessions of the United States, the District of Columbia and the Commonwealth of Puerto Rico. The holder may at his option make protest of any dishonor of any other instrument and in the case of a foreign draft may on insolvency of the acceptor before maturity make protest for better security.

(4) Notwithstanding any provision of this section, neither presentment nor notice of dishonor nor protest is necessary to charge an indorser who has indorsed an instrument after maturity.

§ 3-502. Unexcused Delay; Discharge.

(1) Where without excuse any necessary presentment or notice of dishonor is delayed beyond the time when it is due

(a) any indorser is discharged; and

(b) any drawer or the acceptor of a draft payable at a bank or the maker of a note payable at a bank who because the drawee or payor bank becomes insolvent during the delay is deprived of funds maintained with the drawee or payor bank to cover the instrument may discharge his liability by written assignment to the holder of his rights against the drawee or payor bank in respect of such funds, but such drawer, acceptor or maker is not otherwise discharged.

(2) Where without excuse a necessary protest is delayed beyond the time when it is due any drawer or indorser is discharged.

§ 3-503. Time of Presentment.

(1) Unless a different time is expressed in the instrument the time for any presentment is determined as follows:

(a) where an instrument is payable at or a fixed period after a stated date any presentment for acceptance must be made on or before the date it is payable;

(b) where an instrument is payable after sight it must either be presented for acceptance or negotiated within a reasonable time after date or issue whichever is later;

(c) where an instrument shows the date on which it is payable presentment for payment is due on that date;

(d) where an instrument is accelerated presentment for payment is due within a reasonable time after the acceleration;

(e) with respect to the liability of any secondary party presentment for acceptance or payment of any other instrument is due within a reasonable time after such party becomes liable thereon.

(2) A reasonable time for presentment is determined by the nature of the instrument, any usage of banking or trade and the facts of the particular case. In the case of an uncertified check which is drawn and payable within the United States and which is not a draft drawn by a bank the following are presumed to be reasonable periods within which to present for payment or to initiate bank collection:

(a) with respect to the liability of the drawer, thirty days after date or issue whichever is later; and

(b) with respect to the liability of an indorser, seven days after his indorsement.

(3) Where any presentment is due on a day which is not a full business day for either the person making presentment or the party to pay or accept, presentment is due on the next following day which is a full business day for both parties.

(4) Presentment to be sufficient must be made at a reasonable hour, and if at a bank during its banking day.

§ 3-504. How Presentment Made.

(1) Presentment is a demand for acceptance or payment made upon the maker, acceptor, drawee or other payor by or on behalf of the holder.

(2) Presentment may be made

(a) by mail, in which event the time of presentment is determined by the time of receipt of the mail; or

(b) through a clearing house; or

(c) at the place of acceptance or payment specified in the instrument or if there be none at the place of business or residence of the party to accept or pay. If neither the party to accept or pay nor anyone authorized to act for him is present or accessible at such place presentment is excused.

(3) It may be made

(a) to any of two or more makers, acceptors, drawees or other payors; or

(b) to any person who has authority to make or refuse the acceptance or payment.

(4) A draft accepted or a note made payable at a bank in the United States must be presented at such bank.

(5) In the cases described in Section 4-210 presentment may be made in the manner and with the result stated in that section.

§ 3-505. Rights of Party to Whom Presentment Is Made.

(1) The party to whom presentment is made may without dishonor require

(a) exhibition of the instrument; and

(b) reasonable identification of the person making presentment and evidence of his authority to make it if made for another; and

(c) that the instrument be produced for acceptance or payment at a place specified in it, or if there be none at any place reasonable in the circumstances; and

(d) a signed receipt on the instrument for any partial or full payment and its surrender upon full payment.

(2) Failure to comply with any such requirement invalidates the presentment but the person presenting has a reasonable time in which to comply and the time for acceptance or payment runs from the time of compliance.

§ 3-506. Time Allowed for Acceptance or Payment.

(1) Acceptance may be deferred without dishonor until the close of the next business day following presentment. The holder may also in a good faith effort to obtain acceptance and without either dishonor of the instrument or discharge of secondary parties allow postponement of acceptance for an additional business day.

(2) Except as a longer time is allowed in the case of documentary drafts drawn under a letter of credit, and unless an earlier time is agreed to by the party to pay, payment of an instrument may be deferred without dishonor pending reasonable examination to determine whether it is properly payable, but payment must be made in any event before the close of business on the day of presentment.

§ 3-507. Dishonor; Holder's Right of Recourse; Term Allowing Re-Presentment.

(1) An instrument is dishonored when

(a) a necessary or optional presentment is duly made and due acceptance or payment is refused or cannot be obtained within the prescribed time or in case of bank collections the instrument is seasonably returned by the midnight deadline (Section 4-301); or

(b) presentment is excused and the instrument is not duly accepted or paid.

(2) Subject to any necessary notice of dishonor and protest, the holder has upon dishonor an immediate right of recourse against the drawer and indorsers.

(3) Return of an instrument for lack of proper indorsement is no dishonor.

(4) A term in a draft or an indorsement thereof allowing a stated time for re-presentment in the event of any dishonor of the draft by nonacceptance if a time draft or by nonpayment if a sight draft gives the holder as against any secondary party bound by the term an option to waive the dishonor without affecting the liability of the secondary party and he may present again up to the end of the stated time.

§ 3-508. Notice of Dishonor.

(1) Notice of dishonor may be given to any person who may be liable on the instrument by or on behalf of the holder or any party who has himself received notice, or any other party who can be compelled to pay the instrument. In addition an agent or bank in whose hands the instrument is dishonored may give notice to his principal or customer or to another agent or bank from which the instrument was received.

(2) Any necessary notice must be given by a bank before its midnight deadline and by any other person before midnight of the third business day after dishonor or receipt of notice of dishonor.

(3) Notice may be given in any reasonable manner. It may be oral or written and in any terms which identify the instrument and state that it has been dishonored. A misdescription which does not mislead the party notified does not vitiate the notice. Sending the instrument bearing a stamp, ticket or writing stating that acceptance or payment has been refused or sending a notice of debit with respect to the instrument is sufficient.

(4) Written notice is given when sent although it is not received.

(5) Notice to one partner is notice to each although the firm has been dissolved.

(6) When any party is in insolvency proceedings instituted after the issue of the instrument notice may be given either to the party or to the representative of his estate.

(7) When any party is dead or incompetent notice may be sent to his last known address or given to his personal representative.

(8) Notice operates for the benefit of all parties who have rights on the instrument against the party notified.

§ 3-509. Protest; Noting for Protest.

(1) A protest is a certificate of dishonor made under the hand and seal of a United States consul or vice consul or a notary public or other person authorized to certify dishonor by the law of the place where dishonor occurs. It may be made upon information satisfactory to such person.

(2) The protest must identify the instrument and certify either that due presentment has been made or the reason why it is excused and that the instrument has been dishonored by non-acceptance or non-payment.

(3) The protest may also certify that notice of dishonor has been given to all parties or to specified parties.

(4) Subject to subsection (5) any necessary protest is due by the time that notice of dishonor is due.

(5) If, before protest is due, an instrument has been noted for protest by the officer to make protest, the protest may be made at any time thereafter as of the date of the noting.

§ 3-510. Evidence of Dishonor and Notice of Dishonor. The following are admissible as evidence and create a presumption of dishonor and of any notice of dishonor therein shown:

(a) a document regular in form as provided in the preceding section which purports to be a protest;

(b) the purported stamp or writing of the drawee, payor bank or presenting bank on the instrument or accompanying it stating that acceptance or payment has been refused for reasons consistent with dishonor.

(c) any book or record of the drawee, payor bank, or any collecting bank kept in the usual course of business which shows dishonor, even though there is no evidence of who made the entry.

§ 3-511. Waived or Excused Presentment, Protest or Notice of Dishonor or Delay Therein.

(1) Delay in presentment, protest or notice of dishonor is excused when the party is without notice that it is due or when the delay is caused by circumstances beyond his control and he exercises reasonable diligence after the cause of the delay ceases to operate.

(2) Presentment or notice or protest as the case may be is entirely excused when

(a) the party to be charged has waived it expressly or by implication either before or after it is due; or

(b) such party has himself dishonored the instrument or has countermanded payment or otherwise has no reason to expect or right to require that the instrument be accepted or paid; or

(c) by reasonable diligence the presentment or protest cannot be made or the notice given.

(3) Presentment is also entirely excused when

(a) the maker, acceptor or drawee of any instrument except a documentary draft is dead or in insolvency proceedings instituted after the issue of the instrument; or

(b) acceptance or payment is refused but not for want of proper presentment.

(4) Where a draft has been dishonored by nonacceptance a later presentment for payment and any notice of dishonor and protest for nonpayment are excused unless in the meantime the instrument has been accepted.

(5) A waiver of protest is also a waiver of presentment and of notice of dishonor even though protest is not required.

(6) Where a waiver of presentation or notice or protest is embodied in the instrument itself it is binding upon all parties; but where it is written above the signature of an indorser it binds him only.

Part 6. Discharge

§ 3-601. Discharge of Parties.

(1) The extent of the discharge of any party from liability on an instrument is governed by the sections on

(a) payment or satisfaction (Section 3-603); or

(b) tender of payment (Section 3-604); or

(c) cancellation or renunciation (Section 3-605); or

(d) impairment of right of recourse or of collateral (Section 3-606); or

(e) reacquisition of the instrument by a prior party (Section 3-208); or

(f) fraudulent and material alteration (Section 3-407); or

(g) certification of a check (Section 3-411); or

(h) acceptance varying a draft (Section 3-412); or

(i) unexcused delay in presentment or notice of dishonor or protest (Section 3-502).

(2) Any party is also discharged from his liability on an instrument to another party by any other act or agreement with such party which would discharge his simple contract for the payment of money.

(3) The liability of all parties is discharged when any party who has himself no right of action or recourse on the instrument

(a) reacquires the instrument in his own right; or

(b) is discharged under any provision of this Article, except as otherwise provided with respect to discharge for impairment of recourse or of collateral (Section 3-606).

§ 3-602. Effect of Discharge Against Holder in Due Course.
No discharge of any party provided by this Article is effective against a subsequent holder in due course unless he has notice thereof when he takes the instrument.

§ 3-603. Payment or Satisfaction.

(1) The liability of any party is discharged to the extent of his payment or satisfaction to the holder even though it is made with knowledge of a claim of another person to the instrument unless prior to such payment or satisfaction the person making the claim either supplies indemnity deemed adequate by the party seeking the discharge or enjoins payment or satisfaction by order of a court of competent jurisdiction in an action in which the adverse claimant and the holder are parties. This subsection does not, however, result in the discharge of the liability.

(a) of a party who in bad faith pays or satisfies a holder who acquired the instrument by theft or who (unless having the rights of a holder in due course) holds through one who so acquired it; or

(b) of a party (other than an intermediary bank or a payor bank which is not a depositary bank) who pays or satisfies the holder of an instrument which has been restrictively indorsed in a manner not consistent with the terms of such restrictive indorsement.

(2) Payment or satisfaction may be made with the consent of the holder by any person including a stranger to the instrument. Surrender of the instrument to such a person gives him the rights of a transferee (Section 3-201).

§ 3-604. Tender of Payment.

(1) Any party making tender of full payment to a holder when or after it is due is discharged to the extent of all subsequent liability for interest, costs and attorney's fees.

(2) The holder's refusal of such tender wholly discharges any party who has a right of recourse against the party making the tender.

(3) Where the maker or acceptor of an instrument payable otherwise than on demand is able and ready to pay at every place of payment specified in the instrument when it is due, it is equivalent to tender.

§ 3-605. Cancellation and Renunciation.

(1) The holder of an instrument may even without consideration discharge any party

(a) in any manner apparent on the face of the instrument or the indorsement, as by intentionally cancelling the instrument or the party's signature by destruction or mutilation, or by striking out the party's signature; or

(b) by renouncing his rights by a writing signed and delivered or by surrender of the instrument to the party to be discharged.

(2) Neither cancellation nor renunciation without surrender of the instrument affects the title thereto.

§ 3-606. Impairment of Recourse or of Collateral.

(1) The holder discharges any party to the instrument to the extent that without such party's consent the holder

(a) without express reservation of rights releases or agrees not to sue any person against whom the party has to the knowledge of the holder a right of recourse or agrees to suspend the right to enforce against such person the instrument or collateral or otherwise discharges such person, except that failure or delay in effecting any required presentment, protest or notice of dishonor with respect to any such person does not discharge any party as to whom presentment, protest or notice of dishonor is effective or unnecessary; or

(b) unjustifiably impairs any collateral for the instrument given by or on behalf of the party or any person against whom he has a right of recourse.

(2) By express reservation of rights against a party with a right of recourse the holder preserves

(a) all his rights against such party as of the time when the instrument was originally due; and

(b) the right of the party to pay the instrument as of that time; and

(c) all rights of such party to recourse against others.

Part 7. Advice of International Sight Draft

§ 3-701. Letter of Advice of International Sight Draft.

(1) A "letter of advice" is a drawer's communication to the drawee that a described draft has been drawn.

(2) Unless otherwise agreed when a bank receives from another bank a letter of advice of an international sight draft the drawee bank may immediately debit the drawer's account and stop the running of interest pro tanto. Such a debit and any resulting credit to any account covering outstanding drafts leaves in the drawer full power to stop payment or otherwise dispose of the amount and creates no trust or interest in favor of the holder.

(3) Unless otherwise agreed and except where a draft is drawn under a credit issued by the drawee, the drawee of an international sight draft owes the drawer no duty to pay an unadvised draft but if it does so and the draft is genuine, may appropriately debit the drawer's account.

Part 8. Miscellaneous

§ 3-801. Drafts in a Set.

(1) Where a draft is drawn in a set of parts, each of which is numbered and expressed to be an order only if no other part has been honored, the whole of the parts constitutes one draft but a taker of any part may become a holder in due course of the draft.

(2) Any person who negotiates, indorses or accepts a single part of a draft drawn in a set thereby becomes liable to any holder in due course of that part as if it were the whole set, but as between different holders in due course to whom different parts have been negotiated the holder whose title first accrues has all rights to the draft and its proceeds.

(3) As against the drawee the first presented part of a draft drawn in a set is the part entitled to payment, or if a time draft to acceptance and payment. Acceptance of any subsequently presented part renders the drawee liable thereon under subsection (2). With respect both to a holder and to the drawer payment of a subsequently presented part of a draft payable at sight has the same effect as payment of a check notwithstanding an effective stop order (Section 4-407).

(4) Except as otherwise provided in this section, where any part of a draft in a set is discharged by payment or otherwise the whole draft is discharged.

§ 3-802. Effect of Instrument on Obligation for Which It Is Given.

(1) Unless otherwise agreed where an instrument is taken for an underlying obligation

(a) the obligation is pro tanto discharged if a bank is drawer, maker or acceptor of the instrument and there is no recourse on the instrument against the underlying obligor; and

(b) in any other case the obligation is suspended pro tanto until the instrument is due or if it is payable on demand until its presentment. If the instrument is dishonored action may be maintained on either the instrument or the obligation; discharge of the underlying obligor on the instrument also discharges him on the obligation.

(2) The taking in good faith of a check which is not post-dated does not of itself so extend the time on the original obligation as to discharge a surety.

§ 3-803. Notice to Third Party.
Where a defendant is sued for breach of an obligation for which a third person is answerable over under this Article he may give the third person written notice of the litigation, and the person notified may then give similar notice to any other person who is answerable over to him under this Article. If the notice states that the person notified may come in and defend and that if the person notified does not do so he will in any action against him by the person giving the notice be bound by any determination of fact common to the two litigations, then unless after seasonable receipt of the notice the person notified does come in and defend he is so bound.

§ 3-804. Lost, Destroyed or Stolen Instruments.
The owner of an instrument which is lost, whether by destruction, theft or otherwise, may maintain an action in his own name and recover from any party liable thereon upon due proof of his ownership, the facts which prevent his production of the instrument and its terms. The court may require security indemnifying the defendant against loss by reason of further claims on the instrument.

§ 3-805. Instruments Not Payable to Order or to Bearer.
This Article applies to any instrument whose terms do not preclude transfer and which is otherwise negotiable within this Article but which is not payable to order or to bearer, except that there can be no holder in due course of such an instrument.

ARTICLE 4. BANK DEPOSITS AND COLLECTIONS

Part 1. General Provisions and Definitions

§ 4-101. Short Title.
This Article shall be known and may be cited as Uniform Commercial Code—Bank Deposits and Collections.

§ 4-102. Applicability.

(1) To the extent that items within this Article are also within the scope of Articles 3 and 8, they are subject to the provisions of those Articles. In the event of conflict the provisions of this Article govern those of Article 3 but the provisions of Article 8 govern those of this Article.

(2) The liability of a bank for action or non-action with respect to any item handled by it for purposes of presentment, payment or collection is governed by the law of the place where the bank is located. In the case of action or non-action by or at a branch or separate office of a bank, its liability is governed by the law of the place where the branch or separate office is located.

§ 4-103. Variation by Agreement; Measure of Damages; Certain Action Constituting Ordinary Care.

(1) The effect of the provisions of this Article may be varied by agreement except that no agreement can disclaim a bank's responsibility for its own lack of good faith or failure to exercise ordinary care or can limit the measure of damages for such lack or failure; but the parties may by agreement determine the standards by which such

responsibility is to be measured if such standards are not manifestly unreasonable.

(2) Federal Reserve regulations and operating letters, clearing house rules, and the like, have the effect of agreements under subsection (1), whether or not specifically assented to by all parties interested in items handled.

(3) Action or non-action approved by this Article or pursuant to Federal Reserve regulations or operating letters constitutes the exercise of ordinary care and, in the absence of special instructions, action or non-action consistent with clearing house rules and the like or with a general banking usage not disapproved by this Article, prima facie constitutes the exercise of ordinary care.

(4) The specification or approval of certain procedures by this Article does not constitute disapproval of other procedures which may be reasonable under the circumstances.

(5) The measure of damages for failure to exercise ordinary care in handling an item is the amount of the item reduced by an amount which could not have been realized by the use of ordinary care, and where there is bad faith it includes other damages, if any, suffered by the party as a proximate consequence.

§ 4-104. Definitions and Index of Definitions.

(1) In this Article unless the context otherwise requires

(a) "Account" means any account with a bank and includes a checking, time, interest or savings account;

(b) "Afternoon" means the period of a day between noon and midnight;

(c) "Banking day" means that part of any day on which a bank is open to the public for carrying on substantially all of its banking functions;

(d) "Clearing house" means any association of banks or other payors regularly clearing items;

(e) "Customer" means any person having an account with a bank or for whom a bank has agreed to collect items and includes a bank carrying an account with another bank;

(f) "Documentary draft" means any negotiable or non-negotiable draft with accompanying documents, securities or other papers to be delivered against honor of the draft;

(g) "Item" means any instrument for the payment of money even though it is not negotiable but does not include money;

(h) "Midnight deadline" with respect to a bank is midnight on its next banking day following the banking day on which it receives the relevant item or notice or from which the time for taking action commences to run, whichever is later;

(i) "Properly payable" includes the availability of funds for payment at the time of decision to pay or dishonor;

(j) "Settle" means to pay in cash, by clearing house settlement, in a charge or credit or by remittance, or otherwise as instructed. A settlement may be either provisional or final;

(k) "Suspends payments" with respect to a bank means that it has been closed by order of the supervisory authorities, that a public officer has been appointed to take it over or that it ceases or refuses to make payments in the ordinary course of business.

(2) Other definitions applying to this Article and the sections in which they appear are:

"Collecting bank" Section 4-105.

"Depositary bank" Section 4-105.

"Intermediary bank" Section 4-105.

"Payor bank" Section 4-105.

"Presenting bank" Section 4-105.

"Remitting bank" Section 4-105.

(3) The following definitions in other Articles apply to this Article:

"Acceptance" Section 3-410.

"Certificate of deposit" Section 3-104.

"Certification" Section 3-411.

"Check" Section 3-104.

"Draft" Section 3-104.

"Holder in due course" Section 3-302.

"Notice of dishonor" Section 3-508.

"Presentment" Section 3-504.

"Protest" Section 3-509.

"Secondary party" Section 3-102.

(4) In addition Article 1 contains general definitions and principles of construction and interpretation applicable throughout this Article.

§ 4-105. "Depositary Bank"; "Intermediary Bank"; "Collecting Bank"; "Payor Bank"; "Presenting Bank"; "Remitting Bank." In this Article unless the context otherwise requires:

(a) "Depositary bank" means the first bank to which an item is transferred for collection even though it is also the payor bank;

(b) "Payor bank" means a bank by which an item is payable as drawn or accepted;

(c) "Intermediary bank" means any bank to which an item is transferred in course of collection except the depositary or payor bank;

(d) "Collecting bank" means any bank handling the item for collection except the payor bank;

(e) "Presenting bank" means any bank presenting an item except a payor bank;

(f) "Remitting bank" means any payor or intermediary bank remitting for an item.

§ 4-106. Separate Office of a Bank. A branch or separate office of a bank [maintaining its own deposit ledgers] is a separate bank for the purpose of computing the time within which and determining the place at or to which action may be taken or notices or orders shall be given under this Article and under Article 3.

Note: The brackets are to make it optional with the several states whether to require a branch to maintain its own deposit ledgers in order to be considered to be a separate bank for certain purposes under Article 4. In some states "maintaining its own deposit ledgers" is a satisfactory test. In others branch banking practices are such that this test would not be suitable.

§ 4-107. Time of Receipt of Items.

(1) For the purpose of allowing time to process items, prove balances and make the necessary entries on its books to determine its position for the day, a bank may fix an afternoon hour of 2 P.M. or later as a cut-off hour for the handling of money and items and the making of entries on its books.

(2) Any item or deposit of money received on any day after a cut-off hour so fixed or after the close of the banking day may be treated as being received at the opening of the next banking day.

§ 4-108. Delays.

(1) Unless otherwise instructed, a collecting bank in a good faith effort to secure payment may, in the case of specific items and with or without the approval of any person involved, waive, modify or extend time limits imposed or permitted by this Act for a period not in excess

of an additional banking day without discharge of secondary parties and without liability to its transferor or any prior party.

(2) Delay by a collecting bank or payor bank beyond time limits prescribed or permitted by this Act or by instructions is excused if caused by interruption of communication facilities, suspension of payments by another bank, war, emergency conditions or other circumstances beyond the control of the bank provided it exercises such diligence as the circumstances require.

§ 4-109. Process of Posting.

The "process of posting" means the usual procedure followed by a payor bank in determining to pay an item and in recording the payment including one or more of the following or other steps as determined by the bank:

    (a) verification of any signature;

    (b) ascertaining that sufficient funds are available;

    (c) affixing a "paid" or other stamp;

    (d) entering a charge or entry to a customer's account;

    (e) correcting or reversing an entry or erroneous action with respect to the item.

Part 2. Collection of Items: Depositary and Collecting Banks

§ 4-201. Presumption and Duration of Agency Status of Collecting Banks and Provisional Status of Credits; Applicability of Article; Item Indorsed "Pay Any Bank."

(1) Unless a contrary intent clearly appears and prior to the time that a settlement given by a collecting bank for an item is or becomes final (subsection (3) of Section 4-211 and Sections 4-212 and 4-213) the bank is an agent or subagent of the owner of the item and any settlement given for the item is provisional. This provision applies regardless of the form of indorsement or lack of indorsement and even though credit given for the item is subject to immediate withdrawal as of right or is in fact withdrawn; but the continuance of ownership of an item by its owner and any rights of the owner to proceeds of the item are subject to rights of a collecting bank such as those resulting from outstanding advances on the item and valid rights of setoff. When an item is handled by banks for purposes of presentment, payment and collection, the relevant provisions of this Article apply even though action of parties clearly establishes that a particular bank has purchased the item and is the owner of it.

(2) After an item has been indorsed with the words "pay any bank" or the like, only a bank may acquire the rights of a holder

    (a) until the item has been returned to the customer initiating collection; or

    (b) until the item has been specially indorsed by a bank to a person who is not a bank.

§ 4-202. Responsibility for Collection; When Action Seasonable.

(1) A collecting bank must use ordinary care in

    (a) presenting an item or sending it for presentment; and

    (b) sending notice of dishonor or non-payment or returning an item other than a documentary draft to the bank's transferor [or directly to the depositary bank under subsection (2) of Section 4-212] (see note to Section 4-212) after learning that the item has not been paid or accepted, as the case may be; and

    (c) settling for an item when the bank receives final settlement; and

    (d) making or providing for any necessary protest; and

    (e) notifying its transferor of any loss or delay in transit within a reasonable time after discovery thereof.

(2) A collecting bank taking proper action before its midnight deadline following receipt of an item, notice or payment acts seasonably; taking proper action within a reasonably longer time may be seasonable but the bank has the burden of so establishing.

(3) Subject to subsection (1)(a), a bank is not liable for the insolvency, neglect, misconduct, mistake or default of another bank or person or for loss or destruction of an item in transit or in the possession of others.

§ 4-203. Effect of Instructions.

Subject to the provisions of Article 3 concerning conversion of instruments (Section 3-419) and the provisions of both Article 3 and this Article concerning restrictive indorsements only a collecting bank's transferor can give instructions which affect the bank or constitute notice to it and a collecting bank is not liable to prior parties for any action taken pursuant to such instructions or in accordance with any agreement with its transferor.

§ 4-204. Methods of Sending and Presenting; Sending Direct to Payor Bank.

(1) A collecting bank must send items by reasonably prompt method taking into consideration any relevant instructions, the nature of the item, the number of such items on hand, and the cost of collection involved and the method generally used by it or others to present such items.

(2) A collecting bank may send

    (a) any item direct to the payor bank;

    (b) any item to any non-bank payor if authorized by its transferor; and

    (c) any item other than documentary drafts to any non-bank payor, if authorized by Federal Reserve regulation or operating letter, clearing house rule or the like.

(3) Presentment may be made by a presenting bank at a place where the payor bank has requested that presentment be made.

§ 4-205. Supplying Missing Indorsement; No Notice from Prior Indorsement.

(1) A depositary bank which has taken an item for collection may supply any indorsement of the customer which is necessary to title unless the item contains the words "payee's indorsement required" or the like. In the absence of such a requirement a statement placed on the item by the depositary bank to the effect that the item was deposited by a customer or credited to his account is effective as the customer's indorsement.

(2) An intermediary bank, or payor bank which is not a depositary bank, is neither given notice nor otherwise affected by a restrictive indorsement of any person except the bank's immediate transferor.

§ 4-206. Transfer Between Banks.

Any agreed method which identifies the transferor bank is sufficient for the item's further transfer to another bank.

§ 4-207. Warranties of Customer and Collecting Bank on Transfer or Presentment of Items; Time for Claims.

(1) Each customer or collecting bank who obtains payment or acceptance of an item and each prior customer and collecting bank warrants to the payor bank or other payor who in good faith pays or accepts the item that

    (a) he has a good title to the item or is authorized to obtain payment or acceptance on behalf of one who has a good title; and

    (b) he has no knowledge that the signature of the maker or drawer is unauthorized, except that this warranty is not given by any customer or collecting bank that is a holder in due course and acts in good faith

    (i) to a maker with respect to the maker's own signature; or

    (ii) to a drawer with respect to the drawer's own signature, whether or not the drawer is also the drawee; or

    (iii) to an acceptor of an item if the holder in due course took the item after the acceptance or obtained the acceptance without knowledge that the drawer's signature was unauthorized; and

(c) the item has not been materially altered, except that this warranty is not given by any customer or collecting bank that is a holder in due course and acts in good faith

    (i) to the maker of a note; or

    (ii) to the drawer of a draft whether or not the drawer is also the drawee; or

    (iii) to the acceptor of an item with respect to an alteration made prior to the acceptance if the holder in due course took the item after the acceptance, even though the acceptance provided "payable as originally drawn" or equivalent terms; or

    (iv) to the acceptor of an item with respect to an alteration made after the acceptance.

2) Each customer and collecting bank who transfers an item and receives a settlement or other consideration for it warrants to his transferee and to any subsequent collecting bank who takes the item in good faith that

(a) he has a good title to the item or is authorized to obtain payment or acceptance on behalf of one who has a good title and the transfer is otherwise rightful, and

(b) all signatures are genuine or authorized; and

(c) the item has not been materially altered; and

(d) no defense of any party is good against him; and

(e) he has no knowledge of any insolvency proceeding instituted with respect to the maker or acceptor or the drawer of an unaccepted item.

In addition each customer and collecting bank so transferring an item and receiving a settlement or other consideration engages that upon dishonor and any necessary notice of dishonor and protest he will take up the item.

3) The warranties and the engagement to honor set forth in the two preceding subsections arise notwithstanding the absence of indorsement or words of guaranty or warranty in the transfer or presentment and a collecting bank remains liable for their breach despite remittance to its transferor. Damages for breach of such warranties or engagement to honor shall not exceed the consideration received by the customer or collecting bank responsible plus finance charges and expenses related to the item, if any.

4) Unless a claim for breach of warranty under this section is made within a reasonable time after the person claiming learns of the breach, the person liable is discharged to the extent of any loss caused by the delay in making claim.

§ 4-208. Security Interest of Collecting Bank in Items, Accompanying Documents and Proceeds.

1) A bank has a security interest in an item and any accompanying documents or the proceeds of either

(a) in case of an item deposited in an account to the extent to which credit given for the item has been withdrawn or applied;

(b) in case of an item for which it has given credit available for withdrawal as of right, to the extent of the credit given whether or not the credit is drawn upon and whether or not there is a right of chargeback; or

(c) if it makes an advance on or against the item.

(2) When credit which has been given for several items received at one time or pursuant to a single agreement is withdrawn or applied in part the security interest remains upon all the items, any accompanying documents or the proceeds of either. For the purpose of this section, credits first given are first withdrawn.

(3) Receipt by a collecting bank of a final settlement for an item is a realization on its security interest in the item, accompanying documents and proceeds. To the extent and so long as the bank does not receive final settlement for the item or give up possession of the item or accompanying documents for purposes other than collection, the security interest continues and is subject to the provisions of Article 9 except that

(a) no security agreement is necessary to make the security interest enforceable (subsection (1)(a) of Section 9-203); and

(b) no filing is required to perfect the security interest; and

(c) the security interest has priority over conflicting perfected security interests in the item, accompanying documents or proceeds.

§ 4-209. When Bank Gives Value for Purposes of Holder in Due Course. For purposes of determining its status as a holder in due course, the bank has given value to the extent that it has a security interest in an item provided that the bank otherwise complies with the requirements of Section 3-302 on what constitutes a holder in due course.

§ 4-210. Presentment by Notice of Item Not Payable by, Through or at a Bank; Liability of Secondary Parties.

(1) Unless otherwise instructed, a collecting bank may present an item not payable by, through or at a bank by sending to the party to accept or pay a written notice that the bank holds the item for acceptance or payment. The notice must be sent in time to be received on or before the day when presentment is due and the bank must meet any requirement of the party to accept or pay under Section 3-505 by the close of the bank's next banking day after it knows of the requirement.

(2) Where presentment is made by notice and neither honor nor request for compliance with a requirement under Section 3-505 is received by the close of business on the day after maturity or in the case of demand items by the close of business on the third banking day after notice was sent, the presenting bank may treat the item as dishonored and charge any secondary party by sending him notice of the facts.

§ 4-211. Media of Remittance; Provisional and Final Settlement in Remittance Cases.

(1) A collecting bank may take in settlement of an item

(a) a check of the remitting bank or of another bank on any bank except the remitting bank; or

(b) a cashier's check or similar primary obligation of a remitting bank which is a member of or clears through a member of the same clearing house or group as the collecting bank; or

(c) appropriate authority to charge an account of the remitting bank or of another bank with the collecting bank; or

(d) if the item is drawn upon or payable by a person other than a bank, a cashier's check, certified check or other bank check or obligation.

(2) If before its midnight deadline the collecting bank properly dishonors a remittance check or authorization to charge on itself or presents or forwards for collection a remittance instrument of or on

another bank which is of a kind approved by subsection (1) or has not been authorized by it, the collecting bank is not liable to prior parties in the event of the dishonor of such check, instrument or authorization.

(3) A settlement for an item by means of a remittance instrument or authorization to charge is or becomes a final settlement as to both the person making and the person receiving the settlement

(a) if the remittance instrument or authorization to charge is of a kind approved by subsection (1) or has not been authorized by the person receiving the settlement and in either case the person receiving the settlement acts seasonably before its midnight deadline in presenting, forwarding for collection or paying the instrument or authorization,—at the time the remittance instrument or authorization is finally paid by the payor by which it is payable;

(b) if the person receiving the settlement has authorized remittance by a non-bank check or obligation or by a cashier's check or similar primary obligation of or a check upon the payor or other remitting bank which is not of a kind approved by subsection (1)(b),—at the time of the receipt of such remittance check or obligation; or

(c) if in a case not covered by sub-paragraphs (a) or (b) the person receiving the settlement fails to seasonably present, forward for collection, pay or return a remittance instrument or authorization to it to charge before its midnight deadline,—at such midnight deadline.

§ 4-212. Right of Charge-Back or Refund.

(1) If a collecting bank has made provisional settlement with its customer for an item and itself fails by reason of dishonor, suspension of payments by a bank or otherwise to receive a settlement for the item which is or becomes final, the bank may revoke the settlement given by it, charge back the amount of any credit given for the item to its customer's account or obtain refund from its customer whether or not it is able to return the items if by its midnight deadline or within a longer reasonable time after it learns the facts it returns the item or sends notification of the facts. These rights to revoke, charge-back and obtain refund terminate if and when a settlement for the item received by the bank is or becomes final (subsection (3) of Section 4-211 and subsections (2) and (3) of Section 4-213).

[(2) Within the time and manner prescribed by this section and Section 4-301, an intermediary or payor bank, as the case may be, may return an unpaid item directly to the depositary bank and may send for collection a draft on the depositary bank and obtain reimbursement. In such case, if the depositary bank has received provisional settlement for the item, it must reimburse the bank drawing the draft and any provisional credits for the item between banks shall become and remain final.]

Note: Direct returns are recognized as an innovation that is not yet established bank practice, and therefore, Paragraph 2 has been bracketed. Some lawyers have doubts whether it should be included in legislation or left to development by agreement.

(3) A depositary bank which is also the payor may charge-back the amount of an item to its customer's account or obtain refund in accordance with the section governing return of an item received by a payor bank for credit on its books (Section 4-301).

(4) The right to charge-back is not affected by

(a) prior use of the credit given for the item; or

(b) failure by any bank to exercise ordinary care with respect to the item but any bank so failing remains liable.

(5) A failure to charge-back or claim refund does not affect other rights of the bank against the customer or any other party.

(6) If credit is given in dollars as the equivalent of the value of an item payable in a foreign currency the dollar amount of any charge-back or refund shall be calculated on the basis of the buying sight rate for the foreign currency prevailing on the day when the person entitle to the charge-back or refund learns that it will not receive payment i ordinary course.

§ 4-213. Final Payment of Item by Payor Bank; When Provisional Debits and Credits Become Final; When Certain Credits Become Available for Withdrawal.

(1) An item is finally paid by a payor bank when the bank has don any of the following, whichever happens first:

(a) paid the item in cash; or

(b) settled for the item without reserving a right to revoke the settlement and without having such right under statute, clearing house rule or agreement; or

(c) completed the process of posting the item to the indicate account of the drawer, maker or other person to be charged there with; or

(d) made a provisional settlement for the item and failed to revok the settlement in the time and manner permitted by statute, clearing house rule or agreement.

Upon a final payment under subparagraphs (b), (c) or (d) the payor bank shall be accountable for the amount of the item.

(2) If provisional settlement for an item between the presenting an payor banks is made through a clearing house or by debits or credit in an account between them, then to the extent that provisional debit or credits for the item are entered in accounts between the presenting and payor banks or between the presenting and successive prior collecting banks seriatim, they become final upon final payment of th item by the payor bank.

(3) If a collecting bank receives a settlement for an item which is o becomes final (subsection (3) of Section 4-211, subsection (2) of Section 4-213) the bank is accountable to its customer for the amount of th item and any provisional credit given for the item in an account wit its customer becomes final.

(4) Subject to any right of the bank to apply the credit to an obligatio of the customer, credit given by a bank for an item in an account wit its customer becomes available for withdrawal as of right

(a) in any case where the bank has received a provisional settlemer for the item,—when such settlement becomes final and the bank ha had a reasonable time to learn that the settlement is final;

(b) in any case where the bank is both a depositary bank and payor bank and the item is finally paid,—at the opening of th bank's second banking day following receipt of the item.

(5) A deposit of money in a bank is final when made but, subject t any right of the bank to apply the deposit to an obligation of th customer, the deposit becomes available for withdrawal as of right a the opening of the bank's next banking day following receipt of th deposit.

§ 4-214. Insolvency and Preference.

(1) Any item in or coming into the possession of a payor or collectin bank which suspends payment and which item is not finally paid sha be returned by the receiver, trustee or agent in charge of the close bank to the presenting bank or the closed bank's customer.

(2) If a payor bank finally pays an item and suspends payments withou making a settlement for the item with its customer or the presentin bank which settlement is or becomes final, the owner of the item ha a preferred claim against the payor bank.

(3) If a payor bank gives or a collecting bank gives or receives provisional settlement for an item and thereafter suspends payment the suspension does not prevent or interfere with the settlemer becoming final if such finality occurs automatically upon the lapse

certain time or the happening of certain events (subsection (3) of Section 4-211, subsections (1) (d), (2) and (3) of Section 4-213).

(4) If a collecting bank receives from subsequent parties settlement for an item which settlement is or becomes final and suspends payments without making a settlement for the item with its customer which is or becomes final, the owner of the item has a preferred claim against such collecting bank.

Part 3. Collection of Items: Payor Banks

§ 4-301. Deferred Posting; Recovery of Payment by Returns of Items; Time of Dishonor.

(1) Where an authorized settlement for a demand item (other than a documentary draft) received by a payor bank otherwise than for immediate payment over the counter has been made before midnight of the banking day of receipt the payor bank may revoke the settlement and recover any payment if before it has made final payment (subsection (1) of Section 4-213) and before its midnight deadline it

(a) returns the item; or

(b) sends written notice of dishonor or nonpayment if the item is held for protest or is otherwise unavailable for return.

(2) If a demand item is received by a payor bank for credit on its books it may return such item or send notice of dishonor and may revoke any credit given or recover the amount thereof withdrawn by its customer, if it acts within the time limit and in the manner specified in the preceding subsection.

(3) Unless previous notice of dishonor has been sent an item is dishonored at the time when for purposes of dishonor it is returned or notice sent in accordance with this section.

(4) An item is returned:

(a) as to an item received through a clearing house, when it is delivered to the presenting or last collecting bank or to the clearing house or is sent or delivered in accordance with its rules; or

(b) in all other cases, when it is sent or delivered to the bank's customer or transferor or pursuant to his instructions.

§ 4-302. Payor Bank's Responsibility for Late Return of Item.

In the absence of a valid defense such as breach of a presentment warranty (subsection (1) of Section 4-207), settlement effected or the like, if an item is presented on and received by a payor bank the bank is accountable for the amount of

(a) a demand item other than a documentary draft whether properly payable or not if the bank, in any case where it is not also the depositary bank, retains the item beyond midnight of the banking day of receipt without settling for it or, regardless of whether it is also the depositary bank, does not pay or return the item or send notice of dishonor until after its midnight deadline; or

(b) any other properly payable item unless within the time allowed for acceptance or payment of that item the bank either accepts or pays the item or returns it and accompanying documents.

§ 4-303. When Items Subject to Notice, Stop-Order, Legal Process or Setoff; Order in Which Items May Be Charged or Certified.

(1) Any knowledge, notice or stop-order received by, legal process served upon or setoff exercised by a payor bank, whether or not effective under other rules of law to terminate, suspend or modify the bank's right or duty to pay an item or to charge its customer's account for the item, comes too late to so terminate, suspend or modify such right or duty if the knowledge, notice, stop-order or legal process is received or served and a reasonable time for the bank to act thereon expires or the setoff is exercised after the bank has done any of the following:

(a) accepted or certified the item;

(b) paid the item in cash;

(c) settled for the item without reserving a right to revoke the settlement and without having such right under statute, clearing house rule or agreement;

(d) completed the process of posting the item to the indicated account of the drawer, maker or other person to be charged therewith or otherwise has evidenced by examination of such indicated account and by action its decision to pay the item; or

(e) become accountable for the amount of the item under subsection (1)(d) of Section 4-213 and Section 4-302 dealing with the payor bank's responsibility for late return of items.

(2) Subject to the provisions of subsection (1) items may be accepted, paid, certified or charged to the indicated account of its customer in any order convenient to the bank.

Part 4. Relationship Between Payor Bank and Its Customers

§ 4-401. When Bank May Charge Customer's Account.

(1) As against its customer, a bank may charge against his account any item which is otherwise properly payable from that account even though the charge creates an overdraft.

(2) A bank which in good faith makes payment to a holder may charge the indicated account of its customer according to

(a) the original tenor of his altered item; or

(b) the tenor of his completed item, even though the bank knows the item has been completed unless the bank has notice that the completion was improper.

§ 4-402. Bank's Liability to Customer for Wrongful Dishonor.

A payor bank is liable to its customer for damages proximately caused by the wrongful dishonor of an item. When the dishonor occurs through mistake liability is limited to actual damages proved. If so proximately caused and proved damages may include damages for an arrest or prosecution of the customer or other consequential damages. Whether any consequential damages are proximately caused by the wrongful dishonor is a question of fact to be determined in each case.

§ 4-403. Customer's Right to Stop Payment; Burden of Proof of Loss.

(1) A customer may by order to his bank stop payment of any item payable for his account but the order must be received at such time and in such manner as to afford the bank a reasonable opportunity to act on it prior to any action by the bank with respect to the item described in Section 4-303.

(2) An oral order is binding upon the bank only for fourteen calendar days unless confirmed in writing within that period. A written order is effective for only six months unless renewed in writing.

(3) The burden of establishing the fact and amount of loss resulting from the payment of an item contrary to a binding stop payment order is on the customer.

§ 4-404. Bank Not Obliged to Pay Check More Than Six Months Old.

A bank is under no obligation to a customer having a checking account to pay a check, other than a certified check, which is presented more than six months after its date, but it may charge its customer's account for a payment made thereafter in good faith.

§ 4-405. Death or Incompetence of Customer.

(1) A payor or collecting bank's authority to accept, pay or collect an item or to account for proceeds of its collection if otherwise effective

is not rendered ineffective by incompetence of a customer of either bank existing at the time the item is issued or its collection is undertaken if the bank does not know of an adjudication of incompetence. Neither death nor incompetence of a customer revokes such authority to accept, pay, collect or account until the bank knows of the fact of death or of an adjudication of incompetence and has reasonable opportunity to act on it.

(2) Even with knowledge a bank may for ten days after the date of death pay or certify checks drawn on or prior to that date unless ordered to stop payment by a person claiming an interest in the account.

§ 4-406. Customer's Duty to Discover and Report Unauthorized Signature or Alteration.

(1) When a bank sends to its customer a statement of account accompanied by items paid in good faith in support of the debit entries or holds the statement and items pursuant to a request or instructions of its customer or otherwise in a reasonable manner makes the statement and items available to the customer, the customer must exercise reasonable care and promptness to examine the statement and items to discover his unauthorized signature or any alteration on an item and must notify the bank promptly after discovery thereof.

(2) If the bank establishes that the customer failed with respect to an item to comply with the duties imposed on the customer by subsection (1) the customer is precluded from asserting against the bank

(a) his unauthorized signature or any alteration on the item if the bank also establishes that it suffered a loss by reason of such failure; and

(b) an unauthorized signature or alteration by the same wrongdoer on any other item paid in good faith by the bank after the first item and statement was available to the customer for a reasonable period not exceeding fourteen calendar days and before the bank receives notification from the customer of any such unauthorized signature or alteration.

(3) The preclusion under subsection (2) does not apply if the customer establishes lack of ordinary care on the part of the bank in paying the item(s).

(4) Without regard to care or lack of care of either the customer or the bank a customer who does not within one year from the time the statement and items are made available to the customer (subsection (1)) discover and report his unauthorized signature or any alteration on the face or back of the item or does not within three years from that time discover and report any unauthorized indorsement is precluded from asserting against the bank such unauthorized signature or indorsement or such alteration.

(5) If under this section a payor bank has a valid defense against a claim of a customer upon or resulting from payment of an item and waives or fails upon request to assert the defense the bank may not assert against any collecting bank or other prior party presenting or transferring the item a claim based upon the unauthorized signature or alteration giving rise to the customer's claim.

§ 4-407. Payor Bank's Right to Subrogation on Improper Payment.
If a payor bank has paid an item over the stop payment order of the drawer or maker or otherwise under circumstances giving a basis for objection by the drawer or maker, to prevent unjust enrichment and only to the extent necessary to prevent loss to the bank by reason of its payment of the item, the payor bank shall be subrogated to the rights

(a) of any holder in due course on the item against the drawer or maker; and

(b) of the payee or any other holder of the item against the drawer or maker either on the item or under the transaction out of which the item arose; and

(c) of the drawer or maker against the payee or any other holder of the item with respect to the transaction out of which the item arose.

Part 5. Collection of Documentary Drafts

§ 4-501. Handling of Documentary Drafts; Duty to Send for Presentment and to Notify Customer of Dishonor.
A bank which takes a documentary draft for collection must present or send the draft and accompanying documents for presentment and upon learning that the draft has not been paid or accepted in due course must seasonably notify its customer of such fact even though it may have discounted or bought the draft or extended credit available for withdrawal as of right.

§ 4-502. Presentment of "On Arrival" Drafts.
When a draft or the relevant instructions require presentment "on arrival", "when goods arrive" or the like, the collecting bank need not present until in its judgment a reasonable time for arrival of the goods has expired. Refusal to pay or accept because the goods have not arrived is not dishonor; the bank must notify its transferor of such refusal but need not present the draft again until it is instructed to do so or learns of the arrival of the goods.

§ 4-503. Responsibility of Presenting Bank for Documents and Goods; Report of Reasons for Dishonor; Referee in Case of Need.
Unless otherwise instructed and except as provided in Article 5 a bank presenting a documentary draft

(a) must deliver the documents to the drawee on acceptance of the draft if it is payable more than three days after presentment; otherwise, only on payment; and

(b) upon dishonor, either in the case of presentment for acceptance or presentment for payment, may seek and follow instructions from any referee in case of need designated in the draft or if the presenting bank does not choose to utilize his services it must use diligence and good faith to ascertain the reason for dishonor, must notify its transferor of the dishonor and of the results of its effort to ascertain the reasons therefor and must request instructions.

But the presenting bank is under no obligation with respect to goods represented by the documents except to follow any reasonable instructions seasonably received; it has a right to reimbursement for any expense incurred in following instructions and to prepayment of or indemnity for such expenses.

§ 4-504. Privilege of Presenting Bank to Deal With Goods; Security Interest for Expenses.

(1) A presenting bank which, following the dishonor of a documentary draft, has seasonably requested instructions but does not receive them within a reasonable time may store, sell, or otherwise deal with the goods in any reasonable manner.

(2) For its reasonable expenses incurred by action under subsection (1) the presenting bank has a lien upon the goods or their proceeds, which may be foreclosed in the same manner as an unpaid seller's lien.

ARTICLE 4A. FUNDS TRANSFERS

Part 1. Subject Matter and Definitions

§ 4A-101. Short Title.
This Article may be cited as Uniform Commercial Code—Funds Transfers.

§ 4A-102. Subject Matter.
Except as otherwise provided in Section 4A-108, this Article applies to funds transfers defined in Section 4A-104.

§ 4A-103. Payment Order—Definitions.

(a) In this Article:

(1) "Payment order" means an instruction of a sender to a receiving bank, transmitted orally, electronically, or in writing, to pay, or to cause another bank to pay, a fixed or determinable amount of money to a beneficiary if:

(i) the instruction does not state a condition to payment to the beneficiary other than time of payment,

(ii) the receiving bank is to be reimbursed by debiting an account of, or otherwise receiving payment from, the sender, and

(iii) the instruction is transmitted by the sender directly to the receiving bank or to an agent, funds-transfer system, or communication system for transmittal to the receiving bank.

(2) "Beneficiary" means the person to be paid by the beneficiary's bank.

(3) "Beneficiary's bank" means the bank identified in a payment order in which an account of the beneficiary is to be credited pursuant to the order or which otherwise is to make payment to the beneficiary if the order does not provide for payment to an account.

(4) "Receiving bank" means the bank to which the sender's instruction is addressed.

§ 4A-104. Funds Transfer—Definitions.

In this Article:

(a) "Funds transfer" means the series of transactions, beginning with the originator's payment order, made for the purpose of making payment to the beneficiary of the order. The term includes any payment order issued by the originator's bank or an intermediary bank intended to carry out the originator's payment order. A funds transfer is completed by acceptance by the beneficiary's bank of a payment order for the benefit of the beneficiary of the originator's payment order.

(b) "Intermediary bank" means a receiving bank other than the originator's bank or the beneficiary's bank.

(c) "Originator" means the sender of the first payment order in a funds transfer.

(d) "Originator's bank" means (i) the receiving bank to which the payment order of the originator is issued if the originator is not a bank, or (ii) the originator if the originator is a bank.

§ 4A-105. Other Definitions.

(a) In this Article:

(1) "Authorized account" means a deposit account of a customer in a bank designated by the customer as a source of payment of payment orders issued by the customer to the bank. If a customer does not so designate an account, any account of the customer is an authorized account if payment of a payment order from that account is not inconsistent with a restriction on the use of that account.

(2) "Bank" means a person engaged in the business of banking and includes a savings bank, savings and loan association, credit union, and trust company. A branch or separate office of a bank is a separate bank for purposes of this Article.

(3) "Customer" means a person, including a bank, having an account with a bank or from whom a bank has agreed to receive payment orders.

(4) "Funds-transfer business day" of a receiving bank means the part of a day during which the receiving bank is open for the receipt, processing, and transmittal of payment orders and cancellations and amendments of payment orders.

(5) "Funds-transfer system" means a wire transfer network, automated clearing house, or other communication system of a clearing house or other association of banks through which a payment order

by a bank may be transmitted to the bank to which the order is addressed.

(6) "Good faith" means honesty in fact and the observance of reasonable commercial standards of fair dealing.

(7) "Prove" with respect to a fact means to meet the burden of establishing the fact (Section 1-201(8)).

(b) Other definitions applying to this Article and the sections in which they appear are:

"Acceptance"	Section 4A-209
"Beneficiary"	Section 4A-103
"Beneficiary's bank"	Section 4A-103
"Executed"	Section 4A-301
"Execution date"	Section 4A-301
"Funds transfer"	Section 4A-104
"Funds-transfer system rule"	Section 4A-501
"Intermediary bank"	Section 4A-104
"Originator"	Section 4A-104
"Originator's bank"	Section 4A-104
"Payment by beneficiary's bank to beneficiary"	Section 4A-405
"Payment by originator to beneficiary"	Section 4A-406
"Payment by sender to receiving bank"	Section 4A-403
"Payment date"	Section 4A-401
"Payment order"	Section 4A-103
"Receiving bank"	Section 4A-103
"Security procedure"	Section 4A-201
"Sender"	Section 4A-103

(c) The following definitions in Article 4 apply to this Article:

"Clearing house"	Section 4-104
"Item"	Section 4-104
"Suspends payments"	Section 4-104

(d) In addition Article 1 contains general definitions and principles of construction and interpretation applicable throughout this Article.

§ 4A-106. Time Payment Order Is Received.

(a) The time of receipt of a payment order or communication cancelling or amending a payment order is determined by the rules applicable to receipt of a notice stated in Section 1-201(27). A receiving bank may fix a cut-off time or times on a funds-transfer business day for the receipt and processing of payment orders and communications cancelling or amending payment orders. Different cut-off times may apply to payment orders, cancellations, or amendments, or to different categories of payment orders, cancellations, or amendments. A cut-off time may apply to senders generally or different cut-off times may apply to different senders or categories of payment orders. If a payment order or communication cancelling or amending a payment order is received after the close of a funds-transfer business day or after the appropriate cut-off time on a funds-transfer business day, the receiving bank may treat the payment order or communication as received at the opening of the next funds-transfer business day.

(b) If this Article refers to an execution date or payment date or states a day on which a receiving bank is required to take action, and the date or day does not fall on a funds-transfer business day, the next day that is a funds-transfer business day is treated as the date or day stated, unless the contrary is stated in this Article.

§ 4A-107. Federal Reserve Regulations and Operating Circulars.

Regulations of the Board of Governors of the Federal Reserve System and operating circulars of the Federal Reserve Banks supersede any inconsistent provision of this Article to the extent of the inconsistency.

§ 4A-108. Exclusion of Consumer Transactions Governed by Federal Law.

This Article does not apply to a funds transfer any part of which is governed by the Electronic Fund Transfer Act of 1978 (Title XX, Public Law 95-630, 92 Stat. 3728, 15 U.S.C. § 1693 et seq.) as amended from time to time.

Part 2. Issue and Acceptance of Payment Order

§ 4A-201. Security Procedure.

"Security procedure" means a procedure established by agreement of a customer and a receiving bank for the purpose of (i) verifying that a payment order or communication amending or cancelling a payment order is that of the customer, or (ii) detecting error in the transmission or the content of the payment order or communication. A security procedure may require the use of algorithms or other codes, identifying words or numbers, encryption, callback procedures, or similar security devices. Comparison of a signature on a payment order or communication with an authorized specimen signature of the customer is not by itself a security procedure.

§ 4A-202. Authorized and Verified Payment Orders.

(a) A payment order received by the receiving bank is the authorized order of the person identified as sender if that person authorized the order or is otherwise bound by it under the law of agency.

(b) If a bank and its customer have agreed that the authenticity of payment orders issued to the bank in the name of the customer as sender will be verified pursuant to a security procedure, a payment order received by the receiving bank is effective as the order of the customer, whether or not authorized, if (i) the security procedure is a commercially reasonable method of providing security against unauthorized payment orders, and (ii) the bank proves that it accepted the payment order in good faith and in compliance with the security procedure and any written agreement or instruction of the customer restricting acceptance of payment orders issued in the name of the customer. The bank is not required to follow an instruction that violates a written agreement with the customer or notice of which is not received at a time and in a manner affording the bank a reasonable opportunity to act on it before the payment order is accepted.

(c) Commercial reasonableness of a security procedure is a question of law to be determined by considering the wishes of the customer expressed to the bank, the circumstances of the customer known to the bank, including the size, type, and frequency of payment orders normally issued by the customer to the bank, alternative security procedures offered to the customer, and security procedures in general use by customers and receiving banks similarly situated. A security procedure was chosen by the customer after the bank offered, and the customer refused, a security procedure that was commercially reasonable for that customer, and (ii) the customer expressly agreed in writing to be bound by any payment order, whether or not authorized, issued in its name and accepted by the bank in compliance with the security procedure chosen by the customer.

(d) The term "sender" in this Article includes the customer in whose name a payment order is issued if the order is the authorized order of the customer under subsection (a), or it is effective as the order of the customer under subsection (b).

(e) This section applies to amendments and cancellations of payment orders to the same extent it applies to payment orders.

(f) Except as provided in this section and in Section 4A-203(a)(1), rights and obligations arising under this section or Section 4A-203 may not be varied by agreement.

§ 4A-203. Unenforceability of Certain Verified Payment Orders.

(a) If an accepted payment order is not, under Section 4A-202(a), an authorized order of a customer identified as sender, but is effective as an order of the customer pursuant to Section 4A-202(b), the following rules apply:

(1) By express written agreement, the receiving bank may limit the extent to which it is entitled to enforce or retain payment of the payment order.

(2) The receiving bank is not entitled to enforce or retain payment of the payment order if the customer proves that the order was not caused, directly or indirectly, by a person (i) entrusted at any time with duties to act for the customer with respect to payment orders or the security procedure, or (ii) who obtained access to transmitting facilities of the customer or who obtained, from a source controlled by the customer and without authority of the receiving bank, information facilitating breach of the security procedure, regardless of how the information was obtained or whether the customer was at fault. Information includes any access device, computer software, or the like.

(b) This section applies to amendments of payment orders to the same extent it applies to payment orders.

§ 4A-204. Refund of Payment and Duty of Customer to Report with Respect to Unauthorized Payment Order.

(a) If a receiving bank accepts a payment order issued in the name of its customer as sender which is (i) not authorized and not effective as the order of the customer under Section 4A-202, or (ii) not enforceable, in whole or in part, against the customer under Section 4A-203, the bank shall refund any payment of the payment order received from the customer to the extent the bank is not entitled to enforce payment and shall pay interest on the refundable amount calculated from the date the bank received payment to the date of the refund. However, the customer is not entitled to interest from the bank on the amount to be refunded if the customer fails to exercise ordinary care to determine that the order was not authorized by the customer and to notify the bank of the relevant facts within a reasonable time not exceeding 90 days after the date the customer received notification from the bank that the order was accepted or that the customer's account was debited with respect to the order. The bank is not entitled to any recovery from the customer on account of a failure by the customer to give notification as stated in this section.

(b) Reasonable time under subsection (a) may be fixed by agreement as stated in Section 1-204(1), but the obligation of a receiving bank to refund payment as stated in subsection (a) may not otherwise be varied by agreement.

§ 4A-205. Erroneous Payment Orders.

(a) If an accepted payment order was transmitted pursuant to a security procedure for the detection of error and the payment order (i) erroneously instructed payment to a beneficiary not intended by the sender, (ii) erroneously instructed payment in an amount greater than the amount intended by the sender, or (iii) was an erroneously transmitted duplicate of a payment order previously sent by the sender, the following rules apply:

(1) If the sender proves that the sender or a person acting on behalf of the sender pursuant to Section 4A-206 complied with the security procedure and that the error would have been detected if the receiving bank had also complied, the sender is not obliged to pay the order to the extent stated in paragraphs (2) and (3).

(2) If the funds transfer is completed on the basis of an erroneous payment order described in clause (i) or (iii) of subsection (a), the sender is not obliged to pay the order and the receiving bank is entitled to recover from the beneficiary any amount paid to the beneficiary to the extent allowed by the law governing mistake and restitution.

(3) If the funds transfer is completed on the basis of a payment order described in clause (ii) of subsection (a), the sender is not

obliged to pay the order to the extent the amount received by the beneficiary is greater than the amount intended by the sender. In that case, the receiving bank is entitled to recover from the beneficiary the excess amount received to the extent allowed by the law governing mistake and restitution.

(b) If (i) the sender of an erroneous payment order described in subsection (a) is not obliged to pay all or part of the order, and (ii) the sender receives notification from the receiving bank that the order was accepted by the bank or that the sender's account was debited with respect to the order, the sender has a duty to exercise ordinary care, on the basis of information available to the sender, to discover the error with respect to the order and to advise the bank of the relevant facts within a reasonable time, not exceeding 90 days, after the bank's notification was received by the sender. If the bank proves that the sender failed to perform that duty, the sender is liable to the bank for the loss the bank proves it incurred as a result of the failure, but the liability of the sender may not exceed the amount of the sender's order.

(c) This section applies to amendments to payment orders to the same extent it applies to payment orders.

§ 4A-206. Transmission of Payment Order Through Funds-Transfer or Other Communication System.

(a) If a payment order addressed to a receiving bank is transmitted to a funds-transfer system or other third-party communication system for transmittal to the bank, the system is deemed to be an agent of the sender for the purpose of transmitting the payment order to the bank. If there is a discrepancy between the terms of the payment order transmitted to the system and the terms of the payment order transmitted by the system to the bank, the terms of the payment order of the sender are those transmitted by the system. This section does not apply to a funds-transfer system of the Federal Reserve Banks.

(b) This section applies to cancellations and amendments of payment orders to the same extent it applies to payment orders.

§ 4A-207. Misdescription of Beneficiary.

(a) Subject to subsection (b), if, in a payment order received by the beneficiary's bank, the name, bank account number, or other identification of the beneficiary refers to a nonexistent or unidentifiable person or account, no person has rights as a beneficiary of the order and acceptance of the order cannot occur.

(b) If a payment order received by the beneficiary's bank identifies the beneficiary both by name and by an identifying or bank account number and the name and number identify different persons, the following rules apply:

(1) Except as otherwise provided in subsection (c), if the beneficiary's bank does not know that the name and number refer to different persons, it may rely on the number as the proper identification of the beneficiary of the order. The beneficiary's bank need not determine whether the name and number refer to the same person.

(2) If the beneficiary's bank pays the person identified by name or knows that the name and number identify different persons, no person has rights as beneficiary except the person paid by the beneficiary's bank if that person was entitled to receive payment from the originator of the funds transfer. If no person has rights as beneficiary, acceptance of the order cannot occur.

(c) If (i) a payment order described in subsection (b) is accepted, (ii) the originator's payment order described the beneficiary inconsistently by name and number, and (iii) the beneficiary's bank pays the person identified by number as permitted by subsection (b)(1), the following rules apply:

(1) If the originator is a bank, the originator is obliged to pay its order.

(2) If the originator is not a bank and proves that the person identified by number was not entitled to receive payment from the originator, the originator is not obliged to pay its order unless the originator's bank proves that the originator, before acceptance of the originator's order, had notice that payment of a payment order issued by the originator might be made by the beneficiary's bank on the basis of an identifying or bank account number even if it identifies a person different from the named beneficiary. Proof of notice may be made by any admissible evidence. The originator's bank satisfies the burden of proof if it proves that the originator, before the payment order was accepted, signed a writing stating the information to which the notice relates.

(d) In a case governed by subsection (b)(1), if the beneficiary's bank rightfully pays the person identified by number and that person was not entitled to receive payment from the originator, the amount paid may be recovered from that person to the extent allowed by the law governing mistake and restitution as follows:

(1) If the originator is obliged to pay its payment order as stated in subsection (c), the originator has the right to recover.

(2) If the originator is not a bank and is not obliged to pay its payment order, the originator's bank has the right to recover.

§ 4A-208. Misdescription of Intermediary Bank or Beneficiary's Bank.

(a) This subsection applies to a payment order identifying an intermediary bank or the beneficiary's bank only by an identifying number.

(1) The receiving bank may rely on the number as the proper identification of the intermediary or beneficiary's bank and need not determine whether the number identifies a bank.

(2) The sender is obliged to compensate the receiving bank for any loss and expenses incurred by the receiving bank as a result of its reliance on the number in executing or attempting to execute the order.

(b) This subsection applies to a payment order identifying an intermediary bank or the beneficiary's bank both by name and an identifying number if the name and number identify different persons.

(1) If the sender is a bank, the receiving bank may rely on the number as the proper identification of the intermediary or beneficiary's bank if the receiving bank, when it executes the sender's order, does not know that the name and number identify different persons. The receiving bank need not determine whether the name and number refer to the same person or whether the number refers to a bank. The sender is obliged to compensate the receiving bank for any loss and expenses incurred by the receiving bank as a result of its reliance on the number in executing or attempting to execute the order.

(2) If the sender is not a bank and the receiving bank proves that the sender, before the payment order was accepted, had notice that the receiving bank might rely on the number as the proper identification of the intermediary or beneficiary's bank even if it identifies a person different from the bank identified by name, the rights and obligations of the sender and the receiving bank are governed by subsection (b)(1), as though the sender were a bank. Proof of notice may be made by any admissible evidence. The receiving bank satisfies the burden of proof if it proves that the sender, before the payment order was accepted, signed a writing stating the information to which the notice relates.

(3) Regardless of whether the sender is a bank, the receiving bank may rely on the name as the proper identification of the intermediary or beneficiary's bank if the receiving bank, at the time it executes the sender's order, does not know that the name and number identify different persons. The receiving bank need not determine whether the name and number refer to the same person.

(4) If the receiving bank knows that the name and number identify different persons, reliance on either the name or the number in

executing the sender's payment order is a breach of the obligation stated in Section 4A-302(a)(1).

§ 4A-209. Acceptance of Payment Order.

(a) Subject to subsection (d), a receiving bank other than the beneficiary's bank accepts a payment order when it executes the order.

(b) Subject to subsections (c) and (d), a beneficiary's bank accepts a payment order at the earliest of the following times:

(1) when the bank (i) pays the beneficiary as stated in Section 4A-405(a) or 4A-405(b), or (ii) notifies the beneficiary of receipt of the order or that the account of the beneficiary has been credited with respect to the order unless the notice indicates that the bank is rejecting the order or that funds with respect to the order may not be withdrawn or used until receipt of payment from the sender of the order;

(2) when the bank receives payment of the entire amount of the sender's order pursuant to Section 4A-403(a)(1) or 4A-403(a)(2); or

(3) the opening of the next funds-transfer business day of the bank following the payment date of the order if, at that time, the amount of the sender's order is fully covered by a withdrawable credit balance in an authorized account of the sender or the bank has otherwise received full payment from the sender, unless the order was rejected before that time or is rejected within (i) one hour after that time, or (ii) one hour after the opening of the next business day of the sender following the payment date if that time is later. If notice of rejection is received by the sender after the payment date and the authorized account of the sender does not bear interest, the bank is obliged to pay interest to the sender on the amount of the order for the number of days elapsing after the payment date to the day the sender receives notice or learns that the order was not accepted, counting that day as an elapsed day. If the withdrawable credit balance during that period falls below the amount of the order, the amount of interest payable is reduced accordingly.

(c) Acceptance of a payment order cannot occur before the order is received by the receiving bank. Acceptance does not occur under subsection (b)(2) or (b)(3) if the beneficiary of the payment order does not have an account with the receiving bank, the account has been closed, or the receiving bank is not permitted by law to receive credits for the beneficiary's account.

(d) A payment order issued to the originator's bank cannot be accepted until the payment date if the bank is the beneficiary's bank, or the execution date if the bank is not the beneficiary's bank. If the originator's bank executes the originator's payment order before the execution date or pays the beneficiary of the originator's payment order before the payment date and the payment order is subsequently canceled pursuant to Section 4A-211(b), the bank may recover from the beneficiary any payment received to the extent allowed by the law governing mistake and restitution.

§ 4A-210. Rejection of Payment Order.

(a) A payment order is rejected by the receiving bank by a notice of rejection transmitted to the sender orally, electronically, or in writing. A notice of rejection need not use any particular words and is sufficient if it indicates that the receiving bank is rejecting the order or will not execute or pay the order. Rejection is effective when the notice is given if transmission is by a means that is reasonable in the circumstances. If notice of rejection is given by a means that is not reasonable, rejection is effective when the notice is received. If an agreement of the sender and receiving bank establishes the means to be used to reject a payment order, (i) any means complying the agreement is reasonable and (ii) any means not complying is not reasonable unless no significant delay in receipt of the notice resulted from the use of the noncomplying means.

(b) This subsection applies if a receiving bank other than the beneficiary's bank fails to execute a payment order despite the existence on the execution date of a withdrawable credit balance in an authorized account of the sender sufficient to cover the order. If the sender does not receive notice of rejection of the order on the execution date and the authorized account of the sender does not bear interest, the bank is obliged to pay interest to the sender on the amount of the order for the number of days elapsing after the execution date to the earlier of the day the order is canceled pursuant to Section 4A-211(d) or the day the sender receives notice or learns that the order was not executed, counting the final day of the period as an elapsed day. If the withdrawable credit balance during that period falls below the amount of the order, the amount of interest is reduced accordingly.

(c) If a receiving bank suspends payments, all unaccepted payment orders issued to it are deemed rejected at the time the bank suspends payments.

(d) Acceptance of a payment order precludes a later rejection of the order. Rejection of a payment order precludes a later acceptance of the order.

§ 4A-211. Cancellation and Amendment of Payment Order.

(a) A communication of the sender of a payment order cancelling or amending the order may be transmitted to the receiving bank orally, electronically, or in writing. If a security procedure is in effect between the sender and the receiving bank, the communication is not effective to cancel or amend the order unless the communication is verified pursuant to the security procedure or the bank agrees to the cancellation or amendment.

(b) Subject to subsection (a), a communication by the sender cancelling or amending a payment order is effective to cancel or amend the order if notice of the communication is received at a time and in a manner affording the receiving bank a reasonable opportunity to act on the communication before the bank accepts the payment order.

(c) After a payment order has been accepted, cancellation or amendment of the order is not effective unless the receiving bank agrees or a funds-transfer system rule allows cancellation or amendment without agreement of the bank.

(1) With respect to a payment order accepted by a receiving bank other than the beneficiary's bank, cancellation or amendment is not effective unless a conforming cancellation or amendment of the payment order issued by the receiving bank is also made.

(2) With respect to a payment order accepted by the beneficiary's bank, cancellation or amendment is not effective unless the order was issued in execution of an unauthorized payment order, or because of a mistake by a sender in the funds transfer which resulted in the issuance of a payment order (i) that is a duplicate of a payment order previously issued by the sender, (ii) that orders payment to a beneficiary not entitled to receive payment from the originator, or (iii) that orders payment in an amount greater than the amount the beneficiary was entitled to receive from the originator. If the payment order is canceled or amended, the beneficiary's bank is entitled to recover from the beneficiary any amount paid to the beneficiary to the extent allowed by the law governing mistake and restitution.

(d) An unaccepted payment order is canceled by operation of law at the close of the fifth funds-transfer business day of the receiving bank after the execution date or payment date of the order.

(e) A canceled payment order cannot be accepted. If an accepted payment order is canceled, the acceptance is nullified and no person has any right or obligation based on the acceptance. Amendment of a payment order is deemed to be cancellation of the original order at the time of amendment and issue of a new payment order in the amended form at the same time.

f) Unless otherwise provided in an agreement of the parties or in a funds-transfer system rule, if the receiving bank, after accepting a payment order, agrees to cancellation or amendment of the order by the sender or is bound by a funds-transfer system rule allowing cancellation or amendment without the bank's agreement, the sender, whether or not cancellation or amendment is effective, is liable to the bank for any loss and expenses, including reasonable attorney's fees, incurred by the bank as a result of the cancellation or amendment or attempted cancellation or amendment.

g) A payment order is not revoked by the death or legal incapacity of the sender unless the receiving bank knows of the death or of an adjudication of incapacity by a court of competent jurisdiction and has reasonable opportunity to act before acceptance of the order.

h) A funds-transfer system rule is not effective to the extent it conflicts with subsection (c)(2).

§ 4A-212. Liability and Duty of Receiving Bank Regarding Unaccepted Payment Order.

If a receiving bank fails to accept a payment order that it is obliged by express agreement to accept, the bank is liable for breach of the agreement to the extent provided in the agreement or in this Article, but does not otherwise have any duty to accept a payment order or, before acceptance, to take any action, or refrain from taking action, with respect to the order except as provided in this Article or by express agreement. Liability based on acceptance arises only when acceptance occurs as stated in Section 4A-209, and liability is limited to that provided in this Article. A receiving bank is not the agent of the sender or beneficiary of the payment order it accepts, or of any other party to the funds transfer, and the bank owes no duty to any party to the funds transfer except as provided in this Article or by express agreement.

Part 3. Execution of Sender's Payment Order by Receiving Bank

§ 4A-301. Execution and Execution Date.

a) A payment order is "executed" by the receiving bank when it issues a payment order intended to carry out the payment order received by the bank. A payment order received by the beneficiary's bank can be accepted but cannot be executed.

b) "Execution date" of a payment order means the day on which the receiving bank may properly issue a payment order in execution of the sender's order. The execution date may be determined by instruction of the sender but cannot be earlier than the day the order is received and, unless otherwise determined, is the day the order is received. If the sender's instruction states a payment date, the execution date is the payment date or an earlier date on which execution is reasonably necessary to allow payment to the beneficiary on the payment date.

§ 4A-302. Obligations of Receiving Bank in Execution of Payment Order.

a) Except as provided in subsections (b) through (d), if the receiving bank accepts a payment order pursuant to Section 4A-209(a), the bank has the following obligations in executing the order:

(1) The receiving bank is obliged to issue, on the execution date, a payment order complying with the sender's order and to follow the sender's instructions concerning (i) any intermediary bank or funds-transfer system to be used in carrying out the funds transfer, or (ii) the means by which payment orders are to be transmitted in the funds transfer. If the originator's bank issues a payment order to an intermediary bank, the originator's bank is obliged to instruct the intermediary bank according to the instruction of the originator. An

intermediary bank in the funds transfer is similarly bound by an instruction given to it by the sender of the payment order it accepts.

(2) If the sender's instruction states that the funds transfer is to be carried out telephonically or by wire transfer or otherwise indicates that the funds transfer is to be carried out by the most expeditious means, the receiving bank is obliged to transmit its payment order by the most expeditious available means, and to instruct any intermediary bank accordingly. If a sender's instruction states a payment date, the receiving bank is obliged to transmit its payment order at a time and by means reasonably necessary to allow payment to the beneficiary on the payment date or as soon thereafter as is feasible.

(b) Unless otherwise instructed, a receiving bank executing a payment order may (i) use any funds-transfer system if use of that system is reasonable in the circumstances, and (ii) issue a payment order to the beneficiary's bank or to an intermediary bank through which a payment order conforming to the sender's order can expeditously be issued to the beneficiary's bank if the receiving bank exercises ordinary care in the selection of the intermediary bank. A receiving bank is not required to follow an instruction of the sender designating a funds-transfer system to be used in carrying out the funds transfer if the receiving bank, in good faith, determines that it is not feasible to follow the instruction or that following the instruction would unduly delay completion of the funds transfer.

(c) Unless subsection (a)(2) applies or the receiving bank is otherwise instructed, the bank may execute a payment order by transmitting its payment order by first class mail or by any means reasonable in the circumstances. If the receiving bank is instructed to execute the sender's order by transmitting its payment order by a particular means, the receiving bank may issue its payment order by the means stated or by any means as expeditious as the means stated.

(d) Unless instructed by the sender, (i) the receiving bank may not obtain payment of its charges for services and expenses in connection with the execution of the sender's order by issuing a payment order in an amount equal to the amount of the sender's order less the amount of the charges, and (ii) may not instruct a subsequent receiving bank to obtain payment of its charges in the same manner.

§ 4A-303. Erroneous Execution of Payment Order.

(a) A receiving bank that (i) executes the payment order of the sender by issuing a payment order in an amount greater than the amount of the sender's order, or (ii) issues a payment order in execution of the sender's order and then issues a duplicate order, is entitled to payment of the amount of the sender's order under Section 4A-402(c) if that subsection is otherwise satisfied. The bank is entitled to recover from beneficiary of the erroneous order the excess payment received to the extent allowed by the law governing mistake and restitution.

(b) A receiving bank that executes the payment order of the sender by issuing a payment order in an amount less than the amount of the sender's order is entitled to payment of the amount of the sender's order under Section 4A-402(c) if (i) that subsection is otherwise satisfied and (ii) the bank corrects its mistake by issuing an additional payment order for the benefit of the beneficiary of the sender's order. If the error is not corrected, the issuer of the erroneous order is entitled to receive or retain payment from the sender of the order it accepted only to the extent of the amount of the erroneous order. This subsection does not apply if the receiving bank executes the sender's payment order by issuing a payment order in an amount less than the amount of the sender's order for the purpose of obtaining payment of its charges for services and expenses pursuant to instruction of the sender.

(c) If a receiving bank executes the payment order of the sender by issuing a payment order to a beneficiary different from the beneficiary of the sender's order and the funds transfer is completed on the basis of that error, the sender of the payment order that was erroneously executed and all previous senders in the funds transfer are not obliged to pay the payment orders they issued. The issuer of the erroneous order is entitled to recover from the payment received to the extent allowed by the law governing mistake and restitution.

§ 4A-304. Duty of Sender to Report Erroneously Executed Payment Order.

If the sender of a payment order that is erroneously executed as stated in Section 4A-303 receives notification from the receiving bank that the order was executed or that the sender's account was debited with respect to the order, the sender has a duty to exercise ordinary care to determine, on the basis of information available to the sender, that the order was erroneously executed and to notify the bank of the relevant facts within a reasonable time not exceeding 90 days after the notification from the bank was received by the sender. If the sender fails to perform that duty, the bank is not obliged to pay interest on any amount refundable to the sender under Section 4A-402(d) for the period before the bank learns of the execution error. The bank is not entitled to any recovery from the sender on account of a failure by the sender to perform the duty stated in this section.

§ 4A-305. Liability for Late or Improper Execution or Failure to Execute Payment Order.

(a) If a funds transfer is completed but execution of a payment order by the receiving bank in breach of Section 4A-302 results in delay in payment to the beneficiary, the bank is obliged to pay interest to either the originator or the beneficiary of the funds transfer for the period of delay caused by the improper execution. Except as provided in subsection (c), additional damages are not recoverable.

(b) If execution of a payment order by a receiving bank in breach of Section 4A-302 results in (i) noncompletion of the funds transfer, (ii) failure to use an intermediary bank designated by the originator, or (iii) issuance of a payment order that does not comply with the terms of the payment order of the originator, the bank is liable to the originator for its expenses in the funds transfer and for incidental expenses and interest losses, to the extent not covered by subsection (a), resulting from the improper execution. Except as provided in subsection (c), additional damages are not recoverable.

(c) In addition to the amounts payable under subsections (a) and (b), damages, including consequential damages, are recoverable to the extent provided in an express written agreement of the receiving bank.

(d) If a receiving bank fails to execute a payment order it was obliged by express agreement to execute, the receiving bank is liable to expenses and interest losses resulting from the failure to execute. Additional damages, including consequential damages, are recoverable to the extent provided in an express written agreement of the receiving bank, but are not otherwise recoverable.

(e) Reasonable attorney's fees are recoverable if demand for compensation under subsection (a) or (b) is made and refused before an action is brought on the claim. If a claim is made for breach of an agreement under subsection (d) and the agreement does not provide for damages, reasonable attorney's fees are recoverable if demand for compensation under subsection (d) is made and refused before an action is brought on the claim.

(f) Except as stated in this section, the liability of a receiving bank under subsections (a) and (b) may not be varied by agreement.

Part 4. Payment

§ 4A-401. Payment Date.

"Payment date" of a payment order means the day on which the amount of the order is payable to the beneficiary by the beneficiary's bank. The payment date may be determined by instruction of the

sender but cannot be earlier than the day the order is received by the beneficiary's bank and, unless otherwise determined, is the day the order is received by the beneficiary's bank.

§ 4A-402. Obligation of Sender to Pay Receiving Bank.

(a) This section is subject to Sections 4A-205 and 4A-207.

(b) With respect to a payment order issued to the beneficiary's bank, acceptance of the order by the bank obliges the sender to pay the bank the amount of the order, but payment is not due until the payment date of the order.

(c) This subsection is subject to subsection (e) and to Section 4A-303. With respect to a payment order issued to a receiving bank other than the beneficiary's bank, acceptance of the order by the receiving bank obliges the sender to pay the bank the amount of the sender's order. Payment by the sender is not due until the execution date of the sender's order. Payment by the sender is not completed by acceptance by the beneficiary's bank of a payment order instructing payment to the beneficiary of that sender's payment order.

(d) If the sender of a payment order pays the order and was not obliged to pay all or part of the amount paid, the bank receiving payment is obliged to refund payment to the extent the sender was not obliged to pay. Except as provided in Sections 4A-204 and 4A-304, interest is payable on the refundable amount from the date of payment.

(e) If a funds transfer is not completed as stated in subsection (c) and an intermediary bank is obliged to refund payment as stated in subsection (d) but is unable to do so because not permitted by applicable law or because the bank suspends payments, a sender in the funds transfer that executed a payment order in compliance with an instruction, as stated in Section 4A-302(a)(1), to route the funds transfer through that intermediary bank is entitled to receive or retain payment from the sender of the payment order that it accepted. The first sender in the funds transfer that issued an instruction requiring routing through that intermediary bank is subrogated to the right of the bank that paid the intermediary bank to refund as stated in subsection (d).

(f) The right of the sender of a payment order to be excused from the obligation to pay the order as stated in subsection (c) or to receive refund under subsection (d) may not be varied by agreement.

§ 4A-403. Payment by Sender to Receiving Bank.

(a) Payment of the sender's obligation under Section 4A-402 to pay the receiving bank occurs as follows:

(1) If the sender is a bank, payment occurs when the receiving bank receives final settlement of the obligation through a Federal Reserve Bank or through a funds-transfer system.

(2) If the sender is a bank and the sender (i) credited an account of the receiving bank with the sender, or (ii) caused an account of the receiving bank in another bank to be credited, payment occurs when the credit is withdrawn or, if not withdrawn, at midnight of the day on which the credit is withdrawable and the receiving bank learns of that fact.

(3) If the receiving bank debits an account of the sender with the receiving bank, payment occurs when the debit is made to the extent the debit is covered by a withdrawable credit balance in the account.

(b) If the sender and receiving bank are members of a funds-transfer system that nets obligations multilaterally among participants, the receiving bank receives final settlement when settlement is complete in accordance with the rules of the system. The obligation of the sender to pay the amount of a payment order transmitted through the funds-transfer system may be satisfied, to the extent permitted by the rules of the system, by setting off and applying against the sender's obligation the right of the sender to receive payment from the receiving bank of the amount of any other payment order transmitted to the sender by the receiving bank through the funds-transfer system. The aggregate balance of obligations owed by each sender to each receiving bank in the funds-transfer system may be satisfied, to the extent permitted by the rules of the system, by setting off and applying against that balance the aggregate balance of obligations owed to the sender by other members of the system. The aggregate balance is determined after the right of setoff stated in the second sentence of this subsection has been exercised.

(c) If two banks transmit payment orders to each other under an agreement that settlement of the obligations of each bank to the other under Section 4A-402 will be made at the end of the day or other period, the total amount owed with respect to all orders transmitted by one bank shall be set off against the total amount owed with respect to all orders transmitted by the other bank. To the extent of the setoff, each bank has made payment to the other.

(d) In a case not covered by subsection (a), the time when payment of the sender's obligation under Section 4A-402(b) or 4A-402(c) occurs is governed by applicable principles of law that determine when an obligation is satisfied.

§ 4A-404. Obligation of Beneficiary's Bank to Pay and Give Notice to Beneficiary.

(a) Subject to Sections 4A-211(e), 4A-405(d), and 4A-405(e), if a beneficiary's bank accepts a payment order, the bank is obliged to pay the amount of the order to the beneficiary of the order. Payment is due on the payment date of the order, but if acceptance occurs on the payment date after the close of the funds-transfer business day of the bank, payment is due on the next funds-transfer business day. If the bank refuses to pay after demand by the beneficiary and receipt of notice of particular circumstances that will give rise to consequential damages as a result of nonpayment, the beneficiary may recover damages resulting from the refusal to pay to the extent the bank had notice of the damages, unless the bank proves that it did not pay because of a reasonable doubt concerning the right of the beneficiary to payment.

(b) If a payment order accepted by the beneficiary's bank instructs payment to an account of the beneficiary, the bank is obliged to notify the beneficiary of receipt of the order before midnight of the next funds-transfer business day following the payment date. If the payment order does not instruct payment to an account of the beneficiary, the bank is required to notify the beneficiary only if notice is required by the order. Notice may be given by first class mail or any other means reasonable in the circumstances. If the bank fails to give the required notice, the bank is obliged to pay interest to the beneficiary on the amount of the payment order from the day notice should have been given until the day the beneficiary learned of receipt of the payment order by the bank. No other damages are recoverable. Reasonable attorney's fees are also recoverable if demand for interest is made and refused before an action is brought on the claim.

(c) The right of a beneficiary to receive payment and damages as stated in subsection (a) may not be varied by agreement or a funds-transfer system rule. The right of a beneficiary to be notified as stated in subsection (b) may be varied by agreement of the beneficiary or by a funds-transfer system rule if the beneficiary is notified of the rule before initiation of the funds transfer.

§ 4A-405. Payment by Beneficiary's Bank to Beneficiary.

(a) If the beneficiary's bank credits an account of the beneficiary of a payment order, payment of the bank's obligation under Section 4A-404(a) occurs when and to the extent (i) the beneficiary is notified of the right to withdraw the credit, (ii) the bank lawfully applies the credit to a debt of the beneficiary, or (iii) funds with respect to the order are otherwise made available to the beneficiary by the bank.

(b) If the beneficiary's bank does not credit an account of the beneficiary of a payment order, the time when payment of the bank's obligation under Section 4A-404(a) occurs is governed by principles of law that determine when an obligation is satisfied.

(c) Except as stated in subsections (d) and (e), the beneficiary's bank pays the beneficiary of a payment order under a condition to payment or agreement of the beneficiary giving the bank the right to recover payment from the beneficiary if the bank does not receive payment of the order, the condition to payment or agreement is not enforceable.

(d) A funds-transfer system rule may provide that payments made to beneficiaries of funds transfers made through the system are provisional until receipt of payment by the beneficiary's bank of the payment order it accepted. A beneficiary's bank that makes a payment that is provisional under the rule is entitled to refund from the beneficiary if (i) the rule requires that both the beneficiary and the originator be given notice of the provisional nature of the payment before the funds transfer is initiated, (ii) the beneficiary, the beneficiary's bank and the originator's bank agreed to be bound by the rule, and (iii) the beneficiary's bank did not receive payment of the payment order that it accepted. If the beneficiary is obliged to refund payment to the beneficiary's bank, acceptance of the payment order by the beneficiary's bank is nullified and no payment by the originator of the funds transfer to the beneficiary occurs under Section 4A-406.

(e) This subsection applies to a funds transfer that includes a payment order transmitted over a funds-transfer system that (i) nets obligations multilaterally among participants, and (ii) has in effect a loss-sharing agreement among participants for the purpose of providing funds necessary to complete settlement of the obligations of one or more participants that do not meet their settlement obligations. If the beneficiary's bank in the funds transfer accepts a payment order and the system fails to complete settlement pursuant to its rules with respect to any payment order in the funds transfer, (i) the acceptance by the beneficiary's bank is nullified and no person has any right or obligation based on the acceptance, (ii) the beneficiary's bank is entitled to recover payment from the beneficiary, (iii) no payment by the originator to the beneficiary occurs under Section 4A-406, and (iv) subject to Section 4A-402(e), each sender in the funds transfer is excused from its obligation to pay its payment order under Section 4A-402(c) because the funds transfer has not been completed.

§ 4A-406. Payment by Originator to Beneficiary; Discharge of Underlying Obligation.

(a) Subject to Sections 4A-211(e), 4A-405(d), 4A-405(e), the originator of a funds transfer pays the beneficiary of the originator's payment order (i) at the time a payment order for the benefit of the beneficiary is accepted by the beneficiary's bank in the funds transfer and (ii) in an amount equal to the amount of the order accepted by the beneficiary's bank, but not more than the amount of the originator's order.

(b) If payment under subsection (a) is made to satisfy an obligation the obligation is discharged to the same extend discharge would result from payment to the beneficiary of the same amount in money, unless (i) the payment under subsection (a) was made by a means prohibited by the contract of the beneficiary with respect to the obligation, (ii) the beneficiary, within a reasonable time after receiving notice of receipt of the order by the beneficiary's bank, notified the originator of the beneficiary's refusal of the payment, (iii) funds with respect to the order were not withdrawn by the beneficiary or applied to a debt of the beneficiary, and (iv) the beneficiary would suffer a loss that could reasonably have been avoided if payment had been made by a means complying with the contract. If payment by the originator does not result in discharge under this section, the originator is subrogated to the rights of the beneficiary to receive payment from the beneficiary's bank under Section 4A-404(a).

(c) For the purpose of determining whether discharge of an obligation occurs under subsection (b), if the beneficiary's bank accepts a payment order in an amount equal to the amount of the originator's payment order less charges of one or more receiving banks in the funds transfer, payment to the beneficiary is deemed to be in the amount of the originator's order unless upon demand by the beneficiary the originator does not pay the beneficiary the amount of the deducted charges.

(d) Rights of the originator or of the beneficiary of a funds transfer under this section may be varied only by agreement of the originator and the beneficiary.

Part 5. Miscellaneous Provisions

§ 4A-501. Variation by Agreement and Effect of Funds-Transfer System Rule.

(a) Except as otherwise provided in this Article, the rights and obligations of a party to a funds transfer may be varied by agreement of the affected party.

(b) "Funds-transfer system rule" means a rule of an association of banks (i) governing transmission of payment orders by means of a funds-transfer system of the association or rights and obligations with respect to those orders, or (ii) to the extent the rule governs rights and obligations between banks that are parties to a funds transfer in which a Federal Reserve Bank, acting as an intermediary bank, sends a payment order to the beneficiary's bank. Except as otherwise provided in this Article, a funds-transfer system rule governing rights and obligations between participating banks using the system may be effective even if the rule conflicts with this Article and indirectly affects another party to the funds transfer who does not consent to the rule. A funds-transfer system rule may also govern rights and obligations of parties other than participating banks using the system to the extent stated in Sections 4A-404(c), 4A-405(d), and 4A-507(c).

§ 4A-502. Creditor Process Served on Receiving Bank; Set-off by Beneficiary's Bank.

(a) As used in this section, "creditor process" means levy, attachment, garnishment, notice of lien, sequestration, or similar process issued by or on behalf of a creditor or other claimant with respect to an account.

(b) This subsection applies to creditor process with respect to an authorized account of the sender of a payment order if the creditor process is served on the receiving bank. For the purpose of determining rights with respect to the creditor process, if the receiving bank accepts the payment order the balance in the authorized account is deemed to be reduced by the amount of the payment order to the extent the bank did not otherwise receive payment of the order, unless the creditor process is served at a time and in a manner affording the bank a reasonable opportunity to act on it before the bank accepts the payment order.

(c) If the beneficiary's bank has received a payment order for payment to the beneficiary's account in the bank, the following rules apply:

(1) The bank may credit the beneficiary's account. The amount credited may be set off against an obligation owed by the beneficiary to the bank or may be applied to satisfy creditor process served on the bank with respect to the account.

(2) The bank may credit the beneficiary's account and allow withdrawal of the amount credited unless creditor process with respect to the account is served at a time and in a manner affording the bank a reasonable opportunity to act to prevent withdrawal.

(3) If creditor process with respect to the beneficiary's account has been served and the bank has had a reasonable opportunity to act on it, the bank may not reject the payment order except for a reason unrelated to the service of process.

(d) Creditor process with respect to a payment by the originator to the beneficiary pursuant to a funds transfer may be served only on the beneficiary's bank with respect to the debt owed by that bank to the beneficiary. Any other bank served with the creditor process is not obliged to act with respect to the process.

§ 4A-503. Injunction or Restraining Order With Respect to Funds Transfer.

For proper cause and in compliance with applicable law, a court may restrain (i) a person from issuing a payment order to initiate a funds transfer, (ii) an originator's bank from executing the payment order of the originator, or (iii) the beneficiary's bank from releasing funds to the beneficiary or the beneficiary from withdrawing the funds. A court may not otherwise restrain a person from issuing a payment order, paying or receiving payment of a payment order, or otherwise acting with respect to a funds transfer.

§ 4A-504. Order in Which Items and Payment Orders May Be Charged to Account; Order of Withdrawals From Account.

(a) If a receiving bank has received more than one payment order of the sender or one or more payment orders and other items that are payable from the sender's account, the bank may charge the sender's account with respect to the various orders and items in any sequence.

(b) In determining whether a credit to an account has been withdrawn by the holder of the account or applied to a debt of the holder of the account, credits first made to the account are first withdrawn or applied.

§ 4A-505. Preclusion of Objection to Debit of Customer's Account.

If a receiving bank has received payment from its customer with respect to a payment order issued in the name of the customer as sender and accepted by the bank, and the customer received notification reasonably identifying the order, the customer is precluded from asserting that the bank is not entitled to retain the payment unless the customer notifies the bank of the customer's objection to the payment within one year after the notification was received by the customer.

§ 4A-506. Rate of Interest.

(a) If, under this Article, a receiving bank is obliged to pay interest with respect to a payment order issued to the bank, the amount payable may be determined (i) by agreement of the sender and receiving bank, or (ii) by a funds-transfer system rule if the payment order is transmitted through a funds-transfer system.

(b) If the amount of interest is not determined by an agreement or rule as stated in subsection (a), the amount is calculated by multiplying the applicable Federal Funds rate by the amount on which interest is payable, and then multiplying the product by the number of days for which interest is payable. The applicable Federal Funds rate is the average of the Federal Funds rates published by the Federal Reserve Bank of New York for each of the days for which interest is payable divided by 360. The Federal Funds rate for any day on which a published rate is not available is the same as the published rate for the next preceding day for which there is a published rate. If a receiving bank that accepted a payment order is required to refund payment to the sender of the order because the funds transfer was not completed, but the failure to complete was not due to any fault by the bank, the interest payable is reduced by a percentage equal to the reserve requirement on deposits of the receiving bank.

§ 4A-507. Choice of Law.

(a) The following rules apply unless the affected parties otherwise agree or subsection (c) applies:

(1) The rights and obligations between the sender of a payment order and the receiving bank are governed by the law of the jurisdiction in which the receiving bank is located.

(2) The rights and obligations between the beneficiary's bank and the beneficiary are governed by the law of the jurisdiction in which the beneficiary's bank is located.

(3) The issue of when payment is made pursuant to a funds transfer of the originator to the beneficiary is governed by the law of the jurisdiction in which the beneficiary's bank is located.

(b) If the parties described in each paragraph of subsection (a) have made an agreement selecting the law of a particular jurisdiction to govern rights and obligations between each other, the law of that jurisdiction governs those rights and obligations, whether or not the payment order or the funds transfer bears a reasonable relation to that jurisdiction.

(c) A funds-transfer system rule may select the law of a particular jurisdiction to govern (i) rights and obligations between participating banks with respect to payment orders transmitted or processed through the system, or (ii) the rights and obligations of some or all parties to a funds transfer any part of which is carried out by means of the system. A choice of law made pursuant to clause (i) is binding on participating banks. A choice of law made pursuant to clause (ii) is binding on the originator, other sender, or a receiving bank having notice that the funds-transfer system might be used in the funds transfer and of the choice of law by the system when the originator, other sender, or receiving bank issued or accepted a payment order. The beneficiary of a funds transfer is bound by the choice of law if, when the funds transfer is initiated, the beneficiary has notice that the funds-transfer system might be used in the funds transfer and of the choice of law by the system. The law of a jurisdiction selected pursuant to this subsection may govern, whether or not that law bears a reasonable relation to the matter in issue.

(d) In the event of inconsistency between an agreement under subsection (b) and a choice-of-law rule under subsection (c), the agreement under subsection (b) prevails.

(e) If a funds transfer is made by use of more than one funds-transfer system and there is inconsistency between choice-of-law rules of the systems, the matter in issue is governed by the law of the selected jurisdiction that has the most significant relationship to the matter in issue.

ARTICLE 5. LETTERS OF CREDIT
[TEXT NOT INCLUDED]

ARTICLE 6. BULK SALES

§ 6-101. Short Title.
This Article shall be known and may be cited as Uniform Commercial Code—Bulk Sales.

§ 6-102. Definitions and Index of Definitions.

(1) In this Article, unless the context otherwise requires:

(a) "Assets" means the inventory that is the subject of a bulk sale and any tangible and intangible personal property used or held for use primarily in, or arising from, the seller's business and sold in connection with that inventory, but the term does not include:

(i) fixtures (Section 9-313(1)(a)) other than readily removable factory and office machines;

(ii) the lessee's interest in a lease of real property; or

(iii) property to the extent it is generally exempt from creditor process under nonbankruptcy law.

(b) "Auctioneer" means a person whom the seller engages to direct, conduct, control, or be responsible for a sale by auction.

(c) "Bulk sale" means:

(i) in the case of a sale by auction or a sale or series of sales conducted by a liquidator on the seller's behalf, a sale or series of sales not in the ordinary course of the seller's business of more than half of the seller's inventory, as measured by value on the date of the bulk-sale agreement, if on that date the auctioneer or liquidator has notice, or after reasonable inquiry would have had notice, that the seller will not continue to operate the same or a similar kind of business after the sale or series of sales; and

(ii) in all other cases, a sale not in the ordinary course of the seller's business of more than half the seller's inventory, as measured by value on the date of the bulk-sale agreement, if on that date the buyer has notice, or after reasonable inquiry would have had notice, that the seller will not continue to operate the same or a similar kind of business after the sale.

(d) "Claim" means a right to payment from the seller, whether or not the right is reduced to judgment, liquidated, fixed, matured, disputed, secured, legal, or equitable. The term includes costs of collection and attorney's fees only to the extent that the laws of this state permit the holder of the claim to recover them in an action against the obligor.

(e) "Claimant" means a person holding a claim incurred in the seller's business other than:

(i) an unsecured and unmatured claim for employment compensation and benefits, including commissions and vacation, severance, and sick-leave pay;

(ii) a claim for injury to an individual or to property, or for breach of warranty, unless:

(A) a right of action for the claim has accrued;

(B) the claim has been asserted against the seller; and

(C) the seller knows the identity of the person asserting the claim and the basis upon which the person has asserted it; and

(States To Select One Alternative)

Alternative A

[(iii) a claim for taxes owing to a governmental unit.]

Alternative B

[(iii) a claim for taxes owing to a governmental unit, if:

(A) a statute governing the enforcement of the claim permits or requires notice of the bulk sale to be given to the governmental unit in a manner other than by compliance with the requirements of this Article; and

(B) notice is given in accordance with the statute.]

(f) "Creditor" means a claimant or other person holding a claim.

(g) (i) "Date of the bulk sale" means:

(A) if the sale is by auction or is conducted by a liquidator on the seller's behalf, the date on which more than ten percent of the net proceeds is paid to or for the benefit of the seller; and

(B) in all other cases, the later of the date on which:

(I) more than ten percent of the net contract price is paid to or for the benefit of the seller; or

(II) more than ten percent of the assets, as measured by value, are transferred to the buyer.

(ii) For purposes of this subsection:

(A) Delivery of a negotiable instrument (Section 3-104(1)) to or for the benefit of the seller in exchange for assets constitutes payment of the contract price pro tanto;

(B) To the extent that the contract price is deposited in an escrow, the contract price is paid to or for the benefit of the seller when the seller acquires the unconditional right to receive the deposit or when the deposit is delivered to the seller or for the benefit of the seller, whichever is earlier; and

(C) An asset is transferred when a person holding an unsecured claim can no longer obtain through judicial proceedings rights to the asset that are superior to those of the buyer arising as a result of the bulk sale. A person holding an unsecured claim can obtain those superior rights to a tangible asset at least until the buyer has an unconditional right, under the bulk-sale agreement, to possess the asset, and a person holding an unsecured claim can obtain those superior rights to an intangible asset at least until the buyer has an unconditional right, under the bulk-sale agreement, to use the asset.

(h) "Date of the bulk-sale agreement" means:

(i) in the case of a sale by auction or conducted by a liquidator (subsection (c)(i)), the date on which the seller engages the auctioneer or liquidator; and

(ii) in all other cases, the date on which a bulk-sale agreement becomes enforceable between the buyer and the seller.

(i) "Debt" means liability on a claim.

(j) "Liquidator" means a person who is regularly engaged in the business of disposing of assets for businesses contemplating liquidation or dissolution.

(k) "Net contract price" means the new consideration the buyer is obligated to pay for the assets less:

(i) the amount of any proceeds of the sale of an asset, to the extent the proceeds are applied in partial or total satisfaction of a debt secured by the asset; and

(ii) the amount of any debt to the extent it is secured by a security interest or lien that is enforceable against the asset before and after it has been sold to a buyer. If a debt is secured by an asset and other property of the seller, the amount of the debt secured by a security interest or lien that is enforceable against the asset is determined by multiplying the debt by a fraction, the numerator of which is the value of the new consideration for the asset on the date of the bulk sale and the denominator of which is the value of all property securing the debt on the date of the bulk sale.

(l) "Net proceeds" means the new consideration received for assets sold at a sale by auction or a sale conducted by a liquidator on the seller's behalf less:

(i) commissions and reasonable expenses of the sale;

(ii) the amount of any proceeds of the sale of an asset, to the extent the proceeds are applied in partial or total satisfaction of a debt secured by the asset; and

(iii) the amount of any debt to the extent it is secured by a security interest or lien that is enforceable against the asset before and after it has been sold to a buyer. If a debt is secured by an asset and other property of the seller, the amount of the debt secured by a security interest or lien that is enforceable against the asset is determined by multiplying the debt by a fraction, the numerator of which is the value of the new consideration for the asset on the date of the bulk sale and the denominator of which is the value of all property securing the debt on the date of the bulk sale.

(m) A sale is "in the ordinary course of the seller's business" if the sale comports with usual or customary practices in the kind of business in which the seller is engaged or with the seller's own usual or customary practices.

(n) "United States" includes its territories and possessions and the Commonwealth of Puerto Rico.

(o) "Value" means fair market value.

(p) "Verified" means signed and sworn to or affirmed.

(2) The following definitions in other Articles apply to this Article:

(a) "Buyer."	Section 2-103(1)(a).
(b) "Equipment."	Section 9-109(2).
(c) "Inventory."	Section 9-109(4).
(d) "Sale."	Section 2-106(1).
(e) "Seller."	Section 2-103(1)(d).

(3) In addition, Article 1 contains general definitions and principles of construction and interpretation applicable throughout this Article.

§ 6-103. Applicability of Article.

(1) Except as otherwise provided in subsection (3), this Article applies to a bulk sale if:

(a) the seller's principal business is the sale of inventory from stock; and

(b) on the date of the bulk-sale agreement the seller is located in this state or, if the seller is located in a jurisdiction that is not a part of the United States, the seller's major executive office in the United States is in this state.

(2) A seller is deemed to be located at his [or her] place of business. If a seller has more than one place of business, the seller is deemed located at his [or her] chief executive office.

(3) This Article does not apply to:

(a) a transfer made to secure payment or performance of an obligation;

(b) a transfer of collateral to a secured party pursuant to Section 9-503;

(c) a sale of collateral pursuant to Section 9-504;

(d) retention of collateral pursuant to Section 9-505;

(e) a sale of an asset encumbered by a security interest or lien if (i) all the proceeds of the sale are applied in partial or total satisfaction of the debt secured by the security interest or lien or (ii) the security interest or lien is enforceable against the asset after it has been sold to the buyer and the net contract price is zero;

(f) a general assignment for the benefit of creditors or to a subsequent transfer by the assignee;

(g) a sale by an executor, administrator, receiver, trustee in bankruptcy, or any public officer under judicial process;

(h) a sale made in the course of judicial or administrative proceedings for the dissolution or reorganization of an organization;

(i) a sale to a buyer whose principal place of business is in the United States and who:

(i) not earlier than 21 days before the date of the bulk sale, (A) obtains from the seller a verified and dated list of claimants of whom the seller has notice three days before the seller sends or delivers the list to the buyer or (B) conducts a reasonable inquiry to discover the claimants;

(ii) assumes in full the debts owed to claimants of whom the buyer has knowledge on the date the buyer receives the list of claimants from the seller or on the date the buyer completes the reasonable inquiry, as the case may be;

(iii) is not insolvent after the assumption; and

(iv) gives written notice of the assumption not later than 30 days after the date of the bulk sale by sending or delivering a notice to the claimants identified in subparagraph (ii) or by filing a notice in the office of the [Secretary of State];

(j) a sale to a buyer whose principal place of business is in the United States and who:

(i) assumes in full the debts that were incurred in the seller's business before the date of the bulk sale;

(ii) is not insolvent after the assumption; and

(iii) gives written notice of the assumption not later than 30 days after the date of the bulk sale by sending or delivering a notice to each creditor whose debt is assumed or by filing a notice in the office of the [Secretary of State];

(k) a sale to a new organization that is organized to take over and continue the business of the seller and that has its principal place of business in the United States if:

(i) the buyer assumes in full the debts that were incurred in the seller's business before the date of the bulk sale;

(ii) the seller receives nothing from the sale except an interest in the new organization that is subordinate to the claims against the organization arising from the assumption; and

(iii) the buyer gives written notice of the assumption not later than 30 days after the date of the bulk sale by sending or delivering a notice to each creditor whose debt is assumed or by filing a notice in the office of the [Secretary of State];

(l) a sale of assets having:

(i) a value, net of liens and security interests, of less than $10,000. If a debt is secured by assets and other property of the seller, the net value of the assets is determined by subtracting from their value an amount equal to the product of the debt multiplied by a fraction, the numerator of which is the value of the assets on the date of the bulk sale and the denominator of which is the value of all property securing the debt on the date of the bulk sale; or

(ii) a value of more than $25,000,000 on the date of the bulk-sale agreement; or

(m) a sale required by, and made pursuant to, statute.

(4) The notice under subsection (3)(i)(iv) must state: (i) that a sale that may constitute a bulk sale has been or will be made; (ii) the date or prospective date of the bulk sale; (iii) the individual, partnership, or corporate names and the addresses of the seller and buyer; (iv) the address to which inquiries about the sale may be made, if different from the seller's address; and (v) that the buyer has assumed or will assume in full the debts owed to claimants of whom the buyer has knowledge on the date the buyer receives the list of claimants from the seller or completes a reasonable inquiry to discover the claimants.

(5) The notice under subsections (3)(j)(iii) and (3)(k)(iii) must state: (i) that a sale that may constitute a bulk sale has been or will be made; (ii) the date or prospective date of the bulk sale; (iii) the individual partnership, or corporate names and the addresses of the seller and buyer; (iv) the address to which inquiries about the sale may be made, if different from the seller's address; and (v) that the buyer has assumed or will assume the debts that were incurred in the seller's business before the date of the bulk sale.

(6) For purposes of subsection (3)(l), the value of assets is presumed to be equal to the price the buyer agrees to pay for the assets. However, in a sale by auction or a sale conducted by a liquidator on the seller's behalf, the value of assets is presumed to be the amount the auctioneer or liquidator reasonably estimates the assets will bring at auction or upon liquidation.

§ 6-104. Obligations of Buyer.

(1) In a bulk sale as defined in Section 6-102(1)(c)(ii) the buyer shall:

(a) obtain from the seller a list of all business names and addresses used by the seller within three years before the date the list is sent or delivered to the buyer;

(b) unless excused under subsection (2), obtain from the seller a verified and dated list of claimants of whom the seller has notice three days before the seller sends or delivers the list to the buyer

and including, to the extent known by the seller, the address of and the amount claimed by each claimant;

(c) obtain from the seller or prepare a schedule of distribution (Section 6-106(1));

(d) give notice of the bulk sale in accordance with Section 6-105;

(e) unless excused under Section 6-106(4), distribute the net contract price in accordance with the undertakings of the buyer in the schedule of distribution; and

(f) unless excused under subsection (2), make available the list of claimants (subsection (1)(b)) by:

(i) promptly sending or delivering a copy of the list without charge to any claimant whose written request is received by the buyer no later than six months after the date of the bulk sale;

(ii) permitting any claimant to inspect and copy the list at any reasonable hour upon request received by the buyer no later than six months after the date of the bulk sale; or

(iii) filing a copy of the list in the office of the [Secretary of State] no later than the time for giving a notice of the bulk sale (Section 6-105(5)). A list filed in accordance with this subparagraph must state the individual, partnership, or corporate name and a mailing address of the seller.

(2) A buyer who gives notice in accordance with Section 6-105(2) is excused from complying with the requirements of subsection (1)(b) and (1)(f).

§ 6-105. Notice to Claimants.

(1) Except as otherwise provided in subsection (2), to comply with Section 6-104(1)(d), the buyer shall send or deliver a written notice of the bulk sale to each claimant on the list of claimants (Section 6-104(1)(b)) and to any other claimant of whom the buyer has knowledge at the time the notice of the bulk sale is sent or delivered.

(2) A buyer may comply with Section 6-104(1)(d) by filing a written notice of the bulk sale in the office of the [Secretary of State] if:

(a) on the date of the bulk-sale agreement the seller has 200 or more claimants, exclusive of claimants holding secured or matured claims for employment compensation and benefits, including commissions and vacation, severance, and sick-leave pay; or

(b) the buyer has received a verified statement from the seller stating that, as of the date of the bulk-sale agreement, the number of claimants, exclusive of claimants holding secured or matured claims for employment compensation and benefits, including commissions and vacation, severance, and sick-leave pay, is 200 or more.

(3) The written notice of the bulk sale must be accompanied by a copy of the schedule of distribution (Section 6-106(1)) and state at least:

(a) that the seller and buyer have entered into an agreement for a sale that may constitute a bulk sale under the laws of the State of _____;

(b) the date of the agreement;

(c) the date on or after which more than ten percent of the assets were or will be transferred;

(d) the date on or after which more than ten percent of the net contract price was or will be paid, if the date is not stated in the schedule of distribution;

(e) the name and a mailing address of the seller;

(f) any other business name and address listed by the seller pursuant to Section 6-104(1)(a);

(g) the name of the buyer and an address of the buyer from which information concerning the sale can be obtained;

(h) a statement indicating the type of assets or describing the assets item by item;

(i) the manner in which the buyer will make available the list of claimants (Section 6-104(1)(f)), if applicable; and

(j) if the sale is in total or partial satisfaction of an antecedent debt owed by the seller, the amount of the debt to be satisfied and the name of the person to whom it is owed.

(4) For purposes of subsections (3)(e) and (3)(g), the name of a person is the person's individual, partnership, or corporate name.

(5) The buyer shall give notice of the bulk sale not less than 45 days before the date of the bulk sale and, if the buyer gives notice in accordance with subsection (1), not more than 30 days after obtaining the list of claimants.

(6) A written notice substantially complying with the requirements of subsection (3) is effective even though it contains minor errors that are not seriously misleading.

(7) A form substantially as follows is sufficient to comply with subsection (3):

Notice of Sale

(1) _____, whose address is _____, is described in this notice as the "seller."

(2) _____, whose address is _____, is described in this notice as the "buyer."

(3) The seller has disclosed to the buyer that within the past three years the seller has used other business names, operated at other addresses, or both, as follows: _____.

(4) The seller and the buyer have entered into an agreement dated _____, for a sale that may constitute a bulk sale under the laws of the state of _____.

(5) The date on or after which more than ten percent of the assets that are the subject of the sale were or will be transferred is _____, and [if not stated in the schedule of distribution] the date on or after which more than ten percent of the net contract price was or will be paid is _____.

(6) The following assets are the subject of the sale: _____.

(7) [If applicable] The buyer will make available to claimants of the seller a list of the seller's claimants in the following manner: _____.

(8) [If applicable] The sale is to satisfy $_____ of an antecedent debt owed by the seller to _____.

(9) A copy of the schedule of distribution of the net contract price accompanies this notice.

[End of Notice]

§ 6-106. Schedule of Distribution.

(1) The seller and buyer shall agree on how the net contract price is to be distributed and set forth their agreement in a written schedule of distribution.

(2) The schedule of distribution may provide for distribution to any person at any time, including distribution of the entire net contract price to the seller.

(3) The buyer's undertakings in the schedule of distribution run only to the seller. However, a buyer who fails to distribute the net contract price in accordance with the buyer's undertakings in the schedule of distribution is liable to a creditor only as provided in Section 6-107(1).

(4) If the buyer undertakes in the schedule of distribution to distribute any part of the net contract price to a person other than the seller, and, after the buyer has given notice in accordance with Section 6-105, some or all of the anticipated net contract price is or becomes

unavailable for distribution as a consequence of the buyer's or seller's having complied with an order of court, legal process, statute, or rule of law, the buyer is excused from any obligation arising under this Article or under any contract with the seller to distribute the net contract price in accordance with the buyer's undertakings in the schedule if the buyer:

(a) distributes the net contract price remaining available in accordance with any priorities for payment stated in the schedule of distribution and, to the extent that the price is insufficient to pay all the debts having a given priority, distributes the price pro rata among those debts shown in the schedule as having the same priority;

(b) distributes the net contract price remaining available in accordance with an order of court;

(c) commences a proceeding for interpleader in a court of competent jurisdiction and is discharged from the proceeding; or

(d) reaches a new agreement with the seller for the distribution of the net contract price remaining available, sets forth the new agreement in an amended schedule of distribution, gives notice of the amended schedule, and distributes the net contract price remaining available in accordance with the buyer's undertakings in the amended schedule.

(5) The notice under subsection (4)(d) must identify the buyer and the seller, state the filing number, if any, of the original notice, set forth the amended schedule, and be given in accordance with subsection (1) or (2) of Section 6-105, whichever is applicable, at least 14 days before the buyer distributes any part of the net contract price remaining available.

(6) If the seller undertakes in the schedule of distribution to distribute any part of the net contract price, and, after the buyer has given notice in accordance with Section 6-105, some or all of the anticipated net contract price is or becomes unavailable for distribution as a consequence of the buyer's or seller's having complied with an order of court, legal process, statute, or rule of law, the seller and any person in control of the seller are excused from any obligation arising under this Article or under any agreement with the buyer to distribute the net contract price in accordance with the seller's undertakings in the schedule if the seller:

(a) distributes the net contract price remaining available in accordance with any priorities for payment stated in the schedule of distribution and, to the extent that the price is insufficient to pay all the debts having a given priority, distributes the price pro rata among those debts shown in the schedule as having the same priority;

(b) distributes the net contract price remaining available in accordance with an order of court;

(c) commences a proceeding for interpleader in a court of competent jurisdiction and is discharged from the proceeding; or

(d) prepares a written amended schedule of distribution of the net contract price remaining available for distribution, gives notice of the amended schedule, and distributes the net contract price remaining available in accordance with the amended schedule.

(7) The notice under subsection (6)(d) must identify the buyer and the seller, state the filing number, if any, of the original notice, set forth the amended schedule, and be given in accordance with subsection (1) or (2) of Section 6-105, whichever is applicable, at least 14 days before the seller distributes any part of the net contract price remaining available.

§ 6-107. Liability for Noncompliance.

(1) Except as provided in subsection (3), and subject to the limitation in subsection (4):

(a) a buyer who fails to comply with the requirements of Section 6-104(1)(e) with respect to a creditor is liable to the creditor for damages in the amount of the claim, reduced by any amount that the creditor would not have realized if the buyer had complied; and

(b) a buyer who fails to comply with the requirements of any other subsection of Section 6-104 with respect to a claimant is liable to the claimant for damages in the amount of the claim, reduced by any amount that the claimant would not have realized if the buyer had complied.

(2) In an action under subsection (1), the creditor has the burden of establishing the validity and amount of the claim, and the buyer has the burden of establishing the amount that the creditor would not have realized if the buyer had complied.

(3) A buyer who:

(a) made a good faith and commercially reasonable effort to comply with the requirements of Section 6-104(1) or to exclude the sale from the application of this Article under Section 6-103(3); or

(b) on or after the date of the bulk-sale agreement, but before the date of the bulk sale, held a good faith and commercially reasonable belief that this Article does not apply to the particular sale is not liable to creditors for failure to comply with the requirements of Section 6-104. The buyer has the burden of establishing the good faith and commercial reasonableness of the effort or belief.

(4) In a single bulk sale the cumulative liability of the buyer for failure to comply with the requirements of Section 6-104(1) may not exceed an amount equal to:

(a) if the assets consist only of inventory and equipment, twice the net contract price, less the amount of any part of the net contract price paid to or applied for the benefit of the seller or a creditor; or

(b) if the assets include property other than inventory and equipment, twice the net value of the inventory and equipment less the amount of the portion of any part of the net contract price paid to or applied for the benefit of the seller or a creditor which is allocable to the inventory and equipment.

(5) For the purposes of subsection (4)(b), the "net value" of an asset is the value of the asset less (i) the amount of any proceeds of the sale of an asset, to the extent the proceeds are applied in partial or total satisfaction of a debt secured by the asset and (ii) the amount of any debt to the extent it is secured by a security interest or lien that is enforceable against the asset before and after it has been sold to a buyer. If a debt is secured by an asset and other property of the seller, the amount of the debt secured by a security interest or lien that is enforceable against the asset is determined by multiplying the debt by a fraction, the numerator of which is the value of the asset on the date of the bulk sale and the denominator of which is the value of all property securing the debt on the date of the bulk sale. The portion of a part of the net contract price paid to or applied for the benefit of the seller or a creditor that is "allocable to the inventory and equipment" is the portion that bears the same ratio to that part of the net contract price as the net value of the inventory and equipment bears to the net value of all the assets.

(6) A payment made by the buyer to a person to whom the buyer is, or believes he [or she] is, liable under subsection (1) reduces pro tanto the buyer's cumulative liability under subsection (4).

(7) No action may be brought under subsection (1)(b) by or on behalf of a claimant whose claim is unliquidated or contingent.

(8) A buyer's failure to comply with the requirements of Section 6-104(1) does not (i) impair the buyer's rights in or title to the assets, (ii) render the sale ineffective, void, or voidable, (iii) entitle a creditor to more than a single satisfaction of his [or her] claim, or (iv) create liability other than as provided in this Article.

(9) Payment of the buyer's liability under subsection (1) discharges pro tanto the seller's debt to the creditor.

(10) Unless otherwise agreed, a buyer has an immediate right of reimbursement from the seller for any amount paid to a creditor in partial or total satisfaction of the buyer's liability under subsection (1).

(11) If the seller is an organization, a person who is in direct or indirect control of the seller, and who knowingly, intentionally, and without legal justification fails, or causes the seller to fail, to distribute the net contract price in accordance with the schedule of distribution is liable to any creditor to whom the seller undertook to make payment under the schedule for damages caused by the failure.

§ 6-108. Bulk Sales by Auction; Bulk Sales Conducted by Liquidator.

(1) Sections 6-104, 6-105, 6-106, and 6-107 apply to a bulk sale by auction and a bulk sale conducted by a liquidator on the seller's behalf with the following modifications:

(a) "buyer" refers to auctioneer or liquidator, as the case may be;

(b) "net contract price" refers to net proceeds of the auction or net proceeds of the sale, as the case may be;

(c) the written notice required under Section 6-105(3) must be accompanied by a copy of the schedule of distribution (Section 6-106(1)) and state at least:

(i) that the seller and the auctioneer or liquidator have entered into an agreement for auction or liquidation services that may constitute an agreement to make a bulk sale under the laws of the State of _____;

(ii) the date of the agreement;

(iii) the date on or after the auction began or will begin or the date on or after which the liquidator began or will begin to sell assets on the seller's behalf;

(iv) the date on or after which more than ten percent of the net proceeds of the sale were or will be paid, if the date is not stated in the schedule of distribution;

(v) the name and a mailing address of the seller;

(vi) any other business name and address listed by the seller pursuant to Section 6-104(1)(a);

(vii) the name of the auctioneer or liquidator and an address of the auctioneer or liquidator from which information concerning the sale can be obtained;

(viii) a statement indicating the type of assets or describing the assets item by item;

(ix) the manner in which the auctioneer or liquidator will make available the list of claimants (Section 6-104(1)(f)), if applicable; and

(x) if the sale is in total or partial satisfaction of an antecedent debt owed by the seller, the amount of the debt to be satisfied and the name of the person to whom it is owed; and

(d) in a single bulk sale the cumulative liability of the auctioneer or liquidator for failure to comply with the requirements of this section may not exceed the amount of the net proceeds of the sale allocable to inventory and equipment sold less the amount of the portion of any part of the net proceeds paid to or applied for the benefit of a creditor which is allocable to the inventory and equipment.

(2) A payment made by the auctioneer or liquidator to a person to whom the auctioneer or liquidator is, or believes he [or she] is, liable under this section reduces pro tanto the auctioneer's or liquidator's cumulative liability under subsection (1)(d).

(3) A form substantially as follows is sufficient to comply with subsection (1)(c):

Notice of Sale

(1) _____, whose address is _____, is described in this notice as the "seller."

(2) _____, whose address is _____, is described in this notice as the "auctioneer" or "liquidator."

(3) The seller has disclosed to the auctioneer or liquidator that within the past three years the seller has used other business names, operated at other addresses, or both, as follows: _____.

(4) The seller and the auctioneer or liquidator have entered into an agreement dated _____ for auction or liquidation services that may constitute an agreement to make a bulk sale under the laws of the State of _____.

(5) The date on or after which the auction began or will begin or the date on or after which the liquidator began or will begin to sell assets on the seller's behalf is _____, and [if not stated in the schedule of distribution] the date on or after which more than ten percent of the net proceeds of the sale were or will be paid is _____.

(6) The following assets are the subject of the sale: _____.

(7) [If applicable] The auctioneer or liquidator will make available to claimants of the seller a list of the seller's claimants in the following manner: _____.

(8) [If applicable] The sale is to satisfy $_____ of an antecedent debt owed by the seller to _____.

(9) A copy of the schedule of distribution of the net proceeds accompanies this notice.

[End of Notice]

(4) A person who buys at a bulk sale by auction or conducted by a liquidator need not comply with the requirements of Section 6-104(1) and is not liable for the failure of an auctioneer or liquidator to comply with the requirements of this section.

§ 6-109. What Constitutes Filing; Duties of Filing Officer; Information from Filing Officer.

(1) Presentation of a notice or list of claimants for filing and tender of the filing fee or acceptance of the notice or list by the filing officer constitutes filing under this Article.

(2) The filing officer shall:

(a) mark each notice or list with a file number and with the date and hour of filing;

(b) hold the notice or list or a copy for public inspection;

(c) index the notice or list according to each name given for the seller and for the buyer; and

(d) note in the index the file number and the addresses of the seller and buyer given in the notice or list.

(3) If the person filing a notice or list furnishes the filing officer with a copy, the filing officer upon request shall note upon the copy the file number and date and hour of the filing of the original and send or deliver the copy to the person.

(4) The fee for filing and indexing and for stamping a copy furnished by the person filing to show the date and place of filing is $_____ for the first page and $_____ for each additional page. The fee for indexing each name more than two is $_____.

(5) Upon request of any person, the filing officer shall issue a certificate showing whether any notice or list with respect to a particular seller or buyer is on file on the date and hour stated in the certificate. If a notice or list is on file, the certificate must give the date and hour of filing of each notice or list and the name and address of each seller, buyer, auctioneer, or liquidator. The fee for the certificate is $_____ if the request for the certificate is in the standard form prescribed by the [Secretary of State] and otherwise is $_____. Upon request of any person, the filing officer shall furnish a copy of any filed notice or list for a fee of $_____.

(6) The filing officer shall keep each notice or list for two years after it is filed.

§ 6-110. Limitation of Actions.

(1) Except as provided in subsection (2), an action under this Article against a buyer, auctioneer, or liquidator must be commenced within one year after the date of the bulk sale.

(2) If the buyer, auctioneer, or liquidator conceals the fact that the sale has occurred, the limitation is tolled and an action under this Article may be commenced within the earlier of (i) one year after the person bringing the action discovers that the sale has occurred or (ii) one year after the person bringing the action should have discovered that the sale has occurred, but no later than two years after the date of the bulk sale. Complete noncompliance with the requirements of this Article does not of itself constitute concealment.

(3) An action under Section 6-107(11) must be commenced within one year after the alleged violation occurs.

ARTICLE 7. WAREHOUSE RECEIPTS, BILLS OF LADING AND OTHER DOCUMENTS OF TITLE

Part 1. General

§ 7-101. Short Title.   This Article shall be known and may be cited as Uniform Commercial Code—Documents of Title.

§ 7-102. Definitions and Index of Definitions.

(1) In this Article, unless the context otherwise requires:

(a) "Bailee" means the person who by a warehouse receipt, bill of lading or other document of title acknowledges possession of goods and contracts to deliver them.

(b) "Consignee" means the person named in a bill to whom or to whose order the bill promises delivery.

(c) "Consignor" means the person named in a bill as the person from whom the goods have been received for shipment.

(d) "Delivery order" means a written order to deliver goods directed to a warehouseman, carrier or other person who in the ordinary course of business issues warehouse receipts or bills of lading.

(e) "Document" means document of title as defined in the general definitions in Article 1 (Section 1-201).

(f) "Goods" means all things which are treated as movable for the purposes of a contract of storage or transportation.

(g) "Issuer" means a bailee who issues a document except that in relation to an unaccepted delivery order it means the person who orders the possessor of goods to deliver. Issuer includes any person for whom an agent or employee purports to act in issuing a document if the agent or employee has real or apparent authority to issue documents, notwithstanding that the issuer received no goods or that the goods were misdescribed or that in any other respect the agent or employee violated his instructions.

(h) "Warehouseman" is a person engaged in the business of storing goods for hire.

(2) Other definitions applying to this Article or to specified Parts thereof, and the sections in which they appear are:

"Duly negotiate." Section 7-501.

"Person entitled under the document." Section 7-403(4).

(3) "Definitions in other Articles applying to this Article and the sections in which they appear are:

"Contract for sale." Section 2-106.

"Overseas." Section 2-323.

"Receipt" of goods. Section 2-103.

4) In addition Article 1 contains general definitions and principles of construction and interpretation applicable throughout this Article.

§ 7-103. Relation of Article to Treaty, Statute, Tariff, Classification or Regulation.
To the extent that any treaty or statute of the United States, regulatory statute of this State or tariff, classification or regulation filed or issued pursuant thereto is applicable, the provisions of this Article are subject thereto.

§ 7-104. Negotiable and Non-Negotiable Warehouse Receipt, Bill of Lading or Other Document of Title.
(1) A warehouse receipt, bill of lading or other document of title is negotiable

(a) if by its terms the goods are to be delivered to bearer or to the order of a named person; or

(b) where recognized in overseas trade, if it runs to a named person or assigns.

(2) Any other document is non-negotiable. A bill of lading in which it is stated that the goods are consigned to a named person is not made negotiable by a provision that the goods are to be delivered only against a written order signed by the same or another named person.

§ 7-105. Construction Against Negative Implication.
The omission from either Part 2 or Part 3 of this Article of a provision corresponding to a provision made in the other Part does not imply that a corresponding rule of law is not applicable.

Part 2. Warehouse Receipts: Special Provisions

§ 7-201. Who May Issue a Warehouse Receipt; Storage Under Government Bond.
(1) A warehouse receipt may be issued by any warehouseman.

(2) Where goods including distilled spirits and agricultural commodities are stored under a statute requiring a bond against withdrawal or a license for the issuance of receipts in the nature of warehouse receipts, a receipt issued for the goods has like effect as a warehouse receipt even though issued by a person who is the owner of the goods and is not a warehouseman.

§ 7-202. Form of Warehouse Receipt; Essential Terms; Optional Terms.
(1) A warehouse receipt need not be in any particular form.

(2) Unless a warehouse receipt embodies within its written or printed terms each of the following, the warehouseman is liable for damages caused by the omission to a person injured thereby:

(a) the location of the warehouse where the goods are stored;

(b) the date of issue of the receipt;

(c) the consecutive number of the receipt;

(d) a statement whether the goods received will be delivered to the bearer, to a specified person, or to a specified person or his order;

(e) the rate of storage and handling charges, except that where goods are stored under a field warehousing arrangement a statement of that fact is sufficient on a non-negotiable receipt;

(f) a description of the goods or of the packages containing them;

(g) the signature of the warehouseman, which may be made by his authorized agent;

(h) if the receipt is issued for goods of which the warehouseman is owner, either solely or jointly or in common with others, the fact of such ownership; and

(i) a statement of the amount of advances made and of liabilities incurred for which the warehouseman claims a lien or security interest (Section 7-209). If the precise amount of such advances made or of such liabilities incurred is, at the time of the issue of the receipt, unknown to the warehouseman or to his agent who issues it, a statement of the fact that advances have been made or liabilities incurred and the purpose thereof is sufficient.

(3) A warehouseman may insert in his receipt any other terms which are not contrary to the provisions of this Act and do not impair his obligation of delivery (Section 7-403) or his duty of care (Section 7-204). Any contrary provisions shall be ineffective.

§ 7-203. Liability for Non-Receipt or Misdescription.
A party to or purchaser for value in good faith of a document of title other than a bill of lading relying in either case upon the description therein of the goods may recover from the issuer damages caused by the non-receipt or misdescription of the goods, except to the extent that the document conspicuously indicates that the issuer does not know whether any part or all of the goods in fact were received or conform to the description, as where the description is in terms of marks or labels or kind, quantity or condition, or the receipt or description is qualified by "contents, condition and quality unknown", "said to contain" or the like, if such indication be true, or the party or purchaser otherwise has notice.

§ 7-204. Duty of Care; Contractual Limitation of Warehouseman's Liability.
(1) A warehouseman is liable for damages for loss of or injury to the goods caused by his failure to exercise such care in regard to them as a reasonably careful man would exercise under like circumstances but unless otherwise agreed he is not liable for damages which could not have been avoided by the exercise of such care.

(2) Damages may be limited by a term in the warehouse receipt or storage agreement limiting the amount of liability in case of loss or damage, and setting forth a specific liability per article or item, or value per unit of weight, beyond which the warehouseman shall not be liable; provided, however, that such liability may on written request of the bailor at the time of signing such storage agreement or within a reasonable time after receipt of the warehouse receipt be increased on part or all of the goods thereunder, in which event increased rates may be charged based on such increased valuation, but that no such increase shall be permitted contrary to a lawful limitation of liability contained in the warehouseman's tariff, if any. No such limitation is effective with respect to the warehouseman's liability for conversion to his own use.

(3) Reasonable provisions as to the time and manner of presenting claims and instituting actions based on the bailment may be included in the warehouse receipt or tariff.

(4) This section does not impair or repeal . . .

Note: Insert in subsection (4) a reference to any statute which imposes a higher responsibility upon the warehouseman or invalidates contractual limitations which would be permissible under this Article.

§ 7-205. Title Under Warehouse Receipt Defeated in Certain Cases.
A buyer in the ordinary course of business of fungible goods sold and delivered by a warehouseman who is also in the business of buying and selling such goods takes free of any claim under a warehouse receipt even though it has been duly negotiated.

§ 7-206. Termination of Storage at Warehouseman's Option.
(1) A warehouseman may on notifying the person on whose account the goods are held and any other person known to claim an interest in the goods require payment of any charges and removal of the goods from the warehouse at the termination of the period of storage fixed by the document, or, if no period is fixed, within a stated period not

less than thirty days after the notification. If the goods are not removed before the date specified in the notification, the warehouseman may sell them in accordance with the provisions of the section on enforcement of a warehouseman's lien (Section 7-210).

(2) If a warehouseman in good faith believes that the goods are about to deteriorate or decline in value to less than the amount of his lien within the time prescribed in subsection (2) for notification, advertisement and sale, the warehouseman may specify in the notification any reasonable shorter time for removal of the goods and in case the goods are not removed, may sell them at public sale held not less than one week after a single advertisement or posting.

(3) If as a result of a quality or condition of the goods of which the warehouseman had no notice at the time of deposit the goods are a hazard to other property or to the warehouse or to persons, the warehouseman may sell the goods at public or private sale without advertisement on reasonable notification to all persons known to claim an interest in the goods. If the warehouseman after a reasonable effort is unable to sell the goods he may dispose of them in any lawful manner and shall incur no liability by reason of such disposition.

(4) The warehouseman must deliver the goods to any person entitled to them under this Article upon due demand made at any time prior to sale or other disposition under this section.

(5) The warehouseman may satisfy his lien from the proceeds of any sale or disposition under this section but must hold the balance for delivery on the demand of any person to whom he would have been bound to deliver the goods.

§ 7-207. Goods Must Be Kept Separate; Fungible Goods.

(1) Unless the warehouse receipt otherwise provides, a warehouseman must keep separate the goods covered by each receipt so as to permit at all times identification and delivery of those goods except that different lots of fungible goods may be commingled.

(2) Fungible goods so commingled are owned in common by the persons entitled thereto and the warehouseman is severally liable to each owner for that owner's share. Where because of overissue a mass of fungible goods is insufficient to meet all the receipts which the warehouseman has issued against it, the persons entitled include all holders to whom overissued receipts have been duly negotiated.

§ 7-208. Altered Warehouse Receipts.
Where a blank in a negotiable warehouse receipt has been filled in without authority, a purchaser for value and without notice of the want of authority may treat the insertion as authorized. Any other unauthorized alteration leaves any receipt enforceable against the issuer according to its original tenor.

§ 7-209. Lien of Warehouseman.

(1) A warehouseman has a lien against the bailor on the goods covered by a warehouse receipt or on the proceeds thereof in his possession for charges for storage or transportation (including demurrage and terminal charges), insurance, labor, or charges present or future in relation to the goods, and for expenses necessary for preservation of the goods or reasonably incurred in their sale pursuant to law. If the person on whose account the goods are held is liable for like charges or expenses in relation to other goods whenever deposited and it is stated in the receipt that a lien is claimed for charges or expenses in relation to other goods, the warehouseman also has a lien against him for such charges and expenses whether or not the other goods have been delivered by the warehouseman. But against a person to whom a negotiable warehouse receipt is duly negotiated a warehouseman's lien is limited to charges in an amount or at a rate specified on the receipt or if no charges are so specified then to a reasonable charge for storage of the goods covered by the receipt subsequent to the date of the receipt.

(2) The warehouseman may also reserve a security interest against the bailor for a maximum amount specified on the receipt for charges other than those specified in subsection (1), such as for money advanced and interest. Such a security interest is governed by the Article on Secured Transactions (Article 9).

(3) (a) A warehouseman's lien for charges and expenses under subsection (1) or a security interest under subsection (2) is also effective against any person who so entrusted the bailor with possession of the goods that a pledge of them by him to a good faith purchaser for value would have been valid but is not effective against a person as to whom the document confers no right in the goods covered by it under Section 7-503.

(b) A warehouseman's lien on household goods for charges and expenses in relation to the goods under subsection (1) is also effective against all persons if the depositor was the legal possessor of the goods at the time of deposit. "Household goods" means furniture, furnishings and personal effects used by the depositor in a dwelling.

(4) A warehouseman loses his lien on any goods which he voluntarily delivers or which he unjustifiably refuses to deliver.

§ 7-210. Enforcement of Warehouseman's Lien.

(1) Except as provided in subsection (2), a warehouseman's lien may be enforced by public or private sale of the goods in block or in parcels, at any time or place and on any terms which are commercially reasonable, after notifying all persons known to claim an interest in the goods. Such notification must include a statement of the amount due, the nature of the proposed sale and the time and place of any public sale. The fact that a better price could have been obtained by a sale at a different time or in a different method from that selected by the warehouseman is not of itself sufficient to establish that the sale was not made in a commercially reasonable manner. If the warehouseman either sells the goods in the usual manner in any recognized market thereof, or if he sells at the price current in such market at the time of his sale, or if he has otherwise sold in conformity with commercially reasonable practices among dealers in the type of goods sold, he has sold in a commercially reasonable manner. A sale of more goods than apparently necessary to be offered to insure satisfaction of the obligation is not commercially reasonable except in cases covered by the preceding sentence.

(2) A warehouseman's lien on goods other than goods stored by a merchant in the course of his business may be enforced only as follows:

(a) All persons known to claim an interest in the goods must be notified.

(b) The notification must be delivered in person or sent by registered or certified letter to the last known address of any person to be notified.

(c) The notification must include an itemized statement of the claim, a description of the goods subject to the lien, a demand for payment within a specified time not less than ten days after receipt of the notification, and a conspicuous statement that unless the claim is paid within that time the goods will be advertised for sale and sold by auction at a specified time and place.

(d) The sale must conform to the terms of the notification.

(e) The sale must be held at the nearest suitable place to that where the goods are held or stored.

(f) After the expiration of the time given in the notification, an advertisement of the sale must be published once a week for two weeks consecutively in a newspaper of general circulation where the sale is to be held. The advertisement must include a description of the goods, the name of the person on whose account they are being held, and the time and place of the sale. The sale must take place at least fifteen days after the first publication. If there is no newspaper of general circulation where the sale is to be held, the advertisement must be posted at least ten days before the sale in not less than six conspicuous places in the neighborhood of the proposed sale.

3) Before any sale pursuant to this section any person claiming a right in the goods may pay the amount necessary to satisfy the lien and the reasonable expenses incurred under this section. In that event the goods must not be sold, but must be retained by the warehouseman subject to the terms of the receipt and this Article.

4) The warehouseman may buy at any public sale pursuant to this section.

5) A purchaser in good faith of goods sold to enforce a warehouseman's lien takes the goods free of any rights of persons against whom the lien was valid, despite noncompliance by the warehouseman with the requirements of this section.

(6) The warehouseman may satisfy his lien from the proceeds of any sale pursuant to this section but must hold the balance, if any, for delivery on demand to any person to whom he would have been bound to deliver the goods.

(7) The rights provided by this section shall be in addition to all other rights allowed by law to a creditor against his debtor.

(8) Where a lien is on goods stored by a merchant in the course of his business the lien may be enforced in accordance with either subsection (1) or (2).

(9) The warehouseman is liable for damages caused by failure to comply with the requirements for sale under this section and in case of willful violation is liable for conversion.

Part 3. Bills of Lading: Special Provisions

§ 7-301. Liability for Non-Receipt or Misdescription; "Said to Contain"; "Shipper's Load and Count"; Improper Handling.

(1) A consignee of a non-negotiable bill who has given value in good faith or a holder to whom a negotiable bill has been duly negotiated relying in either case upon the description therein of the goods, or upon the date therein shown, may recover from the issuer damages caused by the misdating of the bill or the non-receipt or misdescription of the goods, except to the extent that the document indicates that the issuer does not know whether any part or all of the goods in fact were received or conform to the description, as where the description is in terms of marks or labels or kind, quantity, or condition or the receipt or description is qualified by "contents or condition of contents of packages unknown", "said to contain", "shipper's weight, load and count" or the like, if such indication be true.

(2) When goods are loaded by an issuer who is a common carrier, the issuer must count the packages of goods if package freight and ascertain the kind and quantity if bulk freight. In such cases "shipper's weight, load and count" or other words indicating that the description was made by the shipper are ineffective except as to freight concealed by packages.

(3) When bulk freight is loaded by a shipper who makes available to the issuer adequate facilities for weighing such freight, an issuer who is a common carrier must ascertain the kind and quantity within a reasonable time after receiving the written request of the shipper to do so. In such cases "shipper's weight" or other words of like purport are ineffective.

(4) The issuer may by inserting in the bill the words "shipper's weight, load and count" or other words of like purport indicate that the goods were loaded by the shipper; and if such statement be true the issuer shall not be liable for damages caused by the improper loading. But their omission does not imply liability for such damages.

(5) The shipper shall be deemed to have guaranteed to the issuer the accuracy at the time of shipment of the description, marks, labels, number, kind, quantity, condition and weight, as furnished by him; and the shipper shall indemnify the issuer against damage caused by inaccuracies in such particulars. The right of the issuer to such indemnity shall in no way limit his responsibility and liability under the contract of carriage to any person other than the shipper.

§ 7-302. Through Bills of Lading and Similar Documents.

(1) The issuer of a through bill of lading or other document embodying an undertaking to be performed in part by persons acting as its agents or by connecting carriers is liable to anyone entitled to recover on the document for any breach by such other persons or by a connecting carrier of its obligation under the document but to the extent that the bill covers an undertaking to be performed overseas or in territory not contiguous to the continental United States or an undertaking including matters other than transportation this liability may be varied by agreement of the parties.

(2) Where goods covered by a through bill of lading or other document embodying an undertaking to be performed in part by persons other than the issuer are received by any such person, he is subject with respect to his own performance while the goods are in his possession to the obligation of the issuer. His obligation is discharged by delivery of the goods to another such person pursuant to the document and does not include liability for breach by any other such persons or by the issuer.

(3) The issuer of such through bill of lading or other document shall be entitled to recover from the connecting carrier or such other person in possession of the goods when the breach of the obligation under the document occurred, the amount it may be required to pay to anyone entitled to recover on the document therefor, as may be evidenced by any receipt, judgment, or transcript thereof, and the amount of any expense reasonably incurred by it in defending any action brought by anyone entitled to recover on the document therefor.

§ 7-303. Diversion; Reconsignment; Change of Instructions.

(1) Unless the bill of lading otherwise provides, the carrier may deliver the goods to a person or destination other than that stated in the bill or may otherwise dispose of the goods on instruction from

(a) the holder of a negotiable bill; or

(b) the consignor on a non-negotiable bill notwithstanding contrary instructions from the consignee; or

(c) the consignee on a non-negotiable bill in the absence of contrary instructions from the consignor, if the goods have arrived at the billed destination or if the consignee is in possession of the bill; or

(d) the consignee on a non-negotiable bill if he is entitled as against the consignor to dispose of them.

(2) Unless such instructions are noted on a negotiable bill of lading, a person to whom the bill is duly negotiated can hold the bailee according to the original terms.

§ 7-304. Bills of Lading in a Set.

(1) Except where customary in overseas transportation, a bill of lading must not be issued in a set of parts. The issuer is liable for damages caused by violation of this subsection.

(2) Where a bill of lading is lawfully drawn in a set of parts, each of which is numbered and expressed to be valid only if the goods have not been delivered against any other part, the whole of the parts constitute one bill.

(3) Where a bill of lading is lawfully issued in a set of parts and different parts are negotiated to different persons, the title of the holder to whom the first due negotiation is made prevails as to both the document and the goods even though any later holder may have

received the goods from the carrier in good faith and discharged the carrier's obligation by surrender of his part.

(4) Any person who negotiates or transfers a single part of a bill of lading drawn in a set is liable to holders of that part as if it were the whole set.

(5) The bailee is obliged to deliver in accordance with Part 4 of this Article against the first presented part of a bill of lading lawfully drawn in a set. Such delivery discharges the bailee's obligation on the whole bill.

§ 7-305. Destination Bills.

(1) Instead of issuing a bill of lading to the consignor at the place of shipment a carrier may at the request of the consignor procure the bill to be issued at destination or at any other place designated in the request.

(2) Upon request of anyone entitled as against the carrier to control the goods while in transit and on surrender of any outstanding bill of lading or other receipt covering such goods, the issuer may procure a substitute bill to be issued at any place designated in the request.

§ 7-306. Altered Bills of Lading.
An unauthorized alteration or filling in of a blank in a bill of lading leaves the bill enforceable according to its original tenor.

§ 7-307. Lien of Carrier.

(1) A carrier has a lien on the goods covered by a bill of lading for charges subsequent to the date of its receipt of the goods for storage or transportation (including demurrage and terminal charges) and for expenses necessary for preservation of the goods incident to their transportation or reasonably incurred in their sale pursuant to law. But against a purchaser for value of a negotiable bill of lading a carrier's lien is limited to charges stated in the bill or the applicable tariffs, or if no charges are stated then to a reasonable charge.

(2) A lien for charges and expenses under subsection (1) on goods which the carrier was required by law to receive for transportation is effective against the consignor or any person entitled to the goods unless the carrier had notice that the consignor lacked authority to subject the goods to such charges and expenses. Any other lien under subsection (1) is effective against the consignor and any person who permitted the bailor to have control or possession of the goods unless the carrier had notice that the bailor lacked such authority.

(3) A carrier loses his lien on any goods which he voluntarily delivers or which he unjustifiably refuses to deliver.

§ 7-308. Enforcement of Carrier's Lien.

(1) A carrier's lien may be enforced by public or private sale of the goods, in block or in parcels, at any time or place and on any terms which are commercially reasonable, after notifying all persons known to claim an interest in the goods. Such notification must include a statement of the amount due, the nature of the proposed sale and the time and place of any public sale. The fact that a better price could have been obtained by a sale at a different time or in a different method from that selected by the carrier is not of itself sufficient to establish that the sale was not made in a commercially reasonable manner. If the carrier either sells the goods in the usual manner in any recognized market therefor or if he sells at the price current in such market at the time of his sale or if he has otherwise sold in conformity with commercially reasonable practices among dealers in the type of goods sold he has sold in a commercially reasonable manner. A sale of more goods than apparently necessary to be offered to ensure satisfaction of the obligation is not commercially reasonable except in cases covered by the preceding sentence.

(2) Before any sale pursuant to this section any person claiming a right in the goods may pay the amount necessary to satisfy the lien and the

reasonable expenses incurred under this section. In that event the goods must not be sold, but must be retained by the carrier subject to the terms of the bill and this Article.

(3) The carrier may buy at any public sale pursuant to this section.

(4) A purchaser in good faith of goods sold to enforce a carrier's lien takes the goods free of any rights of persons against whom the lien was valid, despite noncompliance by the carrier with the requirements of this section.

(5) The carrier may satisfy his lien from the proceeds of any sale pursuant to this section but must hold the balance, if any, for delivery on demand to any person to whom he would have been bound to deliver the goods.

(6) The rights provided by this section shall be in addition to all other rights allowed by law to a creditor against his debtor.

(7) A carrier's lien may be enforced in accordance with either subsection (1) or the procedure set forth in subsection (2) of Section 7-210.

(8) The carrier is liable for damages caused by failure to comply with the requirements for sale under this section and in case of willful violation is liable for conversion.

§ 7-309. Duty of Care; Contractual Limitation of Carrier's Liability.

(1) A carrier who issues a bill of lading whether negotiable or non-negotiable must exercise the degree of care in relation to the goods which a reasonably careful man would exercise under like circumstances. This subsection does not repeal or change any law or rule of law which imposes liability upon a common carrier for damages not caused by its negligence.

(2) Damages may be limited by a provision that the carrier's liability shall not exceed a value stated in the document if the carrier's rates are dependent upon value and the consignor by the carrier's tariff is afforded an opportunity to declare a higher value or a value as lawfully provided in the tariff, or where no tariff is filed he is otherwise advised of such opportunity; but no such limitation is effective with respect to the carrier's liability for conversion to its own use.

(3) Reasonable provisions as to the time and manner of presenting claims and instituting actions based on the shipment may be included in a bill of lading or tariff.

Part 4. Warehouse Receipts and Bills of Lading: General Obligations

§ 7-401. Irregularities in Issue of Receipt or Conduct of Issuer.
The obligations imposed by this Article on an issuer apply to a document of title regardless of the fact that

(a) the document may not comply with the requirements of this Article or of any other law or regulation regarding its issue, form or content; or

(b) the issuer may have violated laws regulating the conduct of his business; or

(c) the goods covered by the document were owned by the bailee at the time the document was issued; or

(d) the person issuing the document does not come within the definition of warehouseman if it purports to be a warehouse receipt.

§ 7-402. Duplicate Receipt or Bill; Overissue.
Neither a duplicate nor any other document of title purporting to cover goods already represented by an outstanding document of the same issuer confers any right in the goods, except as provided in the case of bills in a set, overissue of documents for fungible goods and substitutes for lost, stolen or destroyed documents. But the issuer is liable for damages caused by his overissue or failure to identify a duplicate document as such by conspicuous notation on its face.

§ 7-403. Obligation of Warehouseman or Carrier to Deliver; Excuse.

(1) The bailee must deliver the goods to a person entitled under the document who complies with subsection (2) and (3), unless and to the extent that the bailee establishes any of the following:

(a) delivery of the goods to a person whose receipt was rightful as against the claimant;

(b) damage to or to delay, loss or destruction of the goods for which the bailee is not liable [but the burden of establishing negligence in such cases is on the person entitled under the document];

Note: The brackets in (1)(b) indicate that the State enactments may differ on this point without serious damage to the principle of uniformity.

(c) previous sale or other disposition of the goods in lawful enforcement of a lien or on warehouseman's lawful termination of storage;

(d) the exercise by a seller of his right to stop delivery pursuant to the provisions of the Article on Sales (Section 2-705);

(e) a diversion, reconsignment or other disposition pursuant to the provisions of this Article on Sales (Section 7-303) or tariff regulating such right;

(f) release, satisfaction or any other fact affording a personal defense against the claimant;

(g) any other lawful excuse.

(2) A person claiming goods covered by a document of title must satisfy the bailee's lien where the bailee so requests or where the bailee is prohibited by law from delivering the goods until the charges are paid.

(3) Unless the person claiming is one against whom the document confers no right under Section 7-503(1), he must surrender for cancellation or notation of partial deliveries any outstanding negotiable document covering the goods, and the bailee must cancel the document or conspicuously note the partial delivery thereon or be liable to any person to whom the document is duly negotiated.

(4) "Person entitled under the document" means holder in the case of a negotiable document, or the person to whom delivery is to be made by the terms of or pursuant to written instructions under a non-negotiable document.

§ 7-404. No Liability for Good Faith Delivery Pursuant to Receipt or Bill.

A bailee who in good faith including observance of reasonable commercial standards has received goods and delivered or otherwise disposed of them according to the terms of the document of title or pursuant to this Article is not liable therefor. This rule applies even though the person from whom he received the goods had no authority to procure the document or to dispose of the goods and even though the person to whom he delivered the goods has no authority to receive them.

Part 5. Warehouse Receipts and Bills of Lading: Negotiation and Transfer

§ 7-501. Form of Negotiation and Requirements of "Due Negotiation."

(1) A negotiable document of title running to the order of a named person is negotiated by his indorsement and delivery. After his indorsement in blank or to bearer any person can negotiate it by delivery alone.

(2) (a) A negotiable document of title is also negotiated by delivery alone when by its original terms it runs to bearer.

(b) When a document running to the order of a named person is delivered to him the effect is the same as if the document has been negotiated.

(3) Negotiation of a negotiable document of title after it has been indorsed to a specified person requires indorsement by the special indorsee as well as delivery.

(4) A negotiable document of title is "duly negotiated" when it is negotiated in the manner stated in this section to a holder who purchases it in good faith without notice of any defense against or claim to it on the part of any person and for value, unless it is established that the negotiation is not in the regular course of business or financing or involves receiving the document in settlement or payment of a money obligation.

(5) Indorsement of a non-negotiable document neither makes it negotiable nor adds to the transferee's rights.

(6) The naming in a negotiable bill of a person to be notified of the arrival of the goods does not limit the negotiability of the bill nor constitute notice to a purchaser thereof of any interest of such person in the goods.

§ 7-502. Rights Acquired by Due Negotiation.

(1) Subject to the following section and to the provisions of Section 7-205 on fungible goods, a holder to whom a negotiable document of title has been duly negotiated acquires thereby:

(a) title to the document;

(b) title to the goods;

(c) all rights accruing under the law of agency or estoppel, including rights to goods delivered to the bailee after the document was issued; and

(d) the direct obligation of the issuer to hold or deliver the goods according to the terms of the document free of any defense or claim by him except those arising under the terms of the document or under this Article. In the case of a delivery order the bailee's obligation accrues only upon acceptance and the obligation acquired by the holder is that the issuer and any indorser will procure the acceptance of the bailee.

(2) Subject to the following section, title and rights so acquired are not defeated by any stoppage of the goods represented by the document or by surrender of such goods by the bailee, and are not impaired even though the negotiation or any prior negotiation constituted a breach of duty or even though any person has been deprived of possession of the document by misrepresentation, fraud, accident, mistake, duress, loss, theft, or conversion, or even though a previous sale or other transfer of the goods or document has been made to a third person.

§ 7-503. Document of Title to Goods Defeated in Certain Cases.

(1) A document of title confers no right in goods against a person who before issuance of the document had a legal interest or a perfected security interest in them and who neither

(a) delivered or entrusted them or any document of title covering them to the bailor or his nominee with actual or apparent authority to ship, store or sell or with power to obtain delivery under this Article (Section 7-403) or with power of disposition under this Act (Sections 2-403 and 9-307) or other statute or rule of law; nor

(b) acquiesced in the procurement by the bailor or his nominee of any document of title.

(2) Title to goods based upon an unaccepted delivery order is subject to the rights of anyone to whom a negotiable warehouse receipt or bill of lading covering the goods has been duly negotiated. Such a title may be defeated under the next section to the same extent as the rights of the issuer or a transferee from the issuer.

(3) Title to goods based upon a bill of lading issued to a freight forwarder is subject to the rights of anyone to whom a bill issued by the freight forwarder is duly negotiated; but delivery by the carrier in accordance with Part 4 of this Article pursuant to its own bill of lading discharges the carrier's obligation to deliver.

§ 7-504. Rights Acquired in the Absence of Due Negotiation; Effect of Diversion; Seller's Stoppage of Delivery.

(1) A transferee of a document, whether negotiable or non-negotiable, to whom the document has been delivered but not duly negotiated, acquires the title and rights which his transferor had or had actual authority to convey.

(2) In the case of a non-negotiable document, until but not after the bailee receives notification of the transfer, the rights of the transferee may be defeated.

(a) by those creditors of the transferor who could treat the sale as void under Section 2-402; or

(b) by a buyer from the transferor in ordinary course of business if the bailee has delivered the goods to the buyer or received notification of his rights; or

(c) as against the bailee by good faith dealings of the bailee with the transferor.

(3) A diversion or other change of shipping instructions by the consignor in a non-negotiable bill of lading which causes the bailee not to deliver to the consignee defeats the consignee's title to the goods if they have been delivered to a buyer in ordinary course of business and in any event defeats the consignee's rights against the bailee.

(4) Delivery pursuant to a non-negotiable document may be stopped by a seller under Section 2-705, and subject to the requirement of due notification there provided. A bailee honoring the seller's instructions is entitled to be indemnified by the seller against any resulting loss or expense.

§ 7-505. Indorser Not a Guarantor for Other Parties.
The indorsement of a document of title issued by a bailee does not make the indorser liable for any default by the bailee or by previous indorsers.

§ 7-506. Delivery Without Indorsement: Right to Compel Indorsement.
The transferee of a negotiable document of title has a specifically enforceable right to have his transferor supply any necessary indorsement but the transfer becomes a negotiation only as of the time the indorsement is supplied.

§ 7-507. Warranties on Negotiation or Transfer of Receipt or Bill.
Where a person negotiates or transfers a document of title for value otherwise than as a mere intermediary under the next following section, then unless otherwise agreed he warrants to his immediate purchaser only in addition to any warranty made in selling the goods.

(a) that the document is genuine; and

(b) that he has no knowledge of any fact which would impair its validity or worth; and

(c) that his negotiation or transfer is rightful and fully effective with respect to the title to the document and the goods it represents.

§ 7-508. Warranties of Collecting Bank as to Documents.
A collecting bank or other intermediary known to be entrusted with documents on behalf of another or with collection of a draft or other claim against delivery of documents warrants by such delivery of the documents only its own good faith and authority. This rule applies even though the intermediary has purchased or made advances against the claim or draft to be collected.

§ 7-509. Receipt or Bill: When Adequate Compliance With Commercial Contract.
The question whether a document is adequate to fulfill the obligations of a contract for sale or the conditions of a credit is governed by the Articles on Sales (Article 2) and on Letters of Credit (Article 5).

Part 6. Warehouse Receipts and Bills of Lading: Miscellaneous Provisions

§ 7-601. Lost and Missing Documents.

(1) If a document has been lost, stolen or destroyed, a court may order delivery of the goods or issuance of a substitute document and the bailee may without liability to any person comply with such order. If the document was negotiable the claimant must post security approved by the court to indemnify any person who may suffer loss as a result of nonsurrender of the document. If the document was not negotiable, such security may be required at the discretion of the court. The court may also in its discretion order payment of the bailee's reasonable costs and counsel fees.

(2) A bailee who without court order delivers goods to a person claiming under a missing negotiable document is liable to any person injured thereby, and if the delivery is not in good faith becomes liable for conversion. Delivery in good faith is not conversion if made in accordance with a filed classification or tariff or, where no classification or tariff is filed, if the claimant posts security with the bailee in an amount at least double the value of the goods at the time of posting to indemnify any person injured by the delivery who files a notice of claim within one year after the delivery.

§ 7-602. Attachment of Goods Covered by a Negotiable Document.
Except where the document was originally issued upon delivery of the goods by a person who had no power to dispose of them, no lien attaches by virtue of any judicial process to goods in the possession of a bailee for which a negotiable document of title is outstanding unless the document be first surrendered to the bailee or its negotiation enjoined, and the bailee shall not be compelled to deliver the goods pursuant to process until the document is surrendered to him or impounded by the court. One who purchases the document for value without notice of the process or injunction takes free of the lien imposed by judicial process.

§ 7-603. Conflicting Claims; Interpleader.
If more than one person claims title or possession of the goods, the bailee is excused from delivery until he has had a reasonable time to ascertain the validity of the adverse claims or to bring an action to compel all claimants to interplead and may compel such interpleader, either by defending an action for non-delivery of the goods, or by original action, whichever is appropriate.

ARTICLE 8. INVESTMENT SECURITIES

[TEXT NOT INCLUDED.]

ARTICLE 9. SECURED TRANSACTIONS; SALES OF ACCOUNTS AND CHATTEL PAPER

Part 1. Short Title, Applicability and Definitions

§ 9-101. Short Title.
This Article shall be known and may be cited as Uniform Commercial Code—Secured Transactions.

§ 9-102. Policy and Subject Matter of Article.

(1) Except as otherwise provided in Section 9-104 on excluded transactions, this Article applies

(a) to any transaction (regardless of its form) which is intended to create a security interest in personal property or fixtures including goods, documents, instruments, general intangibles, chattel paper or accounts; and also

(b) to any sale of accounts or chattel paper.

(2) This Article applies to security interests created by contract including pledge, assignment, chattel mortgage, chattel trust, trust deed, factor's lien, equipment trust, conditional sale, trust receipt, other lien

or title retention contract and lease or consignment intended as security. This Article does not apply to statutory liens except as provided in Section 9-310.

(3) The application of this Article to a security interest in a secured obligation is not affected by the fact that the obligation is itself secured by a transaction or interest to which this Article does not apply. Amended in 1972.

Note: The adoption of this Article should be accompanied by the repeal of existing statutes dealing with conditional sales, trust receipts, factor's liens where the factor is given a non-possessory lien, chattel mortgages, crop mortgages, mortgages on railroad equipment, assignment of accounts and generally statutes regulating security interests in personal property.

Where the state has a retail installment selling act or small loan act, that legislation should be carefully examined to determine what changes in those acts are needed to conform them to this Article. This Article primarily sets out rules defining rights of a secured party against persons dealing with the debtor, it does not prescribe regulations and controls which may be necessary to curb abuses arising in the small loan business or in the financing of consumer purchases on credit. Accordingly there is no intention to repeal existing regulatory acts in those fields by enactment or re-enactment of Article 9. See Section 9-203(4) and the Note thereto.

§ 9-103. Perfection of Security Interest in Multiple State Transactions.

(1) Documents, instruments and ordinary goods.

(a) This subsection applies to documents and instruments and to goods other than those covered by a certificate of title described in subsection (2), mobile goods described in subsection (3), and minerals described in subsection (5).

(b) Except as otherwise provided in this subsection, perfection and the effect of perfection or non-perfection of a security interest in collateral are governed by the law of the jurisdiction where the collateral is when the last event occurs on which is based the assertion that the security interest is perfected or unperfected.

(c) if the parties to a transaction creating a purchase money security interest in goods in one jurisdiction understand at the time that the security interest attaches that the goods will be kept in another jurisdiction, then the law of the other jurisdiction governs the perfection and the effect of perfection or nonperfection of the security interest from the time it attaches until thirty days after the debtor receives possession of the goods and thereafter if the goods are taken to the other jurisdiction before the end of the thirty-day period.

(d) When collateral is brought into and kept in this state while subject to a security interest perfected under the law of the jurisdiction from which the collateral was removed, the security interest remains perfected, but if action is required by Part 3 of this Article to perfect the security interest,

(i) if the action is not taken before the expiration of the period of perfection in the other jurisdiction or the end of four months after the collateral is brought into this state, whichever period first expires, the security interest becomes unperfected at the end of that period and is thereafter deemed to have been unperfected as against a person who became a purchaser after removal;

(ii) if the action is taken before the expiration of the period specified in subparagraph (i), the security interest continues perfected thereafter;

(iii) for the purpose of priority over a buyer of consumer goods (subsection (2) of Section 9-307), the period of the effectiveness of a filing in the jurisdiction from which the collateral is removed is governed by the rules with respect to perfection in subparagraphs (i) and (ii).

(2) Certificate of title.

(a) This subsection applies to goods covered by a certificate of title under a statute of this state or of another jurisdiction under the law of which indication of a security interest on the certificate is required as a condition of perfection.

(b) Except as otherwise provided in this subsection, perfection and the effect of perfection or non-perfection of the security interest are governed by the law (including the conflict of laws rules) of the jurisdiction issuing the certificate until four months after the goods are removed from that jurisdiction and therefore until four months after the goods are registered in another jurisdiction, but in any event not beyond surrender of the certificate. After the expiration of that period, the goods are not covered by the certificate of title within the meaning of this section.

(c) Except with respect to the rights of a buyer described in the next paragraph, a security interest, perfected in another jurisdiction otherwise than by notation on a certificate of title issued by this state is subject to the rules stated in paragraph (d) of subsection (1).

(d) If goods are brought into this state while a security interest therein is perfected in any manner under the law of the jurisdiction from which the goods are removed and a certificate of title is issued by this state and the certificate does not show that the goods are subject to the security interest or that they may be subject to security interests not shown on the certificate, the security interest is subordinate to the rights of a buyer of the goods who is not in the business of selling goods of that kind to the extent that he gives value and receives delivery of the goods after issuance of the certificate and without knowledge of the security interest.

(3) Accounts, general intangibles and mobile goods.

(a) This subsection applies to accounts (other than an account described in subsection (5) on minerals) and general intangibles (other than uncertificated securities) and to goods which are mobile and which are of a type normally used in more than one jurisdiction, such as motor vehicles, trailers, rolling stock, airplanes, shipping containers, road building and construction machinery and commercial harvesting machinery and the like, if the goods are equipment or are inventory leased or held for lease by the debtor to others, and are not covered by a certificate of title described in subsection (2).

(b) The law (including the conflict of laws rules) of the jurisdiction in which the debtor is located governs the perfection and the effect of perfection or non-perfection of the security interest.

(c) If, however, the debtor is located in a jurisdiction which is not a part of the United States, and which does not provide for perfection of the security interest by filing or recording in that jurisdiction, the law of the jurisdiction in the United States in which the debtor has its major executive office in the United States governs the perfection and the effect of perfection or non-perfection of the security interest through filing. In the alternative, if the debtor is located in a jurisdiction which is not a part of the United States or Canada and the collateral is accounts or general intangibles for money due or to become due, the security interest may be perfected by notification to the account debtor. As used in this paragraph, "United States" includes its territories and possessions and the Commonwealth of Puerto Rico.

(d) A debtor shall be deemed located at his place of business if he has one, at his chief executive office if he has more than one place of business, otherwise at his residence. If, however, the debtor is a foreign air carrier under the Federal Aviation Act of 1958, as amended, it shall be deemed located at the designated office of the agent upon whom service of process may be made on behalf of the foreign air carrier.

(e) A security interest perfected under the law of the jurisdiction of the location to another jurisdiction, or until perfection would have ceased by the law of the first jurisdiction, whichever period first expires. Unless perfected in the new jurisdiction before the end of that period, it becomes unperfected thereafter and is deemed to have been unperfected as against a person who became a purchaser after the change.

(4) Chattel paper.

The rules stated for goods in subsection (1) apply to a possessory security interest in chattel paper. The rules stated for accounts in subsection (3) apply to a non-possessory security interest in chattel paper, but the security interest may not be perfected by notification to the account debtor.

(5) Minerals.

Perfection and the effect of perfection or non-perfection of a security interest which is created by a debtor who has an interest in minerals or the like (including oil and gas) before extraction and which attaches thereto as extracted, or which attaches to an account resulting from the sale thereof at the wellhead or minehead are governed by the law (including the conflict of laws rules) of the jurisdiction wherein the wellhead or minehead is located.

(6) Uncertificated securities.

The law (including the conflict of laws rules) of the jurisdiction of organization of the issuer governs the perfection and the effect of perfection or non-perfection of a security interest in uncertificated securities.

§ 9-104. Transactions Excluded From Article. This Article does not apply

(a) to a security interest subject to any statute of the United States, to the extent that such statute governs the rights of parties to and third parties affected by transactions in particular types of property; or

(b) to a landlord's lien; or

(c) to a lien given by statute or other rule of law for services or materials except as provided in Section 9-310 on priority of such liens; or

(d) to a transfer of a claim for wages, salary or other compensation of an employee; or

(e) to a transfer by a government or governmental subdivision or agency; or

(f) to a sale of accounts or chattel paper as part of a sale of the business out of which they arose, or an assignment of accounts or chattel paper which is for the purpose of collection only, or a transfer of a right to payment under a contract to an assignee who is also to do the performance under the contract or a transfer of a single account to an assignee in whole or partial satisfaction of a preexisting indebtedness; or

(g) to a transfer of an interest in or claim in or under any policy of insurance, except as provided with respect to proceeds (Section 9-306) and priorities in proceeds (Section 9-312); or

(h) to a right represented by a judgment (other than a judgment taken on a right to payment which was collateral); or

(i) to any right of set-off; or

(j) except to the extent that provision is made for fixtures in Section 9-313, to the creation or transfer of an interest in or lien on real estate, including a lease or rents thereunder; or

(k) to a transfer in whole or in part of any claim arising out of tort; or

(l) to a transfer of an interest in any deposit account (sub-section (1) of Section 9-105) except as provided with respect to proceeds (Section 9-306) and priorities in proceeds (Section 9-312).

§ 9-105. Definitions and Index of Definitions.

(1) In this Article unless the context otherwise requires:

(a) "Account debtor" means the person who is obligated on an account, chattel paper or general intangible;

(b) "Chattel paper" means a writing or writings which evidence both a monetary obligation and a security interest in or a lease of specific goods, but a charter or other contract involving the use or hire of a vessel is not chattel paper. When a transaction is evidenced both by such a security agreement or a lease and by an instrument or a series of instruments, the group of writings taken together constitutes chattel paper;

(c) "Collateral" means the property subject to a security interest, and includes accounts and chattel paper which have been sold;

(d) "Debtor" means the person who owes payment or other performance of the obligation secured, whether or not he owns or has rights in the collateral, and includes the seller of accounts or chattel paper. Where the debtor and the owner of the collateral are not the same person, the term "debtor" means the owner of the collateral in any provision of the Article dealing with the collateral, the obligor in any provision dealing with the obligation, and may include both where the context so requires;

(e) "Deposit account" means a demand, time, savings, passbook or like account maintained with a bank, savings and loan association, credit union or like organization, other than an account evidenced by a certificate of deposit;

(f) "Document" means document of title as defined in the general definitions of Article 1 (Section 1-201), and a receipt of the kind described in subsection (2) of Section 7-201;

(g) "Encumbrance" includes real estate mortgages and other liens on real estate and all other rights in real estate that are not ownership interests;

(h) "Goods" includes all things which are movable at the time the security interest attaches or which are fixtures (Section 9-313), but does not include money, documents, instruments, accounts, chattel paper, general intangibles, or minerals or the like (including oil and gas) before extraction. "Goods" also includes standing timber which is to be cut and removed under a conveyance or contract for sale, the unborn young of animals, and growing crops;

(i) "Instrument" means a negotiable instrument (defined in Section 3-104), or a certificated security (defined in Section 8-102) or any other writing which evidences a right to the payment of money and is not itself a security agreement or lease and is of a type which is in ordinary course of business transferred by delivery with any necessary indorsement or assignment;

(j) "Mortgage" means a consensual interest created by a real estate mortgage, a trust deed on real estate, or the like;

(k) An advance is made "pursuant to commitment" if the secured party has bound himself to make it, whether or not a subsequent event of default or other event not within his control has relieved or may relieve him from his obligation;

(l) "Security agreement" means an agreement which creates or provides for a security interest;

(m) "Secured party" means a lender, seller or other person in whose favor there is a security interest, including a person to whom accounts of chattel paper have been sold. When the holders of obligations issued under an indenture of trust, equipment trust agreement or the like are represented by a trustee or other person, the representative is the secured party;

(n) "Transmitting utility" means any person primarily engaged in the railroad, street railway or trolley bus business, the electric or electronics communications transmission business, the transmission of goods by pipeline, or the transmission or the production and transmission of electricity, steam, gas or water, or the provision of sewer service.

(2) Other definitions applying to this Article and the sections in which they appear are:

"Account". Section 9-106.

"Attach". Section 9-203.

"Construction mortgage". Section 9-313(1).

"Consumer goods". Section 9-109(1).

"Equipment". Section 9-109(2).

"Farm products". Section 9-109(3).

"Fixture". Section 9-313(1).

"Fixture filing". Section 9-313(1).

"General intangibles". Section 9-106.

"Inventory". Section 9-109(4).

"Lien creditor". Section 9-301(3).

"Proceeds". Section 9-306(1).

"Purchase money security interest". Section 9-107.

"United States". Section 9-103.

(3) The following definitions in other Articles apply to this Article:

"Check". Section 3-104.

"Contract for sale". Section 2-106.

"Holder in due course". Section 3-302.

"Note". Section 3-104.

"Sale". Section 2-106.

(4) In addition Article 1 contains general definitions and principles of construction and interpretation applicable throughout this article.

§ 9-106. Definitions: "Account"; "General Intangibles."

"Account" means any right to payment for goods sold or leased or for services rendered which is not evidenced by an instrument or chattel paper, whether or not it has been earned by performance. "General intangibles" means any personal property (including things in action) other than goods, accounts, chattel paper, documents, instruments, and money. All rights to payment earned or unearned under a charter or other contract involving the use or hire of a vessel and all rights incident to the charter or contract are accounts.

§ 9-107. Definitions: "Purchase Money Security Interest." A security interest is a "purchase money security interest" to the extent that it is

(a) taken or retained by the seller of the collateral to secure all or part of its price; or

(b) taken by a person who by making advances or incurring an obligation gives value to enable the debtor to acquire rights in or the use of collateral if such value is in fact so used.

§ 9-108. When After-Acquired Collateral Not Security for Antecedent Debt. Where a secured party makes an advance, incurs an obligation, releases a perfected security interest, or otherwise gives new value which is to be secured in whole or in part by after-acquired property his security interest in the after-acquired collateral shall be deemed to be taken for new value and not as security for an antecedent debt if the debtor acquires his rights in such collateral either in the ordinary course of his business or under a contract of purchase made pursuant to the security agreement within a reasonable time after new value is given.

§ 9-109. Classification of Goods: "Consumer Goods"; "Equipment"; "Farm Products"; "Inventory." Goods are

(1) "consumer goods" if they are used or bought for use primarily for personal, family or household purposes;

(2) "equipment" if they are used or bought for use primarily in business (including farming or a profession) or by a debtor who is a non-profit organization or a governmental subdivision or agency or if the goods are not included in the definitions of inventory, farm products or consumer goods;

(3) "farm products" if they are crops or livestock or supplies used or produced in farming operations or if they are products of crops or livestock in their unmanufactured states (such as ginned cotton, wool-clip, maple syrup, milk and eggs), and if they are in the possession of a debtor engaged in raising, fattening, grazing or other farming operations. If goods are farm products they are neither equipment nor inventory;

(4) "inventory" if they are held by a person who holds them for sale or lease or to be furnished under contracts of service or if he has so furnished them, or if they are raw materials, work in process or materials used or consumed in a business. Inventory of a person is not to be classified as his equipment.

§ 9-110. Sufficiency of Description. For the purposes of this Article any description of personal property or real estate is sufficient whether or not it is specific if it reasonably identifies what is described.

§ 9-111. Applicability of Bulk Transfer Laws. The creation of a security interest is not a bulk transfer under Article 6 (see Section 6-103).

§ 9-112. Where Collateral Is Not Owned by Debtor.

Unless otherwise agreed, when a secured party knows that collateral is owned by a person who is not the debtor, the owner of the collateral is entitled to receive from the secured party any surplus under Section 9-502(2) or under Section 9-504(1), and is not liable for the debt or for any deficiency after resale, and he has the same right as the debtor

(a) to receive statements under Section 9-208;

(b) to receive notice of and to object to a secured party's proposal to retain the collateral in satisfaction of the indebtedness under Section 9-505;

(c) to redeem the collateral under Section 9-506;

(d) to obtain injunctive or other relief under Section 9-507(1); and

(e) to recover losses caused to him under Section 9-208(2).

§ 9-113. Security Interests Arising Under Article on Sales or Under Article on Leases.

A security interest arising solely under the Article on Sales (Article 2) or the Article on Leases (Article 2A) is subject to the provisions of this Article except that to the extent that and so long as the debtor does not have or does not lawfully obtain possession of the goods

(a) no security agreement is necessary to make the security interest enforceable; and

(b) no filing is required to perfect the security interest; and

(c) the rights of the secured party on default by the debtor are governed (i) by the Article on Sales (Article 2) in the case of a security interest arising solely under such Article or (ii) by the Article on Leases (Article 2A) in the case of a security interest arising solely under such Article.

As amended in 1987.

§ 9-114. Consignment.

(1) A person who delivers goods under a consignment which is not a security interest and who would be required to file under this Article by paragraph (3)(c) of Section 2-326 has priority over a secured party who is or becomes a creditor of the consignee and who would have a perfected security interest in the goods if they were the property of the consignee, and also has priority with respect to identifiable cash proceeds received on or before delivery of the goods to a buyer, if

(a) the consignor complies with the filing provision of the Article on Sales with respect to consignments (3)(c) of Section 2-326 before the consignee receives possession of the goods; and

(b) the consignor gives notification in writing to the holder of the security interest if the holder has filed a financing statement covering the same types of goods before the date of the filing made by the consignor; and

(c) the holder of the security interest receives the notification within five years before the consignee receives possession of the goods; and

(d) the notification states that the consignor expects to deliver goods on consignment to the consignee, describing the goods by item or type.

(2) In the case of a consignment which is not a security interest and in which the requirements of the preceding subsection have not been met, a person who delivers goods to another is subordinate to a person who would have a perfected security interest in the goods if they were the property of the debtor.

Part 2. Validity of Security Agreement and Rights of Parties Thereto

§ 9-201. General Validity of Security Agreements.
Except as otherwise provided by this Act a security agreement is effective according to its terms between the parties, against purchasers of the collateral and against creditors. Nothing in this Article validates any charge or practice illegal under any statute or regulation thereunder governing usury, small loans, retail installment sales, or the like, or extends the application of any such statute or regulation to any transaction not otherwise subject thereto.

§ 9-202. Title to Collateral Immaterial.
Each provision of this Article with regard to rights, obligations and remedies applies whether title to collateral is in the secured party or in the debtor.

§ 9-203. Attachment and Enforceability of Security Interest, Proceeds; Formal Requisites.

(1) Subject to the provisions of Section 4-208 on the security interest of a collecting bank, Section 8-321 on security interests in securities and Section 9-113 on a security interest arising under the Article on Sales, a security interest is not enforceable against the debtor or third parties with respect to the collateral and does not attach unless:

(a) the collateral is in the possession of the secured party pursuant to agreement, or the debtor has signed a security agreement which contains a description of the collateral and in addition, when the security interest covers crops growing or to be grown or timber to be cut, a description of the land concerned;

(b) value has been given; and

(c) the debtor has rights in the collateral.

(2) A security interest attaches when it becomes enforceable against the debtor with respect to the collateral. Attachment occurs as soon as all the events specified in subsection (1) have taken place unless explicit agreement postpones the time of attaching.

(3) Unless otherwise agreed a security agreement gives the secured party the rights to proceeds provided by Section 9-306.

(4) A transaction, although subject to this Article, is also subject to . . . .*, and in the case of conflict between the provisions of this Article and any such statute, the provisions of such statute control. Failure to comply with any applicable statute has only the effect which is specified therein.

*Note: At * in subsection (4) insert reference to any local statute regulating small loans, retail installment sales and the like.*

The foregoing subsection (4) is designed to make it clear that certain transactions, although subject to this Article, must also comply with other applicable legislation.

This Article is designed to regulate all the "security" aspects of transactions within its scope. There is, however, much regulatory legislation, particularly in the consumer field, which supplements this Article and should not be repealed by its enactment. Examples are small loan acts, retail installment selling acts and the like. Such acts may provide for licensing and rate regulation and may prescribe particular forms of contract. Such provisions should remain in force despite the enactment of this Article. On the other hand if a retail installment selling act contains provisions on filing, rights on default, etc., such provisions should be repealed as inconsistent with this Article except that inconsistent provisions as to deficiencies, penalties, etc., in the Uniform Consumer Credit Code and other recent related legislation should remain because those statutes were drafted after the substantial enactment of the Article and with the intention of modifying certain provisions of this Article as to consumer credit.

§ 9-204. After-Acquired Property; Future Advances.

(1) Except as provided in subsection (2), a security agreement may provide that any or all obligations covered by the security agreement are to be secured by after-acquired collateral.

(2) No security interest attaches under an after-acquired property clause to consumer goods other than accessions (Section 9-314) when given as additional security unless the debtor acquires rights in them within ten days after the secured party gives value.

(3) Obligations covered by a security agreement may include future advances or other value whether or not the advances or value are given pursuant to commitment (subsection (1) of Section 9-105).

§ 9-205. Use or Disposition of Collateral Without Accounting Permissible.
A security interest is not invalid or fraudulent against creditors by reason of liberty in the debtor to use, commingle or dispose of all or part of the collateral (including returned or repossessed goods) or to collect or compromise accounts or chattel paper, or to accept the return of goods or make repossessions, or to use, commingle or dispose of proceeds, or by reason of the failure of the secured party to require the debtor to account for proceeds or replace collateral. This section does not relax the requirements of possession where perfection of a security interest depends upon possession of the collateral by the secured party or by a bailee.

§ 9-206. Agreement Not to Assert Defenses Against Assignee; Modification of Sales Warranties Where Security Agreement Exists.

(1) Subject to any statute or decision which establishes a different rule for buyers or lessees of consumer goods, an agreement by a buyer or lessee that he will not assert against an assignee any claim or defense which he may have against the seller or lessor is enforceable by an assignee who takes his assignment for value, in good faith and without notice of a claim or defense, except as to defenses of a type which may be asserted against a holder in due course of a negotiable instrument under the Article on Commercial Paper (Article 3). A buyer who as part of one transaction signs both a negotiable instrument and a security agreement makes such an agreement.

(2) When a seller retains a purchase money security interest in goods the Article on Sales (Article 2) governs the sale and any disclaimer, limitation or modification of the seller's warranties.

§ 9-207. Rights and Duties When Collateral is in Secured Party's Possession.

(1) A secured party must use reasonable care in the custody and preservation of collateral in his possession. In the case of an instrument or chattel paper reasonable care includes taking necessary steps to preserve rights against prior parties unless otherwise agreed.

(2) Unless otherwise agreed, when collateral is in the secured party's possession

(a) reasonable expenses (including the cost of any insurance and payment of taxes or other charges) incurred in the custody, preservation, use or operation of the collateral are chargeable to the debtor and are secured by the collateral;

(b) the risk of accidental loss or damage is on the debtor to the extent of any deficiency in any effective insurance coverage;

(c) the secured party may hold as additional security any increase or profits (except money) received from the collateral, but money so received, unless remitted to the debtor, shall be applied in reduction of the secured obligation;

(d) the secured party must keep the collateral identifiable but fungible collateral may be commingled;

(e) the secured party may repledge the collateral upon terms which do not impair the debtor's right to redeem it.

(3) A secured party is liable for any loss caused by his failure to meet any obligation imposed by the preceding subsections but does not lose his security interest.

(4) A secured party may use or operate the collateral for the purpose of preserving the collateral or its value or pursuant to the order of a court of appropriate jurisdiction or, except in the case of consumer goods, in the manner and to the extent provided in the security agreement.

§ 9-208. Request for Statement of Account or List of Collateral.

(1) A debtor may sign a statement indicating what he believes to be the aggregate amount of unpaid indebtedness as of a specified date and may send it to the secured party with a request that the statement be approved or corrected and returned to the debtor. When the security agreement or any other record kept by the secured party identifies the collateral a debtor may similarly request the secured party to approve or correct a list of the collateral.

(2) The secured party must comply with such a request within two weeks after receipt by sending a written correction or approval. If the secured party claims a security interest in all of a particular type of collateral owned by the debtor he may indicate that fact in his reply and need not approve or correct an itemized list of such collateral. If the secured party without reasonable excuse fails to comply he is liable for any loss caused to the debtor thereby; and if the debtor has properly included in his request a good faith statement of the obligation or a list of the collateral or both the secured party may claim a security interest only as shown in the statement against persons misled by his failure to comply. If he no longer has an interest in the obligation or collateral at the time the request is received he must disclose the name and address of any successor in interest known to him as a result of failure to disclose. A successor in interest is not subject to this section until a request is received by him.

(3) A debtor is entitled to such a statement once every six months without charge. The secured party may require payment of a charge not exceeding $10 for each additional statement furnished.

Part 3. Rights of Third Parties; Perfected and Unperfected Security Interests; Rules of Priority

§ 9-301. Persons Who Take Priority Over Unperfected Security Interests; Rights of "Lien Creditor."

(1) Except as otherwise provided in subsection (2), an unperfected security interest is subordinate to the rights of

(a) persons entitled to priority under Section 9-312;

(b) a person who becomes a lien creditor before the security interest is perfected;

(c) in the case of goods, instruments, documents, and chattel paper, a person who is not a secured party and who is a transferee in bulk or other buyer not in ordinary course of business or is a buyer of farm products in ordinary course of business, to the extent that he gives value and receives delivery of the collateral without knowledge of the security interest and before it is perfected;

(d) in the case of accounts and general intangibles, a person who is not a secured party and who is a transferee to the extent that he gives value without knowledge of the security interest and before it is perfected.

(2) If the secured party files with respect to a purchase money security interest before or within ten days after the debtor receives possession of the collateral, he takes priority over the rights of a transferee in bulk or of a lien creditor which arise between the time the security interest attaches and the time of filing.

(3) A "lien creditor" means a creditor who has acquired a lien on the property involved by attachment, levy or the like and includes an assignee for benefit of creditors from the time of assignment, and a trustee in bankruptcy from the date of the filing of the petition or a receiver in equity from the time of appointment.

(4) A person who becomes a lien creditor while a security interest is perfected takes subject to the security interest only to the extent that it secures advances made before he becomes a lien creditor or within 45 days thereafter or made without knowledge of the lien or pursuant to a commitment entered into without knowledge of the lien.

§ 9-302. When Filing Is Required to Perfect Security Interest; Security Interests to Which Filing Provisions of This Article Do Not Apply.

(1) A financing statement must be filed to perfect all security interests except the following:

(a) a security interest in collateral in possession of the secured party under Section 9-305;

(b) a security interest temporarily perfected in instruments or documents without delivery under Section 9-304 or in proceeds for a 10 day period under Section 9-306;

(c) a security interest created by an assignment of a beneficial interest in a trust or a decedent's estate;

(d) a purchase money security interest in consumer goods; but filing is required for a motor vehicle required to be registered; and fixture filing is required for priority over conflicting interests in fixtures to the extent provided in Section 9-313;

(e) an assignment of accounts which does not alone or in conjunction with other assignments to the same assignee transfer a significant part of the outstanding accounts of the assignor;

(f) a security interest of a collecting bank (Section 4-208) or in securities (Section 8-321) or arising under the Article on Sales (see Section 9-113) or covered in subsection (3) of this section;

(g) an assignment for the benefit of all the creditors of the transferor, and subsequent transfers by the assignee thereunder.

(2) If a secured party assigns a perfected security interest, no filing under this Article is required in order to continue the perfected status of the security interest against creditors of and transferees from the original debtor.

(3) The filing of a financing statement otherwise required by this Article is not necessary or effective to perfect a security interest in property subject to

(a) a statute or treaty of the United States which provides for a national or international registration or a national or international certificate of title or which specifies a place of filing different from that specified in this Article for filing of the security interest; or

(b) the following statutes of this state; [list any certificate of title statute covering automobiles, trailers, mobile homes, boats, farm tractors, or the like and any central filing statute*]; but during any period in which collateral is inventory held for sale by a person who is in the business of selling goods of that kind, the filing provisions of this Article (Part 4) apply to a security interest in that collateral created by him as debtor; or

(c) a certificate of title statute of another jurisdiction under the law of which indication of a security interest on the certificate is required as a condition of perfection (subsection (2) of Section 9-103).

(4) Compliance with a statute or treaty described in subsection (3) is equivalent to the filing of a financing statement under this Article, and a security interest in property subject to the statute or treaty can be perfected only by compliance therewith except as provided in Section 9-103 on multiple state transactions. Duration and renewal of perfection of a security interest perfected by compliance with the statute or treaty are governed by the provisions of the statute or treaty; in other respects the security interest is subject to this Article.

*Note: It is recommended that the provisions of certificate of title acts for perfection of security interests by notation on the certificates should be amended to exclude coverage of inventory held for sale.

§ 9-303. When Security Interest Is Perfected; Continuity of Perfection.

(1) A security interest is perfected when it has attached and when all of the applicable steps required for perfection have been taken. Such steps are specified in Sections 9-302, 9-304, 9-305 and 9-306. If such steps are taken before the security interest attaches, it is perfected at the time when it attaches.

(2) If a security interest is originally perfected in any way permitted under this Article and is subsequently perfected in some other way under this Article, without an intermediate period when it was unperfected, the security interest shall be deemed to be perfected continuously for the purposes of this Article.

§ 9-304. Perfection of Security Interest in Instruments, Documents, and Goods Covered by Documents; Perfection by Permissive Filing; Temporary Perfection Without Filing or Transfer of Possessions.

(1) A security interest in chattel paper or negotiable documents may be perfected by filing. A security interest in money or instruments (other than certificated securities or instruments which constitute part of chattel paper) can be perfected only by the secured party's taking possession, except as provided in subsections (4) and (5) of this section and subsections (2) and (3) of Section 9-306 on proceeds.

(2) During the period that goods are in the possession of the issuer of a negotiable document therefor, a security interest in the goods is perfected by perfecting a security interest in the document, and any security interest in the goods otherwise perfected during such period is subject thereto.

(3) A security interest in goods in the possession of a bailee other than one who has issued a negotiable document therefor is perfected by

issuance of a document in the name of the secured party or by the bailee's receipt of notification of the secured party's interest or by filing as to the goods.

(4) A security interest in instruments (other than certificated security) or negotiable documents is perfected without filing or the taking of possession for a period of 21 days from the time it attaches to the extent that it arises for new value given under a written security agreement.

(5) A security interest remains perfected for a period of 21 days without filing where a secured party having a perfected security interest in an instrument (other than a certificated security), a negotiable document or goods in possession of a bailee other than one who has issued a negotiable documents therefor

(a) makes available to the debtor the goods or documents representing the goods for the purpose of ultimate sale or exchange or for the purpose of loading, unloading, storing, shipping, transshipping, manufacturing, processing or otherwise dealing with them in a manner preliminary to their sale or exchange, but priority between conflicting security interests in the goods is subject to subsection (3) of Section 9-312; or

(b) delivers the instrument to the debtor for the purpose of ultimate sale or exchange or of presentation, collection, renewal or registration of transfer.

(6) After the 21 day period of subsections (4) and (5) perfection depends upon compliance with applicable provisions of this Article.

§ 9-305. When Possession by Secured Party Perfects Security Interest Without Filing.

A security interest in letters of credit and advices of credit (subsection (2)(a) of Section 5-116), goods, instruments (other than certificated securities), money, negotiable documents or chattel paper may be perfected by the secured party's taking possession of the collateral. If such collateral other than goods covered by a negotiable document is held by a bailee, the secured party is deemed to have possession from the time the bailee receives notification of the secured party's interest. A security interest is perfected by possession from the time possession is taken without a relation back and continues only so long as possession is retained, unless otherwise specified in this Article. The security interest may be otherwise perfected as provided in this Article before or after the period of possession by the secured party.

§ 9-306. "Proceeds"; Secured Party's Rights on Disposition of Collateral.

(1) "Proceeds" includes whatever is received upon the sale, exchange, collection or other disposition of collateral or proceeds. Insurance payable by reason of loss or damage to the collateral is proceeds, except to the extent that it is payable to a person other than a party to the security agreement. Money, checks, deposit accounts, and the like are "cash proceeds". All other proceeds are "non-cash proceeds".

(2) Except where this Article otherwise provides, a security interest continues in collateral notwithstanding sale, exchange or other disposition thereof unless the disposition was authorized by the secured party in the security agreement or otherwise, and also continues in any identifiable proceeds including collections received by the debtor.

(3) The security interest in proceeds is a continuously perfected security interest if the interest in the original collateral was perfected but it ceases to be a perfected security interest and becomes unperfected ten days after receipt of the proceeds by the debtor unless

(a) a filed financing statement covers the original collateral and the proceeds are collateral in which a security interest may be perfected by filing in the office or offices where the financing statement has been filed and, if the proceeds are acquired with cash proceeds, the description of collateral in the financing statement indicates the types of property constituting the proceeds; or

(b) a filed financing statement covers the original collateral and the proceeds are identifiable cash proceeds; or

(c) the security interest in the proceeds is perfected before the expiration of the ten day period.

Except as provided in this section, a security interest in proceeds can be perfected only by the methods or under the circumstances permitted in this Article for original collateral of the same type.

(4) In the event of insolvency proceedings instituted by or against a debtor, a secured party with a perfected security interest in proceeds has a perfected security interest only in the following proceeds:

(a) in identifiable non-cash proceeds and in separate deposit accounts containing only proceeds;

(b) in identifiable cash proceeds in the form of money which is neither commingled with other money nor deposited in a deposit account prior to the insolvency proceedings;

(c) in identifiable cash proceeds in the form of checks and the like which are not deposited in a deposit account prior to the insolvency proceedings; and

(d) in all cash and deposit accounts of the debtor in which proceeds have been commingled with other funds, but the perfected security interest under this paragraph (d) is

(i) subject to any right to set-off; and

(ii) limited to an amount not greater than the amount of any cash proceeds received by the debtor within ten days before the institution of the insolvency proceedings less the sum of (I) the payments to the secured party on account of cash proceeds received by the debtor during such period and (II) the cash proceeds received by the debtor during such period to which the secured party is entitled under paragraphs (a) through (c) of this subsection (4).

(5) If a sale of goods results in an account or chattel paper which is transferred by the seller to a secured party, and if the goods are returned to or are repossessed by the seller or the secured party, the following rules determine priorities:

(a) If the goods were collateral at the time of sale, for an indebtedness of the seller which is still unpaid, the original security interest attaches again to the goods and continues as a perfected security interest if it was perfected at the time when the goods were sold. If the security interest was originally perfected by a filing which is still effective, nothing further is required to continue the perfected status; in any other case, the secured party must take possession of the returned or repossessed goods or must file.

(b) An unpaid transferee of the chattel paper has a security interest in the goods against the transferor. Such security interest is prior to a security interest asserted under paragraph (a) to the extent that the transferee of the chattel paper was entitled to priority under Section 9-308.

(c) An unpaid transferee of the account has a security interest in the goods against the transferor. Such security interest is subordinate to a security interest asserted under paragraph (a).

(d) A security interest of an unpaid transferee asserted under paragraph (b) or (c) must be perfected for protection against creditors of the transferor and purchasers of the returned or repossessed goods.

§ 9-307. Protection of Buyers of Goods.

(1) A buyer of ordinary course of business (subsection (9) of Section 1-21) other than a person buying farm products from a person engaged in farming operations takes free of a security interest created by his seller even though the security interest is perfected and even though the buyer knows of its existence.

(2) In the case of consumer goods, a buyer takes free of a security interest even though perfected if he buys without knowledge of the security interest, for value and for his own personal, family or household purposes unless prior to the purchase the secured party has filed a financing statement covering such goods.

(3) A buyer other than a buyer in ordinary course of business (subsection (1) of this section) takes free of a security interest to the extent that it secures future advances made after the secured party acquires knowledge of the purchase, or more than 45 days after the purchase, whichever first occurs, unless made pursuant to a commitment entered into without knowledge of the purchase and before the expiration of the 45 day period.

§ 9-308. Purchase of Chattel Paper and Instruments.
A purchaser of chattel paper or an instrument who gives new value and takes possession of it in the ordinary course of his business has priority over a security interest in the chattel paper or instrument

(a) which is perfected under Section 9-304 (permissive filing and temporary perfection) or under Section 9-306 (perfection as to proceeds) if he acts without knowledge that the specific paper or instrument is subject to a security interest; or

(b) which is claimed merely as proceeds of inventory subject to a security interest (Section 9-306) even though he knows that the specific paper or instrument is subject to the security interest.

§ 9-309. Protection of Purchasers of Instruments, Documents and Securities.
Nothing in this Article limits the rights of a holder in due course of a negotiable instrument (Section 3-302) or a holder to whom a negotiable document of title has been duly negotiated (Section 7-501) or a bona fide purchaser of a security (Section 8-302) and the holders or purchasers take priority over an earlier security interest even though perfected. Filing under this Article does not constitute notice of the security interest to such holders or purchasers.

§ 9-310. Priority of Certain Liens Arising by Operation of Law.
When a person in the ordinary course of his business furnishes services or materials with respect to goods subject to a security interest, a lien upon goods in the possession of such person given by statute or rule of law for such materials or services takes priority over a perfected security interest unless the lien is statutory and the statute expressly provides otherwise.

§ 9-311. Alienability of Debtor's Rights: Judicial Process.
The debtor's rights in collateral may be voluntarily or involuntarily transferred (by way of sale, creation of a security interest, attachment, levy, garnishment or other judicial process) notwithstanding a provision in the security agreement prohibiting any transfer or making the transfer constitute a default.

§ 9-312. Priorities Among Conflicting Security Interests in the Same Collateral.

(1) The rules of priority stated in other sections of this part and in the following sections shall govern when applicable: Section 4-208 with respect to the security interests of collecting banks in items being collected, accompanying documents and proceeds; Section 9-103 on security interests related to other jurisdictions; Section 9-114 on consignments.

(2) A perfected security interest in crops for new value given to enable the debtor to produce the crops during the production season and given not more than three months before the crops become growing crops by planting or otherwise takes priority over an earlier perfected security interest to the extent that such earlier interest secures obligations due more than six months before the crops become growing crops by planting or otherwise, even though the person giving new value had knowledge of the earlier security interest.

(3) A perfected purchase money security interest in inventory has priority over a conflicting security interest in the same inventory and also has priority in identifiable cash proceeds received on or before the delivery of the inventory to a buyer if

(a) the purchase money security interest is perfected at the time the debtor receives possession of the inventory; and

(b) the purchase money secured party gives notification in writing to the holder of the conflicting security interest if the holder had filed a financing statement covering the same types of inventory (i) before the date of the filing made by the purchase money secured party, or (ii) before the beginning of the 21 day period where the purchase money security interest is temporarily perfected without filing or possession (subsection (5) of Section 9-304); and

(c) the holder of the conflicting security interest receives the notification within five years before the debtor receives possession of the inventory; and

(d) the notification states that the person giving the notice has or expects to acquire a purchase money security interest in inventory of the debtor, describing such inventory by item or type.

(4) A purchase money security interest in collateral other than inventory has priority over a conflicting security interest in the same collateral or its proceeds if the purchase money security interest is perfected at the time the debtor receives possession of the collateral or within ten days thereafter.

(5) In all cases not governed by other rules stated in this section (including cases of purchase money security interests which do not qualify for the special priorities set forth in subsections (3) and (4) of this section), priority between conflicting security interests in the same collateral shall be determined according to the following rules:

(a) Conflicting security interests rank according to priority in time of filing or perfection. Priority dates from the time a filing is first made covering the collateral or the time the security interest is first perfected, whichever is earlier, provided that there is no period thereafter when there is neither filing nor perfection.

(b) So long as conflicting security interests are unperfected, the first to attach has priority.

(6) For the purposes of subsection (5) a date of filing or perfection as to collateral is also a date of filing or perfection as to proceeds.

(7) If future advances are made while a security interest is perfected by filing, the taking of possession, or under Section 8-321 on securities, the security interest has the same priority for the purposes of subsection (5) with respect to the future advances as it does with respect to the first advance. If a commitment is made before or while the security interest is so perfected, the security interest has the same priority with respect to advances made pursuant thereto. In other cases a perfected security interest has priority from the date the advance is made.

§ 9-313. Priority of Security Interests in Fixtures.

(1) In this section and in the provisions of Part 4 of this Article referring to fixture filing, unless the context otherwise requires

(a) goods are "fixtures" when they become so related to particular real estate that an interest in them arises under real estate law

(b) a "fixture filing" is the filing in the office where a mortgage on the real estate would be filed or recorded of a financing statement covering goods which are or are to become fixtures and conforming to the requirements of subsection (5) of Section 9-402

(c) a mortgage is a "construction mortgage" to the extent that it secures an obligation incurred for the construction of an improvement on land including the acquisition cost of the land, if the recorded writing so indicates.

(2) A security interest under this Article may be created in goods which are fixtures or may continue in goods which become fixtures, but no security interest exists under this Article in ordinary building materials incorporated into an improvement on land.

(3) This Article does not prevent creation of an encumbrance upon fixtures pursuant to real estate law.

(4) A perfected security interest in fixtures has priority over the conflicting interest of an encumbrancer or owner of the real estate where

(a) the security interest is a purchase money security interest, the interest of the encumbrancer or owner arises before the goods become fixtures, the security interest is perfected by a fixture filing before the goods become fixtures or within ten days thereafter, and the debtor has an interest of record in the real estate or is in possession of the real estate; or

(b) the security interest is perfected by a fixture filing before the interest of the encumbrancer or owner is of record, the security interest has priority over any conflicting interest of a predecessor in title of the encumbrancer or owner, and the debtor has an interest of record in the real estate or is in possession of the real estate; or

(c) the fixtures are readily removable factory or office machines or readily removable replacements of domestic appliances which are consumer goods, and before the goods become fixtures the security interest is perfected by any method permitted by this Article; or

(d) the conflicting interest is a lien on the real estate obtained by legal or equitable proceedings after the security interest was perfected by any method permitted by this Article.

(5) A security interest in fixtures, whether or not perfected, has priority over the conflicting interest of an encumbrancer or owner of the real estate where

(a) the encumbrancer or owner has consented in writing to the security interest or has disclaimed an interest in the goods as fixtures; or

(b) the debtor has a right to remove the goods as against the encumbrancer or owner. If the debtor's right terminates, the priority of the security interest continues for a reasonable time.

(6) Notwithstanding paragraph (a) of subsection (4) but otherwise subject to subsections (4) and (5), a security interest in fixtures is subordinate to a construction mortgage recorded before the goods become fixtures if the goods become fixtures before the completion of the construction. To the extent that it is given to refinance a construction mortgage, a mortgage has this priority to the same extent as the construction mortgage.

(7) In cases not within the preceding subsections, a security interest in fixtures is subordinate to the conflicting interest of an encumbrancer or owner of the related real estate who is not the debtor.

(8) When the secured party has priority over all owners and encumbrancers of the real estate, he may, on default, subject to the provisions of Part 5, remove his collateral from the real estate but he must reimburse any encumbrancer or owner of the real estate who is not the debtor and who has not otherwise agreed for the cost of repair of any physical injury, but not for any diminution in value of the real estate caused by the absence of the goods removed or by any necessity of replacing them. A person entitled to reimbursement may refuse permission to remove until the secured party gives adequate security for the performance of this obligation.

§ 9-314. Accessions.

(1) A security interest in goods which attaches before they are installed in or affixed to other goods takes priority as to the goods installed or affixed (called in this section "accessions") over the claims of all persons to the whole except as stated in subsection (3) and subject to Section 9-315(1).

(2) A security interest which attaches to goods after they become part of a whole is valid against all persons subsequently acquiring interests

in the whole except as stated in subsection (3) but is invalid against any person with an interest in the whole at the time the security interest attaches to the goods who has not in writing consented to the security interest or disclaimed an interest in the goods as part of the whole.

(3) The security interests described in subsections (1) and (2) do not take priority over

(a) a subsequent purchaser for value of any interest in the whole; or

(b) a creditor with a lien on the whole subsequently obtained by judicial proceedings; or

(c) a creditor with a prior perfected security interest in the whole to the extent that he makes subsequent advances.

If the subsequent purchase is made, the lien by judicial proceedings obtained or the subsequent advance under the prior perfected security interest is made or contracted for without knowledge of the security interest and before it is perfected. A purchaser of the whole at a foreclosure sale other than the holder of a perfected security interest purchasing at his own foreclosure sale is a subsequent purchaser within this section.

(4) When under subsections (1) or (2) and (3) a secured party has an interest in accessions which has priority over the claims of all persons who have interests in the whole, he may on default subject to the provisions of Part 5 remove his collateral from the whole but he must reimburse any encumbrancer or owner of the whole who is not the debtor and who has not otherwise agreed for the cost of repair of any physical injury but not for any diminution in value of the whole caused by the absence of the goods removed or by any necessity for replacing them. A person entitled to reimbursement may refuse permission to remove until the secured party gives adequate security for the performance of this obligation.

§ 9-315. Priority When Goods Are Commingled or Processed.

(1) If a security interest in goods was perfected and subsequently the goods or a part thereof have become part of a product or mass, the security interest continues in the product or mass if

(a) the goods are so manufactured, processed, assembled or commingled that their identity is lost in the product or mass; or

(b) a financing statement covering the original goods also covers the product into which the goods have been manufactured, processed or assembled.

In a case to which paragraph (b) applies, no separate security interest in that part of the original goods which has been manufactured, processed or assembled into the product may be claimed under Section 9-314.

(2) When under subsection (1) more than one security interest attaches to the product or mass, they rank equally according to the ratio that the cost of the goods to which each interest originally attached bears to the cost of the total product or mass.

§ 9-316. Priority Subject to Subordination. Nothing in this Article prevents subordination by agreement by any person entitled to priority.

§ 9-317. Secured Party Not Obligated on Contract of Debtor. The mere existence of a security interest or authority given to the debtor to dispose of or use collateral does not impose contract or tort liability upon the secured party for the debtor's acts or omissions.

§ 9-318. Defenses Against Assignee; Modification of Contract After Negotiation of Assignment; Term Prohibiting Assignment Ineffective; Identification and Proof of Assignment.

(1) Unless an account debtor has made an enforceable agreement not to assert defenses or claims arising out of a sale as provided in Section 9-206 the rights of an assignee are subject to

(a) all the terms of the contract between the account debtor and assignor and any defense or claim arising therefrom; and

(b) any other defense or claim of the account debtor against the assignor which accrues before the account debtor receives notification of the assignment.

(2) So far as the right to payment or a part thereof under an assigned contract has not been fully earned by performance, and notwithstanding notification of the assignment, any modification of or substitution for the contract made in good faith and in accordance with reasonable commercial standards is effective against an assignee unless the account debtor has otherwise agreed but the assignee acquires corresponding rights under the modified or substituted contract. The assignment may provide that such modification or substitution is a breach by the assignor.

(3) The account debtor is authorized to pay the assignor until the account debtor receives notification that the amount due or to become due has been assigned and that payment is to be made to the assignee. A notification which does not reasonably identify the rights assigned is ineffective. If requested by the account debtor, the assignee must seasonably furnish reasonable proof that the assignment has been made and unless he does so the account debtor may pay the assignor.

(4) A term in any contract between an account debtor and an assignor is ineffective if it prohibits assignment of an account or prohibits creation of a security interest in a general intangible for money due or to become due or requires the account debtor's consent to such assignment or security interest.

Part 4. Filing

§ 9-401. Place of Filing; Erroneous Filing; Removal of Collateral.

First Alternative Subsection (1)

(1) The proper place to file in order to perfect a security interest is as follows:

(a) when the collateral is timber to be cut or is minerals or the like (including oil and gas) or accounts subject to subsection (5) of Section 9-103, or when the financing statement is filed as a fixture filing (Section 9-313) and the collateral is goods which are or are to become fixtures, then in the office where a mortgage on the real estate would be filed or recorded;

(b) in all other cases, in the office of the [Secretary of State].

Second Alternative Subsection (1)

(1) The proper place to file in order to perfect a security interest is as follows:

(a) when the collateral is equipment used in farming operations, or farm products, or accounts or general intangibles arising from or relating to the sale of farm products by a farmer, or consumer goods, then in the office of the . . . . in the county of the debtor's residence or if the debtor is not a resident of this state then in the office of the . . . . in the county where the goods are kept, and in addition when the collateral is crops growing or to be grown in the office of the . . . . in the county where the land is located;

(b) when the collateral is timber to be cut or is minerals or the like (including oil and gas) or accounts subject to subsection (5) of Section 9-103, or when the financing statement is filed as a fixture filing (Section 9-313) and the collateral is goods which are or are to become fixtures, then in the office where a mortgage on the real estate would be filed or recorded;

(c) in all other cases, in the office of the [Secretary of State].

Third Alternative Subsection (1)

(1) The proper place to file in order to perfect a security interest is as follows:

(a) when the collateral is equipment used in farming operations, or farm products, or accounts or general intangibles arising from or relating to the sale of farm products by a farmer, or consumer goods, then in the office of the . . . . in the county of the debtor's residence or if the debtor is not a resident of this state then in the office of the . . . . in the county where the goods are kept, and in addition when the collateral is crops growing or to be grown in the office of the . . . . in the county where the land is located;

(b) when the collateral is timber to be cut or is minerals or the like (including oil and gas) or accounts subject to subsection (5) of Section 9-103, or when the financing statement is filed as a fixture filing (Section 9-313) and the collateral is goods which are or are to become fixtures, then in the office where a mortgage on the real estate would be filed or recorded;

(c) in all other cases, in the office of the [Secretary of State] and in addition, if the debtor has a place of business in only one county of this state, also in the office of . . . . of such county, or, if the debtor has no place of business in this state, but resides in the state, also in the office of . . . . of the county in which he resides.

Note: One of the three alternatives should be selected as subsection (1).

(2) A filing which is made in good faith in an improper place or not in all of the places required by this section is nevertheless effective with regard to any collateral as to which the filing complied with the requirements of this Article and is also effective with regard to collateral covered by the financing statement against any person who has knowledge of the contents of such financing statement.

(3) A filing which is made in the proper place in this state continues effective even though the debtor's residence or place of business or the location of the collateral or its use, whichever controlled the original filing, is therefore changed.

Alternative Subsection (3)

[(3) A filing which is made in the proper county continues effective for four months after a change to another county of the debtor's residence or place of business or the location of the collateral, whichever controlled the original filing. It becomes ineffective thereafter unless a copy of the financing statement signed by the secured party is filed in the new county within said period. The security interest may also be perfected in the new county after the expiration of the four-month period; in such case perfection dates from the time of perfection in the new county. A change in the use of the collateral does not impair the effectiveness of the original filing.]

(4) The rules stated in Section 9-103 determine whether filing is necessary in this state.

(5) Notwithstanding the preceding subsections, and subject to subsection (3) of Section 9-302, the proper place to file in order to perfect a security interest in collateral, including fixtures, of a transmitting utility is the office of the [Secretary of State]. This filing constitutes a fixture filing (Section 9-313) as to the collateral described therein which is or is to become fixtures.

(6) For the purpose of this section, the residence of an organization is its place of business if it has one or its chief executive office if it has more than one place of business.

Note: Subsection (6) should be used only if the state chooses the Second or Third Alternative Section (1).

§ 9-402. Formal Requisites of Financing Statement; Amendments; Mortgage as Financing Statement.

(1) A financing statement is sufficient if it gives the names of the debtor and the secured party, is signed by the debtor, gives an address of the secured party from which information concerning the security interest may be obtained, gives a mailing address of the debtor and contains a statement indicating the types, or describing the items, of collateral. A financing statement may be filed before a security agreement is made or a security interest otherwise attaches. When the financing statement covers crops growing or to be grown, the statement must also contain a description of the real estate concerned. When the financing statement covers timber to be cut or covers minerals or the like (including oil and gas) or accounts subject to subsection (5) of Section 9-103, or when the financing statement is filed as a fixture filing (Section 9-313) and the collateral is goods which are or are to become fixtures, the statement must also comply with subsection (5). A copy of the security agreement is sufficient as a financing statement if it contains the above information and is signed by the debtor. A carbon, photographic or other reproduction of a security agreement or a financing statement is sufficient as a financing statement if the security agreement so provides or if the original has been filed in this state.

(2) A financing statement which otherwise complies with subsection (1) is sufficient when it is signed by the secured party instead of the debtor if it is filed to perfect a security interest in

(a) collateral already subject to a security interest in another jurisdiction when it is brought into this state, or when the debtor's location is changed to this state. Such a financing statement must state that the collateral was brought into this state or that the debtor's location was changed to this state under such circumstances; or

(b) proceeds under Section 9-306 if the security interest in the original collateral was perfected. Such a financing statement must describe the original collateral; or

(c) collateral as to which the filing has lapsed; or

(d) collateral acquired after a change of name, identity or corporate structure of the debtor (subsection (7)).

(3) A form substantially as follows is sufficient to comply with subsection (1):

Name of debtor (or assignor). . . . .
Address. . . . .
Name of secured party (or assignee). . . . .
Address. . . . .
1. This financing statement covers the following types (or items) of property:
(Describe). . . . .
2. (If collateral is crops) The above described crops are growing or are to be grown on:
(Describe Real Estate) . . . .
3. (If applicable) The above goods are to become fixtures on [where appropriate substitute either "The above timber is standing on _____" or "The above minerals or the like (including oil and gas) or accounts will be financed at the wellhead of the well or mine located on _____."
(Describe Real Estate) . . . .
and this financing statement is to be filed [for record] in the real estate records. (If the debtor does not have an interest of record) The name of a record owner is

. . . .

4. (If products of collateral are claimed) Products of the collateral are also covered.

(use whichever signature is applicable)

. . . .
Signature of Debtor (or Assignor)

. . . .
Signature of Secured Party (or Assignee)

(4) A financing statement may be amended by filing a writing signed by both the debtor and the secured party. An amendment does not extend the period of effectiveness of a financing statement. If any amendment adds collateral, it is effective as to the added collateral only from the filing date of the amendment. In this Article, unless the context otherwise requires, the term "financing statement" means the original financing statement and any amendments.

(5) A financing statement covering timber to be cut or covering minerals or the like (including oil and gas) or accounts subject to subsection (5) of Section 9-103, or a financing statement filed as a fixture filing (Section 9-313) where the debtor is not a transmitting utility, must show that it covers this type of collateral, must recite that it is to be filed [for record] in the real estate records, and the financing statement must contain a description of the real estate [sufficient if it were contained in a mortgage of real estate to give constructive notice of the mortgage under the law of this state]. If the debtor does not have an interest or record in the real estate, the financing statement must show the name of a record owner.

(6) A mortgage is effective as a financing statement filed as a fixture filing from the date of its recording if

(a) the goods are described in the mortgage by item or type; and

(b) the goods are or are to become fixtures related to the real estate described in the mortgage; and

(c) the mortgage complies with the requirements for a financing statement in this section other than a recital that it is to be filed in the real estate records; and

(d) the mortgage is duly recorded.

No fee with reference to the financing statement is required other than the regular recording and satisfaction fees with respect to the mortgage.

(7) A financing statement sufficiently shows the name of the debtor if it gives the individual, partnership or corporate name of the debtor, whether or not it adds other trade names or names of partners. Where the debtor so changes his name or in the case of an organization its name, identity or corporate structure that a filed financing statement becomes seriously misleading, the filing is not effective to perfect a security interest in collateral acquired by the debtor more than four months after the change, unless a new appropriate financing statement is filed before the expiration of that time. A filed financing statement remains effective with respect to collateral transferred by the debtor even though the secured party knows of or consents to the transfer.

(8) A financing statement substantially complying with the requirements of this section is effective even though it contains minor errors which are not seriously misleading.

Note: Language in brackets is optional.

Note: Where the state has any special recording system for real estate other than the usual grantor-grantee index (as, for instance, a tract system or a title registration or Torrens system) local adaptations of subsection (5) and Section 9-403(7) may be necessary. See Mass. Gen. Laws Chapter 106, Section 9-409.

§ 9-403. What Constitutes Filing; Duration of Filing; Effect of Lapsed Filing; Duties of Filing Officers.

(1) Presentation for filing of a financing statement and tender of the filing fee or acceptance of the statement by the filing officer constitutes filing under this Article.

(2) Except as provided in subsection (6) a filed financing statement is effective for a period of five years from the date of filing. The effectiveness of a filed financing statement lapses on the expiration of the five year period unless a continuation statement is filed prior to the lapse. If a security interest perfected by filing exists at the time insolvency proceedings are commenced by or against the debtor, the security interest remains perfected until termination of the insolvency proceedings and thereafter for a period of sixty days or until expiration of the five year period, whichever occurs later. Upon lapse the security interest becomes unperfected, unless it is perfected without filing. If the security interest becomes unperfected upon lapse, it is deemed to have been unperfected as against a person who became a purchaser or lien creditor before lapse.

(3) A continuation statement may be filed by the secured party within six months prior to the expiration of the five year period specified in subsection (2). Any such continuation statement must be signed by the secured party, identify the original statement by file number and state that the original statement is still effective. A continuation statement signed by a person other than the secured party of record must be accompanied by a separate written statement of assignment signed by the secured party of record and complying with subsection (2) of Section 9-405, including payment of the required fee. Upon timely filing of the continuation statement, the effectiveness of the original statement is continued for five years after the last date to which the filing was effective whereupon it lapses in the same manner as provided in subsection (2) unless another continuation statement is filed prior to such lapse. Succeeding continuation statements may be filed in the same manner to continue the effectiveness of the original statement. Unless a statute on disposition of public records provides otherwise, the filing officer may remove a lapsed statement from the files and destroy it immediately if he has retained a microfilm or other photographic record, or in other cases after one year after the lapse. The filing officer shall so arrange matters by physical annexation of financing statements to continuation statements or other related filings, or by other means, that if he physically destroys the financing statements of a period more than five years past, those which have been continued by a continuation statement or which are still effective under subsection (6) shall be retained.

(4) Except as provided in subsection (7) a filing officer shall mark each statement with a file number and with the date and hour of filing and shall hold the statement or a microfilm or other photographic copy thereof for public inspection. In addition the filing officer shall index the statement according to the name of the debtor and shall note in the index the file number and the address of the debtor given in the statement.

(5) The uniform fee for filing and indexing and for stamping a copy furnished by the secured party to show the date and place of filing for an original financing statement or for a continuation statement shall be $ . . . . if the statement is in the standard form prescribed by the [Secretary of State] and otherwise shall be $ . . . . , plus in each case, if the financing statement is subject to subsection (5) of Section 9-402, $ . . . . The uniform fee for each name more than one required to be indexed shall be $ . . . . The secured party may at his option show a trade name for any person and an extra uniform indexing fee of $ . . . . shall be paid with respect thereto.

(6) If the debtor is a transmitting utility (subsection (5) of Section 9-401) and a filed financing statement so states, it is effective until a

termination statement is filed. A real estate mortgage which is effective as a fixture filing under subsection (6) of Section 9-402 remains effective as a fixture filing until the mortgage is released or satisfied of record or its effectiveness otherwise terminates as to the real estate.

(7) When a financing statement covers timber to be cut or covers minerals or the like (including oil and gas) or accounts subject to a subsection (5) of Section 9-103, or is filed as a fixture filing, [it shall be filed for record and] the filing officer shall index it under the names of the debtor and any owner of record shown on the financing statement in the same fashion as if they were the mortgagors in a mortgage of the real estate described, and, to the extent that law of this state provides for indexing of mortgages under the name of the mortgagee, under the name of the secured party as if he were the mortgagee thereunder, or where indexing is by description in the same fashion as if the financing statement were a mortgage of the real estate described.

Note: In states in which writings will not appear in the real estate records and indices unless actually recorded the bracketed language in subsection (7) should be used.

§ 9-404. Termination Statement.

(1) If a financing statement covering consumer goods is filed on or after . . . . , then within one month or within ten days following written demand by the debtor after there is no outstanding secured obligation and no commitment to make advances, incur obligations or otherwise give value, the secured party must file with each filing officer with whom the financing statement was filed, a termination statement to the effect that he no longer claims a security interest under the financing statement, which shall be identified by file number. In other cases whenever there is no outstanding secured obligation and no commitment to make advances, incur obligations or otherwise give value, the secured party must on written demand by the debtor send the debtor, for each filing officer with whom the financing statement was filed, a termination statement to the effect that he no longer claims a security interest under the financing statement, which shall be identified by file number. A termination statement signed by a person other than the secured party of record must be accompanied by a separate written statement of assignment signed by the secured party of record complying with subsection (2) of Section 9-405, including payment of the required fee. If the affected secured party fails to file such a termination statement as required by this subsection, or to send such a termination statement within ten days after proper demand therefor, he shall be liable to the debtor for one hundred dollars, and in addition for any loss caused to the debtor by such failure.

(2) On presentation to the filing officer of such a termination statement he must note it in the index. If he has received the termination statement in duplicate, he shall return one copy of the termination statement to the secured party stamped to show the time of receipt thereof. If the filing officer has a microfilm or other photographic record of the financing statement, and of any related continuation statement, statement of assignment and statement of release, he may remove the originals from the files at any time after receipt of the termination statement, or if he has no such record, he may remove them from the files at any time after one year after receipt of the termination statement.

(3) If the termination statement is the standard form prescribed by the [Secretary of State], the uniform fee for filing and indexing the termination statement shall be $ . . . . , and otherwise shall be $ . . . . , plus in each case an additional fee of $ . . . . for each name more than one against which the termination statement is required to be indexed.

Note: The date to be inserted should be the effective date of the revised Article 9.

§ 9-405. Assignment of Security Interest; Duties of Filing Officer; Fees.

(1) A financing statement may disclose an assignment of a security interest in the collateral described in the financing statement by indication in the financing statement of the name and address of the assignee or by an assignment itself or a copy thereof on the face or back of the statement. On presentation to the filing officer of such a financing statement the filing officer shall mark the same as provided in Section 9-403(4). The uniform fee for filing, indexing and furnishing filing data for a financing statement so indicating an assignment shall be $ . . . . if the statement is in the standard form prescribed by the [Secretary of State] and otherwise shall be $ . . . . , plus in each case an additional fee of $ . . . . for each name more than one against which the financing statement is required to be indexed.

(2) A secured party may assign of record all or part of his rights under a financing statement by the filing in the place where the original financing statement was filed of a separate written statement of assignment signed by the secured party of record and setting forth the name of the secured party of record and the debtor, the file number and the date of filing of the financing statement and the name and address of the assignee and containing a description of the collateral assigned. A copy of the assignment is sufficient as a separate statement if it complies with the preceding sentence. On presentation to the filing officer of such a separate statement, the filing officer shall mark such separate statement with the date and hour of the filing. He shall note the assignment on the index of the financing statement, or in the case of a fixture filing, or a filing covering timber to be cut, or covering minerals or the like (including oil and gas) or accounts subject to subsection (5) of Section 9-103, he shall index the assignment under the name of the assignor as grantor and, to the extent that the law of this state provides for indexing the assignment of a mortgage under the name of the assignee, he shall index the assignment of the financing statement under the name of the assignee. The uniform fee for filing, indexing and furnishing filing data about such a separate statement of assignment shall be $ . . . . if the statement is in the standard form prescribed by the [Secretary of State] and otherwise shall be $ . . . . , plus in each case an additional fee of $ . . . . for each name more than one against which the statement of assignment is required to be indexed. Notwithstanding the provisions of this subsection, an assignment of record of a security interest in a fixture contained in a mortgage effective as a fixture filing (subsection (6) of Section 9-402) may be made only by an assignment of the mortgage in the manner provided by the law of this state other than this Act.

(3) After the disclosure or filing of an assignment under this section, the assignee is the secured party of record.

§ 9-406. Release of Collateral; Duties of Filing Officer; Fees.
A secured party of record may by his signed statement release all or a part of any collateral described in a filed financing statement. The statement of release is sufficient if it contains a description of the collateral being released, the name and address of the debtor, the name and address of the secured party, and the file number of the financing statement. A statement of release signed by a person other than the secured party of record must be accompanied by a separate written statement of assignment signed by the secured party of record and complying with subsection (2) of Section 9-405, including payment of the required fee. Upon presentation of such a statement of release to the filing officer he shall mark the statement with the hour and date of filing of the financing statement. The uniform fee for filing and noting such a statement of release shall be $ i

the statement is in the standard form prescribed by the [Secretary of State] and otherwise shall be $ . . . . , plus in each case an additional fee of $ . . . . for each name more than one against which the statement of release is required to be indexed.

[§ 9-407. Information From Filing Officer.]

[(1) If the person filing any financing statement, termination statement, statement of assignment, or statement of release, furnishes the filing officer a copy thereof, the filing officer shall upon request note upon the copy the file number and date and hour of the filing of the original and deliver or send the copy to such person.]

[(2) Upon request of any person, the filing officer shall issue his certificate showing whether there is on file on the date and hour stated therein, any presently effective financing statement naming a particular debtor and any statement of assignment thereof and if there is, giving the names and addresses of each secured party therein. The uniform fee for such a certificate shall be $ . . . . if the request for the certificate is in the standard form prescribed by the [Secretary of State] and otherwise shall be $ . . . . Upon request the filing officer shall furnish a copy of any filed financing statement or statement of assignment for a uniform fee of $ . . . . per page.]

Note: This section is proposed as an optional provision to require filing officers to furnish certificates. Local law and practice should be consulted with regard to the advisability of adoption.

§ 9-408. Financing Statements Covering Consigned or Leased Goods.

A consignor or lessor of goods may file a financing statement using the terms "consignor," "consignee," "lessor," "lessee" or the like instead of the terms specified in Section 9-402. The provisions of this Part shall apply as appropriate to such a financing statement but its filing shall not of itself be a factor in determining whether or not the consignment or lease is intended as security (Section 1-201(37)]. However, if it is determined for other reasons that the consignment or lease is so intended, a security interest of the consignor or lessor which attaches to the consigned or leased goods is perfected by such filing.

Part 5. Default

§ 9-501. Default; Procedure When Security Agreement Covers Both Real and Personal Property.

(1) When a debtor is in default under a security agreement, a secured party has the rights and remedies provided in this Part and except as limited by subsection (3) those provided in the security agreement. He may reduce his claim to judgment, foreclose or otherwise enforce the security interest by any available judicial procedure. If the collateral is documents the secured party may proceed either as to the documents or as to the goods covered thereby. A secured party in possession has the rights, remedies and duties provided in Section 9-207. The rights and remedies referred to in this subsection are cumulative.

(2) After default, the debtor has the rights and remedies provided in this Part, those provided in the security agreement and those provided in Section 9-207.

(3) To the extent that they give rights to the debtor and impose duties on the secured party, the rules stated in the subsections referred to below may not be waived or varied except as provided with respect to compulsory disposition of collateral (subsection (3) of Section 9-504 and Section 9-505) and with respect to redemption of collateral (Section 9-506) but the parties may by agreement determine the standards by which the fulfillment of these rights and duties is to be measured if such standards are not manifestly unreasonable:

  (a) subsection (2) of Section 9-502 and subsection (2) of Section 9-504 insofar as they require accounting for surplus proceeds of collateral;

  (b) subsection (3) of Section 9-504 and subsection (1) of Section 9-505 which deal with disposition of collateral;

  (c) subsection (2) of Section 9-505 which deals with acceptance of collateral as discharge of obligation;

  (d) Section 9-506 which deals with redemption of collateral; and

  (e) subsection (1) of Section 9-507 which deals with the secured party's liability for failure to comply with this Part.

(4) If the security agreement covers both real and personal property, the secured party may proceed under this Part as to the personal property or he may proceed as to both the real and the personal property in accordance with his rights and remedies in respect of the real property in which case the provisions of this Part do not apply.

(5) When a secured party has reduced his claim to judgment the lien of any levy which may be made upon his collateral by virtue of any execution based upon the judgment shall relate back to the date of the perfection of the security interest in such collateral. A judicial sale, pursuant to such execution, is a foreclosure of the security interest by judicial procedure within the meaning of this section, and the secured party may purchase at the sale and thereafter hold the collateral free of any other requirements of this Article.

§ 9-502. Collection Rights of Secured Party.

(1) When so agreed and in any event on default the secured party is entitled to notify an account debtor or the obligor on an instrument to make payment to him whether or not the assignor was theretofore making collections on the collateral, and also to take control of any proceeds to which he is entitled under Section 9-306.

(2) A secured party who by agreement is entitled to charge back uncollected collateral or otherwise to full or limited recourse against the debtor and who undertakes to collect from the account debtors or obligors must proceed in a commercially reasonable manner and may deduct his reasonable expenses of realization from the collections. If the security agreement secures an indebtedness, the secured party must account to the debtor for any surplus, and unless otherwise agreed, the debtor is liable for any deficiency. But, if the underlying transaction was a sale of accounts or chattel paper, the debtor is entitled to any surplus or is liable for any deficiency only if the security agreement so provides.

§ 9-503. Secured Party's Right to Take Possession After Default.

Unless otherwise agreed a secured party has on default the right to take possession of the collateral. In taking possession a secured party may proceed without judicial process if this can be done without breach of the peace or may proceed by action. If the security agreement so provides the secured party may require the debtor to assemble the collateral and make it available to the secured party at a place to be designated by the secured party which is reasonably convenient to both parties. Without removal a secured party may render equipment unusable, and may dispose of collateral on the debtor's premises under Section 9-504.

§ 9-504. Secured Party's Right to Dispose of Collateral After Default; Effect of Disposition.

(1) A secured party after default may sell, lease or otherwise dispose of any or all of the collateral in its then condition or following any commercially reasonable preparation or processing. Any sale of goods is subject to the Article on Sales (Article 2). The proceeds of disposition shall be applied in the order following to

  (a) the reasonable expenses of retaking, holding, preparing for sale or lease, selling, leasing and the like and, to the extent provided for in the agreement and not prohibited by law, the reasonable attorneys' fees and legal expenses incurred by the security party;

(b) the satisfaction of indebtedness secured by the security interest under which the disposition is made;

(c) the satisfaction of indebtedness secured by any subordinate security interest in the collateral if written notification of demand therefor is received before distribution of the proceeds is completed. If requested by the secured party, the holder of a subordinate security interest must seasonably furnish reasonable proof of his interest, and unless he does so, the secured party need not comply with his demand.

(2) If the security interest secures an indebtedness, the secured party must account to the debtor for any surplus, and, unless otherwise agreed, the debtor is liable for any deficiency. But if the underlying transaction was a sale of accounts or chattel paper, the debtor is entitled to any surplus or is liable for any deficiency only if the security agreement so provides.

(3) Disposition of the collateral may be by public or private proceedings and may be made by way of one or more contracts. Sale or other disposition may be as a unit or in parcels and at any time and place and on any terms but every aspect of the disposition including the method, manner, time, place and terms must be commercially reasonable. Unless collateral is perishable or threatens to decline speedily in value or is of a type customarily sold on a recognized market, reasonable notification of the time and place of any public sale or reasonable notification of the time after which any private sale or other intended disposition is to be made shall be sent by the secured party to the debtor, if he has not signed after default a statement renouncing or modifying his right to notification of sale. In the case of consumer goods no other notification need be sent. In other cases notification shall be sent to any other secured party from whom the secured party has received (before sending his notification to the debtor or before the debtor's renunciation of his rights) written notice of a claim of an interest in the collateral. The secured party may buy at any public sale and if the collateral is of a type customarily sold in a recognized market or is of a type which is the subject of widely distributed standard price quotations he may buy at private sale.

(4) When collateral is disposed of by a secured party after default, the disposition transfers to a purchaser for value of all the debtor's rights therein, discharges the security interest under which it is made and any security interest or lien subordinate thereto. The purchaser takes free of all such rights and interests even though the secured party fails to comply with the requirements of this Part or of any judicial proceedings

(a) in the case of a public sale, if the purchaser has no knowledge of any defects in the sale and if he does not buy in collusion with the secured party, other bidders or the person conducting the sale; or

(b) in any other case, if the purchaser acts in good faith.

(5) A person who is liable to a secured party under a guaranty, indorsement, repurchase agreement or the like and who receives a transfer of collateral from the secured party or is subrogated to his rights has thereafter the rights and duties of the secured party. Such a transfer of collateral is not a sale or disposition of the collateral under this Article.

§ 9-505. Compulsory Disposition of Collateral; Acceptance of the Collateral as Discharge of Obligation.

(1) If the debtor has paid sixty per cent of the cash price in the case of a purchase money security interest in consumer goods or sixty per cent of the loan in the case of another security interest in consumer goods, and has not signed after default a statement renouncing or modifying his rights under this Part a secured party who has taken possession of collateral must dispose of it under Section 9-504 and if he fails to do so within ninety days after he takes possession the debtor at his option may recover in conversion or under Section 9-507(1) on secured party's liability.

(2) In any other case involving consumer goods or any other collateral a secured party in possession may, after default, propose to retain the collateral in satisfaction of the obligation. Written notice of such proposal shall be sent to the debtor if he has not signed after default a statement renouncing or modifying his rights under this subsection. In the case of consumer goods no other notice need be given. In other cases notice shall be sent to any other secured party from whom the secured party has received (before sending his notice to the debtor or before the debtor's renunciation of his rights) written notice of a claim of an interest in the collateral. If the secured party receives objection in writing from a person entitled to receive notification within twenty-one days after the notice was sent, the secured party must dispose of the collateral under Section 9-504. In the absence of such written objection the secured party may retain the collateral in satisfaction of the debtor's obligation.

§ 9-506. Debtor's Right to Redeem Collateral.

At any time before the secured party has disposed of collateral or entered into a contract for its disposition under Section 9-504 or before the obligation has been discharged under Section 9-505(2) the debtor or any other secured party may unless otherwise agreed in writing after default redeem the collateral by tendering fulfillment of all obligations secured by the collateral as well as the expenses reasonably incurred by the secured party in retaking, holding and preparing the collateral for disposition, in arranging for the sale, and to the extent provided in the agreement and not prohibited by law, his reasonable attorneys' fees and legal expenses.

§ 9-507. Secured Party's Liability for Failure to Comply With This Part.

(1) If it is established that the secured party is not proceeding in accordance with the provisions of this Part disposition may be ordered or restrained on appropriate terms and conditions. If the disposition has occurred the debtor or any person entitled to notification or whose security interest has been made known to the secured party prior to the disposition has a right to recover from the secured party any loss caused by a failure to comply with the provisions of this Part. If the collateral is consumer goods, the debtor has a right to recover in any event an amount not less than the credit service charge plus ten per cent of the principal amount of the debt or the time price differential plus 10 per cent of the cash price.

(2) The fact that a better price could have been obtained by a sale at a different time or in a different method from that selected by the secured party is not of itself sufficient to establish that the sale was not made in a commercially reasonable manner. If the secured party either sells the collateral in the usual manner in any recognized market therefor or if he sells at the price current in such market at the time of his sale or if he has otherwise sold in conformity with reasonable commercial practices among dealers in the type of property sold he has sold in a commercially reasonable manner. The principles stated in the two preceding sentences with respect to sales also apply as may be appropriate to other types of disposition. A disposition which has been approved in any judicial proceeding or by any bona fide creditors' committee or representative of creditors shall conclusively be deemed to be commercially reasonable, but this sentence does not indicate that any such approval must be obtained in any case nor does it indicate that any disposition not so approved is not commercially reasonable.

ARTICLE 10. EFFECTIVE DATE AND REPEALER

§ 10-101. Effective Date. This Act shall become effective at midnight on December 31st following its enactment. It applies to transactions entered into and events occurring after that date.

§ 10-102. Specific Repealer; Provision for Transition.

(1) The following acts and all other acts and parts of acts inconsistent herewith are hereby repealed:

(Here should follow the acts to be specifically repealed including the following:

Uniform Negotiable Instruments Act

Uniform Warehouse Receipts Act

Uniform Sales Act

Uniform Bills of Lading Act

Uniform Stock Transfer Act

Uniform Conditional Sales Act

Uniform Trust Receipts Act

Also any acts regulating:

Bank collections

Bulk sales

Chattel mortgages

Conditional sales

Factor's lien acts

Farm storage of grain and similar acts

Assignment of accounts receivable)

(2) Transactions validly entered into before the effective date specified in Section 10-101 and the rights, duties and interests flowing from them remain valid thereafter and may be terminated, completed, consummated or enforced as required or permitted by any statute or other law amended or repealed by this Act as though such repeal or amendment had not occurred.

Note: Subsection (1) should be separately prepared for each state. The foregoing is a list of statutes to be checked.

§ 10-103. General Repealer. Except as provided in the following section, all acts and parts of acts inconsistent with this Act are hereby repealed.

§ 10-104. Laws Not Repealed.

[(1) The Article on Documents of Title (Article 7) does not repeal or modify any laws prescribing the form or contents of documents of title or the services or facilities to be afforded by bailees, or otherwise regulating bailees' businesses in respects not specifically dealt with herein; but the fact that such laws are violated does not affect the status of a document of title which otherwise complies with the definition of a document of title (Section 1-201).]

[(2) This Act does not repeal . . . . , cited as the Uniform Act for the Simplification of Fiduciary Security Transfers, and if in any respect there is any inconsistency between that Act and the Article of this Act on investment securities (Article 8) the provisions of the former Act shall control.]

APPENDIX D

United Nations Convention on Contracts for the International Sale of Goods

The States Parties to this Convention,

Bearing in mind the broad objectives in the resolutions adopted by the sixth special session of the General Assembly of the United Nations on the establishment of a New International Economic Order,

Considering that the development of international trade on the basis of equality and mutual benefit is an important element in promoting friendly relations among States,

Being of the opinion that the adoption of uniform rules which govern contracts for the international sale of goods and take into account the different social, economic and legal systems would contribute to the removal of legal barriers in international trade and promote the development of international trade,

Have agreed as follows:

PART I. SPHERE OF APPLICATION AND GENERAL PROVISIONS

Chapter I. Sphere of Application

Article 1

(1) This Convention applies to contracts of sale of goods between parties whose places of business are in different States:

(a) when the States are Contracting States; or

(b) when the rules of private international law lead to the application of the law of a Contracting State.

(2) The fact that the parties have their places of business in different States is to be disregarded whenever this fact does not appear either from the contract or from any dealings between, or from information disclosed by, the parties at any time before or at the conclusion of the contract.

(3) Neither the nationality of the parties nor the civil or commercial character of the parties or of the contract is to be taken into consideration in determining the application of this Convention.

Article 2

This Convention does not apply to sales:

(a) of goods bought for personal, family or household use, unless the seller, at any time before or at the conclusion of the contract, neither knew nor ought to have known that the goods were bought for any such use;

(b) by auction;

(c) on execution or otherwise by authority of law;

(d) of stocks, shares, investment securities, negotiable instruments or money;

(e) of ships, vessels, hovercraft or aircraft;

(f) of electricity.

Article 3

(1) Contracts for the supply of goods to be manufactured or produced are to be considered sales unless the party who orders the goods undertakes to supply a substantial part of the materials necessary for such manufacture or production.

(2) This Convention does not apply to contracts in which the preponderant part of the obligations of the party who furnishes the goods consists in the supply of labour or other services.

Article 4

This Convention governs only the formation of the contract of sale and the rights and obligations of the seller and the buyer arising from such a contract. In particular, except as otherwise expressly provided in this Convention, it is not concerned with:

(a) the validity of the contract or of any of its provisions or of any usage;

(b) the effect which the contract may have on the property in the goods sold.

Article 5

This Convention does not apply to the liability of the seller for death or personal injury caused by the goods to any person.

Article 6

The parties may exclude the application of this Convention or, subject to article 12, derogate from or vary the effect of any of its provisions.

Chapter II. General Provisions

Article 7

(1) In the interpretation of this Convention, regard is to be had to its international character and to the need to promote uniformity in its application and the observance of good faith in international trade.

(2) Questions concerning matters governed by this Convention which are not expressly settled in it are to be settled in conformity with the general principles on which it is based or, in the absence of such principles, in conformity with the law applicable by virtue of the rules of private international law.

Article 8

(1) For the purposes of this Convention statements made by and other conduct of a party are to be interpreted according to his intent where the other party knew or could not have been unaware what that intent was.

(2) If the preceding paragraph is not applicable, statements made by and other conduct of a party are to be interpreted according to the understanding that a reasonable person of the same kind as the other party would have had in the same circumstances.

(3) In determining the intent of a party or the understanding a reasonable person would have had, due consideration is to be given to all relevant circumstances of the case including the negotiations, any practices which the parties have established between themselves, usages and any subsequent conduct of the parties.

Article 9

(1) The parties are bound by any usage to which they have agreed and by any practices which they have established between themselves.

(2) The parties are considered, unless otherwise agreed, to have impliedly made applicable to their contract or its formation a usage of which the parties knew or ought to have known and which in international trade is widely known to, and regularly observed by, parties to contracts of the type involved in the particular trade concerned.

Article 10

For the purposes of this Convention:

(a) if a party has more than one place of business, the place of business is that which has the closest relationship to the contract and its performance, having regard to the circumstances known to or contemplated by the parties at any time before or at the conclusion of the contract;

(b) if a party does not have a place of business, reference is to be made to his habitual residence.

Article 11

A contract of sale need not be concluded in or evidenced by writing and is not subject to any other requirements as to form. It may be proved by any means, including witnesses.

Article 12

Any provision of article 11, article 29 or Part II of this Convention that allows a contract of sale or its modification or termination by agreement or any offer, acceptance or other indication of intention to be made in any form other than in writing does not apply where any party has his place of business in a Contracting State which has made a declaration under article 96 of this Convention. The parties may not derogate from or vary the effect of this article.

Article 13

For the purposes of this Convention "writing" includes telegram and telex.

PART II. FORMATION OF THE CONTRACT

Article 14

(1) A proposal for concluding a contract addressed to one or more specific persons constitutes an offer if it is sufficiently definite and indicates the intention of the offeror to be bound in case of acceptance. A proposal is sufficiently definite if it indicates the goods and expressly or implicitly fixes or makes provision for determining the quantity and the price.

(2) A proposal other than one addressed to one or more specific persons is to be considered merely as an invitation to make offers, unless the contrary is clearly indicated by the person making the proposal.

Article 15

(1) An offer becomes effective when it reaches the offeree.

(2) An offer, even if it is irrevocable, may be withdrawn if the withdrawal reaches the offeree before or at the same time as the offer.

Article 16

(1) Until a contract is concluded an offer may be revoked if the revocation reaches the offeree before he has dispatched an acceptance.

(2) However, an offer cannot be revoked:

(a) if it indicates, whether by stating a fixed time for acceptance or otherwise, that it is irrevocable; or

(b) if it was reasonable for the offeree to rely on the offer as being irrevocable and the offeree has acted in reliance on the offer.

Article 17

An offer, even if it is irrevocable, is terminated when a rejection reaches the offeror.

Article 18

(1) A statement made by or other conduct of the offeree indicating assent to an offer is an acceptance. Silence or inactivity does not in itself amount to acceptance.

(2) An acceptance of an offer becomes effective at the moment the indication of assent reaches the offeror. An acceptance is not effective if the indication of assent does not reach the offeror within the time he has fixed or, if no time is fixed, within a reasonable time, due account being taken of the circumstances of the transaction, including the rapidity of the means of communication employed by the offeror. An oral offer must be accepted immediately unless the circumstances indicate otherwise.

(3) However, if by virtue of the offer or as a result of practices which the parties have established between themselves or of usage, the offeree may indicate assent by performing an act, such as one relating to the dispatch of the goods or payment of the price, without notice to the offeror, the acceptance is effective at the moment the act is performed, provided that the act is performed within the period of time laid down in the preceding paragraph.

Article 19

(1) A reply to an offer which purports to be an acceptance but contains additions, limitations or other modifications is a rejection of the offer and constitutes a counter-offer.

(2) However, a reply to an offer which purports to be an acceptance but contains additional or different terms which do not materially alter the terms of the offer constitutes an acceptance, unless the offeror, without undue delay, objects orally to the discrepancy or dispatches a notice to that effect. If he does not so object, the terms of the contract are the terms of the offer with the modifications contained in the acceptance.

(3) Additional or different terms relating, among other things, to the price, payment, quality and quantity of the goods, place and time of delivery, extent of one party's liability to the other or the statement of disputes are considered to alter the terms of the offer materially.

Article 20

(1) A period of time for acceptance fixed by the offeror in a telegram or a letter begins to run from the moment the telegram is handed in for dispatch or from the date shown on the letter or, if no such date is shown, from the date shown on the envelope. A period of time for acceptance fixed by the offeror by telephone, telex or other means of instantaneous communication, begins to run from the moment that the offer reaches the offeree.

(2) Official holidays or non-business days occurring during the period for acceptance are included in calculating the period. However, if a notice of acceptance cannot be delivered at the address of the offeror on the last day of the period because that day falls on an official holiday or a non-business day at the place of business of the offeror, the period is extended until the first business day which follows.

Article 21

(1) A late acceptance is nevertheless effective as an acceptance if without delay the offeror orally so informs the offeree or dispatches a notice to that effect.

(2) If a letter or other writing containing a late acceptance shows that it has been sent in such circumstances that if its transmission had been normal it would have reached the offeror in due time, the late acceptance is effective as an acceptance unless, without delay, the offeror orally informs the offeree that he considers his offer as having lapsed or dispatches a notice to that effect.

Article 22

An acceptance may be withdrawn if the withdrawal reaches the offeror before or at the same time as the acceptance would have become effective.

Article 23

A contract is concluded at the moment when an acceptance of an offer becomes effective in accordance with the provisions of this Convention.

Article 24

For the purposes of this Part of the Convention, an offer, declaration of acceptance or any other indication of intention "reaches" the addressee when it is made orally to him or delivered by any other means to him personally, to his place of business or mailing address or, if he does not have a place of business or mailing address, to his habitual residence.

PART III. SALE OF GOODS

Chapter I. General Provisions

Article 25

A breach of contract committed by one of the parties is fundamental if it results in such detriment to the other party as substantially to deprive him of what he is entitled to expect under the contract, unless the party in breach did not foresee and a reasonable person of the same kind in the same circumstances would not have foreseen such a result.

Article 26

A declaration of avoidance of the contract is effective only if made by notice to the other party.

Article 27

Unless otherwise expressly provided in this Part of the Convention, if any notice, request or other communication is given or made by a party in accordance with this Part and by means appropriate in the circumstances, a delay or error in the transmission of the communication or its failure to arrive does not deprive that party of the right to rely on the communication.

Article 28

If, in accordance with the provisions of this Convention, one party is entitled to require performance of any obligation by the other party, a court is not bound to enter a judgment for specific performance unless the court would do so under its own law in respect of similar contracts of sale not governed by this Convention.

Article 29

(1) A contract may be modified or terminated by the mere agreement of the parties.

(2) A contract in writing which contains a provision requiring any modification or termination by agreement to be in writing may not be otherwise modified or terminated by agreement. However, a party may be precluded by his conduct from asserting such a provision to the extent that the other party has relied on that conduct.

Chapter II. Obligations of the Seller

Article 30

The seller must deliver the goods, hand over any documents relating to them and transfer the property in the goods, as required by the contract and this Convention.

Section I. Delivery of the Goods and Handing Over of Documents

Article 31

If the seller is not bound to deliver the goods at any other particular place, his obligation to deliver consists:

(a) if the contract of sale involves carriage of the goods—in handling the goods over to the first carrier for transmission to the buyer;

(b) if, in cases not within the preceding subparagraph, the contract relates to specific goods, or unidentified goods to be drawn from a specific stock or to be manufactured or produced, and at the time of the conclusion of the contract the parties knew that the goods were at, or were to be manufactured or produced at, a particular place—in placing the goods at the buyer's disposal at that place;

(c) in other cases—in placing the goods at the buyer's disposal at the place where the seller had his place of business at the time of the conclusion of the contract.

Article 32

(1) If the seller, in accordance with the contract or this Convention, hands the goods over to a carrier and if the goods are not clearly identified to the contract by markings on the goods, by shipping documents or otherwise, the seller must give the buyer notice of the consignment specifying the goods.

(2) If the seller is bound to arrange for carriage of the goods, he must make such contracts as are necessary for carriage to the place fixed by means of transportation appropriate in the circumstances and according to the usual terms for such transportation.

(3) If the seller is not bound to effect insurance in respect of the carriage of the goods, he must, at the buyer's request, provide him with all available information necessary to enable him to effect such insurance.

Article 33

The seller must deliver the goods:

(a) if a date is fixed by or determinable from the contract, on that date;

(b) if a period of time is fixed by or determinable from the contract, at any time within that period unless circumstances indicate that the buyer is to choose a date; or

(c) in any other case, within a reasonable time after the conclusion of the contract.

Article 34

If the seller is bound to hand over documents relating to the goods, he must hand them over at the time and place and in the form required by the contract. If the seller has handed over documents before that time, he may, up to that time, cure any lack of conformity in the documents, if the exercise of this right does not cause the buyer unreasonable inconvenience or unreasonable expense. However, the buyer retains any right to claim damages as provided for in this Convention.

Section II. Conformity of the Goods and Third Party Claims

Article 35

(1) The seller must deliver goods which are of the quantity, quality and description required by the contract and which are contained or packaged in the manner required by the contract.

(2) Except where the parties have agreed otherwise, the goods do not conform with the contract unless they:

(a) are fit for the purposes for which goods of the same description would ordinarily be used;

(b) are fit for any particular purpose expressly or impliedly made known to the seller at the time of the conclusion of the contract, except where the circumstances show that the buyer did not rely, or that it was unreasonable for him to rely, on the seller's skill and judgement;

(c) possess the qualities of goods which the seller has held out to the buyer as a sample or model;

(d) are contained or packaged in the manner usual for such goods or, where there is no such manner, in a manner adequate to preserve and protect the goods.

(3) The seller is not liable under subparagraphs (a) to (d) of the preceding paragraph for any lack of conformity of the goods if at the

time of the conclusion of the contract the buyer knew or could not have been unaware of such lack of conformity.

Article 36

(1) The seller is liable in accordance with the contract and this Convention for any lack of conformity which exists at the time when the risk passes to the buyer, even though the lack of conformity becomes apparent only after that time.

(2) The seller is also liable for any lack of conformity which occurs after the time indicated in the preceding paragraph and which is due to a breach of any of his obligations, including a breach of any guarantee that for a period of time the goods will remain fit for their ordinary purpose or for some particular purpose or will retain specified qualities or characteristics.

Article 37

If the seller has delivered goods before the date for delivery, he may, up to that date, deliver any missing part or make up any deficiency in the quantity of the goods delivered, or deliver goods in replacement of any nonconforming goods delivered or remedy any lack of conformity in the goods delivered, provided that the exercise of this right does not cause the buyer unreasonable inconvenience or unreasonable expense. However, the buyer retains any right to claim damages as provided for in this Convention.

Article 38

(1) The buyer must examine the goods, or cause them to be examined, within as short a period as is practicable in the circumstances.

(2) If the contract involves carriage of the goods, examination may be deferred until after the goods have arrived at their destination.

(3) If the goods are redirected in transit or redispatched by the buyer without a reasonable opportunity for examination by him and at the time of the conclusion of the contract the seller knew or ought to have known of the possibility of such redirection or redispatch, examination may be deferred until after the goods have arrived at the new destination.

Article 39

(1) The buyer loses the right to rely on a lack of conformity of the goods if he does not give notice to the seller specifying the nature of the lack of conformity within a reasonable time after he has discovered it or ought to have discovered it.

(2) In any event, the buyer loses the right to rely on a lack of conformity of the goods if he does not give the seller notice thereof at the latest within a period of two years from the date on which the goods were actually handed over to the buyer, unless this time-limit is inconsistent with a contractual period of guarantee.

Article 40

The seller is not entitled to rely on the provisions of articles 38 and 39 if the lack of conformity relates to facts of which he knew or could not have been unaware and which he did not disclose to the buyer.

Article 41

The seller must deliver goods which are free from any right or claim of a third party, unless the buyer agreed to take the goods subject to that right or claim. However, if such right or claim is based on industrial property or other intellectual property, the seller's obligation is governed by article 42.

Article 42

(1) The seller must deliver goods which are free from any right or claim of a third party based on industrial property or other intellectual property, of which at the time of the conclusion of the contract the seller knew or could not have been unaware, provided that the right or claim is based on industrial property or other intellectual property:

(a) under the law of the State where the goods will be resold or otherwise used, if it was contemplated by the parties at the time of the conclusion of the contract that the goods would be resold or otherwise used in that State; or

(b) in any other case, under the law of the State where the buyer has his place of business.

(2) The obligation of the seller under the preceding paragraph does not extend to cases where:

(a) at the time of the conclusion of the contract the buyer knew or could have been unaware of the right or claim; or

(b) the right or claim results from the seller's compliance with technical drawings, designs, formulae or other such specifications furnished by the buyer.

Article 43

(1) The buyer loses the right to rely on the provisions of article 41 or article 42 if he does not give notice to the seller specifying the nature of the right or claim of the third party within a reasonable time after he has become aware or ought to have become aware of the right or claim.

(2) The seller is not entitled to rely on the provisions of the preceding paragraph if he knew of the right or claim of the third party and the nature of it.

Article 44

Notwithstanding the provisions of paragraph (1) of article 39 and paragraph (1) of article 43, the buyer may reduce the price in accordance with article 50 or claim damages, except for loss of profit, if he has a reasonable excuse for his failure to give the required notice.

Section III. Remedies for Breach of Contract by the Seller

Article 45

(1) If the seller fails to perform any of his obligations under the contract or this Convention, the buyer may:

(a) exercise the rights provided in articles 46 to 52;

(b) claim damages as provided in articles 74 to 77.

(2) The buyer is not deprived of any right he may have to claim damages by exercising his right to other remedies.

(3) No period of grace may be granted to the seller by a court or arbitral tribunal when the buyer resorts to a remedy for breach of contract.

Article 46

(1) The buyer may require performance by the seller of this obligation unless the buyer has resorted to a remedy which is inconsistent with this requirement.

(2) If the goods do not conform with the contract, the buyer may require delivery of substitute goods only if the lack of conformity constitutes a fundamental breach of contract and a request for substitute goods is made either in conjunction with notice given under article 39 or within a reasonable time thereafter.

(3) If the goods do not conform with the contract, the buyer may require the seller to remedy the lack of conformity by repair, unless this is unreasonable having regard to all the circumstances. A request for repair must be made either in conjunction with notice given under article 39 or within a reasonable time thereafter.

Article 47

(1) The buyer may fix an additional period of time of reasonable length for performance by the seller of his obligations.

(2) Unless the buyer has received notice from the seller that he will not perform within the period so fixed, the buyer may not, during that period, resort to any remedy for breach of contract. However, the buyer is not deprived thereby of any right he may have to claim damages for delay in performance.

Article 48

(1) Subject to article 49, the seller may, even after the date for delivery, remedy at his own expense any failure to perform his obligations, if he can do so without unreasonable delay and without causing the buyer unreasonable inconvenience or uncertainty of reimbursement by the seller of expenses advanced by the buyer. However, the buyer retains any right to claim damages as provided for in this Convention.

(2) If the seller requests the buyer to make known whether he will accept performance and the buyer does not comply with the request within a reasonable time, the seller may perform within the time indicated in his request. The buyer may not, during that period of time, resort to any remedy which is inconsistent with performance by the seller.

(3) A notice by the seller that he will perform within a specified period of time is assumed to include a request, under the preceding paragraph, that the buyer make known his decision.

(4) A request or notice by the seller under paragraph (2) or (3) of this article is not effective unless received by the buyer.

Article 49

(1) The buyer may declare the contract avoided:

(a) if the failure by the seller to perform any of his obligations under the contract or this Convention amounts to a fundamental breach of contract; or

(b) in case of non-delivery, if the seller does not deliver the goods within the additional period of time fixed by the buyer in accordance with paragraph (1) of article 47 or declares that he will not deliver within the period so fixed.

(2) However, in cases where the seller has delivered the goods, the buyer loses the right to declare the contract avoided unless he does so:

(a) in respect of late delivery, within a reasonable time after he has become aware that delivery has been made;

(b) in respect of any breach other than late delivery, within a reasonable time:

(i) after he knew or ought to have known of the breach;

(ii) after the expiration of any additional period of time fixed by the buyer in accordance with paragraph (1) of article 47, or after the seller has declared that he will not perform his obligations within such an additional period; or

(iii) after the expiration of any additional period of time indicated by the seller in accordance with paragraph (2) of article 48, or after the buyer has declared that he will not accept performance.

Article 50

If the goods do not conform with the contract and whether or not the price has already been paid, the buyer may reduce the price in the same proportion as the value that the goods actually delivered had at the time of the delivery bears to the value that conforming goods would have had at that time. However, if the seller remedies any failure to perform his obligations in accordance with article 37 or article 48 or if the buyer refuses to accept performance by the seller in accordance with those articles, the buyer may not reduce the price.

Article 51

(1) If the seller delivers only a part of the goods or if only a part of the goods delivered is in conformity with the contract, articles 46 to 50 apply in respect of the part which is missing or which does not conform.

(2) The buyer may declare the contract avoided in its entirety only if the failure to make delivery completely or in conformity with the contract amounts to a fundamental breach of the contract.

Article 52

(1) If the seller delivers the goods before the date fixed, the buyer may take delivery or refuse to take delivery.

(2) If the seller delivers a quantity of goods greater than that provided for in the contract, the buyer may take delivery or refuse to take delivery of the excess quantity. If the buyer takes delivery of all or part of the excess quantity, he must pay for it at the contract rate.

Chapter III. Obligations of the Buyer

Article 53

The buyer must pay the price for the goods and take delivery of them as required by the contract and this Convention.

Section I. Payment of the Price

Article 54

The buyer's obligation to pay the price includes taking such steps and complying with such formalities as may be required under the contract or any laws and regulations to enable payment to be made.

Article 55

Where a contract has been validly concluded but does not expressly or implicitly fix or make provision for determining the price, the parties are considered, in the absence of any indication to the contrary, to have impliedly made reference to the price generally charged at the time of the conclusion of the contract for such goods sold under comparable circumstances in the trade concerned.

Article 56

If the price is fixed according to the weight of the goods, in case of doubt it is to be determined by the net weight.

Article 57

(1) If the buyer is not bound to pay the price at any other particular place, he must pay it to the seller:

(a) at the seller's place of business; or

(b) if the payment is to be made against the handing over of the goods or of documents, at the place where the handing over takes place.

(2) The seller must bear any increase in the expenses incidental to payment which is caused by a change in his place of business subsequent to the conclusion of the contract.

Article 58

(1) If the buyer is not bound to pay the price at any other specific time, he must pay it when the seller places either the goods or documents controlling their disposition at the buyer's disposal in accordance with the contract and this Convention. The seller may make such payment a condition for handing over the goods or documents.

(2) If the contract involves carriage of the goods, the seller may dispatch the goods on terms whereby the goods, or documents controlling their disposition, will not be handed over to the buyer except against payment of the price.

(3) The buyer is not bound to pay the price until he has had an opportunity to examine the goods, unless the procedures for delivery or payment agreed upon by the parties are inconsistent with his having such an opportunity.

Article 59

The buyer must pay the price on the date fixed by or determinable from the contract and this Convention without the need for any request or compliance with any formality on the part of the seller.

Section II. Taking Delivery

Article 60

The buyer's obligation to take delivery consists:

(a) in doing all the acts which could reasonably be expected of him in order to enable the seller to make delivery; and

(b) in taking over the goods.

Section III. Remedies for Breach of Contract by the Buyer

Article 61

(1) If the buyer fails to perform any of his obligations under the contract or this Convention, the seller may:

(a) exercise the rights provided in articles 62 to 65;

(b) claim damages as provided in articles 74 to 77.

(2) The seller is not deprived of any right he may have to claim damages by exercising his right to other remedies.

(3) No period of grace may be granted to the buyer by a court or arbitral tribunal when the seller resorts to a remedy for breach of contract.

Article 62

The seller may require the buyer to pay the price, take delivery or perform his other obligations, unless the seller has resorted to a remedy which is inconsistent with this requirement.

Article 63

(1) The seller may fix an additional period of time of reasonable length for performance by the buyer of his obligations.

(2) Unless the seller has received notice from the buyer that he will not perform within the period so fixed, the seller may not, during that period, resort to any remedy for breach of contract. However, the seller is not deprived thereby of any right he may have to claim damages for delay in performance.

Article 64

(1) The seller may declare the contract avoided:

(a) if the failure by the buyer to perform any of his obligations under the contract or this Convention amounts to a fundamental breach of contract; or

(b) if the buyer does not, within the additional period of time fixed by the seller in accordance with paragraph (1) of article 63, perform his obligation to pay the price or take delivery of the goods, or if he declares that he will not do so within the period so fixed.

(2) However, in cases where the buyer has paid the price, the seller loses the right to declare the contract avoided unless he does so:

(a) in respect of late performance by the buyer, before the seller has become aware that performance has been rendered; or

(b) in respect of any breach other than late performance by the buyer, within a reasonable time:

(i) after the seller knew or ought to have known of the breach; or

(ii) after the expiration of any additional period of time fixed by the seller in accordance with paragraph (1) of article 63, or after the buyer has declared that he will not perform his obligations within such an additional period.

Article 65

(1) If under the contract the buyer is to specify the form, measurement or other features of the goods and he fails to make such specification either on the date agreed upon or within a reasonable time after receipt of a request from the seller, the seller may, without prejudice to any other rights he may have, make the specification himself in accordance with the requirements of the buyer that may be known to him.

(2) If the seller makes the specification himself, he must inform the buyer of the details thereof and must fix a reasonable time within which the buyer may make a different specification. If, after receipt of such a communication, the buyer fails to do so within the time so fixed, the specification made by the seller is binding.

Chapter IV. Passing of Risk

Article 66

Loss of or damage to the goods after the risk has passed to the buyer does not discharge him from his obligation to pay the price, unless the loss or damage is due to an act or omission of the seller.

Article 67

(1) If the contract of sale involves carriage of the goods and the seller is not bound to hand them over at a particular place, the risk passes to the buyer when the goods are handed over to the first carrier for transmission to the buyer in accordance with the contract of sale. If the seller is bound to hand the goods over to a carrier at a particular place, the risk does not pass to the buyer until the goods are handed over to the carrier at that place. The fact that the seller is authorized to retain documents controlling the disposition of the goods does not affect the passage of the risk.

(2) Nevertheless, the risk does not pass to the buyer until the goods are clearly identified to the contract, whether by markings on the goods, by shipping documents, by notice given to the buyer or otherwise.

Article 68

The risk in respect of goods sold in transit passes to the buyer from the time of the conclusion of the contract. However, if the circumstances so indicate, the risk is assumed by the buyer from the time the goods were handed over to the carrier who issued the documents embodying the contract of carriage. Nevertheless, if at the time of the conclusion of the contract of sale the seller knew or ought to have known that the goods had been lost or damaged and did not disclose this to the buyer, the loss or damage is at the risk of the seller.

Article 69

(1) In cases not within articles 67 and 68, the risk passes to the buyer when he takes over the goods or, if he does not do so in due time, from the time the goods are placed at his disposal and he commits a breach of contract by failing to take delivery.

(2) However, if the buyer is bound to take over the goods at a place other than a place of business of the seller, the risk passes when delivery is due and the buyer is aware of the fact that the goods are placed at his disposal at that place.

(3) If the contract relates to goods not then identified, the goods are considered not to be placed at the disposal of the buyer until they are clearly identified to the contract.

Article 70

If the seller has committed a fundamental breach of contract, articles 67, 68 and 69 do not impair the remedies available to the buyer on account of the breach.

Chapter V. Provisions Common to the Obligations of the Seller and of the Buyer

Section I. Anticipatory Breach and Instalment Contracts

Article 71

(1) A party may suspend the performance of his obligations if, after the conclusion of the contract, it becomes apparent that the other party will not perform a substantial part of his obligations as a result of:

(a) a serious deficiency in his ability to perform or in his creditworthiness; or

(b) his conduct in preparing to perform or in performing the contract.

(2) If the seller has already dispatched the goods before the grounds described in the preceding paragraph become evident, he may prevent the handing over of the goods to the buyer even though the buyer holds a document which entitles him to obtain them. The present paragraph relates only to the rights in the goods as between the buyer and the seller.

(3) A party suspending performance, whether before or after dispatch of the goods, must immediately give notice of the suspension to the other party and must continue with performance if the other party provides adequate assurance of his performance.

Article 72

(1) If prior to the date for performance of the contract it is clear that one of the parties will commit a fundamental breach of contract, the other party may declare the contract avoided.

(2) If time allows, the party intending to declare the contract avoided must give reasonable notice to the other party in order to permit him to provide adequate assurance of his performance.

(3) The requirements of the preceding paragraph do not apply if the other party has declared that he will not perform his obligations.

Article 73

(1) In the case of a contract for delivery of goods by instalments, if the failure of one party to perform any of his obligations in respect of any instalment constitutes a fundamental breach of contract with respect to that instalment, the other party may declare the contract avoided with respect to that instalment.

(2) If one party's failure to perform any of his obligations in respect of any instalment gives the other party good grounds to conclude that a fundamental breach of contract will occur with respect to future instalments, he may declare the contract avoided for the future, provided that he does so within a reasonable time.

(3) A buyer who declares the contract avoided in respect of any delivery may, at the same time, declare it avoided in respect of deliveries already made or of future deliveries if, by reason of their interdependence, those deliveries could not be used for the purpose contemplated by the parties at the time of the conclusion of the contract.

Section II. Damages

Article 74

Damages for breach of contract by one party consist of a sum equal to the loss, including loss of profit, suffered by the other party as a consequence of the breach. Such damages may not exceed the loss which the party in breach foresaw or ought to have foreseen at the time of the conclusion of the contract, in the light of the facts and matters of which he then knew or ought to have known, as a possible consequence of the breach of contract.

Article 75

If the contract is avoided and if, in a reasonable manner and within reasonable time after avoidance, the buyer has brought goods in replacement or the seller has resold the goods, the party claiming damages may recover the difference between the contract price and the price in the substitute transaction as well as any further damages recoverable under article 74.

Article 76

(1) If the contract is avoided and there is a current price for the goods, the party claiming damages may, if he has not made a purchase or resale under article 75, recover the difference between the price fixed by the contract and the current price at the time of avoidance as well as any further damages recoverable under article 74. If, however, the party claiming damages has avoided the contract after taking over the goods, the current price at the time of such taking over shall be applied instead of the current price at the time of avoidance.

(2) For the purposes of the preceding paragraph, the current price is the price prevailing at the place where delivery of the goods should have been made or, if there is no current price at that place, the price at such other place as serves as a reasonable substitute, making due allowance for differences in the cost of transporting the goods.

Article 77

A party who relies on a breach of contract must take such measures as are reasonable in the circumstances to mitigate the loss, including loss of profit, resulting from the breach. If he fails to take such measures, the party in breach may claim a reduction in the damages in the amount by which the loss should have been mitigated.

Section III. Interest

Article 78

If a party fails to pay the price or any other sum that is in arrears, the other party is entitled to interest on it, without prejudice to any claim for damages recoverable under article 74.

Section IV. Exemptions

Article 79

(1) A party is not liable for a failure to perform any of his obligations if he proved that the failure was due to an impediment beyond his control and that he could not reasonably be expected to have taken the impediment into account at the time of the conclusion of the contract or to have avoided or overcome it or its consequences.

(2) If the party's failure is due to the failure by a third person whom he has engaged to perform the whole or a part of the contract, that party is exempt from liability only if:

(a) he is exempt under the preceding paragraph; and

(b) the person whom he has so engaged would be so exempt if the provisions of that paragraph were applied to him.

(3) The exemption provided by this article has effect for the period during which the impediment exists.

(4) The party who fails to perform must give notice to the other party of the impediment and its effect on his ability to perform. If the notice is not received by the other party within a reasonable time after the party who fails to perform knew or ought to have known of the impediment, he is liable for damages resulting from such non-receipt.

(5) Nothing in this article prevents either party from exercising any right other than to claim damages under this Convention.

Article 80

A party may not rely on a failure of the other party to perform, to the extent that such failure was caused by the first party's act or omission.

Section V. Effects of Avoidance

Article 81

(1) Avoidance of the contract releases both parties from their obligations under it, subject to any damages which may be due. Avoidance does not affect any provision of the contract for the settlement of disputes or any other provision of the contract governing the rights and obligations of the parties consequent upon the avoidance of the contract.

(2) A party who has performed the contract either wholly or in part may claim restitution from the other party of whatever the first party has supplied or paid under the contract. If both parties are bound to make restitution, they must do so concurrently.

Article 82

(1) The buyer loses the right to declare the contract avoided or to require the seller to deliver substitute goods if it is impossible for him to make restitution of the goods substantially in the condition in which he received them.

(2) The preceding paragraph does not apply:

(a) if the impossibility of making restitution of the goods or of making restitution of the goods substantially in the condition in which the buyer received them is not due to his act or omission;

(b) if the goods or part of the goods have perished or deteriorated as a result of the examination provided for in article 38; or

(c) if the goods or part of the goods have been sold in the normal course of business or have been consumed or transformed by the buyer in the course of normal use before he discovered or ought to have discovered the lack of conformity.

Article 83

A buyer who has lost the right to declare the contract avoided or to require the seller to deliver substitute goods in accordance with article 82 retains all other remedies under the contract and this Convention.

Article 84

(1) If the seller is bound to refund the price, he must also pay interest on it, from the date on which the price was paid.

(2) The buyer must account to the seller for all benefits which he has derived from the goods or part of them:

(a) if he must make restitution of the goods or part of them; or

(b) if it is impossible for him to make restitution of all or part of the goods or to make restitution of all or part of the goods substantially in the condition in which he received them, but he has nevertheless declared the contract avoided or required the seller to deliver substitute goods.

Section VI. Preservation of the Goods

Article 85

If the buyer is in delay in taking delivery of the goods or, where payment of the price and delivery of the goods are to be made concurrently, if he fails to pay the price, and the seller is either in possession of the goods or otherwise able to control their disposition, the seller must take such steps as are reasonable in the circumstances to preserve them. He is entitled to retain them until he has been reimbursed his reasonable expenses by the buyer.

Article 86

(1) If the buyer has received the goods and intends to exercise any right under the contract or this Convention to reject them, he must take such steps to preserve them as are reasonable in the circumstances. He is entitled to retain them until he has been reimbursed his reasonable expenses by the seller.

(2) If goods dispatched to the buyer have been placed at his disposal at their destination and he exercises the right to reject them, he must take possession of them on behalf of the seller, provided that this can be done without payment of the price and without unreasonable inconvenience or unreasonable expense. This provision does not apply if the seller or a person authorized to take charge of the goods on his behalf is present at the destination. If the buyer takes possession of the goods under this paragraph, his rights and obligations are governed by the preceding paragraph.

Article 87

A party who is bound to take steps to preserve the goods may deposit them in a warehouse of a third person at the expense of the other party provided that the expense incurred is not unreasonable.

Article 88

(1) A party who is bound to preserve the goods in accordance with article 85 or 86 may sell them by any appropriate means if there has been an unreasonable delay by the other party in taking possession of the goods or in taking them back or in paying the price or the cost of preservation, provided that reasonable notice of the intention to sell has been given to the other party.

(2) If the goods are subject to rapid deterioration or their preservation would involve unreasonable expense, a party who is bound to preserve the goods in accordance with article 85 or 86 must take reasonable measures to sell them. To the extent possible he must give notice to the other party of his intention to sell.

(3) A party selling the goods has the right to retain out of the proceeds of sale an amount equal to the reasonable expenses of preserving the goods and of selling them. He must account to the other party for the balance.

PART IV. FINAL PROVISIONS

Article 89

The Secretary-General of the United Nations is hereby designated as the depositary for this Convention.

Article 90

This Convention does not prevail over any international agreement which has already been or may be entered into and which contains provisions concerning the matters governed by this Convention, provided that the parties have their places of business in States parties to such agreement.

Article 91

(1) This Convention is open for signature at the concluding meeting of the United Nations Conference on Contracts for the International Sale of Goods and will remain open for signature by all States at the Headquarters of the United Nations, New York until 30 September 1981.

(2) This Convention is subject to ratification, acceptance or approval by the signatory States.

(3) This Convention is open for accession by all States which are not signatory States as from the date it is open for signature.

(4) Instruments of ratification, acceptance, approval and accession are to be deposited with the Secretary-General of the United Nations.

Article 92

(1) A Contracting State may declare at the time of signature, ratification, acceptance, approval or accession that it will not be bound by Part II of this Convention or that it will not be bound by Part III of this Convention.

(2) A Contracting State which makes a declaration in accordance with the preceding paragraph in respect of Part II or Part III of this Convention is not to be considered a Contracting State within para-

graph (1) of article 1 of this Convention in respect of matters governed by the Part to which the declaration applies.

Article 93

(1) If a Contracting State has two or more territorial units in which, according to its constitution, different systems of law are applicable in relation to the matters dealt with in this Convention, it may, at the time of signature, ratification, acceptance, approval or accession, declare that this Convention is to extend to all its territorial units or only to one or more of them, and may amend its declaration by submitting another declaration at any time.

(2) These declarations are to be notified to the depositary and are to state expressly the territorial units to which the Convention extends.

(3) If, by virtue of a declaration under this article, this Convention extends to one or more but not all of the territorial units of a Contracting State, and if the place of business of a party is located in that State, this place of business, for the purposes of this Convention, is considered not to be in a Contracting State, unless it is in a territorial unit to which the Convention extends.

(4) If a Contracting State makes no declaration under paragraph (1) of this article, the Convention is to extend to all territorial units of that State.

Article 94

(1) Two or more Contracting States which have the same or closely declared legal rules on matters governed by this Convention may at any time declare that the Convention is not to apply to contracts of sale or to their formation where the parties have their places of business in those States. Such declarations may be made jointly or by reciprocal unilateral declarations.

(2) A Contracting State which has the same or closely related legal rules on matters governed by this Convention as one or more non-Contracting States may at any time declare that the Convention is not to apply to contracts of sale or to their formation where the parties have their place of business in those States.

(3) If a State which is the object of a declaration under the preceding paragraph subsequently becomes a Contracting State, the declaration made will, as from the date on which the Convention enters into force in respect of the new Contracting State, have the effect of a declaration made under paragraph (1), provided that the new Contracting State joins in such declaration or makes a reciprocal unilateral declaration.

Article 95

Any State may declare at the time of the deposit of its instrument of ratification, acceptance, approval or accession that it will not be bound by subparagraph (1) (b) of article 1 of this Convention.

Article 96

A Contracting State whose legislation requires contracts of sale to be concluded in or evidenced by writing may at any time make a declaration in accordance with article 12 that any provision of article 11, article 29, or Part II of this Convention, that allows a contract of sale or its modification or termination by agreement or any offer, acceptance, or other indication of intention to be made in any form other than in writing, does not apply where any party has his place of business in that State.

Article 97

(1) Declarations made under this Convention at the time of signature are subject to confirmation upon ratification, acceptance or approval.

(2) Declarations and confirmations of declarations are to be in writing and be formally notified to the depositary.

(3) A declaration takes effect simultaneously with the entry into force of this Convention in respect of the State concerned. However, a declaration of which the depositary receives formal notification after such entry into force takes effect on the first day of the month following the expiration of six months after the date of its receipt by the depositary. Reciprocal unilateral declarations under article 94 take effect on the first day of the month following the expiration of six months after the receipt of the latest declaration by the depositary.

(4) Any State which makes a declaration under this Convention may withdraw it at any time by a formal notification in writing addressed to the depositary. Such withdrawal is to take effect on the first day of the month following the expiration of six months after the date of the receipt of the notification by the depositary.

(5) A withdrawal of a declaration made under article 94 renders inoperative, as from the date on which the withdrawal takes effect, any reciprocal declaration made by another State under that article.

Article 98

No reservations are permitted except those expressly authorized in this Convention.

Article 99

(1) This Convention enters into force, subject to the provisions of paragraph (6) of this article, on the first day of the month following the expiration of twelve months after the date of deposit of the tenth instrument of ratification, acceptance, approval or accession, including an instrument which contains a declaration made under article 92.

(2) When a State ratifies, accepts, approves or accedes to this Convention after the deposit of the tenth instrument of ratification, acceptance, approval or accession, this Convention, with the exception of the Part excluded, enters into force in respect of that State, subject to the provisions of paragraph (6) of this article, on the first day of the month following the expiration of twelve months after the date of the deposit of its instrument of ratification, acceptance, approval or accession.

(3) A State which ratifies, accepts, approves or accedes to this Convention and is a party to either or both the Convention relating to a Uniform Law on the Formation of Contracts for the International Sale of Goods done at The Hague on 1 July 1964 (1964 Hague Formation Convention) and the Convention relating to a Uniform Law on the International Sale of Goods done at The Hague on 1 July 1964 (1964 Hague Sales Convention) shall at the same time denounce, as the case may be, either or both the 1964 Hague Sales Convention and the 1964 Hague Formation Convention by notifying the Government of the Netherlands to that effect.

(4) A State party to the 1964 Hague Sales Convention which ratifies, accepts, approves or accedes to the present Convention and declares or has declared under article 92 that it will not be bound by Part II of this Convention shall at the time of ratification, acceptance, approval or accession denounce the 1964 Hague Sales Convention by notifying the Government of the Netherlands to that effect.

(5) A State party to the 1964 Hague Formation Convention which ratifies, accepts, approves or accedes to the present Convention and declares or has declared under article 92 that it will not be bound by Part III of this Convention shall at the time of ratification, acceptance, approval or accession denounce the 1964 Hague Formation Convention by notifying the Government of the Netherlands to that effect.

(6) For the purpose of this article, ratifications, acceptances, approvals and accessions in respect of this Convention by States parties to the 1964 Hague Formation Convention or to the 1964 Hague Sales Convention shall not be effective until such denunciations as may be required on the part of those States in respect of the latter two Conventions have themselves become effective. The depositary of this Convention shall consult with the Government of Netherlands, as the depositary of the 1964 Conventions, so as to ensure necessary coordination in this respect.

Article 100

(1) The Convention applies to the formation of a contract only when the proposal for concluding the contract is made on or after the date when the Convention enters into force in respect of the Contracting States referred to in subparagraph (1) (a) or the Contracting State referred to in subparagraph (1) (b) of article 1.

(2) This Convention applies only to contracts concluded on or after the date when the Convention enters into force in respect of the Contracting States referred to in subparagraph (1) (a) or the Contracting State referred to in subparagraph (1) (b) of article 1.

Article 101

(1) A Contracting State may denounce this Convention, or Part II or Part III of the Convention, by a formal notification in writing addressed to the depositary.

(2) The denunciation takes effect on the first day of the month following the expiration of twelve months after the notification is received by the depositary. Where a longer period for the denunciation to take effect is specified in the notification, the denunciation takes effect upon the expiration of such longer period after the notification is received by the depositary.

DONE AT VIENNA, this day of eleventh day of April, one thousand nine hundred and eighty, in a single original, or which the Arabic, Chinese, English, French, Russian and Spanish texts are equally authentic.

IN WITNESS WHEREOF the undersigned plenipotentiaries, being duly authorized by their respective Governments, have signed this Convention.

APPENDIX E

Revised Model Business Corporation Act (with 1990 Revisions)

CHAPTER 1. GENERAL PROVISIONS

Subchapter A. Short Title and Reservation of Power

§ 1.01. Short Title. This Act shall be known and may be cited as the "[name of state] Business Corporation Act."

§ 1.02. Reservation of Power to Amend or Repeal. The [name of state legislature] has power to amend or repeal all or part of this Act at any time and all domestic and foreign corporations subject to this Act are governed by the amendment or repeal.

Subchapter B. Filing Documents [Text not included.]

Subchapter C. Secretary of State

§ 1.30. Powers. The secretary of state has the power reasonably necessary to perform the duties required of him by this Act.

Subchapter D. Definitions

§ 1.40. Act Definitions. In this Act:

(1) "Articles of incorporation" include amended and restated articles of incorporation and articles of merger.

(2) "Authorized shares" means the shares of all classes a domestic or foreign corporation is authorized to issue.

(3) "Conspicuous" means so written that a reasonable person against whom the writing is to operate should have noticed it. For example, printing in italics or boldface or contrasting color, or typing in capitals or underlined, is conspicuous.

(4) "Corporation" or "domestic corporation" means a corporation for profit, which is not a foreign corporation, incorporated under or subject to the provisions of this Act.

(5) "Deliver" includes mail.

(6) "Distribution" means a direct or indirect transfer of money or other property (except its own shares) or incurrence of indebtedness by a corporation to or for the benefit of its shareholders in respect of any of its shares. A distribution may be in the form of a declaration or payment of a dividend; a purchase, redemption, or other acquisition of shares; a distribution of indebtedness; or otherwise.

(7) "Effective date of notice" is defined in section 1.41.

(8) "Employee" includes an officer but not a director. A director may accept duties that make him also an employee.

(9) "Entity" includes corporation and foreign corporation; not-for-profit corporation; profit and not-for-profit unincorporated association; business trust, estate, partnership, trust, and two or more persons having a joint or common economic interest; and state, United States, and foreign government.

(10) "Foreign corporation" means a corporation for profit incorporated under a law other than the law of this state.

(11) "Governmental subdivision" includes authority, county, district, and municipality.

(12) "Includes" denotes a partial definition.

(13) "Individual" includes the estate of an incompetent or deceased individual.

(14) "Means" denotes an exhaustive definition.

(15) "Notice" is defined in section 1.41.

(16) "Person" includes individual and entity.

(17) "Principal office" means the office (in or out of this state) so designated in the annual report where the principal executive offices of a domestic or foreign corporation are located.

(18) "Proceeding" includes civil suit and criminal, administrative, and investigatory action.

(19) "Record date" means the date established under chapter 6 or 7 on which a corporation determines the identity of its shareholders and their shareholdings for purposes of this Act. The determinations shall be made as of the close of business on the record date unless another time for doing so is specified when the record date is fixed.

(20) "Secretary" means the corporate officer to whom the board of directors has delegated responsibility under section 8.40(c) for custody of the minutes of the meetings of the board of directors and of the shareholders and for authenticating records of the corporation.

(21) "Share" means the unit into which the proprietary interests in a corporation are divided.

(22) "Shareholder" means the person in whose name shares are registered in the records of a corporation or the beneficial owner of shares to the extent of the rights granted by a nominee certificate on file with a corporation.

(23) "State," when referring to a part of the United States, includes a state and commonwealth (and their agencies and governmental subdivisions) and a territory, and insular possession (and their agencies and governmental subdivisions) of the United States.

(24) "Subscriber" means a person who subscribes for shares in a corporation, whether before or after incorporation.

(25) "United States" includes district, authority, bureau, commission, department, and any other agency of the United States.

(26) "Voting group" means all shares of one or more classes or series that under the articles of incorporation or this Act are entitled to vote and be counted together collectively on a matter at a meeting of shareholders. All shares entitled by the articles of incorporation or this Act to vote generally on the matter are for that purpose a single voting group.

§ 1.41. Notice. [Text not included.]

§ 1.42. Number of Shareholders.

(a) For purposes of this Act, the following identified as a shareholder in a corporation's current record of shareholders constitutes one shareholder:

(1) three or fewer coowners;

(2) a corporation, partnership, trust, estate, or other entity;

(3) the trustees, guardians, custodians, or other fiduciaries of a single trust, estate, or account.

(b) For purposes of this Act, shareholdings registered in substantially similar names constitute one shareholder if it is reasonable to believe that the names represent the same person.

CHAPTER 2. INCORPORATION

§ 2.01. Incorporators. One or more persons may act as the incorporator or incorporators of a corporation by delivering articles of incorporation to the secretary of state for filing.

§ 2.02. Articles of Incorporation.

(a) The articles of incorporation must set forth:

(1) a corporate name for the corporation that satisfies the requirements of section 4.01;

(2) the number of shares the corporation is authorized to issue;

(3) the street address of the corporation's initial registered office and the name of its initial registered agent at that office; and

(4) the name and address of each incorporator.

(b) The articles of incorporation may set forth:

(1) the names and addresses of the individuals who are to serve as the initial directors;

(2) provisions not inconsistent with law regarding:

(i) the purpose or purposes for which the corporation is organized;

(ii) managing the business and regulating the affairs of the corporation;

(iii) defining, limiting, and regulating the powers of the corporation, its board of directors, and shareholders;

(iv) a par value for authorized shares or classes of shares;

(v) the imposition of personal liability on shareholders for the debts of the corporation to a specified extent and upon specified conditions;

(3) any provision that under this Act is required or permitted to be set forth in the bylaws and

(4) a provision eliminating or limiting the liability of a director to the corporation or its shareholders for money damages for any action taken, or any failure to take any action, as a director, except liability for (A) the amount of a financial benefit received by a director to which he is not entitled; (B) an intentional infliction of harm on the corporation or the shareholders; (C) a violation of section 8.33; or (D) an intentional violation of criminal law.

(c) The articles of incorporation need not set forth any of the corporate powers enumerated in this Act.

§ 2.03. Incorporation.

(a) Unless a delayed effective date is specified, the corporate existence begins when the articles of incorporation are filed.

(b) The secretary of state's filing of the articles of incorporation is conclusive proof that the incorporators satisfied all conditions precedent to incorporation except in a proceeding by the state to cancel or revoke the incorporation or involuntarily dissolve the corporation.

§ 2.04. Liability for Preincorporation Transactions. All persons purporting to act as or on behalf of a corporation, knowing there was no incorporation under this Act, are jointly and severally liable for all liabilities created while so acting.

§ 2.05. Organization of Corporation.

(a) After incorporation:

(1) If initial directors are named in the articles of incorporation, the initial directors shall hold an organizational meeting, at the call of a majority of the directors, to complete the organization of the corporation by appointing officers, adopting bylaws, and carrying on any other business brought before the meeting;

(2) if initial directors are not named in the articles, the incorporator or incorporators shall hold an organizational meeting at the call of a majority of the incorporators:

(i) to elect directors and complete the organization of the corporation; or

(ii) to elect a board of directors who shall complete the organization of the corporation.

(b) Action required or permitted by this Act to be taken by incorporators at an organizational meeting may be taken without a meeting if the action taken is evidenced by one or more written consents describing the action taken and signed by each incorporator.

(c) An organizational meeting may be held in or out of this state.

§ 2.06. Bylaws.

(a) The incorporators or board of directors of a corporation shall adopt initial bylaws for the corporation.

(b) The bylaws of a corporation may contain any provision for managing the business and regulating the affairs of the corporation that is not inconsistent with law or the articles of incorporation.

§ 2.07. Emergency Bylaws.

(a) Unless the articles of incorporation provide otherwise, the board of directors of a corporation may adopt bylaws to be effective only in an emergency defined in subsection (d). The emergency bylaws, which are subject to amendment or repeal by the shareholders, may make all provisions necessary for managing the corporation during the emergency, including:

(1) procedures for calling a meeting of the board of directors;

(2) quorum requirements for the meeting; and

(3) designation of additional or substitute directors.

(b) All provisions of the regular bylaws consistent with the emergency bylaws remain effective during the emergency. The emergency bylaws are not effective after the emergency ends.

(c) Corporate action taken in good faith in accordance with the emergency bylaws:

(1) binds the corporation; and

(2) may not be used to impose liability on a corporate director, officer, employee, or agent.

(d) An emergency exists for purposes of this section if a quorum of the corporation's directors cannot readily be assembled because of some catastrophic event.

CHAPTER 3. PURPOSES AND POWERS

§ 3.01. Purposes.

(a) Every corporation incorporated under this Act has the purpose of engaging in any lawful business unless a more limited purpose is set forth in the articles of incorporation.

(b) A corporation engaging in a business that is subject to regulation under another statute of this state may incorporate under this Act only if permitted by, and subject to all limitations of, the other statute.

§ 3.02. General Powers. Unless its articles of incorporation provide otherwise, every corporation has perpetual duration and succession in its corporate name and has the same powers as an individual to do all things necessary or convenient to carry out its business and affairs, including without limitation power:

(1) to sue and be sued, complain and defend in its corporate name;

(2) to have a corporate seal, which may be altered at will, and to use it, or a facsimile of it, by impressing or affixing it or in any other manner reproducing it;

(3) to make and amend bylaws, not inconsistent with its articles of incorporation or with the laws of this state, for managing the business and regulating the affairs of the corporation;

(4) to purchase, receive, lease, or otherwise acquire, and own, hold, improve, use, and otherwise deal with, real or personal property, or any legal or equitable interest in property, wherever located;

(5) to sell, convey, mortgage, pledge, lease, exchange, and otherwise dispose of all or any part of its property;

(6) to purchase, receive, subscribe for, or otherwise acquire; own, hold, vote, use, sell, mortgage, lend, pledge, or otherwise dispose of; and deal in and with shares or other interests in, or obligations of, any other entity;

(7) to make contracts and guarantees, incur liabilities, borrow money, issue its notes, bonds, and other obligations (which may be convertible into or include the option to purchase other securities of the corporation), and secure any of its obligations by mortgage or pledge of any of its property, franchises, or income;

(8) to lend money, invest and reinvest its funds, and receive and hold real and personal property as security for repayment;

(9) to be a promoter, partner, member, associate, or manager of any partnership, joint venture, trust, or other entity;

(10) to conduct its business, locate offices, and exercise the powers granted by this Act within or without this state;

(11) to elect directors and appoint officers, employees, and agents of the corporation, define their duties, fix their compensation, and lend them money and credit;

(12) to pay pensions and establish pension plans, pension trusts, profit sharing plans, share bonus plans, share option plans, and benefit or incentive plans for any or all of its current or former directors, officers, employees, and agents;

(13) to make donations for the public welfare or for charitable, scientific, or educational purposes;

(14) to transact any lawful business that will aid governmental policy;

(15) to make payments or donations, or do any other act, not inconsistent with law, that furthers the business and affairs of the corporation.

§ 3.03. Emergency Powers.

(a) In anticipation of or during an emergency defined in subsection (d), the board of directors of a corporation may:

(1) modify lines of succession to accommodate the incapacity of any director, officer, employee, or agent; and

(2) relocate the principal office, designate alternative principal offices or regional offices, or authorize the officers to do so.

(b) During an emergency defined in subsection (d), unless emergency bylaws provide otherwise:

(1) notice of a meeting of the board of directors need be given only to those directors whom it is practicable to reach and may be given in any practicable manner, including by publication and radio; and

(2) one or more officers of the corporation present at a meeting of the board of directors may be deemed to be directors for the meeting, in order of rank and within the same rank in order of seniority, as necessary to achieve a quorum.

(c) Corporate action taken in good faith during an emergency under this section to further the ordinary business affairs of the corporation:

(1) binds the corporation; and

(2) may not be used to impose liability on a corporate director, officer, employee, or agent.

(d) An emergency exists for purposes of this section if a quorum of the corporation's directors cannot readily be assembled because of some catastrophic event.

§ 3.04. Ultra Vires.

(a) Except as provided in subsection (b), the validity of corporate action may not be challenged on the ground that the corporation lacks or lacked power to act.

(b) A corporation's power to act may be challenged:

(1) in a proceeding by a shareholder against the corporation to enjoin the act;

(2) in a proceeding by the corporation, directly, derivatively, or through a receiver, trustee, or other legal representative, against an incumbent or former director, officer, employee, or agent of the corporation; or

(3) in a proceeding by the Attorney General under section 14.30.

(c) In a shareholder's proceeding under subsection (b)(1) to enjoin an unauthorized corporate act, the court may enjoin to set aside the act, if equitable and if all affected persons are parties to the proceeding, and may award damages for loss (other than anticipated profits) suffered by the corporation or another party because of enjoining the unauthorized act.

CHAPTER 4. NAME

§ 4.01. Corporate Name.

(a) A corporate name:

(1) must contain the word "corporation," "incorporated," "company," or "limited," or the abbreviation "corp.," "inc.," "co.," or "ltd.", or words or abbreviations of like import in another language; and

(2) may not contain language stating or implying that the corporation is organized for a purpose other than that permitted by section 3.01 and its articles of incorporation.

(b) Except as authorized by subsections (c) and (d), a corporate name must be distinguishable upon the records of the secretary of state from:

(1) the corporate name of a corporation incorporated or authorized to transact business in this state;

(2) a corporate name reserved or registered under section 4.02 or 4.03;

(3) the fictitious name adopted by a foreign corporation authorized to transact business in this state because its real name is unavailable; and

(4) the corporate name of a not-for-profit corporation incorporated or authorized to transact business in this state.

(c) A corporation may apply to the secretary of state for authorization to use a name that is not distinguishable upon his records from one or more of the names described in subsection (b). The secretary of state shall authorize use of the name applied for if:

(1) the other corporation consents to the use in writing and submits an undertaking in form satisfactory to the secretary of state to change its name to a name that is distinguishable upon the records of the secretary of state from the name of the applying corporation; or

(2) the applicant delivers to the secretary of state a certified copy of the final judgment of a court of competent jurisdiction establishing the applicant's right to use the name applied for in this state.

(d) A corporation may use the name (including the fictitious name) of another domestic or foreign corporation that is used in this state if the other corporation is incorporated or authorized to transact business in this state and the proposed user corporation:

(1) has merged with the other corporation;

(2) has been formed by reorganization of the other corporation; or

(3) has acquired all or substantially all of the assets, including the corporate name, of the other corporation.

(e) This Act does not control the use of fictitious names.

§ 4.02. Reserved Name.

(a) A person may reserve the exclusive use of a corporate name, including a fictitious name for a foreign corporation whose corporate name is not available, by delivering an application to the secretary of state for filing. The application must set forth the name and address of the applicant and the name proposed to be reserved. If the secretary of state finds that the corporate name applied for is available, he shall reserve the name for the applicant's exclusive use for a nonrenewable 120-day period.

(b) The owner of a reserved corporate name may transfer the reservation to another person by delivering to the secretary of state a signed notice of the transfer that states the name and address of the transferee.

§ 4.03. Registered Name. [Text not included.]

CHAPTER 5. OFFICE AND AGENT

§ 5.01. Registered Office and Registered Agent. Each corporation must continuously maintain in this state:

(1) a registered office that may be the same as any of its places of business; and

(2) a registered agent, who may be:

(i) an individual who resides in this state and whose business office is identical with the registered office;

(ii) a domestic corporation or not-for-profit domestic corporation whose business office is identical with the registered office; or

(iii) a foreign corporation or not-for-profit foreign corporation authorized to transact business in this state whose business office is identical with the registered office.

[Text of other sections not included.]

CHAPTER 6. SHARES AND DISTRIBUTIONS

Subchapter A. Shares

§ 6.01. Authorized Shares.

(a) The articles of incorporation must prescribe the classes of shares and the number of shares of each class that the corporation is authorized to issue. If more than one class of shares is authorized, the articles of incorporation must prescribe a distinguishing designation for each class, and prior to the issuance of shares of a class the preferences, limitations, and relative rights of that class must be described in the articles of incorporation. All shares of a class must have preferences, limitations, and relative rights identical with those of other shares of the same class except to the extent otherwise permitted by section 6.02.

(b) The articles of incorporation must authorize (1) one or more classes of shares that together have unlimited voting rights, and (2) one or more classes of shares (which may be the same class or classes as those with voting rights) that together are entitled to receive the net assets of the corporation upon dissolution.

(c) The articles of incorporation may authorize one or more classes of shares that:

(1) have special, conditional, or limited voting rights, or no right to vote, except to the extent prohibited by this Act;

(2) are redeemable or convertible as specified in the articles of incorporation (i) at the option of the corporation, the shareholder,

or another person or upon the occurrence of a designated event; (ii) for cash, indebtedness, securities, or other property; (iii) in a designated amount or in an amount determined in accordance with a designated formula or by reference to extrinsic data or events;

(3) entitle the holders to distributions calculated in any manner, including dividends that may be cumulative, noncumulative, or partially cumulative;

(4) have preference over any other class of shares with respect to distributions, including dividends and distributions upon the dissolution of the corporation.

(d) The description of the designations, preferences, limitations, and relative rights of share classes in subsection (c) is not exhaustive.

§ 6.02. Terms of Class or Series Determined by Board of Directors.

(a) If the articles of incorporation so provide, the board of directors may determine, in whole or part, the preferences, limitations, and relative rights (within the limits set forth in section 6.01) of (1) any class of shares before the issuance of any shares of that class or (2) one or more series within a class before the issuance of any shares of that series.

(b) Each series of a class must be given a distinguishing designation.

(c) All shares of a series must have preferences, limitations, and relative rights identical with those of other shares of the same series and, except to the extent otherwise provided in the description of the series, of those of other series of the same class.

(d) Before issuing any shares of a class or series created under this section, the corporation must deliver to the secretary of state for filing articles of amendment, which are effective without shareholder action, that set forth:

(1) the name of the corporation;

(2) the text of the amendment determining the terms of the class or series of shares;

(3) the date it was adopted; and

(4) a statement that the amendment was duly adopted by the board of directors.

§ 6.03. Issued and Outstanding Shares.

(a) A corporation may issue the number of shares of each class or series authorized by the articles of incorporation. Shares that are issued are outstanding shares until they are reacquired, redeemed, converted, or cancelled.

(b) The reacquisition, redemption, or conversion of outstanding shares is subject to the limitations of subsection (c) of this section and to section 6.40.

(c) At all times that shares of the corporation are outstanding, one or more shares that together have unlimited voting rights and one or more shares that together are entitled to receive the net assets of the corporation upon dissolution must be outstanding.

§ 6.04. Fractional Shares.

(a) A corporation may:

(1) issue fractions of a share or pay in money the value of fractions of a share;

(2) arrange for disposition of fractional shares by the shareholders;

(3) issue scrip in registered or bearer form entitling the holder to receive a full share upon surrendering enough scrip to equal a full share.

(b) Each certificate representing scrip must be conspicuously labeled "scrip" and must contain the information required by section 6.25(b).

(c) The holder of a fractional share is entitled to exercise the rights of a shareholder, including the right to vote, to receive dividends, and to participate in the assets of the corporation upon liquidation. The holder of scrip is not entitled to any of these rights unless the scrip provides for them.

(d) The board of directors may authorize the issuance of scrip subject to any condition considered desirable, including:

(1) that the scrip will become void if not exchanged for full shares before a specified date; and

(2) that the shares for which the scrip is exchangeable may be sold and the proceeds paid to the scripholders.

Subchapter B. Issuance of Shares

§ 6.20. Subscription of Shares Before Incorporation.

(a) A subscription for shares entered into before incorporation is irrevocable for six months unless the subscription agreement provides a longer or shorter period or all the subscribers agree to revocation.

(b) The board of directors may determine the payment terms of subscriptions for shares that were entered into before incorporation, unless the subscription agreement specifies them. A call for payment by the board of directors must be uniform so far as practicable as to all shares of the same class or series, unless the subscription agreement specifies otherwise.

(c) Shares issued pursuant to subscriptions entered into before incorporation are fully paid and nonassessable when the corporation receives the consideration specified in the subscription agreement.

(d) If a subscriber defaults in payment of money or property under a subscription agreement entered into before incorporation, the corporation may collect the amount owed as any other debt. Alternatively, unless the subscription agreement provides otherwise, the corporation may rescind the agreement and may sell the shares if the debt remains unpaid more than 20 days after the corporation sends written demand for payment to the subscriber.

(e) A subscription agreement entered into after incorporation is a contract between the subscriber and the corporation subject to section 6-21.

§ 6.21. Issuance of Shares.

(a) The powers granted in this section to the board of directors may be reserved to the shareholders by the articles of incorporation.

(b) The board of directors may authorize shares to be issued for consideration consisting of any tangible or intangible property or benefit to the corporation, including cash, promissory notes, services performed, contracts for services to be performed, or other securities of the corporation.

(c) Before the corporation issues shares, the board of directors must determine that the consideration received or to be received for shares to be issued is adequate. That determination by the board of directors is conclusive insofar as the adequacy of consideration for the issuance of shares relates to whether the shares are validly issued, fully paid, and nonassessable.

(d) When the corporation receives the consideration for which the board of directors authorized the issuance of shares, the shares issued therefore are fully paid and nonassessable.

(e) The corporation may place in escrow shares issued for a contract for future services or benefits or a promissory note, or make other arrangements to restrict the transfer of the shares, and may credit distributions in respect of the shares against their purchase price, until the services are performed, the note is paid, or the benefits received. If the services are not performed, the note is not paid, or the benefits are not received, the shares escrowed or restricted and the distributions credited may be cancelled in whole or part.

§ 6.22. Liability of Shareholders.

(a) A purchaser from a corporation of its own shares is not liable to the corporation or its creditors with respect to the shares except to pay the consideration for which the shares were authorized to be issued (section 6.21) or specified in the subscription agreement (section 6.20).

(b) Unless otherwise provided in the articles of incorporation, a shareholder of a corporation is not personally liable for the acts or debts of the corporation except that he may become personally liable by reason of his own acts or conduct.

§ 6.23. Share Dividends.

(a) Unless the articles of incorporation provide otherwise, shares may be issued pro rata and without consideration to the corporation's shareholders or to the shareholders of one or more classes or series. An issuance of shares under this subsection is a share dividend.

(b) Shares of one class or series may not be issued as a share dividend in respect of shares of another class or series unless (1) the articles of incorporation so authorize, (2) a majority of the votes entitled to be cast by the class or series to be issued approve the issue, or (3) there are no outstanding shares of the class or series to be issued.

(c) If the board of directors does not fix the record date for determining shareholders entitled to a share dividend, it is the date the board of directors authorizes the share dividend.

§ 6.24. Share Options.
A corporation may issue rights, options, or warrants for the purchase of shares of the corporation. The board of directors shall determine the terms upon which the rights, options, or warrants are issued, their form and content, and the consideration for which the shares are to be issued.

§ 6.25. Form and Content of Certificates.
[Text not included.]

§ 6.26. Shares without Certificates.
[Text not included.]

§ 6.27. Restriction on Transfer of Shares and Other Securities.

(a) The articles of incorporation, bylaws, an agreement among shareholders, or an agreement between shareholders and the corporation may impose restrictions on the transfer or registration of transfer of shares of the corporation. A restriction does not affect shares issued before the restriction was adopted unless the holders of the shares are parties to the restriction agreement or voted in favor of the restriction.

(b) A restriction on the transfer or registration of transfer of shares is valid and enforceable against the holder or a transferee of the holder if the restriction is authorized by this section and its existence is noted conspicuously on the front or back of the certificate or is contained in the information statement required by section 6.26(b). Unless so noted, a restriction is not enforceable against a person without knowledge of the restriction.

(c) A restriction on the transfer or registration of transfer of shares is authorized:

(1) to maintain the corporation's status when it is dependent on the number or identity of its shareholders;

(2) to preserve exemptions under federal or state securities law;

(3) for any other reasonable purpose.

(d) A restriction on the transfer or registration of transfer of shares may:

(1) obligate the shareholder first to offer the corporation or other persons (separately, consecutively, or simultaneously) an opportunity to acquire the restricted shares;

(2) obligate the corporation or other persons (separately, consecutively, or simultaneously) to acquire the restricted shares;

(3) require the corporation, the holders of any class of its shares, or another person to approve the transfer of the restricted shares, if the requirement is not manifestly unreasonable;

(4) prohibit the transfer of the restricted shares to designated persons or classes of persons, if the prohibition is not manifestly unreasonable.

e) For purposes of this section, "shares" includes a security convertible into or carrying a right to subscribe for or acquire shares.

§ 6.28. Expense of Issue. A corporation may pay the expenses of selling or underwriting its shares, and of organizing or reorganizing the corporation, from the consideration received for shares.

Subchapter C. Subsequent Acquisition of Shares by Shareholders and Corporation

§ 6.30. Shareholders' Preemptive Rights.

(a) The shareholders of a corporation do not have a preemptive right to acquire the corporation's unissued shares except to the extent the articles of incorporation so provide.

(b) A statement included in the articles of incorporation that "the corporation elects to have preemptive rights" (or words of similar import) means that the following principles apply except to the extent the articles of incorporation expressly provide otherwise:

(1) The shareholders of the corporation have a preemptive right, granted on uniform terms and conditions prescribed by the board of directors to provide a fair and reasonable opportunity to exercise the right, to acquire proportional amounts of the corporation's unissued shares upon the decision of the board of directors to issue them.

(2) A shareholder may waive his preemptive right. A waiver evidenced by a writing is irrevocable even though it is not supported by consideration.

(3) There is no preemptive right with respect to:

(i) shares issued as compensation to directors, officers, agents, or employees of the corporation, its subsidiaries or affiliates;

(ii) shares issued to satisfy conversion or option rights created to provide compensation to directors, officers, agents, or employees of the corporation, its subsidiaries or affiliates;

(iii) shares authorized in articles of incorporation that are issued within six months from the effective date of incorporation;

(iv) shares sold otherwise than for money.

(4) Holders of shares of any class without general voting rights but with preferential rights to distributions or assets have no preemptive rights with respect to shares of any class.

(5) Holders of shares of any class with general voting rights but without preferential rights to distributions or assets have no preemptive rights with respect to shares of any class with preferential rights to distributions or assets unless the shares with preferential rights are convertible into or carry a right to subscribe for or acquire shares without preferential rights.

(6) Shares subject to preemptive rights that are not acquired by shareholders may be issued to any person for a period of one year after being offered to shareholders at a consideration set by the board of directors that is not lower than the consideration set for the exercise of preemptive rights. An offer at a lower consideration or after the expiration of one year is subject to the shareholders' preemptive rights.

(c) For purposes of this section, "shares" includes a security convertible into or carrying a right to subscribe for or acquire shares.

§ 6.31. Corporation's Acquisition of Its Own Shares.

(a) A corporation may acquire its own shares and shares so acquired constitute authorized but unissued shares.

(b) If the articles of incorporation prohibit the reissue of acquired shares, the number of authorized shares is reduced by the number of shares acquired, effective upon amendment of the articles of incorporation.

(c) Articles of amendment may be adopted by the board of directors without shareholder action, shall be delivered to the secretary of state for filing, and shall set forth:

(1) the name of the corporation;

(2) the reduction in the number of authorized shares, itemized by class and series; and

(3) the total number of authorized shares, itemized by class and series, remaining after reduction of the shares.

Subchapter D. Distributions

§ 6.40. Distributions to Shareholders.

(a) A board of directors may authorize and the corporation may make distributions to its shareholders subject to restriction by the articles of incorporation and the limitation in subsection (c).

(b) If the board of directors does not fix the record date for determining shareholders entitled to a distribution (other than one involving a purchase, redemption, or other acquisition of the corporation's shares), it is the date the board of directors authorizes the distribution.

(c) No distribution may be made if, after giving it effect:

(1) the corporation would not be able to pay its debts as they become due in the usual course of business; or

(2) the corporation's total assets would be less than the sum of its total liabilities plus (unless the articles of incorporation permit otherwise) the amount that would be needed, if the corporation were to be dissolved at the time of the distribution, to satisfy the preferential rights upon dissolution of shareholders whose preferential rights are superior to those receiving the distribution.

(d) The board of directors may base a determination that a distribution is not prohibited under subsection (c) either on financial statements prepared on the basis of accounting practices and principles that are reasonable in the circumstances or on a fair valuation or other method that is reasonable in the circumstances.

(e) Except as provided in subsection (g), the effect of a distribution under subsection (c) is measured:

(1) in the case of distribution by purchase, redemption, or other acquisition of the corporation's shares, as of the earlier of (i) the date money or other property is transferred or debt incurred by the corporation or (ii) the date the shareholder ceases to be a shareholder with respect to the acquired shares;

(2) in the case of any other distribution of indebtedness, as of the date the indebtedness is distributed; and

(3) in all other cases, as of (i) the date the distribution is authorized if the payment occurs within 120 days after the date of authorization or (ii) the date the payment is made if it occurs more than 120 days after the date of authorization.

(f) A corporation's indebtedness to a shareholder incurred by reason of a distribution made in accordance with this section is at parity with the corporation's indebtedness to its general, unsecured creditors except to the extent subordinated by agreement.

(g) Indebtedness of a corporation, including indebtedness issued as a distribution, is not considered a liability for purposes of determinations under subsection (c) if its terms provide that payment of principal and interest are made only if and to the extent that payment of a distribution to shareholders could then be made under this section. If the indebtedness is issued as a distribution, each payment of principal or interest is treated as a distribution, the effect of which is measured on the date the payment is actually made.

CHAPTER 7. SHAREHOLDERS

Subchapter A. Meetings

§ 7.01. Annual Meeting.

(a) A corporation shall hold annually at a time stated in or fixed in accordance with the bylaws a meeting of shareholders.

(b) Annual shareholders' meetings may be held in or out of this state at the place stated in or fixed in accordance with the bylaws. If no place is stated in or fixed in accordance with the bylaws, annual meetings shall be held at the corporation's principal office.

(c) The failure to hold an annual meeting at the time stated in or fixed in accordance with a corporation's bylaws does not affect the validity of any corporate action.

§ 7.02. Special Meeting.

(a) A corporation shall hold a special meeting of shareholders:

(1) on call of its board of directors or the person or persons authorized to do so by the articles of incorporation or bylaws; or

(2) if the holders of at least 10 percent of all the votes entitled to be cast on any issue proposed to be considered at the proposed special meeting sign, date, and deliver to the corporation's secretary one or more written demands for the meeting describing the purpose or purposes for which it is to be held.

(b) If not otherwise fixed under sections 7.03 or 7.07, the record date for determining shareholders entitled to demand a special meeting is the date the first shareholder signs the demand.

(c) Special shareholders' meetings may be held in or out of this state at the place stated in or fixed in accordance with the bylaws. If no place is stated or fixed in accordance with the bylaws, special meetings shall be held at the corporation's principal office.

(d) Only business within the purpose or purposes described in the meeting notice required by section 7.05(c) may be conducted at a special shareholders' meeting.

§ 7.03. Court-Ordered Meeting.

(a) The [name or describe] court of the county where a corporation's principal office (or, if none in this state, its registered office) is located may summarily order a meeting to be held:

(1) on application of any shareholder of the corporation entitled to participate in an annual meeting if an annual meeting was not held within the earlier of 6 months after the end of the corporation's fiscal year or 15 months after its last annual meeting; or

(2) on application of a shareholder who signed a demand for a special meeting valid under section 7.02 if:

(i) notice of the special meeting was not given within 30 days after the date the demand was delivered to the corporation's secretary; or

(ii) the special meeting was not held in accordance with the notice.

(b) The court may fix the time and place of the meeting, determine the shares entitled to participate in the meeting, specify a record date for determining shareholders entitled to notice of and to vote at the meeting, prescribe the form and content of the meeting notice, fix the quorum required for specific matters to be considered at the meeting (or direct that the votes represented at the meeting constitute a quorum for action on those matters), and enter other orders necessary to accomplish the purpose or purposes of the meeting.

§ 7.04. Action Without Meeting.

(a) Action required or permitted by this Act to be taken at a shareholders' meeting may be taken without a meeting if the action is taken by all the shareholders entitled to vote on the action. The action must be evidenced by one or more written consents describing the action taken, signed by all the shareholders entitled to vote on the action, and delivered to the corporation for inclusion in the minutes or filing with the corporate records.

(b) If not otherwise determined under sections 7.03 or 7.07, the record date for determining shareholders entitled to take action without a meeting is the date the first shareholder signs the consent under subsection (a).

(c) A consent signed under this section has the effect of a meeting vote and may be described as such in any document.

(d) If this Act requires that notice of proposed action be given to nonvoting shareholders and the action is to be taken by unanimous consent of the voting shareholders, the corporation must give its nonvoting shareholders written notice of the proposed action at least 10 days before the action is taken. The notice must contain or be accompanied by the same material that, under this Act, would have been required to be sent to nonvoting shareholders in a notice of meeting at which the proposed action would have been submitted to the shareholders for action.

§ 7.05. Notice of Meeting.

(a) A corporation shall notify shareholders of the date, time, and place of each annual and special shareholders' meeting no fewer than 10 nor more than 60 days before the meeting date. Unless this Act or the articles of incorporation require otherwise, the corporation is required to give notice only to shareholders entitled to vote at the meeting.

(b) Unless this Act or the articles of incorporation require otherwise, notice of an annual meeting need not include a description of the purpose or purposes for which the meeting is called.

(c) Notice of a special meeting must include a description of the purpose or purposes for which the meeting is called.

(d) If not otherwise fixed under sections 7.03 or 7.07, the record date for determining shareholders entitled to notice of and to vote at an annual or special shareholders' meeting is the day before the first notice is delivered to shareholders.

(e) Unless the bylaws require otherwise, if an annual or special shareholders' meeting is adjourned to a different date, time, or place, notice need not be given of the new date, time, or place if the new date, time, or place is announced at the meeting before adjournment. If a new record date for the adjourned meeting is or must be fixed under section 7.07, however, notice of the adjourned meeting must be given under this section to persons who are shareholders as of the new record date.

§ 7.06. Waiver of Notice.

(a) A shareholder may waive any notice required by this Act, the articles of incorporation, or bylaws before or after the date and time stated in the notice. The waiver must be in writing, be signed by the shareholder entitled to the notice, and be delivered to the corporation for inclusion in the minutes or filing with the corporate records.

(b) A shareholder's attendance at a meeting:

(1) waives objection to lack of notice or defective notice of the meeting, unless the shareholder at the beginning of the meeting objects to holding the meeting or transacting business at the meeting;

(2) waives objection to consideration of a particular matter at the

meeting that is not within the purpose or purposes described in the meeting notice, unless the shareholder objects to considering the matter when it is presented.

§ 7.07. Record Date.

(a) The bylaws may fix or provide the manner of fixing the record date for one or more voting groups in order to determine the shareholders entitled to notice of a shareholders' meeting, to demand a special meeting, to vote, or to take any other action. If the bylaws do not fix or provide for fixing a record date, the board of directors of the corporation may fix a future date as the record date.

(b) A record date fixed under this section may not be more than 70 days before the meeting or action requiring a determination of shareholders.

(c) A determination of shareholders entitled to notice of or to vote at a shareholders' meeting is effective for any adjournment of the meeting unless the board of directors fixes a new record date, which it must do if the meeting is adjourned to a date more than 120 days after the date fixed for the original meeting.

(d) If a court orders a meeting adjourned to a date more than 120 days after the date fixed for the original meeting, it may provide that the original record date continues in effect or it may fix a new record date.

Subchapter B. Voting

§ 7.20. Shareholders' List for Meeting.

(a) After fixing a record date for a meeting, a corporation shall prepare an alphabetical list of the names of all its shareholders who are entitled to notice of a shareholders' meeting. The list must be arranged by voting group (and within each voting group by class or series of shares) and show the address of and number of shares held by each shareholder.

(b) The shareholders' list must be available for inspection by any shareholder, beginning two business days after notice of the meeting is given for which the list was prepared and continuing through the meeting, at the corporation's principal office or at a place identified in the meeting notice in the city where the meeting will be held. A shareholder, his agent, or attorney is entitled on written demand to inspect and, subject to the requirements of section 16.02(c), to copy the list, during regular business hours and at his expense, during the period it is available for inspection.

(c) The corporation shall make the shareholders' list available at the meeting, and any shareholder, his agent, or attorney is entitled to inspect the list at any time during the meeting or any adjournment.

(d) If the corporation refuses to allow a shareholder, his agent, or attorney to inspect the shareholders' list before or at the meeting (or copy the list as permitted by subsection (b)), the [name or describe] court of the county where a corporation's principal office (or, if none in this state, its registered office) is located, on application of the shareholder, may summarily order the inspection or copying at the corporation's expense and may postpone the meeting for which the list was prepared until the inspection or copying is complete.

(e) Refusal or failure to prepare or make available the shareholders' list does not affect the validity of action taken at the meeting.

§ 7.21. Voting Entitlement of Shares.

(a) Except as provided in subsections (b) and (c) or unless the articles of incorporation provide otherwise, each outstanding share, regardless of class, is entitled to one vote on each matter voted on at a shareholders' meeting. Only shares are entitled to vote.

(b) Absent special circumstances, the shares of a corporation are not entitled to vote if they are owned, directly or indirectly, by a second corporation, domestic or foreign, and the first corporation owns, directly or indirectly, a majority of the shares entitled to vote for directors of the second corporation.

(c) Subsection (b) does not limit the power of a corporation to vote any shares, including its own shares, held by it in a fiduciary capacity.

(d) Redeemable shares are not entitled to vote after notice of redemption is mailed to the holders and a sum sufficient to redeem the shares has been deposited with a bank, trust company, or other financial institution under an irrevocable obligation to pay the holders the redemption price on surrender of the shares.

§ 7.22. Proxies.

(a) A shareholder may vote his shares in person or by proxy.

(b) A shareholder may appoint a proxy to vote or otherwise act for him by signing an appointment form, either personally or by his attorney-in-fact.

(c) An appointment of a proxy is effective when received by the secretary or other officer or agent authorized to tabulate votes. An appointment is valid for 11 months unless a longer period is expressly provided in the appointment form.

(d) An appointment of a proxy is revocable by the shareholder unless the appointment form conspicuously states that it is irrevocable and the appointment is coupled with an interest. Appointments coupled with an interest include the appointment of:

　(1) a pledgee;

　(2) a person who purchased or agreed to purchase the shares;

　(3) a creditor of the corporation who extended it credit under terms requiring the appointment;

　(4) an employee of the corporation whose employment contract requires the appointment; or

　(5) a party to a voting agreement created under section 7.31.

(e) The death or incapacity of the shareholder appointing a proxy does not affect the right of the corporation to accept the proxy's authority unless notice of the death or incapacity is received by the secretary or other officer or agent authorized to tabulate votes before the proxy exercises his authority under the appointment.

(f) An appointment made irrevocable under subsection (d) is revoked when the interest with which it is coupled is extinguished.

(g) A transferee for value of shares subject to an irrevocable appointment may revoke the appointment if he did not know of its existence when he acquired the shares and the existence of the irrevocable appointment was not noted conspicuously on the certificate representing the shares or on the information statement for shares without certificates.

(h) Subject to section 7.24 and to any express limitation on the proxy's authority appearing on the face of the appointment form, a corporation is entitled to accept the proxy's vote or other action as that of the shareholder making the appointment.

§ 7.23. Shares Held by Nominees.

(a) A corporation may establish a procedure by which the beneficial owner of shares that are registered in the name of a nominee is recognized by the corporation as the shareholder. The extent of this recognition may be determined in the procedure.

(b) The procedure may set forth:

　(1) the types of nominees to which it applies;

　(2) the rights or privileges that the corporation recognizes in a beneficial owner;

　(3) the manner in which the procedure is selected by the nominee;

　(4) the information that must be provided when the procedure is selected;

(5) the period for which selection of the procedure is effective; and

(6) other aspects of the rights and duties created.

§ 7.24. Corporation's Acceptance of Votes.

(a) If the name signed on a vote, consent, waiver, or proxy appointment corresponds to the name of a shareholder, the corporation if acting in good faith is entitled to accept the vote, consent, waiver, or proxy appointment and give it effect as the act of the shareholder.

(b) If the name signed on a vote, consent, waiver, or proxy appointment does not correspond to the name of its shareholder, the corporation if acting in good faith is nevertheless entitled to accept the vote, consent, waiver, or proxy appointment and give it effect as the act of the shareholder if:

(1) the shareholder is an entity and the name signed purports to be that of an officer or agent of the entity;

(2) the name signed purports to be that of an administrator, executor, guardian, or conservator representing the shareholder and, if the corporation requests, evidence of fiduciary status acceptable to the corporation has been presented with respect to the vote, consent, waiver, or proxy appointment;

(3) the name signed purports to be that of a receiver or trustee in bankruptcy of the shareholder and, if the corporation requests, evidence of this status acceptable to the corporation has been presented with respect to the vote, consent, waiver, or proxy appointment;

(4) the name signed purports to be that of a pledgee, beneficial owner, or attorney-in-fact of the shareholder and, if the corporation requests, evidence acceptable to the corporation of the signatory's authority to sign for the shareholder has been presented with respect to the vote, consent, waiver, or proxy appointment;

(5) two or more persons are the shareholder as cotenants or fiduciaries and the name signed purports to be the name of at least one of the coowners and the person signing appears to be acting on behalf of all the coowners.

(c) The corporation is entitled to reject a vote, consent, waiver, or proxy appointment if the secretary or other officer or agent authorized to tabulate votes, acting in good faith, has reasonable basis for doubt about the validity of the signature on it or about the signatory's authority to sign for the shareholder.

(d) The corporation and its officer or agent who accepts or rejects a vote, consent, waiver, or proxy appointment in good faith and in accordance with the standards of this section are not liable in damages to the shareholder for the consequences of the acceptance or rejection.

(e) Corporate action based on the acceptance or rejection of a vote, consent, waiver, or proxy appointment under this section is valid unless a court of competent jurisdiction determines otherwise.

§ 7.25. Quorum and Voting Requirements for Voting Groups.

(a) Shares entitled to vote as a separate voting group may take action on a matter at a meeting only if a quorum of those shares exists with respect to that matter. Unless the articles of incorporation or this Act provide otherwise, a majority of the votes entitled to be cast on the matter by the voting group constitutes a quorum of that voting group for action on that matter.

(b) Once a share is represented for any purpose at a meeting, it is deemed present for quorum purposes for the remainder of the meeting and for any adjournment of that meeting unless a new record date is or must be set for that adjourned meeting.

(c) If a quorum exists, action on a matter (other than the election of directors) by a voting group is approved if the votes cast within the voting group favoring the action exceed the votes cast opposing the

action, unless the articles of incorporation or this Act require a greater number of affirmative votes.

(d) An amendment or articles of incorporation adding, changing, or deleting a quorum or voting requirement for a voting group greater than specified in subsection (b) or (c) is governed by section 7.27.

(e) The election of directors is governed by section 7.28.

§ 7.26. Action by Single and Multiple Voting Groups.

(a) If the articles of incorporation or this Act provide for voting by a single voting group on a matter, action on that matter is taken when voted upon by that voting group as provided in section 7.25.

(b) If the articles of incorporation or this Act provide for voting by two or more voting groups on a matter, action on that matter is taken only when voted upon by each of those voting groups counted separately as provided in section 7.25. Action may be taken by one voting group on a matter even though no action is taken by another voting group entitled to vote on the matter.

§ 7.27. Greater Quorum or Voting Requirements.

(a) The articles of incorporation may provide for a greater quorum or voting requirement for shareholders (or voting groups of shareholders) than is provided for by this Act.

(b) An amendment to the articles of incorporation that adds, changes, or deletes a greater quorum or voting requirement must meet the same quorum requirement and be adopted by the same vote and voting groups required to take action under the quorum and voting requirements then in effect or proposed to be adopted, whichever is greater.

§ 7.28. Voting for Directors; Cumulative Voting.

(a) Unless otherwise provided in the articles of incorporation, directors are elected by a plurality of the votes cast by the shares entitled to vote in the election at a meeting at which a quorum is present.

(b) Shareholders do not have a right to cumulate their votes for directors unless the articles of incorporation so provide.

(c) A statement included in the articles of incorporation that "[all] [a designated voting group of] shareholders are entitled to cumulate their votes for directors" (or words of similar import) means that the shareholders designated are entitled to multiply the number of votes they are entitled to cast by the number of directors for whom they are entitled to vote and cast the product for a single candidate or distribute the product among two or more candidates.

(d) Shares otherwise entitled to vote cumulatively may not be voted cumulatively at a particular meeting unless:

(1) the meeting notice or proxy statement accompanying the notice states conspicuously that cumulative voting is authorized; or

(2) a shareholder who has the right to cumulate his votes gives notice to the corporation not less than 48 hours before the time set for the meeting of his intent to cumulate his votes during the meeting, and if one shareholder gives this notice all other shareholders in the same voting group participating in the election are entitled to cumulate their votes without giving further notice.

Subchapter C. Voting Trusts and Agreements

§ 7.30. Voting Trusts.

(a) One or more shareholders may create a voting trust, conferring on a trustee the right to vote or otherwise act for them, by signing an agreement setting out the provisions of the trust (which may include anything consistent with its purpose) and transferring their shares to the trustee. When a voting trust agreement is signed, the trustee shall prepare a list of the names and addresses of all owners of beneficial interests in the trust, together with the number and class of shares each transferred to the trust, and deliver copies of the list and agreement to the corporation's principal office.

(b) A voting trust becomes effective on the date the first shares subject to the trust are registered in the trustee's name. A voting trust is valid for not more than 10 years after its effective date unless extended under subsection (c).

(c) All or some of the parties to a voting trust may extend it for additional terms of not more than 10 years each by signing an extension agreement and obtaining the voting trustee's written consent to the extension. An extension is valid for 10 years from the date the first shareholder signs the extension agreement. The voting trustee must deliver copies of the extension agreement and list of beneficial owners to the corporation's principal office. An extension agreement binds only those parties signing it.

§ 7.31. Voting Agreements.

(a) Two or more shareholders may provide for the manner in which they will vote their shares by signing an agreement for that purpose. A voting agreement created under this section is not subject to the provisions of section 7.30.

(b) A voting agreement created under this section is specifically enforceable.

Subchapter D. Derivative Proceedings

§ 7.40. Subchapter Definitions.

In this subchapter:

(1) "Derivative proceeding" means a civil suit in the right of a domestic corporation or, to the extent provided in section 7.47, in the right of a foreign corporation.

(2) "Shareholder" includes a beneficial owner whose shares are held in a voting trust or held by a nominee on the beneficial owner's behalf.

§ 7.41. Standing.

A shareholder may not commence or maintain a derivative proceeding unless the shareholder:

(1) was a shareholder of the corporation at the time of the act or omission complained of or became a shareholder through transfer by operation of law from one who was a shareholder at that time; and

(2) fairly and adequately represents the interests of the corporation in enforcing the right of the corporation.

§ 7.42 Demand.

No shareholder may commence a derivative proceeding until:

(1) a written demand has been made upon the corporation to take suitable action; and

(2) 90 days have expired from the date the demand was made unless the shareholder has earlier been notified that the demand has been rejected by the corporation or unless irreparable injury to the corporation would result by waiting for the expiration of the 90 day period.

§ 7.43. Stay of Proceeding.

If the corporation commences an inquiry into the allegations made in the demand or complaint, the court may stay any derivative proceeding for such period as the court deems appropriate.

§ 7.44. Dismissal.

(a) A derivative proceeding shall be dismissed by the court on motion by the corporation if one of the groups specified in subsections (b) or (f) has determined in good faith after conducting a reasonable inquiry

upon which its conclusions are based that the maintenance of the derivative proceeding is not in the best interests of the corporation.

(b) Unless a panel is appointed pursuant to subsection (f), the determination in subsection (a) shall be made by:

(1) a majority vote of independent directors present at a meeting of the board of directors if the independent directors constitute a quorum; or

(2) a majority vote of a committee consisting of two or more independent directors appointed by majority vote of independent directors present at a meeting of the board of directors, whether or not such independent directors constituted a quorum.

(c) None of the following shall by itself cause a director to be considered not independent for purposes of this section:

(1) the nomination or election of the director by persons who are defendants in the derivative proceeding or against whom action is demanded;

(2) the naming of the director as a defendant in the derivative proceeding or as a person against whom action is demanded; or

(3) the approval of the director of the act being challenged in the derivative proceeding or demand if the act resulted in no personal benefit to the director.

(d) If a derivative proceeding is commenced after a determination has been made rejecting a demand by a shareholder, the complaint shall allege with particularity facts establishing either (1) that a majority of the board of directors did not consist of independent directors at the time the determination was made or (2) that the requirements of subsection (a) have not been met.

(e) If a majority of the board of directors does not consist of independent directors at the time the determination is made, the corporation shall have the burden of proving that the requirements of subsection (a) have been met. If a majority of the board of directors consists of independent directors at the time the determination is made, the plaintiff shall have the burden of proving that the requirements of subsection (a) have not been met.

(f) The court may appoint a panel of one or more independent persons upon motion by the corporation to make a determination whether the maintenance of the derivative proceeding is in the best interests of the corporation. In such case, the plaintiff shall have the burden of proving that the requirements of subsection (a) have not been met.

§ 7.45. Discontinuance or Settlement.

A derivative proceeding may not be discontinued or settled without the court's approval. If the court determines that a proposed discontinuance or settlement will substantially affect the interests of the corporation's shareholders or a class of shareholders, the court shall direct that notice be given to the shareholders affected.

§ 7.46. Payment of Expenses.

On termination of the derivative proceeding the court may:

(1) order the corporation to pay the plaintiff's reasonable expenses (including counsel fees) incurred in the proceeding if it finds that the proceeding has resulted in a substantial benefit to the corporation;

(2) order the plaintiff to pay any defendant's reasonable expenses (including counsel fees) incurred in defending the proceeding if it finds that the proceeding was commenced or maintained without reasonable cause or for an improper purpose; or

(3) order a party to pay an opposing party's reasonable expenses (including counsel fees) incurred because of the filing of a pleading, motion or other paper, if it finds that the pleading, motion or other paper was not well grounded in fact, after reasonable inquiry, or warranted by existing law or a good faith argument for the extension, modification or reversal of existing law and was interposed for an

improper purpose, such as to harass or to cause unnecessary delay or needless increase in the cost of litigation.

§ 7.47. Applicability to Foreign Corporations.

In any derivative proceeding in the right of a foreign corporation, the matters covered by this subchapter shall be governed by the laws of the jurisdiction of incorporation of the foreign corporation except for sections 7.43, 7.45 and 7.46.

CHAPTER 8. DIRECTORS AND OFFICERS

Subchapter A. Board of Directors

§ 8.01. Requirement for and Duties of Board of Directors.

(a) Except as provided in subsection (c), each corporation must have a board of directors.

(b) All corporate powers shall be exercised by or under the authority of, and the business and affairs of the corporation managed under the direction of, its board of directors, subject to any limitation set forth in the articles of incorporation.

(c) A corporation having 50 or fewer shareholders may dispense with or limit the authority of a board of directors by describing in its articles of incorporation who will perform some or all of the duties of a board of directors.

§ 8.02. Qualifications of Directors.
The articles of incorporation or bylaws may prescribe qualifications for directors. A director need not be a resident of this state or a shareholder of the corporation unless the articles of incorporation or bylaws so prescribe.

§ 8.03. Number and Election of Directors.

(a) A board of directors must consist of one or more individuals, with the number specified in or fixed in accordance with the articles of incorporation or bylaws.

(b) If a board of directors has power to fix or change the number of directors, the board may increase or decrease by 30 percent or less the number of directors last approved by the shareholders, but only the shareholders may increase or decrease by more than 30 percent the number of directors last approved by the shareholders.

(c) The articles of incorporation or bylaws may establish a variable range for the size of the board of directors by fixing a minimum and maximum number of directors. If a variable range is established, the number of directors may be fixed or changed from time to time, within the minimum and maximum, by the shareholders or the board of directors. After shares are issued, only the shareholders may change the range for the size of the board or change from a fixed to a variable-range size board or vice versa.

(d) Directors are elected at the first annual shareholders' meeting and at each annual meeting thereafter unless their terms are staggered under section 8.06.

§ 8.04. Election of Directors by Certain Classes of Shareholders.

If the articles of incorporation authorize dividing the shares into classes, the articles may also authorize the election of all or a specified number of directors by the holders of one or more authorized classes of shares. Each class (or classes) of shares entitled to elect one or more directors is a separate voting group for purposes of the election of directors.

§ 8.05. Terms of Directors Generally.

(a) The terms of the initial directors of a corporation expire at the first shareholders' meeting at which directors are elected.

(b) The terms of all other directors expire at the next annual shareholders' meeting following their election unless their terms are staggered under section 8.06.

(c) A decrease in the number of directors does not shorten an incumbent director's term.

(d) The term of a director elected to fill a vacancy expires at the next shareholders' meeting at which directors are elected.

(e) Despite the expiration of a director's term, he continues to serve until his successor is elected and qualifies or until there is a decrease in the number of directors.

§ 8.06. Staggered Terms for Directors.
If there are nine or more directors, the articles of incorporation may provide for staggering their terms by dividing the total number of directors into two or three groups, with each group containing one-half or one-third of the total, as near as may be. In that event, the terms of directors in the first group expire at the first annual shareholders' meeting after their election, the terms of the second group expire at the second annual shareholders' meeting after their election, and the terms of the third group, if any, expire at the third annual shareholders' meeting after their election. At each annual shareholders' meeting held thereafter, directors shall be chosen for a term of two years or three years, as the case may be, to succeed those whose terms expire.

§ 8.07. Resignation of Directors.

(a) A director may resign at any time by delivering written notice to the board of directors, its chairman, or to the corporation.

(b) A resignation is effective when the notice is delivered unless the notice specifies a later effective date.

§ 8.08. Removal of Directors by Shareholders.

(a) The shareholders may remove one or more directors with or without cause unless the articles of incorporation provide that directors may be removed only for cause.

(b) If a director is elected by a voting group of shareholders, only the shareholders of that voting group may participate in the vote to remove him.

(c) If cumulative voting is authorized, a director may not be removed if the number of votes sufficient to elect him under cumulative voting is voted against his removal. If cumulative voting is not authorized, a director may be removed only if the number of votes cast to remove him exceeds the number of votes cast not to remove him.

(d) A director may be removed by the shareholders only at a meeting called for the purpose of removing him and the meeting notice must state that the purpose, or one of the purposes, of the meeting is removal of the director.

§ 8.09. Removal of Directors by Judicial Proceeding.

(a) The [name or describe] court of the county where a corporation's principal office (or, if none in this state, its registered office) is located may remove a director of the corporation from office in a proceeding commenced either by the corporation or by its shareholders holding at least 10 percent of the outstanding shares of any class if the court finds that (1) the director engaged in fraudulent or dishonest conduct, or gross abuse of authority or discretion, with respect to the corporation and (2) removal is in the best interest of the corporation.

(b) The court that removes a director may bar the director from reelection for a period prescribed by the court.

(c) If shareholders commence a proceeding under subsection (a), they shall make the corporation a party defendant.

§ 8.10. Vacancy on Board.

(a) Unless the articles of incorporation provide otherwise, if a vacancy occurs on a board of directors, including a vacancy resulting from an increase in the number of directors:

(1) the shareholders may fill the vacancy;

(2) the board of directors may fill the vacancy; or

(3) if the directors remaining in office constitute fewer than a quorum of the board, they may fill the vacancy by the affirmative vote of a majority of all the directors remaining in office.

(b) If the vacant office was held by a director elected by a voting group of shareholders, only the holders of shares of that voting group are entitled to vote to fill the vacancy if it is filled by the shareholders.

(c) A vacancy that will occur at a specific later date (by reason of a resignation effective at a later date under section 8.07(b) or otherwise) may be filled before the vacancy occurs but the new director may not take office until the vacancy occurs.

§ 8.11. Compensation of Directors.
Unless the articles of incorporation or bylaws provide otherwise, the board of directors may fix the compensation of directors.

Subchapter B. Meetings and Action of the Board

§ 8.20. Meetings.

(a) The board of directors may hold regular or special meetings in or out of this state.

(b) Unless the articles of incorporation or bylaws provide otherwise, the board of directors may permit any or all directors to participate in a regular or special meeting by, or conduct the meeting through the use of, any means of communication by which all directors participating may simultaneously hear each other during the meeting. A director participating in a meeting by this means is deemed to be present in person at the meeting.

§ 8.21. Action Without Meeting.

(a) Unless the articles of incorporation or bylaws provide otherwise, action required or permitted by this Act to be taken at a board of directors' meeting may be taken without a meeting if the action is taken by all members of the board. The action must be evidenced by one or more written consents describing the action taken, signed by each director, and included in the minutes or filed with the corporate records reflecting the action taken.

(b) Action taken under this section is effective when the last director signs the consent, unless the consent specifies a different effective date.

(c) A consent signed under this section has the effect of a meeting vote and may be described as such in any document.

§ 8.22. Notice of Meeting.

(a) Unless the articles of incorporation or bylaws provide otherwise, regular meetings of the board of directors may be held without notice of the date, time, place, or purpose of the meeting.

(b) Unless the articles of incorporation or bylaws provide for a longer or shorter period, special meetings of the board of directors must be preceded by at least two days' notice of the date, time, and place of the meeting. The notice need not describe the purpose of the special meeting unless required by the articles of incorporation or bylaws.

§ 8.23. Waiver of Notice.

(a) A director may waive any notice required by this Act, the articles of incorporation, or bylaws before or after the date and time stated in the notice. Except as provided by subsection (b), the waiver must be in writing, signed by the director entitled to the notice, and filed with the minutes or corporate records.

(b) A director's attendance at or participation in a meeting waives any required notice to him of the meeting unless the director at the beginning of the meeting (or promptly upon his arrival) objects to holding the meeting or transacting business at the meeting and does not thereafter vote for or assent to action taken at the meeting.

§ 8.24. Quorum and Voting.

(a) Unless the articles of incorporation or bylaws require a greater number, a quorum of a board of directors consists of:

(1) a majority of the fixed number of directors if the corporation has a fixed board size; or

(2) a majority of the number of directors prescribed, or if no number is prescribed the number in office immediately before the meeting begins, if the corporation has a variable-range size board.

(b) The articles of incorporation or bylaws may authorize a quorum of a board of directors to consist of no fewer than one-third of the fixed or prescribed number of directors determined under subsection (a).

(c) If a quorum is present when a vote is taken, the affirmative vote of a majority of directors present is the act of the board of directors unless the articles of incorporation or bylaws require the vote of a greater number of directors.

(d) A director who is present at a meeting of the board of directors or a committee of the board of directors when corporate action is taken is deemed to have assented to the action taken unless: (1) he objects at the beginning of the meeting (or promptly upon his arrival) to holding it or transacting business at the meeting; (2) his dissent or abstention from the action taken is entered in the minutes of the meeting; or (3) he delivers written notice of his dissent or abstention to the presiding officer of the meeting before its adjournment or to the corporation immediately after adjournment of the meeting. The right of dissent or abstention is not available to a director who votes in favor of the action taken.

§ 8.25. Committees.

(a) Unless the articles of incorporation or bylaws provide otherwise, a board of directors may create one or more committees and appoint members of the board of directors to serve on them. Each committee may have two or more members, who serve at the pleasure of the board of directors.

(b) The creation of a committee and appointment of members to it must be approved by the greater of (1) a majority of all the directors in office when the action is taken or (2) the number of directors required by the articles of incorporation or bylaws to take action under section 8.24.

(c) Sections 8.20 through 8.24, which govern meetings, action without meetings, notice and waiver of notice, and quorum and voting requirements of the board of directors, apply to committees and their members as well.

(d) To the extent specified by the board of directors or in the articles of incorporation or bylaws, each committee may exercise the authority of the board of directors under section 8.01.

(e) A committee may not, however:

(1) authorize distributions;

(2) approve or propose to shareholders action that this Act requires to be approved by shareholders;

(3) fill vacancies on the board of directors or on any of its committees;

(4) amend articles of incorporation pursuant to section 10.02;

(5) adopt, amend, or repeal bylaws;

(6) approve a plan of merger not requiring shareholder approval;

(7) authorize or approve reacquisition of shares, except according to a formula or method prescribed by the board of directors; or

(8) authorize or approve the issuance or sale or contract for sale of shares, or determine the designation and relative rights, preferences, and limitations of a class or series of shares, except that the board of directors may authorize a committee (or a senior executive officer of the corporation) to do so within limits specifically prescribed by the board of directors.

(f) The creation of, delegation of authority to, or action by a committee does not alone constitute compliance by a director with the standards of conduct described in section 8.30.

Subchapter C. Standards of Conduct

§ 8.30. General Standards for Directors.

(a) A director shall discharge his duties as a director, including his duties as a member of a committee:

(1) in good faith;

(2) with the care an ordinarily prudent person in a like position would exercise under similar circumstances; and

(3) in a manner he reasonably believes to be in the best interests of the corporation.

(b) In discharging his duties a director is entitled to rely on information, opinions, reports, or statements, including financial statements and other financial data, if prepared or presented by:

(1) one or more officers or employees of the corporation whom the director reasonably believes to be reliable and competent in the matters presented;

(2) legal counsel, public accountants, or other persons as to matters the director reasonably believes are within the person's professional or expert competence; or

(3) a committee of the board of directors of which he is not a member if the director reasonably believes the committee merits confidence.

(c) A director is not acting in good faith if he has knowledge concerning the matter in question that makes reliance otherwise permitted by subsection (b) unwarranted.

(d) A director is not liable for any action taken as a director, or any failure to take action, if he performed the duties of his office in compliance with this section.

§ 8.33. Liability for Unlawful Distributions.

(a) A director who votes for or assents to a distribution made in violation of section 6.40 or the articles of incorporation is personally liable to the corporation for the amount of the distribution that exceeds what could have been distributed without violating section 6.40 or the articles of incorporation if it is established that he did not perform his duties in compliance with section 8.30. In any proceeding commenced under this section, a director has all of the defenses ordinarily available to a director.

(b) A director held liable under subsection (a) for an unlawful distribution is entitled to contribution:

(1) from every other director who could be held liable under subsection (a) for the unlawful distribution; and

(2) from each shareholder for the amount the shareholder accepted knowing the distribution was made in violation of section 6.40 or the articles of incorporation.

(c) A proceeding under this section is barred unless it is commenced within two years after the date on which the effect of the distribution was measured under section 6.40(e) or (g).

Subchapter D. Officers

§ 8.40. Required Officers.

(a) A corporation has the officers described in its bylaws or appointed by the board of directors in accordance with the bylaws.

(b) A duly appointed officer may appoint one or more officers or assistant officers if authorized by the bylaws or the board of directors.

(c) The bylaws or the board of directors shall delegate to one of the officers responsibility for preparing minutes of the directors' and shareholders' meetings and for authenticating records of the corporation.

(d) The same individual may simultaneously hold more than one office in a corporation.

§ 8.41. Duties of Officers.
Each officer has the authority and shall perform the duties set forth in the bylaws or, to the extent consistent with the bylaws, the duties prescribed by the board of directors or by direction of an officer authorized by the board of directors to prescribe the duties of other officers.

§ 8.42. Standards of Conduct for Officers.

(a) An officer with discretionary authority shall discharge his duties under that authority:

(1) in good faith;

(2) with the care an ordinarily prudent person in a like position would exercise under similar circumstances; and

(3) in a manner he reasonably believes to be in the best interests of the corporation.

(b) In discharging his duties an officer is entitled to rely on information, opinions, reports, or statements, including financial statements and other financial data, if prepared or presented by:

(1) one of more officers or employees of the corporation whom the officer reasonably believes to be reliable and competent in the matters presented; or

(2) legal counsel, public accountants, or other persons as to matters the officer reasonably believes are within the person's professional or expert competence.

(c) An officer is not acting in good faith if he has knowledge concerning the matter in question that makes reliance otherwise permitted by subsection (b) unwarranted.

(d) An officer is not liable for any action taken as an officer, or any failure to take any action, if he performed the duties of his office in compliance with this section.

§ 8.43. Resignation and Removal of Officers.

(a) An officer may resign at any time by delivering notice to the corporation. A resignation is effective when the notice is delivered unless the notice specifies a later effective date. If a resignation is made effective at a later date and the corporation accepts the future effective date, its board of directors may fill the pending vacancy before the effective date if the board of directors provides that the successor does not take office until the effective date.

(b) A board of directors may remove any officer at any time with or without cause.

§ 8.44. Contract Rights of Officers.

(a) The appointment of an officer does not itself create contract rights.

(b) An officer's removal does not affect the officer's contract rights, if any, with the corporation. An officer's resignation does not affect the corporation's contract rights, if any, with the officer.

Subchapter E. Indemnification

§ 8.50. Subchapter Definitions. In this subchapter:

(1) "Corporation" includes any domestic or foreign predecessor entity of a corporation in a merger or other transaction in which the predecessor's existence ceased upon consummation of the transaction.

(2) "Director" means an individual who is or was a director of a corporation or an individual who, while a director of a corporation, is or was serving at the corporation's request as a director, officer, partner, trustee, employee, or agent of another foreign or domestic corporation, partnership, joint venture, trust, employee benefit plan, or other enterprise. A director is considered to be serving an employee benefit plan at the corporation's request if his duties to the corporation also impose duties on, or otherwise involve services by, him to the plan or to participants in or beneficiaries of the plan. "Director" includes, unless the context requires otherwise, the estate or personal representative of a director.

(3) "Expenses" include counsel fees.

(4) "Liability" means the obligation to pay a judgment, settlement, penalty, fine (including an excise tax assessed with respect to an employee benefit plan), or reasonable expenses incurred with respect to a proceeding.

(5) "Official capacity" means: (i) when used with respect to a director, the office of director in a corporation; and (ii) when used with respect to an individual other than a director, as contemplated in section 8.56, the office in a corporation held by the officer or the employment or agency relationship undertaken by the employee or agent on behalf of the corporation. "Official capacity" does not include service for any other foreign or domestic corporation or any partnership, joint venture, trust, employee benefit plan, or other enterprise.

(6) "Party" includes an individual who was, is, or is threatened to be made a named defendant or respondent in a proceeding.

(7) "Proceeding" means any threatened, pending, or completed action, suit, or proceeding, whether civil, criminal, administrative, or investigative and whether formal or informal.

§ 8.51. Authority to Indemnify.

(a) Except as provided in subsection (d), a corporation may indemnify an individual made a party to a proceeding because he is or was a director against liability incurred in the proceeding if:

(1) he conducted himself in good faith; and

(2) he reasonably believed:

(i) in the case of conduct in his official capacity with the corporation, that his conduct was in its best interests; and

(ii) in all other cases, that his conduct was at least not opposed to its best interests; and

(3) in the case of any criminal proceeding, he had no reasonable cause to believe his conduct was unlawful.

(b) A director's conduct with respect to an employee benefit plan for a purpose he reasonably believed to be in the interests of the participants in and beneficiaries of the plan is conduct that satisfies the requirement of subsection (a)(2)(ii).

(c) The termination of a proceeding by judgment, order, settlement, conviction, or upon a plea of nolo contendere or its equivalent is not, of itself, determinative that the director did not meet the standard of conduct described in this section.

(d) A corporation may not indemnify a director under this section:

(1) in connection with a proceeding by or in the right of the corporation in which the director was adjudged liable to the corporation; or

(2) in connection with any other proceeding charging improper personal benefit to him, whether or not involving action in his official capacity, in which he was adjudged liable on the basis that personal benefit was improperly received by him.

(e) Indemnification permitted under this section in connection with a proceeding by or in the right of the corporation is limited to reasonable expenses incurred in connection with the proceeding.

§ 8.52. Mandatory Indemnification. Unless limited by its articles of incorporation, a corporation shall indemnify a director who was wholly successful, on the merits or otherwise, in the defense of any proceeding to which he was a party because he is or was a director of the corporation against reasonable expenses incurred by him in connection with the proceeding.

§ 8.53. Advance for Expenses.

(a) A corporation may pay for or reimburse the reasonable expenses incurred by a director who is a party to a proceeding in advance of final disposition of the proceeding if:

(1) the director furnishes the corporation a written affirmation of his good faith belief that he has met the standard of conduct described in section 8.51;

(2) the director furnishes the corporation a written undertaking, executed personally or on his behalf, to repay the advance if it is ultimately determined that he did not meet the standard of conduct; and

(3) a determination is made that the facts then known to those making the determination would not preclude indemnification under this subchapter.

(b) The undertaking required by subsection (a)(2) must be an unlimited general obligation of the director but need not be secured and may be accepted without reference to financial ability to make repayment.

(c) Determinations and authorizations of payments under this section shall be made in the manner specified in section 8.55.

§ 8.54. Court-Ordered Indemnification. Unless a corporation's articles of incorporation provide otherwise, a director of the corporation who is a party to a proceeding may apply for indemnification to the court conducting the proceeding or to another court of competent jurisdiction. On receipt of an application, the court after giving any notice the court considers necessary may order indemnification if it determines:

(1) the director is entitled to mandatory indemnification under section 8.52, in which case the court shall also order the corporation to pay the director's reasonable expenses incurred to obtain court-ordered indemnification; or

(2) the director is fairly and reasonably entitled to indemnification in view of all the relevant circumstances, whether or not he met the standard of conduct set forth in section 8.51 or was adjudged liable as described in section 8.51(d), but if he was adjudged so liable his indemnification is limited to reasonable expenses incurred.

§ 8.55. Determination and Authorization of Indemnification.

(a) A corporation may not indemnify a director under section 8-51 unless authorized in the specific case after a determination has been made that indemnification of the director is permissible in the circumstances because he has met the standard of conduct set forth in section 8.51.

(b) The determination shall be made:

(1) by the board of directors by majority vote of a quorum consisting of directors not at the time parties to the proceeding;

(2) if a quorum cannot be obtained under subdivision (1), by majority vote of a committee duly designated by the board of directors (in which designation directors who are parties may participate), consisting solely of two or more directors not at the time parties to the proceeding;

(3) by special legal counsel:

(i) selected by the board of directors or its committee in the manner prescribed in subdivision (1) or (2); or

(ii) if a quorum of the board of directors cannot be obtained under subdivision (1) and a committee cannot be designated under subdivision (2), selected by majority vote of the full board of directors (in which selection directors who are parties may participate); or

(4) by the shareholders, but shares owned by or voted under the control of directors who are at the time parties to the proceeding may not be voted on the determination.

(c) Authorization of indemnification and evaluation as to reasonableness of expenses shall be made in the same manner as the determination that indemnification is permissible, except that if the determination is made by special legal counsel, authorization of indemnification and evaluation as to reasonableness of expenses shall be made by those entitled under subsection (b)(3) to select counsel.

Subchapter F. Directors' Conflicting Interest Transactions

§ 8.60. Subchapter Definitions.
In this subchapter;

(1) "Conflicting interest" with respect to a corporation means the interest a director of the corporation has respecting a transaction effected or proposed to be effected by the corporation (or by a subsidiary of the corporation or any other entity in which the corporation has a controlling interest) if

(i) whether or not the transaction is brought before the board of directors of the corporation for action, the director knows at the time of commitment that he or a related person is a party to the transaction or has a beneficial financial interest in or so closely linked to the transaction and of such financial significance to the director or a related person that the interest would reasonably be expected to exert an influence on the director's judgment if he were called upon to vote on the transaction; or

(ii) the transaction is brought (or is of such character and significance to the corporation that it would in the normal course be brought) before the board of directors of the corporation for action, and the director knows at the time of commitment that any of the following persons is either a party to the transaction or has a beneficial financial interest in or so closely linked to the transaction and of such financial significance to the person that the interest would reasonably be expected to exert an influence on the director's judgment if he were called upon to vote on the transaction: (A) an entity (other than the corporation) of which the director is a director, general partner, agent, or employee; (B) a person that controls one or more of the entities specified in subclause (A) or an entity that is controlled by, or is under common control with, one or more of the entities specified in subclause (A); or (C) an individual who is a general partner, principal, or employer of the director.

(2) "Director's conflicting interest transaction" with respect to a corporation means a transaction effected or proposed to be effected by the corporation (or by a subsidiary of the corporation or any other entity in which the corporation has a controlling interest) respecting which a director of the corporation has a conflicting interest.

(3) "Related person" of a director means (i) the spouse (or a parent or sibling thereof) of the director, or a child, grandchild, sibling, parent (or spouse of any thereof) of the director, or an individual having the same home as the director, or a trust or estate of which an individual specified in this clause (i) is a substantial beneficiary; or (ii) a trust, estate, incompetent, conservatee, or minor of which the director is a fiduciary.

(4) "Required disclosure" means disclosure by the director who has a conflicting interest of (i) the existence and nature of his conflicting interest, and (ii) all facts known to him respecting the subject matter of the transaction that an ordinarily prudent person would reasonably believe to be material to a judgment about whether or not to proceed with the transaction.

(5) "Time of commitment" respecting a transaction means the time when the transaction is consummated or, if made pursuant to contract, the time when the corporation (or its subsidiary or the entity in which it has a controlling interest) becomes contractually obligated so that its unilateral withdrawal from the transaction would entail significant loss, liability, or other damage.

§ 8.61. Judicial Action.

(a) A transaction effected or proposed to be effected by a corporation (or by a subsidiary of the corporation or any other entity in which the corporation has a controlling interest) that is not a director's conflicting interest transaction may not be enjoined, set aside, or give rise to an award of damages or other sanctions, in a proceeding by a shareholder or by or in the right of the corporation, because a director of the corporation, or any person with whom or which he has a personal, economic, or other association, has an interest in the transaction.

(b) A director's conflicting interest transaction may not be enjoined, set aside, or give rise to an award of damages or other sanctions, in a proceeding by a shareholder or by or in the right of the corporation, because the director, or any person with whom or which he has a personal, economic, or other association, has an interest in the transaction if:

(1) directors' action respecting the transaction was at any time taken in compliance with section 8.62;

(2) shareholders' action respecting the transaction was at any time taken in compliance with section 8.63;

(3) the transaction, judged according to the circumstances at the time of commitment, is established to have been fair to the corporation.

§ 8.62. Directors' Action.

(a) Directors' action respecting a transaction is effective for purposes of section 8.61(b)(1) if the transaction received the affirmative vote of a majority (but no fewer than two) of those qualified directors on the board of directors or on a duly empowered committee of the board who voted on the transaction after either required disclosure to them (to the extent the information was not known by them) or compliance with subsection (b); provided that action by a committee is so effective only if (1) all its members are qualified directors, and (2) its members are either all the qualified directors on the board or are appointed by the affirmative vote of a majority of the qualified directors on the board.

(b) If a director has a conflicting interest respecting a transaction, but neither he nor a related person of the director specified in section 8.60(3)(i) is a party to the transaction, and if the director has a duty under law or professional canon, or a duty of confidentiality to another person, respecting information relating to the transaction such that the director may not make the disclosure described in section 8.60(4)(ii), then disclosure is sufficient for purposes of subsection (a) if the director (1) discloses to the directors voting on the transaction the existence and nature of his conflicting interest and informs them of the character and limitations imposed by that duty before their vote on the trans-

ction, and (2) plays no part, directly or indirectly, in their delibera-
ons or vote.

c) A majority (but no fewer than two) of all the qualified directors on
he board of directors, or on the committee, constitutes a quorum for
urposes of action that complies with this section. Directors' action
hat otherwise complies with this section is not affected by the presence
r vote of a director who is not a qualified director.

d) For purposes of this section, "qualified director" means, with
espect to a director's conflicting interest transaction, any director who
oes not have either (1) a conflicting interest respecting the transaction,
r (2) a familial, financial, professional, or employment relationship
ith a second director who does have a conflicting interest respecting
he transaction, which relationship would, in the circumstances, rea-
onably be expected to exert an influence on the first director's judg-
ent when voting on the transaction.

8.63. Shareholders' Action.

a) Shareholders' action respecting a transaction is effective for pur-
oses of section 8.61(b)(2) if a majority of the votes entitled to be cast
y the holders of all qualified shares were cast in favor of the transaction
fter (1) notice to shareholders describing the director's conflicting
iterest transaction, (2) provision of the information referred to in
ubsection (d), and (3) required disclosure to the shareholders who
oted on the transaction (to the extent the information was not known
y them).

b) For purposes of this section, "qualified shares" means any shares
ntitled to vote with respect to the director's conflicting interest
ansaction except shares that, to the knowledge, before the vote, of
he secretary (or other officer or agent of the corporation authorized
o tabulate votes), are beneficially owned (or the voting of which is
ontrolled) by a director who has a conflicting interest respecting the
ansaction or by a related person of the director, or both.

c) A majority of the votes entitled to be cast by the holders of all
ualified shares constitutes a quorum for purposes of action that
omplies with this section. Subject to the provisions of subsections (d)
nd (e), shareholders' action that otherwise complies with this section
not affected by the presence of holders, or the voting, of shares that
re not qualified shares.

d) For purposes of compliance with subsection (a), a director who
as a conflicting interest respecting the transaction shall, before the
nareholders' vote, inform the secretary (or other office or agent of the
orporation authorized to tabulate votes) of the number, and the
lentity of persons holding or controlling the vote, of all shares that
he director knows are beneficially owned (or the voting of which is
ontrolled) by the director or by a related person of the director, or
oth.

e) If a shareholders' vote does not comply with subsection (a) solely
ecause of a failure of a director to comply with subsection (d), and if
he director establishes that his failure did not determine and was not
itended by him to influence the outcome of the vote, the court may,
ith or without further proceedings respecting section 8.61(b)(3), take
ich action respecting the transaction and the director, and give such
ffect, if any, to the shareholders' vote, as it considers appropriate in
he circumstances.

Text of other sections, Chapter 9 (Reserved) and Chapter 10 (Amend-
ient of Articles of Incorporation and Bylaws) not included.]

CHAPTER 11. MERGER AND SHARE EXCHANGE

11.01. Merger.

a) One or more corporations may merge into another corporation if
he board of directors of each corporation adopts and its shareholders
f required by section 11.03) approve a plan of merger.

(b) The plan of merger must set forth:

(1) the name of each corporation planning to merge and the name
of the surviving corporation into which each other corporation plans
to merge;

(2) the terms and conditions of the merger; and

(3) the manner and basis of converting the shares of each corporation
into shares, obligations, or other securities of the surviving or any
other corporation or into cash or other property in whole or part.

(c) The plan of merger may set forth:

(1) amendments to the articles of incorporation of the surviving
corporation; and

(2) other provisions relating to the merger.

§ 11.02. Share Exchange.

(a) A corporation may acquire all of the outstanding shares of one or
more classes or series of another corporation if the board of directors
of each corporation adopts and its shareholders (if required by section
11.03) approve the exchange.

(b) The plan of exchange must set forth:

(1) the name of the corporation whose shares will be acquired and
the name of the acquiring corporation;

(2) the terms and conditions of the exchange;

(3) the manner and basis of exchanging the shares to be acquired
for shares, obligations, or other securities of the acquiring or any
other corporation or for cash or other property in whole or part.

(c) The plan of exchange may set forth other provisions relating to
the exchange.

(d) This section does not limit the power of a corporation to acquire
all or part of the shares of one or more classes or series of another
corporation through a voluntary exchange or otherwise.

§ 11.03. Action on Plan.

(a) After adopting a plan of merger or share exchange, the board of
directors of each corporation party to the merger, and the board of
directors of the corporation whose shares will be acquired in the share
exchange, shall submit the plan of merger (except as provided in
subsection (g)) or share exchange for approval by its shareholders.

(b) For a plan of merger or share exchange to be approved:

(1) the board of directors must recommend the plan of merger or
share exchange to the shareholders, unless the board of directors
determines that because of conflict of interest or other special
circumstances it should make no recommendation and communicates
the basis for its determination to the shareholders with the plan;
and

(2) the shareholders entitled to vote must approve the plan.

(c) The board of directors may condition its submission of the proposed merger or share exchange on any basis.

(d) The corporation shall notify each shareholder, whether or not
entitled to vote, of the proposed shareholders' meeting in accordance
with section 7.05. The notice must also state that the purpose, or one
of the purposes, of the meeting is to consider the plan of merger or
share exchange and contain or be accompanied by a copy or summary
of the plan.

(e) Unless this Act, the articles of incorporation, or the board of
directors (acting pursuant to subsection (c)) require a greater vote or
a vote by voting groups, the plan of merger or share exchange to be
authorized must be approved by each voting group entitled to vote
separately on the plan by a majority of all the votes entitled to be cast
on the plan by that voting group.

(f) Separate voting by voting groups is required:

(1) on a plan of merger if the plan contains a provision that, if contained in a proposed amendment to articles of incorporation, would require action by one or more separate voting groups on the proposed amendment under section 10.04;

(2) on a plan of share exchange by each class or series of shares included in the exchange, with each class or series constituting a separate voting group.

(g) Action by the shareholders of the surviving corporation on a plan of merger is not required if:

(1) the articles of incorporation of the surviving corporation will not differ (except for amendments enumerated in section 10.02) from its articles before the merger;

(2) each shareholder of the surviving corporation whose shares were outstanding immediately before the effective date of the merger will hold the same number of shares, with identical designations, preferences, limitations, and relative rights, immediately after;

(3) the number of voting shares outstanding immediately after the merger, plus the number of voting shares issuable as a result of the merger (either by the conversion of securities issued pursuant to the merger or the exercise of rights and warrants issued pursuant to the merger), will not exceed by more than 20 percent the total number of voting shares of the surviving corporation outstanding immediately before the merger; and

(4) the number of participating shares outstanding immediately after the merger, plus the number of participating shares issuable as a result of the merger (either by the conversion of securities issued pursuant to the merger or the exercise of rights and warrants issued pursuant to the merger), will not exceed by more than 20 percent the total number of participating shares outstanding immediately before the merger.

(h) As used in subsection (g):

(1) "Participating shares" means shares that entitle their holders to participate without limitation in distributions.

(2) "Voting shares" means shares that entitle their holders to vote unconditionally in elections of directors.

(i) After a merger or share exchange is authorized, and at any time before articles of merger or share exchange are filed, the planned merger or share exchange may be abandoned (subject to any contractual rights), without further shareholder action, in accordance with the procedure set forth in the plan of merger or share exchange or, if none is set forth, in the manner determined by the board of directors.

§ 11.04. Merger of Subsidiary.

(a) A parent corporation owning at least 90 percent of the outstanding shares of each class of a subsidiary corporation may merge the subsidiary into itself without approval of the shareholders of the parent or subsidiary.

(b) The board of directors of the parent shall adopt a plan of merger that sets forth:

(1) the names of the parent and subsidiary; and

(2) the manner and basis of converting the shares of the subsidiary into shares, obligations, or other securities of the parent or any other corporation or into cash or other property in whole or part.

(c) The parent shall mail a copy or summary of the plan of merger to each shareholder of the subsidiary who does not waive the mailing requirement in writing.

(d) The parent may not deliver articles of merger to the secretary of state for filing until at least 30 days after the date it mailed a copy of the plan of merger to each shareholder of the subsidiary who did not waive the mailing requirement.

(e) Articles of merger under this section may not contain amendments to the articles of incorporation of the parent corporation (except for amendments enumerated in section 10.02).

§ 11.05. Articles of Merger or Share Exchange.

(a) After a plan of merger or share exchange is approved by the shareholders, or adopted by the board of directors if shareholder approval is not required, the surviving or acquiring corporation shall deliver to the secretary of state for filing articles of merger or share exchange setting forth:

(1) the plan of merger or share exchange;

(2) if shareholder approval was not required, a statement to that effect;

(3) if approval of the shareholders of one or more corporations party to the merger or share exchange was required:

(i) the designation, number of outstanding shares, and number of votes entitled to be cast by each voting group entitled to vote separately on the plan as to each corporation; and

(ii) either the total number of votes cast for and against the plan by each voting group entitled to vote separately on the plan or the total number of undisputed votes cast for the plan separately by each voting group and a statement that the number cast for the plan by each voting group was sufficient for approval by that voting group.

(b) Unless a delayed effective date is specified, a merger or share exchange takes effect when the articles of merger or share exchange are filed.

§ 11.06. Effect of Merger or Share Exchange.

(a) When a merger takes effect:

(1) every other corporation party to the merger merges into the surviving corporation and the separate existence of every corporation except the surviving corporation ceases;

(2) the title to all real estate and other property owned by each corporation party to the merger is vested in the surviving corporation without reversion or impairment;

(3) the surviving corporation has all liabilities of each corporation party to the merger;

(4) a proceeding pending against any corporation party to the merger may be continued as if the merger did not occur or the surviving corporation may be substituted in the proceeding for the corporation whose existence ceased;

(5) the articles of incorporation of the surviving corporation are amended to the extent provided in the plan of merger; and

(6) the shares of each corporation party to the merger that are to be converted into shares, obligations, or other securities of the surviving or any other corporation or into cash or other property are converted and the former holders of the shares are entitled only to the rights provided in the articles of merger or to their rights under chapter 13.

§ 11.07. Merger or Share Exchange With Foreign Corporation.

(a) One or more foreign corporations may merge or enter into a share exchange with one or more domestic corporations if:

(1) in a merger, the merger is permitted by the law of the state or country under whose law each foreign corporation is incorporated and each foreign corporation complies with that law in effecting the merger;

(2) in a share exchange, the corporation whose shares will be acquired is a domestic corporation, whether or not a share exchange is permitted by the law of the state or country under whose law the acquiring corporation is incorporated;

(3) the foreign corporation complies with section 11.05 if it is the surviving corporation of the merger or acquiring corporation of the share exchange; and

(4) each domestic corporation complies with the applicable provisions of sections 11.01 through 11.04 and, if it is the surviving corporation of the merger or acquiring corporation of the share exchange, with section 11.05.

(b) Upon merger or share exchange taking effect, the surviving foreign corporation of a merger and the acquiring foreign corporation of a share exchange is deemed:

(1) to appoint the secretary of state as its agent for service of process in a proceeding to enforce any obligation or the rights of dissenting shareholders of each domestic corporation party to the merger or share exchange; and

(2) to agree that it will promptly pay to the dissenting shareholders of each domestic corporation party to the merger or share exchange the amount, if any, to which they are entitled under chapter 13.

(c) This section does not limit the power of a foreign corporation to acquire all or part of the shares of one or more classes or series of a domestic corporation through a voluntary exchange or otherwise.

CHAPTER 12. SALE OF ASSETS

§ 12.01. Sale of Assets in Regular Course of Business and Mortgage of Assets.

(a) A corporation may, on the terms and conditions and for the consideration determined by the board of directors:

(1) sell, lease, exchange, or otherwise dispose of all, or substantially all, of its property in the usual and regular course of business,

(2) mortgage, pledge, dedicate to the repayment of indebtedness (whether with or without recourse), or otherwise encumber any or all of its property whether or not in the usual and regular course of business, or

(3) transfer any or all of its property to a corporation all the shares of which are owned by the corporation.

(b) Unless the articles of incorporation require it, approval by the shareholders of a transaction described in subsection (a) is not required.

§ 12.02. Sale of Assets Other Than in Regular Course of Business.

(a) A corporation may sell, lease, exchange, or otherwise dispose of all, or substantially all, of its property (with or without the good will), otherwise than in the usual and regular course of business, on the terms and conditions and for the consideration determined by the corporation's board of directors, if the board of directors proposes and its shareholders approve the proposed transaction.

(b) For a transaction to be authorized:

(1) the board of directors must recommend the proposed transaction to the shareholders unless the board of directors determines that because of conflict of interest or other special circumstances it should make no recommendation and communicates the basis for its determination to the shareholders with the submission of the proposed transaction; and

(2) the shareholders entitled to vote must approve the transaction.

(c) The board of directors may condition its submission of the proposed transaction on any basis.

(d) The corporation shall notify each shareholder, whether or not entitled to vote, of the proposed shareholders' meeting in accordance with section 7.05. The notice must also state that the purpose, or one of the purposes, of the meeting is to consider the sale, lease, exchange, or other disposition of all, or substantially all, the property of the corporation and contain or be accompanied by a description of the transaction.

(e) Unless the articles of incorporation or the board of directors (acting pursuant to subsection (c)) require a greater vote or a vote by voting groups, the transaction to be authorized must be approved by a majority of all the votes entitled to be cast on the transaction.

(f) After a sale, lease, exchange, or other disposition of property is authorized, the transaction may be abandoned (subject to any contractual rights) without further shareholder action.

(g) A transaction that constitutes a distribution is governed by section 6.40 and not by this section.

CHAPTER 13. DISSENTERS' RIGHTS

Subchapter A. Right to Dissent and Obtain Payment of Shares

§ 13.01. Definitions.   In this chapter:

(1) "Corporation" means the issuer of the shares held by a dissenter before the corporate action, or the surviving or acquiring corporation by merger or share exchange of that issuer.

(2) "Dissenter" means a shareholder who is entitled to dissent from corporate action under section 13.02 and who exercises that right when and in the manner required by sections 13.20 through 13.28.

(3) "Fair value," with respect to a dissenter's shares, means the value of the shares immediately before the effectuation of the corporate action to which the dissenter objects, excluding any appreciation or depreciation in anticipation of the corporate action unless exclusion would be inequitable.

(4) "Interest" means interest from the effective date of the corporate action until the date of payment, at the average rate currently paid by the corporation on its principal bank loans, or, if none, at a rate that is fair and equitable under all the circumstances.

(5) "Record shareholder" means the person in whose names shares are registered in the records of a corporation or the beneficial owner of shares to the extent of the rights granted by a nominee certificate on file with a corporation.

(6) "Beneficial shareholder" means the person who is a beneficial owner of shares held in a voting trust or by a nominee as the record shareholder.

(7) "Shareholder" means the record shareholder or the beneficial shareholder.

§ 13.02. Right to Dissent.

(a) A shareholder is entitled to dissent from, and obtain payment of the fair value of his shares in the event of, any of the following corporate actions:

(1) consummation of a plan of merger to which the corporation is a party (i) if shareholder approval is required for the merger by section 11.03 or the articles of incorporation and the shareholder is entitled to vote on the merger or (ii) if the corporation is a subsidiary that is merged with its parent under section 11.04;

(2) consummation of a plan of share exchange to which the corporation is a party as the corporation whose shares will be acquired, if the shareholder is entitled to vote on the plan;

(3) consummation of a sale or exchange of all, or substantially all, of the property of the corporation other than in the usual and regular course of business, if the shareholder is entitled to vote on the sale or exchange, including a sale in dissolution, but not including a sale pursuant to court order or a sale for cash pursuant to a plan by which all or substantially all of the net proceeds of the sale will be distributed to the shareholders within one year after the date of sale;

(4) an amendment of the articles of incorporation that materially

and adversely affects rights in respect of a dissenter's shares because it:

    (i) alters or abolishes a preferential right of the shares;

    (ii) creates, alters, or abolishes a right in respect of redemption, including a provision respecting a sinking fund for the redemption or repurchase, of the shares;

    (iii) alters or abolishes a preemptive right of the holder of the shares to acquire shares or other securities;

    (iv) excludes or limits the right of the shares to vote on any matter, or to cumulate votes, other than a limitation by dilution through issuance of shares or other securities with similar voting rights; or

    (v) reduces the number of shares owned by the shareholder to a fraction of a share if the fractional share so created is to be acquired for cash under section 6.04; or

    (5) any corporate action taken pursuant to a shareholder vote to the extent the articles of incorporation, bylaws, or a resolution of the board of directors provides that voting or nonvoting shareholders are entitled to dissent and obtain payment for their shares.

(b) A shareholder entitled to dissent and obtain payment for his shares under this chapter may not challenge the corporate action creating his entitlement unless the action is unlawful or fraudulent with respect to the shareholder or the corporation.

§ 13.03. Dissent by Nominees and Beneficial Owners [Text not included.].

Subchapter B. Procedure for Exercise of Dissenters' Rights

§ 13.20. Notice of Dissenters' Rights.

(a) If proposed corporate action creating dissenters' rights under section 13.02 is submitted to a vote at a shareholders' meeting, the meeting notice must state that shareholders are or may be entitled to assert dissenters' rights under this chapter and be accompanied by a copy of this chapter.

(b) If corporate action creating dissenters' rights under section 13.02 is taken without a vote of shareholders, the corporation shall notify in writing all shareholders entitled to assert dissenters' rights that the action was taken and send them the dissenters' notice described in section 13.22.

§ 13.21. Notice of Intent to Demand Payment.

(a) If proposed corporate action creating dissenters' rights under section 13.02 is submitted to a vote at a shareholders' meeting, a shareholder who wishes to assert dissenter's rights (1) must deliver to the corporation before the vote is taken written notice of his intent to demand payment for his shares if the proposed action is effectuated and (2) must not vote his shares in favor of the proposed action.

(b) A shareholder who does not satisfy the requirements of subsection (a) is not entitled to payment for his shares under this chapter.

§ 13.22. Dissenters' Notice.

(a) If proposed corporate action creating dissenters' rights under section 13.02 is authorized at a shareholders' meeting, the corporation shall deliver a written dissenters' notice to all shareholders who satisfied the requirements of section 13.21.

(b) The dissenters' notice must be sent no later than 10 days after the corporate action was taken, and must:

    (1) state where the payment demand must be sent and where and when certificates for certificated shares must be deposited;

    (2) inform holders of uncertificated shares to what extent transfer of the shares will be restricted after the payment demand is received;

    (3) supply a form for demanding payment that includes the date of the first announcement to news media or to shareholders of the terms of the proposed corporate action and requires that the person asserting dissenters' rights certify whether or not he acquired beneficial ownership of the shares before that date;

    (4) set a date by which the corporation must receive the payment demand, which date may not be fewer than 30 nor more than 60 days after the date the subsection (a) notice is delivered; and

    (5) be accompanied by a copy of this chapter.

§ 13.23. Duty to Demand Payment.

(a) A shareholder sent a dissenters' notice described in section 13.22 must demand payment, certify whether he acquired beneficial ownership of the shares before the date required to be set forth in the dissenters' notice pursuant to section 13.22(b)(3), and deposit his certificates in accordance with the terms of the notice.

(b) The shareholder who demands payment and deposits his shares under section (a) retains all other rights of a shareholder until these rights are cancelled or modified by the taking of the proposed corporate action.

(c) A shareholder who does not demand payment or deposit his share certificates where required, each by the date set in the dissenters' notice, is not entitled to payment for his shares under this chapter.

§ 13.24. Share Restrictions.

(a) The corporation may restrict the transfer of uncertificated shares from the date the demand for their payment is received until the proposed corporate action is taken or the restrictions released under section 13.26.

(b) The person for whom dissenters' rights are asserted as to uncertificated shares retains all other rights of a shareholder until these rights are cancelled or modified by the taking of the proposed corporate action.

§ 13.25. Payment.

(a) Except as provided in section 13.27, as soon as the proposed corporate action is taken, or upon receipt of a payment demand, the corporation shall pay each dissenter who complied with section 13.23 the amount the corporation estimates to be the fair value of his shares, plus accrued interest.

(b) The payment must be accompanied by:

    (1) the corporation's balance sheet as of the end of a fiscal year ending not more than 16 months before the date of payment, an income statement for that year, a statement of changes in shareholders' equity for that year, and the latest available interim financial statements, if any;

    (2) a statement of the corporation's estimate of the fair value of the shares;

    (3) an explanation of how the interest was calculated;

    (4) a statement of the dissenters' right to demand payment under section 13.28; and

    (5) a copy of this chapter.

§ 13.26. Failure to Take Action.

(a) If the corporation does not take the proposed action within 60 days after the date set for demanding payment and depositing share certificates, the corporation shall return the deposited certificates and release the transfer restrictions imposed on uncertificated shares.

(b) If after returning deposited certificates and releasing transfer restrictions, the corporation takes the proposed action, it must send a new dissenters' notice under section 13.22 and repeat the payment demand procedure.

§ 13.27. After-Acquired Shares.

(a) A corporation may elect to withhold payment required by section 13.25 from a dissenter unless he was the beneficial owner of the shares before the date set forth in the dissenters' notice as the date of the first announcement to news media or to shareholders of the terms of the proposed corporate action.

(b) To the extent the corporation elects to withhold payment under subsection (a), after taking the proposed corporate action, it shall estimate the fair value of the shares, plus accrued interest, and shall pay this amount to each dissenter who agrees to accept it in full satisfaction of his demand. The corporation shall send with its offer a statement of its estimate of the fair value of the shares, an explanation of how the interest was calculated, and a statement of the dissenter's right to demand payment under section 13.28.

§ 13.28. Procedure if Shareholder Dissatisfied with Payment or Offer.

(a) A dissenter may notify the corporation in writing of his own estimate of the fair value of his shares and amount of interest due, and demand payment of his estimate (less any payment under section 13.25), or reject the corporation's offer under section 13.27 and demand payment of the fair value of his shares and interest due, if:

(1) the dissenter believes that the amount paid under section 13.25 or offered under section 13.27 is less than the fair value of his shares or that the interest due is incorrectly calculated;

(2) the corporation fails to make payment under section 13.25 within 60 days after the date set for demanding payment; or

(3) the corporation, having failed to take the proposed action, does not return the deposited certificates or release the transfer restrictions imposed on uncertificated shares within 60 days after the date set for demanding payment.

(b) A dissenter waives his right to demand payment under this section unless he notifies the corporation of his demand in writing under subsection (a) within 30 days after the corporation made or offered payment for his shares.

Subchapter C. Judicial Appraisal of Shares

§ 13.30. Court Action.

(a) If a demand for payment under section 13.28 remains unsettled, the corporation shall commence a proceeding within 60 days after receiving the payment demand and petition the court to determine the fair value of the shares and accrued interest. If the corporation does not commence the proceeding within the 60-day period, it shall pay each dissenter whose demand remains unsettled the amount demanded.

(b) The corporation shall commence the proceeding in the [name or describe] court of the county where a corporation's principal office (or, if none in this state, its registered office) is located. If the corporation is a foreign corporation without a registered office in this state, it shall commence the proceeding in the county in this state where the registered office of the domestic corporation merged with or whose shares were acquired by the foreign corporation was located.

(c) The corporation shall make all dissenters (whether or not residents of this state) whose demands remain unsettled parties to the proceeding as in an action against their shares and all parties must be served with a copy of the petition. Nonresidents may be served by registered or certified mail or by publication as provided by law.

(d) The jurisdiction of the court in which the proceeding is commenced under subsection (b) is plenary and exclusive. The court may appoint one or more persons as appraisers to receive evidence and recommend decision on the question of fair value. The appraisers have the powers described in the order appointing them, or in any amendment to it. The dissenters are entitled to the same discovery rights as parties in other civil proceedings.

(e) Each dissenter made a party to the proceeding is entitled to judgment (1) for the amount, if any, by which the court finds the fair value of his shares, plus interest, exceeds the amount paid by the corporation or (2) for the fair value, plus accrued interest, of his after-acquired shares for which the corporation elected to withhold payment under section 13.27.

§ 13.31. Court Costs and Counsel Fees.

(a) The court in an appraisal proceeding commenced under section 13.30 shall determine all costs of the proceeding, including the reasonable compensation and expenses of appraisers appointed by the court. The court shall assess the costs against the corporation, except that the court may assess costs against all or some of the dissenters, in amounts the court finds equitable, to the extent the court finds the dissenters acted arbitrarily, vexatiously, or not in good faith in demanding payment under section 13.28.

(b) The court may also assess the fees and expenses of counsel and experts for the respective parties, in amounts the court finds equitable:

(1) against the corporation and in favor of any or all dissenters if the court finds the corporation did not substantially comply with the requirements of sections 13.20 through 13.28; or

(2) against either the corporation or a dissenter, in favor of any other party, if the court finds that the party against whom the fees and expenses are assessed acted arbitrarily, vexatiously, or not in good faith with respect to the rights provided by this chapter.

(c) If the court finds that the services of counsel for any dissenter were of substantial benefit to other dissenters similarly situated, and that the fees for those services should not be assessed against the corporation, the court may award to these counsel reasonable fees to be paid out of the amounts awarded the dissenters who were benefited.

CHAPTER 14. DISSOLUTION

Subchapter A. Voluntary Dissolution

§ 14.01. Dissolution by Incorporators or Initial Directors.
A majority of the incorporators or initial directors of a corporation that has not issued shares or has not commenced business may dissolve the corporation by delivering to the secretary of state for filing articles of dissolution that set forth:

(1) the name of the corporation;

(2) the date of its incorporation;

(3) either (i) that none of the corporation's shares has been issued or (ii) that the corporation has not commenced business;

(4) that no debt of the corporation remains unpaid;

(5) that the net assets of the corporation remaining after winding up have been distributed to the shareholders, if shares were issued; and

(6) that a majority of the incorporators or initial directors authorized the dissolution.

§ 14.02. Dissolution by Board of Directors and Shareholders.

(a) A corporation's board of directors may propose dissolution for submission to the shareholders.

(b) For a proposal to dissolve to be adopted:

(1) the board of directors must recommend dissolution to the shareholders unless the board of directors determines that because of conflict of interest or other special circumstances it should make no recommendation and communicates the basis for its determination to the shareholders; and

(2) the shareholders entitled to vote must approve the proposal to dissolve as provided in subsection (e).

(c) The board of directors may condition its submission of the proposal for dissolution on any basis.

(d) The corporation shall notify each shareholder, whether or not entitled to vote, of the proposed shareholders' meeting in accordance with section 7.05. The notice must also state that the purpose, or one of the purposes, of the meeting is to consider dissolving the corporation.

(e) Unless the articles of incorporation or the board of directors (acting pursuant to subsection (c)) require a greater vote or a vote by voting groups, the proposal to dissolve to be adopted must be approved by a majority of all the votes entitled to be cast on that proposal.

§ 14.03. Articles of Dissolution [Text not included].

§ 14.04. Revocation of Dissolution [Text not included].

§ 14.05. Effect of Dissolution.

(a) A dissolved corporation continues its corporate existence but may not carry on any business except that appropriate to wind up and liquidate its business and affairs, including:

(1) collecting its assets;

(2) disposing of its properties that will not be distributed in kind to its shareholders;

(3) discharging or making provision for discharging its liabilities;

(4) distributing its remaining property among its shareholders according to their interests; and

(5) doing every other act necessary to wind up and liquidate its business and affairs.

(b) Dissolution of a corporation does not:

(1) transfer title to the corporation's property;

(2) prevent transfer of its shares or securities, although the authorization to dissolve may provide for closing the corporation's share transfer records;

(3) subject its directors or officers to standards of conduct different from those prescribed in chapter 8;

(4) change quorum or voting requirements for its board of directors or shareholders; change provisions for selection, resignation, or removal of its directors or officers or both; or change provisions for amending its bylaws;

(5) prevent commencement of a proceeding by or against the corporation in its corporate name;

(6) abate or suspend a proceeding pending by or against the corporation on the effective date of dissolution; or

(7) terminate the authority of the registered agent of the corporation.

§ 14.06. Known Claims Against Dissolved Corporation.

(a) A dissolved corporation may dispose of the known claims against it by following the procedures described in this section.

(b) The dissolved corporation shall notify its known claimants in writing of the dissolution at any time after its effective date. The written notice must:

(1) describe information that must be included in a claim;

(2) provide a mailing address where a claim may be sent;

(3) state the deadline, which may not be fewer than 120 days from the effective date of the written notice, by which the dissolved corporation must receive the claim; and

(4) state that the claim will be barred if not received by the deadline.

(c) A claim against the dissolved corporation is barred:

(1) if a claimant who was given written notice under subsection (b)

does not deliver the claim to the dissolved corporation by the deadline;

(2) if a claimant whose claim was rejected by the dissolved corporation does not commence a proceeding to enforce the claim within 90 days from the effective date of the rejection notice.

(d) For purposes of this section, "claim" does not include a contingent liability or a claim based on an event occurring after the effective date of dissolution.

§ 14.07. Unknown Claims Against Dissolved Corporation.

(a) A dissolved corporation may also publish notice of its dissolution and request that persons with claims against the corporation present them in accordance with the notice.

(b) The notice must:

(1) be published one time in a newspaper of general circulation in the county where the dissolved corporation's principal office (or, if none in this state, its registered office) is or was last located;

(2) describe the information that must be included in a claim and provide a mailing address where the claim may be sent; and

(3) state that a claim against the corporation will be barred unless a proceeding to enforce the claim is commenced within five years after the publication of the notice.

(c) If the dissolved corporation publishes a newspaper notice in accordance with subsection (b), the claim of each of the following claimants is barred unless the claimant commences a proceeding to enforce the claim against the dissolved corporation within five years after the publication date of the newspaper notice:

(1) a claimant who did not receive written notice under section 14.06;

(2) a claimant whose claim was timely sent to the dissolved corporation but not acted on;

(3) a claimant whose claim is contingent or based on an event occurring after the effective date of dissolution.

(d) A claim may be enforced under this section:

(1) against the dissolved corporation, to the extent of its undistributed assets; or

(2) if the assets have been distributed in liquidation, against a shareholder of the dissolved corporation to the extent of his pro rata share of the claim or the corporate assets distributed to him in liquidation, whichever is less, but a shareholder's total liability for all claims under this section may not exceed the total amount of assets distributed to him.

Subchapter B. Administrative Dissolution

§ 14.20. Grounds for Administrative Dissolution. The secretary of state may commence a proceeding under section 14.21 to administratively dissolve a corporation if:

(1) the corporation does not pay within 60 days after they are due any franchise taxes or penalties imposed by this Act or other law;

(2) the corporation does not deliver its annual report to the secretary of state within 60 days after it is due;

(3) the corporation is without a registered agent or registered office in this state for 60 days or more;

(4) the corporation does not notify the secretary of state within 60 days that its registered agent or registered office has been changed, that its registered agent has resigned, or that its registered office has been discontinued; or

(5) the corporation's period of duration stated in its articles of incorporation expires.

14.21. Procedure for and Effect of Administrative Dissolution.

a) If the secretary of state determines that one or more grounds exist under section 14.20 for dissolving a corporation, he shall serve the corporation with written notice of his determination under section .04.

b) If the corporation does not correct each ground for dissolution or demonstrate to the reasonable satisfaction of the secretary of state that each ground determined by the secretary of state does not exist within 0 days after service of the notice is perfected under section 5.04, the secretary of state shall administratively dissolve the corporation by signing a certificate of dissolution that recites the ground or grounds or dissolution and its effective date. The secretary of state shall file the original of the certificate and serve a copy on the corporation under section 5.04.

c) A corporation administratively dissolved continues its corporate existence but may not carry on any business except that necessary to wind up and liquidate its business and affairs under section 14.05 and notify claimants under sections 14.06 and 14.07.

d) The administrative dissolution of a corporation does not terminate the authority of its registered agent.

14.22. Reinstatement Following Administrative Dissolution.

a) A corporation administratively dissolved under section 14.21 may apply to the secretary of state for reinstatement within two years after the effective date of dissolution. The application must:

(1) recite the name of the corporation and the effective date of its administrative dissolution;

(2) state that the ground or grounds for dissolution either did not exist or have been eliminated;

(3) state that the corporation's name satisfies the requirements of section 4.01; and

(4) contain a certificate from the [taxing authority] reciting that all taxes owed by the corporation have been paid.

b) If the secretary of state determines that the application contains the information required by subsection (a) and that the information is correct, he shall cancel the certificate of dissolution and prepare a certificate of reinstatement that recites his determination and the effective date of reinstatement, file the original of the certificate, and serve a copy on the corporation under section 5.04.

c) When the reinstatement is effective, it relates back to and takes effect as of the effective date of the administrative dissolution and the corporation resumes carrying on its business as if the administrative dissolution had never occurred.

14.23. Appeal from Denial of Reinstatement.

a) If the secretary of state denies a corporation's application for reinstatement following administrative dissolution, he shall serve the corporation under section 5.04 with a written notice that explains the reason or reasons for denial.

b) The corporation may appeal the denial of reinstatement to the [name or describe] court within 30 days after service of the notice of denial is perfected. The corporation appeals by petitioning the court to set aside the dissolution and attaching to the petition copies of the secretary of state's certificate of dissolution, the corporation's application for reinstatement, and the secretary of state's notice of denial.

c) The court may summarily order the secretary of state to reinstate the dissolved corporation or may take other action the court considers appropriate.

d) The court's final decision may be appealed as in other civil proceedings.

Subchapter C. Judicial Dissolution

§ 14.30. Grounds for Judicial Dissolution.   The [name or describe court or courts] may dissolve a corporation:

(1) in a proceeding by the attorney general if it is established that:

(i) the corporation obtained its articles of incorporation through fraud; or

(ii) the corporation has continued to exceed or abuse the authority conferred upon it by law;

(2) in a proceeding by a shareholder if it is established that:

(i) the directors are deadlocked in the management of the corporate affairs, the shareholders are unable to break the deadlock, and irreparable injury to the corporation is threatened or being suffered, or the business and affairs of the corporation can no longer be conducted to the advantage of the shareholders generally, because of the deadlock;

(ii) the directors or those in control of the corporation have acted, are acting, or will act in a manner that is illegal, oppressive, or fraudulent;

(iii) the shareholders are deadlocked in voting power and have failed, for a period that includes at least two consecutive annual meeting dates, to elect successors to directors whose terms have expired; or

(iv) the corporate assets are being misapplied or wasted;

(3) in a proceeding by a creditor if it is established that:

(i) the creditor's claim has been reduced to judgment, the execution on the judgment returned unsatisfied, and the corporation is insolvent; or

(ii) the corporation has admitted in writing that the creditor's claim is due and owing and the corporation is insolvent; or

(4) in a proceeding by the corporation to have its voluntary dissolution continued under court supervision.

§ 14.31. Procedure for Judicial Dissolution.

(a) Venue for a proceeding by the attorney general to dissolve a corporation lies in [name the county or counties]. Venue for a proceeding brought by any other party named in section 14.30 lies in the county where a corporation's principal office (or, if none in this state, its registered office) is or was last located.

(b) It is not necessary to make shareholders parties to a proceeding to dissolve a corporation unless relief is sought against them individually.

(c) A court in a proceeding brought to dissolve a corporation may issue injunctions, appoint a receiver or custodian pendente lite with all powers and duties the court directs, take other action required to preserve the corporate assets wherever located, and carry on the business of the corporation until a full hearing can be held.

§ 14.32. Receivership or Custodianship. [Text not included.]

§ 14.33. Decree of Dissolution.

(a) If after a hearing the court determines that one or more grounds for judicial dissolution described in section 14.30 exist, it may enter a decree dissolving the corporation and specifying the effective date of the dissolution, and the clerk of the court shall deliver a certified copy of the decree to the secretary of state, who shall file it.

(b) After entering the decree of dissolution, the court shall direct the winding up and liquidation of the corporation's business and affairs in accordance with section 14.05 and the notification of claimants in accordance with sections 14.06 and 14.07.

Subchapter D. Miscellaneous

§ 14.40. Deposit with State Treasurer. Assets of a dissolved corporation that should be transferred to a creditor, claimant, or shareholder of the corporation who cannot be found or who is not competent to receive them shall be reduced to cash and deposited with the state treasurer or other appropriate state official for safekeeping. When the creditor, claimant, or shareholder furnishes satisfactory proof of entitlement to the amount deposited, the state treasurer or other appropriate state official shall pay him or his representative that amount.

CHAPTER 15. FOREIGN CORPORATIONS

Subchapter A. Certificate of Authority

§ 15.01. Authority to Transact Business Required.

(a) A foreign corporation may not transact business in this state until it obtains a certificate of authority from the secretary of state.

(b) The following activities, among others, do not constitute transacting business within the meaning of subsection (a):

(1) maintaining, defending, or settling any proceeding;

(2) holding meetings of the board of directors or shareholders or carrying on other activities concerning internal corporate affairs;

(3) maintaining bank accounts;

(4) maintaining offices or agencies for the transfer, exchange, and registration of the corporation's own securities or maintaining trustees or depositaries with respect to those securities;

(5) selling through independent contractors;

(6) soliciting or obtaining orders, whether by mail or through employees or agents or otherwise, if the orders require acceptance outside this state before they become contracts;

(7) creating or acquiring indebtedness, mortgages, and security interests in real or personal property;

(8) securing or collecting debts or enforcing mortgages and security interests in property securing the debts;

(9) owning, without more, real or personal property;

(10) conducting an isolated transaction that is completed within 30 days and that is not one in the course of repeated transactions of a like nature;

(11) transacting business in interstate commerce.

(c) The list of activities in subsection (b) is not exhaustive.

§ 15.02. Consequences of Transacting Business Without Authority.

(a) A foreign corporation transacting business in this state without a certificate of authority may not maintain a proceeding in any court in this state until it obtains a certificate of authority.

(b) The successor to a foreign corporation that transacted business in this state without a certificate of authority and the assignee of a cause of action arising out of that business may not maintain a proceeding based on that cause of action in any court in this state until the foreign corporation or its successor obtains a certificate of authority.

(c) A court may stay a proceeding commenced by a foreign corporation, its successor, or assignee until it determines whether the foreign corporation or its successor requires a certificate of authority. If it so determines, the court may further stay the proceeding until the foreign corporation or its successor obtains the certificate.

(d) A foreign corporation is liable for a civil penalty of $_____ for each day, but not to exceed a total of $_____ for each year, it transacts business in this state without a certificate of authority. The attorney general may collect all penalties due under this subsection.

(e) Notwithstanding subsections (a) and (b), the failure of a foreign corporation to obtain a certificate of authority does not impair the validity of its corporate acts or prevent it from defending any proceeding in this state.

§ 15.03. Application for Certificate of Authority.

(a) A foreign corporation may apply for a certificate of authority to transact business in this state by delivering an application to the secretary of state for filing. The application must set forth:

(1) the name of the foreign corporation or, if its name is unavailable for use in this state, a corporate name that satisfies the requirements of section 15.06;

(2) the name of the state or country under whose law it is incorporated;

(3) its date of incorporation and period of duration;

(4) the street address of its principal office;

(5) the address of its registered office in this state and the name of its registered agent at that office; and

(6) the names and usual business addresses of its current directors and officers.

(b) The foreign corporation shall deliver with the completed application a certificate of existence (or a document of similar import) duly authenticated by the secretary of state or other official having custody of corporate records in the state or country under whose law it is incorporated.

§ 15.04. Amended Certificate of Authority.

(a) A foreign corporation authorized to transact business in this state must obtain an amended certificate of authority from the secretary of state if it changes:

(1) its corporate name;

(2) the period of its duration; or

(3) the state or country of its incorporation.

(b) The requirements of section 15.03 for obtaining an original certificate of authority apply to obtaining an amended certificate under this section.

§ 15.05. Effect of Certificate of Authority.

(a) A certificate of authority authorizes the foreign corporation to which it is issued to transact business in this state subject, however, to the right of the state to revoke the certificate as provided in this Act.

(b) A foreign corporation with a valid certificate of authority has the same but no greater rights and has the same but no greater privileges as, and except as otherwise provided by this Act is subject to the same duties, restrictions, penalties, and liabilities now or later imposed on a domestic corporation of like character.

(c) This Act does not authorize this state to regulate the organization or internal affairs of a foreign corporation authorized to transact business in this state.

§ 15.06. Corporate Name of Foreign Corporation. [Text not included.]

§ 15.07. Registered Office and Registered Agent of Foreign Corporation. Each foreign corporation authorized to transact business in this state must continuously maintain in this state:

(1) a registered office that may be the same as any of its places of business; and

(2) a registered agent, who may be:

(i) an individual who resides in this state and whose business office is identical with the registered office;

(ii) a domestic corporation or not-for-profit domestic corporation whose business office is identical with the registered office; or

(iii) a foreign corporation or foreign not-for-profit corporation authorized to transact business in this state whose business office is identical with the registered office.

[Text of other sections not included.]

Subchapter B. Withdrawal [Text not included.]

Subchapter C. Revocation of Certificate of Authority

§ 15.30. Grounds for Revocation. The secretary of state may commence a proceeding under section 15.31 to revoke the certificate of authority of a foreign corporation authorized to transact business in this state if:

(1) the foreign corporation does not deliver its annual report to the secretary of state within 60 days after it is due;

(2) the foreign corporation does not pay within 60 days after they are due any franchise taxes or penalties imposed by this Act or other law;

(3) the foreign corporation is without a registered agent or registered office in this state for 60 days or more;

(4) the foreign corporation does not inform the secretary of state under section 15.08 or 15.09 that its registered agent or registered office has changed, that its registered agent has resigned, or that its registered office has been discontinued within 60 days of the change, resignation, or discontinuance;

(5) an incorporator, director, officer, or agent of the foreign corporation signed a document he knew was false in any material respect with intent that the document be delivered to the secretary of state for filing;

(6) the secretary of state receives a duly authenticated certificate from the secretary of state or other official having custody of corporate records in the state or country under whose law the foreign corporation is incorporated stating that it has been dissolved or disappeared as the result of a merger.

§ 15.31. Procedure for and Effect of Revocation.

(a) If the secretary of state determines that one or more grounds exist under section 15.30 for revocation of a certificate of authority, he shall serve the foreign corporation with written notice of his determination under section 15.10.

(b) If the foreign corporation does not correct each ground for revocation or demonstrate to the reasonable satisfaction of the secretary of state that each ground determined by the secretary of state does not exist within 60 days after service of the notice is perfected under section 15.10, the secretary of state may revoke the foreign corporation's certificate of authority by signing a certificate of revocation that recites the ground or grounds for revocation and its effective date. The secretary of state shall file the original of the certificate and serve a copy on the foreign corporation under section 15.10.

(c) The authority of a foreign corporation to transact business in this state ceases on the date shown on the certificate revoking its certificate of authority.

(d) The secretary of state's revocation of a foreign corporation's certificate of authority appoints the secretary of state the foreign corporation's agent for service of process in any proceeding based on a cause of action which arose during the time the foreign corporation was authorized to transact business in this state. Service of process on the secretary of state under this subsection is service on the foreign corporation. Upon receipt of process, the secretary of state shall mail a copy of the process to the secretary of the foreign corporation at its principal office shown in its most recent annual report or in any

subsequent communication received from the corporation stating the current mailing address of its principal office, or, if none are on file, in its application for a certificate of authority.

(e) Revocation of a foreign corporation's certificate of authority does not terminate the authority of the registered agent of the corporation.

§ 15.32. Appeal from Revocation.

(a) A foreign corporation may appeal the secretary of state's revocation of its certificate of authority to the [name or describe] court within 30 days after service of the certificate of revocation is perfected under section 15.10. The foreign corporation appeals by petitioning the court to set aside the revocation and attaching to the petition copies of its certificate of authority and the secretary of state's certificate of revocation.

(b) The court may summarily order the secretary of state to reinstate the certificate of authority or may take any other action the court considers appropriate.

(c) The court's final decision may be appealed as in other civil proceedings.

CHAPTER 16. RECORDS AND REPORTS

Subchapter A. Records

§ 16.01. Corporate Records.

(a) A corporation shall keep as permanent records minutes of all meetings of its shareholders and board of directors, a record of all actions taken by a committee of the board of directors in place of the board of directors on behalf of the corporation.

(b) A corporation shall maintain appropriate accounting records.

(c) A corporation or its agent shall maintain a record of its shareholders, in a form that permits preparation of a list of the names and addresses of all shareholders, in alphabetical order by class of shares showing the number and class of shares held by each.

(d) A corporation shall maintain its records in written form or in another form capable of conversion into written form within a reasonable time.

(e) A corporation shall keep a copy of the following records at its principal office:

(1) its articles or restated articles of incorporation and all amendments to them currently in effect;

(2) its bylaws or restated bylaws and all amendments to them currently in effect;

(3) resolutions adopted by its board of directors creating one or more classes of series of shares, and fixing their relative rights, preferences, and limitations, if shares issued pursuant to those resolutions are outstanding;

(4) the minutes of all shareholders' meetings, and records of all action taken by shareholders without a meeting, for the past three years;

(5) all written communications to shareholders generally within the past three years, including the financial statements furnished for the past three years under section 16.20;

(6) a list of the names and business addresses of its current directors and officers; and

(7) its most recent annual report delivered to the secretary of state under section 16.22.

§ 16.02. Inspection of Records by Shareholders.

(a) A shareholder of a corporation is entitled to inspect and copy, during regular business hours at the corporation's principal office, any of the records of the corporation described in section 16.01(e) if he gives the corporation written notice of his demand at least five business days before the date on which he wishes to inspect and copy.

(b) A shareholder of a corporation is entitled to inspect and copy, during regular business hours at a reasonable location specified by the corporation, any of the following records of the corporation if the shareholder meets the requirements of subsection (c) and gives the corporation written notice of his demand at least five business days before the date on which he wishes to inspect and copy:

(1) excerpts from minutes of any meeting of the board of directors, records of any action of a committee of the board of directors while acting in place of the board of directors on behalf of the corporation, minutes of any meeting of the shareholders, and records of action taken by the shareholders or board of directors without a meeting, to the extent not subject to inspection under section 16.02(a);

(2) accounting records of the corporation; and

(3) the record of shareholders.

(c) A shareholder may inspect and copy the records identified in subsection (b) only if:

(1) his demand is made in good faith and for a proper purpose;

(2) he describes with reasonable particularity his purpose and the records he desires to inspect; and

(3) the records are directly connected with his purpose.

(d) The right of inspection granted by this section may not be abolished or limited by a corporation's articles of incorporation or bylaws.

(e) This section does not affect:

(1) the right of a shareholder to inspect records under section 7.20 or, if the shareholder is in litigation with the corporation, to the same extent as any other litigant;

(2) the power of a court, independently of this Act, to compel the production of corporate records for examination.

(f) For purposes of this section, "shareholder" includes a beneficial owner whose shares are held in a voting trust or by a nominee on his behalf.

[Text of other sections not included.]

Subchapter B. Reports

§ 16.20. Financial Statements for Shareholders.

(a) A corporation shall furnish its shareholders annual financial statements, which may be consolidated or combined statements of the corporation and one or more of its subsidiaries, as appropriate, that include a balance sheet as of the end of the fiscal year, an income statement for that year, and a statement of changes in shareholders' equity for the year unless that information appears elsewhere in the financial statements. If financial statements are prepared for the corporation on the basis of generally accepted accounting principles, the annual financial statements must also be prepared on that basis.

(b) If the annual financial statements are reported upon by a public accountant, his report must accompany them. If not, the statements must be accompanied by a statement of the president or the person responsible for the corporation's accounting records:

(1) stating his reasonable belief whether the statements were pre-

pared on the basis of generally accepted accounting principles and, if not, describing the basis of preparation; and

(2) describing any respects in which the statements were not prepared on a basis of accounting consistent with the statements prepared for the preceding year.

(c) A corporation shall mail the annual financial statements to each shareholder within 120 days after the close of each fiscal year. Thereafter, on written request from a shareholder who was not mailed the statements, the corporation shall mail him the latest financial statements.

§ 16.21. Other Reports to Shareholders.

(a) If a corporation indemnifies or advances expenses to a director under section 8.51, 8.52, 8.53, or 8.54 in connection with a proceeding by or in the right of the corporation, the corporation shall report the indemnification or advance in writing to the shareholders with or before the notice of the next shareholders' meeting.

§ 16.22. Annual Report for Secretary of State.

(a) Each domestic corporation, and each foreign corporation authorized to transact business in this state, shall deliver to the secretary of state for filing an annual report that sets forth:

(1) the name of the corporation and the state or country under whose law it is incorporated;

(2) the address of its registered office and the name of its registered agent at that office in this state;

(3) the address of its principal office;

(4) the names and business addresses of its directors and principal officers;

(5) a brief description of the nature of its business;

(6) the total number of authorized shares, itemized by class and series, if any, within each class; and

(7) the total number of issued and outstanding shares, itemized by class and series, if any, within each class.

(b) Information in the annual report must be current as of the date the annual report is executed on behalf of the corporation.

(c) The first annual report must be delivered to the secretary of state between January 1 and April 1 of the year following the calendar year in which a domestic corporation was incorporated or a foreign corporation was authorized to transact business. Subsequent annual reports must be delivered to the secretary of state between January 1 and April 1 of the following calendar years.

(d) If an annual report does not contain the information required by this section, the secretary of state shall promptly notify the reporting domestic or foreign corporation in writing and return the report to it for correction. If the report is corrected to contain the information required by this section and delivered to the secretary of state within 30 days after the effective date of notice, it is deemed to be timely filed.

CHAPTER 17. TRANSITION PROVISIONS

[Text not included.]

APPENDIX F

Uniform Partnership Act*

Part 1. Preliminary Provisions

§ 1. Name of Act.
This act may be cited as Uniform Partnership Act.

§ 2. Definition of Terms.
In this act, "Court" includes every court and judge having jurisdiction in the case.

"Business" includes every trade, occupation, or profession.

"Person" includes individuals, partnerships, corporations, and other associations.

"Bankrupt" includes bankrupt under the Federal Bankruptcy Act or insolvent under any state insolvent act.

"Conveyance" includes every assignment, lease, mortgage, or encumbrance.

"Real property" includes land and any interest or estate in land.

§ 3. Interpretation of Knowledge and Notice.

(1) A person has "knowledge" of a fact within the meaning of this act not only when he has actual knowledge thereof, but also when he has knowledge of such other facts as in the circumstances shows bad faith.

(2) A person has "notice" of a fact within the meaning of this act when the person who claims the benefit of the notice:

(a) States the fact to such person, or

(b) Delivers through the mail, or by other means of communication, a written statement of the fact to such person or to a proper person at his place of business or residence.

§ 4. Rules of Construction.

(1) The rule that statutes in derogation of the common law are to be strictly construed shall have no application to this act.

(2) The law of estoppel shall apply under this act.

(3) The law of agency shall apply under this act.

(4) This act shall be so interpreted and construed as to effect its general purpose to make uniform the law of those states which enact it.

(5) This act shall not be construed so as to impair the obligations of any contract existing when the act goes into effect, nor to affect any action or proceedings begun or right accrued before this act takes effect.

§ 5. Rules for Cases Not Provided for in This Act.
In any case not provided for in this act the rules of law and equity, including the law merchant, shall govern.

*The text of this act was obtained from the National Conference of Commissioners on Uniform State Laws, and is reprinted with the Commissioner's consent.

Part 2. Nature of Partnership

§ 6. Partnership Defined.

(1) A partnership is an association of two or more persons to carry on as co-owners a business for profit.

(2) But any association formed under any other statute of this state, or any statute adopted by authority, other than the authority of this state, is not a partnership under this act, unless such association would have been a partnership in this state prior to the adoption of this act; but this act shall apply to limited partnerships except in so far as the statutes relating to such partnerships are inconsistent herewith.

§ 7. Rules for Determining the Existence of a Partnership.
In determining whether a partnership exists, these rules shall apply:

(1) Except as provided by section 16 persons who are not partners as to each other are not partners as to third persons.

(2) Joint tenancy, tenancy in common, tenancy by the entireties, joint property, common property, or part ownership does not of itself establish a partnership, whether such co-owners do or do not share any profits made by the use of the property.

(3) The sharing of gross returns does not of itself establish a partnership, whether or not the persons sharing them have a joint or common right or interest in any property from which the returns are derived.

(4) The receipt by a person of a share of the profits of a business is prima facie evidence that he is a partner in the business, but no such inference shall be drawn if such profits were received in payment:

(a) As a debt by installments or otherwise,

(b) As wages of an employee or rent to a landlord,

(c) As an annuity to a widow or representative of a deceased partner,

(d) As interest on a loan, though the amount of payments vary with the profits of the business.

(e) As the consideration for the sale of a good-will of a business or other property by installments or otherwise.

§ 8. Partnership Property.

(1) All property originally brought into the partnership stock or subsequently acquired by purchase or otherwise, on account of the partnership, is partnership property.

(2) Unless the contrary intention appears, property acquired with partnership funds is partnership property.

(3) Any estate in real property may be acquired in the partnership name. Title so acquired can be conveyed only in the partnership name.

(4) A conveyance to a partnership in the partnership name, though without words of inheritance, passes the entire estate of the grantor unless a contrary intent appears.

Part 3. Relations of Partners to Persons Dealing with the Partnership

§ 9. Partner Agent of Partnership as to Partnership Business.

(1) Every partner is an agent of the partnership for the purpose of its business, and the act of every partner, including the execution in the partnership name of any instrument, for apparently carrying on in the usual way the business of the partnership of which he is a member binds the partnership, unless the partner so acting has in fact no authority to act for the partnership in the particular matter, and the person with whom he is dealing has knowledge of the fact that he has no such authority.

(2) An act of a partner which is not apparently for the carrying on of the business of the partnership in the usual way does not bind the partnership unless authorized by the other partners.

(3) Unless authorized by the other partners or unless they have abandoned the business, one or more but less than all the partners have no authority to:

(a) Assign the partnership property in trust for creditors or on the assignee's promise to pay the debts of the partnership,

(b) Dispose of the good-will of the business,

(c) Do any other act which would make it impossible to carry on the ordinary business of a partnership,

(d) Confess a judgment,

(e) Submit a partnership claim or liability to arbitration or reference.

(4) No act of a partner in contravention of a restriction on authority shall bind the partnership to persons having knowledge of the restriction.

§ 10. Conveyance of Real Property of the Partnership.

(1) Where title to real property is in the partnership name, any partner may convey title to such property by a conveyance executed in the partnership name; but the partnership may recover such property unless the partner's act binds the partnership under the provisions of paragraph (1) of section 9, or unless such property has been conveyed by the grantee or a person claiming through such grantee to a holder for value without knowledge that the partner, in making the conveyance, has exceeded his authority.

(2) Where title to real property is in the name of the partnership, a conveyance executed by a partner, in his own name, passes the equitable interest of the partnership, provided the act is one within the authority of the partner under the provisions of paragraph (1) of section 9.

(3) Where title to real property is in the name of one or more but not all the partners, and the record does not disclose the right of the partnership, the partners in whose name the title stands may convey title to such property, but the partnership may recover such property if the partners' act does not bind the partnership under the provisions of paragraph (1) of section 9, unless the purchaser or his assignee, is a holder for value, without knowledge.

(4) Where the title to real property is in the name of one or more of all the partners, or in a third person in trust for the partnership, a conveyance executed by a partner in the partnership name, or in his own name, passes the equitable interest of the partnership, provided the act is one within the authority of the partner under the provisions of paragraph (1) section 9.

(5) Where the title to real property is in the names of all the partners a conveyance executed by all the partners passes all their rights in such property.

§ 11. Partnership Bound by Admission of Partner.

An admission or representation made by any partner concerning partnership affairs within the scope of his authority as conferred by this act is evidence against the partnership.

§ 12. Partnership Charged with Knowledge of or Notice to Partner.

Notice to any partner of any matter relating to partnership affairs, and the knowledge of the partner acting in the particular matter, acquired while a partner or then present to his mind, and the knowledge of any other partner who reasonably could and should have communicated it to the acting partner, operate as notice to or knowledge of the partnership, except in the case of a fraud on the partnership committed by or with the consent of that partner.

§ 13. Partnership Bound by Partner's Wrongful Act.

Where, by any wrongful act or omission of any partner acting in the ordinary course of the business of the partnership or with the authority of his co-partners, loss or injury is caused to any person, not being a partner in the partnership, or any penalty is incurred, the partnership is liable therefor to the same extent as the partner so acting or omitting to act.

§ 14. Partnership Bound by Partner's Breach of Trust.

The partnership is bound to make good the loss:

(a) Where one partner acting within the scope of his apparent authority receives money or property of a third person and misapplies it; and

(b) Where the partnership in the course of its business receives money or property of a third person and the money or property so received is misapplied by any partner while it is in the custody of the partnership.

§ 15. Nature of Partner's Liability.

All partners are liable

(a) Jointly and severally for everything chargeable to the partnership under sections 13 and 14.

(b) Jointly for all other debts and obligations of the partnership; but any partner may enter into a separate obligation to perform a partnership contract.

§ 16. Partner by Estoppel.

(1) When a person, by words spoken or written or by conduct, represents himself, or consents to another representing him to anyone, as a partner in an existing partnership or with one or more persons not actual partners, he is liable to any such person to whom such representation has been made, who has, on the faith of such representation, given credit to the actual or apparent partnership, and if he has made such representation or consented to its being made in a public manner he is liable to such person, whether the representation has or has not been made or communicated to such person so giving credit by or with the knowledge of the apparent partner making the representation or consenting to its being made.

(a) When a partnership liability results, he is liable as though he were an actual member of the partnership.

(b) When no partnership liability results, he is liable jointly with the other persons, if any, so consenting to the contract or representation as to incur liability otherwise separately.

(2) When a person has been thus represented to be a partner in an existing partnership, or with one or more persons not actual partners, he is an agent of the persons consenting to such representation to bind them to the same extent and in the same manner as though he were a partner in fact, with respect to persons who rely upon the representation. Where all the members of the existing partnership consent to the representation, a partnership act or obligation results; but in all other cases it is the joint act or obligation of the person acting and the persons consenting to the representation.

§ 17. Liability of Incoming Partner.

A person admitted as a partner into an existing partnership is liable for all the obligations of the partnership arising before his admission as though he had been a partner when such obligations were incurred, except that this liability shall be satisfied only out of partnership property.

Part 4. Relations of Partners to One Another

§ 18. Rules Determining Rights and Duties of Partners.

The rights and duties of the partners in relation to the partnership shall be determined, subject to any agreement between them, by the following rules:

(a) Each partner shall be repaid his contributions, whether by way of capital or advances to the partnership property and share equally in the profits and surplus remaining after all liabilities, including those to partners, are satisfied; and must contribute towards the losses, whether of capital or otherwise, sustained by the partnership according to his share in the profits.

(b) The partnership must indemnify every partner in respect of payments made and personal liabilities reasonably incurred by him in the ordinary and proper conduct of its business, or for the preservation of its business or property.

(c) A partner, who in aid of the partnership makes any payment or advance beyond the amount of capital which he agreed to contribute, shall be paid interest from the date of the payment or advance.

(d) A partner shall receive interest on the capital contributed by him only from the date when repayment should be made.

(e) All partners have equal rights in the management and conduct of the partnership business.

(f) No partner is entitled to remuneration for acting in the partnership business, except that a surviving partner is entitled to reasonable compensation for his services in winding up the partnership affairs.

(g) No person can become a member of a partnership without the consent of all the partners.

(h) Any difference arising as to ordinary matters connected with the partnership business may be decided by a majority of the partners; but no act in contravention of any agreement between the partners may be done rightfully without the consent of all the partners.

§ 19. Partnership Books.

The partnership books shall be kept, subject to any agreement between the partners, at the principal place of business of the partnership, and every partner shall at all times have access to and may inspect and copy any of them.

§ 20. Duty of Partners to Render Information.

Partners shall render on demand true and full information of all things affecting the partnership to any partner or the legal representative of any deceased partner or partner under legal disability.

§ 21. Partner Accountable as a Fiduciary.

(1) Every partner must account to the partnership for any benefit, and hold as trustee for it any profits derived by him without the consent of the other partners from any transaction connected with the formation, conduct, or liquidation of the partnership or from any use by him of its property.

(2) This section applies also to the representatives of a deceased partner engaged in the liquidation of the affairs of the partnership as the personal representatives of the last surviving partner.

§ 22. Right to an Account.

Any partner shall have the right to a formal account as to partnership affairs:

(a) If he is wrongfully excluded from the partnership business or possession of its property by his copartners,

(b) If the right exists under the terms of any agreement,

(c) As provided by section 21,

(d) Whenever other circumstances render it just and reasonable.

§ 23. Continuation of Partnership Beyond Fixed Term.

(1) When a partnership for a fixed term or particular undertaking is continued after the termination of such term or particular undertaking without any express agreement, the rights and duties of the partners remain the same as they were at such termination, so far as is consistent with a partnership at will.

(2) A continuation of the business by the partners or such of them as habitually acted therein during the term, without any settlement or liquidation of the partnership affairs, is prima facie evidence of a continuation of the partnership.

Part 5. Property Rights of a Partner

§ 24. Extent of Property Rights of a Partner.

The property rights of a partner are (1) his rights in specific partnership property, (2) his interest in the partnership, and (3) his right to participate in the management.

§ 25. Nature of a Partner's Right in Specific Partnership Property.

(1) A partner is co-owner with his partners of specific partnership property holding as a tenant in partnership.

(2) The incidents of this tenancy are such that:

(a) A partner, subject to the provisions of this act and to any agreement between the partners, has an equal right with his partners to possess specific partnership property for partnership purposes; but he has no right to possess such property for any other purpose without the consent of his partners.

(b) A partner's right in specific partnership property is not assignable except in connection with the assignment of rights of all the partners in the same property.

(c) A partner's right in specific partnership property is not subject to attachment or execution, except on a claim against the partnership. When partnership property is attached for a partnership debt the partners, or any of them, or the representatives of a deceased partner, cannot claim any right under the homestead or exemption laws.

(d) On the death of a partner his right in specific partnership property vests in the surviving partner or partners, except where the deceased was the last surviving partner, when his right in such property vests in his legal representative. Such surviving partner or partners, or the legal representative of the last surviving partner, has no right to possess the partnership property for any but a partnership purpose.

(e) A partner's right in specific partnership property is not subject to dower, curtesy, or allowances to widows, heirs, or next of kin.

§ 26. Nature of Partner's Interest in the Partnership.

A partner's interest in the partnership is his share of the profits and surplus, and the same is personal property.

§ 27. Assignment of Partner's Interest.

(1) A conveyance by a partner of his interest in the partnership does not of itself dissolve the partnership, nor, as against the other partners in the absence of agreement, entitle the assignee, during the continuance of the partnership, to interfere in the management or administration of the partnership business or affairs, or to require any information or account of partnership transactions, or to inspect the partnership books; but it merely entitles the assignee to receive in accordance with his contract the profits to which the assigning partner would otherwise be entitled.

(2) In case of a dissolution of the partnership, the assignee is entitled to receive his assignor's interest and may require an account from the date only of the last account agreed to by all the partners.

§ 28. Partner's Interest Subject to Charging Order.

(1) On due application to a competent court by any judgment creditor of a partner, the court which entered the judgment, order, or decree, or any other court, may charge the interest of the debtor partner with payment of the unsatisfied amount of such judgment debt with interest thereon; and may then or later appoint a receiver of his share of the

profits, and of any other money due or to fall due to him in respect of the partnership, and make all other orders, directions, accounts and inquiries which the debtor partner might have made, or which the circumstances of the case may require.

(2) The interest charged may be redeemed at any time before foreclosure, or in the case of a sale being directed by the court may be purchased without thereby causing a dissolution:

(a) With separate property, by any one or more of the partners, or

(b) With partnership property, by any one or more of the partners with the consent of all the partners whose interests are not so charged or sold.

(3) Nothing in this act shall be held to deprive a partner of his right, if any, under the exemption laws, as regards his interest in the partnership.

Part 6. Dissolution and Winding Up

§ 29. **Dissolution Defined.** The dissolution of a partnership is a change in the relation of the partners caused by any partner ceasing to be associated in the carrying on as distinguished from the winding up of the business.

§ 30. **Partnership not Terminated by Dissolution.** On dissolution the partnership is not terminated, but continues until the winding up of partnership affairs is completed.

§ 31. **Causes if Dissolution.**   Dissolution is caused:

(1) Without violation of the agreement between the partners,

(a) By the termination of the definite term or particular undertaking specified in the agreement,

(b) By the express will of any partner when no definite term or particular undertaking is specified,

(c) By the express will of all the partners who have not assigned their interests or suffered them to be charged for their separate debts, either before or after the termination of any specified term or particular undertaking.

(d) By the expulsion of any partner from the business bona fide in accordance with such a power conferred by the agreement between the partners;

(2) In contravention of the agreement between the partners, where the circumstances do not permit a dissolution under any other provision of this section, by the express will of any partner at any time;

(3) By any event which makes it unlawful for the business of the partnership to be carried on or for the members to carry it on in partnership;

(4) By the death of any partner;

(5) By the bankruptcy of any partner or the partnership;

(6) By decree of court under section 32.

§ 32. **Dissolution by Decree of Court.**

(1) On application by or for a partner the court shall decree a dissolution whenever:

(a) A partner has been declared a lunatic in any judicial proceeding or is shown to be of unsound mind,

(b) A partner becomes in any other way incapable of performing his part of the partnership contract,

(c) A partner has been guilty of such conduct as tends to affect prejudicially the carrying on of the business,

(d) A partner willfully or persistently commits a breach of the partnership agreement, or otherwise so conducts himself in matters relating to the partnership business that it is not reasonably practicable to carry on the business in partnership with him,

(e) The business of the partnership can only be carried on at a loss,

(f) Other circumstances render a dissolution equitable.

(2) On the application of the purchaser of a partner's interest under sections 27 or 28:

(a) After the termination of the specified term or particular undertaking,

(b) At any time if the partnership was a partnership at will when the interest was assigned or when the charging order was issued.

§ 33. **General Effect of Dissolution on Authority of Partner.** Except so far as may be necessary to wind up partnership affairs or to complete transactions begun but not then finished, dissolution terminates all authority of any partner to act for the partnership,

(1) With respect to the partners,

(a) When the dissolution is not by the act, bankruptcy or death of a partner; or

(b) When the dissolution is by such act, bankruptcy or death of a partner, in cases where section 34 so requires.

(2) With respect to persons not partners, as declared in section 35.

§ 34. **Right of Partner to Contribution from Co-partners after Dissolution.** Where the dissolution is caused by the act, death or bankruptcy of a partner, each partner is liable to his co-partners for his share of any liability created by any partner acting for the partnership as if the partnership had not been dissolved unless

(a) The dissolution being by act of any partner, the partner acting for the partnership had knowledge of the dissolution, or

(b) The dissolution being by the death or bankruptcy of a partner, the partner acting for the partnership had knowledge or notice of the death or bankruptcy.

§ 35. **Power of Partner to Bind Partnership to Third Persons after Dissolution.**

(1) After dissolution a partner can bind the partnership except as provided in Paragraph (3)

(a) By any act appropriate for winding up partnership affairs or completing transactions unfinished at dissolution;

(b) By any transaction which would bind the partnership if dissolution had not taken place, provided the other party to the transaction

(I) Had extended credit to the partnership prior to dissolution and had no knowledge or notice of the dissolution; or

(II) Though he had not so extended credit, had nevertheless known of the partnership prior to dissolution, and, having no knowledge or notice of dissolution, the fact of dissolution had not been advertised in a newspaper of general circulation in the place (or in each place if more than one) at which the partnership business was regularly carried on.

(2) The liability of a partner under Paragraph (1b) shall be satisfied out of partnership assets alone when such partner had been prior to dissolution

(a) Unknown as a partner to the person with whom the contract is made; and

(b) So far unknown and inactive in partnership affairs that the business reputation of the partnership could not be said to have been in any degree due to his connection with it.

(3) The partnership is in no case bound by any act of a partner after dissolution

(a) Where the partnership is dissolved because it is unlawful to carry on the business, unless the act is appropriate for winding up partnership affairs; or

(b) Where the partner has become bankrupt; or

(c) Where the partner has no authority to wind up partnership affairs; except by a transaction with one who

(I) Had extended credit to the partnership prior to dissolution and had no knowledge or notice of his want of authority; or

(II) Had not extended credit to the partnership prior to dissolution, and, having no knowledge or notice of his want of authority, the fact of his want of authority has not been advertised in the manner provided for advertising the fact of dissolution in Paragraph (1bII).

(4) Nothing in this section shall affect the liability under Section 16 of any person who after dissolution represents himself or consents to another representing him as a partner in a partnership engaged in carrying on a business.

§ 36. Effect of Dissolution on Partner's Existing Liability.

(1) The dissolution of the partnership does not of itself discharge the existing liability of any partner.

(2) A partner is discharged from any existing liability upon dissolution of the partnership by an agreement to that effect between himself, the partnership creditor and the person or partnership continuing the business; and such agreement may be inferred from the course of dealing between the creditor having knowledge of the dissolution and the person or partnership continuing the business.

(3) Where a person agrees to assume the existing obligations of a dissolved partnership, the partners whose obligations have been assumed shall be discharged from any liability to any creditor of the partnership who, knowing of the agreement, consents to a material alteration in the nature or time of payment of such obligations.

(4) The individual property of a deceased partner shall be liable for all obligations of the partnership incurred while he was a partner but subject to the prior payment of his separate debts.

§ 37. Right to Wind Up.
Unless otherwise agreed the partners who have not wrongfully dissolved the partnership or the legal representative of the last surviving partner, not bankrupt, has the right to wind up the partnership affairs; provided, however, that any partner, his legal representative or assignee, upon cause shown, may obtain winding up by the court.

§ 38. Rights of Partners to Application of Partnership Property.

(1) When dissolution is caused in any way, except in contravention of the partnership agreement, each partner, as against his co-partners and all persons claiming through them in respect of their interests in the partnership, unless otherwise agreed, may have the partnership property applied to discharge its liabilities, and the surplus applied to pay in cash the net amount owing to the respective partners. But if dissolution is caused by expulsion of a partner, bona fide under the partnership agreement and if the expelled partner is discharged from all partnership liabilities, either by payment or agreement under section 36(2), he shall receive in cash only the net amount due him from the partnership.

(2) When dissolution is caused in contravention of the partnership agreement the rights of the partners shall be as follows:

(a) Each partner who has not caused dissolution wrongfully shall have,

(I) All the rights specified in paragraph (1) of this section, and

(II) The right, as against each partner who has caused the dissolution wrongfully, to damages for breach of the agreement.

(b) The partners who have not caused the dissolution wrongfully, if they all desire to continue the business in the same name, either by themselves or jointly with others, may do so, during the agreed term for the partnership and for that purpose may possess the partnership property, provided they secure the payment by bond approved by the court, or pay to any partner who has caused the dissolution wrongfully, the value of his interest in the partnership at the dissolution, less any damages recoverable under clause (2aII) of this section, and in like manner indemnify him against all present or future partnership liabilities.

(c) A partner who has caused the dissolution wrongfully shall have:

(I) If the business is not continued under the provisions of paragraph (2b) all the rights of a partner under paragraph (1), subject to clause (2aII), of this section,

(II) If the business is continued under paragraph (2b) of this section the right as against his co-partners and all claiming through them in respect of their interests in the partnership, to have the value of his interest in the partnership, less any damages caused to his co-partners by the dissolution, ascertained and paid to him in cash, or the payment secured by bond approved by the court, and to be released from all existing liabilities of the partnership; but in ascertaining the value of the partner's interest the value of the good-will of the business shall not be considered.

§ 39. Rights Where Partnership Is Dissolved for Fraud or Misrepresentation.
Where a partnership contract is rescinded on the ground of the fraud or misrepresentation of one of the parties thereto, the party entitled to rescind is, without prejudice to any other right, entitled,

(a) To a lien on, or a right of retention of, the surplus of the partnership property after satisfying the partnership liabilities to third persons for any sum of money paid by him for the purchase of an interest in the partnership and for any capital or advances contributed by him; and

(b) To stand, after all liabilities to third persons have been satisfied, in the place of the creditors of the partnership for any payments made by him in respect of the partnership liabilities; and

(c) To be indemnified by the person guilty of the fraud or making the representation against all debts and liabilities of the partnership.

§ 40. Rules for Distribution.
In settling accounts between the partners after dissolution, the following rules shall be observed, subject to any agreement to the contrary:

(a) The assets of the partnership are:

(I) The partnership property,

(II) The contributions of the partners necessary for the payment of all the liabilities specified in clause (b) of this paragraph.

(b) The liabilities of the partnership shall rank in order of payment, as follows:

(I) Those owing to creditors other than partners,

(II) Those owing to partners other than for capital and profits,

(III) Those owing to partners in respect of capital,

(IV) Those owing to partners in respect of profits.

(c) The assets shall be applied in order of their declaration in clause (a) of this paragraph to the satisfaction of the liabilities.

(d) The partners shall contribute, as provided by section 18 (a) the amount necessary to satisfy the liabilities; but if any, but not all, of the partners are insolvent, or, not being subject to process, refuse to contribute, the other partners shall contribute their share of the liabilities, and, in the relative proportions in which they share the profits, the additional amount necessary to pay the liabilities.

(e) An assignee for the benefit of creditors or any person appointed by the court shall have the right to enforce the contributions specified in clause (d) of this paragraph.

(f) Any partner or his legal representative shall have the right to enforce the contributions specified in clause (d) of this paragraph, to the extent of the amount which he has paid in excess of his share of the liability.

(g) The individual property of a deceased partner shall be liable for the contributions specified in clause (d) of this paragraph.

(h) When partnership property and the individual properties of the partners are in possession of a court for distribution, partnership creditors shall have priority on partnership property and separate creditors on individual property, saving the rights of lien or secured creditors as heretofore.

(i) Where a partner has become bankrupt or his estate is insolvent the claims against his separate property shall rank in the following order:

(I) Those owing to separate creditors,

(II) Those owing to partnership creditors,

(III) Those owing to partners by way of contribution.

§ 41. Liability of Persons Continuing the Business in Certain Cases.

(1) When any new partner is admitted into an existing partnership, or when any partner retires and assigns (or the representative of the deceased partner assigns) his rights in partnership property to two or more of the partners, or to one or more of the partners and one or more third persons, if the business is continued without liquidation of the partnership affairs, creditors of the first or dissolved partnerships are also creditors of the partnership so continuing the business.

(2) When all but one partner retire and assign (or the representative of a deceased partner assigns) their rights in partnership property to the remaining partner, who continues the business without liquidation of partnership affairs, either alone or with others, creditors of the dissolved partnership are also creditors of the person or partnership so continuing the business.

(3) When any partner retires or dies and the business of the dissolved partnership is continued as set forth in paragraphs (1) and (2) of this section, with the consent of the retired partners or the representative of the deceased partner, but without any assignment of his right in partnership property, rights of creditors of the dissolved partnership and of the creditors of the person or partnership continuing the business shall be as if such assignment had been made.

(4) When all the partners or their representatives assign their rights in partnership property to one or more third persons who promise to pay the debts and who continue the business of the dissolved partnership, creditors of the dissolved partnership are also creditors of the person or partnership continuing the business.

(5) When any partner wrongfully causes a dissolution and the remaining partners continue the business under the provisions of section 38(2b), either alone or with others, and without liquidation of the partnership affairs, creditors of the dissolved partnership are also creditors of the person or partnership continuing the business.

(6) When a partner is expelled and the remaining partners continue the business either alone or with others, without liquidation of the partnership affairs, creditors of the dissolved partnership are also creditors of the person or partnership continuing the business.

(7) The liability of a third person becoming a partner in the partnership continuing the business, under this section, to the creditors of the dissolved partnership shall be satisfied out of partnership property only.

(8) When the business of a partnership after dissolution is continued under any conditions set forth in this section the creditors of the dissolved partnership, as against the separate creditors of the retiring or deceased partner or the representative of the deceased partner, have a prior right to any claim of the retired partner or the representative of the deceased partner against the person or partnership continuing the business, on account of the retired or deceased partner's interest in the dissolved partnership or on account of any consideration promised for such interest or for his right in partnership property.

(9) Nothing in this section shall be held to modify any right of creditors to set aside any assignment on the ground of fraud.

(10) The use by the person or partnership continuing the business of the partnership name, or the name of a deceased partner as part thereof, shall not of itself make the individual property of the deceased partner liable for any debts contracted by such person or partnership.

§ 42. Rights of Retiring or Estate of Deceased Partner When the Business Is Continued.

When any partner retires or dies, and the business is continued under any of the conditions set forth in section 41(1, 2, 3, 5, 6), or section 38(2b) without any settlement of accounts as between him or his estate and the person or partnership continuing the business, unless otherwise agreed, he or his legal representative as against such persons or partnership may have the value of his interest at the date of dissolution ascertained, and shall receive as an ordinary creditor an amount equal to the value of his interest in the dissolved partnership with interest, or, at his option or at the option of his legal representative, in lieu of interest, the profits attributable to the use of his right in the property of the dissolved partnership, provided that the creditors of the dissolved partnership as against the separate creditors, or the representative of the retired or deceased partner, shall have priority on any claim arising under this section, as provided by section 41(8) of this act.

§ 43. Accrual of Actions.

The right to an account of his interest shall accrue to any partner, or his legal representative, as against the winding up partners or the surviving partners or the person or partnership continuing the business, at the date of dissolution, in the absence of any agreement to the contrary.

Part 7. Miscellaneous Provisions

§ 44. When Act Takes Effect.

This act shall take effect on the . . . . day of . . . . one thousand nine hundred and . . . .

§ 45. Legislation Repealed.

All acts or parts of acts inconsistent with this act are hereby repealed.

APPENDIX G

Revised Uniform Limited Partnership Act (1976), with 1985 Amendments *

ARTICLE 1. GENERAL PROVISIONS

§ 101. Definitions

As used in this [Act], unless the context otherwise requires:

(1) "Certificate of limited partnership" means the certificate referred to in Section 201, and the certificate as amended or restated.

(2) "Contribution" means any cash, property, services rendered, or a promissory note or other binding obligation to contribute cash or property or to perform services, which a partner contributes to a limited partnership in his capacity as a partner.

(3) "Event of withdrawal of a general partner" means an event that causes a person to cease to be a general partner as provided in Section 402.

(4) "Foreign limited partnership" means a partnership formed under the laws of any state other than this State and having as partners one or more general partners and one or more limited partners.

(5) "General partner" means a person who has been admitted to a limited partnership as a general partner in accordance with the partnership agreement and named in the certificate of limited partnership as a general partner.

(6) "Limited partner" means a person who has been admitted to a limited partnership as a limited partner in accordance with the partnership agreement.

(7) "Limited partnership" and "domestic limited partnership" means a partnership formed by two or more persons under the laws of this State and having one or more general partners and one or more limited partners.

(8) "Partner" means a limited or general partner.

(9) "Partnership agreement" means any valid agreement, written or oral, of the partners as to the affairs of a limited partnership and the conduct of its business.

(10) "Partnership interest" means a partner's share of the profits and losses of a limited partnership and the right to receive distribution of partnership assets.

(11) "Person" means a natural person, partnership, limited partnership (domestic or foreign), trust, estate, association, or corporation.

(12) "State" means a state, territory, or possession of the United States, the District of Columbia, or the Commonwealth of Puerto Rico.

*Source: The text of this act was obtained from the National Conference of Commissioners on Uniform State Laws, and is reprinted with the Commissioner's consent.

§ 102. Name

The name of each limited partnership as set forth in its certificate of limited partnership:

(1) shall contain without abbreviation the words "limited partnership";

(2) may not contain the name of a limited partner unless (i) it is also the name of a general partner or the corporate name of a corporate general partner, or (ii) the business of the limited partnership had been carried on under that name before the admission of that limited partner;

(3) may not be the same as, or deceptively similar to, the name of any corporation or limited partnership organized under the laws of this State or licensed or registered as a foreign corporation or limited partnership in this State; and

(4) may not contain the following words [here insert prohibited words].

§ 103. Reservation of Name

(a) The exclusive right to the use of a name may be reserved by:

(1) any person intending to organize a limited partnership under this [Act] and to adopt that name;

(2) any domestic limited partnership or any foreign limited partnership registered in this State which, in either case, intends to adopt that name;

(3) any foreign limited partnership intending to register in this State and adopt that name; and

(4) any person intending to organize a foreign limited partnership and intending to have it register in this State and adopt that name.

(b) The reservation shall be made by filing with the Secretary of State an application, executed by the applicant, to reserve a specified name. If the Secretary of State finds that the name is available for use by a domestic or foreign limited partnership, he [or she] shall reserve the name for the exclusive use of the applicant for a period of 120 days. Once having so reserved a name, the same applicant may not again reserve the same name until more than 60 days after the expiration of the last 120-day period of which that applicant reserved that name. The right to the exclusive use of a reserved name may be transferred to any other person by filing in the office of the Secretary of State a notice of the transfer, executed by the applicant for whom the name was reserved and specifying the name and address of the transferee.

§ 104. Specified Office and Agent

Each limited partnership shall continuously maintain in this State:

(1) an office, which may but need not be a place of its business in this State, at which shall be kept the records required by Section 105 to be maintained; and

(2) an agent for service of process on the limited partnership, which agent must be an individual resident of this State, a domestic corporation, or a foreign corporation authorized to do business in this State.

§ 105. Records to be Kept

(a) Each limited partnership shall keep at the office referred to in Section 104(1) the following:

(1) a current list of the full name and last known business address of each partner, separately identifying the general partners (in alphabetical order) and the limited partners (in alphabetical order);

(2) a copy of the certificate of limited partnership and all certificates of amendment thereto, together with executed copies of any powers of attorney pursuant to which any certificate has been executed;

(3) copies of the limited partnership's federal, state and local income tax returns and reports, if any, for the three most recent years;

(4) copies of any then effective written partnership agreements and

of any financial statements of the limited partnership for the three most recent years; and

(5) unless contained in a written partnership agreement, a writing setting out:

(i) the amount of cash and a description and statement of the agreed value of the other property or services contributed by each partner and which each partner has agreed to contribute;

(ii) the times at which or events on the happening of which any additional contributions agreed to be made by each partner are to be made;

(iii) any right of a partner to receive, or of a general partner to make, distributions to a partner which include a return of all or any part of the partner's contribution; and

(iv) any events upon the happening of which the limited partnership is to be dissolved and its affairs wound up.

(b) Records kept under this section are subject to inspection and copying at the reasonable request and at the expense of any partner during ordinary business hours.

§ 106. Nature of Business

A limited partnership may carry on any business that a partnership without limited partners may carry on except [here designate prohibited activities].

§ 107. Business Transactions of Partner with Partnership

Except as provided in the partnership agreement, a partner may lend money to and transact other business with the limited partnership and, subject to other applicable law, has the same rights and obligations with respect thereto as a person who is not a partner.

ARTICLE 2. FORMATION; CERTIFICATE OF LIMITED PARTNERSHIP

§ 201. Certificate of Limited Partnership

(a) In order to form a limited partnership, a certificate of limited partnership must be executed and filed in the office of the Secretary of State. The certificate shall set forth:

(1) the name of the limited partnership;

(2) the address of the office and the name and address of the agent for service of process required to be maintained by Section 104;

(3) the name and the business address of each general partner;

(4) the latest date upon which the limited partnership is to dissolve; and

(5) any other matters the general partners determine to include therein.

(b) A limited partnership is formed at the time of the filing of the certificate of limited partnership in the office of the Secretary of State or at any later time specified in the certificate of limited partnership if, in either case, there has been substantial compliance with the requirements of this section.

§ 202. Amendment to Certificate

(a) A certificate of limited partnership is amended by filing a certificate of amendment thereto in the office of the Secretary of State. The certificate shall set forth:

(1) the name of the limited partnership;

(2) the date of filing the certificate; and

(3) the amendment to the certificate.

(b) Within 30 days after the happening of any of the following events, an amendment to a certificate of limited partnership reflecting the occurrence of the event or events shall be filed:

(1) the admission of a new general partner;

(2) the withdrawal of a general partner; or

(3) the continuation of the business under Section 801 after an event of withdrawal of a general partner.

(c) A general partner who becomes aware that any statement in a certificate of limited partnership was false when made or that any arrangements or other facts described have changed, making the certificate inaccurate in any respect, shall promptly amend the certificate.

(d) A certificate of limited partnership may be amended at any time for any other proper purpose the general partners determine.

(e) No person has any liability became an amendment to a certificate of limited partnership has not been filed to reflect the occurrence of any event referred to in subsection (b) of this section if the amendment is filed within the 30-day period specified in subsection (b).

(f) A restated certificate of limited partnership may be executed and filed in the same manner as a certificate of amendment.

§ 203. Cancellation of Certificate

A certificate of limited partnership shall be cancelled upon the dissolution and the commencement of winding up of the partnership or at any other time there are no limited partners. A certificate of cancellation shall be filed in the office of the Secretary of State and set forth:

(1) the name of the limited partnership;

(2) the date of filing of its certificate of limited partnership;

(3) the reason for filing the certificate of cancellation;

(4) the effective date (which shall be a date certain) of cancellation if it is not to be effective upon the filing of the certificate; and

(5) any other information the general partners filing the certificate determine.

§ 204. Execution of Certificates

(a) Each certificate required by this Article to be filed in the office of the Secretary of State shall be executed in the following manner:

(1) an original certificate of limited partnership must be signed by all general partners;

(2) a certificate of amendment must be signed by at least one general partner and by each other general partner designated in the certificate as a new general partner; and

(3) a certificate of cancellation must be signed by all general partners.

(b) Any person may sign a certificate by an attorney-in-fact, but a power of attorney to sign a certificate relating to the admission of a general partner must specifically describe the admission.

(c) The execution of a certificate by a general partner constitutes an affirmation under the penalties of perjury that the facts stated therein are true.

§ 205. Execution by Judicial Act

If a person required by Section 204 to execute any certificate fails or refuses to do so, any other person who is adversely affected by the failure or refusal may petition the [designate the appropriate court] to direct the execution of the certificate. If the court finds that it is proper for the certificate to be executed and that any person so designated has failed or refused to execute the certificate, it shall order the Secretary of State to record an appropriate certificate.

§ 206. Filing in Office of Secretary of State

(a) Two signed copies of the certificate of limited partnership and of any certificates of amendment or cancellation (or of any judicial decree of amendment or cancellation) shall be delivered to the Secretary of State. A person who executes a certificate as an agent or fiduciary need not exhibit evidence of his [or her] authority as a prerequisite to filing. Unless the Secretary of State finds that any certificate does not conform to law, upon receipt of all filing fees required by law he [or she] shall:

(1) endorse on each duplicate original the word "Filed" and the day, month and year of the filing thereof;

(2) file one duplicate original in his [or her] office; and

(3) return the other duplicate original to the person who filed it or his [or her] representative.

(b) Upon the filing of a certificate of amendment (or judicial decree of amendment) in the office of the Secretary of State, the certificate of limited partnership shall be amended as set forth therein, and upon the effective date of a certificate of cancellation (or a judicial decree thereof), the certificate of limited partnership is cancelled.

§ 207. Liability for False Statement in Certificate

If any certificate of limited partnership or certificate of amendment or cancellation contains a false statement, one who suffers loss by reliance on the statement may recover damages for the loss from:

(1) any person who executes the certificate, or causes another to execute it on his behalf, and knew, and any general partner who knew or should have known, the statement to be false at the time the certificate was executed; and

(2) any general partner who thereafter knows or should have known that any arrangement or other fact described in the certificate has changed, making the statement inaccurate in any respect within a sufficient time before the statement was relied upon reasonably to have enabled that general partner to cancel or amend the certificate, or to file a petition for its cancellation or amendment under Section 205.

§ 208. Scope of Notice

The fact that a certificate of limited partnership is on file in the office of the Secretary of State is notice that the partnership is a limited partnership and the persons designated therein as general partners are general partners, but it is not notice of any other fact.

§ 209. Delivery of Certificates to Limited Partners

Upon the return by the Secretary of State pursuant to Section 206 of a certificate marked "Filed," the general partners shall promptly deliver or mail a copy of the certificate of limited partnership and each certificate of amendment or cancellation to each limited partner unless the partnership agreement provides otherwise.

ARTICLE 3. LIMITED PARTNERS

§ 301. Admission of Limited Partners

(a) A person becomes a limited partner:

(1) at the time the limited partnership is formed; or

(2) at any later time specified in the records of the limited partnership for becoming a limited partner.

(b) After the filing of a limited partnership's original certificate of limited partnership, a person may be admitted as an additional limited partner:

(1) in the case of a person acquiring a partnership interest directly from the limited partnership, upon compliance with the partnership agreement or, if the partnership agreement does not so provide, upon the written consent of all partners; and

(2) in the case of an assignee of a partnership interest of a partner who has the power, as provided in Section 704, to grant the assignee

the right to become a limited partner, upon the exercise of that power and compliance with any conditions limiting the grant or exercise of the power.

§ 302. Voting

Subject to Section 303, the partnership agreement may grant to all or a specified group of the limited partners the right to vote (on a per capita or other basis) upon any matter.

§ 303. Liability to Third Parties

(a) Except as provided in subsection (d), a limited partner is not liable for the obligations of a limited partnership unless he [or she] is also a general partner or, in addition to the exercise of his [or her] rights and powers as a limited partner, he [or she] participates in the control of the business. However, if the limited partner participates in the control of the business, he [or she] is liable only to persons who transact business with the limited partnership reasonably believing, based upon the limited partner's conduct, that the limited partner is a general partner.

(b) A limited partner does not participate in the control of the business within the meaning of subsection (a) solely by doing one or more of the following:

(1) being a contractor for or an agent or employee of the limited partnership or of a general partner or being an officer, director, or shareholder of a general partner that is a corporation;

(2) consulting with and advising a general partner with respect to the business of the limited partnership;

(3) acting as surety for the limited partnership or guaranteeing or assuming one or more specific obligations of the limited partnership;

(4) taking any action required or permitted by law to bring or pursue a derivative action in the right of the limited partnership;

(5) requesting or attending a meeting of partners;

(6) proposing, approving, or disapproving, by voting or otherwise, one or more of the following matters:

(i) the dissolution and winding up of the limited partnership;

(ii) the sale, exchange, lease, mortgage, pledge, or other transfer of all or substantially all of the assets of the limited partnership;

(iii) the incurrence of indebtedness by the limited partnership other than in the ordinary course of its business;

(iv) a change in the nature of the business;

(v) the admission or removal of a general partner;

(vi) the admission or removal of a limited partner;

(vii) a transaction involving an actual or potential conflict of interest between a general partner and the limited partnership or the limited partners;

(viii) an amendment to the partnership agreement or certificate of limited partnership; or

(ix) matters related to the business of the limited partnership not otherwise enumerated in this subsection (b), which the partnership agreement states in writing may be subject to the approval or disapproval of limited partners;

(7) winding up the limited partnership pursuant to Section 803; or

(8) exercising any right or power permitted to limited partners under this [Act] and not specifically enumerated in this subsection (b).

(c) The enumeration in subsection (b) does not mean that the possession or exercise of any other powers by a limited partner constitutes participation by him [or her] in the business of the limited partnership.

(d) A limited partner who knowingly permits his [or her] name to be used in the name of the limited partnership, except under circumstances permitted by Section 102(2), is liable to creditors who extend credit to the limited partnership without actual knowledge that the limited partner is not a general partner.

§ 304. Person Erroneously Believing Himself [or Herself] Limited Partner

(a) Except as provided in subsection (b), a person who makes a contribution to a business enterprise and erroneously but in good faith believes that he [or she] has become a limited partner in the enterprise is not a general partner in the enterprise and is not bound by its obligations by reason of making the contribution, receiving distributions from the enterprise, or exercising any rights of a limited partner, if, on ascertaining the mistake, he [or she]:

(1) causes an appropriate certificate of limited partnership or a certificate of amendment to be executed and filed; or

(2) withdraws from future equity participation in the enterprise by executing and filing in the office of the Secretary of State a certificate declaring withdrawal under this section.

(b) A person who makes a contribution of the kind described in subsection (a) is liable as a general partner to any third party who transacts business with the enterprise (i) before the person withdraws and an appropriate certificate is filed to show withdrawal, or (ii) before an appropriate certificate is filed to show that he [or she] is not a general partner, but in either case only if the third party actually believed in good faith that the person was a general partner at the time of the transaction.

§ 305. Information

Each limited partner has the right to:

(1) inspect and copy any of the partnership records required to be maintained by Section 105; and

(2) obtain from the general partners from time to time upon reasonable demand (i) true and full information regarding the state of the business and financial condition of the limited partnership, (ii) promptly after becoming available, a copy of the limited partnership's federal, state and local income tax returns for each year, and (iii) other information regarding the affairs of the limited partnership as is just and reasonable.

ARTICLE 4. GENERAL PARTNERS

§ 401. Admission of Additional General Partners

After the filing of a limited partnership's original certificate of limited partnership, additional general partners may be admitted as provided in writing in the partnership agreement or, if the partnership agreement does not provide in writing for the admission of additional general partners, with the written consent of all partners.

§ 402. Events of Withdrawal

Except as approved by the specific written consent of all partners at the time, a person ceases to be a general partner of a limited partnership upon the happening of any of the following events:

(1) the general partner withdraws from the limited partnership as provided in Section 602;

(2) the general partner ceases to be a member of the limited partnership as provided in Section 702;

(3) the general partner is removed as a general partner in accordance with the partnership agreement;

(4) unless otherwise provided in writing in the partnership agreement, the general partner: (i) makes an assignment for the benefit of creditors; (ii) files a voluntary petition in bankruptcy; (iii) is adjudicated a bankrupt or insolvent; (iv) files a petition or answer seeking for himself [or herself] any reorganization, arrangement, composition, readjust-

ment, liquidation, dissolution or similar relief under any statute, law, or regulation; (v) files an answer or other pleading admitting or failing to contest the material allegations of a petition filed against him [or her] in any proceeding of this nature; or (vi) seeks, consents to, or acquiesces in the appointment of a trustee, receiver, or liquidator of the general partner or of all or any substantial part of his [or her] properties;

(5) unless otherwise provided in writing in the partnership agreement, [120] days after the commencement of any proceeding against the general partner seeking reorganization, arrangement, composition, readjustment, liquidation, dissolution or similar relief under any statute, law, or regulation, the proceeding has not been dismissed, or if within [90] days after the appointment without his [or her] consent or acquiescence of a trustee, receiver, or liquidator of the general partner or of all or any substantial part of his [or her] properties, the appointment is not vacated or stayed or within [90] days after the expiration of any such stay, the appointment is not vacated;

(6) in the case of a general partner who is a natural person.

(i) his [or her] death; or

(ii) the entry of an order by a court of competent jurisdiction adjudicating him [or her] incompetent to manage his [or her] person or his [or her] estate;

(7) in the case of a general partner who is acting as a general partner by virtue of being a trustee of a trust, the termination of the trust (but not merely the substitution of a new trustee);

(8) in the case of a general partner that is a separate partnership, the dissolution and commencement of winding up the separate partnership;

(9) in the case of a general partner that is a corporation, the filing of a certificate of dissolution, or its equivalent, for the corporation or the revocation of its charter; or

(10) in the case of an estate, the distribution by the fiduciary of the estate's entire interest in the partnership.

§ 403. General Powers and Liabilities

(a) Except as provided in this [Act] or in the partnership agreement, a general partner of a limited partnership has the rights and powers and is subject to the restrictions of a partner in a partnership without limited partners.

(b) Except as provided in this [Act], a general partner of a limited partnership has the liabilities of a partner in a partnership without limited partners to persons other than the partnership and the other partners. Except as provided in this [Act] or in the partnership agreement, a general partner of a limited partnership has the liabilities of a partner in a partnership without limited partners to the partnership and to the other partners.

§ 404. Contributions by General Partner

A general partner of a limited partnership may make contributions to the partnership and share in the profits and losses of, and in distributions from, the limited partnership as a general partner. A general partner also may make contributions to and share in profits, losses, and distributions as a limited partner. A person who is both a general partner and a limited partner has the rights and powers, and is subject to the restrictions and liabilities, of a general partner and, except as provided in the partnership agreement, also has the powers, and is subject to the restrictions, of a limited partner to the extent of his [or her] participation in the partnership as a limited partner.

§ 405. Voting

The partnership agreement may grant to all or certain identified general partners the right to vote (on a per capita or any other basis), separately or with all or any class of the limited partners, on any matter.

ARTICLE 5. FINANCE

§ 501. Form of Contribution

The contribution of a partner may be in cash, property, or services rendered, or a promissory note or other obligation to contribute cash or property or to perform services.

§ 502. Liability for Contribution

(a) A promise by a limited partner to contribute to the limited partnership is not enforceable unless set out in a writing signed by the limited partner.

(b) Except as provided in the partnership agreement, a partner is obligated to the limited partnership to perform any enforceable promise to contribute cash or property or to perform services, even if he [or she] is unable to perform because of death, disability, or any other reason. If a partner does not make the required contribution of property or services, he [or she] is obligated at the option of the limited partnership to contribute cash equal to that portion of the value, as stated in the partnership records required to be kept pursuant to Section 105, of the stated contribution which has not been made.

(c) Unless otherwise provided in the partnership agreement, the obligation of a partner to make a contribution or return money or other property paid or distributed in violation of this [Act] may be compromised only by consent of all partners. Notwithstanding the compromise, a creditor of a limited partnership who extends credit or otherwise acts in reliance on that obligation after the partner signs a writing which reflects the obligation and before the amendment or cancellation thereof to reflect the compromise may endorce the original obligation.

§ 503. Sharing of Profits and Losses

The profits and losses of a limited partnership shall be allocated among the partners, and among classes of partners, in the manner provided in writing in the partnership agreement. If the partnership agreement does not so provide in writing, profits and losses shall be allocated on the basis of the value, as stated in the partnership records required to be kept pursuant to Section 105, of the contributions made by each partner to the extent they have been received by the partnership and have not been returned.

§ 504. Sharing of Distributions

Distributions of cash or other assets of a limited partnership shall be allocated among the partners and among classes of partners in the manner provided in writing in the partnership agreement. If the partnership agreement does not so provide in writing, distributions shall be made on the basis of the value, as stated in the partnership records required to be kept pursuant to Section 105, of the contributions made by each partner to the extent that they have been received by the partnership and have not been returned.

ARTICLE 6. DISTRIBUTIONS AND WITHDRAWAL

§ 601. Interim Distributions

Except as provided in this Article, a partner is entitled to receive distributions from a limited partnership before his [or her] withdrawal from the limited partnership and before the dissolution and winding up thereof to the extent and at the times or upon the happening of the events specified in the partnership agreement.

§ 602. Withdrawal of General Partner

A general partner may withdraw from a limited partnership at any time by giving written notice to the other partners, but if the withdrawal violates the partnership agreement, the limited partnership may recover from the withdrawing general partner damages for breach of the partnership agreement and offset the damages against the amount otherwise distributable to him [or her].

§ 603. Withdrawal of Limited Partner

A limited partner may withdraw from a limited partnership at the time or upon the happening of events specified in writing in the partnership agreement. If the agreement does not specify in writing the time or the events upon the happening of which a limited partner may withdraw or a definite time for the dissolution and winding up of the limited partnership, a limited partner may withdraw upon not less than six months' prior written notice to each general partner at his [or her] address on the books of the limited partnership at its office in this State.

§ 604. Distribution upon Withdrawal

Except as provided in this Article, upon withdrawal any withdrawing partner is entitled to receive any distribution to which he [or she] is entitled under the partnership agreement and, if not otherwise provided in the agreement, he [or she] is entitled to receive, within a reasonable time after withdrawal, the fair value of his [or her] interest in the limited partnership as of the date of withdrawal based upon his [or her] right to share in distributions from the limited partnership.

§ 605. Distribution in Kind

Except as provided in writing in the partnership agreement, a partner, regardless of the nature of his [or her] contribution, has no right to demand and receive any distribution from a limited partnership in any form other than cash. Except as provided in writing in the partnership agreement, a partner may not be compelled to accept a distribution of any asset in kind from a limited partnership to the extent that the percentage of the asset distributed to him [or her] exceeds a percentage of that asset which is equal to the percentage in which he [or she] shares in distributions from the limited partnership.

§ 606. Right to Distribution

At the time a partner becomes entitled to receive a distribution, he [or she] has the status of, and is entitled to all remedies available to, a creditor of the limited partnership with respect to the distribution.

§ 607. Limitations on Distribution

A partner may not receive a distribution from a limited partnership to the extent that, after giving effect to the distribution, all liabilities of the limited partnership, other than liabilities to partners on account of their partnership interests, exceed the fair value of the partnership assets.

§ 608. Liability upon Return of Contribution

(a) If a partner has received the return of any part of his [or her] contribution without violation of the partnership agreement or this [Act], he [or she] is liable to the limited partnership for a period of one year thereafter for the amount of the returned contribution, but only to the extent necessary to discharge the limited partnership's liabilities to creditors who extended credit to the limited partnership during the period the contribution was held by the partnership.

(b) If a partner has received the return of any part of his [or her] contribution in violation of the partnership agreement or this [Act], he [or she] is liable to the limited partnership for a period of six years thereafter for the amount of the contribution wrongfully returned.

(c) A partner receives a return of his [or her] contribution to the extent that a distribution to him [or her] reduces his [or her] share of the fair value of the net assets of the limited partnership below the value, as set forth in the partnership records required to be kept pursuant to Section 105, of his contribution which has not been distributed to him [or her].

ARTICLE 7. ASSIGNMENT OF PARTNERSHIP INTERESTS

§ 701. Nature of Partnership Interest

A partnership interest is personal property.

§ 702. Assignment of Partnership Interest

Except as provided in the partnership agreement, a partnership interest is assignable in whole or in part. An assignment of a partnership interest does not dissolve a limited partnership or entitle the assignee to become or to exercise any rights of a partner. An assignment entitles the assignee to receive, to the extent assigned, only the distribution to which the assignor would be entitled. Except as provided in the partnership agreement, a partner ceases to be a partner upon assignment of all his [or her] partnership interest.

§ 703. Rights of Creditor

On application to a court of competent jurisdiction by any judgment creditor of a partner, the court may charge the partnership interest of the partner with payment of the unsatisfied amount of the judgment with interest. To the extent so charged, the judgment creditor has only the rights of an assignee of the partnership interest. This [Act] does not deprive any partner of the benefit of any exemption laws applicable to his [or her] partnership interest.

§ 704. Right of Assignee to Become Limited Partner

(a) An assignee of a partnership interest, including an assignee of a general partner, may become a limited partner if and to the extent that (i) the assignor gives the assignee that right in accordance with authority described in the partnership agreement, or (ii) all other partners consent.

(b) An assignee who has become a limited partner has, to the extent assigned, the rights and powers, and is subject to the restrictions and liabilities, of a limited partner under the partnership agreement and this [Act]. An assignee who becomes a limited partner also is liable for the obligations of his [or her] assignor to make and return contributions as provided in Articles 5 and 6. However, the assignee is not obligated for liabilities unknown to the assignee at the time he [or she] became a limited partner.

(c) If an assignee of a partnership interest becomes a limited partner, the assignor is not released from his [or her] liability to the limited partnership under Sections 207 and 502.

§ 705. Power of Estate of Deceased or Incompetent Partner

If a partner who is an individual dies or a court of competent jurisdiction adjudges him [or her] to be incompetent to manage his [or her] person or his [or her] property, the partner's executor, administrator, guardian, conservator, or other legal representative may exercise all the partner's rights for the purpose of settling his [or her] estate or administering his [or her] property, including any power the partner had to give an assignee the right to become a limited partner. If a partner is a corporation, trust, or other entity and is dissolved or terminated, the powers of that partner may be exercised by its legal representative or successor.

ARTICLE 8. DISSOLUTION

§ 801. Nonjudicial Dissolution

A limited partnership is dissolved and its affairs shall be wound up upon the happening of the first to occur of the following:

(1) at the time specified in the certificate of limited partnership;

(2) upon the happening of events specified in writing in the partnership agreement;

(3) written consent of all partners;

(4) an event of withdrawal of a general partner unless at the time there is at least one other general partner and the written provisions of the partnership agreement permit the business of the limited partnership to be carried on by the remaining general partner and that partner does so, but the limited partnership is not dissolved and is not required to be wound up by reason of any event of withdrawal if, within 90 days after the withdrawal, all partners agree in writing to continue the business of the limited partnership and to the appointment of one or more additional general partners if necessary or desired; or

(5) entry of a decree of judicial dissolution under Section 802.

§ 802. Judicial Dissolution

On application by or for a partner the [designate the appropriate court] court may decree dissolution of a limited partnership whenever it is not reasonably practicable to carry on the business in conformity with the partnership agreement.

§ 803. Winding Up

Except as provided in the partnership agreement, the general partners who have not wrongfully dissolved a limited partnership or, if none, the limited partners, may wind up the limited partnership's affairs; but the [designate the appropriate court] court may wind up the limited partnership's affairs upon application of any partner, his [or her] legal representative, or assignee.

§ 804. Distribution of Assets

Upon the winding up of a limited partnership, the assets shall be distributed as follows:

(1) to creditors, including partners who are creditors, to the extent permitted by law, in satisfaction of liabilities of the limited partnership other than liabilities for distribution to partners under Section 601 or 604;

(2) except as provided in the partnership agreement, to partners and former partners in satisfaction of liabilities for distributions under Section 601 or 604; and

(3) except as provided in the partnership agreement, to partners first for the return of their contributions and secondly respecting their partnership interests, in the proportions in which the partners share in distributions.

ARTICLE 9. FOREIGN LIMITED PARTNERSHIPS

§ 901. Law Governing

Subject to the Constitution of this State, (i) the laws of the state under which a foreign limited partnership is organized govern its organization and internal affairs and the liability of its limited partners, and (ii) a foreign limited partnership may not be denied registration by reason of any difference between those laws and the laws of this State.

§ 902. Registration

Before transacting business in this State, a foreign limited partnership shall register with the Secretary of State. In order to register, a foreign limited partnership shall submit to the Secretary of State, in duplicate, an application for registration as a foreign limited partnership, signed and sworn to by a general partner and setting forth:

(1) the name of the foreign limited partnership and, if different, the name under which it proposes to register and transact business in this State;

(2) the State and date of its formation;

(3) the name and address of any agent for service of process on the foreign limited partnership whom the foreign limited partnership elects to appoint; the agent must be an individual resident of this State, a

domestic corporation, or a foreign corporation having a place of business in, and authorized to do business in, this State;

(4) a statement that the Secretary of State is appointed the agent of the foreign limited partnership for service of process if no agent has been appointed under paragraph (3) or, if appointed, the agent's authority has been revoked or if the agent cannot be found or served with the exercise of reasonable diligence;

(5) the address of the office required to be maintained in the state of its organization by the laws of that state or, if not so required, of the principal office of the foreign limited partnership;

(6) the name and business address of each general partner; and

(7) the address of the office at which is kept a list of the names and addresses of the limited partners and their capital contributions, together with an undertaking by the foreign limited partnership to keep those records until the foreign limited partnership's registration in this State is cancelled or withdrawn.

§ 903. Issuance of Registration

(a) If the Secretary of State finds that an application for registration conforms to law and all requisite fees have been paid, he [or she] shall:

(1) endorse on the application the word "Filed," and the month, day and year of the filing thereof;

(2) file in his [or her] office a duplicate original of the application; and

(3) issue a certificate of registration to transact business in this State.

(b) The certificate of registration, together with a duplicate original of the application, shall be returned to the person who filed the application or his [or her] representative.

§ 904. Name

A foreign limited partnership may register with the Secretary of State under any name, whether or not it is the name under which it is registered in its state of organization, that includes without abbreviation the words "limited partnership" and that could be registered by a domestic limited partnership.

§ 905. Changes and Amendments

If any statement in the application for registration of a foreign limited partnership was false when made or any arrangements or other facts described have changed, making the application inaccurate in any respect, the foreign limited partnership shall promptly file in the office of the Secretary of State a certificate, signed and sworn to by a general partner, correcting such statement.

§ 906. Cancellation of Registration

A foreign limited partnership may cancel its registration by filing with the Secretary of State a certificate of cancellation signed and sworn to by a general partner. A cancellation does not terminate the authority of the Secretary of State to accept service of process on the foreign limited partnership with respect to [claims for relief] [causes of action] arising out of the transactions of business in this State.

§ 907. Transaction of Business Without Registration

(a) A foreign limited partnership transacting business in this State may not maintain any action, suit, or proceeding in any court of this State until it has registered in this State.

(b) The failure of a foreign limited partnership to register in this State does not impair the validity of any contract or act of the foreign limited partnership or prevent the foreign limited partnership from defending any action, suit, or proceeding in any court of this State.

(c) A limited partner of a foreign partnership is not liable as a general partner of the foreign limited partnership solely by reason of having transacted business in this State without registration.

(d) A foreign limited partnership, by transacting business in this State without registration, appoints the Secretary of State as its agent for service of process with respect to [claims for relief] [causes of action] arising out of the transaction of business in this State.

§ 908. Action by [Appropriate Official]

The [designate the appropriate official] may bring an action to restrain a foreign limited partnership from transacting business in this State in violation of this Article.

ARTICLE 10. DERIVATIVE ACTION

§ 1001. Right of Action

A limited partner may bring an action in the right of a limited partnership to recover a judgment in its favor if general partners with authority to do so have refused to bring the action or if an effort to cause those general partners to bring the action is not likely to succeed.

§ 1002. Proper Plaintiff

In a derivative action, the plaintiff must be a partner at the time of bringing the action and (i) must have been a partner at the time of the transaction of which he [or she] complains or (ii) his [or her] status as a partner must have devolved upon him [or her] by operation of law or pursuant to the terms of the partnership agreement from a person who was a partner at the time of the transaction.

§ 1003. Pleading

In a derivative action, the complaint shall set forth with particularity the effort of the plaintiff to secure initiation of the action by a general partner or the reasons for not making the effort.

§ 1004. Expenses

If a derivative action is successful, in whole or in part, or if anything is received by the plaintiff as a result of a judgment, compromise or settlement of an action or claim, the court may award the plaintiff reasonable expenses, including reasonable attorney's fees, and shall direct him [or her] to remit to the limited partnership the remainder of those proceeds received by him [or her].

ARTICLE 11. MISCELLANEOUS

§ 1101. Construction and Application

This [Act] shall be so applied and construed to effectuate its general purpose to make uniform the law with respect to the subject of this [Act] among states enacting it.

§ 1102. Short Title

This [Act] may be cited as the Uniform Limited Partnership Act.

§ 1103. Severability

If any provision of this [Act] or its application to any person or circumstance is held invalid, the invalidity does not affect other provisions or applications of the [Act] which can be given effect without the invalid provision or application, and to this end the provisions of this Act are severable.

§ 1104. Effective Date, Extended Effective Date, and Repeal

Except as set forth below, the effective date of this [Act] is _____ and the following acts [list existing limited partnership acts] are hereby repealed:

(1) The existing provisions for execution and filing of certificates of limited partnerships and amendments thereunder and cancellations thereof continue in effect until [specify time required to create central

filing system], the extended effective date, and Sections 102, 103, 104, 105, 201, 202, 203, 204 and 206 are not effective until the extended effective date.

(2) Section 402, specifying the conditions under which a general partner ceases to be a member of a limited partnership, is not effective until the extended effective date, and the applicable provisions of existing law continue to govern until the extended effective date.

(3) Sections 501, 502 and 608 apply only to contributions and distributions made after the effective date of this [Act].

(4) Section 704 applies only to assignments made after the effective date of this [Act].

(5) Article 9, dealing with registration of foreign limited partnerships, is not effective until the extended effective date.

(6) Unless otherwise agreed by the partners, the applicable provisions of existing law governing allocation of profits and losses (rather than the provisions of Section 503), distributions to a withdrawing partner (rather than the provisions of Section 604), and distribution of assets upon the winding up of a limited partnership (rather than the provisions of Section 804) govern limited partnerships formed before the effective date of this [Act].

§ 1105. Rules for Cases Not Provided for in this [Act]

In any case not provided for in this [Act] the provisions of the Uniform Partnership Act govern.

§ 1106. Savings Clause

The repeal of any statutory provision by this Act does not impair, or otherwise affect, the organization or the continued existence of a limited partnership existing at the effective date of this Act, nor does the repeal of any existing statutory provision by this Act impair any contract or affect any right accrued before the effective date of this Act.

Glossary

abatement a proportional reduction of the amount payable under a will when the funds are no longer available to pay in full.

acceptor a drawee who accepts a draft and who agrees to be primarily responsible to pay it.

accession the right of a property owner to keep whatever his property produces (for example, the calves produced by his livestock).

accommodation party one who signs an instrument as drawer, indorser, or acceptor in order to help someone else raise money.

accord and satisfaction the giving of something, usually less than originally required, in satisfaction of a debt or of some other legal entitlement, by which the person to whom the thing is given agrees to release the other from any legal liability.

acquitted absolved of criminal responsibility; verdict of not guilty.

action lawsuit.

act of God a natural event, outside human control.

ademption revocation or cancellation of a legatee's rights under a will by the actions of the testator during his life, often by his having given away assets that the will says are to go to the legatee.

adjudication the process of resolving disputes through litigation in court according to the rules of evidence.

adverse possession method of taking title to land by open and notorious possession adverse to the interests of the original owner.

agency shop a workplace in which an employee is not required to join the union but is required to pay the amount of union dues.

annexation the affixing or attaching of property (fixtures) to land.

answer pleadings filed by the defendant in response to the plaintiff's complaint.

appellant one who appeals the decision of a trial court to a higher court.

appellate jurisdiction the authority of a court to hear appeals from lower courts.

appellee one whose victory in a lower court is being appealed to a higher court by the loser at trial.

appraisal right a right of a stockholder to an appraisal of the fair value of his shares when the corporation is being acquired by or merging with another.

arbitration submission of a dispute, by agreement among the parties, to a private person for resolution in accordance with rules also determined by the parties.

arbitrator a person, usually acting in a private capacity, who resolves a dispute among two or more people.

arraignment a proceeding in which a criminal suspect is brought to court to plead guilty or not guilty to the charges against him.

assignee one to whom an agreement is made.

assignment a transfer of contract rights.

assignor one who makes an assignment.

attractive nuisance a condition of or object on one's land that attracts young children and that therefore requires the owner to take special care to prevent them from being injured by the attraction (such as a swimming pool).

bailee the person to whom property is delivered to hold in bailment.

bailment a delivery of goods to a person who does not have title.

bailor an owner of property who delivers it to another to hold in bailment.

bait and switch an unfair trade practice of offering particular merchandise for sale but denigrating it or displaying other, more expensive merchandise to the shopper.

bequest a gift in a will of personal property.

BFOQ bona fide occupational qualification.

bill of attainder an act of a legislature (unconstitutional in the United States) by which the legislature declares a particular person guilty of a crime.

bill of exchange a written order by one person to another to pay a sum of money to a third person.

blind trust a trust in which the grantor puts assets in trust for himself as beneficiary but in which the trustees are forbidden to tell the grantor how they are managing the trust.

Blue Sky laws state securities laws designed to protect investors from fraud.

bona fide in good faith, with good faith.

boycott the act of preventing someone from doing business with others.

bulk sales the sale of all or almost all of a merchant's stock not in the ordinary course of business.

cause of action a legal claim that is the basis for a lawsuit.

caveat emptor "Let the buyer beware."

caveat venditor "Let the seller beware."

certificated security a share, participation, or other interest in a property, an enterprise, or an obligation of the issuer, that is represented by an instrument issued in registered or bearer form.

certified check a check that has been accepted by the drawee.

certiorari a writ directed to a lower court by a higher appellate court to permit the latter to review a decision of the lower court.

chattel an item of personal property.

chattel paper any writing evidencing both a monetary obligation and a security interest in specific goods.

circuit court in the federal system, an appellate court intermediate between the district (trial) courts and the U.S. Supreme Court.

class action a lawsuit on behalf of many people all asserting a common legal claim against the defendant.

closed shop a workplace in which a

prospective employee is required to belong to a union in order to be hired; unlawful under the federal labor laws.

codicil an addition or amendment to a will.

collateral property given as security for a debt.

common carrier a carrier (railroad, airline, taxicab company, etc.) that holds itself open to any member of the public for a fee.

common law the basic system of law developed by the courts in the absence of legislation.

comparative negligence a measure of negligence by which the plaintiff's recovery is diminished by the degree to which he was at fault.

compensatory damages an award of money to compensate a plaintiff for actual injuries done to him by the defendant.

complaint the pleadings filed by a plaintiff stating his legal claims against the defendant.

composition an agreement between a debtor and his creditors in which the latter accept a payment of less than the amount owed.

condition precedent an event that must happen before the promisor must carry out his obligation or before title will vest.

condition subsequent an event that terminates an existing duty of performance.

condominium a form of ownership in which the common space is held by all tenants in common and the owner has title to a particular space.

confusion of goods a mixture of goods of different owners in such a manner that they cannot be identified.

conscious parallelism in antitrust, an evidentiary rule that holds competitors to be in restraint of trade if they consciously abide by a common scheme to do so, even if they have not directly discussed it.

consent decree a decree of the court, to which the parties have consented without trial, entered after they have negotiated the terms.

consequential damages damages that are not the direct result of the action causing the harm but that are the consequence of special circumstances.

consideration the legal detriment of a promisee bargained for in exchange for a promise.

consignment delivery of goods by owner to another for sale, in which the person undertaking to sell does not take title and is not obligated to pay for the goods if they are not sold.

conspiracy a combination of two or more persons for the undertaking of a criminal act.

contribution the sharing of a loss or payment by two or more persons; such as joint defendants or co-sureties.

contributory negligence negligence on the part of the plaintiff.

cooperative a form of ownership in which the tenants in a building own the entire building in common, and the occupant does not have title to his specific apartment.

countercomplaint a complaint against the plaintiff asserted by the defendant; part of the pleadings.

cross-elasticity of demand in antitrust, a measure of the degree to which one product should be considered as competing with another for the purpose of determining the relevant market.

cumulative voting a system of voting in which each person entitled to vote may divide the number of votes to which he is entitled as he sees fit; because he can concentrate them all on one person, the system permits election of a minority candidate.

curtesy the right of the husband to a share in the deceased wife's property.

cy pres doctrine "as near as possible"; the doctrine in will and trusts that lets the court order that the party's intention, which because of the circumstances might be impossible to carry out, be carried out as nearly as possible.

de facto in fact, actual; something that must be recognized as existing, even though it might technically be illegal.

de jure rightful, legitimate, lawful.

de novo new; starting afresh.

deed the written document that conveys title to real property.

defamation the injuring of a person's reputation, either in writing or orally.

defendant the person or institution being sued.

delectus personae the right of a partner to decide who shall become additional partners.

delegatee one to whom a duty is delegated.

demurrer a defendant's motion to dismiss a complaint on the grounds that even if the plaintiff's claim is true, it does not state a cause of action.

deposition questioning of witness before trial, a common method of discovery.

derivative action a suit filed by stockholder(s) on behalf of the corporation.

detainer the act of withholding from the rightful owner or possessor his land or goods.

devise gift, in a will, of real property.

directed verdict a verdict given by the court before the jury has an opportunity to give its verdict.

discovery the pre-trial process of uncovering the evidence.

dishonor refusal to pay a bill or note when due.

diversity jurisdiction the authority of federal courts to hear common law suits between residents of different states when the amount in dispute exceeds $10,000.

donee beneficiary one who is to have the benefit of the promisor's performance, when the promisee is not indebted to the donee.

double jeopardy the principle that no person can be tried twice for the same offense.

dower the right of a widow to a certain share of the deceased husband's estate.

draft a bill of exchange; an order for the payment of money drawn by one person on another.

drawee the person to whom a draft is addressed and who is ordered to pay the amount indicated.

due diligence a measure of an auditor's obligation to perform his audit in a professional manner.

due process constitutional requirement applicable to both the federal and state governments that they conduct themselves fairly under law and that they avoid arbitrary behavior.

dumping   the sale of goods in a particular market at less than fair value.

earnest money   the down payment given to a seller of real property.

embezzlement   the fraudulent appropriation of property to his own use by one who has been entrusted with it.

eminent domain   the power of government to appropriate private property for public purposes.

entrapment   the act of a government official in inducing someone to commit a crime that he did not contemplate committing.

equal protection clause   the part of the Fourteenth Amendment requiring the states to guarantee to every person "equal protection of the laws."

equitable title   title held by a beneficiary of a trust, legal title to the corpus of which is held by the trustees.

equity   a system of jurisprudence originally administered by courts different from common-law courts, but which today connotes fairness and justice. In real estate, equity refers to the value that the mortgagor would receive from the sale of his property once the mortgage is paid off.

escrow   when a deed or other document is held by a third party for delivery to the buyer or other party once a particular event or occurrence takes place.

estate for years   a leasehold in which the tenant has possession for a fixed term.

estate   a right or interest in real property; in a general sense, a person's estate connotes everything that he owns.

estoppel   a rule of equity invoked by courts that precludes a person from making certain pleas to the court because of something that he said or did.

ex parte   on, by, or on behalf of one side only.

ex-ship   from the carrying vessel; in a destination contract, ex-ship places the risk of loss on the seller.

executor   person appointed by testator to carry out terms of his will. A female executor is sometimes still referred to as an executrix.

executory contract   a contract the terms of which have not yet been performed by either party.

expropriation   the taking of private property, usually by a government, often without paying for it.

exculpatory clause   clause in a contract or other document that excuses one party from liability for certain actions taken.

factor   one who purchases the right to receive income from another.

false pretenses   deliberate misrepresentation intended to defraud someone of his money or property.

fee simple   absolute title to real property.

felony   a serious crime, usually defined as punishable by a jail sentence of a year or more.

fiduciary   one who is held to the highest standard of good faith and trust in dealing on behalf of another, the standard characteristic of a trustee.

field warehouse   when a warehouse service takes control or possession of collateral in the "field"—that is, at the debtor's place of business.

financing statement   document filed in an appropriate state office to perfect a security interest.

fixtures   goods attached to real property.

force majeure   irresistible force; act of God.

forgery   an unauthorized signature.

fraud   false representation of a material fact relied on by the other party to a contract.

freehold   an estate in land without any fixed termination.

grand jury   jury (usually consisting of twenty-three persons) who decide whether to indict a suspect in order to try him for a crime.

habeas corpus   Latin for "you have the body"; a writ issued by a court commanding the jailor to produce a prisoner and give reasons for continuing to incarcerate him.

holder   one who has legally acquired possession of a draft, note, or other negotiable instrument and who is entitled to payment.

holder in due course   one who became a holder of a draft or note or other negotiable instrument, complete and regular on its face, before it became due and without any notice of previous dishonor, and who

took the note in good faith for value without notice of any defect in the title of the negotiator.

holding   the specific legal ground on which a court decides an issue.

homicide   unlawful killing (includes murder and manslaughter).

hot cargo agreement   a provision in a collective bargaining agreement by which an employer agrees to refrain from dealing with certain people.

identification to the contract   marking or segregating specific goods as those described in a contract for their transfer.

indemnity   an assurance of one person to secure another against an anticipated loss; payment by one person to make another whole from a loss already sustained.

indictment   formal charge of the grand jury under which a criminal defendant must stand trial.

indorsement   method by which a holder can negotiate to another a negotiable instrument by signing the holder's name on the back.

information   an authorized public official's formal accusation that someone has committed a crime for which he must be tried; a substitute for an indictment for lesser crimes.

injunction   a court order usually forbidding the defendant from acting in specified ways (but sometimes requiring him to act in a particular way), violation of which is punishable by contempt of court.

insider trading   trading in securities of a corporation by one with a special relationship to the corporation in violation of federal securities laws.

instrument   a written document.

insurable interest   a sufficiently substantial interest in property or someone's life to support a contract to insure it.

intangible property   property with no intrinsic value but which evidences something of value (for example, stocks and bonds).

intellectual property   intangible property that stems from creations of the mind; includes copyrights, patents, and trademarks.

intestacy   the condition of having died without leaving a will.

inverse condemnation   a proceeding in which a property owner asserts that the government has taken his property without paying compensation.

invitee   a person invited to the premises of another, usually for a business purpose.

joint and several liability   liability in which any one of several defendants may be held liable for the entire amount due, even though each is equally responsible.

joint venture   an association of persons to carry on a particular task until completed.

judgment n.o.v.   a judgment given by the judge notwithstanding the jury's verdict.

jurisdiction   the authority of a court to act, either over a particular person or with regard to a particular cause of action.

larceny   the taking of another's personal property with intent to convert it to one's own use.

law merchant   law that developed in the Middle Ages to regulate relations between merchants among different countries.

lease   an agreement for rent of land or equipment.

leasehold   an estate for a fixed term of years.

libel   injury to someone's reputation, done in writing.

lien   an incumbrance upon property to secure a payment.

liquidated damages   damages specified in amount in a contract governing the relationship of the parties.

liquidation   making certain; in bankruptcy, process of converting debtor's assets into cash for distribution to creditors.

lockout   act of employer barring employees from working to force them to settle for terms more advantageous to employer.

long-arm statute   statute subjecting out-of-state parties to jurisdiction of courts within the state.

maker   one who executes a note.

malice   intentional infliction of wrongful act with intent to do harm.

malice aforethought   predetermined intent to commit an act without legal justification.

mandamus   a writ issued by the court directing a public official to take action the law requires him to take.

master   a common-law term for a person who controls the work of servants.

mechanic's lien   a claim allowed to one who furnishes labor, services, or materials to improve real estate.

mediation   the process by which a neutral intermediary attempts to settle a dispute between two adverse parties.

mens rea   guilty mind.

merger   the joining of two entities; absorption of one thing or right into another.

metes and bounds   a type of real estate description using angles and distances.

misdemeanor   a minor crime, usually punishable by a jail sentence of less than one year.

misrepresentation   an assertion to another not in accord with the facts.

mortgage   security in which the collateral is (usually) land.

mortgagee   the party who holds the mortgage (for example, a bank or savings and loan company).

mortgagor   one who gives a mortgage.

negative option   a scheme in which a purchaser automatically is shipped goods and for which he is liable to pay unless he affirmatively notifies the seller that he does not wish them.

negligence   the tort of carelessness; unreasonable behavior leading to injury.

negotiability   commercial paper which meets certain requirements specified in the Uniform Commercial Code.

negotiation   the act of transferring commercial paper, including drafts and notes, to a subsequent holder.

nimble dividend   dividends paid out of net earnings of the current and previous year.

nolo contendere   no contest; a plea that does not admit guilt but that will permit the court to issue a sanction.

note   an instrument committing the maker to pay a definite amount of money at a specified time to a particular person, or to order, or to bearer.

novation   substitution of one person for another, by mutual agreement.

nuisance   a condition or act that disturbs an owner in the use of his property or that renders it unfit for its normal use.

obligee   a person to whom some legal obligation is owed.

obligor   a person who has contractually undertaken to perform an obligation.

opinion   a written statement of the court of reasons for its decision.

option contract   a contract in which the promisee has the option whether to buy or not buy, or sell or not sell, from the promisor.

par value   a value of a share of stock specified in the certificate.

paramount title   superior title.

parens patriae   in antitrust, the power of the attorney general to sue on behalf of the citizens of the state.

parol evidence   oral evidence.

partnership   an association of two or more persons to carry on as co-owners a business for profit.

patent   the right to exclude everyone else from using or selling various types of inventions.

payee   the person who is to receive payment on a draft or note.

penalty   in law of damages, an unreasonably large liquidated damages provision.

per capita   according to the number of individuals, share and share alike; in a distribution per capita, each person named will receive an equal share.

per se rule   an antitrust, unlawful on its face.

per stirpes   by representation; in a distribution *per stirpes*, each class of individuals takes the share to which their deceased would have been entitled.

perfection   process by which a secured party announces to the world that he has taken a security interest in the particular goods.

periodic tenancy   a tenancy for a period of time that is renewed automatically unless either landlord or tenant notifies the other to the contrary.

perjury   an intentional statement under oath that is contrary to the facts and known to the witness to be false.

petit jury   an ordinary jury of twelve (sometimes six) citizens, who try civil and criminal cases.

pirating   intentional violation of

rights secured by copyright or patent; usually occurring when the pirate sells a literary work or markets an invention purportedly as coming from the original author, publisher, manufacturer, or inventor.

plaintiff the one who files a lawsuit in court.

plats maps of land subdivided into lots.

plea bargain a deal struck between the prosecutor and the defendant in a criminal prosecution by which the defendant pleads guilty and avoids trial, in return for which he usually receives a lighter sentence.

pleadings the opening papers in a lawsuit, including the answer, complaint, and countercomplaint, that show the basic charges and defenses.

pledge the delivery of goods to a creditor as security for the debt.

possession control or custody of property.

power of attorney the consent of a person for another to act in his stead, and to sign his name to any legal documents authorized by the power of attorney.

precedent a prior case, the holding of which is the basis for decisions in future cases by the same court.

prima facie on the face of it; at first appearance.

privity direct connection of parties to a contract.

probable cause a reasonable enough belief that a person committed a crime to permit a warrant to be issued for his arrest.

probate the process of proving a will.

promissory estoppel the judicial enforcement, in the interests of justice, of a promise that the promisor should know will induce action on the part of the promisee and that does induce such action.

prospectus a document required to be disseminated by a corporation preparing to sell securities, detailing the nature of the issuance.

protest a certificate, often signed by a notary, that a draft or note was presented for payment and was dishonored.

proximate cause direct or immediate cause, without which an injury would not have occurred, and suf-

ficient to support an action for tort.

proxy a person who is appointed to serve for another; also, the instrument evidencing the appointment.

puffing an expression of opinion (usually overblown) by a seller, not treated as a representation of fact.

punitive damages damages above the actual damages caused by the tortfeasor, assessed as punishment for a willful act.

quantum meruit an award imposed by law, not by contract, in the interests of justice, for work actually performed.

quasi-contract an obligation imposed by law that arises from the actions of one person toward another or from relations between them, similar in character to a contract obligation.

quitclaim deed a deed that conveys to the buyer all that the seller possessed and makes no further representations.

real property land and structures affixed to the land.

rebuttable presumption in evidence, a presumption that will be made unless one of the parties by further proof manages to show that it should not be held.

rebuttal introduction of evidence at trial that contradicts evidence already offered.

receiver a neutral person given authority by the court to take possession of the property in dispute and to manage, preserve, or dispose of it.

reciprocity in antitrust, a practice in which a company buys from its customers as well as sells to them.

reception statute a statute that declares that existing law in a particular place is received into the law of the new state.

recording the process of placing on the public record deeds, mortgages, and other documents.

redlining the alleged practice by banks and other lenders of determining not to lend to people who live within certain geographic boundaries of a city, town, or county.

relevant market in antitrust, the market, whether based on geography or product, within which to

test monopoly power or the effect on competition of an acquisition or merger.

remand to send back; an appellate court remands a case to a lower court when further action is necessary.

replevin an action to recover possession of goods unlawfully held.

res ipsa loquitur the thing speaks for itself; a rebuttable presumption that the defendant was culpable in tort because the instrumentality of injury was in his exclusive control.

res judicata a thing or matter decided; the rule that final decisions by the court to which the case has been taken may not be relitigated.

rescission the remedy in appropriate cases of annulling the contract, putting the parties back to where they were before it was entered into.

restitution restoration; returning goods or providing a sum of money to make a party whole.

restrictive covenant a provision in a deed to land that restricts subsequent purchasers in their use of the land.

reversion a future interest in land that remains with the original transferor or his successor.

riparian a riparian owner is one who owns land along a waterway.

runaway shop the removal of a plant or workplace to a different location to try to break a union.

S corporation a corporation that for federal tax purposes is treated for the most part as if it were a partnership.

scienter intent to deceive, manipulate, or defraud.

seal an impression, on wax or paper, used to attest the formal execution of a document.

search warrant authorization by a court for the police to search particular premises for named persons or things.

secondary boycott a boycott of suppliers or customers of the employer.

securities stocks, bonds, and other evidences of indebtedness of, or right to participate in, the profits of a business.

servant common-law term for an agent whose conduct is controlled by the master.

service of process   the delivery of a summons or related documents to the named party.

settlor   grantor; the one who creates a trust.

shop rights   the rights of a company to exploit an invention made by an employee on company time and with company resources.

slander   oral defamation.

sovereign immunity   the immunity of state, federal, or foreign governments from suit in court.

standing   the legal right of someone to file suit in a particular case.

stare decisis   to stand by what is decided; the principle that cases already decided must serve as precedents to govern later cases.

stated capital   the sum of par value stock and the consideration received for any no-par stock issued.

Statute of Frauds   the statute that requires certain contracts to be in writing to be enforced.

statute of limitations   a statute that dictates a period of years in which a plaintiff must bring suit or thereafter forfeit his right to sue.

statute of repose   in product liability law, a statute that determines how new a machine must be for someone to be permitted to sue its original manufacturer for defects that caused injury.

stay   stopping; a court order that temporarily stops a particular proceeding or legal action.

stock split   the division of one share of stock into two or more.

strict liability   liability imposed even in the absence of negligence; in product liability law, for defective conditions that cause injury.

subrogation   substitution of one person for another who has a legal claim or right.

summary judgment   judgment given by a court when there are no factual issues in the case and only legal issues need to be resolved.

summons   a notice to a person that a legal action has been commenced against him and that requires him to appear in court.

surety   one who undertakes to pay the debt or any other obligation of his principal.

surrebuttal   a response to a rebuttal.

tenancy at will   a tenancy that will last only so long as the landlord and tenant desire.

tenant at sufferance   a tenant who has wrongfully held over beyond his rightful term of possession.

tender offer   an invitation to shareholders to tender their shares at a stipulated price.

third-party beneficiary   a party intended as a beneficiary of a contract made between a promisor and promisee.

timesharing   an arrangement whereby different people own or lease rights to the same property for use on different days and weeks each year.

title insurance   insurance against the risk that the buyer did not acquire rightful title.

tort   a civil wrong, actionable in court for damages or injunction.

tortfeasor   one who commits a tort.

trade secret   a process, chemical formula, mechanism, or plan known only to an employer and those employees who need to know in order to use it in the business.

trade usage   customs generally followed by people in a particular trade.

trademark   a distinctive mark that identifies a product as having been made by a particular manufacturer or having been sold by a particular vendor.

treasury shares   authorized and issued shares of a company held by the company itself.

trespass   wrongful entry onto someone else's land or injury to his property.

trust   the holding of legal title by one party for the benefit of another.

tying   in antitrust, the requirement that a person buy certain goods or services in order to be able to buy certain other goods or services.

ultra vires   beyond one's authority or power; a company that takes actions not permitted under its charter or bylaws is acting *ultra vires*.

undisclosed principal   the principal on behalf of whom an agent is acting when the other party to the transaction is unaware that the agent is in fact an agent for a principal.

unfair labor practice   certain acts of both employers and unions that are made unlawful by federal labor laws.

union shop   a workplace in which an employee must agree to become a member of the union when hired.

usury laws   laws that establish the maximum rate of lawful interest.

uttering   publishing, sending forth, declaring that an instrument is good; presenting a check for payment.

variance   authority to carry on a use that does not conform to zoning requirements.

venue   the proper geographic location of a court.

vicarious liability   the liability of one person for the actions of another.

void contract   a contract which never had legal validity.

voidable contract   a contract that the wronged party may void at his option.

voidable preferences   in bankruptcy, a transfer of assets within a certain period of time that gives one creditor a greater share of the assets than other creditors.

voir dire   the process of selecting a jury.

wage assignments   an agreement by an employee that a creditor may take certain wages as security for a debt.

warranty   a representation or promise that certain facts are true.

watered stock   when inflated consideration received for stock is less than par value.

zoning   a land use plan that sets forth what types of uses may be made of land in different parts of a particular town, city, or county.

References

The references listed in this section are cited in the text by author and year of publication.

American Bar Association (1976). *The proper role of the lawyer in real estate transactions.* Chicago: ABA Press.

American Criminal Law Review (1980). White-collar crime: A survey of law. 18:371.

Beard, M. A. (1962). *A history of business. vol. 2.* Ann Arbor: University of Michigan Press.

The Blade. (1974). Streakers denied insurance coverage. Mar. 24.

Business Insurance. (1979). D & O claims incidence rises. Nov. 12, pp. 18, 19.

Business Week. (1977). The tricks of the trade-off. Apr. 4, p. 72. (1978) When businessmen confess their social sins. Nov. 6, p. 175ff.

Cardozo, B. N. (1921). *The nature of the judicial process.* New Haven: Yale University Press.

Danzig, R. J. (1975). Hadley v. Baxendale: A study in the industrialization of the law. *Journal of Legal Studies,* 4:249.

Dworkin, R. (1978). *Taking Rights Seriously.* Cambridge: Harvard University Press.

The Economist. (1978). Quick, stop them, those men are talking to each other. Apr. 29, pp. 192–230.

Fader, B. (1982). Manville submits bankruptcy filing to halt lawsuits. *New York Times,* Aug. 27, p. 1.

Fortune. (1979). A company that's worth more dead than alive. Feb. 26, pp. 42–45.

Frank, J. (1963). *Law and the modern mind.* New York: Doubleday & Co., Anchor Books.

Friedman, M. (1962). *Capitalism and freedom.* Chicago: University of Chicago Press.

Geisel, J. (1978). Gun firm pays $6.8 million to attorney. *Business Insurance,* Nov. 13, p. 12.

Havighurst, H. D. (1952). Review of Corbin on Contracts. *Yale Law Journal,* 61:1143, 1144–45.

Joseph, R. (1982). Problems have long plagued asbestos firms. *Wall Street Journal,* Aug. 30, p. 15.

Kern, F. (1970). *Kingship and law in the Middle Ages,* trans. by S. B. Chrimes. New York: Harper & Row.

Lewis, Peter H. (1990). When computing power is generated by the lawyers. *New York Times,* July 22, p. 4F.

Lewis, D. (1976). *The public image of Henry Ford.* Detroit: Wayne State University Press.

Lewis, W. D. (1915). The Uniform Partnership Act (review). *Yale Law Journal,* 24:617, 622.

Lieberman, Jethro K. and Henry, James F. (1986). Lessons from the Alternative Dispute Movement. *Univ. of Chicago Law Review,* 53:424.

Macauley, S. (1963). Non-contractual relations in business. *American Sociological Review,* 28:55.

McInturff, P. (1981). Products liability: the impact on California manufacturers. *American Business Law Journal,* 19:343.

Main, J. (1982). When accidents don't happen. *Fortune,* Sept. 6, p. 62ff.

Maine, H. (1930). *Ancient law.* New York: Dutton.

Maslow, J. E. (1975). Products liability comes of age. *Juris Doctor,* Jan., p. 26.

Michigan Daily. (1978). Friction triggers Iacocca ouster. July 15, p. 10.

Morgenthaler, E., and Calame, B. E. (1976). More concerns issue guidelines on ethics in payoffs aftermath. *Wall Street Journal,* Mar. 16, p. 1.

Perkins, R. M. (1969). *Criminal law,* 2d ed. Mineola: Foundation Press.

Posner, R. A. (1973). *Economic analysis of the law.* Boston: Little-Brown.

Prosser, M. (1971). *Torts,* 4th ed. St. Paul: West Publishing Co.

Samuelson, P. A. (1973). *Economics.* New York: McGraw-Hill.

Schwartz, B. (1976). *Administrative law.* Boston: Little-Brown.

Seavey, W. (1964). *Handbook of the law of agency.* St. Paul: West Publishing Co.

Securities & Exchange Commission. (1981). The work of the SEC.

Simpson, L. P. (1965). *Contracts,* 2d ed. St. Paul: West Publishing Co.

Strayer, J. (1970). *On the medieval origins of the modern state.* Princeton: Princeton University Press.

Teger, A. I. (1979). *Too Much Invested to Quit: The Psychology of Conflict.* New York: Pergamon Press.

Wall Street Journal. (1981). Petrogene's tax shelter attracts attention. Dec. 29, p. 23.

White, B. Corporate codes of conduct: a mechanism of internal control, in Mautz, R., et al. (1980). *Internal control in U.S. corporations: the state of the art.* New York: Financial Executives Research Foundation.

Williston, S. (1921). Freedom of contract. *Cornell Law Quarterly,* 6:365.

Wysocki, B. (1976). Manufacturers are hit with more lawsuits. *Wall Street Journal,* June 3, p. 1.

Copyrights and Acknowledgments

Please note there are no pages 659–668.

Index of Cases

Statutory Index

References to Uniform State Laws
[Section number follows main listing]

2.07	922
3.01	922
3.02	947
3.04	948
4.01	921
6.20	921
7.05	951
7.30	954
8.01	957
8.03	958
8.08	952
8.25	958
8.30	958, 963
8.61	960
10.20	922
14.06	1007
14.07	1007
15.01	997

References to Restatements
[Section numbers follow the main listing]

Restatement, Second, of the Law of Agency

2	821
2	822
47	841
379	828
383	830
395	694, 827
396	694
434	831

Restatement, First, of the Law of Contracts, 11, 189

71	270
164	313

Restatement, Second, of the Law of Contracts, 189

Chap. 5	280
pp. 101–102	343
1	188
2	301
3	205
5	218
16 comment b	275
20	270
24	207
32	218
41	217
60	218
69	219
87	225
90	237
162(1)	264
162(2)	264
163 comment a	261
168 comment d	265
171(1)	268
176	258
177	258
177 comment b	259
178	243, 248
186	249
195	253
195(2)(b)	450

197(b)	242
199(b)	242
205	162
207 comment f	290
207 comment h	290
226	319
261	329
283	335
302	301
304	301
315	301
322	311
350	345
520	58

Restatement of the Foreign Relations Law of the United States, 1118
Restatement of the Law of Property, 671
Restatement of Security Law, 605
Restatement, First, of the Law of Torts

46	120
551(2)	1194
757	690, 692
851	716
852	716
853	716

Restatement, Second, of the Law of Torts

344	721
402A	427-30
402A(1)(b)	430
402A(2)(b)	432
552	1196, 1197
552(1)	1195
552(2)(b)	1195
559	137

Restatement, Second, of the Law of Trusts

2	787

Index of Hypothetical Names

Index of Businesses

General Index